McDougal Littell

THE LANGUAGE OF
LITERATURE

AMERICAN LITERATURE

Arthur N. Applebee

Andrea B. Bermúdez

Sheridan Blau

Rebekah Caplan

Peter Elbow

Susan Hynds

Judith A. Langer

James Marshall

McDougal Littell

A HOUGHTON MIFFLIN COMPANY

Evanston, Illinois • Boston • Dallas

Acknowledgments

Unit One

Harcourt Brace & Company: "A Worn Path," from *A Curtain of Green and Other Stories* by Eudora Welty. Copyright 1941 and renewed © 1969 by Eudora Welty. Reprinted by permission of Harcourt Brace & Company.

McGraw-Hill Companies: Excerpt from "The World on the Turtle's Back," from *The Great Tree and the Longhouse* by Hazel W. Hertzberg. Copyright © 1966 by the American Anthropological Association. Reprinted with the permission of The McGraw-Hill Companies.

Excerpt from *The Log of Christopher Columbus* by Christopher Columbus, edited by Robert Fuson, originally published by International Marine Publishing Company. Copyright © 1987 by Robert H. Fuson. All rights reserved. Reprinted with the permission of The McGraw-Hill Companies.

Sunstone Press: "Song of the Sky Loom" from *Songs of the Tewa,* translated by Herbert Joseph Spinden. Courtesy of Sunstone Press, Box 2321, Santa Fe, NM 87504-2321.

University of Nebraska Press: "Coyote and the Buffalo" and "Fox and Coyote and Whale," from *Coyote Stories* by Mourning Dove. Reprinted by permission of the University of Nebraska Press.

Continued on page 1405

ISBN-13: 978-0-618-17047-0   ISBN-10: 0-618-17047-2

14 15 -0868- 09

Senior Consultants

The senior consultants guided the conceptual development for *The Language of Literature* series. They participated actively in shaping prototype materials for major components, and they reviewed completed prototypes and/or completed units to ensure consistency with current research and the philosophy of the series.

Arthur N. Applebee Professor of Education, State University of New York at Albany; Director, Center for the Learning and Teaching of Literature; Senior Fellow, Center for Writing and Literacy

Andrea B. Bermúdez Professor of Studies in Language and Culture; Director, Research Center for Language and Culture; Chair, Foundations and Professional Studies, University of Houston-Clear Lake

Sheridan Blau Senior Lecturer in English and Education and former Director of Composition, University of California at Santa Barbara; Director, South Coast Writing Project; Director, Literature Institute for Teachers; Former President, National Council of Teachers of English

Rebekah Caplan Senior Associate for Language Arts for middle school and high school literacy, National Center on Education and the Economy, Washington, D.C.; served on the California State English Assessment Development Team for Language Arts; former co-director of the Bay Area Writing Project, University of California at Berkeley

Peter Elbow Emeritus Professor of English, University of Massachusetts at Amherst; Fellow, Bard Center for Writing and Thinking

Susan Hynds Professor and Director of English Education, Syracuse University, Syracuse, New York

Judith A. Langer Professor of Education, State University of New York at Albany; Co-director, Center for the Learning and Teaching of Literature; Senior Fellow, Center for Writing and Literacy

James Marshall Professor of English and English Education; Chair, Division of Curriculum and Instruction, University of Iowa, Iowa City

Contributing Consultants

Linda Diamond Executive Vice President, Consortium on Reading Excellence (CORE); co-author of *Building a Powerful Reading Program*

Lucila A. Garza ESL Consultant, Austin, Texas

Jeffrey N. Golub Assistant Professor of English Education, University of South Florida, Tampa

William L. McBride, Ph.D. Reading and Curriculum Specialist; former middle and high school English instructor

Sharon Sicinski-Skeans, Ph.D. Assistant Professor of Reading, University of Houston-Clear Lake; primary consultant on *The InterActive Reader*

Multicultural Advisory Board

The multicultural advisors reviewed literature selections for appropriate content and made suggestions for teaching lessons in a multicultural classroom.

Vikki Pepper Ascuena, Meridian High School, Meridian, Idaho

Dr. Joyce M. Bell, Chairperson, English Department, Townview Magnet Center, Dallas, Texas

Linda F. Bellmore, Livermore High School, Livermore, California

Dr. Eugenia W. Collier, Author; lecturer; Chairperson, Department of English and Language Arts; Teacher of Creative Writing and American Literature, Morgan State University, Maryland

Dr. Bill Compagnone, English Department Chairperson, Lawrence High School, Lawrence, Massachusetts

Kathleen S. Fowler, President, Palm Beach County Council of Teachers of English, Boca Raton Middle School, Boca Raton, Florida

Jan Graham, Cobb Middle School, Tallahassee, Florida

Continued on page 1448

Teacher Review Panels

The following educators provided ongoing review during the development of the tables of contents, lesson design, and key components of the program.

CALIFORNIA
Steve Bass, 8th Grade Team Leader, Meadowbrook Middle School, Ponway Unified School District

Cynthia Brickey, 8th Grade Academic Block Teacher, Kastner Intermediate School, Clovis Unified School District

Continued on page 1449

Manuscript Reviewers

The following educators reviewed prototype lessons and tables of contents during the development of *The Language of Literature* program.

David Adcox, Trinity High School, Euless, Texas

Carol Alves, English Department Chairperson, Apopka High School, Apopka, Florida

Jacqueline Anderson, James A. Foshay Learning Center, Los Angeles, California

Continued on page 1450

Student Board

The student board members read and evaluated selections to assess their appeal for 11th-grade students.

Joanne Cheng, Spanish River High School, Boca Raton, Florida

Sharon Garnett Counts, Lake Worth High School, Lake Worth, Florida

Shericko Davis, Ramsey High School, Birmingham, Alabama

Leigh Ann Gordon, Plantation High School, Plantation, Florida

Jennifer Halbert, Peoria High School, Peoria, Illinois

Denise Harris, Phineas Banning High School, Wilmington, California

Robbie Hay, Butler High School, Louisville, Kentucky

Michael Scott, Westerville North High School, Westerville, Ohio

Calvin Yu, Ramsey Alternative High School, Birmingham, Alabama

The Language of Literature
Overview

UNIT ONE Origins and Encounters
2000 B.C.–A.D. 1620

Part 1 In Harmony with Nature
Part 2 First Encounters

LITERARY FOCUS
Historical Narratives

SKILL FOCUS
Writing Workshop: Eyewitness Report
Grammar: Achieving Sentence Variety
Vocabulary: Building a Stronger Vocabulary

UNIT TWO From Colony to Country 1620–1800

Part 1 Between Heaven and Hell
Part 2 The Right to Be Free

LITERARY FOCUS
The Conventions of Drama

Persuasive Rhetoric

SKILL FOCUS
Writing Workshop: Critical Review, Persuasion
Grammar: Using Gerunds, Using Verb Tenses in Sequence
Vocabulary: Interpreting Analogies; Using Context Clues

UNIT THREE The Spirit of Individualism
1800–1855

Part 1 Celebrations of the Self
Part 2 The Dark Side of Individualism

LITERARY FOCUS
Form in Poetry

SKILL FOCUS
Writing Workshop: Reflective Essay, Short Story
Grammar: Using Adjectives and Adjective Phrases, Using Adverbs and Adverb Phrases
Vocabulary: Analyzing Word Parts— Roots, Using Word Origins to Learn New Words

UNIT FOUR Conflict and Expansion 1850–1900

Part 1 A House Divided
Part 2 Tricksters and Trailblazers

LITERARY FOCUS
Setting in Regional Literature

SKILL FOCUS
Writing Workshop: Literary Interpretation
Communication Workshop: Storytelling
Grammar: Creating Compound Sentences, Using Adjective and Adverb Clauses
Vocabulary: Comprehending Words with Multiple Meanings; Homophones, Homographs, and Homonyms

UNIT FIVE The Changing Face of America
1855–1925

Part 1 Women's Voices, Women's Lives
Part 2 Illusion and Reality

LITERARY FOCUS
Social Themes in Fiction

SKILL FOCUS
Writing Workshop: Comparison-and-Contrast Essay
Grammar: Using Noun Clauses
Vocabulary: Recognizing Denotations and Connotations

UNIT SIX The Modern Age 1910–1940

Part 1 A New Cultural Identity
Part 2 Alienation of the Individual

LITERARY FOCUS
Modernism

SKILL FOCUS
Writing Workshop: Research Report
Grammar: Making Sentence Parts Parallel
Vocabulary: Understanding Informal Language

UNIT SEVEN War Abroad and Conflict at Home
1940–Present

Part 1 Remembering the Wars
Part 2 Integration and Disintegration

LITERARY FOCUS
Tone in Contemporary Literature

SKILL FOCUS
Communication Workshop: Multimedia Exhibit
Grammar: Using Sentence Closers
Vocabulary: Analyzing Word Parts— Affixes

Table of Contents

Student Resource Bank

Reading Handbook
Writing Handbook
Communication Handbook
Grammar Handbook
Glossary of Literary Terms
Glossary of Words to Know in English and Spanish

Literature Connections

Each of the books in the *Literature Connections* series combines a novel or play with related readings—poems, stories, plays, personal essays, articles—that add new perspectives on the theme or subject matter of the longer work.

Listed below are some of the most popular choices to accompany the Grade 11 anthology:

The Scarlet Letter by Nathaniel Hawthorne

The Adventures of Huckleberry Finn by Mark Twain

The Crucible by Arthur Miller

Jubilee by Margaret Walker

My Ántonia by Willa Cather

Ethan Frome by Edith Wharton

A Raisin in the Sun by Lorraine Hansberry

Go Tell It on the Mountain by James Baldwin

The Autobiography of Miss Jane Pittman by Ernest J. Gaines

... And the Earth Did Not Devour Him by Tomás Rivera

Fallen Angels by Walter Dean Myers

Farewell to Manzanar by Jeanne Wakatsuki Houston and James D. Houston

The Souls of Black Folk by W.E.B. Du Bois

THE LANGUAGE OF
LITERATURE

Reading Strategies

Becoming an Active Reader   6
STRATEGIES FOR READING

Reading Literature   8
READING MODEL
   A Worn Path by Eudora Welty

Reading Handbook
READING FOR DIFFERENT PURPOSES   1240
READING DIFFERENT GENRES   1242
READING DIFFERENT FORMATS   1243
ENRICHING YOUR VOCABULARY   1244
READING FOR INFORMATION   1250
   Reading a Textbook   1250
   Reading a Magazine Article   1252
   Reading a Web Page   1253
PATTERNS OF ORGANIZATION   1254
   Main Ideas and Supporting Details   1255
   Chronological Order   1256
   Comparison and Contrast   1257
   Cause and Effect   1258
   Problem-Solution   1259
FUNCTIONAL READING   1260
   Instruction Manual   1260
   Technical Manual   1261
   Product Advertisement   1262
   Product Manual   1263
   Pay Stub   1264
   Medicine Label   1265
   Passport Application   1266

UNIT ONE

Origins and *Encounters*

2000 B.C.–A.D. 1620

16

Native American Traditions
Part 1 **In Harmony with Nature**

INTERNET
CONNECTION

Time Line		18
Historical Background		20
Voices from the Times: PAWNEE		21

Iroquois	**The World on the Turtle's Back**	MYTH	24
Tewa	**Song of the Sky Loom**	SONG	33
Navajo	**Hunting Song/Dinni-e Sin**	SONG	33

Okanogan
retold by **Mourning Dove**
	Coyote Stories
	   Coyote and the Buffalo
	   Fox and Coyote and Whale
	      LITERATURE IN PERFORMANCE VIDEO
		
		FOLK TALE
		FOLK TALE
			39
			40
			43

Comparing Literature
Traditions Across Time: Harmonizing Old and New

Leslie Marmon Silko	**The Man to Send Rain Clouds** (1969)	SHORT STORY	48
N. Scott Momaday	*from* **The Way to Rainy Mountain** (1969)	NONFICTION	55
	Assessment Practice Comparing Literature		64
	Extend Your Reading		65

Accounts of Exploration and Exploitation

Part 2 First Encounters

INTERNET
CONNECTION

Historical Background		66
Voices from the Times: CHRISTOPHER COLUMBUS		67

Learning the Language of Literature: Historical Narratives		70

Álvar Núñez
Cabeza de Vaca — *from* **La Relación** — REPORT — 72

Link Across Cultures
Marco Polo — *from* **The Travels of Marco Polo** — TRAVELOGUE — 77

William Bradford — *from* **Of Plymouth Plantation** — CHRONICLE — 81

from **Women and Children First:
The Mayflower Pilgrims**
• READING FOR INFORMATION — MAGAZINE ARTICLE — 91

Olaudah Equiano — *from* **The Interesting Narrative of the Life
of Olaudah Equiano** — SLAVE NARRATIVE — 93

Comparing Literature
Traditions Across Time: The New Explorers

William Least
Heat Moon — *from* **Blue Highways** (1982) — TRAVELOGUE — 100

Maya Angelou — **My Sojourn in the Lands of My Ancestors** (1986) — AUTOBIOGRAPHY — 109

Assessment Practice Comparing Literature — 118

Extend Your Reading — 119

READING AND WRITING SKILLS
Reading for Information Primary and Secondary Sources — 91
Writing Workshop Eyewitness Report (Observation and Description) — 120
STUDENT MODEL Far from the Land of Opportunity — 121
REVISING SKILL Elaborating with Sensory Details — 124
EDITING SKILL Modifier Placement — 124
Assessment Practice Revising and Editing — 125
Building Vocabulary Building a Stronger Vocabulary — 126
Sentence Crafting Achieving Sentence Variety — 127

UNIT WRAP-UP
Reflect and Assess — 128

UNIT TWO

From *Colony* To *Country*
1620 — 1800

130

The Puritan Tradition
Part 1 Between Heaven and Hell

INTERNET
CONNECTION

Time Line	132
Historical Background	134
Voices from the Times: from *THE NEW ENGLAND PRIMER*	136

Anne Bradstreet	**To My Dear and Loving Husband** • GUIDE FOR READING	POETRY	138
	Upon the Burning of Our House, July 10th, 1666 • GUIDE FOR READING	POETRY	138
Salem Court Documents, 1692	**The Examination of Sarah Good**	DOCUMENTS	144
	History Clashes with Commercialism • READING FOR INFORMATION	NEWSPAPER ARTICLE	150
Jonathan Edwards	*from* **Sinners in the Hands of an Angry God**	SERMON	152

Comparing Literature
Traditions Across Time: Another Look at the Puritans

	Learning the Language of Literature: The Conventions of Drama		161
Arthur Miller	**The Crucible** (1953)	DRAMA	163
	Assessment Practice Comparing Literature		246

Extend Your Reading	247

READING AND WRITING SKILLS

Reading for Information Distinguishing Fact from Opinion	150
Writing Workshop Critical Review (Responding to Literature)	248
PROFESSIONAL MODEL Review of *The Crucible* by Scott Renshaw	249
REVISING SKILL Avoiding Circular Reasoning	252
EDITING SKILL Eliminating Qualifiers	252
Assessment Practice Revising and Editing	253
Building Vocabulary Interpreting Analogies	254
Sentence Crafting Using Gerunds	255

Writers in the Time of Revolution

Part 2 The Right to Be Free

INTERNET
CONNECTION

Historical Background		256
Voices from the Times: THOMAS JEFFERSON, THOMAS PAINE, JOHN ADAMS, BENJAMIN FRANKLIN		257

	Learning the Language of Literature: Persuasive Rhetoric		260
Patrick Henry	**Speech in the Virginia Convention** • GUIDE FOR READING	SPEECH	262
Thomas Jefferson	**The Declaration of Independence** • GUIDE FOR READING	DOCUMENT	270
Olympe de Gouges	*Link Across Cultures* *from* **The Declaration of the Rights of Woman**	DOCUMENT	277
Phillis Wheatley	**Letter to the Rev. Samson Occom**	LETTER	282
Abigail Adams	**Letter to John Adams**	LETTER	282
Michel-Guillaume Jean de Crèvecoeur	**What Is an American?**	ESSAY	289
Benjamin Franklin	*Literary Link* *from* **Poor Richard's Almanack**	APHORISMS	292
Red Jacket	**Lecture to a Missionary**	SPEECH	295

Comparing Literature
Traditions Across Time: Demands for Equal Rights

Martin Luther King, Jr.	*from* **Stride Toward Freedom** (1958)	NONFICTION	300
Malcolm X *interviewed by* **Les Crane**	**Necessary to Protect Ourselves** (1964)	INTERVIEW	300
Rodolfo Gonzales	*from* **I Am Joaquín/Yo Soy Joaquín** (1967)	POETRY	309
	Assessment Practice Comparing Literature		318
	Extend Your Reading		319

READING AND WRITING SKILLS		
Writing Workshop Persuasion		320
STUDENT MODEL Security Cameras in Schools		321
REVISING SKILL Supporting Personal Opinions with Facts		324
EDITING SKILL Pronoun-Antecedent Agreement		324
Assessment Practice Revising and Editing		325
Building Vocabulary Using Context Clues		326
Sentence Crafting Using Verb Tenses in Sequence		327

UNIT WRAP-UP		
Reflect and Assess		328
Reading and Writing for Assessment		330

UNIT THREE

The *Spirit* of *Individualism*
1800–1855

336

Romanticism and Transcendentalism

Part 1 Celebrations of the Self

INTERNET
CONNECTION

Time Line	338
Historical Background	340
Voices from the Times: WILLIAM CULLEN BRYANT, HENRY WADSWORTH	341
LONGFELLOW, WALT WHITMAN, RALPH WALDO EMERSON, HERMAN MELVILLE	

Henry Wadsworth Longfellow	**A Psalm of Life**	POETRY	344
Washington Irving	**The Devil and Tom Walker**	SHORT STORY	349
Ralph Waldo Emerson	*from* **Self-Reliance** • GUIDE FOR READING	ESSAY	363
Margaret Fuller	*Literary Link* *from* **Memoirs**	POETRY	366
Henry David Thoreau	*from* **Civil Disobedience** • GUIDE FOR READING	ESSAY	369
Mohandas K. Gandhi	*Link Across Cultures* **On Civil Disobedience**	SPEECH	377
Henry David Thoreau	*from* **Walden** • GUIDE FOR READING	ESSAY	381
	Learning the Language of Literature: Form in Poetry		394
Walt Whitman	*Selected Poems* **I Hear America Singing** **I Sit and Look Out** • GUIDE FOR READING *from* **Song of Myself** • GUIDE FOR READING	POETRY	396 397 399 400

Pablo Neruda	*Link Across Cultures* **Ode to Walt Whitman**	POETRY	406

Comparing Literature
Traditions Across Time: Whitman's Heirs Express the Self

William Carlos Williams	**Danse Russe** (1916)	POETRY	410
E. E. Cummings	**anyone lived in a pretty how town** (1940)	POETRY	410
Aurora Levins Morales *and* **Rosario Morales**	**Ending Poem** (1986)	POETRY	416
Luis J. Rodriguez	**Tía Chucha** (1991)	POETRY	416
Garrison Keillor	**Gary Keillor** (1993)	SHORT STORY	424
	Assessment Practice Comparing Literature		436
	Extend Your Reading		437

READING AND WRITING SKILLS

Writing Workshop Reflective Essay (Personal and Reflective)	438
STUDENT MODEL Eternally Slow	439
REVISING SKILL Avoiding Clichés	442
EDITING SKILL Possessives and Plurals	442
Assessment Practice Revising and Editing	443
Building Vocabulary Analyzing Word Parts—Roots	444
Sentence Crafting Using Adjectives and Adjective Phrases	445

American Gothic

Part 2　The Dark Side of Individualism

Historical Background		**446**
Voices from the Times: CHARLES BROCKDEN BROWN,		**447**
JAMES KIRKE PAULDING, EDGAR ALLAN POE, NATHANIEL HAWTHORNE, H. P. LOVECRAFT		

Edgar Allan Poe	Author Study		
	Life and Times		450
	INTERNET CONNECTION		
	The Masque of the Red Death	SHORT STORY	454
	• GUIDE FOR READING		
	from **Danse Macabre,** *by* **Stephen King**	ESSAY	464
	The Raven	POETRY	466
	The Fall of the House of Usher	SHORT STORY	473
	• GUIDE FOR READING		
	Link Across Cultures		
NETACTIVITIES: Author Exploration	**Spleen LXXXI,** *by* **Charles Baudelaire**	POETRY	495
	The Author's Style		497
Nathaniel Hawthorne	**Dr. Heidegger's Experiment**	SHORT STORY	500
	• GUIDE FOR READING		
	Literary Link		
Herman Melville	**Monody (Elegy for Nathaniel Hawthorne)**	POETRY	513

Comparing Literature
Traditions Across Time: Southern Gothic

William Faulkner	**A Rose for Emily** (1930)	SHORT STORY	516
	LITERATURE IN PERFORMANCE VIDEO		
Flannery O'Connor	**The Life You Save May Be Your Own** (1953)	SHORT STORY	528
	• ACTIVE READING SUPPORT		
	Assessment Practice Comparing Literature		542
	Extend Your Reading		543

READING AND WRITING SKILLS

Writing Workshop Short Story (Narrative and Literary)	544
STUDENT MODEL Reunited	545
REVISING SKILL Using Dialogue	548
EDITING SKILL Punctuating Dialogue	548
Assessment Practice Revising and Editing	549
Building Vocabulary Using Word Origins to Learn New Words	550
Sentence Crafting Using Adverbs and Adverb Phrases	551

UNIT WRAP-UP

Reflect and Assess	552

UNIT FOUR

Conflict
and *Expansion*
1850–1900

554

Slavery and the Civil War
Part 1 **A House Divided**

INTERNET
CONNECTION

Time Line		556
Historical Background		558
Voices from the Times: HENRY DAVID THOREAU,		559

ROBERT E. LEE, MARY BOYKIN CHESNUT, ABRAHAM LINCOLN,
CLARA BARTON, WILLIAM TECUMSEH SHERMAN, WALT WHITMAN

Frederick Douglass	*from* **Narrative of the Life of Frederick Douglass, an American Slave**	SLAVE NARRATIVE	562
James Russell Lowell	**Stanzas on Freedom**	POETRY	574
Frances Ellen Watkins Harper	**Free Labor**	POETRY	574
Ambrose Bierce	**An Occurrence at Owl Creek Bridge** • ACTIVE READING SUPPORT	SHORT STORY	580
Sullivan Ballou	*Literary Link* **Letter to Sarah Ballou**	LETTER	590
Stephen Crane	**A Mystery of Heroism**	SHORT STORY	593
Abraham Lincoln	**The Gettysburg Address**	SPEECH	605

Comparing Literature
Traditions Across Time: The Civil Rights Movement

Anne Moody	*from* **Coming of Age in Mississippi** (1968)	AUTOBIOGRAPHY	609
Robert Hayden	*Literary Link* **Frederick Douglass** (1962)	POETRY	615
Dudley Randall	**Ballad of Birmingham** (1969)	POETRY	618
	Assessment Practice Comparing Literature		622
	Extend Your Reading		623

XV

READING AND WRITING SKILLS
Writing Workshop Literary Interpretation (Responding to Literature)   624
    STUDENT MODEL *The Red Badge of Courage*   625
    REVISING SKILL Conclusions   628
    EDITING SKILL Verb Tense   628
Assessment Practice Revising and Editing   629
Building Vocabulary Comprehending Words with Multiple Meanings   630
Sentence Crafting Creating Compound Sentences   631

The Vanishing Frontier

Part 2   Tricksters and Trailblazers

INTERNET
CONNECTION

Historical Background   632
Voices from the Times: WHITE THUNDER, BLACK ELK,   633
PAUL ROBERT WALKER

Learning the Language of Literature: Setting in Regional Literature   636

retold by
José Griego y Maestas   **The Indian and the Hundred Cows/**   FOLK TALE   638
translated by   **El Indito de las Cien Vacas**
Rudolfo A. Anaya

Black Elk   **High Horse's Courting**   FOLK TALE   645
told through **John G. Neihardt**   *from* **Black Elk Speaks**

Literary Link
Chief Joseph   **I Will Fight No More Forever**   SPEECH   651

Mark Twain   **Author Study**

   Life and Times   654
     INTERNET CONNECTION

   from **The Autobiography of Mark Twain**   AUTOBIOGRAPHY   658

   from **Life on the Mississippi**   MEMOIR   669
     LITERATURE IN PERFORMANCE VIDEO

   Epigrams   EPIGRAMS   678

   The Notorious Jumping Frog of Calaveras County   SHORT STORY   679

   The First Jumping Frog   NEWSPAPER ARTICLE   684

   The Author's Style   686

NETACTIVITIES:
Author Exploration

Willa Cather   **A Wagner Matinee**   SHORT STORY   688

Elinore Pruitt Stewart   *from* **Letters of a Woman Homesteader**   LETTER   700
   • READING FOR INFORMATION

Comparing Literature
Traditions Across Time: Writing of the New West

Américo Paredes   **The Legend of Gregorio Cortez** (1973)   LEGEND   702

Assessment Practice Comparing Literature   720

Extend Your Reading   721

READING AND WRITING SKILLS
Reading for Information Evaluating an Argument   700
Communication Workshop Storytelling (Speaking and Listening)   722
  A Storyteller in Action   723
  Analyzing a Storytelling Script   724
  Preparing to Tell a Story   725
Assessment Practice Revising and Editing   727
Building Vocabulary Homophones, Homographs, and Homonyms   728
Sentence Crafting Using Adjective and Adverb Clauses   729

UNIT WRAP-UP
Reflect and Assess   730
Reading and Writing for Assessment   732

Cliffs Beyond Abiquiu, Dry Waterfall (1943), Georgia O'Keeffe. Oil on canvas, 76.2 cm × 40.6 cm. The Cleveland (Ohio) Museum of Art, bequest of Georgia O'Keeffe (87.141). Copyright © 1996 The Georgia O'Keeffe Foundation/Artists Rights Society (ARS), New York. Photo Copyright © The Cleveland Museum of Art.

UNIT FIVE The *Changing Face of America* 1855–1925

738

A New Literature

Part 1 Women's Voices, Women's Lives

INTERNET
CONNECTION

Time Line	740
Historical Background	742
Voices from the Times: SOJOURNER TRUTH	743

Emily Dickinson | **Author Study**

Life and Times		746
INTERNET CONNECTION		
Selected Poems		750
• GUIDE FOR READING		
This is my letter to the World	POETRY	751
"Hope" is the thing with feathers—	POETRY	752
Success is counted sweetest	POETRY	753
Much Madness is divinest Sense	POETRY	754
Letter to Thomas Wentworth Higginson	LETTER	755
My life closed twice before its close—	POETRY	756
After great pain, a formal feeling comes—	POETRY	757
I heard a Fly buzz—when I died—	POETRY	758
Because I could not stop for Death—	POETRY	759
The Author's Style		761
LITERATURE IN PERFORMANCE VIDEO		

NETACTIVITIES:
Author Exploration

Learning the Language of Literature: Social Themes in Fiction		763

Charlotte Perkins Gilman	The Yellow Wallpaper	SHORT STORY	765
	• ACTIVE READING SUPPORT		
Barbara Ehrenreich *and* **Deirdre English**	*from* Complaints and Disorders	HISTORICAL BACKGROUND	782
	• READING FOR INFORMATION		
Kate Chopin	The Story of an Hour	SHORT STORY	783
	LITERATURE IN PERFORMANCE VIDEO		

Comparing Literature
Traditions Across Time: A Diversity of Voices

Hisaye Yamamoto	Seventeen Syllables (1949)	SHORT STORY	788
Rita Dove	Adolescence—III (1980)	POETRY	802
Tillie Olsen	I Stand Here Ironing (1956)	SHORT STORY	806
	Literary Link		
Julia Alvarez	Ironing Their Clothes (1986)	POETRY	814
	Assessment Practice Comparing Literature		818

Extend Your Reading			819

READING AND WRITING SKILLS
Reading for Information Finding Evidence			782

Illusion or Reality?
Part 2 The American Dream

INTERNET
CONNECTION

Historical Background		820
Voices from the Times: CARL SANDBURG, ALEXIS DE TOCQUEVILLE,		821

JOHN D. ROCKEFELLER, CALVIN COOLIDGE, THEODORE DREISER,

EUGENE O'NEILL, EMMA LAZARUS, ISRAEL ZANGWILL

Carl Sandburg	**Chicago**	POETRY	824
Edgar Lee Masters	**Lucinda Matlock**	POETRY	824
Edwin Arlington Robinson	**Richard Cory**	POETRY	830
	Miniver Cheevy	POETRY	830
Paul Laurence Dunbar	**We Wear the Mask**	POETRY	835
	Sympathy	POETRY	835
F. Scott Fitzgerald	**Winter Dreams**	SHORT STORY	840
	• ACTIVE READING SUPPORT		
Anzia Yezierska	**America and I**	SHORT STORY	863
	The New Immigrants	HISTORICAL	875
	• READING FOR INFORMATION	BACKGROUND	

Comparing Literature
Traditions Across Time: Dreams Lost and Found

Gish Jen	**In the American Society** (1986)	SHORT STORY	877
	Literary Link		
Naomi Shihab Nye	**My Father and the Figtree** (1980)	POETRY	891
Yvonne Sapia	**Defining the Grateful Gesture** (1986)	POETRY	894
Lorna Dee Cervantes	**Refugee Ship** (1982)	POETRY	894
	Assessment Practice Comparing Literature		900

Extend Your Reading			901

READING AND WRITING SKILLS
Reading for Information Comparing Text and Graphic Information	875
Writing Workshop Comparison-and-Contrast Essay	902
(Informative Exposition)	
STUDENT MODEL Antigua: Almost Paradise	903
REVISING SKILL Parallel Construction	906
EDITING SKILL Modifiers	906
Assessment Practice Revising and Editing	907
Building Vocabulary Recognizing Denotations and Connotations	908
Sentence Crafting Using Noun Clauses	909

UNIT WRAP-UP
Reflect and Assess	910

UNIT SIX The *Modern Age* 1900–1940

912

The Harlem Renaissance
Part 1 A New Cultural Identity

INTERNET
CONNECTION

Time Line	914
Historical Background	916
Voices from the Times: JAMES WELDON JOHNSON,	917

W. E. B. DU BOIS, LANGSTON HUGHES, ALAIN LOCKE, LOUIS ARMSTRONG,
CARL VAN DOREN, MARCUS GARVEY

Langston Hughes	**Author Study**		

NETACTIVITIES:
Author Exploration

Life and Times			920
INTERNET CONNECTION			
Selected Poems			924
I, Too		POETRY	925
A Dream Deferred		POETRY	926
The Weary Blues		POETRY	927
Link Across Cultures			
Flute Players *by* Jean-Joseph Rabéarivelo		POETRY	930
from Love, Langston *by* Dahleen Glanton		NEWSPAPER ARTICLE	931
When the Negro Was in Vogue		MEMOIR	932
The Author's Style			938

James Weldon Johnson	**My City**	POETRY	940
Countee Cullen	**Any Human to Another**	POETRY	940
Claude McKay	**If We Must Die**	POETRY	945
Arna Bontemps	**A Black Man Talks of Reaping**	POETRY	945
Zora Neale Hurston	**How It Feels to Be Colored Me**	ESSAY	950
Alice Walker	*Literary Link* *from* **Zora Neale Hurston: A Cautionary Tale and a Partisan View**	ESSAY	955

Comparing Literature
Traditions Across Time: Reaffirming Cultural Identity

James Baldwin	**My Dungeon Shook: Letter to My Nephew** (1962)	OPEN LETTER	959
Gwendolyn Brooks	**Life for My Child Is Simple** (1949)	POETRY	967
	Primer for Blacks (1980)	POETRY	967
Toni Morrison	**Thoughts on the African-American Novel** (1984)	LITERARY CRITICISM	973
	Assessment Practice Comparing Literature		978

Extend Your Reading	979

READING AND WRITING SKILLS
Writing Workshop Research Report 980
   STUDENT MODEL Zora Neale Hurston 981
    REVISING SKILL Elaborating—Details and Examples 988
    EDITING SKILL Using Commas 988
Assessment Practice Revising and Editing 989
Building Vocabulary Understanding Informal Language 990
Sentence Crafting Making Sentence Parts Parallel 991

Modernism

Part 2   **Alienation of the Individual**

INTERNET
CONNECTION

Historical Background 992
Voices from the Times: EZRA POUND, T. S. ELIOT, SINCLAIR LEWIS, 993
EDNA ST. VINCENT MILLAY, DOROTHY PARKER, THOMAS WOLFE,
ERNEST HEMINGWAY, GERTRUDE STEIN, LILLIAN HELLMAN

Robert Frost	**Author Study**		
	Life and Times		996
	INTERNET CONNECTION		
	Selected Poems		1000
	Acquainted with the Night	POETRY	1001
	Mending Wall	POETRY	1002
	• GUIDE FOR READING		
	"Out, Out—"	POETRY	1004
	The Death of the Hired Man	POETRY	1007
	• GUIDE FOR READING		
	In Praise of Robert Frost *by* **John F. Kennedy**	SPEECH	1012
NETACTIVITIES: Author Exploration	**The Author's Style**		1014
	Learning the Language of Literature: Modernism		1017
Ernest Hemingway	**The End of Something**	SHORT STORY	1018
T. S. Eliot	**The Love Song of J. Alfred Prufrock**	POETRY	1025
	• GUIDE FOR READING		
	Link Across Cultures		
Franz Kafka	*from* **The Diaries**	DIARY	1033
Katherine Anne Porter	**The Jilting of Granny Weatherall**	SHORT STORY	1035
Richard Wright	**The Man Who Was Almost a Man**	SHORT STORY	1045
	LITERATURE IN PERFORMANCE VIDEO		
	Comparing Literature		
	Traditions Across Time: The Lonely Self		
Sylvia Plath	**Mirror** (1963)	POETRY	1057
Anne Sexton	**Self in 1958** (1966)	POETRY	1057
	• GUIDE FOR READING		
	Assessment Practice Comparing Literature		1064
	Extend Your Reading		1065
	UNIT WRAP-UP		
	Reflect and Assess		1066

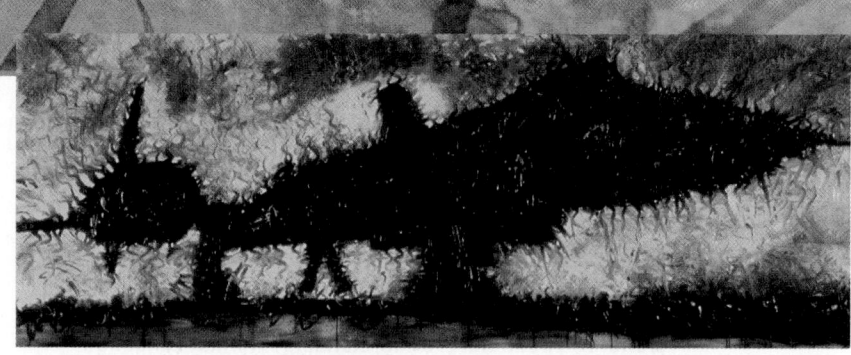

UNIT SEVEN *War Abroad*
and *Conflict at Home*
1940–PRESENT

1068

World War II
Part 1 Remembering the Wars

INTERNET
CONNECTION

Time Line		1070
Historical Background		1072
Voices from the Times: from "THE GOOD WAR":		1073
AN ORAL HISTORY OF WORLD WAR TWO BY STUDS TERKEL		

Bernard Malamud	**Armistice**	SHORT STORY	1076
	Link Across Cultures		
Primo Levi	*from* **Survival in Auschwitz**	MEMOIR	1083
Randall Jarrell	**The Death of the Ball Turret Gunner**	POETRY	1088
John Steinbeck	**Why Soldiers Won't Talk**	ESSAY	1088
Joan Didion	**Letter from Paradise, 21° 19′ N., 157° 52′ W.**	ESSAY	1095
Dwight Okita	**In Response to Executive Order 9066**	POETRY	1095
	Point/Counterpoint: The Japanese-American Internment	HISTORICAL BACKGROUND	1103
	• READING FOR INFORMATION		

Comparing Literature
Traditions Across Time: War in Vietnam

Tim O'Brien	**Ambush** (1990)	SHORT STORY	1105
Yusef Komunyakaa	**Camouflaging the Chimera** (1988)	POETRY	1111
	• GUIDE FOR READING		
Wendy Wilder Larsen and Tran Thi Nga	**Deciding** (1986)	POETRY	1111
	• GUIDE FOR READING		
Denise Levertov	**At the Justice Department, November 15, 1969** (1969)	POETRY	1118
	Assessment Practice Comparing Literature		1122
	Extend Your Reading		1123

READING AND WRITING SKILLS

Reading for Information Analyzing an Issue 1103

Communication Workshop Multimedia Exhibit (Using Technology) 1124

    Analyzing a Multimedia Exhibit 1125

    Creating Your Multimedia Exhibit 1126

Assessment Practice Revising and Editing 1129

Building Vocabulary Analyzing Word Parts—Affixes 1130

Sentence Crafting Using Sentence Closers 1131

Postwar Society

Part 2 Integration and Disintegration

INTERNET
CONNECTION

Historical Background 1132

Voices from the Times: MARTIN LUTHER KING, JR., BETTY FRIEDAN, 1133
WILLIAM H. WHYTE, JR., BOB DYLAN, DR. BENJAMIN SPOCK, WING TEK LUM

Martin Luther King, Jr.	from **Letter from Birmingham Jail**	LETTER	1136
	Literary Link		
Nikki Giovanni	**Revolutionary Dreams**	POETRY	1145
	Learning the Language of Literature: **Tone in Contemporary Literature**		1148
Lanford Wilson	**Wandering**	DRAMA	1150
E. L. Doctorow	**The Writer in the Family**	SHORT STORY	1157
Anne Tyler	**Teenage Wasteland**	SHORT STORY	1168
John Updike	**Separating**	SHORT STORY	1180
Gary Soto	**Mexicans Begin Jogging**	POETRY	1194
Pat Mora	**Legal Alien**	POETRY	1194

Comparing Literature
Traditions Across Time: Continuing Transformation

Joyce Carol Oates	**Hostage** (1991)	SHORT STORY	1200
	Literary Link		
Garrett Hongo	**The Legend** (1988)	POETRY	1210
Amy Tan	**Mother Tongue** (1990)	ESSAY	1215
Judith Ortiz Cofer	**The Latin Deli: An Ars Poetica** (1991)	POETRY	1223
Sandra Cisneros	**Straw into Gold: The Metamorphosis** **of the Everyday** (1987)	ESSAY	1227
	Assessment Practice Comparing Literature		1234
	Extend Your Reading		1235

UNIT WRAP-UP
Reflect and Assess 1236

Student *Resource Bank*

Reading Handbook 1240

    Reading for Different Purposes 1240

    Reading Different Genres 1242

    Reading Different Formats 1243

    Enriching Your Vocabulary 1244

    Reading for Information 1250

    Functional Reading 1260

Writing Handbook 1268

    The Writing Process 1268

    Building Blocks of Good Writing 1272

    Descriptive Writing 1277

    Narrative Writing 1279

    Explanatory Writing 1281

    Persuasive Writing 1285

    Research Report Writing 1287

    Business Writing 1293

Communication Handbook 1295

    Inquiry and Research 1295

    Study Skills and Strategies 1297

    Critical Thinking 1299

    Speaking and Listening 1300

    Viewing and Representing 1302

Grammar Handbook 1305

    Quick Reference: Parts of Speech 1305

    Nouns 1306

    Pronouns 1307

Verbs 1309

Modifiers 1312

Prepositions, Conjunctions, and Interjections 1314

Quick Reference: The Sentence and Its Parts 1316

The Sentence and Its Parts 1317

Phrases 1319

Verbals and Verbal Phrases 1319

Clauses 1321

The Structure of Sentences 1322

Writing Complete Sentences 1323

Subject-Verb Agreement 1324

Quick Reference: Punctuation 1327

Quick Reference: Capitalization 1329

Little Rules That Make a Big Difference 1330

Commonly Confused Words 1334

Grammar Glossary 1335

Glossary of Literary Terms 1342

Glossary of Words to Know in English and Spanish 1366

Pronunciation Key 1384

Index of Fine Art 1385

Index of Skills 1388

Index of Titles and Authors 1401

Acknowledgments 1405

Art Credits 1412

Selections by Genre

Folk Tales and Songs

Coyote and the Buffalo 40
Okanogan

Fox and Coyote and Whale 43
Okanogan

High Horse's Courting *from* **Black Elk Speaks** 645
Black Elk

Hunting Song/Dinni-e Sin 33
Navajo

Song of the Sky Loom 33
Tewa

The World on the Turtle's Back 24
Iroquois

Fiction

Ambush 1105
Tim O'Brien

America and I 863
Anzia Yezierska

Armistice 1076
Bernard Malamud

The Devil and Tom Walker 349
Washington Irving

Dr. Heidegger's Experiment 500
Nathaniel Hawthorne

Hostage 1200
Joyce Carol Oates

The End of Something 1018
Ernest Hemingway

The Fall of the House of Usher 473
Edgar Allan Poe

The First Jumping Frog 684

Gary Keillor 424
Garrison Keillor

I Stand Here Ironing 806
Tillie Olsen

In the American Society 877
Gish Jen

**The Indian and the Hundred Cows/El Indito
de las Cien Vacas** 638
José Griego y Maestas

The Jilting of Granny Weatherall 1035
Katherine Anne Porter

The Legend of Gregorio Cortez 702
Américo Paredes

The Life You Save May Be Your Own 528
Flannery O'Connor

The Man to Send Rain Clouds 48
Leslie Marmon Silko

The Man Who Was Almost a Man 1045
Richard Wright

The Masque of the Red Death 454
Edgar Allan Poe

A Mystery of Heroism 593
Stephen Crane

The Notorious Jumping Frog of Calaveras County . . . 679
Mark Twain

An Occurrence at Owl Creek Bridge 580
Ambrose Bierce

A Rose for Emily 516
William Faulkner

Separating 1180
John Updike

Seventeen Syllables 788
Hisaye Yamamoto

The Story of an Hour 783
Kate Chopin

Teenage Wasteland 1168
Anne Tyler

A Wagner Matinee 688
Willa Cather

Winter Dreams 840
F. Scott Fitzgerald

The Writer in the Family 1157
E. L. Doctorow

A Worn Path 8
Eudora Welty

The Yellow Wallpaper 765
Charlotte Perkins Gilman

Nonfiction

from **The Autobiography of Mark Twain** 658
Mark Twain

from **Blue Highways** 100
William Least Heat-Moon

from **Civil Disobedience** 369
Henry David Thoreau

from **Coming of Age in Mississippi** 609
Anne Moody

from **Complaints and Disorders** 782

from **Danse Macabre** 464
Stephen King

The Declaration of Independence 270
    Thomas Jefferson

from **The Declaration of the Rights of Woman** 277
    Olympe de Gouges

from **The Diaries** 1033
    Franz Kafka

Epigrams 678
    Mark Twain

The Examination of Sarah Good 144

The Gettysburg Address 605
    Abraham Lincoln

History Clashes with Commercialism 150

How It Feels to Be Colored Me 950
    Zora Neale Hurston

I Will Fight No More Forever 651
    Chief Joseph

In Praise of Robert Frost 1012
    John F. Kennedy

from **The Interesting Narrative of the Life
of Olaudah Equiano** 93
    Olaudah Equiano

Lecture to a Missionary 295
    Red Jacket

from **Letter from Birmingham Jail** 1136
    Martin Luther King, Jr.

Letter from Paradise, 21° 19′ N., 157° 52′ W. 1095
    Joan Didion

Letter to John Adams 282
    Abigail Adams

Letter to Sarah Ballou 590
    Sullivan Ballou

**Letter to Thomas Wentworth Higginson
(April 15, 1862)** 755
    Emily Dickinson

Letter to the Rev. Samson Occom 282
    Phillis Wheatley

from **Life on the Mississippi** 669
    Mark Twain

from **Love, Langston** 931
    Dahleen Glanton

Mother Tongue 1215
    Amy Tan

My Dungeon Shook: Letter to My Nephew 959
    James Baldwin

My Sojourn in the Lands of My Ancestors 109
    Maya Angelou

from **Narrative of the Life of Frederick Douglass,
an American Slave** 562
    Frederick Douglass

Necessary to Protect Ourselves 300
    Malcolm X

The New Immigrants 875

from **Of Plymouth Plantation** 81
    William Bradford

On Civil Disobedience 377
    Mohandas K. Gandhi

**Point/Counterpoint: The Japanese-American
Internment** 1103

from **Poor Richard's Almanack** 292
    Benjamin Franklin

from **La Relación** 72
    Álvar Núñez Cabeza de Vaca

from **Self-Reliance** 363
    Ralph Waldo Emerson

from **Sinners in the Hands of an Angry God** 152
    Jonathan Edwards

Speech in the Virginia Convention 262
    Patrick Henry

**Straw into Gold: The Metamorphosis
of the Everyday** 1227
    Sandra Cisneros

from **Stride Toward Freedom** 300
    Martin Luther King, Jr.

from **Survival in Auschwitz** 1083
    Primo Levi

Thoughts on the African-American Novel 973
    Toni Morrison

from **The Travels of Marco Polo** 77

from **Walden** 381
    Henry David Thoreau

from **The Way to Rainy Mountain** 55
    N. Scott Momaday

What Is an American? 289
    Michel-Guillaume Jean de Crèvecoeur

When the Negro Was in Vogue 932
    Langston Hughes

Why Soldiers Won't Talk 1088
    John Steinbeck

Women and Children First: The Mayflower Pilgrims . . 91

from **Zora Neale Hurston: A Cautionary Tale
and a Partisan View** 955
    Alice Walker

Poetry

Acquainted with the Night 1001
  Robert Frost

Adolescence—III 802
  Rita Dove

After great pain, a formal feeling comes— 757
  Emily Dickinson

Any Human to Another 940
  Countee Cullen

anyone lived in a pretty how town 410
  E. E. Cummings

At the Justice Department, November 15, 1969 1118
  Denise Levertov

Ballad of Birmingham 618
  Dudley Randall

Because I could not stop for Death— 759
  Emily Dickinson

A Black Man Talks of Reaping 945
  Arna Bontemps

Camouflaging the Chimera 1111
  Yusef Komunyakaa

Chicago 824
  Carl Sandburg

Danse Russe 410
  William Carlos Williams

The Death of the Ball Turret Gunner 1088
  Randall Jarrell

The Death of the Hired Man 1007
  Robert Frost

Deciding 1111
  Wendy Wilder Larsen and Tran Thi Nga

Defining the Grateful Gesture 894
  Yvonne Sapia

Ending Poem 416
  Aurora Levins Morales and Rosario Morales

Flute Players 930
  Jean Joseph Rabéarivelo

Frederick Douglass 615
  Robert Hayden

Free Labor 574
  Frances Ellen Watkins Harper

Harlem 926
  Langston Hughes

"Hope" is the thing with feathers— 752
  Emily Dickinson

from I Am Joaquín/Yo Soy Joaquín 309
  Rodolfo Gonzales

I Hear America Singing 397
  Walt Whitman

I Heard a Fly buzz—when I died— 758
  Emily Dickinson

I Sit and Look Out 399
  Walt Whitman

I, Too 925
  Langston Hughes

If We Must Die 945
  Claude McKay

In Response to Executive Order 9066 1095
  Dwight Okita

Ironing Their Clothes 814
  Julia Alvarez

The Latin Deli: An Ars Poetica 1223
  Judith Ortiz Cofer

Legal Alien 1194
  Pat Mora

The Legend 1210
  Garrett Hongo

Life for My Child Is Simple 967
  Gwendolyn Brooks

The Love Song of J. Alfred Prufrock 1025
  T. S. Eliot

Lucinda Matlock 824
  Edgar Lee Masters

from Memoirs 366
  Margaret Fuller

Mending Wall 1002
  Robert Frost

Mexicans Begin Jogging 1194
  Gary Soto

Miniver Cheevy 830
  Edwin Arlington Robinson

Mirror 1057
  Sylvia Plath

Monody (Elegy for Nathaniel Hawthorne) 513
  Herman Melville

Much Madness is divinest Sense— 754
  Emily Dickinson

My City 940
  James Weldon Johnson

My Father and the Figtree 891
  Naomi Shihab Nye

My life closed twice before its close— 756
    Emily Dickinson

Ode to Walt Whitman 406
    Pablo Neruda

"Out, Out—" 1004
    Robert Frost

Primer for Blacks 967
    Gwendolyn Brooks

A Psalm of Life 344
    Henry Wadsworth Longfellow

The Raven 466
    Edgar Allan Poe

Refugee Ship 894
    Lorna Dee Cervantes

Revolutionary Dreams 1145
    Nikki Giovanni

Richard Cory 830
    Edwin Arlington Robinson

Self in 1958 1057
    Anne Sexton

from **Song of Myself** 400
    Walt Whitman

Spleen LXXXI 495
    Charles Baudelaire

Stanzas on Freedom 574
    James Russell Lowell

Success is counted sweetest 753
    Emily Dickinson

Sympathy 835
    Paul Laurence Dunbar

Tía Chucha 416
    Luis J. Rodriguez

This is my letter to the World 751
    Emily Dickinson

To My Dear and Loving Husband 138
    Anne Bradstreet

Upon the Burning of Our House, July 10th,1666 138
    Anne Bradstreet

We Wear the Mask 835
    Paul Laurence Dunbar

The Weary Blues 927
    Langston Hughes

Drama

The Crucible 163
    Arthur Miller

Wandering 1150
    Lanford Wilson

Electronic Library

The *Electronic Library* is a CD-ROM that contains additional fiction, nonfiction, poetry, and drama for each unit in *The Language of Literature.* Here is a sampling from the titles included in Grade 11.

What Happened Till the First Supply, *from* The General History of Virginia
    John Smith

Huswifery
    Edward Taylor

from Common Sense
    Thomas Paine

Rip Van Winkle
    Washington Irving

Thanatopsis
    William Cullen Bryant

Hymn at Concord Monument
    Ralph Waldo Emerson

Conclusion, *from* Walden
    Henry David Thoreau

Walden
    E. B. White

The Minster's Black Veil
    Nathaniel Hawthorne

Bartleby, the Scrivener
    Herman Melville

Swing Low, Sweet Chariot
    Negro Spiritual

Farewell to His Army
    Robert E. Lee

O Captain! My Captain!
    Walt Whitman

The Outcasts of Poker Flat
    Bret Harte

The Open Boat
    Stephen Crane

Disappointment Is the Lot of Women
    Lucy Stone

Roman Fever
    Edith Wharton

Beehive
    Jean Toomer

Sophistication
    Sherwood Anderson

He
    Katherine Anne Porter

Special Features in This Book

Author Study

Edgar Allan Poe 450

Mark Twain 654

Emily Dickinson 746

Langston Hughes 920

Robert Frost 996

Learning the Language of Literature

Historical Narratives 70

The Conventions of Drama 161

Persuasive Rhetoric 260

Form in Poetry 394

Setting in Regional Literature 636

Social Themes in Fiction 763

Modernism 1017

Tone in Contemporary Literature . . 1148

Links Across Cultures

from The Travels of Marco Polo 77

from The Declaration of the
Rights of Woman 277
    Olympe de Gouges

On Civil Disobedience 377
    Mohandas K. Gandhi

Ode to Walt Whitman 406
    Pablo Neruda

Spleen LXXXI 495
    Charles Baudelaire

Flute Players 930
    Jean-Joseph Rabéarivelo

from The Diaries 1033
    Franz Kafka

from Survival in Auschwitz 1083
    Primo Levi

Related Readings

Women and Children First:
The Mayflower Pilgrims 91
    Primary and Secondary Sources

History Clashes with
Commercialism 150
    Distinguishing Fact from Opinion

from Letters of a Woman
Homesteader 700
    Evaluating an Argument

from Complaints and Disorders 782
    Finding Evidence

The New Immigrants 875
    Comparing Text and Graphic Information

Point/Counterpoint: The
Japanese-American Internment . . . 1103
    Analyzing an Issue

Writing Workshop

Eyewitness Report 120

Critical Review 248

Persuasion 320

Reflective Essay 438

Short Story 544

Literary Interpretation 624

Comparison-and-Contrast Essay . . . 902

Research Report 980

Communication Workshops

Storytelling 722

Multimedia Exhibit 1124

Building Vocabulary

Building a Stronger Vocabulary 126

Interpreting Analogies 254

Using Context Clues 326

Analyzing Word Parts—Roots 444

Using Word Origins to
Learn New Words 550

Comprehending Words with
Multiple Meanings 630

Homophones, Homographs,
and Homonyms 728

Recognizing Denotations
and Connotations 908

Understanding Informal Language . . 990

Analyzing Word Parts—Affixes . . . 1130

Sentence Crafting

Achieving Sentence Variety 127

Using Gerunds 255

Using Verb Tenses in Sequence 327

Using Adjectives and
Adjective Phrases 445

Using Adverbs and Adverb Phrases . 551

Creating Compound Sentences 631

Using Adjective and
Adverb Clauses 729

Using Noun Clauses 909

Making Sentence Parts Parallel 991

Using Sentence Closers 1131

Assessment Pages

Comparing Literature: Assessment
Practice 64, 118, 246, 318, 436,
    542, 622, 720, 818, 900, 978, 1064,
    1122, 1234

Assessment Practice: Revising
and Editing 125, 253, 325,
    443, 549, 629, 727, 907, 989, 1129

Reading and Writing
for Assessment 330, 732

Traditions Across Time

The legacy of America is a legacy of traditions—trends, themes, and issues that have occurred throughout our history. The literature of America reflects these traditions, serving as a record of the conflicts, failures, and triumphs of a country and its people. Look at the images and quotations below. What kinds of issues and themes are represented?

Clockwise from top: Civil War soldiers; Vietnam War soldiers; World War II soldiers

"A Bayonet's contrition is nothing to the Dead."

Emily Dickinson
19th-century poet

"Never think that war, no matter how necessary, nor how justified, is not a crime."

Ernest Hemingway
20th-century novelist

"Though the flame of liberty may sometimes cease to shine, the coal can never expire."

Thomas Paine
18th-century patriot

Clockwise from top:
Thomas Paine;
Frederick Douglass;
Martin Luther King, Jr.

"Oppressed people cannot remain oppressed forever. The yearning for freedom eventually manifests itself."

Martin Luther King, Jr.
20th-century political activist

- **How can literature teach you about the traditions and issues of American culture?**
- **How can a piece of literature from generations ago still capture our imaginations, our minds, and our emotions?**
- **How can YOU find relevance in literature from earlier times?**

The answers lie on the next few pages.

Get Involved with the Literature

*Think of any activity you enjoy—sports, music, traveling, painting.
How did you really learn to understand and appreciate it? By watching
others, or by participating yourself? Just about any activity is richer, more
interesting, and more exciting when you are actively involved. The same is
true with literature. You can't simply sit back and absorb the words on a page.
You have to jump into the stories and participate.*

Your Reader's Notebook

Almost any kind of notebook can be used to help you
interact with literature. Use your Reader's Notebook
to keep track of what's going on inside your mind as
you read. Here are three ways to interact.

❶ Record Your Thoughts

In your 📖 **READER'S NOTEBOOK**, jot
down ideas, responses, connections,
and questions before, while, and after
you read a selection. (See "Strategies
for Reading," page 7.) Summarize
important passages, and include
sketches and charts, too, if they will
help. If you wish, compare your ideas
with those of a classmate.

*"A Worn Path"
by Eudora Welty*

*(page 7) The old woman closed her eyes, yet she made it
across the log. How was she able to do that?*

*(page 13) On one level, this story makes me feel sorry for
the old woman. But I'm also so amazed at how strong-
willed and determined she is. I feel like she's a real survivor.*

READING MODEL

Alongside "A Worn Path" are transcripts of the spoken comments made by two
11th-grade students, Robert Lewis and Gesenia Veizaga, while they were reading
the story. Their comments provide a glimpse into the minds of readers actively
engaged in the process of reading. You'll notice that in the course of their reading,
Robert and Gesenia quite naturally used the Strategies for Reading that were
introduced on page 7.

To benefit most from this model of active reading, read the story first, jotting
down your own responses in your reading log. (Cover up the side comments with
a sheet of paper if you're tempted to peek.) Then read Robert's and Gesenia's
comments and compare their processes of reading with your own.

A Worn Path
EUDORA WELTY

Detail of *Sharecropper* (1970),
Elizabeth Catlett. Linoleum cut on paper,
National Museum of American Art,
Smithsonian Institution, Washington
D.C./Art Resource, New York.

It was December—a bright frozen day in the early morning. Far out
in the country there was an old Negro woman with her head tied
in a red rag, coming along a path through the pinewoods. Her
name was Phoenix Jackson. She was very old and small and she
walked slowly in the dark pine shadows, moving a little from side
to side in her steps, with the balanced heaviness and lightness of a
pendulum in a grandfather clock. She carried a thin, small cane made
from an umbrella, and with this she kept tapping the frozen earth in
front of her. This made a grave and persistent noise in the still air,
that seemed meditative like the chirping of a solitary little bird.

Robert: *That's a neat image comparing
her to a pendulum. I wonder if that
means she measures time somehow.*
EVALUATING/QUESTIONING

She wore a dark striped dress reaching down to her shoe tops, and
an equally long apron of bleached sugar sacks, with a full pocket: all
neat and tidy, but every time she took a step she might have fallen
over her shoelaces, which dragged from her unlaced shoes. She looked
straight ahead. Her eyes were blue with age. Her skin had a pattern
all its own of numberless branching wrinkles and as though a whole

Gesenia: *But she's so tidy. Why
would she be sloppy with her shoes?*
QUESTIONING

READING MODEL

❷ Improve Your Reading Skills

Complete the specific 📖 READER'S NOTEBOOK activity on the first page of each literature lesson. This activity will help you apply an important skill as you read the selection.

❸ Collect Ideas for Writing

Be aware of intriguing themes, passages, and thoughts of your own as you read or complete follow-up activities. In a special section of your 📖 READER'S NOTEBOOK, jot down anything that may later be a springboard to your own writing.

little tree stood in the middle of her forehead, but a golden color ran underneath, and the two knobs of her cheeks were illumined by a yellow burning under the dark. Under the red rag her hair came down on her neck in the frailest of ringlets, still black, and with an odor like copper.

Now and then there was a quivering in the thicket. Old Phoenix said, "Out of my way, all you foxes, owls, beetles, jack rabbits, coons and wild animals! . . . Keep out from under these feet, little bob-whites. . . . Keep the big wild hogs out of my path. Don't let none of those come running my direction. I got a long way." Under her small black-freckled hand her cane, limber as a buggy whip, would switch at the brush as if to rouse up any hiding things.

On she went. The woods were deep and still. The sun made the pine needles almost too bright to look at, up where the wind rocked. The cones dropped as light as feathers. Down in the hollow was the mourning dove—it was not too late for him.

The path ran up a hill. "Seem like there is chains about my feet, time I get this far," she said, in the voice of argument old people keep to use with themselves. "Something always take a hold of me on this hill—pleads I should stay."

After she got to the top she turned and gave a full, severe look behind her where she had come. "Up through pines," she said at length. "Now down through oaks."

Her eyes opened their widest, and she started down gently. But before she got to the bottom of the hill a bush caught her dress.

Her fingers were busy and intent, but her skirts were full and long, so that before she could pull them free in one place they were caught in another. It was not possible to allow the dress to tear. "I in the thorny bush," she said. "Thorns, you doing your appointed work. Never want to let folks pass, no sir. Old eyes thought you was a pretty little *green* bush."

Finally, trembling all over, she stood free, and for a moment dared to stoop for her cane.

"Sun so high!" she cried, leaning back and looking, while the thick tears went over her eyes. "The time getting all gone here."

At the foot of this hill was a place where a log was laid across the creek.

"Now comes the trial," said Phoenix.

Putting her right foot out, she mounted the log and shut her eyes. Lifting her skirt, leveling her cane fiercely before her, like a festival figure in some parade, she began to march across. Then she opened her eyes and she was safe on the other side.

"I wasn't as old as I thought," she said.

But she sat down to rest. She spread her skirts on the bank around her and folded her hands over her knees. Up above her was a tree in a pearly cloud of mistletoe. She did not dare to close her eyes, and when a little boy brought her a plate with a slice of marble-cake on it

---

Gesenia: You can really picture her skin color from this description.
VISUALIZING

Robert: Phoenix seems like a down-to-earth person. She just goes about her business.
EVALUATING

Robert: Phoenix has made this trip before.
CLARIFYING

Gesenia: This author uses a lot of description. I'd better pay attention to details so I get a clear picture of what's happening in this story.
MONITORING

Gesenia: She's not grumpy like some old people. She sees that the thorns are just doing what they do. It doesn't make her mad.
EVALUATING/CONNECTING

Gesenia: Why would she close her eyes? Usually that's for when you do something for the first time, and she's been here before.
QUESTIONING/CONNECTING

A WORN PATH   **9**

"A Worn Path"
by Eudora Welty

Writing Ideas
The author is so good at describing this woman and what she goes through minute by minute. I'd like to try writing a character sketch of a person and using this much detail. It makes the woman seem so real.

Your Working Portfolio

Artists and writers keep portfolios in which they store works in progress or the works they are most proud of. Your portfolio can be a folder, a box, or a notebook—the form doesn't matter. Just make sure to keep adding to it—with drafts of your writing experiments, summaries of your projects, and your own goals and accomplishments as a reader and writer. Later in this book, on the Reflect and Assess pages, you will choose your best or favorite work to place in a **Presentation Portfolio.**

Become an Active Reader

The strategies you need to become an active reader are already within your grasp. In fact, you use them every day to make sense of the images and the events in your world. And you really exercise them when you are watching a television program or a movie!

Take a look at this photograph. The four strategies shown here—Clarify, Question, Predict, and Evaluate—are among those you can use to understand and interpret the situation portrayed. These and other reading strategies listed on the next page can help you interact with literature as well.

Clarify *From the way the people are dressed, I'd say it was the 1930s.*

Question *I wonder what the little girl is looking at. And why does she seem sad?*

Predict *I wonder if the woman will comfort the girl.*

Evaluate *I like this photo because it leaves you asking a lot of questions.*

Strategies for Reading

Following are specific reading strategies that are introduced and applied throughout this book. Use them when you read and interact with the various literature selections. Occasionally **monitor** how well the strategies are working for you and, if desired, modify them to suit your needs.

PREDICT Try to figure out what will happen next and how the selection might end. Then read on to see how accurate your guesses were.

VISUALIZE Visualize characters, events, and setting to help you understand what's happening. When you read nonfiction, pay attention to the images that form in your mind as you read.

CONNECT Connect personally with what you're reading. Think of similarities between the descriptions in the selection and what you have personally experienced, heard about, and read about.

QUESTION Question what happens while you read. Searching for reasons behind events and characters' feelings can help you feel closer to what you are reading.

CLARIFY Stop occasionally to review what you understand, and expect to have your understanding change and develop as you read on. Reread and use resources to help you clarify your understanding. Also watch for answers to questions you had earlier.

EVALUATE Form opinions about what you read, both while you're reading and after you've finished. Develop your own ideas about characters and events.

On the next page, you will see how two readers applied these strategies to the story "A Worn Path."

Go Beyond the Text If you really become an active reader, your involvement doesn't stop with the last line of the text. Decide what else you'd like to know. Discuss your ideas with others, do some research, or jump on the Internet.

More Online
www.mcdougallittell.com

Alongside "A Worn Path" are transcripts of the spoken comments made by two 11th-grade students, Robert Lewis and Gesenia Veizaga, while they were reading the story. Their comments provide a glimpse into the minds of readers actively engaged in the process of reading. You'll notice that in the course of their reading, Robert and Gesenia quite naturally used the Strategies for Reading that were introduced on page 7.

To benefit most from this model of active reading, read the story first, jotting down your own responses in your reading log. (Cover up the side comments with a sheet of paper if you're tempted to peek.) Then read Robert's and Gesenia's comments and compare their processes of reading with your own.

A Worn Path
EUDORA WELTY

Detail of *Sharecropper* (1970), Elizabeth Catlett. Linoleum cut on paper, National Museum of American Art, Smithsonian Institution, Washington D.C./Art Resource, New York.

It was December—a bright frozen day in the early morning. Far out in the country there was an old Negro woman with her head tied in a red rag, coming along a path through the pinewoods. Her name was Phoenix Jackson. She was very old and small and she walked slowly in the dark pine shadows, moving a little from side to side in her steps, with the balanced heaviness and lightness of a pendulum in a grandfather clock. She carried a thin, small cane made from an umbrella, and with this she kept tapping the frozen earth in front of her. This made a grave and persistent noise in the still air, that seemed meditative like the chirping of a solitary little bird.

She wore a dark striped dress reaching down to her shoe tops, and an equally long apron of bleached sugar sacks, with a full pocket: all neat and tidy, but every time she took a step she might have fallen over her shoelaces, which dragged from her unlaced shoes. She looked straight ahead. Her eyes were blue with age. Her skin had a pattern all its own of numberless branching wrinkles and as though a whole

Robert: *That's a neat image comparing her to a pendulum. I wonder if that means she measures time somehow.*
EVALUATING/QUESTIONING

Gesenia: *But she's so tidy. Why would she be sloppy with her shoes?*
QUESTIONING

little tree stood in the middle of her forehead, but a golden color ran underneath, and the two knobs of her cheeks were illumined by a yellow burning under the dark. Under the red rag her hair came down on her neck in the frailest of ringlets, still black, and with an odor like copper.

Now and then there was a quivering in the thicket. Old Phoenix said, "Out of my way, all you foxes, owls, beetles, jack rabbits, coons and wild animals! . . . Keep out from under these feet, little bob-whites. . . . Keep the big wild hogs out of my path. Don't let none of those come running my direction. I got a long way." Under her small black-freckled hand her cane, limber as a buggy whip, would switch at the brush as if to rouse up any hiding things.

On she went. The woods were deep and still. The sun made the pine needles almost too bright to look at, up where the wind rocked. The cones dropped as light as feathers. Down in the hollow was the mourning dove—it was not too late for him.

The path ran up a hill. "Seem like there is chains about my feet, time I get this far," she said, in the voice of argument old people keep to use with themselves. "Something always take a hold of me on this hill—pleads I should stay."

After she got to the top she turned and gave a full, severe look behind her where she had come. "Up through pines," she said at length. "Now down through oaks."

Her eyes opened their widest, and she started down gently. But before she got to the bottom of the hill a bush caught her dress.

Her fingers were busy and intent, but her skirts were full and long, so that before she could pull them free in one place they were caught in another. It was not possible to allow the dress to tear. "I in the thorny bush," she said. "Thorns, you doing your appointed work. Never want to let folks pass, no sir. Old eyes thought you was a pretty little *green* bush."

Finally, trembling all over, she stood free, and after a moment dared to stoop for her cane.

"Sun so high!" she cried, leaning back and looking, while the thick tears went over her eyes. "The time getting all gone here."

At the foot of this hill was a place where a log was laid across the creek.

"Now comes the trial," said Phoenix.

Putting her right foot out, she mounted the log and shut her eyes. Lifting her skirt, leveling her cane fiercely before her, like a festival figure in some parade, she began to march across. Then she opened her eyes and she was safe on the other side.

"I wasn't as old as I thought," she said.

But she sat down to rest. She spread her skirts on the bank around her and folded her hands over her knees. Up above her was a tree in a pearly cloud of mistletoe. She did not dare to close her eyes, and when a little boy brought her a plate with a slice of marble-cake on it

Gesenia: You can really picture her skin color from this description.
VISUALIZING

Robert: Phoenix seems like a down-to-earth person. She just goes about her business.
EVALUATING

Robert: Phoenix has made this trip before.
CLARIFYING

Gesenia: This author uses a lot of description. I'd better pay attention to details so I get a clear picture of what's happening in this story.
MONITORING

Gesenia: She's not grumpy like some old people. She sees that the thorns are just doing what they do. It doesn't make her mad.
EVALUATING/CONNECTING

Gesenia: Why would she close her eyes? Usually that's for when you do something for the first time, and she's been here before.
QUESTIONING/CONNECTING

she spoke to him. "That would be acceptable," she said. But when she went to take it there was just her own hand in the air.

So she left that tree, and had to go through a barbed-wire fence. There she had to creep and crawl, spreading her knees and stretching her fingers like a baby trying to climb the steps. But she talked loudly to herself: she could not let her dress be torn now, so late in the day, and she could not pay for having her arm or her leg sawed off if she got caught fast where she was.

At last she was safe through the fence and risen up out in the clearing. Big dead trees, like black men with one arm, were standing in the purple stalks of the withered cotton field. There sat a buzzard.

"Who you watching?"

In the furrow she made her way along.

"Glad this not the season for bulls," she said, looking sideways, "and the good Lord made his snakes to curl up and sleep in the winter. A pleasure I don't see no two-headed snake coming around that tree, where it come once. It took a while to get by him, back in the summer."

She passed through the old cotton and went into a field of dead corn. It whispered and shook and was taller than her head. "Through the maze now," she said, for there was no path.

Then there was something tall, black, and skinny there, moving before her.

At first she took it for a man. It could have been a man dancing in the field. But she stood still and listened, and it did not make a sound. It was as silent as a ghost.

"Ghost," she said sharply, "who be you the ghost of? For I have heard of nary death close by."

But there was no answer—only the ragged dancing in the wind.

She shut her eyes, reached out her hand, and touched a sleeve. She found a coat and inside that an emptiness, cold as ice.

"You scarecrow," she said. Her face lighted. "I ought to be shut up for good," she said with laughter. "My senses is gone. I too old. I the oldest people I ever know. Dance, old scarecrow," she said, "while I dancing with you."

She kicked her foot over the furrow, and with mouth drawn down, shook her head once or twice in a little strutting way. Some husks blew down and whirled in streamers about her skirts.

Then she went on, parting her way from side to side with the cane, through the whispering field. At last she came to the end, to a wagon track where the silver grass blew between the red ruts. The quail were walking around like pullets, seeming all dainty and unseen.

"Walk pretty," she said. "This the easy place. This the easy going."

She followed the track, swaying through the quiet bare fields, through the little strings of trees silver in their dead leaves, past cabins silver from weather, with the doors and windows boarded shut, all like old women under a spell sitting there. "I walking in their sleep," she said, nodding her head vigorously.

In a ravine she went where a spring was silently flowing through a hollow log. Old Phoenix bent and drank. "Sweet-gum makes the water sweet," she said, and drank more. "Nobody know who made this well, for it was here when I was born."

The track crossed a swampy part where the moss hung as white as lace from every limb. "Sleep on, alligators, and blow your bubbles." Then the track went into the road.

Deep, deep the road went down between the high green-colored banks. Overhead the live-oaks met, and it was as dark as a cave.

A black dog with a lolling tongue came up out of the weeds by the ditch. She was meditating, and not ready, and when he came at her she only hit him a little with her cane. Over she went in the ditch, like a little puff of milkweed.

Down there, her senses drifted away. A dream visited her, and she reached her hand up, but nothing reached down and gave her a pull. So she lay there and presently went to talking. "Old woman," she said to herself, "that black dog come up out of the weeds to stall you off, and now there he sitting on his fine tail, smiling at you."

A white man finally came along and found her—a hunter, a young man, with his dog on a chain.

"Well, Granny!" he laughed. "What are you doing there?"

"Lying on my back like a June-bug waiting to be turned over, mister," she said, reaching up her hand.

He lifted her up, gave her a swing in the air, and set her down. "Anything broken, Granny?"

"No sir, them old dead weeds is springy enough," said Phoenix, when she had got her breath. "I thank you for your trouble."

"Where do you live, Granny?" he asked, while the two dogs were growling at each other.

"Away back yonder, sir, behind the ridge. You can't even see it from here."

"On your way home?"

"No sir, I going to town."

"Why, that's too far! That's as far as I walk when I come out myself, and I get something for my trouble." He patted the stuffed bag he carried, and there hung down a little closed claw. It was one of the bob-whites, with its beak hooked bitterly to show it was dead. "Now you go on home, Granny!"

"I bound to go to town, mister," said Phoenix. "The time come around."

Georgia Landscape (about 1934–1935), Hale Woodruff. National Museum of American Art, Smithsonian Institution, Washington D.C./Art Resource, New York.

He gave another laugh, filling the whole landscape. "I know you old colored people! Wouldn't miss going to town to see Santa Claus!"

But something held old Phoenix very still. The deep lines in her face went into a fierce and different radiation. Without warning, she had seen with her own eyes a flashing nickel fall out of the man's pocket onto the ground.

"How old are you, Granny?" he was saying.

"There is no telling, mister," she said, "no telling."

Then she gave a little cry and clapped her hands and said, "Git on away from here, dog! Look! Look at that dog!" She laughed as if in admiration. "He ain't scared of nobody. He a big black dog." She whispered, "Sic him!"

"Watch me get rid of that cur," said the man. "Sic him, Pete! Sic him!"

Phoenix heard the dogs fighting, and heard the man running and throwing sticks. She even heard a gunshot. But she was slowly bending forward by that time, further and further forward, the lids stretched down over her eyes, as if she were doing this in her sleep. Her chin was lowered almost to her knees. The yellow palm of her hand came out from the fold of her apron. Her fingers slid down and along the ground under the piece of money with the grace and care they would have in lifting an egg from under a setting hen. Then she slowly straightened up, she stood erect, and the nickel was in her apron pocket. A bird flew by. Her lips moved. "God watching me the whole time. I come to stealing."

The man came back, and his own dog panted about them. "Well, I scared him off that time," he said, and then he laughed and lifted his gun and pointed it at Phoenix.

She stood straight and faced him.

"Doesn't the gun scare you?" he said, still pointing it.

"No, sir, I seen plenty go off closer by, in my day, and for less than what I done," she said, holding utterly still.

He smiled, and shouldered the gun. "Well, Granny," he said, "you must be a hundred years old, and scared of nothing. I'd give you a dime if I had any money with me. But you take my advice and stay home, and nothing will happen to you."

"I bound to go on my way, mister," said Phoenix. She inclined her head in the red rag. Then they went in different directions, but she could hear the gun shooting again and again over the hill.

She walked on. The shadows hung from the oak trees to the road like curtains. Then she smelled wood-smoke, and smelled the river, and she saw a steeple and the cabins on their steep steps. Dozens of little black children whirled around her. There ahead was Natchez shining. Bells were ringing. She walked on.

In the paved city it was Christmas time. There were red and green electric lights strung and crisscrossed everywhere, and all turned on in the daytime. Old Phoenix would have been lost if she had not distrusted her eyesight and depended on her feet to know where to take her.

She paused quietly on the sidewalk where people were passing by. A lady came along in the crowd, carrying an armful of red-, green- and silver-wrapped presents; she gave off perfume like the red roses in hot summer, and Phoenix stopped her.

"Please, missy, will you lace up my shoe?" She held up her foot.

"What do you want, Grandma?"

"See my shoe," said Phoenix. "Do all right for out in the country, but wouldn't look right to go in a big building."

"Stand still then, Grandma," said the lady. She put her packages down on the sidewalk beside her and laced and tied both shoes tightly.

"Can't lace 'em with a cane," said Phoenix. "Thank you, missy. I doesn't mind asking a nice lady to tie up my shoe, when I gets out on the street."

Moving slowly and from side to side, she went into the big building, and into a tower of steps, where she walked up and around and around until her feet knew to stop.

She entered a door, and there she saw nailed up on the wall the document that had been stamped with the gold seal and framed in the gold frame, which matched the dream that was hung up in her head.

"Here I be," she said. There was a fixed and ceremonial stiffness over her body.

"A charity case, I suppose," said an attendant who sat at the desk before her.

But Phoenix only looked above her head. There was sweat on her face, the wrinkles in her skin shone like a bright net.

"Speak up, Grandma," the woman said. "What's your name? We must have your history, you know. Have you been here before? What seems to be the trouble with you?"

Old Phoenix only gave a twitch to her face as if a fly were bothering her.

"Are you deaf?" cried the attendant.

But then the nurse came in.

"Oh, that's just old Aunt Phoenix," she said. "She doesn't come for herself—she has a little grandson. She makes these trips just as regular as clockwork. She lives away back off the Old Natchez Trace." She bent down. "Well, Aunt Phoenix, why don't you just take a seat? We won't keep you standing after your long trip." She pointed.

The old woman sat down, bolt upright in the chair.

"Now, how is the boy?" asked the nurse.

Old Phoenix did not speak.

"I said, how is the boy?"

But Phoenix only waited and stared straight ahead, her face very solemn and withdrawn into rigidity.

"Is his throat any better?" asked the nurse. "Aunt Phoenix, don't you hear me? Is your grandson's throat any better since the last time you came for the medicine?"

With her hands on her knees, the old woman waited, silent, erect and motionless, just as if she were in armor.

"You mustn't take up our time this way, Aunt Phoenix," the nurse said. "Tell us quickly about your grandson, and get it over. He isn't dead, is he?"

At last there came a flicker and then a flame of comprehension across her face, and she spoke.

"My grandson. It was my memory had left me. There I sat and forgot why I made my long trip."

"Forgot?" The nurse frowned. "After you came so far?"

Then Phoenix was like an old woman begging a dignified forgiveness for waking up frightened in the night. "I never did go to school, I was too old at the Surrender," she said in a soft voice. "I'm an old woman without an education. It was my memory fail me. My little grandson, he is just the same, and I forgot it in the coming."

"Throat never heals, does it?" said the nurse, speaking in a loud, sure voice to old Phoenix. By now she had a card with something written on it, a little list. "Yes. Swallowed lye. When was it?—January—two-three years ago—"

Phoenix spoke unasked now. "No, missy, he not dead, he just the same. Every little while his throat begin to close up again, and he not able to swallow. He not get his breath. He not able to help himself. So the time come around, and I go on another trip for the soothing medicine."

"All right. The doctor said as long as you came to get it, you could have it," said the nurse. "But it's an obstinate case."

"My little grandson, he sit up there in the house all wrapped up, waiting by himself," Phoenix went on. "We is the only two left in the world. He suffer and it don't seem to put him back at all. He got a sweet look. He going to last. He wear a little patch quilt and peep out holding his mouth open like a little bird. I remembers so plain now. I not going to forget him again, no, the whole enduring time. I could tell him from all the others in creation."

"All right." The nurse was trying to hush her now. She brought her a bottle of medicine. "Charity," she said, making a check mark in a book.

Old Phoenix held the bottle close to her eyes, and then carefully put it into her pocket.

"I thank you," she said.

"It's Christmas time, Grandma," said the attendant. "Could I give you a few pennies out of my purse?"

"Five pennies is a nickel," said Phoenix stiffly.

"Here's a nickel," said the attendant.

Phoenix rose carefully and held out her hand. She received the nickel and then fished the other nickel out of her pocket and laid it beside the new one. She stared at her palm closely, with her head on one side.

Then she gave a tap with her cane on the floor.

"This is what come to me to do," she said. "I going to the store and buy my child a little windmill they sells, made out of paper. He going to find it hard to believe there such a thing in the world. I'll march myself back where he waiting, holding it straight up in this hand."

She lifted her free hand, gave a little nod, turned around, and walked out of the doctor's office. Then her slow step began on the stairs, going down.

ORIGINS AND ENCOUNTERS

Pleasant it looked,
this newly created world.
Along the entire length and breadth
of the earth, our grandmother,
extended the green reflection
of her covering
and the escaping odors
were pleasant to inhale.

WINNEBAGO
an Algonkian people

Let us... go
to the place that
God will show
us to possess in
peace and plenty,
a land more like
the Garden of
Eden, which the
Lord planted,
than any part else
of all the earth.

REVEREND WILLIAM SYMONDS
Puritan minister

Giovanni da Verrazano becoming the first European
to enter New York Bay, 1524. Lithograph done
in 1868 by an unknown American artist.
The Granger Collection, New York.

ORIGINS AND ENCOUNTERS

EVENTS IN AMERICAN LITERATURE

2000–1000 B.C.	0	A.D. 1000

EVENTS IN NORTH AMERICA

2000–1000 B.C.	0	A.D. 1000

c.2000–1000 B.C. Native Americans in Southwest cultivate maize, a forerunner of corn

c.400 B.C. Olmec civilization begins decline in central Mexico

c.A.D. 500 Native American tribes in Eastern woodlands establish agricultural economy and widespread trade

c.800 Mound Builder culture develops along Mississippi River (to c. 1500s)

c.1000 Anasazi build elaborate, multistory cliff dwellings in Southwest canyons (to c. 1300)

1492 Christopher Columbus sets foot in Bahamas

EVENTS IN THE WORLD

2000–1000 B.C.	0	A.D. 1000

c.1790 B.C. Hammurabi, king of Babylon, codifies set of laws

c.753 B.C. City of Rome founded

483 B.C. The Buddha dies

334 B.C. Alexander the Great begins conquest of Persia (to 323 B.C.)

c.A.D. 30 Jesus crucified

105 Chinese invent paper

c.250 Mayan civilization begins Classic Period (to c. 880)

c.476 Western Roman Empire falls

630 Prophet Muhammad conquers Mecca, which becomes holiest city of Islam

800 Charlemagne unites much of Europe and is crowned Holy Roman Emperor

1095 First of nine "holy wars," known as Crusades, begins

1206 Genghis Khan begins Mongol conquest of Asia (to 1227)

1215 In England, King John agrees to Magna Carta

c.1300 Renaissance begins in Italy

1453 Ottomans conquer Constantinople

1455 Gutenberg Bible produced on printing press

PERIOD PIECES

Compass used for navigation in the 15th century

Pilgrim foot warmer

The Anko Calendar from the Kiowa people

1500   **1600**

1521 Hernándo Cortés writes to king of Spain describing Aztec gifts

1537 Upon returning to Spain, Álvar Núñez Cabeza de Vaca reports to Spanish king about harrowing North American journey

1630 William Bradford describes journey across Atlantic and Pilgrims' settlement in *Of Plymouth Plantation*

1500   **1600**

1502 Amerigo Vespucci returns from second exploration of South America and declares it a New World; the Americas are named after him.

1521 Hernándo Cortés conquers Aztecs and claims territory for Spain

1535 Jacques Cartier explores St. Lawrence River and claims Quebec and Montreal for France

1540 Horses introduced on large scale by Spanish explorers

1607 First permanent English colony set up in Jamestown, Virginia

1618 Virginia governor Samuel Argall declares all colonists who fail to attend church will be locked in guardhouse

1619 Africans first arrive in Virginia as indentured servants

1620 Before landing at Plymouth, Pilgrims sign Mayflower Compact, establishing government by will of majority

---

1500   **1600**

1502 First enslaved Africans taken to the Americas

1517 Martin Luther begins Protestant Reformation

1522 Magellan sails around world

1526 Babur founds Mughal Empire in India

1543 Copernicus publishes theory that sun is center of universe

1588 Spanish Armada sails for England

1603 Tokugawa Ieyasu unites Japan

1613 Michael Romanov elected Russian czar, founding the Romanov dynasty

1615 Italian scientist Galileo Galilei condemned by Inquisition for supporting Copernicus's theory

In Harmony with Nature

Native American Traditions

The first American literature was created by the first people to live here—the Native Americans, who inhabited North America thousands of years before the first Europeans arrived. To be sure, the Native Americans did not think of themselves as living in a single nation, as most Americans do today. Rather, the original native peoples belonged to more than 200 distinct groups who spoke more than 500 different languages. They called themselves names such as Anishinabe, Diné, and Lakota—each of which means "the people." Their ways of life, dictated by their natural surroundings, varied greatly. They had complex religious beliefs, sophisticated political systems, and strong social values, all reflected in their literatures.

Literature is not limited to what is written down in books. Native American literatures were primarily oral, passed down from generation to generation by storytelling and performances.

Some widespread types of Native American oral literature are creation myths, which explain the beginning of the world; tales of heroes and tricksters who transformed the world to its present state; and the ritual songs and chants that are part of ceremonies.

This part of Unit One presents a small sampling of works from Native American oral traditions: a creation myth from the Iroquois of the Northeast, two ancient songs from the Tewa and the Navajo of the Southwest, and two trickster tales from the Okanogan of the Pacific Northwest. Preceding these, in Voices from the Times, is a fable from the Pawnee of the central plains.

As readers of a textbook, you will not be experiencing these works as you would if you belonged to the cultures they came from. You will not be hearing them or seeing them performed; you will be reading them on a page, in a language different from the languages in which they were created. These pieces were collected in the early 1900s and translated into English by anthropologists—or in the case of the Okanogan stories, by a bilingual member of the tribe with the help of white editors. Despite the limitations of translations, they remain the best way to expose a wide audience to the beauty, wisdom, and humor of Native American oral literature.

Although traditional Native American literature has many forms and functions, much of it emphasizes the importance of living in harmony with the natural world. In Native American belief, human beings have a kinship with animals, plants, the land, heavenly bodies, and the elements. All of these things are seen as alive and aware, as when singers address Mother Earth and Father Sky in the Tewa "Song of the Sky Loom." Furthermore, the human and the nonhuman are seen as parts of a sacred whole. To Native Americans, human beings do not have dominion over nature; they are part of nature and must act to maintain a right relationship with the world around them. Notice

THE LESSON OF THE BIRDS
Pawnee

One day a man whose mind was open to the teaching of the powers wandered on the prairie. As he walked, his eyes upon the ground, he spied a bird's nest hidden in the grass, and arrested his feet just in time to prevent stepping on it. He paused to look at the little nest tucked away so snug and warm, and noted that it held six eggs and that a peeping sound came from some of them. While he watched, one moved and soon a tiny bill pushed through the shell, uttering a shrill cry. At once the parent birds answered and he looked up to see where they were. They were not far off; they were flying about in search of food, chirping the while to each other and now and then calling to the little one in the nest.

The homely scene stirred the heart and the thoughts of the man as he stood there under the clear sky, glancing upward toward the old birds and then down to the helpless young in the nest at his feet. As he looked he thought of his people, who were so often careless and thoughtless of their children's needs, and his mind brooded over the matter. After many days he desired to see the nest again. So he went to the place where he had found it, and there it was as safe as when he left it. But a change had taken place. It was now full to overflowing with little birds, who were stretching their wings, balancing on their little legs and making ready to fly, while the parents with encouraging calls were coaxing the fledglings to venture forth.

"Ah!" said the man, "if my people would only learn of the birds, and, like them, care for their young and provide for their future, homes would be full and happy, and our tribe be strong and prosperous."

When this man became a priest, he told the story of the bird's nest and sang its song; and so it has come down to us from the days of our fathers.

Translated by Alice C. Fletcher

Senator Ben Nighthorse Campbell at a news conference

Celebration at the Red Earth Festival in Oklahoma City

this perspective as you read the examples of traditional oral literature in this book.

Traditions Across Time: Harmonizing Old and New

Native Americans and their traditions have not disappeared from this country. Although some cultures were lost to the diseases and violence of the Europeans, others have survived— changed but not destroyed by forced religious conversion, forced relocation, and forced education. Today, Native Americans live in cities and suburbs as well as on reservations. They are keeping oral traditions alive by singing songs and telling stories, but they are also writing in English.

A new generation of such writers is enjoying unprecedented respect and popularity. They include N. Scott Momaday (whose 1969 novel *House Made of Dawn* won a Pulitzer Prize), Leslie Marmon Silko, Paula Gunn Allen, Simon Ortiz, Louise Erdrich, and Michael Dorris.

Most of these writers display a powerful interest in the problems of harmonizing the old and the new. In many of their works, such as Silko's story "The Man to Send Rain Clouds," characters or speakers are shown reconciling old traditions with new practices. Moreover, the structures of the works themselves are often based on a blend of oral techniques and new literary forms. For example, in *The Way to Rainy Mountain*, Momaday braids together mythology, oral history, and personal reflections. His novel *House Made of Dawn* and Silko's novel *Ceremony* both are constructed around traditional Native American ceremonies.

That these writers continue to draw on traditional sources for inspiration and have found such wide acclaim demonstrates the enduring value of our country's first literature.

Native American Traditions

Iroquois	**The World on the Turtle's Back** *How the earth was created*	24
Tewa	**Song of the Sky Loom** *A prayer to Mother Earth and Father Sky*	33
Navajo	**Hunting Song/Dinni-e Sin** *Deer are drawn to this song.*	33

Okanogan *Retold by*
Mourning Dove
	Coyote Stories
	   Coyote and the Buffalo
	   Fox and Coyote and Whale
	Trickster tales from the Northwest
		39
		40
		43

COMPARING LITERATURE
Traditions Across Time: Harmonizing Old and New

Leslie Marmon Silko	**The Man to Send Rain Clouds** (1969) *A ceremony in the desert Southwest*	48
N. Scott Momaday	*from* **The Way To Rainy Mountain** (1969) *The Kiowa journey across the Plains*	55

The World on the Turtle's Back

IROQUOIS (ĭr'ə-kwoi') MYTH

Connect to Your Life

Mysterious Origins In all times and places, people have wondered how the world was created. What different accounts of creation—biblical narratives, scientific theories, or stories from other cultures, for example—have you heard or read? With a group of classmates, summarize as many of these accounts as you know.

Build Background

The Iroquois League "The World on the Turtle's Back" is an Iroquois explanation of how the world was created. The term *Iroquois* refers to a league of five separate Native American peoples—the Seneca, Cayuga, Oneida, Onondaga, and Mohawk—who united in a confederation in the 14th century. (In the 18th century, a sixth group, the Tuscarora, joined the Iroquois League.) The ancestors of today's Iroquois lived in the woodlands of what is now New York State, the region roughly extending from the Hudson River in the east to the Great Lakes in the west.

The Iroquois groups spoke similar languages, held similar beliefs, and followed similar ways of life. They lived in longhouses made of pole frames covered with elm bark, and they built fences around their villages for protection. The women cultivated squash, beans, and corn and gathered berries and nuts. The men hunted, fished, and fought with the neighboring Mahican people. Warfare, an important part of Iroquois culture, gave men power and prestige. The Iroquois League was created primarily to end fighting among the nations that formed the alliance.

WORDS TO KNOW
Vocabulary Preview

contend   succumb
devious   void
ritual

Focus Your Reading

LITERARY ANALYSIS   CREATION MYTHS

A **myth** is a traditional story, passed down through generations, that explains why the world is the way it is. In myths, events usually result from the actions of supernatural beings. A **creation myth** explains how the universe, earth, and life began. As you read this Iroquois creation myth, note the supernatural explanations of the world's origin.

ACTIVE READING   CAUSES AND EFFECTS

Creation myths, to some extent, are imaginative stories of cause and effect. When events have a **cause-and-effect** relationship, one (the cause) directly brings about the other (the effect). In this Iroquois myth, the actions of supernatural beings cause the present features of the world to exist.

READER'S NOTEBOOK As you read, fill in a chart like the one started below to record what caused the existence of various things in the world, according to the myth.

What Exists	What Caused It to Be
The earth	It grew when a woman walked in a circle around dirt brought up from the ocean floor and placed on a turtle's back.

The WORLD on the TURTLE'S BACK

IROQUOIS

In the beginning there was no world, no land, no creatures of the kind that are around us now, and there were no men. But there was a great ocean which occupied space as far as anyone could see. Above the ocean was a great void of air. And in the air there lived the birds of the sea; in the ocean lived the fish and the creatures of the deep. Far above this unpeopled world, there was a Sky-World. Here lived gods who were like people—like Iroquois.

In the Sky-World there was a man who had a wife, and the wife was expecting a child. The woman became hungry for all kinds of strange delicacies, as women do when they are with child. She kept her husband busy almost to distraction finding delicious things for her to eat.

In the middle of the Sky-World there grew a Great Tree which was not like any of the trees that we know. It was tremendous; it had grown there forever. It had enormous roots that spread out from the floor of the Sky-World. And on its branches there were many different kinds of leaves and different kinds of fruits and flowers. The tree was not supposed to be marked or mutilated by any of the beings who dwelt in the Sky-World. It was a sacred tree that stood at the center of the universe.

The woman decided that she wanted some bark from one of the roots of the Great Tree—perhaps as a food or as a medicine, we don't know. She told her husband this. He didn't like the idea. He knew it was wrong. But she insisted, and he gave in. So he dug a hole among the roots of this great sky tree, and he bared some of its roots. But the floor of the Sky-World wasn't very thick, and he broke a hole through it. He was terrified, for he had never expected to find empty space underneath the world.

WORDS TO KNOW   **void** (void) *n.* an empty space

But his wife was filled with curiosity. He wouldn't get any of the roots for her, so she set out to do it herself. She bent over and she looked down, and she saw the ocean far below. She leaned down and stuck her head through the hole and looked all around. No one knows just what happened next. Some say she slipped. Some say that her husband, fed up with all the demands she had made on him, pushed her.

So she fell through the hole. As she fell, she frantically grabbed at its edges, but her hands slipped. However, between her fingers there clung bits of things that were growing on the floor of the Sky-World and bits of the root tips of the Great Tree. And so she began to fall toward the great ocean far below.

To keep the earth growing,
the woman walked as the sun goes,
moving in the direction
that the people still move
in the dance rituals.

The birds of the sea saw the woman falling, and they immediately consulted with each other as to what they could do to help her. Flying wingtip to wingtip they made a great feathery raft in the sky to support her, and thus they broke her fall. But of course it was not possible for them to carry the woman very long. Some of the other birds of the sky flew down to the surface of the ocean and called up the ocean creatures to see what they could do to help. The great sea turtle came and agreed to receive her on his back. The birds placed her gently on the shell of the turtle, and now the turtle floated about on the huge ocean with the woman safely on his back.

The beings up in the Sky-World paid no attention to this. They knew what was happening, but they chose to ignore it.

When the woman recovered from her shock and terror, she looked around her. All that she could see were the birds and the sea creatures and the sky and the ocean.

And the woman said to herself that she would die. But the creatures of the sea came to her and said that they would try to help her and asked her what they could do. She told them that if they could find some soil, she could plant the roots stuck between her fingers, and from them plants would grow. The sea animals said perhaps there was dirt at the bottom of the ocean, but no one had ever been down there so they could not be sure.

If there was dirt at the bottom of the ocean, it was far, far below the surface in the cold deeps. But the animals said they would try to get some. One by one the diving birds and animals tried and failed. They went to the limits of their endurance, but they could not get to the bottom of the ocean. Finally, the muskrat said he would try. He dived and disappeared. All the creatures waited, holding their breath, but he did not return. After a long time, his little body floated up to the surface of the ocean, a tiny crumb of earth clutched in his paw. He seemed to be dead. They pulled him up on the turtle's back and they sang and prayed over him and breathed air into his mouth, and finally, he stirred. Thus it was the muskrat, the Earth-Diver, who brought from the bottom of the ocean the soil from which the earth was to grow.

The woman took the tiny clod of dirt and placed it on the middle of the great sea turtle's back. Then the woman began to walk in a circle around it, moving in the direction that the sun goes. The earth began to grow. When the earth was big enough, she planted the roots she had clutched between her fingers when she fell from the Sky-World. Thus the plants grew on the earth.

To keep the earth growing, the woman walked as the sun goes, moving in the direction that the people still move in the dance <u>rituals</u>. She

WORDS
TO
KNOW   **ritual** (rĭch′ōō-əl) *n.* a ceremonial act or a series of such acts

Creation Legend, Tom (Two Arrows) Dorsey. Philbrook Museum of Art, Tulsa, Oklahoma (46.24).

gathered roots and plants to eat and built herself a little hut. After a while, the woman's time came, and she was delivered of a daughter. The woman and her daughter kept walking in a circle around the earth, so that the earth and plants would continue to grow. They lived on the plants and roots they gathered. The girl grew up with her mother, cut off forever from the Sky-World above, knowing only the birds and the creatures of the sea, seeing no other beings like herself.

One day, when the girl had grown to womanhood, a man appeared. No one knows for sure who this man was. He had something to do with the gods above. Perhaps he was the West Wind. As the girl looked at him, she was filled with terror, and amazement, and warmth, and she fainted dead away. As she lay on the ground, the man reached into his quiver, and he took out two arrows, one sharp and one blunt, and he laid them across the body of the girl, and quietly went away.

When the girl awoke from her faint, she and her mother continued to walk around the earth. After a while, they knew that the girl was to bear a child. They did not know it, but the girl was to bear twins.

Within the girl's body, the twins began to argue and quarrel with one another. There could be no peace between them. As the time approached for them to be born, the twins fought about their birth. The right-handed twin wanted to be born in the normal way, as all children are born. But the left-handed twin said no. He said he saw light in another direction, and said he would be born that way. The right-handed twin beseeched him not to, saying that he would kill their mother. But the left-handed twin was stubborn. He went in the direction where he saw light. But he could not be born through his mother's mouth or her nose. He was born through her left armpit, and killed her. And meanwhile, the right-handed twin was born in the normal way, as all children are born.

The twins met in the world outside, and the right-handed twin accused his brother of murdering their mother. But the grandmother told them to stop their quarreling. They buried their mother. And from her grave grew the plants which the people still use. From her head grew the corn, the beans, and the squash—"our supporters, the three sisters." And from her heart grew the sacred tobacco, which the people still use in the ceremonies and by whose upward-floating smoke they send thanks. The women call her "our mother," and they dance and sing in the rituals so that the corn, the beans, and the squash may grow to feed the people.

But the conflict of the twins did not end at the grave of their mother. And, strangely enough, the grandmother favored the left-handed twin.

The right-handed twin was angry, and he grew more angry as he thought how his brother had killed their mother. The right-handed twin was the one who did everything just as he should. He said what he meant, and he meant what he said. He always told the truth, and he always tried to accomplish what seemed to be right and reasonable. The left-handed twin never said what he meant or meant what he said. He always lied, and he always did things backward. You could never tell what he was trying to do because he always made it look as if he were doing the opposite. He was the <u>devious</u> one.

These two brothers, as they grew up, represented two ways of the world which are in

WORDS
TO
KNOW

devious (dē′vē-əs) *adj.* shifty; not straightforward

all people. The Indians did not call these the right and the wrong. They called them the straight mind and the crooked mind, the upright man and the devious man, the right and the left.

The twins had creative powers. They took clay and modeled it into animals, and they gave these animals life. And in this they <u>contended</u> with one another. The right-handed twin made the deer, and the left-handed twin made the mountain lion which kills the deer. But the right-handed twin knew there would always be more deer than mountain lions. And he made another animal.

The world the twins made
was a balanced
and orderly world,
and this was good.

He made the ground squirrel. The left-handed twin saw that the mountain lion could not get to the ground squirrel, who digs a hole, so he made the weasel. And although the weasel can go into the ground squirrel's hole and kill him, there are lots of ground squirrels and not so many weasels. Next the right-handed twin decided he would make an animal that the weasel could not kill, so he made the porcupine. But the left-handed twin made the bear, who flips the porcupine over on his back and tears out his belly.

And the right-handed twin made berries and fruits of other kinds for his creatures to live on. The left-handed twin made briars and poison ivy, and the poisonous plants like the baneberry and the dogberry, and the suicide root with which people kill themselves when they go out of their minds. And the left-handed twin made medicines, for good and for evil, for doctoring and for witchcraft.

And finally, the right-handed twin made man.

The people do not know just how much the left-handed twin had to do with making man. Man was made of clay, like pottery, and baked in the fire. . . .

The world the twins made was a balanced and orderly world, and this was good. The plant-eating animals created by the right-handed twin would eat up all the vegetation if their number was not kept down by the meat-eating animals, which the left-handed twin created. But if these carnivorous animals ate too many other animals, then they would starve, for they would run out of meat. So the right- and the left-handed twins built balance into the world.

As the twins became men full grown, they still contested with one another. No one had won, and no one had lost. And they knew that the conflict was becoming sharper and sharper, and one of them would have to vanquish the other.

And so they came to the duel. They started with gambling. They took a wooden bowl, and in it they put wild plum pits. One side of the pits was burned black, and by tossing the pits in the bowl and betting on how these would fall, they gambled against one another, as the people still do in the New Year's rites. All through the morning they gambled at this game, and all through the afternoon, and the sun went down. And when the sun went down, the game was done, and neither one had won.

WORDS
TO
KNOW   **contend** (kǝn-tĕnd′) *v.* to compete; vie

29

So they went on to battle one another at the lacrosse[1] game. And they contested all day, and the sun went down, and the game was done. And neither had won.

And now they battled with clubs, and they fought all day, and the sun went down, and the fight was done. But neither had won.

And they went from one duel to another to see which one would <u>succumb</u>. Each one knew in his deepest mind that there was something, somewhere, that would vanquish the other. But what was it? Where to find it?

Each knew somewhere in his mind what it was that was his own weak point. They talked about this as they contested in these duels, day after day, and somehow the deep mind of each entered into the other. And the deep mind of the right-handed twin lied to his brother, and the deep mind of the left-handed twin told the truth.

On the last day of the duel, as they stood, they at last knew how the right-handed twin was to kill his brother. Each selected his weapon. The left-handed twin chose a mere stick that would do him no good. But the right-handed twin picked out the deer antler, and with one touch he destroyed his brother. And the left-handed twin died, but he died and he didn't die. The right-handed twin picked up the body and cast it off the edge of the earth. And some place below the world, the left-handed twin still lives and reigns.

When the sun rises from the east and travels in a huge arc along the sky dome, which rests like a great upside-down cup on the saucer of the earth, the people are in the daylight realm of the right-handed twin. But when the sun slips down in the west at nightfall and the dome lifts to let it escape at the western rim, the people are again in the domain of the left-handed twin—the fearful realm of night.

Having killed his brother, the right-handed twin returned home to his grandmother. And she met him in anger. She threw the food out of the cabin onto the ground and said that he was a murderer, for he had killed his brother. He grew angry and told her she had always helped his brother, who had killed their mother. In his anger, he grabbed her by the throat and cut her head off. Her body he threw into the ocean, and her head, into the sky. There, "Our Grandmother, the Moon" still keeps watch at night over the realm of her favorite grandson.

The right-handed twin has many names. One of them is Sapling. It means smooth, young, green and fresh and innocent, straightforward, straight-growing, soft and pliable, teachable and trainable. These are the old ways of describing him. But since he has gone away, he has other names. He is called "He Holds Up the Skies," "Master of Life," and "Great Creator."

The left-handed twin also has many names. One of them is Flint. He is called the devious one, the one covered with boils. Old Warty. He is stubborn. He is thought of as being dark in color.

These two beings rule the world and keep an eye on the affairs of men. The right-handed twin, the Master of Life, lives in the Sky-World. He is content with the world he helped to create and with his favorite creatures, the humans. The scent of sacred tobacco rising from the earth comes gloriously to his nostrils.

In the world below lives the left-handed twin. He knows the world of men, and he finds contentment in it. He hears the sounds of warfare and torture, and he finds them good.

In the daytime, the people have rituals which honor the right-handed twin. Through the daytime rituals, they thank the Master of Life. In the nighttime, the people dance and sing for the left-handed twin. ❖

---

1. **lacrosse** (lǝ-krôs′): a game of Native American origin, played on a field by two teams, in which participants use long-handled sticks with webbed pouches to maneuver a ball into the opposing team's goal.

WORDS
TO
KNOW

succumb (sǝ-kŭm′) *v.* to give up or give in; yield

Connect to the Literature

1. What Do You Think? What are your thoughts about this creation myth?

> **Comprehension Check**
> - How did the animals help the woman who fell from the sky?
> - What are the differences between the twins?
> - What was the outcome of the duels between the twins?

Think Critically

2. **ACTIVE READING** **CAUSES AND EFFECTS** Look over the chart you made in your **READER'S NOTEBOOK** as you read this **myth.** What caused various things in the world to come into being? Discuss the cause and effect you found most interesting.

3. What are the most important things you learned about the values and way of life of the Iroquois from reading this myth?

> **THINK ABOUT**
> - their attitude toward nature
> - their view of their gods
> - important foods, rituals, and games
> - the roles of men and women

4. Why do you think the Iroquois honor both the left-handed twin and the right-handed twin?

Extend Interpretations

5. Comparing Texts How does this Iroquois creation myth compare with the other accounts of creation that you discussed earlier?

6. Connect to Life How would you relate the left-handed and right-handed twins to your own concept of good and evil?

Literary Analysis

CREATION MYTHS As you recall, a **creation myth** explains how the universe, earth, and life began. Creation myths, like all myths, can be viewed as essentially religious, presenting the cosmic views of the cultural groups that create them. According to the scholar Joseph Campbell, myths have four functions:

- to instill a sense of awe toward the mystery of the universe
- to explain the workings of the natural world
- to support and validate social customs
- to guide people through the trials of living

Cooperative Learning Activity Do you think "The World on the Turtle's Back" serves the functions of myths noted by Joseph Campbell? Meet in small groups to discuss this question. Support your responses with examples from the selection.

Function	Examples
to instill awe	
to explain world	
to support customs	
to guide people	

Writing Options

1. Essay on Harmony The Iroquois, like most native peoples of North America, emphasized the importance of living in harmony with the natural world. Write a short expository essay in which you explain how the Iroquois myth expresses this relationship toward all living things.

Writing Handbook
See page 1283: Analysis

2. Opinion Essay The twins in this myth represent "two ways of the world which are in all people"—the "straight mind" and the "crooked mind." Draft a short reflective essay in which you agree or disagree with this view of human character. Support your opinion with examples.

3. Alternate Ending If the left-handed twin had killed the right-handed twin, what kind of world might have resulted? Write an alternate ending to this Iroquois myth.

Activities & Explorations

1. Oral Storytelling Iroquois traditions, rituals, and history have been passed down orally from generation to generation. Present an oral interpretation of part of this Iroquois myth for the class. ~ **SPEAKING AND LISTENING**

2. Narrative Pictographs Native American groups without written languages often used pictographs—pictures that represent objects and ideas—to help them remember important events and stories. The pictograph shown here, from the Lenni Lenape group, represents the creation of the sun, the moon, and the stars. Create your own pictographs to represent significant events in "The World on the Turtle's Back." Display your work in the classroom. ~ **ART**

3. Food Chain Diagram A food chain shows the sequence of food relationships among plants and animals. In rural areas, for example, some snakes eat mice, which feed on grain. Draw a diagram of a food chain based on the animal and plant life the twins created in the Iroquois myth. Think of each plant and animal as a link in the chain. Refer to diagrams of food chains in a biology textbook or encyclopedia as models. ~ **SCIENCE, ART**

Inquiry & Research

Creation Stories Compared Read or listen to a creation myth from a culture other than the Iroquois—for example, the Navajo from the southwestern United States or the Norse from Scandinavia. In a chart or essay, explore similarities and differences between this myth and the Iroquois myth.

Art Connection

Every Picture Tells a Story Look at the picture *Creation Legend* by Tom (Two-Arrows) Dorsey on page 27. What characters and events from "The World on the Turtle's Back" are portrayed?

Vocabulary in Action

EXERCISE A: ASSESSMENT PRACTICE Review the list of Words to Know. On your paper, write the vocabulary word that is a synonym of each word below. Then write a sentence containing the vocabulary word.

1. dishonest
2. strive
3. vacuum
4. quit
5. ceremony

EXERCISE B With a partner, make up a story that contains at least three of the Words to Know. Then practice telling the story, partly in words and partly in pantomime. Perform the story for your classmates, and have them try to figure out which vocabulary words it contains.

Building Vocabulary
For an in-depth lesson on how to expand your vocabulary, see page 126.

WORDS TO KNOW		
contend	ritual	void
devious	succumb	

Song of the Sky Loom

TEWA (tā′wə) SONG

Hunting Song / Dinni-e Sin

NAVAJO (năv′ə-hō′) SONG

Connect to Your Life

Sacred Words Many cultures have spiritual songs and poetry that are used in worship or thanksgiving. Write down the words of a prayer, psalm, vow, hymn, or some other form of sacred expression in your culture. Study the words carefully. What, in your opinion, distinguishes sacred language from ordinary language?

Build Background

Tewa and Navajo Songs These selections are sacred songs of two Native American groups of the Southwest. The Tewa are a group of Pueblo Indians, so called because they live in pueblos—villages of stone or adobe dwellings. The Tewa live in six pueblos north of Santa Fe, New Mexico: Tesque, Nambe, Pojoaque, San Ildefonso, Santa Clara, and San Juan. "Song of the Sky Loom" is one of many Tewa songs that are sung in religious rituals. The translator, Herbert Spinden, states that *sky loom* refers to "small desert rains which resemble a loom hung from the sky."

   "Dinni-e Sin" ("Hunting Song" in English translation) is a song of the Navajo. The Navajo were originally hunters and gatherers, but after migrating to the Southwest in the 11th century, they gradually adopted a more settled life of herding and farming. According to the Navajo, "Hunting Song" was given to them by Hastyeyalti, the god of the sunrise and of game animals. Navajo men prepared for the hunt by praying and singing hunting songs, in the belief that if they sang well, they would have success.

Focus Your Reading

LITERARY ANALYSIS **REPETITION** **Repetition** is the recurrence of words, phrases, or lines in a piece of literature. Notice the repetition in the following lines from "Hunting Song":

> *Comes the deer to my singing,*
> *Comes the deer to my song,*
> *Comes the deer to my singing.*

Consider how this repetition affects you. Look for other examples of repetition in the songs.

ACTIVE READING **STRATEGIES FOR READING NATIVE AMERICAN SONGS** It is important to remember that the texts you are about to read are not fully representative of these songs. They are lyrics, translated from the original languages, unaccompanied by music and movement, and taken out of the context of the ceremonies they are a part of. Still, there is enough left to appreciate. The following strategies will help you accomplish this:

- Read the songs aloud.
- Try to **visualize** the singers and the occasions for which the songs were sung.
- **Speculate** about the deeper, nonliteral meaning of words such as "garment of brightness."
- Be aware of the feelings the songs express about nature and the universe. Record your impressions in your
  📖 **READER'S NOTEBOOK.**

SONG of the SKY LOOM

TEWA

Oh our Mother the Earth, oh our Father the Sky,
Your children are we, and with tired backs
We bring you the gifts that you love.
Then weave for us a garment of brightness;
5 May the warp[1] be the white light of morning,
May the weft[2] be the red light of evening,
May the fringes be the falling rain,
May the border be the standing rainbow.
Thus weave for us a garment of brightness
10 That we may walk fittingly where birds sing,
That we may walk fittingly where grass is green,
Oh our Mother the Earth, oh our Father the Sky!

---

1. **warp:** the threads that run lengthwise in a woven fabric.
2. **weft:** the threads interlaced at right angles through the warp threads in a woven fabric.

Copyright © School of American Research Press.
Photo by Deborah Flynn.

Thinking Through the Literature

1. What feeling are you left with after reading "Song of the Sky Loom"?

2. The Tewa ask the earth and the sky for a "garment of brightness." What do you think this phrase means?

    THINK ABOUT
    • the four parts of the garment (lines 5–8)
    • why they ask for the garment (lines 10 and 11)

3. How is this sacred song like the examples of sacred expression you wrote down before you read?

Hunting Song

Navajo

Comes the deer to my singing,
Comes the deer to my song,
Comes the deer to my singing.

He, the blackbird, he am I,
5 Bird beloved of the wild deer,
    Comes the deer to my singing.

From the Mountain Black,
From the summit,
Down the trail, coming, coming now,
10   Comes the deer to my singing.

Through the blossoms,
Through the flowers, coming, coming now,
    Comes the deer to my singing.

Through the flower dew-drops,
15   Coming, coming now,
    Comes the deer to my singing.

Through the pollen, flower pollen,
    Coming, coming now,
    Comes the deer to my singing.

(continued)

Dinni-E Sin

Ye shakaikatal, i-ne-yanga,
Ye shakaikatal, ai-ye-lo,
Ye shakaikatal, i-ne-yanga.

Ka' aiyash-te tilyilch-ye
5 Shini shlini ko-lo,
    Ye shakaikatal, i-ne yanga

Dsichl-tilyilch-iye
Bakashte
Ka' ta-adetin 'shte lo,
10   Ye shakaikatal, i-ne yanga

Tshilatra hozhoni-ye
Bitra 'shte lo,
    Ye shakaikatal, i-ne yanga

Bi datro-iye
15 Bitra 'shte lo,
    Ye shakaikatal, i-ne yanga

Ka' bi tradetin-iye
Bitra 'shte lo,
    Ye shakaikatal, i-ne yanga

(continued)

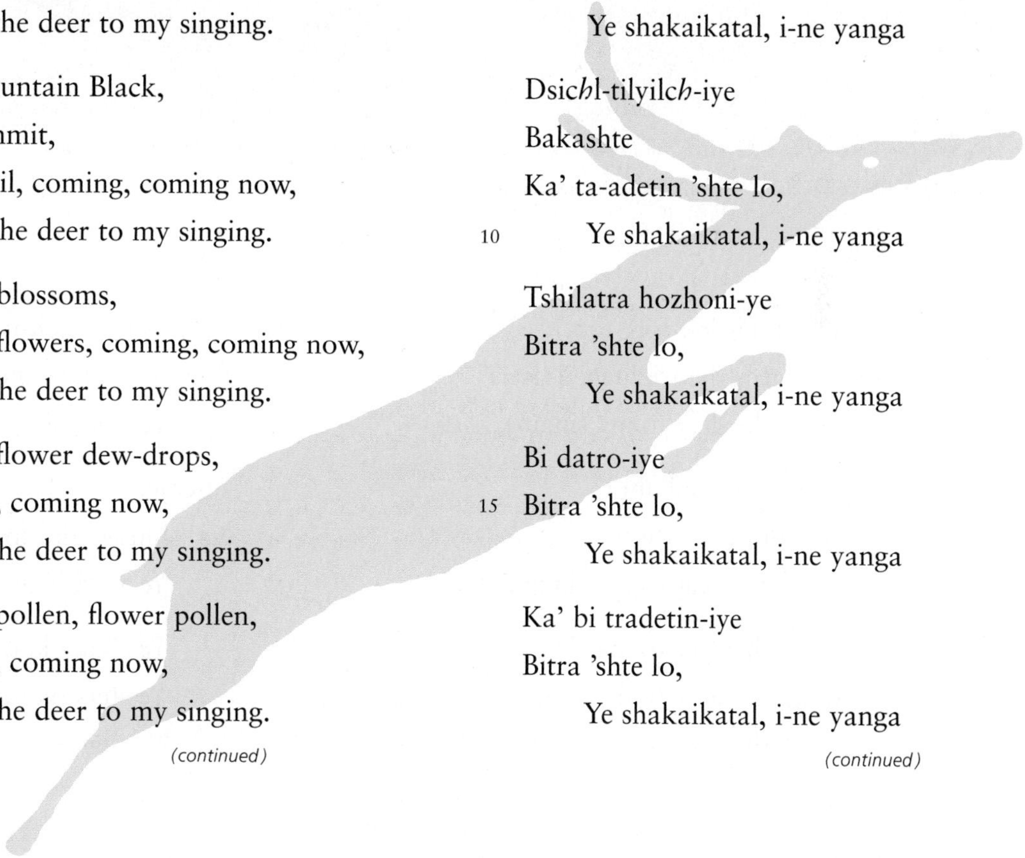

Born Free, Edwin Salomon. Courtesy, Jacques Soussana Graphics, Jerusalem, Israel.

20 Starting with his left fore-foot,
Stamping, turns the frightened deer,
    Comes the deer to my singing.

Quarry mine, blessed am I
In the luck of the chase,
25   Comes the deer to my singing.

    Comes the deer to my singing,
    Comes the deer to my song,
    Comes the deer to my singing.

20 Dinnitshe-beka*n*-iye
Bitzil-le deshklashdji-lo
    Ye shakaikatal, i-ne yanga

Bisedje
Ka' shinosin-ku lo,
25   Ye shakaikatal, i-ne-yanga

    Ye shakaikatal, i-ne-yanga,
    Ye shakaikatal, ai-ye-lo,
    Ye shakaikatal, i-ne-yanga.

Connect to the Literature

1. What Do You Think? What distinctive features of "Hunting Song" did you notice? Discuss your impressions with a classmate.

> **Comprehension Check**
> • What is the purpose of "Hunting Song"?

Think Critically

2. Describe your interpretation of the deer hunt as it is portrayed in the song.

> • what attracts the deer
> • the hunter's comparison of himself to the bird loved by the deer
> • the use of the words "blessed" and "luck"
> • the hunter's feelings about the deer

3. What kinds of movement or what larger rituals do you think accompanied "Hunting Song" and "Song of the Sky Loom"? Describe what you visualized and why.

4. **ACTIVE READING STRATEGIES FOR READING NATIVE AMERICAN SONGS** Refer to the notes you made in your **READER'S NOTEBOOK.** What attitude toward nature and the universe do you see expressed in the songs? Discuss why the Navajo might consider these songs sacred.

Extend Interpretations

5. Comparing Texts How would you compare "Hunting Song" and "Song of the Sky Loom"?

> • the singers
> • the purposes of the songs
> • the attitudes expressed toward nature

6. Comparing Texts How does the relationship between humans and animals suggested in "Hunting Song" compare with the relationship between humans and animals suggested in "The World on the Turtle's Back"?

7. Connect to Life How do the attitudes toward nature expressed in these songs compare with the attitudes toward nature common in American society today?

Literary Analysis

REPETITION One obvious feature of these songs is **repetition**—the recurrence of words, phrases, or lines. For example, the first line of "Song of the Sky Loom" is the same as the last line.

Some songs and poems feature **incremental repetition:** the structure of a line or stanza is repeated a certain number of times, with a slight variation in wording each time. The sequence "May the warp be. . . / May the weft be. . . / May the border be. . ." is an example of incremental repetition. Find examples of incremental repetition in "Hunting Song." Identify any repetition used in the examples of sacred speech and song you noted for the Connect to Your Life activity on page 33.

Cooperative Learning Activity
Scholars of Native American song have proposed that repetition creates a regular rhythm for dancing, reinforces important ideas, makes a song easier to remember, gives power to a song, and has a hypnotic effect on consciousness. Gather in small groups and discuss which of these purposes for repetition is apparent in "Song of the Sky Loom" and "Hunting Song." Write down specific examples to support your answers.

Function of Repetition	Examples
Creates regular rhythm	
Reinforces ideas	
Makes memorable	
Gives power	
Has hypnotic effect	

Writing Options

1. Definition Essay In "Song of the Sky Loom," the Tewa express a wish to "walk fittingly." Draft a definition essay describing how a person might walk fittingly in today's society. Place the essay into your **Working Portfolio.**

2. Siren Song The singer in "Hunting Song" attempts to draw a deer to himself. Compose your own hunting song in which you lure what you most desire to yourself.

3. Reflective Essay Review the ideas about sacred language you recorded in your Reader's Notebook. Has studying these Native American songs given you new ideas about sacred language and how it differs from ordinary language? What comparisons can you make between these songs and forms of sacred expression in your own culture? Share your thoughts in a reflective essay.

My hunting song

Activities & Explorations

1. Oral Reading With a small group of classmates, prepare oral readings of these two songs and perform them for the class. Include movement if you wish. After the performances, ask the class to vote on which reading they liked the best, giving reasons for their choice.
~ SPEAKING AND LISTENING

2. Visual Storytelling Make a sequence of drawings, in panels, that show stages of the deer hunt in "Hunting Song." **~ VIEWING AND REPRESENTING**

Inquiry & Research

1. Mapping the Music Recall that the term *sky loom* refers to desert rains. Point out images in "Song of the Sky Loom" that relate to rain. Why would rain be important to a farming culture in the Southwest? Research the terrain and climate of New Mexico. Draw a map on which you represent the different terrains and climates with various materials. Predict what other things might be subjects of Tewa songs.

2. Thrill of the Hunt Find out how the techniques and attitudes of modern hunters compare with those found in "Hunting Song." Give an oral report to the class based on research you conduct, on an interview with a hunter or local game warden, or on your own personal experiences.

3. Hear My Song If possible, bring in and play a recording of a traditional Tewa or Navajo song. (If you live in Arizona or New Mexico, perhaps you might invite a Tewa or Navajo singer to class.) What is the song about, and when is it usually sung? What aspects of the song could not be captured in a written translation of the lyrics? How does the song compare, in style and theme, to either of the songs you studied?

Coyote Stories

OKANOGAN (ō′kə-nŏg′ən) FOLK TALES
Retold by MOURNING DOVE

Connect to Your Life

Coyotes—Fact and Fiction A coyote is a small, wolflike animal that is native to western North America and found in many other regions of the continent. You might have observed coyotes in the wild or in a zoo, or you might have seen them depicted in Westerns or cartoons. What traits do you associate with coyotes? Record your impressions in a word web, with the word *coyote* in the center of the web.

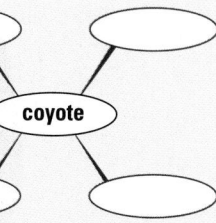

coyote

Build Background

Okanogan Storytelling The homeland of the Okanogan people is north central Washington State and southern British Columbia. Many of the Okanogan now live on the Colville Reservation in Washington. "Coyote and the Buffalo" and "Fox and Coyote and Whale" are two folk tales originally told by Okanogan storytellers who traveled from village to village. They told these stories in Salish, their native language, and referred to places along the Columbia River, where they lived. Mourning Dove's retellings include Salish words and place names, spelled in a way that reflects their pronunciation.

Both tales belong to an oral tradition of the history of the Animal People, a race of supernatural beings believed to have been the first inhabitants of the world. The Animal People had magical powers and could alter their shapes. They usually appeared in animal form but could also take human form. When human beings appeared on earth, the Animal People were changed into different animal species. Coyote, one of the most important Animal People, is a central figure in these stories. He is thought to have made the world habitable for humans by killing monsters and bringing fire and salmon, among other deeds. Coyote stories are told in many Native American cultures across the western states.

Focus Your Reading

LITERARY ANALYSIS TRICKSTER TALES Like myths, **folk tales** are stories handed down, usually by word of mouth, from generation to generation. In fact, some scholars regard myths—religious stories offering supernatural explanations of the world—as a special category of folk tale. **Trickster tales** are folk tales that feature an animal or human character who engages in deceit, violence, and magic. Often trickster tales are mythic, explaining features of the world. As you read these two stories, notice how Coyote demonstrates the trickster's contradictory qualities: he is foolish yet clever, greedy yet helpful, immoral yet moral. Also notice what Coyote creates.

ACTIVE READING STRATEGIES FOR READING TRICKSTER TALES

Using the following strategies as you read will help you get the most from these trickster tales:

- Read them aloud, or imagine a storyteller's voice.
- See the footnotes for explanations of Salish words.
- Accept magical transformations and animals who behave as humans.
- Note mysteries of nature that are explained.
- Infer the social values taught through the characters and situations.
- Note details that reveal other aspects of Okanogan culture.

READER'S NOTEBOOK As you use the last three strategies, jot down your notes in a three-column chart with these headings: **Explanations, Social Values, Cultural Details.**

COYOTE STORIES

OKANOGAN

COYOTE
and the
BUFFALO

Retold by Mourning Dove

Buffalo skull. Private collection.
Photo by John Oldenkamp.

No buffalo ever lived in the *Swah-netk'-qhu*[1] country. That was Coyote's fault. If he had not been so foolish and greedy, the people beside the *Swah-netk'-qhu* would not have had to cross the Rockies to hunt the *quas-peet-za*[2] (curled-hairs).

This is the way it happened:

COYOTE was traveling over the plains beyond the big mountains. He came to a flat. There he found an old buffalo skull. It was the skull of Buffalo Bull. Coyote always had been afraid of Buffalo Bull. He remembered the many times Bull Buffalo had scared him, and he laughed upon seeing the old skull there on the flat.

"Now I will have some fun," Coyote remarked. "I will have revenge for the times Buffalo made me run."

He picked up the skull and threw it into the air; he kicked it and spat on it; he threw dust in the eye sockets. He did these things many times, until he grew tired. Then he went his way. Soon he heard a rumbling behind him. He thought it was thunder, and he looked at the sky. The sky was clear. Thinking he must have imagined the sound, he walked on, singing. He heard the rumbling again, only much closer and louder. Turning around, he saw Buffalo Bull pounding along after him, chasing him. His old enemy had come to life!

Coyote ran, faster than he thought he could run, but Buffalo gained steadily. Soon Buffalo was right at his heels. Coyote felt his hot breath.

"Oh, *Squas-tenk'*,[3] help me!" Coyote

---

1. *Swah-netk'-qhu:* the Salish name for Kettle Falls on the Columbia River or for the river itself.
2. *quas-peet-za:* a Salish word for buffalo.
3. *Squas-tenk':* a Salish word that refers to Coyote's power or spirit helper.

begged, and his power answered by putting three trees in front of him. They were there in the wink of an eye. Coyote jumped and caught a branch of the first tree and swung out of Buffalo's way. Buffalo rammed the tree hard, and it shook as if in a strong wind. Then Buffalo chopped at the trunk with his horns, first with one horn and then the other. He chopped fast, and in a little while over went the tree, and with it went Coyote. But he was up and into the second tree before Buffalo Bull could reach him. Buffalo soon laid that tree low, but he was not quick enough to catch Coyote, who scrambled into the third and last tree.

"Buffalo, my friend, let me talk with you," said Coyote, as his enemy hacked away at the tree's trunk. "Let me smoke my pipe. I like the *kinnikinnick*.[4] Let me smoke. Then I can die more content."

"You may have time for one smoke," grunted Bull Buffalo, resting from his chopping.

Coyote spoke to his medicine-power, and a pipe, loaded and lighted, was given to him. He puffed on it once and held out the pipe to Buffalo Bull.

"No, I will not smoke with you," said that one. "You made fun of my bones. I have enough enemies without you. Young Buffalo is one of them. He killed me and stole all my fine herd."

"My uncle,"[5] said Coyote, "you need new horns. Let me make new horns for you. Then you can kill Young Buffalo. Those old horns are dull and worn."

Bull Buffalo was pleased with that talk. He decided he did not want to kill Coyote. He told Coyote to get down out of the tree and make the new horns. Coyote jumped down and called to his power. It scolded him for getting into trouble, but it gave him a flint knife and a stump of pitchwood.[6] From this stump Coyote carved a pair of fine heavy horns with sharp points. He gave them to Buffalo Bull. All buffalo bulls have worn the same kind of horns since.

BUFFALO BULL was very proud of his new horns. He liked their sharpness and weight and their pitch-black color. He tried them out on what was left of the pitchwood stump. He made one toss and the stump flew high in the air, and he forgave Coyote for his mischief. They became good friends right there. Coyote said he would go along with Buffalo Bull to find Young Buffalo.

They soon came upon Young Buffalo and the big herd he had won from Buffalo Bull. Young Buffalo laughed when he saw his old enemy, and he walked out to meet him. He did not know, of course, about the new horns. It was not much of a fight, that fight between Young Buffalo and Buffalo Bull. With the fine new horns, Buffalo Bull killed the other easily, and then he took back his herd, all his former wives and their children. He gave Coyote a young cow, the youngest cow, and he said:

> **H**e heard the rumbling again, only much closer and louder. Turning around, he saw Buffalo Bull pounding along after him, chasing him. His old enemy had come to life!

"Never kill her, *Sin-ka-lip'*![7] Take good care of her and she will supply you with meat forever. When you get hungry, just slice off some choice fat with a flint knife. Then rub ashes on the wound and the cut will heal at once."

Coyote promised to remember that, and they parted. Coyote started back to his own country, and the cow followed. For a few suns he ate only the fat when he was hungry. But after awhile he became

---

4. *kinnikinnick:* the Salish word for the bearberry, a shrub that is native to North America and Eurasia. The Okanogan toasted bearberry leaves and then crumbled and mixed them with tobacco for pipe smoking.

5. **my uncle:** Native Americans commonly use terms such as *uncle, cousin, brother,* and *sister* to express affection or respect or to flatter someone. Coyote uses this term of endearment to flatter Buffalo Bull.

6. **pitchwood:** the sap-filled wood of a pine or fir tree.

7. *Sin-ka-lip':* the Salish name for Coyote; it means "Imitator."

tired of eating fat, and he began to long for the sweet marrow-bones and the other good parts of the buffalo. He smacked his lips at the thought of having some warm liver.

"Buffalo Bull will never know," Coyote told himself, and he took his young cow down beside a creek and killed her.

As he peeled off the hide, crows and magpies came from all directions. They settled on the carcass and picked at the meat. Coyote tried to chase them away, but there were too many of them. While he was chasing some, others returned and ate the meat. It was not long until they had devoured every bit of the meat.

"Well, I can get some good from the bones and marrow-fat," Coyote remarked, and he built a fire to cook the bones. Then he saw an old woman walking toward him. She came up to the fire.

"Sin-ka-lip'," she said, "you are a brave warrior, a great chief. Why should you do woman's work? Let me cook the bones while you rest."

Vain Coyote! He was flattered. He believed she spoke her true mind. He stretched out to rest and he fell asleep. In his sleep he had a bad dream. It awoke him, and he saw the old woman running away with the marrow-fat and the

VAIN COYOTE!

He was flattered. He believed she spoke her true mind. He stretched out to rest and he fell asleep. In his sleep he had a bad dream.

boiled grease. He looked into the cooking-basket. There was not a drop of soup left in it. He chased the old woman. He would punish her! But she could run, too, and she easily kept ahead of him. Every once in awhile she stopped and held up the marrow-fat and shouted: "Sin-ka-lip', do you want this?"

Finally Coyote gave up trying to catch her. He went back to get the bones. He thought he would boil them again. He found the bones scattered all around, so he gathered them up and put them into the cooking-basket. Needing some more water to boil them in, he went to the creek for it, and when he got back, there were no bones in the basket! In place of the bones was a little pile of tree limbs!

Coyote thought he might be able to get another cow from Buffalo Bull, so he set out to find him. When he came to the herd, he was astonished to see the cow he had killed. She was there with the others! She refused to go with Coyote again, and Buffalo Bull would not give him another cow. Coyote had to return to his own country without a buffalo.

That is why there never have been any buffalo along the *Swah-netk'-qhu*. ❖

Thinking Through the Literature

1. **Comprehension Check** What happens when Coyote disobeys Buffalo Bull's order?

2. Folk tales often serve to teach or explain. In your view, what does "Coyote and the Buffalo" teach or explain? Refer to the chart you made in your
   📖 READER'S NOTEBOOK as you read.

   THINK ABOUT
   - what actions are rewarded or punished
   - what changes occur in the characters
   - the first and last paragraphs of the tale

3. Okanogan storytellers might tell "Coyote and the Buffalo" during a winter night. Why do you think people would want to hear this story over and over again?

OKANOGAN

FOX and COYOTE and WHALE

Retold by Mourning Dove

FOX had a beautiful wife. He was very much in love with her, but she had stopped caring for him. Fox was a great hunter, and every day he brought home food and fine skins for his wife to make into robes and clothing. He did not know that, while he was away hunting, his wife would sit beside the *Swah-netk'-qhu* and sing love songs to the water. Painting her face with bright colors, she would pour out her love thoughts in song.

Coyote came to visit his twin brother, and he soon noticed the strange actions of his sister-in-law. He spoke to Fox. "*Why-ay'-looh,*"[1] he said, "I think your wife is in love with somebody else." But Fox could not believe she loved anyone but him. He was blinded by his love for her. Then, one sun, he and Coyote returned from a hunt and she was not in the lodge. So Fox started to look for her. He walked down toward

the river and there he saw his wife. She was sitting on the river bank, singing a love song. She did not see Fox. He watched her.

As Fox watched, the water began to rise. Slowly it rose, higher and higher, and soon, out of the middle of the river, appeared a big monster of the fish-kind. The monster was *En-hah-et'-qhu*, the Spirit of the Water—Whale. It swam to the shore. As it

Nootka wood whale effigy rattle (about 1870). Courtesy, Morning Star Gallery, Santa Fe, New Mexico. Photo by Addison Doty.

---

1. *Why-ay'-looh:* the Salish name for Fox.

touched dry land, it changed into a tall handsome man with long braided hair. This monster-man made love to the wife of Fox.

Sad at heart, Fox turned away. He went to his lodge. He said nothing, but he wondered how he could win back his wife's love. He worried about her as the suns passed. She grew pale and thin. Nothing that Fox could do pleased her. Her thoughts always were with the man who was not a man but a monster. One day when Fox and Coyote came home from hunting, she was gone, and the fire in the lodge was cold. Fox called and called. He got no answer. His heart was heavy.

A few suns later Fox looked up the river and saw an odd-shaped canoe coming. It was only half of a canoe. Two Water Maidens were standing in it, rocking it from side to side. They were singing:

> We come for food,
> Food for the Chief's stolen wife.
> The water-food does not suit her.
> That is why we come! We come!

As the Water Maidens approached, Fox and Coyote hid in the tepee. The maidens beached the half-canoe and entered the lodge. They began to pick up dried meat to take to the stolen wife. Coyote and Fox sprang from their hiding places and caught the maidens, and Fox asked about his wife—where she was and how to get to her. The maidens were silent. Then the brothers threatened to kill them unless they answered, and the maidens said:

"To find the person who stole her, you must go over the Big Falls[2] and under the water. His lodge is under the falls, under the water—a dangerous trip for Land People. Every trail is watched. Even if you get there, the mighty Whale chief will kill you. He is bad."

The Water Maidens had told all they knew, so Fox broke their necks. He and Coyote dressed in the maidens' robes and started down the river in the half-canoe. Standing on the sides of the strange craft, they rocked it as they had seen the maidens do, and rode it down the river and over the roaring falls. "Let me do all the talking," Fox warned Coyote. "I know better what to say." Down through the pouring, flashing waters they shot with the half-canoe. The thunder of the falls hurt their ears. And then, suddenly, they were landing at a great encampment of Water People, a strange kind of people to them. All of the people were strange except *Gou-kouh-whay'-na*—Mouse. She was there. She knew them and they knew her. Fox jumped ashore. Coyote, following, tripped and touched the water, and Mouse, the Sly One, laughed. "Ha-ha!" said Mouse, "Coyote nearly fell into the water."

"Do not speak," Fox whispered to Mouse. "Say nothing. I will pay you well."

But some of the Water People had heard. "What, *Gou-kouh-whay'-na*, did you say?" they inquired.

"Nothing," Mouse answered. "Nothing of importance. I was just joking."

"Yes, you did say something," said a Water Person. "You said that Coyote nearly fell into the water. You cannot fool me."

MOUSE insisted that she had not said that, and the other Water People believed her. They knew she was a fickle person and giddy, and they did not think much of her because she went everywhere to steal. She went everywhere, and that is why she understood all the different languages.

Carrying packs of dried meat and berries they had brought with them, Coyote and Fox made their way to the lodge of Whale, the chief. He and the stolen wife sat side by side in the lodge. The wife was glad to get the meat and berries, her kind of food.

---

2. **Big Falls:** Kettle Falls on the Columbia River in northeastern Washington.

FOX AND COYOTE kept their robes over their faces until everyone else was asleep. Then, when everything was quiet, Fox slipped up to Whale and cut off the monster's head with a flint knife. At the same time Coyote picked up the stolen wife and ran for the broken canoe. The noise they made awoke the camp, and the people rushed out of their lodges to see Coyote carrying off Fox's wife and Fox close behind, carrying the head of their chief. The people chased them, but the three got into the broken canoe, and Fox quickly put Coyote and the woman into his *shoo'-mesh*[3] pipe. Then Fox pushed the half-canoe into the water and it shot up to the river's surface below the falls. There Fox landed. He took Coyote and his twice-stolen wife out of the medicine pipe, and the head of the Whale Monster he threw toward the setting sun.

"In the Big Salt Water (ocean) shall Whale Monster stay," said Fox. "No longer shall he live in the smaller waters, in the rivers, where he can make love to the wives of men, where he can lure wives from their husbands."

As Fox and his wife and brother walked up the bank to their tepee, the headless body of Whale Monster turned over and over in the depths of the river, making the Big Falls of the *Swah-netk'-qhu* more fearful and thunderous, the way they are today, spilling with such force over the great rocks.

The wife of Fox became contented and happy again, glad to be back in her husband's lodge. But since that day Whale Monster was vanquished the Land People and the Water People have not loved each other. Fox made it so. ❖

Mask for Coyote Dance. Courtesy, University of Texas at Austin. Photo by Donald Codry.

---

3. *shoo'-mesh:* the Salish word for medicine, or magic power.

Connect to the Literature

1. **What Do You Think?** What did you feel was most memorable about "Fox and Coyote and Whale"?

   Comprehension Check
   - Why do Fox and Coyote go to the world of the Water People?
   - What caused the powerful force of Kettle Falls, according to the story?
   - Why don't whales live in fresh waters, according to the story?

Think Critically

2. What might be Okanogan storytellers' purpose for telling this story?

3. **ACTIVE READING** **STRATEGIES FOR READING TRICKSTER TALES** Share details about Okanogan culture that you recorded in your ▌READER'S NOTEBOOK as you read the story. What did you learn about the Okanogan people and their way of life?

   THINK ABOUT
   {
   - their values, attitudes, and beliefs
   - geographical features of their area
   - the ways they adapt to their environment

4. Do you view Coyote as admirable? Explain why or why not.

Extend Interpretations

5. **Comparing Texts** What do these Coyote stories have in common with other folk tales you know?

6. **Different Perspectives** Some Native Americans have argued that stories about the Animal People constitute "the first history of America." Do you agree? Support your opinion.

7. **Connect to Life** Compare Coyote in these stories with your previous mental image of a coyote. Refer to the word web you were asked to make on page 39.

Literary Analysis

TRICKSTER TALE A **trickster tale** is a folk tale about an animal or person who engages in deceit, violence, and magic. Besides Coyote, tricksters in Native American oral traditions also include Raven, Mink, Hare, and Blue Jay. In tales from other world cultures, the trickster is a spider, a rabbit, or a fox. According to the folklorist Stith Thompson, a trickster "may appear in any one of three roles: the beneficent culture hero, the clever deceiver, or the numskull."

Paired Activity Create a three-column chart that classifies tricksters according to Stith Thompson's categories. Then meet with a partner to analyze the roles that Coyote plays in "Coyote and the Buffalo" and "Fox and Coyote and Whale." Fill in the chart with examples to support your findings. In each tale, which role of trickster seems the most dominant?

Culture Hero	Clever Deceiver	Numskull

Writing Options

1. Magazine Article Meet with two other students to brainstorm a list of four tricksters who are popular today. Then compare and contrast them with Coyote. Use your discussion to outline a magazine article about one of these tricksters.

Writing Handbook
See page 1281: Compare and Contrast

2. Updated Trickster Tale Some modern American writers have used the figure of Coyote in their own stories and poetry, updating the traditional tales for their own times. Drawing on the characters and plot structures of the Coyote tales you have just read, write your own contemporary trickster tale.

A Trickster Tale

Activities & Explorations

1. Creative Pantomime It was customary for storytellers to visit different villages and tell stories about the Animal People to children. To help dramatize the stories, the storytellers used facial expressions and gestures. Choose one of the two Coyote tales, and use creative movement and gestures to act it out for your classmates as a partner reads aloud. **~ PERFORMING**

2. Coyote on Video When the Nez Perce anthropologist Archie Phinney recorded his people's animal stories in writing, he felt that their spirit had been lost. He said, "When I read my story mechanically I find only the cold corpse." View the video of storyteller Terry Tafoya's performance of "Coyote's Eyes." What would be lost if the performance were transferred to the printed page? **~ VIEWING AND REPRESENTING**

 Literature in Performance

Mourning Dove
1888?–1936

Other Works
Mourning Dove: A Salishan Autobiography
Mourning Dove's Stories

Echoes of the Past "Mourning Dove" was the pen name of Christine Quintasket, who grew up on the Colville Reservation in north central Washington State. As a child, she listened eagerly to the stories told by her mother, Lucy; her father, Joseph; Broken Nose Abraham; Long Woman; and other storytellers. In the preface to *Coyote Stories,* she reflects on what these storytellers taught her about the Animal People:

> *Vividly I recall old S'whist-kane (Lost-Head), also known as Old Narciss, and how, in the course of a narrative, he would jump up and mimic his characters, speaking or singing in a strong or weak voice, just as the Animal Persons were supposed to have done. And he would dance around the fire in the tule-mat covered lodge until the pines rang with the gleeful shouts of the smallest listeners.*

Determined to Write Mourning Dove not only was educated in her people's oral traditions but also had some formal education at government and Catholic mission schools. Determined to be a writer, she learned to write English and later attended secretarial school in Canada to learn how to type. She drafted a novel in 1912 but put it away for several years, until she met Lucullus Virgil McWhorter, an author and Native American–rights activist, who offered to edit it. *Cogewea, the Half-Blood* was published in 1927.

A Storyteller's Legacy McWhorter encouraged Mourning Dove to record the traditional stories of the Okanogan and the other Colville tribes. Although Mourning Dove was a migrant worker, picking apples ten hours a day, she managed to write at night. *Coyote Stories,* which McWhorter and the journalist Heister Dean Guie helped edit, was published in 1933. By collecting and preserving some of the stories that tell the history of her people, Mourning Dove in her own way carried on the work of the storytellers she had heard as a child.

The Man to Send Rain Clouds

Short Story by LESLIE MARMON SILKO

Comparing Literature

Traditions Across Time: Harmonizing Old and New

"The Man to Send Rain Clouds" is not traditional oral literature but a short story, in a modern setting, by a contemporary Native American writer. Still, like the earlier pieces you have read, the story reflects ancient beliefs and ceremonies.

Points of Comparison As you read, compare the Laguna characters' spiritual views with those expressed in other Native American cultures. Also notice the impact of Christianity on traditional Laguna ways.

Build Background

The story depicts funeral ceremonies held among the Laguna people of western New Mexico. Like the Tewa, the Laguna are a Pueblo group, but they speak a Keresan language. Pueblo groups had settled in the Southwest thousands of years before the first Spanish conquistadors arrived in 1540. The Spanish came to establish a colony and to convert the Pueblos to Catholicism but were driven away in 1680 during the Pueblo Rebellion. The Spanish soon returned, however, completing their re-conquest of New Mexico in 1692. The Laguna pueblo was founded in 1699 by emigrants from other pueblos to the north. In the 1700s and 1800s, the Laguna and other Pueblo groups were harassed by Mexican slavers; raiders from the Navajo, Apache, and Ute tribes; and Protestant settlers from the United States.

Despite being influenced by outside cultures, the Laguna have kept many of their values and beliefs. For example, they perform traditional ceremonies when a person dies because they believe that dead persons' spirits will become Shiwanna —Cloud People—who bring the precious gift of rain.

Focus Your Reading

LITERARY ANALYSIS **CONFLICT** A **conflict** is a struggle between opposing forces that is the basis of a story's plot. A character can be in conflict with an outside force, such as nature, society or another character. One of the conflicts in this story is between the characters Leon and Father Paul. Conflict can also occur within a character. Notice the different kinds of conflict in this story.

ACTIVE READING **MAKING INFERENCES** An **inference** is a logical guess based on evidence. By using information from your reading and from your own experience, you can make inferences about things left unstated in a work of literature.

READER'S NOTEBOOK Use a chart like the one started below to record the ceremonies, or prescribed acts, that people either perform or want performed after Teofilo's death. Use the second or third column to indicate which tradition you infer that the ceremony belongs to, Laguna or European.

Ceremony	Laguna	European
painting on face	X	

THE MAN TO SEND RAIN CLOUDS

Leslie Marmon Silko

THEY FOUND HIM UNDER A BIG COTTONWOOD TREE.
His Levi jacket and pants were faded light-blue so that he had been easy to find. The big cottonwood tree stood apart from a small grove of winterbare cottonwoods which grew in the wide, sandy arroyo. He had been dead for a day or more, and the sheep had wandered and scattered up and down the arroyo. Leon and his brother-in-law, Ken, gathered the sheep and left them in the pen at the sheep camp before they returned to the cottonwood tree. Leon waited under the tree while Ken drove the truck through the deep sand to the edge of the arroyo. He squinted up at the sun and unzipped his jacket—it sure was hot for this time of year. But high and northwest the blue mountains were still deep in snow. Ken came sliding down the low, crumbling bank about fifty yards down, and he was bringing the red blanket.

Before they wrapped the old man, Leon took a piece of string out of his pocket and tied a small gray feather in the old man's long white hair. Ken gave him the paint. Across the brown wrinkled forehead he drew a streak of white and along the high cheekbones he drew a strip of blue paint. He paused and watched Ken throw pinches of corn meal and pollen into the wind that fluttered the small gray feather. Then Leon painted with yellow under the old man's broad nose, and finally, when he had painted green across the chin, he smiled.

"Send us rain clouds, Grandfather." They laid the bundle in the back of the pickup and covered it with a heavy tarp before they started back to the pueblo.

They turned off the highway onto the sandy pueblo road. Not long after they passed the store and post office they saw Father Paul's car coming toward them. When he recognized their faces he slowed his car and waved for them to stop. The young priest rolled down the car window.

"Did you find old Teofilo?" he asked loudly.

Leon stopped the truck. "Good morning, Father. We were just out to the sheep camp. Everything is O.K. now."

49

"Thank God for that. Teofilo is a very old man. You really shouldn't allow him to stay at the sheep camp alone."

"No, he won't do that any more now."

"Well, I'm glad you understand. I hope I'll be seeing you at Mass this week—we missed you last Sunday. See if you can get old Teofilo to come with you." The priest smiled and waved at them as they drove away.

Louise and Teresa were waiting. The table was set for lunch, and the coffee was boiling on the black iron stove. Leon looked at Louise and then at Teresa.

"We found him under a cottonwood tree in the big arroyo near sheep camp. I guess he sat down to rest in the shade and never got up again." Leon walked toward the old man's bed. The red plaid shawl had been shaken and spread carefully over the bed, and a new brown flannel shirt and pair of stiff new Levis were arranged neatly beside the pillow. Louise held the screen door open while Leon and Ken carried in the red blanket. He looked small and shriveled, and after they dressed him in the new shirt and pants he seemed more shrunken.

It was noontime now because the church bells rang the Angelus.[1] They ate the beans with hot bread, and nobody said anything until after Teresa poured the coffee.

Ken stood up and put on his jacket. "I'll see about the gravediggers. Only the top layer of soil is frozen. I think it can be ready before dark."

Leon nodded his head and finished his coffee. After Ken had been gone for a while, the neighbors and clanspeople came quietly to embrace Teofilo's family and to leave food on the table because the gravediggers would come to eat when they were finished.

The sky in the west was full of pale-yellow light. Louise stood outside with her hands in the pockets of Leon's green army jacket that was too big for her. The funeral was over, and the old men had taken their candles and medicine bags[2]

and were gone. She waited until the body was laid into the pickup before she said anything to Leon. She touched his arm, and he noticed that her hands were still dusty from the corn meal that she had sprinkled around the old man. When she spoke, Leon could not hear her.

"What did you say? I didn't hear you."

"I said that I had been thinking about something."

"About what?"

"About the priest sprinkling holy water[3] for Grandpa. So he won't be thirsty."

Leon stared at the new moccasins that Teofilo had made for the ceremonial dances in the summer. They were nearly hidden by the red blanket. It was getting colder, and the wind pushed gray dust down the narrow pueblo road. The sun was approaching the long <u>mesa</u> where it disappeared during the winter. Louise stood there shivering and watching his face. Then he zipped up his jacket and opened the truck door. "I'll see if he's there."

Ken stopped the pickup at the church, and Leon got out; and then Ken drove down the hill to the graveyard where people were waiting. Leon knocked at the old carved door with its symbols of the Lamb. While he waited he looked up at the twin bells from the king of Spain with the last sunlight pouring around them in their tower.

The priest opened the door and smiled when he saw who it was. "Come in! What brings you here this evening?"

The priest walked toward the kitchen, and

---

1. **rang the Angelus** (ăn'jə-ləs): was rung to remind Roman Catholics to recite a prayer in commemoration of the Annunciation, the archangel Gabriel's announcing to the Virgin Mary that she had conceived Jesus, the Son of God.

2. **medicine bags:** pouches containing collections of sacred items believed to possess magical influence.

3. **holy water:** water blessed by a priest and used for religious purposes.

WORDS TO KNOW **mesa** (mā' sə) n. a broad, flat-topped hill with clifflike sides

Between Heaven and Earth; Earth and Sky (1976), Frank LaPena. Acrylic on canvas, 24″ × 18″, WINTU-NOMTIPOM.

Leon stood with his cap in his hand, playing with the earflaps and examining the living room—the brown sofa, the green armchair, and the brass lamp that hung down from the ceiling by links of chain. The priest dragged a chair out of the kitchen and offered it to Leon.

"No thank you, Father. I only came to ask you if you would bring your holy water to the graveyard."

The priest turned away from Leon and looked out the window at the patio full of shadows and the dining-room windows of the nuns' <u>cloister</u> across the patio. The curtains were heavy, and the light from within faintly penetrated; it was impossible to see the nuns inside eating supper. "Why didn't you tell me he was dead? I could have brought the Last Rites[4] anyway."

Leon smiled. "It wasn't necessary, Father."

The priest stared down at his scuffed brown loafers and the worn hem of his <u>cassock</u>. "For a Christian burial it was necessary."

His voice was distant, and Leon thought that his blue eyes looked tired.

"It's O.K. Father, we just want him to have plenty of water."

---

4. **Last Rites:** a sacrament in which a priest anoints a dying person with holy oil and prays for his or her salvation.

He felt good because it was finished, and he was happy about the sprinkling of the holy water; now the old man could send them big thunderclouds for sure.

The priest sank down into the green chair and picked up a glossy missionary magazine. He turned the colored pages full of lepers and pagans without looking at them.

"You know I can't do that, Leon. There should have been the Last Rites and a funeral Mass at the very least."

Leon put on his green cap and pulled the flaps down over his ears. "It's getting late, Father. I've got to go."

When Leon opened the door Father Paul stood up and said, "Wait." He left the room and came back wearing a long brown overcoat. He followed Leon out the door and across the dim churchyard to the adobe steps in front of the church. They both stooped to fit through the low adobe entrance. And when they started down the hill to the graveyard only half of the sun was visible above the mesa.

The priest approached the grave slowly, wondering how they had managed to dig into the frozen ground; and then he remembered that this was New Mexico, and saw the pile of cold loose sand beside the hole. The people stood close to each other with little clouds of steam puffing from their faces. The priest looked at them and saw a pile of jackets, gloves, and scarves in the yellow, dry tumbleweeds that grew in the graveyard. He looked at the red blanket, not sure that Teofilo was so small, wondering if it wasn't some <u>perverse</u> Indian trick—something they did in March to ensure a good harvest—wondering if maybe old Teofilo was actually at sheep camp corralling the sheep for the night. But there he was, facing into a cold dry wind and squinting at the last sunlight, ready to bury a red wool blanket while the faces of his parishioners were in shadow with the last warmth of the sun on their backs.

His fingers were stiff, and it took him a long time to twist the lid off the holy water. Drops of water fell on the red blanket and soaked into dark icy spots. He sprinkled the grave and the water disappeared almost before it touched the dim, cold sand; it reminded him of something— he tried to remember what it was, because he thought if he could remember he might understand this. He sprinkled more water; he shook the container until it was empty, and the water fell through the light from sundown like August rain that fell while the sun was still shining, almost evaporating before it touched the wilted squash flowers.

The wind pulled at the priest's brown Franciscan robe[5] and swirled away the corn meal and pollen that had been sprinkled on the blanket. They lowered the bundle into the ground, and they didn't bother to untie the stiff pieces of new rope that were tied around the ends of the blanket. The sun was gone, and over on the highway the eastbound lane was full of headlights. The priest walked away slowly. Leon watched him climb the hill, and when he had disappeared within the tall, thick walls, Leon turned to look up at the high blue mountains in the deep snow that reflected a faint red light from the west. He felt good because it was finished, and he was happy about the sprinkling of the holy water; now the old man could send them big thunderclouds for sure. ❖

---

5. **Franciscan robe:** the distinctive garment of a Roman Catholic religious order founded by Saint Francis of Assisi in 1209. After Spain established a colony in New Mexico in 1598, Franciscan missionaries began to settle there and build churches in the pueblos.

WORDS TO KNOW **perverse** (pər-vûrs′) *adj.* stubbornly opposed to what is right or reasonable; wrong-headed

Connect to the Literature

1. **What Do You Think?** Did Teofilo have a "good" funeral? Share your impressions.

> **Comprehension Check**
> - Who is Teofilo and what has happened to him?
> - What do Teofilo's relatives want Father Paul to do?
> - Why is it necessary for Teofilo to have plenty of water?

Think Critically

2. Why do you think Leon and Ken do not tell Father Paul about Teofilo's death right away?

3. Louise and Leon want Father Paul to sprinkle holy water on Teofilo's grave. Why do you think this act is so important to them?

4. **ACTIVE READING   MAKING INFERENCES**   Of the two kinds of ceremonies surrounding Teofilo's death—Laguna and European—which do you think is more important to his people? Refer to the chart you were asked to make in your **READER'S NOTEBOOK.**

5. In your opinion, does Father Paul do the right thing at the end of the story? Consider the evidence.

THINK ABOUT {
 - his attitude toward Laguna ceremonies
 - his attitude toward Christian burial
 - possible reasons for his decision

Extend Interpretations

6. **What If?** Suppose Father Paul had been a Laguna man who had lived in the pueblo as a youth, left to study for the priesthood, and then returned. How might the **conflicts** in this story be different?

7. **Connect to Life** Name important ceremonies in your own culture; for example, the passing out of diplomas at a graduation. What do you believe is the function of ceremonies? When do you think a ceremony should be changed, if ever?

8. **Points of Comparison** Judging from this story, how would you describe the Laguna people's spiritual views and relationship to nature? Compare their beliefs with those of the Iroquois, Tewa, or Navajo.

Literary Analysis

CONFLICT   As you recall, the basis of a story's plot is **conflict,** or a struggle between opposing forces. An **external conflict** pits a character against nature, society, or another character. An **internal conflict** is between opposing forces within a character. In "Coyote and the Buffalo," for example, Coyote's struggle to keep Buffalo Bull from killing him is an external conflict, whereas Coyote's struggle to decide whether to kill and eat the buffalo cow is an internal conflict.

Cooperative Learning Activity In a small group, discuss the conflicts you see in "The Man to Send Rain Clouds." Summarize them on a chart like the one below, and classify each as external or internal. Are the conflicts resolved? If so, tell how.

Conflict	Internal or External?	How Resolved

Writing Options

1. Performance Review Assuming the role either of Father Paul's religious superior or of a leader of the Laguna community, write an evaluation of Father Paul, assessing his relationship with the community he serves.

2. Description of Rites Think about a ceremony that is familiar to you, such as graduation, wedding, or coming-of-age ceremony, and write a detailed description of it for someone who has never seen it before. If you can, explain any symbolic actions, garments, or colors associated with the ceremony. Put your writing in your **Working Portfolio.**

Writing Handbook
See page 1277: Description

Activities & Explorations

1. Illustrative Scene Draw or paint a scene from the story, including specific objects and colors mentioned in relation to Teofilo's death. Then display your picture, explaining significant details to the class. ~ **ART**

2. Points of Comparison Listen as a class member reads the first three paragraphs of this story aloud. Discuss how the story differs in style from the traditional oral literature you read earlier in the unit.

Vocabulary in Action

EXERCISE: RELATED WORDS On your paper, fill in each blank with the word or words that belong in each group below. Then with a partner, practice using the words in a conversation.

Group A: irrational, obstinate, ____(1)____
Group B: mission, ____(2)____, ____(3)____
Group C: desert, ____(4)____, ____(5)____

Building Vocabulary
Two of the Words to Know come from Spanish. For an in-depth study of word origins, see page 550.

WORDS TO KNOW		
arroyo	cloister	perverse
cassock	mesa	

Leslie Marmon Silko
1948–

Other Works
Laguna Woman, Ceremony, Almanac of the Dead

Girl from Laguna Leslie Marmon Silko grew up in the pueblo of Old Laguna, about 45 miles west of Albuquerque, New Mexico. Although she is of mixed European, Laguna, and Mexican ancestry, Silko derives inspiration for her stories, poems, and novels from the traditional Native American myths and tales she learned as a child. "I grew up at Laguna listening," she has said, "and I hear the ancient stories, I hear them very clearly in the stories we are telling right now. Most important, I feel the power which the stories still have, to bring us together, especially when there is loss and grief."

Stories as a Natural Resource In *Storyteller*, which was published in 1981 and includes the story "The Man to Send Rain Clouds," Silko pays tribute to Native American storytelling traditions, weaving together poems, photographs, ancient tales, stories about her family, and stories about memorable characters like Father Paul and Leon. As she told an interviewer, "Storytelling for Indians is like a natural resource. Some places have oil, some have a lot of water or timber or gold, but around here, it's the ear that has developed."

Award Winner Silko, who was educated at the University of New Mexico, considered a law career before becoming a writer and a teacher. She has won numerous grants and awards for her poetry and fiction.

Author Activity

Silko the Storyteller Find a copy of Silko's book *Storyteller*, and choose two other stories from it to read aloud in class. As a group, discuss what more you learn about the Laguna people from the stories.

from The Way to Rainy Mountain

Nonfiction by N. SCOTT MOMADAY

Comparing Literature

Traditions Across Time: Harmonizing Old and New

The selection you are about to read is a personal and historical narrative by N. Scott Momaday, one of the most important modern voices of Kiowa culture. Momaday's writing, like Leslie Marmon Silko's, draws on Native American history and traditions and reflects a love of the land.

Points of Comparison Compare Momaday to Silko as you read. Also notice how the stories embedded in Momaday's narrative are similar to the earlier Native American literature you have read.

Build Background

The Kiowa In the 1600s, after a bitter dispute between two chiefs, a band of Kiowa moved from what is now western Montana to South Dakota's Black Hills. About 1785, the Kiowa migrated farther south to escape frequent attacks by neighboring tribes, settling in what is now western Kansas and Oklahoma. Like other Plains Indian groups, the Kiowa hunted buffalo, lived in tepees, had warrior societies, and observed the annual Sun Dance as an important religious ceremony.

With their Comanche allies, the Kiowa ruled the southern Great Plains for about 100 years, until their survival was threatened by deadly smallpox and cholera epidemics, the decline of buffalo herds, and bloody conflicts with other tribes and with U.S. soldiers. One of the last tribes of Plains Indians to be defeated by the U.S. government, the Kiowa surrendered at Fort Sill in 1875 and were forced onto a reservation in the southwestern part of the Indian Territory (now Oklahoma), where today members of the tribe farm and lease mining rights.

WORDS TO KNOW **Vocabulary Preview**

engender	nomadic	servitude
inherently	opaque	unrelenting
linear	preeminently	
luxuriant	profusion	

Focus Your Reading

LITERARY ANALYSIS **SETTING** The **setting** of a literary work consists of the time and place in which the events unfold. Notice how, in the opening sentence of this selection, Momaday uses details to establish the setting:

A single knoll rises out of the plain in Oklahoma, north and west of the Wichita Range.

As you read the selection, be aware that Momaday weaves together events from several different times and places. Use details to help you visualize each time period and landscape that he describes.

ACTIVE READING **UNDERSTANDING STRUCTURE**

The **structure** of a literary work is the arrangement of its parts—its pattern of organization. Momaday interweaves three distinct strands throughout his narrative:

- geographical details about the landscape
- historical details about the rise and fall of the Kiowa
- personal details about his grandmother Aho

READER'S NOTEBOOK Create a three column chart with the following headings: **The Landscape, The Kiowa, Momaday's Grandmother.** As you read each paragraph in this selection, write down one or two things you learn about any of these topics.

from The Way to RAINY MOUNTAIN

N. Scott Momaday

A single knoll[1] rises out of the plain in Oklahoma, north and west of the Wichita Range. For my people, the Kiowas, it is an old landmark, and they gave it the name Rainy Mountain. The hardest weather in the world is there. Winter brings blizzards, hot tornadic winds arise in the spring, and in summer the prairie is an anvil's edge. The grass turns brittle and brown, and it cracks beneath your feet. There are green belts along the rivers and creeks, <u>linear</u> groves of hickory and pecan, willow and witch hazel. At a distance in July or August the steaming foliage seems almost to writhe in fire. Great green and yellow grasshoppers are everywhere in the tall grass, popping up like corn to sting the flesh, and tortoises crawl about on the red earth, going nowhere in the plenty of time. Loneliness is an aspect of the land. All things in the plain are isolate; there is no confusion of objects in the eye, but one hill or one tree or one man. To look upon that landscape in the early morning, with the sun at your back, is to

Wun-Pan-To-Mee, The White Weasel (1836), George Catlin. Watercolor on paper, 5¾″ × 5⅛″. Gilcrease Museum, Tulsa, Oklahoma (0226.1493).

---

1. **knoll** (nōl): a small round hill.

lose the sense of proportion. Your imagination comes to life, and this, you think, is where Creation was begun.

I returned to Rainy Mountain in July. My grandmother had died in the spring, and I wanted to be at her grave. She had lived to be very old and at last infirm. Her only living daughter was with her when she died, and I was told that in death her face was that of a child.

HER FOREBEARS *came down from the high country in western Montana nearly three centuries ago.*

I like to think of her as a child. When she was born, the Kiowas were living the last great moment of their history. For more than a hundred years they had controlled the open range from the Smoky Hill River to the Red, from the headwaters of the Canadian to the fork of the Arkansas and Cimarron. In alliance with the Comanches, they had ruled the whole of the southern Plains. War was their sacred business, and they were among the finest horsemen the world has ever known. But warfare for the Kiowas was <u>preeminently</u> a matter of disposition rather than of survival, and they never understood the grim, <u>unrelenting</u> advance of the U.S. Cavalry. When at last, divided and ill-provisioned, they were driven onto the Staked Plains in the cold rains of autumn, they fell into panic. In Palo Duro Canyon they abandoned their crucial stores to pillage and had nothing then but their lives. In order to save themselves, they surrendered to the soldiers at Fort Sill[2] and were imprisoned in the old stone corral that now stands as a military museum. My grandmother was spared the humiliation of those high gray walls by eight or ten years, but she must have known from birth the affliction of defeat, the dark brooding of old warriors.

Her name was Aho, and she belonged to the last culture to evolve in North America. Her forebears came down from the high country in western Montana nearly three centuries ago. They were a mountain people, a mysterious tribe of hunters whose language has never been positively classified in any major group. In the late seventeenth century they began a long migration to the south and east. It was a journey toward the dawn, and it led to a golden age. Along the way the Kiowas were befriended by the Crows,[3] who gave them the culture and religion of the Plains. They acquired horses, and their ancient <u>nomadic</u> spirit was suddenly free of the ground. They acquired Tai-me, the sacred Sun Dance doll, from that moment the object and symbol of their worship, and so shared in the divinity of the sun. Not least, they acquired the sense of destiny, therefore courage and pride. When they entered upon the southern Plains they had been transformed. No longer were they slaves to the simple necessity of survival; they were a lordly and dangerous society of fighters and thieves, hunters and priests of the sun. According to their origin myth, they entered the world through a hollow log. From one point of view, their migration was the fruit of an old prophecy, for indeed they emerged from a sunless world.

Although my grandmother lived out her long life in the shadow of Rainy Mountain, the immense landscape of the continental interior lay

---

2. **Fort Sill:** a U.S. Army post established in 1869 in the Indian Territory (now Oklahoma).

3. **Crows:** a group of Native Americans who once inhabited the region between the Platte and Yellowstone rivers in the northern Great Plains and who are now settled in Montana.

WORDS TO KNOW	**preeminently** (prē-ĕm′ə-nənt-lē) *adv.* above all; most importantly **unrelenting** (ŭn′rĭ-lĕn′tĭng) *adj.* not stopping or weakening **nomadic** (nō-măd′ĭk) *adj.* without a fixed home; wandering

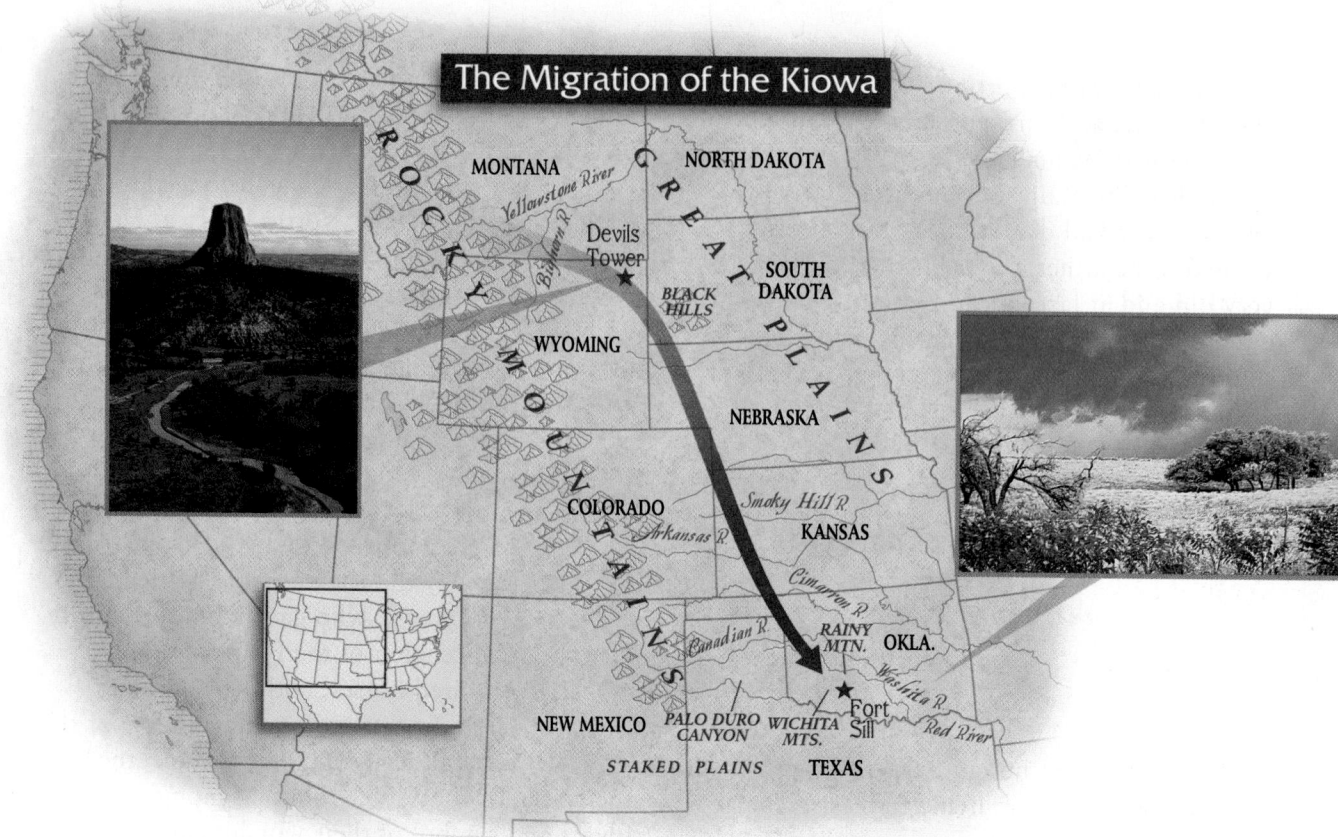

The Migration of the Kiowa

MONTANA

NORTH DAKOTA

Yellowstone River

ROCKY

Devils
Tower
★

BLACK
HILLS

SOUTH
DAKOTA

GREAT

WYOMING

NEBRASKA

PLAINS

Smoky Hill R.

COLORADO

Arkansas R.

KANSAS

MOUNTAINS

Cimarron R.

Canadian R.

RAINY
MTN.

OKLA.

Wichita R.

NEW MEXICO

PALO DURO
CANYON

WICHITA
MTS.

★ Fort
Sill

Red River

STAKED PLAINS

TEXAS

like memory in her blood. She could tell of the Crows, whom she had never seen, and of the Black Hills, where she had never been. I wanted to see in reality what she had seen more perfectly in the mind's eye, and traveled fifteen hundred miles to begin my pilgrimage.

Yellowstone, it seemed to me, was the top of the world, a region of deep lakes and dark timber, canyons and waterfalls. But, beautiful as it is, one might have the sense of confinement there. The skyline in all directions is close at hand, the high wall of the woods and deep cleavages of shade. There is a perfect freedom in the mountains, but it belongs to the eagle and the elk, the badger and the bear. The Kiowas reckoned their stature by the distance they could see, and they were bent and blind in the wilderness.

Descending eastward, the highland meadows are a stairway to the plain. In July the inland

slope of the Rockies is <u>luxuriant</u> with flax and buckwheat, stonecrop and larkspur. The earth unfolds and the limit of the land recedes. Clusters of trees, and animals grazing far in the distance, cause the vision to reach away and wonder to build upon the mind. The sun follows a longer course in the day, and the sky is immense beyond all comparison. The great billowing clouds that sail upon it are shadows that move upon the grain like water, dividing light. Farther down, in the land of the Crows and Blackfeet,[4] the plain is yellow. Sweet clover takes hold of the hills and bends upon itself to cover and seal the soil. There the Kiowas paused on their way; they had come to the place where they must change their lives. The sun is at home

---

4. **Blackfeet:** a group of Native Americans who once inhabited a region now occupied by parts of Montana, Alberta, and Saskatchewan.

WORDS
TO
KNOW   **luxuriant** (lŭg-zhŏŏr′ē-ənt) *adj.* characterized by abundant growth

on the plains. Precisely there does it have the certain character of a god. When the Kiowas came to the land of the Crows, they could see the dark lees[5] of the hills at dawn across the Bighorn River, the profusion of light on the grain shelves, the oldest deity ranging after the solstices.[6] Not yet would they veer southward to the caldron[7] of the land that lay below; they must wean their blood from the northern winter and hold the mountains a while longer in their view. They bore Tai-me in procession to the east.

A dark mist lay over the Black Hills, and the land was like iron. At the top of a ridge I caught sight of Devil's Tower upthrust against the gray sky as if in the birth of time the core of the earth had broken through its crust and the motion of the world was begun. There are things in nature that engender an awful quiet in the heart of man; Devil's Tower is one of them. Two centuries ago, because they could not do otherwise, the Kiowas made a legend at the base of the rock. My grandmother said:

Eight children were there at play, seven sisters and their brother. Suddenly the boy was struck dumb; he trembled and began to run upon his hands and feet. His fingers became claws, and his body was covered with fur. Directly there was a bear where the boy had been. The sisters were terrified; they ran, and the bear after them. They came to the stump of a great tree, and the tree spoke to them. It bade them climb upon it, and as they did so it began to rise into the air. The bear came to kill them, but they were just beyond its reach. It reared against the tree and scored the bark all around with its claws. The seven sisters were borne into the sky, and they became the stars of the Big Dipper.

From that moment, and so long as the legend lives, the Kiowas have kinsmen in the night sky. Whatever they were in the mountains, they could be no more. However tenuous their well-being, however much they had suffered and would suffer again, they had found a way out of the wilderness.

My grandmother had a reverence for the sun, a holy regard that now is all but gone out of mankind. There was a wariness in her, and an ancient awe. She was a Christian in her later years, but she had come a long way about, and she never forgot her birthright. As a child she had been to the Sun Dances; she had taken part in those annual rites, and by them she had learned the restoration of her people in the presence of Tai-me. She was about seven when the last Kiowa Sun Dance was held in 1887 on the Washita River above Rainy Mountain Creek. The buffalo were gone. In order to consummate the ancient sacrifice—to impale the head of a buffalo bull upon the medicine tree—a delegation of old men journeyed into Texas, there to beg and barter for an animal from the Goodnight herd. She was ten when the Kiowas came together for the last time as a living Sun Dance culture. They could find no buffalo; they had to hang an old hide from the sacred tree. Before the dance could begin, a company of soldiers rode out from Fort Sill under orders to disperse the tribe. Forbidden without cause the essential act of their faith, having seen the wild herds slaughtered and left to rot upon the ground, the Kiowas backed away forever from the medicine tree. That was July 20, 1890, at the

---

5. **lees:** sides sheltered from the wind.

6. **solstices** (sŏl′stĭs-ĭz): the times of year—about June 21 and December 21—when days are longest and shortest in the Northern Hemisphere, marking the beginnings of summer and winter.

7. **caldron** (kôl′drən): a large kettle for boiling things—here, the term is used figuratively.

WORDS TO KNOW
profusion (prə-fyoo′zhən) *n.* abundance; lavishness
engender (ĕn-jĕn′dər) *v.* to produce; bring about

59

Kiowa Sun Dance,
Sharron Ahtone.
Photo by Sandy
Settle. Private col-
lection.

great bend of the Washita. My grandmother was there. Without bitterness, and for as long as she lived, she bore a vision of deicide.[8]

Now that I can have her only in memory, I see my grandmother in the several postures that were peculiar to her: standing at the wood stove on a winter morning and turning meat in a great iron skillet; sitting at the south window, bent above her beadwork, and afterwards, when her vision failed, looking down for a long time into the fold of her hands; going out upon a cane, very slowly as she did when the weight of age came upon her; praying. I remember her most often at prayer. She made long, rambling prayers out of suffering and hope, having seen many things. I was never sure that I had the right to hear, so exclusive were they of all mere custom and company. The last time I saw her she prayed standing by the side of her bed at night, naked to the waist, the light of a kerosene lamp moving upon her dark skin. Her long, black hair, always

drawn and braided in the day, lay upon her shoulders and against her breasts like a shawl. I do not speak Kiowa, and I never understood her prayers, but there was something inherently sad in the sound, some merest hesitation upon the syllables of sorrow. She began in a high and descending pitch, exhausting her breath to silence; then again and again—and always the same intensity of effort, of something that is, and is not, like urgency in the human voice. Transported so in the dancing light among the shadows of her room, she seemed beyond the reach of time. But that was illusion; I think I knew then that I should not see her again.

Houses are like sentinels[9] in the plain, old keepers of the weather watch. There, in a very little while, wood takes on the appearance of great age. All colors wear soon away in the wind

---

8. **deicide** (dē'ə-sīd'): the destruction of a god.

9. **sentinels:** sentries; watchmen.

60

and rain, and then the wood is burned gray and the grain appears and the nails turn red with rust. The windowpanes are black and opaque; you imagine there is nothing within, and indeed there are many ghosts, bones given up to the land. They stand here and there against the sky, and you approach them for a longer time than you expect. They belong in the distance; it is their domain.

Once there was a lot of sound in my grandmother's house, a lot of coming and going, feasting and talk. The summers there were full of excitement and reunion. The Kiowas are a summer people; they abide the cold and keep to themselves, but when the season turns and the land becomes warm and vital they cannot hold still; an old love of going returns upon them. The aged visitors who came to my grandmother's house when I was a child were made of lean and leather, and they bore themselves upright. They wore great black hats and bright ample shirts that shook in the wind. They rubbed fat upon their hair and wound their braids with strips of colored cloth. Some of them painted their faces and carried the scars of old and cherished enmities.[10] They were an old council of warlords, come to remind and be reminded of who they were. Their wives and daughters served them well. The women might indulge themselves; gossip was at once the mark and compensation of their servitude. They made loud and elaborate talk among themselves, full of jest and gesture, fright and false alarm. They went abroad in fringed and flowered shawls, bright beadwork and German silver. They were at home in the kitchen, and they prepared meals that were banquets.

There were frequent prayer meetings, and great nocturnal[11] feasts. When I was a child I played with my cousins outside, where the lamplight fell upon the ground and the singing of the old people rose up around us and carried away into the darkness. There were a lot of good things to eat, a lot of laughter and surprise. And afterwards, when the quiet returned, I lay down with my grandmother and could hear the frogs away by the river and feel the motion of the air.

Now there is a funeral silence in the rooms, the endless wake of some final word. The walls have closed in upon my grandmother's house. When I returned to it in mourning, I saw for the first time in my life how small it was. It was late at night, and there was a white moon, nearly full. I sat for a long time on the stone steps by the kitchen door. From there I could see out across the land; I could see the long row of trees by the creek, the low light upon the rolling plains, and the stars of the Big Dipper. Once I looked at the moon and caught sight of a strange thing. A cricket had perched upon the handrail, only a few inches away from me. My line of vision was such that the creature filled the moon like a fossil. It had gone there, I thought, to live and die, for there, of all places, was its small definition made whole and eternal. A warm wind rose up and purled[12] like the longing within me.

The next morning I awoke at dawn and went out on the dirt road to Rainy Mountain. It was already hot, and the grasshoppers began to fill the air. Still, it was early in the morning, and the birds sang out of the shadows. The long yellow grass on the mountain shone in the bright light, and a scissortail[13] hied[14] above the land. There, where it ought to be, at the end of a long and legendary way, was my grandmother's grave. Here and there on the dark stones were ancestral names. Looking back once, I saw the mountain and came away. ❖

---

10. **enmities** (ĕn′mĭ-tēz): hatreds.
11. **nocturnal**: occurring at night.
12. **purled**: flowed with a murmuring sound.
13. **scissortail**: a bird with a long, forked tail, native to the southwestern United States.
14. **hied** (hīd): hurried.

WORDS TO KNOW **opaque** (ō-pāk′) *adj.* not allowing light to pass through
servitude (sûr′vĭ-tōōd′) *n.* the condition of one who is subject to a master; lack of freedom

Connect to the Literature

1. What Do You Think?
What are your impressions of Momaday's grandmother Aho? Describe her in a few words or phrases.

Comprehension Check
- Why does Momaday return to Rainy Mountain?
- What two natural phenomena does the Kiowa story about the seven sisters and their brother explain?
- Why did the Kiowa stop holding the annual Sun Dance ritual?

Think Critically

2. How would you characterize Momaday's relationship with his grandmother?

3. **ACTIVE READING** **UNDERSTANDING STRUCTURE** Review the chart you created in your **READER'S NOTEBOOK**. What are some things you learned about the Kiowa from this selection?

THINK ABOUT

- important events in their history
- their beliefs, traditions, and customs
- their origin myth
- the story about the seven sisters and their brother
- the personal habits of Momaday's grandmother

4. What do you think is the most important insight that Momaday gains during his pilgrimage from Yellowstone to his grandmother's grave at Rainy Mountain? Explain your response.

5. A **symbol** is a person, place, or object that has a concrete meaning in itself and also stands for something beyond itself, such as an idea or a feeling. What might the cricket mentioned at the end of this selection symbolize to Momaday?

Extend Interpretations

6. Connect to Life Momaday values his close relationship with his grandmother. Discuss what young people today can learn or gain from older relatives, giving examples from your own or others' experience.

7. **Points of Comparison** What similarities of **style**, **subject**, or **theme** do you see in the excerpt from *The Way to Rainy Mountain* and Leslie Marmon Silko's story "The Man to Send Rain Clouds"?

Literary Analysis

SETTING In some fiction and nonfiction works, **setting**—the particular time and place in which the action occurs—is no more than a backdrop for events. In others, setting is very important. A writer may use setting to create a mood or may make it a driving force in a story—one that influences events or affects how the characters act and feel. In Momaday's narrative, the Great Plains landscape plays a central role.

Paired Activity With a partner, review the details about the plains landscape and about Kiowa history and culture that you recorded in your **READER'S NOTEBOOK**. In what ways did the landscape influence the lives of the Kiowa? In what ways does it affect Momaday as he travels? Jot down your ideas and share them with other pairs of students.

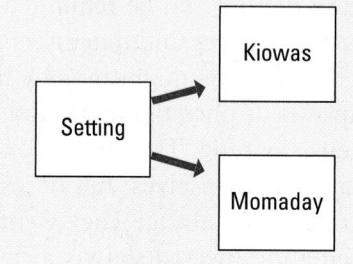

Writing Options

1. A Fitting Eulogy Write a eulogy for Momaday's grandmother Aho or for the culture of the Kiowa as she knew it in her childhood. Deliver the eulogy to classmates, then place it in your **Working Portfolio.**

2. Points of Comparison In an essay, compare the Kiowa values conveyed in the excerpt from *The Way to Rainy Mountain* with the Iroquois values conveyed in "The World on the Turtle's Back."

Activities & Explorations

Points of Comparison Momaday's father, Al, illustrated *The Way to Rainy Mountain.* Create two illustrations of your own—one to accompany this excerpt from Momaday's book and one to accompany another selection in this part of Unit One. Display your artwork in the classroom, along with a brief explanation of how your illustrations reflect the selections' content and the values of different Native American cultures. ~ **ART**

Vocabulary in Action

EXERCISE: ASSESSMENT PRACTICE On your paper, write the vocabulary word that best completes each analogy.

1. GLASS: TRANSPARENT:: paper : _____
2. FARMERS: SETTLED:: herders : _____
3. HAPPILY: JOYFULLY:: especially : _____
4. POVERTY: WEALTH:: freedom : _____
5. DESERT: BARREN:: jungle : _____
6. WHEEL: CIRCULAR:: street : _____
7. INSUFFICIENT: INADEQUATE:: endless : _____
8. OBSERVE: EXAMINE:: produce : _____
9. WEARINESS: VITALITY:: scarcity : _____
10. LARGELY: MOSTLY:: essentially : _____

WORDS TO KNOW	engender luxuriant preeminently unrelenting	inherently nomadic profusion	linear opaque servitude

N. Scott Momaday
1934–

Other Works
Angle of Geese and Other Poems
The Names: A Memoir
The Ancient Child
The Man Made of Words

Native American Roots Born in Lawton, Oklahoma, on February 27, 1934, N. Scott Momaday grew up on Native American reservations in the Southwest. His father, a Kiowa, was a well-known artist and art teacher. His mother, of English, French, and Cherokee ancestry, was a teacher and writer. Although his parents moved away from the Kiowa community when he was two years old, Momaday developed a strong ethnic identity. In his childhood, his parents taught him about the culture, history, and traditions of the Kiowa people, and they took him on a journey to Devils Tower. During the summer months, he frequently returned to Oklahoma to visit his grandfather Mammedaty, his grandmother Aho, and other Kiowa relations.

Voice of the Kiowa Momaday wrote his first poem, a tribute to a pet dog, when he was nine years old. Later he became the first Native American to receive a Pulitzer Prize, which he was awarded for his novel *House Made of Dawn* (1968). In one of his favorite works, *The Way to Rainy Mountain* (1969), he mixes Kiowa myths, legends, and history with autobiographical details. When asked by an interviewer how his heritage has affected his work, Momaday answered, "When I was growing up on the reservations of the Southwest, I saw people who were deeply involved in their traditional life, in the memories of their blood. They had, as far as I could see, a certain strength and beauty that I find missing in the modern world at large. I like to celebrate that involvement in my writing."

Building Vocabulary
For an in-depth lesson on analogies, see page 254.

Comparing Literature: Assessment Practice

Many assessment prompts ask you to compare literary elements in two or more selections. You will now practice writing an essay with a comparison focus.

PART 1 Reading the Prompt

Often you will be asked to write in response to a prompt like the one below. Pay close attention to the wording of the prompt. Look for clues that help you identify the purpose and the scope of your essay and the kind of information to include.

> **Writing Prompt**
>
> In *The Way to Rainy Mountain*, Momaday retells a traditional Kiowa story about seven sisters and their brother. In an essay compare this story and ❶ another traditional Native American story you have read—for example, the Iroquois creation myth or one of the Okanogan Coyote stories. Consider the qualities of the characters, the ❷ transformations that occur, and the explanations offered in the stories. Then generalize about the ❸ relationship between humans and nature that the stories suggest.

STRATEGIES IN ACTION

❶ **Compare,** or find similarities in, two stories.

❷ Notice the **features** you will be comparing.

❸ **Generalize,** making a statement that applies to more than one example.

PART 2 Planning a Comparison Essay

- In a graphic, note details about features you will compare—characters, transformations, and explanations.

- Identify similarities to make a general statement about humans and nature.

Stories Being Compared

Features	Kiowa Story	Iroquois or Okanogan Story	
characters			Generalization about humans and nature
transformations			
explanations			

PART 3 Drafting Your Essay

Introduction State the two stories you will compare and the features you will examine in each.

Organization You might write a **subject-by-subject** comparison in which you write about one story first and then the other. Or, you might write a **feature-by-feature** comparison in which you discuss the characters in both stories, the transformations in both stories, and so on.

Conclusion Summarize what you learned from the comparison. Write a general statement about the relationship between humans and nature in the two stories.

Revision Allow time to review your work. Make sure it is clear, well-supported, and free from mistakes.

Writing Handbook
See page 1281: Compare and Contrast

Fools Crow

JAMES WELCH

Set in Montana during the late 19th century, this coming-of-age story features a young warrior, Fools Crow, whose haunting vision foretells the dying culture of Native Americans. As a member of the Blackfeet, Fools Crow will face a key decision—either to defend his people's land and way of life or to suffer an immense loss of cultural identity. Loosely based on true events, the novel portrays the world of James Welch's ancestors—their landscape and their history.

American Indian Myths and Legends

EDITED BY RICHARD ERDOES AND ALFONSO ORTIZ

This collection of 160 Native American tales keeps the past alive. Drawing from a rich oral tradition, the editors have captured the voices of storytellers from a wide range of tribal groups across the United States. These stories provide a glimpse into Native Americans' diverse cultural heritage—their views of human behavior and relationships, the mysterious origins of life, heroes and war, animals, and the natural environment.

And Even *More* . . .

Books

Growing Up Native American
EDITED BY PATRICIA RILEY
An anthology of stories and personal histories about the passage of youth to maturity, told from the perspective of Native Americans.

The Way to Rainy Mountain
N. SCOTT MOMADAY
This autobiographical work inventively mixes poetry, legend, history, and artwork.

Native American Almanac
ARLENE HIRSCHFELDER AND MARTHA KREIPE DE MONTANO
Comprehensive information and fascinating facts on Native American history, culture, and perspectives.

Other Media

Smoke Signals
This 1998 feature film—the first written, directed, and produced by Native Americans—explores the lives of two men from an Idaho reservation. Miramax Films. (VIDEOCASSETTE)

More Than Bows and Arrows
Author N. Scott Momaday narrates this critically acclaimed documentary focusing on Native American culture. Camera One. (VIDEOCASSETTE)

The American Indian
This product presents a panoramic view of Native American history through audio clips, images, and text. Facts on File. (CD-ROM)

Spider Woman's Granddaughters

EDITED BY PAULA GUNN ALLEN

Remnants of the past and the realities of the present are brought to life in this anthology of tales, essays, and short stories. Louise Erdrich and Leslie Marmon Silko are among the contributors who give voice to the experiences of Native American women.

First Encounters

Accounts of Exploration and Exploitation

*W*hen Christopher Columbus landed on a tiny Caribbean island in 1492, he called the inhabitants Indians because he thought he was near the East Indies. One of the first men to try to communicate with Columbus inadvertently cut his hand on Columbus's sword because he didn't know what a sword was. Such events—mistaken identity and injury—marked the first recorded encounter between the native people of the Americas and the Europeans who were to come in increasing numbers over the next 500 years.

Although the first explorers' motivations for coming to the Americas were complex, many came for the reason people often seek out dangers and challenges: a desire for fame and adventure. In addition, the early explorers expected to find great riches. European rulers had already sent explorers to India and China to bring back spices, silks, gold, jewelry, and other luxuries. Columbus, of course, was looking for a shortcut to these countries when he unexpectedly bumped into a new world. Once the European monarchs realized that Columbus had led the way to two previously unknown continents, they put their best explorers to work finding out what wealth they could gain from these new lands.

Not all motivations for coming to the Americas were selfish ones, however. Reports of the existence of people in the Americas stirred many to come to spread Christianity. Others, such as the English Puritans, came seeking the religious freedom that they were denied in their homeland. Nevertheless, for both Catholics and Protestants, Christianity was the only true religion. People who

The Landing of Columbus at San Salvador (Guanahani), October 12, 1492. The Granger Collection.

were not Christian had to be converted by persuasion or by force. Those who rejected Christianity were considered enemies of God, suitable only for enslavement or death.

The story of cultural contact, like the story of America itself, would not be complete without the experiences of the Africans who were brought here as slaves. The European trade in enslaved Africans had been started by the Portuguese during the 1400s, and enslaved Africans accompanied most of the Spanish and Portuguese explorers in the Americas. In fact, one of the three men who survived with Cabeza de Vaca on his disastrous journey was an enslaved African named Estéban.

Africans were first brought in large numbers to the West Indies to provide labor for the vast sugar plantations. At first, the Spanish plantation owners had tried to use Indian labor, but the native peoples proved too susceptible to European diseases and unable to withstand the harsh treatment of their masters. Africans took their place. Before long, English colonists were also participating in the slave trade. In 1619, twelve years after the founding of Jamestown, Virginia—the first permanent English

Voices *from the* Times

from *The Log of Christopher Columbus*

Friday, October 12, 1492

No sooner had we concluded the formalities of taking possession of the island than people began to come to the beach, all as naked as their mothers bore them, and the women also, although I did not see more than one very young girl. All those that I saw were young people, none of whom was over 30 years old. They are very well-built people, with handsome bodies and very fine faces, though their appearance is marred somewhat by very broad heads and foreheads, more so than I have ever seen in any other race. Their eyes are large and very pretty, and their skin is the color of Canary Islanders or of sunburned peasants, not at all black, as would be expected because we are on an east-west line with Hierro in the Canaries. These are tall people and their legs, with no exceptions, are quite straight, and none of them has a paunch. They are, in fact, well proportioned. Their hair is not kinky, but straight, and coarse like horsehair. They wear it short over the eyebrows, but they have a long hank in the back that they never cut. Many of the natives paint their faces; others paint their whole bodies; some, only the eyes or nose. Some are painted black, some white, some red; others are of different colors.

The people here called this island *Guanahaní* in their language, and their speech is very fluent, although I do not understand any of it. They are friendly and well-dispositioned people who bear no arms except for small spears, and they have no iron. I showed one my sword, and through ignorance he grabbed it by the blade and cut himself. Their spears are made of wood, to which they attach a fish tooth at one end, or some other sharp thing.

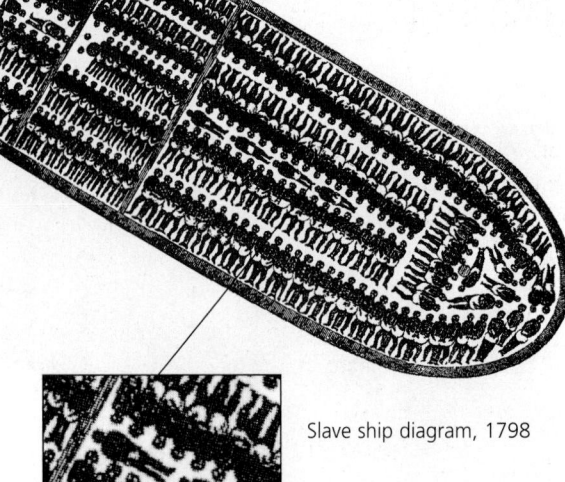

Slave ship diagram, 1798

I want the natives to develop a friendly attitude toward us because I know that they are a people who can be made free and converted to our Holy Faith more by love than by force. I therefore gave red caps to some and glass beads to others. They hung the beads around their necks, along with some other things of slight value that I gave them. And they took great pleasure in this and became so friendly that it was a marvel. They traded and gave everything they had with good will, but it seems to me that they have very little and are poor in everything. I warned my men to take nothing from the people without giving something in exchange.

This afternoon the people of San Salvador[1] came swimming to our ships and in boats made from one log. They brought us parrots, balls of cotton thread, spears, and many other things, including a kind of dry leaf[2] that they hold in great esteem. For these items we swapped them little glass beads and hawks' bells.

Many of the men I have seen have scars on their bodies, and when I made signs to them to find out how this happened, they indicated that people from other nearby islands come to San Salvador to capture them; they defend themselves the best they can. I believe that people from the mainland come here to take them as slaves. They ought to make good and skilled servants, for they repeat very quickly whatever we say to them. I think they can easily be made Christians, for they seem to have no religion. If it pleases Our Lord, I will take six of them to Your Highnesses when I depart, in order that they may learn our language.

Translated by Robert H. Fuson

---

1. **San Salvador** (săn săl'və-dôr'): the name that Columbus gave the island he first landed on; it means "Holy Savior" in Spanish.

2. **dry leaf**: tobacco

settlement in the Americas—20 Africans were brought there as indentured servants. Eighteen years later, the first American-built slave ship, the *Desire,* set sail from Marblehead, Massachusetts.

One of the few firsthand accounts of the perilous two months that enslaved Africans spent packed in ships bound for the Americas is that of Olaudah Equiano. You will read about his experiences in this part of the unit.

Traditions Across Time: The New Explorers

The tradition of writing about the exploration of a new place and what is encountered there has continued up to the present day. But what, you might ask, is left to explore in a world of jet propulsion, TV, computers, and fiber optics? In the remaining selections in this part of Unit One, you will read about some contemporary explorations: William Least Heat-Moon's exploration of forgotten areas of his own country, and Maya Angelou's journey across the ocean to discover the Africa of her ancestors.

Accounts of Exploration and Exploitation

Álvar Núñez Cabeza de Vaca   *from* **La Relación**   72
Struggles to survive in an unknown land

LINK ACROSS CULTURES
Marco Polo   *from* **The Travels of Marco Polo**   77
Five months stranded on the island of Sumatra

William Bradford   *from* **Of Plymouth Plantation**   81
The Pilgrims find a new home.

RELATED READING
Alicia Crane Williams   *from* **Women and Children First: The Mayflower Pilgrims**   91
Something personal about the Pilgrims

Olaudah Equiano   *from* **The Interesting Narrative of the Life of Olaudah Equiano**   93
Harrowing experiences aboard a slave ship

COMPARING LITERATURE
Traditions Across Time: The New Explorers

William Least Heat-Moon   *from* **Blue Highways** (1982)   100
Making discoveries in your own land

Maya Angelou   **My Sojourn in the Lands of My Ancestors** (1986)   109
An American finds sorrow and joy in her African heritage.

Historical Narratives

Recording the American Experience

Imagine living in a world with no electronic media. For many of us, it would be quite a stretch to imagine living like that. However, for all people, this was the basic condition of life more than 400 years ago, when people from very different parts of the world first interacted with each other in America.

Many records of these interactions still exist and provide insights into the past. **Historical narratives** are accounts of real-life historical experiences, given either by a person who experienced those events or by someone who has studied or observed them. In many cases, the narratives are key historical documents, existing as our principal record of events. Historical narratives take two basic forms:

PRIMARY SOURCES Historical narratives can take the form of documents, such as letters, diaries, journals, and autobiographies, that present direct, firsthand knowledge of a subject; these are known as a primary sources.

SECONDARY SOURCES These types of narratives provide indirect, secondhand knowledge. Histories and biographies are examples of secondary sources.

Records of Real Life

The first Americans, the Native Americans, had been recording information for thousands of years through picture symbols (in the form of pictographs, animal skin drawings, Mayan *glyphs,* and wampum belts), and through oral language. The myth "The World on the Turtle's Back"

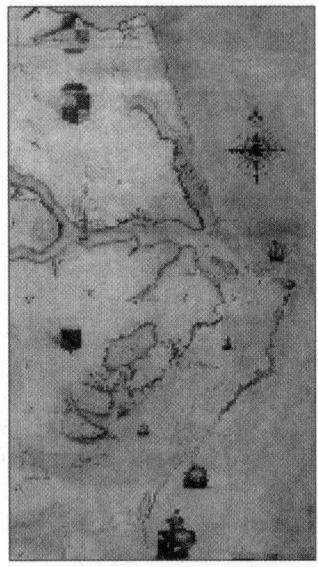

John White and Thomas Harriot, Roanoke colonists, rendered this map of Virginia in about 1588. Copyright © British Museum.

(page 24), the sacred song "Song of the Sky Loom" (page 33), and the selection of coyote stories (page 39) represent a tiny part of the wealth of this oral tradition.

In the late 15th century, Europeans began voyages by ship to the Americas and reported news of their explorations and settlement. Many historical narratives of these times were survivors' tales, gripping adventure stories written down in journals and letters. Álvar Núñez Cabeza de Vaca was one of many explorers who sailed to the New World after Christopher Columbus. The historical narrative *La Relación* was Cabeza de Vaca's report to the King of Spain. Note the details conveyed in this passage:

> When night fell, only the navigator and I remained able to tend the barge. Two hours after dark he told me I must take over; he believed he was going to die that night.
>
> —Álvar Núñez Cabeza de Vaca

The use of vivid, sensory details makes historical narratives come to life. In 1620, the Puritans survived a journey across the Atlantic in *The Mayflower* and landed at Cape Cod. In 1630, William Bradford, the Plymouth Colony's second governor, began writing *Of Plymouth Plantation,* a chronicle of his colony's experiences. This is Bradford's description of the colony's first winter:

> The weather was very cold and it froze so hard as the spray of the sea lighting on their coats, they were as if they had been glazed.
>
> —William Bradford

As American colonies expanded from the 16th through the 18th centuries, the slave trade expanded as well. Olaudah Equiano, one of the millions of Africans captured and transported to the Americas, survived his ordeal and published his autobiography in 1789. (It is also a slave narrative, a literary form that is discussed in detail in the box on the right). These lines from *The Interesting Narrative of the Life of Olaudah Equiano* describe his first reactions to going below the decks of a slave ship:

> There I received such a salutation in my nostrils as I had never experienced in my life; so that, with the loathsomeness of the stench, and crying together, I became so sick and low that I was not able to eat, nor had I the least desire to taste anything.
>
> —Olaudah Equiano

YOUR TURN On the basis of these three excerpts, what personal qualities do you think the writers share?

"Remarkable Productions"

The **slave narrative** is an American literary genre that portrays the daily life of slaves as written by the slaves themselves after having gained their freedom. Some 6,000 slave narratives are known to exist. The Reverend Ephraim Peabody, writing in 1849 about five recently published slave narratives, wrote:

> We place these volumes without hesitation among the most remarkable productions of the age—remarkable as being pictures of slavery by the slave, remarkable as disclosing under a new light the mixed elements of American civilization, and not less remarkable as a vivid exhibition of the force and working of the native love of freedom in the individual mind.
>
> —The Reverend Ephraim Peabody

Probably the most influential example of the genre is the autobiography of Frederick Douglass, *Narrative of the Life of Frederick Douglass, an American Slave* (1845). Harriet Tubman's *Scenes in the Life of Harriet Tubman* (1869) is another important example of the genre.

Strategies for Reading: Historical Narratives

1. Look for clues to a narrative's organization, such as the use of headings and bold type.
2. Determine a document's origin. Check for the use of ellipses [. . .], a clue that words or lines have been cut from the original narrative. Be aware of the original audience and purpose.
3. Keep track of the events described. If necessary, make a time line.
4. Reread and paraphrase (restate in your own words) to help you understand unfamiliar words or sentence structures.
5. Let yourself "experience" the narrative.
6. Briefly state the main idea of the narrative in your own words.
7. Take into account the time a work was written, and try to understand the background, perspective, and even the motives of the writer.
8. Remember to use your Strategies for Active Reading: **monitor, predict, visualize, connect, question, clarify,** and **evaluate.**

from La Relación

***Report by* ÁLVAR NÚÑEZ CABEZA DE VACA**
(äl'vär nōō'nyěs kä-bě'sä dě vä'kä)

Connect to Your Life

Conquistadors—Popular Images Lured by the prospect of vast lands filled with gold and silver, Spanish explorers known as conquistadors (conquerors) took to the seas to claim new colonies for Spain. What image do you have of conquistadors? What did they look like? How did they act? Share your ideas with classmates.

Build Background

A Doomed Expedition In 1527, Pánfilo de Narváez, a Spanish conquistador, led a five-ship, 600-man expedition to Florida. His second in command was Álvar Núñez Cabeza de Vaca. The expedition was a disaster from the moment the Spaniards entered the Caribbean. After the loss of two ships in a hurricane and over 200 men by drowning and desertion, the Narváez expedition finally made its way to the west coast of Florida. Against the advice of Cabeza de Vaca, Narváez separated 300 of his men from the ships and marched these forces overland. Narváez intended for the ships to meet the land forces at a Spanish settlement on the coast of central Mexico, but he had grossly underestimated the vastness of the territory and the difficulty of crossing it. Eventually, overwhelmed by hunger, disease, and Indian attacks, the land forces decided to build five crude barges to get them to Mexico more quickly. These barges, each carrying about 50 men, soon drifted apart, and the one commanded by Cabeza de Vaca was shipwrecked on Galveston Island, off the coast of what is now Texas.

Ultimately, Cabeza de Vaca and three companions were the only survivors of the Narváez expedition. They wandered for more than eight years before reaching Mexico City and thus became the first Europeans to cross North America. After returning to Spain in 1537, Cabeza de Vaca wrote *La Relación,* a report addressed to the king of Spain.

> **WORDS TO KNOW**
> **Vocabulary Preview**
>
> beseech   ingratiate
> cauterize   inundate
> comply   placate
> embody   lament
> infirmity   scoff

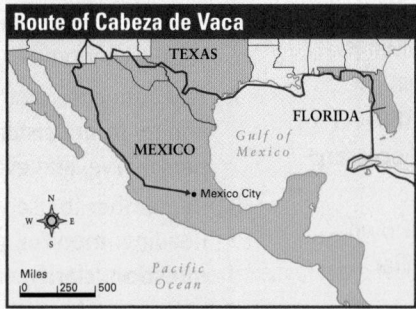

Route of Cabeza de Vaca

Focus Your Reading

LITERARY ANALYSIS | **AUDIENCE**

The **audience** for a piece of writing is the person or persons intended to read it. Cabeza de Vaca wrote *La Relación* for a specific audience—the king of Spain. As you read, notice how Cabeza de Vaca's sense of audience determined the content, format, and organization of his report.

ACTIVE READING | **USING TEXT ORGANIZERS**

Aids—such as italics, boldfaced headings, and colored type—that help emphasize, clarify, or structure ideas in a piece of writing are called **text organizers.** For example, in *La Relación* the italicized paragraphs on pages 73 and 76 provide important background information and introduce the excerpts. The boldfaced headings organize the report by breaking it down into topics. Each heading announces what the section is about.

READER'S NOTEBOOK As you read this report, turn each boldfaced heading into a question. Then take notes, searching for the key details that answer the question and jotting them down.

Álvar Núñez Cabeza de Vaca

from

La Relación

At this point in the account, Narvaez's barge has abandoned the rest, and Cabeza de Vaca's barge has joined one commanded by two other officers. The next three chapters describe the crew's shipwreck on Galveston Island and their encounter with the Karankawa Indians who lived there.

A Sinking and a Landing

Our two barges continued in company for four days, each man eating a ration of half a handful of raw corn a day. Then the other barge was lost in a storm. Nothing but God's great mercy kept us from going down, too.

It was winter and bitterly cold, and we had suffered hunger and the heavy beating of the waves for many days. Next day, the men began to collapse. By sunset, all in my barge had fallen over on one another, close to death. Few were any longer conscious. Not five could stand. When night fell, only the navigator and I remained able to tend the barge. Two hours after dark he told me I must take over; he believed he was going to die that night.

So I took the tiller.[1] After midnight I moved over to see if he were dead. He said no, in fact was better, and would steer till daylight. In that hour I would have welcomed death rather than see so many around me in such a condition. When I had returned the helm[2] to the navigator, I lay down to rest—but without much rest, for nothing was farther from my mind than sleep.

Near dawn I seemed to hear breakers[3] resounding; the coast lying low, they roared louder. Surprised at this, I called to the navigator, who said he thought we were coming close to land. We sounded[4] and found ourselves in seven fathoms.[5] The navigator felt we should stay clear of the shore till daylight; so I took an oar and pulled it on the shore side, wheeling the stern to seaward about a league[6] out.

As we drifted into shore, a wave caught us and heaved the barge a horseshoe-throw [about 42 feet] out of the water. The jolt when it hit brought the dead-looking men to. Seeing land at hand, they crawled through the surf to some rocks. Here we made a fire and parched some of our corn. We also found rain water. The men began to regain their senses, their locomotion, and their hope.

This day of our landing was November 6.

What Befell Oviedo with the Indians

After we ate, I ordered Lope de Oviedo, our strongest man, to climb one of the trees not far off and ascertain the lay of the land. He complied and found out from the treetop that we were on

---

1. **tiller:** a lever used to turn a rudder and steer a boat.
2. **helm:** the steering gear of a boat.
3. **breakers:** waves breaking against a shoreline.
4. **sounded:** measured the depth of the water.
5. **fathoms** (făth′əmz): units used in measuring the depth of water; a fathom is equal to 6 feet (1.83 meters).
6. **league:** a unit of distance; Cabeza de Vaca probably used the Spanish league, equal to 3.1 miles (5 kilometers).

WORDS TO KNOW

comply (kəm-plī′) *v.* to obey another's command, request, rule, or wish

Indians forced to carry baggage and supplies of the Spanish invaders (1590), Theodor de Bry. Rare Books and Manuscripts Division, The New York Public Library, Astor, Lenox, and Tilden Foundations.

not half a dozen of us could even stand up.

The Inspector [Solís] and I walked out and greeted them. They advanced, and we did our best to placate and ingratiate. We gave them beads and bells, and each one of them gave us an arrow in pledge of friendship. They told us by signs that they would return at sunrise and bring food, having none then.

an island. [This was Galveston Island.] He also said that the ground looked as if cattle had trampled it and therefore that this must be a country of Christians.

I sent him back for a closer look, to see if he could find any worn trails, but warned him not to risk going too far. He went and came upon a path which he followed for half a league to some empty huts. The Indians were gone to shoal-flats[7] [to dig roots]. He took an earthen pot, a little dog, and a few mullets[8] and started back.

We had begun to worry what might have happened to him, so I detailed another two men to check. They met him shortly and saw three Indians with bows and arrows following him. The Indians were calling to him and he was gesturing them to keep coming. When he reached us, the Indians held back and sat down on the shore.

Half an hour later a hundred bowmen reinforced the first three individuals. Whatever their stature, they looked like giants to us in our fright. We could not hope to defend ourselves;

The Indians' Hospitality Before and After a New Calamity

As the sun rose next morning, the Indians appeared as they promised, bringing an abundance of fish and of certain roots which taste like nuts, some bigger than walnuts, some smaller, mostly grubbed from the water with great labor.

That evening they came again with more fish and roots and brought their women and children to look at us. They thought themselves rich with the little bells and beads we gave them, and they repeated their visits on other days.

Being provided with what we needed, we thought to embark again. It was a struggle to dig our barge out of the sand it had sunk in, and another struggle to launch her. For the work in the water while launching, we stripped and stowed our clothes in the craft.

---

7. **shoal-flats:** stretches of level ground under shallow water.
8. **mullets** (mŭl′ĭts): a kind of edible fish.

WORDS TO KNOW

placate (plā′kāt′) *v.* to soothe another's feelings; appease
ingratiate (ĭn-grā′shē-āt′) *v.* to gain another's favor by deliberate effort

74

Quickly clambering in and grabbing our oars, we had rowed two crossbow shots from shore when a wave <u>inundated</u> us. Being naked and the cold intense, we let our oars go. The next big wave capsized the barge. The Inspector and two others held fast, but that only carried them more certainly underneath, where they drowned.

A single roll of the sea tossed the rest of the men into the rushing surf and back onto shore half-drowned.

We lost only those the barge took down; but the survivors escaped as naked as they were born, with the loss of everything we had. That was not much, but valuable to us in that bitter November cold, our bodies so emaciated we could easily count every bone and looked the very picture of death. I can say for myself that from the month of May I had eaten nothing but corn, and that sometimes raw. I never could bring myself to eat any of the horse-meat at the time our beasts were slaughtered; and fish I did not taste ten times. On top of everything else, a cruel north wind commenced to complete our killing.

The Lord willed that we should find embers while searching the remnants of our former fire. We found more wood and soon had big fires raging. Before them, with flowing tears, we prayed for mercy and pardon, each filled with pity not only for himself but for all his wretched fellows.

At sunset the Indians, not knowing we had gone, came again with food. When they saw us looking so strangely different, they turned back in alarm. I went after them calling, and they returned, though frightened. I explained to them by signs that our barge had sunk and three of our number drowned. They could see at their feet two of the dead men who had washed ashore. They could also see that the rest of us were not far from joining these two.

The Indians, understanding our full plight, sat down and <u>lamented</u> for half an hour so loudly they could have been heard a long way off. It was amazing to see these wild, untaught savages

Indian man of Florida, after Jacques Le Moyne de Morgues (about 1585–1593), John White. Copyright © British Museum.

howling like brutes in compassion for us. It intensified my own grief at our calamity and had the same effect on the other victims.

When the cries died down, I conferred with the Christians about asking the Indians to take us to their homes. Some of our number who had been to New Spain warned that the Indians would sacrifice us to their idols.[9] But death being surer and nearer if we stayed where we were, I

---

9. **New Spain . . . their idols:** New Spain included what is now the southwest United States, Mexico, Central America north of Panama, and some West Indian islands. In Mexico, conquistadors had encountered Aztecs who practiced human sacrifice.

---

went ahead and <u>beseeched</u> the Indians. They were delighted. They told us to tarry a little while, then they would do as we wished.

Presently thirty of them gathered loads of wood and disappeared to their huts, which were a long walk away; while we waited with the remainder until near nightfall. Then, supporting us under our arms, they hurried us from one to another of the four big fires they had built along the path. At each fire, when we regained a little warmth and strength, they took us on so swiftly our feet hardly touched ground.

Thus we made their village, where we saw they had erected a hut for us with many fires inside. An hour later they began a dance celebration that lasted all night. For us there was no joy, feasting, or sleep, as we waited the hour they should make us victims.

In the morning, when they brought us fish and roots and acted in every way hospitably, we felt reassured and somewhat lost our anxiety of the sacrificial knife.

CABEZA DE VACA *learned that men from one of the other barges had also landed on the island, bringing the number of Europeans there to about 90. In a matter of weeks, all but 16 of them died of disease, which spread to the Karankawas and killed half of them as well. Some of the Karankawas wanted to put the remaining Europeans to death but were dissuaded by Cabeza de Vaca's host. Cabeza de Vaca and his men were later forced to act as healers.*

How We Became Medicine-Men

The islanders wanted to make physicians of us without examination or a review of diplomas. Their method of cure is to blow on the sick, the breath and the laying-on of hands supposedly casting out the <u>infirmity</u>. They insisted we should do this too and be of some use to them. We <u>scoffed</u> at their cures and at the idea we knew how to heal. But they withheld food from us until we complied. An Indian told me I knew not whereof I spoke in saying their methods had no effect. Stones and other things growing about in the fields, he said, had a virtue whereby passing a pebble along the stomach could take away pain and heal; surely extraordinary men like us <u>embodied</u> such powers over nature. Hunger forced us to obey, but disclaiming any responsibility for our failure or success.

An Indian, falling sick, would send for a medicine-man, who would apply his cure. The patient would then give the medicine-man all he had and seek more from his relatives to give. The medicine-man makes incisions over the point of the pain, sucks the wound, and <u>cauterizes</u> it. This remedy enjoys high repute among the Indians. I have, as a matter of fact, tried it on myself with good results. The medicine-men blow on the spot they have treated, as a finishing touch, and the patient regards himself relieved.

Our method, however, was to bless the sick, breathe upon them, recite a *Pater noster* and *Ave Maria*,[10] and pray earnestly to God our Lord for their recovery. When we concluded with the sign of the cross, He willed that our patients should directly spread the news that they had been restored to health.

In consequence, the Indians treated us kindly. They deprived themselves of food to give to us, and presented us skins and other tokens of gratitude. ❖

Translated by Cyclone Covey

---

10. *Pater noster* (pä′tər-nŏs′tər) **and** *Ave Maria* (ä′vä mə-rē′ə): the Lord's Prayer and the Hail Mary, so called from the prayers' opening words in Latin.

from The Travels of Marco Polo

In 1271, when he was about 17 years old, the Italian trader Marco Polo began his famous journey to Asia. He spent 17 years in China as a guest of the emperor, Kublai Khan; visited islands in the Pacific and Indian oceans; and traveled to India and Persia before returning to Venice in 1295. The first printed version of The Travels of Marco Polo *appeared in 1477. This book of colorful stories inspired Columbus and other European explorers and served as a model for later travel accounts, such as* La Relación.

Of the third kingdom, named Samara.

Leaving Basman, you enter the kingdom of Samara,[1] being another of those into which the island is divided. In this Marco Polo resided five months, during which, exceedingly against his inclination, he was detained by contrary winds. The north star is not visible here, nor even the stars that are in the wain.[2] The people are idolaters[3]; they are governed by a powerful prince, who professes himself the vassal of the grand khan.[4]

As it was necessary to continue for so long a time at this island Marco Polo established himself on shore, with a party of about 2,000 men; and in order to guard against mischief from the savage natives, who seek for opportunities of seizing stragglers, putting them to death, and eating them, he caused a large and deep ditch to be dug around him on the land side, in such manner that each of its extremities terminated in the port, where the shipping lay. This ditch he strengthened by erecting several blockhouses or redoubts[5] of wood, the country affording an abundant supply of that material; and being defended by this kind of fortification, he kept the party in complete security during the five months of their residence. Such was the confidence inspired amongst the natives, that they furnished supplies of victuals[6] and other necessary articles according to an agreement made with them.

No finer fish for the table can be met with in any part of the world than are found here. There is no wheat produced, but the people live upon rice. Wine is not made; but from a species of tree resembling the date-bearing palm they procure an excellent beverage in the following manner. They cut off a branch, and put over the place a vessel to receive the juice as it distils from the wound, which is filled in the course of a day and a night. So wholesome are the qualities of this liquor, that it affords relief in dropsical complaints,[7] as well as in those of the lungs and of the spleen. When these shoots that have been cut are perceived not to yield any more juice, they contrive to water the trees, by bringing from the river, in pipes or channels, so much water as is sufficient for the purpose; and upon this being done, the juice runs again as it did at first. Some trees naturally yield it of a reddish, and others of a pale colour. The Indian nuts[8] also grow here, of the size of a man's head, containing an edible substance that is sweet and pleasant to the taste, and white as milk.

---

1. **Basman . . . Samara:** kingdoms on the island of Sumatra (now part of Indonesia).

2. **the wain:** the group of stars more commonly known as the Big Dipper—so called because its shape resembles that of a wain, or farm wagon.

3. **idolaters** (ī-dŏl′ə-tərz): people who worship idols. Polo uses the term to refer to various sorts of non-Christians.

4. **the vassal of the grand khan:** a lord subject to the authority of Kublai Khan, the Mongol emperor of China.

5. **blockhouses or redoubts:** forts.

6. **victuals** (vĭt′lz): food.

7. **dropsical complaints:** symptoms of dropsy, an illness characterized by a buildup of fluids in body tissues.

8. **Indian nuts:** coconuts.

Connect to the Literature

1. **What Do You Think?** What event or idea in Cabeza de Vaca's account did you find the most surprising?

Comprehension Check
- What happened when the Spaniards tried to leave Galveston Island on their barge?
- Why were the Spaniards afraid to go to the Karankawa village?
- How did the Native Americans force the Spaniards to be useful to them?

Think Critically

2. **ACTIVE READING   USING TEXT ORGANIZERS**   Share with a classmate the headings that you rewrote as questions in your **READER'S NOTEBOOK**, and compare your responses. How did these questions act as guides for reading the text?

3. How closely do Cabeza de Vaca and his men fit your image of conquistadors?

4. What can you **infer** about the feelings of Cabeza de Vaca and his men as they went through their ordeals?

5. How would you say Cabeza de Vaca and his men viewed themselves in relation to the Karankawa Indians they met?

   THINK ABOUT
   - the reason Lope de Oviedo assumed that the island was a country of Christians
   - the terms Cabeza de Vaca uses to describe his men, and those he uses to describe the Karankawas
   - Cabeza de Vaca's opinion of the Karankawas' method of healing

6. How do you think the Karankawas viewed Cabeza de Vaca and his men? What parts of the report support your interpretation?

Extend Interpretations

7. **Comparing Texts** Read the excerpt from *The Travels of Marco Polo* on page 77, and compare Cabeza de Vaca's and Marco Polo's encounters with native peoples. What similarities and differences do you see in their attitudes?

8. **Connect to Life** Sixteenth-century conquistadors described, mapped, and claimed territory that was previously unknown to them. They also replaced traditional belief systems with their own. Who are the present-day equivalents of conquistadors, and what do they explore or conquer?

Literary Analysis

AUDIENCE   In writing *La Relación*, Cabeza de Vaca was keenly aware of his **audience**—the king of Spain. To gain insight into the relationship between the writer and his audience, imagine that Cabeza de Vaca considered the following questions while he was drafting his report:
- What does the king already know about my situation?
- What more do I want him to know and why?
- What **details** would he find most interesting?
- How can I make the information easy for him to follow?
- What kind of language will be most appropriate?

The form Cabeza de Vaca chose, the details he included, the level of **diction** he used, and the attitude he expressed toward his subject all were determined by his knowledge of who his reader would be.

Paired Activity   How might Cabeza de Vaca's account have been changed if he had chosen a different audience? Imagine he had decided to tell about one of his ordeals in a letter to his wife. Choose a brief passage from the selection to rewrite as a personal letter. Exchange your letter with a partner, and discuss the differences between the rewritten passage and the original account.

REVIEW   SETTING   As you recall, **setting** is the time and place of the action in a literary work. How does the physical setting determine the events that Cabeza de Vaca recounts in this selection?

Writing Options

1. Firsthand Account Imagine you are a member of Cabeza de Vaca's expedition. Write a firsthand account of the most difficult ordeal you endure. Include details from one of the passages of *La Relación.* Put your account in your **Working Portfolio.**

2. Essay on Leadership From your reading of this selection, do you think Cabeza de Vaca was a good leader? Draft a short persuasive essay in which you state your opinion and support it with reasons.

A Good Leader

3. Report to the President Imagine you are an astronaut who has just returned from a daring space mission. Using *La Relación* as a model, write a brief report describing your exploration to the president of the United States.

Activities & Explorations

1. Miniseries Storyboard Imagine that you are planning a television miniseries based on the adventures of Cabeza de Vaca. Prepare a storyboard—a series of rough sketches—depicting any scene from this selection.

Combine your work with classmates' to make a bulletin-board display. ~ **ART**

2. Karankawa Speech Speaking as one of the Karankawas who met the shipwrecked Spaniards, make an informal speech to members of a neighboring clan, giving your impressions of the strangers.
~ **SPEAKING AND LISTENING**

3. Informal Debate With a small group of classmates, stage an informal debate in which you discuss the pros and cons of whether the Karankawas should take the shipwrecked strangers to their homes. ~ **SPEAKING AND LISTENING**

4. Bar Graph Working with a partner, create a bar graph like the one started below. List five physical or mental challenges that Cabeza de Vaca and his men faced and numbers to indicate

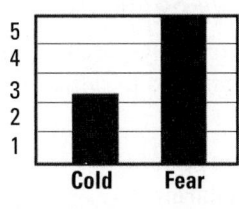

degrees of success. Then draw bars to show the degrees to which the men were able to overcome the challenges.
~ **VIEWING AND REPRESENTING**

Inquiry & Research

Early Explorers Research the following 16th-century Spanish explorers: Juan Ponce de Leon, Vasco Nuñez de Balboa, Hernando Cortés, Ferdinand Magellan, Francisco Pizarro, and Hernando de Soto. Organize your findings in a chart with the following headings: *Explorer, Date of Exploration, Goal,* and *Achievement.*

 More Online: Research Starter www.mcdougallittell.com

Art Connection

History Through Art Like the reports of 16th-century European explorers, the renderings by European artists who came to America served a documentary purpose. For instance, English artist John White made drawings of native people, plants, and wildlife (see his painting of a Florida man on page 75). Theodor de Bry, a Flemish artist, made engravings based on the works of White and others (see page 74). Discuss what these works document—what can you tell about the man in White's painting? What do you learn from de Bry's scene?

Indians forced to carry baggage and supplies of the Spanish invaders (1590).

Vocabulary in Action

EXERCISE: CONTEXT CLUES Write the vocabulary word that is closest in meaning to the italicized word or phrase in each sentence.

1. The Indians learned to *burn* a wound to make it stop bleeding.
2. Starvation caused *illness* among many of the conquistadors.
3. Huge waves threatened to *flood* the barges and capsize them.
4. Why did the navigator *beg* Cabeza de Vaca to take control of the barge?
5. Cabeza de Vaca did not expect the Indians to *express sorrow* for the conquistadors' predicament.
6. The conquistadors learned not to *sneer* at the Indians' healing methods.

7. Cabeza de Vaca seems to *personify* many positive qualities.
8. When Cabeza de Vaca gave an order, his men had no choice but to *obey*.
9. How did the conquistadors *calm* the Indians who were carrying bows?
10. The conquistadors gave away bells and beads to *gain favor for* themselves with the Indians.

WORDS TO KNOW			
	comply	lament	embody
	placate	beseech	cauterize
	ingratiate	infirmity	
	inundate	scoff	

Building Vocabulary
For an in-depth lesson on context clues, see page 326.

Álvar Núñez Cabeza de Vaca
1490?–1557?

A Rising Star As a young man, Cabeza de Vaca joined the Spanish army and fought in many battles. His military successes eventually led to his appointment as an officer of the Narváez expedition to Florida. His report of this ill-fated expedition, *La Relación,* describes his adventures as he crossed the North American continent, living with various Native American tribes and trading shells, beads, skins, and other items to survive. He was the first European to describe a Caribbean hurricane, the Mississippi River, and herds of buffalo.

A Fallen Hero In 1540, Cabeza de Vaca returned to the Americas as governor of the province of Río de la Plata in South America. While there, he led a yearlong expedition 1,000 miles across the continent, becoming the first European to cross both North and South America on foot. As governor, he prohibited the mistreatment of Native Americans by Spaniards. For that reason and others, he was thrown out of office by a group of rebels in 1543 and sent back to Spain two years later. In 1551 he was tried and found guilty of the charges that the rebels had brought against him. He was sentenced to an eight-year exile in Africa, stripped of his titles, and ordered to pay damages to his accusers. In 1556 the king of Spain pardoned him and awarded him a small pension, but his last years were marked by illness and poverty.

Author Activity

Just Like Fiction The scholar William T. Pilkington writes, "*La Relación* possesses many of the attributes of a good novel, especially its subtle presentation of character and its dramatic tension." Read other passages from *La Relación,* and find examples of characterization and plot development that resemble the techniques a novelist uses in writing a well-crafted story.

from Of Plymouth Plantation

Chronicle by WILLIAM BRADFORD

Connect to Your Life

The Pilgrims What do you know about the Pilgrims? How, when, and why did they come to North America? With a small group of classmates, discuss facts and images that come to mind when you think of the Pilgrims. Collect the group's impressions in a cluster diagram.

Build Background

In England during the 1500s and 1600s, a group of Protestants called Puritans led a movement to "purify" the Church of England. One group of Puritans, the Separatists, wanted to withdraw from the established church. Separatist groups were declared illegal, and members faced arrest for practicing their beliefs. One congregation of Separatists, known today as the Pilgrims, fled from England to Holland and eventually migrated to America. In September 1620, this group sailed across the Atlantic on the *Mayflower*. Blown off course, the *Mayflower* reached the tip of Cape Cod, in what is now Massachusetts, in early November. While the ship was moored in Provincetown Harbor, some of the group set out in a smaller boat to search for a good place to build a settlement. About a month later, the colonists built their first shelter at Plymouth.

Nearly half of the colonists died during the first brutal winter, but the entire colony might have perished without the aid of the Wampanoag and other Native American groups. Under Governor William Bradford's leadership, the colony not only survived but also grew to about 300 people by 1630. Bradford wrote about the Pilgrims' long journey and their settlement at Plymouth.

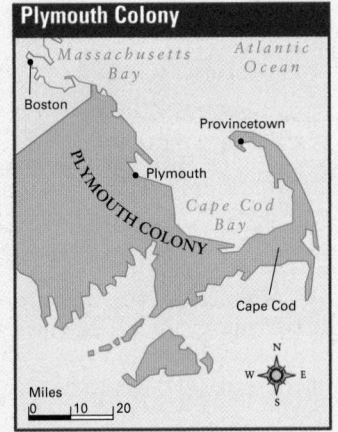

Plymouth Colony

Massachusetts Bay

Atlantic Ocean

Boston

Provincetown

Plymouth

PLYMOUTH COLONY

Cape Cod Bay

Cape Cod

N W E S

Miles
0   10   20

WORDS TO KNOW
Vocabulary Preview

aloof	providence
commodity	procure
desolate	sentinel
feigned	solace
hue	vanquish

Focus Your Reading

LITERARY ANALYSIS   **PRIMARY SOURCES**

Primary sources are written or created by people who observed or participated in an historical event. Primary sources include letters, diaries, speeches, newspaper articles, and eyewitness accounts. *Of Plymouth Plantation,* William Bradford's chronicle of Pilgrim settlers in North America, is an example of a primary source. The passages you are about to read provide direct, firsthand knowledge about a small band of Pilgrims who founded Plymouth colony. As you read this primary source for factual information, also note Bradford's opinions, biases, assumptions, and point of view.

ACTIVE READING   **SUMMARIZING**

Summarizing means condensing what you read into fewer words. As you summarize, you restate the main ideas and most important details. Summarizing helps clarify your understanding of the key information in a piece of writing. The process will be especially useful for reading *Of Plymouth Plantation,* in which the long, complex sentences may divert you from grasping the most essential points.

READER'S NOTEBOOK This selection has five sections, each labeled with a boldfaced heading. Copy the boldfaced headings onto a page of your notebook, leaving writing space below each one. Then, as you read, write a one- or two-sentence summary of each section. Restate the key ideas in your own words.

OF PLYMOUTH PLANTATION

WILLIAM BRADFORD

THEIR SAFE ARRIVAL AT CAPE COD

But to omit other things (that I may be brief) after long beating at sea they[1] fell with that land which is called Cape Cod; the which being made and certainly known to be it, they were not a little joyful. . . .

Being thus arrived in a good harbor, and brought safe to land, they fell upon their knees and blessed the God of Heaven who had brought them over the vast and furious ocean, and delivered them from all the perils and miseries thereof, again to set their feet on the firm and stable earth, their proper element. . . .

But here I cannot but stay and make a pause, and stand half amazed at this

---

1. **they:** Bradford refers to the Pilgrims in the third person even though he is one of them.

poor people's present condition; and so I think will the reader, too, when he well considers the same. Being thus passed the vast ocean, and a sea of troubles before in their preparation (as may be remembered by that which went before), they had now no friends to welcome them nor inns to entertain or refresh their weatherbeaten bodies; no houses or much less towns to repair to, to seek for succor.[2] It is recorded in Scripture as a mercy to the Apostle and his shipwrecked company, that the barbarians showed them no small kindness in refreshing them,[3] but these savage barbarians, when they met with them (as after will appear) were readier to fill their sides full of arrows than otherwise. And for the season it was winter, and they that know the winters of that country know them to be sharp and violent, and subject to cruel and fierce storms, dangerous to travel to known places, much more to search an unknown coast. Besides, what could they see but a hideous and desolate wilderness, full of wild beasts and wild men—and what multitudes there might be of them they knew not. Neither could they, as it were, go up to the top of Pisgah[4] to view from this wilderness a more goodly country to feed their hopes; for which way soever they turned their eyes (save upward to the heavens) they could have little solace or content in respect of any outward objects. For summer being done, all things stand upon them with a weatherbeaten face, and the whole country, full of woods and thickets, represented a wild and savage hue. If they looked behind them, there was the mighty ocean which they had passed and was now as a main bar and gulf to separate them from all the civil parts of the world. . . .

THE FIRST ENCOUNTER

Being thus arrived at Cape Cod the 11th of November, and necessity calling them to look out a place for habitation (as well as the master's and mariners' importunity); they having brought a large shallop[5] with them out of England, stowed in quarters in the ship, they now got her out and set their carpenters to work to trim her up; but being much bruised and shattered in the ship with foul weather, they saw she would be long in mending. Whereupon a few of them tendered themselves to go by land and discover those nearest places, whilst the shallop was in mending; . . .

After this, the shallop being got ready, they set out again for the better discovery of this place, and the master of the ship desired to go himself. So there went some thirty men but found it to be no harbor for ships but only for boats. There was also found two of their [the Indians'] houses covered with mats, and sundry of their implements in them, but the people were run away and could not be seen. Also there was found more of their corn and of their beans of various colors; the corn and beans they [the English] brought away, purposing to give them [the Indians] full satisfaction when they should meet with any of them as, about some six months afterward they did, to their good content.[6]

And here is to be noted a special providence of God, and a great mercy to this poor people, that here they got seed to plant them corn the next year, or else they might have starved, for they had none nor any likelihood to get any till

---

2. **succor** (sŭk′ər): help; relief.

3. **It is . . . refreshing them:** a reference to the biblical account of the courteous reception of Paul and his companions by the inhabitants of Malta (Acts 27:41–28:2).

4. **Pisgah** (pĭz′gə): the mountain from whose peak Moses saw the Promised Land (Deuteronomy 34:1–4).

5. **shallop** (shăl′əp): an open boat usually used in shallow waters.

6. **purposing . . . content:** intending to repay the Nauset Indians whose corn and beans they took, as they in fact did, to the Indians' satisfaction, six months later.

WORDS TO KNOW

desolate (dĕs′ə-lĭt) *adj.* without inhabitants; barren
solace (sŏl′ĭs) *n.* comfort in sorrow or distress
hue (hyōō) *n.* appearance; color
providence (prŏv′ĭ-dəns) *n.* an instance of divine care or guidance

View of Plymouth (1627), Cal Sachs. American Heritage Picture Collection, New York.

the season had been past, as the sequel did manifest. Neither is it likely they had had this, if the first voyage had not been made, for the ground was now all covered with snow and hard frozen; but the Lord is never wanting unto His in their greatest needs; let His holy name have all the praise.

The month of November being spent in these affairs, and much foul weather falling in, the 6th of December they sent out their shallop again with ten of their principal men and some seamen, upon further discovery, intending to circulate that deep bay of Cape Cod. The weather was very cold and it froze so hard as the spray of the sea lighting on their coats, they were as if they had been glazed. . . . [The next night

they landed and] made them a barricado[7] as usually they did every night, with logs, stakes, and thick pine boughs, the height of a man, leaving it open to leeward,[8] partly to shelter them from the cold and wind (making their fire in the middle and lying round about it) and partly to defend them from any sudden assaults of the savages, if they should surround them; so being very weary, they betook them to rest. But about midnight they heard a hideous and great cry, and their <u>sentinel</u> called "Arm! arm!" So they bestirred them and stood to their arms and

---

7. **barricado** (băr´ĭ-kā´dō): a barrier for defense.

8. **to leeward** (lē´wərd): on the side sheltered from the wind.

WORDS	
TO	**sentinel** (sĕn´tə-nəl) *n.* a guard
KNOW	

shot off a couple of muskets, and then the noise ceased. They concluded it was a company of wolves or such like wild beasts, for one of the seamen told them he had often heard such a noise in Newfoundland.

So they rested till about five of the clock in the morning; for the tide, and their purpose to go from thence, made them be stirring betimes. So after prayer they prepared for breakfast, and it being day dawning it was thought best to be carrying things down to the boat. But some said it was not best to carry the arms down, others said they would be the readier, for they had lapped them up in their coats from the dew; but some three or four would not carry theirs till they went themselves. Yet as it fell out, the water being not high enough, they laid them down on the bank side and came up to breakfast.

But presently, all on the sudden, they heard a great and strange cry, which they knew to be the same voices they heard in the night, though they varied their notes; and one of their company being abroad came running in and cried, "Men, Indians! Indians!" And withal, their arrows came flying amongst them. Their men ran with all speed to recover their arms, as by the good providence of God they did. In the meantime, of those that were there ready, two muskets were discharged at them, and two more stood ready in the entrance of their rendezvous[9] but were commanded not to shoot till they could take full aim at them. And the other two charged again with all speed, for there were only four had arms there, and defended the barricado, which was first assaulted. The cry of the Indians was dreadful, especially when they [the Indians] saw their men [the English] run out of the rendezvous toward the shallop to recover their arms, the Indians wheeling about upon them. But some running out with coats of mail on, and cutlasses[10] in their hands, they [the English] soon got their arms and let fly amongst them [the Indians] and quickly stopped their violence. . . .

Thus it pleased God to vanquish their enemies and give them deliverance; and by His special providence so to dispose that not any one of them were either hurt or hit, though their arrows came close by them and on every side [of] them; and sundry of their coats, which hung up in the barricado, were shot through and through. Afterwards they gave God solemn thanks and praise for their deliverance, and gathered up a bundle of their arrows and sent them into England afterward by the master of the ship, and called that place the First Encounter. . . .

THE STARVING TIME

But that which was most sad and lamentable was, that in two or three months' time half of their company died, especially in January and February, being the depth of winter, and wanting houses and other comforts; being infected with the scurvy[11] and other diseases which this long voyage and their inaccommodate condition had brought upon them. So as there died some times two or three of a day in the foresaid time, that of 100 and odd persons, scarce fifty remained. And of these, in the time of most distress, there was but six or seven sound persons who to their great commendations, be it spoken, spared no pains night nor day, but with abundance of toil and hazard of their own health fetched them wood, made them fires, dressed them meat, made their beds, washed their loathsome clothes, clothed and unclothed them. . . . In a word, did all the homely and necessary offices for them which dainty and queasy stomachs cannot endure to hear named; and all this willingly and cheerfully, without any grudging in the least, showing herein their true love unto their friends

---

9. **rendezvous** (rän′dā-vōō′): a gathering place; here used to denote the Pilgrims' encampment.

10. **coats of mail . . . and cutlasses:** armor made of joined metal links, and short curved swords.

11. **scurvy** (skûr′vē): a disease caused by lack of vitamin C.

and brethren; a rare example and worthy to be remembered. Two of these seven were Mr. William Brewster, their reverend Elder, and Myles Standish, their Captain and military commander, unto whom myself and many others were much beholden in our low and sick condition. And yet the Lord so upheld these persons as in this general calamity they were not at all infected either with sickness or lameness. . . .

INDIAN RELATIONS

All this while the Indians came skulking about them, and would sometimes show themselves aloof off, but when any approached near them, they would run away; and once they [the Indians] stole away their [the colonists'] tools where they had been at work and were gone to dinner. But about the 16th of March, a certain Indian came boldly amongst them and spoke to them in broken English, which they could well understand but marveled at it. At length they understood by discourse with him, that he was not of these parts, but belonged to the eastern parts where some English ships came to fish, with whom he was acquainted and could name sundry of them by their names, amongst whom he had got his language. He became profitable to them in acquainting them with many things concerning the state of the country in the east parts where he lived, which was afterwards profitable unto them; as also of the people here, of their names, number and strength, of their situation and distance from this place, and who was chief amongst them. His name was Samoset. He told them also of another Indian whose name was Squanto, a native of this place, who had been in England and could speak better English than himself.

Being, after some time of entertainment and gifts dismissed, a while after he came again, and five more with him, and they brought again all the tools that were stolen away before, and made

way for the coming of their great Sachem,[12] called Massasoit. Who, about four or five days after, came with the chief of his friends and other attendance, with the aforesaid Squanto. With whom, after friendly entertainment and some gifts given him, they made a peace with him (which hath now continued this 24 years) in these terms:

1. That neither he nor any of his should injure or do hurt to any of their people.

2. That if any of his did hurt to any of theirs, he should send the offender, that they might punish him.

3. That if anything were taken away from any of theirs, he should cause it to be restored; and they should do the like to his.

4. If any did unjustly war against him, they would aid him; if any did war against them, he should aid them.

5. He should send to his neighbors confederates to certify them of this, that they might not wrong them, but might be likewise comprised in the conditions of peace.[13]

6. That when their men came to them, they should leave their bows and arrows behind them.

After these things he returned to his place called Sowams,[14] some 40 miles from this place, but Squanto continued with them and was their interpreter and was a special instrument sent of God for their good beyond their expectation. He directed them how to set their corn, where to take fish, and to procure other commodities, and was also their pilot to bring them to unknown places for their profit, and never left them till he died.

---

12. **Sachem** (sā′chəm): chief.

13. **He should . . . peace:** Massasoit was to send representatives to inform other tribes of the compact with the Pilgrims so other tribes might also keep peace with them.

14. **Sowams** (sō′ämz): near the site of present-day Barrington, Rhode Island.

WORDS	**aloof** (ə-lōōf′) *adj.* distant
TO	**procure** (prō-kyŏŏr′) *v.* to get by special effort; obtain
KNOW	**commodity** (kə-mŏd′ĭ-tē) *n.* something useful; an article of commerce

The Bettmann Archive, New York.

FIRST THANKSGIVING

They began now to gather in the small harvest they had, and to fit up their houses and dwellings against winter, being all well recovered in health and strength and had all things in good plenty. For as some were thus employed in affairs abroad, others were exercised in fishing, about cod and bass and other fish, of which they took good store, of which every family had their portion. All the summer there was no want; and now began to come in store of fowl, as winter approached, of which this place did abound when they came first (but afterward decreased by degrees). And besides waterfowl there was great store of wild turkeys, of which they took many, besides venison, etc. Besides they had about a peck[15] a meal a week to a person, or now since harvest, Indian corn to that proportion. Which made many afterwards write so largely of their plenty here to their friends in England, which were not <u>feigned</u> but true reports. ❖

---

15. **peck:** a unit of measurement equal to eight dry quarts.

WORDS TO KNOW **feigned** (fānd) *adj.* not real; pretended

Connect to the Literature

1. What Do You Think?
What is your impression of the Pilgrims after reading these excerpts from *Of Plymouth Plantation*?

Comprehension Check
- How did the Pilgrims view the landscape of Cape Cod when they first arrived?
- What kind of weather did the Pilgrims face after they landed?
- How did the Native Americans help the Pilgrims survive?

Think Critically

2. **ACTIVE READING** **SUMMARIZING** Share your section **summaries** from your **READER'S NOTEBOOK** with a partner. Do they include the most important information? Were all unnecessary details dropped?

3. On the basis of these excerpts, what conclusions can you draw about the Pilgrims' way of looking at the world?

   THINK ABOUT
   - their attitude toward nature
   - their attitude toward God
   - their attitude toward Native Americans

4. Do you think the treaty between the Wampanoag and the Pilgrims was fair? Why or why not? Support your answers with references from the selection.

Extend Interpretations

5. **What If?** What do you think might have happened if Squanto had not helped the Pilgrims? Explain your opinion, using evidence from the selection.

6. **Comparing Texts** Both *Of Plymouth Plantation* and *La Relación* describe Europeans' encounters with Native Americans. Compare the ways in which the Pilgrims and Cabeza de Vaca's men interacted with the Native Americans they met. What do you think accounts for any similarities or differences?

7. **Connect to Life** Religious persecution forced the Pilgrims to flee from England to Holland and later to settle in North America. Think of another group of people who faced persecution for their religious or political beliefs. Briefly explain what happened to them, and compare and contrast their experiences with the Pilgrims' ordeals.

Literary Analysis

PRIMARY SOURCES **Primary sources,** such as diaries and personal histories, often reveal the beliefs and motives of the people involved in an historical event, their ability to overcome obstacles, and the distinctive features of time and place in which they lived. *Of Plymouth Plantation* provides a glimpse of the past through the eyes of William Bradford. As governor of the Plymouth colony and eyewitness to the events he describes, William Bradford is considered a reliable source of information.

Paired Activity Work with a partner to analyze *Of Plymouth Plantation* as a primary source. Consider Bradford's purpose (reason for writing), point of view (narrative perspective from which events are told), assumptions (preconceived ideas) and biases (personal prejudices). Make and fill in a chart like the one shown to record your analyses.

Source	Purpose	Point of View	Assumptions	Biases
Of Plymouth Plantation				

REVIEW **CONFLICT** **Conflict,** as you remember, is a struggle between opposing forces. **Internal conflicts** are within a character; **external conflicts** pit a character against nature, society, or another character. What conflicts are described in this excerpt from *Of Plymouth Plantation*. Are they mostly internal or external?

Writing Options

1. Squanto's Diary Imagine that you are Squanto. Write a diary entry that reveals why you helped the Pilgrims and chose to live with them.

2. Eyewitness Account How do you think the majority of the Wampanoags viewed the arrival and settlement of the Pilgrims? From the Native Americans' point of view, write an eyewitness account of any incident in this selection. Then place the account in your **Working Portfolio.**

3. Interview Questions If you could speak to one of the Pilgrims or Native Americans you have read about, what would you ask him or her? Write five interview questions that you might ask William Bradford, Samoset, or another person. Then write the answers that the person might give.

Activities & Explorations

1. Pilgrim Memorial Design a memorial—such as a statue, monument, or historical marker—for the Pilgrims who died either aboard the *Mayflower* or during the first winter at Plymouth. Then work with classmates to display your memorial designs. ~ **ART**

2. Musical Soundtrack Think about the mood conveyed by each of the excerpts from *Of Plymouth Plantation.* Then work with a partner to create and record a musical soundtrack that evokes these different moods. ~ **MUSIC**

3. Time Line Create a time line, beginning in November 1620 and ending in March 1621, to show important events that happened after the Pilgrims reached Cape Cod. ~ **HISTORY**

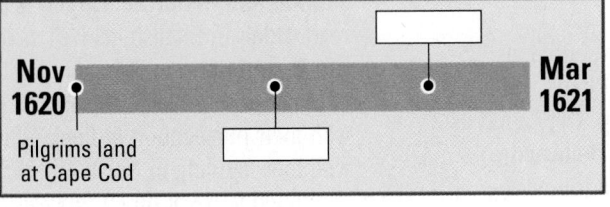

Inquiry & Research

The Voyage of the Pilgrims Find out more about the Pilgrims' voyage on the *Mayflower.* For example, to get a sense of how crowded the 102 passengers were, you might find estimates of the ship's dimensions, make an outline of the deck, and invite other classes to stand with you inside the outline. Learn how women and children fared on the journey by turning to the Related Reading on page 91.

Art Connection

Look at the illustration of the Plymouth colony in 1627 on page 84. Notice where the Puritans set up their military fortification. Why do you think they had it so far inland instead of near the sea?

Choices & CHALLENGES

Vocabulary in Action

EXERCISE A: MATCHING MEANINGS Write the vocabulary word that most clearly relates to the situation expressed by each sentence below.

1. The Pilgrims were able to drive the hostile Indians away.
2. The Pilgrims brought with them some necessities, such as flour for baking bread.
3. The Pilgrims felt that God had helped the colony survive through the first harsh winter.
4. At first, the Indians were reluctant to have contact with the Pilgrims and so didn't come near them.
5. When the Pilgrims explored Cape Cod, some of the men kept watch while the others slept.
6. Vast stretches of seemingly uninhabitable wilderness greeted the Pilgrims.
7. In the fall, the leaves on the trees turned scarlet, orange, and golden yellow.
8. Squanto comforted the Pilgrims by befriending them and helping them learn about the new land.
9. Historians generally believe William Bradford's account and do not think he misrepresented anything.
10. Fortunately, after the first winter the Pilgrims were able to get what they needed to survive by hunting and farming.

EXERCISE B: With a small group of classmates, play a game of charades, acting out the words *desolate, sentinel, vanquish, aloof,* and *feigned.*

Building Vocabulary

For an in-depth lesson on word connotation and denotation, see page 908.

WORDS TO KNOW				
	aloof	feigned	providence	vanquish
	commodity	hue	sentinel	
	desolate	procure	solace	

William Bradford
1590–1657

Other Works
Dialogues

Religious Rebel When the Pilgrims settled at Plymouth, William Bradford was 30 years old and had already endured grave hardship. Orphaned as a young child, he ran off to join an outlawed religious group when he was 12. He joined the Separatists at the age of 16 and two years later followed them to Holland. In 1620, Bradford was among the Separatists and non-Separatists who set sail on the *Mayflower* to start a colony in North America. Bradford likely helped write the Mayflower Compact, the agreement that set up the government of the colony.

Political Leader Bradford joined the initial expeditions to explore Cape Cod but returned from his exploration to find that his young wife, Dorothy May, had drowned while the *Mayflower* was moored in Provincetown Harbor. Despite his difficulties, Bradford kept his faith in God and in the struggling colony. In the spring of 1621, he was elected governor, a post he held for 30 years. Under his leadership, the colony grew into a thriving community.

Scholar and Historian Largely self-taught, Bradford read widely in English, as well as in Dutch, French, Greek, and Hebrew. He wrote the first ten chapters of his history of the Separatists in 1630, beginning with their persecution in England and concluding with their landing in North America in 1620. He continued to work on *Of Plymouth Plantation* over the next 17 years, but his 500-page manuscript remained unpublished until 1856.

Author Activity

Profiles in Courage Historian Samuel Eliot Morison described *Of Plymouth Plantation* as "a story of simple people inspired by an ardent faith to a dauntless courage in danger, a resourcefulness in dealing with new problems . . . ." Read additional selections from *Of Plymouth Plantation,* and find examples that support Morison's claim.

from

Women and Children First: The Mayflower Pilgrims

by Alicia Crane Williams

When the ship *Mayflower* sailed from Plymouth, England, in September 1620 on her voyage into history, she carried 102 passengers, of which nearly half were women and children. Eighteen of the passengers were wives accompanying their husbands to the New World; with them they brought thirty-one children ranging in age from a nursing infant to teenagers. In addition, at least three of the women were pregnant during the voyage. . . .

① Elizabeth Hopkins gave birth to her son Oceanus at sea while also mothering her two-year-old daughter Damaris and her stepchildren, thirteen-year-old Constance and ten-year-old Giles. Miraculously, all survived the voyage and the first winter, though Oceanus and Damaris did not live to adulthood. Five more children eventually were born to the Hopkinses in this inhospitable new land. . . .

In early December 1620, Susanna White gave birth to her son Peregrine on board the *Mayflower* while it was anchored in the shelter of Cape Cod. Two months later her husband William died, leaving her with the baby and their five-year-old son Resolved. In May, Susanna married Edward Winslow, whose first wife had died during the winter. Susanna and Edward's marriage, the first **②** performed in the new colony, produced five children, though only two survived their childhoods. Resolved and Peregrine lived to adulthood, married women of the colony, and fathered fifteen children between them.

Dorothy Bradford, William's wife, left behind her only child, two-year-old John, when she accompanied her husband to the New World. She fell overboard from the *Mayflower*, anchored near Cape Cod, while William was away searching for a settlement site. Although Bradford and his contemporaries recorded the event as accidental, rumors persist to the present day that Dorothy actually committed suicide. . . .

Reading for Information

Curious about the past? Much of our knowledge about past events comes from primary and secondary sources.

- **Primary Source** William Bradford's *Of Plymouth Plantation* is a primary source. It offers firsthand information on the Pilgrims.

- **Secondary Source** In 1993, genealogist Alicia Crane Williams wrote on the same topic. Unlike Bradford, however, Williams did not experience the events she describes. Her article is a secondary source.

PRIMARY AND SECONDARY SOURCES Secondary sources are more likely than primary sources to present a longer view of the history of events. To help you get the most from Williams's article, use these suggestions and activities:

① **Comparing Sources** Bradford himself would have known most of the details that Williams provides about Elizabeth and her children. What information does Williams give that Bradford may not have known?

② Williams has chosen to focus on the women and children among the Pilgrims. What can you infer about her choice, based on the details she provides?

Forty-one-year-old Elinor Billington and her family numbered among the "Strangers" aboard the *Mayflower*. Bradford called the Billingtons "one of the profanest families among us" and could not imagine how they "shuffled into [our] company." John Billington constantly quarreled with Bradford and other leaders and kept company with troublemakers. In 1630 he was convicted of murder, gaining the distinction of being the first person executed by hanging in the New World.

The Billingtons' two sons—John, sixteen years old, and Francis, some years younger—apparently terrorized the other passengers throughout the voyage. Francis endangered the ship by firing his father's fowling piece, igniting a fire that almost spread to nearby barrels of gunpowder. And young John got lost in the woods in May 1621, only to be rescued by Indians and returned to a ten-man search party sent from the colony. The troublesome youth died a few years later, but Francis survived to marry and father nine children.

Priscilla Mullins—today probably the best-known of all the *Mayflower* colonists—would have been about sixteen years old when she supposedly attracted the simultaneous attention of friends John Alden, a cooper hired by the company in Southampton, and Miles Standish, a man of military experience who looked after the colony's defense. Priscilla had arrived in New England with her parents, William and Alice, and her brother Joseph, all of whom perished during that first winter. Captain Standish, who was one of only two people not afflicted with the illness that took so many lives, had lost his wife Rose to the epidemic.

Henry Wadsworth Longfellow's poem *The Courtship of Miles Standish* immortalized the legend of how Standish asked Alden to carry his marriage proposal to Priscilla, who replied, "Why don't you speak for yourself, John?" Married soon after, John and Priscilla had ten children, who in turn produced sixty-nine grandchildren and nearly four hundred great-grandchildren. Miles Standish found a bride elsewhere and fathered seven children.

③ The Billingtons, Williams quotes from Bradford, are "one of the profanest families among us." What does the quotation from Bradford's account add to Williams's own account of the Billington family?

④ Bradford's narrative comes alive with interpretive commentary based on his observations of events, while Williams's is an objective, factual narrative. How would you account for the differences in tone between the two narratives?

Comparing Texts After reading Bradford's account and Williams's narrative, what is your reaction to the experiences of the Plymouth colonists? Did you find one of the accounts more informative than the other? more interesting? more moving? Record your responses.

Detail of *The Slave Ship* (1956),
Robert Riggs.

from The Interesting Narrative of the Life of Olaudah Equiano

Slave Narrative by OLAUDAH EQUIANO (ō-lou′də ĕk′wē-än′ō)

Connect to Your Life

The Slave Trade From the 1500s to the 1800s, millions of Africans were seized from their homelands and brought to the Americas on slave ships. What do you imagine it felt like to be on a slave ship? On what sources—books, movies, magazine articles—do you base your ideas and images? Discuss your ideas in a small group.

Build Background

The Middle Passage The expansion of European colonies in North and South America led to the growth of the transatlantic slave trade. Large plantations needed great numbers of workers to produce sugar, tobacco, and cotton for sale in Europe. Following a triangular route, traders carried manufactured goods (such as cloth and guns) from Europe to Africa, slaves from Africa to the Americas, and raw materials from the Americas to Europe.

Historians estimate that between 10 million and 20 million Africans were enslaved to work in the Americas. During the Middle Passage, the horrific two-month voyage from Africa to the West Indies, millions of enslaved Africans died from the effects of overcrowding, bad food, harsh treatment, disease, and despair. Chained in the dark, airless holds of slave ships, the Africans lay packed side by side. They were allowed on deck only briefly. Olaudah Equiano was one of those who survived the Middle Passage. In the following excerpts, he tells what happened when, as a child, he was shipped to the island of Barbados in the West Indies.

WORDS TO KNOW Vocabulary Preview

anguish	copious	pestilential
apprehension	countenance	stench
avarice	nominal	wretched
consternation		

Focus Your Reading

LITERARY ANALYSIS   SLAVE NARRATIVES
Slave narratives are autobiographical accounts by persons who suffered the horrors of slavery. Equiano's book was one of the earliest American slave narratives. As you read, use your imagination to recreate the horrors he described.

ACTIVE READING   ANALYZING DETAILS
Descriptive details in pieces of writing help readers to imagine and understand characters' experiences. In this selection, Olaudah Equiano uses **sensory details**—ones that appeal to the five senses—to bring to life his first encounter with white men and his ordeal aboard a slave ship.

READER'S NOTEBOOK As you read, use a chart similar to the one shown to jot down the sensory details that make his experience come alive for you.

Sensory Details
Hearing: shrieks of the women
Sight:
Taste:
Smell:
Touch:

from

The INTERESTING NARRATIVE *of the* Life of OLAUDAH EQUIANO

OLAUDAH EQUIANO

When Olaudah Equiano was eleven years old, he and his sister were kidnapped while the adults in his village were working in the fields. After being forced to travel for several days, Equiano and his sister were separated. For the next six or seven months, Equiano was sold to several African masters in different countries. He was eventually taken to the west coast of Africa and carried aboard a slave ship bound for the West Indies.

THE FIRST OBJECT WHICH SALUTED MY EYES WHEN I ARRIVED ON THE COAST, WAS THE SEA, AND A SLAVE SHIP, WHICH WAS THEN RIDING AT ANCHOR, AND WAITING FOR ITS CARGO. THESE filled me with astonishment, which was soon converted into terror, when I was carried on board. I was immediately handled, and tossed up to see if I were sound, by some of the crew; and I was now persuaded that I had gotten into a world of bad spirits, and that they were going to kill me. Their complexions, too, differing so much from ours, their long hair, and the language they spoke (which was very different from any I had ever heard), united to confirm me in this belief. Indeed, such were the horrors of my views and fears at the moment, that, if ten thousand worlds had been my own, I would have freely parted with them all to have exchanged my condition with that of the meanest slave in my own country. When I looked round the ship too, and saw a large furnace of copper boiling, and a multitude of black people of every description chained together, every one of their countenances expressing dejection and sorrow, I no longer doubted of my fate; and, quite overpowered with horror and anguish, I fell motionless on the deck and fainted. When I recovered a little, I found some black people about me, who I believed were some of those who had brought me on board, and had been receiving their pay; they talked to me in order to cheer me, but all in vain. I asked them if we were not to be eaten by those white men with horrible looks, red faces, and long hair. They told me I was not, and one of the crew brought me a small portion of spirituous liquor in a wine glass; but, being afraid of him, I would not take it out of his hand. One of the blacks, therefore, took it from him and gave it to me, and I took a little down my palate, which, instead of reviving me, as they thought it would, threw me into the greatest consternation at the strange feeling it produced, having never tasted any such liquor before. Soon after this, the blacks who brought me on board went off, and left me abandoned to despair.

I now saw myself deprived of all chance of returning to my native country, or even the least glimpse of hope of gaining the shore, which I now considered as friendly; and I even wished for my former slavery in preference to my present situation, which was filled with horrors of every kind, still heightened by my ignorance of what I was to undergo. I was not long suffered to indulge my grief; I was soon put down under the decks, and there I received such a salutation in my nostrils as I had never experienced in my life; so that, with the loathsomeness of the <u>stench</u>, and crying together, I became so sick and low that I was not able to eat, nor had I the least desire to taste anything. I now wished for the last friend, death, to relieve me; but soon, to my grief, two of the white men offered me eatables; and, on my refusing to eat, one of them held me fast by the hands, and laid me across, I think, the windlass,[1] and tied my feet, while the other flogged[2] me severely. I had never experienced anything of this kind before, and, although not being used to the water, I naturally feared that element the first time I saw it, yet, nevertheless, could I have got over the nettings,[3] I would have jumped over the side, but I could not; and besides, the crew used to watch us very closely who were not chained down to the decks, lest we should leap into the water; and I have seen some of these poor African prisoners most severely cut, for attempting to do so, and hourly whipped for not eating. This indeed was often the case with myself. In a little time after, amongst the poor chained men, I found some of my own nation, which in a small degree gave ease to my mind. I inquired of these what was to be done with us? They gave me to understand, we were to be carried to these white people's country to work for them. I then was a little revived, and thought, if it were no worse than working, my situation was not so desperate; but still I feared I should be put to death, the white people looked and acted, as I thought, in so savage a manner; for I had never seen among any people such instances of brutal cruelty; and this not only shown towards us blacks, but also to some of the whites themselves. One white man in particular I saw, when we were permitted to be on deck, flogged so unmercifully with a large rope near the foremast,[4] that he died in consequence of it; and they tossed him over the side as they would have done a brute. This made me fear these people the more; and I expected nothing less than to be treated in the same manner. I could not help expressing my fears and <u>apprehensions</u> to some of my countrymen; I asked them if these people had no country, but lived in this hollow place (the ship)? They told me they did not, but came from a distant one. "Then," said I, "how comes it in all our country we never heard of them?" They told me because they lived so very far off. I then asked where were their women? had they any like themselves? I was told they had. "And why," said I, "do we not see them?" They answered, because they were left behind. I asked how the vessel could go? They told me they could not tell; but that there was cloth put upon the masts by the help of the ropes I saw, and then the vessel went on; and the white men had some spell or magic they put in the water when they liked, in order to stop the vessel. I was exceedingly amazed at this account, and really thought they were spirits. I therefore wished much to be from amongst them, for I expected they would sacrifice me; but my wishes were vain—for we were so quartered that it was impossible for any of us to make our escape. . . .

---

1. **windlass** (wĭnd'ləs): a device for raising and lowering a ship's anchor.
2. **flogged**: beat severely with a whip or rod.
3. **nettings**: networks of small ropes on the sides of a ship used for various purposes, such as to prevent boarding or to stow sails. On slave ships, the nettings helped keep slaves from jumping overboard.
4. **foremast** (fôr'məst): the mast (tall pole that supports sails and rigging) nearest the forward end of a sailing ship.

WORDS TO KNOW

stench (stĕnch) *n.* a strong, foul odor
apprehension (ăp'rĭ-hĕn'shən) *n.* a suspicion of future evil; dread

Detail of *The Slave Ship* (1956), Robert Riggs, N.A. Courtesy of Les Mansfield, Cincinnati, Ohio.

At last, when the ship we were in, had got in all her cargo, they made ready with many fearful noises, and we were all put under deck, so that we could not see how they managed the vessel. But this disappointment was the least of my sorrow. The stench of the hold while we were on the coast was so intolerably loathsome, that it was dangerous to remain there for any time, and some of us had been permitted to stay on the deck for the fresh air; but now that the whole ship's cargo were confined together, it became absolutely <u>pestilential</u>. The closeness of the place, and the heat of the climate, added to the number in the ship, which was so crowded that each had scarcely room to turn himself, almost suffocated us. This produced <u>copious</u> perspirations, so that the air soon became unfit for respiration, from a variety of loathsome smells, and brought on a sickness among the slaves, of which many died. . . . This <u>wretched</u> situation was again aggravated by the galling[5] of the chains. . . . The shrieks of the women, and the groans of the dying, rendered the whole a scene of horror almost inconceivable. Happily perhaps, for myself, I was soon reduced so low here that it was thought necessary to keep me almost always on deck; and from my extreme youth I was not put in fetters.[6] In this situation I expected every hour to share the fate of my companions, some

---

5. **galling** (gô'lĭng): causing skin sores by rubbing.
6. **fetters:** chains or shackles for the ankles.

of whom were almost daily brought upon deck at the point of death, which I began to hope would soon put an end to my miseries. . . .

One day they had taken a number of fishes; and when they had killed and satisfied themselves with as many as they thought fit, to our astonishment who were on deck, rather than give any of them to us to eat, as we expected, they tossed the remaining fish into the sea again, although we begged and prayed for some as well as we could, but in vain; and some of my countrymen, being pressed by hunger, took an opportunity, when they thought no one saw them, of trying to get a little privately; but they were discovered, and the attempt procured them some very severe floggings. One day, when we had a smooth sea and moderate wind, two of my wearied countrymen who were chained together (I was near them at the time), preferring death to such a life of misery, somehow made through the nettings and jumped into the sea; immediately, another quite dejected fellow, who, on account of his illness, was suffered to be out of irons, also followed their example; and I believe many more would very soon have done the same, if they had not been prevented by the ship's crew, who were instantly alarmed. . . .

During the rest of his voyage to the West Indies, Equiano continued to endure hardships. After the ship anchored on the coast of Barbados, Equiano and the other slaves were brought ashore and herded together in a slave merchant's yard to be sold.

WE WERE NOT MANY DAYS IN THE MERCHANT'S CUSTODY, BEFORE WE WERE SOLD AFTER THEIR USUAL MANNER, WHICH IS THIS: ON A SIGNAL GIVEN (as the beat of a drum), the buyers rush at once into the yard where the slaves are confined, and make choice of that parcel[7] they like best. The noise and clamor with which this is attended, and the eagerness visible in the <u>countenances</u> of the buyers, serve not a little to increase the apprehension of terrified Africans, who may well be supposed to consider them as the ministers of that destruction to which they think themselves devoted. In this manner, without scruple, are relations and friends separated, most of them never to see each other again. I remember, in the vessel in which I was brought over, in the men's apartment, there were several brothers, who, in the sale, were sold in different lots; and it was very moving on this occasion, to see and hear their cries at parting. O, ye <u>nominal</u> Christians! might not an African ask you—Learned you this from your God, who says unto you, Do unto all men as you would men should do unto you? Is it not enough that we are torn from our country and friends, to toil for your luxury and lust of gain? Must every tender feeling be likewise sacrificed to your <u>avarice</u>? Are the dearest friends and relations now rendered more dear by their separation from their kindred, still to be parted from each other, and thus prevented from cheering the gloom of slavery, with the small comfort of being together, and mingling their sufferings and sorrows? Why are parents to lose their children, brothers their sisters, or husbands their wives? Surely, this is a new refinement in cruelty, which . . . thus aggravates distress, and adds fresh horrors even to the wretchedness of slavery. ❖

---

7. **parcel:** group of slaves offered for sale.

WORDS TO KNOW

countenance (koun′tə-nəns) *n.* the face, especially as an indicator of emotion
nominal (nŏm′ə-nəl) *adj.* in name but not in reality
avarice (ăv′ə-rĭs) *n.* greed

Connect to the Literature

1. **What Do You Think?** What impact did this selection have on you? Share your response with others.

> **Comprehension Check**
> • What does Equiano think will happen to him when he is brought on board ship?
> • Why is Equiano allowed to be kept on deck rather than in the hold?
> • What new "refinement in cruelty" does Equiano accuse his captors of practicing?

Think Critically

2. Recall some of the ideas about slave ships you discussed before reading this selection. How did reading Equiano's account affect your view of the slave trade?

3. **ACTIVE READING** **ANALYZING DETAILS** Look back in your **READER'S NOTEBOOK** at the chart that lists the **sensory details** you found most gripping. Which of the experiences that Equiano described would be hardest for you to endure? Explain why.

4. Why do you think the captive Africans were treated so brutally?

 THINK ABOUT
> • how the crew probably viewed them
> • how the number of crew members compared with the number of Africans
> • how the Africans reacted to their situation

5. Who do you think are the "nominal Christians" that Equiano refers to in the last paragraph? Do you agree with his **epithet?** Support your answer with evidence from the selection.

6. What qualities do you think the captured Africans needed in order to survive the Middle Passage?

Extend Interpretations

7. **Comparing Texts** How would you compare the experiences of captured Africans brought to North America on slave ships with the experiences of the Pilgrims or Cabeza de Vaca's men?

8. **Connect to Life** At what age do you think American students should learn about slavery in the United States, and what do you think they should be told?

Literary Analysis

SLAVE NARRATIVES Equiano's book is an example of a **slave narrative,** or an autobiographical account by someone who suffered the misery of slavery and lived to write about it. Writers of slave narratives often use sensory details to recreate their experiences. For example, to depict the horror of confinement in the hold of a slave ship, Equiano gives the reader such details as "the galling of the chains" and "the groans of the dying."

Cooperative Learning Activity Working in a small group, go back through this selection and choose a passage that you think gives an especially vivid picture of slavery. As a guide, use the chart that you completed in your **READER'S NOTEBOOK.** Select the details that you find most vivid and discuss why they are so effective. Then prepare a **choral reading** of the passage to convey the power of Equiano's details to the class.

REVIEW **AUDIENCE** Who do you suppose was Equiano's intended audience? Support your opinion with evidence.

REVIEW **PRIMARY AND SECONDARY SOURCES**
Primary sources, such as Equiano's narrative, are written or created by people who observed or participated in a historical event. **Secondary sources,** such as scholarly articles or textbooks, are written after the event, by nonparticipants. Compare what you learn about Equiano from his own words with what you learn about him from the biography on page 99.

Writing Options

1. Song of Freedom Imagine that you are Equiano or another captured African chained below deck on a slave ship. Write a song to express your feelings about freedom.

2. Narrative Summary Write a summary of this selection for someone who has not read it and wants to know what Equiano's experience was like.

Writing Handbook
See page 1279: Narrative Writing

Activities & Explorations

Museum Exhibit In a small group, plan and sketch a museum exhibit designed to show some of the horrors of the Middle Passage that you learned about in this selection. In your sketch, include the pictures, models, and artifacts you would use, and write descriptions of any nonvisual features, such as sound recordings. ~ **VIEWING AND REPRESENTING**

Vocabulary in Action

EXERCISE: ASSESSMENT PRACTICE On your paper, write the vocabulary word that belongs in each group of synonyms below.

1. dread, anxiety, _____
2. odor, _____, stink
3. _____, torment, agony
4. deplorable, terrible, _____
5. _____, plentiful, ample
6. selfishness, _____, greed
7. _____, diseased, polluted
8. alarm, _____, dismay
9. _____, so-called, ostensible
10. expression, visage, _____

Building Vocabulary
For an in-depth lesson on how to expand your vocabulary, see page 126.

WORDS TO KNOW	anguish	copious	pestilential
	apprehension	countenance	stench
	avarice	nominal	wretched
	consternation		

Olaudah Equiano
1745?–1797

A Leader's Son Olaudah Equiano grew up in the West African kingdom of Benin in the area that is now eastern Nigeria. His father ruled the village of Essaka, which Equiano himself would have ruled one day had he not been kidnapped by African slave traders and sent first to Barbados, then to colonial Virginia.

Traveling the World After a short time in Virginia, Equiano was sold to a British naval officer, with whom he traveled as far as Nova Scotia, London, and the Mediterranean. In 1763, he was sold again, to a merchant from Philadelphia who allowed him to work as a clerk and captain's assistant on slave and merchant ships. With the extra money that he was able to earn, Equiano bought his freedom in 1766. Working as a barber, sailor, and free servant, he traveled extensively, from England to the Arctic, but never returned to Africa.

A Voice of Protest During his years of captivity, Equiano had learned to speak and read English. As a free man, he became involved in the antislavery movement, lecturing against British slave holders. From 1787 to 1788 he worked on his autobiography, *The Interesting Narrative of the Life of Olaudah Equiano, or Gustavus Vassa, the African*, which was first published in London in 1789 and quickly became popular.

Author Activity

Personal and Political Discuss the reasons that Equiano's account and other slave narratives were so important to the antislavery movement.

from Blue Highways

Travelogue by WILLIAM LEAST HEAT-MOON

Comparing Literature

Traditions Across Time: The New Explorers

Like early voyagers to America, the contemporary writer William Least Heat-Moon undertook his own journey of discovery—to explore the heart of rural America. He traveled the backroads of this country in a pickup truck, stopping in small towns and talking to ordinary people. In this excerpt from *Blue Highways,* he describes an interview with Kendrick Fritz, a Hopi medical student who reveals his people's values and standards of conduct.

Points of Comparison As you read about this encounter between two strangers, compare it with the other first encounters you read about earlier.

Build Background

This selection describes some cultural traditions of the Hopi (hō′pē) of northeastern Arizona. For more than four centuries, the Hopi have been pressured to adopt European ways, first by Spanish colonizers and Catholic missionaries, then by settlers from the United States. In response to the Hopi's appeal, the U.S. government made Hopi lands a protected reservation in 1882. However, the government also forced Hopi children to attend government schools, a policy that threatened the Hopi way of life and created a division between traditional and progressive Hopi that still exists today. Despite these pressures, the Hopi have kept alive many of their cultural traditions.

WORDS TO KNOW **Vocabulary Preview**

begrudge	evolve	precipitately
contempt	genetic	theology
emergence	materialism	variant
ethical		

Focus Your Reading

LITERARY ANALYSIS **AUTHOR'S PURPOSE** The **author's purpose** is the author's reason for writing: to entertain, to inform, to express himself or herself, or to persuade, for example. Frequently an author writes to accomplish two or more of these purposes. To help you determine Heat-Moon's primary purpose for writing, notice the incidents he recounts, the people he describes, and language that indicates his stance toward his subject.

ACTIVE READING **ORGANIZING DETAILS** In this selection, Kendrick Fritz gives the reader an insider's view of Hopi culture, providing details about important foods, objects, practices, beliefs, and concepts—what Fritz calls the Hopi Way.

READER'S NOTEBOOK
As you read, create a cluster diagram like the one started here to organize these details. You will use them later as you discuss the Hopi Way.

Kahopi — Hopi Way
Piki — Harmony
Blue Corn
Considered "Mother" — Viewed as Compass

Road Past the View I (1964), Georgia O'Keeffe. Oil on canvas, 24″ × 30″. Copyright © 1996 The Georgia O'Keeffe Foundation/Artists Rights Society (ARS), New York. Photo Copyright © Malcolm Varon.

from

BLUE HIGHWAYS

William Least Heat Moon

When William Least Heat Moon set out on a long circular trip around the United States, he drove the back roads—the two-lane highways that were colored blue on old road maps. His goal was to learn about America by seeing the small towns and talking to the people he met there. He was not always successful, however. In Tuba City, Arizona, for instance, he failed to strike up a conversation with several Navajos. This chapter begins a few days later, with Heat Moon at the top of a snowy mountain pass in Utah. He has slept in his van overnight rather than risk driving down the mountain in the dark.

irty and hard, the morning light could have been old concrete. Twenty-nine degrees inside. I tried to figure a way to drive down the mountain without leaving the sleeping bag. I was stiff—not from the cold so much as from having slept coiled like a grub. Creaking open and pinching toes and fingers to check for frostbite, I counted to ten (twice) before shouting and leaping for my clothes. Shouting distracts the agony. Underwear, trousers, and shirt so cold they felt wet.

I went outside to relieve myself. . . . Then to work chipping clear the windows. Somewhere off this mountain, people still lay warm in their blankets and not yet ready to get up to a hot breakfast. So what if they spent the day selling imprinted ballpoint pens? Weren't they down off mountains?

Down. I had to try it. And down it was, Utah 14 a complication of twists and drops descending the west side more precipitately than the east. A good thing I hadn't attempted it in the dark. After a mile, snow on the pavement became slush, then water, and finally at six thousand feet, dry and sunny blacktop.

Cedar City, a tidy Mormon town, lay at the base of the mountains on the edge of the Escalante Desert. Ah, desert! I pulled in for gas, snow still melting off my rig. "See you spent the night in the Breaks," the attendant said. "You people never believe the sign at the bottom."

"I believed, but it said something about winter months. May isn't winter."

"It is up there. You Easterners just don't know what a mountain is."

I didn't say anything, but I knew what a mountain was: a high pile of windy rocks with its own weather.

In the cafeteria of Southern Utah State College, I bought a breakfast of scrambled eggs, pancakes, bacon, oatmeal, grapefruit, orange juice, milk, and a cinnamon roll. A celebration of being alive. I was full of victory.

Across the table sat an Indian student named Kendrick Fritz, who was studying chemistry and wanted to become a physician. He had grown up in Moenkopi, Arizona, just across the highway from Tuba City. I said, "Are you Navajo or Hopi?"

"Hopi. You can tell by my size. Hopis are smaller than Navajos."

His voice was gentle, his words considered, and smile timid. He seemed open to questions. "Fritz doesn't sound like a Hopi name."

"My father took it when he was in the Army in the Second World War. Hopis usually have Anglo[1] first names and long Hopi last names that are hard for other people to pronounce."

I told him of my difficulty in rousing a conversation in Tuba City. He said, "I can't speak for Navajos about prejudice, but I know Hopis who believe we survived Spaniards, missionaries, a thousand years of other Indians, even the BIA.[2] But tourists?" He smiled. "Smallpox would be better."

"Do you—yourself—think most whites are prejudiced against Indians?"

"About fifty-fifty. Half show contempt because they saw a drunk squaw at the Circle K. Another half think we're noble savages—they may be worse because if an Indian makes a mistake they hate him for being human. Who wants to be somebody's ideal myth?"

"My grandfather used to say the Big Vision made the Indian, but the white man invented him."

"Relations are okay here, but I wouldn't call them good, and I'm not one to go around looking for prejudice. I try not to."

"Maybe you're more tolerant of Anglo ways than some others."

---

1. **Anglo:** European-American.
2. **BIA:** the Bureau of Indian Affairs, established in 1824 by the United States government to supervise Native American reservations; many Native Americans feel that the bureau has interfered too much in their lives.

WORDS TO KNOW | **precipitately** (prĭ-sĭp′ĭ-tĭt-lē) *adv.* steeply
contempt (kən-tĕmpt′) *n.* scorn; disdain

"Could be. I mean, I *am* studying to be a doctor and not a medicine man. But I'm no apple Indian—red outside and white underneath. I lived up in Brigham City, Utah, when I went to the Intermountain School run by the BIA. It was too easy though. Too much time to goof around. So I switched to Box Elder—that's a public school. I learned there. And I lived in Dallas a few months. What I'm saying is that I've lived on Hopi land and I've lived away. I hear Indians talk about being red all the way through criticizing others for acting like Anglos, and all the time they're sitting in a pickup at a drive-in. But don't tell them to trade the truck for a horse."

"The Spanish brought the horse."

He nodded. "To me, being Indian means being responsible to my people. Helping with the best tools. Who invented penicillin doesn't matter."

"What happens after you finish school?"

"I used to want out of Tuba, but since I've been away, I've come to see how our land really is our Sacred Circle—it's our strength. Now, I want to go back and practice general medicine. At the Indian hospital in Tuba where my mother and sister are nurse's aides, there aren't any Indian M.D.'s, and that's no good. I don't respect people who don't help themselves. Hopi land is no place to make big money, but I'm not interested anyway."

"You don't use the word *reservation.*"

"We don't think of it as a reservation since we were never ordered there. We found it through Hopi prophecies. We're unusual because we've always held onto our original land—most of it anyway. One time my grandfather pointed out the old boundaries to me. We were way up on a mesa. I've forgotten what they are except for the San Francisco Peaks. But in the last eighty years, the government's given a lot of our land to Navajos, and now we're in a hard spot—eight thousand Hopis are surrounded and outnumbered twenty-five to one. I don't begrudge the Navajo anything, but I think Hopis should be in on making the decisions. Maybe you know that Congress didn't even admit Indians to citizenship until about nineteen twenty. Incredible—live someplace a thousand years and then find out you're a foreigner."

"I know an Osage who says, 'Don't Americanize me and I won't Americanize you.' He means everybody in the country came from someplace else."

"Hopi legends are full of migrations."

"Will other Hopis be suspicious of you when you go home as a doctor?"

"Some might be, but not my family. But for a

"To me, being Indian means being responsible to my people. Helping with the best tools. Who invented penicillin doesn't matter."

Kendrick Fritz in Cedar City, Utah. From *Blue Highways* by William Least Heat-Moon.

lot of Hopis, the worst thing to call a man is *kahopi*, 'not Hopi.' Nowadays, though, we all have to choose either the new ways or the Hopi way, and it's split up whole villages. A lot of us try to find the best in both places. We've always learned from other people. If we hadn't, we'd be extinct like some other tribes."

"Medicine's a pretty good survival technique."

"Sure, but I also like Jethro Tull and the Moody Blues.[3] That's not survival."

"Is the old religion a survival technique?"

"If you live it."

"Do you?"

"Most Hopis follow our religion, at least in some ways, because it reminds us who we are and it's part of the land. I'll tell you, in the rainy season when the desert turns green, it's beautiful there. The land is medicine too."

"If you don't mind telling me, what's the religion like?"

"Like any religion in one way—different clans believe different things."

"There must be something they all share, something common."

"That's hard to say."

"Could you try?"

Human existence is essentially a series of journeys, and the emergence symbol is a kind of map of the wandering soul, an image of a process.

He thought a moment. "Maybe the idea of harmony. And the way a Hopi prays. A good life, a harmonious life, is a prayer. We don't just pray for ourselves, we pray for all things. We're famous for the Snake Dances, but a lot of people don't realize those ceremonies are prayers for rain and crops, prayers for life. We also pray for rain by sitting and thinking about rain. We sit and picture wet things like streams and clouds. It's sitting in pictures."

He picked up his tray to go. "I could give you a taste of the old Hopi Way. But maybe you're too full after that breakfast. You always eat so much?"

"The mountain caused that." I got up. "What do you mean by 'taste'?"

"I'll show you."

We went to his dormitory room. Other than several Kachina dolls[4] he had carved from cottonwood and a picture of a Sioux warrior, it was just another collegiate dorm room—maybe cleaner than most. He pulled a shoebox from under his bed and opened it carefully. I must have been watching a little wide-eyed because he said, "It isn't live rattlesnakes." From the box he took a long cylinder wrapped in waxed paper and held it as if trying not to touch it. "Will you eat this? It's very special." He was smiling. "If you won't, I can't share the old Hopi Way with you."

"Okay, but if it's dried scorpions, I'm going to speak with a forked tongue."

"Open your hands." He unwrapped the cylinder and ever so gently laid across my palms an airy tube the color of a thunderhead. It was about ten inches long and an inch in diameter. "There you go," he said.

"You first."

"I'm not having any right now."

So I bit the end off the blue-gray tube. It was many intricately rolled layers of something with less substance than butterfly wings. The bite crumbled to flakes that stuck to my lips. "Now tell me what I'm eating."

"Do you like it?"

"I think so. Except it disappears like cotton candy just as I get ready to chew. But I think I taste corn and maybe ashes."

"Hopis were eating that before horses came to America. It's piki. Hopi bread you might say. Made from blue-corn flour and ashes from

---

3. **Jethro Tull . . . Moody Blues:** British rock bands popular from the 1960s to the 1980s.

4. **Kachina** (kə-chēˊnə) **dolls:** dolls representing kachinas—spirits of Hopi ancestors that the Hopi believe live in mountains near their lands.

greasewood or sagebrush. Baked on an oiled stone by my mother. She sends piki every so often. It takes time and great skill to make. We call it Hopi cornflakes."

"Unbelievably thin." I laid a piece on a page of his chemistry book. The words showed through.

"We consider corn our mother. The blue variety is what you might call our compass—wherever it grows, we can go. Blue corn directed our migrations. Navajos cultivate a yellow species that's soft and easy to grind, but ours is hard. You plant it much deeper than other corns, and it survives where they would die. It's a genetic variant the Hopi developed."

"Why is it blue? That must be symbolic."

"We like the color blue. Corn's our most important ritual ingredient."

"The piki's good, but it's making me thirsty. Where's a water fountain?"

When I came back from the fountain, Fritz said, "I'll tell you what I think the heart of our religion is—it's the Four Worlds."

Over the next hour, he talked about the Hopi Way, and showed pictures and passages from *Book of the Hopi.* The key seemed to be emergence. Carved in a rock near the village of Shipolovi is the ancient symbol for it:

With variations, the symbol appears among other Indians of the Americas. Its lines represent the course a person follows on his "road of life" as he passes through birth, death, rebirth. Human existence is essentially a series of journeys, and the emergence symbol is a kind of map of the wandering soul, an image of a process; but it is also, like most Hopi symbols and ceremonies, a reminder of cosmic patterns that all human beings move in.

The Hopi believes mankind has evolved through four worlds: the first a shadowy realm of contentment; the second a place so comfortable the people forgot where they had come from and began worshipping material goods. The third world was a pleasant land too, but the people, bewildered by their past and fearful for their future, thought only of their own earthly plans. At last, the Spider Grandmother, who oversees the emergences, told them: "You have forgotten what you should have remembered, and now you have to leave this place. Things will be harder." In the fourth and present world, life is difficult for mankind, and he struggles to remember his source because materialism and selfishness block a greater vision. The newly born infant comes into the fourth world with the door of his mind open (evident in the cranial soft spot[5]), but as he ages, the door closes and he must work at remaining receptive to the great forces. A human being's grandest task is to keep from breaking with things outside himself.

"A Hopi learns that he belongs to two families," Fritz said, "his natural clan and that of all things. As he gets older, he's supposed to move closer to the greater family. In the Hopi Way, each person tries to recognize his part in the whole."

"At breakfast you said you hunted rabbits and pigeons and robins, but I don't see how you can

---

5. **cranial** (krā′nē-əl) **soft spot:** the soft area on top of an infant's head, a result of the as yet incomplete formation of the bones of the skull (cranium).

	genetic (jə-nĕt′ĭk) *adj.* relating to genes, the units that determine and transmit hereditary characteristics
WORDS	variant (vâr′ē-ənt) *n.* something that differs slightly from others of its kind
TO	emergence (ĭ-mûr′jəns) *n.* the process of coming forth or coming into existence
KNOW	evolve (ĭ-vŏlv′) *v.* to develop gradually
	materialism (mə-tîr′ē-ə-lĭz′əm) *n.* a preoccupation with worldly rather than spiritual concerns

shoot a bird if you believe in the union of life."

"A Hopi hunter asks the animal to forgive him for killing it. Only life can feed life. The robin knows that."

"How does robin taste, by the way?"

"Tastes good."

"The religion doesn't seem to have much of an ethical code."

"It's there. We watch what the Kachinas say and do. But the Spider Grandmother did give two rules. To all men, not just Hopis. If you look at them, they cover everything. She said, 'Don't go around hurting each other,' and she said, 'Try to understand things.'"

"I like them. I like them very much."

"Our religion keeps reminding us that we aren't just will and thoughts. We're also sand and wind and thunder. Rain. The seasons. All those things. You learn to respect everything because you *are* everything. If you respect yourself, you respect all things. That's why we have so many songs of creation to remind us where we came from. If the fourth world forgets that, we'll disappear in the wilderness like the third world, where people decided they had created themselves."

"Pride's the deadliest of the Seven Deadly Sins in old Christian theology."

"It's *kahopi* to set yourself above things. It causes divisions."

Fritz had to go to class. As we walked across campus, I said, "I guess it's hard to be a Hopi in Cedar City—especially if you're studying biochemistry."

"It's hard to be a Hopi anywhere."

"I mean, difficult to carry your Hopi heritage into a world as technological as medicine is."

"Heritage? My heritage is the Hopi Way, and that's a way of the spirit. Spirit can go anywhere. In fact, it has to go places so it can change and emerge like in the migrations. That's the whole idea." ❖

Kachina doll representing the divine ancestral corn spirit in Hopi religious practices. Reprinted with permission by K. C. DenDooven, KC Publications.

"The Spider Grandmother
did give two rules.
To all men, not just Hopis.
If you look at them, they cover everything.
She said,
'Don't go around hurting each other,'
and she said,
'Try to understand things.'"

WORDS
TO
KNOW

ethical (ĕth′ĭ-kəl) *adj.* dealing with principles of right and wrong; moral
theology (thē-ŏl′ə-jē) *n.* a system of religious beliefs

Connect to the Literature

1. What Do You Think?
What interests you most about Kendrick Fritz? Discuss your impressions with your classmates.

Comprehension Check
- Why does Fritz invite the author to his room?
- What does Fritz say is the heart of the Hopi religion?
- What two rules did the Spider Grandmother give?

Think Critically

2. **ACTIVE READING** **ORGANIZING DETAILS** Review the cluster diagram you created in your 📖**READER'S NOTEBOOK.** In your own words, tell what you learned about the Hopi Way.

3. What is your opinion of the Hopi Way? For example, what ways would be easy for you to follow and what ways would be difficult?

4. Fritz says, "It's hard to be a Hopi anywhere." What do you think makes it difficult to be a Hopi?

THINK ABOUT
- how most whites view Native Americans
- how some Native Americans view others for "acting like Anglos"
- how the Hopi and other Native Americans have historically been treated

5. The author mentions his grandfather's statement that "the Big Vision made the Indian, but the white man invented him." How would you explain this distinction?

6. At the end of the selection, the author tells Fritz that it is difficult to carry his Hopi heritage "into a world as technological as medicine is." How successful do you think Fritz will be in remaining true to the Hopi Way as a doctor? Explain your views.

Extend Interpretations

7. Connect to Life How would you compare the Hopi experience with that of other minority groups in the United States?

8. **Points of Comparison** How would you compare the experiences and attitudes of William Least Heat Moon, William Bradford, and Álvar Núñez Cabeza de Vaca as they explored America?

Literary Analysis

AUTHOR'S PURPOSE A writer usually writes for one or more of the following **purposes:** to inform, to entertain, to express himself or herself, or to persuade readers to believe or do something. For example, in *The Interesting Narrative of the Life of Olaudah Equiano*, the author's purpose is primarily to inform readers about the horrors of the Middle Passage.

Cooperative Learning Activity
Review the selection and identify two or more reasons why you think Heat Moon wrote it. For each reason you identify, record the evidence on a chart like the one shown. Then get together with a group of classmates to compare charts and to discuss your choices. What would you say is Heat Moon's primary purpose for writing this selection?

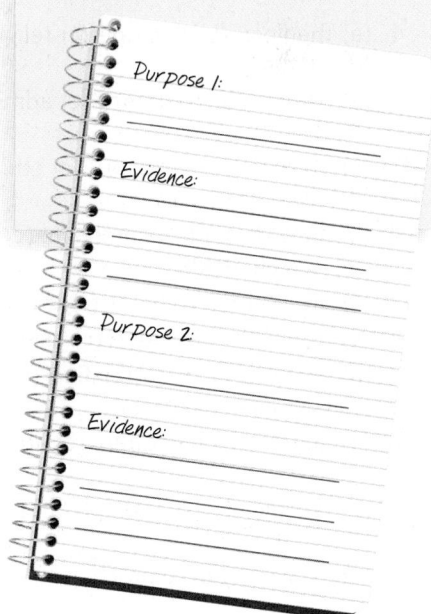

Purpose 1:

Evidence:

Purpose 2:

Evidence:

Writing Options

1. Hopi Dialogue Write an imagined dialogue among three speakers: Kendrick Fritz, an older Hopi with traditional values, and a young Hopi who plans to move away from Hopi lands.

2. Personal Essay on Beliefs Draft a personal essay about an aspect of Hopi belief described in this selection. You might compare the belief with one of your own beliefs or explain how the belief applies to your own experience.

Writing Handbook
See page 1281: Explanatory Writing

3. Points of Comparison Consider the standards of conduct that the Spider Grandmother gave to humans. By these standards, how would you evaluate Squanto's conduct toward the Pilgrims, as recounted in *Of Plymouth Plantation*? Present your evaluations as a report card with comments.

Vocabulary in Action

EXERCISE: RELATED WORDS On your paper, write the letter of the word that does not belong in the group.

1. (a) theology (b) doctrine (c) religion (d) unbelief

2. (a) respect (b) contempt (c) admiration (d) regard

3. (a) immoral (b) improper (c) ethical (d) dishonest

4. (a) materialism (b) spirituality (c) greed (d) consumerism

5. (a) duplicate (b) variant (c) twin (d) replica

6. (a) resent (b) begrudge (c) esteem (d) envy

7. (a) extinction (b) termination (c) emergence (d) disappearance

8. (a) genetic (b) hereditary (c) artificial (d) inheritable

9. (a) precipitately (b) steeply (c) abruptly (d) gradually

10. (a) evolve (b) develop (c) perish (d) unfold

WORDS TO KNOW		
begrudge	evolve	theology
contempt	genetic	variant
emergence	materialism	
ethical	precipitately	

William Least Heat Moon
1939–

Other Works
PrairyErth

His Pen Name "William Least Heat Moon" is the pen name of William Trogdon, who is of mixed European-American and Native American ancestry. As he explains in *Blue Highways*, "My father calls himself Heat Moon, my elder brother Little Heat Moon. I, coming last, am therefore Least." Heat Moon says that his father advised him to use his Anglo name for official business, such as paying taxes, and his Native American name for spiritual matters. His choice of pen name therefore indicates the spiritual quality of the journey that he recorded in *Blue Highways*.

His Odyssey Feeling isolated and tired of the commercialism he saw in mainstream American culture, Heat Moon traveled in search of "places where change did not mean ruin and where time and men and deeds connected." He made his three-month, 13,000-mile journey in a Ford van that he named Ghost Dancing, a reference to a ceremony of the Plains Indians in which they danced for the return of their old, harmonious way of life. Equipped with a tape recorder, a camera, notebooks, Walt Whitman's *Leaves of Grass*, and John Neihardt's *Black Elk Speaks*, Heat Moon followed the back roads, interviewing people he met along the way.

Literary Success After compiling his interviews, Heat Moon spent the next four years editing his tapes and notebooks to capture "the details of ordinary lives that shape, control, and reveal the nature of an existence." His compelling portrait of rural America, *Blue Highways*, won several awards, became a bestseller, and earned critical acclaim.

My Sojourn in the Lands of My Ancestors

Autobiography by MAYA ANGELOU

Comparing Literature

Traditions Across Time: The New Explorers

Earlier you read Olaudah Equiano's account of his terrible journey from Africa to America in a slave ship. More than 200 years later, the African-American writer Maya Angelou made a reverse journey—to West Africa, the land of her enslaved ancestors.

Points of Comparison As you read Angelou's account, notice how she remains affected by the events of history.

Build Background

African Slave Trade In the 1400s, Europeans began to come to West Africa to trade for pepper, gold, and ivory. Over the years, they built more than 40 massive forts along the African coast to protect their trade and to store goods. As the slave trade grew, these European forts were also used to house enslaved Africans, who were branded, chained, and crowded into hot, dark, bat-infested dungeons for months at a time until they were shipped to colonies in the Americas. Two such forts are Elmina Castle and Cape Coast Castle in Ghana. Today, both forts are popular tourist attractions.

WORDS TO KNOW **Vocabulary Preview**

careen	mincing	reverberate	wane
environs	purging	suffuse	
impervious	rebuff	surreptitious	

Focus Your Reading

LITERARY ANALYSIS **AUTOBIOGRAPHY** An **autobiography** is the story of a person's life, written by that person. Generally told from the first-person point of view, autobiographies vary in style from straightforward chronological accounts to impressionistic narratives. The following autobiographical selection focuses on Maya Angelou's experiences as she searches for her roots to the past. You will notice how her account jumps unexpectedly from narration of events to description of her own inner thoughts and reactions.

ACTIVE READING **STRATEGIES FOR READING AUTOBIOGRAPHY**
When you read an autobiography, you learn something about the author as an individual. To discover what "My Sojourn in the Lands of My Ancestors" reveals about Maya Angelou, ask these questions as you read:

- What events has Angelou chosen to describe?
- What feelings and associations do these events trigger in her mind?
- How do these events change her?

READER'S NOTEBOOK Fill in a chart like the one started below to show how the events Angelou writes about reveal the kind of person she is.

Event	Reaction	Impact
Viewing Cape Coast Castle	Imagining her ancestors imprisoned there	Realizing the legacy of slavery

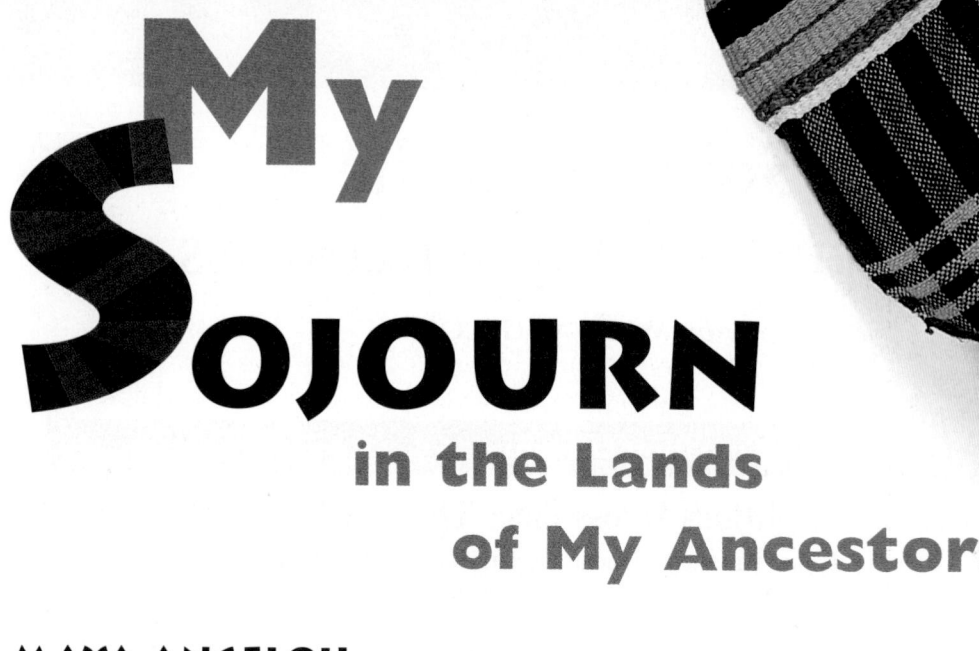

My SOJOURN in the Lands of My Ancestors

MAYA ANGELOU

During the early sixties in New York City, I met, fell in love with, and married a South African Freedom Fighter who was petitioning the United Nations over the issue of apartheid.[1] A year later, my 15-year-old son, Guy, and I followed my new husband to North Africa. I worked as a journalist in Cairo and managed a home that was a haven to Freedom Fighters still trying to rid their countries of colonialism. I was a moderately good mother to a growingly distant teenager and a faithful, if not loving, wife. I watched my romance *wane* and my marriage end in the shadows of the Great Pyramid.

In 1962, my son and I left Egypt for Ghana, where he was to enter the university and I was to continue to a promised job in Liberia.[2] An automobile accident left Guy with a broken neck and me with the responsibility of securing work and a place for him to recover. Within months I did have a job, a house, and a circle of black American friends who had come to Africa before me. With them I, too, became a hunter for that elusive and much longed-for place the heart could call home.

Despite our sincerity and eagerness, we were often *rebuffed*. The pain of rejection in Africa caused the spiritual that black slaves sang about their oppressors to come to my mind:

I'm going to tell God
How you treat me
When I get home.

On the delicious and rare occasions when we were accepted, our ecstasy was boundless, and we could have said with our foreparents in the words of another spiritual:

1. **apartheid** (ə-pärt′hīt′): an official policy of racial segregation practiced from 1948 to 1991 in South Africa, involving discrimination against nonwhites.
2. **Liberia** (lī-bîr′ē-ə): a West African country; it is on the Atlantic coast to the west of Ghana.

WORDS
TO
KNOW

wane (wān) v. to decrease in size, intensity, or degree
rebuff (rĭ-bŭf′) v. to reject bluntly; snub

Afi Negble, Asenema, Ghana, 1964, Paul Strand. Copyright © 1971, Aperture Foundation Inc., Paul Strand Archive.

My soul got happy
When I came out of the wilderness
Came out of the wilderness
Came out of the wilderness.
My soul got happy
When I came out of the wilderness
And up to the welcome table.

I had a long weekend, money in my purse, and working command of Fanti.[3] After a year in Accra,[4] I needed country quiet, so I decided to travel into the bush. I bought roasted plantain stuffed with boiled peanuts, a quart of Club beer, and headed my little car west. The stretch was a highway from Accra to Cape Coast, filled with trucks and private cars passing from lane to lane with abandon. People hung out of windows of the crowded mammie lorries,[5] and I could hear singing and shouting when the drivers careened

those antique vehicles up and down hills as if each was a little train out to prove it could.

I stopped in Cape Coast only for gas. Although many black Americans had headed for the town as soon as they touched ground in Ghana, I successfully avoided it for a year. Cape Coast Castle and the nearby Elmina Castle had been holding forts for captured slaves. The captives had been imprisoned in dungeons beneath the massive buildings, and friends of mine who had felt called upon to make the trek reported that they felt the thick stone walls still echoed with old cries.

The palm-tree-lined streets and fine white-stone buildings did not tempt me to remain any longer than necessary. Once out of the town and again onto the tarred roads, I knew I had not made a clean escape. Despite my hurry, history had invaded my little car. Pangs of self-pity and a sorrow for my unknown relatives suffused me. Tears made the highway waver and were salty on my tongue.

What did they think and feel, my grandfathers, caught on those green savannas, under the baobab trees? How long did their families search for them? Did the dungeon wall feel chilly and its slickness strange to my grand-mothers, who were used to the rush of air against bamboo huts and the sound of birds rattling their green roofs?

I had to pull off the road. Just passing near Cape Coast Castle had plunged me back into the eternal melodrama.

There would be no purging, I knew, unless I asked all the questions. Only then

---

3. **Fanti** (făn'tē): the dialect of the Fanti, one of the many ethnic groups who inhabit Ghana.

4. **Accra** (ăk'rə): the capital and largest city of Ghana.

5. **mammie lorries**: small trucks or open-sided buses used for public transportation in West Africa.

111

would the spirits understand that I was feeding them. It was a crumb, but it was all I had.

I allowed the shapes to come to my imagination; children passed, tied together by ropes and chains, tears abashed, stumbling in a dull exhaustion, then women, hair un-combed, bodies gritted with sand, and sagging in defeat. Men, muscles without memory, minds dimmed, plodding, leaving bloodied footprints in the dirt. The quiet was awful. None of them cried, or yelled, or bellowed. No moans came from them. They lived in a mute territory, dead to feeling and protest. These were the legions, sold by sisters, stolen by brothers, bought by strangers, enslaved by the greedy, and betrayed by history.

For a long time I sat as in an open-air auditorium watching a troupe of tragic players enter and exit the stage.

The visions faded as my tears ceased. Light returned and I started the car, turned off the main road, and headed for the interior. Using rutted track roads, and lanes a little larger than footpaths, I found the River Pra. The black water moving quietly, ringed with the tall trees, seemed enchanted. A fear of snakes kept me in the car, but I parked and watched the bright sun turn the water surface into a rippling cloth of lamé.[6] I passed through villages that were little more than collections of thatch huts, with goats and small children wandering in the lanes. The noise of my car brought smiling adults out to wave at me.

In the late afternoon I reached the thriving town that was my destination. A student whom I had met at Legon (where the University of Ghana is located) had spoken to me often of the gold-mining area, of Dunkwa, his birthplace. His reports had so glowed with the town's virtues, I had chosen that spot for my first journey.

My skin color, features, and the Ghana cloth I wore would make me look like any young Ghanaian woman. I could pass if I didn't talk too much.

As usual, in the towns of Ghana, the streets were filled with vendors selling their wares of tinned pat milk, hot spicy Killi Willis (fried, ripe plantain chips), Pond's cold cream, and antimosquito incense rings. Farmers were returning home, children returning from school. Young boys grinned at mincing girls, and always there were the market women, huge and impervious. I searched for a hotel sign in vain and as the day lengthened, I started to worry. I didn't have enough gas to get to Koforidua, a large town east of Dunkwa, where there would certainly be hotels, and I didn't have the address of my student's family. I parked the car a little out of the town center and stopped a woman carrying a bucket of water on her head and a baby on her back.

"Good day." I spoke in Fanti and she responded. I continued, "I beg you, I am a stranger looking for a place to stay."

She repeated, "Stranger?" and laughed. "You are a stranger? No. No."

To many Africans, only whites could be strangers. All Africans belonged somewhere, to some clan. All Akan[7]-speaking people belong to one of eight blood lines (Abosua) and one of eight spirit lines (Ntoro).

I said, "I am not from here."

For a second, fear darted in her eyes. There was the possibility that I was a witch or some unhappy ghost from the country of the dead. I quickly said, "I am from Accra." She gave me a good smile. "Oh, one Accra. Without a home." She laughed. The Fanti word Nkran, for which

---

6. **lamé** (lă-mā′): a glittering fabric containing metallic threads.

7. **Akan** (ä′kän′): a language spoken in southern Ghana, of which Fanti is a dialect.

WORDS TO KNOW	**mincing** (mĭn′sĭng) *adj.* acting refined or dainty **impervious** (ĭm-pûr′vē-əs) *adj.* incapable of being affected

the capital was named, means the large ant that builds 10-foot-high domes of red clay and lives with millions of other ants.

"Come with me." She turned quickly, steadying the bucket on her head, and led me between two corrugated tin shacks. The baby bounced and slept on her back, secured by the large piece of cloth wrapped around her body. We passed a compound where women were pounding the dinner *foo foo*[8] in wooden bowls.

The woman shouted, "Look what I have found. One Nkran which has no place to sleep tonight." The women laughed and asked, "One Nkran? I don't believe it."

"Are you taking it to the old man?"

"Of course."

"Sleep well, alone, Nkran, if you can." My guide stopped before a small house. She put the water on the ground and told me to wait while she entered the house. She returned immediately, followed by a man who rubbed his eyes as if he had just been awakened.

He walked close and peered hard at my face. "This is the Nkran?" The woman was adjusting the bucket on her head.

"Yes, Uncle. I have brought her." She looked at me, "Good-bye, Nkran. Sleep in peace. Uncle, I am going." The man said, "Go and come, child," and resumed studying my face. "You are not Ga."[9] He was reading my features.

A few small children had collected around his knees. They could barely hold back their giggles as he interrogated me.

Samuel J. K. Essoun, Shama, Ghana, 1963, Paul Strand. Copyright © 1976, Aperture Foundation Inc., Paul Strand Archive.

"Aflao?"
I said, "No."
"Brong-ahafo?"
I said, "No. I am . . ."
I meant to tell him the truth, but he said, "Don't tell me. I will soon know." He continued staring at me. "Speak more. I will know from your Fanti."

"Well, I have come from Accra and I need to rent a room for the night. I told that woman that I was a stranger . . ."

He laughed. "And you are. Now, I know. You are Bambara from Liberia. It is clear you are Bambara." He laughed again. "I always can tell. I am not easily fooled." He shook my hand. "Yes, we will find you a place for the night. Come." He touched a boy at his right. "Find Patience Aduah and bring her to me."

The children laughed, and all ran away as the man led me into the house. He pointed me to a seat in the neat little parlor and shouted, "Foriwa, we have a guest. Bring beer." A small black woman with an imperial air entered the room. Her knowing face told me that she had witnessed the scene in her front yard.

She spoke to her husband. "And, Kobina, did

---

8. *foo foo*: a starchy dough made from mashed yams, cassavas, or plantains.

9. **Ga** (gä): like *Aflao*, *Brong-ahafo*, and *Bambara* in the following sentences, the name of a West African ethnic group.

you find who the stranger was?" She walked to me. I stood and shook her hand. "Welcome, stranger." We both laughed. "Now don't tell me, Kobina, I have ears, also. Sit down, sister, beer is coming. Let me hear you speak."

We sat facing each other while her husband stood over us smiling. "You, Foriwa, you will never get it."

I told her my story, adding a few more words I had recently learned. She laughed grandly. "She is Bambara. I could have told you when Abaa first brought her. See how tall she is? See her head? See her color? Men, huh. They only look at a woman's shape."

Two children brought beer and glasses to the man, who poured and handed the glasses around. "Sister, I am Kobina Artey; this is my wife, Foriwa, and some of my children."

I introduced myself, but because they had taken such relish in detecting my tribal origin I couldn't tell them that they were wrong. Or, less admirably, at the moment I didn't want to remember that I was an American. For the first time since my arrival, I was very nearly home. Not a Ghanaian, but at least accepted for an African. The sensation was worth a lie.

Voices came to the house from the yard.

"Brother Kobina," "Uncle," "Auntie."

Foriwa opened the door to a group of people, who entered, speaking fast and looking at me.

"So this is the Bambara woman? The stranger?" They looked me over and talked with my hosts. I understood some of their conversation. They said that I was nice-looking and old enough to have a little wisdom. They announced that my car was parked a few blocks away. Kobina told them that I would spend the night with the newlyweds, Patience and Kwame Duodu. Yes, they could see clearly that I was a Bambara.

"Give us the keys to your car, sister; someone will bring your bag."

I gave up the keys and all resistance. I was either at home with friends or I would die wishing that to be so.

Later, Patience, her husband, Kwame, and I sat out in the yard around a cooking fire near to their thatched house, which was much smaller than the Artey bungalow. They explained that Kobina Artey was not a chief, but a member of the village council, and all small matters in that area of Dunkwa were taken to him. As Patience stirred the stew in the pot that was balanced over the fire, children and women appeared sporadically out of the darkness carrying covered plates. Each time Patience thanked the bearers and directed them to the house, I felt the distance narrow between my past and present.

In the United States, during segregation, black American travelers, unable to stay in hotels restricted to white patrons, stopped at churches and told the black ministers or

Nana Oparabea, High Priestess, Larteh, Ghana, 1963, Paul Strand. Copyright © 1976, Aperture Foundation Inc., Paul Strand Archive.

deacons of their predicaments. Church officials would select a home and then inform the unexpecting hosts of the decision. There was never a protest, but the new hosts relied on the generosity of their neighbors to help feed and even entertain their guests. After the travelers were settled, surreptitious knocks would sound on the back door.

In Stamps, Arkansas, I heard so often, "Sister Henderson, I know you've got guests. Here's a pan of biscuits."

"Sister Henderson, Mama sent a half a cake for your visitors."

"Sister Henderson, I made a lot of macaroni and cheese. Maybe this will help with your visitors."

My grandmother would whisper her thanks and finally when the family and guests sat down at the table, the offerings were so different and plentiful, it appeared that days had been spent preparing the meal.

Patience invited me inside, and when I saw the table I was confirmed in my earlier impression. Groundnut stew, garden egg stew, hot pepper soup, *kenke, kotomre,* fried plantain, *dukuno,* shrimp, fish cakes, and more, all crowded together on variously patterned plates.

In Arkansas, the guests would never suggest, although they knew better, that the host had not prepared every scrap of food, especially for them.

I said to Patience, "Oh, sister, you went to such trouble."

She laughed. "It is nothing, sister. We don't want our Bambara relative to think herself a stranger anymore. Come let us wash and eat."

After dinner, I followed Patience to the outdoor toilet; then they gave me a cot in a very small room.

In the morning, I wrapped my cloth under my arms, sarong fashion, and walked with Patience to the bathhouse. We joined about 20 women in a walled enclosure which had no ceiling. The greetings were loud and cheerful as we soaped ourselves and poured buckets of water over our shoulders.

Patience introduced me. "This is our Bambara sister."

"She's a tall one, all right. Welcome, sister."

"I like her color."

"How many children, sister?" The woman was looking at my breasts.

I apologized, "I only have one."

"One?"

"One?"

"One!" Shouts reverberated over the splashing water. I said, "One, but I'm trying."

They laughed. "Try hard, sister. Keep trying."

We ate leftovers from the last night feast, and I said a sad good-bye to my hosts. The children walked me back to my car, with the oldest boy carrying my bag. I couldn't offer money to my hosts, Arkansas had taught me that, but I gave change to the children. They bobbed and jumped and grinned.

"Good-bye, Bambara Auntie."

"Go and come, Auntie."

"Go and come."

I drove into Cape Coast before I thought of the gruesome castle and out of its environs before the ghosts of slavery caught me. Perhaps their attempts had been halfhearted. After all, in Dunkwa, although I had let a lie speak for me, I had proved that one of their descendants, at least one, could just briefly return to Africa, and that despite cruel betrayals, bitter ocean voyages, and hurtful centuries, we were still recognizable. ❖

WORDS	**surreptitious** (sûr′əp-tĭsh′əs) *adj.* secret; stealthy
TO	**reverberate** (rĭ-vûr′bə-rāt′) *v.* to echo
KNOW	**environs** (ĕn-vī′rənz) *n.* a surrounding region

Connect to the Literature

1. **What Do You Think?** What thoughts or feelings do you have about Angelou's experiences in Dunkwa? Describe your impressions to a classmate.

Comprehension Check
- Why did Angelou leave Egypt and move to Ghana?
- What was the historical significance of the two castles located on the Cape Coast?
- How did the people of Dunkwa welcome Angelou?

Think Critically

2. Why do you think it matters to Angelou that she "had proved that one of their descendants, at least one, could just briefly return to Africa, and that despite cruel betrayals, bitter ocean voyages, and hurtful centuries, we were still recognizable"?

3. What makes Dunkwa seem like home to Angelou?

4. Do you think Angelou should have revealed that she was an American? Explain your opinion.

5. How do you interpret Angelou's strong reaction the first time she passed by Cape Coast Castle?

   THINK ABOUT
   - why she avoided the town for a year
   - the scenes from the past she imagined
   - her references to "purging" and "feeding the spirits"

6. **ACTIVE READING** **STRATEGIES FOR READING AUTOBIOGRAPHY** Review the chart you made in your **READER'S NOTEBOOK.** Which events had the greatest impact on Angelou? How do you think they changed her?

Extend Interpretations

7. **Connect to Life** While living in Africa, Angelou explored the lands of her ancestors. If you could visit the home of your ancestors, what would you most like to find out? Why?

8. **Points of Comparison** Imagine a conversation between Maya Angelou and Olaudah Equiano, the African who was kidnapped and sent to the Americas on a slave ship (see page 93). What do you think they might say to each other?

Literary Analysis

AUTOBIOGRAPHY As you recall, an **autobiography** is the story of a person's life, written by that person. Writers of autobiographies draw from moments in their lives that are especially compelling, dramatic, or exciting. In "My Sojourn in the Lands of My Ancestors," Angelou recounts some of her powerful memories and explores their personal meaning. Like all writers of autobiographies, she is both a storyteller and an interpreter of events.

Paired Activity Imagine that Maya Angelou considered the following question as she was writing this autobiographical selection: Will the telling of these memories reveal something significant about who I am? Working with a partner, create a personality profile of Angelou, based on what you have learned about her.

REVIEW **AUTHOR'S PURPOSE** What do you think is Angelou's purpose for writing this selection? How does her purpose compare with William Least Heat-Moon's purpose in *Blue Highways*?

Choices & CHALLENGES

Writing Options

1. Description of Place What makes a place feel like home? Write a description of a place (other than your own home) that feels like home to you. Use sensory details—details that appeal to the five senses—to make the place come to life for your readers.

2. Poetry of Experience Angelou was moved by her journey to her ancestors' lands. Draft a poem that captures her feelings about Cape Coast Castle, her visit to Dunkwa, or some other aspect of her experiences. As an alternative, you might draft a poem about your own response to Angelou's journey.

3. Points of Comparison Based on your answer to discussion question 8, write an imagined dialogue between Angelou and Equiano.

Vocabulary in Action

EXERCISE: MATCHING MEANINGS On a piece of paper, write the word that most clearly relates to each phrase below. Then write a sentence containing both the phrase and the vocabulary word.

1. an out-of-control car
2. a map of Accra and its suburbs
3. the light at sunset
4. a stone that is undamaged by harsh weather
5. a slave's secret plan of escape
6. the villagers' loud singing
7. an unwanted offer of money
8. the scent of hot pepper soup
9. sorrow that needs release
10. villagers who try to act sophisticated in front of strangers

Building Vocabulary
For an in-depth lesson on word connotation and denotation, see page 908.

WORDS TO KNOW				
careen	mincing	reverberate	wane
environs	purging	suffuse	
impervious	rebuff	surreptitious	

Maya Angelou
1928–

Other Works
I Know Why the Caged Bird Sings, The Heart of a Woman, The Complete Collected Poems of Maya Angelou

Unlimited Potential Maya Angelou's formal education ended with high school, but she has continued to search for knowledge of herself and the world around her. Her search has taken her from rural Stamps, Arkansas, where as a child she lived with her grandmother, to as far away as Ghana and Egypt. She has said in *Black Women Writers at Work*, "I believe all things are possible for a human being, and I don't think there's anything in the world I can't do." Angelou's life bears witness that she lives by this philosophy.

Performing Artist After high school, Angelou studied dance in New York City, where she eventually worked under the celebrated performer and teacher Martha Graham. She soon made her mark as a dancer, actress, singer, director, and producer, both in the United States and abroad.

Versatile Writer Angelou, who began writing in the 1960s, has written poems, plays, songs, short stories, screenplays, articles, and television specials. She has also written five autobiographical works, including *All God's Children Need Traveling Shoes,* the source of this selection. "I had not consciously come to Ghana to find the roots of my beginnings," Angelou states in this book, "but I had continually and accidentally tripped over them or fallen upon them in my everyday life." One of the highlights of Angelou's career was composing and reciting the poem "On the Pulse of Morning" for President Bill Clinton's inauguration in 1993.

Comparing Literature: Assessment Practice

In writing assessment, you will sometimes be asked to synthesize, or pull together, information from a number of selections and make a generalization about what you've learned. You are now going to practice writing an essay with this kind of focus.

PART 1 ## Reading the Prompt

Often you will be asked to write in response to a prompt like the one below. First, read the entire prompt carefully. Then read through it again, looking for key words that help you identify the purpose of the essay and decide how to approach it.

> **Writing Prompt**
>
> Think about the encounters between people of different cultures in "My Sojourn in the Lands of My Ancestors" and two other selections you have read in Unit One, Part Two. Using examples from the three selections, develop recommendations for anyone wanting to have a positive cross-cultural encounter.

STRATEGIES IN ACTION

1 Consider your **topic**— cross-cultural encounters.

2 Cite **examples** of behavior from three selections.

3 **Synthesize,** or pull together, information to set guidelines for cross-cultural encounters.

PART 2 ## Planning a Synthesis Essay

- Create a diagram to organize your sources of information.

- In each selection, identify the passages related to your topic—cross-cultural encounters.

- Look for examples of positive behavior to imitate or negative behavior to avoid.

- Draw parallels among the various examples.

- Make generalizations and recommendations about positive cross-cultural encounters.

My Sojourn	Other Selection	Other Selection
Positive Examples	Positive Examples	Positive Examples
Negative Examples	Negative Examples	Negative Examples

Generalizations / Recommendations

PART 3 ## Drafting Your Essay

Introduction Begin by stating your topic— guidelines for cross-cultural encounters. Identify the three selections you will use for illustration.

Organization Present your recommendations in a logical order, perhaps from most important to least important, or from those followed at first contact to those followed later. Use examples from all three selections to support your recommendations.

Conclusion End your essay by restating the topic of your paper and summarizing your recommendations.

Revision Allow time to review your work. Make sure it is clear, well-supported, and free from mistakes.

Writing Handbook
See page 1281: Explanatory Writing

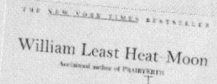

The Great Explorers

SAMUEL ELIOT MORISON

The voyages of Christopher Columbus, Ferdinand Magellan, Sir Francis Drake, and other famous European navigators come alive in Morison's critically acclaimed book. A notable historian and scholar, Morison details the enormous challenges of their hazardous sea journeys, their courage to explore the unknown, and their extraordinary navigational achievements. The book also includes several maps showing the routes of historic voyages.

Blue Highways

WILLIAM LEAST HEAT-MOON

Go beyond the excerpt on page 100 and read more from *Blue Highways,* Heat-Moon's chronicle of his 13,000-mile road trip through the United States. Riding in a van he named "Ghost Dancing," Heat-Moon takes the scenic route, traveling down rural roads and meeting a colorful cast of small-town characters. Heat-Moon's eloquent descriptions provide a panoramic view of the American landscape.

And Even *More* . . .

Books

The Buried Mirror
CARLOS FUENTES
Illustrated essay on Spain's influence in the New World.

The Whole World Guide to Culture Learning
J. DANIEL HESS
Informative book for contemporary travelers who encounter people from new cultures.

Endangered Peoples
ART DAVIDSON
The voices and faces of diverse native peoples who caution against destroying their cultures.

Other Media

1492: Conquest of Paradise
A feature film portraying the history-making explorations of Christopher Columbus. Panavision. (VIDEOCASSETTE)

A Son of Africa: The Slave Narrative of Olaudah Equiano
A film adaptation of Equiano's autobiography chronicling his experiences from his abduction in Africa to his role in the anti-slavery movement. California Newsreel. (VIDEOCASSETTE)

Lewis and Clark
A documentary by Ken Burns dramatizing moments from the historic expedition. Florentine Films and WETA, Washington, D.C. (VIDEOCASSETTE)

The Journals of Lewis and Clark

EDITED BY BERNARD DE VOTO

Imagine a cross-country trip from Missouri to Oregon—without a car or a map. In their journals, explorers Meriwether Lewis and William Clark vividly record their 1804–1806 expedition to find a western route to the Pacific coast.

Writing Workshop

Describing what you have seen . . .

From Reading to Writing Upon arriving in North America for the first time, William Bradford described the land as "a hideous and desolate wilderness, full of wild beasts." Bradford's **eyewitness report** is a firsthand account of the events he observed and experienced as an English colonist in North America. Writers of eyewitness reports use compelling details and sensory language to describe events. Today, eyewitness accounts written by professional journalists are published daily in newspapers and magazines.

For Your Portfolio

WRITING PROMPT Write an eyewitness report describing an event that has personal or historical significance.

Purpose: To inform
Audience: Classmates, family, or general readers

Basics in a Box

Eyewitness Report at a Glance

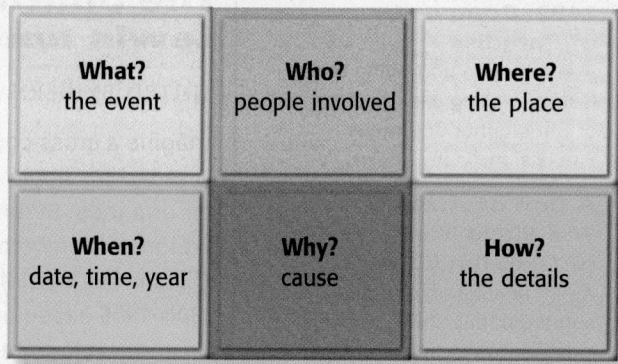

What? the event	Who? people involved	Where? the place
When? date, time, year	Why? cause	How? the details

= **Re-creation of Event**

RUBRIC Standards for Writing

A successful eyewitness report should

- focus on an event that has personal or historical significance
- answer the five *W*'s: *who, what, when, where,* and *why*
- create a sense of immediacy using precise language and sensory images
- present events in a clear, logical order
- capture the mood of the event

Analyzing a Student Model

Joseph Saroufim
West End High School

Far from the Land of Opportunity

On July 27, 1993, my family and I journeyed to the Middle East to the small country of Lebanon, my father's birthplace. On the day of our departure, Lebanon had just been hit with a massive air, land, and sea attack, and our plane landed on a runway made invisible by thick black smoke. As we waited for the jammed cargo doors of the plane to be forcibly opened to claim our luggage, I went in search of a bathroom. Things were not looking good. The bathroom looked even worse. Because of the ongoing war in Lebanon, much was in disrepair and this bathroom was no exception. The doors to the stalls were torn off and the room was completely pitch black. Toilet paper seemed to be considered a luxury. My most memorable summer vacation had begun.

My father had always told us that he grew up in the countryside of Lebanon. Throughout the one-hour ride at high speed on winding mountain roads that overlooked sheer drops of 10,000 feet, I imagined a peaceful village with hens and chickens, and maybe a lamb or two. When we arrived, I was amazed to see that the house was on the main road connecting Beirut, the capital of Lebanon, to Damascus, the capital of Syria. It was like living on the median strip of a major highway. That night, it was impossible to sleep. We were all crowded in the same room with our good friends, the transparent lizards and the bloodsucking mosquitoes. After finally dozing before dawn, I was wakened by the sounds of the Moslem call to prayer at a nearby mosque, a distant bomb, a caravan of large trucks, and a rooster. Well, this was the country, right? Day two, and I was ready to return home.

The incident that occurred the next morning was highly unexpected. As my family was getting ready to go out, we heard a startling bang and shatter. We all rushed to the front balcony. On the busy street in front of our house we saw a tightly compressed blue BMW with red blotches on the windshield belonging to the driver. Lying on its side in front of the car was a giant potato truck. The road was covered with smashed potatoes and little old ladies screaming at something and scurrying to pick up potatoes for a free dinner. As we found out, this would be one of the small surprises in our exciting vacation.

RUBRIC IN ACTION

❶ This writer sets the scene by telling *who, what, when,* and *where.*

❷ Uses precise language and sensory details to create a vivid picture

❸ Includes sound images to recreate the scene for the reader

❹ Orders events chronologically

❺ Uses precise words and images to present a vivid picture

Lebanon is the most beautiful country that I have ever seen, but the war has taken its toll. During our four-week stay, we had no hot water, no drinking water that we didn't have to boil, and electricity for six-hour intervals. Much of our socializing was done with flashlights and candles. Besides these inconveniences, what disturbed me was the lack of personal freedom. In Lebanon, you cannot drive on the road for more than five miles without arriving at an army checkpoint where your papers are examined and, in some cases, your entire car is searched. Male Lebanese citizens over the age of 18 are pulled out of their vehicles and immediately put in the service of the army.

❻ Gives examples to develop a point—the lack of personal freedom

Besides the lack of freedom and the lack of amenities, what bothered me even more was the lack of safety. It seemed as if there were no laws. There were 12-year-old kids driving cars, and there were no stop signs or traffic signals. This might seem like a fantasy for many teenagers in the United States, but as a cautious ten-year-old I was as nervous as can be.

❼ Captures the fearful mood with specific details

We decided to visit the old Lebanese city of Baalbek. There were beautiful pieces of architecture and carved stones, not to mention breathtaking cliffs and bottomless pits just lying in the middle of the dehydrating walk-through tour. My two-year-old cousin nearly ran into a deep hole but, luckily, my aunt caught her in the nick of time.

However, what struck me the most was the resilience of the Lebanese people. Throughout all of these hardships, they faced each day with a smile and a song. Listening to them play music on their rhythmical drums brought a joyful smile to my face. No matter how little they may have, they will always have that little extra for a relative or a friend. They laugh, they sing, they dance, and they make the most of what God has given them. We, in the land of opportunity, should take a long hard look at our Middle Eastern neighbors and learn that we have much to be thankful for and little to complain about. No matter how down or deprived I sometimes feel, whether I'm grounded, can't watch TV, or can't play sports, I look back at my Lebanon summer and realize that I really have a lot to live for.

❽ Summarizes the personal significance of the experience in the conclusion

Other Options:
· Begin the report by explaining the significance.
· Comment throughout the report on what the experiences mean.

Writing Your Eyewitness Report

❶ Prewriting

I can only report on what I know.
Max Frisch, Swiss writer

Eyewitness reporting is about being there and being aware. Jot down school, community, and family events that are coming up in the near future. Ask yourself whether any of these events are newsworthy. Might you have a unique opportunity to witness something that few others experience? Plan to attend those events that seem interesting.

When you go to an event, attend as a keen observer. In your notebook, record details, sensory images, snippets of conversations, and anything else that will help you re-create this experience for your readers. See the **Idea Bank** for more suggestions. Then choose one event and follow the steps below.

Planning Your Eyewitness Report

▶ **1. Get the facts.** Use a chart like the one at the right to record the basic facts about the event.

Who?	
What?	
When?	
Where?	
Why?	

▶ **2. Capture the mood.** Sensory details and vivid images will help you capture the mood of the event. Think about the sights, sounds, smells, tastes, and textures that you experience.

▶ **3. Record what is said.** Direct quotations can often give readers a sense of being at the event.

▶ **4. Make it clear why this is significant.** Reflect on what happens and why it is important to you or to others. Make sure you let your reader know the significance of the event.

❷ Drafting

Use your notes to get going. You might pick a real attention grabber—such as a startling image or a humorous quote—to capture your readers' attention early in your report.

Many eyewitness reports use **chronological order**—telling events in the order they occurred. This structure makes the experience easy for readers to follow. You might want to create a sense of intrigue by starting at the end and then filling in what happened to get there. Think about your choices and try different approaches until one works for you. To get started, look for examples of eyewitness reports in newspapers and magazines. Study one or two reports to see how they are organized and what kinds of details are included.

IDEABank

1. Your Working Portfolio
Build on one of the Writing Options you completed earlier in this unit:
• **Firsthand Account,** p. 79
• **Eyewitness Account,** p. 89

2. Calendar Check
Check a community, school, or sports calendar for interesting upcoming events. Plan to attend one of them and write an eyewitness account.

3. Ace Reporter
For the next week, carry a notebook. Report on both planned and spontaneous events. Take notes!

Have a question?
See the **Writing Handbook,** p. 1278

Ask Your Peer Reader

• What event am I describing? When and where does it take place?
• Why do you think I chose to report on the event?
• How would you describe the mood of the event?
• Which details made the greatest impression on you? Why?
• Which details, if any, seem unnecessary?
• Is the order of events clear?

Need revising help?

Review the **Rubric,**
p. 120.

Consider **peer reader**
comments.

Check **Revising, Editing,**
and Proofreading,
p. 1269.

❸ Revising

TARGET SKILL ▸ ELABORATING WITH SENSORY DETAILS In descriptive
writing, such as an eyewitness report, try to use details that appeal to the senses—sights,
sounds, smells, textures, and flavors. Concrete nouns, and strong verbs and adjectives,
help make images vivid.

> *like being on a film set when the director calls, "Action!"*
> Standing on a busy street during rush hour in New York City is ~~an~~
> ~~amazing experience.~~ Taxis ~~drive~~ by constantly. Bicycle messengers *speed* *bleating their horns* ^
>
> weave in and out of pedestrian traffic on the sidewalks. Pedestrians
> *like a huge herd of cattle on the verge of a stampede.*
> walk down the block ~~in huge groups.~~ ^
>
> *The smells of asphalt and exhaust mingle with*
> *that of hot dogs roasting at outdoor stands.*

❹ Editing and Proofreading

TARGET SKILL ▸ MODIFIER PLACEMENT After adding well-chosen details, be sure
to check the placement of modifiers. In general, you should place modifiers as close as
possible to the words they modify. Two common errors are **misplaced modifiers,** which are
placed too far from the words they modify, and **dangling modifiers,** which do not clearly
modify any noun or pronoun in the sentence.

Maddened by
modifiers?

See the **Grammar**
Handbook,
pp. 1312–1314.

> *I noticed that*
> Looking at people in the city, a few styles of dress stand out. ^
>
> Businessmen and women look serious in their dark suits and white
>
> shirts <u>walking into office buildings.</u> Young people wear everything
>
> from long flowered skirts and tank tops to baggy pants and neon-
>
> colored shirts <u>in trendy restaurants.</u> <u>Wearing comfortable jeans or</u>
>
> <u>shorts,</u> midtown Manhattan is full of tourists like myself.

Publishing
IDEAS

• Publish your eyewit-
  ness report in your
  school or community
  newspaper.

• E-mail your report to
  friends or pen pals.

More Online:
Publishing Options
www.mcdougallittell.com

❺ Reflecting

FOR YOUR WORKING PORTFOLIO What did you learn about being a good observer while
writing your eyewitness report? How did writing the report help you become a better
observer? Attach your answer to your finished work. Save your eyewitness report in
your **Working Portfolio.**

Read this passage from the first draft of an eyewitness report. The underlined sections may include the following kinds of errors:

- **lack of detail**
- **correctly written sentences that should be combined**
- **misplaced modifiers**
- **double negatives**

For each underlined phrase or sentence, choose the revision that most improves the writing.

> From my vantage point I saw the entire incident on the bridge. The first
> (1)
> thing I noticed was white smoke rising from the boat's engine. Then came the
> (2)
> smell. I called to the passengers. The passengers did not hear me. Then the motor
> (3)
> burst into flames. At first the passengers stood motionless in panic, but that
> didn't last long. The captain soon took control and checked that everyone was on
> (4)
> the boat wearing a life jacket . One crew member used the fire extinguisher, but
> it wasn't ineffective against the growing fire. I heard the captain shout. One by
> (5)   (6)
> one, the passengers jumped into the icy lake.

1. **A.** From my vantage point on the bridge, I saw the entire incident.
   B. From my vantage point I saw the entire incident from the bridge.
   C. On the bridge, I saw the entire incident from my vantage point.
   D. Correct as is

2. **A.** Then came the smell from the mist.
   B. Then came the sharp smell of smoke and gas.
   C. Then the smell came quickly.
   D. Correct as is

3. **A.** I called to the passengers, they did not hear me.
   B. I called to the passengers but the passengers did not hear me.
   C. I called to the passengers, but they did not hear me.
   D. Correct as is

4. **A.** everyone was wearing a life jacket on the boat.
   B. on the boat everyone was wearing a life jacket.
   C. everyone on the boat was wearing a life jacket.
   D. Correct as is

5. **A.** was ineffective
   B. was effective
   C. wasn't hardly effective
   D. Correct as is

6. **A.** I heard the captain's shout.
   B. I heard the captain shout the order to abandon ship.
   C. I barely heard the captain shout the order.
   D. Correct as is

Need extra help?

See the **Grammar Handbook:**

Modifiers, p. 1312;

The Sentence and Its Parts, p. 1316.

Expanding Word Power

Building an extensive vocabulary is like building stronger muscles—it helps to have a workout strategy. When you encounter an unfamiliar word, there are certain strategies you can use to determine its meaning and make the word your own. For instance, what words and phrases serve as clues to help you determine the meaning of *ascertain* in the passage on the right?

Details like "ordered . . . to climb one of the trees," "the lay of the land," and "found out . . . we were on an island" can help you infer that *ascertain* probably

> After we ate, I ordered Lope de Oviedo, our strongest man, to climb one of the trees not far off and ascertain the lay of the land. He complied and found out from the treetop that we were on an island.
> —Álvar Núñez Cabeza de Vaca, *La Relación*

means "to find out" or "to discover." Remember that strategies like noting context clues can help you ascertain the meanings of many unfamiliar words as you read.

Strategies for Building Vocabulary

There are a number of useful strategies you can use to strengthen your vocabulary.

❶ **Consider the Context** Inference clues, like those that were used to infer the meaning of *ascertain,* are one type of context clue that can help you learn new words. Others include definition or restatement clues, comparison or contrast clues, description clues, and example clues. For more information on using context clues, see page 326.

❷ **Recognize Word Parts** Sometimes the familiar roots or affixes in words will suggest their meanings. For example, in *The Interesting Narrative of the Life of Olaudah Equiano,* Equiano speaks of a man who was "flogged unmercifully." *Unmercifully* contains the base word *mercy.* The prefix *un-* means "not," and the suffix *-ly* indicates that the word is an adverb and therefore describes an action. You can use what you know about roots and affixes to conclude that the man was flogged without mercy. To learn more about roots and affixes, see pages 444 and 1130.

❸ **Build Word Families** Words that are built from the same base word or root can be grouped together as a "family." For example, the words *incision, precision,* and *concise* all contain the root *cise,* which comes from the Latin verb *caedere,* "to cut." It is useful to know that the sense of the root *cise* has survived in these words: the meaning of each is based on an idea of physical or mental sharpness. Try to make connections like these as

you encounter new words. For more about roots and word families, see page 444.

❹ **Check a Dictionary** Even if you have guessed the meaning of an unfamiliar word, a dictionary can still help you to refine your understanding of the word's meaning, usage, and parts. Of course, it will also tell you if your guess was wrong. See page 990 for more about using reference aids to unlock word meanings.

❺ **Record and Use New Words** A good way to remember new words is to make diagrams like the one below in your ▯ **READER'S NOTEBOOK.** Make it a point to review your word diagrams frequently and to use the words in your conversation and writing until they are a natural part of your vocabulary.

NAVIGATOR

Definition: one who plans and monitors a ship's course

Etymology: *navis* "ship" + *agere* "to drive" + *-or* "one who"

Example: I called to the navigator, who said we were coming close to land.

Related Words: naval, navigable, navigate, navy

EXERCISE Create diagrams like the one above to record five words, from the selections you have read in this book, that you would like to add to your vocabulary.

Grammar from Literature

Experienced writers add interest and rhythm to their writing by using a variety of sentence types and sentences of different lengths. Look at the following passage. The sentence types are identified by color. They are paired with the definitions below.

> It was winter and bitterly cold, and we had suffered hunger and the heavy beating of the waves for many days. Next day the men began to collapse. By sunset, all had fallen over on one another, close to death. Few were any longer conscious. Not five could stand. When night fell, only the navigator and I remained able to tend the barge. Two hours after dark he told me I must take over; he believed he was going to die that night.
>
> —*La Relación*, translated by Cyclone Covey

Notice that the translator of this work used all of the four kinds of sentences in English.

A **simple** sentence has one independent clause or main clause. An independent clause can stand alone as a complete thought.

A **compound** sentence contains two or more independent clauses joined by a conjunction or semicolon.

A **complex** sentence has one independent clause and one or more subordinate clauses, or clauses that cannot stand alone as a sentence.

A **compound complex** sentence has two or more independent clauses and one or more subordinate clauses.

Using Sentence Variety in Your Writing As you revise your own writing, look at the kind and the length of sentences you have used. If many of your sentences are short, experiment with combining ideas.

> LACKING SENTENCE VARIETY
> **The Pilgrims arrived on November 11. Soon they set about repairing the boat. They saw the extensive damage. They knew the repair would take a long time.**
>
> REVISED
> **Soon after the Pilgrims arrived on November 11, they set about mending the boat. They saw the extensive damage, and they knew the repair would take a long time.**

Usage Tip As you try using various types of sentences, avoid sentence fragments. Be sure each sentence has a subject, has a verb, and expresses a complete thought. Remember that although a subordinate clause has a subject and verb, it does not express a complete thought and cannot stand alone as a sentence.

> INCORRECT
> verb   verb
> **Gave the Spaniards shelter and fed them. (no subject)**
>
> CORRECT
>   subject   verb   verb
> **The Indians gave the Spaniards shelter and fed them.**

> INCORRECT
> **As we drifted into shore. (A subordinate clause cannot stand alone.)**
>
> CORRECT
> **As we drifted into shore, a wave pushed us forward.**

WRITING EXERCISE Combine each pair of simple sentences following the directions in parentheses.

1. Is Oviedo lost? Has he been captured? (Form a compound sentence by joining with a comma and a conjunction such as *and, but,* or *or.*)
2. The Pilgrims sailed across the Atlantic. They arrived at Cape Cod in November. (Form a compound sentence.)
3. Conditions were very hard the first year. Many of the colonists died. (Form a complex sentence. Begin with *because,* and put a comma after the first clause.)
4. Maya Angelou followed her husband to North Africa and supported his efforts. Her marriage failed in spite of her efforts. (Form a compound sentence.)
5. Olaudah Equiano saw whites for the first time. He thought they were evil spirits. (Form a complex sentence. Begin with *when,* and put a comma after the first clause.)

GRAMMAR EXERCISE Rewrite these sentences, changing fragments into sentences. You may need to add words.

1. The Spanish explorer Cabeza de Vaca.
2. Because the Pilgrims were weakened during their first winter.
3. Sailed from England to gain more religious freedom.
4. Although Olaudah Equiano survived a voyage on a slave ship.
5. To the Cape Coast Castle and nearby Elmina Castle.

Origins and Encounters

What did you learn about Native American culture from reading this unit? Did you find out anything new about the first Europeans and Africans to come to this continent? Choose one or more of the options in each of these sections to help you explore how your thinking has developed.

Reflecting on the Unit

OPTION 1

Old Beliefs, New Literature Consider how the ancient Native American selections relate to the more contemporary ones in the first part of this unit. What traditions—such as values, beliefs, and forms of storytelling—do you see continuing into the present? How have these traditions been adapted, or changed, to fit contemporary needs? Write a few paragraphs to explain your ideas.

OPTION 2

Explorers and Exploiters Think back over the selections in Part 2 of this unit. What things was each author encountering for the first time? What similarities and differences between the different encounters do you notice? Do any of the selections seem unrelated to the title "First Encounters"? Get together with a partner to discuss these questions, and jot down your conclusions.

OPTION 3

Different World Views How do the attitudes expressed in Part 1, "In Harmony with Nature," differ from those expressed in Part 2, "First Encounters"? With a small group of classmates, discuss the differences.

THINK ABOUT
- ideas about nature
- ideas about good and evil
- ideas about how human beings should behave

Self ASSESSMENT

 READER'S NOTEBOOK

To explore how your understanding has developed as you read this unit, create a two-column chart. In the first column, list what you knew about Native Americans and explorers before you read the selections. In the second column, list important facts and concepts you discovered.

Reviewing Literary Concepts

OPTION 1 **Considering Conflict** You know that conflict forms the basis of a plot and that the resolution of the conflict often concludes a story. To help you analyze the conflicts in the stories that you read in this unit, make a chart like the one shown. Then write a few sentences telling why you particularly liked the way one or two of the conflicts were resolved. Write a few more sentences, telling which resolutions, if any, you found unsatisfying and giving reasons for your opinion.

Selection	Conflict	How Conflict Is Resolved
"The World on the Turtle's Back"	Twins struggle to overcome each other.	Straight-minded twin kills his brother, but both continue to have power over different parts of the world.

OPTION 2 **Oral Literature and Historical Narratives** In this unit you have read not only Native American oral literature—myths, tales, and songs— but also historical narratives written by some of the first nonnative people in North America. How do these two kinds of literature differ? With a small group of classmates, discuss what each kind of literature contributes to your understanding of early America.

Self ASSESSMENT

READER'S NOTEBOOK

Did you understand *conflict, oral literature,* and *historical narratives* well enough to complete one of the options at left? Copy the following list of literary terms introduced in this unit. Next to each, rate your understanding of the concept from 1 (none at all) to 5 (absolute mastery). Review the terms you are not sure about in the **Glossary of Literary Terms** (page 1342).

myth

creation myth

repetition

folk tale

trickster tale

setting

primary and secondary sources

slave narrative

author's purpose

audience

autobiography

Building Your Portfolio

- **QuickWrites** Several of the Writing Options in this unit asked you to relate the ideas presented in selections to your own ideas and experiences. Choose two pieces that you feel present particularly insightful or interesting connections. Write a cover note explaining your choices. Then attach your note to the pieces and add them to your **Presentation Portfolio.**

- **Writing Workshop** In this unit you wrote an Eyewitness Report about an event of personal or historical significance. Reread the report and assess the quality of your writing. Where is your writing most vivid? Attach a note with your thoughts about your work, and place the report in your **Presentation Portfolio.**

- **Additional Activities** Review the assignments you completed under **Activities & Explorations** and **Inquiry & Research**. Keep a record in your portfolio of any assignments that you think are representative of your best work.

Self ASSESSMENT

At this point, you may just be beginning your **Presentation Portfolio.** Are the pieces you have included so far ones you think you'll keep, or do you think you will replace them as the year goes on?

Setting GOALS

As you thought about the selections in this unit, did you want to know more about the original inhabitants of North America and about the Europeans and Africans who came later? Jot down a few questions you would like to investigate on your own.

UNIT TWO

From Colony to Country

A *Morning View of Blue Hill Village* (1824), Jonathan Fisher. William A Farnsworth Library and Art Museum, Rockland, Maine, museum purchase, 1965 (1465.134).

The Lord will make our name a praise and glory, so that men shall say of succeeding plantations: "The Lord make it like that of New England." For we must consider that we shall be like a City upon a Hill; the eyes of all people are on us.

JOHN WINTHROP
First Governor of the Massachusetts Bay Colony

From Colony to Country

EVENTS IN AMERICAN LITERATURE

1620   1700

1624 Captain John Smith writes *General History in Virginia*

1640 *Bay Psalm Book* is first book printed in America

1666 Anne Bradstreet, first notable colonial poet, writes "Upon the Burning of Our House"

1678 Bradstreet publishes "To My Dear and Loving Husband," not originally intended for "public view"

1704 *Boston Newsletter*, first American newspaper is established

1732 Benjamin Franklin initiates a circulating library in Philadelphia; Franklin's *Poor Richard's Almanack* is published

1741 Jonathan Edwards delivers sermon called "Sinners in the Hands of an Angry God"

EVENTS IN NORTH AMERICA

1620   1700

1630 About 1,000 Puritans establish Massachusetts Bay Colony

1676 Puritans' victory in King Philip's War ends Native American resistance in New England colonies

1682 Quakers led by William Penn begin living in peace with Native Americans in Pennsylvania (to c. 1752)

1688 Quakers voice opposition to slavery

1691 New charter provides for religious tolerance in Massachusetts, weakening Puritans' control

1692 Witchcraft trials take place in Salem, Massachusetts

1763 British defeat French in French and Indian War, and claim land east of Mississippi River, including Canada

1765 British Parliament passes Stamp Act, which levies tax on colonies to help pay off British debts

EVENTS IN THE WORLD

1620   1700

1632 Indian emperor Shah Jahan builds Taj Mahal, over the next 22 years

1643 Louis XIV begins 72-year reign in France

1649 Oliver Cromwell and Puritans execute King Charles I of England

1687 Sir Isaac Newton presents law of gravity

1721 Edo (Tokyo) in Japan becomes world's largest city

1748 French philosopher Baron de Montesquieu publishes *Spirit of the Laws*

PERIOD PIECES

Paul Revere silver tea pot

Popular style of wig in the 18th century

Puritan pocket watch

1773 In London, Phillis Wheatley's *Poems on Various Subjects, Religious and Moral* appears, the first book of poetry published by an African American

1775 In speech to the Second Virginia Convention, Patrick Henry makes plea for armed resistance against British

1776 Thomas Paine publishes *Common Sense,* claiming that independence from England is "destiny"; Declaration of Independence is written by Thomas Jefferson; Abigail Adams proclaims power of "ladies" in letter to husband John

1782 Michel-Guillaume Jean de Crèvecoeur publishes *Letters from an American Farmer*, a collection of 12 essays on life in America

1789 *The Interesting Narrative of the Life of Olaudah Equiano* is published

1773 To protest new British tax on tea, enraged colonists stage Boston Tea Party, dumping huge amounts of tea into Boston Harbor

1775 "Shot heard round the world" is fired on Lexington Green in Massachusetts, starting Revolutionary War

1781 British surrender to General George Washington at Yorktown, ending Revolutionary War

1789 George Washington is elected first president of United States (to 1797)

1791 Bill of Rights becomes part of U.S. Constitution

1793 Eli Whitney invents cotton gin

1796 Washington declines to run for third term and establishes presidential succession

1762 Catherine the Great begins rule of Russia (to 1796)

1776 Adam Smith publishes *The Wealth of Nations*

1789 French Revolution begins (to 1794)

1793 French King Louis XVI is executed by guillotine

1795 Poland disappears from map of Europe after last partition

Between Heaven and Hell

The Puritan Tradition

Puritans too often have the reputation of being black-clad moralists self-righteously proclaiming the values of thrift and hard work. According to the American writer and humorist H. L. Mencken, a Puritan is one who suspects that "somewhere someone is having a good time." To call someone a puritan is usually not a compliment.

This negative image, however, is based on a stereotype of the 16th-century Puritans that, like most stereotypes, is full of half-truths and misconceptions. True, the Puritans did value hard work and self-sacrifice, but they also honored material success. Wealth was considered to be the reward of a virtuous life. Some Puritans, especially the early Pilgrims, wore severe black clothing because that was all they had. Those who settled the Massachusetts Bay Colony after 1630, however, were better off financially. They could afford decorative and colorful clothing—when they could find it in the colony, that is. These Puritans were even known to drink beer and other alcoholic beverages on occasion.

Puritans also valued family life, community service, art, and literature. They were the first in the colonies to establish a printing press, free public grammar schools, and a college (Harvard).

On the other hand, the Puritans *were* arrogant in their religious faith and completely intolerant of viewpoints different from their own. Puritans who remained in England

Tombstone design from Puritan New England

Mrs. Freake and Baby Mary (1674), unknown artist. The Granger Collection, New York.

participated in a revolution that not only toppled the king but had him beheaded as well. Those who had come to North America had even freer rein for their beliefs. With supreme confidence and self-consciousness, they went about setting up their institutions as though not only God but the whole world were watching. "The eyes of all people are on us," proclaimed John Winthrop, the first governor of the Massachusetts Bay

Puritan Beliefs

The key to the Puritan heart and soul is religious belief. What follows is a brief explanation of the Puritans' basic convictions:

• *Human beings are inherently evil and so must struggle to overcome their sinful nature.* This belief in original sin was one of the first things a Puritan child learned. "In Adam's fall / We sinned all" is the rhyme that teaches the letter *A* in *The New England Primer*.

• *Personal salvation depends solely on the grace of God, not on individual effort.* Puritans believed in predestination, the doctrine that only those people who are "elected" by God are saved and go to heaven. The only way an individual could know that he or she was saved was by directly experiencing God's grace in a religious conversion.

• *The Bible is the supreme authority on earth.* Puritans argued that the Bible was the sole guide not only in governing the moral and spiritual life but also in governing the church and society as a whole. One effect of this belief was to make Puritan churches more democratic, organized around their congregations rather than around ruling bishops. On the other hand, it led the Puritans to be more repressive in their political systems and more intolerant of others. For example, they used the Bible to justify their occupation of the land and their use of force against Native Americans: "Whosoever therefore resisteth the power, resisteth the ordinance of God: and they that resist shall receive to themselves damnation" (Romans 13:2). In short, the Puritans saw themselves as God's chosen people, like the "children of Israel" in the Old Testament.

from *The New England Primer*

The New England Primer is a famous American schoolbook that dates from before 1690. The sale of more than 2 million copies of the book during the 18th century is an indication of how widely the primer was used.

A — In *Adam's* Fall We Sinned all.

B — Thy Life to Mend This *Book* Attend.

C — The *Cat* doth play And after flay.

D — A *Dog* will bite A Thief at night.

E — An *Eagles* flight Is out of fight.

F — The Idle *Fool* Is whipt at School.

G — As runs the *Glafs* Mans life doth pafs.

H — My *Book* and *Heart* Shall never part.

J — *Job* feels the Rod Yet bleffes GOD.

K — Our *K I N G* the good No man of blood.

L — The *Lion* bold The *Lamb* doth hold.

M — The *Moon* gives light In time of night.

N — *Nightingales* fing In Time of Spring.

O — The *Royal Oak* it was the Tree That fav'd His Royal Majeftie.

P — *Peter* denies His Lord and cries

Q — Queen *Efther* comes in Royal State To Save the JEWS from difmal Fate.

R — *Rachel* doth mourn For her firft born.

S — *Samuel* anoints Whom God appoints:

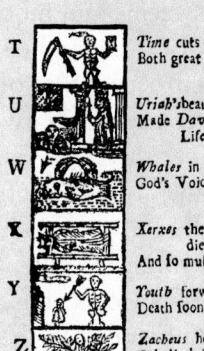

T — *Time* cuts down all Both great and fmall.

U — *Uriah's* beauteous Wife Made *David* feek his Life.

W — *Whales* in the Sea God's Voice obey.

X — *Xerxes* the great did die, And fo muft you & I,

Y — *Youth* forward flips Death fooneft nips.

Z — *Zacheus* he Did climb the Tree His Lord to fee,

Colony. And so it was that in New England during the 1600s Puritanism gained its fullest and perhaps purest development.

The selections in this part of Unit Two represent the Puritan tradition over a span of approximately 100 years. The poet Anne Bradstreet gives a sense of what ordinary Puritan lives were like. Her voice expresses the view of a heaven ruled by a just God—a goal to which all Puritans aspired. The grace of Bradstreet's voice is followed by the harshness of the judges' voices at the Salem witch trials, an example of the darker aspects of Puritanism. The last Puritan represented is the passionate minister Jonathan Edwards, threatening his congregation with the torments of hell in an excerpt from his famous sermon "Sinners in the Hands of an Angry God."

Traditions Across Time: Another Look at the Puritans

Many American writers have been fascinated by the Puritans. Nathaniel Hawthorne, one of whose ancestors had been a presiding judge at the Salem witch trials, set his novel *The Scarlet Letter* and many of his short stories in Puritan times to explore the psychological effects of sin and guilt.

In the 1950s, the playwright Arthur Miller dramatized the Salem witchcraft trials in *The Crucible*. The play was written partly in response to the anti-Communist "witch hunts" of the period. Miller's drama not only personalizes the events of Salem but also warns against similar injustices in our own time.

The Puritan Tradition

Anne Bradstreet	**To My Dear and Loving Husband**	138
	Upon the Burning of Our House, July 10th, 1666	138
	A personal voice from Puritan times	
Salem Court Documents, 1692	**The Examination of Sarah Good**	144
	Chilling testimony from the original witch trials	
	RELATED READING	
	History Clashes with Commercialism	150
	A news article about today's Salem	
Jonathan Edwards	*from* **Sinners in the Hands of an Angry God**	152
	A sermon designed to make you change your ways	

COMPARING LITERATURE
Traditions Across Time: Another Look at the Puritans

| Arthur Miller | **The Crucible** (1953) | 163 |
| | *Salem's "witches" on the modern stage* | |

Detail of chair-seat cover (about 1725), embroidered by a member of Anne Bradstreet's family.

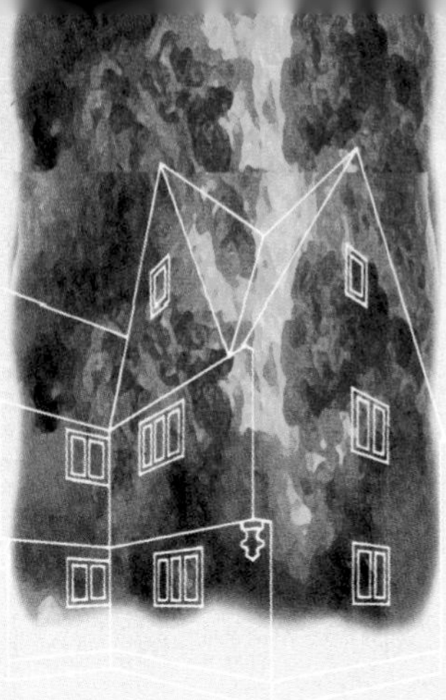

To My Dear and Loving Husband

and

Upon the Burning of Our House, July 10th, 1666

Poetry by ANNE BRADSTREET

Connect to Your Life

Prized Persons and Possessions Think about a person or a possession that means a lot to you. What comparison would express the emotions you feel toward this person or thing? On a sheet of paper, complete the following sentence:
_________ means more to me than _________.

Build Background

Puritan Poetry You may be surprised to learn that Anne Bradstreet was not only the first notable American woman poet—she was essentially the first notable American poet. In the two poems presented here, Bradstreet expresses her intense feelings about her husband and about the loss of her home in a destructive fire. Although Bradstreet's poetic language may seem a bit stiff to you, you'll be able to understand the recognizable emotions of love and sadness she expresses.

Poetry in 17th-century New England was almost exclusively devotional in nature and, as such, was highly recommended reading for the Puritan community. What sets Bradstreet's poems apart from other Puritan verse is their personal subject matter. She focused primarily on the realities of her life—her husband, her children, and her house, for example. However, like any conscientious Puritan, Bradstreet always viewed her life within a spiritual context: every event, no matter how trivial, bore a divine message; every misfortune served to remind her of God's will and the path to salvation. In her poetry, Bradstreet gave us a lasting impression of what it felt like to be a Puritan.

Focus Your Reading

LITERARY ANALYSIS **METER** If you read Bradstreet's two poems aloud, you will hear a distinct rhythm. **Meter** is the repetition of a regular rhythmic unit in a line of poetry. Each unit, known as a foot, has one stressed syllable (indicated by a ´) and either one or two unstressed syllables (indicated by a ˘). Read the beginning lines of both poems aloud, tapping out the rhythm. Note which words or syllables are stressed and how many stresses there are.

ACTIVE READING **CLARIFYING MEANING**
Archaic language consists of words that were once commonly used in the past but are now considered old-fashioned or out-of-date. For example, note that Bradstreet uses the pronouns *thee, ye,* and *thou,* rather than *you.* Also, like other early American poets, Bradstreet often uses **inverted syntax**—meaning that she reverses the expected order of words. In the first line of "Upon the Burning of Our House," for example, she writes "when rest I took" rather than "when I took rest."

READER'S NOTEBOOK As you read "Upon the Burning of Our House," note other lines with archaic language and inverted syntax, and paraphrase (restate) them using contemporary vocabulary and conventional word order.

A N N E   B R A D S T R E E T

To My and **DEAR LOVING** Husband

Chair-seat cover (about 1725), embroidered by a member of the Bradstreet family. Cotton threads, linen warp, wool embroidery, 43 cm × 47 cm. Gift of Samuel Bradstreet, courtesy of Museum of Fine Arts, Boston.

If ever two were one, then surely we.
If ever man were loved by wife, then thee;
If ever wife was happy in a man,
Compare with me, ye women, if you can.
5 I prize thy love more than whole mines of gold
Or all the riches that the East doth hold.
My love is such that rivers cannot quench,
Nor ought but love from thee, give recompense.
Thy love is such I can no way repay,
10 The heavens reward thee manifold, I pray.
Then while we live, in love let's so persevere
That when we live no more, we may live ever.

GUIDE FOR READING

8 recompense (rĕk'əm-pĕns'): payment in return for something, such as a service.

9–12 What relationship is seen between earthly love and eternal life?

11 persevere: In Bradstreet's time, *persevere* would have been pronounced pûr-sĕv'ər, which rhymes with *ever.*

Thinking Through the Literature

1. **Comprehension Check** What is valued more than gold in this poem?
2. What do you think Bradstreet is saying in the last two lines of the poem?
3. What emotions does Bradstreet express toward her husband? Point out the words that make you think so.
4. Do you know any couples who regard each other as Bradstreet and her husband do? Describe them.

ANNE BRADSTREET

Upon the Burning of Our House,

July 10th, 1666

In silent night when rest I took
For sorrow near I did not look
I wakened was with thund'ring noise
And piteous shrieks of dreadful voice.
5   That fearful sound of "Fire!" and "Fire!"
Let no man know is my desire.

I, starting up, the light did spy,
And to my God my heart did cry
To strengthen me in my distress
10 And not to leave me succorless.
Then, coming out, beheld a space
The flame consume my dwelling place.

GUIDE FOR READING

10 succorless (sŭk'ər-lĭs): without help or relief.

And when I could no longer look,
I blest His name that gave and took,
That laid my goods now in the dust:
Yea, so it was, and so 'twas just.
It was His own, it was not mine,
Far be it that I should repine;

He might of all justly bereft,
But yet sufficient for us left.
When by the ruins oft I past,
My sorrowing eyes aside did cast,
And here and there the places spy
Where oft I sat and long did lie:

Here stood that trunk and there that chest,
There lay that store I counted best.
My pleasant things in ashes lie,
And them behold no more shall I.
Under thy roof no guest shall sit,
Nor at thy table eat a bit.

No pleasant tale shall e'er be told,
Nor things recounted done of old.
No candle e'er shall shine in thee,
Nor bridegroom's voice e'er heard shall be.
In silence ever shalt thou lie;
Adieu, Adieu, all's vanity.

Then straight I 'gin my heart to chide,
And did thy wealth on earth abide?
Didst fix thy hope on mold'ring dust?
The arm of flesh didst make thy trust?
Raise up thy thoughts above the sky
That dunghill mists away may fly.

Thou hast an house on high erect,
Framed by that mighty Architect,
With glory richly furnishéd,
Stands permanent though this be fled.
It's purchaséd and paid for too
By Him who hath enough to do.

A price so vast as is unknown
Yet by His gift is made thine own;
There's wealth enough, I need no more,
Farewell, my pelf, farewell my store.
The world no longer let me love,
My hope and treasure lies above.

15

20

25

30

35

40

45

50

14 I . . . took: an allusion to Job 1:21—"The Lord gave, and the Lord hath taken away; blessed be the name of the Lord."

13–18 How does Bradstreet view her loss?

18 repine: to complain or fret; to long for something.

21–36 What does Bradstreet miss about her house?

36 all's vanity: an allusion to Ecclesiastes 1:2, "All is vanity," meaning that all is temporary and meaningless.

37 chide: to scold mildly so as to correct or improve.

43–54 What is Bradstreet comparing to a house? What ideas are suggested by this comparison?

52 pelf: wealth or riches, especially when dishonestly acquired.

Connect to the Literature

1. What Do You Think
What do you make of Bradstreet's reaction to her loss? Share your thoughts with a classmate.

Comprehension Check
- What is Bradstreet's initial reaction when she learns her house is on fire?
- What does she conclude about the reason for the fire?
- Where does she expect to find a permanent home?

Think Critically

2. Explain in your own words why Bradstreet feels the way she does at the end of the poem.

THINK ABOUT { • her attitude toward wealth and material goods
• her religious beliefs and values

3. What different emotions does Bradstreet express at various points in the poem? Point out lines in the poem that support your ideas.

4. If Bradstreet had lost her husband in the fire, how might the poem be different?

5. What did you learn about Bradstreet's daily life from reading this poem?

6. | ACTIVE READING | CLARIFYING MEANING | Share lines from the poem that you paraphrased using contemporary language and conventional word order. How do your versions compare with the original lines? By changing Bradstreet's syntax, how did you alter the **rhyme scheme**— the pattern of rhyme at the end of each line?

Extend Interpretations

7. Comparing Texts On the basis of "To My Dear and Loving Husband" and "Upon the Burning of Our House," how would you describe Bradstreet's views of God and heaven?

8. Connect to Life Think of someone you know whose spiritual values are a source of strength during trying times. Briefly describe that person, and compare him or her to the speaker in "Upon the Burning of Our House."

Literary Analysis

METER Bradstreet's two poems follow a regular pattern, or **meter,** of accented and unaccented syllables. In a poetic line, each unit, known as a foot, has one stressed syllable (indicated by a ´) and either one or two unstressed syllables (indicated by a ˘), as shown in the chart below:

Foot	Syllables	Example
iamb	unstressed, stressed	tŏdáy
trochee	stressed, unstressed	látĕr
anapest	unstressed, unstressed, stressed	ĭntĕrfére
dactyl	stressed, unstressed, unstressed	pérmănĕnt

Two words are used to identify the meter of a line. The first word describes the type of metrical foot— iambic, trochaic, anapestic, or dactylic— and the second word describes the number of feet in a line, as follows:

one foot: **monometer**   four feet: **tetrameter**
two feet: **dimeter**   five feet: **pentameter**
three feet: **trimeter**   six feet: **hexameter**

If you were to analyze, or scan, line 2 of "To My Dear and Loving Husband," it would look like this:

If évĕr mán | wĕre lovĕd bў | wífe thĕn thĕe
　　1　　　2　　　3　　　4　　　5

"To My Dear and Loving Husband" is an example of **iambic pentameter**, the most common meter in English poetry.

Paired Activity What is the meter of "Upon the Burning of Our House"? Working with a partner, scan the first two lines, count the stressed syllables, and refer to the charts. Then write two lines of poetry that duplicate the meter of either Bradstreet poem.

Choices & CHALLENGES

Writing Options

1. Lyric Poem Both of Bradstreet's poems are called lyric poems because they are short and express the thoughts and feelings of one speaker. Write a lyric poem that expresses your emotions toward the person or possession you described for the Connect to Your Life activity on page 138. Imitate Bradstreet's style if you wish.

2. Personal Analogy In the last two stanzas of "Upon the Burning of Our House," Bradstreet compares heaven to a house. Develop an analogy, an extended comparison of two things that have certain similarities, to explain your personal view of one of the following concepts: heaven, love, home, loss, marriage, wealth.

Activities & Explorations

1. Storyboard Illustrations Working with a small group of classmates, create a series of drawings to illustrate the sentiments in "To My Dear and Loving Husband" or the events in "Upon the Burning of Our House." Show your storyboard to the class, identifying specific lines that you illustrated. ~ **ART**

2. Musical Adaptation Bradstreet's poetry was influenced by a book of biblical psalms set to the melodies of familiar hymns. Create a song by setting one of Bradstreet's poems to music with an appropriate rhythm and mood. Make a tape recording of the song, and share it with the class. ~ **MUSIC**

Inquiry & Research

1. Puritan Women The Puritan emphasis on reading the Bible encouraged a higher rate of literacy among Puritan women in New England than in England or other British colonies. Locate information on the education of Puritan women and the roles they played in the Puritan community.

2. Puritan Homes Puritans were artistic interior decorators. For instance, the women wove beautifully designed bedspreads and embroidered colorful chair-seat covers, such as the one shown on page 139. Find out more about the beautiful objects that adorned Puritan homes.

Anne Bradstreet
(1612?–1672)

Other Works
"Before the Birth of One of Her Children"
"As Weary Pilgrim"
"To My Dear Children"

A Privileged Upbringing The first noteworthy poet in the American colonies, Anne Dudley Bradstreet was born in England. She grew up among educated aristocrats because her father, Thomas Dudley, was steward, or manager of affairs, for the Earl of Lincoln. Bradstreet's father provided her with tutors and access to the Earl's extensive library, and he taught her Greek, Latin, Hebrew, and French.

Life in the Colonies In 1628, 16-year-old Anne married Simon Bradstreet. Two years later, the young couple sailed for the Massachusetts Bay Colony. The Bradstreets eventually settled in North Andover, where they raised eight children. Despite Anne Bradstreet's domestic and religious responsibilities and persistent illnesses, she managed to find time to write.

America's First English-Speaking Poet In 1647, Bradstreet's brother-in-law, John Woodbridge, went to England with verses that she had copied for members of her family. Without her knowledge, he had the verses published in London in 1650, in a volume titled *The Tenth Muse Lately Sprung Up in America*. A second edition, published in 1678, contained Bradstreet's corrections and personal poems, including "To My Dear and Loving Husband," which she had not intended for "public view." A third edition, printed in 1867, contained additional poems, including "Upon the Burning of Our House."

The Examination of Sarah Good

SALEM COURT DOCUMENTS, 1692

> ### Connect to Your Life
>
> **Justice Denied** Have you ever been accused of doing something that you didn't do, or do you know of someone else who was falsely accused? If so, how did you feel about the accusation? Why do you think it was made? Was it ever disproved? With your classmates, discuss the causes and effects of false accusations.

Build Background

Mass Hysteria in Salem In 1692, the Massachusetts Bay Colony settlement of Salem was gripped by panic after a group of adolescent girls suffered mysterious symptoms such as convulsive fits, hallucinations, loss of appetite, and the temporary loss of hearing, sight, and speech. Diagnosed as being victims of witchcraft, the girls denounced certain townspeople for this crime, including a woman named Sarah Good. The selection you will read consists of excerpts from the court records of Sarah Good's preliminary examination on March 1, 1692, at the Salem meeting house. Good was later jailed, tried in court, and found guilty; she was hanged on July 19, 1692.

Between 1692 and 1693, more than 400 people in Salem and nearby towns were accused of being witches. Ultimately, 19 men and women were found guilty and hanged. When Puritan leaders began to doubt the accusers and their evidence, the Salem witch trials finally ended. Over the next 20 years, most of those falsely accused were pardoned and awarded financial compensation.

Focus Your Reading

LITERARY ANALYSIS **TRANSCRIPT** A **transcript** is a written record of information communicated orally, such as a **speech**, an **interview**, or **legal testimony**. The transcript of Sarah Good's examination provides the actual questions she was asked and the answers she gave. Think of this document as the script of a real-life drama. Imagine the voices of Sarah Good and her questioners and the motives for their remarks. Also notice how the introductory summary, a brief description of events written by those who questioned Good, differs from the transcript as a source of information.

ACTIVE READING **DETECTING BIAS** A **bias** is a prejudice or mental leaning toward or against some topic, issue, or person. Writers can reveal their biases by using **loaded language,** words with strong emotional associations. The description "poor tormented children" reveals the writer's sympathetic attitude, or positive bias, toward the accusing girls. Similarly, interrogators can reveal their biases by asking **loaded questions**—questions that make unwarranted presumptions or that force a certain answer. For example, the question, "Why do you hurt these children?" assumes Good's guilt.

READER'S NOTEBOOK As you read, note examples of loaded language or loaded questions that reveal the biases of court officials.

The EXAMINATION of SARAH GOOD

SALEM COURT DOCUMENTS, 1692

SUMMARY

SALEM VILLAGE, MARCH THE 1ST, 1691–92.

Sarah Good, the wife of William Good of Salem Village, Laborer. Brought before us by George Locker, Constable in Salem, to Answer, Joseph Hutchinson, Thomas Putnam, etc., of Salem Village, yeomen[1] (Complainants[2] on behalf of their Majesties) against said Sarah Good for

Suspicion of witchcraft by her Committed and thereby much Injury done to the Bodies of Elizabeth Parris, Abigail Williams, Ann Putnam, and Elizabeth Hubbard, all of Salem Village aforesaid according to their Complaints as per warrants.

---

1. **yeomen** (yō'mən): farmers who cultivate their own land.
2. **complainants** (kəm-plā'nənts): people who make a complaint or file a formal charge in court.

Sarah Good upon Examination denieth the matter of fact (viz.) that she ever used any witchcraft or hurt the abovesaid children or any of them.

The above-named Children being all present positively accused her of hurting of them Sundry[3] times with this two months and also that morning.

Sarah Good denied that she had been at their houses in said time or near them, or had done them any hurt. All the abovesaid children then present accused her face to face, upon which they were all dreadfully tortured and tormented for a short space of time, and the affliction and tortures being over, they charged said Sarah Good again that she had then so tortured them, and came to them and did it, although she was personally then kept at a Considerable distance from them.

Sarah Good being Asked if, that she did not then hurt them who did it. And the children being again tortured, she looked upon them And said that it was one of them we brought into the house with us. We Asked her who it was: She then Answered and said it was Sarah Osborne, and Sarah Osborne was then under Custody and not in the house; And the children being quickly after recovered out of their fit said that it was Sarah Good and also Sarah Osborne that then did hurt & torment or afflict them—although both of them at the same time at a distance or Remote from them personally—there were also sundry other Questions put to her and Answers given thereunto by her according as is also given in.

JOHN HATHORNE
JONATHAN CORWIN
} ASSISTANTS

---

3. **sundry** (sŭn′drē): various.

TRANSCRIPT

THE EXAMINATION OF SARAH GOOD BEFORE THE WORSHIPFUL ASSISTANTS JOHN HATHORNE, JONATHAN CORWIN.

Q. Sarah Good, what evil Spirit have you familiarity with?

A. None.

Q. Have you made no contract with the Devil?

Good answered no.

Q. Why do you hurt these children?

A. I do not hurt them. I scorn it.

Q. Who do you employ then to do it?

A. I employ nobody.

Q. What creature do you employ then?

A. No creature, but I am falsely accused.

Q. Why did you go away muttering from Mr. Parris, his house?

A. I did not mutter, but I thanked him for what he gave my child.

Q. Have you made no contract with the devil?

A. No.

H[athorne] desired the children, all of them, to look upon her and see if this were the person that had hurt them, and so they all did look upon her and said this was one of the persons that did torment them—presently they were all tormented.

Q. Sarah Good, do you not see now what you have done? Why do you not tell us the truth? Why do you thus torment these poor children?

A. I do not torment them.

Q. Who do you employ then?

A. I employ nobody. I scorn it.

Q. How came they thus tormented?

A. What do I know? You bring others here and now you charge me with it.

Q. Why, who was it?

A. I do not know, but it was some you brought into the meeting house with you.

Q. We brought you into the meeting house.

A. But you brought in two more.

Q. Who was it then that tormented the children?

A. It was Osborne.

Q. What is it you say when you go muttering away from persons' houses?

A. If I must tell, I will tell.

Q. Do tell us then.

A. If I must tell, I will tell. It is the commandments. I may say my commandments I hope.

Q. What commandment is it?

A. If I must tell, I will tell. It is a psalm.

Q. What psalm?

After a long time she muttered over some part of a psalm.

Q. Who do you serve?

> **Q.** *Why do you hurt these children?*
> **A.** *I do not hurt them. I scorn it.*

A. I serve God.

Q. What God do you serve?

A. The God that made heaven and earth, though she was not willing to mention the word *God*. Her answers were in a very wicked spiteful manner, reflecting and retorting against the authority with base and abusive words, and many lies she was taken in. It was here said that her husband had said that he was afraid that she either was a witch or would be one very quickly. The worshipful Mr. Hathorne asked him his reason why he said so of her, whether he had ever seen anything by her. He answered no, not in this nature, but it was her bad carriage[4] to him and indeed, said he, I may say with tears that she is an enemy to all good.

SALEM VILLAGE, MARCH THE 1ST, 1691–92

WRITTEN BY EZEKIEL CHEEVER

---

4. **carriage:** conduct.

Connect to the Literature

1. What Do You Think?
What is your reaction to Sarah Good's examination?

Comprehension Check
- Who are Sarah Good's alleged victims?
- What charges made against her does Good deny?

Think Critically

2. **ACTIVE READING** **DETECTING BIAS** How would you describe the court officials' attitude toward Sarah Good? Support your answer with evidence from your
 READER'S NOTEBOOK.

> **THINK ABOUT**
> - the questions Good is asked
> - the comments made about her at the end of the transcript

3. What do you think accounts for the court officials' attitude?

4. Why do you think Sarah Good accuses Sarah Osborne of being a witch?

5. Why do you think Sarah Good's husband testifies against her?

6. What explanation can you offer for the apparent torments suffered by the girls who accuse Sarah Good?

Extend Interpretations

7. Different Perspectives In the preface to her book on the Salem witch trials, the 20th-century historian Marion L. Starkey writes, "Who in my day has a right to be indignant with people in Salem of 1692?" Why might she have made this comment? Do you agree that people of our time cannot or should not make judgments about people of earlier times?

8. Connect to Life Do you think that something similar to the Salem witch trials could happen in your community today? Why or why not? Consider the Connect to Your Life activity in which you discussed false accusations.

Literary Analysis

TRANSCRIPT A **transcript** is a written record of information that was originally spoken aloud. The **summary** of Sarah Good's examination you read first provides a brief narrative account of what occurred in the courtroom. The transcript that followed shows what was actually said in the courtroom. The phrasing of the questions and answers are in the interrogators' and Good's own words. Did reading the transcript change your view of the trial?

Activity Compare and contrast the summary and the transcript. What did you learn or infer from the transcript that you didn't learn from the summary? What did the summary tell you that the questions and answers on the transcript did not? What parts of the summary accurately reflect the transcript, in your view? Record differences and similarities in a large Venn diagram, as shown. Then decide which document seems to be the more **credible,** or trustworthy, source of information about the trial. Consider the possible **motivations** of the persons who wrote each document and the kind of information included. Discuss your opinion with classmates.

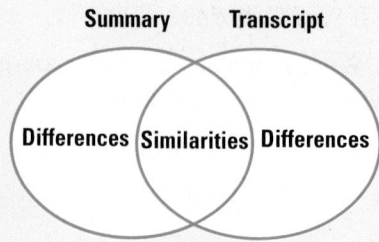

Choices & CHALLENGES

Writing Options

1. Courtroom Drama Rewrite part of the transcript as a dramatic scene from a play. Using a script form, include the name of each character who is speaking and stage directions that show the character's tone of voice, feelings, gestures, or actions.

2. Plea for Mercy Write a letter of appeal asking panel members to reconsider their decision to hang Sarah Good. Tell why the court documents you have read do not convince you of her guilt. Save your writing in your **Working Portfolio.**

3. Explanation of Motives Write a brief essay in which you explain the possible motivations of either the girls who accused Good of witchcraft, the men who pressed charges against Good, or the men who conducted Good's preliminary examination.

Writing Handbook
See page 1283: Analysis

Activities & Explorations

1. Courtroom Sketches Assume the duties of a courtroom artist and draw sketches of the people and events involved in Good's examination. ~
ART

2. Media Coverage With a group of classmates, create a newscast in which you report on Sarah Good's examination. At the beginning of the newscast, have a news anchor recap what has happened so far. Then have reporters interview Sarah Good, the examiners, the afflicted girls, and Salem residents. If possible, make a videotape of the interviews. ~ **SPEAKING AND LISTENING**

Dear Panel Members:
Sarah Good does not deserve hanging.

3. Legal Discussion A basic premise of the U.S. legal system is that a person charged with a crime is presumed innocent until proven guilty. Also, the Bill of Rights in the Constitution provides that a defendant is not required to testify against himself or herself. Meet in a small group to discuss why you think such ideas became so important in our legal system. Base your discussion on Sarah Good's experiences with the justice system in Puritan New England. ~ **GOVERNMENT**

Inquiry & Research

1. Salem Witch Trials Find out more about the Salem witch trials, researching questions such as these:

- Which girls in the community were afflicted?
- Whom else did they accuse?
- How many people confessed?
- How was a person's guilt proven in court?

Report your findings to the class.

2. Salem Memorials Find out how the town of Salem has memorialized those people who were executed as witches. You might research the memorial park that was built in 1992, exactly 300 years after the trials. Also look at the Related Reading on page 150, which describes a clash over ways to commemorate Salem's history.

 More Online: Research Starter
www.mcdougallittell.com

Art Connection

Mental Picture The engraving on page 145 depicts the examination of an accused witch in Salem. How closely does it match the image of the courtroom you formed as you read about Sarah Good's examination?

THE EXAMINATION OF SARAH GOOD / SALEM COURT DOCUMENTS, 1692

History Clashes with Commercialism

by Craig Wilson
USA TODAY

*Salem, Massachusetts, has been the scene of a conflict between two citizens'
groups. One group, capitalizing on the fame of Salem's 17th-century
witchcraft trials, has staged an annual money-making Halloween festival in
the town. According to the other group, such commercialism serves only to
tarnish Salem's historical heritage. Craig Wilson wrote this article about the
controversy in* USA Today.

SALEM, MA *(USA Today)*–One a historic New England seaport, home
to Nathaniel Hawthorne, Federal-style homes, and the infamous 1692
witch trials.

1 The other a tacky tourist town, rife with hot dog vendors, second rate
wax museums, and fly-by-night haunted houses. And shops. Shops
selling everything from $300 witches' capes and herbal potions to
T-shirts that proclaim "Born-Again Pagan."

Both are Salem, Massachusetts.

2 This is also a tale of history vs. commercialism, and some here think
Salem's rich heritage is coming up the loser.

Salem's 24-day Haunted Happenings peaks next weekend when
thousands will flock here for Halloween. As many as 200,000 overrun
this town of 38,000 during the annual event, which in 15 years has
grown from a one-night Halloween party to a three-week carnival. It
now brings in $5 million . . . .

Salem's struggle between revenue for today and reverence for
yesterday has become so touchy several people refused to go on the
record about the flourishing witch business.

And *Witch City*, a documentary that takes an unflattering look at
Salem's "witch industry," has only added fuel to the fire. The film has
become an unwelcome guest at the party.

Filmmaker Joe Cultrera, a native son who now lives in New York,
calls Salem "a company town," the company being the witch-related
tourism that he says does much to line the pockets of local merchants
but little to tell the true story of the 20 people executed here in 1692
during the witch trials.

To tourism director Mariellen Norris that's a bunch of bunk.

"This isn't about the witch hysteria, it's about Halloween," she says.
"It's about fun. . . . What we're trying to do here is make it a wholesome
family event."

Reading for Information

Journalists often resemble tightrope
walkers at a circus: both strive for
balance to accomplish their tasks.
Reporters need balance in their
writing so that readers can form
clear judgments about the news.

DISTINGUISHING FACT FROM OPINION
News reports are filled with facts
and opinions that readers must be
able to recognize and evaluate. Use
the questions and activities below to
help you distinguish between fact
and opinion in this article.

1 One guide to a writer's opinion
or bias is the writer's **word
choice,** or **diction**—especially the
connotations of (feelings associated with) the words he or she
uses. Examine the adjectives
Wilson used in describing the
two views of Salem. Did his
word choice influence your initial
reaction to the conflict? Why or
why not? How might the introduction be changed to make it
seem more evenhanded?

2 A **fact** is something that can be
proved to be true or untrue. One
fact in the article is that the
Halloween festival takes place in
Salem. An **opinion** is something
a person believes, such as
"Salem's rich heritage is coming
up the loser." Make a two-column
chart, with one column headed
"Facts" and the other "Opinions."
Then reread the article, and list
the facts and opinions it contains
in the appropriate columns. Next
to each entry identify the person
responsible for the statement.

Helen Gifford, city editor of *The Salem Evening News*, agrees. Earlier this month she told her readers to lighten up.

"Shall we all observe Halloween in Salem by holding candlelight vigils at the Witch Trials Memorial, while we recall our ancestral sins of bigotry and intolerance?" she asked.

Salem Mayor Neil Harrington, meanwhile, is running for re-election and trying desperately to steer clear of the whole topic. When asked about the documentary, he says he only knew "a Salem native had made a movie."

"But I don't know anything about it," he quickly adds, despite the fact *Witch City* is the talk of Salem, and stories about it have run everywhere from *The Boston Globe* to the front page of Salem's *Evening News*. . . .

Norris says it [the movie] "doesn't really tell us what Salem is about."

Others say it shows present-day Salem all too clearly.

❸ Donna Vinson, a Salem resident and history professor at Salem State College, is one.

"I don't think they care about Salem's historical legacy," she says of Salem's elected officials and witch-industry promoters. "They don't know anything about it, and they don't care to know. . . ."

"There are a lot of people in town who care and want to do the right thing," says Patty MacLeod, director of the Salem Witch Museum, which gets 350,000 visitors a year. "It's in our best interest to do the best job we can or they won't come."

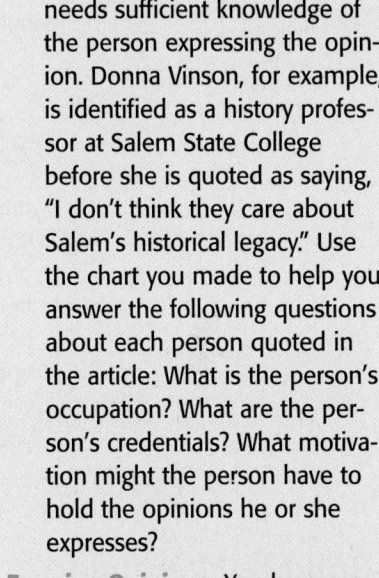

The Salem Witch Museum

Many in town have complained that the four-year-old Salem Wax Museum of Witches & Seafarers, adjacent to the city's 1637 Old Burying Point Cemetery, blares haunted house sounds from its rooftop and has rubber-masked employees dressed as ghouls and goblins at the entrance to the historic cemetery and the adjoining memorial.

Wax museum director Barbara Fanning admits "it's like a carnival this time of year," but adds, "it's good for Salem.". . .

Tad Baker, another history professor at Salem State whose specialty is witchcraft, says he's concerned. . . .

"When you go to the {witch trial} memorial you should get that—that people were willing to die for their beliefs. . . . That's an important story, but you don't get that story, you get spectacle and gross generalizations and haunted house music. . . . That's what a lot of people here object to."

❸ **Analyzing Opinions** To be able to judge an opinion, a reader needs sufficient knowledge of the person expressing the opinion. Donna Vinson, for example, is identified as a history professor at Salem State College before she is quoted as saying, "I don't think they care about Salem's historical legacy." Use the chart you made to help you answer the following questions about each person quoted in the article: What is the person's occupation? What are the person's credentials? What motivation might the person have to hold the opinions he or she expresses?

Forming Opinions You have now identified the facts and the opinions in the article. Which side of the argument would you be on if you lived in Salem? Why? What facts and opinions in the article helped you form your opinion?

from Sinners in the Hands of an Angry God

Sermon by JONATHAN EDWARDS

Connect to Your Life

Power of Persuasion Think about someone who recently persuaded you to do something—perhaps a parent, friend, teacher, coach, or salesperson. What method of persuasion did this person use? For example, what was emphasized—the benefits of taking the action or the drawbacks of not taking the action? Did this person appeal to your emotions, such as love, fear, or pride? Or did this person appeal to principles, such as justice, efficiency, or frugality? Write down what you were persuaded to do, and analyze the method of persuasion that worked on you. With your classmates, talk about effective methods of persuasion.

Build Background

Great Awakening One hundred years after a group of Puritans came to colonial America for religious freedom, some Puritans felt that their congregations had grown too complacent, or self-satisfied. To rekindle the fervor that the early settlers had, Jonathan Edwards and other Puritan ministers led the Great Awakening, a religious revival that swept through New England from 1734 to 1750. Edwards's most famous sermon, "Sinners in the Hands of an Angry God," was delivered in Enfield, Connecticut, in 1741. In it he warned his congregation that being church members would not automatically save them from hell. He tried to persuade them that they had to personally experience conversion, a transforming moment in which they felt God's grace.

WORDS TO KNOW	
Vocabulary Preview	
abhor	incense
abominable	inconceivable
appease	loathsome
ascribe	mitigation
deliverance	wrath

Focus Your Reading

LITERARY ANALYSIS PERSUASIVE WRITING Edwards's sermon is an example of **persuasive writing,** which is intended to convince a reader to adopt a particular opinion or to perform a certain action. Persuasive writing can take many forms, including sermons, political speeches, newspaper editorials, and advertisements. As you read Edwards's sermon, analyze his methods of persuasion: What does he want his audience to do and why does he want them to do it?

ACTIVE READING ANALYZING EMOTIONAL LANGUAGE Persuasive writing often contains **loaded language**—words with strong connotations, or emotional associations. For example, contrast the word *child* with the more loaded words *brat* and *cherub*. A writer would use *brat* to create a negative feeling in the reader and *cherub* to create a positive feeling. Part of what makes Edwards's sermon so effective is his choice of loaded words.

READER'S NOTEBOOK Monitor how you feel as you read the sermon. Create a chart like the one below to list examples of specific words, phrases, and images that Edwards uses to achieve the greatest emotional effect on his audience.

Example	Emotional Impact

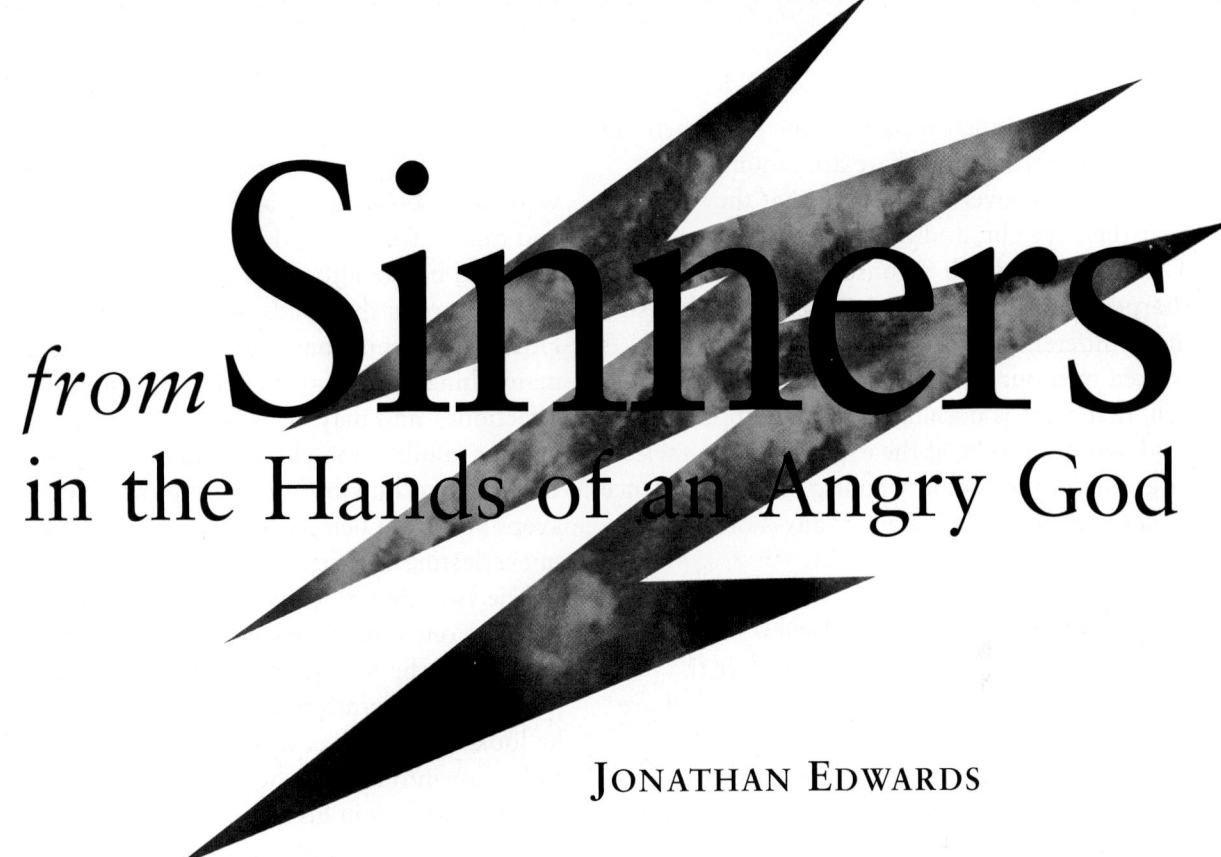

from Sinners
in the Hands of an Angry God

JONATHAN EDWARDS

We find it easy to tread on and crush a worm that we see crawling on the earth; so it is easy for us to cut or singe a slender thread that any thing hangs by; thus easy is it for God when he pleases to cast his enemies down to hell. . . .

They[1] are now the objects of that very same *anger* and <u>wrath</u> of God, that is expressed in the torments of hell. And the reason why they do not go down to hell at each moment, is not because God, in whose power they are, is not then very angry with them; as angry as he is with many miserable creatures now tormented in hell, who there feel and bear the fierceness of his wrath. Yea, God is a great deal more angry with great numbers that are now on earth; yea, doubtless, with many that are now in this congregation,[2] who it may be are at ease, than he is with many of those who are now in the flames of hell.

So that it is not because God is unmindful of their wickedness, and does not resent it, that he does not let loose his hand and cut them off. God is not altogether such an one as themselves, though they may imagine him to be so. The wrath of God burns against them, their damnation does not slumber; the pit is prepared, the fire is made ready, the furnace is now hot, ready to receive them; the flames do now rage and glow. The glittering sword is whet,[3] and held over them, and the pit hath opened its mouth under them. . . .

---

1. **they:** Earlier in the sermon, Edwards refers to all "unconverted men," whom he considers God's enemies. Unconverted men are people who have not been "born again," meaning that they have not accepted Jesus Christ and consequently have not experienced a sense of God's grace and an assurance of salvation.

2. **this congregation:** the Puritans attending the church service at which Edwards spoke.

3. **whet:** sharpened.

Unconverted men walk over the pit of hell on a rotten covering, and there are innumerable places in this covering so weak that they will not bear their weight, and these places are not seen. The arrows of death fly unseen at noonday; the sharpest sight cannot discern them. God has so many different unsearchable ways of taking wicked men out of the world and sending them to hell, that there is nothing to make it appear, that God had need to be at the expense of a miracle, or go out of the ordinary course of his providence, to destroy any wicked man, at any moment. . . .

So that, thus it is that natural men[4] are held in the hand of God, over the pit of hell; they have deserved the fiery pit, and are already sentenced to it; and God is dreadfully provoked, his anger is as great towards them as to those that are actually suffering the executions of the fierceness of his wrath in hell; and they have done nothing in the least to appease or abate that anger, neither is God in the least bound by any promise to hold them up one moment; the devil is waiting for them, hell is gaping for them, the flames gather and flash about them, and would fain[5] lay hold on them, and swallow them up; the fire pent up in their own hearts is struggling to break out: and they have no interest in any Mediator,[6] there are no means within reach that can be any security to them. In short, they have no refuge, nothing to take hold of. . . .

The bow of God's wrath is bent, and the arrow made ready on the string, and justice bends the arrow at your heart, and strains the bow, and it is nothing but the mere pleasure of God, and that of an angry God, without any promise or obligation at all, that keeps the arrow one moment from being made drunk with your blood. Thus all you that never passed under a great change of heart, by the mighty power of the Spirit of God upon your souls; all you that were never born again, and made new creatures, and raised from being dead in sin, to a state of new, and before altogether unexperienced light and life, are in the hands of an angry God. However you may have reformed your life in many things, and may have had religious affections,[7] and may keep up a form of religion in your families and closets,[8] and in the house of God, it is nothing but his mere pleasure that keeps you from being this moment swallowed up in everlasting destruction. . . .

The God that holds you over the pit of hell, much as one holds a spider, or some loathsome insect over the fire, abhors you, and is dreadfully provoked: his wrath towards you burns like fire; he looks upon you as worthy of nothing else, but to be cast into the fire; he is of purer eyes than to bear to have you in his sight; you are ten thousand times more abominable in his eyes, than the most hateful venomous serpent is in ours. You have offended him infinitely more than ever a stubborn rebel did his prince; and yet it is nothing but his hand that holds you from falling into the fire every moment. It is to be ascribed to nothing else, that you did not go to hell the last night; that you was suffered[9] to awake again in this world, after you closed your eyes to sleep. And there is no other reason to be given, why you have not dropped into hell since you arose in the morning, but that God's hand has held you up. There is no other reason to be given why you

---

4. **natural men:** people who have not been "born again."

5. **fain:** rather.

6. **Mediator:** Jesus Christ, who mediates, or is the means of bringing about, salvation.

7. **affections:** feelings or emotions.

8. **closets:** private rooms for meditation.

9. **suffered:** permitted.

WORDS TO KNOW

appease (ə-pēz') v. to bring peace, quiet, or calm to; soothe
loathsome (lōth'səm) adj. arousing great dislike
abhor (ăb-hôr') v. to regard with disgust
abominable (ə-bŏm'ə-nə-bəl) adj. thoroughly detestable
ascribe (ə-skrīb') v. to attribute to a specified cause or source

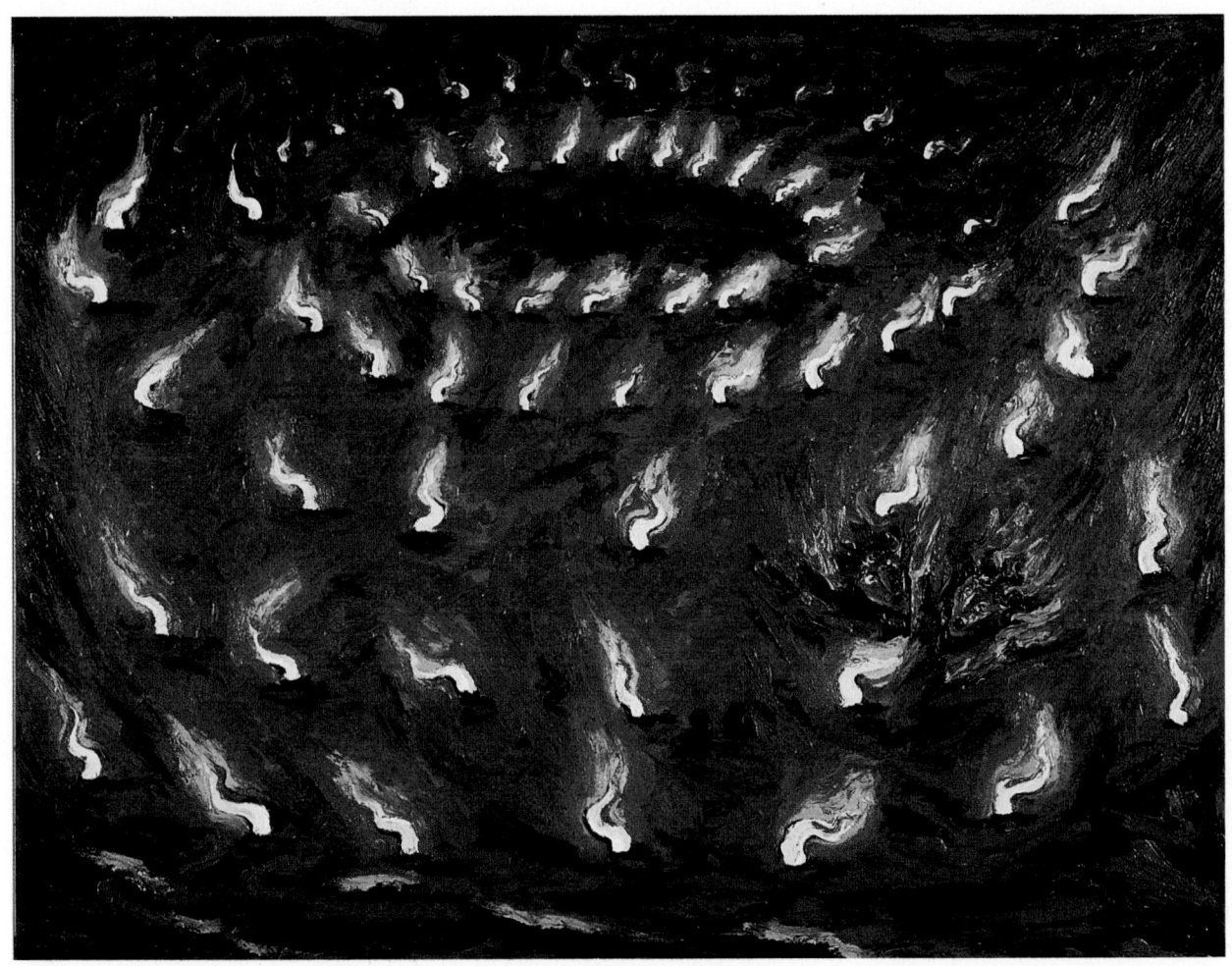

Un quadro di fuochi preziosi [A painting of precious fires] (1983), Enzo Cucchi. Oil on canvas with neon, 117½″ × 153½″, private collection, courtesy of Sperone Westwater, New York.

The pit is prepared,
the fire is made ready,
the furnace is now hot,
ready to receive them;
the flames do now
rage and glow.

have not gone to hell, since you have sat here in the house of God, provoking his pure eyes by your sinful wicked manner of attending his solemn worship. Yea, there is nothing else that is to be given as a reason why you do not this very moment drop down into hell.

O sinner! Consider the fearful danger you are in: it is a great furnace of wrath, a wide and bottomless pit, full of the fire of wrath, that you are held over in the hand of that God, whose wrath is provoked and <u>incensed</u> as much against you, as against many of the damned in hell. You hang by a slender thread, with the flames of divine wrath flashing about it, and ready every moment to singe it, and burn it asunder;[10] and you have no interest in any Mediator, and nothing to lay hold of to save yourself, nothing to keep off the flames of wrath, nothing of your own, nothing that you ever have done, nothing that you can do, to induce God to spare you one moment. . . .

It is *everlasting* wrath. It would be dreadful to suffer this fierceness and wrath of Almighty God one moment; but you must suffer it to all eternity. There will be no end to this exquisite[11] horrible misery. When you look forward, you shall see a long forever, a boundless duration before you, which will swallow up your thoughts, and amaze your soul; and you will absolutely despair of ever having any <u>deliverance</u>, any end, any <u>mitigation</u>, any rest at all. You will know certainly that you must wear out long ages, millions of millions of ages, in wrestling and conflicting with this almighty merciless vengeance; and then when you have so done, when so many ages have actually been spent by you in this manner, you will know that all is but a point to what remains. So that your punishment will indeed be infinite. Oh, who can express what the state of a soul in such circumstances is! All that we can possibly say about it, gives but a very feeble, faint representation of it; it is inexpressible and <u>inconceivable</u>: For "who knows the power of God's anger?"[12]

How dreadful is the state of those that are daily and hourly in the danger of this great wrath and infinite misery! But this is the dismal case of every soul in this congregation that has not been born again, however moral and strict, sober and religious, they may otherwise be. . . .

And now you have an extraordinary opportunity, a day wherein Christ has thrown the door of mercy wide open, and stands in the door calling and crying with a loud voice to poor sinners; a day wherein many are flocking to him, and pressing into the kingdom of God. Many are daily coming[13] from the east, west, north, and south; many that were very lately in the same miserable condition that you are in, are now in a happy state, with their hearts filled with love to him who has loved them, and washed them from their sins in his own blood, and rejoicing in hope of the glory of God. How awful is it to be left behind at such a day! To see so many others feasting, while you are pining and perishing! To see so many rejoicing and singing for joy of heart, while you have cause to mourn for sorrow of heart, and howl for vexation of spirit! How can you rest one moment in such a condition? . . .

Therefore, let every one that is out of Christ, now awake and fly from the wrath to come. . . . ❖

---

10. **asunder** (ə-sŭn′dər): into separate parts or pieces.
11. **exquisite** (ĕk′skwĭ-zĭt): sharply intense.
12. **"who knows . . . anger?":** an allusion to Psalm 90:11, "Who knoweth the power of thine anger?"
13. **Many . . . coming:** Edwards is referring to the hundreds of people who were being converted during the Great Awakening.

WORDS
TO
KNOW

incense (ĭn-sĕns′) v. to cause to be extremely angry
deliverance (dĭ-lĭv′ər-əns) n. rescue from danger
mitigation (mĭt′ĭ-gā′shən) n. lessening of something that causes suffering
inconceivable (ĭn′kən-sē′və-bəl) adj. not able to be understood or imagined

The God that holds you over the pit of **hell**,

much as one holds a **spider**,

or some loathsome insect over the **fire**,

abhors you...

his wrath toward you burns like **fire**;

he looks upon you as worthy of nothing else,

but to be cast into the **fire**.

Thinking through the LITERATURE

Connect to the Literature

1. **What Do You Think?** Describe the most vivid image from this sermon and how it made you feel.

   Comprehension Check
   - According to this sermon, what is a constant threat to all human beings?
   - According to this sermon, which people are spared God's wrath?
   - What does Edwards say sinners can do to save themselves?

Think Critically

2. Would you want to hear another of Edwards's sermons? Explain why or why not.

3. **ACTIVE READING / ANALYZING EMOTIONAL LANGUAGE** Review your list of loaded words and phrases, and identify two that you think are the most emotionally charged. Discuss with a classmate their intended effect on the audience. How do you think Edwards's choice of words affects the overall impact of his message?

4. Why do you think people were persuaded to change their lives as a result of Edwards's sermon?

   THINK ABOUT
   - what he wants his congregation to do and why
   - the emotions he appeals to in the first paragraphs and in the last paragraphs of the excerpt

5. What conclusions can you draw about the spiritual beliefs and values of the people who belonged to Edwards's congregation?

6. How would you describe the view of human beings and the view of God presented in this sermon?

Extend Interpretations

7. **Comparing Texts** In your view, is Jonathan Edwards's conception of God consistent with Anne Bradstreet's conception of God? Explain your opinion.

8. **Connect to Life** Are Edwards's methods of persuasion ones that are likely to work on you? Consider what you wrote for the Connect to Your Life activity on page 152.

Literary Analysis

PERSUASIVE WRITING The goal of **persuasive writing** is to convince a reader to adopt a particular opinion or perform a certain action. The overriding purpose of Edwards's sermon is to change the behavior of his audience and to show them the path toward salvation. Generally, persuasive writing uses both logical and emotional appeals. **Logical appeals** imply that if the readers are reasonable people, they will do or think what the writer desires. **Emotional appeals** sometimes contain very little factual information and instead often rely on highly charged language that triggers intense feelings, such as fear, insecurity, and so on.

Cooperative Learning Activity
Reread Edwards's sermon and find examples of emotional appeals. Responding to criticism of his appeal to emotions rather than reason, Edwards said: "I think it is a reasonable thing to fright persons away from hell. They stand upon its brink, and are just ready to fall into it, and are senseless of their danger. Is it not a reasonable thing to fright a person out of a house on fire?" Meet in small groups to debate whether or not you believe his use of scare tactics is justified, considering his goal.

Choices & CHALLENGES

Writing Options

1. Letter of Opinion Draft a letter to Edwards, giving your personal response to the religious views presented in his sermon.

2. Vivid Comparison Edwards compares a sinful human being to "a spider, or some loathsome insect" held over a fire. Develop a comparison to describe your own view of human beings.

Humans are like ____

3. Public Service Announcement Take a strong moral stand on an issue that concerns you, such as high school dropouts or a social injustice. Using Edwards's sermon as a model, write a public service announcement in which you motivate the audience to adopt your views.

Activities & Explorations

1. Live Performance Jonathan Edwards reportedly read his sermon in a calm, level voice, with his sermon book in his left hand. Imagine what he would do if he had his own television ministry and were giving the sermon today. Present part of this sermon as an oral performance, making it as powerful as you can for a contemporary audience.
~ SPEAKING AND LISTENING

2. Jacket Cover If you were going to publish "Sinners in the Hands of an Angry God" as a religious tract, how would you illustrate it? Design a cover that suggests important ideas in the sermon. **~ ART**

Inquiry & Research

1. Inspirational Speakers Find out more about a modern-day religious or political leader whose powerful speeches have swayed audiences. Compare this leader with Edwards.

2. Artistic Visions Examine paintings, such as Peter Brueghel's *Dulle Griest* (Mad Meg) or Michelangelo's mural on the Sistine Chapel, that depict the fate of evildoers. Compare the mood and images in the paintings with Edwards's sermon.

Vocabulary in Action

EXERCISE: ASSESSMENT PRACTICE Decide if the following pairs of words are synonyms or antonyms. Number your paper from 1 to 10, and write *S* for synonyms or *A* for antonyms.

  1. alleviation—mitigation
  2. upset—appease
  3. inconceivable—knowable
  4. damnation—deliverance
  5. pleasant—loathsome
  6. blessing—wrath
  7. attribute—ascribe
  8. adore—abhor
  9. agreeable—abominable
  10. enrage—incense

Building Vocabulary
For an in-depth lesson on word denotation and connotation, see page 908.

WORDS TO KNOW				
abhor	appease	deliverance	inconceivable	mitigation
abominable	ascribe	incense	loathsome	wrath

Jonathan Edwards
1703–1758

Other Works
Images or Shadows of Divine Things
Personal Narrative

Brilliant Beginnings Jonathan Edwards, the only son in a family of 11 children, was born in East Windsor, Connecticut. Intellectually curious as a child, Edwards wrote "Of Insects," a study of the behavior of spiders, when he was 11 years old. Just before turning 13, Edwards entered what is now Yale University. While a graduate student there, he had a conversion experience that greatly influenced his religious views.

Religious Calling In 1722, after finishing his education, Edwards launched a career in ministry, following the path of his father and his maternal grandfather, both of whom were Puritan ministers. In 1726, Edwards assisted his grandfather as a minister at the church in Northampton, Massachusetts, and three years later became the church's pastor after his grandfather's death. There, he developed a reputation as a powerful preacher. After his accounts of some "surprising conversions" in Northampton from 1734 to 1735, Edwards found himself at the center of a religious revival, the Great Awakening.

Righteous Works Throughout his life, Edwards wrote sermons, as well as philosophical and religious works. In his most famous sermon, "Sinners in the Hands of an Angry God," Edwards captured the intensity of the Great Awakening. Although Edwards inspired thousands, he was dismissed from the Northampton church in 1750 because he wanted to limit church membership to those who had undergone conversion, or had been "born again." A year later, Edwards and his family moved to Stockbridge, where he became a missionary to a Native American settlement. In 1757, Edwards accepted an appointment as president of what is now Princeton University.

Author Activity

A Vision of Terror and Beauty Read Edwards's essay "The Beauty of the World" in *Images or Shadows of Divine Things*. Do the ideas that Edwards expresses in this piece change your impression of him? Explain.

The Conventions of Drama

The Rise of American Drama

Have you ever acted in a school play or been spellbound by an award-winning film? If so, then you've already experienced the thrill of dramatic performances. **Drama** is a form of literature that is written to be performed for an audience, whether on stage or in front of cameras. The two main types of drama are tragedy and comedy: a **tragedy** unveils the downfall of a main character, and a **comedy** is light and often humorous in tone. Many dramas combine elements of both tragedy and comedy.

Drama was one of the last of the literary genres to develop in the United States. The Puritans in New England regarded theatrical performances as frivolous, so few plays were staged in the 1600s. During the 18th and 19th centuries, drama gradually became an accepted form of entertainment. However, most of the plays performed in the United States were imported from Europe or were adapted from novels.

In 1920 the Broadway production of Eugene O'Neill's *Beyond the Horizon* marked a turning point. This important play used a realistic setting to present true-to-life characters who were struggling to understand their lives. Building on O'Neill's achievement, American playwrights Thornton Wilder, Lillian Hellman, Tennessee Williams, and Arthur Miller created dramas in the 1930s and 1940s that met with critical and popular success. Following World War II, American dramatists Edward Albee and Lorraine Hansberry made significant contributions to the theater. Today, hit plays by contemporary

Arthur Miller's *Death of a Salesman* (1949) explores the tragic aspects of the American Dream.

playwrights, including Sam Shepard, David Mamet, August Wilson, Wendy Wasserstein, and Tony Kushner, are performed in theaters across the country. Drama has become a thriving art form in the United States.

Conventions of Drama

Most dramas follow similar conventions, or rules, in how they are presented. An understanding of basic dramatic conventions can help you imagine the staging of the performance as you read. You may recognize that drama and fiction share a common set of elements: **plot, setting, character,** and **theme.**

ACTS AND SCENES Dramatic plots are divided into **acts** and **scenes,** with each scene establishing a different time or place. As in fiction, the **plot** in a drama introduces interactions that produce a **conflict,** or struggle, between opposing forces. The action intensifies, reaches a peak, and is eventually resolved. The elements of plot in drama—**exposition, rising action, climax, falling action,** and **resolution**—parallel those in fiction.

THE CAST OF CHARACTERS A play lists the **cast of characters** in the beginning, before the action starts. Many of the same types of characters that populate fiction are also found in drama. The **protagonist** is the central character of the play. This character is at the center of the conflict and often undergoes radical changes during the course of the play. The **antagonist** is the character who opposes the main character. Some plays also include a **foil,** a minor character whose traits contrast sharply with those of the main character. The interplay among these characters heightens the dramatic tension as the play develops.

STAGE DIRECTIONS The italicized instructions in a play are written by the **playwright,** or author, and are called **stage directions.** Stage directions describe the **setting** of the play and suggest the use of props, lighting, scenery, sound effects, and costumes. Stage directions also describe the entrances and the exits of characters, and how the characters look, speak, and react to events or to others. Excerpted below are stage directions from *The Crucible* that describe the stage set at the beginning of Act Four.

(*A cell in Salem jail, that fall.*)

(*At the back is a high barred window; near it, a great, heavy door. Along the walls are two benches.*)

(*The place is in darkness but for the moonlight seeping through the bars. It appears empty. Presently footsteps are heard coming down a corridor beyond the wall, keys rattle, and the door swings open.* Marshal Herrick *enters with a lantern.*)

YOUR TURN What is the effect of the marshal's entrance on the scene?

SPEECH DEVICES In drama, the playwright develops the story line through the characters' actions and dialogue. **Dialogue,** or conversation between characters, is the lifeblood of drama. Virtually everything of consequence—from the plot details to the character revelations—flows from dialogue.

Other **speech devices** used by playwrights, in addition to dialogue, include

- the **monologue:** a long speech spoken by a single character to himself or herself, or to the audience;
- the **soliloquy:** a monologue in which a character speaks his or her private thoughts aloud and appears to be unaware of the audience;
- the **aside:** a short speech or comment that is delivered by a character to the audience, but that is beyond the hearing of other characters who are present.

Strategies for Reading: Drama

1. Review the cast of characters and read the opening stage directions carefully. Remember that the opening scene usually introduces the main conflict.

2. Try to picture the characters and the action as if you were watching the play being performed. Use stage directions to help you "see" the setting and characters, and use dialogue to help you "hear" how characters speak.

3. Follow the dialogue to keep track of the plot

and to learn more about the characters.

4. Analyze how the characters interact. What motivates their actions and speech?

5. First read the play silently; then read parts of it aloud to yourself or with others.

6. **Monitor** your reading strategies and modify them when your understanding breaks down. Remember to use your Strategies for Active Reading: **predict, visualize, connect, question, clarify,** and **evaluate.**

The Crucible

Drama by ARTHUR MILLER

Comparing Literature

Traditions Across Time: Another Look at the Puritans

The Crucible, a modern play by Arthur Miller, is based on the witch trials that took place in Salem, Massachusetts, in 1692. The play is faithful to the historical period and to Puritan beliefs. Miller actually visited Salem in the course of his research for *The Crucible,* and most of the characters in the play were drawn from those named in the Salem court documents.

Points of Comparison As you read *The Crucible,* use your knowledge of history and of Puritan beliefs to help you interpret the characters' motives and actions.

Build Background

The Puritan Mindset In the Salem witch trials, spectral evidence—the testimony of a church member who claimed to have seen a person's spirit performing witchcraft—was enough to sentence the accused to death. Innocent people were tried and convicted on "evidence" that certain things they did caused children to become sick. Belief in witchcraft fueled a climate of hysteria and suspicion, turning neighbor against neighbor, casting doubts even on those of spotless reputation. Miller vividly depicts this climate in this play.

WORDS TO KNOW
Vocabulary Preview

afflicted	fanatic
arbitrate	immaculate
ascertain	inaudibly
calamity	indictment
contentious	indignant
deposition	iniquity
disproportionate	plaintiff
effrontery	predilection
empower	subservient
excommunication	unintelligible

Focus Your Reading

LITERARY ANALYSIS STAGE DIRECTIONS Located at the beginning of a script and throughout, **stage directions** may identify the setting; tell actors how to speak and move; or describe the characters, the scenery, or the arrangement of props. In *The Crucible,* Miller also uses the stage directions to convey historical background, occasionally drawing parallels to the American political scene of the 1950s.

ACTIVE READING USING A GRAPHIC ORGANIZER **Graphic organizers**—visual representations of information in a text—include charts, diagrams, and time lines. By using a graphic organizer as you read, you can keep track of details and relationships.

READER'S NOTEBOOK Create a chart like this one for each of the following characters: John Proctor, Abigail Williams, and Reverend Hale. Fill in the charts by jotting down important character traits and evidence that reveals these traits. This evidence may be from the characters' actions or dialogue or from the stage directions. As you continue to read the play, add information to your charts and create new charts for the important characters you meet in later acts: Elizabeth Proctor and Deputy Governor Danforth.

John Proctor	

Trait: _____	Trait: _____
Evidence:	Evidence:

The CRUCIBLE

ARTHUR MILLER

Cast of Characters (order of appearance)

Reverend Samuel Parris	Thomas Putnam	Ezekiel Cheever
Betty Parris	Mercy Lewis	Marshal Herrick
Tituba	Mary Warren	Judge Hathorne
Abigail Williams	Rebecca Nurse	Martha Corey
John Proctor	Giles Corey	Deputy Governor Danforth
Elizabeth Proctor	Reverend John Hale	Girls of Salem
Susanna Walcott	Francis Nurse	Sarah Good
Mrs. Ann Putnam		

ACT ONE

An Overture

(A small upper bedroom in the home of Reverend Samuel Parris, Salem, Massachusetts, in the spring of the year 1692.)

(There is a narrow window at the left. Through its leaded panes the morning sunlight streams. A candle still burns near the bed, which is at the right. A chest, a chair, and a small table are the other furnishings. At the back a door opens on the landing of the stairway to the ground floor. The room gives off an air of clean spareness. The roof rafters are exposed, and the wood colors are raw and unmellowed.)

(As the curtain rises, Reverend Parris is discovered kneeling beside the bed, evidently in prayer. His daughter, Betty Parris, aged ten, is lying on the bed, inert.)

At the time of these events Parris was in his middle forties. In history he cut a villainous path, and there is very little good to be said for him. He believed he was being persecuted wherever he went, despite his best efforts to win people and God to his side. In meeting, he felt insulted if someone rose to shut the door without first asking his permission. He was a widower with no interest in children, or talent with them. He regarded them as young adults, and until this strange crisis he, like the rest of Salem, never conceived that the children were anything but thankful for being permitted to walk straight, eyes slightly lowered, arms at the sides, and mouths shut until bidden to speak.

His house stood in the "town"—but we today would hardly call it a village. The meeting house[1] was nearby, and from this point outward—toward the bay or inland—there were a few small-windowed, dark houses snuggling against the raw Massachusetts winter. Salem had been established hardly forty years before. To the European world the whole province was a barbaric frontier inhabited by a sect of <u>fanatics</u> who, nevertheless, were shipping out products of slowly increasing quantity and value.

No one can really know what their lives were like. They had no novelists—and would not have permitted anyone to read a novel if one were handy. Their creed forbade anything resembling a theater or "vain enjoyment." They did not celebrate Christmas, and a holiday from work meant only that they must concentrate even more upon prayer.

Which is not to say that nothing broke into this strict and somber way of life. When a new farmhouse was built, friends assembled to "raise the roof," and there would be special foods cooked and probably some potent cider passed around. There was a good supply of ne'er-do-wells in Salem, who dallied at the shovelboard[2] in Bridget Bishop's tavern. Probably more than the creed, hard work kept the morals of the place from spoiling, for the people were forced to fight the land like heroes for every grain of corn, and no man had very much time for fooling around.

That there were some jokers, however, is indicated by the practice of appointing a two-man patrol whose duty was to "walk forth in the time of God's worship to take notice of such as either lye about the meeting house, without attending to the word and ordinances, or that lye at home or in the fields without giving good account thereof, and to take the names of such persons, and to present them to the magistrates, whereby they may be accordingly proceeded against." This <u>predilection</u> for minding other people's business was time-honored among the people of Salem, and it undoubtedly created many of the suspicions which were to feed the coming madness. It was also, in my opinion, one of the things that a John Proctor would rebel against, for the time of the armed camp had almost passed, and since the country was reasonably—although not wholly—safe, the old disciplines were beginning to rankle. But, as in all such matters, the issue was not clear-cut, for danger was still a possibility, and in unity still lay the best promise of safety.

The edge of the wilderness was close by. The American continent stretched endlessly west, and it was full of mystery for them. It stood, dark and threatening, over their shoulders night and day, for out of it Indian tribes marauded[3] from time to time, and Reverend Parris had parishioners who had lost relatives to these heathen.

The parochial snobbery of these people was partly responsible for their failure to convert the Indians. Probably they also preferred to take land from heathens rather than from fellow Christians. At any rate, very few Indians were converted, and the Salem folk believed that the virgin forest was the Devil's last preserve, his home base and the citadel of his final stand. To the best of their knowledge the American forest was the last place on earth that was not paying homage to God.

For these reasons, among others, they carried about an air of innate resistance, even of persecution. Their fathers had, of course, been persecuted in England. So now they and their church found it necessary to deny any other sect its freedom, lest their New Jerusalem[4] be defiled and corrupted by wrong ways and deceitful ideas.

---

1. **meeting house:** the most important building in a Puritan community, used both for worship and for meetings.
2. **shovelboard:** a game in which a coin or disc is shoved across a board by hand.
3. **marauded** (mə-rôd'ĭd): attacked and raided.
4. **New Jerusalem:** in Christianity, a heavenly city and the last resting place of the souls saved by Jesus. It was considered the ideal city, and Puritans modeled their communities after it.

WORDS TO KNOW	**fanatic** (fē-năt'ĭk) *n.* a person possessed by an excessive and irrational zeal, especially for a religious or political cause **predilection** (prĕd'l-ĕk'shən) *n.* a personal preference

They believed, in short, that they held in their steady hands the candle that would light the world. We have inherited this belief, and it has helped and hurt us. It helped them with the discipline it gave them. They were a dedicated folk, by and large, and they had to be to survive the life they had chosen or been born into in this country.

The proof of their belief's value to them may be taken from the opposite character of the first Jamestown settlement, farther south, in Virginia. The Englishmen who landed there were motivated mainly by a hunt for profit. They had thought to pick off the wealth of the new country and then return rich to England. They were a band of individualists, and a much more ingratiating group than the Massachusetts men. But Virginia destroyed them. Massachusetts tried to kill off the Puritans, but they combined; they set up a communal society which, in the beginning, was little more than an armed camp with an autocratic and very devoted leadership. It was, however, an autocracy by consent, for they were united from top to bottom by a commonly held ideology whose perpetuation was the reason and justification for all their sufferings. So their self-denial, their purposefulness, their suspicion of all vain pursuits, their hardhanded justice, were altogether perfect instruments for the conquest of this space so antagonistic to man.

But the people of Salem in 1692 were not quite the dedicated folk that arrived on the Mayflower. A vast differentiation had taken place, and in their own time a revolution had unseated the royal government and substituted a junta[5] which was at this moment in power. The times, to their eyes, must have been out of joint, and to the common folk must have seemed as insoluble and complicated as do ours today. It is not hard to see how easily many could have been led to believe that the time of confusion had been brought upon them by deep and darkling forces. No hint of such speculation appears on the court record, but social disorder in any age breeds such mystical suspicions, and when, as in Salem, wonders are brought forth from below the social surface, it is too much to expect people to hold back very long from laying on the victims with all the force of their frustrations.

The Salem tragedy, which is about to begin in these pages, developed from a paradox.[6] It is a paradox in whose grip we still live, and there is no prospect yet that we will discover its resolution. Simply, it was this: for good purposes, even high purposes, the people of Salem developed a theocracy, a combine of state and religious power whose function was to keep the community together, and to prevent any kind of disunity that might open it to destruction by material or ideological enemies. It was forged for a necessary purpose and accomplished that purpose. But all organization is and must be grounded on the idea of exclusion and prohibition, just as two objects cannot occupy the same space. Evidently the time came in New England when the repressions of order were heavier than seemed warranted by the dangers against which the order was organized. The witch-hunt was a perverse manifestation of the panic which set in among all classes when the balance began to turn toward greater individual freedom.

When one rises above the individual villainy displayed, one can only pity them all, just as we shall be pitied someday. It is still impossible for man to organize his social life without repressions, and the balance has yet to be struck between order and freedom.

The witch-hunt was not, however, a mere repression. It was also, and as importantly, a long overdue opportunity for everyone so inclined to express publicly his guilt and sins, under the cover of accusations against the victims. It suddenly became possible—and patriotic and holy—for a man to say that Martha Corey had come into his bedroom at night, and that, while his wife was sleeping at his side, Martha laid herself down on

---

5. **junta** (hŏŏn′tə): a Spanish term meaning a small, elite ruling council; in this case the group that led England's Glorious Revolution of 1688–1689.

6. **paradox:** a seemingly contradictory statement that is in fact true.

his chest and "nearly suffocated him." Of course it was her spirit only, but his satisfaction at confessing himself was no lighter than if it had been Martha herself. One could not ordinarily speak such things in public.

Long-held hatreds of neighbors could now be openly expressed, and vengeance taken, despite the Bible's charitable injunctions.[7] Land-lust which had been expressed before by constant bickering over boundaries and deeds, could now be elevated to the arena of morality; one could cry witch against one's neighbor and feel perfectly justified in the bargain. Old scores could be settled on a plane of heavenly combat between Lucifer and the Lord; suspicions and the envy of the miserable toward the happy could and did burst out in the general revenge. 🍂

(Reverend Parris *is praying now, and, though we cannot hear his words, a sense of his confusion hangs about him. He mumbles, then seems about to weep; then he weeps, then prays again; but his daughter does not stir on the bed.*)

(*The door opens, and his Negro slave enters.* Tituba *is in her forties.* Parris *brought her with him from Barbados,[8] where he spent some years as a merchant before entering the ministry. She enters as one does who can no longer bear to be barred from the sight of her beloved, but she is also very frightened because her slave sense has warned her that, as always, trouble in this house eventually lands on her back.*)

Tituba (*already taking a step backward*). My Betty be hearty soon?

Parris. Out of here!

Tituba (*backing to the door*). My Betty not goin' die . . .

Abigail

Parris (*scrambling to his feet in a fury*). Out of my sight! (*She is gone.*) Out of my—(*He is overcome with sobs. He clamps his teeth against them and closes the door and leans against it, exhausted.*) Oh, my God! God help me! (*Quaking with fear, mumbling to himself through his sobs, he goes to the bed and gently takes Betty's hand.*) Betty. Child. Dear child. Will you wake, will you open up your eyes! Betty, little one . . .

(*He is bending to kneel again when his niece,* Abigail Williams, *seventeen, enters—a strikingly beautiful girl, an orphan, with an endless capacity for dissembling.[9] Now she is all worry and apprehension and propriety.*)

Abigail. Uncle? (*He looks to her.*) Susanna Walcott's here from Doctor Griggs.

Parris. Oh? Let her come, let her come.

Abigail (*leaning out the door to call to Susanna, who is down the hall a few steps*). Come in, Susanna.

(Susanna Walcott, *a little younger than* Abigail, *a nervous, hurried girl, enters.*)

Parris (*eagerly*). What does the doctor say, child?

Susanna (*craning around Parris to get a look at Betty*). He bid me come and tell you, reverend sir, that he cannot discover no medicine for it in his books.

Parris. Then he must search on.

Susanna. Aye, sir, he have been searchin' his books since he left you, sir. But he bid me tell you, that you might look to unnatural things for the cause of it.

---

7. **injunctions** (ĭn-jŭngk′shənz): commands; orders.

8. **Barbados** (bär-bā′dōs′): an island in the West Indies under British rule until 1966.

9. **dissembling:** disguising the truth about something.

Parris (*his eyes going wide*). No—no. There be no unnatural cause here. Tell him I have sent for Reverend Hale of Beverly, and Mr. Hale will surely confirm that. Let him look to medicine and put out all thought of unnatural causes here. There be none.

Susanna. Aye, sir. He bid me tell you. (*She turns to go.*)

Abigail. Speak nothin' of it in the village, Susanna.

Parris. Go directly home and speak nothing of unnatural causes.

Susanna. Aye, sir. I pray for her. (*She goes out.*)

Abigail. Uncle, the rumor of witchcraft is all about; I think you'd best go down and deny it yourself. The parlor's packed with people, sir. I'll sit with her.

Parris (*pressed, turns on her*). And what shall I say to them? That my daughter and my niece I discovered dancing like heathen in the forest?

Abigail. Uncle, we did dance; let you tell them I confessed it—and I'll be whipped if I must be. But they're speakin' of witchcraft. Betty's not witched.

Parris. Abigail, I cannot go before the congregation when I know you have not opened with me. What did you do with her in the forest?

Abigail. We did dance, uncle, and when you leaped out of the bush so suddenly, Betty was frightened and then she fainted. And there's the whole of it.

Parris. Child, sit you down.

Abigail (*quavering, as she sits*). I would never hurt Betty. I love her dearly.

Parris. Now look you, child, your punishment will come in its time. But if you trafficked with[10] spirits in the forest I must know it now, for surely my enemies will, and they will ruin me with it.

Abigail. But we never conjured spirits.

Parris. Then why can she not move herself since midnight? This child is desperate! (Abigail *low-*

ers her eyes.) It must come out—my enemies will bring it out. Let me know what you done there. Abigail, do you understand that I have many enemies?

Abigail. I have heard of it, uncle.

Parris. There is a faction that is sworn to drive me from my pulpit. Do you understand that?

Abigail. I think so, sir.

Parris. Now then, in the midst of such disruption, my own household is discovered to be the very center of some obscene practice. Abominations[11] are done in the forest—

Abigail. It were sport, uncle!

Parris (*pointing at* Betty). You call this sport? (*She lowers her eyes. He pleads*). Abigail, if you know something that may help the doctor, for God's sake tell it to me. (*She is silent.*) I saw Tituba waving her arms over the fire when I came on you. Why was she doing that? And I heard a screeching and gibberish coming from her mouth. She were swaying like a dumb beast over that fire!

Abigail. She always sings her Barbados songs, and we dance.

Parris. I cannot blink what I saw, Abigail, for my enemies will not blink it. I saw a dress lying on the grass.

Abigail (*innocently*). A dress?

Parris (*it is very hard to say*). Aye, a dress. And I thought I saw—someone naked running through the trees!

Abigail (*in terror*). No one was naked! You mistake yourself, uncle!

Parris (*with anger*). I saw it! (*He moves from her. Then, resolved*). Now tell me true, Abigail. And I pray you feel the weight of truth upon you, for now my ministry's at stake, my ministry and perhaps your cousin's life. Whatever abomina-

---

10. **trafficked with:** met.

11. **abominations:** dreadful and immoral things.

tion you have done, give me all of it now, for I dare not be taken unaware when I go before them down there.

Abigail. There is nothin' more. I swear it, uncle.

Parris (*studies her, then nods, half convinced*). Abigail, I have fought here three long years to bend these stiff-necked people to me, and now, just now when some good respect is rising for me in the parish, you compromise my very character. I have given you a home, child, I have put clothes upon your back—now give me upright answer. Your name in the town—it is entirely white, is it not?

Abigail (*with an edge of resentment*). Why, I am sure it is, sir. There be no blush about my name.[12]

Parris (*to the point*). Abigail, is there any other cause than you have told me, for your being discharged from Goody[13] Proctor's service? I have heard it said, and I tell you as I heard it, that she comes so rarely to the church this year for she will not sit so close to something soiled. What signified that remark?

Abigail. She hates me, uncle, she must, for I would not be her slave. It's a bitter woman, a lying, cold, sniveling woman, and I will not work for such a woman!

Parris. She may be. And yet it has troubled me that you are now seven month out of their house, and in all this time no other family has ever called for your service.

Abigail. They want slaves, not such as I. Let them send to Barbados for that. I will not black my face for any of them! (*With ill-concealed resentment at him.*) Do you begrudge my bed, uncle?

---

12. **There be . . . my name:** There is nothing wrong with my reputation.

13. **Goody:** short for Goodwife, the Puritan equivalent of Mrs.

Parris. No—no.

Abigail (*in a temper*). My name is good in the village! I will not have it said my name is soiled! Goody Proctor is a gossiping liar!

(*Enter* Mrs. Ann Putnam. *She is a twisted soul of forty-five, a death-ridden woman, haunted by dreams.*)

Parris (*as soon as the door begins to open*). No—no, I cannot have anyone. (*He sees her, and a certain deference springs into him, although his worry remains.*) Why, Goody Putnam, come in.

Mrs. Putnam (*full of breath, shiny-eyed*). It is a marvel. It is surely a stroke of hell upon you.

Parris. No, Goody Putnam, it is—

Mrs. Putnam (*glancing at* Betty). How high did she fly, how high?

Parris. No, no, she never flew—

Mrs. Putnam (*very pleased with it*). Why, it's sure she did. Mr. Collins saw her goin' over Ingersoll's barn, and come down light as bird, he says!

Parris. Now, look you, Goody Putnam, she never—(*Enter* Thomas Putnam, *a well-to-do, hardhanded landowner, near fifty.*) Oh, good morning, Mr. Putnam.

Putnam. It is a providence[14] the thing is out now! It is a providence. (*He goes directly to the bed.*)

Parris. What's out, sir, what's—?

(Mrs. Putnam *goes to the bed.*)

Putnam (*looking down at* Betty). Why, her eyes is closed! Look you, Ann.

Mrs. Putnam. Why, that's strange. (*To* Parris). Ours is open.

Parris (*shocked*). Your Ruth is sick?

Mrs. Putnam (*with vicious certainty*). I'd not call it sick; the Devil's touch is heavier than sick. It's death, y'know, it's death drivin' into them, forked and hoofed.

Parris. Oh, pray not! Why, how does Ruth ail?

Mrs. Putnam. She ails as she must—she never waked this morning, but her eyes open and she walks, and hears naught, sees naught, and cannot eat. Her soul is taken, surely.

(Parris *is struck.*)

Putnam (*as though for further details*). They say you've sent for Reverend Hale of Beverly?

Parris (*with dwindling conviction now*). A precaution only. He has much experience in all demonic arts, and I—

Mrs. Putnam. He has indeed; and found a witch in Beverly last year, and let you remember that.

Parris. Now, Goody Ann, they only thought that were a witch, and I am certain there be no element of witchcraft here.

Putnam. No witchcraft! Now look you, Mr. Parris—

Parris. Thomas, Thomas, I pray you, leap not to witchcraft. I know that you—you least of all, Thomas, would ever wish so disastrous a charge laid upon me. We cannot leap to witchcraft. They will howl me out of Salem for such corruption in my house.

A word about Thomas Putnam. He was a man with many grievances, at least one of which appears justified. Some time before, his wife's brother-in-law, James Bayley, had been turned down as minister of Salem. Bayley had all the qualifications, and a two-thirds vote into the bargain, but a faction stopped his acceptance, for reasons that are not clear.

Thomas Putnam was the eldest son of the richest man in the village. He had fought the Indians at Narragansett, and was deeply interested in parish affairs. He undoubtedly felt it poor payment that the village should so blatantly disregard his candidate for one of its more important offices, especially since he regarded himself as the intellectual superior of most of the people around him.

---

14. **providence** (prŏv′ĭ-dəns): sign of good fortune.

His vindictive[15] nature was demonstrated long before the witchcraft began. Another former Salem minister, George Burroughs, had had to borrow money to pay for his wife's funeral, and, since the parish was remiss in his salary, he was soon bankrupt. Thomas and his brother John had Burroughs jailed for debts the man did not owe. The incident is important only in that Burroughs succeeded in becoming minister where Bayley, Thomas Putnam's brother-in-law, had been rejected; the motif of resentment is clear here. Thomas Putnam felt that his own name and the honor of his family had been smirched[16] by the village, and he meant to right matters however he could.

Another reason to believe him a deeply embittered man was his attempt to break his father's will, which left a disproportionate amount to a stepbrother. As with every other public cause in which he tried to force his way, he failed in this.

So it is not surprising to find that so many accusations against people are in the handwriting of Thomas Putnam, or that his name is so often found as a witness corroborating the supernatural testimony, or that his daughter led the crying-out at the most opportune junctures of the trials, especially when—But we'll speak of that when we come to it. 🌿

Putnam (*at the moment he is intent upon getting* Parris, *for whom he has only contempt, to move toward the abyss*). Mr. Parris, I have taken your part in all contention here, and I would continue; but I cannot if you hold back in this. There are hurtful, vengeful spirits layin' hands on these children.

Parris. But, Thomas, you cannot—

Putnam. Ann! Tell Mr. Parris what you have done.

Mrs. Putnam. Reverend Parris, I have laid seven babies unbaptized in the earth. Believe me, sir, you never saw more hearty babies born. And yet, each would wither in my arms the very night of their birth. I have spoke nothin', but my heart has clamored intimations.[17] And now, this year, my Ruth, my only—I see her turning strange. A secret child she has become this year, and shrivels like a sucking mouth were pullin' on her life too. And so I thought to send her to your Tituba—

Parris. To Tituba! What may Tituba—?

Mrs. Putnam. Tituba knows how to speak to the dead, Mr. Parris.

Parris. Goody Ann, it is a formidable sin to conjure up the dead!

Mrs. Putnam. I take it on my soul, but who else may surely tell us what person murdered my babies?

Parris (*horrified*). Woman!

Mrs. Putnam. They were murdered, Mr. Parris! And mark this proof! Mark it! Last night my Ruth were ever so close to their little spirits; I know it, sir. For how else is she struck dumb now except some power of darkness would stop her mouth? It is a marvelous sign, Mr. Parris!

Putnam. Don't you understand it, sir? There is a murdering witch among us, bound to keep herself in the dark. (Parris *turns to* Betty, *a frantic terror rising in him.*) Let your enemies make of it what they will, you cannot blink it more.

Parris (*to* Abigail). Then you were conjuring spirits last night.

Abigail (*whispering*). Not I, sir—Tituba and Ruth.

Parris (*turns now, with new fear, and goes to* Betty, *looks down at her, and then, gazing off*). Oh, Abigail, what proper payment for my charity! Now I am undone.[18]

---

15. **vindictive:** vengeful; eager to get even when wronged.

16. **smirched:** soiled; reduced in value.

17. **clamored intimations** (klăm′ərd ĭn′tə-mā′shənz): nagging suspicions.

18. **undone:** ruined.

Putnam. You are not undone! Let you take hold here. Wait for no one to charge you—declare it yourself. You have discovered witchcraft—

Parris. In my house? In my house, Thomas? They will topple me with this! They will make of it a—

(*Enter* Mercy Lewis, *the Putnams' servant, a fat, sly, merciless girl of eighteen.*)

Mercy. Your pardons. I only thought to see how Betty is.

Putnam. Why aren't you home? Who's with Ruth?

Mercy. Her grandma come. She's improved a little, I think—she give a powerful sneeze before.

Mrs. Putnam. Ah, there's a sign of life!

Mercy. I'd fear no more, Goody Putnam. It were a grand sneeze; another like it will shake her wits together, I'm sure. (*She goes to the bed to look.*)

Parris. Will you leave me now, Thomas? I would pray a while alone.

Abigail. Uncle, you've prayed since midnight. Why do you not go down and—

Parris. No—no. (*To* Putnam). I have no answer for that crowd. I'll wait till Mr. Hale arrives. (*To get* Mrs. Putnam *to leave.*) If you will, Goody Ann . . .

Putnam. Now look you, sir. Let you strike out against the Devil, and the village will bless you for it! Come down, speak to them—pray with them. They're thirsting for your word, Mister! Surely you'll pray with them.

Parris (*swayed*). I'll lead them in a psalm, but let you say nothing of witchcraft yet. I will not discuss it. The cause is yet unknown. I have had enough contention since I came; I want no more.

Mrs. Putnam. Mercy, you go home to Ruth, d'y'-hear?

Mercy. Aye, mum.

(Mrs. Putnam *goes out.*)

Parris (*to* Abigail). If she starts for the window, cry for me at once.

Abigail. I will, uncle.

Parris (*to* Putnam). There is a terrible power in her arms today. (*He goes out with* Putnam.)

Abigail (*with hushed trepidation*).[19] How is Ruth sick?

Mercy. It's weirdish, I know not—she seems to walk like a dead one since last night.

Abigail (*turns at once and goes to* Betty, *and now, with fear in her voice*). Betty? (Betty *doesn't move. She shakes her.*) Now stop this! Betty! Sit up now!

(Betty *doesn't stir.* Mercy *comes over.*)

Mercy. Have you tried beatin' her? I gave Ruth a good one and it waked her for a minute. Here, let me have her.

Abigail (*holding* Mercy *back*). No, he'll be comin' up. Listen, now; if they be questioning us, tell them we danced—I told him as much already.

Mercy. Aye. And what more?

Abigail. He knows Tituba conjured Ruth's sisters to come out of the grave.

Mercy. And what more?

Abigail. He saw you naked.

Mercy (*clapping her hands together with a frightened laugh*). Oh, Jesus!

(*Enter* Mary Warren, *breathless. She is seventeen, a* subservient, *naive, lonely girl.*)

Mary Warren. What'll we do? The village is out! I just come from the farm; the whole country's talkin' witchcraft! They'll be callin' us witches, Abby!

Mercy (*pointing and looking at* Mary Warren). She means to tell, I know it.

Mary Warren. Abby, we've got to tell. Witchery's a hangin' error, a hangin' like they done in

---

19. **trepidation** (trĕp´ĭ-dā´shən): alarm or dread.

Boston two year ago! We must tell the truth, Abby! You'll only be whipped for dancin', and the other things!

Abigail. Oh, we'll be whipped!

Mary Warren. I never done none of it, Abby. I only looked!

Mercy (*moving menacingly toward Mary*). Oh, you're a great one for lookin', aren't you, Mary Warren? What a grand peeping courage you have!

(Betty, *on the bed, whimpers.* Abigail *turns to her at once.*)

Abigail. Betty? (*She goes to* Betty.) Now, Betty, dear, wake up now. It's Abigail. (*She sits* Betty *up and furiously shakes her.*) I'll beat you, Betty! (*Betty whimpers.*) My, you seem improving. I talked to your papa and I told him everything. So there's nothing to—

Betty (*darts off the bed, frightened of* Abigail, *and flattens herself against the wall*). I want my mama!

Abigail (*with alarm, as she cautiously approaches* Betty). What ails you, Betty? Your mama's dead and buried.

Betty. I'll fly to Mama. Let me fly! (*She raises her arms as though to fly, and streaks for the window, gets one leg out.*)

Abigail (*pulling her away from the window*). I told him everything; he knows now, he knows everything we—

Betty. You drank blood, Abby! You didn't tell him that!

Abigail. Betty, you never say that again! You will never—

Betty. You did, you did! You drank a charm to kill John Proctor's wife! You drank a charm to kill Goody Proctor!

Abigail (*smashes her across the face*). Shut it! Now shut it!

Betty (*collapsing on the bed*). Mama, Mama! (*She dissolves into sobs.*)

Abigail. Now look you. All of you. We danced. And Tituba conjured Ruth Putnam's dead sisters. And that is all. And mark this. Let either of you breathe a word, or the edge of a word, about the other things, and I will come to you in the black of some terrible night and I will bring a pointy reckoning that will shudder you.[20] And you know I can do it; I saw Indians smash my dear parents' heads on the pillow next to mine, and I have seen some reddish work done at night, and I can make you wish you had never seen the sun go down! (*She goes to* Betty *and roughly sits her up.*) Now, you— sit up and stop this!

(*But* Betty *collapses in her hands and lies inert on the bed.*)

Mary Warren (*with hysterical fright*). What's got her? (Abigail *stares in fright at* Betty.) Abby, she's going to die! It's a sin to conjure, and we—

Abigail (*starting for* Mary). I say shut it, Mary Warren!

(*Enter* John Proctor. *On seeing him,* Mary Warren *leaps in fright.*)

Proctor was a farmer in his middle thirties. He need not have been a partisan of any faction in the town, but there is evidence to suggest that he had a sharp and biting way with hypocrites. He was the kind of man—powerful of body, even-tempered, and not easily led—who cannot refuse support to partisans without drawing their deepest resentment. In Proctor's presence a fool felt his foolishness instantly—and a Proctor is always marked for calumny[21] therefore.

But as we shall see, the steady manner he displays does not spring from an untroubled soul. He is a sinner, a sinner not only against the moral fashion of the time, but against his own vision of decent conduct. These people had no ritual for the

---

20. **bring . . . shudder you:** inflict a terrifying punishment on you.

21. **calumny** (kăl′əm-nē): slander; lies about someone.

washing away of sins. It is another trait we inherited from them, and it has helped to discipline us as well as to breed hypocrisy among us. Proctor, respected and even feared in Salem, has come to regard himself as a kind of fraud. But no hint of this has yet appeared on the surface, and as he enters from the crowded parlor below it is a man in his prime we see, with a quiet confidence and an unexpressed, hidden force. Mary Warren, his servant, can barely speak for embarrassment and fear. ❧

Mary Warren. Oh! I'm just going home, Mr. Proctor.

Proctor. Be you foolish, Mary Warren? Be you deaf? I forbid you leave the house, did I not? Why shall I pay you? I am looking for you more often than my cows!

Mary Warren. I only come to see the great doings in the world.

Proctor. I'll show you a great doin' on your arse one of these days. Now get you home; my wife is waitin' with your work! (*Trying to retain a shred of dignity, she goes slowly out.*)

John Proctor

Mercy Lewis (*both afraid of him and strangely titillated*). I'd best be off. I have my Ruth to watch. Good morning, Mr. Proctor.

(Mercy *sidles out. Since* Proctor's *entrance,* Abigail *has stood as though on tiptoe, absorbing his presence, wide-eyed. He glances at her, then goes to* Betty *on the bed.*)

Abigail. Gah! I'd almost forgot how strong you are, John Proctor!

Proctor (*looking at* Abigail *now, the faintest suggestion of a knowing smile on his face*). What's this mischief here?

Abigail (*with a nervous laugh*). Oh, she's only gone silly somehow.

Proctor. The road past my house is a pilgrimage[22] to Salem all morning. The town's mumbling witchcraft.

Abigail. Oh, posh! (*Winningly she comes a little closer, with a confidential, wicked air.*) We were dancin' in the woods last night, and my uncle leaped in on us. She took fright, is all.

Proctor (*his smile widening*). Ah, you're wicked yet, aren't y'! (*A trill of expectant laughter escapes her, and she dares come closer, feverishly looking into his eyes.*) You'll be clapped in the stocks before you're twenty.

(*He takes a step to go, and she springs into his path.*)

Abigail. Give me a word, John. A soft word. (*Her concentrated desire destroys his smile.*)

Proctor. No, no, Abby. That's done with.

Abigail (*tauntingly*). You come five mile to see a silly girl fly? I know you better.

Proctor (*setting her firmly out of his path*). I come to see what mischief your uncle's brewin' now. (*With final emphasis.*) Put it out of mind, Abby.

Abigail (*grasping his hand before he can release her*). John—I am waitin' for you every night.

Proctor. Abby, I never give you hope to wait for me.

Abigail (*now beginning to anger—she can't believe it*). I have something better than hope, I think!

Proctor. Abby, you'll put it out of mind. I'll not be comin' for you more.

---

22. **pilgrimage:** a journey to a religious shrine, often made in groups.

Abigail. You're surely sportin' with me.

Proctor. You know me better.

Abigail. I know how you clutched my back behind your house and sweated like a stallion whenever I come near! Or did I dream that? It's she put me out, you cannot pretend it were you. I saw your face when she put me out, and you loved me then and you do now!

Proctor. Abby, that's a wild thing to say—

Abigail. A wild thing may say wild things. But not so wild, I think. I have seen you since she put me out; I have seen you nights.

Proctor. I have hardly stepped off my farm this sevenmonth.

Abigail. I have a sense for heat, John, and yours has drawn me to my window, and I have seen you looking up, burning in your loneliness. Do you tell me you've never looked up at my window?

Proctor. I may have looked up.

Abigail (*now softening*). And you must. You are no wintry man. I know you, John. I know you. (*She is weeping.*) I cannot sleep for dreamin'; I cannot dream but I wake and walk about the house as though I'd find you comin' through some door. (*She clutches him desperately*).

Proctor (*gently pressing her from him, with great sympathy but firmly*). Child—

Abigail (*with a flash of anger*). How do you call me child!

Proctor. Abby, I may think of you softly from time to time. But I will cut off my hand before I'll ever reach for you again. Wipe it out of mind. We never touched, Abby.

Abigail. Aye, but we did.

Proctor. Aye, but we did not.

Abigail (*with a bitter anger*). Oh, I marvel how such a strong man may let such a sickly wife be—

Proctor (*angered—at himself as well*). You'll speak nothin' of Elizabeth!

Abigail. She is blackening my name in the village! She is telling lies about me! She is a cold, sniveling woman, and you bend to her! Let her turn you like a—

Proctor (*shaking her*). Do you look for whippin'?

(*A psalm is heard being sung below.*)

Abigail (*in tears*). I look for John Proctor that took me from my sleep and put knowledge in my heart! I never knew what pretense Salem was, I never knew the lying lessons I was taught by all these Christian women and their covenanted[23] men! And now you bid me tear the light out of my eyes? I will not, I cannot! You loved me, John Proctor, and whatever sin it is, you love me yet! (*He turns abruptly to go out. She rushes to him.*) John, pity me, pity me!

(*The words "going up to Jesus" are heard in the psalm, and* Betty *claps her ears suddenly and whines loudly.*)

Abigail. Betty? (*She hurries to* Betty, *who is now sitting up and screaming.* Proctor *goes to* Betty *as* Abigail *is trying to pull her hands down, calling "Betty!"*)

Proctor (*growing unnerved*). What's she doing? Girl, what ails you? Stop that wailing!

(*The singing has stopped in the midst of this, and now* Parris *rushes in.*)

Parris. What happened? What are you doing to her? Betty! (*He rushes to the bed, crying, "Betty, Betty!"* Mrs. Putnam *enters, feverish with curiosity, and with her* Thomas Putnam *and* Mercy Lewis. Parris, *at the bed, keeps lightly slapping* Betty's *face, while she moans and tries to get up.*)

Abigail. She heard you singin' and suddenly she's up and screamin'.

Mrs. Putnam. The psalm! The psalm! She cannot bear to hear the Lord's name!

---

23. **covenanted** (kŭv'ə-nən'tĭd): in Puritan religious practice, the men of a congregation would make an agreement, or a covenant, to govern the community.

Parris. No. God forbid. Mercy, run to the doctor! Tell him what's happened here! (*Mercy Lewis rushes out.*)

Mrs. Putnam. Mark it for a sign, mark it!

(*Rebecca Nurse, seventy-two, enters. She is white-haired, leaning upon her walking-stick.*)

Putnam (*pointing at the whimpering* Betty). That is a notorious sign of witchcraft afoot, Goody Nurse, a prodigious[24] sign!

Mrs. Putnam. My mother told me that! When they cannot bear to hear the name of—

Parris (*trembling*). Rebecca, Rebecca, go to her, we're lost. She suddenly cannot bear to hear the Lord's—

(*Giles Corey, eighty-three, enters. He is knotted with muscle, canny, inquisitive, and still powerful.*)

Rebecca. There is hard sickness here, Giles Corey, so please to keep the quiet.

Giles. I've not said a word. No one here can testify I've said a word. Is she going to fly again? I hear she flies.

Putnam. Man, be quiet now!

(*Everything is quiet. Rebecca walks across the room to the bed. Gentleness exudes from her. Betty is quietly whimpering, eyes shut. Rebecca simply stands over the child, who gradually quiets.*)

And while they are so absorbed, we may put a word in for Rebecca. Rebecca was the wife of Francis Nurse, who, from all accounts, was one of those men for whom both sides of the argument had to have respect. He was called upon to arbitrate disputes as though he were an unofficial judge, and Rebecca also enjoyed the high opinion most people had for him. By the time of the delusion,[25] they had three hundred acres, and their children were settled in separate homesteads within the same estate. However, Francis had originally rented the land, and one theory has it

that, as he gradually paid for it and raised his social status, there were those who resented his rise.

Another suggestion to explain the systematic campaign against Rebecca, and inferentially against Francis, is the land war he fought with his neighbors, one of whom was a Putnam. This squabble grew to the proportions of a battle in the woods between partisans of both sides, and it is said to have lasted for two days. As for Rebecca herself, the general opinion of her character was so high that to explain how anyone dared cry her out for a witch—and more, how adults could bring themselves to lay hands on her—we must look to the fields and boundaries of that time.

As we have seen, Thomas Putnam's man for the Salem ministry was Bayley. The Nurse clan had been in the faction that prevented Bayley's taking office. In addition, certain families allied to the Nurses by blood or friendship, and whose farms were contiguous with the Nurse farm or close to it, combined to break away from the Salem town authority and set up Topsfield, a new and independent entity whose existence was resented by old Salemites.

That the guiding hand behind the outcry was Putnam's is indicated by the fact that, as soon as it began, this Topsfield-Nurse faction absented themselves from church in protest and disbelief. It was Edward and Jonathan Putnam who signed the first complaint against Rebecca; and Thomas Putnam's little daughter was the one who fell into a fit at the hearing and pointed to Rebecca as her attacker. To top it all, Mrs. Putnam—who is now staring at the bewitched child on the bed—soon accused Rebecca's spirit of "tempting her to iniquity," a charge that had more truth in it than Mrs. Putnam could know. 🍂

---

24. **prodigious** (prə-dĭj′əs): extraordinary.
25. **delusion** (dĭ-lo͞o′zhən): witchcraft.

WORDS TO KNOW

arbitrate (är′bĭ-trāt) *v.* to judge or act as referee
iniquity (ĭ-nĭk′wĭ-tē) *n.* wickedness; immorality

Mrs. Putnam (*astonished*). What have you done?

(Rebecca, *in thought, now leaves the bedside and sits.*)

Parris (*wondrous and relieved*). What do you make of it, Rebecca?

Putnam (*eagerly*). Goody Nurse, will you go to my Ruth and see if you can wake her?

Rebecca (*sitting*). I think she'll wake in time. Pray calm yourselves. I have eleven children, and I am twenty-six times a grandma, and I have seen them all through their silly seasons, and when it come on them they will run the Devil bow-legged keeping up with their mischief. I think she'll wake when she tires of it. A child's spirit is like a child, you can never catch it by running after it; you must stand still, and, for love, it will soon itself come back.

Proctor. Aye, that's the truth of it, Rebecca.

Mrs. Putnam. This is no silly season, Rebecca. My Ruth is bewildered, Rebecca; she cannot eat.

Rebecca. Perhaps she is not hungered yet. (*To Parris*) I hope you are not decided to go in search of loose spirits, Mr. Parris. I've heard promise of that outside.

Parris. A wide opinion's running in the parish that the Devil may be among us, and I would satisfy them that they are wrong.

Proctor. Then let you come out and call them wrong. Did you consult the wardens[26] before you called this minister to look for devils?

Parris. He is not coming to look for devils!

Proctor. Then what's he coming for?

Putnam. There be children dyin' in the village, Mister!

---

26. **wardens:** officers appointed to keep order.

The Nurse House

Proctor. I seen none dyin'. This society will not be a bag to swing around your head, Mr. Putnam. (*To* Parris) Did you call a meeting before you—?

Putnam. I am sick of meetings; cannot the man turn his head without he have a meeting?

Proctor. He may turn his head, but not to Hell!

Rebecca. Pray, John, be calm. (*Pause. He defers to her.*) Mr. Parris, I think you'd best send Reverend Hale back as soon as he come. This will set us all to arguin' again in the society, and we thought to have peace this year. I think we ought rely on the doctor now, and good prayer.

Mrs. Putnam. Rebecca, the doctor's baffled!

Rebecca. If so he is, then let us go to God for the cause of it. There is prodigious danger in the seeking of loose spirits. I fear it, I fear it. Let us rather blame ourselves and—

Putnam. How may we blame ourselves? I am one of nine sons; the Putnam seed have peopled this province. And yet I have but one child left of eight—and now she shrivels!

Rebecca. I cannot fathom that.

Mrs. Putnam (*with a growing edge of sarcasm*). But I must! You think it God's work you should never lose a child, nor grandchild either, and I bury all but one? There are wheels within wheels in this village, and fires within fires!

Putnam (*to* Parris). When Reverend Hale comes, you will proceed to look for signs of witchcraft here.

Proctor (*to* Putnam). You cannot command Mr. Parris. We vote by name in this society, not by acreage.

Putnam. I never heard you worried so on this society, Mr. Proctor. I do not think I saw you at Sabbath meeting since snow flew.

Proctor. I have trouble enough without I come five mile to hear him preach only hellfire and bloody damnation. Take it to heart, Mr. Parris. There are many others who stay away from church these days because you hardly ever mention God any more.

Parris (*now aroused*). Why, that's a drastic charge!

Rebecca. It's somewhat true; there are many that quail[27] to bring their children—

Parris. I do not preach for children, Rebecca. It is not the children who are unmindful of their obligations toward this ministry.

Rebecca. Are there really those unmindful?

Parris. I should say the better half of Salem village—

Putnam. And more than that!

Parris. Where is my wood? My contract provides I be supplied with all my firewood. I am waiting since November for a stick, and even in November I had to show my frostbitten hands like some London beggar!

Giles. You are allowed six pound a year to buy your wood, Mr. Parris.

Parris. I regard that six pound as part of my salary. I am paid little enough without I spend six pound on firewood.

Proctor. Sixty, plus six for firewood—

Parris. The salary is sixty-six pound, Mr. Proctor! I am not some preaching farmer with a book under my arm; I am a graduate of Harvard College.

Giles. Aye, and well instructed in arithmetic!

Parris. Mr. Corey, you will look far for a man of my kind at sixty pound a year! I am not used to this poverty; I left a thrifty business in the Barbados to serve the Lord. I do not fathom it, why am I persecuted here? I cannot offer one proposition but there be a howling riot of argument. I have often wondered if the Devil be in it somewhere; I cannot understand you people otherwise.

Proctor. Mr. Parris, you are the first minister ever did demand the deed to this house—

---

27. **quail:** fear.

Parris. Man! Don't a minister deserve a house to live in?

Proctor. To live in, yes. But to ask ownership is like you shall own the meeting house itself; the last meeting I were at you spoke so long on deeds and mortgages I thought it were an auction.

Parris. I want a mark of confidence, is all! I am your third preacher in seven years. I do not wish to be put out like the cat whenever some majority feels the whim. You people seem not to comprehend that a minister is the Lord's man in the parish; a minister is not to be so lightly crossed and contradicted—

Putnam. Aye!

Parris. There is either obedience or the church will burn like Hell is burning!

Proctor. Can you speak one minute without we land in Hell again? I am sick of Hell!

Parris. It is not for you to say what is good for you to hear!

Proctor. I may speak my heart, I think!

Parris (*in a fury*). What, are we Quakers?[28] We are not Quakers here yet, Mr. Proctor. And you may tell that to your followers!

Proctor. My followers!

Parris (*now he's out with it*). There is a party in this church. I am not blind; there is a faction and a party.

Proctor. Against you?

Putnam. Against him and all authority!

Proctor. Why, then I must find it and join it.

(*There is shock among the others.*)

Rebecca. He does not mean that.

Putnam. He confessed it now!

Proctor. I mean it solemnly, Rebecca; I like not the smell of this "authority."

Rebecca. No, you cannot break charity[29] with your minister. You are another kind, John. Clasp his hand, make your peace.

Proctor. I have a crop to sow and lumber to drag home. (*He goes angrily to the door and turns to Corey with a smile.*) What say you, Giles, let's find the party. He says there's a party.

Giles. I've changed my opinion of this man, John. Mr. Parris, I beg your pardon. I never thought you had so much iron in you.

Parris (*surprised*). Why, thank you, Giles!

Giles. It suggests to the mind what the trouble be among us all these years. (*To all*) Think on it. Wherefore is everybody suing everybody else? Think on it now, it's a deep thing, and dark as a pit. I have been six time in court this year—

Proctor (*familiarly, with warmth, although he knows he is approaching the edge of Giles' tolerance with this*). Is it the Devil's fault that a man cannot say you good morning without you clap him for defamation?[30] You're old, Giles, and you're not hearin' so well as you did.

Giles (*he cannot be crossed*). John Proctor, I have only last month collected four pound damages for you publicly sayin' I burned the roof off your house, and I—

Proctor (*laughing*). I never said no such thing, but I've paid you for it, so I hope I can call you deaf without charge. Now come along, Giles, and help me drag my lumber home.

Putnam. A moment, Mr. Proctor. What lumber is that you're draggin', if I may ask you?

Proctor. My lumber. From out my forest by the riverside.

Putnam. Why, we are surely gone wild this year. What anarchy[31] is this? That tract is in my bounds, it's in my bounds, Mr. Proctor.

Proctor. In your bounds! (*Indicating* Rebecca) I bought that tract from Goody Nurse's husband five months ago.

---

28. **Quakers:** a radical English religious sect, much hated by the Puritans, who often "spoke their heart" during their religious meetings.

29. **break charity:** break off; end the relationship.

30. **clap . . . defamation** (klăp . . . děf′ə-mā′shən): imprison him for slander.

31. **anarchy** (ăn′ər-kē): disorder and confusion.

Putnam. He had no right to sell it. It stands clear in my grandfather's will that all the land between the river and—

Proctor. Your grandfather had a habit of willing land that never belonged to him, if I may say it plain.

Giles. That's God's truth; he nearly willed away my north pasture but he knew I'd break his fingers before he'd set his name to it. Let's get your lumber home, John. I feel a sudden will to work coming on.

Putnam. You load one oak of mine and you'll fight to drag it home!

Giles. Aye, and we'll win too, Putnam—this fool and I. Come on! (*He turns to* Proctor *and starts out.*)

Putnam. I'll have my men on you, Corey! I'll clap a writ on you!

(*Enter* Reverend John Hale *of Beverly.*)

Reverend Hale

Mr. Hale is nearing forty, a tight-skinned, eager-eyed intellectual. This is a beloved errand for him; on being called here to <u>ascertain</u> witchcraft he felt the pride of the specialist whose unique knowledge has at last been publicly called for. Like almost all men of learning, he spent a good deal of his time pondering the invisible world, especially since he had himself encountered a witch in his parish not long before. That woman, however, turned into a mere pest under his searching scrutiny, and the child she had allegedly been afflicting recovered her normal behavior after Hale had given her his kindness and a few days of rest in his own house. However, that experience never raised a doubt in his mind as to the reality of the underworld or the existence of Lucifer's many-faced lieutenants. And his belief is not to his discredit. Better minds than Hale's were—and still are—convinced that there is a society of spirits beyond our ken. One cannot help noting that one of his lines has never yet raised a laugh in any audience that has seen this play; it is his assurance that "We cannot look to superstition in this. The Devil is precise." Evidently we are not quite certain even now whether diabolism is holy and not to be scoffed at. And it is no accident that we should be so bemused.

Like Reverend Hale and the others on this stage, we conceive the Devil as a necessary part of a respectable view of cosmology.[32] Ours is a divided empire in which certain ideas and emotions and actions are of God, and their opposites are of Lucifer. It is as impossible for most men to conceive of a morality without sin as of an earth without "sky." Since 1692 a great but superficial change has wiped out God's beard and the Devil's horns, but the world is still gripped between two diametrically opposed absolutes. The concept of unity, in which positive and negative are attributes of the same force, in which good and evil are relative, ever-changing, and always joined to the same phenomenon—such a concept is still reserved to the physical sciences and to the few who have grasped the history of ideas. When it is recalled that until the Christian era the underworld was never regarded as a hostile area, that all gods were useful and essentially friendly to man despite occasional lapses; when we see the steady and methodical inculcation into humanity of the idea

---

32. **cosmology** (kŏz-mŏl'ə-jē): a branch of philosophy dealing with the structure of the universe.

WORDS
TO
KNOW   **ascertain** (ăs'ər-tān') v. to find out

of man's worthlessness—until redeemed—the necessity of the Devil may become evident as a weapon, a weapon designed and used time and time again in every age to whip men into a surrender to a particular church or church-state.

Our difficulty in believing the—for want of a better word—political inspiration of the Devil is due in great part to the fact that he is called up and damned not only by our social antagonists but by our own side, whatever it may be. The Catholic Church, through its Inquisition,[33] is famous for cultivating Lucifer as the arch-fiend, but the Church's enemies relied no less upon the Old Boy to keep the human mind enthralled. Luther[34] was himself accused of alliance with Hell, and he in turn accused his enemies. To complicate matters further, he believed that he had had contact with the Devil and had argued theology with him. I am not surprised at this, for at my own university a professor of history—a Lutheran, by the way—used to assemble his graduate students, draw the shades, and commune in the classroom with Erasmus.[35] He was never, to my knowledge, officially scoffed at for this, the reason being that the university officials, like most of us, are the children of a history which still sucks at the Devil's teats. At this writing, only England has held back before the temptations of contemporary diabolism. In the countries of the Communist ideology, all resistance of any import is linked to the totally malign capitalist succubi, and in America any man who is not reactionary in his views is open to the charge of alliance with the Red hell. Political opposition, thereby, is given an inhumane overlay which then justifies the abrogation of all normally applied customs of civilized intercourse. A political policy is equated with moral right, and opposition to it with diabolical malevolence. Once such an equation is effectively made, society becomes a congerie of plots and counterplots, and the main role of government changes from that of the arbiter to that of the scourge of God.

The results of this process are no different now from what they ever were, except sometimes in the degree of cruelty inflicted, and not always even in that department. Normally the actions and deeds of a man were all that society felt comfortable in judging. The secret intent of an action was left to the ministers, priests, and rabbis to deal with. When diabolism rises, however, actions are the least important manifests of the true nature of a man. The Devil, as Reverend Hale said, is a wily one, and, until an hour before he fell, even God thought him beautiful in Heaven.

The analogy, however, seems to falter when one considers that, while there were no witches then, there are Communists and capitalists now, and in each camp there is certain proof that spies of each side are at work undermining the other. But this is a snobbish objection and not at all warranted by the facts. I have no doubt that people *were* communing with, and even worshiping, the Devil in Salem, and if the whole truth could be known in this case, as it is in others, we should discover a regular and conventionalized propitiation of the dark spirit. One certain evidence of this is the confession of Tituba, the slave of Reverend Parris, and another is the behavior of the children who were known to have indulged in sorceries with her.

There are accounts of similar *klatches* in Europe, where the daughters of the towns would assemble at night and, sometimes with fetishes, sometimes with a selected young man, give themselves to love, with some bastardly results. The Church, sharp-eyed as it must be when gods long dead are brought to life, condemned these orgies as witchcraft and interpreted them, rightly, as a resurgence of the Dionysiac[36] forces it had crushed long before. Sex, sin, and the Devil were early

---

33. **Inquisition** (in′kwĭ-zĭsh′ən): a tribunal in the Roman Catholic Church dedicated to the discovery and punishment of heresy.

34. **Luther:** Martin Luther (1483–1546), the German theologian who led the Protestant Reformation.

35. **Erasmus** (ĭ-răz′məs): Desiderius Erasmus (1466?–1536), a Dutch scholar and humanist who sought to restore simple Christian faith by a study of the Scriptures and classical texts.

36. **Dionysiac** (dī′-ə-nĭs′ē-ăk′) **wild and chaotic;** refers to Dionysus, the Greek god of wine and madness.

linked, and so they continued to be in Salem, and are today. From all accounts there are no more puritanical mores in the world than those enforced by the Communists in Russia, where women's fashions, for instance, are as prudent and all-covering as any American Baptist would desire. The divorce laws lay a tremendous responsibility on the father for the care of his children. Even the laxity of divorce regulations in the early years of the revolution was undoubtedly a revulsion from the nineteenth-century Victorian immobility of marriage and the consequent hypocrisy that developed from it. If for no other reasons, a state so powerful, so jealous of the uniformity of its citizens, cannot long tolerate the atomization of the family. And yet, in American eyes at least, there remains the conviction that the Russian attitude toward women is lascivious. It is the Devil working again, just as he is working within the Slav[37] who is shocked at the very idea of a woman's disrobing herself in a burlesque show. Our opposites are always robed in sexual sin, and it is from this unconscious conviction that demonology gains both its attractive sensuality and its capacity to infuriate and frighten.

Coming into Salem now, Reverend Hale conceives of himself much as a young doctor on his first call. His painfully acquired armory of symptoms, catchwords, and diagnostic procedures are now to be put to use at last. The road from Beverly is unusually busy this morning, and he has passed a hundred rumors that make him smile at the ignorance of the yeomanry[38] in this most precise science. He feels himself allied with the best minds of Europe—kings, philosophers, scientists, and ecclesiasts[39] of all churches. His goal is light, goodness and its preservation, and he knows the exaltation of the blessed whose intelligence, sharpened by minute examinations of enormous tracts, is finally called upon to face what may be a bloody fight with the Fiend himself. 🔥

(He appears loaded down with half a dozen heavy books.)

Hale. Pray you, someone take these!

Parris (*delighted*). Mr. Hale! Oh! it's good to see you again! (*Taking some books*) My, they're heavy!

Hale (*setting down his books*). They must be; they are weighted with authority.

Parris (*a little scared*). Well, you do come prepared!

Hale. We shall need hard study if it comes to tracking down the Old Boy. (*Noticing* Rebecca) You cannot be Rebecca Nurse?

Rebecca. I am, sir. Do you know me?

Hale. It's strange how I knew you, but I suppose you look as such a good soul should. We have all heard of your great charities in Beverly.

Parris. Do you know this gentleman? Mr. Thomas Putnam. And his good wife Ann.

Hale. Putnam! I had not expected such distinguished company, sir.

Putnam (*pleased*). It does not seem to help us today, Mr. Hale. We look to you to come to our house and save our child.

Hale. Your child ails too?

Mrs. Putnam. Her soul, her soul seems flown away. She sleeps and yet she walks . . .

Putnam. She cannot eat.

Hale. Cannot eat! (*Thinks on it. Then, to* Proctor *and* Giles Corey) Do you men have afflicted children?

Parris. No, no, these are farmers. John Proctor—

Giles Corey. He don't believe in witches.

Proctor (*to* Hale). I never spoke on witches one way or the other. Will you come, Giles?

Giles. No—no, John, I think not. I have some few queer questions of my own to ask this fellow.

---

37. **Slav** (släv): a generic reference to Russians and other Slavic-speaking peoples of Eastern Europe who were under the control of the former Soviet Union.

38. **yeomanry** (yō′mən-rē): the farmers; common people.

39. **ecclesiasts** (ĭ-klē′zē-ăsts): religious officials; clergy.

Proctor. I've heard you to be a sensible man, Mr. Hale. I hope you'll leave some of it in Salem.

(*Proctor goes.* Hale *stands embarrassed for an instant.*)

Parris (*quickly*). Will you look at my daughter, sir? (*Leads* Hale *to the bed.*) She has tried to leap out the window; we discovered her this morning on the highroad, waving her arms as though she'd fly.

Hale (*narrowing his eyes*). Tries to fly.

Putnam. She cannot bear to hear the Lord's name, Mr. Hale; that's a sure sign of witchcraft afloat.

Hale (*holding up his hands*). No, no. Now let me instruct you. We cannot look to superstition in this. The Devil is precise; the marks of his presence are definite as stone, and I must tell you all that I shall not proceed unless you are prepared to believe me if I should find no bruise of hell upon her.

Parris. It is agreed, sir—it is agreed—we will abide by your judgment.

Hale. Good then. (*He goes to the bed, looks down at* Betty. *To* Parris) Now, sir, what were your first warning of this strangeness?

Parris. Why, sir—I discovered her—(*indicating* Abigail) and my niece and ten or twelve of the other girls, dancing in the forest last night.

Hale (*surprised*). You permit dancing?

Parris. No, no, it were secret—

Mrs. Putnam (*unable to wait*). Mr. Parris's slave has knowledge of conjurin', sir.

Parris (*to* Mrs. Putnam). We cannot be sure of that, Goody Ann—

Mrs. Putnam (*frightened, very softly*). I know it, sir. I sent my child—she should learn from Tituba who murdered her sisters.

Rebecca (*horrified*). Goody Ann! You sent a child to conjure up the dead?

Mrs. Putnam. Let God blame me, not you, not you, Rebecca! I'll not have you judging me any more! (*To* Hale) Is it a natural work to lose seven children before they live a day?

Parris. Sssh!

(Rebecca, *with great pain, turns her face away. There is a pause.*)

Hale. Seven dead in childbirth.

Mrs. Putnam (*softly*). Aye. (*Her voice breaks; she looks up at him. Silence.* Hale *is impressed.* Parris *looks to him. He goes to his books, opens one, turns pages, then reads. All wait, avidly.*)

Parris (*hushed*). What book is that?

Mrs. Putnam. What's there, sir?

Hale (*with a tasty love of intellectual pursuit*). Here is all the invisible world, caught, defined, and calculated. In these books the Devil stands stripped of all his brute disguises. Here are all your familiar spirits—your incubi and succubi;[40] your witches that go by land, by air, and by sea; your wizards of the night and of the day. Have no fear now—we shall find him out if he has come among us, and I mean to crush him utterly if he has shown his face! (*He starts for the bed.*)

Rebecca. Will it hurt the child, sir?

Hale. I cannot tell. If she is truly in the Devil's grip we may have to rip and tear to get her free.

Rebecca. I think I'll go, then. I am too old for this. (*She rises.*)

Parris (*striving for conviction*). Why, Rebecca, we may open up the boil of all our troubles today!

Rebecca. Let us hope for that. I go to God for you, sir.

Parris (*with trepidation—and resentment*). I hope you do not mean we go to Satan here! (*Slight pause.*)

Rebecca. I wish I knew. (*She goes out; they feel resentful of her note of moral superiority.*)

Putnam (*abruptly*). Come, Mr. Hale, let's get on. Sit you here.

---

40. **incubi** (ĭn′kyə-bī′) **and succubi** (sŭk′yə-bī′): male and female demons.

Giles. Mr. Hale, I have always wanted to ask a learned man—what signifies the readin' of strange books?

Hale. What books?

Giles. I cannot tell; she hides them.

Hale. Who does this?

Giles. Martha, my wife. I have waked at night many a time and found her in a corner, readin' of a book. Now what do you make of that?

Hale. Why, that's not necessarily—

Giles. It discomfits me! Last night—mark this—I tried and tried and could not say my prayers. And then she close her book and walks out of the house, and suddenly—mark this—I could pray again!

Old Giles must be spoken for, if only because his fate was to be so remarkable and so different from that of all the others. He was in his early eighties at this time, and was the most comical hero in the history. No man has ever been blamed for so much. If a cow was missed, the first thought was to look for her around Corey's house; a fire blazing up at night brought suspicion of arson to his door. He didn't give a hoot for public opinion, and only in his last years—after he had married Martha—did he bother much with the church. That she stopped his prayer is very probable, but he forgot to say that he'd only recently learned any prayers and it didn't take much to make him stumble over them. He was a crank and a nuisance, but withal a deeply innocent and brave man. In court once, he was asked if it were true that he had been frightened by the strange behavior of a hog and had then said he knew it to be the Devil in an animal's shape. "What frighted you?" he was asked. He forgot everything but the word "frighted," and instantly replied, "I do not know that I ever spoke that word in my life."

Hale. Ah! The stoppage of prayer—that is strange. I'll speak further on that with you.

Giles. I'm not sayin' she's touched the Devil, now, but I'd admire to know what books she reads and why she hides them. She'll not answer me, y' see.

Hale. Aye, we'll discuss it. (*To all*) Now mark me, if the Devil is in her you will witness some frightful wonders in this room, so please to keep your wits about you. Mr. Putnam, stand close in case she flies. Now, Betty, dear, will you sit up? (Putnam *comes in closer, ready-handed.* Hale *sits* Betty *up, but she hangs limp in his hands.*) Hmmm. (*He observes her carefully. The others watch breathlessly.*) Can you hear me? I am John Hale, minister of Beverly. I have come to help you, dear. Do you remember my two little girls in Beverly? (*She does not stir in his hands.*)

Parris (*in fright*). How can it be the Devil? Why would he choose my house to strike? We have all manner of licentious[41] people in the village!

Hale. What victory would the Devil have to win a soul already bad? It is the best the Devil wants, and who is better than the minister?

Giles. That's deep, Mr. Parris, deep, deep!

Parris (*with resolution now*). Betty! Answer Mr. Hale! Betty!

Hale. Does someone afflict you, child? It need not be a woman, mind you, or a man. Perhaps some bird invisible to others comes to you— perhaps a pig, a mouse, or any beast at all. Is there some figure bids you fly? (*The child remains limp in his hands. In silence he lays her back on the pillow. Now, holding out his hands toward her, he intones*) In nomine Domini Sabaoth sui filiique ite ad infernos.[42] (*She does not stir. He turns to* Abigail, *his eyes narrowing.*) Abigail, what sort of dancing were you doing with her in the forest?

---

41. **licentious** (lī-sĕn′shəs): lacking moral restraint.

42. **In . . . infernos** *Latin:* "In the name of the Father and Son, get thee back to Hell."

Abigail. Why—common dancing is all.

Parris. I think I ought to say that I—I saw a kettle in the grass where they were dancing.

Abigail. That were only soup.

Hale. What sort of soup were in this kettle, Abigail?

Abigail. Why, it were beans—and lentils, I think, and—

Hale. Mr. Parris, you did not notice, did you, any living thing in the kettle? A mouse, perhaps, a spider, a frog—?

Parris (*fearfully*). I—do believe there were some movement—in the soup.

Abigail. That jumped in, we never put it in!

Hale (*quickly*). What jumped in?

Abigail. Why, a very little frog jumped—

Parris. A frog, Abby!

Hale (*grasping* Abigail). Abigail, it may be your cousin is dying. Did you call the Devil last night?

Abigail. I never called him! Tituba, Tituba . . .

Parris (*blanched*).[43] She called the Devil?

Hale. I should like to speak with Tituba.

Parris. Goody Ann, will you bring her up? (*Mrs. Putnam exits.*)

Hale. How did she call him?

Abigail. I know not—she spoke Barbados.

Hale. Did you feel any strangeness when she called him? A sudden cold wind, perhaps? A trembling below the ground?

Abigail. I didn't see no Devil! (*Shaking* Betty) Betty, wake up. Betty! Betty!

Hale. You cannot evade me, Abigail. Did your cousin drink any of the brew in that kettle?

Abigail. She never drank it!

Hale. Did you drink it?

Abigail. No, sir!

Hale. Did Tituba ask you to drink it?

Abigail. She tried, but I refused.

Hale. Why are you concealing? Have you sold yourself to Lucifer?

Abigail. I never sold myself! I'm a good girl! I'm a proper girl!

(Mrs. Putnam *enters with* Tituba, *and instantly* Abigail *points at* Tituba.)

Abigail. She made me do it! She made Betty do it!

Tituba (*shocked and angry*). Abby!

Abigail. She makes me drink blood!

Parris. Blood!!

Mrs. Putnam. My baby's blood?

Tituba. No, no, chicken blood. I give she chicken blood!

Hale. Woman, have you enlisted these children for the Devil?

Tituba. No, no, sir, I don't truck with no Devil!

Hale. Why can she not wake? Are you silencing this child?

Tituba. I love me Betty!

Hale. You have sent your spirit out upon this child, have you not? Are you gathering souls for the Devil?

Abigail. She sends her spirit on me in church; she makes me laugh at prayer!

Parris. She have often laughed at prayer!

Abigail. She comes to me every night to go and drink blood!

Tituba. You beg me to conjure! She beg me make charm—

Abigail. Don't lie! (*To* Hale) She comes to me while I sleep; she's always making me dream corruptions![44]

Tituba. Why you say that, Abby?

Abigail. Sometimes I wake and find myself standing in the open doorway and not a stitch on my body! I always hear her laughing in my sleep. I hear her singing her Barbados songs and tempting me with—

---

43. **blanched:** turned pale with shock or fear.

44. **corruptions:** evil, immoral thoughts.

Tituba. Mister Reverend, I never—

Hale (*resolved now*). Tituba, I want you to wake this child.

Tituba. I have no power on this child, sir.

Hale. You most certainly do, and you will free her from it now! When did you compact with the Devil?

Tituba. I don't compact with no Devil!

Parris. You will confess yourself or I will take you out and whip you to your death, Tituba!

Putnam. This woman must be hanged! She must be taken and hanged!

Tituba (*terrified, falls to her knees*). No, no, don't hang Tituba! I tell him I don't desire to work for him, sir.

Parris. The Devil?

Hale. Then you saw him! (Tituba *weeps*.) Now Tituba, I know that when we bind ourselves to Hell it is very hard to break with it. We are going to help you tear yourself free—

Tituba (*frightened by the coming process*). Mister Reverend, I do believe somebody else be witchin' these children.

Hale. Who?

Tituba. I don't know, sir, but the Devil got him numerous witches.

Hale. Does he! It is a clue. Tituba, look into my eyes. Come, look into me. (*She raises her eyes to his fearfully.*) You would be a good Christian woman, would you not, Tituba?

Tituba. Aye, sir, a good Christian woman.

Hale. And you love these little children?

Tituba. Oh, yes, sir, I don't desire to hurt little children.

Hale. And you love God, Tituba?

Tituba. I love God with all my bein'.

Hale. Now, in God's holy name—

Tituba. Bless Him. Bless Him. (*She is rocking on her knees, sobbing in terror.*)

Hale. And to His glory—

Tituba. Eternal glory. Bless Him—bless God . . .

Hale. Open yourself, Tituba—open yourself and let God's holy light shine on you.

Tituba. Oh, bless the Lord.

Hale. When the Devil comes to you does he ever come—with another person? (*She stares up into his face.*) Perhaps another person in the village? Someone you know.

Parris. Who came with him?

Putnam. Sarah Good? Did you ever see Sarah Good with him? Or Osburn?

Parris. Was it man or woman came with him?

Tituba. Man or woman. Was—was woman.

Parris. What woman? A woman, you said. What woman?

Tituba. It was black dark, and I—

Parris. You could see him, why could you not see her?

Tituba. Well, they was always talking; they was always runnin' round and carryin' on—

Parris. You mean out of Salem? Salem witches?

Tituba. I believe so, yes, sir.

(*Now* Hale *takes her hand. She is surprised.*)

Hale. Tituba. You must have no fear to tell us who they are, do you understand? We will protect you. The Devil can never overcome a minister. You know that, do you not?

Tituba (*kisses Hale's hand*). Aye, sir, oh, I do.

Hale. You have confessed yourself to witchcraft, and that speaks a wish to come to Heaven's side. And we will bless you, Tituba.

Tituba (*deeply relieved*). Oh, God bless you, Mr. Hale!

Hale (*with rising exaltation*). You are God's instrument put in our hands to discover the Devil's agents among us. You are selected, Tituba, you are chosen to help us cleanse our village. So speak utterly, Tituba, turn your back on him and face God—face God, Tituba, and God will protect you.

Tituba (*joining with him*). Oh, God, protect Tituba!

Hale (*kindly*). Who came to you with the Devil? Two? Three? Four? How many?

(Tituba *pants, and begins rocking back and forth again, staring ahead.*)

Tituba. There was four. There was four.

Parris (*pressing in on her*). Who? Who? Their names, their names!

Tituba (*suddenly bursting out*). Oh, how many times he bid me kill you, Mr. Parris!

Parris. Kill me!

Tituba (*in a fury*). He say Mr. Parris must be kill! Mr. Parris no goodly man, Mr. Parris mean man and no gentle man, and he bid me rise out of my bed and cut your throat! (*They gasp.*) But I tell him "No! I don't hate that man. I don't want kill that man." But he say, "You work for me, Tituba, and I make you free! I give you pretty dress to wear, and put you way high up in the air, and you gone fly back to Barbados!" And I say, "You lie, Devil, you lie!" And then he come one stormy night to me, and he say, "Look! I have white people belong to me." And I look—and there was Goody Good.

Parris. Sarah Good!

Tituba (*rocking and weeping*). Aye, sir, and Goody Osburn.

Mrs. Putnam. I knew it! Goody Osburn were midwife to me three times. I begged you, Thomas, did I not? I begged him not to call Osburn because I feared her. My babies always shriveled in her hands!

Hale. Take courage, you must give us all their names. How can you bear to see this child suffering? Look at her, Tituba. (*He is indicating Betty on the bed.*) Look at her God-given innocence; her soul is so tender; we must protect her, Tituba; the Devil is out and preying on her like a beast upon the flesh of the pure lamb. God will bless you for your help.

(Abigail *rises, staring as though inspired, and cries out.*)

Abigail. I want to open myself! (*They turn to her, startled. She is enraptured, as though in a pearly light.*) I want the light of God, I want the sweet love of Jesus! I danced for the Devil; I saw him; I wrote in his book; I go back to Jesus; I kiss His hand. I saw Sarah Good with the Devil! I saw Goody Osburn with the Devil! I saw Bridget Bishop with the Devil!

(As *she is speaking, Betty is rising from the bed, a fever in her eyes, and picks up the chant.*)

Betty (*staring too*). I saw George Jacobs with the Devil! I saw Goody Howe with the Devil!

Parris. She speaks! (*He rushes to embrace Betty.*) She speaks!

Hale. Glory to God! It is broken, they are free!

Betty (*calling out hysterically and with great relief*). I saw Martha Bellows with the Devil!

Abigail. I saw Goody Sibber with the Devil! (*It is rising to a great glee.*)

Putnam. The marshal, I'll call the marshal!

(Parris *is shouting a prayer of thanksgiving.*)

Betty. I saw Alice Barrow with the Devil!

(*The curtain begins to fall.*)

Hale (*as Putnam goes out*). Let the marshal bring irons![45]

Abigail. I saw Goody Hawkins with the Devil!

Betty. I saw Goody Bibber with the Devil!

Abigail. I saw Goody Booth with the Devil!

(*On their ecstatic cries*)

the curtain falls

---

45. **irons:** iron chains and manacles for criminals.

Thinking *through the* LITERATURE

Connect to the Literature

1. **What Do You Think?** Do you believe the accusations made at the end of this act? Why or why not?

> **Comprehension Check**
> - Who discovers Betty and the other girls dancing in the forest?
> - Name one symptom shown by the afflicted girls—Betty Parris and Ruth Putnam.
> - Why does Reverend Hale come to Salem?

Think Critically

2. Why do you think Tituba admits so quickly to having practiced witchcraft?

3. **ACTIVE READING   USING A GRAPHIC ORGANIZER** Refer to the chart you made in your **📖 READER'S NOTEBOOK.** How would you describe Abigail Williams's most important **character traits?**

 THINK ABOUT
- her conduct in the woods
- her attitude toward Reverend Parris
- her comments about Elizabeth Proctor
- her conversation with John Proctor
- her accusations at the end of this act

4. Is John Proctor basically an admirable **character,** or not? Support your opinion with evidence from this act.

5. Throughout this act, Miller includes information about land disputes, lawsuits, and job appointments. What effect do you predict this new crisis of suspected witchcraft will have on the community?

Extend Interpretations

6. **What If?** What do you think would have happened if Tituba had not confessed to practicing witchcraft?

7. **Connect to Life** At the end of this act, Tituba, Abigail, and others accuse some of their neighbors of afflicting them. Give examples of individuals or groups today who accuse others of causing their problems. How would you evaluate their accusations?

8. **Points of Comparison** Consider the Puritan beliefs that you explored while reading and discussing the excerpt from Jonathan Edwards's sermon "Sinners in the Hands of an Angry God." Which of those beliefs do you see reflected in Reverend Hale's motives and actions?

Literary Analysis

STAGE DIRECTIONS The **stage directions** of a play—the instructions for the director, the performers, and the stage crew—provide information about any or all of the following:

- the time and place of the action
- how characters look, move, speak, and feel
- the scenery, props, lighting, costumes, music, and other sound effects used in a performance

In *The Crucible,* Miller's stage directions sometimes become "mini-essays," providing historical background about the Puritans and their beliefs, biographical information about the historical figures upon whom the characters are based, or social commentary drawing parallels between circumstances in Salem and those in America after World War II. For example, in the stage directions just after Reverend Hale's entrance, Miller provides social commentary, observing that in the America of his day "any man who is not reactionary in his views is open to the charge of alliance with the Red hell."

Cooperative Learning Activity
Get together with a small group of classmates and review the stage directions for this act. Then create a chart with two columns. In the first column, list at least three details that helped you imagine one of the important characters in the play, such as Abigail Williams or John Proctor. In the second column, list three or more insights about America after the second world war that Miller conveys to his readers. Share your charts with other groups.

Act Two

(*The common room of* Proctor's *house, eight days later.*)

(*At the right is a door opening on the fields outside. A fireplace is at the left, and behind it a stairway leading upstairs. It is the low, dark, and rather long living room of the time. As the curtain rises, the room is empty. From above,* Elizabeth *is heard softly singing to the children. Presently the door opens and* John Proctor *enters, carrying his gun. He glances about the room as he comes toward the fireplace, then halts for an instant as he hears her singing. He continues on to the fireplace, leans the gun against the wall as he swings a pot out of the fire and smells it. Then he lifts out the ladle and tastes. He is not quite pleased. He reaches to a cupboard, takes a pinch of salt, and drops it into the pot. As he is tasting again, her footsteps are heard on the stair. He swings the pot into the fireplace and goes to a basin and washes his hands and face.* Elizabeth *enters.*)

Elizabeth. What keeps you so late? It's almost dark.

Proctor. I were planting far out to the forest edge.

Elizabeth. Oh, you're done then.

Proctor. Aye, the farm is seeded. The boys asleep?

Elizabeth. They will be soon. (*And she goes to the fireplace, proceeds to ladle up stew in a dish.*)

Proctor. Pray now for a fair summer.

Elizabeth. Aye.

Proctor. Are you well today?

Elizabeth. I am. (*She brings the plate to the table, and, indicating the food*) It is a rabbit.

Proctor (*going to the table*). Oh, is it! In Jonathan's trap?

Elizabeth. No, she walked into the house this afternoon; I found her sittin' in the corner like she come to visit.

Proctor. Oh, that's a good sign walkin' in.

Elizabeth. Pray God. It hurt my heart to strip her, poor rabbit. (*She sits and watches him taste it.*)

Proctor. It's well seasoned.

Elizabeth (*blushing with pleasure*). I took great care. She's tender?

Proctor. Aye. (*He eats. She watches him.*) I think we'll see green fields soon. It's warm as blood beneath the clods.

Elizabeth. That's well.

(Proctor *eats, then looks up.*)

Proctor. If the crop is good I'll buy George Jacob's heifer. How would that please you?

Elizabeth. Aye, it would.

Proctor (*with a grin*). I mean to please you, Elizabeth.

Elizabeth (*it is hard to say*). I know it, John.

(*He gets up, goes to her, kisses her. She receives it. With a certain disappointment, he returns to the table.*)

Proctor (*as gently as he can*). Cider?

Elizabeth (*with a sense of reprimanding herself for having forgot*). Aye! (*She gets up and goes and pours a glass for him. He now arches his back.*)

Proctor. This farm's a continent when you go foot by foot droppin' seeds in it.

Elizabeth (*coming with the cider*). It must be.

Proctor (*drinks a long draught, then, putting the glass down*). You ought to bring some flowers in the house.

Elizabeth. Oh! I forgot! I will tomorrow.

Proctor. It's winter in here yet. On Sunday let you come with me, and we'll walk the farm together;

I never see such a load of flowers on the earth. (*With good feeling he goes and looks up at the sky through the open doorway.*) Lilacs have a purple smell. Lilac is the smell of nightfall, I think. Massachusetts is a beauty in the spring!

Elizabeth. Aye, it is.(*There is a pause. She is watching him from the table as he stands there absorbing the night. It is as though she would speak but cannot. Instead, now, she takes up his plate and glass and fork and goes with them to the basin. Her back is turned to him. He turns to her and watches her. A sense of their separation rises.*)

Proctor. I think you're sad again. Are you?

Elizabeth (*she doesn't want friction, and yet she must*). You come so late I thought you'd gone to Salem this afternoon.

Proctor. Why? I have no business in Salem.

Elizabeth. You did speak of going, earlier this week.

Proctor (*he knows what she means*). I thought better of it since.

Elizabeth. Mary Warren's there today.

Proctor. Why'd you let her? You heard me forbid her go to Salem any more!

Elizabeth. I couldn't stop her.

Proctor (*holding back a full condemnation of her*). It is a fault, it is a fault, Elizabeth—you're the mistress here, not Mary Warren.

Elizabeth. She frightened all my strength away.

Proctor. How may that mouse frighten you, Elizabeth? You—

Elizabeth. It is a mouse no more. I forbid her go, and she raises up her chin like the daughter of a prince and says to me, "I must go to Salem, Goody Proctor; I am an official of the court!"

Proctor. Court! What court?

Elizabeth. Aye, it is a proper court they have now. They've sent four judges out of Boston, she says, weighty magistrates of the General Court, and at the head sits the Deputy Governor of the Province.

Proctor (*astonished*). Why, she's mad.

Elizabeth. I would to God she were. There be fourteen people in the jail now, she says. (Proctor *simply looks at her, unable to grasp it.*) And they'll be tried, and the court have power to hang them too, she says.

Proctor (*scoffing, but without conviction*). Ah, they'd never hang—

Elizabeth. The Deputy Governor promise hangin' if they'll not confess, John. The town's gone wild, I think. She speak of Abigail, and I thought she were a saint, to hear her. Abigail brings the other girls into the court, and where she walks the crowd will part like the sea for Israel. And folks are brought before them, and if they scream and howl and fall to the floor— the person's clapped in the jail for bewitchin' them.

Proctor (*wide-eyed*). Oh, it is a black mischief.

Elizabeth. I think you must go to Salem, John. (*He turns to her.*) I think so. You must tell them it is a fraud.

Proctor (*thinking beyond this*). Aye, it is, it is surely.

Elizabeth. Let you go to Ezekiel Cheever—he knows you well. And tell him what she said to you last week in her uncle's house. She said it had naught to do with witchcraft, did she not?

Proctor (*in thought*). Aye, she did, she did. (*Now, a pause.*)

Elizabeth (*quietly, fearing to anger him by prodding*). God forbid you keep that from the court, John. I think they must be told.

Proctor (*quietly, struggling with his thought*). Aye, they must, they must. It is a wonder they do believe her.

Elizabeth. I would go to Salem now, John—let you go tonight.

Proctor. I'll think on it.

Elizabeth (*with her courage now*). You cannot keep it, John.

Proctor (*angering*). I know I cannot keep it. I say I will think on it!

Elizabeth (*hurt, and very coldly*). Good, then, let you think on it. (*She stands and starts to walk out of the room.*)

Elizabeth Proctor

Proctor. I am only wondering how I may prove what she told me, Elizabeth. If the girl's a saint now, I think it is not easy to prove she's fraud, and the town gone so silly. She told it to me in a room alone—I have no proof for it.

Elizabeth. You were alone with her?

Proctor (*stubbornly*). For a moment alone, aye.

Elizabeth. Why, then, it is not as you told me.

Proctor (*his anger rising*). For a moment, I say. The others come in soon after.

Elizabeth (*quietly—she has suddenly lost all faith in him*). Do as you wish, then. (*She starts to turn.*)

Proctor. Woman. (*She turns to him.*) I'll not have your suspicion any more.

Elizabeth (*a little loftily*). I have no—

Proctor. I'll not have it!

Elizabeth. Then let you not earn it.

Proctor (*with a violent undertone*). You doubt me yet?

Elizabeth (*with a smile, to keep her dignity*). John, if it were not Abigail that you must go to hurt, would you falter now? I think not.

Proctor. Now look you—

Elizabeth. I see what I see, John.

Proctor (*with solemn warning*). You will not judge me more, Elizabeth. I have good reason to think before I charge fraud on Abigail, and I will think on it. Let you look to your own improvement before you go to judge your husband any more. I have forgot Abigail, and—

Elizabeth. And I.

Proctor. Spare me! You forget nothin' and forgive nothin'. Learn charity, woman. I have gone tiptoe in this house all seven month since she is gone. I have not moved from there to there without I think to please you, and still an everlasting funeral marches round your heart. I cannot speak but I am doubted, every moment judged for lies, as though I come into a court when I come into this house!

Elizabeth. John, you are not open with me. You saw her with a crowd, you said. Now you—

Proctor. I'll plead my honesty no more, Elizabeth.

Elizabeth (*now she would justify herself*). John, I am only—

Proctor. No more! I should have roared you down when first you told me your suspicion. But I wilted, and, like a Christian, I confessed. Confessed! Some dream I had must have mistaken you for God that day. But you're not, you're not, and let you remember it! Let you look sometimes for the goodness in me, and judge me not.

Elizabeth. I do not judge you. The magistrate sits in your heart that judges you. I never thought you but a good man, John—(*with a smile*)—only somewhat bewildered.

Proctor (*laughing bitterly*). Oh, Elizabeth, your justice would freeze beer![46] (*He turns suddenly toward a sound outside. He starts for the door as* Mary Warren *enters. As soon as he sees her, he goes directly to her and grabs her by her cloak, furious.*) How do you go to Salem when I forbid it? Do you mock me? (*Shaking her.*) I'll whip you if you dare leave this house again!

(*Strangely, she doesn't resist him, but hangs limply by his grip.*)

Mary Warren. I am sick, I am sick, Mr. Proctor. Pray, pray, hurt me not. (*Her strangeness throws him off, and her evident pallor and weakness. He frees her.*) My insides are all shuddery; I am in the proceedings all day, sir.

Proctor (*with draining anger—his curiosity is draining it*). And what of these proceedings here? When will you proceed to keep this house, as you are paid nine pound a year to do—and my wife not wholly well?

(*As though to compensate,* Mary Warren *goes to* Elizabeth *with a small rag doll.*)

Mary Warren. I made a gift for you today, Goody Proctor. I had to sit long hours in a chair, and passed the time with sewing.

Elizabeth (*perplexed, looking at the doll*). Why, thank you, it's a fair poppet.[47]

Mary Warren (*with a trembling, decayed voice*). We must all love each other now, Goody Proctor.

Elizabeth (*amazed at her strangeness*). Aye, indeed we must.

Mary Warren (*glancing at the room*). I'll get up early in the morning and clean the house. I must sleep now. (*She turns and starts off.*)

Proctor. Mary. (*She halts.*) Is it true? There be fourteen women arrested?

Mary Warren. No, sir. There be thirty-nine now— (*She suddenly breaks off and sobs and sits down, exhausted.*)

Elizabeth. Why, she's weepin'! What ails you, child?

Mary Warren. Goody Osburn—will hang!

(*There is a shocked pause, while she sobs.*)

---

46. **your justice . . . beer:** alcoholic beverages freeze at very low temperatures, so Proctor is sarcastically calling his wife cold-hearted.

47. **fair poppet:** pretty doll.

Proctor. Hang! (*He calls into her face.*) Hang, y'say?

Mary Warren (*through her weeping*). Aye.

Proctor. The Deputy Governor will permit it?

Mary Warren. He sentenced her. He must. (*To ameliorate[48] it.*) But not Sarah Good. For Sarah Good confessed, y'see.

Proctor. Confessed! To what?

Mary Warren. That she—(*in horror at the memory*)—she sometimes made a compact with Lucifer, and wrote her name in his black book—with her blood—and bound herself to torment Christians till God's thrown down—and we all must worship Hell forevermore.

(*Pause.*)

Proctor. But—surely you know what a jabberer she is. Did you tell them that?

Mary Warren. Mr. Proctor, in open court she near to choked us all to death.

Proctor. How, choked you?

Mary Warren. She sent her spirit out.

Elizabeth. Oh, Mary, Mary, surely you—

Mary Warren (*with an indignant edge*). She tried to kill me many times, Goody Proctor!

Elizabeth. Why, I never heard you mention that before.

Mary Warren. I never knew it before. I never knew anything before. When she come into the court I say to myself, I must not accuse this woman, for she sleep in ditches, and so very old and poor. But then—then she sit there, denying and denying, and I feel a misty coldness climbin' up my back, and the skin on my skull begin to creep, and I feel a clamp around my neck and I cannot breathe air; and then—(*entranced*)—I hear a voice, a screamin' voice, and it were my voice—and all at once I remembered everything she done to me!

Proctor. Why? What did she do to you?

Mary Warren (*like one awakened to a marvelous secret insight*). So many time, Mr. Proctor, she come to this very door, beggin' bread and a cup of cider—and mark this: whenever I turned her away empty, she mumbled.

Elizabeth. Mumbled! She may mumble if she's hungry.

Mary Warren. But what does she mumble? You must remember, Goody Proctor. Last month—a Monday, I think—she walked away, and I thought my guts would burst for two days after. Do you remember it?

Elizabeth. Why—I do, I think, but—

Mary Warren. And so I told that to Judge Hathorne, and he asks her so. "Sarah Good," says he, "what curse do you mumble that this girl must fall sick after turning you away?" (*And then she replies—mimicking an old crone*)—"Why, your excellence, no curse at all. I only say my commandments;[49] I hope I may say my commandments," says she!

Elizabeth. And that's an upright answer.

Mary Warren. Aye, but then Judge Hathorne say, "Recite for us your commandments!"—(*leaning avidly toward them*)—and of all the ten she could not say a single one. She never knew no commandments, and they had her in a flat lie!

Proctor. And so condemned her?

Mary Warren (*now a little strained, seeing his stubborn doubt*). Why, they must when she condemned herself.

Proctor. But the proof, the proof!

Mary Warren (*with greater impatience with him*). I told you the proof. It's hard proof, hard as rock, the judges said.

Proctor (*pauses an instant, then*). You will not go to court again, Mary Warren.

---

48. **ameliorate** (ə-mēl′yə-rāt′): improve.
49. **commandments:** the biblical Ten Commandments.

WORDS TO KNOW   **indignant** (ĭn-dĭg′nənt) *adj.* filled with anger caused by something unjust or mean

Mary Warren. I must tell you, sir, I will be gone every day now. I am amazed you do not see what weighty work we do.

Proctor. What work you do! It's strange work for a Christian girl to hang old women!

Mary Warren. But, Mr. Proctor, they will not hang them if they confess. Sarah Good will only sit in jail some time—(*recalling*)—and here's a wonder for you; think on this. Goody Good is pregnant!

Elizabeth. Pregnant! Are they mad? The woman's near to sixty!

Mary Warren. They had Doctor Griggs examine her, and she's full to the brim. And smokin' a pipe all these years, and no husband either! But she's safe, thank God, for they'll not hurt the innocent child. But be that not a marvel? You must see it, sir, it's God's work we do. So I'll be gone every day for some time. I'm—I am an official of the court, they say, and I—(*She has been edging toward offstage.*)

Proctor. I'll official you! (*He strides to the mantel, takes down the whip hanging there.*)

Mary Warren (*terrified, but coming erect, striving for her authority*). I'll not stand whipping any more!

Elizabeth (*hurriedly, as* Proctor *approaches*). Mary, promise now you'll stay at home—

Mary Warren (*backing from him, but keeping her erect posture, striving, striving for her way*). The Devil's loose in Salem, Mr. Proctor; we must discover where he's hiding!

Proctor. I'll whip the Devil out of you! (*With whip raised he reaches out for her, and she streaks away and yells.*)

Mary Warren (*pointing at* Elizabeth). I saved her life today!

(*Silence. His whip comes down.*)

Elizabeth (*softly*). I am accused?

Mary Warren (*quaking*). Somewhat mentioned. But I said I never see no sign you ever sent your spirit out to hurt no one, and seeing I do live so closely with you, they dismissed it.

Elizabeth. Who accused me?

Mary Warren. I am bound by law, I cannot tell it. (*To* Proctor) I only hope you'll not be so sarcastical no more. Four judges and the King's deputy sat to dinner with us but an hour ago. I—I would have you speak civilly to me, from this out.

Proctor (*in horror, muttering in disgust at her*). Go to bed.

Mary Warren (*with a stamp of her foot*). I'll not be ordered to bed no more, Mr. Proctor! I am eighteen and a woman, however single!

Proctor. Do you wish to sit up? Then sit up.

Mary Warren. I wish to go to bed!

Proctor (*in anger*). Good night, then!

Mary Warren. Good night. (*Dissatisfied, uncertain of herself, she goes out. Wide-eyed, both,* Proctor *and* Elizabeth *stand staring.*)

Elizabeth (*quietly*). Oh, the noose, the noose is up!

Proctor. There'll be no noose.

Elizabeth. She wants me dead. I knew all week it would come to this!

Proctor (*without conviction*). They dismissed it. You heard her say—

Elizabeth. And what of tomorrow? She will cry me out until they take me!

Proctor. Sit you down.

Elizabeth. She wants me dead, John, you know it!

Proctor. I say sit down! (*She sits, trembling. He speaks quietly, trying to keep his wits.*) Now we must be wise, Elizabeth.

Elizabeth (*with sarcasm, and a sense of being lost*). Oh, indeed, indeed!

Proctor. Fear nothing. I'll find Ezekiel Cheever. I'll tell him she said it were all sport.

Elizabeth. John, with so many in the jail, more than Cheever's help is needed now, I think. Would you favor me with this? Go to Abigail.

Proctor (*his soul hardening as he senses . . .*). What have I to say to Abigail?

Elizabeth (*delicately*). John—grant me this. You have a faulty understanding of young girls. There is a promise made in any bed—

Proctor (*striving against his anger*). What promise!

Elizabeth. Spoke or silent, a promise is surely made. And she may dote on it now—I am sure she does—and thinks to kill me, then to take my place.

(*Proctor's anger is rising; he cannot speak.*)

Elizabeth. It is her dearest hope, John, I know it. There be a thousand names; why does she call mine? There be a certain danger in calling such a name—I am no Goody Good that sleeps in ditches, nor Osburn, drunk and half-witted. She'd dare not call out such a farmer's wife but there be monstrous[50] profit in it. She thinks to take my place, John.

Proctor. She cannot think it! (*He knows it is true.*)

Elizabeth (*"reasonably"*). John, have you ever shown her somewhat of contempt? She cannot pass you in the church but you will blush—

Proctor. I may blush for my sin.

Elizabeth. I think she sees another meaning in that blush.

Proctor. And what see you? What see you, Elizabeth?

Elizabeth (*"conceding"*). I think you be somewhat ashamed, for I am there, and she so close.

Proctor. When will you know me, woman? Were I stone I would have cracked for shame this seven month!

Elizabeth. Then go and tell her she's a whore. Whatever promise she may sense—break it, John, break it.

Proctor (*between his teeth*). Good, then. I'll go. (*He starts for his rifle.*)

Elizabeth (*trembling, fearfully*). Oh, how unwillingly!

Proctor (*turning on her, rifle in hand*). I will curse her hotter than the oldest cinder in hell. But pray, begrudge me not my anger!

Elizabeth. Your anger! I only ask you—

Proctor. Woman, am I so base?[51] Do you truly think me base?

Elizabeth. I never called you base.

Proctor. Then how do you charge me with such a promise? The promise that a stallion gives a mare I gave that girl!

Elizabeth. Then why do you anger with me when I bid you break it?

Proctor. Because it speaks deceit, and I am honest! But I'll plead no more! I see now your spirit twists around the single error of my life, and I will never tear it free!

Elizabeth (*crying out*). You'll tear it free—when you come to know that I will be your only wife, or no wife at all! She has an arrow in you yet, John Proctor, and you know it well!

(*Quite suddenly, as though from the air, a figure appears in the doorway. They start slightly. It is Mr. Hale. He is different now—drawn a little, and there is a quality of deference, even of guilt, about his manner now.*)

Hale. Good evening.

Proctor (*still in his shock*). Why, Mr. Hale! Good evening to you, sir. Come in, come in.

Hale (*to* Elizabeth). I hope I do not startle you.

Elizabeth. No, no, it's only that I heard no horse—

Hale. You are Goodwife Proctor.

Proctor. Aye; Elizabeth.

Hale (*nods, then*). I hope you're not off to bed yet.

Proctor (*setting down his gun*). No, no. (Hale *comes further into the room. And* Proctor, *to explain his nervousness*) We are not used to visitors after dark, but you're welcome here. Will you sit you down, sir?

---

50. **monstrous:** tremendous.

51. **base:** having low moral standards.

Hale. I will. (*He sits.*) Let you sit, Goodwife Proctor.

(*She does, never letting him out of her sight. There is a pause as* Hale *looks about the room.*)

Proctor (*to break the silence*). Will you drink cider, Mr. Hale?

Hale. No, it rebels[52] my stomach; I have some further traveling yet tonight. Sit you down, sir. (Proctor *sits.*) I will not keep you long, but I have some business with you.

Proctor. Business of the court?

Hale. No—no, I come of my own, without the court's authority. Hear me. (*He wets his lips.*) I know not if you are aware, but your wife's name is—mentioned in the court.

Proctor. We know it, sir. Our Mary Warren told us. We are entirely amazed.

Hale. I am a stranger here, as you know. And in my ignorance I find it hard to draw a clear opinion of them that come accused before the court. And so this afternoon, and now tonight, I go from house to house—I come now from Rebecca Nurse's house and—

Elizabeth (*shocked*). Rebecca's charged!

Hale. God forbid such a one be charged. She is, however—mentioned somewhat.

Elizabeth (*with an attempt at a laugh*). You will never believe, I hope, that Rebecca trafficked with the Devil.

Hale. Woman, it is possible.

Proctor (*taken aback*). Surely you cannot think so.

Hale. This is a strange time, Mister. No man may longer doubt the powers of the dark are gathered in monstrous attack upon this village. There is too much evidence now to deny it. You will agree, sir?

Proctor (*evading*). I—have no knowledge in that line. But it's hard to think so pious[53] a woman be secretly a Devil's bitch after seventy year of such good prayer.

Hale. Aye. But the Devil is a wily one, you cannot deny it. However, she is far from accused, and

I know she will not be. (*Pause.*) I thought, sir, to put some questions as to the Christian character of this house, if you'll permit me.

Proctor (*coldly, resentful*). Why, we—have no fear of questions, sir.

Hale. Good, then. (*He makes himself more comfortable.*) In the book of record that Mr. Parris keeps, I note that you are rarely in the church on Sabbath Day.

Proctor. No, sir, you are mistaken.

Hale. Twenty-six time in seventeen month, sir. I must call that rare. Will you tell me why you are so absent?

Proctor. Mr. Hale, I never knew I must account to that man for I come to church or stay at home. My wife were sick this winter.

Hale. So I am told. But you, Mister, why could you not come alone?

Proctor. I surely did come when I could, and when I could not I prayed in this house.

Hale. Mr. Proctor, your house is not a church; your theology must tell you that.

Proctor. It does, sir, it does; and it tells me that a minister may pray to God without he have golden candlesticks upon the altar.

Hale. What golden candlesticks?

Proctor. Since we built the church there were pewter candlesticks upon the altar; Francis Nurse made them, y'know, and a sweeter hand never touched the metal. But Parris came, and for twenty week he preach nothin' but golden candlesticks until he had them. I labor the earth from dawn of day to blink of night, and I tell you true, when I look to heaven and see my money glaring at his elbows—it hurt my prayer, sir, it hurt my prayer. I think, sometimes, the man dreams cathedrals, not clapboard meetin' houses.

---

52. **rebels:** upsets.

53. **pious** (pī′əs): religious.

Hale (*thinks, then*). And yet, Mister, a Christian on Sabbath Day must be in church. (*Pause.*) Tell me—you have three children?

Proctor. Aye. Boys.

Hale. How comes it that only two are baptized?

Proctor (*starts to speak, then stops, then, as though unable to restrain this*). I like it not that Mr. Parris should lay his hand upon my baby. I see no light of God in that man. I'll not conceal it.

Hale. I must say it, Mr. Proctor; that is not for you to decide. The man's ordained, therefore the light of God is in him.

Proctor (*flushed with resentment but trying to smile*). What's your suspicion, Mr. Hale?

Hale. No, no, I have no—

Proctor. I nailed the roof upon the church, I hung the door—

Hale. Oh, did you! That's a good sign, then.

Proctor. It may be I have been too quick to bring the man to book,[54] but you cannot think we ever desired the destruction of religion. I think that's in your mind, is it not?

Hale (*not altogether giving way*). I—have—there is a softness in your record, sir, a softness.

Elizabeth. I think, maybe, we have been too hard with Mr. Parris. I think so. But sure we never loved the Devil here.

Hale (*nods, deliberating this. Then, with the voice of one administering a secret test*). Do you know your Commandments, Elizabeth?

Elizabeth (*without hesitation, even eagerly*). I surely do. There be no mark of blame upon my life, Mr. Hale. I am a convenanted Christian woman.

Hale. And you, Mister?

Proctor (*a trifle unsteadily*). I—am sure I do, sir.

Hale (*glances at her open face, then at John, then*). Let you repeat them, if you will.

Proctor. The Commandments.

Hale. Aye.

Proctor (*looking off, beginning to sweat*). Thou shalt not kill.

Hale. Aye.

Proctor (*counting on his fingers*). Thou shalt not steal. Thou shalt not covet thy neighbor's goods, nor make unto thee any graven image. Thou shalt not take the name of the Lord in vain; thou shalt have no other gods before me. (*With some hesitation.*) Thou shalt remember the Sabbath Day and keep it holy. (*Pause. Then.*) Thou shalt honor thy father and mother. Thou shalt not bear false witness. (*He is stuck. He counts back on his fingers, knowing one is missing.*) Thou shalt not make unto thee any graven image.

Hale. You have said that twice, sir.

Proctor (*lost*). Aye. (*He is flailing[55] for it.*)

Elizabeth (*delicately*). Adultery, John.

Proctor (*as though a secret arrow had pained his heart*). Aye. (*Trying to grin it away—to* Hale) You see, sir, between the two of us we do know them all. (Hale *only looks at* Proctor, *deep in his attempt to define this man.* Proctor *grows more uneasy.*) I think it be a small fault.

Hale. Theology, sir, is a fortress; no crack in a fortress may be accounted small. (*He rises; he seems worried now. He paces a little, in deep thought.*)

Proctor. There be no love for Satan in this house, Mister.

Hale. I pray it, I pray it dearly. (*He looks to both of them, an attempt at a smile on his face, but his misgivings are clear.*) Well, then—I'll bid you good night.

Elizabeth (*unable to restrain herself*). Mr. Hale. (*He turns.*) I do think you are suspecting me somewhat? Are you not?

Hale (*obviously disturbed—and evasive*). Goody Proctor, I do not judge you. My duty is to add

---

54. **bring the man to book:** judge the man.
55. **flailing:** struggling.

what I may to the godly wisdom of the court. I pray you both good health and good fortune. (*To* John) Good night, sir. (*He starts out.*)

Elizabeth (*with a note of desperation*). I think you must tell him, John.

Hale. What's that?

Elizabeth (*restraining a call*). Will you tell him?

(*Slight pause. Hale looks questioningly at* John.)

Proctor (*with difficulty*). I—I have no witness and cannot prove it, except my word be taken. But I know the children's sickness had naught to do with witchcraft.

Hale (*stopped, struck*). Naught to do—?

Proctor. Mr. Parris discovered them sportin' in the woods. They were startled and took sick.

(*Pause.*)

Hale. Who told you this?

Proctor (*hesitates, then*). Abigail Williams.

Hale. Abigail!

Proctor. Aye.

Hale (*his eyes wide*). Abigail Williams told you it had naught to do with witchcraft!

Proctor. She told me the day you came, sir.

Hale (*suspiciously*). Why—why did you keep this?

Proctor. I never knew until tonight that the world is gone daft[56] with this nonsense.

Hale. Nonsense! Mister, I have myself examined Tituba, Sarah Good, and numerous others that have confessed to dealing with the Devil. They have confessed it.

Proctor. And why not, if they must hang for denyin' it? There are them that will swear to anything before they'll hang; have you never thought of that?

Hale. I have. I—I have indeed. (*It is his own suspicion, but he resists it. He glances at* Elizabeth, *then at* John.) And you—would you testify to this in court?

Proctor. I—had not reckoned with goin' into court. But if I must I will.

Hale. Do you falter[57] here?

Proctor. I falter nothing, but I may wonder if my story will be credited in such a court. I do wonder on it, when such a steady-minded minister as you will suspicion such a woman that never lied, and cannot, and the world knows she cannot! I may falter somewhat, Mister; I am no fool.

Hale (*quietly—it has impressed him*). Proctor, let you open with me now, for I have a rumor that troubles me. It's said you hold no belief that there may even be witches in the world. Is that true, sir?

Proctor (*he knows this is critical, and is striving against his disgust with* Hale *and with himself for even answering*). I know not what I have said, I may have said it. I have wondered if there be witches in the world—although I cannot believe they come among us now.

Hale. Then you do not believe—

Proctor. I have no knowledge of it; the Bible speaks of witches, and I will not deny them.

Hale. And you, woman?

Elizabeth. I—I cannot believe it.

Hale (*shocked*). You cannot!

Proctor. Elizabeth, you bewilder him!

Elizabeth (*to* Hale). I cannot think the Devil may own a woman's soul, Mr. Hale, when she keeps an upright way, as I have. I am a good woman, I know it; and if you believe I may do only good work in the world, and yet be secretly bound to Satan, then I must tell you, sir, I do not believe it.

Hale. But, woman, you do believe there are witches in—

Elizabeth. If you think that I am one, then I say there are none.

---

56. **daft:** crazy; mad.
57. **falter:** hesitate.

Hale. You surely do not fly against the Gospel,[58] the Gospel—

Proctor. She believe in the Gospel, every word!

Elizabeth. Question Abigail Williams about the Gospel, not myself!

(Hale *stares at her.*)

Proctor. She do not mean to doubt the Gospel, sir, you cannot think it. This be a Christian house, sir, a Christian house.

Hale. God keep you both; let the third child be quickly baptized, and go you without fail each Sunday in to Sabbath prayer; and keep a solemn, quiet way among you. I think—

(Giles Corey *appears in doorway.*)

Giles. John!

Proctor. Giles! What's the matter?

Giles. They take my wife.

(Francis Nurse *enters.*)

Giles. And his Rebecca!

Proctor (*to* Francis). Rebecca's in the jail!

Francis. Aye, Cheever come and take her in his wagon. We've only now come from the jail, and they'll not even let us in to see them.

Elizabeth. They've surely gone wild now, Mr. Hale!

Francis (*going to* Hale). Reverend Hale! Can you not speak to the Deputy Governor? I'm sure he mistakes these people—

Hale. Pray calm yourself, Mr. Nurse.

Francis. My wife is the very brick and mortar of the church, Mr. Hale—(*indicating* Giles)—and Martha Corey, there cannot be a woman closer yet to God than Martha.

Hale. How is Rebecca charged, Mr. Nurse?

Francis (*with a mocking, half-hearted laugh*). For murder, she's charged! (*Mockingly quoting the warrant*) "For the marvelous and supernatural murder of Goody Putnam's babies." What am I to do, Mr. Hale?

Hale (*turns from* Francis, *deeply troubled, then*). Believe me, Mr. Nurse, if Rebecca Nurse be tainted, then nothing's left to stop the whole green world from burning. Let you rest upon the justice of the court; the court will send her home, I know it.

Francis. You cannot mean she will be tried in court!

Hale (*pleading*). Nurse, though our hearts break, we cannot flinch; these are new times, sir. There is a misty plot afoot so subtle we should be criminal to cling to old respects and ancient friendships. I have seen too many frightful proofs in court—the Devil is alive in Salem, and we dare not quail to follow wherever the accusing finger points!

Proctor (*angered*). How may such a woman murder children?

Hale (*in great pain*). Man, remember, until an hour before the Devil fell, God thought him beautiful in Heaven.[59]

Giles. I never said my wife were a witch, Mr. Hale; I only said she were reading books!

Hale. Mr. Corey, exactly what complaint were made on your wife?

Giles. That bloody mongrel Walcott charge her. Y'see, he buy a pig of my wife four or five year ago, and the pig died soon after. So he come dancin' in for his money back. So my Martha, she says to him, "Walcott, if you haven't the wit to feed a pig properly, you'll not live to own many," she says. Now he goes to court and claims that from that day to this he cannot keep a pig alive for more than four weeks because my Martha bewitch them with her books!

(*Enter* Ezekiel Cheever. *A shocked silence.*)

Cheever. Good evening to you, Proctor.

Proctor. Why, Mr. Cheever. Good evening.

---

58. **the Gospel:** in the Bible, the first four books of the New Testament.

59. **an hour . . . Heaven:** alludes to the Christian belief that Satan was God's favorite angel until Satan rebelled and was cast out of heaven.

Cheever. Good evening, all. Good evening, Mr. Hale.

Proctor. I hope you come not on business of the court.

Cheever. I do, Proctor, aye. I am clerk of the court now, y'know.

(*Enter* Marshal Herrick, *a man in his early thirties, who is somewhat shamefaced at the moment.*)

Giles. It's a pity, Ezekiel, that an honest tailor might have gone to Heaven must burn in Hell. You'll burn for this, do you know it?

Cheever. You know yourself I must do as I'm told. You surely know that, Giles. And I'd as lief[60] you'd not be sending me to Hell. I like not the sound of it, I tell you; I like not the sound of it. (*He fears* Proctor, *but starts to reach inside his coat.*) Now believe me, Proctor, how heavy be the law, all its tonnage I do carry on my back tonight. (*He takes out a warrant.*) I have a warrant for your wife.

Proctor (*to* Hale). You said she were not charged!

Hale. I know nothin' of it. (*To* Cheever) When were she charged?

Cheever. I am given sixteen warrant tonight, sir, and she is one.

Proctor. Who charged her?

Cheever. Why, Abigail Williams charge her.

Proctor. On what proof, what proof?

Cheever (*looking about the room*). Mr. Proctor, I have little time. The court bid me search your house, but I like not to search a house. So will you hand me any poppets that your wife may keep here?

Proctor. Poppets?

Elizabeth. I never kept no poppets, not since I were a girl.

Cheever (*embarrassed, glancing toward the mantel where sits* Mary Warren's *poppet*). I spy a poppet, Goody Proctor.

Elizabeth. Oh! (*Going for it:*) Why, this is Mary's.

Cheever (*shyly*). Would you please to give it to me?

Elizabeth (*handing it to him, asks* Hale). Has the court discovered a text in poppets now?

Cheever (*carefully holding the poppet*). Do you keep any others in this house?

Proctor. No, nor this one either till tonight. What signifies a poppet?

Cheever. Why, a poppet—(*he gingerly turns the poppet over*)—a poppet may signify—Now, woman, will you please to come with me?

Proctor. She will not! (*To* Elizabeth) Fetch Mary here.

Cheever (*ineptly reaching toward* Elizabeth). No, no, I am forbid to leave her from my sight.

Proctor (*pushing his arm away*). You'll leave her out of sight and out of mind, Mister. Fetch Mary, Elizabeth. (Elizabeth *goes upstairs.*)

Hale. What signifies a poppet, Mr. Cheever?

Cheever (*turning the poppet over in his hands*). Why, they say it may signify that she—(*He has lifted the poppet's skirt, and his eyes widen in astonished fear.*) Why, this, this—

Proctor (*reaching for the poppet*). What's there?

Cheever. Why—(*He draws out a long needle from the poppet*)—it is a needle! Herrick, Herrick, it is a needle!

(Herrick *comes toward him.*)

Proctor (*angrily, bewildered*). And what signifies a needle!

Cheever (*his hands shaking*). Why, this go hard with her, Proctor, this—I had my doubts, Proctor, I had my doubts, but here's calamity. (*To* Hale, *showing the needle*) You see it, sir, it is a needle!

Hale. Why? What meanin' has it?

---

60. **as lief** (ăz lēf): rather.

Cheever (*wide-eyed, trembling*). The girl, the Williams girl, Abigail Williams, sir. She sat to dinner in Reverend Parris's house tonight, and without word nor warnin' she falls to the floor. Like a struck beast, he says, and screamed a scream that a bull would weep to hear. And he goes to save her, and, stuck two inches in the flesh of her belly, he draw a needle out. And demandin' of her how she come to be so stabbed, she—(*to Proctor now*)—testify it were your wife's familiar spirit[61] pushed it in.

Proctor. Why, she done it herself! (*To Hale*) I hope you're not takin' this for proof, Mister!

(Hale, *struck by the proof, is silent.*)

Cheever. 'Tis hard proof! (*To Hale*) I find here a poppet Goody Proctor keeps. I have found it, sir. And in the belly of the poppet a needle's stuck. I tell you true, Proctor, I never warranted to see such proof of Hell, and I bid you obstruct me not, for I—

(*Enter Elizabeth with Mary Warren. Proctor, seeing Mary Warren, draws her by the arm to Hale.*)

Proctor. Here now! Mary, how did this poppet come into my house?

Mary Warren (*frightened for herself, her voice very small*). What poppet's that, sir?

Proctor (*impatiently, pointing at the doll in Cheever's hand*). This poppet, this poppet.

Mary Warren (*evasively, looking at it*). Why, I—I think it is mine.

Proctor. It is your poppet, is it not?

Mary Warren (*not understanding the direction of this*). It—is, sir.

Proctor. And how did it come into this house?

Mary Warren (*glancing about at the avid faces*). Why—I made it in the court, sir, and—give it to Goody Proctor tonight.

Proctor (*to Hale*). Now, sir—do you have it?

Hale. Mary Warren, a needle have been found inside this poppet.

Mary Warren (*bewildered*). Why, I meant no harm by it, sir.

Proctor (*quickly*). You stuck that needle in yourself?

Mary Warren. I—I believe I did, sir, I—

Proctor (*to Hale*). What say you now?

Hale (*watching Mary Warren closely*). Child, you are certain this be your natural memory? May it be, perhaps, that someone conjures you even now to say this?

Mary Warren. Conjures me? Why, no, sir, I am entirely myself, I think. Let you ask Susanna Walcott—she saw me sewin' it in court. Or better still: Ask Abby, Abby sat beside me when I made it.

Proctor (*to Hale, of Cheever*). Bid him begone. Your mind is surely settled now. Bid him out, Mr. Hale.

Elizabeth. What signifies a needle?

Hale. Mary—you charge a cold and cruel murder on Abigail.

Mary Warren. Murder! I charge no—

Hale. Abigail were stabbed tonight; a needle were found stuck into her belly—

Elizabeth. And she charges me?

Hale. Aye.

Elizabeth (*her breath knocked out*). Why—! The girl is murder! She must be ripped out of the world!

Cheever (*pointing at Elizabeth*). You've heard that, sir! Ripped out of the world! Herrick, you heard it!

Proctor (*suddenly snatching the warrant out of Cheever's hands*). Out with you.

Cheever. Proctor, you dare not touch the warrant.

Proctor (*ripping the warrant*). Out with you!

Cheever. You've ripped the Deputy Governor's warrant, man!

Proctor. Damn the Deputy Governor! Out of my house!

---

61. **familiar spirit:** the spirit or demon, most usually in the form of an animal such as a black cat, that was a companion and helper to a witch.

Hale. Now, Proctor, Proctor!

Proctor. Get y'gone with them! You are a broken minister.

Hale. Proctor, if she is innocent, the court—

Proctor. If she is innocent! Why do you never wonder if Parris be innocent, or Abigail? Is the accuser always holy now? Were they born this morning as clean as God's fingers? I'll tell you what's walking Salem—vengeance is walking Salem. We are what we always were in Salem, but now the little crazy children are jangling the keys of the kingdom, and common vengeance writes the law! This warrant's vengeance! I'll not give my wife to vengeance!

Elizabeth. I'll go, John—

Proctor. You will not go!

Herrick. I have nine men outside. You cannot keep her. The law binds me, John, I cannot budge.

Proctor (*to* Hale, *ready to break him*). Will you see her taken?

Hale. Proctor, the court is just—

Proctor. Pontius Pilate![62] God will not let you wash your hands of this!

Elizabeth. John—I think I must go with them. (*He cannot bear to look at her.*) Mary, there is bread enough for the morning; you will bake, in the afternoon. Help Mr. Proctor as you were his daughter—you owe me that, and much more. (*She is fighting her weeping. To* Proctor) When the children wake, speak nothing of witchcraft—it will frighten them. (*She cannot go on.*)

Proctor. I will bring you home. I will bring you soon.

Elizabeth. Oh, John, bring me soon!

Proctor. I will fall like an ocean on that court! Fear nothing, Elizabeth.

Elizabeth (*with great fear*). I will fear nothing. (*She looks about the room, as though to fix it in her mind.*) Tell the children I have gone to visit someone sick.

(*She walks out the door,* Herrick *and* Cheever *behind her. For a moment,* Proctor *watches from the doorway. The clank of chain is heard.*)

Proctor. Herrick! Herrick, don't chain her! (*He rushes out the door. From outside*) Damn you, man, you will not chain her! Off with them! I'll not have it! I will not have her chained!

(*There are other men's voices against his.* Hale, *in a fever of guilt and uncertainty, turns from the door to avoid the sight;* Mary Warren *bursts into tears and sits weeping.* Giles Corey *calls to* Hale.)

Giles. And yet silent, minister? It is fraud, you know it is fraud! What keeps you, man?

(Proctor *is half braced, half pushed into the room by two deputies and* Herrick.)

Proctor. I'll pay you, Herrick, I will surely pay you!

Herrick (*panting*). In God's name, John, I cannot help myself. I must chain them all. Now let you keep inside this house till I am gone! (*He goes out with his deputies.*)

(Proctor *stands there, gulping air. Horses and a wagon creaking are heard.*)

Hale (*in great uncertainty*). Mr. Proctor—

Proctor. Out of my sight!

Hale. Charity, Proctor, charity. What I have heard in her favor, I will not fear to testify in court. God help me, I cannot judge her guilty or innocent—I know not. Only this consider: the world goes mad, and it profit nothing you should lay the cause to the vengeance of a little girl.

Proctor. You are a coward! Though you be ordained in God's own tears, you are a coward now!

Hale. Proctor, I cannot think God be provoked so grandly by such a petty cause. The jails are packed—our greatest judges sit in Salem now—

---

62. **Pontius Pilate** (pŏn'chəs pī'lət): the Roman governor who presided over the trial and sentencing of Christ. Pilate publicly washed his hands to absolve himself of responsibility for Christ's death.

and hangin's promised. Man, we must look to cause proportionate. Were there murder done, perhaps, and never brought to light? Abomination? Some secret blasphemy that stinks to Heaven? Think on cause, man, and let you help me to discover it. For there's your way, believe it, there is your only way, when such confusion strikes upon the world. *(He goes to* Giles *and* Francis.*)* Let you counsel among yourselves; think on your village and what may have drawn from heaven such thundering wrath upon you all. I shall pray God open up our eyes.

(Hale goes out.)

Francis *(struck by* Hale's *mood).* I never heard no murder done in Salem.

Proctor *(he has been reached by* Hale's *words).* Leave me, Francis, leave me.

Giles *(shaken).* John—tell me, are we lost?

Proctor. Go home now, Giles. We'll speak on it tomorrow.

Giles. Let you think on it. We'll come early, eh?

Proctor. Aye. Go now, Giles.

Giles. Good night, then.

(Giles Corey goes out. After a moment)

Mary Warren *(in a fearful squeak of a voice).* Mr. Proctor, very likely they'll let her come home once they're given proper evidence.

Proctor. You're coming to the court with me, Mary. You will tell it in the court.

Mary Warren. I cannot charge murder on Abigail.

Proctor *(moving menacingly toward her).* You will tell the court how that poppet come here and who stuck the needle in.

Mary Warren. She'll kill me for sayin' that! *(Proctor continues toward her.)* Abby'll charge lechery[63] on you, Mr. Proctor!

Proctor *(halting).* She's told you!

Mary Warren. I have known it, sir. She'll ruin you with it, I know she will.

Proctor *(hesitating, and with deep hatred of himself).* Good. Then her saintliness is done with. *(Mary backs from him.)* We will slide together into our pit; you will tell the court what you know.

Mary Warren *(in terror).* I cannot, they'll turn on me—

(Proctor strides and catches her, and she is repeating, "I cannot, I cannot!")

Proctor. My wife will never die for me! I will bring your guts into your mouth but that goodness will not die for me!

Mary Warren *(struggling to escape him).* I cannot do it, I cannot!

Proctor *(grasping her by the throat as though he would strangle her).* Make your peace with it! Now Hell and Heaven grapple[64] on our backs, and all our old pretense is ripped away—make your peace! *(He throws her to the floor, where she sobs, "I cannot, I cannot . . ." And now, half to himself, staring, and turning to the open door)* Peace. It is a providence, and no great change; we are only what we always were, but naked now. *(He walks as though toward a great horror, facing the open sky.)* Aye, naked! And the wind, God's icy wind, will blow!

(And she is over and over again sobbing, "I cannot, I cannot, I cannot," as)

the curtain falls

---

63. **lechery** (lĕch′ə-rē): excessive or illicit sexual activity.
64. **grapple:** struggle.

Connect to the Literature

1. **What Do You Think?** How did you react to Elizabeth Proctor's arrest at the end of this act?

Comprehension Check
- What object does Mary Warren give Elizabeth Proctor?
- What does Reverend Hale ask John Proctor to recite?
- Whom does Ezekiel Cheever arrest besides Elizabeth Proctor?

Think Critically

2. What do you think is the most important thing that John Proctor learns about himself by the end of this act? Explain your answer, using details from the play.

3. **ACTIVE READING** **USING A GRAPHIC ORGANIZER** How would you describe Elizabeth Proctor's **character traits?** Refer to the chart you made for her character in your **READER'S NOTEBOOK.**

4. Evaluate the relationship between Elizabeth and John Proctor. Who is more to blame for their marital problems?

5. Do you think Reverend Hale believes that Elizabeth Proctor is practicing witchcraft? Support your opinion.

6. Why do you suppose so many people have been arrested? What do you think is motivating the officials of Salem?

> **THINK ABOUT**
> - who is making the accusations and why
> - why no one speaks out against the accusers
> - the types of women who have been accused and how the pattern of accusation has changed
> - which **characters** seem sincere in their beliefs about witches

Extend Interpretations

7. **Critic's Corner** Critic Sheila Huftel points out that Miller is not content with simply writing a dramatic story about the Salem witch trials but seems to find it "necessary to explain why these things take place and how, in fact, people come to believe in witches." Based on the evidence in the first two acts, how do people come to suspect others of being witches?

8. **What If?** What, if anything, do you think John Proctor might have done to prevent his wife's arrest? Explain.

9. **Connect to Life** Puritan society pressured individuals to adhere to strict standards of conduct and belief. To what extent do you think society expects you to conform today? Explain.

Literary Analysis

DIALOGUE **Dialogue** is written conversation between two or more **characters.** Found in all forms of literature but most important in drama, dialogue moves the **plot** forward and provides clues about characters' motives and relationships. For example, consider the following dialogue between Elizabeth and John Proctor.

> **Elizabeth.** You were alone with her [Abigail Williams]?
>
> **Proctor.** (*stubbornly*): For a moment alone, aye.
>
> **Elizabeth.** Why, then, it is not as you told me.

Why does Elizabeth react so strongly to the news that John was alone with Abigail? What does Proctor's stubborn reply reveal about him? You might infer that John and Elizabeth are both uneasy about John's relationship with Abigail—John feels guilty about what happened between them, and Elizabeth does not trust her husband.

Cooperative Learning Activity With two classmates, examine other passages of dialogue in Act Two: the exchanges between Mary Warren, Proctor, and Elizabeth in which Mary reveals Sarah Good's confession of witchcraft (page 195); the exchanges between Mr. Hale, Proctor, and Elizabeth in which Proctor tries to recite the Commandments (page 199); the exchange between Proctor and Mary Warren at the end of the act (page 205). Read these exchanges aloud. Then discuss with the rest of the class how the dialogue moves the plot forward or what it reveals about the characters.

ACT THREE

(The vestry room[65] of the Salem meeting house, now serving as the ante-room of the General Court.)

(As the curtain rises, the room is empty, but for sunlight pouring through two high windows in the back wall. The room is solemn, even forbidding. Heavy beams jut out, boards of random widths make up the walls. At the right are two doors leading into the meeting house proper, where the court is being held. At the left another door leads outside.)

(There is a plain bench at the left, and another at the right. In the center a rather long meeting table, with stools and a considerable armchair snugged up to it.)

(Through the partitioning wall at the right we hear a prosecutor's voice, Judge Hathorne's, *asking a question; then a woman's voice,* Martha Corey's, *replying.)*

Hathorne's Voice. Now, Martha Corey, there is abundant evidence in our hands to show that you have given yourself to the reading of fortunes. Do you deny it?

Martha Corey's Voice. I am innocent to a witch. I know not what a witch is.

Hathorne's Voice. How do you know, then, that you are not a witch?

Martha Corey's Voice. If I were, I would know it.

Hathorne's Voice. Why do you hurt these children?

Martha Corey's Voice. I do not hurt them. I scorn it!

Giles' Voice *(roaring).* I have evidence for the court!

---

65. **vestry room:** a room in a church used for nonreligious meetings or church business.

(*Voices of townspeople rise in excitement.*)

Danforth's Voice. You will keep your seat!

Giles' Voice. Thomas Putnam is reaching out for land!

Danforth's Voice. Remove that man, Marshal!

Giles' Voice. You're hearing lies, lies!

(*A roaring goes up from the people.*)

Hathorne's Voice. Arrest him, excellency!

Giles' Voice. I have evidence. Why will you not hear my evidence?

(*The door opens and* Giles *is half carried into the vestry room by* Herrick.)

Giles. Hands off, damn you, let me go!

Herrick. Giles, Giles!

Giles. Out of my way, Herrick! I bring evidence—

Herrick. You cannot go in there, Giles; it's a court!

(*Enter* Hale *from the court.*)

Hale. Pray be calm a moment.

Giles. You, Mr. Hale, go in there and demand I speak.

Hale. A moment, sir, a moment.

Giles. They'll be hangin' my wife!

(Judge Hathorne *enters. He is in his sixties, a bitter, remorseless Salem judge.*)

Hathorne. How do you dare come roarin' into this court! Are you gone daft, Corey?

Giles. You're not a Boston judge yet, Hathorne. You'll not call me daft!

(*Enter* Deputy Governor Danforth *and, behind him,* Ezekiel Cheever *and* Parris. *On his appearance, silence falls.* Danforth *is a grave man in his sixties, of some humor and sophistication that does not, however, interfere with an exact loyalty to his position and his cause. He comes down to* Giles, *who awaits his wrath.*)

Danforth (*looking directly at* Giles). Who is this man?

Parris. Giles Corey, sir, and a more <u>contentious</u>—

Giles (*to* Parris). I am asked the question, and I am old enough to answer it! (*To* Danforth, *who impresses him and to whom he smiles through his strain*) My name is Corey, sir, Giles Corey. I have six hundred acres, and timber in addition. It is my wife you be condemning now. (*He indicates the courtroom.*)

Danforth. And how do you imagine to help her cause with such contemptuous riot?[66] Now be gone. Your old age alone keeps you out of jail for this.

Giles (*beginning to plead*). They be tellin' lies about my wife, sir, I—

Danforth. Do you take it upon yourself to determine what this court shall believe and what it shall set aside?

Giles. Your Excellency, we mean no disrespect for—

Danforth. Disrespect indeed! It is disruption, Mister. This is the highest court of the supreme government of this province, do you know it?

Giles (*beginning to weep*). Your Excellency, I only said she were readin' books, sir, and they come and take her out of my house for—

Danforth (*mystified*). Books! What books?

Giles (*through helpless sobs*). It is my third wife, sir; I never had no wife that be so taken with books, and I thought to find the cause of it, d'y'see, but it were no witch I blamed her for. (*He is openly weeping.*) I have broke charity with the woman, I have broke charity with her. (*He covers his face, ashamed.* Danforth *is respectfully silent.*)

Hale. Excellency, he claims hard evidence for his wife's defense. I think that in all justice you must—

Danforth. Then let him submit his evidence in proper affidavit. You are certainly aware of our

---

66. **contemptuous** (kən-tĕmp′chōō-əs) **riot:** disrespectful, outrageous behavior.

WORDS
TO
KNOW

contentious (kən-tĕn′shəs) *adj.* quarrelsome

procedure here, Mr. Hale. (*To* Herrick) Clear this room.

Herrick. Come now, Giles. (*He gently pushes* Corey *out.*)

Francis. We are desperate, sir; we come here three days now and cannot be heard.

Danforth. Who is this man?

Francis. Francis Nurse, Your Excellency.

Hale. His wife's Rebecca that were condemned this morning.

Danforth. Indeed! I am amazed to find you in such uproar. I have only good report of your character, Mr. Nurse.

Hathorne. I think they must both be arrested in contempt, sir.

Danforth (*to* Francis). Let you write your plea, and in due time I will—

Francis. Excellency, we have proof for your eyes; God forbid you shut them to it. The girls, sir, the girls are frauds.

Danforth. What's that?

Francis. We have proof of it, sir. They are all deceiving you.

(Danforth *is shocked, but studying* Francis.)

Hathorne. This is contempt, sir, contempt!

Danforth. Peace, Judge Hathorne. Do you know who I am, Mr. Nurse?

Francis. I surely do, sir, and I think you must be a wise judge to be what you are.

Danforth. And do you know that near to four hundred are in the jails from Marblehead to Lynn,[62] and upon my signature?

Francis. I—

Danforth. And seventy-two condemned to hang by that signature?

Francis. Excellency, I never thought to say it to such a weighty judge, but you are deceived.

(*Enter* Giles Corey *from left. All turn to see as he beckons in* Mary Warren *with* Proctor. Mary *is keeping her eyes to the ground;* Proctor *has her elbow as though she were near collapse.*)

Parris (*on seeing her, in shock*). Mary Warren! (*He goes directly to bend close to her face.*) What are you about here?

Proctor (*pressing* Parris *away from her with a gentle but firm motion of protectiveness*). She would speak with the Deputy Governor.

Danforth (*shocked by this, turns to* Herrick). Did you not tell me Mary Warren were sick in bed?

Herrick. She were, Your Honor. When I go to fetch her to the court last week, she said she were sick.

Giles. She has been strivin' with her soul all week, Your Honor; she comes now to tell the truth of this to you.

Danforth. Who is this?

Proctor. John Proctor, sir. Elizabeth Proctor is my wife.

Parris. Beware this man, Your Excellency, this man is mischief.

Hale (*excitedly*). I think you must hear the girl, sir, she—

Danforth (*who has become very interested in* Mary Warren *and only raises a hand toward* Hale). Peace. What would you tell us, Mary Warren?

(Proctor *looks at her, but she cannot speak.*)

Proctor. She never saw no spirits, sir.

Danforth (*with great alarm and surprise, to* Mary). Never saw no spirits!

Giles (*eagerly*). Never.

Proctor (*reaching into his jacket*). She has signed a deposition, sir—

Danforth (*instantly*). No, no, I accept no depositions. (*He is rapidly calculating this; he turns from her to* Proctor.) Tell me, Mr. Proctor, have you given out this story in the village?

Proctor. We have not.

Parris. They've come to overthrow the court, sir! This man is—

Danforth. I pray you, Mr. Parris. Do you know, Mr. Proctor, that the entire contention of the state in these trials is that the voice of Heaven is speaking through the children?

Proctor. I know that, sir.

Danforth (*thinks, staring at* Proctor, *then turns to* Mary Warren). And you, Mary Warren, how came you to cry out people for sending their spirits against you?

Mary Warren. It were pretense, sir.

Danforth. I cannot hear you.

Proctor. It were pretense, she says.

Danforth. Ah? And the other girls? Susanna Walcott, and—the others? They are also pretending?

Mary Warren. Aye, sir.

Danforth (*wide-eyed*). Indeed. (*Pause. He is baffled by this. He turns to study* Proctor's *face.*)

Parris (*in a sweat*). Excellency, you surely cannot think to let so vile a lie be spread in open court!

Danforth. Indeed not, but it strike hard upon me that she will dare come here with such a tale. Now, Mr. Proctor, before I decide whether I shall hear you or not, it is my duty to tell you this. We burn a hot fire here; it melts down all concealment.

Proctor. I know that, sir.

---

67. **Marblehead to Lynn:** two coastal towns in Massachusetts, near Salem.

WORDS
TO
KNOW

deposition (dĕp′ə-zĭsh′ən) *n.* a written statement by a witness

Danforth. Let me continue. I understand well, a husband's tenderness may drive him to extravagance in defense of a wife. Are you certain in your conscience, Mister, that your evidence is the truth?

Proctor. It is. And you will surely know it.

Danforth. And you thought to declare this revelation in the open court before the public?

Proctor. I thought I would, aye—with your permission.

Danforth (*his eyes narrowing*). Now, sir, what is your purpose in so doing?

Proctor. Why, I—I would free my wife, sir.

Danforth. There lurks nowhere in your heart, nor hidden in your spirit, any desire to undermine this court?

Proctor (*with the faintest faltering*). Why, no, sir.

Cheever (*clears his throat, awakening*). I—Your Excellency.

Danforth. Mr. Cheever.

Cheever. I think it be my duty, sir—(*Kindly, to* Proctor) You'll not deny it, John. (*To* Danforth) When we come to take his wife, he damned the court and ripped your warrant.

Parris. Now you have it!

Danforth. He did that, Mr. Hale?

Hale (*takes a breath*). Aye, he did.

Proctor. It were a temper, sir. I knew not what I did.

Danforth (*studying him*). Mr. Proctor.

Proctor. Aye, sir.

Danforth (*straight into his eyes*). Have you ever seen the Devil?

Proctor. No, sir.

Danforth. You are in all respects a Gospel Christian?[68]

Proctor. I am, sir.

Parris. Such a Christian that will not come to church but once in a month!

Danforth (*restrained—he is curious*). Not come to church?

Proctor. I—I have no love for Mr. Parris. It is no secret. But God I surely love.

Cheever. He plow on Sunday, sir.

Danforth. Plow on Sunday!

Cheever (*apologetically*). I think it be evidence, John. I am an official of the court, I cannot keep it.

Proctor. I—I have once or twice plowed on Sunday. I have three children, sir, and until last year my land give little.

Giles. You'll find other Christians that do plow on Sunday if the truth be known.

Hale. Your Honor, I cannot think you may judge the man on such evidence.

Danforth. I judge nothing. (*Pause. He keeps watching* Proctor, *who tries to meet his gaze.*) I tell you straight, Mister—I have seen marvels in this court. I have seen people choked before my eyes by spirits; I have seen them stuck by pins and slashed by daggers. I have until this moment not the slightest reason to suspect that the children may be deceiving me. Do you understand my meaning?

Proctor. Excellency, does it not strike upon you that so many of these women have lived so long with such upright reputation, and—

Parris. Do you read the Gospel, Mr. Proctor?

Proctor. I read the Gospel.

Parris. I think not, or you should surely know that Cain were an upright man, and yet he did kill Abel.

Proctor. Aye, God tells us that. (*To* Danforth.) But who tells us Rebecca Nurse murdered seven babies by sending out her spirit on them? It is the children only, and this one will swear she lied to you.

---

68. **a Gospel Christian:** a true Christian.

(Danforth *considers, then beckons* Hathorne *to him.* Hathorne *leans in, and he speaks in his ear.* Hathorne *nods.*)

Hathorne. Aye, she's the one.

Danforth. Mr. Proctor, this morning, your wife send me a claim in which she states that she is pregnant now.

Proctor. My wife pregnant!

Danforth. There be no sign of it—we have examined her body.

Proctor. But if she say she is pregnant, then she must be! That woman will never lie, Mr. Danforth.

Danforth. She will not?

Proctor. Never, sir, never.

Danforth. We have thought it too convenient to be credited. However, if I should tell you now that I will let her be kept another month; and if she begin to show her natural signs, you shall have her living yet another year until she is delivered—what say you to that? (John Proctor *is struck silent.*) Come now. You say your only purpose is to save your wife. Good, then, she is saved at least this year, and a year is long. What say you, sir? It is done now. (*In conflict*, Proctor *glances at* Francis *and* Giles.) Will you drop this charge?

Proctor. I—I think I cannot.

Danforth (*now an almost imperceptible hardness in his voice*). Then your purpose is somewhat larger.

Parris. He's come to overthrow this court, Your Honor!

Proctor. These are my friends. Their wives are also accused—

Danforth (*with a sudden briskness of manner*). I judge you not, sir. I am ready to hear your evidence.

Proctor. I come not to hurt the court; I only—

Danforth (*cutting him off*). Marshal, go into the court and bid Judge Stoughton and Judge Sewall declare recess for one hour. And let them go to the tavern, if they will. All witnesses and prisoners are to be kept in the building.

Herrick. Aye, sir. (*Very deferentially*) If I may say it, sir, I know this man all my life. It is a good man, sir.

Danforth (*it is the reflection on himself he resents*). I am sure of it, Marshal. (Herrick *nods, then goes out.*) Now, what deposition do you have for us, Mr. Proctor? And I beg you be clear, open as the sky, and honest.

Proctor (*as he takes out several papers*). I am no lawyer, so I'll—

Danforth. The pure in heart need no lawyers. Proceed as you will.

Proctor (*handing* Danforth *a paper*). Will you read this first, sir? It's a sort of testament. The people signing it declare their good opinion of Rebecca, and my wife, and Martha Corey. (Danforth *looks down at the paper.*)

Parris (*to enlist* Danforth's *sarcasm*). Their good opinion! (*But* Danforth *goes on reading, and* Proctor *is heartened.*)

Proctor. These are all landholding farmers, members of the church. (*Delicately, trying to point out a paragraph*). If you'll notice, sir—they've known the women many years and never saw no sign they had dealings with the Devil.

(Parris *nervously moves over and reads over* Danforth's *shoulder.*)

Danforth (*glancing down a long list*). How many names are here?

Francis. Ninety-one, Your Excellency.

Parris (*sweating*). These people should be summoned. (Danforth *looks up at him questioningly.*) For questioning.

Francis (*trembling with anger*). Mr. Danforth, I gave them all my word no harm would come to them for signing this.

Parris. This is a clear attack upon the court!

Hale (*to* Parris, *trying to contain himself*). Is every defense an attack upon the court? Can no one—?

Parris. All innocent and Christian people are happy for the courts in Salem! These people are gloomy for it. (*To* Danforth *directly*) And I think you will want to know, from each and every one of them, what discontents them with you!

Hathorne. I think they ought to be examined, sir.

Danforth. It is not necessarily an attack, I think. Yet—

Francis. These are all covenanted Christians, sir.

Danforth. Then I am sure they may have nothing to fear. (*Hands* Cheever *the paper.*) Mr. Cheever, have warrants drawn for all of these— arrest for examination. (*To* Proctor) Now, Mister, what other information do you have for us? (Francis *is still standing, horrified.*) You may sit, Mr. Nurse.

Francis. I have brought trouble on these people; I have—

Danforth. No, old man, you have not hurt these people if they are of good conscience. But you must understand, sir, that a person is either with this court or he must be counted against it, there be no road between. This is a sharp time, now, a precise time—we live no longer in the dusky afternoon when evil mixed itself with good and befuddled the world. Now, by God's grace, the shining sun is up, and them that fear not light will surely praise it. I hope you will be one of those. (Mary Warren *suddenly sobs.*) She's not hearty,[69] I see.

Proctor. No, she's not, sir. (*To* Mary, *bending to her, holding her hand, quietly*) Now remember what the angel Raphael said to the boy Tobias.[70] Remember it.

Mary Warren (*hardly audible*). Aye.

Proctor. "Do that which is good, and no harm shall come to thee."

Mary Warren. Aye.

Danforth. Come, man, we wait you.

(Marshal Herrick *returns, and takes his post at the door.*)

Giles. John, my deposition, give him mine.

Proctor. Aye. (*He hands* Danforth *another paper.*) This is Mr. Corey's deposition.

Danforth. Oh? (*He looks down at it. Now* Hathorne *comes behind him and reads with him.*)

Hathorne (*suspiciously*). What lawyer drew this, Corey?

Giles. You know I never hired a lawyer in my life, Hathorne.

Danforth (*finishing the reading*). It is very well phrased. My compliments. Mr. Parris, if Mr. Putnam is in the court, will you bring him in? (Hathorne *takes the deposition, and walks to the window with it.* Parris *goes into the court.*) You have no legal training, Mr. Corey?

Giles (*very pleased*). I have the best, sir—I am thirty-three time in court in my life. And always plaintiff, too.

Danforth. Oh, then you're much put-upon.

Giles. I am never put-upon; I know my rights, sir, and I will have them. You know, your father tried a case of mine—might be thirty-five year ago, I think.

Danforth. Indeed.

Giles. He never spoke to you of it?

Danforth. No, I cannot recall it.

Giles. That's strange, he give me nine pound damages. He were a fair judge, your father. Y'see, I had a white mare that time, and this fellow

---

69. **She's not hearty:** She's not well.

70. **what the angel said . . . to Tobias:** from the Book of Tobit in the Apocrypha; Tobit's son Tobias was attacked on the Tigris River by a fish, which he caught at the bidding of the angel Raphael. Raphael cured Tobit's blindness by applying the gall of the fish to Tobit's eyes. When Tobit and Tobias were about to reward Raphael, the angel revealed his identity and returned to Heaven.

come to borrow the mare—(*Enter* Parris *with* Thomas Putnam. *When he sees* Putnam, Giles' *ease goes; he is hard*.) Aye, there he is.

Danforth. Mr. Putnam, I have here an accusation by Mr. Corey against you. He states that you coldly prompted your daughter to cry witchery upon George Jacobs that is now in jail.

Putnam. It is a lie.

Danforth (*turning to* Giles). Mr. Putnam states your charge is a lie. What say you to that?

Giles (*furious, his fists clenched*). A fart on Thomas Putnam, that is what I say to that!

Danforth. What proof do you submit for your charge, sir?

Giles. My proof is there! (*Pointing to the paper*.) If Jacobs hangs for a witch he forfeit up his property—that's law! And there is none but Putnam with the coin to buy so great a piece. This man is killing his neighbors for their land!

Danforth. But proof, sir, proof.

Giles (*pointing at his deposition*). The proof is there! I have it from an honest man who heard Putnam say it! The day his daughter cried out on Jacobs, he said she'd given him a fair gift of land.

Hathorne. And the name of this man?

Giles (*taken aback*). What name?

Hathorne. The man that give you this information.

Giles (*hesitates, then*). Why, I—I cannot give you his name.

Hathorne. And why not?

Giles (*hesitates, then bursts out*). You know well why not! He'll lay in jail if I give his name!

Hathorne. This is contempt of the court, Mr. Danforth!

Danforth (*to avoid that*). You will surely tell us the name.

Giles. I will not give you no name. I mentioned my wife's name once and I'll burn in hell long enough for that. I stand mute.

Danforth. In that case, I have no choice but to arrest you for contempt of this court, do you know that?

Giles. This is a hearing; you cannot clap me for contempt of a hearing.

Danforth. Oh, it is a proper lawyer![71] Do you wish me to declare the court in full session here? Or will you give me good reply?

Giles (*faltering*). I cannot give you no name, sir, I cannot.

Danforth. You are a foolish old man. Mr. Cheever, begin the record. The court is now in session. I ask you, Mr. Corey—

Proctor (*breaking in*). Your Honor—he has the story in confidence, sir, and he—

Parris. The Devil lives on such confidences! (*To* Danforth) Without confidences there could be no conspiracy, Your Honor!

Hathorne. I think it must be broken, sir.

Danforth (*to* Giles). Old man, if your informant tells the truth let him come here openly like a decent man. But if he hide in anonymity I must know why. Now sir, the government and central church demand of you the name of him who reported Mr. Thomas Putnam a common murderer.

Hale. Excellency—

Danforth. Mr. Hale.

Hale. We cannot blink it more. There is a prodigious fear of this court in the country—

Danforth. Then there is a prodigious guilt in the country. Are you afraid to be questioned here?

Hale. I may only fear the Lord, sir, but there is fear in the country nevertheless.

Danforth (*angered now*). Reproach me not with the fear in the country; there is fear in the country because there is a moving plot[72] to topple Christ in the country!

---

71. **Oh . . . lawyer:** Oh, he thinks he is a real lawyer.

72. **moving:** active.

Hale. But it does not follow that everyone accused is part of it.

Danforth. No uncorrupted man may fear this court, Mr. Hale! None! (*To Giles.*) You are under arrest in contempt of this court. Now sit you down and take counsel with yourself, or you will be set in the jail until you decide to answer all questions.

(*Giles Corey makes a rush for Putnam. Proctor lunges and holds him.*)

Proctor. No, Giles!

Giles (*over Proctor's shoulder at Putnam*). I'll cut your throat, Putnam, I'll kill you yet!

Proctor (*forcing him into a chair*). Peace, Giles, peace. (*Releasing him.*) We'll prove ourselves. Now we will. (*He starts to turn to Danforth.*)

Giles. Say nothin' more, John. (*Pointing at Danforth.*) He's only playin' you! He means to hang us all!

(*Mary Warren bursts into sobs.*)

Danforth. This is a court of law, Mister. I'll have no <u>effrontery</u> here!

Proctor. Forgive him, sir, for his old age. Peace, Giles, we'll prove it all now. (*He lifts up Mary's chin.*) You cannot weep, Mary. Remember the angel, what he say to the boy. Hold to it, now; there is your rock. (*Mary quiets. He takes out a paper, and turns to Danforth.*) This is Mary Warren's deposition. I—I would ask you remember, sir, while you read it, that until two week ago she were no different than the other children are today. (*He is speaking reasonably, restraining all his fears, his anger, his anxiety.*) You saw her scream, she howled, she swore familiar spirits choked her; she even testified that Satan, in the form of women now in jail, tried to win her soul away, and then when she refused—

Danforth. We know all this.

Proctor. Aye, sir. She swears now that she never saw Satan; nor any spirit, vague or clear, that Satan may have sent to hurt her. And she declares her friends are lying now.

(*Proctor starts to hand Danforth the deposition, and Hale comes up to Danforth in a trembling state.*)

Hale. Excellency, a moment. I think this goes to the heart of the matter.

Danforth (*with deep misgivings*). It surely does.

Hale. I cannot say he is an honest man; I know him little. But in all justice, sir, a claim so weighty cannot be argued by a farmer. In God's name, sir, stop here; send him home and let him come again with a lawyer—

Danforth (*patiently*). Now look you, Mr. Hale—

Hale. Excellency, I have signed seventy-two death warrants; I am a minister of the Lord, and I dare not take a life without there be a proof so <u>immaculate</u> no slightest qualm of conscience may doubt it.

Danforth. Mr. Hale, you surely do not doubt my justice.

Hale. I have this morning signed away the soul of Rebecca Nurse, Your Honor. I'll not conceal it, my hand shakes yet as with a wound! I pray you, sir, this argument let lawyers present to you.

Danforth. Mr. Hale, believe me; for a man of such terrible learning you are most bewildered—I hope you will forgive me. I have been thirty-two year at the bar, sir, and I should be confounded were I called upon to defend these people. Let you consider, now—(*To Proctor and the others.*) And I bid you all do likewise. In an ordinary crime, how does one defend the accused? One calls up witnesses to prove his innocence. But witchcraft is ipso facto,[73] on its face and by its nature, an invisible crime, is it not? Therefore, who may possibly be witness to

---

73. **ipso facto** *Latin:* by that very fact.

WORDS TO KNOW

effrontery (ĭ-frŭn′tə-rē) *n.* disrespectful and insulting boldness
immaculate (ĭ-măk′yə-lĭt) *adj.* without stain; pure

215

it? The witch and the victim. None other. Now we cannot hope the witch will accuse herself; granted? Therefore, we must rely upon her victims—and they do testify, the children certainly do testify. As for the witches, none will deny that we are most eager for all their confessions. Therefore, what is left for a lawyer to bring out? I think I have made my point. Have I not?

Hale. But this child claims the girls are not truthful, and if they are not—

Danforth. That is precisely what I am about to consider, sir. What more may you ask of me? Unless you doubt my probity?[74]

Hale (*defeated*). I surely do not, sir. Let you consider it, then.

Danforth. And let you put your heart to rest. Her deposition, Mr. Proctor.

(Proctor *hands it to him.* Hathorne *rises, goes beside* Danforth, *and starts reading.* Parris *comes to his other side.* Danforth *looks at* John Proctor, *then proceeds to read.* Hale *gets up, finds position near the judge, reads too.* Proctor *glances at* Giles. Francis *prays silently, hands pressed together.* Cheever *waits placidly, the sublime official, dutiful.* Mary Warren *sobs once.* John Proctor *touches her head reassuringly. Presently* Danforth *lifts his eyes, stands up, takes out a kerchief and blows his nose. The others stand aside as he moves in thought toward the window.*)

Parris (*hardly able to contain his anger and fear*). I should like to question—

Danforth (*his first real outburst, in which his contempt for* Parris *is clear*). Mr. Parris, I bid you be silent! (*He stands in silence, looking out the window. Now, having established that he will set the gait.*) Mr. Cheever, will you go into the court and bring the children here? (Cheever *gets up and goes out upstage.* Danforth *now turns to* Mary.) Mary Warren, how came you to this turnabout? Has Mr. Proctor threatened you for this deposition?

Mary Warren. No, sir.

Danforth. Has he ever threatened you?

Mary Warren (*weaker*). No, sir.

Danforth (*sensing a weakening*). Has he threatened you?

Mary Warren. No, sir.

Danforth. Then you tell me that you sat in my court, callously lying, when you knew that people would hang by your evidence? (*She does not answer.*) Answer me!

Mary Warren (*almost inaudibly*). I did, sir.

Danforth. How were you instructed in your life? Do you not know that God damns all liars? (*She cannot speak.*) Or is it now that you lie?

Mary Warren. No, sir—I am with God now.

Danforth. You are with God now.

Mary Warren. Aye, sir.

Danforth (*containing himself*). I will tell you this— you are either lying now, or you were lying in the court, and in either case you have committed perjury and you will go to jail for it. You cannot lightly say you lied, Mary. Do you know that?

Mary Warren. I cannot lie no more. I am with God, I am with God.

(*But she breaks into sobs at the thought of it, and the right door opens, and enter* Susanna Walcott, Mercy Lewis, Betty Parris, *and finally* Abigail. Cheever *comes to* Danforth.)

Cheever. Ruth Putnam's not in the court, sir, nor the other children.

Danforth. These will be sufficient. Sit you down, children. (*Silently they sit.*) Your friend, Mary Warren, has given us a deposition. In which she swears that she never saw familiar spirits, apparitions, nor any manifest of the Devil. She claims as well that none of you have seen these

---

74. **probity** (prō′bĭ-tē): complete honesty; integrity.

WORDS
TO
KNOW

inaudibly (ĭn-ô′də-blē) *adv.* unable to be heard clearly

things either. (*Slight pause.*) Now, children, this is a court of law. The law, based upon the Bible, and the Bible, writ by Almighty God, forbid the practice of witchcraft, and describe death as the penalty thereof. But likewise, children, the law and Bible damn all bearers of false witness. (*Slight pause.*) Now then. It does not escape me that this deposition may be devised to blind us; it may well be that Mary Warren has been conquered by Satan, who sends her here to distract our sacred purpose. If so, her neck will break for it. But if she speak true, I bid you now drop your guile and confess your pretense, for a quick confession will go easier with you. (*Pause.*) Abigail Williams, rise. (Abigail *slowly rises.*) Is there any truth in this?

Abigail. No, sir.

Danforth (*thinks, glances at* Mary, *then back to* Abigail). Children, a very auger[75] bit will now be turned into your souls until your honesty is proved. Will either of you change your positions now, or do you force me to hard questioning?

Abigail. I have naught to change, sir. She lies.

Danforth (*to* Mary). You would still go on with this?

Mary Warren (*faintly*). Aye, sir.

Danforth (*turning to* Abigail). A poppet were discovered in Mr. Proctor's house, stabbed by a needle. Mary Warren claims that you sat beside her in the court when she made it, and that you saw her make it and witnessed how she herself stuck her needle into it for safe-keeping. What say you to that?

Abigail (*with a slight note of indignation*). It is a lie, sir.

Danforth (*after a slight pause*). While you worked for Mr. Proctor, did you see poppets in that house?

Abigail. Goody Proctor always kept poppets.

Proctor. Your Honor, my wife never kept no poppets. Mary Warren confesses it was her poppet.

Cheever. Your Excellency.

Danforth. Mr. Cheever.

Cheever. When I spoke with Goody Proctor in that house, she said she never kept no poppets. But she said she did keep poppets when she were a girl.

Proctor. She has not been a girl these fifteen years, Your Honor.

Hathorne. But a poppet will keep fifteen years, will it not?

Proctor. It will keep if it is kept, but Mary Warren swears she never saw no poppets in my house, nor anyone else.

Parris. Why could there not have been poppets hid where no one ever saw them?

Proctor (*furious*). There might also be a dragon with five legs in my house, but no one has ever seen it.

Parris. We are here, Your Honor, precisely to discover what no one has ever seen.

Proctor. Mr. Danforth, what profit this girl to turn herself about? What may Mary Warren gain but hard questioning and worse?

Danforth. You are charging Abigail Williams with a marvelous cool plot to murder, do you understand that?

Proctor. I do, sir. I believe she means to murder.

Danforth (*pointing at* Abigail, *incredulously*). This child would murder your wife?

Proctor. It is not a child. Now hear me, sir. In the sight of the congregation she were twice this year put out of this meetin' house for laughter during prayer.

Danforth (*shocked, turning to* Abigail). What's this? Laughter during—!

Parris. Excellency, she were under Tituba's power at that time, but she is solemn now.

Giles. Aye, now she is solemn and goes to hang people!

Danforth. Quiet, man.

---

75. **auger** (ô'gər) **bit:** sharp drill.

Hathorne. Surely it have no bearing on the question, sir. He charges contemplation of murder.

Danforth. Aye. (*He studies* Abigail *for a moment, then*) Continue, Mr. Proctor.

Proctor. Mary. Now tell the Governor how you danced in the woods.

Parris (*instantly*). Excellency, since I come to Salem this man is blackening my name. He—

Danforth. In a moment, sir. (*To* Mary Warren, *sternly, and surprised.*) What is this dancing?

Mary Warren. I—(*She glances at* Abigail, *who is staring down at her remorselessly. Then, appealing to* Proctor) Mr. Proctor—

Proctor (*taking it right up*). Abigail leads the girls to the woods, Your Honor, and they have danced there naked—

Parris. Your Honor, this—

Proctor (*at once*). Mr. Parris discovered them himself in the dead of night! There's the "child" she is!

Danforth (*it is growing into a nightmare, and he turns, astonished, to* Parris). Mr. Parris—

Parris. I can only say, sir, that I never found any of them naked, and this man is—

Danforth. But you discovered them dancing in the woods? (*Eyes on* Parris, *he points at* Abigail.) Abigail?

Hale. Excellency, when I first arrived from Beverly, Mr. Parris told me that.

Danforth. Do you deny it, Mr. Parris?

Parris. I do not, sir, but I never saw any of them naked.

Danforth. But she have *danced?*

Parris (*unwillingly*). Aye, sir.

(Danforth, *as though with new eyes, looks at* Abigail.)

Hathorne. Excellency, will you permit me? (*He points at* Mary Warren.)

Danforth (*with great worry*). Pray, proceed.

Hathorne. You say you never saw no spirits, Mary, were never threatened or <u>afflicted</u> by any manifest of the Devil or the Devil's agents.

Mary Warren (*very faintly*). No, sir.

Hathorne (*with a gleam of victory*). And yet, when people accused of witchery confronted you in court, you would faint, saying their spirits came out of their bodies and choked you—

Mary Warren. That were pretense, sir.

Danforth. I cannot hear you.

Mary Warren. Pretense, sir.

Parris. But you did turn cold, did you not? I myself picked you up many times, and your skin were icy. Mr. Danforth, you—

Danforth. I saw that many times.

Proctor. She only pretended to faint, Your Excellency. They're all marvelous pretenders.

Hathorne. Then can she pretend to faint now?

Proctor. Now?

Parris. Why not? Now there are no spirits attacking her, for none in this room is accused of witchcraft. So let her turn herself cold now, let her pretend she is attacked now, let her faint. (*He turns to* Mary Warren.) Faint!

Mary Warren. Faint?

Parris. Aye, faint. Prove to us how you pretended in the court so many times.

Mary Warren (*looking to* Proctor). I—cannot faint now, sir.

Proctor (*alarmed, quietly*). Can you not pretend it?

Mary Warren. I—(*She looks about as though searching for the passion to faint.*) I—have no sense of it now, I—

Danforth. Why? What is lacking now?

Mary Warren. I—cannot tell, sir, I—

Danforth. Might it be that here we have no afflicting spirit loose, but in the court there were some?

Mary Warren. I never saw no spirits.

---

afflict (ə-flĭkt′) *v.* to trouble or attack, causing physical or mental suffering

Parris. Then see no spirits now, and prove to us that you can faint by your own will, as you claim.

Mary Warren (*stares, searching for the emotion of it, and then shakes her head*). I—cannot do it.

Parris. Then you will confess, will you not? It were attacking spirits made you faint!

Mary Warren. No, sir, I—

Parris. Your Excellency, this is a trick to blind the court!

Mary Warren. It's not a trick! (*She stands.*) I—I used to faint because I—I thought I saw spirits.

Danforth. Thought you saw them!

Mary Warren. But I did not, Your Honor.

Hathorne. How could you think you saw them unless you saw them?

Mary Warren. I—I cannot tell how, but I did. I—I heard the other girls screaming, and you, Your Honor, you seemed to believe them, and I—It were only sport in the beginning, sir, but then the whole world cried spirits, spirits, and I—I promise you, Mr. Danforth, I only thought I saw them but I did not.

(*Danforth peers at her.*)

Parris (*smiling, but nervous because* Danforth *seems to be struck by* Mary Warren's *story*). Surely Your Excellency is not taken by this simple lie.

Danforth (*turning worriedly to* Abigail). Abigail. I bid you now search your heart and tell me this—and beware of it, child, to God every soul is precious and His vengeance is terrible on them that take life without cause. Is it possible, child, that the spirits you have seen are illusion only, some deception that may cross your mind when—

Abigail. Why, this—this—is a base question, sir.

Danforth. Child, I would have you consider it—

Abigail. I have been hurt, Mr. Danforth; I have seen my blood runnin' out! I have been near to murdered every day because I done my duty pointing out the Devil's people—and this is my reward? To be mistrusted, denied, questioned like a—

Danforth (*weakening*). Child, I do not mistrust you—

Abigail (*in an open threat*). Let you beware, Mr. Danforth. Think you to be so mighty that the power of Hell may not turn your wits? Beware of it! There is—(*Suddenly, from an accusatory attitude, her face turns, looking into the air above—it is truly frightened.*)

Danforth (*apprehensively*). What is it, child?

Abigail (*looking about in the air, clasping her arms about her as though cold*). I—I know not. A wind, a cold wind, has come. (*Her eyes fall on* Mary Warren.)

Mary Warren (*terrified, pleading*). Abby!

Mercy Lewis (*shivering*). Your Honor, I freeze!

Proctor. They're pretending!

Hathorne (*touching* Abigail's *hand*). She is cold, Your Honor, touch her!

Mercy Lewis (*through chattering teeth*). Mary, do you send this shadow on me?

Mary Warren. Lord, save me!

Susanna Walcott. I freeze, I freeze!

Abigail (*shivering visibly*). It is a wind, a wind!

Mary Warren. Abby, don't do that!

Danforth (*himself engaged and entered by* Abigail). Mary Warren, do you witch her? I say to you, do you send your spirit out?

(*With a hysterical cry* Mary Warren *starts to run.* Proctor *catches her.*)

Mary Warren (*almost collapsing*). Let me go, Mr. Proctor, I cannot, I cannot—

Abigail (*crying to Heaven*). Oh, Heavenly Father, take away this shadow!

(*Without warning or hesitation,* Proctor *leaps at* Abigail *and, grabbing her by the hair, pulls her to her feet. She screams in pain.* Danforth, *astonished, cries, "What are you about?" and* Hathorne *and* Parris *call, "Take your hands off her!" and out of it all comes* Proctor's *roaring voice.*)

Proctor. How do you call Heaven! Whore! Whore! (Herrick *breaks* Proctor *from her.*)

Herrick. John!

Danforth. Man! Man, what do you—

Proctor (*breathless and in agony*). It is a whore!

Danforth (*dumfounded*).[76] You charge—?

Abigail. Mr. Danforth, he is lying!

Proctor. Mark her! Now she'll suck a scream to stab me with, but—

Danforth. You will prove this! This will not pass!

Proctor (*trembling, his life collapsing about him*). I have known her, sir. I have known her.

Danforth. You—you are a lecher?

Francis (*horrified*). John, you cannot say such a—

Proctor. Oh, Francis, I wish you had some evil in you that you might know me! (*To* Danforth) A man will not cast away his good name. You surely know that.

Danforth (*dumfounded*). In—in what time? In what place?

Proctor (*his voice about to break, and his shame great*). In the proper place—where my beasts are bedded. On the last night of my joy, some eight months past. She used to serve me in my house, sir. (*He has to clamp his jaw to keep from weeping.*) A man may think God sleeps, but God sees everything, I know it now. I beg you, sir, I beg you—see her what she is. My wife, my dear good wife, took this girl soon after, sir, and put her out on the highroad. And being what she is, a lump of vanity, sir—(*He is being overcome.*) Excellency, forgive me, forgive me. (*Angrily against himself, he turns away from the* Governor *for a moment. Then, as though to cry out is his only means of speech left.*) She thinks to dance with me on my wife's

---

76. **dumfounded:** shocked.

grave! And well she might, for I thought of her softly. God help me, I lusted, and there is a promise in such sweat. But it is a whore's vengeance, and you must see it; I set myself entirely in your hands. I know you must see it now.

Danforth (*blanched, in horror, turning to* Abigail). You deny every scrap and tittle[77] of this?

Abigail. If I must answer that, I will leave and I will not come back again!

(Danforth *seems unsteady*.)

Proctor. I have made a bell of my honor! I have rung the doom of my good name—you will believe me, Mr. Danforth! My wife is innocent, except she knew a whore when she saw one!

Abigail (*stepping up to* Danforth). What look do you give me? (Danforth *cannot speak*.) I'll not have such looks! (*She turns and starts for the door*.)

Danforth. You will remain where you are! (Herrick *steps into her path. She comes up short, fire in her eyes*.) Mr. Parris, go into the court and bring Goodwife Proctor out.

Parris (*objecting*). Your Honor, this is all a—

Danforth (*sharply to* Parris). Bring her out! And tell her not one word of what's been spoken here. And let you knock before you enter. (Parris *goes out*.) Now we shall touch the bottom of this swamp. (*To* Proctor) Your wife, you say, is an honest woman.

Proctor. In her life, sir, she have never lied. There are them that cannot sing, and them that cannot weep—my wife cannot lie. I have paid much to learn it, sir.

Danforth. And when she put this girl out of your house, she put her out for a harlot?[78]

Proctor. Aye, sir.

Danforth. And knew her for a harlot?

Proctor. Aye, sir, she knew her for a harlot.

Danforth. Good then. (*To* Abigail) And if she tell me, child, it were for harlotry, may God spread His mercy on you! (*There is a knock. He calls to the door*.) Hold! (*To* Abigail) Turn your back. Turn your back. (*To* Proctor) Do likewise. (*Both turn their backs—*Abigail *with indignant slowness*.) Now let neither of you turn to face Goody Proctor. No one in this room is to speak one word, or raise a gesture aye or nay. (*He turns toward the door, calls*.) Enter! (*The door opens.* Elizabeth *enters with* Parris. Parris *leaves her. She stands alone, her eyes looking for* Proctor.) Mr. Cheever, report this testimony in all exactness. Are you ready?

Cheever. Ready, sir.

Danforth. Come here, woman. (Elizabeth *comes to him, glancing at* Proctor's *back*.) Look at me only, not at your husband. In my eyes only.

Elizabeth (*faintly*). Good, sir.

Danforth. We are given to understand that at one time you dismissed your servant, Abigail Williams.

Elizabeth. That is true, sir.

Danforth. For what cause did you dismiss her? (*Slight pause. Then* Elizabeth *tries to glance at* Proctor.) You will look in my eyes only and not at your husband. The answer is in your memory and you need no help to give it to me. Why did you dismiss Abigail Williams?

Elizabeth (*not knowing what to say, sensing a situation, wetting her lips to stall for time*). She—dissatisfied me. (*Pause*.) And my husband.

Danforth. In what way dissatisfied you?

Elizabeth. She were—(*She glances at* Proctor *for a cue*.)

Danforth. Woman, look at me! (Elizabeth *does*.) Were she slovenly?[79] Lazy? What disturbance did she cause?

Elizabeth. Your Honor, I—in that time I were sick. And I—My husband is a good and righteous man. He is never drunk as some are, nor

---

77. **tittle:** tiniest bit.

78. **harlot** (här′lət): a woman of low morals.

79. **slovenly:** untidy.

View and Compare
The Crucible

What can the film version of *The Crucible* show you about the setting and characters that a stage version cannot?

The 1996 American film version of *The Crucible,* with Winona Ryder.

A 1990 British production of *The Crucible* by the National Theatre, London.

wastin' his time at the shovelboard, but always at his work. But in my sickness—you see, sir, I were a long time sick after my last baby, and I thought I saw my husband somewhat turning from me. And this girl—(*She turns to* Abigail.)

Danforth. Look at me.

Elizabeth. Aye, sir. Abigail Williams—(*She breaks off.*)

Danforth. What of Abigail Williams?

Elizabeth. I came to think he fancied her. And so one night I lost my wits, I think, and put her out on the highroad.

Danforth. Your husband—did he indeed turn from you?

Elizabeth (*in agony*). My husband—is a goodly man, sir.

Danforth. Then he did not turn from you.

Elizabeth (*starting to glance at* Proctor). He—

Danforth (*reaches out and holds her face, then*). Look at me! To your own knowledge, has John Proctor ever committed the crime of lechery? (*In a crisis of indecision she cannot speak.*) Answer my question! Is your husband a lecher!

Elizabeth (*faintly*). No, sir.

Danforth. Remove her, Marshal.

Proctor. Elizabeth, tell the truth!

Danforth. She has spoken. Remove her!

Proctor (*crying out*). Elizabeth, I have confessed it!

Elizabeth. Oh, God! (*The door closes behind her.*)

Proctor. She only thought to save my name!

Hale. Excellency, it is a natural lie to tell; I beg you, stop now before another is condemned! I may shut my conscience to it no more—private vengeance is working through this testimony! From the beginning this man has struck me true. By my oath to Heaven, I believe him now, and I pray you call back his wife before we—

Danforth. She spoke nothing of lechery, and this man has lied!

Hale. I believe him! (*Pointing at* Abigail). This girl has always struck me false! She has—

(Abigail, *with a weird, wild, chilling cry, screams up to the ceiling.*)

Abigail. You will not! Begone! Begone, I say!

Danforth. What is it, child? (*But* Abigail, *pointing with fear, is now raising up her frightened eyes, her awed face, toward the ceiling—the girls are doing the same—and now* Hathorne, Hale, Putnam, Cheever, Herrick, *and* Danforth *do the same.*) What's there? (*He lowers his eyes from the ceiling, and now he is frightened; there is real tension in his voice.*) Child! (*She is transfixed[80]—with all the girls, she is whimpering open-mouthed, agape at the ceiling.*) Girls! Why do you—?

Mercy Lewis (*pointing*). It's on the beam! Behind the rafter!

Danforth (*looking up*). Where!

Abigail. Why—? (*She gulps.*) Why do you come, yellow bird?

Proctor. Where's a bird? I see no bird!

Abigail (*to the ceiling*). My face? My face?

Proctor. Mr. Hale—

Danforth. Be quiet!

Proctor (*to* Hale). Do you see a bird?

Danforth. Be quiet!!

Abigail (*to the ceiling, in a genuine conversation with the "bird," as though trying to talk it out of attacking her*). But God made my face; you cannot want to tear my face. Envy is a deadly sin, Mary.

Mary Warren (*on her feet with a spring, and horrified, pleading*). Abby!

Abigail (*unperturbed, continuing to the "bird"*). Oh, Mary, this is a black art[81] to change your shape. No, I cannot, I cannot stop my mouth; it's God's work I do.

Mary Warren. Abby, I'm here!

Proctor (*frantically*). They're pretending, Mr. Danforth!

Abigail (*now she takes a backward step, as though in fear the bird will swoop down momentarily*). Oh, please, Mary! Don't come down.

Susanna Walcott. Her claws, she's stretching her claws!

Proctor. Lies, lies.

Abigail (*backing further, eyes still fixed above*). Mary, please don't hurt me!

Mary Warren (*to* Danforth). I'm not hurting her!

Danforth (*to* Mary Warren). Why does she see this vision?

Mary Warren. She sees nothin'!

Abigail (*now staring full front as though hypnotized, and mimicking the exact tone of* Mary Warren's *cry*). She sees nothin'!

Mary Warren (*pleading*). Abby, you mustn't!

Abigail and All the Girls (*all transfixed*). Abby, you mustn't!

Mary Warren (*to all the girls*). I'm here, I'm here!

Girls. I'm here, I'm here!

Danforth (*horrified*). Mary Warren! Draw back your spirit out of them!

Mary Warren. Mr. Danforth!

Girls (*cutting her off*). Mr. Danforth!

Danforth. Have you compacted[82] with the Devil? Have you?

Mary Warren. Never, never!

Girls. Never, never!

Danforth (*growing hysterical*). Why can they only repeat you?

Proctor. Give me a whip—I'll stop it!

Mary Warren. They're sporting.[83] They—!

Girls. They're sporting!

Mary Warren (*turning on them all hysterically and stamping her feet*). Abby, stop it!

Girls (*stamping their feet*). Abby, stop it!

Mary Warren. Stop it!

Girls. Stop it!

Mary Warren (*screaming it out at the top of her*

---

80. **transfixed:** paralyzed with horror or shock.
81. **a black art:** sorcery.
82. **compacted:** made an agreement.
83. **sporting:** playing a game.

lungs, and raising her fists). Stop it!!

Girls (*raising their fists*). Stop it!!

(Mary Warren, *utterly confounded, and becoming overwhelmed by* Abigail's—*and the girls'—utter conviction, starts to whimper, hands half raised, powerless, and all the girls begin whimpering exactly as she does.*)

Danforth. A little while ago you were afflicted. Now it seems you afflict others; where did you find this power?

Mary Warren (*staring at* Abigail). I—have no power.

Girls. I have no power.

Proctor. They're gulling you,[84] Mister!

Danforth. Why did you turn about this past two weeks? You have seen the Devil, have you not?

Hale (*indicating* Abigail *and the girls*). You cannot believe them!

Mary Warren. I—

Proctor (*sensing her weakening*). Mary, God damns all liars!

Danforth (*pounding it into her*). You have seen the Devil, you have made compact with Lucifer, have you not?

Proctor. God damns liars, Mary!

(Mary *utters something* unintelligible, *staring at* Abigail, *who keeps watching the "bird" above.*)

Danforth. I cannot hear you. What do you say? (Mary *utters again unintelligibly.*) You will confess yourself or you will hang! (*He turns her roughly to face him.*) Do you know who I am? I say you will hang if you do not open with me!

Proctor. Mary, remember the angel Raphael—do that which is good and—

---

84. **gulling:** deceiving.

Abigail (*pointing upward*). The wings! Her wings are spreading! Mary, please, don't, don't—!

Hale. I see nothing, Your Honor!

Danforth. Do you confess this power! (*He is an inch from her face.*) Speak!

Abigail. She's going to come down! She's walking the beam!

Danforth. Will you speak!

Mary Warren (*staring in horror*). I cannot!

Girls. I cannot!

Parris. Cast the Devil out! Look him in the face! Trample him! We'll save you, Mary, only stand fast against him and—

Abigail (*looking up*). Look out! She's coming down!

(*She and all the girls run to one wall, shielding their eyes. And now, as though cornered, they let out a gigantic scream, and Mary, as though infected, opens her mouth and screams with them. Gradually Abigail and the girls leave off, until only Mary is left there, staring up at the "bird," screaming madly. All watch her, horrified by this evident fit. Proctor strides to her.*)

Proctor. Mary, tell the Governor what they—(*He has hardly got a word out, when, seeing him coming for her, she rushes out of his reach, screaming in horror.*)

Mary Warren. Don't touch me—don't touch me! (*At which the girls halt at the door.*)

Proctor (*astonished*). Mary!

Mary Warren (*pointing at* Proctor). You're the Devil's man! (*He is stopped in his tracks.*)

Parris. Praise God!

Girls. Praise God!

Proctor (*numbed*). Mary, how—?

Mary Warren. I'll not hang with you! I love God, I love God.

Danforth (*to* Mary). He bid you do the Devil's work?

Mary Warren (*hysterically, indicating* Proctor). He come at me by night and every day to sign, to sign, to—

Danforth. Sign what?

Parris. The Devil's book? He come with a book?

Mary Warren (*hysterically, pointing at* Proctor, *fearful of him*). My name, he want my name. "I'll murder you," he says, "if my wife hangs! We must go and overthrow the court," he says!

(Danforth's *head jerks toward* Proctor, *shock and horror in his face.*)

Proctor (*turning, appealing to* Hale). Mr. Hale!

Mary Warren (*her sobs beginning*). He wake me every night, his eyes were like coals and his fingers claw my neck, and I sign, I sign . . .

Hale. Excellency, this child's gone wild!

Proctor (*as Danforth's wide eyes pour on him*). Mary, Mary!

Mary Warren (*screaming at him*). No, I love God; I go your way no more. I love God, I bless God. (*Sobbing, she rushes to* Abigail.) Abby, Abby, I'll never hurt you more! (*They all watch, as* Abigail, *out of her infinite charity, reaches out and draws the sobbing* Mary *to her, and then looks up to* Danforth.)

Danforth (*to* Proctor). What are you? (*Proctor is beyond speech in his anger.*) You are combined with anti-Christ,[85] are you not? I have seen your power; you will not deny it! What say you, Mister?

Hale. Excellency—

Danforth. I will have nothing from you, Mr. Hale! (*To* Proctor) Will you confess yourself befouled with Hell, or do you keep that black allegiance yet? What say you?

Proctor (*his mind wild, breathless*). I say—I say—God is dead!

Parris. Hear it, hear it!

---

85. **combined with anti-Christ:** working with the Devil.

Proctor (*laughs insanely, then*). A fire, a fire is burning! I hear the boot of Lucifer, I see his filthy face! And it is my face, and yours, Danforth! For them that quail to bring men out of ignorance, as I have quailed, and as you quail now when you know in all your black hearts that this be fraud—God damns our kind especially, and we will burn, we will burn together!

Danforth. Marshal! Take him and Corey with him to the jail!

Hale (*starting across to the door*). I denounce these proceedings!

Proctor. You are pulling Heaven down and raising up a whore!

Hale. I denounce these proceedings, I quit this court! (*He slams the door to the outside behind him.*)

Danforth (*calling to him in a fury*). Mr. Hale! Mr. Hale!

the curtain falls

Connect to the Literature

1. **What Do You Think?** What event or speech in this act made the strongest impression on you? Why?

> **Comprehension Check**
> - What testimony about the girls' behavior does Mary Warren give the court?
> - What sin does John Proctor admit that he committed?
> - Why is Proctor arrested at the end of the act?

Think Critically

2. Why do you suppose Mary Warren changes her testimony at the end of this act?

3. Why does Elizabeth Proctor lie to Danforth about her husband's relationship with Abigail?

THINK ABOUT
- her feelings toward her husband
- her reputation in Salem
- the social and religious consequences of adultery

4. How would you account for the way Reverend Hale has changed since the beginning of the play?

5. Evaluate Giles Corey's behavior in court. Do you think he handles himself well or recklessly? Cite lines from the play to support your opinion.

Extend Interpretations

6. **What If?** What do you think might have happened if Elizabeth Proctor had told the court the truth about her husband's relationship with Abigail?

7. **Connect to Life** Mary Warren is subjected to intense peer pressure from Abigail Williams and the other girls. How would you compare the intensity of the peer pressure she faces with that exerted on many young people today?

8. **Points of Comparison** Judging from your reading of the Salem court documents earlier in the unit, how accurately do you think Arthur Miller portrays the court proceedings? Discuss any additional insights you have gained about the participants' behavior.

Literary Analysis

FOIL A **foil** is a character who provides a striking contrast to another character. A writer might use a foil to emphasize certain traits of another character or simply to set off or enhance this character through contrast. For example, consider contrasts between Reverend Parris and Reverend Hale, two Puritan ministers. Reverend Parris, paranoid and self-centered, is obsessed with maintaining his position in Salem and is supportive of the witch trials. On the other hand, Reverend Hale is an outsider who, at first deeply disturbed by the mounting evidence of witchcraft, eventually comes to doubt the afflicted girls' credibility.

Paired Activity Working with a partner, consider ways that Elizabeth Proctor and Abigail Williams contrast. Refer to the charts of each **character's traits** that you made in your **READER'S NOTEBOOK**. Then create a new chart like the one below, jotting down details about how these characters differ in personality, values, and their feelings for John Proctor. After you have completed the chart, discuss what Miller emphasizes about Elizabeth by presenting Abigail as her foil.

	Elizabeth	Abigail
Personality		
Values		
Feelings for Proctor		

ACT FOUR

(A cell in Salem jail, that fall.)

(At the back is a high barred window; near it, a great, heavy door. Along the walls are two benches.)

(The place is in darkness but for the moonlight seeping through the bars. It appears empty. Presently footsteps are heard coming down a corridor beyond the wall, keys rattle, and the door swings open. Marshal Herrick enters with a lantern.)

(He is nearly drunk, and heavy-footed. He goes to a bench and nudges a bundle of rags lying on it.)

Herrick. Sarah, wake up! Sarah Good! (*He then crosses to the other bench.*)

Sarah Good (*rising in her rags*). Oh, Majesty! Comin', comin'! Tituba, he's here, His Majesty's come!

Herrick. Go to the north cell; this place is wanted now. (*He hangs his lantern on the wall. Tituba sits up.*)

Tituba. That don't look to me like His Majesty; look to me like the marshal.

Herrick (*taking out a flask*). Get along with you now, clear this place. (*He drinks, and Sarah Good comes and peers up into his face.*)

Sarah Good. Oh, is it you, Marshal! I thought sure you be the devil comin' for us. Could I have a sip of cider for me goin'-away?

Herrick (*handing her the flask*). And where are you off to, Sarah?

Tituba (*as Sarah drinks*). We goin' to Barbados, soon the Devil gits here with the feathers and the wings.

Herrick. Oh? A happy voyage to you.

Sarah Good. A pair of bluebirds wingin' southerly, the two of us! Oh, it be a grand transformation, Marshal! (*She raises the flask to drink again.*)

Herrick (*taking the flask from her lips*). You'd best give me that or you'll never rise off the ground. Come along now.

Tituba. I'll speak to him for you, if you desires to come along, Marshal.

Herrick. I'd not refuse it, Tituba; it's the proper morning to fly into Hell.

Tituba. Oh, it be no Hell in Barbados. Devil, him be pleasureman in Barbados, him be singin' and dancin' in Barbados. It's you folks—you riles him up 'round here; it be too cold 'round here for that Old Boy. He freeze his soul in Massachusetts, but in Barbados he just as sweet and—(*A bellowing cow is heard, and* Tituba *leaps up and calls to the window.*) Aye, sir! That's him, Sarah!

Sarah Good. I'm here, Majesty! (*They hurriedly pick up their rags as* Hopkins, *a guard, enters.*)

Hopkins. The Deputy Governor's arrived.

Herrick (*grabbing* Tituba). Come along, come along.

Tituba (*resisting him*). No, he comin' for me. I goin' home!

Herrick (*pulling her to the door*). That's not Satan, just a poor old cow with a hatful of milk. Come along now, out with you!

Tituba (*calling to the window*). Take me home, Devil! Take me home!

Sarah Good (*following the shouting* Tituba *out*). Tell him I'm goin', Tituba! Now you tell him Sarah Good is goin' too!

(*In the corridor outside* Tituba *calls on*—"*Take me home, Devil; Devil take me home!*" *and* Hopkins' *voice orders her to move on.* Herrick *returns and begins to push old rags and straw into a corner. Hearing footsteps, he turns, and enter* Danforth *and Judge Hathorne. They are in great-coats and wear hats against the bitter cold. They* are followed in by Cheever, *who carries a dispatch case*[86] *and a flat wooden box containing his writing materials.*)

Herrick. Good morning, Excellency.

Danforth. Where is Mr. Parris?

Herrick. I'll fetch him. (*He starts for the door.*)

Danforth. Marshal. (Herrick *stops.*) When did Reverend Hale arrive?

Herrick. It were toward midnight, I think.

Danforth (*suspiciously*). What is he about here?

Herrick. He goes among them that will hang, sir. And he prays with them. He sits with Goody Nurse now. And Mr. Parris with him.

Danforth. Indeed. That man have no authority to enter here, Marshal. Why have you let him in?

Herrick. Why, Mr. Parris command me, sir. I cannot deny him.

Danforth. Are you drunk, Marshal?

Herrick. No, sir; it is a bitter night, and I have no fire here.

Danforth (*containing his anger*). Fetch Mr. Parris.

Herrick. Aye, sir.

Danforth. There is a prodigious stench in this place.

Herrick. I have only now cleared the people out for you.

Danforth. Beware hard drink, Marshal.

Herrick. Aye, sir. (*He waits an instant for further orders. But* Danforth, *in dissatisfaction, turns his back on him, and* Herrick *goes out. There is a pause.* Danforth *stands in thought.*)

Hathorne. Let you question Hale, Excellency; I should not be surprised he have been preaching in Andover lately.

Danforth. We'll come to that; speak nothing of Andover. Parris prays with him. That's strange. (*He blows on his hands, moves toward the window, and looks out.*)

---

86. **dispatch case:** a case for carrying documents.

Hathorne. Excellency, I wonder if it be wise to let Mr. Parris so continuously with the prisoners. (Danforth *turns to him, interested.*) I think, sometimes, the man has a mad look these days.

Danforth. Mad?

Hathorne. I met him yesterday coming out of his house, and I bid him good morning—and he wept and went his way. I think it is not well the village sees him so unsteady.

Danforth. Perhaps he have some sorrow.

Cheever (*stamping his feet against the cold*). I think it be the cows, sir.

Danforth. Cows?

Cheever. There be so many cows wanderin' the highroads, now their masters are in the jails, and much disagreement who they will belong to now. I know Mr. Parris be arguin' with farmers all yesterday—there is great contention,[87] sir, about the cows. Contention make him weep, sir; it were always a man that weep for contention. (*He turns, as do* Hathorne *and* Danforth, *hearing someone coming up the corridor.* Danforth *raises his head as* Parris *enters. He is gaunt, frightened, and sweating in his greatcoat.*)

Parris (*to* Danforth, *instantly*). Oh, good morning, sir, thank you for coming, I beg your pardon wakin' you so early. Good morning, Judge Hathorne.

Danforth. Reverend Hale have no right to enter this—

Parris. Excellency, a moment. (*He hurries back and shuts the door.*)

Hathorne. Do you leave him alone with the prisoners?

Danforth. What's his business here?

Parris (*prayerfully holding up his hands*). Excellency, hear me. It is a providence. Reverend Hale has returned to bring Rebecca Nurse to God.

Danforth (*surprised*). He bids her confess?

Parris (*sitting*). Hear me. Rebecca have not given me a word this three month since she came. Now she sits with him, and her sister and Martha Corey and two or three others, and he pleads with them, confess their crimes and save their lives.

Danforth. Why—this is indeed a providence. And they soften, they soften?

Parris. Not yet, not yet. But I thought to summon you, sir, that we might think on whether it be not wise, to—(*He dares not say it.*) I had thought to put a question, sir, and I hope you will not—

Danforth. Mr. Parris, be plain, what troubles you?

Parris. There is news, sir, that the court—the court must reckon with. My niece, sir, my niece—I believe she has vanished.

Danforth. Vanished!

Parris. I had thought to advise you of it earlier in the week, but—

Danforth. Why? How long is she gone?

Parris. This be the third night. You see, sir, she told me she would stay a night with Mercy Lewis. And next day, when she does not return, I send to Mr. Lewis to inquire. Mercy told him she would sleep in my house for a night.

Danforth. They are both gone?!

Parris (*in fear of him*). They are, sir.

Danforth (*alarmed*). I will send a party for them. Where may they be?

Parris. Excellency, I think they be aboard a ship. (Danforth *stands agape.*) My daughter tells me how she heard them speaking of ships last week, and tonight I discover my—my strongbox[88] is broke into. (*He presses his fingers against his eyes to keep back tears.*)

Hathorne (*astonished*). She have robbed you?

Parris. Thirty-one pound is gone. I am penniless. (*He covers his face and sobs.*)

---

87. **contention:** controversy.

88. **strongbox:** a reinforced box for storing valuables.

Danforth. Mr. Parris, you are a brainless man! (*He walks in thought, deeply worried.*)

Parris. Excellency, it profit nothing you should blame me. I cannot think they would run off except they fear to keep in Salem any more. (*He is pleading.*) Mark it, sir, Abigail had close knowledge of the town, and since the news of Andover has broken here—

Danforth. Andover is remedied.[89] The court returns there on Friday, and will resume examinations.

Parris. I am sure of it, sir. But the rumor here speaks rebellion in Andover, and it—

Danforth. There is no rebellion in Andover!

Parris. I tell you what is said here, sir. Andover have thrown out the court, they say, and will have no part of witchcraft. There be a faction here, feeding on that news, and I tell you true, sir, I fear there will be riot here.

Hathorne. Riot! Why at every execution I have seen naught but high satisfaction in the town.

Parris. Judge Hathorne—it were another sort that hanged till now. Rebecca Nurse is no Bridget that lived three year with Bishop before she married him. John Proctor is not Isaac Ward that drank his family to ruin. (*To Danforth*) I would to God it were not so, Excellency, but these people have great weight yet in the town. Let Rebecca stand upon the gibbet[90] and send up some righteous prayer, and I fear she'll wake a vengeance on you.

Hathorne. Excellency, she is condemned a witch. The court have—

Danforth (*in deep concern, raising a hand to Hathorne*). Pray you. (*To Parris.*) How do you propose, then?

Parris. Excellency, I would postpone these hangin's for a time.

Danforth. There will be no postponement.

Parris. Now Mr. Hale's returned, there is hope, I think—for if he bring even one of these to God, that confession surely damns the others in the public eye, and none may doubt more that they are all linked to Hell. This way, unconfessed and claiming innocence, doubts are multiplied, many honest people will weep for them, and our good purpose is lost in their tears.

Danforth (*after thinking a moment, then going to Cheever*). Give me the list.

(Cheever *opens the dispatch case, searches.*)

Parris. It cannot be forgot, sir, that when I summoned the congregation for John Proctor's excommunication there were hardly thirty people come to hear it. That speak a discontent, I think, and—

Danforth (*studying the list*). There will be no postponement.

Parris. Excellency—

Danforth. Now, sir—which of these in your opinion may be brought to God? I will myself strive[91] with him till dawn. (*He hands the list to Parris, who merely glances at it.*)

Parris. There is not sufficient time till dawn.

Danforth. I shall do my utmost. Which of them do you have hope for?

Parris (*not even glancing at the list now, and in a quavering voice, quietly*). Excellency—a dagger—(*He chokes up.*)

Danforth. What do you say?

Parris. Tonight, when I open my door to leave my house—a dagger clattered to the ground. (*Silence. Danforth absorbs this. Now Parris cries out.*) You cannot hang this sort. There is danger for me. I dare not step outside at night!

(Reverend Hale *enters. They look at him for an instant in silence. He is steeped in sorrow, exhausted, and more direct than he ever was.*)

---

89. **remedied:** no longer a problem.

90. **gibbet** (jĭb′ĭt): a structure for hanging criminals; the gallows.

91. **strive:** struggle (in prayer).

Danforth. Accept my congratulations, Reverend Hale; we are gladdened to see you returned to your good work.

Hale (*coming to* Danforth *now*). You must pardon them. They will not budge.

(Herrick *enters, waits.*)

Danforth (*conciliatory*).[92] You misunderstand, sir; I cannot pardon these when twelve are already hanged for the same crime. It is not just.

Parris (*with failing heart*). Rebecca will not confess?

Hale. The sun will rise in a few minutes. Excellency, I must have more time.

Danforth. Now hear me, and beguile[93] yourselves no more. I will not receive a single plea for pardon or postponement. Them that will not confess will hang. Twelve are already executed; the names of these seven are given out, and the village expects to see them die this morning. Postponement now speaks a floundering on my part; reprieve or pardon must cast doubt upon the guilt of them that died till now. While I speak God's law, I will not crack its voice with whimpering. If retaliation is your fear, know this—I should hang ten thousand that dared to rise against the law, and an ocean of salt tears could not melt the resolution of the statutes. Now draw yourselves up like men and help me, as you are bound by Heaven to do. Have you spoken with them all, Mr. Hale?

Hale. All but Proctor. He is in the dungeon.

Danforth (*to* Herrick). What's Proctor's way now?

Herrick. He sits like some great bird; you'd not know he lived except he will take food from time to time.

Danforth (*after thinking a moment*). His wife—his wife must be well on with child now.

Herrick. She is, sir.

Danforth. What think you, Mr. Parris? You have closer knowledge of this man; might her presence soften him?

Parris. It is possible, sir. He have not laid eyes on her these three months. I should summon her.

Danforth (*to* Herrick). Is he yet adamant? Has he struck at you again?

Herrick. He cannot, sir, he is chained to the wall now.

Danforth (*after thinking on it*). Fetch Goody Proctor to me. Then let you bring him up.

Herrick. Aye, sir. (Herrick *goes. There is silence.*)

Hale. Excellency, if you postpone a week and publish to the town that you are striving for their confessions, that speak mercy on your part, not faltering.

Danforth. Mr. Hale, as God have not empowered me like Joshua to stop this sun from rising,[94] so I cannot withhold from them the perfection of their punishment.

Hale (*harder now*). If you think God wills you to raise rebellion, Mr. Danforth, you are mistaken!

Danforth (*instantly*). You have heard rebellion spoken in the town?

Hale. Excellency, there are orphans wandering from house to house; abandoned cattle bellow on the highroads, the stink of rotting crops hangs everywhere, and no man knows when the harlots' cry will end his life—and you wonder yet if rebellion's spoke? Better you should marvel how they do not burn your province!

Danforth. Mr. Hale, have you preached in Andover this month?

Hale. Thank God they have no need of me in Andover.

Danforth. You baffle me, sir. Why have you returned here?

---

92. **conciliatory** (kən-sĭl′ə-tôr′ē): showing goodwill to end an argument.

93. **beguile** (bĭ-gīl′): deceive.

94. **like Joshua . . . rising:** According to the Bible, after the death of Moses, Joshua became the leader of the Israelites, defeating the Amorites and leading his people to the Promised Land while the sun stood still.

Hale. Why, it is all simple. I come to do the Devil's work. I come to counsel Christians they should belie[95] themselves. (*His sarcasm collapses.*) There is blood on my head! Can you not see the blood on my head!!

Parris. Hush! (*For he has heard footsteps. They all face the door.* Herrick *enters with* Elizabeth. *Her wrists are linked by heavy chain, which* Herrick *now removes. Her clothes are dirty; her face is pale and gaunt.* Herrick *goes out.*)

Danforth (*very politely*). Goody Proctor. (*She is silent.*) I hope you are hearty?

Elizabeth (*as a warning reminder*). I am yet six month before my time.

Danforth. Pray be at your ease, we come not for your life. We—(*uncertain how to plead, for he is not accustomed to it.*) Mr. Hale, will you speak with the woman?

Hale. Goody Proctor, your husband is marked to hang this morning.

(*Pause.*)

Elizabeth (*quietly*). I have heard it.

Hale. You know, do you not, that I have no connection with the court? (*She seems to doubt it.*) I come of my own, Goody Proctor. I would save your husband's life, for if he is taken I count myself his murderer. Do you understand me?

Elizabeth. What do you want of me?

Hale. Goody Proctor, I have gone this three month like our Lord into the wilderness.[96] I have sought a Christian way, for damnation's doubled on a minister who counsels men to lie.

Hathorne. It is no lie, you cannot speak of lies.

Hale. It is a lie! They are innocent!

Danforth. I'll hear no more of that!

Hale (*continuing to* Elizabeth). Let you not mistake your duty as I mistook my own. I came into this village like a bridegroom to his beloved, bearing gifts of high religion; the very crowns of holy law I brought, and what I touched with my bright confidence, it died; and where I turned the eye of my great faith, blood flowed up. Beware, Goody Proctor—cleave to no faith when faith brings blood. It is mistaken law that leads you to sacrifice. Life, woman, life is God's most precious gift; no principle, however glorious, may justify the taking of it. I beg you, woman, prevail upon your husband to confess. Let him give his lie. Quail not before God's judgment in this, for it may well be God damns a liar less than he that throws his life away for pride. Will you plead with him? I cannot think he will listen to another.

Elizabeth (*quietly*). I think that be the Devil's argument.

Hale (*with a climactic desperation*). Woman, before the laws of God we are as swine! We cannot read His will!

Elizabeth. I cannot dispute with you, sir; I lack learning for it.

Danforth (*going to her*). Goody Proctor, you are not summoned here for disputation. Be there no wifely tenderness within you? He will die with the sunrise. Your husband. Do you understand it? (*She only looks at him.*) What say you? Will you contend with him? (*She is silent.*) Are you stone? I tell you true, woman, had I no other proof of your unnatural life, your dry eyes now would be sufficient evidence that you delivered up your soul to Hell! A very ape would weep at such calamity! Have the devil dried up any tear of pity in you? (*She is silent.*) Take her out. It profit nothing she should speak to him!

Elizabeth (*quietly*). Let me speak with him, Excellency.

Parris (*with hope*). You'll strive with him? (*She hesitates.*)

Danforth. Will you plead for his confession or will you not?

Elizabeth. I promise nothing. Let me speak with him.

---

95. **belie:** slander; defame.

96. **like our Lord . . . wilderness:** According to the New Testament, Jesus spent 40 days wandering in the wilderness.

(*A sound—the sibilance*[97] *of dragging feet on stone. They turn. A pause.* Herrick *enters with* John Proctor. *His wrists are chained. He is another man, bearded, filthy, his eyes misty as though webs had overgrown them. He halts inside the doorway, his eye caught by the sight of* Elizabeth. *The emotion flowing between them prevents anyone from speaking for an instant. Now* Hale, *visibly affected, goes to* Danforth *and speaks quietly.*)

Hale. Pray, leave them, Excellency.

Danforth (*pressing* Hale *impatiently aside*). Mr. Proctor, you have been notified, have you not? (Proctor *is silent, staring at* Elizabeth.) I see light in the sky, Mister; let you counsel with your wife, and may God help you turn your back on Hell. (Proctor *is silent, staring at* Elizabeth.)

Hale (*quietly*). Excellency, let—

(Danforth *brushes past* Hale *and walks out.* Hale *follows.* Cheever *stands and follows,* Hathorne *behind.* Herrick *goes.* Parris, *from a safe distance, offers*)

Parris. If you desire a cup of cider, Mr. Proctor, I am sure I—(Proctor *turns an icy stare at him, and he breaks off.* Parris *raises his palms toward* Proctor.) God lead you now. (Parris *goes out.*)

(*Alone.* Proctor *walks to her, halts. It is as though they stood in a spinning world. It is beyond sorrow, above it. He reaches out his hand as though toward an embodiment not quite real, and as he touches her, a strange soft sound, half laughter, half amazement, comes from his throat. He pats her hand. She covers his hand with hers. And then, weak, he sits. Then she sits, facing him.*)

Proctor. The child?

Elizabeth. It grows.

Proctor. There is no word of the boys?

Elizabeth. They're well. Rebecca's Samuel keeps them.

Proctor. You have not seen them?

Elizabeth. I have not. (*She catches a weakening in herself and downs it.*)

Proctor. You are a—marvel, Elizabeth.

Elizabeth. You—have been tortured?

Proctor. Aye. (*Pause. She will not let herself be drowned in the sea that threatens her.*) They come for my life now.

Elizabeth. I know it.

(*Pause.*)

Proctor. None—have yet confessed?

Elizabeth. There be many confessed.

Proctor. Who are they?

Elizabeth. There be a hundred or more, they say. Goody Ballard is one; Isaiah Goodkind is one. There be many.

Proctor. Rebecca?

Elizabeth. Not Rebecca. She is one foot in Heaven now; naught may hurt her more.

Proctor. And Giles?

Elizabeth. You have not heard of it?

Proctor. I hear nothin', where I am kept.

Elizabeth. Giles is dead.

(*He looks at her incredulously.*)

Proctor. When were he hanged?

Elizabeth (*quietly, factually*). He were not hanged. He would not answer aye or nay to his indictment; for if he denied the charge they'd hang him surely, and auction out his property. So he stand mute, and died Christian under the law. And so his sons will have his farm. It is the law, for he could not be condemned a wizard without he answer the <u>indictment</u>, aye or nay.

Proctor. Then how does he die?

Elizabeth (*gently*). They press him, John.

Proctor. Press?

---

97. **sibilance:** a hissing sound.

WORDS TO KNOW **indictment** (ĭn-dīt′mənt) *n.* accusation

Elizabeth. Great stones they lay upon his chest until he plead aye or nay. (*With a tender smile for the old man.*) They say he give them but two words. "More weight," he says. And died.

Proctor (*numbed—a thread to weave into his agony*). "More weight."

Elizabeth. Aye. It were a fearsome[98] man, Giles Corey.

(*Pause.*)

Proctor (*with great force of will, but not quite looking at her*). I have been thinking I would confess to them, Elizabeth. (*She shows nothing.*) What say you? If I give them that?

Elizabeth. I cannot judge you, John.

(*Pause.*)

Proctor (*simply—a pure question*). What would you have me do?

Elizabeth. As you will, I would have it. (*Slight pause.*) I want you living, John. That's sure.

Proctor (*pauses, then with a flailing of hope*). Giles' wife? Have she confessed?

Elizabeth. She will not.

(*Pause.*)

Proctor. It is a pretense, Elizabeth.

Elizabeth. What is?

Proctor. I cannot mount the gibbet like a saint. It is a fraud. I am not that man. (*She is silent.*) My honesty is broke, Elizabeth; I am no good man. Nothing's spoiled by giving them this lie that were not rotten long before.

Elizabeth. And yet you've not confessed till now. That speak goodness in you.

Proctor. Spite only keeps me silent. It is hard to give a lie to dogs. (*Pause, for the first time he turns directly to her.*) I would have your forgiveness, Elizabeth.

Elizabeth. It is not for me to give, John, I am—

Proctor. I'd have you see some honesty in it. Let them that never lied die now to keep their souls. It is pretense for me, a vanity that will

not blind God nor keep my children out of the wind. (*Pause.*) What say you?

Elizabeth (*upon a heaving sob that always threatens*). John, it come to naught that I should forgive you, if you'll not forgive yourself. (*Now he turns away a little, in great agony.*) It is not my soul, John, it is yours. (*He stands, as though in physical pain, slowly rising to his feet with a great immortal longing to find his answer. It is difficult to say, and she is on the verge of tears.*) Only be sure of this, for I know it now: Whatever you will do, it is a good man does it. (*He turns his doubting, searching gaze upon her.*) I have read my heart this three month, John. (*Pause.*) I have sins of my own to count. It needs a cold wife to prompt lechery.

Proctor (*in great pain*). Enough, enough—

Elizabeth (*now pouring out her heart*). Better you should know me!

Proctor. I will not hear it! I know you!

Elizabeth. You take my sins upon you, John—

Proctor (*in agony*). No, I take my own, my own!

Elizabeth. John, I counted myself so plain, so poorly made, no honest love could come to me! Suspicion kissed you when I did; I never knew how I should say my love. It were a cold house I kept! (*In fright, she swerves, as Hathorne enters.*)

Hathorne. What say you, Proctor? The sun is soon up.

(Proctor, *his chest heaving, stares, turns to* Elizabeth. *She comes to him as though to plead, her voice quaking.*)

Elizabeth. Do what you will. But let none be your judge. There be no higher judge under Heaven than Proctor is! Forgive me, forgive me, John— I never knew such goodness in the world! (*She covers her face, weeping.*)

(Proctor *turns from her to* Hathorne; *he is off the earth, his voice hollow.*)

---

98. **fearsome:** courageous.

Proctor. I want my life.

Hathorne (*electrified, surprised*). You'll confess yourself?

Proctor. I will have my life.

Hathorne (*with a mystical tone*). God be praised! It is a providence! (*He rushes out the door, and his voice is heard calling down the corridor.*) He will confess! Proctor will confess!

Proctor (*with a cry, as he strides to the door*). Why do you cry it? (*In great pain he turns back to her.*) It is evil, is it not? It is evil.

Elizabeth (*in terror, weeping*). I cannot judge you, John, I cannot!

Proctor. Then who will judge me? (*Suddenly clasping his hands.*) God in Heaven, what is John Proctor, what is John Proctor? (*He moves as an animal, and a fury is riding in him, a tantalized search.*) I think it is honest, I think so; I am no saint. (*As though she had denied this he calls angrily at her.*) Let Rebecca go like a saint; for me it is fraud!

(*Voices are heard in the hall, speaking together in suppressed excitement.*)

Elizabeth. I am not your judge, I cannot be. (*As though giving him release.*) Do as you will, do as you will!

Proctor. Would you give them such a lie? Say it. Would you ever give them this? (*She cannot answer.*) You would not; if tongs of fire were singeing you you would not! It is evil. Good, then—it is evil, and I do it!

(Hathorne *enters with* Danforth, *and, with them,* Cheever, Parris, *and* Hale. *It is a businesslike, rapid entrance, as though the ice had been broken.*)

Danforth (*with great relief and gratitude*). Praise to God, man, praise to God; you shall be blessed in Heaven for this. (Cheever *has hurried to the bench with pen, ink, and paper.* Proctor *watches him.*) Now then, let us have it. Are you ready, Mr. Cheever?

Proctor (*with a cold, cold horror at their efficiency*). Why must it be written?

Danforth. Why, for the good instruction of the village, Mister; this we shall post upon the church door! (*To* Parris, *urgently.*) Where is the marshal?

Parris (*runs to the door and calls down the corridor*). Marshal! Hurry!

Danforth. Now, then, Mister, will you speak slowly, and directly to the point, for Mr. Cheever's sake. (*He is on record now, and is really dictating to* Cheever, *who writes.*) Mr. Proctor, have you seen the Devil in your life? (Proctor's *jaws lock.*) Come, man, there is light in the sky; the town waits at the scaffold; I would give out this news. Did you see the Devil?

Proctor. I did.

Parris. Praise God!

Danforth. And when he come to you, what were his demand? (Proctor *is silent.* Danforth *helps.*) Did he bid you to do his work upon the earth?

Proctor. He did.

Danforth. And you bound yourself to his service? (Danforth *turns, as* Rebecca Nurse *enters, with* Herrick *helping to support her. She is barely able to walk.*) Come in, come in, woman!

Rebecca (*brightening as she sees* Proctor). Ah, John! You are well, then, eh?

(Proctor *turns his face to the wall.*)

Danforth. Courage, man, courage—let her witness your good example that she may come to God herself. Now hear it, Goody Nurse! Say on, Mr. Proctor. Did you bind yourself to the Devil's service?

Rebecca (*astonished*). Why, John!

Proctor (*through his teeth, his face turned from* Rebecca). I did.

Danforth. Now, woman, you surely see it profit nothin' to keep this conspiracy any further. Will you confess yourself with him?

Rebecca. Oh, John—God send his mercy on you!

Danforth. I say, will you confess yourself, Goody Nurse?

Rebecca. Why, it is a lie, it is a lie; how may I damn myself? I cannot, I cannot.

Danforth. Mr. Proctor. When the Devil came to you did you see Rebecca Nurse in his company? (Proctor *is silent*.) Come, man, take courage— did you ever see her with the Devil?

Proctor (*almost inaudibly*). No.

(Danforth, *now sensing trouble, glances at* John *and goes to the table, and picks up a sheet—the list of condemned*.)

Danforth. Did you ever see her sister, Mary Easty, with the Devil?

Proctor. No, I did not.

Danforth (*his eyes narrow on* Proctor). Did you ever see Martha Corey with the Devil?

Proctor. I did not.

Danforth (*realizing, slowly putting the sheet down*). Did you ever see anyone with the Devil?

Proctor. I did not.

Danforth. Proctor, you mistake me. I am not empowered to trade your life for a lie. You have most certainly seen some person with the Devil. (Proctor *is silent*.) Mr. Proctor, a score of people have already testified they saw this woman with the Devil.

Proctor. Then it is proved. Why must I say it?

Danforth. Why "must" you say it! Why, you should rejoice to say it if your soul is truly purged of any love for Hell!

Proctor. They think to go like saints. I like not to spoil their names.

Danforth (*inquiring, incredulous*).[99] Mr. Proctor, do you think they go like saints?

---

99. **incredulous:** disbelieving.

WORDS
TO
KNOW
empower (ĕm-pou′ər) *v.* to invest with authority

Proctor (*evading*). This woman never thought she done the Devil's work.

Danforth. Look you, sir. I think you mistake your duty here. It matters nothing what she thought—she is convicted of the unnatural murder of children, and you for sending your spirit out upon Mary Warren. Your soul alone is the issue here, Mister, and you will prove its whiteness or you cannot live in a Christian country. Will you tell me now what persons conspired with you in the Devil's company? (Proctor *is silent.*) To your knowledge was Rebecca Nurse ever—

Proctor. I speak my own sins; I cannot judge another. (*Crying out, with hatred*) I have no tongue for it.

Hale (*quickly to* Danforth). Excellency, it is enough he confess himself. Let him sign it, let him sign it.

Parris (*feverishly*). It is a great service, sir. It is a weighty name; it will strike the village that Proctor confess. I beg you, let him sign it. The sun is up, Excellency!

Danforth (*considers; then with dissatisfaction*). Come, then, sign your testimony. (*To* Cheever) Give it to him. (Cheever *goes to* Proctor, *the confession and a pen in hand.* Proctor *does not look at it.*) Come, man, sign it.

Proctor (*after glancing at the confession*). You have all witnessed it—it is enough.

Danforth. You will not sign it?

Proctor. You have all witnessed it; what more is needed?

Danforth. Do you sport with me? You will sign your name or it is no confession, Mister! (*His breast heaving with agonized breathing,* Proctor *now lays the paper down and signs his name.*)

Parris. Praise be to the Lord!

(Proctor *has just finished signing when* Danforth *reaches for the paper. But* Proctor *snatches it up, and now a wild terror is rising in him, and a boundless anger.*)

Danforth (*perplexed, but politely extending his hand*). If you please, sir.

Proctor. No.

Danforth (*as though* Proctor *did not understand*). Mr. Proctor, I must have—

Proctor. No, no. I have signed it. You have seen me. It is done! You have no need for this.

Parris. Proctor, the village must have proof that—

Proctor. Damn the village! I confess to God, and God has seen my name on this! It is enough!

Danforth. No, sir, it is—

Proctor. You came to save my soul, did you not? Here! I have confessed myself; it is enough!

Danforth. You have not con—

Proctor. I have confessed myself! Is there no good penitence[100] but it be public? God does not need my name nailed upon the church! God sees my name; God knows how black my sins are! It is enough!

Danforth. Mr. Proctor—

Proctor. You will not use me! I am no Sarah Good or Tituba, I am John Proctor! You will not use me! It is no part of salvation that you should use me!

Danforth. I do not wish to—

Proctor. I have three children—how may I teach them to walk like men in the world, and I sold my friends?

Danforth. You have not sold your friends—

Proctor. Beguile me not! I blacken all of them when this is nailed to the church the very day they hang for silence!

Danforth. Mr. Proctor, I must have good and legal proof that you—

Proctor. You are the high court, your word is good enough! Tell them I confessed myself; say Proctor broke his knees and wept like a woman; say what you will, but my name cannot—

---

100. **penitence:** regret for one's sins.

Danforth (*with suspicion*). It is the same, is it not? If I report it or you sign to it?

Proctor (*he knows it is insane*). No, it is not the same! What others say and what I sign to is not the same!

Danforth. Why? Do you mean to deny this confession when you are free?

Proctor. I mean to deny nothing!

Danforth. Then explain to me, Mr. Proctor, why you will not let—

Proctor (*with a cry of his whole soul*). Because it is my name! Because I cannot have another in my life! Because I lie and sign myself to lies! Because I am not worth the dust on the feet of them that hang! How may I live without my name? I have given you my soul; leave me my name!

Danforth (*pointing at the confession in* Proctor's *hand*). Is that document a lie? If it is a lie I will not accept it! What say you? I will not deal in lies, Mister! (Proctor *is motionless.*) You will give me your honest confession in my hand, or I cannot keep you from the rope. (Proctor *does not reply.*) Which way do you go, Mister?

(*His breast heaving, his eyes staring,* Proctor *tears the paper and crumples it, and he is weeping in fury, but erect.*)

Danforth. Marshal!

Parris (*hysterically, as though the tearing paper were his life*). Proctor, Proctor!

Hale. Man, you will hang! You cannot!

Proctor (*his eyes full of tears*). I can. And there's your first marvel, that I can. You have made your magic now, for now I do think I see some shred of goodness in John Proctor. Not enough to weave a banner with, but white enough to keep it from such dogs. (Elizabeth, *in a burst of terror, rushes to him and weeps against his hand.*) Give them no tear! Tears pleasure them! Show honor now, show a stony heart and sink them with it! (*He has lifted her, and kisses her now with great passion.*)

Rebecca. Let you fear nothing! Another judgment waits us all!

Danforth. Hang them high over the town! Who weeps for these, weeps for corruption! (*He sweeps out past them.* Herrick *starts to lead* Rebecca, *who almost collapses, but* Proctor *catches her, and she glances up at him apologetically.*)

Rebecca. I've had no breakfast.

Herrick. Come, man.

(Herrick *escorts them out,* Hathorne *and* Cheever *behind them.* Elizabeth *stands staring at the empty doorway.*)

Parris (*in deadly fear, to* Elizabeth). Go to him, Goody Proctor! There is yet time!

(*From outside a drumroll strikes the air.* Parris *is startled.* Elizabeth *jerks about toward the window.*)

Parris. Go to him! (*He rushes out the door, as though to hold back his fate.*) Proctor! Proctor!

(*Again, a short burst of drums.*)

Hale. Woman, plead with him! (*He starts to rush out the door, and then goes back to her.*) Woman! It is pride, it is vanity. (*She avoids his eyes, and moves to the window. He drops to his knees.*) Be his helper!—What profit him to bleed? Shall the dust praise him? Shall the worms declare his truth? Go to him, take his shame away!

Elizabeth (*supporting herself against collapse, grips the bars of the window, and with a cry*). He have his goodness now. God forbid I take it from him!

(*The final drumroll crashes, then heightens violently.* Hale *weeps in frantic prayer, and the new sun is pouring in upon her face, and the drums rattle like bones in the morning air.*)

the curtain falls

View and Compare
The Crucible

In your opinion, which movie poster better reflects the content and atmosphere of *The Crucible?*

Poster for the 1996 film version of *The Crucible*.

Poster for a 1957 French film based on *The Crucible*.

Thinking through the LITERATURE

Connect to the Literature

1. **What Do You Think?** What was your reaction to John Proctor's final choice?

Comprehension Check
- What becomes of Abigail Williams and Mercy Lewis?
- How is Giles Corey killed?
- What does John Proctor do when asked to sign a confession?

Think Critically

2. At the end of the play, Elizabeth Proctor says that her husband has "his goodness now." What do you think she means?

THINK ABOUT

- why he at first agrees to confess after having resisted so long
- why he believes his signed confession would blacken his friends' reputations
- what gives him the strength to die

3. Explain, in your own words, why Reverend Hale urges the prisoners to confess to a lie. What does this suggest to you about the way he has changed?

4. Who do you think is the most courageous **character** in the play, and why?

5. The word *crucible* means "a severe test or trial." Why do you think Miller chose to give his play this **title**?

Extend Interpretations

6. **Critic's Corner** According to critic Penelope Curtis, "The most interesting feature of *The Crucible* is that it is so impressively a play about evil forces, despite the fact that it *seems* to be a play discrediting belief in such forces." How would you describe the evil forces that Miller presents in this play?

7. **Different Perspectives** *The Crucible* was first produced in 1953, during Senator Joseph McCarthy's congressional investigations to root out suspected Communists in the State Department, the entertainment industry, and the U.S. Army. In his pursuit of Communists, McCarthy sometimes accused individuals on the basis of flimsy evidence and innuendo. In what ways do you think *The Crucible* is a criticism of McCarthy and his ways? Support your opinion with details from the play.

8. **Connect to Life** Think of a 20th-century person who suffered or died for his or her beliefs, and compare this person to John Proctor.

Literary Analysis

PLOT AND CONFLICT The **plot** is the sequence of events in a literary work. Generally, plots are built around a **conflict**—a struggle between opposing forces. An **external conflict** pits a character against nature, society, or another character. For example, the courtroom confrontation between Mary Warren and Abigail Williams over who is telling the truth is an external conflict. An **internal conflict** is a struggle between opposing forces within a character. For example, Reverend Hale at first supports the proceedings in Salem. Soon, however, he doubts whether the afflicted girls are truthful. As more and more people are accused, his doubts grow, and he eventually quits the court.

In a plot structure, the **climax** is the moment when interest and emotional force reach a peak. Usually occurring toward the end of a story or a drama, the climax often results in a change in the characters or a solution to a conflict.

Paired Activity Working with a partner, create a diagram to show the internal and the external conflicts of John Proctor. Then create a second diagram for Elizabeth Proctor. After you complete both diagrams, identify the conflict that is resolved at the climax. Discuss whether the other conflicts are resolved by the end of the play.

Writing Options

1. Points of Comparison
Think about the views of Puritan life you formed after reading Jonathan Edwards's sermon "Sinners in the Hands of an Angry God," on pages 152–156. In what ways did reading *The Crucible* confirm or challenge these views? Write a personal response to answer this question, using the diagram below to structure your writing.

Edwards's sermon	Miller's play
↓	↓

My views of Puritan life	What confirms or changes my views
1.	1.
2.	2.
3.	3.

2. Missing Scene Act Two of *The Crucible* originally consisted of two scenes. The second scene dramatized a meeting between John Proctor and Abigail Williams. Miller later omitted this scene from the published version, and it is not usually performed. Write your own scene between Proctor and Abigail to serve as a bridge between Acts Two and Three.

3. Editorial on Hysteria Write a newspaper editorial expressing your opinion about the causes of the witchcraft hysteria in Salem more than 300 years ago. For evidence, draw upon events in Miller's play and your own knowledge of the witchcraft hysteria.

4. Capsule Review Write a brief evaluation of *The Crucible,* telling what you think the play achieved or did not achieve. Support your opinion with evidence. Save your review in your **Working Portfolio.**

Activities & Explorations

1. Historical Fashions Create a costume design for one of the characters in a production of *The Crucible.* To make your design as historically accurate as possible, research 17th-century American fashions typically worn by Puritans, ministers, judges, household servants, farmers, and so forth. ~ **HISTORY, ART**

2. Set Design With a small group of classmates, create a three-dimensional diorama of one of the sets for the play. First, review details given in the stage directions to visualize the setting. Then consult reference books on colonial homes in New England for ideas on decor. Display your finished diorama in the classroom. ~ **HISTORY, ART**

3. Dramatic Reading Readers Theater requires no props, no costumes, and no memorization. Instead, performers read aloud from a script, using only their voices to convey their interpretations of characters and events. With a group of classmates, stage a Readers Theater performance of a favorite passage from this play. Use the stage directions to help you determine how the characters act and speak. Then rehearse your reading and present it to the class. ~ **PERFORMING**

4. Salem Game Show With a small group, create a television game show in which contestants answer questions relating to events or characters in Miller's play. One student should act as emcee and the other members of the group as contestants. ~ **SPEAKING AND LISTENING**

Inquiry & Research

1. Drama v. History Do some historical research to find out how faithfully Miller depicts the actual people and events from the Salem witch trials. For example, did you know that the real Abigail Williams was only 11 years old at the time? Present an oral report to share your findings.

 More Online: Research Starter www.mcdougallittell.com

2. McCarthyism The McCarthy hearings of the 1950s, often described as "witch hunts," inspired Miller's writing of *The Crucible.* With a small group of classmates, find out more about what led to the hearings, how they were conducted, and what happened to the accused.

Vocabulary in Action

EXERCISE A: CONTEXT CLUES Review the Words to Know on page 163. On your paper, write the vocabulary word that best answers each riddle.

1. I am a terrible event that harms many people.
2. I describe the behavior of an ideal butler.
3. I will do anything in support of my beliefs.
4. I am issued against a suspected criminal.
5. I am a punishment for religious wrongdoing.
6. I describe something clean and without blemish.
7. I might be a person who accuses you of crime.
8. I am the statement of a witness.
9. I describe something that cannot be understood.
10. I fill the soul of a wicked person.

EXERCISE B: ASSESSMENT PRACTICE Write the vocabulary word that fits best in each group.

1. authorize, grant, entitle, _____
2. troublesome, contrary, argumentative, _____
3. boldness, rudeness, impudence, _____
4. distress, torment, harass, _____
5. partiality, taste, liking, _____
6. irregular, unbalanced, unfair, _____
7. decide, negotiate, judge, _____
8. angry, outraged, insulted, _____
9. learn, discern, discover, _____
10. silently, soundlessly, quietly, _____

Arthur Miller
1915–

Other Works
All My Sons
Death of a Salesman
A View from the Bridge

Growing Up in the Depression Arthur Miller was born in New York City on October 17, 1915. As a boy, he showed little interest in writing or reading literature. Instead, he played football, baseball, and other sports. When he was 13, his father suffered business losses during the Great Depression, and the family was forced to move from a large apartment in Harlem to a tiny house in Brooklyn. Miller graduated from high school in 1932, but his parents could not afford to send him to college. For the next two years, he worked at a variety of odd jobs, including shipping clerk in an automobile parts warehouse. While riding the subway to and from work, he read voraciously.

Aspiring Playwright After saving money for college, Miller enrolled as a journalism student at the University of Michigan. After graduating in 1938, He returned to New York. Following his debut on Broadway with *The Man Who Had All the Luck* in

1944, Miller's career began to soar. His play *All My Sons* (1947) captured numerous awards. The drama introduced one of his main motifs—the haunting influence of a guilty past. This motif also informed his next work, *Death of a Salesman* (1949), a Pulitzer Prize-winning play that met with enormous critical and popular acclaim.

On Trial The inspiration for Miller's next play, *The Crucible* (1953), came from the McCarthy era in American politics. Miller wrote the play to warn against mass hysteria and to plead for freedom and tolerance. Ironically, Miller himself was subpoenaed to appear before McCarthy's committee in 1956 and was questioned about his activities with the American Communist Party. Miller refused to provide testimony that might implicate others. He said, "My conscience will not permit me to use the name of another person and bring trouble to him." For his refusal, he was cited for contempt of Congress—a conviction that was later overturned.

Years of Triumph Since the mid-1960s, Miller has published more than a dozen plays. *Broken Glass*, his play about an American Jewish couple's reaction to Nazi atrocities during World War II, appeared on Broadway in 1994—50 years after his first Broadway play premiered.

Comparing Literature: Assessment Practice

In writing assessments, you will often be asked to compare and contrast two works of literature. The purpose of the comparison may be to evaluate the works against a standard. You will now practice writing a comparison-contrast essay with an evaluative focus.

PART 1 Reading the Prompt

Often you will be asked to write in response to a prompt like the one below. Examine the wording carefully to see what is required in your response.

Writing Prompt

Both Arthur Miller's play *The Crucible* and Anne Bradstreet's poem "To My Dear and Loving Husband" depict a husband-and-wife relationship in Puritan times. In an essay, compare and contrast ① these relationships. Consider such qualities as the ② following: the depth of love, the degree of commitment, and the amount of personal fulfillment. Conclude by telling which relationship better ③ reflects the Puritan ideal—a love that brings the individual closer to God.

> **STRATEGIES IN ACTION**
>
> ① **Compare** and **contrast**, stating similarities and differences.
>
> ② Notice the **qualities**, or characteristics, of relationships you will examine.
>
> ③ **Evaluate** the relationships against a given standard.

PART 2 Planning a Comparison-Contrast Essay

- Create a Venn diagram to organize similarities and differences.

- Write characteristics shared by both relationships in the overlapping area, and write characteristics not shared outside this area.

- Evaluate each relationship against the criteria in the prompt. Decide which relationship brings the partners closer to God.

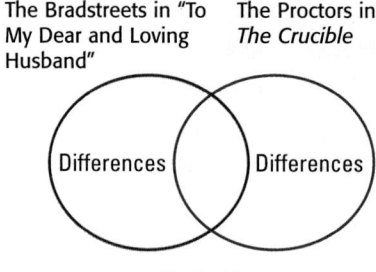

The Bradstreets in "To My Dear and Loving Husband"

The Proctors in *The Crucible*

Differences

Differences

Similarities

PART 3 Drafting Your Essay

Introduction Introduce the subject—husband-and-wife relationships in the two selections—and describe the ideal against which you will evaluate the relationships.

Organization You might first describe one relationship, then describe the other, and then explain their similarities and differences. Or, you might present first all the similarities and then all the differences. Include examples from the play and the poem to illustrate your ideas. Use transitional words and phrases such as *similarly* or *however* to connect ideas within and between paragraphs.

Conclusion State an opinion about which relationship is closer to the Puritan ideal.

Revision Allow some time to review your work. Make sure it is clear, well-supported, and free from mistakes.

Writing Handbook
See page 1281: Compare and Contrast.

LITERATURE CONNECTIONS

The Scarlet Letter

NATHANIEL HAWTHORNE

These thematically related readings are provided along with *The Scarlet Letter:*

For each ecstatic instant / Mine Enemy is growing old
EMILY DICKINSON

The Lottery
SHIRLEY JACKSON

Concerns Raised on "Scarlet Letter" for Drunk Drivers
TONY LOCY

Muddy Brains
JOHN DUNTON

from **The Classics Reclassified**
RICHARD ARMOUR

A Respectable Woman
KATE CHOPIN

The Crucible

ARTHUR MILLER

These thematically related readings are provided along with *The Crucible:*

Conversation with an American Writer
YEVGENY YEVTUSHENKO

Guilt
CLIFFORD LINDSEY ALDERMAN

How to Spot a Witch
ADAM GOODHEART

Young Goodman Brown
NATHANIEL HAWTHORNE

The Great Fear
J. RONALD OAKLEY

Justice Denied in Massachusetts
EDNA ST. VINCENT MILLAY

The Very Proper Gander
JAMES THURBER

A Piece of String
GUY DE MAUPASSANT

And Even *More* . . .

Books

Hester: A Novel About the Early Hester Prynne
CHRISTOPHER BIGSBY
This imaginative prequel to *The Scarlet Letter* recounts the beginnings of Hester and Dimmesdale's relationship and their years of separation.

Everyday Life in Early America
DAVID FREEMAN HAWKES
A fascinating assortment of details about the daily routines of 17th-century American colonists covers such topics as housing, foods, fashions, and superstitions.

Salem-Village Witchcraft
PAUL BOYER AND STEPHEN NISSENBAUM
This highly informative book provides a documentary record of the witchcraft hysteria that gripped colonial New England.

Other Media

The Scarlet Letter
A PBS production of the novel, starring Meg Foster and John Heard. WGBH Boston.
(VIDEOCASSETTE)

The Puritan Experience: Making of a New World
A brief videodisc providing insights into the Puritans and the communities they founded. LCA Releases. (VIDEODISC)

McCarthy: Death of a Witch Hunter
The downfall of the famous 1950s anti-communist activist. Film Archives. (VIDEOCASSETTE)

The Witchcraft of Salem Village

SHIRLEY JACKSON

This versatile author, who often explored supernatural happenings and the sinister side of human nature in her fiction, investigates Salem's outbreak of witchcraft hysteria in this intriguing nonfiction work.

Writing Workshop

You be the judge . . .

From Reading to Writing Both *The Crucible* and "The Examination of Sarah Good" are writings that excite strong reader responses—either positive or negative. You can present your response to books, movies, or performances in a **critical review** of the work. In writing a review, you use evidence from the work to support your opinion. You already form opinions of what you read and see every day. In this workshop, you will learn to put them on paper.

For Your Portfolio

WRITING PROMPT Write a review of a piece of literature or a film you feel strongly about. You will establish evaluation criteria and express your opinion of the piece.

Purpose: To share your opinion
Audience: Your classmates or a reading group

Basics in a Box

Critical Review at a Glance

Introduction
• Identify author and subject
• State overall evaluation

Body
• Briefly summarize selection
• Establish criteria for judging work
• Give evidence to support evaluation

Conclusion
Make a recommendation

RUBRIC **Standards for Writing**

A successful critical review should
• identify and give a brief summary of the work
• state your opinion of the work and make clear the criteria you used to judge it
• support your opinion with well-chosen details and examples from the text
• organize arguments and supporting details in a way that is easy to follow
• conclude with a recommendation to the reader regarding the work

Analyzing a Professional Model

Scott Renshaw
Movie Reviewer

To demonstrate my empathy with the themes of *The Crucible,* I'm going to engage in a bit of heresy of my own: I don't think Arthur Miller's play is particularly good. I'm not suggesting that it is dated, as other critics have done. Irrational fear and extremism are alive and well in America today. The ideas in *The Crucible* were never the issue, but those weighty issues overwhelmed underdeveloped characters. Productions of *The Crucible* have lived or died on the ability of the actors to invest the material with feeling missing from the page, and this first English-language film of the play is no different. Fortunately, the cast is very strong, and the conventions of cinema give the energy level a much-needed boost. Flawed as it may be, *The Crucible* still has moments of undeniable power.

Set in 1692 in Salem, Massachusetts, *The Crucible* begins with a gathering in the woods where several young girls, led by Abigail Williams (Winona Ryder) play at conjuring spirits. The fun ends when they are discovered by Reverend Parris (Bruce Davison) and the Reverend's own daughter is frightened into a catatonic state. To save themselves from punishment, the girls begin accusing Salem's women of witchcraft, naming names indiscriminately. Abigail, however, has one specific name in mind: Elizabeth Proctor (Joan Allen), wife of her former employer and lover, John Proctor (Daniel Day-Lewis). As Salem becomes a town ruled by paranoia, Judge Danforth (Paul Scofield) arrives to try the accused witches. Only a few men like Proctor are brave enough to challenge the court.

Miller's 1953 play is well-known as an allegory for the "Red Scare" and the blacklisting of the 1950s, but Miller's own screen adaptation attempts to make the story less specific to that era, while also making it more visual. The girls' ritual gathering, only described by other characters in the play, is shown in graphic detail, as is an incident in which Abigail stabs herself with a needle and accuses Elizabeth of hexing her. The scenes are not included simply for shock value, but to emphasize the active hypocrisy of the accusers. They also make Abigail less a creature of youthful spite and more a deeply disturbed young woman caught up in the attention and admiration she receives for pointing out the witches of Salem. Winona

---

RUBRIC IN ACTION

❶ Identifies the work to be evaluated

❷ This writer hooks the reader with a bold statement.
Other Options:
- Quote a professional critic about the work
- Describe a striking scene from the work

❸ States his overall evaluation

❹ Summarizes the story without giving away the ending

❺ Clearly states first supporting point and illustrates it with details from the film

Ryder does some of her best work ever in the role, shedding the restrained quality of her previous period-film performances. Here she lets loose like an animal—desperate, haunted, and dangerous.

Ryder is one part of a cast that gives its all to *The Crucible*, beginning with Paul Scofield as Danforth. Scofield brings a commanding, weathered presence to the role of Salem's Grand Inquisitor and a conviction that the judge's work is good and proper. He also gives lines a punch few other actors could muster; when he announces that he intends to "touch the bottom of this swamp" of accusations and counter-accusations, he utters the word "swamp" with a fearsome authority. Joan Allen's steady, cool Elizabeth is just what the part calls for, and she shows that passive-aggressive behavior is not a uniquely 20th-century phenomenon. Surprisingly, the weak link in the cast is Daniel Day-Lewis. In both the play and the movie, Proctor is an underwritten role. However, in the movie there is too much self-righteous heroism in Day-Lewis's reading. When he delivers his final plea to avoid a public confession, literally foaming at the mouth, he almost seems to believe he deserves special consideration.

❻ Makes second supporting point and illustrates it with details and examples

Underwritten characters and underdeveloped relationships are the main faults of *The Crucible* as a text; at times, it feels nearly as plot-driven as a Michael Crichton novel. The story is meant to provoke outrage at the lives destroyed by false accusers and complicit authority figures, but it only takes a couple of scenes to make this point. After this, the children's accusations begin to seem repetitive. Still, there are a couple of scenes in *The Crucible* which can get any audience to hold its breath, notably a tense questioning of Elizabeth for which there can be no correct answer. Director Nicholas Hytner (*The Madness of King George*) offers an interpretation which isn't in the least iconoclastic, but he knows where to use George Fenton's score or a lingering close-up to give a scene added weight. *The Crucible* is a good (though not great) adaptation of a good (though not great) play which still has the ability to cast its own spell.

❼ Summarizes the criteria for his review.

❽ Concludes by making a recommendation

Writing Your Critical Review

❶ Prewriting

It is as hard to find a neutral critic as it is a neutral country in time of war. I suppose if a critic were neutral, he wouldn't trouble to write anything.

Katherine Anne Porter, short story writer

Begin by choosing a piece of literature or a film that strongly affected you—either positively or negatively. Perhaps you want to examine a film based on a literary work. You might select a work you've read for class, another selection by an author you liked, or a memorable piece of literature you've read in the past. See the **Idea Bank** in the margin for more suggestions. After you've chosen a subject, follow the steps below.

IDEABank

1. Your Working Portfolio 📁
Look for ideas in this **Writing Option** which you completed earlier in this unit:
• Capsule Review, p. 244

2. Screen the Screen
Look at the movie section of your local newspaper or visit a video store to remind yourself of movies you've seen.

3. Jog Your Memory
Look in your Readers Notebook to find a story you felt strongly about.

Planning Your Evaluation

▶ **1. Explore your overall reaction to the work.** Did you generally feel positively or negatively? Why? If you had both positive and negative reactions, which were stronger? Discuss your impressions with a friend. How did his or her reactions differ from yours?

▶ **2. List the criteria you will use to judge the work.** How did you judge elements of the work such as plot, characters, language, setting and visual elements, or theme? For example, do the characters seem realistic? Does the setting make sense with the plot?

▶ **3. Gather evidence from the work to support your review.** What facts, examples, quotations, and other details from the work support your opinion of each element? If you find evidence that contradicts your view, will you include and respond to it in your review? You might create a chart like the one below to list your evaluation and your evidence.

Element	Criteria	Critical Evaluation	Supporting Evidence
plot			
characters			
language			
setting			
theme			

▶ **4. Evaluate and organize your evidence.** For which criteria do you have the strongest evidence? Which less strongly supported criteria might you not want to include in your review?

❷ Drafting

You might want to begin your draft by **freewriting** about each of your criteria, one by one. At some point, you will also need to state your **overall opinion** of the work and think of an interest-grabbing way to begin your review. In the body of the review, you will present your **criteria for judgment** and the **evidence** that supports them. Start with your freewriting and organize and refine it. You can either begin with your strongest point or build to it at the end of your review. Try to give a balanced view of the work by including a discussion of both its strengths and its weaknesses. Be sure to include a **clear recommendation** in your conclusion.

Ask Your Peer Reader

- What criteria for evaluation was I using?
- Which parts of my review are most convincing?
- Which of my statements need additional support?
- How can I improve my organization?

Need revising help?

Review the **Rubric**, p. 248

Consider **peer reader** comments

Check **Revision Guidelines**, p. 1269

❸ Revising

TARGET SKILL ▶ AVOIDING CIRCULAR REASONING To be convincing, your review must show clear thinking. Avoid circular reasoning or trying to prove a statement merely by restating it in different words. Be sure to include detailed evidence to support your statements.

> Winona Ryder does some of her best work ever in the role ~~because~~ *shedding the restrained quality of* ~~she never acted as well in~~ her previous period-film performances.
> Here she lets loose like an animal—~~totally beastlike~~ *desperate, haunted, and dangerous.*

❹ Editing and Proofreading

TARGET SKILL ▶ ELIMINATING QUALIFIERS When writing a review, you should state your opinions firmly and clearly. Eliminate unnecessary qualifiers—such as the conditional verbs *could* and *might;* the adverbs *nearly, somewhat, possibly,* and *probably;* and phrases like *It seems to me*—that express indecision and weaken your message.

> ~~It seems to me that~~ the scenes are ~~probably~~ not included simply for shock value, but ~~possibly~~ to emphasize the ~~somewhat~~ active hypocrisy of the accusers.

Publishing IDEAS

- Submit your review to an online journal with literary or film reviews.
- Meet with classmates who wrote reviews of the same work or a work by the same author. Analyze your classmates' reviews and compare them to your own reactions.

More Online: Publishing Options www.mcdougallittell.com

❺ Reflecting

FOR YOUR WORKING PORTFOLIO How did your opinions change as you wrote your review? What will you do differently the next time you write a review? Write answers to these questions and save them with your review in your **Working Portfolio.**

Assessment Practice Revising & Editing

Read this paragraph from the first draft of a review. The underlined sections may include the following kinds of errors:

- **capitalization errors**
- **comma errors**
- **unnecessary qualifiers**
- **sentence fragments**

For each underlined section, choose the revision that most improves the writing.

> Nathaniel Hawthorne's <u>daughter, Una provided</u> inspiration for the
> (1)
> character of <u>Pearl in *the Scarlet letter.*</u> Pearl's wild and willful nature <u>seems to</u>
> (2)   (3)
> <u>be</u> an exaggerated version of Una's lively personality. <u>In his journal. Hawthorne</u>
> (4)
> <u>describes Una and her brother play-acting.</u> "There is something that almost
> frightens me about the child," he writes. "I know not whether elfish or angelic,
> but, at all events, supernatural." In my opinion, the parallels between Una and
> Pearl are <u>pretty clear.</u> <u>Pearl's behavior like Una's can be described as</u>
>   (5)   (6)
> <u>supernatural.</u>

1. **A.** daughter Una provided
   B. daughter. Una, provided
   C. daughter Una, provided
   D. Correct as is

2. **A.** pearl in *the Scarlet Letter*
   B. Pearl in *The Scarlet letter*
   C. Pearl in *The Scarlet Letter*
   D. Correct as is

3. **A.** must surely be
   B. is almost
   C. is
   D. Correct as is

4. **A.** In his journal, Hawthorne describes Una and her brother play-acting.
   B. In his journal Hawthorne describes Una and her brother, play-acting.
   C. In his journal Hawthorne describes Una, and her brother, play-acting.
   D. Correct as is

5. **A.** fairly clear
   B. clear
   C. pretty
   D. Correct as is

6. **A.** Pearl's behavior like Una's, can be described as supernatural.
   B. Pearl's behavior, like Una's, can be described as supernatural.
   C. Pearl's behavior, like Una's can be described, as supernatural.
   D. Correct as is

Need extra help?

See the **Grammar Handbook**

Capitalization Chart, p. 1329

Punctuation Chart, pp. 1327–1328

Correcting Fragments, p. 1323

Recognizing Relationships

When we encounter a new thing, we mentally connect and compare it with things we already know and understand. One type of comparison between objects or situations is called an **analogy**.

The Puritans of colonial Massachusetts constantly compared their own lives, communities, and behavior to those recorded in the Bible, and they often used analogies to make those comparisons clear. For example, in the excerpt at the right, the poet Anne Bradstreet likens heaven to "a house on high erect."

> Thou hast an house on high erect,
> Framed by that mighty Architect,
> With glory richly furnishéd,
> Stands permanent though this be fled.
> —Anne Bradstreet,
> "Upon the Burning of Our House"

She is saying, in effect, that just as a house shelters those who live in it, so heaven shelters saved souls. Metaphors like this one compare things or ideas that have certain similarities.

Strategies for Building Vocabulary

Not only are analogies the basis of literary metaphors; expressed as word formulas, they can be used to test your ability to make logical connections. For example, an analogy comparing the lava that flows from a volcano to ketchup that flows from a bottle would be expressed as follows:

LAVA : VOLCANO :: ketchup : bottle

To read this, you would say, "Lava is to a volcano as ketchup is to a bottle."

❶ **Determine Word Relationships** The first step in analyzing an analogy is to determine the relationship between the first pair of words in the analogy. What, for example, do you think is the relationship between these two words?

PURITANISM : PROTESTANTISM

Once you see that the relationship is one of classification (Puritanism is a type of Protestantism), you can determine which of the following word pairs best completes this analogy. Which pair would you choose?

(A) joy : rapture   (C) anarchy : order
(B) leaf : plant   (D) dirge : song

Although each pair expresses a relationship, pair D best completes the analogy, since a dirge is classified as a type of song.

❷ **Distinguish Types of Analogies** Many standardized tests include items that require you to complete analogies. This chart will help you become familiar with some of the more common types of analogies.

Common Relationships in Analogies

Type	Example	Relationship
Classification	COTTAGE : HOUSE	is a type of
Description	INTOLERANT : FANATIC	describes
Worker to Creation	MINISTER : SERMON	is one who creates or makes
Sequence or Time	CHILDHOOD : ADOLESCENCE	occurs before (or after)
Synonyms	AFFLUENCE : PROSPERITY	means the same as
Part to Whole	MAST : SAILBOAT	is a part of
Cause to Effect	CRIME : PUNISHMENT	results in or leads to
Action to Object	CULTIVATE : PLANTS	is what you do to
Grammar	WHO : WHOM	is a grammatical form related to

EXERCISE Complete and classify these five analogies.

1. PROVOKE : INFLAME :: appease : _____
2. REDUCE : PRESSURE :: mitigate : _____
3. ARMY : SOLDIER :: congregation: _____
4. BIGOTRY : PERSECUTION :: empathy : _____
5. BELIEF : CONVICTION :: indifference : _____

Grammar from Literature

Notice the words in blue in the passages below from *The Crucible* by Arthur Miller. At first glance they may appear to be verbs. A closer look reveals that they are verb forms used as nouns; in other words, they are gerunds.

> gerund as subject
> **The singing has stopped in the midst of this, and now Parris rushes in.**
>
> gerund as direct object
> **And I heard a screeching and gibberish coming from her mouth.**
>
> gerund as object of a preposition
> **Oh, you're a great one for lookin' aren't you, Mary Warren?**
>
> gerund phrase as object of a preposition
> **This predilection for minding other people's business was time-honored among the people of Salem.**

Gerunds can take the form of single words or phrases. A gerund phrase may consist of a gerund with modifiers, objects, or complements. In the example above, the gerund *minding* is followed by a direct object, *business.*

You can see from the examples above that writers use gerunds and gerund phrases in all the ways that they use nouns and noun phrases.

Using Gerunds in Your Writing Sometimes, you can eliminate awkwardness and be more concise by using a gerund. Longer phrases and clauses can be reduced to a gerund. The examples at the top of the next column show ways this can be done.

> ORIGINAL
> **Jonathan Edwards paints a vivid picture of the consequences when someone commits a sin.**
>
> REVISED USING A GERUND
> **Jonathan Edwards paints a vivid picture of the consequences of sinning.**
>
> ORIGINAL
> **Proctor finds the fact that he must sign his name to the confession very difficult and very distasteful.**
>
> REVISED USING A GERUND
> **Proctor finds signing his name to the confession very difficult and very distasteful.**

Usage Tip A pronoun that modifies a gerund must be in the possessive case. Similarly, a proper noun in the possessive case is used to modify a gerund.

> INCORRECT
>   proper noun gerund
> **The Nurse family prevents Bayley taking office.**
>   pronoun gerund
> **The Nurse family prevents him taking office.**
>
> CORRECT
>   possessive gerund
> **The Nurse family prevents Bayley's taking office.**
>   possessive gerund
> **The Nurse family prevents his taking office.**

Punctuation When you combine two short sentences that have gerund subjects be careful to avoid comma splices. Remember that you cannot join two complete ideas with just a comma. Use a semicolon or use a comma and a coordinating conjunction.

> INCORRECT
> **Suspecting is bad, knowing is worse.**
>
> CORRECT
> **Suspecting is bad; knowing is worse.**

WRITING EXERCISE Rewrite each sentence, changing the underlined words to a gerund or gerund phrase.
1. Prior to the time when he became a minister, Samuel Parris was a merchant in Barbados.
2. Abigail seems to enjoy it when she taunts John Proctor.
3. Acts of prayer and acts of worship are regular parts of Parris's daily life.
4. The fact that the girls danced in the woods outrages Parris.
5. In the talk that she has with the other girls, Abigail reveals her true nature.

GRAMMAR EXERCISE Rewrite these sentences, correcting any errors in punctuation and usage.
1. Believing is fine, taking action is even better.
2. Samuel Parris praying has little effect on the unconscious child.
3. Mrs. Putnam offers a reason for the child screaming.
4. Lying to friends and family is one thing, lying on the witness stand is quite another.
5. The other men are rattled by him arriving at that moment.

The Right to Be Free

Writers in the Time of Revolution

"*No* taxation without representation!" "Give me liberty, or give me death!" "We hold these truths to be self-evident. . . ." "We the people . . ." Many famous phrases have come from the rhetoric of the American Revolution, along with many of our favorite national anecdotes—the Boston Tea Party, "the shot heard round the world," and George Washington at Valley Forge. Behind the rhetoric and the mythologizing of the Revolution, however, lie major philosophical ideas that not only transformed 13 British colonies into a nation but laid the groundwork for democratic institutions throughout the world.

Statue of John Locke in the classical style

On the surface, the conflict between England and her American colonies was about money—specifically, what the colonists considered unlawful taxation. On a deeper level, what gave the rebellious colonists the mental preparedness and moral strength needed for such a dangerous undertaking as revolution came essentially from two sources: the writings of English philosopher John Locke and the Bible.

Central to John Locke's theory was the notion of "natural rights." In addition to life and liberty, the right to own property was considered a natural right. If any government abridged that right to property—by levying taxes without the consent of the property owners, for example—then the people could organize a new government.

You can see the spirit of Locke reflected in Jefferson's eloquent opening to the Declaration of Independence. Locke's ideas of property rights were echoed in the wording of the U.S. Constitution. The Revolutionary writers in this part of Unit Two—particularly Patrick Henry, Phillis Wheatley, Abigail Adams, and Michel-Guillaume Jean de Crèvecoeur—all appealed to natural rights in their arguments for freedom.

The American Revolution was not solely the enterprise of learned

Portrait of Thomas Jefferson

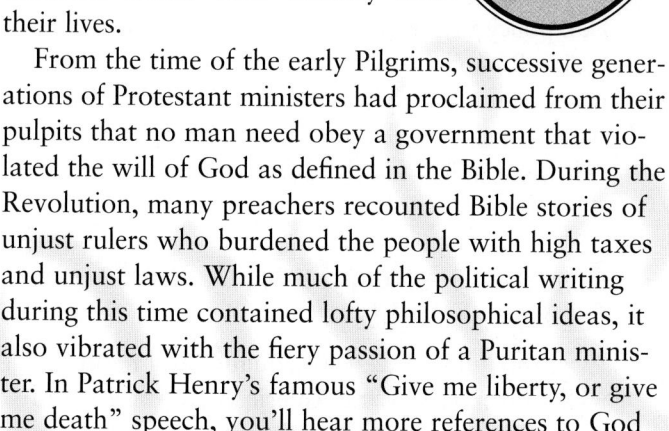
Silhouette of Abigail Adams

men and women of the day, however. Ordinary people were caught up in the struggle and used the Bible to help them make hard decisions about their country and their lives.

From the time of the early Pilgrims, successive generations of Protestant ministers had proclaimed from their pulpits that no man need obey a government that violated the will of God as defined in the Bible. During the Revolution, many preachers recounted Bible stories of unjust rulers who burdened the people with high taxes and unjust laws. While much of the political writing during this time contained lofty philosophical ideas, it also vibrated with the fiery passion of a Puritan minister. In Patrick Henry's famous "Give me liberty, or give me death" speech, you'll hear more references to God and the Bible than to Locke's ideas of natural rights.

The philosophical and religious ideas that spurred the American Revolution also raised other important issues—the most important being slavery. The philosophy of democracy is as much an attack on the institution of slavery as it is on political tyranny. However, the entire plantation economy of the South was dependent on slaves, who were considered the property of plantation owners. As powerful Southern landowners exerted their influence in the new government, reform that might have prohibited slavery was halted.

Another issue for the Founding Fathers was what to do about Native Americans. In the early years of the nation, the policy of the U.S. government was to assimilate Native Americans

The United States of America have exhibited, perhaps, the first example of governments erected on the simple principles of nature; and if men are now sufficiently enlightened to disabuse themselves of artifice, imposture, hypocrisy, and superstition, they will consider this event as an era in their history.

John Adams
from Defense of the Constitutions
of Government of the
United States of America

When Israel was in Egypt's land,
　　Let my people go;
Oppressed so hard they could
　　not stand,
Let my people go.
　　　CHORUS
Go down, Moses, way down
　　in Egypt's land;
Tell old Pharaoh, to let my people go.

Anonymous Negro spiritual

Benjamin Franklin created this woodcut in 1754 to warn the colonies to unite in their common defense.

into Anglo culture. To this end, government officials worked with existing missions set up by the principal churches of the time to teach Native Americans Christian theology, reading, and writing as well as to train them in agriculture.

Although some Native Americans resisted such efforts—most notably Seneca chief Red Jacket—the U.S. policy worked for a while. However in 1830, U.S. policy toward Native Americans changed. The Indian Removal Act authorized the relocation of tribes from the Southeastern states to land west of the Mississippi River, in order to free up the well-cultivated Indian farmland for white settlers.

Traditions Across Time: Demands for Equal Rights

Even though the ideals of equality and natural rights promised by the American Revolution did not fully materialize after the war, the noble words had been written—and they remained to haunt the country. The conflicts also remained for subsequent generations of Americans to resolve— first during the Civil War and later in the civil rights movement of the 20th century. When you read the words of Martin Luther King, Jr., and Malcolm X as they contemplate the meaning of equal rights in their own time, you'll be able to recognize the American tradition of political thought that dates back to the beginnings of our country.

Rodolfo Gonzales in his 1967 poem *I Am Joaquín* speaks as eloquently for his people—Chicanos— as Patrick Henry did for his.

Writers in the Time of Revolution

Patrick Henry — **Speech in the Virginia Convention** — 262
A fiery call to arms

Thomas Jefferson — **The Declaration of Independence** — 270
Life, liberty, and the pursuit of happiness

LINK ACROSS CULTURES

Olympe de Gouges — from **The Declaration of the Rights of Woman** — 277
A French revolutionary demands equality for women.

Phillis Wheatley — **Letter to the Rev. Samson Occom** — 282
An early African-American poet has her say.

Abigail Adams — **Letter to John Adams** — 282
A Revolutionary woman speaks her mind.

Michel-Guillaume Jean de Crèvecoeur — **What Is an American?** — 289
Early ideas about the melting pot

LITERARY LINK

Benjamin Franklin — from **Poor Richard's Almanack** — 292
Wit and wisdom from an American original

Red Jacket — **Lecture to a Missionary** — 295
A Seneca chief talks back.

COMPARING LITERATURE
Traditions Across Time: Demands for Equal Rights

Martin Luther King, Jr. — from **Stride Toward Freedom** (1958) — 300
The classic call for nonviolent resistance

Malcolm X
Interviewed by Les Crane — **Necessary to Protect Ourselves** (1964) — 300
A counter call to do "whatever is necessary" for protection

Rodolfo Gonzales — from **I Am Joaquín/Yo Soy Joaquín** (1967) — 309
An assertion of Chicano identity and pride

Persuasive Rhetoric

Beyond "Please!"

If old news footage of speeches by John F. Kennedy or Martin Luther King, Jr., never fails to capture your attention, you have experienced the power of persuasive language. The aim of persuasive writing or speaking is to convince people to adopt an opinion, perform an action, or both. **Rhetoric** is the art of communicating ideas. **Persuasive rhetoric** consists of reasoned arguments in favor of or against particular beliefs or courses of action.

The pamphlets of Thomas Paine (1737-1809) urged American colonists to seek independence.

The Workings of an Argument

To be effectively persuasive, a work generally has to engage both the mind and the emotions of its audience, making them think that the problem the work deals with is important enough for them to care how it is resolved. (See "Persuasion in Action" below.) Furthermore, the writer needs to show that his or her position has a firm moral basis. The Declaration of Independence (page 270) provides examples of the three basic types of appeals used in persuasive arguments:

LOGICAL APPEALS Generally based on sets of assumptions, **logical appeals** provide rational arguments to support writers' claims—for instance, the assumption that "all men are created equal"—and are supported with objective evidence, such as the list of "injuries and usurpations" committed by King George III. A writer can develop an argument **deductively,** by beginning with a **generalization,** or **premise,** and proceeding to marshal examples and facts that support it (as in the Declaration of Independence), or **inductively,** by beginning with examples or facts and proceeding to draw a

---

Persuasion in Action

To be effective, a persuasive writer:

- clearly states the issue and a position

- gives an opinion and supports it with facts and reasons

- takes opposing views into account

- uses sound logic and effective language

- concludes by summing up reasons or calling for action

"When, in the course of human events, it becomes necessary for one people to dissolve . . . political bands . . . they should declare the causes which impel them to the separation."
—Thomas Jefferson

"I cannot say that I think you are very generous to the ladies; for, whilst you are proclaiming peace and good-will to men, emancipating all nations, you insist upon retaining an absolute power over wives."
—Abigail Adams

"With nonviolent resistance, no individual or group need submit to any wrong, nor need anyone resort to violence in order to right a wrong."
—Martin Luther King, Jr.

YOUR TURN Pick one of the quotes above. Identify which of the bulleted standards to the left apply.

conclusion from them. Analyzing the reasoning of an argument can help you evaluate its soundness.

EMOTIONAL APPEALS Appeals to emotion are often based on specific examples of suffering or potential threats, as in Jefferson's statement that King George is attempting "to complete the works of death, desolation, and tyranny." Emotional appeals can also include "loaded language"—language that is rich in connotations and vivid images.

ETHICAL APPEALS Based on shared moral values, ethical appeals call forth the audience's sense of right, justice, and virtue. Jefferson, for example, reminded people that independence was a last resort, after the failure of other measures: "In every stage of these oppressions we have petitioned for redress, in the most humble terms; our repeated petitions have been answered only by repeated injury."

Styles of Persuasion

Persuasive writers and speakers use a number of techniques.

ELEVATED LANGUAGE Formal words and phrases can lend a serious tone to a discussion. In her "Declaration of the Rights of Woman" (page 277), written during the French Revolution, Olympe de Gouges used the political terminology of the time to stir women to action: "The powerful empire of nature is no longer surrounded by prejudice, fanaticism, superstition, and lies. The flame of truth has dispersed all the clouds of folly and usurpation."

RHETORICAL QUESTIONS Think of these as questions that don't require answers. Writers pose rhetorical questions to show that their arguments make the answers obvious. Patrick Henry's speech in the Virginia Convention (page 262), for example, includes a variety of questions whose answers Henry considers self-evident, such as "Is life so dear, or peace so sweet, as to be purchased at the price of chains and slavery?"

REPETITION Repeating a point tells the audience that it is especially important; repeating a form of expression tells the audience that the ideas expressed in the same way are related. **Parallelism,** a form of repetition, is used very effectively in the Declaration of Independence. Notice the parallel clauses beginning with *that* in the following famous passage.

> We hold these truths to be self-evident:—That all men are created equal; that they are endowed by their Creator with certain unalienable rights; that among these are life, liberty, and the pursuit of happiness.
>
> —Thomas Jefferson

Strategies for Reading: Persuasive Rhetoric

1. Identify the problem that is addressed and the solution that is proposed. Restate them in your own words.

2. Analyze the writer's presentation of his or her argument. What rhetorical tools does the writer use?

3. Analyze the evidence used to support the argument. What facts support the writer's opinions?

4. Consider how the writer appeals to the logic, emotions, and ethics of the audience.

5. Evaluate the credibility of the writer. What motivations might lie behind the work?

6. **Monitor** your reading strategies and modify them when your understanding breaks down. Remember to use the Strategies for Active Reading: **predict, visualize, connect, question, clarify,** and **evaluate.**

Speech in the Virginia Convention

Speech by PATRICK HENRY

Build Background

Heading Toward War Until the mid-1700s, American colonists largely had been content to be under British rule. However, tension grew between Great Britain and her American colonies after the end of the French and Indian War in 1763. Although Britain had defeated the French and their Indian allies, thousands of British troops remained quartered in the colonies, which caused resentment among the colonists. Their resentment increased and angry protests ensued when, beginning in 1764, the British Parliament passed a series of harsh laws and taxes.

To discuss the growing crisis, the First Continental Congress, composed of delegates from all 13 colonies except Georgia, met in Philadelphia in 1774. The delegates held out hope that they could restore the colonies' relationship with Great Britain, and they sent formal petitions to King George III and the British people, asking for their rights as British subjects. Six months after this meeting, in March 1775, the Second Virginia Provincial Convention was called to vote on whether Virginia should take up arms to defend against a feared British attack. Patrick Henry, the most famous orator of the American Revolution, delivered a fiery speech to convince delegates of the need for armed resistance.

WORDS TO KNOW **Vocabulary Preview**

adversary	irresolution	tyrannical
formidable	martial	vigilant
insidious	subjugation	
invincible	spurn	

Focus Your Reading

LITERARY ANALYSIS | **ALLUSION**

An **allusion** is an indirect reference to a person, place, event, or literary work with which the author believes the reader will be familiar. Refer to the Guide for Reading for an explanation of the allusions in Patrick Henry's speech. Consider what this technique contributes to Henry's argument.

ACTIVE READING | **RHETORICAL QUESTIONS AND PERSUASION**

A **rhetorical question** is a question to which no answer is expected because the answer is obvious. Rhetorical questions are often used in persuasive writing to emphasize a point or create an emotional effect. For example, Patrick Henry asks this rhetorical question in his speech: "Is life so dear, or peace so sweet, as to be purchased at the price of chains and slavery?" The obvious answer is no, and the effect of the question is to stir his listeners to act decisively against the British.

READER'S NOTEBOOK As you read Henry's famous speech, list some examples of rhetorical questions.

SPEECH *in the*

VIRGINIA CONVENTION

PATRICK HENRY

March 23, 1775

Mr. President: No man thinks more highly than I do of the patriotism, as well as abilities, of the very worthy gentlemen who have just addressed the House. But different men often see the same subject in different lights; and, therefore, I hope that it will not be
5 thought disrespectful to those gentlemen, if, entertaining as I do opinions of a character very opposite to theirs, I shall speak forth my sentiments freely and without reserve. This is no time for ceremony. The question before the House is one of awful moment to this country. For my own part I consider it as nothing less than a
10 question of freedom or slavery; and in proportion to the magnitude of the subject ought to be the freedom of the debate. It is only in this way that we can hope to arrive at truth, and fulfill the great responsibility which we hold to God and our country. Should I keep back my opinions at such a time, through fear of giving
15 offense, I should consider myself as guilty of treason towards my country, and of an act of disloyalty towards the majesty of heaven, which I revere above all earthly kings.

Mr. President, it is natural to man to indulge in the illusions of hope. We are apt to shut our eyes against a painful truth, and lis-
20 ten to the song of that siren, till she transforms us into beasts. Is this the part of wise men, engaged in a great and arduous struggle for liberty? Are we disposed to be of the number of those who,

GUIDE FOR READING

1 Mr. President: the president of the Virginia Convention, Peyton Randolph.

5 entertaining: holding in mind.

1–7 Henry states his respect for the previous speakers, a technique called "concession to the opposition." What effect might this have on the audience?

8 The question before the House: Henry proposed resolutions to prepare the Virginia colony for war and gave this speech to support those resolutions.

20 song . . . beasts: an allusion to Homer's *Odyssey*. The sirens' seductive song lured sailors to their deaths. The goddess Circe lured men to her island and then magically transformed them into pigs. Henry compares "the illusions of hope" to these dangerous mythical creatures.

having eyes, see not, and having ears, hear not, the things which so nearly concern their temporal salvation? For my part, whatever anguish of spirit it may cost, I am willing to know the whole truth—to know the worst and to provide for it.

I have but one lamp by which my feet are guided; and that is the lamp of experience. I know of no way of judging of the future but by the past. And judging by the past, I wish to know what there has been in the conduct of the British ministry for the last ten years, to justify those hopes with which gentlemen have been pleased to solace themselves and the House? Is it that insidious smile with which our petition has been lately received? Trust it not, sir; it will prove a snare to your feet. Suffer not yourselves to be betrayed with a kiss.

Ask yourselves how this gracious reception of our petition comports with these warlike preparations which cover our waters and darken our land. Are fleets and armies necessary to a work of love and reconciliation? Have we shown ourselves so unwilling to be reconciled that force must be called in to win back our love? Let us not deceive ourselves, sir. These are the implements of war and subjugation—the last arguments to which kings resort. I ask gentlemen, sir, what means this martial array, if its purpose be not to force us to submission? Can gentlemen assign any other possible motives for it? Has Great Britain any enemy, in this quarter of the world, to call for all this accumulation of navies and armies? No, sir, she has none. They are meant for us; they can be meant for no other. They are sent over to bind and rivet upon us those chains which the British ministry have been so long forging.

And what have we to oppose to them? Shall we try argument? Sir, we have been trying that for the last ten years. Have we anything new to offer on the subject? Nothing. We have held the subject up in every light of which it is capable; but it has been all in vain. Shall we resort to entreaty and humble supplication? What terms shall we find which have not been already exhausted? Let us not, I beseech you, sir, deceive ourselves longer.

Sir, we have done everything that could be done to avert the storm which is now coming on. We have petitioned; we have remonstrated; we have supplicated; we have prostrated ourselves before the throne, and have implored its interposition to arrest the tyrannical hands of the ministry and Parliament. Our petitions have been slighted; our remonstrances have produced additional violence and insult; our supplications have been disregarded; and we have been spurned, with contempt, from the foot of the throne.

23 having eyes . . . hear not: an allusion to Ezekiel 12:2.

24 temporal: worldly.

32 solace (sŏl´ĭs): comfort.

34 snare: trap.

35 betrayed with a kiss: a biblical allusion to the Apostle Judas, who betrayed Jesus. When soldiers came to arrest Jesus, Judas identified him by kissing him.

38–49 What does Henry say is the reason for the British military buildup in America?

50–55 Notice how Henry uses rhetorical questions to anticipate the arguments of his opponents. How effective is this technique?

54 entreaty (ĕn-trē´tē): earnest request; plea; **supplication** (sŭp´lĭ-kā´shən): the act of asking for something humbly or earnestly.

59 remonstrated (rĭ-mŏn´strā-tĭd): objected.

60 interposition: intervention.

WORDS TO KNOW	**insidious** (ĭn-sĭd´ē-əs) *adj.* treacherous
	subjugation (sŭb´jə-gā´shən) *n.* control by conquering
	martial (mär´shəl) *adj.* warlike
	tyrannical (tĭ-răn´ĭ-kəl) *adj.* harsh; oppressive
	spurn (spûrn) *v.* to reject scornfully

Patrick Henry Before the Virginia House of Burgesses (1851), Peter F. Rothermel. Red Hill,
The Patrick Henry National Memorial, Brookneal, Virginia.

65 In vain, after these things, may we indulge the fond hope of peace and reconciliation. There is no longer any room for hope.

If we wish to be free—if we mean to preserve inviolate those inestimable privileges for which we have been so long contend-
70 ing—if we mean not basely to abandon the noble struggle in which we have been so long engaged, and which we have pledged our-selves never to abandon until the glorious object of our contest shall be obtained, we must fight! I repeat it, sir, we must fight! An appeal to arms and to the God of Hosts is all that is left us!

They tell us, sir, that we are weak—unable to cope with so
75 formidable an adversary. But when shall we be stronger? Will it be the next week, or the next year? Will it be when we are totally disarmed, and when a British guard shall be stationed in every house? Shall we gather strength by irresolution and inaction? Shall we acquire the means of effectual resistance, by lying supinely on
80 our backs, and hugging the delusive phantom of hope, until our enemies shall have bound us hand and foot?

Sir, we are not weak, if we make a proper use of those means which the God of nature hath placed in our power. Three millions of people, armed in the holy cause of liberty, and in such a coun-
85 try as that which we possess, are invincible by any force which our enemy can send against us. Besides, sir, we shall not fight our bat-tles alone. There is a just God who presides over the destinies of nations, and who will raise up friends to fight our battles for us. The battle, sir, is not to the strong alone; it is to the vigilant, the
90 active, the brave. Besides, sir, we have no election. If we were base enough to desire it, it is now too late to retire from the contest. There is no retreat but in submission and slavery! Our chains are forged! Their clanking may be heard on the plains of Boston! The war is inevitable—and let it come! I repeat it, sir, let it come!
95 It is in vain, sir, to extenuate the matter. Gentlemen may cry, "Peace! peace!"—but there is no peace. The war is actually begun! The next gale that sweeps from the north will bring to our ears the clash of resounding arms! Our brethren are already in the field! Why stand we here idle? What is it that gentlemen wish? What
100 would they have? Is life so dear, or peace so sweet, as to be pur-chased at the price of chains and slavery? Forbid it, Almighty God! I know not what course others may take; but as for me, give me liberty, or give me death! ❖

67 **inviolate** (ĭn-vī′ə-lĭt): not violated; intact.

68 **inestimable** (ĭn-ĕs′tə-mə-bəl): extremely valuable.

69 **basely** (bās′lē): dishonorably.

72–73 Henry has reached the main point of his speech. What is Henry trying to convince his listeners to do?

74–94 In these two paragraphs, what reasons does Henry give for taking military action now?

89 **battle . . . strong alone:** an allusion to Ecclesiastes 9:11— "the race is not to the swift, nor the battle to the strong."

90 **election:** choice.

95 **extenuate** (ĭk-stĕn′yōō-āt′): to lessen the seriousness of, especially by providing partial excuses.

97 **the next gale . . . north:** Some colonists in Massachusetts had already shown open resistance to the British and were on the brink of war.

102–103 What emotions does Henry appeal to with the last lines of his speech?

WORDS TO KNOW	**formidable** (fôr′mĭ-də-bəl) *adj.* difficult to defeat
	adversary (ăd′vər-sĕr′ē) *n.* an opponent
	irresolution (ĭ-rĕz′ə-lōō′shən) *n.* uncertainty; indecision
	invincible (ĭn-vĭn′sə-bəl) *adj.* unbeatable
	vigilant (vĭj′ə-lənt) *adj.* alert; watchful

Thinking through the LITERATURE

Connect to the Literature

1. What Do You Think?
After hearing Henry's speech, would you have voted to prepare for war?

Comprehension Check
- What does Henry warn the colonists about?
- What does Henry urge the colonists to do?

Think Critically

2. In your view, what is the most convincing point Henry makes in his argument?

THINK ABOUT
- the main points he makes in the speech
- whether his reason for wanting to fight is the one you circled as the most compelling

3. ACTIVE READING RHETORICAL QUESTIONS AND PERSUASION
Review the examples of rhetorical questions you copied in your READER'S NOTEBOOK. Choose one of these rhetorical questions and reread the passage of the speech in which it is found. How does the use of a rhetorical question strengthen the persuasive force of this passage?

4. Think about Henry's famous statement, "Give me liberty, or give me death!" Do you agree that liberty is more important than life itself? Explain your answer.

Extend Interpretations

5. Different Perspectives Imagine how each of these people might have responded to Henry's speech:

- an American-born colonist whose grandparents were British
- a Loyalist, meaning an American colonist who sides with the British
- an African enslaved in the Virginia colony
- a Native American

6. Comparing Texts How would you compare Patrick Henry's speech and Jonathan Edwards's sermon as examples of persuasion? Consider the purpose of each speech and the emotions to which it appeals.

7. Connect to Life Patrick Henry argued that the actions of King George III and the British Parliament posed major threats to the liberty of the American colonists. In your opinion, what are the major threats to the liberty of Americans today?

Literary Analysis

ALLUSION An **allusion** is an indirect reference to a person, place, event, or literary work with which the author believes the reader will be familiar. Many works contain allusions to the Bible, classical mythology, or other works of literature. By using allusions, writers tap the knowledge and memory of the reader, drawing upon associations already in the reader's mind. For example, Patrick Henry warns colonists not to be "betrayed with a kiss." This biblical allusion refers to the Apostle Judas, who betrayed Jesus by kissing him. Henry used this brief, powerful allusion to suggest that there might be something sinister behind Great Britain's friendly gestures.

Paired Activity Work with a partner to investigate Henry's allusions in this speech. Review the Guide for Reading notes that explain the allusions to Homer's *Odyssey* and to Ecclesiastes. Each of you should choose one of these allusions to research, locating the particular passage in the original source, reading it carefully, and then expanding the note given in the Guide for Reading. Share your new note with your partner and with the rest of the class.

REVIEW REPETITION Reread the paragraph that begins "Sir, we have done everything . . ." (pages 264–266). What words, phrases, and sentence patterns are repeated in this paragraph? What effect does this repetition have?

Choices & CHALLENGES

Writing Options

1. Newspaper Report Write the first paragraphs of a newspaper report about Henry's speech that might have been published in the colonial *Virginia Gazette.* Describe the speech and its probable effect on the audience.

2. Character Sketch It has been said that history is written by the winners. Patrick Henry is regarded as a patriot today, but if the British had won the Revolutionary War, how would he be described? Write a brief sketch of Henry as it might appear in a current British history textbook.

3. Rebuttal Speech Draft a rebuttal opposing Henry's point of view. Offer a counterargument in favor of peaceful compromise with the British. Place this piece in your **Working Portfolio.**

Writing Handbook
See page 1285: Persuasive Writing

Activities & Explorations

1. Political Advertisement Plan a political advertisement for television that promotes one or more ideas from Henry's speech. Select fitting visual images, music, or slogans to use in the ad. Then share your TV spot with classmates. ~ **VIEWING AND REPRESENTING**

2. Liberty Poster Which images in Henry's speech do you think are the most powerful? Create a poster that conveys Henry's message, using illustrations and quotations that best capture the spirit of his speech. Use a computer to experiment with different type fonts and type sizes for your poster. ~ **ART**

3. Dramatic Reading Prepare and give a dramatic reading of Henry's speech, using gestures and varying your tone of voice to make the speech effective.
~ **PERFORMING**

4. Independence Discussion Take part in a roundtable discussion in which you identify groups of people who have recently fought or are now fighting for independence from another nation. What arguments have they used to support their cause? What do they stand to lose or gain?
~ **SPEAKING AND LISTENING**

Art Connection

Patrick Henry earned fame as an orator long before he made the speech reprinted here. In the painting on page 265, Peter F. Rothermel portrays Henry giving a speech in Virginia's House of Burgesses, which was Virginia's colonial legislature before the Revolution. Look for techniques that make this scene dramatic. What features of the painting focus attention on Henry?

Inquiry & Research

Countdown to Revolution What events led up to the conflict between Great Britain and the American colonists? What events happened after Patrick Henry called for war on March 23, 1775? Use an encyclopedia or an American history textbook to find out about important events that occurred before and after Henry gave his speech. Then make a time line of these events to share with the class.

 More Online: Research Starter
www.mcdougallittell.com

Vocabulary in Action

EXERCISE: CLASSIFYING WORDS On your paper, copy the chart shown. Then review the Words to Know. Which vocabulary words best fit the American colonists' view of the British? Write these words in the first column of the chart. Which words best fit the colonists' view of themselves? Write them in the second column. Be ready to explain your choices in class.

British	Colonists

WORDS TO KNOW			
	adversary	irresolution	tyrannical
	formidable	martial	vigilant
	insidious	spurn	
	invincible	subjugation	

Patrick Henry
1736–1799

Fiery Orator American patriot Patrick Henry was a self-taught lawyer whose gift of oration helped spark the American Revolution. In acknowledging Henry's gift, fellow Virginian Thomas Jefferson said: "Call it oratory or what you will, but I never heard anything like it. He had more command over the passions than any man I ever knew." An eloquent defender of colonial rights, Henry spent more than 30 years in public life and took part in the creation of a new nation.

A Voice of Protest In 1765, at the age of 28, Henry joined the House of Burgesses, the lower house of Virginia's colonial legislature. Just nine days after becoming a burgess, Henry introduced the Stamp Act Resolves. He opposed the Stamp Act, which required colonists to buy stamps to put on taxable paper items, on the grounds that only the colonial legislature—not the British Parliament—had the right to tax colonists. Virginia became the first colony to officially protest the Stamp Act.

Revolutionary Activities Ten years later, Henry again proposed resolutions that led toward American independence. At the Second Virginia Provincial Convention, he gave the impassioned speech you have just read. His resolutions to prepare for war passed by five votes, and he was named chairman of a committee to implement the plan to arm Virginia. In 1776, while the American Revolution raged, Henry helped draw up Virginia's first state constitution and was elected Virginia's first governor.

Later Years After the Revolution had ended and the U.S. Constitution had been ratified, Henry resumed his law practice. Then, in 1794, he retired to his Virginia estate, Red Hill. Although he was offered a U.S. Senate seat, posts as minister to Spain and to France, and the positions of Secretary of State and Chief Justice, he did not return to politics until George Washington urged him to run for representative in the Virginia state legislature in 1799. Henry won the election, but he died before taking office.

Declaration of Independence

Document by THOMAS JEFFERSON

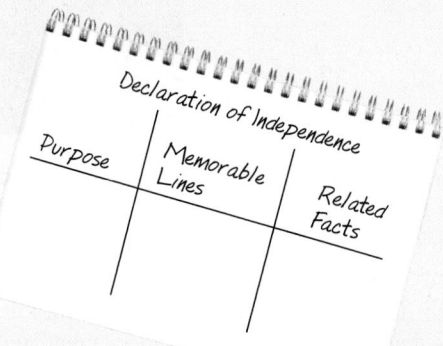

(Connect to Your Life)

A Treasured Document With a small group of your classmates, explore what you already know about the Declaration of Independence by filling in a chart like this one. Then read this selection to find out more about the Declaration of Independence.

Build Background

Let Freedom Ring In 1775, simmering tensions between Great Britain and her American colonies exploded in violent clashes. By the spring of 1776, many colonial Americans believed that the only solution to the conflict was to break away from British rule. At the Second Continental Congress held in Philadelphia, a five-member committee was appointed to draft an official statement of the reasons for independence. Thomas Jefferson, a 33-year-old Virginia lawyer with a keen talent for writing, prepared the first draft. After voting for independence on July 2, the full Congress debated the Declaration for two days, making a few more changes before adopting it on July 4.

The final version of the Declaration has four main parts:

- a preamble, or foreword, that announces the reason for the document
- a declaration of people's natural rights and relationship to government
- a long list of complaints against George III, the British king
- a conclusion that formally states America's independence

WORDS TO KNOW **Vocabulary Preview**

abdicate   impel   mercenary
arbitrary   insurrection

Focus Your Reading

LITERARY ANALYSIS   PARALLELISM When a writer uses similar grammatical forms or sentence patterns to express ideas of equal importance, this technique is called **parallelism.** Patrick Henry's famous line, "Give me liberty, or give me death!" is an example of parallelism. Notice other examples in the Declaration of Independence.

ACTIVE READING   PARAPHRASING A **paraphrase** restates someone else's ideas in simpler words. To paraphrase a passage, determine its main idea and replace difficult words with easier ones. Consider the following passage from the Declaration of Independence:

Prudence, indeed, will dictate that governments long established should not be changed for light and transient causes.

Here is a paraphrase of the same passage that restates the main idea in simpler language:

Common sense tells us that governments that have existed for a long time should not be changed for minor reasons.

READER'S NOTEBOOK As you read the Declaration of Independence, pause from time to time to paraphrase difficult passages, replacing difficult words with easier ones.

The DECLARATION of *Independence*

Thomas Jefferson
In Congress,
July 4, 1776

Jefferson drafted the Declaration of Independence on the portable writing desk he designed.

When, in the course of human events, it becomes necessary for one people to dissolve the political bands which have connected them with another, and to assume, among the powers of the earth, the separate and equal station to
5 which the laws of nature and of nature's God entitle them, a decent respect to the opinions of mankind requires that they should declare the causes which <u>impel</u> them to the separation.

GUIDE FOR READING

[Part 1: The Preamble]

1–8 The colonists felt they must explain their reasons to the world. Why?

WORDS TO KNOW	**impel** (ĭm-pĕl′) v. to drive forward; force

We hold these truths to be self-evident:—That all men are created equal; that they are endowed by their Creator with certain unalienable rights; that among these are life, liberty, and the pursuit of happiness. That, to secure these rights, governments are instituted among men, deriving their just powers from the consent of the governed; that, whenever any form of government becomes destructive of these ends, it is the right of the people to alter or to abolish it, and to institute a new government, laying its foundation on such principles, and organizing its powers in such form, as to them shall seem most likely to effect their safety and happiness. Prudence, indeed, will dictate that governments long established should not be changed for light and transient causes; and, accordingly, all experience hath shown that mankind are more disposed to suffer, while evils are sufferable, than to right themselves by abolishing the forms to which they are accustomed. But, when a long train of abuses and usurpations, pursuing invariably the same object, evinces a design to reduce them under absolute despotism, it is their right, it is their duty, to throw off such government, and to provide new guards for their future security. Such has been the patient sufferance of these colonies; and such is now the necessity that constrains them to alter their former systems of government. The history of the present King of Great Britain is a history of repeated injuries and usurpations, all having, in direct object, the establishment of an absolute tyranny over these States. To prove this, let facts be submitted to a candid world.

He has refused his assent to laws the most wholesome and necessary for the public good.

He has forbidden his Governors to pass laws of immediate and pressing importance, unless suspended in their operation till his assent should be obtained; and, when so suspended, he has utterly neglected to attend to them.

He has refused to pass other laws for the accommodation of large districts of people, unless these people would relinquish the right of representation in the legislature—a right inestimable to them, and formidable to tyrants only.

He has called together legislative bodies at places unusual, uncomfortable, and distant from the depository of their public records, for the sole purpose of fatiguing them into compliance with his measure.

He has dissolved representative houses repeatedly, for opposing, with manly firmness, his invasions on the rights of the people.

[Part 2: A Declaration of Rights]

11 unalienable (un āl′ yən ə bəl): that may not be taken away.

12–14 What is the purpose of government?

15–17 When is it right to overthrow a government?

20–22 When is it not right to change a government?

22 transient (trăn′shənt): passing away with time; temporary.

26 usurpations (yo͞o′sər-pā′shənz): acts of wrongfully taking over a right or power that belongs to someone else.

33 the present King of Great Britain: George III, who reigned from 1760 to 1820.

36 candid: fair; impartial.

[Part 3: A List of Complaints]

37–42 Laws passed in the colonies needed the king's approval; sometimes it took years for laws to be approved or rejected.

39–59 Royal colonial governors created hardships for the colonial assemblies. What were some of these hardships?

39 Governors: officials appointed by the king to govern individual colonies.

Signing the Declaration of Independence, John Trumbull. Corbis-Bettmann.

He has refused, for a long time after such dissolutions,
to cause others to be elected; whereby the legislative powers,
incapable of annihilation, have returned to the people at
large for their exercise; the State remaining, in the meantime,
exposed to all dangers of invasion from without, and
convulsions within.

He has endeavored to prevent the population of these
States; for that purpose obstructing the laws for the natural
ization of foreigners; refusing to pass others to encourage
their migration hither, and raising the conditions of new
appropriations of lands.

He has obstructed the administration of justice, by
refusing his assent to laws for establishing judiciary powers.

He has made judges dependent on his will alone for the
tenure of their offices, and the amount and payment of their
salaries.

He has erected a multitude of new offices, and sent hither
swarms of officers to harass our people and eat out their
substance.

60–64 The king had decreed that no more immigrants to America could become citizens, and he had raised the purchase price of frontierland.

65–69 The British had created hardships for the colonial courts. What were these hardships?

66 judiciary (jōō-dĭsh′ē-ĕr′ē): relating to courts of law.

67–68 the tenure (tĕn′yər) **of their offices:** their job security.

71 officers: tax gatherers and law enforcers.

71–72 eat out their substance: use up their resources.

The signature of John Hancock, president of the Continental Congress, is followed by 55 other signatures.

He has kept among us, in times of peace, standing armies, without the consent of our legislatures.

75 He has affected to render the military independent of, and superior to, the civil power.

He has combined with others to subject us to a jurisdiction foreign to our constitutions, and unacknowledged by our laws; giving his assent to their acts of pretended

80 legislation:

For quartering large bodies of armed troops among us;

For protecting them, by a mock trial, from punishment for any murders which they should commit on the inhabitants of these States;

85 For cutting off our trade with all parts of the world;

For imposing taxes on us without our consent;

For depriving us, in many cases, of the benefits of trial by jury;

For transporting us beyond the seas, to be tried for

90 pretended offenses;

For abolishing the free system of English laws in a neighboring province, establishing there an <u>arbitrary</u> government, and enlarging its boundaries, so as to render it at once an

77–79 Parliament had passed the Declaratory Act in 1766, stating that the King and Parliament could make all the laws for the colonies.

81–84 What objections did the colonists have about British soldiers in America?

85–101 What additional hardships were put on colonial lawmakers?

91-92 a neighboring province: the province of Quebec, which at the time extended south to the Ohio River and west to the Mississippi.

WORDS TO KNOW
arbitrary (är'bĭ-trĕr'ē) adj. based on unpredictable decisions rather than on reason or law

example and fit instrument for introducing the same
absolute rule into these colonies;

For taking away our charters, abolishing our most valuable laws, and altering, fundamentally, the forms of our governments;

For suspending our own legislatures, and declaring themselves invested with power to legislate for us in all cases whatsoever.

He has <u>abdicated</u> government here, by declaring us out of his protection, and waging war against us.

He has plundered our seas, ravaged our coasts, burnt our towns, and destroyed the lives of our people.

He is at this time transporting large armies of foreign <u>mercenaries</u> to complete the works of death, desolation, and tyranny, already begun with circumstances of cruelty and perfidy scarcely paralleled in the most barbarous ages, and totally unworthy the head of a civilized nation.

He has constrained our fellow citizens, taken captive on the high seas, to bear arms against their country, to become the executioners of their friends and brethren, or to fall themselves by their hands.

104–105 American seaports, such as Norfolk, Virginia, had already been shelled.

106–107 The British hired thirty thousand German soldiers to fight in America.

109 perfidy (pûr'fĭ-dē): betrayal; treachery.

We mutually pledge to each other our lives, our fortunes, and our sacred honor.

The signers used this silver inkwell, made by Philip Syng in 1752.

WORDS
TO
KNOW

abdicate (ăb'dĭ-kāt') v. to give up responsibility for
mercenary (mûr'sə-nĕr'ē) n. a professional soldier hired to fight in a foreign army

275

115   He has excited domestic <u>insurrection</u> amongst us, and has endeavored to bring on the inhabitants of our frontiers the merciless Indian savages, whose known rule of warfare is an undistinguished destruction of all ages, sexes, and conditions.

120   In every stage of these oppressions we have petitioned for redress, in the most humble terms; our repeated petitions have been answered only by repeated injury. A prince whose character is thus marked by every act which may define a tyrant is unfit to be the ruler of a free people.

125   Nor have we been wanting in our attentions to our British brethren. We have warned them, from time to time, of attempts by their legislature to extend an unwarrantable jurisdiction over us. We have reminded them of the circumstances of our emigration and settlement here. We

130 have appealed to their native justice and magnanimity; and we have conjured them, by the ties of our common kindred, to disavow these usurpations, which would inevitably interrupt our connections and correspondence.

    They, too, have been deaf to the voice of justice and of

135 consanguinity. We must, therefore, acquiesce in the necessity which denounces our separation; and hold them, as we hold the rest of mankind, enemies in war, in peace friends.

    WE, THEREFORE, THE REPRESENTATIVES OF THE UNITED STATES OF AMERICA, in General Congress assembled,

140 appealing to the Supreme Judge of the world for the rectitude of our intentions, do, in the name and by the authority of the good people of these colonies, solemnly publish and declare, that these United Colonies are, and of right ought to be, FREE AND INDEPENDENT STATES; that they are absolved

145 from all allegiance to the British crown, and that all political connection between them and the state of Great Britain is, and ought to be, totally dissolved; and that, as free and independent states, they have full power to alliances, establish commerce, and to do all other acts and

150 things which independent states may of right do. And, for the support of this declaration, with a firm reliance on the protection of Divine Providence, we mutually pledge to each other our lives, our fortunes, and our sacred honor. ❖

115 domestic insurrection: George III had encouraged slaves to rebel against their masters.

121 redress: the correction of a wrong.

130 native: natural; inborn.

[Part 4: A Statement of Independence]

131 conjured: appealed to.

135 consanguinity (kŏn'săn-gwĭn'ĭ-tē): blood relationship.

135–136 acquiesce (ăk'wē-ĕs') **in the necessity which denounces:** recognize that we must demand.

138–139 Some historians believe that this is the first appearance of the name "United States of America" in a document.

140 Supreme Judge of the world: God.

144 Notice the word *states*. America would not become one united country until 1789.

152 Divine Providence: God in his role of controller and guardian of the world.

from THE DECLARATION OF THE RIGHTS OF WOMAN

Olympe de Gouges (ô-lamp' də gōōzh')

The Declaration of Independence asserted that the people could overthrow a government if it did not protect their natural rights. In 1789, the common people in France did just that, rebelling against their king and setting up a government of their own. In August of that year, the Declaration of the Rights of Man and of the Citizen proclaimed the ideals that inspired the French Revolution. Responding to this document in 1791, the French writer and revolutionary Olympe de Gouges urged that political rights be extended to women.

Preamble

Mothers, daughters, sisters [and] representatives of the nation demand to be constituted into a national assembly. Believing that ignorance, omission, or scorn for the rights of woman are the only causes of public misfortunes and of the corruption of governments, [the women] have resolved to set forth in a solemn declaration the natural, inalienable,[1] and sacred rights of woman in order that this declaration, constantly exposed before all the members of the society, will ceaselessly remind them of their rights and duties; in order that the authoritative acts of women and the authoritative acts of men may be at any moment compared with and respectful of the purpose of all political institutions; and in order that citizens' demands, henceforth based on simple and incontestable principles, will always support the constitution, good morals, and the happiness of all.

Consequently, the sex that is as superior in beauty as it is in courage during the sufferings of maternity recognizes and declares in the presence and under the auspices of the Supreme Being, the following Rights of Woman and of Female Citizens.

Article I. Woman is born free and lives equal to man in her rights. Social distinctions can be based only on the common utility.

Article II. The purpose of any political association is the conservation of the natural and imprescriptible[2] rights of woman and man; these rights are liberty, property, security, and especially resistance to oppression.

Article III. The principle of all sovereignty rests essentially with the nation, which is nothing but the union of woman and man; no body and no individual can exercise any authority which does not come expressly from it [the nation].

Article IV. Liberty and justice consist of restoring all that belongs to others; thus, the only limits on the exercise of the natural rights of woman are perpetual male tyranny; these limits are to be reformed by the laws of nature and reason.

Article V. Laws of nature and reason proscribe all acts harmful to society; everything which is not prohibited by these wise and divine laws cannot be prevented, and no one can be constrained to do what they do not command.

Article VI. The law must be the expression of the general will; all female and male citizens must contribute either personally or through their representatives to its formation; it must be the same for all: male and female citizens, being equal in the eyes of the law, must be equally admitted to all honors, positions, and public employment according to their capacity and without other distinctions besides those of their virtues and talents.

---

1. **inalienable** (ĭn-āl'yə-nə-bəl): not to be taken away.
2. **imprescriptible** (ĭm'prē-skrĭp'tə-bəl): inalienable.

Article VII. No woman is an exception; she is accused, arrested, and detained in cases determined by law. Women, like men, obey this rigorous law.

Article VIII. The law must establish only those penalties that are strictly and obviously necessary, and no one can be punished except by virtue of a law established and promulgated[3] prior to the crime and legally applicable to women.

Article IX. Once any woman is declared guilty, complete rigor is [to be] exercised by the law.

Article X. No one is to be disquieted for his very basic opinions; woman has the right to mount the scaffold; she must equally have the right to mount the rostrum,[4] provided that her demonstrations do not disturb the legally established public order.

Article XI. The free communication of thoughts and opinions is one of the most precious rights of woman, since that liberty assures the recognition of children by their fathers. Any female citizen thus may say freely, I am the mother of a child which belongs to you, without being forced by a barbarous prejudice to hide the truth; [an exception may be made] to respond to the abuse of this liberty in cases determined by the law.

Article XII. The guarantee of the rights of woman and the female citizen implies a major benefit; this guarantee must be instituted for the advantage of all, and not for the particular benefit of those to whom it is entrusted.

Article XIII. For the support of the public force and the expenses of administration, the contributions of woman and man are equal; she shares all the duties [*corvées*] and all the painful tasks; therefore, she must have the same share in the distribution of positions, employment, offices, honors, and jobs [*industrie*].

Article XIV. Female and male citizens have the right to verify, either by themselves or through their representatives, the necessity of the public contribution. . . .

Article XV. The collectivity of women, joined for tax purposes to the aggregate of men, has the right to demand an accounting of his administration from any public agent.

Article XVI. No society has a constitution without the guarantee of rights and the separation of powers; the constitution is null if the majority of individuals comprising the nation have not cooperated in drafting it.

Article XVII. Property belongs to both sexes whether united or separate; for each it is an inviolable and sacred right; no one can be deprived of it, since it is the true patrimony[5] of nature, unless the legally determined public need obviously dictates it, and then only with a just and prior indemnity.[6]

Postscript

Woman, wake up; the tocsin[7] of reason is being heard throughout the whole universe; discover your rights. The powerful empire of nature is no longer surrounded by prejudice, fanaticism, superstition, and lies. The flame of truth has dispersed all the clouds of folly and usurpation. Enslaved man has multiplied his strength and needs recourse to yours to break his chains. Having become free, he has become unjust to his companion. Oh, women, women! When will you cease to be blind? What advantage have you received from the Revolution? . . . Regardless of what barriers confront you, it is in your power to free yourselves; you have only to want to.

---

3. **promulgated** (prŏm′əl-gā′tĭd): announced publicly.
4. **rostrum** (rŏs′trəm): a raised platform for public speaking.
5. **patrimony** (păt′rə-mō′nē): inheritance; legacy.
6. **indemnity** (ĭn-dĕm′nĭ-tē): compensation for loss.
7. **tocsin** (tŏk′sĭn): alarm bell.

Thinking through the LITERATURE

Connect to the Literature

1. What Do You Think? What did you learn about the Declaration of Independence that you didn't know before?

Comprehension Check
- What main reason for writing the Declaration is stated in the Preamble?
- According to the Declaration, what three rights do all people have?
- What are three complaints the colonists had against the king?

Think Critically

2. Which reason for breaking away from British rule strikes you as most important, and why?

THINK ABOUT

- the colonists' philosophical ideals
- the economic and political hardships colonists suffered as a result of British policies
- the king's response to colonists' complaints

3. Jefferson makes it clear that America has complaints against George III, not against the British people. In what ways does the Declaration emphasize this difference, and why do you think this distinction was made?

4. The Enlightenment, or the Age of Reason, was a period in which logic, reason, and rational thought prevailed. What phrases and sentences in the Declaration suggest that this document was a product of the Age of Reason?

5. **ACTIVE READING PARAPHRASING** Read aloud a passage that you paraphrased in your **READER'S NOTEBOOK** and compare the paraphrase with the original passage. How does the effect on the reader change?

6. How do you think the statement "all men are created equal" was interpreted at the time it was written? How do Americans interpret the words today?

Extend Interpretations

7. Comparing Texts What influences from the Declaration of Independence do you see on Olympe de Gouges's Declaration of the Rights of Woman (page 277)? How do the two documents differ?

8. Connect to Life The Declaration of Independence states the purpose of government and the conditions under which a government should be changed. How would you evaluate your local government or the present federal government, based on Jefferson's standards?

Literary Analysis

PARALLELISM The use of similar grammatical forms or sentence patterns to express ideas of equal importance is called **parallelism.** Parallelism generally makes both written and spoken expression more concise and powerful. In the Declaration of Independence, for example, Jefferson uses the parallel constructions *He has refused . . . , He has forbidden . . . , He has dissolved . . .* in his list of complaints against George III. By using parallelism, Jefferson emphasizes that each of the colonists' grievances is equally important, and he cumulatively builds a case against the king.

Paired Activity Work with a partner to find three or more sets of parallel phrases in the Declaration of Independence. Then create a diagram like the one shown for each set of parallelisms that you find. Later, find examples of parallelism in modern political speeches or advertisements.

Writing Options

1. Modern Paraphrase Looking back at the passages you paraphrased in your

📖 READER'S NOTEBOOK , write a more polished paraphrase of one section of the Declaration of Independence. Choose either the preamble, the declaration of rights, or the conclusion. Then share your paraphrase with the class.

2. Teenager's Declaration With a small group of classmates, write a declaration of independence for teenagers, following Jefferson's or de Gouges's style. Include a brief declaration of teen rights, a list of at least ten complaints, and a concluding statement of independence. Have a member of your group read the declaration to the class.

3. Personal Response Choose a famous phrase from the Declaration of Independence—"all men are created equal" or "life, liberty, and the pursuit of happiness"—and explore what the phrase means to you in a personal essay. You might tell how you interpret the words or whether you believe them.

Activities & Explorations

1. Taking Sides With your classmates, role play an informal debate between colonists who support independence and those who feel loyal to Great Britain, using points brought out in the Declaration to frame your argument. ~ SPEAKING AND LISTENING

2. First Draft Blues Thomas Jefferson spent two weeks writing a draft of the Declaration of Independence. Imagine that he used the same writing process as you do. Present a one-person skit for your class that shows Jefferson talking to himself as he writes. Use your own writing experiences as a guide. ~ PERFORMING

3. Colonial Cartoon Imagine that you are an 18th-century cartoonist who either supports or rejects the ideas in the Declaration of Independence. Draw an editorial cartoon that expresses your point of view. Then display your cartoon on a classroom bulletin board. ~ ART

Vocabulary in Action

EXERCISE: CONTEXT CLUES For each sentence, determine whether the boldfaced word is used correctly or incorrectly. Write *correct* or *incorrect* on your paper.

1. Jefferson believed that King George needed to **abdicate** Benjamin Franklin in France.

2. Jefferson wrote the Declaration of Independence during a colonial **insurrection** against the king.

3. The British troops tried to **impel** their cannons at the Battle of Lexington.

4. Colonists felt that many British actions were **arbitrary,** or taken without justification.

5. Many a colonial family was forced to provide lodging to a **mercenary** in the British army.

Building Vocabulary

For an in-depth lesson on context clues, see page 326.

WORDS TO KNOW	abdicate	arbitrary	impel	insurrection	mercenary

Thomas Jefferson
1743–1826

Renaissance Man Few in American history have better fit the ideal of the Renaissance man, or a man who develops talents in many areas, than Thomas Jefferson. He was a lawmaker and writer, the author of the Virginia laws on religious freedom and of the Declaration of Independence. He was a talented scientist, with notable accomplishments in botany and agriculture. He was an architect whose Virginia home—Monticello—is considered an architectural masterpiece. An inventor, he designed such practical devices as the dumbwaiter, a revolving music stand, a better type of plow, a machine that made copies of letters, and a portable writing desk on which he probably drafted the Declaration.

A Man of Contradictions Jefferson was not only versatile, but he was also a complex man who often showed contradictions in his actions. He was one of the young radicals who pushed for a break with Great Britain, but he had no interest in the military, and he did not fight in the Revolutionary War. He spoke out frequently against slavery, yet he owned slaves all his life. Although he was a wealthy landowner from a prominent Southern family, he neglected to pay his debts and was plagued by financial troubles, and he passionately championed the rights of the small farmer and the average citizen.

Early Years Jefferson was born in Albermarle County, Virginia, on April 13, 1743. His father was a successful planter, surveyor, and mapmaker, and his mother was a member of a respected Virginia family. As a young man, he was educated at small, private schools and attended the College of William and Mary in Williamsburg. After finishing college, Jefferson studied law. He launched a successful career as a lawyer in 1767, practicing until the American Revolution closed the courts in 1774. A few years after establishing his law practice, he married a wealthy young widow, Martha Skelton. Tragically, after only ten years of marriage, Mrs. Jefferson died, and four of the couple's six children died in childhood. Jefferson did not marry again but devoted his energies to his two surviving daughters and to public life.

The Statesman Jefferson distinguished himself in politics. At the age of 26, he was elected to Virginia's colonial legislature, where he befriended Patrick Henry and became an outspoken advocate of American rights. As a delegate to the Second Continental Congress, he was chosen to draft the Declaration of Independence. During the Revolutionary War, Jefferson was elected Virginia's governor in 1779. He later served as United States minister to France during the unfolding French Revolution, as the nation's first secretary of state, and as vice-president under John Adams before being elected the third president of the United States in 1800. Among his accomplishments as president were the Louisiana Purchase, which nearly doubled the size of the United States, and the Lewis and Clark expedition, which brought back invaluable scientific and cultural information about the West.

Later Years After two terms in office, Jefferson retired to Monticello in 1809, where he read voraciously, studied mathematics, conducted scientific experiments in farming, played the violin, and collected paintings. He founded the University of Virginia, designing the course of study as well as many of the buildings. To prevent plunging into bankruptcy, he sold his 10,000-volume library to the United States; his library formed the basis of the Library of Congress. With dramatic appropriateness, Thomas Jefferson died just hours before fellow patriot John Adams on July 4, 1826, the 50th anniversary of the adoption of the Declaration of Independence.

Letter to the Rev. Samson Occom

by PHILLIS WHEATLEY

Letter to John Adams

by ABIGAIL ADAMS

Connect to Your Life

What Freedom Means What ideas and phrases come to mind when you think of the words *liberty* and *freedom?* What kinds of liberty and freedom do you believe people should have? Should all people have the same liberties and freedoms? Discuss your thoughts with a small group of classmates.

Build Background

Letters by Colonial Women The two letters you are about to read are concerned with the issues of liberty and freedom. Both were written at the time of the American Revolution and provide insights into colonial life during the struggle for independence. The first letter is by Phillis Wheatley, a former slave in Boston who was the first African American to have a book of poetry published. It is believed that she was writing to her friend the Reverend Samson Occom, a converted Mohegan Indian minister, in response to his written protest against slave-owning ministers. This letter was dated February 11, 1774, and was published later in the *Connecticut Gazette* and other colonial newspapers.

The second letter is by Abigail Adams, the wife of John Adams, who became the second president of the United States. It was written to her husband shortly before the Declaration of Independence was signed. He had left their Massachusetts home in 1774 to become a delegate to the First Continental Congress in Philadelphia, and they saw each other only rarely in the ten years afterward. During this time, however, they exchanged more than 300 letters, including the one you will read. A grandson saved the letters and first published them in 1840.

> **WORDS TO KNOW**
> **Vocabulary Preview**
>
> acquiescing
> countenance
> dispensation
> emancipate
> lethargy
>
> precept
> probity
> ruminating
> solicitous
> vindication

Focus Your Reading

LITERARY ANALYSIS FIGURATIVE LANGUAGE

Language that communicates ideas beyond the literal meaning of words is known as **figurative language.** Both Wheatley's and Adams's letters contain figurative language. For example, a line from Adams's letter states that one's country is a "secondary god" and the "first and greatest parent." Notice other examples of figurative language in the letters.

ACTIVE READING LITERARY LETTERS

A **literary letter** is a personal letter that has been published because a well-known figure wrote it and/or because it provides information about the period in which it was written. Not only do literary letters reveal a writer's personal concerns, but they may also cast light on public issues of the writer's time.

READER'S NOTEBOOK As you read each letter, fill in a diagram like the one shown to separate the private and public issues that are addressed.

Public
Private

Letter

to the
Rev. Samson Occom

Phillis Wheatley

An engraving of Phillis Wheatley. Reproduced from the collections of the Library of Congress.

Reverend and honored sir,

"I have this day received your obliging kind epistle,[1] and am greatly satisfied with your reasons respecting the negroes, and think highly reasonable what you offer in <u>vindication</u> of their natural rights: Those that invade them cannot be insensible[2] that the divine light is chasing away the thick darkness which broods over the land of Africa;[3] and the chaos which has reigned so long, is converting into beautiful order, and reveals more and more clearly the glorious

---

1. **epistle:** letter.
2. **insensible:** unaware.
3. **divine light . . . Africa:** Wheatley is referring to the spread of Christianity to areas of Africa where it had not been practiced.

For in every human breast God has implanted a principle, which we call love of freedom.

dispensation of civil and religious liberty, which are so inseparably united, that there is little or no enjoyment of one without the other: Otherwise, perhaps, the Israelites had been less solicitous for their freedom from Egyptian slavery;[4] I do not say they would have been contented without it, by no means; for in every human breast God has implanted a principle, which we call love of freedom; it is impatient of oppression, and pants for deliverance; and by the leave of our modern Egyptians[5] I will assert, that the same principle lives in us. God grant deliverance in his own way and time, and get him honor upon all those whose avarice impels them to countenance and help forward the calamities of their fellow creatures. This I desire not for their hurt, but to convince them of the strange absurdity of their conduct, whose words and actions are so diametrically opposite. How well the cry for liberty, and the reverse disposition for the exercise of oppressive power over others agree—I humbly think it does not require the penetration[6] of a philosopher to determine."—

---

4. **Israelites . . . Egyptian slavery:** a biblical allusion to the enslaved Jews who were led out of Egypt by Moses sometime between 1300 and 1200 B.C.

5. **modern Egyptians:** this comparison refers to the owners of African slaves.

6. **penetration:** understanding; insight.

Thinking Through the Literature

1. **Comprehension Check** Paraphrase the last sentence of this letter. You could begin the paraphrase with "It doesn't take a rocket scientist. . . ."

2. How would you describe Wheatley's attitude toward Occom? toward slaveholders? Support your answer with evidence from the text.

3. How would you evaluate the case that Wheatley makes against slavery?

THINK ABOUT
- what she says is happening in Africa
- what relationship she sees between civil and religious liberty
- what she hopes God will do

WORDS TO KNOW
dispensation (dĭs´pən-sā´shən) *n.* distribution; giving out
solicitous (sə-lĭs´ĭ-təs) *adj.* full of desire; eager
countenance (koun´tə-nəns) *v.* to give or express approval; support

Letter
to
John Adams

Abigail Adams

This 1775 British cartoon ridicules a group of North Carolina women who, in support of the patriot cause, signed a pledge not to drink tea. Courtesy of the State Department of Cultural Resources, Divison of Archives and History, Raleigh, North Carolina.

Braintree, 7 May, 1776.

How many are the solitary hours I spend, ruminating upon the past, and anticipating the future, whilst you, overwhelmed with the cares of state, have but a few moments you can devote to any individual. All domestic pleasures and enjoyments are absorbed in the great and important duty you owe your country, "for our country is, as it were, a secondary god, and the first and greatest parent. It is to be preferred to parents, wives, children, friends, and all things, the gods only excepted; for, if our country perishes, it is as impossible to save an individual, as to preserve one of the fingers of a mortified[1] hand." Thus do I suppress every wish, and silence every murmur, acquiescing in a painful separation from the companion of my youth, and the friend of my heart.

I believe 't is near ten days since I wrote you a line. I have not felt in a humor to entertain you if I had taken up my pen. Perhaps some unbecoming invective[2] might have fallen from it. The eyes of our rulers have been closed, and a lethargy has seized almost every member. I fear a fatal security has taken possession of them. Whilst the building is in flames, they tremble at the expense of water to quench it. In short, two months have elapsed since the evacuation of

---

1. **mortified:** decayed; having gangrene.
2. **invective:** abusive language.

WORDS TO KNOW	
ruminating (rōō′mə-nā-tǐng) *adj.* turning a matter over and over in the mind **ruminate** *v.*
acquiescing (ăk′wē-ĕs′ǐng) *adj.* consenting passively or without protest **acquiesce** *v.*
lethargy (lĕth′ər-jē) *n.* a state of sluggishness and inactivity

Boston,[3] and very little has been done in that time to secure it, or the harbor, from future invasion. The people are all in a flame, and no one among us, that I have heard of, even mentions expense. They think, universally, that there has been an amazing neglect somewhere. Many have turned out as volunteers to work upon Noddle's Island, and many more would go upon Nantasket, if the business was once set on foot. "'T is a maxim of state,[4] that power and liberty are like heat and moisture. Where they are well mixed, every thing prospers; where they are single, they are destructive."

A government of more stability is much wanted in this colony, and they are ready to receive it from the hands of the Congress. And since I have begun with maxims of state, I will add another, namely, that a people may let a king[5] fall, yet still remain a people; but, if a king let his people slip from him, he is no longer a king. And as this is most certainly our case, why not proclaim to the world, in decisive terms, your own importance?

Shall we not be despised by foreign powers, for hesitating so long at a word?

I cannot say that I think you are very generous to the ladies; for, whilst you are proclaiming peace and good-will to men, emancipating all nations, you insist upon retaining an absolute power over wives. But you must remember, that arbitrary power is like most other things which are very hard, very liable to be broken; and, notwithstanding all your wise laws and maxims, we have it in our power, not only to free ourselves, but to subdue our masters, and, without violence, throw both your natural and legal authority at our feet;—

"Charm by accepting, by submitting sway,
Yet have our humor most when we obey."[6]

I thank you for several letters which I have received since I wrote last; they alleviate a tedious absence, and I long earnestly for a Saturday evening, and experience a similar pleasure to that which I used to find in the return of my friend upon that day after a week's absence. The idea of a year dissolves all my philosophy.

Our little ones, whom you so often recommend to my care and instruction, shall not be deficient in virtue or probity, if the precepts of a mother have their desired effect; but they would be doubly enforced, could they be indulged with the example of a father alternately before them. I often point them to their sire,
"engaged in a corrupted state,
Wrestling with vice and faction."[7]

A Adams

---

3. **two months . . . Boston:** British troops under General William Howe and more than a thousand Loyalists evacuated Boston on March 17, 1776.

4. **maxim of state:** rule or short saying related to government.

5. **king:** Adams is referring to the British king George III, who ignored colonists' protests and put Massachusetts under military rule.

6. **"Charm . . . obey":** a couplet taken from Alexander Pope's poem *Moral Essays*.

7. **vice and faction:** corruption and conflict within a nation.

WORDS
TO
KNOW

emancipate (ĭ-măn′sə-pāt′) *v.* to free; liberate
probity (prō′bĭ-tē) *n.* honesty; integrity
precept (prē′sĕpt′) *n.* a rule or principle prescribing a particular course of action

Connect to the Literature

1. What Do You Think?
What impression of Abigail Adams do you get from her letter? Share your ideas with classmates.

Comprehension Check
- What does Adams warn will result from the congressmen's treatment of the ladies?
- According to Adams, what should take precedence, public responsibilities or personal concerns?

Think Critically

2. | ACTIVE READING | LITERARY LETTERS | What private issues and what public issues do you see addressed in Adams's letter? Refer to the diagram you made in your **READER'S NOTEBOOK**.

3. How would you describe Adams's attitude toward her husband and his work? Support your answer with evidence from the letter.

4. What can you **infer** about Adams's views on public issues?

THINK ABOUT
- her description of the local colonial government
- her maxim about power and liberty
- her maxim about people and a king
- her comments about women

Extend Interpretations

5. Comparing Texts How similar are the purposes of Wheatley's letter and Adams's letter? Consider the private and public issues they address.

6. What If? If Phillis Wheatley or Abigail Adams were living today, what public issues do you think they would have addressed? What stand do you think they would have taken on these issues?

7. Connect to Life Adams and Wheatley did not intend their letters to be published, but many people have read and enjoyed them. Name a contemporary woman whose letters or diaries you think might be read 200 years from now, and explain why.

Literary Analysis

| FIGURATIVE LANGUAGE |

Figurative language is language that communicates ideas beyond the literal meaning of words. Two common forms of figurative language—metaphors and similes—make comparisons between two unlike things that have something in common. A **metaphor** makes the comparison directly: "Our country is a parent," for example. A **simile** states the comparison using *like* or *as:* "Our country is like a parent." Metaphors and similes in prose can make descriptions more interesting and also make unfamiliar ideas easier to understand.

Cooperative Learning Activity
Working with a small group of classmates, find three or four examples of figurative language in these two letters. Copy each one into a chart like the one shown. Classify each example as a simile or a metaphor, and explain what ideas the comparison suggests. Share your chart with other groups.

Example	Simile or Metaphor?	Ideas Suggested

Choices & CHALLENGES

Writing Options

Literary Letter Write your own literary letter addressing the topic of liberty. As a starting point, use the comments you made in the Connect to Your Life activity (page 282). Then consider the ideas that the letters by Wheatley and Adams suggest to you. Publish your letter by displaying it in the classroom or by submitting it to the school newspaper or literary magazine. Place this piece in your **Working Portfolio.**

Activities & Explorations

Talk Show With other members of your class, stage a colonial talk show with guests Phillis Wheatley and Abigail Adams. The host can introduce the guests and ask a few questions, then open up the questioning to the rest of the audience. ~ **SPEAKING AND LISTENING**

Vocabulary in Action

EXERCISE: ASSESSMENT PRACTICE Read this fictitious letter by an 18th-century patriot. Rewrite the letter, replacing the underlined word or phrase with the vocabulary word that is a synonym.

I am <u>eager</u> to learn your views on the burning issue of freedom. While I do not <u>favor</u> violence, I do think there is <u>justification</u> for recent events. It is a fundamental <u>law</u> that those who are attacked must defend themselves if they wish to escape destruction. We must shake off our <u>drowsiness</u> and prepare for war. We should neither be politely <u>consenting</u> to the king's taxes nor blindly trusting his <u>honesty</u> as he says one thing to us and does another. What choice do we have left but to prepare for freeing ourselves from his choking grasp? He will offer no <u>kind gift</u> of freedom, to be sure. While <u>thinking</u> about possible conflict, I pray for God's guidance.

Building Vocabulary
Most of the Words to Know in this lesson come from Latin. For an in-depth study of word origins, see page 550.

WORDS TO KNOW			
acquiescing	lethargy		
countenance	precept	solicitous	
dispensation	probity	vindication	
emancipate	ruminating		

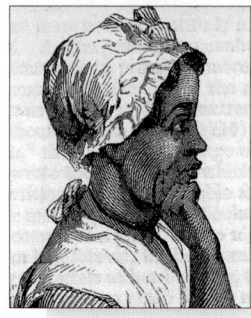

Phillis Wheatley
1753?–1784

African-born Poet After being kidnapped by slave traders in 1761, Phillis Wheatley was brought from Africa to Boston on the slave ship *Phillis* and was bought by Susanna Wheatley, the wife of a wealthy merchant. While living at the Wheatleys, she learned English and Latin and studied literature, and she began to write poetry at about age 12. Her only book, *Poems on Various Subjects, Religious and Moral,* was published in London in 1773. That same year, she received her freedom, and a short time later she wrote the antislavery letter you have just read.

Abigail Adams
1744–1818

Colonial Commentator Abigail Adams was the wife of President John Adams and the mother of President John Quincy Adams. Educated at home, Adams studied the works of John Milton, Alexander Pope, and William Shakespeare. When she was 15, she met John Adams, a 26-year-old Massachusetts lawyer. Five years later, in 1764, they were married. From 1774 to 1784, John was often away from home, serving first as a delegate to the Continental Congress in Philadelphia and later as a diplomat in Europe. During this period, Abigail raised four children, managed family business matters, and carried on a lively correspondence with her husband. Her letters today provide us with a vivid portrait of 18th-century life as a new nation was being born.

What Is an American?

Essay by MICHEL-GUILLAUME JEAN DE CRÈVECOEUR
(mē-shĕl′ gē-yōm′ zhäɴ də-krĕv-kœr′)

Connect to Your Life

Defining an American What words and phrases come to mind when you hear the word *American*? What different traits or qualities do you associate with Americans? Create a word web to explore your associations. Then as a class, discuss the question, What is an American?

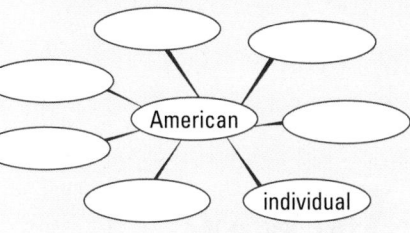

Build Background

An Immigrant's Impressions During the mid-1700s, many people left Europe for the opportunity and challenge of North America. Some came to escape crowded cities, to own their own land, and to earn a better living. Others came in search of religious freedom, a life with less government interference, and the chance to have a greater voice in government.

Michel-Guillaume Jean de Crèvecoeur was a French immigrant who arrived in New York in 1759. For ten years, he traveled widely throughout the British colonies as a surveyor and a trader, finally settling on a farm he bought in New York. There, he began to write down his impressions of life in America. In 1782, under the name of J. Hector St. John, he published a collection of 12 essays called *Letters from an American Farmer.* These letters were very well received in Europe and were read by many people—some considering the voyage to America and some just curious. The selection you will read is an excerpt from one of the best known of these letters, in which de Crèvecoeur offers his definition of an American.

WORDS TO KNOW
Vocabulary Preview
allurement
despotic
kindred
servile
subsistence

Focus Your Reading

LITERARY ANALYSIS **THEME** The **theme** of a literary work is the central idea the writer wishes to share with the reader. For example, the theme of Phillis Wheatley's "Letter to the Rev. Samson Occom" is that the love of freedom is inborn in all humans. As you read this essay, consider de Crèvecoeur's ideas and think about which one is most important.

ACTIVE READING **ANALYZING CONTRAST** "What Is an American?" is structured as a series of contrasts: de Crèvecoeur contrasts America and Americans with Europe and Europeans. To **contrast** two things is to state or show how they are dissimilar.

READER'S NOTEBOOK Copy in your notebook the chart shown. Then as you read de Crèvecoeur's essay, complete the chart by noting the contrasts he makes.

Category	Europe/European	America/American
Government	"despotic prince"	a new government
Work		
Quality of Life		
Ethnic Background		
Religion		

What Is an ? American?

Michel-Guillaume Jean de Crèvecoeur

In this great American asylum,[1] the poor of Europe have by some means met together, and in consequence of various causes; to what purpose should they ask one another, what countrymen they are? Alas, two-thirds of them had no country. Can a wretch who wanders about, who works and starves, whose life is a continual scene of sore affliction or pinching penury[2]—can that man call England or any other kingdom his country? A country that had no bread for him, whose fields procured him no harvest, who met with nothing but the frowns of the rich, the severity of the laws, with jails and punishments, who owned not a single foot of the extensive surface of this planet? No! urged by a variety of motives, here they came. Everything has tended to regenerate them: new laws, a new mode of living, a new social system. Here they are become men; in Europe they were as so many useless plants, wanting vegetative mold[3] and refreshing showers; they withered and were mowed down by want, hunger, and war. But now, by the power of transplantation, like all other plants, they have taken root and flourished! Formerly they were not numbered in any civil list of their country, except in those of the poor; here they rank as citizens. . . .

What attachment can a poor European emigrant have for a country where he had nothing? The knowledge of the language, the love of a few

---

1. **asylum** (ə-sī′ləm): a shelter.
2. **penury** (pĕn′yə-rē): extreme poverty.
3. **vegetative mold:** loose, crumbly soil that is rich in nutrients and helps plants grow.

Van Bergen Overmantel (1732–1733), attributed to John Heaten. Oil on wood (fireboard), 15¼″ × 73½″, New York State Historical Association, Cooperstown, New York. Photo Copyright © New York State Historical Association, Cooperstown, New York.

kindred as poor as himself were the only cords that tied him. His country is now that which gives him land, bread, protection, and consequence.[4] *Ubi panis ibi patria* [where my bread is earned, there is my country] is the motto of all emigrants. What then is the American, this new man? He is either a European or the descendant of a European; hence that strange mixture of blood which you will find in no other country. I could point out to you a man whose grandfather was an Englishman, whose wife was Dutch, whose son married a French woman, and whose present four sons have now four wives of different nations. *He* is an American who, leaving behind him all his ancient prejudices and manners, receives new ones from the new mode of life he has embraced, the new government he obeys, and the new rank he holds. He becomes an American by being received in the broad lap of our great alma mater.[5]

Here individuals of all nations are melted into a new race of men, whose labors and posterity will one day cause great change in the world. Americans are the western pilgrims who are carrying along with them that great mass of arts, sciences, vigor, and industry[6] which began long since in the east; they will finish the great circle. The Americans were once scattered all over Europe; here they are incorporated into one of the finest systems of population which has ever appeared, and which will hereafter become distinct by the power of the different climates they inhabit. The American ought, therefore, to love this country much better than that wherein either he or his forefathers were born. Here the rewards of his industry follow with equal steps the progress of his labor; his labor is founded on the basis of nature, self-interest. Can it want a stronger allurement? Wives and children, who before in vain demanded of him a morsel of bread, now, fat and frolicsome, gladly help their father to clear those fields whence exuberant crops are to arise to feed and to clothe them all, without any part being claimed, either by a despotic prince, a rich abbot,[7] or a mighty lord. Here, religion demands but little of him; a small voluntary salary to the minister, and gratitude to God. Can he refuse these?

The American is a new man, who acts upon new principles; he must, therefore, entertain new ideas and form new opinions. From involuntary idleness, servile dependence, penury, and useless labor he has passed to toils of a very different nature, rewarded by ample subsistence. This is an American. ❖

---

4. **consequence:** importance.

5. **alma mater** (ăl′mə mä′tər): A Latin phrase that literally means "nourishing mother."

6. **industry:** energetic devotion to a task or endeavor; diligence.

7. **abbot** (ăb′ət): the head of a monastery.

WORDS TO KNOW

kindred (kĭn′drĭd) *n.* relatives or family
allurement (ə-lōōr′mənt) *n.* attraction; enticement
despotic (dĭ-spŏt′ĭk) *adj.* like a dictator
servile (sûr′vəl) *adj.* humbly submissive; slavish
subsistence (səb-sĭs′təns) *n.* livelihood

from
Poor Richard's Almanack
Benjamin Franklin

He that cannot obey cannot command.

Don't count your chickens
before they are hatched.

A mob's a monster;
heads enough but no
brains.

Well done is better
than well said.

Lost time is never
found again.

Early to bed,
early to rise,
makes a man healthy,
wealthy and wise.

If you would know the worth of money,
go and try to borrow some.

A friend in need is
a friend indeed.

Fish and visitors smell in three days.

Love your neighbor; yet don't pull
down your hedge.

God helps them that help themselves.

If you would keep your secret from
an enemy, tell it not to a friend.

Be slow in choosing a friend,
slower in changing.

Don't throw stones at your neighbors',
if your own windows are glass.

Eat to live and not live to eat.

Love your enemies, for they
tell you your faults.

Better slip with foot
than tongue.

Three may keep a secret,
if two of them are dead.

Never leave that till tomorrow,
which you can do today.

A penny saved is a
penny earned.

A rolling stone
gathers no moss.

Make hay while
the sun shines.

Beware of little expenses;
a small leak will sink a great ship.

He that goes a borrowing
goes a sorrowing.

Honesty is the best policy.

Little strokes fell big oaks.

He that lies down with dogs
shall rise up with fleas.

Thinking through the LITERATURE

Connect to the Literature

1. What Do You Think?
What impressions of America and Americans do you get from de Crèvecoeur's essay?

> **Comprehension Check**
> - What does de Crèvecoeur say life was like for the poor of Europe?
> - According to de Crèvecoeur, why should Americans love their country?

Think Critically

2. `ACTIVE READING` `ANALYZING CONTRAST` Refer to the chart you made in your **READER'S NOTEBOOK** to discuss the contrasts de Crèvecoeur sees between America and Europe. What do you think is the main reason that de Crèvecoeur prefers America to Europe?

3. Why do you think de Crèvecoeur feels that the American must be a "new man"?

4. To what extent do you think de Crèvecoeur's definition of an American still applies today?

> **THINK ABOUT**
> - groups that Crèvecoeur does not mention
> - goals and lifestyles popular in America today
> - how you and your classmates defined an American in the Connect to Your Life activity

Extend Interpretations

5. Comparing Texts Consider what the proverbs from *Poor Richard's Almanack* (page 292) suggest about the concerns of 18th-century Americans. Is Franklin's picture of Americans consistent with de Crèvecoeur's? Explain your opinion.

6. Critic's Corner Critics have noted that when de Crèvecoeur writes, "Here individuals of all nations are melted into a new race," he anticipates the "melting pot" **metaphor** commonly used to describe America. Do you think "melting pot" is a good metaphor for this country? Explain why or why not. What other metaphors can you think of to describe America?

7. Connect to Life How similar are the motives of 18th-century immigrants and today's immigrants to the United States? Support your answer.

Literary Analysis

`THEME` As you recall, the **theme** of a literary work is the central idea the writer wishes to share with the reader. This idea may be a lesson about life or about people and their actions. Sometimes, writers state the theme directly. Often, however, the reader must infer the central message. Different readers may even discover different themes in the same work. Sometimes, the title of a literary work may provide a clue about its theme.

Paired Activity Working with a partner, review the chart of contrasts you made in your
📖**READER'S NOTEBOOK.**
Based on these contrasts, discuss what you think is the central idea of "What Is an American?" Then write a statement that expresses de Crèvecoeur's theme. Share this statement with other pairs of classmates.

`REVIEW` `FIGURATIVE LANGUAGE`
Point out the figurative language that de Crèvecoeur uses to convey his ideas about life in Europe and America. Do you think he makes good comparisons?

Writing Options

1. Draft of Article Review the word web you created for the Connect to Your Life activity. Write a draft of a magazine article comparing and contrasting de Crèvecoeur's definition of an American with your own definition.

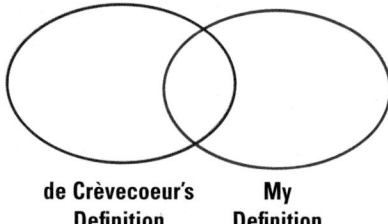

de Crèvecoeur's   My
Definition   Definition

2. Local Definition Using "What Is an American?" as a model, write a short letter to a friend who lives outside your state, defining what it means to be a resident of your area. You might answer the question "What Is a Texan?" or "What Is a Detroiter?" for example.

Writing Handbook
See page 1281: Explanatory Writing

Vocabulary in Action

EXERCISE: CONTEXT CLUES Read the sentences below. On your paper, write the vocabulary word that best completes each sentence.

1. Immigrants found being rewarded fairly for their labor a great _____.

2. Fertile land and good weather offered farmers a good _____.

3. Colonists gladly left behind their _____ existence in Europe.

4. Immigrants often left countries that were ruled by a _____ government.

5. American colonists were frequently separated from their _____ forever.

Building Vocabulary
For an in-depth study of context clues see page 326.

WORDS TO KNOW			
	allurement	kindred	subsistence
	despotic	servile	

Michel-Guillaume Jean de Crèvecoeur
1735–1813

Other Works
Sketches of Eighteenth Century America

Coming to America Born in Caen, France, Michel-Guillaume Jean de Crèvecoeur was educated in a Jesuit school and traveled to England as a young man. In 1755, he left England for Canada, where he enlisted in the French militia. During the French and Indian War, he served as a surveyor and a mapmaker. In 1759, de Crèvecoeur came to New York; ten years later, he married an American woman and settled down to farm.

A Perceptive Essayist During the period in which de Crèvecoeur lived on his farm in New York, he wrote the essays that were published in 1782 in *Letters from an American Farmer*. An immediate success in Europe, de Crèvecoeur's book provided an eyewitness account of American life in places ranging from Massachusetts to South Carolina.

Tragic Upheavals During the American Revolution, both the patriots and the British suspected de Crèvecoeur's loyalty because he seemed sympathetic to the British side but would not openly state his feelings. He was arrested as a spy and imprisoned by the British army in New York before sailing for Europe with his elder son in 1780. It was not until 1783, after being appointed French consul to New York, New Jersey, and Connecticut, that de Crèvecoeur was able to return to America. He found his farm burned, his wife dead, and his two other children housed with strangers in Boston. Reunited with his children in 1784, de Crèvecoeur remained in America until 1790. In that year, the "American farmer" returned to France, where he spent the last 23 years of his life.

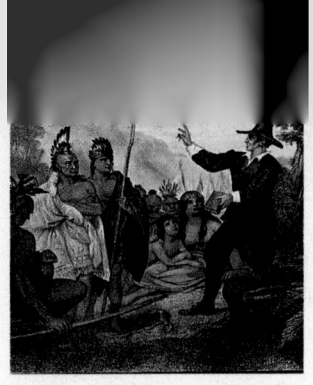

Lecture to a Missionary

Speech by RED JACKET

Connect to Your Life

Europeans and Native Americans What do you know about the history of relations between Native Americans and white settlers? How would you describe the relationship between Native Americans and other Americans today? Discuss your ideas with a group of classmates.

Build Background

A Clash of Cultures Early relations between Native Americans and white settlers were marked by the missionary impulse. In the mid-1600s, Catholic missionaries from Spain and France and Puritans from England sought to convert Native Americans to Christianity. As the United States became a nation in the late 1700s and early 1800s, a number of Protestant missionary societies sent workers to establish churches and schools on Iroquois reservations. At the time, the Iroquois consisted of six separate nations: the Seneca, Cayuga, Oneida, Onondaga, Mohawk, and Tuscarora. In the summer of 1805, Reverend Cram of the Boston Missionary Society met with Iroquois chiefs assembled at Buffalo Creek in New York and offered to instruct the Iroquois on "how to worship the Great Spirit agreeably." In the speech you are about to read, Red Jacket, a Seneca chief, responds to this offer.

Focus Your Reading

LITERARY ANALYSIS **TONE** **Tone** is a writer's attitude toward his or her subject. A writer's tone might be respectful, angry, or amused, for example. Tone can be communicated through word connotations, choice of details, and direct statements of a writer's position. Consider the tone established in the first words of this speech:

> *Friend and Brother, it was the will of the Great Spirit that we should meet together this day.*

What seems to be Red Jacket's attitude toward Missionary Cram and his offer?

ACTIVE READING **DRAWING CONCLUSIONS ABOUT TONE**
To **draw a conclusion** is to pull together pieces of information from your reading and your own experiences to make some final decision or judgment. To draw conclusions about tone, look for word connotations, revealing details, and direct statements that express the writer's or speaker's attitude. These clues may become more obvious to you if you read the speech aloud, noting the emotions you convey.

📖 **READER'S NOTEBOOK** As you read, jot down specific words, revealing details, and direct statements that suggest Red Jacket's tone.

RED JACKET

LECTURE TO A MISSIONARY

Friend and Brother, it was the will of the Great Spirit that we should meet together this day. He orders all things, and has given us a fine day for our Council. He has taken his garment from before the sun, and caused it to shine with brightness upon us. Our eyes are opened, that we see clearly; our ears are unstopped, that we have been able to hear distinctly the words you have spoken. For all these favors we thank the Great Spirit and Him only.

Brother, this council fire was kindled by you. It was at your request that we came together at this time. We have listened with attention to what you have said. You requested us to speak our minds freely. This gives us great joy; for we now consider that we stand upright before you, and can speak what we think. All have heard your voice, and all speak to you now as one man. Our minds are agreed.

Brother, you say you want an answer to your talk before you leave this place. It is right you should have one; as you are a great distance from home, and we do not wish to detain you. But we will first look back a little, and tell you what our fathers have told us, and what we have heard from the white people.

Brother, listen to what we say. There was a time when our forefathers owned this great island. Their seats extended from the rising to the setting sun. The Great Spirit had made it for the use of Indians. He had created the buffalo, the deer, and other animals for food. He had made the bear and the beaver. Their skins served us for clothing. He had scattered them over the country, and taught us how to take them. He had caused the earth to produce corn for bread. All this He had done for his red children, because he loved them. If we had some disputes about our hunting ground, they were generally settled without the shedding of much blood. But an evil day came upon us. Your forefathers crossed the great water and landed on this island. Their numbers were small. They found friends and not enemies. They told us they had fled from their own country for fear of wicked men, and had come here to enjoy their religion. They asked for a small seat. We took pity on them; granted their request; and they sat down amongst us. We gave them corn and meat; they gave us poison [rum] in return.

The white people, Brother, had now found our country. Tidings were carried back, and more came amongst us. Yet we did not fear them. We took them to be friends. They called us brothers. We believed them and gave them a larger seat. At length their numbers had greatly increased. They wanted more land; they wanted our country. Our eyes were opened, and our minds became uneasy. Wars took place. Indians were hired to fight against Indians, and many of our people were destroyed. They also brought strong liquor amongst us. It was strong and powerful, and has slain thousands.

Brother, our seats were once large and yours were small. You have now become a great people, and we have scarcely a place left to spread our blankets. You have got our country, but are not

satisfied; you want to force your religion upon us.

Brother, continue to listen. You say that you are sent to instruct us how to worship the Great Spirit agreeably to his mind, and, if we do not take hold of the religion which you white people teach, we shall be unhappy hereafter. You say that you are right and we are lost. How do we know this to be true? We understand that your religion is written in a book. If it was intended for us as well as you, why has not the Great Spirit given to us, and not only to us, but why did he not give to our forefathers, the knowledge of that book, with the means of understanding it rightly? We only know what you tell us about it. How shall we know when to believe, being so often deceived by the white people?

Brother, you say there is but one way to worship and serve the Great Spirit. If there is but one religion, why do you white people differ so much about it? Why not all agreed, as you can all read the book?

Brother, we do not understand these things. We are told that your religion was given to your forefathers, and has been handed down from father to son. We also have a religion, which was given to our forefathers, and has been handed down to us their children. We worship in that way. It teaches us to be thankful for all the favors we receive; to love each other, and to be united. We never quarrel about religion.

Brother, the Great Spirit has made us all, but He has made a great difference between his white and red children. He has given us different complexions and different customs. To you

He has given the arts. To these He has not opened our eyes. We know these things to be true. Since He has made so great a difference between us in other things, why may we not conclude that he has given us a different religion according to our understanding? The Great Spirit does right. He knows what is best for his children; we are satisfied.

Brother, we do not wish to destroy your religion, or take it from you. We only want to enjoy our own.

Brother, you say you have not come to get our land or our money, but to enlighten our minds. I will now tell you that I have been at your meetings, and saw you collect money from the meeting. I cannot tell what this money was intended for, but suppose that it was for your minister, and if we should conform to your way of thinking, perhaps you may want some from us.

Brother, we are told that you have been preaching to the white people in this place. These people are our neighbors. We are acquainted with them. We will wait a little while, and see what effect your preaching has upon them. If we find it does them good, makes them honest and less disposed to cheat Indians, we will then consider again of what you have said.

Brother, you have now heard our answer to your talk, and this is all we have to say at present. As we are going to part, we will come and take you by the hand, and hope the Great Spirit will protect you on your journey, and return you safe to your friends. ❖

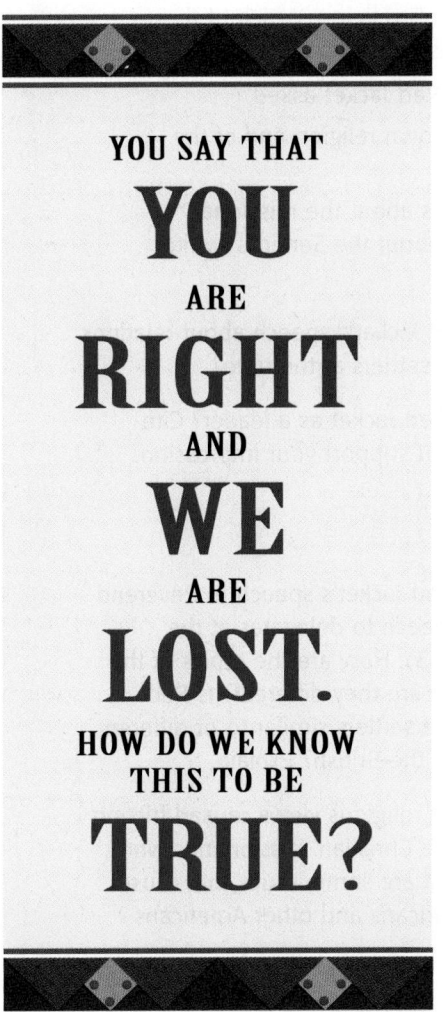

YOU SAY THAT

YOU

ARE

RIGHT

AND

WE

ARE

LOST.

HOW DO WE KNOW THIS TO BE

TRUE?

Connect to the Literature

1. What Do You Think?
What did you think of Red Jacket's lecture? Share some comments with your classmates.

Comprehension Check
- What does Reverend Cram want the Iroquois to do?
- State one "evil" that the Europeans brought to the Iroquois, according to Red Jacket.

Think Critically

2. **ACTIVE READING** **DRAWING CONCLUSIONS ABOUT TONE**
Review the words and passages you copied into your **READER'S NOTEBOOK** as clues to **tone.** How would you describe Red Jacket's overall attitude toward Reverend Cram and his proposal?

3. In your own words, explain Red Jacket's reasons for not converting to Reverend Cram's religion. Which of these reasons seems most persuasive to you?

> **THINK ABOUT**
> - the questions Red Jacket asked
> - his view of his own religion and of the Great Spirit
> - his observations about the missionary's meetings and about the Senecas' white neighbors

4. What can you **infer** from Red Jacket's speech about relations between Senecas and white settlers at the time?

5. What is your impression of Red Jacket as a leader? Cite passages from his speech that support your impression.

Extend Interpretations

6. Comparing Texts Compare Red Jacket's speech to Reverend Cram with Patrick Henry's speech to delegates at the Virginia Convention (page 263). How are the topics of the two speeches alike, and how are they different? Is Red Jacket's attitude toward white settlers similar to or different from Henry's attitude toward the British? Explain.

7. Connect to Life Differences in religious views caused friction between the Senecas and the Christian missionaries who sought to convert them. What are some issues that cause conflict between Native Americans and other Americans today?

Literary Analysis

TONE As you recall, **tone** is a writer's attitude toward a subject. De Crèvecoeur's tone in "What Is an American?" was enthusiastic; Abigail Adams's tone in her letter to her husband was alternately loving and critical, depending on the subject she was discussing. Tone is conveyed by what a writer says about a subject as well as how he or she says it. For example, de Crèvecoeur's enthusiasm for America was conveyed by his inclusion of details about free, productive farmers instead of slaves or indentured servants. His use of positive terms such as "new man" also helped convey his tone.

Activity Again review the clues to tone—word connotations, revealing details, and direct statements—that you put in your **READER'S NOTEBOOK.** Then imagine you are Red Jacket's speech-writing consultant. If Red Jacket wanted to express a friendlier tone, what changes would you suggest? If he wanted to express a more defiant tone, what would you suggest? Share your recommendations with classmates.

REVIEW **THEME** How would you state the theme, or central idea, of Red Jacket's speech in a single sentence?

Writing Options

1. Mediator's Recommendations Consider the points of conflict between the Senecas and their white neighbors as revealed in Red Jacket's speech. Then think about ways that relations between the two groups could be improved. Write a list of recommendations that you would propose.

Recommendations
1
2
3

2. Cram's Response After Red Jacket spoke, he and other Senecas walked over to shake hands with Reverend Cram. The missionary refused to shake hands with them, saying there was "no fellowship between the religion of God and the devil." If, the next day, Cram had written a response to Red Jacket, what do you think he might have said? Draft a response that tries to answer Red Jacket's objections.

3. Tolerance Pamphlet Create a pamphlet that argues for religious tolerance. Refer to or quote Red Jacket's speech within the pamphlet.

Writing Handbook
See page 1285: Persuasive Writing

Activities & Explorations

1. Re-created Speech Do a dramatic reading of this lecture for your class. As you prepare, keep in mind the occasion for Red Jacket's speech, and the words and phrases that most strongly communicate his tone.
~ SPEAKING AND LISTENING

2. Mural of Seneca History Draw a sketch that depicts an aspect of the history of the Senecas as recounted by Red Jacket in his speech. Then work with your classmates to design a mural.
~ ART

Red Jacket
1756?–1830

Seneca Orator Red Jacket, whose Iroquois name, Sagoyewatha, means "He Keeps Them Awake," was a Seneca chief known for eloquent oratory. Although he did not distinguish himself in battle, he did use his oratorical skills to wage war against the European influence on Iroquois culture. Vehemently opposed to efforts to convert the Iroquois to Christianity, he led the effort to evict a local missionary after the New York legislature passed a law in 1821 forbidding white settlers from living on reservation lands.

His English Name During the American Revolution, the Senecas and most other Iroquois nations sided with the British. Sagoyewatha came to be known as Red Jacket after he began wearing the red military coats that British soldiers gave him. After the war, he advocated peace with the Americans. In 1792, he went to Philadelphia with other Iroquois chiefs to meet President George Washington, who gave him a silver medal.

Ironic End Toward the end of his life, Red Jacket experienced much turmoil. He left his wife for a few months after she became a Christian. As his power waned and his dependence on alcohol grew, he lost his chieftainship in 1827. When he died, Red Jacket, despite his wishes to the contrary, was given a Christian funeral and was buried in a missionary cemetery.

from Stride Toward Freedom

Nonfiction
by MARTIN LUTHER KING, JR.

Necessary to Protect Ourselves

Interview with MALCOLM X
by Les Crane

Comparing Literature

Traditions Across Time: Demands for Equal Rights

In the time of the American Revolution, Patrick Henry, Thomas Jefferson, Abigail Adams, and others passionately voiced the ideas of equality and natural rights. Inspired by these ideas, Martin Luther King, Jr., and Malcolm X led a crusade for racial justice in the 1950s and 1960s.

Points of Comparison As you read, compare King's and Malcolm X's views about responding to oppression with the views of the founders of this country.

Build Background

Fighting for Racial Justice Southern states in our country once had segregation laws—that is, laws that imposed social separation of races. African Americans were forced to attend separate schools and to sit in separate sections of buses and trains. Many public buildings, such as restaurants, movie theaters, and hotels, were also segregated. Through boycotts, sit-ins, and marches, African Americans and their supporters challenged segregation laws, sought better housing and jobs, and fought for voting rights in the 1950s and 1960s.

The first selection is an excerpt from *Stride Toward Freedom,* King's 1958 book about the Montgomery, Alabama, bus boycott. The second is a transcript of a 1964 television interview with Malcolm X.

WORDS TO KNOW **Vocabulary Preview**

anarchy	indiscriminately	repudiate
corroding	legacy	synthesis
exploitation	oppressed	tacitly
glib		

Focus Your Reading

LITERARY ANALYSIS **HISTORICAL CONTEXT** One way to increase your understanding of a literary work is to relate it to its **historical context,** or the social conditions that influenced its creation. As you read these selections, apply what you know about the crusade for racial justice.

ACTIVE READING **ANALYZING THE STRUCTURE OF ARGUMENTS** Analyzing the **structure** of a persuasive argument involves identifying the main ideas you are being asked to accept and the details (facts, examples, and reasons) that support these ideas.

READER'S NOTEBOOK As you read the excerpt from *Stride Toward Freedom,* complete a diagram like the one shown, noting King's ideas about methods of responding to oppression.

Response 1: Acquiescence	Response 2: Violence
Problems	Problems

Response 3: _____
Advantages

from

stride toward freedom

Oppressed people deal with their oppression in three characteristic ways. One way is acquiescence: the oppressed resign themselves to their doom. They tacitly adjust themselves to oppression, and thereby become conditioned to it. In every movement toward freedom some of the oppressed prefer to remain oppressed. Almost 2800 years ago Moses set out to lead the children of Israel from the slavery of Egypt to the freedom of the promised land.[1] He soon discovered that slaves do not always welcome their deliverers. They become accustomed to being slaves. They would rather bear those ills they have, as Shakespeare pointed out, than flee to others that they know not of.[2] They prefer the "fleshpots of Egypt" to the ordeals of emancipation.

There is such a thing as the freedom of exhaustion. Some people are so worn down by the yoke of oppression that they give up. A few years ago in the slum areas of Atlanta, a Negro guitarist used to sing almost daily: "Been down so long that down don't bother me." This is the type of negative freedom and resignation that often engulfs the life of the oppressed.

But this is not the way out. To accept passively an unjust system is to cooperate with that system; thereby the oppressed become as evil as

Martin Luther King, Jr.

the oppressor. Noncooperation with evil is as much a moral obligation as is cooperation with good. The oppressed must never allow the conscience of the oppressor to slumber. Religion reminds every man that he is his brother's keeper.[3] To accept injustice or segregation passively is to say to the oppressor that his actions are morally right. It is a way of allowing his

---

1. **promised land:** in general, a longed-for place where complete satisfaction and happiness will be achieved. In the Old Testament of the Bible, the Promised Land is the land of Canaan, promised by the Lord to Abraham's descendants.

2. **bear those ills they have . . . know not of:** an allusion to a line in Act III, Scene I, of *Hamlet* by William Shakespeare.

3. **his brother's keeper:** an allusion to the biblical story of the brothers Cain and Abel. After Cain murdered Abel, God asked him where his brother was. Cain replied, "I know not; am I my brother's keeper?" In general, the saying refers to people's reluctance to accept responsibility for the welfare of others.

WORDS
TO
KNOW

oppressed (ə-prĕst′) *adj.* kept down by severe and unjust use of force or authority **oppress** *v.*
tacitly (tăs′ĭt-lē) *adv.* silently

conscience to fall asleep. At this moment the oppressed fails to be his brother's keeper. So acquiescence—while often the easier way—is not the moral way. It is the way of the coward. The Negro cannot win the respect of his oppressor by acquiescing; he merely increases the oppressor's arrogance and contempt. Acquiescence is interpreted as proof of the Negro's inferiority. The Negro cannot win the respect of the white people of the South or the peoples of the world if he is willing to sell the future of his children for his personal and immediate comfort and safety.

A second way that oppressed people sometimes deal with oppression is to resort to physical violence and corroding hatred. Violence often brings about momentary results. Nations have frequently won their independence in battle. But in spite of temporary victories, violence never brings permanent peace. It solves no social problem; it merely creates new and more complicated ones.

Violence as a way of achieving racial justice is both impractical and immoral. It is impractical because it is a descending spiral ending in destruction for all. The old law of an eye for an eye[4] leaves everybody blind. It is immoral because it seeks to humiliate the opponent rather than win his understanding; it seeks to annihilate rather than to convert. Violence is immoral because it thrives on hatred rather than love. It destroys community and makes brotherhood impossible. It leaves society in monologue rather than dialogue. Violence ends by defeating itself. It creates bitterness in the survivors and brutality in the destroyers. A voice echoes through time saying to every potential Peter, "Put up your sword."[5] History is cluttered with the wreckage of nations that failed to follow this command.

If the American Negro and other victims of oppression succumb to the temptation of using violence in the struggle for freedom, future generations will be the recipients of a desolate night of bitterness, and our chief legacy to them will be an endless reign of meaningless chaos. Violence is not the way.

The third way open to oppressed people in their quest for freedom is the way of nonviolent resistance. Like the synthesis in Hegelian philosophy,[6] the principle of nonviolent resistance seeks to reconcile the truths of two opposites—acquiescence and violence—while avoiding the extremes and immoralities of both. The nonviolent resister agrees with the person who acquiesces that one should not be physically aggressive toward his opponent but he balances the equation by agreeing with the person of violence that evil must be resisted. He avoids the nonresistance of the former and the violent resistance of the latter. With nonviolent resistance, no individual or group need submit to any wrong, nor need anyone resort to violence in order to right a wrong.

It seems to me that this is the method that must guide the actions of the Negro in the present crisis in race relations. Through nonviolent resistance the Negro will be able to rise to the noble height of opposing the unjust system while loving the perpetrators of the system. The Negro must work passionately and unrelentingly for full stature as a citizen, but he must not use inferior methods to gain it. He

---

4. **an eye for an eye:** an allusion to Exodus 21:23–25— "You shall give life for life, eye for eye, tooth for tooth, hand for hand, foot for foot."

5. **Peter . . . sword:** Peter, one of the 12 disciples of Jesus, drew his sword to protect Jesus from the soldiers who came to arrest him in the Garden of Gethsemane, but Jesus condemned Peter's use of violence.

6. **Hegelian** (hā-gā′lē-ĭn) **philosophy:** Georg Hegel (1770–1831) was a German philosopher who proposed the theory that for each idea or situation there is an opposite and that these two will eventually merge to form a unified whole.

WORDS TO KNOW

corroding (kə-rō′dĭng) *adj.* gradually destructive **corrode** *v.*
legacy (lĕg′ə-sē) *n.* something handed down from an ancestor or a predecessor or from the past
synthesis (sĭn′thĭ-sĭs) *n.* the combining of separate elements or substances to form a coherent whole

"To accept passively an *unjust* system is to cooperate with that system; thereby the oppressed become as *evil* as the oppressor."

Martin Luther King, Jr., on the march from Selma to Montgomery, Alabama, in 1965 to protest voting restrictions on African Americans.
Copyright © Bruce Davidson/Magnum Photos.

must never come to terms with falsehood, malice, hate, or destruction.

Nonviolent resistance makes it possible for the Negro to remain in the South and struggle for his rights. The Negro's problem will not be solved by running away. He cannot listen to the glib suggestion of those who would urge him to migrate en masse[7] to other sections of the country. By grasping his great opportunity in the South he can make a lasting contribution to the moral strength of the nation and set a sublime example of courage for generations yet unborn.

By nonviolent resistance, the Negro can also enlist all men of good will in his struggle for equality. The problem is not a purely racial one, with Negroes set against whites. In the end, it is not a struggle between people at all, but a tension between justice and injustice. Nonviolent resistance is not aimed against oppressors but against oppression. Under its banner consciences, not racial groups, are enlisted.

If the Negro is to achieve the goal of integration, he must organize himself into a militant and nonviolent mass movement. All three elements are indispensable. The movement for equality and justice can only be a success if it has both a mass and militant character; the barriers to be overcome require both. Nonviolence is an imperative in order to bring about ultimate community.

A mass movement of a militant quality that is not at the same time committed to nonviolence tends to generate conflict, which in turn breeds anarchy. The support of the participants and the sympathy of the uncommitted are both inhibited by the threat that bloodshed will engulf the community. This reaction in turn encourages the opposition to threaten and resort to force. When, however, the mass movement repudiates violence while moving resolutely toward its goal, its opponents are revealed as the instigators and practitioners of violence if it occurs. Then public support is magnetically attracted to the advocates of nonviolence, while those who employ violence are literally disarmed by overwhelming sentiment against their stand. ❖

---

7. **en masse** (ŏn măs′): in one group or body; all together.

Thinking Through the Literature

1. **Comprehension Check** Which two methods of responding to oppression does King oppose, and which does he support?

2. **ACTIVE READING** | **ANALYZING STRUCTURE** Refer to the diagram you made in your 📖 **READER'S NOTEBOOK.** What are King's reasons for opposing the first two methods he discusses?

3. Of the reasons King favors the third response to oppression, which reason do you find the most persuasive, and why?

WORDS
TO
KNOW
glib (glĭb) *adj.* showing little thought, preparation, or concern
anarchy (ăn′ər-kē) *n.* absence of any form of political authority
repudiate (rĭ-pyōō′dē-āt′) *v.* to reject the validity or authority of

necessary to protect ourselves

Malcolm X

Interviewed by Les Crane

Crane: You've been a critic of some of the Negro leadership in this country—Martin Luther King, Roy Wilkins, Abernathy,[1] and others—have you changed in your feelings toward them of late?

Malcolm X: I think all of us should be critics of each other. Whenever you can't stand criticism you can never grow. I don't think that it serves any purpose for the leaders of our people to waste their time fighting each other needlessly. I think that we accomplish more when we sit down in private and iron out whatever differences that may exist and try and then do something constructive for the benefit of our people. But on the other hand, I don't think that we should be above criticism. I don't think that anyone should be above criticism.

Crane: Violence or the threat of violence has always surrounded you. Speeches that you've made have been interpreted as being threats. You have made statements reported in the press about how the Negroes should go out and arm themselves, form militias of their own. I read a thing once, a statement I believe you made that every Negro should belong to the National Rifle Association—

Malcolm X: No, I said this: That in areas of this country where the government has proven its— either its inability or its unwillingness to protect the lives and property of our people, then it's only fair to expect us to do whatever is necessary

to protect ourselves. And in situations like Mississippi, places like Mississippi where the government actually has proven its inability to protect us—and it has been proven that ofttimes the police officers and sheriffs themselves are involved in the murder that takes place against our people—then I feel, and I say that anywhere, that our people should start doing what is necessary to protect ourselves. This doesn't mean that we should buy rifles and go out and initiate attacks <u>indiscriminately</u> against whites. But it does mean that we should get whatever is necessary to protect ourselves in a country or in an area where the governmental ability to protect us has broken down—

---

1. **Roy Wilkins, Abernathy:** Roy Wilkins (1901–1981) was executive secretary of the National Association for the Advancement of Colored People (NAACP) from 1955 to 1977. Ralph Abernathy (1926–1990) was a close friend of Martin Luther King, Jr., and helped him found the Southern Christian Leadership Conference to combat racism.

WORDS
TO
KNOW

indiscriminately (ĭn'dĭ-skrĭm'ə-nĭt-lē) *adv.* randomly

"My belief in brotherhood would never restrain me in any way from protecting myself in a society from a people whose disrespect for brotherhood makes them feel inclined to put my neck on a tree at the end of a rope."

Malcolm X with his daughters Qubilah and Attallah in 1962. Photo by Robert L. Haggins.

Crane: Therefore you do not agree with Dr. King's Gandhian philosophy[2]—

Malcolm X: My belief in brotherhood would never restrain me in any way from protecting myself in a society from a people whose disrespect for brotherhood makes them feel inclined to put my neck on a tree at the end of a rope.[3] *[Applause]*

Crane: Well, it sounds as though you could be preaching a sort of an anarchy—

Malcolm X: No, no. I respect government and respect law. But does the government and the law respect us? If the FBI, which is what people depend upon on a national scale to protect the morale and the property and the lives of the people, can't do so when the property and lives of Negroes and whites who try and help Negroes are concerned, then I think that it's only fair to expect elements to do whatever is necessary to protect themselves.

And this is no departure from normal procedure. Because right here in New York City you have vigilante committees[4] that have been set up by groups who see where their neighborhood community is endangered and the law can't do anything about it. So—and even their lives aren't at stake. So—but the fear, Les, seems to come into existence only when someone says Negroes should form vigilante committees to protect their lives and their property.

I'm not advocating the breaking of any laws. But I say that our people will never be respected as human beings until we react as other normal, intelligent human beings do. And this country came into existence by people who were tired of tyranny and oppression and <u>exploitation</u> and the brutality that was being inflicted upon them by powers higher than they, and I think that it is only fair to expect us, sooner or later, to do likewise. ❖

---

2. **Gandhian** (gän'dē-ĭn) **philosophy:** Mohandas Gandhi (1869–1948) was an Indian nationalist and spiritual leader who developed the practice of nonviolent civil disobedience that forced Great Britain to grant independence to India in 1947.

3. **put my neck . . . rope:** an allusion to the practice of lynching. Many African Americans were executed by whites without due process of law, especially by hanging.

4. **vigilante** (vĭj'ə-lăn'tē) **committees:** volunteer groups of citizens that without lawful authority assume powers such as pursuing and punishing suspected criminals or offenders.

WORDS TO KNOW | **exploitation** (ĕk'sploi-tā'shən) *n.* use of another person or group for selfish purposes

306

Thinking through the LITERATURE

Connect to the Literature

1. **What Do You Think?**
   What is your response to the ideas Malcolm X expresses in this interview? Share your first thoughts in a small group.

   Comprehension Check
   - According to Malcolm X, when is violence justifiable?
   - In explaining what to expect from African Americans, to what historical event does Malcolm X refer?

Think Critically

2. **ACTIVE READING** **ANALYZING STRUCTURE** What are the main positions Malcolm X takes in this interview, and what are his supporting reasons? Create a diagram to represent his argument.

3. Malcolm X compares the oppression of African Americans with that of American colonists under King George III. He believes that "it is only fair to expect" African Americans to react to tyranny as the revolutionaries did. Do you agree?

4. Based on these two selections, which leader do you regard as more persuasive—King or Malcolm X?

    THINK ABOUT
   - each leader's intellectual arguments
   - each leader's emotional appeals
   - each leader's **tone,** or attitude

5. Which leader do you think is more revolutionary—King or Malcolm X?

    THINK ABOUT
   - what "revolutionary" means to you
   - each leader's arguments and results

6. In your view, are the similarities between King and Malcolm X more important, or are the differences? Explain.

Extend Interpretations

7. **Connect to Life** Both King and Malcolm X fought for justice for African Americans in the 1950s and 1960s. Name political, religious, or social causes that people are fighting for in the United States today. What are the most effective methods used to promote these causes?

8. **Points of Comparison** Based on "Speech in the Virginia Convention," what do you imagine Patrick Henry might have said about King's advocacy of nonviolent resistance?

Literary Analysis

HISTORICAL CONTEXT
The **historical context** of a literary work refers to the social conditions that inspired or influenced its creation. Patrick Henry, for example, protested against the British military buildup in the colonies in his "Speech in the Virginia Convention" on page 263. In *Stride Toward Freedom,* King uses the phrase "the present crisis in race relations." To understand this phrase, readers must apply what they know about the civil rights struggle of the 1950s and 1960s. This struggle sought to overturn segregation laws in the South—laws which, as you learned in Build Background on page 300, sanctioned racial separation.

Cooperative Learning Activity
Working in a small group, reread "Necessary to Protect Ourselves." Identify sentences in the selection that refer to events or conditions at the time of the interview or to public figures that Malcolm X is reacting to. To interpret comments in their historical context, research each of these events, conditions, or individuals. Then write a note that provides useful background information. Compile the notes in a Guide for Reading, modeled on the one that accompanies "Speech in the Virginia Convention," on page 263.

REVIEW **ALLUSION** Identify the Biblical **allusions** in the excerpt from *Stride Toward Freedom.* How do they make King's writing more persuasive? Which one do you think is most important to the selection, and why?

Choices & CHALLENGES

Writing Options

Points of Comparison Write notes and organize them for a persuasive essay about the use of violence to achieve a goal. As you develop your views, consider the ideas of King and Malcolm X as well as those of Patrick Henry. Place this piece in your **Working Portfolio.**

Writing Handbook
See page 1285: Persuasive Writing

Vocabulary in Action

EXERCISE: WORD KNOWLEDGE For each vocabulary word, write a sentence describing a situation in which the word could be applied.

1. oppressed
2. tacitly
3. corroding
4. legacy
5. synthesis

6. glib
7. anarchy
8. repudiate
9. indiscriminately
10. exploitation

Building Vocabulary
For an in-depth lesson on how to expand your vocabulary, see page 126.

Martin Luther King, Jr.
1929–1968

Other Works
"Letter from Birmingham Jail" (See excerpt on pages 1137–1145.)
Why We Can't Wait
Where Do We Go from Here

Malcolm X
1925–1965

Other Works
The Autobiography of Malcolm X
Malcolm X Talks to Young People

Called to Leadership The Reverend Dr. Martin Luther King, Jr., was the pastor of a Baptist church in Montgomery, Alabama, in 1955 when a woman named Rosa Parks was arrested for refusing to give up her bus seat to a white passenger as the local segregation law then required. Civil rights activists in Montgomery organized a boycott of buses by African Americans and selected King as their leader. A little over a year after the boycott began, the U.S. Supreme Court determined that segregated seating on public buses in Montgomery violated the Constitution.

Crusader for Justice The successful Montgomery bus boycott launched King's career in the civil rights movement. He went on to develop a reputation as a powerful leader and a brilliant orator. In his most famous speech, "I Have a Dream," he electrified more than 200,000 demonstrators gathered for the March on Washington in August 1963. The following year, Congress passed the landmark Civil Rights Act of 1964, and King received the Nobel Peace Prize. For the rest of his life, King continued to work for justice and equality. He was killed by an assassin's bullet on April 4, 1968, in Memphis, Tennessee.

Symbolic Name While in prison for burglary from 1946 to 1952, Malcolm Little converted to the faith of the Nation of Islam (popularly known as the Black Muslims), a militant religious and cultural community that believed in black separatism. Like many members of that group, he took the name "X" as a symbol of his lost African name.

Dynamic Speaker Malcolm X was one of the most powerful speakers of his time, and he won many converts to the Nation of Islam. However, in 1964, after a disagreement with Nation of Islam leader Elijah Muhammad, Malcolm X left the sect and founded his own organization. On a pilgrimage to Mecca, he saw Muslims of all races joined in common faith and soon embraced the possibility of cooperation among races.

Final Years The rivalry between Malcolm X and the Nation of Islam grew, resulting in violence and threats against his life. On February 21, 1965, some members of the organization shot Malcolm X to death as he spoke at a rally in Harlem.

from I Am Joaquín / Yo Soy Joaquín

Poetry by RODOLFO GONZALES

Comparing Literature

Traditions Across Time: Demands for Equal Rights

"The Declaration of Independence" proclaimed the basic rights of all citizens to life, liberty, and the pursuit of happiness. To extend these rights to African Americans, Martin Luther King, Jr., Malcolm X, and others spearheaded the civil rights movement in the 1950s and 1960s. Inspired by this movement, other minority groups asserted their right to equality. *I Am Joaquín / Yo Soy Joaquín,* by Rodolfo Gonzales, is a famous poem associated with the Chicano movement.

Points of Comparison   Consider what this poem has to do with revolution and what it has in common with the other selections in this part of Unit Two.

Build Background

During the 1960s, Chicanos—residents of the United States who trace their ancestry to Mexico—demanded economic justice and equal rights. In California, Cesar Chavez organized the United Farm Workers Union and led a successful strike against grape growers. New political groups such as the Alianza in New Mexico, La Raza Unida in Texas, and the Crusade for Justice in Colorado spoke out for the rights of Chicanos. Groups of Chicano students throughout the southwestern states that were once part of Mexico protested unfair treatment and promoted pride in their Chicano heritage.

The Chicano movement inspired much new poetry, prose, and drama. *I Am Joaquín/Yo Soy Joaquín* is one of the earliest and most widely read works associated with the movement. Reprinted here are excerpts from the beginning and the end of this book-length poem by social activist Rodolfo Gonzales. In its entirety the poem describes the modern dilemma of Chicanos in the 1960s, then outlines 2,000 years of Mexican and Mexican-American history, highlighting the different, often opposing strains that make up the Chicano heritage.

Focus Your Reading

LITERARY ANALYSIS EPIC POEM   An **epic** is a long narrative poem on a serious subject presented in an elevated or formal style. Ancient epic poems, such as *The Odyssey,* trace the adventures of a hero who performs courageous, even superhuman deeds. As you read *I Am Joaquín,* a modern epic poem, consider what makes the speaker heroic.

ACTIVE READING STRATEGIES FOR READING EPIC POETRY   The length of an epic poem poses challenges to the reader, who must keep track of many events and details. One way to increase your understanding of Gonzales's poem is to identify its epic characteristics.

READER'S NOTEBOOK While reading, fill in a chart like the one shown. Jot down evidence from the poem for each of the characteristics listed.

Epic Characteristics	Evidence
1. Hero with high ideals	
2. Courageous deeds	
3. Large-scale setting	
4. Universal ideas	

I AM JOAQUÍN

Rodolfo Gonzales

from **I Am Joaquín**

I am Joaquín,
lost in a world of confusion,
caught up in the whirl of a
        gringo society,
5 confused by the rules,
scorned by attitudes,
suppressed by manipulation,
and destroyed by modern society.
My fathers
10   have lost the economic battle
and won
    the struggle of cultural survival.
And now!
    I must choose
15   between
    the paradox of
victory of the spirit,
despite physical hunger,
        or
20   to exist in the grasp
of American social neurosis,
sterilization of the soul
    and a full stomach. . . .

de **Yo Soy Joaquín**

Yo soy Joaquín,
perdido en un mundo de confusión,
enganchado en el remolino de una
        sociedad gringa,
5 confundido por las reglas,
despreciado por las actitudes,
sofocado por manipulaciones,
y destrozado por la sociedad moderna.
Mis padres
10   perdieron la batalla económica
y conquistaron
    la lucha de supervivencia cultural.
Y ¡ahora!
    yo tengo que escojer
15   en medio
    de la paradoja de
triunfo del espíritu,
a despecho de hambre física,
        o
20   existir en la empuñada
de la neurosis social americana,
esterilización del alma
    y un estómago repleto. . . .

Detail of *The Farmworkers of Guadalupe* (1990), Judith F. Baca. From *The Guadalupe Mural*, acrylic on plywood, 8′ × 7′. Copyright © J. Baca, photo by R. Rolle.

I shed the tears of anguish
25 as I see my children disappear
behind the shroud of mediocrity,
never to look back to remember me.
I am Joaquín.
    I must fight
30   and win this struggle
       for my sons, and they
       must know from me
       who I am.

Lloro lágrimas de angustia
25 cuando veo a mis hijos desaparecer
detrás de la mortaja de mediocridad,
para jamás reflexionar o acordarse de mí.
Yo soy Joaquín.
    Debo pelear
30   y ganar la lucha
       para mis hijos, y ellos
       deben saber de mí,
       quien soy yo.

Part of the blood that runs deep in me
35 could not be vanquished by the Moors.[1]
I defeated them after five hundred years,
and I endured.
      Part of the blood that is mine
      has labored endlessly four hundred
40   years under the heel of lustful
      Europeans.[2]
         I am still here!
I have endured in the rugged mountains
  of our country.
45 I have survived the toils and slavery
  of the fields.
        I have existed
in the barrios of the city
in the suburbs of bigotry
50 in the mines of social snobbery
in the prisons of dejection
in the muck of exploitation
and
in the fierce heat of racial hatred.
55 And now the trumpet sounds,
the music of the people stirs the
      revolution.
Like a sleeping giant it slowly
rears its head
60 to the sound of
         tramping feet
        clamoring voices
        mariachi strains
        fiery tequila explosions
65   the smell of chile verde and
      soft brown eyes of expectation for a
            better life.

---

1. **Moors** (mŏŏrz): followers of the religion of Islam
who conquered Spain during the 700s and who lost
most of their territory there by the late 1200s.

2. **labored . . . Europeans:** In 1521, Hernándo Cortés, a
Spanish conquistador, conquered the Aztec empire,
located in the area around present-day Mexico City.
The speaker suggests that the native population has
been dominated by Europeans ever since.

Parte de la sangre que corre hondo en mí
35 no pudo ser vencida por los moros.
Los derroté después de quinientos años,
y yo perduré.
      La parte de sangre que es mía
      ha obrado infinitamente cuatrocientos
40   años debajo el talón de europeos
          lujuriosos.
              ¡Yo todavía estoy aquí!
He perdurado en las montañas escarpadas
   de nuestro país.
45 He sobrevivido los trabajos y esclavitud
   de los campos.
         Yo he existido
en los barrios de la ciudad
en los suburbios de intolerancia
50 en las minas de snobismo social
en las prisiones de desaliento
en la porquería de explotación
y
en el calor feroz de odio racial.
55 Y ahora suena la trompeta,
la música de la gente incita la
       revolución.
Como un gigantón soñoliento lentamente
alza su cabeza
60 al sonido de
          patulladas
        voces clamorosas
       tañido de mariachis
      explosiones ardientes de tequila
65   el aroma de chile verde y
   ojos morenos, esperanzosos de una
              vida mejor.

And in all the fertile farmlands,
                    the barren plains,
70 the mountain villages,
    smoke-smeared cities,
                    we start to MOVE.
        La Raza!³
    Méjicano!
75   Español!
            Latino!
                Hispano!
                Chicano!
    or whatever I call myself,
80   I look the same
                I feel the same
                I cry
                    and
                sing the same.
85 I am the masses of my people and
    I refuse to be absorbed.
                    I am Joaquín.
    The odds are great
    but my spirit is strong,
90   my faith unbreakable,
                    my blood is pure.
    I am Aztec prince and Christian Christ.
                I SHALL ENDURE!
                I WILL ENDURE!

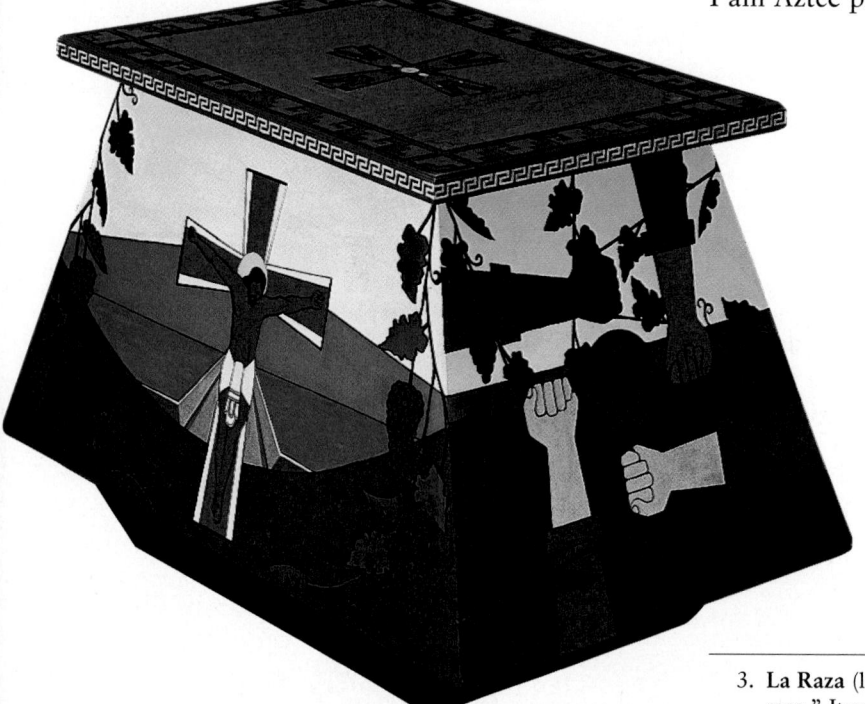

Farm Workers' Altar (1967), Emanuel
Martinez. Acrylic on wood, 37½″ × 53″
× 35½″, UCLA at The Armand Hammer
Museum of Art and Cultural Center,
Los Angeles.

---

3. **La Raza** (lä rä′sä): literally, the term means "the
race." It refers to people who trace their heritage
to Mexico.

Y en todos los terrenos fértiles,
           los llanos áridos,
70 los pueblos montañeros,
ciudades ahumadas,
        empezamos a AVANZAR.
   ¡La Raza!
¡Méjicano!
75   ¡Español!
    ¡Latino!
     ¡Hispano!
      ¡Chicano!
o lo que me llame yo,
80   yo parezco lo mismo
        yo siento lo mismo
        yo lloro
         y
        canto lo mismo.
85 Yo soy el bulto de mi gente y
yo renuncio ser absorbido.
      Yo soy Joaquín.
Las desigualdades son grandes
pero mi espíritu es firme,
90   mi fé impenetrable,
         mi sangre pura.
Soy príncipe azteca y Cristo cristiano.
      ¡YO PERDURARÉ!
      ¡YO PERDURARÉ!

Connect to the Literature

1. **What Do You Think?**
What immediate thoughts or questions do you have after reading these excerpts? Share them in class.

Comprehension Check
- According to the speaker, what struggle have his fathers won and what struggle have they lost?
- What does the speaker wish for his children?

Think Critically

2. What kind of revolution do you think the speaker is calling for? Explain.

3. **ACTIVE READING STRATEGIES FOR READING EPIC POETRY**
What evidence do you see that Joaquín is a hero with high ideals? Refer to the chart you made in your **READER'S NOTEBOOK.** Then tell whom or what you think Joaquín represents.

THINK ABOUT {
- who the speaker says he is
- the references to the past and future

4. In lines 9–23, the speaker suggests that economic success is incompatible with cultural and spiritual survival. Do you agree with this view? Give reasons to support your opinion.

5. Analyze this poem as an effort to persuade. Who do you believe is the intended audience, and what do you think the poet wants the audience to do, think, or feel?

Extend Interpretations

6. **Critic's Corner** In his introduction to *I Am Joaquín/Yo Soy Joaquín,* Rodolfo Gonzales has written, "Ultimately, there are no revolutions without poets." What do you think he means by this? In what way would his poem contribute to a revolution?

7. **Points of Comparison** Both "What Is an American?" and *I Am Joaquín/Yo Soy Joaquín* attempt to define a new race of people. Compare and contrast the "new men" idealized in each work, paying special attention to the forces that created them.

Literary Analysis

EPIC POEM *I Am Joaquín/Yo Soy Joaquín* is subtitled *An Epic Poem.* As you remember, an **epic poem** is a long narrative poem on a serious subject presented in an elevated or formal style. An epic poem traces the adventures of a hero who performs courageous, even superhuman, deeds. Such deeds often represent the ideals and values of a group of people, such as a nation or a race.

For example, Odysseus, the hero of Homer's ancient epic *The Odyssey,* is supremely clever, defeating monsters and other enemies by tricking them. He also is a great warrior, killing all the men who have pursued his wife while he was away. Odysseus' deeds show that the ancient Greeks valued wit, fighting skill, and fidelity.

Cooperative Learning Activity
Get together with a small group of classmates to review the charts you made in your **READER'S NOTEBOOK.** Then discuss Joaquín's deeds—his triumphs and sufferings. What can you conclude about the ideals and values of Mexican Americans, based on Joaquín's deeds? Write a group statement and share it with other groups. If you are ambitious, you might obtain the full text of *I Am Joaquín* to better see its epic elements.

Choices & CHALLENGES

Writing Options

1. Book Review *I Am Joaquín/Yo Soy Joaquín* was first published in 1967. Based on the excerpts you have read, how relevant do you believe the poem is today? Explain your opinion in a book review.

2. **Points of Comparison** Of the other works in this part of the unit, "The Right to Be Free," which do think is closest in spirit to Gonzales's poem? Defend your choice in a brief essay,

pointing out the connections you see. Place this piece in your **Working Portfolio.**

Activities & Explorations

1. Choral Reading Many theater groups have performed dramatizations of *I Am Joaquín/ Yo Soy Joaquín.* With a group of classmates, plan and present a dramatic reading of these excerpts from the poem. Consider assigning

different voices or groups of voices to different phrases or verses.
~ SPEAKING AND LISTENING

2. Language Study Compare the English and Spanish versions of the poem. Do you notice words that are similar in two languages? Are there similarities in word order? If you know Spanish, evaluate how well this poem has been translated. Are there lines you would render differently in English? **~ WORLD LANGUAGES**

Rodolfo Gonzales
1928–

Chicano Voice A poet and a leader of the Chicano movement, Rodolfo "Corky' Gonzales has devoted his life to promoting the pride and power of the Chicano people. He founded the Crusade for Justice, an organization based in Denver, Colorado, to promote political action among Chicano youth. During the 1968 Poor People's March, Gonzales presented the "Plan of the Barrio," a declaration demanding rights for Chicanos. Later, the Crusade for Justice proposed "The Spiritual Plan of Aztlán," which identified the Southwestern United States as Aztlán, the mythical place of origin of the Aztecs. By linking Chicano identity to pre-Columbian history, Gonzales connected modern Chicano concerns to the long history of the Chicano people.

Former Boxer Born in Denver to a family of migrant workers, Gonzales began working in the fields in the spring and summer by the time he was ten. During the fall and winter, he went to

public school in Denver, graduating from high school at age 16. Gonzales, a skilled boxer, won a Golden Gloves championship and a National Amateur Athletic Union championship, then turned professional. Before he retired from the ring in 1955, he was a contender for the world featherweight championship.

Social Activist After he left professional boxing, Gonzales became active in politics. He organized the Viva Kennedy presidential campaign in Colorado during the 1960 elections and subsequently served in a variety of government posts. In 1966, however, he left government service to devote himself full time to promoting Chicano issues.

Author Activity

Think again about Gonzales's statement, "Ultimately, there are no revolutions without poets." Discuss other individuals who merge art with social activism as Gonzales does.

Comparing Literature: Assessment Practice

In writing assessment, you will often be asked to evaluate, or judge, pieces of writing. You are now going to practice writing an essay with an evaluative focus.

PART 1 Reading the Prompt

Often you will be asked to write an essay in response to a prompt like the one below. Read the entire prompt carefully, looking for key words that help you identify the purpose of the essay and decide how to approach it.

Writing Prompt

I Am Joaquín and the other selections in Unit Two, Part 2, all are concerned with group struggles for freedom. Choose three selections from this part of the unit. In an essay, evaluate ❶ the three and decide which you found to be the most persuasive call for freedom. Cite evidence ❷ from the selections to support your evaluation. ❸

STRATEGIES
IN ACTION

❶ **Evaluate** the selections, judging them against standards or criteria.

❷ Notice the general **quality** you are evaluating.

❸ Include **examples** or **quotations** from the selections.

PART 2 Planning an Evaluative Essay

- Choose your three selections. (Pick those with which you are most familiar or those to which you had strong positive or negative reactions.)

- Choose your criteria for persuasiveness. You might be moved most by appeals to reason, appeals to emotion, or the moral standing of the writer, for example.

- For each selection, create an evaluation matrix like the one shown. As you apply each criterion in the first column, note an example and check off a value in one of the last three columns.

- Decide which selection is most persuasive overall.

Which is the most persuasive selection?

Criterion	Example	Strong	Medium	Weak

PART 3 Drafting Your Essay

Introduction Begin by clearly stating your thesis—your opinion about which selection is most persuasive.

Organization You could evaluate each selection individually or take one criterion at a time and relate it to all three selections. Connect back to your thesis as you go along. Include strong examples from the selections to illustrate your points.

Conclusion Restate your thesis and leave the reader with a final idea about writing and freedom.

Revision If possible, allow time to review your work. Make sure it is clear, well-supported, and free from mistakes.

Writing Handbook
See page 1283: Analysis.

The Autobiography of Benjamin Franklin

Benjamin Franklin—inventor, writer, statesman, and diplomat—tells his life history with wit, charm, and intellect. An American success story, Franklin describes his climb from anonymity and poverty to fame and fortune. Full of concrete suggestions and ideas on how to achieve moral perfection, *The Autobiography* stands as a monument to the ideals of reason, order, and human perfectibility that typified Enlightenment thought of the 18th century. Franklin wrote this book as a model that might guide readers to follow his example.

The American Revolutionaries: A History in Their Own Words

EDITED BY MILTON MELTZER

A sweeping collection of primary sources, this book captures the spirit of '76 through the voices of people who joined the struggle for independence. A cross-section of American society—for example, teenagers in combat, women revolutionaries, commanding officers, religious leaders, immigrants, and slaves—provide firsthand accounts of this critical time in the nation's history. They show how the Revolutionary War touched the lives of all Americans, not just the troops fighting on the battlefield and the leaders forging a democratic government.

And Even *More* . . .

Books
The Poems of Phillis Wheatley
PHILLIS WHEATLEY
A collection of Wheatley's poems on a broad range of topics, including patriotic themes.

Angel in the Whirlwind: The Triumph of the American Revolution
BENSON BOBRICK
Engaging historical account, filled with interesting quotations from key political and military leaders.

The American Revolution in Drawings and Prints
COMPILED BY DONALD H. CRESSWELL
A pictorial history of the struggle for independence.

Other Media
1776
Film version of a smash-hit Broadway musical, tracing events that spurred the American colonies to declare their independence from Britain. Columbia. (VIDEOCASSETTE)

Liberty! The American Revolution
A documentary of the dramatic events that culminated in the founding of a new nation. PBS Home Video. (VIDEOCASSETTE)

Thomas Jefferson
A film by Ken Burns profiling Jefferson's life and political career. PBS Home Video.
(VIDEOCASSETTE)

April Morning

HOWARD FAST
This historical novel focuses on Adam Cooper, a 15-year-old boy who comes to grips with his fears during the Revolutionary War. Fast skillfully weaves fact with fiction. Through Adam's eyes, readers experience the real-life Battle of Lexington, fought in April 1775.

Writing Workshop

Writing to Persuade Others . . .

From Reading to Writing Thomas Jefferson, Martin Luther King, Jr., and Malcolm X had powerful ideas about political and social problems, and they believed that one way to solve them was by persuading others to think and act as they did. All **persuasive writing** serves this basic purpose, although it is not always about such world-shaking issues. Advertising, fund-raising campaigns, editorials, and political speeches are examples of persuasive writing.

For Your Portfolio

WRITING PROMPT Write a persuasive essay about an issue that concerns you.

Purpose: To express your opinion and to convince others to agree with you and possibly to take some action

Audience: Your classmates and friends; members of your community

---

Basics in a Box

Persuasive Essay at a Glance

WHAT I BELIEVE

Opinion or belief — Introduction

WHY YOU SHOULD BELIEVE IT

Supporting evidence | Supporting evidence | Supporting evidence — Body

Summary of opinion
What readers should do — Conclusion

RUBRIC Standards for Writing

A successful persuasive essay should

- state the issue and your position on it clearly in the introduction
- be geared to the audience you're trying to convince
- support your position with evidence, such as facts, statistics, and examples
- answer possible objections to your position
- show clear reasoning
- conclude with a summary of your position or a call to action

Analyzing a Student Model

Jim Meyer
Fenwick High School

Security Cameras in Schools

Today, reports of improved test scores and of successful community service projects are only one part of the news from our public schools. Frequently, it seems, we also hear reports of dangers faced by students and teachers, from violence to drugs to vandalism. There's no question that students and faculty should feel safe at school and that whenever safety is in doubt, the quality of education is jeopardized. So how do you provide the needed security? Some schools have installed security cameras to ensure safety among faculty and students. However, the idea of security cameras is not universally accepted. While some students feel the cameras are a violation of their rights, I maintain their right to learn and work in a safe environment is more important.

According to a study published by the Office of the Attorney General in the state of South Carolina, the top offenses in schools since 1995 included controlled substance violations, possession of pagers, weapons offenses, aggravated assaults, thefts, vandalism, and threatening students and school officials. Security cameras can reduce these crimes significantly. Alan Page, systems engineer for North Miami Beach High School, reports that the rate of theft and vandalism dropped 85 percent in those Miami-area schools where security cameras had been installed. The students also reported feeling safer with the cameras watching over the school.

Opponents of security cameras claim they are too expensive. I do not agree. A proper installation costs from $10,000 to $20,000—less than the annual salary of one security guard according to *American School and University,* Oct. 1996. Security cameras don't need fringe benefits, vacations, or retirement, either. The money schools would save on property insurance premiums alone would more than cover the cost of installation. For example, an article in *Security Management,* March 1996, notes that the Huntsville, Alabama, school district installed an elaborate microwave-based surveillance system throughout the district for $1.7 million. That's a huge investment, but in just two years, the district saved $700,000 on insurance premiums alone. The installation cost of a security system is, at best, a weak argument for not having cameras watching over the school.

RUBRIC IN ACTION

❶ This writer introduces the issue with a straightforward statement of the problem.
Other Options:
- Quote an expert
- Present an anecdote
- Cite an example or give statistics

❷ Clearly states position on the issue

❸ Gives statistics and an example to support the position

❹ States opposing view

❺ Answers opposing view with facts and statistics

The fact is, cameras can actually save money for a school district. The same *Security Management* article reported that one high school in Chicago was spending $35,000 each year just to paint over graffiti. After cameras were installed, the annual cost dropped to $2,000. The savings are being used for school beautification projects. This same school also had a long history of students transferring to other schools because students and parents considered it dangerous. Because of the cameras, that perception has changed. The school is now seen as a safe learning environment and the student population is again growing.

Students in some California schools have objected to security cameras on the grounds that they are an invasion of privacy. They claim the cameras create a prison-like atmosphere in the school. The students feel security cameras in every hallway convey the feeling that Big Brother is watching every move they make. They say having the cameras is like having a prison guard observing them constantly, waiting for them to make a mistake. I might concede this point if the cameras were installed in a private area, but I fail to see what could possibly be private about a public area like a hallway. Do the security cameras in local department stores create a prison-like atmosphere that drives customers away? I fully support the Constitution of the United States, but I question the students' interpretation of the rights the Constitution guarantees. There is no privacy in an area intended for public use.

The American Civil Liberties Union, a staunch and untiring guardian of American rights, has, in fact, raised some questions about the legal use of cameras in schools and how much or how little they infringe on the rights of students. But even the ACLU has stated that surveillance cameras, when properly installed and used in correct situations, are neither illegal nor bad policy.

Although some students and faculty in the United States feel security cameras are a bad idea, other schools are installing these systems in order to improve their schools. Whether the argument is about a prison-like atmosphere or too much spending, without security measures teachers will have to take on more responsibility for the safety of students. They will have less time for teaching. The right to learn is one of the most powerful rights Americans have. This right should not be taken away from us because some feel their need for privacy is more important. I believe in my right to learn in a safe environment, and cameras will help to ensure safety for every student who is under their watchful eye.

6 Provides additional facts and statistics to answer opposing view

7 Presents and answers another opposing view

8 Gives additional facts to refute opposing view

9 This writer concludes by summing up arguments and restating his position.
Another Option:
· Urge readers to take action.

Writing Your Persuasive Essay

❶ Prewriting

Writing comes more easily if you have something to say.
Sholem Asch, novelist

Look for an issue that's important to you and about which people disagree. Try brainstorming for ideas with a friend or looking for controversial issues in the news. See the **Idea Bank** in the margin for more suggestions. After you've chosen an issue, follow the steps below.

Planning Your Persuasive Essay

▶ **1. Clarify your position.** What do you believe about your topic? Why do you hold that belief?

▶ **2. Identify your audience.** What do they know about the topic? What is their position on it? How can you answer opposing views?

▶ **3. Use evidence to support your arguments.** What facts, statistics, and examples support your position? What reference books or experts will offer more information?

❷ Drafting

Continue exploring your ideas as you begin drafting. Don't be afraid to rethink or revise your opinion as you work. At some point, you must state your position clearly and support it with evidence, such as **facts, statistics, examples, observations, anecdotes,** or **quotations.** Make your case strongly, but beware of using unfair language and faulty reasoning. Watch out for these illogical arguments and faulty and deceptive uses of language.

- **circular reasoning**—just restating something in other words without offering proof (We need a new traffic light at the corner because it's necessary.)

- **over-generalization**—making a statement that's too broad to prove (Everybody likes chocolate.)

- **either-or fallacy**—stating that there are only two possible alternatives (Either I get into Ivy League U. or my future is ruined.)

- **cause-and-effect fallacy**—assuming that because event B followed event A, A caused B (I flunked the test because I wore my unlucky shirt.)

- **bandwagon appeal**—trying to persuade people to follow the crowd (Everyone wears Spike brand of athletic shoes.)

- **name-calling**—attacking the person, not the idea (Joe won't be a good representative because he is a nerd.)

IDEABank

1. Your Working Portfolio
Look for ideas in the **Writing Options** you completed earlier in this unit:

- **Rebuttal Speech,** p. 268
- **Literary Letter,** p. 288
- **Points of Comparison,** p. 308
- **Points of Comparison,** p. 317

2. What's Your Opinion?
Interview several classmates and adults to find out what current issue they think is most important and controversial.

3. Fill in the Blanks.
Complete this statement: If we don't do something about _____ soon, _____.

Have you used language fairly?

See the **Writing Handbook** Persuasive Writing, pp. 1285–1286

Ask Your Peer Reader

- What is my position on this issue?
- What more do you need to know to understand the issue?
- What arguments do you find most convincing?
- What arguments are not convincing?

Need revising help?

Review the **Rubric**, p. 320

Consider **peer reader** comments

Check **Revision Guidelines**, p. 1269

❸ Revising

TARGET SKILL ▶ **SUPPORTING PERSONAL OPINIONS WITH FACTS**
While experts' opinions can provide strong support for your arguments, you must back up your own opinions with facts.

> Opponents of security cameras claim they are too expensive. I do not
>
> *A proper installation costs from $10,000 to $20,000—less than*
> agree. The installation cost of a security system is, at best, a weak
> ^
>
> *the annual salary of one security guard.*
> argument for not having cameras watching over the school.

Stumped by pronoun-antecedent agreement?

See the **Grammar Handbook**, p. 1307

❹ Editing and Proofreading

TARGET SKILL ▶ **PRONOUN–ANTECEDENT AGREEMENT** In doing persuasive writing, you're focusing on solid reasoning and objective arguments, and it's easy to over-look pronoun-antecedent agreement. When you edit and proofread, make sure pronouns agree with their antecedents in number, gender, and person so your writing is clear and unambiguous.

> This right should not be taken away from us because some feel ~~our~~ *their*
> ^
>
> need for privacy is more important. I believe in my right to learn in a
>
> safe environment, and cameras will help ensure safety for every
>
>   *their*
> student who is under ~~its~~ watchful eye.
>   ^

Publishing IDEAS

• Submit your essay to your local or school newspaper.

• Post your essay on your school's Web page.

More Online: Publishing Options
www.mcdougallittell.com

❺ Reflecting

FOR YOUR WORKING PORTFOLIO What do I like most about my finished essay? How has my opinion on this issue been changed by writing about it? Which aspect of this writing assignment was most difficult for me? Write responses to these questions and keep them with your persuasive essay in your **Working Portfolio.**

Assessment Practice Revising & Editing

Read this paragraph from the first draft of a persuasive essay. The underlined sections may include the following kinds of errors:

- **unsupported opinions**
- **lack of subject-verb agreement**
- **lack of pronoun-antecedent agreement**
- **incorrect possessive forms**

For each underlined section, choose the revision that most improves the writing.

> School uniforms unfairly restrict students's freedom of choice and
> <u>(1)</u>
> expression. <u>Restricting free choice isn't good.</u> Everyone has a right to choose
> <u>(2)</u>
> <u>their</u> own clothes, and <u>uniforms take away</u> this right. Teens who are allowed to
> <u>(3)</u> <u>(4)</u>
> wear whatever they choose can pick clothes that <u>reflects their personality and</u>
> <u>(5)</u>
> <u>judgment.</u> On the other hand, a teen who must wear a uniform is denied <u>the</u>
> <u>(6)</u>
> <u>chance to make their own decisions.</u>

1. **A.** student's
   B. students'
   C. students
   D. Correct as is

2. **A.** Restricting free choice isn't good because it prevents students from practicing real-world decision-making skills.
   B. Restricting free choice isn't good because it's harmful to students.
   C. In my opinion, restricting free choice isn't good.
   D. Correct as is

3. **A.** theirs
   B. his or her
   C. your
   D. Correct as is

4. **A.** a uniform takes away
   B. a uniform take away
   C. uniform's take aways
   D. Correct as is

5. **A.** reflects his or her personality and judgment
   B. are reflecting their personality and judgment
   C. reflect their personality and judgment
   D. Correct as is

6. **A.** the chance to make his or her own decisions
   B. the chance to make its own decision
   C. the chance to make your own decisions
   D. Correct as is

Need extra help?

See the **Grammar Handbook**

Pronouns, p. 1307

Subject-Verb Agreement, p. 1324

Possessives, p. 1306

Meaning from Details

By now you have developed a variety of strategies to help you figure out the meanings of unfamiliar words. Often, you can find hints to the meaning of a word in the words and sentences that surround it. These hints are called **context clues.** For example, you can determine that *acquiescence* in the quotation on the right means "resignation" or "giving in" because Martin Luther King, Jr., restates his meaning immediately after the word appears.

> **Oppressed people deal with their oppression in three characteristic ways. One way is acquiescence: the oppressed resign themselves to their doom.**
> —Martin Luther King, Jr., *Stride Toward Freedom*

Strategies for Building Vocabulary

Familiarity with context clues like the ones explained in the following paragraphs can help you expand your vocabulary.

❶ **Definition or Restatement Clues** The passage quoted above demonstrates that a writer sometimes provides a clue to a word's meaning by restating the meaning in a simpler and defining way. Words like *or, that is, in other words,* and *also called* often signal definition or restatement clues.

❷ **Example Clues** Sometimes a writer follows an unfamiliar word with examples that illustrate its meaning. At other times, an unfamiliar word may occur within a series of examples and be explained by the other examples that surround it. In the passage below, the phrases "to be underpaid for the work they do," "tied to menial jobs," and "to be used" help you determine that *exploitation* means "a selfish and unfair use of a person or group".

> Some groups in society fail to appreciate the effects of exploitation. They do not know what it is like to be underpaid for the work they do or to be tied to the most menial jobs. They do not know what it feels like to be used.

❸ **Comparison and Contrast Clues** A word's meaning may also be clarified by comparing or contrasting it with a more familiar word. Comparisons are often signaled by words like *like, as,* and *than;* contrasts, by words like *although, but, yet, however,* and *on the other hand.* For example,

in the sentence "He called for order rather than anarchy," the words *rather than* signal that *anarchy* contrasts with *order.*

❹ **Inference Clues** The meaning of a word is sometimes clarified by the general sense of the words and sentences that surround it. For example, in lines 20–22 of the Declaration of Independence, Jefferson writes that "Prudence, indeed, will dictate that governments long established should not be changed for light and transient causes." The reference to the "long established" governments and Jefferson's warning that they should not be changed for "light and transient causes" helps you to infer that *transient* means "temporary."

EXERCISE Explain the meaning of the italicized word in each sentence. Then identify the type of context clue and the details that helped you to define it.

1. The colonists presented their proposals for changes in the laws, but the angry king refused his *assent.*
2. Jefferson considered the king to be a *tyrant,* an oppressor.
3. The speaker's response was *glib.* She joked about the issues and showed no knowledge of the facts.
4. While some people *tacitly* accept oppression, others speak out against it.
5. To *repudiate* authority is to reject its values.

Grammar from Literature

Writers use different verb tenses in the same sentence for a variety of reasons.

- To establish a time frame for events—past, present, or future.
- To show a chronological or conditional relationship.

Notice in the following sentences how different forms of the verbs, or tenses, have been used to show variations in the time of action or state of being.

> simple present
> **It becomes necessary for one people to dissolve the**
> present perfect
> **political bands which have connected them with another.**
> —The Declaration of Independence
>
> present progressive   simple future
> **As we are going to part, we will come and take you by the hand.**   —Red Jacket, "Lecture to a Missionary"

When writing about events that happened at different times, it is important to use the right combination of verb tenses. The order of the verb tenses within a sentence is called the **sequence of tenses.**

In the first example, Thomas Jefferson begins by relating a present situation and then switches to the present perfect tense to talk about a continuing action that began in the past. In the second passage, Red Jacket switches to the future tense to talk about something that will happen after the first action mentioned in the sentence (*are going*).

Writers also use shifts in tense to express conditional relationships—that is, relationships in which one event will occur only if another does. In the following sentence, the shift in tense shows that the action indicated by *will fight* will occur after the action indicated by *continues*.

> **If the tyranny continues, we will fight.**

Remember that all verbs have three simple tenses and three perfect tenses. The list below illustrates forms of the verb walk in the simple and perfect verb tenses.

Simple Tenses	Regular Verb	Irregular Verb
Present	walk	begin
Past	walked	began
Future	(shall) will walk	(shall) will begin
Perfect Tenses		
Present Perfect	has walked	has or have begun
Past Perfect	had walked	had begun
Future Perfect	will have walked	will have begun

Using Verb Sequences in Your Writing Many writing situations involve recording actions that happened at various times. By carefully structuring the sequence of the tenses you choose, you can avoid confusion and give your reader a clear picture of events and relationships.

> **Letters and journal entries give us a picture of events that happened in day to day life over two centuries ago, but events in the future will tell if we have learned anything from history.**

Usage Tip If one event in the past clearly happened before another, use the past perfect tense for the event that happened first. Form the past perfect tense by combining the word *had* with the past participle of the verb.

> INCORRECT
> simple past   simple past
> **They told us they fled from their own country for fear of wicked men.**
>
> CORRECT
> simple past   past perfect
> **They told us they had fled from their own country for fear of wicked men.**
>
> —Red Jacket, "Lecture to a Missionary"

WRITING EXERCISE Rewrite the following sentences, correcting errors in sequence of verb tenses.

1. Patrick Henry had felt that under some circumstances it is better to die than to live.
2. The words of the Declaration of Independence will remain a model for nations who sought democracy.
3. Phillis Wheatley will say that some people have oppressed others in the name of liberty.
4. If we read carefully the words of Martin Luther King, Jr., we come to understand his greatness.
5. Dr. King discussed the three ways in which people dealt with oppression in the past.

From Colony to Country

A Morning View of Blue Hill Village (1824), Jonathan Fisher. William A. Farnsworth Library and Art Museum, Rockford, Maine.

As a result of reading the selections in this unit, have you gained any new insights into the principles and beliefs of the Puritans and the American revolutionaries? What did you learn about the power of persuasion as you read the examples of persuasive writing? Choose one or more of the options in each of the following sections to explore what you've learned.

Reflecting on the Unit

OPTION 1

Strong Beliefs Many of the selections in this unit express the strong religious and political beliefs held by early Americans. List some of these beliefs, noting the people or groups who supported them. Which of the beliefs do you agree with most? Which do you disagree with? In a few paragraphs, identify your choices and explain why you chose them.

OPTION 2

The American Way With a small group of classmates, discuss the principles and values that you believe were the most important in the creation of the United States as a nation. Are those principles and values still important today? Use examples from the selections to support your opinions, but also draw on your previous knowledge.

OPTION 3

To Form a More Perfect Union Choose four or more writers from this unit, both historical and contemporary, that have had the greatest influence on your opinions about the values central to American democracy. Using the ideas of these writers as support, write a letter to the President of the United States, commenting on the current government's political and moral policies.

Self ASSESSMENT

📖 **READER'S NOTEBOOK**

To document what you have learned by reading the selections in this unit, make a list of the insights into the development of the nation that you have gained.

Reviewing Literary Concepts

Analyzing Drama In this unit, you read *The Crucible*, a modern play, and learned literary concepts associated with drama. To test your understanding, write one or two sentences applying each of the following literary terms to *The Crucible:* **setting, internal conflict, external conflict, plot, climax, resolution, characters, protagonist, antagonist, foil, dialogue, stage directions.** For example, you might write, "The **setting** of *The Crucible* is Salem, Massachusetts, in 1692." To extend your knowledge further, apply the same terms to a film or television show you saw recently.

OPTION 2

Understanding Persuasion Most of the selections in this unit contain persuasive arguments. Make a chart like the one shown here, noting the main points of the writer's argument in each selection you have read. Also note how each writer attempts to persuade the reader—for example, by appeals to reason or emotion, by biblical allusions, by loaded language, or by rhetorical questions. Then write a short paragraph explaining which two or three arguments you found most persuasive and why.

Selection	Points Argued For	Author's Persuasive Tactics
"Speech in the Virginia Convention"	The need to arm and fight the British	Biblical allusions, rhetorical questions, appeals to patriotism, appeals to reason

Self ASSESSMENT

📖 READER'S NOTEBOOK

In addition to dramatic terms, other literary terms were discussed in Unit Two. Copy this list and place an X next to those terms you understand well. Review the terms you are not sure about in the **Glossary of Literary Terms** (page 1244).

meter	metaphor
iambic pentameter	simile
transcript	theme
allusion	tone
rhetorical question	historical context
parallelism	epic poem
figurative language	

📁 Building Your Portfolio

- **Writing Options** Several of the Writing Options in this unit asked for your personal responses to the beliefs and principles presented in the selections. Choose the response that best expresses your opinion about a belief or principle important to you, and explain your choice in a cover note. Attach the note to the response and put them in your **Presentation Portfolio.** 📁

- **Writing Workshop** In this unit, you wrote a Review of a literary work or a film. You also wrote a Persuasive Essay about an issue important to you. Reread these pieces and decide which is more successful at presenting and defending your opinions. Explain your choice in a note attached to the preferred one. Place this piece in your **Presentation Portfolio.** 📁

- **Additional Activities** Think back to any of the assignments you completed under **Activities & Explorations** and **Inquiry & Research.** Keep a record in your portfolio of any assignments you would like to do further work on in the future.

Self ASSESSMENT

Now that you have some pieces of writing in your **Presentation Portfolio,** 📁 look them over and decide which kinds of writing contain your strongest work. What kinds of writing would you like more practice in as the year goes on?

Setting GOALS

Look back through this unit's selections, your portfolio, and your notebook, identifying the literary genres that you would like to read more examples of or would like to experiment within your writing.

Reading & Writing for Assessment

Throughout high school, you will be tested on your ability to read and understand many different kinds of reading selections. These tests will assess your basic understanding of ideas and knowledge of vocabulary. They will also check your ability to analyze and evaluate both the message of the text and the techniques the writer uses in getting that message across.

The following pages will give you test-taking strategies. Practice applying these strategies by working through each of the models provided.

PART 1 How to Read a Test Selection

In many tests, you will read a passage and then answer multiple-choice questions about it. Applying the basic test-taking strategies that follow, taking notes, and highlighting or underscoring passages as you read can help you focus on the information you will need to know.

STRATEGIES FOR READING A TEST SELECTION

▶ **Before you begin reading, skim the questions that follow the passage.** These can help focus your reading.

▶ **Use your active reading strategies such as analyzing, predicting, and questioning.** Make notes in the margin to help you focus your reading. You may do this only if the test directions allow you to mark on the test itself.

▶ **Think about the title.** What does it suggest about the overall message or theme of the selection?

▶ **Look for main ideas.** These are often stated at the beginnings or ends of paragraphs. Sometimes they are implied, not stated. After reading each paragraph, ask "What was this passage about?"

▶ **Note the literary elements and techniques used by the writer.** You might consider structure, the writer's portrayal of people, or techniques the writer used to create humor or suspense. Then ask yourself what effect the writer achieves with each choice.

▶ **Unlock word meanings.** Use context clues and word parts to help you unlock the meaning of unfamiliar words.

▶ **Think about the message or theme.** What larger lesson can you draw from the passage? Can you infer anything or make generalizations about other similar situations, human beings, or life in general?

A Boy's School Project Aims to Revise History: New Focus on Case of a 1945 War Disaster

By Lizette Alvarez

1   It took the cruiser *Indianapolis* just 12 minutes to go down, pierced by three Japanese torpedoes in the Pacific on July 30, 1945. Hundreds of the ship's 1,169 crewmen managed to scurry overboard and spent four days and five nights fending off sharks and hallucinations.

2   For 53 years, the 316 survivors of the single worst disaster at sea in American naval history have pursued one goal: to wipe clean the 1946 court-martial conviction of Capt. Charles Butler McVay 3d, their skipper. Now a 12-year-old Florida boy could be the impetus for the ❶ exoneration of a captain whose crew considered him a scapegoat for the Navy's own culpability.

3   The boy, Hunter Scott of Cantonment, on the outskirts of Pensacola, a Navy town in the Florida panhandle, was watching the movie *Jaws* when he got the inspiration for a history project. Now through a combination of luck, gumption and the appeal only a 12-year-old could carry off, ❷ Hunter has become a sensation, attracting the interest of politicians, reporters and documentarians around the world.

4   "We have tried and tried and it didn't get anywhere," said Maurice G. Bell, 73, one of the 150 remaining survivors of the *Indianapolis,* the ship that ferried the atom bomb Little Boy to Guam. "And here you've got this young 12-year-old boy and they listen to him a little bit better. This is the best chance we've ever had. If we don't get it now, I don't think we ever will."

5   Last week, with Hunter in Washington, Representative Joe Scarborough, whose district includes the town where Hunter lives, introduced a bill to exonerate Captain McVay.

6   Hunter toted his hundreds of letters, interviews, documents and newspaper clippings around the Capitol, meeting with numerous lawmakers, including Speaker Newt Gingrich, who was instantly smitten and told the boy he expected to push for the bill after a review by the House National Security Committee. Senator Daniel K. Inouye, Democrat of Hawaii, said he would sponsor the bill in the Senate, and Senator Robert C. Smith, Republican of New Hampshire, said he would help.

7   "Is your evidence solid?" Senator Smith asked Hunter, during their one-on-one chat.

8   "Like a rock, sir," Hunter replied, without missing a beat.

9   Wise to the ways of Washington, Hunter even made his pitch at a full-fledged news conference there, ❸ shrugging off microphones that all but obscured his head.

❶ **Use context clues to understand vocabulary.**

ONE STUDENT'S THOUGHTS

"Exoneration must mean that Captain McVay's name would be cleared if his court-martial conviction is set aside."

❷ **Note literary elements that build interest.**

"I've read three paragraphs and all I have are questions. Why has Hunter become a sensation? Why was Captain McVay court-martialed?"

YOUR TURN

What questions do the first three paragraphs leave you with? Why would the writer want you to ask these questions?

❸ **Note how the writer shows character traits.**

"Hunter must be very confident—all those microphones would make me nervous!"

YOUR TURN

What else does the writer show about Hunter by telling us how Hunter reacted to the microphones?

10   To the chagrin of the Navy, Hunter, who cannot help winding up his sentences with "ma'am" and "sir," has stayed resolutely "on-message."

11   Back home, he said: "A lot of people in the Navy don't want to reopen this. That's politics. ❹ They had to have a scapegoat to appease the public and they chose Captain McVay. I'm not going to let that stop me."

12   In a statement yesterday, a Navy spokesman said that in 1996 the Navy had reviewed the court-martial proceeding and concluded that it was "accurate," and that "no further actions are appropriate."

13   ❺ And what exactly has Hunter learned from his blockbuster history project? "I found out how hard it is to right an injustice," he said. . . .

14   The Navy has long maintained that Captain McVay was at fault for failing to follow a zigzag course in a submarine-infested patch of the Pacific. He was convicted of that charge, although the Secretary of the Navy, taking note of Captain McVay's illustrious record, remitted the sentence and gave him a desk job. The Navy refused, however, to expunge his conviction.

15   Subsequent evidence, though, cast doubt on the Government's position. One 1993 report, for example, indicated that the Navy knew there were Japanese submarines in the area but never told Mr. McVay and sent the ship to sea unescorted. ❻ The Navy disputes that conclusion. . . .

16   Hunter, a seventh-grader at Ransom Middle School, spent what seemed like a lifetime to him—"since sixth grade"—compiling all the information he could get his hands on.

17   Mr. Scarborough exhibited Hunter's research in his office, and in no time, word spread about the project.

18   None of this has fazed Hunter, who says he never gets nervous, even when he makes the rounds on morning television news programs and tells his story to the BBC.

19   The idea for the project zapped Hunter while he watched *Jaws,* and heard Quint, the scurrilous shark hunter, recount his hair-raising battle with sharks after the *Indianapolis* went down. Hunter's father suggested he start a research project, and Hunter put an advertisement in the local Navy newspaper seeking survivors. . . .

20   His schoolmates predict that Hunter will be President one day. But Hunter has other plans. He wants to join the Navy as a doctor or lawyer, then "get a bunch of land in New Mexico and hunt and fish every day."

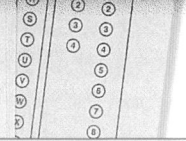

PART 2   How to Answer Multiple Choice Questions

Use the strategies in the box and notes in the side column to
help you answer the questions below and on the following pages.

> **STRATEGIES** FOR ANSWERING
> MULTIPLE-CHOICE QUESTIONS

> ▸ **Ask questions** that help you
> eliminate some of the choices.
> ▸ **Pay attention to choices** such as
> "all of the above" or "none of the
> above." To eliminate them, all you
> need to find is one answer that
> doesn't fit.
> ▸ **Skim your notes.** Details you
> noticed as you read may provide
> answers.

Based on the selection you have just read, choose the best
answer for each of the following questions.

1. The main idea expressed by this selection is that
   A. the Indianapolis disaster was a great tragedy.
   B. Captain McVay was scapegoated by the Navy.
   C. The survivors of the Indianapolis have been ignored.
   D. Hunter Scott is a good student.

2. Why do you think that the writer chooses to tell us that
   Hunter "cannot help winding up his sentences with 'ma'am'
   and 'sir'"?
   A. to show that Hunter is respectful
   B. to make fun of Hunter
   C. to show Hunter's youth
   D. all of the above

3. Hunter tells Senator Smith that his evidence is as solid as a
   rock. Why does the writer include this detail in the selection?
   A. to show that Hunter will say anything to make his case
   B. to show that Hunter has a sense of humor
   C. to show that Hunter feels intimidated by the Senator
   D. to show that Hunter feels confident about stating his case

4. What literary element does the writer add to the selection by
   telling us that the time period "since sixth grade" seems like
   a lifetime to Hunter?
   A. plot
   B. foreshadowing
   C. humor
   D. suspense

5. Which of the following might be one of the larger lessons the
   writer hopes to convey through this story?
   A. It's never too late to reverse an injustice.
   B. With a fresh approach, a child may succeed where adults
      have failed.
   C. It's hard to fight a large institution.
   D. All of the above.

STRATEGIES
IN ACTION

**Pay attention to choices such as "all of
the above."**

**ONE STUDENT'S
THOUGHTS**

"The writer seems to admire Hunter—I
don't think she would make fun of him.
*So I can eliminate choice B. That
means I can also eliminate choice D.*"

YOUR TURN
What other choice doesn't make sense?

Skim your notes.

**ONE STUDENT'S
THOUGHTS**

"The writer doesn't go on to say
anything that would suggest Hunter is
likely to spend a lifetime on this project.
I don't think this detail is foreshadowing
anything. *So I can eliminate choice B.*"

YOUR TURN
*Which of the three remaining choices
makes the most sense?*

How To Respond in Writing

You may also be asked to write answers to questions about a reading passage. Short-answer questions usually ask you to answer in a sentence or two. Essay questions require a fully developed piece of writing.

Short-Answer Question

STRATEGIES FOR RESPONDING TO SHORT-ANSWER QUESTIONS

▶ **Identify the key words** in the writing prompt that tell you the ideas to discuss. Make sure you know what is meant by each.
▶ **State your response directly** and to the point.
▶ **Support your ideas** by using evidence from the selection.
▶ **Use correct grammar.**

> **Sample Question**
>
> Answer the following question in one or two sentences.
>
> Why does the writer not tell Hunter's story in chronological order? How does the writer's decision to save important information for the end of the article affect the reader?

Essay Question

STRATEGIES FOR ANSWERING ESSAY QUESTIONS

▶ **Look for direction words** in the writing prompt, such as *essay, analyze, describe,* or *compare and contrast,* that tell you how to respond directly to the prompt.
▶ **List the points** you want to make before beginning to write.
▶ **Write an interesting introduction** that presents your main point.
▶ **Develop your ideas** by using evidence from the selection that supports the statements you make.
▶ **Present the ideas** in a logical order.
▶ **Write a conclusion** that summarizes your points.
▶ **Check your work** for correct grammar.

> **Sample Prompt**
>
> The writer describes Hunter as having a combination of "luck, gumption, and appeal." Write an essay in which you analyze Hunter's character using evidence provided by the writer.

STRATEGIES IN ACTION

Identify the key words.

ONE STUDENT'S THOUGHTS

"This question is asking about the structure of the selection. The key words seem to be *chronological* and *important information.*"

YOUR TURN

What is the important information at the end of the article? Why isn't it put at the beginning?

Develop your ideas by using evidence from the selection.

ONE STUDENT'S THOUGHTS

"The writer says that Hunter compiled a file containing letters, interviews, documents, and newspaper clippings. Hunter must have worked on this project a long time. He must have been very determined—and organized."

YOUR TURN

What other details does the writer provide that suggest insights into Hunter's character?

How to Revise and Edit a Test Selection

Here is a student's first draft in response to the writing prompt at the bottom of page 334. Read it and answer the multiple-choice questions that follow.

1	Hunter is a determined kid. He has worked on his project for a
2	year and has taken his case to Washington. To be that determined,
3	he must really think that Captain McVay is innocent and should
4	have his name cleared. He seems to care about truth and justice—
5	and he doesn't think much of politics.
6	Hunter not only cares about this project, but he also has what
7	it takes. The character traits that might help him to succeed. He
8	is organized, confident, and ready to talk to people. Hunter seems
9	to want to make his case through hard evidence and polite words.
10	He doesn't want to stir people up with inflamed rhetoric.

▶ **Read the passage carefully.**
▶ **Note the parts that are confusing** or don't make sense. What kinds of errors would that signal?
▶ **Look for errors** in grammar, usage, spelling, and capitalization. Common errors include:
  • run-on sentences
  • sentence fragments
  • subject-verb agreement
  • unclear pronoun antecedents
  • lack of transition words

1. What is the BEST way to revise the sentence in lines 2–4 to make it clear who is referred to by the pronoun "his"? ("To be... must...name cleared.")

   A. He must really think that Captain McVay is innocent and should have McVay's name cleared.

   B. Hunter must really think Captain McVay is innocent and should have his name cleared.

   C. Hunter must want Captain McVay's name to be cleared because he (McVay) is innocent.

   D. Make no change.

2. What is the BEST change, if any, to the sentences in lines 6 and 7? ("Hunter not only...to succeed.")

   A. Hunter not only cares about this project, but he also has what it takes; the character traits that might help him to succeed.

   B. Hunter not only cares about this project, but he also has: the character traits that might help him to succeed.

   C. Hunter not only cares about this project, but he also has the character traits that might help him to succeed.

   D. Make no change.

3. What is the BEST way to combine the sentences in lines 8–10? ("Hunter seems...inflamed rhetoric.")

   A. Hunter uses hard evidence and polite words to make his case. Never inflamed rhetoric.

   B. Hunter wants to make his case using hard evidence, but not using inflamed rhetoric, and using polite words.

   C. Hunter seems to want to make his case through hard evidence and polite words, not with inflamed rhetoric.

   D. Make no change.

The Spirit of Individualism

If a man does not keep pace

with his companions,

perhaps it is because

he hears a different drummer.

Let him step to the music

which he hears, however measured

or far away.

HENRY DAVID THOREAU

Naturalist and writer

The Wanderer (1818), Caspar
David Friedrich. Kunsthalle, Hamburg,
Germany, Bridgeman/Art Resource,
New York.

The
Spirit
of
Individualism

EVENTS IN AMERICAN LITERATURE

1800   **1810**   **1820**

1809 Washington Irving publishes *A History of New York*

1824 Irving's "The Devil and Tom Walker" is published

1826 James Fenimore Cooper publishes *The Last of the Mohicans*

1827 *Freedom's Journal*, first African-American newspaper, is founded

1828 *American Dictionary of the English Language* is published by Noah Webster

EVENTS IN THE UNITED STATES

1800   **1810**   **1820**

1801 Thomas Jefferson becomes president

1803 Jefferson doubles size of United States by buying Louisiana territory from France

1804 Meriwether Lewis and William Clark begin explorations of Louisiana territory and beyond to Pacific coast (to 1806)

1807 Robert Fulton launches *Clermont*, the first steamboat

1808 United States bans slave trade

1812 United States declares war on Great Britain

1814 After witnessing naval battle during War of 1812, Francis Scott Key composes "The Star Spangled Banner"

1820 Missouri Compromise prohibits slavery in western territory north of Missouri's southern border and allows slavery in Arkansas territory and Louisiana

1821 Sequoyah develops a system for writing the Cherokee language

1823 President James Monroe issues Monroe Doctrine, banning European colonization in Americas

1825 Erie Canal, a 363-mile waterway linking Lake Erie with the Hudson River, is opened

EVENTS IN THE WORLD

1800   **1810**   **1820**

1804 Napoleon crowned emperor of France

1807 British slave trade is abolished

1812 Napoleon invades Russia

1815 Napoleon is defeated at Battle of Waterloo

1819 Zulu kingdom controls southeastern Africa

1821 Mexico declares independence from Spain

1823 Beethoven completes Ninth Symphony

PERIOD PIECES

The cotton gin invented by Eli Whitney in 1793

Levi Strauss designed the first blue jeans, which were worn by prospectors in the 1850s

Mahogany tall-case clock

1830 | 1840 | 1850

1835 Ralph Waldo Emerson, Henry David Thoreau, Margaret Fuller, and others form the Transcendental Club

1838 Henry Wadsworth Longfellow's "A Psalm of Life" is published

1839 Edgar Allan Poe's "The Fall of the House of Usher" is published

1845 Henry David Thoreau begins living on shore of Walden Pond (to 1847)

1846 Herman Melville's first novel, *Typee*, is published

1847 Thoreau publishes essay later known as "Civil Disobedience"

1850 Nathaniel Hawthorne's *The Scarlet Letter* is published

1855 Walt Whitman publishes poetry collection *Leaves of Grass*

1830 | 1840 | 1850

1830 Indian Removal Act authorizes relocation of southeastern Native American tribes—including the Cherokee, Chickasaw, Choctaw, Creek, and Seminole—to territories west of Mississippi River

1837 John Deere produces first steel-bladed plow, which makes large-scale farming possible in heavy soil in Midwest and West

1844 Samuel F. B. Morse sends first telegraph message from Baltimore to Washington, D.C.

1848 United States defeats Mexico in Mexican War and claims land that is now Nevada, California, and part of New Mexico and Arizona

1848 Gold discoveries in California lead to first gold rush

1850 Congress passes Fugitive Slave Act, forcing officials in Northern states to return escaped slaves to owners; Compromise of 1850 is passed, which supposedly settles controversy over slavery between slave and free states

1830 | 1840 | 1850

1839 Britain and China fight first Opium War

1848 Mass of revolutions sweep Europe; Karl Marx and Friedrich Engels publish *Communist Manifesto*

1850 Taiping rebellion in China begins (to 1864)

Celebrations of the Self

Romanticism and Transcendentalism

"Good men must not obey the laws too well," Ralph Waldo Emerson said. His aphorism illustrates a vital key to the American character—after all, if the original colonists *had* obeyed the laws, the American Revolution would never have occurred, and the country might never have existed. This rebelliousness—so much a part of our heritage—reflects an essential aspect of Emerson's philosophy of transcendentalism, a distinctively American offshoot of the romantic movement.

Around the beginning of the 19th century, the movement known as romanticism sprang up in both Europe and America as a reaction to everything that had come before it: the rationalism of the 18th-century

Ralph Waldo Emerson

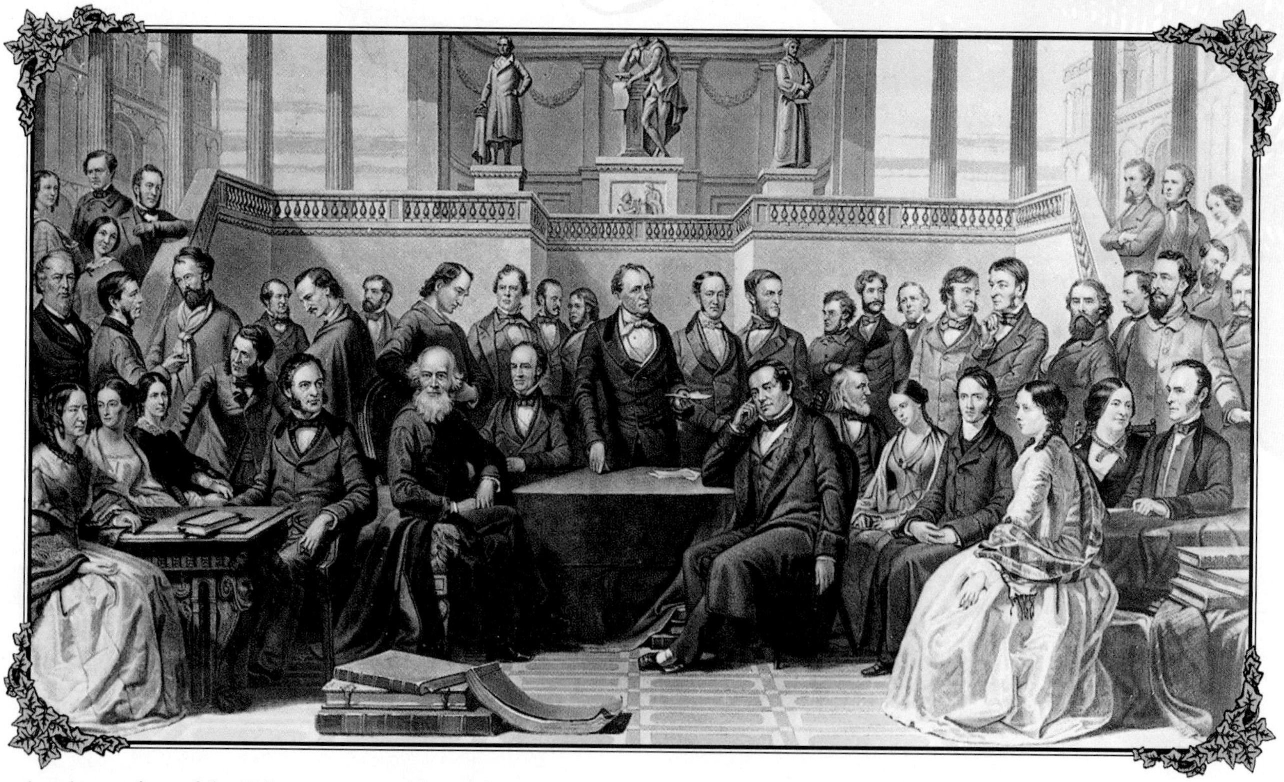

American authors of the 19th century. *Seated from left:* Henry Wadsworth Longfellow, William Cullen Bryant, Washington Irving (at the end of the table), and Margaret Fuller (slightly behind Irving). *Seated in right foreground:* Harriet Beecher Stowe.

Standing from left: Edgar Allan Poe (in profile facing left) and Nathaniel Hawthorne (in profile facing right).
Standing from right: James Russell Lowell (with beard facing front) and Ralph Waldo Emerson. The Bettmann Archive.

Age of Reason and, especially in America, the strict doctrines of Puritanism. Romantic artists, philosophers, and writers saw the limitations of reason and celebrated instead the glories of the individual spirit, the emotions, and the imagination as basic elements of human nature. The splendors of nature inspired the romantics more than the fear of God, and some of them felt a fascination with the supernatural.

In the first half of the century, as the U.S. population exploded and the country's borders spread westward, the romantic spirit guided American writers in their efforts to capture the energy and character of the new country. Henry Wadsworth Longfellow and Washington Irving were by far the most popular American writers of the time. Their works exhibit a typical romantic preoccupation with atmosphere, sentiment, and optimism.

Henry Wadsworth Longfellow

Although Washington Irving was the first American writer to achieve international fame, the first really distinctive American literature came from the transcendentalists. The philosophy of transcendentalism, derived in part from German romanticism, was based on a belief that "transcendent forms" of truth exist beyond reason and experience. However, Ralph Waldo Emerson gave this philosophy a peculiarly American spin: he said that every individual is capable of discovering this higher truth on his or her own, through intuition.

Washington Irving

Voices *from the* TIMES

The groves were God's first temples.
    Ere man learned
To hew the shaft, and lay the architrave,
And spread the roof above them—ere
    he framed
The lofty vault, to gather and roll back
The sound of anthems; in the darkling
    wood,
Amid the cool and silence, he knelt down,
And offered to the Mightiest solemn thanks
And supplication.

    William Cullen Bryant
    from "A Forest Hymn"

By the shores of Gitche Gumee,
By the shining Big-Sea-Water,
Stood the wigwam of Nokomis,
Daughter of the Moon, Nokomis.
Dark behind it rose the forest,
Rose the black and gloomy pine-trees,
Rose the firs with cones upon them;
Bright before it beat the water,
Beat the clear and sunny water,
Beat the shining Big-Sea-Water.

    Henry Wadsworth Longfellow
    from *The Song of Hiawatha*

I know I am august,
I do not trouble my spirit to vindicate
    itself or be understood,
I see that the elementary laws never
    apologize,
(I reckon I behave no prouder than
    the level I plant my house by,
    after all.)

    Walt Whitman
    from "Song of Myself"

It was a high counsel that I once heard given to a young person, "Always do what you are afraid to do."

Ralph Waldo Emerson

Call me Ishmael. Some years ago—never mind how long precisely—having little or no money in my purse, and nothing particular to interest me on shore, I thought I would sail about a little and see the watery part of the world. It is a way I have of driving off the spleen, and regulating the circulation. Whenever I find myself growing grim about the mouth; whenever it is a damp, drizzly November in my soul; whenever I find myself involuntarily pausing before coffin warehouses, and bringing up the rear of every funeral I meet; and especially whenever my hypos [hypochondria] get such an upper hand of me, that it requires a strong moral principle to prevent me from deliberately stepping into the street, and methodically knocking people's hats off—then, I account it high time to get to sea as soon as I can.

Herman Melville
from *Moby-Dick*

Henry David Thoreau, Emerson's young friend and colleague, proved a prickly but brilliant embodiment of transcendentalist ideals as, militantly turning his back on material rewards, he devoted his life to the study of nature and his own individual spirit. His *Walden,* an account of the two years he lived alone in a one-room shack in the country (although dining regularly at Emerson's Boston house), remains a genuine American masterwork.

Walt Whitman was championed at the beginning of his career by Emerson for the ideas and style that Emerson believed the new American poetry required. Still, influential as Whitman has been in the 20th century, he waited a long time for his contribution to be recognized by the larger public in his own time. In 1855 he had to print the first collection of his poems, *Leaves of Grass,* himself. Able to sell only a few copies of the book, he gave virtually all of the 795 copies away. Meanwhile, in that same year, Longfellow published *The Song of Hiawatha,* which like his earlier books of poetry, sold thousands and became a bestseller.

Traditions Across Time: Whitman's Heirs Express the Self

The celebration of individualism that began with romanticism and flourished with transcendentalism has remained at the core of American literature to the present day. During the first half of the 20th century, the poetry of William Carlos Williams and E. E. Cummings, among others, emphasized the spirit and power of solitary individuals. Contemporary writers, however, tend to temper their celebrations of the individual with more ambiguity. Rosario and Aurora Morales, for instance, try to find a new unity in their separate voices as mother and daughter, and the poet Luis J. Rodriguez makes readers view his eccentric aunt with a mixture of admiration and shock. The down-home voice of Garrison Keillor is shaped by the humorous ironies that are a trademark of our time.

PART 1 Celebrations of the Self

Romanticism and Transcendentalism

Henry Wadsworth Longfellow — **A Psalm of Life** — 344
The purpose of life expressed in rhyme and meter

Washington Irving — **The Devil and Tom Walker** — 349
A tempting proposition

Ralph Waldo Emerson — *from* **Self-Reliance** — 363
Wise words from an American philosopher

Margaret Fuller — LITERARY LINK
from **Memoirs** — 366
Nothing but the truth will do.

Henry David Thoreau — *from* **Civil Disobedience** — 369
The power of the individual conscience

Mohandas K. Gandhi — LINK ACROSS CULTURES
On Civil Disobedience — 377
A 20th-century leader echoes Thoreau.

Henry David Thoreau — *from* **Walden** — 381
A famous nonconformist's experiment in simple living

Walt Whitman — *Selected Poems* — 396
    I Hear America Singing — 397
    I Sit and Look Out — 399
    from **Song of Myself** — 400
An American original

Pablo Neruda — LINK ACROSS CULTURES
Ode to Walt Whitman — 406
A celebration of Whitman's legacy

COMPARING LITERATURE
Traditions Across Time: Whitman's Heirs Express the Self

William Carlos Williams — **Danse Russe** (1916) — 410
A "happy genius" has some fun.

E. E. Cummings — **anyone lived in a pretty how town** (1940) — 410
An unusual telling of a love story

Aurora Levins Morales and Rosario Morales — **Ending Poem** (1986) — 416
Separate voices unite in one poem.

Luis J. Rodriguez — **Tía Chucha** (1991) — 416
How would you feel if Tía Chucha were your aunt?

Garrison Keillor — **Gary Keillor** (1993) — 424
Share the last laugh with the author.

A Psalm of Life

Poetry by HENRY WADSWORTH LONGFELLOW

Connect to Your Life

What Life Is All About Each of the quotations on this page presents a way of looking at life. Which one comes closest to expressing your own philosophy of life?

> The life which is unexamined is not worth living.
> *Plato*

> To be what we are, and to become what we are capable of becoming, is the only end of life.
> *Robert Louis Stevenson*

> Life is far too important a thing ever to talk seriously about.
> *Oscar Wilde*

> Life is like a box of chocolates. You never know what you're going to get.
> *Forrest Gump*

Build Background

Uplifting Poetry Henry Wadsworth Longfellow was the most popular and famous member of a group of New England romantic writers known as the Fireside Poets—a group that also included Oliver Wendell Holmes, James Russell Lowell, and John Greenleaf Whittier. The name of the group refers to a popular family pastime of the period: reading poetry aloud in front of the fireplace after dinner. Longfellow and his fellow Fireside Poets wrote poems that were morally uplifting and often sentimental.

One summer morning, Longfellow wrote "A Psalm of Life" in the blank spaces of an invitation. After it was published in *Knickerbocker* magazine in October 1838, the poem swept the country and became known around the world. Although widely parodied, even by Longfellow himself, it celebrates an optimistic view of life and reflects the aims of Americans at the time.

Focus Your Reading

LITERARY ANALYSIS STANZA AND RHYME SCHEME A **stanza** is a group of lines that form a unit in a poem. "A Psalm of Life" is written in four-line stanzas. A **rhyme scheme** is the pattern of end rhyme (rhyming of words at the end of lines) in a stanza or an entire poem. Traditional poems, such as "A Psalm of Life," contain stanzas with a regular rhyme scheme. In addition to having a regular rhyme scheme, much of the poetry written by the Fireside Poets has a regular **meter** (a repeated sequence of stressed and unstressed syllables).

ACTIVE READING STRATEGIES FOR READING TRADITIONAL POETRY To appreciate the musical qualities of "A Psalm of Life," try these strategies:

- Read the poem silently to understand the basic meaning.
- Then read the poem aloud, paying attention to its patterns of sound. Notice the pattern of end rhymes in each stanza.
- Tap out the meter, or the rhythm of the poem.

En Mer [At sea] (1898), Max Bohm. Courtesy of Alfred J. Walker Fine Art, Boston.

A Psalm of Life

HENRY
WADSWORTH
LONGFELLOW

*What the Heart of the Young Man
Said to the Psalmist*[1]

Tell me not, in mournful numbers,[2]
    Life is but an empty dream!—
For the soul is dead that slumbers,
    And things are not what they seem.

5   Life is real! Life is earnest!
    And the grave is not its goal;
Dust thou art, to dust returnest,
    Was not spoken of the soul.

Not enjoyment, and not sorrow,
10   Is our destined end or way;
But to act, that each tomorrow
    Find us farther than today.

---

1. **Psalmist** (sä′mĭst): the author of the poems in the
   biblical Book of Psalms, many of which comment on
   the fleeting nature of life. Traditionally, most of the
   psalms have been ascribed to King David of Israel.
2. **numbers:** metrical feet or lines; verses.

Art is long, and Time is fleeting,
　　And our hearts, though stout and brave,
15　Still, like muffled drums, are beating
　　Funeral marches to the grave.

In the world's broad field of battle,
　　In the bivouac[3] of Life,
Be not like dumb, driven cattle!
20　Be a hero in the strife!

Trust no Future, howe'er pleasant!
　　Let the dead Past bury its dead!
Act—act in the living Present!
　　Heart within, and God o'erhead!

25　Lives of great men all remind us
　　We can make our lives sublime,[4]
And, departing, leave behind us
　　Footprints on the sands of time;

Footprints, that perhaps another,
30　Sailing o'er life's solemn main,[5]
A forlorn and shipwrecked brother,
　　Seeing, shall take heart again.

Let us, then, be up and doing,
　　With a heart for any fate;
35　Still achieving, still pursuing,
　　Learn to labor and to wait.

---

3. **bivouac** (bĭv′o͞o-ăk′): a temporary encampment of troops.

4. **sublime:** of high spiritual, moral, or intellectual worth.

5. **main:** open ocean.

Connect to the Literature

1. What Do You Think? What are your thoughts about the form or the message of this poem?

> **Comprehension Check**
> What, according to the speaker, is "our destined end," or purpose?

Think Critically

2. How does the **speaker's** view of life compare with your own view?

> **THINK ABOUT**
> - what the speaker says life is not
> - the command "Act—act in the living Present!" (line 23)
> - the last four lines of the poem
> - the quotation you chose as closest to your philosophy

3. In your own words, summarize what the speaker says about the value of the lives of great people (lines 25–32). Do you agree with the speaker? Explain.

4. **ACTIVE READING** **STRATEGIES FOR READING TRADITIONAL POETRY** Read the poem aloud in class, with a different person taking each stanza. If the poem were to be sung, what style of music do you think would fit best with its **meter** and **theme?** Explain your choice.

Extend Interpretations

5. Comparing Texts How do you think a Puritan writer such as Anne Bradstreet (page 139) or Jonathan Edwards (page 152) might have responded to the ideas presented in "A Psalm of Life"?

6. What If? Imagine that Longfellow were a counselor at your school. Based on the message of "A Psalm of Life," do you think he would be a successful counselor or not? Explain your opinion.

7. Connect to Life Do you think that Americans today still share the values expressed in "A Psalm of Life"? Point out lines in the poem that you think contemporary Americans might or might not agree with.

Literary Analysis

STANZA AND RHYME SCHEME
You can mark the **rhyme scheme** of a stanza or a poem by using letters (beginning with *a*) to designate the lines, assigning the same letter to lines that end with the same sound. Here is the first stanza of an Anne Bradstreet poem:

In silent night when rest I <u>took</u>	a
For sorrow near I did not <u>look</u>	a
I wakened was with thund'ring <u>noise</u>	b
And piteous shrieks of dreadful <u>voice</u>.	b
That fearful sound of "Fire!" and "<u>Fire!</u>"	c
Let no man know is my <u>desire</u>.	c

Notice that the letters change each time the end rhyme changes. The rhyme scheme of this stanza is *aabbcc*.

Paired Activity Working with a partner, identify the rhyme scheme used in "A Psalm of Life" by marking it for the first two stanzas. Then look at the poem as a whole. What words or ideas does the rhyme scheme emphasize?

REVIEW A **metaphor** is a figure of speech that compares two things that have something in common. Consider the metaphor in lines 17–18. How is the world like a field of battle? How is life like a bivouac in this battlefield?

Writing Options

1. Personal Response How do you think life should be lived? Think about the quotation you chose and the ideas you discussed in responding to question 2. Then in a personal response to Longfellow, perhaps in the form of a poem, explain your philosophy of life. Place this piece in your **Working Portfolio.**

2. Longfellow Parody "A Psalm of Life" is among the most parodied poems in the English language. Here is an example by Harriet Fleischman:

> *Lives of great men all remind us*
> *As we history's pages turn*
> *That we often leave behind us*
> *Letters which we ought to burn.*

Write a stanza or two of parody in the style of "A Psalm of Life."

Activities & Explorations

1. Photo Collage Find a photograph or an illustration that suggests an idea or theme in "A Psalm of Life." Combine the images found by the class to create a bulletin-board collage.
~ VIEWING AND REPRESENTING

2. Bumper Sticker Work with a partner to design a bumper sticker that expresses the philosophy of life suggested by the poem. Present your design to the class and explain why it is appropriate. **~ ART**

Philosophy of Life

Longfellow's Views	My Views

Henry Wadsworth Longfellow
1807–1882

Other Works
The Courtship of Miles Standish
Evangeline
The Song of Hiawatha
"Paul Revere's Ride"
"The Wreck of the Hesperus"
"The Village Blacksmith"

Aspiring Poet Henry Wadsworth Longfellow, the most famous American poet of the 1800s, had a career that spanned more than 50 years. His first poem was published in a Maine newspaper when he was 13. Two years later, he entered Bowdoin College, where, like his classmate Nathaniel Hawthorne, he decided to become a writer. From college, Longfellow wrote his father, "I most eagerly aspire after further eminence in literature." Eventually he was to fulfill his aspirations.

College Professor A brilliant scholar, the 18-year-old Longfellow was offered Bowdoin's first established professorship in modern languages when he graduated in 1825. Since the field was so new, he had to create his own textbooks. Several years later he accepted a similar position at Harvard, where he remained until 1854, when he resigned to write full time.

Literary Eminence Longfellow's first book of poetry, *Voices of the Night,* was published when he was 32. As his popularity grew, many of his poems became household favorites. A beloved poet and a scholar able to speak and read ten languages, Longfellow was respected all over the world. He was the first American writer to be honored with a bust in the Poets' Corner of London's Westminster Abbey.

Author Activity

Do you recognize any of the other Longfellow works listed? Can you quote lines from them? Discuss what has made Longfellow's poetry so popular.

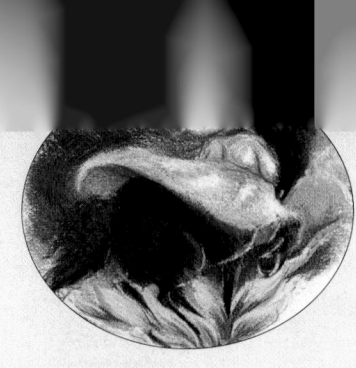

The Devil and Tom Walker

Short Story by WASHINGTON IRVING

Connect to Your Life

Money Matters Should people pursue wealth? Why or why not? How important is wealth to you? What limits, if any, would you put on your own pursuit of wealth? Discuss your answers to these questions with a small group of classmates.

Build Background

The Faust Legend The first American writer esteemed abroad, Washington Irving is known for his humorous essays and stories. In "The Devil and Tom Walker," Irving adapted the Germanic legend of Johann Faust, a 16th-century magician and alchemist who was said to have sold his soul to the devil in exchange for worldly power and wealth. For his comic retelling, Irving created an American character who strikes the same bargain and faces the same consequences in an American setting. The story takes place in the environs of Boston in the early 1700s, when the Puritans still dominated Massachusetts society.

WORDS TO KNOW
Vocabulary Preview

abode	ostentation	prowess
censurer	parsimony	repose
daunted	peculiar	resolute
dolefully	piety	singular
melancholy	propitious	surmise

Focus Your Reading

LITERARY ANALYSIS IMAGERY Imagery is words and phrases that appeal to the five senses, helping you to imagine precisely what people, places, and events in a literary work are like. The majority of images are visual, serving to stimulate pictures in your mind. Consider this descriptive paragraph from Irving's story:

> *. . . there lived near this place a meager, miserly fellow, of the name of Tom Walker. He had a wife as miserly as himself. . . . They lived in a forlorn-looking house that stood alone and had an air of starvation. A few straggling savin trees, emblems of sterility, grew near it; no smoke ever curled from its chimney; no traveler stopped at its door. A miserable horse, whose ribs were as articulate as the bars of a gridiron, stalked about a field.*

The images of the forlorn house, the straggling trees, and the starved horse show you just how miserly Tom and his wife are.

ACTIVE READING VISUALIZING Irving provides much description in "The Devil and Tom Walker," so an understanding of the imagery is crucial to an understanding of the story—and to an enjoyment of its humor.

READER'S NOTEBOOK As you read, try to visualize, or form mental pictures of, the characters, settings, and events. Jot down some of the images that describe Tom and the character trait that each image helps you to picture.

The Devil and Tom Walker

Washington Irving

A few miles from Boston in Massachusetts, there is a deep inlet, winding several miles into the interior of the country from Charles Bay, and terminating in a thickly wooded swamp or morass. On one side of this inlet is a beautiful dark grove; on the opposite side the land rises abruptly from the water's edge into a high ridge, on which grow a few scattered oaks of great age and immense size. Under one of these gigantic trees, according to old stories, there was a great amount of treasure buried by Kidd the pirate. The inlet allowed a facility to bring the money in a boat secretly and at night to the very foot of the hill; the elevation of the place permitted a good lookout to be kept that no one was at hand; while the remarkable trees formed good landmarks by which the place might easily be found again. The old stories add, moreover, that the devil presided at the hiding of the money and took it under his guardianship; but this, it is well-known, he always does with buried treasure, particularly when it has been ill-gotten. Be that as it may, Kidd never returned to recover his wealth; being shortly after seized at Boston, sent out to England, and there hanged for a pirate.

About the year 1727, just at the time that earthquakes were prevalent in New England, and shook many tall sinners down upon their knees, there lived near this place a meager, miserly fellow, of the name of Tom Walker. He had a wife as miserly as himself: they were so miserly that they even conspired to cheat each other. Whatever the woman could lay hands on, she hid away; a hen could not cackle but she was on the alert to secure the new-laid egg. Her husband was continually prying about to detect her secret hoards, and many and fierce were the conflicts that took place about what ought

to have been common property. They lived in a forlorn-looking house that stood alone and had an air of starvation. A few straggling savin trees, emblems of sterility, grew near it; no smoke ever curled from its chimney; no traveler stopped at its door. A miserable horse, whose ribs were as articulate as the bars of a gridiron,[1] stalked about a field, where a thin carpet of moss, scarcely covering the ragged beds of pudding-stone,[2] tantalized and balked his hunger; and sometimes he would lean his head over the fence, look piteously at the passerby and seem to petition deliverance from this land of famine.

The house and its inmates had altogether a bad name. Tom's wife was a tall termagant,[3] fierce of temper, loud of tongue, and strong of arm. Her voice was often heard in wordy warfare with her husband; and his face sometimes showed signs that their conflicts were not confined to words. No one ventured, however, to interfere between them. The lonely wayfarer shrunk within himself at the horrid clamor and clapper-clawing;[4] eyed the den of discord askance;[5] and hurried on his way, rejoicing, if a bachelor, in his celibacy.

One day that Tom Walker had been to a distant part of the neighborhood, he took what he considered a shortcut homeward, through the swamp. Like most shortcuts, it was an ill-chosen route. The swamp was thickly grown with great

---

1. **as articulate . . . gridiron:** as clearly separated as the bars of a grill.
2. **puddingstone:** a rock consisting of pebbles and gravel cemented together.
3. **termagant** (tûr′mə-gənt): a quarrelsome, scolding woman.
4. **clapper-clawing:** scratching or clawing with the fingernails.
5. **eyed . . . askance** (ə-skăns′): looked disapprovingly at the house filled with arguing.

gloomy pines and hemlocks, some of them ninety feet high, which made it dark at noonday, and a retreat for all the owls of the neighborhood. It was full of pits and quagmires, partly covered with weeds and mosses, where the green surface often betrayed the traveler into a gulf of black, smothering mud; there were also dark and stagnant pools, the <u>abodes</u> of the tadpole, the bullfrog, and the water snake; where the trunks of pines and hemlocks lay half-drowned, half-rotting, looking like alligators sleeping in the mire.

Tom had long been picking his way cautiously through this treacherous forest; stepping from tuft to tuft of rushes and roots, which afforded precarious footholds among deep sloughs; or pacing carefully, like a cat, along the prostrate trunks of trees; startled now and then by the sudden screaming of the bittern,[6] or the quacking of wild duck rising on the wind from some solitary pool. At length he arrived at a firm piece of ground, which ran out like a peninsula into the deep bosom of the swamp. It had been one of the strongholds of the Indians during their wars with the first colonists. Here they had thrown up a kind of fort, which they had looked upon as almost impregnable, and had used as a place of refuge for their squaws and children. Nothing remained of the old Indian fort but a few embankments,

gradually sinking to the level of the surrounding earth, and already overgrown in part by oaks and other forest trees, the foliage of which formed a contrast to the dark pines and hemlocks of the swamp.

It was late in the dusk of evening when Tom Walker reached the old fort, and he paused there awhile to rest himself. Anyone but he would have felt unwilling to linger in this lonely, <u>melancholy</u> place, for the common people had a bad opinion of it, from the stories handed down from the time of the Indian wars, when it was asserted that the savages held incantations[7] here, and made sacrifices to the evil spirit.

Tom Walker, however, was not a man to be troubled with any fears of the kind. He <u>reposed</u> himself for some time on the trunk of a fallen hemlock, listening to the boding cry of the tree toad, and delving with his walking staff into a mound of black mold at his feet. As he turned up the soil unconsciously, his staff struck against something hard. He raked it out of the vegetable mold, and lo! a cloven skull, with an Indian tomahawk buried deep in it, lay before him. The rust on the weapon showed the time that had elapsed since this death-blow had been given. It was a dreary memento of the fierce struggle that had taken place in this last foothold of the Indian warriors.

"Humph!" said Tom Walker, as he gave it a kick to shake the dirt from it.

"Let that skull alone!" said a gruff voice. Tom lifted up his eyes, and beheld a great black man seated directly opposite him, on the stump of a tree. He was exceedingly surprised, having neither heard nor seen anyone approach; and he was still more perplexed on observing, as well as the gathering gloom would permit, that the stranger was neither Negro nor Indian. It is true he was dressed in a rude half-Indian garb, and

---

6. **bittern:** a wading bird with mottled, brownish plumage and a deep, booming cry.

7. **incantations:** verbal charms or spells recited to produce a magic effect.

had a red belt or sash swathed round his body;
but his face was neither black nor copper-
color, but swarthy and dingy, and begrimed
with soot, as if he had been accustomed to toil
among fires and forges. He had a shock of coarse
black hair, that stood out from his head in all
directions, and bore an ax on his shoulder.

He scowled for a moment at Tom with a pair
of great red eyes.

"What are you doing on my grounds?" said
the black man, with a hoarse, growling voice.

"Your grounds!" said Tom, with a sneer, "no
more your grounds than mine; they belong to
Deacon Peabody."

"Deacon Peabody be d—d," said the stranger,
"as I flatter myself he will be, if he does not look
more to his own sins and less to those of his
neighbors. Look yonder, and see how Deacon
Peabody is faring."

Tom looked in the direction that the stranger
pointed, and beheld one of the great trees, fair
and flourishing without, but rotten at the core,
and saw that it had been nearly hewn through,
so that the first high wind was likely to blow
it down. On the bark of the tree was scored
the name of Deacon Peabody, an eminent man,
who had waxed wealthy by driving shrewd
bargains with the Indians. He now looked
around, and found most of the tall trees marked
with the name of some great man of the colony,
and all more or less scored by the ax. The one
on which he had been seated, and which had
evidently just been hewn down, bore the name of
Crowninshield; and he recollected a mighty rich
man of that name, who made a vulgar display of
wealth, which it was whispered he had acquired
by buccaneering.[8]

"He's just ready for burning!" said the black
man, with a growl of triumph. "You see, I am
likely to have a good stock of firewood for
winter."

"But what right have you," said Tom, "to cut
down Deacon Peabody's timber?"

8. **buccaneering:** robbing ships at sea; piracy.

"The right of a prior claim," said the other. "This woodland belonged to me long before one of your white-faced race put foot upon the soil."

"And pray, who are you, if I may be so bold?" said Tom.

"Oh, I go by various names. I am the wild huntsman in some countries; the black miner in others. In this neighborhood I am he to whom the red men consecrated this spot, and in honor of whom they now and then roasted a white man, by way of sweet-smelling sacrifice. Since the red men have been exterminated by you white savages, I amuse myself by presiding at the persecutions of Quakers and Anabaptists;[9] I am the great patron and prompter of slave dealers, and the grand master of the Salem witches."

"The upshot of all which is that, if I mistake not," said Tom, sturdily, "you are he commonly called Old Scratch."[10]

"The same, at your service!" replied the black man, with a half-civil nod.

Such was the opening of this interview, according to the old story; though it has almost too familiar an air to be credited. One would think that to meet with such a singular personage, in this wild, lonely place, would have shaken any man's nerves; but Tom was a hard-minded fellow, not easily daunted, and he had lived so long with a termagant wife that he did not even fear the devil.

It is said that after this commencement they had a long and earnest conversation together, as Tom returned homeward. The black man told him of great sums of money buried by Kidd the pirate, under the oak trees on the high ridge, not far from the morass. All these were under his command, and protected by his power, so that none could find them but such as propitiated his favor. These he offered to place within Tom Walker's reach, having conceived an especial kindness for him; but they were to be had only on certain conditions. What these conditions were may be easily surmised, though Tom never disclosed them publicly. They must have been very hard, for he required time to think of them, and he was not a man to stick at trifles when money was in view. When they had reached the edge of the swamp, the stranger paused. "What proof have I that all you have been telling me is true?" said Tom. "There's my signature," said the black man, pressing his finger on Tom's forehead. So saying, he turned off among the thickets of the swamp, and seemed, as Tom said, to go down, down, down, into the earth, until nothing but his head and shoulders could be seen, and so on, until he totally disappeared.

When Tom reached home, he found the black print of a finger burnt, as it were, into his forehead, which nothing could obliterate.

The first news his wife had to tell him was the sudden death of Absalom Crowninshield, the rich buccaneer. It was announced in the papers

---

9. **presiding . . . Anabaptists:** exercising authority over the oppression of Christian groups that the Puritans considered radical.

10. **Old Scratch:** a nickname for the devil.

WORDS
TO
KNOW

singular (sĭng′gyə-lər) *adj.* unusual or remarkable; unique
daunted (dôn′tĭd) *adj.* intimidated or frightened **daunt** *v.*
surmise (sər-mīz′) *v.* to guess

with the usual flourish that "a great man had fallen in Israel."[11]

Tom recollected the tree which his black friend had just hewn down and which was ready for burning. "Let the freebooter[12] roast," said Tom; "who cares!" He now felt convinced that all he had heard and seen was no illusion.

He was not prone to let his wife into his confidence; but as this was an uneasy secret, he willingly shared it with her. All her avarice was awakened at the mention of hidden gold, and she urged her husband to comply with the black man's terms, and secure what would make them wealthy for life. However Tom might have felt disposed to sell himself to the devil, he was determined not to do so to oblige his wife; so he flatly refused, out of the mere spirit of contradiction. Many and bitter were the quarrels they had on the subject; but the more she talked, the more <u>resolute</u> was Tom not to be damned to please her.

At length she determined to drive the bargain on her own account, and if she succeeded, to keep all the gain to herself. Being of the same fearless temper as her husband, she set off for the old Indian fort toward the close of a summer's day. She was many hours absent. When she came back, she was reserved and sullen in her replies. She spoke something of a black man, whom she met about twilight hewing at the root of a tall tree. He was sulky, however, and would not come to terms; she was to go again with a propitiatory offering, but what it was she forbore to say.

The next evening she set off again for the swamp, with her apron heavily laden. Tom waited and waited for her, but in vain; midnight came, but she did not make her appearance; morning, noon, night returned, but still she did not come. Tom now grew uneasy for her safety, especially as he found she had carried off in her apron the silver teapot and spoons, and every portable article of value. Another night elapsed,

another morning came; but no wife. In a word, she was never heard of more.

What was her real fate nobody knows, in consequence of so many pretending to know. It is one of those facts which have become confounded by a variety of historians. Some asserted that she lost her way among the tangled mazes of the swamp, and sank into some pit or slough; others, more uncharitable, hinted that she had eloped with the household booty and made off to some other province; while others surmised that the tempter had decoyed her into a dismal quagmire, on the top of which her hat was found lying. In confirmation of this, it was said a great black man, with an ax on his shoulder, was seen late that very evening coming out of the swamp, carrying a bundle tied in a check apron, with an air of surly triumph.

The most current and probable story, however, observes that Tom Walker grew so anxious about the fate of his wife and his property that he set out at length to seek them both at the Indian fort. During a long summer's afternoon he searched about the gloomy place, but no wife was to be seen. He called her name repeatedly, but she was nowhere to be heard. The bittern alone responded to his voice, as they flew screaming by; or the bullfrog croaked <u>dolefully</u> from a neighboring pool. At length, it is said, just in the brown hour of twilight, when the owls began to hoot, and the bats to flit about, his attention was attracted by the clamor of carrion crows[13] hovering about a cypress tree. He looked up, and beheld a bundle tied in a check apron, and hanging in the branches of the tree, with a great vulture perched hard by, as if

---

11. **a great man . . . Israel:** a biblical reference—"Know ye not that there is a prince and a great man fallen this day in Israel?" (2 Samuel 3:38)—used, with unconscious irony, by the papers to mean that an important member of God's people on earth has passed away.

12. **freebooter:** pirate.

13. **carrion crows:** crows that feed on dead or decaying flesh.

keeping watch upon it. He leaped with joy; for he recognized his wife's apron and supposed it to contain the household valuables.

"Let us get hold of the property," said he consolingly to himself, "and we will endeavor to do without the woman."

As he scrambled up the tree, the vulture spread its wide wings, and sailed off screaming into the deep shadows of the forest. Tom seized the checked apron, but, woeful sight! found nothing but a heart and liver tied up in it!

Such, according to this most authentic old story, was all that was to be found of Tom's wife. She had probably attempted to deal with the black man as she had been accustomed to deal with her husband; but though a female scold is generally considered a match for the devil, yet in this instance she appears to have had the worst of it. She must have died game, however; for it is said Tom noticed many prints of cloven feet stamped upon the tree, and found handfuls of hair that looked as if they had been plucked from the coarse black shock of the woodman. Tom knew his wife's prowess by experience. He shrugged his shoulders, as he looked at the signs of a fierce clapper-clawing. "Egad," said he to himself, "Old Scratch must have had a tough time of it!"

Tom consoled himself for the loss of his property with the loss of his wife, for he was a man of fortitude. He even felt something like gratitude towards the black woodman, who, he considered, had done him a kindness. He sought, therefore, to cultivate a further acquaintance with him, but for some time without success; the old blacklegs played shy, for, whatever people may think, he is not always to be had for calling for: he knows how to play his cards when pretty sure of his game.

At length, it is said, when delay had whetted Tom's eagerness to the quick, and prepared him to agree to anything rather than not gain the promised treasure, he met the black man one evening in his usual woodsman's dress, with his ax on his shoulder, sauntering along the swamp, and humming a tune. He affected to receive Tom's advances with great indifference, made brief replies, and went on humming his tune.

By degrees, however, Tom brought him to business, and they began to haggle about the terms on which the former was to have the pirate's treasure. There was one condition which need not be mentioned, being generally understood in all cases where the devil grants favors; but there were others about which, though of less importance, he was inflexibly obstinate. He insisted that the money found through his means should be employed in his service. He proposed, therefore, that Tom should employ it in the black traffic; that is to say, that he should fit out a slave ship. This, however, Tom resolutely refused: he was bad enough in all conscience; but the devil himself could not tempt him to turn slave trader.

Finding Tom so squeamish on this point, he did not insist upon it, but proposed, instead, that he should turn usurer;[14] the devil being extremely

---

14. **usurer** (yo͞o′zhər-ər): one who lends money, especially at an unusually or unlawfully high rate of interest.

WORDS
TO
KNOW   **prowess** (prou′ĭs) *n.* superior strength, courage, or daring, especially in battle

anxious for the increase of usurers, looking upon them as his <u>peculiar</u> people.

To this no objections were made, for it was just to Tom's taste.

"You shall open a broker's shop in Boston next month," said the black man.

"I'll do it tomorrow, if you wish," said Tom Walker.

"You shall lend money at two percent a month."

"Egad, I'll charge four!" replied Tom Walker.

"You shall extort bonds, foreclose mortgages, drive the merchants to bankruptcy—"

"I'll drive them to the d——l," cried Tom Walker.

"You are the usurer for my money!" said blacklegs with delight. "When will you want the rhino[15]?"

"This very night."

"Done!" said the devil.

"Done!" said Tom Walker. So they shook hands and struck a bargain.

A few days' time saw Tom Walker seated behind his desk in a countinghouse[16] in Boston.

His reputation for a ready-moneyed man, who would lend money out for a good consideration, soon spread abroad. Everybody remembers the time of Governor Belcher, when money was particularly scarce. It was a time of paper credit. The country had been deluged with government bills; the famous Land Bank[17] had been established; there had been a rage for speculating; the people had run mad with schemes for new settlements; for building cities in the wilderness; land-jobbers[18] went about with maps of grants, and townships, and Eldorados[19] lying nobody knew where, but which everybody was ready to purchase. In a word, the great speculating fever, which breaks out every now and then in the country, had raged to an alarming degree, and everybody was dreaming of making sudden fortunes from nothing. As usual the fever had subsided; the dream had gone off, and the imaginary fortunes with it; the patients were left in doleful plight, and the whole country resounded with the consequent cry of "hard times."

At this <u>propitious</u> time of public distress did Tom Walker set up as usurer in Boston. His door was soon thronged by customers. The needy and adventurous, the gambling speculator, the dreaming land-jobber, the thriftless tradesman, the merchant with cracked credit; in short, everyone driven to raise money by desperate means and desperate sacrifices hurried to Tom Walker.

Thus Tom was the universal friend of the needy and acted like a "friend in need"; that is to say, he always exacted good pay and good security. In proportion to the distress of the applicant was the hardness of his terms. He accumulated bonds and mortgages; gradually squeezed his customers closer and closer; and sent them at length, dry as a sponge, from his door.

In this way he made money hand over hand, became a rich and mighty man, and exalted his cocked hat upon 'Change.[20] He built himself, as usual, a vast house, out of <u>ostentation</u>; but left the greater part of it unfinished and unfurnished,

---

15. **rhino:** a slang term for money.

16. **countinghouse:** an office in which a business firm conducts its bookkeeping, correspondence, and similar activities.

17. **Land Bank:** Boston merchants organized the Land Bank in 1739. Landowners could take out mortgages on their property and then repay the loans with cash or manufactured goods. When the Land Bank was outlawed in 1741, many colonists lost money.

18. **land-jobbers:** people who buy and sell land for profit.

19. **Eldorados:** places of fabulous wealth or great opportunity. Early Spanish explorers sought a legendary country named El Dorado, which was rumored to be rich with gold.

20. **exalted . . . 'Change:** proudly raised himself to a position of importance as a trader on the stock exchange.

WORDS
TO
KNOW

peculiar (pĭ-kyōōl′yər) *adj.* belonging particularly or primarily to one person, group, or kind

propitious (prə-pĭsh′əs) *adj.* helpful or advantageous; favorable

ostentation (ŏs′tĕn-tā′shən) *n.* display meant to impress others; boastful showiness

357

out of parsimony. He even set up a carriage in the fullness of his vainglory,[21] though he nearly starved the horses which drew it; and as the ungreased wheels groaned and screeched on the axletrees, you would have thought you heard the souls of the poor debtors he was squeezing.

As Tom waxed old, however, he grew thoughtful. Having secured the good things of this world, he began to feel anxious about those of the next. He thought with regret on the bargain he had made with his black friend, and set his wits to work to cheat him out of the conditions. He became, therefore, all of a sudden, a violent churchgoer. He prayed loudly and strenuously, as if heaven were to be taken by force of lungs. Indeed, one might always tell when he had sinned most during the week, by the clamor of his Sunday devotion. The quiet Christians who had been modestly and steadfastly traveling Zionward[22] were struck with self-reproach at seeing themselves so suddenly outstripped in their career by this new-made convert. Tom was as rigid in religious as in money matters; he was a stern supervisor and censurer of his neighbors, and seemed to think every sin entered up to their account became a credit on his own side of the page. He even talked of the expediency of reviving the persecution of Quakers and Anabaptists. In a word, Tom's zeal became as notorious as his riches.

Still, in spite of all this strenuous attention to forms, Tom had a lurking dread that the devil, after all, would have his due.[23] That he might not be taken unawares, therefore, it is said he always carried a small Bible in his coat pocket. He had also a great folio Bible on his countinghouse desk, and would frequently be found reading it when people called on business; on such occasions he would lay his green spectacles in the book, to mark the place, while he turned round to drive some usurious bargain.

Some say that Tom grew a little crackbrained

Tom's zeal became as notorious as his riches.

in his old days, and that fancying his end approaching, he had his horse new shod, saddled and bridled, and buried with his feet uppermost; because he supposed that at the last day the world would be turned upside down; in which case he should find his horse standing ready for mounting, and he was determined at the worst to give his old friend a run for it. This, however, is probably a mere old wives' fable. If he really did take such a precaution, it was totally superfluous; at least so says the authentic old legend, which closes his story in the following manner:

One hot summer afternoon in the dog days, just as a terrible black thundergust was coming up, Tom sat in his countinghouse, in his white linen cap and India silk morning gown. He was on the point of foreclosing a mortgage, by which he would complete the ruin of an unlucky land speculator for whom he had professed the greatest friendship. The poor land-jobber begged him to grant a few months' indulgence. Tom had grown testy and irritated, and refused another day.

"My family will be ruined and brought upon the parish," said the land-jobber. "Charity begins at home," replied Tom; "I must take care of myself in these hard times."

"You have made so much money out of me," said the speculator.

---

21. **vainglory:** boastful, undeserved pride in one's accomplishments or qualities.
22. **Zionward:** toward heaven.
23. **the devil . . . due:** a reference to the proverb "Give the devil his due," used to mean "Give even a disagreeable person the credit he or she deserves." Here, of course, the expression is used literally rather than figuratively.

WORDS TO KNOW

parsimony (pär′sə-mō′nē) *n.* extreme economy; stinginess
censurer (sĕn′shər-ər) *n.* one who expresses strong disapproval or harsh criticism

Tom lost his patience and his <u>piety</u>. "The devil take me," said he, "if I have made a farthing!"[24]

Just then there were three loud knocks at the street door. He stepped out to see who was there. A black man was holding a black horse, which neighed and stamped with impatience.

"Tom, you're come for," said the black fellow, gruffly. Tom shrank back, but too late. He had left his little Bible at the bottom of his coat pocket, and his big Bible on the desk buried under the mortgage he was about to foreclose; never was a sinner taken more unawares. The black man whisked him like a child into the saddle, gave the horse the lash, and away he galloped, with Tom on his back, in the midst of the thunderstorm. The clerks stuck their pens behind their ears, and stared after him from the windows. Away went Tom Walker, dashing down the streets; his white cap bobbing up and down, his morning gown fluttering in the wind, and his steed striking fire out of the pavement at every bound. When the clerks turned to look for the black man, he had disappeared.

Tom Walker never returned to foreclose the mortgage. A countryman, who lived on the border of the swamp, reported that in the height of the thundergust he had heard a great clattering of hoofs and a howling along the road, and running to the window caught sight of a figure, such as I have described, on a horse that galloped like mad across the fields, over the hills, and down into the black hemlock swamp toward the old Indian fort; and that shortly after a thunderbolt falling in that direction seemed to set the whole forest in a blaze.

The good people of Boston shook their heads and shrugged their shoulders, but had been so much accustomed to witches and goblins, and tricks of the devil, in all kinds of shapes, from the first settlement of the colony, that they were not so much horror-struck as might have been expected. Trustees were appointed to take charge of Tom's effects. There was nothing, however, to administer upon. On searching his coffers[25] all his bonds and mortgages were found reduced to cinders. In place of gold and silver, his iron chest was filled with chips and shavings; two skeletons lay in his stable instead of his half-starved horses, and the very next day his great house took fire and burnt to the ground.

Such was the end of Tom Walker and his ill-gotten wealth. Let all griping money brokers lay this story to heart. The truth of it is not to be doubted. The very hole under the oak trees whence he dug Kidd's money is to be seen to this day; and the neighboring swamp and old Indian fort are often haunted in stormy nights by a figure on horseback, in morning gown and white cap, which is doubtless the troubled spirit of the usurer. In fact the story has resolved itself into a proverb so prevalent throughout New England, of "The Devil and Tom Walker." ❖

---

24. **farthing:** a coin worth one-fourth of a penny, formerly used throughout the British Empire.

25. **coffers:** safes or strongboxes designed to hold money or other valuable items.

WORDS TO KNOW   **piety** (pī′ĭ-tē) *n.* religious devotion; reverence for God

359

Thinking through the LITERATURE

Connect to the Literature

1. **What Do You Think?**
   What comments do you have about the ending of this story? Share them with classmates.

   Comprehension Check
   • What does Old Scratch offer Tom and what does he want in return?
   • How does Tom try to get out of his bargain?
   • What happens to Tom at the end?

Think Critically

2. In your opinion, could Tom Walker have escaped the consequences of his bargain with Old Scratch? Explain?

3. **ACTIVE READING VISUALIZING** How did you visualize Tom Walker from the **images** used to describe him? What **character traits** are suggested by these images? Refer to the notes from your **READER'S NOTEBOOK.**

4. Do you consider Tom Walker better or worse than the other prominent Puritans in Boston? Consider the evidence.

   THINK ABOUT
   • the Puritans' treatment of Native Americans, Quakers, and Anabaptists
   • what the marked trees in the swamp suggest about some respected Puritans
   • why land speculators have "run mad with schemes for new settlements"
   • how other Christians react to Tom's religious zeal

5. What do you think was Irving's **purpose** in writing this story?

Extend Interpretations

6. **Critic's Corner** It has been noted that Washington Irving received critical acclaim as a writer because in his stories he managed to impart insights about human nature that were amusing without being too moralistic. Agree or disagree, basing your answer on "The Devil and Tom Walker."

7. **The Writer's Style** Writers use a variety of elements to create humor, including ridiculous characters, absurd situations and images, exaggeration, understatement, and **situational irony.** What makes this story humorous?

8. **Connect to Life** Driven by greed, Tom Walker literally sells his soul to gain wealth. What real person or fictional character reminds you of Tom Walker? Explain your choice.

Literary Analysis

IMAGERY For the Active Reading activity on page 349, you were asked to pay close attention to Irving's **imagery**—the descriptive words and phrases a writer uses to re-create sensory experiences. Think of imagery as a multimedia presentation in your mind. The pictures, sounds, physical sensations, and sometimes tastes and smells that you imagine as you read help you interpret what is going on in a story.

Cooperative Activity Identify the imagery in the following passages, and discuss how it supports **characterization, plot,** or **theme.**
• the description of the trees marked with the names of men in the colony (page 353)
• the description of Tom's search for his wife in the forest (pages 355–356)
• the description of Tom's house, horses, and carriage (pages 357–358)
• the description of Tom's being carried off by the devil (page 359)

NARRATOR Another interesting element of this story is its **omniscient** (all-knowing) **narrator,** who stands outside the action of the story and reports what different characters are thinking. What seems to be the narrator's attitude toward the events of the story? What does Irving gain by using this type of narrator rather than having Tom relate the events?

Choices & CHALLENGES

Writing Options

1. Reflective Essay on Wealth Drawing on your reading of this story and on your notes for Connect to Your Life activity on page 349, draft a reflective essay on the pursuit of wealth. Place this piece in your **Working Portfolio.**

2. Fitting Proverbs Write a set of three proverbs—such as "Money is the root of all evil"—that help explain the lesson or moral of "The Devil and Tom Walker."

3. Updated Faust Legend Write your own version of the Faust legend, as Irving did. Create a modern character in a present-day setting who makes a bargain he or she shouldn't.

Three proverbs
1.
2.
3.

Activities & Explorations

Board Game With a small group of classmates, design a board game, a video game, or a computer game based on the major events and characters in "The Devil and Tom Walker." Use the imagery in the story to help you depict specific settings, such as Deacon Peabody's woods. In class, show the game and explain the rules.
~ VIEWING AND REPRESENTING

Vocabulary in Action

EXERCISE A: ASSESSMENT PRACTICE Review the Words to Know. Then, for each item below, write the letter of the word pair that expresses a relationship similar to that of the capitalized pair.

1. ABODE : COTTAGE ::
  (a) nest : bird   (c) vehicle : car
  (b) nail : hammer (d) trumpet : music

2. SINGULAR : ORDINARY ::
  (a) whole : complete (c) warm : hot
  (b) chapter : book   (d) flexible : rigid

3. PIETY : NUN ::
  (a) poverty : banker (c) warmth : humidity
  (b) dishonesty : crook (d) simplicity : puzzle

4. DOLEFULLY : GRIEVE ::
  (a) loudly : whisper (c) joyfully : celebrate
  (b) humbly : brag   (d) rapidly : stroll

5. OSTENTATION : FLAUNT ::
  (a) cowardice : sneak (c) give : generosity
  (b) love : emotion   (d) humility : boast

Building Vocabulary
For an in-depth lesson on analogies, see page 254.

EXERCISE B: MEANING CLUES Write the vocabulary word, not used in Exercise A, that is suggested by each description below.

1. If you don't give way, give in, or give an inch, and you never say die, this describes you.

2. Facing a vicious dog or having to perform a solo could make a person feel this way.

3. Walking five miles to buy beans at a discount is an example of this.

4. This is someone who finds fault, comes down hard, and rakes people over the coals.

5. This is what sunny skies are for picnic planners, storm clouds are for farmers in need of rain.

6. Clues help a detective do this about a suspect's guilt.

7. Listening to mournful music on a gray, cloudy day could make you feel this way.

8. Odysseus, Crazy Horse, Davy Crockett, and Hercules all had plenty of this.

9. One could tell workers to do this by saying "Take a break."

10. This could describe an accent, a style of dressing, or a way of celebrating a holiday.

WORDS TO KNOW	abode	dolefully	parsimony	propitious	resolute
	censurer	melancholy	peculiar	prowess	singular
	daunted	ostentation	piety	repose	surmise

Washington Irving
1783–1859

Other Works
Diedrich Knickerbocker's History of New York
Tales of a Traveller

Literary Pioneer Born at the end of the American Revolution and named after our first president, Washington Irving made many contributions to American literature. He set an example for humorous writing, pioneered the short story as a literary form, influenced important writers—particularly Nathaniel Hawthorne—and put America on the literary map.

An Eye for Detail While growing up in a large, prosperous New York family, Irving came to know American society intimately. Besides learning to appreciate literature, art, theater, and opera, he loved to explore the countryside along the Hudson River. Gifted with an eye for the pictorial, he considered painting as a career but instead used his talent to write about the American landscapes he knew so well.

World Traveler Ironically, this first notable American writer spent much of his life abroad. After studying law for 6 years, Irving joined the family exporting business and was sent to work in its British office in 1815. Although the business failed, he stayed in Europe for the next 17 years, traveling extensively and serving as a U.S. diplomat.

Creator of Classic Tales Irving captured his European experiences in much of his writing, but American life provided him with some of his richest stories and most memorable characters. In *The Sketch Book of Geoffrey Crayon, Gent.* (1819–1820), he created the first distinctively American tales, such as "Rip Van Winkle" and "The Legend of Sleepy Hollow." Irving spent the last years of his life at his New York estate, Sunnyside, near his beloved Hudson River.

Author Activity

Tales Compared Recall or reread "Rip Van Winkle" and "The Legend of Sleepy Hollow." What do these stories have in common with "The Devil and Tom Walker"?

from **Self-Reliance**

Essay by RALPH WALDO EMERSON

(**Connect to Your Life**)

Self-Reliance Defined What do you think *self-reliance* means? Which people in the world today seem to have this quality? What are some advantages and disadvantages of being self-reliant? Discuss these questions with a small group of classmates.

Build Background

Voice of Transcendentalism Ralph Waldo Emerson was one of 19th-century America's greatest writers and thinkers. In 1836, Emerson formed the Transcendental Club with a group of friends, including Henry David Thoreau and the feminist writer and critic Margaret Fuller. As the intellectual leader of the transcendentalists, he defined many of his original ideas in lectures, poems, and essays. Part of the appeal of Emerson's lectures and essays was his poetic style and elegant way with words. This excerpt from the essay "Self-Reliance" is a series of loosely related thoughts and extracts from lectures and journals that Emerson had written in the years between 1832 and 1840. Published in 1841, the essay elaborates Emerson's belief in the importance of the individual.

WORDS TO KNOW **Vocabulary Preview**
absolve	aversion	bestowed
nonconformist	predominate	

Focus Your Reading

LITERARY ANALYSIS   APHORISM   An **aphorism** is a brief statement, usually one sentence long, that expresses a general principle or truth about life. For example, in *Poor Richard's Almanack,* Franklin uses several aphorisms, such as "Honesty is the best policy." Notice Emerson's aphorisms in this essay.

ACTIVE READING   SUMMARIZING   To summarize a piece of writing is to state its main ideas briefly in your own words, omitting less important details. These guidelines will help you summarize Emerson's essay.

- In each paragraph, identify the one or two most important phrases or statements.
- Write a sentence of your own to express the main idea of each statement you identified.
- Pull your sentences together into a single summary.

READER'S NOTEBOOK   After reading this excerpt from "Self-Reliance," summarize Emerson's main ideas in a few sentences.

Self-Reliance

RALPH
WALDO
EMERSON

There is a time in every man's education when he arrives at the conviction that envy is ignorance; that imitation is suicide; that he must take himself for better for worse as his portion; that though the wide universe is full of good, no kernel of nourishing corn can come to him but through his toil <u>bestowed</u> on that plot of ground which is given to him to till. . . .

Trust thyself: every heart vibrates to that iron string. Accept the place the divine providence has found for you, the society of your contemporaries, the connection of events. Great men have always done so, and confided themselves childlike to the genius of their age, betraying their perception that the absolutely trustworthy was seated at their heart, working through their hands, <u>predominating</u> in all their being. . . .

Whoso would be a man, must be a <u>nonconformist</u>. He who would gather immortal palms must not be hindered by the name of goodness, but must explore if it be goodness. Nothing is at last sacred but the integrity of your own mind. <u>Absolve</u> you to yourself, and you shall have the suffrage of the world. I remember an answer which when quite young I was prompted to make to a valued adviser who was wont to importune me with the dear old doctrines of the church. On my saying, "What have I to do with the sacredness of traditions, if I live wholly from within?" my friend suggested—"But these impulses may be from below, not from above." I replied, "They do not seem to me to be such; but if I am the Devil's child, I will live then from the Devil." No law can be sacred to me but that of my nature. Good and bad are but names very readily transferable to that or this; the only right is what is after my constitution; the only wrong what is against it. . . .

9 the divine providence: God.

12–13 betraying . . . trustworthy: revealing their awareness that God.

16 immortal palms: everlasting triumph and honor. In ancient times, people carried palm leaves as a symbol of victory, success, or joy.

19 suffrage: approval; support.

21 wont to importune me: accustomed to trouble me.

26–29 What is implied by Emerson's use of the word *sacred?* Why does he believe that one should follow his or her own nature?

29 after my constitution: consistent with my physical and mental nature.

WORDS
TO
KNOW

bestowed (bĭ-stōd') *adj.* applied; used **bestow** *v.*
predominate (prĭ-dŏm'ə-nāt') *v.* to have controlling power or influence
nonconformist (nŏn'kən-fôr'mĭst) *n.* one who does not follow generally accepted beliefs, customs, or practices
absolve (əb-zŏlv') *v.* to clear of guilt or blame

Kindred Spirits (1849), Asher B. Durand. Oil on canvas, collection of The New York Public Library, Astor, Lenox and Tilden Foundations.

30 What I must do is all that concerns me, not what the people think. This rule, equally arduous in actual and in intellectual life, may serve for the whole distinction between greatness and meanness. It is the harder because you will always find those who think they know what is your duty
35 better than you know it. It is easy in the world to live after the world's opinion; it is easy in solitude to live after our own; but the great man is he who in the midst of the crowd keeps with perfect sweetness the independence of solitude. . . .

33 meanness: the state of being inferior in quality, character, or value.

35–38 What does Emerson say is easy to do? What does he say a great person is able to do?

For nonconformity the world whips you with its displeasure.
And therefore a man must know how to estimate a sour
face. The by-standers look askance on him in the public
street or in the friend's parlor. If this aversion had its origin in
contempt and resistance like his own he might well go home
with a sad countenance; but the sour faces of the multitude, like
their sweet faces, have no deep cause, but are put on and off as
the wind blows and a newspaper directs. . . .

The other terror that scares us from self-trust is our consistency; a reverence for our past act or word because the eyes of
others have no other data for computing our orbit than our past
acts, and we are loth to disappoint them. . . .

A foolish consistency is the hobgoblin of little minds, adored
by little statesmen and philosophers and divines. With consistency a great soul has simply nothing to do. He may as well
concern himself with his shadow on the wall. Speak what you
think now in hard words and to-morrow speak what to-morrow
thinks in hard words again, though it contradict every thing you
said today.—"Ah, so you shall be sure to be misunderstood."—
Is it so bad then to be misunderstood? Pythagoras was misunderstood, and Socrates, and Jesus, and Luther, and Copernicus,
and Galileo, and Newton, and every pure and wise spirit that
ever took flesh. To be great is to be misunderstood. ❖

39–42 What does Emerson say is one consequence of being a nonconformist?

41 askance (ə-skǎns'): with disapproval, suspicion, or distrust.

47–52 Why does consistency scare us from trusting ourselves?

50 loth (lōth): unwilling; reluctant.

51 hobgoblin: a source of fear or dread. Notice that Emerson does not criticize all consistency, only "foolish" consistency that does not allow for change or progress.

52 divines: religious leaders.

58–60 Pythagoras . . . Newton: great thinkers whose radical theories and viewpoints caused controversy.

LITERARY LINK

from Memoirs

MARGARET FULLER

In the chamber
of death, I prayed
in very early years,
"Give me truth;
cheat me by no illusion."
O, the granting of
this prayer is
sometimes terrible to me!

I walk over the
burning ploughshares,[1]
and they sear[2]
my feet. Yet nothing but
the truth will do.

---

1. **ploughshares** (plou'shârz'): the cutting blades of plows.
2. **sear:** scorch; burn.

WORDS
TO
KNOW
   aversion (ə-vûr'zhən) *n.* a strong dislike

Thinking through the LITERATURE

Connect to the Literature

1. What Do You Think?
What kind of impact did this essay have on you? Share your reaction with your classmates.

Comprehension Check
- Which does Emerson value more—original thought or traditional wisdom?
- According to Emerson, which virtue does society demand most—truth, conformity, creativity, or self-reliance?
- What is the only law that Emerson says can be sacred to him?

Think Critically

2. **ACTIVE READING** **SUMMARIZING** How did you summarize Emerson's main ideas in this excerpt? Share what you wrote in your **READER'S NOTEBOOK**.

3. Describe situations or aspects of your own life in which Emerson's ideas about the importance of the individual might apply.

> **THINK ABOUT**
> - his idea that all people should be nonconformists
> - his disregard for consistency in thought and deed
> - peer pressures to conform to certain standards of appearance or behavior

4. If you had heard this essay as a public lecture, what questions would you have liked to ask Emerson directly about his philosophy?

Extend Interpretations

5. Critic's Corner The noted writer Henry James said that Emerson "had no great sense of wrong… no sense of the dark, the foul, the base." How do you think Emerson might have defended his views against this charge?

6. What If? If Emerson had specifically addressed the institution of slavery in this essay, what do you think he would have said about it?

7. Comparing Texts How do Margaret Fuller's ideas in the Literary Link poem on page 366 compare with Emerson's ideas in "Self-Reliance"?

8. Connect to Life Refer to the ideas you wrote about self-reliance for the Connect to Your Life activity on page 363. How do the ideas in Emerson's essay compare with your own?

Literary Analysis

APHORISM "Self-Reliance" is sprinkled with memorable sayings or **aphorisms**—brief statements, usually one sentence long, that express a general principle or truth about life. "A foolish consistency is the hobgoblin of little minds" is one of the most frequently quoted aphorisms from American literature. Emerson's aphorisms are interesting for their shock value. They proclaim his radical ideas in clear, concise sentences. His idea about consistency, for example, is distilled into one easy-to-remember aphorism and thereby immortalized.

Cooperative Learning Activity With a small group of classmates, identify at least three other aphorisms from "Self-Reliance," then list them on a sheet of paper. Compare your list with those of other groups. How similar are the ideas expressed in different aphorisms?

Emerson's Aphorisms
1.
2.
3.

Writing Options

1. Personal Essay Choose your favorite aphorism from "Self-Reliance," and draft a personal essay to explain why it is significant to you. Support your explanation with examples drawn from your life. Place this piece in your **Working Portfolio.**

2. Update of Emerson Imagine that Emerson has come to you and asked for your help in bringing his message about the importance of the individual to an audience of contemporary teenagers. Paraphrase his ideas for a teenage audience and provide up-to-date examples.

Inquiry & Research

History In the last paragraph of the selection, Emerson names several historical figures who were misunderstood. Choose one to learn more about and present your findings in an oral report.

Vocabulary in Action

EXERCISE: MEANING CLUES Review the Words to Know and then answer the following questions.

1. Would you be most likely to **bestow** a great deal of thought on a matter that revolted you, one that puzzled you, or one that bored you?

2. What is likely to be most important to a **nonconformist**—tradition, independence, or approval?

3. Is a person who **predominates** in too many situations wimpy, sneaky, or bossy?

4. If you have an **aversion** to a person, are you most likely to avoid the person, ignore the person, or seek the person out?

5. Is a judge most likely to **absolve** an accused criminal if the judge knows that the accused is guilty but sorry, guilty and not sorry, or completely innocent?

Building Vocabulary

For an in-depth study of word parts and root words, see page 444.

Ralph Waldo Emerson
1803–1882

Other Works
The Poet
The American Scholar
Concord Hymn

Early Struggles The distinguished poet, essayist, and lecturer Ralph Waldo Emerson was born in Boston, Massachusetts. As a child, he experienced illness, poverty, and the death of a parent. His father, a Unitarian minister, died when Emerson was 8 years old, and his mother struggled to raise five boys—including a mentally retarded son—alone. With the aid of several grants, however, Emerson was able to enter Harvard College when he was 14. To pay for other expenses, he worked as a tutor, a messenger, and a waiter at the college.

Spiritual Challenges After graduating, Emerson taught for several years at his brother's school for girls. He returned to Harvard to study for the ministry and became a Unitarian minister in 1829. Unfortunately, his brief career as a minister was marred by religious doubt and by his wife's death in 1831. Because he felt that he could no longer perform certain church rituals in good faith, he resigned his ministry in 1832.

Popular Lecturer After traveling in Europe for a year, Emerson returned to the United States to devote himself to lecturing and writing. In 1835, he remarried and settled in Concord, and a year later he celebrated the birth of his first child as well as the publication of his first book, *Nature*.

Author Activity

Emerson was the most important spiritual voice of his generation. Find out which other writers Emerson influenced, in addition to Thoreau and Fuller. Which writers rejected his beliefs?

from Civil Disobedience

Essay by HENRY DAVID THOREAU

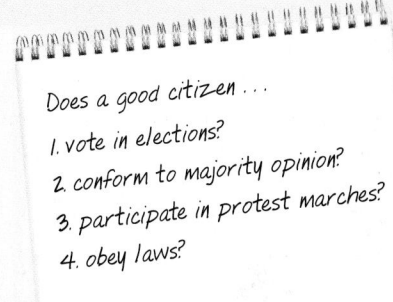
Build Background

Nonviolent Resistance Henry David Thoreau put into practice the ideas expressed in Emerson's "Self-Reliance." Thoreau spent a night in jail for refusing to pay a poll tax used to finance a government that condoned the institution of slavery and waged war against Mexico. Like many Americans at the time, Thoreau viewed the Mexican War (1846–1848) as a conflict in which a stronger country sought to overpower a weaker one simply to expand its own borders. Inspired by his experience in jail, Thoreau in 1847 published an essay originally titled "Resistance to Civil Government." In this essay, which became popularly known as "Civil Disobedience," Thoreau affirmed individual conscience and advocated nonviolent acts of political resistance to protest government policy.

WORDS TO KNOW
Vocabulary Preview

blunder	flourish
conclude	inexpedient
confront	meditation
conscientious	multitude
endeavor	unscrupulous

Focus Your Reading

LITERARY ANALYSIS ESSAY An **essay** is a short work of nonfiction that deals with a single subject, usually presenting the personal views of the writer. "Civil Disobedience" is a persuasive essay. It presents political ideas that Thoreau hopes his readers will adopt, and at the same time, it reveals much about Thoreau's personality.

ACTIVE READING STRATEGIES FOR READING ESSAYS Using these strategies will help you get the most from this essay:

- Keep the **historical context** in mind.
- Use the Guide for Reading alongside the text.
- Keep reading a paragraph even if a sentence stumps you, but read the entire essay more than once.
- Throughout, notice what Thoreau favors and opposes.
- Keep track of the **main ideas** and the **supporting details** that develop them.

READER'S NOTEBOOK One of Thoreau's main ideas in this excerpt is that there are three ways in which citizens serve the state. As you read, identify the three ways on a chart like the one shown. Fill in examples of each, and mark what Thoreau believes is the best way.

Ways to Serve the State

1. _____	2. _____	3. _____

from

Civil Disobedience
Henry David Thoreau

Nelson Mandela, imprisoned for 27 years by the South African government for his antiapartheid activities, recalls his confinement in this 1994 photo.

I heartily accept the motto, "That government is best which governs least;" and I should like to see it acted up to more rapidly and systematically. Carried out, it finally amounts
5 to this, which also I believe,—"That government is best which governs not at all;" and when men are prepared for it, that will be the kind of government which they will have. Government is at best but an expedient; but most governments are usually, and all governments are sometimes, <u>inexpedient</u>. The objections
10 which have been brought against a standing army, and they are many and weighty, and deserve to prevail, may also at last be brought against a standing government. The standing army is only an arm of the standing government. The government itself, which is only the mode which the people have chosen to
15 execute their will, is equally liable to be abused and perverted before the people can act through it. Witness the present Mexican war, the work of comparatively a few individuals using the standing government as their tool; for, in the outset, the people would not have consented to this measure. . . .

GUIDE FOR READING

8 expedient (ĭk-spē′dē-ənt): a means to an end.

1–9 How would you restate Thoreau's attitude toward government?

16–17 the present Mexican war: the 1846–1848 war between the United States and Mexico.

WORDS
TO
KNOW
inexpedient (ĭn′ĭk-spē′dē-ənt) adj. not useful for achieving a goal

370

20 But, to speak practically and as a citizen, unlike those who
call themselves no-government men, I ask for, not at once
no government, but *at once* a better government. Let every man
make known what kind of government would command his
respect, and that will be one step toward obtaining it.

25   After all, the practical reason why, when the power is once in
the hands of the people, a majority are permitted, and for a
long period continue, to rule is not because they are most likely
to be in the right, nor because this seems fairest to the minority,
but because they are physically the strongest. But a government
30 in which the majority rule in all cases cannot be based on
justice, even as far as men understand it. Can there not be a
government in which majorities do not virtually decide right
and wrong, but conscience?—in which majorities decide only
those questions to which the rule of expediency is applicable?
35 Must the citizen ever for a moment, or in the least degree,
resign his conscience to the legislator? Why has every man a

29–37 What position does Thoreau
take on the conflict between
majority rule and individual
conscience?

In Tianenmen Square in 1989, Chinese
demonstrators support prodemocracy
students on a hunger strike.

A young man strapped to logs protests
the cutting of California redwoods in
1990.

conscience, then? I think that we should be men first, and subjects afterward. It is not desirable to cultivate a respect for the law, so much as for the right. The only obligation which I have a right to assume is to do at any time what I think right. It is truly enough said, that a corporation has no conscience; but a corporation of <u>conscientious</u> men is a corporation *with* a conscience. Law never made men a whit more just; and, by means of their respect for it, even the well-disposed are daily made the agents of injustice. A common and natural result of an undue respect for law is, that you may see a file of soldiers, colonel, captain, corporal, privates, powder-monkeys, and all, marching in admirable order over hill and dale to the wars, against their wills, ay, against their common sense and consciences, which makes it very steep marching indeed, and produces a palpitation of the heart. They have no doubt that it is a damnable business in which they are concerned; they are all peaceably inclined. Now, what are they? Men at all? or small movable forts and magazines, at the service of some <u>unscrupulous</u> man in power? Visit the Navy-Yard, and behold a marine, such a man as an American government can make, or such as it can make a man with its black arts—a mere shadow and reminiscence of humanity, a man laid out alive and standing, and already, as one may say, buried under arms with funeral accompaniments, though it may be,—

> "Not a drum was heard, not a funeral note,
>   As his corse to the rampart we hurried;
> Not a soldier discharged his farewell shot
>   O'er the grave where our hero we buried."

The mass of men serve the state thus, not as men mainly, but as machines, with their bodies. They are the standing army, and the militia, jailers, constables, *posse comitatus,* etc. In most cases there is no free exercise whatever of the judgment or of the moral sense; but they put themselves on a level with wood and earth and stones; and wooden men can perhaps be manufactured that will serve the purpose as well. Such command no more respect than men of straw or a lump of dirt. They have the same sort of worth only as horses and dogs. Yet such as these even are commonly esteemed good citizens. Others—as most legislators, politicians, lawyers, ministers, and office-holders—serve the state chiefly with their heads; and, as they rarely make any moral distinctions, they are as likely to serve the Devil, without *intending* it, as God. A very few—as heroes, patriots, martyrs, reformers in the great

42 corporation: group.

43 a whit: the least bit.

43–45 What can be the consequences of having too much respect for the law?

47 powder-monkeys: boys with the job of carrying gunpowder to artillery crews.

51 palpitation (păl'pĭ-tā'shən): irregular, rapid beating.

54 magazines: places where ammunition is stored.

57 black arts: witchcraft.

61–64 "Not a drum . . . we buried": the opening lines of "The Burial of Sir John Moore After Corunna" by the Irish poet Charles Wolfe.

65–82 Which way of serving the state does Thoreau approve of? Which ways does he condemn?

67 *posse comitatus* (pŏs'ē kŏm'ĭ-tŏt'əs) *Latin:* power of the county—a term used to refer to the group of people that can be called on by a sheriff to help enforce the law.

WORDS TO KNOW

conscientious (kŏn'shē-ĕn'shəs) *adj.* guided by conscience; honest
unscrupulous (ŭn-skrōō'pyə-ləs) *adj.* without principles; dishonorable

80 sense, and *men*—serve the state with their consciences also, and so necessarily resist it for the most part; and they are commonly treated as enemies by it. . . .

Unjust laws exist: shall we be content to obey them, or shall we <u>endeavor</u> to amend them, and obey them until we have 85 succeeded or shall we transgress them at once? Men generally, under such a government as this, think that they ought to wait until they have persuaded the majority to alter them. They think that, if they should resist, the remedy would be worse than the evil. But it is the fault of the government itself that the 90 remedy *is* worse than the evil. *It* makes it worse. Why is it not more apt to anticipate and provide for reform? Why does it not cherish its wise minority? Why does it cry and resist before it is hurt? Why does it not encourage its citizens to be on the alert to point out its faults, and *do* better than it would have them? 95 Why does it always crucify Christ, and excommunicate Copernicus and Luther, and pronounce Washington and Franklin rebels? . . .

```
Let your life be

a counter-friction

to stop the machine.
```

If the injustice is part of the necessary friction of the machine of government, let it go, let it go: perchance it will wear smooth, —certainly
105 the machine will wear out. If the injustice has a spring, or a pulley, or a rope, or a crank, exclusively for itself, then perhaps you may consider whether the remedy will not be worse than the evil; but if it is of such a nature that it requires you to be the agent of injustice to another, then, I say, break the law. Let
110 your life be a counter-friction to stop the machine. What I have to do is to see, at any rate, that I do not lend myself to the wrong which I condemn. . . .

I meet this American government, or its representative, the state government, directly, and face to face, once a year—
115 no more—in the person of its tax-gatherer; this is the only mode in which a man situated as I am necessarily meets it; and it then says distinctly, Recognize me; and the simplest, most effectual, and, in the present posture of affairs, the indispensablest
120 mode of treating with it on this head, of expressing your little satisfaction with and love for it, is to deny it then. My civil neighbor, the tax-gatherer, is the very man I have to deal with,—

96-97 Copernicus (kō-pûr′nə-kəs) **and Luther:** Nicolaus Copernicus (1473–1543), a Polish astronomer who theorized that the sun rather than the earth is the center of our planetary system, and Martin Luther (1483–1546), a German theologian who was a leader in the Protestant Reformation. Both men were excommunicated (barred from participation in religious rites) by the Roman Catholic Church.

100-106 In this metaphor Thoreau compares injustice within government to friction in the workings of a machine—both are often unavoidable byproducts of the workings of a complex system.

114-122 What does Thoreau consider the most effective way of expressing his displeasure with the government?

119 posture of affairs: situation.

for it is, after all, with men and not with parchment that I quarrel,—and he has voluntarily chosen to be an agent of the government. How shall he ever know well what he is and does as an officer of the government, or as a man, until he is obliged to consider whether he shall treat me, his neighbor, for whom he has respect, as a neighbor and well-disposed man, or as a maniac and disturber of the peace, and see if he can get over this obstruction to his neighborliness without a ruder and more impetuous thought or speech corresponding with his action. I know this well, that if one thousand, if one hundred, if ten men whom I could name,—if ten *honest* men only,—ay, if *one* HONEST man, in this State of Massachusetts, *ceasing to hold slaves*, were actually to withdraw from this copartnership, and be locked up in the county jail therefor, it would be the abolition of slavery in America. For it matters not how small the beginning may seem to be: what is once well done is done forever. But we love better to talk about it: that we say is our mission. Reform keeps many scores of newspapers in its service, but not one man. . . .

Under a government which imprisons any unjustly, the true place for a just man is also a prison. The proper place today, the only place which Massachusetts has provided for her freer and less desponding spirits, is in her prisons, to be put out and locked out of the State by her own act, as they have already put themselves out by their principles. It is there that the fugitive slave, and the Mexican prisoner on parole, and the Indian come to plead the wrongs of his race should find them; on that separate, but more free and honorable ground, where the State places those who are not *with* her, but *against* her,— the only house in a slave State in which a free man can abide with honor. If any think that their influence would be lost there, and their voices no longer afflict the ear of the State, that they would not be as an enemy within its walls, they do not know by how much truth is stronger than error, nor how much more eloquently and effectively he can combat injustice who has experienced a little in his own person. Cast your whole vote, not a strip of paper merely, but your whole influence. A minority is powerless while it conforms to the majority; it is not even a minority then; but it is irresistible when it clogs by its whole weight. If the alternative is to keep all just men in prison, or give up war and slavery, the State will not hesitate which to choose. If a thousand men were not to pay their tax bills this year, that would not be a violent and bloody measure, as it would be to pay them, and enable the State to commit violence and shed innocent blood. This is, in fact, the definition

132-139 Note that Thoreau advocates refusing to go along with the "copartnership of the individual and government if the government acts against an individual's conscience." Although abolitionists in Thoreau's time did not act on his suggestion, civil rights leaders more than one hundred years later, in the 1960s, staged protests and went to jail to oppose unjust segregation laws and practices.

of a peaceable revolution, if any such is possible. If the tax-
gatherer, or any other public officer, asks me, as one has done,
"But what shall I do?" my answer is, "If you really wish to do
anything, resign your office." When the subject has refused
allegiance, and the officer has resigned his office, then the
revolution is accomplished. But even suppose blood should flow.
Is there not a sort of blood shed when the conscience is
wounded? Through this wound a man's real manhood and
immortality flow out, and he bleeds to an everlasting death. I
see this blood flowing now. . . .

I have paid no poll-tax for six years. I was put into a jail
once on this account, for one night; and, as I stood
considering the walls of solid stone, two or three feet thick, the
door of wood and iron, a foot thick, and the iron grating
which strained the light, I could not help being struck with the
foolishness of that institution which treated me as if I were
mere flesh and blood and bones, to be locked up. I wondered
that it should have <u>concluded</u> at length that this was the best
use it could put me to, and had never thought to avail itself of
my services in some way. I saw that, if there was a wall of
stone between me and my townsmen, there was a still more
difficult one to climb or break through before they could get to
be as free as I was. I did not for a moment feel confined, and

170
175
180
185
190

A 1981 march for nuclear
disarmament in London's West End.

Rosa Parks, whose arrest for refusing
to move to the back of a segregated
bus touched off the Montgomery,
Alabama, bus boycott in 1955.

In the early 1900s, suffragists
demonstrate for women's voting
rights outside Buckingham Palace
in London.

178–205 Why do you think
Thoreau includes this personal
anecdote about his one night in
jail?

178 poll-tax: a tax that one had to
pay in order to vote.

the walls seemed a great waste of stone and mortar. I felt as if I alone of all my townsmen had paid my tax. They plainly did not know how to treat me, but behaved like persons who are underbred. In every threat and in every compliment there was a
195 blunder; for they thought that my chief desire was to stand the other side of that stone wall. I could not but smile to see how industriously they locked the door on my meditations, which followed them out again without let or hindrance, and *they* were really all that was dangerous. As they could not reach me,
200 they had resolved to punish my body; just as boys, if they cannot come at some person against whom they have a spite, will abuse his dog. I saw that the State was half-witted, that it was timid as a lone woman with her silver spoons, and that it did not know its friends from its foes, and I lost all my
205 remaining respect for it, and pitied it.

Thus the State never intentionally confronts a man's sense, intellectual or moral, but only his body, his senses. It is not armed with superior wit or honesty, but with superior physical strength. I was not born to be forced. I will breathe after my
210 own fashion. Let us see who is the strongest. What force has a multitude? They only can force me who obey a higher law than I. They force me to become like themselves. I do not hear of *men* being *forced* to live this way or that by masses of men. What sort of life were that to live? When I meet a government
215 which says to me, "Your money or your life," why should I be in haste to give it my money? It may be in a great strait, and not know what to do: I cannot help that. It must help itself; do as I do. It is not worth the while to snivel about it. I am not responsible for the successful working of the machinery of
220 society. I am not the son of the engineer. I perceive that, when an acorn and a chestnut fall side by side, the one does not remain inert to make way for the other, but both obey their own laws, and spring and grow and flourish as best they can, till one, perchance, overshadows and destroys the other. If a
225 plant cannot live according to its nature, it dies; and so a man.

194 underbred: ill-mannered.

198 without let or hindrance (hĭn'drəns): without encountering obstacles.

201 spite: grudge.

220–225 What message does Thoreau convey through this example of the acorn and the chestnut?

If a plant cannot live according to its nature; it dies;
and so a man.

ON CIVIL DISOBEDIENCE

Mohandas K. Gandhi

Mohandas K. Gandhi (1869-1948), called Mahatma ("Great Soul"), helped free India of British rule. As a student, he greatly admired Thoreau's essay "Civil Disobedience." Thoreau's ideas helped shape Gandhi's key principle—satyagraha (sə-tyä' grə-hə), or "truth-force." In the following excerpt from a 1916 speech, Gandhi describes this powerful weapon for fighting oppression.

July 27, 1916

There are two ways of countering injustice. One way is to smash the head of the man who perpetrates injustice and to get your own head smashed in the process. All strong people in the world adopt this course. Everywhere wars are fought and millions of people are killed. The consequence is not the progress of a nation but its decline. . . . No country has ever become, or will ever become, happy through victory in war. A nation does not rise that way, it only falls further. In fact, what comes to it is defeat, not victory. And if, perchance, either our act or our purpose was ill-conceived, it brings disaster to both belligerents.[1]

But through the other method of combating injustice, we alone suffer the consequences of our mistakes, and the other side is wholly spared. This other method is *satyagraha*.[2] One who resorts to it does not have to break another's head; he may merely have his own head broken. He has to be prepared to die himself suffering all the pain. In opposing the atrocious laws of the Government of South Africa, it was this method that we adopted. We made it clear to the said Government that we would never bow to its outrageous laws. No clapping is possible without two hands to do it, and no quarrel without two persons to make it. Similarly, no State is possible without two entities, the rulers and the ruled. You are our sovereign, our Government, only so long as we consider ourselves your subjects. When we are not subjects, you are not the sovereign either. So long as it is your endeavour to control us with justice and love, we will let you to do so. But if you wish to strike at us from behind, we cannot permit it. Whatever you do in other matters, you will have to ask our opinion about the laws that concern us. If you make laws to keep us suppressed in a wrongful manner and without taking us into confidence, these laws will merely adorn the statute-books.[3] We will never obey them. Award us for it what punishment you like, we will put up with it. Send us to prison and we will live there as in a paradise. Ask us to mount the scaffold[4] and we will do so laughing. Shower what sufferings you like upon us, we will calmly endure all and not hurt a hair of your body. We will gladly die and will not so much as touch you. But so long as there is yet life in these our bones, we will never comply with your arbitrary laws.

1. **belligerents** (bə-lĭj'ər-ənts): participants in a war.
2. **satyagraha** (sə-tyä'''grə-hə) *Sanskrit:* insistence on truth—a term used by Gandhi to describe his policy of seeking reform by means of nonviolent resistance.
3. **statute-books:** books of laws.
4. **scaffold:** a platform on which people are executed by hanging.

Connect to the Literature

1. **What Do You Think?**
What is your first reaction to Thoreau's views on civil disobedience, or nonviolent resistance?

Comprehension Check
- According to Thoreau, what should be respected more than the law?
- What should a citizen do about an unjust law?
- How does Thoreau respond to being jailed?

Think Critically

2. How convincing do you find Thoreau's argument?

THINK ABOUT

- Thoreau's comment that a man must live according to his nature
- circumstances under which he advocates breaking the law
- his views on majority rule

3. **ACTIVE READING** **STRATEGIES FOR READING ESSAYS** Refer to the chart you made in your 📖 **READER'S NOTEBOOK**. How important to Thoreau's argument is his idea about the different ways of serving the state? Explain your answer.

4. What might some find threatening about Thoreau's ideas?

Extend Interpretations

5. **The Writer's Style** A **paradox** is a statement that seems to contradict itself but may nevertheless suggest an important truth. "Civil Disobedience" is based on the paradox that a good citizen must be a lawbreaker under certain circumstances. Find other paradoxes in the essay that reinforce and extend this basic paradox.

6. **Critic's Corner** Critic Leon Edel states that Thoreau's theory of nonviolent resistance does not work in all conditions and that it "presupposes . . . a society which has moved beyond barbarism." Explain what you think Edel means. Does his view affect your opinion of Thoreau's argument?

7. **Comparing Texts** Thoreau's ideas influenced many 20th-century reformers, notably Mohandas Gandhi, the Indian nationalist and spiritual leader. What connections do you see between Thoreau's views and Gandhi's in the excerpt "On Civil Disobedience," on page 377?

8. **Connect to Life** How would you compare Thoreau's views on good citizenship with your own?

Literary Analysis

ESSAY An **essay** is a short work of nonfiction that deals with a single subject. The term comes from the French word *essai*, meaning "attempt." The purpose of an essay may be to express ideas and feelings, to analyze, to inform, to entertain, or to persuade. For example, de Crèvecoeur's essay "What Is an American?" was written to inform Europeans about a new breed of people, the Americans. Thoreau's purpose in "Civil Disobedience," on the other hand, is to persuade his audience to use nonviolent resistance to oppose unjust laws.

Even when they discuss serious ideas, essays are often informal, loosely structured, and highly personal. Consider the picture you get of Thoreau the man as you digest the political views in his essay.

Cooperative Learning Activity
Working in small groups, locate passages in which Thoreau refers to himself—identifying his personal opinions or recounting personal experiences, such as the night he spent in jail. How do these passages influence your acceptance of his arguments? Discuss what effect omitting these passages would have on the essay.

Choices & CHALLENGES

Writing Options

1. Comparison of Emerson and Thoreau
Ralph Waldo Emerson was Thoreau's mentor and friend. Compare Thoreau's and Emerson's messages about the importance of the individual, as expressed in "Civil Disobedience" and "Self-Reliance." From their writings, make a generalization about the romantic view of the individual.

Writing Handbook
See page 1281: Comparison and Contrast

2. Personal Response
Select a paradox you identified for question 5 on the Writer's Style (page 378). Then write a personal response, explaining what this paradox means to you.

3. Essay on Citizenship
Imagine that a local civic group is sponsoring an essay contest about good citizenship. Drawing upon your views and Thoreau's, write an essay exploring ways to serve the community or the nation with your conscience.

Good Citizenship

A good citizen tries to create a good environment for all.

Activities & Explorations

1. Group Discussion
Thoreau acted on his beliefs by going to jail rather than paying taxes to help finance the war against Mexico or slavery in the South. What present-day causes do you think Thoreau might have supported? With five or six classmates, explore this question in a discussion. Choose one of the causes, and in a chart list two strategies that you believe Thoreau would have used to support this cause and two that he would not have used.
~ **SPEAKING AND LISTENING**

Cause: _____	
Strategies to Use	Strategies to Avoid

2. Drama in a Jailhouse
With a small group of classmates, stage a reenactment of Thoreau's arrest, his night in jail, and his subsequent release. Feel free to add imaginative touches such as an interview by a journalist questioning Thoreau about his motives or a visit by one of Thoreau's friends, such as Emerson. Make sure that your characterization of Thoreau is consistent with the message of this essay. ~ **PERFORMING**

3. Political Poster
Design a political poster based on your reading of this essay. Include a slogan and visual images that convey Thoreau's political views. Display your poster in the classroom. ~ **ART**

Inquiry & Research

Resisting Injustice Working with a small group, research situations in which protesters have used nonviolent resistance as a means of opposing injustice. Consider situations in the following countries:

- India in the 1920s and 1930s
- Germany in the late 1930s
- the United States in the 1960s
- the Philippines in 1987
- China in 1989

Gather information from resources such as history books and print or on-line encyclopedias. Then, based on your group's research, form an opinion about the effectiveness of nonviolent resistance. Present an oral report to share your findings.

 More Online: Research Starter
www.mcdougallittell.com

Vocabulary in Action

EXERCISE A: CONTEXT CLUES Write the Word to Know that best completes the meaning of each sentence.

1. Thoreau's "Civil Disobedience" is a _____ on the relationship between citizen and government.

2. Thoreau believes that government leaders sometimes find it _____ to do what is morally right.

3. Thoreau wants a society in which individual liberty would _____ .

4. Thoreau says that Americans should _____ to change unjust laws.

5. Some might _____ that Thoreau wants a revolution.

EXERCISE B: SYNONYMS AND ANTONYMS For each pair of words, write *S* if the words are synonyms or *A* if they are antonyms.

1. blunder—error
2. conscientious—principled
3. multitude—individual
4. confront—encounter
5. unscrupulous—honorable

WORDS TO KNOW	blunder conclude confront conscientious	endeavor flourish inexpedient	meditation multitude unscrupulous

Building Vocabulary
For an in-depth lesson on context clues, see page 326.

Henry David Thoreau
1817–1862

Other Works
Walden
*A Week on the Concord and
    Merrimack Rivers*
*The Collected Poems of Henry
    Thoreau*

Philosopher and Scholar Henry David Thoreau was born and raised in Concord, Massachusetts, where he lived almost all of his life. He studied classics and natural history at Harvard University. After graduating at the age of 20, he returned to Concord to teach school. Although some of Thoreau's neighbors viewed him as a cranky eccentric, he was a careful observer and a deep thinker, who recorded his thoughts and observations in his journal. Taking to heart the ideas of Ralph Waldo Emerson, Thoreau tried to live by his own values rather than society's values, which he considered materialistic.

Dedicated Nonconformist Thoreau's life was full of examples of his independent spirit. As a Harvard student, he was required to wear a black coat but sported a green one instead. In his first year of teaching, he refused to punish his students physically and resigned his post. In 1845, he conducted his famous experiment, living simply and frugally in a small cabin that he had built himself on the shores of Walden Pond. In 1846, he was arrested and spent a night in jail for refusing to pay a poll tax.

Social Reformer Despite his love of solitude and country life, Thoreau took an active part in social causes. During the 1840s and 1850s, he became passionately involved in the abolitionist movement. He lectured at antislavery rallies and served as a conductor on the Underground Railroad, hiding fugitive slaves in his family's house. Although he did not advocate violence, he publicly defended John Brown, the fiery abolitionist who had led a bloody raid on Harpers Ferry.

Posthumous Praise During his lifetime, Thoreau published only two books, both of which sold poorly. In the years since his death, however, his reputation has grown tremendously. His observations about nature, the importance of the individual, and the value of a simple life are more and more relevant today, as environmental abuses multiply, the pressure to conform increases, and the pace of life continues to speed up.

from **Walden**

Essay by HENRY DAVID THOREAU

(Connect to Your Life)

Future Experiences What do you want to experience in your life? Think of some experiences you look forward to, such as working for the Peace Corps, learning to play the guitar, inventing a computer game, seeing the Rocky Mountains, or appearing on TV. Pick three of the experiences and explain to a small group of your classmates why you want to have each one.

Build Background

Thoreau's Experiment Like Ralph Waldo Emerson and other transcendentalists, Thoreau felt a need to confirm his unity with nature. On July 4, 1845, he began his famous experiment in what he thought of as "essential" living—living simply, studying the natural world, and seeking truth within himself. On land owned by Emerson near Concord, Massachusetts, Thoreau built a small cabin by Walden Pond and lived there for more than two years, writing and studying nature. *Walden*—a mixture of philosophy, autobiography, and meditation upon nature—is the record of Thoreau's experiences at the pond.

WORDS TO KNOW
Vocabulary Preview

abject	magnanimity	resignation
congenial	mean	rudiment
deliberately	misgiving	serenity
disreputable	perennial	sublime
dissipation	perturbation	vulgar

Focus Your Reading

LITERARY ANALYSIS **NATURE WRITING** The term **nature writing** describes a type of essay in which the writer uses firsthand observations to explore his or her relationship with the natural world. *Walden* is one of the best known examples of nature writing. Find out what Thoreau learns from his experiences with nature.

ACTIVE READING **EVALUATING AUTHOR'S OBSERVATIONS**
Good readers look for connections between what they read and their own experiences. They also challenge the text, forming their own opinions about the writer's observations. As Emerson did in "Self-Reliance," Thoreau often uses aphorisms—brief statements that express general principles or truths about life—to convey his observations.

READER'S NOTEBOOK
As you read, jot down some of Thoreau's aphorisms. Then, after you finish reading, write a brief evaluation of each aphorism, explaining whether or not you agree with it.

Aphorism	Do I Agree?
"An honest man has hardly need to count more than his ten fingers."	

FROM

Walden

HENRY DAVID THOREAU

FROM

Where I Lived, and What I Lived For

When first I took up my abode in the woods, that is, began to spend my nights as well as days there, which, by accident, was on Independence day, or the fourth of July, 1845, my house was not finished for winter, but was
5   merely a defense against the rain, without plastering or chimney, the walls being of rough weather-stained boards, with wide chinks, which made it cool at night. The upright
10 white hewn studs and freshly planed door and window casings gave it a clean and airy look, especially in the morning, when its timbers were saturated with dew, so that I fancied that by noon some sweet gum would exude from them. . . .

15 I was seated by the shore of a small pond, about a mile and a half south of the village of Concord and somewhat higher than it, in the midst of an extensive wood between that town and Lincoln, and about two miles south of that our only field known to fame, Concord Battle Ground; but I was so low in the

20 woods that the opposite shore, half a mile off, like the rest, covered with wood, was my most distant horizon. For the first week, whenever I looked out on the pond it impressed me like a tarn high up on the side of a mountain, its bottom far above the surface of other lakes, and, as the sun arose, I saw it throwing off its nightly clothing of mist, and here and there, by degrees,

25 its soft ripples or its smooth reflecting surface was revealed, while the mists, like ghosts, were stealthily withdrawing in every direction into the woods, as at the breaking up of some nocturnal conventicle. The very dew seemed to hang upon the trees later into the day than usual, as on the sides of mountains. . . .

30 I went to the woods because I wished to live deliberately, to front only the essential facts of life, and see if I could not learn what it had to teach, and not, when I came to die, discover that I had not lived. I did not wish to live what was not life, living is so dear; nor did I wish to practice resignation, unless it was

35 quite necessary. I wanted to live deep and suck out all the marrow of life, to live so sturdily and Spartan-like as to put to rout all that was not life, to cut a broad swath and shave close, to drive life into a corner, and reduce it to its lowest terms, and, if it proved to be mean, why then to get the whole and genuine

40 meanness of it, and publish its meanness to the world; or if it were sublime, to know it by experience, and be able to give a true account of it in my next excursion. For most men, it appears to me, are in a strange uncertainty about it, whether it is of the devil or of God, and have *somewhat hastily* concluded

45 that it is the chief end of man here to "glorify God and enjoy him forever."

Still we live meanly, like ants; though the fable tells us that we were long ago changed into men; like pygmies we fight with cranes; it is error upon error, and clout upon clout, and our best

50 virtue has for its occasion a superfluous and evitable wretchedness. Our life is frittered away by detail. An honest man has hardly need to count more than his ten fingers, or in extreme cases he may add his ten toes, and lump the rest. Simplicity, simplicity, simplicity! I say, let your affairs be as two or three,

55 and not a hundred or a thousand; instead of a million count

22 tarn: a small mountain lake or pool.

27–28 nocturnal conventicle (kən-věn′tĭ-kəl): a secret religious meeting held at night.

30–42 What are Thoreau's reasons for moving to the woods?

35–36 marrow: the central, most essential part; literally, the soft tissue inside a bone.

36 Spartan-like: in a simple, economical, and disciplined way, like the inhabitants of the ancient Greek city-state of Sparta.

37 cut a broad swath and shave close: gather as much of the essence of life as possible.

45 chief end of man here: most important purpose of human life on earth.

47 the fable: a Greek myth in which Zeus changes ants into men.

48–49 like pygmies . . . cranes: a reference to a legend, mentioned in Homer's *Iliad,* about the continual battles fought by a race of dwarfs against cranes.

50 evitable (ěv′ĭ-tə-bəl): avoidable.

53–54 What is Thoreau's remedy for our hectic, detail-crowded lives?

WORDS
TO
KNOW

deliberately (dĭ-lĭb′ər-ĭt-lē) *adv.* in an unhurried and thoughtful manner
resignation (rěz′ĭg-nā′shən) *n.* an acceptance of something as unavoidable
mean (mēn) *adj.* inferior in quality, value, or importance
sublime (sə-blīm′) *adj.* of high spiritual, moral, or intellectual worth; noble

half a dozen, and keep your accounts on your thumbnail. In the
midst of this chopping sea of civilized life, such are the clouds
and storms and quicksands and thousand-and-one items to be
allowed for, that a man has to live, if he would not founder and
60   go to the bottom and not make his port at all, by dead reckoning, and he must be a great calculator indeed who succeeds.
Simplify, simplify. Instead of three meals a day, if it be necessary
eat but one; instead of a hundred dishes, five; and reduce other
things in proportion. . . .

65   Why should we live with such hurry and waste of life? We
are determined to be starved before we are hungry. Men say
that a stitch in time saves nine, and so they take a thousand
stitches today to save nine to-morrow. As for *work,* we haven't
any of any consequence. We have the Saint Vitus' dance, and
70   cannot possibly keep our heads still. If I should only give a few
pulls at the parish bell-rope, as for a fire, that is, without setting
the bell, there is hardly a man on his farm in the outskirts of
Concord, notwithstanding that press of engagements which was
his excuse so many times this morning, nor a boy, nor a
75   woman, I might almost say, but would forsake all and follow
that sound, not mainly to save property from the flames, but, if
we will confess the truth, much more to see it burn, since burn
it must, and we, be it known, did not set it on fire,—or to see it
put out, and have a hand in it, if that is done as handsomely;
80   yes, even if it were the parish church itself. Hardly a man takes
a half hour's nap after dinner, but when he wakes he holds up
his head and asks, "What's the news?" as if the rest of mankind
had stood his sentinels. Some give directions to be waked every
half hour, doubtless for no other purpose; and then, to pay for
85   it, they tell what they have dreamed. After a night's sleep the
news is as indispensable as the breakfast. "Pray tell me any
thing new that has happened to a man any where on this
globe,"—and he reads it over his coffee and rolls, that a man
has had his eyes gouged out this morning on the Wachito River;
90   never dreaming the while that he lives in the dark unfathomed
mammoth cave of this world, and has but the <u>rudiment</u> of an
eye himself.

For my part, I could easily do without the post-office. I think
that there are very few important communications made
95   through it. To speak critically, I never received more than one or
two letters in my life—I wrote this some years ago—that were
worth the postage. The penny-post is, commonly, an institution
through which you seriously offer a man that penny for his

59 founder: to sink like a ship.

60–61 dead reckoning: guesswork.
The term, used by sailors, describes
a method of estimating a ship's
position when the stars cannot be
seen.

69 Saint Vitus' (vī′təs) **dance:** a
disorder of the nervous system,
characterized by rapid, jerky,
involuntary movements.

80–92 What situation is Thoreau
exaggerating here?

89 Wachito River: a river (now
called the Ouachita) in northern
Louisiana and southern Arkansas.
In Thoreau's time, it was believed
that violent men went to that
region to escape from the law.

97–99 Thoreau jokingly connects
the postage rate (a penny per
letter at the time) with the phrase
"a penny for your thoughts." What
is the point of his joke?

WORDS
TO   **rudiment** (rōō′də-mənt) *n.* an imperfect or undeveloped form
KNOW

Photo by Ernst Haas. Copyright © Tony Stone Images

thoughts which is so often safely offered in jest. And I am sure
100 that I never read any memorable news in a newspaper. If we
read of one man robbed, or murdered, or killed by accident, or
one house burned, or one vessel wrecked, or one steamboat
blown up, or one cow run over on the Western Railroad, or one
mad dog killed, or one lot of grasshoppers in the winter,—we
105 never need read of another. One is enough. . . .

Let us spend one day as deliberately as Nature, and not be
thrown off the track by every nutshell and mosquito's wing that
falls on the rails. Let us rise early and fast, or break fast, gently
and without <u>perturbation</u>; let company come and let company
110 go, let the bells ring and the children cry,—determined to make
a day of it. . . .

Time is but the stream I go a-fishing in. I drink at it; but
while I drink I see the sandy bottom and detect how shallow it

112–126 Thoreau says that we do
not have much time on earth.
What does he say he wants to
spend his time trying to understand? How does he feel that he
can find some of the answers
he seeks?

> WORDS
> TO   **perturbation** (pûr′tər-bā′shən) *n.* a disturbance of the emotions; agitation; uneasiness
> KNOW

is. Its thin current slides away, but eternity remains. I would
drink deeper; fish in the sky, whose bottom is pebbly with stars.
I cannot count one. I know not the first letter of the alphabet. I
have always been regretting that I was not as wise as the day I
was born. The intellect is a cleaver; it discerns and rifts its way
into the secret of things. I do not wish to be any more busy with
my hands than is necessary. My head is hands and feet. I feel all
my best faculties concentrated in it. My instinct tells me that my
head is an organ for burrowing, as some creatures use their
snout and fore-paws, and with it I would mine and burrow my
way through these hills. I think that the richest vein is somewhere hereabouts; so by the divining rod and thin rising vapors
I judge; and here I will begin to mine.

115

120

125

125 divining rod: a forked stick
that is believed to indicate the
presence of underground water.

FROM

Solitude

This is a delicious evening,
when the whole body is one
sense, and imbibes delight
through every pore. I go and
come with a strange liberty
in Nature, a part of herself.
As I walk along the stony
shore of the pond in my shirt
sleeves, though it is cool as
well as cloudy and windy, and I see nothing special to attract me,
all the elements are unusually <u>congenial</u> to me. The bullfrogs
trump to usher in the night, and the note of the whippoorwill is
borne on the rippling wind from over the water. Sympathy with
the fluttering alder and poplar leaves almost takes away my
breath; yet, like the lake, my <u>serenity</u> is rippled but not ruffled.
These small waves raised by the evening wind are as remote
from storm as the smooth reflecting surface. Though it is now
dark, the wind still blows and roars in the wood, the waves still
dash, and some creatures lull the rest with their notes. The
repose is never complete. The wildest animals do not repose, but
seek their prey now; the fox, and skunk, and rabbit, now roam
the fields and woods without fear. They are Nature's watchmen,—links which connect the days of animated life. . . .

130

135

140

145

130–145 What does Thoreau say
he is part of, and why does he feel
as he does?

WORDS
TO
KNOW

congenial (kən-gēn′yəl) *adj.* suited to one's needs or nature; agreeable
serenity (sə-rĕn′ĭ-tē) *n.* a mental and spiritual calm; tranquillity

150   Men frequently say to me, "I should think you would feel lonesome down there, and want to be nearer to folks, rainy and snowy days and nights especially." I am tempted to reply to such,—This whole earth which we inhabit is but a point in space. How far apart, think you, dwell the two most distant

155 inhabitants of yonder star, the breadth of whose disk cannot be appreciated by our instruments? Why should I feel lonely? Is not our planet in the Milky Way? This which you put seems to me not to be the most important question. What sort of space is that which separates a man from his fellows and makes him

160 solitary? I have found that no exertion of the legs can bring two minds much nearer to one another. . . .

153–160 Thoreau suggests that because we are all in this life together, the physical distance between us is insignificant.

FROM
The Pond in Winter

    Every winter the liquid and trembling surface of the pond, which was so sensitive to every breath, and reflected every light and shadow, becomes solid to the depth of a foot or a foot and a

165 half, so that it will support the heaviest teams, and perchance the snow covers it to an equal depth, and it is not to be distinguished from any level field. Like the marmots in the surrounding hills, it closes its eye-lids and becomes dormant for three months or more. Standing on the snow-covered plain, as if in a pasture

170 amid the hills, I cut my way first through a foot of snow, and then a foot of ice, and open a window under my feet, where, kneeling to drink, I look down into the quiet parlor of the fishes, pervaded by a softened light as through a

167 marmots: rodents that hibernate in the winter; groundhogs.

175 window of ground glass, with its bright sanded floor the same as in summer; there a <u>perennial</u> waveless

180 serenity reigns as in the amber twilight sky, corresponding to the cool and even temperament of the inhabitants. Heaven is

185 under our feet as well as over our heads. . . .

WORDS
TO   **perennial** (pə-rĕn′ē-əl) *adj.* lasting through the year or through many years; enduring
KNOW

FROM *Spring*

One attraction in coming to the woods to live was that I should
have leisure and opportunity to see the spring come in. The ice
in the pond at length begins to be honey-combed, and I can set
190 my heel in it as I walk. Fogs and rains and warmer suns are
gradually melting the snow; the days have grown sensibly
longer; and I see how I shall get through the winter without
adding to my woodpile, for large fires are no longer necessary.
I am on the alert for the first signs of spring, to hear the chance
195 note of some arriving bird, or the striped squirrel's chirp, for his
stores must be now nearly exhausted, or see the woodchuck
venture out of his winter quarters. . . .

   The change from storm and winter to serene and mild weather, from dark and sluggish hours to bright and elastic ones, is a
200 memorable crisis which all things proclaim. It is seemingly
instantaneous at last. Suddenly an influx of light filled my
house, though the evening was at hand, and the clouds of winter still overhung it, and the eaves were dripping with sleety
rain. I looked out the window, and lo! where yesterday was cold
205 gray ice there lay the transparent pond already calm and full of
hope as in a summer evening, reflecting a summer evening sky
in its bosom, though none was visible overhead, as if it had
intelligence with some remote horizon. . . .

191 sensibly: noticeably.

200 crisis: turning point.

FROM *Conclusion*

I left the woods for as good a reason as I went there. Perhaps it
210 seemed to me that I had several more lives to live, and could
not spare any more time for that one. It is remarkable how easily and insensibly we fall into a particular route, and make a
beaten track for ourselves. I had not lived there a week before
my feet wore a path from my door to the pond-side; and though
215 it is five or six years since I trod it, it is still quite distinct. It is
true, I fear that others may have fallen into it, and so helped to
keep it open. The surface of the earth is soft and impressible by
the feet of men; and so with the paths which the mind travels.
How worn and dusty, then, must be the highways of the world,
220 how deep the ruts of tradition and conformity! I did not wish to
take a cabin passage, but rather to go before the mast and on

209–211 Why does Thoreau leave
the woods?

220–223 On a sailing ship,
passengers stayed in private
compartments near the middle of
the ship, while the crew shared
living quarters at the front
("before the mast"). What is
Thoreau comparing here? How
does he want to live his life?

Photo by Ernst Haas. Copyright © Tony Stone Images

the deck of the world, for there I could best see the moonlight amid the mountains. I do not wish to go below now.

I learned this, at least, by my experiment; that if one
225 advances confidently in the direction of his dreams, and endeavors to live the life which he has imagined, he will meet with a success unexpected in common hours. He will put some things behind, will pass an invisible boundary; new, universal, and more liberal laws will begin to establish themselves around and
230 within him; or the old laws be expanded, and interpreted in his favor in a more liberal sense, and he will live with the license of a higher order of beings. In proportion as he simplifies his life, the laws of the universe will appear less complex, and solitude will not be solitude, nor poverty poverty, nor weakness weak-
235 ness. If you have built castles in the air, your work need not be lost; that is where they should be. Now put the foundations under them. . . .

Why should we be in such desperate haste to succeed, and in such desperate enterprises? If a man does not keep pace with his companions, perhaps it is because he hears a different drummer. Let him step to the music which he hears, however measured or far away. It is not important that he should mature as soon as an appletree or an oak. Shall he turn his spring into summer? If the condition of things which we were made for is not yet, what were any reality which we can substitute? We will not be ship-wrecked on a vain reality. Shall we with pains erect a heaven of blue glass over ourselves, though when it is done we shall be sure to gaze still at the true ethereal heaven far above, as if the former were not? . . .

However mean your life is, meet it and live it; do not shun it and call it hard names. It is not so bad as you are. It looks poorest when you are richest. The fault-finder will find faults even in paradise. Love your life, poor as it is. You may perhaps have some pleasant, thrilling, glorious hours, even in a poorhouse. The setting sun is reflected from the windows of the almshouse as brightly as from the rich man's abode; the snow melts before its door as early in the spring. I do not see but a quiet mind may live as contentedly there, and have as cheering thoughts, as in a palace. The town's poor seem to me often to live the most independent lives of any. May be they are simply great enough to receive without misgiving. Most think that they are above being supported by the town; but it oftener happens that they are not above supporting themselves by dishonest means, which should be more disreputable. Cultivate poverty like a garden herb, like sage. Do not trouble yourself much to get new things, whether clothes or friends. Turn the old; return to them. Things do not change; we change. Sell your clothes and keep your thoughts. God will see that you do not want society. If I were confined to a corner of a garret all my days, like a spider, the world would be just as large to me while I had my thoughts about me. The philosopher said: "From an army of three divisions one can take away its general, and put it in disorder; from the man the most abject and vulgar one cannot take away his thought." Do not seek so anxiously to be developed, to subject yourself to many influences to be played on; it is all dissipation. Humility like darkness reveals the heavenly lights. The shadows of poverty and meanness gather around us, "and lo! creation widens to our view." We are often reminded that if there were bestowed on us

240

245

250

255

260

265

270

275

239–242 This is one of the most famous passages in Thoreau's writings. The "different drummer" evolved from one of his journal entries describing an 1839 river voyage when he had fallen asleep to the sound of someone's beating a drum "alone in the silence and the dark." The phrase "marching to the beat of a different drummer" became popular in the nonconformist 1960s. What does it mean to hear a different drummer?

255 almshouse: poorhouse.

255–260 What similarities between poverty and wealth does Thoreau find? What benefits of poverty does Thoreau see?

WORDS
TO
KNOW

misgiving (mĭs-gĭv′ĭng) *n.* a feeling of doubt, mistrust, or uncertainty
disreputable (dĭs-rĕp′yə-tə-bəl) *adj.* lacking respectability of character or behavior
abject (ăb′jĕkt′) *adj.* low; contemptible; wretched
vulgar (vŭl′gər) *adj.* coarse; common
dissipation (dĭs′ə-pā′shən) *n.* a reckless waste of resources; wastefulness

the wealth of Croesus, our aims must still be the same, and our means essentially the same. Moreover, if you are restricted in your range by poverty, if you cannot buy books and newspapers, for instance, you are but confined to the most significant and vital experiences; you are compelled to deal with the material which yields the most sugar and the most starch. It is life near the bone where it is sweetest. You are defended from being a trifler. No man loses ever on a lower level by magnanimity on a higher. Superfluous wealth can buy superfluities only. Money is not required to buy one necessary of the soul. . . .

The life in us is like the water in the river. It may rise this year higher than man has ever known it, and flood the parched uplands; even this may be the eventful year, which will drown out all our muskrats. It was not always dry land where we dwell. I see far inland the banks which the stream anciently washed, before science began to record its freshets. Every one has heard the story which has gone the rounds of New England, of a strong and beautiful bug which came out of the dry leaf of an old table of apple-tree wood, which had stood in a farmer's kitchen for sixty years, first in Connecticut, and afterward in Massachusetts,—from an egg deposited in the living tree many years earlier still, as appeared by counting the annual layers beyond it; which was heard gnawing out for several weeks, hatched perchance by the heat of an urn. Who does not feel his faith in a resurrection and immortality strengthened by hearing of this? Who knows what beautiful and winged life, whose egg has been buried for ages under many concentric layers of woodenness in the dead dry life of society, deposited at first in the alburnum of the green and living tree, which has been gradually converted into the semblance of its well-seasoned tomb,—heard perchance gnawing out now for years by the astonished family of man, as they sat round the festive board,—may unexpectedly come forth from amidst society's most trivial and handselled furniture, to enjoy its perfect summer life at last!

I do not say that John or Jonathan will realize all this; but such is the character of that morrow which mere lapse of time can never make to dawn. The light which puts out our eyes is darkness to us. Only that day dawns to which we are awake. There is more day to dawn. The sun is but a morning star. ❖

279 Croesus (krē′səs): a king of Lydia (now part of Turkey) in the sixth century B.C. who became legendary for his great wealth.

299–317 What is the message of this famous parable of the "strong and beautiful bug"?

312 alburnum (ăl-bûr′nəm): the part of a tree's trunk through which sap flows.

316 handselled: cheap; discounted; bought from a traveling salesman.

318 John or Jonathan: the common man. Thoreau's use of familiar given names here is similar to that in the expression "every Tom, Dick, and Harry."

WORDS
TO   **magnanimity** (măg′nə-nĭm′ĭ-tē) *n.* generosity
KNOW

Thinking through the LITERATURE

Connect to the Literature

1. **What Do You Think?**
Would you like to live in a cabin in the woods as Thoreau did? Share your thoughts with a classmate.

Comprehension Check
• What does Thoreau advise people to do so that their lives will not be "frittered away by detail"?
• What is Thoreau's advice to the poor?

Think Critically

2. How would you explain Thoreau's reasons for leaving Walden Pond?

THINK ABOUT
• the meaning of the statement "I had several more lives to live"
• the parable of the bug in the apple-tree
• Thoreau's ideas about tradition, conformity, and success

3. What do you think is the most valuable lesson that Thoreau learned from his experience of living in the woods?

4. In these excerpts from *Walden*, Thoreau frequently discusses what is not important. What do you think *was* important to him?

5. **ACTIVE READING** **EVALUATING AUTHOR'S OBSERVATIONS**
Look over the aphorisms you copied into your **READER'S NOTEBOOK** and your evaluations of them. Which one comes closest to expressing one of your own views about life? Which one is most opposed to your views? Explain your answers.

Extend Interpretations

6. **The Writer's Style** Thoreau is fond of **paradoxes,** statements that seem to contradict themselves but are nevertheless true. For example, he writes, "I did not wish to live what was not life" (page 383) and "We are determined to be starved before we are hungry" (page 384). Tell what you think he means by each of these statements. What other paradoxes can you find in these excerpts?

7. **Comparing Texts** What connections do you see between the ideas expressed in *Walden* and those expressed in "Civil Disobedience" or Emerson's "Self-Reliance"?

8. **Connect to Life** Consider the experiences that you identified for the Connect to Your Life activity on page 381. How do your desires compare with Thoreau's wish to live simply and deliberately in the woods?

Literary Analysis

NATURE WRITING **Nature writing** is a term for a type of essay in which the writer uses firsthand observations to explore the mysteries of the human relationship with nature. According to Frank Stewart in *A Natural History of Nature Writing,* nature writers are "moved by the joyous, wild, and dazzling beauty in the world." Thoreau, the father of American nature writing, was renowned for his understanding of nature's ways through patient, frequent, careful observations of his surroundings. He used richly poetic language to convey what he learned from his observations.

Cooperative Learning Activity Work with a small group to read aloud and discuss one or more passages from *Walden,* such as the excerpt "Solitude," on pages 386–387. Then discuss Thoreau's observations of nature and his insights about life. Finally, list two or three words you would use to describe Thoreau's relationship with nature.

REVIEW **FIGURATIVE LANGUAGE** Thoreau was a poet as well as an essayist, and in *Walden* he used striking figurative language to express abstract concepts. Consider the **metaphor** "Time is but the stream I go a-fishing in." Try to convey the same idea without using figurative language. Find other good examples of figurative language—**metaphor, simile,** and **personification**—in these excerpts from *Walden.*

Writing Options

1. Letter from Walden Pond

Imagine that you are Thoreau and that you have been living at Walden Pond for one month. Your parents have asked you to come back to town, get a real job, and settle down. Write a letter to them explaining why you want to continue living at Walden Pond.

2. Interpretive Essay

One of the well-known quotations from Walden is "Our lives are frittered away by detail." Write an essay explaining what you think this quotation means. Use examples to elaborate your ideas.

3. Nature Writing

Spend one hour alone closely observing nature. You might go to a forest preserve or sit in your own backyard. Draft an informal essay, modeled on *Walden,* to describe your thoughts and feelings.

Activities & Explorations

Photo Essay Take a series of photographs of a pond or forest at different times of the day. Mount the photos on poster board. Try to convey the feeling of Thoreau's experience at Walden. Use quotations from Thoreau as captions for some of your photos. ~ **VIEWING AND REPRESENTING**

Inquiry & Research

Walden Today Walden Pond is now a state reservation where thousands swim, fish, and hike each year. Some people believe that overuse is destroying Walden Pond and that the area should be made into a limited-use nature preserve. Others say that Walden should remain freely accessible to everyone. Research the current condition of Walden Pond and hold a debate on this issue.

 More Online: Research Starter
www.mcdougallittell.com

Vocabulary in Action

EXERCISE A: ASSESSMENT PRACTICE For each group of words below, write the letter of the word that is an antonym of the boldfaced vocabulary word.

1. **vulgar:** (a) classy, (b) ordinary, (c) popular
2. **abject:** (a) appropriate, (b) accidental, (c) lofty
3. **disreputable:** (a) honorable, (b) famous, (c) noticeable
4. **mean:** (a) predictable, (b) superior, (c) basic
5. **congenial:** (a) illegal, (b) sophisticated, (c) incompatible
6. **magnanimity:** (a) selfishness, (b) rejection, (c) fragility
7. **sublime:** (a) exciting, (b) average, (c) excessive
8. **rudiment:** (a) completion, (b) estimation, (c) delicacy
9. **serenity:** (a) stupidity, (b) chaos, (c) peace
10. **dissipation:** (a) greed, (b) honesty, (c) thrift

EXERCISE B: IDIOMS Write the vocabulary word, not used in Exercise A, that is suggested by each set of familiar expressions.

1. That's the way the cookie crumbles. You can't fight city hall. Like it or lump it.
2. ants in your pants; on pins and needles; climbing the walls
3. Haste makes waste. Look before you leap. Wear your thinking cap.
4. year in, year out; for a month of Sundays; not a flash in the pan
5. smell a rat; think something's fishy; have second thoughts

Building Vocabulary
Several Words to Know in this lesson have multiple meanings. For an in-depth lesson on choosing the right meaning, see page 630.

WORDS TO KNOW				
abject	disreputable	mean	perturbation	serenity
congenial	dissipation	misgiving	resignation	sublime
deliberately	magnanimity	perennial	rudiment	vulgar

Form in Poetry

The Shapes and Sounds of Poetry

All works of art have form, a particular organization of parts to make a whole. **Form,** or **structure,** in poetry refers to the way the words are arranged in lines, the way the lines are arranged in stanzas, and the way the units of sound are organized in rhythm and rhyme. In general, poetic forms fall into two categories: conventional form and organic form.

CONVENTIONAL FORM Poems in conventional form follow certain fixed rules: for example, they have a limited number of lines, a specified meter and rhyme scheme, and a definite structure. Such poems are also called **fixed form** poems, and include the **sonnet,** the **ballad,** the **epic,** the **elegy,** the **ode,** the **villanelle,** and **blank verse.** The great English poets before the 19th century, such as William Shakespeare and John Milton, used conventional poetic forms, as did American poets.

ORGANIC FORM The organic form of poetry, also known as **irregular form,** developed in the early 19th century. The English romantic poets wanted more flexible verse forms to fit the new content of their poetry. Unlike the conventional form that provides an ideal pattern for poems to follow, the **organic form** takes its shape and pattern from the content of the poem itself. That is, the form of a poem "grows" naturally out of what the poem says.

Poetic Form in Action

One way to understand the difference between conventional and organic forms is to compare the poetry of Henry Wadsworth Longfellow and Emily Dickinson. Longfellow was somewhat conventional in most of his poems, as shown in the following stanza from "A Psalm of Life." You can hear the regular beat of the poem even without scanning its meter: stressed syllables alternate with unstressed syllables four times in each line. This metrical pattern is called **trochaic tetrameter.** (See the chart on page 142.) The excerpted lines below have a regular meter (even the dash in the second line counts as an unstressed syllable). Longfellow's poems also have a predictable alternating rhyme scheme and punctuation.

> *from* "A Psalm of Life"
>
> Tell me not, in mournful numbers,   *a*
>
> Life is but an empty dream!—   *b*
>
> For the soul is dead that slumbers,   *a*
>
> And things are not what they seem.   *b*
>
> —Henry Wadsworth Longfellow

Now look at the first stanza of a poem by Emily Dickinson. The meter of her poem is also trochaic tetrameter, but notice the missing beat at the end of the second and fourth lines. This rhythmical variation—combined with the first line running on to the second, the unaccented dashes, and the simple rhyme scheme—gives the poem a forward acceleration, even a breathless quality, that fits perfectly with the speaker's feelings of joy and excitement.

> *from* "Exultation is the going"
>
> Exultation is the going   *a*
>
> Of an inland soul to sea,   *b*
>
> Past the houses—past the headlands—   *c*
>
> Into deep Eternity—   *b*
>
> —Emily Dickinson

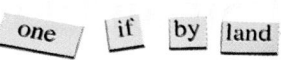

Free Verse

Free verse, also known by its French name *vers libre,* is different from conventional and other organic forms in its lack of regular meter and rhyme. The freedom of free verse extends only so far. Free verse still uses rhythm, although not in the regular patterns of meter. It also depends largely on other sound devices besides rhyme to achieve musical effects, such as various types of repetition.

The great master of free verse in American poetry is Walt Whitman. At a time when all American poetry (and most English poetry) sounded like Longfellow, Whitman created a new form of poetic song:

> ### from "I Hear America Singing"
>
> I hear America **singing**, the varied carols I hear,
>
> Those of mechanics, each one **singing** his as it should be blithe and strong,
>
> The carpenter **singing** his as he measures his plank or beam,
>
> —Walt Whitman

Although Whitman's poem lacks meter, it has a recognizable cadence provided by the repetition of *singing* and the parallel phrasing of the lines themselves. Whitman also uses a related technique called **anaphora** in which the same word or phrase is repeated at the beginning of two or more lines, like this:

> ### from "Song of Myself"
>
> **Or** I guess the grass is itself a child, the produced babe of the vegetation.
>
> **Or** I guess it is a uniform hieroglyphic,
>
> —Walt Whitman

Ironically, repetitive devices such as parallelism and anaphora, like free verse itself, were developed very long ago. You can find evidence of them in the Twenty-third Psalm, for instance. Whitman's resurrection of these ancient devices freed future poets from the conventions that had been layered onto poetic expression for so many centuries and threatened to drain the life out of poetry.

Whitman's revolutionary poems were first published in 1855, but it took most English-language poets until the 20th century to catch up. This part of Unit Three includes poetry by Whitman and by some 20th-century poets who followed his lead.

YOUR TURN Now that you've explored two major poetic forms, do you prefer the conventional form or free verse poetry? Explain.

Strategies for Reading: Understanding Poetic Form

1. Read each poem at least three times: first to get an overall sense of the meaning; then to clarify or deepen the meaning; and finally to study the form. Be sure to read the poem aloud, too.

2. For conventional and organic poems, scan for meter and identify the rhyme scheme. Review the Literary Analysis activities on meter (page 142) and on rhyme scheme (page 347).

3. For free verse poems, identify devices of repetition and parallelism that substitute for patterns of meter and rhyme.

4. **Monitor** your reading strategies and modify them when your understanding breaks down. Remember to use your Strategies for Active Reading: **predict, visualize, connect, question, clarify,** and **evaluate.**

I Hear America Singing
I Sit and Look Out
from Song of Myself

Poetry by WALT WHITMAN

Connect to Your Life

Images of America Many of Walt Whitman's poems contain vivid images of America in the mid-1800s. What images do you think capture the spirit and reality of America today? Share descriptions or sketches with a small group of classmates.

Build Background

A Revolution in Poetry Walt Whitman's first book of poems, *Leaves of Grass,* was so revolutionary in content and form that publishers would not publish it. After Whitman printed the book himself in 1855, many established poets and critics disparaged it. In 1856, the *Saturday Review* suggested that "if the *Leaves of Grass* should come into anybody's possession, our advice is to throw them instantly behind the fire."

Doubtless Whitman was shocked and hurt by such a reception, for he saw himself as capturing the spirit of his country and his times. In the preface to *Leaves of Grass* he wrote, "The United States themselves are essentially the greatest poem." Whitman's images encompass all of American life, including the common and "vulgar." His lines are long and rambling, like the vastly expanding country. His language reflects the vigor and tang of American speech, resounding with new, distinctively American, rhythms. Most of his poems are marked by optimism, vitality, and a love of nature, free expression, and democracy—values often associated with the America of his day.

Focus Your Reading

LITERARY ANALYSIS **FREE VERSE** Walt Whitman is generally credited with bringing free verse to American poetry. **Free verse** is poetry without regular patterns of rhyme and meter. Whitman, however, does use the following poetic devices to create rhythm:

> **Catalog** There are frequent lists of people, things, and attributes.
> **Repetition** Words or phrases are repeated at the beginning of two or more lines.
> **Parallelism** Related ideas are phrased in similar ways.

ACTIVE READING **STRATEGIES FOR READING FREE VERSE**
Use the following strategies as you read Whitman's free verse:
- Read the poems aloud, and listen to the rhythm of the lines.
- Notice where he uses the devices of catalog, repetition, and parallelism.
- Do not spend too much time on any one line; instead, appreciate the sweep of his images and ideas.
- The speaker can be identified with Whitman himself. Build a mental image of the speaker, particularly as you read "Song of Myself."

I Hear America Singing

WALT WHITMAN

I hear America singing, the varied carols I hear,
Those of mechanics, each one singing his as it should be blithe[1] and
    strong,
The carpenter singing his as he measures his plank or beam,
The mason singing his as he makes ready for work, or leaves off work,
5   The boatman singing what belongs to him in his boat, the deckhand
    singing on the steamboat deck,
The shoemaker singing as he sits on his bench, the hatter singing as
    he stands,
The wood-cutter's song, the ploughboy's on his way in the morning, or
    at noon intermission or at sundown,
The delicious singing of the mother, or of the young wife at work, or
    of the girl sewing or washing,
Each singing what belongs to him or her and to none else,
10   The day what belongs to the day—at night the party of young fellows,
    robust, friendly,
Singing with open mouths their strong melodious songs.

---

1. **blithe** (blī*th*): carefree and lighthearted.

Thinking Through the Literature

1. **Comprehension Check** Name two of the people singing in "I Hear America Singing."

2. What do you think singing represents in this poem? Consider who the singers are and what they might be singing about.

3. Why do you think Whitman does not mention wealthy entrepreneurs, prominent leaders, or powerful politicians in this poem?

Cliff Dwellers (1913), George Bellows. Oil on canvas. 40 ⁄₁₆″ × 42 ⁄₁₆″. Los Angeles County Museum of Art, Los Angeles County Fund. Copyright © 1995 Museum Associates, Los Angeles County Museum of Art, all rights reserved.

I Sit and Look Out

WALT WHITMAN

I sit and look out upon all the sorrows of the world, and
    upon all oppression and shame,
I hear secret convulsive sobs from young men at anguish
    with themselves, remorseful after deeds done,
I see in low life the mother misused by her children, dying,
    neglected, gaunt, desperate,
I see the wife misused by her husband, I see the
    treacherous seducer of young women,
5 I mark the ranklings of jealousy and unrequited love
    attempted to be hid, I see these sights on the earth,
I see the workings of battle, pestilence, tyranny, I see
    martyrs and prisoners,
I observe a famine at sea, I observe the sailors casting lots
    who shall be kill'd to preserve the lives of the rest,
I observe the slights and degradations cast by arrogant persons
    upon laborers, the poor, and upon negroes, and the like;
All these—all the meanness and agony without end I
    sitting look out upon,
10 See, hear, and am silent.

GUIDE FOR READING

2 convulsive: intense and uncontrolled.

2–8 Notice how many sorrows the speaker lists in this poem. What effect might this have on a reader?

3 low life: the life of the lower classes.

5 ranklings: bitter feelings or resentments; **unrequited:** not returned.

7 casting lots: deciding by means of a random choice of objects (as in drawing straws).

Thinking Through the Literature

1. **Comprehension Check** Name one of the social injustices described in this poem.

2. How do you evaluate the speaker's response to the sorrows of the world?

 THINK ABOUT
- what the speaker sees and hears
- why the speaker might respond with silence
- whether you think silence is the appropriate response

3. If Whitman were to write this poem today, do you think he would list the same sorrows or different ones? Explain your opinion.

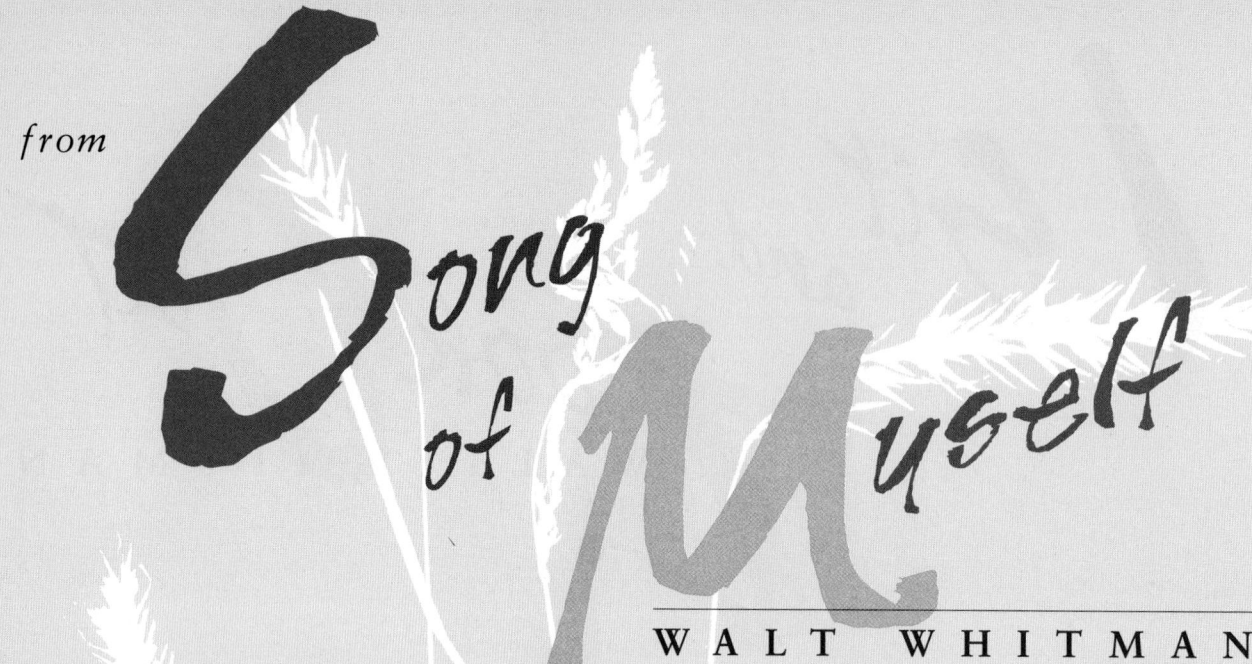

from

Song of Myself

WALT WHITMAN

1

I celebrate myself, and sing myself,
And what I assume you shall assume,
For every atom belonging to me as good belongs to you.

I loaf and invite my soul,
5 I lean and loaf at my ease observing a spear of summer grass.

My tongue, every atom of my blood, form'd from this soil,
    this air,
Born here of parents born here from parents the same, and
    their parents the same,
I, now thirty seven years old in perfect health begin,
Hoping to cease not till death.

10 Creeds and schools in abeyance,
Retiring back a while sufficed at what they are, but never
    forgotten,
I harbor for good or bad, I permit to speak at every
    hazard,
Nature without check with original energy.

GUIDE FOR READING

1–3 Why do you think the speaker identifies the reader with himself at the very beginning of the poem?

10 in abeyance (ə-bā′əns): temporarily set aside.

11 sufficed at: satisfied with.

6

A child said *What is the grass?* fetching it to me with full
    hands,
15 How could I answer the child? I do not know what it is
    any more than he.
I guess it must be the flag of my disposition, out of hopeful
    green stuff woven.

Or I guess it is the handkerchief of the Lord,
A scented gift and remembrancer designedly dropt,
Bearing the owner's name someway in the corners, that we
    may see and remark, and say *Whose?*

20 Or I guess the grass is itself a child, the produced babe of
    the vegetation.
Or I guess it is a uniform hieroglyphic,
And it means, Sprouting alike in broad zones and narrow
    zones,
Growing among black folks as among white,
Kanuck, Tuckahoe, Congressman, Cuff, I give them the
    same, I receive them the same.

25 And now it seems to me the beautiful uncut hair of graves.
Tenderly will I use you curling grass,
It may be you transpire from the breasts of young men,
It may be if I had known them I would have loved them,
It may be you are from old people, or from offspring taken
    soon out of their mothers' laps,
30 And here you are the mothers' laps.

16–25 What metaphors does the speaker use to describe what grass means to him?

18 remembrancer designedly dropt: a purposely dropped token of affection.

21 hieroglyphic: a system of symbols that represent meanings or speech sounds.

24 Kanuck, Tuckahoe, . . . Cuff: slang terms for various groups of people. A Kanuck (now spelled Canuck) is a Canadian, especially a French Canadian; a Tuckahoe is someone from the coast of Virginia; and a Cuff is an African American.

25–33 The speaker presents the grass as "the uncut hair of graves." Who are the dead that he includes in this extended metaphor?

27 transpire: emerge; ooze out.

This grass is very dark to be from the white heads of old
    mothers,
Darker than the colorless beards of old men,
Dark to come from under the faint red roofs of mouths.

O I perceive after all so many uttering tongues,
35 And I perceive they do not come from the roofs of mouths
    for nothing.

I wish I could translate the hints about the dead young
    men and women,
And the hints about old men and mothers, and the
    offspring taken soon out of their laps.

What do you think has become of the young and old men?
And what do you think has become of the women and
    children?

40 They are alive and well somewhere,
The smallest sprout shows there is really no death,
And if ever there was it led forward life, and does not wait
    at the end to arrest it,
And ceas'd the moment life appear'd.

All goes onward and outward, nothing collapses,
45 And to die is different from what any one supposed, and
    luckier.

38–45 What concept of death does
the speaker express in these lines?

45 Why does the speaker think
that to die is "luckier" than what
people suppose?

52

The spotted hawk swoops by and accuses me, he complains
    of my gab and my loitering.

I too am not a bit tamed, I too am untranslatable,
I sound my barbaric yawp over the roofs of the world.

The last scud of day holds back for me,
50 It flings my likeness after the rest and true as any on the
    shadow'd wilds,
It coaxes me to the vapor and the dusk.

I depart as air, I shake my white locks at the runaway sun,
I effuse my flesh in eddies, and drift it in lacy jags.

I bequeath myself to the dirt to grow from the grass I love,
55 If you want me again look for me under your boot-soles.

You will hardly know who I am or what I mean,
But I shall be good health to you nevertheless,
And filter and fibre your blood.

Failing to fetch me at first keep encouraged,
60 Missing me one place search another,
I stop somewhere waiting for you.

48 yawp: loud, rough speech.

49 scud: wind-blown cloud.

53 effuse . . . eddies: scatter my flesh in swirling currents.

54 bequeath: hand over, as if in a will.

61 Why do you think the speaker says he's "waiting for you"?

Connect to the Literature

1. **What Do You Think?** What do you like or dislike or wonder about "Song of Myself"? Share your responses with a partner.

   Comprehension Check
   - In section 6, what does a child ask the speaker to define?
   - To what does the speaker compare himself at the beginning of section 52?

Think Critically

2. Describe your impression of the speaker in this poem. Is he justified in celebrating himself?

   THINK ABOUT
   - the speaker's view of himself
   - the speaker's view of death
   - the speaker's relationships with the reader and with others

3. What do you think grass **symbolizes,** or represents, in this poem?

4. **ACTIVE READING** **STRATEGIES FOR READING FREE VERSE**
   Did you find Whitman's poems easier or more difficult to read than traditional, metered poems such as "A Psalm of Life"? Discuss the reading strategies you found most useful.

5. Review the characteristics of romanticism on page 341. What romantic qualities do you see in Whitman's poems? Cite lines as evidence.

Extend Interpretations

6. **Critic's Corner** Ralph Waldo Emerson, one of Walt Whitman's few early supporters, described *Leaves of Grass* as "the most extraordinary piece of wit and wisdom that America has yet contributed." On the basis of what you know of Emerson from reading "Self-Reliance," what do you think he liked about Whitman's poems?

7. **Comparing Texts** "Ode to Walt Whitman" (pages 406–409) is a tribute to Whitman by the Chilean poet Pablo Neruda. What does Neruda celebrate about Whitman, and how does the style of Neruda's poem imitate Whitman's?

8. **Connect to Life** How would you compare Whitman's images of America in the mid-1800s with the images of today's America you described or sketched earlier?

Literary Analysis

FREE VERSE Whitman is often considered the master of **free verse**—poetry without regular patterns of rhyme and meter. For example, consider lines 3 and 4 from "I Hear America Singing":

The carpenter singing his as he measures his plank or beam, The mason singing his as he makes ready for work, or leaves off work,

These lines flow more naturally than do rhymed, metrical lines and sound more like human speech—precisely the effect Whitman intended. Though free verse lacks meter, it does exhibit a variety of rhythmical devices. For example, in the quoted lines Whitman creates rhythm with **repetition** of the word *singing* and with **parallelism** in phrasing: "The carpenter singing his as he . . . / The mason singing his as he . . . ."

Cooperative Learning Activity With a few classmates, take turns reading aloud passages from "Song of Myself." Identify instances of repetition and parallelism, and of **catalog**—lists of people, things, or attributes. Discuss the appropriateness of free verse for a poem celebrating the self.

Writing Options

1. Literary Review Write a short review of the three Whitman poems, explaining whether you see consistency or contradiction in them. Read or display your review in class.

"I Hear America Singing"

"I Sit and Look Out"

"Song of Myself"

2. Free-Verse Poem Using Whitman's three poems as a model, write a free-verse poem about America today. As a starting point, you might develop one or more of the images you came up with for the Connect to Your Life activity on page 396. Share your poem with the class.

Activities & Explorations

1. Collage of Images Using photos, drawings, or other images, create a collage that captures the spirit of one of the Whitman poems you have read. If you have a drawing program on your computer and access to a scanner, you can combine images you create with ones scanned from magazines or other sources. You might even include lines from the poem in your collage. Display your work in the classroom. **~ VIEWING AND REPRESENTING**

2. Interpretive Dance Create and perform a dance interpretation of one of Whitman's poems. Let the movements of the dance suggest the mood and content of the poem. **~ PERFORMING**

Walt Whitman
1819–1892

Other Works
Democratic Vistas
Specimen Days

Early Experiences "I am large. I contain multitudes," says Walt Whitman in "Song of Myself." It is a fitting description of a man whose writing touches on all aspects of life—the unique and the commonplace, the beautiful and the ugly. Whitman knew country life as well as city life, having grown up in rural Long Island and then in crowded Brooklyn. His varied work life included jobs as an office boy, a typesetter and printer, a school teacher, a carpenter, a newspaper editor and journalist, a nurse during the Civil War, and a government clerk in the Bureau of Indian Affairs.

Revolutionary Poetry His true life's work, however, was a book of poems called *Leaves of Grass,* which he began to work on in 1848. Whitman quit his job, moved in with his parents, and worked part-time as a carpenter while writing his poems. In 1855, unable to find a firm that would publish his 12-poem book, he had it printed at his own expense. Throughout his lifetime, Whitman rewrote, revised, and expanded *Leaves of Grass*; the ninth and final edition in 1891 contained nearly 400 poems.

Literary Recognition Many critics thought the poems in *Leaves of Grass* "barbaric" and "noxious." They were shocked by the poems' radical style and suspicious of the poems' subject matter, particularly the vivid sexual imagery. Other readers, most notably Ralph Waldo Emerson, praised Whitman. Gradually, the literary world recognized the brilliance of the book. By the time the fifth edition was published in 1871, many well-known writers in England and America were traveling to Whitman's home in Camden, New Jersey, to visit him. Today *Leaves of Grass* is often regarded as the greatest, most influential book of poetry in American literature.

Author Activity

Neruda's Whitman Point out lines from the three Whitman poems that support Pablo Neruda's view of Whitman as a friend to the downtrodden and a promoter of "brotherhood on earth."

Ode to Walt Whitman

Pablo Neruda

Walt Whitman's celebration of life reached beyond U.S. shores and inspired modern poets worldwide. Whitman's literary heirs include Pablo Neruda (1904–1973), the Nobel Prize–winning poet from Chile. In a speech delivered in 1972, Neruda expressed his gratitude to Whitman: "I was barely fifteen when I discovered Walt Whitman, my primary creditor. I stand among you today still owing this marvelous debt that has helped me live." The following poem by Neruda echoes Whitman's joyful poetic voice.

I do not remember
at what age
nor where:
in the great damp South
5   or on the fearsome
coast, beneath the brief
cry of the seagulls,
I touched a hand and it was
the hand of Walt Whitman.
10   I trod the ground
with bare feet,
I walked on the grass,
on the firm dew
of Walt Whitman.

15 *D*uring
my entire
youth
I had the company of that hand,
that dew,
20   its firmness of patriarchal pine, its
prairie-like expanse,
and its mission of circulatory peace.

*N*ot
disdaining
the gifts
25   of the earth,
nor the copious
curving of the column's capital,[1]
nor the purple
initial
30   of wisdom,
you taught me
to be an American,
you raised
my eyes
35   to books,
towards
the treasure
of the grains:
broad,
40   in the clarity
of the plains,
you made me see
the high
tutelary[2]
45   mountain. From subterranean
echoes,
you gathered
for me
everything;
50   everything that came forth
was harvested by you,
galloping in the alfalfa,
picking poppies for me,
visiting
55   the rivers,
coming into the kitchens
in the afternoon.

*B*ut not only
soil
60   was brought to light
by your spade:
you unearthed
man,
and the
65   slave
who was humiliated
with you, balancing
the black dignity of his stature,
walked on, conquering
70   happiness.

*T*o the fireman
below,
in the stoke-hole,[3]
you sent
75   a little basket
of strawberries.
To every corner of your town
a verse
of yours arrived for a visit,
80   and it was like a piece
of clean body,
the verse that arrived,
like
your own fisherman beard
85   or the solemn tread of your acacia
legs.

---

1. **column's capital:** the ornamental top part of a column.
2. **tutelary** (tōōt′l-ĕr´ē): serving as a guardian or protector.
3. **fireman below in the stoke-hole:** On steamships, firemen are the workers who shovel coal to fuel the fires that heat the boilers; the rooms in which they work are called stokeholes.

Your silhouette
passed among the soldiers:
the poet, the wound-dresser,
90 the night attendant
who knows
the sound
of breathing in mortal agony
and awaits with the dawn
95 the silent
return
of life.

Good baker!
Elder first cousin
100 of my roots,
araucaria's
cupola,[4]
it is
now
105 a hundred
years
that over your grass
and its germinations,
the wind
110 passes
without wearing out your eyes

New
and cruel years in your Fatherland:
persecutions,
115 tears,
prisons,
poisoned weapons
and wrathful wars
have not crushed
120 the grass of your book;
the vital fountainhead
of its freshness.
And, alas!
those
125 who murdered
Lincoln
now
lie in his bed.
They felled
130 his seat of honor
made of fragrant wood,
and raised a throne
spattered
with misfortune and blood.

---

4. **araucaria's cupola** (ăr′ô-kăr′ē-əz kyōō′pə-lə): the projecting top of a South American evergreen tree.

135 But
       your voice
       sings
       in the suburban
       stations,
140   in
       the
       vespertine[5]
       wharfs,
       your word
145   splashes
       like
       dark water.
       Your people,
       white
150   and black,
       poor
       people,
       simple people
       like
155   all
       people
       do not forget
       your bell:
       They congregate singing
160   beneath
       the magnitude
       of your spacious life.
       They walk among the peoples with your love
       caressing
165   the pure development
       of brotherhood on earth.

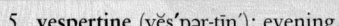

5. **vespertine** (vĕs′pər-tīn′): evening.

Danse Russe

Poetry by WILLIAM CARLOS WILLIAMS

anyone lived in a pretty how town

Poetry by E. E. CUMMINGS

Comparing Literature

Traditions Across Time: Whitman's Heirs Express the Self

E. E. Cummings once remarked, "So far as I'm concerned, poetry and every other art was and is and forever will be strictly and distinctly a question of individuality." Like their literary forefather, Whitman, E. E. Cummings and fellow poet William Carlos Williams prized individuality and self-expression.

Points of Comparison As you read "Danse Russe" and "anyone lived in a pretty how town," notice how these poems, like Whitman's, spotlight the unique perceptions of individuals.

Build Background

Poetic Rebels E. E. Cummings and William Carlos Williams defied many of the conventions of traditional poetry and ushered in innovative techniques and approaches. Both used the American idiom—our characteristic speech—in their poetry, rather than the formal diction of traditional poetry. Williams avoided symbolism and figurative language, instead concentrating on the use of specific concrete images to re-create experience. He wrote the poem "Danse Russe" in 1916, after seeing a performance of the Ballets Russes, a famous Russian ballet company that performed in New York that year. The company featured Vaslav Nijinsky, whose emotional expressiveness, perfect body control, and spectacular leaps led audiences to proclaim him a genius.

Cummings turned poetry upside down, inside out, and on its side. He created striking effects by violating rules of punctuation, spelling, grammar, and capitalization. His poem "anyone lived in a pretty how town," first published in the 1940 volume *50 Poems*, is actually a love story about two people.

Focus Your Reading

LITERARY ANALYSIS **EXPERIMENTAL POETRY** Poetry of the kind you will read—in which the poets explore unusual subjects, invent new forms, order words in unexpected ways, or create striking effects through language—is often labeled **experimental poetry.** Keeping traditional poetry in mind, look for ways in which these poems by Williams and Cummings "break the rules."

ACTIVE READING **MAKING INFERENCES** Making inferences involves "reading between the lines"—making logical guesses based on evidence in the text to figure out what is not directly stated. Reading "anyone lived in a pretty how town" demands that you make many inferences. Consider the first stanza:

> *anyone lived in a pretty how town*
> *(with up so floating many bells down)*
> *spring summer autumn winter*
> *he sang his didn't he danced his did*

READER'S NOTEBOOK
You might record your inferences, and the evidence on which you base them, in a chart like the one shown. Continue to do this as you read.

Inferences	Evidence
"anyone" is a man	the words "he" and "his" in line 4

danse russe

William Carlos Williams

If I when my wife is sleeping
and the baby and Kathleen[1]
are sleeping
and the sun is a flame-white disc
5 in silken mists
above shining trees,—
if I in my north room
dance naked, grotesquely
before my mirror
10 waving my shirt round my head
and singing softly to myself:
"I am lonely, lonely.
I was born to be lonely,
I am best so!"
15 If I admire my arms, my face,
my shoulders, flanks, buttocks
against the yellow drawn shades,—

Who shall say I am not
the happy genius of my household?

---

1. **Kathleen:** the nursemaid for the Williamses'
   children.

Thinking Through the Literature

1. What overall feeling do you get from the poem? Describe this feeling
   to your classmates.
2. Did the last two lines surprise you? Explain what you think they mean.
3. Why do you think the speaker dances and sings, "I am lonely"?
4. How well does the poem fit your ideas about loneliness?

anyone lived in a pretty how town

E. E. Cummings

anyone lived in a pretty how town
(with up so floating many bells down)
spring summer autumn winter
he sang his didn't he danced his did.

5   Women and men(both little and small)
cared for anyone not at all
they sowed their isn't they reaped their
   same
sun moon stars rain

children guessed(but only a few
10   and down they forgot as up they grew
autumn winter spring summer)
that noone loved him more by more

when by now and tree by leaf
she laughed his joy she cried his grief
15   bird by snow and stir by still
anyone's any was all to her

someones married their everyones
laughed their cryings and did their dance
(sleep wake hope and then)they
20   said their nevers they slept their dream

stars rain sun moon
(and only the snow can begin to explain
how children are apt to forget to remember
with up so floating many bells down)

25   one day anyone died i guess
(and noone stooped to kiss his face)
busy folk buried them side by side
little by little and was by was

all by all and deep by deep
30   and more by more they dream their sleep
noone and anyone earth by april
wish by spirit and if by yes.

Women and men(both dong and ding)
summer autumn winter spring
35   reaped their sowing and went their came
sun moon stars rain

Icarus (1947), Henri Matisse. Plate VIII from *Jazz,* École des Beaux Arts, Paris/Art Resource,
New York. Copyright © 1995 Succession H. Matisse/Artists Rights Society (ARS), New York.

Connect to the Literature

1. What Do You Think? Share with a classmate any questions or comments you have about "anyone lived in a pretty how town."

> **Comprehension Check**
> • Who are "anyone" and "noone"?
> • How do the children in the town change when they grow up?

Think Critically

2. Retell in your own words the story that unfolds in this poem. What, in your view, is the point of the story?

THINK ABOUT
> • how "anyone" compares with the other people who live in the town
> • how you would describe the relationship between "anyone" and "noone"

3. **ACTIVE READING** **MAKING INFERENCES** On what evidence did you base some of the inferences you made as you read this poem? Review the chart you created in your **READER'S NOTEBOOK**. Compare your chart and interpretations with those of your classmates.

4. Notice the **refrains**—lines in which the same words are repeated—in this poem. What ideas do they suggest to you?

Extend Interpretations

5. Critic's Corner Williams believed that the goal of a poem must be "to refine, to clarify, to intensify that eternal moment in which we alone live." Do you think "Danse Russe" clarifies a particular moment? Would Cummings agree with Williams's description of the goal of poetry? Defend your opinions.

6. Connect to Life Describe a real-life situation in which a person's individuality is stifled because of peer group pressure to conform. What advice do you think "anyone" in Cummings's poem would offer this person?

7. **Points of Comparison** Of "Danse Russe," "anyone lived in a pretty how town," "I Hear America Singing," and "Song of Myself"—which poem presents the most idealized view of individuality? Explain your opinion.

Literary Analysis

EXPERIMENTAL POETRY Poetry described as **experimental** is often full of surprises—comic situations, conversational speech, playful use of words, descriptions of ordinary objects, and other distinctive elements not found in traditional verse forms.

William Carlos Williams belonged to a group of experimental poets known as the Imagists. Their poems contained sharp, clear images of striking beauty, such as the description of the sun above the trees in "Danse Russe." E. E. Cummings's "anyone lived in a pretty how town" reflects his poetic experiments, such as arranging words in scrambled order.

Paired Activity With a partner, choose about three stanzas of "anyone lived in a pretty how town" to rewrite, using standard capitalization, punctuation, diction and syntax (word order). Share your revision with the rest of the class. In your view, do Cummings's experiments with language and form add to or detract from the meaning of the poem?

Choices & CHALLENGES

Writing Options

1. Diary Confession Assume the identity of the speaker of "Danse Russe" and write a diary entry about the incident presented in the poem, making sure to explain why you are lonely.

2. Headstone Inscription In the style of E. E. Cummings, write an epitaph for the headstone of "anyone."

3. Points of Comparison
Think about the unique personalities you read about in "I Hear America Singing," "Song of Myself," "Danse Russe," and "anyone lived in a pretty how town." Write a reflective essay giving your personal response to the varied ways that people in these poems express their individuality.

Activities & Explorations

Animation, Anyone? Imagine you are planning an animated film based on "anyone lived in a pretty how town." Draw sketches to show how to visualize "anyone" and the world he lives in. Refer to details in the poem for ideas. ~ **ART**.

William Carlos Williams
1883–1963
Other Works
Paterson
In the American Grain
Spring and All

E. E. Cummings
1894–1962
Other Works
&
1 x 1
95 Poems

Poet and Physician Williams was born in Rutherford, New Jersey, to an English father and a Puerto Rican mother. He received his medical degree in 1906 from the University of Pennsylvania, where he met the painter Charles Demuth and the poets H.D. and Ezra Pound. After completing his internship and spending a year in Europe, Williams established his medical practice in Rutherford in 1910.

Keen Observer of the Ordinary Williams wrote when he could, often jotting down ideas on prescription pads or composing poetry on a typewriter hidden in his desk. Convinced that poetry should be grounded in immediate reality, he wrote about the industrialized, urban world of northern New Jersey. Williams published more than 40 books during his lifetime, including poetry, plays, stories, novels, essays, and an autobiography. In 1963, he was posthumously awarded a Pulitzer Prize.

Gifted Child Edward Estlin Cummings, the son of a well-known Unitarian minister, was born in Cambridge, Massachusetts. Raised in a nurturing environment, Cummings began writing at age six and often illustrated his own stories.

Bold Poet During World War I, Cummings served as an ambulance driver in France. His surrealistic and savage account of his war experiences—*The Enormous Room,* published in 1922—propelled him into the public eye. The next year, his first volume of poetry, *Tulips and Chimneys,* was published. After the war, Cummings lived in Paris and then in New York's Greenwich Village, where he spent his days painting and writing. By the 1950s, Cummings's playful, innovative style had made him one of the most popular of American poets. His pioneering experiments with language remain a significant influence on poetry today.

Author Activity

Williams on Video View the videotape featuring William Carlos Williams from the *Voices and Visions* series, available at many public libraries.

Author Activity

Cummings's Voice When Cummings read his poems aloud, he had a powerful effect on his listeners. Find and play audiotapes of his poems.

Ending Poem

Poetry by AURORA LEVINS MORALES *and* ROSARIO MORALES

Tía Chucha

Poetry by LUIS J. RODRIGUEZ

Comparing Literature

Traditions Across Time: Whitman's Heirs Express the Self

In "Song of Myself," Whitman celebrates a distinct individual who also represents the nation at large. The poems you are about to read echo "Song of Myself" in that they too are celebrations of identity—either cultural or individual.

Points of Comparison As you read these poems, consider particular characteristics they have in common with Whitman's poetry.

Build Background

Celebrating Identity "Ending Poem" was written by Aurora Levins Morales and her mother, Rosario Morales, poets of Puerto Rican ancestry. They created this poem to conclude a reading they did together in San Francisco. Rosario Morales explains: "We used lines from the poems we were performing to create a new whole that reflected . . . our differing yet clearly similar experiences as women, as immigrants and children of immigrants." She adds that the poem also reflects "our connection in spirit and community with the children of other migrations." This poem also appears at the end of a book the Moraleses co-authored, *Getting Home Alive.*

In "Tía Chucha," Luis J. Rodriguez celebrates individual identity rather than cultural identity. It is a portrait of the poet's eccentric aunt, who greatly influenced him when he was a child. *Tía* is Spanish for "aunt"; *chucha* is a Spanish nickname that may mean either "sweetheart" or "sly and foxy."

Focus Your Reading

LITERARY ANALYSIS **SPEAKER** Similar to the narrator in fiction, the **speaker** of a poem is the voice that talks to the reader. In some poems, this voice may be the poet's; in other poems, the voice is that of someone or something other than the poet. Try to form a mental picture of the speaker when reading these two poems.

ACTIVE READING **STRUCTURE AND FORM IN POETRY**
The **structure** of a literary work is the way it is put together— the arrangement of its parts. **Form** is a structural term that refers to the arrangement of words and lines in poetry.

"Ending Poem" has an unusual form: notice that every other line is printed in italic type. It is a collaborative poem, with some lines contributed by Aurora and others by Rosario. According to the poets, the alternating typefaces do not signal whose line is whose but instead "blur origins and authorship," making the speaker a "new entity, a collective voice."

To get a sense of this collective voice, try reading the poem aloud, alternating lines with a partner. Also use the form of the second poem to help you focus on each different aspect of the speaker's Tía Chucha.

Aurora Levins Morales

and Rosario Morales

ending poem

I am what I am.
A child of the Americas.
A light-skinned mestiza[1] of the Caribbean.
A child of many diaspora,[2] born into this continent at a crossroads.
5 I am Puerto Rican. I am U.S. American.
I am New York Manhattan and the Bronx.
A mountain-born, country-bred, homegrown jíbara[3] child,
up from the shtetl,[4] a California Puerto Rican Jew.
A product of the New York ghettos I have never known.

10 *I am an immigrant*
and the daughter and granddaughter of immigrants.
We didn't know our forbears'[5] names with a certainty.
They aren't written anywhere.
First names only, or mija, negra, ne,[6] honey, sugar, dear.

15 I come from the dirt where the cane was grown.
My people didn't go to dinner parties. They weren't invited.
I am caribeña,[7] island grown.
Spanish is in my flesh, ripples from my tongue, lodges in my hips,
the language of garlic and mangoes.
20 *Boricua.[8] As Boricuas come from the isle of Manhattan.*
I am of latinoamerica, rooted in the history of my continent.
I speak from that body. Just brown and pink and full of drums inside.

Untitled [The Wedding Quilt] (1981), Rosario Morales.

1. **mestiza** (mĕs-tē′sä) *Spanish:* a woman of mixed racial ancestry, especially one of mixed European and Native American ancestry.

2. **diaspora** (dī-ăs′pər-ə): a migration or scattering of a group of people (here used as a plural).

3. **jíbara** (hē′bä-rä) *Spanish:* a girl or woman of rural Puerto Rico; female peasant.

4. **shtetl** (shtĕt′l): one of the small Jewish communities formerly found in Eastern Europe.

5. **forbears:** ancestors (a variant spelling of *forebears*).

6. **mija** (mē′hä), **negra** (nĕ′grä), **ne** (nĕ) *Spanish:* affectionate terms for girls or women.

7. **caribeña** (kä-rē-bĕ′nyä) *Spanish:* a girl or woman of the Caribbean islands.

8. **Boricua** (bô-rē′kwä) *Spanish:* Puerto Rican.

I am not African.
Africa waters the roots of my tree, but I cannot return.

25 I am not Taína.[9]
I am a late leaf of that ancient tree,
and my roots reach into the soil of two Americas.
Taíno is in me, but there is no way back.

I am not European, though I have dreamt of those cities.
30 *Each plate is different,*
wood, clay, papier mâché, metal, basketry, a leaf, a coconut shell.
Europe lives in me but I have no home there.

The table has a cloth woven by one, dyed by another,
embroidered by another still.
35 I am a child of many mothers.
They have kept it all going
All the civilizations erected on their backs.
All the dinner parties given with their labor.

We are new.
40 *They gave us life, kept us going,*
brought us to where we are.
Born at a crossroads.
Come, lay that dishcloth down. Eat, dear, eat.
History made us.
45 We will not eat ourselves up inside anymore.

And we are whole.

In My Grandmother's Garden (1982),
Rosario Morales.

---

9. **Taína** (tä-ē'nä) *Spanish:* a girl or woman of the
Caribbean Taino Indians. The first native people
encountered by Columbus, the Taino were wiped out
during the Spanish colonization of the 16th century.

Thinking Through the Literature

1. Pick a line from this poem that you like or wonder about. Discuss this line with your classmates.

2. What do you think the **images** of roots, trees, and leaves in lines 24–28 might represent?

3. How do you interpret the last two lines of the poem?

4. Suggest a reason for the title "Ending Poem" other than the writers' use of the poem to end a poetry reading and a book.

Woman with Turban (1985), Gilberto Ruiz. Mixed media on fabric, 36″ × 52″, courtesy of Barbara Gillman Gallery, Miami Beach, Florida.

tía chucha

Luis J. Rodriguez

*E*very few years
Tía Chucha would visit the family
in a tornado of song
and open us up
5   as if we were an overripe avocado.
She was a dumpy, black-haired
creature of upheaval,
who often came unannounced
with a bag of presents
10 including home-made perfumes and colognes
that smelled something like
rotting fish
on a hot day at the tuna cannery.

I didn't learn guitar, but I learned something about her craving for the new, the unbroken ...so she could break it.

They said she was crazy.
15 Oh sure, she once ran out naked
to catch the postman
with a letter that didn't belong to us.
I mean, she had this annoying habit
of boarding city buses
20 and singing at the top of her voice
(one bus driver even refused to go on
until she got off).
But crazy?

To me, she was the wisp
25 of the wind's freedom,
a music-maker
who once tried to teach me guitar
but ended up singing
and singing,
30 me listening,
and her singing
until I put the instrument down
and watched the clock
click the lesson time away.

35 I didn't learn guitar,
but I learned something
about her craving
for the new, the unbroken
. . . so she could break it.
40 Periodically she banished
herself from the family
and was the better for it.

I secretly admired Tía Chucha.
She was always quick with a story,
45 another "Pepito" joke,
or a hand-written lyric
that she would produce
regardless of the occasion.

She was a despot[1]
50 of desire;
uncontainable
as a splash of water
on a varnished table.

I wanted to remove
55 the layers
of unnatural seeing
the way Tía Chucha beheld
the world, with first eyes,
like an infant
60 who can discern
the elixir[2]
within milk.

I wanted to be
one of the prizes
65 she stuffed into
her rumpled bag.

---

1. **despot** (dĕs'pət): a ruler with absolute power.
2. **elixir** (ĭ-lĭk'sər): a medicine believed to have the power to cure all ills.

Connect to the Literature

1. **What Do You Think?**
   What are your impressions of Tía Chucha? Discuss them with your classmates.

   Comprehension Check
   Name one unusual thing that Tía Chucha does.

Think Critically

2. Which lines of the poem do you think describe Tía Chucha most effectively?

3. Do you think you would appreciate or disapprove of a relative like Tía Chucha? Explain your answer.

   THINK ABOUT

   - how her visits affect the speaker's family
   - how others, such as the bus driver, view her
   - what happens when she tries to teach the speaker to play the guitar
   - the way she sees the world

4. As you learned from Build Background on page 416, the Spanish word *chucha* can mean either "sweetheart" or "sly and foxy." What connections can you make between this word's meanings and the speaker's aunt?

5. **ACTIVE READING** **STRUCTURE AND FORM IN POETRY**
   Think about the effect created by the arrangement of lines in "Tía Chucha." How would the effect have been different if Rodriguez had instead described his aunt in prose paragraphs?

Extend Interpretations

6. **Connect to Life** It is sometimes said that people who are "crazy" see the world more clearly than do others. Do you agree or disagree? Explain your opinion, making reference to Tía Chucha and to someone else—for example, a character in a movie or TV show—who reminds you of her.

7. **Points of Comparison** What common characteristics do you see in "Ending Poem," "Tía Chucha," and "Song of Myself"(page 400)?

Literary Analysis

SPEAKER The speaker of a poem, like the narrator of a story, is the voice that talks to the reader. In "Ending Poem," the speaker is a collective voice rather than an individual. The opening line "I am what I am" suggests the speaker's attitude toward herself. She accepts herself unconditionally, making no apologies for herself. In the rest of the poem, the speaker reveals the main source of her self-esteem: her embodiment of an African, European, and Taíno heritage.

Cooperative Learning Activity With a small group of classmates, reread "Tía Chucha." Discuss what you learn or can infer about the speaker. Try rewriting the poem, omitting the references to the speaker, and then decide what is lost or gained in the new version. Prepare a statement about why you think Rodriguez chose to make the speaker such a prominent part of the poem. Share your statement with other groups.

REVIEW **TONE** **Tone** is a writer's attitude toward his or her subject. A writer can communicate tone through **diction** (word choice), choice of details, and direct statements of his or her position. Compare the tone of "Ending Poem" with that of "Tía Chucha." In each poem, what attitude is expressed toward the subject? How intimately is the reader addressed?

Choices & CHALLENGES

Writing Options

1. **Points of Comparison**
Write a dialogue in which the speaker of "Song of Myself" and Tía Chucha exchange views about expressing individuality.

2. **Autobiographical Sketch or Poem** Define your own identity in an autobiographical sketch or poem titled "I Am What I Am." If you like, write a collaborative poem with a partner, modeled on "Ending Poem." Place this piece in your **Working Portfolio.**

3. **Contrast Essay** Consider again the ideas about viewing the world that you discussed for question 6. Then develop those ideas in an essay that contrasts the "crazy" and the so-called normal ways of seeing.

Ways of Seeing	
Normal	**Crazy**
indifferent	full of wonder
perceptive	imaginative

Activities & Explorations

1. **Paired Reading** With a partner, perform a dramatic reading of "Ending Poem" for the class. Include appropriate gestures or pantomimed scenes in your performance. If necessary, ask a Spanish-speaking classmate to help you with difficult pronunciations.
~ SPEAKING AND LISTENING

2. **Monologue** Assume the character of Tía Chucha and perform a monologue in which you express your feelings about your life and your family.
~ PERFORMING

3. **Self-Representation** In "Ending Poem," identity and heritage are described in terms of a tree and a dinner table. Create your own self-representation—perhaps a drawing or a collage of objects to show what contributes to your identity. **~ ART**

Art Connection

Look at the reproduction of Gilberto Ruiz's painting *Woman with Turban* below. What similarities do you see between the woman in the painting and Tía Chucha? What differences?

Woman with Turban (1985), Gilberto Ruiz. Mixed media on fabric, 36″ × 52″, courtesy of Barbara Gillman Gallery, Miami Beach, Florida.

Inquiry & Research

Puerto Rican History Working with a small group of classmates, investigate the history of Puerto Rico. What events caused there to be so many different strains of ancestry among its people? What is the connection between Puerto Rico and New York City?

 More Online: Research Starter
www.mcdougallittell.com

Aurora Levins Morales
1954–

Rosario Morales
1930–

Luis J. Rodriguez
1954–

Other Works
The Concrete River
America Is Her Name
Poems Across the Pavement
Trochemoche

A Blend of Cultures Rosario Morales, a child of Puerto Rican immigrants, grew up in New York City. She married Richard Levins, a son of Jewish immigrants, and in 1951 returned to Puerto Rico with him to learn about the land she felt to be "both mine and not mine." In the early 1960s, she moved back to the U.S. mainland with her husband and her young daughter Aurora. Aurora Levins Morales was raised in New York and Chicago. She was influenced by the rich stories of her parents and her Puerto Rican and Jewish grandparents.

Exploring Identity Both Rosario and Aurora wrote as young children and were inspired to resume writing by the women's liberation movement of the early 1970s. In 1986 they co-authored *Getting Home Alive*, a dialogue in prose and poetry. This book explored their cultural, political, generational, and geographical identities. Aurora's recent books include *Medicine Stories, Writings on Cultural Activism,* and *Remedios,* which presents the history of the Atlantic world through the lives of Puerto Rican women.

Surviving the Streets A son of Mexican immigrants, Luis J. Rodriguez was born in El Paso, Texas, and raised in Los Angeles, California. Growing up surrounded by violence, he barely escaped to reach adulthood and explore his creativity as a writer. In the 1960s and 1970s, Rodriguez became involved with Hispanic gangs in Los Angeles. In *Always Running: La Vida Loca— Gang Days in L.A.,* he describes how he eventually left gang life behind through the help of a counselor.

Becoming a Creative Writer After finishing high school, Rodriguez attended college and at various times worked as a school-bus driver, a truck driver, a factory worker, a carpenter, and a journalist. In addition to writing poetry and his memoirs, he has written articles, reviews, short stories, essays, and screenplays, including one of *Always Running*. Rodriguez told an interviewer, "Despite great odds, today I'm a poet and writer. . . . We all have the capabilities of great art and poetry. It's a matter of tapping into that creative reservoir we contain as human beings. Once tapped, this reservoir is inexhaustible." In 1989, Rodriguez founded Tía Chucha Press, named for his aunt, to publish the first works of emerging young poets.

Gary Keillor

Autobiographical Story by GARRISON KEILLOR

Comparing Literature

Traditions Across Time: Whitman's Heirs Express the Self

Garrison Keillor is a popular radio host and writer. His story "Gary Keillor" is about a love-smitten teenager out to impress the girl of his dreams. Though this light story is a departure in style from the pieces in the first part of this subunit, it too celebrates the self.

Points of Comparison Consider this story's message about individuality and self-expression. Try to connect Keillor's ideas to those of Whitman, Emerson, and Thoreau.

Build Background

Whitman's Elegy for Lincoln The assassination of Abraham Lincoln in 1865, shortly after the close of the Civil War, shocked and grieved the nation. To honor Lincoln's memory, Walt Whitman wrote "O Captain! My Captain!" In this poem Whitman compared Lincoln to a ship's captain who falls dead after guiding his ship safely through a horrific storm. Whitman's elegy figures prominently in the story you are about to read.

Like the main character in Keillor's story, generations of students have memorized Whitman's elegy for Lincoln. Some, like the students in the film *The Dead Poets' Society*, have even declaimed it to the delight of their peers. Here is the first stanza:

> *O Captain! my captain! our fearful trip is done,*
> *The ship has weathered every rack, the prize we sought is won.*
> *The port is near, the bells I hear, the people all exulting,*
> *While follow eyes the steady keel, the vessel grim and daring;*
>   *But O heart! heart! heart!*
>   *O the bleeding drops of red,*
>   *Where on the deck my Captain lies,*
>   *Fallen cold and dead.*

Focus Your Reading

LITERARY ANALYSIS **HUMOR** A literary work that is intended to induce laughter or amusement in the reader is said to be humorous. If you laugh while reading this story, think about why.

ACTIVE READING **PURPOSE FOR READING** In school you are asked to read for a variety of purposes—to find out information, to understand a period in history, to interpret a theme, to take action on an issue, or to discover models for writing. This time your purpose is different. Read this story for enjoyment.

READER'S NOTEBOOK After you finish the story, take a few minutes to make notes about the parts you found most entertaining.

gary keillor

Garrison Keillor

When I was sixteen years old, I stood six feet two inches tall and weighed a hundred and forty pounds. I was intense and had the metabolism[1] of a wolverine. I ate two or three lunches a day and three full dinners at night, as my family sat around the kitchen table and observed, and I cleaned off their plates too when they had poor appetites or were finicky. There was no food I disliked except muskmelon, which smelled rotten and loathsome. Everything else I ate. (It was Minnesota so we didn't have seafood, except fish sticks, of course.) I was a remarkable person. I was a junior in high school, Class of 1960. I was smart, so smart that poor grades didn't bother me in the slightest; I considered them no reflection on my intelligence. I read four books a week, and I sometimes walked home from school, all twelve miles, so I could relive favorite chapters out loud, stride along the shoulder of the highway past the potato farms, and say brilliant and outrageous things, and sing in a big throbbing voice great songs like "Til There Was You" and "Love Me Tender."

I had no wish to sing in front of an audience, songs were a private thing with me. I was an intense person, filled with powerful feelings, and I assumed that I would live alone for the rest of my life, perhaps in a monastery, silent, swishing around in a cassock,[2] my heart broken by a tragic love affair with someone like Natalie Wood,[3] my life dedicated to God.

I was a lucky boy. I had learned this two years before on a car trip to Colorado. My Uncle Earl and Aunt Myrna drove there that summer—he had been stationed in Colorado Springs during the war—along with my cousins Gordon and Mel, and I got to go too. I won that trip by dropping over to their house and being extremely nice. I'd say, "Here, let me wash those dishes." I'd say, "Boy, I'm sure in a mood to mow a lawn." And then she'd offer me a glass of nectar and a piece of angel food cake and I'd eat it and say, "Boy, I was looking at *National Geographic* the other night and they had a big article on Colorado. It was so interesting. Just the different rock formations and things. I don't see how people can look at those mountains and not know there's a God." And she'd smile at me, a good boy who mowed lawns and whose faith was pure, and I got to go. Of course my brothers and sisters were fit to be tied. "How come he gets to go? We never get to go. Oh no, we have

---

1. **metabolism** (mĭ-tăb′ə-lĭz′əm): the set of processes by which food is transformed into energy.
2. **cassock:** an ankle-length garment worn by clergymen.
3. **Natalie Wood:** a glamorous American movie star.

to stay here all summer and work in the garden while he goes riding out to Colorado." They just didn't get it. Trips to Colorado don't fall in your lap. You've got to go out and earn Colorado.

We took off on the trip, and I was a very good passenger. I sat in the favored front seat between my aunt and uncle, looking at the scenery for hours, no stains on my clothes, my face clean, a good strong bladder, never got carsick, and had a subtle sideways technique for picking my nose—you'd never see it even if you looked straight at me. Far off, the mountains appeared, shining on the horizon for almost a whole day, and then we rose up into them—snowcapped peaks, like the last scene in a western in which justice and romance prevail, and when we reached Denver (*EL.5280,* the sign said, exactly a mile), we ate dinner at a Chinese restaurant and my fortune cookie said: "You are enter-prising[4]—take advantage of it." Well, there it was in a nutshell.

The mountains were startling in their whiteness and steepness, the valleys dark in the late afternoon, the peaks glittering in pure sunlight, beautiful stands of light gray-green aspen floating like fog, and my aunt took a picture of me with trees and mountains behind me. Just me, tall and intense. You would never guess I was from Minnesota. I thought, "This is my lucky picture. I'll keep it the rest of my life."

My family lived in the country, along the Mississippi River between Minneapolis and Tryon, and I attended New Tryon High School, which was bulging under a tidal wave of children from new subdivisions on the other side of the river, places with names like Riverview Estates and Woodlawn and Forest Hills. Our side, South Tryon Township, along the West River Road, was still rural, truck farms, and scattered houses on big rolling tracts, and we West River Roaders were the cream of the school. The editor of the school paper, *The Beacon,* Elaine Eggert, was one of us; so were the stars of the debate team and the speech team, three of the class officers, and the chairperson of the spring talent show, Dede Petersen, who rode on my bus.

I had been in love with Dede for two years, in an intense and secret way. She had bouncy blonde hair and wore soft sweaters, plaid skirts, penny loafers and knee socks. One winter day I wrote her a fourteen-page letter (single-spaced) saying that she was my ideal of womanhood, a person of pure taste, excellent judgment, stunning beauty, and natural intelligence, a woman to whom I could pledge myself in a spiritual friendship that would last forever no matter what. If the friendship should turn into physical love, good, and if not, fine. We would be friends for the rest of our lives, our souls communing[5] over vast distances.

I did not, after long thought, give her the letter. I guessed that she might laugh at it and also that her boyfriend Bill Swenson might pound me into the ground. He was an intense person too.

One afternoon riding home on the bus, sitting behind her, I heard her complain to her pal Marcy about the miseries of planning the April talent show. Bill Swenson would be in it, lip-synching "All Shook Up," and he was terrific, but there wasn't much other talent around, nothing compared to last year, when all those guys sang "Bali Hai" with the coconuts on their chests,[6] and the skit about school lunch when the kids pretended to vomit and out came green confetti, and of course last year there had been Barbara Lee. Barbara Lee was the most talented person ever to graduate from our school. She danced, she sang, she did the splits, she played

---

4. **enterprising:** willing to undertake new projects; ambitious.

5. **communing** (kə-myoo′nĭng): talking or meeting in close understanding.

6. **guys sang . . . chests:** In the musical *South Pacific,* sailors stationed on a remote island sing about women while wearing coconut shells (to imitate breasts) and grass skirts; later, a woman sings "Bali Hai," a song about a beautiful, magical island.

Detail of *Play Within a Play* (1963), David Hockney. Oil on canvas and plexiglass, 72″ × 78″. Copyright © David Hockney.

the marimba.[7] She was Broadway bound, no doubt about it.

I leaned forward and said, "Well, I think we have lots of talent." Oh? like who, for example? she said. I said, "Well, I could do something." *You?* she said. "Or I could get together with some other kids and we could do a skit." *Like what?* she said. I said, "Oh, I don't know. Something about the school burning down. It all depends."

"That doesn't sound funny to me," she said.

Marcy didn't think it was funny either.

What burned my toast was her saying *"You?"* when I volunteered to be in her talent show. I was only being helpful, I was not claiming to be another Barbara Lee. I had no interest in the stage at all until I heard her incredulity[8] and amusement—*"You?"*—and then I was interested

---

7. **marimba** (mə-rĭm′bə): a large wooden percussion instrument resembling a xylophone.

8. **incredulity** (ĭn′krĭ-dōō′lĭ-tē): disbelief.

in being interested. A spiritual friendship with Dede was out of the question, if she thought I was the sort of guy you could say "*You?*" to.

No one in our family sang or performed for entertainment, only for the glory of God and only in groups, never solo. We were Christian people; we did not go in for show. But I was an intense young man. Intensity was my guiding principle. And when I thought about joining that monastery after Natalie Wood rejected me and spending my life in the woodshop making sturdy chairs and tables, I thought that perhaps I ought to get in the talent show at New Tryon High first, get a whiff of show business before I gave my life to God.

"Never give up on beauty," she said. "Never compromise your standards out of fear that someone may not understand." Teachers were full of useless advice like that.

It was one of those ugly and treacherous springs in the Midwest, when winter refuses to quit, like a big surly[9] drunk who heads for home and then staggers back for another round and a few more songs that everyone has heard before. It was cold and wet, and we sat day after day in dim airless classrooms, the fluorescent lights turned on at midday, the murky sky and bare trees filling the big classroom windows, pools of oil-slicked rain in the parking lot, the grass in front dead, the Stars and Stripes hanging limp and wet like laundry. In plane geometry, I was lost in the wilderness, had been lost since Christmas, and in history, we were slogging through World War I, and in English class, we were memorizing poems. "These are treasures you will carry with you forever," said Miss Rasmussen, a big woman in a blue knit suit. In her wanderings around the classroom as she talked about poetry and metaphor, she often stopped in the aisle and stood looming above me, her voice overhead, her hand resting on my desk, her puffy white hand and red knuckles and short ringless fingers. Her stopping there

indicated, I knew, her fondness for me. I was the only student of hers who wrote poems. She had even suggested that I memorize and recite one of my own poems. I declined. Part of the memorization assignment was reciting the poem in front of the class. My poems were far too intense and personal to be said out loud in front of people. I was memorizing Whitman's elegy[10] on the death of Abraham Lincoln, "O Captain! My Captain!" I walked home through the rain one cold day crying out, "O Captain! my Captain! our fearful trip is done,/The ship has weather'd every rack,[11] the prize we sought is won."

One day a fuel oil truck backed into our driveway and got stuck in the mud and the driver put it into forward gear and got dug in deeper. He gunned it in reverse and gunned it forward and rocked the truck loose and pulled forward and unwound his hose and started filling our fuel oil tank, but meanwhile he had left deep ruts in my mother's garden and the front yard. She was home alone, washing clothes. She heard the grinding and roaring from down in the laundry room and came outdoors to find her garden dug up and the tulips and irises destroyed, and the driver looked at her and said, "You ought to do something about your driveway." Not a word of apology, acted like it was the driveway's fault. My mother was the quietest, politest person ever, she felt that raising your voice indicated a flawed character, but she put her hands on her hips and said, "Mister, if

---

9. **surly:** bad-tempered; rude.

10. **elegy** (ĕl'ə-jē): a poem lamenting a person's death.

11. **rack:** buffeting (as by a storm).

you can't figure out how to drive a truck, then they oughta find you a job you'd be able to handle." And she told him to get out and she would be sending the company a bill for the flower garden. And he did. And she did. And the company sent us a check and an apology from the general manager, a Harold L. Bergstrom.

It was the first time in my memory that my mother had fought back and raised her voice to a stranger, a watershed[12] moment for me. I heard the story from our neighbor, Mr. Couture, and I admired her so much for standing up to the jerk and defending our family's honor. Her principles had always told her to be quiet and polite and turn the other cheek and never make trouble, but there comes a time to let go of principle and do the right thing. To me, this seemed to open the door to show business.

And then, about a week before the talent show, suddenly I was in. The real power behind the show wasn't Dede, it was Miss Rasmussen, my teacher, the adviser to the talent show, and the day I stood before the class and recited "O Captain! My Captain!" she told Dede to put me in the show. The next day, Miss Rasmussen had me stand up in class and recite it again. It was one of the finest pieces of oral interpretation she had ever seen, she said. She sat in a back corner of the room, her head bowed, her eyes closed, as I stood in front and with dry mouth launched the Captain's ship again, and she did not see the kids smirking and gagging and retching and pulling long invisible skeins of snot from their nostrils when my Captain died and I got to "O the bleeding drops of red,/Where on the deck my Captain lies,/Fallen cold and dead," they rolled their eyes and clutched at their hearts and died. Then, when she stood up, her eyes moist, and clapped, they all clapped too. "Wasn't that good!" she cried. "You really liked it, didn't you! Oh, I'm glad you did! He's going to recite it in the talent show, too! Won't that be nice!" A couple of boys in front clapped their hands over their mouths and pretended to lose

their lunch. They seemed to speak for most of the class.

So I was in the talent show, which I wanted to be, but with an inferior piece of material. I suggested to Miss Rasmussen that "O Captain! My Captain!" might not be right for the talent show audience, that maybe I could find a humorous poem, and she said, "Oh, it'll be just fine," not realizing the gravity[13] of the situation. "Never give up on beauty," she said. "Never compromise your standards out of fear that someone may not understand." Teachers were full of useless advice like that.

I tried not to think about "O Captain." I experimented with combing my hair a new way, with the part on the right. I was handsome at certain angles, I thought, and a right-hand part would emphasize a good angle. I stood at the bathroom mirror, a small mirror in my hand, and experimented holding my head cocked back and aimed up and to the right, a pose favored by seniors in their graduation pictures, which looked good from either side, and reciting "O Captain" with my head at that angle. I had good skin except when it flared up, which it did two days before the show, and it took a long time to repair the damage. There were six children in our family and only one bathroom, but I spent fifteen minutes behind a locked door doing surgery and applying alcohol and cold packs and skin-toned cream. The little kids stood banging on the door, pleading to use the toilet. I said, "Well, how bad do you have to go?" I was the one in show business, after all.

I worked on "O Captain" so that every line was set in my head. I recited it to myself in the mirror ("O Captain! O Captain! the fateful day is done,/Your blemishes have disappeared, the skin you sought is won") and for my mother, who said I was holding my head at an unnatural angle, and then, the Friday night before the

---

12. **watershed:** marking an important turning point.

13. **gravity:** seriousness or importance.

show, I recited it at a party at Elaine Eggert's house, and there my interpretation of "O Captain! My Captain!" took a sharp turn toward the English stage.

Miss Rasmussen loved a recording of Sir John Gielgud[14] reading "Favourites of English Poetry" and she played it once for our class, a whole hour of it, and from that day, all the boys in the class loved to do English accents. A little lisp, endless dramatic pauses, inflections including shrill birdlike tones of wonderment, and instead of the vowel *o* that delicious English *aaoooww,* a bleating sound not found anywhere in American speech. In the cafeteria, when my friend Ralph Moody came to the table where all of us West River Road rats sat, he stood holding his tray, peering down at us and the welter of milk cartons and comic books and ice cream wrappers and uneaten macaroni-cheese lunches, and after a long pause he cried "Aaaaooooowww," with a shudder, a great man forced to sit among savages. So at the party, surrounded by kids from the debate team and the newspaper, the cream of West River Road society, when Elaine had said for the sixth time, "Do the poem you're going to do on Monday," I reached back for Ralph's *Aaoooww* and did "O Captain" as Sir John might have done it:

Aoowww Cap-tin, myyyyy Cap-tin,
aower _____ feeah-fool twip eez
    done!
Th' sheep has wethah'd _____ eviddy
    rack!
th' priiiiiiize we sot _____ eez won!
But _____ aaaooooooooowwwww
th' bleeeeeeeding drrrops _____ of
    rrred _____
wheahhhh _____
on th' deck _____
myyyy Captin liiiiiiies _____
fallin _____
caaaooooowwwwld _____
and _____ ded!

It was a good party poem. I recited it in the basement, and then everyone upstairs had to come down and hear it, and then Elaine had to call up a friend of hers in the city and I did it on the phone. It got better. "Miss Rasmussen is going to burst a blood vessel," said Elaine. She was a true rebel, despite the editorials she wrote extolling[15] the value of team play and school spirit. I was starting to see some of the virtues in her that I had previously imagined in Dede Petersen.

bill Swenson had worked for weeks on "All Shook Up," and he looked cool and capable backstage before the curtain went up. His hair was slicked down, he wore heavy eye makeup, and he was dressed in a white suit with gold trim, without a single wrinkle in it. He stood, holding his arms out to the sides, avoiding wrinkling, and practiced moving his lips to "A-wella bless my soul, what'sa wrong with me? I'm itching like a man on a fuzzy tree." Dede knelt, shining his black shoes.

He pretended to be surprised to see me. "What are you doing here? You running the p.a. or what?"

I told him I would be in the show, reciting a poem by Walt Whitman.

"Who? Twitman?" No. Whitman, I said.

"Well, I'm glad I don't have to follow that," he said, with heavy sarcasm. He glanced at my outfit, brown corduroy pants, a green plaid cotton shirt, a charcoal gray sweater vest, and said, "You better change into your stage clothes though."

"These are my stage clothes," I said.

"Oh," he said, his eyebrows raised. "Oh." He smiled. "Well, good luck." He did not know

---

14. **Sir John Gielgud:** a highly respected British actor and director.

15. **extolling** (ĭk-stō′lĭng): praising highly.

Illustration by Todd Schorr.

how much luck I had. I had my lucky picture in my pocket, the one of me in the mountains.

Dede brushed his forehead with face powder and poofed up his hair. She gave him a light kiss on the lips. "You're going to be great," she said. He smiled. He had no doubt about that. She had put him high on the program, right after "America the Beautiful," a dramatic choral reading from *Antigone*,[16] a solo trumpet rendition of "Nobody Knows the Trouble I've Seen," and a medley of Rodgers and Hammerstein songs performed on the piano by Cheryl Ann Hansen. Then Bill would electrify the crowd with "All Shook Up," and then I would do "O Captain."

He was Mr. Cool. After Cheryl Ann Hansen's interminable[17] medley, which kids clapped and cheered for only because they knew that her mother had recently died of cancer, Bill grinned at Dede and bounced out on stage and yelled, "Helllll-ooo baby!" in a Big Bopper[18] voice, and the audience clapped and yelled, "Helllooo baby!" and he yelled, "You knowwwwwwww what I like!" and he was a big hit in the first five seconds. He said it again, "Hellllllllllooo baby!" and the audience yelled back, "Hellllllllllooo baby!" And then Dede carefully set the phono-

---

16. *Antigone* (ăn-tĭg′ə-nē): an ancient Greek tragedy by Sophocles.

17. **interminable** (ĭn-tûr′mə-nə-bəl): endless.

18. **Big Bopper:** a popular singer of the late 1950s.

graph needle on the record of "All Shook Up" and Elvis's hoody voice blasted out in the auditorium and Bill started shimmying across the stage and tossing his head like a dustmop. "My friends say I'm acting queer as a bug, I'm in love—huh! I'm all shook up," and on the *huh* he stuck both arms in the air and threw his hip to the left, *huh,* and the audience sang along on the "hmm hmm hmm—oh—yeah yeah"—he was the star of the show right there. Dede ran to look out through a hole in the curtain, leaving me standing by the record player. She was so thrilled, she hopped up and down and squealed.

I could see part of him out there, his white suit hanging loose, the red socks flashing, him pulling out the red satin hanky and tossing it into the audience, *hmmm hmmm hmmm oh yeah yeah,* and at the end the whole auditorium stood up and screamed. He came off stage bright with sweat, grinning, and went back out and made three deep bows, and threw his hip, *huh,* and came off and Dede wiped his face with a towel and kissed him, and the audience was still screaming and whistling and yelling, "More! More!" and right then Bill made his fateful decision. He went out and did his other number.

It was "Vaya con Dios" by the Conquistadores.[19] Dede put the needle down and the guitars throbbed, and the audience clapped, but Bill hadn't worked as hard on "Vaya con Dios" as on "All Shook Up" and his lips didn't synch very well, but the main problem was that "Vaya con Dios" was "Vaya con Dios," and after "All Shook Up" it seemed like a joke, especially since the Conquistadores were a trio and Bill wasn't. Kids started to laugh, and Bill got mad—perhaps "Vaya con Dios" meant a lot to him personally—and his grim face and his clenched fists made "Vaya con Dios" seem even zanier.

> **"More! More!" and right then Bill made his fateful decision. He went out and did his other number.**

Dede ran to the hole in the curtain to see where the hooting and light booing were coming from, and there, standing by the record player, I thought I would help poor Bill out by lightly touching the record with my finger and making the music go flat and sour for a moment.

I t was miraculous, the effect this had, like pressing a laugh button. I touched the black vinyl rim and the music warbled, and fifty feet away, people erupted in fits of happiness. I did it again. How wonderful to hear people laugh! and to be able to give them this precious gift of laughter so easily. Then I discovered a speed control that let me slow it down and speed it up. The singers sounded demented,[20] in love one moment, carsick the next. The audience thought this was a stitch. But Bill sort of went to pieces. One prime qualification for a show business career, I would think, is the ability to improvise and go with the audience, but Bill Swenson did not have that ability. Here he was, rescued from his drippy encore, magically transformed into comedy, and he was too rigid to recognize what a hit he was. His lips stopped moving. He shook his fist at someone in the wings, perhaps me, and yelled a common vulgar expression at someone in the crowd, and wheeled around and walked off.

I didn't care to meet him, so I walked fast right past him onto the stage, and coming out of the bright light into the dark, he didn't see me until I

---

19. **"Vaya con Dios"** (vī′ä kôn dē′ôs) **by the Conquistadores:** A song (whose title is a Spanish expression of farewell, literally "Go with God") that was the biggest hit for this singing group of the 1950s and 1960s.

20. **demented:** mentally ill; insane.

was out of reach. There was still some heavy booing when I arrived at the microphone, and I made a deep English-actor type of bow, with princely flourishes and flutters, and they laughed, and then they were mine all the way. I held on to them for dear life for the next two minutes. I sailed into "O Captain," in my ripest accent, with roundhouse[21] gestures, outflung arms, hand clapped to the forehead _____ I cried:

> AOOWWW CAP-TIN, MYYYYY CAP-TIN,
> AOWER _____ FEEAH-FOOL
>   TWIP EEZ DONE!
> TH' SHEEP HAS WETHAH'D
>   _____ EVIDDY RACK!
> TH' PRIIIIIIIZE WE SOT _____
>   EEZ WON!
> BUT _____ _____
>   AAAAOOOOOOOWWWWW
> TH' BLLEEEEEEEDING DRRROPS
>
> _____
> OF RRRED _____
> WHEAHH _____
> ON TH' DECK _____
> BEEEL SWEN-SON LIIIIIIIES
>
> _____
> FALLIN _____
> CAAAOOOOWWWLD
> _____ AND _____
> _____ DED!

It wasn't a kind or generous thing to do, but it was successful, especially the "AAAAAOOOOO OOWWWWW" and also the part about Bill Swenson, and at the end there was shouting and whistling and pandemonium, and I left the stage with the audience wanting more, but I had witnessed the perils of success, and did not consider an encore. "Go out and take a bow," said Miss Rasmussen, and out I went, and came back off. Dede and Bill were gone. Dede was not feeling well, said Miss Rasmussen.

I watched the rest of the show standing at the back of the auditorium. The act after me was a girl from the wrong side of the river who did a humorous oral interpretation entitled "Granny on the Phone with Her Minister." The girl had painted big surprise eyebrows and a big red mouth on her so we would know it was comedy, and as the sketch went on, she shrieked to remind us that it was humorous. The joke was that Granny was hard-of-hearing and got the words wrong. Then came an accordionist, a plump young man named David Lee, Barbara's cousin, who was a little overambitious with "Lady of Spain" and should have left out two or three of the variations, and a tap dancer who tapped to a recording of "Nola" and who made the mistake of starting the number all over again after she had made a mistake. I enjoyed watching these dogs, strictly from a professional point of view. And then the choir returned to sing "Climb Every Mountain," and then Miss Rasmussen stood and spoke about the importance of encouraging those with talent and how lucky we should feel to have them in our midst to bring beauty and meaning to our lives. And then the lights came up, and my classmates piled into the aisles and headed for the door and saw me standing in back, modest me, looking off toward the stage. Almost every one of them said how good I was as they trooped past— clapped my shoulder, said, hey, you were great, you should've done more, that was funny—and I stood and patiently endured their attention until the auditorium was empty and then I went home.

"You changed the poem a little," Miss Rasmussen said the next day. "Did you forget the line?" "Yes," I said. "Your voice sounded funny," she said. I told her I was nervous. "Oh well," she said, "they seemed to like it anyway."

"Thank you," I said, "thank you very much." ❖

---

21. **roundhouse:** wide and sweeping.

Connect to the Literature

1. What Do You Think? What was your reaction to the outcome of the talent show? Share your comments with classmates.

> **Comprehension Check**
> - What is Gary Keillor's lucky picture?
> - What is Gary's act in the talent show?
> - What does Gary do to Bill Swenson at the talent show?

Think Critically

2. **ACTIVE READING** **PURPOSE FOR READING** What part or parts of this story did you enjoy the most, and why?

3. At the end of the story, why does Gary say to Miss Rasmussen, "Thank you, thank you very much"?

4. How would you describe the most important way in which Gary changes as a result of participating in the talent show?

THINK ABOUT
- his description of himself as an "intense person" early in the story
- his popularity with other students before and after the talent show
- his attitude toward Bill Swenson

5. Consider the important female **characters** in Gary's life: Dede Petersen, Miss Rasmussen, and his mother. Which of them do you think influences him the most? Explain the reasons for your choice.

6. Miss Rasmussen says that talented people "bring beauty and meaning to our lives." Explain whether you agree with her opinion.

Extend Interpretations

7. What If? Suppose Gary had recited Whitman's elegy in a serious way. Would his performance have been so successful? Why or why not?

8. Connect to Life How would you compare Gary's experiences of performing in front of the class with your own experiences?

9. **Points of Comparison** What connections do you see between Gary's conduct in this story and Emerson's ideas in the excerpt from "Self-Reliance"?

Literary Analysis

HUMOR Humor is a term applied to a literary work whose purpose is to entertain and to evoke laughter. In literature there are three basic types of humor, all of which may involve exaggeration or irony. **Humor of situation** is derived from the plot of a work. It usually involves exaggerated events or situational irony, which occurs when something happens that is different from what was expected. **Humor of character** is often based on exaggerated personalities or on characters who fail to recognize their own flaws, a form of dramatic irony. **Humor of language** may include sarcasm, exaggeration, puns, or verbal irony, which occurs when what is said is not what is meant.

Paired Activity Get together with a partner and review your answers to question 2, about the parts of the story that you enjoyed the most. Then choose a passage that you find particularly funny. Reread the passage carefully and identify the source or sources of its humor: plot, character, or language. Then prepare an oral presentation of the passage for your class. As you practice reading the passage, keep in mind that the way the story is told is an important part of its humor. Record and then critique your presentation and those of your classmates.

Writing Options

1. Points of Comparison
How do you imagine Whitman would have responded to Gary's comic recitation of his immortal poem? Write a dialogue between Whitman and Gary, showing Whitman's response. Be true to the ideas about individuality that Whitman expressed in his poetry.

2. Story Sequel Write a sequel to this story showing what happens when Gary and Dede Petersen or Bill Swenson meet the next time.

3. Literary Review In commenting on Lake Wobegon, Keillor's fictional home town, newspaper columnist Mary T. Schmich observed, "[It is] a town that lies not on any map but somewhere along the border of his imagination and his memory." Which elements in "Gary Keillor" might have been based on actual memories? Which might have been a product of Keillor's imagination? Write a review of the story, expressing your views.

Activities & Explorations

1. Drawn-Out Story With a small group, paint or sketch a series of scenes that recapture the major incidents of the story. ~ **ART**

2. Comic Recitation Choose another poem that has become a classic, and perform a comic recitation of it for your classmates. ~ **PERFORMING**

Art Connection

David Hockney's paintings use the stage and stage curtains as intriguing metaphors. Look again at *Detail of Play Within a Play* on page 427. What feelings about performing on stage does this painting suggest? How would you compare these feelings with Gary's in this story?

Garrison Keillor
1942–

Other Works
Lake Wobegon Days
Happy to Be Here
Leaving Home
We Are Still Married
WLT: A Radio Romance

A Lover of Language The storyteller, writer, and radio-show host Garrison Keillor (kē′ lər) was born in Minnesota. He and his family were members of the Plymouth Brethren, a strict religious sect that frowned on dancing, card playing, and other forms of entertainment. As a child, however, Keillor fell in love with both the written and the spoken word. He enjoyed listening to religious parables and tales told by his relatives and other adults, and he developed a keen appetite for reading and writing. "When I was fourteen, I was happy to read all day every day and into the night." In the eighth grade, he submitted poems to the school paper under the name Garrison instead of his given name, Gary, "to hide behind a name that meant strength."

Radio Career In addition to reading and writing, Keillor's other childhood passion was listening to the radio. While attending the University of Minnesota, he worked for the campus radio station, and after graduating from college, he became the host of a classical music show on Minnesota Public Radio. In 1974, Keillor launched the immensely popular radio show *A Prairie Home Companion*, set in the mythical Midwestern town of Lake Wobegon.

Celebrity and Writer In addition to working as the host and writer of *A Prairie Home Companion*, Keillor has written several books. "Gary Keillor" is taken from his 1993 collection of stories, *The Book of Guys*.

Author Activity

Good Humor Keillor is acclaimed for his storytelling skills. Listen to a recording of a humorous story he told on his radio show, *A Prairie Home Companion*. Compare the sources of humor in this oral performance with those in "Gary Keillor."

Comparing Literature: Assessment Practice

Some assessment prompts ask you to synthesize, or pull together, information from several selections to make a generalization about a literary movement or genre. You will now practice writing an essay with this focus.

PART 1 Reading the Prompt

Study the wording of the prompt carefully. Look for clues to help you identify the selections to examine and the basis on which you will examine them.

Writing Prompt

One issue important to 19th-century romantic writers—and to some 20th-century writers they inspired—was the relationship between the individual and society. Summarize the romantic ❶ view of the individual, supporting your ideas with ❷ examples from the works of Thoreau, Whitman, ❸ and other writers you read in Unit 3, Part 1.

STRATEGIES IN ACTION

❶ To **summarize** is to reduce something to its most important features.

❷ Notice the **concept** you will examine and summarize.

❸ Include **details** and **quotations** from selections to illustrate each feature of the concept.

PART 2 Planning a Synthesis Essay

- Create a graphic to record examples.

- Identify lines and passages from romantic writers that relate to your concept—individuality.

- Look for connections among the examples. Determine what three or four features of the concept are suggested by the examples.

- Pull your examples together into a summary statement, or generalization, about the romantic view of the individual.

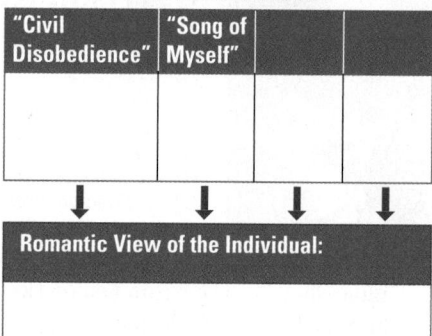

PART 3 Drafting Your Essay

Introduction State your thesis—your main point about the romantic view of the individual. Define "romantic" and name writers in this category.

Organization Present your ideas and examples in a logical way. You might begin with the earliest romantic writers and end with contemporary ones. Or you might discuss the idea about individuality shared by most of the writers and then go on to ideas linked only to one writer.

Conclusion Restate your main point, and leave the reader with a parting thought about the concept, perhaps about its relevance today.

Revision Allow time to review your work. Make sure it is clear, well-supported, and free from mistakes.

Writing Handbook: See page 1278: Order of Importance.

My First Summer in the Sierra

JOHN MUIR

In the tradition of the Romantics' reverence toward the natural world, John Muir (1838–1914) describes his experiences as a sheep herder in the Sierra Nevada Mountains. Muir—a famous naturalist, environmentalist, and writer—detailed the breathtaking scenery of this area, which later would become Yosemite National Park. Muir's book also contains several photographs and his own original sketches.

Pilgrim at Tinker Creek

ANNIE DILLARD

In the same way that Thoreau closely observed Walden Pond, Dillard examines Tinker Creek in Virginia and the creatures that live there. This Pulitzer Prize-winning book is filled with striking descriptions of wildlife and unique insights about the wonders of nature.

And Even *More* . . .

Books

The Enormous Room
E. E. CUMMINGS
A savage and surrealistic account of Cummings's experiences in a French prisoner-of-war camp during World War I.

Leaves of Grass
WALT WHITMAN
Whitman's poetry collection, considered one of the most influential works in American literature.

The Transcendentalists: An Anthology
EDITED BY PERRY MILLER
A wide-ranging collection of works by representative writers of this literary movement.

Other Media

Voices & Visions: Walt Whitman
A documentary about the poet, including dramatic readings of his works. Mystic Fire Video. (VIDEOCASSETTE)

Garrison Keillor's Comedy Theater
Witty monologues and songs from Keillor's live broadcasts that show his talent for self-expression. St. Paul, MN: High Bridge. (SOUND RECORDING)

Gandhi
Academy Award-winning film about India's celebrated leader who used civil disobedience to achieve independence from British rule. Columbia Home Video. (VIDEOCASSETTE)

The Night Thoreau Spent in Jail

JEROME LAWRENCE AND ROBERT E. LEE

Issues of moral and civic responsibility take center stage in this play dramatizing the risks Thoreau took to follow his conscience. As the curtain rises, Thoreau is behind bars—his punishment for committing an act of civil disobedience. When Ralph Waldo Emerson, the famous transcendentalist, visits him, Thoreau challenges him to defy a government that fosters injustice.

Writing Workshop

Sharing your experience. . .

From Reading to Writing In their essays, Emerson and Thoreau reflect on some basic truths about life that they derived from personal experience. Emerson's words, "Whoso would be a man, must be a nonconformist," still prod us to examine our lives today. Like Emerson and Thoreau, you too have personal experiences from which you learn important lessons. A **reflective essay** describes a personal experience and explores its significance. Autobiographies, letters, and memoirs often include reflective writing that gives insight into the writer's actions.

For Your Portfolio

WRITING PROMPT Write an essay in which you reflect on an experience that taught you an important lesson.

Purpose: To share what the experience means to you

Audience: Your classmates, friends, or family

Basics in a Box

Reflective Essay at a Glance

personal experience

thoughts
observations
connections

lesson
learned

RUBRIC Standards for Writing

A successful reflective essay should

- be written in the first person
- describe an important experience in your life or in the life of someone you admire
- use figurative language, dialogue, sensory details, or other techniques to re-create the experience for the reader
- explain the significance of the event
- make an observation about life based on the experience
- encourage readers to think about the significance of the experience in light of their own lives

Analyzing a Student Model

Stephanie Lauer
Bexley High School

Eternally Slow

I am a slow cross-country runner. Not a slow track runner, thank you very much, because anyone can be a slow track runner. After all, running around an oval twice in shorts split up to the waist can only last around five minutes. I'm talking about cross-country running. Over the river and through the woods. For 3.1 miles, and 3.1 miles isn't over in anything like five minutes, especially for those of us who start out with eight-minute miles and get progressively slower on good days.

I will never be fast. But fortunately, I have fellow slow runners to keep me company. There is a special bond between us because we are so obviously not running for awards, or record-breaking times, or even to show off our unathletic legs. We run simply because we love to run, and we love to be part of a team. This love is what keeps us going through five-mile practices that we finish after everyone else has gone home, and through races we finish after the clock has been turned off because we got sick but we had to finish, just to finish. This love is what keeps us going when we start up our 6th hill as the guys are coming down their 15th. But we keep going, and every year a few people who always considered themselves eternally slow discover they can charge up those hills just as fast as anyone else.

Then they become runners with a purpose in addition to love. They still cheer for me and my companions and make jokes about being slow, but they've moved up. They've become someday-varsity runners, the ones coaches look at when they talk about the future. These are the runners who talk about pasta and debate the merits of sports drinks. Exceed and Gatorade become the drinks of choice, replacing the trusty old H_2O preferred by the eternally slow. Someday-varsities are concerned with shoes. The trusty Nikes left over from junior high don't have the gel pads or air capsules or heel counters needed when you're improving by leaps and bounds. And times improve minute by minute as each race they push a little harder and find hidden reserves, allowing them to sprint just a little faster, to push up a hill a little stronger.

RUBRIC IN ACTION

❶ Immediately engages reader by making an unexpected statement

❷ Begins to introduce the theme of the essay

❸ Includes strong examples to show how important running is to the writer

❹ Begins to explain what she learned from her years on the team

❺ This writer uses precise language and images to describe the experiences of runners.
Another Option:
• Use dialogue.

And eventually, the someday-varsities become varsities. They run to be good. Their races are what count for the team. When I watch them at the start with game faces on and toes to the line, I wonder what it would be like to be fast. I might even daydream about it a little, seeing myself pass one, then two, then three people in my sprint to the finish. But as I've grown older and my friends have become the varsity runners, I've realized that in a way, I'm lucky to be slow. Lucky because the coaches don't yell at me to pass another person when my legs are lead weights, even though I try anyway. Lucky because I don't cry before and/or after every race because I could/did let my team down.

But don't get me wrong. The good probably does outweigh the bad for fast runners. I'll never know what it's like to cross the finish line with every other runner behind me. I'll never feel the complete exhaustion and euphoria coming after a championship. And I'll never be able to look at my time and think, "Man, am I good!"

But I don't love running any less. And I think I have a clearer perspective than most because I stay in one place as I watch the somedays become todays, and so-called slow runners become somedays. We all understand that running is about being the best. The best you can be with the body you have. Some of my friends, swimmers and basketball players, ask me why I compete if I never get better. I always tell them it's because of the team and because I am accepted for being my best. Slow runners, fast runners, and all the runners in between give unconditional support. And we are all true cross-country runners—some of us just need a little extra time to get where we're going.

6 Continues telling about her experiences as a runner

7 States the lesson learned from the experience

8 Ends by making an observation about life based on the experience

Writing Your Reflective Essay

❶ Prewriting

To find ideas for your essay, try listing some memorable experiences and think about why you remember them. You might look through **family photograph** albums to help jog your memory.

Here are some other approaches you may wish to try. Make a list of people who inspire you. What have these people done to earn your admiration? Jot down some notes about an incident from each person's life that shows his or her special qualities. See the **Idea Bank** in the margin for more suggestions. After you have selected your experience, follow the steps below.

Planning Your Reflective Essay

▶ **1. Think about your experience.** Why do you remember this experience more clearly than others? What different emotions did you go through during the experience? Did your emotions change?

▶ **2. Explore the significance.** What is the significance of your experience? What is the most obvious meaning to you? What else did your experience teach you? Keep exploring to uncover as many levels of meaning as you can.

▶ **3. Decide on the scope of your essay.** Will you dwell on one example in depth or relate several events to create the impression you want?

▶ **4. Decide on the message you want to convey.** How can you encourage your readers to apply the meaning of the experience to their own lives?

❷ Drafting

A writer's material is what he cares about.

John Gardner

Begin Writing

You might write about your experience as though you were writing a journal entry. Or, you may want to begin your draft by trying out a variety of ideas. Either way, keep writing and let your ideas flow even though you sense problems you'll need to address later.

Organize Your Essay

You might start your paper with an account of your experience and then explain its significance. From that point, go on to discuss the larger lesson about life that the experience has taught you.

Or, you might begin with the larger lesson you want to share with your readers and then go on to describe the experience that helped you learn this lesson.

IDEABank

1. Your Working Portfolio 📁
Look for ideas in the **Writing Options** you completed earlier in this unit:

- **Personal Repsonse,** p. 348
- **Reflective Essay on Wealth,** p. 361
- **Personal Essay,** p. 368
- **Autobiographical Sketch or Poem,** p. 422

2. Brainstorming Maxims
Think about some of the maxims or lessons you learned about life. How did you learn each lesson? Choose one as the subject of your essay.

3. Fables and Proverbs
In a small group, think of all the proverbs and all the fable morals that you can. Discuss how the lessons taught by each might apply to your own experiences.

Writer's Choice

Will your essay focus on telling about the experience in detail, or will you briefly describe the experience and spend most of your essay reflecting upon its significance?

Elaborate on Ideas

Precise, vivid language will help you convey the lesson about life you want to explain. Stephanie Lauer uses precise details about sports drinks and shoes and about coaches and daydreams to add spice to her essay.

After you write a rough draft of your whole essay, set it aside for a while before you go back to revise it. Taking a fresh look will help you see problems that you may have overlooked.

> **Ask Your Peer Reader**
>
> - How would you describe the main point of my essay?
> - Why is this experience important to me?
> - How does this experience relate to something you have thought about?
> - Is any part confusing? Which part?
> - If your interest lagged at some point, what could I do to make that part more interesting?

❸ Revising

TARGET SKILL ▶ AVOIDING CLICHÉS You have worked to use vivid language in your reflective essay. Now make sure that none of your images are clichés, expressions that were once fresh and powerful but have since been worn out through overuse.

> *talk about pasta and debate*
> *the merits of sports drinks.*
> These are the runners who ~~begin to think they know it all.~~
> ^

❹ Editing and Proofreading

TARGET SKILL ▶ POSSESSIVES AND PLURALS As you revise your reflective essay, be sure that you have formed plurals and possessives correctly. To form the possessive of a plural noun that ends in -s, add an apostrophe only. To form the possessive of a plural noun that does not end in -s, add both an apostrophe and an -s.

> They still cheer for our crowds' turtle brigade and make jokes
> *their*
> about ~~they're~~ own slowness, but they've moved up. They've
>
> become someday-varsity runners, the ones in the coaches'
>
> plans for the future.

❺ Reflecting

FOR YOUR WORKING PORTFOLIO How did writing this essay influence your thinking about your experience? What went well as you were writing this piece? What problems did you encounter? Attach your answer to your finished work. Save your essay in your **Working Portfolio.** 🗂

Need revising help?

Review the **Rubric,** p. 438.

Consider **peer reader** comments.

Check **Revising, Editing, and Proofreading,** p. 1269.

Perplexed by possessives?

See the **Grammar Handbook,** p. 1306.

Publishing IDEAS

- Begin a collection of essays about your experiences in order to understand your feelings and give others insight into who you are.
- Submit the essay to your school newspaper or magazine.

More Online: Publishing Options www.mcdougallittell.com

Read this paragraph from the first draft of a reflective essay. The underlined sections may include the following kinds of errors:

- **capitalization errors**
- **incorrect possessive forms**
- **incorrect plural forms**
- **verb tense errors**

For each underlined section, choose the revision that most improves the writing.

It was after midnight when I <u>hear</u> Mr. Pinsky, my neighbor, start to play his
(1)
saxophone. After a few sweet saxophone cries, I recognized the tune of "<u>mood</u>
<u>indigo</u>." This is my favorite of Duke Ellington's <u>melodies</u>. The familiar strains
(2)   (3)
made me <u>forgot</u> my worries, and I fell asleep listening to the sad, lingering
(4)
tones. When I bumped into Mr. Pinsky the next day, I couldn't help myself. I
raved about his playing and <u>had told</u> him I thought he was amazing. Then it
(5)
was <u>Mr. Pinskys</u> turn to amaze me: he offered to give me saxophone lessons!
(6)

---

1. **A.** heared
   B. was hearing
   C. heard
   D. Correct as is

2. **A.** "Mood indigo"
   B. "Mood Indigo"
   C. "mood Indigo"
   D. Correct as is

3. **A.** melody
   B. melodyes
   C. melodys
   D. Correct as is

4. **A.** forgetting
   B. forget
   C. forgotten
   D. Correct as is

5. **A.** told
   B. was telling
   C. has told
   D. Correct as is

6. **A.** Mr. Pinskies
   B. Mr. Pinskys'
   C. Mr. Pinsky's
   D. Correct as is

Need extra help?

See the **Grammar Handbook**

Capitalization Chart, p. 1329

Possessive Nouns, p. 1306

Verb Tense, pp. 1310–1311

Enriching Your Vocabulary

Many modern English words you use daily are based on languages such as Latin and Greek that are thousands of years old. For example, look at the word *consistency* in the quotation to the right.

Consistency, which in this case refers to a steadfastness of thought over time, comes from the Latin root *sist*, meaning "to take a stand." A **root** is the core word part, to which other word parts can be added to create new words. Notice how the idea of

> **A foolish consistency is the hobgoblin of little minds, adored by little statesmen and philosophers and divines.**
> —Ralph Waldo Emerson, "Self-Reliance"

"taking a stand" or never veering from a particular path or vision is at the core of this meaning of *consistency*.

Strategies for Building Vocabulary

Learning how to break up a word into its parts and recognizing the meanings of roots can help you enrich your vocabulary.

❶ **Break Up a Word into Parts** All complex words are ultimately built on roots. Prefixes (like *con-, de-, in-, un-*), and suffixes (such as *-ent, -en, -gy, -tion*) may also be added to a root to form new words. For example, the word *nonconformist* is made up of several word parts:

Prefixes		Root		Suffix
non- + con-	+	form	+	-ist
(not) (same)		(shape)		(person who believes in or does a certain thing)

So, the literal meaning of *nonconformist* is "not-same-shape-person." At first this might look silly, but a closer look shows that a nonconformist is, indeed, someone whose behavior does not "fit in" with the accepted or popular look, custom, or way of thinking. Knowing the meaning of a word's root can often help you determine the meaning of the word.

❷ **Build Word Families** Words that derive from the same roots are known as a **word family.** It is useful to know that the meanings of words in a family are also related to the meaning of the root. For instance, using the information about the root of *nonconformist* in Strategy 1, what can you tell about the meaning of the words below?

uniform, deform, cuneiform, format, formulate

If you guessed that all five words derive from the Latin root *form* and that their meanings all have to do with "shape," you were right! The more roots

you know, the better you will be at deciphering unfamiliar words. Study the charts on this page to learn more about Greek and Latin roots.

Greek Root	Meaning	Word Family
crat	power, strength	autocrat, bureaucrat
phil, philo	having a preference for, loving	philanthropic, philharmonic
phon	sound	phonetics, telephone
phys	nature	physics, physique
poli, polis	city	politics, politician, police
therm	heat	thermometer, thermal

Latin Root	Meaning	Word Family
anim	life, spirit, soul	animated, animosity
dict	say, speak	contradict, edict
domin	master	dominion, predominate
div	divide	dividend, indivisible
(s)pend, pens, pond	hang, weight	pendant, pensive, suspend, appendage
sent, sens	feel	sentiment, sensibility
vid, vis	see	evident, providence, visual

EXERCISE Identify the common root for each word pair below. Then explain how the meaning of the root relates to the meaning of each word in the pair.

1. formative — formal
2. visage — visionary
3. animator — animato
4. division — divorce
5. megaphone — phonograph

Grammar from Literature

Writers use adjectives in both prose and poetry for a variety of reasons.

- To make description more accurate and specific.
- To make writing more colorful and interesting.
- To describe and create characters and settings.

Notice how the adjectives in the following passage add detail and precision while creating a powerful image.

> There a perennial waveless serenity reigns as in the amber twilight sky, corresponding to the cool and even temperament of the inhabitants.
> —Henry David Thoreau, *Walden*

Phrases can also be used as adjectives. In the first example below, a prepositional phrase modifies the noun *waste.* In the second example, *at anguish* modifies *men.*

> I did not for a moment feel confined, and the walls
> prepositional phrase
> seemed a great waste of stone and mortar.
> —Thoreau, "Civil Disobedience"
>
> prepositional phrases
> I hear secret convulsive sobs from young men at anguish with themselves.
> —Walt Whitman, "I Sit and Look Out"

Adjectives also take the form of participles and participial phrases. You may recall that a participle is an *-ing* or *-ed* verb form used as an adjective. In the first example at the top of the next column, the participial phrase and the single-word participles modify *mother.* In the second example, the participial phrase modifies the pronoun *I:*

> participial phrase
> I see in low life the mother misused by her children,
> single-word participles
> dying, neglected, gaunt, desperate.
> —Whitman, "I Sit and Look Out"
>
> participial phrase
> Standing on the snow-covered plain, as if in a pasture amid the hills, I cut my way first through a foot of snow, and then a foot of ice.
> —Thoreau, *Walden*

Using Adjectives in Your Writing Look for opportunities in your writing to add precision by adding detail. Which modifiers will make the picture clearer for your reader? Which ones will make people and places more vivid and believable?

> Imagine a meadow of spring green and a glassy pond in the fading sunlight. The unbroken stillness gives way to the insistent call of a lovesick bullfrog.

Usage Tip To avoid confusion, place an adjective phrase close to the noun it modifies.

> CONFUSING
> Acting bravely, Whitman was inspired by Lincoln.
> CLEAR
> Acting bravely, Lincoln inspired Whitman.

Punctuation Tip Use a comma after an introductory adjective phrase if there is a chance of misreading.

> CONFUSING
> Written near a pond *Walden* is a famous book.
> CLEAR
> Written near a pond, *Walden* is a famous book.

WRITING EXERCISE Rewrite each sentence, adding an adjective or adjective phrase that modifies the underlined word. Use participle forms twice.

1. <u>Writers</u> such as Thoreau stress the importance of individual responsibility.
2. Thoreau describes how <u>people</u> make all of the government's decisions.
3. Sometimes <u>people</u> march off to war because they do not question the laws.
4. Thoreau's <u>book</u> has been an inspiration for many.
5. Thoreau got drinking water by chopping through the <u>ice</u>.

GRAMMAR EXERCISE Rewrite the following sentences, correcting any errors in usage.

1. Traveling across America, ordinary people inspired Walt Whitman.
2. Singing in the mill workers make their spirit heard.
3. Thoreau showed his opposition to government in a jail cell in Massachusetts.
4. Read by students throughout the world "I Hear America Singing" is a powerful expression of democracy.
5. Wishing not to get bogged down in the details of life, Walden was the answer for Thoreau.

The Dark Side of Individualism

American Gothic

Set in an ancient castle where strange and terrifying events take place, Horace Walpole's *The Castle of Otranto* (1765) spawned the Gothic tradition in English fiction. Eighteenth-century readers fell in love with the novel's weird setting and macabre plot, and over the next century, Gothic novels of varying literary quality poured from the presses. In them, some of the greatest creatures of all time were born—including the repulsive monster created from human body parts in Mary Shelley's *Frankenstein* (1818) and the dangerously attractive count in Bram Stoker's *Dracula* (1897). Today, Anne Rice's sexy vampire Lestat owes his immortal life to the Gothic tradition.

The spirit and imagery of the Gothic literary tradition came in part from the Gothic architecture of the Middle Ages. Cavernous Gothic cathedrals with their irregularly placed towers and their high stained-glass windows were intended to inspire awe and fear in religious worshipers. Gargoyles—those carvings of small deformed creatures squatting at the corners and crevices of Gothic cathedrals—were supposed to ward off evil spirits, but they often looked more like demonic spirits themselves. Think of a gargoyle—a grotesque creature—as the mascot of Gothic, and you will get a good idea of the kind of imaginative distortion of reality that Gothic represents.

Another force that gave rise to Gothic literature was the romantic movement. As you have already learned, romanticism developed as a reaction against the rationalism of the Age of Reason. Once the romantics freed the imagination from the lordship of reason, they could follow the imagination wherever it might lead them. For some romantic writers, the imagination led to the threshold of the unknown— that shadowy region where the fantastic, the demonic, and the insane reside. This is Gothic territory. Because of this perspective, the Gothic tradition can be called the dark side of individualism. When romantics looked at the individual, they saw hope (think of Longfellow's "A Psalm of Life"); but when Gothic

Gargoyles on the Cathedral of Notre Dame, Paris. Copyright © Van Phillips/Leo de Wys, Inc.

Bodiam Castle in East Sussex, England. Copyright © Penny Tweedie/Tony Stone Images.

writers looked at the individual, they saw potential evil (think of anything you've ever read by Edgar Allan Poe). While romantic writers were extolling the beauties of nature, the Gothic writers were peering into the darkness at the supernatural.

The Gothic tradition was firmly established in Europe before American writers had made names for themselves. By the 19th century, however, Edgar Allan Poe and Nathaniel Hawthorne, and to a lesser extent Washington Irving and Herman Melville, were using Gothic elements in their fiction.

Edgar Allan Poe, of course, was the master of the Gothic form in the United States. In many of his stories, dark medieval castles or decaying ancient estates provide the setting for weird and terrifying events. Many of Poe's male narrators are insane; his female characters, beautiful and dead (or dying). His plots involve extreme situations— not just murder, but live burials, physical and mental torture, and retribution from beyond the grave. For Poe, it was only in such extreme situations that people revealed their true natures. The Gothic dimension of his fictional world offered him a way to explore the human mind in these extreme situations and so arrive at an essential truth.

Hawthorne also used Gothic elements in his fiction to express what he felt were important truths. However, instead of looking at the mind and its functions (or dysfunctions) as Poe did, Hawthorne examined the human heart under various conditions of fear, greed, vanity, mistrust, and betrayal.

Moonlight, in a familiar room, falling so white upon the carpet, and showing all its figures so distinctly—making every object so minutely visible, yet so unlike a morning or noontide visibility— . . . [has created] a neutral territory, somewhere between the real world and fairyland, where the Actual and the Imaginary may meet, and each imbue itself with the nature of the other. Ghosts might enter here, without affrighting us.

Nathaniel Hawthorne
from *The Scarlet Letter*

The oldest and strongest emotion of mankind is fear, and the oldest and strongest kind of fear is fear of the unknown.

H. P. Lovecraft
from *Supernatural Horror in Literature*

Traditions Across Time: Southern Gothic

After the real horrors of the Civil War, the popularity of Gothic writing waned in the United States. Realism replaced romanticism as the preferred American literary style. The Gothic spirit had to wait until the 20th century before it again found fertile ground for its particular brand of truth telling. That ground was the American South.

Modern Southern writers as diverse as William Faulkner, Carson McCullers, Truman Capote, and Flannery O'Connor are sometimes grouped together in the category of Southern Gothic because of the gloom and pessimism of their fiction. For William Faulkner, the crumbling medieval castle of 19th-century Gothic fiction became the decaying plantation, with its fallen aristocratic family isolated in time and place. Instead of ghostly figures stalking noble heroines, Faulkner gave us the ghost of the past hounding his not-so-noble characters to madness and death.

Coming after Faulkner, Flannery O'Connor saw the pressures of modern life making grotesques of us all. Like Hawthorne, O'Connor was interested in the human heart and its potential for evil. In her view, the old moral and religious order was crumbling. Criminals, con men, and fools—rather than ghosts and goblins—were unleashed upon the world.

Although this part of Unit Three focuses on the Gothic, you can see Gothic aspects in the work of writers in other units, such as Ambrose Bierce in Unit Four, Charlotte Perkins Gilman in Unit Five, and Sylvia Plath in Unit Six. Try identifying what's Gothic about the next horror movie you see or the next Stephen King or Anne Rice novel you read.

American Gothic

Edgar Allan Poe	*A*UTHOR *S*TUDY	450
Edgar Allan Poe	**The Masque of the Red Death**	454
Stephen King	*from* **Danse Macabre**	464
Edgar Allan Poe	**The Raven**	466
	The Fall of the House of Usher	473
Charles Baudelaire	LINK ACROSS CULTURES **Spleen LXXXI**	495

Works by the master of melancholy and two writers he influenced

Nathaniel Hawthorne	**Dr. Heidegger's Experiment** *Is the fountain of youth an illusion?*	500
Herman Melville	LITERARY LINK **Monody** *Mourning Hawthorne's death*	513

COMPARING LITERATURE
Traditions Across Time: Southern Gothic

William Faulkner	**A Rose for Emily** (1930) *The secrets of a human heart*	516
Flannery O'Connor	**The Life You Save May Be Your Own** (1953) *A deceiver is deceived.*	528

EDGAR ALLAN POE

OVERVIEW

Life and Times   450

The Masque of the Red Death
~ SHORT STORY   454

from Danse Macabre by
Stephen King ~ ESSAY   464

The Raven ~ POETRY   466

The Fall of the House of
Usher ~ SHORT STORY   473

Spleen LXXXI by Charles
Baudelaire ~ POETRY   495

The Author's Style   497

Author Study Project   499

"What a strange, though enormously talented writer, that Edgar Poe!"

—Feodor Dostoyevsky

Edgar A Poe

HIS LIFE
HIS TIMES

A Talented, Tormented Writer

During a life marked by pain and loss, Edgar Allan Poe wrote haunting tales in which he explored the dark side of the human mind. A well-read man with a taste for literature, Poe was cursed with a morbidly sensitive nature and made his feelings of sadness and depression the basis of a distinctive body of literary work. Through this Author Study, you will explore the life and work of a mysterious American master.

1809–1849

"AMBITIOUS TO EXCEL" Edgar Allan Poe was born in Boston, Massachusetts, in 1809, one of three children of a couple who toured the East as actors. Before he reached the age of three, however, his father abandoned the family and his mother died of tuberculosis.

John and Frances Allan, a well-to-do merchant and his wife who were both theater fans, took Poe into their Richmond, Virginia, home and became his foster parents. In 1815 the Allans moved to England. Poe's stay in England lasted only

1809
Is born in Boston on January 19

1811
Death of mother; taken in by the Allans

Elizabeth Arnold Poe, mother

1820
Returns from a five-year stay in England

1810   **1815**   **1820**

1812
U.S. declares war on Great Britain.

1819
Washington Irving publishes "Rip Van Winkle."

five years. Mrs. Allan's ill health and the failure of the London branch of her husband's business forced the family to return to Richmond.

Poe continued his education in the United States, showing a flair for languages, particularly Latin and French. Schoolmates noted that he was "ambitious to excel." He started writing poems and by the time he was 16 had enough to fill a book.

A RESTLESS SPIRIT In Poe's young adulthood, the pattern of his life became established: periods of personal difficulty would alternate with promises of a fresh start. In 1826 he began attending the University of Virginia, where his reckless spending habits led to heavy debts. Poe was forced to leave the school. He fled to Boston, attracted by the city's literary activity, and it was there that the anonymous *Tamerlane and Other Poems*, his first book, was published in 1827. Flat broke, the 18-year-old Poe enlisted in the army, but he continued to read widely and to experiment with poetry.

When Frances Allan died in 1829, the grief-stricken John Allan arranged for Poe's release from the army and secured him a place as a cadet in the U.S. Military Academy at West Point. Poe, however, found life at the academy confining and still had his eye on a writing career. By deliberately misbehaving, he managed to get himself expelled.

LITERARY *Contributions*

Best known as a literary critic during his lifetime, today Poe is renowned for his poems and stories in the Gothic tradition (which is discussed in detail on pages 446–448).

Poetic Pioneer Poe regarded his poems as his greatest works. He believed that poetry should be musical, be expressive of beauty, and be composed logically. The following poems reflect Poe's strong views:

> **"The Raven"** (1845)
> **"For Annie"** (1849)
> **"Annabel Lee"** (1849)

Founder of the Short Story Prior to Poe's time, short fiction consisted primarily of loose, rambling tales. It was Poe who insisted that a story or poem should create a single effect, containing no details or incidents that do not contribute to the effect—an idea that would have an enormous influence on subsequent writers. Among the stories in which he put his theory into practice are

> **"The Pit and the Pendulum"** (1842)
> **"The Tell-Tale Heart"** (1843)
> **"The Cask of Amontillado"** (1846)

Originator of the Detective Story With the publication of "The Murders in the Rue Morgue" in 1841, Poe gave birth to a new genre: the detective story. His hero, who solves crimes solely by means of logic, has been the model for scores of later fictional detectives.

1825	1826	1827	1829	1830	1831
A large inheritance restores John Allan's wealth.	Briefly attends the University of Virginia	Publishes *Tamerlane and Other Poems*	Frances Allan dies.	Enters West Point	Expelled from West Point; publishes *Poems*

1825   1830

1821	1825	1826	1828	1830
Charles Baudelaire is born in France.	Erie Canal opens.	Thomas Jefferson and John Adams die on July 4.	Andrew Jackson is elected president.	Emily Dickinson is born.

Charles Baudelaire

A MAN OF LETTERS Poe now began to embark on a literary career in earnest. In 1831, shortly after leaving West Point, he published *Poems,* then moved to Baltimore to live with his aunt Maria Clemm and her young daughter Virginia. There, he began writing short stories, and in 1833 one of these, "MS. Found in a Bottle," won him a sorely needed $50 prize in a literary contest.

In 1834 John Allan died, leaving nothing to his foster son. The next year, Poe moved to Richmond to work for a periodical, the *Southern Literary Messenger.* The popularity of his book reviews in the *Messenger* led to a great increase in the magazine's circulation. In May 1836, now editor of the *Messenger,* Poe married his cousin Virginia; but before eight months had passed, a dispute with the magazine's publisher led him to resign his editorship and move his household to New York City. There, he published the short novel *The Narrative of Arthur Gordon Pym* before deciding to move again in search of work, this time to Philadelphia.

Poe's years in Philadelphia, though not without conflict, would be his most productive. In 1839, he became an editor of *Burton's Gentleman's Magazine,* to which he contributed both stories and reviews. The end of that year also saw the publication of the first collection of his short stories, called *Tales of the Grotesque and Arabesque.* Once again, Poe found himself at odds with his publisher, and he was fired from *Burton's* in mid-1840. In 1841, having failed in an attempt to start his own literary magazine, he accepted a job as editor of *Graham's Magazine,* for which he wrote the ground-breaking detective story "The Murders in the Rue Morgue."

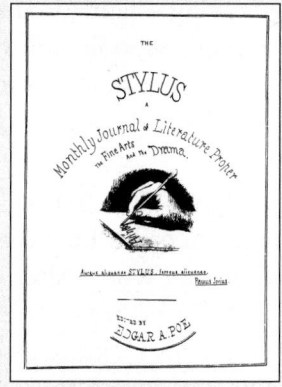

This is Poe's suggested design for the cover of *The Stylus,* his short-lived magazine.

TROUBLES DILUTE SUCCESS Poe's fame increased when a Philadelphia newspaper awarded him a $100 prize for "The Gold Bug" in 1843; and "The Raven," published in 1845, was an enormous success, bringing him the recognition as a poet he had long desired. But personal difficulties continued to dog Poe. Then, in early 1847, he was hit with a major blow: Virginia, who had been in poor health since 1842, died.

1834
Death of John Allan

1835
Becomes editor of the *Southern Literary Messenger*

1836
Marries Virginia Clemm

Virginia Clemm

1839
Becomes an editor of *Burton's Gentleman's Magazine;* publishes *Tales of the Grotesque and Arabesque*

1835   **1840**

1833
Charles Dickens's first works are published in Britain.

1836
Alamo falls; Texas becomes a republic.

1837
Nathaniel Hawthorne publishes first series of *Twice-Told Tales.*

1838
Cherokee driven west along the "Trail of Tears."

1839
Daguerreotype (an early type of photograph) is invented.

In the years following Virginia's death, Poe struggled with despair as well as with his own deteriorating health. In 1849 he became engaged to Elmira Royster Shelton, a widow who had been his boyhood sweetheart. Late that year, he left Richmond for Baltimore, where his health declined quickly. He collapsed on a Baltimore street and was taken to a hospital, where he died a few days later.

POE'S REPUTATION Poe's work generated strong responses: critics either loved him or hated him. Shortly after his death, a one-time friend published a biography that included harsh attacks on Poe's personal life. This work established the view of Poe as a gifted but socially unacceptable writer that would taint his reputation in America for many years. The French poet Charles Baudelaire, however, recognized and championed Poe's achievements, and eventually Baudelaire's favorable view began to influence thinking in the United States. Today, Poe is recognized as a master of poetry, a superb writer of short stories, and a profound explorer of the torments of the human soul.

 More Online: Author Link
www.mcdougallittell.com

Poe's Death: The Mystery Continues

The exact reason for Poe's death in 1849 has never been established, although the most common theory is that he died from heart failure after consuming too much alcohol. In 1996, however, a Baltimore physician came up with a new solution of the mystery. A noted cardiologist and assistant professor of medicine, he was given a description of Poe's last four days but not told the patient's name. After careful study, the physician came up with his diagnosis—the victim, he said, was suffering from a classic case of rabies, caused by the bite of an infected animal. Poe's last days may never be unraveled to everyone's satisfaction, but if this theory is true, his reputation is cleared of at least one dark spot.

Poe's grave in Baltimore, Maryland

1841	1845		1847	1849
Writes "The Murders in the Rue Morgue"	Becomes famous overnight after publication of "The Raven"	Poe lived in this house in New York City.	Death of Virginia	Dies in Baltimore on October 7

1845 — **1850**

1841	1844	1846	1847	1848	1849
A utopian community is established at Brook Farm.	Alexandre Dumas publishes *The Three Musketeers*.	U.S. goes to war with Mexico.	Frederick Douglass founds antislavery paper *The North Star*.	Women's rights convention is held in Seneca Falls, New York.	California gold rush begins.

The Masque of the Red Death

Short Story by EDGAR ALLAN POE

Connect to Your Life

Facing an Epidemic Imagine that your city or town has been struck by an epidemic of a deadly disease that seems to be incurable. The disease spreads rapidly but has not yet reached your neighborhood. How do you think you, other members of your family, and your neighbors would react? With a small group of classmates, discuss some actions that you could take in the crisis, both to protect yourself and to help other people.

Build Background

Plague A deadly disease seems just the thing to inspire Poe's haunted imagination. Before the advances of 20th-century medicine, when people had no antibiotics and little knowledge about how diseases spread, an outbreak of disease could be a source of great terror. Poe's story may have been inspired by an outbreak of bubonic plague that killed about 25 million people in Europe (more than a quarter of the continent's population) in the mid-14th century. Victims experienced high fever, vomiting, pain, and swellings that oozed blood, and they were usually dead within three to five days. In "The Masque of the Red Death," Poe's characters try to find a place of refuge from a similar disease.

A depiction of the Great Plague of London. The Granger Collection, New York.

WORDS TO KNOW **Vocabulary Preview**

contagion	dauntless	impetuosity	pervade	tangible
courtier	grotesque	license	sagacious	untenanted

Focus Your Reading

LITERARY ANALYSIS **ALLEGORY** This story can be read as an **allegory,** a work with two layers of meaning. In an allegorical tale, most of the persons, objects, and events stand for abstract ideas or qualities. For example, a bird might represent freedom. As you read the story, take note of the characters, objects, and events that Poe describes. Think about what each might represent.

ACTIVE READING **CLARIFYING MEANING**

In "The Masque of the Red Death," Poe uses unusual, archaic vocabulary, partly to reinforce the story's setting in the past. The following strategies can help you **clarify** the meanings of particular words and passages:

- Use the Guide for Reading notes, which explain difficult words and passages.
- Reread difficult sentences or passages slowly and carefully. Try to **paraphrase** them—that is, to restate them in your own words.
- **Summarize** difficult passages.
- Use **context clues**—clues in the surrounding phrases—to help you figure out the meanings of unfamiliar words.

READER'S NOTEBOOK Record any questions you have about words or passages as you read the story.

EDGAR ALLAN POE

The Masque of the Red Death

Il ridotto [The foyer] (about 1757–1760), Pietro Longhi. Oil on canvas, 62.5 cm × 51 cm, Fondazione Scientifica Querini Stampaglia, Venice, Italy, Erich Lessing/Art Resource, New York.

THE "RED DEATH" HAD LONG DEVASTATED THE COUNTRY. NO PESTILENCE HAD EVER BEEN SO FATAL, OR SO HIDEOUS. BLOOD WAS ITS

2 **devastated** (dĕv'ə-stā'tĭd): laid waste to.

3 **pestilence** (pĕs'tə-ləns): a very destructive infectious disease.

Avatar and its seal—the redness and horror of blood. There were
sharp pains, and sudden dizziness, and then profuse bleeding at
the pores, with dissolution. The scarlet stains upon the body, and
especially upon the face of the victim, were the pest ban which
shut him out from the aid and from the sympathy of his fellow
men. And the whole seizure, progress, and termination of the disease were the incidents of half an hour.

But the Prince Prospero was happy and <u>dauntless</u> and
<u>sagacious</u>. When his dominions were half depopulated, he sum-
moned to his presence a thousand hale and lighthearted friends
from among the knights and dames of his court, and with these
retired to the deep seclusion of one of his castellated abbeys. This
was an extensive and magnificent structure, the creation of the
prince's own eccentric yet august taste. A strong and lofty wall
girded it in. This wall had gates of iron. The <u>courtiers</u>, having
entered, brought furnaces and massy hammers and welded the
bolts. They resolved to leave means neither of ingress or egress to
the sudden impulses of despair or of frenzy from within. The
abbey was amply provisioned. With such precautions the courtiers
might bid defiance to <u>contagion</u>. The external world could take
care of itself. In the meantime it was folly to grieve, or to think.
The prince had provided all the appliances of pleasure. There were
buffoons, there were improvisatori, there were ballet-dancers,
there were musicians, there was Beauty, there was wine. All these
and security were within. Without was the "Red Death."

It was toward the close of the fifth or sixth month of his seclusion, and while the pestilence raged most furiously abroad, that
the Prince Prospero entertained his thousand friends at a masked
ball of the most unusual magnificence.

It was a voluptuous scene, that masquerade. But first let me tell
of the rooms in which it was held. There were seven—an imperial suite. In many palaces, however, such suites form a long and
straight vista, while the folding doors slide back nearly to the
walls on either hand, so that the view of the whole extent is
scarcely impeded. Here the case was very different; as might have
been expected from the duke's love of the *bizarre*. The apartments
were so irregularly disposed that the vision embraced but little
more than one at a time. There was a sharp turn at every twenty
or thirty yards, and at each turn a novel effect. To the right and
left, in the middle of each wall, a tall and narrow Gothic window
looked out upon a closed corridor which pursued the windings of
the suite. These windows were of stained glass whose color

5 **Avatar** (ăv'ə-tär'): an appearance
in physical form of an unseen force.

7 **dissolution:** death.

8 **pest ban:** a proclamation announcing that a person is afflicted with
the plague.

1–29 How is life outside the abbey
different from life inside?

16 **castellated abbey** (kăs'tə-lā'tĭd
ăb'ē): a fortified building formerly
used as, or built to resemble, a
monastery.

21 **ingress** (ĭn'grĕs') **or egress**
(ē'grĕs'): entry or exit.

23 **provisioned:** provided with
supplies.

27 **improvisatori** (ĭm-prŏv'ĭ-zə-
tôr'ē): poets who recite verses that
they make up as they go along.

34–72 If you are having trouble
visualizing the setting, try drawing
a floor plan of the abbey's suite
of seven rooms and labeling their
colors. The arrangement of the
rooms will be important later on.

varied in accordance with the prevailing hue of the decorations of the chamber into which it opened. That at the eastern extremity was hung, for example, in blue—and vividly blue were its windows. The second chamber was purple in its ornaments and tapestries, and here the panes were purple. The third was green throughout, and so were the casements. The fourth was furnished and lighted with orange—the fifth with white—the sixth with violet. The seventh apartment was closely shrouded in black velvet tapestries that hung all over the ceiling and down the walls, falling in heavy folds upon a carpet of the same material and hue. But in this chamber only, the color of the windows failed to correspond with the decorations. The panes here were scarlet—a deep blood color. Now in no one of the seven apartments were there any lamp or candelabrum amid the profusion of golden ornaments that lay scattered to and fro or depended from the roof. There was no light of any kind emanating from lamp or candle within the suite of chambers. But in the corridors that followed the suite, there stood, opposite to each window, a heavy tripod, bearing a brazier of fire that projected its rays through the tinted glass and so glaringly illumined the room. And thus were produced a multitude of gaudy and fantastic appearances. But in the western or black chamber the effect of the firelight that streamed upon the dark hangings through the blood-tinted panes, was ghastly in the extreme, and produced so wild a look upon the countenances of those who entered, that there were few of the company bold enough to set foot within its precincts at all.

It was in this apartment, also, that there stood against the western wall a gigantic clock of ebony. Its pendulum swung to and fro with a dull, heavy, monotonous clang; and when the minute hand made the circuit of the face, and the hour was to be stricken, there came from the brazen lungs of the clock a sound which was clear and loud and deep and exceedingly musical, but of so peculiar a note and emphasis that, at each lapse of an hour, the musicians of the orchestra were constrained to pause, momentarily, in their performance, to hearken to the sound; and thus the waltzers perforce ceased their evolutions; and there was a brief disconcert of the whole gay company; and, while the chimes of the clock yet rang, it was observed that the giddiest turned pale, and the more aged and sedate passed their hands over their brows as if in confused reverie or meditation. But when the echoes had fully ceased, a light laughter at once pervaded the assembly; the musicians looked at each other and smiled as if at their own nervousness and folly, and made whispering vows, each to the other, that the

65 brazier (brā′zhər): metal pan for holding a fire.

71 countenances (koun′tə-nən-səz): faces.

74 ebony (ĕb′ə-nē): a hard, very dark wood.

77 brazen: brass.

79–94 How do you explain the effect of the ebony clock's chimes on the assembled guests?

82 evolutions: intricate patterns of movement.

WORDS TO KNOW **pervade** (pər-vād′) v. to spread throughout

next chiming of the clock should produce in them no similar emotion; and then, after the lapse of sixty minutes (which embrace
three thousand and six hundred seconds of the Time that flies),
there came yet another chiming of the clock, and then were the
same disconcert and tremulousness and meditation as before.

But in spite of these things, it was a gay and magnificent revel.
The tastes of the duke were peculiar. He had a fine eye for colors
and effects. He disregarded the *decora* of mere fashion. His plans
were bold and fiery, and his conceptions glowed with barbaric
luster. There are some who would have thought him mad. His followers felt that he was not. It was necessary to hear and see and
touch him to be *sure* that he was not.

He had directed, in great part, the movable embellishments of
the seven chambers, upon occasion of this great *fête*; and it was
his own guiding taste which had given character to the masqueraders. Be sure they were grotesque. There were much glare and
glitter and piquancy and phantasm—much of what has been seen
since in *Hernani*. There were arabesque figures with unsuited
limbs and appointments. There were delirious fancies such as the
madman fashions. There was much of the beautiful, much of the
wanton, much of the *bizarre*, something of the terrible, and not a
little of that which might have excited disgust. To and fro in the
seven chambers there stalked, in fact, a multitude of dreams. And
these—the dreams—writhed in and about, taking hue from the
rooms, and causing the wild music of the orchestra to seem as the
echo of their steps. And, anon, there strikes the ebony clock
which stands in the hall of velvet. And then, for a moment, all is
still, and all is silent save the voice of the clock. The dreams are
stiff-frozen as they stand. But the echoes of the chime die away—
they have endured but an instant—and a light, half-subdued
laughter floats after them as they depart. And now again the
music swells, and the dreams live, and writhe to and fro more
merrily than ever, taking hue from the many-tinted windows
through which stream the rays of the tripods. But to the chamber
which lies most westwardly of the seven, there are now none of
the maskers who venture; for the night is waning away; and there
flows a ruddier light through the blood-colored panes; and the
blackness of the sable drapery appalls; and to him whose foot
falls upon the sable carpet, there comes from the near clock of
ebony a muffled peal more solemnly emphatic than any which
reaches *their* ears who indulge in the more remote gaieties of the
other apartments.

But these other apartments were densely crowded, and in them

94 disconcert: confusion.

97 *decora*: fine things.

102–123 Notice the comparison of the masqueraders to dreams, phantasms, and a madman's fancies. How do such comparisons help you imagine the scene?

107 *Hernani* (ĕr'nä-nē): a play by Victor Hugo, first staged in 1830, notable for its use of color and spectacle; **arabesque** (ăr'ə-bĕsk'): characterized by complicated decorations.

124–131 Why do you think none of the revellers venture into the seventh room?

WORDS
TO
KNOW   **grotesque** (grō-tĕsk') *adj.* having a bizarre, fantastic appearance

beat feverishly the heart of life. And the revel went whirlingly on, until at length there commenced the sounding of midnight upon
135 the clock. And then the music ceased, as I have told; and the evolutions of the waltzes were quieted; and there was an uneasy cessation of all things as before. But now there were twelve strokes to be sounded by the bell of the clock;
140 and thus it happened, perhaps, that more of thought crept, with more of time, into the meditations of the thoughtful among those who reveled. And thus,
145 too, it happened, perhaps, that before the last echoes of the last chime had utterly sunk into silence,
150 there were many individuals in the crowd who had found leisure to become aware of the presence of a masked fig-
155 ure which had arrested the attention of no single individual before. And the rumor of this new presence having spread itself whisper-
160 ingly around, there arose at length from the whole company a buzz, or murmur, expressive of disapprobation and surprise—then, finally of terror, of horror, and of
165 disgust.

   In an assembly of phantasms such as I have painted, it may well be supposed that no ordinary appearance could have excited such sensation. In truth the masquerade <u>license</u>
170 of the night was nearly unlimited; but the figure in question had out-Heroded Herod, and gone beyond the bounds of even the prince's indefinite decorum. There are chords in the hearts of the most reckless which cannot be touched without emotion. Even with the utterly
175 lost, to whom life and death are equally jests, there are matters of

144–165 What effect does the strange figure who appears at the stroke of midnight have on the revellers?

Detail of *Adoration of the Magi: Lorenzo il Magnifico as Youngest of Magi* (1459), Benozzo Gozzoli. Palazzo Medici Riccardi, Florence, Italy, Erich Lessing/Art Resource, New York.

171–172 out-Heroded Herod: been more extreme than the biblical king Herod, who ordered the deaths of all male babies up to two years old in an effort to kill the infant Jesus. This expression is used in Shakespeare's *Hamlet*.

WORDS
TO   **license** (līˈsəns) *n.* a lack of restrictions on behavior; freedom
KNOW

which no jest can be made. The whole company, indeed, seemed now deeply to feel that in the costume and bearing of the stranger neither wit nor propriety existed. The figure was tall and gaunt, and shrouded from head to foot in the habiliments of the grave. The mask which concealed the visage was made so nearly to resemble the countenance of a stiffened corpse that the closest scrutiny must have difficulty in detecting the cheat. And yet all this might have been endured, if not approved, by the mad revellers around. But the mummer had gone so far as to assume the type of the Red Death. His vesture was dabbed in *blood*—and his broad brow, with all the features of the face, was besprinkled with the scarlet horror.

When the eyes of Prince Prospero fell upon this spectral image (which with a slow and solemn movement, as if more fully to sustain its *role*, stalked to and fro among the waltzers), he was seen to be convulsed, in the first moment with a strong shudder either of terror or distaste; but, in the next, his brow reddened with rage.

"Who dares?" he demanded hoarsely of the courtiers who stood near him—"who dares insult us with this blasphemous mockery? Seize him and unmask him—that we may know whom we have to hang at sunrise, from the battlements!"

It was in the eastern or blue chamber in which stood the Prince Prospero as he uttered these words. They rang throughout the seven rooms loudly and clearly—for the prince was a bold and robust man, and the music had become hushed at the waving of his hand.

It was in the blue room where stood the prince, with a group of pale courtiers by his side. At first, as he spoke, there was a slight rushing movement of this group in the direction of the intruder, who at the moment was also near at hand, and now, with deliberate and stately step, made closer approach to the speaker. But from a certain nameless awe with which the mad assumptions of the mummer had inspired the whole party, there were found none who put forth a hand to seize him; so that, unimpeded, he passed within a yard of the prince's person; and, while the vast assembly, as if with one impulse, shrank from the centers of the rooms to the walls, he made his way uninterruptedly, but with the same solemn and measured step which had distinguished him from the first, through the blue chamber to the purple—through the purple to the green—through the green to the orange—through this again to the white—and even thence to the violet, ere a decided movement had been made to arrest him. It was then, however, that the Prince Prospero, maddening with rage and the shame of his own momentary cowardice, rushed hurriedly through the six chambers while none followed him on

179 habiliments (hə-bĭl′ə-mənts): clothing.

180 visage (vĭz′ĭj): face.

184 mummer: a person dressed for a masquerade.

188–196 Why does Prince Prospero get so mad?

207–217 Why do you think the masked figure is allowed to walk the length of the rooms uninterrupted?

account of a deadly terror that had seized upon all. He bore aloft a drawn dagger, and had approached, in rapid impetuosity, to within three or four feet of the retreating figure, when the latter, having attained the extremity of the velvet apart-

225 ment, turned suddenly and confronted his pursuer. There was a sharp cry—and the dagger dropped gleaming upon the sable carpet, upon which, instantly after- wards, fell prostrate in death the

230 Prince Prospero. Then, summoning the wild courage of despair, a throng of the revellers at once threw themselves into the black apartment, and seizing the mum-

235 mer, whose tall figure stood erect and motionless within the shad- ow of the ebony clock, gasped in unutterable horror at finding the grave-cerements and corpselike

240 mask, which they handled with so violent a rudeness, untenanted by any tangible form.

And now was acknowledged the presence of the Red Death. He

245 had come like a thief in the night. And one by one dropped the rev- ellers in the blood-bedewed halls of their revel, and died each in the despairing posture of his fall. And the life of the ebony

250 clock went out with that of the last of the gay. And the flames of the tripods expired. And Darkness and Decay and the Red Death held illimitable dominion over all. ❖

Skull (19th or 20th century), artist unknown. Carved and painted wood, 8 ⅞″ × 5 ⅛″ × 6 ½″, National Museum of American Art, gift of Herbert Waide Hemphill, Jr., and museum purchase made possible by Ralph Cross Johnson, Smithsonian Institution, Washington, D.C./Art Resource, New York.

230–242 Poe's language is hard to understand here. Essentially, he says that when a group of revellers rip off the figure's costume, there is nothing underneath.

239 cerements (sĕr′ə-mənts): cloth wrappings for the dead.

253 illimitable dominion (ĭ-lĭm′ĭ-tə-bəl də-mĭn′yən): unlimited power.

WORDS	impetuosity (ĭm-pĕch′oo-ŏs′ĭ-tē) *n.* unthinking action
TO	untenanted (ŭn-tĕn′ən-tĭd) *adj.* not occupied
KNOW	tangible (tăn′jə-bəl) *adj.* able to be touched or felt

Connect to the Literature

1. **What Do You Think?**
   How did you react to the masked figure's first appearance?

   Comprehension Check
   - Why does Prince Prospero close himself and his courtiers off in the abbey?
   - Why does the masked figure's presence cause such a sensation?
   - What happens to the prince and the revellers?

Think Critically

2. What feeling do you think Poe wanted readers to have at the end of the story? Give reasons for your opinion.

3. **ACTIVE READING** | **CLARIFYING MEANING** Refer to questions you may have recorded in your **READER'S NOTEBOOK** about words or passages. Look again at lines 21–29, and recall the techniques you used to clarify your understanding of this passage. How does the passage set up the basic plot of the story?

4. The ebony clock, when it chimes, has the ability to silence the revellers. What might their thoughts be during these still moments?

5. What are your impressions of Prince Prospero?

   THINK ABOUT
   - his plan to escape the Red Death
   - the decorated rooms of the party suite
   - why he becomes angry

6. What message or messages do you see in this story?

   THINK ABOUT
   - what literally happens to the revellers
   - what the Red Death might stand for

Extend Interpretations

7. **Comparing Texts** Compare this story with "The Devil and Tom Walker" (page 349). Which story did you find more horrifying? Cite evidence to support your choice.

8. **Connect to Life** Recall your earlier discussion about what you might do when faced with an epidemic, and think about how people today react to epidemic diseases. Bearing these things in mind, give your opinion of Prospero's reactions.

Literary Analysis

ALLEGORY "The Masque of the Red Death" can be read as an **allegory,** a literary work in which most of the people, objects, and events stand for abstract qualities. Here are some important things to know about allegories:

- An allegory usually has a second level of meaning in addition to its literal meaning.
- Some allegories are intended to teach moral lessons. In the fable of the tortoise and the hare, for example, the actions of the tortoise—the slow, focused, character—are shown as more admirable than those of the cunning but easily distracted hare.
- Stories that are not formal allegories may nevertheless contain some allegorical elements—some objects, people, or events that stand for abstract ideas or qualities.

Paired Activity Review the story to find elements that might have allegorical meanings. Explain what you think is the meaning of each element, as well as how Poe used the elements to convey a moral lesson. You might use a chart like this one to record your interpretations. Compare charts with a partner, and defend your interpretations.

Person, Object, Event	Possible Meaning	Possible Lesson of Story
The prince		
The abbey		
The series of seven rooms		
The clock		
The stranger		

Writing Options

1. Newspaper Editorial Prospero and his friends escape to the abbey after half the people in his lands have died. Pretend that you are a newspaper editor in the prince's domain, and write an editorial giving your opinion of this action.

2. Poetic Retelling In a ballad or another type of narrative poem, retell the story of the prince and his friends. Make sure that you include all the key events.

3. Archaeological Report In the role of an archaeologist who has excavated the remains of Prospero's abbey, write a descriptive report about the remains you have found and the conclusions you have drawn from them.

What I think about Prospero and his friends:

Activities & Explorations

1. A Fantastic Set Design the set for a television version of "The Masque of the Red Death." You can either make drawings or make a model of the set representing the suite of rooms.
~ **ART**

2. Radio Drama Work with a group of classmates to create a radio dramatization of the story. Figure out how you might turn some of the narration into dialogue. You might also include sound effects (chimes, the laughter of revellers) and music to make your dramatization more effective.
~ **PERFORMING**

Inquiry & Research

Medical Detective Find out more about the great outbreak of plague in Europe during the mid-1300s. What caused it? What parts of Europe were affected? How did people try to contain it? Present your findings to the class in an oral report.

 More Online: Research Starter
www.mcdougallittell.com

What caused the plague in the 1300s?

What parts of Europe were affected?

How did people deal with the plague?

Vocabulary in Action

EXERCISE A: WORD KNOWLEDGE In the chart shown here, the Words to Know are grouped under headings that refer to elements in the story. Use each group of words to write two or more sentences about the person or thing named by its heading. You may also want to include in your sentences words that you looked up on your own.

Red Death	Masked Ball	Prince Prospero
contagion	courtier	dauntless
pervade	grotesque	sagacious
untenanted	license	impetuosity
tangible		

EXERCISE B Work with classmates to act out some of the sentences you created for Exercise A.

Building Vocabulary
Many of the Words to Know in this lesson are from French or Latin. For an in-depth lesson on word origins, see page 550.

WORDS TO KNOW				
contagion	grotesque	pervade	tangible	
courtier	impetuosity	sagacious	untenanted	
dauntless	license			

from Danse

Essay by **STEPHEN KING**

Preparing to Read

Build Background

Stephen King is probably the best-known writer of horror fiction since Poe. In 1981, after making a name for himself with a number of bestselling novels, King wrote *Danse Macabre,* a nonfiction work in which he discussed horror in literature and film and examined the psychology of terror. The book's title is a reference to the "Dance of Death," a symbolic representation of Death, in the form of a skeleton, leading people to their graves. In the Middle Ages and the Renaissance, the Dance of Death was a common decoration on cemetery walls and the subject of many artworks. In this excerpt from the book, King discusses the inner tensions that are triggered by spine-tingling tales.

I want to say something about imagination purely as a tool in the art and science of scaring people. The idea isn't original with me; I heard it expressed by William F. Nolan at the 1979 World Fantasy Convention. Nothing is so frightening as what's behind the closed door, Nolan said. You approach the door in the old, deserted house, and you hear something scratching at it. The audience holds its breath along with the protagonist as she or he (more often she) approaches that door. The protagonist throws it open, and there is a ten-foot-tall bug. The audience screams, but this particular scream has an oddly relieved sound to it. "A bug ten feet tall is pretty horrible," the audience thinks, "but I can deal with a ten-foot-tall bug. I was afraid it might be a *hundred* feet tall.". . .

Bill Nolan was speaking as a screenwriter when he offered the example of the big bug behind the door, but the point applies to all media. What's behind the door or lurking at the top of the stairs is never as frightening as the door or the staircase itself. And because of this, comes the paradox: the artistic work of horror is almost always a disappointment. It is the classic no-win situation. You can scare people with the unknown for a long, long time (the classic example, as Bill Nolan also pointed out, is the Jacques Tourneur film with Dana Andrews, *Curse of the Demon*), but sooner or later, as in poker, you have to turn your down cards up. You have to open the door and show the audience what's behind it. And if what happens to be behind it is a bug, not ten but a hundred feet tall, the audience heaves a sigh of relief (or utters a scream of relief) and thinks, "A bug a hundred feet tall is pretty horrible, but I can deal with that. I was afraid it might be a *thousand* feet tall.". . .

The danse macabre is a waltz with death. This is a truth we cannot afford to shy away from.

Macabre

Like the rides in the amusement park which mimic violent death, the tale of horror is a chance to examine what's going on behind doors which we usually keep double-locked. Yet the human imagination is not content with locked doors. Somewhere there is another dancing partner, the imagination whispers in the night—a partner in a rotting ball gown, a partner with empty eyesockets, green mold growing on her elbow-length gloves, maggots squirming in the thin remains of her hair. To hold such a creature in our arms? Who, you ask me, would be so mad? Well . . . ?

"You will not want to open this door," Bluebeard tells his wife in that most horrible of all horror stories, "because your husband has forbidden it." But this, of course, only makes her all the more curious. . . . and at last, her curiosity is satisfied.

"You may go anywhere you wish in the castle," Count Dracula tells Jonathan Harker, "except where the doors are locked, where of course you will not wish to go." But Harker goes soon enough.

And so do we all. Perhaps we go to the forbidden door or window willingly because we understand that a time comes when we must go whether we want to or not . . . and not just to look, but to be pushed through. Forever.

Thinking Through the Literature

1. How do you think King's ideas explain the appeal of Poe's work?

2. What do King's feelings seem to be about the "dancing partner" that the imagination seeks?

3. How might an audience react if a writer or filmmaker did not "open the door and show the audience what's behind it"?

The Raven

Poetry by EDGAR ALLAN POE

(Connect to Your Life)

The Pain of Loss The speaker of "The Raven," one of the most famous poems in American literature, is a man grieving over the death of his beloved, Lenore. To understand the speaker's feelings, think about a time when you or someone you know lost a loved one—a person or a pet—through death or separation. Write a brief account of how you or the other person handled the loss.

Build Background

The Raven's Reputation The raven that visits the poem's speaker lands on a bust of the ancient Greek goddess of wisdom, Athena. To the ancient Greeks, the raven was a bird of prophecy. In Western culture, ravens have long been associated with mystery, evil omens, and death. When writing his poem about loss, Poe first considered using an owl or a parrot as his mysterious visitor, but because of its cultural associations, the raven became his choice.

> WORDS TO KNOW
> **Vocabulary Preview**
>
> | | |
> |---|---|
> | beguiling | implore |
> | decorum | ominous |
> | dirge | placid |
> | discourse | respite |
> | divining | tempest |

Focus Your Reading

LITERARY ANALYSIS **SOUND DEVICES** One distinctive feature of "The Raven" is Poe's handling of **rhyme,** the repetition of similar sounds. Poe used rhymes in the following ways to produce musical effects in the poem:

- **End rhyme:** similar or identical sounds at the ends of lines
- **Internal rhyme:** rhymes within a line
- **Rhyme scheme:** the basic pattern of the end rhymes

Read "The Raven" aloud to better appreciate Poe's use of rhyme and other sound devices. As you read, notice how Poe maintains the rhyme scheme.

ACTIVE READING **DRAWING CONCLUSIONS** Readers **draw conclusions** by using their own knowledge and experiences to make logical guesses about characters and events in what they read. As you read "The Raven," try to draw conclusions about the speaker. Consider the following:

- the events he describes
- his physical condition when the events take place
- his intense sorrow about his loss

In your **READER'S NOTEBOOK,** list your conclusions about the speaker, and explain how you arrived at them.

THE RAVEN

EDGAR

ALLAN

POE

Once upon a midnight dreary, while I pondered, weak and weary,
Over many a quaint and curious volume of forgotten lore—
While I nodded, nearly napping, suddenly there came a tapping,
As of someone gently rapping, rapping at my chamber door.
5   "'Tis some visitor," I muttered, "tapping at my chamber door—
                           Only this and nothing more."

Ah, distinctly I remember it was in the bleak December;
And each separate dying ember wrought its ghost upon the floor.
Eagerly I wished the morrow;—vainly I had sought to borrow
10   From my books surcease[1] of sorrow—sorrow for the lost Lenore—
For the rare and radiant maiden whom the angels name Lenore—
                           Nameless *here* forevermore.

And the silken, sad, uncertain rustling of each purple curtain
Thrilled me—filled me with fantastic terrors never felt before;
15   So that now, to still the beating of my heart, I stood repeating
"'Tis some visitor entreating entrance at my chamber door;—
Some late visitor entreating entrance at my chamber door;—
                         That it is and nothing more."

---

1. **surcease:** an end.

Presently my soul grew stronger; hesitating then no longer,
20   "Sir," said I, "or Madam, truly your forgiveness I <u>implore</u>;
But the fact is I was napping, and so gently you came rapping,
And so faintly you came tapping, tapping at my chamber door,
That I scarce was sure I heard you"—here I opened wide the door;—
                    Darkness there and nothing more.

25   Deep into that darkness peering, long I stood there wondering, fearing,
Doubting, dreaming dreams no mortal ever dared to dream before;
But the silence was unbroken, and the stillness gave no token,
And the only word there spoken was the whispered word, "Lenore!"
This I whispered, and an echo murmured back the word "Lenore!"
30   Merely this and nothing more.

Back into the chamber turning, all my soul within me burning,
Soon again I heard a tapping somewhat louder than before.
"Surely," said I, "surely that is something at my window lattice;
Let me see, then, what thereat is, and this mystery explore—
35   Let my heart be still a moment and this mystery explore;—
                    'Tis the wind and nothing more!"

Open here I flung the shutter, when, with many a flirt and flutter,
In there stepped a stately Raven of the saintly days of yore.[2]
Not the least obeisance[3] made he; not a minute stopped or stayed he;
40   But, with mien[4] of lord or lady, perched above my chamber door—
Perched upon a bust of Pallas[5] just above my chamber door—
                    Perched, and sat, and nothing more.

Then this ebony bird <u>beguiling</u> my sad fancy into smiling,
By the grave and stern <u>decorum</u> of the countenance it wore,
45   "Though thy crest be shorn and shaven, thou," I said, "art sure no craven,[6]
Ghastly grim and ancient Raven wandering from the Nightly shore—
Tell me what thy lordly name is on the Night's Plutonian[7] shore!"
                    Quoth the Raven, "Nevermore."

---

2. **saintly days of yore:** sacred days of the past.

3. **obeisance** (ō-bā′səns): a polite gesture of respect, such as a bow.

4. **mien** (mēn): a way of carrying oneself; appearance.

5. **bust of Pallas:** statue of the head and shoulders of Athena, the Greek goddess of wisdom.

6. **craven:** cowardly person.

7. **Plutonian:** having to do with Pluto, the Roman god of the dead and ruler of the underworld.

WORDS TO KNOW
implore (ĭm-plôr′) v. to beg; earnestly ask for
beguiling (bĭ-gī′lĭng) adj. charming or delighting **beguile** v.
decorum (dĭ-kôr′əm) n. proper and dignified behavior

Much I marveled this ungainly fowl to hear discourse so plainly,
50 Though its answer little meaning—little relevancy bore;
For we cannot help agreeing that no living human being
Ever yet was blessed with seeing bird above his chamber door—
Bird or beast upon the sculptured bust above his chamber door,
        With such name as "Nevermore."

55 But the Raven, sitting lonely on the placid bust, spoke only
That one word, as if his soul in that one word he did outpour.
Nothing farther then he uttered—not a feather then he fluttered—
Till I scarcely more than muttered "Other friends have flown before—
On the morrow *he* will leave me, as my hopes have flown before."
60   Then the bird said, "Nevermore."

Startled at the stillness broken by reply so aptly spoken,
"Doubtless," said I, "what it utters is its only stock and store
Caught from some unhappy master whom unmerciful Disaster
Followed fast and followed faster till his songs one burden bore—
65 Till the dirges of his Hope that melancholy burden bore
        Of 'Never—nevermore.'"

But the Raven still beguiling all my fancy into smiling,
Straight I wheeled a cushioned seat in front of bird and bust and door;
Then, upon the velvet sinking, I betook myself to linking
70 Fancy unto fancy, thinking what this ominous bird of yore—
What this grim, ungainly, ghastly, gaunt, and ominous bird of yore
        Meant in croaking, "Nevermore."

This I sat engaged in guessing, but no syllable expressing
To the fowl whose fiery eyes now burned into my bosom's core;
75 This and more I sat divining, with my head at ease reclining
On the cushion's velvet lining that the lamp-light gloated o'er,
But whose velvet violet lining with the lamp-light gloating o'er,
        She shall press, ah, nevermore!

WORDS
TO
KNOW

discourse (dĭ-skôrs′) *v.* to speak
placid (plăs′ĭd) *adj.* undisturbed; calm or quiet
dirge (dûrj) *n.* a slow, mournful piece of music; a funeral hymn
ominous (ŏm′ə-nəs) *adj.* threatening; menacing
divining (dĭ-vī′nĭng) *adj.* finding out through intuition; guessing from incomplete
  evidence **divine** *v.*

Then, methought, the air grew denser, perfumed from an unseen censer[8]

80 Swung by Seraphim[9] whose foot-falls tinkled on the tufted floor.
"Wretch," I cried, "thy God hath lent thee—by these angels he hath sent thee
Respite—respite and nepenthe[10] from thy memories of Lenore;
Quaff,[11] oh quaff this kind nepenthe and forget this lost Lenore!"
                              Quoth the Raven, "Nevermore."

85 "Prophet!" said I, "thing of evil!—prophet still, if bird or devil!—
Whether Tempter[12] sent, or whether tempest tossed thee here ashore,
Desolate yet all undaunted, on this desert land enchanted—
On this home by Horror haunted—tell me truly, I implore—
Is there—*is* there balm in Gilead?[13]—tell me—tell me, I implore!"
90   Quoth the Raven, "Nevermore."

"Prophet!" said I, "thing of evil!—prophet still, if bird or devil!
By that Heaven that bends above us—by that God we both adore—
Tell this soul with sorrow laden if, within the distant Aidenn,[14]
It shall clasp a sainted maiden whom the angels name Lenore—
95 Clasp a rare and radiant maiden whom the angels name Lenore."
                              Quoth the Raven, "Nevermore."

"Be that word our sign of parting, bird or fiend!" I shrieked, upstarting—
"Get thee back into the tempest and the Night's Plutonian shore!
Leave no black plume as a token of that lie thy soul hath spoken!
100 Leave my loneliness unbroken!—quit the bust above my door!
Take thy beak from out my heart, and take thy form from off my door!"
                              Quoth the Raven, "Nevermore."

And the Raven, never flitting, still is sitting, *still* is sitting
On the pallid[15] bust of Pallas just above my chamber door;
105 And his eyes have all the seeming of a demon's that is dreaming,
And the lamp-light o'er him streaming throws his shadow on the floor;
And my soul from out that shadow that lies floating on the floor
                              Shall be lifted—nevermore!

---

8. **censer:** a container in which incense is burned, especially during religious services.

9. **Seraphim** (sĕr'ə-fĭm): angels of the highest rank.

10. **nepenthe** (nĭ-pĕn'thē): a drug that eases grief or sorrow by causing forgetfulness.

11. **quaff:** drink deeply.

12. **Tempter:** the Devil.

13. **balm** (bäm) **in Gilead** (gĭl'ē-əd): relief from suffering. The phrase comes from the Bible (Jeremiah 8:22) and refers to a soothing ointment from Gilead, a region of Palestine.

14. **Aidenn** (ād'n): heaven (from the Arabic form of the word *Eden*).

15. **pallid:** pale.

WORDS TO KNOW
respite (rĕs'pĭt) *n.* a brief period of rest or relief from pain or labor
tempest (tĕm'pĭst) *n.* a violent storm

Connect to the Literature

1. **What Do You Think?**
   What three words would you use to describe the raven?

   Comprehension Check
   - When do the events in the poem take place?
   - Where does the speaker look to find the source of the sound he hears?
   - What is the raven's response to all the speaker's questions?

Think Critically

2. **ACTIVE READING** **DRAWING CONCLUSIONS** Refer to the **conclusions** about the **speaker** that you recorded in your **READER'S NOTEBOOK**. What conclusions did you draw about his mental state?

3. What meaning or meanings do you think the word *nevermore* has in the poem? What effect does the **repetition** of the word have on you?

4. How do you explain the raven and its visit?

   THINK ABOUT {
   - why the bird comes to the speaker
   - whether the bird is real or an illusion

Extend Interpretations

5. **Critic's Corner** The poet James Russell Lowell wrote this couplet: "There comes Poe, with his raven, like Barnaby Rudge, / Three-fifths of him genius and two-fifths sheer fudge." (Barnaby Rudge is a character in a Charles Dickens novel who walks about with a pet raven on his back.) Do you agree with Lowell's view of Poe? Explain your opinion, referring to what you know about Poe's life and writings.

6. **Connect to Life** Recall your thoughts about the way in which you or someone you know handled a loss. What useful advice do you think you could give the speaker of "The Raven"?

Stanza	Rhyme Scheme
Stanza 1	
Stanza 2	

Literary Analysis

SOUND DEVICES Much of the musical quality of "The Raven" is produced by Poe's use of **rhyme,** the repetition of similar or identical sounds, to drive the poem's rhythm forward. Rhyme is employed by poets in various ways.

- **End rhyme** is the use of words with similar or identical sounds at the ends of lines:

. . . tapping at my chamber door—
Only this and nothing more.

- **Internal rhyme** is the use of rhyming words within a line:

Back into the chamber turning, all
my soul within me burning

- A **rhyme scheme** (pattern of end rhymes in a stanza or poem) can be identified by assigning a letter, starting with *a*, to each line, with lines that rhyme being given the same letter. Here is an example from Poe's poem "Annabel Lee":

It was many and many a year ago,	a
In a kingdom by the sea.	b
That a maiden there lived whom you may know	a
By the name of Annabel Lee;—	b

Cooperative Learning Activity Get together with a group of classmates, and have each member of the group record the rhyme scheme, along with any uses of internal rhyme, in a different stanza of "The Raven." Gather your information in a simple chart like the one shown here, and then compare findings. Does the rhyme scheme change from stanza to stanza, or does it stay the same? How does Poe's use of rhyme scheme affect the overall atmosphere of the poem?

Writing Options

1. Prose Description Write a prose description of the setting of "The Raven." Use words and phrases that evoke the same overall atmosphere as the poem itself.

2. Speaker's Diary Entry Writing as the speaker, compose a diary entry for a day one week after the events described in the poem. What does the speaker think and feel now? What has happened to the raven?

3. Poetic Parody A parody is an imitation (usually intended to be humorous) of a literary or artistic work. Write one or two stanzas of a parody of "The Raven." You might use another bird or animal in place of the raven, change the reason for the speaker's sorrow, or invent a new message for the intruder to utter. Whatever you change, try to follow Poe's meter and rhyme schemes so that your parody will be recognizable. Place the parody in your **Working Portfolio.**

Activities & Explorations

1. Dramatic Reading With other members of your class, take turns performing dramatic readings of the poem. You might make video or audio recordings of the readings. ~ **PERFORMING**

2. Image of the Study Make an illustration of the speaker's study, including him and the raven. Try to capture the mood of Poe's poem through your use of details and color. ~ **ART**

Inquiry & Research

Psychological View Modern psychology—the systematic study of human behavior—did not develop until several decades after Poe's death. In the 20th century, however, it became common for literary critics to discuss characters' actions in psychological terms. Find out some basic information about psychology—and in particular about psychotic disorders and psychotherapy. Then discuss the speaker of "The Raven" in terms of his possible psychological condition.

Vocabulary in Action

EXERCISE A: MEANING CLUES Read each magazine article title below and write the vocabulary word you would expect to find in the article.

1. "Wild Weather: Protecting Yourself from the Elements"
2. "How to Ask for Forgiveness . . . and Get It"
3. "Vacation Spots for When You Really Need a Break"
4. "Psychics and Fortunetellers: Help or Hype?"
5. "Modern Manners for Modern Times"
6. "Flee or Fight? What to Do When You're in Danger"
7. "Avoiding the Wrong Music for Your Wedding"
8. "Tossing and Turning? You Too Can Sleep Like a Rock"
9. "How to Hold Up Your End of the Conversation"
10. "Putting That Certain Someone Under Your Spell"

EXERCISE B With a partner, take turns acting out the meanings of the words *implore, decorum, placid, ominous, divine,* and *respite.* (In some cases, you may be able to communicate the meaning with a single gesture.

WORDS TO KNOW	beguiling	discourse	ominous	respite
	decorum	divining	placid	tempest
	dirge	implore		

Building Vocabulary
For an in-depth lesson on word connotation and denotation, see page 908.

The Fall of the House of Usher

Short Story by EDGAR ALLAN POE

Connect to Your Life

Nothing to Fear but Fear Roderick Usher, the main character in this story, claims that his greatest fear is that he will lose his life and sanity to fear. Many people have found that when fear takes over, it prevents them from reacting in an effective manner. Have you ever witnessed a situation in which someone showed fear? How did the fear seem to affect the person's judgment and ability to handle the situation? Jot down your thoughts.

Build Background

From Fear to Terror "The Fall of the House of Usher" was written in 1839, when Poe was developing his literary theories. In "The Philosophy of Composition" (1846), he asserted that the writer of a literary work must plot the work out completely before beginning to write—an assertion at odds with the views of the literary community of his day. Poe crafted his works to achieve "unity of effect," with every part of each work, every detail, designed to contribute to a single overall feeling. Poe's particular genius was for exploring the strange and fantastic, conveying psychological terror through carefully chosen details and events.

WORDS TO KNOW
Vocabulary Preview

affinity	insipid
aghast	insoluble
alleviation	interment
annihilate	narrative
deficiency	obstinate
emaciated	terrestrial
fitfully	vivacious
futility	

Focus Your Reading

LITERARY ANALYSIS MOOD Throughout this story, Poe develops an atmosphere that plays a vivid role in the tale's development. **Mood** is the feeling or atmosphere that a writer conveys with his or her words. Here are three of Poe's mood-building techniques:

- detailed descriptions of settings though the use of imagery and figurative language
- precisely chosen words and phrases
- the use of a narrator who both observes and participates in the events recounted

As you read, notice how these features of the story work to create a mood. What effect does the mood have on you?

ACTIVE READING UNDERSTANDING COMPLEX SENTENCES In this story, Poe makes frequent use of **complex sentences,** piling detail upon detail to describe scenes or convey emotions. Use these techniques to help you understand a complex sentence:

- Look for the **main idea.** Locate the subject and the verb that form the basic kernel of the sentence.
- If the subject and verb are in inverted order, rearrange them.
- Temporarily disregard modifiers that do not seem crucial to the meaning.
- Read on. A confusing sentence might be followed by a sentence or two that clarifies it.

Take notes in your ▯▯ READER'S NOTEBOOK about words or passages that you find especially difficult. After finishing the story, try applying a variety of strategies to clarify your understanding of those passages.

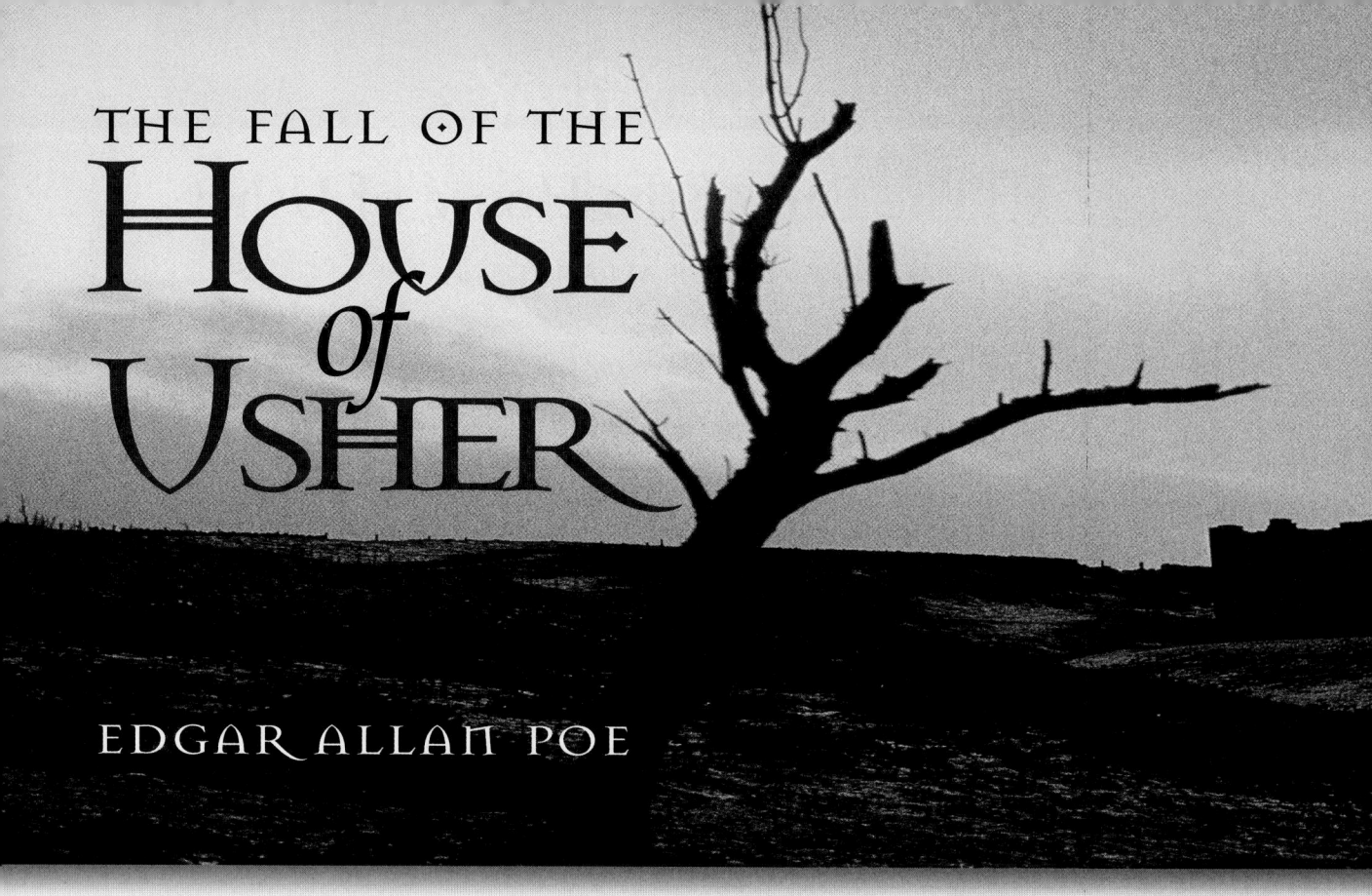

THE FALL OF THE
HOUSE
of
USHER

EDGAR ALLAN POE

Son coeur est un luth suspendu;
Sitôt qu'on le touche il résonne.
—De Béranger

GUIDE FOR READING

Son coeur . . . résonne *French*: His
heart is a hanging lute; / As soon
as one touches it, it sounds (lines
from a poem by the 19th-century
French poet Pierre Jean de
Béranger).

During the whole of a dull, dark, and soundless day in the
autumn of the year, when the clouds hung oppressively
low in the heavens, I had been passing alone, on horseback, through a singularly dreary tract of country, and
5 at length found myself, as the shades of the evening
drew on, within view of the melancholy House of Usher.
I know not how it was—but, with the first glimpse of
the building, a sense of insufferable gloom pervaded my
spirit. I say insufferable; for the feeling was unrelieved by any of
10 that half-pleasurable, because poetic, sentiment with which the
mind usually receives even the sternest natural images of the desolate or terrible. I looked upon the scene before me—upon the mere
house, and the simple landscape features of the domain—upon the
bleak walls—upon the vacant eye-like windows—upon a few rank
15 sedges—and upon a few white trunks of decayed trees—with an
utter depression of soul which I can compare to no earthly sensation more properly than to the after-dream of the reveller upon
opium—the bitter lapse into every-day life—the hideous dropping

off of the veil. There was an iciness, a sinking, a sickening of the
heart—an unredeemed dreariness of thought which no goading of
the imagination could torture into aught of the sublime. What was
it—I paused to think—what was it that so unnerved me in the
contemplation of the House of Usher? It was a mystery all
<u>insoluble</u>; nor could I grapple with the shadowy fancies that
crowded upon me as I pondered. I was forced to fall back upon
the unsatisfactory conclusion, that while, beyond doubt, there *are*
combinations of very simple natural objects which have the power
of thus affecting us, still the analysis of this power lies among
considerations beyond our depth. It was possible, I reflected, that
a mere different arrangement of the particulars of the scene, of the
details of the picture, would be sufficient to modify, or perhaps to
<u>annihilate</u> its capacity for sorrowful impression; and, acting upon
this idea, I reined my horse to the precipitous brink of a black and
lurid tarn that lay in unruffled lustre by the dwelling, and gazed
down—but with a shudder even more thrilling than before—upon
the remodelled and inverted images of the gray sedge, and the
ghastly tree-stems, and the vacant and eye-like windows.

34 tarn: a small mountain lake.

WORDS TO KNOW   **insoluble** (ĭn-sŏl′yə-bəl) *adj.* having no solution; unsolvable
annihilate (ə-nī′ə-lāt′) *v.* to destroy completely; wipe out

475

Nevertheless, in this mansion of gloom I now proposed to myself a sojourn of some weeks. Its proprietor, Roderick Usher, had been one of my boon companions in boyhood; but many years had elapsed since our last meeting. A letter, however, had lately reached me in a distant part of the country—a letter from him—which, in its wildly importunate nature, had admitted of no other than a personal reply. The MS. gave evidence of nervous agitation. The writer spoke of acute bodily illness—of a mental disorder which oppressed him—and of an earnest desire to see me, as his best and indeed his only personal friend, with a view of attempting, by the cheerfulness of my society, some <u>alleviation</u> of his malady. It was the manner in which all this, and much more, was said—it was the apparent *heart* that went with his request—which allowed me no room for hesitation; and I accordingly obeyed forthwith what I still considered a very singular summons.

Although, as boys, we had been even intimate associates, yet I really knew little of my friend. His reserve had been always excessive and habitual. I was aware, however, that his very ancient family had been noted, time out of mind, for a peculiar sensibility of temperament, displaying itself, through long ages, in many works of exalted art, and manifested, of late, in repeated deeds of munificent yet unobtrusive charity, as well as in a passionate devotion to the intricacies, perhaps even more than to the orthodox and easily recognizable beauties, of musical science. I had learned, too, the very remarkable fact, that the stem of the Usher race, all time-honored as it was, had put forth, at no period, any enduring branch; in other words, that the entire family lay in the direct line of descent, and had always, with very trifling and very temporary variation, so lain. It was this <u>deficiency</u>, I considered, while running over in thought the perfect keeping of the character of the premises with the accredited character of the people, and while speculating upon the possible influence which the one, in the long lapse of centuries, might have exercised upon the other—it was this deficiency, perhaps, of collateral issue, and the consequent undeviating transmission, from sire to son, of the patrimony with the name, which had, at length, so identified the two as to merge the original title of the estate in the quaint and equivocal appellation of the "House of Usher"—an appellation which seemed to include, in the minds of the peasantry who used it, both the family and the family mansion.

I have said that the sole effect of my somewhat childish experiment—that of looking down within the tarn—had been to

44 had admitted of no other than: had required.

45 MS.: an abbreviation of *manuscript.*

72 collateral (kə-lăt′ər-əl) **issue:** relatives not in the direct line of descent.

76 equivocal appellation (ĭ-kwĭv′ə-kəl ăp′ə-lā′shən): ambiguous name.

54–78 Summarize what the narrator already knows about Roderick Usher and his family estate.

WORDS TO KNOW	**alleviation** (ə-lē′vē-ā′shən) *n.* a decrease in severity; relief **deficiency** (dĭ-fĭsh′ən-sē) *n.* a lack

deepen the first singular impression. There can be no doubt that the consciousness of the rapid increase of my superstition—for why should I not so term it?—served mainly to accelerate the increase itself. Such, I have long known, is the paradoxical law of all sentiments having terror as a basis. And it might have been for this reason only, that, when I again uplifted my eyes to the house itself, from its image in the pool, there grew in my mind a strange fancy—a fancy so ridiculous, indeed, that I but mention it to show the vivid force of the sensations which oppressed me. I had so worked upon my imagination as really to believe that about the whole mansion and domain there hung an atmosphere peculiar to themselves and their immediate vicinity—an atmosphere which had no affinity with the air of heaven, but which had reeked up from the decayed trees, and the gray wall, and the silent tarn—a pestilent and mystic vapor, dull, sluggish, faintly discernible, and leaden-hued.

Shaking off from my spirit what *must* have been a dream, I scanned more narrowly the real aspect of the building. Its principal feature seemed to be that of an excessive antiquity. The discoloration of ages had been great. Minute fungi overspread the whole exterior, hanging in a fine tangled web-work from the eaves. Yet all this was apart from any extraordinary dilapidation. No portion of the masonry had fallen; and there appeared to be a wild inconsistency between its still perfect adaptation of parts, and the crumbling condition of the individual stones. In this there was much that reminded me of the specious totality of old woodwork which has rotted for long years in some neglected vault, with no disturbance from the breath of the external air. Beyond this indication of extensive decay, however, the fabric gave little token of instability. Perhaps the eye of a scrutinizing observer might have discovered a barely perceptible fissure, which, extending from the roof of the building in front, made its way down the wall in a zigzag direction, until it became lost in the sullen waters of the tarn.

Noticing these things, I rode over a short causeway to the house. A servant in waiting took my horse, and I entered the Gothic archway of the hall. A valet, of stealthy step, thence conducted me, in silence, through many dark and intricate passages in my progress to the *studio* of his master. Much that I encountered on the way contributed, I know not how, to heighten the vague sentiments of which I have already spoken. While the objects around me—while the carvings of the ceilings, the sombre

79–96 Consider the narrator's description of his first impressions of the house. What are your impressions of the narrator?

106 specious totality (spē'shəs tō-tăl'ĭ-tē): false appearance of soundness.

117 Gothic (gŏth'ĭk) **archway**: a doorway topped by an arch with a pointed peak, characteristic of Gothic architecture.

WORDS
TO   **affinity** (ə-fĭn'ĭ-tē) *n.* a kinship or likeness
KNOW

477

tapestries of the walls, the ebon blackness of the floors, and the phantasmagoric armorial trophies which rattled as I strode, were
125 but matters to which, or to such as which, I had been accustomed from my infancy—while I hesitated not to acknowledge how familiar was all this—I still wondered to find how unfamiliar were the fancies which ordinary images were stirring up. On one of the staircases, I met the physician of the family. His counte-
130 nance, I thought, wore a mingled expression of low cunning and perplexity. He accosted me with trepidation and passed on. The valet now threw open a door and ushered me into the presence of his master.

The room in which I found myself was very large and lofty.
135 The windows were long, narrow, and pointed, and at so vast a distance from the black oaken floor as to be altogether inaccessible from within. Feeble gleams of encrimsoned light made their way through the trellissed panes, and served to render sufficiently distinct the more prominent objects around; the eye, however,
140 struggled in vain to reach the remoter angles of the chamber, or the recesses of the vaulted and fretted ceiling. Dark draperies hung upon the walls. The general furniture was profuse, comfortless, antique, and tattered. Many books and musical instruments lay scattered about, but failed to give any vitality to the scene. I
145 felt that I breathed an atmosphere of sorrow. An air of stern, deep, and irredeemable gloom hung over and pervaded all.

Upon my entrance, Usher arose from a sofa on which he had been lying at full length, and greeted me with a vivacious warmth which had much in it, I at first thought, of an overdone
150 cordiality—of the constrained effort of the *ennuyé* man of the world. A glance, however, at his countenance convinced me of his perfect sincerity. We sat down; and for some moments, while he spoke not, I gazed upon him with a feeling half of pity, half of awe. Surely, man had never before so terribly altered, in so brief
155 a period, as had Roderick Usher! It was with difficulty that I could bring myself to admit the identity of the wan being before me with the companion of my early boyhood. Yet the character of his face had been at all times remarkable. A cadaverousness of complexion; an eye large, liquid, and luminous beyond compar-
160 ison; lips somewhat thin and very pallid, but of a surpassingly beautiful curve; a nose of a delicate Hebrew model, but with a breadth of nostril unusual in similar formations; a finely moulded chin, speaking, in its want of prominence, of a want of moral energy; hair of a more than web-like softness and tenuity;—these
165 features, with an inordinate expansion above the regions of the

124 phantasmagoric armorial (făn-tăz′mə-gôr′ĭk är-môr′ē-əl) **trophies:** looming wall decorations bearing coats of arms.

134–146 How does the description of the room contribute to the mood of the story?

150 ennuyé (äN-wē-ā′) *French:* bored.

158 cadaverousness (kə-dăv′ər-əs-nĭs): corpselike appearance.

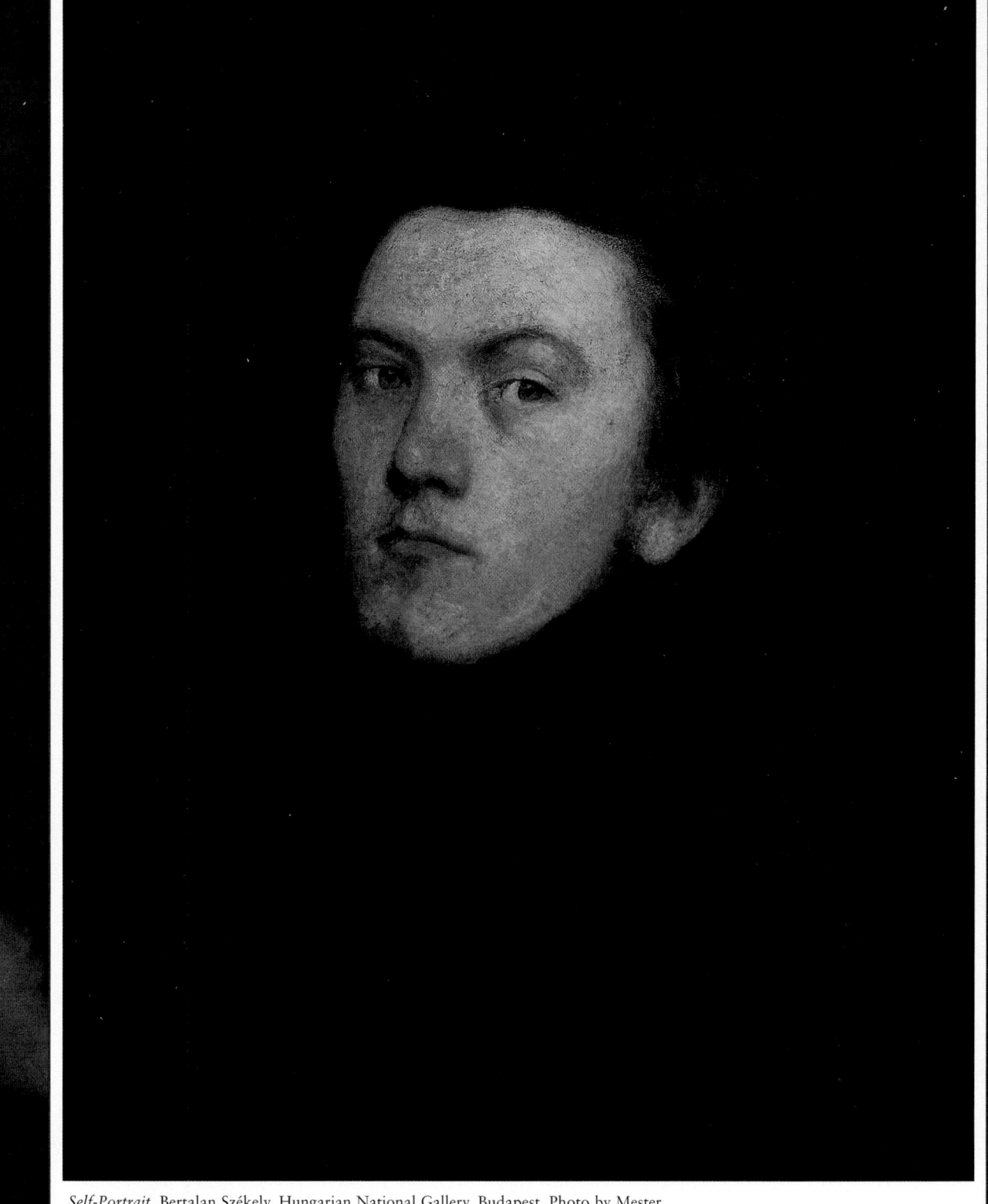

Self-Portrait, Bertalan Székely. Hungarian National Gallery, Budapest. Photo by Mester Tibor Foto, Budapest.

temple, made up altogether a countenance not easily to be forgotten. And now in the mere exaggeration of the prevailing character of these features, and of the expression they were wont to convey, lay so much of change that I doubted to whom I spoke. The now ghastly pallor of the skin, and the now miraculous lustre of the eye, above all things startled and even awed me. The silken hair, too, had been suffered to grow all unheeded, and as, in its wild gossamer texture, it floated rather than fell about the face, I could not, even with effort, connect its Arabesque expression with any idea of simple humanity.

In the manner of my friend I was at once struck with an incoherence—an inconsistency; and I soon found this to arise from a series of feeble and futile struggles to overcome an habitual trepidancy—an excessive nervous agitation. For something of this nature I had indeed been prepared, no less by his letter, than by reminiscences of certain boyish traits, and by conclusions deduced from his peculiar physical conformation and temperament. His action was alternately vivacious and sullen. His voice varied rapidly from a tremulous indecision (when the animal spirits seemed utterly in abeyance) to that species of energetic concision—that abrupt, weighty, unhurried, and hollow-sounding enunciation—that leaden, self-balanced, and perfectly modulated guttural utterance, which may be observed in the lost drunkard, or the irreclaimable eater of opium, during the periods of his most intense excitement.

It was thus that he spoke of the object of my visit, of his earnest desire to see me, and of the solace he expected me to afford him. He entered, at some length, into what he conceived to be the nature of his malady. It was, he said, a constitutional and a family evil, and one for which he despaired to find a remedy—a mere nervous affection, he immediately added, which would undoubtedly soon pass off. It displayed itself in a host of unnatural sensations. Some of these, as he detailed them, interested and bewildered me; although, perhaps, the terms and the general manner of their narration had their weight. He suffered much from a morbid acuteness of the senses; the most insipid food was alone endurable; he could wear only garments of certain texture; the odors of all flowers were oppressive; his eyes were tortured by even a faint light; and there were but peculiar sounds, and these from stringed instruments, which did not inspire him with horror.

To an anomalous species of terror I found him a bounden slave. "I shall perish," said he, "I *must* perish in this deplorable folly. Thus, thus, and not otherwise, shall I be lost. I dread the

174 Arabesque (ăr'ə-bĕsk'): intricately interwoven (like the design on an Oriental carpet).

186 concision (kən-sĭzh'ən): briefness of communication; terseness.

204 but peculiar: only certain.

WORDS TO KNOW

insipid (ĭn-sĭp'ĭd) *adj.* lacking in flavor; bland

events of the future, not in themselves, but in their results. I shudder at the thought of any, even the most trivial, incident, which may operate upon this intolerable agitation of soul. I have, indeed, no abhorrence of danger, except in its absolute effect—in terror. In this unnerved, in this pitiable, condition I feel that the period will sooner or later arrive when I must abandon life and reason together, in some struggle with the grim phantasm, FEAR."

I learned, moreover, at intervals, and through broken and equivocal hints, another singular feature of his mental condition. He was enchained by certain superstitious impressions in regard to the dwelling which he tenanted, and whence, for many years, he had never ventured forth—in regard to an influence whose supposititious force was conveyed in terms too shadowy here to be re-stated—an influence which some peculiarities in the mere form and substance of his family mansion had, by dint of long sufferance, he said, obtained over his spirit—an effect which the *physique* of the gray walls and turrets, and of the dim tarn into which they all looked down, had, at length, brought about upon the *morale* of his existence.

He admitted, however, although with hesitation, that much of the peculiar gloom which thus afflicted him could be traced to a more natural and far more palpable origin—to the severe and long-continued illness—indeed to the evidently approaching dissolution—of a tenderly beloved sister, his sole companion for long years, his last and only relative on earth. "Her decease," he said, with a bitterness which I can never forget, "would leave him (him, the hopeless and the frail) the last of the ancient race of the Ushers." While he spoke, the lady Madeline (for so was she called) passed through a remote portion of the apartment, and, without having noticed my presence, disappeared. I regarded her with an utter astonishment not unmingled with dread; and yet I found it impossible to account for such feelings. A sensation of stupor oppressed me as my eyes followed her retreating steps. When a door, at length, closed upon her, my glance sought instinctively and eagerly the countenance of the brother; but he had buried his face in his hands, and I could only perceive that a far more than ordinary wanness had overspread the <u>emaciated</u> fingers through which trickled many passionate tears.

The disease of the lady Madeline had long baffled the skill of her physicians. A settled apathy, a gradual wasting away of the person, and frequent although transient affections of a partially cataleptical character were the unusual diagnosis. Hitherto she

207–216 In your own words, sum up Usher's view of his situation.

222 supposititious (sə-pŏz'ĭ-tĭsh'əs): supposed. How does the narrator seem to regard Usher's condition?

224 dint: force; power.

237–241 Why do you think the narrator's first glimpse at Madeline Usher is so startling?

251 cataleptical (kăt'l-ĕp'tĭ-kəl): involving paralysis and unconsciousness; trancelike.

WORDS
TO
KNOW

emaciated (ĭ-mā'shē-ā'tĭd) *adj.* excessively thin; wasted away **emaciate** *v.*

481

Head of Ophelia, study (about 1897), Edwin Austin Abbey. Oil on wood, 14" x 9⅝". Edwin Austin Abbey Memorial Collection, Yale University Art Gallery, New Haven, Connecticut.

had steadily borne up against the pressure of her malady, and had not betaken herself finally to bed; but on the closing in of the evening of my arrival at the house, she succumbed (as her brother told me at night with inexpressible agitation) to the prostrating power of the destroyer; and I learned that the glimpse I had obtained of her person would thus probably be the last I should obtain—that the lady, at least while living, would be seen by me no more.

255

259 Where, probably, is Madeline at this point?

**F**or several days ensuing, her name was unmentioned by either Usher or myself; and during this period I was busied in earnest endeavors to alleviate the melancholy of my friend. We painted and read together, or I listened, as if in a dream, to the wild improvisations of his speaking guitar. And thus, as a closer and still closer intimacy admitted me more unreservedly into the recesses of his spirit, the more bitterly did I perceive the <u>futility</u> of all attempt at cheering a mind from which darkness, as if an inherent positive quality, poured forth upon all objects of the moral and physical universe in one unceasing radiation of gloom.

I shall ever bear about me a memory of the many solemn hours I thus spent alone with the master of the House of Usher. Yet I should fail in any attempt to convey an idea of the exact character of the studies, or of the occupations, in which he involved me, or led me the way. An excited and highly distempered ideality threw a sulphureous lustre over all. His long improvised dirges will ring forever in my ears. Among other things, I hold painfully in mind a certain singular perversion and amplification of the wild air of the last waltz of Von Weber. From the paintings over which his elaborate fancy brooded, and which grew, touch by touch, into vagueness at which I shuddered the more thrillingly, because I shuddered knowing not why—from these paintings (vivid as their images now are before me) I would in vain endeavor to educe more than a small portion which should lie within the compass of merely written words. By the utter simplicity, by the nakedness of his designs, he arrested and overawed attention. If ever mortal painted an ideal, that mortal was Roderick Usher. For me at least, in the circumstances then surrounding me, there arose out of the pure abstractions which the hypochondriac contrived to throw upon his canvas, an intensity of intolerable awe, no shadow of which felt I ever yet in the contemplation of the certainly glowing yet too concrete reveries of Fuseli.

One of the phantasmagoric conceptions of my friend, partaking not so rigidly of the spirit of abstraction, may be shadowed forth, although feebly, in words. A small picture presented the interior of an immensely long and rectangular vault or tunnel, with low walls, smooth, white, and without interruption or device. Certain accessory points of the design served well to convey the idea that this excavation lay at an exceeding depth below the surface of the earth. No outlet was observed in any portion of its vast extent, and no torch or other artificial source

275 distempered ideality (ĭ′dē-ăl′ĭ-tē): diseased creativity.

276 sulphureous (sŭl-fyōōr′ē-əs) **luster:** lurid glow; nightmarish quality.

279 Von Weber (fôn vā′bər): the German romantic composer Karl Maria von Weber.

288 What do the narrator's observations about Roderick Usher reveal about his own personality?

293 Fuseli (fyōō′zə-lē′): the Swiss-born British painter Henry Fuseli, many of whose works feature fantastic or gruesome elements.

of light was discernible; yet a flood of intense rays rolled throughout, and bathed the whole in a ghastly and inappropriate splendor.

296–305 What does this picture suggest to you?

I have just spoken of that morbid condition of the auditory nerve which rendered all music intolerable to the sufferer, with the exception of certain effects of stringed instruments. It was, perhaps, the narrow limits to which he thus confined himself upon the guitar which gave birth, in great measure, to the fantastic character of his performances. But the fervid *facility* of his *impromptus* could not be so accounted for. They must have been, and were, in the notes, as well as in the words of his wild fantasias (for he not unfrequently accompanied himself with rhymed verbal improvisations), the result of that intense mental collectedness and concentration to which I have previously alluded as observable only in particular moments of the highest artificial excitement. The words of one of these rhapsodies I have easily remembered. I was, perhaps, the more forcibly impressed with it as he gave it, because, in the under or mystic current of its meaning, I fancied that I perceived, and for the first time, a full consciousness on the part of Usher of the tottering of his lofty reason upon her throne. The verses, which were entitled "The Haunted Palace," ran very nearly, if not accurately, thus:—

312 *impromptus* (ăn-prônp-tü′) *French:* musical pieces made up as they are played.

I.

In the greenest of our valleys,
    By good angels tenanted,
Once a fair and stately palace—
    Radiant palace—reared its head.
In the monarch Thought's dominion—
    It stood there!
Never seraph spread a pinion
    Over fabric half so fair.

332–333 Never seraph (sĕr′əf) . . . **half so fair:** No angel ever spread its wing over half as beautiful a structure.

II.

Banners yellow, glorious, golden,
    On its roof did float and flow
(This—all this—was in the olden
    Time long ago);
And every gentle air that dallied,
    In that sweet day,
Along the ramparts plumed and pallid,
    A winged odor went away.

III.

Wanderers in that happy valley
    Through two luminous windows saw

Spirits moving musically
    To a lute's well-tunèd law;
Round about a throne, where sitting
    (Porphyrogene!)
In state his glory well befitting,
    The ruler of the realm was seen.

349 porphyrogene (pôr-fîr′ə-jēn′): a son born to a ruling king.

IV.

And all with pearl and ruby glowing
    Was the fair palace door,
Through which came flowing, flowing, flowing
    And sparkling evermore,
A troop of Echoes whose sweet duty
    Was but to sing,
In voices of surpassing beauty,
    The wit and wisdom of their king.

V.

But evil things, in robes of sorrow,
    Assailed the monarch's high estate;
(Ah, let us mourn, for never morrow
    Shall dawn upon him, desolate!)
And, round about his home, the glory
    That blushed and bloomed
Is but a dim-remembered story
    Of the old time entombed.

VI.

And travellers now within that valley,
    Through the red-litten windows see
Vast forms that move fantastically
    To a discordant melody;
While, like a rapid ghastly river,
    Through the pale door;
A hideous throng rush out forever,
    And laugh—but smile no more.

326–378 How does the poem contribute to the story's mood?

I well remember that suggestions arising from this ballad led us into a train of thought wherein there became manifest an opinion of Usher's which I mention not so much on account of its novelty (for other men have thought thus), as on account of the pertinacity with which he maintained it. This opinion, in its general form, was that of the sentience of all vegetable things. But, in his disordered fancy, the idea had assumed a more daring character, and trespassed, under certain conditions, upon the kingdom of inorganization. I lack words to express the full extent, or the earnest *abandon* of his persuasion. The belief, however, was connected (as I have previously hinted) with the gray stones of the

382–383 pertinacity (pûr′tn-ăs′ĭ-tē): stubbornness.

384 sentience (sĕn′shəns) **of all vegetable things:** consciousness of all growing things.

home of his forefathers. The conditions of the sentence had been here, he imagined, fulfilled in the method of collocation of these stones—in the order of their arrangement, as well as in that of the many *fungi* which overspread them, and of the decayed trees which stood around—above all, in the long undisturbed endurance of this arrangement, and in its reduplication in the still waters of the tarn. Its evidence—the evidence of the sentience—was to be seen, he said (and I here started as he spoke), in the gradual yet certain condensation of an atmosphere of their own about the waters and the walls. The result was discoverable, he added, in that silent yet importunate and terrible influence which for centuries had moulded the destinies of his family, and which made *him* what I now saw him—what he was. Such opinions need no comment, and I will make none.

Our books—the books which, for years, had formed no small portion of the mental existence of the invalid—were, as might be supposed, in strict keeping with this character of phantasm. We pored together over such works as the "Ververt et Chartreuse" of Gresset; the "Belphegor" of Machiavelli; the "Heaven and Hell" of Swedenborg; the "Subterranean Voyage of Nicholas Klimm" of Holberg; the "Chiromancy" of Robert Flud, of Jean D'Indaginé, and of Dela Chambre; the "Journey into the Blue Distance" of Tieck; and the "City of the Sun" of Campanella. One favorite volume was a small octavo edition of the "Directorium Inquisitorium," by the Dominican Eymeric de Gironne; and there were passages in Pomponius Mela, about the old African Satyrs and Aegipans, over which Usher would sit dreaming for hours. His chief delight, however, was found in the perusal of an exceedingly rare and curious book in quarto Gothic—the manual of a forgotten church—the *Vigiliae Mortuorum secundum Chorum Ecclesiae Maguntinae.*

I could not help thinking of the wild ritual of this work, and of its probable influence upon the hypochondriac, when, one evening, having informed me abruptly that the lady Madeline was no more, he stated his intention of preserving her corpse for a fortnight (previously to its final <u>interment</u>), in one of the numerous vaults within the main walls of the building. The worldly reason, however, assigned for this singular proceeding, was one which I did not feel at liberty to dispute. The brother had been led to his resolution (so he told me) by consideration of the unusual character of the malady of the deceased, of certain obtrusive and eager inquiries on the part of her medical men, and of the remote and exposed situation of the burial-ground of the family. I will not

379–403 What comment would you make about Usher's opinion?

407–415 "Ververt et Chartreuse" . . . **Pomponius Mela:** extravagantly imaginative works of fiction, theology, philosophy, and geography.

419–420 Vigiliae Mortuorum secundum Chorum Ecclesiae Maguntinae (wĭ-gĭl'ē-ī môr-tōō-ôr'ŏŏm sĕ-kŏŏn'dŏŏm kôr'ŏŏm ĕ-klā'sē-ī mä-gŏŏn-tē'nī) *Latin:* Wakes for the Dead, in the Manner of the Choir of the Church of Mainz.

WORDS TO KNOW **interment** (ĭn-tûr'mənt) *n.* burial

deny that when I called to mind the sinister countenance of the person whom I met upon the staircase, on the day of my arrival at the house, I had no desire to oppose what I regarded as at best but a harmless, and by no means an unnatural, precaution.

At the request of Usher, I personally aided him in the arrangements for the temporary entombment. The body having been encoffined, we two alone bore it to its rest. The vault in which we placed it (and which had been so long unopened that our torches, half smothered in its oppressive atmosphere, gave us little opportunity for investigation) was small, damp, and entirely without means of admission for light; lying, at great depth, immediately beneath that portion of the building in which was my own sleeping apartment. It had been used, apparently, in remote feudal times, for the worst purpose of a donjonkeep, and, in later days, as a place of deposit for powder, or some other highly combustible substance, as a portion of its floor, and the whole interior of a long archway through which we reached it, were carefully sheathed with copper. The door, of massive iron, had

446 **donjonkeep** (dŏn'jən-kēp'): dungeon.

been, also, similarly protected. Its immense weight caused an unusually sharp, grating sound, as it moved upon its hinges.

Having deposited our mournful burden upon tressels within this region of horror, we partially turned aside the yet unscrewed lid of the coffin, and looked upon the face of the tenant. A striking similitude between the brother and sister now first arrested my attention; and Usher, divining, perhaps, my thoughts, murmured out some few words from which I learned that the deceased and himself had been twins, and that sympathies of a scarcely intelligible nature had always existed between them. Our glances, however, rested not long upon the dead—for we could not regard her unawed. The disease which had thus entombed the lady in the maturity of youth, had left, as usual in all maladies of a strictly cataleptical character, the mockery of a faint blush upon the bosom and the face, and that suspiciously lingering smile upon the lip which is so terrible in death. We replaced and screwed down the lid, and, having secured the door of iron, made our way, with toil, into the scarcely less gloomy apartments of the upper portion of the house.

 nd now, some days of bitter grief having elapsed, an observable change came over the features of the mental disorder of my friend. His ordinary manner had vanished. His ordinary occupations were neglected or forgotten. He roamed from chamber to chamber with hurried, unequal, and objectless step. The pallor of his countenance had assumed, if possible, a more ghastly hue—but the luminousness of his eye had utterly gone out. The once occasional huskiness of his tone was heard no more; and a tremulous quaver, as if of extreme terror, habitually characterized his utterance. There were times, indeed, when I thought his unceasingly agitated mind was laboring with some oppressive secret, to divulge which he struggled for the necessary courage. At times, again, I was obliged to resolve all into the mere inexplicable vagaries of madness, for I beheld him gazing upon vacancy for long hours, in an attitude of the profoundest attention, as if listening to some imaginary sound. It was no wonder that his condition terrified—that it infected me. I felt creeping upon me, by slow yet certain degrees, the wild influences of his own fantastic yet impressive superstitions.

It was, especially, upon retiring to bed late in the night of the seventh or eighth day after the placing of the lady Madeline within the donjon, that I experienced the full power of such feelings. Sleep came not near my couch—while the hours waned and waned away. I struggled to reason off the nervousness which had

470–489 What do you infer about the changes in Usher's behavior?

493 couch: bed.

495 dominion over me. I endeavored to believe that much, if not all of what I felt, was due to the bewildering influence of the gloomy furniture of the room—of the dark and tattered draperies, which, tortured into motion by the breath of a rising tempest, swayed fitfully to and fro upon the walls, and rustled uneasily about the

500 decorations of the bed. But my efforts were fruitless. An irrepressible tremor gradually pervaded my frame; and, at length, there sat upon my very heart an incubus of utterly causeless alarm. Shaking this off with a gasp and a struggle, I uplifted myself upon the pillows, and, peering earnestly within the intense

505 darkness of the chamber, hearkened—I know not why, except that an instinctive spirit prompted me—to certain low and indefinite sounds which came, through the pauses of the storm, at long intervals, I knew not whence. Overpowered by an intense sentiment of horror, unaccountable yet unendurable, I threw on

510 my clothes with haste (for I felt that I should sleep no more during the night), and endeavored to arouse myself from the pitiable condition into which I had fallen, by pacing rapidly to and fro through the apartment.

I had taken but few turns in this manner, when a light step on

515 an adjoining staircase arrested my attention. I presently recognized it as that of Usher. In an instant afterward he rapped, with a gentle touch, at my door, and entered, bearing a lamp. His countenance was, as usual, cadaverously wan—but, moreover, there was a species of mad hilarity in his eyes—an evidently

520 restrained *hysteria* in his whole demeanor. His air appalled me—but any thing was preferable to the solitude which I had so long endured, and I even welcomed his presence as a relief.

"And you have not seen it?" he said abruptly, after having stared about him for some moments in silence—"you have not

525 then seen it?—but, stay! you shall." Thus speaking, and having carefully shaded his lamp, he hurried to one of the casements, and threw it freely open to the storm.

The impetuous fury of the entering gust nearly lifted us from our feet. It was, indeed, a tempestuous yet sternly beautiful night,

530 and one wildly singular in its terror and its beauty. A whirlwind had apparently collected its force in our vicinity; for there were frequent and violent alterations in the direction of the wind; and the exceeding density of the clouds (which hung so low as to press upon the turrets of the house) did not prevent our perceiving the

535 life-like velocity with which they flew careering from all points against each other, without passing away into the distance. I say that even their exceeding density did not prevent our perceiving

495–500 Which of the narrator's experiences in the Usher mansion might have led to his conclusion?

502 incubus (ĭn'kyə-bəs): burden.

525 stay: wait.

WORDS
TO
KNOW

fitfully (fĭt'fə-lē) *adv.* in an irregular way; unsteadily

this—yet we had no glimpse of the moon or stars, nor was there any flashing forth of the lightning. But the under surfaces of the huge masses of agitated vapor, as well as all <u>terrestrial</u> objects immediately around us, were glowing in the unnatural light of a faintly luminous and distinctly visible gaseous exhalation which hung about and enshrouded the mansion.

"You must not—you shall not behold this!" said I, shuddering, to Usher, as I led him, with a gentle violence, from the window to a seat. "These appearances, which bewilder you, are merely electrical phenomena not uncommon—or it may be that they have their ghastly origin in the rank miasma of the tarn. Let us close this casement;—the air is chilling and dangerous to your frame. Here is one of your favorite romances. I will read, and you shall listen:—and so we will pass away this terrible night together."

The antique volume which I had taken up was the "Mad Trist" of Sir Launcelot Canning; but I had called it a favorite of Usher's more in sad jest than in earnest; for, in truth, there is little in its uncouth and unimaginative prolixity which could have had interest for the lofty and spiritual ideality of my friend. It was, however, the only book immediately at hand; and I indulged a vague hope that the excitement which now agitated the hypochondriac, might find relief (for the history of mental disorder is full of similar anomalies) even in the extremeness of the folly which I should read. Could I have judged, indeed, by the wild overstrained air of vivacity with which he hearkened, or apparently hearkened, to the words of the tale, I might well have congratulated myself upon the success of my design.

I had arrived at that well-known portion of the story where Ethelred, the hero of the Trist, having sought in vain for peaceable admission into the dwelling of the hermit, proceeds to make good an entrance by force. Here, it will be remembered, the words of the narrative run thus:

"And Ethelred, who was by nature of a doughty heart, and who was now mighty withal, on account of the powerfulness of the wine which he had drunken, waited no longer to hold parley with the hermit, who, in sooth, was of an <u>obstinate</u> and maliceful turn, but, feeling the rain upon his shoulders, and fearing the rising of the tempest, uplifted his mace outright, and, with blows, made quickly room in the plankings of the door for his gauntleted hand; and now pulling therewith sturdily, he so cracked, and ripped, and tore all asunder, that the noise of the dry and hollow-sounding wood alarumed and reverberated throughout the forest."

540

545

550

555

560

565

570

575

548 miasma (mī-ăz′mə): poisonous vapors.

555 prolixity (prō-lĭk′sĭ-tē): tedious length; wordiness.

572 hold parley (pär′lē) **with**: converse with.

573 in sooth: truly.

580   At the termination of this sentence I started and, for a moment, paused; for it appeared to me (although I at once concluded that my excited fancy had deceived me)—it appeared to me that, from some very remote portion of the mansion, there came, indistinctly, to my ears, what might have been, in its exact similarity
585 of character, the echo (but a stifled and dull one certainly) of the very cracking and ripping sound which Sir Launcelot had so particularly described. It was, beyond doubt, the coincidence alone which had arrested my attention; for, amid the rattling of the sashes of the casements, and the ordinary commingled noises
590 of the still increasing storm, the sound, in itself, had nothing, surely, which should have interested or disturbed me. I continued the story:

591 How would you describe the mood of the story at this point?

"But the good champion Ethelred, now entering within the door, was sore enraged and amazed to perceive no signal of the
595 maliceful hermit; but, in the stead thereof, a dragon of a scaly and prodigious demeanor, and of a fiery tongue, which sate in guard before a palace of gold, with a floor of silver; and upon the wall there hung a shield of shining brass with this legend enwritten—

     Who entereth herein, a conqueror hath bin;
600   *Who slayeth the dragon, the shield he shall win.*

And Ethelred uplifted his mace, and struck upon the head of the dragon, which fell before him, and gave up his pesty breath, with a shriek so horrid and harsh, and withal so piercing, that Ethelred had fain to close his ears with his hands against the dreadful noise of it, the like whereof was never before heard."

Here again I paused abruptly, and now with a feeling of wild amazement—for there could be no doubt whatever that, in this instance, I did actually hear (although from what direction it proceeded I found it impossible to say) a low and apparently distant, but harsh, protracted, and most unusual screaming or grating sound—the exact counterpart of what my fancy had already conjured up for the dragon's unnatural shriek as described by the romancer.

Oppressed, as I certainly was, upon the occurrence of this second and most extraordinary coincidence, by a thousand conflicting sensations, in which wonder and extreme terror were predominant, I still retained sufficient presence of mind to avoid exciting, by any observation, the sensitive nervousness of my companion. I was by no means certain that he had noticed the sounds in question; although, assuredly, a strange alteration had, during the last few minutes, taken place in his demeanor. From a position fronting my own, he had gradually brought round his chair, so as to sit with his face to the door of the chamber; and thus I could but partially perceive his features, although I saw that his lips trembled as if he were murmuring inaudibly. His head had dropped upon his breast—yet I knew that he was not asleep, from the wide and rigid opening of the eye as I caught a glance of it in profile. The motion of his body, too, was at variance with this idea—for he rocked from side to side with a gentle yet constant and uniform sway. Having rapidly taken notice of all this, I resumed the narrative of Sir Launcelot, which thus proceeded:

"And now, the champion, having escaped from the terrible fury of the dragon, bethinking himself of the brazen shield, and of the breaking up of the enchantment which was upon it, removed the carcass from out of the way before him, and approached valorously over the silver pavement of the castle to where the shield was upon the wall; which in sooth tarried not for his full coming, but fell down at his feet upon the silver floor, with a mighty great and terrible ringing sound."

No sooner had these syllables passed my lips, than—as if a shield of brass had indeed, at the moment, fallen heavily upon a floor of silver—I became aware of a distinct, hollow, metallic, and clangorous, yet apparently muffled, reverberation. Completely unnerved, I leaped to my feet; but the measured rocking move-

602 pesty: poisonous.

613 romancer: storyteller.

614 What effect do the passages from the "Mad Trist" have on the events of the story?

631–638 What do you predict will happen?

605

610

615

620

625

630

635

640

WORDS
TO
KNOW

narrative (năr′ə-tĭv) *n.* a story

ment of Usher was undisturbed. I rushed to the chair in which he
sat. His eyes were bent fixedly before him, and throughout his
whole countenance there reigned a stony rigidity. But, as I placed
my hand upon his shoulder, there came a strong shudder over his
whole person; a sickly smile quivered about his lips; and I saw
that he spoke in a low, hurried, and gibbering murmur, as if
unconscious of my presence. Bending closely over him, I at length
drank in the hideous import of his words.

"Not hear it?—yes, I hear it, and *have* heard it. Long—long—
long—many minutes, many hours, many days, have I heard it—
yet I dared not—oh, pity me, miserable wretch that I am!—I
dared not—I *dared* not speak! *We have put her living in the
tomb!* Said I not that my senses were acute? I *now* tell you that I
heard her first feeble movements in the hollow coffin. I heard
them—many, many days ago—yet I dared not—*I dared not
speak!* And now—to-night—Ethelred—ha ha!—the breaking of
the hermit's door, and the death-cry of the dragon, and the
clangor of the shield—say, rather, the rending of her coffin, and
the grating of the iron hinges of her prison, and her struggles
within the coppered archway of the vault! Oh! whither shall I fly?
Will she not be here anon? Is she not hurrying to upbraid me for
my haste? Have I not heard her footstep on the stair? Do I not
distinguish that heavy and horrible beating of her heart?
Madman!"—here he sprang furiously to his feet, and shrieked
out his syllables, as if in the effort he were giving up his soul—
"Madman! I tell you that she now stands without the door!"

As if in the superhuman energy of his utterance there had been
found the potency of a spell, the huge antique panels to which the
speaker pointed threw slowly back, upon the instant, their
ponderous and ebony jaws. It was the work of the rushing gust—
but then without those doors there *did* stand the lofty and
enshrouded figure of the lady Madeline of Usher. There was
blood upon her white robes, and the evidence of some bitter
struggle upon every portion of her emaciated frame. For a
moment she remained trembling and reeling to and fro upon the
threshold—then, with a low moaning cry, fell heavily inward
upon the person of her brother, and in her violent and now final
death-agonies, bore him to the floor a corpse, and a victim to the
terrors he had anticipated.

From that chamber, and from that mansion, I fled aghast. The
storm was still abroad in all its wrath as I found myself crossing
the old causeway. Suddenly there shot along the path a wild light,
and I turned to see whence a gleam so unusual could have issued;

652–669 On the basis of what Usher is saying, what do you expect to happen next?

WORDS
TO
KNOW   **aghast** (ə-găst′) *adj.* overcome with fear; terrified

for the vast house and its shadows were alone behind me. The radiance was that of the full, setting, and blood-red moon, which now shone vividly through that once barely discernible fissure, of
690   which I have spoken as extending from the roof of the building, in a zigzag direction, to the base. While I gazed, this fissure rapidly widened—there came a fierce breath of the whirlwind—the entire orb of the satellite burst at once upon my sight—my brain reeled as I saw the mighty walls rushing asunder—there was a long
695   tumultuous shouting sound like the voice of a thousand waters— and the deep and dank tarn at my feet closed sullenly and silently over

the

fragments

700   of

the

"HOUSE

OF

USHER."

Spleen

Charles Baudelaire

*The renowned French poet Charles Baudelaire (1821–1867) found a soul
mate in Edgar Allan Poe. In translating Poe's short stories and poems,
Baudelaire discovered the artistic bonds they shared: "The first time I opened
a book of his I saw, with horror and delight, not just subjects I had dreamt
of, but sentences I had thought of, and written by him twenty years before."
The first stanza of "Spleen LXXXI" mirrors the first sentence of "The Fall
of the House of Usher" (page 474).*

LXXXI

When the low heavy sky weighs like a lid
Upon the spirit aching for the light
And all the wide horizon's line is hid
By a black day sadder than any night;

5 When the changed earth is but a dungeon
     dank
Where batlike Hope goes blindly fluttering
And, striking wall and roof and moldered
     plank,
Bruises his tender head and timid wing;

When like grim prison bars stretch down
     the thin,
10 Straight, rigid pillars of the endless rain,
And the dumb throngs of infamous
     spiders spin
Their meshes in the caverns of the brain,

Suddenly, bells leap forth into the air,
Hurling a hideous uproar to the sky
15 As 'twere a band of homeless spirits who fare
Through the strange heavens, wailing
     stubbornly.

And hearses, without drum or instrument,
File slowly through my soul; crushed,
     sorrowful
Weeps Hope, and Grief, fierce and
     omnipotent,
20 Plants his black banner on my drooping skull.

—*Translated by Sir John Squire*

Connect to the Literature

1. **What Do You Think?** After you finished the story, what image in it remained most vivid in your mind?

Comprehension Check
- Why does the narrator visit the House of Usher?
- Why do the narrator and his friend go to a vault below the mansion?
- What happens to the house at the end of the story?

Think Critically

2. What thoughts or unanswered questions about what took place at the House of Usher still linger in your mind?

3. **ACTIVE READING** **UNDERSTANDING COMPLEX SENTENCES**
   Review your **READER'S NOTEBOOK** notes about difficult passages in the story. Then read the sentence in lines 62–67 (page 476). Explain what the sentence means and what useful information it gives you about the Usher family.

4. What are your impressions of Roderick Usher?

   THINK ABOUT
   - his family background
   - his condition when the narrator arrives
   - his final revelations

5. How deeply do you think Roderick Usher's state of mind influences the **narrator**'s? Give reasons for your answer.

Extend Interpretations

6. **Comparing Texts** Compare the first stanza of Baudelaire's poem "Spleen LXXXI" with the opening lines of "The Fall of the House of Usher." What similarities and differences do you see?

7. **Critic's Corner** In his critical commentary *Danse Macabre,* Stephen King states, "The tale of horror is a chance to examine what's going on behind doors which we usually keep double-locked." On the basis of the works you've read in this Author Study, how well do you think Edgar Allan Poe understood what goes on behind the locked doors of the human mind? Cite evidence from the works to support your views.

8. **Connect to Life** Recall the important points in your earlier discussion about fear. Then think about the role fear plays in each of the Poe selections. Choose one of Poe's characters, and tell what chance he or she might have had to overcome fear before a situation became worse.

Literary Analysis

MOOD One of the most prominent features of this story is its **mood,** the feeling or atmosphere that the writer's words convey to the reader. In this classic tale of horror, Poe developed a gloomy and frightening mood in a variety of ways:

- His detailed descriptions of the setting through the use of **imagery,** or words or phrases that re-create sensory experiences—"vacant eye-like windows," "black and lurid tarn," "decayed trees"—help build up an impression of a place where it is impossible for happiness to exist.
- His precisely chosen words and phrases—"dreary," "bleak," "rank," "extensive decay"—create a gloomy, oppressive picture.
- His choice of a narrator who takes part in the events heightens the sense of fear by allowing the narrator to present his immediate reactions, as when he speaks of "a strange fancy" growing in his mind.

Paired Activity With another student, fill in a chart like the one shown, listing the **moods** conveyed by specific details in the story. Then review the information about Poe's theory of "unity of effect" under Build Background on page 473. Referring to your chart, try to identify the overall feeling and effect Poe may have wanted to convey in "The Fall of the House of Usher."

Descriptive Detail	Effect of Description
"clouds hung oppressively low"	depression, dread

THE AUTHOR'S STYLE
Poe's Painstaking Prose

Style is the particular way that a writer expresses himself or herself. A writer's style involves such characteristics as diction, or word choice; sentence length and construction; the presence or absence of figurative language; and tone. Edgar Allan Poe's style has delighted—and frightened—readers for over a century.

Key Aspects of Poe's Style

- a use of dashes or other interrupters in sentences to suggest hurried or excited speech
- a strong rhythm (even in prose works), produced by a repetition of phrases and word patterns
- a frequent use of figurative language, particularly similes and metaphors
- formal language that is suited to upper-class settings or intellectual characters

Analysis of Style

On the right are passages from three other stories by Poe. Study the chart above, and read each passage carefully. Then complete the following activities:

- Find several examples of each stylistic feature in the three passages. Decide what Poe was trying to achieve stylistically.
- Find at least two additional stylistic features in the passages. Describe them and give examples of each.
- Look again at the Poe stories in the Author Study. With a partner, find and list examples of some of their stylistic features.

Applications

1. Comparing Points of View "The Masque of the Red Death" is told from the third-person point of view; "The Fall of the House of Usher," from a first-person point of view. How does the point of view affect each story's emotional intensity?

2. Style in Action Choose a story, not by Poe, that you have read in this book. Rewrite a passage of it in an imitation of Poe's style. How does your retelling change the nature of the story?

3. Speaking and Listening With a group of classmates, read aloud passages chosen from the selections in this Author Study. What differences in the passages reflect differences in the works' purposes? What similarities are regular characteristics of Poe's style?

---

from "The Imp of the Perverse"

We have a task before us which must be speedily performed. We know that it will be ruinous to make delay. The most important crisis of our life calls, trumpet-tongued, for immediate energy and action. We glow, we are consumed with eagerness to commence the work, with the anticipation of whose glorious result our whole souls are on fire. It must, it shall be undertaken today, and yet we put it off until tomorrow; and why? There is no answer, except that we feel *perverse.* . . .

I have said thus much, that in some measure I may answer your question—that I may explain to you why I am here. . . . Had I not been thus prolix, you might either have misunderstood me altogether, or, with the rabble, have fancied me mad.

from "William Wilson"

But the house!—how quaint an old building was this!—to me how veritably a palace of enchantment! There was really no end to its windings—to its incomprehensible subdivisions. It was difficult, at any given time, to say with certainty upon which of its two stories one happened to be.

from "Ligeia"

I trembled not—I stirred not—for a crowd of unutterable fancies connected with the air, the stature, the demeanor, of the figure, rushing hurriedly through my brain, had paralyzed—h chilled me into stone. I stirred not—but gaze upon the apparition. There was a mad disorde in my thoughts—a tumult unappeasable.

Writing Options

1. Roderick Usher's Letter The narrator of "The Fall of the House of Usher" tells of the persuasive letter that Usher wrote, inviting him to the house. Write your own version of that letter. Be sure to convey Usher's emotional state.

2. Comparing Ushers In a comparison-contrast essay, discuss Roderick Usher and his ancestral home. In what ways are the two similar? Alternatively, compare Roderick and Madeline Usher. Why do you think Poe made the brother and sister twins?

Writing Handbook
See page 1281: Compare and Contrast.

3. Madeline's Retelling In a few paragraphs, briefly retell the story as it might be told by Madeline after she awakens in the vault. Try using Poe's style. Put your story in your **Working Portfolio.**

Activities & Explorations

1. Eerie Pantomime Join with other members of your class to create and perform a pantomime or an interpretive dance that tells the story of the House of Usher without the use of words.
~ PERFORMING

2. Usher Poster Imagine that you're part of a team that is making a movie version of the story. Create a poster to attract a new generation of Poe fans.
~ ART

Roderick

Madeline Usher

3. Charting Usher Events To clarify the plot of the story, make a flow chart that shows the sequence of events in it. You can use the following chart as a model.
~ VIEWING AND REPRESENTING

Inquiry & Research

Science Usher tells the narrator that he and his sister were twins who shared "sympathies of a scarcely intelligible nature." Psychologists have conducted interesting research into twins and the characteristics they share. Look into popular magazines and psychology textbooks to find out what psychologists have learned, and report your find-ings to the class.

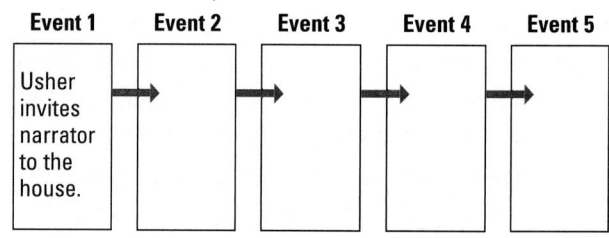

Event 1	Event 2	Event 3	Event 4	Event 5
Usher invites narrator to the house.				

Vocabulary in Action

EXERCISE A: CONTEXT CLUES Read the following sentences, and decide which Word to Know would best replace the underlined word or phrase.

1. People in the 1800s must have been <u>horribly shocked</u> at the events depicted in "The Fall of the House of Usher."

2. Many must have slept <u>badly, waking up often</u>, after reading the story.

3. In the days when there were few drugs for the <u>reduction</u> of physical pain, Poe's descriptions of disease and suffering probably struck a responsive chord.

4. In this <u>tale</u> Poe exploits people's anxieties about death and decay.

5. In Poe's time there was widespread fear about the <u>laying to rest</u> of people who were not really dead.

EXERCISE B: MEANING CLUES On your paper write the Word to Know that best matches each description.

1. two objects or people alike in many ways
2. a diet that lacks enough nutrients
3. a hurricane that leaves an entire town in ruins
4. unsuccessful efforts to accomplish something
5. a dog whose ribs are showing
6. a bird that can't fly, such as an ostrich
7. a cheerleader with a lot of spirit
8. a plain, boring meal
9. a mule that will not budge
10. problems without answers

WORDS TO KNOW			
	affinity	emaciated	interment
	aghast	fitfully	narrative
	alleviation	futility	obstinate
	annihilate	insipid	terrestrial
	deficiency	insoluble	vivacious

Building Vocabulary

For an in-depth lesson on context clues, see page 326.

Go To:

Edgar Allan Poe

Author Study Project

A CRITICAL SCRAPBOOK ON POE

Document : Done.

Edgar Allan Poe's reputation as a writer has varied greatly. During his lifetime, some critics condemned him for his strange tales, but Poe had his champions as well. In the decades since his death, critics have continued a fierce debate about Poe's writing ability. Working alone or with a group, create a scrapbook of critical and popular views of Poe's work. You might also include critical reviews of Poe by your classmates. The following are some sources you might uses in your research.

Books and Periodicals Look for opinions about Poe's writings in reviews and critical biographies. Be sure to note whose opinions they are and when they were expressed. Find out whether any of the opinions were motivated by nonliterary considerations. Focus especially on the opinions of well-known writers who were Poe's contemporaries, such as James Russell Lowell, Ralph Waldo Emerson, and Elizabeth Barrett Browning.

Computer Resources See if you can find any CD-ROMs that contain comments about Poe. Look for Poe newsgroups and Web sites on the Internet.

Survey Devise a set of questions that you can use to interview students, friends, and family members about their views of Poe. You might want to bring along some samples of Poe's work for them to look over before you ask your questions. Present your results in a graph or chart.

 More Online: Research Starter
www.mcdougallittell.com

Dr. Heidegger's Experiment

Short Story by NATHANIEL HAWTHORNE

Connect to Your Life

Aging Gracefully What do you like most about being the age you are right now? What aspects of growing older do you look forward to? What aspects of growing older are undesirable to you? Do you think youth and age should be measured by the years a person has lived or by a person's behavior and outlook? With a small group of classmates, discuss these questions about youth and aging.

Build Background

Forever Young You may have heard about the Spanish explorer Ponce de León (pŏns' də lē-ōn') and his travels throughout Florida in search of the Fountain of Youth. People believed that water from this fountain would make old people young again. Although the fountain was a myth, the belief in a magic liquid that could bring the dead to life or that could confer immortality has a long history. During the Middle Ages, alchemists (early chemists who combined science and magic) sought the "elixir of life," a substance they believed would prolong life indefinitely. Nathaniel Hawthorne was fascinated by the concept of immortality, and in several stories—including "Dr. Heidegger's Experiment"—he wrote about men who possessed the secret elixir of life.

WORDS TO KNOW
Vocabulary Preview

decrepit	exultingly
deferential	stigma
dispute	transient
efface	tremulous
exhilaration	venerable

Focus Your Reading

LITERARY ANALYSIS **FORESHADOWING** While watching a movie or television show, have you ever accurately guessed other events that were going to happen? A writer's use of hints or clues to indicate events that will occur later in a story is called **foreshadowing.** Foreshadowing creates suspense and at the same time prepares the reader for what is to come. As you read "Dr. Heidegger's Experiment," look for clues that might help you guess how the story will unfold.

ACTIVE READING **INTERPRETING ALLEGORY** As you recall, an **allegory** is a work of literature in which people, objects, and events stand for abstract qualities, such as evil, compassion, or greed. For example, the four guests in "Dr. Heidegger's Experiment" are not realistic, fully developed characters. Instead, they seem more like representations of ideas. Allegories are written not only to entertain but also to teach lessons or moral principles.

READER'S NOTEBOOK Draw a chart like the one below, and complete it as you read the story or right after you finish reading it. Identify an abstract quality or idea that each of the four guests in the story might represent.

Character	What he or she loses or wastes	What happens when he or she is given a second youth	What he or she might represent
Mr. Medbourne	wealth	schemes to make money again	greed
Col. Killigrew			
Mr. Gascoigne			
Widow Wycherly			

Dr. Heidegger's Experiment

NATHANIEL
HAWTHORNE

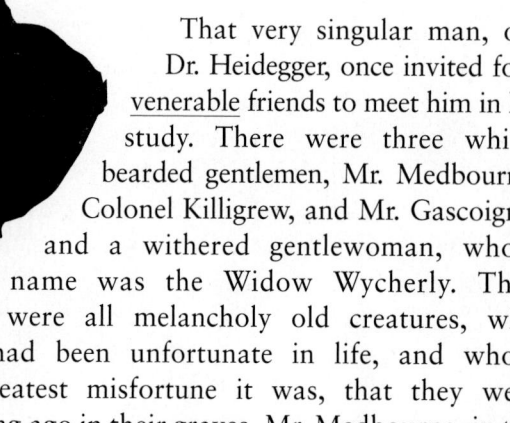

That very singular man, old Dr. Heidegger, once invited four <u>venerable</u> friends to meet him in his study. There were three white-bearded gentlemen, Mr. Medbourne, Colonel Killigrew, and Mr. Gascoigne, and a withered gentlewoman, whose name was the Widow Wycherly. They were all melancholy old creatures, who had been unfortunate in life, and whose greatest misfortune it was, that they were not long ago in their graves. Mr. Medbourne, in the vigor of his age, had been a prosperous merchant, but had lost his all by a frantic speculation, and was now little better than a mendicant. Colonel Killigrew had wasted his best years, and his health and substance, in the pursuit of sinful pleasures, which had given birth to a brood of pains, such as the gout, and divers other torments of soul and body. Mr. Gascoigne was a ruined politician, a man of evil fame, or at least had been so, till time had buried him from the knowledge of the present generation, and made him obscure instead of infamous. As for the Widow Wycherly, tradition tells us that she was a great beauty in her day; but, for a long while past, she had lived in deep seclusion, on account of certain scandalous stories, which had prejudiced the gentry of the town against her. It is a circumstance worth mentioning, that each of these three old gentlemen, Mr. Medbourne, Colonel Killigrew, and Mr. Gascoigne, were early lovers of the Widow Wycherly, and had once been on the point of cutting each other's throats for her sake. And, before proceeding farther, I will merely hint, that Dr. Heidegger and all his four guests were sometimes thought to be a little beside themselves; as is not unfrequently the case with old people, when worried either by present troubles or woeful recollections.

"My dear old friends," said Dr. Heidegger, motioning them to be seated, "I am desirous of your assistance in one of those little experiments with which I amuse myself here in my study."

If all stories were true, Dr. Heidegger's study must have been a very curious place. It was a dim, old-fashioned chamber, festooned with cobwebs, and besprinkled with antique dust. Around the walls stood several oaken book-cases, the lower shelves of which were filled with rows of gigantic folios, and black-letter quartos, and the upper with little parchment covered duodecimos. Over the central book-case was a bronze bust of

GUIDE FOR READING

12–25 What has each of these four characters wasted or lost?

15 mendicant (mĕn′dĭ-kənt): beggar.

17 gout: a painful disease of the joints, once thought to be caused by eating too much rich food.

21 obscure instead of infamous (ĭn′fə-məs): little known rather than well-known for wickedness.

25 gentry: respectable or socially high-ranking people.

25–28 What relationship did the four guests have in their youth?

37–60 Notice the details included in this Gothic description of Dr. Heidegger's study. What mood is established by this description?

39 festooned: decorated in draping curves.

41–43 folios . . . quartos . . . duodecimos: books of different sizes.

WORDS
TO
KNOW

venerable (vĕn′ər-ə-bəl) *adj.* worthy of respect because of age, dignity, or character

Hippocrates, with which, according to some authorities, Dr. Heidegger was accustomed to hold consultations, in all difficult cases of his practice. In the obscurest corner of the room stood a tall and narrow oaken closet, with its door ajar, within which doubtfully appeared a skeleton. Between two of the book-cases hung a looking-glass, presenting its high and dusty plate within a tarnished gilt frame. Among many wonderful stories related of this mirror, it was fabled that the spirits of all the doctor's deceased patients dwelt within its verge, and would stare him in the face whenever he looked thitherward. The opposite side of the chamber was ornamented with the full length portrait of a young lady, arrayed in the faded magnificence of silk, satin, and brocade, and with a visage as faded as her dress. Above half a century ago, Dr. Heidegger had been on the point of marriage with this young lady; but, being affected with some slight disorder, she had swallowed one of her lover's prescriptions, and died on the bridal evening.

44 Hippocrates (hĭ-pŏk′rə-tēz′): a Greek physician, considered to be the father of medicine.

48–50 This is no ordinary mirror. Watch what it reveals as the story continues.

52 verge: border.

53 thitherward: in that direction.

56 visage (vĭz′ĭj): face.

> "**I** am desirous of your assistance in one of those little experiments with which I amuse myself here in my study."

The greatest curiosity of the study remains to be mentioned: it was a ponderous folio volume, bound in black leather, with massive silver clasps. There were no letters on the back, and nobody could tell the title of the book. But it was well known to be a book of magic; and once, when a chambermaid had lifted it, merely to brush away the dust, the skeleton had rattled in its closet, the picture of the young lady had stepped one foot upon the floor, and several ghastly faces had peeped forth from the mirror; while the brazen head of Hippocrates frowned, and said—"Forbear!"

Such was Dr. Heidegger's study. On the summer afternoon of our tale, a small round table, as black as ebony, stood in the center of the room, sustaining a cut-glass vase, of beautiful form and elaborate workmanship. The sunshine came through the window, between the heavy festoons of two faded damask curtains, and fell directly across this vase; so that a mild splendor was reflected

70 forbear: stop; cease.

from it on the ashen visages of the five old people who sat around. Four champagne glasses were also on the table.

"My dear old friends," repeated Dr. Heidegger, "may I reckon on your aid in performing an exceedingly curious experiment?"

Now Dr. Heidegger was a very strange old gentleman, whose eccentricity had become the nucleus for a thousand fantastic stories. Some of these fables, to my shame be it spoken, might possibly be traced back to mine own veracious self; and if any passages of the present tale should startle the reader's faith, I must be content to bear the <u>stigma</u> of a fiction-monger.

When the doctor's four guests heard him talk of his proposed experiment, they anticipated nothing more wonderful than the murder of a mouse in an air-pump, or the examination of a cobweb by the microscope, or some similar nonsense, with which he was constantly in the habit of pestering his intimates. But without waiting for a reply, Dr. Heidegger hobbled across the chamber, and returned with the same ponderous folio, bound in black leather, which common report affirmed to be a book of magic. Undoing the silver clasps, he opened the volume, and took from among its black-letter pages a rose, or what was once a rose, though now the green leaves and crimson petals had assumed one brownish hue, and the ancient flower seemed ready to crumble to dust in the doctor's hands.

"This rose," said Dr. Heidegger, with a sigh, "this same withered and crumbling flower, blossomed five-and-fifty years ago. It was given me by Sylvia Ward, whose portrait hangs yonder; and I meant to wear it in my bosom at our wedding. Five-and-fifty years it has been treasured between the leaves of this old volume. Now, would you deem it possible that this rose of half a century could ever bloom again?"

"Nonsense!" said the Widow Wycherly, with a peevish toss of her head. "You might as well ask whether an old woman's wrinkled face could ever bloom again."

"See!" answered Dr. Heidegger.

He uncovered the vase, and threw the faded rose into the water which it contained. At first, it lay lightly on the surface of the fluid, appearing to imbibe none of its moisture. Soon, however, a singular change began to be visible. The crushed and dried petals stirred, and assumed a deepening tinge of crimson, as if the flower were reviving from a death-like slumber; the slender stalk and twigs of foliage became green; and there was the rose of half a century, looking as fresh as when Sylvia Ward had first given it to her lover. It was scarcely full-blown; for some of its delicate

83–86 The narrator admits to having told fables about Dr. Heidegger in the past.

84 veracious: truthful.

86 fiction-monger: liar.

107 peevish: irritable.

113 imbibe: absorb.

119 full-blown: completely open.

WORDS
TO
KNOW

stigma (stĭg′mə) *n.* a mark of disgrace

504

Déjeuner [Luncheon] (1876), Gustave Caillebotte. Oil on canvas, 52 cm × 75 cm, private collection.

𝒯he crushed and dried petals stirred, . . . as if the

flower were reviving from a death-like slumber.

red leaves curled modestly around its moist bosom, within which two or three dewdrops were sparkling.

"That is certainly a very pretty deception," said the doctor's friends; carelessly, however, for they had witnessed greater miracles at a conjurer's show: "pray how was it effected?"

128 conjurer's: magician's.

"Did you never hear of the 'Fountain of Youth,'" asked Dr. Heidegger, "which Ponce De Leon, the Spanish adventurer, went in search of, two or three centuries ago?"

"But did Ponce De Leon ever find it?" said the Widow Wycherly.

"No," answered Dr. Heidegger, "for he never sought it in the
135 right place. The famous Fountain of Youth, if I am rightly informed, is situated in the southern part of the Floridian peninsula, not far from Lake Macaco. Its source is overshadowed by several gigantic magnolias, which, though numberless centuries old, have been kept as fresh as violets, by the virtues of this won-
140 derful water. An acquaintance of mine, knowing my curiosity in such matters, has sent me what you see in the vase."

"Ahem!" said Colonel Killigrew, who believed not a word of the doctor's story: "and what may be the effect of this fluid on the human frame?"

145 "You shall judge for yourself, my dear colonel," replied Dr. Heidegger; "and all of you, my respected friends, are welcome to so much of this admirable fluid, as may restore to you the bloom of youth. For my own part, having had much trouble in growing old, I am in no hurry to grow young again. With your permission,
150 therefore, I will merely watch the progress of the experiment."

While he spoke, Dr. Heidegger had been filling the four champagne glasses with the water of the Fountain of Youth. It was apparently impregnated with an effervescent gas, for little bubbles were continually ascending from the depths of the glasses,
155 and bursting in silvery spray at the surface. As the liquor diffused a pleasant perfume, the old people doubted not that it possessed cordial and comfortable properties; and, though utter skeptics as to its rejuvenescent power, they were inclined to swallow it at once. But Dr. Heidegger besought them to stay a moment.

160 "Before you drink, my respectable old friends," said he, "it would be well that, with the experience of a life-time to direct you, you should draw up a few general rules for your guidance, in passing a second time through the perils of youth. Think what a sin and shame it would be, if, with your peculiar advantages,

148–149 What do you think of Dr. Heidegger's reason for not wanting to be young again?

152–153 was apparently . . . gas: seemed to have a bubbling gas dissolved in it.

157 cordial (kôr´jəl): stimulating.

158 rejuvenescent (rĭ-jōō´və-nĕs´ənt): producing renewed youth.

159 besought them to stay: begged them to wait.

160–166 What warning does Dr. Heidegger give his guests?

165 you should not become patterns of virtue and wisdom to all the young people of the age!"

The doctor's four venerable friends made him no answer, except by a feeble and <u>tremulous</u> laugh; so very ridiculous was the idea, that, knowing how closely repentance treads behind the

170 steps of error, they should ever go astray again.

"Drink, then," said the doctor, bowing: "I rejoice that I have so well selected the subjects of my experiment."

With palsied hands, they raised the glasses to their lips. The liquor, if it really possessed such virtues as Dr. Heidegger

175 imputed to it, could not have been bestowed on four human beings who needed it more woefully. They looked as if they had never known what youth or pleasure was, but had been the offspring of Nature's dotage, and always the gray, <u>decrepit</u>, sapless, miserable creatures, who now sat stooping round the doctor's

180 table, without life enough in their souls or bodies to be animated even by the prospect of growing young again. They drank off the water, and replaced their glasses on the table.

Assuredly there was an almost immediate improvement in the aspect of the party, not unlike what might have been produced by

185 a glass of generous wine, together with a sudden glow of cheerful sunshine, brightening over all their visages at once. There was a healthful suffusion on their cheeks, instead of the ashen hue that had made them look so corpselike. They gazed at one another, and fancied that some magic power had really begun to smooth

190 away the deep and sad inscriptions which Father Time had been so long engraving on their brows. The Widow Wycherly adjusted her cap, for she felt almost like a woman again.

167–170 Should the guests feel so confident that they will not repeat the errors of the past?

171–172 What do you think is the purpose of Dr. Heidegger's experiment?

173 palsied: trembling.

175 imputed: attributed; credited.

178 dotage (dō′tĭj): feebleness due to old age.

184 aspect: appearance.

187 healthful suffusion: rosy glow of health.

> "Drink, then," said the doctor, bowing: "I rejoice that I have so well selected the subjects of my experiment."

"Give us more of this wondrous water!" cried they, eagerly. "We are younger—but we are still too old! Quick!—give us more!"

195 "Patience, patience!" quoth Dr. Heidegger, who sat watching the experiment, with philosophic coolness. "You have been a long

WORDS TO KNOW	**tremulous** (trĕm′yə-ləs) *adj.* marked by trembling, quivering, or shaking **decrepit** (dĭ-krĕp′ĭt) *adj.* weakened, worn out, or broken down by old age or hard use

time growing old. Surely, you might be content to grow young in half an hour! But the water is at your service."

Again he filled their glasses with the liquor of youth, enough of which still remained in the vase to turn half the old people in the city to the age of their own grand-children. While the bubbles were yet sparkling on the brim, the doctor's four guests snatched their glasses from the table, and swallowed the contents at a single gulp. Was it delusion? Even while the draught was passing down their throats, it seemed to have wrought a change on their whole systems. Their eyes grew clear and bright; a dark shade deepened among their silvery locks; they sat around the table, three gentlemen of middle age, and a woman, hardly beyond her buxom prime.

"My dear widow, you are charming!" cried Colonel Killigrew, whose eyes had been fixed upon her face, while the shadows of age were flitting from it like darkness from the crimson day-break.

The fair widow knew, of old, that Colonel Killigrew's compliments were not always measured by sober truth; so she started up and ran to the mirror, still dreading that the ugly visage of an old woman would meet her gaze. Meanwhile, the three gentlemen behaved in such a manner, as proved that the water of the Fountain of Youth possessed some intoxicating qualities; unless, indeed, their <u>exhilaration</u> of spirits were merely a lightsome dizziness, caused by the sudden removal of the weight of years. Mr. Gascoigne's mind seemed to run on political topics, but whether relating to the past, present, or future, could not easily be determined, since the same ideas and phrases have been in vogue these fifty years. Now he rattled forth full-throated sentences about patriotism, national glory, and the people's right; now he muttered some perilous stuff or other, in a sly and doubtful whisper, so cautiously that even his own conscience could scarcely catch the secret; and now, again, he spoke in measured accents, and a deeply <u>deferential</u> tone, as if a royal ear were listening to his well-turned periods. Colonel Killigrew all this time had been trolling forth a jolly bottle-song, and ringing his glass in symphony with the chorus, while his eyes wandered towards the buxom figure of the Widow Wycherly. On the other side of the

207–215 Is the effect of the water physical or psychological? Watch how the narrator blurs the line between what is real and what is an illusion throughout the story.

219–257 How do the guests begin to behave as soon as their youth is restored?

WORDS TO KNOW	**exhilaration** (ĭg-zĭl′ə-rā′shən) *n.* a lively delight
	deferential (dĕf′ə-rĕn′shəl) *adj.* extremely respectful

table, Mr. Medbourne was involved in a calculation of dollars and cents, with which was strangely intermingled a project for supplying the East Indies with ice, by harnessing a team of whales to the polar icebergs.

As for the Widow Wycherly, she stood before the mirror, curtseying and simpering to her own image, and greeting it as the friend whom she loved better than all the world beside. She thrust her face close to the glass, to see whether some long-remembered wrinkle or crow's-foot had indeed vanished. She examined whether the snow had so entirely melted from her hair, that the venerable cap could be safely thrown aside. At last, turning briskly away, she came with a sort of dancing step to the table.

"My dear old doctor," cried she, "pray favor me with another glass!"

"Certainly, my dear madam, certainly!" replied the complaisant doctor; "See! I have already filled the glasses."

There, in fact, stood the four glasses, brim full of this wonderful water, the delicate spray of which, as it effervesced from the surface, resembled the tremulous glitter of diamonds. It was now so nearly sunset, that the chamber had grown duskier than ever; but a mild and moon-like splendor gleamed from within the vase, and rested alike on the four guests, and on the doctor's venerable figure. He sat in a high-backed, elaborately-carved, oaken armchair, with a gray dignity of aspect that might have well befitted

The doctor's four guests snatched their glasses from the table, and swallowed the contents at a single gulp.

that very Father Time, whose power had never been <u>disputed</u>, save by this fortunate company. Even while quaffing the third draught of the Fountain of Youth, they were almost awed by the expression of his mysterious visage.

But, the next moment, the exhilarating gush of young life shot through their veins. They were now in the happy prime of youth. Age, with its miserable train of cares, and sorrows, and diseases, was remembered only as the trouble of a dream, from which they

245 simpering: smiling in a silly, self-conscious way.

254-255 complaisant (kəm-plā'sənt): willing to please.

265 quaffing (kwŏf'ĭng): drinking heartily.

WORDS
TO   **dispute** (dĭ-spyo͞ot') v. to question or doubt
KNOW

had joyously awoke. The fresh gloss of the soul, so early lost, and without which the world's successive scenes had been but a gallery of faded pictures, again threw its enchantment over all their prospects. They felt like new-created beings, in a new-created universe.

"We are young! We are young!" they cried, <u>exultingly</u>.

Youth, like the extremity of age, had <u>effaced</u> the strongly marked characteristics of middle life, and mutually assimilated them all. They were a group of merry youngsters, almost maddened with the exuberant frolicksomeness of their years. The most singular effect of their gayety was an impulse to mock the infirmity and decrepitude of which they had so lately been the victims. They laughed loudly at their old-fashioned attire, the wide-skirted coats and flapped waistcoats of the young men, and the ancient cap and gown of the blooming girl. One limped across the floor, like a gouty grandfather; one set a pair of spectacles astride of his nose, and pretended to pore over the black-letter pages of the book of magic; a third seated himself in an arm-chair, and strove to imitate the venerable dignity of Dr. Heidegger. Then all shouted mirthfully, and leaped about the room. The Widow Wycherly—if so fresh a damsel could be called a widow—tripped up to the doctor's chair, with a mischievous merriment in her rosy face.

"Doctor, you dear old soul," cried she, "get up and dance with me!" And then the four young people laughed louder than ever, to think what a queer figure the poor old doctor would cut.

"Pray excuse me," answered the doctor, quietly. "I am old and rheumatic, and my dancing days were over long ago. But either of these gay young gentlemen will be glad of so pretty a partner."

"Dance with me, Clara!" cried Colonel Killigrew.

"No, no, I will be her partner!" shouted Mr. Gascoigne.

"She promised me her hand, fifty years ago!" exclaimed Mr. Medbourne.

They all gathered round her. One caught both her hands in his passionate grasp—another threw his arm about her waist—the third buried his hand among the glossy curls that clustered beneath the widow's cap. Blushing, panting, struggling, chiding, laughing, her warm breath fanning each of their faces by turns, she strove to disengage herself, yet still remained in their triple embrace. Never was there a livelier picture of youthful rivalship, with bewitching beauty for the prize. Yet, by a strange deception, owing to the duskiness of the chamber, and the antique dresses which they still wore, the tall mirror is said to have reflected the figures of the three old, gray, withered grand-sires, ridiculously contending for the skinny ugliness of a shrivelled grand-dam.

278–280 How does the narrator say youth and old age are alike?

279 assimilated: absorbed.

281–296 Whom or what are the guests mocking, and why?

291 mirthfully: joyfully.

298 rheumatic (rōō-măt′ĭk): made stiff by a condition such as arthritis.

309 strove to disengage herself: struggled to free herself.

311–315 The narrator is unclear about whether the reflection is real or an illusion. Why? What does the image in the mirror reveal?

314–315 grand-sires . . . grand-dam: old men . . . old woman.

WORDS TO KNOW	**exultingly** (ĭg-zŭl′tĭng-lē) *adv.* in a joyful and triumphant way **efface** (ĭ-fās′) *v.* to rub or wipe out; erase

Age, with its miserable train of cares, and sorrows, and diseases, was remembered only as the trouble of a dream, from which they had joyously awoke.

La danse à la campagne [The country dance] (1883),
Pierre Auguste Renoir. Private collection.

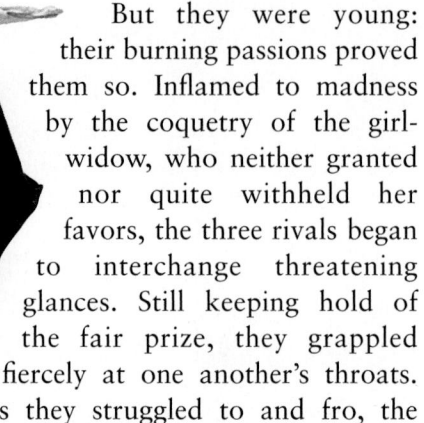

But they were young: their burning passions proved them so. Inflamed to madness by the coquetry of the girl-widow, who neither granted nor quite withheld her favors, the three rivals began to interchange threatening glances. Still keeping hold of the fair prize, they grappled fiercely at one another's throats. As they struggled to and fro, the table was overturned, and the vase dashed into a thousand fragments. The precious Water of Youth flowed in a bright stream across the floor, moistening the wings of a butterfly, which, grown old in the decline of summer, had alighted there to die. The insect fluttered lightly through the chamber, and settled on the snowy head of Dr. Heidegger.

"Come, come, gentlemen!—come, Madam Wycherly," exclaimed the doctor, "I really must protest against this riot."

They stood still, and shivered; for it seemed as if gray Time were calling them back from their sunny youth, far down into the chill and darksome vale of years. They looked at old Dr. Heidegger, who sat in his carved arm-chair, holding the rose of half a century, which he had rescued from among the fragments of the shattered vase. At the motion of his hand, the four rioters resumed their seats; the more readily, because their violent exertions had wearied them, youthful though they were.

"My poor Sylvia's rose!" ejaculated Dr. Heidegger, holding it in the light of the sunset clouds: "it appears to be fading again."

And so it was. Even while the party were looking at it, the flower continued to shrivel up, till it became as dry and fragile as when the doctor had first thrown it into the vase. He shook off the few drops of moisture which clung to its petals.

"I love it as well thus, as in its dewy freshness," observed he, pressing the withered rose to his withered lips. While he spoke, the butterfly fluttered down from the doctor's snowy head, and fell upon the floor.

His guests shivered again. A strange chillness, whether of the body or spirit they could not tell, was creeping gradually over them all. They gazed at one another, and fancied that each fleeting moment snatched away a charm, and left a deepening furrow where none had been before. Was it an illusion? Had the changes of a life-time been crowded into so brief a space, and were they

319 coquetry (kō'kǐ-trē): flirtatious behavior.

318–329 How does the characters' behavior in this scene compare with that of their youth?

338 vale: valley.

344 ejaculated: exclaimed.

350–353 Can you infer how Dr. Heidegger feels about old age from the way he regards the rose?

360 now four aged people, sitting with their old friend, Dr. Heidegger?

"Are we grown old again, so soon!" cried they, dolefully.

In truth, they had. The Water of Youth possessed merely a virtue more <u>transient</u> than that of wine. The delirium which it cre-
365 ated had effervesced away. Yes! they were old again. With a shud-dering impulse, that showed her a woman still, the widow clasped her skinny hands before her face, and wished that the coffin-lid were over it, since it could be no longer beautiful.

"Yes, friends, ye are old again," said Dr. Heidegger; "and lo!
370 the Water of Youth is all lavished on the ground. Well—I bemoan it not; for if the fountain gushed at my very doorstep, I would not stoop to bathe my lips in it—no, though its delirium were for years instead of moments. Such is the lesson ye have taught me!"

But the doctor's four friends had taught no such lesson to
375 themselves. They resolved forthwith to make a pilgrimage to Florida, and quaff at morning, noon, and night, from the Fountain of Youth. ❖

364 delirium: a temporary state of mental confusion and clouded consciousness.

369-373 What lesson has Dr. Heidegger learned?

LITERARY LINK

𝔐ONODY

(Elegy for Nathaniel Hawthorne)

HERMAN MELVILLE

Herman Melville (1819–1891), best known for his famous sea story Moby-Dick, *became friends with Nathaniel Hawthorne around 1850. Though their relationship grew strained, Melville's admiration for Hawthorne was enduring. In "Monody" the speaker of the poem mourns Hawthorne's death.*

To have known him, to have loved him
    After loneness long;
And then to be estranged in life,
    And neither in the wrong;
And now for death to set his seal—
5   Ease me, a little ease, my song!
By wintry hills his hermit-mound[1]
    The sheeted snow-drifts drape,
And houseless there the snow-bird flits
    Beneath the fir-trees' crape:[2]
10 Glazed now with ice the cloistral[3] vine
    That hid the shyest grape.

---

1. **hermit-mound:** the burial mound where the dead man rests in isolation, like a hermit.
2. **crape:** a black cloth used in funeral decorations.
3. **cloistral** (kloi′strəl): secluded.

WORDS
TO
KNOW
   transient (trăn′shənt) *adj.* lasting or existing for only a short time

Thinking through the LITERATURE

Connect to the Literature

1. What Do You Think? What are your thoughts about the ending of this story?

> **Comprehension Check**
> - Why does Dr. Heidegger invite his friends to his chamber?
> - What warning does the doctor give his guests?
> - What do the four guests resolve to do at the end of the story?

Think Critically

2. ACTIVE READING INTERPRETING ALLEGORY

Look over the **character** chart you made in your READER'S NOTEBOOK. What lesson or lessons do you think Hawthorne intended this story to teach?

THINK ABOUT
- what qualities the characters might represent
- what Dr. Heidegger is testing
- why Dr. Heidegger says he would not drink from the Fountain of Youth

3. Compare your attitudes toward youth and aging with those expressed by the **characters** in this story.

THINK ABOUT
- Dr. Heidegger's comments about the withered rose (page 512)
- the guests' behavior when restored to youth
- the guests' desire to find the Fountain of Youth

4. The narrator is deliberately unclear about whether the guests are actually restored to youth. What do you think? Support your answer.

Extend Interpretations

5. What If? What do you think would have happened if the Water of Youth had not spilled?

6. Different Perspectives A year before his death at the age of 59, Hawthorne wrote, "Everything is beautiful in youth—all things are allowed it." How do you think each of the characters in "Dr. Heidegger's Experiment" would respond to this viewpoint?

7. Comparing Texts Reread Melville's poem "Monody" on page 513. Compare the speaker's regrets with the characters' regrets in "Dr. Heidegger's Experiment."

8. Connect to Life If people could regain their youth again, do you think they would make the same mistakes? Explain.

Literary Analysis

FORESHADOWING

Foreshadowing is a writer's use of hints or clues to indicate events that will occur later in a story. For example, the former rivalry for the Widow Wycherly that is mentioned on page 502 foreshadows the rivalry that occurs later in Dr. Heidegger's study (page 510). Foreshadowing is a technique that helps build suspense and arouse the reader's curiosity.

Paired Activity Working with a partner, scan the story for two other examples of foreshadowing. Did Hawthorne's use of foreshadowing add to or detract from your enjoyment of the story? Share your response with classmates.

REVIEW MOOD How would you describe the **mood** of this story, or the atmosphere conveyed to the reader? What elements make the mood similar to or different from the mood of "The Fall of the House of Usher"?

Writing Options

1. **Warning Label** Hazardous products carry labels that caution consumers about their use. Write a warning label that might appear on a bottle of water from the Fountain of Youth.

2. **Science News** Write a summary of Dr. Heidegger's experiment for a popular scientific or medical journal.

3. **Story Ending** If you could be ten years old again, knowing what you know now, would you turn back the clock? Give your answer as the concluding paragraphs of a story about a teenager who chooses to become ten years old again. Save your writing in your **Working Portfolio.**

Activities & Explorations

Product Chart Look for magazine and TV ads promising people that they can look and feel younger. Then, in a chart, record the names of the products or services advertised and what they claim to do. How do these products or services compare to the Water of Youth? What advice would you give a consumer? ~ **VIEWING AND REPRESENTING**

Vocabulary in Action

EXERCISE: ASSESSMENT PRACTICE Write the letter of the word that is an antonym of the boldfaced word.

1. **efface:** (a) mock, (b) preserve, (c) disguise
2. **stigma:** (a) award, (b) beauty, (c) hero
3. **decrepit:** (a) large, (b) fashionable, (c) sturdy
4. **venerable:** (a) dishonorable, (b) famous, (c) pale
5. **transient:** (a) wealthy, (b) permanent, (c) feeble
6. **deferential:** (a) similar, (b) accepting, (c) contemptuous
7. **exhilaration:** (a) gloom, (b) delay, (c) anticipation
8. **dispute:** (a) accept, (b) challenge, (c) admire
9. **tremulous:** (a) tired, (b) steady, (c) tiny
10. **exultingly:** (a) quietly, (b) arrogantly, (c) sadly

Nathaniel Hawthorne
1804–1864

Other Works
The Scarlet Letter
The House of the Seven Gables
"The Minister's Black Veil"
"Rappaccini's Daughter"

The Sorrows of Youth Nathaniel Hawthorne was born in Salem, Massachusetts. His childhood was not especially happy. His father, a sea captain, died when Hawthorne was four years old, and his grieving mother became reclusive. After graduating from Bowdoin College in Maine, where one of his classmates was Henry Wadsworth Longfellow, Hawthorne secluded himself at his mother's home in Salem for 12 years. He dedicated himself to writing and reading, hoping to develop his craft.

A Flair for Writing Hawthorne, a descendant of a prominent Massachusetts Bay Colony settler and of a Salem witch trial judge, was fascinated by the society of his Puritan ancestors and studied colonial New England history during his long seclusion. Many of Hawthorne's stories are drawn from the darker aspects of his Puritan heritage. In 1837, Hawthorne published his first collection of short stories, *Twice-Told Tales.* In 1842, he married and settled in Concord, Massachusetts. In 1850, with the publication of *The Scarlet Letter*, Hawthorne gained acclaim as a writer. Despite his success, he made little money.

An Unhappy Ending Eventually, Hawthorne became despondent over money, his poor health, and his inability to write. Hawthorne died in 1864 while visiting New Hampshire with his old friend, the former U.S. president Franklin Pierce. Among the pallbearers at Hawthorne's funeral were Longfellow, Ralph Waldo Emerson, Oliver Wendell Holmes, and James Russell Lowell.

A Rose for Emily

Short Story by WILLIAM FAULKNER

Comparing Literature

Traditions Across Time: Southern Gothic

Critics often place William Faulkner, along with writers such as Flannery O'Connor and Truman Capote, in the literary tradition known as Southern Gothic. The elements of Gothic fiction include disturbed or unbalanced characters, strange or terrifying events, and gloomy or rundown settings. Faulkner's story "A Rose for Emily" is particularly interesting to compare with Edgar Allan Poe's 19th-century Gothic tale, "The Fall of the House of Usher."

Points of Comparison As you read, compare the two stories in terms of their settings and other Gothic elements noted above.

Build Background

Art Imitates Life The first-person narrator of "A Rose for Emily" speaks for an entire community—the fictional town of Jefferson, Mississippi. Jefferson is the county seat of William Faulkner's fictional Yoknapatawpha (yŏk'nə-pə-tô'fə) County. Over a span of more than 30 years, Faulkner wrote novels and short stories about the land and the people of Jefferson and Yoknapatawpha County, creating a complete world that was patterned after his own home of Oxford. Many of the inhabitants of Faulkner's fictional world are based on real people.

Faulkner's writing preserves the manners of Southern life at an earlier time; be warned that the narrator refers to African Americans with a term that is offensive to contemporary readers.

WORDS TO KNOW **Vocabulary Preview**

circumvent	edict	profoundly
coquettish	encroach	tedious
dank	obliterate	temerity
diffident	obscure	thwart
divulge	pallid	virulent

Focus Your Reading

LITERARY ANALYSIS **CHARACTERIZATION** The methods a writer uses to portray a **character** are called **characterization.** For example, one technique that Faulkner uses to acquaint you with Miss Emily is to show her behavior over the course of her lifetime. As you read, note what her actions reveal about her.

ACTIVE READING **SEQUENCING EVENTS** Faulkner often used **flashbacks** in his stories, shuffling the order of events. His unusual approach to **sequencing events** was based on his notion of the fluidity of time, in which the past and the future seem to merge. Sentences beginning with the words *when, after,* and *during* help the reader note any time shifts.

READER'S NOTEBOOK As you read, keep a time line showing the sequence of events in Miss Emily's life. After you finish reading each section, jot down the important moments in chronological order. The sample timeline below lists two events from the first section.

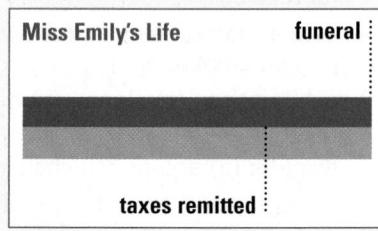

Miss Emily's Life   funeral

taxes remitted

A ROSE for EMILY

William Faulkner

I

When Miss Emily Grierson died, our whole town went to her funeral: the men through a sort of respectful affection for a fallen monument, the women mostly out of curiosity to see the inside of her house, which no one save an old manservant—a combined gardener and cook—had seen in at least ten years.

It was a big, squarish frame house that had once been white, decorated with cupolas and spires and scrolled balconies in the heavily lightsome style of the seventies,[1] set on what had once been our most select street. But garages and cotton gins had encroached and obliterated even the august names of that neighborhood; only Miss Emily's house was left, lifting its stubborn and coquettish decay above the cotton wagons and the gasoline pumps—an eyesore among eyesores. And now Miss Emily had gone to join the representatives of those august names where they lay in the cedar-bemused[2] cemetery among the ranked and anonymous graves of Union and Confederate soldiers who fell at the battle of Jefferson.

Alive, Miss Emily had been a tradition, a duty, and a care; a sort of hereditary obligation upon the town, dating from that day in 1894 when

Colonel Sartoris, the mayor—he who fathered the edict that no Negro woman should appear on the streets without an apron—remitted her taxes, the dispensation dating from the death of her father on into perpetuity.[3] Not that Miss Emily would have accepted charity. Colonel Sartoris invented an involved tale to the effect that Miss Emily's father had loaned money to the town, which the town, as a matter of business, preferred this way of repaying. Only a man of Colonel Sartoris' generation and thought could have invented it, and only a woman could have believed it.

When the next generation, with its more modern ideas, became mayors and aldermen, this arrangement created some little dissatisfaction. On the first of the year they mailed her a tax notice. February came, and there was no reply. They wrote her a formal letter, asking her to call at the sheriff's office at her convenience. A week

---

1. **the seventies:** the 1870s.
2. **cedar-bemused:** almost lost in cedar trees (literally, confused by cedars).
3. **remitted . . . perpetuity:** released her from paying taxes forever after the time of her father's death.

517

later the mayor wrote her himself, offering to call or to send his car for her, and received in reply a note on paper of an archaic shape, in a thin, flowing calligraphy[4] in faded ink, to the effect that she no longer went out at all. The tax notice was also enclosed, without comment.

They called a special meeting of the Board of Aldermen. A deputation[5] waited upon her, knocked at the door through which no visitor had passed since she ceased giving china-painting lessons eight or ten years earlier. They were admitted by the old Negro into a dim hall from which a stairway mounted into still more shadow. It smelled of dust and disuse—a close, <u>dank</u> smell. The Negro led them into the parlor. It was furnished in heavy, leather-covered furniture. When the Negro opened the blinds of one window, they could see that the leather was cracked; and when they sat down, a faint dust rose sluggishly about their thighs, spinning with slow motes[6] in the single sun-ray. On a tarnished gilt easel before the fireplace stood a crayon portrait of Miss Emily's father.

They rose when she entered—a small, fat woman in black, with a thin gold chain descending to her waist and vanishing into her belt, leaning on an ebony cane with a tarnished gold head. Her skeleton was small and spare; perhaps that was why what would have been merely plumpness in another was obesity in her. She looked bloated, like a body long submerged in motionless water, and of that <u>pallid</u> hue. Her eyes, lost in the fatty ridges of her face, looked like two small pieces of coal pressed into a lump of dough as they moved from one face to another while the visitors stated their errand.

She did not ask them to sit. She just stood in the door and listened quietly until the spokesman

German Teapot (1994), Charles Warren Mundy. Oil on canvas, 14″ × 18″.

came to a stumbling halt. Then they could hear the invisible watch ticking at the end of the gold chain.

Her voice was dry and cold. "I have no taxes in Jefferson. Colonel Sartoris explained it to me. Perhaps one of you can gain access to the city records and satisfy yourselves."

"But we have. We are the city authorities, Miss Emily. Didn't you get a notice from the sheriff, signed by him?"

"I received a paper, yes," Miss Emily said. "Perhaps he considers himself the sheriff . . . I have no taxes in Jefferson."

"But there is nothing on the books to show that, you see. We must go by the—"

"See Colonel Sartoris. I have no taxes in Jefferson."

"But, Miss Emily—"

"See Colonel Sartoris." (Colonel Sartoris had been dead almost ten years.) "I have no taxes in Jefferson. Tobe!" The Negro appeared. "Show these gentlemen out."

---

4. **calligraphy:** beautiful handwriting.

5. **deputation:** a small group representing a larger one.

6. **motes:** specks.

II

So she vanquished them, horse and foot, just as she had vanquished their fathers thirty years before about the smell. That was two years after her father's death and a short time after her sweetheart—the one we believed would marry her—had deserted her. After her father's death she went out very little; after her sweetheart went away, people hardly saw her at all. A few of the ladies had the <u>temerity</u> to call, but were not received, and the only sign of life about the place was the Negro man—a young man then—going in and out with a market basket.

"Just as if a man—any man—could keep a kitchen properly," the ladies said; so they were not surprised when the smell developed. It was another link between the gross, teeming world and the high and mighty Griersons.

A neighbor, a woman, complained to the mayor, Judge Stevens, eighty years old.

"But what will you have me do about it, madam?" he said.

"Why, send her word to stop it," the woman said. "Isn't there a law?"

"I'm sure that won't be necessary," Judge Stevens said. "It's probably just a snake or a rat that nigger of hers killed in the yard. I'll speak to him about it."

The next day he received two more complaints, one from a man who came in <u>diffident</u> deprecation.[7] "We really must do something about it, Judge. I'd be the last one in the world to bother Miss Emily, but we've got to do something." That night the Board of Aldermen met—three graybeards and one younger man, a member of the rising generation.

"It's simple enough," he said. "Send her word to have her place cleaned up. Give her a certain time to do it in, and if she don't . . ."

"Dammit, sir," Judge Stevens said, "will you accuse a lady to her face of smelling bad?"

So the next night, after midnight, four men crossed Miss Emily's lawn and slunk about the house like burglars, sniffing along the base of the brickwork and at the cellar openings while one of them performed a regular sowing motion with his hand out of a sack slung from his shoulder. They broke open the cellar door and sprinkled lime there, and in all the outbuildings. As they recrossed the lawn, a window that had been dark was lighted and Miss Emily sat in it, the light behind her, and her upright torso motionless as

> "We really must do something about it, Judge. I'd be the last one in the world to bother Miss Emily, but we've got to do something."

that of an idol. They crept quietly across the lawn and into the shadow of the locusts that lined the street. After a week or two the smell went away.

That was when people had begun to feel really sorry for her. People in our town, remembering how old lady Wyatt, her great-aunt, had gone completely crazy at last, believed that the Griersons held themselves a little too high for what they really were. None of the young men were quite good enough for Miss Emily and such. We had long thought of them as a tableau,[8] Miss Emily a slender figure in white in the background, her father a spraddled silhouette in

---

7. **deprecation:** disapproval.

8. **tableau** (tăb′lō′): dramatic scene or picture.

WORDS TO KNOW   **temerity** (tə-mĕr′ĭ-tē) *n.* foolish boldness
  diffident (dĭf′ĭ-dənt) *adj.* shy and timid; lacking self-confidence

519

the foreground, his back to her and clutching a horsewhip, the two of them framed by the back-flung front door. So when she got to be thirty and was still single, we were not pleased exactly, but vindicated; even with insanity in the family she wouldn't have turned down all of her chances if they had really materialized.

When her father died, it got about that the house was all that was left to her; and in a way, people were glad. At last they could pity Miss Emily. Being left alone, and a pauper, she had become humanized. Now she too would know the old thrill and the old despair of a penny more or less.

The day after his death all the ladies prepared to call at the house and offer condolence and aid, as is our custom. Miss Emily met them at the door, dressed as usual and with no trace of grief on her face. She told them that her father was not dead. She did that for three days, with the ministers calling on her, and the doctors, trying to persuade her to let them dispose of the body. Just as they were about to resort to law and force, she broke down, and they buried her father quickly.

White frame house in Holly Springs, Mississippi

We did not say she was crazy then. We believed she had to do that. We remembered all the young men her father had driven away, and we knew that with nothing left, she would have to cling to that which had robbed her, as people will.

III

She was sick for a long time. When we saw her again, her hair was cut short, making her look like a girl, with a vague resemblance to those angels in colored church windows—sort of tragic and serene.

The town had just let the contracts for paving the sidewalks, and in the summer after her father's death they began the work. The construction company came with niggers and mules and machinery, and a foreman named Homer Barron, a Yankee—a big, dark, ready man, with a big voice and eyes lighter than his face. The little boys would follow in groups to hear him cuss the niggers, and the niggers singing in time to the rise and fall of picks. Pretty soon he knew everybody in town. Whenever you heard a lot of laughing anywhere about the square, Homer Barron would be in the center of the group.

Presently we began to see him and Miss Emily on Sunday afternoons driving in the yellow-wheeled buggy and the matched team of bays from the livery stable.

At first we were glad that Miss Emily would have an interest, because the ladies all said, "Of course a Grierson would not think seriously of a Northerner, a day laborer." But there were still others, older people, who said that even grief could not cause a real lady to forget *noblesse oblige*[9]—without calling it *noblesse oblige*. They just said, "Poor Emily. Her kinsfolk should come to her." She had some kin in Alabama; but years ago her father had fallen out with them over the estate of old lady Wyatt, the crazy woman, and there was no communication between the two families. They had not even been represented at the funeral.

And as soon as the old people said, "Poor Emily," the whispering began. "Do you suppose it's really so?" they said to one another. "Of course it is. What else could . . ." This behind their hands; rustling of craned[10] silk and satin behind jalousies[11] closed upon the sun of Sunday afternoon as the thin, swift clop-clop-clop of the matched team passed: "Poor Emily."

She carried her head high enough—even when we believed that she was fallen. It was as if she demanded more than ever the recognition of her dignity as the last Grierson; as if it had wanted that touch of earthiness to reaffirm her imperviousness. Like when she bought the rat poison, the arsenic. That was over a year after they had begun to say "Poor Emily," and while the two female cousins were visiting her.

"I want some poison," she said to the druggist. She was over thirty then, still a slight woman, though thinner than usual, with cold, haughty black eyes in a face the flesh of which was strained across the temples and about the eye-sockets as you imagine a lighthouse-keeper's face ought to look. "I want some poison," she said.

"Yes, Miss Emily. What kind? For rats and such? I'd recom—"

"I want the best you have. I don't care what kind."

The druggist named several. "They'll kill anything up to an elephant. But what you want is—"

"Arsenic," Miss Emily said. "Is that a good one?"

"Is . . . arsenic? Yes, ma'am. But what you want—"

"I want arsenic."

The druggist looked down at her. She looked back at him, erect, her face like a strained flag. "Why, of course," the druggist said. "If that's what you want. But the law requires you to tell what you are going to use it for."

Miss Emily just stared at him, her head tilted back in order to look him eye for eye, until he looked away and went and got the arsenic and wrapped it up. The Negro delivery boy brought her the package; the druggist didn't come back. When she opened the package at home there was written on the box, under the skull and bones: "For rats."

---

9. *noblesse oblige* (nō-blĕs′ ō-blēzh′): the responsibility of people of high social position to behave in a noble fashion.

10. **craned:** stretched.

11. **jalousies** (jăl′ə-sēz): doors or windows containing overlapping slats that can be opened or closed.

IV

So the next day we all said, "She will kill herself"; and we said it would be the best thing. When she had first begun to be seen with Homer Barron, we had said, "She will marry him." Then we said, "She will persuade him yet," because Homer himself had remarked—he liked men, and it was known that he drank with the younger men in the Elks' Club—that he was not a marrying man. Later we said, "Poor Emily" behind the jalousies as they passed on Sunday afternoon in the glittering buggy, Miss Emily with her head high and Homer Barron with his hat cocked and a cigar in his teeth, reins and whip in a yellow glove.

Then some of the ladies began to say that it was a disgrace to the town and a bad example to the young people. The men did not want to interfere, but at last the ladies forced the Baptist minister—Miss Emily's people were Episcopal—to call upon her. He would never divulge what happened during that interview, but he refused to go back again. The next Sunday they again drove about the streets, and the following day the minister's wife wrote to Miss Emily's relations in Alabama.

So she had blood-kin under her roof again and we sat back to watch developments. At first nothing happened. Then we were sure that they were to be married. We learned that Miss Emily had been to the jeweler's and ordered a man's toilet set in silver, with the letters H. B. on each piece. Two days later we learned that she had bought a complete outfit of men's clothing, including a nightshirt, and we said, "They are married." We were really glad. We were glad because the two female cousins were even more Grierson than Miss Emily had ever been.

So we were not surprised when Homer Barron—the streets had been finished some time since—was gone. We were a little disappointed that there was not a public blowing-off,[12] but we believed that he had gone on to prepare for Miss Emily's coming, or to give her a chance to get rid of the cousins. (By that time it was a cabal,[13] and we were all Miss Emily's allies to help circumvent the cousins.) Sure enough, after another week they departed. And, as we had expected all along, within three days Homer Barron was back in town. A neighbor saw the

> We learned that Miss Emily had been to the jeweler's and ordered a man's toilet set in silver, with the letters H. B. on each piece.

Negro man admit him at the kitchen door at dusk one evening.

And that was the last we saw of Homer Barron. And of Miss Emily for some time. The Negro man went in and out with the market basket, but the front door remained closed. Now and then we would see her at a window for a moment, as the men did that night when they sprinkled the lime, but for almost six months she did not appear on the streets. Then we knew that this was to be expected too; as if that quality of her father which had thwarted her woman's life

---

12. **blowing-off:** celebration.
13. **cabal** (kə-băl'): a group united in a secret plot.

so many times had been too <u>virulent</u> and too furious to die.

When we next saw Miss Emily, she had grown fat and her hair was turning gray. During the next few years it grew grayer and grayer until it attained an even pepper-and-salt iron-gray, when it ceased turning. Up to the day of her death at seventy-four it was still that vigorous iron-gray, like the hair of an active man.

From that time on her front door remained closed, save for a period of six or seven years, when she was about forty, during which she gave lessons in china-painting. She fitted up a studio in one of the downstairs rooms, where the daughters and granddaughters of Colonel Sartoris' contemporaries were sent to her with the same regularity and in the same spirit that they were sent to church on Sundays with a twenty-five-cent piece for the collection plate. Meanwhile her taxes had been remitted.

Then the newer generation became the backbone and the spirit of the town, and the painting pupils grew up and fell away and did not send their children to her with boxes of color and <u>tedious</u> brushes and pictures cut from the ladies' magazines. The front door closed upon the last one and remained closed for good. When the town got free postal delivery, Miss Emily alone refused to let them fasten the metal numbers above her door and attach a mailbox to it. She would not listen to them.

Daily, monthly, yearly we watched the Negro grow grayer and more stooped, going in and out with the market basket. Each December we sent her a tax notice, which would be returned by the post office a week later, unclaimed. Now and then we would see her in one of the downstairs windows—she had evidently shut up the top floor of the house—like the carven torso of an idol in a niche,[14] looking or not looking at us, we could never tell which. Thus she passed from generation to generation—dear, inescapable,

impervious, tranquil, and perverse.

And so she died. Fell ill in the house filled with dust and shadows, with only a doddering Negro man to wait on her. We did not even know she was sick; we had long since given up trying to get any information from the Negro. He talked to no one, probably not even to her, for his voice had grown harsh and rusty, as if from disuse.

She died in one of the downstairs rooms, in a heavy walnut bed with a curtain, her gray head propped on a pillow yellow and moldy with age and lack of sunlight.

V

The Negro met the first of the ladies at the front door and let them in, with their hushed, sibilant[15] voices and their quick, curious glances, and then he disappeared. He walked right through the house and out the back and was not seen again.

The two female cousins came at once. They held the funeral on the second day, with the town coming to look at Miss Emily beneath a mass of bought flowers, with the crayon face of her father musing <u>profoundly</u> above the bier[16] and the ladies sibilant and macabre; and the very old men—some in their brushed Confederate uniforms—on the porch and the lawn, talking of Miss Emily as if she had been a contemporary of theirs, believing that they had danced with her and courted her perhaps, confusing time with its mathematical progression, as the old do, to whom all the past is not a diminishing road but, instead, a huge meadow which no winter ever quite

---

14. **niche** (nĭch): an indented space in a wall.

15. **sibilant** (sĭb′ə-lənt): making a hissing sound.

16. **bier** (bîr): a platform for a coffin.

WORDS TO KNOW	**virulent** (vîr′yə-lənt) *adj.* extremely poisonous or harmful **tedious** (tē′dē-əs) *adj.* boring because of dullness **profoundly** (prə-found′lē) *adv.* deeply; intensely

touches, divided from them now by the narrow bottleneck of the most recent decade of years.

Already we knew that there was one room in that region above stairs which no one had seen in forty years, and which would have to be forced. They waited until Miss Emily was decently in the ground before they opened it.

The violence of breaking down the door seemed to fill this room with pervading dust. A thin, acrid pall[17] as of the tomb seemed to lie everywhere upon this room decked and furnished as for a bridal:[18] upon the valance curtains of faded rose color, upon the rose-shaded lights, upon the dressing table, upon the delicate array of crystal and the man's toilet things backed with tarnished silver, silver so tarnished that the monogram was <u>obscured</u>. Among them lay a collar and tie, as if they had just been removed, which, lifted, left

Woman in Distress (1882), James Ensor. Musée d'Orsay, Paris, Giraudon/Art Resource. Copyright © Estate of James Ensor/VAGA, New York.

upon the surface a pale crescent in the dust. Upon a chair hung the suit, carefully folded; beneath it the two mute shoes and the discarded socks.

The man himself lay in the bed.

For a long while we just stood there, looking down at the profound and fleshless grin. The body had apparently once lain in the attitude of an embrace, but now the long sleep that outlasts love, that conquers even the grimace of love, had cuckolded him.[19] What was left of him, rotted beneath what was left of the nightshirt, had become inextricable from the bed in which he lay;

and upon him and upon the pillow beside him lay that even coating of the patient and biding dust.

Then we noticed that in the second pillow was the indentation of a head. One of us lifted something from it, and leaning forward, that faint and invisible dust dry and acrid in the nostrils, we saw a long strand of iron-gray hair. ❖

---

17. **acrid pall** (ăk′rĭd pôl′): bitter-smelling covering.
18. **bridal:** wedding.
19. **cuckolded him:** made his wife or lover unfaithful to him.

524

Connect to the Literature

1. **What Do You Think?** Were you surprised by the ending of this story? Talk about your reaction.

   Comprehension Check
   - How did Emily's father treat young men who wanted to date her?
   - What is the reason Homer Barron disappears?

Think Critically

2. What do you think motivates Miss Emily to commit murder?

   THINK ABOUT
   - her father's reaction to her previous suitors
   - what Homer Barron's intentions toward Miss Emily might have been
   - what Miss Emily's deepest feelings and hidden longings might have been
   - the appearance of the upstairs room and the bed when discovered

3. How would you judge the way the community responds to Miss Emily throughout her life? Support your opinion.

4. How much responsibility, if any, do you think the community bears for Miss Emily's crime?

5. **ACTIVE READING   SEQUENCING EVENTS** Use the time line you made in your **READER'S NOTEBOOK** to retell the story to another student. Do you think relating the events in strict chronological order weakens or improves the story?

Extend Interpretations

6. **Different Perspectives** What might the servant, Tobe, say if he were the telling the story?

7. **Critic's Corner** The critic Cleanth Brooks stated, "Miss Emily's story constitutes a warning against the sin of pride: heroic isolation pushed too far ends in homicidal madness." Do you agree with his summary? Explain why or why not. What other possible meanings can you draw from Miss Emily's story?

8. **Connect to Life** How do you think Miss Emily compares with people who have committed shocking crimes in recent years?

9. **Points of Comparison** What are the similarities between Miss Emily's home and the mansion in "The Fall of the House of Usher?" How do each of these places set the stage for the events that occur?

Literary Analysis

CHARACTERIZATION

Characterization refers to the techniques a writer uses to develop characters. A writer may reveal a character through one or more of the following ways:
- the character's physical description
- the character's actions, words, and feelings
- a narrator's direct comments about the character's nature
- other characters' actions, words, and feelings

Paired Activity Which techniques does Faulkner use most effectively to reveal the character of Miss Emily? With a partner, find at least three specific examples of characterization that help you learn more about her. Then compare your examples with those of other groups.

REVIEW   FORESHADOWING

Foreshadowing is the writer's use of hints or clues that prepare the readers for events that occur later in the story. For example, Emily's denial of her father's death and her refusal to bury him foreshadows her response to Homer Barron's death. What other instances of foreshadowing are there in this story? Find details that give clues about events to come.

Writing Options

1. Obituary for Miss Emily Drawing on details in the story, write Miss Emily's obituary for the *Jefferson Enquirer.* Use examples of newspaper obituaries as models.

2. Secret Diary Suppose that Miss Emily's diary were found in the locked room after her death. Write three entries that might be found in the diary, describing Miss Emily's feelings about her courtship by Homer Barron, her father's death, her encounter with the aldermen, or her decision to buy arsenic.

3. Points of Comparison
Imagine you are a detective investigating the deaths of Madeline in "The Fall of the House of Usher" and Homer Barron in a "A Rose for Emily." Write a set of police reports summarizing the circumstances surrounding each death.

4. Points of Comparison
What specifically does "A Rose for Emily" have in common with other Gothic works you read in this part of Unit Three? Would you say that Faulkner is closer in spirit to Hawthorne or Poe? Write your responses to these two questions as lecture notes to deliver to the class. Include details from the stories to support your views.

Activities & Explorations

1. Short Story Video View the video of "A Rose for Emily" provided with the program. Did the characters and the setting in the video match your mental picture of what they would be like? Discuss this question with a small group of classmates. ~ **VIEWING AND REPRESENTING**

 **Literature in Performance**

2. Theatrical Performance With a partner, rehearse a dramatic scene showing what might have happened the night Homer Barron was last seen entering Miss Emily's kitchen. What did Homer and Miss Emily say to each other? Perform your scene for classmates. ~ **PERFORMING**

Inquiry & Research

The "New South" While Miss Emily resists change and clings to the traditions of the "Old South"— the South before the Civil War—her town takes strides to become more modern. Toward the end of the 1800s, a "New South," built on the foundation of business and industry, was emerging. Locate more information about this shift and the clashing values between the "Old South" and the "New South." Summarize your findings.

Art Connection

Southern Mansion The house pictured on pages 520–521 is near Faulkner's hometown of Oxford, Mississippi, and exemplifies the kind of house he was familiar with. How closely does this house match your mental image of Miss Emily's house?

Vocabulary in Action

EXERCISE: CONTEXT CLUES Write the vocabulary word that best completes each sentence.

1. Miss Emily's life held little interest—it consisted merely of one _____ day after another.

2. The mayor had issued a foolish _____ that Miss Emily would not have to pay taxes.

3. Instead of directly offering financial help to her, he took another route by making up an involved story to _____ the problem.

4. When a new administration tried to make her pay, the obstructions created by her stubbornness made her able to _____ every attempt.

5. When Miss Emily insisted on something, no one in town had the _____ to argue with her.

6. Closed shutters and moist air gave her house an unpleasantly _____ atmosphere.

7. Miss Emily never sunned, and her complexion became _____.

8. Perhaps the judge was normally bold, but he reacted to the foul smell from Miss Emily's house with _____ hesitation.

9. The townspeople thought that sprinkling lime might destroy, or _____, the source of the smell.

10. Miss Emily had always been a no-nonsense kind of woman, not the type to behave in a _____ fashion toward any man.

11. Although the town realized that she kept company with Homer Barron, no one knew just how _____ in love she had been.

12. Only after her death did anyone dare to _____ on the privacy of the upstairs room.

13. Enough tarnish had formed on the silver of the men's toilet things to _____ the monogram.

14. Was it Homer's plans to leave town that made Miss Emily react in such a _____ fashion?

15. Did she know that a clue on the pillow would _____ her closely kept secret?

Building Vocabulary

For an in-depth lesson on context clues, see page 326.

WORDS TO KNOW				
encroach	edict	temerity	circumvent	tedious
obliterate	dank	diffident	thwart	profoundly
coquettish	pallid	divulge	virulent	obscure

William Faulkner
1897–1962

Other Works
As I Lay Dying
The Sound and the Fury
Intruder in the Dust

Aimless Youth William Faulkner, the great-grandson of a colorful Civil War hero, was nurtured on legends of the honor and gallantry of his Mississippi ancestors. Though a high school dropout, Faulkner read widely. For years, he drifted aimlessly. He traveled, did odd jobs, and attended the University of Mississippi for one year as a special student.

Focus on Writing By the late 1920s, Faulkner had published his first two novels. In 1929, his writing career blossomed. In a 13-year period, he published 15 books—novels and collections of short stories—including his masterworks *Light in August* (1932) and *Absalom, Absalom!* (1936). Faulkner focused his considerable talents on the land and people of northern Mississippi. His challenging experiments with stream of consciousness and fractured chronology cost him a wide audience, however. To earn a living, he worked as a Hollywood screenwriter during the 1930s and 1940s.

Prestige and Fame After World War II, Faulkner's critical reputation and popularity grew, and in 1949 he won the Nobel Prize in literature. By the time he died, Faulkner was widely regarded as one of America's greatest writers.

The Life You Save May Be Your Own

Short Story by FLANNERY O'CONNOR

Comparing Literature

Traditions Across Time: Southern Gothic

Influenced by Edgar Allan Poe and Nathaniel Hawthorne, Flannery O'Connor wrote stories filled with sinister characters and bizarre situations. Like these two earlier writers of Gothic literature, she vividly portrays the experiences of isolated, self-absorbed people set against the backdrop of a grotesque world.

Points of Comparison As you read "The Life You Save May Be Your Own," compare the characters with those in Poe's and Hawthorne's stories.

Build Background

Southern Sideshow As a child, Flannery O'Connor had a pet chicken that could either walk backward or forward, and some news reporters came to photograph the animal. This experience, she later said, marked her for life, for it began her preoccupation with the grotesque—a fascination she shares with other writers of her region who are often classified as belonging to the literary tradition known as Southern Gothic. "Southern writers are fond of 'writing about freaks,' " she remarked, "because we are still able to recognize one." O'Connor's fictional world—the 1940s and 1950s South—is populated with misfits, fanatics, and con artists. O'Connor believed that "distortion was the only way to make people see." In twisting reality, she used elements of the grotesque to convey a message about the need for spiritual renewal.

> WORDS TO KNOW
> **Vocabulary Preview**
> composed   morose
> gaunt   rue
> list

Focus Your Reading

LITERARY ANALYSIS | **IRONY** Irony is a contrast between what is expected and what actually exists or happens. In literature, **situational irony** is a contrast between what a character expects to happen and what actually happens. **Dramatic irony** occurs when readers know more about a situation in a story than the characters do. Look for examples of irony in this story.

ACTIVE READING | **DRAWING CONCLUSIONS ABOUT CHARACTERS**

O'Connor never tells the reader directly whether her **characters** are good or evil. Instead, she allows the reader to **draw conclusions** about characters based on clues, such as the characters' thoughts, words, and actions. The names O'Connor gives characters and the **imagery** she uses to describe them also provide hints about characters and their moral conduct.

READER'S NOTEBOOK To help you draw conclusions about the characters, use the reading-strategy questions inserted throughout the selection. Write your responses in your notebook.

THE LIFE YOU SAVE MAY BE YOUR OWN

FLANNERY O'CONNOR

The old woman and her daughter were sitting on their porch when Mr. Shiftlet came up their road for the first time. The old woman slid to the edge of her chair and leaned forward, shading her eyes from the piercing sunset with her hand. The daughter could not see far in front of her and continued to play with her fingers. Although the old woman lived in this desolate spot with only her daughter and she had never seen Mr. Shiftlet before, she could tell, even from a distance, that he was a tramp and no one to be afraid of. His left coat sleeve was folded up to show there was only half an arm in it, and his gaunt figure listed slightly to the side as if the breeze were pushing him. He had on a black town suit and a brown felt hat that was turned up in the front and down in the back and he carried a tin toolbox by a handle. He came on, at an amble, up her road, his face turned toward the sun which appeared to be balancing itself on the peak of a small mountain.

The old woman didn't change her position until he was almost into her yard; then she rose with one hand fisted on her hip. The daughter, a large girl in a short blue organdy dress, saw him all at once and jumped up and began to stamp and point and make excited speechless sounds.

Mr. Shiftlet stopped just inside the yard and set his box on the ground and tipped his hat at her as if she were not in the least afflicted; then he turned toward the old woman and swung the hat all the way off. He had long black slick hair that hung flat from a part in the middle to beyond the tips of his ears on either side. His face descended in forehead for more than half its length and ended suddenly with his features just balanced over a jutting steel-trap jaw. He seemed to be a young man but he had a look of composed

---

WORDS
TO
KNOW

gaunt (gônt) *adj.* thin and bony
list (lĭst) *v.* to lean or tilt to one side
composed (kəm-pōzd´) *adj.* calm; cool and collected

dissatisfaction as if he understood life thoroughly.

"Good evening," the old woman said. She was about the size of a cedar fence post and she had a man's gray hat pulled down low over her head.

The tramp stood looking at her and didn't answer. He turned his back and faced the sunset. He swung both his whole and his short arm up slowly so that they indicated an expanse of sky and his figure formed a crooked cross. The old woman watched him with her arms folded across her chest as if she were the owner of the sun, and the daughter watched, her head thrust forward and her fat helpless hands hanging at the wrists. She had long pink-gold hair and eyes as blue as a peacock's neck.

He held the pose for almost fifty seconds and then he picked up his box and came on to the porch and dropped down on the bottom step. "Lady," he said in a firm nasal voice, "I'd give a fortune to live where I could see me a sun do that every evening."

"Does it every evening," the old woman said and sat back down. The daughter sat down too and watched him with a cautious, sly look as if he were a bird that had come up very close. He leaned to one side, rooting in his pants pocket, and in a second he brought out a package of chewing gum and offered her a piece. She took it and unpeeled it and began to chew without taking her eyes off him. He offered the old woman a piece but she only raised her upper lip to indicate she had no teeth.

Mr. Shiftlet's pale, sharp glance had already passed over everything in the yard—the pump near the corner of the house and the big fig tree that three or four chickens were preparing to roost in—and had moved to a shed where he saw the square rusted back of an automobile. "You ladies drive?" he asked.

"That car ain't run in fifteen year," the old woman said. "The day my husband died, it quit running."

"Nothing is like it used to be, lady," he said. "The world is almost rotten."

"That's right," the old woman said. "You from around here?"

"Name Tom T. Shiftlet," he murmured, looking at the tires.

"I'm pleased to meet you," the old woman said. "Name Lucynell Crater and daughter Lucynell Crater. What you doing around here, Mr. Shiftlet?"

He judged the car to be about a 1928 or '29 Ford. "Lady," he said, and turned and gave her his full attention, "lemme tell you something. There's one of these doctors in Atlanta that's taken a knife and cut the human heart—the human heart," he repeated, leaning forward, "out of a man's chest and held it in his hand," and he held his hand out, palm up, as if it were slightly weighted with the human heart, "and studied it like it was a day-old chicken, and lady," he said, allowing a long significant pause in which his head slid forward and his clay-colored eyes brightened, "he don't know no more about it than you or me."

"That's right," the old woman said.

"Why, if he was to take that knife and cut into every corner of it, he still wouldn't know no more than you or me. What you want to bet?"

"Nothing," the old woman said wisely. "Where you come from, Mr. Shiftlet?"

He didn't answer. He reached into his pocket and brought out a sack of tobacco and a package of cigarette papers and rolled himself a cigarette, expertly with one hand, and attached it in a hanging position to his upper lip. Then he took a box of wooden matches from his pocket and struck one on his shoe. He held the burning match as if he were studying the mystery of flame while it traveled dangerously toward his skin. The daughter began to make loud noises and to point to his hand and shake her finger at him, but when the flame was just before touching him, he leaned down with his hand cupped over it as if he were going to set fire to his nose and lit the cigarette.

He flipped away the dead match and blew a stream of gray into the evening. A sly look came

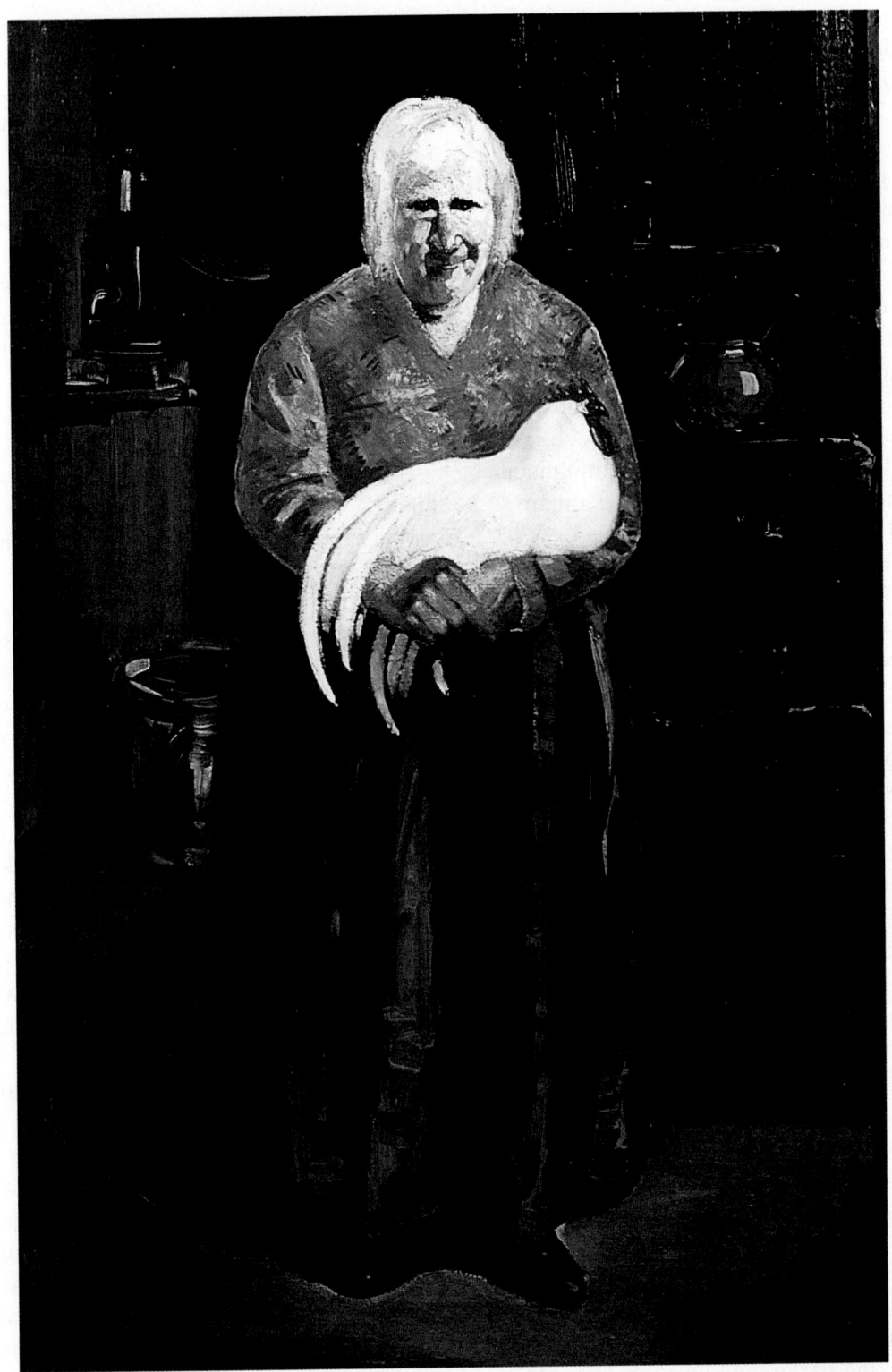

Mrs. Gamely (1930), George Luks. Oil on canvas, 66″ × 48″, collection of Whitney Museum of American Art, purchase (31.289). Copyright © 1995 Whitney Museum of American Art.

over his face. "Lady," he said, "nowadays, people'll do anything anyways. I can tell you my name is Tom T. Shiftlet and I come from Tarwater, Tennessee, but you never have seen me before: how you know I ain't lying? How you know my name ain't Aaron Sparks, lady, and I come from Singleberry, Georgia, or how you know it's not George Speeds and I come from Lucy, Alabama, or how you know I ain't Thompson Bright from Toolafalls, Mississippi?"

"I don't know nothing about you," the old woman muttered, irked.

"Lady," he said, "people don't care how they lie. Maybe the best I can tell you is, I'm a man; but listen lady," he said and paused and made his tone more ominous still, "what is a man?"

The old woman began to gum a seed. "What you carry in that tin box, Mr. Shiftlet?" she asked.

"Tools," he said, put back. "I'm a carpenter."

"Well, if you come out here to work, I'll be able to feed you and give you a place to sleep but I can't pay. I'll tell you that before you begin," she said.

There was no answer at once and no particular expression on his face. He leaned back against the two-by-four that helped support the porch roof. "Lady," he said slowly, "there's some men that some things mean more to them than money." The old woman rocked without comment and the daughter watched the trigger that moved up and down in his neck. He told the old woman then that all most people were interested in was money, but he asked what a man was made for. He asked her if a man was made for money, or what. He asked her what she thought she was made for but she didn't answer, she only sat rocking and wondered if a one-armed man could put a new roof on her garden house. He asked a lot of questions that she didn't answer. He told her that he was twenty-eight years old and had lived a varied life. He had been a gospel singer, a foreman on the railroad, an assistant in an undertaking parlor, and he come over the radio for three months with Uncle Roy and his Red Creek Wranglers. He said he had fought and bled in the Arm Service of his country and visited every foreign land and that everywhere he had seen people that didn't care if they did a thing one way or another. He said he hadn't been raised thataway.

A fat yellow moon appeared in the branches of the fig tree as if it were going to roost there with the chickens. He said that a man had to escape to the country to see the world whole and that he wished he lived in a desolate place like this where he could see the sun go down every evening like God made it to do.

"Are you married or are you single?" the old woman asked.

There was a long silence. "Lady," he asked finally, "where would you find you an innocent woman today? I wouldn't have any of this trash I could just pick up."

The daughter was leaning very far down, hanging her head almost between her knees watching him through a triangular door she had made in her overturned hair; and she suddenly fell in a heap on the floor and began to whimper. Mr. Shiftlet straightened her out and helped her get back in the chair.

"Is she your baby girl?" he asked.

"My only," the old woman said, "and she's the sweetest girl in the world. I would give her up for nothing on earth. She's smart too. She can sweep the floor, cook, wash, feed the chickens, and hoe. I wouldn't give her up for a casket of jewels."

"No," he said kindly, "don't ever let any man take her away from you."

"Any man come after her," the old woman said, " 'll have to stay around the place."

Mr. Shiftlet's eye in the darkness was focused on a part of the automobile bumper that glittered in the distance. "Lady," he said, jerking his short arm up as if he could point with it to her house and yard and pump, "there ain't a broken thing on this plantation that I couldn't fix for you, one-arm jackleg[1] or not. I'm a

---

1. **jackleg:** someone who does work he or she has not been trained to do.

man," he said with a sullen dignity, "even if I ain't a whole one. I got," he said, tapping his knuckles on the floor to emphasize the immensity of what he was going to say, "a moral intelligence!" and his face pierced out of the darkness into a shaft of door light and he stared at her as if he were astonished himself at this impossible truth.

ACTIVE READING

EVALUATE How would you characterize Mr. Shiftlet? Mrs. Crater? her daughter, Lucynell?

The old woman was not impressed with the phrase. "I told you you could hang around and work for food," she said, "if you don't mind sleeping in that car yonder."

"Why listen, lady," he said with a grin of delight, "the monks of old slept in their coffins!"

"They wasn't as advanced as we are," the old woman said.

The next morning he began on the roof of the garden house while Lucynell, the daughter, sat on a rock and watched him work. He had not been around a week before the change he had made in the place was apparent. He had patched the front and back steps, built a new hog pen, restored a fence, and taught Lucynell, who was completely deaf and had never said a word in her life, to say the word bird. The big rosy-faced girl followed him everywhere, saying "Burrttddt ddbirrrttdt," and clapping her hands. The old woman watched from a distance, secretly pleased. She was ravenous for a son-in-law.

Mr. Shiftlet slept on the hard narrow back seat of the car with his feet out the side window. He had his razor and a can of water on a crate that served him as a bedside table and he put up a piece of mirror against the back glass and kept his coat neatly on a hanger that he hung over one of the windows.

In the evenings he sat on the steps and talked while the old woman and Lucynell rocked violently in their chairs on either side of him.

The old woman's three mountains were black against the dark blue sky and were visited off and on by various planets and by the moon after it had left the chickens. Mr. Shiftlet pointed out that the reason he had improved this plantation was because he had taken a personal interest in it. He said he was even going to make the automobile run.

He had raised the hood and studied the mechanism, and he said he could tell that the car had been built in the days when cars were really built. You take now, he said, one man puts in one bolt and another man puts in another bolt and another man puts in another bolt so that it's a man for a bolt. That's why you have to pay so much for a car: you're paying all those men. Now if you didn't have to pay but one man, you could get you a cheaper car and one that had had a personal interest taken in it, and it would be a better car. The old woman agreed with him that this was so.

Mr. Shiftlet said that the trouble with the world was that nobody cared, or stopped and took any trouble. He said he never would have been able to teach Lucynell to say a word if he hadn't cared and stopped long enough.

"Teach her to say something else," the old woman said.

"What you want her to say next?" Mr. Shiftlet asked.

The old woman's smile was broad and toothless and suggestive. "Teach her to say 'sugarpie,'" she said.

ACTIVE READING

CLARIFY What do you think is on the old woman's mind?

Mr. Shiftlet already knew what was on her mind.

The next day he began to tinker with the automobile, and that evening he told her that if she would buy a fan belt, he would be able to make the car run.

The old woman said she would give him the money. "You see that girl yonder?" she asked, pointing to Lucynell who was sitting on the floor a foot away, watching him, her eyes blue even in the dark. "If it was ever a man wanted to take her away, I would say, 'No man on earth is going to take that sweet girl of mine away from me!' but if he was to say, 'Lady, I don't want to take her away, I want her right here,' I would say, 'Mister, I don't blame you none. I wouldn't pass up a chance to live in a permanent place and get the sweetest girl in the world myself. You ain't no fool,' I would say."

"How old is she?" Mr. Shiftlet asked casually.

"Fifteen, sixteen," the old woman said. The girl was nearly thirty but because of her innocence it was impossible to guess.

"It would be a good idea to paint it too," Mr. Shiftlet remarked. "You don't want it to rust out."

"We'll see about that later," the old woman said.

The next day he walked into town and returned with the parts he needed and a can of gasoline. Late in the afternoon, terrible noises issued from the shed and the old woman rushed out of the house, thinking Lucynell was somewhere having a fit. Lucynell was sitting on a chicken crate, stamping her feet and screaming, "Burrddtttt! bddurrddtttt!" but her fuss was drowned out by the car. With a volley of blasts it emerged from the shed, moving in a fierce and stately way. Mr. Shiftlet was in the driver's seat, sitting very erect. He had an expression of serious modesty on his face as if he had just raised the dead.

That night, rocking on the porch, the old woman began her business, at once. "You want you an innocent woman, don't you?" she asked sympathetically. "You don't want none of this trash."

"No'm, I don't," Mr. Shiftlet said.

"One that can't talk," she continued, "can't sass you back or use foul language. That's the kind for you to have. Right there," and she pointed to Lucynell sitting cross-legged in her chair, holding both feet in her hands.

"That's right," he admitted. "She wouldn't give me any trouble."

"Saturday," the old woman said, "you and her and me can drive into town and get married."

Mr. Shiftlet eased his position on the steps.

"I can't get married right now," he said. "Everything you want to do takes money and I ain't got any."

"What you need with money?" she asked.

"It takes money," he said. "Some people'll do anything anyhow these days, but the way I think, I wouldn't marry no woman that I couldn't take on a trip like she was somebody. I mean take her to a hotel and treat her. I wouldn't marry the Duchesser Windsor," he said firmly, "unless I could take her to a hotel and giver something good to eat.

"I was raised thataway and there ain't a thing I can do about it. My old mother taught me how to do."

"Lucynell don't even know what a hotel is," the old woman muttered. "Listen here, Mr. Shiftlet," she said, sliding forward in her chair, "you'd be getting a permanent house and a deep well and the most innocent girl in the world. You don't need no money. Lemme tell you something: there ain't any place in the world for a poor, disabled, friendless drifting man."

The ugly words settled in Mr. Shiftlet's head like a group of buzzards in the top of a tree. He didn't answer at once. He rolled himself a cigarette and lit it and then he said in an even voice, "Lady, a man is divided into two parts, body and spirit."

The old woman clamped her gums together.

"A body and a spirit," he repeated. "The body, lady, is like a house: it don't go anywhere; but the spirit, lady, is like a automobile: always on the move, always . . . ."

"Listen, Mr. Shiftlet," she said, "my well never goes dry and my house is always warm in the winter and there's no mortgage on a thing about this place. You can go to the courthouse and see for yourself. And yonder under that shed is a fine automobile." She laid the bait carefully. "You can have it painted by Saturday. I'll pay for the paint."

The Interloper (1958), Billy Morrow Jackson. Collection of Mrs. Virginia Penofsky.

"THE SPIRIT IS LIKE A AUTOMOBILE: ALWAYS ON THE MOVE, ALWAYS."

"THE BODY IS LIKE A HOUSE: IT DON'T GO ANYWHERE."

"A MAN IS DIVIDED INTO TWO PARTS, BODY AND SPIRIT."

In the darkness, Mr. Shiftlet's smile stretched like a weary snake waking up by a fire. After a second he recalled himself and said, "I'm only saying a man's spirit means more to him than anything else. I would have to take my wife off for the weekend without no regards at all for cost. I got to follow where my spirit says to go."

"I'll give you fifteen dollars for a weekend trip," the old woman said in a crabbed voice. "That's the best I can do."

"That wouldn't hardly pay for more than the gas and the hotel," he said. "It wouldn't feed her."

"Seventeen-fifty," the old woman said. "That's all I got so it isn't any use you trying to milk me. You can take a lunch."

Mr. Shiftlet was deeply hurt by the word *milk*. He didn't doubt that she had more money sewed up in her mattress, but he had already told her he was not interested in her money. "I'll make that do," he said and rose and walked off without treating[2] with her further.

ACTIVE READING

CONCLUDE What can you conclude about Mr. Shiftlet's intentions from these negotiations?

On Saturday the three of them drove into town in the car that the paint had barely dried on, and Mr. Shiftlet and Lucynell were married in the Ordinary's[3] office while the old woman witnessed. As they came out of the courthouse, Mr. Shiftlet began twisting his neck in his collar. He looked <u>morose</u> and bitter as if he had been insulted while someone held him. "That didn't satisfy me none," he said. "That was just something a woman in an office did, nothing but paperwork and blood tests. What do they know about my blood? If they was to take my heart and cut it out," he said, "they wouldn't know a thing about me. It didn't satisfy me at all."

"It satisfied the law," the old woman said sharply.

"The law," Mr. Shiftlet said and spit. "It's the law that don't satisfy me."

He had painted the car dark green with a yellow band around it just under the windows. The three of them climbed in the front seat and the old woman said, "Don't Lucynell look pretty? Looks like a baby doll." Lucynell was dressed up in a white dress that her mother had uprooted from a trunk and there was a Panama hat on her head with a bunch of red wooden cherries on the brim. Every now and then her placid expression was changed by a sly isolated little thought like a shoot of green in the desert. "You got a prize!" the old woman said.

Mr. Shiftlet didn't even look at her.

They drove back to the house to let the old woman off and pick up the lunch. When they were ready to leave, she stood staring in the window of the car, with her fingers clenched around the glass. Tears began to seep sideways out of her eyes and run along the dirty creases in her face. "I ain't ever been parted with her for two days before," she said.

Mr. Shiftlet started the motor.

"And I wouldn't let no man have her but you because I seen you would do right. Goodbye, Sugarbaby," she said, clutching at the sleeve of the white dress. Lucynell looked straight at her and didn't seem to see her there at all. Mr. Shiftlet eased the car forward so that she had to move her hands.

The early afternoon was clear and open and surrounded by pale blue sky. Although the car would go only thirty miles an hour, Mr. Shiftlet imagined a terrific climb and dip and swerve that went entirely to his head so that he forgot his morning bitterness. He had always wanted an automobile, but he had never been able to afford one before. He drove very fast because he wanted to make Mobile by nightfall.

---

2. **treating:** discussing terms; negotiating.
3. **Ordinary's:** judge's.

WORDS TO KNOW   **morose** (mə-rōs´) *adj.* gloomy and ill-tempered

Occasionally he stopped his thoughts long enough to look at Lucynell in the seat beside him. She had eaten the lunch as soon as they were out of the yard and now she was pulling the cherries off the hat one by one and throwing them out the window. He became depressed in spite of the car. He had driven about a hundred miles when he decided that she must be hungry again and at the next small town they came to, he stopped in front of an aluminum-painted eating place called The Hot Spot and took her in and ordered her a plate of ham and grits. The ride had made her sleepy and as soon as she got up on the stool, she rested her head on the counter and shut her eyes. There was no one in The Hot Spot but Mr. Shiftlet and the boy behind the counter, a pale youth with a greasy rag hung over his shoulder. Before he could dish up the food, she was snoring gently.

"Give it to her when she wakes up," Mr. Shiftlet said. "I'll pay for it now."

The boy bent over her and stared at the long pink-gold hair and the half-shut sleeping eyes. Then he looked up and stared at Mr. Shiftlet. "She looks like an angel of Gawd," he murmured.

"Hitchhiker," Mr. Shiftlet explained. "I can't wait. I got to make Tuscaloosa."

The boy bent over again and very carefully touched his finger to a strand of the golden hair, and Mr. Shiftlet left.

Road to Rhome (1934), Alexandre Hogue. Oil on canvas. Private collection.

ACTIVE READING

QUESTION Why do you think Mr. Shiftlet feels "more depressed than ever"?

He was more depressed than ever as he drove on by himself. The late afternoon had grown hot and sultry and the country had flattened out. Deep in the sky a storm was preparing very slowly and without thunder as if it meant to drain every drop of air from the earth before it broke. There were times when Mr. Shiftlet preferred not to be alone. He felt too that a man with a car had a responsibility to others, and he kept his eye out for a hitchhiker. Occasionally he saw a sign that warned: "Drive carefully. The life you save may be your own."

The narrow road dropped off on either side into dry fields, and here and there a shack or a filling station stood in a clearing. The sun began to set directly in front of the automobile. It was a reddening ball that through his windshield was slightly flat on the bottom and top. He saw a boy in overalls and a gray hat standing on the edge of the road and he slowed the car down and stopped in front of him. The boy didn't have his hand raised to thumb the ride, he was only standing there, but he had a small card-board suitcase and his hat was set on his head in a way to indicate that he had left somewhere for good. "Son," Mr. Shiftlet said, "I see you want a ride."

The boy didn't say he did or he didn't but he opened the door of the car and got in, and Mr. Shiftlet started driving again. The child held the suitcase on his lap and folded his arms on top of it. He turned his head and looked out the window away from Mr. Shiftlet. Mr. Shiftlet felt oppressed. "Son," he said after a minute, "I got the best old mother in the world so I reckon you only got the second best."

The boy gave him a quick dark glance and then turned his face back out the window.

"It's nothing so sweet," Mr. Shiftlet continued, "as a boy's mother. She taught him his first prayers at her knee, she give him love when no other would, she told him what was right and what wasn't, and she seen that he done the right thing. Son," he said, "I never <u>rued</u> a day in my life like the one I rued when I left that old mother of mine."

The boy shifted in his seat but he didn't look at Mr. Shiftlet. He unfolded his arms and put one hand on the door handle.

"My mother was a angel of Gawd," Mr. Shiftlet said in a very strained voice. "He took her from heaven and giver to me and I left her."

ACTIVE READING

QUESTION Why do you think Mr. Shiftlet is speaking this way to the hitchhiker?

His eyes were instantly clouded over with a mist of tears. The car was barely moving.

The boy turned angrily in the seat. "You go to the devil!" he cried. "My old woman is a fleabag and yours is a stinking polecat!" and with that he flung the door open and jumped out with his suitcase into the ditch.

Mr. Shiftlet was so shocked that for about a hundred feet he drove along slowly with the door still open. A cloud, the exact color of the boy's hat and shaped like a turnip, had descended over the sun, and another, worse looking, crouched behind the car. Mr. Shiftlet felt that the rottenness of the world was about to engulf him. He raised his arm and let it fall again to his breast. "Oh Lord!" he prayed. "Break forth and wash the slime from this earth!"

The turnip continued slowly to descend. After a few minutes there was a guffawing peal of thunder from behind and fantastic raindrops, like tin-can tops, crashed over the rear of Mr. Shiftlet's car. Very quickly he stepped on the gas, and with his stump sticking out the window, he raced the galloping shower into Mobile. ❖

WORDS
TO
KNOW

rue (r$\overline{oo}$) *v.* to regret

538

Connect to the Literature

1. **What Do You Think?** What is your opinion of Mr. Shiftlet? Jot down your feelings and share them with the class.

> **Comprehension Check**
> - What are Lucynell's disabilities?
> - What does Mr. Shiftlet do while living on the farm?
> - Why do the three main characters go to town together?

Think Critically

2. Do you blame Mrs. Crater for what happens to Lucynell? Why or why not?

3. At what point did you first suspect Mr. Shiftlet of manipulating Mrs. Crater? Why do you think he is successful?

4. How do you interpret the story's title?

    THINK ABOUT
   - the road sign Mr. Shiftlet sees
   - whose life needs to be saved
   - who is a potential savior

5. **ACTIVE READING** **DRAWING CONCLUSIONS ABOUT CHARACTERS** Review your responses to the reading-strategy questions that you jotted down in your **READER'S NOTEBOOK**. What did you find the most striking about each of the three main characters? What conclusions can you draw about their sense of morality?

Extend Interpretations

6. **What If?** Suppose the story ended right after Mr. Shiftlet leaves The Hot Spot and before he meets the hitchhiker. How might your perceptions of him be different?

7. **Critic's Corner** The critic Dorothy Walters notes that "the grotesque, in many of its forms, relies for effect upon a balance between the two contrary impulses of the terrible and the comic." What in O'Connor's story do you see as terrible, and what do you see as comic? Does O'Connor achieve a satisfactory balance to you?

8. **Connect to Life** In what ways does Mr. Shiftlet resemble real-life con artists you know about?

9. **Points of Comparison** Think about the stories by Hawthorne and Poe that you read earlier. Which character most reminds you of Mr. Shiftlet?

Literary Analysis

IRONY As you have learned, **irony** is the contrast between what is expected and what actually exists or happens. In "The Life You Save May Be Your Own," O'Connor skillfully uses **situational irony** to emphasize the startling gap between her characters' expectations and the events that actually unfold. For example, at the end of this story, Mr. Shiftlet prays that the world's rottenness—slime—be washed away, and a rain shower soon chases *him*. **Dramatic irony** occurs when readers learn information that remains unknown to certain characters. For example, readers detect what the counter boy at The Hot Spot does not—that Lucynell, the "angel of Gawd," will be a major problem when she wakes up.

Paired Activity Working with a partner, find other examples of each kind of irony in the story. What view of the world does O'Connor suggest with these ironies?

REVIEW **CHARACTERIZATION**
Which techniques of characterization does O'Connor use most effectively in this story—physical description; presentation of a character's actions, words, or feelings; direct comments by the narrator; or the reactions of other characters? Support your answer with examples.

Writing Options

1. Letter of Opinion In 1957, an adaptation of this story was broadcast on television. In the TV version, the ending was changed, according to O'Connor, "by having Shiftlet suddenly get a conscience and come back for the girl." Write a letter to the network that presented the show, either protesting or supporting this change. Give reasons for your opinion.

2. Sequel: The Saga Continues Extend the story by writing a brief episode revealing what happens to Lucynell after Mr. Shiftlet leaves her at The Hot Spot or what Mr. Shiftlet encounters when he reaches Mobile. Save your writing in your **Working Portfolio.** 🗁

3. Points of Comparison "Dr. Heidegger's Experiment" is an **allegory,** a work of literature in which people, objects, and events stand for abstract qualities, such as evil, compassion, or greed. Do you think that "The Life You Save May Be Your Own" can also be thought of as an allegory? Write your response in a comparison-and-contrast essay.

Writing Handbook
See page 1281: Compare and Contrast.

Activities & Explorations

1. Wanted Poster By hand or with the help of a computer, improve this wanted poster for Mr. Shiftlet. Include comments on his appearance, behavior, and manipulative techniques. ~ **ART**

2. Points of Comparison Sketch caricatures to depict the grotesqueness of the characters in Gothic tales. Choose characters from "The Life You Save May Be Your Own" and from one of Poe's or Hawthorne's short stories in this unit. Are there similarities in your portrayals? ~ **ART**

Inquiry & Research

1. Con Artists Locate information about real-life con artists and the manipulative techniques they use to dupe people. Summarize your findings in a brief report.

2. Antisocial Personalities Find out more about the personality traits of misfits, such as Mr. Shiftlet, in a psychology textbook and other sources. Write a case study, based on your research, that profiles the behavior of an antisocial individual.

WANTED

$$$$ REWARD $$$$ $$$$ REWARD $$$$

MR. SHIFTLET
For Abandoning The Daughter of Ms. Lucynell Crater. Was Last Seen Driving A Dark Green Ford.

$$ REWARD $$

Vocabulary in Action

EXERCISE: ASSESSMENT PRACTICE Write the letter of the word pair that expresses a relationship similar to that expressed by the capitalized pair.

1. LIST : TOPPLE :: (a) need : want, (b) damage : ruin, (c) laugh : cry, (d) irritate : annoy

2. GAUNT : SKELETON :: (a) tall : giant, (b) timid : lion, (c) bold : villain, (d) mountainous : hill

3. COMPOSED : EXCITED :: (a) proud : arrogant, (b) hesitant : foolish, (c) careful : skillful, (d) cowardly : brave

4. MOROSE : PARTY POOPER :: (a) sassy : smart aleck, (b) clumsy : athlete, (c) rich : hero, (d) lazy : student

5. RUE : SORROW :: (a) admire : scorn, (b) yearn : superiority, (c) trust : confidence, (d) appreciate : adoration

Building Vocabulary

For an in-depth lesson on analogies, see page 254.

WORDS TO KNOW		
	composed	morose
	gaunt	rue
	list	

Flannery O'Connor
1925–1964

Other Works
Everything That Rises Must Converge
A Good Man Is Hard to Find
The Violent Bear It Away
The Habit of Being: Letters

A Flair for Writing Flannery O'Connor lived a short, brilliant life. Born in Savannah, Georgia, O'Connor began drawing cartoons and writing as a young girl. In her high school yearbook, she wrote that her chief hobby was "collecting rejection slips." After high school, O'Connor attended college in Georgia and the Writers' Workshop at the University of Iowa.

Personal Triumphs In 1950, while completing her first novel, *Wise Blood*, O'Connor learned that she was suffering from lupus, the degenerative disease that had killed her father when she was 15. O'Connor returned to Milledgeville, Georgia, to live with her mother on a farm for the last 14 years of her life. Despite her debilitating illness and the specter of an early death, O'Connor continued to write, producing two acclaimed volumes of short stories and a second novel.

Biting Humor As a writer, O'Connor is noted for her intense Catholic faith and her comic portrayal of grotesque characters obsessed with sin and salvation. O'Connor's grim humor is at once her writing's most disturbing feature and its strength, allowing the reader to acknowledge the severe human faults of her characters while at the same time extending them sympathy. O'Connor herself commented, "I like [my stories] better than anybody and read them over and over and laugh and laugh."

Author Activity

The Writer's Eye Read O'Connor's views about writing in her book, *The Habit of Being: Letters.* Based on her comments, write the script for an interview, using a question-and-answer format. Working with a partner, create an audiotape of the interview to present to the class.

In writing assessments, you will often be asked to analyze a story in order to clarify its meaning. You are now going to practice writing an analytical essay in which you investigate the connections between two literary elements.

PART 1 **Reading the Prompt**

Often you will be asked to write in response to a prompt like the one below. First, read the entire prompt carefully. Then read through it again, looking for key words that help you identify the purpose of the essay and decide how to approach it.

Writing Prompt

Choose a 19th-century Gothic tale and another 20th-century Gothic tale from this unit. Write a literary analysis that explores the relationship ❶ between the setting and the characters in both ❷ works. How do the settings reflect or shape the characters?

STRATEGIES IN ACTION

❶ **Analysis** involves looking at parts in relation to a whole.

❷ Notice the two **elements** you will relate—setting and character.

PART 2 **Planning an Analytical Essay**

- Pick two Gothic tales to analyze. For each story, create a diagram to organize details.

- Make notes about relevant story elements. Write physical descriptions of the setting and main character(s) in each story, and identify emotional qualities suggested by the descriptions.

- Look for connections between the elements you are analyzing.

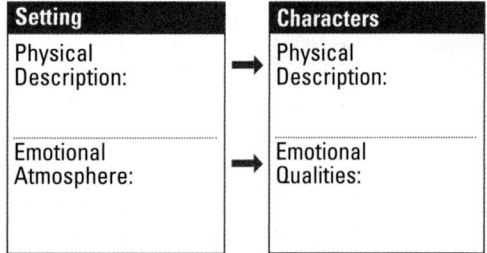

Setting		Characters
Physical Description:	➡	Physical Description:
Emotional Atmosphere:	➡	Emotional Qualities:

PART 3 **Drafting Your Essay**

Introduction Begin by explaining the focus of your analysis—the relationship between setting and character in two Gothic tales. Identify the stories.

Organization In the body of your paper, point out resemblances between the setting and characters in one story. Then discuss setting and characters in the other story.

Conclusion Make a comparison between the two stories. If possible, end with a generalization about the relationship between character and setting in Gothic stories.

Revision Allow time to review your work for mistakes and unclear wording.

Writing Handbook
See page 1283: Analysis

Billy Budd

HERMAN MELVILLE

Good and evil collide in this allegorical tale, set on the battleship *Indomitable.* Melville's short novel centers on the relationship of three men serving in the British Navy. Billy Budd, the angelic "Handsome Sailor," is pitted against the diabolical Claggart, a petty officer, who falsely accuses him of plotting a mutiny. Following a violent confrontation between these two men, Captain Vere, the commander, must uphold the truth and administer justice.

Intruder in the Dust

WILLIAM FAULKNER

Race relations in the deep South form the backdrop of Faulkner's novel, set in his mythical Yoknapatawpha County. Lucas Beauchamp, an elderly African-American farmer, is framed for the shooting death of a white man. After his arrest, a mob gathers at the jail house, hoping for a lynching. Charles ("Chick") Mallison, a white teenager, rises to Lucas's defense and helps unravel this chilling murder mystery.

And Even *More* . . .

Books

The Fall of the House of Usher and Other Stories
EDGAR ALLAN POE
More tales of bizarre and extraordinary events.

The Complete Stories
FLANNERY O'CONNOR
A collection of short stories in the Southern Gothic literary tradition.

Selected Writings of Truman Capote
TRUMAN CAPOTE
A sampling of the critically acclaimed author's literary works, including his Gothic tale "Miriam."

Other Media

Rappaccini's Daughter
Film adaptation of Hawthorne's eerie tale about an exotically beautiful young woman and the fatal flowers that bloom in her father's garden. PBS *The American Short Story* video series. (VIDEOCASSETTE)

Intruder in the Dust
Film adaptation of Faulkner's novel. MGM/UA Home Video.
(VIDEOCASSETTE)

The Haunting
Film adaptation of Shirley Jackson's Gothic novel *The Haunting of Hill House.* MGM/UA Home Video. (VIDEOCASSETTE)

American Gothic Tales

EDITED BY JOYCE CAROL OATES

Oates's anthology of haunting tales shows the far reaches of the Gothic imagination in American literature. This collection includes the short stories of nearly 50 writers from the past two

Writing Workshop

Creating your own story. . .

From Reading to Writing Stories such as "The Masque of the Red Death" may horrify you, while other stories delight you with humor, suspense, or surprises. You not only have the opportunity to read the stories of others, but you can also create stories of your own that will affect others. A **short story** uses characters, action, and setting to explore a conflict and create an experience that engages readers. Like all literary works worth reading, short stories entertain us and touch our feelings at the same time they teach us something worth remembering.

For Your Portfolio

WRITING PROMPT Write a short story. You might choose to use a surprise ending or twist.

Purpose: To engage and entertain readers

Audience: Your classmates, friends, family, or a wider audience

---

Basics in a Box

Short Story at a Glance

Introduction	Body	Conclusion
Sets the stage by • introducing the **characters** • describing the **setting**	**Develops the plot by** • introducing the **conflict** • telling a sequence of **events** • developing **main characters** • building toward a **climax**	**Finishes the story by** • resolving the **conflict** • telling the **last event**

RUBRIC Standards for Writing

A successful short story should

• use the elements of character, setting, and plot to create a convincing world

• use techniques such as vivid sensory language, concrete details, and dialogue to create believable characters and setting

• develop and resolve a central conflict

• present a clear sequence of events

• maintain a consistent point of view

Analyzing a Student Model

Sarah Mossberger
North Posey High School

Reunited

"You missed the turn," said Mom.

"How do you know?" Dad asked.

"Well, the sign back there said, 'Turn here for Gettysburg, 5 miles.' I'd say that was a pretty subtle hint."

We were on our way to Gettysburg and had been driving all day. Dad had taken the "scenic route." Mom was in a bad mood. Well, we all were. I was probably in the worst mood. Going to some stupid old battlefield wasn't exactly my idea of the perfect summer vacation.

* * *

"Come on," said Dad, "let's all stretch our legs a while. We can go to the museum first. Then we'll go on the car tour later. I want to get some fresh air before we have to get back into that car again."

We went through the museum for an hour or so. It wasn't all that bad. In fact, I learned some things from the displays. A museum attendant dressed in a Civil War-era business suit told us that several Civil War battles would be reenacted on the battlefields around the museum.

After lunch, we got back into the car to drive around the grounds. A one-way road led us to different battlefields, look-out towers, and memorials. There were areas by the sides of the road where we could park our car, get out, and walk around. From these places we watched some of the battle reenactments. . . .

About mid-afternoon, Dad pulled over for what seemed like the umpteenth time, and we got out of the car. I wandered off by myself. All of a sudden, I looked up. Standing in front of me was a boy, probably fourteen or fifteen years old. He was dressed in North colors, blue. He had on a jacket, and it was buttoned up the front. His outfit looked really old, like it was an actual soldier's uniform. It was in really good condition, and he even had a gun with him. He didn't have on a hat, so I could see his blondish-brown hair. He had bright blue eyes and was just a little taller than I am.

"Hi," I said softly, and I felt myself blush. He was kind of cute.

"Hi," he said just as softly.

"Are you working here for the summer?" I asked.

"Well, not exactly," he answered slowly.

"My name's Sarah Williams."

"Mine's Seth Roberts, and I'm looking for my brother Caleb."

"Is he dressed as a soldier too?"

"Sarah, come on," said my mom. "We're ready!"

"Coming!" I hollered. "Well, I hope you find your brother. Good luck."

"Thank you. Maybe I'll see you again."

RUBRIC
IN ACTION

❶ This writer begins with dialogue to introduce the characters and setting.

Other Options:
· Start the story with the central conflict.
· Start with the first event.

❷ Introduces a character with detailed description

❸ Uses dialogue to introduce the story's conflict

"I hope so," I said.

"Listen, if you see my brother, tell him to meet me at . . . the bottom of Little Round Top around 5:00, okay?"

"Sure, anything to help," I said, "but how will I know your brother when I see him?"

"Trust me, you'll know. We're twins," he answered.

★ ★ ★

"Mom," I said as I caught up with my parents, "couldn't you see I was in the middle of a conversation?"

"You were?" asked my mom. "With who? Casper?"

"Funny, Mom. Didn't you see the boy?"

"No."

"Honestly?"

"Yes. I'm sorry if I embarrassed you."

We got back into the car and continued the tour. At every stop I watched for Seth. Later in the afternoon, I thought I saw Seth again, but this time he was wearing grey, the South's colors. I realized it must be his brother Caleb, so I walked over to him. "Are you by chance Caleb Roberts?" I asked.

"Yes! Yes, I am. Why?" he asked.

"I sort of know your brother. He wants you to meet him."

"Okay," he said. "Where?"

"At the bottom of Little Round Top at 5:00."

"Thank you," he said, his eyes shining. "I've been looking for him. Good-bye."

"Bye," I said as he walked off.

★ ★ ★

At about 4:45 my family and I were at Little Round Top, and there was Seth, waiting. I looked down at my watch. It was 5:00 when Caleb walked up.

"Oh Seth, it's you! I'm so sorry! I didn't mean to shoot you. I didn't mean to kill you. And then I got hit, too. But I think that was for the best. I knew I wouldn't have been able to live with what I'd done." Seth embraced Caleb.

"Shhh, it's okay, Caleb. I know you didn't mean it. That's why I've kept looking for you. I love you, Caleb."

What did Caleb mean? He'd killed Seth and then been killed himself? How could they be dead? They were standing right there. Then it hit me—my mother hadn't seen Seth.

"Thank you, Sarah," cried Caleb.

"Yeah, thank you," said Seth. "Without you, I couldn't have found him. Thank you again. Good-bye."

"Good-bye," I said. I felt a lump in my throat. A ray of light fell onto them. As if they were floating on the beam, they slowly faded away. I began to cry, not because I was sad, but out of happiness for Seth. He had finally found his brother.

❹ Foreshadows story twist

❺ Maintains a consistent point of view with narrator relating the events

❻ Spells out story twist

❼ This writer resolves the conflict between fantastic and real with Sarah's explanation.

Other Options:
• End with the climax.
• Describe the setting to suggest the character's feelings.

Writing Your Short Story

❶ Prewriting

To imagine yourself inside another person . . . is what a story writer does in every piece of work . . . .
Eudora Welty

As you look for ideas for your story, you might try listing interesting settings, characters, and conflicts. Then mix and match them, or ask yourself what story each might lead to. Other possible sources of writing ideas include your daydreams, news stories, or experiences from your life. See the **Idea Bank** in the margin for additional ideas. After you have chosen your story idea, follow the steps below.

Planning Your Short Story

▶ **1. Imagine the characters and setting.** Who will be in the story and how will you show their personality traits? What setting will you use?

▶ **2. Think through the plot.** What are the main events? What is the conflict? Will the conflict be resolved? If so, how? You might make a sequence chart like this one to help you organize your ideas.

▶ **3. Choose a narrator.** Who will tell your story? Will the story be told from the first-person or third-person point of view?

▶ **4. Create a mood.** Will your story be frightening? humorous? mysterious?

▶ **5. Identify your goals and audience.** Are you writing for children, your peers, or a general audience?

❷ Drafting

Begin your story wherever you like: at the beginning, the conclusion, or the incident that triggers the conflict. You can rearrange the sections later. Many good stories begin in the middle and then go back to the beginning to provide more information. Remember, however, that the order of events must be clear.

Flesh Out the Characters Use **description**, **dialogue**, and **action** to make your characters real.

- Describe a character's physical appearance, habits, or talents.
- Tell what the character says and how the words are spoken.
- Show the character's actions. How does the character react to other people and events?

Use Description to Show Rather Than Tell Your Story For instance, instead of telling the readers that Seth and Caleb disappeared, the writer uses description to show them disappearing: "A ray of light fell onto them. As if they were floating on the beam, they slowly faded away."

IDEABank

1. Your Working Portfolio
Build on one of the **Writing Options** you completed earlier in this unit:

- **Madeline's Retelling,** p. 498
- **Story Ending,** p. 515
- **Sequel: The Saga Continues,** p. 540

2. A Picture Tells 1,000 Words
Look at paintings or photographs and ask yourself what story a picture is telling or might tell.

3. What If?
Set your imagination free by asking "What if?" questions. What if time travel were possible? What if guns magically disappeared?

Have a question?

See the **Writing Handbook**
Narrative Writing, pp. 1279–1280

Organize the Events A natural way to organize events in a story is to use **chronological order**—the order in which the events occur. Another choice is to use **flashback**—a recalling of past events After the flashback, return to the present and continue telling the story. Just be sure that the sequence of events and the connections between ideas are clear.

Ask Your Peer Reader

- What is the central conflict in my story?
- How would you describe the main character?
- When and where does the story take place?
- Was there any part that was hard to follow? What would make it clearer?

❸ Revising

TARGET SKILL ▶ USING DIALOGUE Dialogue can add suspense to your story and help readers get to know your characters. Good dialogue shows the most important things characters say to each other. Notice how the writer sometimes avoided direct responses, such as "yes" and "no," to keep the dialogue moving.

> "Mom," I said as I caught up with my parents, "couldn't you see I was in the middle of a conversation?"
>
> *You were? asked*
> "~~No~~," ~~said~~ my mom. "With who? Casper?"
>
> *Funny, Mom.*
> "~~No.~~ Didn't you see the boy?"

Need revising help?

Review the **Rubric**, p. 544

Consider **peer reader** comments

Check **Revision Guidelines**, p. 1269

Daunted by punctuating dialogue?

See the **Grammar Handbook**, p. 1327

❹ Editing and Proofreading

TARGET SKILL ▶ PUNCTUATING DIALOGUE In writing dialogue, remember to start a new paragraph each time the speaker changes. Also, use single quotation marks to indicate a quote within a quote. Here is how the writer above used this technique in her story:

> "Didn't you see the boy?" I asked. ¶My mother looked puzzled, too.
>
> "No, what did he say?"
>
> "He wants me to find his brother. He said, 'Tell him to meet me at the bottom of Little Round Top around 5:00.'"

❺ Reflecting

FOR YOUR WORKING PORTFOLIO How did you decide to end your story? What other endings did you consider, and why did you pick the one you did? Attach your answers to your finished work. Save your short story in your **Working Portfolio.**

Publishing IDEAS

- Submit your story to the school literary magazine. or a popular magazine for teens.
- Adapt your story to make a reader's theater script and present it with the help of classmates.

More Online: Publishing Options www.mcdougallittell.com

Read this passage from the first draft of a short story. The underlined sections may include the following kinds of errors:

- **lack of pronoun-antecedent agreement**
- **correctly written sentences that should be combined**
- **punctuation errors**
- **misplaced modifiers**

For each underlined section, choose the revision that most improves the writing.

Ms. Padrone ran her hardware store like a prison ward. <u>Their</u> rules were
(1)

strict and unbending. "One sale item per customer," read one sign. "No

layaways," read another. <u>"No exceptions," said Ms. Padrone.</u>
(2)

<u>"Nate, said Dad,</u> one windy autumn day, "we need two new rakes. Please
(3)

run down to Padrone's and buy a couple." <u>I tried to get out of it. I couldn't get</u>
(4)

<u>out of it.</u>

<u>So there I stood asking for two rakes in front of the counter.</u> Just my luck,
(5)

rakes were on sale.

"You want TWO rakes?" Ms. Padrone snapped. "Well, you can't have <u>it</u>! The
(6)

sign says only one per customer and that's final."

---

1. A. Its
   B. His
   C. Her
   D. Correct as is

2. A. "No exceptions", said
   B. "No exceptions" said
   C. "No exceptions, said
   D. Correct as is

3. A. "Nate," said Dad, one windy autumn day, "we
   B. "Nate said Dad, one windy autumn day, "we
   C. "Nate", said Dad, one windy autumn day, we
   D. Correct as is

4. A. I tried to get out of it, but I couldn't.
   B. I tried to get out of it, I couldn't get out of it.
   C. I tried to get out of it, I couldn't.
   D. Correct as is

5. A. So asking for two rakes there, I stood in front of the counter.
   B. So there I stood, in front of the counter, asking for two rakes.
   C. So I asked for two rakes in front of the counter, and there I stood.
   D. Correct as is

6. A. theirs.
   B. this!
   C. them!
   D. Correct as is

Need extra help?

See the **Grammar Handbook:**

Pronoun Agreement, p. 1307

Punctuation Chart, p. 1327

Writing Complete Sentences, p. 1323

Using Modifiers Correctly, p. 1313

Finding the Sources of Words

Exploring word histories can help you remember words' meanings and expand your understanding of the English language. For example, in the excerpt on the right, Edgar Allan Poe used the word *grotesque* to mean "having a bizarre, fantastic appearance," and the history of the word sheds a good deal of light on how it came to have that meaning.

The adjective *grotesque* has been part of the English language for about 400 years. During the Renaissance, when ancient Roman buildings were being excavated in Italy, the Italians used the word *grotte,* meaning "caves," to refer to the subterranean chambers they uncovered. The fanciful wall paintings that were found in the chambers were called *pitture grottesche* (literally "cave paintings") and the adjective came to be applied to a similarly fanciful style of contemporary art. The word passed into French in the form *grotesque* and thence into English, gradually acquiring the extended senses of "distorting natural forms in an absurd or ugly way" and "exotic or bizarre in appearance."

> He had directed, in great part, the movable embellishments of the seven chambers, upon occasion of this great *fête;* and it was his own guiding taste which had given character to the masqueraders. Be sure they were grotesque.　—Edgar Allan Poe,
> "The Masque of the Red Death"

Strategies for Building Vocabulary

The strategies that follow can help you use information about words' etymology—their origin and history—as a tool for inferring meanings, enriching vocabulary, and improving spelling.

❶ Word Parts Learning the meanings of word parts such as affixes and roots can give you insights into words' meanings. When trying to determine the meaning of a word, first break the word into its parts, then combine the meanings of the parts to produce a possible definition, as in this example:

embellishment

word parts
em + bellish + ment

Latin origins
in- + bellus + -mentum

meanings of parts
"to cause to be" + "beautiful" + "a means of"

definition
something that beautifies

❷ Word Families Words derived from a single linguistic "ancestor" form what is known as a word family. If you know the meaning of one word in such a family, you can often figure out the meanings of other words in the family. For example, the word *tangible* contains the root of the Latin word *tangere,* "to touch." The following list shows some other members of the *tangere* family.

Words Derived from Latin *Tangere*

English Word	Meaning
tangent	touching at a single point
tangible	able to be perceived by the sense of touch
tact	skill and grace in dealing with others
tactile	relating to the sense of touch
contact	a coming together or touching
contagious	communicable by contact

❸ Spelling In many cases, a knowledge of word families can help you spell more accurately. The word *perspiration,* for example, contains *spir,* the root of the Latin verb *spīrāre,* "to blow or breathe." This root is also found in *spirit, transpire, inspire, respiration,* and *inspiration.* Notice that the root's spelling is the same in all of the words, even though its pronunciation varies.

EXERCISE Use a dictionary to trace the origin of each of these words. Then explain how the word's etymology relates to its meaning.

1. venerable
2. shrouded
3. disconcert
4. termination
5. magnificence
6. divulge
7. transient
8. dispute
9. virulent
10. circumvent

Grammar from Literature

Adverbs provide a way to improve precision in your writing. They describe, clarify, and qualify. Notice how Edgar Allan Poe uses adverbs both to add rhythm to his writing and to tell how and when actions occur.

>   adverb   adverb
> **While I nodded, nearly napping, suddenly there came a tapping,**
>   adverb
> **As of someone gently rapping, rapping on my chamber door.**
>   —Edgar Allan Poe, "The Raven"

Adverbs modify not only verbs; they can be used to qualify adjectives and other adverbs. By carefully choosing adverbs, Flannery O'Conner is able to make her description very exact.

>   adverbs
> **The daughter was leaning very far down, hanging her**
>   adverb
> **head almost between her knees.**
> —Flannery O'Connor, "The Life You Save May Be Your Own"

Adverbs can take the form of prepositional phrases. The following sentence contains a pair of prepositional phrases that tell where Miss Emily died.

>   prepositional phrases
> **She died in one of the downstairs rooms, in a heavy walnut bed with a curtain.**
>   —William Faulkner, "A Rose for Emily"

Infinitive phrases can also function as adverbs. In the sentence below, an infinitive phrase modifies the verb *invited*.

> **That very singular man, old Dr. Heidegger, once**
>   infinitive phrase
> **invited four venerable friends to meet him in his study.**
>   —Nathaniel Hawthorne, "Dr. Heidegger's Experiment"

Using Adverbs in Your Writing When you revise, examine your verbs and modifiers. Would the addition of an adverb that tells *how, when,* or *where* make your writing more precise or accurate? Notice the difference adverbs make in this portion of a synopsis of "A Rose for Emily."

> LACKING DETAIL
> **Emily was poor. She was seeing a burly construction foreman. Rumors began. No one could have guessed the truth.**

> REVISED USING ADVERBS
> **After her father's death, Emily was somewhat poor. Soon, she was regularly seeing a rather burly construction foreman. In no time, rumors began to fly around town about their relationship. No one, however, could have ever guessed the truth.**

Usage Tip Remember, only adverbs can modify adjectives and other adverbs. Confusion about this fact can lead to errors in usage.

> INCORRECT   adjective
> **Poe is a master at creating real scary stories.**
> CORRECT   adverb
> **Poe is a master at creating really scary stories.**

WRITING EXERCISE Rewrite these sentences, adding adverbs and adverb phrases that modify the underlined words. Follow the directions in parentheses.

1. The cut-glass vase <u>stands</u> in the sunlight. (Tell where it stands.)
2. Dr. Heidegger <u>pours</u> the magical water. (Add two adverb elements. Tell how and where he pours the water.)
3. Dr. Heidegger nods as his guests <u>leap</u> energetically. (Add two adverb elements. Tell how he nods and where the guests leap.)
4. The ancient rose is <u>dry</u> and <u>faded.</u> (Add three adverb elements. Tell when and how the rose is dry and how it is faded.)
5. Now that they are old again, the guests are <u>anxious.</u> (Add an infinitive phrase that tells how or for what the guests are anxious.)

PROOFREADING EXERCISE Rewrite these sentences, correcting errors in usage. If a sentence contains no error, write *Correct.*

1. Hawthorne explores some real interesting aspects of human nature.
2. The revelers were near exhausted by the end of the ball.
3. The guests found the guest who resembled a victim of the Red Death awful frightening.
4. Gothic writers certainly achieve a mood of gloom.
5. If you haven't read "The Fall of the House of Usher," you sure should.

The Spirit of Individualism

Do you feel you have gained a deeper understanding of the American philosophy of individualism as it developed in the 19th century? Has reading 19th-century literature sharpened your reading skills? To explore what you've learned from the selections in this unit, choose one or more of the options in each of the following sections.

Detail of *The Wanderer* (1818), Caspar David Friedrich, Kunsthalle, Hamburg, Germany, Bridgeman/Art Resource, New York.

Reflecting on the Unit

OPTION 1

The Concept of the Individual The selections in this unit reflect two different concepts of the individual. To illustrate the difference, create two portraits of individuals—one representing the romantic and transcendentalist view, the other representing the Gothic view. Choose your own medium for the portrait: an illustration, an oral description, a written character sketch, or any combination of these.

OPTION 2

Roundtable Discussion Reread the quotation from Thoreau that begins this unit (page 336). Do you think the other writers in this unit—especially the 20th-century writers—would agree with Thoreau? Get together with a group of five classmates, with each student choosing a writer from the unit to role-play. Make sure your group represents writers from both centuries and from both parts of the unit. Then participate in a group discussion about individual freedom, evaluating Thoreau's statement from the point of view of the writer you are playing. During the discussion, pay attention to the writers' different attitudes toward individual freedom.

OPTION 3

Visions of Good and Evil Compare and contrast the portrayals of human nature in the two parts of the unit: "Celebrations of the Self" and "The Dark Side of Individualism." What generalizations about the views of romantic and transcendentalist writers can you infer from the selections in Part 1? Compile a list of them, then come up with a similar list for the Gothic writers in Part 2. Write a few paragraphs explaining which vision of human nature you agree with more.

Self ASSESSMENT

📖 **READER'S NOTEBOOK**

To show how your understanding has deepened as you have read this unit, create a cluster diagram or list in which you identify about five key characteristics of American individualism. For each characteristic, indicate which of the writers represented in the unit would consider it admirable.

Reviewing Literary Concepts

Analyzing Imagery The 19th-century writers represented in this unit used imagery for a variety of purposes: to illustrate ideas; to enhance descriptions of character and setting; to create moods; to reflect psychological realities—the inner workings of characters' minds. Go back through the selections in the unit and identify, in a chart like the one shown, which of these purposes each writer's imagery primarily serves.

Selection	Primary Use of Imagery	Example of Imagery
"A Psalm of Life"	to illustrate ideas	"Footprints on the sands of time" (line 28)
"The Devil and Tom Walker"	to enhance description and to create mood	"The swamp was thickly grown with great gloomy pines and hemlocks . . ." (pp. 351-352)

Understanding Form in Poetry With a partner, review all the poems in the unit (including the Literary Links and Links Across Cultures) and classify them. Which are traditional in form, written in stanzas with a regular meter and rhyme scheme? Which are nontraditional in form? Of the nontraditional poems, which are written in free verse? Which would you label *experimental,* and why? After you classify the poems, draw conclusions about the strengths and weaknesses of traditional and nontraditional forms. What is gained or lost by using each form? Which form do you prefer?

Building Your Portfolio

- **Writing Options** Many of the Writing Options in this unit asked you to give your personal response to a writer's ideas. Choose the two responses which you believe were the most thorough and interesting examinations of a writer's ideas. Write a cover note explaining your choices, and place these pieces in your **Presentation Portfolio.**

- **Writing Workshops** In this unit you wrote a Reflective Essay about a learning experience. You also wrote a Short Story. Which do you think was a more successful piece of writing, and why? Attach a note explaining your evaluation, and put the work in your **Presentation Portfolio.**

- **Additional Activities** Review the assignments you completed under **Activities & Explorations** and **Inquiry & Research.** Keep a record in your portfolio of any assignments that you think are worthy of expanding into a larger project.

Self ASSESSMENT

READER'S NOTEBOOK

From the following list of literary terms discussed in this unit, select the ones that you think you need to know more about. Jot down those terms and their definitions. Refer to the **Glossary of Literary Terms** (page 1342).

narrator	Gothic
omniscient narrator	allegory
aphorism	end rhyme
essay	internal rhyme
paradox	mood
nature writing	foreshadowing
catalog	characterization
repetition	flashback
parallelism	situational irony
speaker	dramatic irony
humor	

Self ASSESSMENT

Look over the pieces you have added to your **Presentation Portfolio** so far. Is there enough variety in the writing and activities you've selected? Make a note of ways to add more diversity as the year goes on.

Setting GOALS

Jot down ideas or issues that you'd like to explore further as you read literature from the second half of the 19th century in the next unit.

UNIT FOUR

CONFLICT *and* EXPANSION

We all declare for liberty; but in using the same word we do not mean the same thing.

Abraham Lincoln
*16th president
of the
United States*

If the Indians had tried to make the whites live like them, the whites would have resisted, and it was the same way with many Indians.

Wamditanka
*(Big Eagle)
Santee Sioux*

Pictorial quilt (1895–1898), Harriet Powers. Pieced and appliquéd cotton embroidered with plain and metallic yarns, 69″ × 105″, bequest of Maxim Karolik, courtesy of Museum of Fine Arts, Boston.

CONFLICT *and*
EXPANSION

EVENTS IN AMERICAN LITERATURE

1850   1860   1870

1851 Herman Melville's *Moby-Dick* is published

1852 Harriet Beecher Stowe publishes *Uncle Tom's Cabin*, increasing tension between proslavery and antislavery forces

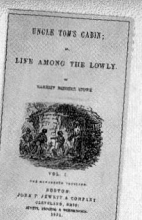

1863 Abraham Lincoln delivers Gettysburg Address

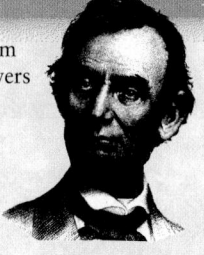

1876 Mark Twain publishes *The Adventures of Tom Sawyer* and begins writing *The Adventures of Huckleberry Finn*

EVENTS IN THE UNITED STATES

1850   1860   1870

1851 Former slave Sojourner Truth speaks at women's rights convention

1857 Supreme Court's Dred Scott decision declares slaves and former slaves are not U.S. citizens and thus not entitled to basic rights

1859 Abolitionist John Brown is hanged for treason after leading raid on federal arsenal at Harpers Ferry

1860 Abraham Lincoln is elected president; in response, South Carolina secedes from Union, followed eventually by ten other Southern states

1863 Lincoln signs Emancipation Proclamation

1865 Civil War ends; Lincoln is assassinated; 13th Amendment to Constitution abolishes slavery

1868 Congress passes 14th Amendment to Constitution, prohibiting discrimination against African Americans

1873 Colt's Manufacturing Company introduces Peacemaker revolver, most famous sidearm of West

1874 Joseph F. Glidden patents barbed wire, key development in settlement of West

1876 At Battle of Little Bighorn, several thousand Sioux and Cheyenne warriors defeat and kill about 200 U.S. Army troops commanded by Lieutenant George Armstrong Custer

1877 Chief Joseph of Nez Perce tribe surrenders to U.S. Army

EVENTS IN THE WORLD

1850   1860   1870

1852 David Livingstone explores Zambezi River in central Africa

1857 Sepoys rebel against British rule in India

1861 Czar Alexander II of Russia frees serfs

1867 Alfred Nobel invents dynamite; Meiji era in Japan begins period of modernization

1869 Suez Canal is completed in Egypt

1870 Italy is unified

1871 Franco-Prussian War ends; Germany is unified

1872 Critics coin term *impressionism* after Claude Monet's painting "Impression: Sunrise"

PERIOD PIECES

Confederate money

Steam engine

Decorative carriage
clock from 1870

1880   **1890**   **1900**

1882 Frederick Douglass completes autobiography

1883 Twain's *Life on the Mississippi* is published

1891 Ambrose Bierce publishes "An Occurrence at Owl Creek Bridge"

1895 Stephen Crane's fictional account of the Civil War, *The Red Badge of Courage,* is published

1897 In Pittsburgh, Willa Cather hears her first Wagnerian opera and becomes passionate fan of the German composer

---

1880   **1890**   **1900**

1883 "Buffalo Bill" Cody organizes Wild West show and begins touring United States and Europe

1890 At Wounded Knee Creek, South Dakota, U.S. soldiers kill more than 200 Sioux in last battle of Indian Wars

1893 Henry Ford develops gasoline-powered automobile

1896 Supreme Court upholds "separate but equal" doctrine of Jim Crow laws, widely used to discriminate against African Americans

1898 Spanish-American War results in United States gaining control of Guam, Puerto Rico, and the Philippines

---

1880   **1890**   **1900**

1885 At Berlin Conference, 14 European nations lay down rules for division of Africa

1893 France takes over Indochina

1895 Japanese defeat Chinese in Sino-Japanese War

1896 Menelik II maintains Ethiopian independence after victory over Italians at Battle of Adowa

1900 Boxer Rebellion protests foreign influence in China

A House Divided

Slavery and the Civil War

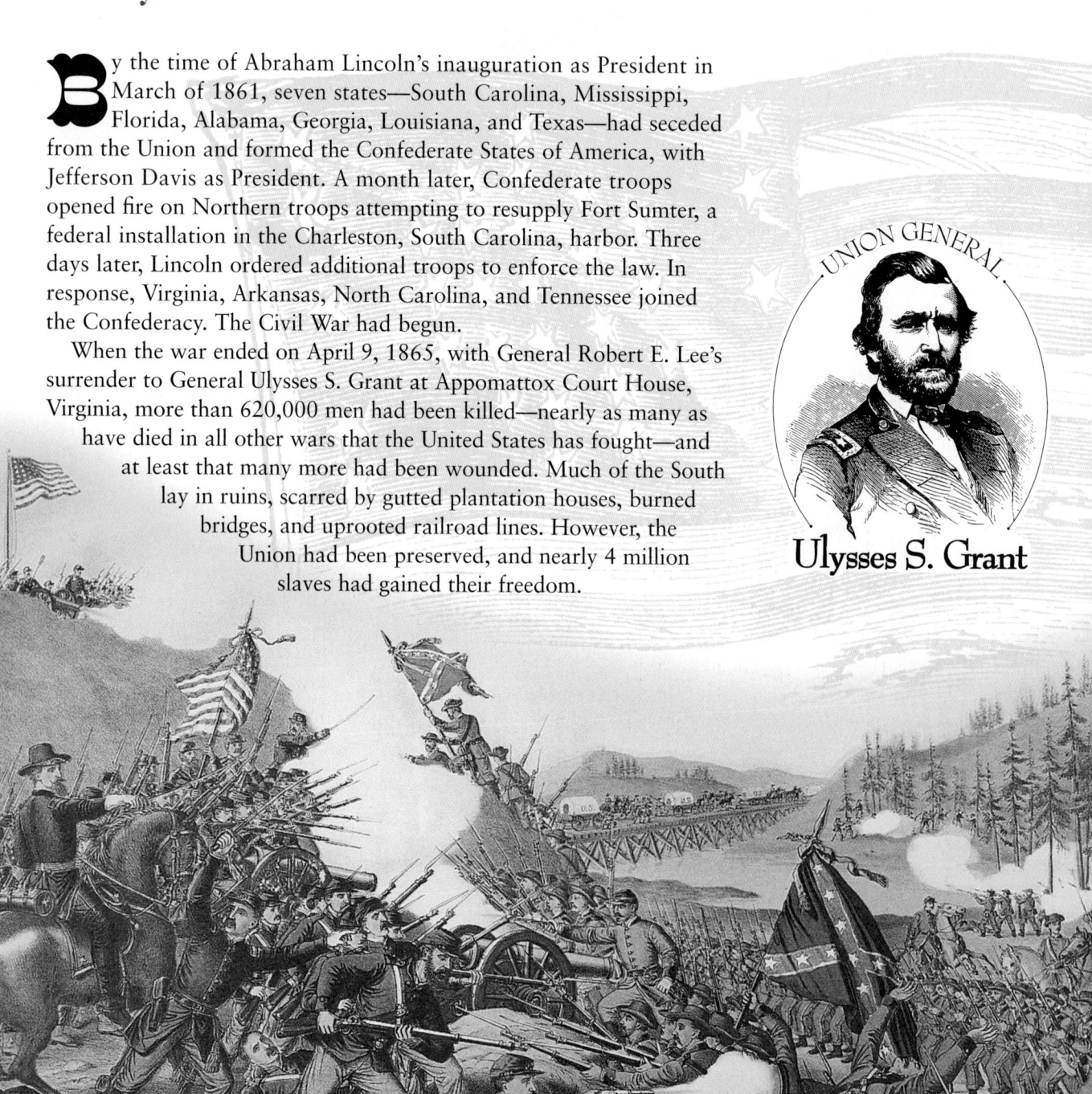

By the time of Abraham Lincoln's inauguration as President in March of 1861, seven states—South Carolina, Mississippi, Florida, Alabama, Georgia, Louisiana, and Texas—had seceded from the Union and formed the Confederate States of America, with Jefferson Davis as President. A month later, Confederate troops opened fire on Northern troops attempting to resupply Fort Sumter, a federal installation in the Charleston, South Carolina, harbor. Three days later, Lincoln ordered additional troops to enforce the law. In response, Virginia, Arkansas, North Carolina, and Tennessee joined the Confederacy. The Civil War had begun.

When the war ended on April 9, 1865, with General Robert E. Lee's surrender to General Ulysses S. Grant at Appomattox Court House, Virginia, more than 620,000 men had been killed—nearly as many as have died in all other wars that the United States has fought—and at least that many more had been wounded. Much of the South lay in ruins, scarred by gutted plantation houses, burned bridges, and uprooted railroad lines. However, the Union had been preserved, and nearly 4 million slaves had gained their freedom.

UNION GENERAL

Ulysses S. Grant

Before the Civil War, *United States* had been a plural noun. People were used to saying "The United States *are* . . . ," with the emphasis on the individual *states* more than the *united* interests of all. However, a strong belief in states' rights ultimately threatened the union itself and allowed the institution of slavery a longer history in the Southern states than in the

CONFEDERATE GENERAL

Robert E. Lee

Northern states and in most of Latin America and Europe as well. "A house divided against itself cannot stand," maintained Abraham Lincoln. "I believe this government cannot endure permanently half slave and half free." After the Civil War, the United States had become irrevocably one country. People began saying "The United States *is* . . ."

In the years before the war, slavery was a major subject engaging a large number of writers. Public lectures were a forum by which many writers supported themselves. Henry David Thoreau, as active in the political and social world as he was in the literary, lectured on the individual's responsibility to take action against unjust laws. His lecture, published as the essay "Civil Disobedience" (page 369) in 1849, has since become famous, providing some of the basis for the American tradition of nonviolent protest that took hold about 100 years later during the civil rights movement.

This crucial time period also generated some of the first important literature by African Americans. Frances Ellen Watkins Harper became the first popular African-American poet, as she traveled throughout the North lecturing to substantial audiences in favor of abolition and punctuating her lectures with recitations of her poems. Most eloquent of all, however, was Frederick Douglass, the escaped slave who taught himself to read and write and later became a champion of the abolitionist cause and woman suffrage. Douglass's

Mary Chesnut

I know this well, that if one thousand, if one hundred, if ten men whom I could name—if ten *honest* men only—ay, if *one* HONEST man, in this State of Massachusetts, *ceasing to hold slaves*, were actually to withdraw from this copartnership [with government by refusing to pay taxes], and be locked up in the county jail therefor, it would be the abolition of slavery in America. For it matters not how small the beginning may seem to be: what is once well done is done forever.

Henry David Thoreau
from "Civil Disobedience"

The South, in my opinion, has been aggrieved by the acts of the North, as you say. I feel the aggression, and am willing to take every proper step for redress. . . . As an American citizen, I take great pride in my country, her prosperity and institutions, and would defend any State, if her rights were invaded. But I can anticipate no greater calamity for the country than a dissolution of the Union. It would be an accumulation of all the evils we complain of, and I am willing to sacrifice everything but honor for its preservation.

Robert E. Lee
from a letter to his son
three months before the war

This Southern Confederacy must be supported now by calm determination and cool brains. We have risked all and we must play our best, for the stake is life or death.

Mary Boykin Chesnut
from her diary

Both parties deprecated war, but one of them would make war rather than let the nation survive, and the other would accept war rather than let it perish. And the war came.

Abraham Lincoln
from *Second Inaugural Address*

Clara Barton

I saw, crowded into one old sunken hotel, lying upon its bare, wet, bloody floors, 500 fainting men hold up their cold, blood-less, dingy hands as I passed, and beg me in Heaven's name for a cracker to keep them from starving (and I had none); or to give them a cup that they might have something to drink water from, if they could get it (and I had no cup and could get none).

Clara Barton
on wounded soldiers awaiting
transfer to hospitals

War is hell.
William Tecumseh Sherman

Look down fair moon and bathe this scene,
Pour softly down night's nimbus floods
 on faces ghastly, swollen, purple,
On the dead on their backs with arms toss'd wide,
Pour down your unstinted nimbus
 sacred moon.

Walt Whitman
"Look Down Fair Moon"

autobiography re-mains one of the most moving, authentic accounts we have of the bitter history of slavery.

As always during periods of great change, it is the expe-rience of individuals caught up in large his-torical forces that finally gives life to events and makes them real. Walt Whitman worked as an army nurse in New York and Washington and on the front lines during the first three years of the war. Many of his poems written at this time are painfully personal. His famous elegies for Abraham Lincoln, "When Lilacs Last in the Dooryard Bloom'd" and "O Captain! My Captain!" express the grief of a nation still mourning the losses of the Civil War. Ambrose Bierce's story "An Occurrence at Owl Creek Bridge" has its origins in his own experience as a foot soldier in the war. The strange twists of that story, like oth-ers he wrote, prefigure his own mysterious disappearance years later in Mexico. Stephen Crane's story "A Mystery of Heroism" describes the forces—external and internal—that impel a soldier in battle.

Traditions Across Time: The Civil Rights Movement

Though the horrors of slavery cannot be minimized, its end turned out to be only the first step in a long, arduous struggle for equal rights for African Americans. With publications and speeches by Martin Luther King, Jr., Malcolm X, and others, the civil rights movement of the 1950s and 1960s gener-ated some of the most memorable work. Included in this part of Unit Four is Anne Moody's graphic and vivid account of one of the first sit-ins in Mississippi. Also, in the tradition of James Russell Lowell, Frances Ellen Watkins Harper, and other abolitionist poets, Robert Hayden and Dudley Randall address the struggle in historical as well as personal terms.

Slavery and the Civil War

Frederick Douglass   *from* **Narrative of the Life of Frederick Douglass, an American Slave**   562
The grueling experience of a field slave

James Russell Lowell   **Stanzas on Freedom**   574
A new definition of slavery

Frances Ellen Watkins Harper   **Free Labor**   574
Taking a stand with what you wear

Ambrose Bierce   **An Occurrence at Owl Creek Bridge**   580
The last thoughts of a condemned man

LITERARY LINK
Sullivan Ballou   **Letter to Sarah Ballou**   590
Tender feelings from a soldier going off to battle

Stephen Crane   **A Mystery of Heroism**   593
A hero or a fool?

Abraham Lincoln   **Gettysburg Address**   605
A brief speech—a timeless message

COMPARING LITERATURE
Traditions Across Time: The Civil Rights Movement

Anne Moody   *from* **Coming of Age in Mississippi** (1968)   609
College students challenge segregation.

LITERARY LINK
Robert Hayden   **Frederick Douglass** (1962)   615
A tribute to a great man

Dudley Randall   **Ballad of Birmingham** (1969)   618
A tragedy remembered

Detail of *A Load of Brush* (1912), Louis Paul Dessar.

from Narrative of the Life of Frederick Douglass, an American Slave

Slave Narrative by FREDERICK DOUGLASS

Connect to Your Life

Land of the Free? What do you know about slavery in the United States? Get together with a group of classmates and share what you have learned from slave narratives such as the one by Olaudah Equiano (page 94), from movies such as *Amistad,* from TV programs, or from history books. Record your group's knowledge about slavery in a word web.

Build Background

From Slave to Hero After escaping from slavery in 1838, Frederick Douglass gave public lectures about his experiences. To convince skeptics who doubted that such an eloquent speaker could have ever been a slave, Douglass decided to write his autobiography, *Narrative of the Life of Frederick Douglass.* The book became one of the most famous slave narratives ever. As a boy, Douglass was a servant in the home of Hugh Auld of Baltimore, where Mrs. Auld taught Douglass the alphabet and some simple spelling. After Mr. Auld commanded his wife to stop educating the boy, Douglass taught himself to read with the help of white playmates. When Douglass was 16, he was sent back to his first home to live with Hugh Auld's brother, Thomas. Thomas Auld believed that Douglass had been too spoiled as a house slave to be useful on a plantation and decided it was necessary to break the young man's spirit. Auld rented Douglass for a year to Edward Covey, who had a reputation as a slave breaker. This excerpt from Douglass's narrative covers the time that Douglass spent with Covey.

WORDS TO KNOW
Vocabulary Preview
faculty   intimate   sundry
interpose   languish

Focus Your Reading

LITERARY ANALYSIS   AUTOBIOGRAPHY AND STYLE

As you recall, an **autobiography** is the story of a person's life, written by that person. The style of an autobiography is as individual as its author. **Style** is not what is said but how it is said. For example, style can be described as formal or conversational, concise or elaborate, objective (matter-of-fact) or subjective (personal and emotional). Among the elements contributing to style are word choice, sentence length, tone, figurative language, and use of dialogue. Notice such elements as you read Douglass's narrative, and think about how you would describe his style.

ACTIVE READING   AUTHOR'S PURPOSE   Authors may write for any number of reasons, such as to inform, to entertain, or simply to express themselves. Frederick Douglass published his autobiography in 1845 primarily as a protest of slavery, with the hope that those who read his book would support the cause of freedom. Consider how readers of the time might have responded to this excerpt.

READER'S NOTEBOOK   Divide a page from your notebook into the areas shown. As you read, note your reactions to the slaves and masters presented in the selection. Primarily, you will be reacting to Douglass himself and to Covey, but also jot down your thoughts about Sandy, Bill, and Master Thomas.

Slaves	Masters
Douglass	Covey
Sandy	Master Thomas
Bill	

from Narrative of the Life of Frederick Douglass

Frederick Douglass

I left Master Thomas's house, and went to live with Mr. Covey, on the 1st of January, 1833. I was now, for the first time in my life, a field hand. In my new employment, I found myself even more awkward than a country boy appeared to be in a large city. I had been at my new home but one week before Mr. Covey gave me a very severe whipping, cutting my back, causing the blood to run, and raising ridges on my flesh as large as my little finger. The details of this affair are as follows: Mr. Covey sent me, very early in the morning of one of our coldest days in the month of January, to the woods, to get a load of wood. He gave me a team of unbroken oxen. He told me which was the in-hand ox, and which the off-hand[1] one. He then tied the end of a large rope around the horns of the in-hand ox, and gave me the other end of it, and told me, if the oxen started to run, that I must hold on upon the rope. I had never driven oxen before, and of course I was very awkward. I, however, succeeded in getting to the edge of the woods with little difficulty; but I had got a very few rods into the woods, when the oxen took fright, and started full tilt, carrying the cart against trees, and over stumps, in the most frightful manner. I expected every moment that my brains would be dashed out against the trees. After running thus for a considerable distance, they finally upset the cart, dashing it with great force against a tree, and threw themselves into a dense thicket.

How I escaped death, I do not know. There I was, entirely alone, in a thick wood, in a place new to me. My cart was upset and shattered, my oxen were entangled among the young trees, and there was none to help me. After a long spell of effort, I succeeded in getting my cart righted, my oxen disentangled, and again yoked to the cart. I now proceeded with my team to the place where I had, the day before, been chopping wood, and loaded my cart pretty heavily, thinking in this way to tame my oxen. I then proceeded on my way home. I had now consumed one half of the day. I got out of the woods safely, and now felt out of danger. I stopped my oxen to open the woods gate; and just as I did so, before I could get hold of my ox rope, the oxen again started, rushed through the gate, catching it between the wheel and the body of the cart, tearing it to pieces, and coming within a few inches of crushing me against the gate-post. Thus twice, in one short day, I escaped death by the merest chance. On my return, I told Mr. Covey what had happened, and how it happened. He ordered me to return to the woods again immediately. I did so, and he followed on after me. Just as I got into the

---

1. **in-hand . . . off-hand:** In a team of animals used for pulling loads, the animal trained to work on the left side is the in-hand one; the animal on the right is the off-hand one.

A Load of Brush (1912), Louis Paul Dessar. Oil on canvas, 28 ¼" × 36 ¼", National Museum of American Art, gift of John Gellatly, Smithsonian Institution, Washington, D.C./Art Resource, New York.

almost always his excuse for whipping me. We were worked fully up to the point of endurance. Long before day we were up, our horses fed, and by the first approach of day we were off to the field with our hoes and ploughing teams. Mr. Covey gave us enough to eat, but scarce time to eat it. We were often less than five minutes taking our meals. We were often in the field from the first approach of day till its last lingering ray had left us; and at saving-fodder time, midnight often caught us in the field binding blades.[2]

Covey would be out with us. The way he used to stand it, was this. He would spend the most of his afternoons in bed. He would then come out fresh in the evening, ready to urge us on with his words, example, and frequently with the whip. Mr. Covey was one of the few slaveholders who could and did work with his hands. He was a hard-working man. He knew by himself just what a man or a boy could do. There was no deceiving him. His work went on in his absence almost as well as in his presence; and he had the <u>faculty</u> of making us feel that he was ever present with us. This he did by surprising us. He seldom approached the spot where we were at work openly, if he could do it secretly. He always aimed at taking us by surprise. Such was his cunning, that we used to call him, among ourselves, "the snake." When we were at work in

woods, he came up and told me to stop my cart, and that he would teach me how to trifle away my time, and break gates. He then went to a large gum-tree, and with his axe cut three large switches, and, after trimming them up neatly with his pocket-knife, he ordered me to take off my clothes. I made him no answer, but stood with my clothes on. He repeated his order. I still made him no answer, nor did I move to strip myself. Upon this he rushed at me with the fierceness of a tiger, tore off my clothes, and lashed me till he had worn out his switches, cutting me so savagely as to leave the marks visible for a long time after. This whipping was the first of a number just like it, and for similar offenses.

I lived with Mr. Covey one year. During the first six months, of that year, scarce a week passed without his whipping me. I was seldom free from a sore back. My awkwardness was

---

2. **saving-fodder . . . binding blades:** They are gathering and bundling ("binding") corn-plant leaves ("blades") to use as food for livestock ("fodder").

the cornfield, he would sometimes crawl on his hands and knees to avoid detection, and all at once he would rise nearly in our midst, and scream out, "Ha, ha! Come, come! Dash on, dash on!" This being his mode of attack, it was never safe to stop a single minute. His comings were like a thief in the night. He appeared to us as being ever at hand. He was under every tree, behind every stump, in every bush, and at every window, on the plantation. He would sometimes mount his horse, as if bound to St. Michael's, a distance of seven miles, and in half an hour afterwards you would see him coiled up in the corner of the wood-fence, watching every motion of the slaves. He would, for this purpose, leave his horse tied up in the woods. Again, he would sometimes walk up to us, and give us orders as though he was upon the point of starting on a long journey, turn his back upon us, and make as though he was going to the house to get ready; and, before he would get half way thither, he would turn short and crawl into a fence-corner, or behind some tree, and there watch us till the going down of the sun. . . .

If at any one time of my life more than another, I was made to drink the bitterest dregs of slavery, that time was during the first six months of my stay with Mr. Covey. We were worked in all weathers. It was never too hot or too cold; it could never rain, blow, hail, or snow, too hard for us to work in the field. Work,

My awkwardness was almost always his excuse for whipping me.

work, work, was scarcely more the order of the day than of the night. The longest days were too short for him, and the shortest nights too long for him. I was somewhat unmanageable when I first went there, but a few months of this discipline tamed me. Mr. Covey succeeded in breaking me. I was broken in body, soul, and spirit. My natural elasticity was crushed, my intellect languished, the disposition to read departed, the cheerful spark that lingered about my eye died; the dark night of slavery closed in upon me; and behold a man transformed into a brute!

Sunday was my only leisure time. I spent this in a sort of beast-like stupor, between sleep and wake, under some large tree. At times I would rise up, a flash of energetic freedom would dart through my soul, accompanied with a faint beam of hope, that flickered for a moment, and then vanished. I sank down again, mourning over my wretched condition. I was sometimes prompted to take my life, and that of Covey, but was prevented by a combination of hope and fear. My sufferings on this plantation seem now like a dream rather than a stern reality. . . .

I have already intimated that my condition was much worse, during the first six months of my stay at Mr. Covey's, than in the last six. The circumstances leading to the change in Mr. Covey's course toward me form an epoch in my humble history. You have seen how a man was made a slave; you shall see how a slave was made a man. On one of the hottest days of the month of August, 1833, Bill Smith, William Hughes, a slave named Eli, and myself, were engaged in fanning wheat.[3] Hughes was clearing the fanned wheat from before the fan. Eli was turning, Smith was feeding, and I was carrying wheat to the fan. The work was simple, requiring strength rather than intellect; yet, to one entirely unused to such work, it came very hard. About three o'clock of that day, I broke down; my strength failed me; I was seized with a violent aching of the head, attended with extreme dizziness; I trembled in every limb. Finding what was coming, I nerved myself up, feeling it would never do to stop work. I stood as long as I could stagger to the hopper[4] with grain. When I could stand no longer, I fell, and felt as if held down by an immense weight. The fan of course stopped; every one had his own work to do; and no one could do the work of the other, and have his own go on at the same time.

Mr. Covey was at the house, about one hundred yards from the treading-yard where we were fanning. On hearing the fan stop, he left immediately, and came to the spot where we were. He hastily inquired what the matter was. Bill answered that I was sick, and there was no one to bring wheat to the fan. I had by this time crawled away under the side of the post and rail-fence by which the yard was enclosed, hoping to find relief by getting out of the sun. He then asked where I was. He was told by one of the hands. He came to the spot, and, after looking at me awhile, asked me what was the matter. I told him as well as I could, for I scarce had strength to speak. He then gave me a savage kick in the side, and told me to get up. I tried to do so, but fell back in the attempt. He gave me another kick, and again told me to rise. I again tried, and succeeded in gaining my feet; but, stooping to get the tub with which I was feeding the fan, I again staggered and fell. While down in this situation, Mr. Covey took up the hickory slat with which Hughes had been striking off the half-bushel measure, and with it gave me a

heavy blow upon the head, making a large wound, and the blood ran freely; and with this again told me to get up. I made no effort to comply, having now made up my mind to let him do his worst. In a short time after receiving this blow, my head grew better. Mr. Covey had now left me to my fate. At this moment I resolved, for the first time, to go to my master, enter a complaint, and ask his protection. In order to do this, I must that afternoon walk seven miles; and this, under the circumstances, was truly a severe undertaking. I was exceedingly feeble; made so as much by the kicks and blows which I received, as by the severe fit of sickness to which I had been subjected. I, however, watched my chance, while Covey was looking in an opposite direction, and started for St. Michael's. I succeeded in getting a considerable distance on my way to the woods, when Covey discovered me, and called after me to come back, threatening what he would do if I did not come. I disregarded both his calls and his threats, and made my way to the woods as fast as my feeble state would allow; and thinking I might be overhauled by him if I kept the road, I walked through the woods, keeping far enough from the road to avoid detection, and near enough to prevent losing my way. I had not gone far before my little strength again failed me. I could go no farther. I fell down, and lay for a considerable time. The blood was yet oozing from the wound on my head. For a time I thought I should bleed to death; and think now that I should have done so, but that the blood so matted my hair as to stop the wound. After lying there about three quarters of an hour, I nerved myself up again, and started on my way, through bogs and briers, barefooted and bareheaded, tearing my feet sometimes at nearly every step; and after a journey of about seven miles, occupying some five hours to perform it, I arrived at master's

3. **fanning wheat:** using a machine that blows air to separate grains of wheat from the unusable husks.

4. **hopper:** a funnel-shaped container for storing grain.

Head of a Negro (1777–1778), John Singleton Copley. Paint on canvas, 53.3 cm × 41.3 cm.
The Detroit Institute of Arts, Founders Society Purchase, Gibbs-Williams Fund.

store. I then presented an appearance enough to affect any but a heart of iron. From the crown of my head to my feet, I was covered with blood. My hair was all clotted with dust and blood; my shirt was stiff with blood. My legs and feet were torn in sundry places with briers and thorns, and were also covered with blood. I suppose I looked like a man who had escaped a den of wild beasts, and barely escaped them. In this state I appeared before my master, humbly entreating him to interpose his authority for my protection. I told him all the circumstances as well as I could, and it seemed, as I spoke, at times to affect him. He would then walk the floor, and seek to justify Covey by saying he expected I deserved it. He asked me what I wanted. I told him, to let me get a new home; that as sure as I lived with Mr. Covey again, I should live with but to die with him; that Covey would surely kill me; he was in a fair way for it. Master Thomas ridiculed the idea that there was any danger of Mr. Covey's killing me, and said that he knew Mr. Covey; that he was a good man, and that he could not think of taking me from him; that, should he do so, he would lose the whole year's wages; that I belonged to Mr. Covey for one year, and that I must go back to him, come what might; and that I must not trouble him with any more stories, or that he would himself *get hold of me*. After threatening me thus, he gave me a very large dose of salts,[5] telling me that I might remain in St. Michael's that night, (it being quite late,) but that I must be off back to Mr. Covey's early in the morning; and that if I did not, he would *get hold of me*,

I resolved to fight; and, suiting my action to the resolution, I seized Covey hard by the throat.

which meant that he would whip me. I remained all night, and, according to his orders, I started off to Covey's in the morning, (Saturday morning,) wearied in body and broken in spirit. I got no supper that night, or breakfast that morning. I reached Covey's about nine o'clock; and just as I was getting over the fence that divided Mrs. Kemp's fields from ours, out ran Covey with his cowskin, to give me another whipping. Before he could reach me, I succeeded in getting to the cornfield; and as the corn was very high, it afforded me the means of hiding. He seemed very angry, and searched for me a long time. My behavior was altogether unaccountable. He finally gave up the chase, thinking, I suppose, that I must come home for something to eat; he would give himself no further trouble in looking for me. I spent that day mostly in the woods, having the alternative before me,—to go home and be whipped to death, or stay in the woods and be starved to death. That night, I fell in with Sandy Jenkins, a slave with whom I was somewhat acquainted. Sandy had a free wife who lived about four miles from Mr. Covey's; and it being Saturday, he was on his way to see her. I told him my circumstances, and he very kindly invited me to go home with him. I went home with him, and talked this whole matter over, and got his advice as to what course it was best for me to pursue. I found Sandy an old adviser. He told

---

5. **salts:** mineral salts used to relieve faintness and headache or reduce swelling.

WORDS TO KNOW

sundry (sŭn′drē) *adj.* various; miscellaneous
interpose (ĭn′tər-pōz′) *v.* to interfere in order to help; intervene

me, with great solemnity, I must go back to Covey; but that before I went, I must go with him into another part of the woods, where there was a certain *root,* which, if I would take some of it with me, carrying it *always on my right side,* would render it impossible for Mr. Covey, or any other white man, to whip me. He said he had carried it for years; and since he had done so, he had never received a blow, and never expected to while he carried it. I at first rejected the idea, that the simple carrying of a root in my pocket would have any such effect as he had said, and was not disposed to take it; but Sandy impressed the necessity with much earnestness, telling me it could do no harm, if it did no good. To please him, I at length took the root, and, according to his direction, carried it upon my right side. This was Sunday morning. I immediately started for home; and upon entering the yard gate, out came Mr. Covey on his way to meeting.[6] He spoke to me very kindly, bade me drive the pigs from a lot near by, and passed on towards the church. Now, this singular conduct of Mr. Covey really made me begin to think that there was something in the *root* which Sandy had given me; and had it been on any other day than Sunday, I could have attributed the conduct to no other cause than the influence of that root; and as it was, I was half inclined to think the *root* to be something more than I at first had taken it to be. All went well till Monday morning. On this morning, the virtue of the *root* was fully tested. Long before daylight, I was called to go and rub, curry, and feed, the horses. I obeyed, and was glad to obey. But whilst thus engaged, whilst in the act of throwing down some blades from the loft, Mr. Covey entered the stable with a long rope; and just as I was half out of the loft, he caught hold of my legs, and was about tying me. As soon as I found what he was up to, I gave a sudden spring, and as I did so, he holding to my legs, I was brought sprawling on the stable floor. Mr. Covey seemed now to think he had me, and could do what he pleased; but at

this moment—from whence came the spirit I don't know—I resolved to fight; and, suiting my action to the resolution, I seized Covey hard by the throat; and as I did so, I rose. He held on to me, and I to him. My resistance was so entirely unexpected, that Covey seemed taken all aback.[7] He trembled like a leaf. This gave me assurance, and I held him uneasy, causing the blood to run where I touched him with the ends of my fingers. Mr. Covey soon called out to Hughes for help. Hughes came, and, while Covey held me, attempted to tie my right hand. While he was in the act of doing so, I watched my chance, and gave him a heavy kick close under the ribs. This kick fairly sickened Hughes, so that he left me in the hands of Mr. Covey. This kick had the effect of not only weakening Hughes, but Covey also. When he saw Hughes bending over with pain, his courage quailed. He asked me if I meant to persist in my resistance. I told him I did, come what might; that he had used me like a brute for six months, and that I was determined to be used so no longer. With that, he strove to drag me to a stick that was lying just out of the stable door. He meant to knock me down. But just as he was leaning over to get the stick, I seized him with both hands by his collar, and brought him by a sudden snatch to the ground. By this time, Bill came. Covey called upon him for assistance. Bill wanted to know what he could do. Covey said, "Take hold of him, take hold of him!" Bill said his master hired him out to work, and not to help to whip me; so he left Covey and myself to fight our own battle out. We were at it for nearly two hours. Covey at length let me go, puffing and blowing at a great rate, saying that if I had not resisted, he would not have whipped me half so much. The truth was, that he had not whipped me at all. I considered him as getting entirely the worst end of the bargain; for he had drawn no

---

6. **meeting:** church service.

7. **taken all aback:** so surprised as to be unable to move or respond.

blood from me, but I had from him. The whole six months afterwards, that I spent with Mr. Covey, he never laid the weight of his finger upon me in anger. He would occasionally say, he didn't want to get hold of me again. "No," thought I, "you need not; for you will come off worse than you did before."

This battle with Mr. Covey was the turning-point in my career as a slave. It rekindled the few expiring embers of freedom, and revived within me a sense of my own manhood. It recalled the departed self-confidence, and inspired me again with a determination to be free. The gratification afforded by the triumph was a full compensation for whatever else might follow, even death itself. He only can understand the deep satisfaction which I experienced, who has himself repelled by force the bloody arm of slavery. I felt as I never felt before. It was a glorious resurrection, from the tomb of slavery, to the heaven of freedom. My long-crushed spirit rose, cowardice departed, bold defiance took its place; and I now resolved that, however long I might remain a slave in form, the day had passed forever when I could be a slave in fact. I did not hesitate to let it be known of me, that the white man who expected to succeed in whipping, must also succeed in killing me.

From this time I was never again what might be called fairly whipped, though I remained a slave four years afterwards. I had several fights, but was never whipped. ❖

Connect to the Literature

1. **What Do You Think?** What are your impressions of Frederick Douglass?

> **Comprehension Check**
> - What was Covey's first reason for beating Douglass?
> - How did Master Thomas respond when Douglass asked for protection from Covey?
> - How did Douglass keep Covey from beating him again?

Think Critically

2. Explain what you think Douglass means when he states, "However long I might remain a slave in form, the day had passed forever when I could be a slave in fact" (page 570).

3. What do Douglass's choices reveal to you about his character?

   - his resolve to ask Master Thomas for protection
   - his agreeing to take the root from Sandy
   - his decision to fight Covey

4. What would you say freedom means to Douglass?

5. **ACTIVE READING** | **AUTHOR'S PURPOSE** | Think about your reactions to Douglass and his fellow slaves, on the one hand, and to Covey and Master Thomas on the other. How does Douglass's writing make his **audience** feel about slavery? Explain.

6. What do the **conflicts** between Douglass and Covey reveal about slavery's effects on both slaves and masters?

Extend Interpretations

7. **Comparing Texts** Reread the next-to-last paragraph, in which Douglass describes his feelings of freedom and manhood after resisting Covey's brutality. Cite specific examples to compare Douglass's ideas with Emerson's philosophy in the excerpt from "Self-Reliance" on page 364.

8. **Connect to Life** In what situations today might a person be inspired by Douglass's life story?

Literary Analysis

AUTOBIOGRAPHY AND STYLE

The **style** of a literary work is the distinctive way in which it was written. Douglass's style in this autobiography is formal and elegant. Often his diction, or choice of words, is elevated ("whilst thus engaged"). His tone is restrained, as opposed to furious. He uses little direct dialogue. What other features of his style did you notice?

Critics often comment that Douglass is surprisingly **objective**—he can be quite factual and unemotional, given the brutality he describes. Consider this example:

We were worked fully up to the point of endurance. . . . Mr. Covey gave us enough to eat, but scarce time to eat it.

Yet at times Douglass can also be **subjective,** describing his personal feelings in emotionally charged words and figurative expressions:

It was a glorious resurrection, from the tomb of slavery, to the heaven of freedom.

Cooperative Learning Activity
With a group of classmates, choose three passages that you think give an especially telling picture of slavery. Decide whether the passages are primarily objective, subjective, or a combination of both. Discuss how Douglass's style might suit his **purpose** of convincing a largely white audience to abolish slavery.

Choices & CHALLENGES

Writing Options

1. Closing Statement Imagine that Covey had Douglass arrested for fighting him. As Douglass's attorney, write a closing statement for the trial. Use both objective evidence and subjective language to persuade a jury that Douglass was right to defend himself.

Writing Handbook
See page 1283: Analysis.

2. Antislavery Editorial Douglass founded an antislavery newspaper, the *North Star.* Based on your reading of this excerpt, write an outline for an editorial about slavery that you would write for his paper.

3. Comparison of Slave Narratives In an essay, compare and contrast the excerpts from the narratives of Douglass and Olaudah Equiano (page 94). Focus on the content, style, theme, and purpose of each selection.

Writing Handbook
See page 1281: Compare and Contrast.

	Douglass	Equiano
Content		
Style		
Theme		
Purpose		

4. Autobiographical Sketch
Douglass's fight with Covey was a turning point for him. Think of an incident from your own life that you would describe as a turning point.

Write about this incident in a short autobiographical sketch, explaining why it changed your life.

Activities & Explorations

1. Living to Tell As Douglass, retell an episode from this selection as a short speech to the Anti-Slavery Society. ~ **PERFORMING**

2. Story in Pictures Collaborate with several classmates on a picture book for young readers. Recount Douglass's time with Covey, simplifying the language and illustrating important scenes. Then share the picture book with younger readers at home or in your school. ~ **ART**

3. Discussion of Covey Gather in a small group to discuss why Covey never again whipped Douglass. Speculate about why Covey did not tell authorities about Douglass's resistance and have him punished. Draw on your own experiences with bullies to come up with reasons. Share notes from your discussion with the rest of the class. ~ **SPEAKING AND LISTENING**

Inquiry & Research

1. Another View Find another slave narrative, such as *Incidents in the Life of a Slave Girl,* by Harriet Jacobs, or *The History of Mary Prince, a West Indian Slave.* How does the writer's experience of slavery compare to Frederick Douglass's experience? Make comparisons in an oral presentation.

2. Slave Laws States where slavery was legal had special laws restricting the activities of slaves. Research these laws, using published or electronic sources, and hang a poster in your classroom that lists ten of the harshest laws.

 More Online: Research Starter
www.mcdougallittell.com

Art Connection

The 18th-century portrait on page 567 does not depict Frederick Douglass but an unnamed man, perhaps a servant of the artist, John Singleton Copley. Realistic portraits of African Americans were rare during the 18th and 19th centuries. What seems to be this man's state of mind? If you had to pull out a line from the Frederick Douglass selection to go with this painting, which line would you choose, and why?

Head of a Negro (1777–1778), John Singleton Copley. Paint on canvas, 53.3 cm × 41.3 cm. The Detroit Institute of Arts, Founders Society Purchase, Gibbs-Williams Fund.

Vocabulary in Action

EXERCISE A: MEANING CLUES Read each magazine article title below and write the vocabulary word that you would expect to find in that article.

1. "Sibling Rivalry: When to Step In"
2. "Making the Most of Your Natural Talents"
3. "Energy Boosters: Some Perfect Pick-Me-Ups"
4. "How to Get What You Want Without Having to Ask"
5. "Too Much Junk? How to Have a Successful Garage Sale"

Building Vocabulary

Some of the Words to Know have more than one meaning. For an in-depth lesson on words with multiple meanings, see page 630.

EXERCISE B: Team up with a partner to write a sentence that uses as many of the Words to Know as possible. Describing a humorous or unlikely situation is fine, as long as the words are used accurately. Then either act out this sentence as someone reads it to the class, or draw an illustration of it to show to your classmates.

WORDS TO KNOW	faculty	intimate	sundry
	interpose	languish	

Frederick Douglass
1817?–1895

Other Works
My Bondage and My Freedom
The Life and Times of Frederick Douglass
"What to the Slave Is the Fourth of July?"
"The Color Line"

Lecturing to the World After having grown up in slavery in Maryland, Frederick Douglass escaped when he was 21 and fled to New York City disguised as a sailor. Three years later, Douglass spoke so eloquently to the Massachusetts Anti-Slavery Society that they hired him to lecture about his experiences. Soon after that he became one of the country's most prominent antislavery speakers, devoting his life to fighting for abolition, suffrage and civil rights. The publication of his autobiography, *Narrative of the Life of Frederick Douglass, an American Slave* (1845), resulted in widespread publicity and the possibility of recapture by his former owner. To remove himself from this dangerous situation, Douglass embarked on a two-year speaking tour in England, Scotland, Wales and Ireland.

Publisher and Statesman During Douglass's trip abroad, two friends raised the money to purchase his freedom. After returning to America in 1847 as a free man, Douglass settled in Rochester, New York, and founded an antislavery newspaper called the *North Star.* He continued lecturing against slavery and in 1848 addressed the first Women's Rights Convention in Seneca Falls, New York. As the Civil War began, Douglass was instrumental in recruiting the first African-American troops—including his own sons—for the 54th Massachusetts Volunteers. During the war, he advised President Abraham Lincoln. Douglass held several government positions after the war, including the post of Minister to Haiti. Throughout his life, Douglass continued to champion civil rights for African Americans and for women.

Author Activity

Poetic Tribute Read Robert Hayden's poem "Frederick Douglass" on page 615. Is Hayden justified in his praise of Douglass? Use evidence from Douglass's life and autobiography to support your answer.

Stanzas on Freedom

Poetry by JAMES RUSSELL LOWELL

Free Labor

Poetry by FRANCES ELLEN WATKINS HARPER

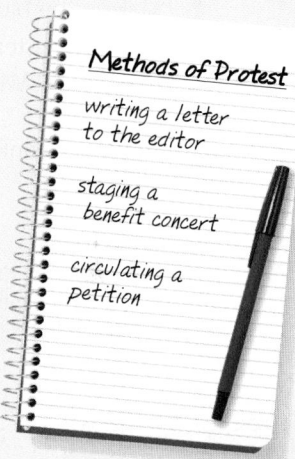

Methods of Protest
writing a letter to the editor
staging a benefit concert
circulating a petition

Connect to Your Life

Standing for Justice Name a current social or political situation you think should be protested. How would you attempt to generate public interest in solving this problem? With a group of classmates, brainstorm ten ways to publicize issues, adding to the list shown here. Then rate the effectiveness of the methods you listed on a scale of 1 to 10, with 10 being the most effective.

Build Background

Demand for Change These two poems were written before the Civil War to protest slavery. In the United States, public opposition to slavery began in the 1680s when Quakers criticized slavery on religious grounds. Although the antislavery movement grew steadily in the 1700s, it gained momentum in the decades prior to the Civil War. By 1840, there were more than 2,000 antislavery societies and at least a dozen abolitionist newspapers. At the height of the movement, abolitionists in the North not only gave public lectures that denounced slavery but also published antislavery almanacs, magazines, and pamphlets. These publications often featured antislavery poems. In 1843, poet James Russell Lowell, a lifelong abolitionist, published "Stanzas on Freedom." Frances Ellen Watkins Harper, an antislavery lecturer and the most popular African-American poet of her time, published "Free Labor" in 1857.

Focus Your Reading

LITERARY ANALYSIS **SYMBOL** A **symbol** is a person, place, object, or activity that has a concrete meaning but also stands for something beyond itself. Familiar symbols include a heart (symbolizing love), a dove (symbolizing peace), and a handshake (symbolizing friendship). The symbols in a poem are usually more original and complex; interpreting them is essential to understanding and enjoying the work. Look for words used as symbols in "Stanzas on Freedom" and "Free Labor."

ACTIVE READING **STRATEGIES FOR READING PROTEST POETRY**
These works are examples of **protest poetry,** written less to express personal feelings than to persuade readers to support a certain cause. You might approach these poems as you approached the political speeches, letters, and essays in the second part of Unit Two, "The Right to Be Free."

- **First reading** Get a sense of the general ideas and overall feeling of each poem.
- **Second reading** Be more analytical. Determine the intended audience.
- **Third reading** Analyze what the poet wants readers to feel. Pay attention to your emotional reactions and the symbols, images, or devices that trigger them.

READER'S NOTEBOOK Begin to take notes as you first read the poem, and add to your notes as you read a second and a third time.

Stanzas on Freedom

James Russell Lowell

Men! whose boast it is that ye
Come of fathers brave and free,
If there breathe on earth a slave,
Are ye truly free and brave?
5 If ye do not feel the chain,
When it works a brother's pain,
Are ye not base[1] slaves indeed,
Slaves unworthy to be freed?

Women! who shall one day bear
10 Sons to breathe New England air,
If ye hear, without a blush,
Deeds to make the roused blood rush
Like red lava through your veins,
For your sisters now in chains,—
15 Answer! are ye fit to be
Mothers of the brave and free?

Is true Freedom but to break
Fetters[2] for our own dear sake,
And, with leathern hearts, forget
20 That we owe mankind a debt?
No! true freedom is to share
All the chains our brothers wear,
And, with heart and hand, to be
Earnest to make others free!

25 They are slaves who fear to speak
For the fallen and the weak;
They are slaves who will not choose
Hatred, scoffing, and abuse,
Rather than in silence shrink
30 From the truth they needs must think;
They are slaves who dare not be
In the right with two or three.

---

1. **base:** having little or no honor, courage, or decency; low or inferior.
2. **fetters:** chains or other bonds.

Thinking Through the Literature

1. **Comprehension Check** What does Lowell call those who are afraid to speak?

2. Judging from this poem, how do you think Lowell would define *freedom* and *slavery?*

   THINK ABOUT
   - his view of the "free" men and women he addresses in the first and second stanzas
   - his definition of "true freedom" in the third stanza
   - whom he describes as slaves in the last stanza

3. **ACTIVE READING** **PROTEST POETRY** What kind of people do you believe Lowell is speaking to in this poem, and what does he want them to do?

4. Think again about the way Lowell uses the term *slaves* in the last stanza. Who in present-day America might Lowell view as slaves in this sense?

Free Labor

FRANCES ELLEN WATKINS HARPER

I wear an easy garment,
    O'er it no toiling slave
Wept tears of hopeless anguish,
    In his passage to the grave.

5 And from its ample folds
    Shall rise no cry to God,
Upon its warp and woof[1] shall be
    No stain of tears and blood.

Oh, lightly shall it press my form,
10   Unladened[2] with a sigh,
I shall not 'mid its rustling hear,
    Some sad despairing cry.

This fabric is too light to bear
    The weight of bondsmen's[3] tears,
15 I shall not in its texture trace
    The agony of years.

Too light to bear a smother'd sigh,
    From some lorn[4] woman's heart,
Whose only wreath of household love
20   Is rudely torn apart.

Then lightly shall it press my form,
    Unburden'd by a sigh;
And from its seams and folds shall rise,
    No voice to pierce the sky,

25 And witness at the throne of God,
    In language deep and strong,
That I have nerv'd[5] Oppression's hand,
    For deeds of guilt and wrong.

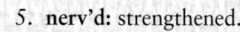

1. **warp and woof:** In weaving cloth, the lengthwise threads ("warp") pass over and under the crosswise threads ("woof").
2. **unladened:** unburdened.
3. **bondsmen's:** slaves'.
4. **lorn:** forlorn; lonely and unhappy.
5. **nerv'd:** strengthened.

Collection of The New York Historical Society.

From the collections of the Library of Congress.

Thinking through the LITERATURE

Connect to the Literature

1. **What Do You Think?**
   Describe the images that the poem "Free Labor" creates in your mind.

   > **Comprehension Check**
   > • What kind of garment won't the speaker wear?
   > • Whose voice would rise from this garment, and what would it say to God?

Think Critically

2. **ACTIVE READING** **PROTEST POETRY** In your own words, explain how "Free Labor" protests slavery.

   THINK ABOUT
   - what the **title** might mean
   - what makes the speaker's garment "easy" and "light"
   - what it means to "have nerv'd Oppression's hand"
   - what specific action the poet might want her audience to take

3. What kind of person might the speaker in this poem be? What would you guess about the speaker's past?

4. Which do you think are the most effective lines in this poem? Explain your choice.

Extend Interpretations

5. **Comparing Texts** If both "Stanzas on Freedom" and "Free Labor" had been read widely before the Civil War, which one do you think would be more likely to stir people to take a stand against slavery? Why?

6. **Connect to Life** What examples of art today do you think are comparable to the antislavery poems of the 19th century?

Literary Analysis

SYMBOL As you know, a **symbol** has a concrete meaning in itself while also standing for something else, such as an idea or a feeling. In the story "Dr. Heidegger's Experiment," for example, the blooming and fading rose symbolizes human life. What do you think the chains in "Stanzas on Freedom" symbolize? In "Free Labor," what might the garment stand for?

Cooperative Learning Activity Work as a small group to paraphrase each of these poems as a short speech. Instead of using symbols, spell out what Lowell and Harper mean in literal terms. Read the speeches aloud to the class. Are they as effective as the poems? What are some advantages of using symbols to express ideas?

Symbol	Ideas
Chains	
Garment	

Writing Options

1. New Stanza The first and second stanzas of "Stanzas on Freedom" begin "Men!" and "Women!" Imagine that the next stanza begins "Youths!" Complete such a stanza, writing what you believe would reflect a teenager's situation in those times. Read your stanza to classmates.

2. Protest Poem Write a protest poem to influence people to take a stand on some contemporary issue, perhaps the one you named in the Connect to Your Life activity on page 574.

Activities & Explorations

Political Poster Create a poster to persuade people in the 1850s to take a stand against slavery. As an alternative, create a poster urging people today to take a stand against a modern injustice. ~ **ART**

James Russell Lowell
1819–1891

Other Works
Poems
A Fable for Critics
My Study Windows
Under the Willows

Literary Activist James Russell Lowell, a member of a prominent Massachusetts family, had achieved fame for his poetry and essays by the time he was 30. A well-known abolitionist, he wrote editorials for the antislavery newspaper, the *Pennsylvania Freeman,* and also contributed to the *National Anti-Slavery Standard* and other periodicals. In addition to "Stanzas on Freedom," Lowell also wrote other antislavery poems, including "On the Capture of Fugitive Slaves Near Washington," and dealt with this subject in The Biglow Papers, a collection of poetic letters attributed to the fictional Hosea Biglow.

Tragedy and Achievement While Lowell's literary reputation grew, his life took a tragic turn when his wife and three of his four children died within six years of one another. In 1856 he became professor of modern languages at Harvard, succeeding Henry Wadsworth Longfellow in that post. A year later, he accepted the editorship of the newly founded magazine *Atlantic Monthly,* and he remarried. In 1877 Lowell was appointed U.S. Minister to Spain and took a similar post in England three years later. After the death of his second wife in 1885, Lowell returned home, where he remained for the rest of his life.

Frances Ellen Watkins Harper
1825–1911

Other Works
"The Slave Mother"
Poems on Miscellaneous Subjects
Iola Leroy

A Gifted Orphan Later known as the "Bronze Muse," poet, novelist, lecturer, and social reformer Frances Ellen Watkins Harper was born free in the slave city of Baltimore, Maryland. Orphaned at the age of three, she was raised by her aunt and uncle and attended her uncle's private school until she was 13. Harper then began working as a housekeeper. Because the family for whom she worked owned a bookstore, Harper was able to read books in her spare time. When she was fourteen, she began to write poems and essays.

On Freedom's Road In 1850, Harper moved to Ohio and became a teacher, but she soon decided to devote herself to the abolitionist cause. She traveled throughout the North and the Midwest giving lectures on the evils of slavery. Harper, who combined her artistic and political lives by reciting her poems during her speeches, wrote to a friend: "You would be amused to hear some of the remarks which my lectures call forth. 'She is a man,' again 'She is not colored, she is white. She is painted.'" After marrying in 1860, Harper settled on a farm in Ohio. Following her husband's death in 1864, she began lecturing on the topic of equal rights for the newly freed.

An Occurrence at Owl Creek Bridge

Short Story by AMBROSE BIERCE

Connect to Your Life

Final Thoughts This story is about a man who is facing death. It is often said that when people have a close brush with death, their life flashes before their eyes. What do you think might be the last thoughts of someone about to die? Would such a person think about the meaning of life, the loved ones left behind, or the immediate situation? Discuss the possibilities with a group of your classmates.

Build Background

Writing What He Knew Ambrose Bierce enlisted in the Union Army at 18 and fought bravely in several major battles of the Civil War. After the war, he moved to San Francisco and began an equally distinguished career as a journalist. In this story, Bierce fictionalizes a real hanging that took place in 1862 during the bloody battle of Shiloh in Tennessee. Bierce's firsthand knowledge of the war and his training as a reporter can be seen in the opening two paragraphs of the story, in which he objectively describes the setting for a hanging that is about to occur.

WORDS TO KNOW
Vocabulary Preview

apprise	ludicrous
evade	perceptibly
inaccessible	interminable
preternaturally	subordinate
ineffable	summarily

Focus Your Reading

LITERARY ANALYSIS   POINT OF VIEW   The **point of view** in a story is the narrative perspective from which it is told. In the **first-person** point of view, the narrator is a character in the work who describes events using the pronouns *I, me,* and *my.* In the **third-person** point of view, events are related by a voice outside the action, who uses such pronouns as *he, she,* and *they.* The third-person point of view may be **omniscient** (aware of all characters' thoughts) or **limited** (focused on one character's thoughts). Try to identify the point of view in Bierce's story.

ACTIVE READING   ANALYZING STRUCTURE   The **structure** of a literary work is the arrangement of its parts. This story is arranged in three numbered sections. A change of section signals a change in time. To ensure your understanding as you read, be aware of when the events in each section take place.

📖 **READER'S NOTEBOOK** To help you follow the sequence of events and clarify what happens in each section, use the reading strategy questions inserted throughout the story. Write down answers to the questions in your Reader's Notebook. Also, jot down other ideas that come to you, especially those relating to the main character's last thoughts.

AN OCCURRENCE AT OWL CREEK BRIDGE

Ambrose Bierce

I

A man stood upon a railroad bridge in northern Alabama, looking down into the swift water twenty feet below. The man's hands were behind his back, the wrists bound with a cord. A rope closely encircled his neck. It was attached to a stout cross-timber above his head and the slack fell to the level of his knees. Some loose boards laid upon the sleepers[1] supporting the metals of the railway supplied a footing for him and his executioners—two private soldiers of the Federal army, directed by a sergeant who in civil life may have been a deputy sheriff. At a short remove upon the same temporary platform was an officer in the uniform of his rank, armed. He was a captain. A sentinel at each end of the bridge stood with his rifle in the position known as "support," that is to say, vertical in front of the left shoulder, the hammer resting on the forearm thrown straight across the chest—a formal and unnatural position, enforcing an erect carriage of the body. It did not appear to be the duty of these two men to know what was occurring at the center of the bridge; they merely blockaded the two ends of the foot planking that traversed it.

Beyond one of the sentinels nobody was in sight; the railroad ran straight away into a forest for a hundred yards, then, curving, was lost to view. Doubtless there was an outpost farther along. The other bank of the stream was open ground—a gentle acclivity topped with a stockade of vertical tree trunks, loopholed for rifles, with a single embrasure through which protruded the muzzle of a brass cannon commanding the

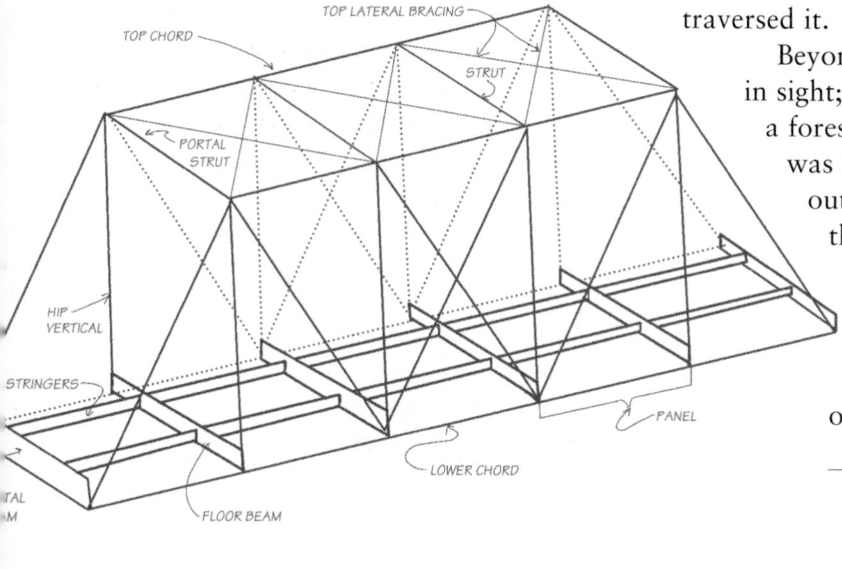

TOP LATERAL BRACING
TOP CHORD
STRUT
PORTAL STRUT
HIP VERTICAL
STRINGERS
PANEL
LOWER CHORD
FLOOR BEAM

---

1. **sleepers:** railroad ties.

Union soldiers. From the collections of the Library of Congress.

announced is to be received with formal manifestations of respect, even by those most familiar with him. In the code of military etiquette silence and fixity are forms of deference.

The man who was engaged in being hanged was apparently about thirty-five years of age. He was a civilian, if one might judge from his habit, which was that of a planter. His features were good—a straight nose, firm mouth, broad forehead, from which his long, dark hair was combed straight back, falling behind his ears to the collar of his well-fitting frock-coat. He wore a mustache and pointed beard, but no whiskers; his eyes were large and dark gray, and had a kindly expression which one would hardly have expected in one whose neck was in the hemp. Evidently this was no vulgar assassin. The liberal military code makes provision for hanging many kinds of persons, and gentlemen are not excluded.

The preparations being complete, the two private soldiers stepped aside and each drew away the plank upon which he had been standing. The sergeant turned to the captain, saluted and placed himself immediately behind that officer, who in turn moved apart one pace. These movements left the condemned man and the sergeant standing on the two ends of the same plank, which spanned three of the cross-ties of the bridge. The end upon which the civilian stood almost, but not quite, reached a fourth. This plank had been held in place by the weight of the captain; it was now held by that of the sergeant. At a signal from the former the latter would step aside, the plank would tilt and the condemned man go down between two ties. The arrangement commended itself to his judgment as simple and effective. His face

bridge. Midway of the slope between bridge and fort were the spectators—a single company of infantry in line, at "parade rest," the butts of the rifles on the ground, the barrels inclining slightly backward against the right shoulder, the hands crossed upon the stock. A lieutenant stood at the right of the line, the point of his sword upon the ground, his left hand resting upon his right. Excepting the group of four at the center of the bridge, not a man moved. The company faced the bridge, staring stonily, motionless. The sentinels, facing the banks of the stream, might have been statues to adorn the bridge. The captain stood with folded arms, silent, observing the work of his <u>subordinates</u>, but making no sign. Death is a dignitary who when he comes

WORDS
TO
KNOW

subordinate (sə-bôr′dn-ĭt) *n.* one who is lower in rank

had not been covered nor his eyes bandaged. He looked a moment at his "unsteadfast footing,"

ACTIVE READING

QUESTION Whose thoughts and feelings does the narrator relate?

then let his gaze wander to the swirling water of the stream racing madly beneath his feet. A piece of dancing driftwood caught his attention and his eyes followed it down the current. How slowly it appeared to move! What a sluggish stream!

He closed his eyes in order to fix his last thoughts upon his wife and children. The water, touched to gold by the early sun, the brooding mists under the banks at some distance down the stream, the fort, the soldiers, the piece of drift— all had distracted him. And now he became conscious of a new disturbance. Striking through the thought of his dear ones was a sound which he could neither ignore nor understand, a sharp, distinct, metallic percussion like the stroke of a blacksmith's hammer upon the anvil; it had the same ringing quality. He wondered what it was, and whether immeasurably distant or near by— it seemed both. Its recurrence was regular, but as slow as the tolling of a death knell.[2] He awaited each stroke with impatience and—he knew not why—apprehension. The intervals of silence grew progressively longer; the delays became maddening. With their greater infrequency the sounds increased in strength and sharpness. They hurt his ear like the thrust of a knife; he feared he would shriek. What he heard was the ticking of his watch.

He unclosed his eyes and saw again the water below him. "If I could free my hands," he thought, "I might throw off the noose and spring into the stream. By diving I could evade the bullets and, swimming vigorously, reach the bank, take to the woods and get away home. My home, thank God, is as yet outside their lines; my wife and little ones are still beyond the invader's farthest advance."

As these thoughts, which have here to be set down in words, were flashed into the doomed man's brain rather than evolved from it the captain nodded to the sergeant. The sergeant stepped aside.

ACTIVE READING

CLARIFY What does the captain's nod mean?

II

Peyton Farquhar was a well-to-do planter, of an old and highly respected Alabama family. Being a slave owner and like other slave owners a politician he was naturally an original secessionist[3] and ardently devoted to the Southern cause. Circumstances of an imperious nature, which it is unnecessary to relate here, had prevented him from taking service with the gallant army that had fought the disastrous campaigns ending with the fall of Corinth,[4] and he chafed under the inglorious restraint, longing for the release of his energies, the larger life of the soldier, the opportunity for distinction. That opportunity, he felt, would come, as it comes to all in war time. Meanwhile he did what he could. No service was too humble for him to perform in aid of the South, no adventure too perilous for him to undertake if consistent with the character of a civilian who was at heart a soldier, and who in good faith and without too much qualification assented to at least a part of the frankly villainous dictum that all is fair in love and war.

One evening while Farquhar and his wife were sitting on a rustic bench near the entrance to his grounds, a gray-clad soldier rode up to the gate and asked for a drink of water. Mrs. Farquhar

---

2. **tolling of a death knell:** the slow, steady ringing of a bell at a funeral or to indicate death.

3. **secessionist** (sĭ-sĕsh'ə-nĭst): one who supported the withdrawal of Southern states from the Union.

4. **Corinth:** a town in Mississippi that was the site of a Civil War battle in 1862.

WORDS TO KNOW   **evade** (ĭ-vād') *v.* to escape or avoid

was only too happy to serve him with her own white hands. While she was fetching the water her husband approached the dusty horseman and inquired eagerly for news from the front.

"The Yanks are repairing the rail-roads," said the man, "and are getting ready for another advance. They have reached the Owl Creek bridge, put it in order and built a stockade on the north bank. The commandant has issued an order, which is posted every-where, declaring that any civilian caught interfering with the railroad, its bridges, tunnels or trains will be <u>summarily</u> hanged. I saw the order."

"How far is it to the Owl Creek bridge?" Farquhar asked.

"About thirty miles."

"Is there no force on this side the creek?"

"Only a picket post[5] half a mile out, on the railroad, and a single sentinel at this end of the bridge."

"Suppose a man—a civilian and student of hanging—should elude the picket post and perhaps get the better of the sentinel," said Farquhar, smiling, "what could he accomplish?"

The soldier reflected. "I was there a month ago," he replied. "I observed that the flood of last winter had lodged a great quantity of driftwood against the wooden pier at this end of the bridge. It is now dry and would burn like tow."[6]

The lady had now brought the water, which the soldier drank. He thanked her ceremoniously, bowed to her husband and rode away. An hour later, after nightfall, he repassed the plantation, going northward in the direction from which he had come. He was a Federal scout.

ACTIVE READING

ANALYZE When do these events occur and what do they explain?

<hr>

—— III ——

As Peyton Farquhar fell straight downward through the bridge he lost consciousness and was as one already dead. From this state he was awakened—ages later, it seemed to him—by the pain of a sharp pressure upon his throat, followed by a sense of suffocation. Keen, poignant[7] agonies seemed to shoot from his neck downward through every fiber of his body and limbs. These pains appeared to flash along well-defined lines of ramification[8] and to beat with an inconceivably rapid periodicity. They seemed like streams of pulsating fire heating him to an intolerable temperature. As to his head, he was conscious of nothing but a feeling of fullness—of congestion. These sensations were unaccompanied by thought. The intellectual part of his nature was already effaced; he had power only to feel, and feeling

<hr>

5. **picket post:** the camp of soldiers who are assigned to guard against a surprise attack.

6. **tow:** coarse, dry fiber.

7. **poignant** (poin'yənt): physically painful.

8. **flash . . . ramification:** spread out rapidly along branches from a central point.

WORDS
TO
KNOW

summarily (sə-mĕr′ə-lē) *adv.* in a way that is quick and bypasses usual procedures

was torment. He was conscious of motion. Encompassed in a luminous cloud, of which he was now merely the fiery heart, without material substance, he swung through unthinkable arcs of oscillation, like a vast pendulum. Then all at once, with terrible suddenness, the light about him shot upward with the noise of a loud plash; a frightful roaring was in his ears, and all was cold and dark. The power of thought was restored; he knew that the rope had broken and he had fallen into the stream. There was no additional strangulation; the noose about his neck was already suffocating him and kept the water from his lungs. To die of hanging at the bottom of a river!—the idea seemed to him <u>ludicrous</u>. He opened his eyes in the darkness and saw above him a gleam of light, but how distant, how <u>inaccessible</u>! He was still sinking, for the light became fainter and fainter until it was a mere glimmer. Then it began to grow and brighten, and he knew that he was rising toward the surface—knew it with reluctance, for he was now very comfortable. "To be hanged and drowned," he thought, "that is not so bad; but I do not wish to be shot. No; I will not be shot; that is not fair."

ACTIVE READING

EVALUATE Would these be the thoughts of a man on the brink of death?

He was not conscious of an effort, but a sharp pain in his wrist <u>apprised</u> him that he was trying to free his hands. He gave the struggle his attention, as an idler might observe the feat of a juggler, without interest in the outcome. What splendid effort!—what magnificent, what superhuman strength! Ah, that was a fine endeavor! Bravo! The cord fell away; his arms parted and floated upward, the hands dimly seen on each side in the growing light. He watched them with a new interest as first one and then the other pounced upon the noose at his neck. They tore it away and thrust it fiercely aside, its undulations resembling those of a water-snake. "Put it back, put it back!" He thought he shouted these words to his hands, for the undoing of the noose had been succeeded by the direst pang that he had yet experienced. His neck ached horribly; his brain was on fire; his heart, which had been fluttering faintly, gave a great leap, trying to force itself out at his mouth. His whole body was racked and wrenched with an insupportable anguish![9] But his disobedient hands gave no heed to the command. They beat the water vigorously with quick, downward strokes, forcing him to the surface. He felt his head emerge; his eyes were blinded by the sunlight; his chest expanded convulsively, and with a supreme and crowning agony his lungs engulfed a great draught of air, which instantly he expelled in a shriek!

He was now in full possession of his physical senses. They were, indeed, <u>preternaturally</u> keen and alert. Something in the awful disturbance of his organic system had so exalted and refined them that they made record of things never before perceived. He felt the ripples upon his face and heard their separate sounds as they struck. He looked at the forest on the bank of the stream, saw the individual trees, the leaves and the veining of each leaf—saw the very insects upon them: the locusts, the brilliant-bodied flies, the gray spiders stretching their webs from twig to twig. He noted the prismatic colors in all the dewdrops upon a million blades of grass. The humming of the gnats that danced above the eddies of the stream, the beating of the dragon-flies' wings, the strokes of the water-spiders' legs, like oars which had lifted their boat—all these made audible music. A fish slid along beneath his eyes and he heard the rush of its body parting the water.

---

9. **racked . . . anguish:** stretched and twisted with unendurable physical pain.

WORDS TO KNOW

ludicrous (lōō′dĭ-krəs) *adj.* laughably absurd; ridiculous
inaccessible (ĭn′ăk-sĕs′ə-bəl) *adj.* not obtained easily, if at all; unreachable
apprise (ə-prīz′) *v.* to give notice to; inform
preternaturally (prē′tər-năch′ər-əl-ē) *adv.* more than naturally; extraordinarily

He had come to the surface facing down the stream; in a moment the visible world seemed to wheel slowly round, himself the pivotal point, and he saw the bridge, the fort, the soldiers upon the bridge, the captain, the sergeant, the two privates, his executioners. They were in silhouette against the blue sky. They shouted and gesticulated, pointing at him. The captain had drawn his pistol, but did not fire; the others were unarmed. Their movements were grotesque and horrible, their forms gigantic.

Suddenly he heard a sharp report and something struck the water smartly within a few inches of his head, spattering his face with spray. He heard a second report, and saw one of the sentinels with his rifle at his shoulder, a light cloud of blue smoke rising from the muzzle. The man in the water saw the eye of the man on the bridge gazing into his own through the sights of the rifle. He observed that it was a gray eye and remembered having read that gray eyes were keenest, and that all famous marksmen had them. Nevertheless, this one had missed.

A counter-swirl had caught Farquhar and turned him half round; he was again looking into the forest on the bank opposite the fort. The sound of a clear, high voice in a monotonous singsong now rang out behind him and came across the water with a distinctness that pierced and subdued all other sounds, even the beating of the ripples in his ears. Although no soldier, he had frequented camps enough to know the dread significance of that deliberate, drawling, aspirated chant; the lieutenant on shore was taking a part in the morning's work. How coldly and pitilessly—with what an even, calm intonation, presaging,[10] and enforcing tranquillity in the men—with what accurately measured intervals fell those cruel words:

"Attention, company! . . . Shoulder arms! . . . Ready! . . . Aim! . . . Fire!"

Farquhar dived—dived as deeply as he could. The water roared in his ears like the voice of Niagara, yet he heard the dulled thunder of the volley and, rising again toward the surface, met shining bits of metal, singularly flattened, oscillating slowly downward. Some of them touched him on the face and hands, then fell away, continuing their descent. One lodged between his collar and neck; it was uncomfortably warm and he snatched it out.

As he rose to the surface, gasping for breath, he saw that he had been a long time under water; he was perceptibly farther down stream—nearer to safety. The soldiers had almost finished reloading; the metal ramrods flashed all at once in the sunshine as they were drawn from the barrels, turned in the air, and thrust into their sockets. The two sentinels fired again, independently and ineffectually.

The hunted man saw all this over his shoulder; he was now swimming vigorously with the current. His brain was as energetic as his arms and legs; he thought with the rapidity of lightning.

"The officer," he reasoned, "will not make that martinet's[11] error a second time. It is as easy to dodge a volley as a single shot. He has probably already given the command to fire at will. God help me, I cannot dodge them all!"

An appalling plash within two yards of him was followed by a loud, rushing sound, *diminuendo*,[12] which seemed to travel back through the air to the fort and died in an explosion which stirred the very river to its deeps! A rising sheet of water curved over him, fell down upon him, blinded him, strangled him! The cannon had taken a hand in the game. As he shook his head free from the commotion of the smitten water he heard the deflected shot humming through the air ahead, and in an

---

10. **presaging** (prĕs′ĭj-ĭng): predicting.

11. **martinet** (mär′tn-ĕt′): strict disciplinarian; one who demands that regulations be followed exactly.

12. *diminuendo* (dĭ-mĭn′yōo-ĕn′dō) *Italian*: gradually decreasing in loudness.

perceptibly (pər-sĕp′tə-blē) *adv.* in a way that can be perceived by the senses or the mind; noticeably

20'

instant it was cracking and smashing the branches in the forest beyond.

"They will not do that again," he thought; "the next time they will use a charge of grape.[13] I must keep my eye upon the gun; the smoke will apprise me—the report arrives too late; it lags behind the missile. That is a good gun."

Suddenly he felt himself whirled round and round—spinning like a top. The water, the banks, the forests, the now distant bridge, fort and men—all were commingled and blurred. Objects were represented by their colors only; circular horizontal streaks of color—that was all he saw. He had been caught in a vortex and was being whirled on with a velocity of advance and gyration that made him giddy and sick. In a few moments he was flung upon the gravel at the foot of the left bank of the stream—the southern bank—and behind a projecting point which concealed him from his enemies. The sudden arrest of his motion, the abrasion of one of his hands on the gravel, restored him, and he wept with delight. He dug his fingers into the sand, threw it over himself in handfuls and audibly blessed it. It looked like diamonds, rubies, emeralds; he could think of nothing beautiful which it did not resemble. The trees upon the bank were giant garden plants; he noted a definite order in their arrangement, inhaled the fragrance of their blooms. A strange, roseate light shone through the spaces among their trunks and the wind made in their branches the music of æolian harps.[14] He had no wish to perfect his escape—was content to remain in that enchanting spot until retaken.

A whiz and rattle of grapeshot among the branches high above his head roused him from his dream. The baffled cannoneer had fired him a random farewell. He sprang to his feet, rushed up the sloping bank, and plunged into the forest.

All that day he traveled, laying his course by the rounding sun. The forest seemed interminable; nowhere did he discover a break in it, not even a woodman's road. He had not known that he lived in so wild a region. There was something uncanny in the revelation.

By night fall he was fatigued, footsore, famishing. The thought of his wife and children urged him on. At last he found a road which led him in what he knew to be the right direction. It was as wide and straight as a city street, yet it seemed untraveled. No fields bordered it, no dwelling anywhere. Not so much as the barking of a dog suggested human habitation. The black bodies of the trees formed a straight wall on both sides, terminating on the horizon in a point, like a diagram in a lesson in perspective. Overhead, as he looked up through this rift in the wood, shone great golden stars looking unfamiliar and grouped in strange constellations. He was sure they were arranged in some order which had a secret and malign[15] significance. The wood on either side was full of singular noises, among which—once, twice, and again, he distinctly heard whispers in an unknown tongue.

ACTIVE READING

EVALUATE Can you account for the changes in the surroundings?

His neck was in pain and lifting his hand to it he found it horribly swollen. He knew that it had a circle of black where the rope had bruised it. His eyes felt congested; he could no longer close them. His tongue was swollen with thirst; he relieved its fever by thrusting it forward from between his teeth into the cold air. How softly the turf had carpeted the untraveled avenue—he could no longer feel the roadway beneath his feet!

Doubtless, despite his suffering, he had fallen asleep while walking, for now he sees another scene—perhaps he has merely recovered from a

---

13. **grape:** short for *grapeshot*, a cluster of several small iron balls fired in one shot from a cannon.
14. **music of æolian** (ē-ō′lē-ən) **harps:** heavenly, or unearthly, music.
15. **malign** (mə-līn′): evil; harmful; threatening harm or evil.

WORDS
TO   **interminable** (ĭn-tûr′mə-nə-bəl) *adj.* endless
KNOW

Copyright © Ed Simpson/Tony Stone Images.

delirium.[16] He stands at the gate of his own home. All is as he left it, and all bright and beautiful in the morning sunshine. He must have traveled the entire night. As he pushes open the gate and passes up the wide white walk, he sees a flutter of female garments; his wife, looking fresh and cool and sweet, steps down from the veranda to meet him. At the bottom of the steps she stands waiting, with a smile of ineffable joy, an attitude of matchless grace and dignity. Ah, how beautiful she is! He springs forward with extended arms. As he is about to clasp her he feels a stunning blow upon the back of the neck; a blinding white light blazes all about him with a sound like the shock of a cannon—then all is darkness and silence!

Peyton Farquhar was dead; his body, with a broken neck, swung gently from side to side beneath the timbers of the Owl Creek bridge. ❖

ACTIVE READING

CLARIFY What kills Farquhar?

---

16. **delirium** (dĭ-lîr′ē-əm): a temporary state of extreme mental confusion, marked by hallucinations.

WORDS
TO
KNOW
    ineffable (ĭn-ĕf′ə-bəl) *adj.* unable to be expressed in words

Letter to Sarah Ballou

SULLIVAN BALLOU

Major Sullivan Ballou of the 2nd Rhode Island regiment wrote the following letter to his wife on July 14, 1861. He was killed about a week later at the first battle of Bull Run.

My very dear Sarah:

The indications are very strong that we shall move in a few days—perhaps tomorrow. Lest I should not be able to write again, I feel impelled to write a few lines that may fall under your eye when I shall be no more. . . .

I have no misgivings about, or lack of confidence in the cause in which I am engaged, and my courage does not halt or falter. I know how strongly American Civilization now leans on the triumph of the Government, and how great a debt we owe to those who went before us through the blood and sufferings of the Revolution. And I am willing—perfectly willing—to lay down all my joys in this life, to help maintain this Government, and to pay that debt. . . .

Sarah my love for you is deathless, it seems to bind me with mighty cables that nothing but Omnipotence could break; and yet my love of Country comes over me like a strong wind and bears me unresistibly on with all these chains to the battle field.

The memories of the blissful moments I have spent with you come creeping over me, and I feel most gratified to God and to you that I have enjoyed them so long. And hard it is for me to give them up and burn to ashes the hopes of future years, when, God willing, we might still have lived and loved together, and seen our sons grown up to honorable manhood, around us. I have, I know, but few and small claims upon Divine Providence, but something whispers to me—perhaps it is the wafted prayer of my little Edgar, that I shall return to my loved ones unharmed. If I do not my dear Sarah, never forget how much I love you, and when my last breath escapes me on the battle field, it will whisper your name. Forgive my many faults, and the many pains I have caused you. How thoughtless and foolish I have often times been! How gladly would I wash out with my tears every little spot upon your happiness. . . .

But, O Sarah! if the dead can come back to this earth and flit unseen around those they loved, I shall always be near you; in the gladdest days and in the darkest nights . . . *always, always,* and if there be a soft breeze upon your cheek, it shall be my breath, as the cool air fans your throbbing temple, it shall be my spirit passing by. Sarah do not mourn me dead; think I am gone and wait for thee, for we shall meet again. . . .

Thinking through the LITERATURE

Connect to the Literature

1. What Do You Think? Did you like the ending of this story, or dislike it? Share your reaction with classmates.

Comprehension Check
- What is Peyton Farquhar's background?
- What does Farquhar do after he falls through the bridge?
- How does Farquhar die?

Think Critically

2. How did the ending change the way you interpreted events in the story?

3. Why do you think Peyton Farquhar has the last thoughts he does before he dies?

4. What is the Union soldiers' reason for hanging Farquhar? Cite evidence from section II to support your view.

5. **ACTIVE READING** **ANALYZING STRUCTURE** Tell when the events in each numbered section take place. How would changing the order of the three sections affect the story and your understanding of events?

6. Judging from this story, how do you think the author, Ambrose Bierce, views war?

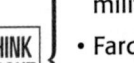

- the statement about hanging and "the liberal military code" (page 582)
- Farquhar's sentiments about the Southern cause, and the result of these sentiments
- the action of the Federal scout who visits Farquhar

Extend Interpretations

7. Comparing Texts Read the letter from Sullivan Ballou, an actual Civil War soldier, on page 590. Compare his thoughts to Farquhar's as he faces death.

8. Connect to Life Were the thoughts of Farquhar and Ballou similar to those you imagined a person would have when facing death?

Literary Analysis

POINT OF VIEW The perspective from which events in a story are narrated is called **point of view.** Notice that the first three paragraphs of this story are told from a **third-person omniscient,** or all-knowing, point of view, as though the narrator is an objective observer of the entire scene. Then, in the fourth paragraph, the perspective subtly shifts to focus on Peyton Farquhar's personal thoughts and sensations. This focus on one character's inner life is called **third-person limited** point of view.

Paired Activity With a partner, analyze the point of view in sections II and III of the story. Where does the point of view shift? How do the shifts affect the level of suspense? Discuss possible reasons why Bierce did not write the story entirely from the third-person omniscient point of view or entirely from the third-person limited point of view.

Writing Options

1. Evaluation of Bierce Draft an evaluation of Ambrose Bierce as a storyteller, based on "An Occurrence at Owl Creek Bridge." Consider how convincing you find his description of Farquhar's last thoughts, how you feel about the ending, and what meaning you draw from the story. Place your writing in your **Working Portfolio.**

Writing Handbook
See page 1283: Analysis.

2. Comparison Essay Ambrose Bierce is thought to have been influenced by Edgar Allan Poe. In a brief essay, explore similarities and differences you see in their styles and concerns.

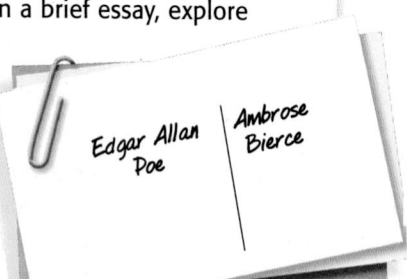

Edgar Allan Poe | Ambrose Bierce

Vocabulary in Action

EXERCISE A: SYNONYMS For each phrase in the first column, write the letter of the synonymous phrase from the second column.

1. dodge the servant
2. favored the ludicrous
3. interminable noise
4. notify the secret agents
5. bet on the general's subordinate

a. apprise the spies
b. wager on the major
c. evade the maid
d. preferred the absurd
e. ceaseless peacelessness

EXERCISE B: Draw cartoons that illustrate the meaning of the following vocabulary words: *ineffable, inaccessible, preternaturally, perceptibly, summarily.*

Building Vocabulary
Several of the Words to Know contain prefixes and suffixes. For an in-depth study of affixes, see page 1130.

Ambrose Bierce
1842-1914?

Other Works
*Black Beetles in Amber
Can Such Things Be?
The Devil's Dictionary*

In the Line of Fire Ambrose Bierce was born into a large, poor, intensely religious family and spent his early years on an Indiana farm. After a miserable childhood, he left home for good at 15 and landed a job at a newspaper setting type. Three years later he enlisted in the Union Army, and received several citations for bravery after fighting in some of the war's fiercest battles. After the war, Bierce worked as a surveyor in the West. He moved to San Francisco in 1866, where he worked for a newspaper and published some of his short stories. He married in 1872 and lived in London for several years with his wife. He earned the nickname "Bitter Bierce" for his cynical humor and cruel wit. His finest stories, such as "An Occurrence at Owl Creek Bridge," published in *Tales of Soldiers and Civilians* in 1891, concern the ironic futility of war.

Vanished During the latter part of his life, Bierce continued to publish short stories, essays, and poems and to work as a political reporter and columnist for the San Francisco *Examiner.* At 71, Bierce revisited Civil War battle sites where he had fought and then went to Mexico to report on the Mexican Revolution as an observer with Pancho Villa's rebel army. He never returned to the United States, and all trace of him disappeared. Before he left, he wrote to a niece, "If you hear of my being stood up against a Mexican stone wall and shot to rags, please know that I think that a pretty good way to depart this life. It beats old age, disease or falling down the cellar stairs."

A Mystery of Heroism

Short Story by STEPHEN CRANE

Connect to Your Life

Heroes and Fine Deeds What does the term *heroism* mean to you? With a small group of classmates, brainstorm a list of personal heroes and heroic actions. Then try to agree on a definition of the term.

Build Background

Civil War Tales Following the remarkable success of his Civil War novel, *The Red Badge of Courage,* Stephen Crane wrote a series of sketches about battles in the Civil War. He did careful research, interviewing veterans and visiting the site where a battle had been fought in Virginia. "A Mystery of Heroism" appeared in *The Little Regiment and Other Episodes of the American Civil War* in 1896. Set on a battlefield, this short story focuses on the motives and actions of Fred Collins, a Union soldier. In this story, Crane uses **dialect** ("Dern yeh! I ain't afraid t' go.") to reflect how soldiers might actually speak and, like an impressionistic painter, provides vivid details to capture the soldiers' sensations in the heat of battle.

WORDS TO KNOW
Vocabulary Preview

eloquence	tousled
furtive	provisional
futile	retraction
genial	stupendous
incessant	sullenly

Focus Your Reading

LITERARY ANALYSIS **NATURALISM** Stephen Crane represents a literary movement known as **naturalism,** an offshoot of realism. Like realistic writers, naturalists sought to portray common people and ordinary life accurately. The naturalists, however, also sought to describe the effect of natural and social forces—such as instinct and environment—on the individual. Consider how these forces affect Fred Collins in this story.

ACTIVE READING **VISUALIZING** **Visualizing** is the process of forming mental pictures as you read. Good readers use the details supplied by writers to picture characters, settings, and events in their mind. For example, notice how Crane's details in this passage help you experience what a soldier under fire might hear, see, and smell:

> *There was the blaring thunder of a shell. Crimson light shone through the swift-boiling smoke and made a pink reflection on part of the wall of the well.*

READER'S NOTEBOOK As you read, use Crane's descriptive details to visualize the setting, the characters, and the events. Create a chart like this one to record your impressions.

Impressions		
Setting	Characters	Events

Battle of Chancellorsville, unknown artist. Corbis-Bettmann.

A Mystery of Heroism

★ ★ ★ ★ ★ ★ ★ ★ ★ ★ ★

Stephen Crane

★ ★ ★ ★ ★ ★ ★ ★ ★ ★ ★ ★ ★ ★ ★ ★ ★ ★ ★ ★

The dark uniforms of the men were so coated with dust from the incessant wrestling of the two armies that the regiment almost seemed a part of the clay bank which shielded them from the shells. On the top of the hill a battery[1] was arguing in tremendous roars with some other guns and to the eye of the infantry, the artillerymen, the guns, the caissons,[2] the horses, were distinctly outlined upon the blue sky. When a piece was fired a red streak as round as a log flashed low in the heavens, like a monstrous bolt of lightning. The men of the battery wore white duck trousers, which somehow emphasized their legs, and when they ran and crowded in little groups at the bidding of the shouting officers, it was more impressive than usual to the infantry.

---

1. **battery:** group of cannons.
2. **caissons** (kā′sŏnz′): horse-drawn wagons used to carry ammunition.

WORDS TO KNOW

incessant (ĭn-sĕs′ənt) *adj.* ceaseless; continual

Fred Collins of A Company was saying: "Thunder, I wisht I had a drink. Ain't there any water round here?" Then somebody yelled: "There goes th'bugler!"

As the eyes of half of the regiment swept in one machine-like movement there was an instant's picture of a horse in a great convulsive leap of a death wound and a rider leaning back with a crooked arm and spread fingers before his face. On the ground was the crimson terror of an exploding shell, with fibres of flame that seemed like lances. A glittering bugle swung clear of the rider's back as fell headlong the horse and the man. In the air was an odor as from a conflagration.[3]

Sometimes they of the infantry looked down at a fair little meadow which spread at their feet. Its long, green grass was rippling gently in a breeze. Beyond it was the grey form of a house half torn to pieces by shells and by the busy axes of soldiers who had pursued firewood. The line of an old fence was now dimly marked by long weeds and by an occasional post. A shell had blown the well-house to fragments. Little lines of grey smoke ribboning upward from some embers indicated the place where had stood the barn.

From beyond a curtain of green woods there came the sound of some stupendous scuffle as if two animals of the size of islands were fighting. At a distance there were occasional appearances of swift-moving men, horses, batteries, flags, and, with the crashing of infantry volleys were heard, often, wild and frenzied cheers. In the midst of it all, Smith and Ferguson, two privates of A Company, were engaged in a heated discussion, which involved the greatest questions of the national existence.

The battery on the hill presently engaged in a frightful duel. The white legs of the gunners scampered this way and that way and the officers redoubled their shouts. The guns, with their demeanors of stolidity and courage, were typical of something infinitely self-possessed in this clamor of death that swirled around the hill.

One of a "swing" team was suddenly smitten quivering to the ground and his maddened brethren dragged his torn body in their struggle to escape from this turmoil and danger. A young soldier astride one of the leaders swore and fumed in his saddle and furiously jerked at the bridle. An officer screamed out an order so violently that his voice broke and ended the sentence in a falsetto[4] shriek.

The leading company of the infantry regiment was somewhat exposed and the colonel ordered it moved more fully under the shelter of the hill. There was the clank of steel against steel.

A lieutenant of the battery rode down and passed them, holding his right arm carefully in his left hand. And it was as if this arm was not at all a part of him, but belonged to another man. His sober and reflective charger[5] went slowly. The officer's face was grimy and perspiring and his uniform was tousled as if he had been in direct grapple with an enemy. He smiled grimly when the men stared at him. He turned his horse toward the meadow.

Collins of A Company said: "I wisht I had a drink. I bet there's water in that there ol' well yonder!"

"Yes; but how you goin' to git it?"

For the little meadow which intervened was now suffering a terrible onslaught of shells. Its green and beautiful calm had vanished utterly. Brown earth was being flung in monstrous handfuls. And there was a massacre of the young blades of grass. They were being torn, burned, obliterated. Some curious fortune of the battle had made this gentle little meadow the object of the red hate of the shells and each one as it

---

3. **conflagration** (kŏn′flə-grā′shən): huge fire.

4. **falsetto:** at a pitch higher than the normal vocal range.

5. **charger:** warhorse.

exploded seemed like an imprecation[6] in the face of a maiden.

The wounded officer who was riding across this expanse said to himself: "Why, they couldn't shoot any harder if the whole army was massed here!"

A shell struck the grey ruins of the house and as, after the roar, the shattered wall fell in fragments, there was a noise which resembled the flapping of shutters during a wild gale of winter. Indeed the infantry paused in the shelter of the bank, appeared as men standing upon a shore contemplating a madness of the sea. The angel of calamity had under its glance the battery upon the hill. Fewer white-legged men labored about the guns. A shell had smitten one of the pieces and after the flare, the smoke, the dust, the wrath of this blow was gone, it was possible to see white legs stretched horizontally upon the ground. And at that interval to the rear, where it is the business of battery horses to stand with their noses to the fight awaiting the command to drag their guns out of the destruction or into it or wheresoever these incomprehensible humans demanded with whip and spur—in this line of passive and dumb spectators, whose fluttering hearts yet would not let them forget the iron laws of man's control of them—in this rank of brute-soldiers there had been relentless and hideous carnage. From the ruck[7] of bleeding and prostrate horses, the men of the infantry could see one animal raising its stricken body with its fore-legs and turning its nose with mystic and profound eloquence toward the sky.

Some comrades joked Collins about his thirst. "Well, if yeh want a drink so bad, why don't yeh go git it?"

"Well, I will in a minnet if yeh don't shut up."

A lieutenant of artillery floundered his horse straight down the hill with as great concern as if it were level ground. As he galloped past the colonel of the infantry, he threw up his hand in swift salute. "We've got to get out of that," he roared angrily. He was a black-bearded officer, and his eyes, which resembled beads, sparkled like those of an insane man. His jumping horse sped along the column of infantry.

The fat major standing carelessly with his sword held horizontally behind him and with his legs far apart, looked after the receding horseman and laughed. "He wants to get back with orders pretty quick or there'll be no batt'ry left," he observed.

The wise young captain of the second company hazarded[8] to the lieutenant colonel that the enemy's infantry would probably soon attack the hill, and the lieutenant colonel snubbed him.

A private in one of the rear companies looked out over the meadow and then turned to a companion and said: "Look there, Jim." It was the wounded officer from the battery, who some time before had started to ride across the meadow, supporting his right arm carefully with his left hand. This man had encountered a shell apparently at a time when no one perceived him and he could now be seen lying face downward with a stirruped foot stretched across the body of his dead horse. A leg of the charger extended slantingly upward precisely as stiff as a stake. Around this motionless pair the shells still howled.

---

6. **imprecation** (ĭm′prĭ-kā′shən): curse; oath.

7. **ruck**: crowd; jumble.

8. **hazarded**: ventured a guess.

There was a quarrel in A Company. Collins was shaking his fist in the faces of some laughing comrades. "Dern yeh! I ain't afraid t' go. If yeh say much, I will go!"

"Of course, yeh will! Yeh'll run through that there medder, won't yeh?"

Collins said, in a terrible voice: "You see, now!" At this ominous threat his comrades broke into renewed jeers.

Collins gave them a dark scowl and went to find his captain. The latter was conversing with the colonel of the regiment.

"Captain," said Collins, saluting and standing at attention. In those days all trousers bagged at the knees. "Captain, I want t' git permission to go git some water from that there well over yonder!"

The colonel and the captain swung about simultaneously and stared across the meadow. The captain laughed. "You must be pretty thirsty, Collins?"

"Yes, sir; I am."

"Well—ah," said the captain. After a moment he asked: "Can't you wait?"

"No, sir."

The colonel was watching Collins's face. "Look here, my lad," he said, in a pious[9] sort of a voice. "Look here, my lad." Collins was not a lad. "Don't you think that's taking pretty big risks for a little drink of water?"

"I dunno," said Collins, uncomfortably. Some of the resentment toward his companions, which perhaps had forced him into this affair, was beginning to fade. "I dunno wether 'tis."

The colonel and the captain contemplated him for a time.

"Well," said the captain finally.

"Well," said the colonel, "if you want to go, why go."

Collins saluted. "Much obliged t' yeh."

As he moved away the colonel called after him. "Take some of the other boys' canteens with you an' hurry back now."

"Yes, sir. I will."

The colonel and the captain looked at each other then, for it had suddenly occurred that they could not for the life of them tell whether Collins wanted to go or whether he did not.

They turned to regard Collins and as they perceived him surrounded by gesticulating[10] comrades the colonel said: "Well, by thunder! I guess he's going."

Collins appeared as a man dreaming. In the midst of the questions, the advice, the warnings, all the excited talk of his company mates, he maintained a curious silence.

They were very busy in preparing him for his ordeal. When they inspected him carefully it was somewhat like the examination that grooms give a horse before a race; and they were amazed, staggered by the whole affair. Their astonishment found vent in strange repetitions.

"Are yeh sure a-goin'?" they demanded again and again.

"Certainly I am," cried Collins, at last furiously.

He strode sullenly away from them. He was swinging five or six canteens by their cords. It seemed that his cap would not remain firmly on his head, and often he reached and pulled it down over his brow.

There was a general movement in the compact column. The long animal-like thing moved slightly. Its four hundred eyes were turned upon the figure of Collins.

"Well, sir, if that ain't th' derndest thing. I never thought Fred Collins had the blood in him for that kind of business."

---

9. **pious** (pī′əs): high-minded; solemn.
10. **gesticulating** (jĕ-stĭk′yə-lā′tĭng): gesturing.

WORDS
TO
KNOW   **sullenly** (sŭl′ən-lē) *adv.* resentfully; sulkily

"What's he goin' to do, anyhow?"

"He's goin' to that well there after water."

"We ain't dyin' of thirst, are we? That's fool-ishness."

"Well, somebody put him up to it an' he's doin' it."

"Say, he must be a desperate cuss."

When Collins faced the meadow and walked away from the regiment he was vaguely conscious that a chasm, the deep valley of all prides, was suddenly between him and his comrades. It was provisional, but the provision was that he return as a victor. He had blindly been led by quaint emotions and laid himself under an obligation to walk squarely up to the face of death.

But he was not sure that he wished to make a retraction even if he could do so without shame. As a matter of truth he was sure of very little. He was mainly surprised.

It seemed to him supernaturally strange that he had allowed his mind to maneuver his body into such a situation. He understood that it might be called dramatically great.

However, he had no full appreciation of anything excepting that he was actually conscious of being dazed. He could feel his dulled mind groping after the form and color of this incident.

Too, he wondered why he did not feel some keen agony of fear cutting his sense like a knife. He wondered at this because human expression had said loudly for centuries that men should feel afraid of certain things and that all men who did not feel this fear were phenomena,[11] heroes.

He was then a hero. He suffered that disappointment which we would all have if we discovered that we were ourselves capable of

those deeds which we most admire in history and legend. This, then, was a hero. After all, heroes were not much.

No, it could not be true. He was not a hero. Heroes had no shames in their lives and, as for him, he remembered borrowing fifteen dollars from a friend and promising to pay it back the next day, and then avoiding that friend for ten months. When at home his mother had aroused him for the early labor of his life on the farm, it had often been his fashion to be irritable, childish, diabolical, and his mother had died since he had come to the war.

He saw that in this matter of the well, the canteens, the shells, he was an intruder in the land of fine deeds.

He was now about thirty paces from his comrades. The regiment had just turned its many faces toward him.

From the forest of terrific noises there suddenly emerged a little uneven line of men. They fired fiercely and rapidly at distant foliage on which appeared little puffs of white smoke. The spatter of skirmish firing was added to the thunder of the guns on the hill. The little line of men ran forward. A color-sergeant[12] fell flat with his flag as if he had slipped on ice. There was hoarse cheering from this distant field.

Collins suddenly felt that two demon fingers were pressed into his ears. He could see nothing but flying arrows, flaming red. He lurched from the shock of this explosion, but he made a mad rush for the house, which he viewed as a man

★ ★ ★ ★ ★ ★ ★ ★ ★

"Don't you think that's taking pretty big risks for a little drink of water?"

★ ★ ★ ★ ★ ★ ★ ★ ★

---

11. **phenomena** (fĭ-nŏm′ə-nə): exceptional or remarkable people.

12. **color-sergeant**: a soldier who carries a military unit's flag, or "colors," into battle.

WORDS TO KNOW   **provisional** (prə-vĭzh′ə-nəl) *adj.* temporary
retraction (rĭ-trăk′shən) *n.* a taking back of something said

599

submerged to the neck in a boiling surf might view the shore. In the air, little pieces of shell howled and the earthquake explosions drove him insane with the menace of their roar. As he ran the canteens knocked together with a rhythmical tinkling.

As he neared the house each detail of the scene became vivid to him. He was aware of some bricks of the vanished chimney lying on the sod. There was a door which hung by one hinge.

Rifle bullets called forth by the insistent skirmishers came from the far-off bank of foliage. They mingled with the shells and the pieces of shells until the air was torn in all directions by hootings, yells, howls. The sky was full of fiends who directed all their wild rage at his head.

When he came to the well he flung himself face downward and peered into its darkness. There were <u>furtive</u> silver glintings some feet from

the surface. He grabbed one of the canteens and, unfastening its cap, swung it down by the cord. The water flowed slowly in with an indolent gurgle.

And now as he lay with his face turned away he was suddenly smitten with the terror. It came upon his heart like the grasp of claws. All the power faded from his muscles. For an instant he was no more than a dead man.

The canteen filled with a maddening slowness in the manner of all bottles. Presently he recovered his strength and addressed a screaming oath to it. He leaned over until it seemed as if he intended to try to push water into it with his hands. His eyes as he gazed down into the well shone like two pieces of metal and in their expression was a great appeal and a great curse. The stupid water derided[13] him.

There was the blaring thunder of a shell. Crimson light shone through the swift-boiling smoke and made a pink reflection on part of the wall of the well. Collins jerked out his arm and canteen with the same motion that a man would use in withdrawing his head from a furnace.

He scrambled erect and glared and hesitated. On the ground near him lay the old well bucket, with a length of rusty chain. He lowered it swiftly into the well. The bucket struck the water and then turning lazily over, sank.

When, with hand reaching tremblingly over hand, he hauled it out, it knocked often against the walls of the well and spilled some of its contents.

In running with a filled bucket, a man can adopt but one kind of gait. So through this terrible field over which screamed practical[14] angels of death Collins ran in the manner of a farmer chased out of a dairy by a bull.

---

13. **derided:** mocked.
14. **practical:** virtual.

His face went staring white with anticipation—anticipation of a blow that would whirl him around and down. He would fall as he had seen other men fall, the life knocked out of them so suddenly that their knees were no more quick to touch the ground than their heads. He saw the long blue line of the regiment, but his comrades were standing looking at him from the edge of an impossible star. He was aware of some deep wheel ruts and hoof prints in the sod beneath his feet.

The artillery officer who had fallen in this meadow had been making groans in the teeth of the tempest of sound. These <u>futile</u> cries, wrenched from him by his agony, were heard only by shells, bullets. When wild-eyed Collins came running, this officer raised himself. His face contorted and blanched[15] from pain, he was about to utter some great beseeching cry. But suddenly his face straightened and he called: "Say, young man, give me a drink of water, will you?"

Collins had no room amid his emotions for surprise. He was mad from the threats of destruction.

"I can't," he screamed, and in this reply was a full description of his quaking apprehension. His cap was gone and his hair was riotous. His clothes made it appear that he had been dragged over the ground by the heels. He ran on.

The officer's head sank down and one elbow crooked. His foot in its brass-bound stirrup still stretched over the body of his horse and the other leg was under the steed.

But Collins turned. He came dashing back. His face had now turned grey and in his eyes was all terror. "Here it is! Here it is!"

The officer was as a man gone in drink. His arm bended like a twig. His head drooped as if his neck was of willow. He was sinking to the ground, to lie face downward.

Collins grabbed him by the shoulder. "Here it is. Here's your drink. Turn over! Turn over, man, for God's sake!"

With Collins hauling at his shoulder, the officer twisted his body and fell with his face turned toward that region where lived the unspeakable noises of the swirling missiles. There was the faintest shadow of a smile on his lips as he looked at Collins. He gave a sigh, a little primitive breath like that from a child.

Collins tried to hold the bucket steadily, but his shaking hands caused the water to splash all over the face of the dying man. Then he jerked it away and ran on.

The regiment gave him a welcoming roar. The grimed faces were wrinkled in laughter.

His captain waved the bucket away. "Give it to the men!"

The two <u>genial</u>, sky-larking[16] young lieutenants were the first to gain possession of it. They played over it in their fashion.

When one tried to drink the other teasingly knocked his elbow. "Don't, Billie! You'll make me spill it," said the one. The other laughed.

Suddenly there was an oath, the thud of wood on the ground, and a swift murmur of astonishment from the ranks. The two lieutenants glared at each other. The bucket lay on the ground empty. ❖

---

15. **blanched:** turned white.
16. **sky-larking:** playful; fun-loving.

> ★ ★ ★ ★ ★ ★ ★ ★ ★
>
> ## His face went staring white with anticipation— anticipation of a blow that would whirl him around and down.
>
> ★ ★ ★ ★ ★ ★ ★ ★

Connect to the Literature

1. What Do You Think? How did you react to the ending of this story?

> **Comprehension Check**
> - How do the other soldiers feel about Collins's attempt to get water?
> - Who asks Collins for a drink of water on his way back from the well?
> - What happens to the bucket of water at the end of the story?

Think Critically

2. Why do you think Fred Collins is not mentioned in the last three paragraphs of this story? Explain your answer.

3. How would you explain what Collins learns from his brush with death?

4. Do you consider Collins a hero? Cite evidence to support your answer.

THINK ABOUT
- the risks he takes and why he takes them
- his emotions in the heat of battle
- how he treats the dying artillery officer

5. **ACTIVE READING** **VISUALIZING** Review the details you listed in your **READER'S NOTEBOOK**. What words would you use to describe the picture of war that you formed in your imagination?

6. How would you explain the **title** of this story?

Extend Interpretations

7. The Writer's Style Often Crane uses figurative language—**similes, metaphors,** and **personification**—to describe a soldier's sensations. Which figures of speech in the story strike you as especially vivid?

8. What If? If Collins had been killed, how would the effect of this story be different?

9. Comparing Texts Which **character** do you think shows more courage, Collins in Crane's story or Peyton Farquhar in "An Occurrence at Owl Creek Bridge," on page 581? Explain the reasons for your choice.

10. Connect to Life How do Collins and his deeds compare with the heroes and heroic actions you listed for the Connect to Your Life activity on page 593?

Literary Analysis

NATURALISM As a literary movement, **naturalism** originated in France in the late 1800s with the grisly, extreme realism of novelist Émile Zola. Naturalistic writers sought not only to render common people and ordinary life accurately but also to describe how instinct and environment affect human behavior.

Many of the naturalists' ideas reflected intellectual trends emerging in Europe in biology, economics, and psychology. For example, the writings of Charles Darwin strongly influenced naturalistic thought. In *The Origin of Species* (1859), Darwin proposed his theory that species evolve through a process of natural selection, whereby only those with the most favorable traits adapt and survive. The naturalists, too, tended to believe that the fate of humans, like that of any other species in nature, was determined by forces beyond individual control.

Cooperative Learning Activity With a small group of classmates, debate to what extent Collins's actions are determined by forces beyond his control. Cite passages to support your opinion. On a scale like the one below, place a mark to record your group's view about his degree of freedom. Then compare your scale with other groups' scales.

Collins's Actions

Totally Free	Totally Predetermined

REVIEW **IRONY** **Irony** refers to a contrast between what is expected and what actually exists or happens. What do you find ironic about Collins's deeds? Explain your answer.

Choices & CHALLENGES

Writing Options

1. Letter Home As Collins, write a letter to a friend or a relative in civilian life. Explain your views about war, your relationship with your comrades, your act of "heroism," and what you learned from your brush with death.

2. Literary Analysis To what extent is "The Mystery of Heroism" a good example of naturalistic fiction? Using what you learned about **naturalism** on pages 593 and 602, write a brief critique of this story. As a prewriting task, look again at the scale you created for the Literary Analysis activity. Place your critique in your **Working Portfolio.**

3. Different Ending What are some other ways that this story might have ended? Draft an alternative ending to the story, and read it aloud to classmates.

Writing Handbook
See page 1279: Narrative Writing.

Characteristics of Naturalism	Present?
1.	☐
2.	☐
3.	☐

Activities & Explorations

1. Combat Sketch Using details from your Active Reading chart, draw a sketch to accompany the story. ~ **ART**

2. War Songs Find and listen to a recording of Civil War songs, such as "Tenting on the Old Camp Ground" or "The Old Union Wagon." What aspects of war do the song lyrics address? Choose a song that you think fits the mood and events of Crane's story, play the recording for your classmates, and then point out the connections you see. ~ **MUSIC**

3. Interview with Collins With a partner, role-play a journalist interviewing Collins about his conduct on the battlefield. In the interview, be faithful to Collins's perspective on events and try to imitate his dialect.
~ **SPEAKING AND LISTENING**

Inquiry & Research

Photo Gallery Crane himself never served in the Civil War. He relied on resources such as newspaper and magazine accounts, veterans' tales, and combat photographs to re-create the grim reality of battle. Crane was impressed by the riveting photographs taken by Mathew B. Brady, a photographer who had traveled with the Union army. Find reproductions of Brady's photographs in history books and biographies such as *Mr. Lincoln's Camera Man* by Roy Meredith and *Mathew Brady* by Barry Pritzker. With a group of classmates, prepare an exhibit of these photographs. Then present a guided tour of the exhibit, explaining what each photo reveals.

 More Online: Research Starter
www.mcdougallittell.com

Mathew Brady in the field with his darkroom wagon.

Vocabulary in Action

EXERCISE: MEANING CLUES On your paper, write the Word to Know whose meaning is suggested by each sentence.

1. The battle resulted in a tremendous number of deaths.
2. The soldiers looked as if they had been swept up by a tornado.
3. The two armies did not need to exchange words; the cannons expressed their feelings very well.
4. The army had to endure continual fire from enemy artillery.
5. Many men, forced to charge the enemy, obeyed orders unwillingly.
6. Several sergeants relieved their stress by joking around with one another.
7. The major came up with a plan to use until he got new orders.
8. The soldier who asked to be allowed to go to the well knew that it was too late to change his mind.
9. It was useless to try to save the badly wounded man.
10. Both sides sent scouts to spy on the enemy.

WORDS TO KNOW	eloquence furtive futile genial	incessant provisional retraction	stupendous sullenly tousled

Stephen Crane
1871–1900

Other Works
The Red Badge of Courage
"The Bride Comes to Yellow Sky"
"The Open Boat"

Naturalistic Writer As both a resident of the urban slums and a newspaper reporter, Crane walked the mean streets of New York City, recording the struggles and hopelessness of the people who lived there. His first novel, *Maggie: A Girl of the Streets* (1893), was rejected by publishers for its shocking depiction of the degradation and immorality of slum life. Crane had to borrow money to have the novel published independently. Later hailed by critics and writers alike, *Maggie* has been called America's "first truly naturalistic novel." Crane's second naturalistic novel, *The Red Badge of Courage* (1895), exposed American readers, for the first time, to a brutally realistic account of a young soldier's experiences in the Civil War. These and other works broke new ground in choice of subject, point of view, and style.

Foreign Correspondent In his short lifetime, Crane undertook a series of far-flung writing assignments. In 1895, under contract with a newspaper syndicate, he toured Mexico and the American West, settings for "The Blue Hotel" and "The Bride Comes to Yellow Sky." Later, as a war correspondent, he covered the Spanish-American War in Cuba and Puerto Rico and the Greco-Turkish War in Greece. These experiences affected his health.

Early Death By the age of 25, Crane was a star reporter and literary phenomenon. Settling in London in 1897, he came to know Joseph Conrad, Henry James, H. G. Wells, and other writers. However, as he wrote feverishly to pay off debts, his health steadily deteriorated. At the age of 28, Crane died of tuberculosis in Germany.

Author Activity

War Stories Read Crane's masterpiece, *The Red Badge of Courage*. Then compare the picture of war in the novel with that in "A Mystery of Heroism."

The Gettysburg Address

Speech by ABRAHAM LINCOLN

Connect to Your Life

President Lincoln What words come to mind when you think of Abraham Lincoln? With classmates, discuss what you know about Lincoln, creating a word web like the one started here. List words and phrases that you associate with Lincoln's early life, his presidency, his appearance, his character, his leadership during the Civil War, and his death.

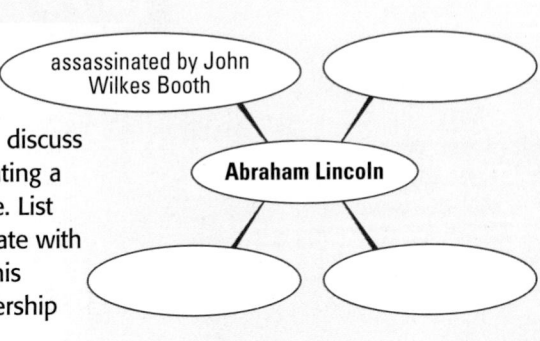

assassinated by John Wilkes Booth

Abraham Lincoln

Build Background

Gettysburg The Battle of Gettysburg, the turning point of the Civil War, began over shoes. The advancing Confederate army needed shoes; to get them, some Confederate soldiers were sent to nearby Gettysburg, Pennsylvania, where they accidentally encountered Union soldiers. Soon, two huge forces began to maneuver for battle—the 75,000 Confederate troops of General Robert E. Lee and the 90,000 Union army troops under General George Meade. For three days—July 1–3, 1863—the two sides fought a horrendous battle. In the end, the Union won, but the losses on both sides were staggering—28,000 Confederate soldiers and 23,000 Union soldiers killed or wounded. On November 19, 1863, President Lincoln spoke at the dedication of the National Soldiers' Cemetery at the Gettysburg battlefield. Though Lincoln spoke for little more than two minutes, his words still echo through the ages.

WORDS TO KNOW
Vocabulary Preview

conceive   devotion
consecrate   resolve
detract

Focus Your Reading

LITERARY ANALYSIS   **STYLE**   As you recall, the distinctive way in which a work of literature is written is its **style.** One technique of style is **repetition,** or the recurrence of words, phrases, or lines. For example, Patrick Henry used repetition for emphasis in his speech on pages 263–266:

> *The war is inevitable—and <u>let it come!</u> I repeat it, sir, <u>let it come!</u>*

Notice repetition and other features of Lincoln's style in the address.

ACTIVE READING   **INTERPRETING HISTORICAL CONTEXT**   When you read a speech, keep in mind the **historical context**—the occasion, the audience, and the purpose of the speech. Lincoln delivered this speech shortly after the Battle of Gettysburg. At a solemn dedication ceremony held at the battle site, a crowd of some 15,000 mourners listened to the eloquent main speaker, Edward Everett, deliver a two-hour speech. Then Lincoln, barely glancing at his handwritten address, spoke for roughly two minutes.

Try to imagine yourself in the audience as you read this speech. Lincoln does not explain things that he assumes his listeners already know. For example, "Four score and seven years ago" means 87 years before, in 1776, when the Declaration of Independence was signed.

READER'S NOTEBOOK   As you go through each paragraph, fill in the blanks, so to speak. What has occurred recently? What is happening as Lincoln speaks? Define any terms or references that a person unfamiliar with American history would not understand.

ABRAHAM LINCOLN
THE GETTYSBURG ADDRESS

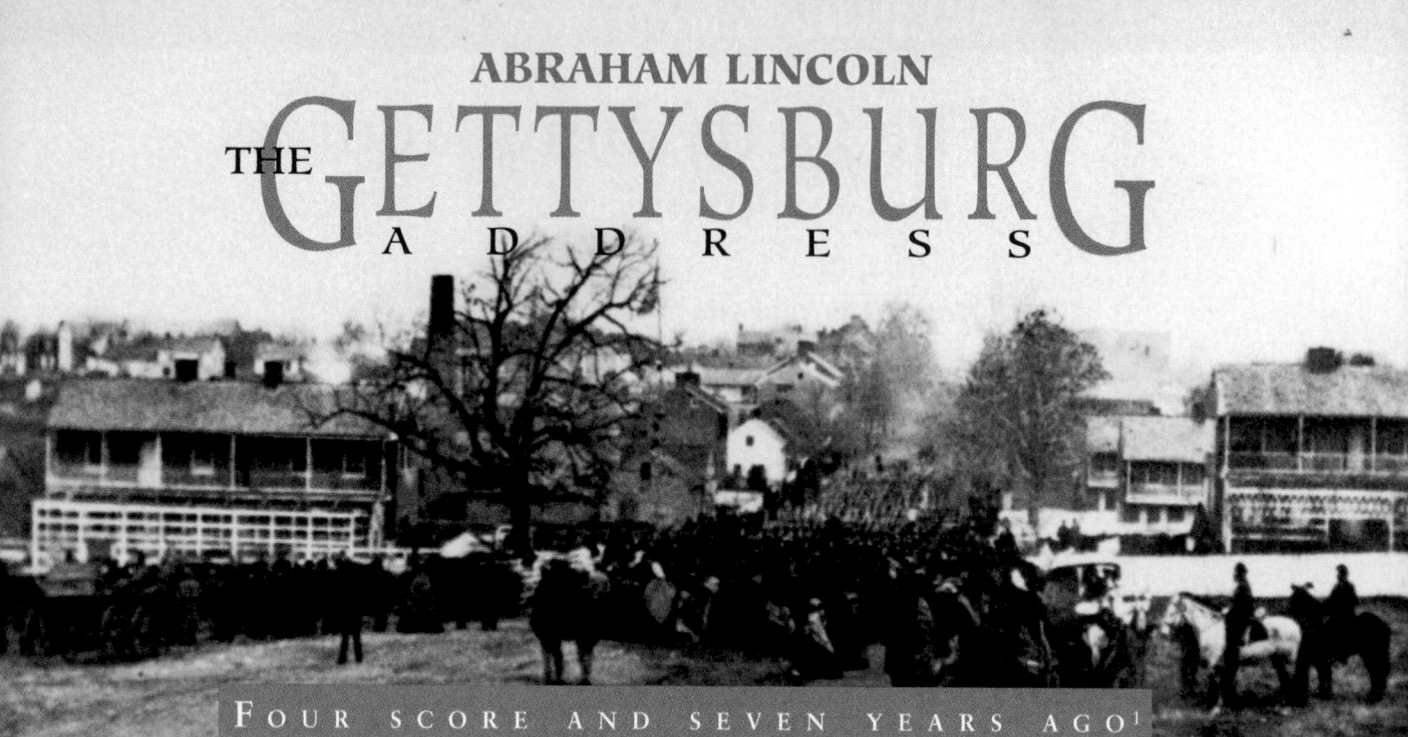

Gettysburg on the day that Lincoln spoke.

FOUR SCORE AND SEVEN YEARS AGO[1]

our fathers brought forth on this continent a new nation, <u>conceived</u> in liberty, and dedicated to the proposition that all men are created equal. Now we are engaged in a great civil war, testing whether that nation, or any nation so conceived and so dedicated, can long endure. We are met on a great battlefield of that war. We have come to dedicate a portion of that field as a final resting place for those who here gave their lives that that nation might live. It is altogether fitting and proper that we should do this. But, in a larger sense, we cannot dedicate—we cannot <u>consecrate</u>—we cannot hallow[2] —this ground. The brave men, living and dead, who struggled here have consecrated it far above our poor power to add or <u>detract</u>. The world will little note nor long remember what we say here, but it can never forget what they did here. It is for us, the living, rather, to be dedicated here to the unfinished work which they who fought here have thus far so nobly advanced. It is rather for us to be here dedicated to the great task remaining before us— that from these honored dead we take increased devotion to that cause for which they gave the last full measure of <u>devotion</u>; that we here highly <u>resolve</u> that these dead shall not have died in vain; that this nation, under God, shall have a new birth of freedom; and that government of the people, by the people, for the people, shall not perish from the earth.

---

1. **four score and seven years ago:** 87 years ago—that is, in 1776. (*Score* means "a group of twenty.")

2. **hallow:** set apart as holy.

WORDS TO KNOW

conceived (kən-sēvd´) *adj.* originated **conceive** *v.*
consecrate (kŏn´sĭ-krāt´) *v.* to declare sacred
detract (dĭ-trăkt´) *v.* to take away; diminish
devotion (dĭ-vō´shən) *n.* earnest dedication
resolve (rĭ-zŏlv´) *v.* to make a firm decision

Thinking through the LITERATURE

Connect to the Literature

1. **What Do You Think?** What words, phrases, or sentences stand out most in your mind? Share your choices with a partner.

Comprehension Check
- According to Lincoln, to which proposition is the nation dedicated?
- For what cause does Lincoln say the soldiers died?

Think Critically

2. **ACTIVE READING** **INTERPRETING HISTORICAL CONTEXT** Given what you know about the historical context of the speech, define the "unfinished work" left for the living to complete. Pretend you are explaining it to a foreign friend who has never studied American history.

3. What kind of person do you think Lincoln was? Use evidence from this speech to explain your opinion.

THINK ABOUT
- the emotions his speech stirs
- his attitude toward those who fought at Gettysburg
- the goals he sets for his audience
- his vision of the nation

4. Lincoln was mistaken when he said "The world will little note, nor long remember what we say here. . . ." Why do you think the world still remembers this speech?

Extend Interpretations

5. **What If?** How would your reaction to this speech be different if Lincoln had mentioned the Confederate forces as the enemy?

6. **Critic's Corner** Edward Everett, the main speaker at Gettysburg, later sent Lincoln this note: "I should be glad if I could flatter myself that I had come as near to the central idea of the occasion in two hours as you did in two minutes." How would you express "the central idea of the occasion" that Lincoln's speech captured?

7. **Connect to Life** Of what value to Americans today are the ideas Lincoln expressed at Gettysburg? In explaining your opinion, cite lines from Lincoln's speech.

Literary Analysis

STYLE **Style** is the distinctive way in which a work of literature is written. Several elements contribute to style, such as word choice, sentence length, tone, and imagery, as well as particular techniques such as **repetition.** In the Gettysburg Address, Lincoln repeats words such as *dedicate, consecrate, devotion,* and *people* to emphasize key ideas. Sometimes he combines this technique with **parallelism**—the use of the same grammatical form to express ideas of equal importance—as in this sentence:

But, in a larger sense, we cannot dedicate—we cannot consecrate—we cannot hallow—this ground.

The parallel phrases "we cannot dedicate," "we cannot consecrate," "we cannot hallow" give the sentence a rhythmic cadence and drive home the point.

Cooperative Learning Activity In a small group, reread Lincoln's speech, looking for more examples of repetition and parallelism. Discuss the effect that these techniques create. To appreciate the effect, try rewriting a sentence without using the technique, and then compare your version with Lincoln's. For example, what happens to the last sentence if you remove the parallel structure?

Writing Options

1. Modern Paraphrase Write a paraphrase of the Gettysburg Address in modern language. To prepare, you might review the definitions you wrote for an uninformed audience in your **READER'S NOTEBOOK.**

2. Letter to Lincoln Imagine that you are a parent who has lost a son at Gettysburg, fighting for either the Union or the Confederate army. Write a letter to Lincoln in response to his speech.

Inquiry & Research

Battle Report With a group of classmates, research the Battle of Gettysburg and its significance in the Civil War. Gather information from encyclopedias, Civil War history books, and electronic sources. Share your findings in a report.

More Online: Research Starter
www.mcdougallittell.com

Vocabulary in Action

EXERCISE: CONTEXT CLUES Decide whether the boldfaced vocabulary word is used correctly or incorrectly in each sentence. Write correct or incorrect on your paper.

1. The federal government decided to **consecrate** the ground at Gettysburg by making it a cemetery for the men who had died there.

2. Lincoln asked the audience to imitate the soldiers' **devotion** to the cause of liberty.

3. The president gazed out upon the **detract** where the battle had been fought.

4. He wanted to ensure that a nation **conceived** in liberty would endure.

5. The Union Army had tried to **resolve** the Confederate Army.

Building Vocabulary
For an in-depth lesson on context clues, see page 326.

Abraham Lincoln
1809–1865

Humble Origin Abraham Lincoln rose from a simple beginning to become president of the United States. The son of illiterate parents, he was born in a log cabin and raised on the Kentucky and Indiana frontier. Young Lincoln had almost no formal schooling; he educated himself by diligent study of the few books available to him. Encouraged by his stepmother, Lincoln read and reread the Bible, John Bunyan's *Pilgrim's Progress*, Aesop's *Fables*, and Daniel Defoe's *Robinson Crusoe*, as well as history books and biographies.

President of the United States Lincoln's election as president coincided with the first secessions of Southern states from the Union. During his first term in office, he led the nation through its most divisive period—the Civil War. Despite strong opposition, he issued the historic Emancipation Proclamation in 1863, freeing the slaves in Confederate-held territory. The letters and speeches of Lincoln's presidency are characterized by a simple, touching eloquence. "In times like the present," Lincoln told a wartime Congress, "men should utter nothing for which they would not willingly be responsible through time and in eternity."

Assassination A few weeks into Lincoln's second term, and five days after General Robert E. Lee surrendered to General Ulysses S. Grant at Appomattox, Lincoln was shot and killed by John Wilkes Booth while attending a theatrical performance in Washington.

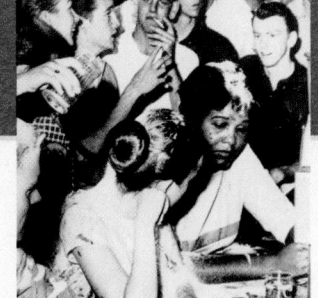

from Coming of Age in Mississippi

Autobiography by ANNE MOODY

Comparing Literature

Traditions Across Time: The Civil Rights Movement

Though the Thirteenth Amendment officially abolished slavery in 1865, new "Jim Crow" laws that discriminated against African Americans were eventually established by whites in many Southern states. Such laws denied African Americans the right to vote, the right to attend state universities, even the right to use public facilities like swimming pools, restrooms, and lunch counters. This firsthand account by civil-rights activist Anne Moody describes an attempt to overturn Jim Crow laws a hundred years after the Civil War.

Points of Comparison As you read, compare the social climate of Moody's time with the climate that produced Frederick Douglass and the protest poets James Russell Lowell and Frances E. W. Harper. Also compare the writers' purposes for writing.

Build Background

Uniting for Change *Coming of Age in Mississippi* is Anne Moody's true account of her experiences as a college student in the civil rights movement of the 1960s. During this time, volunteers in the South registered African-American voters at risk of their lives; "freedom riders" braved beatings and killings to desegregate interstate buses and bus stations; and protesters took part in sit-ins to integrate lunch counters, parks, and theaters. The result of the movement was the Civil Rights Act of 1964, the most far-reaching civil rights legislation in American history.

Focus Your Reading

LITERARY ANALYSIS **EYEWITNESS REPORT** This selection is an account of a 1963 sit-in at a lunch counter in Jackson, Mississippi. A newspaper article of the time might have reported: "Today three Negro college students sat down at a segregated Woolworth's lunch counter and were attacked by an angry white mob." Notice how much more you learn from this **eyewitness report** by Moody, a participant in the sit-in.

ACTIVE READING **CHRONOLOGICAL ORDER** Eyewitness reports are usually narrated in **chronological order,** or time order. (The ancient Greek word *chronos* means "time.") A chronological pattern of organization, or text structure, helps put the reader in the writer's place, experiencing events as they unfold.

READER'S NOTEBOOK To help you understand and recall what happens from the time the sit-in begins until it ends, create a sequence chain like the one begun here. In the boxes, summarize significant events in the order that they occur.

Anne, Pearlena, and Memphis take seats at lunch counter. → →

Coming of Age

I had counted on graduating in the spring of 1963, but as it
turned out, I couldn't because some of my credits still had to
be cleared with Natchez College. A year before, this would
have seemed like a terrible disaster, but now I hardly even felt
disappointed. I had a good excuse to stay on campus for the summer
and work with the Movement, and this was what I really wanted to
do. I couldn't go home again anyway, and I couldn't go to New
Orleans—I didn't have money enough for bus fare.

During my senior year at Tougaloo, my family hadn't sent me one
penny. I had only the small amount of money I had earned at Maple
Hill. I couldn't afford to eat at school or live in the dorms, so I had
gotten permission to move off campus. I had to prove that I could
finish school, even if I had to go hungry every day. I knew Raymond
and Miss Pearl were just waiting to see me drop out. But something
happened to me as I got more and more involved in the Movement.
It no longer seemed important to prove anything. I had found
something outside myself that gave meaning to my life.

I had become very friendly with my social science professor,
John Salter, who was in charge of NAACP[1] activities on campus.
All during the year, while the NAACP conducted a boycott of the
downtown stores in Jackson, I had been one of Salter's most faithful

---

1. **NAACP:** the National Association for the Advancement
   of Colored People, an organization that works to end
   discrimination against African Americans and other
   minority groups.

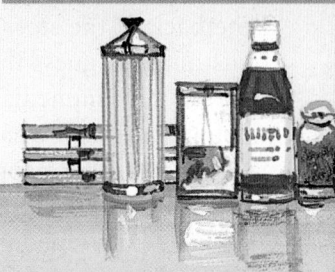

in Mississippi

ANNE MOODY

canvassers[2] and church speakers. During the last week of school, he told me that sit-in demonstrations were about to start in Jackson and that he wanted me to be the spokesman for a team that would sit-in at Woolworth's lunch counter. The two other demonstrators would be classmates of mine, Memphis and Pearlena. Pearlena was a dedicated NAACP worker, but Memphis had not been very involved in the Movement on campus. It seemed that the organization had had a rough time finding students who were in a position to go to jail. I had nothing to lose one way or the other. Around ten o'clock the morning of the demonstrations, NAACP headquarters alerted the news services. As a result, the police department was also informed, but neither the policemen nor the newsmen knew exactly where or when the demonstrations would start. They stationed themselves along Capitol Street and waited.

To divert attention from the sit-in at Woolworth's, the picketing started at J. C. Penney's a good fifteen minutes before. The pickets were allowed to walk up and down in front of the store three or four times before they were arrested. At exactly 11 A.M., Pearlena, Memphis, and I entered Woolworth's from the rear entrance. We separated as soon as we stepped into the store, and made small purchases from various counters. Pearlena had given Memphis her watch. He was to let us know when it was 11:14. At 11:14 we were to join him near the lunch counter and at exactly 11:15 we were to take seats at it.

Seconds before 11:15 we were occupying three seats at the previously segregated Woolworth's lunch counter. In the beginning the waitresses seemed to ignore us, as if they really didn't know what was going on. Our waitress walked past us a couple of times before she noticed we had started to write our own orders down and realized we wanted service. She asked us what we wanted. We began to read to her from our order slips. She told us that we would be served at the back counter, which was for Negroes.

"We would like to be served here," I said.

---

2. **canvassers:** people who canvass, or go door to door to get support for a cause or gather opinions on an issue.

The waitress started to repeat what she had said, then stopped in the middle of the sentence. She turned the lights out behind the counter, and she and the other waitresses almost ran to the back of the store, deserting all their white customers. I guess they thought that violence would start immediately after the whites at the counter realized what was going on. There were five or six other people at the counter. A couple of them just got up and walked away. A girl sitting next to me finished her banana split before leaving. A middle-aged white woman who had not yet been served rose from her seat and came over to us. "I'd like to stay here with you," she said, "but my husband is waiting."

The newsmen came in just as she was leaving. They must have discovered what was going on shortly after some of the people began to leave the store. One of the newsmen ran behind the woman who spoke to us and asked her to identify herself. She refused to give her name, but said she was a native of Vicksburg and a former resident of California. When asked why she had said what she had said to us, she replied, "I am in sympathy with the Negro movement." By this time a crowd of cameramen and reporters had gathered around us taking pictures and asking questions, such as Where were we from? Why did we sit-in? What organization sponsored it? Were we students? From what school? How were we classified?

I told them that we were all students at Tougaloo College, that we were represented by no particular organization, and that we planned to stay there even after the store closed.

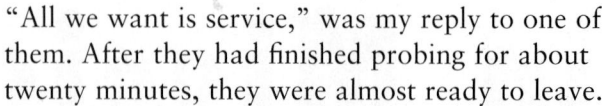

"All we want is service," was my reply to one of them. After they had finished probing for about twenty minutes, they were almost ready to leave.

At noon, students from a nearby white high school started pouring in to Woolworth's. When they first saw us they were sort of surprised. They didn't know how to react. A few started to heckle and the newsmen became interested again. Then the white students started chanting all kinds of anti-Negro slogans. We were called a little bit of everything. The rest of the seats except the three we were occupying had been roped off to prevent others from sitting down. A couple of the boys took one end of the rope and made it into a hangman's noose. Several attempts were made to put it around our necks. The crowds grew as more students and adults came in for lunch.

We kept our eyes straight forward and did not look at the crowd except for occasional glances to see what was going on. All of a sudden I saw a face I remembered—the drunkard from the bus station sit-in. My eyes lingered on him just long enough for us to recognize each other. Today he was drunk too, so I don't think he remembered where he had seen me before. He took out a knife, opened it, put it in his pocket, and then began to pace the floor. At this point, I told Memphis and Pearlena what was going on. Memphis suggested that we pray. We bowed our heads, and all hell broke loose. A man rushed forward, threw Memphis from his seat, and slapped my face. Then another man who worked in the store threw me against an adjoining counter.

Down on my knees on the floor, I saw Memphis lying near the lunch counter with blood running out of the corners of his mouth. As he tried to protect his face, the man who'd thrown him down kept kicking him against the head. If he had worn hard-soled shoes instead of sneakers, the first kick probably would have killed Memphis. Finally a man dressed in plain clothes identified himself as a police officer and arrested Memphis and his attacker.

On May 23, 1963, Anne Moody (right), John R. Salter (left), and Joan Trumpauer (middle) are harassed during a sit-in demonstration at a lunch counter in Jackson, Mississippi. AP/Wide World Photos.

Pearlena had been thrown to the floor. She and I got back on our stools after Memphis was arrested. There were some white Tougaloo teachers in the crowd. They asked Pearlena and me if we wanted to leave. They said that things were getting too rough. We didn't know what to do. While we were trying to make up our minds, we were joined by Joan Trumpauer. Now there were three of us and we were integrated. The crowd began to chant, "Communists, Communists, Communists." Some old man in the crowd ordered the students to take us off the stools.

"Which one should I get first?" a big husky boy said.

"That white nigger," the old man said.

The boy lifted Joan from the counter by her waist and carried her out of the store. Simultaneously, I was snatched from my stool by two high school students. I was dragged about thirty feet toward the door by my hair when someone made them turn me loose. As I was getting up off the floor, I saw Joan coming back inside. We started back to the center of the counter to join Pearlena. Lois Chaffee, a white Tougaloo faculty member, was now sitting next to her. So Joan and I just climbed across the rope at the front end of the counter and sat down. There were now four of us, two whites and two Negroes, all women. The mob started smearing us with ketchup, mustard, sugar, pies, and everything on the counter. Soon Joan and I were joined by John Salter, but the moment he sat down he was hit on the jaw with what appeared to be brass knuckles. Blood gushed from his face and someone threw salt into the open wound. Ed King, Tougaloo's chaplain, rushed to him.

At the other end of the counter, Lois and Pearlena were joined by George Raymond, a CORE[3] field worker and a student from Jackson State College. Then a Negro high school boy sat down next to me. The mob took spray paint from the counter and sprayed it on the new demonstrators. The high school student had on a white shirt; the word "nigger" was written on his back with red spray paint.

We sat there for three hours taking a beating when the manager decided to close the store because the mob had begun to go wild with stuff from other counters. He begged and begged everyone to leave. But even after fifteen minutes of begging, no one budged. They would not leave until we did. Then Dr. Beittel, the president of Tougaloo College, came running in. He said he had just heard what was happening.

About ninety policemen were standing outside the store; they had been watching the whole thing through the windows, but had not come in to stop the mob or do anything. President Beittel went outside and asked Captain Ray to come and escort us out. The captain refused, stating the manager had to invite him in before he could enter the premises, so Dr. Beittel himself brought us out. He had told the police that they had better protect us after we were outside the store. When we got outside, the policemen formed a single line that blocked the mob from us. However, they were allowed to throw at us everything they had collected. Within ten minutes, we were picked up by Reverend King in his station wagon and taken to the NAACP headquarters on Lynch Street.

After the sit-in, all I could think of

was how sick Mississippi whites were. They believed so much in the segregated Southern way of life, they would kill to preserve it. I sat there in the NAACP office and thought of how many times they had killed when this way of life was threatened. I knew that the killing had just begun. "Many more will die before it is over with," I thought. Before the sit-in, I had always hated the whites in Mississippi. Now I knew it was impossible for me to hate sickness. The whites had a disease, an incurable disease in its final stage. What were our chances against such a disease? I thought of the students, the young Negroes who had just begun to protest, as young interns.[4] When these young interns got older, I thought, they would be the best doctors in the world for social problems.

Before we were taken back to campus, I wanted to get my hair washed. It was stiff with dried mustard, ketchup and sugar. I stopped in at a beauty shop across the street from the NAACP office. I didn't have on any shoes because I had lost them when I was dragged across the floor at Woolworth's. My stockings were sticking to my legs from the mustard that had dried on them. The hairdresser took one look at me and said, "My land, you were in the sit-in, huh?"

"Yes," I answered. "Do you have time to wash my hair and style it?"

"Right away," she said, and she meant right away. There were three other ladies already waiting, but they seemed glad to let me go ahead of them. The hairdresser was real nice. She even took my stockings off and washed my legs while my hair was drying.

There was a mass rally that night at the Pearl Street Church in Jackson, and the place was packed. People were standing two abreast in the aisles. Before the speakers began, all the sit-inners

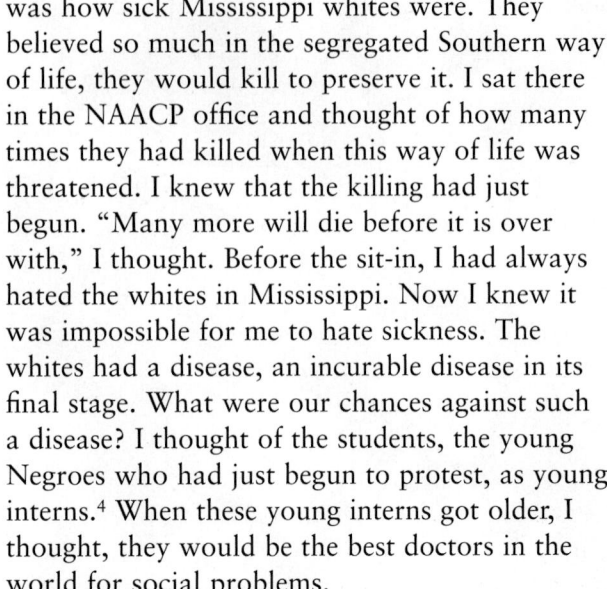

---

3. **CORE:** the Congress of Racial Equality, a civil rights organization that coordinated marches and demonstrations in the 1960s.

4. **interns:** students or recent graduates who are undergoing practical training, particularly medical training.

walked out on the stage and were introduced by Medgar Evers.[5] People stood and applauded for what seemed like thirty minutes or more. Medgar told the audience that this was just the beginning of such demonstrations. He asked them to pledge themselves to unite in a massive offensive against segregation in Jackson, and throughout the state. The rally ended with "We Shall Overcome" and sent home hundreds of determined people. It seemed as though Mississippi Negroes were about to get together at last.

Before I demonstrated, I had written Mama. She wrote me back a letter, begging me not to take part in the sit-in. She even sent ten dollars for bus fare to New Orleans. I didn't have one penny, so I kept the money. Mama's letter made me mad. I had to live my life as I saw fit. I had made that decision when I left home. But it hurt to have my family prove to me how scared they were. It hurt me more than anything else—I knew the whites had already started the threats and intimidations. I was the first Negro from my hometown who had openly demonstrated, worked with the NAACP, or anything. When Negroes threatened to do anything in Centreville, they were either shot like Samuel O'Quinn or run out of town, like Reverend Dupree.

I didn't answer Mama's letter. Even if I had written one, she wouldn't have received it before she saw the news on TV or heard it on the radio. I waited to hear from her again. And I waited to hear in the news that someone in Centreville had been murdered. If so, I knew it would be a member of my family. ❖

---

5. **Medgar Evers:** a civil rights leader and major organizer and supervisor for the NAACP in Mississippi from 1954 until he was killed by a sniper in 1963.

FREDERICK DOUGLASS
Robert Hayden

When it is finally ours, this freedom, this liberty, this beautiful
and terrible thing, needful to man as air,
usable as earth; when it belongs at last to all,
when it is truly instinct, brain matter, diastole, systole,[1]
5   reflex action; when it is finally won; when it is more
than the gaudy mumbo jumbo of politicians:
this man, this Douglass, this former slave, this Negro
beaten to his knees, exiled, visioning a world
where none is lonely, none hunted, alien,
10   this man, superb in love and logic, this man
shall be remembered. Oh, not with statues' rhetoric,
not with legends and poems and wreaths of bronze alone,
but with the lives grown out of his life, the lives
fleshing his dream of the beautiful, needful thing.

Frederick Douglass (about 1850), unknown photographer. Daguerreotype, 3⅛″ × 2¾″, National Portrait Gallery, Smithsonian Institution/Art Resource, New York.

---

1. **diastole** (dī-ăs′tə-lē), **systole** (sĭs′tə-lē): The heart pumps blood in two steps. Diastole refers to the heart's enlargement when it fills with blood; systole refers to the heart's contraction when the blood pumps out.

Connect to the Literature

1. What Do You Think?
What is your opinion of Anne Moody's actions? Discuss your thoughts with classmates.

Comprehension Check
- Why were Anne Moody and her fellow students sitting at the Woolworth's lunch counter?
- Name one of the things that happened to them after they sat down.
- What positive effect did their action have on African Americans in Mississippi?

Think Critically

2. **ACTIVE READING** **CHRONOLOGICAL ORDER**
Using the sequence chain you created in your **READER'S NOTEBOOK**, summarize what happens during the sit-in. How clearly did you understand what was happening?

3. How do you explain the behavior of the store manager and the police during the sit-in?

4. Moody describes Mississippi whites' racism as "an incurable disease in its final stage" and the protesters as "interns." Do you think these are good metaphors? Explain your answer.

5. How would you describe Moody to someone who has not read this selection?

6. Do you think you would have been able to take such a risk as Moody did?

THINK ABOUT
- the cause for which she is protesting
- the violence she witnesses and endures
- her belief that someone in her family could be murdered

Extend Interpretations

7. Connect to Life What forms does the fight against racism presently take in this country? Tell whether you believe this fight is closer to being won today than it was when Anne Moody was writing. Support your opinion.

8. **Points of Comparison** How would you compare Anne Moody with Frederick Douglass? Think about how he is portrayed in his autobiography and also in the poem by Robert Hayden on page 615.

Literary Analysis

EYEWITNESS REPORT This excerpt from Anne Moody's autobiography recounts an actual historical event: a sit-in at a Woolworth's lunch counter in 1963. An **eyewitness report** is a firsthand account of an event written by someone who directly observed it or participated in it. (As such, an eyewitness account is a primary source.) Eyewitness reports are narrated from the first-person point of view; this single point of view is maintained throughout. Eyewitness reports almost always include:

- objective **facts** about an event (the 5 W's: *who, what, when, where,* and *why*)
- a **chronological** (time-order) pattern of organization or text structure
- vivid **sensory details** that bring the scene to life
- **direct quotations** from people who were present
- description of the writer's **subjective feelings** and interpretations

Cooperative Learning Activity
Gather in small groups and, on a chart, record examples from the selection that show these characteristics of eyewitness reports. After you have compiled your chart, imagine that the group is researching student participation in civil rights protests of the 1960s. What would Moody's eyewitness report tell you? What wouldn't it tell you? Discuss these questions.

Writing Options

1. Mother's Letter, Anne's Reply
Write the letter that you think Anne Moody's mother sent to her. Then write the reply Anne might have written.

2. Points of Comparison
In an analytical essay, point out connections you see between Anne Moody and the antislavery writers you read earlier in Unit 4. You might explore their purposes for writing and the social climates in which they wrote.

Writing Handbook
See page 1283: Analysis.

3. Eyewitness Account
Attend a political rally, sporting event, or performance and write an eyewitness account of the event. Include relevant facts and vivid sensory details that will help your readers share your experiences. As an experiment, you and another classmate might attend the same event and compare your accounts. Do your facts and details match?

Writing Handbook
See page 1280: Chronological Order.

Activities & Explorations

On the Scene With several classmates, videotape imaginary interviews for a documentary about the sit-in. Explore the viewpoints and motivations of participants, bystanders, and authorities. Share your videotape.
~ SPEAKING AND LISTENING

Art Connection

Under Siege What does the photo of the sit-in on page 613 reveal that Moody's description of the same scene does not?

Anne Moody
1940–

Other Works
Mr. Death: Four Stories

Burning Memory When Anne Moody was growing up as the daughter of poor sharecroppers in rural Mississippi, she saw a neighboring family killed when their house was set on fire. The violence was brought about by a white citizens' guild, an organization dedicated to intimidating African Americans who in some way threatened whites' power. Moody's mother advised her, "Just act like you don't know nothing." Moody slowly came to realize that her mother's advice might be the safest course, but it was one that Anne herself could not follow.

Student Activist In her teens, Moody spent summers working in a factory, carefully saving money to make her dream of college a reality. She earned a basketball scholarship to Natchez Junior College but transferred to Tougaloo College, where she became involved with the civil rights movement. She was a volunteer for the Congress of Racial Equality (CORE) and a civil rights coordinator at Cornell University—a position in which she faced constant threats to her life. She worked for voting rights, on literacy projects, and for an end to segregated public facilities. Her experiences in the civil rights movement became the basis for a book that is widely considered to be a masterpiece of the movement, *Coming of Age in Mississippi,* from which this selection is taken.

Lasting Creed Although Moody eventually left the civil rights movement, her heart has never deserted the battle for human rights. She explains, "I realized that the universal fight for human rights, dignity, justice, equality, and freedom is . . . the right of every ethnic and racial minority, every suppressed and exploited person, every one of the millions who daily suffer one or another of the indignities of the powerless and voiceless masses."

Author Activity

Read more of *Coming of Age in Mississippi.* Find out what other protests Anne took part in and how they compare to the sit-in.

Ballad of Birmingham

Poetry by DUDLEY RANDALL

Comparing Literature

Traditions Across Time: The Civil Rights Movement

Earlier in this part of Unit 4 you read poems that protested slavery. The following selection, Dudley Randall's "Ballad of Birmingham," is also a protest poem. Inspired by an actual historical event—the 1963 bombing of the 16th Street Baptist Church in Birmingham—this poem protests the violence inflicted on participants in the civil rights movement.

Points of Comparison As you read, think again how poetry can be an instrument of political change. Try to see connections between Randall's poem and the antislavery poems by Harper and Lowell.

Build Background

City of "Bombingham"
Birmingham is Alabama's largest city. In the spring of 1963, Dr. Martin Luther King, Jr., led a huge demonstration to protest racial discrimination in Birmingham, which was then considered one of the most segregated cities of the South. Police dogs and fire hoses were used against the peaceful protesters, including children. Later that year, four young African-American girls were killed when the 16th Street Baptist Church was bombed. A white supremacist, Robert Chambliss, was finally convicted of the murders in 1977.

Focus Your Reading

LITERARY ANALYSIS **BALLADS** A **ballad** is a narrative poem that was originally meant to be sung. Traditional folk ballads are forms of oral literature, composed anonymously and passed down through performance. Early ballads often commemorated tragedies—ill-fated love affairs, wars, shipwrecks, and murders. Literary ballads imitate the style of folk ballads but are composed by one individual and written down as they are created. "Ballad of Birmingham" is a literary ballad. Notice how it resembles a song, and consider how it might make a tragic event live on in memory.

ACTIVE READING **READING NARRATIVE POETRY** A **narrative poem** is one that tells a story. Like a work of fiction it has characters, setting, and plot. However, a narrative poem, particularly a ballad, tells a story in a much more condensed form, without many of the details that aid a reader. You will have to make inferences as you read. The following strategies will help you get the most from the "Ballad of Birmingham."

- Read the poem aloud to appreciate its patterns of rhythm and rhyme.
- Infer who is speaking. Often ballads are structured as a conversation between two people.
- Watch for abrupt shifts in time. In ballads there are often no transitions to indicate that time has passed.
- Bring your background knowledge to the poem. The poet assumes his readers already know what happened in Birmingham.

READER'S NOTEBOOK If, after reading, you have questions about the events or references in the poem, write them down in your notebook.

Ballad of Birmingham

DUDLEY RANDALL

"Mother dear, may I go downtown
instead of out to play,
and march the streets of Birmingham
in a freedom march today?"

5 "No, baby, no, you may not go,
for the dogs are fierce and wild,
and clubs and hoses, guns and jails
ain't good for a little child."

"But, mother, I won't be alone.
10 Other children will go with me,
and march the streets of Birmingham
to make our country free."

"No, baby, no, you may not go,
for I fear those guns will fire.
15 But you may go to church instead,
and sing in the children's choir."

She has combed and brushed her nightdark hair,
and bathed rose petal sweet,
and drawn white gloves on her small brown hands,
20 and white shoes on her feet.

The mother smiled to know her child
was in the sacred place,
but that smile was the last smile
to come upon her face.

25 For when she heard the explosion,
her eyes grew wet and wild.
She raced through the streets of Birmingham
calling for her child.

She clawed through bits of glass and brick,
30 then lifted out a shoe.
"O, here's the shoe my baby wore,
but, baby, where are you?"

Flip Flops and Lace (1991), Stephen Scott Young.
Copyright © Stephen Scott Young. Courtesy of
John H. Surovek Gallery, Palm Beach, Florida.

Thinking through the LITERATURE

Connect to the Literature

1. What Do You Think?
What was the first emotion you felt after reading the poem?

Comprehension Check
- Who is speaking in the poem?
- What do the speakers disagree about?
- What has happened at the end of the poem?

Think Critically

2. ACTIVE READING | **READING NARRATIVE POETRY** | What details did you have to infer because they were not directly explained in the poem?

3. What questions do you still have about the events in the poem?

4. What **ironies** do you see in the poem?

THINK ABOUT
- what the child would rather do than play
- what the mother fears
- why the mother smiles
- what happens to the child

Extend Interpretations

5. The Writer's Style How well do you think the traditional **style** of the poem fits its subject?

6. Connect to Life Why should the tragedy in Birmingham still be remembered today? Name a recent tragedy that you think will be remembered 40 years from now.

7. **Points of Comparison** Compare Randall's **purpose** and **audience** with the purpose and audience for "Stanzas on Freedom" (page 575) and "Free Labor" (page 576).

Literary Analysis

BALLADS As you recall, a **ballad** is a narrative poem that was originally meant to be sung. "Barbara Allan" and "John Henry" are traditional folk ballads. A literary ballad you may have studied is Longfellow's "The Wreck of the Hesperus," about a young woman killed in a shipwreck. A ballad typically has the following characteristics:

- It focuses on a single incident, beginning in the middle of a crisis and proceeding directly to the resolution, with only the sketchiest background information, character development, or descriptive detail.
- It consists of four-line stanzas, or **quatrains,** with **end rhyme** in the second and fourth lines.
- Each stanza has a regular **meter,** usually with four stressed syllables in the first and third lines and three stressed syllables in the second and fourth lines.
- Action is developed through **dialogue.**
- There is often **repetition** of words, phrases, and lines to emphasize ideas and to create suspense.

Paired Activity With a partner, go through the "Ballad of Birmingham" and note which of these ballad characteristics it shows. Be prepared to give examples. Then collaborate in writing your own ballad stanza, on any subject you choose. Share your stanza with the class.

Choices & CHALLENGES

Writing Options

1. Original Ballad Using what you have learned about the ballad form, write your own ballad to commemorate a true event. You might finish the ballad you began for the Literary Analysis activity.

2. Points of Comparison
Evaluate "Ballad of Birmingham" against either "Stanzas on Freedom" or "Free Labor." In a critical essay, tell which you believe is a more effective protest poem, and why.

Writing Handbook
See page 1281: Compare and Contrast

Activities & Explorations

1. Learned by Heart Memorize "Ballad of Birmingham" and perform it for an audience who has never heard it. Monitor yourself as you prepare. What makes the poem easy to memorize? What lines do you want to emphasize for dramatic effect? ~ **SPEAKING AND LISTENING**

2. Sorrowful Song Set "Ballad of Birmingham" to music, either composing your own melody or adapting an existing one. Perform your song for the class. ~ **MUSIC**

3. Ballads of Today What contemporary rock, rap, or pop songs qualify as ballads? Bring in a recording of one such song, and in a lecture-demonstration, explain what elements make it a ballad. ~ **MUSIC**

Inquiry and Research

Find out more about the bombing of the 16th Street Baptist Church and the events in Birmingham that led up to and followed it. Spike Lee's 1997 documentary "Four Little Girls" is an excellent source of information. You might also consult Martin Luther King's "Letter from Birmingham Jail" (page 1136).

Dudley Randall
1914-

Other Works
A Litany of Friends
After the Killing
Broadside Memories: Poets I Have Known

Poet of All Trades Dudley Randall, the first poet laureate of Detroit, Michigan, wrote his earliest poem when he was four years old. His first published poems appeared in the *Detroit Free Press* when he was only 13. Randall, who received his education at Wayne University (now Wayne State University), the University of Michigan, and the University of Ghana, worked for many years at different jobs before becoming a book publisher and an editor. He was employed as a foundry worker for 5 years, a mail carrier for 13 years, and a librarian for 24 years.

Four Little Girls "Ballad of Birmingham" was Randall's response to the 1963 church bombing that killed four young girls in that city. This poem eventually led to the birth of Broadside Press,

which Randall founded and operated until 1977. As he explains, "Folk singer Jerry Moore of New York had it ["Ballad of Birmingham"] set to music, and I wanted to protect the rights to the poem by getting it copyrighted." After Randall learned that leaflets could be copyrighted, he printed his poem on a single sheet of paper called a broadside. "Ballad of Birmingham" was the first title published by Broadside Press.

Publishing for the People As a publisher, Randall provided an important forum for numerous African-American poets. Under Randall's direction, Broadside published nearly sixty books by such distinguished writers as Gwendolyn Brooks, Sonia Sanchez, Nikki Giovanni, Haki Madhubuti (Don L. Lee), and Etheridge Knight.

Author Activity

If you can, obtain some books published by Broadside Press. What do the concerns and styles of the authors tell you about the period in which Randall was publishing?

Comparing Literature: Assessment Practice

Some assessment prompts ask you to compare and contrast different literary selections. You will now practice writing an essay with a comparison-contrast focus.

PART 1 Reading the Prompt

Often you will be asked to write in response to a prompt like the one below. First, read the entire prompt carefully. Then read through it again, looking for key words that help you identify the purpose of the essay and what it must include.

Writing Prompt

Compare and contrast literature of the 19th-century antislavery movement with literature of the 1960s civil rights movement. Point out important similarities and differences you see between works by Douglass, Lowell, and Harper, and later works by Moody and Randall. Concentrate on purpose, audience, theme, tone, and style. Draw a conclusion about which is more significant—the parallels or the divergences between the movements.

STRATEGIES IN ACTION

1 **Compare and contrast** literature from two different periods, stating how it is alike and different.

2 Cite **examples** from the selections named.

3 Focus on five **literary elements**.

4 **Conclude,** or make a decision supported by evidence

PART 2 Planning a Comparison-Contrast Essay

- Create a chart with a row for each literary element you will discuss.

- For each selection, make notes related to these literary elements. (Recall your answers to relevant discussion questions.)

- Identify and mark similarities and differences among selections.

- Decide which seem more important, the similarities or the differences.

	Antislavery			Civil Rights	
	Douglass	Lowell	Harper	Moody	Randall
Purpose					
Audience					
Theme					
Tone					
Style					

PART 3 Drafting Your Essay

Introduction Begin by stating your purpose—to compare and contrast antislavery and civil rights literature.

Organization Summarize characteristics of antislavery literature, giving examples to support your ideas. Show how selections from the civil rights movement resemble antislavery works, then show how they differ.

Conclusion End your essay by stating an opinion about the relative importance of the resemblances and differences. Be sure your points lead to this conclusion.

Revision Allow time to review your work. Make sure it is clear, well-supported, and free from mistakes.

Writing Handbook
See page 1281: Compare and Contrast

Jubilee

Margaret Walker

These thematically related readings are provided along with *Jubilee*:

Come Up from the Fields Father
Walt Whitman

The Sheriff's Children
Charles Waddell Chestnutt

Traveling the Long Road to Freedom
Donovan Webster

To the University of Cambridge, in New England
Phillis Wheatley

To Phillis Wheatley
Lisa Clayton

Virginia Portrait
Sterling A. Brown

***from* Incidents in the Life of a Slave Girl**
Harriet A. Jacobs

Raise a Ruckus Tonight
Many Thousand Gone
Two slave songs

And Even *More* . . .

Books
The Red Badge of Courage
Stephen Crane
A gripping novel about a young Civil War soldier's initiation into battle.

Battle Cry of Freedom
James M. McPherson
A Pulitzer Prize-winning book on the history of the Civil War.

Lincoln at Gettysburg
Garry Wills
A critically acclaimed book examining the impact of the Gettysburg Address on America's democratic ideals.

Other Media
Frederick Douglass: When the Lion Wrote History
Three-part documentary about the eloquent speaker and writer whose words shaped people's views on slavery and the rights of African Americans. WETA/ROJA Productions (VIDEOCASSETTE)

The Civil War
A compelling six-part documentary produced by Ken Burns. PBS. (VIDEOCASSETTE)

Walt Whitman's Civil War
Dramatic readings of the renowned poet's war literature are intertwined with combat scenes from movies. Churchill. (VIDEOCASSETTE)

The Souls of Black Folk

W. E. B. Du Bois

These thematically related readings are provided along with *The Souls of Black Folk*:

Atlanta Exposition Address
Booker T. Washington

Booker T. and W. E. B.
Dudley Randall

Address to the 4th International Convention of the Negro Peoples of the World
Marcus Garvey

***from* Coming of Age in Mississippi**
Anne Moody

***from* Warriors Don't Cry**
Melba Patillo Beals

After Dreaming of President Johnson
Howard Gordon

Communication and Reality
Malcolm X

***from* Sushi and Grits: Ethnic Identity and Conflict in a Newly Multicultural America**
Itabari Njeri

Civil War Women

Edited by Frank D. McSherry, Charles G. Waugh, and Martin Harry Greenberg
The varied roles women played during the Civil War come to life in this collection of short stories by distinguished women writers. Among the contributors are Louisa May Alcott, Kate Chopin, and Eudora Welty.

Writing Workshop

Finding meaning . . .

From Reading to Writing After reading a powerful work of literature like Ambrose Bierce's "An Occurrence at Owl Creek Bridge" or Stephen Crane's "A Mystery of Heroism," you may be filled with questions about its meaning. Writing a **literary interpretation** is a good way to explore your own ideas about the meaning of a literary work and to analyze the elements in the work that communicate the meaning.

For Your Portfolio

WRITING PROMPT Write an interpretation of a literary work in which you explain its meaning.

Purpose: To explain your interpretation

Audience: Others who are familiar with the work

Basics in a Box

Literary Interpretation at a Glance

Introduction
Introduces the literary work and includes a clear thesis statement that introduces the interpretation

Body
Supports the interpretation with evidence from the literary work

- Explanation
- Evidence
- Evidence
- Evidence

Conclusion
Summarizes the interpretation

RUBRIC   Standards for Writing

A successful literary interpretation should

- clearly identify the title and author of the literary work
- give a clearly stated interpretation at or near the beginning of the essay
- present evidence and quotations from the text to support the interpretation
- take into account other interpretations and contradictory evidence

---

Analyzing a Student Model

Molly Ball
Cherry Creek High School

The Red Badge of Courage

Stephen Crane's *The Red Badge of Courage* (1895) owes many of its ideas to the Naturalist movement of the late 19th century; likewise, a good understanding of the ideas of Naturalism can be drawn from the ideas in *The Red Badge of Courage*. Crane uses the setting of the American Civil War to illustrate two important naturalistic concepts: that the natural world is indifferent to the affairs of its creatures, including humans, and that humans and their struggles are therefore insignificant.

The Red Badge of Courage rejects the Romantic idea that nature is a sympathetic mirror of human emotion. Instead, the natural world, as presented in the book, is completely indifferent to human struggles. Henry, upon viewing a battle scene, is surprised "that Nature had gone tranquilly on with her golden process in the midst of so much devilment." He expects something dark, cloudy, and appropriately sinister to reflect the evil he sees because he is still too naive to understand that Nature is more than just a backdrop for human affairs. He does not realize that Nature is a force much larger than he or his species, a machine whose mysterious workings will continue regardless of the squabbles in its midst. As Henry matures, he comes to understand this. Pondering his own actions, he comforts himself with the knowledge that "the sky would forget. . . . The imperturbable sun shines on insult and worship." Nature, Crane shows us, cannot be truthfully personified. In reality, it is wholly impassive to humankind. It is not sensitive to us, and it cannot be affected by us.

Logically, a natural world so completely indifferent must cherish (or not cherish) all of its creatures equally; thus, man cannot justify feeling superior to any other species. Crane implies this when Henry sees the dead soldier, "black ants swarming greedily upon the gray face." If we are disgusted by the image of the ants, we must be more disgusted by the battle scenes, in which humans swarm upon each other with no regard for the

---

RUBRIC IN ACTION

❶ Identifies the title and author of the work

❷ States the interpretation

❸ Cites a quotation that supports the interpretation

❹ Explains the interpretation in more detail

❺ Uses a strong quotation as further support

death or life of their prey. The parallel between the soldiers and the ants is striking, and it shows that human behavior is no more sophisticated than that of insects. This natural equality also is apparent when Henry enters battle: "Into the youth's eyes there came a look that one can see in the orbs of a jaded horse." If man is no more noble than any other animal, it makes sense that Henry's fear should take the same form as that of a horse. By showing the similarities between human and animal action, Crane illustrates his naturalistic view that all species are basically equal in significance.

So here we find Henry, in the middle of a struggle for his very existence; yet the world around him will continue whether he lives or dies, just as if he were a horse or an ant. What, then, can this struggle amount to? Not much, says Crane. Ultimately, human effort, especially war, is futile; even the lives of men who strive toward lofty goals are fleeting and insignificant. "The youth could not tell from the battle flags flying like crimson foam in many directions which color of cloth was winning." But what difference can it make when all that is at stake are pieces of cloth? The battle begins to seem absurd and silly, much like the silliness of the image of the lunging men being "bandied about like light toys between the contending forces." Crane presents a picture of human effort as ultimately futile and meaningless, and of humankind as insignificant on any objective scale.

Clearly, Stephen Crane presents his interpretation of Naturalism in *The Red Badge of Courage* by displaying a man in a setting and context where he is undeniably an unimportant part of something much larger. Through this lens, the human race seems tiny in the vastness of nature and time, as do all other creatures. Ultimately, human actions are altogether inconsequential.

❻ Draws a conclusion from quoted evidence to support the interpretation

❼ Reinforces her interpretation by asking a rhetorical question and answering it as she believes the author would

❽ This writer concludes by restating the interpretation.
Other Options:
· End with a summary of the evidence.
· End with a quotation from the text.

Writing Your Literary Interpretation

❶ Prewriting

Begin by choosing a work of literature to write about. You might select a work that you especially liked or one you had problems with in some way. See the **Idea Bank** in the margin for more suggestions. Then follow the steps below.

Planning Your Literary Interpretation

▶ **1. Develop an interpretation.** Read the story more than once, taking notes in your Reader's Notebook. Freewrite about the literary elements in the work. What are the main character's most significant thoughts or actions? What is the central conflict? What is the theme? Write your interpretation of the story as a tentative thesis statement.

▶ **2. Gather evidence to support your interpretation.** Use a chart to list significant passages from the text and how they support your interpretation.

Evidence from the text	How it supports interpretation

▶ **3. Test your interpretation.** Does the evidence support your interpretation? What contradictory evidence did you find? How can you revise your interpretation to account for more of the evidence?

❷ Drafting

If everybody is thinking alike then somebody isn't thinking.
General George S. Patton, U.S. Army

Try out your interpretation by just writing down your ideas. A good way to start is to try to get through an entire first draft without stopping. When you get stuck, leave a blank or write yourself a note but keep going. You can revise form and style later. Eventually, you should organize your writing into the following parts:

- **Introduction**—identifies the author and title of the work and briefly states the main point of the interpretation
- **Body**—presents evidence from the text to support the interpretation
- **Conclusion**—restates the interpretation and summarizes the evidence

Ask Your Peer Reader

- What is the main point of my interpretation?
- What evidence did I present for my interpretation?
- Are you convinced that my interpretation is reasonable? Why or why not?
- What other points should I include to clarify my interpretation?

IDEABank

1. Your Working Portfolio 📁
Build on one of the **Writing Options** you completed earlier in this unit:

- **Evaluation of Bierce,** p. 592
- **Literary Analysis,** p. 603

2. Favorite Authors
Make a list of your favorite authors. Go to the library and look for new, different, or unfamiliar selections by these authors.

3. Freewriting
Look through the Table of Contents of your literature book and consider two or three possible selections to interpret. Then freewrite on these pieces to help you decide which one you want to continue working with.

Need revising help?

Review the **Rubric,**
p. 624.

Consider **peer reader**
comments.

Check **Revising, Editing,
and Proofreading**
p. 1269.

❸ Revising

TARGET SKILL ▶ CONCLUSIONS A good conclusion in a literary interpretation summarizes what was presented in the body of the paper, does not introduce anything new, and leaves the reader with a sense of closure and something to think about.

> *Clearly, Stephen Crane presents his interpretation of Naturalism*
> ⌃In *The Red Badge of Courage* ~~Stephen Crane offers a psychological study~~
>
> ~~of fear all the more remarkable because he had never actually seen a battle~~
>
> *by displaying a*   *a*
> ~~at the time. He also wants to display~~ man in ~~his~~ setting and context, where
>
> he is undeniably an unimportant part of something much larger. Through
>
> this lens, the human race seems tiny in the vastness of nature and time, as
>
> do all other creatures.   *Ultimately, human actions are*
> ⌃   *altogether inconsequential.*

❹ Editing and Proofreading

TARGET SKILL ▶ VERB TENSE When writing about a literary work, use the present tense (called the historical present); that is, write about a past action as if it were happening now. However, keep the verbs in quotations in the tense in which they were written.

> *can*   *says*
> What, then, ~~could~~ this struggle amount to? Not much, ~~said~~ Crane.
>
> *is*
> Ultimately, human effort especially war ~~was~~ futile; even the lives of men
>
> *strive*   *are*
> who ~~strove~~ toward lofty goals ~~were~~ fleeting and insignificant. "The youth
>
> could not tell from the battle flags flying like crimson foam in many
>
> directions which color of cloth was winning."

**Stumped by verb
tenses?**

See the **Grammar
Handbook,** p. 1396.

Publishing
IDEAS

• Read your interpreta-
tion aloud, preferably to
an audience that has
read the story.

• Collect interpretations
of works by a particular
author in one book.
Keep it as a classroom
reference source.

**More Online:
Publishing Options**
www.mcdougallittell.com

❺ Reflecting

FOR YOUR WORKING PORTFOLIO What helped you the most in developing your literary interpretation? How did your interpretation change as you wrote? Attach your answers to your finished work. Save your literary interpretation in your **Working Portfolio.**

Read this opening from the first draft of a literary analysis. The underlined sections may include the following kinds of errors:

- **lack of parallel structure**
- **verb tenses errors**
- **sentence fragments**
- **comma errors**

For each underlined section, choose the revision that most improves the writing.

"Flowers for Algernon," written by Daniel Keyes, questions the relationship between <u>intelligent and happiness</u>. As the story <u>began</u>, Charlie Gordon is an
(1)   (2)
eager and happy worker with a limited intellect. After an experimental operation, Charlie's intelligence triples. <u>He develops many new insights. Which
(3)
are often disturbing to him.</u> Charlie becomes less <u>optimistic, as he</u> learns more
(4)
about the world. <u>When Charlie's new intelligence finally fades, he returns to his
(5)
earlier life.</u> By the end of the story, Charlie's previous happiness <u>vanished</u> as
(6)
well.

---

1. **A.** can you be intelligent and happiness
   B. intelligence and being happy
   C. intelligence and happiness
   D. Correct as is

2. **A.** begins
   B. begun
   C. has begun
   D. Correct as is

3. **A.** He develops many new insights, which are often disturbing to him.
   B. He develops many new insights which disturbing him.
   C. He develops many new insights are often disturbing to him.
   D. Correct as is

4. **A.** optimistic as he,
   B. optimistic as, he
   C. optimistic as he
   D. Correct as is

5. **A.** When Charlie's new intelligence finally fades he, then, returns to his earlier life.
   B. When Charlie's new intelligence finally fades. He returns to his earlier life.
   C. When Charlie's new intelligence finally fades he returns to his earlier life.
   D. Correct as is

6. **A.** was vanished
   B. has vanished
   C. did vanish
   D. Correct as is

Need extra help?

See the **Grammar Handbook:**

Verb Tense, p. 1310

Correcting Fragments, p. 1323

Punctuation Chart, pp. 1327–1328

Finding the Right Meaning

The English language is huge and diverse. The *Oxford English Dictionary* lists about 500,000 words, and another half-million technical and scientific terms have not yet been added to the dictionary. Despite this wealth of words, a single word often has multiple meanings, making it difficult, sometimes, to determine which meaning is intended in a particular context.

Consider the use of the words *works* and *base* in the excerpt on the right. The word *work* has more than 20 meanings. In this excerpt, *works* means "steadily increasing influence." If you were to look up

base in a dictionary, you would find two entries, each with several meanings, such as "a foundation," "a headquarters," or "morally bad." The meaning for *base* used in this excerpt can be found in the second entry—the word means "low and inferior."

> If ye do not feel the chain,
> When it works a brother's pain,
> Are ye not base slaves indeed,
> Slaves unworthy to be freed?
> —James Russell Lowell, "Stanzas on Freedom"

Strategies for Building Vocabulary

Because many words have multiple meanings, it is important to know how to determine which meaning a writer intends. Here are two methods for doing this.

❶ Determine Meaning from Context First try to figure out the meaning of the word from the context. Consider the word *light* in this excerpt from "Free Labor."

> This fabric is too light to bear
>   The weight of bondsmen's tears,
> I shall not in its texture trace
>   The agony of years.
> —Frances Ellen Watkins Harper, "Free Labor"

Do you think *light* means "having little weight" or "electromagnetic radiation"? Since in this context *light* is used as an adjective describing fabric, and fabric is more likely to be lightweight than to glow in the dark, the context helps you infer that *light* means "having little weight."

❷ Consider Dictionary Meanings When context clues don't help with meaning, consult a dictionary. For example, in "An Occurrence at Owl Creek Bridge," the narrator states, "Some loose boards laid upon the sleepers supporting the metals of the railway supplied a footing for him and his executioners." If you look up *sleeper* in a dictionary,

you'll find several meanings. At first glance, a definition like "a sleeping car on a railroad train" might seem to be relevant.

However, a train car would most likely *not* be "supporting the metals of the railway," so that meaning makes no sense. If you read on, you will find a definition like "a heavy beam used as a support for rails in a railroad track." Given the context, this definition seems to make the most sense.

Always read *all* the definitions for a word before deciding which meaning is intended. If you have trouble deciding which definition is correct, try choosing the one you think works best and reading it aloud in the sentence in place of the unfamiliar word.

EXERCISE Use a dictionary to define each underlined word in these excerpts from "Occurrence at Owl Creek Bridge."

1. He was a civilian, if one might judge from his <u>habit</u>, which was that of a planter.

2. He chafed under the inglorious restraint, longing for the release of his energies, the larger life of the soldier, the opportunity for <u>distinction</u>.

3. At a short <u>remove</u> upon the same temporary platform was an officer.

4. Suddenly he heard a sharp <u>report</u> and something struck the water smartly within a few inches of his head.

5. A single company of infantry [were] in line, at "parade rest," the butts of the rifles on the ground, . . . the hands crossed upon the <u>stock</u>.

Sentence Crafting — Creating Compound Sentences

Grammar from Literature

A compound sentence is a sentence that consists of two or more independent clauses. Look at the sentence below. Notice that independent clauses can stand alone as sentences.

> independent clause   independent clause
> **You have seen how a man was made a slave; you shall see how a slave was made a man.**
> —*Narrative of the Life of Frederick Douglass, an African Slave*

Compound sentences can show a number of types of relationships between ideas. Here are some examples from " An Occurrence at Owl Creek Bridge."

> SEQUENCE OF EVENTS
> **This plank had been held in place by the weight of the captain; it was now held by that of the sergeant.**

> SIMULTANEOUS EVENTS
> **The intervals of silence grew progressively longer; the delays became maddening.**

> EXPLANATION
> **The hunted man saw all this over his shoulder; he was now swimming vigorously with the current.**

Notice that in each of the preceding examples the independent clauses are linked by a semicolon. Independent clauses can also be linked by a comma and a coordinating conjunction, such as *and, or, nor, but, yet, for,* or *so.*

> CAUSE AND EFFECT
> **There was a mass rally that night at the Pearl Street Church in Jackson, and the place was packed.**
> —Anne Moody, *Coming of Age in Mississippi*

Using Compound Sentences in Your Writing Showing connections between ideas is a key element of effective writing. As you revise your writing, look for related ideas and consider combining them in compound sentences. By doing so, you may also eliminate repetition and wordiness. If you use coordinating conjunctions, be sure to choose ones that clearly express the relationships between the ideas.

> RELATED IDEAS
> **Ambrose Bierce was a journalist. He had a reporter's eye for detail.**

> COMPOUND SENTENCE
> **Ambrose Bierce was a journalist, so he had a reporter's eye for detail.**

Usage Tip When a pronoun in the second clause of a compound sentence refers to a noun in the first clause, be sure there is no confusion about which noun the pronoun replaces.

> UNCLEAR
> noun   noun   pronoun
> **The captain nods to the sergeant, and he steps aside.**

Note that in this sentence it is not clear whether the captain or the sergeant steps aside. There are several ways in which the sentence can be rewritten to clarify its meaning. Here are two possibilities:

> CLEAR
> **The captain nods to the sergeant, and the sergeant steps aside.**

> CLEAR
> **The captain nods to the sergeant, who steps aside.**

WRITING EXERCISE For items 1 and 2, join the sentences to form compound sentences. For items 3–5, make each simple sentence into a compound sentence by adding another independent clause. Use *and* as a connector only once.

1. The executioners stand quietly. They are deeply affected by the gravity of the situation.
2. Farquhar stands on one end of a plank. A sergeant stands on the other.
3. A sentinel stands on each end of the bridge.
4. The prisoner feels pressure on his throat.
5. At first he imagines his body is sinking into the river.

GRAMMAR EXERCISE Rewrite the sentences so that it is clear which noun the pronoun replaces.

1. Farquhar welcomes the scout; he is in disguise.
2. The increasing number of desertions resulted in more frequent hangings, yet they didn't seem to solve anything.
3. Farquhar's escape begins at the bridge, but it is only imaginary.
4. Bierce provides readers with believable characters and interesting plot twists, and they are held in keen suspense.
5. Farquhar travels a lonely road to his home; it grows stranger and stranger.

631

Tricksters and Trailblazers

The Vanishing Frontier

Before white settlers in large numbers had pushed west of the Mississippi, the vast frontier was populated by many tribes of Native Americans. The Sioux (so͞o), the Cheyenne (shī-ĕn′), the Arapaho (ə-răp′e-hō′), the Kiowa (kī′ə-wô′), and the Comanche (kə-măn′chē) on the Great Plains had developed a way of life that depended almost exclusively on the large herds of buffalo, estimated at 15 million head in 1865. In the Southwest, the Apache had fought against the Spanish for 250 years; but other southwestern tribes, such as the Navajo, had adopted Spanish ways and were raising sheep and goats and cultivating crops. The Nez Perce (nĕz′ pûrs′) of the Pacific Northwest had coexisted peacefully with white traders and trappers since Lewis and Clark first explored their vast territory in 1805.

In 1841 the first caravan of covered wagons brought pioneers across the Great Plains, heading for fertile territories in California and Oregon. Within two years, more than 1,000 people had made the journey. During the California gold rush of 1849, the dream of riches lured thousands of miners west. Within 30 years of that first discov-

A 19th-centry artist's rendition of a Native American chief's refusal to allow a wagon train to pass through his country.

ery, gold or silver had been found in every Western state and territory.

By the 1860s, the plains themselves began to be settled. The free land granted by the Homestead Act of 1862 attracted thousands of settlers west. Newly constructed railroads transported more than 8 million settlers in two decades alone.

This relatively rapid settlement of the West doomed the Native American way of life. White settlers believed that they were bringing civilization to the wilderness, and few considered the Indians as having any legitimate claim to the land. One by one the tribes of the Northwest and of the Great Plains were forced—either through armed conflict or signed treaties—to give up their territories to the U.S. government. The tribes were often relocated onto cramped reservations, on land so poor that no white settlers wanted it.

This part of Unit Four includes a variety of selections to give you an idea of what was lost and gained during this dramatic episode in

No white person or persons shall be permitted to settle upon or occupy any portion of the territory, or without the consent of the Indians to pass through the same.

Treaty of 1868

Our land here is the dearest thing on earth to us. Men take up land and get rich on it, and it is very important for us Indians to keep it.

White Thunder
48th U.S. Congress, 1st session
Senate Report 283

I did not know then how much was ended. When I look back now from this high hill of my old age, I can still see the butchered women and children lying heaped and scattered all along the crooked gulch as plain as when I saw them with eyes still young. And I can see that something else died there in the bloody mud, and was buried in the blizzard. A people's dream died there. It was a beautiful dream.

Black Elk
recalling the Battle of Wounded Knee
in *Black Elk Speaks*

The dead man lay stretched out on the pool table, right in the middle of the saloon/courtroom. The grizzled old judge walked around the body as if he were measuring it for size. No one knew the dead man's name, so the judge searched his pockets for identification. He found out the man's name was O'Brien. He also found $40 and a six-shooter.

The judge stepped back and thumbed his old dusty law book, the *Revised Statutes of Texas* for 1879. After thinking about the situation for a while, he turned to the coroner's jury and the other men hanging around the saloon.

"Gentlemen," he said, "that man fell from the bridge and that's all there is about it. But there is one thing that is not so plain, and that is what was he doing with that gun? Of course he's dead and can't explain, but that ain't the fault of the law; it's his own misfortune. Justice is justice, and law is law, and as he can't offer no satisfactory explanation of the matter I shall be obliged to fine him forty dollars for carrying a concealed weapon."

Welcome to the court of Judge Roy Bean, the Law West of the Pecos. Not to mention the coroner and the best saloonkeeper. For 20 years, Roy Bean was a legend throughout the Southwest. Texas Rangers, Mexican shepherds, and New York tourists came to his combination courtroom and saloon for justice, whiskey, and entertainment. The justice and whiskey were a little on the shady side, but the entertainment was first rate.

Paul Robert Walker
from *Judge Roy Bean: Law West of the Pecos*

American history. You'll recognize the Native American trickster tradition in the two tales "The Indian and the Hundred Cows" and "High Horse's Courting." You'll also see tricksters in the humorous excerpt from Mark Twain's autobiography and in the tale "The Notorious Jumping Frog of Calaveras County." On a more serious note, Willa Cather takes a very unromantic view of life on the plains in her story of hardship and longing, "A Wagner Matinee."

After the Civil War and by the time the West was being settled, American literature was also changing. Realism replaced romanticism as the dominant literary style, in part because people wanted to read more truthful accounts of ordinary life rather than the sentimentality of much romantic fiction. The new regional diversity that sprang up among the mining camps, cattle ranches, farming communities, and frontier towns in the West gave rise to new regional literature called local-color realism. Mark Twain, who once lived in a mining camp, was foremost among the local-color realists. Later in the century, Willa Cather carried on the spirit of local-color realism with increasing sophistication. When you read Twain and Cather, think about the difference between their writing and the writing of Poe, Hawthorne, and Thoreau, who wrote earlier in the century, and you'll understand the direction American literature was going.

Traditions Across Time: Writing of the New West

America's unique relationship with the frontier has continued to influence our literature and character, engaging our writers and thinkers to the present day. Although the days of the "Wild West" are gone, its mythic lure of freedom remains a powerful force. Américo Paredes incorporates the trickster tradition into his modern retelling of a Mexican-American folk song, "The Legend of Gregorio Cortez."

The Vanishing Frontier

Retold by **José Griego y Maestas** Translated by **Rudolfo A. Anaya**
The Indian and the Hundred Cows/ El indito de las cien vacas 638
God helps those who help themselves.

Black Elk Retold through **John G. Neihardt**
High Horse's Courting 645
from **Black Elk Speaks**
Gallantry and trickery on the Great Plains

LITERARY LINK
Chief Joseph
I Will Fight No More Forever 651
The heartbreaking voice of defeat

Mark Twain $\mathcal{A}$UTHOR $\mathcal{S}$TUDY

from **The Autobiography of Mark Twain** 658
from **Life on the Mississippi** 669
Epigrams 678
The Notorious Jumping Frog of Calaveras County 679
The First Jumping Frog 684

Selections from America's favorite humorist

Willa Cather
A Wagner Matinee 688
A touching portrait of a pioneer woman

RELATED READING
Elinore Pruitt Stewart
from **Letters of a Woman Homesteader** 700
The joys of homesteading

COMPARING LITERATURE
Traditions Across Time: Writing of the New West

Américo Paredes
The Legend of Gregorio Cortez (1973) 702
A legendary hero who would not bend

Setting in Regional Literature

Pride of Place

Sports fans scream for the home team; people wave flags and wear T-shirts proclaiming their allegiance to specific localities and schools. Almost everybody today exhibits some kind of pride in a specific region of the country. The same enthusiasm for place can be found in the regional writing that sprang up in the United States during the second half of the 19th century and has continued to the present day.

The Growth of Regional Literature

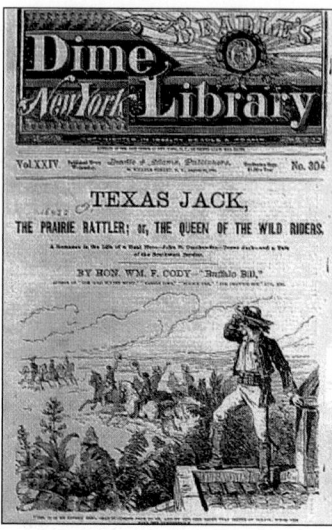

Dime novels similar to this one became popular in the late 1800s.

Regional literature arose from an effort to represent accurately the speech, manners, habits, history, folklore, and beliefs of people in specific geographical areas. Regionalism has been part of American literature from the beginning. Washington Irving's tales of Dutch New York and Nathaniel Hawthorne's stories of Puritan New England are just two examples. After the Civil War, however, when realism became the dominant literary movement, writers began to focus on the lives of ordinary people and to avoid the supernaturalism and sentimentality found in much of the work of Irving, Hawthorne, and Poe.

A factor that contributed to the growth of regional writing was the boom in publishing in the late 1800s. Popular magazines started up all over the United States to meet the demand for news about the rest of the country. Mark Twain's "The Notorious Jumping Frog of Calaveras County" was first published in a New York magazine and became an immediate sensation.

The Importance of Setting

The effectiveness of regional writing depends to a large extent on the depiction of setting. Setting—

basically, the time and place in which a story's events occur—includes several key elements:

- Geographical location and physical features—such as a river, a camp, a house, or a car (Remember how important the car is in Flannery O'Connor's "The Life You Save May Be Your Own"?)

- The time in which the events are embedded—a season of the year or a historical period (What would *The Crucible* be without its historical setting?)

- The jobs and daily activities of the characters (In Faulkner's "A Rose for

Local Color Realism

In 1868, a popular story about the California gold rush—Bret Harte's "The Luck of Roaring Camp"—launched a specific form of regional writing called **local color realism.** Mark Twain, with his memorable characters, was a master of local color. Other local color realists at this time include Joel Chandler Harris in the South and Sarah Orne Jewett in New England. Later regional writers, such as Willa Cather, William Faulkner, and Flannery O'Connor, developed sophisticated ways of making universal statements about the human condition while focusing on the local and the particular.

The Jolly Flatboatmen in Port, (1857), George Caleb Bingham.

Emily," the disappearance of students for Miss Emily's china-painting lessons tells a lot about the changing lives of Southern women after the Civil War.)

- The culture of the characters, including their religious and moral beliefs and the social and economic conditions in which they live (Think about the cultural differences between the characters in Hawthorne's "Dr. Heidegger's Experiment" and those in "The Life You Save May Be Your Own.")

A Closer Look

Two means of conveying setting that are commonly found in regional literature are (1) dialects—distinctive forms of language spoken in particular areas or by particular groups of people—and (2) detailed descriptions of location. Take a look at the beginning of Simon Wheeler's rambling tale in Twain's "The Notorious Jumping Frog of Calaveras County":

> "Rev. Leonidas W. H'm, Reverend Le— Well, there was a feller here once by the name of Jim Smiley, in the winter of '49—or maybe it was the spring of '50—I don't recollect exactly, somehow, though what makes me think it was one or the other is because I remember the big flume warn't finished when he first come to the camp. . . ."
>
> —Mark Twain, "The Notorious Jumping Frog of Calaveras County"

The pronunciations indicated by the spellings *feller* and *warn't*, the expression "I don't recollect," and the use of *come* rather than *came* all contribute to the regional flavor of the piece.

YOUR TURN Rewrite the passage in the dialect of another region or in the sort of language you speak with your friends. How does the change in dialect alter the story?

Now look at this description from Cather's "A Wagner Matinee," in which the narrator recalls the Nebraska farm where he grew up:

> I saw again the tall, naked house on the prairie, black and grim as a wooden fortress; the black pond where I had learned to swim, its margin pitted with sun-dried cattle tracks; the rain gullied clay banks about the naked house, the four dwarf ash seedlings where the dish-cloths were always hung to dry before the kitchen door.
>
> —Willa Cather, "A Wagner Matinee"

Notice the lack of color and the harshness of the setting described: both the landscape and the evidences of human habitation are black, pitted, and bare.

YOUR TURN What feeling about life on the frontier do you get from the description? How could you rewrite the passage to change that feeling?

Strategies for Reading: Regional Literature

1. Determine what the details of **setting** reveal about the particular region and time period.
2. Notice how the **characters** exemplify the values of their particular culture or time period.
3. Think about why the story was created in the first place. What was the writer aiming at?
4. **Monitor** your reading strategies and modify them when your understanding breaks down. Remember to use the Strategies for Active Reading: **predict, visualize, connect, question, clarify,** and **evaluate.**

The Indian and the Hundred Cows / El indito de las cien vacas

Folk Tale retold by JOSÉ GRIEGO Y MAESTAS
(hô-sě′ grē-yě′gô ē mä-ěs′täs)
Translated by RUDOLFO A. ANAYA (rōō-dôl′fô ä-nä′yä)

Connect to Your Life

Communication Breakdown Think of a time when you misunderstood or misinterpreted something that someone told you. What do you think caused this breakdown in communication? What was the result of the misunderstanding? Jot down your thoughts about this experience.

Build Background

Cultural Contact Since the earliest Spanish settlements, the Native American and Mexican populations in the Southwest had come into close contact. Before Mexico won its independence in 1821, Spain's system of Roman Catholic missions in California, New Mexico, and Colorado was staffed with Franciscan priests who tried to convert Native Americans to Catholicism and settle them on mission lands.

A conflict erupts between a fictional priest and a Native American member of his congregation in "The Indian and the Hundred Cows," published in *Cuentos: Tales from the Hispanic Southwest.* The tales in this collection were selected and adapted in Spanish by the scholar José Griego y Maestas and were translated into English by the novelist Rudolfo A. Anaya. The English version of the tale appears on page 639; the Spanish version, on page 641. Anaya wrote: "My English variations of these old, old *cuentos* are my versions. . . . I started with José Griego's adaptations from the literal transcriptions originally compiled by Juan B. Rael, and I worked from Spanish into English to suit my own rhythm."

Focus Your Reading

LITERARY ANALYSIS **CUENTO** As you know, a **folk tale** is a short, simple story that is handed down, usually by word of mouth, from generation to generation. "The Indian and the Hundred Cows" is a *cuento,* a traditional folk tale that comes from the oral tradition of New Mexico and southern Colorado. Early settlers and their descendants told *cuentos* to entertain, to reinforce cultural values, and to teach traditional customs and beliefs to their children.

ACTIVE READING **DETERMINING THEME** Theme is the central idea or ideas that the writer wishes to share with the reader. In simple stories, such as folk tales and fables, the theme is called the **moral**—a lesson about life or about people and their actions. Sometimes the moral is directly stated at the end of the story, while in others the moral is implied. Making inferences about the significance of plot events and characters' actions can help you figure out the theme or moral.

READER'S NOTEBOOK In "The Indian and the Hundred Cows," you can infer the moral based on what the main characters learn when they resolve a problem. To help you discover the central theme of the story, create a diagram like the one shown, and fill it in as you read.

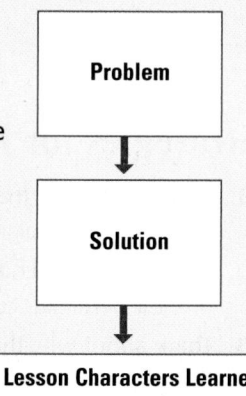

Problem

↓

Solution

↓

Lesson Characters Learned

The Indian and the Hundred Cows

translated by rudolfo a. anaya

In a small pueblo there once lived an Indian who was so devoted to the church he never missed mass on Sunday. One Sunday, during his homily,[1] the priest said:

"Have charity, my children. Give alms[2] to the poor. If you expect God's help it is necessary that you also help the church. You know that when you make a donation to God, He returns it a hundredfold."

The Indian, who was listening carefully, decided to give a cow that he had to the priest. That afternoon he brought his cow to the church and told the priest, "Padre,[3] I have brought you my cow so that God will give me a hundred cows."

"Yes, yes, my son," the priest answered. "Have faith in God and He will repay your gift." Then the priest took the cow and added it to his own herd.

The Indian returned home very satisfied and he began to build a large corral where he could keep his hundred cows when they arrived. When he finished his corral he sat down to wait for the cows. He waited some time and then thought, "Perhaps the cows don't come on their own, maybe I should go for them." So he set out to look for his promised hundred cows. Near the church he came upon a large herd which he drove home and locked securely in his corral.

Later that afternoon the two *vaqueros*[4] who took care of the priest's herd rode to the Indian's home.

"Why do you have these cattle locked up?" they asked gruffly. "Have they done some damage?"

"No, they haven't done any damage," the Indian answered. "I have them locked up because they're mine. I gave the priest a cow and he promised me God would give me a hundred, and here they are!"

"These are the priest's cattle, not yours," the cowboys answered.

"No, these are mine because he promised me a hundred for one!" the Indian insisted.

The cowboys returned to tell the priest what had happened. When he heard the news the

---

1. **homily** (hŏm′ə-lē): sermon.
2. **alms:** money or goods given as charity to the poor.
3. **Padre** (pä′drĕ) *Spanish:* Father; used as a form of address for a priest.
4. *vaqueros* (vä-kĕ′rôs) *Spanish:* cowboys.

Castle Mission, John Runne. Copyright © John Runne, Evergreen Art Company, Evergeen, Colorado.

priest became very angry. He got on his mule and the three rode to the Indian's home. When they arrived at the corral the Indian was sitting by the gate, his bow and quiver of arrows ready.

"Why have you locked up my cattle in your corral!" the priest shouted. "Is this the way you show your gratitude?"

"But these are my cows," the Indian answered.

"And who gave them to you?"

"You did. You said at mass whoever gave one cow would get a hundred in return!"

"That's not what I meant, you thief!" the

priest cried angrily. "You are a thief and you must turn my cattle loose." He got down from his mule to open the gate but stopped when he saw the Indian put an arrow to his bow.

"Padre, if you dare touch the lock I will stick this arrow into your heart. Then the devils in hell will give you a hundred more."

The priest backed away. He realized the Indian meant to make him keep the promise he had made in church, and there was nothing he could do. So he got on his mule and quietly rode home, reminding himself to be more careful with what he said in his sermons. ❖

El Indito de Las Cien Vacas

interpretado por josé griego y maestas

Habia un indio del pueblo muy devoto que no faltaba a misa nunca. Y un domingo en el sermón que les echó el padre, les dijo:

"Hagan caridades, hijos. Den limosna. Miren que para que Dios les ayude, es menester que ustedes también le den a la iglesia, porque han de saber que el que le hace una donación a Dios, Dios le devuelve ciento por uno."

El indito, que estaba escuchando, de una vez intentó traerle al padre una vaquita que tenía. En la tarde le trujo la vaquita y le dijo, "Tata padre, aquí te traigo esta vaquita para que Dios me de cien por una vaquita."

"Sí, sí, hijo. Ten fe en que Dios te va a recompensar esta limosna."

El indito se volvió a su casa muy satisfecho y empezó a hacer un corral grande para cuando le vinieran las cien vacas. Acabó su corral y se puso a esperar las vacas. El miraba para todos rumbos a ver por donde venían y viendo que no venían, ya se puso en camino a buscarlas. Pensó, "Quizás las vacas no venir solas. Quizás yo ir por ellas." Pues el primer hatajo de vacas que encontró lo arreó para su corral y lo encerró y atrincó bien la puerta.

Detail of *Castle Mission*, John Runne.

Más tarde cayeron los que cuidaban las vacas y eran de tata padre las vacas y le dijeron al indio:

"¿Por qué tienes estas vacas encerradas? ¿Qué te hicieron daño?"

"No, no me hicieron daño, pero yo le di a tata padre mi vaquita y él me prometió que Dios me daría cien, y estas son."

"Estas son del padre y no tuyas," le decían los vaqueros.

"No son. Estas son mías porque él me prometió darme el ciento por uno."

Los vaqueros se fueron a avisarle al padre. Luego el padre se enojó, montó en su mula y se fueron los tres junto. Cuando llegaron al corral de las vacas, ya el indito estaba allí en la puerta con su arco y su carcaje.

"Pero, indio grosero, ¿por qué tienes mis vacas encerradas aquí?"

"Porque estas son mías, tata padre."

"¿Quién te las dio?"

"Tú me las distes. Tú decir allá en misa que el que te diera una vaca, tú le dabas cien."

"Pero indio embustero, tú eres un ladrón y estas vacas voy a echarlas." El padre se apeó a abrir la puerta y el indito puso una flecha en su arco.

"Tata padre, si tú mueves una tranca, te ensarto esta flecha en el mero corazón."

"No, no, hijo, con las armas no se juega. Si así quieres, está bien."

Pues le dejó el padre las vacas al indio y se fue el padre muy callado a su casa, recordando que en otra ocasión, valía más escoger sus palabras con cuidado. ❖

Thinking through the LITERATURE

Connect to the Literature

1. **What Do You Think?** Did you enjoy this *cuento?* Share your opinion with classmates.

   .... **Comprehension Check** ....
   - What misunderstanding arises between the priest and the Indian?
   - What does the Indian do when a hundred cows don't show up?
   - What does the Indian threaten to do if the priest opens up the gate?

Think Critically

2. Should the priest have let the Indian keep the hundred cows? Give reasons for your answer.

3. Why do you think the Indian and the priest misunderstand one another?

    THINK ABOUT
   - what the priest means when he tells the churchgoers that God returns gifts a hundredfold
   - what makes the Indian believe he can take the cows

4. **ACTIVE READING** | **DETERMINING THEME** | Review the diagram you made earlier that showed how plot events point to the theme. What do you think is the moral, or **theme,** of this *cuento?* Is the moral a guiding principle that might apply to most people's lives? Why or why not?

Extend Interpretations

5. **Comparing Texts** The two Native American Coyote stories you read in Unit One were trickster tales. Would you say that "The Indian and the Hundred Cows" is a trickster tale in the same way that the Coyote stories are? Explain your opinion.

6. **The Writer's Style** Rudolfo A. Anaya, the translator of this tale, retold the *cuentos* in written form and then translated them into English to suit his own "rhythm." What do you think might be gained or lost through this process? If you know some Spanish, evaluate how Anaya's English version of "The Indian and the Hundred Cows" differs from the Spanish.

7. **Connect to Life** At the heart of this *cuento* is a misunderstanding that arises because of differences between cultures. What cultural differences might cause misunderstandings among people who live in your community? Was the misunderstanding you described in the Connect to Your Life activity on page 638 the result of cultural differences?

Literary Analysis

CUENTO Folk tales, such as this *cuento,* often serve to teach family obligations or societal values. First brought to the southwestern part of the United States by Spanish and Mexican settlers, *cuentos* were further shaped and influenced by the landscape and by Native American cultures in this area. By reading *cuentos* such as "The Indian and the Hundred Cows," you can learn about the culture of this region.

Cooperative Learning Activity Meet with a small group and hold a panel discussion in which you address these questions about "The Indian and the Hundred Cows":
- What did you learn about the frontier Southwest, where the tale originated?
- What values do you think this tale might teach?
- Are there tales that reveal the ways of living or the values of your community?

Writing Options

1. Sermon on Charity Imagine that the priest again speaks to churchgoers about the importance of charity when he delivers his next homily, on the Sunday after the incident in the story. Write part of the sermon he might give that day.

2. Comic Tale Draft a humorous folk tale in which a figurative statement is taken literally. If the misunderstanding you described in the Connect to Your Life activity on page 638 is applicable here, you might use it as the basis for your folk tale. Place your story in your **Working Portfolio.**

Activities & Explorations

Mural Art Working with a small group, create a mural, a traditional Mexican art form, that depicts a scene from this *cuento.* Paint the images on oversized sheets of paper. Tape the completed mural to a wall in the classroom.

Inquiry & Research

Translations from Spanish Some words in English are similar to Spanish words. These words— such as *Indian* and *indio, deity* and *Dios*— often have common roots that are based on words with Latin origins.

Choose five words from the Spanish version of "The Indian and the Hundred Cows," and use an English-Spanish dictionary to translate them. Then make a chart showing each Spanish word and its English equivalent. If you can think of any related English words that seem to share a common Latin root with the Spanish word, add them to the chart, as in the example shown.

Spanish Word	English Equivalent	From Common Root
ciento	hundred	cent, century, centennial

Building Vocabulary
For an in-depth lesson on root words, see page 444.

Rudolfo A. Anaya
1937–

Other Works
Bless Me, Ultima
Heart of Aztlán
Tortuga
Alburquerque

Celebrating the Past Rudolfo A. Anaya, one of the most widely read Mexican-American writers in the United States, was born, raised, and educated in New Mexico. In his novels, short stories, plays, and poetry, he draws on the rich culture and history of his native Southwest and on the myths and legends of the Spanish *cuentos.* As Anaya has observed, "each community has art to offer, and now we've come to a place in American history where we celebrate that." Until his retirement in 1993, Anaya taught creative writing and literature at the University of New Mexico.

José Griego y Maestas

An Ear for Language José Griego y Maestas adapted "The Indian and the Hundred Cows" from the original Spanish version gathered by Juan B. Rael from Southwestern storytellers. Griego, who received his master's degree in Spanish literature from the University of New Mexico, has taught at the College of Santa Fe. An expert in the field of bilingual education, he has directed and administered New Mexico's bilingual education program. Griego has also served as the director of the Guadalupe Historic Foundation in Santa Fe.

High Horse's Courting *from* Black Elk Speaks

Folk Tale by BLACK ELK, *told through* JOHN G. NEIHARDT

(**Connect to Your Life**)

For Richer or for Poorer In a small group, share ideas about how important wealth or earning ability is in courtship. Do you believe money should be an important consideration in deciding whom to marry? Do you think some parents would have different ideas than you and your classmates have? Share your group's ideas with the rest of the class.

Build Background

Sioux Courtship Black Elk was an Oglala Sioux medicine man who was born in the 19th century, before his people were driven from their lands in the northern Great Plains onto reservations. "High Horse's Courting" is a story that Black Elk learned from Watanye, an older member of his tribe, and later passed on to Nebraska writer John G. Neihardt, who preserved it in the book *Black Elk Speaks.* The story deals with courtship in the context of traditional Sioux beliefs and customs. Usually, before marrying, a Sioux man had to prove himself in war or hunting. Having many horses increased a man's status, and a man's offer of horses to a woman's family signaled a marriage proposal. If the horses were accepted, the wedding would take place a few days later.

Focus Your Reading

LITERARY ANALYSIS **ORAL LITERATURE** Folk tales, fables, myths, legends, chants, and oral histories are examples of **oral literature—** literature that is passed from one generation to another by performance or word of mouth. As you read "High Horse's Courting" from *Black Elk Speaks,* notice words and phrases that sound like conversational speech. By giving voice to their cultural heritage, storytellers like Black Elk keep the past alive.

ACTIVE READING **IDENTIFYING AUTHOR'S PURPOSE** Black Elk explained one of his purposes in telling his oral stories to John G. Neihardt: "There is so much to teach you. What I know was given to me for men and it is true and it is beautiful." When speakers and writers communicate, they have different **purposes,** or goals, in mind—for example, to inform, to entertain, to persuade, or to express feelings. A reading selection, such as Black Elk's story, may have more than one purpose.

READER'S NOTEBOOK To help identify the various purposes of "High Horse's Courting," fill in a questionnaire like the following as you read. Jot down reasons to support your responses.

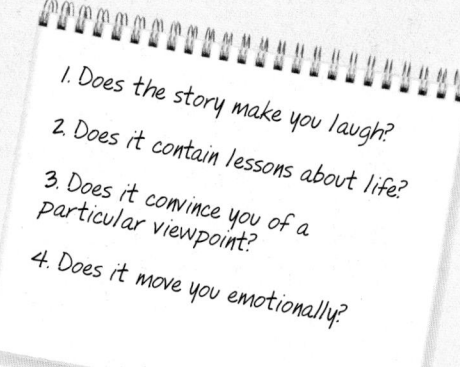

1. Does the story make you laugh?

2. Does it contain lessons about life?

3. Does it convince you of a particular viewpoint?

4. Does it move you emotionally?

HIGH HORSE'S COURTING

YOU KNOW, IN THE OLD DAYS, IT WAS NOT SO VERY EASY TO GET A GIRL WHEN

you wanted to be married. Sometimes it was hard work for a young man and he had to stand a great deal. Say I am a young man and I have seen a young girl who looks so beautiful to me that I feel all sick when I think about her. I cannot just go and tell her about it and then get married if she is willing. I have to be a very sneaky fellow to talk to her at all, and after I have managed to talk to her, that is only the beginning.

Probably for a long time I have been feeling sick about a certain girl because I love her so much, but she will not even look at me, and her parents keep a good watch over her. But I keep feeling worse and worse all the time; so maybe I sneak up to her tepee in the dark and wait until she comes out. Maybe I just wait there all night and don't get any sleep at all and she does not come out. Then I feel sicker than ever about her.

Maybe I hide in the brush by a spring where she sometimes goes to get water, and when she comes by, if nobody is looking, then I jump out and hold her and just make her listen to me. If she likes me too, I can tell that from the way she acts, for she is very bashful and maybe will not say a word or even look at me the first time. So I let her go, and then maybe I sneak around until I can see her father alone, and I tell him how many horses I can give him for his beautiful girl, and by now I am feeling so sick that maybe I would give him all the horses in the world if I had them.

Well, this young man I am telling about was called High Horse, and there was a girl in the village who looked so beautiful to him that he was just sick all over from thinking about her so much and he was getting sicker all the time. The girl was very shy, and her parents thought a great deal of her because they were not young anymore and this was the only child they had. So they watched her all day long, and they fixed it so that she would be safe at night, too, when they were asleep. They thought so much of her that they had made a rawhide bed for her to sleep in, and after they knew that High Horse was sneaking around after her, they took rawhide thongs and tied the girl in bed at night so that nobody could steal her when they were asleep, for they were not sure but that their girl might really want to be stolen.

Wild Horses of Nevada (1927), Maynard Dixon. Oil, 44″ × 50″, courtesy of the William A. Karges Family Trust.

Well, after High Horse had been sneaking around a good while and hiding and waiting for the girl and getting sicker all the time, he finally caught her alone and made her talk to him. Then he found out that she liked him maybe a little. Of course this did not make him feel well. It made him sicker than ever, but now he felt as brave as a bison bull, and so he went right to her father and said he loved the girl so much that he would give two good horses for her—one of them young and the other one not so very old.

But the old man just waved his hand, meaning for High Horse to go away and quit talking foolishness like that.

High Horse was feeling sicker than ever about it; but there was another young fellow who said he would loan High Horse two ponies and when he got some more horses, why, he could just give them back for the ones he had borrowed.

Then High Horse went back to the old man and said he would give four horses for the girl— two of them young and the other two not hardly old at all. But the old man just waved his hand and would not say anything.

So High Horse sneaked around until he could talk to the girl again, and he asked her to run away with him. He told her he thought he would just fall over and die if she did not. But she said she would not do that; she wanted to be bought like a fine woman. You see she thought a great deal of herself too.

That made High Horse feel so very sick that he could not eat a bite, and he went around with his head hanging down as though he might just fall down and die any time.

Red Deer was another young fellow, and he and High Horse were great comrades, always doing things together. Red Deer saw how High Horse was acting, and he said: "Cousin, what is the matter? Are you sick in the belly? You look as though you were going to die."

Then High Horse told Red Deer how it was, and said he thought he could not stay alive much longer if he could not marry the girl pretty quick.

Red Deer thought awhile about it, and then he said: "Cousin, I have a plan, and if you are man enough to do as I tell you, then everything will be all right. She will not run away with you; her old man will not take four horses; and four horses are all you can get. You must steal her and run away with her. Then afterwhile you can come back and the old man cannot do anything because she will be your woman. Probably she wants you to steal her anyway."

SO **THEY PLANNED WHAT HIGH HORSE HAD TO DO, AND HE SAID HE** loved the girl so much that he was man enough to do anything Red Deer or anybody else could think up.

So this is what they did.

That night late they sneaked up to the girl's tepee and waited until it sounded inside as though the old man and the old woman and the girl were sound asleep. Then High Horse crawled under the tepee with a knife. He had to cut the rawhide thongs first, and then Red Deer, who was pulling up the stakes around that side of the tepee, was going to help drag the girl outside and gag her. After that, High Horse could put her across his pony in front of him and hurry out of there and be happy all the rest of his life.

When High Horse had crawled inside, he felt so nervous that he could hear his heart drumming, and it seemed so loud he felt sure it would 'waken the old folks. But it did not, and afterwhile he began cutting the thongs. Every time he cut one it made a pop and nearly scared him to death. But he was getting along all right and all the thongs were cut down as far as the girl's thighs, when he became so nervous that his knife slipped and stuck the girl. She gave a big, loud yell. Then the old folks jumped up and yelled too. By this time High Horse was outside, and he and Red Deer were running away like antelope. The old man and some other people chased the young men but they got away in the dark and nobody knew who it was.

Well, if you ever wanted a beautiful girl you will know how sick High Horse was now. It was very bad the way he felt, and it looked as though he would starve even if he did not drop over dead sometime.

Red Deer kept thinking about this, and after a few days he went to High Horse and said: "Cousin, take courage! I have another plan, and I am sure, if you are man enough, we can steal her this time." And High Horse said: "I am man enough to do anything anybody can think up, if I can only get that girl."

So this is what they did.

They went away from the village alone, and Red Deer made High Horse strip naked. Then he painted High Horse solid white all over, and after that he painted black stripes all over the white and put black rings around High Horse's eyes. High Horse looked terrible. He looked so terrible that when Red Deer was through painting and took a good look at what he had done, he said it scared even him a little.

"Now," Red Deer said, "if you get caught again, everybody will be so scared they will think you are a bad spirit and will be afraid to chase you."

So when the night was getting old and everybody was sound asleep, they sneaked back to the girl's tepee. High Horse crawled in with his knife, as before, and Red Deer waited outside, ready to drag the girl out and gag her when High Horse had all the thongs cut.

High Horse crept up by the girl's bed and began cutting at the thongs. But he kept thinking, "If they see me they will shoot me because I look so terrible." The girl was restless and kept squirming around in bed, and when a thong was cut, it popped. So High Horse worked very slowly and carefully.

But he must have made some noise, for suddenly the old woman awoke and said to her old man: "Old Man, wake up! There is somebody in this tepee!" But the old man was sleepy and didn't want to be bothered. He said: "Of course there is somebody in this tepee. Go to sleep and don't bother me." Then he snored some more.

But High Horse was so scared by now that he lay very still and as flat to the ground as he could. Now, you see, he had not been sleeping very well for a long time because he was so sick about the girl. And while he was lying there waiting for the old woman to snore, he just forgot everything, even how beautiful the girl was. Red Deer, who was lying outside ready to do his part, wondered and wondered what had happened in there, but he did not dare call out to High Horse.

Afterwhile the day began to break and Red Deer had to leave with the two ponies he had staked there for his comrade and girl, or somebody would see him.

So he left.

Home Is the Hunter (1994), Gary Kapp. Oil, 34″ × 46″.

Now when it was getting light in the tepee, the girl awoke and the first thing she saw was a terrible animal, all white with black stripes on it, lying asleep beside her bed. So she screamed, and then the old woman screamed and the old man yelled. High Horse jumped up, scared almost to death, and he nearly knocked the tepee down getting out of there.

People were coming running from all over the village with guns and bows and axes, and everybody was yelling.

By now High Horse was running so fast that he hardly touched the ground at all, and he looked so terrible that the people fled from him and let him run. Some braves wanted to shoot at him, but the others said he might be some sacred being and it would bring bad trouble to kill him.

High Horse made for the river that was near, and in among the brush he found a hollow tree and

Night Horse (1992), C. J. Wells. Oil, 70″ × 60″, courtesy of Joan Marcus Fine Art.

dived into it. Afterwhile some braves came there and he could hear them saying that it was some bad spirit that had come out of the water and gone back in again.

That morning the people were ordered to break camp and move away from there. So they did, while High Horse was hiding in his hollow tree.

Now Red Deer had been watching all this from his own tepee and trying to look as though he were as much surprised and scared as all the others. So when the camp moved, he sneaked back to where he had seen his comrade disappear. When he was down there in the brush, he called, and High Horse answered, because he knew his friend's voice. They washed off the paint from High Horse and sat down on the river bank to talk about their troubles.

High Horse said he never would go back to the village as long as he lived and he did not

care what happened to him now. He said he was going to go on the war-path all by himself. Red Deer said: "No, cousin, you are not going on the war-path alone, because I am going with you."

So Red Deer got everything ready, and at night they started out on the war-path all alone. After several days they came to a Crow camp just about sundown, and when it was dark they sneaked up to where the Crow horses were grazing, killed the horse guard, who was not thinking about enemies because he thought all the Lakotas were far away, and drove off about a hundred horses.

They got a big start because all the Crow horses stampeded and it was probably morning before the Crow warriors could catch any horses to ride. Red Deer and High Horse fled with their herd three days and nights before they reached the village of their people. Then they drove the whole herd right into the village and up in front of the girl's tepee. The old man was there, and High Horse called out to him and asked if he thought maybe that would be enough horses for his girl. The old man did not wave him away

that time. It was not the horses that he wanted. What he wanted was a son who was a real man and good for something.

So High Horse got his girl after all, and I think he deserved her. ❖

LITERARY LINK

I Will Fight No More Forever

Chief Joseph

Below is the famous surrender speech made in 1877 by Chief Joseph of the Nez Perce (něz′ pûrs′). In that year, Chief Joseph and his people, after being forced from their traditional lands in northeastern Oregon, had won several battles with U.S. Army forces led by General Oliver O. Howard. However, their only recourse lay in retreat. Chief Joseph and his remaining group of 750 traveled more than 1,000 miles and were only 40 miles from the Canadian border when they were surrounded by more U.S. troops. Following a five-day siege in which several chieftains were killed, including his own brother, Chief Joseph handed over his rifle.

Chief Joseph. Courtesy of the Heye Foundation, National Museum of the American Indian, Smithsonian Institution (33738).

Tell General Howard I know his heart. What he told me before I have in my heart. I am tired of fighting. Our chiefs are killed. Looking Glass is dead. Toohoolhoolzote is dead. The old men are all dead. It is the young men who say yes or no. He who led on the young men is dead. It is cold and we have no blankets. The little children are freezing to death. My people, some of them, have run away to the hills, and have no blankets, no food; no one knows where they are—perhaps freezing to death. I want to have time to look for my children and see how many of them I can find. Maybe I shall find them among the dead. Hear me, my chiefs! I am tired; my heart is sick and sad. From where the sun now stands I will fight no more forever.

Thinking through the LITERATURE

Connect to the Literature

1. **What Do You Think?**
   What thoughts came to mind as you read this tale of courtship? Share your reaction with a partner.

   Comprehension Check
   - What goes wrong the first time High Horse tries to steal the girl?
   - How does High Horse finally win the girl?

Think Critically

2. Do you think High Horse deserved to marry the girl he loved? Give reasons for your answer.

3. How might things have worked out if High Horse had just stolen the girl, as he had first planned to do?

   THINK ABOUT
   - how he and the girl might have felt about each other afterward
   - how the girl's parents and others might have viewed him

4. **ACTIVE READING   IDENTIFYING AUTHOR'S PURPOSE**
   Based on the questionnaire you made in your
   READER'S NOTEBOOK, what do you think were Black Elk's two most important purposes for telling this story? Cite evidence to support your answer.

5. "He was always teaching me things," Black Elk said of Watanye, who told him this story. In your opinion, what values does "High Horse's Courting" teach?

Extend Interpretations

6. **Comparing Texts** In one section of *Black Elk Speaks,* Black Elk mourns what the Sioux lost after the massacre at Wounded Knee (see quotation on page 633), much as Chief Joseph, on page 651, mourns what the Nez Perce lost in their final battle with U.S. Army forces. If you were a spiritual leader of a group, as these men were, how would you help your people survive such a defeat?

7. **The Writer's Style** What makes this story sound as if it were being told to someone, instead of read from a book? Support your answer with examples.

8. **Connect to Life** Compare and contrast the courtship customs of the Sioux with those praticed among your own circle of friends and family.

Literary Analysis

ORAL LITERATURE "High Horse's Courting" is an example of **oral literature,** literature that is passed from one generation to another by performance or word of mouth. *Black Elk Speaks* was written primarily to record the traditional Sioux way of life that was destroyed with the coming of whites. Stories that are communicated orally are alive in a way that written stories are not. When a story is committed to paper it becomes fixed—it is set in print. In contrast, oral stories change because they are often retold in slightly different ways, depending on who the speaker is, what he or she remembers about the story, and the words he or she chooses in the retelling.

Cooperative Learning Activity
Divide this tale among the members of a small group of classmates. Have each group member retell a portion of the tale in his or her own words. Use gestures and vary the tone of voice to make the story come alive. How was the story altered during the performance?

Choices & CHALLENGES

Writing Options

Modernizing a Story Write a story outline that adapts this tale to a modern setting. What obstacles might a young person today have to overcome to win his or her love? What would he or she offer instead of horses? Save your outline in your **Working Portfolio.**

Activities & Explorations

Talk Show Act out a talk-show interview with High Horse, the girl he loved, the girl's father, and Red Deer. The audience should ask questions about the characters' reasons for acting and feeling as they did at specific points in the tale. ~ **SPEAKING AND LISTENING**

Inquiry & Research

Sioux Culture Find out more about traditional Sioux (Lakota) courtship and marriage customs or research any other aspects of Sioux culture that interest you, such as bison hunting or spirituality. Share your knowledge in an oral presentation.

Black Elk
1863–1950

Other Works
The Sacred Pipe

John G. Neihardt
1881–1973

Other Works
Collected Poems
Indian Tales and Others
When the Tree Flowered

A Boyhood Vision At age 9, Black Elk had a vision in which he was given the power to help his fellow Oglala Sioux. He later interpreted his vision to mean that he should help his people survive the coming of white settlers—a belief that grew stronger as he witnessed the defeat of General George Custer's troops at the Battle of Little Bighorn.

Betrayal and Violence In his 20s, Black Elk joined Buffalo Bill's Wild West Show, hoping to learn from the whites something that would benefit his people. In 1889, after touring Europe with the show, he returned home to find that a new treaty had deprived his tribe of half its land. Tensions between the Sioux and the U.S. Army led, in the following year, to the Battle of Wounded Knee, in which soldiers massacred nearly 300 unarmed Sioux men, women, and children.

Reflections of the Past For the rest of his life, Black Elk lived on the Pine Ridge Reservation in South Dakota, saddened that he had failed to save his people. In 1931 he told the story of his life and visions to John G. Neihardt, who helped him write his life story, *Black Elk Speaks.*

The Stamp of the Frontier John G. Neihardt grew up in the frontier town of Wayne, Nebraska. From 1901 to 1907, he lived near the Omaha Indian Reservation. His experiences with the Omaha and other tribes that lived on the Great Plains influenced his poetry and fiction.

Literary Achievements Between 1915 and 1941, Neihardt published a five-part epic poem, *The Cycle of the West,* about the displacement of Native Americans by white settlers in the 1800s. While doing research for the final part of this epic—*The Song of the Messiah*—he met with Black Elk. The result of their talks was Neihardt's most popular book, *Black Elk Speaks.*

Career Highlights From 1943 to 1948, Neihardt served with the Bureau of Indian Affairs. In earlier years, he had worked as the literary editor of the *Minneapolis Journal* and the *St. Louis Post-Dispatch.* He also taught poetry at the University of Nebraska and at the University of Missouri. Neihardt was named Nebraska's poet laureate in 1921.

Author Study
Mark Twain

OVERVIEW

Life and Times   654

from The Autobiography of
Mark Twain ~ AUTOBIOGRAPHY   658

from Life on the
Mississippi ~ MEMOIR   669

Epigrams   678

The Notorious Jumping
Frog of Calaveras County
~ SHORT STORY   679

The First Jumping Frog
~ ARTICLE   684

The Author's Style   686

Author Study Project   687

"The human race has one really effective weapon, and that is laughter."

—*Mark Twain*

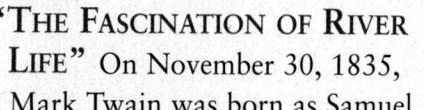

HIS LIFE
HIS TIMES

An American Legend

For generations of readers, Mark Twain has embodied the spirit of America. A poor boy who worked his way to international fame, Twain used his comic genius to comment on human nature and the pretensions of his day. Read more about this American spokesman who made people laugh even as he made them think about themselves and their society.

1835–1910

"THE FASCINATION OF RIVER LIFE" On November 30, 1835, Mark Twain was born as Samuel Langhorne Clemens in Florida, Missouri. When Clemens was four years old, his family moved some 30 miles to the Mississippi River town of Hannibal, a bustling port of about 500 people. When he was 11, his father died of pneumonia. To help support the family, Clemens took jobs as a grocery clerk and delivery boy. When he was 13, a local print shop hired him as an apprentice, and a few years

1835
Is born Nov. 30 as Samuel Langhorne Clemens in Florida, Missouri

1839
Moves with family to Hannibal, Missouri

1846
Clemens's father dies

1830   **1840**

1835
Halley's comet appears.

1836
Martin Van Buren is elected president.

1838
Native Americans walk the Trail of Tears.

1848
Gold is discovered in California.

later, he became a pressman at his brother Orion's newspaper. Before long, he was writing comic sketches for the newspaper and itching to travel.

Clemens left Hannibal at the age of 18. Four years later, he decided to seek his fortune in South America. He boarded a Mississippi River steamboat for New Orleans, but along the way, he made a life-changing decision. Horace Bixby, a veteran steamboat pilot whom Clemens met on the voyage, taught him "how to steer the boat and thus made the fascination of river life more potent than ever" for Clemens. Under Bixby's stern guidance, Clemens became a licensed riverboat pilot. He reveled in a job that suited his love of freedom. And he got an education. Clemens wrote later, "When I find a well-drawn character in fiction or biography I generally take a warm personal interest in him, for the reason that I have known him before—met him on the river."

The steamboat caught the imagination of young Sam Clemens.

LITERARY Contributions

Many writers and critics hail Mark Twain as an author whose work has had a lasting effect on 20th-century fiction. One of them, Ernest Hemingway, remarked that "all modern American literature comes from one book by Mark Twain, called *Huckleberry Finn*." Twain's ability to bring ordinary American voices into the realm of art is demonstrated in these major works:

Novels
The Gilded Age (1873)
The Adventures of Tom Sawyer (1876)
The Prince and the Pauper (1881)
The Adventures of Huckleberry Finn (1884)

Tales and Sketches
The Celebrated Jumping Frog of Calaveras County, and Other Sketches (1867)
Mark Twain's Sketches, New and Old (1875)
The Stolen White Elephant and Other Stories (1882)

Travel Sketches
The Innocents Abroad (1869)

Other Works
Roughing It (1872)
Life on the Mississippi (1883)
How to Tell a Story and Other Essays (1897)
Mark Twain's Autobiography (incomplete at his death; published posthumously in 1924)

1851
Takes job at his brother Orion's newspaper

Clemens as a young man

1859
Becomes Mississippi riverboat pilot

1863
Starts using the pen name Mark Twain

1865
Earns national fame with "The Notorious Jumping Frog of Calaveras County"

1869
Publishes *The Innocents Abroad*, based on his travels

1850   **1860**

1852
Harriet Beecher Stowe publishes *Uncle Tom's Cabin.*

1860
Abraham Lincoln is elected president.

1861
The Civil War begins.

1863
Lincoln issues the Emancipation Proclamation.

1865
The Confederacy surrenders at Appomattox; Lincoln is assassinated.

1868
President Johnson is impeached; Grant is elected president.

Author Study: *Mark Twain*

"A PICNIC ON A GRAND SCALE" In 1861, when the Civil War halted shipping on the Mississippi, 26-year-old Clemens traveled west to Nevada with his brother. At first, he tried mining and prospecting for gold and silver—a dismal failure that turned him back to writing. In 1862, he took a $25-a-week job as a journalist for the Virginia City *Territorial Enterprise*. In 1863, he published his first article under the pen name "Mark Twain," riverboat jargon for water two fathoms, or 12 feet, deep—water just deep enough to keep a steamboat safely afloat. By the time Twain left the West three years later, his star was rising. He debuted as a stage performer, riveting audiences with his entertaining stories. Even more important, he had won national fame with his humorous tale "The Notorious Jumping Frog of Calaveras County."

Twain sailed to Europe and the Middle East in 1867, enjoying "a picnic on a grand scale," as he put it. Along the way, he supplied irreverent newspaper articles about his fellow travelers and foreign manners to papers in California and New York City. Later, Twain expanded the articles into his first and highly successful book, *The Innocents Abroad*. But the trip had another important consequence, too. Aboard ship, Twain met Charley Langdon, the 18-year-old son of a wealthy New York coal merchant. One day Charley showed Twain a picture of his handsome older sister, Olivia, and from that moment, Twain was charmed.

Twain and Olivia Langdon were married in 1870, and the couple settled in Hartford, Connecticut. Over the next two decades, Twain focused his talents and energies on serious writing, producing his greatest works. Among the most important were *The Adventures of Tom Sawyer* (1876), *Life on the Mississippi* (1883), and his masterpiece, *The Adventures of Huckleberry Finn* (1885). It was also during these years that Twain matured into America's first celebrity author.

As America developed a national identity, people looked to writers like Twain to create true-to-life images of Americans. Twain's characters reflected the reality of a new nation that was growing rapidly. His realism, his truthful imitation of real life, won him national favor. All over the country, people felt they knew this shaggy-haired, drawling

1870
Marries Olivia Langdon

1876
Publishes
The Adventures of Tom Sawyer

1884
Launches a publishing company

1885
Publishes
The Adventures of Huckleberry Finn

1870

1880

1876
George Custer is killed at Little Bighorn.

1879
F. W. Woolworth opens his five-and-ten-cent store.

1880
John D. Rockefeller's Standard Oil Company of Ohio controls U.S. refining business.

1886
Statue of Liberty is dedicated.

character who made a splash in his trademark white suit.

"A VAST EMPTINESS" In the last decades of his life, Twain suffered one painful loss after another. A publishing business he began in the 1880s failed in 1894, forcing him to declare bankruptcy. For several years, Twain wrote and lectured abroad at a grueling pace in order to repay his debts and rebuild his fortune. Between 1896 and 1910, the loss of his cherished Hartford mansion and the death of his wife and two of his daughters plunged him into despair. Twain wrote intensely during this painful period, but his humor grew more biting. After the death of his daughter Jean on Christmas Eve, 1909, Twain fell ill. Feeling lost in "a vast emptiness," he died a few months later, on April 21.

More Online: Author Link
www.mcdougallittell.com

The Gilded Age

The last three decades of the 19th century were characterized by an explosive growth in technology, which was accompanied by a growth in corruption in politics, business, and society. Between 1870 and 1890, the gap between the rich and the poor grew wider than ever before. For example, on one side of New York City, elegant and ornate hotels and mansions flourished, yet many people in the city were living in shanty towns or tenements. Mark Twain dubbed this period "the Gilded Age"—a satirical commentary on the extravagant displays of the wealthy.

Mrs. Jay Gould, 1908

1894
Publishing company goes bankrupt

1895
Begins overseas lecture tour to raise money

1901
Death of Olivia on June 5

1910
Dies April 21 at Redding, Connecticut

1890

1900

1910

1890
Immigration to America by Europeans soars.

1903
W. E. B. Du Bois publishes *The Souls of Black Folk.*

1904
Theodore Roosevelt is elected president.

1909
National Association for the Advancement of Colored People forms.

1910
Halley's comet returns.

from The Autobiography of Mark Twain

Connect to Your Life

Deception! In this selection, Mark Twain describes how he once talked his way into a hypnotist's act and pretended to be hypnotized. Have you ever pretended to be something you're not? If so, why did you do it? What did you say to convince other people to believe you? How did you eventually feel about deceiving other people? Jot down the incident.

Build Background

The Mesmerizer The events in this excerpt from Twain's autobiography take place around 1850, when Americans had no televisions, radios, computer games, compact discs, or movies for entertainment. Small-town people like Twain turned to local talent or traveling minstrel shows and steamboat performances for amusement. The showmen drew crowds with magic shows and performances by ventriloquists and mesmerizers, or hypnotists. As you probably know, a hypnotist places a person in a suggestible, trancelike state; the hypnotist then may order the person to perform antics.

WORDS TO KNOW
Vocabulary Preview

collusion	implacable
confederate	odious
credulity	rapt
dissemble	unassailable
gullible	usurping

Focus Your Reading

LITERARY ANALYSIS **IRONY** One element that adds tension and humor to Twain's story is **irony,** the contrast between appearance and actuality. At the mesmerizer's show, the young Twain, already a ham, is eager to show off his imagination and intellect by pretending to be hypnotized. He expects to relish the success of his exploits but is instead disappointed by the deception and trickery of hypnotism:

> *The truth is I did not have to wait long to get tired of my triumphs. . . . The glory which is built upon a lie soon becomes a most unpleasant incumbrance.*

Watch for other examples of irony as you read Twain's story.

ACTIVE READING **PREDICTING** **Predicting** is the process of using text clues to make a reasonable guess about what will happen in a story. Sometimes a story's twist will surprise you; sometimes your predictions will hit the mark. Either way, watching for text clues can help you to find the irony in Twain's story. For example, what clues in the passage below could help you predict what will happen next?

> *When I saw the "subjects" perform their foolish antics on the platform and make the people laugh and shout and admire I had a burning desire to be a subject myself.*

READER'S NOTEBOOK As you read, use a chart like this one to record your predictions and the clues from the text that led you to make an educated guess. Here's an example:

Predictions	Text Clues
I predict he'll find a way to get involved.	Twain says he can't resist the temptation to be a subject.

from THE AUTOBIOGRAPHY OF MARK TWAIN

MARK TWAIN

An exciting event in our village was the arrival of the mesmerizer.[1] I think the year was 1850. As to that I am not sure but I know the month—it was May; that detail has survived the wear of fifty years. A pair of connected little incidents of that month have served to keep the memory of it green for me all this time; incidents of no consequence and not worth embalming, yet my memory has preserved them carefully and flung away things of real value to give them space and make them comfortable. The truth is, a person's memory has no more sense than his conscience and no appreciation whatever of values and proportions. However, never mind those trifling incidents; my subject is the mesmerizer now.

He advertised his show and promised marvels. Admission as usual: 25 cents, children half price. The village had heard of mesmerism in a general way but had not encountered it yet. Not many people attended the first night but next day they had so many wonders to tell that everybody's curiosity was fired and after that for a fortnight the magician had prosperous times. I was fourteen or fifteen years old, the age at which a boy is willing to endure all things, suffer all things short of death by fire, if thereby he may be conspicuous and show off before the public; and so, when I saw the "subjects" perform their foolish antics on the platform and make the people laugh and shout and admire I had a burning desire to be a subject myself.

Every night for three nights I sat in the row of candidates on the platform and held the magic disk[2] in the palm of my hand and gazed at it and tried to get sleepy, but it was a failure; I remained wide awake and had to retire defeated, like the majority. Also, I had to sit there and be gnawed with envy of Hicks, our journeyman;[3] I had to sit there and see him scamper and jump when Simmons the enchanter exclaimed, "See the snake! See the snake!" and hear him say, "My, how beautiful!" in response to the suggestion that he was observing a splendid sunset; and so on—the whole insane business. I couldn't laugh, I couldn't applaud; it filled me with bitterness to have others do it and to have people make a hero of Hicks and crowd around him when the show was over and ask him for more and more particulars of the wonders he had seen in his visions and manifest in many ways that they were proud to be acquainted

---

1. **mesmerizer** (mĕz′mə-rī′zər): hypnotist; from the name of an Austrian physician, Franz Anton Mesmer, who popularized hypnotism in the 1770s.
2. **magic disk:** object used by the mesmerizer to focus a subject's attention, helping him or her to achieve the hypnotic state.
3. **journeyman:** sound and experienced, but not brilliant, craftsman or performer.

with him. Hicks—the idea! I couldn't stand it; I was getting boiled to death in my own bile.[4]

On the fourth night temptation came and I was not strong enough to resist. When I had gazed at the disk a while I pretended to be sleepy and began to nod. Straightway came the professor and made passes over my head and down my body and legs and arms, finishing each pass with a snap of his fingers in the air to discharge the surplus electricity;[5] then he began to "draw" me with the disk, holding it in his fingers and telling me I could not take my eyes off it, try as I might; so I rose slowly, bent and gazing, and followed that disk all over the place, just as I had seen the others do. Then I was put through the other paces. Upon suggestion I fled from snakes, passed buckets at a fire, became excited over hot steamboat-races, made love to imaginary girls and kissed them, fished from the platform and landed mud cats[6] that outweighed me—and so on, all the customary marvels. But not in the customary way. I was cautious at first and watchful, being afraid the professor would discover that I was an impostor and drive me from the platform in disgrace; but as soon as I realized that I was not in danger, I set myself the task of terminating Hicks's usefulness as a subject and of <u>usurping</u> his place.

It was a sufficiently easy task. Hicks was born honest, I without that incumbrance[7]—so some people said. Hicks saw what he saw and reported accordingly, I saw more than was visible and added to it such details as could help. Hicks had no imagination; I had a double supply. He was born calm, I was born excited. No vision could start a rapture in him and he was constipated as to language, anyway; but if I saw a vision I emptied the dictionary onto it and lost the remnant of my mind into the bargain.

At the end of my first half-hour Hicks was a thing of the past, a fallen hero, a broken idol, and I knew it and was glad and said in my heart, "Success to crime!" Hicks could never have been mesmerized to the point where he could kiss an imaginary girl in public or a real one either, but I was competent. Whatever Hicks had failed in, I made it a point to succeed in, let the cost be what it might, physically or morally. He had shown several bad defects and I had made a note of them. For instance, if the magician asked, "What do you see?" and left him to invent a vision for himself, Hicks was dumb and blind, he couldn't see a thing nor say a word, whereas the magician soon found out that when it came to seeing visions of a stunning and marketable sort I could get along better without his help than with it.

Then there was another thing: Hicks wasn't worth a tallow dip[8] on mute mental suggestion. Whenever Simmons stood behind him and gazed at the back of

---

4. **bile** (bīl): bitterness; ill humor.

5. **discharge . . . electricity:** It was once believed, wrongly, that hypnosis was linked to electricity and magnetism.

6. **mud cats:** catfish.

7. **incumbrance:** burden; obligation.

8. **wasn't worth a tallow dip:** wasn't any good. A tallow dip was an inexpensive candle.

his skull and tried to drive a mental suggestion into it, Hicks sat with vacant face and never suspected. If he had been noticing he could have seen by the rapt faces of the audience that something was going on behind his back that required a response. Inasmuch as I was an impostor I dreaded to have this test put upon me, for I knew the professor would be "willing" me to do something, and as I couldn't know what it was, I should be exposed and denounced. However, when my time came, I took my chance. I perceived by the tense and expectant faces of the people that Simmons was behind me willing me with all his might. I tried my best to imagine what he wanted but nothing suggested itself. I felt ashamed and miserable then. I believed that the hour of my disgrace was come and that in another moment I should go out of that place disgraced. I ought to be ashamed to confess it but my next thought was not how I could win the compassion of kindly hearts by going out humbly and in sorrow for my misdoings, but how I could go out most sensationally and spectacularly.

There was a rusty and empty old revolver lying on the table among the "properties"[9] employed in the performances. On May Day two or three weeks before there had been a celebration by the schools and I had had a quarrel with a big boy who was the school bully and I had not come out of it with credit.[10] That boy was now seated in the middle of the house, halfway down the main aisle. I crept stealthily and impressively toward the table, with a dark and murderous scowl on my face, copied from a popular romance, seized the revolver suddenly, flourished it, shouted the bully's name, jumped off the platform and made a rush for him and chased him out of the house before the paralyzed people could interfere to save him. There was a storm of applause, and the magician, addressing the house, said, most impressively—

"That you may know how really remarkable this is and how wonderfully developed a subject we have in this boy, I assure you that without a single spoken word to guide him he has carried out what I mentally commanded him to do, to the minutest detail. I could have stopped him at a moment in his vengeful career by a mere exertion of my will, therefore the poor fellow who has escaped was at no time in danger."

So I was not in disgrace. I returned to the platform a hero and happier than I have ever been in this world since. As regards mental suggestion, my fears of it were gone. I judged that in case I failed to guess what the professor might be willing me to do, I could count on putting up something that would answer just as well. I was right, and exhibitions of unspoken suggestion became a favorite with the public. Whenever I perceived that I was being willed to do something I got up and did something—anything that occurred to me—and the magician, not being a fool, always ratified it.

> Hicks had no IMAGINATION; I HAD A DOUBLE SUPPLY. HE WAS BORN CALM, I WAS BORN EXCITED.

---

9. **"properties"**: articles, other than costumes and scenery, that are used on the stage during a dramatic performance.

10. **credit**: honor or distinction.

THE MESMERIZER

When people asked me, "How *can* you tell what he is willing you to do?" I said, "It's just as easy," and they always said admiringly, "Well, it beats *me* how you can do it."

Hicks was weak in another detail. When the professor made passes over him and said "his whole body is without sensation now—come forward and test him, ladies and gentlemen," the ladies and gentlemen always complied eagerly and stuck pins into Hicks, and if they went deep Hicks was sure to wince, then that poor professor would have to explain that Hicks "wasn't sufficiently under the influence." But I didn't wince; I only suffered and shed tears on the inside. The miseries that a conceited boy will endure to keep up his "reputation"! And so will a conceited man; I know it in my own person and have seen it in a hundred thousand others. That professor ought to have protected me and I often hoped he would, when the tests were unusually severe, but he didn't. It may be that he was deceived as well as the others, though I did not believe it nor think it possible. Those were dear good people but they must have carried simplicity and <u>credulity</u> to the limit. They would stick a pin in my arm and bear on it until they drove it a third of its length in, and then be lost in wonder that by a mere exercise of will power the professor could turn my arm to iron and make it insensible to pain. Whereas it was not insensible at all; I was suffering agonies of pain.

After that fourth night, that proud night, that triumphant night, I was the only subject. Simmons invited no more candidates to the platform. I performed alone every night the rest of the fortnight. Up to that time a dozen wise old heads, the intellectual aristocracy of the town, had held out as <u>implacable</u> unbelievers. I was as hurt by this as if I were engaged in some honest occupation.

There is nothing surprising about this. Human beings feel dishonor the most, sometimes, when they most deserve it. That handful of overwise old gentlemen kept on shaking their heads all the first week and saying they had seen no marvels there that could not have been produced by <u>collusion</u>; and they were pretty vain of their unbelief too and liked to show it and air it and be superior to the ignorant and the <u>gullible</u>. Particularly old Dr. Peake, who was the ringleader of the irreconcilables and very formidable; for he was an F.F.V.,[11] he was learned, white-haired and venerable, nobly and richly clad in the fashions of an earlier and a courtlier day, he was large and stately, and he not only seemed wise but was what he seemed in that regard. He had great influence and his opinion upon any matter was worth much more than that of any other person in the community. When I conquered him at last, I knew I was undisputed master of the field; and now after more than fifty years I acknowledge with a few dry old tears that I rejoiced without shame.

In 1847 we were living in a large white house on the corner of Hill and Main Streets—a house that still stands but isn't large now although it hasn't lost a plank; I saw it a year ago and noticed that shrinkage. My father died in it in March of the year mentioned but our family did not move out of it until some months afterward. Ours was not the only family in the house; there was another, Dr. Grant's. One day Dr. Grant and Dr. Reyburn argued a matter on the street with sword canes and Grant was brought home

---

11. **F.F.V.:** First Family of Virginia. Dr. Peake has high social status because his ancestors were among the first settlers of Virginia.

multifariously punctured. Old Dr. Peake caulked the leaks and came every day for a while to look after him.

The Grants were Virginians, like Peake, and one day when Grant was getting well enough to be on his feet and sit around in the parlor and talk, the conversation fell upon Virginia and old times. I was present but the group were probably unconscious of me, I being only a lad and a negligible quantity.[12] Two of the group— Dr. Peake and Mrs. Crawford, Mrs. Grant's mother—had been of the audience when the Richmond theater burned down thirty-six years before, and they talked over the frightful details of that memorable tragedy. These were eye-witnesses, and with their eyes I saw it all with an intolerable vividness: I saw the black smoke rolling and tumbling toward the sky, I saw the flames burst through it and turn red, I heard the shrieks of the despairing, I glimpsed their faces at the windows, caught fitfully through the veiling smoke, I saw them jump to their death or to mutilation worse than death. The picture is before me yet and can never fade.

In due course they talked of the colonial mansion of the Peakes, with its stately columns and its spacious grounds, and by odds and ends I picked up a clearly defined idea of the place. I was strongly interested, for I had not before heard of such palatial things from the lips of people who had seen them with their own eyes. One detail, casually dropped, hit my imagination hard. In the wall by the great front door there was a round hole as big as a saucer—a British cannon ball had made it in the war of the Revolution. It was breathtaking; it made history real; history had never been real to me before.

Very well, three or four years later, as already mentioned, I was king bee and sole "subject" in the mesmeric show; it was the beginning of the second week; the performance was half over; just then the majestic Dr. Peake with his ruffled bosom and wrist-bands and his gold-headed cane entered, and a deferential citizen vacated his seat beside the Grants and made the great chief take it. This happened while I was trying to invent something fresh in the way of vision, in response to the professor's remark— "Concentrate your powers. Look—look attentively. There—don't you see something? Concentrate—concentrate! Now then—describe it."

Without suspecting it, Dr. Peake, by entering the place, had reminded me of the talk of three years before. He had also furnished me capital and was become my <u>confederate</u>, an accomplice in my frauds. I began on a vision, a vague and dim one (that was part of the game at the beginning of a vision; it isn't best to see it too clearly at first, it might look as if you had come loaded with it). The vision developed by degrees and gathered swing, momentum, energy. It was the Richmond fire. Dr. Peake was cold at first and his fine face had a trace of polite scorn in it; but when he began to recognize that fire, that

---

12. **negligible quantity:** something insignificant or unimportant; nothing.

THE GLORY WHICH IS BUILT UPON A LIE SOON BECOMES A MOST UNPLEASANT INCUMBRANCE.

WORDS TO KNOW

confederate (kən-fĕd′ər-ĭt) *n.* one who assists in a plot; associate

expression changed and his eyes began to light up. As soon as I saw that, I threw the valves wide open and turned on all the steam and gave those people a supper of fire and horrors that was calculated to last them one while! They couldn't gasp when I got through—they were petrified. Dr. Peake had risen and was standing—and breathing hard. He said, in a great voice:

"My doubts are ended. No collusion could produce that miracle. It was totally impossible for him to know those details, yet he has described them with the clarity of an eyewitness—and with what <u>unassailable</u> truthfulness God knows I know!"

I saved the colonial mansion for the last night and solidified and perpetuated Dr. Peake's conversion with the cannon-ball hole. He explained to the house that I could never have heard of that small detail, which differentiated this mansion from all other Virginian mansions and perfectly identified it, therefore the fact stood proven that I had *seen* it in my vision. Lawks![13]

It is curious. When the magician's engagement closed there was but one person in the village who did not believe in mesmerism and I was the one. All the others were converted but I was to remain an implacable and unpersuadable disbeliever in mesmerism and hypnotism for close upon fifty years. This was because I never would examine them, in after life. I couldn't. The subject revolted me. Perhaps it brought back to me a passage in my life which for pride's sake I wished to forget; though I thought, or persuaded myself I thought, I should never come across a "proof" which wasn't thin and cheap and probably had a fraud like me behind it.

The truth is I did not have to wait long to get tired of my triumphs. Not thirty days, I think. The glory which is built upon a lie soon becomes a most unpleasant incumbrance. No doubt for a while I enjoyed having my exploits told and retold and told again in my presence and wondered over and exclaimed about, but I quite distinctly remember that there presently came a time when the subject was wearisome and <u>odious</u> to me and I could not endure the disgusting discomfort of it. I am well aware that the world-glorified doer of a deed of great and real splendor has just my experience; I know that he deliciously enjoys hearing about it for three or four weeks and that pretty soon after that he begins to dread the mention of it and by and by wishes he had been with the damned before he ever thought of doing that deed. I remember how General Sherman[14] used to rage and swear over "While we were marching through Georgia," which was played at him and sung at him everywhere he went; still, I think I suffered a shade more than the legitimate hero does, he being privileged to soften his misery with the reflection that his glory was at any rate golden and reproachless[15] in its origin, whereas I had no such privilege, there being no possible way to make mine respectable.

How easy it is to make people believe a lie and how hard it is to undo that work again! Thirty-five years after those evil exploits of mine I visited my old mother, whom I had not seen for ten years; and being moved by what seemed to me a rather noble and perhaps heroic impulse, I thought I would humble myself and confess my ancient fault. It cost me a great effort to make up my mind; I dreaded the sorrow that would rise in her face and the shame that would look out of her eyes; but after long and troubled reflection, the sacrifice seemed due and

---

13. **Lawks!:** an expression of wonder or amusement, shortened from "Lord, have mercy!"

14. **General Sherman:** William Tecumseh Sherman, the Union commander who led a destructive march from Atlanta, Georgia, to the Atlantic Ocean, cutting the Confederacy in two.

15. **reproachless:** so good and upright as to make any criticism impossible.

WORDS TO KNOW

unassailable (ŭn′ə-sā′lə-bəl) *adj.* impossible to dispute or disprove; undeniable
odious (ō′dē-əs) *adj.* arousing, or worthy of, strong dislike

right and I gathered my resolution together and made the confession.

To my astonishment there were no sentimentalities, no dramatics, no George Washington effects; she was not moved in the least degree; she simply did not believe me and said so! I was not merely disappointed, I was nettled[16] to have my costly truthfulness flung out of the market in this placid and confident way when I was expecting to get a profit out of it. I asserted and reasserted, with rising heat, my statement that every single thing I had done on those long-vanished nights was a lie and a swindle; and when she shook her head tranquilly and said she knew better, I put up my hand and *swore* to it— adding a triumphant, "*Now* what do you say?"

It did not affect her at all; it did not budge her the fraction of an inch from her position. If this was hard for me to endure, it did not begin with the blister she put upon the raw[17] when she began to put my sworn oath out of court with *arguments* to prove that I was under a delusion and did not know what I was talking about. Arguments! Arguments to show that a person on a man's outside can know better what is on his inside than he does himself. I had cherished some contempt for arguments before, I have not enlarged my respect for them since. She refused to believe that I had invented my visions myself; she said it was folly: that I was only a child at the time and could not have done it. She cited the Richmond fire and the colonial mansion and said they were quite beyond my capacities. Then I saw my chance! I said she was right—I didn't invent those; I got them from Dr. Peake. Even this great shot did not damage. She said Dr. Peake's evidence was better than mine, and he had said in plain words that it was impossible for me to have heard about those things. Dear, dear, what a grotesque and unthinkable situation: a confessed swindler convicted of honesty and condemned to acquittal by circum-stantial evidence furnished by the swindled!

I realized with shame and with impotent vexation that I was defeated all along the line. I had but one card left but it was a formidable one. I played it and stood from under. It seemed ignoble to demolish her fortress after she had defended it so valiantly but the defeated know not mercy. I played that master card. It was the pin-sticking. I said solemnly—

"I give you my honor, a pin was never stuck into me without causing me cruel pain."

She only said—

"It is thirty-five years. I believe you do think that now but I was there and I know better. You never winced."

She was so calm! and I was so far from it, so nearly frantic.

"Oh, my goodness!" I said, "let me *show* you that I am speaking the truth. Here is my arm; drive a pin into it—drive it to the head—I shall not wince."

She only shook her gray head and said with simplicity and conviction—

"You are a man now and could <u>dissemble</u> the hurt; but you were only a child then and could not have done it."

And so the lie which I played upon her in my youth remained with her as an unchallengeable truth to the day of her death. Carlyle[18] said "a lie cannot live." It shows that he did not know how to tell them. If I had taken out a life policy on this one the premiums would have bankrupted me ages ago. ❖

---

16. **nettled:** irritated; annoyed.

17. **the blister . . . raw:** a bad thing made even worse.

18. **Carlyle:** Thomas Carlyle, a British historian and essayist.

WORDS
TO
KNOW

dissemble (dĭ-sĕm′bəl) *v.* to disguise or conceal behind a false appearance

Connect to the Literature

1. **What Do You Think?** What did you find humorous about this selection? Explain.

Comprehension Check
- What prompted Twain to become a subject?
- What weaknesses made Hicks a bad subject?
- Why did Twain's feelings change after the mesmerizer left town?

Think Critically

2. How would you describe Twain's attitude toward himself as a boy and toward the people in his hometown?

3. Do you think it was wrong for young Twain to deceive people by pretending to be mesmerized? Explain your opinion.

THINK ABOUT
- why Twain decides to deceive people
- how he feels about deceiving
- his later failure to make his mother believe the truth

4. Do you agree with the statements Twain makes about human nature in the story? Consider Carlyle's statement that "a lie cannot live" and Twain's opposing viewpoint. Give reasons for your opinion.

5. **ACTIVE READING** **PREDICTING** Review your list of **predictions** and **clues.** Were you able to predict everything that happened? Or were you surprised by how some aspects of the story developed? Support your answer with evidence from the story.

Extend Interpretations

6. **Critic's Corner** Elmer J. Joseph, a member of our student advisory board, complained about this selection: "Much is left unsaid about what happened to the mesmerizer and whether he knew how much of an impostor the narrator was." Do you think the mesmerizer knew the young Twain was faking? Share your conclusions with other students, giving reasons for your views.

7. **Connect to Life** Twain wrote that the incidents in his autobiography "must interest the average human being because [these incidents] are of a sort which he is familiar with in his own life." Can you easily relate this story to your own life? Consider what you wrote for the Connect to Your Life.

Literary Analysis

IRONY **Irony** is the contrast between what we expect and what actually happens. In ironic situations, appearances are often deceiving and outcomes are usually surprising. The ugly duckling turns into a beautiful swan. The trusted friend turns out to be a phony.

In this selection, Twain relies on situational irony to poke fun at society and himself. In a story that uses **situational irony,** things turn out to be the opposite of what we expect, and characters are surprised by what actually happens.

Twain expects to enjoy the thrill of celebrity but soon finds his victory is hollow and worthless:

No doubt for a while I enjoyed having my exploits told and retold and told again in my presence . . . but . . . there presently came a time when the subject was wearisome and odious to me and I could not endure the disgusting discomfort of it.

Paired Activity Work with a partner to identify two or three other examples of situational irony in this story. Discuss what makes each example both ironic and humorous. You might use a chart like this one to organize your information.

Twain's Situational Irony	
What Twain Expects	**What Happens**
To enjoy the thrill of being the subject of hypnotism.	He is the only one in town who is not interested in hypnotism.

Writing Options

1. Screenplay Script If you were writing a screenplay of this excerpt, how would you have Twain tell the story of the Richmond Theater fire? Analyze Twain's account of hearing the story. Then write the lines that Twain would deliver. Put your script in your **Working Portfolio.**

2. Instruction Manual Working in a small group, put together tips for an instruction manual called *How to Be a Good Mesmerizer.* Base your tips on the practices of Simmons (the mesmerizer) and his model "subject," the young Mark Twain.

3. Newspaper Report Imagine you're a reporter for the *Hannibal Chronicle* in 1850. Last night you saw the mesmerizer's show and watched Twain perform under hypnosis. You were so amazed that you couldn't wait to describe the events. Write an engaging article about the performance that captivated the audience.

Activities & Explorations

1. Stage Directions How would you stage a performance of the mesmerist and Twain's convincing performance? Pick one dramatic scene from the selection and write stage directions for it. Use the diagram below to show how the action progresses. ~ VIEWING AND REPRESENTING

2. Advertising Flyer Pretend that Twain goes on the road with the mesmerizer. Design a flyer advertising an upcoming performance in another Mississippi River town. ~ ART

Wings (off-stage)	Upstage Right	Upstage Center	Upstage Left	Wings (off-stage)
	Right	Center	Left	
	Downstage Right	Downstage Center	Downstage Left	

AUDIENCE

Inquiry & Research

Science Twain pretended to be hypnotized by the mesmerizer. But could he have really been hypnotized? Find out more about hypnosis using scientific journals, psychology journals, encyclopedias, and on-line resources. What is hypnosis? Does it really work? How is someone hypnotized? Is it dangerous? Report what you find to the class.

 More Online: Research Starter www.mcdougallittell.com

Vocabulary in Action

EXERCISE: ASSESSMENT PRACTICE For each group of words below, write the letter of the word that is the best synonym for the boldfaced word.

1. usurping (a) seizing, (b) defeating, (c) borrowing

2. rapt (a) hidden, (b) casual, (c) spellbound

3. unassailable (a) leaky, (b) unquestionable, (c) mistaken

4. gullible (a) doubtful, (b) overtrusting, (c) excitable

5. collusion (a) conspiracy, (b) mixture, (c) idea

6. dissemble (a) feel, (b) disconnect, (c) hide

7. implacable (a) quiet, (b) indecisive, (c) unyielding

8. credulity (a) payment, (b) trust, (c) respect

9. odious (a) disgusting, (b) secretive, (c) humble

10. confederate (a) falsity, (b) accomplice, (c) team

WORDS TO KNOW					
	collusion	credulity	gullible	odious	unassailable
	confederate	dissemble	implacable	rapt	usurping

Building Vocabulary

Several Words to Know in this lesson contain prefixes and suffixes. For an in-depth study of word parts, see page 1130.

from Life on the Mississippi

Memoir by MARK TWAIN

Connect to Your Life

A Change of Heart In this excerpt, Twain recalls how his view of the Mississippi River changed as he became a riverboat pilot. Have you ever experienced a change of heart as you learned more about a person, an activity, a place, or a subject? What characteristics fascinated you in the beginning? Why? How did your feelings change as you became more knowledgeable? Describe such a situation with a group of classmates.

Build Background

Dangerous Expedition! In Twain's day, piloting a paddle steamboat was tricky because the Mississippi was constantly changing. South of St. Louis, Missouri, the huge brown river meanders, curving and looping back on itself, looking like "a long, pliant apple paring," as Twain put it. The powerful current would move from one side to the other, changing course often. Along this twisting course lurked hidden sandbars and submerged wrecks. Depending on the season, low water or floods added more dangers. Riverboat pilots constantly swapped precious information about the changing river as they sailed its perilous length.

Focus Your Reading

LITERARY ANALYSIS **DESCRIPTION** Twain brings the Mississippi River to life by using **description**—writing that helps a reader picture scenes, events, and people. By using colorful comparisons and vivid details, Twain helps us see the river as he did. Many of the details Twain uses appeal to our senses, like those in his description of sunset on the river.

> *A broad expanse of the river was turned to blood; in the middle distance the red hue brightened into gold. . . .*

Watch for more examples of descriptive details and comparisons as you read.

ACTIVE READING **VISUALIZING** When writers skillfully describe a scene or a character, they help readers **visualize,** or form a mental picture based on their written descriptions. The more precise the **details** a writer supplies about a person, setting, or event, the more vivid the picture you can form in your mind's eye. For example, what details make it so easy to visualize the part of the river described in this passage?

> *High above the forest wall a clean-stemmed dead tree waved a single leafy bough that glowed like a flame. . . .*

READER'S NOTEBOOK As you read, record the details and comparisons that help you to clearly visualize the Mississippi. Here's an example:

Mississippi Descriptions	
Details	**Comparison**
the red hue brightened into gold	leafy bough glows like a flame

from LIFE ON THE Mississippi

MARK TWAIN

A CUB-PILOT'S EXPERIENCE

What with lying on the rocks four days at Louisville, and some other delays, the poor old *Paul Jones* fooled away about two weeks in making the voyage from Cincinnati to New Orleans. This gave me a chance to get acquainted with one of the pilots, and he taught me how to steer the boat, and thus made the fascination of river life more potent than ever for me. . . .

I soon discovered two things. One was that a vessel would not be likely to sail for the mouth of the Amazon under ten or twelve years; and the other was that the nine or ten dollars still left in my pocket would not suffice for so impossible an exploration as I had planned, even if I could afford to wait for a ship. Therefore it followed that I must contrive a new career. The *Paul Jones* was now bound for St. Louis. I planned a siege against my pilot, and at the end of three hard days he surrendered. He agreed to teach me the

Mississippi River from New Orleans to St. Louis for five hundred dollars, payable out of the first wages I should receive after graduating. I entered upon the small enterprise of "learning" twelve or thirteen hundred miles of the great Mississippi River with the easy confidence of my time of life. If I had really known what I was about to require of my faculties,[1] I should not have had the courage to begin. I supposed that all a pilot

---

1. **faculties:** abilities.

had to do was to keep his boat in the river, and I did not consider that that could be much of a trick, since it was so wide.

The boat backed out from New Orleans at four in the afternoon, and it was "our watch" until eight. Mr. Bixby, my chief, "straightened her up," plowed her along past the sterns of the other boats that lay at the Levee,[2] and then said, "Here, take her; shave those steamships as close as you'd peel an apple." I took the wheel, and my heartbeat fluttered up into the hundreds; for it seemed to me that we were about to scrape the side off every ship in the line, we were so close. I held my breath and began to claw the boat away from the danger; and I had my own opinion of the pilot who had known no better than to get us into such peril, but I was too wise to express it. In half a minute I had a wide margin of safety intervening between the *Paul Jones* and the ships; and within ten seconds more I was set aside in disgrace, and Mr. Bixby was going into danger again and flaying me alive with abuse of my cowardice. I was stung, but I was obliged to admire the easy confidence with which my chief loafed from side to side of his wheel, and trimmed the ships so closely that disaster seemed ceaselessly imminent.[3] When he had cooled a little he told me that the easy water was close ashore and the current outside, and therefore we must hug the bank, upstream, to get the benefit of the former, and stay well out, downstream, to take advantage of the latter. In my own mind I resolved to be a downstream pilot and leave the upstreaming to people dead to prudence.[4]

---

2. **Levee** (lĕv′ē): a landing place for boats on a river.
3. **imminent** (ĭm′ə-nənt): about to happen.
4. **dead to prudence:** lacking good judgment.

Mark Twain at age fifteen.

yawed[5] too far from shore, and so dropped back into disgrace again and got abused.

The watch was ended at last, and we took supper and went to bed. At midnight the glare of a lantern shone in my eyes, and the night watchman said, "Come, turn out!" And then he left. I could not understand this extraordinary procedure; so I presently gave up trying to, and dozed off to sleep. Pretty soon the watchman was back again, and this time he was gruff. I was annoyed. I said,

"What do you want to come bothering around here in the middle of the night for? Now, as like as not, I'll not get to sleep again to-night."

The watchman said, "Well, if this ain't good, I'm blessed."

HELLO, WATCHMAN! AIN'T THE NEW CUB TURNED OUT YET?

Now and then Mr. Bixby called my attention to certain things. Said he, "This is Six-Mile Point." I assented. It was pleasant enough information, but I could not see the bearing of it. I was not conscious that it was a matter of any interest to me. Another time he said, "This is Nine-Mile Point." Later he said, "This is Twelve-Mile Point." They were all about level with the water's edge; they all looked about alike to me; they were monotonously unpicturesque. I hoped Mr. Bixby would change the subject. But no; he would crowd up around a point, hugging the shore with affection, and then say: "The slack water ends here, abreast this bunch of China trees; now we cross over." So he crossed over. He gave me the wheel once or twice, but I had no luck. I either came near chipping off the edge of a sugar plantation, or I

The "offwatch" was just turning in, and I heard some brutal laughter from them, and such remarks as "Hello, watchman! ain't the new cub turned out yet? He's delicate, likely. Give him some sugar in a rag, and send for the chambermaid to sing 'Rock-a-by Baby' to him."

About this time Mr. Bixby appeared on the scene. Something like a minute later I was climbing the pilothouse steps with some of my

5. **yawed:** swerved.

clothes on and the rest in my arms. Mr. Bixby was close behind, commenting. Here was something fresh[6]—this thing of getting up in the middle of the night to go to work. It was a detail in piloting that had never occurred to me at all. I knew that boats ran all night, but somehow I had never happened to reflect that somebody had to get up out of a warm bed to run them. I began to fear that piloting was not quite so romantic as I had imagined it was; there was something very real and worklike about this new phase of it. . . .

Mr. Bixby made for the shore and soon was scraping it, just the same as if it had been daylight. And not only that, but singing:

Father in heaven, the day is declining, etc.

It seemed to me that I had put my life in the keeping of a peculiarly reckless outcast. Presently he turned on me and said, "What's the name of the first point above New Orleans?"

I was gratified to be able to answer promptly, and I did. I said I didn't know.

"Don't *know*?"

This manner jolted me. I was down at the foot[7] again, in a moment. But I had to say just what I had said before.

"Well, you're a smart one!" said Mr. Bixby. "What's the name of the *next* point?"

Once more I didn't know.

"Well, this beats anything. Tell me the name of *any* point or place I told you."

I studied awhile and decided that I couldn't.

"Look here! What do you start out from, above Twelve-Mile Point, to cross over?"

"I—I—don't know."

"You—you—don't know?" mimicking my drawling manner of speech. "What *do* you know?"

"I—I—nothing, for certain."

"By the great Caesar's ghost, I believe you! You're the stupidest dunderhead I ever saw or ever heard of, so help me Moses! The idea of *you* being a pilot—you! Why, you don't know enough to pilot a cow down a lane."

Oh, but his wrath was up! He was a nervous man, and he shuffled from one side of his wheel to the other as if the floor was hot. He would boil awhile to himself, and then overflow and scald me again.

"Look here! What do you suppose I told you the names of those points for?"

I tremblingly considered a moment, and then the devil of temptation provoked me to say, "Well to—to—be entertaining, I thought."

This was a red rag to the bull. He raged and stormed so (he was crossing the river at the time) that I judged it made him blind, because he ran over the steering oar of a trading scow.[8] Of course the traders sent up a volley of red-hot profanity. Never was a man so grateful as Mr. Bixby was, because he was brimful, and here were subjects who could *talk back*. He threw open a window, thrust his head out, and such an irruption followed as I never had heard before. The fainter and farther away the scowmen's curses drifted, the higher Mr. Bixby lifted his voice and the weightier his adjectives grew. When he closed the window he was empty. You could have drawn a seine[9] through his system and not caught curses enough to disturb your mother with. Presently he said to me in the gentlest way, "My boy, you must get a little memorandum book; and every time I tell you a thing, put it down right away. There's only one way to be a pilot, and that is to get this entire river by heart. You have to know it just like A B C."

That was a dismal revelation to me, for my memory was never loaded with anything but blank cartridges. However, I did not feel discouraged long. I judged that it was best to

---

6. **fresh:** new.
7. **down at the foot:** at the bottom of the class.
8. **scow:** a flat-bottomed boat used chiefly to transport freight.
9. **seine** (sān): large fishing net.

make some allowances, for doubtless Mr. Bixby was "stretching."[10] . . .

By the time we had gone seven or eight hundred miles up the river, I had learned to be a tolerably plucky upstream steersman, in daylight; and before we reached St. Louis I had made a trifle of progress in night work, but only a trifle. I had a notebook that fairly bristled with the names of towns, "points," bars, islands, bends, reaches, etc.; but the information was to be found only in the notebook—none of it was in my head. It made my heart ache to think I had only got half of the river set down; for as our watch was four hours off and four hours on, day and night, there was a long four-hour gap in my book for every time I had slept since the voyage began. . . .

———✦———

. . . The face of the water, in time, became a wonderful book—a book that was a dead language to the uneducated passenger, but which told its mind to me without reserve, delivering its most cherished secrets as clearly as if it uttered them with a voice. And it was not a book to be read once and thrown aside, for it had a new story to tell every day. Throughout the long twelve hundred miles there was never a page that was void of interest, never one that you could leave unread without loss, never one that you would want to skip, thinking you could find higher enjoyment in some other thing. There never was so wonderful a book written by man; never one whose interest was so absorbing, so unflagging, so sparklingly renewed with every reperusal.[11] The passenger who could not read it was charmed with a peculiar sort of faint dimple on its surface (on the rare occasions when he did not overlook it altogether); but to the pilot that was an *italicized* passage; indeed, it was more than that, it was a legend of the largest capitals,[12] with a string of shouting exclamation points at the end of it, for it meant that a wreck or a rock was buried there that could tear the life out of the strongest vessel that ever floated. It is the faintest and simplest expression the water ever makes, and the most hideous to a pilot's eye. In truth, the passenger who could not read this book saw nothing but all manner of pretty pictures in it, painted by the sun and shaded by the clouds, whereas to the trained eye these were not pictures at all, but the grimmest and most dead earnest of reading matter.

Now when I had mastered the language of this water, and had come to know every trifling feature that bordered the great river as familiarly as I knew the letters of the alphabet, I had made a valuable acquisition. But I had lost something, too. I had lost something which could never be restored to me while I lived. All the grace, the beauty, the poetry, had gone out of the majestic river! I still kept in mind a certain wonderful sunset which I witnessed when steamboating was new to me. A broad expanse of the river was turned to blood; in the middle distance the red hue brightened into gold, through which a solitary log came floating, black and conspicuous; in one place a long, slanting mark lay sparkling upon the water; in another the surface was broken by boiling, tumbling rings, that were as many-tinted as an opal; where the ruddy flush was faintest, was a smooth spot that was covered with graceful circles and radiating lines, ever so delicately traced; the shore on our left was densely wooded, and the somber shadow that fell from this forest was broken in one place by a long, ruffled trail that shone like silver; and high above the forest wall a clean-stemmed dead tree waved a single leafy bough that glowed like a flame in the unobstructed splendor that was flowing from the sun. There were graceful curves, reflected images, woody heights, soft distances; and over the whole scene, far and near, the dissolving lights drifted steadily,

---

10. **"stretching":** exaggerating.

11. **reperusal** (rē′pə-roō′zəl): rereading.

12. **a legend of the largest capitals:** an inscription in large capital letters.

A. If I must tell, I will tell. It is the command-ments. I may say my commandments I hope.

Q. What commandment is it?

A. If I must tell, I will tell. It is a psalm.

Q. What psalm?

After a long time she muttered over some part of a psalm.

Q. Who do you serve?

Q. **Why do you hurt these children?**
A. **I do not hurt them. I scorn it.**

A. I serve God.

Q. What God do you serve?

A. The God that made heaven and earth, though she was not willing to mention the word *God*. Her answers were in a very wicked spiteful manner, reflecting and retorting against the authority with base and abusive words, and many lies she was taken in. It was here said that her husband had said that he was afraid that she either was a witch or would be one very quickly. The worshipful Mr. Hathorne asked him his reason why he said so of her, whether he had ever seen anything by her. He answered no, not in this nature, but it was her bad carriage[4] to him and indeed, said he, I may say with tears that she is an enemy to all good.

SALEM VILLAGE, MARCH THE 1ST, 1691–92

WRITTEN BY EZEKIEL CHEEVER

---

4. **carriage:** conduct.

[left column, partially torn]

...m for

...h the devil?

..., all of them, to
...vere the person
...hey all did look
...one of the persons
...esently they were all

...not

...t tell
... you
...oor

...nt them.

...employ then?

...ody. I scorn it.

...they thus tormented?

...know? You bring others here and
...rge me with it.

...ho was it?

...t know, but it was some you brought
...eeting house with you.

...rought you into the meeting house.

...you brought in two more.

...o was it then that tormented the
...n?

...as Osborne.

...at is it you say when you go muttering
...rom persons' houses?

...must tell, I will tell.

...tell us then.

Thinking through the LITERATURE

Connect to the Literature

1. **What Do You Think?**
   What is your reaction to Sarah Good's examination?

   Comprehension Check
   - Who are Sarah Good's alleged victims?
   - What charges made against her does Good deny?

Think Critically

2. **ACTIVE READING** **DETECTING BIAS** How would you describe the court officials' attitude toward Sarah Good? Support your answer with evidence from your **READER'S NOTEBOOK**.

   THINK ABOUT
   - the questions Good is asked
   - the comments made about her at the end of the transcript

3. What do you think accounts for the court officials' attitude?

4. Why do you think Sarah Good accuses Sarah Osborne of being a witch?

5. Why do you think Sarah Good's husband testifies against her?

6. What explanation can you offer for the apparent torments suffered by the girls who accuse Sarah Good?

Extend Interpretations

7. **Different Perspectives** In the preface to her book on the Salem witch trials, the 20th-century historian Marion L. Starkey writes, "Who in my day has a right to be indignant with people in Salem of 1692?" Why might she have made this comment? Do you agree that people of our time cannot or should not make judgments about people of earlier times?

8. **Connect to Life** Do you think that something similar to the Salem witch trials could happen in your community today? Why or why not? Consider the Connect to Your Life activity in which you discussed false accusations.

a
oce
trans
was a
The ph
answers
and Good
the transc
the trial?

Activity Com
summary and
did you learn o
transcript that yo
the summary? Wh
summary tell you
and answers on the
not? What parts of th
accurately reflect the
your view? Record dif
similarities in a large V
as shown. Then decide
document seems to be t
credible, or trustworthy,
information about the trial
the possible **motivations**
persons who wrote each do
and the kind of information
included. Discuss your opinio
classmates.

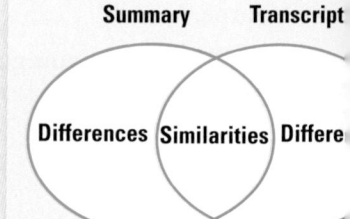

Summary   Transcript

Differences Similarities Differe

enriching it every passing moment with new marvels of coloring.

I stood like one bewitched. I drank it in, in a speechless rapture. The world was new to me, and I had never seen anything like this at home. But as I have said, a day came when I began to cease from noting the glories and the charms which the moon and the sun and the twilight wrought upon the river's face; another day came when I ceased altogether to note them. Then, if that sunset scene had been repeated, I should have looked upon it without rapture, and should have commented upon it, inwardly, after this fashion: "This sun means that we are going to have wind tomorrow; that floating log means that the river is rising, small thanks to it; that slanting mark on the water refers to a bluff reef[13] which is going to kill somebody's steamboat one of these nights, if it keeps on stretching out like that; those tumbling 'boils' show a dissolving bar and a changing channel there; the lines and circles in the slick water over yonder are a warning that that troublesome place is shoaling up[14] dangerously; that silver streak in the shadow of the forest is the 'break' from a new snag, and he has located himself in the very best place he could have found to fish for steamboats; that tall dead tree, with a single living branch, is not going to last long, and then how is a body ever going to get through this blind place at night without the friendly old landmark?"

No, the romance and beauty were all gone from the river. All the value any feature of it had for me now was the amount of usefulness it could furnish toward compassing the safe

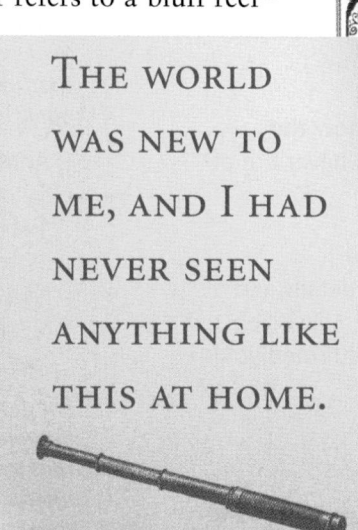

THE WORLD WAS NEW TO ME, AND I HAD NEVER SEEN ANYTHING LIKE THIS AT HOME.

Pilot's certificate issued to Mark Twain in 1859.

piloting of a steamboat. Since those days, I have pitied doctors from my heart. What does the lovely flush in a beauty's cheek mean to a doctor but a "break" that ripples above some deadly disease? Are not all her visible charms sown thick with what are to him the signs and symbols of hidden decay? Does he ever see her beauty at all, or doesn't he simply view her professionally, and comment upon her unwholesome condition all to himself? And doesn't he sometimes wonder whether he has gained most or lost most by learning his trade? ❖

---

13. **bluff reef:** an underwater ridge of rock.

14. **shoaling up:** becoming too shallow for safe navigation, because of a buildup of sand or silt in the riverbed.

Connect to the Literature

1. **What Do You Think?**
   What opinion of Mark Twain do you form from this selection? Support your opinion.

   Comprehension Check
   - What is the *Paul Jones?*
   - Why did Bixby think Twain was "the stupidest dunderhead"?
   - Why does Twain fear that the romance of the river is gone for him?

Think Critically

2. What are your impressions of the job of a riverboat pilot?

    THINK ABOUT
   - Twain's first impressions of piloting on the river
   - what changes Twain had to make in his everyday habits
   - the kinds of things Twain had to memorize and use on the job
   - the nature of the river

3. Do you think Twain convincingly explains how the Mississippi was like a book that one could never tire of reading? Defend your answer.

4. **ACTIVE READING** **VISUALIZING** Review your **READER'S NOTEBOOK** record of the details and comparisons that helped you **visualize** the Mississippi. Which details or comparisons changed or affirmed your previous impression of the river?

Extend Interpretations

5. **Comparing Texts** In his *Autobiography* and in *Life on the Mississippi,* Twain retells different episodes of his life. Which work do you prefer? Discuss your preferences in a small group. Cite evidence to support your opinion.

6. **What If?** Imagine that Twain gave up the idea of riverboat piloting after the first trip with Mr. Bixby. How might his view of the river have been different?

7. **Connect to Life** Recall your discussion, in the Connect to Your Life activity on page 669, about your own experiences with a change of heart. Do you think what you learned outweighed any sense of loss you felt? Explain.

Literary Analysis

DESCRIPTION **Description** is the process by which a writer creates a picture in words of a scene, an event, or a character. Two descriptive devices include:

- **Imagery,** or descriptive words and phrases a writer uses to re-create sensory experience. Sensory details appeal to the reader's senses of sight, hearing, smell, taste, and touch. For example, Twain uses the image of a jewel to help readers visualize the restless river:

In another [place] the surface was broken by boiling, tumbling rings, that were as many-tinted as an opal. . . .

- **Analogies,** which show the similarities between two things that are otherwise unlike each other. To help readers understand his fascination with the Mississippi, Twain compared the river to a book:

The face of the water, in time, became a wonderful book—a book that was a dead language to the uneducated passenger, but which told its mind to me without reserve, delivering its most cherished secrets. . . .

Paired Activity With a partner, look for additional examples of these descriptive devices in the selection. Use a chart like the one below to identify each example as imagery or analogy, and record the effects of each example on you as a reader.

Twain's Descriptions		
Detail	Descriptive Device	Effect

Writing Options

1. Diary Entry Twain says he would not have had the courage to learn the duties of a riverboat pilot had he known at the start what would be required of him. Write a diary entry describing the chores, routines, responsibilities—and rewards—of a pilot as Twain presents them in his memoir.

2. Magazine Article In October 1874, Twain wrote to the *Atlantic Monthly's* editor, William Dean Howells, about an idea he had for a series in the magazine, capturing the "old Mississippi days of steamboating glory and grandeur as I saw them." Pretend that you are Twain, and write a short article about your life on the Mississippi. Include details about the scenery along the riverbanks, the crowds of people you met, and the adventures you encountered.

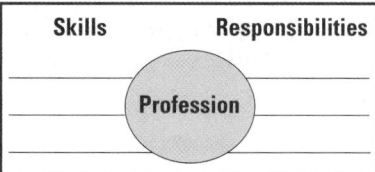

Writer
Mark Twain.

Activities & Explorations

1. Occupational Outlook Twain agreed to pay Mr. Bixby $500 for his apprenticeship. Today, most people learn the specific tasks and responsibilities of their professions while on the job. On a diagram like this one, identify another profession that would require on-the-job training. Be sure to include specific skills and responsibilities that an apprentice would gain. Present your diagram to the class.
~ SPEAKING AND LISTENING

2. Video Adaptation View the videotaped excerpt of *Life on the Mississippi* provided as a part of this program. Focus on the inter-action between Twain and Mr. Bixby. How is it similar to or different from their interaction in Twain's memoir? Does it realistically depict the actions in the memoir? In a class discussion, compare the videotape portrayals with those in the selection.
~ VIEWING AND REPRESENTING

 Literature in Performance

Inquiry & Research

A view of downtown , Hannibal, Missouri, on the Mississipi River, hometown of writer Mark Twain.

Geography Write a brief report on the Mississippi River as it is today. What effect does the river have on the people who live near it? Does it continue to be a thriving avenue of commerce, or has it been replaced? How has the river's physical appearance changed over the years?

 More Online: Research Starter
www.mcdougallittell.com

EPIGRAMS

MARK TWAIN

☼ Don't, like the cat, try to get more out of an experience than there is in it. The cat, having sat upon a hot stove lid, will not sit upon a hot stove lid again. Nor upon a cold stove lid.

☼ It is by the goodness of God that in our country we have those three unspeakably precious things: freedom of speech, freedom of conscience, and the prudence never to practice either of them.

☼ Man is the only animal that blushes. Or needs to.

☼ I am an old man and have known a great many troubles, but most of them have never happened.

☼ Nothing so needs reforming as other people's habits.

☼ When I was a boy of fourteen, my father was so ignorant I could hardly stand to have the old man around. But when I got to be twenty-one, I was astonished at how much the old man had learned in seven years.

☼ There are several good protections against temptations, but the surest is cowardice.

☼ Courage is resistance to fear, mastery of fear—not absence of fear.

☼ If you pick up a starving dog and make him prosperous, he will not bite you. This is the principal difference between a dog and a man.

☼ Put all your eggs in one basket, and—watch the basket.

☼ Good breeding consists in concealing how much we think of ourselves and how little we think of the other person.

☼ To promise not to do a thing is the surest way in the world to make a body want to go and do that very thing.

☼ Habit is habit, and not to be flung out of the window by any man, but coaxed downstairs a step at a time.

☼ One of the most striking differences between a cat and a lie is that a cat only has nine lives.

☼ Each person is born to one possession which outvalues all the others—his last breath.

☼ Everyone is a moon, and has a dark side which he never shows to anybody.

The Notorious Jumping Frog of Calaveras County

Short Story by MARK TWAIN

Connect to Your Life

Telling Tales The narrator of this story asks an old Westerner if he knows anything about a man named Smiley. The old man corners him and tells him an incredible tale about a wager on a jumping frog. Think about a situation in which you heard someone tell an outlandish story that others believed. What made the tale so convincing? Discuss this situation with a group of classmates.

Build Background

Western Humor Twain got the idea for this story in the gold hills outside San Francisco in 1865. While there, he mined for gold and spent time listening to local storytellers, who told this tale and others without ever cracking a smile. From these story-tellers, Twain learned two truths about humor writing that he used for the rest of his life: one, the manner in which a person tells a story is what makes it funny; and two, a successful humorist should always pretend to be dead serious.

WORDS TO KNOW
Vocabulary Preview

cavorting	infamous
commission	lattice
dilapidated	recommence
enterprising	tranquil
inclination	vagabond

Focus Your Reading

LITERARY ANALYSIS | TALL TALE | This story by Twain is an example of a **tall tale,** a distinctively American form of humorous story that features exaggeration. Much of a tall tale's rich humor comes from its use of **local color,** or writing that truthfully imitates ordinary life and brings a region alive by portraying its typical dress, mannerisms, customs, character types, and **dialects.** In Twain's tale, dialect, or local language, plays a crucial role, as seen in this passage:

> *Smiley was monstrous proud of his frog, and well he might be for fellers that had traveled and been everywheres all said he laid over any frog that ever* they see.

As you read, be on the lookout for the characteristics of a tall tale.

ACTIVE READING | UNDERSTANDING DIALECT | Sometimes **dialects** are so different from familiar language that they can be hard to understand. Moreover, writers often reproduce the sound of words in a dialect by using unconventional spellings. As you read Twain's tale, use these techniques to decode difficult passages of dialect:

• Read slowly. Listen to the words as if someone were speaking them. You might try reading the story aloud to help you recognize unusual words as you pronounce them.

• Use **context clues** to figure out the meaning of unfamiliar words. For example, Twain writes, "You'd see that frog whirling in the air like a doughnut—see him turn one summerset. . . ." Twain restates the meaning of the unfamiliar word *summerset*. He uses the phrase "whirling in the air like a doughnut" to indicate that *summerset* must be the word *somersault*.

📖 READER'S NOTEBOOK As you read, jot down unfamiliar words and expressions and what you think they mean. Here's an example:

DIALECT	
Well, thish-yer Smiley had rat terriers	Thish-yer = this here

The NOTORIOUS Jumping Frog of CALAVERAS COUNTY

Mark Twain

In compliance with the request of a friend of mine who wrote me from the East, I called on good-natured, garrulous[1] old Simon Wheeler and inquired after my friend's friend, Leonidas W. Smiley, as requested to do, and I hereunto append[2] the result. I have a lurking suspicion that *Leonidas W. Smiley* is a myth, that my friend never knew such a personage, and that he only conjectured that if I asked old Wheeler about him, it would remind him of his infamous *Jim* Smiley and he would go to work and bore me to death with some exasperating reminiscence of him as long and as tedious as it should be useless to me. If that was the design, it succeeded.

I found Simon Wheeler dozing comfortably by the barroom stove of the dilapidated tavern in the decayed mining camp of Angel's, and I noticed that he was fat and baldheaded and had an expression of winning gentleness and simplicity upon his tranquil countenance. He roused up and gave me good day. I told him that a friend of mine had commissioned me to make some inquiries about a cherished companion of his boyhood named *Leonidas W. Smiley—Rev. Leonidas W.* Smiley, a young minister of the Gospel, who he had heard was at one time a resident of Angel's Camp. I added that if Mr. Wheeler could tell me anything about this Rev. Leonidas W. Smiley, I would feel under many obligations to him.

Simon Wheeler backed me into a corner and blockaded me there with his chair, and then sat down and reeled off the monotonous narrative which follows this paragraph. He never smiled, he never frowned, he never changed his voice from the gentle-flowing key to which he tuned his initial sentence, he never betrayed the slightest suspicion of enthusiasm, but all through the interminable[3] narrative there ran a vein of impressive earnestness and sincerity which showed me plainly that, so far from his imagining that there was anything ridiculous or funny about his story, he regarded it as a really important matter and admired its two heroes as men of transcendent genius in finesse.[4] I let him go on in his own way and never interrupted him once.

"Rev. Leonidas W. H'm, Reverend Le—Well, there was a feller here once by the name of *Jim* Smiley, in the winter of '49—or maybe it was the spring of '50—I don't recollect exactly, somehow, though what makes me think it was one or the other is because I remember the big flume[5] warn't finished when he first come to the camp; but anyway, he was the curiousest man about always betting on anything that turned up you ever see, if he could get anybody to bet on the other side, and if he couldn't he'd change sides. Any way that

---

1. **garrulous** (găr′ə-ləs): extremely talkative.
2. **hereunto append:** add to this document.
3. **interminable** (ĭn-tûr′mə-nə-bəl): seemingly endless.
4. **men of . . . finesse** (fə-něs′): exceptionally brilliant men.
5. **flume:** a wooden trough built as a channel for running water—used in gold mining to separate particles of gold.

suited the other man would suit *him*—any way just so's he got a bet, *he* was satisfied. But still he was lucky, uncommon lucky; he most always come out winner. He was always ready and laying for a chance; there couldn't be no solit'ry thing mentioned but that feller'd offer to bet on it and take ary side you please, as I was just telling you. If there was a horse race, you'd find him flush or you'd find him busted at the end of it; if there was a dogfight, he'd bet on it; if there was a cat fight, he'd bet on it; if there was a chicken fight, he'd bet on it; why, if there was two birds setting on a fence, he would bet you which one would fly first; or if there was a camp meeting, he would be there reg'lar to bet on Parson Walker, which he judged to be the best exhorter about here, and so he was too, and a good man. If he even see a straddlebug start to go anywheres, he would bet you how long it would take him to get to—to wherever he was going to, and if you took him up, he would foller that straddlebug to Mexico but what he would find out where he was bound for and how long he was on the road. Lots of the boys here has seen that Smiley and can tell you about him. Why, it never made no difference to *him*—he'd bet on *any* thing—the dangdest feller. Parson Walker's wife laid very sick once for a good while, and it seemed as if they warn't going to save her; but one morning he come in and Smiley up and asked him how she was, and he said she was considerable better—thank the Lord for his inf'nite mercy—and coming on so smart that with the blessing of Prov'dence she'd get well yet; and Smiley, before he thought, says, 'Well, I'll resk two-and-a-half she don't anyway.'

"Thish-yer Smiley had a mare—the boys called her the fifteen-minute nag but that was only in fun, you know, because of course she was faster than that—and he used to win money on that horse, for all she was so slow and always had the asthma, or the distemper, or the consumption,[6] or something of that kind. They used to give her two or three hundred yards' start and then pass her underway, but always at the fag end of the race she'd get excited and desperatelike, and come cavorting and straddling up and scattering her legs around limber, sometimes in the air and sometimes out to one side among the fences, and kicking up m-o-r-e dust and raising m-o-r-e racket with her coughing and sneezing and blowing her nose—and always fetch up at the stand just about a neck ahead, as near as you could cipher it down.[7]

"And he had a little small bull-pup, that to look at him you'd think he warn't worth a cent but to set around and look ornery and lay for a chance to steal something. But as soon as money was up on him he was a different dog; his underjaw'd begin to stick out like the fo'castle[8] of a steamboat and his teeth would uncover and shine like the furnaces. And a dog might tackle him and bullyrag[9] him, and bite him and throw him over his shoulder two or three times, and Andrew Jackson—which was the name of the pup—Andrew Jackson would never let on but what *he* was satisfied and hadn't expected nothing else—and the bets being doubled and doubled on the other side all the time, till the money was all up; and then all of a sudden he would grab that other dog jest by the j'int of his hind leg and freeze to it—not chaw, you understand, but only just grip and hang on till they threw up the sponge,[10] if it

He was always ready and laying for a chance.

---

6. **distemper . . . consumption:** diseases of mammals.

7. **cipher** (sī'fər) **it down:** calculate it; figure it.

8. **fo'castle** (fōk'səl): forecastle—the part of a steamboat in front of the superstructure.

9. **bullyrag:** harass.

10. **throwed up the sponge:** gave up.

was a year. Smiley always come out winner on that pup till he harnessed a dog once that didn't have no hind legs, because they'd been sawed off in a circular saw, and when the thing had gone along far enough and the money was all up and he come to make a snatch for his pet holt,[11] he see in a minute how he'd been imposed on and how the other dog had him in the door, so to speak, and he 'peared surprised, and then he looked sorter discouragedlike and didn't try no more to win the fight, and so he got shucked out bad. He give Smiley a look, as much as to say his heart was broke, and it was *his* fault for putting up a dog that hadn't no hind legs for him to take holt of, which was his main dependence in a fight, and then he limped off a piece and laid down and died. It was a good pup, was that Andrew Jackson, and would have made a name for hisself if he'd lived, for the stuff was in him and he had genius—I know it, because he hadn't no opportunities to speak of, and it don't stand to reason that a dog could make such a fight as he could under them circumstances if he hadn't no talent. It always makes me feel sorry when I think of that last fight of his'n and the way it turned out.

"Well, thish-yer Smiley had rat terriers, and chicken cocks, and tomcats and all them kind of things till you couldn't rest, and you couldn't fetch nothing for him to bet on but he'd match you. He ketched a frog one day and took him home, and said he cal'lated[12] to educate him; and so he never done nothing for three months but set in his back yard and learn that frog to jump. And you bet you he *did* learn him, too. He'd give him a little punch behind, and the next minute you'd see that frog whirling in the air like a doughnut—see him turn one summerset, or maybe a couple if he got a good start, and come down flatfooted and all right, like a cat. He got him up so in the matter of ketching flies, and kep' him in practice so constant, that he'd nail a fly every time as fur as he could see

him. Smiley said all a frog wanted was education and he could do 'most anything—and I believe him. Why, I've seen him set Dan'l Webster down here on this floor—Dan'l Webster was the name of the frog—and sing out, 'Flies, Dan'l, flies!' and quicker'n you could wink he'd spring straight up and snake a fly off'n the counter there, and flop down on the floor ag'in as solid as a gob of mud, and fall to scratching the side of his head with his hind foot as indifferent as if he hadn't no idea he'd been doin' any more'n any frog might do. You never see a frog so modest and straight-for'ard as he was, for all he was so gifted. And when it come to fair and square jumping on a deadlevel, he could get over more ground at one straddle than any animal of his breed you ever see. Jumping on a dead level was his strong suit, you understand; and when it come to that, Smiley would ante up money on him as long as he had a red.[13] Smiley was monstrous proud of his frog, and well he might be for fellers that had traveled and been everywheres all said he laid over any frog that ever *they* see.

"Well, Smiley kep' the beast in a little <u>lattice</u> box, and he used to fetch him downtown sometimes and lay for a bet. One day a feller—a stranger in the camp, he was—come acrost him with his box and says:

"'What might it be that you've got in the box?'

"And Smiley says, sorter indifferentlike, 'It might be a parrot, or it might be a canary, maybe, but it ain't—it's only just a frog.'

"And the feller took it and looked at it careful, and turned it round this way and that, and says, 'H'm—so 'tis. Well, what's *he* good for?'

"'Well,' Smiley says, easy and careless, 'he's good enough for *one* thing, I should judge—he can outjump any frog in Calaveras County.'

"The feller took the box again and took another long, particular look, and give it back to Smiley

---

11. **pet holt:** favorite grip.
12. **cal'lated** (kăl'lā´tĭd): calculated; intended.
13. **red:** red cent (slang for a penny).

lattice (lăt'ĭs) *n.* an open framework made of spaced, crisscrossed strips

and says, very deliberate, 'Well,' he says, 'I don't see no p'ints[14] about that frog that's any better'n any other frog.'

"'Maybe you don't,' Smiley says. 'Maybe you understand frogs and maybe you don't understand 'em; maybe you've had experience and maybe you ain't only a amature, as it were. Anyways, I've got *my* opinion, and I'll resk forty dollars that he can outjump any frog in Calaveras County.'

"And the feller studied a minute and then says, kinder sadlike, 'Well, I'm only a stranger here and I ain't got no frog; but if I had a frog, I'd bet you.'"

"And then Smiley says, 'That's all right—that's all right—if you'll hold my box a minute, I'll go and get you a frog.' And so the feller took the box and put up his forty dollars along with Smiley's, and set down to wait.

"So he set there a good while thinking and thinking to himself, and then he got the frog out and prized his mouth open and took a teaspoon and filled him full of quail shot[15]—filled him pretty near up to his chin—and set him on the floor. Smiley he went to the swamp and slopped around in the mud for a long time, and finally he ketched a frog and fetched him in and give him to this feller, and says:

"'Now, if you're ready, set him alongside of Dan'l, with his forepaws just even with Dan'l's, and I'll give the word.' Then he says, 'One—two—three—*git!*' and him and the feller touched up the frogs from behind, and the new frog hopped off lively, but Dan'l give a heave and hysted up his shoulders—so—like a Frenchman, but it warn't no use—he couldn't budge; he was planted as solid as a church, and he couldn't no more stir than if he was anchored out. Smiley was a good deal surprised, and he was disgusted too, but he didn't have no idea what the matter was, of course.

"The feller took the money and started away, and when he was going out at the door, he sorter jerked his thumb over his shoulder—so—at Dan'l and says again, very deliberate, 'Well,' he says, 'I

don't see no p'ints about that frog that's any better'n any other frog.'

"Smiley he stood scratching his head and looking down at Dan'l a long time, and at last he says, 'I do wonder what in the nation that frog throw'd off for—I wonder if there ain't something the matter with him—he 'pears to look mighty baggy, somehow.' And he ketched Dan'l by the nap of the neck and hefted him, and says, 'Why, blame my cats if he don't weigh five pound!' and turned him upside down and he belched out a double handful of shot. And then he see how it was, and he was the maddest man—he set the frog down and took out after that feller, but he never ketched him. And—"

[Here Simon Wheeler heard his name called from the front yard and got up to see what was wanted.] And turning to me as he moved away, he said: "Just set where you are, stranger, and rest easy—I ain't going to be gone a second."

But, by your leave, I did not think that a continuation of the history of the <u>enterprising vagabond</u> *Jim* Smiley would be likely to afford me much information concerning the Rev. *Leonidas W.* Smiley and so I started away.

At the door I met the sociable Wheeler returning, and he buttonholed[16] me and <u>recommenced</u>:

"Well, thish-yer Smiley had a yaller one-eyed cow that didn't have no tail, only just a short stump like a bannanner, and—"

However, lacking both time and <u>inclination</u>, I did not wait to hear about the afflicted cow but took my leave.

---

14. **p'ints:** points.
15. **quail shot:** small lead pellets for firing from a shotgun.
16. **buttonholed:** detained for conversation.

WORDS TO KNOW	**enterprising** (ĕn′tər-prī′zĭng) *adj.* possessing imagination and initiative **vagabond** (văg′ə-bŏnd′) *n.* a wanderer; drifter **recommence** (rē′kə-mĕns′) *v.* to begin again **inclination** (ĭn′klə-nā′shən) *n.* a favorable disposition; desire

THE FIRST JUMPING FROG

Preparing to Read

Build Background

Ever wonder where Mark Twain came up with the idea for his famous "The Notorious Jumping Frog of Calaveras County"? Here's an article that appeared in the Sonora, California, *Herald* on June 11, 1853—fourteen years before Twain wrote his short story.

Twain on his frog, colored caricature by Frederick Waddy (1872)

A toad story.—A long stupid-looking fellow used to frequent a [California] gambling saloon, some time since, and was in the habit of promenading up and down, but never speaking. The boys began to play with him, at last, and in down-east drawl he gave them Rolands for their Olivers[1] till they left him alone. At night he spread out his blankets on an empty monte table and lived like a gambler, except that he talked to no one nor gambled a cent. He became, at length, an acknowledged character, slunk in and out, and the boys tittered as they saw him pass. One day he came in with an important air, and said:

"I have got a toad that'll leap further than any toad you can scare up."

They soon surrounded him, and roared and laughed.

"Yes," says he, "I'll bet money on it. Barkeeper, give me a cigar box to hold my toad in."

The fun was great, and the oddity was the talk of all hands. A gambler, in the evening, happened to come across a big frog, fetched him to the gambling house, and offered to jump him against the Yankee's toad.

"Well," says Yank, "I'll bet liquors on it." A chalk line was made and the toad put down. They struck the boards behind the toad and he leaped six feet, then the frog jumped seven. Yank paid the liquors; but, next morning, he says aloud:

"My toad waren't beat. No man's toad can leap with my toad. I have two ounces and two double eagles, and all of them I bet on my toad." The boys bet with him again, and his toad leaped six feet, but the frog leaped only two feet.

"The best two out of three," said the gamblers.

"Very well," says Yank. But still the frog could not go over two feet. Yank pocketed the bets.

"My frog is darn heavy this morning," says the gambler.

"I reckoned it would be, stranger," says the Yankee, "for I rolled a pound of shot into him last night."

---

1. **Gave them Rolands for their Olivers:** gave them punch for punch.

Connect to the Literature

1. What Do You Think?
Do you think the narrator of this story had a good sense of humor? Explain your opinion.

Comprehension Check
- How did the narrator get involved with Simon Wheeler?
- Why did Wheeler refer to Smiley as "the curiousest man"?
- Why did Smiley lose his bet on Dan'l Webster?

Think Critically

2. **ACTIVE READING** **UNDERSTANDING DIALECT** Review your notes in your **READER'S NOTEBOOK** on unusual words and expressions in Twain's story. What does Wheeler's **dialect** tell you about his character? Cite examples from the story to support your conclusion.

3. What sort of person is Jim Smiley?

THINK ABOUT {
- his relationship with his animals
- how he deals with the loss of his wager

4. How did Twain's use of **exaggeration** make this tale amusing? Use examples from the story to support your views.

Extend Interpretations

5. Critic's Corner According to writer John Gerber, Twain's organization of this tale "seems wholly directionless," yet "actually, it is carefully molded for climax." Do you agree that Wheeler seems to tell a rambling tale when in fact it carefully builds to a climax? Use examples from the story to support your ideas.

6. Comparing Texts Twain believed that good humor writing depended more on how a story was told than on the subject matter of the story. Based on your reading of both jumping frog versions, do you agree? Support your ideas with examples from both versions of the jumping frog story.

7. Connect to Life Refer to your notes and review the situation in which you observed someone fooling other people with an outrageous tale. Did the storyteller in the situation you observed use any of the same techniques that Twain did in his tale about the frog? Describe any similarities and differences between the two tales.

Literary Analysis

TALL TALE A **tall tale** is a distinctively American type of humorous story characterized by **exaggeration.** Tall tales and practical jokes have a similar kind of humor. In both, someone gets fooled, to the amusement of the person or persons who know the truth. In this tall tale, Twain uses both exaggeration and **dialect** for comic effect.

- **Exaggeration** involves stretching the truth to an unrealistic extent. Here, Twain exaggerates the lengths to which Smiley would go to make a bet:

He would foller that straddlebug to Mexico but what he would find out where he was bound for and how long he was on the road.

- **Dialect** is the distinct form of a language spoken in one geographic area by a particular social or ethnic group. A group's dialect is reflected in its characteristic pronunciation, vocabulary, expressions, and grammatical constructions. Throughout the story of the jumping frog, Twain reproduces the dialect spoken in California around the time of the Civil War, as seen here:

And he had a little small bull-pup, that to look at him you'd think he warn't worth a cent but to set around and look ornery and lay for a chance to steal something.

Paired Activity Find in this story three or four examples of Twain's combining dialect and exaggeration. Then share your examples with a partner, explaining how you think the combination of dialect and exaggeration creates a humorous effect.

THE AUTHOR'S STYLE
Twain's Witty Writing

Style is the distinctive way in which a work of literature is written. Style refers not so much to what is said but to how it is said. Word choice, imagery, sentence structure, and tone all contribute to a writer's style. Twain masterfully employed witty devices that contributed to his lively personal style.

Key Aspects of Twain's Style

- comic exaggeration
- humorous and entertaining subject matter
- rambling and indirect narratives, often involving the use of more words than necessary to express an idea
- offbeat **similes, metaphors,** and **irony**
- use of **analogies** to deepen meaning and understanding
- use of **dialect** and **idioms**—the vocabulary of the ordinary person

Analysis of Style

At the right are excerpts from three of Twain's stories. Study the list above, then read each excerpt carefully. Complete the following activities:

- Find examples of Twain's key stylistic devices in the excerpts. Think about the effect that is created by each device.
- Find examples of other devices you see at work in the excerpts.
- Review the other reading selections in this Author Study. Choose one, and discuss with others the stylistic devices that Twain has used in it.

Applications

1. Imitating the Style Choose one excerpt, and write another paragraph for the story using Twain's style. Share your work by reading it to the class.

2. Changing the Style Choose one excerpt, and rewrite it in your own humorous style. Then, with a partner, read your versions and the originals aloud, and compare them.

3. Speaking and Listening In small groups, take turns reading each excerpt aloud to hear the unique American voices Twain brought to literature. What **character** do you imagine telling each story? What **mood** does each excerpt convey? Discuss the differences you hear in each of these oral interpretations.

---

from A Connecticut Yankee in King Arthur's Court

Vast as the show-grounds were, there were no vacant spaces in them. . . . The mammoth grandstand was clothed in flags, streamers, and rich tapestries and packed with several acres of small-fry tributary kings, their suites, and the British aristocracy; with our own royal gang in the chief place, and each and every individual a flashing prism of gaudy silks and velvets—well, I never saw anything to begin with it but a fight between an Upper Mississippi sunset and the aurora borealis.

from The Notorious Jumping Frog of Calaveras County

He ketched a frog one day and took him home, and said he cal'lated to educate him; and so he never done nothing for three months but set in his back yard and learn that frog to jump. And you bet you he *did* learn him, too. He'd give him a little punch behind, and the next minute you'd see that frog whirling in the air like a doughnut—see him turn one summerset, or maybe a couple if he got a good start. . . . Smiley said all a frog wanted was education and he could do 'most anything—and I believe him.

from A Tramp Abroad

I am persuaded that the average ant is a sham . . . ; he is the hardest working creature in the world,—when anybody is looking,— but his leather-headedness is the point I make against him. He goes out foraging, he makes a capture, and then what does he do? Go home? No,—he goes anywhere but home. . . . He makes his capture, as I have said; . . . comes to a weed; it never occurs to him to go around it; no, he must climb it; and he does climb it, dragging his worthless property to the top—which is as bright a thing to do as it would be for me to carry a sack of flour from Heidelberg to Paris by way of Strasburg steeple.

Writing Options

1. The Stranger's Tale Rewrite part of "The Notorious Jumping Frog of Calaveras County" as if you were the stranger who outwitted Jim Smiley. Try to use local color and dialect. Place your writing in your **Working Portfolio.**

2. Local Storytelling Obtain a copy of Twain's sketches and tales, and choose a tale to rewrite for a younger audience.

3. Dialects Today Find out more about dialects spoken in the United States today. What are some major dialects? Where are they spoken? Write a brief report of your findings.

Vocabulary in Action

EXERCISE A: MEANING CLUES For each sentence, write *T* or *F* to indicate whether the statement is true or false.

1. An **enterprising** character would know how to help his frog jump highest.

2. An **infamous** person usually has a good reputation.

3. If you **recommence** telling a story, you are starting over from the beginning.

4. A **dilapidated** mining office is in excellent condition.

5. **Lattice** is a good source of several vitamins.

EXERCISE B: WORD KNOWLEDGE Design a crossword puzzle, using all of the Words to Know below, plus other words if you wish. Then exchange puzzles with a classmate and solve his or her puzzle.

commission   tranquil   inclination
cavorting   vagabond

WORDS TO KNOW	cavorting	inclination	recommence
	commission	infamous	tranquil
	dilapidated	lattice	vagabond
	enterprising		

Mark Twain

Author Study Project

CREATING A MULTIMEDIA BIOGRAPHY

Work with a small group, a partner, or alone to create a multimedia biography of Mark Twain, emphasizing his gifts as a humorist. To focus your work, think about some aspect of Twain's travels, jobs, performances, or personal life that fascinates you. Then choose a form you'd like your biography to take. You might tell a tall tale, make a video or a Web page, stage an interview or a talk show, or combine any of these possibilities. The following suggestions will help you with your research:

Films and Impersonations Several videos look at aspects of Twain's life and the America of his day. Hal Holbrook, an actor well known for his impersonations of Mark Twain, has filmed *Mark Twain Gives an Interview.* Watch the performance and pay attention to Holbrook's portrayal of Mark Twain.

Books and Periodicals Search these materials for images of Twain, his family, his homes in Hannibal and Hartford, documents and publications related to his life, and the changing society around him. Many biographies of Twain provide a rich store of anecdotes and quotations. An especially useful book is *Mark Twain and His World* by Justin Kaplan.

Computer Resources Search for nonprint materials for your presentation. Use CD-ROMs and the Internet as resources. Contact museums in Hannibal and Hartford as well as organizations like the Mark Twain Association of New York.

 More Online: Research Starter www.mcdougallittell.com

A Wagner Matinee

Short Story by WILLA CATHER

Connect to Your Life

Turning Points Recall a time when you had to choose between two things that were very important to you. What were your choices? What factors did you weigh in making your decision? Looking back, do you think you made the right choice?

Build Background

Cultural Backdrop The story you are about to read is set in Boston around 1900. At that time, many city dwellers were able to enjoy cultural opportunities, such as art museums and concerts featuring music by great European composers. In contrast, Easterners who made the choice to go west, like Aunt Georgiana in this story, left such worldly pleasures behind. Instead, these homesteaders faced long hours of strenuous labor and endured natural disasters such as drought, flood, and prairie fires.

This story contains several references to operas by the German composer Richard Wagner (väg′nər). It also mentions other operas and composers as well as musical terms such as *prelude, motive, overture, solo,* and *chorus.* It is not necessary to be familiar with these musical references to understand the story. However, if you do have a knowledge of classical music, you might briefly describe Wagner's operas and explain the musical terms to other students before they read.

WORDS TO KNOW **Vocabulary Preview**

callow	pathetic	sordid
conjecture	pious	superficially
excruciatingly	reproach	trepidation
inexplicable		

Focus Your Reading

LITERARY ANALYSIS **SETTING** The setting of a story refers to the time and place in which the action occurs. In some stories, setting may greatly influence plot events and shape the characters' lives. For example, in "A Wagner Matinee," the contrasting settings of turn-of-the-century Boston and the Nebraska frontier have a strong impact on both the narrator of the story and his aunt. As you read, note the details of each location.

ACTIVE READING **DRAWING CONCLUSIONS ABOUT CHARACTER** Understanding a character in a story is often like getting to know a real person. You **draw conclusions,** or make logical decisions, about the person by combining the impressions you have already formed with new facts you have discovered. To become better acquainted with Aunt Georgiana, the main character in "A Wagner Matinee," look closely at the details as you read the story, note what they suggest about the kind of person she is, and then draw conclusions that are solidly based on evidence.

READER'S NOTEBOOK To help you gather evidence as you read, create a chart like the one below, and fill it in with details about Aunt Georgiana. Then consider the evidence as you draw conclusions.

Observations	What They Reveal
Physical appearance	
Major decisions	
Actions and reactions	

A Wagner Matinee

Willa Cather

I received one morning a letter, written in pale ink on glassy, blue-lined note-paper, and bearing the postmark of a little Nebraska village. This communication, worn and rubbed, looking as though it had been carried for some days in a coat pocket that was none too clean, was from my Uncle Howard and informed me that his wife had been left a small legacy by a bachelor relative who had recently died, and that it would be necessary for her to go to Boston to attend to the settling of the estate. He requested me to meet her at the station and render her whatever services might be necessary. On examining the date indicated as that of her arrival, I found it no later than tomorrow. He had characteristically delayed writing until, had I been away from home for a day, I must have missed the good woman altogether.

The name of my Aunt Georgiana called up not alone her own figure, at once <u>pathetic</u> and grotesque, but opened before my feet a gulf of recollection so wide and deep, that, as the letter dropped from my hand, I felt suddenly a stranger to all the present conditions of my existence, wholly ill at ease and out of place amid the familiar surroundings of my study. I became, in short, the gangling farmer-boy my aunt had known, scourged with chilblains[1] and bashfulness, my hands cracked and sore from the corn husking. I felt the knuckles of my thumb tentatively, as though they were raw again. I sat again before her parlor organ, fumbling the scales with my stiff, red hands, while she, beside me, made canvas mittens for the huskers.[2]

The next morning, after preparing my landlady somewhat, I set out for the station. When the train arrived I had some difficulty in finding my aunt. She was the last of the passengers to alight, and it was not until I got her into the carriage that she seemed really to recognize me. She had come all the way in a day coach; her linen duster had become black with soot and her black bonnet grey with dust during the journey. When we arrived at my boarding-house the landlady put her to bed at once and I did not see her again until the next morning.

Whatever shock Mrs. Springer experienced at my aunt's appearance, she considerately concealed. As for myself, I saw my aunt's misshapen figure with that feeling of awe and respect with which we behold explorers who have left their ears and fingers north of Franz-Josef-Land,[3] or their health somewhere along the Upper Congo.[4] My Aunt Georgiana had been a music teacher at the Boston Conservatory, somewhere back in the latter sixties. One summer, while visiting in the little village among the Green Mountains where her ancestors had dwelt for generations, she had kindled the callow fancy of the most idle and shiftless of all the village lads, and had conceived for this Howard Carpenter one of those extrava-

gant passions which a handsome country boy of twenty-one sometimes inspires in an angular, spectacled woman of thirty. When she returned to her duties in Boston, Howard followed her, and the upshot of this inexplicable infatuation was that she eloped with him, eluding the reproaches of her family and the criticisms of her friends by going with him to the Nebraska frontier. Carpenter, who, of course, had no money, had taken a homestead in Red Willow County, fifty miles from the railroad. There they had measured off their quarter section themselves by driving across the prairie in a wagon, to the wheel of which they had tied a red cotton handkerchief, and counting off its revolutions. They built a dugout in the red hillside, one of those cave dwellings whose inmates so often reverted to primitive conditions. Their water they got from the lagoons where the buffalo drank, and their slender stock of provisions was always at the mercy of bands of roving Indians. For thirty years my aunt had not been further than fifty miles from the homestead.

But Mrs. Springer knew nothing of all this, and must have been considerably shocked at what was left of my kinswoman. Beneath the soiled linen duster which, on her arrival, was the most conspicuous

> **For thirty years my aunt had not been further than fifty miles from the homestead.**

---

1. **chilblains:** painful swelling or sores on the feet or hands, caused by exposure to the cold.
2. **huskers:** farm workers who remove cornhusks by hand.
3. **Franz-Josef-Land:** a group of small, mostly ice-covered islands in the Arctic Ocean north of Russia.
4. **Upper Congo:** river in central Africa, now called the Zaire (zä-îr′) River.

feature of her costume, she wore a black stuff dress, whose ornamentation showed that she had surrendered herself unquestioningly into the hands of a country dressmaker. My poor aunt's figure, however, would have presented astonishing difficulties to any dressmaker. Originally stooped, her shoulders were now almost bent together over her sunken chest. She wore no stays, and her gown, which trailed unevenly behind, rose in a sort of peak over her abdomen. She wore ill-fitting false teeth, and her skin was as yellow as a Mongolian's from constant exposure to a pitiless wind and to the alkaline water which hardens the most transparent cuticle into a sort of flexible leather.

I owed to this woman most of the good that ever came my way in my boyhood, and had a reverential affection for her. During the years when I was riding herd for my uncle, my aunt, after cooking the three meals—the first of which was ready at six o'clock in the morning—and putting the six children to bed, would often stand until midnight at her ironing-board with me at the kitchen table beside her, hearing me recite Latin declensions and conjugations, gently shaking me when my drowsy head sank down over a page of irregular verbs. It was to her, at her ironing or mending, that I read my first Shakespeare, and her old text-book on mythology was the first that ever came into my empty hands. She taught me my scales and exercises, too—on the little parlor organ, which her husband had bought her after fifteen years,

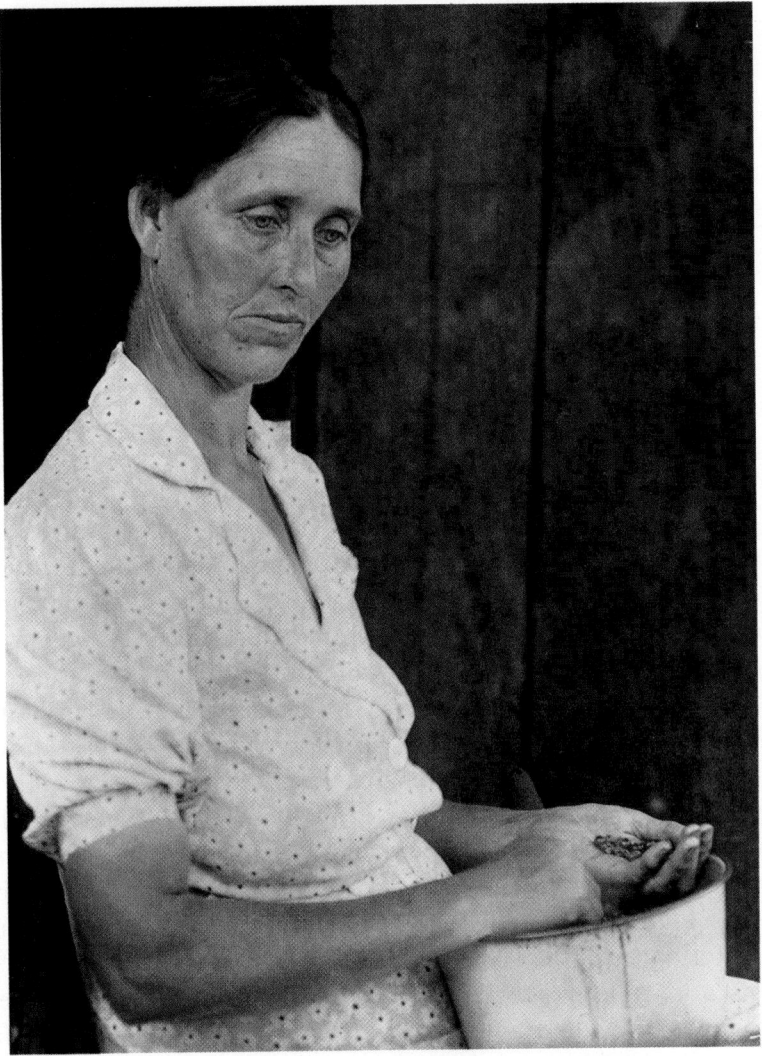

Mrs. Stewart, Housewife and Singer, Brasstown, North Carolina, Doris Ulmann. Doris Ulmann Collection, #635, Special Collections, University of Oregon Library.

during which she had not so much as seen any instrument, but an accordion that belonged to one of the Norwegian farmhands. She would sit beside me by the hour, darning and counting while I struggled with the "Joyous Farmer," but she seldom talked to me about music, and I understood why. She was a pious woman; she had the consolations of religion and, to her at least, her martyrdom was not wholly sordid. Once when I had been doggedly beating out some easy passages from an old score of

---

WORDS TO KNOW

pious (pī′əs) *adj.* having or showing reverence for God
sordid (sôr′dĭd) *adj.* wretched; dirty; morally degraded

691

Euryanthe[5] I had found among her music books, she came up to me and, putting her hands over my eyes, gently drew my head back upon her shoulder, saying tremulously, "Don't love it so well, Clark, or it may be taken from you. Oh! dear boy, pray that whatever your sacrifice may be, it be not that."

When my aunt appeared on the morning after her arrival, she was still in a semi-somnambulant state. She seemed not to realize that she was in the city where she had spent her youth, the place longed for hungrily half a lifetime. She had been so wretchedly train-sick throughout the journey that she had no recollection of anything but her discomfort, and, to all intents and purposes, there were but a few hours of nightmare between the farm in Red Willow County and my study on Newbury Street. I had planned a little pleasure for her that afternoon, to repay her for some of the glorious moments she had given me when we used to milk together in the straw-thatched cowshed and she, because I was more than usually tired, or because her husband had spoken sharply to me, would tell me of the splendid performance of the *Huguenots*[6] she had seen in Paris, in her youth. At two o'clock the Symphony Orchestra was to give a Wagner program, and I intended to take my aunt; though, as I conversed with her, I grew doubtful about her enjoyment of it. Indeed, for her own sake, I could only wish her taste for such things quite dead, and the long struggle mercifully ended at last. I suggested our visiting the Conservatory and the Common[7] before lunch, but she seemed altogether too timid to wish to venture out. She questioned me absently about various changes in the city, but she was chiefly concerned that she had forgotten to leave instructions about feeding half-skimmed milk to a certain weakling calf, "old Maggie's calf, you know, Clark," she explained, evidently having forgotten how long I had been away. She was further troubled because she had neglected to tell her daughter about the freshly-opened kit of mackerel in the cellar, which would spoil if it were not used directly.

I asked her whether she had ever heard any of the Wagnerian operas,[8] and found that she had not, though she was perfectly familiar with their respective situations, and had once possessed the piano score of *The Flying Dutchman*. I began to think it would have been best to get her back to Red Willow County without waking her, and regretted having suggested the concert.

From the time we entered the concert hall, however, she was a trifle less passive and inert, and for the first time seemed to perceive her surroundings. I had felt some <u>trepidation</u> lest she might become aware of the absurdities of her attire, or might experience some painful embarrassment at stepping suddenly into the world to which she had been dead for a quarter of a century. But, again, I found how <u>superficially</u> I had judged her. She sat looking about her with eyes as impersonal, almost as stony, as those with which the granite Rameses[9] in a museum watches the froth and fret that ebbs and flows[10] about his pedestal—separated from it by the lonely stretch of centuries. I have seen this same aloofness in old miners who drift into the Brown hotel at Denver, their pockets full of bullion,[11] their linen soiled, their haggard faces unshaven; standing in the thronged corridors

---

5. *Euryanthe* (yo͞o′rē-ăn′thē): an opera by the German composer Carl Maria von Weber.

6. *Huguenots* (hyo͞o′gə-nŏts′): an opera by the German composer Giacomo Meyerbeer.

7. the Common: Boston Common, a public park.

8. Wagnerian operas: The orchestra will play selections from several operas composed by Wagner, including *The Flying Dutchman, Tannhauser, Tristan and Isolde*, and a cycle of four operas called *The Ring of the Nibelung*.

9. Rameses (răm′sēz′): one of the ancient kings of Egypt of that name.

10. froth . . . flows: happiness and sadness that comes and goes.

11. bullion: gold.

WORDS TO KNOW

trepidation (trĕp′ĭ-dā′shən) *n.* fearful uncertainty or worry

superficially (so͞o′pər-fĭsh′ə-lē) *adv.* in a shallow way; concerned with only what is obvious

The Opera, Paris (about 1924), Raoul Dufy. Watercolor and gouache on paper, 19″ × 25″, The Phillips Collection, Washington, D.C.

as solitary as though they were still in a frozen camp on the Yukon,[12] conscious that certain experiences have isolated them from their fellows by a gulf no haberdasher could bridge.

We sat at the extreme left of the first balcony, facing the arc of our own and the balcony above us, veritable hanging gardens, brilliant as tulip beds. The matinée audience was made up chiefly of women. One lost the contour of faces and figures, indeed any effect of line whatever, and there was only the color of bodices past counting, the shimmer of fabrics soft and firm, silky and sheer; red, mauve, pink, blue, lilac, purple, ecru, rose, yellow, cream, and white, all

the colors that an impressionist[13] finds in a sunlit landscape, with here and there the dead shadow of a frock coat. My Aunt Georgiana regarded them as though they had been so many daubs of tube-paint on a palette.

When the musicians came out and took their places, she gave a little stir of anticipation and looked with quickening interest down over the rail at that invariable grouping, perhaps the first

---

12. **Yukon** (yoo′kŏn′): a river in the Yukon Territory, in northwest Canada.

13. **impressionist:** member of a movement in French painting that emphasized the play of light and color.

wholly familiar thing that had greeted her eye since she had left old Maggie and her weakling calf. I could feel how all those details sank into her soul, for I had not forgotten how they had sunk into mine when I came fresh from ploughing forever and forever between green aisles of corn, where, as in a treadmill, one might walk from daybreak to dusk without perceiving a shadow of change. The clean profiles of the musicians, the gloss of their linen, the dull black of their coats, the beloved shapes of the instruments, the patches of yellow light thrown by the green shaded lamps on the smooth, varnished bellies of the 'cellos and the bass viols in the rear, the restless, wind-tossed forest of fiddle necks and bows—I recalled how, in the first orchestra I had ever heard, those long bow strokes seemed to draw the heart out of me, as a conjurer's stick reels out yards of paper ribbon from a hat.

The first number was the *Tannhauser* overture. When the horns drew out the first strain of the Pilgrim's chorus, my Aunt Georgiana clutched my coat sleeve. Then it was I first realized that for her this broke a silence of thirty years; the inconceivable silence of the plains. With the battle between the two motives, with the frenzy of the Venusberg theme and its ripping of strings, there came to me an overwhelming sense of the waste and wear we are so powerless to combat; and I saw again the tall, naked house on the prairie, black and grim as a wooden fortress; the black pond where I had learned to swim, its margin pitted with sun-dried cattle tracks; the rain gullied clay banks about the naked house, the four dwarf ash seedlings where the dish-cloths were always hung to dry before the kitchen door.

> She sat staring at the orchestra through a dullness of thirty years

The world there was the flat world of the ancients; to the east, a cornfield that stretched to daybreak; to the west, a corral that reached to sunset; between, the conquests of peace, dearer bought than those of war.

The overture closed, my aunt released my coat sleeve, but she said nothing. She sat staring at the orchestra through a dullness of thirty years, through the films made little by little by each of the three hundred and sixty-five days in every one of them. What, I wondered, did she get from it? She had been a good pianist in her day I knew, and her musical education had been broader than that of most music teachers of a quarter of a century ago. She had often told me of Mozart's operas and Meyerbeer's, and I could remember hearing her sing, years ago, certain melodies of Verdi's. When I had fallen ill with a fever in her house she used to sit by my cot in the evening—when the cool, night wind blew in through the faded mosquito netting tacked over the window and I lay watching a certain bright star that burned red above the cornfield—and sing "Home to our mountains, O, let us return!" in a way fit to break the heart of a Vermont boy near dead of homesickness already.

I watched her closely through the prelude to *Tristan and Isolde*, trying vainly to <u>conjecture</u> what that seething turmoil of strings and winds might mean to her, but she sat mutely staring at the violin bows that drove obliquely downward, like the pelting streaks of rain in a summer shower. Had this music any message for her? Had she enough left to at all comprehend this power which had kindled the world since she

WORDS TO KNOW	**conjecture** (kən-jĕk′chər) *v.* to make a judgment on the basis of uncertain evidence; guess

had left it? I was in a fever of curiosity, but Aunt Georgiana sat silent upon her peak in Darien.[14] She preserved this utter immobility throughout the number from *The Flying Dutchman*, though her fingers worked mechanically upon her black dress, as though, of themselves, they were recalling the piano score they had once played. Poor old hands! They had been stretched and twisted into mere tentacles to hold and lift and knead with; the palms unduly swollen, the fingers bent and knotted—on one of them a thin, worn band that had once been a wedding ring. As I pressed and gently quieted one of those groping hands, I remembered with quivering eyelids their services for me in other days.

Soon after the tenor began the "Prize Song," I heard a quick drawn breath and turned to my aunt. Her eyes were closed, but the tears were glistening on her cheeks, and I think, in a moment more, they were in my eyes as well. It never really died, then—the soul that can suffer so <u>excruciatingly</u> and so interminably; it withers to the outward eye only; like that strange moss which can lie on a dusty shelf half a century and yet, if placed in water, grows green again. She wept so throughout the development and elaboration of the melody.

During the intermission before the second half of the concert, I questioned my aunt and found that the "Prize Song" was not new to her. Some years before there had drifted to the farm in Red Willow County a young German, a tramp cow puncher, who had sung the chorus at Bayreuth,[15] when he was a boy, along with the other peasant boys and girls. Of a Sunday morning he used to sit on his gingham-sheeted bed in the hands' bedroom which opened off the kitchen, cleaning the leather of his boots and saddle, singing the "Prize Song," while my aunt went about her work in the kitchen. She had hovered about him until she had prevailed upon him to join the country church, though his sole fitness for this step, in so far as I could gather, lay in his boyish

face and his possession of this divine melody. Shortly afterward he had gone to town on the Fourth of July, been drunk for several days, lost his money at a faro[16] table, ridden a saddled Texas steer on a bet, and disappeared with a fractured collar-bone. All this my aunt told me huskily, wanderingly, as though she were talking in the weak lapses of illness.

"Well, we have come to better things than the old *Trovatore*[17] at any rate, Aunt Georgie?" I queried, with a well meant effort at jocularity.

Her lip quivered and she hastily put her handkerchief up to her mouth. From behind it she murmured, "And you have been hearing this ever since you left me, Clark?" Her question was the gentlest and saddest of reproaches.

The second half of the program consisted of four numbers from the *Ring*, and closed with Siegfried's funeral march. My aunt wept quietly, but almost continuously, as a shallow vessel overflows in a rainstorm. From time to time her dim eyes looked up at the lights which studded the ceiling, burning softly under their dull glass globes; doubtless they were stars in truth to her. I was still perplexed as to what measure of musical comprehension was left to her, she who had heard nothing but the singing of Gospel Hymns at Methodist services in the square frame school-house on Section Thirteen for so many years. I was wholly unable to gauge how much of it had been dissolved in soapsuds, or worked into bread, or milked into the bottom of a pail.

---

14. **peak in Darien** (dâr′ē-ĕn′): an allusion to a poem by the English poet John Keats, in which Keats describes Spanish explorers on a mountain in Darien, a region that is now Panama. The Spaniards stand silent and amazed as they become the first Europeans to view the Pacific Ocean.

15. **Bayreuth** (bī-roit′): the Bayreuth Festival, an annual international music festival in Germany that presents Wagner's operas.

16. **faro**: a gambling game.

17. *Trovatore* (trô′vä-tô′rĕ): *Il Trovatore* is an opera by the Italian composer Giuseppe Verdi.

House in Winter (1941), Wright Morris. Photo taken near Lincoln, Nebraska.

The deluge of sound poured on and on; I never knew what she found in the shining current of it; I never knew how far it bore her, or past what happy islands. From the trembling of her face I could well believe that before the last numbers she had been carried out where the myriad graves are, into the grey, nameless burying grounds of the sea; or into some world of death vaster yet, where, from the beginning of the world, hope has lain down with hope and dream with dream and, renouncing,[18] slept.

The concert was over; the people filed out of the hall chattering and laughing, glad to relax and find the living level again, but my kinswoman made no effort to rise. The harpist slipped its green felt cover over his instrument;

the flute-players shook the water from their mouthpieces; the men of the orchestra went out one by one, leaving the stage to the chairs and music stands, empty as a winter cornfield.

I spoke to my aunt. She burst into tears and sobbed pleadingly. "I don't want to go, Clark, I don't want to go!"

I understood. For her, just outside the door of the concert hall, lay the black pond with the cattle-tracked bluffs; the tall, unpainted house, with weather-curled boards; naked as a tower, the crook-backed ash seedlings where the dishcloths hung to dry; the gaunt, molting turkeys picking up refuse about the kitchen door. ❖

---

18. **renouncing:** giving up.

Connect to the Literature

1. **What Do You Think?**
   What thoughts do you have about Aunt Georgiana? Discuss them with a classmate.

   > **Comprehension Check**
   > • Why is Aunt Georgiana on her way to Boston?
   > • Why is Clark grateful to his aunt?
   > • How does Clark expect his aunt to react to the concert?

Think Critically

2. Do you think that Aunt Georgiana will be tempted to stay in Boston and not return to her home in Nebraska? Why?

3. In your opinion, was it a good idea for Clark to take Aunt Georgiana to the concert? Defend your view.

4. **ACTIVE READING** **DRAWING CONCLUSIONS ABOUT CHARACTER**
   Based on the diagram you made about Aunt Georgiana in your **READER'S NOTEBOOK**, what details from the story present the strongest evidence about the kind of person she is? From the choices that Aunt Georgiana has made in her life, what conclusions can you draw about her character?

   THINK ABOUT
   - the circumstances of her elopement
   - how she feels about life on the farm
   - how she treated Clark as a child in her home
   - your own insights into making difficult choices

5. What new insights do you think Clark gains over the course of the story? Explain your answer.

Extend Interpretations

6. **Different Perspectives** If the events were described by Aunt Georgiana rather than Clark, how might the story differ?

7. **Critic's Corner** "A Wagner Matinee" created a stir when it appeared in *Everybody's Magazine* in 1904. Cather's family objected to the fictional portrait of her real-life aunt Franc. One of her friends criticized the writer's portrayal of Nebraska: "The stranger to this state will associate Nebraska with the aunt's wretched figure, her ill-fitting false teeth, her skin yellowed by the weather." Is Cather's portrait of Aunt Georgiana too unflattering? Do you think her portrayal of Nebraska is too harsh? Support your answers with details.

8. **Connect to Life** What do you think Aunt Georgiana would say to a young person who believed love could overcome all problems in a marriage? Explain your answer.

Literary Analysis

SETTING As you recall, the **setting** of a story refers to the time and place in which the action occurs. In "A Wagner Matinee," Cather sharply distinguishes between two places—a Nebraska homestead and the Boston concert hall—that have a profound effect on Aunt Georgiana. The elegance and vibrancy of the concert hall are contrasted with the barrenness of Red Willow County and the "tall, naked house on the prairie, black and grim as a wooden fortress." How do the descriptions of the two settings highlight the sacrifices Aunt Georgiana made when she chose to marry?

Activity Go back through the story and record details describing the Nebraska farm and the Boston concert hall. Then, acting as a set designer for a movie, TV program, or play based on the story, sketch the two settings described. Compare your depictions with those of other students.

Choices & CHALLENGES

Writing Options

1. Cause-and-Effect Analysis Draft a short cause-and-effect analysis, explaining why Aunt Georgiana chose to marry and move to the Nebraska frontier and what impact this choice had on her life.

2. Telegram from Boston Imagine that you are Clark. Write a telegram to be sent to your uncle, Howard Carpenter, explaining what has happened to Aunt Georgiana during her visit to Boston.

3. Interview: Personal Sacrifices Aunt Georgiana gave up a life of music that she loved. Ask a friend or family member to reveal to you his or her feelings about something he or she has given up in life. Then write up your interview with that person.

Explorations & Activities

1. Real Estate Ad Create a real estate advertisement to "sell" the virtues of life on the frontier, using details from your reading of "A Wagner Matinee." As an alternative, you may want to create an ad discouraging people from moving to the frontier.

2. Opera Poster Using music reference books and recordings, research the music of Richard Wagner. Use what you learn to create a poster advertising the performance that Clark and Aunt Georgiana attend.

Inquiry & Research

Music Appreciation Find recordings of operas by Richard Wagner. Then play one or two of the excerpts that Aunt Georgiana hears performed at the concert in Boston, and explain how you think she may have reacted to each piece of music. You may also want to find and play music by other composers mentioned in the story, such as Mozart and Verdi.

Vocabulary in Action

EXERCISE A: CONTEXT CLUES Write the vocabulary word that best completes each sentence.

1. If you think of Wagner as the composer of operas featuring large blonds wearing helmets with horns sticking out of them, you might _____ that his music is not relevant to your life.

2. However, bear in mind that it is easy to dismiss or ridicule things that we look at only _____, without considering them in depth.

3. In reacting to opera, to literature, or to art, a person who is scornful of what he or she is unfamiliar with deserves _____.

4. Wagner's music is filled with familiar emotions; one whole opera was composed while he was hopelessly and _____ in love with a woman who could never be his.

5. Brilliant as he was, Wagner was a careless student with childish attitudes who showed many signs of being _____.

6. His continuing financial irresponsibility makes it difficult to pity him and view his money troubles as _____.

7. Puzzled by his music, which was far ahead of its time, many opera lovers at first found his work _____.

8. Financial problems and a lack of quick success may well have filled Wagner with a sense of _____ about the future.

9. Although some musical dramas, called oratorios, involve biblical characters, Wagner's work does not have these _____ connections.

10. Even if the theme of his work is not religiously spiritual, listening to it can lift one out of the petty, mean, and _____ events of the world and provide a glimpse of purity and beauty.

EXERCISE B Try acting out the Words to Know by using only a facial expression and gestures.

WORDS TO KNOW	callow	pathetic	sordid
	conjecture	pious	superficially
	excruciatingly	reproach	trepidation
	inexplicable		

Building Vocabulary

For an in-depth lesson on context clues, see page 326.

Willa Cather
1873–1947

Other Works
Death Comes for the Archbishop
One of Ours
The Song of the Lark

The Making of a Writer Willa Cather believed that "the most basic material a writer works with is acquired before the age of fifteen. . . . Those years determine whether one's work will be poor and thin or rich and fine." Born in Back Creek Valley, Virginia, Cather moved to the prairies of Nebraska when she was nine years old. The land there—and the pioneers who lived on it—gave Cather her distinctive voice. Her acclaimed novels *O Pioneers!* and *My Àntonia* are set on her beloved prairie.

Cultural Influences As a child, Cather enjoyed a rich cultural life despite the limitations of growing up in the young frontier town of Red Cloud. She had fine books in her home and excellent teachers at school. Among her Nebraska neighbors were educated European immigrants who introduced her to French and German literature, taught her to read classical Latin and Greek, and taught her the history and appreciation of classical music and opera. The railroad brought traveling stock companies to the opera house in Red Cloud, where Cather saw plays and light operas; she herself wrote, staged, and performed in amateur plays.

Career Path After studying journalism at the University of Nebraska, Cather went to Pittsburgh, where she worked as a magazine editor, a critic, and a teacher. From 1906 on, far from the wild Nebraska frontier of her childhood, Cather lived in New York City, supporting herself as a novelist.

Author Activity

Read another short story from her collection *Youth and the Bright Medusa* or *Obscure Destinies*. Prepare a comparison chart in which you show the realistic details of setting and characters in the story you chose and in "A Wagner Matinee."

from
LETTERS OF A WOMAN HOMESTEADER
Elinore Pruitt Stewart

In 1909, Elinore Pruitt Stewart (formerly Rupert) left Denver and became a homesteader, a person who received public land free of charge under the Homestead Act of 1862. She moved to Burnt Fork, Wyoming, and wrote the following letter about her new life.

January 23, 1913

Dear Mrs. Coney,—

❶ I am afraid all my friends think I am very forgetful and that you think I am ungrateful as well, but I am going to plead not guilty. Right after Christmas Mr. Stewart came down with *la grippe*[1] and was so miserable that it kept me busy trying to relieve him. Out here where we can get no physician we have to dope ourselves, so that I had to be housekeeper, nurse, doctor, and general overseer. That explains my long silence.

And now I want to thank you for your kind thought in prolonging our Christmas. The magazines were much appreciated. They relieved some weary night-watches, and the box did Jerrine more good than the medicine I was having to give her for *la grippe*. She was content to stay in bed and enjoy the contents of her box.

When I read of the hard times among the Denver poor, I feel like urging them every one to get out and file on land. I am very enthusiastic about women homesteading. It really requires less strength and labor to raise plenty to satisfy a large family than it does to go out to wash, with the added satisfaction of knowing that their job will not be lost to them if they care to keep it. Even if improving the place does go slowly, it is that ❷ much done to stay done. Whatever is raised is the homesteader's own, and there is no house-rent to pay. This year Jerrine cut and dropped enough potatoes to raise a ton of fine potatoes. She wanted to try, so we let her, and you will remember that she is but six years old. We had a man to break the ground and

---

1. *la grippe* (lä-grēp') *French:* the flu; influenza.

Reading for Information

Have you ever received a letter or an e-mail from a friend who has moved away? Like Stewart, did he or she attempt to justify the new circumstances by explaining how much better his or her life is now than before? Letters are more than just personal correspondence; they are also primary sources that reveal details and personal observations of the life and times of the writer.

EVALUATING AN ARGUMENT

In her letter, Stewart discusses the benefits of homesteading and gives reasons to support those opinions. Use the questions and activities below to help you evaluate her argument.

❶ In the beginning of the letter, Stewart explains why she hasn't written. To whom is she writing? What does her **tone** suggest about the purpose of the letter?

❷ **Analyzing the Evidence** Stewart describes aspects of homesteading that she likes, such as "Whatever is raised is the homesteader's own." She also tells of things she dislikes. Make a chart similar to the one below and list Stewart's pros and cons of homesteading.

HOMESTEADING	
Pros	Cons
no rent	loneliness

cover the potatoes for her and the man irrigated them once. That was all that was done until digging time, when they were ploughed out and Jerrine picked them up. Any woman strong enough to go out by the day could have done every bit of the work and put in two or three times that much, and it would have been so much more pleasant than to work so hard in the city and then be on starvation rations in the winter.

❸ To me, homesteading is the solution of all poverty's problems, but I realize that temperament has much to do with success in any undertaking, and persons afraid of coyotes and work and loneliness had better let ranching alone. At the same time, any woman who can stand her own company, can see the beauty of the sunset, loves growing things, and is willing to put in as much time at careful labor as she does over the washtub, will certainly succeed; will have independence, plenty to eat all the time, and a home of her own in the end.

Experimenting need cost the homesteader no more than the work, because by applying to the Department of Agriculture at Washington he can get enough of any seed and as many kinds as he wants to make a thorough trial, and it doesn't even cost postage. Also one can always get bulletins from there and from the Experiment Station of one's own State concerning any problem or as many problems as may come up. I would not, for anything, allow Mr. Stewart to do anything toward improving my place, for I want the fun and the experience myself. And I want to be able to speak from experience when I tell others what they can do. Theories are very beautiful, but facts are what must be had, and what I intend to give some time.

❹ Here I am boring you to death with things that cannot interest you! You'd think I wanted you to homestead, wouldn't you? But I am only thinking of the troops of tired, worried women, sometimes even cold and hungry, scared to death of losing their places to work, who could have plenty to eat, who could have good fires by gathering the wood, and comfortable homes of their own, if they but had the courage and determination to get them.

I must stop right now before you get so tired you will not answer. With much love to you from Jerrine and myself, I am

Yours affectionately,

Elinore Rupert Stewart

Westly Potato Camp, Edison, California, Dorothea Lange (1895–1965). Copyright © 1982. The Dorothea Lange Collection, The Oakland Museum of California, The City of Oakland, gift of Paul S. Taylor.

❸ Stewart states that "temperament has much to do with success in any undertaking." What do you think she means? She then describes the qualities of a person who she thinks will dislike homesteading and those of a person she thinks will like it. How do these descriptions support her overall argument that homesteading is better than city life?

❹ **Concluding the Letter** Reread the next-to last paragraph of the letter, and explain whether you think this conclusion effectively ends her argument in favor of homesteading.

Evaluating You've analyzed the pros and cons of homesteading and learned Stewart's reasons for leaving Denver. If you had been living in that city in 1913 and read this letter, would it move you to take up homesteading? Explain.

The Legend of Gregorio Cortez

Fiction by AMÉRICO PAREDES

Comparing Literature

Traditions Across Time: Writing of the New West

The *cuento* "The Indian and the Hundred Cows" teaches important cultural values of the Southwestern frontier, while Black Elk's retelling of "High Horse's Courting" portrays distinctive customs and beliefs of the Sioux who lived in the northern Great Plains. "The Legend of Gregorio Cortez," a modern prose retelling of an old ballad, gives some clues about the ideals of Mexican Americans living in the Texas border region during the early 1900s.

Points of Comparison As you read, compare the cultural values revealed in this legend with those evident in the *cuento* and the Sioux tale.

Build Background

The Man Behind the Legend "The Legend of Gregorio Cortez" is a prose retelling of a *corrido,* a fast-paced ballad from the Mexican oral tradition. Both the original *corrido* and this retelling are based on the life of Gregorio Cortez, who was born in Mexico in 1875. On June 12, 1901, while Cortez was living in Karnes County, Texas, he shot and killed Sheriff Brack Morris just after the

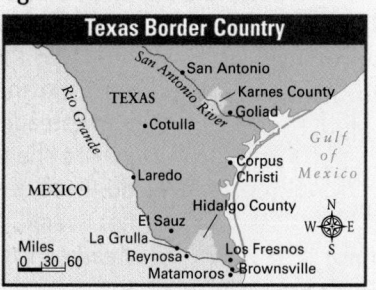

sheriff shot Cortez's brother. In his flight to the border, Cortez walked more than 100 miles and rode another 400 miles. On the way, he killed another sheriff and eluded several posses, some with as many as 300 men. He was finally captured—out of ammunition and on foot—near the border town of Laredo. After a three-year legal battle, Cortez was acquitted of killing the first sheriff but sentenced to life for killing the second. He spent about 12 years in prison before being pardoned by the governor of Texas in 1913. Cortez died three years later of unknown causes.

Focus Your Reading

LITERARY ANALYSIS LEGEND A **legend** is a story passed down orally from generation to generation and popularly believed to have a historical basis. Many legends, such as "The Legend of Gregorio Cortez," feature a **cultural hero**—a larger-than-life figure who reflects the values of a people. The cultural hero's role is to provide a noble image that will inspire and guide the actions of all who share that culture.

ACTIVE READING MAKING JUDGMENTS ABOUT TEXT Like many legends, this retelling of the *corrido* about Gregorio Cortez mixes fact, exaggeration, and fiction, much as a tall tale does, to create an unforgettable hero. To determine how much this legend stretches the truth, **make judgments** about, or evaluate, the accuracy of the details and situations as you read.

READER'S NOTEBOOK Make judgments as to which details and situations in "The Legend of Gregorio Cortez" are factual, exaggerated, or fictional. Use a diagram like the one shown to record your judgments.

Details and Events

Factual	Exaggerated	Fictional

The Legend of
Gregorio Cortez

Américo Paredes

THEY still sing of him—in the *cantinas*[1] and the country stores, in the ranches when men gather at night to talk in the cool dark, sitting in a circle, smoking and listening to the old songs and the tales of other days. Then the *guitarreros*[2] sing of the border raids and the skirmishes, of the men who lived by the phrase, "I will break before I bend."

They sing with deadly-serious faces, throwing out the words of the song like a challenge, tearing savagely with their stiff, callused fingers at the strings of the guitars.

And that is how, in the dark quiet of the ranches, in the lighted noise of the saloons, they sing of Gregorio Cortez.

After the song is sung there is a lull. Then the old men, who have lived long and seen almost everything, tell their stories. And when they tell about Gregorio Cortez, the telling goes like this:

---

1. *cantinas* (kän-tē′näs) *Spanish:* taverns or bars.
2. *guitarreros* (gē-tä-rĕ′rôs) *Spanish:* guitar players.

How Gregorio Cortez Came to Be in the County of El Carmen

That was good singing, and a good song; give the man a drink. Not like these pachucos[3] nowadays, mumbling damn-foolishness into a microphone; it is not done that way. Men should sing with their heads thrown back, with their mouths wide open and their eyes shut. Fill your lungs, so they can hear you at the pasture's farther end. And when you sing, sing songs like *El Corrido de Gregorio Cortez*. There's a song that makes the hackles rise. You can almost see him there—Gregorio Cortez, with his pistol in his hand.

He was a man, a Border man. What did he look like? Well, that is hard to tell. Some say he was short and some say he was tall; some say he was Indian brown and some say he was blond like a newborn cockroach. But I'd say he was not too dark and not too fair, not too thin and not too fat, not too short and not too tall; and he looked just a little bit like me. But does it matter so much what he looked like? He was a man, very much of a man; and he was a Border man. Some say he was born in Matamoros; some say Reynosa; some say Hidalgo county on the other side. And I guess others will say other things. But Matamoros, or Reynosa, or Hidalgo, it's all the same Border; and short or tall, dark or fair, it's the man that counts. And that's what he was, a man.

Not a gunman, no, not a bravo. He never came out of a cantina wanting to drink up the sea at one gulp. Not that kind of man, if you can call that kind a man. No, that wasn't Gregorio Cortez at all. He was a peaceful man, a hard-working man like you and me.

He could shoot. Forty-four and thirty-thirty, they were the same to him. He could put five bullets into a piece of board and not make but one hole, and quicker than you could draw a good deep breath. Yes, he could shoot. But he could also work.

He was a vaquero,[4] and a better one there has not ever been from Laredo to the mouth. He could talk to horses, and they would understand. They would follow him around, like dogs, and no man knew a good horse better then Gregorio Cortez. As for cattle, he could set up school for your best caporal.[5] And if an animal was lost, and nobody could pick up a trail, they would send for Gregorio Cortez. He could always find a trail. There was no better tracker in all the Border country, nor a man who could hide his tracks better if he wanted to. That was Gregorio Cortez, the best vaquero and range man that there ever was.

But that is not all. You farmers, do you think that Gregorio Cortez did not know your business too? You could have told him nothing about cotton or beans or corn. He knew it all. He could look into the sky of a morning and smell it, sniff it the way a dog sniffs, and tell you what kind of weather there was going to be. And he would take a piece of dirt in his hands and rub it back and forth between his fingers—to see if the land had reached its point—and you would say he was looking into it. And perhaps he was, for Gregorio Cortez was the seventh son of a seventh son.[6]

You piddling modern farmers, vain of yourselves when you make a bale! You should have seen the crops raised by Gregorio Cortez. And when harvesting came, he was in there with the rest. Was it shucking corn? All you could see was the shucks fly and the pile grow, until you didn't know there was a man behind the pile. But he was even better at cotton-picking time. He would bend down and never raise his head till he came out the other end, and he would

---

3. **pachucos** (pä-chōō′kôs) *Spanish:* young toughs.
4. **vaquero** (vä-kě′rō) *Spanish:* cowboy.
5. **caporal** (kä-pô-räl′) *Spanish:* boss of a ranch.
6. **seventh son of a seventh son:** According to the folklore of several cultures, the seventh son of a seventh son is always lucky and may be gifted with certain supernatural powers.

be halfway through another row before the next man was through with his. And don't think the row he went through wasn't clean. No flags, no streamers, nothing left behind, nothing but clean, empty burrs where he had passed. It was the same when clearing land. There were men who went ahead of him, cutting fast along their strip in the early morning, but by noontime the man ahead was always Gregorio Cortez, working at his own pace, talking little and not singing very much, and never acting up.

FOR Gregorio Cortez was not of your noisy, hell-raising type. That was not his way. He always spoke low, and he was always polite, whoever he was speaking to. And when he spoke to men older than himself he took off his hat and held it over his heart. A man who never raised his voice to parent or elder brother, and never disobeyed. That was Gregorio Cortez, and that was the way men were in this country along the river. That was the way they were before these modern times came, and God went away.

He should have stayed on the Border; he should not have gone up above, into the North. But it was going to be that way, and that was the way it was. Each man has a certain lot in life, and no other thing but that will be his share. People were always coming down from places in the North, from Dallas and San Antonio and Corpus and Foro West. And they would say, "Gregorio Cortez, why don't you go north? There is much money to be made. Stop eating

New Mexico Peon (1945), Ernest L. Blumenschein. Oil on canvas, 40″ × 25″, collection of Kathleen and Gerald Peters, Santa Fe, New Mexico.

beans and tortillas and that rubbery jerked beef. One of these days you're going to put out one of your eyes, pull and pull with your teeth on that stuff and it suddenly lets go. It's a wonder all you Border people are not one-eyed. Come up above with us, where you can eat white bread and ham."

Román was just like the young men of today,...

But Gregorio Cortez would only smile, because he was a peaceful man and did not take offense. He did not like white bread and ham; it makes people flatulent and dull. And he liked it where he was. So he always said, "I like this country. I will stay here."

But Gregorio Cortez had a brother, a younger brother named Román. Now Román was just like the young men of today, loud-mouthed and discontented. He was never happy where he was, and to make it worse he loved a joke more than any other thing. He would think nothing of playing a joke on a person twice his age. He had no respect for anyone, and that is why he ended like he did. But that is yet to tell.

Román talked to Gregorio and begged him that they should move away from the river and go up above, where there was much money to be made. And he talked and begged so, that finally Gregorio Cortez said he would go with his brother Román, and they saddled their horses and rode north.

Well, they did not grow rich, though things went well with them because they were good workers. Sometimes they picked cotton; sometimes they were vaqueros, and sometimes they cleared land for the Germans. Finally they came to a place called El Carmen, and there they settled down and farmed. And that was how Gregorio Cortez came to be in the county of El Carmen, where the tragedy took place.

Román's Horse Trade and What Came of It

Román owned two horses, two beautiful sorrels[7] that were just alike, the same color, the same markings, and the same size. You could not have told them apart, except that one of them was lame. There was an American who owned a little sorrel mare. This man was dying to get Román's sorrel—the good one—and every time they met he would offer to swap the mare for the horse. But Román did not think much of the mare. He did not like it when the American kept trying to make him trade.

"I wonder what this Gringo[8] thinks," Román said to himself. "He takes me for a fool. But I'm going to make him such a trade that he will remember me forever."

And Román laughed a big-mouthed laugh. He thought it would be a fine joke, besides being a good trade. There were mornings when the American went to town in his buggy along a narrow road. So Román saddled the lame sorrel, led him a little way along the road, and stopped under a big mesquite[9] that bordered on the fence. He fixed it so the spavined[10] side was against the mesquite. Román waited a little while, and soon he heard the buggy coming along the road. Then he got in the saddle and began picking mesquites off the tree and eating them. When the American came around the bend, there was Román on his sorrel horse. The American stopped his buggy beside Román and looked at the horse with much admiration.

---

7. **sorrels:** horses of a light reddish brown.

8. **gringo** (grēng′gô) *Spanish:* slang term for a foreigner, especially someone from the United States.

9. **mesquite** (mĕ-skēt′): thorny, shrublike tree with sweet seeds.

10. **spavined** (spăv′ĭnd): afflicted with spavin, a disease in which a horse's hind leg joint becomes enlarged, resulting in lameness.

It was a fine animal, exactly like the other one, but the American could not see the spavined leg.

"Changed your mind?" the American said.

Román stopped chewing on a mesquite and said, "Changed my mind about what?"

"About trading that horse for my mare."

"You're dead set on trading your mare for this horse of mine?" Román said.

"You know I am," the American said. "Are you ready to come round?"

"I'm in a trading mood," said Román. "With just a little arguing you might convince me to trade this horse for that worthless mare of yours. But I don't know; you might go back on the deal later on."

"I never go back on my word," the American said. "What do you think I am, a Mexican?"

"We'll see, we'll see," said Román. "How much are you willing to give in hand?"

"Enough to give you the first square meal you've had in your life," the American said.

ROMÁN just laughed, and it was all he could do to keep from guffawing. He knew who was getting the best of things.

So they made the deal, with Román still sitting on his spavined horse under the tree, chewing on mesquites.

"Where's the mare?" Román said.

"She's in my yard," said the American, "hung to a tree. You go get her and leave the horse there for me because I'm in a hurry to get to town."

That was how Román had figured it, so he said, "All right, I'll do it, but when I finish with these mesquites."

"Be sure you do, then," the American said.

"Sure, sure," said Román. "No hurry about it, is there?"

"All right," the American said, "take your time." And he drove off leaving Román still sitting on his horse under the mesquite, and as he drove off the American said, "Now isn't that just like a Mexican. He takes his time."

Román waited until the American was gone, and then he stopped eating mesquites. He got off and led the horse down the road to the American's yard and left him there in place of the little sorrel mare. On the way home Román almost fell off his saddle a couple of times, just laughing and laughing to think of the sort of face the American would pull when he came home that night.

The next morning, when Gregorio Cortez got up he said to his brother Román, "Something is going to happen today."

"Why do you say that?" asked Román.

"I don't know," said Gregorio Cortez. "I just know that something is going to happen today. I feel it. Last night my wife began to sigh for no reason at all. She kept sighing and sighing half the night, and she didn't know why. Her heart was telling her something, and I know some unlucky thing will happen to us today."

But Román just laughed, and Gregorio went inside the house to shave. Román followed him into the house and stood at the door while Gregorio shaved. It was a door made in two sections; the upper part was open and Román was leaning on the lower part, like a man leaning out of a window or over a fence. Román began to tell Gregorio about the horse trade he had made the day before, and he laughed pretty loud about it, because he thought it was a good

...loud-mouthed and discontented.

joke. Gregorio Cortez just shaved, and he didn't say anything.

When what should pull in at the gate but a buggy, and the American got down, and the Major Sheriff of the county of El Carmen got down too. They came into the yard and up to where Román was leaning over the door, looking out.

The American had a very serious face. "I came for the mare you stole yesterday morning," he said.

Román laughed a big-mouthed laugh. "What did I tell you, Gregorio?" he said. "This Gringo . . . has backed down on me." . . .

Just as the word "Gringo . . ." came out of Román's mouth, the sheriff whipped out his pistol and shot Román. He shot Román as he stood there with his head thrown back, laughing at his joke. The sheriff shot him in the face, right in the open mouth, and Román fell away from the door, at the Major Sheriff's feet.

AND then Gregorio Cortez stood at the door, where his brother had stood, with his pistol in his hand. Now he and the Major Sheriff met, each one pistol in hand, as men should meet when they fight for what is right. For it is a pretty thing to see, when two men stand up for their right, with their pistols in their hands, front to front and without fear. And so it was, for the Major Sheriff also was a man.

Yes, the Major Sheriff was a man; he was a gamecock[11] that had won in many pits, but in Gregorio Cortez he met a cockerel[12] that pecked his comb. The Major Sheriff shot first, and he missed; and Gregorio Cortez shot next, and he didn't miss. Three times did they shoot, three times did the Major Sheriff miss, and three times did Gregorio Cortez shoot the sheriff of El Carmen. The Major Sheriff fell dead at the feet of Gregorio Cortez, and it was in this way that Gregorio Cortez killed the first sheriff of many that he was to kill.

When the Major Sheriff fell, Gregorio Cortez looked up, and the other American said, "Don't kill me; I am unarmed."

"I will not kill you," said Gregorio Cortez. "But you'd better go away."

So the American went away. He ran into the brush and kept on running until he came to town and told all the other sheriffs that the Major Sheriff was dead.

Meanwhile, Gregorio Cortez knew that he too must go away. He was not afraid of the law; he knew the law, and he knew that he had the right. But if he stayed, the Rangers[13] would come, and the Rangers have no regard for law. You know what kind of men they are. When the Governor of the State wants a new Ranger, he asks his sheriffs, "Bring all the criminals to me." And from the murderers he chooses the Ranger, because no one can be a Ranger who has not killed a man. So Gregorio Cortez knew that the best thing for him was to go away, and his first thought was of the Border, where he had been born. But first he must take care of his brother, so he put Román in the buggy and drove into town, where his mother lived.

Now there was a lot of excitement in town. All the Americans were saddling up and loading rifles and pistols, because they were going out to kill Cortez. When all of a sudden, what should come rolling into town but the buggy, driven by Gregorio Cortez. They met him on the edge of town, armed to the teeth, on horseback and afoot, and he on the buggy, holding the reins lightly in his hands. Román was in the back, shot in the mouth. He could neither speak nor move, but just lay there like one who is dead.

They asked him, "Who are you?"

And he said to them, "I am Gregorio Cortez."

They all looked at him and were afraid of him, because they were only twenty or twenty-

---

11. **gamecock:** rooster trained for fighting.
12. **cockerel:** young rooster.
13. **Rangers:** mounted riflemen organized to protect Anglo ranchers and settlers in Texas.

Chama Running Red (1925), John Sloan. Courtesy of The Anschutz Collection. Photo by James O. Milmoe.

five, and they knew that they were not enough. So they stepped aside and let him pass and stood talking among themselves what would be the best thing to do. But Gregorio Cortez just drove ahead, slowly, without seeming to care about the men he left behind. He came to his mother's house, and there he took down his brother and carried him in the house. He stayed there until dawn, and during the night groups of armed men would go by the house and say, "He's in there. He's in there." But none of them ever went in.

At dawn Gregorio Cortez came out of his mother's house. There were armed men outside, but they made no move against him. They just watched as he went down the street, his hands resting on his belt. He went along as if he was taking a walk, and they stood there watching until he reached the brush and he jumped into it and disappeared. And then they started shooting at him with rifles, now that he was out of pistol range.

"I must get me a rifle," said Gregorio Cortez, "a rifle and a horse."

They gathered in a big bunch and started after him in the brush. But they could not catch Gregorio Cortez. No man was ever as good as

They'll never catch me like that,...

him in hiding his own tracks, and he soon had them going around in circles, while he doubled back and headed for home to get himself a rifle and a horse.

How Gregorio Cortez Rode the Little Sorrel Mare All of Five Hundred Miles

He went in and got his thirty-thirty, and then he looked around for the best horse he had. It is a long way from El Carmen to the Border, all of five hundred miles. The first thing he saw in the corral was the little sorrel mare. Gregorio Cortez took a good look at her, and he knew she was no ordinary mare.

"You're worth a dozen horses," said Gregorio Cortez, and he saddled the little mare.

But by then the whole wasp's nest was beginning to buzz. The President of the United States offered a thousand dollars for him, and many men went out to get Gregorio Cortez. The Major Sheriffs of the counties and all their sheriffs were out. There were Rangers from the counties, armed to the teeth, and the King Ranch Rangers from the Capital, the meanest of them all, all armed and looking for Cortez. Every road was blocked and every bridge guarded. There were trackers out with those dogs they call hounds, that can follow a track better than the best tracker. They had railroad cars loaded with guns and ammunition and with men, moving up and down trying to head him off. The women and children stayed in the houses, behind locked doors, such was the fear they all had of Gregorio Cortez. Every town from the Capital to the Border was watching out for him. The brush and the fields were full of men, trying to pick up his trail. And Gregorio Cortez rode out for the Border, through brush and fields and barbed wire fences, on his little sorrel mare.

He rode and rode until he came to a great broad plain, and he started to ride across. But just as he did, one of the sheriffs saw him. The sheriff saw him, but he hid behind a bush, because he was afraid to take him on alone. So he called the other sheriffs together and all the Rangers he could find, and they went off after Gregorio Cortez just as he came out upon the plain.

Gregorio Cortez looked back and saw them coming. There were three hundred of them.

"We'll run them a little race," said Gregorio Cortez.

Away went the mare, as if she had been shot from a gun, and behind her came the sheriffs and the Rangers, all shooting and riding hard. And so they rode across the plain, until one by one their horses foundered and fell to the ground and died. But still the little mare ran on, as fresh as a lettuce leaf, and pretty soon she was running all alone.

"They'll never catch me like that," said Gregorio Cortez, "not even with those dogs called hounds."

Another big bunch of sheriffs rode up, and they chased him to the edge of the plain, and into the brush went Cortez, with the trackers after him, but they did not chase him long. One moment there was a trail to follow, and next moment there was none. And the dogs called hounds sat down and howled, and the men scratched their heads and went about in circles looking for the trail. And Gregorio Cortez went on, leaving no trail, so that people thought he was riding through the air.

There were armed men everywhere, and he could not stop to eat or drink, because wherever he tried to stop armed men were there before him. So he had to ride on and on. Now they saw him, now they lost him, and so the chase went on. Many more horses foundered, but the mare still ran, and Gregorio Cortez rode on and on, pursued by hundreds and fighting hundreds every place he went.

"So many mounted Rangers," said Gregorio Cortez, "to catch just one Mexican."

It was from the big bunches that he ran. Now and again he would run into little ones of ten or a dozen men, and they were so scared of him that they would let him pass. Then, when he was out of range they would shoot at him, and he would shoot back at them once or twice, so they could go back and say, "We met up with Gregorio Cortez, and we traded shots with him." But from the big ones he had to run. And it was the little sorrel mare that took him safe away, over the open spaces and into the brush, and once in the brush, they might as well have been following a star.

So it went for a day, and when night fell Cortez arrived at a place named Los Fresnos and called at a Mexican house. When the man of the house came out, Cortez told him, "I am Gregorio Cortez."

That was all he had to say. He was given to eat and drink, and the man of the house offered Gregorio Cortez his own horse and his rifle and his saddle. But Cortez would not take them. He thanked the man, but he would not give up his little sorrel mare. Cortez was sitting there, drinking a cup of coffee, when the Major Sheriff of Los Fresnos came up with his three hundred men. All the other people ran out of the house and hid, and no one was left in the house, only Gregorio Cortez, with his pistol in his hand.

Then the Major Sheriff called out, in a weepy voice, as the corrido says. He sounded as if he wanted to cry, but it was all done to deceive Gregorio Cortez.

"Cortez," the Major Sheriff said, "hand over your weapons. I did not come to kill you. I am your friend."

"If you come as my friend," said Gregorio Cortez, "why did you bring three hundred men? Why have you made me a corral?"

The Major Sheriff knew that he had been caught in a lie, and the fighting began. He killed the Major Sheriff and the second sheriff under him, and he killed many sheriffs more. Some of the sheriffs got weak in the knees, and many ran away.

"Don't go away," said Gregorio Cortez. "I am the man you are looking for. I am Gregorio Cortez."

They were more than three hundred, but he jumped their corral, and he rode away again, and those three hundred did not chase him any more.

He rode on and on, until he came to a river called the San Antonio. It is not much of a river, but the banks are steep and high, and he could not find a ford. So he rode to a ranch house nearby, where they were holding a *baile*[14] because the youngest child of the house had been baptized that day, and he asked the man of the house about a ford.

"There are only two fords," the man said. "One is seven miles upstream and the other is seven miles down."

---

14. *baile* (bäy'lĕ) *Spanish:* dance.

...not even with those dogs called hounds.

"I will take another look at the river," said Gregorio Cortez. He left the baile and rode slowly to the river. It was steep, and far below he could see the water flowing; he could barely see it because it was so dark. He stood there thinking, trying to figure out a way, when he heard the music at the baile stop.

He knew the Rangers were at the baile now. So he leaned over in his saddle and whispered in the mare's ear. He talked to her, and she understood. She came to the edge of the bank, with soft little steps, because she was afraid. But Gregorio Cortez kept talking to her and talking to her, and finally she jumped. She jumped far out and into the dark water below, she and Gregorio Cortez.

The other bank was not so high, but it was just as steep. Gregorio Cortez took out his reata,[15] and he lassoed a stump high on the bank. He climbed up the rope and got a stick, and with the stick he worked on the bank as fast as he could, for he could hear the racket of the dogs. The ground was soft, and he knocked off part of the top, until he made something like a slope. Then he pulled and talked until the mare struggled up the bank to where he was. After that they rested up a bit and waited for the Rangers. Up they came with their dogs, to the spot where the mare had jumped. When they came up to the river's edge, Cortez fired a shot in the air and yelled at them, "I am Gregorio Cortez!"

Then he rode away, leaving them standing there on the other side, because none of them

Cliffs Beyond Abiquiu, Dry Waterfall (1943), Georgia O'Keeffe. Oil on canvas, 76.2 cm × 40.6 cm, The Cleveland (Ohio) Museum of Art, bequest of Georgia O'Keeffe (87.141). Copyright © 1996 The Georgia O'Keeffe Foundation/Artists Rights Society (ARS), New York. Photo Copyright © The Cleveland Museum of Art.

was brave enough to do what Cortez had done.

He rode on and on, and sometimes they chased him and sometimes he stood and fought. And every time he fought he would kill them a Ranger or two. They chased him across the Arroyo del Cíbolo and into an oak grove, and there they made him a corral. Then they sent the dogs away and sat down to wait, for they wanted to catch him asleep. Gregorio Cortez thought for a little while what he should do. Then he made his mare lie down on the ground, so she would not be hurt. After that Gregorio Cortez began talking to himself and answering himself in different voices, as if he had many men. This made the Rangers say to one another, "There is a whole army of men with Gregorio Cortez." So they broke up their corral and went away, because they did not think there were enough of them to fight Gregorio Cortez and all the men he had. And Gregorio Cortez rode away, laughing to himself.

He kept riding on and on, by day and by night, and if he slept the mare stood guard and she would wake him up when she heard a noise. He had no food or cigarettes, and his ammunition was running low. He was going along a narrow trail with a high barbed wire fence on one side and a nopal[16] thicket on the other, and right before he hit a turn he heard

---

15. **reata** (rĕ-ä′tä) *Spanish:* lasso or lariat.

16. **nopal** (nô-päl′) *Spanish:* kind of cactus.

horses ahead. The first man that came around the turn ran into Gregorio Cortez, with his pistol in his hand. There was a whole line of others behind the first, all armed with rifles, but they had to put the rifles away. Then Gregorio Cortez knocked over a tall nopal plant with his stirrup and made just enough room for his mare to back into while the Rangers filed by. He stopped the last one and took away his tobacco, matches, and ammunition. And then he rode away.

He rode on to La Grulla, and he was very thirsty, because he had not had water in a long time, and the mare was thirsty too. Near La Grulla there was a dam where the vaqueros watered their stock. But when Gregorio Cortez got there, he saw twenty armed men resting under the trees that grew close to the water. Gregorio Cortez stopped and thought what he could do. Then he went back into the brush and began rounding up cattle, for this was cattle country and steers were everywhere. Pretty soon he had two hundred head, and he drove them to water and while the cattle drank he and the mare drank too. After he had finished, some of the Rangers that were resting under the trees came over and helped him get the herd together again, and Gregorio Cortez rode off with the herd, laughing to himself.

HE rode on and on, and by now he knew that the Rio Grande was near. He rode till he came to Cotulla, and there he was chased again. The little mare was tired, and now she began to limp. She had cut her leg and it was swelling up. Gregorio Cortez rode her into a thicket, and the Rangers made him a corral. But once in the brush, Gregorio Cortez led the mare to a *coma*[17] tree and tied her there. He unsaddled her and hung the saddle to the tree, and he patted her and talked to her for a long while. Then he slipped out of the thicket, and the Rangers didn't see him because they were waiting for him to ride out. They waited for three days and finally they crept in and found only the mare and the saddle.

How El Teco Sold Gregorio Cortez for a Morral[18] Full of Silver Dollars

Gregorio Cortez was gone. While all the armed men were guarding the thicket where the mare was tied, he walked into Cotulla itself. He walked into town and mixed with the Mexicans there. He sat on the station platform and listened to other men while they talked of all the things that Gregorio Cortez had done. Then he went to a store and bought himself new clothes and walked out of the town. He went to the river and took a bath and then swam across, because the bridge was guarded. That sort of man was Gregorio Cortez. They don't make them like him any more.

He had only three cartridges left, one for one pistol and two for the other, and he had left his rifle with the mare. But he was very near the Rio Grande, and he expected to cross it soon. Still he needed ammunition, so he walked into El Sauz and tried to buy some, but they did not sell cartridges in that town. Then he thought of trying some of the houses, and chose one in which there was a pretty girl at the door because he knew it would be easier if he talked to a girl. There was not a woman that did not like Gregorio Cortez.

The girl was alone, and she invited him into the house. When he asked for ammunition, she told him she had none.

"My father has taken it all," she said. "He is out looking for a man named Gregorio Cortez."

Gregorio Cortez was embarrassed because he could see that the girl knew who he was. But she did not let on and neither did he. He stayed at the house for a while, and when he left she told him how to get to the Rio Grande by the quickest way.

---

17. *coma* (kô′mä) *Spanish:* kind of thorn tree.
18. *morral* (mô-räl′) *Spanish:* large bag or pouch.

Now all the people along the river knew that Gregorio Cortez was on the Border, and that he would soon cross, but no one told the sheriffs what they knew. And Gregorio Cortez walked on, in his new clothes, with his pistols in a morral, looking like an ordinary man, but the people he met knew that he was Gregorio Cortez. And he began to talk to people along the way.

SOON he met a man who told him, "You'll be on the other side of the river tonight, Gregorio Cortez."

"I think I will," he said.

"You'll be all right then," said the man.

"I guess so," said Gregorio Cortez.

"But your brother won't," the man said. "He died in the jail last night."

"He was badly wounded," said Gregorio Cortez. "It was his lot to die, but I have avenged his death."

"They beat him before he died," the man said. "The Rangers came to the jail and beat him to make him talk."

This was the first news that Gregorio Cortez had heard, and it made him thoughtful.

He walked on, and he met another man who said, "Your mother is in the jail, Gregorio Cortez."

"Why?" said Gregorio Cortez. "Why should the sheriffs do that to her?"

"Because she is your mother," the man said. "That's why. Your wife is there too, and so are your little sons."

Gregorio Cortez thought this over, and he walked on. Pretty soon he met another man who said, "Gregorio Cortez, your own people are suffering, and all because of you."

"Why should my own people suffer?" said Cortez. "What have I done to them?"

"You have killed many sheriffs, Gregorio Cortez," said the man. "The Rangers cannot catch you, so they take it out on other people like you. Every man that's given you a glass of water has been beaten and thrown in jail. Every man who has fed you has been hanged from a tree branch, up and down, up and down, to make him tell where you went, and some have died rather than tell. Lots of people have been shot and beaten because they were your people. But you will be safe, Gregorio Cortez; you will cross the river tonight."

"I did not know these things," said Gregorio Cortez.

And he decided to turn back, and to give himself up to the Governor of the State so that his own people would not suffer because of him.

He turned and walked back until he came to a place called Goliad, where he met eleven Mexicans, and among them there was one that called himself his friend. This man was a vaquero named El Teco, but Judas should have been his name. Gregorio Cortez was thirsty, and he came up to the eleven Mexicans to ask for water, and when El Teco saw Gregorio Cortez he thought how good it would be if he could get the thousand-dollar reward. So he walked up to Cortez and shook his hand and told the others, "Get some water for my friend Gregorio Cortez."

Then El Teco asked Gregorio Cortez to let him see the pistols he had, and that he would get him some ammunition. Gregorio Cortez smiled, because he knew. But he handed over the guns to El Teco, and El Teco looked at them and put them in his own morral. Then El Teco called the sheriffs to come and get Gregorio Cortez.

Every man that's given you a glass of water...

...has been beaten and thrown in jail.

When Gregorio Cortez saw what El Teco had done, he smiled again and said to him, "Teco, a man can only be what God made him. May you enjoy your reward."

But El Teco did not enjoy the reward, though the sheriffs gave him the money, one thousand dollars in silver, more than a morral could hold. He did not enjoy it because he could not spend it anywhere. If he went to buy a taco at the market place, the taco vender would tell him that tacos were worth two thousand dollars gold that day. People cursed him in the streets and wished that he would be killed or die. So El Teco became very much afraid. He buried the money and never spent it, and he never knew peace until he died.

How Gregorio Cortez Went to Prison, but Not for Killing the Sheriffs

When the sheriffs came to arrest Gregorio Cortez, he spoke to them and said, "I am not your prisoner yet. I will be the prisoner only of the Governor of the State. I was going to the Capital to give myself up, and that is where I'll go."

The sheriffs saw that he was in the right, so they went with him all the way to the Capital, and Cortez surrendered himself to the Governor of the State.

Then they put Cortez in jail, and all the Americans were glad, because they no longer were afraid. They got together, and they tried to lynch him. Three times they tried, but they could not lynch Gregorio Cortez.

And pretty soon all the people began to see that Gregorio Cortez was in the right, and they did not want to lynch him any more. They brought him gifts to the jail, and one day one of the judges came and shook the hand of Gregorio Cortez and said to him, "I would have done the same."

But Gregorio Cortez had many enemies, for he had killed many men, and they wanted to see him hanged. So they brought him to trial for killing the Major Sheriff of the county of El Carmen. The lawyer that was against him got up and told the judges that Cortez should die, because he had killed a man. Then Gregorio Cortez got up, and he spoke to them.

"Self-defense is allowed to any man," said Gregorio Cortez. "It is in your own law, and by your own law do I defend myself. I killed the sheriff, and I am not sorry, for he killed my brother. He spilled my brother's blood, which was also my blood. And he tried to kill me too. I killed the Major Sheriff defending my right."

And Gregorio Cortez talked for a long time to the judges, telling them about their own law. When he finished even the lawyer who was against him at the start was now for him. And all the judges came down from their benches and shook hands with Gregorio Cortez.

The judges said, "We cannot kill this man."

They took Gregorio Cortez all over the State, from town to town, and in each town he was tried before the court for the killing of a man. But in every court it was the same. Gregorio Cortez spoke to the judges, and he told them about the law, and he proved that he had the right. And each time the judges said, "This man was defending his right. Tell the sheriffs to set him free."

And so it was that Gregorio Cortez was not found guilty of any wrong because of the sheriffs he had killed. And he killed many of them, there is no room for doubt. No man has killed more sheriffs than did Gregorio Cortez, and he always fought alone. For that is the way the real men fight, always on their own. There are young men around here today, who think that they are brave. Dangerous men they call themselves, and it takes five or six of them to jump a fellow and slash him in the arm. Or they hide in the brush and fill him full of buckshot as he goes by. They are not men. But that was not the way with Gregorio Cortez, for he was a real man.

Now the enemies of Gregorio Cortez got together and said to each other, "What are we going to do? This man is going free after killing so many of our friends. Shall we kill ourselves? But we would have to catch him asleep, or shoot him in the back, because if we meet him face to face there will be few of us left."

Then one of them thought of the little sorrel mare, and there they had a plan to get Gregorio Cortez. They brought him back to court, and the lawyer who was against him asked, "Gregorio Cortez, do you recognize this mare?"

"I do," said Gregorio Cortez. "And a better little mare there never was."

Then the lawyer asked him, "Have you ridden this mare?"

And Gregorio Cortez answered, "She carried me all the way from El Carmen to the Border, a distance of five hundred miles."

T**HEN** the lawyer asked him, "Is this mare yours?"

And Gregorio Cortez saw that they had him, but there was nothing he could do, because he was an honest man and he felt that he must tell the truth. He said no, the mare did not belong to him.

Then the judges asked Gregorio Cortez, "Is this true, Gregorio Cortez? Did you take this mare that did not belong to you?"

And Gregorio Cortez had to say that the thing was true.

So they sentenced Gregorio Cortez, but not for killing the sheriffs, as some fools will tell you even now, when they ought to know better. No, not for killing the sheriffs but for stealing the little sorrel mare. The judge sentenced him to ninety-nine years and a day. And the enemies of Gregorio Cortez were happy then, because they thought Cortez would be in prison for the rest of his life.

How President Lincoln's Daughter Freed Gregorio Cortez, and How He Was Poisoned and Died

But Gregorio Cortez did not stay in prison long. Inside of a year he was free, and this is the way it came about. Every year at Christmastime, a pretty girl can come to the Governor of the State and ask him to give her a prisoner as a Christmas present. And the Governor then has to set the prisoner free and give him to the girl. So it happened to Cortez. One day President Lincoln's daughter visited the prison, and she saw Gregorio Cortez. As soon as she saw him she went up and spoke to him.

"I am in love with you, Gregorio Cortez," President Lincoln's daughter said, "and if you promise to marry me I will go to the Governor next Christmas and tell him to give you to me."

Gregorio Cortez looked at President Lincoln's daughter, and he saw how beautiful she was. It made him thoughtful, and he did not know what to say.

"I have many rich farms," President Lincoln's daughter said. "They are all my own. Marry me and we will farm together."

Gregorio Cortez thought about that. He could see himself already like a German, sitting on the gallery, full of ham and beer, and belching and breaking wind while a half-dozen little blond cockroaches played in the yard. And he was tempted. But then he said to himself, "I can't marry a Gringo girl. We would not make a matching pair."

So he decided that President Lincoln's daughter was not the woman for him, and he told her, "I thank you very much, but I cannot marry you at all."

But President Lincoln's daughter would not take his no. She went to the Governor and said, "I would like to have a prisoner for Christmas."

And the Governor looked at her and saw she was a pretty girl, so he said, "Your wish is granted. What prisoner do you want?"

And President Lincoln's daughter said, "I want Gregorio Cortez."

The Governor thought for a little while and then he said, "That's a man you cannot have. He's the best prisoner I got."

But President Lincoln's daughter shook her head and said, "Don't forget that you gave your word."

"So I did," the Governor said, "and I cannot go back on it."

And that was how Gregorio Cortez got out of prison, where he had been sentenced to ninety-nine years and a day, not for killing the sheriffs, as some fools will tell you, but for stealing the little sorrel mare. Gregorio Cortez kept his word, and he did not marry President Lincoln's daughter, and when at last she lost her hopes she went away to the north.

Still, the enemies of Gregorio Cortez did not give up. When they heard that he was getting out of prison they were scared and angry, and they started thinking of ways to get revenge. They got a lot of money together and gave it to a man who worked in the prison, and this man gave Cortez a slow poison just before Gregorio Cortez got out of jail.

And that was how he came to die, within a year from the day he got out of jail. As soon as he came out and his friends saw him, they said to each other, "This man is sick. This man will not last the year."

And so it was. He did not last the year. He died of the slow poison they gave him just before he was let out, because his enemies did not want to see him free.

AND that was how Gregorio Cortez came to die. He's buried in Laredo some place, or maybe it's Brownsville, or Matamoros, or somewhere up above. To tell the truth, I don't know. I don't know the place where he is buried any more than the place where he was born. But he was born and lived and died, that I do know. And a lot of Rangers could also tell you that.

So does the corrido; it tells about Gregorio Cortez and who he was. They started singing the corrido soon after he went to jail, and there was a time when it was forbidden in all the United States, by order of the President himself. Men sometimes got killed or lost their jobs because they sang *El Corrido de Gregorio Cortez*. But everybody sang it just the same, because it spoke about things that were true.

Now it is all right to sing *El Corrido de Gregorio Cortez*, but not everybody knows it any more. And they don't sing it as it used to be sung. These new singers change all the old songs a lot. But even so, people still remember Gregorio Cortez. And when a good singer sings the song— good and loud and clear—you can feel your neck-feathers rise, and you can see him standing there, with his pistol in his hand. ❖

Thinking through the LITERATURE

Connect to the Literature

1. What Do You Think?
Did you enjoy this retelling of the *corrido?* Discuss your opinions with classmates.

Comprehension Check
- Why is Cortez being pursued?
- Why does El Teco betray Cortez?
- For what crime is Cortez finally sentenced to prison?

Think Critically

2. Which of Gregorio Cortez's personal qualities do you find most admirable? Why?

3. What do the comments and attitudes of the **speaker** in this retelling reveal about cultural conflicts between Anglos and Mexicans in the Texas border area during this time period?

> **THINK ABOUT**
> - the portrayal of the sheriffs and the Texas Rangers
> - the number of men required to capture Gregorio Cortez
> - the conversation between Román and the American who owns the mare
> - the treatment Cortez receives in U.S. courts

4. Do you think Gregorio Cortez was right to live by the code "I will break before I bend"? Defend your opinion.

5. **ACTIVE READING** **MAKING JUDGMENTS ABOUT TEXT** Refer to the diagram you made in your **READER'S NOTEBOOK.** Which details and events in this story seem especially realistic and which appear to be purely fictional?

Extend Interpretations

6. Critic's Corner Some readers argue that because Gregorio Cortez kills many people, he is an inappropriate person to present as a hero. Argue for or against that position.

7. Connect to Life Think of other heroes you have encountered in movies, TV programs, books, cartoons, or newspaper and magazine articles. Which of them resemble Gregorio Cortez, and in what ways?

8. Points of Comparison What cultural values revealed in "The Legend of Gregorio Cortez" are also highly regarded in "The Indian and the Hundred Cows" and "High Horse's Courting"? Support your answer with examples from all three stories.

Literary Analysis

LEGEND Like myths, fables, and folk tales, **legends** belong to the oral tradition of literature. A mix of both fact and fiction, "The Legend of Gregorio Cortez" centers on a **cultural hero,** who embodies the values of early 20th-century Mexican Americans from the Texas border region. This kind of hero is not the creation of a single writer, but rather evolves from communal tales—told orally or sung to musical accompaniment—that were passed down from one generation to the next.

Cooperative Learning Activity
Review the biographical information about Gregorio Cortez in the Build Background feature on page 702. Why do you think singers and storytellers might have exaggerated or invented certain events in Cortez's life? Share your response with a small group of classmates.

Choices & CHALLENGES

Writing Options

1. Farewell Letter Write a farewell letter from Gregorio to his young sons in which he explains the reasons for his actions and gives them advice for living their lives.

2. Points of Comparison
Imagine a meeting between Gregorio Cortez and High Horse, the lovesick young man in "High Horse's Courting." Write a fictional dialogue in which they discuss the ideals of manhood that are prized in each of their cultures. Both characters should explain how their behavior illustrates these ideals. Refer to the stories for examples.

Activities & Explorations

1. Map of the Setting Copy and enlarge the map of the Texas border region on page 702 to locate some of the places mentioned in this story. Write a brief description explaining the importance of these sites. Then draw the escape route followed by Gregorio Cortez as he tried to elude the Texas Rangers and the sheriffs. How likely is it that the *real* Gregorio Cortez followed the route described in the story? **~ GEOGRAPHY**

2. TV Newscast With a small group, report the story of Gregorio Cortez for a national evening news broadcast. Include spot interviews to make your report lively. **~ SPEAKING AND LISTENING**

Inquiry & Research

Colorful Folk Songs This story is a prose retelling of a Mexican folk song, "El Corrido de Gregorio Cortez." If possible, find recordings of *corridos* about Cortez or other heroes, such as Pancho Villa or José Mosqueda. Play your favorites for the class.

Américo Paredes
1915–

Other Works
Corridos and Calaveras
Between Two Worlds
The Hammon and the Beans and Other Stories
A Texas-Mexican Cancionero

Resounding Mexican Voices Américo Paredes, the son of a rancher, grew up near Brownsville, Texas, along the Mexican border. During this time, he absorbed the colorful traditions, songs, and legends of the area. This early experience with these traditions shaped Paredes's lifework. In describing his fascination with Mexican *corridos* and other folk songs, he said, "I started 'collecting' these songs around 1920, when I first became aware of them on the lips of the *guitarreros* and other people of the ranchos and the towns."

Scholarly Pursuits After serving in the U.S. Army during World War II, Paredes attended the University of Texas, where he earned his bachelor's, master's, and doctoral degrees. In 1954 he joined the faculty at the university, where he has served as the director of the Center for Intercultural Studies in Folklore and Oral History and of the Mexican-American Studies program.

Impressive Credentials While a professor of English and anthropology at the University of Texas, Paredes published numerous books documenting Mexican-American folk traditions. Among his best-known works are *"With His Pistol in His Hand": A Border Ballad and Its Hero* (1958), from which "The Legend of Gregorio Cortez" is taken, and *Folktales of Mexico* (1970). Paredes also has been the editor of the *Journal of American Folklore* and has edited many works on cultural anthropology. For his achievement in preserving the Mexican-American folk tradition, Paredes has received several important awards, among them the Order of the Aztec Eagle, Mexico's highest award to foreigners.

Author Activity

The Storyteller's Voice Read a selection from *Folktales from Mexico* by Paredes, and perform it orally for the class. Use gestures and props to make the story come alive.

Comparing Literature: Assessment Practice

In writing assessments, you will often be asked to evaluate the quality or merit of a literary work. You are now going to practice writing an essay with this kind of evaluative focus.

PART 1 ## Reading the Prompt

Often you will be asked to write in response to a prompt like the one below. First, read the entire prompt carefully. Then read through it again, looking for key words that help you identify the purpose of the essay and decide how to approach it.

> **Writing Prompt**
>
> Many of the selections from Unit Four, Part Two are intended to entertain audiences. Choose three of these pieces to explore. In an essay, (evaluate) ❶ the three and decide which you found to be the most entertaining. Justify your ratings with ❷ (evidence) from the literary selections. ❸

STRATEGIES IN ACTION

❶ **Evaluate**—form a judgment based on a set of standards, or criteria.

❷ Notice the **quality** you must create standards for and judge.

❸ Include **examples** or **quotations** from the selections.

PART 2 ## Planning an Evaluative Essay

- Determine your criteria—the key literary elements and devices that make stories entertaining.

- For each selection, create an evaluation grid like the example shown.

- Rate your responses to each of the criteria by filling in where they fall on the continuum.

- Note which selection received the highest ratings and why.

Criteria	Not successful Very successful
Amusing characters	████████████
Surprising plot	█████████████

PART 3 ## Drafting Your Essay

Introduction Begin by identifying the three selections you are judging. Then state your general opinion about which one is the most entertaining. Quickly summarize the criteria you used to make your decision.

Organization Evaluate each selection individually, or focus on one criterion at a time and apply it to all three selections. Remember to maintain the focus of your essay as you write. Support your judgments with examples, quotations, and details from the stories.

Conclusion Sum up your general impression of the most entertaining selection, and restate your key points.

Revision Allow time to review your work. Make sure it is clear, well-supported, and free from mistakes.

Writing Handbook See page 1283: Analysis

The Adventures of Huckleberry Finn

MARK TWAIN

These thematically related readings are provided along with *The Adventures of Huckleberry Finn*:

from **Life on the Mississippi**
MARK TWAIN

The Negro Speaks of Rivers
LANGSTON HUGHES

Narrative of Daniel Fisher
DANIEL FISHER

Three Days of Forest, A River, Free
RITA DOVE

The Outlaws
SELMA LAGERLÖF

from **Nine Pounds of Luggage**
MAUD PARRISH

Freedom
WILLIAM STAFFORD

from **Mississippi Solo**
EDDY HARRIS

My Ántonia

WILLA CATHER

These thematically related readings are provided along with *My Ántonia*:

Prairie Town
WILLIAM STAFFORD

If There Be Sorrow
MARI EVANS

On the Divide
WILLA CATHER

from **The Quilters**
NORMA BRADLEY BUFERD

Night on the Prairies
WALT WHITMAN

The Chrysanthemums
JOHN STEINBECK

And Even *More* . . .

Books

Giants in the Earth
OLE EDVART RÖLVAAG
A heroic tale focusing on Norwegian pioneers who settled in South Dakota.

Bury My Heart at Wounded Knee: An Indian History of the American West
DEE BROWN
A powerful chronicle of the West from a Native American perspective.

Remington and Russell: Artists of the West
WILLIAM C. KETCHUM, JR.
Profiles of two artists best known for their creative depictions of the West.

Other Media

Life on the Mississippi
Television adaptation of Mark Twain's autobiographical work about his apprenticeship on a riverboat. Films Inc. (VIDEOCASSETTE)

Shane
A classic Western adapted from Jack Schaefer's novel about homesteaders and the heroic gunfighter who protects them. Paramount Home Video. (VIDEOCASSETTE)

Mexican-American Folklore

JOHN O. WEST
This sweeping collection contains fascinating examples that reflect the rich culture of the American Southwest—legends, songs, festivals, proverbs, riddles, superstitions, crafts, tales of saints and revolutionaries, and more.

Communication Workshop Storytelling

Presenting an engaging tale . . .

From Reading to Presenting Long ago, folk tales such as "The Indian and the Hundred Cows" were passed down by word of mouth through **storytelling**. Early storytellers combined music, dance, stories, and poetry to pass on important information. Today, many folk tales have been written down, but professional storytellers still perform these and other stories at schools, libraries, and festivals. Professional story-tellers use costumes, props, gestures, and expressions to entertain their audiences. When you tell your friends about something exciting that happened to you, you are telling a story too.

For Your Portfolio

WRITING PROMPT Prepare a script or notes in which you plan how to tell a story. Then tell the story.

Purpose: To entertain
Audience: Classmates, hospital patients or nursing home residents, listeners at a library story hour

---

Basics in a Box

GUIDELINES & STANDARDS Storytelling

To prepare a useful script
- select or prepare a written version of the story
- mark individual lines with appropriate gestures, movements, and tone of voice

- indicate changes in mood and scene
- include a description of the setting, props, and costumes

To present a successful performance
- memorize the story (though not necessarily word for word from the script)
- consider the needs and interests of the audience members and maintain eye contact with them

- speak clearly, varying your voice as necessary
- incorporate body movements, facial expressions, props, and costumes as needed

A Storyteller in Action

- Storyteller begins speaking while sitting
- Tells story from memory
- Uses beads to create a simple costume that connects to story
- Uses gesture and voice to grab audience's interest immediately

- Moves to a standing position to shift the mood and maintain the audience's attention
- Makes dramatic movements and facial expressions to build tension

- Maintains eye contact to keep audience involved
- Performs specific actions to help the audience visualize the story

Analyzing a Storytelling Script

The Warrior Maiden:
An Oneida Folk Tale

Sit on stool; pause before beginning; make a wide, sweeping gesture with both arms

Costume: purple and white beaded necklaces, black clothes; props: feathery branch to represent woodbine, vine to represent honeysuckle

❶ Describes the costume and props needed

Long ago, in the days before the white settlers came to this continent, the Oneida people were beset by their

menacingly

old enemies, the Mingoes. The invaders attacked the

Stand up

Oneida villages, stormed their palisades, set fire to their

Pretend to throw spear

longhouses, laid waste to the land, destroyed the corn-fields, killed men and boys, and abducted the women

❷ Gives body move-ment and vocal cues

Motion of letting grains of sand fall from one hand to the other

and girls. There was no resisting the Mingoes, because their numbers were like grains of sand, like pebbles on a lake shore.

sadly

The villages of the Oneida lay deserted, their fields untended, the ruins of their homes blackened. The men had taken the women, the old people, the young boys and girls into the deep forests, hiding them in secret places among rocks, in caves, and on desolate moun-tains. The Mingoes searched for victims, but could not find them. The Great Spirit himself helped the people to hide and shielded their places of refuge from the eyes of their enemies.

❸ Uses gestures to act out story images

Put hands on stomach to show hunger

Thus the Oneida people were safe in their inaccessible retreats, but they were also starving. Whatever food they

Hold out one palm

had been able to save was soon eaten up. They could

Hold out the other palm

either stay in their hideouts and starve, or leave them in search of food and be discovered by their enemies. The warrior chiefs and sachems met in council but could find no other way out.

Change to hopeful tone

Then a young girl stepped forward in the council and said that the good spirits had sent her a dream showing

❹ Adjusts voice to change mood

Hands on hips

her how to save the Oneida. Her name was Aliquipiso

deliberately

and she was not afraid to give her life for her people. . . .

Preparing to Tell a Story

❶ Planning Your Performance

Choose a story you would love to tell. For instance, you might choose a favorite fable, folk tale, or legend. You also might choose to tell your own story about something that happened to you. Be sure to choose a story that strongly interests you. See the **Idea Bank** for other suggestions. After you select a story, follow the steps below.

Developing Your Performance

▶ **1. Tighten the plot.** Outline your own story or work with a published one. Analyze the story for any subplots that you need to get rid of in order to concentrate on a single, clearly developed theme.

▶ **2. Learn your story.** You don't need to memorize every word in the story you plan to tell. However, you should read the story or your outline several times so you know it very well.

▶ **3. Think of the story as a series of movie scenes.** Like a movie director, you must interpret the characters and events in the story to make them come to life. Identify the opening scene, the middle scenes, and the ending scene. How does each scene look and sound? How might you change your voice to indicate different characters? What facial expressions and movements would enhance the story? What costumes and props could you use?

▶ **4. Signal the ending.** How can you make sure the audience recognizes the ending? You might change the tone of your voice or use a statement such as "The moral of this fable is . . ."

❷ Developing Your Script

After choosing a story to tell and planning how to shape it, you should prepare a script to guide your performance.

Preparing the Script

▶ **1. Write out the story as a script.** After planning the story and making sure the plot is tightly focused, you need to prepare a script. Write out your own story or photocopy a published story. Leave large margins and extra space between the lines, if possible.

▶ **2. Give an overview of any props or costumes needed.** At the top of the script, describe any props or costumes you want to use.

▶ **3. Mark up the script.** Add directions for gestures, tone of voice, facial expressions, and movements to specific sections of the story.

IDEABank

1. Your Working Portfolio 🗀
Look for ideas in the **Writing Options** you completed earlier in this unit:
- **Comic tale,** p. 644
- **Modernizing a Story,** p. 653
- **Screenplay Script,** p. 668

2. Observe a Storyteller
Find out where a story-teller is performing in your area and arrange to watch the performance.

3. Listen to Storytellers
Check out audiotapes from your library that feature storytellers or short story readers.

Practicing Tip

You might have someone videotape your performance so you can check your movements and expressions, or you may audiotape it to check your voice.

❸ Practicing and Presenting

Practice reading your story aloud several times, possibly in front of a mirror. Change any words that sound awkward. Eventually, you should be able to tell your story without looking at your script. Your goal is not to memorize the story word for word, but to learn it so well that you can comfortably tell it to others. Then find a **practice audience** of one or two people and rehearse your story. Consider these guidelines for your performance.

- Use your body movement or position to get the audience's attention before you begin.
- Make eye contact with the audience.
- Speak clearly at a comfortable pace.
- Use a different voice for each character.
- Use props that are large enough to be seen from the back of the room.

Ask Your Peer Reviewers

- Which parts of the story interested you most?
- Which voices, gestures, and facial expressions were most effective?
- Were the characters real to you? Why or why not?
- How did my pacing affect the story?

❹ Refining Your Performance

TARGET SKILL ▶ EVALUATING YOUR INTERPRETIVE CHOICES

Think about the choices you made as you performed your story. Do these choices make your interpretation work? Here are some items to consider.

- **Pacing.** Is the pace too fast? too slow? Should some parts be delivered more slowly than others? If so, which ones?
- **Volume.** Is your voice loud enough? too loud?
- **Props and costumes.** Do the props and costumes help your audience understand the story?
- **Movements and expression.** Are your body movements and facial expressions effective? Are there any others that might help make the story more enjoyable?

Now revise your performance to include any needed changes.

Publishing IDEAS

- Offer to tell your story during a story hour at the public library or at your school library.
- Ask someone to videotape you as you tell your story to your classmates.

More Online: Publishing Options
www.mcdougallittell.com

❺ Reflecting

FOR YOUR WORKING PORTFOLIO What did you discover about telling a story? How did telling the story help you understand it better? Attach your answers to your story script. Save your story script in your **Working Portfolio.**

Read this paragraph from the first draft of a story. The underlined sections may include the following kinds of errors:

- **comma errors**
- **correctly written sentences that should be combined**
- **sentence fragments**
- **verb-tense errors**

For each underlined section, choose the revision that most improves the writing.

> Many years ago, our town was the setting for a truly supernatural event. <u>The moon was full. It was shining. It was bright.</u> <u>It is exactly midnight</u>
> (1)   (2)
> <u>when</u> a strange wind began to stir. <u>It blew strong and cold. The wind was like</u>
>   (3)
> <u>and icy fist.</u> Then the noise started. At first it was a quiet hum, but it changed.
> <u>The single chord harmonic and beautiful grew louder and louder.</u> The sound
> (4)
> became almost overwhelming <u>and then, it suddenly stopped.</u> <u>Although some</u>
>   (5)   (6)
> <u>people say that it was the wind in the trees.</u> This is not true. Only I know the
> real story.

1. A. The moon was shining and full and bright.

   B. The moon was full and shining and bright.

   C. The full moon was shining brightly.

   D. Correct as is

2. A. It will be exactly midnight when

   B. It was exactly midnight when

   C. It had been exactly midnight when

   D. Correct as is

3. A. The wind blew strong and cold, like an icy fist.

   B. The wind blew strong and cold. The wind was like an icy fist.

   C. Strong and cold. The wind blew like an icy fist.

   D. Correct as is

4. A. The single chord harmonic and beautiful, grew louder and louder.

   B. The single chord, harmonic and beautiful, grew louder and louder.

   C. The single chord, harmonic and beautiful grew louder and louder.

   D. Correct as is

5. A. and then it suddenly, stopped.

   B. and, then it suddenly stopped.

   C. and then it suddenly stopped.

   D. Correct as is

6. A. Even though some people say that it was the wind in the trees.

   B. Although some people say that, it was the wind in the trees.

   C. Some people say that it was the wind in the trees.

   D. Correct as is

Need extra help?

See the **Grammar Handbook**

Correcting Fragments, p. 1323

Punctuation Chart, pp. 1327–1328

Verb Tense, p. 1310

Words That Sound and Look Alike

Imagine you are listening to someone read the excerpt on the right. How might you misinterpret the word *rapt* if it were unfamiliar to you?

Might you momentarily think of the word *wrapped* and imagine the audience sitting with their heads covered up like mummies? In Twain's world anything is possible, but in this case the context helps you know that *wrapped* is incorrect. The actual word, *rapt*, means "deeply moved, delighted, or absorbed."

> Whenever Simmons stood behind him and gazed at the back of his skull and tried to drive a mental suggestion into it, Hicks sat with vacant face and never suspected. If he had been noticing he could have seen by the **rapt** faces of the audience that something was going on behind his back that required a response.
> —*The Autobiography of Mark Twain*

Rapt and *wrapped* are **homophones**, different words that sound the same.

Strategies for Building Vocabulary

In addition to homophones, homonyms and homographs may cause confusion for English speakers and writers. Use the etymologies of these terms, which come from the Greek language, to help you remember their meanings.

❶ Homophones The term *homophone* comes from the Greek words *homos* ("same") and *phōnē* ("sound"). Homophones like *rapt* and *wrapped* can cause comprehension errors and spelling mistakes because they are pronounced the same but spelled differently. Learning sets of homophones can help you choose the correct word. The chart below provides some examples.

Homophones

Alike in	Different in	Examples
pronunciation	meanings and spellings	*past/passed; weigh/way/whey; boarder/border*

❷ Homonyms Words that have the same pronunciation and spelling but different meanings are called **homonyms.** The term comes from the Greek words *homos* ("same") and *onuma* ("name"). When, for example, the narrator of Willa Cather's "A Wagner Matinee" states, "The deluge of sound poured on and on; . . . I never knew how far it bore her, or past what happy islands," the reader must recognize that *bore* is the word meaning "carried" rather than, for example, the word meaning "to drill a hole."

Unlike multiple meanings of a single word, homonyms have separate entries in dictionaries because they have different derivations—their being spelled and pronounced alike is only coincidence.

Bore, the past tense of *bear,* comes from a form of the Old English word *beran,* whereas *bore* meaning "to drill a hole" comes from a different Old English word, *borian.* See the chart for more examples.

Homonyms

Alike in	Different in	Examples
pronunciation and spelling	meaning	*story* (tale)/*story* (floor of a building)
		lock (length of hair)/*lock* (device for securing a door)

❸ Homographs The term *homograph* comes from the Greek words *homos* and *graphē* ("writing"). **Homographs** are words with the same spelling but with different pronunciations and meanings, such as *present* (prĕz'ənt) and *present* (prĭ-zĕnt'). Practice can help you remember the different pronunciations and meanings. See the chart below for more examples.

Homographs

Alike in	Different in	Examples
spelling	pronunciation and meaning	*wind* (wĭnd)/*wind* (wīnd); *incense* (ĭn'sĕns')/*incense* (ĭn-sĕns')

EXERCISE Use a dictionary to identify the meanings, pronunciations, and origins of the words in each pair. Then classify the words as homophones, homonyms, or homographs and use each in a sentence.

1. *heard* and *herd*
2. *invalid* and *invalid*
3. *loom* and *loom*
4. *pour* and *pore* (verb)
5. *quiver* and *quiver*

Grammar from Literature

Writers use complex sentences when they want to link two or more ideas that are related but not of equal importance. Complex sentences consist of one independent clause and one or more subordinate clauses. The less important ideas are expressed in subordinate clauses, which cannot stand alone as sentences. Look at the examples below.

> adverb subordinate clause
> **When the horns drew out the first strain of the**
> independent clause
> **Pilgrim's chorus,** my Aunt Georgiana clutched my coat
> sleeve. —Willa Cather, "A Wagner Matinee"
>
> adverb clause
> **I was hurt by this as if I were engaged in some honest**
> **occupation.**
> —Mark Twain, *The Autobiography of Mark Twain*
>
> adjective clause
> The Indian, **who was listening carefully,** decided to
> adjective clause
> give a cow **that he had** to the priest.
> —"The Indian and the Hundred Cows,"
> translated by Rudolfo A. Anaya

Each subordinate clause functions as a single part of speech—in the examples as an adverb or adjective.

Using Adjective and Adverb Clauses in Your Writing
Examine your own writing for related ideas that could be more clearly expressed by using adjective or adverb clauses in complex sentences. Look for places where added detail is needed or where wording could be streamlined. Decide which idea you wish to emphasize. Usually the less important idea is placed in the adjective or adverb clause. Notice the difference in emphasis in the examples below.

> adverb clauses
> **Samuel Clemens tried out the names Jefferson Snodgrass**
> **and simply Josh** before he settled on Mark Twain as a pen
> name.
>
> **Samuel Clemens settled on Mark Twain as a pen name**
> after he tried out the names Jefferson Snodgrass and
> simply Josh.

The first example focuses on names Clemens tried out; the second draws attention to the name Clemens chose.

Usage Tip Since a subordinate clause contains a subject and verb, you might mistakenly confuse it with a sentence. The introductory word in a subordinate clause, such as *although, after, because, if,* or *where,* causes the clause to be an incomplete thought. A subordinate clause is a fragment until it is joined to an independent clause.

> INCORRECT
> **When Clark received the letter.**
>
> CORRECT
> **When Clark received the letter, he realized his aunt was**
> **arriving in just one day.**

Punctuation Tip Use a comma to set off an adverbial clause at the beginning of a sentence.

> When Aunt Georgiana arrived at the train station, her
> clothes were covered with dust.
>
> Aunt Georgiana's clothes were covered with dust when she
> arrived at the train station.

WRITING EXERCISE Combine each pair of sentences in items 1–3 by expressing the less important idea as a subordinate clause. In sentences 4–5, add subordinate clauses as indicated in parentheses.

1. Aunt Georgiana was visiting relatives in the Green Mountains. She met Harold Carpenter.
2. Their homestead was lonely and primitive. The reason for this was that it lay fifty miles from the railroad.
3. The couple moved to Nebraska. Land was free and available there.
4. They built a dugout to live in. (Add an adverb clause at the start of the sentence.)
5. Boston seemed exciting to someone from the West. (Add an adjective clause describing Boston. Set the clause off in commas.)

GRAMMAR EXERCISE Both fragments and sentences are listed below. Rewrite the fragments as sentences. Correct errors in punctuation in the sentences.

1. If a young couple wanted adventure.
2. When the railroad was completed in 1850.
3. Travelers on wagon trains took time to regain their energy, after they had completed such long journeys.
4. Although the lure of gold drew many people.
5. When the concert ended Georgiana did not want to leave.

Conflict and Expansion

Did your assumptions about slavery, the Civil War, the civil rights movement, and the development of the West change as you read this unit? As you complete one or more of the options in each of the following sections, think about how your ideas have developed.

Detail of pictorial quilt (1895–1898), Harriet Powers. Pieced and appliquéd cotton embroidered with plain and metallic yarns, 69" × 105", bequest of Maxim Karolik, courtesy of Museum of Fine Arts, Boston.

Reflecting on the Unit

OPTION 1

What Is Liberty? Think about Abraham Lincoln's words on the first page of this unit: "We all declare for liberty; but in using the same word we do not all mean the same thing." How do you think the writers represented in this unit would define *liberty?* Write a series of statements describing what you think liberty means to each author. Then write what liberty means to you.

OPTION 2

Life in the West The selections in Part 2 of this unit deal with the ways of life of different peoples in the American West—from Native Americans to Hispanic and Anglo settlers to people facing new conflicts and challenges in the 20th century. What insights into the development of the West have the selections given you? With a small group of classmates, role-play three or four characters from the selections and discuss what was gained and what was lost as the frontier was gradually settled.

OPTION 3

Irrepressible Conflicts In the second half of the 19th century, the United States faced wrenching conflicts—over slavery, over preserving the Union, and over the settlement of the West. Some of these conflicts even spilled over into the 20th century. Write a few paragraphs about one of the major conflicts dealt with in this unit's selections, explaining your opinion of the way the conflict was resolved at the time and telling what further progress, if any, needs to be made.

Self ASSESSMENT

READER'S NOTEBOOK

Make a list of the selections in this unit that impressed you the most. Briefly explain how and why you were affected by each one. Which ones taught you something you didn't know before?

Reviewing Literary Concepts

OPTION 1

Examining Point of View Work with a partner—one of you listing the selections in this unit that are told from the first-person point of view, the other listing the selections that are told from the third-person point of view. Compare the lists, then discuss the following questions:

• Why do you think the author of each selection chose the point of view that he or she used?

• How would each selection be different if it were told from a different point of view?

OPTION 2

Analyzing Setting The selections in this unit take place in a variety of settings, from a slave plantation in Maryland to the Texas-Mexico border early in the 20th century. Which selections gave you the most detailed picture of a particular time, place, and culture? Choose three or four selections in which you visualized the setting most clearly. For each one, write details you recall about setting in a chart like the one shown. What kinds of details make setting come alive?

Time	Place	Culture

Self ASSESSMENT

READER'S NOTEBOOK

In this unit, you have read autobiographies, folk tales, and works of local-color realism. Write down some distinguishing characteristics of each of these kinds of writing, then list a selection from the unit that is a good example of each kind.

Building Your Portfolio

• **Writing Options** Several of the Writing Options asked you to imitate literary forms you read, such as the protest poem, ballad, or comic tale. Review your examples of creative writing and choose one that you think is particularly strong. Write a cover note describing what you like about the piece, and add both the note and the piece to your **Presentation Portfolio.**

• **Writing and Communication Workshops** In this unit you wrote a Literary Interpretation in which you explained the meaning a work had for you. You also wrote a Storytelling Script with directions for performing a story. Which of these pieces is ready for an audience? Attach a cover letter with ideas for publishing or performing the piece, then add it to your **Presentation Portfolio.**

• **Additional Activities** Reflect on the various assignments you completed under **Activities & Explorations** and **Inquiry & Research.** Which activity taught you the most? Write a note explaining your choice and add it to your portfolio.

Self ASSESSMENT

At this point your **Presentation Portfolio** contains a substantial amount of your work. Review the work it contains and decide which pieces show your thinking and writing abilities best. What other kinds of writing would you like to try as the year goes on?

Setting GOALS

Look back through your assignments and notebook to identify writing skills and thinking skills you would like to strengthen. Select three or four skills to improve as you study the next unit.

Reading & Writing for Assessment

When you studied strategies for reading a test selection on pages 330–335, you practiced techniques for success on reading and writing assessments. These kinds of tests are often important end-of-course examinations. The following pages will give you more practice with test-taking strategies. Work through the models to practice applying each of the following strategies.

PART 1 How to Read a Test Selection

Here are the basic strategies you studied earlier along with several new ones based on a different type of reading selection. By applying basic test-taking strategies, by taking notes, and by highlighting or underscoring passages as you read, you can focus on the key information you need to know.

> ### STRATEGIES FOR READING A TEST SELECTION
>
> ▷ **Before you begin reading, skim the questions that follow the passage.** These can help focus your reading.
>
> ▷ **Think about the title.** What does it suggest about the overall message and tone of the passage?
>
> ▷ **Use your active reading strategies, such as analyzing, predicting, and questioning.** Make notes in the margin to help you focus your reading. You may do this only if the test directions allow you to mark on the test itself.
>
> ▷ **Look for main ideas.** These are often stated at the beginnings or ends of paragraphs. Sometimes main ideas are implied, not stated. After reading each paragraph, ask "What was this passage about?"
>
> ▷ **Note the literary elements and techniques used by the writer.** You might consider the tone (writer's attitude toward the subject), the structure (how the writer organizes details into a single message), or the use of techniques like foreshadowing or depiction of people. Then ask yourself what effect the writer achieves with each choice.
>
> ▷ **Examine the sequence of ideas.** Are the ideas developed in chronological order, presented in order of importance, or organized in some other way? What does the sequence of ideas suggest about the writer's message?
>
> ▷ **Think about the message and writer's purpose.** What questions does the selection answer? What new questions does it imply? Can you make any generalizations?

Reading Selection

An English Foothold in North America

1   England's first significant attempt to carve out a colony of its own in North America (after an earlier failed attempt at Roanoke) nearly collapsed, as disease and starvation threatened the new settlement. However, through the determination of its colonists and the development of a marketable crop, ❶ England's first permanent settlement in North America took shape.

2   **The Business of Colonization** The rulers of England—unlike the Spanish—decided not to fund the risky venture of colonizing the Americas. Instead, King James I in 1606 granted a charter, or official permit, to two joint-stock companies, the Virginia companies of London and Plymouth. Numerous investors had pooled their wealth in order to finance the trip to North America. The Virginia Company of Plymouth soon disbanded, leaving only the Virginia Company of London, later simply called the Virginia Company.

3   ❷ The Virginia Company had lured financial supporters with the chance of reaping wealth in the form of gold or silver for a relatively small investment. England was to get something from the expedition, too. The King's charter guaranteed that the English monarch would receive one-fifth of all gold and silver found by the colonists.

4   In April of 1607, nearly four months after the Virginia Company's three ships—and nearly 150 passengers and crew members—had pushed out of an English harbor, the North American shore rose on the horizon. Reaching the coast of Virginia, the vessels slipped into a broad coastal river and sailed inland until they reached a small peninsula. There, the colonists climbed off their ships and claimed the land as theirs. They named the settlement Jamestown and the river the James, in honor of their king.

5   **A Disastrous Start** ❸ John Smith sensed trouble from the beginning. Nearly all of the settlers seemed to be consumed by one thought—the discovery of gold. Because the investors in the colony demanded a quick return on their investment, the colonists directed much of their energy toward searching the land for riches. As Smith later put it, "There was no talk, no hope, no work, but dig gold, wash gold, refine gold, load gold." Smith warned of disaster, but few listened to the arrogant captain, who had made few friends on the voyage over.

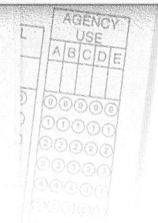

6   Disease from infected river water struck first. Hunger soon followed. ❹ The colonists, many of whom were unaccustomed to a life of labor, had refused to clear fields, plant crops, or even gather shellfish from the river's edge. After several months, one settler described the terrifying predicament.

7   Thus we lived for the space of five months in this miserable distress...our men night and day groaning in every corner of the fort, most pitiful to hear. If there were any conscience in men, it would make their hearts to bleed to hear the pitiful murmurings and outcries of our sick men for relief, every night and day for the space of six weeks: ❺ some departing out of the World, many times three or four in a night; in the morning their bodies trailed out of their cabins like dogs, to be buried.

8   By the winter of 1607 only 38 colonists remained alive. Standing among them was John Smith, who took control of the settlement. ❻ "You see that power now rests wholly with me," he announced. "You must now obey this law,...he that will not work shall not eat." Smith held the colony together by forcing the colonists to farm. He also received food and support from nearby Powhatan peoples, who had watched warily as the English established their settlement. Smith, a seasoned soldier, knew the Powhatan easily could wipe out the settlement. So he flattered and negotiated his way into winning an uneasy friendship with the group's leader, Chief Powhatan.

9   Just as Jamestown began to look like a real village, tragedy struck. A stray spark ignited a gunpowder bag Smith was wearing and set him on fire. Badly burned, Smith headed back to England, leaving Jamestown to fend for itself.

10 In the spring of 1609, the Virginia Company dispatched another 600 colonists, including women and children, to Jamestown. The newcomers arrived to find a settlement of disorganized colonists who were being threatened by angry Powhatan. Fearing the growing English presence, the Powhatan killed much of the colonists' livestock and harassed those settlers who attempted to hunt or farm. ❼ By the winter of 1609, conditions in Jamestown had deteriorated to the point of famine. In what became known as the "starving time," colonists ate roots, rats, snakes, and even boiled shoe leather. Of the hundreds of settlers who began the winter, only about 60 survived to see the relief ship that arrived in the spring.

STRATEGIES
IN ACTION

❹ **Think about the message or theme.**

"Even if the settlers found plenty of gold, it would do them no good unless they returned to England. You can't eat gold."

YOUR TURN
What larger lesson does the writer intend for readers to draw from this passage?

❺ **Look for main ideas.**

"Based on what this colonist said, it's amazing that anyone in Jamestown survived."

YOUR TURN
What main ideas of the selection are supported by this quotation?

❻ **Note the techniques the writer uses to portray character.**

"Here, the writer shows us Smith's character by providing the words Smith said, as well as telling us Smith's actions."

❼ **Examine the sequence of ideas.**

"This selection describes events dating from 1606–1609—the time it took for the English to develop a 'foothold in North America.'"

How to Answer Multiple Choice Questions

Use the strategies in the box and notes in the side column to help you answer the questions below and on the following pages. Based on the selection you have just read, choose the best answer for each of the following questions.

▶ Ask questions that help you eliminate some of the choices.

▶ Pay attention to choices such as "all of the above" or "none of the above." To eliminate them, all you need is to find is one answer that doesn't fit.

▶ **Skim your notes.** Details you noticed as you read may provide answers.

1. Which of the following statements is a theme of this selection?

   A. Courage and a sense of adventure can overcome the harshest adversities.

   B. Soldiers make the best leaders.

   C. Success comes to those who work hard, not to those who are lazy.

   D. Greed is not a good motivation for action.

2. The settlers got into trouble because they

   A. were too sick to work.

   B. didn't plant crops for food.

   C. didn't have enough supplies.

   D. had poor leadership.

3. The tone of paragraphs 5-9 is mostly

   A. personal.

   B. angry.

   C. judgmental.

   D. objective.

4. What is the writer's opinion of John Smith?

   A. The writer admires Smith's leadership ability.

   B. The writer considers Smith to be overbearing.

   C. all of the above

   D. none of the above

5. The writer characterizes the Powhatan as

   A. indifferent.

   B. fearful.

   C. greedy.

   D. lacking in resources.

STRATEGIES IN ACTION

Ask questions. What kind of men were these settlers?

ONE STUDENT'S THOUGHTS

"The writer says in paragraph 5 that John Smith is arrogant. That doesn't sound very objective. So I can eliminate choice D."

YOUR TURN

What other choices do not accurately reflect the tone of the writer?

Skim your notes.

ONE STUDENT'S THOUGHTS

"The writer says the Powhatan killed the settlers' livestock. If they were greedy or lacking in resources, they would have taken the livestock for themselves. So I can eliminate choices C and D."

YOUR TURN

What other choice is not supported by the evidence in the selection?

How to Respond in Writing

You may also be asked to write answers to questions about a reading passage. Short-answer questions usually ask you to answer in a sentence or two. Essay questions require a fully developed piece of writing.

Short-Answer Question

STRATEGIES FOR RESPONDING TO SHORT-ANSWER QUESTIONS

▶ **Identify the key words** in the writing prompt that tell you the ideas to discuss. Make sure you know what is meant by each.
▶ **State your response directly** and to the point.
▶ **Support your ideas** by using evidence from the selection.
▶ **Use correct grammar.**

> **Sample Question**
>
> Answer the following question in one or two sentences.
>
> The factual information in the quotation from the Jamestown colonist could be summarized in a single sentence. Why is it more effective for the writer to use a quotation than to summarize the information it provides?

STRATEGIES IN ACTION

Support your ideas by using evidence from the selection.

ONE STUDENT'S THOUGHTS

"The colonist expresses much more emotion than the writer does. For example, the colonist says the cries of the settlers would make your heart bleed."

YOUR TURN

How else is the tone of the quotation different from that of the selection?

Essay Question

STRATEGIES FOR ANSWERING ESSAY QUESTIONS

▶ **Look for direction words** in the writing prompt, such as *essay, analyze, describe,* or *compare and contrast* that tell you how to respond directly to the prompt.
▶ **List the points** you want to make before beginning to write.
▶ **Write an interesting introduction** that presents your main point.
▶ **Develop your ideas** by using evidence from the selection that supports the statements you make. Present the ideas in a logical order.
▶ **Write a conclusion** that summarizes your points.
▶ **Check your work** for correct grammar.

> **Sample Prompt**
>
> In the opinion of the writer, could John Smith have prevented "the starving time"? Write an essay in which you analyze the writer's characterization of John Smith's leadership skills.

Look for direction words.

ONE STUDENT'S THOUGHTS

"The important words are analyze, characterization, and leadership skills. My essay will have to use evidence from the selection about John Smith's character to argue that the writer thinks Smith could or could not have prevented 'the starving time.'"

YOUR TURN

What does the writer say about John Smith's character?

How to Revise and Edit a Test Selection

Here is a student's first draft in response to the writing prompt on page 736. Read it and answer the multiple-choice questions that follow.

> 1   The writer seems to think that John Smith could indeed prevent
> 2 "the starving time." The writer creates the impression that many of
> 3 the colonists' problems were brought on by laziness and lack of
> 4 leadership. For example, the writer says the colonists did not spend
> 5 any time clearing fields, planting crops, or fishing.
> 6   The writer describes John Smith as an intelligent, hard-
> 7 working soldier who predicted trouble from the beginning. The
> 8 writer says that Smith's return to England was a tragedy for
> 9 Jamestown. Without Smith's leadership, the settlers could not
>   even manage to keep farming.

> **STRATEGIES** FOR REVISING, EDITING, AND PROOFREADING
>
> ▶ Read the passage carefully.
> ▶ Note the parts that are confusing or don't make sense. What kinds of errors would that signal?
> ▶ Look for errors in grammar, usage, spelling, and capitalization. Common errors include:
> • run-on sentences
> • sentence fragments
> • no subject-verb agreement
> • unclear pronoun antecedents
> • lack of transition words

1. The BEST way to make it clear that "the starving time" occurred in the past, not in the future, would be to change the sentence in lines 1 and 2 ("The writer...'the starving time.'") in which of the following ways?

   A. The writer seems to think that John Smith could indeed have prevented "the starving time."

   B. The writer seems to think that John Smith would indeed prevent "the starving time."

   C. The writer seems to think that John Smith did indeed prevent "the starving time."

   D. Make no change.

2. The BEST way to make the connection between paragraphs clearer would be to add which of the following sentences to the beginning of line 6 ("The writer...from the beginning.")?

   A. John Smith was different from the rest of the colonists.

   B. Only a few colonists remained alive after the first winter.

   C. The Powhatan could have wiped out the settlement.

   D. Make no change.

3. The BEST way to summarize and conclude this essay would be to add which of the following sentences to the end of line 9 ("Without Smith's leadership...keep farming.")?

   A. Only a few settlers survived "the starving time" and lived to see the spring relief ship.

   B. During "the starving time," the colonists even ate boiled shoe leather.

   C. The writer implies that with strong leadership, Jamestown could have avoided "the starving time."

   D. Make no change.

THE CHANGING FACE OF AMERICA

If we
are to
achieve
a richer
culture,
rich in
contrasting
values,
we must
recognize
the whole
gamut of
human
potentialities.

MARGARET MEAD
anthropologist

Mr. and Mrs. Isaac Newton Phelps Stokes (1897),
John Singer Sargent. Oil on canvas, 85¼″ × 39¾″, The
Metropolitan Museum of Art, bequest of Edith
Minturn Phelps Stokes (Mrs. I. N.), 1938. (38.104).
Copyright © 1989 The Metropolitan Museum of Art.

THE CHANGING
FACE
OF AMERICA

EVENTS IN AMERICAN LITERATURE

1855   **1867**   **1879**

1856 *New York Tribune* publishes letters by Margaret Fuller about her travels in Europe, making her America's first woman foreign correspondent

1862 Emily Dickinson writes 366 poems within the year

1869 Louisa May Alcott completes writing of *Little Women*

1870 Bret Harte publishes story collection *The Luck of Roaring Camp, and Other Sketches*

1883 Emma Lazarus writes sonnet "The New Colossus," dedicated to Statue of Liberty

1890 Charlotte Perkins Gilman writes "The Yellow Wallpaper," which describes the emotional and intellectual decline of a young wife and mother

EVENTS IN THE UNITED STATES

1855   **1879**

1857 Elizabeth Blackwell establishes New York Infirmary for women and children, the first medical clinic of its kind

1870 John D. Rockefeller founds Standard Oil Company

1872 Susan B. Anthony is arrested and fined for leading a group of women to test their right to vote

1876 Alexander Graham Bell patents first telephone

1879 Thomas Edison invents first practical light bulb

1882 Congress passes Chinese Exclusion Act, suspending Chinese immigration for ten years

1883 First metal-framed skyscraper, ten stories high, is built in Chicago

1886 Statue of Liberty is dedicated in New York Harbor; trade unionists organize American Federation of Labor (AFL)

EVENTS IN THE WORLD

1855   **1867**   **1879**

1855 Florence Nightingale, British nurse, introduces hygienic standards into military hospitals during Crimean War

1856 Two states of Australia introduce modern secret-voting procedure known as Australian ballot

1868 Remains of Cro-Magnon man discovered in Europe

1870 After a troubled reign, Queen Isabella II of Spain abdicates throne in favor of her son, Alfonso XII

1885 Karl Benz of Germany builds single-cylinder engine for motor car

PERIOD PIECES

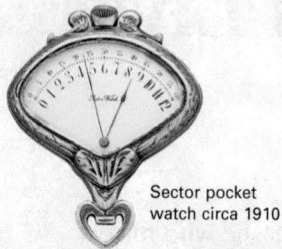

Sector pocket watch circa 1910

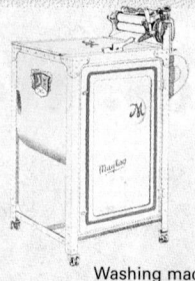

Washing machine from the 1920s

Charlie Chaplin popularizes silent movies.

1891 1903 1915

1893 Paul Laurence Dunbar publishes first volume of poetry, *Oak and Ivy,* while working as elevator operator

1897 Edward Arlington Robinson publishes "Richard Cory"

1898 Henry James publishes *The Turn of the Screw*

1899 Kate Chopin publishes her novel, *The Awakening*

1911 Edith Wharton publishes the tragic novel *Ethan Frome*

1914 Carl Sandburg writes the poem "Chicago," an energetic celebration of life early in the 20th century

1915 Edgar Lee Masters writes "Lucinda Matlock," part of *Spoon River Anthology*

1922 F. Scott Fitzgerald publishes short story "Winter Dreams"

1925 Eugene O'Neill publishes *Desire Under the Elms,* a play based on a Greek tragedy that explores family conflicts

1891 1903 1915

1892 Ellis Island in New York Harbor becomes chief U.S. immigration station

1898 Spanish-American War begins in the Caribbean

1901 President McKinley is assassinated

1903 Near Kitty Hawk, North Carolina, Orville and Wilbur Wright make first flight in engine-powered airplane

1907 Japan limits emigration to U.S. in response to hostility toward Japanese laborers

1913 Ford Motor Company puts first moving assembly line into place and is soon producing 1,000 Model T automobiles a day

1920 Congress passes 19th Amendment, giving women right to vote

1924 Ending centuries of nearly open admissions, Congress passes Immigration Act of 1924 that limits number of immigrants from outside of Western Hemisphere

1891 1903 1915

1893 New Zealand becomes first country to grant women suffrage

1896 Italian physicist Guglielmo Marconi creates first radio

1898 Pierre and Marie Curie discover radium and polonium

1901 After 64 years as ruler of Great Britain, Queen Victoria dies

1903 Emmeline Pankhurst founds Women's Social and Political Union in England to further woman suffrage

1912 "Unsinkable" English ship *Titanic* sinks on maiden voyage, killing 1,513; African National Congress formed in South Africa

1914 World War I breaks out in Europe

1915 Albert Einstein postulates general theory of relativity

1918 Women aged 30 and over gain suffrage in England

1919 Gandhi becomes leader of Indian independence movement

Women's Voices, Women's Lives

A New Literature

"*The* power of a woman is in her refinement, gentleness and elegance; it is she who makes etiquette, and it is she who preserves the order and decency of society. Without women, men soon resume the savage state, and the comfort and the graces of the home are exchanged for the misery of the mining camp." So said a popular book of etiquette in 1880, voicing a widely held notion about women's place in society. At the same time, however, the movement to give women the right to vote was reemerging after a period of inactivity in the years following the Civil War. Both before and after the war, however, the woman's suffrage movement was only the most public aspect of a growing force for women to have a voice in both politics and literature. Sojourner Truth's eloquent speech articulating the realities of women's lives, delivered at one women's rights convention (see Voices from the Times), resonated in the hearts of many 19th-century women.

One important factor in the growth of the women's movement was the spread of university education among women of the era, although popular newspapers of the time trumpeted the dangers: "Are We Destroying Woman's Beauty? The Startling Warning of a Great English Physician Against Higher Education of Women. How Intellectual Work Destroys Beauty" proclaimed a *New York Journal* headline in 1896.

A suffragist struggles with police in 1913 (above) and suffragists argue for the vote before a congressional committee in 1871 (below).

Emily Dickinson

The 1890s also saw the emergence of the poetry of Emily Dickinson—the first major American woman poet—although emergence may not be the right word to apply to a body of work that has become widely known only in the last 40 years. A near contemporary of Walt Whitman, and just as important in the development of a uniquely American literary voice, Dickinson was virtually unknown during her lifetime. Her anonymity was due in large part to the difficulties she would have experienced in trying to overcome prevailing attitudes about a woman's proper place. When Dickinson's sister published a collection of her poetry in 1890, after Dickinson's death, most critical reviews were negative, objecting especially to what was considered an odd poetic style, with its unusual imagery, untraditional meters, inexact rhymes, and grammatical errors. Nonetheless, a century later, Dickinson looms as one of our most important poets, not only of her time but of any time.

Around the same time, Charlotte Perkins Gilman—related on her father's side to a noted family of writers and social reformers that included Harriet Beecher Stowe, the author of *Uncle Tom's Cabin*—became one of the most noted advocates for women. Fleeing her own repressive marriage, she moved from the East Coast to California, where she wrote and spoke out on behalf of women's rights and against male domination.

Harriet Beecher Stowe

Kate Chopin's fiction articulates the frustrations of generations of women that were confined to a sort of extended childhood by the men in their lives. Her gentle stories depicting some of the most obvious of women's difficulties were extremely popular in the 1890s. Her 1899 novel *The Awakening*, however, stepped over the line in its portrayal of a woman's hidden passion, arousing a public protest so vigorous that Chopin ceased writing completely.

Voices *from the* TIMES

Ain't I a Woman?
Sojourner Truth

This speech was given by the ex-slave Sojourner Truth at a women's rights convention at Akron, Ohio, in 1851. Prior to her speech, male speakers had argued in favor of men's superior rights and privileges on the grounds of their superior intellect and the manhood of Christ. As the convention was heating up, the dignified Sojourner Truth—who was in her 60s at the time—rose slowly from her seat in a corner of the room. Amid shouts of "Don't let her speak!" and hissing, she moved to the front, laid her bonnet down, and began this unprepared speech. A profound hush settled over the crowd as she began to speak.

Well, children, where there is so much racket there must be something out of kilter. I think that 'twixt the Negroes of the South and the women at the North all talking about rights, the white men will be in a fix pretty soon. But what's all this here talking about?

That man over there says that women need to be helped into carriages, and lifted over ditches, and to have the best place everywhere. Nobody ever helps me into carriages, or over mud puddles, or gives me any best place! And ain't I a woman? Look at me! Look at my arm! I have ploughed, and planted, and gathered into barns, and no man could head me. And ain't I a woman? I could work as much and eat as much as a man—when I could get it—and bear the lash as well! And ain't I a woman? I have borne thirteen children, and seen most all sold off to slavery, and when I cried out with my mother's grief, none but Jesus heard me! And ain't I a woman?

Then they talk about this thing in the head; what's this they call it? ["Intellect," someone whispers.] That's it, honey. What's that got to do with women's rights or Negroes' rights? If my cup won't hold but a pint, and yours holds a quart, wouldn't you be mean not to let me have my little half-measure full?

Then that little man in black there, he says women can't have as much rights as men, 'cause Christ wasn't a woman! Where did your Christ come from? From God and a woman! Man had nothing to do with Him.

If the first woman God ever made was strong enough to turn the world upside down all alone, these women together ought to be able to turn it back, and get it right side up again! And now they is asking to do it, the men better let them.

Obliged to you for hearing me, and now old Sojourner hasn't got nothing more to say.

Sojourner Truth

Traditions Across Time: A Diversity of Voices

In 1920 the 19th Amendment to the Constitution gave women the right to vote, but suffrage heralded no great revolution. Women did not unite at the polls to gain reforms for themselves; instead, many voted like their fathers or husbands or didn't vote at all. This political failure combined with the cultural changes rocking the 1920s—the rise of advertising, Hollywood glamour, and the flapper image of woman —to further inhibit women's intellectual and literary development. The playwright Lillian Hellman, one of the few American women writing successfully in the 1930s and 1940s, summed up her generation this way: "By the time I grew up, the fight for the emancipation of women, their rights under the law, in the office, in bed, was stale stuff. My generation didn't think much about the place or the problems of women."

Only after the eruption of the feminist movement in the late 1960s were large numbers of women again inspired to examine the quality of their lives and find voices of their own. With the renewed confidence of women came a desire to rediscover female writers of the more recent past. Hence Hisaye Yamamoto's "Seventeen Syllables" and Tillie Olsen's "I Stand Here Ironing"—both stories about women struggling with oppressive conditions—are more popular today than when they were written.

The legacy of 19th-century women writers lives on in the richness and diversity of contemporary women's writing. Women of all ages and ethnic groups are writing today, giving voice to a multitude of experiences and concerns. Julia Alvarez's poem "Ironing Their Clothes" expresses loving feelings associated with a household chore, while Rita Dove's poem "Adolescence—III" portrays a young girl on the verge of becoming a woman.

A New Literature

Emily Dickinson | *A*UTHOR *S*TUDY

This is my letter to the World	751
"Hope" is the thing with feathers—	752
Success is counted sweetest	753
Much Madness is divinest Sense	754
Letter to T. W. Higginson (April 15, 1862)	755
My life closed twice before its close—	756
After great pain, a formal feeling comes—	757
I heard a Fly buzz—when I died—	758
Because I could not stop for Death—	759

Selected poems and a letter

Charlotte Perkins Gilman | The Yellow Wallpaper — 765
Who is trapped in the wallpaper?

RELATED READING

Barbara Ehrenreich and Deirdre English | from **Complaints and Disorders** — 782
A look at 19th-century women and their doctors

Kate Chopin | The Story of an Hour — 783
What a difference an hour makes.

COMPARING LITERATURE
Traditions Across Time: A Diversity of Voices

Hisaye Yamamoto | Seventeen Syllables (1949) — 788
Conflicts and kisses in a teenage girl's life

Rita Dove | Adolescence—III (1980) — 802
A girl's daydreams of womanhood

Tillie Olsen | I Stand Here Ironing (1956) — 806
Summing up a daughter's life

LITERARY LINK

Julia Alvarez | Ironing Their Clothes (1986) — 814
Loving feelings spread out on an ironing board

Author Study
Emily Dickinson

OVERVIEW

Life and Times	746
This is my letter to the World	751
"Hope" is the thing with feathers—	752
Success is counted sweetest	753
Much Madness is divinest Sense—	754
Letter to Thomas Wentworth Higginson ~ LETTER	755
My life closed twice before its close—	756
After great pain, a formal feeling comes—	757
I heard a Fly buzz—when I died—	758
Because I could not stop for Death—	759
The Author's Style	761
Author Study Project	762

> *"If I read a book [and] it makes my whole body so cold no fire ever can warm me I know that is poetry."*
>
> —Emily Dickinson

A Life of Insight and Isolation

Although she chose to withdraw from society, Emily Dickinson became one of the most prominent American poets. Her contribution of 1,775 poems was virtually unknown during her lifetime, which was partly due to her anonymity. She once wrote, "Publication—is the Auction / Of the Mind of Man—" and later asked that all her poems be burned upon her death. This startlingly innovative poet left the world pondering her untold secrets. As you read this Author Study, discover the fully realized life that Emily Dickinson's poetry reveals.

1830–1886

"THE FAIREST HOME I EVER KNEW" Emily Dickinson was born on December 10, 1830, in Amherst, Massachusetts. She spent her entire life in this small New England farming community, taking fewer than a dozen extended trips away from home. As a young girl, she enjoyed exploring the countryside, playing the piano, singing, and attending social gatherings with friends and relatives.

The center of Dickinson's existence was her family. Her father, Edward, was a prominent businessman and lawyer.

HER LIFE
HER TIMES

1830 Is born Dec. 10 in Amherst, Massachusetts	Emily with siblings	1840 Enters Amherst Academy	1847 Attends Mount Holyoke Female Seminary	

1830   **1840**   **1850**

1841 Utopian community Brook Farm is founded in Massachusetts.	1845 Henry David Thoreau lives at Walden Pond.	1848 Seneca Falls women's rights convention is held.

Although he was stern and aloof, Dickinson greatly admired his "pure and terrible" heart. On the other hand, she criticized her mother, Emily Norcross Dickinson, and once bitterly observed that she never had a mother. Dickinson and her mother developed a more intimate relationship after Mrs. Dickinson suffered a paralyzing stroke.

Dickinson felt particularly close to her older brother, Austin, and her younger sister, Lavinia, or Vinnie. With Austin, who moved next door after his marriage, she shared a quick-witted sense of humor and a passion for learning. Like Emily, Vinnie remained unmarried and helped run the household. Devoted and loyal, Vinnie shared her sister's secrets and protected her privacy.

"SUCH ARE THE INLETS OF THE MIND" Dickinson's father frowned on books that might "joggle" his daughter's mind, but he encouraged her education. She attended Amherst Academy and then enrolled at Mount Holyoke Female Seminary in nearby South Hadley when she was 16.

Dickinson's home in Amherst, Massachusetts

While she was still a student, Dickinson experienced a religious crisis. Pressured to join a church, she wrestled with doubt.

LITERARY Contributions

Emily Dickinson chose privacy over fame. During her lifetime she consented to one or two publications of her poems—others were published without her permission. It wasn't until after her death that numerous collections of her poems were published. The genius of her poetry—her innovative style, verbal precision, and sharp observations—has influenced generations of poets and delighted generations of readers.

A Unique Voice In 1890, the book *Poems by Emily Dickinson* was edited by Mabel Loomis Todd and T. W. Higginson. This first collection of Dickinson's poems was altered to make the poems, which the editors thought "too crude in form," more presentable.

The Authoritative Version Dickinson's talent was not widely recognized until a complete, unaltered edition of her poetry was published in 1955. Edited by Thomas H. Johnson, *The Poems of Emily Dickinson, Including Variant Readings Critically Compared With All Known Manuscripts* was the first book to eliminate the tamperings of earlier editors.

Avid Correspondent Dickinson wrote more than 1,000 letters to family and friends, which illustrate her original style and reveal the richness of her day-to-day life. *The Letters of Emily Dickinson,* edited by Thomas H. Johnson and Theodora Ward, appeared in 1958.

1852
First poem is published in Springfield *Daily Republican*

1861
"I taste a liquor never brewed—" published

1862
Begins correspondence with Thomas W. Higginson

1864–1865
Visits Boston twice for eye treatments

1860

1870

1855
Walt Whitman publishes *Leaves of Grass.*

1857
R. W. Emerson lectures at Amherst, visits Austin Dickinson.

1860
Abraham Lincoln is elected president.

1861
U.S. Civil War begins.

1865
Thirteenth Amendment to U.S. Constitution abolishes slavery.

By her late 20s, she stopped attending church services altogether. Many of her poems reflect the conflict she experienced between her own convictions and those that surrounded her.

After one year at Mount Holyoke, Dickinson returned home. Although her formal schooling had ended, she continued to educate herself. During her late teens or early 20s, Dickinson found her calling—she began to write poetry. While doing household chores, she jotted down her thoughts on scraps of paper, old recipes, and the backs of envelopes. She wrote late at night by candlelight. Inspired by intense sufferings of loss, loneliness, and death, she composed a remarkable number of short, profound, gemlike poems.

"THE SOUL SELECTS HER OWN SOCIETY"
The year 1862 marked a turning point in Dickinson's life. That year the Reverend Charles Wadsworth—an older, married man whom Dickinson admired and reportedly loved—took a position in California. In the same year, she wrote 366 poems. Perhaps as a consequence of grief over lost love or as a result of a new-found focus on her writing, Dickinson, now in her 30s, gradually withdrew from the world.

By the time she reached middle age, Dickinson rarely ventured beyond her house and garden. Still, she maintained contact with friends and family by means of a prolific correspondence. Furthermore, the self-imposed isolation did not prohibit her from forming an alliance with the neighborhood children. It was typical of her to lower, by a cord, small baskets of baked goods and fruit from her bedroom window.

"THIS IS MY LETTER TO THE WORLD"
After living in seclusion for almost 20 years, Dickinson fell ill in 1884. She suffered from Bright's disease, a gradual failure of the kidneys, and died on May 15, 1886. A short time later Vinnie carried out her sister's wishes and burned nearly all of her correspondence from family and friends. Fortunately, Vinnie rescued a box full of poems bound neatly into homemade booklets that Emily had stored.

Of the 1,775 poems Dickinson wrote, only seven were published, anonymously, while she was alive. As a result of Vinnie's persistence, the first volume of Dickinson's poetry was published four years after her death. Even though she was reclusive, her poems, according to the 20th-century American poet Allen Tate, reveal a life that was "one of the richest and deepest ever lived on this continent."

More Online: Author Link
www.mcdougallittell.com

LaserLinks: Background for Reading
Author Background

1874
Her father dies in Boston. In 1875, her mother dies.

Edward Dickinson

1883
Her favorite nephew, Gilbert, dies of typhoid.

1884
Suffers first attack of kidney disease

1886
Dies in Amherst on May 15

1890
Poems are published by Emily's sister

Lavinia Dickinson

1880

1890

1876
Alexander Graham Bell invents the telephone.

1879
Edison invents the light bulb.

1887
Interstate Commerce Act is passed.

Dickinson's Legacy Today

The life of Emily Dickinson inspired several contemporary playwrights. *Alison's House* (1931), a Pulitzer Prize-winning play by Susan Glaspell, explores what happens to a poet's unpublished poems when her family discovers them after her death. William Luce's two-act play based on Dickinson's life, *The Belle of Amherst,* opened on Broadway on April 28, 1976. In the 1980 film version of the play, Julie Harris re-created the starring role that had earned her a Tony Award.

The following is a dramatization from *The Belle of Amherst* that captures Emily's thoughts and feelings about her neighbors, particularly Henrietta Sweetser:

Julie Harris as Emily Dickinson in *The Belle of Amherst*

> *Here in Amherst, I'm known as Squire Edward Dickinson's half-cracked daughter. Well, I am! The neighbors can't figure me out. I don't cross my father's ground to any house or town. I haven't left the house for years.*
>
> *The Soul selects her own society—then—shuts the door.*
>
> *Why should I socialize with village gossips?* (Emily turns to the window. . . .)
>
> *There goes one of them now—Henrietta Sweetser—everyone knows Henny. Look at her! She's strolling by the house, trying to catch a glimpse of me. Would you like that?*
>
> *So I give them something to talk about. I dress in white all year round, even in winter. "Bridal white," Henny calls it.*
>
> (She mimics back-fence gossips.)
>
> *"Dear, dear? Dresses in bridal white, she does, every day of the blessed year. Year in, year out. Disappointed in love as a girl, so I hear. Poor creature. All so very sad. And her sister, Lavinia, a spinster too. Didn't you know? Oh, yes. Stayed unmarried just to be at home and take care of Miss Emily. Two old maids in that big house. What a lonely life, to shut yourself away from good people like us."*
>
> *Indeed!*

Selected poems by Emily Dickinson

Connect to Your Life

Poetic Subjects Emily Dickinson's poems are like diary entries in that they explore the private realm of thought, feeling, and imagination. The following poems convey fresh observations about some of life's timeless concerns: nature, hope, success, madness, pain, and death. Use a graphic like this one to explore the emotions such concepts trigger in you.

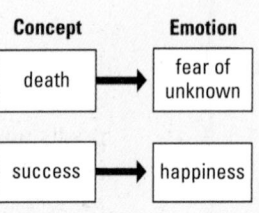

Concept		Emotion
death	→	fear of unknown
success	→	happiness

Build Background

A Unique Style Emily Dickinson's observations are as poignant and personal as her poetic style. One of the originators of modern American poetry, Dickinson departed from the poetic traditions of the 19th century in her inventive treatment of rhyme, punctuation, capitalization, and sentence structure. Dickinson's poems are also short, usually no longer than 20 lines. She wrote most of her poetry in dense **quatrains** (four-line stanzas) that echo the simple rhythms of the church hymns she knew and loved. However, she added a fresh twist with **slant rhymes,** or words that do not rhyme exactly, and used dashes to highlight important words and help break up the singsong rhythm of her poems.

Focus Your Reading

LITERARY ANALYSIS **FIGURATIVE LANGUAGE** Dickinson used fresh and original **figurative language** to communicate ideas beyond the literal meaning of words, including the following:

Simile: a figure of speech that compares two things that have something in common, using *like* or *as*
> *The Nerves sit ceremonious, like Tombs—*

Metaphor: a figure of speech that directly states a comparison between two things
> *"Hope" is the thing with feathers—*

Personification: a figure of speech in which an object, animal, or idea is given human characteristics
> *The simple News that Nature told—*

ACTIVE READING **STRATEGIES FOR READING POETRY** The following suggestions can help you increase your understanding and enjoyment of Dickinson's poetry:

- Read each poem once for overall impression, then again for meaning. Then read it at least one more time, this time aloud, to appreciate Dickinson's unique **style, rhythm,** and **imagery.**
- Think about Dickinson's use of **figurative language.** Pay close attention to words that are capitalized for emphasis.
- Pause when you encounter dashes, just as you do when you come to commas or periods in a poem.

READER'S NOTEBOOK As you read, jot down any questions you may have about any poetic element or device at work within a poem.

Emily Dickinson

This is my letter to the World

This is my letter to the World
That never wrote to Me—
The simple News that Nature told—
With tender Majesty

5   Her Message is committed
To Hands I cannot see—
For love of Her—Sweet—countrymen—
Judge tenderly—of Me

GUIDE FOR READING

1 this: Dickinson's poetry, or this particular poem.

3 What might Nature's "simple News" be?

5 committed: given over; entrusted.

6 Whose might be the "Hands" that the speaker cannot see?

Thinking Through the Literature

1. What is your impression of the speaker of this poem?

2. Dickinson sees her poem as her "letter to the World." Based on your reading of the poem, what can you infer about the message she wants to share with others?

3. Dickinson says that her message is "The simple News that Nature told." What does this suggest about Dickinson's feelings for nature?

THINK ABOUT

- in line 4, the "tender Majesty" with which nature communicates
- in line 7, the feeling she hopes her readers will have about nature

4. Most of Dickinson's poems were not published during her lifetime. Do you think she expected that other people would ever read them? What lines in this poem lead you to your conclusion?

"Hope" is the thing with feathers

"Hope" is the thing with feathers—
That perches in the soul—
And sings the tune without the words—
And never stops—at all—

5 And sweetest—in the Gale—is heard—
And sore must be the storm—
That could abash the little Bird
That kept so many warm—

I've heard it in the chillest land—
10 And on the strangest Sea—
Yet, never, in Extremity,
It asked a crumb—of Me.

GUIDE FOR READING

1–4 What qualities of hope are suggested by this image?

6 sore: severe.

7 abash: frustrate; baffle.

11 Extremity: greatest need or peril.

Thinking Through the Literature

1. On a sheet of paper, sketch the images that came to you as you read the poem.

2. Why do you think Dickinson pictures hope as a bird?

   THINK ABOUT { • the qualities of a bird
   • the qualities of hope that are similar to those of a bird

3. How do you interpret the last two lines?

Emily Dickinson

Success is counted sweetest

Success is counted sweetest
By those who ne'er succeed.
To comprehend a nectar
Requires sorest need.

5 Not one of all the purple Host
Who took the Flag today
Can tell the definition
So clear of Victory

As he defeated—dying—
10 On whose forbidden ear
The distant strains of triumph
Burst agonized and clear!

GUIDE FOR READING

2 ne'er: never.

1–2 Who prizes success most?

3 comprehend: fully appreciate;
nectar: a sweet beverage.

5 Host: army.

6 took the Flag: captured the
enemy's flag as a token of victory.

Thinking Through the Literature

1. What were you thinking as you finished reading this poem?
2. How do you interpret lines 3 and 4? Explain how they relate to lines 1 and 2.
3. In this poem, Dickinson uses the image of a battlefield to make her point. Why might the defeated soldier be better able to appreciate victory than a winning soldier?

Much Madness is divinest Sense

Much Madness is divinest Sense
To a discerning Eye—
Much Sense—the starkest Madness—
'Tis the Majority
5   In this, as All, prevail—
Assent—and you are sane—
Demur—you're straightway dangerous—
And handled with a Chain—

GUIDE FOR READING

2 discerning: having keen insight and good judgment.

4 Majority: the community at large; the society.

1–4 According to the speaker, what are the meanings of madness and sense?

6 assent: agree.

7 demur (dĭ-mûr'): voice opposition; object.

8 handled with a Chain: In the 19th century, those who were considered insane were often kept chained in asylums.

Thinking Through the Literature

1. What impact did this poem have on you? Jot down some thoughts.

2. What might Dickinson have been feeling when she wrote this poem?

  • the speaker's own views about madness and sense
  • the meanings of madness and sense in the larger society

3. Do you agree with the speaker's attitudes about madness and sense? Support your opinion, citing examples from your own observations and experiences.

Letter to
THOMAS WENTWORTH HIGGINSON

Emily Dickinson

Preparing to Read

Build Background

In April 1862 critic and literary editor Thomas Wentworth Higginson published an essay, "Letter to a Young Contributor," in the *Atlantic Monthly.* He offered practical advice to beginning writers on how to break into print, urging them, "Charge your style with life." One young writer who responded to Higginson's essay was Emily Dickinson, who was 32 years old at the time. She submitted four poems along with the following unsigned letter. Characteristically, she broke with tradition, enclosing a signed calling card in its own envelope in place of a signature.

Unfortunately, Higginson's reply to Dickinson's letter no longer exists. Apparently, he offered criticism of her poems —which she referred to as "surgery"—and asked about her education, her family and friends, and books she had read. Although Dickinson's letter sparked an important literary correspondence that lasted more than 20 years, she steadfastly ignored Higginson's advice on how to improve her poems.

Letter to Mr. T. W. Higginson
April 15, 1862

Mr. Higginson,

Are you too deeply occupied to say if my verse is alive?

The Mind is so near itself—it cannot see, distinctly—and I have none to ask. Should you think it breathed—and had you the leisure to tell me, I should feel quick gratitude—

If I make the mistake—that you dared to tell me—would give me sincerer honor toward you—

I enclosed my name—asking you, if you please—Sir—to tell me what is true? That you will not betray me—it is needless to ask—since honor is its own pawn—

Miss Emily E. Dickinson

Emily Dickinson

My life closed twice before its close

My life closed twice before its close—
It yet remains to see
If Immortality unveil
A third event to me

5   So huge, so hopeless to conceive
As these that twice befell.
Parting is all we know of heaven,
And all we need of hell.

GUIDE FOR READING

6 befell (bǐ-fĕl'): happened.

5–8 How does the speaker feel about the loss of a loved one?

Thinking Through the Literature

1. What kind of "parting" might Dickinson be referring to in the last two lines of the poem?

2. What does this poem reveal about Dickinson's attitude toward death?

 THINK ABOUT
   • the human quality she gives to immortality (line 3)
   • the use of the descriptive phrases "so huge" and "so hopeless to conceive," and what they describe

3. Would a reader who has recently experienced the loss of a loved one be disturbed or comforted by this poem? Explain your answer.

Emily Dickinson

After great pain, a formal feeling comes

After great pain, a formal feeling comes—
The Nerves sit ceremonious, like Tombs—
The stiff Heart questions was it He, that bore,
And Yesterday, or Centuries before?

5 The Feet, mechanical, go round—
Of Ground, or Air, or Ought—
A Wooden way
Regardless grown,
A Quartz contentment, like a stone—

10 This is the Hour of Lead—
Remembered, if outlived,
As Freezing persons, recollect the Snow—
First—Chill—then Stupor—then the letting go—

GUIDE FOR READING

3 He, that bore: the heart that felt the pain.

6 Ought: anywhere.

8 regardless: unmindful.

1–9 What different responses to mental anguish are described in these lines?

10–13 How is someone who experiences emotional pain similar to "Freezing persons"?

Thinking Through the Literature

1. What emotions do you think the speaker is trying to convey? Jot down your impressions.

2. In this poem, Dickinson uses **metaphors** that leave an image of the "formal feeling" that follows pain. How do the metaphors reveal this formal feeling of loss?

3. Why do you think the speaker focuses on the numbed feelings after a loss rather than on the agony and pain?

Emily Dickinson

I heard a Fly buzz when I died

I heard a Fly buzz—when I died—
The Stillness in the Room
Was like the Stillness in the Air—
Between the Heaves of Storm—

5   The Eyes around—had wrung them dry—
And Breaths were gathering firm
For that last Onset—when the King
Be witnessed—in the Room—

I willed my Keepsakes—Signed away
10 What portion of me be
Assignable—and then it was
There interposed a Fly—

With Blue—uncertain stumbling Buzz—
Between the light—and me—
15 And then the Windows failed—and then
I could not see to see—

GUIDE FOR READING

4 Heaves: risings and fallings.

7 the King: God.

5–8 In the 19th century, people usually died at home in the presence of friends and family.

12 interposed: came between.

13–16 What are the dying person's last sensations?

Thinking Through the Literature

1. What is your reaction to the way the poem ends? Briefly describe your reactions to a classmate.

2. How would you describe the view of death presented in the poem?

   THINK ABOUT
   - the moments just before death described in the first and last stanzas
   - the meaning of lines 5–8

3. Look closely at Dickinson's last stanza. What does she do to make the portrayal of death a realistic one?

Emily Dickinson

Because I could not stop for Death

Because I could not stop for Death—
He kindly stopped for me—
The Carriage held but just Ourselves—
And Immortality.

5   We slowly drove—He knew no haste
And I had put away
My labor and my leisure too,
For His Civility—

We passed the School, where Children strove
10 At Recess—in the Ring—
We passed the Fields of Gazing Grain—
We passed the Setting Sun—

Or rather—He passed Us—
The Dews drew quivering and chill—
15 For only Gossamer, my Gown—
My Tippet—only Tulle—

We paused before a House that seemed
A Swelling of the Ground—
The Roof was scarcely visible—
20 The Cornice—in the Ground—

Since then—'tis Centuries—and yet
Feels shorter than the Day
I first surmised the Horses' Heads
Were toward Eternity—

GUIDE FOR READING

8 Civility: politeness.

1–8 How is Death portrayed in these lines?

11 Gazing Grain: grain leaning toward the sun.

15 Gossamer: a thin, light cloth.

16 Tippet: shawl; **Tulle** (tool): fine netting.

20 Cornice (kôr′ nĭs): the molding around the top of a building.

17–20 What do you think this house represents?

21–24 How does the speaker seem to feel about the length of time that has passed?

Connect to the Literature

1. **What Do You Think?**
   What image of death do you get from "Because I could not stop for Death—"?

   > **Comprehension Check**
   > • What has happened to the speaker?
   > • What does Death's carriage hold?
   > • What has happened to time?

Think Critically

2. In the third stanza of "Because I could not stop for Death—" the carriage passes the school, fields of grain, and the setting sun. What might these objects **symbolize?**

3. **ACTIVE READING** **STRATEGIES FOR READING POETRY** Reread lines 17–20. What does the house in this stanza represent? Refer to your **READER'S NOTEBOOK** to review any questions or reactions that you may have recorded about the stanza. Explain what strategy you used to help you arrive at this meaning.

4. In "This is my letter to the World" Dickinson, in effect, states that the poem is her letter. Do you think the other poems are additional "letters" from Dickinson? Consider the evidence.

   THINK ABOUT
   - what you can conclude about her personality
   - what the poems suggest about what she values
   - what the poems suggest about her view of the world

5. Based on the eight poems you've read, what are your impressions of Emily Dickinson as a person? Give reasons for your answer.

Extend Interpretations

6. **Critic's Corner** Read Dickinson's quotation on the definition of poetry (page 746). In your opinion, do the poems in this Author Study meet the standards expressed by this definition? Explain.

7. **Connect to Life** How did discovering Dickinson's observations about nature, hope, success, and death affect your feelings about these topics that you recorded for the graphic shown on page 750?

Literary Analysis

FIGURATIVE LANGUAGE

Figurative language consists of groups of words that express ideas beyond the literal meaning of the words. Dickinson's poetry features some common figures of speech.

Similes compare two unlike things that have something in common, using *like* or *as.* The following lines from "I heard a Fly buzz—when I died—" compare the tense atmosphere of a death to the short periods of calm that occur in the midst of a violent storm:

The Stillness in the Room
Was like the Stillness in the Air—

A **metaphor** directly compares two unlike things. An **extended metaphor** compares two things at some length and in several ways. The extended metaphor in "'Hope' is the thing with feathers—" compares hope to a bird.

Personification is a figure of speech in which an object, animal, or idea is given human characteristics. In "Because I could not stop for Death—" death is personified as a kind gentleman.

Cooperative Learning Activity In small groups, choose an abstract concept (such as victory or truth) and compose your own definition by using figures of speech. Determine what is being compared. What ideas does the comparison bring out?

REVIEW **PARADOX** A **paradox** is a statement that seems to contradict itself but may suggest the truth. Note the paradox here:

Success is counted sweetest
By those who ne'er succeed.

THE AUTHOR'S STYLE
Dickinson's Stylistic Experiments

Emily Dickinson's style is as unique and personal as her observations about the world. In her inventive treatment of rhyme, punctuation, capitalization, and sentence structure, she rebelled against the poetic traditions of the 1800s.

Key Aspects of Dickinson's Style

- short, untitled lyric poems, usually no longer than 20 lines
- dense **quatrains,** or four-line stanzas, that echo the simple rhythms of church hymns
- **slant rhymes,** or words that do not rhyme exactly
- dashes used to highlight important words and to break up the singsong rhythm of her poems
- unconventional capitalization and inverted syntax to emphasize words
- omission of conjunctions, pronouns, prepositions, or articles to heighten the effect of compression

Analysis of Style

At the right are **quatrains** of three well-known Dickinson poems. Study the chart above, and then complete the following activities:

- Find examples of **slant rhyme,** inverted syntax, and omission of different parts of speech.

- Find at least two or three additional stylistic devices that you see at work in any of the three examples. What effect do they create?

- Look again at the eight poems in this Author Study. Choose one, and discuss with other readers the stylistic devices you see at work.

Applications

1. Changing Style Until 1955, volumes of Dickinson's poetry consisted of "corrected" versions of her poems. Acting as a 19th-century editor, rewrite one of Dickinson's poems, using standard punctuation and capitalization. Share your version with the class.

2. Imitation of Style Write a **quatrain** (four-line stanza) on any subject, imitating Dickinson's style. Copy your quatrain onto a page with the opening quatrains of other poems by Dickinson, and see if your classmates or your teacher can pick yours out.

3. Speaking and Listening Obtain a copy of *The Complete Poems of Emily Dickinson* edited by Thomas H. Johnson. In a small group, share a reading of Dickinson's poems. Discuss the strengths and weaknesses of each.

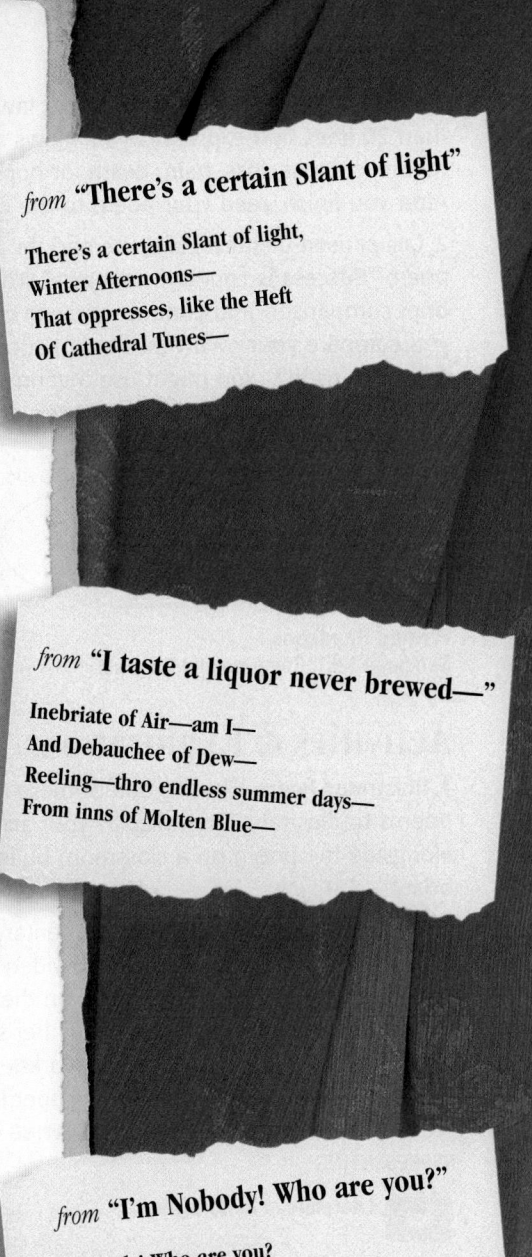

from **"There's a certain Slant of light"**

There's a certain Slant of light,
Winter Afternoons—
That oppresses, like the Heft
Of Cathedral Tunes—

from **"I taste a liquor never brewed—"**

Inebriate of Air—am I—
And Debauchee of Dew—
Reeling—thro endless summer days—
From inns of Molten Blue—

from **"I'm Nobody! Who are you?"**

I'm Nobody! Who are you?
Are you—Nobody—Too?
Then there's a pair of us?
Don't tell! they'd advertise—you know!

Writing Options

1. Mini Poem Create a short poem of fewer than 20 lines that expresses your views about nature, success, loss, pain, death, or hope. After you finish, read your poem to the class.

2. Comparison-Contrast Essay Reread the poem "Success is counted sweetest." Write a brief comparison-and-contrast essay in which you compare your own views about success with Dickinson's. You might use a Venn diagram like this one. Place your essay in your **Working Portfolio.**

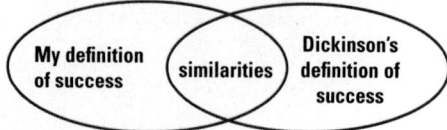

My definition of success — similarities — Dickinson's definition of success

Writing Handbook
See page 1281: Compare and Contrast.

Activities & Explorations

1. Illustrated Poem Choose one of these poems to illustrate. Then display your art alongside the poem on a classroom bulletin board. ~ **ART**

2. Video Adaptation View the documentary *Finished Knowing,* included on the video provided with this program. Focus on the filmmaker's message as she threads her story with lines from Emily Dickinson's works. Compare this film with Dickinson's poem "This is my letter to the World." ~ **VIEWING AND REPRESENTING**

VIDEO Literature in Performance

Inquiry & Research

Historical Connection Find out more about life in 19th-century rural New England. What values and beliefs did people hold? What kinds of challenges did they face? Then present a brief oral report with visual aids.

More Online: Research Starter
www.mcdougallittell.com

Netscape: Welcome to Netscape

Back | Forward | Home | Reload | Images | Open | Print | Find | Stop

Go To:

Emily Dickinson

Author Study Project
PRESENTING A POETRY SLAM

Since the 1990s, poetry slams have become a popular form of entertainment in schools and cafés and on college campuses. With your classmates, plan a reading of Dickinson's poems and letters. The following suggestions can help you launch a successful event:

Plan the Event First, choose several Dickinson poems or letters to read aloud. Next, determine the order in which the poems and letters will be read. For example, you may want to present the works in chronological order, or you may group them by theme. To heighten the dramatic effect, consider using props, sound effects, or music to accompany the reading.

Create a Program Guide Use a computer to create a program guide. Include the following:
- a brief biographical sketch about Dickinson's life and work
- titles of poems in the appropriate order
- the names of the readers
- illustrations of Emily Dickinson

Include the Ingredients In addition to readers, you will need the following:
- **MC.** A master of ceremonies to introduce readers and engage the audience.
- **Audience.** A group of people who cheer, boo, weep, laugh, or make clever remarks—depending on the quality of the presentations.
- **Judges.** A panel of three or four people who rate the readers on a scale of 1 to 10. The rating is determined partly by audience reaction.

Hold the Reading Presenters should read slowly and clearly, make eye contact with the audience, and pace the reading according to the punctuation of the material. You may want to videotape the reading for future audiences.

Social Themes in Fiction

Issues for Us All

Social issues are issues that affect groups of people trying to live together peacefully, in a nation, for example, or in a religious community, a geographical region, or a neighborhood. Today, crime is a social issue; so are all forms of discrimination.

American writers have always shown an interest in how society is organized. The dynamics of Puritan society, for instance—with its strictly enforced rules and punishments—have inspired great literary works from Nathaniel Hawthorne's *The Scarlet Letter* (1850) to Arthur Miller's *The Crucible* (1953). Although both of these works focus on the Puritans, Hawthorne explored the effects of Puritan morality on individual lives, whereas Miller, by exposing wrongs committed in the name of righteousness during the Salem witch trials, sought to suggest parallels to events of his own time.

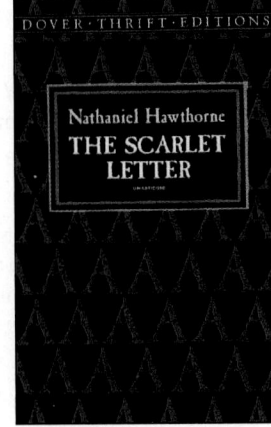

Nathaniel Hawthorne's
The Scarlet Letter (1850)

novel *Uncle Tom's Cabin* and the poetry of James Russell Lowell and Frances Ellen Watkins Harper.

As the nation expanded westward after the Civil War, another social issue gained prominence: Native Americans' presence on lands coveted by white settlers. Unlike the issue of slavery, however, the conflict between white settlement and the Native American way of life did not become the focus of a large body of American literature— although the tension simmering below the surface is evident in folk tales such as "The Indian and the Hundred Cows." That tale has a basically social theme, dealing as it does with the interaction between Native Americans and European settlers. You can infer from the tale that even Christianity, which promised to bind the two cultures together in common faith, was ironically a source of conflict. This simple folk tale demonstrates how effectively fiction can illuminate a large social problem by dramatizing conflicts between characters.

Dramatizing Social Issues

One issue that pervaded American life in the 19th century was slavery. Strong antislavery themes appear in such works as Harriet Beecher Stowe's

Identifying Social Themes

A social issue that emerged in the second half of the 19th century is the role of women in society. All of the selections in this part of Unit Five

---

The Spark that Ignited the Fire

Perhaps the most famous American novel with a social theme is Harriet Beecher Stowe's *Uncle Tom's Cabin,* published in 1852. Intending to expose slavery's evil effects on society as a whole, Stowe portrayed not

Harriet Beecher Stowe's *Uncle Tom's Cabin* (1852)

only the suffering of the enslaved characters but also the moral degradation of the slaveholder. More than a million copies of Stowe's powerful novel had been sold by the end of 1853, and it helped convince many Northerners that slavery had to end. Years later, when Stowe visited the White House during the Civil War, President Abraham Lincoln greeted her by saying, "So this is the little lady who made the big war."

address this issue in one way or another. As you read them, look for the following characteristics to help you identify social themes:

- Works that address social issues often focus on people who have few, if any, rights and privileges in society. The first-person narrator of "The Yellow Wallpaper," although comfortably middle-class, has no control over her life. Early in the story, she explains her complete submission to her doctor and her husband.

> So I take phosphates . . . and tonics, and journeys, and air, and exercise, and am absolutely forbidden to "work" until I am well again.
>
> Personally, I disagree with their ideas.
>
> Personally, I believe that congenial work, with excitement and change, would do me good.
>
> But what is one to do?
>
> —Charlotte Perkins Gilman,
> "The Yellow Wallpaper"

YOUR TURN What would you do if you found yourself in disagreement with your doctor and your spouse?

- Some works dealing with social themes contain direct statements that are clues to their themes. In "The Story of an Hour," the main character, after hearing that her husband is dead, reflects on the control he has exercised over her.

> There would be no powerful will bending hers in that blind persistence with which men and women believe they have a right to impose a private will upon a fellow creature.
>
> —Kate Chopin,
> "The Story of an Hour"

YOUR TURN How is this character's attitude different from that expressed in the passage from "The Yellow Wallpaper"?

- Many works with social themes portray characters struggling against poverty, prejudice, or other social obstacles. The narrator of "I Stand Here Ironing," for example, runs up against the emotional and financial limitations of being a single mother.

Strategies for Reading: Social Themes in Literature

1. Look for characters who have little power and ask yourself what social factors contribute to their situations.
2. Clarify the conflicts in the story and determine to what extent they are caused by forces beyond the characters' control.
3. Evaluate direct statements of the characters' opinions to see whether they provide clues to a theme.
4. Think about the author's reason for writing the story. What was he or she trying to achieve?
5. **Monitor** your reading strategies and modify them when your understanding breaks down. Remember to use the Strategies for Active Reading: **predict, visualize, connect, question, clarify,** and **evaluate.**

The Yellow Wallpaper

Short Story by CHARLOTTE PERKINS GILMAN

(**Connect to Your Life**)

Medical Practices This is a story about a woman who undergoes medical treatment for a "nervous condition" more than a hundred years ago. In a small group, discuss some medical treatments of the past that are no longer prescribed. List them on a word web like the one shown.

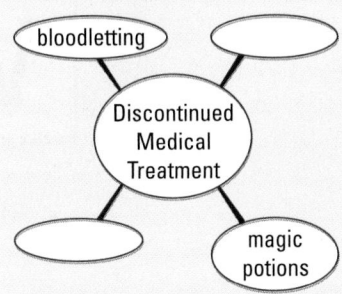

Build Background

"Women's Disorders" This story was written in 1890, when many women—especially nonworking middle-class and upper-class women—suffered from a variety of physical and mental disorders, such as fatigue and depression. If they sought medical treatment and no organic cause could be determined, their ills were often diagnosed as vague, trivial "nervous conditions," curable through isolation and prolonged rest. Although today it is believed that some of these disorders may have been caused by the stress of living within the rigid social roles to which women were confined, doctors in the late 1800s typically felt that the root of many women's illnesses was their gender. They assumed that women were weak and emotionally unstable, and thus by their very nature predisposed to illness.

WORDS TO KNOW
Vocabulary Preview

atrocious	impertinence	querulous
basely	inanimate	undulating
derision	patent	
felicity	perseverance	

Focus Your Reading

LITERARY ANALYSIS **FIRST-PERSON NARRATOR** The **narrator** of a story is the character or voice that relates the story's events to the reader. When a story is told from the first-person point of view, the narrator is a character in the story. "The Yellow Wallpaper" is told from the first-person point of view, and the narrator is an unnamed woman diagnosed with a nervous condition.

ACTIVE READING **MAKING INFERENCES ABOUT THE NARRATOR** The narrator in this story writes journal entries about her experiences. Much of what happens seems distorted or is unexplained; to understand the events, therefore, you must make **inferences,** or logical guesses, based on the details the narrator provides and what you know about life. As you read, allow yourself to perceive things as the narrator does. Occasionally, though, stand back from her to examine her perceptions and actions with a critical eye.

READER'S NOTEBOOK Record your responses to the questions inserted throughout this story. Also jot down other inferences you make about the narrator and the evidence on which you base your inferences.

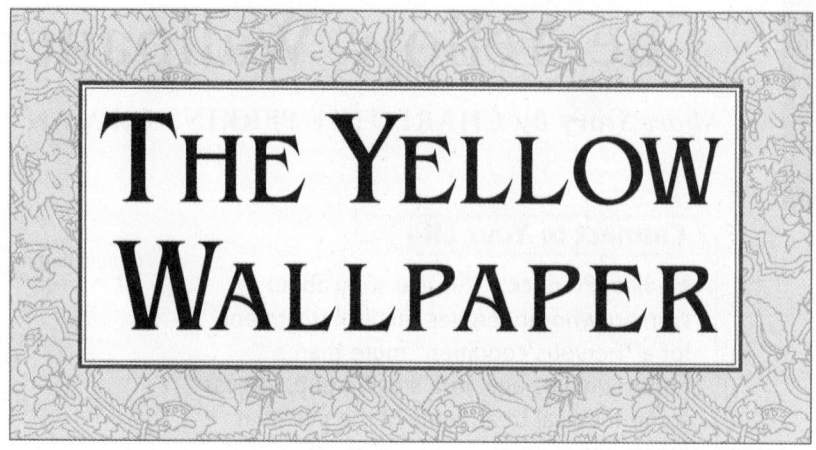

THE YELLOW WALLPAPER

CHARLOTTE PERKINS GILMAN

It is very seldom that mere ordinary people like John and myself secure ancestral halls for the summer.

A colonial mansion, a hereditary estate, I would say a haunted house, and reach the height of romantic felicity—but that would be asking too much of fate!

Still I will proudly declare that there is something queer about it.

Else, why should it be let so cheaply? And why have stood so long untenanted?

John laughs at me, of course, but one expects that in marriage.

John is practical in the extreme. He has no patience with faith, an intense horror of superstition, and he scoffs openly at any talk of things not to be felt and seen and put down in figures.

John is a physician, and *perhaps*—(I would not say it to a living soul, of course, but this is dead paper and a great relief to my *mind*)—*perhaps* that is one reason I do not get well faster.

You see he does not believe I am sick!

And what can one do?

If a physician of high standing, and one's own husband, assures friends and relatives that there is really nothing the matter with one but temporary nervous depression—a slight hysterical[1] tendency—what is one to do?

My brother is also a physician, and also of high standing, and he says the same thing.

So I take phosphates or phosphites—whichever it is, and tonics, and journeys, and air, and exercise, and am absolutely forbidden to "work" until I am well again.

Personally, I disagree with their ideas.

---

1. **hysterical:** Hysteria is the presence of a physical ailment with no underlying physical cause.

WORDS TO KNOW

felicity (fĭ-lĭs′ĭ-tē) *n.* happiness; bliss

A Woman Sewing in an Interior (about 1900), Wilhelm Hammershøi. Christie's, London, Bridgeman/Art Resource, New York.

Personally, I believe that congenial work, with excitement and change, would do me good.

But what is one to do?

I did write for a while in spite of them; but it *does* exhaust me a good deal—having to be so sly about it, or else meet with heavy opposition.

ACTIVE READING

CLARIFY Why is the narrator writing in secret?

I sometimes fancy that in my condition if I had less opposition and more society and stimulus—but John says the very worst thing I can do is to think about my condition, and I confess it always makes me feel bad.

So I will let it alone and talk about the house.

The most beautiful place! It is quite alone, standing well back from the road, quite three miles from the village. It makes me think of English places that you read about, for there are hedges and walls and gates that lock, and lots of separate little houses for the gardeners and people.

There is a *delicious* garden! I never saw such a garden—large and shady, full of box-bordered paths, and lined with long grape-covered arbors with seats under them.

There were greenhouses, too, but they are all broken now.

There was some legal trouble, I believe, something about the heirs and coheirs; anyhow, the place has been empty for years.

That spoils my ghostliness, I am afraid, but I don't care—there is something strange about the house—I can feel it.

I even said so to John one moonlight evening, but he said what I felt was a draft, and shut the window.

I get unreasonably angry with John sometimes. I'm sure I never used to be so sensitive. I think it is due to this nervous condition.

But John says if I feel so, I shall neglect proper self-control; so I take pains to control myself—before him, at least, and that makes me very tired.

I don't like our room a bit. I wanted one downstairs that opened on the piazza and had roses all over the window, and such pretty old-fashioned chintz hangings! but John would not hear of it.

He said there was only one window and not room for two beds, and no near room for him if he took another.

He is very careful and loving, and hardly lets me stir without special direction.

I have a schedule prescription for each hour in the day; he takes all care from me, and so I feel basely ungrateful not to value it more.

He said we came here solely on my account, that I was to have perfect rest and all the air I could get. "Your exercise depends on your strength, my dear," said

ACTIVE READING

EVALUATE Describe the relationship between the narrator and her husband.

he, "and your food somewhat on your appetite; but air you can absorb all the time." So we took the nursery at the top of the house.

It is a big, airy room, the whole floor nearly, with windows that look all ways, and air and sunshine galore. It was nursery first and then playroom and gymnasium, I should judge; for the windows are barred for little children, and there are rings and things in the walls.

The paint and paper look as if a boys' school had used it. It is stripped off—the paper—in great patches all around the head of my bed, about as far as I can reach, and in a great place on the other side of the room low down. I never saw a worse paper in my life.

One of those sprawling flamboyant patterns committing every artistic sin.

It is dull enough to confuse the eye in following, pronounced enough to constantly irritate and provoke study, and when you follow the lame uncertain curves for a little distance they suddenly commit suicide—plunge off at outrageous angles, destroy themselves in unheard of contradictions.

WORDS TO KNOW

basely (bās′lē) *adv.* dishonorably; meanly

The color is repellent, almost revolting; a smouldering unclean yellow, strangely faded by the slow-turning sunlight.

It is a dull yet lurid orange in some places, a sickly sulphur tint in others.

No wonder the children hated it! I should hate it myself if I had to live in this room long.

There comes John, and I must put this away,—he hates to have me write a word.

We have been here two weeks, and I haven't felt like writing before, since that first day.

I am sitting by the window now, up in this atrocious nursery, and there is nothing to hinder my writing as much as I please, save lack of strength.

John is away all day, and even some nights when his cases are serious.

I am glad my case is not serious!

But these nervous troubles are dreadfully depressing.

John does not know how much I really suffer. He knows there is no *reason* to suffer, and that satisfies him.

Of course it is only nervousness. It does weigh on me so not to do my duty in any way!

I meant to be such a help to John, such a real rest and comfort, and here I am a comparative burden already!

Nobody would believe what an effort it is to do what little I am able,—to dress and entertain, and order things.

It is fortunate Mary is so good with the baby. Such a dear baby!

And yet I *cannot* be with him, it makes me so nervous.

I suppose John never was nervous in his life. He laughs at me so about this wallpaper!

At first he meant to repaper the room, but afterwards he said that I was letting it get the better of me, and that nothing was worse for a nervous patient than to give way to such fancies.

He said that after the wallpaper was changed

ACTIVE READING

CONNECT What do the details about the room suggest about its function?

it would be the heavy bedstead, and then the barred windows, and then that gate at the head of the stairs, and so on.

"You know the place is doing you good," he said, "and really, dear, I don't care to renovate the house just for a three months' rental."

"Then do let us go downstairs," I said, "there are such pretty rooms there."

Then he took me in his arms and called me a blessed little goose, and said he would go down to the cellar, if I wished, and have it white-washed into the bargain.

But he is right enough about the beds and windows and things.

It is an airy and comfortable room as any one need wish, and, of course, I would not be so silly as to make him uncomfortable just for a whim.

I'm really getting quite fond of the big room, all but that horrid paper.

Out of one window I can see the garden, those mysterious deepshaded arbors, the riotous old-fashioned flowers, and bushes and gnarly trees.

Out of another I get a lovely view of the bay and a little private wharf belonging to the estate. There is a beautiful shaded lane that runs down there from the house. I always fancy I see people walking in these numerous paths and arbors, but John has cautioned me not to give way to fancy in the least. He says that with my imaginative power and habit of story-making, a nervous weakness like mine is sure to lead to all manner of excited fancies, and that I ought to use my will and good sense to check the tendency. So I try.

I think sometimes that if I were only well enough to write a little it would relieve the press of ideas and rest me.

But I find I get pretty tired when I try.

It is so discouraging not to have any advice and companionship about my work. When I get really well, John says we will ask Cousin Henry and

WORDS
TO
KNOW

atrocious (ə-trō′shəs) *adj.* shockingly bad or lacking in taste; awful

Julia down for a long visit; but he says he would as soon put fireworks in my pillowcase as to let me have those stimulating people about now.

I wish I could get well faster.

But I must not think about that. This paper looks to me as if it knew what a vicious influence it had!

There is a recurrent spot where the pattern lolls like a broken neck and two bulbous eyes stare at you upside down.

I get positively angry with the impertinence of it and the everlastingness. Up and down and sideways they crawl, and those absurd, unblinking eyes are everywhere. There is one place where two breadths didn't match, and the eyes go all up and down the line, one a little higher than the other.

I never saw so much expression in an inanimate thing before, and we all know how much expression they have! I used to lie awake as a child and get more entertainment and terror out of blank walls and plain furniture than most children could find in a toystore.

I remember what a kindly wink the knobs of our big, old bureau used to have, and there was one chair that always seemed like a strong friend.

I used to feel that if any of the other things looked too fierce I could always hop into that chair and be safe.

The furniture in this room is no worse than inharmonious, however, for we had to bring it all from downstairs. I suppose when this was used as a playroom they had to take the nursery things out, and no wonder! I never saw such ravages as the children have made here.

The wallpaper, as I said before, is torn off in spots, and it sticketh closer than a brother—they must have had perseverance as well as hatred.

Then the floor is scratched and gouged and splintered, the plaster itself is dug out here and there, and this great heavy bed which is all we found in the room, looks as if it had been through the wars.

But I don't mind it a bit—only the paper.

There comes John's sister. Such a dear girl as she is, and so careful of me! I must not let her find me writing.

She is a perfect and enthusiastic housekeeper, and hopes for no better profession. I verily believe she thinks it is the writing which made me sick!

But I can write when she is out, and see her a long way off from these windows.

There is one that commands the road, a lovely shaded winding road, and one that just looks off over the country. A lovely country, too, full of great elms and velvet meadows.

This wallpaper has a kind of sub-pattern in a different shade, a particularly irritating one, for you can only see it in certain lights, and not clearly then.

But in the places where it isn't faded and where the sun is just so—I can see a strange, provoking, formless sort of figure, that seems to skulk about behind that silly and conspicuous front design.

ACTIVE READING

CLARIFY Describe the effect the wallpaper is having on the narrator.

There's sister on the stairs!

Well, the Fourth of July is over! The people are all gone and I am tired out. John thought it might do me good to see a little company, so we just had mother and Nellie and the children down for a week.

Of course I didn't do a thing. Jennie sees to everything now.

But it tired me all the same.

John says if I don't pick up faster he shall send me to Weir Mitchell[2] in the fall.

---

2. **Weir Mitchell:** Dr. Silas Weir Mitchell, famous for his "rest cure" for nervous diseases, which is no longer considered effective.

WORDS
TO
KNOW
impertinence (ĭm-pûr'tn-əns) *n.* improper boldness; rudeness
inanimate (ĭn-ăn'ə-mĭt) *adj.* not alive; lifeless
perseverance (pûr'sə-vîr'əns) *n.* persistence in the face of difficulty; determination

Stairway (1949), Edward Hopper. Oil on wood, 16″ × 11 ⅞″, Collection of Whitney Museum of American Art, New York, Josephine N. Hopper Bequest (70.1265). Copyright © 1995 Whitney Museum of American Art. Photo by Geoffrey Clements.

But I don't want to go there at all. I had a friend who was in his hands once, and she says he is just like John and my brother, only more so!

Besides, it is such an undertaking to go so far.

I don't feel as if it was worth while to turn my hand over for anything, and I'm getting dreadfully fretful and querulous.

I cry at nothing, and cry most of the time.

Of course I don't when John is here, or anybody else, but when I am alone.

And I am alone a good deal just now. John is kept in town very often by serious cases, and Jennie is good and lets me alone when I want her to.

So I walk a little in the garden or down that lovely lane, sit on the porch under the roses, and lie down up here a good deal.

I'm getting really fond of the room in spite of the wallpaper. Perhaps *because* of the wallpaper.

It dwells in my mind so!

I lie here on this great immovable bed—it is nailed down, I believe—and follow that pattern about by the hour. It is as good as gymnastics, I assure you. I start, we'll say, at the bottom, down in the corner over there where it has not been touched, and I determine for the thousandth time that I *will* follow that pointless pattern to some sort of a conclusion.

I know a little of the principle of design, and I know this thing was not arranged on any laws of radiation, or alternation, or repetition, or symmetry, or anything else that I ever heard of.

It is repeated, of course, by the breadths, but not otherwise.

Looked at in one way each breadth stands alone, the bloated curves and flourishes—a kind of "debased Romanesque"[3] with *delirium tremens*[4]—go waddling up and down in isolated columns of fatuity.[5]

But, on the other hand, they connect diagonally, and the sprawling outlines run off in great slanting waves of optic horror, like a lot of wallowing seaweeds in full chase.

The whole thing goes horizontally, too, at least

it seems so, and I exhaust myself in trying to distinguish the order of its going in that direction.

They have used a horizontal breadth for a frieze, and that adds wonderfully to the confusion.

There is one end of the room where it is almost intact, and there, when the crosslights fade and the low sun shines directly upon it, I can almost fancy radiation after all,—the interminable grotesques seem to form around a common center and rush off in headlong plunges of equal distraction.

It makes me tired to follow it. I will take a nap I guess.

I don't know why I should write this.

I don't want to.

I don't feel able.

And I know John would think it absurd. But I *must* say what I feel and think in some way—it is such a relief!

But the effort is getting to be greater than the relief.

Half the time now I am awfully lazy, and lie down ever so much.

John says I mustn't lose my strength, and has me take cod liver oil and lots of tonics and things, to say nothing of ale and wine and rare meat.

Dear John! He loves me very dearly, and hates to have me sick. I tried to have a real earnest reasonable talk with him the other day, and tell him how I wish he would let me go and make a visit to Cousin Henry and Julia.

But he said I wasn't able to go, nor able to stand it after I got there; and I did not make out a very good case for myself, for I was crying before I had finished.

It is getting to be a great effort for me to think straight. Just this nervous weakness I suppose.

And dear John gathered me up in his arms, and

---

3. **Romanesque:** an artistic style characterized by simple ornamentation.

4. *delirium tremens:* violent trembling and hallucinations caused by excessive drinking.

5. **fatuity** (fə-tōō′ĭ-tē): foolishness; smug stupidity.

WORDS
TO
KNOW

querulous (kwĕr′ə-ləs) *adj.* given to complaining

just carried me upstairs and laid me on the bed, and sat by me and read to me till it tired my head.

He said I was his darling and his comfort and all he had, and that I must take care of myself for his sake, and keep well.

He says no one but myself can help me out of it, that I must use my will and self-control and not let any silly fancies run away with me.

There's one comfort, the baby is well and happy, and does not have to occupy this nursery with the horrid wallpaper.

If we had not used it, that blessed child would have! What a fortunate escape! Why, I wouldn't have a child of mine, an impressionable little thing, live in such a room for worlds.

I never thought of it before, but it is lucky that John kept me here after all, I can stand it so much easier than a baby, you see.

Of course I never mention it to them any more—I am too wise,—but I keep watch of it all the same.

There are things in that paper that nobody knows but me, or ever will.

Behind that outside pattern the dim shapes get clearer every day.

It is always the same shape, only very numerous.

And it is like a woman stooping down and creeping about behind that pattern. I don't like it a bit. I wonder—I begin to think—I wish John would take me away from here!

ACTIVE READING

EVALUATE How do you explain the figure beginning to appear in the wallpaper?

It is so hard to talk with John about my case, because he is so wise, and because he loves me so.

But I tried it last night.

It was moonlight. The moon shines in all around just as the sun does.

I hate to see it sometimes, it creeps so slowly, and always comes in by one window or another.

John was asleep and I hated to waken him, so I kept still and watched the moonlight on that undulating wallpaper till I felt creepy.

The faint figure behind seemed to shake the pattern, just as if she wanted to get out.

I got up softly and went to feel and see if the paper *did* move, and when I came back John was awake.

"What is it, little girl?" he said. "Don't go walking about like that—you'll get cold."

I thought it was a good time to talk, so I told him that I really was not gaining here, and that I wished he would take me away.

"Why darling!" said he, "our lease will be up in three weeks, and I can't see how to leave before.

"The repairs are not done at home, and I cannot possibly leave town just now. Of course if you were in any danger, I could and would, but you really are better, dear, whether you can see it or not. I am a doctor, dear, and I know. You are gaining flesh and color, your appetite is better, I feel really much easier about you."

"I don't weigh a bit more," said I, "nor as much; and my appetite may be better in the evening when you are here, but it is worse in the morning when you are away!"

"Bless her little heart!" said he with a big hug, "she shall be as sick as she pleases! But now let's improve the shining hours[6] by going to sleep, and talk about it in the morning!"

"And you won't go away?" I asked gloomily.

"Why, how can I, dear? It is only three weeks more and then we will take a nice little trip of a few days while Jennie is getting the house ready. Really dear you are better!"

"Better in body perhaps—" I began, and stopped short, for he sat up straight and looked at me with such a stern, reproachful look that I could not say another word.

---

6. **improve the shining hours:** make good use of time (an allusion to the poem "Against Idleness and Mischief" by Isaac Watts: "How doth the little busy bee / Improve each shining hour, / And gather honey all the day / From every opening flower!").

WORDS TO KNOW

undulating (ŭn′jə-lā′tĭng) *adj.* moving with a wavelike motion **undulate** *v.*

"My darling," said he, "I beg of you, for my sake and for our child's sake, as well as for your own, that you will never for one instant let that idea enter your mind! There is nothing so dangerous, so fascinating, to a temperament like yours. It is a false and foolish fancy. Can you not trust me as a physician when I tell you so?"

ACTIVE READING

INFER What is the "idea" that John says the narrator should not "let . . . enter your mind"?

So of course I said no more on that score, and we went to sleep before long. He thought I was asleep first, but I wasn't, and lay there for hours trying to decide whether that front pattern and the back pattern really did move together or separately.

On a pattern like this, by daylight, there is a lack of sequence, a defiance of law, that is a constant irritant to a normal mind.

The color is hideous enough, and unreliable enough, and infuriating enough, but the pattern is torturing.

You think you have mastered it, but just as you get well underway in following, it turns a back-somersault and there you are. It slaps you in the face, knocks you down, and tramples upon you. It is like a bad dream.

The outside pattern is a florid arabesque,[7] reminding one of a fungus. If you can imagine a toadstool in joints, an interminable string of toadstools, budding and sprouting in endless convolutions—why, that is something like it.

That is, sometimes!

There is one marked peculiarity about this paper, a thing nobody seems to notice but myself, and that is that it changes as the light changes.

When the sun shoots in through the east window—I always watch for that first long, straight ray—it changes so quickly that I never can quite believe it.

That is why I watch it always.

By moonlight—the moon shines in all night when there is a moon—I wouldn't know it was the same paper.

At night in any kind of light, in twilight, candle light, lamplight, and worst of all by moonlight, it becomes bars! The outside pattern I mean, and the woman behind it is as plain as can be.

I didn't realize for a long time what the thing was that showed behind, that dim sub-pattern, but now I am quite sure it is a woman.

By daylight she is subdued, quiet. I fancy it is the pattern that keeps her so still. It is so puzzling. It keeps me quiet by the hour.

I lie down ever so much now. John says it is good for me, and to sleep all I can.

Indeed he started the habit by making me lie down for an hour after each meal.

It is a very bad habit I am convinced, for you see I don't sleep.

And that cultivates deceit, for I don't tell them I'm awake—O no!

The fact is I am getting a little afraid of John.

He seems very queer sometimes, and even Jennie has an inexplicable look.

It strikes me occasionally, just as a scientific hypothesis,—that perhaps it is the paper!

I have watched John when he did not know I was looking, and come into the room suddenly on the most innocent excuses, and I've caught him several times *looking at the paper!* And Jennie too. I caught Jennie with her hand on it once.

She didn't know I was in the room, and when I asked her in a quiet, a very quiet voice, with the most restrained manner possible, what she was doing with the paper—she turned around as if she had been caught stealing, and looked quite angry—asked me why I should frighten her so!

Then she said that the paper stained everything it touched, that she had found yellow smooches[8] on all my clothes and John's, and she wished we would be more careful!

Did not that sound innocent? But I know she was studying that pattern, and I am determined that nobody shall find it out but myself!

---

7. **florid arabesque:** an elaborate interwoven pattern.

8. **smooches:** dirty marks or spots; smudges.

Life is very much more exciting now than it used to be. You see I have something more to expect, to look forward to, to watch. I really do eat better, and am more quiet than I was.

John is so pleased to see me improve! He laughed a little the other day, and said I seemed to be flourishing in spite of my wallpaper.

I turned it off with a laugh. I had no intention of telling him it was *because* of the wallpaper—he would make fun of me. He might even want to take me away.

I don't want to leave now until I have found it out. There is a week more, and I think that will be enough.

ACTIVE READING

PREDICT The narrator's attitude seems to have changed. Do you think she will get better?

I'm feeling ever so much better! I don't sleep much at night, for it is so interesting to watch developments; but I sleep a good deal in the daytime.

In the daytime it is tiresome and perplexing.

There are always new shoots on the fungus, and new shades of yellow all over it. I cannot keep count of them, though I have tried conscientiously.

It is the strangest yellow, that wallpaper! It makes me think of all the yellow things I ever saw—not beautiful ones like buttercups, but old foul, bad yellow things.

But there is something else about that paper—the smell! I noticed it the moment we came into the room, but with so much air and sun it was not bad. Now we have had a week of fog and rain, and whether the windows are open or not, the smell is here.

It creeps all over the house.

I find it hovering in the dining room, skulking in the parlor, hiding in the hall, lying in wait for me on the stairs.

It gets into my hair.

Even when I go to ride, if I turn my head suddenly and surprise it—there is that smell!

Such a peculiar odor, too! I have spent hours in trying to analyze it, to find what it smelled like.

It is not bad—at first, and very gentle, but quite the subtlest, most enduring odor I ever met.

In this damp weather it is awful, I wake up in the night and find it hanging over me.

It used to disturb me at first. I thought seriously of burning the house—to reach the smell.

But now I am used to it. The only thing I can think of that it is like is the *color* of the paper! A yellow smell.

There is a very funny mark on this wall, low down, near the mopboard. A streak that runs round the room. It goes behind every piece of furniture, except the bed, a long, straight, even *smooch*, as if it had been rubbed over and over.

I wonder how it was done and who did it, and what they did it for. Round and round and round—round and round and round—it makes me dizzy!

I really have discovered something at last.

Through watching so much at night, when it changes so, I have finally found out.

The front pattern *does* move—and no wonder! The woman behind shakes it!

Sometimes I think there are a great many women behind, and sometimes only one, and she crawls around fast, and her crawling shakes it all over.

Then in the very bright spots she keeps still, and in the very shady spots she just takes hold of the bars and shakes them hard.

And she is all the time trying to climb through. But nobody could climb through that pattern—it strangles so; I think that is why it has so many heads.

They get through, and then the pattern strangles them off and turns them upside down, and makes their eyes white!

If those heads were covered or taken off it would not be half so bad.

I think that woman gets out in the daytime!

And I'll tell you why—privately—I've seen her!

I can see her out of every one of my windows!

It is the same woman, I know, for she is always creeping, and most women do not creep by daylight.

I see her on that long road under the trees, creeping along, and when a carriage comes she hides under the blackberry vines.

I don't blame her a bit. It must be very humiliating to be caught creeping by daylight!

I always lock the door when I creep by daylight. I can't do it at night, for I know John would suspect something at once.

And John is so queer now, that I don't want to irritate him. I wish he would take another room! Besides, I don't want anybody to get that woman out at night but myself.

I often wonder if I could see her out of all the windows at once.

But, turn as fast as I can, I can only see out of one at one time.

And though I always see her, she may be able to creep faster than I can turn! I have watched her sometimes away off in the open country, creeping as fast as a cloud shadow in a high wind.

ACTIVE READING

EVALUATE What is the narrator's condition?

If only that top pattern could be gotten off from the under one! I mean to try it, little by little.

I have found out another funny thing, but I shan't tell it this time! It does not do to trust people too much.

There are only two more days to get this paper off, and I believe John is beginning to notice. I don't like the look in his eyes.

And I heard him ask Jennie a lot of professional questions about me. She had a very good report to give.

She said I slept a good deal in the daytime.

John knows I don't sleep very well at night, for all I'm so quiet!

He asked me all sorts of questions, too, and pretended to be very loving and kind.

As if I couldn't see through him!

Still, I don't wonder he acts so, sleeping under this paper for three months.

It only interests me, but I feel sure John and Jennie are secretly affected by it.

Hurrah! This is the last day, but it is enough. John to stay in town over night, and won't be out until this evening.

Jennie wanted to sleep with me—the sly thing! but I told her I should undoubtedly rest better for a night all alone.

That was clever, for really I wasn't alone a bit! As soon as it was moonlight and that poor thing began to crawl and shake the pattern, I got up and ran to help her.

I pulled and she shook, I shook and she pulled, and before morning we had peeled off yards of that paper.

A strip about as high as my head and half around the room.

And then when the sun came and that awful pattern began to laugh at me, I declared I would finish it today!

We go away tomorrow, and they are moving all my furniture down again to leave things as they were before.

Jennie looked at the wall in amazement, but I told her merrily that I did it out of pure spite at the vicious thing.

She laughed and said she wouldn't mind doing it herself, but I must not get tired.

How she betrayed herself that time!

But I am here, and no person touches this paper but me,—not *alive!*

She tried to get me out of the room—it was too patent! But I said it was so quiet and empty and clean now that I believed I would lie down again and sleep all I could; and not to wake me even for dinner—I would call when I woke.

So now she is gone, and the servants are gone, and the things are gone, and there is nothing left but that great bedstead nailed down, with the canvas mattress we found on it.

We shall sleep downstairs tonight, and take the boat home tomorrow.

WORDS
TO   **patent** (păt'nt) *adj.* obvious; apparent
KNOW

I quite enjoy the room, now it is bare again.
How those children did tear about here!
This bedstead is fairly gnawed!
But I must get to work.
I have locked the door and thrown the key down into the front path.
I don't want to go out, and I don't want to have anybody come in, till John comes.
I want to astonish him.
I've got a rope up here that even Jennie did not find. If that woman does get out, and tries to get away, I can tie her!
But I forgot I could not reach far without anything to stand on!
This bed will *not* move!
I tried to lift and push it until I was lame, and then I got so angry I bit off a little piece at one corner—but it hurt my teeth.
Then I peeled off all the paper I could reach standing on the floor. It sticks horribly and the pattern just enjoys it! All those strangled heads and bulbous eyes and waddling fungus growths just shriek with <u>derision</u>!
I am getting angry enough to do something desperate. To jump out of the window would be admirable exercise, but the bars are too strong even to try.
Besides I wouldn't do it. Of course not. I know well enough that a step like that is improper and might be misconstrued.

ACTIVE READING

CLARIFY What does the narrator now believe?

I don't like to *look* out of the windows even— there are so many of those creeping women, and they creep so fast.
I wonder if they all come out of that wallpaper as I did?
But I am securely fastened now by my well-hidden rope—you don't get *me* out in the road there!
I suppose I shall have to get back behind the pattern when it comes night, and that is hard!
It is so pleasant to be out in this great room and creep around as I please!

I don't want to go outside. I won't, even if Jennie asks me to.
For outside you have to creep on the ground, and everything is green instead of yellow.
But here I can creep smoothly on the floor, and my shoulder just fits in that long smooch around the wall, so I cannot lose my way.
Why there's John at the door!
It is no use, young man, you can't open it!
How he does call and pound!
Now he's crying for an axe.
It would be a shame to break down that beautiful door!
"John dear!" said I in the gentlest voice, "the key is down by the front steps, under a plantain leaf!"
That silenced him for a few moments.
Then he said—very quietly indeed, "Open the door, my darling!"
"I can't," said I. "The key is down by the front door under a plantain leaf!"
And then I said it again, several times, very gently and slowly, and said it so often that he had to go and see, and he got it of course, and came in. He stopped short by the door.
"What is the matter?" he cried. "What are you doing!"
I kept on creeping just the same, but I looked at him over my shoulder.
"I've got out at last," said I, "in spite of you and Jane.[9] And I've pulled off most of the paper, so you can't put me back!"
Now why should that man have fainted? But he did, and right across my path by the wall, so that I had to creep over him every time! ❖

---

9. **in spite of you and Jane:** This reference to a previously unmentioned Jane is a point of debate. It could be an error made by the original printer for the name of the sister-housekeeper Jennie or Cousin Julia. It is also possible, however, that Jane is the narrator, here freeing herself from both her husband and her commonplace, wifely "Jane" self.

WORDS
TO
KNOW   **derision** (dĭ-rĭzh′ən) *n.* harsh ridicule or mockery; scorn

Thinking through the LITERATURE

Connect to the Literature

1. **What Do You Think?** What unanswered questions do you have about this story?

Comprehension Check
- What treatment has been prescribed for the narrator?
- What is unusual about the yellow wallpaper?
- What is the narrator doing at the end of the story?

Think Critically

2. **ACTIVE READING | MAKING INFERENCES ABOUT THE NARRATOR** Review the **inferences** about the narrator that you listed in your **READER'S NOTEBOOK.** Based on these inferences, how do you explain the narrator's behavior at the end of the story?

3. Why do you think the **narrator** becomes so obsessed with the wallpaper?

   THINK ABOUT
   - the descriptions of the patterns and colors
   - the amount of time she spends in the room
   - the changes the narrator finds in the wallpaper

Extend Interpretations

4. **Critic's Corner** Over the years, "The Yellow Wallpaper" has been interpreted in different ways: as a Gothic horror tale like those of Edgar Allan Poe, as a semiautobiographical account of a mental breakdown (see the writer's biography on page 781), and as a symbolic presentation of the effects of social and economic oppression on women. What aspects of the story do you think prompted each of these interpretations? State which interpretation you favor, and explain your reasons.

5. **Comparing Texts** From reading the excerpt from *Complaints and Disorders* on page 782, do you think Dr. S. Weir Mitchell would have found the narrator of this story to be an ideal patient? Explain.

6. **The Writer's Style** As the story progresses, the narrator's paragraphs become increasingly short, sometimes consisting of just a single sentence or sentence fragment. What reason might Gilman have had for using this curt, choppy style? What effect does the style have on you as a reader?

7. **Connect to Life** Which of the narrator's traits would be considered normal in a woman today?

Literary Analysis

FIRST PERSON NARRATOR The **narrator** relates a story's events to the reader and, in the first-person point of view, is a character in the story. A first-person narrator engages the reader, communicating a sense of immediacy and personal concern. The reader may even identify with such a narrator. Sometimes, however, the credibility, or the trustworthiness, of the narrator is open to question. In Poe's "The Fall of the House of Usher," for example, the reader is not quite sure about the narrator's credibility. Did the events he described really happen, or are they mere figments of his imagination?

In "The Yellow Wallpaper," the first-person narrator begins to see **images** in the wallpaper: bars, bulbous eyes, a creeping woman, and more. If the wallpaper reflects the narrator's psychological state, you can use it as evidence to draw conclusions about her feelings and preoccupations.

Cooperative Learning Activity Working with a small group of classmates, go back through the story and list the images that describe the wallpaper. Try to interpret each image, associating it with some aspect of the narrator's life. (There are no definite answers.) What general statement can your group make about the narrator's problem? What are the advantages and disadvantages of using a first-person narrator to tell this story, especially in light of the narrator's condition?

Choices & CHALLENGES

Writing Options

1. Advertising Copy Write a few sentences of advertising copy that you think would intrigue people enough to make them want to read this story.

2. Letter to Editor When Gilman first tried to get "The Yellow Wallpaper" published, she sent the story to the famous author William Dean Howells, who passed it along to H. E. Scudder, editor of the *Atlantic Monthly*. In rejecting Gilman's story, Scudder wrote her this response: "Mr. Howells has handed me this story. I could not forgive myself if I made others as miserable as I have made myself. " Do you agree that this story makes readers miserable? Would you recommend it to your friends? Write a letter to the editor, expressing your views.

3. Extend the Story Write a sequel to the story, showing what will happen to the narrator and her husband, or a prequel, describing what their courtship was like. Save your story in your **Working Portfolio**.

Activities & Explorations

1. Dramatic Scene With a partner, improvise a dramatic scene in which the narrator and her husband discuss her illness and treatment. In your scene, have the narrator attempt to explain how she feels and what she needs in order to recover, and have her husband explain to her why his treatment is the preferred therapy. ~ **PERFORMING**

2. Wallpaper Design Re-create the infamous yellow wallpaper. Go back through the story to pinpoint some of its specific characteristics, but also base your work on the narrator's impressions of it. Use markers, paints, or crayons—or any combination—on oversized paper or poster board. ~ **ART**

3. Top Story How might a television station cover the final scene as a sensationalized news story? Write and perform a newscast of the events, including interviews with John, Jennie, Cousin Henry and Julia, and the narrator herself. ~ **SPEAKING AND LISTENING**

Inquiry & Research

Depression A modern clinician might say that after the birth of her child, the narrator of this story experiences a postpartum depression that later develops into postpartum psychosis. Find out more about these illnesses. What causes them? What are their symptoms, and which of the symptoms does the narrator exhibit? How are the conditions treated today?

Vocabulary in Action

EXERCISE A: MEANING CLUES Review the Words to Know in the boxes at the bottom of the selection pages. Answer the following questions.

1. Would a child show **impertinence** by being sleepy, by being sassy, or by being shy?

2. Which would most likely be described as **atrocious**—something gross, something elegant, or something amusing?

3. Would a **querulous** person be likely to respond to an unpleasant situation by whining, by suffering in silence, or by making the best of it?

4. Is a **patent** lie one that is unnecessary, one that is highly creative, or one that is evident?

5. Which facial expression communicates **derision**—a wink, a sneer, or a yawn?

6. Does a person who has **perseverance** possess the quality of stick-to-itiveness, of quick-wittedness, or of open-mindedness?

7. Would you see the water in a lake **undulating** as a result of freezing weather, of a jumping fish, or of serious pollution?

8. Which is **inanimate**—a sleeping person, a barking dog, or a shining rock?

9. Would someone experiencing **felicity** be most likely to smile, to glare, or to sob?

10. If you thought someone had behaved **basely**, would you feel critical, jealous, or respectful?

EXERCISE B Working with a partner, act out the meaning of these vocabulary words—*felicity, impertinence, perseverance,* and *derision*—while another pair of students tries to guess them.

Building Vocabulary
For an in-depth lesson on word connotation and denotation, see page 908.

Charlotte Perkins Gilman
1860–1935

Other Works
Herland
*The Living of Charlotte Perkins Gilman: An
Autobiography*

Mental Illness After reading "The Yellow Wallpaper," a doctor wrote to Charlotte Perkins Gilman, praising the story's "detailed account of incipient insanity." Of course, he assumed she had not herself experienced what she had written about. Unfortunately, she had. After the birth of her daughter in 1885, Gilman suffered from severe depression, a condition known today as postpartum depression. She consulted the noted neurologist Dr. S. Weir Mitchell, who advised her: "Live as domestic a life as possible. Have your child with you all the time. . . . Lie down an hour after each meal. Have but two hours' intellectual life a day. And never touch pen, brush or pencil as long as you live." By following Mitchell's orders, Gilman became even more depressed.

Triumph Eventually, Gilman saved herself from a total mental breakdown by ignoring her doctor's advice. Gilman wrote "The Yellow Wallpaper" in 1890 to protest doctors' "rest cures" for women. Learning that Dr. Mitchell had changed his treatment after reading her story, Gilman said, "If

that is a fact, I have not lived in vain." In 1894 she divorced her first husband, Charles Stetson, and sent her daughter to live with him and his new wife. An artist and art teacher, she resumed painting and teaching. She gave lectures about women's issues, started a magazine, *The Forerunner,* and began publishing poems and articles. Within a ten-year period, Gilman wrote her best-known work of nonfiction, *Women and Economics* (1898), as well as *Concerning Children* (1900), *The Home: Its Work and Influence* (1903), and *Human Work* (1904).

Final Years At the age of 72, Gilman was diagnosed with incurable cancer. She continued writing for three more years; but when the pain of the disease began to prevent her from working, she committed suicide.

from

Complaints and Disorders

by Barbara Ehrenreich and Deirdre English

In 1900 there were 173 doctors (engaged in primary patient care) per 100,000 population, compared to 50 per 100,000 today. So, it was in the interests of doctors to cultivate the illnesses of their patients with frequent home visits and drawn-out "treatments." A few dozen well-heeled lady customers were all that a doctor needed for a successful urban practice. Women—at least, women whose husbands could pay the bills—became a natural "client caste"[1] to the developing medical profession.

❶   In many ways, the upper-middle-class woman was the ideal patient: her illnesses—and her husband's bank account—seemed almost inexhaustible. Furthermore, she was usually submissive and obedient to the 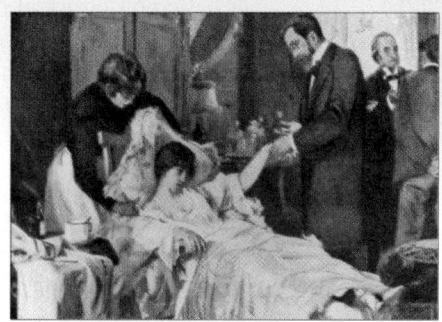 "doctor's orders." The famous Philadelphia doctor S. Weir Mitchell expressed his profession's deep appreciation of the female invalid in 1888:

> With all her weakness, her unstable emotionality, her tendency to morally warp when long nervously ill, she is then far easier to deal with, far more amenable to reason, far more sure to be comfortable as a patient, than the man who is relatively in a like position. The reasons for this are too obvious to delay me here, and physicians accustomed to deal with both sexes as sick people will be apt to justify my position.

❷   In Mitchell's mind women were not only easier to relate to, but sickness was the very key to femininity: "The man who does not know sick women does not know women."

---

1. **caste** (kăst): a group or class of people.

Reading for Information

In the 20th century, women have asserted their rights at home, in the workplace, and even in the field of medicine, but conditions were very different in the 19th century. The story "The Yellow Wallpaper" provides a glimpse of the way in which female patients were treated at that time. How do you think this treatment reflected the limitations of women's role in society? This excerpt can help you support your opinion.

FINDING EVIDENCE

When you research a topic, it is helpful to keep in mind the questions you are trying to answer or the conclusions you are trying to prove or validate. Then, as you read, you can look for statistics, primary sources, and quotations that tell you what you need to know. Use the activities below to examine the evidence in this article.

❶ **Evaluating Evidence** The writers explain why "the upper-middle-class woman was the ideal patient." What evidence do they use to support this claim? What is your reaction to their evidence?

❷ What can you infer about the writers by their choice of subject and the nature of their comments?

Comparing Texts Do you think Dr. S. Weir Mitchell would have found the narrator of "The Yellow Wallpaper" to be an ideal patient? Explain your opinion.

The Story of an Hour

Short Story by KATE CHOPIN

(Connect to Your Life)

Marriage Guidelines "The Story of an Hour" reveals a young woman's private thoughts about her life and marriage. What kind of relationship do you expect to have with a spouse? What are some guidelines for a good marriage? With a small group of classmates, discuss your thoughts about and expectations of marriage.

Build Background

Status of Women This story takes place about 100 years ago, near the turn of the century, when the status of women was very different from what it is today. Both custom and law severely limited women's actions and their control over their own lives. Because women could not vote, they had almost no political or legal power; and because they could not own property and their educational and employment opportunities were limited, they had little or no financial independence. Few careers were open to middle-class and upper-class single women, and even fewer to married women—like Mrs. Mallard in this story— who were expected to be supported by their husbands. Those who did work had to turn their wages over to their fathers or their husbands. In most American marriages of the time, the husband was the undisputed head of the household and made all the important decisions.

Focus Your Reading

LITERARY ANALYSIS **PLOT** The **plot** of a literary work is the sequence of actions and events. Generally, plots are built around a **conflict**—a problem or a struggle between two or more opposing forces. The plot of this story is built around Mrs. Mallard's inner conflict. Notice the opposing forces within her.

ACTIVE READING **PREDICTING** Using what you already know to figure out what might happen is called **predicting.** To make a prediction, you gather clues as you read and then use them to make reasonable guesses about what will occur in the story. For example, the first sentence of this story provides a detail about Mrs. Mallard's health and an unexpected piece of news. Use these clues and others to make predictions as you read. Feel free to revise your predictions as you come upon new clues.

READER'S NOTEBOOK On a chart like the one shown, jot down the clues you find and the predictions you make.

Clues	Predictions

THE STORY OF AN HOUR

Kate Chopin

Knowing that Mrs. Mallard was afflicted with a heart trouble, great care was taken to break to her as gently as possible the news of her husband's death.

It was her sister Josephine who told her, in broken sentences; veiled hints that revealed in half concealing. Her husband's friend Richards was there, too, near her. It was he who had been in the newspaper office when intelligence of the railroad disaster was received, with Brently Mallard's name leading the list of "killed." He had only taken the time to assure himself of its truth by a second telegram, and had hastened to forestall any less careful, less tender friend in bearing the sad message.

> What could love, the unsolved mystery, count for in face of this possession of self-assertion which she suddenly recognized as the strongest impulse of her being!

She did not hear the story as many women have heard the same, with a paralyzed inability to accept its significance. She wept at once, with sudden, wild abandonment, in her sister's arms. When the storm of grief had spent itself she went away to her room alone. She would have no one follow her.

There stood, facing the open window, a comfortable, roomy armchair. Into this she sank, pressed down by a physical exhaustion that haunted her body and seemed to reach into her soul.

She could see in the open square before her house the tops of trees that were all aquiver with the new spring life. The delicious breath of rain was in the air. In the street below a peddler was crying his wares. The notes of a distant song which someone was singing reached her faintly, and countless sparrows were twittering in the eaves.

There were patches of blue sky showing here and there through the clouds that had met and piled one above the other in the west facing her window.

She sat with her head thrown back upon the cushion of the chair, quite motionless, except when a sob came up into her throat and shook her, as a child who has cried itself to sleep continues to sob in its dreams.

She was young, with a fair, calm face, whose lines bespoke repression and even a certain strength. But now there was a dull stare in her eyes, whose gaze was fixed away off yonder on one of those patches of blue sky. It was not a glance of reflection, but rather indicated a suspension of intelligent thought.

There was something coming to her and she was waiting for it, fearfully. What was it? She did not know; it was too subtle and elusive to name. But she felt it, creeping out of the sky, reaching toward her through the sounds, the scents, the color that filled the air.

Now her bosom rose and fell tumultuously. She was beginning to recognize this thing that was approaching to possess her, and she was striving to beat it back with her will—as powerless as her two white slender hands would have been.

When she abandoned herself, a little whispered word escaped her slightly parted lips. She said it over and over under her breath: "free, free, free!" The vacant stare and the look of terror that had followed it went from her eyes. They stayed keen and bright. Her pulses beat fast, and the coursing blood warmed and relaxed every inch of her body.

She did not stop to ask if it were or were not a monstrous joy that held her. A clear and exalted perception enabled her to dismiss the suggestion as trivial.

She knew that she would weep again when she saw the kind, tender hands folded in death; the face that had never looked save with love upon her, fixed and gray and dead. But she saw beyond that bitter moment a long procession of years to come that would belong to her absolutely. And she opened and spread her arms out to them in welcome.

There would be no one to live for her during those coming years; she would live for herself. There would be no powerful will bending hers in that blind persistence with which men and women believe they have a right to impose a private will upon a fellow creature. A kind intention or a cruel intention made the act seem no less a crime as she looked upon it in that brief moment of illumination.

And yet she had loved him—sometimes. Often she had not. What did it matter! What could love, the unsolved mystery, count for in face of this possession of self-assertion which she suddenly recognized as the strongest impulse of her being!

"Free! Body and soul free!" she kept whispering.

Josephine was kneeling before the closed door with her lips to the keyhole, imploring for admission. "Louise, open the door! I beg; open the door—you will make yourself ill. What are

Morning Glories (1873), Winslow Homer. Private Collection.

you doing, Louise? For heaven's sake open the door."

"Go away. I am not making myself ill." No; she was drinking in a very elixir of life[1] through that open window.

Her fancy was running riot along those days ahead of her. Spring days, and summer days, and all sorts of days that would be her own. She breathed a quick prayer that life might be long. It was only yesterday she had thought with a shudder that life might be long.

She arose at length and opened the door to her sister's importunities. There was a feverish triumph in her eyes, and she carried herself unwittingly like a goddess of Victory. She clasped her sister's waist, and together they descended the stairs. Richards stood waiting for them at the bottom.

Someone was opening the front door with a latchkey. It was Brently Mallard who entered, a little travel-stained, composedly carrying his grip-sack[2] and umbrella. He had been far from the scene of accident, and did not know there had been one. He stood amazed at Josephine's piercing cry; at Richards's quick motion to screen him from the view of his wife.

But Richards was too late.

When the doctors came they said she had died of heart disease—of joy that kills. ❖

---

1. **elixir of life:** a medicine that restores vigor or the essence of life.

2. **grip-sack:** a small traveling bag or satchel.

Connect to the Literature

1. What Do You Think? How did you react to the ending of this story?

Comprehension Check
- What disease afflicts Mrs. Mallard?
- What news does Mrs. Mallard receive at the beginning of the story, and how does she react?
- What does Mrs. Mallard learn at the end of the story?

Think Critically

2. ACTIVE READING PREDICTING What **predictions** did you make as you read, and what clues did you use to make them? Refer to the chart you made in your READER'S NOTEBOOK. Tell whether your predictions were accurate.

3. How would you explain the cause of Mrs. Mallard's death?

4. What are your impressions of Mrs. Mallard?

THINK ABOUT
{
- how Richards and Josephine treat her
- her initial reaction to the news of her husband's death
- why she says under her breath "free, free, free!"
- how she reacts when her husband arrives
}

5. How would you describe Mrs. Mallard's relationship with her husband?

Extend Interpretations

6. What If? What might the future have been like for the Mallards if Mrs. Mallard had lived?

7. The Writer's Style Reread the fifth and sixth paragraphs of the story, which describe what Mrs. Mallard sees and hears from her open window after learning of her husband's death. What do you think the **imagery** in these paragraphs contributes to the story?

8. Comparing Texts Both "The Story of an Hour" and "The Yellow Wallpaper" were written in the 1890s. How would you compare the **themes** of the two stories? Which story do you prefer, and why?

9. Connect to Life How would you compare Mrs. Mallard's view of marriage with your own?

Literary Analysis

PLOT AND SURPRISE ENDING
In "The Story of an Hour," the **plot,** or the sequence of events, focuses on Mrs. Mallard's inner conflict. Though she feels deep grief over her husband's death, she cannot help looking forward to the freedom that widowhood will bring. The plot begins with a surprise announcement—the death of Mr. Mallard—and then builds toward a **surprise ending**—Mr. Mallard's return and Mrs. Mallard's sudden death. A surprise ending is an unexpected plot twist at the conclusion of a story.

Cooperative Learning Activity In this story the events of the plot occur within the span of an hour. With a group of classmates, draw the outline of a clock. Note the events in the order in which they occur and Mrs. Mallard's feelings about them. Then discuss the surprise ending. Do you find it clever and fitting? a masterstroke of irony? a cheap trick? Share your conclusions with other groups.

REVIEW IRONY Surprise endings, almost by definition, are ironic. Mr. Mallard's return and Mrs. Mallard's death are examples of situational irony. What other examples of situational irony or dramatic irony do you see in this story? Discuss them in class.

Writing Options

1. Husband's Monologue What feelings do you think Brently Mallard will have about his wife's sudden death? Will his feelings be similar to or different from her feelings about his supposed death? Write a monologue expressing his feelings.

2. Wife's Epitaph Write an appropriate epitaph for Mrs. Mallard, commenting on her life or the circumstances of her death. Remember to draw on your knowledge of her private thoughts.

3. Different Ending Imagine that Brently Mallard indeed dies in the train wreck. Write a brief summary of an alternative ending for the story, and share it with your classmates.

4. Essay About Marriage Alexis de Tocqueville wrote, "In America, the independence of woman is irrecoverably lost in the bonds of matrimony." Write a persuasive essay, supporting or challenging this opinion. Use details from "The Story of an Hour" in your essay.

Writing Handbook
See page 1285: Persuasive Writing

Activities & Explorations

Story and Video View the video of "The Story of an Hour," provided with this program. Which version—the oral interpretation or the dramatization—impressed you more, and why? What changes did you notice between the original story and the dramatization? Why do you think the director chose to make those changes? ~ **VIEWING AND REPRESENTING**

 Literature in Performance

Kate Chopin
1851–1904

Other Works
At Fault
Bayou Folk
A Night in Acadie

Early Years Kate Chopin was born Catherine O'Flaherty in St. Louis, Missouri. When she was five years old, her father was killed in a railroad disaster similar to the one described in "The Story of an Hour," leaving her mother a 27-year-old widow. As a student at Sacred Heart Academy, Chopin exhibited "gifts as a teller of marvelous stories," and as a young woman she was a belle of St. Louis society. In 1870 she married Oscar Chopin, a Creole businessman, and settled with him in New Orleans.

Family and Work In 1879 financial problems forced the Chopins and their five young sons to move to rural Louisiana, where their sixth child, a daughter, was born. In 1882 Oscar Chopin died of malaria, leaving his family in debt. Before she returned home to St. Louis in 1884, Chopin raised her children alone and managed her husband's business.

Moments of Inspiration In 1889 Chopin's first poem and first story were published. Over the next ten years, she published two novels, more than a hundred short stories, and many reviews and poems. According to her son Felix, Chopin would "go weeks and weeks without an idea, then suddenly grab her pencil and old lapboard . . . , and in a couple of hours her story was complete and off to the publisher."

Literary Concerns Chopin's local-color stories about the Creoles, Cajuns, African Americans, and Indians whom she had known in Louisiana won her acclaim, but her stories about women seeking to be free often aroused protest. Severe criticism was directed at her second novel, *The Awakening* (1899), for its depiction of a woman's adulterous affair. That novel and Chopin's other works dealing with women's issues have since received greater appreciation.

Seventeen Syllables

Short Story by HISAYE YAMAMOTO (hē-sa'yĕ ya'ma-mō'tō)

Comparing Literature

Traditions Across Time: A Diversity of Voices

"Seventeen Syllables" is a modern short story by a Japanese-American writer. Set in California in the 1930s, this story explores conflicts between a Japanese-born husband and wife and between them and Rosie, their American-born daughter. Like the stories you read in the first part of this section, this story describes a married woman's struggles to reach her potential.

Points of Comparison Compare the husband-and-wife relationship in this story with the one in "The Yellow Wallpaper."

Build Background

Japanese Immigrants Early Japanese immigrants were mostly single men, who, after settling in America, often sought to get married. In accordance with Japanese custom, family members arranged marriages for them with Japanese women, who then immigrated. While facing the challenges of adjusting to a radically different culture, these couples also struggled to bridge the cultural differences that separated them from their American-born children.

After coming to the United States, many Japanese immigrants maintained an interest in Japanese literature. Groups were formed to write and study traditional forms of Japanese poetry, and numerous Japanese-language anthologies and magazines were devoted to this literature. In this story, the main character's mother writes haiku—poems with only 17 syllables.

WORDS TO KNOW **Vocabulary Preview**

adamant	irrevocable	unobtrusive
delectable	preoccupied	untoward
dubious	repercussion	vacillating
indiscretion		

Focus Your Reading

LITERARY ANALYSIS **COMING-OF-AGE STORY** A **coming-of-age story** portrays an adolescent in the process of growing up. The main character faces conflicts, makes difficult decisions, and gains new awareness of self and others. In "Seventeen Syllables," Rosie matures as she faces conflicts and struggles to understand them.

ACTIVE READING **UNDERSTANDING CONFLICTS**
Understanding Rosie's conflicts is critical to understanding this story. Use these strategies:

- Review the definition of **conflict.** (See Glossary of Literary Terms, page 1247.)
- As you read, write down conflicts (internal and external) involving Rosie and also conflicts between her parents.
- Ask these questions about each conflict: How does it affect Rosie? How is it resolved?

READER'S NOTEBOOK In your notebook, record the conflicts you identify, their effects on Rosie, and their resolutions (if resolved).

SEVENTEEN SYLLABLES

● Hisaye Yamamoto

Consolation (1961), Ruth Gikow. 30″ × 18″, collection of Dr. Violet Friedman.

The first Rosie knew that her mother had taken to writing poems was one evening when she finished one and read it aloud for her daughter's approval. It was about cats, and Rosie pretended to understand it thoroughly and appreciate it no end, partly because she hesitated to disillusion her mother about the quantity and quality of Japanese she had learned in all the years now that she had been going to Japanese school every Saturday (and Wednesday, too, in the summer). Even so, her mother must have been skeptical about the depth of Rosie's understanding, because she explained afterwards about the kind of poem she was trying to write.

See, Rosie, she said, it was a *haiku*, a poem in which she must pack all her meaning into seventeen syllables only, which were divided into three lines of five, seven, and five syllables. In the one she had just read, she had tried to capture the charm of a kitten, as well as comment on the superstition that owning a cat of three colors meant good luck.

"Yes, yes, I understand. How utterly lovely," Rosie said, and her mother, either satisfied or seeing through the deception and resigned, went back to composing.

> • *It was a* **haiku**, *a poem in which she must pack all her meaning into seventeen syllables only.*

The truth was that Rosie was lazy; English lay ready on the tongue but Japanese had to be searched for and examined, and even then put forth tentatively (probably to meet with laughter). It was so much easier to say yes, yes, even when one meant no, no. Besides, this was what was in her mind to say: I was looking through one of your magazines from Japan last night, Mother, and towards the back I found some *haiku* in English that delighted me. There was one that made me giggle off and on until I fell asleep—

It is morning, and lo!
I lie awake, comme il faut,[1]
sighing for some dough.

Now, how to reach her mother, how to communicate the melancholy song? Rosie knew

formal Japanese by fits and starts, her mother had even less English, no French. It was much more possible to say yes, yes.

It developed that her mother was writing the *haiku* for a daily newspaper, the *Mainichi Shimbun,*[2] that was published in San Francisco. Los Angeles, to be sure, was closer to the farming community in which the Hayashi[3] family lived and several Japanese vernaculars[4] were printed there, but Rosie's parents said they preferred the tone of the northern paper. Once a week, the *Mainichi* would have a section devoted to *haiku,* and her mother became an extravagant contributor, taking for herself the blossoming pen name, Ume Hanazono.[5]

So Rosie and her father lived for awhile with two women, her mother and Ume Hanazono. Her mother (Tome Hayashi by name) kept house, cooked, washed, and, along with her husband and the Carrascos, the Mexican family hired for the harvest, did her ample share of picking tomatoes out in the sweltering fields and boxing them in tidy strata in the cool packing shed. Ume Hanazono, who came to life after the dinner dishes were done, was an earnest, muttering stranger who often neglected speaking when spoken to and stayed busy at the parlor table as late as midnight scribbling with pencil on scratch paper or

---

1. *comme il faut* (kôm′ ēl fō′) *French:* as is proper; as usual.
2. *Mainichi Shimbun* (mī-nē′chē shēm′bŏŏn).
3. **Hayashi** (hä-yä′shē).
4. **Japanese vernaculars:** newspapers in the Japanese language.
5. **Ume Hanazono** (ŏŏ′mĕ hä′nä-zō′nō).

carefully copying characters on good paper with her fat, pale green Parker.

The new interest had some <u>repercussions</u> on the household routine. Before, Rosie had been accustomed to her parents and herself taking their hot baths early and going to bed almost immediately afterwards, unless her parents challenged each other to a game of flower cards or unless company dropped in. Now if her father wanted to play cards, he had to resort to solitaire (at which he always cheated fearlessly), and if a group of friends came over, it was bound to contain someone who was also writing *haiku*, and the small assemblage would be split in two, her father entertaining the non-literary members and her mother comparing ecstatic notes with the visiting poet.

If they went out, it was more of the same thing. But Ume Hanazono's life span, even for a poet's, was very brief—perhaps three months at most.

One night they went over to see the Hayano family in the neighboring town to the west, an adventure both painful and attractive to Rosie. It was attractive because there were four Hayano girls, all lovely and each one named after a season of the year (Haru, Natsu, Aki, Fuyu),[6] painful because something had been wrong with Mrs. Hayano ever since the birth of her first child. Rosie would sometimes watch Mrs. Hayano, reputed to have been the belle of her native village, making her way about a room, stooped, slowly shuffling, violently trembling (*always* trembling), and she would be reminded that this woman, in this same condition, had carried and given issue to three babies. She would look wonderingly at Mr. Hayano, handsome, tall, and strong, and she would look at her four pretty friends. But it was not a matter she could come to any decision about.

On this visit, however, Mrs. Hayano sat all evening in the rocker, as motionless and unobtrusive as it was possible for her to be, and Rosie found the greater part of the evening practically anaesthetic.[7] Too, Rosie spent most of it in the girls' room, because Haru, the garrulous[8] one, said almost as soon as the bows and other greetings were over, "Oh, you must see my new coat!"

It was a pale plaid of grey, sand, and blue, with an enormous collar, and Rosie, seeing nothing special in it, said, "Gee, how nice."

"Nice?" said Haru, indignantly. "Is that all you can say about it? It's gorgeous! And so cheap, too. Only seventeen-ninety-eight, because it was a sale. The saleslady said it was twenty-five dollars regular."

"Gee," said Rosie. Natsu, who never said much and when she said anything said it shyly, fingered the coat covetously and Haru pulled it away.

"Mine," she said, putting it on. She minced in the aisle between the two large beds and smiled happily. "Let's see how your mother likes it."

She broke into the front room and the adult conversation and went to stand in front of Rosie's mother, while the rest watched from the door. Rosie's mother was properly envious. "May I inherit it when you're through with it?"

Haru, pleased, giggled and said yes, she could, but Natsu reminded gravely from the door, "You promised me, Haru."

Everyone laughed but Natsu, who shame-facedly retreated into the bedroom. Haru came in laughing, taking off the coat. "We were only kidding, Natsu," she said. "Here, you try it on now."

After Natsu buttoned herself into the coat, inspected herself solemnly in the bureau mirror,

---

6. **Haru** (hä′rōō), **Natsu** (nät′sōō), **Aki** (ä′kē), **Fuyu** (fōō′yōō): the Japanese words for spring, summer, autumn, and winter, respectively.

7. **anaesthetic:** causing sleep; boring.

8. **garrulous** (găr′ə-ləs): talkative.

WORDS TO KNOW

repercussion (rē′pər-kŭsh′ən) *n.* a far-reaching effect
unobtrusive (ŭn′əb-trōō′sĭv) *adj.* not noticeable; not calling attention to oneself

791

and reluctantly shed it, Rosie, Aki, and Fuyu got their turns, and Fuyu, who was eight, drowned in it while her sisters and Rosie doubled up in amusement. They all went into the front room later, because Haru's mother quaveringly called to her to fix the tea and rice cakes and open a can of sliced peaches for everybody. Rosie noticed that her mother and Mr. Hayano were talking together at the little table—they were discussing a *haiku* that Mr. Hayano was planning to send to the *Mainichi*, while her father was sitting at one end of the sofa looking through a copy of *Life,* the new picture magazine. Occasionally, her father would comment on a photograph, holding it toward Mrs. Hayano and speaking to her as he always did—loudly, as though he thought someone such as she must surely be at least a trifle deaf also.

The five girls had their refreshments at the kitchen table, and it was while Rosie was showing the sisters her trick of swallowing peach slices without chewing (she chased each slippery crescent down with a swig of tea) that her father brought his empty teacup and untouched saucer to the sink and said, "Come on, Rosie, we're going home now."

"Already?" asked Rosie.

"Work tomorrow," he said.

He sounded irritated, and Rosie, puzzled, gulped one last yellow slice and stood up to go, while the sisters began protesting, as was their wont.

"We have to get up at five-thirty," he told them, going into the front room quickly, so that they did not have their usual chance to hang onto his hands and plead for an extension of time.

Rosie, following, saw that her mother and Mr. Hayano were sipping tea and still talking together, while Mrs. Hayano concentrated, quivering, on raising the handleless Japanese cup to her lips with both her hands and lowering it back to her lap. Her father, saying nothing, went out the door, onto the bright porch, and down the steps. Her mother looked up and asked, "Where is he going?"

"Where is he going?" Rosie said. "He said we were going home now."

"Going home?" Her mother looked with embarrassment at Mr. Hayano and his absorbed wife and then forced a smile. "He must be tired," she said.

Haru was not giving up yet. "May Rosie stay overnight?" she asked, and Natsu, Aki, and Fuyu came to reinforce their sister's plea by helping her make a circle around Rosie's mother. Rosie, for once having no desire to stay, was relieved when her mother, apologizing to the perturbed Mr. and Mrs. Hayano for her father's abruptness at the same time, managed to shake her head no at the quartet, kindly but <u>adamant</u>, so that they broke their circle and let her go.

Rosie's father looked ahead into the windshield as the two joined him. "I'm sorry," her mother said. "You must be tired." Her father, stepping on the starter, said nothing. "You know how I get when it's *haiku*," she continued, "I forget what time it is." He only grunted.

As they rode homeward silently, Rosie, sitting between, felt a rush of hate for both—for her mother for begging, for her father for denying her mother. I wish this old Ford would crash, right now, she thought, then immediately, no, no, I wish my father would laugh, but it was too late: already the vision had passed through her mind of the green pick-up crumpled in the dark against one of the mighty eucalyptus trees they were just riding past, of the three contorted, bleeding bodies, one of them hers.

Rosie ran between two patches of tomatoes, her heart working more rambunctiously than she had ever known it to. How lucky it was that Aunt Taka and Uncle Gimpachi[9] had come tonight, though, how very lucky. Otherwise she

---

9. **Aunt Taka** (tä′kä) . . . **Uncle Gimpachi** (gēm-pä′chē).

Japanese-American family in the 1930s. Photo by Russell Lee. Underwood Photo Archives, San Francisco.

might not have really kept her half-promise to meet Jesus Carrasco. Jesus was going to be a senior in September at the same school she went to, and his parents were the ones helping with the tomatoes this year. She and Jesus, who hardly remembered seeing each other at Cleveland High where there were so many other people and two whole grades between them, had become great friends this summer—he always had a joke for her when he periodically drove the loaded pickup up from the fields to the shed where she was usually sorting while her mother and father did the packing, and they laughed a great deal together over infinitesimal repartee[10] during the afternoon break for chilled watermelon or ice cream in the shade of the shed.

What she enjoyed most was racing him to see which could finish picking a double row first. He, who could work faster, would tease her by slowing down until she thought she would surely pass him this time, then speeding up furiously to leave her several sprawling vines behind. Once he had made her screech hideously by crossing over, while her back was turned, to place atop the tomatoes in her green-stained bucket a truly monstrous, pale green worm (it had looked more like an infant snake). And it was when they had finished a contest this morning, after she had

---

10. **infinitesimal repartee** (ĭn´fĭ-nĭ-tĕs´ə-məl rĕp´ər-tē´): an attempt at witty conversation about trivial matters (a humorous exaggeration of the term *small talk*).

pantingly pointed a green finger at the immature tomatoes evident in the lugs[11] at the end of his row and he had returned the accusation (with justice), that he had startlingly brought up the matter of their possibly meeting outside the range of both their parents' dubious eyes.

"What for?" she had asked.

"I've got a secret I want to tell you," he said.

"Tell me now," she demanded.

"It won't be ready till tonight," he said.

She laughed. "Tell me tomorrow then."

"It'll be gone tomorrow," he threatened.

"Well, for seven hakes,[12] what is it?" she had asked, more than twice, and when he had suggested that the packing shed would be an appropriate place to find out, she had cautiously answered maybe. She had not been certain she was going to keep the appointment until the arrival of mother's sister and her husband. Their coming seemed a sort of signal of permission, of grace, and she had definitely made up her mind to lie and leave as she was bowing them welcome.

So as soon as everyone appeared settled back for the evening, she announced loudly that she was going to the privy outside, "I'm going to the *benjo!*" and slipped out the door. And now that she was actually on her way, her heart pumped in such an undisciplined way that she could hear it with her ears. It's because I'm running, she told herself, slowing to a walk. The shed was up ahead, one more patch away, in the middle of the fields. Its bulk, looming in the dimness, took on a sinisterness that was funny when Rosie reminded herself that it was only a wooden frame with a canvas roof and three canvas walls that made a slapping noise on breezy days.

Jesus was sitting on the narrow plank that was the sorting platform and she went around to the other side and jumped backwards to seat herself on the rim of a packing stand. "Well, tell me," she said without greeting, thinking her voice

All that remained intact now was

yes

and

no

and

oh,

and even these few sounds would not easily out.

sounded reassuringly familiar.

"I saw you coming out the door," Jesus said. "I heard you running part of the way, too."

"Uh-huh," Rosie said. "Now tell me the secret."

"I was afraid you wouldn't come," he said.

Rosie delved around on the chicken-wire bottom of the stall for number two tomatoes, ripe, which she was sitting beside, and came up with a left-over that felt edible. She bit into it and began sucking out the pulp and seeds. "I'm here," she pointed out.

"Rosie, are you sorry you came?"

"Sorry? What for?" she said. "You said you were going to tell me something."

---

11. **lugs:** shallow boxes in which fruit is shipped.

12. **for seven hakes:** a play on the phrase "for heaven's sake."

"I will, I will," Jesus said, but his voice contained disappointment, and Rosie fleetingly felt the older of the two, realizing a brand-new power which vanished without category under her recognition.

"I have to go back in a minute," she said. "My aunt and uncle are here from Wintersburg. I told them I was going to the privy."

Jesus laughed. "You funny thing," he said. "You slay me!"

"Just because you have a bathroom *inside,*" Rosie said. "Come on, tell me."

Chuckling, Jesus came around to lean on the stand facing her. They still could not see each other very clearly, but Rosie noticed that Jesus became very sober again as he took the hollow tomato from her hand and dropped it back into the stall. When he took hold of her empty hand, she could find no words to protest; her vocabulary had become distressingly constricted and she thought desperately that all that remained intact now was yes and no and oh, and even these few sounds would not easily out. Thus, kissed by Jesus, Rosie fell for the first time entirely victim to a helplessness <u>delectable</u> beyond speech. But the terrible, beautiful sensation lasted no more than a second, and the reality of Jesus' lips and tongue and teeth and hands made her pull away with such strength that she nearly tumbled.

Rosie stopped running as she approached the lights from the windows of home. How long since she had left? She could not guess, but gasping yet, she went to the privy in back and locked herself in. Her own breathing deafened her in the dark, close space, and she sat and waited until she could hear at last the nightly calling of the frogs and crickets. Even then, all she could think to say was oh, my, and the pressure of Jesus' face against her face would not leave.

No one had missed her in the parlor, however, and Rosie walked in and through quickly, announcing that she was next going to take a bath. "Your father's in the bathhouse," her mother said, and Rosie, in her room, recalled that she had not seen him when she entered. There had been only Aunt Taka and Uncle Gimpachi with her mother at the table, drinking tea. She got her robe and straw sandals and crossed the parlor again to go outside. Her mother was telling them about the *haiku* competition in the *Mainichi* and the poem she had entered.

Rosie met her father coming out of the bathhouse. "Are you through, Father?" she asked. "I was going to ask you to scrub my back."

"Scrub your own back," he said shortly, going toward the main house.

"What have I done now?" she yelled after him. She suddenly felt like doing a lot of yelling. But he did not answer, and she went into the bathhouse. Turning on the dangling light, she removed her denims and T-shirt and threw them in the big carton for dirty clothes standing next to the washing machine. Her other things she took with her into the bath compartment to wash after her bath. After she had scooped a basin of hot water from the square wooden tub, she sat on the grey cement of the floor and soaped herself at exaggerated leisure, singing "Red Sails in the Sunset" at the top of her voice and using da-da-da where she suspected her words. Then, standing up, still singing, for she was possessed by the notion that any attempt now to analyze would result in spoilage and she believed that the larger her volume the less she would be able to hear herself think, she obtained more hot water and poured it on until she was free of lather. Only then did she allow herself to step into the steaming vat, one leg first, then the remainder of her body inch by inch until the water no longer stung and she could move around at will.

She took a long time soaking, afterwards remembering to go around outside to stoke the embers of the tin-lined fireplace beneath the tub and to throw on a few more sticks so that the water might keep its heat for her mother, and when she finally returned to the parlor, she found her mother still talking *haiku* with her aunt and uncle, the three of them on another round of tea. Her father was nowhere in sight.

At Japanese school the next day (Wednesday, it was), Rosie was grave and giddy by turns. Preoccupied at her desk in the row for students on Book Eight, she made up for it at recess by performing wild mimicry for the benefit of her friend Chizuko.[13] She held her nose and whined a witticism or two in what she considered was the manner of Fred Allen; she assumed intoxication and a British accent to go over the climax of the Rudy Vallee recording of the pub conversation about William Ewart Gladstone; she was the child Shirley Temple piping, "On the Good Ship Lollipop"; she was the gentleman soprano of the Four Inkspots trilling, "If I Didn't Care."[14] And she felt reasonably satisfied when Chizuko wept and gasped, "Oh, Rosie, you ought to be in the movies!"

Her father came after her at noon, bringing her sandwiches of minced ham and two nectarines to eat while she rode, so that she could pitch right into the sorting when they got home. The lugs were piling up, he said, and the ripe tomatoes in them would probably have to be taken to the cannery tomorrow if they were not ready for the produce haulers tonight. "This heat's not doing them any good. And we've got no time for a break today."

It was hot, probably the hottest day of the year, and Rosie's blouse stuck damply to her back even under the protection of the canvas. But she worked as efficiently as a flawless machine and kept the stalls heaped, with one part of her mind listening in to the parental murmuring about the heat and the tomatoes and with another part planning the exact words she would say to Jesus when he drove up with the

first load of the afternoon. But when at last she saw that the pick-up was coming, her hands went berserk and the tomatoes started falling in the wrong stalls, and her father said, "Hey, hey! Rosie, watch what you're doing!"

"Well, I have to go to the *benjo,*" she said, hiding panic.

"Go in the weeds over there," he said, only half-joking.

"Oh, Father!" she protested.

"Oh, go on home," her mother said. "We'll make out for awhile."

In the privy Rosie peered through a knothole toward the fields, watching as much as she could of Jesus. Happily she thought she saw him look in the direction of the house from time to time before he finished unloading and went back toward the patch where his mother and father worked. As she was heading for the shed, a very presentable black car purred up the dirt driveway to the house and its driver motioned to her. Was this the Hayashi home, he wanted to know. She nodded. Was she a Hayashi? Yes, she said, thinking that he was a good-looking man. He got out of the car with a huge, flat package and she saw that he warmly wore a business suit. "I have something here for your mother then," he said, in a more elegant Japanese than she was used to.

She told him where her mother was and he came along with her, patting his face with an immaculate white handkerchief and saying something about the coolness of San Francisco. To her surprised mother and father, he bowed and introduced himself as, among other things,

---

13. **Chizuko** (chē-zōō′kō).

14. **Fred Allen . . . "If I Didn't Care":** The comedian Fred Allen had a radio show during the 1930s and 1940s. Rudy Vallee was a singer popular during the 1920s and 1930s, who performed a comedy routine featuring a conversation about Gladstone, a 19th-century British prime minister. Shirley Temple was a famous child star of the 1930s. "If I Didn't Care" was a hit record for the Four Inkspots, a popular African-American singing group, in 1939.

Returning Sails to Gyotoku (about 1837–1838) Ichiryusai Hiroshige. From the series *Eight Views of the Edo Suburbs,* woodblock print, 23.5 cm × 36 cm., Edo Period, Japan. The Art Institute of Chicago, Clarence Buckingham Collection (1943.708). Photo Copyright © 1995 The Art Institute of Chicago, all rights reserved.

the *haiku* editor of the *Mainichi Shimbun,* saying that since he had been coming as far as Los Angeles anyway, he had decided to bring her the first prize she had won in the recent contest.

"First prize?" her mother echoed, believing and not believing, pleased and overwhelmed. Handed the package with a bow, she bobbed her head up and down numerous times to express her utter gratitude.

"It is nothing much," he added, "but I hope it will serve as a token of our great appreciation for your contributions and our great admiration of your considerable talent."

"I am not worthy," she said, falling easily into his style. "It is I who should make some sign of my humble thanks for being permitted to contribute."

"No, no, to the contrary," he said, bowing again.

But Rosie's mother insisted, and then saying that she knew she was being unorthodox, she asked if she might open the package because her curiosity was so great. Certainly she might. In fact, he would like her reaction to it, for personally, it was one of his favorite Hiroshiges.[15]

Rosie thought it was a pleasant picture, which looked to have been sketched with delicate quickness. There were pink clouds, containing some graceful calligraphy, and a sea that was a pale blue except at the edges, containing four sampans[16] with indications of people in them.

---

15. **Hiroshiges** (hē′rō-shē′gĕz): works by Hiroshige, master designer of color prints, considered one of Japan's most important artists. (See art on this page.)

16. **sampans:** small boats, used in Japan, that can be either sailed or rowed.

Pines edged the water and on the far-off beach there was a cluster of thatched huts towered over by pine-dotted mountains of grey and blue. The frame was scalloped and gilt.

After Rosie's mother pronounced it without peer and somewhat prodded her father into nodding agreement, she said Mr. Kuroda[17] must at least have a cup of tea after coming all this way, and although Mr. Kuroda did not want to impose, he soon agreed that a cup of tea would be refreshing and went along with her to the house, carrying the picture for her.

"Ha, your mother's crazy!" Rosie's father said, and Rosie laughed uneasily as she resumed judgment on the tomatoes. She had emptied six lugs when he broke into an imaginary conversation with Jesus to tell her to go and remind her mother of the tomatoes, and she went slowly.

"Tell him I shall only be a minute," her mother said, speaking the language of Mr. Kuroda.

When Rosie carried the reply to her father, he did not seem to hear and she said again, "Mother says she'll be back in a minute."

"All right, all right," he nodded, and they worked again in silence. But suddenly, her father uttered an incredible noise, exactly like the cork of a bottle popping, and the next Rosie knew, he was stalking angrily toward the house, almost running in fact, and she chased after him crying, "Father! Father! What are you going to do?"

He stopped long enough to order her back to the shed. "Never mind!" he shouted. "Get on with the sorting!"

And from the place in the fields where she stood, frightened and vacillating, Rosie saw her father enter the house. Soon Mr. Kuroda came out alone, putting on his coat. Mr. Kuroda got into his car and backed out down the driveway onto the highway. Next her father emerged, also alone, something in his arms (it was the picture, she realized), and, going over to the bathhouse woodpile, he threw the

• "Do you know why I married your father?"...

"No," said Rosie.... Don't tell me now, she wanted to say, tell me tomorrow, tell me next week, don't tell me today.

Mr. Kuroda was in his shirtsleeves expounding some *haiku* theory as he munched a rice cake, and her mother was rapt. Abashed in the great man's presence, Rosie stood next to her mother's chair until her mother looked up inquiringly, and then she started to whisper the message, but her mother pushed her gently away and reproached, "You are not being very polite to our guest."

"Father says the tomatoes . . ." Rosie said aloud, smiling foolishly.

picture on the ground and picked up the axe. Smashing the picture, glass and all (she heard the explosion faintly), he reached over for the kerosene that was used to encourage the bath fire and poured it over the wreckage. I am dreaming, Rosie said to herself, I am dreaming, but her father, having made sure that his act of cremation was irrevocable, was even then returning to the fields.

---

17. **Kuroda** (kŏŏ-rō′dä).

Rosie ran past him and toward the house. What had become of her mother? She burst into the parlor and found her mother at the back window watching the dying fire. They watched together until there remained only a feeble smoke under the blazing sun. Her mother was very calm.

"Do you know why I married your father?" she said without turning.

"No," said Rosie. It was the most frightening question she had ever been called upon to answer. Don't tell me now, she wanted to say, tell me tomorrow, tell me next week, don't tell me today. But she knew she would be told now, that the telling would combine with the other violence of the hot afternoon to level her life, her world to the very ground.

It was like a story out of the magazines illustrated in sepia,[18] which she had consumed so greedily for a period until the information had somehow reached her that those wretchedly unhappy autobiographies, offered to her as the testimonials of living men and women, were largely inventions: Her mother, at nineteen, had come to America and married her father as an alternative to suicide.

At eighteen she had been in love with the first son of one of the well-to-do families in her village. The two had met whenever and wherever they could, secretly, because it would not have done for his family to see him favor her—her father had no money; he was a drunkard and a gambler besides. She had learned she was with child; an excellent match had already been arranged for her lover. Despised by her family, she had given premature birth to a stillborn son, who would be seventeen now. Her family did not turn her out, but she could no longer project herself in any direction without refreshing in them the memory of her <u>indiscretion</u>. She wrote to Aunt Taka, her favorite sister in America, threatening to kill herself if Aunt Taka would

not send for her. Aunt Taka hastily arranged a marriage with a young man of whom she knew, but lately arrived from Japan, a young man of simple mind, it was said, but of kindly heart. The young man was never told why his unseen betrothed was so eager to hasten the day of meeting.

The story was told perfectly, with neither groping for words nor <u>untoward</u> passion. It was as though her mother had memorized it by heart, reciting it to herself so many times over that its nagging vileness had long since gone.

"I had a brother then?" Rosie asked, for this was what seemed to matter now; she would think about the other later, she assured herself, pushing back the illumination which threatened all that darkness that had hitherto been merely mysterious or even glamorous. "A half-brother?"

"Yes."

"I would have liked a brother," she said.

Suddenly, her mother knelt on the floor and took her by the wrists. "Rosie," she said urgently, "promise me you will never marry!" Shocked more by the request than the revelation, Rosie stared at her mother's face. Jesus, Jesus, she called silently, not certain whether she was invoking the help of the son of the Carrascos or of God, until there returned sweetly the memory of Jesus' hand, how it had touched her and where. Still her mother waited for an answer, holding her wrists so tightly that her hands were going numb. She tried to pull free. Promise, her mother whispered fiercely, promise. Yes, yes, I promise, Rosie said. But for an instant she turned away, and her mother, hearing the familiar glib agreement, released her. Oh, you, you, you, her eyes and twisted mouth said, you fool. Rosie, covering her face, began at last to cry, and the embrace and consoling hand came much later than she expected. ❖

---

18. **sepia** (sē′pē-ə): a dark, reddish-brown color.

Thinking through the LITERATURE

Connect to the Literature

1. **What Do You Think?** What character were you most concerned about as you finished reading the story?

> **Comprehension Check**
> - In what circumstances do Rosie and Jesus Carrasco become friends?
> - What happens to the prize Rosie's mother receives for writing haiku?
> - What does Rosie's mother make Rosie promise at the end of the story?

Think Critically

2. **ACTIVE READING   UNDERSTANDING CONFLICTS**   Think about the conversation between Rosie and her mother after the burning of the picture. How does this conversation relate to the other **conflicts** in the story? Refer to the conflict you listed in your 📖 **READER'S NOTEBOOK.**

3. Do you think Rosie is more likely to follow her mother's advice not to marry or to follow her own way? Cite evidence from the story to support your opinion.

4. How would you describe Rosie's feelings after Jesus Carrasco kisses her?

5. Why does Rosie's father's react as he does to his wife's writing?

> - the changes in the family's routine and social life
> - the intensity of the farm work
> - the prize awarded Mrs. Hayashi

6. Can Mrs. Hayashi do anything to resolve the **conflict** between her husband's needs and her own desires? Explain your answer.

Extend Interpretations

7. **What If?** How would the effect of the story be different if the visit to the Hayano family were not included?

8. **Connect to Life** Like Mrs. Hayashi in this story, many women today are torn between family obligations and creative work. What advice would you give to someone trying to meet her obligations and still achieve her potential?

9. **Points of Comparison**   What similarities and differences do you see between Mrs. Hayashi's situation and that of the unnamed narrator in "The Yellow Wallpaper"?

Literary Analysis

COMING-OF-AGE STORY

A coming-of-age story is a story about growing up. The **plot** describes a rite of passage, or the experiences that lead the main character to a new level of maturity. In "Seventeen Syllables," two related plot lines operate simultaneously. The development of Rosie's relationship with Jesus Carrasco forms one plot line. In this part of the story, Yamamoto explores the conflicting emotions that often surround such a relationship. The second plot line involves Mrs. Hayashi's haiku writing and the **conflicts** she and her husband experience because of it.

Paired Activity With a partner, create two time lines, one above the other. Indicate events related to Rosie's romance with Jesus Carrasco on the top line and events connected with Mrs. Hayashi's haiku writing on the bottom one. Circle points on the time lines where the two plots overlap at crucial points. Then write a statement that answers this question: What does Yamamoto communicate about Rosie and her adolescent awakening? Share your time line and thematic statement with other pairs of students.

Writing Options

1. **Points of Comparison** Write a dialogue in which Mrs. Hayashi and the narrator of "The Yellow Wallpaper" exchange views about writing as a tool for self-expression. For your prewriting notes, list some of the points you discussed in answering question 9.

2. **Character Sketch** Imagine that a book of haiku by Mrs. Hayashi—under her pen name Ume Hanazono—is soon to be published. Write a biographical note about the author that might appear on the book's cover.

Vocabulary in Action

EXERCISE: CONTEXT CLUES Write the word that best completes each of the following sentences.

1. In the early 1800s, European paintings tended to be quite realistic, showing gorgeous flowers and _____ fruit.

2. Japanese prints were quite detailed but more subtle and _____ than European works.

3. The arrival of some of these prints in Europe had a surprising impact, with long-lasting _____.

4. The impressionists abandoned classic Western painting styles, becoming _____ with some of the Japanese techniques.

5. Skeptical critics were _____ about paintings that depicted "impressions" of reality.

6. Still, the course the impressionists took was not a _____ one; it remained focused and steady.

7. Unswayed by criticism, the impressionists were _____ in their attempts to convey the effects of light and shadow and capture fleeting moments.

8. One critic scorned Renoir's paintings for what he considered an _____ use of color.

9. This critic ridiculed Renoir for his _____ as an artist.

10. The influence of the impressionists and the Japanese printmakers who inspired them proved _____, persisting even today.

Building Vocabulary

For an in-depth lesson on context clues, see page 326.

WORDS TO KNOW		
adamant	irrevocable	untoward
delectable	preoccupied	vacillating
dubious	repercussion	
indiscretion	unobtrusive	

Hisaye Yamamoto
1921–

Other Works
"Yoneko's Earthquake"
"Wilshire Bus"

Japanese-American Writer The daughter of Japanese immigrants, like her character Rosie, Yamamoto was born in Redondo Beach, California. Along with many other Japanese Americans, she was interned by the U.S. government during World War II. While she was in the detention camp, the interest in writing that she had developed as a teenager led her to write a column for the camp newspaper and to publish a serialized mystery. For three years after the war, she worked as a columnist for the *Los Angeles Tribune*, an African-American weekly. Later, she received a John Hay Whitney Foundation Opportunity Fellowship that allowed her to write fiction full time for a year.

Literary Focus Yamamoto has had a relatively small literary output. She has published only one collection in the United States—*Seventeen Syllables and Other Stories*—yet she continues to receive critical acclaim. In 1986 she received a lifetime achievement award from the Before Columbus Foundation. Her work, which features Japanese-American protagonists, often focuses on encounters between representatives of different races and cultures. Using irony and realistic detail, Yamamoto shows the oppression caused by racism and sexism.

Mother's Influence "Seventeen Syllables," which was first published in 1949, was inspired by the life of Yamamoto's mother, who had published senryu, a traditional form of Japanese poetry, in Japanese-language newspapers. According to Yamamoto, her mother, like most women, did not have a chance to fulfill her potential. "She had us kids to look after, on top of all the housework and working alongside my father in the fields."

Adolescence—III

Poetry by RITA DOVE

Traditions Across Time: A Diversity of Voices

The speaker of "Adolescence—III," a modern poem by an African-American writer, is at an awkward age. She is not yet a woman, but no longer a child. Still, she has a distinct personality and a rich inner life. She may bring to mind the unnamed narrator in "The Yellow Wallpaper," the main character in "The Story of an Hour," and the speakers in Emily Dickinson's poems. As you read this poem, consider connections between the speaker and these selections.

Build Background

Rita Dove's Poetry
"Adolescence—III" is the third in a series of three poems about being young that Rita Dove wrote for *The Yellow House on the Corner,* her first volume of poetry. Dove often gives public readings of her poems and intends them to be read aloud. Her language is restrained and concise, and she lets the images in her poems speak for themselves. She often creates speakers who are displaced—living, as she puts it, in "two different worlds."

Focus Your Reading

LITERARY ANALYSIS | **IMAGERY** | **Imagery** is language that represents sensory experience. To help bring the poem inside the reader, poets choose words that help readers see, hear, feel, taste, and smell what's being described. For example, in the opening lines of this poem, Dove uses this image to describe rows of tomatoes: "they glowed orange in sunlight / And rotted in shadow."

ACTIVE READING | **VISUALIZING** | **Visualizing** is the process of forming mental pictures from a written description. Use these tips as you read Dove's poem:

- Let the words and phrases conjure up pictures and sensations in your imagination.
- Relate these pictures and sensations to your own experiences and feelings.
- Look for contrasting images. Some images describe things in the real world; others describe things in the speaker's dreams.

READER'S NOTEBOOK As you read, list the images you visualize on a chart like the one below. Classify them according to what they describe.

Images	
Real World	**Speaker's Dreams**

ADOLESCENCE — III

**RITA
DOVE**

With Dad gone, Mom and I worked
The dusky rows of tomatoes.
As they glowed orange in sunlight
And rotted in shadow, I too
5   Grew orange and softer, swelling out
Starched cotton slips.

The texture of twilight made me think of
Lengths of Dotted Swiss.[1] In my room
I wrapped scarred knees in dresses
10   That once went to big-band dances;
I baptized my earlobes with rosewater.
Along the window-sill, the lipstick stubs
Glittered in their steel shells.

Looking out at the rows of clay
15   And chicken manure, I dreamed how it would happen:
He would meet me by the blue spruce,
A carnation over his heart, saying,
"I have come for you, Madam;
I have loved you in my dreams."
20   At his touch, the scabs would fall away.
Over his shoulder, I see my father coming toward us:
He carries his tears in a bowl,
And blood hangs in the pine-soaked air.

---

1. **Dotted Swiss:** a crisp, sheer cotton fabric decorated
   with raised dots.

Connect to the Literature

1. **What Do You Think?** What is your reaction to the speaker of this poem?

   ....
   Comprehension Check
   - What task do the speaker and her mother do?
   - What does the speaker dream will happen to her?
   ....

Think Critically

2. What do the last two lines of this poem mean to you?

3. What conclusions can you draw about the speaker?

   THINK ABOUT
   {
   - her comparison of herself to the tomatoes
   - her feelings about her absent father
   - how she dresses up in her room
   - the figures in her dreams

4. **ACTIVE READING** **VISUALIZING** Based on the **images** you listed in your **READER'S NOTEBOOK**, how would you describe the contrast between the "two different worlds" the speaker lives in—the real world and that of her dreams?

Extend Interpretations

5. **Critic's Corner** In commenting on her poetry, Dove has stated, "Obviously, as a black woman, I am concerned with race. . . . But certainly not every poem of mine mentions the fact of being black. They are poems about humanity, and sometimes humanity happens to be black. I cannot run from, I won't run from any kind of truth." How would you describe the truths about adolescence that this poem conveys?

6. **Points of Comparison** Compare the **speaker** of this poem with a **speaker, narrator,** or **character** from any selection in the first part of this subunit. Support the comparison with evidence from both works.

Literary Analysis

IMAGERY **Imagery** refers to the words and phrases that re-create sensory experiences for the reader. Though the majority of images are visual, stimulating pictures in the reader's mind, images can appeal to any of the other senses—hearing, smell, taste, and touch. For example, in the first stanza, the speaker uses this image to describe herself: "swelling out / Starched cotton slips." This image appeals to the senses of sight and touch. It suggests growth and maturity.

Paired Activity With a partner, make a chart like the one shown. List two or more images that you find especially vivid in this poem. For each one, identify the sense or senses appealed to and tell what the image suggests to you. Share your chart with other pairs of students.

Image	Appeals to...	Suggests

Choices & CHALLENGES

Writing Options

1. **Points of Comparison** In an essay, compare and contrast the imagery in this poem with that in an Emily Dickinson poem, such as "Success is counted sweetest" (page 753). Use the chart you made for the Literary Analysis activity on page 804 to help you get started.

Writing Handbook
See page 1281: Compare and Contrast.

2. Rosie's Diary Entry Both Rosie in "Seventeen Syllables" (page 789) and the speaker in this poem are on the threshold of adulthood. Moreover, they both work in tomato fields and have troubled feelings about their fathers. Imagine

Dear Diary, Today I read a poem about a girl like me.

that Rosie has just read this poem. Write a diary entry from her point of view, relating the speaker's situation to her own.

3. Write a Review Dove says that in her poems she tries "very hard to create characters who are seen as individuals—not only as Blacks or as women, or whatever, but as a Black woman with her own particular problems. Does the speaker in "Adolescence—III" come across as an individual or as a typical teenager? Write a review, explaining your views.

Activities & Explorations

1. Sketch Make sketches of the speaker, the figure in her dreams, and the different settings for a book jacket of Rita Dove's poems. Refer to the images you listed in your **READER'S NOTEBOOK.** ~ ART

2. Oral Interpretation With a partner read the poem aloud to the class. Decide on the method for your oral reading, such as alternating stanzas, alternating lines, or alternating readings of the entire poem. Vary the pitch and volume of your voices and the pace of the reading to express the speaker's emotions. ~ SPEAKING AND LISTENING

Rita Dove
1952–

Other Works
Fifth Sunday
Grace Notes
Museum
Through the Ivory Gate
Mother Love

Poet Laureate Rita Dove has said, "Poetry is language at its most distilled and most powerful. It's like a bouillon cube: you carry it around and then it nourishes you when you need it." In October 1993 she became the seventh poet laureate of the United States—the youngest person and the first African American so honored. Serving as poet laureate until 1995, she used this post to cultivate a wider appreciation of poetry, especially among children and teenagers.

A Lover of Books Dove grew up in Akron, Ohio, where her father was the first African-American

chemist at the Goodyear Tire and Rubber Company. As a child, she wrote plays and stories, created a comic book with her brother, took cello lessons, and listened to music every day with her family. Although her parents restricted her television viewing, they allowed her to visit the library as often as she wished. She would "rush into the local public library with the same eagerness other children reserved for the candy store, thrilled at the prospect of finding many and varied worlds waiting between the covers of all those books."

Professor and Poet Educated at Miami University in Ohio and the University of Iowa, Dove also studied drama and poetry in Germany as a Fulbright scholar. She taught English at Arizona State University for eight years and is currently the Commonwealth Professor of English at the University of Virginia. In 1987 Dove won a Pulitzer Prize for *Thomas and Beulah* (1986), a book of poems based on the lives of her maternal grandparents.

I Stand Here Ironing

Short Story by TILLIE OLSEN

Comparing Literature

Traditions Across Time: A Diversity of Voices

"I Stand Here Ironing" is a story about a mother-and-daughter relationship. While ironing, the narrator recalls the events that helped shape her daughter Emily's personality and her own struggles to support her family during and after the Great Depression. Like the stories in the first part of this subunit, this story reflects the circumstances shared by countless women at a specific period in history.

Points of Comparison As you read, consider the narrator's struggles. Contrast them with those of the narrator in "The Yellow Wallpaper."

Build Background

Hard Times During the Great Depression of the 1930s and World War II and its aftermath in the 1940s, many parents had to struggle to raise their families. After the stock market crashed in 1929 and the American economy collapsed, millions were left without jobs. Work was so scarce that Secretary of Labor Frances Perkins urged women to give up their jobs so that more men could be employed. Working mothers who kept their jobs often relied on government-supported nurseries for child care or on relatives.

As industry expanded to manufacture the equipment needed to fight World War II, thousands of workers found jobs. Even in the new prosperity, however, families faced problems. With their husbands serving in the armed forces, many women had to care for their children alone. At the same time, the wartime demand for workers brought about 6 million women into the work force. The government built large daycare centers to care for children while their mothers worked. Families now had money to spend, but the war brought shortages of meat, sugar, and other important goods.

WORDS TO KNOW
Vocabulary Preview

anonymity	dredge
articulate	laceration
coherent	preening
compound	prestige
denunciation	ravaged

Focus Your Reading

LITERARY ANALYSIS INTERIOR MONOLOGUE **Interior monologue** refers to the direct presentation of a character's thoughts in a short story or a poem. "I Stand Here Ironing" is an example of an interior monologue. As the narrator relates anecdotes and observations about her daughter Emily's childhood, her mind moves between the past and the present.

ACTIVE READING MAKING JUDGMENTS ABOUT CHARACTER One way to understand the narrator better is to make judgments about her character and support them with reasons.

- Set up standards, for judging her as a parent.
- Gather evidence about how she treats her daughter.
- Measure the narrator's conduct against the standards and state your final judgment about her as a parent.

READER'S NOTEBOOK On a chart like the one shown, list the qualities of a good parent, examples of the narrator's conduct, and your judgment about her character.

Qualities of a Good Parent	Narrator's Treatment of Emily

Judgment _____

I Stand Here Ironing

Tillie Olsen

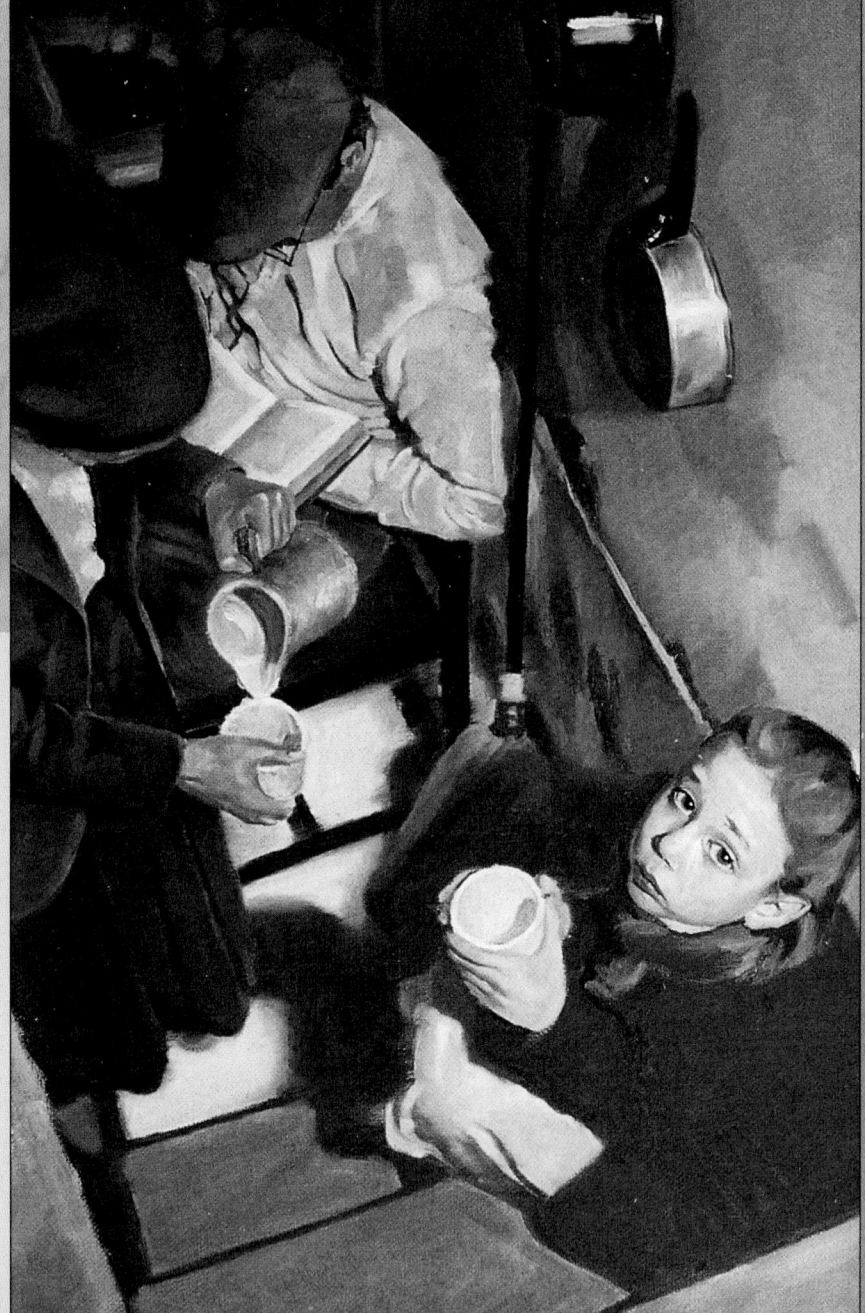

Illustration by Mike Dooling from *Mary McLean and the St. Patrick's Day Parade* by Steven Kroll. Illustration Copyright © 1990 by Mike Dooling, reprinted by permission of Scholastic Inc.

I stand here ironing, and what you asked me moves tormented back and forth with the iron.

"I wish you would manage the time to come in and talk with me about your daughter. I'm sure you can help me understand her. She's a youngster who needs help and whom I'm deeply interested in helping."

"Who needs help." . . . Even if I came, what good would it do? You think because I am her mother I have a key, or that in some way you could use me as a key? She has lived for nineteen years. There is all that life that has happened outside of me, beyond me.

And when is there time to remember, to sift, to weigh, to estimate, to total? I will start and there will be an interruption and I will have to gather it all together again. Or I will become engulfed with all I did or did not do, with what should have been and what cannot be helped.

She was a beautiful baby. The first and only one of our five that was beautiful at birth. You do not guess how new and uneasy her tenancy[1] in her now-loveliness. You did not know her all those years she was thought homely, or see her poring over her baby pictures, making me tell her over and over how beautiful she had been— and would be, I would tell her—and was now, to the seeing eye. But the seeing eyes were few or nonexistent. Including mine.

I nursed her. They feel that's important now-adays. I nursed all the children, but with her, with all the fierce rigidity of first motherhood, I did like the books then said. Though her cries battered me to trembling and my breasts ached with swollenness, I waited till the clock decreed.

Why do I put that first? I do not even know if it matters, or if it explains anything.

She was a beautiful baby. She blew shining bubbles of sound. She loved motion, loved light, loved color and music and textures. She would lie on the floor in her blue overalls patting the surface so hard in ecstasy her hands and feet would blur. She was a miracle to me, but when she was eight months old I had to leave her daytimes with the woman downstairs to whom she was no miracle at all, for I worked or looked for work and for Emily's father, who "could no longer endure" (he wrote in his good-bye note) "sharing want with us."

I was nineteen. It was the pre-relief, pre-WPA[2]

world of the depression. I would start running as soon as I got off the streetcar, running up the stairs, the place smelling sour, and awake or asleep to startle awake, when she saw me she would break into a clogged weeping that could not be comforted, a weeping I can hear yet.

After a while I found a job hashing[3] at night so I could be with her days, and it was better. But it came to where I had to bring her to his family and leave her.

It took a long time to raise the money for her fare back. Then she got chicken pox and I had to wait longer. When she finally came, I hardly knew her, walking quick and nervous like her father, looking like her father, thin, and dressed in a shoddy red that yellowed her skin and glared at the pockmarks. All the baby loveliness gone.

She was two. Old enough for nursery school they said, and I did not know then what I know now—the fatigue of the long day, and the lacerations of group life in the kinds of nurseries that are only parking places for children.

Except that it would have made no difference if I had known. It was the only place there was. It was the only way we could be together, the only way I could hold a job.

And even without knowing, I knew. I knew the teacher that was evil because all these years it has curdled into my memory, the little boy hunched in the corner, her rasp, "why aren't you outside, because Alvin hits you? that's no reason, go out, scaredy." I knew Emily hated it even if she did not clutch and implore "don't go Mommy" like the other children, mornings.

---

1. **tenancy** (tĕn′ən-sē): residence.
2. **pre-relief, pre-WPA:** preceding the creation of the welfare and employment programs—such as the Works Progress Administration (WPA)—by which the U.S. government tried to ease the effects of the Great Depression.
3. **hashing:** a slang term for working as a waitress, especially at a diner.

She always had a reason why we should stay home. Momma, you look sick. Momma, I feel sick. Momma, the teachers aren't there today, they're sick. Momma, we can't go, there was a fire there last night. Momma, it's a holiday today, no school, they told me.

But never a direct protest, never rebellion. I think of our others in their three-, four-year-oldness—the explosions, the tempers, the denunciations, the demands—and I feel suddenly ill. I put the iron down. What in me demanded that goodness in her? And what was the cost, the cost to her of such goodness?

The old man living in the back once said in his gentle way: "You should smile at Emily more when you look at her." What *was* in my face when I looked at her? I loved her. There were all the acts of love.

It was only with the others I remembered what he said, and it was the face of joy, and not of care or tightness or worry I turned to them—too late for Emily. She does not smile easily, let alone almost always as her brothers and sisters do. Her face is closed and somber, but when she wants, how fluid. You must have seen it in her pantomimes, you spoke of her rare gift for comedy on the stage that rouses a laughter out of the audience so dear they applaud and applaud and do not want to let her go.

Where does it come from, that comedy? There was none of it in her when she came back to me that second time, after I had had to send her away again. She had a new daddy now to learn to love, and I think perhaps it was a better time.

Except when we left her alone nights, telling ourselves she was old enough.

"Can't you go some other time, Mommy, like tomorrow?" she would ask. "Will it be just a little while you'll be gone? Do you promise?"

The time we came back, the front door open, the clock on the floor in the hall. She rigid awake. "It wasn't just a little while. I didn't cry.

Three times I called you, just three times, and then I ran downstairs to open the door so you could come faster. The clock talked loud. I threw it away, it scared me what it talked."

She said the clock talked loud again that night I went to the hospital to have Susan. She was delirious with the fever that comes before red measles, but she was fully conscious all the week I was gone and the week after we were home when she could not come near the new baby or me.

She did not get well. She stayed skeleton thin, not wanting to eat, and night after night she had nightmares. She would call for me, and I would rouse from exhaustion to sleepily call back: "You're all right, darling, go to sleep, it's just a dream," and if she still called, in a sterner voice, "now go to sleep, Emily, there's nothing to hurt you." Twice, only twice, when I had to get up for Susan anyhow, I went in to sit with her.

Now when it is too late (as if she would let me hold and comfort her like I do the others) I get up and go to her at once at her moan or restless stirring. "Are you awake, Emily? Can I get you something?" And the answer is always the same: "No, I'm all right, go back to sleep, Mother."

They persuaded me at the clinic to send her away to a convalescent home in the country where "she can have the kind of food and care you can't manage for her, and you'll be free to concentrate on the new baby." They still send children to that place. I see pictures on the society page of sleek young women planning affairs to raise money for it, or dancing at the affairs, or decorating Easter eggs or filling Christmas stockings for the children.

They never have a picture of the children so I do not know if the girls still wear those gigantic red bows and the ravaged looks on the every other Sunday when parents can come to visit "unless otherwise notified"—as we were notified the first six weeks.

| WORDS TO KNOW | **denunciation** (dĭ-nŭn′sē-ā′shən) *n.* an act of condemning or accusing another; accusation |
| | **ravaged** (răv′ĭjd) *adj.* devastated; ruined **ravage** *v.* |

Girl Skipping Rope (1943), Ben Shahn. Tempera on board, 15¼″ × 23½″, gift of the Stephen and Sybil Stone Foundation, Museum of Fine Arts, Boston (1971.702). Copyright © 1996 Estate of Ben Shahn/Licensed by VAGA, New York.

Oh she had physical

lightness and brightness…

bouncing like a ball

up and down up and down

over the jump rope…

but these were

momentary.

Oh it is a handsome place, green lawns and tall trees and fluted flower beds. High up on the balconies of each cottage the children stand, the girls in their red bows and white dresses, the boys in white suits and giant red ties. The parents stand below shrieking up to be heard and the children shriek down to be heard, and between them the invisible wall "Not to Be Contaminated by Parental Germs or Physical Affection."

There was a tiny girl who always stood hand in hand with Emily. Her parents never came. One visit she was gone. "They moved her to Rose Cottage," Emily shouted in explanation. "They don't like you to love anybody here."

She wrote once a week, the labored writing of a seven-year-old. "I am fine. How is the baby. If I write my leter nicly I will have a star. Love."

There never was a star. We wrote every other day, letters she could never hold or keep but only hear read—once. "We simply do not have room for children to keep any personal possessions," they patiently explained when we pieced one Sunday's shrieking together to plead how much it would mean to Emily, who loved so to keep things, to be allowed to keep her letters and cards.

Each visit she looked frailer. "She isn't eating," they told us.

(They had runny eggs for breakfast or mush with lumps, Emily said later, I'd hold it in my mouth and not swallow. Nothing ever tasted good, just when they had chicken.)

It took us eight months to get her released home, and only the fact that she gained back so little of her seven lost pounds convinced the social worker.

I used to try to hold and love her after she came back, but her body would stay stiff, and after a while she'd push away. She ate little. Food sickened her, and I think much of life too. Oh she had physical lightness and brightness, twinkling by on skates, bouncing like a ball up and down up and down over the jump rope, skimming over the hill; but these were momentary.

She fretted about her appearance, thin and dark and foreign-looking at a time when every little girl was supposed to look or thought she should look a chubby blonde replica of Shirley Temple.[4] The doorbell sometimes rang for her, but no one seemed to come and play in the house or be a best friend. Maybe because we moved so much.

There was a boy she loved painfully through two school semesters. Months later she told me how she had taken pennies from my purse to buy him candy. "Licorice was his favorite and I brought him some every day, but he still liked Jennifer better'n me. Why, Mommy?" The kind of question for which there is no answer.

School was a worry to her. She was not glib or quick in a world where glibness and quickness were easily confused with ability to learn. To her overworked and exasperated teachers she was an overconscientious "slow learner" who kept trying to catch up and was absent entirely too often.

I let her be absent, though sometimes the illness was imaginary. How different from my now-strictness about attendance with the others. I wasn't working. We had a new baby, I was home anyhow. Sometimes, after Susan grew old enough, I would keep her home from school, too, to have them all together.

Mostly Emily had asthma, and her breathing, harsh and labored, would fill the house with a curiously tranquil sound. I would bring the two old dresser mirrors and her boxes of collections to her bed. She would select beads and single earrings, bottle tops and shells, dried flowers and pebbles, old postcards and scraps, all sorts of oddments; then she and Susan would play Kingdom, setting up landscapes and furniture, peopling them with action.

Those were the only times of peaceful companionship between her and Susan. I have edged away from it, that poisonous feeling between them, that terrible balancing of hurts and needs I had to do between the two, and did so badly, those earlier years.

Oh there are conflicts between the others too, each one human, needing, demanding, hurting, taking—but only between Emily and Susan, no, Emily toward Susan that corroding resentment. It seems so obvious on the surface, yet it is not obvious. Susan, the second child, Susan, golden- and curly-haired and chubby, quick and <u>articulate</u> and assured, everything in appearance and manner. Emily was not; Susan, not able to resist Emily's precious things, losing or sometimes clumsily breaking them; Susan telling jokes and riddles to company for applause while Emily sat silent (to say to me later: that was *my* riddle, Mother, I told it to Susan); Susan,

---

4. **Shirley Temple:** a famous child star of the 1930s.

WORDS TO KNOW   **articulate** (är-tĭk′yə-lĭt) *adj.* clear and effective in speech

who for all the five years' difference in age was just a year behind Emily in developing physically.

I am glad for that slow physical development that widened the difference between her and her contemporaries, though she suffered over it. She was too vulnerable for that terrible world of youthful competition, of <u>preening</u> and parading, of constant measuring of yourself against every other, of envy, "If I had that copper hair," "If I had that skin. . . ." She tormented herself enough about not looking like the others, there was enough of the unsureness, the having to be conscious of words before you speak, the constant caring—what are they thinking of me? without having it all magnified by the merciless physical drives.

Ronnie is calling. He is wet and I change him. It is rare there is such a cry now. That time of motherhood is almost behind me when the ear is not one's own but must always be racked and listening for the child cry, the child call. We sit for a while and I hold him, looking out over the city spread in charcoal with its soft aisles of light. *"Shoogily,"* he breathes and curls closer. I carry him back to bed, asleep. *Shoogily.* A funny word, a family word, inherited from Emily, invented by her to say: *comfort.*

In this and other ways she leaves her seal, I say aloud. And startle at my saying it. What do I mean? What did I start to gather together, to try and make <u>coherent</u>? I was at the terrible, growing years. War years. I do not remember them well. I was working, there were four smaller ones now, there was not time for her. She had to help be a mother, and housekeeper, and shopper. She had to set her seal. Mornings of crisis and near hysteria trying to get lunches packed, hair combed, coats and shoes found, everyone to school or Child Care on time, the baby ready for transportation. And always the paper scribbled on by a smaller one, the book looked at by Susan then mislaid,

the homework not done. Running out to that huge school where she was one, she was lost, she was a drop; suffering over the unpreparedness, stammering and unsure in her classes.

There was so little time left at night after the kids were bedded down. She would struggle over books, always eating (it was in those years she developed her enormous appetite that is legendary in our family) and I would be ironing, or preparing food for the next day, or writing V-mail[5] to Bill, or tending the baby. Sometimes, to make me laugh, or out of her despair, she would imitate happenings or types at school.

I think I said once: "Why don't you do something like this in the school amateur show?" One morning she phoned me at work, hardly understandable through the weeping: "Mother, I did it. I won, I won; they gave me first prize; they clapped and clapped and wouldn't let me go."

Now suddenly she was Somebody, and as imprisoned in her difference as she had been in <u>anonymity</u>.

She began to be asked to perform at other high schools, even in colleges, then at city and statewide affairs. The first one we went to, I only recognized her that first moment when thin, shy, she almost drowned herself into the curtains. Then: Was this Emily? The control, the command, the convulsing and deadly clowning, the spell, then the roaring, stamping audience, unwilling to let this rare and precious laughter out of their lives.

Afterwards: You ought to do something about her with a gift like that—but without money or knowing how, what does one do? We have left it all to her, and the gift has as often eddied[6] inside,

---

5. **V-mail:** letters sent to and by soldiers in World War II. The mail was photographed on microfilm to make it easier to transport; enlarged prints were made for reading by the recipients.

6. **eddied:** whirled in circles, without progressing forward.

WORDS
TO
KNOW

preening (prē′nĭng) *n.* dressing and grooming oneself with excessive care; primping **preen** *v.*
coherent (kō-hîr′ənt) *adj.* understandable; logically consistent
anonymity (ăn′ə-nĭm′ĭ-tē) *n.* a state of being unknown or unrecognized, without special or distinguishing qualities

clogged and clotted, as been used and growing.

She is coming. She runs up the stairs two at a time with her light graceful step, and I know she is happy tonight. Whatever it was that occasioned your call did not happen today.

"Aren't you ever going to finish the ironing, Mother? Whistler[7] painted his mother in a rocker. I'd have to paint mine standing over an ironing board." This is one of her communicative nights and she tells me everything and nothing as she fixes herself a plate of food out of the icebox.

She is so lovely. Why did you want me to come in at all? Why were you concerned? She will find her way.

She starts up the stairs to bed. "Don't get me up with the rest in the morning." "But I thought you were having midterms." "Oh, those," she comes back in, kisses me, and says quite lightly, "in a couple of years when we'll all be atom-dead they won't matter a bit."

She has said it before. She *believes* it. But because I have been <u>dredging</u> the past, and all that <u>compounds</u> a human being is so heavy and meaningful in me, I cannot endure it tonight.

I will never total it all. I will never come in to say: She was a child seldom smiled at. Her father left me before she was a year old. I had to work her first six years when there was work, or I sent her home and to his relatives. There were years she had care she hated. She was dark and thin and foreign-looking in a world where the <u>prestige</u> went to blondeness and curly hair and dimples, she was slow where glibness was prized. She was a child of anxious, not proud, love. We were poor and could not afford for her the soil of easy growth. I was a young mother, I was a distracted mother. There were the other children pushing up, demanding. Her younger sister seemed all that she was not. There were years she did not want me to touch her. She kept too much in herself, her life was such she had to

The Brown Sweater (1952), Raphael Soyer. Oil on canvas, 50″ × 34″, Collection of Whitney Museum of American Art, New York, purchase and gift of Gertrude Vanderbilt Whitney by exchange (53.53). Copyright © 1995 Whitney Museum of American Art. Photo by Geoffrey Clements.

keep too much in herself. My wisdom came too late. She has much to her and probably nothing will come of it. She is a child of her age, of depression, of war, of fear.

Let her be. So all that is in her will not bloom —but in how many does it? There is still enough left to live by. Only help her to know—help make it so there is cause for her to know—that she is more than this dress on the ironing board, helpless before the iron. ❖

---

7. **Whistler:** James Abbot McNeill Whistler, a 19th-century American painter and etcher. His best-known painting is a portrait of his mother in her chair.

813

Ironing

Their

Clothes

Julia Alvarez

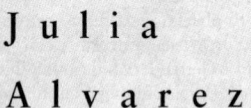

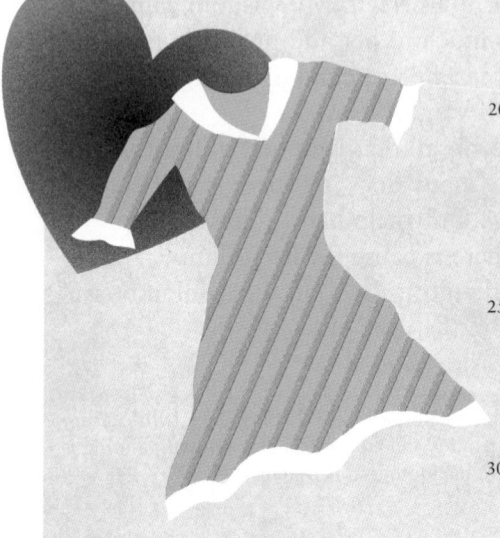

With a hot glide up, then down, his shirts,
I ironed out my father's back, cramped
and worried with work. I stroked the yoke,
the breast pocket, collar and cuffs,
5   until the rumpled heap relaxed into the shape
of my father's broad chest, the shoulders shrugged off
the world, the collapsed arms spread for a hug.
And if there'd been a face above the buttondown neck,
I would have pressed the forehead out, I would
10 have made a boy again out of that tired man!

If I clung to her skirt as she sorted the wash
or put out a line, my mother frowned,
a crease down each side of her mouth.
This is no time for love! But here
15 I could linger over her wrinkled bedjacket,
kiss at the damp puckers of her wrists
with the hot tip. Here I caressed complications
of darts, scallops, ties, pleats which made
her outfits test of the patience of my passion.
20 Here I could lay my dreaming iron on her lap. . . .

The smell of baked cotton rose from the board
and blew with a breeze out the window
to the family wardrobe drying on the clothesline,
all needing a touch of my iron. Here I could tickle
25 the underarms of my big sister's petticoat
or secretly pat the backside of her pajamas.
For she too would have warned me not to muss
her fresh blouses, starched jumpers, and smocks,
all that my careful hand had ironed out,
30 forced to express my excess love on cloth.

Thinking through the LITERATURE

Connect to the Literature

1. **What Do You Think?** What mental picture do you have of the narrator of this story?

   Comprehension Check
   - Why is Emily separated from her family?
   - What talent does Emily develop?

Think Critically

2. Who is the "you" the **narrator** addresses, and why has that person asked for her help in understanding Emily? Speculate about what Emily might have said or done to prompt the person's call.

3. What problems do you think Emily might have, and how might her past experiences have contributed to them?

   THINK ABOUT
   - her stiffness when her mother would try to hold her
   - her resentment toward her sister Susan
   - her differences from others her age
   - the summary in the next-to-last paragraph

4. What events in Emily's life might have contributed to her talent for performance?

5. **ACTIVE READING** | **MAKING JUDGMENTS ABOUT CHARACTER** How do you **evaluate** Emily's mother as a parent? Explain the reasons for your answer. Refer to the chart in your ▮▮ READER'S NOTEBOOK.

Extend Interpretations

6. **Critic's Corner** One critic has pointed out that Olsen writes about people who are victims of harsh social, economic, familial, and political conditions. How well does "I Stand Here Ironing" fit this description? Who are the victims in the story? What conditions have oppressed them?

7. **Connect to Life** Do you think an individual's personality is mostly inborn, or mostly determined by parents and environment? Explain your answer, taking into consideration Emily's personality as well as those of people you know.

8. **Points of Comparison** Who do you think struggles against greater obstacles, the narrator in this story or the one in "The Yellow Wallpaper"? Cite examples in your answer.

Literary Analysis

INTERIOR MONOLOGUE In a drama, the speech of a character who is alone on stage, voicing his or her thoughts, is known as a soliloquy or a monologue. In a short story or novel, the direct presentation of a character's unspoken thoughts is called an **interior monologue.** An interior monologue may jump back and forth between past and present, displaying thoughts, memories, and impressions just as they might occur to a person's mind. Events follow one another because of the way they fit together in the character's mind, not necessarily because they happened in that order.

Cooperative Learning Activity With a small group of students, discuss these questions: What does the interior monologue reveal about the driving forces in the narrator's life? Why is it significant that the narrator tells this story while ironing? How would the effect have been different if the events were told from the third-person point of view and in chronological order, beginning with Emily's birth? Choose one member to write a brief summary of the group's discussion. Share the summary with other groups.

REVIEW | **METAPHOR** What does the mother mean when she says, in the last sentence of the story, "Only help her [Emily] to know . . . that she is more than this dress on the ironing board, helpless before the iron"? What is being compared to the iron? How appropriate is the comparison?

Choices & CHALLENGES

Writing Options

1. **Points of Comparison**
Both this story and "The Yellow Wallpaper" are told from the first-person point of view. Write an essay comparing these first-person narrators. Fill in a chart like this one for your prewriting notes.

	narrator of "I Stand Here Ironing"	narrator of "The Yellow Wallpaper"
circumstances in life		
challenges faced		
qualities shown		

2. **Story Sequel** What do you think will happen next to Emily? What will the mother and daughter be like ten years later? Write a sequel to this story in the form of an interior monologue by Emily or her mother.

3. **Response to Relationships** Write a personal response to the family relationships described in this story, in "Seventeen Syllables" (page 789), and in the poem "Ironing Their Clothes" (page 814).

4. **Emily's Interview** Imagine that Emily has become a star comedienne and that a reporter for a fan magazine has said to her, "Tell me about your mother. How has she influenced your life?" Write Emily's response as part of an interview. Save your writing in your **Working Portfolio.**

Activities & Explorations

1. **Guidelines for Parents** Design a poster to display guidelines for good parenting. Refer to the qualities you listed. ~ **ART**

2. **Informal Discussion** In what ways has Emily suffered because of the period in United States history in which she was born? Explore this question with a small group of classmates and record your conclusions. ~ **SPEAKING AND LISTENING**

3. **Role-Play** In *Walden,* Henry David Thoreau makes some observations about poverty (page 390, lines 255–257), including that "the setting sun is reflected from the windows of the almshouse as brightly as from the rich man's abode." Role-play a conversation in which Thoreau and the narrator of "I Stand Here Ironing" debate the advantages of poverty. ~ **PERFORMING**

Art Connection

Look again at the paintings shown on pages 807, 810, and 813. What stories do you read into these paintings? Why does the child in the first painting look so sad? What has happened to the red building in the second painting? In the third painting, what is the relationship between the girl in the foreground and the people in the background? Finally, how would you relate these artworks to the story "I Stand Here Ironing"?

Inquiry & Research

1. **Sibling Rivalry** Emily resents her younger sister Susan. Is this a common attitude? Find out what child-development experts say about sibling rivalry—conflicts among brothers and sisters. You might search a computer database for current magazine articles on the topic. What contributes to sibling rivalry? What can parents do to lessen it? Report your findings to the class.

2. **Oral History** Interview a person who lived through the Great Depression or World War II, asking what family life was like at that time. Were any of the person's experiences similar to Emily's and her mother's? If possible, tape-record the interview and play the tape for the class.

 More Online: Research Starter
www.mcdougallittell.com

Illustration by Mike Dooling from *Mary McLean and the St. Patrick's Day Parade* by Steven Krull.

Vocabulary in Action

EXERCISE: MEANING CLUES Write the word described by each clue below.

1. A whip can cause this; so can a cruel comment.
2. You may do this to buried treasure or to almost-forgotten memories.
3. A mirror isn't required for this activity, but it is helpful.
4. The President has a lot of this; so does a Nobel Prize winner.
5. If a building's design is this, you can probably find your way around in it.
6. Warfare, plague, or famine can cause a nation to be described as this.
7. A secret agent wants and needs this quality; a person seeking fame does not.
8. It is almost impossible to be this if you try to talk with a mouth full of mashed potatoes.
9. One common response to this is "I did not!"; another is "Oh, yeah? Prove it!"
10. Dirt and water do this with respect to mud.

Building Vocabulary

Several of the Words to Know have Greek or Latin roots. For an in-depth lesson on root words, see page 444.

WORDS TO KNOW				
anonymity articulate	coherent compound	denunciation dredge	laceration preening	prestige ravaged

Tillie Olsen
1913–

Other Works
Yonnondio: From the Thirties

Working Mother Tillie Olsen began writing as a teenager in the 1930s, during the Great Depression, but stopped to marry and raise a family. A mother of four daughters, she helped support her family by working as a waitress and a secretary, all the time carrying the desire to write "within her" while riding the bus, doing household chores, and working long hours at a job. She has explained, "It is no accident that the first work I considered publishable began: 'I stand here ironing, and what you asked me moves tormented back and forth with the iron.'"

A Writer at Last For years hampered in her efforts to write by the struggle to earn a living, Olsen resumed her career only after receiving a fellowship from Stanford University in 1956. She was in her late 40s before she was able to publish *Tell Me a Riddle* (1961), a collection of short stories. Immediately acclaimed, Olsen's book

earned her fellowships and university teaching assignments. A high school dropout in the 11th grade, Olsen has nevertheless taught at various schools, including the University of Massachusetts, Stanford University, Amherst College, and the Massachusetts Institute of Technology.

Literary Concerns Olsen writes of people who have known economic hardships and whose lives are lived for others. In *Silences* (1978), a book of essays, she explores some of the social, political, and economic conditions that have adversely affected writers—especially women—and the creation of literature throughout history. Through her own personal experiences, Olsen has gained insight into the "thwarting of what struggles to come into being but cannot." Through her writing, she has given voice to those who might otherwise be silent.

Author Activity

According to Olson, her method of writing involves "trying to be inside the people whom I am writing about." To what extent do you think Olsen succeeded in getting inside Emily's mother in "I Stand Here Ironing"?

Comparing Literature: Assessment Practice

PART 1 Reading the Prompt

Read the writing prompt carefully, more than once. Look for key words that help you identify the purpose of the essay and decide how to approach it.

> **Writing Prompt**
>
> In Unit Five, Part 1, several works deal with the issue of self-fulfillment for women. In an essay, relate the ideas about women's self-fulfillment presented in three selections you have read—from both the 19th and 20th centuries. What overall perspective on female self-fulfillment do these selections suggest? Cite evidence to support your ideas.

STRATEGIES IN ACTION

❶ Bring together, or **synthesize,** ideas from three selections.

❷ State a new idea—a **generalization** applying to all three selections.

❸ Gather relevant **details** from the selections.

PART 2 Planning a Synthesis Essay

- Choose three selections to examine: for example, "The Yellow Wallpaper," "The Story of an Hour," and "Seventeen Syllables."

- Create a diagram like the one shown.

- Jot down details about women's self-fulfillment in these selections.

- Identify patterns among these details.

- Based on these patterns, make a broad statement about self-fulfillment in women.

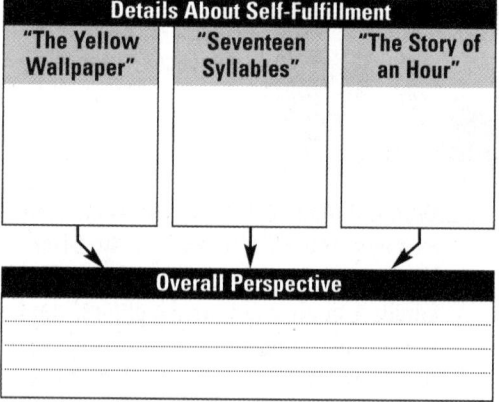

Details About Self-Fulfillment		
"The Yellow Wallpaper"	"Seventeen Syllables"	"The Story of an Hour"

Overall Perspective

PART 3 Drafting Your Essay

Introduction Begin by stating the thesis of your essay—the perspective on women's self-fulfillment that the selections share.

Organization Present the evidence in a logical way. For example, in each middle paragraph, you might state a supporting idea and then explain it with details.

Conclusion Restate your thesis and state a final thought.

Revision Allow time to review your work. Make sure it is clear, well-supported, and free from mistakes.

Writing Handbook
See page 1281: Explanatory Writing.

LITERATURE CONNECTIONS

Ethan Frome

EDITH WHARTON

These thematically related readings are provided along with *Ethan Frome*:

The Snow Man
WALLACE STEVENS

Confessions of a Hypochondriac
BARBARA GRAHAM

Adventure
SHERWOOD ANDERSON

The Painted Door
SINCLAIR ROSS

Mirage
CHRISTINA ROSSETTI

Desert Places
ROBERT FROST

Dreams
MARIE G. LEE

The Awakening

KATE CHOPIN

This ground-breaking novel dramatizes the artistic and emotional awakening of Edna Pontellier, a 28-year-old woman who feels trapped by marriage and motherhood. Her true identity lies beyond the roles that society has imposed on her. In her quest for self-discovery, Edna willingly defies convention and takes enormous risks.

And Even *More . . .*

Books

Mother Love
RITA DOVE
A book of poems exploring mother-daughter relationships.

The Madwoman in the Attic: The Woman Writer and the Nineteenth-Century Literary Imagination
SANDRA M. GILBERT
Insightful study of notable women writers, including Emily Dickinson.

A History of Women in America
CAROLYN HYMOWITZ AND MICHAELE WEISSMAN
Overview of the shifting roles of women in American society.

Other Media

Cross Creek
Feature film about writer Marjorie Kinnan Rawlings and her search for self-discovery in the backwoods of Florida.
(VIDEOCASSETTE)

Ethan Frome
Film adaptation of the novel, starring Liam Neeson. Touchstone Home Video.
(VIDEOCASSETTE)

The Belle of Amherst
Televised version of William Luce's play about Emily Dickinson. International Film Exchange. (VIDEOCASSETTE)

Reena and Other Stories

PAULE MARSHALL
Marshall's collection of stories feature women and their relationships. Tillie Olsen highly praised this work, commending Marshall for her rare gift of creating "characters with such passionate understanding and radiant art that they remain with us permanently."

The American Dream

Illusion or Reality?

In the United States, the closing decades of the 19th century were a time of rapid change and sharp contrasts. Great entrepreneurs—such as Andrew Carnegie, J. P. Morgan, John D. Rockefeller, and Cornelius Vanderbilt—amassed vast fortunes by exploiting cheap labor in the cities and creating giant companies that controlled entire industries. Urban manufacturing centers swelled with the influx of immigrants from Europe and people from rural areas in search of work. Almost half of the U.S. population was crowded in about a dozen cities, and the majority of all U.S. workers were industrial laborers sweating in factories.

As the new century dawned, the belief in America as a unique place where work and merit, rather than social privilege, determined one's fate remained a powerful ideal. Everyone knew of Abraham Lincoln's rise from his early life in a simple log cabin in rural Illinois. Many also knew that the millionaire newspaperman Joseph Pulitzer had come to America as a poor young German-speaking immigrant, recruited to fight in the Civil War. Stories of people who had risen, through their own efforts, from humble beginnings to achieve fabulous success were told and retold.

For many writers, however, the underside of this ideal— the flaws hidden beneath its optimistic simplicity—became a preoccupation. In the novel *Sister Carrie*, Theodore Dreiser challenged the notion of self-improvement by depicting a heroine crushed by forces she cannot control. In *The Jungle*,

The republic is a dream
Nothing happens unless first a dream.
Carl Sandburg
from "Washington Monument
by Night"

Upton Sinclair exposed the appalling working conditions of immigrants in the Chicago stockyards. The poet and folksinger Carl Sandburg presented the seamy side of urban industrialization—the poverty, the crime, the corruption—even as he celebrated the courage and resilience of everyday men and women in the face of these blights.

In their poetry, Edgar Lee Masters and Edwin Arlington Robinson turned their gaze away from the cities to look at the changes surging through rural areas at this time. Each investigated, in a different way, the currents of discontent running beneath the surface stability of small-town life.

Paul Laurence Dunbar, the first African American to earn his living solely by his writing, made his own sharp points in America's picturesque veneer by exposing the truth behind popular racial stereotypes of the day.

The American dream of material success was nowhere so minutely explored as in the stories and novels of F. Scott Fitzgerald. Nearly all of his works concern the tension between the very wealthy and those—like him—who were attracted to them. In following the lives of characters whose fates are determined by their responses to wealth and to those who possess it, he gave us intimate insights into the American preoccupation with money.

For the more than 20 million immigrants who came to America in the years between 1870 and 1920, the American dream was not just a compelling ideal but a last chance at survival. Many found work

The love of wealth is therefore to be traced, as either a principal or accessory motive, at the bottom of all that the Americans do; this gives to all their passions a sort of family likeness. . . . It may be said that it is the vehemence of their desires that makes the Americans so methodical; it perturbs their minds, but it disciplines their lives.
Alexis de Tocqueville
from *Democracy in America*

God gave me my money. I believe the power to make money is a gift from God . . . to be developed and used to the best of our ability for the good of mankind.

John D. Rockefeller

The business of America is business.
Calvin Coolidge

In your rocking chair by your window shall you dream such happiness as you may never feel.

Theodore Dreiser
from *Sister Carrie*

Yuh don't belong, get me! Look at me, why don't youse dare? I belong, dat's me! *(pointing to a skyscraper across the street which is in process of construction—with bravado)* See dat building goin' up dere? See de steel work? Steel, dat's me! Youse guys live on it and tink yuh're somep'n. But I'm in it, see! I'm de hoistin' engine dat makes it go up! I'm it—de inside and bottom of it! Sure! I'm steel and steam and smoke and de rest of it! It moves—speed—twenty-five stories up—and me at de top and bottom—movin'! Youse simps don't move. Yuh're on'y dolls I winds up to see 'm spin.

Eugene O'Neill
from *The Hairy Ape*

"Give me your tired, your poor,
Your huddled masses yearning to
    breathe free,
The wretched refuse of your teeming
    shore.
Send these, the homeless, tempest-
    tossed to me:
I lift my lamp beside the golden door!"

Emma Lazarus
from "The New Colossus,"
inscribed at the base
of the Statue of Liberty

America is God's Crucible, the great Melting-Pot where all the races of Europe are melting and re-forming!

Israel Zangwill
from *The Melting Pot*

building skyscrapers, bridges, subways, and trolley lines in the growing cities. Anzia Yezierska's moving account of disillusion and persistence in her story "America and I" provides a glimpse of what life was like for immigrants in the sweatshops of New York City's garment district.

Traditions Across Time: Dreams Lost and Found

Although the great waves of immigrants from Europe subsided during the 1920s—after the passage of restrictive quota laws—and during the Great Depression of the 1930s, the United States continued to be a "land of opportunity" for those in need. In the 1960s quotas based on nationality were lifted, and another wave of immigration began. The immigrants came mainly from Asia and the West Indies rather than from Europe.

These new immigrants came for the same reason as their predecessors a century before—to make a better life for themselves and their families—but some were also escaping homelands scarred by war and political persecution. Gish Jen's story "In the American Society" and Naomi Shihab Nye's poem "My Father and the Figtree" treat the immigrant experience with humor. Yvonne Sapia's poem "Defining the Grateful Gesture" and Lorna Dee Cervantes' poem "Refugee Ship" look at generational differences in immigrant families.

PART 2   The American Dream

Illusion or Reality?

Carl Sandburg	**Chicago** *Not one of those little soft cities*	824
Edgar Lee Masters	**Lucinda Matlock** *A woman who took what life had to offer*	824
Edwin Arlington Robinson	**Richard Cory** *Appearances can be deceiving.*	830
	Miniver Cheevy *He escapes into the legendary past.*	830
Paul Laurence Dunbar	**We Wear the Mask** *A mask to hide the hurt*	835
	Sympathy *Understanding the plight of a caged bird*	835
F. Scott Fitzgerald	**Winter Dreams** *Can happiness be more than just a dream?*	840
Anzia Yezierska	**America and I** *Finding the true America*	863
The Americans	RELATED READING **The New Immigrants** *Millions seek a better life in the United States.*	875

COMPARING LITERATURE
Traditions Across Time: Dreams Lost and Found

Gish Jen	**In the American Society** (1986) *Smart guys think in advance.*	877
Naomi Shihab Nye	LITERARY LINK **My Father and the Figtree** (1980) *A dreamer's imaginings come true.*	891
Yvonne Sapia	**Defining the Grateful Gesture** (1986) *Plates heaped with food and gratitude*	894
Lorna Dee Cervantes	**Refugee Ship** (1982) *Orphaned from her Spanish name*	894

Chicago

Poetry by CARL SANDBURG

Lucinda Matlock

Poetry by EDGAR LEE MASTERS

Connect to Your Life

Ideal Settings Where would you prefer to live—the city or the country? Why? Which environment do you think would let you live your life to the fullest? List some positive and negative features of city life and of country life. Then, as you read these poems, compare your own ideas with those of the speakers.

Build Background

The American Spirit Carl Sandburg and Edgar Lee Masters wrote poetry that captured the vitality of America in the early 20th century. What Sandburg found when he moved to Chicago in 1913 was a metropolis of bustling industry and appalling slums, cultural achievements and criminal activity. From the ruins of a devastating 1871 fire, Chicago had risen to become the railroad hub of the nation and a center of meatpacking and manufacturing. At the same time, the city's population had increased explosively as people moved there from small towns in the Midwest and the South to find work. Written in 1914, "Chicago" catalogs both the negative and the positive aspects of the city, reflecting the energy and enthusiasm of its citizens in the early 1900s.

"Lucinda Matlock" is from Masters's *Spoon River Anthology,* a collection of 244 free-verse monologues spoken by deceased inhabitants of the fictional rural town of Spoon River. They disclose the joys and tragedies of their lives as they speak from the grave. Masters patterned these characters on the people he had observed while growing up in Lewistown, near the Spoon River of central Illinois. His model for Lucinda Matlock was his grandmother Lucinda, who died in 1910 at the age of 96.

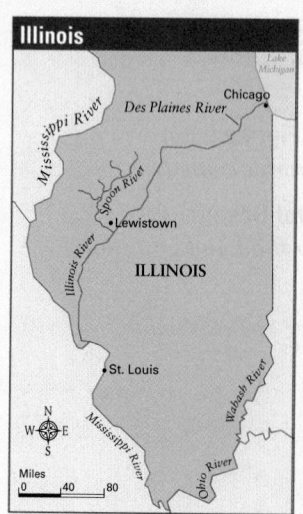

Focus Your Reading

LITERARY ANALYSIS **TONE** **Tone** is the attitude a writer takes toward his or her subject. A writer can communicate tone through diction (word choice) and choice of details. Read these two poems aloud to help you identify the tone. The emotions conveyed in your voice should provide you with clues that hint at the tone.

ACTIVE READING **SYNTHESIZING DETAILS**
"Chicago" catalogs, or lists, the attributes of a city, while "Lucinda Matlock" sums up the key moments of a woman's life. To bring these details into focus, synthesize the information. **Synthesizing** involves putting together clues, facts, and details to form an overall picture of a person, place, or event.

READER'S NOTEBOOK For each poem, use a spider diagram, like the example shown, to help you gather details as you read. Then note recurring patterns or relationships among the details you collected.

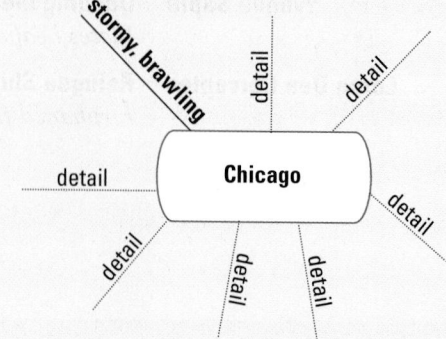

ght handler to the nation, stormy, husky, brawling, city of the b ulders, hog butcher, tool maker, stacker of wheat, player with ra ds, freight handler to the nation, stormy, husky, brawling, city e big shoulders, hog butcher, tool maker, stacker of wheat, play th railroads

City Building (1930), Thomas Hart Benton. From *America Today,* distemper and egg tempera on gessoed linen with oil glaze, 92″ × 117″. Copyright © The Equitable Life Assurance Society of the United States. Copyright © 1996 T.H. Benton & R.P. Benton Testamentary Trusts/Licensed by VAGA, New York. Photo Copyright © 1988 Dorothy Zeidman.

CHICAGO

Carl Sandburg

Hog Butcher for the World,
Tool Maker, Stacker of Wheat,
Player with Railroads and the Nation's Freight Handler;
Stormy, husky, brawling,
5   City of the Big Shoulders:

They tell me you are wicked and I believe them, for I have seen your
painted women under the gas lamps luring the farm boys.

And they tell me you are crooked and I answer: Yes, it is true I have
     seen the gunman kill and go free to kill again.
And they tell me you are brutal and my reply is: On the faces of
     women and children I have seen the marks of wanton hunger.
And having answered so I turn once more to those who sneer at this
     my city, and I give them back the sneer and say to them:
10   Come and show me another city with lifted head singing so proud to
     be alive and coarse and strong and cunning.
Flinging magnetic curses amid the toil of piling job on job, here is a
     tall bold slugger set vivid against the little soft cities;
Fierce as a dog with tongue lapping for action, cunning as a savage
     pitted against the wilderness,
Bareheaded,
Shoveling,
15   Wrecking,
Planning,
Building, breaking, rebuilding,
Under the smoke, dust all over his mouth, laughing with white teeth,
Under the terrible burden of destiny laughing as a young man laughs,
20   Laughing even as an ignorant fighter laughs who has never lost a
     battle,
Bragging and laughing that under his wrist is the pulse, and under his
     ribs the heart of the people,
                         Laughing!
Laughing the stormy, husky, brawling laughter of Youth, half-naked,
     sweating, proud to be Hog Butcher, Tool Maker, Stacker of
     Wheat, Player with Railroads and Freight Handler to the Nation.

Thinking Through the Literature

1. Would you like to live in a city like the one depicted in this poem? Share your ideas with a classmate.

2. In your opinion, what are the best and worst aspects of the Chicago presented in the poem?

3. How well do you think Sandburg's poetic **style** suits his subject?

   THINK ABOUT
   - how you would characterize his use of rhythm
   - the effectiveness of descriptive names like "Tool Maker" in helping you picture Chicago
   - how the repetition in the last three lines affects your impression of the city
   - how the city would seem different if described in formal, rhymed stanzas

4. **ACTIVE READING** **SYNTHESIZING DETAILS** Review the spider diagram you created in your 📖 **READER'S NOTEBOOK.** Based on these details, what is the overall picture of Chicago presented in this poem?

Lucinda Matlock

Edgar Lee Masters

Country Dance (1928), Thomas Hart Benton. Oil on panel, 30″ × 25″, private collection. Copyright © 1996 T.H. Benton & R.P. Benton Testamentary Trusts/Licenses by VAGA, New York.

I went to the dances at Chandlerville,
And played snap-out at Winchester.
One time we changed partners,
Driving home in the moonlight of middle June,
5 And then I found Davis.
We were married and lived together for seventy years,
Enjoying, working, raising the twelve children,
Eight of whom we lost
Ere I had reached the age of sixty.
10 I spun, I wove, I kept the house, I nursed the sick,
I made the garden, and for holiday
Rambled over the fields where sang the larks,
And by Spoon River gathering many a shell,
And many a flower and medicinal weed—
15 Shouting to the wooded hills, singing to the green valleys.
At ninety-six I had lived enough, that is all,
And passed to a sweet repose.
What is this I hear of sorrow and weariness,
Anger, discontent and drooping hopes?
20 Degenerate sons and daughters,
Life is too strong for you—
It takes life to love Life.

2 snap-out: a game—similar to crack the whip—in which players join hands in a line, then run about trying to shake off those at the end of the line.

17 repose: rest (here the reference is to death, viewed as a quiet, serene sleep).

20 degenerate (dĭ-jĕn′ər-ĭt): showing a decline in vigor or moral strength.

Connect to the Literature

1. **What Do You Think?**
   What is your opinion of Lucinda Matlock's life?

   Comprehension Check
   • How did Lucinda Matlock meet her husband?
   • What happened to most of her children?

Think Critically

2. **ACTIVE READING SYNTHESIZING DETAILS** Refer to the details in the spider diagram from your  **READER'S NOTEBOOK.** What were the sources of both joy and pain in her life?

3. How would you describe Lucinda Matlock's approach to life?

4. Do you think Lucinda is fair in her judgment of the "degenerate sons and daughters"? Explain your opinion.

   THINK ABOUT
   • the attitudes she attributes to them in lines 18–19
   • what she might mean by her statements in lines 21–22

5. What portrait of small-town life do you get from this poem? Explain.

Extend Interpretations

6. **Comparing Texts** How is Lucinda Matlock similar to and different from the people that the speaker of "Chicago" admires? Support your answer.

7. **Critic's Corner** In a review of *Spoon River Anthology,* Carl Sandburg wrote, "The people whose faces look out from the pages of the book are the people of life itself, each trait of them as plain or as mysterious as in the old home valley where the writer came from." Do you think his remark accurately describes Lucinda Matlock, as she is characterized in the poem? Explain.

8. **Connect to Life** Would you rather live in Sandburg's Chicago or Lucinda Matlock's Spoon River? Consider the positive and negative aspects of country and city life you recorded for the Connect to Your Life activity on page 824.

Literary Analysis

TONE Like tone of voice, the **tone** of a poem may reveal the speaker's feelings or the poet's attitude toward the subject of the poem. Tone often relies on the poet's choice of words and selection of details. For example, the tone of "Chicago" might be described as brash and spirited. Calling Chicago "Hog Butcher of the World" and "Tool Maker, Stacker of Wheat" suggests the energetic tone that the speaker is trying to convey. The words *shouting* and *singing* in line 15 of "Lucinda Matlock" suggest the speaker's deep and joyful relationship with the natural world.

Paired Activity Reread "Lucinda Matlock" aloud to a partner, and discuss how the speaker's tone shifts toward the end of the poem. Cite words and details that reveal a change in the speaker's feelings.

REVIEW PERSONIFICATION
Personification is a figure of speech in which an object, animal, place, or idea is given human characteristics. For example, starting at line 10 in "Chicago," Sandburg personifies the city as a proud man. If you were to personify your own city or town, what kind of person would it be?

Writing Options

1. Hometown Poems Write a poem about your own city or town. You might imitate the style of "Chicago," using epithets, or descriptive names, and personification to depict the town. You might prefer to present the town indirectly, through a character sketch of a typical resident, as in "Lucinda Matlock." Gather the class's poems into a booklet of poems about communities.

2. Comparison-Contrast Essay Draft an essay in which you compare and contrast city life and country life. Place this piece in your **Working Portfolio.**

Writing Handbook
See page 1281: Compare and Contrast

Carl Sandburg
1878–1967

Other Works
The People, Yes
Always the Young Strangers

Edgar Lee Masters
1868?–1950

Other Works
Poems of People
Illinois Poems
Across Spoon River: An Autobiography

The Winding Road to Success The renowned poet, award-winning historian, and popular folk musician Carl Sandburg was born in Galesburg, Illinois. Forced to leave school when he was 13 in order to find work, he roamed the Midwest as a youth, working at various jobs—including house painting and brick making. Eventually, he turned to journalism. After moving to Chicago in 1913, he became a reporter, editorial writer, and columnist for the *Chicago Daily News.*

The People's Poet The poem "Chicago" was one of Sandburg's earliest literary successes. His verse collections *Chicago Poems, Cornhuskers,* and *Smoke and Steel* established his fame as a poet of the people. Because he gave popular public readings around the country, it has been said that no other American writer was so widely read and heard at the same time.

Literary Prizes Sandburg won a number of awards and honors, including the 1951 Pulitzer Prize for poetry for *Complete Poems* and the 1939 Pulitzer Prize for history for *Abraham Lincoln: The War Years,* the last four volumes of a six-volume biography.

Bridging Two Centuries Born with one foot in the nineteenth century and one foot in the twentieth, Edgar Lee Masters seemed at ease with both the old and the new. His poetry reflects his ties to small-town traditions and his awareness of the changing face of American culture in the early 1900s.

The Birth of a Masterpiece Edgar Lee Masters had already published 12 books of poetry, essays, and plays before he began writing his masterpiece, *Spoon River Anthology,* which he originally conceived as a work of prose. For the names of the poems' characters, Masters drew on "both the Spoon river and the Sangamon river neighborhoods, combining first names here with surnames there, and taking some also from the constitutions and State papers of Illinois."

Critical Acclaim The publication of *Spoon River Anthology* in 1915 immediately established Masters as an important American poet. In 1920, Masters gave up the Chicago law practice at which he had worked for 30 years and moved to New York City to write full time. He wrote more than 50 books, but none of his later works achieved the critical and popular success of *Spoon River Anthology.*

Richard Cory
Miniver Cheevy

Poetry by EDWIN ARLINGTON ROBINSON

(**Connect to Your Life**)

Life's Disappointments What do you think causes some people to feel regretful about their lives? How might they try to escape their unhappiness? With a small group of classmates, discuss these questions. Brainstorm a list of both positive and negative ways of coping with disappointing experiences.

Build Background

Tilbury Town Edwin Arlington Robinson's "Richard Cory" and "Miniver Cheevy" are from a famous series of poems depicting the inner lives of imaginary residents in Tilbury Town, a fictional community modeled on Robinson's hometown of Gardiner, Maine. Tilbury Town, a typical small town in New England at the turn of the century, is a place where individuality and creativity are stifled. Though some members of this community chase after the American dream, it remains out of their reach. In most of his Tilbury Town poems, Robinson paints a complex psychological portrait of isolated individuals—often misfits and failures. "The failures are much more interesting," Robinson said. Along with his fascination with failed lives, Robinson also explores how his characters try to overcome their personal defeats and shortcomings.

Focus Your Reading

LITERARY ANALYSIS   CHARACTERIZATION IN NARRATIVE POETRY

Narrative poetry tells a story using elements of character, setting, and plot to develop a theme. To portray characters in narrative poems, poets may adapt the methods of **characterization** typically used in fiction:

- physical description
- the character's own actions, words, thoughts, and feelings
- other characters' actions, words, thoughts, and feelings
- the speaker's own direct comments

As you read "Richard Cory" and "Miniver Cheevy," note how you get to know the characters.

ACTIVE READING   EVALUATING CHARACTER   Robinson does not directly state how to view the characters in his poems. Are they good or bad? weak or strong? likable or unlikable? He leaves these **evaluations,** or judgments, up to the reader. Robinson provides you with clues that will shape your impressions of the characters' personalities and behavior.

READER'S NOTEBOOK   To form valid opinions about Richard Cory and Miniver Cheevy, note the descriptive details Robinson uses to portray them. As you read each poem, jot down details you learned about the characters. Use a chart like the one shown.

	Richard Cory	Miniver Cheevy
Traits		
Behavior		
Outlook on Life		

Richard Cory

Edwin
Arlington
Robinson

Whenever Richard Cory went down town,
We people on the pavement looked at him:
He was a gentleman from sole to crown,
Clean favored, and imperially slim.

5   And he was always quietly arrayed,
And he was always human when he talked;
But still he fluttered pulses when he said,
"Good-morning," and he glittered when he walked.

And he was rich—yes, richer than a king—
10   And admirably schooled in every grace:
In fine, we thought that he was everything
To make us wish that we were in his place.

So on we worked, and waited for the light,
And went without the meat, and cursed the bread;
15   And Richard Cory, one calm summer night,
Went home and put a bullet through his head.

4 clean favored: having a tidy appearance; **imperially:** majestically; royally.

5 arrayed: dressed.

10 schooled in every grace: extremely well-mannered and cultured.

11 In fine: in short

Thinking Through the Literature

1. What is your reaction to the ending of "Richard Cory"?

2. How do the townspeople seem to feel about Richard Cory? Support your ideas with details from the poem.

3. **ACTIVE READING** **EVALUATING CHARACTER** Review the chart in your **READER'S NOTEBOOK.** What is your opinion of Richard Cory?

   THINK ABOUT
   - his physical appearance and other traits
   - his speech and behavior toward the townspeople
   - his apparent outlook on life

4. Why do you think Richard Cory kills himself?

5. What would you say is the **theme** of this poem?

Miniver Cheevy, child of scorn,
    Grew lean while he assailed the seasons;
He wept that he was ever born,
    And he had reasons.

5 Miniver loved the days of old
    When swords were bright and steeds
    were prancing;
The vision of a warrior bold
    Would set him dancing.

Miniver sighed for what was not,
10   And dreamed, and rested from his labors;
He dreamed of Thebes and Camelot,
    And Priam's neighbors.

Miniver mourned the ripe renown
    That made so many a name so fragrant;
15 He mourned Romance, now on the town,
    And Art, a vagrant.

Miniver loved the Medici,
    Albeit he had never seen one;
He would have sinned incessantly
20   Could he have been one.

Miniver cursed the commonplace
    And eyed a khaki suit with loathing;
He missed the medieval grace
    Of iron clothing.

25 Miniver scorned the gold he sought,
    But sore annoyed was he without it;
Miniver thought, and thought, and thought,
    And thought about it.

Miniver Cheevy, born too late,
30   Scratched his head and kept on thinking;
Miniver coughed, and called it fate,
    And kept on drinking.

Miniver Cheevy

Edwin Arlington Robinson

11 Thebes (thēbz): a city of ancient Greece, the setting of many famous legends; **Camelot:** King Arthur's legendary castle.

12 Priam's (prī'əmz) **neighbors:** the participants in the Trojan War (during which Priam was king of Troy).

17 Medici (měd'ə-chē'): a powerful Italian noble family, among whose members were several cruel and immoral rulers of Florence during the Renaissance.

18 albeit (ôl-bē'ĭt): even though.

Connect to the Literature

1. What Do You Think? What is your impression of Miniver Cheevy? Share your thoughts with a classmate.

Comprehension Check
- What is Miniver Cheevy's position in society?
- What does Miniver Cheevy daydream about?
- How does Miniver Cheevy respond to the disappointments in his life?

Think Critically

2. How would you describe Miniver Cheevy's view of the past? Why do you think he holds this view?

THINK ABOUT
- the content of his daydreams
- why he is disappointed with his own life
- how he deals with his "fate"

3. How do you think the speaker of the poem feels about Miniver Cheevy? Cite lines from poem that suggest the speaker's attitude.

4. How does the final stanza of the poem influence your opinion of Miniver Cheevy?

5. **ACTIVE READING** **EVALUATING CHARACTER** Review the chart you made in your ▮▮ **READER'S NOTEBOOK.** Do you think Miniver Cheevy is a sympathetic or an unsympathetic character? Defend your view.

Extend Interpretations

6. Comparing Texts How would you relate "Richard Cory" and "Miniver Cheevy" to the idea of the American dream?

7. What If? If Miniver Cheevy had lived during medieval times, do you think he would have found happiness? Why or why not?

8. Connect to Life Both Miniver Cheevy and Richard Cory solve their problems in self-destructive ways. In your opinion, what are some positive ways of coping with life's disappointments? Think about your discussion with classmates in the Connect to Your Life activity on page 830.

Literary Analysis

CHARACTERIZATION IN NARRATIVE POETRY Like a short story or novel, **narrative poetry,** such as "Richard Cory" and "Miniver Cheevy," relies on literary elements, such as character, setting, plot, and point of view, to tell a story. Robinson adapts techniques of **characterization** to create compelling portraits of imaginary townspeople. For example, the speaker in "Richard Cory" and "Miniver Cheevy" acts as a narrator who reports information about the main character. The speaker in each of these poems provides you with a glimpse of the character's actions, appearance, feelings, and ideas.

Activity Create personality profiles of Richard Cory and Miniver Cheevy based on the specific details revealed about them in the poems. Use a format like the one shown.

> Character's Name:
> Physical Description
> Actions:
> Feelings:
> Thoughts:

REVIEW **RHYME AND METER**
Rhyme is the occurrence of a similar or identical sound at the ends of words. **Meter** is the pattern of stressed and unstressed syllables in each line. How do you think the arrangement of rhyming lines and the meter of "Miniver Cheevy" contribute to the overall effect of the poem?

Choices & CHALLENGES

Writing Options

1. Miniver's Monologue Write a monologue from Miniver Cheevy's point of view in which he glorifies moments from the past. Refer to images from the poem for ideas.

2. Farewell Note Compose a note that Richard Cory might have left, expressing his view of the townspeople and explaining why he took his life.

3. Interview Questions Imagine you are reporter who writes a news column profiling Tilbury Town residents. Write a list of ten interview questions you would ask either Richard Cory or Miniver Cheevy.

Activities & Explorations

Musical Adaptation Listen to the song "Richard Cory" on Simon and Garfunkel's 1966 album *Sounds of Silence*. Compare the depiction of Richard Cory in the song with that in Robinson's poem. Which do you prefer? Why? Then create your own musical version of "Miniver Cheevy," composing original lyrics and music or setting the words of the poem to the tune of a familiar song that captures the poem's mood.
~ MUSIC

Edwin Arlington Robinson
1869–1935

Other Works
Tristram; Merlins; The Selected Poems of Edwin Arlington Robinson

New England Poet A descendant of Anne Bradstreet, New England's first colonial poet, Edwin Arlington Robinson grew up in the river town of Gardiner, Maine. He began writing poetry when he was 11 and had already started to publish poems and translations before he entered Harvard in 1891. In 1893, after the death of his father, he returned to Gardiner, where he worked as a freelance writer, farmed, and worked on poems. His first collection, *The Torrent and The Night Before,* was privately printed in 1896. Although Robinson had intended the book to be a surprise for his mother, she died a week before the book was published.

Life of Poverty Following his mother's death, Robinson later moved to Greenwich Village in New York City, where he worked at a variety of menial jobs. Although living in poverty and obscurity, Robinson nevertheless continued to pursue his literary ambitions.

President's Praise Fortunately, Robinson's second volume of poems, the self-published *The Children of the Night,* came to the attention of President Theodore Roosevelt, who admired the book so much that he lent the struggling poet a hand by offering him a position as a clerk in the New York Customs House. Robinson gratefully accepted, working there from 1905 until 1909, when he was finally able to begin writing full time.

Recognition and Rewards Concentrating on his craft, Robinson slowly began to earn a living as a writer. His financial worries were eased by a small inheritance and a trust fund set up by an anonymous group of friends. As he became more able to devote himself to his poetry, Robinson gained a reputation as one of the country's most accomplished narrative poets. He was ultimately rewarded with a popular following and Pulitzer Prizes for *Collected Poems* (1921), *The Man Who Died Twice* (1924), and the best-selling *Tristram* (1927).

Author Activity

Locate other Tilbury Town poems in a volume of Robinson's work or in a poetry anthology. Working with a small group, create an illustrated booklet of his poems. Group members should select about six poems and add accompanying illustrations, such as portraits of characters or a map of Maine.

We Wear the Mask
Sympathy

Poetry by PAUL LAURENCE DUNBAR

Connect to Your Life

Social Barriers What social barriers sometimes keep people from becoming or showing who they really are? What happens to individuals who are prevented from realizing their potential? Discuss these questions with classmates.

Build Background

Turn-of-the-Century Race Relations "We Wear the Mask" and "Sympathy" reflect the climate of racial prejudice that existed during Paul Laurence Dunbar's time. At the turn of the 19th century, African Americans faced legal discrimination, such as voting restrictions and segregation in schools and transportation. African Americans were also compelled to follow informal rules and customs, called racial etiquette, that reinforced their status as second-class citizens. For example, most white people never shook hands with African Americans, a gesture that would imply equality.

In "We Wear the Mask," the speaker reveals the pain that racial stereotyping caused African Americans. This poem was composed in the 1890s when a popular form of entertainment was the minstrel show, in which white men with blackened faces performed comedy and variety acts. In an exaggerated mimicry of African-American speech and behavior, blackface minstrels danced and sang sentimental songs while playing banjos, violins, and tambourines.

In "Sympathy," also composed in the 1890s, the speaker's attention is on a caged bird. The situation is perhaps reminiscent of Dunbar's own experiences of operating an elevator cage, the only job he could find after graduating high school. He was denied positions in business and journalism because of his race.

Focus Your Reading

LITERARY ANALYSIS **SYMBOL** A **symbol** is a person, place, or object that has a concrete meaning in itself and also stands for something beyond itself, such as an idea or feeling. For example, a dove is not only a kind of bird but also a symbol of peace. Look for the central symbol in "We Wear the Mask" and "Sympathy." Note recurring descriptions of a person, place, or object that seems to have broader meanings within the context of the poem.

ACTIVE READING **INTERPRETING SYMBOLS** Interpreting symbols involves discovering what they might represent. On your second reading of "We Wear the Mask" and "Sympathy," follow these strategies to help you figure out the symbolic meanings in the poems:

- Identify a possible symbol.
- Consider the qualities of the symbolic object.
- Note the ideas or feelings the poet associates with the symbol.
- Consider the associations the symbol seems to trigger in you.
- Make a guess about what the symbol might represent.

READER'S NOTEBOOK To help you organize your thoughts about symbols as you reread the poems, create a chart like the one shown and fill it in.

	Object	Qualities	Symbol of . . .
"We Wear the Mask"			
"Sympathy"			

WE WEAR THE MASK

Paul Laurence Dunbar

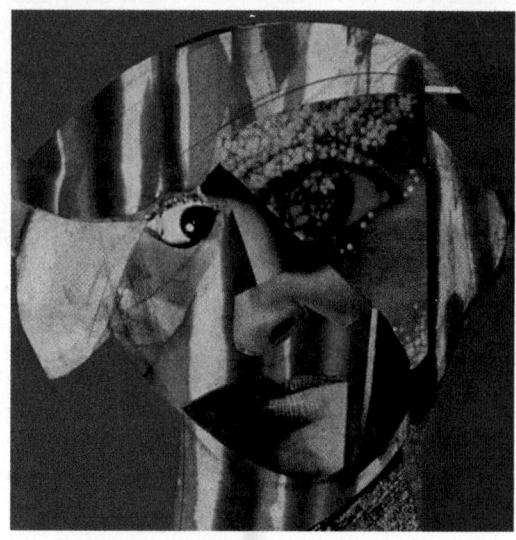

Detail of *Three Folk Musicians* (1967), Romare Bearden.
Collage on canvas on board, 50″ × 60″. Copyright © Romare Bearden/VAGA, New York.

We wear the mask that grins and lies,
It hides our cheeks and shades our eyes,—
This debt we pay to human guile;
With torn and bleeding hearts we smile,
5   And mouth with myriad subtleties.

Why should the world be overwise,
In counting all our tears and sighs?
Nay, let them only see us, while
    We wear the mask.

10   We smile, but, O great Christ, our cries
To Thee from tortured souls arise.
We sing, but oh, the clay is vile
Beneath our feet, and long the mile;
But let the world dream otherwise,
15   We wear the mask.

3 guile: slyness and craftiness in dealing with others.

5 myriad subtleties: countless artful statements.

12 vile: disgusting or objectionable.

Thinking Through the Literature

1. **Comprehension Check** Who is the speaker of the poem?

2. **ACTIVE READING** | **INTERPRETING SYMBOLS**
   Review the chart you made in your 📖 **READER'S NOTEBOOK**. In your own words, explain what wearing a mask represents in the poem.

   THINK ABOUT
   - the description of wearing the mask as a "debt we pay to human guile"
   - who is wearing the mask and why
   - the feelings that the mask hides

3. Is "We Wear the Mask" relevant to people other than African Americans? Why or why not?

Sympathy

Paul Laurence Dunbar

I know what the caged bird feels, alas!
　　When the sun is bright on the upland slopes;
When the wind stirs soft through the springing grass,
And the river flows like a stream of glass;
5　　When the first bird sings and the first bud opes,
And the faint perfume from its chalice steals—
I know what the caged bird feels!

I know why the caged bird beats his wing
　　Till its blood is red on the cruel bars;
10　For he must fly back to his perch and cling
When he fain would be on the bough a-swing;
　　And a pain still throbs in the old, old scars
And they pulse again with a keener sting—
I know why he beats his wing!

15　I know why the caged bird sings, ah me,
　　When his wing is bruised and his bosom sore,—
When he beats his bars and he would be free;
It is not a carol of joy or glee,
　　But a prayer that he sends from his heart's deep core,
20　But a plea, that upward to Heaven he flings—
I know why the caged bird sings!

Connect to the Literature

1. **What Do You Think?** What was your reaction to the bird's plight?

....
Comprehension Check
- What is the season and the scene described in the first stanza of the poem?
- Where would the caged bird rather be perched?
- What kind of song does the caged bird finally sing?
....

Think Critically

2. What do you think the poem reveals about the speaker's inner longings?

3. What do you think is the significance of the title?

4. How would you explain the progression of ideas in the poem?

   THINK ABOUT
   - the situation described in each stanza
   - what central ideas the speaker builds on
   - the first and last line of each stanza

5. **ACTIVE READING** **INTERPRETING SYMBOLS** Refer to your the chart you made in your **READER'S NOTEBOOK.** What do you think the caged bird symbolizes? Support your interpretation with evidence.

Extend Interpretations

6. **Comparing Texts** How did the historical information presented in the Build Background section on page 835 influence your interpretation of both "We Wear the Mask" and "Sympathy"? In what ways do these poems reflect turn-of-the-century race relations in the United States?

7. **Different Perspectives** In 1895, Booker T. Washington, one of the most prominent African-American leaders of his day, remarked, "No race can prosper till it learns that there is as much dignity in tilling a field as in writing a poem. It is at the bottom of life we must begin, and not at the top." Do you think the speaker in "Sympathy" would agree with this statement? Why or why not?

8. **Writer's Style** "Sympathy" is a **lyric poem,** or short poem in which a single speaker expresses thoughts and feelings in intensely emotional language. Which descriptive details from the poem did you find the most deeply moving? Why?

9. **Connect to Life** What oppressed groups around the world might identify with the bird's plight in "Sympathy"?

Literary Analysis

SYMBOL A **symbol** is a person, place, or object that represents something beyond itself. Symbols in literature generally have several possible interpretations, rather than one precise meaning, and often communicate complex, abstract ideas. For example, a symbolic mask is more meaningful than an ordinary mask; a symbolic bird is more meaningful than an ordinary bird. Clues to the meaning of a particular symbol are usually found within the work itself.

Activity Think of other symbols besides the mask and the caged bird that could represent a similar idea in these poems. For example, Dunbar might have described camouflage, rather than a mask, or a prisoner, rather than a caged bird. Share your symbols with the class and then discuss whether any of them would work as well as the ones Dunbar used in his poems.

REVIEW **TONE** Describe the **tone** of these poems—the attitude expressed toward the subject. Point out words that suggest the tone you describe. How similar are the poems in tone?

Choices & CHALLENGES

Writing Options

1. Narrative Sequel Imagine that the bird in "Sympathy" is released from its cage. Write a narrative sequel to the poem titled "I Know What the Freed Bird Feels," describing the bird's emotions after its long captivity. You might want to connect the bird's liberation to the freedoms gained by African Americans after the civil rights movement.

Writing Handbook
See page 1279: Narrative Writing

2. Lyrics of a Songbird Write the lyrics to the plea that the bird sings in the final stanza of the poem. Share your lyrics with classmates.

Activities & Explorations

1. Personal Mask Create your own mask, designing it to reflect the role that you think society, your friends, or your family expects you to play. Display your mask in the classroom. ~ **ART**

2. Political Cartoon Draw a political cartoon that illustrates Dunbar's view of racism as reflected in "We Wear the Mask" or "Sympathy." Consider using phrases from the poem as captions and labels. Study cartoons from newspaper editorial pages as models. ~ **VIEWING AND REPRESENTING**

Paul Laurence Dunbar
1872–1906

Other Works
Lyrics of Lowly Life
Poems of Cabin and Field
Lyrics of Sunshine and Shadow

Literary Beginnings The son of former slaves, Paul Laurence Dunbar was born in Dayton, Ohio, and began to write when he was 12 years old. While in high school, he became editor of the school newspaper and contributed to a newspaper published by one of the Wright brothers, who later invented the airplane. Considered the class poet, he also published his first poems in the *Dayton Herald*.

Budding Career After high school, Dunbar took a job as an elevator operator, the only work he could find. His literary career was launched when a former teacher asked him to read a poem before a writers' convention. Dunbar published his first volume of poetry, *Oak and Ivy*, in 1893. The publication of his second volume, *Majors and Minors*, in 1896 attracted the attention of the noted writer William Dean Howells, whose favorable review helped establish Dunbar's career.

Bittersweet Success Despite earning critical acclaim, Dunbar felt disappointed that his serious lyric poems were not as popular as his African-American dialect poems. He told a friend, "I didn't start with dialect, but dialect is what [white] people want. They won't let me do anything else, no matter how much I try. I've got to write dialect if I want them to listen."

Failing Health While his popularity continued to grow, Dunbar's health began to deteriorate. Following several bouts of pneumonia, Dunbar died from tuberculosis at the age of 33. By the time of his death, he had written four novels, four collections of short stories, more than ten volumes of poetry, and several musicals. He unfortunately did not live to see his lyric poems, such as "We Wear the Mask" and "Sympathy," win lasting respect.

Author Activity

The Music of Poetry Excerpts from the following poems by Dunbar—"Twell de Night Is Pas'," "When I Gits Home," "An Antebellum Sermon," and "Ode to Ethiopia"—were used as the prologues to *Afro-American Symphony* by composer William Grant Still. Read these four poems, and then listen to a sound recording of Still's symphony, available at many libraries. How does the music capture the spirit of the poems?

Winter Dreams

Short Story by F. SCOTT FITZGERALD

Connect to Your Life

Dream Keepers This story involves a young man from a small Midwestern town who pursues his dreams. What are your own aspirations? List some of them as labels on a bar graph like the one shown. Then draw bars to indicate, on a rising scale of 0 to 10, the importance you attach to achieving each aspiration.

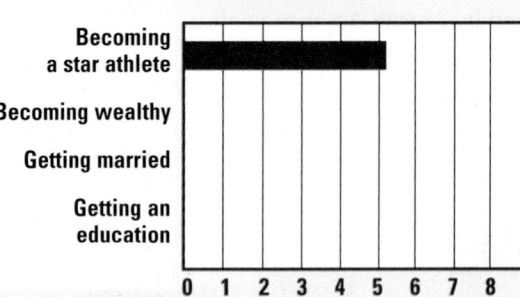

Build Background

Reckless Youth F. Scott Fitzgerald coined the term *Jazz Age* to convey the glitter and glamour of the 1920s, when many Americans threw themselves into the pursuit of fun, excitement, money, and social status. Fitzgerald and his wife, Zelda, themselves enjoyed the high life, moving among fashionable hotels and resorts in the United States and Europe, giving and attending lavish parties, and engaging in reckless stunts, such as riding on the hoods of taxicabs and jumping into fountains. First published in 1922, "Winter Dreams" provides a glimpse of the wealthy in the United States around the time of World War I. The Minnesota setting is drawn from Fitzgerald's adolescence and early adulthood among the country-club set of St. Paul.

WORDS TO KNOW **Vocabulary Preview**

blatantly	malicious	precarious
grimace	petulance	sully
incorrigible	poignant	surfeit
ingenuous		

Focus Your Reading

LITERARY ANALYSIS **CHARACTERS** **Characters** are the people—and sometimes animals or creatures—who take part in the action of a story or a novel. **Static** characters remain unchanged by their experiences as the story progresses, while **dynamic** characters change. As the plot of "Winter Dreams" unfolds, note whether or not the two main characters—Dexter Green and Judy Jones—mature and develop as individuals.

ACTIVE READING **EVALUATING CHARACTER** The characters introduced in the first section of this story are people you will have to **evaluate,** or make judgments about, as the plot unfolds. When the story begins, Dexter Green is a teenager and Judy Jones is an 11-year-old girl. As you read, decide what you like and what you dislike about them. Also, try to figure out why they act as they do. Pay particular attention to the dreams Dexter Green has for his life, forming your own opinions about his aspirations.

📖 **READER'S NOTEBOOK** To help you evaluate the characters, use the reading-strategy questions inserted throughout the selection. Write your responses in your notebook.

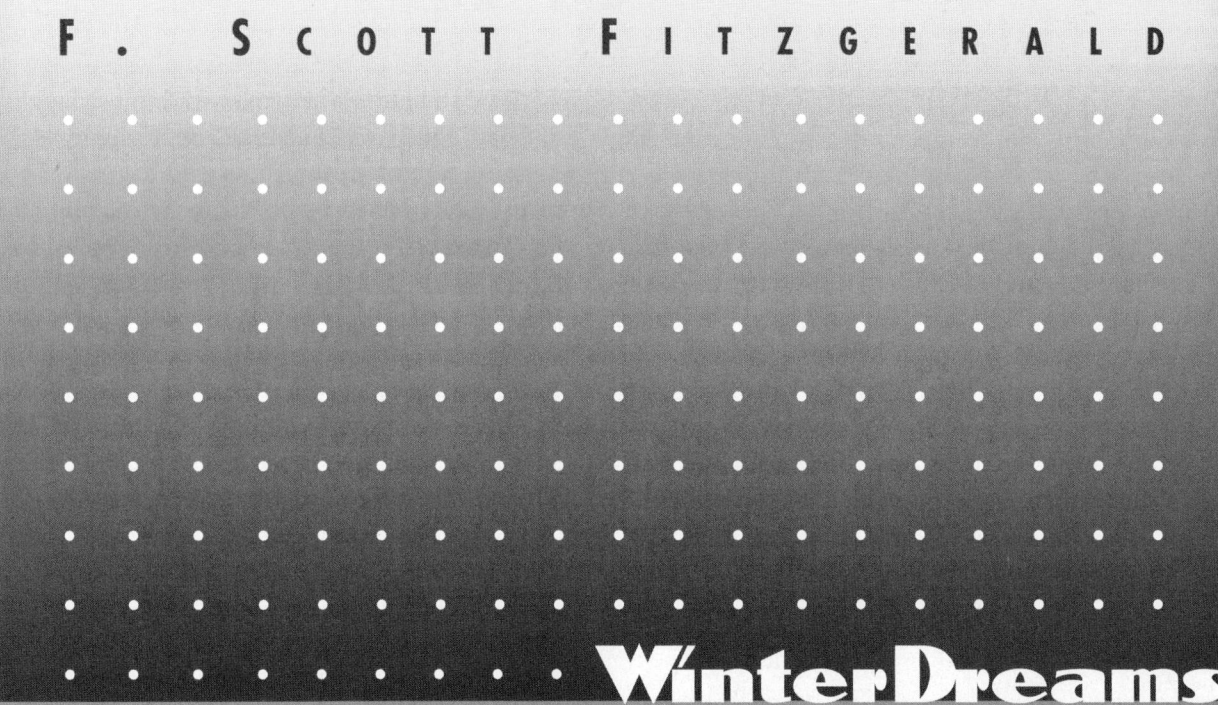

F. SCOTT FITZGERALD

WinterDreams

Some of the caddies were poor as sin and lived in one-room houses with a neurasthenic[1] cow in the front yard, but Dexter Green's father owned the second best grocery-store in Black Bear—the best one was "The Hub," patronized by the wealthy people from Sherry Island—and Dexter caddied only for pocket-money.

In the fall when the days became crisp and gray, and the long Minnesota winter shut down like the white lid of a box, Dexter's skis moved over the snow that hid the fairways of the golf course. At these times the country gave him a feeling of profound melancholy—it offended him that the links should lie in enforced fallowness,[2] haunted by ragged sparrows for the long season. It was dreary, too, that on the tees where the gay colors fluttered in summer there were now only the desolate sand-boxes knee-deep in crusted ice. When he crossed the hills the wind blew cold as misery, and if the sun was out he tramped with his eyes squinted up against the hard dimensionless glare.

In April the winter ceased abruptly. The snow ran down into Black Bear Lake scarcely tarrying for the early golfers to brave the season with red and black balls. Without elation, without an interval of moist glory, the cold was gone.

Dexter knew that there was something dismal about this Northern spring, just as he knew there was something gorgeous about the fall. Fall made him clinch his hands and tremble and repeat idiotic sentences to himself, and make brisk abrupt gestures of command to imaginary audiences and armies. October filled him with hope which November raised to a sort of ecstatic triumph, and in this mood the fleeting brilliant impressions of the summer at Sherry Island were ready grist to his mill.[3] He became a golf champion and defeated Mr. T. A. Hedrick in a marvelous match played a hundred times over the fairways of his imagination, a match each detail of which he changed about untiringly—

---

1. **neurasthenic** (nŏŏr´əs-thĕn´ĭk): weak and lacking in vigor.
2. **fallowness**: disuse.
3. **grist to his mill**: something that he could make good use of.

Illustration Copyright © 1995 Bart Forbes.

Sometimes he won

with almost

laughable ease,

sometimes he came

up magnificently

from behind.

sometimes he won with almost laughable ease, sometimes he came up magnificently from behind. Again, stepping from a Pierce-Arrow[4] automobile, like Mr. Mortimer Jones, he strolled frigidly into the lounge of the Sherry Island Golf Club—or perhaps, surrounded by an admiring crowd, he gave an exhibition of fancy diving from the spring-board of the club raft. . . . Among those who watched him in open-mouthed wonder was Mr. Mortimer Jones.

And one day it came to pass that Mr. Jones—himself and not his ghost—came up to Dexter with tears in his eyes and said that Dexter was the — — best caddy in the club, and wouldn't he decide not to quit if Mr. Jones made it worth his while, because every other — — caddy in the club lost one ball a hole for him— regularly—

"No, sir," said Dexter decisively, "I don't want to caddy any more." Then, after a pause, "I'm too old."

"You're not more than fourteen. Why the devil did you decide just this morning that you wanted to quit? You promised that next week you'd go over to the State tournament with me."

"I decided I was too old."

Dexter handed in his "A Class" badge, collected what money was due him from the caddy-master, and walked home to Black Bear Village.

"The best — — caddy I ever saw," shouted Mr. Mortimer Jones over a drink that afternoon. "Never lost a ball! Willing! Intelligent! Quiet! Honest! Grateful!"

---

4. **Pierce-Arrow:** a luxury automobile of the day.

The little girl who had done this was eleven—beautifully ugly as little girls are apt to be who are destined after a few years to be inexpressibly

ACTIVE READING

CLARIFY How does the little girl make Dexter quit?

lovely and bring no end of misery to a great number of men. The spark, however, was perceptible. There was a general ungodliness in the way her lips twisted down at the corners when she smiled, and in the—Heaven help us!—in the almost passionate quality of her eyes. Vitality is born early in such women. It was utterly in evidence now, shining through her thin frame in a sort of glow.

She had come eagerly out onto the course at nine o'clock with a white linen nurse and five small new golf-clubs in a white canvas bag which the nurse was carrying. When Dexter first saw her she was standing by the caddy house, rather ill at ease and trying to conceal the fact by engaging her nurse in an obviously unnatural conversation graced by startling and irrelevant grimaces from herself.

"Well, it's certainly a nice day, Hilda," Dexter heard her say. She drew down the corners of her mouth, smiled, and glanced furtively around, her eyes in transit falling for an instant on Dexter.

Then to the nurse:

"Well, I guess there aren't very many people out here this morning, are there?"

The smile again—radiant, blatantly artificial—convincing.

"I don't know what we're supposed to do now," said the nurse, looking nowhere in particular.

"Oh, that's all right. I'll fix it up."

Dexter stood perfectly still, his mouth slightly ajar. He knew that if he moved forward a step his stare would be in her line of vision—if he moved backward he would lose his full view of her face. For a moment he had not realized how young she was. Now he remembered having seen her several times the year before—in bloomers.[5]

Suddenly, involuntarily, he laughed, a short abrupt laugh—then, startled by himself, he turned and began to walk quickly away.

"Boy!"

Dexter stopped.

"Boy—"

Beyond question he was addressed. Not only that, but he was treated to that absurd smile, that preposterous smile—the memory of which at least a dozen men were to carry into middle age.

"Boy, do you know where the golf teacher is?"

"He's giving a lesson."

"Well, do you know where the caddy-master is?"

"He isn't here yet this morning."

"Oh." For a moment this baffled her. She stood alternately on her right and left foot.

"We'd like to get a caddy," said the nurse. "Mrs. Mortimer Jones sent us out to play golf, and we don't know how without we get a caddy."

Here she was stopped by an ominous glance from Miss Jones, followed immediately by the smile.

"There aren't any caddies here except me," said Dexter to the nurse, "and I got to stay here in charge until the caddy-master gets here."

"Oh."

Miss Jones and her retinue[6] now withdrew, and at a proper distance from Dexter became involved in a heated conversation, which was concluded by Miss Jones taking one of the clubs and hitting it on the ground with violence. For further emphasis she raised it again and was about to bring it down smartly upon the nurse's bosom, when the nurse seized the club and twisted it from her hands.

---

5. **bloomers:** baggy pants that end just below the knee, formerly worn by young girls.

6. **retinue** (rĕt'n-o͞o'): a group of attendants or followers; entourage.

WORDS TO KNOW

grimace (grĭm'ĭs) *n.* a twisting or distortion of the face

blatantly (blāt'nt-lē) *adv.* in an extremely obvious way; conspicuously

"You damn little mean old *thing!*" cried Miss Jones wildly.

Another argument ensued. Realizing that the elements of comedy were implied in the scene, Dexter several times began to laugh, but each time restrained the laugh before it reached audibility. He could not resist the monstrous conviction that the little girl was justified in beating the nurse.

The situation was resolved by the fortuitous appearance of the caddy-master, who was appealed to immediately by the nurse.

"Miss Jones is to have a little caddy, and this one says he can't go."

"Mr. McKenna said I was to wait here till you came," said Dexter quickly.

"Well, he's here now." Miss Jones smiled cheerfully at the caddy-master. Then she dropped her bag and set off at a haughty mince[7] toward the first tee.

"Well?" The caddy-master turned to Dexter. "What you standing there like a dummy for? Go pick up the young lady's clubs."

"I don't think I'll go out today," said Dexter.

"You don't—"

"I think I'll quit."

The enormity of his decision frightened him. He was a favorite caddy, and the thirty dollars a month he earned through the summer were not to be made elsewhere around the lake. But he had received a strong emotional shock, and his perturbation required a violent and immediate outlet.

It is not so simple as that, either. As so frequently would be the case in the future, Dexter was unconsciously dictated to by his winter dreams.

Now, of course, the quality and the seasonability of these winter dreams varied, but the stuff of them remained. They persuaded Dexter several years later to pass up a business course at the State university—his father, prospering now, would have paid his way—for the precarious advantage of attending an older and more famous university in the East, where he was bothered by his scanty funds. But do not get the impression, because his winter dreams happened to be concerned at first with musings on the rich, that there was anything merely snobbish in the boy. He wanted not association with glittering things and glittering people—he wanted the glittering things themselves. Often he reached out for the best without knowing why he wanted it—and sometimes he ran up against the mysterious denials and prohibitions in which life indulges. It is with one of those denials and not with his career as a whole that this story deals.

He made money. It was rather amazing. After college he went to the city from which Black Bear Lake draws its wealthy patrons. When he was only twenty-three and had been there not quite two years, there were already people who liked to say: "Now *there's* a boy—" All about him rich men's sons were peddling bonds precariously, or investing patrimonies[8] precariously, or plodding through the two dozen volumes of the "George Washington Commercial Course," but Dexter borrowed a thousand dollars on his college degree and his confident mouth, and bought a partnership in a laundry.

It was a small laundry when he went into it but Dexter made a specialty of learning how the

---

7. **mince:** an artificial, dainty way of walking with short steps.

8. **patrimonies:** estates or money inherited from ancestors.

Illustration by Todd Leonardo.

English washed fine woolen golf-stockings without shrinking them, and within a year he was catering to the trade that wore knickerbockers.[9] Men were insisting that their Shetland hose and sweaters go to his laundry just as they had insisted on a caddy who could find golf-balls. A little later he was doing their wives' lingerie as well—and running five branches in different parts of the city. Before he was twenty-seven he owned the largest string of laundries in his section of the country. It was then that he sold out and went to New York. But the part of his story that concerns us goes back to the days when he was making his first big success.

When he was twenty-three Mr. Hart—one of the gray-haired men who liked to say "Now there's a boy"—gave him a guest card to the Sherry Island Golf Club for a weekend. So he signed his name one day on the register, and that afternoon played golf in a foursome with Mr. Hart and Mr. Sandwood and Mr. T. A. Hedrick. He did not consider it necessary to remark that he had once carried Mr. Hart's bag over this same links, and that he knew every trap and gully with his eyes shut—but he found himself glancing at the four caddies who trailed them, trying to catch a gleam or gesture that would remind him of himself, that would lessen the gap which lay between his present and his past.

It was a curious day, slashed abruptly with fleeting, familiar impressions. One minute he had the sense of being a trespasser—in the next he was impressed by the tremendous superiority he felt toward Mr. T. A. Hedrick, who was a bore and not even a good golfer any more.

Then, because of a ball Mr. Hart lost near the fifteenth green, an enormous thing happened. While they were searching the stiff grasses of the rough there was a clear call of "Fore!" from behind a hill in their rear. And as they all turned abruptly from their search a bright new ball sliced abruptly over the hill and caught Mr. T. A. Hedrick in the abdomen.

"By Gad!" cried Mr. T. A. Hedrick, "they ought to put some of these crazy women off the course. It's getting to be outrageous."

A head and a voice came up together over the hill:

"Do you mind if we go through?"

"You hit me in the stomach!" declared Mr. Hedrick wildly.

"Did I?" The girl approached the group of men. "I'm sorry. I yelled 'Fore!'"

Her glance fell casually on each of the men—then scanned the fairway for her ball.

"Did I bounce into the rough?"

It was impossible to determine whether this question was <u>ingenuous</u> or <u>malicious</u>. In a moment, however, she left no doubt, for as her partner came up over the hill she called cheerfully:

"Here I am! I'd have gone on the green except that I hit something."

As she took her stance for a short mashie[10] shot, Dexter looked at her closely. She wore a blue gingham dress, rimmed at throat and shoulders with a white edging that accentuated her tan. The quality of exaggeration, of thinness, which had made her passionate eyes and down-turning mouth absurd at eleven, was gone now. She was arrestingly beautiful. The color in her cheeks was centered like the color in a picture—it was not a "high" color, but a sort of fluctuating and feverish warmth, so shaded that it seemed at any moment it would recede and disappear. This color and the mobility of her mouth gave a continual impression of flux,[11] of intense life, of passionate vitality—balanced only partially by the sad luxury of her eyes.

---

9. **knickerbockers:** loose pants that end in a gathering just below the knee and are worn with long socks—formerly popular as golf wear.

10. **mashie:** an old name for the golf club now known as a five iron.

11. **flux:** change.

846

She swung her mashie impatiently and without interest, pitching the ball into a sand-pit on the other side of the green. With a quick, insincere smile and a careless "Thank you!" she went on after it.

"That Judy Jones!" remarked Mr. Hedrick on the next tee, as they waited—some moments—for her to play on ahead. "All she needs is to be turned up and spanked for six months and then to be married off to an old-fashioned cavalry captain."

"My God, she's good-looking!" said Mr. Sandwood, who was just over thirty.

"Good-looking!" cried Mr. Hedrick contemptuously, "she always looks as if she wanted to be kissed! Turning those big cow-eyes on every calf in town!"

It was doubtful if Mr. Hedrick intended a reference to the maternal instinct.

"She'd play pretty good golf if she'd try," said Mr. Sandwood.

ACTIVE READING

EVALUATE What is your opinion of Judy Jones?

"She has no form," said Mr. Hedrick solemnly.

"She has a nice figure," said Mr. Sandwood.

"Better thank the Lord she doesn't drive a swifter ball," said Mr. Hart, winking at Dexter.

Later in the afternoon the sun went down with a riotous swirl of gold and varying blues and scarlets, and left the dry, rustling night of Western summer. Dexter watched from the veranda of the Golf Club, watched the even overlap of the waters in the little wind, silver molasses under the harvest-moon. Then the moon held a finger to her lips and the lake became a clear pool, pale and quiet. Dexter put on his bathing-suit and swam out to the farthest raft, where he stretched dripping on the wet canvas of the springboard.

There was a fish jumping and a star shining and the lights around the lake were gleaming. Over on a dark peninsula a piano was playing the songs of last summer and of summers before that—songs from "Chin-Chin" and "The Count of Luxemburg" and "The Chocolate Soldier"[12]— and because the sound of a piano over a stretch of water had always seemed beautiful to Dexter he lay perfectly quiet and listened.

The tune the piano was playing at that moment had been gay and new five years before when Dexter was a sophomore at college. They had played it at a prom once when he could not afford the luxury of proms, and he had stood outside the gymnasium and listened. The sound of the tune precipitated in him a sort of ecstasy and it was with that ecstasy he viewed what happened to him now. It was a mood of intense appreciation, a sense that, for once, he was magnificently attuned to life and that everything about him was radiating a brightness and a glamour he might never know again.

A low, pale oblong detached itself suddenly from the darkness of the Island, spitting forth the reverberated sound of a racing motor-boat. Two white streamers of cleft water rolled themselves out behind it and almost immediately the boat was beside him, drowning out the hot tinkle of the piano in the drone of its spray. Dexter raising himself on his arms was aware of a figure standing at the wheel, of two dark eyes regarding him over the lengthening space of water—then the boat had gone by and was sweeping in an immense and purposeless circle of spray round and round in the middle of the lake. With equal eccentricity one of the circles flattened out and headed back toward the raft.

"Who's that?" she called, shutting off her motor. She was so near now that Dexter could see her bathing-suit, which consisted apparently of pink rompers.[13]

The nose of the boat bumped the raft, and as the latter tilted rakishly he was precipitated toward her. With different degrees of interest they recognized each other.

---

12. "Chin-Chin" . . . "The Chocolate Soldier": three popular Broadway musicals, first performed in 1914, 1912, and 1909 respectively.

13. rompers: a loose-fitting one-piece garment with bloomerlike pants.

"Aren't you one of those men we played through this afternoon?" she demanded.

He was.

"Well, do you know how to drive a motor-boat? Because if you do I wish you'd drive this one so I can ride on the surf-board behind. My name is Judy Jones"—she favored him with an absurd smirk—rather, what tried to be a smirk, for, twist her mouth as she might, it was not grotesque, it was merely beautiful—"and I live in a house over there on the Island, and in that house there is a man waiting for me. When he drove up at the door I drove out of the dock because he says I'm his ideal."

There was a fish jumping and a star shining and the lights around the lake were gleaming. Dexter sat beside Judy Jones and she explained how her boat was driven. Then she was in the water, swimming to the floating surf-board with a sinuous crawl. Watching her was without effort to the eye, watching a branch waving or a sea-gull flying. Her arms, burned to butternut, moved sinuously among the dull platinum ripples, elbow appearing first, casting the forearm back with a cadence of falling water, then reaching out and down, stabbing a path ahead.

They moved out into the lake; turning, Dexter saw that she was kneeling on the low rear of the now uptilted surf-board.

"Go faster," she called, "fast as it'll go."

Obediently he jammed the lever forward and the white spray mounted at the bow. When he looked around again the girl was standing up on the rushing board, her arms spread wide, her eyes lifted toward the moon.

"It's awful cold," she shouted. "What's your name?"

He told her.

"Well, why don't you come to dinner tomorrow night?"

His heart turned over like the fly-wheel of the boat, and, for the second time, her casual whim gave a new direction to his life.

3

Next evening while he waited for her to come downstairs, Dexter peopled the soft deep summer room and the sun-porch that opened from it with the men who had already loved Judy Jones. He knew the sort of men they were—the men who when he first went to college had entered from the great prep schools with graceful clothes and the deep tan of healthy summers. He had seen that, in one sense, he was better than these men. He was newer and stronger. Yet in acknowledging to himself that he wished his children to be like them he was admitting that he was but the rough, strong stuff from which they eternally sprang.

When the time had come for him to wear good clothes, he had known who were the best tailors in America, and the best tailors in America had made him the suit he wore this evening. He had acquired that particular reserve peculiar to his university, that set it off from other universities. He recognized the value to him of such a mannerism and he had adopted it; he knew that to be careless in dress and manner required more confidence than to be careful. But carelessness was for his children. His mother's name had been Krimslich. She was a Bohemian of the peasant class and she had talked broken English to the end of her days. Her son must keep to the set patterns.

At a little after seven Judy Jones came downstairs. She wore a blue silk afternoon dress, and he was disappointed at first that she had not put on something more elaborate. This feeling was accentuated when, after a brief greeting, she went to the door of a butler's pantry and pushing it open called: "You can serve dinner, Martha." He had rather expected that a butler would announce dinner, that there would be a cocktail. Then he put these thoughts behind him as they sat down side by side on a lounge and looked at each other.

"Father and mother won't be here," she said thoughtfully.

He remembered the last time he had seen her father, and he was glad the parents were not to be here tonight—they might wonder who he was. He had been born in Keeble, a Minnesota village fifty miles farther north, and he always gave Keeble as his home instead of Black Bear Village. Country towns were well enough to come from if they weren't inconveniently in sight and used as footstools by fashionable lakes.

They talked of his university, which she had visited frequently during the past two years, and of the near-by city which supplied Sherry Island with its patrons, and whither Dexter would return next day to his prospering laundries.

During dinner she slipped into a moody depression which gave Dexter a feeling of uneasiness. Whatever <u>petulance</u> she uttered in her throaty voice worried him. Whatever she smiled at—at him, at a chicken liver, at nothing—it disturbed him that her smile could have no root in mirth, or even in amusement. When the scarlet corners of her lips curved down, it was less a smile than an invitation to a kiss.

Then, after dinner, she led him out on the dark sun-porch and deliberately changed the atmosphere.

"Do you mind if I weep a little?" she said.

"I'm afraid I'm boring you," he responded quickly.

"You're not. I like you. But I've just had a terrible afternoon. There was a man I cared about, and this afternoon he told me out of a clear sky that he was poor as a church-mouse. He'd never even hinted it before. Does this sound horribly mundane?"

"Perhaps he was afraid to tell you."

"Suppose he was," she answered. "He didn't start right. You see, if I'd thought of him as poor—well, I've been mad about loads of poor men, and fully intended to marry them all. But in this case, I hadn't thought of him that way, and my interest in him wasn't strong enough to survive the shock. As if a girl calmly informed her fiancé that she was a widow. He might not object to widows, but—

"Let's start right," she interrupted herself suddenly. "Who are you, anyhow?"

For a moment Dexter hesitated. Then:

"I'm nobody," he announced. "My career is largely a matter of futures."

"Are you poor?"

"No," he said frankly, "I'm probably making more money than any man my age in the Northwest. I know that's an obnoxious remark, but you advised me to start right."

There was a pause. Then she smiled and the corners of her mouth drooped and an almost imperceptible sway brought her closer to him, looking up into his eyes. A lump rose in Dexter's throat, and he waited breathless for the experiment, facing the unpredictable compound that would form mysteriously from the elements of their lips. Then he saw—she communicated her excitement to him, lavishly, deeply, with kisses that were not a promise but a fulfillment. They aroused in him not hunger demanding renewal but <u>surfeit</u> that would demand more surfeit . . . kisses that were like charity, creating want by holding back nothing at all.

It did not take him many hours to decide that he had wanted Judy Jones ever since he was a proud, desirous little boy.

It began like that—and continued, with varying shades of intensity, on such a note right up to the dénouement.[14] Dexter surrendered a part of himself to the most direct and unprincipled personality with which he had ever come in contact. Whatever Judy wanted, she went after with the full pressure of her charm. There was no divergence of method, no jockeying for position or premeditation of effects—there was a very little mental side to any of her affairs. She simply made men conscious to the highest degree of her physical loveliness. Dexter had no desire to change her. Her deficiencies were knit up with a passionate energy that transcended and justified them.

When, as Judy's head lay against his shoulder that first night, she whispered, "I don't know what's the matter with me. Last night I thought I was in love with a man and tonight I think I'm in love with you—"—it seemed to him a beautiful and romantic thing to say. It was the exquisite excitability that for the moment he controlled and owned. But a week later he was compelled to view this same quality in a different light. She took him in her roadster[15] to a picnic supper, and after supper she disappeared, likewise in her roadster, with another man. Dexter became enormously upset and was scarcely able to be decently civil to the other people present. When she assured him that she had not kissed the other man, he knew she was lying—yet he was glad that she had taken the trouble to lie to him.

He was, as he found before the summer ended, one of a varying dozen who circulated about her. Each of them had at one time been favored above all others—about half of them still basked in the solace of occasional sentimental revivals. Whenever one showed signs of dropping out through long neglect, she granted him a brief honeyed hour, which encouraged him to tag along for a year or so longer. Judy made these forays[16] upon the helpless and defeated without malice, indeed half unconscious that there was anything mischievous in what she did.

When a new man came to town every one dropped out—dates were automatically canceled.

The helpless part of trying to do anything about it was that she did it all herself. She was not a girl who could be "won" in the kinetic[17] sense—she was proof against cleverness, she was proof against charm; if any of these assailed her too strongly she would immediately resolve the affair to a physical basis, and under the magic of her physical splendor the strong as well as the brilliant played her game and not their own. She was entertained only by the gratification of her desires and by the direct exercise of her own charm. Perhaps from so much youthful love, so many youthful lovers, she had come, in self-defense, to nourish herself wholly from within.

Succeeding Dexter's first exhilaration came restlessness and dissatisfaction. The helpless ecstasy of losing himself in her was opiate rather than tonic.[18] It was fortunate for his work during the winter that those moments of ecstasy came infrequently. Early in their acquaintance it had seemed for a while that there was a deep and spontaneous mutual attraction—that first August, for example—three days of long evenings on her dusky veranda, of strange wan[19] kisses through the late afternoon, in shadowy alcoves or behind the protecting trellises of the garden arbors, of mornings when she was fresh as a dream and almost shy at meeting him in the clarity of the rising day. There was all the ecstasy of an engagement about it, sharpened by his realization that there was no engagement. It was

---

14. **dénouement** (dā´nōō-mäN´): the resolution of the conflicts in a story's plot; a final outcome.
15. **roadster:** a sporty, two-seat open automobile.
16. **forays:** sudden attacks or raids.
17. **kinetic:** involving action.
18. **opiate . . . tonic:** deadening rather than stimulating.
19. **wan** (wŏn): weary or melancholy.

during those three days that, for the first time, he had asked her to marry him. She said "maybe some day," she said "kiss me," she said "I'd like to marry you," she said "I love you"—she said—nothing.

The three days were interrupted by the arrival of a New York man who visited at her house for half September. To Dexter's agony, rumor engaged them. The man was the son of the president of a great trust company. But at the end of a month it was reported that Judy was yawning. At a dance one night she sat all evening in a motor-boat with a local beau, while the New Yorker searched the club for her frantically. She told the local beau that she was bored with her visitor, and two days later he left. She was seen with him at the station, and it was reported that he looked very mournful indeed.

ACTIVE READING

CONNECT Do you know anyone like Judy? What motivates her behavior?

On this note the summer ended. Dexter was twenty-four, and he found himself increasingly in a position to do as he wished. He joined two clubs in the city and lived at one of them. Though he was by no means an integral part of the stag-lines at these clubs, he managed to be on hand at dances where Judy Jones was likely to appear. He could have gone out socially as much as he liked—he was an eligible young man, now, and popular with downtown fathers. His confessed devotion to Judy Jones had rather solidified his position. But he had no social aspirations and rather despised the dancing men who were always on tap for the Thursday or Saturday parties and who filled in at dinners with the younger married set. Already he was playing with the idea of going East to New York. He wanted to take Judy Jones with him. No disillusion as to the world in which she had grown up could cure his illusion as to her desirability.

Remember that—for only in the light of it can what he did for her be understood.

Eighteen months after he first met Judy Jones he became engaged to another girl. Her name was Irene Scheerer, and her father was one of the men who had always believed in Dexter. Irene was light-haired and sweet and honorable, and a little stout, and she had two suitors whom she pleasantly relinquished when Dexter formally asked her to marry him.

Summer, fall, winter, spring, another summer, another fall—so much he had given of his active life to the incorrigible lips of Judy Jones. She had treated him with interest, with encouragement, with malice, with indifference, with contempt. She had inflicted on him the innumerable little slights and indignities possible in such a case—as if in revenge for having ever cared for him at all. She had beckoned him and yawned at him and beckoned him again and he had responded often with bitterness and narrowed eyes. She had brought him ecstatic happiness and intolerable agony of spirit. She had caused him untold inconvenience and not a little trouble. She had insulted him, and she had ridden over him, and she had played his interest in her against his interest in his work—for fun. She had done everything to him except to criticize him—this she had not done—it seemed to him only because it might have sullied the utter indifference she manifested and sincerely felt toward him.

When autumn had come and gone again it occurred to him that he could not have Judy Jones. He had to beat this into his mind but he convinced himself at last. He lay awake at night for a while and argued it over. He told himself the trouble and the pain she had caused him, he enumerated her glaring deficiencies as a wife. Then he said to himself that he loved her, and after a while he fell asleep. For a week, lest he

---

WORDS TO KNOW   **incorrigible** (ĭn-kôr′ĭ-jə-bəl) *adj.* impossible to correct or reform; uncontrollable
sully (sŭl′ē) *v.* to spoil; tarnish

imagine her husky voice over the telephone or her eyes opposite him at lunch, he worked hard and late, and at night he went to his office and plotted out his years.

At the end of a week he went to a dance and cut in on her once. For almost the first time since they had met he did not ask her to sit out with him or tell her that she was lovely. It hurt him that she did not miss these things—that was all. He was not jealous when he saw that there was a new man tonight. He had been hardened against jealousy long before.

He stayed late at the dance. He sat for an hour with Irene Scheerer and talked about books and about music. He knew very little about either. But he was beginning to be master of his own time now, and he had a rather priggish[20] notion that he—the young and already fabulously successful Dexter Green—should know more about such things.

That was in October, when he was twenty-five. In January, Dexter and Irene became engaged. It was to be announced in June, and they were to be married three months later.

ACTIVE READING

EVALUATE Do you approve of Dexter's decision to marry Irene?

The Minnesota winter prolonged itself interminably, and it was almost May when the winds came soft and the snow ran down into Black Bear Lake at last. For the first time in over a year Dexter was enjoying a certain tranquillity of spirit. Judy Jones had been in Florida, and afterward in Hot Springs, and somewhere she had been engaged, and somewhere she had broken it off. At first, when Dexter had definitely given her up, it had made him sad that people still linked them together and asked for news of her, but when he began to be placed at dinner next to Irene Scheerer people didn't ask him about her any more—they told him about her. He ceased to be an authority on her.

May at last. Dexter walked the streets at night when the darkness was damp as rain, wondering that so soon, with so little done, so much of ecstasy had gone from him. May one year back had been marked by Judy's poignant, unforgivable, yet forgiven turbulence—it had been one of those rare times when he fancied she had grown to care for him. That old penny's worth of happiness he had spent for this bushel of content. He knew that Irene would be no more than a curtain spread behind him, a hand moving among gleaming tea-cups, a voice calling to children . . . fire and loveliness were gone, the magic of nights and the wonder of the varying hours and seasons . . . slender lips, downturning, dropping to his lips and bearing him up into a heaven of eyes. . . . The thing was deep in him. He was too strong and alive for it to die lightly.

In the middle of May when the weather balanced for a few days on the thin bridge that led to deep summer he turned in one night at Irene's house. Their engagement was to be announced in a week now—no one would be surprised at it. And tonight they would sit together on the lounge at the University Club and look on for an hour at the dancers. It gave him a sense of solidity to go with her—she was so sturdily popular, so intensely "great."

He mounted the steps of the brownstone house and stepped inside.

"Irene," he called.

Mrs. Scheerer came out of the living-room to meet him.

"Dexter," she said, "Irene's gone upstairs with a splitting headache. She wanted to go with you but I made her go to bed."

"Nothing serious, I—"

"Oh, no. She's going to play golf with you in the morning. You can spare her for just one night, can't you, Dexter?"

---

20. **priggish:** smug; conceited.

Autoportrait (about 1925), Tamara de Lempicka. Oil on wood, 35 × 26 cm, private collection. Copyright © SPADEM/Kizette de Lempicka Foxhall.

Her smile was kind. She and Dexter liked each other. In the living-room he talked for a moment before he said good night.

Returning to the University Club, where he had rooms, he stood in the doorway for a moment and watched the dancers. He leaned against the door-post, nodded at a man or two—yawned.

"Hello, darling."

The familiar voice at his elbow startled him. Judy Jones had left a man and crossed the room to him—Judy Jones, a slender enameled doll in cloth of gold: gold in a band at her head, gold in two slipper points at her dress's hem. The fragile glow of her face seemed to blossom as she smiled at him. A breeze of warmth and light blew through the room. His hands in the pockets of his dinner-jacket tightened spasmodically. He was filled with a sudden excitement.

"When did you get back?" he asked casually.

"Come here and I'll tell you about it."

She turned and he followed her. She had been away—he could have wept at the wonder of her return. She had passed through enchanted streets, doing things that were like provocative music. All mysterious happenings, all fresh and quickening hopes, had gone away with her, come back with her now.

She turned in the doorway.

"Have you a car here? If you haven't, I have."

"I have a coupé."

In then, with a rustle of golden cloth. He slammed the door. Into so many cars she had stepped—like this—like that—her back against the leather, so-—her elbow resting on the door—waiting. She would have been soiled long since had there been anything to soil her—except herself—but this was her own self-outpouring.

With an effort he forced himself to start the car and back into the street. This was nothing, he must remember. She had done this before, and he had put her behind him, as he would have crossed a bad account from his books.

He drove slowly downtown and, affecting abstraction,[21] traversed the deserted streets of the business section, peopled here and there where a movie was giving out its crowd or where consumptive or pugilistic[22] youth lounged in front of pool halls. The clink of glasses and the slap of hands on the bars issued from saloons, cloisters[23] of glazed glass and dirty yellow light.

She was watching him closely and the silence was embarrassing, yet in this crisis he could find no casual word with which to profane the hour. At a convenient turning he began to zigzag back toward the University Club.

"Have you missed me?" she asked suddenly.

"Everybody missed you."

He wondered if she knew of Irene Scheerer. She had been back only a day—her absence had been almost contemporaneous with his engagement.

"What a remark!" Judy laughed sadly—without sadness. She looked at him searchingly. He became absorbed in the dashboard.

A perfect wave of emotion washed over him, carrying off with it a sediment of wisdom, of convention, of doubt, of honor.

▼

---

21. **affecting abstraction:** pretending to be lost in thought.

22. **consumptive or pugilistic** (pyoō′jə-lĭs′tĭk): sickly or aggressive.

23. **cloisters:** places of religious retreat, such as convents and monasteries (here used metaphorically to refer to places of escape from life's problems).

"You're handsomer than you used to be," she said thoughtfully. "Dexter, you have the most rememberable eyes."

He could have laughed at this, but he did not laugh. It was the sort of thing that was said to sophomores. Yet it stabbed at him.

"I'm awfully tired of everything, darling." She called every one darling, endowing the endearment with careless, individual camaraderie. "I wish you'd marry me."

The directness of this confused him. He should have told her now that he was going to marry another girl, but he could not tell her. He could as easily have sworn that he had never loved her.

"I think we'd get along," she continued, on the same note, "unless probably you've forgotten me and fallen in love with another girl."

Her confidence was obviously enormous. She had said, in effect, that she found such a thing impossible to believe, that if it were true he had merely committed a childish indiscretion—and probably to show off. She would forgive him, because it was not a matter of any moment but rather something to be brushed aside lightly.

"Of course you could never love anybody but me," she continued, "I like the way you love me. Oh, Dexter, have you forgotten last year?"

"No, I haven't forgotten."

"Neither have I!"

Was she sincerely moved—or was she carried along by the wave of her own acting?

"I wish we could be like that again," she said, and he forced himself to answer:

"I don't think we can."

"I suppose not. . . . I hear you're giving Irene Scheerer a violent rush."

There was not the faintest emphasis on the name, yet Dexter was suddenly ashamed.

"Oh, take me home," cried Judy suddenly; "I don't want to go back to that idiotic dance—with those children."

Then, as he turned up the street that led to the residence district, Judy began to cry quietly to herself. He had never seen her cry before.

The dark street lightened, the dwellings of the rich loomed up around them, he stopped his coupé in front of the great white bulk of the Mortimer Joneses' house, somnolent, gorgeous, drenched with the splendor of the damp moonlight. Its solidity startled him. The strong walls, the steel of the girders, the breadth and beam and pomp of it were there only to bring out the contrast with the young beauty beside him. It was sturdy to accentuate her slightness—as if to show what a breeze could be generated by a butterfly's wing.

He sat perfectly quiet, his nerves in wild clamor, afraid that if he moved he would find her irresistibly in his arms. Two tears had rolled down her wet face and trembled on her upper lip.

"I'm more beautiful than anybody else," she said brokenly, "why can't I be happy?" Her moist eyes tore at his stability—her mouth turned slowly downward with an exquisite sadness: "I'd like to marry you if you'll have me, Dexter. I suppose you think I'm not worth having, but I'll be so beautiful for you, Dexter."

ACTIVE READING

EVALUATE How sincere does Judy seem?

A million phrases of anger, pride, passion, hatred, tenderness fought on his lips. Then a perfect wave of emotion washed over him, carrying off with it a sediment of wisdom, of convention, of doubt, of honor. This was his girl who was speaking, his own, his beautiful, his pride.

"Won't you come in?" He heard her draw in her breath sharply.

Waiting.

"All right," his voice was trembling, "I'll come in."

It was strange that neither when it was over nor a long time afterward did he regret that night. Looking at it from the perspective of ten years, the fact that Judy's flare for him endured just one month seemed of little importance. Nor did it matter that by his yielding he subjected himself to a deeper agony in the end and gave serious hurt to Irene Scheerer and to Irene's parents, who had befriended him. There was nothing sufficiently pictorial about Irene's grief to stamp itself on his mind.

Dexter was at bottom hard-minded. The attitude of the city on his action was of no importance to him, not because he was going to leave the city, but because any outside attitude on the situation seemed superficial. He was completely indifferent to popular opinion. Nor, when he had seen that it was no use, that he did not possess in himself the power to move fundamentally or to hold Judy Jones, did he bear any malice toward her. He loved her, and he would love her until the day he was too old for loving—but he could not have her. So he tasted the deep pain that is reserved only for the strong, just as he had tasted for a little while the deep happiness.

Even the ultimate falsity of the grounds upon which Judy terminated the engagement—that she did not want to "take him away" from Irene—Judy, who had wanted nothing else—did not revolt him. He was beyond any revulsion or any amusement.

ACTIVE READING

EVALUATE What do you think of Dexter's response to Judy's betrayal?

He went East in February with the intention of selling out his laundries and settling in New York—but the war came to America in March and changed his plans. He returned to the West, handed over the management of the business to his partner, and went into the first officers' training-camp in late April. He was one of those young thousands who greeted the war with a certain amount of relief, welcoming the liberation from webs of tangled emotion.

Illustration by Joseph Lyendecker. Courtesy of Cluett, Peabody & Co., Inc.

He tasted the deep pain

that is reserved

only for the strong,

just as he had tasted

for a little while

the deep happiness.

6

This story is not his biography, remember, although things creep into it which have nothing to do with those dreams he had when he was young. We are almost done with them and with him now. There is only one more incident to be related here, and it happens seven years farther on.

It took place in New York, where he had done well—so well that there were no barriers too high for him. He was thirty-two years old, and, except for one flying trip immediately after the war, he had not been West in seven years. A man named Devlin from Detroit came into his office to see him in a business way, and then and there this incident occurred, and closed out, so to speak, this particular side of his life.

"So you're from the Middle West," said the man Devlin with careless curiosity. "That's funny—I thought men like you were probably born and raised on Wall Street. You know—wife of one of my best friends in Detroit came from your city. I was an usher at the wedding."

Dexter waited with no apprehension of what was coming.

"Judy Simms," said Devlin with no particular interest; "Judy Jones she was once."

"Yes, I knew her." A dull impatience spread over him. He had heard, of course, that she was married—perhaps deliberately he had heard no more.

"Awfully nice girl," brooded Devlin meaninglessly, "I'm sort of sorry for her."

"Why?" Something in Dexter was alert, receptive, at once.

"Oh, Lud Simms has gone to pieces in a way. I don't mean he ill-uses her, but he drinks and runs around—"

"Doesn't she run around?"

"No. Stays at home with her kids."

"Oh."

"She's a little too old for him," said Devlin.

"Too old!" cried Dexter. "Why, man, she's only twenty-seven."

He was possessed with a wild notion of rushing out into the streets and taking a train to Detroit. He rose to his feet spasmodically.

"I guess you're busy," Devlin apologized quickly. "I didn't realize—"

"No, I'm not busy," said Dexter, steadying his voice. "I'm not busy at all. Not busy at all. Did you say she was—twenty-seven? No, I said she was twenty-seven."

"Yes, you did," agreed Devlin dryly.

"Go on, then. Go on."

"What do you mean?"

"About Judy Jones."

Devlin looked at him helplessly.

"Well, that's—I told you all there is to it. He treats her like the devil. Oh, they're not going to get divorced or anything. When he's particularly outrageous she forgives him. In fact, I'm inclined to think she loves him. She was a pretty girl when she first came to Detroit."

A pretty girl! The phrase struck Dexter as ludicrous.

"Isn't she—a pretty girl, any more?"

"Oh, she's all right."

"Look here," said Dexter, sitting down suddenly. "I don't understand. You say she was a 'pretty girl' and now you say she's 'all right.' I don't understand what you mean—Judy Jones wasn't a pretty girl, at all. She was a great beauty. Why, I knew her, I knew her. She was—"

Devlin laughed pleasantly.

"I'm not trying to start a row,[24]" he said. "I think Judy's a nice girl and I like her. I can't understand how a man like Lud Simms could fall madly in love with her, but he did." Then he added: "Most of the women like her."

ACTIVE READING

QUESTION Why do you think Judy married Lud Simms?

Dexter looked closely at Devlin, thinking wildly that there must be a reason for this, some insensitivity in the man or some private malice.

---

24. **row** (rou): a noisy argument or dispute.

"Lots of women fade just like *that*," Devlin snapped his fingers. "You must have seen it happen. Perhaps I've forgotten how pretty she was at her wedding. I've seen her so much since then, you see. She has nice eyes."

A sort of dullness settled down upon Dexter. For the first time in his life he felt like getting very drunk. He knew that he was laughing loudly at something Devlin had said, but he did not know what it was or why it was funny. When, in a few minutes, Devlin went he lay down on his lounge and looked out the window at the New York sky-line into which the sun was sinking in dull lovely shades of pink and gold.

He had thought that having nothing else to lose he was invulnerable at last—but he knew that he had just lost something more, as surely as if he had married Judy Jones and seen her fade away before his eyes.

The dream was gone. Something had been taken from him. In a sort of panic he pushed the palms of his hands into his eyes and tried to bring up a picture of the waters lapping on Sherry Island and the moonlit veranda, and gingham on the golf-links and the dry sun and the gold color

of her neck's soft down. And her mouth damp to his kisses and her eyes plaintive with melancholy and her freshness like new fine linen in the morning. Why, these things were no longer in the world! They had existed and they existed no longer.

For the first time in years the tears were streaming down his face. But they were for himself now. He did not care about mouth and eyes and moving hands. He wanted to care, and he could not care. For he had gone away and he could never go back any more. The gates were closed, the sun was gone down, and there was no beauty but the gray beauty of steel that withstands all time. Even the grief he could have borne was left behind in the country of illusion, of youth, of the richness of life, where his winter dreams had flourished.

ACTIVE READING

CLARIFY What makes Dexter so sad?

"Long ago," he said, "long ago, there was something in me, but now that thing is gone. Now that thing is gone, that thing is gone. I cannot cry. I cannot care. That thing will come back no more." ❖

The gates were closed,

the sun was gone down,

and there was no beauty

but the **gray beauty** of **steel**

that withstands all time.

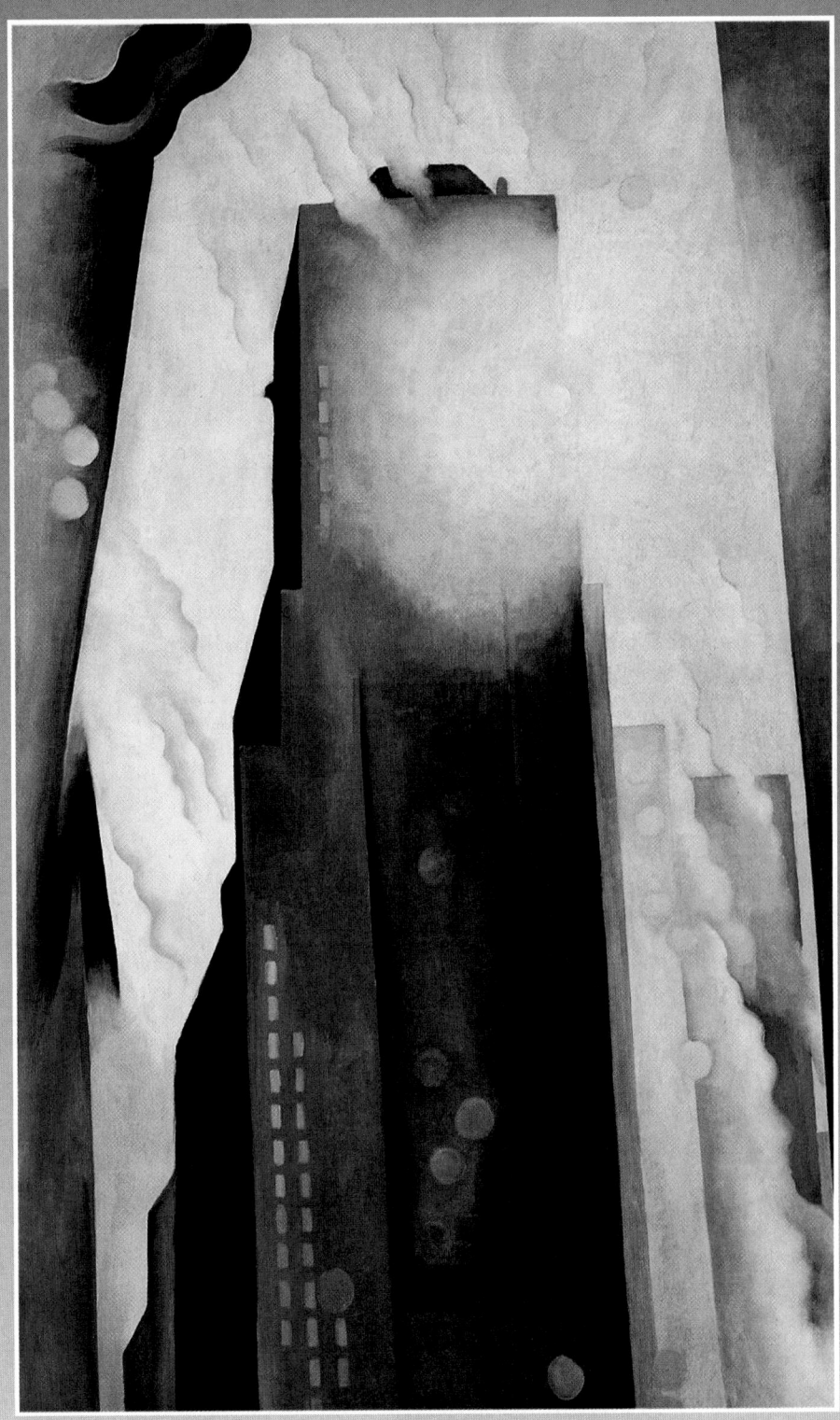

The Shelton with Sunspots (1926), Georgia O'Keeffe. Oil on canvas, 123.1 cm × 76.8 cm, The Art Institute of Chicago, gift of Leigh B. Block (1985.206). Photo Copyright © 1994 The Art Institute of Chicago, all rights reserved.

Connect to the Literature

1. **What Do You Think?** Describe how you felt about Dexter Green as you finished reading the story.

> **Comprehension Check**
> - Where does Dexter first meet Judy?
> - Why does Dexter become engaged to Irene?
> - What does Dexter learn about Judy some years later?

Think Critically

2. Are your feelings about what has happened to Judy Jones the same as Dexter's? Explain your answer.

3. How do you account for Dexter and Judy's attraction?

4. **ACTIVE READING** **EVALUATING CHARACTER** Review your responses to the reading-strategy questions that you jotted down in your **READER'S NOTEBOOK.** Do you approve or disapprove of the way Judy Jones and Dexter Green treat other people? What else do you like or dislike about them? Defend your views.

5. How worthwhile do you find Dexter's "winter dreams"?

> **THINK ABOUT**
> - what the dreams are
> - what he gains from the dreams
> - what he loses because of the dreams

Extend Interpretations

6. **Critic's Corner** In the essay, "Scott Fitzgerald: The Apprentice Fiction," literary critic Marius Bewley notes, "Fitzgerald's ultimate subject is the character of the American Dream in which, in their respective ways, his principal heroes are all trapped." How well do you think this statement applies to "Winter Dreams"? Use examples from the story to support your opinion.

7. **What If?** If Dexter and Judy had married, what do you think their life together would have been like?

8. **The Writer's Style** Fitzgerald is admired for his use of **figurative language**—language (such as metaphors, similes, and personification) that communicates ideas or feelings beyond the literal meaning of the words. Find some examples of figurative language in the story, and explain what ideas or feelings you think each conveys.

9. **Connect to Life** How do the dreams you listed for the Connect to Your Life activity on page 840 compare with Dexter Green's "winter dreams"?

Literary Analysis

CHARACTERS **Characters**—the imaginary people or creatures who inhabit the world of fiction—may be classified as either static or dynamic. **Static characters** tend to stay in a fixed position over the course of the story. They do not experience life-altering moments and seem to act the same, even though their situation changes. In contrast, **dynamic characters** evolve as individuals. They learn from their experiences and grow emotionally.

Paired Activity Working with a partner, classify Dexter Green and Judy Jones as either a static character or a dynamic character. To help you make a judgment, discuss the following questions:
- What were they like in the beginning of the story?
- Do they cling to the same behavior patterns as they become adults?
- How do they respond to the mistakes they have made in their lives?

REVIEW **SYMBOL** As you recall, a **symbol** is a person, place, or object that represents something beyond itself. What does the setting sun seem to symbolize at the end of "Winter Dreams"?

Choices & CHALLENGES

Writing Options

1. Psychological Evaluation
Pretend that you are a relationship counselor. Write a brief evaluation of Dexter and Judy's relationship.

2. Dexter's Résumé Write a draft of Dexter Green's résumé. Summarize his work experience, beginning with his job as a caddy.

Writing Handbook
See page 1294: Résumé.

3. Personal Lecture If you could offer advice to Dexter at the end of the story, what would you tell him? Outline the lecture that you would give him.

Activities & Explorations

Illustrated Calendar Work with a small group of classmates to create a "Winter Dreams" illustrated calendar of the seasons. On the calendar, indicate what feelings Dexter associates with each season and what happens to him during the seasons. Use the calendar to help you investigate Fitzgerald's use of seasonal imagery in the story. What do winter and summer seem to represent? ~ **ART**

Inquiry & Research

Clothing Styles Locate information about fashions of the period around World War I. Then sketch costume designs for a movie version of the story and display them in class. Alternatively, put on a fashion show with some of your classmates, modeling clothing of the time. Play popular music from this era in the background.

Experience
Caddy--Sherry
Island Golf
Club

Art Connection

The self-portrait by the European artist Tamara de Lempicka shown on page 853 is representative of the Art Deco style of the 1920s and 1930s—consciously "modern" with its angularity, streamlined forms, and glorification of machines and technology. The automobile is an important element in this painting, as the punning title *Autoportrait* suggests. In what ways does the artwork remind you of Judy Jones in "Winter Dreams"?

Detail of *Autoportrait* (about 1925), Tamara de Lempicka. Oil on wood, 35 cm x 26 cm, private collection. Copyright © SPADEM/Kizette de Lempicka Foxhall.

Choices & CHALLENGES

Vocabulary in Action

EXERCISE A: SYNONYMS For each phrase in the first column, write the letter of the synonymous phrase in the second column.

1. a surfeit of change
2. mar the ravine
3. fool the ingenuous
4. comically hazardous
5. blatantly wishing
6. pathetic pig sounds
7. incorrigible filthiness
8. grimace during hugs
9. wary and evil
10. petulance and poor muscle tone

a. sully the gully
b. poignant oinking
c. hopeless soaplessness
d. suspicious and malicious
e. deceive the naive
f. too many pennies
g. openly hoping
h. crabbiness and flabbiness
i. hilariously precarious
j. make faces at embraces

> WORDS TO KNOW
>
> blatantly   incorrigible   malicious   poignant   sully
> grimace   ingenuous   petulance   precarious surfeit

EXERCISE B See how quickly you can communicate some of the vocabulary words to a partner by saying things—other than synonyms—that call the words to mind. For *poignant,* for example, you might say "a hungry child; a sad song; Mother's Day cards; tearjerker movies; a puppy's whimper; nostalgic memories . . . ," continuing until the correct word is guessed.

Building Vocabulary
For an in-depth lesson on word connotation and denotation, see page 908.

F. Scott Fitzgerald
1896–1940

Other Works
All the Sad Young Men
Tales of the Jazz Age
The Great Gatsby
Tender Is the Night

Stormy Romance Francis Scott Key Fitzgerald experienced, and depicted in his fiction, the material success and eventual disillusionment that characterized the decade he dubbed the *Jazz Age.* While in army training in Alabama, he fell in love with Zelda Sayre, the beautiful and high-spirited daughter of an Alabama Supreme Court judge. They had a tumultuous courtship, with Zelda refusing to marry the aspiring writer until he was financially secure. Fortunately, his first novel, *This Side of Paradise* (1920), met with immediate success, and the couple were married within a week of the book's publication.

Whirlwind Success In the decade that followed, Fitzgerald's career flourished as he published two more novels, three short story collections, and a play. His 1925 novel of overindulgent lives, *The Great Gatsby*—of which "Winter Dreams" was a sort of rough draft—became famous. By 1929 he was selling stories for as much as $3,600 each. Then everything seemed to go wrong.

A Turn of Fortune In 1930, at the onset of the Great Depression, Zelda suffered the first of a number of mental breakdowns that would keep her hospitalized for much of the remainder of her life. At the same time, Fitzgerald was battling alcoholism, which, along with his need to earn money for Zelda's care, caused him to produce poor, hastily written fiction. Readers now rejected his subject matter, the lives of the wealthy, and by 1940 he was no longer a major writer. He died that year in Hollywood, leaving a "comeback" novel—*The Last Tycoon*—unfinished.

Redeemed Reputation After World War II, though, prosperity brought nostalgia for the 1920s and new respect for Fitzgerald's work. Today he is considered a major 20th-century writer whose stories make the Jazz Age come alive.

America and I

Short Story by ANZIA YEZIERSKA (ənz-yä′ yĭ-zyĭr′skə)

(Connect to Your Life)

Life in a New Land How do you think people who emigrate from their homelands feel? What challenges and opportunities await them in their new countries? Why do you think immigrants come to America? Share your thoughts about immigration with a small group of classmates. Then, as you read this story, compare your group's ideas with those of the narrator.

Build Background

A Wave of Immigrants The Jewish narrator of "America and I" emigrates from Russia to the United States in the late 1800s. Between 1870 and 1920, millions of immigrants from around the world entered the United States. Although their countries of origin might have differed, these immigrants shared a great deal in terms of experience. Many had left their homelands to escape wars, religious persecution, poverty, and, in some cases, starvation. After arriving in the United States, they had to face the challenges of learning English and finding housing and work. Many settled in ethnic neighborhoods in cities, where they lived in dark, crowded tenements with inadequate sanitation. Those immigrants who were uneducated, unskilled, and poor often had to work under dangerous conditions in sweatshops, toiling long hours for low wages.

WORDS TO KNOW
Vocabulary Preview

avid	pestilence
delve	simper
indomitable	

Focus Your Reading

LITERARY ANALYSIS **VOICE** The term *voice* refers to a writer's unique use of language that allows a reader to "hear" a human personality in the writing. The elements of style that determine a writer's voice include diction, sentence structure, and tone. The term can be applied not only to the writer of a selection but also to the narrator of a story. As you read "America and I," try to hear the first-person narrator's voice and form an image of this young immigrant woman.

ACTIVE READING **UNDERSTANDING ANALOGIES** An **analogy** is an extended, point-by-point comparison of two things that have certain similarities. Its purpose is usually to make the less familiar of the two things more comprehensible. For example, the narrator of "America and I" draws an analogy between her experiences in America and those of the Pilgrims. As you read the analogy, note the points of comparison.

READER'S NOTEBOOK To help you grasp the meaning of the narrator's analogy on page 872, read it a second time. Create a chart like the one shown, and fill it as you reread.

	Narrator's Experiences	Pilgrims' Experiences
Ocean voyage		
View of America		
Cross-cultural encounters		
Expectations		

AMERICA AND I

★ ★ ★ ★

I was in America, among the Americans, but not of them.

Anzia Yezierska

As one of the dumb, voiceless ones I speak. One of the millions of immigrants beating, beating out their hearts at your gates for a breath of understanding.

Ach! America! From the other end of the earth from where I came, America was a land of living hope, woven of dreams, aflame with longing and desire.

Choked for ages in the airless oppression of Russia, the Promised Land rose up—wings for my stifled spirit—sunlight burning through my darkness—freedom singing to me in my prison—deathless songs tuning prison-bars into strings of a beautiful violin.

I arrived in America. My young, strong body, my heart and soul pregnant with the unlived lives of generations clamoring for expression.

What my mother and father and their mother and father never had a chance to give out in Russia, I would give out in America. The hidden sap of centuries would find release; colors that never saw light—songs that died unvoiced—romance that never had a chance to blossom in the black life of the Old World.

In the golden land of flowing opportunity I was to find my work that was denied me in the sterile village of my forefathers. Here I was to be free from the dead drudgery for bread that held me down in Russia. For the first time in America, I'd cease to be a slave of the belly. I'd be a creator, a giver, a human being! My work would be the living joy of fullest self-expression.

But from my high visions, my golden hopes, I had to put my feet down on earth. I had to have food and shelter. I had to have the money to pay for it.

I was in America, among the Americans, but not of them. No speech, no common language, no way to win a smile of understanding from them, only my young, strong body and my untried faith. Only my eager, empty hands, and my full heart shining from my eyes!

God from the world! Here I was with so much richness in me, but my mind was not wanted without the language. And my body, unskilled, untrained, was not even wanted in the factory. Only one of two chances was left open to me: the kitchen, or minding babies.

My first job was as a servant in an American-ized family. Once, long ago, they came from the same village from where I came. But they were so well-dressed, so well-fed, so successful in America, that they were ashamed to remember their mother tongue.

"What were to be my wages?" I ventured timidly, as I looked up to the well-fed, well-dressed "American" man and woman.

They looked at me with a sudden coldness. What have I said to draw away from me their warmth? Was it so low from me to talk of wages? I shrank back into myself like a low-down bargainer. Maybe they're so high up in well-being they can't any more understand my low thoughts for money.

From his rich height the man preached down to me that I must not be so grabbing for wages. Only just landed from the ship and already thinking about money when I should be thankful to associate with "Americans."

The woman, out of her smooth, smiling fatness assured me that this was my chance for a summer vacation in the country with her two lovely children. My great chance to learn to be a civilized being, to become an American by living with them.

So, made to feel that I was in the hands of American friends, invited to share with them their home, their plenty, their happiness, I pushed out from my head the worry for wages. Here was my first chance to begin my life in the sunshine, after my long darkness. My laugh was all over my face as I said to them: "I'll trust myself to you. What I'm worth you'll give me." And I entered their house like a child by the hand.

The best of me I gave them. Their house cares were my house cares. I got up early. I worked till late. All that my soul hungered to give I put into the passion with which I scrubbed floors, scoured pots, and washed clothes. I was so grateful to mingle with the American people, to hear the music of the American language, that I never knew tiredness.

There was such a freshness in my brains and such a willingness in my heart that I could go on and on—not only with the work of the house, but work with my head—learning new words from the children, the grocer, the butcher, the iceman. I was not even afraid to ask for words from the policeman on the street. And every new word made me see new American things with American eyes. I felt like a Columbus, finding new worlds through every new word.

But words alone were only for the inside of me. The outside of me still branded me for a steerage[1] immigrant. I had to have clothes to forget myself that I'm a stranger yet. And so I had to have money to buy these clothes.

The month was up. I was so happy! Now I'd have money. *My own, earned* money. Money to buy a new shirt on my back—shoes on my feet. Maybe yet an American dress and hat!

Ach! How high rose my dreams! How plainly

---

1. **steerage:** the section of a passenger ship containing the cheapest accommodations.

I saw all that I would do with my visionary wages shining like a light over my head!

In my imagination I already walked in my new American clothes. How beautiful I looked as I saw myself like a picture before my eyes! I saw how I would throw away my immigrant rags tied up in my immigrant shawl. With money to buy—free money in my hands—I'd show them that I could look like an American in a day.

Like a prisoner in his last night in prison, counting the seconds that will free him from his chains, I trembled breathlessly for the minute I'd get the wages in my hand.

Before dawn I rose.

I shined up the house like a jewel-box.

I prepared breakfast and waited with my heart in my mouth for my lady and gentleman to rise. At last I heard them stirring. My eyes were jumping out of my head to them when I saw them coming in and seating themselves by the table.

Like a hungry cat rubbing up to its boss for meat, so I edged and simpered around them as I passed them the food. Without my will, like a beggar, my hand reached out to them.

The breakfast was over. And no word yet from my wages.

"*Gottuniu!*"[2] I thought to myself. "Maybe they're so busy with their own things they forgot it's the day for my wages. Could they who have everything know what I was to do with my first American dollars? How could they, soaking in plenty, how could they feel the longing and the fierce hunger in me, pressing up through each visionary dollar? How could they know the gnawing ache of my avid fingers for the feel of my own, earned dollars? *My* dollars that I could spend like a free person. *My* dollars that would make me feel with everybody alike!

Breakfast was long past.

Lunch came. Lunch past.

Oi-i weh![3] Not a word yet about my money.

It was near dinner. And not a word yet about my wages.

I began to set the table. But my head—it swam away from me. I broke a glass. The silver dropped from my nervous fingers. I couldn't stand it any longer. I dropped everything and rushed over to my American lady and gentleman.

"*Oi weh!* The money—my money—my wages!" I cried breathlessly.

Four cold eyes turned on me.

"Wages? Money?" The four eyes turned into hard stone as they looked me up and down. "Haven't you a comfortable bed to sleep, and three good meals a day? You're only a month here. Just came to America. And you already think about money. Wait till you're worth any money. What use are you without knowing English? You should be glad we keep you here. It's like a vacation for you. Other girls pay money yet to be in the country."

It went black for my eyes. I was so choked no words came to my lips. Even the tears went dry in my throat.

I left. Not a dollar for all my work.

For a long, long time my heart ached and ached like a sore wound. If murderers would have robbed me and killed me it wouldn't have hurt me so much. I couldn't think through my pain. The minute I'd see before me how they looked at me, the words they said to me—then everything began to bleed in me. And I was helpless.

For a long, long time the thought of ever working in an "American" family made me tremble with fear, like the fear of wild wolves. No—never again would I trust myself to an "American" family, no matter how fine their language and how sweet their smile.

It was blotted out in me all trust in friendship from "Americans." But the life in me still burned to live. The hope in me still craved to hope. In

---

2. *Gottuniu!* (gôt′ŏŏn-yōō) *Yiddish:* Oh, my God!
3. *Oi-i weh!* (oi′ vā′) *Yiddish:* Oh, woe! (a common expression of dismay or resignation).

WORDS TO KNOW

simper (sĭm′pər) *v.* to smile in a shy or self-conscious way
avid (ăv′ĭd) *adj.* having an intense desire or craving

"Where is America?
Is there an America?
What is this wilderness
in which I'm lost?"

darkness, in dirt, in hunger and want, but only to live on!

There had been no end to my day—working for the "American" family.

Now rejecting false friendships from higher-ups in America, I turned back to the Ghetto,[4] I worked on a hard bench with my own kind on either side of me. I knew before I began what my wages were to be. I knew what my hours were to be. And I knew the feeling of the end of the day.

From the outside my second job seemed worse than the first. It was in a sweatshop of a Delancey Street basement, kept up by an old, wrinkled woman that looked like a black witch of greed. My work was sewing on buttons. While the morning was still dark I walked into a dark basement. And darkness met me when I turned out of the basement.

Day after day, week after week, all the contact I got with America was handling dead buttons. The money I earned was hardly enough to pay for bread and rent. I didn't have a room to myself. I didn't even have a bed. I slept on a mattress on the floor in a rat-hole of a room occupied by a dozen other immigrants. I was always hungry—oh, so hungry! The scant meals I could afford only sharpened my appetite for real food. But I felt myself better off than working in the "American" family, where I had three good meals a day and a bed to myself. With all the hunger and darkness of the sweatshop, I had at least the evening to myself. And all night was mine. When all were asleep, I used to creep up on the roof of the tenement and talk out my heart in silence to the stars in the sky.

"Who am I? What am I? What do I want with my life? Where is America? Is there an America? What is this wilderness in which I'm lost?"

I'd hurl my questions and then think and think. And I could not tear it out of me, the feeling that America must be somewhere,

---

4. **Ghetto:** the part of New York City where Jewish immigrants lived and worked.

somehow—only I couldn't find it—*my America*, where I would work for love and not for a living. I was like a thing following blindly after something far off in the dark!

"*Oi weh!*" I'd stretch out my hand up in the air. "My head is so lost in America! What's the use of all my working if I'm not in it? Dead buttons is not me."

Then the busy season started in the shop. The mounds of buttons grew and grew. The long day stretched out longer. I had to begin with the buttons earlier and stay with them till later in the night. The old witch turned into a huge greedy maw for wanting more and more buttons.

For a glass of tea, for a slice of herring over black bread, she would buy us up to stay another and another hour, till there seemed no end to her demands.

One day, the light of self-assertion broke into my cellar darkness.

"I don't want the tea. I don't want your herring," I said with terrible boldness. "I only want to go home. I only want the evening to myself!"

"You fresh mouth, you!" cried the old witch. "You learned already too much in America. I want no clock-watchers in my shop. Out you go!"

I was driven out to cold and hunger. I could no longer pay for my mattress on the floor. I no longer could buy the bite in the mouth. I walked the streets. I knew what it is to be alone in a strange city, among strangers.

But I laughed through my tears. So I learned

I burned to give,

to give something,

to do something,

to be something.

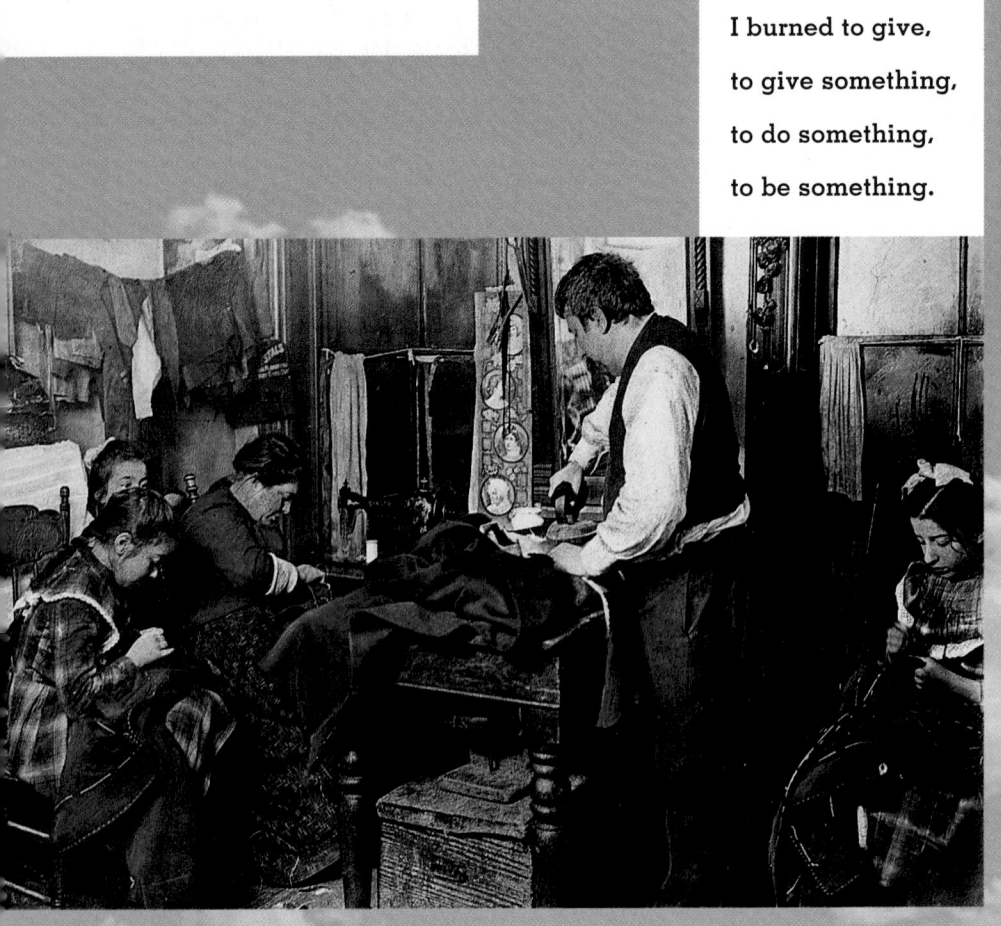

too much already in America because I wanted the whole evening to myself? Well America has yet to teach me still more: how to get not only the whole evening to myself, but a whole day a week like the American workers.

That sweatshop was a bitter memory but a good school. It fitted me for a regular factory. I could walk in boldly and say I could work at something, even if it was only sewing on buttons.

Gradually, I became a trained worker. I worked in a light, airy factory, only eight hours a day. My boss was no longer a sweater and a blood-squeezer. The first freshness of the morning was mine. And the whole evening was mine. All day Sunday was mine.

Now I had better food to eat. I slept on a better bed. Now, I even looked dressed up like the American-born. But inside of me I knew that I was not yet an American. I choked with longing when I met an American-born, and I could say nothing.

Something cried dumb in me. I couldn't help it. I didn't know what it was I wanted. I only knew I wanted. I wanted. Like the hunger in the heart that never gets food.

An English class for foreigners started in our factory. The teacher had such a good, friendly face, her eyes looked so understanding, as if she could see right into my heart. So I went to her one day for an advice:

"I don't know what is with me the matter," I began. "I have no rest in me. I never yet done what I want."

"What is it you want to do, child?" she asked me.

"I want to do something with my head, my feelings. All day long, only with my hands I work."

"First you must learn English." She patted me as if I was not yet grown up. "Put your mind on that, and then we'll see."

So for a time I learned the language. I could almost begin to think with English words in my head. But in my heart the emptiness still hurt. I burned to give, to give something, to do some-

thing, to be something. The dead work with my hands was killing me. My work left only hard stones on my heart.

Again I went to our factory teacher and cried out to her: "I know already to read and write the English language, but I can't put it into words what I want. What is it in me so different that can't come out?"

She smiled at me down from her calmness as if I were a little bit out of my head. "What do *you want* to do?"

"I feel. I see. I hear. And I want to think it out. But I'm like dumb in me. I only feel I'm different—different from everybody."

She looked at me close and said nothing for a minute. "You ought to join one of the social clubs of the Women's Association," she advised.

"What's the Women's Association?" I implored greedily.

"A group of American women who are trying to help the working-girl find herself. They have a special department for immigrant girls like you."

I joined the Women's Association. On my first evening there they announced a lecture: "The Happy Worker and His Work," by the Welfare director of the United Mills Corporation.

"Is there such a thing as a happy worker at his work?" I wondered. "Happiness is only by working at what you love. And what poor girl can ever find it to work at what she loves? My old dreams about my America rushed through my mind. Once I thought that in America everybody works for love. Nobody has to worry for a living. Maybe this welfare man came to show me the *real* America that till now I sought in vain.

With a lot of polite words the head lady of the Women's Association introduced a higher-up that looked like the king of kings of business. Never before in my life did I ever see a man with such a sureness in his step, such power in his face, such friendly positiveness in his eye as when he smiled upon us.

"Efficiency is the new religion of business," he began. "In big business houses, even in up-to-date factories, they no longer take the first comer and give him any job that happens to stand empty. Efficiency begins at the employment office. Experts are hired for the one purpose, to find out how best to fit the worker to his work. It's economy for the boss to make the worker happy." And then he talked a lot more on efficiency in educated language that was over my head.

I didn't know exactly what it meant—efficiency—but if it was to make the worker happy at his work, then that's what I had been looking for since I came to America. I only felt from watching him that he was happy by his job. And as I looked on this clean, well-dressed, successful one, who wasn't ashamed to say he rose from an office-boy, it made me feel that I, too, could lift myself up for a person.

He finished his lecture, telling us about the Vocational Guidance Center that the Women's Association started.

The very next evening I was at the Vocational Guidance Center. There I found a young, college-looking woman. Smartness and health shining from her eyes! She, too, looked as if she knew her way in America. I could tell at the first glance: here is a person that is happy by what she does.

"I feel you'll understand me," I said right away.

She leaned over with pleasure in her face: "I hope I can."

"I want to work by what's in me. Only, I don't know what's in me. I only feel I'm different."

She gave me a quick, puzzled look from the corner of her eyes. "What are you doing now?"

"I'm the quickest shirtwaist[5] hand on the floor. But my heart wastes away by such work. I think and think, and my thoughts can't come out."

"Why don't you think out your thoughts in shirtwaists? You could learn to be a designer. Earn more money."

"I don't want to look on waists. If my hands are sick from waists, how could my head learn to put beauty into them?"

"But you must earn your living at what you

know, and rise slowly from job to job."

I looked at her office sign: "Vocational Guidance." "What's your vocational guidance?" I asked. "How to rise from job to job—how to earn more money?"

The smile went out from her eyes. But she tried to be kind yet. "What *do* you want?" she asked, with a sigh of last patience.

"I want America to want me."

She fell back in her chair, thunderstruck with my boldness. But yet, in a low voice of educated self-control, she tried to reason with me:

"You have to *show* that you have something special for America before America has need of you."

"But I never had a chance to find out what's in me, because I always had to work for a living. Only, I feel it's efficiency for America to find out what's in me so different, so I could give it out by my work."

Her eyes half closed as they bored through me. Her mouth opened to speak, but no words came from her lips. So I flamed up with all that was choking in me like a house on fire:

"America gives free bread and rent to criminals in prison. They got grand houses with sunshine, fresh air, doctors and teachers, even for the crazy ones. Why don't they have free boarding-schools for immigrants—strong people—willing people? Here you see us burning up with something different, and America turns her head away from us."

Her brows lifted and dropped down. She shrugged her shoulders away from me with the look of pity we give to cripples and hopeless lunatics.

"America is no Utopia.[6] First you must become efficient in earning a living before you can indulge in your poetic dreams."

I went away from the vocational guidance

---

5. **shirtwaist:** a tailored blouse, usually with a collar and cuffs.

6. **Utopia:** an ideal place of perfect justice and social harmony.

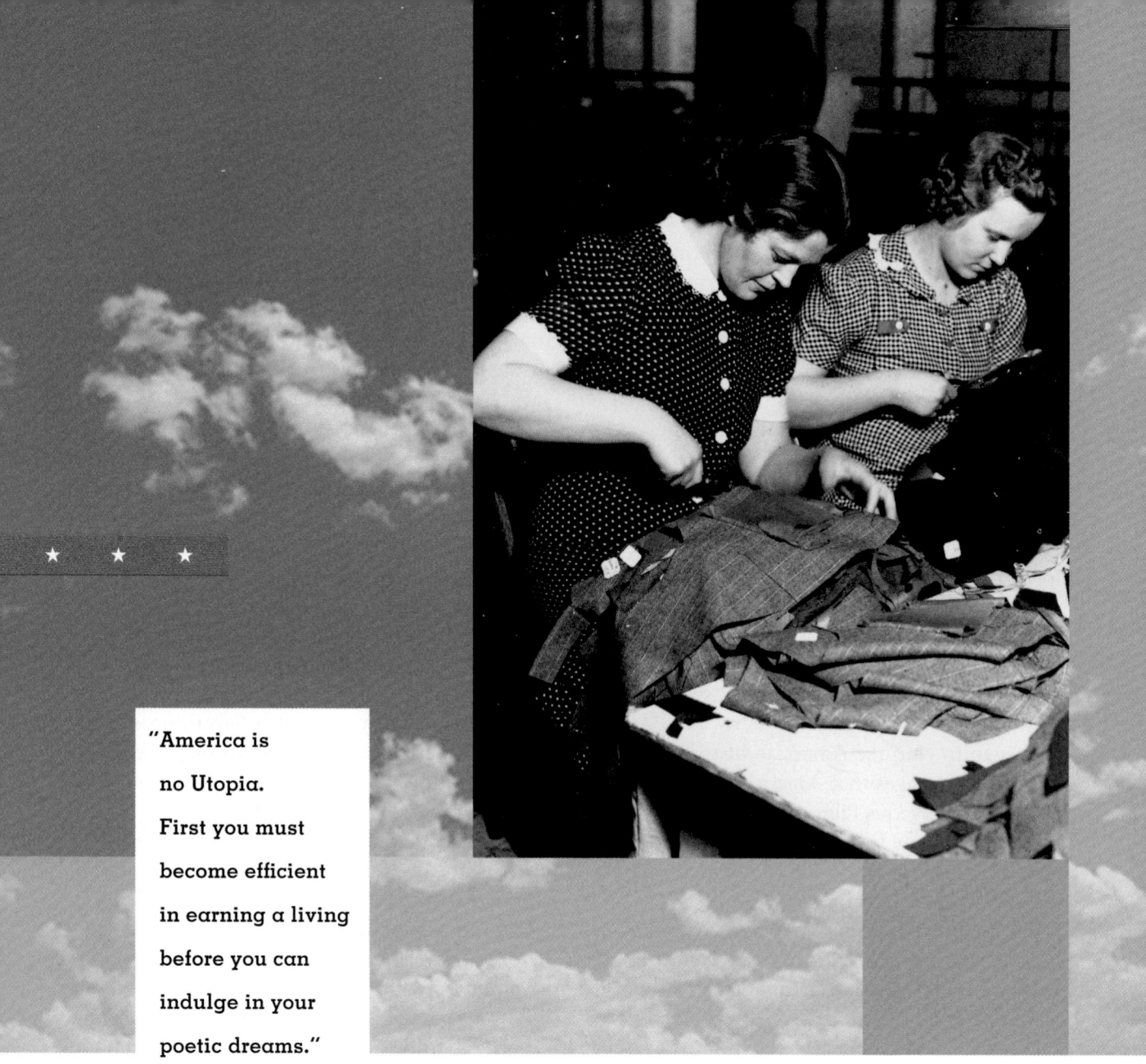

> "America is no Utopia. First you must become efficient in earning a living before you can indulge in your poetic dreams."

office with all the air out of my lungs. All the light out of my eyes. My feet dragged after me like dead wood.

Till now there had always lingered a rosy veil of hope over my emptiness, a hope that a miracle would happen. I would open up my eyes some day and suddenly find the America of my dreams. As a young girl hungry for love sees always before her eyes the picture of lover's arms around her, so I saw always in my heart the vision of Utopian America.

But now I felt that the America of my dreams never was and never could be. Reality had hit me on the head as with a club. I felt that the America that I sought was nothing but a shadow—an echo—a chimera[7] of lunatics and crazy immigrants.

---

7. **chimera** (kǐ-mîr′ə): an illusion of the mind; fantasy.

Stripped of all illusion, I looked about me. The long desert of wasting days of drudgery stared me in the face. The drudgery that I had lived through, and the endless drudgery still ahead of me rose over me like a withering wilderness of sand. In vain were all my cryings, in vain were all frantic efforts of my spirit to find the living waters of understanding for my perishing lips. Sand, sand was everywhere. With every seeking, every reaching out I only lost myself deeper and deeper in a vast sea of sand.

I knew now the American language. And I knew now, if I talked to the Americans from morning till night, they could not understand what the Russian soul of me wanted. They could not understand *me* any more than if I talked to them in Chinese. Between my soul and the American soul were worlds of difference that no words could bridge over. What was that difference? What made the Americans so far apart from me?

I began to read the American history. I found from the first pages that America started with a band of Courageous Pilgrims. They had left their native country as I had left mine. They had crossed an unknown ocean and landed in an unknown country, as I.

But the great difference between the first Pilgrims and me was that they expected to make America, build America, create their own world of liberty. I wanted to find it ready made.

I read on. I delved deeper down into the American history. I saw how the Pilgrim Fathers came to a rocky desert country, surrounded by Indian savages on all sides. But undaunted, they pressed on—through danger—through famine, pestilence, and want—they pressed on. They did not ask the Indians for sympathy, for understanding. They made no demands on anybody, but on their own indomitable spirit of persistence.

And I—I was forever begging a crumb of sympathy, a gleam of understanding from strangers who could not sympathize, who could not understand.

I, when I encountered a few savage Indian scalpers, like the old witch of the sweatshop, like my "Americanized" countryman, who cheated me of my wages—I, when I found myself on the lonely, untrodden path through which all seekers of the new world must pass, I lost heart and said: "There is no America!"

Then came a light—a great revelation! I saw America—a big idea—a deathless hope—a world still in the making. I saw that it was the glory of America that it was not yet finished. And I, the last comer, had her share to give, small or great, to the making of America, like those Pilgrims who came in the *Mayflower*.

Fired up by this revealing light, I began to build a bridge of understanding between the American-born and myself. Since their life was shut out from such as me, I began to open up my life and the lives of my people to them. And life draws life. In only writing about the Ghetto I found America.

Great chances have come to me. But in my heart is always a deep sadness. I feel like a man who is sitting down to a secret table of plenty, while his near ones and dear ones are perishing before his eyes. My very joy in doing the work I love hurts me like secret guilt, because all about me I see so many with my longings, my burning eagerness, to do and to be, wasting their days in drudgery they hate, merely to buy bread and pay rent. And America is losing all that richness of the soul.

The Americans of to-morrow, the America that is every day nearer coming to be, will be too wise, too open-hearted, too friendly-handed, to let the least last-comer at their gates knock in vain with his gifts unwanted. ❖

WORDS **delve** (dĕlv) *v.* to conduct an investigation; search
TO   **pestilence** (pĕs′tə-ləns) *n.* any epidemic disease that is usually fatal
KNOW   **indomitable** (ĭn-dŏm′ĭ-tə-bəl) *adj.* not easily discouraged or defeated

Thinking through the LITERATURE

Connect to the Literature

1. What Do You Think
Describe the narrator and your attitude toward her.

> **Comprehension Check**
> • Why does the narrator leave her first job as a housekeeper and nanny?
> • What kind of work does the narrator do in the sweatshop?

Think Critically

2. What is your reaction to the **narrator's** ideas about America?

> **THINK ABOUT**
> • how she hopes immigrants will be treated in the future
> • her "revelation" that America is still being made
> • her understanding of American history
> • what she expects America to provide for her

3. What do you think the narrator learns from her encounters with employers, teachers, and advisers?

4. In your opinion, what is the most important step the narrator takes in learning to live in America?

5. Do you think the American dream is an illusion or a reality for the narrator of this story? Explain.

6. **ACTIVE READING** **UNDERSTANDING ANALOGIES** Review the chart you made in your
 READER'S NOTEBOOK. What similarities does the narrator see between herself and the Pilgrims? What conclusion does she reach on the basis of her **analogy?**

Extend Interpretations

7. Comparing Texts How does the narrator's account of the Pilgrims (page 872) compare with William Bradford's account of the Pilgrims' arrival in America (page 82)? Do you think the narrator's analogy between her experience and that of the Pilgrims is a valid one? Cite evidence to support your answer.

8. Different Perspectives In "What Is an American?" (page 290), de Crèvecoeur offers this vision of America: "Here individuals of all nations are melted into a new race of men, whose labors and posterity will one day cause great change in the world." Do you think the narrator of "America and I" shares this view? Why or why not?

9. Connect to Life How might a social worker have evaluated the narrator's progress in making a satisfying life for herself in America?

Literary Analysis

VOICE **Voice** is the writer's stamp of originality—the distinctive way he or she uses language. Anzia Yezierska gives voice to her immigrant experience by writing about a character like herself who adapts to an alien culture. The conversational language of the first-person narrator in "America and I" contributes to her "stage presence." For example, the way the narrator tells anecdotes about her jobs almost sounds as though she is delivering a monologue to an audience. The narrator's melodramatic tone in recounting moments in her life further heightens the story's theatrical quality—another stylistic element that characterizes the voice of the piece.

Activity Reread the story and find examples of the following stylistic elements that characterize the narrator's voice:
• speech that reflects the narrator's immigrant background
• vivid anecdotes
• diction, or choice of words, that is intensely emotional
Share your examples with the class.

Choices & CHALLENGES

Vocabulary in Action

EXERCISE: CONTEXT CLUES Write the vocabulary word that best completes each sentence below.

1. Is greed contagious—a _____ like smallpox or the plague?

2. Yezierska wondered this as she tried to _____ into what it meant to be an American.

3. Not content to _____ with pretended gratitude for food and a bed, she pursued her dream, even sacrificing security for independence.

4. Although she was disheartened, her desire for fulfillment remained _____ and could not be crushed.

5. Today, _____ scholars of Yezierska's life and writings labor excitedly to bring her works to wide attention.

WORDS TO KNOW		
avid	pestilence	
delve	simper	
indomitable		

Writing Options

1. Tips for Newcomers Think about the narrator's positive and negative experiences in this story. Write at least five tips to help recent immigrants adjust to life in America.

2. Letter to Russia Imagine that the narrator receives a letter from a friend back in Russia. Write the narrator's reply, answering questions about America, explaining what has happened to her since she arrived, and describing her feelings about her experiences.

3. Looking Back: A Memoir Compose a passage for a memoir you might someday write, describing an experience that was "a bitter memory but a good school" for you. Be sure to tell what you learned from it.

Building Vocabulary
For an in-depth lesson on context clues, see page 326.

Anzia Yezierska
1885?–1970

Other Works
Bread Givers
Children of Loneliness

New Beginnings Born, like the narrator of "America and I," in a village of Russian Poland, Anzia Yezierska migrated with her family to the United States in the late 1800s. The family settled in a tenement in New York City's Lower East Side, where Yezierska briefly attended public school until she was old enough to work to help support her family. She later worked as a cook, a servant, a waitress, and a needle-worker, sewing on buttons in a sweatshop.

Lofty Ambitions Although Jewish tradition discouraged the education of women, Yezierska rebelled against her family and went to college. Supporting herself by working at a laundry before and after classes, she began attending Columbia University in 1904. Her studies were designed to make a cooking teacher of her, but she decided to be a writer instead.

The Lure of Hollywood In 1920 Yezierska published her first short story collection, *Hungry Hearts.* Paying her $10,000 for the film rights and hiring her to write the script, the Hollywood producer Samuel Goldwyn turned the book into a silent film. Called "the sweat-shop Cinderella," Yezierska instantly became famous. She moved to Hollywood, intending to become a screenwriter, but found herself unable to write so far away from the colorful New York neighborhoods that had first inspired her.

Literary Achievements Within a year Yezierska returned to New York, and in 1922 she published her first novel, *Salome of the Tenements,* which was followed, over the next 10 years, by three more novels and a second book of short stories. In 1950, after a silence of 18 years, she published the autobiographical novel *Red Ribbon on a White Horse* to critical acclaim. However, it failed to regain for her the fame and success she had experienced in the 1920s, and she spent the last years of her life in obscurity.

The New Immigrants

❶ Millions of immigrants entered the United States in the late 19th and early 20th centuries because they were lured by the promise of a better life. Some of these immigrants sought to escape difficult conditions—such as poverty, famine, land shortages, or religious or political persecution—in their native countries. Others, known as "birds of passage," intended to immigrate temporarily in order to make money and then return to their homelands.

❷ **Immigrants from Europe** Between 1870 and 1920, approximately 20 million Europeans arrived in the United States. Before 1890, most immigrants came from countries in western and northern Europe, including Great Britain, Ireland, and Germany. Beginning in the 1890s, however, increasing numbers came from southern and eastern Europe, especially Italy, Austria-Hungary, and Russia. In 1905 alone, nearly a million people arrived from these countries to the land of opportunity.

Many of these new immigrants left their homelands to escape religious persecution. Whole villages of Jews—businesspeople, intellectuals, workers, and farmers—were driven out of Russia by pogroms. These were organized anti-Semitic campaigns that led to the massacre of Jews during the early 1880s and early 1900s.

Other Europeans left because of rising population. Between 1800 and 1900, the population in Europe more than doubled to 432 million. This population explosion resulted in a lack of land available for farming. Farmers as well as laborers often found themselves competing for too few industrial jobs. Some emigrated to the United States, where jobs were supposedly plentiful.

Where They Came From and Where They Settled, 1900

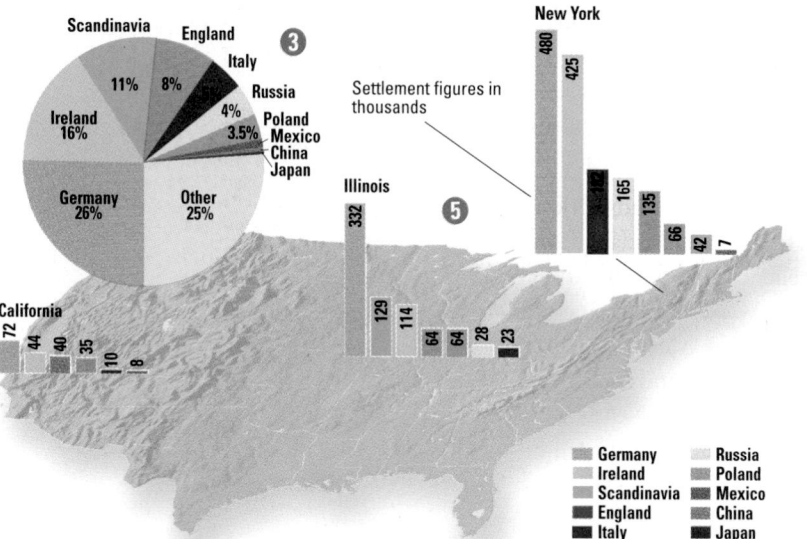

Reading for Information

Think about how long your family has been in the United States. Were your ancestors' reasons for coming to America similar to those of the people this article describes?

COMPARING TEXT AND GRAPHIC INFORMATION

Historical articles contain an array of facts, figures, and information. Certain kinds of information are best presented in written text. Other kinds are easier to grasp when presented visually. Use the questions and activities below to examine two different forms of presentation.

❶ Try using a graphic device like this one to convey the information presented in this paragraph. What information cannot be included?

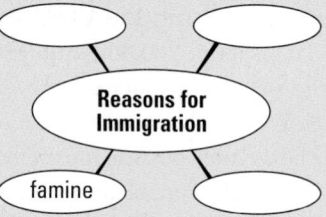

❷ This paragraph explains that millions of Europeans came to the United States during a 50-year period. What additional details do the bar graphs on this page provide about immigration during that period?

❸ Graphic devices can be combined to show how groups of data are related. Here, a pie graph (at the left) is combined with several small bar graphs and a map.

875

Finally, there was a spirit of reform and revolt in Europe, especially after the political disturbances in France, Germany, Italy, and elsewhere in the late 1840s. Many young European men and women were still influenced by the spirit of these movements and sought to start independent lives in the United States.

Immigrants from China and Japan While waves of Europeans arrived on the shores of the East Coast, Chinese immigrants came to the West Coast in smaller numbers. Between 1851 and 1883, about 200,000 Chinese arrived. Many came to seek their fortunes after the discovery of gold in 1848 sparked the California gold rush. The Chinese helped build the nation's first transcontinental railroad as well as other railroads in the West. When the railroads were completed, they turned to farming, mining, and domestic service. Chinese immigration was sharply limited by a congressional act in 1882.

④ In 1884, the Japanese government allowed Hawaiian planters to recruit Japanese workers, and a Japanese emigration boom began. When the United States annexed Hawaii in 1898, Japanese emigration to the West Coast increased. As word of comparatively high American wages spread in Japan, the number of Japanese who entered the United States each year reached about 10,000. By 1920, more than 200,000 Japanese lived on the West Coast.

Immigrants from the West Indies and Mexico Between 1880 and 1920, about 260,000 immigrants arrived in the eastern and southeastern United States from the West Indies. They came from Jamaica, Cuba, Puerto Rico, and other islands. Many West Indians left their homelands because jobs were scarce.

The Mexican population in the United States also increased. Unlike the Europeans, Asians, and West Indians, however, some Mexicans became U.S. residents without even leaving home. As a result of the statehood of Texas in 1845 and the end of the Mexican War in 1848, the United States acquired vast territories from Mexico. Many of the residents of these territories chose to become American citizens.

Other Mexicans immigrated to the United States to find work or to flee political turmoil. As a result of the 1902 National Reclamation Act (also known as the Newlands Act), which encouraged the irrigation of arid land, new farmland was created in many Western states, including Texas, Arizona, and California. This farmland drew Mexican farm workers northward to seek jobs. After 1910, political and social upheavals in Mexico prompted even more immigration. Nearly a million people—7 percent of the population of Mexico at the time— came to the United States over the next 20 years.

What general information is presented in each of these graphic devices?

④ **Creating a Graphic Device** Create a graphic device—such as a bar graph, a line graph, or a table—that presents the numerical information in this paragraph. Which presentation of the information—graphic or textual—do you find more understandable? Explain your opinion.

⑤ Look at the bar graphs on the previous page for Illinois and New York. Write a paragraph explaining the 1900 immigration statistics for these states. Then compare your paragraph with the bar graphs. Which medium provides a better way of presenting the information?

Comparing Texts Review the article and the graphic devices. How effective would the article be without the graphic devices? How do the graphic devices contribute to your understanding of the article?

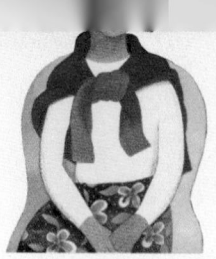

In the American Society

Short Story by GISH JEN

Traditions Across Time: Dreams Lost and Found

In this short story, a Chinese-American girl describes her immigrant parents' struggles to adjust to American society. Each of her parents clings to secret ambitions and personal dreams—like Dexter Green in "Winter Dreams" and the narrator of "America and I."

Points of Comparison As you read, think about how the challenges that the narrator's family faces contrast with those faced by the narrator of "America and I."

Build Background

Chinese Immigrants in American Society Chinese immigrants have often had difficulty being accepted in American society. In the mid-1800s, large numbers of Chinese men came to California to work in the gold mines and on the Central Pacific railroad. When an economic depression struck in the 1870s, Americans who viewed Chinese workers as unfair, lower-paid competitors for jobs raised such an outcry that in 1882 Congress passed the Chinese Exclusion Act, prohibiting immigration from China to the United States.

The lifting of this ban in 1943 led to a new wave of Chinese immigration after World War II. Many Chinese came to the United States in the late 1940s to escape the bitter civil war between the Communists and the Nationalists in their homeland. After the Communists took over mainland China in 1949, Chinese immigrants—like the character Booker in this story—came mainly from Nationalist China on the island of Taiwan. The family in the story discovers, however, that even though the immigration policy has changed, Chinese Americans still face more subtle forms of prejudice.

WORDS TO KNOW **Vocabulary Preview**

amicably	contrite	intercede	largesse	recalcitrant
cajole	forte	jubilant	panache	scrutinize

Focus Your Reading

LITERARY ANALYSIS **STRUCTURE** The **structure** of a work of literature is the way in which it is put together—the arrangement of its parts. "In the American Society" is divided into two sections. Consider why the author structured the story this way.

ACTIVE READING **MAKING INFERENCES ABOUT MOTIVATIONS** A character's **motivations** are the reasons why he or she acts, feels, or thinks in a certain way. Often you must make inferences—logical guesses or conclusions based on the evidence you find in a story—to determine these reasons. For example, while reading "In the American Society," think about the characters' actions in the story. Then combine clues from the story with what you already know from your experiences to infer the reasons for those actions.

READER'S NOTEBOOK For each of the narrator's parents, make a chart like the one shown. List several of the character's actions, the motivations you infer, and the clues you used to make your inferences.

Actions	Motivations	Clues

IN THE AMERICAN SOCIETY

GISH JEN

I. HIS OWN SOCIETY

When my father took over the pancake house, it was to send my little sister Mona and me to college. We were only in junior high at the time, but my father believed in getting a jump on things. "Those Americans always saying it," he told us. "Smart guys thinking in advance." My mother elaborated, explaining that businesses took bringing up, like children. They could take years to get going, she said, years.

In this case, though, we got rich right away. At two months we were breaking even, and at four, those same hotcakes that could barely withstand the weight of butter and syrup were supporting our family with ease. My mother bought a station wagon with air conditioning, my father an oversized, red vinyl recliner for the back room; and as time went on and the business continued to thrive, my father started to talk about

his grandfather and the village he had reigned over in China—things my father had never talked about when he worked for other people. He told us about the bags of rice his family would give out to the poor at New Year's, and about the people who came to beg, on their hands and knees, for his grandfather to intercede for the more wayward of their relatives. "Like that Godfather in the movie," he would tell us as, his feet up, he distributed paychecks. Sometimes an employee would get two green envelopes instead of one, which meant that Jimmy needed a tooth pulled, say, or that Tiffany's husband was in the clinker again.

"It's nothing, nothing," he would insist, sinking back into his chair. "Who else is going to take care of you people?"

My mother would mostly just sigh about it.

WORDS
TO
KNOW

intercede (ĭn'tər-sēd') v. to plead on behalf of another or mediate in a dispute

"Your father thinks this is China," she would say, and then she would go back to her mending. Once in a while, though, when my father had given away a particularly large sum, she would exclaim, outraged, "But this here is the U—S—of—A!"— this apparently having been what she used to tell immigrant stock boys when they came in late.

She didn't work at the supermarket anymore; but she had made it to the rank of manager before she left, and this had given her not only new words and phrases, but new ideas about herself, and about America, and about what was what in general. She had opinions, now, on how downtown should be zoned; she could pump her own gas and check her own oil; and for all she used to chide Mona and me for being "copycats," she herself was now interested in espadrilles,[1] and wallpaper, and most recently, the town country club.

"So join already," said Mona, flicking a fly off her knee.

My mother enumerated the problems as she sliced up a quarter round of watermelon: There was the cost. There was the waiting list. There was the fact that no one in our family played either tennis or golf.

"So what?" said Mona.

"It would be waste," said my mother.

"Me and Callie can swim in the pool."

"Plus you need that recommendation letter from a member."

"Come *on*," said Mona. "Annie's mom'd write you a letter in *sec*."

My mother's knife glinted in the early summer sun. I spread some more newspaper on the picnic table.

"*Plus* you have to eat there twice a month. You know what that means." My mother cut another, enormous slice of fruit.

"No, I *don't* know what that means," said Mona.

"It means Dad would have to wear a jacket, dummy," I said.

"Oh! Oh! Oh!" said Mona, clasping her hand to her breast. "Oh! Oh! Oh! Oh! Oh!"

> FOR IN MY FATHER'S MIND, A FAMILY OWED ITS HEAD A DEGREE OF LOYALTY THAT LEFT NO ROOM FOR DISSENT. TO EMBRACE WHAT HE EMBRACED WAS TO LOVE; AND TO EMBRACE SOMETHING ELSE WAS TO BETRAY HIM.

We all laughed: my father had no use for nice clothes, and would wear only ten-year-old shirts, with grease-spotted pants, to show how little he cared what anyone thought.

"Your father doesn't believe in joining the American society," said my mother. "He wants to have his own society."

"So go to dinner without him." Mona shot her seeds out in long arcs over the lawn. "Who cares what he thinks?"

But of course we all did care, and knew my mother could not simply up and do as she pleased. For in my father's mind, a family owed its head a degree of loyalty that left no room for dissent. To embrace what he embraced was to love; and to embrace something else was to betray him.

---

1. **espadrilles** (ĕs′pə-drĭlz′): casual shoes with cloth uppers and soles of twisted rope.

He demanded a similar sort of loyalty of his workers, whom he treated more like servants than employees. Not in the beginning, of course. In the beginning all he wanted was for them to keep on doing what they used to do, and to that end he concentrated mostly on leaving them alone. As the months passed, though, he expected more and more of them, with the result that for all his largesse, he began to have trouble keeping help. The cooks and busboys complained that he asked them to fix radiators and trim hedges, not only at the restaurant, but at our house; the waitresses that he sent them on errands and made them chauffeur him around. Our head waitress, Gertrude, claimed that he once even asked her to scratch his back.

"It's not just the blacks don't believe in slavery," she said when she quit.

My father never quite registered her complaint, though, nor those of the others who left. Even after Eleanor quit, then Tiffany, then Gerald, and Jimmy, and even his best cook, Eureka Andy, for whom he had bought new glasses, he remained mostly convinced that the fault lay with them.

"All they understand is that assembly line," he lamented. "Robots, they are. They want to be robots."

There *were* occasions when the clear running truth seemed to eddy,[2] when he would pinch the vinyl of his chair up into little peaks and wonder if he were doing things right. But with time he would always smooth the peaks back down; and when business started to slide in the spring, he kept on like a horse in his ways.

By the summer our dishboy was overwhelmed with scraping. It was no longer just the hashbrowns that people were leaving for trash, and the service was as bad as the food. The waitresses served up French pancakes instead of German, apple juice instead of orange, spilt things on laps, on coats. On the Fourth of July some greenhorn[3] sent an entire side of fries slaloming[4] down a lady's *massif centrale*.[5]

Meanwhile in the back room, my father labored through articles on the economy.

"What is housing starts?"[6] he puzzled. "What is GNP?"[7]

Mona and I did what we could, filling in as busgirls and bookeepers and, one afternoon, stuffing the comments box that hung by the cashier's desk. That was Mona's idea. We rustled up a variety of pens and pencils, checked boxes for an hour, smeared the cards up with coffee and grease, and waited. It took a few days for my father to notice that the box was full, and he didn't say anything about it for a few days more. Finally, though, he started to complain of fatigue; and then he began to complain that the staff was not what it could be. We encouraged him in this—pointing out, for instance, how many dishes got chipped—but in the end all that happened was that, for the first time since we took over the restaurant, my father got it into his head to fire someone. Skip, a skinny busboy who was saving up for a sportscar, said nothing as my father mumbled on about the price of dishes. My father's hands shook as he wrote out the severance check;[8] and he spent the rest of the day napping in his chair once it was over.

As it was going on midsummer, Skip wasn't easy to replace. We hung a sign in the window

---

2. **eddy:** form a whirlpool.

3. **greenhorn:** beginner.

4. **slaloming:** skiing in a zigzag path.

5. *massif centrale* (mä-sēf' sĕn-träl') *French:* central mass (usually used to refer to the highest group of peaks in a mountain range).

6. **housing starts:** the number of new houses on which construction began during a given period.

7. **GNP:** gross national product—the value of all the goods and services produced in a country during a given period. (As a measure of the strength of the national economy, the U.S. government now uses gross domestic product, or GDP, which is based on a somewhat different set of calculations.)

8. **severance check:** payment given to an employee who is dismissed.

WORDS
TO
KNOW

largesse (lär-zhĕs') *n.* generosity

880

Diner Interior with Coffee Urns (1984), Ralph Goings. Oil on canvas, 44″ × 66″, courtesy of O. K. Harris Works of Art, New York. Photo Copyright © 1985 D. James Dee.

and advertised in the paper, but no one called the first week, and the person who called the second didn't show up for his interview. The third week, my father phoned Skip to see if he would come back, but a friend of his had already sold him a Corvette for cheap.

Finally a Chinese guy named Booker turned up. He couldn't have been more than thirty, and was wearing a lighthearted seersucker suit, but he looked as though life had him pinned: his eyes were bloodshot and his chest sunken, and the muscles of his neck seemed to strain with the effort of holding his head up. In a single dry breath he told us that he had never bussed tables but was willing to learn, and that he was on the lam from the deportation authorities.[9]

"I do not want to lie to you," he kept saying.

He had come to the United States on a student visa, had run out of money, and was now in a bind. He was loath[10] to go back to Taiwan, as it happened—he looked up at this point, to be sure my father wasn't pro-KMT[11]—but all he had was a phony social security card and a willingness to absorb all blame, should anything untoward come to pass.

"I do not think, anyway, that it is against law to hire me, only to be me," he said, smiling faintly.

Anyone else would have examined him on

---

9. **on the lam from the deportation authorities:** running away from immigration officials with the power to send illegal immigrants back to their own countries.

10. **loath:** unwilling.

11. **pro-KMT:** on the side of the Kuomintang, or Nationalist Party, which controls the government of Taiwan.

Illustration Copyright © Darryl Zudeck.

this, but my father conceived of laws as speed bumps rather than curbs. He wiped the counter with his sleeve, and told Booker to report the next morning.

"I will be good worker," said Booker.

"Good," said my father.

"Anything you want me to do, I will do."

My father nodded.

Booker seemed to sink into himself for a moment. "Thank you," he said finally. "I am appreciate your help. I am very, very appreciate for everything." He reached out to shake my father's hand.

My father looked at him. "Did you eat today?" he asked in Mandarin.

Booker pulled at the hem of his jacket.

"Sit down," said my father. "Please, have a seat."

My father didn't tell my mother about Booker, and my mother didn't tell my father about the country club. She would never have applied, except that Mona, while over at Annie's, had let it drop that our mother wanted to join. Mrs. Lardner came by the very next day.

"Why, I'd be honored and delighted to write you people a letter," she said. Her skirt billowed around her.

"Thank you so much," said my mother. "But it's too much trouble for you, and also my husband is . . ."

"Oh, it's no trouble at all, no trouble at all. I tell you." She leaned forward so that her chest freckles showed. "I know just how it is. It's a secret of course, but you know, my natural father was Jewish. Can you see it? Just look at my skin."

"My husband," said my mother.

"I'd be honored and delighted," said Mrs. Lardner with a little wave of her hands. "Just honored and delighted."

Mona was triumphant. "See, Mom," she said, waltzing around the kitchen when Mrs. Lardner left. "What did I tell you? 'I'm just honored and delighted, just honored and delighted.'" She waved her hands in the air.

"You know, the Chinese have a saying," said my mother. "To do nothing is better than to overdo. You mean well, but you tell me now what will happen."

"I'll talk Dad into it," said Mona, still waltzing. "Or I bet Callie can. He'll do anything Callie says."

"I can try, anyway," I said.

"Did you hear what I said?" said my mother. Mona bumped into the broom closet door. "You're not going to talk anything; you've already made enough trouble." She started on the dishes with a clatter.

Mona poked diffidently at a mop.

I sponged off the counter. "Anyway," I ventured. "I bet our name'll never even come up."

"That's if we're lucky," said my mother.

"There's all these people waiting," I said.

"Good," she said. She started on a pot.

I looked over at Mona, who was still cowering in the broom closet. "In fact, there's some black family's been waiting so long, they're going to sue," I said.

My mother turned off the water. "Where'd you hear that?"

"Patty told me."

She turned the water back on, started to wash a dish, then put it back down and shut the faucet.

"I'm sorry," said Mona.

"Forget it," said my mother. "Just forget it."

Booker turned out to be a model worker, whose boundless gratitude translated into a willingness to do anything. As he also learned quickly, he soon knew not only how to bus, but how to cook, and how to wait table, and how to keep the books. He fixed the walk-in door so that it stayed shut, reupholstered the torn seats in the dining room, and devised a system for tracking inventory. The only stone in the rice was that he tended to be sickly; but, reliable even in illness, he would always send a friend to take his place. In this way we got to know Ronald, Lynn, Dirk, and Cedric, all of whom, like Booker, had problems with their legal status and were anxious to please. They weren't all as capable as Booker, though, with the exception of Cedric, whom my father often hired even when Booker was well. A round wag of a man who called Mona and me *shou hou*—skinny monkeys—he was a professed nonsmoker who was nevertheless always begging drags off of other people's cigarettes. This last habit drove our head cook, Fernando, crazy, especially since, when refused a hit, Cedric would occasionally snitch one. Winking impishly at Mona and me, he would steal up to an ashtray, take a quick puff, and then break out laughing so that the smoke came rolling out of his mouth in a great incriminatory cloud. Fernando accused him of stealing fresh cigarettes too, even whole packs.

"Why else do you think he's weaseling around in the back of the store all the time," he said. His face was blotchy with anger. "The man is a thief."

Other members of the staff supported him in this contention and joined in on an "Operation Identification," which involved numbering and initialing their cigarettes—even though what they seemed to fear for wasn't so much their cigarettes as their jobs. Then one of the cooks quit; and rather than promote someone, my father hired Cedric for the position. Rumors flew that he was taking only half the normal salary, that Alex had been pressured to resign, and that my father was looking for a position with which to placate Booker, who had been bypassed because of his health.

The result was that Fernando categorically refused to work with Cedric.

"The only way I'll cook with that piece of slime," he said, shaking his huge tattooed fist, "is if he's frying on the grill."

My father cajoled and cajoled, to no avail, and in the end was simply forced to put them on different schedules.

The next week Fernando got caught stealing a carton of minute steaks. My father would not tell even Mona and me how he knew to be standing by the back door when Fernando was on his way out, but everyone suspected Booker. Everyone but Fernando, that is, who was sure Cedric had been the tip-off. My father held a staff meeting in which he tried to reassure everyone that Alex had left on his own, and that he had no intention of firing anyone. But though he was careful not to mention Fernando, everyone was so amazed that he was being allowed to stay that Fernando was incensed nonetheless.

"Don't you all be putting your bug eyes on me," he said. "*He's* the crook." He grabbed Cedric by the collar.

Cedric raised an eyebrow. "Cook, you mean," he said.

At this Fernando punched Cedric in the mouth; and the words he had just uttered notwithstanding, my father fired him on the spot.

With everything that was happening, Mona and I were ready to be getting out of the restaurant. It was almost time: the days were still stuffy with summer, but our window shade had started flapping in the evening as if gearing up to go out. That year the breezes were full of salt, as they sometimes were when they came in from the East, and they blew anchors and docks through my mind like so many tumbleweeds, filling my dreams with wherries[12] and lobsters and grainy-faced men who squinted, day in and day out, at the sky.

It was time for a change, you could feel it; and yet the pancake house was the same as ever. The day before school started my father came home with bad news.

"Fernando called police," he said, wiping his hand on his pant leg.

My mother naturally wanted to know what police; and so with much coughing and hawing, the long story began, the latest installment of which had the police calling immigration, and immigration sending an investigator. My mother sat stiff as whalebone as my father described how the man summarily refused lunch on the house and how my father had admitted, under pressure, that he knew there were "things" about his workers.

"So now what happens?"

My father didn't know. "Booker and Cedric went with him to the jail," he said. "But me, here I am." He laughed uncomfortably.

The next day my father posted bail for "his boys" and waited apprehensively for something to happen. The day after that he waited again, and the day after that he called our neighbor's law student son, who suggested my father call the immigration department under an alias. My father took his advice; and it was thus that he discovered that Booker was right: it was illegal for aliens to work, but it wasn't to hire them.[13]

In the happy interval that ensued, my father apologized to my mother, who in turn confessed about the country club, for which my father had no choice but to forgive her. Then he turned his attention back to "his boys."

My mother didn't see that there was anything to do.

---

12. **wherries:** light rowboats.

13. **it wasn't to hire them:** Although this statement was true at the time, U.S. law now prohibits the hiring of illegal aliens.

WORDS
TO
KNOW   **cajole** (kə-jōl′) *v.* to persuade by pleasant words or flattery; coax

WITH EVERYTHING
THAT WAS HAPPENING,
MONA AND I WERE READY
TO BE GETTING OUT
OF THE RESTAURANT.
IT WAS ALMOST TIME:
THE DAYS WERE STILL
STUFFY WITH SUMMER,
BUT OUR WINDOW SHADE
HAD STARTED FLAPPING
IN THE EVENING AS IF
GEARING UP TO GO OUT.

"I like to talking to the judge," said my father.

"This is not China," said my mother.

"I'm only talking to him. I'm not give him money unless he wants it."

"You're going to land up in jail."

"So what else I should do?" My father threw up his hands. "Those are my boys."

"Your boys!" exploded my mother. "What about your family? What about your wife?"

My father took a long sip of tea. "You know," he said finally. "In the war my father sent our cook to the soldiers to use. He always said it— the province comes before the town, the town comes before the family."

"A restaurant is not a town," said my mother.

My father sipped at his tea again. "You know, when I first come to the United States, I also had to hide-and-seek with those deportation guys. If people did not helping me, I'm not here today."

My mother <u>scrutinized</u> her hem.

After a minute I volunteered that before seeing a judge, he might try a lawyer.

He turned. "Since when did you become so afraid like your mother?"

I started to say that it wasn't a matter of fear, but he cut me off.

"What I need today," he said, "is a son."

My father and I spent the better part of the next day standing in lines at the immigration office. He did not get to speak to a judge, but with much persistence he managed to speak to a judge's clerk, who tried to persuade him that it was not her place to extend him advice. My father, though, shamelessly plied her with compliments and offers of free pancakes until she finally conceded that she personally doubted anything would happen to either Cedric or Booker.

"Especially if they're 'needed workers,'" she said, rubbing at the red marks her glasses left on her nose. She yawned. "Have you thought about sponsoring them to become permanent residents?"

Could he do that? My father was overjoyed. And what if he saw to it right away? Would she

perhaps put in a good word with the judge?

She yawned again, her nostrils flaring. "Don't worry," she said. "They'll get a fair hearing."

My father returned <u>jubilant</u>. Booker and Cedric hailed him as their savior, their Buddha incarnate. He was like a father to them, they said; and laughing and clapping, they made him tell the story over and over, sorting over the details like jewels. And how old was the assistant judge? And what did she say?

That evening my father tipped the paperboy a dollar and bought a pot of mums for my mother, who suffered them to be placed on the dining room table. The next night he took us all out to dinner. Then on Saturday, Mona found a letter on my father's chair at the restaurant.

Dear Mr. Chang,
You are the grat boss. But, we do not like to trial, so will runing away now. Plese to excus us. People saying the law in America is fears like dragon. Here is only $140. We hope some day we can pay back the rest bale. You will getting intrest, as you diserving, so grat a boss you are. Thank you for every thing. In next life you will be burn in rich family, with no more pancaks.

Yours truley,
Booker + Cedric

In the weeks that followed my father went to the pancake house for crises, but otherwise hung around our house, fiddling idly with the sump pump and boiler in an effort, he said, to get ready for winter. It was as though he had gone into retirement, except that instead of moving South, he had moved to the basement. He even took to showering my mother with little attentions, and to calling her "old girl," and when we finally heard that the club had entertained all the applications it could for the year, he was so sympathetic that he seemed more disappointed than my mother.

Mrs. Lardner tempered the bad news with an invitation to a bon voyage[14] "bash" she was throwing for a friend of hers who was going to Greece for six months.

"Do come," she urged. "You'll meet everyone, and then, you know, if things open up in the spring . . ." She waved her hands.

My mother wondered if it would be appropriate to show up at a party for someone they didn't know, but "the honest truth" was that this was an annual affair. "If it's not Greece, it's Antibes," sighed Mrs. Lardner. "We really just do it because his wife left him and his daughter doesn't speak to him, and poor Jeremy just feels so *unloved.*"

She also invited Mona and me to the goings on, as "*demi*-guests" to keep Annie out of the champagne. I wasn't too keen on the idea, but before I could say anything, she had already thanked us for so generously agreeing to honor her with our presence.

"A pair of little princesses, you are!" she told us. "A pair of princesses!"

The party was that Sunday. On Saturday, my mother took my father out shopping for a suit. As it was the end of September, she insisted that he buy a worsted rather than a seersucker, even though it was only ten, rather than fifty percent off. My father protested that it was as hot out as ever, which was true—a thick Indian summer had cozied murderously up to us—but to no avail. Summer clothes, said my mother, were not properly worn after Labor Day.

The suit was unfortunately as extravagant in length as it was in price, which posed an additional quandary, since the tailor wouldn't be in until Monday. The salesgirl, though, found a way of tacking it up temporarily.

"Maybe this suit not fit me," fretted my father.

"Just don't take your jacket off," said the salesgirl. He gave her a tip before they left, but when he got home refused to remove the price tag.

"I like to asking the tailor about the size," he insisted.

"You mean you're going to *wear* it and then return it?" Mona rolled her eyes.

"I didn't say I'm return it," said my father stiffly. "I like to asking the tailor, that's all."

The party started off swimmingly, except that most people were wearing bermudas or wrap skirts. Still, my parents carried on, sharing with great feeling the complaints about the heat. Of course my father tried to eat a cracker full of shallots[15] and burnt himself in an attempt to help Mr. Lardner turn the coals of the barbeque; but on the whole he seemed to be doing all right. Not nearly so well as my mother, though, who had accepted an entire cupful of Mrs. Lardner's magic punch, and seemed indeed to be under some spell. As Mona and Annie skirmished over whether some boy in their class inhaled when he smoked, I watched my mother take off her shoes, laughing and laughing as a man with a beard regaled her with navy stories by the pool. Apparently he had been stationed in the Orient and remembered a few words of Chinese, which made my mother laugh still more. My father excused himself to go to the men's room then drifted back and weighed anchor at the hors d'oeuvres table, while my mother sailed on to a group of women, who tinkled at length over the clarity of her complexion. I dug out a book I had brought.

Just when I'd cracked the spine, though, Mrs. Lardner came by to bewail her shortage of servers. Her caterers were criminals, I agreed; and the next thing I knew I was handing out bits of marine life, making the rounds as amicably as I could.

"Here you go, Dad," I said when I got to the hors d'oeuvres table.

---

14. **bon voyage** (bôn′ vwä-yäzh′): a farewell to a traveler.

15. **shallots:** small garliclike onions.

"Everything is fine," he said.

I hesitated to leave him alone; but then the man with the beard zeroed in on him, and though he talked of nothing but my mother, I thought it would be okay to get back to work. Just that moment, though, Jeremy Brothers lurched our way, an empty, albeit corked, wine bottle in hand. He was a slim, well-proportioned man, with a Roman nose and small eyes and a nice manly jaw that he allowed to hang agape.

"Hello," he said drunkenly. "Pleased to meet you."

"Pleased to meeting you," said my father.

"Right," said Jeremy. "Right. Listen. I have this bottle here, this most <u>recalcitrant</u> bottle. You see that it refuses to do my bidding. I bid it open sesame, please, and it does nothing." He pulled the cork out with his teeth, then turned the bottle upside down.

My father nodded.

"Would you have a word with it please?" said Jeremy. The man with the beard excused himself. "Would you please have a damned word with it?"

My father laughed uncomfortably.

"Ah!" Jeremy bowed a little. "Excuse me, excuse me, excuse me. You are not my man, not my man at all." He bowed again and started to leave, but then circled back. "Viticulture[16] is not your <u>forte</u>, yes I can see that, see that plainly. But may I trouble you on another matter? Forget the damned bottle." He threw it into the pool, and winked at the people he splashed. "I have another matter. Do you speak Chinese?"

My father said he did not, but Jeremy pulled out a handkerchief with some characters on it anyway, saying that his daughter had sent it from Hong Kong and that he thought the characters might be some secret message.

"Long life," said my father.

"But you haven't looked at it yet."

"I know what it says without looking." My father winked at me.

"You do?"

"Yes, I do."

"You're making fun of me, aren't you?"

"No, no, no," said my father, winking again.

"Who are you anyway?" said Jeremy.

His smile fading, my father shrugged.

"Who are you?"

My father shrugged again.

Jeremy began to roar. "This is my party, *my party*, and I've never seen you before in my life." My father backed up as Jeremy came toward him. "*Who are you? WHO ARE YOU?*"

Just as my father was going to step back into the pool, Mrs. Lardner came running up. Jeremy informed her that there was a man crashing his party.

"Nonsense," said Mrs. Lardner. "This is Ralph Chang, who I invited extra especially so he could meet you." She straightened the collar of Jeremy's peach-colored polo shirt for him.

"Yes, well we've had a chance to chat," said Jeremy.

She whispered in his ear; he mumbled something; she whispered something more.

"I do apologize," he said finally.

My father didn't say anything.

"I do." Jeremy seemed genuinely <u>contrite</u>. "Doubtless you've seen drunks before, haven't you? You must have them in China."

"Okay," said my father.

As Mrs. Lardner glided off, Jeremy clapped his arm over my father's shoulders. "You know, I really am quite sorry, quite sorry."

My father nodded.

"What can I do, how can I make it up to you?"

"No thank you."

"No, tell me, tell me," wheedled Jeremy. "Tickets to casino night?" My father shook his head. "You don't gamble. Dinner at Bartholomew's?" My father shook his head again.

---

16. **viticulture**: the growing of grapevines.

WORDS TO KNOW

recalcitrant (rǐ-kăl′sǐ-trənt) *adj.* stubborn; hard to deal with
forte (fôrt) *n.* something in which a person excels
contrite (kən-trīt′) *adj.* sorrowful for one's wrongdoing; repentant

The Splash (1966), David Hockney. Acrylic on canvas, 72″ × 72″.
Copyright © David Hockney.

"WHO ARE YOU?

WHO ARE YOU?"

"You don't eat." Jeremy scratched his chin. "You know, my wife was like you. Old Annabelle could never let me make things up— never, never, never, never, never."

My father wriggled out from under his arm.

"How about sport clothes? You are rather over-dressed, you know, excuse me for saying so. But here." He took off his polo shirt and folded it up. "You can have this with my most profound apologies." He ruffled his chest hairs with his free hand.

"No thank you," said my father.

"No, take it, take it. Accept my apologies." He thrust the shirt into my father's arms. "I'm so very sorry, so very sorry. Please, try it on."

Helplessly holding the shirt, my father searched the crowd for my mother.

"Here, I'll help you off with your coat."

My father froze.

Jeremy reached over and took his jacket off. "Milton's, one hundred twenty-five dollars reduced to one hundred twelve-fifty," he read. "What a bargain, what a bargain!"

"Please give it back," pleaded my father. "Please."

"Now for your shirt," ordered Jeremy.

Heads began to turn.

"Take off your shirt."

"I do not take orders like a servant," announced my father.

"Take off your shirt, or I'm going to throw this jacket right into the pool, just right into this little pool here." Jeremy held it over the water.

"Go ahead."

"One hundred twelve-fifty," taunted Jeremy. "One hundred twelve . . ."

My father flung the polo shirt into the water with such force that part of it bounced back up into the air like a fluorescent fountain. Then it settled into a soft heap on top of the water. My mother hurried up.

"You're a sport!" said Jeremy, suddenly breaking into a smile and slapping my father on the back. "You're a sport! I like that. A man with spirit, that's what you are. A man with panache. Allow me to return to you your jacket." He handed it back to my father. "Good value you got on that, good value."

My father hurled the coat into the pool too. "We're leaving," he said grimly. "Leaving!"

"Now, Ralphie," said Mrs. Lardner, bustling up; but my father was already stomping off.

"Get your sister," he told me. To my mother: "Get your shoes."

"That was *great*, Dad," said Mona as we walked down to the car. "You were *stupendous*."

"Way to show 'em," I said.

"What?" said my father offhandedly.

Although it was only just dusk, we were in a gulch, which made it hard to see anything except the gleam of his white shirt moving up the hill ahead of us.

"It was all my fault," began my mother.

"Forget it," said my father grandly. Then he said, "The only trouble is I left those keys in my jacket pocket."

"Oh *no*," said Mona.

"Oh no is right," said my mother.

"So we'll walk home," I said.

"But how're we going to get into the *house*," said Mona.

The noise of the party churned through the silence.

"Someone has to going back," said my father.

"Let's go to the pancake house first," suggested my mother. "We can wait there until the party is finished, and then call Mrs. Lardner."

Having all agreed that that was a good plan, we started walking again.

"God, just think," said Mona. "We're going to have to *dive* for them."

My father stopped a moment. We waited.

"You girls are good swimmers," he said finally. "Not like me."

Then his shirt started moving again, and we trooped up the hill after it, into the dark. ❖

WORDS TO KNOW **panache** (pə-năsh′) *n.* a sense of style; flair

My Father and the Figtree

Naomi Shihab Nye

For other fruits my father was indifferent.
He'd point at the cherry trees and say,
"See those? I wish they were figs."
In the evenings he sat by my bed
weaving folktales like vivid little scarves.
They always involved a figtree.
Even when it didn't fit, he'd stick it in.
Once Joha was walking down the road and he saw a figtree.
Or, he tied his camel to a figtree and went to sleep.
Or, later when they caught and arrested him,
his pockets were full of figs.

At age six I ate a dried fig and shrugged.
"That's not what I'm talking about!" he said,
"I'm talking about a fig straight from the earth—
gift of Allah!—on a branch so heavy it touches the ground.
I'm talking about picking the largest fattest sweetest fig
in the world and putting it in my mouth."
(Here he'd stop and close his eyes.)

Years passed, we lived in many houses, none had figtrees.
We had lima beans, zucchini, parsley, beets.
"Plant one!" my mother said, but my father never did.
He tended garden half-heartedly, forgot to water, let the okra get too big.
"What a dreamer he is. Look how many things he starts
and doesn't finish."

The last time he moved, I got a phone call.
My father, in Arabic, chanting a song I'd never heard.
"What's that?"
"Wait till you see!"

He took me out to the new yard.
There, in the middle of Dallas, Texas,
a tree with the largest, fattest, sweetest figs in the world.
"It's a figtree song!" he said,
plucking his fruits like ripe tokens,
emblems, assurance
of a world that was always his own.

Thinking through the LITERATURE

Connect to the Literature

1. What Do You Think? As you finished reading this story, what did you think of the Chang family? Share your comments with the class.

> **Comprehension Check**
> - What does the narrator's mother want to join?
> - Why are Booker and Cedric arrested?
> - What does the father do with Jeremy's shirt and his own jacket?

Think Critically

2. **ACTIVE READING** **MAKING INFERENCES ABOUT MOTIVATIONS** How would you explain why Mr. Chang hurls his coat into the pool at Mrs. Lardner's party? Share some other inferences you made about the motivations for characters' behavior.

3. What is your opinion of the way the members of Mr. Chang's family treat him?

4. What does fitting into American society seem to mean to Mr. Chang? to Mrs. Chang?

5. How would you describe the American society that the Changs encounter?

6. In your view, is Mr. Chang more effective in his own society (Section I) or in the American society (Section II)?

THINK ABOUT
- the way he treats his employees
- his efforts to help Booker and Cedric
- his encounter with Jeremy Brothers

Extend Interpretations

7. What If? What do you think might have happened if Mr. Chang had returned to Mrs. Lardner's party to retrieve his keys?

8. Connect to Life For Mrs. Chang, joining the country club is an important sign of success in American society. What do you consider signs of success?

9. **Points of Comparison** How would you contrast the challenges that the Changs face in America with those faced by the narrator of "America and I" (page 864)?

Literary Analysis

STRUCTURE The **structure** of a work of literature is the way in which it is put together—the arrangement of its parts. Prose writing is most often structured either by idea or by incident. Gish Jen uses a two-part structure for her story, giving each section its own title: "I. His Own Society" and "II. In the American Society."

Cooperative Learning Activity With a small group of classmates, create a chart that lists similarities and differences between the two sections of this story. Then discuss these questions: What is the focus of each section? What do the sections tell together that neither tells alone? Share your chart with another group.

	setting	characters	events	conflicts
Section I				
Section II				

REVIEW **CHARACTERS** Earlier you learned that **static** characters remain the same over the course of a story, while **dynamic** characters learn and grow. Would you classify Mr. and Mrs. Chang as static or dynamic characters? Explain.

Choices & CHALLENGES

Writing Options

1. **Points of Comparison**

How would Mr. or Mrs. Chang define the American dream? Write an essay comparing his or her definition with Dexter Green's in "Winter Dreams" (page 841). Place this piece in your **Working Portfolio.**

Writing Handbook
See page 1281: Compare and Contrast

2. Argument about Assimilation

Outline an argument for or against assimilation—the process of adapting one's values and expectations in order to fit into the prevailing society. Keep in mind issues such as cultural identity, personal integrity, and economic necessity, and support your argument with reasons and examples drawn from this story and from the poem "My Father and the Figtree" (page 891).

3. Critical Review

Did reading this story make you want to read another work by Gish Jen? In a draft of a critical review, discuss an aspect of the story—such as **tone, characterization,** or **theme**—that you particularly admired or disliked. Quote passages from the story to illustrate your ideas.

Vocabulary in Action

EXERCISE A: ASSESSMENT PRACTICE For each group of words below, write the letter of the word that is a synonym of the boldfaced word.

1. **cajole:** (a) coax, (b) support, (c) control
2. **recalcitrant:** (a) ignorant, (b) unlucky, (c) headstrong
3. **forte:** (a) talent, (b) security, (c) sensitivity
4. **amicably:** (a) intensely, (b) pleasantly, (c) efficiently
5. **contrite:** (a) shallow, (b) clever, (c) apologetic

EXERCISE B: MEANING CLUES Write the vocabulary word, not used in Exercise A, that is suggested by each set of idioms.

1. walking on air, feeling one's heart sing, being A-OK
2. giving the shirt off one's back, being openhanded, showering blessings upon
3. take up the case of, be a go-between, pave the way
4. pore over, dig into, comb through
5 carry it off with style, show a lot of dash, strut one's stuff

Building Vocabulary

Most of the Words to Know in this lesson come from French. For an in-depth lesson on word origins, see page 550.

WORDS TO KNOW	amicably cajole contrite forte	intercede jubilant largesse panache	recalcitrant scrutinize

Gish Jen
1956?–

Other Works
Mona in the Promised Land
"What Means Switch"
"The Water-Faucet Vision"

Cultural Conflicts Gish Jen, the daughter of Chinese immigrants, grew up in Scarsdale, New York, where hers was the only Asian family in the neighborhood. Like Ralph Chang's daughters in "In the American Society," Jen often felt ill at ease growing up in American society: "I'd learn all these manners from my parents . . . and then I found I didn't have the right manners for this society, and so I then had to learn this whole other set of right manners for this place where we were living."

First Novel In 1991 Jen published her first novel, *Typical American*, which was nominated for a National Book Critics Circle Award. The novel grew out of several short stories, including "In the American Society," as well as her experiences during a nine-month stay in China, when she taught English to coal-mining engineers.

Defining the Grateful Gesture

Poetry by YVONNE SAPIA

Refugee Ship

Poetry by LORNA DEE CERVANTES

Comparing Literature

Traditions Across Time: Dreams Lost and Found

"Defining the Grateful Gesture" and "Refugee Ship" are modern poems about the conflicts experienced in some immigrant families. The speakers in these poems are American-born children of immigrant parents. Like the narrator in "America and I," these speakers describe conflicts that are part of the process of adapting to a different culture.

Points of Comparison As you read, think about the speakers' conflicts. How would you compare them with the narrator's in "America and I"?

Build Background

Hispanic Immigrants Many recent immigrants to the United States are from Spanish-speaking countries. Like immigrants of the past, they left their native lands for economic, social, or political reasons. In search of a better future in America, they have had to adjust to a new life and a different culture. Sometimes, this process can trigger family conflict. For example, immigrant parents may cling to their native languages, foods, and customs; their American-born children, on the other hand, may prefer American ways and feel distant from their parents' culture.

Focus Your Reading

LITERARY ANALYSIS **THEME AND TITLE** The **theme** of a literary work is the central idea or ideas the writer wishes to share with the reader. Sometimes the **title** of a work may provide clues about the writer's message. Think about what the titles of these poems suggest about their messages.

ACTIVE READING **DRAWING CONCLUSIONS ABOUT THEME** In these poems, the **theme** is not stated directly. Instead, the reader must **draw conclusions** about the central idea based on evidence discovered in the poem. Use these tips to gather the evidence you need:

- Read the poem more than once, silently and aloud, without trying to figure out the central idea; instead, use your imagination to recreate the speaker's experiences, and try to relate them to your own.
- Note the details that impress you most.
- Describe the speaker's conflict in your own words.

READER'S NOTEBOOK For each poem, fill in a chart listing connections between the speaker's experience and your own, key details, and a description of the speaker's conflict.

Connections	Key Details	Speaker's Conflict

Defining the Grateful Gesture

Yvonne Sapia

*A*ccording to our mother,
when she was a child
what was placed before her
for dinner was not a feast,
5   but she would eat it
to gain back the strength
taken from her by long hot days
of working in her mother's house
and helping her father make
10 candy in the family kitchen.
No idle passenger
traveling through life was she.

And that's why she resolved
to tell stories about
15 the appreciation for satisfied hunger.
When we would sit down
for our evening meal
of arroz con pollo[1]
or frijoles negros con plátanos[2]

---

1. **arroz con pollo** (ä-rôs′ kôn pô′yô) *Spanish:*
   rice with chicken.
2. **frijoles negros con plátanos** (frē-hô′lĕs
   nĕ′grôs kôn plä′tä-nôs) *Spanish:* black beans
   with plantains (banana-like fruits).

Analogía IV (1972)), Victor Grippo.
59 cm × 76 cm × 94.5 cm, collection
of Jorge and Marion Helft.

20 she would expect us
    to be reverent to the sources
    of our undeserved nourishment,
    and to strike a thankful pose
    before each lift of the fork
25 or swirl of the spoon.

    For the dishes she prepared
    we were ungrateful,
    she would say, and repeat
    her archetypal[3] tale about the Perez
30 brothers from her girlhood town of Ponce,[4]
    who looked like ripe mangoes,
    their cheeks rosed despite poverty.
    My mother would then tell us about the
        day
    she saw Mrs. Perez searching
35 the neighborhood garbage,
    picking out with a missionary's care
    the edible potato peels, the plantain skins,

    the shafts of old celery to take
    home to her muchachos[5]
40 who required more food
    than she could afford.

    Although my brothers and I never
    quite mastered the ritual
    of obedience our mother craved,
45 and as supplicants failed
    to feed her with our worthiness,
    we'd sit like solemn loaves of bread,
    sighing over the white plates
    with a sense of realization, or relief,
50 guilty about possessing appetite.

---

3. **archetypal** (är´kĭ-tī´pəl): serving as an ideal example.
4. **Ponce** (pôn´sā): a seaport city of Puerto Rico.
5. **muchachos** (mōō-chä´chôs) *Spanish:* boys.

Thinking Through the Literature

1. **Comprehension Check** What did Mrs. Perez do to get more food for her children?

2. How would you evaluate the speaker's mother?

    THINK ABOUT
   - her attitude toward her children
   - the values she tries to give them
   - why she tells stories about her life in Puerto Rico

3. **ACTIVE READING** **DRAWING CONCLUSIONS ABOUT THEME**
   How would you state the theme of this poem? Use the evidence you listed in
   your **READER'S NOTEBOOK**.

Femme Violette, Wifredo Lam. Photo courtesy of Sotheby's, New York.

Refugee Ship

LORNA

DEE

CERVANTES

Like wet cornstarch, I slide
past my grandmother's eyes. Bible
at her side, she removes her glasses.
The pudding thickens.

5   Mama raised me without language.
I'm orphaned from my Spanish name.
The words are foreign, stumbling
on my tongue. I see in the mirror
my reflection: bronzed skin, black hair.

10 I feel I am a captive
aboard the refugee ship.
The ship that will never dock.
El barco que nunca atraca.[1]

---

1. *El barco que nunca atraca* (ĕl bär′kô kĕ
   nōōn′kä ä-trä-kä′): This is a translation,
   in Spanish, of the previous line.

Thinking through the LITERATURE

Connect to the Literature

1. What Do You Think?
What are your impressions of the speaker? Share them with your classmates.

> **Comprehension Check**
> • What language does the speaker use with difficulty?

Think Critically

2. Why do you think the **speaker** ends this poem with the Spanish translation of the line "The ship that will never dock"?

3. How would you describe the speaker's situation?

 {
• her comparison of herself to a captive aboard a refugee ship
• her attitude toward her Hispanic heritage

4. What, if anything, might the speaker do to improve her situation? Explain your answer.

5. **ACTIVE READING** **DRAWING CONCLUSIONS ABOUT THEME** How would you state the **theme** of this poem? Is the central idea similar to or different from the central idea of "Defining the Grateful Gesture"? Explain your answer by citing evidence listed in your 📖 **READER'S NOTEBOOK.**

Extend Interpretations

6. Connect to Life Why is it important that children appreciate their ethnic heritage?

7. **Points of Comparison** How would you compare the speaker's conflicts with the narrator's in "America and I"? (page 864)

Literary Analysis

THEME AND TITLE The **theme** is the central idea or message of a literary work. Theme should not be confused with subject—or what a work is about. Rather, theme is a perception about life or human nature, sometimes directly stated, but often only implied. At times, different readers may discover different themes in the same work.

The **title** of a work may suggest its theme. For example, "Winter Dreams," the title of F. Scott Fitzgerald's short story (page 841), emphasizes Dexter's dreams of youth rather than his later disillusionment. The title suggests that the theme of the story concerns the nature of youthful dreams.

Cooperative Learning Activity With a small group of classmates, discuss the appropriateness of the titles of these poems, "Defining the Grateful Gesture" and "Refugee Ship." Think about connections between title and theme, and brainstorm alternative titles for each poem. Then list two or more reasons why you think each poet chose the title she did. Share your list with other groups.

Choices & CHALLENGES

Writing Options

1. **Points of Comparison** The process of adapting to American life has consequences—both good and bad—for immigrants and their children. Describe these consequences in an essay, using examples from these poems and "America and I"

(page 864). Place this piece in your **Working Portfolio.** 📁

Writing Handbook
See page 1281: Compare and Contrast

2. Review of Sapia's Language
Yvonne Sapia has described her goals as a poet: "In order to understand what is happening to all of us in a world we have become too busy to observe significantly, I try to convey the

intense emotion of illuminating experience with sparse and carefully chosen language." Write a review about her choice of language in "Defining the Grateful Gesture." For example, you might describe the effects she creates by choosing words with religious connotations, such as "reverent," "ritual," "supplicants," and "solemn."

Yvonne Sapia
1946–

Other Works
The Fertile Crescent

Writer and Teacher Born in New York City, poet and novelist Yvonne Sapia received a bachelor's degree from Florida Atlantic University, a master's degree from the University of Florida, and a doctorate from Florida State University. She has worked as a reporter for the *Village Post* in Miami, taught at Florida state prisons, and conducted poetry workshops for gifted children and the elderly. She also has taught English at Lake City Community College in Florida.

Literary Awards Sapia received the Samuel French Morse Poetry Prize for her collection *Valentino's Hair*, which includes "Defining the Grateful Gesture." In 1991 she won the Charles H. and N. Mildred Nilon Excellence in Minority Fiction Award for her first novel, also entitled *Valentino's Hair.* The daughter of a Puerto Rican barber, Sapia was inspired by her father's real-life experience of cutting the hair of Rudolph Valentino, a silent-movie idol of the 1920s. Besides writing fiction and poetry, Sapia has also tried her hand at playwriting, finding plays "a way to free the voices of my characters."

Lorna Dee Cervantes
1954–

Other Works
From the Cables of Genocide: Poems on Love and Hunger

Cultural Background Feminist poet and editor Lorna Dee Cervantes was born in San Francisco, California. Of Native American and Mexican ancestry, she grew up in a Mexican-American *barrio* in San Jose and was active in the Chicano movement in the 1970s. In poems such as "Refugee Ship," she addresses the conflict of cultures that many Americans of Mexican descent experience. She also founded a small press called Mango Publications to publish the work of Chicano writers.

Literary Acclaim Cervantes's first book of poetry, *Emplumada* (1981), won the American Book Award from the Before Columbus Foundation. Using bold, simple imagery, she traces her own life—from her experiences living in the *barrio* through her discovery of "books, those staunch, upright men." The recipient of two National Endowment for the Arts grants, Cervantes won the Paterson Poetry Prize for her second book, *From the Cables of Genocide: Poems on Love and Hunger* (1991).

Comparing Literature: Assessment Practice

In writing assessments, you will sometimes be asked to analyze a work of literature, or examine its parts. You are now going to practice writing an analytical essay in which you focus on one literary element.

PART 1 Reading the Prompt

First, read the entire prompt carefully. Then read through it again, looking for key words and phrases that help you identify the purpose of the essay and ways to approach it.

Writing Prompt

Choose two selections from Unit 5, Part 2—one from the early 20th century and one from the late 20th century. Analyze how the characters are affected by the American dream of wealth and social success. Support your ideas with evidence. ➊

➋

STRATEGIES IN ACTION

➊ **To analyze** is to look at parts and relationships. You must identify different ways that characters are influenced by the American dream.

➋ Include **examples** and **quotations** from the selections.

PART 2 Planning an Analytical Essay

- Pick two selections to analyze, and create a diagram for each main character.
- Look for descriptions of characters' responses to wealth and social success.
- Cite examples of goals, achievements, and disappointments that reflect the influence of the American dream.
- Link examples that illustrate the same point.

How does American Dream Affect . . .		
Goals?	Achievements?	Disappointments?

PART 3 Drafting Your Essay

Introduction State the focus of your essay—how the American dream shapes the characters in the two selections you have chosen. Identify the authors and titles, and briefly present the characters you will analyze.

Organization Arrange the supporting evidence logically. Choose instances that most strongly illustrate your points.

Conclusion In the final paragraph, try to draw a conclusion about the overall impact of the American dream on the characters' lives.

Revision Make sure your work is clear, well-supported, and free of mistakes.

Writing Handbook
See page 1283: Analysis

PART 2 Extend Your *Reading*

LITERATURE CONNECTIONS

A Raisin in the Sun

LORRAINE HANSBERRY

These thematically related readings are provided along with *A Raisin in the Sun*:

Queens, 1963
JULIA ALVAREZ

Everything That Rises Must Converge
FLANNERY O'CONNOR

Dreams
LANGSTON HUGHES

Judith's Fancy
AUDRE LORDE

Emerald City: Third & Pike
CHARLOTTE WATSON SHERMAN

Running from Racists
SUZANNE SEIXAS

The Beach Umbrella
CYRUS COLTER

What Is Africa to Me?—A Question of Identity
PAULI MURRAY

The Great Gatsby

F. SCOTT FITZGERALD

Fitzgerald's novel, set in New York during the 1920s, echoes the themes and motifs of his story "Winter Dreams." Though Jay Gatsby has achieved material success, his flighty dream girl, Daisy Buchanan, remains out of reach. Daisy, her brash husband Tom, and the other characters inhabit the glittering world of the Jazz Age, where wealth and glamour reign.

And Even *More . . .*

Books

Spoon River Anthology
EDGAR LEE MASTERS
A collection of 244 free-verse monologues spoken by the deceased residents of a fictional town.

American Dreams, Lost and Found
STUDS TERKEL
The Pulitzer Prize-winning author's interviews with people who present their views of the American Dream.

The Immigrant Experience: The Anguish of Becoming American
EDITED BY THOMAS C. WHEELER
Nine first-person accounts of the immigrant experience.

Other Media

Carl Sandburg Reading Cool Tombs and Other Poems
Oral interpretations from the celebrated poet. Caedmon. (AUDIOCASSETTE)

A Raisin in the Sun
Film adaptation of Lorraine Hansberry's play, starring Sidney Poitier. Columbia Home Pictures Video. (VIDEOCASSETTE)

The Women of Brewster Place
Film adaptation of Gloria Naylor's novel about seven African-American women struggling to surmount the obstacles that thwart their hopes and dreams. Phoenix Entertainment Group, Inc. (VIDEOCASSETTE)

Imagining America: Stories from the Promised Land

EDITED BY WESLEY BROWN AND AMY LING
In this anthology of short stories, the voices of 20th-century writers from diverse cultures share their visions of American society. Fictional immigrants and migrants struggle to adapt to alien cultures and to discover the meaning of their identities as Americans.

Writing Workshop

Examining similarities and differences. . .

From Reading to Writing In F. Scott Fitzgerald's story "Winter Dreams," the narrator observes, "Dexter Green's father owned the second best grocery-store in Black Bear—the best one was 'The Hub,' patronized by the wealthy people from Sherry Island." The comparisons in this passage help readers understand more about Dexter's life. You can use **comparison and contrast** any time you want to analyze the similarities and differences between objects, people, experiences, or effects.

For Your Portfolio

WRITING PROMPT Write a comparison-and-contrast essay in which you explore the similarities and differences between two or more subjects that interest you.

Purpose: To explain, illustrate, or clarify
Audience: People interested in the subjects being compared

Basics in a Box

Comparison-and-Contrast Essay at a Glance

Introduction
• Identifies the **subjects** being compared
• Tells the **purpose** for the comparison

Body

Subject A only   Both Subjects   Subject B only

Explains similarities and differences

Conclusion
Restates the **main idea** or draws a **conclusion**

RUBRIC Standards for Writing

A successful comparison-and-contrast essay should
• identify the subjects being compared
• establish a clear reason for the comparison
• include both similarities and differences and support them with specific examples and details
• follow a clear organizational pattern
• use transitional words and phrases to make the relationships among ideas clear
• summarize the comparison in the conclusion

Analyzing a Student Model

Jillian Braithwaite
Evander Childs High School

Antigua: Almost Paradise

"Gad e cold!" was my first thought after going through Customs and walking outside. People were walking around the airport in shorts and tank tops and there I was, shivering in my borrowed coat. Making the transition from the weather in Antigua to the weather in New York was one experience I could have done without. Even though it was August, I was freezing.

I had been to New York a couple of times before, and it wasn't very dear to my heart. On one visit, my cousin and I were returning from the park one day, and as we were going into the elevator, a man got on with us. When the doors opened on the fifth floor, he snatched my chain. He was never caught. New York still owes me a 14-karat-gold necklace.

New York is a great city, but it's nowhere near as beautiful as Antigua, a small island in the Caribbean. My whole country could fit in the borough of Queens and there would still be room left over. But it has room for 365 beaches, one for every day of the year. (When it's a leap year, you take a shower on the extra day and repeat the process all over.)

The water in Antigua is a beautiful clear blue-green, and the sands are white and gold. When you walk, you feel the warmth right through your soul. So you walk more slowly. At New York beaches the water is much darker—it's so murky you can't even see your feet—and the sand is just a few shades lighter. It's more difficult to find a reason to linger.

I grew up in St. John's, Antigua's capital. Every Saturday morning I used to wake up early to go to market. When I arrived, I saw people coming off buses from all over the island to buy fruits, vegetables, meat, and fish. The market is like a huge kaleidoscope—reds of apples and beets; greens of okra, cabbage, fresh figs, and papaya; oranges of carrots, sweet potatoes, and pumpkins; and yellows of grapefruits, pineapples, and bananas.

The meat and fish market is in a separate building. Here you see butchers in their stalls chopping up whole cows, their once-white smocks all bloodstained. Sometimes you have to hold your nose. Other vendors sit with big baskets filled with doctor fish, angelfish, snappers, barracuda, shark, crab, shellfish, and all types of seafood.

In Antigua we use what Mother Nature provides as best we can and try not to waste anything. I used to have mango, coconut, lime, tangerine, orange, passion fruit, soursop, and pear trees right in my backyard.

I miss being able to go out back and pick a fruit, wash it, and then eat it. In New York I can only dream of doing things like that. The people in my building use the little yard at the back as a convenient garbage dump.

RUBRIC IN ACTION

❶ This writer begins with an anecdote.

Another Option:
· Begin with a statement of the reason for the comparison.

❷ Introduces the two subjects being compared and contrasted: New York and Antigua

❸ This writer examines the two subjects feature-by-feature.

Other Options:
· Discuss one subject completely, then the next.
· Discuss all the subjects' similarities first and then their differences (or vice versa).

❹ Uses vivid sensory details to show the setting

❺ Contrasts another feature of both places—backyards

But in some ways, life in New York is easier. Students here are always complaining about how unfair the school system is, that they can't do anything they want. <u>But in comparison</u> to the school system in Antigua, you people are living in the lap of luxury. Here I'll sit in class and watch students insult their teachers and think to myself, "They wouldn't last a day in Antigua. They'd have more welts on their backs than a tiger has stripes."

Teachers there don't take any lip from students. In my old school if you had so much as the top button of your uniform (that's right—uniform) open, you received one demerit. Three demerits equaled one detention and every Thursday at 4 P.M., that's where you'd find me.

In the primary school that I attended, two bells were rung after recess. At the sound of the first you were supposed to freeze, stop whatever you were doing. When the second bell rang you went back to class. No side trips to the bathroom, and—as I found out the hard way—no side trips to buy candy. The first and last time I tried doing that, the headmaster caught me and I got three lashes across my back with his infamous belt.

One reason I like New York is because if a teacher tried to do something like that, it would be the last time she raised her hand to anyone.

Parents in the United States are not as strict with their children as Antiguan parents either. American parents encourage their daughters' interest in boys. They allow them to wear makeup at 13 or 14 and let them bring their boyfriends home to meet the family.

If you're an Antiguan girl, you don't talk to your parents about makeup before 16 or, in some cases, 18, and you don't talk to them about boys ever.

For the last four years I've been living in the Bronx and I must admit, I do enjoy being able to do certain things that I wouldn't have dared to do in Antigua—like walking out of school anytime I want to without having to ask permission. But then I remember the things I miss most about Antigua—like all the open space. In New York all you see are big, ugly buildings and some garbage here and there to brighten the place up.

If Antigua had all the opportunities that New York has, I would be back there so fast that Superman would be the one asking if I was a bird or a plane.

❻ Uses a transitional phrase to signal a comparison

❼ Supports statements with specific examples

❽ Contrasts another feature of both places— parents

❾ This writer ends by drawing a conclusion from the comparison.
Other Options:
· Restate the main idea.
· Summarize the main points.

Writing Your Comparison-and-Contrast Essay

❶ Prewriting

Resemblances are the shadows of differences.
Different people see different similarities and differences.
Vladimir Nabokov, Russian novelist

Think about why you might want to compare two things. Do you have a choice or decision to make? Do you want to convince someone that one thing is better than another? Maybe you and your friends disagree about the best running shoes, movies, or food. **List** ideas that come to mind. See the **Idea Bank** in the margin for more suggestions. After you choose your subjects, follow the steps below.

Planning Your Comparison-and-Contrast Essay

▶ 1. **Decide what features you will compare or contrast.** Think about the main idea of the essay. Focus on similarities and differences that are important to this main idea.

▶ 2. **Choose an organizational pattern.** There are two basic patterns for organizing comparisons: subject-by-subject and feature-by-feature. The following chart shows the two patterns.

Subject-by-Subject	Feature-by-Feature
Introduction	Introduction
Subject A	Feature 1
Feature 1	Subject A
Feature 2	Subject B
Subject B	Feature 2
Feature 1	Subject A
Feature 2	Subject B
Conclusion	Conclusion

❷ Drafting

Begin writing by identifying the subjects you are comparing. You can work on creating a lively **introduction** now or you can do it during the revision stage. Stick to the **organizational pattern** you chose, and be sure to give the most specific and interesting examples and details to support your comparisons.

You can help your reader keep track of your ideas by using **transitional words and phrases,** such as *both, similarly, but, instead, in contrast,* and *however,* to indicate similarities and differences. Finally, write a **conclusion,** or brief summarizing paragraph.

IDEABank

1. Your Working Portfolio 📁
Look for ideas in the **Writing Options** you completed earlier in this unit:

- **Comparison-Contrast Essay,** p. 829
- **Points of Comparison,** pp. 893, 899

2. Which Is Better?
Think of topics such as sports teams or school activities that you and your friends disagree about. Choose two specific items to compare and contrast.

3. Then and Now
Skim magazines and newspapers. Look for a current event to compare with a past one or a new form of technology to compare with an older one.

Need more help with comparison and contrast?

See the **Writing Handbook,** pp. 1281-1282.

Ask Your Peer Reader

- What is my reason for comparing and contrasting these subjects?

- What parts of my essay did you find most and least interesting? Why?

- What parts were confusing?

Need revising help?

Review the **Rubric**, p. 902

Consider **peer reader** comments

Check **Revision Guidelines**, p. 1269

❸ Revising

TARGET SKILL ▶ PARALLEL CONSTRUCTION Writers often use parallel construction, or **parallelism**, to emphasize similarities and differences. They repeat similar grammatical structures or sentence patterns to link similar or contrasting ideas. The key is to make sure the repeated sentence elements are the same.

> Spending the summer in England gave me the opportunity
> to study a foreign language. ~~I learned~~ *Learning* new words for familiar
> things (tube for subway), discovering new words for familiar
> foods (biscuit for cracker), and ~~I stumbled~~ *stumbling* over odd pronun-
> ciations (Bet you can't pronounce Cholmondeley!) ~~These~~
> were all part of my education.

Confused by comparative forms of modifiers?

See the **Grammar Handbook,** p. 1313

❹ Editing and Proofreading

TARGET SKILL ▶ MODIFIERS Use comparative forms of modifiers to compare two people, places, ideas, or actions. Some modifiers add the suffix *-er* to make their comparative forms, and others use the word *more* with the basic form of the adjective or adverb. Be sure you use the proper form.

> I also learned that the English are ~~more nice~~ *nicer* than I had
> expected. Once, when I was lost and desperate *more* than usual,
> I found that Londoners were ~~more~~ quick*er* than most New
> Yorkers to help a puzzled tourist.

Publishing IDEAS

- If you compared two products, submit your essay to a consumer's guide.
- If you compared two movies, share your essay with others interested in the movies.

More Online: Publishing Options www.mcdougallittell.com

❺ Reflecting

FOR YOUR WORKING PORTFOLIO What did you learn about the two subjects you chose by analyzing their similarities and differences? What would you do differently the next time you compare and contrast two subjects? Attach your answers to your finished work. Save your comparison-and-contrast essay in your **Working Portfolio.**

Assessment Practice Revising & Editing

Read this paragraph from the first draft of a student essay. The underlined sections may include the following kinds of errors:

- **lack of parallel structure**
- **incorrect comparative forms**
- **capitalization errors**
- **run-on sentences**

For each underlined section, choose the revision that most improves the writing.

<u>Just because two women are sisters this doesn't mean they have a lot in</u>
<u>common.</u> Although Stella and Blanche are sisters in <u>Tennessee williams's play</u>
(2)
<u>*a streetcar named Desire,*</u> they are <u>different</u> than they are alike. <u>Stella is</u>
(3)   (4)
<u>satisfied and earthy, she has a realistic view of the world.</u> <u>Blanche is a dreamer</u>
(5)
<u>and hopelessly romantic.</u> The sisters' desires tell the reader a lot about each
character. Blanche aspires to a luxurious life. <u>She likes parties, music, and to</u>
(6)
<u>dance.</u> Stella, on the other hand, is content with her humble life.

---

1. A. Just because two women are sisters. This doesn't mean they have a lot in common.

  B. Just because two women are sisters doesn't mean they have a lot in common.

  C. Just because two women are sisters, this doesn't mean they have a lot in common.

  D. Correct as is

2. A. Tennessee Williams's play *a Streetcar Named Desire*

  B. Tennessee Williams's Play *A Streetcar named Desire*

  C. Tennessee Williams's play *A Streetcar Named Desire*

  D. Correct as is

3. A. more different

  B. most different

  C. more differently

  D. Correct as is

4. A. Stella is satisfied and earthy; She has a realistic view of the world.

  B. Stella is satisfied and earthy she has a realistic view of the world.

  C. Stella is satisfied and earthy. She has a realistic view of the world.

  D. Correct as is

5. A. Blanche is a dreamer and a hopeless romantic.

  B. Blanche is a dreamer and hopeless.

  C. Blanche is a dreamer and a hopelessly romantic.

  D. Correct as is

6. A. She likes parties, music, and to go dancing.

  B. She likes parties, music, and dancing.

  C. She likes parties, music, and dance.

  D. Correct as is

Need extra help?

See the **Grammar Handbook**

Capitalization Chart, p. 1329

Correcting Run-on Sentences, p. 1323

Regular Comparison, p. 1313

The Power of Words

Good writers recognize the power of language and choose words carefully for maximum impact. They consider both the **denotation,** or the precise meaning, of a word and its **connotations,** or implied meanings and overtones. For example, in his poem "Chicago," Carl Sandburg depends on the denotations and connotations of his chosen words to express both the negative and positive aspects of the city. Notice the word *cunning* in the lines on the right. What meanings does the word hold for you?

Although the word *cunning* has the denotation of "artfully clever," the word has negative connotations of slyness and craftiness often associated with predatory

> . . . here is a tall bold slugger set vivid
>   against the little soft cities;
> Fierce as a dog with tongue lapping for
>   action, cunning as a savage pitted against
>   the wilderness.
> —Carl Sandburg, "Chicago"

creatures, such as foxes and wolves. On the other hand, it also carries the positive connotations of intelligence and a will to survive. If Sandburg had instead chosen a **synonym** (a word with a similar meaning) for *cunning,* such as *tricky* or *artful,* he would have lost the combined implications of intelligence, deceitful cleverness, and predation for the sake of survival that *cunning* connotes.

Strategies for Building Vocabulary

Sensitivity to differences between denotation and connotation will enrich your understanding of literature and sharpen your powers of expression. The strategies that follow can help you become aware of the power of words.

❶ **Watch for Words with Impact** As you read, consider both the denotation and connotations of words. Ask yourself what associations a word brings to mind and what emotions it evokes. Look for meanings that are implied but not directly stated. For example, consider the different connotations of such similar words as *inexpensive, cheap,* and *bargain.*

❷ **Identify the Author's Purpose** Consider the author's purpose for writing and the audience for which the work is intended. What feelings is the author trying to convey? How does the choice of words affect the tone of the work? For example, in the excerpt below, the word *steel* is quite emotive, or charged with a number of associations. *Steel* implies a powerful strength and coldness, mirroring the feelings of Dexter.

> He wanted to care, and he could not care. . . .
> The gates were closed, the sun was gone down,
> and there was no beauty but the gray beauty of
> steel that withstands all time.
> —F. Scott Fitzgerald, "Winter Dreams"

❸ **Choose Words Carefully** When you write, remember that synonyms are not always interchangeable. For example, although *aspiration* and *illusion* are both synonyms for *dream,* the meaning of the phrase "the American dream" changes greatly when it becomes "the American aspiration" or "the American illusion." To test the power of connotation, think about the meanings that are implied by each synonym, as in the example that follows.

1. He is an intelligent individual.
   (*Intelligent* implies that the person has considerable mental ability.)

2. He is a brilliant individual.
   (*Brilliant* connotes that the person is exceptionally intelligent, perhaps even a genius.)

3. He is a knowing individual.
   (*Knowing* connotes that the person possesses intelligence and also a clever awareness of the world.)

EXERCISE Write a sentence for each word that follows. Then rewrite the sentence, substituting a synonym for the word. Explain how the meaning of the sentence changes when a synonym is used.

1. retort   3. contrite   5. malicious
2. cajole   4. ingenuous

Grammar from Literature

Read the excerpts below from F. Scott Fitzgerald's "Winter Dreams." The blue passages in the examples below are subordinate clauses. They are functioning as nouns in the sentences.

noun clauses as direct objects
He did not know **what it was** or **why it was funny.**

The helpless part of trying to do anything about it
noun clause as predicate nominative
was **that she did it all herself.**

noun clause as object of preposition
Dexter waited with no apprehension of **what was coming.**

A noun clause can function in the same ways that a single-word noun does—as subject, direct object, predicate nominative, indirect object, or object of a preposition.

A noun clause can be introduced by a pronoun (*who, whom, whose, which, that, whoever, whomever, what, whatever*) or by a subordinating conjunction (such as *how, that, when, where, whether, why*). Sometimes the introductory word *that* is understood rather than stated at the beginning of a noun clause.

noun clause
She whispered, . . ."Last night I thought **I was in love with**
noun clause
[another] man and tonight I think **I'm in love with you.**"

Using Noun Clauses in Your Writing When you create a subordinate clause, you clarify and sometimes emphasize the relationship between or among ideas. Using noun clauses may also improve sentence variety.

In addition, using noun clauses sometimes eliminates awkward wording and improves the flow of your writing.

ORIGINAL
Don't characters like Judy make you wonder about the motivations of people? Are some people just incapable of loyalty?

REWRITTEN
Don't characters like Judy make you wonder
noun clause as direct object
whether some people are incapable of loyalty?

ORIGINAL
The method the character will use to overcome his or her conflict is unknown. The information is not apparent until the denouement.

REWRITTEN   noun clause as subject
How the character will overcome his or her conflict is not apparent until the denouement.

Usage Tip The choice about whether to use *who* or *whom* often causes confusion. The choice depends on how *who* or *whom* is functioning within a clause. *Who* is the nominative form of the pronoun and is used as a subject or predicate nominative. *Whom* is the objective form and is used as a direct object, indirect object, or object of prepositions.

subject of the noun clause
Who loved Judy was no mystery.

direct object in a noun clause
Whom Judy loved was another matter altogether.

subject of the noun clause
Judy seemed capable of being attracted by whoever was passing.

direct object of the noun clause
Dexter was annoyed by whomever Judy chased.

WRITING EXERCISE Create a complex sentence by rewriting each pair of sentences below. Add introductory words if necessary, and rewrite the underlined portion as a noun clause. Eliminate words in italics.

1. A reader might wonder *about the outcome*. Dexter will forget Judy and get on with his life.
2. Social position was judged by *a number of things*. Whom you married counted and the place you lived.
3. Judy has a certain kind of behavior. *This* is quite acceptable to Dexter.
4. As you read, you must make decisions. What do you like and dislike about the characters?

5. Make no mistake: Judy is aware *of something important*. She has control over men.

GRAMMAR EXERCISE Rewrite the sentences below, correcting any errors in pronoun usage. If there is no error, write *Correct*.

1. Who Judy hurt was of no importance to her.
2. At "cut-in" dances, a girl danced with whomever cut in.
3. Irene was the girl to whom Dexter was engaged.
4. He knew now who was speaking.
5. A friend of Fitzgerald's friend Ginevera King is who Fitzgerald used as an inspiration for the character Judy.

The Changing Face of America

What do you feel you've learned about the social position of American women in the past? What new thoughts do you have about the American dream? Choose one or more of the following options in each section and complete the activities to help determine what knowledge you've gained.

Detail of *Mr. and Mrs. Isaac Newton Phelps Stokes* (1897), John Singer Sargent. Oil on canvas, 85¼″ × 39¾″, The Metropolitan Museum of Art, bequest of Edith Minturn Phelps Stokes (Mrs. I. N.), 1938. (38.104). Copyright © 1989 The Metropolitan Museum of Art.

Reflecting on the Unit

OPTION 1

A Woman's Proper Place Many of the selections in the first part of this unit show American women's struggles with social constraints, stereotypes, and inequalities. Review the ways in which the female characters in these selections respond to oppression or limitation. Which character did you find it easiest to identify with? Which character did you find it most difficult to identify with? Jot down a couple of paragraphs explaining your choices.

OPTION 2

The American Dream Think about the American dream in relation to the selections in the second part of this unit. Which characters would classify the American dream as an illusion? Which would view it as a reality? Form a group of four or five, with each member role-playing a different character. In a discussion of equality and economic opportunity in the United States, each student should classify the American dream as illusion or reality and defend that position according to the point of view of the character he or she is playing.

Self ASSESSMENT

📖 **READER'S NOTEBOOK**

To illustrate what you've learned about the concerns that native-born and immigrant men and women had at the end of the 19th century, write down their concerns in a diagram like the one shown. Then underline any concerns that do not seem relevant today.

	Women	Men
Native born		
Immigrants		

Reviewing Literary Concepts

OPTION 1

Understanding Figurative Language Many writers in this unit use figurative language—for example, simile, metaphor, and personification—to communicate ideas, feelings, character qualities, or states of mind. Select one example of figurative language from five different selections in the unit. Classify the type of figurative language used in each example and the primary idea or feeling conveyed.

Selection	Example of Figurative Language	Type of Figurative Language	Idea, Feeling, or State of Mind Conveyed

OPTION 2

Analyzing Social Themes Social themes in fiction are insights or messages about large problems in society. Go back through the seven short stories you read in the unit, and list the social themes they deal with. How are these themes conveyed—are they expressed through direct statements or suggested through conflicts faced by characters? Which themes are the most obvious, and which are the most subtle? Which themes seem most relevant in today's American society?

📁 Portfolio Building

- **Writing Options** Several Writing Options in this unit involved writing from the perspective of a character. Which character did you come to understand most deeply in this way? Attach a cover note to the assignment explaining what you learned from assuming the role of a character. Place the assignment in your **Presentation Portfolio.** 📁

- **Writing Workshop** In this unit you wrote a Comparison-Contrast Essay that explored similarities and differences between two subjects. Evaluate your essay. How interesting were the subjects you chose? How original were the comparisons and contrasts you made? Decide whether you want to add your essay to your **Presentation Portfolio.** 📁 If you do, attach a cover sheet telling what makes it worthy.

- **Additional Activities** Think about the various assignments you completed under **Activities & Explorations** and **Inquiry & Research.** Pick one that you felt was very challenging. Write a note explaining how the assignment challenged you and what you did to rise to the challenge. Add the note to your portfolio.

Self ASSESSMENT

📖 **READER'S NOTEBOOK.**
Copy the following list of literary terms. Place a check next to each item you were able to define. For those you couldn't define, look up the definition in the **Glossary of Literary Terms** (page 1244).

quatrains	tone
slant rhyme	narrative poetry
first-person narrator	characterization
plot	symbol
surprise ending	lyric poem
coming-of-age story	static and dynamic characters
interior monologue	voice
imagery	analogy

Self ASSESSMENT

By now you should have quite a few pieces in your **Presentation Portfolio.** 📁 Are you satisfied with the pieces you've chosen so far? If so, why? Or would you like to replace some? If so, which ones, and why?

Setting GOALS

After completing this unit's reading and writing activities, what topics would you like to continue learning about? Look back through the selections, your portfolios, and notebook. Jot down one or two topics you would like to read more about.

THE MODERN AGE

make it new!

Ezra Pound
poet and critic

Rush Hour, New York (1915), Max Weber. Oil on canvas, 36¼″ × 30¼″. National Gallery of Art, Washington, D.C., gift of the Avalon Foundation (1970.6.1 PA).

THE MODERN AGE

EVENTS IN AMERICAN LITERATURE

1910   **1920**

1912 Harriet Monroe founds *Poetry* magazine, which would introduce many modernist poets

1915 Early poem by T. S. Eliot, "The Love Song of J. Alfred Prufrock," first appears in *Poetry*

1916 Robert Frost's "The Road Not Taken" is published

1917 The first collection of *The Cantos* by Ezra Pound is published in *Poetry*

1919 Claude McKay writes "If We Must Die" during summer wave of violence against African Americans

1920s Harlem Renaissance is in its heyday

1922 Groundbreaking anthology, *The Book of American Negro Poetry,* is compiled by James Weldon Johnson

EVENTS IN THE UNITED STATES

1910   **1920**

1909 Sixty prominent black and white citizens found National Association for the Advancement of Colored People (NAACP) to end discrimination and prevent violence against black people

1913 Armory Show in New York City exhibits modern art to large crowds and horrified critics

Nude Descending a Staircase by Marcel Duchamp

1917 United States enters World War I, ensuring the Allied victory a year later

1919 Congress ratifies 18th Amendment, which prohibits manufacture, transportation, and sale of alcoholic beverages, ushering in Prohibition

1920 U.S. Bureau of Census reports that for the first time the nation's rural population is less than half of total population

1921 First radio coverage of World Series demonstrates radio's growing popularity

1922 Louis Armstrong joins King Oliver's Creole Jazz Band in Chicago, heralding Jazz Age

EVENTS IN THE WORLD

1910   **1920**

1912 Qing Dynasty, in power in China since 1644, is overthrown by nationalist revolt in favor of a republic

1914 War erupts in Europe between Central Powers (Germany and Austria-Hungary) and Allies (Great Britain, France, and Russia)

1917 V. I. Lenin leads Bolshevik Revolution that topples Russian czar

1918 The Allies, with U.S. help, defeat Central Powers, ending World War I; Bolsheviks become Russian Communist Party

1919 The Treaty of Versailles is signed by Allies and Associated Powers and by Germany

1920 Hitler takes control of new National Socialist German Workers' (Nazi) Party

1921 Mao Zedong co-founds China's Communist Party

PERIOD PIECES

The fashion of the 1920s

1936 Crosley Radio
Corporation's "Majestic"

Art deco wristwatch

1930

1925 Countee Cullen publishes his first book of poetry, *Color*

1926 Langston Hughes publishes *The Weary Blues*, depicting life in Harlem in the 1920s; Ernest Hemingway publishes his first novel, *The Sun Also Rises*

1928 Zora Neale Hurston publishes "How It Feels to Be Colored Me"

1930 Katherine Anne Porter's "The Jilting of Granny Weatherall" appears in collection titled *Flowering Judas*

1931 Arna Bontemps's first novel, *God Sends Sunday,* is published

1933 Gertrude Stein publishes *The Autobiography of Alice B. Toklas*

1934 Dorothy West founds *Challenge*, a literary magazine for African-American writers

1936 Dorothy Parker publishes *Collected Poems: Not So Deep as a Well*

1930

1923 Performance of the Charleston in musical *Runnin' Wild* starts nationwide dance craze

1927 Charles Lindbergh is first to fly solo across Atlantic, nonstop from New York to Paris; Babe Ruth hits season record of 60 home runs (since surpassed); first "talking" movie, *The Jazz Singer,* is released

1929 Stock-market crash on Wall Street plunges nation into Great Depression

1931 Empire State Building is completed, the world's then-tallest building at 102 stories

1932 Franklin Delano Roosevelt is elected president at height of Depression, with nearly one-third of work force unemployed

1938 Congress passes Fair Labor Standards Act, which establishes minimum wage and provides for adoption of 40-hour workweek

1939 First regular television broadcasts begin

1930

1928 Joseph Stalin becomes dictator of Communist Russia

1930 Nationalists and Communists fight civil war in China

1932 Saudi Arabia declares itself a single kingdom

1933 Hitler and Nazis seize dictatorial control of Germany

1937 Japan invades China

1938 English prime minister claims "peace in our time" after ceding parts of Czechoslovakia to Hitler

1939 Germany invades Poland and World War II begins

A New Cultural Identity

The Harlem Renaissance

"*The* Harlem Renaissance was an unprecedented period of literary, musical, and artistic production among African Americans that reached its peak in the 1920s. This movement was centered in the Harlem section of Manhattan in New York City—a magnet for thousands of blacks migrating from the South, the Midwest, and even the West Indies. Southern blacks, in particular, were fleeing poverty and growing racial violence, hoping to find more economic and personal freedom in the North. Politically, the Renaissance years were an extremely difficult time for African Americans. During the "Red Summer" of 1919, there were bloody antiblack riots in 26 cities, including Chicago and Washington, D.C. In the 1920s, membership in the terrorist, white-supremacist Ku Klux Klan rose to more than 4 million nationwide.

Not only a magnet for blacks, Harlem drew whites as well—tourists flocked to nightspots such as the Cotton Club to hear the new jazz music played by Louis Armstrong and Duke Ellington. And white writers, publishers, and patrons of the arts developed a keen interest in Harlem residents and their culture.

For African Americans a new cultural identity crystallized during the Harlem Renaissance; it was the time of "The New Negro," in the words of philosopher Alain Locke, who first defined the movement. "New

Harlem in the 1920s: a young couple out on the town (top), Lenox Avenue (below)

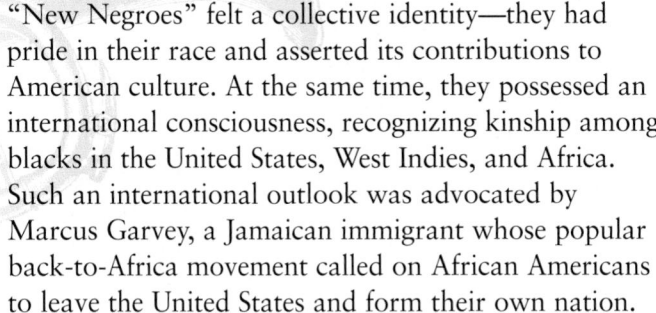

The Cotton Club

Negroes" rejected beastlike or sentimental stereotypes, claiming the right to define themselves and defend themselves against attack. "New Negroes" felt a collective identity—they had pride in their race and asserted its contributions to American culture. At the same time, they possessed an international consciousness, recognizing kinship among blacks in the United States, West Indies, and Africa. Such an international outlook was advocated by Marcus Garvey, a Jamaican immigrant whose popular back-to-Africa movement called on African Americans to leave the United States and form their own nation.

The writers of the Harlem Renaissance embodied these "New Negroes." Langston Hughes was one of the most original and important. In 1925, he published his first poetry collection, *The Weary Blues*, following it with dozens of volumes of poetry, fiction, plays, and essays over a career lasting into the 1960s. He praised blackness, embraced common people as subjects, and blended elements of blues and jazz into his work. The exuberant Zora Neale Hurston, raised in a small, all-black Florida town and trained in anthropology at Barnard College, also drew upon African-American folk traditions. Her stories, novels, essays, and folklore collections reflect a love of black language and manners. Hurston was one of the first writers to present African Americans as complete, multifaceted human beings. Other important Renaissance writers were James Weldon Johnson, Claude McKay, Countee Cullen, and Arna Bontemps, all of whom showed mastery of traditional literary forms and poured into them new expressions of individual and collective feeling. Yet another significant figure was Jean Toomer, whose experimental *Cane* (1923) blended poetry and prose to evoke the beautiful, terrible South of black experience.

Voices from the TIMES

Lift every voice and sing
Till earth and heaven ring,
Ring with the harmonies of Liberty;
Let our rejoicing rise
High as the listening skies,
Let it resound loud as the rolling sea.
Sing a song full of the faith that the
   dark past has taught us,
Sing a song full of the hope that the
   present has brought us,
Facing the rising sun of our new day
   begun
Let us march on till victory is won.
         James Weldon Johnson
         "Lift Every Voice and Sing"
         (the "Negro national anthem,"
         first performed in 1900)

All art is propaganda and ever must be, despite the wailing of the purists. I stand in utter shamelessness and say that whatever art I have for writing has been used always for propaganda for gaining the right of black folk to love and enjoy.

         W. E. B. Du Bois
         from "Criteria of Negro Art"

I had an overwhelming desire to see Harlem. More than Paris, or the Shakespeare country, or Berlin, or the Alps, I wanted to see Harlem, the greatest Negro city in the world.

         Langston Hughes
         from *The Big Sea*

Voices from the Times

Traditions Across Time: Reaffirming Cultural Identity

The Great Depression of the 1930s brought an end to the Harlem Renaissance, causing many of the writers who had gathered in Harlem to scatter and take other jobs to support themselves. But their work planted seeds that continue to generate important writing from the African-American experience.

In 1950, the poet Gwendolyn Brooks became the first African American to win a Pulitzer Prize. Throughout the 1950s and 1960s, James Baldwin, who left the United States and the racism he felt here to live in Paris, gave us some of the most important essays of the period, essays based on his experiences and struggles with racial identity. And in contemporary times, Toni Morrison has become one of the most accomplished American novelists, winning nearly every important literary award, including the Nobel Prize for literature. In her essay in this part of Unit Six, Morrison demonstrates the continuing effort to find and present the essentials of African-American life.

Toni Morrison accepting the 1993 Nobel Prize for literature in Stockholm, Sweden (above), and a close-up of the prize itself (at right)

The Harlem Renaissance

Langston Hughes	*A*UTHOR *S*TUDY	
	I, Too	925
	Harlem	926
	The Weary Blues	927
	LINK ACROSS CULTURES	
Jean-Joseph Rabéarivelo	Flute Players	930
Dahleen Glanton	*from* Love, Langston	931
Langston Hughes	When the Negro Was in Vogue	932

Meet Harlem's "poet laureate"—a fine translator and a dear cousin.

James Weldon Johnson	My City	940
Countee Cullen	Any Human to Another	940
Claude McKay	If We Must Die	945
Arna Bontemps	A Black Man Talks of Reaping	945
Zora Neale Hurston	How It Feels to Be Colored Me	950
	LITERARY LINK	
Alice Walker	*from* Zora Neale Hurston: A Cautionary Tale and a Partisan View	955

C OMPARING L ITERATURE
Traditions Across Time: Reaffirming Cultural Identity

James Baldwin	My Dungeon Shook: Letter to My Nephew (1962)	959
Gwendolyn Brooks	Life for My Child Is Simple (1949)	967
	Primer for Blacks (1980)	967
Toni Morrison	Thoughts on the African-American Novel (1984)	973

Author Study
Langston Hughes

OVERVIEW

Life and Times   920

I, Too ~ POETRY   925

Harlem ~ POETRY   926

The Weary Blues ~ POETRY   927

Link Across Cultures—
Flute Players by Jean-Joseph
Rabéarivelo ~ POETRY   930

from Love, Langston
~ NEWSPAPER ARTICLE   931

When the Negro Was in
Vogue ~ MEMOIR   932

The Author's Style   938

Author Study Project   939

*"Life is a big sea
full of many fish.
I let down my
nets and pull."*

—*Langston Hughes*

1902–1967

Harlem's Poet Laureate

*A man who had worked as a bus-
boy, a truck farmer, and a sailor,
Langston Hughes understood
and loved working class and poor
African Americans. As a writer,
Hughes vividly portrayed the
lives of those people—whom literature had mostly ignored.*

*Hughes was one of the leading
voices of the Harlem Renaissance
in the 1920s. He never lost his emotional tie to Harlem.
Through his poems, plays, novels, and essays, he brought
that community to life for the world.*

A WANDERING CHILDHOOD James Mercer Langston
Hughes was born on February 1, 1902, in Joplin, Missouri.
Shortly afterward, his parents separated. His father
emigrated to Mexico to escape racial discrimination in the
United States and had little contact with Hughes for 11
years. His mother, a teacher, struggled to support herself
and her son. She frequently moved in search of decent jobs,

1902
Is born on
February 1
in Joplin,
Missouri

1915
Reads his
first poem
at 8th-grade
graduation

HIS LIFE
HIS TIMES

1900

1910

1903
W.E.B. Du Bois
publishes *The
Souls of Black
Folk*.

The Crisis was a tool of
expression for Hughes
and other writers.

1909
NAACP is
founded.

1914
World
War I
begins in
Europe.

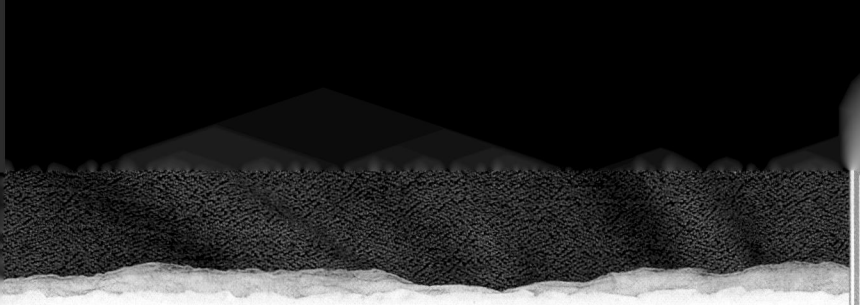

leaving Hughes in the care of relatives or family friends. From the ages of 7 to 12, Hughes lived in Lawrence, Kansas, with his maternal grandmother.

After his grandmother's death in 1915, Hughes rejoined his mother and her second husband in Lincoln, Illinois, where he completed grammar school. While Hughes was in seventh grade, his classmates elected him class poet, even though he had never written a poem in his life! Hughes took his duties seriously, composing multiple verses about his teachers and classmates.

The family moved again in 1916—this time to Cleveland, Ohio. There, Hughes attended Central High School. A popular student, he was elected to class offices, acted in school plays, and joined the track-and-field team. He also wrote dialect poems in the style of Paul Laurence Dunbar and free-verse poems in the style of Carl Sandburg.

WORLD TRAVELER After graduating from high school, Hughes visited his father in Mexico and lived with him for a year. On the train trip there, Hughes observed the Mississippi River and composed what was ultimately to become one of his most famous poems, "The Negro Speaks of Rivers." Hughes had found his distinctive poetic voice and began to publish in magazines.

After convincing his father to send him to Columbia University, Hughes left for New York City in 1921. Unhappy at college, he dropped out after one year.

LITERARY *Contributions*

During his life-long career as a writer, Hughes published over 40 books, including poetry, novels, fiction, nonfiction, autobiographies, and children's stories. He also wrote 30 plays and translated poetry by international poets. Hughes's versatility and his staggering output of literary work during his lifetime earned him the nickname "Harlem's Shakespeare."

Poetry Collections
The Weary Blues (1926)
Fine Clothes to the Jew (1927)
Shakespeare in Harlem (1942)
Fields of Wonder (1947)
One-Way Ticket (1949)
Montage of a Dream Deferred (1951)
Ask Your Mama: 12 Moods for Jazz (1961)
The Panther and the Lash: Poems of Our Times (1967)

Novels
Not Without Laughter (1930)
Tambourines to Glory (1958)

Short Story Collections
The Ways of White Folks (1934)
Laughing to Keep from Crying (1952)
Something in Common and Other Stories (1963)

Autobiographies
The Big Sea (1940)
I Wonder As I Wander (1956)

1920 Finishes high school, and lives in Mexico with father

1923 Works aboard a freighter bound for Africa

1926 Publishes first collection of poetry, *The Weary Blues*

1929 Graduates from Lincoln University in Pennsylvania

1935 Receives Guggenheim Fellowship; play *Mulatto* is staged on Broadway

1937 Reports on the Spanish Civil War

1920

1930

1918 By end of World War I, thousands of African Americans move to northern cities.

1922 The Harlem Renaissance begins.

1929 The Great Depression begins; African-American artists start to leave Harlem.

1934 *Jonah's Gourd Vine* by Zora Neale Hurston is published.

Zora Neale Hurston

Fascinated by the sights and sounds of Harlem, he remained in New York and supported himself as best he could.

In 1923 Hughes found work as a cabin boy on a freighter bound for Africa, a trip that moved him profoundly. He also sailed to Europe aboard another freighter and decided to remain there for awhile. In the fall of 1924, with only 25 cents in his pocket, Hughes returned to the United States to pursue his career as a writer.

SUDDEN FAME By winning a literary contest with "The Weary Blues" in 1925, Hughes won the support of a prominent critic. He also gained public notice through an encounter with Vachel Lindsay, a famous poet of the day. When Lindsay came to the hotel restaurant in Washington, D.C., where Hughes worked as a busboy, Hughes slipped three poems—including "The Weary Blues"—beside Lindsay's plate. The next morning the newspapers reported that Lindsay had "discovered" a busboy poet.

After receiving a scholarship, Hughes enrolled at Pennsylvania's Lincoln University in 1926, the same year in which his first collection of poems, *The Weary Blues*, was published. A second

collection, *Fine Clothes to the Jew,* appeared in 1927. In response to African-American critics who disliked Hughes's gritty depiction of the lives of ordinary working people, Hughes said, "I didn't know the upper-class Negroes well enough to write much about them. I knew only the people I had grown up with, and they weren't people whose shoes were always shined, who had been to Harvard, or who had heard of Bach. But they seemed to me good people, too."

AN INFLUENTIAL CAREER Hughes played a key role in the Harlem Renaissance. In his writing, he portrayed both the nightlife and the everyday experiences of Harlem. He championed the right of African-American artists to express their own culture. He also used his writing to protest racial discrimination, especially the form of legal segregation commonly known as Jim Crow laws.

The first African American to earn a living solely from writing, Hughes went on to publish more than 40 books. His efforts to re-create the structures and rhythms of blues and jazz music in poetic works, such as *Montage of a Dream Deferred* (1951), demonstrate his desire to use

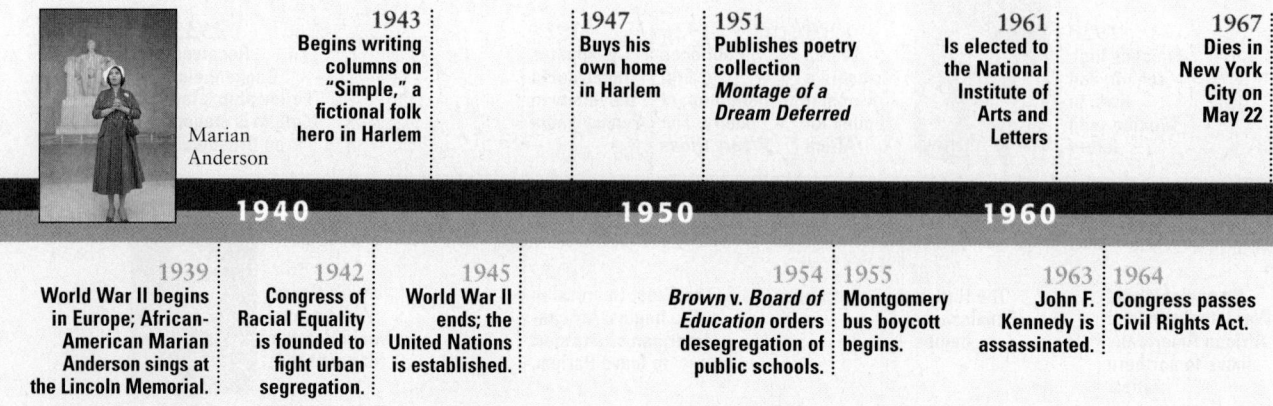

Marian Anderson

1943
Begins writing columns on "Simple," a fictional folk hero in Harlem

1947
Buys his own home in Harlem

1951
Publishes poetry collection *Montage of a Dream Deferred*

1961
Is elected to the National Institute of Arts and Letters

1967
Dies in New York City on May 22

1940 **1950** **1960**

1939
World War II begins in Europe; African-American Marian Anderson sings at the Lincoln Memorial.

1942
Congress of Racial Equality is founded to fight urban segregation.

1945
World War II ends; the United Nations is established.

1954
Brown v. *Board of Education* orders desegregation of public schools.

1955
Montgomery bus boycott begins.

1963
John F. Kennedy is assassinated.

1964
Congress passes Civil Rights Act.

poetry to immortalize other African-American art forms. After a long and varied career, Hughes died in New York City in 1967.

Many have been encouraged by Hughes's poems of racial pride, such as the poets of the négritude movement—the French-speaking African poets who affirmed black culture. Succeeding generations of writers have been enormously influenced by Hughes, who has been called the "Poet Laureate of Harlem."

More Online: Author Link
www.mcdougallittell.com

The Negro Looks Ahead (1940), Richmond Barthe. Bronze, 16″ × 10½″ × 10½″. Art & Artifacts Division, Schomburg Center for Research in Black Culture, The New York Public Library, Astor, Lenox, and Tilden Foundations. Photo by Manu Sassoonian.

Goals of the Harlem Renaissance

In 1926 African-American journalist George S. Schuyler published "The Negro-Art Hokum," in which he ridiculed the idea of black and white cultural differences in the United States and argued that "any attempt on the part of the black American to aim at the production of any art distinctively Negro borders on self-deception." Responding to Schuyler, Hughes wrote "The Negro Artist and the Racial Mountain," an essay in which he laid out the goals of the writers and artists of the Harlem Renaissance. The final paragraph of the essay, which was published in *The Nation* in 1926, follows:

We younger Negro artists who create now intend to express our individual dark-skinned selves without fear or shame. If white people are pleased we are glad. If they are not, it doesn't matter. We know we are beautiful. And ugly too. The tom-tom cries and the tom-tom laughs. If colored people are pleased we are glad. If they are not, their displeasure doesn't matter either. We build our temples for tomorrow, strong as we know how, and we stand on top of the mountain, free within ourselves.

Selected Poems

by LANGSTON HUGHES

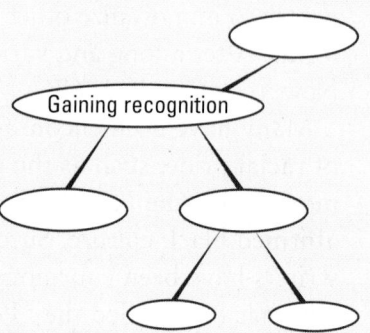

Gaining recognition

Connect to Your Life

Gaining Recognition Think about a time when you wanted to win recognition from a group or an individual. What accomplishment or quality were you hoping would be noticed? What strategies did you use to gain recognition? Use a cluster diagram like the one shown to explore the idea of gaining recognition. Then share your thoughts with a classmate.

Build Background

Poet of Blues and Jazz When Langston Hughes began to write, many African-American poets tried to sound like the white poets they had read in school. Instead of following that practice, Hughes incorporated the patterns of African-American speech and the rhythms of African-American music into his poetry. By doing so, Hughes hoped to gain recognition for the beauty of his culture. He also wrote protest poems, such as "I, Too," to expose the injustice of Jim Crow laws that imposed segregation upon African Americans.

Both "The Weary Blues" and "Harlem" are influenced by music. "The Weary Blues" draws on the blues, a style of music that African Americans developed in the late 19th century. Blues lyrics, which typically express sorrow or melancholy, often consist of three-line verses in which the second line repeats the first and the third expresses a response to the other two. "Harlem" draws on bebop jazz of the 1940s. Jazz evolved from ragtime and blues in the early 20th century. The music is characterized by syncopation, heavily accented rhythms, and improvisation on tunes and chord patterns. Bebop jazz has more complicated melodies and faster rhythmic changes than traditional jazz.

Focus Your Reading

LITERARY ANALYSIS **MOOD** The **mood** of a poem is the emotional feeling or atmosphere that the poet creates for a reader. Poets create mood through their use of **imagery, figurative language, sound devices, rhythm,** and **description.** For example, the following line from "The Weary Blues" helps create a feeling of tiredness:

> *By the pale dull pallor of an old gas light*

As you read each of the following poems, pay attention to the different moods that Hughes creates and the elements he uses to create them.

ACTIVE READING **DETECTING RHYTHM IN POETRY** Inspired by the blues and jazz he heard in Harlem nightclubs, Hughes tried to write poetry with the distinctive **rhythms** of these types of music. As you read the poems, try to detect the different rhythms that Hughes creates through his arrangement of stressed and unstressed syllables in a line. Use one or more of the following suggestions:

- Read the poems aloud, listening for the rhythm.
- Tap the rhythm out as you read the poems silently to yourself.
- Imagine how the poems would sound recited over a background of music, such as blues or jazz.

READER'S NOTEBOOK As you read the poems, copy lines whose rhythm appeals to you. Put accent marks over the syllables that you think should be stressed.

I, Too

LANGSTON HUGHES

I, too, sing America.

I am the darker brother.
They send me to eat in the kitchen
When company comes,
5 But I laugh,
And eat well,
And grow strong.

Tomorrow,
I'll be at the table
10 When company comes.
Nobody'll dare
Say to me,
"Eat in the kitchen,"
Then.

15 Besides,
They'll see how beautiful I am
And be ashamed—

I, too, am America.

Jim, Selma Burke. Art and Artifacts Division, Schomburg Center for Research in Black Culture, The New York Public Library, Astor, Lenox and Tilden Foundations.

Thinking Through the Literature

1. What is your opinion of the **speaker**? Share your thoughts with a classmate.

2. What do you believe the poem is saying about America?

   THINK ABOUT
   - the first and last lines
   - the identities of the speaker and the "they," in lines 3 and 16
   - what is meant by "when company comes," in line 4
   - what the speaker wants other people to recognize

3. How do you think the speaker expects to move from the "kitchen" to the "table"? How do you view his expectations?

A Dream Deferred

Langston Hughes

What happens to a dream deferred?

   Does it dry up
   like a raisin in the sun?
   Or fester like a sore—
5 And then run?
   Does it stink like rotten meat?
   Or crust and sugar over—
   like a syrupy sweet?

   Maybe it just sags
10 like a heavy load.

   Or does it explode?

Black Manhattan 1969 Romare Bearden.
Collage and Synthetic Polymer on board, 25 3/8" x 21".
Schomburg Center for Research in Black Culture,
Art & Artifacts Division, New York Public Library,
Astor, Lenox and Tilden Foundations.
Photo by Manu Sassoonian. Copyright @ Romare Bearden
Foundation/Licensed by VAGA, New York.

Thinking Through the Literature

1. What is your response to the last line? Share your reaction with a classmate.

2. What do you think is the poem's main message, or **theme**?

    THINK ABOUT
   - the **title**
   - what the speaker's dream might be and why it might "explode"
   - your own experiences of a dream that has been "deferred," or postponed

3. Do you agree or disagree with the speaker's opinion of what happens to a dream deferred? Explain your answer by citing details from the poem and from your own observations of life.

The Weary Blues

LANGSTON HUGHES

Droning a drowsy syncopated[1] tune,
Rocking back and forth to a mellow croon,[2]
   I heard a Negro play.
Down on Lenox Avenue the other night
5 By the pale dull pallor[3] of an old gas light
   He did a lazy sway. . . .
   He did a lazy sway. . . .
To the tune o' those Weary Blues.
With his ebony hands on each ivory key
10 He made that poor piano moan with melody.
   O Blues!
Swaying to and fro on his rickety stool
He played that sad raggy tune like a musical fool.
   Sweet Blues!
15 Coming from a black man's soul.
   O Blues!
In a deep song voice with a melancholy tone
I heard that Negro sing, that old piano moan—
   "Ain't got nobody in all this world,
20   Ain't got nobody but ma self.
   I's gwine to quit ma frownin'
   And put ma troubles on the shelf."
Thump, thump, thump, went his foot on the floor.
He played a few chords then he sang some more—
25   "I got the Weary Blues
   And I can't be satisfied.
   Got the Weary Blues
   And can't be satisfied—
   I ain't happy no mo'
30   And I wish that I had died."
And far into the night he crooned that tune.
The stars went out and so did the moon.
The singer stopped playing and went to bed
While the Weary Blues echoed through his head.
35 He slept like a rock or a man that's dead.

---

1. **syncopated** (sĭng'kə-pā'tĭd): characterized by a shifting of stresses from normally strong to normally weak beats.

2. **croon:** a soft humming or singing.

3. **pallor** (păl'ər): lack of color.

Connect to the Literature

1. What Do You Think? What vision of the musician did you develop as you read "The Weary Blues"? Describe your image of him.

Comprehension Check
- Who are the characters in "The Weary Blues"?
- What instrument does the singer play?
- What type of song does the singer sing?

Think Critically

2. How does the **speaker** seem to feel about the musician and about blues music? Cite evidence from the poem.

3. **ACTIVE READING** | **DETECTING RHYTHM IN POETRY**
Which lines in "The Weary Blues" have the most heavily accented **rhythms?**

THINK ABOUT

- the rhythm of the lines that you copied into your **📖 READER'S NOTEBOOK**
- how the rhythms of the long and the short lines differ

4. What aspects of African-American culture or African-American identity do you think Hughes wanted to gain recognition for in this poem? Explain.

5. What differences do you see between the two blues verses (lines 19–22 and 25–30) in "The Weary Blues" and the rest of the poem? How well do you think the two styles work together?

6. "The Weary Blues," "I, Too," and "Harlem" may be read as describing different ways of responding to discrimination. Which response do you think is more effective? Give reasons for your answer.

Extend Interpretations

7. Comparing Texts How would you compare the vision of America suggested in "I, Too" with that in Walt Whitman's poem "I Hear America Singing" on page 397?

8. Connect to Life If Hughes were writing today, what features of contemporary African-American culture do you think he would portray in his poetry? Explain the aspects of African-American culture that Hughes might think deserve more recognition.

Literary Analysis

MOOD In each of these poems, Hughes creates a certain **mood,** or emotional feeling or atmosphere. **Imagery, figurative language, description,** and **sound devices** contribute to the mood of each poem, as does the **rhythm** of the language Hughes uses. For example, in the poem "Harlem," the **similes** "fester like a sore" and "stink like rotten meat" convey a sense of disease and decay. This causes the reader to have negative feelings about the idea of deferring dreams.

Paired Activity Work with a partner to identify the mood of each of the three Hughes poems—"I, Too," "Harlem," and "The Weary Blues." Then list the elements—imagery, figurative language, sound devices, description, and rhythm—that contribute to the mood of each poem. Use a chart like the one shown to record your findings. Then share your perceptions in class.

	Mood of Poem	Elements that Contribute to Mood
"I, Too"		
"Harlem"		
"The Weary Blues"		

Writing Options

1. Congratulatory Letter "The Weary Blues," which Hughes referred to as his "lucky" poem, was the winning entry in a literary contest sponsored by *Opportunity* magazine. Draft a letter of congratulation to Hughes, telling him why his poem won first prize.

2. Musical Poem Begin writing a poem that in some way suggests a particular style of music you enjoy, as Hughes did in "I, Too," "Harlem," and "The Weary Blues." Have a classmate read it and guess what kind of music inspired you.

3. Compare-Contrast Essay Reread "I, Too," "Harlem," and "The Weary Blues." In an essay, compare and contrast the different responses to discrimination that are presented in these three poems. Before you begin, create a compare-and-contrast chart like this one to organize your ideas.

Poem	Response to Discrimination
"I, Too"	
"Harlem"	
"The Weary Blues"	

Writing Handbook
See page 1281: Compare and Contrast.

Activities & Explorations

1. Oral Readings With a small group of classmates, plan an oral reading of one of the three poems by Hughes. Choose appropriate volumes, phrasings, pitches, and gestures. Decide whether the poem should be read by a single voice or by several voices and whether you will read with jazz accompaniment. Present your reading to the class. ~ **SPEAKING AND LISTENING/MUSIC**

2. Poem Illustration Create an illustration to accompany either "I, Too," "Harlem," or "The Weary Blues." Use images and colors that convey the mood of the poem. Then display your artwork in the classroom. ~ **ART**

3. Map of Harlem The blues singer in "The Weary Blues" and other African-American musicians played in clubs on Lenox Avenue in Harlem during the Harlem Renaissance. With a partner, use a map of New York City to locate Harlem and Lenox Avenue. Create an illustrated map of Harlem to accompany Hughes's poem. ~ **GEOGRAPHY**

4. Blues Adaptation Perform your own interpretation of the "weary blues," adapting or inventing a blues melody and making up additional lyrics. ~ **MUSIC**

Inquiry & Research

The Blues In "The Weary Blues," Hughes incorporated the first blues lyrics he had ever heard when he was a child in Kansas. Find out more about the blues, using a print or on-line encyclopedia, a book about blues music, or the Internet. Look for answers to the following questions:

Blues musician Muddy Waters

What are the roots of blues music? Who are some well-known blues musicians? How has the blues influenced other popular forms of music? Answer these questions in a presentation to the class, accompanied by some recordings of blues music.

 More Online: Research Starter
www.mcdougallittell.com

FLUTE PLAYERS

Jean-Joseph Rabéarivelo

Jean-Joseph Rabéarivelo (1910–1937), from Madagascar, was one of the négritude poets inspired and championed by Langston Hughes. This poem, translated by Hughes, is close in spirit to "The Weary Blues."

Your flute
you carved from the shinbone of a mighty bull
and polished it on barren hills beaten by sun.

His flute
he carved from a reed trembling in the breeze
and cut in it little holes beside a flowing brook
drunk on dreams of moonlight.

Together
you made music in the late afternoon
as if to hold back the round boat
sinking on the shores of the sky
to save it from its fate:
but are your plaintive incantations
heeded by the gods of the wind,
of the earth, of the forest, and the sand?

Your flute
throws out a beat like the march of an angry bull
toward the desert—
but who comes back running,
burned by thirst and hunger
and defeated by weariness
at the foot of a shadeless tree
with neither leaves nor fruit.

His flute
is like a reed that bends
beneath the weight of a passing bird in flight—
not a bird captured by a child
whose feathers are caressed,
but a bird lost from other birds
who looks at his own shadow for solace
in the flowing water.

Your flute and his
regret their beginnings
in the songs of both your sorrows.

Margrett Ann Duncan,
Hughes's cousin

Preparing to Read

Build Background

Imagine discovering that you have a celebrity in your family! That's what happened to Margrett Ann Duncan. For years, her Aunt Jessie had claimed to be related to Langston Hughes, but no one believed the elderly woman. Then after Aunt Jessie's death, Duncan discovered that she was indeed a cousin of Hughes. This article, printed in the *Chicago Tribune* on July 8, 1998, describes what happened after the two met—and how the celebrity benefited from the relationship as much as his stay-at-home cousin.

Newspaper Article
by Dahleen Glanton

She was a homemaker from Joliet who had never ventured out of the Midwest. He was a world-renowned poet who had traveled around the globe five times before they ever met.

It was her search through the family's bloodline that in 1958 led Margrett Ann Duncan to Langston Hughes, her first cousin once removed. But it was their fondness and admiration for each other that kept them close for almost a decade.

She baked maple nut cakes and mailed them to him in an aluminum pan. The sweet token would be waiting for him at his East 127th Street apartment in Harlem when he returned from a trip to Paris or San Francisco or the West Indies. Afterward, he would return the pan filled with autographed books of his writings, candy for her four children, and always a friendly note expressing his gratitude.

On her birthday, Valentine's Day, and Christmas, the arrival of flowers, cards, or sometimes a singing telegram became an annual ritual that she cherished as much as his almost-monthly letters. On green-and-white stationery, Hughes shared almost every aspect of his life with the woman he fondly called his "No. 1 Coz." He wrote of his travels, his lectures, his performances, and the people he had met in faraway places. He spoke of his family, inquired about hers, and promised to visit as soon as he could. She pre-served every memento in a brown vinyl scrapbook kept locked away in a safe deposit box.

When his work brought him to Chicago, Hughes often stayed with Duncan and her husband in an 11-room home in Joliet she had inherited from her Aunt Jessie. Normally, Hughes would read poetry or perform readings to the accompaniment of a jazz quartet, but Duncan's favorite performance was when he appeared on stage in Chicago with gospel singer Mahalia Jackson. When her cousin was in town, the family partied into the early morning hours, then spent the rest of the day exchanging life stories. . . .

Duncan gave Hughes something he'd never had—knowledge about his father's family. His parents separated shortly after his birth, and he lived with his maternal grandmother in Lawrence, Kansas, until he was 12. When she died he moved to Lincoln, Illinois, with his mother and after high school lived a year with his father in Mexico. Among Duncan's vast collection of antiques and family heirlooms handed down from Aunt Jessie was a picture of Langston's grandfather, a man he had never seen. He borrowed the photograph from Duncan, she said, and never returned it. . . .

Duncan and her brother grew up much like their cousin. Their parents, too, separated when they were young. She and her brother clung to each other, and Langston Hughes clung to them.

When the Negro Was in Vogue

Essay by LANGSTON HUGHES

Connect to Your Life

What's "In"? Think about current fads that are popular with your classmates. What is the latest craze in fashion, music, or dance? Which celebrities—artists, authors, musicians, actors, and so on—are hot? Brainstorm with a small group of classmates and create a list of who and what is "in" at your school. As you read Hughes's essay, consider who and what were trendy in the 1920s during the Harlem Renaissance.

Build Background

Hughes in Harlem Hughes first became acquainted with Harlem in 1921 while he was a student at Columbia University. Initially dazzled by Harlem's vibrant nightlife, Hughes later perceived the underlying economic and social problems that existed there. As an eyewitness to Harlem's renaissance, he captures the neighborhood's rich African-American cultural life as well as the hypocrisy and racism of the time in his essay "When the Negro Was in Vogue." The essay first appeared in the final section of Hughes's autobiography *The Big Sea* (1940).

Focus Your Reading

LITERARY ANALYSIS **TONE** The **tone** of a literary work is an expression of a writer's attitude toward his or her subject. A writer conveys tone by *what* he or she says about a subject as well as *how* he or she says it. For example, in the following excerpt from "When the Negro Was in Vogue," Hughes displays a critical tone toward nightclub owners:

> *Some of the owners of Harlem clubs, delighted at the flood of white patronage, made the grievous error of barring their own race, after the manner of the famous Cotton Club.*

ACTIVE READING **DRAWING CONCLUSIONS ABOUT AUTHOR'S PERSPECTIVE** To get the most out of reading a work of nonfiction, try to **draw conclusions** about the **author's perspective,** or view of the events and people described. Some authors adopt the perspective of an objective observer. Others identify emotionally with one or more of their subjects and try to express that person's point of view. To determine an author's perspective, pay attention to the facts that the author includes and to the emotions and opinions that the author expresses.

READER'S NOTEBOOK In your notebook, create a chart like the one shown. As you read the essay, record the facts that Hughes mentions and the emotions and opinions he expresses about each group of people.

	African-American Entertainers	Residents of Harlem	White Tourists
Facts			
Opinions and Emotions			

WHEN THE NEGRO WAS IN VOGUE

LANGSTON HUGHES

The 1920's were the years of Manhattan's black Renaissance. It began with *Shuffle Along, Running Wild,* and the Charleston. Perhaps some people would say even with *The Emperor Jones,* Charles Gilpin, and the tom-toms at the Provincetown. But certainly it was the musical revue, *Shuffle Along,* that gave a scintillating send-off to that Negro vogue in Manhattan, which reached its peak just before the crash of 1929, the crash that sent Negroes, white folks, and all rolling down the hill toward the Works Progress Administration.[1]

Shuffle Along was a honey of a show. Swift, bright, funny, rollicking, and gay, with a dozen danceable, singable tunes. Besides, look who were in it: The now famous choir director, Hall Johnson, and the composer, William Grant Still, were a part of the orchestra. Eubie Blake and Noble Sissle wrote the music and played and acted in the show. Miller and Lyles were the comics. Florence Mills skyrocketed to fame in the second act. Trixie Smith sang "He May Be Your Man But He Comes to See Me Sometimes." And Caterina Jarboro, now a European prima donna, and the internationally celebrated Josephine Baker were merely in the chorus. Everybody was in the audience—including me. People came back to see it innumerable times. It was always packed.

To see *Shuffle Along* was the main reason I wanted to go to Columbia. When I saw it, I was thrilled and delighted. From then on I was in the gallery of the Cort Theatre every time I got a chance. That year, too, I saw Katharine Cornell in *A Bill of Divorcement,* Margaret Wycherly in *The Verge,* Maugham's *The Circle* with Mrs. Leslie Carter, and the Theatre Gild production of Kaiser's *From Morn Till Midnight.* But I remember

Shuffle Along best of all. It gave just the proper push—a pre-Charleston kick—to that Negro vogue of the 20's that spread to books, African sculpture, music, and dancing.

Put down the 1920's for the rise of Roland Hayes, who packed Carnegie Hall, the rise of Paul Robeson[2] in New York and London, of Florence Mills over two continents, of Rose McClendon in Broadway parts that never measured up to her, the booming voice of Bessie Smith and the low moan of Clara on thousands of records, and the rise of that grand comedienne of song, Ethel Waters, singing: "Charlie's elected now! He's in right for sure!" Put down the 1920's for Louis Armstrong and Gladys Bentley and Josephine Baker.[3]

White people began to come to Harlem in droves. For several years they packed the expensive Cotton Club on Lenox Avenue. But I was never there, because the Cotton Club was a Jim Crow[4] club for gangsters and monied whites. They were not cordial to Negro patronage, unless you were a celebrity like Bojangles. So Harlem Negroes did not like the Cotton Club and never appreciated its Jim Crow policy in the very heart of their dark community. Nor did ordinary Negroes like the growing influx of whites toward Harlem after sundown, flooding the little cabarets and bars where formerly only colored people laughed and sang, and where now

---

1. **Works Progress Administration:** an agency formed to help create jobs for the unemployed during the Depression.
2. **Paul Robeson** (rōb'sən): an actor, singer, and activist.
3. **Louis Armstrong . . . Josephine Baker:** Louis Armstrong was a pioneering jazz trumpeter; Gladys Bentley was a pianist and singer; and Josephine Baker was a singer, dancer, and movie actress.
4. **Jim Crow:** racially segregated.

the strangers were given the best ringside tables to sit and stare at the Negro customers—like amusing animals in a zoo.

The Negroes said: "We can't go downtown and sit and stare at you in your clubs. You won't even let us in your clubs." But they didn't say it out loud—for Negroes are practically never rude to white people. So thousands of whites came to Harlem night after night, thinking the Negroes loved to have them there, and firmly believing that all Harlemites left their houses at sundown to sing and dance in cabarets, because most of the whites saw nothing but the cabarets, not the houses.

Some of the owners of Harlem clubs, delighted at the flood of white patronage, made the grievous error of barring their own race, after the manner of the famous Cotton Club. But most of these quickly lost business and folded up, because they failed to realize that a large part of the Harlem attraction for downtown New Yorkers lay in simply watching the colored customers amuse themselves. And the smaller clubs, of course, had no big floor shows or a name band like the Cotton Club, where Duke Ellington[5] usually held forth, so, without black patronage, they were not amusing at all.

Some of the small clubs, however, had people like Gladys Bentley, who was something worth discovering in those days, before she got famous, acquired an accompanist, specially written material, and conscious vulgarity. But for two or three amazing years, Miss Bentley sat, and played a big piano all night long, literally all night, without stopping—singing songs like "The St. James Infirmary," from ten in the evening until dawn, with scarcely a break between the notes, sliding from one song to another, with a powerful and continuous underbeat of jungle rhythm. Miss Bentley was an amazing exhibition of musical energy—a large, dark, masculine lady, whose feet pounded the floor while her fingers pounded the keyboard—a perfect piece of African sculpture, animated by her own rhythm.

But when the place where she played became too well known, she began to sing with an accompanist, became a star, moved to a larger place, then downtown, and is now in Hollywood. The old magic of the woman and the piano and the night and the rhythm being one is gone. But everything goes, one way or another. The '20's are gone and lots of fine things in Harlem night life have disappeared like snow in the sun—since it became utterly commercial, planned for the downtown tourist trade, and therefore dull.

---

5. **Duke Ellington:** a gifted pianist, bandleader, and composer who helped advance jazz music.

ETHEL WATERS

LOUIS ARMSTRONG'S HOT FIVE

BESSIE SMITH

The lindy-hoppers at the Savoy[6] even began to practise acrobatic routines, and to do absurd things for the entertainment of the whites, that probably never would have entered their heads to attempt merely for their own effortless amusement. Some of the lindy-hoppers had cards printed with their names on them and became dance professors teaching the tourists. Then Harlem nights became show nights for the Nordics.

Some critics say that that is what happened to certain Negro writers, too—that they ceased to write to amuse themselves and began to write to amuse and entertain white people, and in so doing distorted and over-colored their material, and left out a great many things they thought would offend their American brothers of a lighter complexion. Maybe—since Negroes have writer-racketeers, as has any other race. But I have known almost all of them, and most of the good ones have tried to be honest, write honestly, and express their world as they saw it.

All of us know that the gay and sparkling life of the so-called Negro Renaissance of the '20's was not so gay and sparkling beneath the surface as it looked. Carl Van Vechten,[7] in the character of Byron in *Nigger Heaven,* captured some of the bitterness and frustration of literary Harlem that Wallace Thurman later so effectively poured into his *Infants of the Spring*—the only novel by a Negro about that fantastic period when Harlem was in vogue.

It was a period when, at almost every Harlem upper-crust dance or party, one would be introduced to various distinguished white celebrities there as guests. It was a period when almost any Harlem Negro of any social importance at all would be likely to say casually: "As I was remarking the other day to Heywood—," meaning Heywood Broun. Or: "As I said to George—," referring to George Gershwin.[8] It was a period when local and visiting royalty were not at all uncommon in Harlem. And when the parties of A'Lelia Walker, the Negro heiress, were filled with guests whose names would turn any Nordic social climber green with envy. It was a period when Harold Jackman, a handsome young Harlem school teacher of modest means, calmly announced one day that he was sailing for the Riviera for a fortnight, to attend Princess Murat's yachting party. It was a period when Charleston preachers opened up shouting churches as sideshows for

---

6. **lindy-hoppers at the Savoy:** people often did a popular 1920s dance, the lindy hop, at the Savoy, a famous Harlem ballroom.

7. **Carl Van Vechten** (văn vĕk′tən): Carl Van Vechten was a white photographer and writer who promoted and publicized the works of his African-American friends.

8. **Heywood . . . Gershwin:** Heywood Broun (hā′wŏŏd brŏŏn) was a New York City newspaper columnist and social critic; George Gershwin was a famous composer.

JOSEPHINE BAKER

PAUL ROBESON

white tourists. It was a period when at least one charming colored chorus girl, amber enough to pass for a Latin American, was living in a pent house, with all her bills paid by a gentleman whose name was banker's magic on Wall Street. It was a period when every season there was at least one hit play on Broadway acted by a Negro cast. And when books by Negro authors were being published with much greater frequency and much more publicity than ever before or since in history. It was a period when white writers wrote about Negroes more successfully (commercially speaking) than Negroes did about themselves. It was the period (God help us!) when Ethel Barrymore[9] appeared in blackface in *Scarlet Sister Mary!* It was the period when the Negro was in vogue.

I was there. I had a swell time while it lasted. But I thought it wouldn't last long. (I remember the vogue for things Russian, the season the Chauve-Souris[10] first came to town.) For how could a large and enthusiastic number of people be crazy about Negroes forever? But some Harlemites thought the millennium had come. They thought the race problem had at last been solved through Art plus Gladys Bentley. They were sure the New Negro would lead a new life from then on in green pastures of tolerance created by Countee Cullen, Ethel Waters, Claude McKay, Duke Ellington, Bojangles, and Alain Locke.[11]

I don't know what made any Negroes think that—except that they were mostly intellectuals doing the thinking. The ordinary Negroes hadn't heard of the Negro Renaissance. And if they had, it hadn't raised their wages any. As for all those white folks in the speakeasies[12] and night clubs of Harlem—well, maybe a colored man could find *some* place to have a drink that the tourists hadn't yet discovered.

Then it was that house-rent parties began to flourish—and not always to raise the rent either. But, as often as not, to have a get-together of one's own, where you could do the black-bottom[13] with no stranger behind you trying to

do it, too. Non-theatrical, non-intellectual Harlem was an unwilling victim of its own vogue. It didn't like to be stared at by white folks. But perhaps the downtowners never knew this—for the cabaret owners, the entertainers, and the speakeasy proprietors treated them fine—as long as they paid.

The Saturday night rent parties that I attended were often more amusing than any night club, in small apartments where God knows who lived—because the guests seldom did—but where the piano would often be augmented by a guitar, or an odd cornet, or somebody with a pair of drums walking in off the street. And where awful bootleg whiskey and good fried fish or steaming chitterling were sold at very low prices. And the dancing and singing and impromptu entertaining went on until dawn came in at the windows.

These parties, often termed whist parties or dances, were usually announced by brightly colored cards stuck in the grille of apartment house elevators. Some of the cards were highly entertaining in themselves.

Almost every Saturday night when I was in Harlem I went to a house-rent party. I wrote lots of poems about house-rent parties, and ate thereat many a fried fish and pig's foot—with liquid refreshments on the side. I met ladies' maids and truck drivers, laundry workers and shoe shine boys, seamstresses and porters. I can still hear their laughter in my ears, hear the soft slow music, and feel the floor shaking as the dancers danced. ❖

---

9. **Ethel Barrymore:** a famous American actress.

10. **Chauve-Souris** (shōv-sōō-rē′): a Paris-based cabaret act featuring actors who formerly lived in Russia.

11. **Countee Cullen . . . Alain Locke:** Countee Cullen was a leading poet; Ethel Waters was a popular singer and actress; Claude McKay was a best-selling author and political activist; Bill "Bojangles" Robinson was considered the greatest tap dancer of the era; Alain Locke (ä′lăn lŏk) was the editor of the anthology *The New Negro.*

12. **speakeasies:** illegal prohibition-era bars.

13. **the black-bottom:** an enormously popular 1920s dance.

Connect to the Literature

1. **What Do You Think?**
   What impressions of Harlem in the 1920s did you get from reading this essay? Jot down words and phrases, or draw a sketch of Harlem.

   Comprehension Check
   - When did the Harlem Renaissance take place?
   - How did many blacks feel about whites who flocked to Harlem clubs?
   - Name two African-American celebrities to whom Hughes refers in his essay.

Think Critically

2. Why do you think white America suddenly became fascinated by Harlem?

   THINK ABOUT
   - the connotation of the word "vogue"
   - the different cultural attractions that Hughes describes
   - the reason Hughes gives for the closing of many Jim Crow clubs
   - the state of race relations in the 1920s

3. What **irony** do you see in the situations described in this essay?

4. **ACTIVE READING** **DRAWING CONCLUSIONS ABOUT AUTHOR'S PERSPECTIVE**

   Determine whether Hughes is objective in his writing or whether he seems sympathetic to any particular group. Support your conclusion with evidence from the chart you made in your **READER'S NOTEBOOK** and from the essay.

Extend Interpretations

5. **What If?** How might the **perspective** of this essay be different if it had been written by one of the whites who "came to Harlem night after night" rather than by Hughes?

6. **Comparing Texts** How do you think the **speaker** of "We Wear the Mask" by Paul Laurence Dunbar (page 836) might react to this essay? Explain your answer.

7. **Connect to Life** In this essay, Hughes mentions some of the African-American cultural achievements and celebrities of the Harlem Renaissance. What specific cultural achievements or important celebrities might you include in an essay about African Americans today?

Literary Analysis

TONE The **tone** of a work of literature reflects the attitude of the writer toward the subject he or she is writing about. For example, a writer's tone can be serious, comical, ironic, or bitter. A writer can communicate tone through his or her choice of words, choice of details, and direct statements of his or her position about a subject. For example, Hughes displays a sarcastic tone toward white tourists by listing wealthy people and gangsters together as equals:

But I was never there, because the Cotton Club was a Jim Crow club for gangsters and monied whites.

Cooperative Learning Activity With a small group of classmates, go back through the essay and identify Hughes's tone toward the different groups of people he describes, such as entertainers, nightclub owners, Harlem residents, and white tourists. For each group, list words and phrases that reveal Hughes's tone. When you have finished, share your findings with the class.

THE AUTHOR'S STYLE
Hughes's Love Song to His People

When Langston Hughes's first book was published, one critic described him as "intensely subjective, passionate, keenly sensitive to beauty, and possessed of an unfaltering musical sense." Those qualities—as well as a great love for African-American culture—would characterize Hughes's style throughout his writing career. The following stylistic devices appear frequently in Hughes's work.

Key Aspects of Hughes's Style

- use of dialect that is characteristic of African Americans in the urban North
- a passionate tone, often one of love, sympathy, or melancholy
- use of irony, satire, and paradox to expose racial problems and self-deceptions
- vivid imagery of the African-American experience, particularly life in Harlem
- rhythms that are taken from speech and music

Analysis of Style

At the right are three excerpts from Hughes's work. Study the chart above, and then complete the following activities:

- Identify examples of different aspects of Hughes's style, such as his use of dialect, irony, or imagery.
- Compare the style of Hughes's poems with that of his essay.
- Go back through the selections in this Author Study, and find other examples of these key aspects of Hughes's style.

Applications

1. Changing Style Working with a partner, rewrite a paragraph from "When the Negro Was in Vogue" in a more formal style. For example, change any dialect or slang to standard English. Discuss how the changes affect your feeling about the piece.

2. Imitation of Style Draft an original poem about discrimination and prejudice, using elements of Hughes's poetic style, such as irony or dialect.

3. Speaking and Listening With a small group of classmates, locate and read aloud another poem or piece of prose by Hughes. Discuss the stylistic devices that you hear in the work.

from "The Weary Blues"

With his ebony hands on each ivory key
He made that poor piano moan with melody.
    O Blues!
Swaying to and fro on his rickety stool
He played that sad raggy tune like a musical fool.
    Sweet Blues!
Coming from a black man's soul.
    O Blues!

from "Mother to Son"

Well, son, I'll tell you:
Life for me ain't been no crystal stair.
It's had tacks in it,
And splinters,
And boards torn up,
And places with no carpet on the floor—
Bare.

from "When the Negro Was in Vogue"

I was there. I had a swell time while it lasted. But I thought it wouldn't last long. (I remember the vogue for things Russian, the season the Chauve-Souris first came to town.) For how could a large and enthusiastic number of people be crazy about Negroes forever? But some Harlemites thought the millennium had come. They thought the race problem had at last been solved through Art plus Gladys Bentley. They were sure the New Negro would lead a new life from then on in green pastures of tolerance created by Countee Cullen, Ethel Waters, Claude McKay, Duke Ellington, Bojangles, and Alain Locke.

Choices & CHALLENGES

Writing Options

1. Autobiographical Essay Draft an auto-biographical essay, modeled on Hughes's, in which you express your opinions of a current trend.

2. Documentary Plan Imagine that you have been asked to produce a documentary about the Harlem Renaissance. Write notes about how you would cover the subject. List the film footage, photographs, and musical recordings you would need. Also, note which of the celebrities, tourists, and residents mentioned by Hughes you would like to interview. Place your notes in your **Working Portfolio.**

Activities & Explorations

1. Music of the 1920s Find and listen to a recording of one of the musicians associated with the Harlem Renaissance, such as Duke Ellington, Louis Armstrong, Ethel Waters, or Bessie Smith. Then discuss with your classmates some of the qualities that you think made this music so popular in the 1920s. ~ **MUSIC/SPEAKING AND LISTENING**

2. Do the Lindy Find out how to do the lindy hop, a popular Harlem dance that was named after the aviation hero Charles A. Lindbergh. With a partner, demonstrate the steps for the class. ~ **DANCE**

Inquiry & Research

The Harlem Renaissance Find out more about the literary and artistic movement called the Harlem Renaissance. Using literature anthologies, history books, and encyclopedias, investigate some of the important writers, artists, musicians, and performers who are associated with this movement. Then work with your classmates to create an informational bulletin board about the Harlem Renaissance.

Netscape: Welcome to Netscape

Langston Hughes

Author Study Project
CREATING A MULTIMEDIA TOUR

Working with a small group, create a multimedia tour of Harlem during the 1920s. You may wish to focus on the shows, the nightclubs, or the daily life of the area. Your guided tour might take the form of a video, a web page, a slide show, or some combination of these. Draw on the information you gathered during the Inquiry & Research activity to get started. Then use the following suggestions to complete your research.

Photography of the Renaissance Look in books and periodicals for photography of the era. You may want to investigate the work of famous photographers, such as James Van Der Zee. Try to find photographs of both celebrities and ordinary citizens of Harlem.

Musical Recordings Find recordings of the musical artists of the Harlem Renaissance. Since the Harlem Renaissance flourished during the early 20th century, you may want to locate records in public libraries or vintage record shops, as well as explore recordings reissued on CDs.

Writings Try to find other written descriptions of Harlem during the 1920s. You might want to try autobiographies, essays, newspaper articles, and collections of letters by famous individuals of the time. Check the Internet to see if there are web sites devoted to the Harlem Renaissance. Look for short, descriptive passages that can be used in your multimedia tour.

 More Online: Research Starter
www.mcdougallittell.com

My City

Poetry by JAMES WELDON JOHNSON

Any Human to Another

Poetry by COUNTEE CULLEN

(Connect to Your Life)

Impressions of New York With a small group of classmates, brainstorm what you know about New York City. Use a cluster diagram to list your thoughts about and attitudes toward this city. Share them with the rest of the class.

Build Background

African-American Migration New York City stirred strong feelings among the African Americans who migrated there in the early 20th century. To some, New York was a charismatic place, representing freedom and opportunities for self-fulfillment. To others, the harsh realities of urban living—such as overcrowding, prejudice, and unemployment—frustrated the expectations that originally had prompted their migration. In "My City," James Weldon Johnson expresses deep feelings about Manhattan, the New York City borough where Harlem is located.

During the Harlem Renaissance, many African-American writers focused on the racism and injustice that, they felt, denied them their rights and opportunities. Countee Cullen, however, believed that instead of restricting themselves to matters related to race, African-American writers should explore more deeply the human condition. In his poem "Any Human to Another," Cullen emphasizes the commonality of the human experience.

Focus Your Reading

LITERARY ANALYSIS **SONNET** A **sonnet** is a lyric poem of 14 lines. Some sonnets have a two-part structure: the first eight lines form one part, and the last six lines form another. Consider how the two parts of "My City" are related.

ACTIVE READING **DETERMINING MAJOR IDEAS IN A POEM**
Use these tips to identify the major ideas in "My City" and "Any Human to Another":

• Read the poems—silently and aloud—more than once.
• Remember that the end of a line may or may not signal the end of a complete thought. Look for periods, question marks, and exclamation points. These marks tell you that you have come to the end of a complete thought. Commas help you separate the different parts of a complete idea.
• Consider the **structure** of each poem. The way a poem is organized or divided gives a clue about where its **major ideas** reside. For example, the two-part structure of "My City" suggests that the poem has two "chunks" of meaning. "Any Human to Another," on the other hand, is divided into five stanzas, each of which conveys a major idea.
• For each part into which a poem is divided, first identify the **subject,** or the focus; then try to state the related major idea.

READER'S NOTEBOOK As you read "My City," fill in a chart like the one shown. Then for "Any Human to Another," create a different chart to list the major idea of each stanza.

	Subject	Major Idea
lines 1–8		
lines 9–14		

My City

JAMES WELDON JOHNSON

New York Harbor/Paris (about 1925),
Jan Matulka. Photo courtesy of Norfolk
Southern Corporation.

When I come down to sleep death's endless night,
The threshold of the unknown dark to cross,
What to me then will be the keenest loss,
When this bright world blurs on my fading sight?
5 Will it be that no more I shall see the trees
Or smell the flowers or hear the singing birds
Or watch the flashing streams or patient herds?
No, I am sure it will be none of these.

But, ah! Manhattan's sights and sounds, her smells,
10 Her crowds, her throbbing force, the thrill that comes
From being of her a part, her subtle spells,
Her shining towers, her avenues, her slums—
O God! the stark, unutterable pity,
To be dead, and never again behold my city!

Thinking Through the Literature

1. **Comprehension Check** What is the one thing the speaker most regrets about death?

2. **ACTIVE READING** **DETERMINING MAJOR IDEAS IN A POEM** What relationship do you see between the main ideas in the two parts of this poem? Refer to the chart you made in your **READER'S NOTEBOOK**.

3. Is the speaker's description of New York City appealing? Is it accurate?

Any Human to Another

COUNTEE CULLEN

The ills I sorrow at
Not me alone
Like an arrow,
Pierce to the marrow,
5 Through the fat
And past the bone.

Your grief and mine
Must intertwine
Like sea and river,
10 Be fused and mingle,
Diverse yet single,
Forever and forever.

Let no man be so proud
And confident,
15 To think he is allowed
A little tent
Pitched in a meadow
Of sun and shadow
All his little own.

20 Joy may be shy, unique,
Friendly to a few,
Sorrow never scorned to speak
To any who
Were false or true.

25 Your every grief
Like a blade
Shining and unsheathed[1]
Must strike me down.
Of bitter aloes[2] wreathed,
30 My sorrow must be laid
On your head like a crown.

---

1. **unsheathed:** removed from its protective case.

2. **bitter aloes** (ăl'ōz): a spiny-leaved plant from the juice of which a bad-tasting medicine is made.

Shotgun, Third Ward #1 (1966), John T. Biggers. Oil on canvas, 76.2 × 121.9 cm, National Museum of American Art, Washington, D.C./Art Resource, New York.

Connect to the Literature

1. **What Do You Think?** What lines from "Any Human to Another" appeal to you the most, and why? Share your response with your classmates.

> **Comprehension Check**
> According to the speaker, which emotion—joy or sorrow—is more common?

Think Critically

2. **ACTIVE READING** | **DETERMINING MAJOR IDEAS IN A POEM**
   How would you describe the major idea of each stanza in this poem? What **theme** do these ideas suggest? Refer to the chart in your **READER'S NOTEBOOK.**

3. What is your opinion of the speaker's ideas about sorrow and grief?

   THINK ABOUT
   - "Your grief and mine / Must intertwine…" (lines 7–8)
   - "Sorrow never scorned to speak / To any…" (lines 22–23)
   - "My sorrow must be laid / On your head like a crown" (lines 30–31)

4. How do the human qualities that the speaker attributes to joy and sorrow differ?

Extend Interpretations

5. **What If?** How might you have responded to "Any Human to Another" if the speaker had expressed a defeatist attitude?

6. **Comparing Texts** Which poem do you think shows greater affection for other people—"My City" or "Any Human to Another"? Support your answer by citing lines from each poem.

7. **Connect to Life** What might individuals do to help make the speaker's dream for humanity in "Any Human to Another" come to pass?

Literary Analysis

SONNET A **sonnet** is a 14-line lyric poem that follows any of several rhyme schemes. One type of sonnet is the **Petrarchan** (pĭ-trär´kən) **sonnet** (named after Francesco Petrarch, 14th-century, the poet who perfected the form in Italian). It consists of two parts. The first eight lines, called the octave, usually have the rhyme scheme *abbaabba.* In the last six lines, called the sestet, the rhyme scheme may be *cdecde, cdcdcd,* or some other variation. Generally, the octave tells a story, introduces a situation, or raises a question. The sestet, in turn, comments on the story, situation, or question. Sonnets are commonly written in **iambic pentameter,** a metrical line of five feet, each of which is made up of two syllables, the first unstressed and the second stressed. By scanning the first line of "My City," you can see that the five feet are iambic:

When I | come down | to sleep | death's end | less night,

Paired Activity With a partner, reread "My City" and then discuss the characteristics that make it a Petrarchan sonnet, charting the rhyme scheme and describing the relationship between the octave and the sestet.

REVIEW | **FIGURATIVE LANGUAGE**
Figurative language communicates ideas beyond the literal meaning of the words. Among the most common types of figurative language are **simile, metaphor,** and **personification.** Find examples of figurative language in "Any Human to Another."

Choices & CHALLENGES

Writing Options

1. Slogan About New York The speaker of "My City" has a strong reaction to New York City. Using the poem and the ideas you listed for the Connect to Your Life activity (page 940) as a basis, write a slogan that celebrates the city.

2. Write a Review Read the following quotation from Dr. Martin Luther King, Jr.: "True altruism is more than the capacity to pity; it is the capacity to empathize… Empathy is fellow feeling for the person in need—his pain, agony, and burdens." Write a review that relates this definition of altruism to the speaker's ideas in "Any Human to Another."

Inquiry & Research

Art Find out about artists who were associated with the Harlem Renaissance, such as the sculptors Meta Warrick Fuller and Richmond Barthé, the painters Jacob Lawrence and Palmer C. Hayden, and the illustrator Aaron Douglas. Identify a particular work of art that you think suits "My City" or "Any Human to Another" in mood or images, and share it with the class.

James Weldon Johnson
1871–1938
Other Works
Autobiography of an Ex-Colored Man
Fifty Years and Other Poems
God's Trombones

Countee Cullen
1903–1946
Other Works
The Ballad of the Brown Girl
The Black Christ and Other Poems
Copper Sun

Multitalented Leader James Weldon Johnson was one of the most prominent African-American leaders of his time. Born into a middle-class family in Jacksonville, Florida, Johnson was a precocious child who read the books of Charles Dickens and Sir Walter Scott. After graduating from Atlanta University, he became a school principal, founded a daily newspaper, and became the first African-American lawyer to be admitted to the Florida bar. In 1902, after his newspaper folded and his school burned down, Johnson decided to go to New York, where he and his brother J. Rosamond became successful Broadway songwriters. Their song "Lift Every Voice and Sing" became known as the African-American "national anthem" (see page 917).

Writer and Cultural Activist During his writing career, Johnson published in all genres of literature. He also wrote *Black Manhattan*, a book about African-American history, and compiled the groundbreaking anthology *The Book of American Negro Poetry* (1922).

Esteemed Poet In 1925, while still an undergraduate at New York University, Countee Cullen published his first poetry collection, *Color*, which established his reputation as a poet. A superb student, he also won several poetry prizes. After graduating from college in 1925, Cullen went on to earn a master's degree at Harvard University.

Literary Influences Cullen was influenced by the English romantic poets, especially John Keats. In his introduction to the anthology *Caroling Dusk*, he stated his belief that African-American poets "may have more to gain from the rich background of English and American poetry than from any . . . yearnings towards an African inheritance." This philosophy is apparent in his own verse.

Later Career In the 1930s and 1940s, Cullen wrote a novel, *One Way to Heaven*, as well as children's books, translations, and (in collaboration with Arna Bontemps) a musical. He taught French at Frederick Douglass Junior High School until his death.

If We Must Die

Poetry by CLAUDE McKAY

A Black Man Talks of Reaping

Poetry by ARNA BONTEMPS (bôn-tän′)

Connect to Your Life

Racial Injustice In the early decades of the 20th century, African Americans suffered many injustices as a result of racial discrimination and prejudice. With a group of classmates, discuss a time when you witnessed someone being treated unfairly. Tell what you think provoked this treatment—was it race, age, gender, religion, income, or some other factor? How did the victim of injustice respond to the unfair treatment? Was the response, in your opinion, effective?

Build Background

Fighting Oppression While still facing widespread discrimination and violence in the 1920s, some writers in Harlem denounced the injustices African Americans endured in a predominantly white society. Claude McKay wrote the poem "If We Must Die" in response to a wave of violence against African Americans during the so-called Red Summer of 1919, when escalating racial tension resulted in 26 bloody riots across the country. In "A Black Man Talks of Reaping," Arna Bontemps condemned the economic exploitation African Americans suffered even after the end of slavery.

Focus Your Reading

LITERARY ANALYSIS **EXTENDED METAPHOR** An **extended metaphor** is a comparison between two things that is developed at some length and in several ways. In the poems you are about to read, notice the comparisons that describe the unfair treatment experienced by African Americans in the early 20th century.

ACTIVE READING **DISTINGUISHING FIGURATIVE AND LITERAL MEANING** **Figurative language** is language that communicates ideas beyond the literal meanings of words. The words in a figurative expression are not literally true; rather, they create impressions in the reader's mind. For example, in the first line of "My City," the poet uses the figurative expression "to sleep death's endless night." This expression compares the experience of death to a sleep that never ends, creating impressions such as peacefulness, darkness, and stillness. As you read "If We Must Die" and "A Black Man Talks of Reaping," use these tips to explore their figurative language:

- Read each poem once to grasp its overall meaning.
- Next reread the poems, noting important words and phrases.
- Ask questions about the comparisons you notice. For example, as you read "If We Must Die," ask yourself, Who are like hogs? What resembles being hunted and penned? As you read "A Black Man Talks of Reaping," ask yourself, What is comparable to *sowing* and *reaping*?

READER'S NOTEBOOK On a chart similar to the one shown, list examples of figurative language in each poem, and describe the impressions created in your mind.

Figurative Language	
Example	Impression

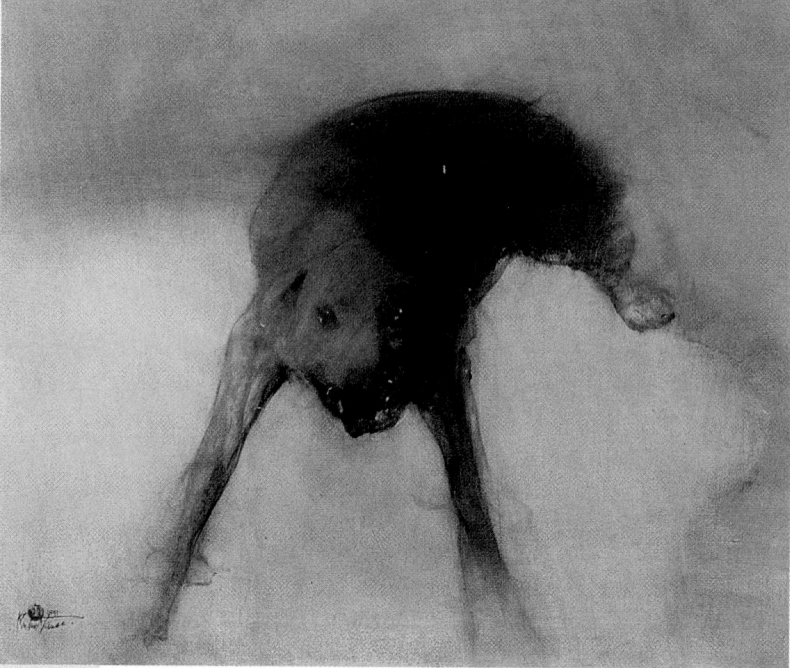

Copyright © Herbert Tauss.

IF WE MUST DIE

CLAUDE McKAY

If we must die, let it not be like hogs
Hunted and penned in an inglorious[1] spot,
While round us bark the mad and hungry dogs,
Making their mock at our accursed lot.
5 If we must die, O let us nobly die,
So that our precious blood may not be shed
In vain; then even the monsters we defy
Shall be constrained[2] to honor us though dead!
O kinsmen! we must meet the common foe!
10 Though far outnumbered let us show us brave,
And for their thousand blows deal one deathblow!
What though before us lies the open grave?
Like men we'll face the murderous, cowardly pack,
Pressed to the wall, dying, but fighting back!

---

1. **inglorious:** shameful; disgraceful.
2. **constrained:** forced.

Thinking Through the Literature

1. **Comprehension Check** What type of death does the speaker argue for or against?

2. Whom is the speaker addressing? Support your answer.

3. **ACTIVE READING** **DISTINGUISHING FIGURATIVE AND LITERAL MEANING** Which figurative expressions created strong impressions in your mind? Refer to your chart.

I have sown beside all waters in my day.
I planted deep, within my heart the fear
That wind or fowl would take the grain away.
I planted safe against this stark, lean year.

5   I scattered seed enough to plant the land
In rows from Canada to Mexico,
But for my reaping only what the hand
Can hold at once is all that I can show.

Yet what I sowed and what the orchard yields
10   My brother's sons are gathering stalk and root,
Small wonder then my children glean[1] in fields
They have not sown, and feed on bitter fruit.

---

1. **glean:** gather grain left behind by reapers.

Photo by Arthur Rothstein.
From the collections of the
Library of Congress.

Connect to the Literature

1. What Do You Think?
What feelings does "A Black Man Talks of Reaping" evoke in you?

> **Comprehension Check**
> • How much has the speaker reaped from all the seed he has scattered?

Think Critically

2.

ACTIVE READING	DISTINGUISHING FIGURATIVE AND LITERAL MEANING

Interpret examples of figurative language you listed on the chart in your **READER'S NOTEBOOK**. What do you think *sowing* and *reaping* mean in this poem?

3. How would you state the **theme,** or the main message, of this poem?

> **THINK ABOUT**
> • the figurative meanings of "sown," "reaping," "my brother's sons," "glean," and "bitter fruit"
> • the difference between reaping and gleaning
> • why the speaker has reaped so little

4. How would you compare the wrongs the speakers face in these two poems and their responses to unfair treatment?

Extend Interpretations

5. Critic's Corner When McKay's poem "If We Must Die" was published in 1919, it was read as a protest against white violence and a call for African Americans to resist oppression. After learning that a white American soldier who died in World War II had carried the poem with him, however, McKay said, "I felt assurance that 'If We Must Die' was just what I intended it to be, a universal poem." In your opinion, does this poem have a universal meaning? Explain your answer.

6. Comparing Texts How do you think Martin Luther King, Jr. (page 301) or Malcolm X (page 305) might respond to the ideas expressed by the speaker of "If We Must Die" or "A Black Man Talks of Reaping"?

7. Connect to Life Which of these poems do you think is more relevant to African Americans today, and why?

Literary Analysis

EXTENDED METAPHOR A **metaphor** is a figure of speech that makes a comparison between two things that have something in common. An **extended metaphor** draws that comparison out and compares the two things in many ways. For example, an extended metaphor that compares life to a journey might be expressed in this way: Different ages in a person's life are signposts along life's journey, marked by high points such as graduation, marriage, and childbirth and by obstacles such as illness.

Paired Activity With a partner, reread "A Black Man Talks of Reaping." Then on a chart like the one shown, identify and interpret the parts of the extended metaphor comparing the African-American race to a farmer.

Parts of the Metaphor	Interpretation

REVIEW SONNET As you may recall, a **sonnet** is a 14-line lyric poem. "My City" (page 941) is an example of a Petrarchan sonnet. A second kind of sonnet, the **Shakespearean sonnet,** is divided into three quatrains (groups of four lines) and a couplet (two rhyming lines). Its rhyme scheme is *abab cdcd efef gg.* The couplet usually expresses a response to the important issue developed in the three quatrains. With a small group, explain how "If We Must Die" shows the features of a Shakespearean sonnet.

Writing Options

1. Problem-Solution Essay What should a group do when it is a target of violence or economic exploitation by another group? Write an essay proposing and developing a solution, based on your interpretation of these poems and your personal philosophy or your knowledge of current events. Place this piece in your **Working Portfolio.**

Writing Handbook
See page 1283: Problem-Solution

2. Write a Sonnet Try writing a sonnet on any subject—perhaps the instance of unfair treatment you discussed for the Connect to Your Life activity on page 945. Use either the Shakespearean or the Petrarchan form, and remember that the end must somehow answer or comment on the beginning. Share a draft of your poem with a partner for comment.

Activities & Explorations

Activist Poster With a small group of classmates, design a poster with print and art for each of the speakers of "If We Must Die" and "A Black Man Talks of Reaping." Each poster should feature a motto that expresses a goal, principle, or action advocated by the speaker for whom it is designed. ~ **VIEWING AND REPRESENTING**

Claude McKay
1890?–1948

Other Works
Banana Bottom
Banjo
Harlem: Negro Metropolis
A Long Way from Home

Harlem Renaissance Figure Born and raised on the island of Jamaica, Claude McKay came to the United States in 1912. With the publication in 1922 of his major collection of poetry, *Harlem Shadows,* McKay helped launch the Harlem Renaissance.

Militant Writer Called "the poet of rebellion" by James Weldon Johnson, McKay protested racial injustice in both poetry and prose. His powerful sonnet "If We Must Die," first published in *The Liberator* in July 1919, is still one of the best-known African-American poems. The popularity of his novel *Home to Harlem,* about a soldier's life after World War I, made McKay the first best-selling African-American novelist.

Universal Themes McKay spent most of the 1920s abroad, living for 12 years in the Soviet Union, France, Spain, and Morocco. He once said, "I have always felt that my gift of song was something bigger than the narrow confined limits of any one people and its problems."

Arna Bontemps
1902–1973

Other Works
The Old South
Personals

Inspired by Marcus Garvey Through his poetry, novels, and plays, Arna Bontemps made a significant contribution to the development of African-American identity. Bontemps was born in Alexandria, Louisiana, the son of a teacher and a brick mason. While attending Pacific Union College, he heard the Jamaican social reformer Marcus Garvey speak in Los Angeles and learned about the flourishing Harlem Renaissance.

At Work in Harlem After graduating from college in 1923, Bontemps moved to Harlem to "see what all the excitement was about." What he discovered was "a foretaste of paradise." While earning a living by teaching, he concentrated as much as possible on his writing and within a year of his arrival in New York City began publishing poems in *Crisis* magazine. His first novel, *God Sends Sunday,* published in 1931, is considered by some to have been the final product of the Harlem Renaissance movement.

How It Feels to Be Colored Me

Essay by ZORA NEALE HURSTON

(Connect to Your Life)

Your Individuality Imagine that you are filling out a college application and that one of the questions asks you to describe what makes you a unique individual. On a sheet of paper, list three or four qualities that you would attribute to yourself in such a description. Compare your list with a partner's.

Build Background

Flamboyant Personality From the time she moved to Harlem in 1925 until her death in 1960, Zora Neale Hurston was the most prolific African-American woman writer. She was also a popular figure on the social scene during the Harlem Renaissance. According to her biographer Robert Hemenway, Hurston "acquired an instant reputation in New York for her high spirits and side-splitting tales of Eatonville," her Florida hometown. Like other writers of the Harlem Renaissance, such as Langston Hughes and Claude McKay, Hurston searched within herself for her identity rather than defining herself according to the racial stereotypes of her day. In this essay, first published in 1928, she uses several unique images to convey her individuality.

WORDS TO KNOW
Vocabulary Preview

deplore	rend	veneer
extenuating	specter	

Focus Your Reading

LITERARY ANALYSIS **AUTOBIOGRAPHICAL ESSAY** An essay is a short work of nonfiction that deals with a single subject. In an **autobiographical essay,** that subject is some aspect of the writer's life. The subject of Hurston's essay is her sense of herself as an individual and an African American.

ACTIVE READING **DRAWING CONCLUSIONS ABOUT AUTHOR'S PURPOSES** A writer usually writes for one or more **purposes**—to inform, to entertain, to express himself or herself, or to persuade readers to believe or do something. In this autobiographical essay, Hurston writes for multiple purposes. To **draw conclusions** about them, use these tips:

- Identify passages that affect you strongly.
- In these passages, consider the kinds of experiences she relates—for example, painful ones or generally happy ones—and the descriptive details she provides. Note especially her direct statements and comparisons.
- Ask yourself why she includes these passages, and state your own conclusions.

READER'S NOTEBOOK As you read, use a chart to gather data about selected passages from the beginning, middle, and end of this essay. Then state your conclusion about Hurston's purposes for writing each one.

Hurston's Essay

Passages	Purposes
1. Childhood in Eatonville	
2. Experiencing Live Jazz	
3. Comparison of People to Stuffed Bags	

How It Feels to Be Colored Me

ZORA NEALE HURSTON

I am colored but I offer nothing in the way of extenuating circumstances except the fact that I am the only Negro in the United States whose grandfather on the mother's side was *not* an Indian chief.

I remember the very day that I became colored. Up to my thirteenth year I lived in the little Negro town of Eatonville, Florida. It is exclusively a colored town. The only white people I knew passed through the town going to or coming from Orlando. The native whites rode dusty horses; the Northern tourists chugged down the sandy village road in automobiles. The town knew the Southerners and never stopped cane chewing when they passed. But the Northerners were something else again. They were peered at cautiously from behind curtains by the timid. The more venturesome would come out on the porch to watch them go past and got just as much pleasure out of the tourists as the tourists got out of the village.

The front porch might seem a daring place for the rest of the town, but it was a gallery seat for me. My favorite place was atop the gatepost. Proscenium box[1] for a born first-nighter.[2] Not only did I enjoy the show, but I didn't mind the actors knowing that I liked it. I usually spoke to them in passing. I'd wave at them and when they returned my salute, I would say something like this: "Howdy-do-well-I-thank-you-where-you-goin'?" Usually the automobile or the horse paused at this, and after a queer exchange of compliments, I would probably "go a piece of the way" with them, as we say in farthest Florida. If one of my family happened to come to the front in time to see me, of course negotiations would be rudely broken off. But even so, it is clear that I was the first "welcome-to-our-state" Floridian, and I hope the Miami Chamber of Commerce will please take notice.

During this period, white people differed from colored to me only in that they rode through town and never lived there. They liked to hear me "speak pieces" and sing and wanted to see me dance the parse-me-la, and gave me generously of their small silver for doing these things,

---

1. **proscenium** (prō-sē′nē-əm) **box:** a box seat near the stage.
2. **first-nighter:** a person who attends the opening performance of a play, an opera, or a similar show.

Skipping Along, Stephen Scott Young. Copyright © Stephen Scott Young. Photo courtesy of John H. Surovek Gallery, Palm Beach, Flordia.

which seemed strange to me, for I wanted to do them so much that I needed bribing to stop. Only they didn't know it. The colored people gave no dimes. They <u>deplored</u> any joyful tendencies in me, but I was their Zora nevertheless. I belonged to them, to the nearby hotels, to the county—everybody's Zora.

But changes came in the family when I was thirteen, and I was sent to school in Jacksonville. I left Eatonville, the town of the oleanders,[3] as Zora. When I disembarked from the riverboat at Jacksonville, she was no more. It seemed that I had suffered a sea change.[4] I was not Zora of Orange County any more, I was now a little colored girl. I found it out in certain ways. In my heart as well as in the mirror, I became a fast brown—warranted not to rub nor run.

But I am not tragically colored. There is no great sorrow dammed up in my soul, nor lurking behind my eyes. I do not mind at all. I do not belong to the sobbing school of Negrohood who hold that nature somehow has given them a lowdown dirty deal and whose feelings are all

hurt about it. Even in the helter-skelter skirmish that is my life, I have seen that the world is to the strong regardless of a little pigmentation[5] more or less. No, I do not weep at the world—I am too busy sharpening my oyster knife.[6]

Someone is always at my elbow reminding me that I am the granddaughter of slaves. It fails to register depression with me. Slavery is sixty years in the past. The operation was successful and the patient is doing well, thank you. The terrible struggle that made me an American out of a potential slave said, "On the line!" The Reconstruction said, "Get set!" and the generation before said, "Go!" I am off to a flying start and I must not halt in the stretch to look behind and weep. Slavery is the price I paid for civilization, and the choice was not with me. It is a bully[7] adventure and worth all that I have paid through my ancestors for it. No one on earth ever had a greater chance for glory. The world to be won and nothing to be lost. It is thrilling to think—to know that for any act of mine, I shall get twice as much praise or twice as much blame. It is quite exciting to hold the center of the national stage, with the spectators not knowing whether to laugh or to weep.

The position of my white neighbor is much more difficult. No brown <u>specter</u> pulls up a chair beside me when I sit down to eat. No dark ghost thrusts its leg against mine in bed. The game of keeping what one has is never so exciting as the game of getting.

---

3. **oleanders** (ō′lē-ăn′dərz): evergreen shrubs with fragrant flowers.

4. **sea change:** complete transformation.

5. **pigmentation:** darkness of skin coloration.

6. **oyster knife:** a reference to the saying "The world is my oyster," implying that the world contains treasure waiting to be taken, like the pearl in an oyster.

7. **bully:** excellent; splendid.

I do not always feel colored. Even now I often achieve the unconscious Zora of Eatonville before the Hegira.[8] I feel most colored when I am thrown against a sharp white background.

For instance at Barnard.[9] "Beside the waters of the Hudson"[10] I feel my race. Among the thousand white persons, I am a dark rock surged upon, and overswept, but through it all, I remain myself. When covered by the waters, I am; and the ebb but reveals me again.

Sometimes it is the other way around. A white person is set down in our midst, but the contrast is just as sharp for me. For instance, when I sit in the drafty basement that is The New World Cabaret with a white person, my color comes. We enter chatting about any little nothing that we have in common and are seated by the jazz waiters. In the abrupt way that jazz orchestras have, this one plunges into a number. It loses no time in circumlocutions,[11] but gets right down to business. It constricts the thorax and splits the heart with its tempo and narcotic harmonies. This orchestra grows rambunctious, rears on its hind legs and attacks the tonal veil with primitive fury, <u>rending</u> it, clawing it until it breaks through to the jungle beyond. I follow those heathen—follow them exultingly. I dance wildly inside myself; I yell within, I whoop; I shake my assegai[12] above my head, I hurl it true to the mark *yeeeeoooww!* I am in the jungle and living in the jungle way. My face is painted red and yellow and my body is painted blue. My pulse is throbbing like a war drum. I want to slaughter something—give pain, give death to what, I do not know. But the piece ends. The men of the orchestra wipe their lips and rest their fingers. I creep back slowly to the <u>veneer</u> we call civilization with the last tone and find the white friend sitting motionless in his seat, smoking calmly.

"Good music they have here," he remarks, drumming the table with his fingertips.

Music. The great blobs of purple and red emotion have not touched him. He has only heard what I felt. He is far away and I see him but dimly across the ocean and the continent that have fallen between us. He is so pale with his whiteness then and I am *so* colored.

At certain times I have no race. I am *me*. When I set my hat at a certain angle and saunter down Seventh Avenue, Harlem City, feeling as snooty as the lions in front of the Forty-Second Street Library, for instance. So far as my feelings are concerned, Peggy Hopkins Joyce on the Boule Mich with her gorgeous raiment, stately carriage,[13] knees knocking together in a most aristocratic manner, has nothing on me. The cosmic[14] Zora emerges. I belong to no race nor time. I am the eternal feminine with its string of beads.

I have no separate feeling about being an American citizen and colored. I am merely a fragment of the Great Soul that surges within the boundaries. My country, right or wrong.

Sometimes, I feel discriminated against, but it does not make me angry. It merely astonishes

---

8. **Hegira** (hĭ-jī'rə): journey (from the name given to Mohammed's journey from Mecca to Medina in 622).

9. **Barnard:** the college in New York City from which Hurston graduated in 1928.

10. **"Beside the waters of the Hudson":** a reference to the first line of Barnard's school song.

11. **circumlocutions** (sûr'kəm-lō-kyōo'shənz): unnecessary elaboration or "beating around the bush."

12. **assegai** (ăs'ə-gī'): a light spear, especially one with a short shaft and long blade, used in southern Africa.

13. **Peggy Hopkins Joyce . . . carriage:** one of the richest women of Hurston's day, walking along the Boulevard Saint-Michel in Paris, dressed in beautiful clothes, carrying herself like a queen.

14. **cosmic:** of or belonging to the universe.

WORDS TO KNOW

rend (rĕnd) *v.* to tear or split apart violently
veneer (və-nîr') *n.* a thin surface layer that conceals what is below

Bal Jeunesse (about 1927), Palmer Hayden. Watercolor on paper, 14″ × 17″, collection of Meredith and Gail Wright Sirmans.

me. How *can* any deny themselves the pleasure of my company? It's beyond me.

But in the main, I feel like a brown bag of miscellany propped against a wall. Against a wall in company with other bags, white, red, and yellow. Pour out the contents, and there is discovered a jumble of small things priceless and worthless. A first-water[15] diamond, an empty spool, bits of broken glass, lengths of string, a key to a door long since crumbled away, a rusty knife blade, old shoes saved for a road that never was and never will be, a nail bent under the weight of things too heavy for any nail, a dried flower or two still a little fragrant. In your hand is the brown bag. On the ground before you is the jumble it held—so much like the jumble in the bags, could they be emptied, that all might be dumped in a single heap and the bags refilled without altering the content of any greatly. A bit of colored glass more or less would not matter. Perhaps that is how the Great Stuffer of Bags filled them in the first place—who knows? ❖

---

15. **first-water:** of the highest quality or purity.

from
Zora Neale Hurston: A Cautionary Tale and a Partisan View

ALICE WALKER

Novelist Alice Walker was responsible for rediscovering the writings of Zora Neale Hurston in the 1970s and bringing her to the attention of a new generation of readers. In the following excerpt from an essay on Hurston, Walker discusses the impact of Hurston's collection of black folktales, Mules and Men, *first published in 1935.*

ZORA NEALE HURSTON

AUTHOR OF THEIR EYES WERE WATCHING GOD

MULES AND MEN

"Simply the most exciting book on black folklore and culture I have eve read."
—Roger D. Abraham

. . . When I read *Mules and Men* I was delighted. Here was this perfect book! The "perfection" of which I immediately tested on my relatives, who are such typical black Americans they are useful for every sort of political, cultural, or economic survey. Very regular people from the South, rapidly forgetting their Southern cultural inheritance in the suburbs and ghettos of Boston and New York, they sat around reading the book themselves, listening to me read the book, listening to each other read the book, and a kind of paradise was regained. For what Zora's book did was this: it gave them back all the stories they had forgotten or of which they had grown ashamed (told to us years ago by our parents and grandparents—not one of whom could *not* tell a story to make you weep, or laugh) and showed how marvelous, and, indeed, priceless, they are. This is not exaggerated. No matter how they read the stories Zora had collected, no matter how much distance they tried to maintain between themselves, as new sophisticates, and the lives their parents and grandparents lived, no matter how they tried to remain cool toward all Zora revealed, in the end they could not hold back the smiles, the laughter, the joy over who she was showing them to be: descendants of an inventive, joyous, courageous, and outrageous people; loving drama, appreciating wit, and, most of all, relishing the pleasure of each other's loquacious[1] and *bodacious*[2] company.

This was my first indication of the quality I feel is most characteristic of Zora's work: racial health; a sense of black people as complete, complex, *undiminished* human beings, a sense that is lacking in so much black writing and literature. (In my opinion, only Du Bois[3] showed an equally consistent delight in the beauty and spirit of black people, which is interesting when one considers that the angle of his vision was completely the opposite of Zora's.) Zora's pride in black people was so pronounced in the ersatz[4] black twenties that it made other blacks suspicious and perhaps uncomfortable (after all, *they* were still infatuated[5] with things European). Zora was interested in Africa, Haiti, Jamaica, and—for a little racial diversity (Indians)—Honduras. She also had a confidence in herself as an individual that few people (anyone?), black or white, understood. This was because Zora grew up in a community of black people who had enormous respect for themselves and for their ability to govern themselves. Her own father had written the Eatonville town laws. This community affirmed her right to exist, and loved her as an extension of its self. For how many other black Americans is this true? It certainly isn't true for any that I know. In her easy self-acceptance, Zora was more like an uncolonized African than she was like her contemporary American blacks, most of whom believed, at least during their formative years, that their blackness was something wrong with them.

On the contrary, Zora's early work shows she grew up pitying whites because the ones she saw lacked "light" and soul. It is impossible to imagine Zora envying anyone (except tongue in cheek), and least of all a white person for being white. Which is, after all, if one is black, a clear and present calamity of the mind.

Condemned to a desert island for life, with an allotment of ten books to see me through, I would choose, unhesitatingly, two of Zora's: *Mules and Men*, because I would need to be able to pass on to younger generations the life of American blacks as legend and myth; and *Their Eyes Were Watching God*, because I would want to enjoy myself while identifying with the black heroine, Janie Crawford, as she acted out many roles in a variety of settings, and functioned (with spectacular results!) in romantic and sensual love. *There is no book more important to me than this one. . . .* ❖

---

1. **loquacious** (lō-kwā′shəs): very talkative.
2. *bodacious* (bō-dā′shəs): a Southern dialect term meaning "remarkable" or "spirited."
3. **Du Bois** (dōō bois′): the U.S. civil rights leader, editor, and author W. E. B. Du Bois (1868–1963).
4. ersatz (ĕr′zäts′): artificial; imitation.
5. infatuated (ĭn-făch′ōō-ā′tĭd): carried away by a foolish attraction.

Connect to the Literature

1. What Do You Think?
If you had met Zora Neale Hurston, would you have liked her?

> **Comprehension Check**
> - What kind of community was Eatonville, Florida?
> - What was the "sea change" Zora suffered at the age of 13?

Think Critically

2. ACTIVE READING DRAWING CONCLUSIONS ABOUT AUTHOR'S PURPOSES What conclusions did you draw about Hurston's purposes for writing this essay? Refer to the chart in your READER'S NOTEBOOK to support your conclusions.

3. Why do you think Hurston concludes this essay by comparing people to stuffed bags?

4. What do you think Hurston's cultural identity meant to her?

> **THINK ABOUT**
> - her statement "I am not tragically colored"
> - when she was aware of her color and when she forgot it
> - her views of slavery, discrimination, and the United States
> - her response to jazz

Extend Interpretations

5. Comparing Texts In the Literary Link on page 955, Alice Walker identifies qualities she feels are characteristic of Hurston's writing. Which, if any, of these qualities do you detect in Hurston's essay? Explain your answer.

6. Critic's Corner Alice Walker, one of Hurston's greatest admirers, had this to say about Hurston's essay:

> *"How It Feels to Be Colored Me" is an excellent example of Zora Neale Hurston at her most exasperating. Published in 1928, near the beginning of Hurston's career, this essay presents two stereotypes: the "happy darky" who sings and dances for white folks, for money and for joy; and the educated black person who is, underneath the thin veneer of civilization, still a "heathen."*

Do you agree with Walker's views? Why or why not?

7. Connect to Life Which of the ideas expressed in Hurston's essay do you think might be controversial today?

Literary Analysis

AUTOBIOGRAPHICAL ESSAY An **autobiographical essay** is a short work of nonfiction that focuses on an aspect of the writer's life. One of the challenges is to combine objective description with the expression of subjective feelings. For example, at the beginning of this essay, Hurston uses objective language to describe the white people passing through Eatonville: "The native whites rode dusty horses; the Northern tourists chugged down the sandy village road in automobiles." In contrast, when relating her own subjective feelings about watching these people, Hurston uses a figurative expression and emotionally charged words: "My favorite place was atop the gatepost. Proscenium box for a born first-nighter. Not only did I enjoy the show, but I didn't mind the actors knowing that I liked it."

Activity Reread the passage in which Hurston describes her reaction to jazz at The New World Cabaret. Then fill in a chart like the following, distinguishing the objective description from the subjective expression.

Objective Description	Subjective Expression

REVIEW TONE What **tone** is conveyed by Hurston's comparisons of life to a "show," a "game," and a "bully adventure"? Compare her attitude toward being African American with the attitudes of the other Harlem Renaissance writers you've read.

Choices & CHALLENGES

Writing Options

1. Proposal for School Assembly Write a proposal to a committee planning a school assembly in honor of famous African Americans. In your proposal, present reasons why Hurston's essay should be read at the assembly.

Writing Handbook
See page 1285: Persuasive Writing.

2. Autobiographical Essay Imagine that an organization whose purpose is to foster racial or ethnic pride will award a scholarship to the applicant who best expresses an appreciation of his or her heritage. Draft an autobiographical essay, modeled after Hurston's, expressing your views about your heritage.

Vocabulary in Action

EXERCISE: MEANING CLUES Answer these questions.

1. What attraction at an amusement park would probably involve a **specter**—a roller coaster, a ring-toss game, or a haunted house?

2. If you said that someone had a **veneer** of friendliness, would you be suggesting that the person was eager, was hesitant, or was insincere?

3. If you were to **rend** a curtain, would you be closing it, ripping it, or hanging it?

4. Which would be an **extenuating** circumstance for being tardy for school—that you dawdled on the way, that the bus broke down, or that you thought it was Saturday?

5. Is an action that you **deplore** one that you find horrible, one that you find amusing, or one that you find boring?

Building Vocabulary
For an in-depth study of word connotation and denotation, see page 908.

Zora Neale Hurston
1891?–1960

Other Works
Jonah's Gourd Vine
Moses, Man of the Mountain
Tell My Horse
"Sweat"
"The Gilded Six-Bits"

Arrival in Harlem Born in the all-black town of Eatonville, Florida, Zora Neale Hurston took her mother's advice to "jump at de sun" and overcome poverty and prejudice. She entered Harlem society in 1925, arriving with "$1.50, no job, no friends, and a lot of hope." After she had won two second prizes—one for a short story and one for a play—in a literary contest sponsored by *Opportunity* magazine, Hurston came to the attention of the leaders of the Harlem Renaissance. In the New York City of the 1920s, Hurston soon became known for her flamboyant, theatrical personality as well as for her short stories.

Folklorist In 1928, after graduating from Barnard College, where she had studied with the renowned anthropologist Franz Boas, Hurston returned to her native South to collect African-American folklore. "I had to go back, dress as they did, talk as they did, live their life," she said, "so I could get into my stories the world I knew as a child."

Literary Success Over the next two decades, Hurston built her reputation as the best African-American woman writer of her time with a steady stream of publications. Among her prominent works were the folklore collection *Mules and Men,* the novel *Their Eyes Were Watching God,* and her autobiography, *Dust Tracks on a Road.*

Final Years During the last 20 years of her life, Hurston struggled with financial and health problems. She died in poverty and was buried in an unmarked grave in Fort Pierce, Florida. Many readers have rediscovered Hurston in recent years, however—largely because of the African-American writer Alice Walker's efforts to publicize her life and work.

Author Activity

Give a dramatic reading of one of the folktales in Hurston's *Mules and Men,* a book that Alice Walker said she would take with her to a desert island.

My Dungeon Shook:
Letter to My Nephew on the One Hundredth Anniversary of the Emancipation

Open Letter by JAMES BALDWIN

Comparing Literature

Traditions Across Time: Reaffirming Cultural Identity

Like the writers of the Harlem Renaissance, James Baldwin explores African-American cultural identity. He wrote this essay as a letter to his nephew, advising him to discover for himself who he really is.

Points of Comparison Compare and contrast Baldwin's views about race relations with those of Harlem Renaissance writers.

Build Background

Effects of Racism In this essay, written 100 years after Abraham Lincoln's Emancipation Proclamation, Baldwin refers to the harsh social conditions under which some African Americans lived, particularly the conditions he himself had witnessed while growing up in Harlem. The center of African-American culture in the 1920s, Harlem later became a bleak ghetto from which residents had little hope of escaping and which they had even less hope of improving. In the 1960s the sense of despair pervading decayed urban neighborhoods like Harlem fueled an atmosphere of violence. From 1964 to 1967, more than 100 race riots erupted in major cities across the United States.

WORDS TO KNOW
Vocabulary Preview

aspire	monumental
constitute	paradox
devastation	perspective
impertinent	truculent
mediocrity	whence

Focus Your Reading

LITERARY ANALYSIS **OPEN LETTER** An **open letter** is addressed to a specific person but published for a wider readership. Consider the larger audience that Baldwin targets in "My Dungeon Shook."

ACTIVE READING **ANALYZING CHARACTERISTICS OF CLEARLY WRITTEN TEXTS** In this letter, Baldwin explores the complexity of race relations in the United States. Use these strategies to help you understand his ideas:

- Complex ideas sometimes require complex sentences. When you come upon these sentences, pay attention to the **syntax**—or the arrangement of the sentence parts. Identify the subject (the person, place, thing, or idea about which something is said) and the predicate (the part that tells or asks something about the subject).
- Watch for paradoxes and other thought-provoking statements. A **paradox** is a statement that appears to be a contradiction. For example, Baldwin writes, "It is the innocence which constitutes the crime." When you come upon such a statement, ask yourself what words signal a possible double meaning. Then try to figure out the underlying truth that the apparent contradiction conveys. In the paradox above, you probably associate innocence with the absence of wrongdoing. So in order to understand this sentence, you must determine what kind of innocence Baldwin means.

READER'S NOTEBOOK List and interpret thought-provoking statements in this letter, including the paradox discussed above.

MY DUNGEON SHOOK

Letter to My Nephew on the One Hundredth Anniversary of the Emancipation

James Baldwin

Dear James:

I have begun this letter five times and torn it up five times. I keep seeing your face, which is also the face of your father and my brother. Like him, you are tough, dark, vulnerable, moody—with a very definite tendency to sound truculent because you want no one to think you are soft. You may be like your grandfather in this, I don't know, but certainly both you and your father resemble him very much physically. Well, he is dead, he never saw you, and he had a terrible life; he was defeated long before he died because, at the bottom of his heart, he really believed what white people said about him. This is one of the reasons that he became so holy.[1] I am sure that your father has told you something about all that. Neither you nor your father exhibit any tendency towards holiness: you really *are* of another era, part of what happened when the Negro left the land and came into what the late E. Franklin Frazier called "the cities of destruction." You can only be destroyed by believing that you really are what the white world calls a *nigger*. I tell you this because I love you, and please don't you ever forget it.

I have known both of you all your lives, have carried your Daddy in my arms and on my shoulders, kissed and spanked

Copyright © Julian Allen.

him and watched him learn to walk. I don't know if you've known anybody from that far back; if you've loved anybody that long, first as an infant, then as a child, then as a man, you gain a strange perspective on time and human pain and effort. Other people cannot see what I see whenever I look into your father's face, for behind your father's face as it is today are all those other faces which were his. Let him laugh and I see a cellar your father does not remember and a house he does not remember and I hear in his present laughter his laughter as a child. Let him curse and I remember him falling down the cellar steps, and howling, and I remember, with pain, his tears, which my hand or your grandmother's so easily wiped away. But no one's hand can wipe away those tears he sheds invisibly today, which one hears in his laughter and in his speech and in his songs. I know what the world has done to my brother and how narrowly he has survived it. And I know, which is much worse, and this is the crime of which I accuse my country and my countrymen, and for which neither I nor time nor history will ever

---

1. **so holy:** Baldwin's stepfather was a minister who raised his children in a strict, conservative, religious atmosphere.

forgive them, that they have destroyed and are destroying hundreds of thousands of lives and do not know it and do not want to know it. One can be, indeed one must strive to become, tough and philosophical concerning destruction and death, for this is what most of mankind has been best at since we have heard of man. (But remember: *most* of mankind is not *all* of mankind.) But it is not permissible that the authors of <u>devastation</u> should also be innocent. It is the innocence which <u>constitutes</u> the crime.

Now, my dear namesake, these innocent and well-meaning people, your countrymen, have caused you to be born under conditions not very far removed from those described for us by Charles Dickens in the London of more than a hundred years ago. (I hear the chorus of the innocents screaming, "No! This is not true! How *bitter* you are!"—but I am writing this letter to *you,* to try to tell you something about how to handle *them,* for most of them do not yet really know that you exist. I *know* the conditions under which you were born, for I was there. Your countrymen were *not* there, and haven't made it yet. Your grandmother was also there, and no one has ever accused her of being bitter. I suggest that the innocents check with her. She isn't hard to find. Your countrymen don't know that *she* exists, either, though she has been working for them all their lives.)

Well, you were born, here you came, something like fifteen years ago; and though your father and mother and grandmother, looking about the streets through which they were carrying you, staring at the walls into which

they brought you, had every reason to be heavyhearted, yet they were not. For here you were, Big James, named for me—you were a big baby, I was not—here you were: to be loved. To be loved, baby, hard, at once, and forever, to strengthen you against the loveless world. Remember that: I know how black it looks today, for you. It looked bad that day, too, yes, we were trembling. We have not stopped trembling yet, but if we had not loved each other none of us would have survived. And now you must survive because we love you, and for the sake of your children and your children's children.

This innocent country set you down in a ghetto in which, in fact, it intended that you should perish. Let me spell out precisely what I mean by that, for the heart of the matter is here, and the root of my dispute with my country. You were born where you were born and faced the future that you faced because you were black and *for no other reason.* The limits of your ambition were, thus, expected to be set forever. You were born into a society which spelled out with brutal clarity, and in as many ways as possible, that you were a worthless human being. You were not expected to <u>aspire</u> to excellence: you were expected to make peace with <u>mediocrity</u>. Wherever you have turned, James, in your short time on this earth, you have been told where you could go and what you could do (and *how* you could do it) and where you could live and whom you could marry. I know your countrymen do not agree with me about this, and I hear them saying, "You exaggerate." They do not know Harlem, and I do. So do you. Take no one's word for anything, including mine—but trust your experience.

It is the innocence which constitutes the crime.

WORDS
TO
KNOW

devastation (dĕv'ə-stā'shən) *n.* complete destruction
constitute (kŏn'stĭ-tōōt') *v.* to amount to; equal
aspire (ə-spīr') *v.* to seek to achieve; strive
mediocrity (mē'dē-ŏk'rĭ-tē) *n.* a state of being only average in quality; moderate inferiority

My Brother (1942), John Wilson. Oil on panel, 12″ × 10 ⅝″, Smith College Museum of Art, Northampton, Massachusetts, purchased 1943.

t

Know whence you came. If you know whence you came, there is really no limit to where you can go. The details and symbols of your life have been deliberately constructed to make you believe what white people say about you. Please try to remember that what they believe, as well as what they do and cause you to endure, does not testify to your inferiority but to their inhumanity and fear. Please try to be clear, dear James, through the storm which rages about your youthful head today, about the reality which lies behind the words *acceptance* and *integration*. There is no reason for you to try to become like white people and there is no basis whatever for their impertinent assumption that *they* must accept *you*. The really terrible thing, old buddy, is that *you* must accept *them*. And I mean that very seriously. You must accept them and accept them with love. For these innocent people have no other hope. They are, in effect, still trapped in a history which they do not understand; and until they understand it, they cannot be released from it. They have had to believe for many years, and for innumerable reasons, that black men are inferior to white men. Many of them, indeed, know better, but, as you will discover, people find it very difficult to act on what they know. To act is to be committed, and to be committed is to be in danger. In this case, the danger, in the minds of most white Americans, is the loss of their identity. Try to imagine how you would feel if you woke up one morning to find the sun shining and all the stars aflame. You would be frightened because it is out of the order of nature. Any upheaval in the universe is terrifying because it so profoundly attacks one's sense of one's own reality. Well, the black man has functioned in the white man's world as a fixed star, as an immovable pillar: and as he moves out of his place, heaven and earth are shaken to their foundations. You, don't be afraid. I said that it was intended that you should perish in the ghetto, perish by never being allowed to go behind the white man's definitions, by never being allowed to spell your proper name. You have, and many of us have, defeated this intention; and, by a terrible law, a terrible paradox, those innocents who believed that your imprisonment made them safe are losing their grasp of reality. But these men are your brothers —your lost, younger brothers. And if the word *integration* means anything, this is what it means: that we, with love, shall force our brothers to see themselves as they are, to cease fleeing from reality and begin to change it. For this is your home, my friend, do not be driven from it; great men have done great things here, and will again, and we can make America what America must become. It will be hard, James, but you come from sturdy, peasant stock, men who picked cotton and dammed rivers and built railroads, and, in the teeth of the most terrifying odds, achieved an unassailable and monumental dignity. You come from a long line of great poets, some of the greatest poets since Homer. One of them said, *The very time I thought I was lost, My dungeon shook and my chains fell off.*[2]

You know, and I know, that the country is celebrating one hundred years of freedom one hundred years too soon. We cannot be free until they are free. God bless you, James, and Godspeed.

Your uncle,

James

---

2. *The very time . . . fell off:* a quotation from the traditional spiritual "My Dungeon Shook." It contains an allusion to the biblical story of Paul and Silas (Acts 16), who were freed from an unjust imprisonment by an earthquake that broke their chains and opened the prison doors.

WORDS
TO
KNOW

whence (hwĕns) *adv.* from where
impertinent (ĭm-pûr′ tn ənt) *adj.* rude, ill-mannered
paradox (păr′ə-dŏks′) *n.* a seemingly contradictory statement that may nevertheless be true
monumental (mŏn′yə-mĕn′tl) *adj.* great and lasting

Connect to the Literature

1. **What Do You Think?**
   If you were Baldwin's nephew, how would you feel about receiving this letter?

   Comprehension Check
   • According to Baldwin, what defeated James's grandfather?
   • What does Baldwin say *integration* means?

Think Critically

2. What do you think Baldwin hoped his nephew would gain from the advice in the letter?

3. Do you believe that Baldwin was bitter, as he says his countrymen would claim?

4. **ACTIVE READING** | **ANALYZING CHARACTERISTICS OF CLEARLY WRITTEN TEXTS** Explain what you think Baldwin meant by "It is the innocence which constitutes the crime." Refer to the interpretation you wrote in your **READER'S NOTEBOOK.** Discuss your interpretations of other thought-provoking statements.

5. What ideas about cultural identity do you get from Baldwin's letter?

   THINK ABOUT
   • what he claims can destroy his nephew
   • what he attributes his family's survival to
   • what he says is the root of his dispute with his country
   • what he says white Americans fear and why he thinks they have those fears
   • what he says *integration* means
   • how he describes young James's ancestors

Extend Interpretations

6. **Critic's Corner** In *Soul on Ice* (1968), the African-American activist Eldridge Cleaver wrote, "There is in James Baldwin's work the most grueling, agonizing, total hatred of the blacks, particularly of himself, and the most shameful, fanatical, fawning, sycophantic love of the whites that one can find in the writing of any black American writer of note in our time." Support or refute this opinion with evidence from the essay.

7. **Connect to Life** How do you think Baldwin would view racial attitudes in American society today?

8. **Points of Comparison** Compare and contrast Baldwin's views about race relations with the views expressed by any of the Harlem Renaissance writers you have read.

Literary Analysis

OPEN LETTER "My Dungeon Shook" is an **open letter,** addressed to a specific person but published for a wider readership. What in the letter suggests that Baldwin intended it not only for James but for the general public, particularly white Americans? How do you think he wanted them to respond?

Cooperative Learning Activity
With a small group of classmates, brainstorm responses that young James might have to his uncle's advice and ideas and the responses that a white American might have. Then draft two letters of response—one in James's voice and the other in the voice of a white American. Share your letters with other groups.

REVIEW **ANALOGY** Baldwin draws an analogy between his nephew's probable reaction to seeing the stars shining while the sun is out and whites' reaction to blacks moving out of their fixed places. How does this analogy help you understand Baldwin's ideas about racism better? With a classmate, write your own analogy to illustrate your ideas about a social or political issue that is important to you.

Writing Options

1. Points of Comparison

Imagine that you are the host of a radio show featuring a panel discussion with Zora Neale Hurston and James Baldwin. With two other students, write some questions about race relations in the United States, as well as the comments that each writer might make in response. For your prewriting notes, use some of the ideas you discussed for question 8 on page 964. Re-create the panel discussion for the class.

2. Personal Response

Write a personal response to Baldwin's letter, reacting to one or more of his paradoxical or thought-provoking statements.

How can being innocent be criminal?

3. Compare-Contrast Essay

How do you think the social conditions described in Baldwin's letter compare with the conditions under which African Americans live today? Using specific examples from the news and from your own observation, draft a comparison-contrast essay to answer this question. Place this piece in your **Working Portfolio.**

Writing Handbook
See page 1281: Compare and Contrast

Activities & Explorations

1. Commencement Address

Turn some of the ideas expressed by Baldwin in this letter into a commencement address that he might deliver at a high school graduation. Present the speech to the class. ~ **SPEAKING AND LISTENING**

2. Photo Gallery of Harlem

Research photographs of Harlem in the 1960s. Choose several that you think best illustrate Baldwin's letter to his nephew, and show them to the class.
~ **VIEWING AND REPRESENTING**

3. Group Discussion

In a small-group discussion, talk about a time when others' beliefs about you—either positive or negative—influenced your behavior or self-perception. Would you say that Baldwin's warning not to listen to negative messages from society applies more to young African-American men than to others? If you have a computer, extend the discussion through electronic mail, asking for opinions from friends or groups you belong to. ~ **SPEAKING AND LISTENING**

Art Connection

An interesting aspect of John Wilson's painting *My Brother* (page 962) is that the face is painted in detail, whereas the background is barely sketched in. What do you think the artist achieves by this contrast? What is your impression of his brother?

Detail of *My Brother* (1942), John Wilson

Inquiry & Research

Music Spirituals, such as the one Baldwin quotes at the end of his letter, express the pain caused by the oppression of slavery, as well as a hope for freedom. Find a recording of "My Dungeon Shook," the spiritual quoted by Baldwin, and play it for the class; or perform the song yourself, alone or with a group. Why do you think Baldwin alluded to the song in his title?

Vocabulary in Action

ACTIVITY: CONTEXT CLUES Write the vocabulary word that best completes each sentence.

1. Abraham Lincoln has been praised by some and condemned by others, but virtually no one has accused him of _____

2. The Emancipation Proclamation he issued in 1863 had a _____ effect on the North's ability to win the Civil War.

3. Many Northerners thought that the nation should _____ to become a true "land of the free."

4. The South, fearing the _____ of its way of life, had seceded from the Union rather than risk losing the power to decide about slavery.

5. Lincoln thought slavery was wrong, but it was his _____ on the war—not on slavery—that caused him to issue the Emancipation Proclamation.

6. He knew that the border states, which were not fighting against the Union, could change their attitude toward the North to a _____ one if he declared that all slaves were free.

7. This concern resulted in the _____ that slaves were freed by the Union only in the areas outside any Union control.

8. To achieve freedom, then, a slave who reached Union lines would have to declare _____ he or she had come.

9. Lincoln's belief was that freeing Southern slaves and allowing them to enlist with Union forces could _____ a significant advantage for the North.

10. Does it show an _____ disrespect for Lincoln to suggest that his proclamation was too limited?

WORDS TO KNOW	aspire	constitute	devastation	impertinent	mediocrity
	monumental	paradox	perspective	truculent	whence

Building Vocabulary
For an in-depth study of context clues, see page 326.

James Baldwin
1924–1987

Other Works
Nobody Knows My Name
The Price of the Ticket
The Amen Corner
"Sonny's Blues"

Inspired Youth Born and raised in Harlem, James Baldwin had to endure not only terrible poverty but harsh treatment by his stepfather and the burden of taking care of eight younger siblings while his mother worked. Baldwin realized later that "my teachers somehow made me believe that I could learn. And when I could scarcely see for myself any future at all, my teachers told me that the future was mine... everything was up to me."

Preacher Turned Writer When he was 14, Baldwin became a successful preacher, but he had quit preaching by the time he graduated from high school. Determined to become a writer, he moved to Greenwich Village in 1944.

Settles in Paris In 1948, tormented by the racial discrimination he saw around him, Baldwin moved to Paris, where he remained for most of his life.

Critic of Society Although Baldwin's fiction, especially the novel *Go Tell It on the Mountain*, was well received, it was his eloquent nonfiction— such as *Notes of a Native Son* and *The Fire Next Time*—that made him famous. In many of his essays, he took the role of "disturber of the peace," urging whites to face their racism and the damage it did. Baldwin never stopped challenging the country he loved to live up to its democratic ideals.

Life for My Child Is Simple ❦ Primer for Blacks

Poetry by GWENDOLYN BROOKS

Comparing Literature

Traditions Across Time: Reaffirming Cultural Identity

As a child, Gwendolyn Brooks met James Weldon Johnson and Langston Hughes, two of the distinguished poets of the Harlem Renaissance. Throughout her long career, Brooks's poetry has reflected the influence of this movement, particularly its affirmation of African-American cultural identity. The two poems you are about to read—"Life for My Child Is Simple" and "Primer for Blacks"—explore the importance of self-esteem and racial pride, respectively.

Points of Comparison Consider how Brooks's ideas about African-American cultural identity compare with those of the other writers in this part of Unit Six.

Build Background

Thematic Shift At the start of her career, Gwendolyn Brooks often wrote about the effects of racism and poverty on individuals' self-esteem. "Life for My Child Is Simple," from her Pulitzer Prize-winning collection *Annie Allen,* is one of a series of poems that trace the life of a fictitious African-American woman from infancy through motherhood and maturity. Although the speaker is Annie Allen, Brooks drew on her own experiences of raising her son, Henry, in writing this poem.

From 1967 on, Brooks became increasingly committed to political and social issues. Shifting her focus from the individual to African Americans in general, Brooks began to address, in poems such as "Primer for Blacks" and "To Those of My Sisters Who Kept Their Naturals," the lack of black unity and self-esteem that she perceived.

Focus Your Reading

LITERARY ANALYSIS STYLE **Style** is the distinctive way in which a work of literature is written. Style refers not so much to what is said but how it is said. Two elements contributing to style are **diction** (word choice) and **tone** (writer's attitude). Consider ways in which these poems differ in style.

ACTIVE READING COMPARING AND CONTRASTING POEMS
Brooks wrote "Life for My Child Is Simple" early in her career and "Primer for Blacks" many years later. To determine the similarities and differences in the poems, try these tips:

- Ask yourself what is the focus or subject of each poem.
- List each speaker's main qualities.
- Describe each speaker's tone.
- Consider the diction in each poem. Are the words simple or difficult, common or unusual, concrete or abstract?
- Identify the theme of each poem—the approach to life it suggests.

READER'S NOTEBOOK On a compare/contrast matrix like the one shown, chart the attributes of these two poems.

	"Life for My Child Is Simple"	"Primer for Blacks"
Subject		
Speaker		
Tone		
Diction		
Theme		

Life for My Child Is Simple

GWENDOLYN BROOKS

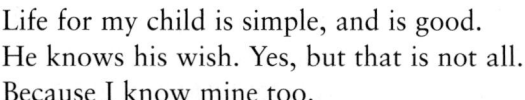

Life for my child is simple, and is good.
He knows his wish. Yes, but that is not all.
Because I know mine too.
And we both want joy of undeep and unabiding[1] things,
5   Like kicking over a chair or throwing blocks out of a window
Or tipping over an ice box pan
Or snatching down curtains or fingering an electric outlet
Or a journey or a friend or an illegal kiss.
No. There is more to it than that.
10   It is that he has never been afraid.
Rather, he reaches out and lo the chair falls with a beautiful crash,
And the blocks fall, down on the people's heads,
And the water comes slooshing sloppily out across the floor.
And so forth.
15   Not that success, for him, is sure, infallible.[2]
But never has he been afraid to reach.
His lesions are legion.[3]
But reaching is his rule.

---

1. **unabiding:** not lasting; continually changing.
2. **infallible** (ĭn-făl′ə-bəl): foolproof.
3. **His lesions are legion:** His injuries are many.

Thinking Through the Literature

1. **Comprehension Check** Name one quality that the speaker admires about her son.
2. Why do you think the speaker's son is not "afraid to reach"?
3. What do you think "reaching" means to the speaker of this poem?
4. How would you describe the speaker's feelings for her child? Cite lines to support your answer.

Primer
for
Blacks

GWENDOLYN BROOKS

Blackness
is a title,
is a preoccupation,
is a commitment Blacks
5   are to comprehend---
and in which you are
to perceive your Glory.

The conscious shout
of all that is white is
10 "It's Great to be white."
The conscious shout
of the slack in Black is
"It's Great to be white."
Thus all that is white
15 has white strength and yours.

The word Black
has geographic power,
pulls everybody in:
Blacks here--
20 Blacks there---
Blacks wherever they may be.
And remember, you Blacks, what they told you---
remember your Education:
"one Drop---one Drop
25 maketh a brand new Black."

3 preoccupation: something that takes one's full attention.

12 slack: lack of force.

24 one Drop: Historically in the United States, a person has been considered black if he or she has only "one drop" of African blood.

Oh mighty Drop.
And because they have given us kindly
so many more of our people
Blackness
30 stretches over the land.
Blackness—
the Black of it,
the rust-red of it,
the milk and cream of it,
35 the tan and yellow-tan of it,
the deep-brown middle-brown high-brown of it,
the "olive" and ochre of it—
Blackness
marches on.

40 The huge, the pungent object of our prime out-ride
is to Comprehend,
to salute and to Love the fact that we are Black,
which *is* our "ultimate Reality,"
which is the lone ground
45 from which our meaningful metamorphosis,
from which our prosperous staccato,
group or individual, can rise.

Self-shriveled Blacks.
Begin with gaunt and marvelous concession:
50 YOU are our costume and our fundamental bone.

All of you—
you COLORED ones,
you NEGRO ones,
those of you who proudly cry
55 "I'm half INDian"—
those of you who proudly screech
"I'VE got the blood of George WASHington in MY veins"—
ALL of you—
    you proper Blacks,
60 you half-Blacks,
you wish-I-weren't Blacks,
Niggeroes and Niggerenes.

You.

37 ochre (ō'kər): brownish orange-yellow.

40 pungent (pŭn'jənt): sharp and intense, like a powerful odor; **prime out-ride:** literally "principal riding out," perhaps here meaning "main effort."

43 "ultimate Reality": Here Brooks is quoting the activist Ron Karenga.

46 staccato (stə-kä'tō): the playing of musical notes in a crisp, disconnected way.

Connect to the Literature

1. **What Do You Think?** What emotions does "Primer for Blacks" stir in you? Share your response with your classmates.

> **Comprehension Check**
> • What does the speaker say should be the main effort of black people?

Think Critically

2. Whom do you think the speaker is addressing at the end of the poem, and how do you think they are meant to feel?

3. What points about "Blackness" do you think the speaker makes in this poem?

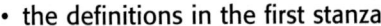

THINK ABOUT
- the definitions in the first stanza
- the comparison with whiteness in the second stanza
- what "geographic power" might mean (line 17)
- the different colors mentioned in lines 32–39
- what can rise from "the fact that we are Black" (lines 42–47)
- what the "concession" asked for in line 49 might be

4. Do you agree with the speaker's ideas about blackness?

5. **ACTIVE READING** **COMPARING AND CONTRASTING POEMS** In your opinion, do "Life for My Child Is Simple" and "Primer for Blacks" suggest similar ways or different ways of approaching life? In explaining your response, refer to the compare/contrast matrix in your **READER'S NOTEBOOK**.

Extend Interpretations

6. **Connect to Life** How important do you think it is to develop self-esteem and racial pride?

7. **Points of Comparison** Of the other writers represented in this part of Unit Six, whose ideas about African-American cultural identity are closest to Brooks's? Whose are farthest from hers? Support your views.

Literary Analysis

STYLE **Style** is the way in which a piece of literature is written. Style refers not so much to what is said but how it is said. Many elements contribute to style—for example, tone, word choice, and imagery; sound devices such as repetition, rhyme, and alliteration; as well as the use of capitalization and punctuation. One type of repetition is **anaphora** (ə-nǎf′ər-ə), or the repetition of a word or words at the beginning of successive lines, clauses, or sentences.

In "Primer for Blacks," for example, notice the use of anaphora in lines 2–4: "is a title / is a preoccupation / is a commitment…" This repetition creates a cadence in which the definitions of "Blackness" build in importance—from a mere designation ("a title") to an abiding concern ("a preoccupation") to total devotion ("a commitment").

Cooperative Learning Activity On the basis of these two poems, in what ways would you say Brooks's style changed in the 30 years between "Life for My Child Is Simple" and "Primer for Blacks"? In what ways did it remain the same? In a small group, discuss these questions. Consider the forms of the poems; the use of sound devices such as repetition, rhyme, and alliteration; and the use of capitalization and punctuation. Record your findings on a chart, and share it with other groups.

Writing Options

1. Points of Comparison

Write a proposal for a research paper based on the ideas you discussed for question 7 on page 971. Place this piece in your **Working Portfolio.**

Writing Handbook
See page 1287: Research Report Writing

2. Yearbook Biography

What do you think the young boy described in "Life for My Child Is Simple" will be like as he grows older? Write a list of accomplishments to accompany his high school yearbook picture.

3. Summary of Brooks's Message

Brooks calls "Primer for Blacks" a "preachment"—a statement intended to teach and to inspire to action. Write an abstract of the poem, summarizing the main points of the lesson that Brooks teaches.

Activities & Explorations

1. T-shirt Emblem

Design a T-shirt to illustrate the theme of "Life for My Child Is Simple" or "Primer for Blacks." If possible, actually make the T-shirt and wear it to class. ~ **ART**

2. Preach a Sermon

Prepare a sermon based on "Primer for Blacks," and deliver it to the class. Try to reflect the speaker's tone in your delivery and to make each member of your audience feel as if you were speaking directly to him or her. ~ **SPEAKING AND LISTENING**

Gwendolyn Brooks
1917–2000

Other Works
Maud Martha
The Bean Eaters
To Disembark
The Near-Johannesburg Boy and Other Poems

Childhood Influences Gwendolyn Brooks was born in Topeka, Kansas, but was taken as an infant to Chicago, which became her permanent home and a frequent setting for her poems. In her family's creative household, her early interest in writing poetry was nurtured by her mother, who told her that she would be the "lady Paul Laurence Dunbar" and took her to meet the Harlem Renaissance writers James Weldon Johnson and Langston Hughes. Her first published poem appeared in a children's magazine when she was 13.

Early Works After graduating from junior college, Brooks continued to write. In the early 1940s, she attended a poetry workshop taught by Inez Cunningham Stark, a socialite who was a reader for *Poetry* magazine, where Brooks was introduced to the work of such modernist poets as T. S. Eliot. She published her first poetry collection, *A Street in Bronzeville,* in 1945, and with her second book, *Annie Allen,* she became the first African-American author to win a Pulitzer Prize.

Watershed Event A pivotal point in Brooks's career came in 1967, when she attended the Second Black Writers' Conference at Fisk University. After meeting younger, more militant African-American poets there, Brooks began responding in her poems to the social upheavals of the time, dealing with such subjects as Malcolm X, urban riots, and street-gang warfare. She has said, "Until 1967 my own blackness did not confront me with a shrill spelling of itself."

Honored Poet Among the honors Brooks has received are appointments as poet laureate of Illinois in 1968 and as poetry consultant to the Library of Congress in 1985. She has also received more than 50 honorary doctorates and in 1980 read her poetry at the White House.

Author Activity

Read additional poems by Brooks—such as "Kitchenette Building," "One wants a Teller in a time like this," and "Horses Graze"—and analyze the style of each one.

Thoughts on the African-American Novel

Literary Criticism by TONI MORRISON

Comparing Literature

Traditions Across Time: Reaffirming Cultural Identity

During the Harlem Renaissance, writers, artists, and musicians depicted the realities of African-American life. Toni Morrison, a Nobel Prize winner, carries on this work in the late 20th century. In "Thoughts on the African-American Novel," she presents her views about African-American literature.

Points of Comparison As you read, think about Morrison's views and consider how to apply them to other works in this part of Unit 6.

Build Background

Community and Language

Toni Morrison grew up in an African-American community during the Depression. That community and its language—vivid, rhythmic, and magical—helped shape her writing: "I'm completely informed by that community, by my extended family, the language particularly. Not just the survival, but the way they spoke… this incredible merging of new language and Biblical language and sermonic language and street language and standard that created a third thing for me." In the selection you are about to read, Morrison describes the importance of oral language to the African-American novel.

Focus Your Reading

LITERARY ANALYSIS LITERARY CRITICISM **Literary criticism** refers to a piece of writing—usually an essay—that focuses on a literary work or genre, describing some aspect of it, such as its origin, its characteristics, or its appeal. Consider what makes "Thoughts on the African-American Novel" a work of literary criticism.

ACTIVE READING IDENTIFYING MAJOR IDEAS In this piece, Toni Morrison discusses novels in general and the African-American novel in particular, describing its characteristics. Use these tips to identify the **major ideas,** or the ones that she considers important.

- First read the entire piece to get an overview of Morrison's ideas.
- Then reread each paragraph, and separate the major idea from the supporting details. The major idea is what the whole paragraph is about. The **supporting details** are the words, phrases, and sentences that tell something about the major idea.
- Remember that writers sometimes state the major idea as a topic sentence: other times, the major idea is implied, or suggested, by the details in the paragraph.

READER'S NOTEBOOK As you read "Thoughts on the African-American Novel," use a chart like the one shown to list the major idea of each paragraph.

Paragraph	Major Idea
1	
2	
3	

Thoughts on the African-American Novel

Toni Morrison

The label "novel" is useful in technical terms because I write prose that is longer than a short story. My sense of the novel is that it has always functioned for the class or the group that wrote it. The history of the novel as a form began when there was a new class, a middle class, to read it; it was an art form that they needed. The lower classes didn't need novels at that time because they had an art form already: they had songs, and dances, and ceremony, and gossip, and celebrations. The aristocracy didn't need it because they had the art that they had patronized,[1] they had their own pictures painted, their own houses built, and they made sure their art separated them from the rest of the world. But when the industrial revolution began, there emerged a new class of people who were neither peasants nor aristocrats. In large measure they had no art form to tell them how to behave in this new situation. So they produced an art form: we call it the novel of manners, an art form designed to tell people something they didn't know. That is, how to behave in this new world, how to distinguish between the good guys and the bad guys. How to get married. What a good living was. What would happen if you strayed from the fold. So that early works such as *Pamela,* by Samuel Richardson, and the Jane Austen material provided social rules and explained behavior, identified outlaws, identified the people, habits, and customs that one should approve of. They were didactic[2] in that sense. That, I think, is probably why the novel was not missed among the so-called peasant cultures. They didn't need it, because they were clear about what their responsibilities were and who and where was evil, and where was good.

But when the peasant class, or lower class, or what have you, confronts the middle class, the city, or the upper classes, they are thrown a little bit into disarray.[3] For a long time, the art form

that was healing for Black people was music. That music is no longer *exclusively* ours, we don't have exclusive rights to it. Other people sing it and play it; it is the mode of contemporary music everywhere. So another form has to take that place, and it seems to me that the novel is needed by African-Americans now in a way that it was not needed before—and it is following along the lines of the function of novels everywhere. We don't live in places where we can hear those stories anymore; parents don't sit around and tell their children those classical, mythological archetypal[4] stories that we heard years ago. But new information has got to get out, and there are several ways to do it. One is in the novel. I regard it as a way to accomplish certain very strong functions—one being the one I just described.

It should be beautiful, and powerful, but it should also *work*. It should have something in it that enlightens; something in it that opens the door and points the way. Something in it that suggests what the conflicts are, what the problems are. But it need not solve those problems because it is not a case study, it is not a recipe. There are things that I try to incorporate into my fiction that are directly and deliberately related to what I regard as the major characteristics of Black art, wherever it is. One of which is the ability to be both print and oral literature: to combine those two aspects so that the stories can be read in silence, of course, but one should be able to hear them as well. It should try deliberately to make you stand up and make you feel something profoundly in the same way that a

---

1. **patronized** (pāʹtrə-nīzdʹ): sponsored and supported.
2. **didactic** (dī-dăkʹtĭk): intended to instruct.
3. **disarray** (dĭsʹə-rāʹ): disorder; confusion.
4. **archetypal** (ärʹkĭ-tīʹpəl): serving as a pattern for later examples.

Black preacher requires his congregation to speak, to join him in the sermon, to behave in a certain way, to stand up and to weep and to cry and to accede[5] or to change and to modify—to expand on the sermon that is being delivered. In the same way that a musician's music is enhanced when there is a response from the audience. Now in a book, which closes, after all—it's of some importance to me to try to make that connection—to try to make that happen also. And, having at my disposal only the letters of the alphabet and some punctuation, I have to provide the places and spaces so that the reader can participate. Because it is the affective[6] and participatory relationship between the artist or the speaker and the audience that is of primary importance, as it is in these other art forms that I have described.

To make the story appear oral, meandering, effortless, spoken—to have the reader *feel* the narrator without *identifying* that narrator, or hearing him or her knock about, and to have the reader work *with* the author in the construction of the book—is what's important. What is left out is as important as what is there. To describe sexual scenes in such a way that they are not clinical, not even explicit[7]—so that the reader brings his own sexuality to the scene and thereby participates in it in a very personal way. And owns it. To construct the dialogue so that it is heard. So that there are no adverbs attached to them: "loudly," "softly," "he said menacingly." The menace should be in the sentence. To use, even formally, a chorus. The real presence of a chorus. Meaning the community or the reader at large, commenting on the action as it goes ahead.

In the books that I have written, the chorus has changed but there has always been a choral note, whether it is the "I" narrator of *Bluest Eye*, or the town functioning as a character in *Sula*, or the neighborhood and the community that responds in the two parts of town in *Solomon*. Or, as extreme as I've gotten, all of nature thinking and feeling and watching and responding to the action going on in *Tar Baby*, so that they are in the story: the trees hurt, fish are afraid, clouds report, and the bees are alarmed. Those are the ways in which I try to incorporate, into that traditional genre the novel, unorthodox novelistic characteristics—so that it is, in my view, Black, because it uses the characteristics of Black art. I am not suggesting that some of these devices have not been used before and elsewhere—only the reason why I do. I employ them as well as I can. And those are just some; I wish there were ways in which such things could be talked about in the criticism. My general disappointment in some of the criticism that my work has received has nothing to do with approval. It has something to do with the vocabulary used in order to describe these things. I don't like to find my books condemned as bad or praised as good, when that condemnation or that praise is based on criteria from other paradigms[8]. I would much prefer that they were dismissed or embraced based on the success of their accomplishment within the culture out of which I write.

I don't regard Black literature as simply books written *by* Black people, or simply as literature written *about* Black people, or simply as literature that uses a certain mode of language in which you just sort of drop g's. There is something very special and very identifiable about it and it is my struggle to *find* that elusive but identifiable style in the books. My joy is when I think that I have approached it; my misery is when I think I can't get there. ❖

---

5. **accede** (ăk-sēd′): agree.

6. **affective:** emotional.

7. **not clinical, not even explicit:** not coldly impersonal or even clearly detailed.

8. **paradigms** (păr′ə-dīmz′): theoretical frameworks.

Connect to the Literature

1. **What Do You Think?** What are your impressions of Toni Morrison from this essay? Share your comments with your classmates.

Think Critically

2. **ACTIVE READING** **IDENTIFYING MAJOR IDEAS**
Review the chart in your ▐▐ **READER'S NOTEBOOK**. Based on this chart, how would you summarize Morrison's ideas in this essay?

3. How would you describe the way Morrison views her relationship with her readers?

4. Based on this essay, how would you explain the major characteristics of African-American literature?

THINK ABOUT
- Morrison's ideas about how novels function
- her comparisons of a writer to a preacher and a musician
- the statement "what is left out is as important as what is there"
- her views about dialogue

5. To what extent do you think Morrison's comments about the African-American novel might apply to other kinds of novels as well?

6. After reading her essay, would you be interested in reading Morrison's novels? Why or why not?

Extend Interpretations

7. **Connect to Life** Morrison says that a novel should have "something in it that enlightens... that opens the door and points the way." Think about novels you have read or stories you have heard. Which one opened a door for you, and how?

8. **Points of Comparison** Based on her ideas about African-American literature, which of the selections in this part of Unit 6 do you think Morrison might praise the most? Explain your choice.

Literary Analysis

LITERARY CRITICISM **Literary criticism** is a category of writing that focuses on a literary work or a genre, describing some aspect of it, such as its origin, its characteristics, or its effects. Works of literary criticism expand knowledge or enhance appreciation. Often, they put a literary work in a historical or a literary context and describe standards against which to measure its excellence.

Cooperative Learning Activity According to Toni Morrison, an important standard for evaluating a work of African-American literature is whether or not the reader hears its language and responds to it personally. With a small group, choose two or three passages from Zora Neale Hurston's "How It Feels to Be Colored Me," on page 950, to read aloud. Then discuss whether each passage meets Morrison's standard. If so, identify the words, phrases, and sentences that pull you into it; if not, tell what you think the passage lacks. Then choose a member to give an oral interpretation of your favorite passage to the class.

Writing Options

1. Letter to Toni Morrison Write a letter to Toni Morrison responding to her ideas about African-American literature.

2. Points of Comparison

Create a dialogue in which Toni Morrison and a writer of your choice from Unit 6 share their views about African-American cultural identity.

3. Essay About Art Form In an essay modeled on Morrison's,

Adventure Movies
• must take viewers away from ordinary life

describe the function and the characteristics of a form of entertainment other than the novel—for example, adventure movies, musicals, cartoons, talk shows, interpretive dances, rock concerts, or situation comedies. Put this piece in your **Working Portfolio.**

Activities & Explorations

Illustration Design a poster to accompany Morrison's essay or an African-American novel of your choice. ~ **ART**

Inquiry & Research

Origin of the Novel Morrison traces the novel to the rise of the middle class during the Industrial Revolution. With a small group, research the origins of the novel in the 18th century. Compile a list of the early novelists, and describe the characteristics of the first novels. Present an oral report to share your findings.

More Online: Research Starter
www.mcdougallittell.com

Toni Morrison
1931–

Other Works
The Bluest Eye
Sula
Tar Baby
Jazz
Paradise

Literary Focus Drawing on her childhood in the small town of Lorain, Ohio, Toni Morrison vividly re-creates the African-American experience in her acclaimed novels. Much of her writing is set in fictional Midwestern African-American communities at various times in history. She has created several unforgettable characters—notably, African-American women who, like Pecola Breedlove in *The Bluest Eye,* suffer the effects of poverty, racism, and violence.

Novelist, Educator, Editor After receiving a bachelor's degree from Howard University and a master's degree from Cornell University, Morrison taught college English for nine years. Then she worked for 20 years at Random House in New York City, editing works by such African Americans as Muhammad Ali, Toni Cade Bambara, Angela Davis, and Andrew Young. In 1989 she was appointed to the Robert F. Goheen Chair in the Council of the Humanities at Princeton University.

Literary Acclaim Morrison has won numerous awards and honors. In 1977 she won the prestigious National Book Critics Circle Award for her third novel, *Song of Solomon,* and she was awarded the 1988 Pulitzer Prize for *Beloved.* In 1993 she became the first African American to win the Nobel Prize in literature.

Author Activity

Read one of Toni Morrison's novels, and then evaluate it according to her own standards for the African-American novel.

Comparing Literature: Assessment Practice

In writing assessments you will sometimes be asked to compare and contrast two works in terms of certain literary elements. You are now going to practice writing a comparison-contrast essay that ends with an evaluation.

PART 1   Reading the Prompt

To respond to a prompt like the one below, read it carefully more than once. Look for key words that help you identify the purpose of the essay and what you must do.

Writing Prompt

Throughout the 20th century, African-American writers have explored racial identity. In an essay, compare and contrast a work written during the Harlem Renaissance with one written later in the 20th century. Consider the theme, the tone, and the use of figurative language. In your conclusion, tell which work appeals to you more, and why.

STRATEGIES IN ACTION

❶ **Compare and contrast,** or find similarities and differences in, a Harlem Renaissance work and a later work.

❷ Focus on three **literary elements**.

❸ **Conclude** with an opinion about which work is more appealing.

PART 2   Planning a Comparison-Contrast Essay

- Choose two works to compare and contrast.

- Create a compare-and-contrast chart like the one shown.

- On this chart, jot down notes about the theme, tone, and figurative language in each work. Mark similarities and differences.

- Decide which work you prefer.

	Harlem Renaissance Selection	Later Selection
Theme		
Tone		
Figurative Language		

PART 3   Drafting Your Essay

Introduction State the purpose of your essay—to compare and contrast two works of African-American literature.

Organization Choose a logical method to present the information. For example, you might devote one paragraph to each literary element or you might cover all the elements in one work in the first part of the essay and all the elements in the other work in the second part.

Conclusion Briefly explain why you think one work is more appealing than the other. Be sure your earlier comparisons lead to this conclusion.

Revision Allow time to review your work. Make sure it is clear, well-supported, and free from mistakes.

Writing Handbook
See page 1281: Compare and Contrast

The Autobiography of Miss Jane Pittman

ERNEST J. GAINES

These thematically related readings are provided along with *The Autobiography of Miss Jane Pittman:*

A Conspiracy of Grace
ETHEL MORGAN SMITH

Keeping the Thing Going While Things Are Stirring
SOJOURNER TRUTH

"It's Such a Pleasure to Learn"
WALLACE TERRY

To be of use
MARGE PIERCY

Booker T. and W. E. B.
DUDLEY RANDALL

from **Having Our Say: The Delany Sisters' First Hundred years**
SARAH AND A. ELIZABETH DELANY WITH AMY HILL HEARTH

The First Time I Sat in a Restaurant
JO CARSON

The Great White Myth
ANNA QUINDLEN

The Old Demon
PEARL S. BUCK

Go Tell It on the Mountain

JAMES BALDWIN

These thematically related readings are provided along with *Go Tell It on the Mountain:*

Notes of a Native Son
JAMES BALDWIN

The Whipping
ROBERT HAYDEN

The Revelation
JAMES WRIGHT

Bright Thursdays
OLIVE SENIOR

The Man of Adamant
NATHANIEL HAWTHORNE

The Pot Maker
MARITA BONNER

Forgiveness in Families
ALICE MUNRO

from **A Bintel Brief**
JEWISH DAILY FORWARD

The Old Demon
PEARL S. BUCK

And Even *More* . . .

Books

Selected Poems of Claude McKay
CLAUDE MCKAY
A sampling of this Harlem Renaissance poet's works.

Harlem Renaissance: Art of Black America
EDITED BY DAVID C. DRISKELL
An overview of the artwork produced by painters and sculptors of this period.

The Portable Harlem Renaissance Reader
EDITED BY DAVID LEVERING LEWIS
Short stories, novel excerpts, essays, speeches, and other works by 45 Harlem Renaissance writers.

Other Media

Against the Odds: The Artists of the Harlem Renaissance
A documentary exploring this artistic and literary movement. PBS Video. (VIDEOCASSETTE)

Go Tell It on the Mountain
TV adaptation of Baldwin's novel, starring Paul Winfield and Alfre Woodard. Monterey Home Video. (VIDEOCASSETTE)

Gwendolyn Brooks Reading Her Poetry
Dramatic oral interpretations by this critically acclaimed poet. Caedmon. (SOUND RECORDING)

Zora Neale Hurston: Folklore, Memoirs, and Other Writings

ZORA NEALE HURSTON

This compilation of Zora Neale Hurston's nonfiction features the original version of her autobiography *Dust Tracks on a Road,* as well as *Mules and Men,* her ground-breaking collection of African-American folklore. Also included are selected articles and Hurston's book on religious practices in the Americas.

Writing Workshop

Researching the history of an era . . .

From Reading to Writing We get a mere glimpse of the richness of the cultural scene during the Harlem Renaissance in this unit. It was a time when African Americans used a variety of means to show pride in their race and in the contributions they had made to American culture. This period offers a rich variety of choices for a **research report**—an academic paper that presents and interprets information collected through reading and other research. When you write a research report, you not only deepen your knowledge but you also sharpen your research skills.

WRITING PROMPT Write a historical research report about some aspect of the Harlem Renaissance or on another topic that your teacher has approved.

Purpose: To share information and to reach a conclusion about your topic

Audience: Your classmates, teacher, or anyone else interested in your topic

---

Basics in a Box

Research Report at a Glance

THESIS

INTRODUCTION
Presents the thesis statement

BODY
Presents evidence that supports the thesis statement

CONCLUSION
Restates the thesis

WORKS CITED
Lists the sources of information

RESEARCH

RUBRIC Standards for Writing

A successful research report should

- provide a strong introduction with a clear thesis statement
- use evidence from primary and secondary sources to develop and support ideas
- credit sources of information

- follow a logical pattern of organization, using transitions between ideas
- synthesize ideas with a satisfying conclusion
- provide a correctly formatted Works Cited list at the end of the paper

Analyzing a Student Model

Izada Chan
Ms. VanVuren
English III
15 October

Zora Neale Hurston

Zora Neale Hurston was a black writer who single-mindedly and eloquently spoke for her people and the black culture of the rural South. In reading about her, it is easy to get the impression that she was simply such an indomitable spirit that nothing could silence her or put her down. Basically, that is true, but the whole picture of her life is also much more complicated than that. In fact, she herself was so complicated that one writer titled an essay about her "Zora Neale Hurston: A Woman Half in Shadow" Through an examination of Zora Neale Hurston's work, it will become evident that she was a talented and complex woman with conflicting sides to her personality.

Hurston was a popular figure on the Harlem Renaissance scene from almost the first moment she moved to Harlem in 1925. She was so colorful that "for a long time she was remembered more as a *character* of the Renaissance than as one of the most serious and gifted artists to emerge during this period" (Williams ix).

A prolific and gifted writer, she published her first story, "John Redding Goes to Sea," in 1921. By the time she died on January 28, 1960, she had written seven books—four novels, two books of folklore, and an autobiography—and over 50 shorter works including a dozen short stories, two plays, and many essays, articles, and newspaper columns. Yet, in spite of the fact that she won many prizes, including two Guggenheims and the Ainsfield-Wolf Book Award in Race Relations, and received much critical acclaim for her work, she died in poverty at the St. Lucie County Welfare Home in Fort Pierce, Florida. She was buried in an unmarked grave in the Garden of Heavenly Rest in Fort Pierce (Gates 289, 298, 311).

Hurston might well have remained unknown to most readers if it hadn't been for Alice Walker, a famous modern black writer. Walker fell in love with Hurston's work when she read *Mules and Men,* a collection of black folktales, Hurston's second book. Walker found Hurston's grave and put a marker on it in 1973. She published an article called "In Search of Zora Neale Hurston" in *Ms.* in 1975. That article led to a revival of interest in Hurston's work. According to Henry Louis Gates, "More people have read Hurston's works since 1975 than did between that date and the publication of her first novel, in 1934" (Gates 294).

RUBRIC IN ACTION

1 This writer begins with a provocative statement to capture the reader's attention.
Other Options:
· Begin with a quotation.
• Relate an anecdote.

2 Presents the thesis statement

3 This writer supports a key idea with a direct quotation.
Other Options:
· Paraphrase a quotation.
· Summarize information.

4 Credits sources using parenthetical documentation

5 This writer presents information in a chronological order.
Another Option:
· Present information in a way that highlights causes and effects.

Hurston was born in 1891 in a small town called Eatonville, about five miles from Orlando, Florida. As Hurston put it, "Eatonville, Florida, is, and was at the time of my birth, a pure Negro town—charter, mayor, council, town marshall and all. It was not the first Negro community in America, but it was the first to be incorporated, the first attempt at organized self-government on the part of Negroes in America" (Hurston 1).

Growing up in Eatonville meant that Hurston not only was sheltered from much of the rampant racial prejudice of her day but also that she got to see African Americans in control of things, making up their own minds instead of waiting for white people to tell them what to do.

❻ Uses a transitional phrase between paragraphs to connect ideas

Works Cited

Dickinson, Laurie. "Zora Neale Hurston." Voices from the Gaps: Women Writers of Color. Minneapolis: U of Minnesota. 15 June 1998. <http://www-engl.cla.umn.edu.//kd/vfg/Authors/ZoraNeale Hurston1>.

Gates, Henry Louis, Jr. Afterword. Tell My Horse: Voodoo and Life in Haiti and Jamaica. By Zora Neale Hurston. New York: Harper & Row, 1990. 289–311

"Harlem Renaissance." Grolier Multimedia Encyclopedia. 10th ed. CD-ROM. Danbury: Arolier, 1998.

McKissack, Patricia, and Fredrick McKissack. Zora Neale Hurston: Writer and Storyteller. Hillside: Enslow, 1992.

Hemenway, Robert E. Introduction. Dust Tracks on a Road: An Autobiography. By Zora Neale Hurston. Urbana: U of Illinois P, 1984. ix–xxxix.

Hurston, Zora Neale. Dust Tracks on a Road: An Autobiography. Urbana: U of Illinois P, 1984.

Pierpont, Claudia Roth. "A Society of One: Zora Neale Hurston, American Contrarian." The New Yorker 17 Feb. 1997: 80–91.

Walker, Alice. Foreword. Zora Neale Hurston: A Literary Biography. By Robert E. Hemenway. Urbana: U of Illinois P, 1977. xi–xviii.

Williams, Sherley Ann. Foreword. Their Eyes Were Watching God. By Zora Neale Hurston. Urbana: U of Illinois P, 1978. v–xv.

Works Cited
- Identifies sources of information used in researching the paper
- Alphabetizes entries by author's last name
- Lists complete publication information
- Punctuates entries correctly
- Double spaces entire list
- Follows a preferred style

Need help with Works Cited?

See pages 1290–1292 in the **Writing Handbook**.

Writing a Research Report

The important thing is not to stop questioning.
Albert Einstein

❶ Prewriting and Exploring

If you are writing your research report on the Harlem Renaissance, you might begin by looking in the library for books or articles not only on the Harlem Renaissance, but also on the 1920s, on individuals whose works appear in this unit, on famous African Americans, on black history, on American jazz, or on American literature. See the **Idea Bank** in the margin for more suggestions on finding a subject. The steps below will also help you choose your subject and define your goal.

Planning Your Research Report

▶ **1. Choose a topic.** What subjects really intrigue you? What would you like to learn about one of them? Make a list of ideas that appeal to you and then choose the topic that interests you most. You might also try making a word web like this one to generate ideas.

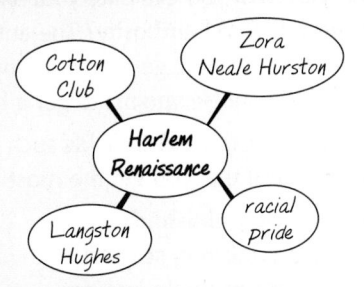

▶ **2. Narrow your topic.** Is your topic too broad for the research report you plan to write? Can it be divided into smaller parts? You could do some preliminary research in an encyclopedia, or look in the tables of contents and indexes of relevant books to see how they divide the subject into subtopics.

▶ **3. Decide on your goal.** What do you want to achieve with your report? Do you want to prove a point, draw a conclusion, or just learn and share information about the subject?

▶ **4. Consider your audience.** What do they already know about the subject? What extra background might they need?

▶ **5. Write a thesis statement.** Your thesis statement is a sentence that explains what your paper will be about. It will guide your research and help you sort out relevant and irrelevant information on your topic. Be flexible enough to consider reworking your thesis if your research leads you in new directions.

IDEA Bank

1. Your Working Portfolio
Look for ideas in the **Writing Options** you completed earlier in the unit:
- **Documentary Plan** p. 939
- **Problem-Solution Essay** p. 949
- **Points of Comparison** p. 972

2. Follow the News
Look in the newspaper and on news broadcasts for issues, people, or events that intrigue you. Choose one to research and develop.

3. Surf the Net
Check out the Internet for ideas that interest you. Try a subject search using various search engines. Choose one topic and explore it further.

Research Tip

Use primary sources when they are available and suit your purpose. Use secondary sources to explain difficult, hard-to-read, or hard-to-find material from primary sources.

❷ Researching

Begin your research by making a list of relevant, interesting, and researchable questions. Use these questions to guide your review of reliable sources. You might look in general reference books, such as encyclopedias, and then examine books, periodicals, and on-line databases for more specific information.

Source	Type of Information	Examples
Primary Sources	Direct, firsthand knowledge	letters, journals, diaries, original manuscripts
Secondary Sources	Secondhand information gathered from primary sources	encyclopedias, books, newspapers, magazines

Evaluate Your Source Material

These guidelines can help you evaluate your sources.

- **Is the author an unbiased authority?** The author's viewpoint may be influenced by his or her political position, gender, or ethnic background. Be sure to read material from a variety of viewpoints to get a balanced picture.

- **How up-to-date is the source?** In fields such as medicine or technology, rapid changes make it crucial that you get the most up-to-date information.

- **Where was the article published?** Newspapers that specialize in scandal or sensational stories, for example, are not reliable sources of information.

- **What is the intended audience?** Is the material written for a general audience? Some sources may provide oversimplified information, while other sources may be too technical.

Make Source Cards

Make source cards to keep track of the information you find. Use index cards to record publishing information for each source you decide to use. Study the cards at the right and follow the format for each type of source card. Number each source card and refer to it when you take notes. You will then use these source cards to credit sources in your

Be Wary on the Internet

Evaluate information you find on the Internet the same way you would evaluate print material. Information from a government agency (.gov) or an educational institution (.edu) usually will be reputable. Material on someone's personal Web page may or may not be reliable.

Research Tip

For each note card you write, be sure to include a reference to the source and the page number where you found the information.

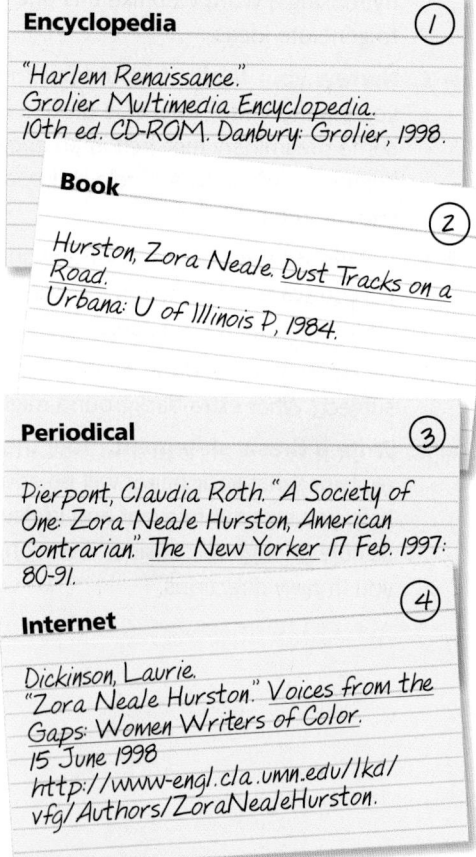

Encyclopedia ①

"Harlem Renaissance."
Grolier Multimedia Encyclopedia.
10th ed. CD-ROM. Danbury: Grolier, 1998.

Book ②

Hurston, Zora Neale. Dust Tracks on a Road.
Urbana: U of Illinois P, 1984.

Periodical ③

Pierpont, Claudia Roth. "A Society of One: Zora Neale Hurston, American Contrarian." The New Yorker 17 Feb. 1997: 80-91.

Internet ④

Dickinson, Laurie.
"Zora Neale Hurston." Voices from the Gaps: Women Writers of Color.
15 June 1998
http://www-engl.cla.umn.edu/lkd/vfg/Authors/ZoraNealeHurston.

report and to write your Works Cited list.

Read Your Sources and Take Notes

As you read, keep your thesis statement and the questions you want answered in mind. Use a separate index card for each piece of information you record. Write the number of the source on each note card. Use the following techniques.

- **Paraphrase.** Restate the material in your own words.

- **Quotation.** Copy the original text word for word, including all punctuation marks. Use quotation marks to indicate the beginning and end of the quotation. Use this form to emphasize a point or when the author's words are well phrased.

Need help documenting sources?

See the **Writing Handbook,** pp. 1290–1292

Source Number

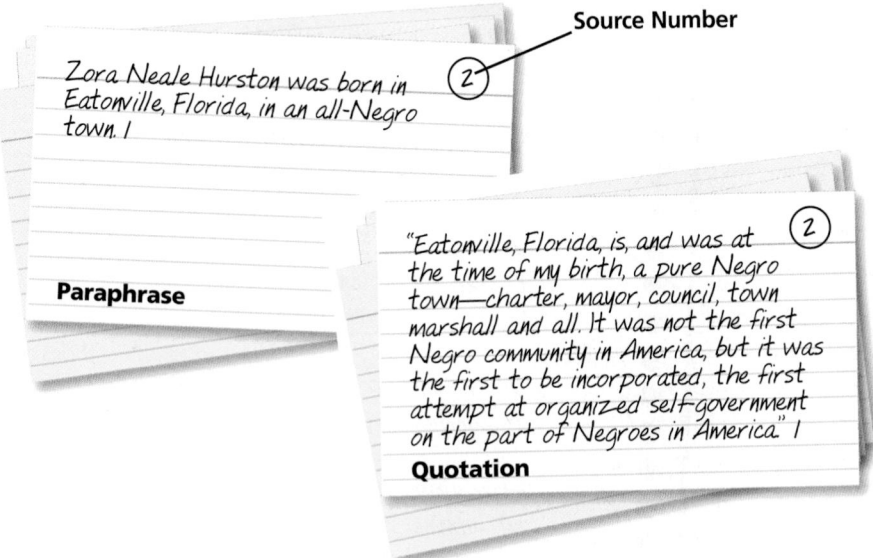

Zora Neale Hurston was born in Eatonville, Florida, in an all-Negro town. 1

Paraphrase

"Eatonville, Florida, is, and was at the time of my birth, a pure Negro town—charter, mayor, council, town marshall and all. It was not the first Negro community in America, but it was the first to be incorporated, the first attempt at organized self-government on the part of Negroes in America." 1

Quotation

More OnLine: Research Starter
www.mcdougallittell.com

Get Organized

Once you have gathered a quantity of material, begin to organize it. It is a good idea to make an outline that will provide the framework for the information you have collected.

Begin by grouping your note cards according to the main ideas on the cards. Then determine the best way to arrange those main ideas. You might want to use **chronological order, comparison-and-contrast order,** or **cause-and-effect order,** depending upon your subject. Now write your outline based on your arrangement of the main ideas and subpoints in your stacks of note cards. An example of a format you can follow is on the next page.

Using Note Cards to Create an Outline

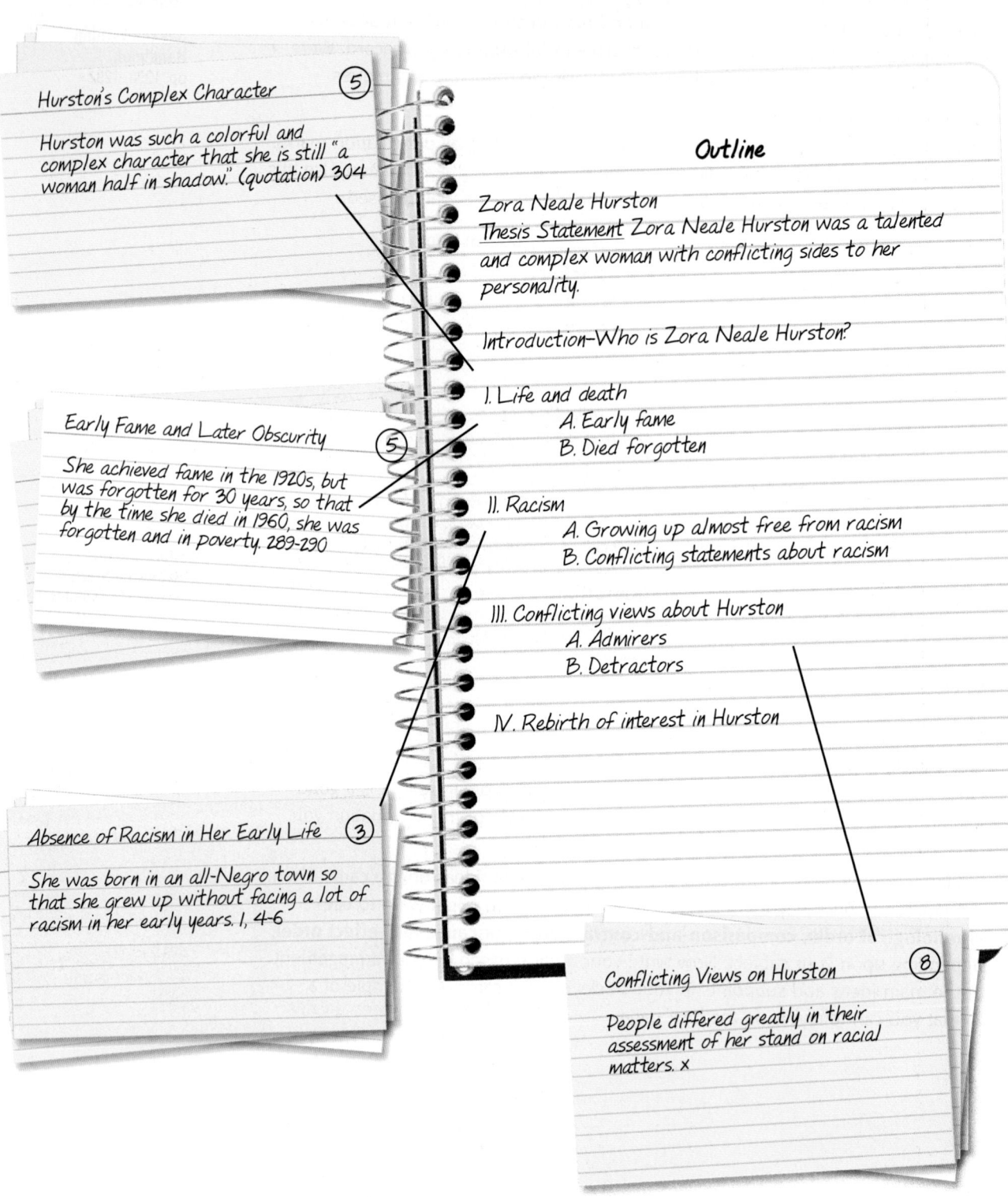

Hurston's Complex Character ⑤

Hurston was such a colorful and complex character that she is still "a woman half in shadow." (quotation) 304

Early Fame and Later Obscurity ⑤

She achieved fame in the 1920s, but was forgotten for 30 years, so that by the time she died in 1960, she was forgotten and in poverty. 289-290

Absence of Racism in Her Early Life ③

She was born in an all-Negro town so that she grew up without facing a lot of racism in her early years. 1, 4-6

Outline

Zora Neale Hurston
Thesis Statement Zora Neale Hurston was a talented and complex woman with conflicting sides to her personality.

Introduction—Who is Zora Neale Hurston?

I. Life and death
    A. Early fame
    B. Died forgotten

II. Racism
    A. Growing up almost free from racism
    B. Conflicting statements about racism

III. Conflicting views about Hurston
    A. Admirers
    B. Detractors

IV. Rebirth of interest in Hurston

Conflicting Views on Hurston ⑧

People differed greatly in their assessment of her stand on racial matters. x

❸ Drafting

Use your outline as a guide to begin writing. The first part of your report should state your main idea, or thesis. You will need to end with a conclusion that restates the thesis and summarizes your main points. The rest of your report should be organized according to your outline.

Craft Your Thesis Statement

Now that you have researched your topic and written your outline, you should have a better understanding of what your report will accomplish. Shape your thesis statement to tell what your paper will prove.

Stay Flexible As You Write Your Draft

In the drafting stage, concentrate on using clear, natural language to get your ideas on paper. Follow your outline and refer to your note cards as you write, but feel free to reorganize your material any time you collect new information or discover a different way of connecting ideas.

Add Your Own Analysis. Your report should not just be a collection of information from your sources. You must make inferences and interpret evidence to reach a conclusion. Use facts, quotations, statistics, and examples from your research to draw your own conclusions about your topic.

Give Credit Where Credit Is Due. If you do not credit the sources of information in your report, you are guilty of **plagiarism**—the unlawful use of another's words or ideas. To credit your sources, use parenthetical documentation. Within the text of the report, briefly identify the source. For example, after each quotation, paraphrase, or summary, list in parenthesis the author's name (or title, if no name is given) and the page number. Include a Works Cited list at the end of the report.

Need more help with parenthetical documentation?

See the **Writing Handbook,** pp. 1290–1292.

Take Another Look

Take a break from your writing—a few days if possible. Then review your draft. Asking the following questions can help:

- How can I make my thesis statement clearer?
- What additional information would support my thesis statement?
- What information, if any, is irrelevant?
- How can I improve my organization?
- What facts and documentation do I need to check?

Ask Your Peer Reader

- What did you like most about my report?
- What did you learn about my topic?
- Which ideas need more explanation?
- Does the order in which I've presented my ideas make sense? Would another type of organization work better?
- What impression were you left with when you read my conclusion?

❹ Revising

TARGET SKILL ▶ ELABORATING—DETAILS AND EXAMPLES Your report
will be more authorative and more interesting if you provide facts and statistics to
support your point.

> —*four novels, two books of folklore,
> and an autobiography—*
>
> By the time she died on January 28, 1960, she had written
>
> seven books, and over 50 shorter works ~~such as~~ essays, articles,
>
> and newspaper columns. *, including a dozen short
> stories, two plays, and many*

❺ Editing and Proofreading

TARGET SKILL ▶ USING COMMAS Reports include a great deal of information.
The correct use of commas can help your readers better understand the relationship
between ideas.

> Yet, in spite of the fact that she won many prizes, including
>
> two Guggenheims and the Ainsfield-Wolf book award in race
>   *c*
> relations, and received much critical aclaim for her work, she died
>
> in poverty at the St. Lucie county welfare home in Fort Pierce,
>
> Florida.

❻ Making a Works Cited List

When you have finished revising and editing your report, make a **Works Cited** list
and attach it to the end of your paper. See pages 1290–1292 in the **Writing Handbook**
for the correct format.

❼ Reflecting

FOR YOUR WORKING PORTFOLIO What new questions do you have about your
topic? Create a list of relevant questions for study. Attach your questions to your
research report and save your report in your **Working Portfolio.**

Read this paragraph from the first draft of a research report. The underlined sections may include the following kinds of errors:

- **facts that need to be elaborated**
- **comma errors**
- **incorrect possessive forms**
- **verb tense errors**

For each underlined section, choose the revision that most improves the writing.

> Industrialization in the United States changed many <u>peoples</u> lives. Skilled
> (1)
> craftspeople could no longer compete with mass production, which required that
> each worker perform <u>one, small task over, and over.</u> Factory workers often <u>work</u>
> (2)   (3)
> 10 to 15 hours a day. Industrialization also meant that the need for unskilled
> workers <u>is increasing</u> dramatically. Between 1877 and 1890, <u>6.3 million people</u>
> (4)   (5)
> <u>mostly poor and unskilled came to the United States</u> from Europe. In 1840, the
> population of the United States was 17 million. <u>By 1900, it had jumped.</u>
> (6)

1. **A.** people's
   B. peoples's
   C. people
   D. Correct as is

2. **A.** one small task over and over
   B. one, small task over and over
   C. one small task over, and over
   D. Correct as is

3. **A.** working
   B. was working
   C. worked
   D. Correct as is

4. **A.** were increasing
   B. was increasing
   C. was increasingly
   D. Correct as is

5. **A.** 6.3 million people, mostly poor and unskilled came to the United States
   B. 6.3 million people mostly poor, and unskilled came to the United States
   C. 6.3 million people, mostly poor and unskilled, came to the United States
   D. Correct as is

6. **A.** By 1900, it was higher.
   B. By 1900, it had jumped higher.
   C. By 1900, it had jumped to over 76 million.
   D. Correct as is

Need extra help?

See the **Grammar Handbook**

Possessive Nouns, p. 1306

Verb Tense, p. 1310

Punctuation Chart, p. 1327–1328

It's Too Cool—or Is It Hot?

The dynamism of the English language is both a blessing and a curse. Wonderful nonstandard words and expressions enter the language every day, while others, once popular and widely used, disappear. For example, look at the once-common expressions highlighted on the right, in the excerpt from Zora Neale Hurston's essay "How It Feels to Be Colored Me."

The phrases "howdy do" and "go a piece" are **regionalisms**—that is, phrases you would most likely hear only in a certain area of a country. Informal language, slang terms, regionalisms, and foreign terms all begin their life outside of mainstream, standard

> I usually spoke to [Northern tourists] in passing. . . . I would say something like this: "Howdy-do-well-I-thank-you-where-you-goin'?" Usually the automobile or the horse paused at this, and after a queer exchange of compliments, I would probably "go a piece of the way" with them, as we say in farthest Florida.   —Zora Neale Hurston,
> "How It Feels to Be Colored Me"

English. Over time, however, many of these words become established in the language.

Strategies for Building Vocabulary

Because English is so fertile and changeable, you are bound to encounter terms that are new to you. When you do, the strategies that follow can help you make sense of those words.

❶ **Consider the Big Picture** In her essay Hurston summarizes her life in this way: "It is a bully adventure and worth all I have paid through my ancestors for it." The slang term *bully* was very popular when Hurston wrote her essay, but it is probably not one with which you are familiar. From the context—Hurston's descriptions of her life and adventures—you might infer that *bully* means "exciting or great."

❷ **Look Up the Word** To check the accuracy of your inferences, look up the word in a dictionary. Read the different meanings of *bully* in the dictionary entry that follows, and choose the one you think Hurston intended.

> **bul•ly** (bŏŏl′ ē) *n., pl.* -lies. 1. A person who is habitually cruel to smaller or weaker people. 2. A hired ruffian. 3. *Archaic.* A fine person. 4. *Archaic.* A sweetheart. –**bully** *v.* -lied, -ly•ing, -lies. –*tr.* To intimidate with superior size or strength. –*intr.* To behave like a bully. –**bully** *adj.* Excellent; splendid. –**bully** *interj.* Used to express approval: *Bully for you!* [Possibly from Middle Dutch *boele*, sweetheart.]

In this case, *bully* is an adjective meaning "excellent" or "splendid." Note that in most large,

comprehensive dictionaries, such as *The American Heritage Dictionary* or *The Oxford English Dictionary*, regional, slang, obsolete, or archaic usages appear after the standard definitions. You might also find information about a word in dictionaries of slang or other books that discuss the etymology of nonstandard words.

As you study the denotations and etymologies of words, you might find that some words, called **portmanteaus,** are formed by blending two or more existing words. For example, in her essay "Zora Neale Hurston: A Cautionary Tale and a Partisan View," Alice Walker describes her own ancestors as "relishing the pleasure of each other's loquacious and bodacious company."

Bodacious, meaning "intrepidly bold or daring," is a combination of *bold* and *audacious.* It began life as a regionalism and was popularized through the comic strip *Snuffy Smith.* Today the word is used throughout the United States. Perhaps in the future, if it survives, dictionaries will no longer label it a regionalism.

EXERCISE Use a dictionary to look up the words and phrases below. For each one, use your own words to write about its usage, origin, and meaning.

1. funky   3. carte blanche   5. (sit) a spell
2. grungy   4. bummer

Grammar from Literature

Writers use parallel construction for a number of reasons:

- To group ideas of equal importance.
- To compare and contrast ideas.
- To create rhythm and a poetic effect.

Parallelism is the use of sentence parts that are similar in meaning and structure. One way to achieve parallelism is to use lists or series. The following example contains a series of prepositional phrases.

> **I belonged** to them, to the nearby hotels, to the country
> —everybody's Zora.
>> —Zora Neale Hurston, "How It Feels to Be Colored Me"

Writers also use parallelism when making comparisons. In the following passage about African-American writers in the 1920s, Langston Hughes uses parallel infinitive phrases.

> **They ceased** to write to amuse themselves **and began** to write to amuse and entertain white people.
>> —Langston Hughes, "When the Negro Was in Vogue"

Using Parallelism in Your Writing The use of parallelism is an effective tool for creating emphasis. In your writing, when you make a point or support an argument, look for places where parallel structures will capture your reader's attention. Use the rhythm of parallelism in both prose and poetry to add flow and grace to your writing. Look at the difference in the passages below.

> ORIGINAL
> **A number of elements contribute to the musical quality of poetry. Stressed syllables and repeated words create rhythm. Rhyming words and sound devices contribute to rhythm too.**

> REVISED USING PARALLELISM
> **The rhythm of repeated words, the rhythm of stressed syllables, the rhythm of rhyming words, the rhythm of sound devices—all these make the music in poetry.**

Usage Tip When you group sentence parts in a series, make sure the items in the series are all the same type of grammatical structure.

> INCORRECT
> **The Harlem Renaissance saw significant achievement** in literature, in fine art, **and** writing music.

In the example above, the first two items in the series are phrases composed of prepositions and objects. The last item is a gerund phrase. Changing the last item to a prepositional phrase makes the series parallel.

> CORRECT
> **The Harlem Renaissance saw significant achievement** in literature, in fine art, **and** in music.

WRITING EXERCISE Rewrite each of the items below creating a series. Be sure your structures are parallel.

1. Whites enjoyed the clubs. These were places where black owners welcomed them. Black performers entertained. Audience members might participate.
2. Gladys Bentley wowed audiences with her singing. She did a little foot stomping too. She played the piano.
3. Later, she began to sing with an accompanist. She started performing in larger clubs, and soon was enjoying her stardom.
4. The blues, one of the forms of music that originated in the Americas, and which was inspired by African-American spirituals, gave rise to jazz, rock, and soul music.
5. Langston Hughes criticizes some African Americans for trying to please whites by practicing acrobatics. He feels they wrote dishonestly and were responsible for segregating night clubs.

GRAMMAR EXERCISE Rewrite the sentences below, correcting any errors in parallelism. If a sentence contains no error, write *Correct.*

1. At rent parties Langston Hughes liked to hear people's laughter, enjoyed listening to the slow music, and relished feeling the floor shaking.
2. New York in the 1920s had many faces for African Americans: to some it held opportunities, to others it was a place of freedom, and to still more it was a place of self-fulfillment.
3. Rent parties offered lively entertainment, good food, and people who were interesting.
4. The literary devices Hughes uses in "When the Negro Was in Vogue" include satire, figurative language, and irony.
5. Many Harlem residents delighted in meeting celebrities, seeing black performers on Broadway, and they profited from the white tourists.

Alienation of the Individual

Modernism

World War I remade the map of Europe, but that was only the most visible sign of a monumental change in the lives of nations and individuals. The four-year conflict, involving a total of 32 nations, devastated Europe. It was the first large-scale modern war, utilizing the savage new weapons of modern technology—poison gas, submarines, armored tanks, airplanes, and machine guns. By the time the war ended in 1918, nearly 10 million soldiers and almost as many civilians had been killed. Even though the United States did not enter the war until 1917, Americans shared the sense that civilization, as they had known it, was being destroyed. Uncertainty about what was to result from this political breakdown became a distinguishing characteristic of the age.

Weeping Woman (1937), Pablo Picasso. Tate Gallery, London/Art Resource, New York. Copyright © 1996 Artists Rights Society, (ARS), New York/SPA-DEM, Paris.

The end of the war signaled an end of idealism and ushered in an era marked by economic growth, technological advancement, and new ways to have fun. During the Roaring Twenties, as the decade of the 1920s is called, people had more money and more things to buy. An increasing number of radios carried the new strains of jazz into American homes. The availability of cars gave people more mobility and freedom. More people went out to nightclubs and to speakeasies, where illegal alcohol was plentiful. Movies became a popular form of entertainment. At the same time, political corruption was rampant;

gangsters flourished with the profits from the sale of illegal alcohol; and Americans, in general, grew distrustful of foreigners and intolerant of political dissent.

The literary movement known as modernism was a direct response to these social and cultural changes. Disillusioned by the war and appalled by the materialism of the age, the new generation of writers searched for different literary forms to express what they understood as the modern consciousness. "Make it new!" was the rallying cry that the poet and critic Ezra Pound inspired in these writers. And they did.

Although the writers in this part of the unit have their own individual styles, they share certain characteristics that have come to be identified with modernism. First of all, they felt that individuals, especially artists, were becoming increasingly threatened by and isolated amid the mass society that was developing at the time. Characters in modernist works are almost always alienated—withdrawn, unresponsive, hurt by unnamed forces.

A second characteristic shared by these modernist writers is experimentation. Katherine Anne Porter used stream-of-consciousness as a fictional technique to dramatize the interior life of her characters, especially their meandering patterns of thinking. In order to reflect the fragmentation of their experience, fiction writers such as Ernest Hemingway and Richard Wright composed short, fragmentary stories that didn't have traditional beginnings and endings. Poets such as Ezra Pound and T. S. Eliot created verse out of the fragments of modern experience—pieces of dreams, feelings, dialogue, images, and literary allusions. The great modern artists of the 20th century—Picasso, Matisse, and Duchamp, for example—visually captured this fragmentary nature of modern experience in their cubist designs, cutouts, and collages.

Finally, modernist writers are as notable for what they leave out of their writing as for what they put in. There is no narrative voice guiding the reader with explanations or details. The reader is left alone to figure

The apparition of these faces in the
    crowd;
Petals on a wet, black bough.

Ezra Pound
"In a Station of the Metro"

Poets in our civilization, as it exists at present, must be *difficult*. . . . The poet must become more and more comprehensive, more allusive, more indirect, in order to force, to dislocate if necessary, language into its meaning.

T. S. Eliot
from "The Metaphysical Poets"

Every compulsion is put upon writers to become safe, polite, obedient, and sterile. In protest, I declined election to the National Institute of Arts and Letters some years ago, and now I must decline the Pulitzer Prize.

Sinclair Lewis
from his letter declining
the Pulitzer Prize

My candle burns at both ends;
It will not last the night;
But, ah, my foes, and, oh, my friends—
It gives a lovely light.

Edna St. Vincent Millay
"First Fig"

Edna St. Vincent Millay

Four be the things I am wiser to know:
Idleness, sorrow, a friend, and a foe.
Four be the things I'd been better
    without:
Love, curiosity, freckles, and doubt.

Dorothy Parker
from "Inventory"

Which of us has known his brother?
Which of us has looked into his father's
heart? Which of us has not remained
forever prison-pent? Which of us is not
forever a stranger and alone?

Thomas Wolfe
from *Look Homeward, Angel*

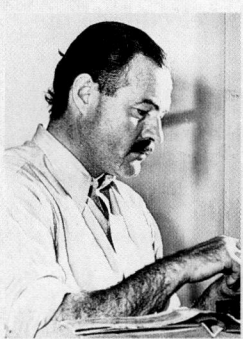

Ernest Hemingway

The further you go
in writing, the more
alone you are.
Ernest Hemingway
from an interview

You are all a lost generation.

Gertrude Stein
spoken to Ernest Hemingway

There are people who eat the earth
and eat all the people on it like in the
Bible with the locusts. And other people who stand around and watch them
eat it.

Lillian Hellman
from *The Little Foxes*

out what is going on in a story or a poem and what
a character or speaker is feeling or thinking. These
omissions place more demands on the reader to put
together the pieces of the characters' experience.

Traditions Across Time: The Lonely Self

Modernism dominated the arts and literature
throughout the 20th century. The generation
that came of age around World War II faced
alienation similar to that experienced by the
early modernists. Some of the great plays of
Tennessee Williams and Arthur Miller feature
characters—most notably, Blanche DuBois in
A Streetcar Named Desire and Willy Loman in
Death of a Salesman—who are trapped by their
own inadequacies and pushed aside by stronger,
more brutal forces in society. In the poems of
Sylvia Plath and Anne Sexton in this part of the
unit, you can see a hostile reaction to the pressures
placed on women to conform to established roles
during the 1950s and early 1960s.

A scene from the play *A Streetcar Named Desire,* starring
Marlon Brando and Jessica Tandy. Copyright © Eileen Darby.

Modernism

Robert Frost   *A*UTHOR *S*TUDY

	Acquainted with the Night	1001
	Mending Wall	1002
	"Out, Out—"	1004
	The Death of the Hired Man	1007
John F. Kennedy	**In Praise of Robert Frost**	1012
	Selected poems and a presidential commentary	
Ernest Hemingway	**The End of Something**	1018
	Breaking up is hard to do.	
T. S. Eliot	**The Love Song of J. Alfred Prufrock**	1025
	A man haunted by an "overwhelming question"	

LINK ACROSS CULTURES

Franz Kafka	*from* **The Diaries**	1033
	The shrinking world of a bachelor	
Katherine Anne Porter	**The Jilting of Granny Weatherall**	1035
	A haunting memory of rejection	
Richard Wright	**The Man Who Was Almost a Man**	1045
	All the wrong moves toward maturity	

COMPARING LITERATURE
Traditions Across Time: The Lonely Self

Sylvia Plath	**Mirror** (1963)	1057
	The reflection of a woman's fears	
Anne Sexton	**Self in 1958** (1966)	1057
	A disturbing sense of self	

Author Study
ROBERT FROST

OVERVIEW

Life and Times   996

Acquainted with the Night
~ POETRY   1000

Mending Wall ~ POETRY   1002

"Out, Out—" ~ POETRY   1004

The Death of the Hired
Man ~ POETRY   1006

In Praise of Robert
Frost by John F. Kennedy
~ SPEECH   1012

The Author's Style   1014

Author Study Project   1015

> "Because of Robert
> Frost's life and
> work, . . . our hold
> on this planet has
> increased."
>
> –John F. Kennedy

Robert Frost

1874–1963

A Simple but Resonant Voice

Robert Frost is probably the most popular American poet; certainly he is one of America's very best. But in many ways he is a poet of surprises. Poems like "The Road Not Taken" have created a popular image of Frost as a writer of simple poems about country life. However, his work is filled with deep questions about modern society and the way we live. In this Author Study, you will learn more about the life and career of this great 20th-century poet.

"I WAS LOST WHEN I WROTE THAT FIRST POEM"

As a boy, Robert Frost was devoted to playing baseball. "I was so interested in baseball," he once recalled, "that my family was afraid I'd waste my life and be a pitcher. Later, they were afraid I'd waste my life and be a poet. . . . They were right."

1874	1885		1895
Is born on March 26 in San Francisco	Moves with mother and sister to New England		Marries Elinor White

HIS LIFE
HIS TIMES

1870   **1880**   **1890**

1879	1892
Thomas Edison invents the light bulb.	Ellis Island opens as immigrant entry point.

In popular imagination, Robert Frost is nearly always associated with rural New England. However, he was born in 1874 in San Francisco, California, and lived there for 11 years. It was not until after his father's death that Frost, his mother, and his sister moved east—eventually settling in Salem, New Hampshire.

At age 14, Frost began attending high school in the industrial community of Lawrence, Massachusetts, where his grandparents lived. In 1890, he wrote the ballad "La Noche Trist" ("The Sad Night"). To his delight, this first poem was published by the *Bulletin*, the school newspaper. The following year, Frost became editor himself and continued playing baseball and other sports. In his heart, Frost already knew his future. He would be a poet. As he would reveal years later, "I was lost when I wrote that first poem in ballad form."

LIFE ON DERRY FARM Frost's early manhood was filled with changes in direction. He enrolled at both Dartmouth College and Harvard University, but did not take a degree. For several years he drifted from occupation to occupation, working as a mill hand, a school teacher, and a reporter. In 1894 he sold a poem, "My Butterfly: An Elegy," to *The Independent*, a New York magazine. After this, he was able to sell a poem occasionally, mostly to local newspapers. During these

LITERARY Contributions

After a shaky start, Robert Frost became one of America's best-known poets. However, he was not simply a grand-fatherly-looking poet of the people. In many ways he rebelled against his age and forged a new kind of distinctly American poetry.

His Own Modernism Some of Frost's contemporaries, such as T. S. Eliot and Ezra Pound, wrote dense, difficult poems, using experimental poetic forms and often treating obscure subject matter. Frost, however, preferred to write tightly structured poems about familiar, everyday topics. Yet much of his writing is serious and probing: families argue, accidents happen, people die. Frost used older poetic forms, such as blank verse, adapting them to the rhythms of everyday speech. No other poet can make conversation sound so natural within such a strict structure. His best-known poems include

  "The Death of the Hired Man" (1914)
  "Mending Wall" (1914)
  "The Road Not Taken" (1914)
  "Stopping by Woods on a Snowy Evening" (1923)
  "'Out, Out—'" (1936)
  "The Gift Outright" (1942)

Poet of the Countryside Many of Frost's poems are set in New England and give a sharp, generally unsentimental picture of rural American life. But the truths they tell about fear, isolation, and longing extend far beyond their limited setting.

Edition of *New Hampshire*

| 1900 Moves to a farm near Derry, New Hampshire | 1912 Moves with his wife and four children to England | 1913 Publication of *A Boy's Will* | 1914 Publication of *North of Boston* | 1915 Returns to New Hampshire as a famous poet | 1924 Receives Pulitzer Prize for the collection *New Hampshire* |

1900   **1910**   **1920**

| 1898 Spanish-American War begins. | 1903 Wright brothers make their first airplane flight. | 1912 *Titanic* sinks. | 1914 World War I begins. | 1922 T. S. Eliot's *The Waste Land* is published. | 1927 Lindbergh flies across the Atlantic. |

Frost in 1913

years, one stabilizing event in his life was his marriage to Elinor White, his high school sweetheart, whom he'd convinced to marry him in 1895.

In 1900, Frost's grandfather bought a farm for Frost and Elinor near Derry, New Hampshire. In this simple setting, during what was one of the richest periods of his life, Frost spent time with his growing family, taking walks, reading aloud great works of literature, and picnicking. He enjoyed encounters with other farmers, in which he absorbed the straightforward attitudes about life that would inspire his most important works. Frost worked the farm for 12 years but was unsuccessful. He began teaching school in 1906 to help support his family. (The Frosts had six children, two of whom died in early childhood.)

In 1911, Frost figured out that 20 years of writing poems had earned him around $200. Determined to make a living from writing, he sold the farm and in 1912 moved his family to England, where it was reportedly cheaper to live. The move proved to be the turning point in his life.

RECOGNITION IN ENGLAND Less than two months after his arrival in England, Frost found a publisher for his first book of poems. *A Boy's Will* was published in 1913 and was well received. His second collection, *North of Boston* (1914), included "Mending Wall" and "After Apple-Picking," two poems that reflected his memories of farm life. The beginning of World War I forced the family to return to the United States early in 1915, but Frost came home a famous man. Thanks to the U.S. publication of his two poetry collections, Frost found himself in demand for lectures and readings. His third book, *Mountain Interval* (1916), solidified his reputation. Frost bought a new farm at Franconia, New Hampshire, and began teaching at Amherst College in Massachusetts.

In 1924 his collection *New Hampshire* won the Pulitzer Prize, the first of four that Frost would receive. His position as one of America's leading writers was unmistakable.

"ACQUAINTED WITH THE NIGHT" Despite his public success, Frost was to face a series of personal tragedies. In 1934, his youngest daughter, Marjorie, died of a fever contracted in childbirth. Four years later, his wife died

| 1931 Receives Pulitzer Prize for *Collected Poems* | Frost's home in New Hampshire | 1937 Receives Pulitzer Prize for *A Further Range* | 1938 Death of Elinor Frost | 1943 Receives Pulitzer Prize for *A Witness Tree* |

1930   **1940**

| 1929 Stock market crashes; Great Depression begins. | 1932 Franklin Delano Roosevelt is elected president. | 1939 World War II begins. | 1941 U.S. enters World War II. | 1945 World War II ends; Harry S. Truman becomes president when Roosevelt dies. |

The Best-Laid Plans

Reading his poem at John F. Kennedy's inauguration was a crowning moment of Frost's career. But things didn't go as planned. Frost had composed a new poem, "Dedication: For John F. Kennedy His Inauguration," and intended to read it aloud. But the day was extremely cold, and the sun was very bright. He began to read but could hardly see in the sun's glare; an unidentified official used his hat to try to create some shade. Frost finally gave up, saving an awkward moment by reciting "The Gift Outright," which he knew by heart. Later, Frost's friend Louis Untermeyer said of the Kennedy poem: "It was a good thing he couldn't read [it]; it was the worst thing he ever wrote."

Frost attempting to read at President Kennedy's 1961 inauguration

suddenly of a heart attack. His only son, Carol, committed suicide in 1940. Understandably, Frost's 1942 collection *A Witness Tree* has a darkness of tone that reflects his anguish.

In the years after World War II, Frost wrote fewer poems and spent more time in his public role as a renowned writer. Sharing his standards for good poetry, Frost once said,

> A poem is never a put-up job, so to speak. It begins as a lump in the throat, a sense of wrong, a homesickness, a lovesickness. It is never a thought to begin with. It is at its best when it is a tantalizing vagueness. It finds its thought and succeeds; or doesn't find it and comes to nothing.

One of Frost's final public appearances was at the inauguration of President John F. Kennedy in 1961, where he read his poem "The Gift Outright" before a national audience. It was one of the highest honors ever given to an American poet. Frost died in Boston in January 1963, at the age of 88.

 More Online: Author Link
www.mcdougallittell.com

1950	1955	1961	1962	1963
U.S. Senate passes resolution honoring Frost.	State of Vermont names a mountain after Frost.	Reads at President Kennedy's inauguration	Receives the Congressional Medal of Honor	Dies on January 29 in Boston

1950   **1960**   **1970**

1955	1957	1962	1963
Bus boycott begins in Montgomery, Alabama.	Soviet satellite *Sputnik* goes into orbit.	Cuban missile crisis increases U.S.-Soviet tensions.	John F. Kennedy is assassinated.

Selected Poems

Poetry by ROBERT FROST

(Connect to Your Life)

Alone or Together? The idea of being alone or somehow separated from others runs through many of Frost's poems. Yet often people choose to be alone. Think about times when you need companionship and times when you choose to be alone. What happens if you want other people around and no one chooses to be with you? Jot down your ideas. You may then discuss your ideas with a partner.

Build Background

Poetry of Frost Robert Frost is perhaps the most widely read American poet of the 20th century. In many ways, he is a transitional figure between the 19th and 20th centuries. Like Emerson, Thoreau, and the other transcendentalists, Frost loved nature and wrote about the lone individual making choices about how to live. Like the modernists who were his contemporaries, Frost portrayed the forces in modern society that served to isolate people. Many of his poems portray tensions in relationships as well as the advantages and disadvantages of being alone.

Focus Your Reading

LITERARY ANALYSIS **MOOD IN POETRY** **Mood** is the overall feeling or atmosphere that a writer creates for the reader. Frost uses a variety of devices to set the mood, including

- **imagery**—descriptive phrases that appeal to the senses
- **rhythm**—the pattern or flow of words and lines in a poem
- **repetition**—the repeated use of a word or phrase for emphasis

As you read each poem, decide what mood is communicated and what techniques Frost has used to get it across.

ACTIVE READING **ANALYZING WORD CHOICE** Be aware of the writer's **word choice.** Focus on the words and phrases that Frost uses to create **mood.** To increase your awareness, try these strategies:

- Read the poems aloud to help you notice mood-setting words or phrases.
- If a word catches your attention, stop and consider its meaning, your emotional response to it, and the effect it creates.

READER'S NOTEBOOK Fill in a chart like this one as you read each poem.

"Acquainted with the Night"	
Word, phrase, or line	line 1
Effect	loneliness, sadness

Acquainted with the Night

ROBERT FROST

I have been one acquainted with the night.
I have walked out in rain—and back in rain.
I have outwalked the furthest city light.

I have looked down the saddest city lane.
5 I have passed by the watchman on his beat
And dropped my eyes, unwilling to explain.

I have stood still and stopped the sound of feet
When far away an interrupted cry
Came over houses from another street,

10 But not to call me back or say good-by;
And further still at an unearthly height
One luminary[1] clock against the sky

Proclaimed the time was neither wrong nor right.
I have been one acquainted with the night.

---

1. **luminary:** giving off light.

Illustration © Litjiun Wong.

Thinking Through the Literature

1. How would you describe the **speaker** of this poem? Write down a series of adjectives.

2. Do you feel sorry for the speaker? Explain why or why not.

3. How do you think the speaker feels about being alone at night? Cite phrases or lines from the poem that suggest his feelings.

4. Describe the mood of the poem. Cite words, phrases, and images that contribute to the **mood.**

THINK ABOUT
- the expressiveness of words like *furthest, saddest,* and *unearthly*
- the effect of the very regular rhythm of the poem
- Frost's repetition of "I have . . ."

Mending Wall

ROBERT FROST

Something there is that doesn't love a wall,
That sends the frozen-ground-swell under it
And spills the upper boulders in the sun,
And makes gaps even two can pass abreast.
5 The work of hunters is another thing:
I have come after them and made repair
Where they have left not one stone on a stone,
But they would have the rabbit out of hiding,
To please the yelping dogs. The gaps I mean,
10 No one has seen them made or heard them made,
But at spring mending-time we find them there.
I let my neighbor know beyond the hill;
And on a day we meet to walk the line
And set the wall between us once again.
15 We keep the wall between us as we go.
To each the boulders that have fallen to each.
And some are loaves and some so nearly balls
We have to use a spell to make them balance:

GUIDE FOR READING

1–4 In some parts of New England, the farms are separated by low walls made of stones that are simply piled up, not mortared together. During the winter, moisture in the ground freezes and makes the earth expand, causing portions of the wall to topple.

12–14 Notice that it is the speaker who lets the neighbor know it is time to mend the wall.

"Stay where you are until our backs are turned!"
20 We wear our fingers rough with handling them.
Oh, just another kind of outdoor game,
One on a side. It comes to little more:
There where it is we do not need the wall:
He is all pine and I am apple orchard.
25 My apple trees will never get across
And eat the cones under his pines, I tell him.
He only says, "Good fences make good neighbors."
Spring is the mischief in me, and I wonder
If I could put a notion in his head:
30 "*Why* do they make good neighbors? Isn't it
Where there are cows? But here there are no cows.
Before I built a wall I'd ask to know
What I was walling in or walling out,
And to whom I was like to give offense.
35 Something there is that doesn't love a wall,
That wants it down." I could say "Elves" to him,
But it's not elves exactly, and I'd rather
He said it for himself. I see him there,
Bringing a stone grasped firmly by the top
40 In each hand, like an old-stone savage armed.
He moves in darkness as it seems to me,
Not of woods only and the shade of trees.
He will not go behind his father's saying,
And he likes having thought of it so well
45 He says again, "Good fences make good neighbors."

23–26 According to the speaker, why is there no practical need for the wall?

27 What need does the neighbor see for the wall?

36–38 Notice the speaker's playful, teasing tone here.

38–42 What is the speaker's opinion of his neighbor?

Thinking Through the Literature

1. Which man in "Mending Wall" would you prefer as a neighbor? Why?

2. How do the **speaker** of the poem and his neighbor differ?

   THINK ABOUT {
   - how each feels about the wall and the job of rebuilding it
   - the image the speaker has of his neighbor in lines 38–42

3. Explain what you think the wall represents in each of the following statements:

   THINK ABOUT {
   - "Something there is that doesn't love a wall."
   - "We keep the wall between us as we go."
   - "Before I built a wall I'd ask to know / What I was walling in or walling out."
   - "He says again, 'Good fences make good neighbors.'"

4. Does the wall separate the neighbors or bring them closer together? Explain.

"Out, Out—"

ROBERT FROST

The buzz saw snarled and rattled in the yard
And made dust and dropped stove-length sticks of wood,
Sweet-scented stuff when the breeze drew across it.
And from there those that lifted eyes could count
5 Five mountain ranges one behind the other
Under the sunset far into Vermont.
And the saw snarled and rattled, snarled and rattled,
As it ran light, or had to bear a load.
And nothing happened: day was all but done.
10 Call it a day, I wish they might have said
To please the boy by giving him the half hour
That a boy counts so much when saved from work.
His sister stood beside them in her apron
To tell them 'Supper.' At the word, the saw,
15 As if to prove saws knew what supper meant,
Leaped out at the boy's hand, or seemed to leap—
He must have given the hand. However it was,
Neither refused the meeting. But the hand!
The boy's first outcry was a rueful[1] laugh,
20 As he swung toward them holding up the hand
Half in appeal, but half as if to keep
The life from spilling. Then the boy saw all—
Since he was old enough to know, big boy
Doing a man's work, though a child at heart—
25 He saw all spoiled. 'Don't let him cut my hand off—
The doctor, when he comes. Don't let him, sister!'
So. But the hand was gone already.
The doctor put him in the dark of ether.
He lay and puffed his lips out with his breath.
30 And then—the watcher at his pulse took fright.
No one believed. They listened at his heart.
Little—less—nothing!—and that ended it.
No more to build on there. And they, since they
Were not the one dead, turned to their affairs.

---

1. **rueful** (rōō′fəl): expressing sorrow or regret.

Connect to the Literature

1. What Do You Think?
What is your reaction to the accident in "'Out, Out—'"?

Comprehension Check
- What is the setting and time of day of the poem?
- How does the accident happen?
- What is the nature of the boy's injury?

Think Critically

2. **ACTIVE READING** **ANALYZING WORD CHOICE** **READER'S NOTEBOOK** Briefly review the charts in your **READER'S NOTEBOOK** that you used to analyze **word choice** in each poem. Reread lines 19–22 of "'Out, Out—.'" What effect do they convey? What specific words and phrases help create this effect?

3. How does the **speaker** of the poem seem to feel about the boy's death?

> **THINK ABOUT**
> - the speaker's expression of personal feelings, as in lines 10–12
> - how the speaker describes the saw in lines 14–18
> - the speaker's comment in the last three lines

4. The title of this poem is an **allusion**, or indirect reference, to a famous speech in Shakespeare's *Macbeth* (Act Five, Scene 5). How do you think the following quotation from this play relates to the poem?

> *. . . Out, out, brief candle!*
> *Life's but a walking shadow, a poor player*
> *That struts and frets his hour upon the stage*
> *And then is heard no more.*

Extend Interpretations

5. Comparing Texts Reread the poems, focusing on the speakers. Then draw and fill in a Venn diagram to compare and contrast the speakers' characteristics.

6. Connect to Life In which poem is the portrayal of aloneness most closely related to an event or situation you yourself have experienced? Did reading the poem give you a new understanding of your reactions to the experience? Explain.

Literary Analysis

MOOD IN POETRY **Mood** is the overall feeling or atmosphere that a writer creates. To create mood in his poems, Frost uses **imagery,** descriptive phrases that re-create sensory experiences for the reader. Imagery usually appeals to one of the five senses. In lines 39–40 of "Mending Wall," Frost creates a visual picture that helps the reader sense that the men are involved in more than a pleasant spring ritual.

Frost also uses **rhythm,** the pattern or flow of sound created by the arrangement of stressed and unstressed syllables in a line. He sometimes breaks the rhythm to introduce tension by inserting a dash, forcing the reader to pause briefly. A good example of this is in line 2 of "Acquainted with the Night."

Repetition is the repeated use of a word or phrase for emphasis and rhythmic effect. In "Acquainted with the Night," the repetition of the phrase "I have . . ." gives the poem a mood of growing despair.

Activity Imagery, rhythm, and repetition all contribute to the mood of Frost's poems. Create a chart like this one in which you list examples of these devices from all three poems.

	"Acquainted with . . ."	"Mending Wall"	"'Out, Out—'"
Imagery			
Rhythm			
Repetition			

The Death of the Hired Man

Poetry by ROBERT FROST

Connect to Your Life

The Idea of Home How would you define the idea of home? Do you think it is an actual physical place, or does it have more to do with the people at home and their attitudes toward you? How do you think your idea of home will change when you go to college or begin living on your own? Discuss your thoughts with a partner.

Build Background

A Hired Hand You are about to read a **dramatic poem,** or a poem that tells a story. In this case, the story is about farmers who provide workers with temporary homes. In the first half of the 20th century, farming was a major source of employment in the United States. Since life on a farm is cyclical, based on the growing season, farmers needed to hire additional help at the busiest times, particularly the fall harvest. Workers generally saved their pay for the winter season, when there was no work to be done. In states where farming was an important industry (and particularly in New England and the South), a pool of itinerant labor existed. So important was the cycle of planting and harvesting—and having enough "hands" to help out—that the schedule of the school year was developed around it.

WORDS TO KNOW
Vocabulary Preview

abide	harbor
assurance	taut
beholden	

Focus Your Reading

LITERARY ANALYSIS **BLANK VERSE** "The Death of the Hired Man" is written in a verse form known as blank verse. **Blank verse** is unrhymed poetry written in iambic pentameter. *Iambic* describes a basic pattern of an unstressed syllable (˘) followed by a stressed syllable (´): *the dóve. Pentameter* means that each line contains five such pairs of syllables:

> *The dóve takes flíght with gráce that's éffortless.*

As you read, try to recognize how the blank verse imitates the natural rhythms of English speech. Note also that sometimes Frost does not exactly follow this rhythmic pattern.

ACTIVE READING **UNDERSTANDING FORM IN POETRY** **Form** is the placement of a poem's lines on the page and the grouping of those lines into **stanzas.** The blank-verse **form** of "The Death of the Hired Man" may make it difficult for you to keep track of the **dialogue.** As you read, watch for devices that Frost has used to help you, including

- **quotation marks:** Double quotation marks indicate the beginning and end of each speech. Single quotation marks indicate quotations within a speech.
- **line breaks:** Frost generally leaves a blank line when the speaker changes and never presents Mary's and Warren's speeches on the same line.
- **point of view:** The narrator always speaks in the third person ("Mary sat," "Warren returned"); in the dialogue, first and second person are used.

READER'S NOTEBOOK Using a graphic like this one, record any part of the poem that causes you to pause to identify the speaker.

Line(s) from Poem	Who I Think Is Speaking	Why I Think So

Philo Bound (about 1965), Billy Morrow Jackson. Oil on masonite. Illinois State Museum, Springfield.

The DEATH of the HIRED MAN

ROBERT FROST

Mary sat musing on the lamp-flame at the table,
Waiting for Warren. When she heard his step,
She ran on tiptoe down the darkened passage
To meet him in the doorway with the news
5   And put him on his guard. "Silas is back."
She pushed him outward with her through the door
And shut it after her. "Be kind," she said.
She took the market things from Warren's arms
And set them on the porch, then drew him down
10   To sit beside her on the wooden steps.

"When was I ever anything but kind to him?
But I'll not have the fellow back," he said.
"I told him so last haying, didn't I?
If he left then, I said, that ended it.
15   What good is he? Who else will <u>harbor</u> him
At his age for the little he can do?
What help he is there's no depending on.
Off he goes always when I need him most.
He thinks he ought to earn a little pay,
20   Enough at least to buy tobacco with,
So he won't have to beg and be <u>beholden</u>.
'All right,' I say, 'I can't afford to pay
Any fixed wages, though I wish I could.'
'Someone else can.' 'Then someone else will have to.'
25   I shouldn't mind his bettering himself
If that was what it was. You can be certain,
When he begins like that, there's someone at him

Trying to coax him off with pocket money—
In haying time, when any help is scarce.
30   In winter he comes back to us. I'm done."

"Sh! not so loud: he'll hear you," Mary said.

"I want him to: he'll have to soon or late."

"He's worn out. He's asleep beside the stove.
When I came up from Rowe's I found him here,
35   Huddled against the barn door fast asleep,
A miserable sight, and frightening, too—
You needn't smile—I didn't recognize him—
I wasn't looking for him—and he's changed.
Wait till you see."

          "Where did you say he'd been?"

40   "He didn't say. I dragged him to the house,
And gave him tea and tried to make him smoke.
I tried to make him talk about his travels.
Nothing would do: he just kept nodding off."

"What did he say? Did he say anything?"

45   "But little."

                "Anything? Mary, confess
He said he'd come to ditch the meadow for me."

"Warren!"

          "But did he? I just want to know."

"Of course he did. What would you have him say?
Surely you wouldn't grudge the poor old man
50   Some humble way to save his self-respect.
He added, if you really care to know,
He meant to clear the upper pasture, too.
That sounds like something you have heard before?
Warren, I wish you could have heard the way
55   He jumbled everything. I stopped to look
Two or three times—he made me feel so queer—
To see if he was talking in his sleep.
He ran on Harold Wilson—you remember—
The boy you had in haying four years since.
60   He's finished school, and teaching in his college.
Silas declares you'll have to get him back.
He says they two will make a team for work:

32 **soon or late:** sooner or later; eventually.

46 **ditch:** plow.

Between them they will lay this farm as smooth!
The way he mixed that in with other things.
65 He thinks young Wilson a likely lad, though daft
On education—you know how they fought
All through July under the blazing sun,
Silas up on the cart to build the load,
Harold along beside to pitch it on."

70 "Yes, I took care to keep well out of earshot."

"Well, those days trouble Silas like a dream.
You wouldn't think they would. How such things linger!
Harold's young college-boy's <u>assurance</u> piqued him.
After so many years he still keeps finding
75 Good arguments he sees he might have used.
I sympathize. I know just how it feels
To think of the right thing to say too late.
Harold's associated in his mind with Latin.
He asked me what I thought of Harold's saying
80 He studied Latin, like the violin,
Because he liked it—that an argument!
He said he couldn't make the boy believe
He could find water with a hazel prong—
Which showed how much good school had ever done him
85 He wanted to go over that. But most of all
He thinks if he could have another chance
To teach him how to build a load of hay—"

"I know, that's Silas' one accomplishment.
He bundles every forkful in its place.
90 And tags and numbers it for future reference,
So he can find and easily dislodge it
In the unloading. Silas does that well.
He takes it out in bunches like big birds' nests.
You never see him standing on the hay
95 He's trying to lift, straining to lift himself."
"He thinks if he could teach him that, he'd be
Some good perhaps to someone in the world.
He hates to see a boy the fool of books.
Poor Silas, so concerned for other folk,
100 And nothing to look backward to with pride,
And nothing to look forward to with hope,
So now and never any different."

WORDS TO KNOW   **assurance** (ə-shŏŏr′əns) *n.* self-confidence

Part of a moon was falling down the west,
Dragging the whole sky with it to the hills.
105 Its light poured softly in her lap. She saw it
And spread her apron to it. She put out her hand
Among the harplike morning-glory strings,
Taut with the dew from garden bed to eaves,
As if she played unheard some tenderness
110 That wrought on him beside her in the night.

110 **wrought** (rôt) **on:** worked on.

"Warren," she said, "he has come home to die:
You needn't be afraid he'll leave you this time."

"Home," he mocked gently.

                              "Yes, what else but home?
It all depends on what you mean by home.
115 Of course he's nothing to us, any more
Than was the hound that came a stranger to us
Out of the woods, worn out upon the trail."

"Home is the place where, when you have to go there,
They have to take you in."

                              "I should have called it
120 Something you somehow haven't to deserve."

Warren leaned out and took a step or two,
Picked up a little stick, and brought it back
And broke it in his hand and tossed it by.
"Silas has better claim on us you think
125 Than on his brother? Thirteen little miles
As the road winds would bring him to his door.
Silas has walked that far no doubt today.
Why doesn't he go there? His brother's rich,
A somebody—director in the bank."

130 "He never told us that."

                              "We know it, though."

"I think his brother ought to help, of course.
I'll see to that if there is need. He ought of right
To take him in, and might be willing to—
He may be better than appearances.

121–123 What words would you use to describe Warren's reaction?

134 **better than appearances:** better than he looks.

135　But have some pity on Silas. Do you think
　　If he had any pride in claiming kin
　　Or anything he looked for from his brother,
　　He'd keep so still about him all this time?"

　　"I wonder what's between them."

　　　　　　　　　　　　　　　　"I can tell you.
140　Silas is what he is—we wouldn't mind him—
　　But just the kind that kinsfolk can't <u>abide</u>.
　　He never did a thing so very bad.
　　He don't know why he isn't quite as good
　　As anybody. Worthless though he is,
145　He won't be made ashamed to please his brother."

　　"I can't think Si ever hurt anyone."

　　"No, but he hurt my heart the way he lay
　　And rolled his old head on the sharp-edged chair-back.
　　He wouldn't let me put him on the lounge.　　　　　　**149 lounge:** couch
150　You must go in and see what you can do.
　　I made the bed up for him there tonight.
　　You'll be surprised at him—how much he's broken.
　　His working days are done; I'm sure of it."

　　"I'd not be in a hurry to say that."

155　"I haven't been. Go, look, see for yourself.
　　But, Warren, please remember how it is:
　　He's come to help you ditch the meadow.
　　He has a plan. You mustn't laugh at him.
　　He may not speak of it, and then he may.
160　I'll sit and see if that small sailing cloud
　　Will hit or miss the moon."

　　　　　　　　　　　　　　It hit the moon.
　　Then there were three there, making a dim row,
　　The moon, the little silver cloud, and she.

　　Warren returned—too soon, it seemed to her—
165　Slipped to her side, caught up her hand and waited.

　　"Warren?" she questioned.
　　　　　　　　　　　　　"Dead," was all he answered.

WORDS
TO　　　**abide** ((e-bīd´) *v.* to put up with
KNOW

1011

In Praise of
Robert Frost

Speech by JOHN F. KENNEDY

Preparing to Read

Build Background

Frost and Kennedy In January 1961, President-elect John F. Kennedy asked Robert Frost to read a poem at his inauguration. It was the first time such an invitation had ever been extended. Kennedy was a great admirer of Frost's poetry, and the two became friends. Frost died in January of 1963, and on October 27 of that year, Kennedy spoke at Amherst College at a ceremony honoring the poet and his literary achievement.

This day, devoted to the memory of Robert Frost, offers an opportunity for reflection which is prized by politicians as well as by others and even by poets. For Robert Frost was one of the granite figures of our time in America. He was supremely two things—an artist and an American.

A nation reveals itself not only by the men it produces but also by the men it honors, the men it remembers.

In America our heroes have customarily run to men of large accomplishments. But today this college and country honor a man whose contribution was not to our size but to our spirit; not to our political beliefs but to our insight; not to our self-esteem, but to our self-comprehension.

In honoring Robert Frost we therefore can pay honor to the deepest sources of our national strength. That strength takes many forms and the most obvious forms are not always the most significant.

The men who create power make an indispensable contribution to the nation's greatness. But the men who question power make a contribution just as indispensable, especially when that questioning is disinterested.

For they determine whether we use power or power uses us. Our national strength matters; but the spirit which informs and controls our strength matters just as much. This was the special significance of Robert Frost. . . .

"I have been," he wrote, "one acquainted with the night."

And because he knew the midnight as well as the high noon, because he understood the ordeal as well as the triumph of the human spirit, he gave his age strength with which to overcome despair. . . .

For art establishes the basic human truths which must serve as the touchstones of our judgment. The artist, however faithful to his personal vision of reality, becomes the last champion of the individual mind and sensibility against an intrusive society and an officious state.

The great artist is thus a solitary figure. He has, as Frost said, "a lover's quarrel with the world." In pursuing his perceptions of reality he must often sail against the currents of his time. This is not a popular role. . . .

In serving his vision of the truth the artist best serves his nation. And the nation which disdains the mission of art invites the fate of Robert Frost's hired man—the fate of having "nothing to look backward to with pride and nothing to look forward to with hope."

I look forward to a great future for America—a future in which our country will match its military strength with our moral restraint, its wealth with our wisdom, its power with our purpose. . . .

And I look forward to a world which will be safe not only for democracy and diversity but also for personal distinction.

Robert Frost was often skeptical about projects for human improvement. Yet I do not think he would disdain this hope.

Connect to the Literature

1. **What Do You Think?** What reactions do you have to the poem's ending?

> **Comprehension Check**
> - Why is Warren angry at Silas?
> - What does Harold Wilson represent to Silas?
> - What changes Warren's mind about Silas's return?

Think Critically

2. **ACTIVE READING** **UNDERSTANDING FORM IN POETRY**

   In your **READER'S NOTEBOOK**, check any notes you made at points in the poem where you had to stop and think about who was speaking. What helped you figure out who the speaker was?

3. Whose position about Silas do you agree with, Mary's or Warren's? Why?

4. In lines 139–145, Mary explains Silas's relationship with his rich brother. What do you think she means by the last line?

5. Compare Warren's definition of home (lines 118–119) with Mary's (lines 119–120). How do you think each definition fits its speaker's personality?

Extend Interpretations

6. **What If?** Suppose Silas had not died at the end of the poem. Do you think Mary would have been able to talk Warren into letting him stay? Why or why not?

7. **Critic's Corner** The poet Ezra Pound, reviewing Frost's second book of poetry, wrote, "I know more of farm life than I did before I had read his poems. That means I know more of 'Life.'" Think of the poems you've read in this Author Study. What do you think Pound meant by his statement? Do you agree with his praise of Frost's poetry?

8. **Connect to Life** Think about how you defined the idea of home in Connect to Your Life. How does your definition compare with the definitions Frost includes in "The Death of the Hired Man" (lines 118–120)? Is your idea of home closer to Warren's or to Mary's?

Literary Analysis

BLANK VERSE Much of "The Death of the Hired Man" is written in **blank verse,** lines of unrhymed **iambic pentameter.** Blank verse, especially when handled by a master such as Frost, imitates the natural rhythms of English speech and thus sounds very much like the way people talk. A line of blank verse has five iambic feet, each consisting of an unstressed syllable followed by a stressed syllable. (*Penta-* comes from a Greek word meaning "five.")

> *Some humble way to save*
>
> *his self-respect.*

Good blank verse does not have a singsong quality; in fact, a reader may not even notice the use of the form. A period or comma within a line, by making the reader briefly pause, can help break up the regular rhythm and make the line sound more natural:

> *"He's worn out. He's asleep beside the stove."*

The use of common phrases and expressions also makes blank verse more closely resemble speech:

> *"He added, if you really care to know,"*

Paired Activity Review the text of "The Death of the Hired Man" one more time. Find lines in iambic pentameter that sound to you like natural speech and read them aloud to a partner. See if your partner agrees with your choices. Remember that not every line in the poem is in iambic pentameter.

THE AUTHOR'S STYLE
Frost's Sly Simplicity

At a time when modern poetry was moving toward difficult, experimental writing, Robert Frost was able to create poems that still seem simple and natural to the reader. Yet complexity lies beneath the simple surface of his poems.

Key Aspects of Frost's Style

- use of plain language to reflect the simple lives of New England farmers
- use of blank verse to achieve the natural rhythms of everyday speech
- use of metaphors that change commonplace ideas into experiences of deeper meaning
- use of repetition, dialogue, and dialect
- unusual word order for emphasis

Analysis of Style

At the right are lines from four of Frost's poems. Study the chart above, and then read each excerpt carefully. Complete the following activities with a small group of classmates:

- Read the excerpts aloud, and discuss the rhythm of each. In which excerpt is the rhythm closest to the way you speak?
- Describe the word choice in the excerpts. What sort of words catch your eye? Are there any confusing word usages?
- Which excerpt do you think contains the most vivid image? What makes it easy to see what Frost is describing?

Applications

1. Imitating Style Choose one of the four excerpts, and write a word-for-word imitation of its style: copy the grammatical structure of the original, replacing every noun with a noun, every verb with a verb, and so on. Compare your version with a partner's.

2. Changing Style Choose either "Nothing Gold Can Stay" or "Fire and Ice." Rewrite the excerpt as a short prose piece. Keep as many of Frost's original words as you can, but add words that fill in the meaning.

3. Speaking and Listening Decide who might be the speaker in "The Gift Outright," "After Apple-Picking," and "Fire and Ice." Then prepare a reading of each excerpt that reflects how you think the speaker might deliver the lines.

---

from **The Gift Outright**

The land was ours before we were the land's.
She was our land more than a hundred years
Before we were her people. . . .

---

from **After Apple-Picking**

My long two-pointed ladder's sticking through a tree
Toward heaven still,
And there's a barrel that I didn't fill
Beside it, and there may be two or three
Apples I didn't pick upon some bough.

---

from **Nothing Gold Can Stay**

Nature's first green is gold,
Her hardest hue to hold.
Her early leaf's a flower;
But only so an hour.

---

from **Fire and Ice**

Some say the world will end in fire,
Some say in ice.
From what I've tasted of desire
I hold with those who favor fire.

Writing Options

Neighborly Editorial Assume the role of either the narrator or the neighbor in "Mending Wall." Write an editorial for the local paper explaining why you agree or disagree with the statement "Good fences make good neighbors."

Activities & Explorations

New England Collage Collect a series of pictures of the New England landscape. You should be able to get images from the tourist office of each state and from magazines and travel guides. Use these images to create a collage depicting the landscape that inspired Frost's poetry. ~ **ART**

Inquiry & Research

Farm Life Research the changes technology has brought to farming in this century. Consider these questions: What was life on a farm like in 1900? What is it like today? When did the need for "hired men" begin to fade? Put your report in your **Working Portfolio.**

Vocabulary in Action

EXERCISE: SYNONYMS Choose the Word to Know that best fits in each word group.

1. tolerate, endure, accept, _____
2. certainty, _____, poise, conviction
3. _____, obliged, indebted, obligated
4. rigid, stretched, tense, _____
5. secure, shield, _____, defend

WORDS TO KNOW	abide	beholden	taut
	assurance	harbor	

Building Vocabulary
Some of the Words to Know have more than one meaning. For an in-depth lesson on words with multiple meanings, see page 630.

Robert Frost

Author Study Project
LIVING MUSEUM PRESENTATION

In small groups, research and represent different stages of Frost's life. Either singly or in groups, actors will portray Frost and others from his world and dramatize a few events. Each group can focus on a different section below, or group members can each cover an area. For more details about Frost, refer to the Internet and to such other sources as biographies and letter collections. The goal is to get a well-rounded picture of Frost as a way of more fully appreciating his writing.

Frost on the Farm The farm in Derry was where Frost produced some of his earliest writing and where his children were born. What was family life like in the Frost household? What incidents became topics for poems?

Frost in England It was not until Frost moved his family to England in 1912 that his literary career began to take off. What happened there to make him a success? Who were some of the literary figures he met, and what influence did they have on his career?

Frost on the Lecture Circuit After he returned from England, Frost gave public presentations in which he talked about writing and read from his works. How was Frost received on the lecture circuit? What are some interesting statements he made about writing? about his fellow poets? about life?

More Online: Research Starter
www.mcdougallittell.com

Modernism

Imagine a world full of contradictions—a world of disillusion and hope, of crumbling traditions and explosive creative energy, of self-doubt and self-discovery. This is the modern world, the world that young European and American writers in the early decades of the century first struggled to come to terms with in their art.

Making It New

Ernest Hemingway, F. Scott Fitzgerald, William Faulkner, Katherine Anne Porter, T. S. Eliot, Ezra Pound, and William Carlos Williams were part of a generation of writers who created new ways of writing to respond to the new post-World War I realities. The loss of stability that was felt so strongly between 1914 and 1945 was reflected in the structure of their literature.

A comparison between Ernest Hemingway and Willa Cather can help you see the difference between a modernist work and a more traditionally structured one. Cather included in her works many modernist themes, such as the effects of alienation. But her method of storytelling is fairly traditional. For example, in "A Wagner Matinee" (page 688), the narrator directly explains the significance of his relationship with his aunt.

The Great Gatsby (1925) captured the emptiness of modern life.

The novels and short stories of Ernest Hemingway reflected Americans' shifting attitudes about the violence and upheaval of the modern world. His work is characterized by spare description and dialogue. In contrast to Willa Cather, Ernest Hemingway gives very little explanation about the relationship between his characters in "The End of Something" (page 1018). The story begins with a description of "a lumbering town" that was depleted of timber and thus abandoned by the lumber company. Into the description of the ruined lumber mill, Hemingway introduces his characters.

> The one-story bunk houses, the eating-house, the company store, the mill offices, and the big mill itself stood deserted in the acres of sawdust that covered the swampy meadow by the shore of the bay.
>
> Ten years later there was nothing of the mill left except the broken white limestone of its foundations showing through the swampy second growth as Nick and Marjorie rowed along the shore.
>
> — Ernest Hemingway, "The End of Something"

YOUR TURN What might be the connection between the ruined mill and Nick and Marjorie?

The Defining Features of Modernism

Modernism comprises a vast diversity of individual styles. Yet there are some defining features of the literature that show a distinct break with the past.

- **A rejection of traditional themes and subject matter.** Instead of love, many modernists wrote of the inability to commit to, or even communicate with, others. Instead of marriage and the community, they often wrote of broken relationships and broken lives.

> I owed to this woman most of the good that ever came my way in my boyhood, and had a reverential affection for her. During the years when I was riding herd for my uncle, my aunt, after cooking three meals . . . and putting the six children to bed, would often stand until midnight at her ironing-board with me at the kitchen table beside her, hearing me recite Latin declensions and conjugations, gently shaking me when my drowsy head sank down over a page of irregular verbs.
>
> — Willa Cather, "A Wagner Matinee"

YOUR TURN What details explain Aunt Georgiana's character and the narrator's feelings about her?

- **A focus on alienated individuals rather than "heroes" who stood for the values of the society.** The protagonist of T. S. Eliot's poem "The Love Song of J. Alfred Prufrock" (page 1025) is no heroic Gregorio Cortez but an insecure, lonely man who is consumed by self-doubt.

- **Frequent themes of impermanence and change.** For most modernists, nothing lasted—neither human institutions nor human attachments. Remember the loss of youthful dreams and beauty in F. Scott Fitzgerald's "Winter Dreams" (page 840).

- **The use of understatement and irony to reveal important emotions and ideas.** The modernists no longer felt confident to state universal truths directly in their works as the romantics and transcendentalists had before them. For example, Robert Frost ends "Out, Out—" (page 1004) with the acknowledgment that, essentially, life goes on. But instead of making a direct statement, he understates this truth by showing the bystanders calmly returning "to their affairs" because "they were not the one dead."

- **The use of symbols and images that suggest meanings rather than statements that explain meanings.** The speaker in Frost's "Acquainted with the Night" (page 1001) never admits that he's lonely or sad; the images in the poem tell you that.

- **The use of a stream-of-consciousness technique to show what's going on both inside and outside the characters.** Eliot's "The Love Song of J. Alfred Prufrock" and Porter's "The Jilting of Granny Weatherall" (pages 1025 and 1034) are both structured on the central characters' sometimes disconnected, but revealing, inner thoughts, feelings, and dreams.

The Tip of the ℐceberg

Although modernist writers often describe the characters' actions, feelings, and thoughts, they do not interpret the significance of these for the reader. Hemingway, for example, does not directly connect the mill to the main events of "The End of Something." He never explains why the characters speak to each other as they do. The reader is left to infer how they feel about each other from their actions and from what they do not say to each other as much as from what they do say.

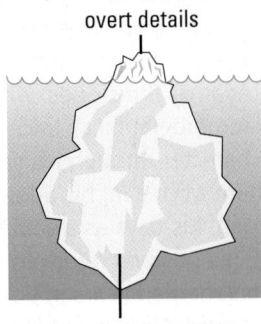

overt details

what must be inferred

Hemingway once explained such omissions this way: "I always try to write on the principle of the iceberg. There is seven-eighths of it under water for every part that shows."

Strategies for Reading: Modernist Literature

1. Make inferences from detailed descriptions, especially of the setting, to understand the characters' feelings and attitudes.

2. Analyze how images relate to character and express complex emotions or ideas.

3. Watch for ironic situations that may point to larger themes.

4. In a stream-of-consciousness narrative, keep track of the twists and turns of a character's thoughts to understand what he or she is reacting to.

5. **Monitor** your reading strategies and modify them when your understanding breaks down. Remember to use your Strategies for Active Reading: **predict, visualize, connect, question, clarify,** and **evaluate.**

The End of Something

Short Story by ERNEST HEMINGWAY

Connect to Your Life

Troubled Romance This story depicts a young couple whose relationship is ending. Their troubles raise the question, Why do people fall out of love? In a small group, discuss various answers to this question and come up with a list of possible reasons. Share your list with those of other groups. Then, as you read the story, try to find out why the couple breaks up.

Build Background

The Nick Adams Stories "The End of Something" is one of a series of Hemingway stories about the character Nick Adams. The stories, which are semiautobiographical, trace the life of this character through his youth in northern Michigan, his adolescence on the road, his days as a soldier in World War I, his postwar return to Michigan, and his married years in Europe. In this story, Nick is a young war veteran struggling to make sense of his life and the end of his love for a young woman. The story is set in Hortons Bay, a resort town on Lake Michigan, where Hemingway himself spent his childhood summers. Like Nick, Hemingway returned to the Hortons Bay area during the summer of 1919 to recover from his war wounds. Although the events of the story are fictional, Nick's pain, loneliness, and disillusionment with the world of adulthood were problems that Hemingway and other young men confronted upon returning from the war.

Focus Your Reading

LITERARY ANALYSIS **STYLE** **Style** is the distinctive way in which a piece of literature is written. Style refers not so much to what is said but how it is said. Word choice, sentence length, tone, imagery, and the use of dialogue all contribute to a writer's style. One of the hallmarks of Hemingway's straightforward style is his simple, clipped dialogue. As you read "The End of Something," note the repetitions and omissions in the characters' speech that resemble real-life conversations.

ACTIVE READING **MAKING INFERENCES** The scenes in "The End of Something" consist almost entirely of **dialogue** between the main characters—Nick and Marjorie. As they speak, the narrator gives little direct information about how they feel or think. Hemingway's sparse style challenges readers to fill in the gaps. You will need to make **inferences,** or logical guesses, to discover the suggested meanings behind the characters' spoken words. Their remarks provide you with clues about their relationship.

READER'S NOTEBOOK To help you make inferences as you read, create a chart like the one shown and fill it in with moments of Nick and Marjorie's dialogue that seem meaningful. Then consider what their comments reveal.

Dialogue Clues	What They Reveal
Nick's comments	
Marjorie's comments	

Illustration Copyright © D. J. McKay.

The End of Something

Ernest Hemingway

In the old days Hortons Bay was a lumbering town. No one who lived in it was out of sound of the big saws in the mill by the lake. Then one year there were no more logs to make lumber. The lumber schooners came into the bay and were loaded with the cut of the mill that stood stacked in the yard. All the piles of lumber were carried away. The big mill building had all its machinery that was removable taken out and hoisted on board one of the schooners by the men who had worked in the mill. The schooner moved out of the bay toward the open lake carrying the two great saws, the travelling carriage that hurled the logs against the revolving, circular saws and all the rollers, wheels, belts, and iron piled on a hull-deep load of lumber. Its open hold covered with canvas and lashed tight, the sails of the schooner filled and it moved out into the open lake, carrying with it everything that had made the mill a mill and Hortons Bay a town.

The one-story bunk houses, the eating-house, the company store, the mill offices, and the big mill itself stood deserted in the acres of sawdust that covered the swampy meadow by the shore of the bay.

Ten years later there was nothing of the mill left except the broken white limestone of its foundations showing through the

Canoe (1957), David Park. Oil on canvas, 36″ × 48″, Thomas C. Woods Memorial Collection,
Sheldon Memorial Art Gallery, University of Nebraska-Lincoln.

swampy second growth as Nick and Marjorie rowed along the shore. They were trolling[1] along the edge of the channel-bank where the bottom dropped off suddenly from sandy shallows to twelve feet of dark water. They were trolling on their way to the point to set night lines for rainbow trout.

"There's our old ruin, Nick," Marjorie said.

Nick, rowing, looked at the white stone in the green trees.

"There it is," he said.

"Can you remember when it was a mill?" Marjorie asked.

"I can just remember," Nick said.

"It seems more like a castle," Marjorie said.

Nick said nothing. They rowed on out of sight of the mill, following the shore line. Then Nick cut across the bay.

"They aren't striking," he said.

"No," Marjorie said. She was intent on the rod all the time they trolled, even when she talked. She loved to fish. She loved to fish with Nick.

Close beside the boat a big trout broke the surface of the water. Nick pulled hard on one oar so the boat would turn and the bait spinning far behind would pass where the trout was feeding. As the trout's back came up out of the water the minnows jumped wildly. They sprinkled the surface like a handful of shot thrown into the water. Another trout broke water, feeding on the other side of the boat.

"They're feeding," Marjorie said.

"But they won't strike," Nick said.

He rowed the boat around to troll past both the feeding fish, then headed it for the point. Marjorie did not reel in until the boat touched the shore.

They pulled the boat up the beach and Nick lifted out a pail of live perch. The perch swam in the water in the pail. Nick caught three of them with his hands and cut their heads off and skinned them while Marjorie chased with her hands in the bucket, finally caught a perch, cut its head off and skinned it. Nick looked at her fish.

"You don't want to take the ventral fin[2] out,"

he said. "It'll be all right for bait but it's better with the ventral fin in."

He hooked each of the skinned perch through the tail. There were two hooks attached to a leader[3] on each rod. Then Marjorie rowed the boat out over the channel-bank, holding the line in her teeth, and looking toward Nick, who stood on the shore holding the rod and letting the line run out from the reel.

"That's about right," he called.

"Should I let it drop?" Marjorie called back, holding the line in her hand.

"Sure. Let it go." Marjorie dropped the line overboard and watched the baits go down through the water.

She came in with the boat and ran the second line out the same way. Each time Nick set a heavy slab of driftwood across the butt of the rod to hold it solid and propped it up at an angle with a small slab. He reeled in the slack line so the line ran taut out to where the bait rested on the sandy floor of the channel and set the click on the reel. When a trout, feeding on the bottom, took the bait it would run with it, taking line out of the reel in a rush and making the reel sing with the click on.

Marjorie rowed up the point a little way so she would not disturb the line. She pulled hard on the oars and the boat went way up the beach. Little waves came in with it. Marjorie stepped out of the boat and Nick pulled the boat high up the beach.

"What's the matter, Nick?" Marjorie asked.

"I don't know," Nick said, getting wood for a fire.

They made a fire with driftwood. Marjorie went to the boat and brought a blanket. The

---

1. **trolling:** a method of fishing in which a line and baited hook trail along behind a slow-moving boat.
2. **ventral fin:** fin on the underside of a fish.
3. **leader:** short length of line by which a hook is fastened to a fishing line.

evening breeze blew the smoke toward the point, so Marjorie spread the blanket out between the fire and the lake.

Marjorie sat on the blanket with her back to the fire and waited for Nick. He came over and sat down beside her on the blanket. In back of them was the close second-growth timber[4] of the point and in front was the bay with the mouth of Hortons Creek. It was not quite dark. The fire-light went as far as the water. They could both see the two steel rods at an angle over the dark water. The fire glinted on the reels.

Marjorie unpacked the basket of supper.

"I don't feel like eating," said Nick.

"Come on and eat, Nick."

"All right."

They ate without talking, and watched the two rods and the fire-light in the water.

"There's going to be a moon tonight," said Nick. He looked across the bay to the hills that were beginning to sharpen against the sky. Beyond the hills he knew the moon was coming up.

"I know it," Marjorie said happily.

"You know everything," Nick said.

"Oh, Nick, please cut it out! Please, please don't be that way!"

"I can't help it," Nick said. "You do. You know everything. That's the trouble. You know you do."

Marjorie did not say anything.

"I've taught you everything. You know you do. What don't you know, anyway?"

"Oh, shut up," Marjorie said. "There comes the moon."

They sat on the blanket without touching each other and watched the moon rise.

"You don't have to talk silly," Marjorie said. "What's really the matter?"

"I don't know."

"Of course you know."

"No I don't."

"Go on and say it."

Nick looked on at the moon, coming up over the hills.

"It isn't fun any more."

He was afraid to look at Marjorie. Then he looked at her. She sat there with her back toward him. He looked at her back. "It isn't fun any more. Not any of it."

She didn't say anything. He went on. "I feel as though everything was gone to hell inside of me. I don't know, Marge. I don't know what to say."

He looked on at her back.

"Isn't love any fun?" Marjorie said.

"No," Nick said. Marjorie stood up. Nick sat there his head in his hands.

"I'm going to take the boat," Marjorie called to him. "You can walk back around the point."

"All right," Nick said. "I'll push the boat off for you."

"You don't need to," she said. She was afloat in the boat on the water with the moonlight on it. Nick went back and lay down with his face in the blanket by the fire. He could hear Marjorie rowing on the water.

He lay there for a long time. He lay there while he heard Bill come into the clearing walking around through the woods. He felt Bill coming up to the fire. Bill didn't touch him, either.

"Did she go all right?" Bill said.

"Yes," Nick said, lying, his face on the blanket.

"Have a scene?"

"No, there wasn't any scene."

"How do you feel?"

"Oh, go away, Bill! Go away for a while."

Bill selected a sandwich from the lunch basket and walked over to have a look at the rods. ❖

---

4. **second-growth timber:** trees that cover an area after the original, "old growth" trees have been cut or burned.

Thinking through the LITERATURE

Connect to the Literature

1. **What Do You Think?**
Which character do you feel the most sympathy for? Why? Share your thoughts with a classmate.

Comprehension Check
- How has Hortons Bay changed over the past ten years?
- What do Nick and Marjorie do in the first part of the story?
- Where does the final scene of the story occur?

Think Critically

2. **ACTIVE READING** **MAKING INFERENCES** Review the chart you made in your **READER'S NOTEBOOK.** What lines of Nick and Marjorie's dialogue hint at the problems in their relationship? How would you describe the way they communicate to each other?

   THINK ABOUT
   - what they say to each other
   - what they do not say to each other

3. Why do you think Nick wants to break up with Marjorie?

4. How do you think Nick feels at the end of the story?

   THINK ABOUT
   - his actions after Marjorie leaves
   - his remark "Oh, go away, Bill! Go away for a while."

5. How would you describe Nick's attitude toward the natural environment in this story? Support your answer with evidence.

Extend Interpretations

6. **Critic's Corner** In an article published in the *Kenyon Review,* critic George Hemphill wrote that Hemingway's story fails "because no necessary connection (other than biographical, perhaps) between the end of the boy and girl affair between Nick and Marjorie and the end of the old lumbering days in Michigan is suggested." What is your response to Hemphill's criticism? Do you think a connection between the Hortons Bay setting and Nick and Marjorie's relationship is implied or not? Discuss your ideas with your classmates.

7. **Different Perspectives** How did the information about Nick Adams presented in the Build Background feature on page 1018 influence your interpretation of the story? Do you think Nick's behavior can be attributed to his experiences as a young war veteran? Defend your view.

8. **Connect to Life** How does this ending of a relationship compare with breakups you have witnessed or experienced?

Literary Analysis

STYLE Before becoming a novelist and short story writer, Hemingway earned his living as a journalist. "The End of Something" reflects the simple, direct **style** of a newspaper reporter—short sentences, close attention to detail, unadorned descriptions, precise language, detached point of view, and matter-of-fact tone. Note the conciseness of the following paragraph about Nick and Marjorie's breakup:

He was afraid to look at Marjorie. Then he looked at her. She sat there with her back toward him. He looked back at her. "It isn't fun any more. Not any of it."

Hemingway's ear for authentic-sounding dialogue is also a keynote of his distinctive style.

Cooperative Learning Activity In a small group, rewrite a passage of the story and include Nick's feelings and thoughts. Share your rewrite with the class, and discuss differences between Hemingway's style and that of your rewrite. Do the additional details add or detract from the story?

Choices & CHALLENGES

Writing Options

1. Personal Ad What do you think happens to Nick and Marjorie after the end of their relationship? Write a personal ad that either Marjorie or Nick might send to a local newspaper, describing the kind of person she or he would like to meet. Read your ad aloud to the class.

2. Advice Letters Write a letter from Marjorie to an advice columnist, asking for advice about how to deal with Nick and their crumbling relationship. Then write the columnist's response to Marjorie.

3. TV Script Imagine that you and a small group of your classmates are head writers for a TV soap opera called *Hortons Bay.* Write the script for an episode based on this story.

Activities & Explorations

1. Story Illustrations Imagine that you have been asked to illustrate "The End of Something" for a collection of Hemingway's stories. Choose one scene from the story, and draw or paint it.
~ **ART**

2. Survey of Romantic Breakups What is the best way to end a relationship? Conduct an informal survey of ten males and ten females in your school or neighborhood. Record their responses, and report your findings to the class.
~ **PSYCHOLOGY**

	Male	Female
1		
2		
3		
4		
5		
6		
7		
8		
9		
10		

Ernest Hemingway
1899–1961

Other Works
The Nick Adams Stories; A Farewell to Arms; Death in the Afternoon; The Sun Also Rises; For Whom the Bell Tolls; The Old Man and the Sea

The Faces of War War punctuated Ernest Hemingway's life and career, from the World War I passages of *In Our Time,* his first book of short stories, to his journalistic accounts of chasing German U-boats with his yacht in the Caribbean during World War II. Hemingway found war the ultimate theater, where an artist could observe human nature and what he called "grace under pressure."

On the Frontlines At the age of 18, with the onset of World War I, Hemingway volunteered as a Red Cross ambulance driver, serving on the frontlines. After three weeks, he was severely wounded. He had a lengthy recovery in an Italian hospital and a love affair with an American nurse. What he experienced during that momentous year—the closeness of death, courage, physical and emotional pain, and romantic love—informs many of his novels and short stories.

The Lure of Adventure Other events of Hemingway's adventurous life also found their way into his fiction. In his highly acclaimed novel *The Sun Also Rises,* he depicted the members of what Gertrude Stein had dubbed the "lost generation"—young people, like himself, who were disillusioned by World War I and living a rather aimless life abroad in the 1920s. His desire for action led him to serve as a war correspondent during the Spanish civil war of the 1930s and during World War II. Out of these war experiences came a highly successful novel, *For Whom the Bell Tolls,* and a much criticized one, *Across the River and Into the Trees.* An avid sports enthusiast, Hemingway also wrote about bullfighting in Spain, big-game hunting in Africa, and deep-sea fishing in Florida.

Tragic Ending In 1953 Hemingway won the Pulitzer Prize for *The Old Man and the Sea,* and in 1954 he received the Nobel Prize in literature. However, the final years of his life were not happy. Suffering from the effects of alcoholism, injuries sustained in two plane crashes, and an emotional breakdown, he committed suicide in 1961.

The Love Song of J. Alfred Prufrock

Poetry by T. S. ELIOT

> **Connect to Your Life**
>
> **Partygoer's Dilemma** In this poem, J. Alfred Prufrock, on his way to a party, is trying to decide what to say to a woman who will be there. Imagine that you are at a party and see someone you would like to get better acquainted with. You do not know how this person feels about you. Would you reach out to this person by starting a conversation, or would you hold back? Jot down the thoughts you might have as you try to decide what to do.

Build Background

Romantics Versus Modernists In 1914 the poet Ezra Pound read "The Love Song of J. Alfred Prufrock" for the first time and enthusiastically wrote to Harriet Monroe, editor of *Poetry* magazine: "Eliot . . . has sent in the best poem I have yet had or seen from an American. . . . He has actually trained himself and modernized himself on his own." Modernist poets like Eliot and Pound sought to make a clear break with the poetic traditions of the past, especially 19th-century romanticism. Whereas romantic poets celebrated the individual and nature, Eliot portrayed the loneliness and alienation of the individual living in a dingy modern city. While romantic poets believed that poems should be written in everyday language for common people, Eliot used elevated diction and classical allusions to separate himself from the masses.

> WORDS
> TO KNOW
> **Vocabulary Preview**
> digress
> malinger
> meticulous
> obtuse
> presume

Focus Your Reading

LITERARY ANALYSIS **IMAGERY** **Imagery** consists of words and phrases that appeal to any of the five senses and that help the reader imagine precisely what the writer is describing. The object of Eliot's modernist style in "The Love Song of J. Alfred Prufrock" is to create a verbal collage of society by weaving together the fragmentary images of the city, the tea party, and the beach. As Prufrock moves through each of these three scenes, note the scattered images that flood his mind.

ACTIVE READING **UNDERSTANDING STREAM OF CONSCIOUSNESS**

Stream of consciousness is a technique developed by the modernists to present the flow of the seemingly unconnected thoughts, responses, and sensations as they occur in a character's mind. Eliot uses this technique to reveal the jumble of images, ideas, feelings, and daydreams that flow through Prufrock's mind. As the poem begins, Prufrock addresses a silent listener, perhaps someone who accompanies him to the party. Pretend you are the listener who hears Prufrock thinking aloud. As you read, pay attention to Prufrock's different associations and feelings about a decision he is trying to make.

READER'S NOTEBOOK To help you follow the structure of Prufrock's random train of thought about his decision, create a chart like the one shown, and fill it in with relevant details as you read.

Part 1: Prufrock's musings about asking the "overwhelming question" (lines 1–83)	
Part 2: Prufrock's decision (lines 84–86)	
Part 3: Prufrock's justification for his decision (lines 87–110)	

The Love Song of J. Alfred Prufrock

T. S. ELIOT

S'io credessi che mia risposta fosse
a persona che mai tornasse al mondo,
questa fiamma staria senza più scosse.
Ma per ciò che giammai di questo fondo
non tornò vivo alcun, s'i'odo il vero,
senza tema d'infamia ti rispondo.

Let us go then, you and I,
When the evening is spread out against the sky
Like a patient etherized upon a table;
Let us go, through certain half-deserted streets,
5   The muttering retreats
Of restless nights in one-night cheap hotels
And sawdust restaurants with oyster-shells:
Streets that follow like a tedious argument
Of insidious intent
10 To lead you to an overwhelming question . . .
Oh, do not ask, "What is it?"
Let us go and make our visit.

In the room the women come and go
Talking of Michelangelo.

15 The yellow fog that rubs its back upon the window-panes,
The yellow smoke that rubs its muzzle on the window-panes,
Licked its tongue into the corners of the evening,
Lingered upon the pools that stand in drains,
Let fall upon its back the soot that falls from chimneys,
20 Slipped by the terrace, made a sudden leap,
And seeing that it was a soft October night,
Curled once about the house, and fell asleep.

And indeed there will be time
For the yellow smoke that slides along the street
25 Rubbing its back upon the window-panes;
There will be time, there will be time
To prepare a face to meet the faces that you meet;
There will be time to murder and create,
And time for all the works and days of hands
30 That lift and drop a question on your plate;
Time for you and time for me,
And time yet for a hundred indecisions,
And for a hundred visions and revisions,
Before the taking of a toast and tea.

35 In the room the women come and go
Talking of Michelangelo.

And indeed there will be time
To wonder, "Do I dare?" and, "Do I dare?"
Time to turn back and descend the stair,
40 With a bald spot in the middle of my hair—
(They will say: "How his hair is growing thin!")
My morning coat, my collar mounting firmly to the chin,
My necktie rich and modest, but asserted by a simple pin—
(They will say: "But how his arms and legs are thin!")
45 Do I dare
Disturb the universe?
In a minute there is time
For decisions and revisions which a minute will reverse.

For I have known them all already, known them all—
50 Have known the evenings, mornings, afternoons,
I have measured out my life with coffee spoons;
I know the voices dying with a dying fall
Beneath the music from a farther room.
    So how should I presume?

55 And I have known the eyes already, known them all—
The eyes that fix you in a formulated phrase,
And when I am formulated, sprawling on a pin,
When I am pinned and wriggling on the wall,
Then how should I begin
60 To spit out all the butt-ends of my days and ways?
    And how should I presume?

23–34 This stanza reveals part of Prufrock's problem. Look for clues as you read.

26–27 What is Prufrock's idea of how people behave at parties or, perhaps, at any time?

37–48 In this stanza, Prufrock seems to grow increasingly insecure. The repeated question "Do I dare?" suggests that he wants to do something extraordinary at the party. What do you think he wants to do?

55–58 Prufrock recalls being scrutinized by women at other parties. The image of himself is one of a live insect that has been classified, labeled, and mounted for display.

56 formulated: reduced to a formula or prepared according to a formula.

WORDS
TO
KNOW

presume (prĭ-zōōm′) *v.* to act overconfidently; go beyond the proper limits; dare

And I have known the arms already, known them all—
Arms that are braceleted and white and bare
(But in the lamplight, downed with light brown hair!)
65 Is it perfume from a dress
That makes me so digress?
Arms that lie along a table, or wrap about a shawl.
    And should I then presume?
    And how should I begin?

          ● ● ● ● ●

70 Shall I say, I have gone at dusk through narrow streets
And watched the smoke that rises from the pipes
Of lonely men in shirt-sleeves, leaning out of windows? . . .

I should have been a pair of ragged claws
Scuttling across the floors of silent seas.

          ● ● ● ● ●

75 And the afternoon, the evening, sleeps so peacefully!
Smoothed by long fingers,
Asleep . . . tired . . . or it malingers,
Stretched on the floor, here beside you and me.
Should I, after tea and cakes and ices,
80 Have the strength to force the moment to its crisis?
But though I have wept and fasted, wept and prayed,
Though I have seen my head (grown slightly bald) brought in
    upon a platter,
I am no prophet—and here's no great matter;
I have seen the moment of my greatness flicker,
85 And I have seen the eternal Footman hold my coat, and snicker,
And in short, I was afraid.

And would it have been worth it, after all,
After the cups, the marmalade, the tea,
Among the porcelain, among some talk of you and me,
90 Would it have been worth while,
To have bitten off the matter with a smile,
To have squeezed the universe into a ball
To roll it towards some overwhelming question,
To say: "I am Lazarus, come from the dead,
95 Come back to tell you all, I shall tell you all"—
If one, settling a pillow by her head,
    Should say: "That is not what I meant at all.
    That is not it, at all."

62–67 How would you describe Prufrock's attitude toward the women at the party? Notice that he wants to say something but doesn't know how.

70–72 Why do you think Prufrock wants to talk about "lonely men"?

73–74 Prufrock has presented an image of himself as an insect (lines 57–58) and, here, as a crab or lobster. What do these images suggest about Prufrock's self-esteem?

81–83 These lines allude to the biblical story of John the Baptist, who is imprisoned by King Herod (Matthew 14; Mark 6). To gratify his stepdaughter Salome, Herod orders the Baptist's head cut off and brought to him on a platter.

85 Who or what do you think is "the eternal Footman"?

86 Who or what do you think Prufrock was afraid of?

87–110 In these two stanzas, Prufrock rationalizes his failure to ask the "overwhelming question."

94 Lazarus: In the biblical story (John 11:17–44), Lazarus lay dead in his tomb for four days before Jesus brought him back to life. Why do you think Prufrock compares himself to a character who returns from the dead?

WORDS	digress (dĭ-grĕs′) *v.* to wander away from the main subject in a conversation
TO	or in writing; ramble
KNOW	malinger (mə-lĭng′gər) *v.* to pretend illness in order to avoid duty or work

And would it have been worth it, after all,
100 Would it have been worth while,
After the sunsets and the dooryards and the sprinkled streets,
After the novels, after the teacups, after the skirts that trail along
    the floor—
And this, and so much more?—
It is impossible to say just what I mean!
105 But as if a magic lantern threw the nerves in patterns on a
    screen:
Would it have been worth while
If one, settling a pillow or throwing off a shawl,
And turning toward the window, should say:
    "That is not it at all,
110   That is not what I meant, at all."

No! I am not Prince Hamlet, nor was meant to be;
Am an attendant lord, one that will do
To swell a progress, start a scene or two,
Advise the prince; no doubt, an easy tool,
115 Deferential, glad to be of use,
Politic, cautious, and meticulous;
Full of high sentence, but a bit obtuse;
At times, indeed, almost ridiculous—
Almost, at times, the Fool.

120 I grow old . . . I grow old . . .
I shall wear the bottoms of my trousers rolled.

Shall I part my hair behind? Do I dare to eat a peach?
I shall wear white flannel trousers, and walk upon the beach.
I have heard the mermaids singing, each to each.

125 I do not think that they will sing to me.

I have seen them riding seaward on the waves
Combing the white hair of the waves blown back
When the wind blows the water white and black.

We have lingered in the chambers of the sea
130 By sea-girls wreathed with seaweed red and brown
Till human voices wake us, and we drown.

105 The magic lantern was a forerunner of the slide projector. In this image, the "nerves" may be Prufrock's inner self exposed for all to see.

111–119 Notice that Prufrock resigns himself to playing a supporting role rather than a starring one in life.

115 deferential (dĕf'ə-rĕn'shəl): yielding to someone else's opinion.

116 politic (pŏl'ĭ-tĭk): skillful in dealing with others; diplomatic.

124–128 In mythology, mermaids attract mortal men by their beauty and their singing, sometimes allowing men to live with them in the sea. What might the mermaids represent to Prufrock?

129–131 Whom do you think "we" refers to? What does the metaphor of waking and drowning suggest?

WORDS
TO
KNOW

meticulous (mĭ-tĭk'yə-ləs) *adj.* extremely careful and precise about details
obtuse (ŏb-tōōs') *adj.* slow to understand; dull

1029

Thinking through the LITERATURE

Connect to the Literature

1. **What Do You Think?** What are your impressions of Prufrock and his dilemma?

Comprehension Check
- In the beginning of the poem, to what does Prufrock compare the evening?
- What does Prufrock look like and about how old is he?
- What creatures will not sing to Prufrock?

Think Critically

2. How do you think Prufrock feels at the end of the poem?

3. **ACTIVE READING** **UNDERSTANDING STREAM OF CONSCIOUSNESS** Review the chart you made in your **READER'S NOTEBOOK.** Based on Prufrock's meandering thoughts, what do you think his "overwhelming question" is? Why does Prufrock decide not to ask it?

THINK ABOUT
- what leads him to think about this question
- to whom the question might be directed
- why the question might "disturb the universe"
- what the question might have to do with the "lonely men in shirt-sleeves" in line 72
- the response he anticipates in lines 97–98 and 109–110

4. Do you think Prufrock makes the right decision in not asking his "overwhelming question"? Defend your view.

5. How would you judge the women at the tea party Prufrock attends? Support your opinion with evidence.

6. Do you think Prufrock is like or unlike most people?

Extend Interpretations

7. **Comparing Texts** Read the excerpt from Kafka's *Diaries* on page 1033. In what ways do you think the bachelor described resembles Prufrock?

8. **Critic's Corner** Although now considered a classic modernist poem, "The Love Song of J. Alfred Prufrock" was not an immediate success. Several well-known American and British literary critics described the poem as dreadful and unpoetic. How would you respond to these critics?

9. **Connect to Life** Why do you think this poem is called a love song? How does it compare with love songs you know?

Literary Analysis

IMAGERY In keeping with other modernists, Eliot uses powerful **imagery—** vivid "word pictures"— to convey complex ideas and emotions. For example, the image of the evening as "a patient etherized upon a table" is richly suggestive of the general ill health and languor in Prufrock's world. The "yellow fog" depicted as an aimless alley cat is another striking image that conveys the atmosphere of Prufrock's city.

Paired Activity Most of the images in the poem are associated with Prufrock himself and reveal his fears, his self-consciousness, and his sustaining dreams. Meet with a partner to study these images. Create a chart like the one shown. In the first column, list images that Prufrock associates with himself, such as a man growing bald and skinny (lines 40–44). In the second column, list images that Prufrock uses in contrast to himself, such as the image of the prophet John the Baptist (lines 81–83). After you have charted several images of Prufrock, analyze what they tell you about him.

Images that Describe Prufrock	Images that Contrast with Prufrock
	1.
A face to meet other faces (line 27)	1. John the Baptist (lines 81–83)
2.	2.
3.	

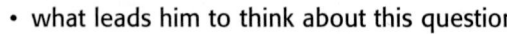

Choices & CHALLENGES

Writing Options

1. Letter to Prufrock If you were the person addressed in the poem, what advice would you give Prufrock? Write Prufrock a personal letter in which you counsel him.

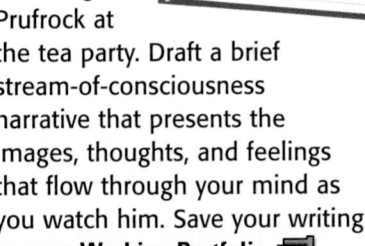

He seems intelligent— not like the others here.

2. Partygoer's Narrative Imagine you are a woman who has been watching Prufrock at the tea party. Draft a brief stream-of-consciousness narrative that presents the images, thoughts, and feelings that flow through your mind as you watch him. Save your writing in your **Working Portfolio.**

3. Social Commentary Write a newspaper commentary about the social scene at the party that Prufrock attends. Include details from the poem about the party guests, their conversations, the refreshments, and so on.

Writing Handbook
See page 1283: Analysis

Activities & Explorations

1. Improvisational Scene With a partner, improvise a scene between Prufrock and the woman he wants to speak with. Add material of your own, but keep it consistent with Prufrock's character and the kind of woman he says will attend the party.
~ PERFORMING

2. Prufrock's Caricature A caricature is a drawing of a person that exaggerates features to satirize that person or to highlight some aspect of his or her character. Draw a caricature of Prufrock based on details in the poem. Display your drawing for the class. **~ ART**

3. Radio Talk Show Imagine that you run a radio show on the arts and that T. S. Eliot will appear as your guest to publicize his new book, *Prufrock and Other Observations.* What questions would you ask him in order to help your listeners understand "The Love Song of J. Alfred Prufrock," and what might he answer? With a partner, prepare the interview and perform it for the class. **~ SPEAKING AND LISTENING**

Inquiry & Research

Michelangelo's Artistic Genius In "The Love Song of J. Alfred Prufrock," Eliot repeats the lines "In the room the women come and go / Talking of Michelangelo." Research Michelangelo's life and work. Then present your findings in a written report illustrated with pictures of some of Michelangelo's most important paintings and sculptures. Discuss with classmates why you think Eliot alludes to this great artist in his poem.

Michelangelo's David

Vocabulary in Action

EXERCISE A: SYNONYMS For each phrase in the first column, write the letter of the synonymous phrase from the second column.

1. meticulous yard work
2. to venture to eat
3. to scheme to malinger
4. as dull-witted as a fowl
5. to get way off track

A. as obtuse as a goose
B. to digress to excess
C. painstaking raking
D. to presume to consume
E. to plan faking some aching

WORDS TO KNOW	digress meticulous presume malinger obtuse

EXERCISE B Work with four other classmates to develop a short dramatic scene using five characters. Your scene can deal with any situation. The important thing is to portray each character in such a way that by the end of the scene, he or she has become associated with one of the five vocabulary words without anyone's having used that word in the scene. An association with the word can be developed through each character's actions and dialogue, as well as through other characters' actions toward, or dialogue about, him or her. Perform your dramatic scene for the rest of your classmates, and have them guess which vocabulary word is associated with each character.

Building Vocabulary

Several Words to Know come from Latin. For an in-depth lesson on word origins, see page 550.

T. S. Eliot
1888–1965

Other Works
The Waste Land
"The Hollow Men"
Murder in the Cathedral
Old Possum's Book of Practical Cats

Two National Identities An American who transformed himself into an Englishman, Thomas Stearns Eliot was born in St. Louis, Missouri, and died in London, England, where he had become a British subject in 1927. Eliot's whole career shows a movement back and forth between what the United States and England each represented to him—the modern and the traditional, the popular and the elite, the secular and the religious, democracy and monarchy. Even his poetry is both learned and colloquial, highly sophisticated yet laced with slang.

Breakthroughs in Poetry Eliot's early poems, such as "The Love Song of J. Alfred Prufrock" and *The Waste Land*, were original, inventive, and irreverent depictions of the decay of civilization. Although Eliot proclaimed a firm belief in tradition, his poems

helped create a break with tradition and establish a new modernist poetic voice.

Varied Professions While his poems, plays, and critical essays were critically acclaimed, Eliot did not make enough money from his writing to live on. He worked in England as a teacher, a bank clerk, and an editor for a British publisher. As the founder and editor of *The Criterion,* a literary magazine, he was able to help younger writers, such as Marcel Proust, get a start in their careers.

Critical Acclaim Eliot won the Nobel Prize in literature in 1948. Two years after his death, Eliot was honored by a memorial tablet placed in the Poets' Corner of Westminster Abbey.

Author Activity

Broadway Smash Hit Meet in a small group, and play cuts from a sound recording of *Cats,* Andrew Lloyd Webber's Broadway musical based on T. S. Eliot's *Old Possum's Book of Practical Cats.* As you listen closely to the lyrics, jot down your impressions.

from

The Diaries

FRANZ KAFKA

Czech-born writer Franz Kafka (1883–1924) shared T. S. Eliot's disillusionment with modern civilization in the 20th century. The characters in Kafka's imaginative stories and novels are plagued by anxiety, loneliness, alienation, and futility. In the following diary entry, Kafka profiles a bachelor who resembles J. Alfred Prufrock.

The unhappiness of the bachelor, whether seeming or actual, is so easily guessed at by the world around him that he will curse his decision, at least if he has remained a bachelor because of the delight he takes in secrecy. He walks around with his coat buttoned, his hands in the upper pockets of his jacket, his arms akimbo,[1] his hat pulled down over his eyes, a false smile that has become natural to him is supposed to shield his mouth as his glasses do his eyes, his trousers are tighter than seem proper for his thin legs. But everyone knows his condition, can detail his sufferings. A cold breeze breathes upon him from within and he gazes inward with the even sadder half of his double face. He moves incessantly,[2] but with predictable regularity, from one apartment to another. The farther he moves away from the living, for whom he must still—and this is the worst mockery—work like a conscious slave who dare not express his consciousness, so much the smaller a space is considered sufficient for him. While it is death that must still strike down the others, though they may have spent all their lives in a sickbed—for even though they would have gone down by themselves long ago from their own weakness, they nevertheless hold fast to their loving, very healthy relatives by blood and marriage—he, this bachelor, still in the midst of life, apparently of his own free will resigns himself to an ever smaller space, and when he dies the coffin is exactly right for him.

---

1. **akimbo** (ə-kĭm′bō): with the elbows pointed outward.
2. **incessantly**: continually.

The Jilting of Granny Weatherall

Short Story by KATHERINE ANNE PORTER

Connect to Your Life

Haunting Memories In the story you are about to read, Granny Weatherall is unable to shake the memory of an event that occurred 60 years earlier. Think about memories that replay again and again in your mind. Which of these do you recall so vividly that you can almost relive the moments? Discuss your responses with a small group of classmates.

Build Background

The Art of Storytelling Katherine Anne Porter claimed to have thrown away trunkloads of manuscripts, allowing only her best work to be published. One of her early stories, "The Jilting of Granny Weatherall," shows Porter's masterly skill in capturing a character with a few concise details and creating a rich experience out of a central episode. The word *jilting* in the title of this story means "a desertion or betrayal, especially by a prospective bride or bridegroom shortly before a wedding." As the story begins, Granny Weatherall lies in bed as a doctor examines her. The second sentence plunges the reader into Granny's mind, where most of the story unfolds. Granny's mind readily moves from present to past and back again.

WORDS TO KNOW
Vocabulary Preview

embroidered	rummage
intently	tactful
plague	

Focus Your Reading

LITERARY ANALYSIS   STREAM OF CONSCIOUSNESS   **Stream of consciousness** is a literary technique that was developed by modernist writers to present the flow of a character's seemingly unconnected thoughts, responses, and sensations. A stream-of-consciousness narrative is not structured into a coherent, logical presentation of events. Rather, the connections are associative, with one impression suggesting another. Note Granny Weatherall's rambling patterns of thinking as she lies on her deathbed.

ACTIVE READING   SEQUENCING   In this stream-of-consciousness narrative, Porter shuffles the past and the present to show the distorted way that a dying person perceives the **sequence,** or time order, of events. The reader experiences Granny's sense of time as she imaginatively travels backward and forward through her life, re-creating dramatic moments. Look for time jumps in the story as you read.

READER'S NOTEBOOK Create a time line like the one shown to help you untangle the main events of Granny Weatherall's life. Jot down the key moments in chronological order. The sample timeline below lists two events.

Jilting
by George

Examination
by Dr. Harry

The JILTING of Granny Weatherall

KATHERINE ANNE PORTER

She flicked her wrist neatly out of Doctor Harry's pudgy careful fingers and pulled the sheet up to her chin. The brat ought to be in knee breeches.[1] Doctoring around the country with spectacles on his nose! "Get along now, take your schoolbooks and go. There's nothing wrong with me."

Doctor Harry spread a warm paw like a cushion on her forehead where the forked green vein danced and made her eyelids twitch. "Now, now, be a good girl, and we'll have you up in no time."

"That's no way to speak to a woman nearly eighty years old just because she's down. I'd have you respect your elders, young man."

"Well, Missy, excuse me." Doctor Harry patted her cheek. "But I've got to warn you, haven't I? You're a marvel, but you must be careful or you're going to be good and sorry."

"Don't tell me what I'm going to be. I'm on my feet now, morally speaking. It's Cornelia. I had to go to bed to get rid of her."

Her bones felt loose, and floated around in her skin, and Doctor Harry floated like a balloon around the foot of the bed. He floated and pulled down his waistcoat and swung

La mere morte de l'artiste [The artist's mother in death], James Ensor. Stedelijk Museum, Ostend, Belgium. Copyright © SABAM.

---

1. **knee breeches:** short pants or knickers worn by young boys.

Portrait of Ambroise Vollard (1909), Pablo Picasso. Pushkin Museum of Fine Arts, Moscow/Giraudon/Art Resource, New York. Copyright © Artist's Rights Society ARS), New York.

his glasses on a cord. "Well, stay where you are, it certainly can't hurt you."

"Get along and doctor your sick," said Granny Weatherall. "Leave a well woman alone. I'll call for you when I want you. . . . Where were you forty years ago when I pulled through milk-leg[2] and double pneumonia? You weren't even born. Don't let Cornelia lead you on," she shouted, because Doctor Harry appeared to float up to the ceiling and out. "I pay my own bills, and I don't throw my money away on nonsense!"

She meant to wave good-by, but it was too much trouble. Her eyes closed of themselves, it was like a dark curtain drawn around the bed. The pillow rose and floated under her, pleasant as a hammock in a light wind. She listened to the leaves rustling outside the window. No, somebody was swishing newspapers: no, Cornelia and Doctor Harry were whispering together. She leaped broad awake, thinking they whispered in her ear.

"She was never like this, *never* like this!" "Well, what can we expect?" "Yes, eighty years old. . . ."

Well, and what if she was? She still had ears. It was like Cornelia to whisper around doors. She always kept things secret in such a public way. She was always being <u>tactful</u> and kind. Cornelia was dutiful; that was the trouble with her. Dutiful and good: "So good and dutiful," said Granny, "that I'd like to spank her." She saw herself spanking Cornelia and making a fine job of it.

"What'd you say, Mother?"

Granny felt her face tying up in hard knots.

"Can't a body think, I'd like to know?"

"I thought you might want something."

"I do. I want a lot of things. First off, go away and don't whisper."

She lay and drowsed, hoping in her sleep that the children would keep out and let her rest a minute. It had been a long day. Not that she was tired. It was always pleasant to snatch a minute now and then. There was always so much to be done, let me see: tomorrow.

---

2. **milk-leg:** a painful swelling of the leg experienced by some women after giving birth.

Tomorrow was far away and there was nothing to trouble about. Things were finished somehow when the time came; thank God there was always a little margin over for peace: then a person could spread out the plan of life and tuck in the edges orderly. It was good to have everything clean and folded away, with the hair brushes and tonic bottles sitting straight on the white embroidered linen: the day started without fuss and the pantry shelves laid out with rows of jelly glasses and brown jugs and white stone-china jars with blue whirligigs[3] and words painted on them: coffee, tea, sugar, ginger, cinnamon, allspice: and the bronze clock with the lion on top nicely dusted off. The dust that lion could collect in twenty-four hours! The box in the attic with all those letters tied up, well, she'd have to go through that tomorrow. All those letters—George's letters and John's letters and her letters to them both—lying around for the children to find afterwards made her uneasy. Yes, that would be tomorrow's business. No use to let them know how silly she had been once.

While she was rummaging around she found death in her mind and it felt clammy and unfamiliar. She had spent so much time preparing for death there was no need for bringing it up again. Let it take care of itself now. When she was sixty she had felt very old, finished, and went around making farewell trips to see her children and grandchildren, with a secret in her mind: This is the very last of your mother, children! Then she made her will and came down with a long fever. That was all just a notion like a lot of other things, but it was lucky too, for she had once for all got over the idea of dying for a long time. Now she couldn't be worried. She hoped she had better sense now. Her father had lived to be one hundred and two years old and had drunk a noggin of strong hot toddy[4] on his last birthday. He told the reporters it was his daily habit, and he owed his long life to that. He had made quite

a scandal and was very pleased about it. She believed she'd just plague Cornelia a little.

"Cornelia! Cornelia!" No footsteps, but a sudden hand on her cheek. "Bless you, where have you been?"

"Here, Mother."

"Well, Cornelia, I want a noggin of hot toddy."

"Are you cold, darling?"

"I'm chilly, Cornelia. Lying in bed stops the circulation. I must have told you that a thousand times."

Well, she could just hear Cornelia telling her husband that Mother was getting a little childish and they'd have to humor her. The thing that most annoyed her was that Cornelia thought she was deaf, dumb, and blind. Little hasty glances and tiny gestures tossed around her and over her head saying, "Don't cross her, let her have her way, she's eighty years old," and she sitting there as if she lived in a thin glass cage. Sometimes Granny almost made up her mind to pack up and move back to her own house where nobody could remind her every minute that she was old. Wait, wait, Cornelia, till your own children whisper behind your back!

In her day she had kept a better house and had got more work done. She wasn't too old yet for Lydia to be driving eighty miles for advice when one of the children jumped the track, and Jimmy still dropped in and talked things over: "Now, Mammy, you've a good business head, I want to know what you think of this? . . ." Old. Cornelia couldn't change the furniture around without asking. Little things, little things! They had been so sweet when they were little. Granny wished the old days were back again with the

---

3. **stone-china . . . whirligigs** (hwûr′lĭ-gĭgz′): jars made of thick pottery with blue spiral designs.

4. **noggin . . . toddy:** mug of a strong, hot alcoholic drink.

children young and everything to be done over. It had been a hard pull, but not too much for her. When she thought of all the food she had cooked, and all the clothes she had cut and sewed, and all the gardens she had made—well, the children showed it. There they were, made out of her, and they couldn't get away from that. Sometimes she wanted to see John again and point to them and say, Well, I didn't do so badly, did I? But that would have to wait. That was for tomorrow. She used to think of him as a man, but now all the children were older than their father, and he would be a child beside her if she saw him now. It seemed strange and there was something wrong in the idea. Why, he couldn't possibly recognize her. She had fenced in a hundred acres once, digging the post holes herself and clamping the wires with just a negro boy to help. That changed a woman. John would be looking for a young woman with the peaked Spanish comb in her hair and the painted fan. Digging post holes changed a woman. Riding country roads in the winter when women had their babies was another thing: sitting up nights with sick horses and sick negroes and sick children and hardly ever losing one. John, I hardly ever lost one of them! John would see that in a minute, that would be something he could understand, she wouldn't have to explain anything!

It made her feel like rolling up her sleeves and putting the whole place to rights again. No matter if Cornelia was determined to be everywhere at once, there were a great many things left undone on this place. She would start tomorrow and do them. It was good to be strong enough for everything, even if all you made melted and changed and slipped under your hands, so that by the time you finished you almost forgot what you were working for. What was it I set out to do? she asked herself <u>intently</u>, but she could not remember. A fog rose over the valley, she saw it marching across the creek swallowing the trees and moving up the hill like an army of ghosts. Soon it would be at the near edge of the orchard, and then it was time to go in and light the lamps. Come in, children, don't stay out in the night air.

Lighting the lamps had been beautiful. The children huddled up to her and breathed like little calves waiting at the bars in the twilight. Their eyes followed the match and watched the flame rise and settle in a blue curve, then they moved away from her. The lamp was lit, they didn't have to be scared and hang on to mother any more. Never, never, never more. God, for all my life I thank Thee. Without Thee, my God, I could never have done it. Hail, Mary, full of grace.[5]

I want you to pick all the fruit this year and see that nothing is wasted. There's always someone who can use it. Don't let good things rot for want of using. You waste life when you waste good food. Don't let things get lost. It's bitter to lose things. Now, don't let me get to thinking, not when I am tired and taking a little nap before supper. . . .

The pillow rose about her shoulders and pressed against her heart and the memory was being squeezed out of it: oh, push down the pillow, somebody: it would smother her if she tried to hold it. Such a fresh breeze blowing and such a green day with no threats in it. But he had not come, just the same. What does a woman do when she has put on the white veil and set out the white cake for a man and he doesn't come? She tried to remember. No, I swear he never harmed me but in that. He never harmed me but in that. . .and what if he did? There was the day, the day, but a whirl of dark

---

5. **Hail . . . grace:** the beginning of a Roman Catholic prayer to the Virgin Mary.

smoke rose and covered it, crept up and over into the bright field where everything was planted so carefully in orderly rows. That was hell, she knew hell when she saw it. For sixty years she had prayed against remembering him and against losing her soul in the deep pit of hell, and now the two things were mingled in one and the thought of him was a smoky cloud from hell that moved and crept in her head when she had just got rid of Doctor Harry and was trying to rest a minute. Wounded vanity, Ellen, said a sharp voice in the top of her mind. Don't let your wounded vanity get the upper hand of you. Plenty of girls get jilted. You were jilted, weren't you? Then stand up to it. Her eyelids wavered and let in streamers of blue-gray light like tissue paper over her eyes. She must get up and pull the shades down or she'd never sleep. She was in bed again and the shades were not down. How could that happen? Better turn over, hide from the light, sleeping in the light gave you nightmares. "Mother, how do you feel now?" and a stinging wetness on her forehead. But I don't like having my face washed in cold water!

Don't let your wounded vanity get the upper hand of you.

Hapsy? George? Lydia? Jimmy? No, Cornelia, and her features were swollen and full of little puddles. "They're coming, darling, they'll all be here soon." Go wash your face, child, you look funny.

Instead of obeying, Cornelia knelt down and put her head on the pillow. She seemed to be talking but there was no sound. "Well, are you tongue-tied? Whose birthday is it? Are you going to give a party?"

Cornelia's mouth moved urgently in strange shapes. "Don't do that, you bother me, daughter."

"Oh, no, Mother. Oh, no. . . ."

Nonsense. It was strange about children. They disputed your every word. "No what, Cornelia?"

"Here's Doctor Harry."

"I won't see that boy again. He just left five minutes ago."

"That was this morning, Mother. It's night now. Here's the nurse."

"This is Doctor Harry, Mrs. Weatherall. I never saw you look so young and happy!"

"Ah, I'll never be young again—but I'd be happy if they'd let me lie in peace and get rested."

She thought she spoke up loudly, but no one answered. A warm weight on her forehead, a warm bracelet on her wrist, and a breeze went on whispering, trying to tell her something. A shuffle of leaves in the everlasting hand of God, He blew on them and they danced and rattled. "Mother, don't mind, we're going to give you a little hypodermic."[6] "Look here, daughter, how do ants get in this bed? I saw sugar ants yesterday." Did you send for Hapsy too?

It was Hapsy she really wanted. She had to go a long way back through a great many rooms to find Hapsy standing with a baby on her arm. She seemed to herself to be Hapsy also, and the baby on Hapsy's arm was Hapsy and himself and herself, all at once, and there was no surprise in the meeting. Then Hapsy melted from within and turned flimsy as gray gauze and the baby was a gauzy shadow, and Hapsy came up close and said, "I thought you'd never come," and looked at her very searchingly and said, "You haven't changed a bit!" They leaned forward to kiss, when Cornelia began whispering

---

6. **hypodermic** (hī′pə-dûr′mĭk): injection.

from a long way off, "Oh, is there anything you want to tell me? Is there anything I can do for you?"

Yes, she had changed her mind after sixty years and she would like to see George. I want you to find George. Find him and be sure to tell him I forgot him. I want him to know I had my husband just the same and my children and my house like any other woman. A good house too and a good husband that I loved and fine children out of him. Better than I hoped for even. Tell him I was given back everything he took away and more. Oh, no, oh, God, no, there was something else besides the house and the man and the children. Oh, surely they were not all? What was it? Something not given back. . . . Her breath crowded down under her ribs and grew into a monstrous frightening shape with cutting edges; it bored up into her head, and the agony was unbelievable: Yes, John, get the Doctor now, no more talk, my time has come.

When this one was born it should be the last. The last. It should have been born first, for it was the one she had truly wanted. Everything came in good time. Nothing left out, left over. She was strong, in three days she would be as well as ever. Better. A woman needed milk in her to have her full health.

"Mother, do you hear me?"

"I've been telling you—"

"Mother, Father Connolly's here."

"I went to Holy Communion only last week. Tell him I'm not so sinful as all that."

"Father just wants to speak to you."

He could speak as much as he pleased. It was like him to drop in and inquire about her soul as if it were a teething baby, and then stay on for a cup of tea and a round of cards and gossip. He always had a funny story of some sort, usually

Tell him I was given back everything he took away and more.

about an Irishman who made his little mistakes and confessed them, and the point lay in some absurd thing he would blurt out in the confessional showing his struggles between native piety and original sin. Granny felt easy about her soul. Cornelia, where are your manners? Give Father Connolly a chair. She had her secret comfortable understanding with a few favorite saints who cleared a straight road to God for her. All as surely signed and sealed as the papers for the new Forty Acres. Forever. . . . heirs and assigns[7] forever. Since the day the wedding cake was not cut, but thrown out and wasted. The whole bottom dropped out of the world, and there she was blind and sweating with nothing under her feet and the walls falling away. His hand had caught her under the breast, she had not fallen, there was the freshly polished floor with the green rug on it, just as before. He had cursed like a sailor's parrot and said, "I'll kill him for you." Don't lay a hand on him, for my sake leave something to God. "Now, Ellen, you must believe what I tell you. . . ."

So there was nothing, nothing to worry about any more, except sometimes in the night one of the children screamed in a nightmare, and they both hustled out shaking and hunting for the matches and calling, "There, wait a minute, here we are!" John, get the doctor now, Hapsy's time has come. But there was Hapsy standing by the bed in a white cap. "Cornelia, tell Hapsy to take off her cap. I can't see her plain."

Her eyes opened very wide and the room stood out like a picture she had seen somewhere.

---

7. **assigns:** people to whom property is transferred in a will or other legal document.

Yvonne and Magdaleine Torn in Tatters (1911), Marcel Duchamp. Oil on canvas, 23¾" × 28⅞". Philadelphia Museum of Art, Louise and Walter Arensberg Collection (1950-134-53).

Dark colors with the shadows rising towards the ceiling in long angles. The tall black dresser gleamed with nothing on it but John's picture, enlarged from a little one, with John's eyes very black when they should have been blue. You never saw him, so how do you know how he looked? But the man insisted the copy was perfect, it was very rich and handsome. For a picture, yes, but it's not my husband. The table by the bed had a linen cover and a candle and a crucifix.[8] The light was blue from Cornelia's silk lampshades. No sort of light at all, just frippery. You had to live forty years with kerosene lamps to appreciate honest electricity. She felt very strong and she saw Doctor Harry with a rosy nimbus[9] around him.

"You look like a saint, Doctor Harry, and I vow that's as near as you'll ever come to it."

"She's saying something."

"I heard you, Cornelia. What's all this carrying-on?"

"Father Connolly's saying—"

Cornelia's voice staggered and bumped like a cart in a bad road. It rounded corners and turned back again and arrived nowhere. Granny stepped up in the cart very lightly and reached for the reins, but a man sat beside her and she knew him by his hands, driving the cart. She did

---

8. **crucifix** (kroo'sə-fĭks'): a cross bearing a sculptured representation of the crucified Christ.

9. **nimbus**: halo of light.

not look in his face, for she knew without seeing, but looked instead down the road where the trees leaned over and bowed to each other and a thousand birds were singing a Mass. She felt like singing too, but she put her hand in the bosom of her dress and pulled out a rosary,[10] and Father Connolly murmured Latin in a very solemn voice and tickled her feet. My God, will you stop that nonsense? I'm a married woman. What if he did run away and leave me to face the priest by myself? I found another a whole world better. I wouldn't have exchanged my husband for anybody except St. Michael himself, and you may tell him that for me with a thank you in the bargain.

Light flashed on her closed eyelids, and a deep roaring shook her. Cornelia, is that lightning? I hear thunder. There's going to be a storm. Close all the windows. Call the children in. . . . "Mother, here we are, all of us." "Is that you, Hapsy?" "Oh, no, I'm Lydia. We drove as fast as we could." Their faces drifted above her, drifted away. The rosary fell out of her hands and Lydia put it back. Jimmy tried to help, their hands fumbled together, and Granny closed two fingers around Jimmy's thumb. Beads wouldn't do, it must be something alive. She was so amazed her thoughts ran round and round. So, my dear Lord, this is my death and I wasn't even thinking about it. My children have come to see me die. But I can't, it's not time. Oh, I always hated surprises. I wanted to give Cornelia the amethyst set—Cornelia, you're to have the amethyst set, but Hapsy's to wear it when she wants, and, Doctor Harry, do shut up. Nobody sent for you. Oh, my dear Lord, do wait a minute. I meant to do something about the Forty Acres, Jimmy doesn't need it and Lydia will later on, with that worthless husband of hers. I meant to finish the altar cloth and send six bottles of wine to Sister Borgia for her dyspepsia.[11] I want to send six bottles of wine to Sister Borgia, Father Connolly, now don't let me forget.

Cornelia's voice made short turns and tilted over and crashed. "Oh, Mother, oh, Mother, oh, Mother . . . ."

"I'm not going, Cornelia. I'm taken by surprise. I can't go."

You'll see Hapsy again. What about her? "I thought you'd never come." Granny made a long journey outward, looking for Hapsy. What if I don't find her? What then? Her heart sank down and down, there was no bottom to death, she couldn't come to the end of it. The blue light from Cornelia's lampshade drew into a tiny point in the center of her brain, it flickered and

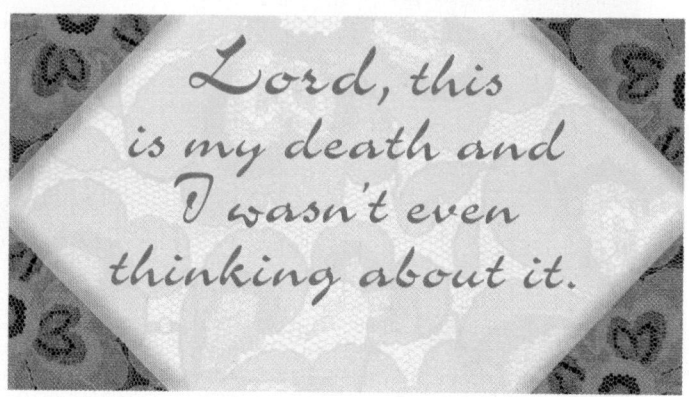

Lord, this is my death and I wasn't even thinking about it.

winked like an eye, quietly it fluttered and dwindled. Granny lay curled down within herself, amazed and watchful, staring at the point of light that was herself; her body was now only a deeper mass of shadow in an endless darkness and this darkness would curl around the light and swallow it up. God, give a sign!

For the second time there was no sign. Again no bridegroom and the priest in the house. She could not remember any other sorrow because this grief wiped them all away. Oh, no, there's nothing more cruel than this—I'll never forgive it. She stretched herself with a deep breath and blew out the light. ❖

---

10. **rosary** (rō′zə-rē): a string of beads used by Roman Catholics to count their prayers.

11. **dyspepsia** (dĭs-pĕp′shə): indigestion.

Thinking through the LITERATURE

Connect to the Literature

1. **What Do You Think?**
   What did you find the most memorable about Granny? Share your thoughts with a partner.

   Comprehension Check
   - Which characters mentioned in the story are mainly figures from Granny's past?
   - What role did George play in Granny's life?
   - Which of her daughters does Granny most want to see?

Think Critically

2. **ACTIVE READING** **SEQUENCING EVENTS** Use the time line you made in your **READER'S NOTEBOOK** to retell the key events of Granny's life in chronological order. How do you picture her in the various stages of her life—young girl, wife and mother, and old widow?

3. Do you think Granny's moment of death—symbolized by her blowing out the light at the end of the story—is an act of resignation or an act of defiance? Explain your response.

4. How would you compare Granny's experience of death with her jilting by George 60 years before?

   THINK ABOUT
   - her expectations and surprises on each occasion
   - her feelings about each experience
   - her thoughts about God that relate to her jilting experience

5. Of all the relationships in her life, which one do you think means the most to Granny? Why?

6. What do you think Granny's rather unusual last name—Weatherall—suggests about her character?

Extend Interpretations

7. **Critic's Corner** The writer Eudora Welty has remarked, "All the stories she [Porter] has written are moral stories about love and the hate that is love's twin. . . ." Do you think that assessment applies to this story? Explain.

8. **Comparing Texts** How would you compare the portrayal of death in this story with Emily Dickinson's portrayal of death in her poems "I heard a Fly buzz—when I died—" (page 758) and "Because I could not stop for Death—" (pages 759)?

9. **Connect to Life** Based on this story and your own experiences, how would you describe the power of memory in shaping people's lives?

Literary Analysis

STREAM OF CONSCIOUSNESS

The term *stream of consciousness* was coined by American psychologist William James to characterize the unbroken flow of thought that occurs in the waking mind. Later the term was adopted to describe a narrative method in modern works of literature. Porter uses stream of consciousness to dramatize Granny's interior life—her memories, secret longings, unsatisfied wishes. This approach allows the reader to develop an intimacy with Granny that would not be possible if the story dramatized only the external events that take place in the sickroom.

Activity Imitate Porter's fictional technique by writing a short stream-of-consciousness narrative in which George recalls jilting Granny Weatherall shortly before his own death. Include the random images, thoughts, and feelings he associates with this event. Share your narrative with classmates.

Writing Options

1. Eulogy for Granny Write a eulogy for Granny Weatherall that Cornelia might present to commemorate her mother. Include details from Granny's life that are mentioned in the story. Put your eulogy in your **Working Portfolio.**

2. Psychological Profile Write a psychological profile of strong elderly women. Use Granny Weatherall as a case study.

Activities & Explorations

1. Story Illustration Sketch an illustration for this story. Choose a sentence or part of a sentence as a caption for your drawing. ~ **ART**

2. Tabloid Interview Working with a partner, role-play a reporter and George, the man who jilted Granny Weatherall. Conduct an interview with George for a tabloid article in which he reveals his motives for jilting Granny. ~ **SPEAKING AND LISTENING**

Vocabulary in Action

EXERCISE: ANALOGIES On your paper, write the vocabulary word that best completes each analogy.

1. JUDGE : FAIR :: diplomat : _____
2. POTTERY : GLAZED :: cloth : _____
3. UNPLEASANTLY : HORRIBLY :: carefully : _____
4. HELP : HINDER :: comfort : _____
5. RETREAT : WITHDRAW :: sift : _____

Building Vocabulary
For an in-depth lesson on analogies, see page 254.

WORDS TO KNOW			
embroidered	plague		tactful
intently	rummage		

Katherine Anne Porter
1890–1980

Other Works
Ship of Fools
Pale Horse, Pale Rider
The Never-Ending Wrong

Difficult Childhood Katherine Anne Porter was born Callie Russell Porter in Indian Creek, Texas. The fourth of five children in a poor family, she later described herself as a "precocious, nervous, rebellious, unteachable" child. When she was two, her mother died. Porter was raised by her grandmother, who probably served as the model for Granny in "The Jilting of Granny Weatherall."

Restless Years Porter was educated at home and in various Catholic convent schools in the South. She always considered herself a "roving spirit." Porter remarked in an interview, "At sixteen I ran away and got married. And at twenty-one I bolted again, went to Chicago, got a newspaper job, and went into the movies." She later worked as a journalist in Chicago, Denver, and Fort Worth, Texas. When she went to Mexico in 1920 on assignment for a magazine, she arrived in the middle of a revolution. Porter's observations of this conflict later became the subject of several short stories in her highly praised first collection, *Flowering Judas* (1930), which launched her literary career.

Emblems of Success In the midst of three marriages, travel, and miscellaneous jobs, Porter produced the small body of work on which her reputation rests: five novellas, three volumes of short stories, and one long novel, *Ship of Fools* (1962), which took her 25 years to write. In 1966, she won the Pulitzer Prize and National Book Award for her *Collected Stories.*

The Man Who Was Almost a Man

Short Story by RICHARD WRIGHT

(**Connect to Your Life**)

Coming of Age The main character in this story, 17-year-old Dave Saunders, is on the threshold of adulthood. Think about the adults in your family, your school, or your community. What do you think it takes to be an adult? How do people display maturity in their attitudes and actions? With a partner, share your thoughts about what it means to be an adult.

Build Background

Rural Poverty in the Deep South The abolishment of slavery in the South after the Civil War did not end the economic oppression of African Americans there. Landowners divided large plantations into smaller farms, which they rented to both white and black laborers who worked for a share of the earnings from the crop. Under the brutal systems of tenant farming and sharecropping, many African-American families—like the Saunders family in this story—endured a life of grinding poverty. Neither tenants nor sharecroppers earned enough money to escape a cycle of debt or to buy their own land and become economically independent.

Richard Wright's father was a cotton sharecropper in Mississippi in the early 1900s, about the time "The Man Who Was Almost a Man" takes place. In the story, young Dave works in the fields during the summer for his white employer, Mr. Hawkins, and earns a meager wage. Be warned that Dave occasionally uses offensive language, including a racist term for his fellow African Americans. Wright's intention is to lend realism to a character who is immature and lacking in awareness.

Focus on Reading

LITERARY ANALYSIS **POINT OF VIEW** **Point of view** refers to the narrative perspective from which events in a story or novel are told. "The Man Who Was Almost a Man" is told from the **third-person limited point of view**—the narrator stands outside the action and focuses on one character's thoughts, observations, and feelings. Note how you see the story through two pairs of eyes—the narrator's and Dave's.

ACTIVE READING **MAKING JUDGMENTS** As the story opens, Dave is grumbling to himself about an earlier incident that occurred between him and the other field hands on the Hawkins plantation. The narrator reveals Dave's thoughts and feelings, but offers no opinions about his behavior. Wright expects the reader to **make judgments,** or evaluate, the character's conduct. As you read, evaluate the quality of Dave's decisions when he finds himself in difficult or frustrating situations.

READER'S NOTEBOOK To help you make judgments about Dave's decisions, create a diagram like the one shown, and fill it in as you read the story. Evaluate the decisions as good or bad.

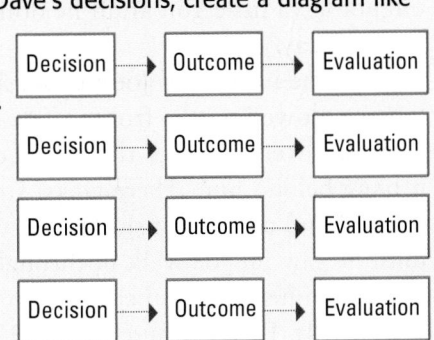

THE MAN WHO WAS

ave struck out across the fields, looking homeward through paling light. Whut's the use talkin wid em niggers in the field? Anyhow, his mother was putting supper on the table. Them niggers can't understan nothing. One of these days he was going to get a gun and practice shooting, then they couldn't talk to him as though he were a little boy. He slowed, looking at the ground. Shucks, Ah ain scareda them even ef they are biggern me! Aw, Ah know whut Ahma do. Ahm going by ol Joe's sto n git that Sears Roebuck catlog n look at them guns. Mebbe Ma will lemme buy one when she gits mah pay from ol man Hawkins. Ahma beg her t gimme some money. Ahm ol ernough to hava gun. Ahm seventeen. Almost a man. He strode, feeling his long loose-jointed limbs. Shucks, a man oughta hava little gun aftah he done worked hard all day.

He came in sight of Joe's store. A yellow lantern glowed on the front porch. He mounted steps and went through the screen door, hearing it bang behind him. There was a strong smell of coal oil and mackerel fish. He felt very confident until he saw fat Joe walk in through the rear door, then his courage began to ooze.

"Howdy, Dave! Whutcha want?"

"How yuh, Mistah Joe? Aw, Ah don wanna buy nothing. Ah jus wanted t see ef yuhd lemme look at tha catlog erwhile."

"Sure! You wanna see it here?"

"Nawsuh. Ah wans t take it home wid me. Ah'll bring it back termorrow when Ah come in from the fiels."

"You plannin on buying something?"

"Yessuh."

"Your ma lettin you have your own money now?"

"Shucks. Mistah Joe, Ahm gittin t be a man like anybody else!"

Joe laughed and wiped his greasy white face with a red bandanna.

"Whut you plannin on buyin?"

Dave looked at the floor, scratched his head, scratched his thigh, and smiled. Then he looked up shyly.

"Ah'll tell yuh, Mistah Joe, ef yuh promise yuh won't tell."

"I promise."

"Waal, Ahma buy a gun."

"A gun? Whut you want with a gun?"

"Ah wanna keep it."

"You ain't nothing but a boy. You don't need a gun."

"Aw, lemme have the catlog, Mistah Joe.

ALMOST A MAN RICHARD WRIGHT

Ah'll bring it back."

Joe walked through the rear door. Dave was elated.[1] He looked around at barrels of sugar and flour. He heard Joe coming back. He craned his neck to see if he were bringing the book. Yeah, he's got it. Gawddog, he's got it!

"Here, but be sure you bring it back. It's the only one I got."

"Sho, Mistah Joe."

"Say, if you wanna buy a gun, why don't you buy one from me? I gotta gun to sell."

"Will it shoot?"

"Sure it'll shoot."

"Whut kind is it?"

"Oh, it's kinda old . . . a left-hand Wheeler. A pistol. A big one."

"Is it got bullets in it?"

"It's loaded."

"Kin Ah see it?"

"Where's your money?"

"Whut yuh wan fer it?"

"I'll let you have it for two dollars."

"Just two dollahs? Shucks, Ah could buy tha when Ah git mah pay."

"I'll have it here when you want it."

"Awright, suh. Ah be in fer it."

He went through the door, hearing it slam again behind him. Ahma git some money from Ma n buy me a gun! Only two dollahs! He tucked the thick catalogue under his arm and hurried.

"Where yuh been, boy?" His mother held a steaming dish of black-eyed peas.

"Aw, Ma, Ah jus stopped down the road t talk wid the boys."

"Yuh know bettah t keep suppah waitin."

He sat down, resting the catalogue on the edge of the table.

"Yuh git up from there and git to the well n wash yosef! Ah ain feedin no hogs in mah house!"

She grabbed his shoulder and pushed him. He stumbled out of the room, then came back to get the catalogue.

"Whut this?"

"Aw, Ma, it's jusa catlog."

"Who yuh git it from?"

"From Joe, down at the sto."

"Waal, thas good. We kin use it in the outhouse."

"Naw, Ma." He grabbed for it. "Gimme ma catlog, Ma."

She held onto it and glared at him.

---

1. **elated:** proud and joyful.

"Quit hollerin at me! Whut's wrong wid yuh? Yuh crazy?"

"But Ma, please. It ain mine! It's Joe's! He tol me t bring it back t im termorrow."

She gave up the book. He stumbled down the back steps, hugging the thick book under his arm. When he had splashed water on his face and hands, he groped back to the kitchen and fumbled in a corner for the towel. He bumped into a chair; it clattered to the floor. The catalogue sprawled at his feet. When he had dried his eyes he snatched up the book and held it again under his arm. His mother stood watching him.

"Now, ef yuh gonna act a fool over that ol book, Ah'll take it n burn it up."

"Naw, Ma, please."

"Waal, set down n be still!"

He sat down and drew the oil lamp close. He thumbed page after page, unaware of the food his mother set on the table. His father came in. Then his small brother.

"Whutcha got there, Dave?" his father asked.

"Jusa catlog," he answered, not looking up.

"Yeah, here they is!" His eyes glowed at blue-and-black revolvers. He glanced up, feeling sudden guilt. His father was watching him. He eased the book under the table and rested it on his knees. After the blessing was asked, he ate. He scooped up peas and swallowed fat meat without chewing. Buttermilk helped to wash it down. He did not want to mention money before his father. He would do much better by cornering his mother when she was alone. He looked at his father uneasily out of the edge of his eye.

"Boy, how come yuh don quit foolin wid tha book n eat yo suppah?"

"Yessuh."

"How you n ol man Hawkins gitten erlong?"

"Suh?"

"Can't yuh hear? Why don yuh lissen? Ah ast yu how wuz yuh n ol man Hawkins gittin erlong?"

"Oh, swell, Pa. Ah plows mo lan than anybody over there."

"Waal, yuh oughta keep yo mind on whut yuh doin."

"Yessuh."

He poured his plate full of molasses and sopped it up slowly with a chunk of cornbread. When his father and brother had left the kitchen, he still sat and looked again at the guns in the catalogue, longing to muster courage enough to present his case to his mother. Lawd, ef Ah only had tha pretty one! He could almost feel the slickness of the weapon with his fingers. If he had a gun like that he would polish it and keep it shining so it would never rust. N Ah'd keep it loaded, by Gawd!

"Ma?" His voice was hesitant.

"Hunh?"

"Ol man Hawkins give yuh mah money yit?"

"Yeah, but ain no usa yuh thinking bout throwin nona it erway. Ahm keepin tha money sos yuh kin have cloes t go to school this winter."

He rose and went to her side with the open catalogue in his palms. She was washing dishes, her head bent low over a pan. Shyly he raised the book. When he spoke, his voice was husky, faint.

"Ma, Gawd knows Ah wans one of these."

"One of whut?" she asked, not raising her eyes.

"One of these," he said again, not daring even to point. She glanced up at the page, then at him with wide eyes.

"Nigger, is yuh gone plumb crazy?"

"Aw, Ma—"

"Git outta here! Don yuh talk t me bout no gun! Yuh a fool!"

"Ma, Ah kin buy one fer two dollahs."

"Not ef Ah knows it, yuh ain!"

"But yuh promised me one—"

"Ah don care whut Ah promised! Yuh ain nothing but a boy yit!"

"Ma, ef yuh lemme buy one Ah'll *never* ast yuh fer nothing no mo."

"Ah tol yuh t git outta here! Yuh ain gonna toucha penny of tha money fer no gun! Thas how come Ah has Mistah Hawkins t pay yo wages t me, cause Ah knows yuh ain got no sense."

"But, Ma, we needa gun. Pa ain got no gun. We needa gun in the house. Yuh kin never tell whut might happen."

"Now don yuh try to maka fool outta me, boy! Ef we did hava gun, yuh wouldn't have it!"

He laid the catalogue down and slipped his arm around her waist.

"Aw, Ma, Ah done worked hard alla summer n ain ast yuh fer nothin, is Ah, now?"

"Thas whut yuh spose t do!"

"But Ma, Ah wans a gun. Yuh kin lemme have two dollahs outta mah money. Please, Ma. I kin give it to Pa . . . Please, Ma! Ah loves yuh, Ma."

When she spoke her voice came soft and low.

"Whut yu wan wida gun, Dave? Yuh don need no gun. Yuh'll git in trouble. N ef yo pa jus thought Ah let yuh have money t buy a gun he'd hava fit."

"Ah'll hide it, Ma. It ain but two dollahs."

"Lawd, chil, whut's wrong wid yuh?"

"Ain nothin wrong, Ma. Ahm almos a man now. Ah wans a gun."

"Who gonna sell yuh a gun?"

"Ol Joe at the sto."

"N it don cos but two dollahs?"

"Thas all, Ma. Jus two dollahs. Please, Ma."

She was stacking the plates away; her hands moved slowly, reflectively. Dave kept an anxious silence. Finally, she turned to him.

"Ah'll let yuh git tha gun ef yuh promise me one thing."

"Whut's tha, Ma?"

"Yuh bring it straight back t me, yuh hear? It be fer Pa."

"Yessum! Lemme go now, Ma."

She stooped, turned slightly to one side, raised the hem of her dress, rolled down the top of her stocking, and came up with a slender wad of bills.

"Here," she said. "Lawd knows yuh don need no gun. But yer pa does. Yuh bring it right back t me, yuh hear? Ahma put it up. Now ef yuh don, Ahma have yuh pa lick yuh so hard yuh won fergit it."

"Yessum."

He took the money, ran down the steps, and across the yard.

"Dave! Yuuuuuh Daaaaave!"

He heard, but he was not going to stop now. "Naw, Lawd!"

The first movement he made the following morning was to reach under his pillow for the gun. In the gray light of dawn he held it loosely, feeling a sense of power. Could kill a man with a gun like this. Kill anybody, black or white. And if he were holding his gun in his hand, nobody could run over him; they would have to respect him. It was a big gun, with a long barrel and a heavy handle. He raised and lowered it in his hand, marveling at its weight.

He had not come straight home with it as his mother had asked; instead he had stayed out in the fields, holding the weapon in his hand, aiming it now and then at some imaginary foe. But he had not fired it; he had been afraid that his father might hear. Also he was not sure he knew how to fire it.

To avoid surrendering the pistol he had not come into the house until he knew that they were all asleep. When his mother had tiptoed to his bedside late that night and demanded the gun, he had first played possum; then he had told her that the gun was hidden outdoors, that he would bring it to her in the morning. Now he lay turning it slowly in his hands. He broke it,[2] took out the cartridges, felt them, and then put them back.

He slid out of bed, got a long strip of old flannel from a trunk, wrapped the gun in it, and

---

2. **broke it:** opened the cartridge chamber.

tied it to his naked thigh while it was still loaded. He did not go in to breakfast. Even though it was not yet daylight, he started for Jim Hawkins' plantation. Just as the sun was rising he reached the barns where the mules and plows were kept.

"Hey! That you, Dave?"

He turned. Jim Hawkins stood eying him suspiciously.

"What're yuh doing here so early?"

"Ah didn't know Ah wuz gittin up so early, Mistah Hawkins. Ah wuz fixin t hitch up ol Jenny n take her t the fiels."

"Good. Since you're so early, how about plowing that stretch down by the woods?"

"Suits me, Mistah Hawkins."

"O.K. Go to it!"

He hitched Jenny to a plow and started across the fields. Hot dog! This was just what he wanted. If he could get down by the woods, he could shoot his gun and nobody would hear. He walked behind the plow, hearing the traces[3] creaking, feeling the gun tied tight to his thigh.

When he reached the woods, he plowed two whole rows before he decided to take out the gun. Finally, he stopped, looked in all directions, then untied the gun and held it in his hand. He turned to the mule and smiled.

"Know whut this is, Jenny? Naw, yuh wouldn know! Yuhs jusa ol mule! Anyhow, this is a gun, n it kin shoot, by Gawd!"

He held the gun at arm's length. Whut t hell, Ahma shoot this thing! He looked at Jenny again.

"Lissen here, Jenny! When Ah pull this ol trigger, Ah don wan yuh t run n acka fool now!"

Jenny stood with head down, her short ears pricked straight. Dave walked off about twenty feet, held the gun far out from him at arm's length, and turned his head. Hell, he told himself, Ah ain afraid. The gun felt loose in his fingers; he waved it wildly for a moment. Then he shut his eyes and tightened his forefinger. Bloom! A report half deafened him and he thought his right hand was torn from his arm. He heard Jenny whinnying and galloping over the field, and he found himself on his knees, squeezing his fingers hard

between his legs. His hand was numb; he jammed it into his mouth, trying to warm it, trying to stop the pain. The gun lay at his feet. He did not quite know what had happened. He stood up and stared at the gun as though it were a living thing. He gritted his teeth and kicked the gun. Yuh almos broke mah arm! He turned to look for Jenny; she was far over the fields, tossing her head and kicking wildly.

"Hol on there, ol mule!"

When he caught up with her she stood trembling, walling[4] her big white eyes at him. The plow was far away; the traces had broken. Then Dave stopped short, looking, not believing. Jenny was bleeding. Her left side was red and wet with blood. He went closer. Lawd, have mercy! Wondah did Ah shoot this mule? He grabbed for Jenny's mane. She flinched, snorted, whirled, tossing her head.

"Hol on now! Hol on."

Then he saw the hole in Jenny's side, right between the ribs. It was round, wet, red. A crimson stream streaked down the front leg, flowing fast. Good Gawd! Ah wuzn't shootin at tha mule. He felt panic. He knew he had to stop that blood, or Jenny would bleed to death. He had never seen so much blood in all his life. He chased the mule for half a mile, trying to catch her. Finally she stopped, breathing hard, stumpy tail half arched. He caught her mane and led her back to where the plow and gun lay. Then he stooped and grabbed handfuls of damp black earth and tried to plug the bullet hole. Jenny shuddered, whinnied, and broke from him.

"Hol on! Hol on now!"

He tried to plug it again, but blood came anyhow. His fingers were hot and sticky. He rubbed dirt into his palms, trying to dry them. Then again he attempted to plug the bullet hole, but Jenny shied away, kicking her heels high. He stood helpless. He had to do something. He ran

---

3. **traces:** side straps or chains connecting the mule to the plow.

4. **walling:** rolling.

at Jenny; she dodged him. He watched a red stream of blood flow down Jenny's leg and form a bright pool at her feet.

"Jenny . . . Jenny," he called weakly.

His lips trembled. She's bleeding t death! He looked in the direction of home, wanting to go back, wanting to get help. But he saw the pistol lying in the damp black clay. He had a queer feeling that if he only did something, this would not be; Jenny would not be there bleeding to death.

When he went to her this time, she did not move. She stood with sleepy, dreamy eyes; and when he touched her she gave a low-pitched whinny and knelt to the ground, her front knees slopping in blood.

"Jenny . . . Jenny . . ." he whispered.

For a long time she held her neck erect; then her head sank, slowly. Her ribs swelled with a mighty heave and she went over.

Dave's stomach felt empty, very empty. He picked up the gun and held it gingerly between his thumb and forefinger. He buried it at the foot of a tree. He took a stick and tried to cover the pool of blood with dirt—but what was the use? There was Jenny lying with her mouth open and her eyes walled and glassy. He could not tell Jim Hawkins he had shot his mule. But he had to tell something. Yeah, Ah'll tell em Jenny started gittin wil n fell on the point of the plow. . . . But that would hardly happen to a mule. He walked across the field slowly, head down.

It was sunset. Two of Jim Hawkins' men were over near the edge of the woods digging a hole in which to bury Jenny. Dave was surrounded by a knot of people, all of whom were looking down at the dead mule.

"I don't see how in the world it happened," said Jim Hawkins for the tenth time.

The crowd parted and Dave's mother, father, and small brother pushed into the center.

"Where Dave?" his mother called.

"There he is," said Jim Hawkins.

His mother grabbed him.

"Whut happened, Dave? Whut yuh done?"

"Nothin."

"C mon, boy, talk," his father said.

Dave took a deep breath and told the story he knew nobody believed.

"Waal," he drawled. "Ah brung ol Jenny down here sos Ah could do mah plowin. Ah plowed bout two rows, just like yuh see." He stopped and pointed at the long rows of upturned earth. "Then somethin musta been wrong wid ol Jenny. She wouldn ack right a-tall. She started snortin n kickin her heels. Ah tried t hol her, but she pulled erway, rearin n goin in. Then when the point of the plow was stickin up in the air, she swung erroun n twisted herself back on it . . . She stuck herself n started t bleed. N fo Ah could do anything, she wuz dead."

"Did you ever hear of anything like that in all your life?" asked Jim Hawkins.

There were white and black standing in the crowd. They murmured. Dave's mother came close to him and looked hard into his face. "Tell the truth, Dave," she said.

"Looks like a bullet hole to me," said one man.

"Dave, whut yuh do wid the gun?" his mother asked.

The crowd surged in, looking at him. He jammed his hands into his pockets, shook his head slowly from left to right, and backed away. His eyes were wide and painful.

"Did he hava gun?" asked Jim Hawkins.

"By Gawd, Ah tol yuh tha wuz a gun wound," said a man, slapping his thigh.

His father caught his shoulders and shook him till his teeth rattled.

"Tell whut happened, yuh rascal! Tell whut . . ."

Dave looked at Jenny's stiff legs and began to cry.

"Whut yuh do wid tha gun?" his mother asked.

"Whut wuz he doin wida gun?" his father asked.

"Come on and tell the truth," said Hawkins. "Ain't nobody going to hurt you . . ."

His mother crowded close to him.

"Did yuh shoot tha mule, Dave?"

Roy Stryker Collection, Photographic Archives, University of Louisville, Kentucky, Negative 78.9.225.

All the crowd was laughing now. They stood on tiptoe and poked heads over one another's shoulders.

"Well, boy, looks like yuh done bought a dead mule! Hahaha!"

"Ain tha ershame."

"Hohohohoho."

Dave stood, head down, twisting his feet in the dirt.

"Well, you needn't worry about it, Bob," said Jim Hawkins to Dave's father. "Just let the boy keep on working and pay me two dollars a month."

"Whut yuh wan fer yo mule, Mistah Hawkins?"

Jim Hawkins screwed up his eyes.

Dave cried, seeing blurred white and black faces.

"Ahh ddinn gggo tt sshooot hher . . . Ah ssswear ffo Gawd Ahh ddin. . . . Ah wuz a-tryin t sssee ef the old gggun would sshoot—"

"Where yuh git the gun from?" his father asked.

"Ah got it from Joe, at the sto."

"Where yuh git the money?"

"Ma give it t me."

"He kept worryin me, Bob. Ah had t. Ah tol im t bring the gun right back t me . . . It was fer yuh, the gun."

"But how yuh happen to shoot that mule?" asked Jim Hawkins.

"Ah wuzn shootin at the mule, Mistah Hawkins. The gun jumped when Ah pulled the trigger . . . N fo Ah knowed anythin Jenny was there a-bleedin."

Somebody in the crowd laughed. Jim Hawkins walked close to Dave and looked into his face.

"Well, looks like you have bought you a mule, Dave."

"Ah swear fo Gawd, Ah didn go t kill the mule, Mistah Hawkins!"

"But you killed her!"

"Fifty dollars."

"Whut yuh do wid tha gun?" Dave's father demanded.

Dave said nothing.

"Yuh wan me t take a tree n beat yuh till yuh talk!"

"Nawsuh!"

"Whut yuh do wid it?"

"Ah throwed it erway."

"Where?"

"Ah . . . Ah throwed it in the creek."

"Waal, c mon home. N firs thing in the mawnin git to tha creek n fin tha gun."

"Yessuh."

"What yuh pay fer it?"

"Two dollahs."

"Take tha gun n git yo money back n carry it t Mistah Hawkins, yuh hear? N don fergit Ahma lam you black bottom good fer this! Now march yosef on home, suh!"

Dave turned and walked slowly. He heard people laughing. Dave glared, his eyes welling with tears. Hot anger bubbled in him. Then he swallowed and stumbled on.

THE MAN WHO WAS ALMOST A MAN   **1053**

That night Dave did not sleep. He was glad that he had gotten out of killing the mule so easily, but he was hurt. Something hot seemed to turn over inside him each time he remembered how they had laughed. He tossed on his bed, feeling his hard pillow. *N Pa says he's gonna beat me . . .* He remembered other beatings, and his back quivered. *Naw, naw, Ah sho don wan im t beat me tha way no mo. Dam em all!* Nobody ever gave him anything. All he did was work. *They treat me like a mule, n then they beat me.* He gritted his teeth. *N Ma had t tell on me.*

Well, if he had to, he would take old man Hawkins that two dollars. But that meant selling the gun. And he wanted to keep that gun. Fifty dollars for a dead mule.

He turned over, thinking how he had fired the gun. He had an itch to fire it again. *Ef other men kin shoota gun, by Gawd, Ah kin!* He was still, listening. *Mebbe they all sleepin now.* The house was still. He heard the soft breathing of his brother. *Yes, now!* He would go down and get that gun and see if he could fire it! He eased out of bed and slipped into overalls.

The moon was bright. He ran almost all the way to the edge of the woods. He stumbled over the ground, looking for the spot where he had buried the gun. *Yeah, here it is.* Like a hungry dog scratching for a bone, he pawed it up. He puffed his black cheeks and blew dirt from the trigger and barrel. He broke it and found four cartridges unshot. He looked around; the fields were filled with silence and moonlight. He clutched the gun stiff and hard in his fingers. But, as soon as he wanted to pull the trigger, he shut his eyes and turned his head. *Naw, Ah can't shoot wid mah eyes closed n mah head turned.* With effort he held his eyes open; then he

squeezed. *Blooooom!* He was stiff, not breathing. The gun was still in his hands. *Dammit, he'd done it.* He fired again. *Blooooom!* He smiled. *Blooooom! Blooooom! Click, click.* There! It was empty. *If anybody could shoot a gun, he could.* He put the gun into his hip pocket and started across the fields.

When he reached the top of a ridge he stood straight and proud in the moonlight, looking at Jim Hawkins' big white house, feeling the gun sagging in his pocket. *Lawd, ef Ah had just one mo bullet Ah'd taka shot at tha house. Ah'd like t scare ol man Hawkins jusa little . . . Jusa enough t let im know Dave Saunders is a man.*

To his left the road curved, running to the tracks of the Illinois Central. He jerked his head, listening. From far off came a faint *hoooof-hoooof; hoooof-hoooof; hoooof-hoooof. . . .* He stood rigid. *Two dollahs a mont. Les see now . . . Tha means it'll take bout two years. Shucks! Ah'll be dam!*

He started down the road, toward the tracks. *Yeah, here she comes!* He stood beside the track and held himself stiffly. *Here she comes, erroun the ben . . . C mon, yuh slow poke! C mon!* He had his hand on his gun; something quivered in his stomach. Then the train thundered past, the gray and brown box cars rumbling and clinking. He gripped the gun tightly; then he jerked his hand out of his pocket. *Ah betcha Bill wouldn't do it! Ah betcha . . .* The cars slid past, steel grinding upon steel. *Ahm ridin yuh ternight, so hep me Gawd!* He was hot all over. He hesitated just a moment; then he grabbed, pulled atop of a car, and lay flat. He felt his pocket; the gun was still there. Ahead the long rails were glinting in the moonlight, stretching away, away to somewhere, somewhere where he could be a man . . . . ❖

Thinking through the LITERATURE

Connect to the Literature

1. What Do You Think? How did you respond to the ending of this story? Share your ideas with your classmates.

Comprehension Check
- How does Dave account for the accident with the mule?
- How does the crowd respond to Dave's mistake?
- What are Dave's reasons for getting out of town?

Think Critically

2. **ACTIVE READING** **MAKING JUDGMENTS** Review the diagram you made in your **READER'S NOTEBOOK**. How would you judge Dave's ability to make sound decisions? Does he behave like an adult? Support your judgments.

3. Does owning a gun give Dave what he wants? Explain.

> THINK ABOUT
> - why Dave wants to own a gun
> - how he handles the responsibility of a gun
> - how others treat him after he buys a gun
> - how he deals with consequences

4. Do you feel sorry for Dave? Explain why or why not. How do you think Richard Wright feels about him?

5. What do you predict might happen to Dave in the future?

Extend Interpretations

6. What If? What would Dave's life have been like if he had not shot the mule?

7. Different Perspectives "Almos' A Man," an earlier version of "The Man Who Was Almost a Man," features an adult character with a wife and child. How would you view Dave's actions at the end of the story if he were a husband and father?

8. Critic's Corner Richard Wright is generally viewed as a protest writer. In this story, what do you think he is fighting for or against?

9. Comparing Texts Think about James Baldwin's advice in "My Dungeon Shook: Letter to My Nephew" on page 959. What advice might Baldwin have for Dave Saunders?

10. Connect to Life Discuss other cultural customs and practices that signify the passage of youth to maturity.

Literary Analysis

POINT OF VIEW One reason that the reader gains insight into Dave's character is that the story is told from **third-person limited point of view,** a narrative perspective used by many modernist fiction writers. The narrator acts as a reporter with inside information. In "The Man Who Was Almost a Man," the narrator not only recounts the external events of the story but also gives voice to the inner workings of Dave's mind, expressed in **dialect.**

Paired Activity Reread the first paragraph of the story, and notice the way Richard Wright weaves dialect into the narration. Point out where the narration stops and Dave's thoughts begin. With a partner, read the first paragraph aloud, with one of you reading the narration and the other reading Dave's thoughts. What effect does Wright achieve by setting up his story this way? What if Dave's thoughts were not included in the story at all? Discuss these questions with your partner.

REVIEW **IRONY** **Irony** is a contrast between what is expected and what actually exists or happens. **Dramatic irony** occurs when readers know more about a situation in a story than the characters do. **Situational irony** is a contrast between what a character expects to happen and what actually happens. Discuss the many instances of situational irony in this story. For example, look at the ways in which owning a gun backfires, so to speak, on Dave.

Choices & CHALLENGES

Writing Options

1. Defining Adulthood What does it mean to be an adult? Write a definition of adulthood based on your reading of this story and on your own observations and experiences. Share your definition with the class.

2. Letter Home At the end of the story, Dave hops on a train to go "somewhere where he could be a man." Write the letter that Dave might eventually send to his family.

3. Editorial: Dave's Situation Write an editorial in which you agree or disagree with the following statement: Dave is merely a victim of circumstances. Support your position with evidence.

Activities & Explorations

1. Dramatic Reading Wright uses dialect to capture the way his characters talk. To appreciate the sound of the characters' spoken words, work with a small group of classmates to plan and present a dramatic reading of this story. ~ **PERFORMING**

2. Charting Expenses Dave is paid $2.00 a month, roughly equivalent to $100.00 a month today. If Dave were a teenager today, how long would he have to work to buy the following items: a pair of sneakers, a CD or tape, a meal at a fast-food restaurant, a concert ticket? Record your findings in a chart or a graph. ~ **MATH AND ECONOMICS**

3. Film Critics' Circle View the video based on the story "The Man Who Was Almost a Man." How well do you think the film version succeeds in bringing the story to life? What moments did you find especially realistic? Discuss your responses.

~ **VIEWING AND REPRESENTING**

VIDEO Literature in Performance

Item	Cost
Pair of sneakers	
CD or tape	
Fast food	
Concert ticket	

Richard Wright
1908–1960

Other Works
Native Son
Lawd Today
Black Boy
White Man, Listen!
American Hunger

Barriers of Prejudice and Poverty Richard Wright, the son of a poor sharecropper, was born in Mississippi. He endured a childhood marked by gnawing hunger, physical beatings, and an intense internal struggle against the religious and racial restrictions imposed on him by his family and his culture. To escape the poverty of the rural South, his father moved the family to Memphis, Tennessee. Unable to find work, however, Wright's frustrated father abandoned the family, and Wright was raised by his ailing mother and later by his stern grandmother. Often left alone while his relatives worked, Wright encountered the violence of the ghetto streets at age 6. He wrote later that it was only through books that he managed to stay alive, books that he got by borrowing a white man's library card.

Literary Fame Wright's first story was published in an African-American newspaper when he was 15. After winning first prize in a writing contest sponsored by *Story* magazine, he published his first collection of stories, *Uncle Tom's Children*. Two years later in 1940, Wright gained international fame for his novel *Native Son*. His fiction and his autobiographies, *Black Boy* and *American Hunger*, expose the brutal racism in American life.

Author Activity

The Creation of Characters Read "How 'Bigger' Was Born," the introduction to *Native Son* in which Wright describes the real-life models for Bigger Thomas, the main character in the novel. Compare Dave to Wright's various portraits of Bigger.

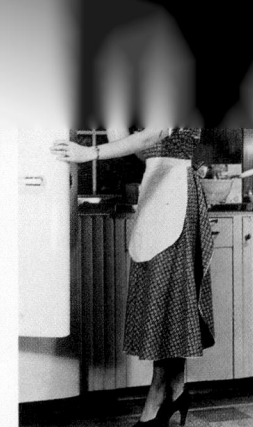

Mirror

Poetry by SYLVIA PLATH

Self in 1958

Poetry by ANNE SEXTON

Comparing Literature

Traditions Across Time: The Lonely Self

T.S. Eliot's "The Love Song of J. Alfred Prufrock," which was first published in 1915, features a character who is painfully aware of himself. This sort of modernist character reappears in "Mirror" and "Self in 1958." Both poems portray self-conscious women who fret over their identities.

Points of Comparison As you read, compare the modernist characters in all three of these poems, noting the troubling emotions that preoccupy their thoughts.

Build Background

True Confessions Both Sylvia Plath and Anne Sexton broke new ground by writing openly and honestly about the reality of their lives in the 1950s and early 1960s. Like Charlotte Perkins Gilman and, to some extent, Kate Chopin before them, Plath and Sexton expressed turbulent and often violent emotions. Their poems read like confessions in which they expose their troubled lives in startling images that some readers still find shocking. "Mirror" begins very much like a riddle, asking the reader to figure out who is speaking, and then explores a woman's feelings about aging. Plath wrote the poem just four days before her 29th birthday and a few months before the birth of her second child. In "Self in 1958," Sexton expresses her feelings about her life two years after a suicide attempt and the first of several hospitalizations for psychiatric problems.

Focus Your Reading

LITERARY ANALYSIS **SPEAKER** The **speaker** of a poem, like the narrator of a story, is the voice that talks to the reader. In "Mirror" and "Self in 1958," the speaker is someone or something other than the poet. In each of these poems, the speaker is a **persona,** a character of the poet's invention who likely acts as a disguise for some aspect of the poet's personality. Note that the speaker in Plath's poem is a mirror and in Sexton's poem, a doll.

ACTIVE READING **LINKING TITLE AND THEME** The **title** of a literary work often suggests its **theme,** or the main idea that explains the underlying meaning of the work. As you read "Mirror" and "Self in 1958," think about how these titles provide you with clues that hint at the central message expressed in the poems.

READER'S NOTEBOOK Create cluster diagrams like the ones shown and fill them in with details from the poems that seem to point to key ideas suggested by the titles.

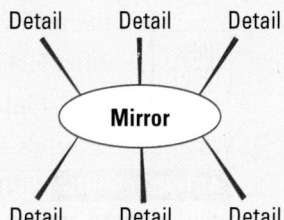

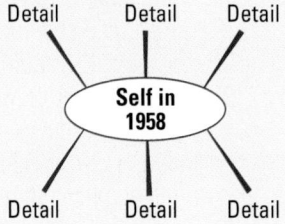

Mirror

S Y L V I A   P L A T H

I am silver and exact. I have no preconceptions.[1]
Whatever I see I swallow immediately
Just as it is, unmisted by love or dislike.
I am not cruel, only truthful—
5   The eye of a little god, four-cornered.
Most of the time I meditate on the opposite wall.
It is pink, with speckles. I have looked at it so long
I think it is a part of my heart. But it flickers.
Faces and darkness separate us over and over.

10   Now I am a lake. A woman bends over me,
Searching my reaches for what she really is.
Then she turns to those liars, the candles or the moon.
I see her back, and reflect it faithfully.
She rewards me with tears and an agitation of hands.
15   I am important to her. She comes and goes.
Each morning it is her face that replaces the darkness.
In me she has drowned a young girl, and in me an old woman
Rises toward her day after day, like a terrible fish.

---

1. **preconceptions:** opinions formed before adequate
   knowledge or understanding is achieved.

Thinking Through the Literature

1. What images from the poem linger in your mind?

2. Why do you think the mirror is so important to the woman?

3. In your opinion, is the mirror "not cruel, only truthful"?

   THINK ABOUT
   - the reality it reflects
   - what feelings it has
   - how it interprets the woman's reflection

4. What is the mirror's attitude toward the woman?

5. **ACTIVE READING   LINKING TITLE AND THEME**   In what ways did the title help you zero in on the **theme?** Review the cluster diagram you made in your READER'S NOTEBOOK.

SELF IN 1958

ANNE SEXTON

What is reality?
I am a plaster doll; I pose
with eyes that cut open without landfall or nightfall
upon some shellacked and grinning person,
5 eyes that open, blue, steel, and close.
Am I approximately an I. Magnin transplant?
I have hair, black angel,
black-angel-stuffing to comb,
nylon legs, luminous arms
10 and some advertised clothes.

GUIDE FOR READING

6 I. Magnin: a department store that sells expensive clothing.

1–10 What image of the speaker do you form from these first ten lines of the poem? How would you describe her self-image?

I live in a doll's house
with four chairs,
a counterfeit table, a flat roof
and a big front door.
15 Many have come to such a small crossroad.
There is an iron bed,
(Life enlarges, life takes aim)
a cardboard floor,
windows that flash open on someone's city,
20 and little more.

Someone plays with me,
plants me in the all-electric kitchen,
Is this what Mrs. Rombauer said?
Someone pretends with me—
25 I am walled in solid by their noise—
or puts me upon their straight bed.
They think I am me!
Their warmth? Their warmth is not a friend!
They pry my mouth for their cups of gin
30 and their stale bread.

What is reality
to this synthetic doll
who should smile, who should shift gears,
should spring the doors open in a wholesome disorder,
35 and have no evidence of ruin or fears?
But I would cry,
rooted into the wall that
was once my mother,
if I could remember how
40 and if I had the tears.

15 *Crossroad* can refer to an intersection or to a crucial point. What is the crossroad referred to here?

11–20 How does the speaker seem to feel about her home?

23 **Mrs. Rombauer:** Irma Rombauer, author of *The Joy of Cooking,* a classic cookbook containing advice and instruction as well as recipes.

21–30 Who do you think is the "someone" (and the "they") that plays with and walls in the speaker?

Thinking *through the* LITERATURE

Connect to the Literature

1. **What Do You Think?**
   What do you think of the speaker's description of herself in "Self in 1958"?

   Comprehension Check
   - How would you describe the speaker's physical appearance?
   - What keeps the speaker from crying?
   - How is the speaker's home furnished?

Think Critically

2. Why do you think the speaker describes herself as a doll? Why can't she be herself?

   THINK ABOUT
   - how the speaker looks and acts
   - the limitations of her existence in her house
   - the expectations that others have of her
   - the feelings she has but cannot express

3. Why do you think the speaker has lost the ability to cry?

4. The speaker questions the reality of her existence because she feels so "synthetic," or fake. What might make her life more authentic, or real?

5. **ACTIVE READING** **LINKING TITLE AND THEME**
   Review the cluster diagram you made in your **READER'S NOTEBOOK**. Based on the details you recorded, expand the title into a general statement that explains the theme, or main idea, of the poem.

Extend Interpretations

6. **Different Perspectives** Confessional poetry in general has sometimes been attacked for its excessive emotional and overly personal content. Do you find these flaws in "Self in 1958"? Why or why not? Defend your view.

7. **Critic's Corner** Anne Sexton once remarked that poetry "should be a shock to the senses. It should also hurt." Do you think this statement holds true for "Self in 1958"? Cite phrases or lines from the poem to support your view.

8. **Connect to Life** Do you think "Self in 1958" expresses issues that still concern women today? Support your response.

9. **Points of Comparison** What aspects of their lives do Prufrock in "The Love Song of J. Alfred Prufrock," the woman in "Mirror" and the speaker in "Self in 1958" find especially disturbing? Which of these characters do you think is the most self-conscious? Explain.

Literary Analysis

SPEAKER *Persona* is a Latin word meaning "actor's mask." In each of these poems, the poet invents a fictional character, or a **persona,** to play the role of the **speaker.** Surprisingly, the persona in "Mirror" and "Self in 1958" is not a human, but rather an inanimate object, capable of speech and thought. Plath and Sexton use a persona in these poems to provide a different and original perspective on a woman's self-image.

Activity If the speakers of "Mirror" and "Self in 1958" were women, instead of inanimate objects, how might the poems be different? Rewrite a stanza from each of these poems so that a woman is the speaker. Then read aloud the original stanzas and your revisions to the class. Discuss which versions are more inventive and surprising.

Writing Options

1. Diary of a Housewife Write a series of journal entries from the point of view of the speaker in "Self in 1958." Record her confessions about her daily life. Refer to the poem for ideas.

2. Poetic Riddle Using "Mirror" as a model, write a poem in the form of a riddle. Use the first-person "I" as you speak in the voice of an inanimate object. Include clues that will help the reader guess your identity. Save your poem in your **Working Portfolio.**

3. Points of Comparison
Write a brief essay in which you compare and contrast ideas about fears of growing old as expressed in "Mirror" and "The Love Song of J. Alfred Prufrock." Cite evidence from both poems to support your ideas.

Writing Handbook
See page 1281: Compare and Contrast

Activities & Explorations

1. Face-to-Face Conversation With a partner, act out a conversation between the woman in "Mirror" and the speaker of "Self in 1958."
~ PERFORMING

2. A Doll's House Sketch a portrait of the speaker of "Self in 1958" in her house, based on details she provides in the poem. Share your portrait with the class.
~ ART

> "Prufrock"
> worries
> about
> baldness
>
> Woman in "Mirror" cries at her reflection

Inquiry & Research

1. Women's Roles Both of these poems touch upon the reality of women's lives in the 1950s and early 1960s. Do research and interview women in your family or community to find out about women's roles at that time. Report your findings to the class.

2. Confessional Poets Find out what other poets are classified with Plath and Sexton as confessional poets. Read several poems by one of these poets, then choose one to present to the class. Discuss what the poem reveals about the poet's private life.

Sylvia Plath
1932–1963

Other Works
The Colossus
Crossing the Water
Winter Trees
Ariel

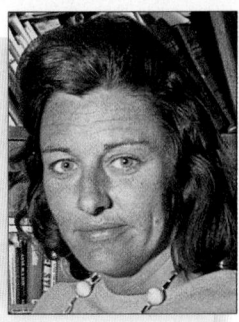

Anne Sexton
1928–1974

Other Works
All My Pretty Ones
The Awful Rowing Toward God
The Book of Folly

Turbulent Emotions Sylvia Plath was described by the poet Robert Lowell, one of her teachers, as having an "air of maddening docility." Beneath that obedient surface, however, simmered the rage and rebellion that was to inform her best work—and that also triggered bouts of depression.

Talented Coed When she was a junior at Smith College, Plath won *Mademoiselle's* fiction contest and was given a month's apprenticeship at the magazine's New York editorial offices. Shortly after her apprenticeship, she became seriously depressed and attempted suicide—an experience detailed in her only novel, *The Bell Jar.* After psychiatric treatment, Plath eventually returned to Smith and graduated with high honors.

Poetic Outburst After graduation, Plath studied at Cambridge University in England, where she met and married the British poet Ted Hughes. Unfortunately, the marriage deteriorated, and in 1962 Plath left Hughes and took her two children to live in a London flat. As a result of the stress, Plath's buried anger rose to the surface, and she expressed her intense feelings in a frenzy of writing.

Fatal Impulses In February 1963, Plath again experienced acute depression, and this time ended her life. Her last poems, considered her best work, were published in *Ariel* after her death. Plath was posthumously awarded a Pulitzer Prize for *Collected Poems.*

Buried Self Anne Sexton graduated from junior college, worked as a fashion model, married at 19, settled in a Boston suburb, and had two daughters. Despite the seeming normality of her life, Sexton suffered repeated mental breakdowns and was haunted by thoughts of suicide. "Until I was twenty-eight," she said, "I had a kind of buried self who didn't know she could do anything but make white sauce and diaper babies. I didn't know I had any creative depths. I was a victim of the American Dream, the bourgeois, middle-class dream. All I wanted was a little piece of life, to be married, to have children. I thought the nightmares, the visions, the demons would go away if there was enough love to put them down. . . . But one can't build little white picket fences to keep nightmares out."

Poetry as Therapy At the suggestion of her psychiatrist, Sexton began writing poetry in her late 20s. In 1958 she attended Robert Lowell's poetry workshop at Boston University, where she and Sylvia Plath became friends. Sexton's first volume of poetry, *To Bedlam and Part Way Back*, details her initial mental breakdown, subsequent hospital stay, and attempt to reconcile with her family upon her return home. Struggling with depression all her life, Sexton still managed to publish ten books of poetry before her death from suicide just shy of her 46th birthday.

Comparing Literature: Assessment Practice

In writing assessments, you will sometimes be asked to synthesize, or put together, information from a variety of selections to form an overall picture. You are now going to practice writing an essay with this focus.

PART 1 **Reading the Prompt**

Read the entire prompt carefully. Then read through it again, looking for key words that help you identify the purpose of the essay and decide how to approach it.

Writing Prompt

Many of the literary selections in Unit 6, Part 2, portray characters in despair. Describe the plight ❶ of the modernist character, pulling together examples from two selections by early modernists ❷ and one by a later modernist—Sexton or Plath.

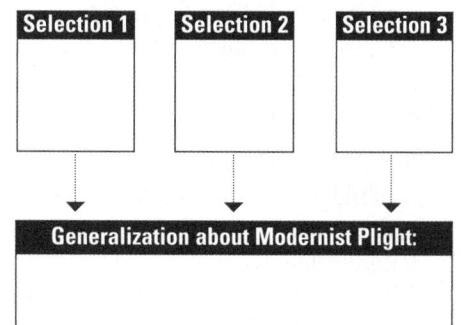

STRATEGIES
IN ACTION

❶ **Describe,** or name, important aspects of the modernist character's plight.

❷ Gather **details** about different characters' unhappy circumstances and find connections.

PART 2 **Planning a Synthesis Essay**

- Choose three selections to explore.

- Create a diagram like the one shown and fill it in with details about the characters' unhappiness.

- Note recurring patterns.

- State a generalization about the modernist character's plight that covers the examples you have chosen.

What Makes Characters Unhappy?

Selection 1	Selection 2	Selection 3

Generalization about Modernist Plight:

PART 3 **Drafting Your Essay**

Introduction Begin by stating your subject—the plight of the modernist character. Identify the authors and titles of the three selections you are exploring.

Organization Arrange the literary examples logically. For instance, you might first cite examples from the early modernist selections, followed by an example from the later modernist selection. Cite details that most strongly illustrate the characters' unhappiness.

Conclusion Bring the details you presented into focus by stating what the characters have in common.

Revision Allow time to review your work. Make sure it is clear, well-supported, and free from mistakes.

Writing Handbook
See page 1281: Explanatory Writing

The Nick Adams Stories

ERNEST HEMINGWAY

A boy goes on a camping trip with his father in Michigan. A young man is held hostage inside a cafe by two thugs. A soldier fights on the battlefields of World War I. A troubled veteran tries to heal his war wounds. These are just a sampling of Nick Adams's experiences depicted in the short stories from this collection, featuring one of the most memorable characters in American fiction.

Invisible Man

RALPH ELLISON

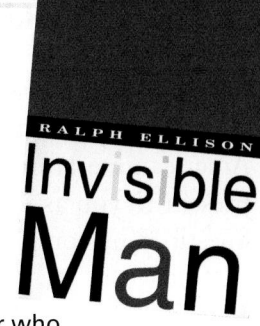

The unnamed narrator, an African-American man, announces, "I am invisible, understand, simply because others refuse to see me." Ellison's critically acclaimed novel centers on the narrator's odyssey to discover who he is in a blind, uncaring world. His search for his identity is a complex quest, which takes him from the deep South to the North.

And Even *More* . . .

Books

The Portable Dorothy Parker
DOROTHY PARKER
A collection of literary works by this modernist writer, known for her biting wit.

A Long Day's Journey into Night
EUGENE O'NEILL
A drama about a troubled family and fractured relationships.

A Streetcar Named Desire
TENNESSEE WILLIAMS
A drama about a woman trapped by her own inadequacies.

Other Media

Tom and Viv
Feature film about T. S. Eliot's marriage to his first wife, starring Willem Dafoe and Miranda Richardson. Miramax Films. (VIDEOCASSETTE)

Black Boy
A documentary exploring the life and literary career of Richard Wright. Mississippi Educational Television/BBC. (VIDEOCASSETTE)

Voices & Visions: Sylvia Plath
A documentary of the poet, including dramatic readings of her works. Mystic Fire Video. (VIDEOCASSETTE)

The Heart Is a Lonely Hunter

CARSON MCCULLERS

Four isolated people—a young aspiring composer, a would-be labor organizer, a cafe owner, and an African-American doctor—find comfort in their relationship with John Singer, who cannot hear or speak. This moving novel about loneliness is set in a small Southern community.

The Modern Age

How does the literature from the Harlem Renaissance writers and other modern writers differ from earlier American literature? What new challenges did this unit present to you as a reader and a writer? Explore these questions by completing one or more of the options below.

Rush Hour, New York (1915), Max Weber. Oil on canvas, 36¼″ × 30¼″. National Gallery of Art, Washington, D.C., gift of the Avalon Foundation (1970.6.1 PA).

Reflecting on the Unit

OPTION 1

Ways to Respond to Prejudice Review the selections in Part 1, "A New Cultural Identity." What possible responses to prejudice and mistreatment do they suggest? Think about the range of responses to prejudice shown in the selections. Then, with a small group of classmates, discuss which responses to prejudice you think are the most effective.

OPTION 2

What's New? Recall the opening quotation of this unit: "Make it new!" What do you think the writers in this unit have done to make their writing different from earlier American literature? Jot down your ideas about each selection, and then, in a paragraph, explain which selection seems most innovative to you.

THINK ABOUT
- the use of rhyme and other techniques in the poetry selections
- the subject matter of all the selections
- the attitudes expressed
- the writers' styles

OPTION 3

The Iceberg Principle Recall Ernest Hemingway's comment that in his writing, seven-eighths of the story is concealed. Is that true for other selections in Part 2 of this unit? Working with a small group, create an iceberg chart for each selection, with a line dividing the iceberg into one-eighth above and seven-eighths below. Above the line, write what is stated or shown about the characters. Below the line, write what the reader must infer. Which selections require readers to make the most inferences?

Self ASSESSMENT

 READER'S NOTEBOOK

To explore how your understanding of modern literature has developed over the course of the unit, jot down words and phrases that you associate with this literature. Then circle at least three words and phrases that you think describe modern literature most accurately. Pair up with a classmate and compare your list with your partner's, explaining your choices.

Reviewing Literary Concepts

OPTION 1

Modernist Characters and Techniques What defines a modernist character? What are modernist literary techniques? For each selection from Part 2, identify modernist qualities of the main character(s) and/or modernist techniques used by the writer, such as understatement, irony, or stream of consciousness. Provide examples from the selections. Then write two paragraphs summarizing modernist character traits and literary techniques.

OPTION 2

Comparing Poets' Styles You have read several important American poets in this unit: Langston Hughes, Robert Frost, T. S. Eliot, and Gwendolyn Brooks. In fact, you have read more than one work by Hughes, Frost, and Brooks. What is distinctive about the styles of these four poets? Gather in a small group and list recognizable features of each poet's work in a chart. To test your knowledge, find another poem by one of these authors, circulate it without a title or author name, and see if your classmates can guess who wrote it.

Self ASSESSMENT

📖 READER'S NOTEBOOK

Thinking back over the literary concepts discussed in this unit, look for connections and distinctions between them. If you are unsure of any of these concepts, consult the **Glossary of Literary Terms** (page 1342) for definitions.

rhythm	literary criticism
iambic pentameter	blank verse
	form
extended metaphor	stream of consciousness
figurative language	imagery
autobiographical essay	third-person limited point of view
open letter	dramatic irony
paradox	situational irony
analogy	speaker
diction	persona

🗀 Building Your Portfolio

- **Writing Options** For several of the Writing Options in this unit, you either wrote a personal response to an author's ideas or imagined how two authors would respond to each other. Which of these assignments best demonstrates your understanding of an author? Explain in a cover letter and add the assignment to your **Presentation Portfolio.** 🗀

- **Writing Workshop** Earlier in the unit you wrote an Historical Research Report about the Harlem Renaissance or some other topic of interest. Evaluate your report—what was the most interesting discovery you made as you researched? What more would you like to find out? How clear is your presentation of facts? Answer these questions in an attached cover note and place your research report in your **Presentation Portfolio.** 🗀

- **Additional Activities** Review the assignments you completed under **Activities & Explorations** and **Inquiry & Research.** Keep a record in your portfolio of any you feel are representative of your best work.

Self ASSESSMENT

At this point your **Presentation Portfolio** 🗀 probably has a considerable variety of your work. Think about what abilities you have developed since the beginning of the year and what kinds of writing or activities you would like to experiment with before the end of the year.

Setting GOALS

As you read the selections in this unit, you might have wondered how economic, social, or historical events affected the way the literature was written. How can you use the knowledge you have gained from other subjects to broaden your understanding of the first four decades of the 20th century? Think of a few questions you would like to have answered.

UNIT SEVEN

War

ABROAD and Conflict

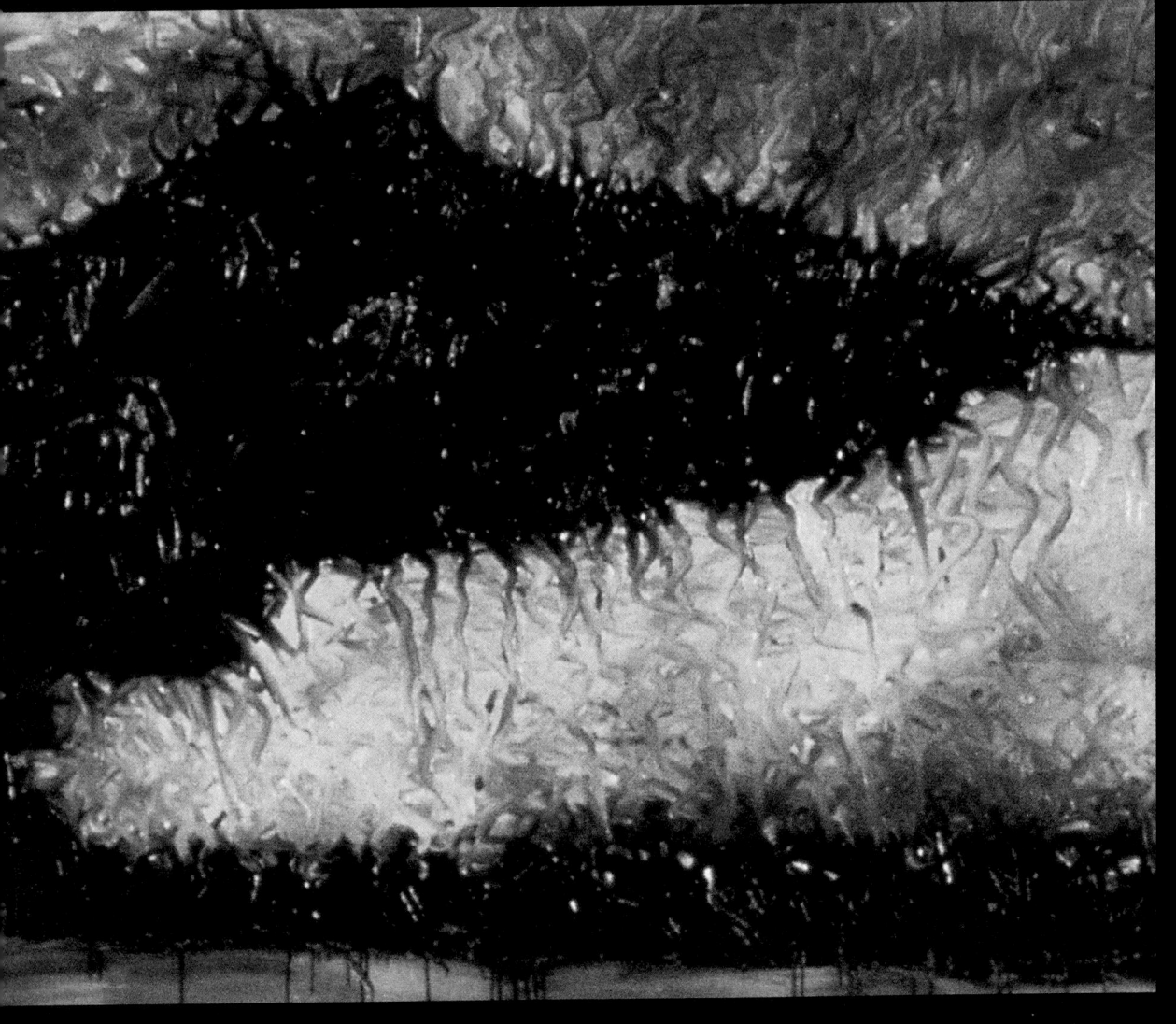

at HOME →

War is a poor chisel
to carve out tomorrows.

MARTIN LUTHER KING, JR.

MINISTER AND CIVIL RIGHTS LEADER

Ominous Omen (1987), Rupert Garcia. Chalk, linseed oil, oil paint on canvas, 47″ × 130″, courtesy of Rupert Garcia; Rena Bransten Gallery, San Francisco; and Galerie Claude Samuel, Paris. Copyright © Rupert Garcia.

War
ABROAD and Conflict at HOME

EVENTS IN AMERICAN LITERATURE

1940 — **1960**

1940 John Steinbeck wins Pulitzer Prize in fiction for *The Grapes of Wrath*

1945 Richard Wright details coming of age in *Black Boy*; Randall Jarrell publishes poem "The Death of the Ball Turret Gunner"

1947 Tennessee Williams's *A Streetcar Named Desire* is first produced

1951 J. D. Salinger's novel *Catcher in the Rye* is published

1952 Bernard Malamud publishes baseball novel, *The Natural*

1953 Arthur Miller's *The Crucible*, set during the Salem witch trials in 1692, explores contemporary events surrounding McCarthy hearings

1961 Joseph Heller's satirical war novel, *Catch-22*, is published

1962 John Steinbeck wins Nobel Prize for literature

1963 Joyce Carol Oates publishes her first book

1969 Kurt Vonnegut publishes *Slaughterhouse-Five*; N. Scott Momaday's *House Made of Dawn* wins Pulitzer Prize

EVENTS IN THE UNITED STATES

1940 — **1960**

1941 The Japanese bomb Pearl Harbor, bringing United States into World War II

1945 United States drops two atomic bombs on Japan, ending war in Pacific

1950 Senator Joseph McCarthy claims Communist spies have infiltrated government bureaus; thousands of people are falsely accused of treasonous acts

1953 Korean War ends after three years of fighting between Communist troops and UN-sponsored international forces.

1954 Ruling in *Brown* v. *Board of Education*, Supreme Court declares segregated schools unconstitutional

1963 President John F. Kennedy is assassinated in Dallas

1964 Congress passes Civil Rights Act of 1964

1965 First U.S. combat forces land in Vietnam; Malcolm X is assassinated

1967 Thurgood Marshall becomes first African-American justice on Supreme Court

1968 Assassinations of Martin Luther King, Jr., and Robert F. Kennedy

EVENTS IN THE WORLD

1940 — **1960**

1940 German forces conquer much of Europe

1945 Germany surrenders to Allies

1948 State of Israel is founded; South African policy of apartheid begins

1949 Communists gain control of China

1957 Soviet Union launches *Sputnik*, first space satellite

1960 Seventeen African countries gain independence

1966 Mao Zedong launches Cultural Revolution in China (to 1976)

1967 Six-Day War erupts between Israel and Arab nations

PERIOD PIECES

Console TV from 1948

The look of the 1960s

Early digital watch

1980

1970 Maya Angelou publishes autobiographical *I Know Why the Caged Bird Sings*

1983 *The House on Mango Street* by Sandra Cisneros is published

1985 Anne Tyler publishes *The Accidental Tourist*

1989 Amy Tan's *The Joy Luck Club* is published

1990 Tim O'Brien's *The Things They Carried* is published

1993 Toni Morrison wins Nobel Prize for literature

1980

1969 U.S. astronauts land on moon

1974 President Richard M. Nixon resigns to avoid impeachment over Watergate scandal

1975 First successful home VCR appears

1977 First practical home computer, Apple II, hits market

1981 First space shuttle, *Columbia*, is launched; Sandra Day O'Connor is first woman appointed to U.S. Supreme Court

1989 Oil tanker *Exxon Valdez* runs aground, creating huge oil spill along Alaskan coast

1991 Persian Gulf War breaks out, and United States leads Allied coalition against Iraq

1995 Murrah Federal Building in Oklahoma City is bombed

1996 Madeleine Albright becomes first woman secretary of state

1997 Unmanned probe *Pathfinder* lands on Mars and sends back stunning pictures

1980

1975 South Vietnam surrenders as North Vietnamese troops occupy Saigon

1979 Egypt's Anwar Sadat and Israel's Menachem Begin sign treaty ending war between Egypt and Israel; Soviet Union invades Afghanistan

1985 Mikhail Gorbachev comes to power in Soviet Union and initiates reforms

1987 Palestinians begin *intifada* ("shaking off") against Israeli rule

1989 Student demonstrators in China are killed in Tiananmen Square

1991 Soviet Union breaks up into 15 republics; South Africa begins repeal of apartheid laws

1992 Serbs begin war against Muslims and Croats in former Yugoslavia

1994 Nelson Mandela is elected president of South Africa

Remembering the Wars

World War II

World War II was a catastrophe of epic dimensions. Never before had so many soldiers fought. Never before had such whole-sale slaughter occurred. When the war finally ended in 1945, more than 78 million people had been killed or wounded. For the first time in history, more civilians than soldiers had died in a war. Adolf Hitler and the National Socialist German Workers' party, commonly called the Nazis, came to power in 1933, at the height of the Great Depression. Full of passionate intensity, Hitler set out to avenge Germany's defeat in World War I and to create a new German state called the Third Reich. He told his followers, "Close your eyes to pity! Act brutally!" Like a tidal wave, the German army overran Europe. By June 1940, British troops had retreated from Dunkirk across the English Channel.

As the Nazis surged across Europe, Hitler targeted certain groups for extermination—political dissenters, homosexuals, mental patients, Gypsies, Poles, Slavs, and especially Jews. Sometimes Jews were confined in squalid ghettoes, but most of the time they were herded into cattle cars for removal to concentration camps. By late 1942, the Nazis had set up six death camps in Poland, where thousands of Jews were gassed each day. In all, approximately 6 million Jews were systematically murdered in what became known as the Holocaust. Included in this part of the unit is Bernard Malamud's chilling story "Armistice." Set in New York City while the war rages in

Images from World War II: U.S. troops roll through Europe (far right); a U.S. war propaganda poster (above); the yellow patch that European Jews were forced to wear (right); and the bombing of Pearl Harbor (below).

KEEP THESE HANDS OFF!

BUY the New VICTORY BONDS

Jood

Europe, the story reveals the roots of the kind of racial hatred that fueled the Holocaust. The armistice, or truce, between the two American characters at the end of the story seems unsatisfactory and temporary, just like the armistice signed by Germany and the allied European and U.S. forces at the end of World War I.

On December 7, 1941, Japanese bombers struck the American naval base at Pearl Harbor, Hawaii, killing approximately 2,000 sailors. This tragedy, which brought the United States into the war, is the occasion of Joan Didion's "Letter from Paradise." Didion describes her feelings as she visits Pearl Harbor a quarter of a century later, views the still-submerged battleships, and recalls the young men who died in the Sunday-morning sneak attack. Dwight Okita's poem "In Response to Executive Order 9066" recalls the reaction of the U.S. government to the fear engendered by Japanese aggression: the rounding up and banishing to internment camps of thousands of Japanese Americans.

The U.S. entry into the war turned the tide in favor of the Allies, but it was a long, hard fight. Two selections in this part of the unit deal with the experience of ordinary combat soldiers. Randall Jarrell's jolting poem "The Death of the Ball Turret Gunner" recalls the terror of aerial warfare, in which combatants felt painfully vulnerable under the fire of a faceless enemy. The prize-winning novelist John Steinbeck, whose work always speaks with sympathy for the common people, also reflects the point of view of the fighting soldier in his essay "Why Soldiers Won't Talk."

Voices
from the TIMES

from
"The Good War": An Oral History of World War Two
by Studs Terkel

We were on our way to the movies on Sunday afternoon. I was twelve at the time. My dad loved Abbott and Costello. We were going to a matinee. We saw them all. On the way to the theater, the car radio was on. "Oh, my God!" my father said, "Pearl Harbor!" I said, "What's a Pearl Harbor?"

"We can't go to the movies," he said. He turned around right away. There was an outcry from the back seat: "We wanna see Abbott and Costello!" My two sisters were eight and six.

Jean Bartlett

On the morning of December 16, we were suddenly under a fantastic barrage. Every tank in Europe came over the hill, all the panzers in the world. We had no tanks at all. The weather was such that we had no air support. They went over our rifles like they weren't even there. We were completely cut off and surrounded. We ran through the hills, firing at anything. . . .

So there I am wandering around with the whole German army shooting at me, and all I've got is a .45 automatic. There were ample opportunities, however, because every place you went there were bodies and soldiers laying around. Mostly Americans. At one time or another, I think I had in my hands every weapon the United States Army manufactured. You'd run out of ammunition with that one, you'd throw it away and try to find something else. One time I had a submachine gun, first experience I ever had with one.

Richard M. "Red" Prendergast
remembering the Battle of the Bulge

The only thing that kept you going was your faith in your buddies. It wasn't just a case of friendship. I never heard of self-inflicted wounds out there. Fellows from other services said they saw this in Europe. Oh, there were plenty of times when I wished I had a million-dollar wound. [Laughs softly.] Like maybe shootin' a toe off. What was worse than death was the indignation of your buddies. You couldn't let 'em down. It was stronger than flag and country.

With the Japanese, the battle was all night long. Infiltratin' the lines, slippin' up and throwin' in grenades. Or runnin' in with a bayonet or saber. They were active all night. Your buddy would try to get a little catnap and you'd stay on watch. Then you'd switch off. It went on, day in and day out. A matter of simple survival. The only way you could get it over with was to kill them off before they killed you. The war I knew was totally savage.

E. B. "Sledgehammer" Sledge
remembering the war in the Pacific

I first became aware of it when I was twelve or thirteen. It was one of the most important experiences of my life. In the school library, I was looking at photographs of the Holocaust. They were oversized books. I can still see the bindings and the mottled green cloth. It wasn't an assignment. Why was I doing this? It was a new library, new furniture, clean floors. The sun was coming through on the Appalachian hills. In contrast to the photographs, which were grainy, fuzzy. Parents wouldn't want their children to see these photographs.

In those grainy photos, you first think it's cords of wood piled up. You look again, it shows you human beings. You never get the picture out of your eye.

Nora Watson

A U.S. soldier in Vietnam

Traditions Across Time: War in Vietnam

Most Americans supported U.S. participation in World War II. Twenty years later, however, the Vietnam War split the American people into so-called hawks and doves—supporters and opponents of the war.

The United States intervened in South Vietnam to help that republic resist the Viet Cong—South Vietnamese Communist rebels—and the North Vietnamese army. The U.S. government wanted to stop the spread of communism in Southeast Asia, whereas the Vietnamese soldiers fighting U.S. troops wanted an independent nation free of foreign interference.

The war in Vietnam bred a degree of domestic conflict unseen since the Civil War. As the war dragged on and more U.S. soldiers died—approximately 58,000 in all—many Americans at home began to doubt the wisdom of continuing the U.S. presence in Vietnam. Indignant students, pacifists, and some returning Vietnam War veterans marched in the streets, calling for an end to the war. The literature of the time reflects the conflicts within the country, as well as within the ranks of the U.S. military. From Tim O'Brien's "Ambush," with its painful memory of an encounter with the enemy, to Denise Levertov's poem "At the Justice Department," a participant's account of an antiwar protest, these selections introduce the troublesome issues plaguing the people who were involved in the longest war in American history.

World War II

Bernard Malamud **Armistice** 1076
It was only a temporary truce.

LINK ACROSS CULTURES
Primo Levi *from* **Survival in Auschwitz** 1083
Life and death in a Nazi concentration camp

Randall Jarrell **The Death of the Ball Turret Gunner** 1088
The terror of aerial combat

John Steinbeck **Why Soldiers Won't Talk** 1088
They won't, or they can't?

Joan Didion **Letter from Paradise, 21° 19′ N., 157° 52′ W.** 1095
When looking at the half-submerged Arizona,
everyone is quiet.

Dwight Okita **In Response to Executive Order 9066** 1095
Evacuation day for a 14-year-old girl

RELATED READING
Point/Counterpoint: The Japanese-American Internment 1103
Opposing views of the government's action

COMPARING LITERATURE
Traditions Across Time: War in Vietnam

Tim O'Brien **Ambush** (1990) 1105
A haunting memory of Vietnam

Yusef Komunyakaa **Camouflaging the Chimera** (1988) 1111
Lying in wait for the enemy

Wendy Wilder Larsen **Deciding** (1986) 1111
and Tran Thi Nga *Do you leave your home when the bombs*
start falling?

Denise Levertov **At the Justice Department, November 15, 1969** (1969) 1118
Tear-gassed and proud of it

Armistice

Short Story by BERNARD MALAMUD

(**Connect to Your Life**)

Preconceived Notions Prejudice is the suspicion, dislike, or hatred of a particular group of people based on preconceived ideas about them. Think about a person you know who is prejudiced, however slightly, against a certain group. What is the group? Why do you think this person is prejudiced against this group? How does he or she demonstrate this prejudice? When is he or she most likely to show this prejudice? Discuss your thoughts with a classmate.

Build Background

Roots of Anti-Semitism Anti-Semitism, prejudice against Jews, plays a major role in "Armistice," a story set during World War II before the United States entered the conflict. When Hitler came to power in Germany in 1933, he made anti-Semitism an official policy of the Nazi government, and during World War II, he instituted a program to exterminate all European Jews. As the Nazis conquered territories, as they did France in 1940, they rounded up the Jews of the area and sent them to concentration camps. Hitler carried anti-Semitism to a terrifying extreme, but the roots of anti-Semitism extend much further back in European history than the 1940s. Since ancient times both Christian and Muslim nations have persecuted and expelled Jews. Originally, Jews were persecuted for not following the dominant religion, but later they were also blamed for society's ills whenever economic or social conditions deteriorated.

WORDS TO KNOW **Vocabulary Preview**

contemptuously	inflict	pretense
derive	overwrought	

Focus Your Reading

LITERARY ANALYSIS **THEME AND TITLE** As you know, **theme** refers to the central idea that a writer wishes to share with a reader of a literary work. Most themes are not stated and must be figured out by the reader. One detail that can help suggest the theme of a story is its **title.** As you read "Armistice," consider what the title tells you about the story's theme.

ACTIVE READING **DRAWING CONCLUSIONS ABOUT CHARACTER MOTIVATION**

As you may recall, **motivation** refers to the forces impelling a **character's** actions. There are two main characters in this story: Morris, who is of Russian Jewish descent, and Gus, who is of German descent. As you read the story, think about why the two characters act as they do, particularly toward each other. Look for clues that will help you **draw conclusions** about their motivations and behaviors.

READER'S NOTEBOOK Being aware of characters' memories, dreams, and imaginings can provide clues to their motivations. Use a chart like the one shown to list the two main characters' memories, dreams, and imaginings.

	Morris	Gus
Memories		
Dreams		
Imaginings		

Bernard Malamud

ARMSTICE

When he was a boy, Morris Lieberman saw a burly Russian peasant seize a wagon wheel that was lying against the side of a blacksmith's shop, swing it around, and hurl it at a fleeing Jewish sexton.[1] The wheel caught the Jew in the back, crushing his spine. In speechless terror, he lay on the ground before his burning house, waiting to die.

Thirty years later Morris, a widower who owned a small grocery and delicatessen store in a Scandinavian neighborhood in Brooklyn, could recall the scene of the pogrom[2] with the twisting fright that he had felt at fifteen. He often experienced the same fear since the Nazis had come to power.

The reports of their persecution of the Jews that he heard over the radio filled him with dread, but he never stopped listening to them. His fourteen-year-old son, Leonard, a thin, studious boy, saw how overwrought his father became and tried to shut off the radio, but the grocer would not allow him to. He listened, and at night did not sleep, because in listening he shared the woes inflicted upon his race.

When the war began, Morris placed his hope for the salvation of the Jews in his trust of the French army. He lived close to his radio, listening to the bulletins and praying for a French victory in the conflict which he called "this righteous war."

On the May day in 1940 when the Germans ripped open the French lines at Sedan, his long-growing anxiety became intolerable. Between waiting on customers, or when he was preparing salads in the kitchen at the rear of the store, he switched on the radio and heard, with increasing dismay, the flood of reports which never seemed to contain any good news. The Belgians surrendered. The British retreated at Dunkerque,[3] and in mid-June, the Nazis, speeding toward Paris in their lorries,[4] were passing large herds of conquered Frenchmen resting in the fields.

Day after day, as the battle progressed, Morris sat on the edge of the cot in the kitchen listening to the additions to his sorrow, nodding his head the way the Jews do in mourning, then rousing himself to hope for the miracle that would save the French as it had saved the Jews in the wilderness. At three o'clock, he shut off the radio, because Leonard came home from school

---

1. **sexton:** caretaker of a synagogue or church.
2. **pogrom** (pə-grŏm′): organized persecution or massacre of a minority group, especially one conducted against Jews.
3. **Dunkerque** (dœN-kĕrk′): also spelled *Dunkirk;* a seaport in northern France. In 1940, more than 330,000 Allied troops, under enemy fire, were forced to evacuate the beaches there.
4. **lorries:** a British term for motor trucks.

WORDS TO KNOW
overwrought (ō′vər-rôt′) *adj.* excessively nervous or excited
inflict (ĭn-flĭkt′) *v.* to cause to have or suffer; impose

A butcher at a deli in New York City. Photo by Victor Laredo.

about then. The boy, seeing the harmful effect of the war on his father's health, had begun to plead with him not to listen to so many news broadcasts, and Morris pacified him by pretending that he no longer thought of the war. Each afternoon Leonard remained behind the counter while his father slept on the cot. From the dream-filled, raw sleep of these afternoons, the grocer managed to <u>derive</u> enough strength to endure the long day and his own bitter thoughts.

The salesmen from the wholesale grocery houses and the drivers who served Morris were amazed at the way he suffered. They told him that the war had nothing to do with America and that he was taking it too seriously. Some of the others made him the object of their ridicule outside the store. One of them, Gus Wagner, who delivered the delicatessen meats and provisions, was not afraid to laugh at Morris to his face.

Gus was a heavy man, with a strong, full head and a fleshy face. Although born in America, and a member of the AEF[5] in 1918, his imagination was fired by the Nazi conquests and he believed that they had the strength and power to conquer the world. He kept a scrapbook filled with clippings and pictures of the German army. He was deeply impressed by the Panzer divisions,[6] and when he read accounts of battles in which they tore through the enemy's lines, his mind glowed with excitement. He did not reveal his feelings directly because he considered his business first. As it was, he poked fun at the grocer for wanting the French to win.

Each afternoon, with his basket of liverwursts and bolognas on his arm, Gus strode into the store and swung the basket onto the table in the kitchen. The grocer as usual was sitting on the cot, listening to the radio.

---

5. **AEF:** American Expeditionary Forces; the 2 million U.S. soldiers sent overseas during World War I.

6. **Panzer divisions:** German armored forces, consisting largely of tanks.

WORDS
TO
KNOW

derive (dĭ-rīv′) v. to obtain; get; receive

"Hello, Morris," Gus said, pretending surprise. "What does it say on the radio?" He sat down heavily and laughed.

When things were going especially well for the Germans, Gus dropped his attitude of pretense and said openly, "You better get used to it, Morris. The Germans will wipe out the Frenchmen."

Morris disliked these remarks, but he said nothing. He allowed Gus to talk as he did because he had known the meat man for nine years. Once they had nearly been friends. After the death of Morris's wife four years ago, Gus stayed longer than usual and joined Morris in a cup of coffee. Occasionally he repaired a hole in the screen door or fixed the plug for the electric slicing machine.

Leonard had driven them apart. The boy disliked the meat man and always tried to avoid him. He was nauseated by Gus's laughter, which he called a cackle, and he would not allow his father to do business with Gus in the kitchen when he was having his milk and crackers after school.

Gus knew how the boy felt about him and he was deeply annoyed. He was angered too when the boy added up the figures on the meat bills and found errors. Gus was careless in arithmetic, which often caused trouble. Once Morris mentioned a five-dollar prize that Leonard had won in mathematics and Gus said, "You better watch out, Morris. He's a skinny kid. If he studies too much, he'll get consumption."[7]

Morris was frightened. He felt that Gus was wishing harm upon Leonard. Their relations became cooler, and after that Gus spoke more freely about politics and the war, often expressing his contempt for the French.

The Germans took Paris and pushed on toward the west and south. Morris, drained of his energy, prayed that the ordeal would soon be over. Then the Reynaud cabinet fell. Marshal Pétain[8] addressed a request to the Germans for "peace with honor." In the dark Compiègne forest, Hitler sat in Marshal Foch's railroad car, listening to his terms being read to the French delegation.[9]

That night, after closing his store, Morris disconnected the radio and carried it upstairs. In his bedroom, the door shut tightly so Leonard would not be awakened, he tuned in softly to the midnight broadcast and learned that the French had accepted Hitler's terms and would sign the armistice tomorrow. Morris shut off the radio. An age-old weariness filled him. He wanted to sleep but he knew that he could not.

Morris turned out the lights, removed his shirt and shoes in the dark, and sat smoking in the large bedroom that had once belonged to him and his wife.

The door opened softly, and Leonard looked into the room. By the light of the street lamp which shone through the window, the boy could

...the Germans ripped open the French lines at Sedan...

---

7. **consumption:** tuberculosis.

8. **Reynaud** (rā-nō′) . . . **Marshal Pétain** (pā-tăN′): Reynaud was the premier of France at the time of its surrender to Germany in June 1940. After the Germans had occupied most of France, Pétain became premier of the unoccupied southern third of the nation. (Marshal is the highest rank in the French army.)

9. **In the dark Compiègne** (kôN-pyĕn′yə) **forest . . . delegation:** This meeting represents a cruel turnabout of Germany's surrender at the end of World War I. In 1918 a German delegation had heard the Allies' peace terms in a railroad car in this same forest. Leading the Allied delegation at that time was France's Marshal Ferdinand Foch (fôsh).

---

see his father in the chair. It made him think of the time when his mother was in the hospital and his father sat in the chair all night.

Leonard entered the bedroom in his bare feet. "Pa," he said, putting his arm around his father's shoulders, "go to sleep."

"I can't sleep, Leonard."

"Pa, you got to. You work sixteen hours."

"Oh, my son," cried Morris, with sudden emotion, putting his arms around Leonard, "what will become of us?"

The boy became afraid.

"Pa," he said, "go to sleep. Please, you got to."

"All right, I'll go," said Morris. He crushed his cigarette in the ashtray and got into bed. The boy watched him until he turned over on his right side, which was the side he slept on; then he returned to his room.

Later Morris rose and sat by the window, looking into the street. The night was cool. The breeze swayed the street lamp, which creaked and moved the circle of light that fell upon the street.

"What will become of us?" he muttered to himself. His mind went back to the days when he was a boy studying Jewish history. The Jews lived in an interminable exodus.[10] Long lines trudged forever with their bundles on their shoulders.

He dozed and dreamed that he had fled from Germany into France. The Nazis had found out where he lived in Paris. He sat in a chair in a dark room waiting for them to come. His hair had grown grayer. The moonlight fell on his sloping shoulders, then moved into the darkness. He rose and climbed out onto a ledge overlooking the lighted city of Paris. He fell. Something clumped to the sidewalk. Morris groaned and awoke. He heard the purring of a truck's motor and he knew that the driver was dropping the bundles of morning newspapers in front of the stationery store on the corner.

The dark was soft with gray. Morris crawled into bed and began to dream again. It was Sunday at suppertime. The store was crowded with customers. Suddenly Gus was there. He waved a copy of *Social Justice* and cried out, "The Protocols of Zion![11] The Protocols of Zion!" The customers began to leave. "Gus," Morris pleaded, "the customers, the customers—"

He awoke shivering and lay awake until the alarm rang.

After he had dragged in the bread and milk boxes and had waited on the deaf man who always came early, Morris went to the corner for a paper. The armistice was signed. Morris looked around to see if the street had changed, but everything was the same, though he could hardly understand why. Leonard came down for his coffee and roll. He took fifty cents from the till and left for school.

The day was warm and Morris was tired. He grew uneasy when he thought of Gus. He knew that today he would have difficulty controlling himself if Gus made some of his remarks.

At three o'clock, when Morris was slicing small potatoes for potato salad, Gus strode into the store and swung his basket onto the table.

"Well, Morris"—he laughed—"why don't you turn the radio on? Let's hear the news."

Morris tried to control himself, but his bitterness overcame him. "I see you're happy today, Gus. What great cause has died?"

The meat man laughed, but he did not like that remark.

"Come on, Morris," he said, "let's do business before your skinny kid comes home and wants the bill signed by a certified public accountant."

"He looks out for my interests," answered Morris. "He's a good mathematics student," he added.

"That's the sixth time I heard that," said Gus.

---

10. **exodus:** a departure or emigration, usually of a large number of people.

11. **The Protocols of Zion:** anti-Jewish writings concerning an alleged conspiracy to establish a world government ruled by Jews (a notion that has been shown to be completely false). Zion is a name for Israel or the people of Israel, and *protocols*, here, means "agreements or treaties."

"You'll never hear it about your children."

Gus lost his temper. "What the hell's the matter with you Jews?" he asked. "Do you think you own all the brains in the world?"

"Gus," Morris cried, "you talk like a Nazi."

"I'm a hundred percent American. I fought in the war," answered Gus.

Leonard came into the store and heard the loud voices. He ran into the kitchen and saw the two men arguing. A feeling of shame and nausea overcame him.

"Pa," he begged, "don't fight."

Morris was still angry. "If you're not a Nazi," he said to Gus, "why are you so glad the French lost?"

"Who's glad?" asked Gus. Suddenly he felt proud and he said, "They deserved to lose, the way they starved the German people. Why the hell do you want them to win?"

"Pa," said Leonard again.

"I want them to win because they are fighting for democracy."

"Like hell," said Gus. "You want them to win because they're protecting the Jews—like that lousy Léon Blum."[12]

"You Nazi, you," Morris shouted angrily, coming from behind the table. "You Nazi! You don't deserve to live in America!"

"Papa," cried Leonard, holding him, "don't fight, please, please."

"Mind your own business, you little . . . ,"

A mother and her children in Yugoslavia in 1943, three of the 10 million Europeans displaced by the war. Photo by George Skrigin.

said Gus, pushing Leonard away.

A sob broke from Leonard's throat. He began to cry.

Gus paused, seeing that he had gone too far. Morris Lieberman's face was white. He put his

---

12. **Léon Blum** (blo͞om): the first Socialist and the first Jew to become, in 1936, premier of France. His social reforms and opposition to the Nazis before and during the war led his enemies to adopt the slogan "Better Hitler than Blum."

arm around the boy and kissed him again and again.

"No, no. No more, Leonard. Don't cry. I'm sorry. I give you my word. No more."

Gus looked on without speaking. His face was still red with anger, but he was afraid that he would lose Morris's business. He pulled two liverwursts and a bologna from his basket.

"The meat's on the table," he said. "Pay me tomorrow."

Gus glanced contemptuously at the grocer comforting his son, who was quiet now, and he walked out of the store. He threw the basket into his truck, got in, and drove off.

As he rode amid the cars on the avenue, he thought of the boy crying and his father holding him. It was always like that with the Jews. Tears and people holding each other. Why feel sorry for them?

Gus sat up straight at the wheel, his face grim. He thought of the armistice and imagined that he was in Paris. His truck was a massive tank rumbling with the others through the wide boulevards. The French, on the sidewalks, were overpowered with fear.

He drove tensely, his eyes unsmiling. He knew that if he relaxed the picture would fade. ❖

Hitler and his advisors parade in Paris ten days after Nazi troops took the city. UPI/Bettmann.

from SURVIVAL IN AUSCHWITZ

Primo Levi

In Malamud's story "Armistice," the main character is alarmed by radio broadcasts about Nazi persecution of Jews. The following selection describes the true experiences of Primo Levi, an Italian chemist who survived the horrors of Auschwitz, a Nazi concentration camp in Poland.

Today is working Sunday, *Arbeitssonntag*: we work until 1 P.M., then we return to camp for the shower, shave and general control for skin diseases and lice. And in the yards, everyone knew mysteriously that the selection would be today.

The news arrived, as always, surrounded by a halo of contradictory or suspect details: the selection in the infirmary took place this morning; the percentage was seven per cent of the whole camp, thirty, fifty per cent of the patients. At Birkenau,[1] the crematorium chimney has been smoking for ten days. Room has to be made for an enormous convoy arriving from the Poznan ghetto.[2] The young tell the young that all the old ones will be chosen. The healthy tell the healthy that only the ill will be chosen. Specialists will be excluded. German Jews will be excluded. Low Numbers[3] will be excluded. You will be chosen. I will be excluded.

At 1 P.M. exactly the yard empties in orderly fashion, and for two hours the gray unending army files past the two control stations where, as on every day, we are counted and recounted, and past the military band which for two hours without interruption plays, as on every day, those marches to which we must synchronize our steps at our entrance and our exit.

It seems like every day, the kitchen chimney smokes as usual, the distribution of the soup is already beginning. But then the bell is heard, and at that moment we realize that we have arrived.

Because this bell always sounds at dawn, when it means the reveille;[4] but if it sounds during the day, it means *"Blocksperre,"* enclosure in huts, and this happens when there is a selection to prevent anyone avoiding it, or when those selected leave for the gas, to prevent anyone seeing them leave.

Our *Blockältester*[5] knows his business. He has made sure that we have all entered, he has the door locked, he has given everyone his card with his number, name, profession, age and nationality and he has ordered everyone to undress completely, except for shoes. We wait like this, naked, with the card in our hands, for the commission to reach our hut. We are hut 48, but one can never tell if they

---

1. **Birkenau** (bîr′kə-nou′): Also known as Auschwitz II, this camp stood about two miles from an older camp, called Auschwitz I. Between 1 million and 4 million people were murdered at Auschwitz-Birkenau during the years 1942–1945.
2. **Poznan** (pôz′năn′) **ghetto:** the area of the Polish city of Poznan in which Jews were forced to live.
3. **Low Numbers:** prisoners with low identification numbers.
4. **reveille** (rĕv′ə-lē): a signal used to awaken people.
5. *Blockältester* (blôk′ĕl′tə-stər) *German:* block elder—a prisoner cooperating with the German guards by serving as the head of a block, or barracks.

are going to begin at hut 1 or hut 60. At any rate, we can rest quietly at least for an hour, and there is no reason why we should not get under the blankets on the bunk and keep warm.

Many are already drowsing when a barrage of orders, oaths and blows proclaims the imminent arrival of the commission. The *Blockältester* and his helpers, starting at the end of the dormitory, drive the crowd of frightened, naked people in front of them and cram them in the *Tagesraum* which is the Quartermaster's office.[6] The *Tagesraum* is a room seven yards by four: when the drive is over, a warm and compact human mass is jammed into the *Tagesraum*, perfectly filling all the corners, exercising such a pressure on the wooden walls as to make them creak. . . .

The *Blockältester* has closed the connecting-door and has opened the other two which lead from the dormitory and the *Tagesraum* outside. Here, in front of the two doors, stands the arbiter[7] of our fate, an SS subaltern.[8] On his right is the *Blockältester*, on his left, the quartermaster of the hut. Each one of us, as he comes naked out of the *Tagesraum* into the cold October air, has to run the few steps between the two doors, give the card to the SS man and enter the dormitory door. The SS man, in the fraction of a second between two successive crossings, with a glance at one's back and front, judges everyone's fate, and in turn gives the card to the man on his right or his left, and this is the life or death of each of us. In three or four minutes a hut of two hundred men is "done," as is the whole camp of twelve thousand men in the course of the afternoon.

Jammed in the charnel-house[9] of the *Tagesraum*, I gradually felt the human pressure around me slacken, and in a short time it was my turn. Like everyone, I passed by with a brisk and elastic step, trying to hold my head high, my chest forward and my muscles contracted and conspicuous. With the corner of my eye I tried to look behind my shoulders, and my card seemed to end on the right.

As we gradually come back into the dormitory we are allowed to dress ourselves. Nobody yet knows with certainty his own fate, it has first of all to be established whether the condemned cards were those on the right or the left. By now there is no longer any point in sparing each other's feelings with superstitious scruples. Everybody crowds around the oldest, the most wasted-away, and most "muselmann";[10] if their cards went to the left, the left is certainly the side of the condemned.

Even before the selection is over, everybody knows that the left was effectively the *"schlechte Seite,"* the bad side. There have naturally been some irregularities: René, for example, so young and robust, ended on the left; perhaps it was because he has glasses, perhaps because he walks a little stooped like a myope,[11] but more probably because of a simple mistake. . . .

There is nothing surprising about these mistakes: the examination is too quick and summary, and in any case, the important thing for the Lager[12] is not that the most useless prisoners be eliminated, but that free posts be quickly created, according to a certain percentage previously fixed.

---

6. **Quartermaster's office:** the office of the person who distributes food and clothing to the prisoners.

7. **arbiter** (är′bĭ-tər): judge; decider.

8. **SS subaltern:** a low-ranking officer in the Nazi special security force.

9. **charnel-house:** vault for the bones of the dead (here used figuratively).

10. **"muselmann"** (mōō′zəl-măn′): concentration-camp slang for a person near death from starvation.

11. **myope** (mī′ōp′): nearsighted person.

12. **Lager** (lä′gər) *German:* camp.

Connect to the Literature

1. What Do You Think?
What was your reaction to Gus's daydream at the end of the story? Share your thoughts with classmates.

Comprehension Check
- Why does Gus make fun of Morris?
- What event causes the argument between Gus and Morris at the end of the story?
- After his fight with Morris, what does Gus imagine he is doing?

Think Critically

2. Why do you think news of the war affects Morris as it does?

 THINK ABOUT
- his memories of the pogrom in Russia
- the two dreams he has

3. In your view, should Morris be as involved in the war as he is?

 THINK ABOUT
- how his health is affected
- what he might mean when he cries "What will become of us?"

4. **ACTIVE READING** **DRAWING CONCLUSIONS ABOUT CHARACTER MOTIVATION** Look over the chart you created in your **READER'S NOTEBOOK**. How would you characterize Morris's memories and dreams? How would you describe Gus's imaginings? How do their different dreams and imaginings help explain their actions?

Extend Interpretations

5. Critic's Corner Many critics have noted the focus on moral concerns in Bernard Malamud's writing. Evelyn Gross Avery writes: "Malamud defines Jewishness as a willingness to honor the Covenant by sacrificing and suffering for freedom and justice. A good Jew assumes responsibility for all the needy, but has a special obligation to his people. A good Jew awakens others to iniquities." How does Avery's comment affect your understanding of Morris Lieberman?

6. Comparing Texts Compare Morris Lieberman's impression of the Nazis and their treatment of Jews with Primo Levi's actual account of his experiences in a Nazi concentration camp in *Survival in Auschwitz* (page 1083). What descriptions of Levi's life in Auschwitz might surprise Morris? What descriptions would probably not surprise him?

7. Connect to Life How much anti-Semitism do you think exists in the United States today? Support your answer.

Literary Analysis

THEME AND TITLE A story's **title** may provide clues to the work's **theme,** or message. In "Armistice," the title alludes to the armistice in Europe as well as to the one between Morris and Gus. The following passage describes Gus's thoughts and feelings after Morris promises his son that there will be no more fighting:

Gus looked on without speaking. His face was still red with anger, but he was afraid that he would lose Morris's business. He pulled two liverwursts and a bologna from his basket.

"The meat's on the table," he said. "Pay me tomorrow."

Gus glanced contemptuously at the grocer comforting his son, who was quiet now, and he walked out of the store. He threw the basket into his truck, got in, and drove off.

How does the armistice in Europe mirror the one reached between Gus and Morris?

Paired Activity Get together with a classmate and discuss theme in "Armistice." What central idea do you think is suggested by the story's title? What other themes do you see in the story? Write out statements to express these themes, and then share them with other student pairs.

REVIEW **POINT OF VIEW**
Malamud frequently uses the **third-person omniscient point of view,** in which the narrator reveals the thoughts of different characters. What do you think would have been lost if "Armistice" had been narrated only from Morris's viewpoint?

Writing Options

1. Dream Analysis Write a dream interpretation analyzing the meaning of Morris's two dreams the night before his fight with Gus. Be sure to explain what you think certain actions symbolize and what the dreams reveal about Morris's state of mind.

Writing Handbook
See page 1283: Analysis.

2. Letter to the Editor Put yourself in Morris's place. Draft a letter to the editor of a newspaper explaining why you consider World War II a "righteous war."

3. Eventful Paragraph Write a paragraph about another event abroad that inflamed prejudices and affected how people perceived each other in the United States.

4. World War II Presentation Create an outline for a multimedia exhibit that captures the World War II era. Take notes on images that illustrate key events, people, and social trends during the war. Identify and list recordings of music that were popular at the time. Be sure to indicate how you would arrange and use these images and recordings in an exhibit. Place the outline in your **Working Portfolio.**

Activities & Explorations

1. Readers Theater Performance Practice and present a Readers Theater performance of this story, with readers taking the parts of Morris, Gus, Leonard, and the narrator. You might use a few items of classroom furniture or some simple props to suggest the setting. ~ **VIEWING AND REPRESENTING/PERFORMING**

2. Memory Illustration Create an illustration, perhaps a painting or a collage, to depict Morris's memories of Jewish persecution and his fears for the future. ~ **ART**

Inquiry & Research

1. History of Anti-Semitism Since ancient times, and in many countries, prejudice against Jews has resulted in discrimination and persecution. Investigate the history of anti-Semitism in Germany, Russia, France, Spain, or some other country, or research details about the Holocaust during World War II. In an oral report, share your knowledge with your classmates.

2. German Victory Find out more about the German victory over France during World War II, including how it was achieved and what resulted from it. Report your findings in class.

 More Online: Research Starter www.mcdougallittell.com

Art Connection

Conflicting Impressions The photo on page 1081 shows a refugee

family fleeing during World War II. The photo on page 1082 depicts Hitler and his entourage marching through Paris. What emotions and ideas do these pictures call to mind for you? How would you contrast the two processions in the photos?

Vocabulary in Action

EXERCISE A: CONTEXT CLUES Use a vocabulary word to complete each sentence.

1. We Americans can become _____ upon hearing about the tragic results of ethnic discrimination around the world while at the same time failing to recognize our own guilt in this area.

2. During World War II, Americans responded with horror to the Nazis' eagerness to _____ terrible misery on Jews and other minorities.

3. In the novel *Gentleman's Agreement,* published soon after World War II, a journalist uses the _____ that he is Jewish to explore how Jews are treated in the United States.

4. Used to being respected in his dealings with other people, the journalist is dismayed by how _____ he is often treated when he is thought to be Jewish.

5. The conclusions he is able to _____ from his experiment are that anti-Semitism is unfair, destructive, and shockingly widespread in the United States.

EXERCISE B Tell a "round robin" story in which one person begins a story and must keep talking until he or she has used one of the vocabulary words. Another person continues the story until he or she uses another word, and so on, until all the words are used.

WORDS TO KNOW		
contemptuously	inflict	pretense
derive	overwrought	

Building Vocabulary
For an in-depth lesson on context clues, see page 326

Bernard Malamud
1914–1986

Other Works
The Assistant
The Magic Barrel
A New Life
Pictures of Fidelman: An Exhibition
The Tenants

Impact of Early Experiences Bernard Malamud grew up in a non-Jewish neighborhood in Brooklyn, New York, where his Russian Jewish immigrant parents owned a grocery store. Like Morris Lieberman in "Armistice," Malamud's father worked long hours just to make a meager living. Noting the close connection between his experience and his writing, Malamud said in an interview published in the *New York Times:* "People say I write so much about misery, but you write about what you write best. As you are grooved, so you are grieved. And the grieving is that no matter how much happiness or success you collect, you cannot obliterate your early experience."

Teacher, Writer, Moralist During his 12 years at Oregon State College, where he taught three days a week and wrote the other four, Malamud produced three novels and a collection of short stories. His first novel, *The Natural,* about a baseball player, was later made into a movie by the same name. In 1961 Malamud began teaching at Bennington College in Vermont. By 1967, when his novel *The Fixer* won both the Pulitzer Prize and the National Book Award, Malamud had become, according to one critic, "one of the foremost writers of moral fiction in America." Throughout his career, he wrote about the need for love, understanding, and responsibility and about the destructiveness of ignorance and hatred. Malamud wrote: "Literature, since it values man by describing him, tends toward morality."

Author Activity

Grave Pronouncement The inscription on Malamud's grave reads: "Art celebrates life and gives us our measure." How do these words apply to "Armistice"?

The Death of the Ball Turret Gunner

Poetry by RANDALL JARRELL

Why Soldiers Won't Talk

Essay by JOHN STEINBECK

Connect to Your Life

Combat! The following selections bring to life the old cliché "War is hell." Imagine for a moment, as best you can, what the experience of combat must be like. Visualize yourself as a soldier, suddenly thrust into the nightmare of battle. Then hypothesize an answer to the question John Steinbeck asks: Why do soldiers avoid talking about their combat experience? Share your thoughts with a small group of classmates.

Build Background

War Experiences Both Randall Jarrell and John Steinbeck had war-related experiences during World War II. Jarrell served in the U.S. Army Air Force, teaching flight navigation in Arizona. He thus gained firsthand experience with fighter planes and gunners. A ball turret, mentioned in the title of his poem, was a Plexiglas bubble on the underside of certain planes. From it, a machine gunner fired at the enemy during combat. John Steinbeck gained combat experience while working as a news correspondent during World War II. To gather information for his dispatches, he spent time with a Flying Fortress unit in England, reported from North Africa, and accompanied frontline troops during the Allied invasion of Italy.

Focus Your Reading

LITERARY ANALYSIS **IMAGERY AND TONE** As you may recall, **tone** is the attitude a writer takes toward a subject. Tone is communicated partly through **imagery,** that is, words and phrases that appeal to the senses. As you read the two selections, consider how imagery conveys tone.

ACTIVE READING **ADJUSTING READING STRATEGIES** When you read literary works from different genres, you need to make adjustments in your reading strategies. For example, when you read a poem, such as "The Death of the Ball Turret Gunner," you might use these strategies:

- Read the poem two or three times.
- Use footnotes and the dictionary to find the meanings of unfamiliar words or terms.
- Try to picture the poem's images and think about what they convey.

When you read Steinbeck's essay "Why Soldiers Won't Talk," follow these strategies:

- Identify the essay's main idea.
- Evaluate the reasons and opinions used to support the main idea.
- Determine your own position on the subject.

READER'S NOTEBOOK As you read, use these strategies and any others that work for you. Jot down notes about the poem's imagery and meaning and the development of the main idea in the essay.

THE DEATH OF THE BALL TURRET GUNNER

From my mother's sleep I fell into the State,
And I hunched in its belly till my wet fur froze.
Six miles from earth, loosed from its dream of life,
I woke to black flak[1] and the nightmare fighters.
5   When I died they washed me out of the turret with a hose.

_____

1. **flak:** the fire of antiaircraft guns.

RANDALL JARRELL

A.F.T.A.D.–"Memphis Belle" B-17 (1943), Stow Wegenroth,
by permission of the Estate of Stow Wegenroth.

Thinking Through the Literature

1. What is your reaction to the last line of this poem? Share your reaction with your classmates.

2. In reference to this poem, Randall Jarrell wrote that the gunner, who sat hunched up and revolved with the turret, looked like a fetus in the womb. With this **image** in mind, try to interpret the first four lines of the poem.

   THINK ABOUT { • what the phrase "fell into the State" might refer to
   • what sleeping, dreaming, and waking might mean

3. How would you describe the **speaker's** attitude toward his death?

4. What does this poem say to you about war and combat?

WHY SOLDIERS WON'T TALK

John Steinbeck

During the years between the last war and this one, I was always puzzled by the reticence[1] of ex-soldiers about their experiences in battle. If they had been reticent men it would have been different, but some of them were talkers and some were even boasters. They would discuss their experiences right up to the time of battle and then suddenly they wouldn't talk any more. This was considered heroic in them. It was thought that what they had seen or done was so horrible that they didn't want to bring it back to haunt them or their listeners. But many of these men had no such consideration in any other field.

Only recently have I found what seems to be a reasonable explanation, and the answer is simple. They did not and do not remember—and the worse the battle was, the less they remember.

In all kinds of combat the whole body is battered by emotion. The ductless glands pour their fluids into the system to make it able to stand up to the great demand on it. Fear and ferocity are products of the same fluid. Fatigue toxins[2] poison the system. Hunger followed by wolfed food distorts the metabolic pattern already distorted by the adrenaline[3] and fatigue. The body and the mind so disturbed are really ill and fevered. But in addition to these ills, which come from the inside of a man and are given him so that he can temporarily withstand pressures beyond his ordinary ability, there is the further stress of explosion.

Under extended bombardment or bombing the nerve ends are literally beaten. The eardrums are tortured by blast and the eyes ache from the constant hammering.

This is how you feel after a few days of constant firing. Your skin feels thick and insensitive. There is a salty taste in your mouth. A hard, painful knot is in your stomach where

---

1. **reticence:** the tendency to be silent or say little.
2. **toxins:** poisons produced by the body that are capable of causing disease. Fatigue may be a symptom of a toxic infection.
3. **adrenaline** (ə-drĕn′ə-lĭn): a substance, also called epinephrine, secreted by the adrenal gland in response to stress. It speeds up the heartbeat and thereby increases bodily energy and resistance to fatigue.

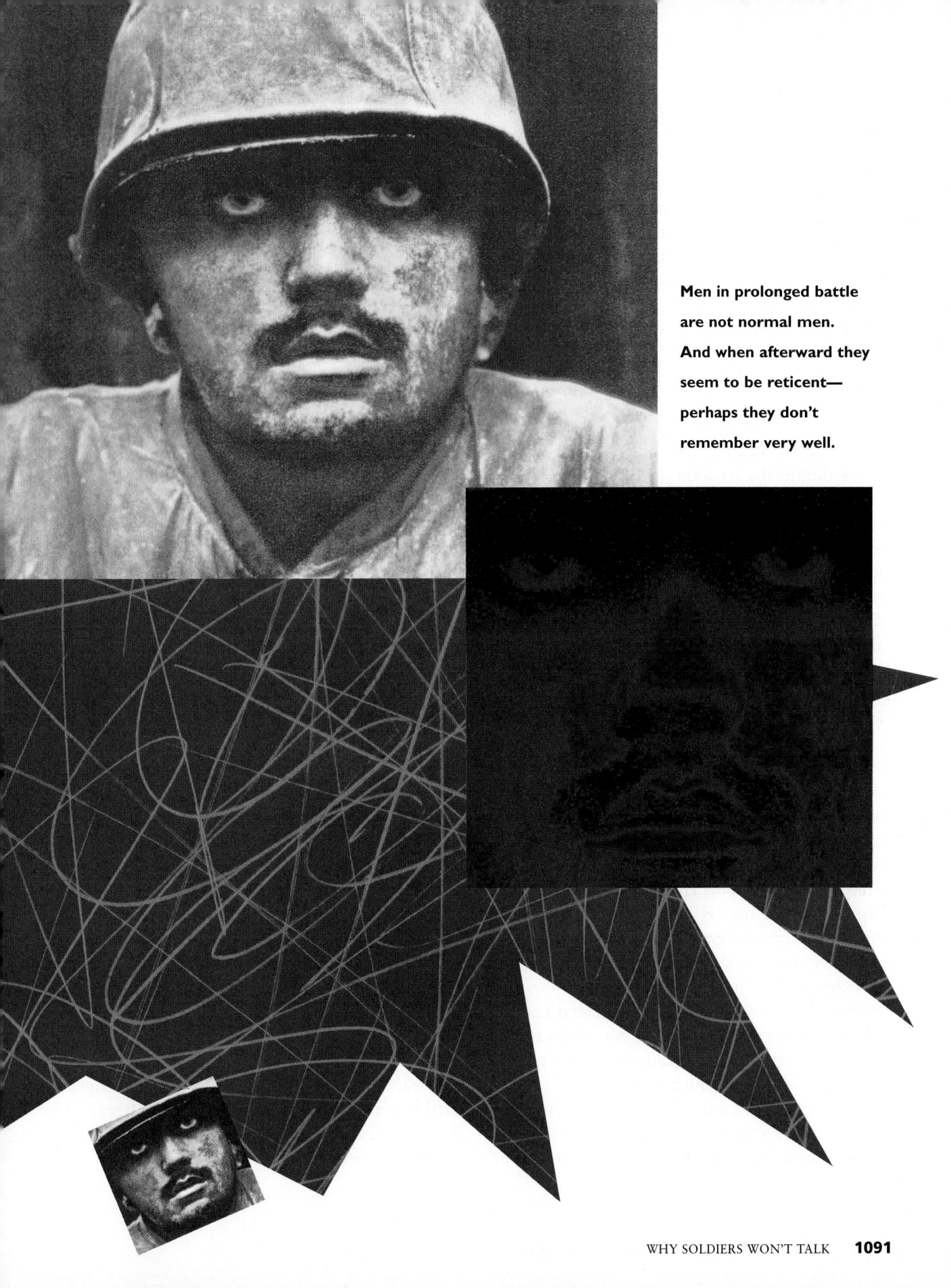

Men in prolonged battle
are not normal men.
And when afterward they
seem to be reticent—
perhaps they don't
remember very well.

the food is undigested. Your eyes do not pick up much detail and the sharp outlines of objects are slightly blurred. Everything looks a little unreal. When you walk, your feet hardly seem to touch the ground and there is a floaty feeling all over your body. Even the time sense seems to be changed. Men who are really moving at a normal pace seem to take forever to pass a given point. And when you move it seems to you that you are very much slowed down, although actually you are probably moving more quickly than you normally do.

Under the blast your eyeballs are so beaten that the earth and the air seem to shudder. At first your ears hurt, but then they become dull and all your other senses become dull, too. There are exceptions, of course. Some men cannot protect themselves this way and they break, and they are probably the ones we call shell-shock cases.

In the dullness all kinds of emphases change. Even the instinct for self-preservation is dulled so that a man may do things which are called heroic when actually his whole fabric of reaction is changed. The whole world becomes unreal. You laugh at things which are not ordinarily funny and you become enraged at trifles. During this time a kind man is capable of great cruelties and a timid man of great bravery, and nearly all men have resistance to stresses beyond their ordinary ability.

Then sleep can come without warning and like a drug. Gradually your whole body seems to be packed in cotton. All the main nerve trunks are deadened, and out of the battered cortex curious dreamlike thoughts emerge. It is at this time that many men see visions. The eyes fasten on a cloud and the tired brain makes a face of it, or an

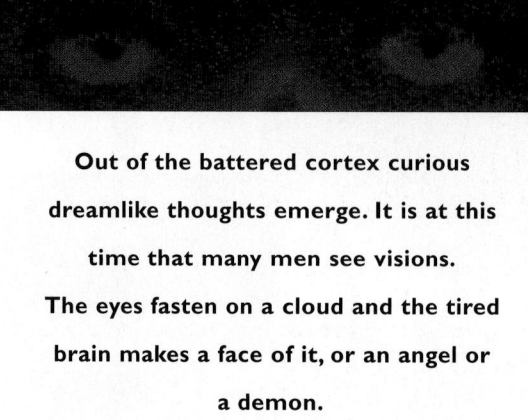

Out of the battered cortex curious dreamlike thoughts emerge. It is at this time that many men see visions. The eyes fasten on a cloud and the tired brain makes a face of it, or an angel or a demon.

angel or a demon. And out of the hammered brain strange memories are jolted loose, scenes and words and people forgotten, but stored in the back of the brain. These may not be important things, but they come back with startling clarity into the awareness that is turning away from reality. And these memories are almost visions.

And then it is over. You can't hear, but there is a rushing sound in your ears. And you want sleep more than anything, but when you do sleep you are dream-ridden, your mind is uneasy and crowded with figures. The anesthesia your body has given you to protect you is beginning to wear off, and, as with most anesthesia, it is a little painful.

And when you wake up and think back to the things that happened they are already becoming dreamlike. Then it is not unusual that you are frightened and ill. You try to remember what it was like, and you can't quite manage it. The outlines in your memory are vague. The next day the memory slips farther, until very little is left at all. A woman is said to feel the same way when she tries to remember what childbirth was like. And fever leaves this same kind of vagueness on the mind. Perhaps all experience which is beyond bearing is that way. The system provides the shield and then removes the memory, so that a woman can have another child and a man can go into combat again.

It slips away so fast. Unless you made notes on the spot you could not remember how you felt or the way things looked. Men in prolonged battle are not normal men. And when afterward they seem to be reticent—perhaps they don't remember very well. ❖

Connect to the Literature

1. What Do You Think? Were you surprised at Steinbeck's explanation of why soldiers don't talk about their combat experiences?

> **Comprehension Check**
> - According to Steinbeck, why don't soldiers talk about combat?
> - What physical changes occur during combat?

Think Critically

2. **ACTIVE READING** **ADJUSTING READING STRATEGIES** With a partner, discuss the notes you wrote down in your **READER'S NOTEBOOK** on the poem and essay. Which strategy was most valuable when you read "The Death of the Ball Turret Gunner"? Which was most helpful when you read "Why Soldiers Won't Talk"?

3. How are you affected by Steinbeck's use of the second-person "you" in his recounting of the physical effects of combat?

4. Steinbeck explains the physical experience of combat as a series of **causes** and **effects.** Do you think this is an effective method? Explain why or why not.

5. Does Steinbeck's explanation seem plausible to you?

THINK ABOUT

- the causes and effects he cites
- your own physical reactions to stress
- your own memory of stressful events
- other possible reasons why soldiers might not talk

Extend Interpretations

6. Comparing Texts Do you think that Jarrell and Steinbeck offer consistent or conflicting accounts of what combat feels like? Explain your answer.

7. Connect to Life Think about the adjustments veterans must make when they return from combat. What does society do to help ease their transition back into civilian life? What else do you think could be done?

Literary Analysis

IMAGERY AND TONE A writer sometimes conveys **tone,** his or her attitude toward a subject, through imagery. **Imagery** consists of the descriptive words and phrases used to re-create sensory experiences. In "The Death of the Ball Turret Gunner," notice the mental picture of a soldier created by the images "hunched in its belly" and "my wet fur froze." In "Why Soldiers Won't Talk," Steinbeck uses imagery to convey his attitude toward soldiers:

This is how you feel after a few days of constant firing. Your skin feels thick and insensitive. There is a salty taste in your mouth. A hard, painful knot is in your stomach where the food is undigested.

Paired Activity Get together with a partner and discuss imagery in the two selections. List images from Jarrell's poem and Steinbeck's essay. From these images, what would you say is Jarrell's attitude toward the soldier? What is Steinbeck's attitude toward combat and its effect on soldiers? How would you characterize the tone in each piece? Do Jarrell and Steinbeck seem to have the same attitude toward war as a whole?

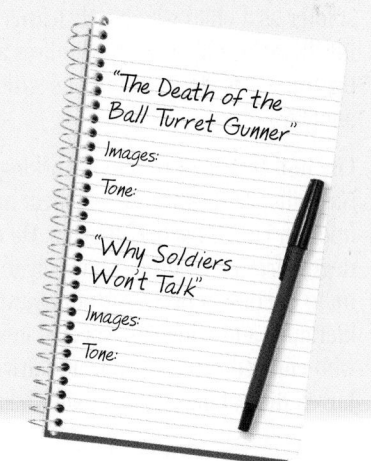

Writing Options

1. Grave Inscriptions Write two epitaphs—brief inscriptions on a tombstone—for the ball turret gunner. Write one that an official of "the State" might compose for him and one that the gunner might write for himself if he could.

2. Personal Narrative Write a personal narrative describing a situation in which you experienced extreme fear or stress. Focus on the physical reactions you had to the stress.

Activities & Explorations

1. Interview with a Veteran Set up an interview with a combat veteran of Vietnam, Desert Storm, or any other world conflict. Does the veteran avoid talking in detail about actual battle experience? If permitted, tape-record your interview and share it with the class. ~ **SPEAKING AND LISTENING**

2. Model Plane Study the picture of the B-17 on page 1089, or any photograph of a B-17 or B-24 with a ball turret. Create a model of the plane with a gunner inside. Show your model to the class, sharing your own thoughts about what it would feel like to be inside such a plane. ~ **ART**

Inquiry & Research

Shell Shock Investigate the condition known as *shell shock,* which is also called *battle fatigue* or *combat fatigue.* In an oral report, describe the symptoms of this condition to your classmates.

Randall Jarrell
1914–1965

Other Works
Losses
Pictures from an Institution
The Woman at the Washington Zoo
Complete Poems

Foremost WWII Poet Randall Jarrell has been called "America's foremost poet of World War II." He drew upon his four years of army service and upon news dispatches from the war front in writing *Little Friend, Little Friend,* the collection in which some of his best-known poems appear. In praise of the collection, critic Suzanne Ferguson wrote, "The motif of the soldier as a child who barely learns the meaning of his life before he loses it, who lives and dies in a dream, . . . is developed in one striking poem after another."

Life and Death Born into a working-class family in Nashville, Tennessee, Jarrell spent much of his child-hood in Long Beach, California. He earned a master's degree from Vanderbilt University in 1939 and went on to become a professor of creative writing and literature and a highly respected literary critic. A man who enjoyed playing tennis and driving sports cars, Jarrell died at the age of 51 after being struck by a car.

John Steinbeck
1902–1968

Other Works
Tortilla Flat
In Dubious Battle
Of Mice and Men
Cannery Row
East of Eden

The Writer's Charge In 1962 John Steinbeck became the sixth American to win the Nobel Prize in literature. In his acceptance speech, he said: "Literature is as old as speech. It grew out of human need for it, and it has not changed except to become more needed. . . . The ancient commission of the writer has not changed. He is charged with exposing our many grievous faults and failures, with dredging up to the light our dark and dangerous dreams, for the purpose of improvement." In his classic novel *The Grapes of Wrath,* Steinbeck brought to light the suffering and exploitation of Depression-era migrant laborers.

Living Simply Steinbeck's life spanned both world wars, the Korean War, and the Vietnam War, in which one of his sons served. Steinbeck avoided publicity, preferring to live simply and casually. As a young man, he held jobs as a ranch hand, a factory worker, and a construction worker.

Letter from Paradise, 21° 19′ N., 157° 52′ W.

Essay by JOAN DIDION

In Response to Executive Order 9066

Poetry by DWIGHT OKITA

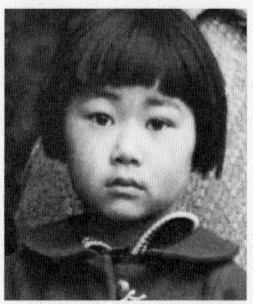

Connect to Your Life

Acts of War "Yesterday, December 7, 1941—a date which will live in infamy—the United States of America was suddenly and deliberately attacked by naval and air forces of the Empire of Japan." With those words, President Franklin D. Roosevelt, in response to the Japanese bombing of the U.S. naval base at Pearl Harbor in Oahu, Hawaii, began his request to Congress to declare war against Japan. What do you know about the attack on Pearl Harbor? What do you know about the later internment, or confinement, of Japanese Americans living on the West Coast of the United States? Brainstorm with a small group of classmates in order to share your knowledge.

Build Background

Effects of Pearl Harbor When the first Japanese bombs struck Pearl Harbor shortly before eight in the morning, the American forces were utterly unprepared. Anchored ships, such as the *Nevada,* the *Utah,* and the *Arizona,* provided easy targets for bombs and torpedoes. Most American airplanes, parked in orderly rows, were destroyed on the ground. In the attack, 18 ships were sunk or damaged, nearly 200 planes were destroyed, and thousands of people were killed.

The attack spawned American hatred and fear of Japan—and of Japanese Americans. Fearing that Japanese Americans would cooperate with the enemy, people on the West Coast of the United States sought to have all persons of Japanese ancestry—citizens and noncitizens alike—removed from coastal areas. Such a removal was authorized by President Roosevelt in Executive Order 9066. During 1942 more than 110,000 Japanese Americans living along the West Coast were forcibly removed from their homes and sent to internment camps called "relocation centers."

Read Joan Didion's essay, which describes her visit to Pearl Harbor 25 years after the attack, and Dwight Okita's poem, which gives a Japanese-American girl's response to the relocation order, to gauge the repercussions of that "day of infamy" in 1941.

Focus Your Reading

LITERARY ANALYSIS **MOOD** As you know, **mood** is the feeling or atmosphere that the writer creates for the reader. **Imagery, setting, dialogue,** and **figurative language** all contribute to the mood of a work, as do the sound and the **rhythm** of the language used. As you read the selections, think about the mood the writer conveys in each one.

ACTIVE READING **COMPARING MOOD** One way to compare two different selections is to compare the mood in each piece. As noted above, the images, dialogue, and figurative language in a literary work contribute to its mood.

READER'S NOTEBOOK As you read "Letter from Paradise," use a chart like the one shown to record the images, dialogue, and figurative language that contribute to the essay's mood. Create and fill out a similar chart for "In Response to Executive Order 9066."

Images	Dialogue	Figurative Language

Joan Didion

Every afternoon now, twenty-five years after the fact, the bright pink tour boats leave Kewalo Basin for Pearl Harbor. It has a kind of sleazy[1] festivity, the prospect of an outing on a fine day, the passengers comparing complaints about their tour directors and their accommodations and the food at Canlis' Charcoal Broiler, the boys diving for coins around the boats; "Hey Mister Big," they scream. "How's about a coin." Sometimes a woman will throw a bill, and then be outraged when the insolent brown bodies pluck it from the air and jeer at her expectations. As the boat leaves the basin the boys swim back, their cheeks stuffed with money, and the children pout that they would rather be at the beach, and the women in their new Liberty House[2] shifts and leftover leis[3] sip papaya juice and study a booklet billed as *An Ideal Gift—Picture Story of December 7*.

It is, after all, a familiar story that we have come to hear—familiar even to the children, for of course they have seen John Wayne and John Garfield at Pearl Harbor, have spent countless rainy afternoons watching Kirk Douglas and Spencer Tracy and Van Johnson[4] wonder out loud why Hickam[5] does not answer this morning—and no one listens very closely to the guide. Sugar cane now blows where the *Nevada* went aground. An idle figure practices putting on Ford Island.[6] The concessionaire breaks out more papaya juice. It is hard to remember what we came to remember.

And then something happens. I took that bright pink boat to Pearl Harbor on two afternoons, but I still do not know what I went to find out, which is how other people respond a quarter of a century later. I do not know because there is a point at which I began to cry, and to notice no one else. I began to cry at the place where the *Utah* lies in fifty feet of water, water neither turquoise nor bright blue here but the grey of harbor waters everywhere, and I did not stop until after the pink boat had left the *Arizona,* or what is visible of the *Arizona:* the rusted after-gun turret[7] breaking the grey water, the flag at full mast because the Navy considers the *Arizona* still in commission, a full crew aboard, 1,102 men from forty-nine states. All I know about how other people respond is what I am told: that everyone is quiet at the *Arizona.*

---

1. **sleazy:** shabby; cheap; shoddy.
2. **Liberty House:** a major department store in Hawaii.
3. **leis** (lāz): wreaths made of large colorful flowers and worn around the neck.
4. **John Wayne . . . Van Johnson:** Hollywood actors who starred in films dramatizing the attack on Pearl Harbor.
5. **Hickam:** Hickam Air Force Base, near Pearl Harbor. It also was attacked on December 7.
6. **Ford Island:** an island within Pearl Harbor.
7. **after-gun turret:** a low, revolving gun mount located in the "aft," or rear part, of a ship.

A few days ago someone just four years younger than I am told me that he did not see why a sunken ship should affect me so, that John Kennedy's assassination, not Pearl Harbor, was the single most indelible event of what he kept calling "our generation." I could tell him only that we belonged to different generations, and I did not tell him what I want to tell you, about a place in Honolulu that is quieter still than the *Arizona:* the National Memorial Cemetery of the Pacific. They all seem to be twenty years old, the boys buried up there in the crater of an extinct volcano named Punchbowl, twenty and nineteen and eighteen and sometimes not that old.

Copyright © 1991 P.J. Griffiths/Magnum Photos Inc.

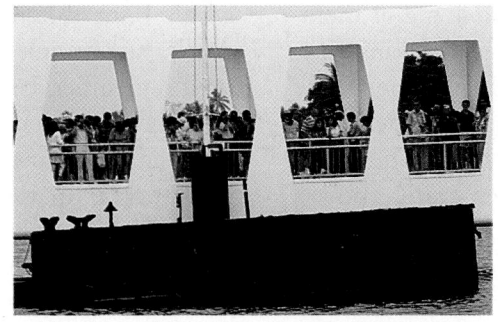

"SAMUEL FOSTER HARMON," one stone reads. "PENNSYLVANIA. PVT 27 REPL DRAFT 5 MARINE DIV. WORLD WAR II. APRIL 10 1928—MARCH 25 1945." Samuel Foster Harmon died, at Iwo Jima,[8] fifteen days short of his seventeenth birthday. Some of them died on 7 December, and some of them died after the *Enola Gay* had

8. **Iwo Jima** (ē′wə jē′mə): Iwo Jima and Okinawa (ō′kĭ-nä′wə), mentioned later, are islands that lie several hundred miles south of Japan. They were the sites of the last two major World War II battles in the Pacific. In 1942 a battle on the island of Guadalcanal (gwŏd′l-ka-năl′), east of New Guinea, raged for six months. Together, the three battles produced more than 80,000 casualties.

The battleship *Arizona,* sunk in the Pearl Harbor attack. From the white platform (seen from the side in the photo above), observers look down at the submerged wreck. Copyright © 1991 H.K. Owen/Black Star.

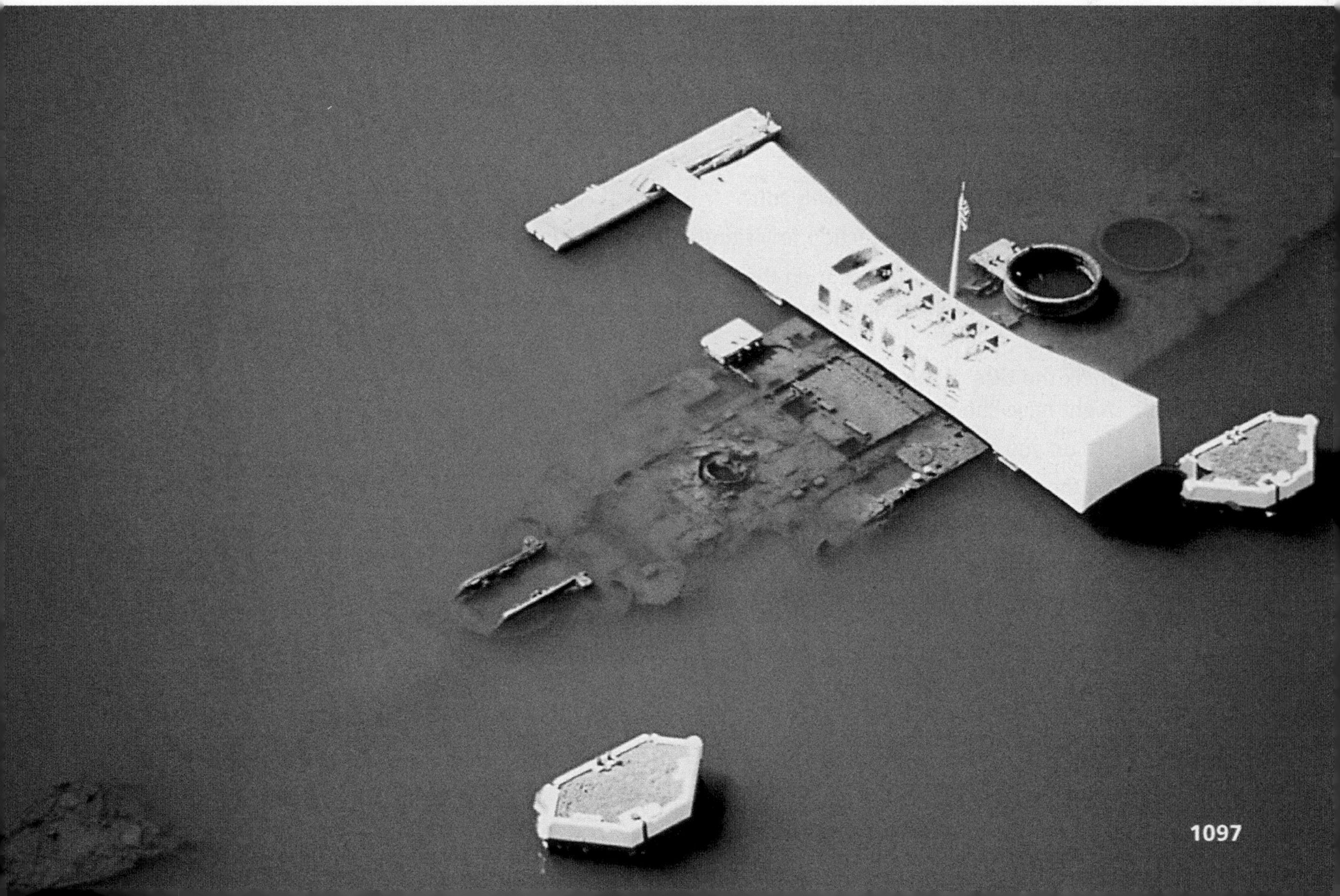

already bombed Hiroshima, and some of them died on the dates of the landings at Okinawa and Iwo Jima and Guadalcanal, and one whole long row of them, I am told, died on the beach of an island we no longer remember. There are 19,000 graves in the vast sunken crater above Honolulu.

I would go up there quite a bit. If I walked to the rim of the crater, I could see the city, look down over Waikiki[9] and the harbor and the jammed arterials,[10] but up there it was quiet, and high enough into the rain forest so that a soft mist falls most of the day. One afternoon a couple came and left three plumeria[11] leis on the grave of a California boy who had been killed, at nineteen, in 1945. The leis were already wilting by the time the woman finally placed them on the grave, because for a long time she only stood there and twisted them in her hands. On the whole I am able to take a very long view of death, but I think a great deal about what there is to remember, twenty-one years later, of a boy who died at nineteen. I saw no one else there but the men who cut the grass and the men who dig new graves, for they are bringing in bodies now from Vietnam. The graves filled last week and the week before that and even last month do not yet have stones, only plastic identification cards, streaked by the mist and splattered with mud. The earth is raw and trampled in that part of the crater, but the grass grows fast, up there in the rain cloud. ❖

---

9. **Waikiki** (wī′kĭ-kē′): a beach and resort district near Honolulu, on the Hawaiian island of Oahu.

10. **arterials:** major streets and highways.

11. **plumeria** (plōō-mîr′ē-ə): a tropical tree bearing large fragrant, colorful flowers.

Thinking Through the Literature

1. **Comprehension Check** What does Didion see when she visits Pearl Harbor? when she visits the National Memorial Cemetery of the Pacific?

2. What **images** from this essay stay with you?

3. How do you explain Didion's reaction to visiting Pearl Harbor?

4. Didion first describes Pearl Harbor, then the National Memorial Cemetery of the Pacific. What links do you see between the two places?

5. Do you think the **title** of this essay is a good one? Offer reasons why Didion might have chosen it.

6. What point do you think Didion is making in this essay?

   THINK ABOUT { • the last lines of the selection
   • any **ironies** you see in the details she includes

7. If you have ever visited a war memorial, or any other memorial to the dead, how did your reaction compare with Didion's in this essay?

In Response to Executive Order 9066:

ALL AMERICANS OF JAPANESE DESCENT

MUST REPORT TO RELOCATION CENTERS

Dwight Okita

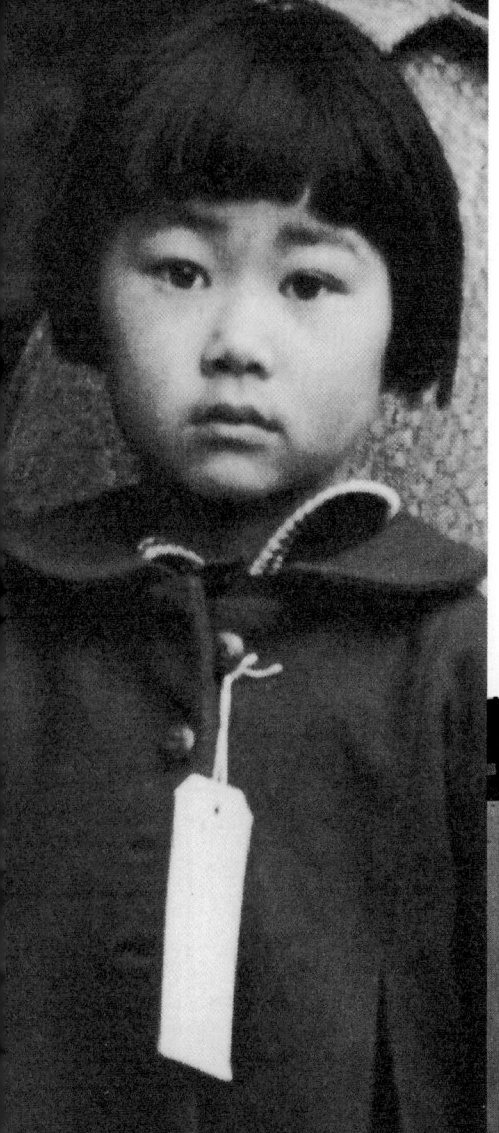

Dear Sirs:
    Of course I'll come. I've packed my galoshes
    and three packets of tomato seeds. Denise calls them
    love apples. My father says where we're going
5   they won't grow.

    I am a fourteen-year-old girl with bad spelling
    and a messy room. If it helps any, I will tell you
    I have always felt funny using chopsticks
    and my favorite food is hot dogs.
10   My best friend is a white girl named Denise—
    we look at boys together. She sat in front of me
    all through grade school because of our names:
    O'Connor, Ozawa. I know the back of Denise's head very
      well.

Clockwise from top: a woman and her children arriving at the relocation center in Manzanar, California; men in Manzanar; a young girl on evacuation day

1099

I tell her she's going bald. She tells me I copy on tests.
15 We're best friends.

I saw Denise today in Geography class.
She was sitting on the other side of the room.
"You're trying to start a war," she said, "giving
    secrets
away to the Enemy, Why can't you keep your big
20 mouth shut?"

I didn't know what to say.
I gave her a packet of tomato seeds
and asked her to plant them for me, told her
when the first tomato ripened
25 she'd miss me.

Clockwise from top: a car carrying a family to Manzanar; schoolgirls reciting the Pledge of Allegiance a few weeks before evacuation; a sign posted on the boundary of a relocation center; barracks at Manzanar

Connect to the Literature

1. **What Do You Think?** What thoughts and feelings do you have about the speaker in Okita's poem?

> **Comprehension Check**
> • Who is the speaker's best friend?
> • What does the speaker give her friend?

Think Critically

2. What do the details that the **speaker** mentions communicate to you about her?

3. If you had been in the speaker's situation, would your attitude toward the executive order have been similar to hers? Explain.

4. How do you interpret what the speaker's friend Denise says to her?

5. What do you think the tomato seeds might represent in the poem?

THINK ABOUT
> • what Denise calls them
> • where they will not grow
> • what the speaker says Denise will do when they ripen

6. **ACTIVE READING COMPARING MOOD** Use the charts you created in your 📖 **READER'S NOTEBOOK** to identify the overall **mood** of "Letter from Paradise" and "In Response to Executive Order 9066." Then compare the mood of Didion's essay with that of Okita's poem. Which piece do you think conveys mood more powerfully? Share your ideas with a classmate.

Extend Interpretations

7. **The Writer's Style** Both Didion and Okita write in an understated style, not boldly offering their opinions but instead carefully piling up descriptive details. Which do you think are the most telling details included in each piece? Consider ones that are particularly informative or ironic. Explain your choice of details, telling what important ideas you believe the writer is suggesting with them.

8. **Connect to Life** Imagine that the United States was suddenly attacked by a foreign country. How do you suppose Americans would react? Would they support an immediate declaration of war? How would they treat citizens who had originally come from the attacking country, or whose relatives lived there?

Literary Analysis

MOOD   Mood is the feeling or atmosphere a writer creates for the reader. The mood within a literary work can change. In "Letter from Paradise," for example, notice the light, informal mood of this passage, which describes the tour boats that leave for Pearl Harbor:

> *It has a kind of sleazy festivity, the prospect of an outing on a fine day, the passengers comparing complaints about their tour directors and their accommodations and the food at Canlis' Charcoal Broiler, the boys diving for coins around the boats; "Hey Mister Big," they scream. "How's about a coin."*

Compare the boisterous mood in the above passage with the somber, contemplative mood conveyed by Didion's description of the setting of the National Memorial Cemetery:

> *If I walked to the rim of the crater, I could see the city, look down over Waikiki and the harbor and the jammed arterials, but up there it was quiet, and high enough into the rain forest so that a soft mist falls most of the day.*

Activity Answer these questions: How would you describe the mood Didion creates in the first paragraph of her essay? When does the mood change, and what changes it? Does it change again, or does it stay the same throughout the rest of the selection? What mood does Okita create in the first 15 lines of his poem? How does the mood change in the last 10 lines? Why do you think both authors chose to create different moods within their work?

Choices & CHALLENGES

Writing Options

Family Memoir In her essay, Didion says, "I think a great deal about what there is to remember, twenty-one years later, of a boy who died at nineteen." In your mind, re-create this 19-year-old boy, giving him a name as well as physical and personal characteristics. Then write a short memoir detailing what a parent or a sister might remember most about him.

Activities & Explorations

Contrasting Cartoons Make two cartoon sketches of the speaker in "In Response to Executive Order 9066." The first should depict her as she views herself, and the second should show her as she is perceived by other Americans after the attack on Pearl Harbor. Base your images on details and dialogue from the poem. ~ ART

Inquiry & Research

Japanese-American Internment Find out more about the internment of Japanese Americans. What were some of the social and economic effects of imprisonment? Present your findings to the class. See the Related Reading on page 1103 for opposing views of the internment.

 More Online: Research Starter www.mcdougallittell.com

Joan Didion
1934–

Other Works
Run River
Salvador
After Henry
Miami

A Distinctive Style Joan Didion has received as much acclaim for her essays as she has for her best-selling novels. Critic Robert Towers describes her distinctive talent as "an instinct for details that continue to emit pulsations in the reader's memory and a style that is spare, subtly musical in its phrasing and exact." Like "Letter from Paradise," her essays tend to have a personal, confessional tone. In her collections *Slouching Towards Bethlehem* and *The White Album*, Didion deals with the themes of personal and cultural loss, disorder, and anxiety.

Reasons for Writing A screenwriter as well as a journalist and novelist, Didion was born and raised in California, where she has lived most of her life. She is married to the writer John Gregory Dunne, with whom she sometimes collaborates on screenplays. Of her writing, Didion says, "I write entirely to find out what I'm thinking, what I'm looking at, what I see and what it means. What I want and what I fear."

Dwight Okita
1958–

Other Works
Crossing with the Light
The Rainy Season
Salad Bowl Dance

Early Promise A Japanese American and a native Chicagoan, Dwight Okita has been writing poetry since first grade. When given writing assignments in school, he had difficulty creating "linear compositions," and so he would add rhymed poems at the end of his assignments. His teachers started grading both his assigned compositions and his poems—giving him poor grades for the compositions but good grades for his poems. In high school, Okita took an interest in writing, acting, and music. Today, he combines these interests by giving dramatic readings of his poetry, which he often sets to music.

Poetic Test In writing "In Response to Executive Order 9066," Okita adopted the voice of his mother, who, as a youngster during World War II, was sent to an internment camp. He imagined how she might have said goodbye to her classmates before being taken away. Okita's play *Letters I Never Wrote* began as a spinoff of this poem.

POINT / COUNTERPOINT:

THE JAPANESE-AMERICAN INTERNMENT

The Japanese bombing of Pearl Harbor in 1941 sparked war with the United States and spread fear that Japanese Americans would aid Japan during World War II. As a result, Executive Order 9066 was issued, and more than 110,000 Japanese Americans living on the West Coast of the United States were placed in internment camps. The following pieces present the arguments for and against internment.

JAPANESE-AMERICAN INTERNMENT
❶ WAS NECESSARY FOR NATIONAL DEFENSE.

The United States was still reeling from the Japanese attack on Pearl Harbor that had brought it into World War II—a threat, some felt, to its very existence. Tom Clark, assistant to the commanding general of the U.S. Army's Western Defense Command and later associate justice of the Supreme Court, offered a justification for internment. "Soon after Pearl Harbor I was deluged by demands that, regardless of citizenship, every person of Japanese descent must be removed from the West Coast," he explained. "The threatening public attitude . . . would permit nothing less than total mass relocation."

❷ Chief Justice Earl Warren pointed out, on the other hand, that many Japanese Americans held dual citizenship and were educated in both Japan and the United States. "Their affiliation in time of war worried us," he explained.

War correspondent Walter Lippman offered more concrete reasons. "It is the fact that the Japanese navy has been reconnoitering[1] the Pacific Coast. . . . It is the fact that communication takes place between the enemy at sea and the enemy agents on land."

❸ Historians Donald Pike and Roger Olmsted observe that only Japan among the Axis nations had attacked the United States, and "suddenly the Japanese . . . threatened our very national existence."

---

1. **reconnoitering** (rē'kə-noi' tər-ĭng): making a military inspection of an area.

Reading for Information

At various points in American history, the threat of war has heightened feelings of suspicion and fear. Even ordinary citizens were viewed as threatening, particularly those who came from Japan, a nation that had attacked the United States at Pearl Harbor. What security measures—severe or relaxed—should a nation take under such circumstances? It's important to consider all sides before deciding which viewpoint seems more reasonable.

ANALYZING AN ISSUE

An issue is a topic, policy, or action that is a matter of concern or debate. **Analyzing an issue** involves examining different points of view to evaluate each side of the argument and to make an informed judgment about the issue. Use the activities below to help you examine the issue of Japanese-American internment.

❶ Position Statement Notice that the first argument begins with a position statement supporting the internment of Japanese Americans.

❷ Identify the reasons for interning Japanese Americans. What justifications did the U.S. government use for internment?

❸ Analyzing Evidence Which reason supporting internment seems strongest to you? What evidence is provided to support that reason?

JAPANESE-AMERICAN INTERNMENT WAS AN UNNECESSARY AND A RACIST ACT.

"Our unjust imprisonment was the result of two closely related emotions: racism and hysteria," says Edison Tomimaro Uno, a former internee. Uno says the claim that Japanese Americans were relocated for their own protection was "sheer hypocrisy" and denies that Japanese Americans posed a national security threat. Instead, he calls the relocation a crime attributable to "racism [and] economic and political opportunism."

"War makes for harsh measures," notes the historian Cary McWilliams, "but we cannot justify the evacuation even as a war measure. No such measure was taken against German or Italian nationals."[2]

Another historian, Henry Steele Commager, comments, "It is sobering to recall that the record does not disclose a single case of Japanese disloyalty or sabotage during the whole war." In fact, more than 25,000 Japanese Americans served in the armed forces during World War II, and the all-Japanese-American 442nd combat team inflicted more casualties and received more decorations than any other comparable army unit.

Relocation left many Americans with a legacy of shame. Chief Justice Earl Warren confessed in his autobiography that he "deeply regretted" his testimony in favor of internment. Tom Clark said, "It was a sad day in our constitutional history."

Japanese-American children wait for a train to take them to the Manzanar internment camp.

---

2. **German or Italian nationals:** people living in the United States who were born in Germany or Italy.

❹ The second argument quotes Edison Tomimaro Uno, a Japanese-American internee, who states that the relocation was "attributable to 'racism [and] economic and political opportunism.'" What effect does including an internee's comment have on the **credibility** (believability) of the argument against internment? What effect do Uno's statements have on the "emotional appeal" of the argument?

❺ What reasons are given to support the position that internment was an unnecessary and unjust act? What evidence is used to support those reasons?

Evaluating Arguments Which side of the debate over Japanese-American internment do you believe presents the most convincing case? Give reasons to support your opinion.

Ambush

Short Story by TIM O'BRIEN

Comparing Literature

Traditions Across Time: War in Vietnam

The Vietnam War lasted nine years, claimed about 58,000 American lives, and left another 365,000 wounded. Night after night during that war, Americans at home watched footage of shocking combat scenes on the evening news programs. Like the soldiers described in John Steinbeck's essay, "Why Soldiers Won't Talk," the soldiers in Vietnam endured horrors—death, injury, physical hardship, and emotional trauma. In this story, Tim O'Brien recounts an incident in one soldier's combat experience and its effects on his life.

Points of Comparison As you read, look for the similarities and differences in the ways war and its effects are portrayed in "Ambush" and in "Why Soldiers Won't Talk."

Build Background

Uncertainties of War During the Vietnam War, even though the American soldiers were better equipped and better trained than the enemy, they fought in a foreign land they did not understand and for a cause that became increasingly unpopular at home. The Vietnamese Communists were skilled at guerilla warfare, using small armies in surprise raids. Their knowledge of the land enabled them to disappear whenever the U.S. forces attacked. These tactics often created a climate of frustration and fear among American soldiers. Tim O'Brien, who served 14 months as an infantryman during the war, presents one soldier's response to the fear and confusion in Vietnam and the troubling memories that haunt him after the war.

Focus Your Reading

LITERARY ANALYSIS **INTERNAL CONFLICT** **External conflict**—the struggle between a character and some outside force—is usually easy to identify in a work of fiction. **Internal conflict**—a struggle within a character—may be more subtle and complex. For example, an internal conflict may revolve around a decision a character has to make, or it may be reflected in behavior that is contradictory. As you read this story, watch for the development of internal conflicts in the main character.

ACTIVE READING **CONNECTING TO EXPERIENCE** Unlike many stories, this story presents a situation—a combat zone during the Vietnam War—that is unfamiliar to most readers. In order to enter into the experiences being related, you can use the following strategies:

- Pay attention to all the details the writer gives.
- Try to imagine what being a soldier in combat might be like.
- Call to mind any movies, books, or articles about the Vietnam War that give you some idea of what being in that war was like.
- Recall any situation involving extended conflict—living in a high-crime area, for example—that you have encountered or heard about. Think about what similarities are present in all conflicts.

READER'S NOTEBOOK As you read, keep notes about which details in the story you can connect with in some way. Also note any aspects of the story with which you find it difficult to relate.

AMBUSH

TIM O'BRIEN

When she was nine, my daughter Kathleen asked if I had ever killed anyone. She knew about the war; she knew I'd been a soldier. "You keep writing these war stories," she said, "so I guess you must've killed somebody." It was a difficult moment, but I did what seemed right, which was to say, "Of course not," and then to take her onto my lap and hold her for a while. Someday, I hope, she'll ask again. But here I want to pretend she's a grown-up. I want to tell her exactly what happened, or what I remember happening, and then I want to say to her that as a little girl she was absolutely right. This is why I keep writing war stories:

He was a short, slender young man of about twenty. I was afraid of him—afraid of something—and as he passed me on the trail I threw a grenade that exploded at his feet and killed him.

Or to go back:

Shortly after midnight we moved into the ambush site outside My Khe.[1] The whole platoon was there, spread out in the dense brush along the trail, and for five hours nothing at all happened. We were working in two-man teams —one man on guard while the other slept, switching off every two hours —and I remember it was still dark when Kiowa shook me awake for the final watch. The night was foggy and hot. For the first few moments I felt lost, not sure about directions, groping for my helmet and weapon. I reached out and found three grenades and lined them up in front of me; the pins had

> "YOU KEEP WRITING THESE WAR STORIES SO I GUESS YOU MUST'VE KILLED SOMEBODY."

---

1. **My Khe** (mĭ'kĕ').

Fenixes (1984), Rupert Garcia. Pastel on paper, 40″ × 78¾″, courtesy of Rupert Garcia; Rena Bransten Gallery, San Francisco; and Galerie Claude Samuel, Paris. Copyright © Rupert Garcia.

already been straightened for quick throwing. And then for maybe half an hour I kneeled there and waited. Very gradually, in tiny slivers, dawn began to break through the fog, and from my position in the brush I could see ten or fifteen meters up the trail. The mosquitoes were fierce. I remember slapping at them, wondering if I should wake up Kiowa and ask for some repellent, then thinking it was a bad idea, then looking up and seeing the young man come out of the fog. He wore black clothing and rubber sandals and a gray ammunition belt. His shoulders were slightly stooped, his head cocked to the side as if listening for something. He seemed at ease. He carried his weapon in one hand, muzzle down, moving without any hurry up the center of the trail. There was no sound at all—none that I can remember. In a way, it seemed, he was part of the morning fog, or my own imagination, but there was also the reality of what was happening in my stomach. I had already pulled the pin on a grenade. I had come

up to a crouch. It was entirely automatic. I did not hate the young man; I did not see him as the enemy; I did not ponder issues of morality or politics or military duty. I crouched and kept my head low. I tried to swallow whatever was rising from my stomach, which tasted like lemonade, something fruity and sour. I was terrified. There were no thoughts about killing. The grenade was to make him go away—just evaporate—and I leaned back and felt my mind go empty and then felt it fill up again. I had already thrown the grenade before telling myself to throw it. The brush was thick and I had to lob it high, not aiming, and I remember the grenade seeming to freeze above me for an instant, as if a camera had clicked, and I remember ducking down and holding my breath and seeing little wisps of fog rise from the earth. The grenade bounced once and rolled across the trail. I did not hear it, but there must've been a sound, because the young man dropped his weapon and began to run, just two or three quick steps, then he hesitated,

EVEN NOW I HAVEN'T FINISHED SORTING IT OUT. SOMETIMES I FORGIVE MYSELF, OTHER TIMES I DON'T.

swiveling to his right, and he glanced down at the grenade and tried to cover his head but never did. It occurred to me then that he was about to die. I wanted to warn him. The grenade made a popping noise—not soft but not loud either—not what I'd expected—and there was a puff of dust and smoke—a small white puff—and the young man seemed to jerk upward as if pulled by invisible wires. He fell on his back. His rubber sandals had been blown off. There was no wind. He lay at the center of the trail, his right leg bent beneath him, his one eye shut, his other eye a huge star-shaped hole.

It was not a matter of live or die. There was no real peril. Almost certainly the young man would have passed by. And it will always be that way.

Later, I remember, Kiowa tried to tell me that the man would've died anyway. He told me that it was a good kill, that I was a soldier and this was a war, that I should shape up and stop staring and ask myself what the dead man would've done if things were reversed.

None of it mattered. The words seemed far too complicated. All I could do was gape at the fact of the young man's body.

Even now I haven't finished sorting it out. Sometimes I forgive myself, other times I don't. In the ordinary hours of life I try not to dwell on it, but now and then, when I'm reading a newspaper or just sitting alone in a room, I'll look up and see the young man coming out of the morning fog. I'll watch him walk toward me, his shoulders slightly stooped, his head cocked to the side, and he'll pass within a few yards of me and suddenly smile at some secret thought and then continue up the trail to where it bends back into the fog. ❖

Thinking through the LITERATURE

Connect to the Literature

1. **What Do You Think?**
   What aspect of this story had the strongest impact on you?

   ### Comprehension Check
   - What was the young Vietnamese man doing before the narrator killed him?
   - What does the dead soldier "do" when he "reappears" to the narrator?

Think Critically

2. Why do you think the narrator kills the man?

   THINK ABOUT
   - the narrator's mental and physical state as the man nears
   - Kiowa's remarks to the narrator
   - the narrator's statement that "there was no real peril"

3. How would you describe the narrator's initial reactions after the killing?

4. Why do you think the narrator keeps writing war stories?

5. **ACTIVE READING   CONNECTING TO EXPERIENCE** Look back at the notes you made in your ⬛ **READER'S NOTEBOOK** about connecting to the experiences described in this story. What details drew you into the experiences the narrator relates? Were there any experiences that you could not relate to? Explain your answers.

Extend Interpretations

6. **The Writer's Style** "Ambush" is a work of fiction, but the story reads like a nonfiction account of a true event. Why do you think O'Brien used this style? Do you think it is effective? Why or why not?

7. **Connect to Life** The fear and uncertainty of war can affect a person's ability to think clearly and make decisions. Think of other situations that might generate a level of anxiety and stress that would have similar consequences. Do you think decisions made under these circumstances should be judged in the same way as decisions made under ordinary circumstances? Explain your answer.

8. **Points of Comparison** "Ambush" and "Why Soldiers Won't Talk" both portray the effects of war on the soldiers who fight in them. Which of these selections seems most realistic and convincing to you? Support your answer with evidence from the selection.

Literary Analysis

INTERNAL CONFLICT

An **external conflict** involves opposition with an outside force. The setting of "Ambush"—the Vietnam War—is a major external conflict between opposing nations and armies. Within that larger conflict the story focuses on the **internal conflicts**—the inner struggles—of the narrator. Internal conflicts may center on a decision a character must make or on problems that draw out contradictory behavior in the character. Internal conflicts often arise out of situations that are ambiguous—that can be interpreted in more than one way.

From the opening lines of the story, the narrator faces situations that generate internal conflicts for him. For example, when his daughter asks whether he has ever killed anyone, he does not know whether he should tell her the truth or not. He says, "It was a difficult moment, but I did what seemed right."

Paired Activity With a partner, identify another internal conflict the narrator experiences. Describe the conflict and the circumstances that lead to it. Tell whether you agree with the way the narrator tries to resolve the conflict.

REVIEW   TITLE The **title** of a work often carries more than one level of meaning. It may summarize a theme, raise a question, or make an ironic comment. Think about the meaning of the word *ambush*. Is more than one kind of ambush portrayed in this story? What is the main connection between the title and the story?

Choices & CHALLENGES

Writing Options

1. Exhibit Proposal Draw up a proposal for a multimedia exhibit on Vietnam for your public library. Briefly describe the parts of the exhibit, including any technology components. Also include materials you think will be needed, a possible schedule for producing the exhibit, and a list of staff needs. Place the proposal in your **Working Portfolio.**

2. Points of Comparison
Write a brief essay in which you analyze what happens in "Ambush" in terms of Steinbeck's ideas in "Why Soldiers Won't Talk." Consider how the two pieces might be considered to be in conflict as well as how Steinbeck's observations might help to explain what the narrator describes.

Writing Handbook
See page 1283: Analysis.

Activities & Explorations

Movie Score Think about what episodes might go into a short movie based on "Ambush." Then look for pieces of music that would reflect the varying episodes and moods in such a movie. Put together the pieces in a sequence that could serve as a score for the film. If possible, get recordings of the works and play them for the class, explaining your choices. ~ **MUSIC/SPEAKING AND LISTENING**

Inquiry & Research

Guerrilla Tactics Investigate the tactics used by the Vietcong guerrillas in the Vietnam War. Find out how their operations and attitudes created major obstacles for the American forces. Present your findings to the class, and discuss how the guerrilla tactics relate to what happens in "Ambush."

 More Online: Research Starter
www.mcdougallittell.com

Tim O'Brien
1946–

Other Works
If I Die in a Combat Zone, Box Me Up and Ship Me Home
Northern Lights
Going After Cacciato
The Nuclear Age
The Things They Carried
In the Lake of the Woods

War and Writing In 1968, immediately after graduating from college with a bachelor's degree in political science, Tim O'Brien was drafted into the army. He was wounded in Vietnam, earning a Purple Heart. Discharged from the army as a sergeant, he accepted a full scholarship to Harvard University as a graduate student in government. While studying at Harvard, O'Brien wrote *If I Die in a Combat Zone, Box Me Up and Ship Me Home*, a book of memoirs about his combat experiences. He subsequently left Harvard to pursue writing as a full-time career.

Major Awards O'Brien's third book, *Going After Cacciato*, won the National Book Award in 1979.

Inspired by O'Brien's own struggle with the choice of whether to go to Vietnam or flee the country, the novel tells about a soldier who decides to escape from Vietnam and the army. *The Things They Carried*, O'Brien's fifth book, won the 1990 National Book Critics Circle Award as best novel of the year.

Novelist's Focus Although he writes about war, O'Brien does not consider himself a war novelist. The true concern of his writing, he says, is "the exploration of substantive, important human values." Regarding his most acclaimed novel, O'Brien said in an interview, "It's not really Vietnam that I was concerned about when I wrote *Cacciato;* rather, it was to have readers care about what's right and wrong and about the difficulty of doing right, the difficulty of saying no to a war."

Author Activity

Real-Life Experiences Read some sections of O'Brien's memoirs, *If I Die in a Combat Zone, Box Me Up and Ship Me Home.* Share with the class any insights you gain into "Ambush" from O'Brien's reflections on his own experience.

Camouflaging the Chimera

Poetry by YUSEF KOMUNYAKAA
(yōō′sĕf kō′mōōn-yä′kä)

Deciding

Poetry by WENDY WILDER LARSEN
and TRÂN THI NGA (drän thē nyä)

Comparing Literature

Traditions Across Time: War in Vietnam

These poems present strong personal images of the Vietnam War from two perspectives—that of an American combat soldier and that of a Vietnamese civilian. Both pieces convey the upheaval of the war and bring to life its frightening realities.

Points of Comparison Compare the speaker in these poems with the characters and speakers in the World War II selections. Think about the turmoil and divisions experienced by people in both wars, and note similarities and differences in their attitudes toward war, life, and death.

Build Background

Evocative Titles The word *chimera* in the title of the first poem has several meanings. It is the name of a mythical fire-breathing monster, a composite of a lion, a goat, and a serpent. The word also refers to a plant created from a mixture of cells of different species. In addition, *chimera* can mean a fantastic or terrible creation of the imagination.

The title of the second poem, "Deciding," refers to the difficult situation the speaker of the poem finds herself in. The speaker is a Vietnamese worker in an American office in Saigon who must decide whether to stay or flee after the United States has withdrawn its troops and the fall of South Vietnam appears imminent. She fears how she will be treated by the Communist victors from North Vietnam.

Focus Your Reading

LITERARY ANALYSIS **SPEAKER IN POETRY** The **speaker** of a poem, like the narrator of a story, is the voice that talks to the reader. In some poems, the speaker can be identified with the poet. However, in many poems, the speaker is someone or something other than the poet. As you read "Camouflaging the Chimera" and "Deciding," think about the role of the speaker in the two poems.

ACTIVE READING **STRUCTURE IN POETRY** In poetry, **structure** refers to the arrangement of words, lines, and stanzas to produce a desired effect. The structure of a poem usually emphasizes important aspects of content and **mood.** In "Camouflaging the Chimera," for example, the staccato lines and brief, free verse stanzas help create a tense, wary mood.

READER'S NOTEBOOK As you read the poems, write down what you notice about the stanza structure in each one. Notice line length, the number of lines in each stanza, and the relationship between stanzas and the ends of sentences. Also, think about how the variety of stanza structure relates to the poem's mood and ideas.

Camouflaging the Chimera

Yusef Komunyakaa

We tied branches to our helmets.
We painted our faces & rifles
with mud from a riverbank,

blades of grass hung from the pockets
5   of our tiger suits. We wove
ourselves into the terrain,
content to be a hummingbird's target.

We hugged bamboo & leaned
against a breeze off the river,
10   slow-dragging with ghosts

from Saigon to Bangkok,
with women left in doorways
reaching in from America.
We aimed at dark-hearted songbirds.

15   In our way station of shadows
rock apes tried to blow our cover,
throwing stones at the sunset. Chameleons

crawled our spines, changing from day
to night: green to gold,
20   gold to black. But we waited
till the moon touched metal,

till something almost broke
inside us. VC struggled
with the hillside, like black silk

25   wrestling iron through grass.
We weren't there. The river ran
through our bones. Small animals took refuge
against our bodies; we held our breath,

ready to spring the L-shaped
30   ambush, as a world revolved
under each man's eyelid.

GUIDE FOR READING

1–6 How do you visualize the soldiers from this description?

5 tiger suits: camouflage uniforms with black and green stripes.

7 What might it mean to be "a hummingbird's target"?

10–14 What is revealed about the soldiers' state of mind from their slow-dragging, or dancing, with ghosts and their aiming at songbirds?

11 Saigon (sī-gŏn′): formerly the capital of South Vietnam. **Bangkok** (băng′kŏk′): the capital of Thailand.

15 way station: a station between main stations, as on a railroad line. In what sense is the soldiers' position a "way station"?

16 rock apes: mountain-dwelling monkeys.

16–21 Notice how the passage of time is suggested through these images of nature. In what ways are the soldiers like the chameleons?

23–24 VC . . . silk: The Viet Cong, Communist rebels who fought U.S. soldiers, typically wore black for camouflage during nighttime operations in the jungle.

20–25 How were the American soldiers able to spot the VC?

26–28 How well were the soldiers camouflaged?

Members of a long-range reconnaissance patrol unit in Vietnam. Photo by John Olson for *Life* Magazine. Copyright © Time Inc.

Thinking Through the Literature

1. **Comprehension Check** What are the soldiers in the poem doing?

2. What did you think or feel as you visualized the **images** of the Vietnam War presented in this poem?

3. How do you interpret the last image in the poem?

4. What do you imagine the soldiers thought and felt in their "way station of shadows"? Support your answer with lines from the poem.

5. In line 26, how do you interpret the statement "We weren't there"?

6. Offer your explanation of the **title** "Camouflaging the Chimera."

THINK ABOUT
{
- which definition of chimera seems to best fit the poem (see page 1111)
- the visual image brought to your mind by the title

Deciding

Wendy Wilder Larsen and Tran Thi Nga

We went to the office every day.
Though the situation was critical,
people at work said nothing.
Province Chiefs were running.
5　We told the Big Boss our country would be lost.
We told him we would blow ourselves up
if we could not leave.

I sat at my desk doing the financial report.
My thoughts went round and round.

10　Should I leave?
Should I go alone?
Should I take my mother?
She did not want to go.
She feared they wouldn't let her chew the betel.
15　Should I leave my children?
How would I make a living?
What would happen when the communists came?

When I made up my mind,
pictures of my childhood floated to the surface
20　as clear and strong as dreams.

Our old house in Hadong.
The bamboo in the backyard.
We ate the shoots.
The soldiers made a fence from the stalks.
25　My sister and I painted the fence
first white, then blue, then her favorite yellow.
The small antigonon vine we planted
with its pink blossoms in spring.

GUIDE FOR READING

1–9 Who are "we"? What state of mind are these people in?

12–14 Who are "they"? What are other reasons the mother might not want to leave?

14 betel (bēt'l): Many Asians chew nuts from the betel palm tree as a mild stimulant.

18–20 Can you tell what the speaker has decided?

21 Hadong (hä'döng'): a town in North Vietnam.

21–34 What can you tell about the speaker's childhood from these images?

27 antigonon (ăn-tǐ'gə-nän').

People running for a U.S. helicopter during the fall of Saigon in April 1975. Copyright © 1975 Nik Wheeler/Black Star.

Our ponds.
30 The many steps down
to the small bridge
where we'd sit hour after hour
letting our hands dip into the water
trying to catch the silver-brown fish.

35 Airplanes bombing
running from our house
people dying, people calling from outside the walls
don't take me. I'm not dead yet.
The family hiding together in our house in Cholon
40 sunlight coming through the bullet holes.

39 Cholon (chō-lŏn'): the Chinese section of Saigon, in South Vietnam.

35–40 What mood is created by these images?

Connect to the Literature

1. What Do You Think?
If you had been the speaker in "Deciding," would you have stayed or fled?

··
Comprehension Check
• What does the speaker of "Deciding" have to decide?
• What memories does the speaker recall?
··

Think Critically

2. How do you think the speaker's childhood memories influenced her decision?

3. What message do you draw from the final image of sunlight shining through bullet holes?

4. Judging only from these poems, whose experience of war do you think was worse, the American soldiers' or the Vietnamese civilians'?

THINK ABOUT
{
• the soldiers' feelings as they wait in ambush and what you imagine the attack will be like
• the memories of the speaker in "Deciding" and the decision she is forced to make

5. ACTIVE READING STRUCTURE IN POETRY Review the notes you wrote down in your READER'S NOTEBOOK. What did you notice about the stanzas and line lengths in "Camouflaging the Chimera" and "Deciding"? How does the structure of each poem relate to the ideas and **mood** in each one?

Extend Interpretations

6. Connect to Life Imagine that you are faced with the necessity of fleeing your country, possibly never to return. What images of your own life would fill your mind?

7. Points of Comparison "Deciding," "Armistice," and "Executive Order 9066" all deal with the turmoil and divisions experienced by civilians as a result of war. In what ways are the divisions described in the three pieces similar? In your opinion, which of the three situations described creates the most turmoil? Explain your answer.

Literary Analysis

SPEAKER IN POETRY The **speaker** in a poem is sometimes a distant observer and at other times is intimately involved with the experiences and ideas being expressed. In both "Camouflaging the Chimera" and "Deciding," the use of first-person pronouns indicate that the speakers are active participants in the thoughts and actions described. In the following passage from "Camouflaging the Chimera," notice how the repeated use of the pronouns "we" and "our" emphasizes the speaker's identification with the group:

We weren't there. The river ran through our bones. Small animals took refuge against our bodies; we held our breath,...

In "Deciding," the speaker also identifies with a group—"we"—which she distinguishes from another group—"they." The speaker reveals her own thoughts and memories but also refers throughout the poem to the words and feelings of others:

Airplanes bombing running from our house people dying, people calling from outside the walls don't take me. I'm not dead yet.

Cooperative Learning Activity In a small group, discuss the speaker in each poem. Why do you think the poets made the speakers participants in the action? What would be lost if a detached observer had related a soldier's experience or a civilian's dilemma? What is the effect of each speaker's identification with his or her particular group?

Writing Options

Points of Comparison Write a dialogue between the soldier in "The Death of the Ball Turret Gunner" and one of the soldiers on patrol in "Camouflaging the Chimera." Have the soldiers discuss their attitude toward war, death, and the enemy. Use images from the poems to develop their conversation.

Inquiry & Research

Environmental Effects of War Both of these poems give a sense of Vietnam's unique physical environment. Investigate the effects of the war on the natural environment in Vietnam. Create an illustrated and annotated map of the country, detailing the environmental damage wrought.

Wendy Wilder Larsen
1940–

Encounter in Saigon Born in Boston, Wendy Wilder Larsen lived in Saigon from 1970 to 1971 with her husband, who was head of the local bureau of *Time* magazine. While in Saigon, she taught English literature and met Tran Thi Nga, a Vietnamese bookkeeper in the *Time* office. In 1975 Larsen encountered Nga again, in New York, after Nga had fled from Saigon with three of her four children and a grandchild. Over lunch, Larsen began to learn about Nga's amazing life.

Yusef Komunyakaa
1947–

Other Works
Lost in the Bonewheel Factory
Copacetic
Thieves of Paradise

Portrait of a Poet Born in Bogalusa, Louisiana, Yusef Komunyakaa entered the army at age 18, immediately after graduating from high school. After returning from Vietnam, where he earned a Bronze Star, Komunyakaa attended college in Colorado and eventually earned a master of fine arts degree in creative writing from the University of California at Irvine. He has lived in a number of countries for short periods, including Australia, Puerto Rico, and Japan. He is currently professor of English at Indiana University in Bloomington and travels across the United States and abroad to read his poetry. "Camouflaging the Chimera" is the first poem in his collection *Dien Cai Dau,* the title of which is Vietnamese slang for "crazy." Komunyakaa won the 1994 Pulitzer Prize for poetry for his book *Neon Vernacular: New and Selected Poems.*

Tran Thi Nga
1927–

Turbulent Times Nga was born in China, where her Vietnamese father had been sent to teach. Her family returned to North Vietnam to live when she was still very young. During the Chinese occupation of North Vietnam, 18-year-old Nga married a Chinese general in order to save her father's life. Her husband died in battle, and Nga became the second wife of her sister's husband, who was the man she had originally loved. In 1954, when Vietnam was divided into North and South, Nga's family moved to Saigon. In 1975, as South Vietnam fell, Nga narrowly escaped with her family; they eventually settled in Connecticut.

Verse Collaboration Larsen and Nga decided to work together to write Nga's story, to be combined with the story of Larsen's experiences in Saigon. The result was a book in verse, *Shallow Graves: Two Women and Vietnam,* from which "Deciding" comes.

At the Justice Department, November 15, 1969

Poetry by DENISE LEVERTOV

Comparing Literature

Traditions Across Time: War in Vietnam

The Vietnam War created deep divisions between those Americans who supported the government's policy in Vietnam and those who felt that the war was wrong. "At the Justice Department, November 15, 1969" describes what happens when these two sides clash during an antiwar demonstration.

Points of Comparison As you read the poem, compare the speaker's response to the Vietnam War with the public response to World War II described in "Armistice" and "Letter from Paradise."

Build Background

War Moratorium Levertov's poem was written in response to a specific protest march. The New Mobilization to End the War in Vietnam, a coalition committee of antiwar groups, organized two major demonstrations called moratoriums in the fall of 1969. One of the moratoriums took place in Washington, D.C., on November 13–15. The protests were, for the most part, peaceful. On a Thursday, a single file of protesters formed a procession from Arlington National Cemetery, each carrying a candle and a poster with the name of an American killed in Vietnam or the name of a Vietnamese village destroyed by U.S. troops. Each paused at the White House to call out the name on his or her poster, then went on to the Capitol to deposit the poster in a coffin. Two days later, the largest group of protesters to have ever gathered in the nation's capital up to that point—crowd estimates varied from 200,000 to 800,000—assembled peacefully at the Washington Monument to demonstrate their opposition to the war. That evening, a group of a few thousand militants tried to raise the Viet Cong flag in front of the Justice Department. When the demonstration became violent, police used tear gas against the crowd.

Focus Your Reading

LITERARY ANALYSIS STYLE **Style** is the particular way in which a piece of literature is written. Style refers not to what is said but how it is said. **Word choice, sentence length, rhythm,** and **imagery** all contribute to a writer's style. Notice the elements of style Levertov uses in her poem.

ACTIVE READING MAKING INFERENCES ABOUT MEANING When you read a poem, you usually need to make **inferences** to figure out what is unstated yet implied. You can make inferences about the meaning of a poem by thinking about its descriptive details. Notice details related to the following categories:

- the description of the tear gas
- the speaker's description of the incident and what she would like it to be
- the relationship among the protesters
- the relationship between the protesters and the police

READER'S NOTEBOOK List the poem's descriptive details as you read. Write down details related to the above categories as well as any other details that help you infer the poem's meaning.

At the Justice Department, November 15, 1969

Denise Levertov

Antiwar demonstrators march to the Washington Monument on Nov. 15, 1969. Photo by John Olson for *Life* Magazine. Copyright © Time Inc.

Brown gas-fog, white
beneath the street lamps.
Cut off on three sides, all space filled
with our bodies.
5   Bodies that stumble
in brown airlessness, whitened
in light, a mildew glare,
      that stumble
hand in hand, blinded, retching.
10 Wanting it, wanting
to be here, the body believing it's
dying in its nausea, my head
clear in its despair, a kind of joy,
knowing this is by no means death,
15 is trivial, an incident, a
fragile instant.   Wanting it, wanting
      with all my hunger this anguish,
      this knowing in the body
the grim odds we're
20 up against, wanting it real.
Up that bank where gas
curled in the ivy, dragging each other
up, strangers, brothers
and sisters.   Nothing
25 will do but
to taste the bitter
taste. No life
other, apart from.

Thinking *through the* LITERATURE

Connect to the Literature

1. **What Do You Think?** How do the images in the poem compare with the images you have formed about antiwar marches in the 1960s?

Comprehension Check
- What is the speaker's physical response to the tear gas?
- What does the speaker think about when she's being tear-gassed?

Think Critically

2. Describe the speaker's response to being tear-gassed. How do you explain her response?

> **THINK ABOUT** {
> - what she says she wants
> - what she calls the protesters

3. How do you interpret the last words of the poem: "No life other, apart from"?

4. **ACTIVE READING** **MAKING INFERENCES ABOUT MEANING**
Look over the notes you wrote down in your **READER'S NOTEBOOK.** What can you infer about the poem's meaning? What might the tear gas represent? Why does the speaker call the incident "trivial"? What do you think she means by "wanting it real"?

Extend Interpretations

5. **Different Perspectives** In the poem, the speaker doesn't mention the police officers who threw the tear gas into the crowd of antiwar protesters. How do you think the officers felt when they faced the protesters? Why do you think they felt compelled to tear-gas the demonstrators?

6. **Connect to Life** Think about a time you protested a policy or practice at home, at school, or in your community. What means did you use to express your dissatisfaction? Did your protest effect any change?

7. **Points of Comparison** Compare Morris's response to World War II in "Armistice" with the speaker's response to the Vietnam War. How does Morris's stand on the war affect his life? How does the speaker's stand affect her life? Who seems happier? Who suffers more? Why do you think that is?

Literary Analysis

STYLE **Style** is the writer's uniquely individual way of communicating ideas. In Denise Levertov's "At the Justice Department, November 15, 1969," **word choice, sentence length, rhythm,** and **imagery** all help convey the poet's style. The style of the poem is also influenced by its subject and meaning. Notice the connection between style and subject in the following passage from the poem:

> *Bodies that stumble*
> *in brown airlessness, whitened*
> *in light, a mildew glare,*
> *   that stumble*
> *hand in hand, blinded, retching.*

The short, chaotic lines, choppy rhythm, and images of sightlessness help convey the experience of being tear-gassed.

Paired Activity With a partner, read aloud each sentence from the poem. Discuss what you notice about the word choice, sentence length, rhythm, and imagery in each one. You might want to use a chart like the one shown to list your ideas about these elements. Then answer these questions: How would you describe Levertov's style in the poem? What overall connection do you see between the style of the poem and its subject?

Word Choice	Sentence Length	Rhythm	Imagery

Writing Options

1. TV Script Sketch out the script for a TV news report about the incident described in "At the Justice Department, November 15, 1969."

2. Antiwar Storyboard Create a storyboard chronicling the antiwar movement of the 1960s. Write a brief paragraph describing each image you use to tell the movement's story. Be sure to include images and notes about antiwar singers and their songs. Place the storyboard in your **Working Portfolio.**

3. Points of Comparison In Joan Didion's "Letter from Paradise," the author shows great compassion for American soldiers who died during World War II. In Levertov's poem, the speaker protests against the efforts of American soldiers. Write an exchange of letters between Didion and the poem's speaker in which both explain and defend their positions.

Activities & Explorations

1. Opinion Poster Create a poster that could be carried by an antiwar protester or by a supporter of the war. Use slogans and images to express your opinion of the Vietnam War. ~ **ART**

2. War Debate Stage a debate between antiwar protesters and those who supported the war. Participants on both sides of the debate should research and prepare strong arguments to defend their positions. ~ **SPEAKING AND LISTENING**

Inquiry & Research

Impact of Antiwar Protests Find out what impact the antiwar protests of the 1960s had on American policy in Vietnam. In particular, what effect did the protest demonstrations have on American troop withdrawal from Vietnam? Share your findings with your classmates.

Denise Levertov
1923–1997

Other Works
The Jacob's Ladder
O Taste and See
The Sorrow Dance
Relearning the Alphabet
Breathing the Water
Evening Train

Unusual Upbringing Denise Levertov grew up in England, where she had an unusual home life. Her father, a Russian Jew who became an Anglican priest, trained Denise in religious philosophy and filled the house with theologians, booksellers, priests, and opera singers. Her mother, the daughter of a Welsh mystic, imparted to her a love of nature and spirituality.

Young Poet Although Levertov received no formal education—she was schooled at home by her mother—she never lacked the nerve or eloquence to speak out. Her poetic career began at age 5, when she declared she would become a poet. At age 12, she sent some poems to T. S. Eliot, who responded with two pages of criticism and encouragement.

Passionate Activist Never a passive observer, Levertov combined poetry and political activism to speak against social injustices. Some critics called her poetry preachy, while she criticized others for "mealy-mouthed" apathy in the face of social ills. In 1965, she cofounded the Writers and Artists Protest against the War in Vietnam. She participated in antiwar demonstrations in the 1960s and was jailed for protesting. In the 1980s she protested against U.S. involvement in civil wars in El Salvador, Honduras, and Nicaragua and spoke against nuclear armament and environmental abuse. According to her editor, Barbara Epler, "she was very 19th-century with her vision of what poetry was and how total a calling it was."

Comparing Literature: Assessment Practice

In writing assessments you will sometimes be asked to analyze how the details in a work of literature are used to develop the main ideas. You are now going to practice writing an analytical essay with this kind of focus.

PART 1 Reading the Prompt

Read the wording of the prompt carefully. Identify the selections you will be writing about, the type of writing you will be doing, and the topic of your essay.

Writing Prompt

Several of the selections in Unit Seven, Part 1, portray the experiences of soldiers in combat. Choose one of the selections from World War II and one from the Vietnam War. Analyze how the details described in each work reveal the difficult realities of life on the battlefield and the impact of those realities on the soldiers.

1

2

STRATEGIES
IN ACTION

1 To **analyze** is to look at parts in relation to a whole and to discover patterns, relationships, and recurring ideas.

2 Notice the **topic** of your analysis—the realities of combat and their impact on soldiers.

PART 2 Planning an Analytical Essay

- After choosing your two selections, think about ways to classify details that relate to your topic. For this essay, you might consider the different circumstances, people, actions, and attitudes experienced by a soldier in combat.

- For each selection, organize your details in a diagram. Note the realities and their effects.

- Look for patterns and relationships among the details.

- Draw conclusions from your analysis of the details.

Types of Details			
Circumstances	People	Actions	Attitudes

PART 3 Drafting Your Essay

Introduction Begin by clearly stating your topic—for this essay, how details reveal the realities of combat and the impact of those realities on the soldiers. Identify the selections you will be analyzing.

Organization Present the evidence of your analysis in a clear, logical way. For example, you might choose the most forceful examples from each selection for each of the categories you are examining.

Conclusion In the final paragraph, state your conclusions. Tell the reader what you think the details in the two selections reveal about life on the battlefield and its effects on soldiers.

Revision Allow time to review your work. Make sure it is clear, well-supported, and free from mistakes.

Writing Handbook See page 1283: Analysis.

Fallen Angels

WALTER DEAN MYERS

These thematically related readings are provided along with *Fallen Angels*:

In the Forest at Night
DUC THANH, TRANSLATED BY THANH T. NGUYEN AND BRUCE WEIGL

What Were They Like?
DENISE LEVERTOV

The Things They Carried
TIM O'BRIEN

from Dear America: Letters Home from Vietnam
GEORGE OLSEN

look at this)
E. E. CUMMINGS

The Spoils of War
LYNNE SHARON SCHWARTZ

from Ghosts in the Wall
KRIS HARDIN

Farewell to Manzanar

JEANNE WAKATSUKI HOUSTON AND JAMES D. HOUSTON

These thematically related readings are provided along with *Farewell to Manzanar*:

from Legends from Camp
LAWSON FUSAO INADA

Sleep in the Mojave Desert
SYLVIA PLATH

I Remember Pearl Harbor: Dealing with the "Problem Race"
CHARLES SHIRO INOUYE

Wilshire Bus
HISAYE YAMAMOTO

Trains at Night
ALBERTO ALVARO RIOS

Visiting Home
KEVIN YOUNG

from Unto the Sons
GAY TALESE

Lectures on How You Never Lived Back Home
M. EVELINA GALANG

And Even *More* . . .

Books
Night
ELIE WIESEL
A survivor's moving account of the Holocaust.

A Rumor of War
PHILIP CAPUTO
Considered among the best nonfiction accounts of the Vietnam War.

Fire in the Lake: The Vietnamese and the Americans in Vietnam
FRANCES FITZGERALD
A Pulitzer Prize–winning book about the U.S. military's role in Vietnam and Vietnamese cultural history.

Other Media
Tora! Tora! Tora!
Film about the attack of Pearl Harbor as seen from two viewpoints—American and Japanese. 20th Century-Fox.
(VIDEOCASSETTE)

The Best Years of Our Lives
Academy Award-winning film about veterans adapting to civilian life after World War II. Embassy Home Entertainment.
(VIDEOCASSETTE)

No Time for Tears—The Women Who Served
A documentary filled with personal accounts of women Vietnam veterans—nurses, doctors, and teachers. West End Films. (VIDEOCASSETTE)

Writers on World War II

EDITED BY MORDECAI RICHER

This sweeping collection of nearly 150 writers, such as Randall Jarrell, John Cheever, and Primo Levi, documents the viewpoints of eyewitnesses and soldiers. Included are fictional excerpts, shocking observations, and poignant letters that convey the grim horror of World War II.

Communication Workshop

Presenting text, sound, and images . . .

From Reading to Exhibiting In his story "Ambush," Tim O'Brien examines his experiences as a soldier during the Vietnam War and concludes, "Even now I haven't finished sorting it out. Sometimes I forgive myself. Other times I don't." It may be difficult to understand the strong feelings people have about war unless you know something about this emotional topic. One way to explore complex subjects is through **multimedia exhibits.** In such exhibits, video recordings, music, visuals, artifacts, and other media are used to engage viewers and teach them about particular topics.

For Your Portfolio

PROMPT Create a multimedia exhibit about a topic that interests you.

Purpose: To describe and inform
Audience: Classmates, members of your community, people with similar interests

---

Basics in a Box

GUIDELINES & STANDARDS Multimedia Exhibit

A successful multimedia exhibit should

- attract viewers' attention with appealing visuals, interesting artifacts, and clear text

- present information about a topic logically and clearly

- contain a variety of objects and materials appropriate to the subject

- include specific and accurate written information

- lead viewers along an easy-to-follow pathway, with clearly labeled beginning and ending points

Analyzing a Multimedia Exhibit

America at War

Large and engaging visuals capture viewers' attention.

A variety of appropriate materials—including photographs, text, a map, and military supply crates—teach viewers about the topic.

Guidelines IN ACTION

An interactive computer display offers more information about the topic and involves viewers in the exhibit.

Text and visuals concerning specific events are arranged in a logical sequence.

Artifacts such as the protest buttons, dramatic magazine cover, and posters shown here engage viewers and bring the subject to life.

Captions and short descriptions give viewers background information about the items displayed.

1. Your Working Portfolio 📁

Look for ideas in the **Writing Options** you completed earlier in this unit:

• **World War II Presentation,** p. 1086
• **Exhibit Proposal,** p. 1110
• **Antiwar Storyboard,** p. 1121

2. Inspirational Exhibits

Visit an art, science, or natural history museum and look for topic ideas in the exhibits you find there.

3. Online Museums

Visit a few museum Web sites to see what kinds of topics are covered there and to help you get ideas for your own exhibit.

TECHTutor

Consider the following options when you are deciding which media to use in your exhibit:

• Audiotapes and CDs
• Posters, photos, slides, charts, maps, and graphs
• Videos
• Artifacts and other objects

Creating Your Multimedia Exhibit

❶ Planning Your Exhibit

Since your exhibit will probably be a group effort, you might begin by brainstorming possible exhibit topics with a small group of your classmates. Try to come up with broad topics—such as sports, war, peace, and childhood—that you can later refine. See the **Idea Bank** in the margin for other suggestions. Then choose a topic that all group members are interested in. After you have selected a topic, follow the steps below.

Planning Your Multimedia Exhibit

▶ **1. Narrow the focus of your subject.** You will need to break down your topic into more specific parts. Use a web to list various elements of your subject that you might cover, then pick one or two elements as your focus.

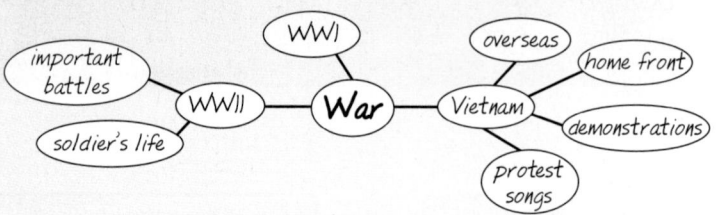

▶ **2. Brainstorm a list of materials.** What objects, materials, and media are most appropriate to your content and focus? Where will you find these things? Check the library and the Internet for books, photographs, audiotapes, and videos. Ask family members and friends for objects and artifacts that will fit in your exhibit. Are there any items you need that you will have to make yourself?

▶ **3. Conduct research.** Make some notes on what you already know about your topic and what you need to find out. Conduct library research to identify key ideas, dates, and facts that relate to your topic. As you research, consider what will interest your audience. What might they already know about this topic?

▶ **4. Sketch a rough floor plan.** Where will you set up your exhibit? Draw a sketch of the area and imagine how you might arrange items in it. Keep in mind the flow of traffic through your exhibit. To avoid traffic jams, make sure you put enough space between items in your exhibit. Also think about how many electrical outlets are available and where they are.

❷ Preparing Your Exhibit

After you have gathered all of your materials, use these steps to prepare your exhibit.

Preparing Your Multimedia Exhibit

▶ 1. **Revise your floor plan.** Depending on what materials you've gathered, you may need to revise your initial sketch. Will you group your materials chronologically? thematically? Which organization will offer the clearest and most interesting path through your exhibit?

▶ 2. **Create visuals.** You may need to create charts, graphs, or maps for your exhibit. Make sure the visuals you create are neat, clear, and accurate. If necessary, conduct research to ensure accuracy. Also make sure your visuals are large enough.

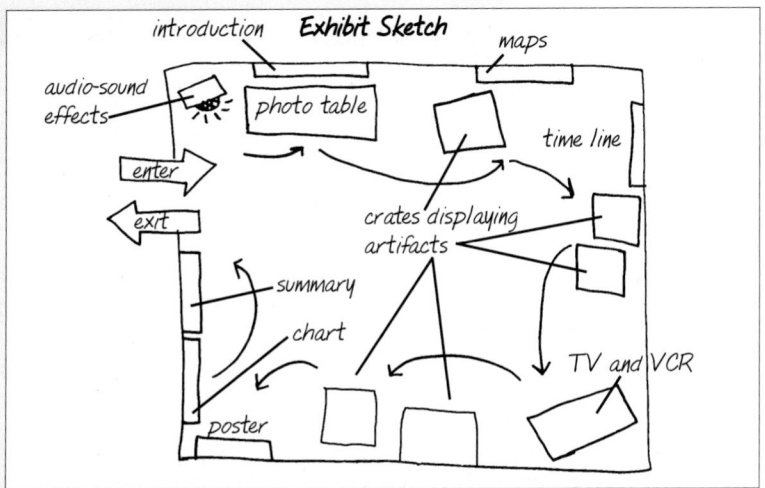

▶ 3. **Write the text.** For the beginning point of your exhibit, create a sign that includes the title of the exhibit and a paragraph explaining what viewers are about to see or why you created the exhibit. Also create labels that identify the items in the exhibit, pointing out their important features and explaining their significance. Finally, write a paragraph for the end of your exhibit, summarizing what viewers have seen. Your text should be clear, specific, and accurate.

▶ 4. **Proofread the text.** Although your exhibit may not include a lot of text, everything you write should be grammatically correct. Share the task of editing and proofreading with other group members. Refer to the **Grammar Handbook,** pages 1305–1341, to help you fix any grammatical errors.

▶ 5. **Arrange your materials.** You may want to experiment with the layout, but use your final sketch to guide you in setting up your exhibit.

Need help with your exhibit?

See the
Communication Handbook

Making Multimedia Presentations, p. 1304

Understanding Visual Messages, p. 1302

Using Visual Representations, p. 1303

Need revising help?

Review the **Guidelines & Standards**, p. 1124

Consider **peer reviewers'** comments

Check **Revision Guidelines**, p. 1269

Unsure about visuals?

See the **Communication Handbook**

Using Visual Representations, p. 1303

❸ Refining Your Exhibit

After you have constructed your exhibit, ask several friends or classmates to walk through it and share their impressions. Use their feedback to make your exhibit as interesting, informative, and clear as possible. The following points can help you review your work:

- **Look at the exhibit as a whole.** Consider how well your materials work together. Does everything fit in the exhibit space? Does the order of the items make sense? Do any of the media you chose overpower other points of the exhibit?

- **Evaluate your information.** Have you presented enough information about the items? Have you presented too much? Are your facts accurate? Is the writing specific and clear?

- **Review your media choices.** Audiences often ignore lengthy text in favor of visuals. Do you have a good mix of sound, visuals, and text? Look for places where a visual would present your information more effectively than text. The example below shows one way to create a visual from text.

Ask Your Peer Reviewers

- What did you like best about the exhibit?
- What was confusing, unnecessary, or out of place?
- What else would you like to know about the topic?
- What changes in the arrangement of the exhibit would make it easier to follow?

Original

The United States began sending combat troops to Vietnam in 1965. By 1967, the troop strength was over 400,000. It remained at that level for two years, but began falling after 1969. In 1971, there were approximately 200,000 U.S. troops in Vietnam. All U.S. troops were withdrawn in 1973.

Revised

Combat Troops Involved

Troops (in thousands): 1,000 / 800 / 600 / 400 / 200 / 0

1961 1963 1965 1967 1969 1971 1973 1975

■ S.Vietnam ■ N. Vietnam ■ U.S.

Publishing IDEAS

- Invite other classes or families and friends to view your exhibit.
- Make a video of a group member proceeding through and explaining the exhibit.

More Online: Publishing Options
www.mcdougallittell.com

❹ Reflecting

FOR YOUR WORKING PORTFOLIO What did you discover about your topic while creating your exhibit? What did you learn about the strengths and weaknesses of the media themselves? Attach your reflections to any notes you made when preparing your exhibit. Save your notes in your **Working Portfolio.**

Read this passage from the first draft of a multimedia exhibit brochure. The underlined sections may include the following kinds of errors:

- incorrect verb forms
- incorrect possessive forms
- sentence fragments
- correctly written sentences that should be combined

For each underlined section, choose the revision that most improves the writing.

The new exhibit at the Lewiston Museum is called "The Watchful Eye." The exhibit showcases the work of Joanna Wing, an artist who <u>have contributed</u> a
(1)
great deal to the world of photography. <u>Here you will see her early photographs.</u>
(2)
<u>As well as samples of her recent work.</u> <u>You will see videos. You will hear sound</u>
(3)
<u>effects. She recorded them.</u>

In a recent interview, Joanna explained that an important lesson she <u>have</u>
(4)
<u>learned</u> is to carry a camera at all times. She never knows when something will
catch her eye. <u>A beautiful sunset or a sudden rainstorm.</u> <u>Joanna Wing's</u> work
(5)   (6)
will be on display during the month of October.

---

1. **A.** has contributed
   B. was contributed
   C. had contributed
   D. Correct as is

2. **A.** Here you will see her early photographs and samples of her recent work.
   B. Here you will see her early photographs, samples of her recent work.
   C. Here you will see her early photographs. Samples of her recent work, too.
   D. Correct as is

3. **A.** You will see videos, too. You will hear sound effects.
   B. You will see videos and hear sound effects that she recorded.
   C. She has made some videos. She has recorded a few sound effects.
   D. Correct as is

4. **A.** was learning
   B. will have learned
   C. has learned
   D. Correct as is

5. **A.** A beautiful sunset or a sudden rainstorm may inspire her to take a picture.
   B. Perhaps a beautiful sunset or a sudden rainstorm.
   C. Like a beautiful sunset or a rainstorm suddenly occurs.
   D. Correct as is

6. **A.** Joanna Wings'
   B. Joanna Wing
   C. Joanna Wings
   D. Correct as is

Need extra help?

See the **Grammar Handbook**

Correcting Fragments, p. 1323

Possessive Nouns, p. 1306

Verb Tense, p. 1310

Creating Words from Word Parts

What's in a word? While some words, called **base words,** cannot be further broken down, many English words are made up of two or more word parts. In the passage on the right, which words do you think are combinations of word parts?

Two examples are the nouns *assassination* and *generation.* They are formed by adding the word part *-ation* to a root derived from the Arabic *hassasin* and to the Latin root *gener.* Another word in the passage, the adjective *sunken,* is formed by adding the word part *-en* to the base word *sunk,* which is the past

> A few days ago someone just four years younger than I am told me that he did not see why a sunken ship should affect me so, that John Kennedy's assassination, not Pearl Harbor, was the single most indelible event of what he kept calling "our generation."
>
> —Joan Didion, "Letter from Paradise, 21° 19' N., 157° 52' W."

participle of the verb *sink.* Other examples include *younger, indelible,* and *calling.* Recognizing word parts and knowing their meanings can help you decode unfamiliar words.

Strategies for Building Vocabulary

There are two types of word parts: roots and affixes. A **root** is a core word part that cannot stand alone, like *gener* or *onym.* The root, as the term implies, carries the fundamental meaning of the word. For example, *gener* means "birth" and *onym* means "name."

An **affix** is a word part that can be added to the beginning or end of a root or base word to change its meaning. An affix at the beginning of a word is called a **prefix,** while one at the end is called a **suffix.** The word *incessant,* for example, is made up of three word parts:

Prefix	Root	Suffix
in-	+ cess +	-ant
"not"	"to stop"	"in a state of"

Together the parts mean "continuous" or "not ceasing."

❶ **Look for Prefixes** The prefix *in-* is part of many words in this subunit. For example, the word *inflict,* meaning "to deal out" or "to impose," is formed by adding the prefix *in-* ("on") to the Latin root *flict* ("to strike"). Note that the prefix *in-* can mean either "not" or "on." The chart on the right presents several common prefixes.

❷ **Identifying Suffixes** Adding a suffix to a base word often changes the word from one part of speech to another. For example, the suffix *-ation* changes the verb *generate* to the noun *generation.*

You can learn more about suffixes by studying the suffix chart below.

Prefix	Meaning	Words
cata-	in accordance with, down, against	catalogue, catastrophe
de-	to come down from, to remove from	derive, denounce
ex-, e-, ef-	out of, to drive out	exterminate, eject, effigy
inter-	between	intervene, intercede
mal-	badly, poorly	malnutrition, malevolent
prot-, proto-	first	protagonist, prototype

Suffix	Meaning	Words
-ate	having, characterized by, resembling, to act upon	denigrate, radiate, laminate, subjugate
-en	made of, to make	silken, sunken
-ence	an action, the state or quality of	violence, belligerence
-fy	to make	simplify, notify
-ure	action, process, or condition	exposure, failure

EXERCISE Identify the word parts that make up each word below. Use the meanings of the word parts to help define the word. Then use the word in a sentence. Use a dictionary to check your work.

1. depopulate   3. interference   5. expunge
2. cataclysm   4. malform

Grammar from Literature

Experienced writers sometimes draw attention to details by adding modifying phrases or series of words to the ends of sentences. A sentence closer, as such a word group is called, may add information about the word immediately preceding it or may add information to the sentence as a whole. The examples below demonstrate the variety of structures that can be used as sentence closers.

> adjective prepositional phrase
> **Gus was a heavy man,** with a strong, full head and a fleshy face. —Bernard Malamud, "Armistice"
>
> **Here, in front of the two doors, stands the arbiter of**
> appositive phrase
> **our fate,** an SS subaltern.
> —Primo Levi, *Survival in Auschwitz*
>
> **The graves filled last week . . . do not yet have stones,**
> participial phrases
> **only plastic identification cards,** streaked by the mist and splattered with mud. —Joan Didion, "Letter from Paradise"

Subordinate clauses can also be used as closers, as in these examples:

> adverb clause
> **The next day the memory slips farther,** until very little is left at all. —John Steinbeck, "Why Soldiers Don't Talk"
> adjective clauses
> **The breeze swayed the street lamp,** which creaked and moved the circle of light that fell upon the street.
> —"Armistice"

A writer sometimes begins a sentence with an independent clause that is vague and follows it with a sentence closer that fills in the details. In this way, the writer generates interest by raising readers' curiosity as they read the sentence. Notice how Joan Didion does this in the following example.

> **They all seem to be twenty years old,** the boys buried up there in the crater of an extinct volcano named Punchbowl, twenty and nineteen and eighteen and sometimes not that old. —"Letter from Paradise"

Using Sentence Closers in Your Writing As you revise your writing, look for places where sentence closers could be used to add interesting details or vary your sentence structures. You can choose from a variety of structures that serve well as closers.

Punctuation Tip A sentence closer is usually separated from the rest of the sentence by a comma or a dash.

> ORIGINAL
> **Joan Didion establishes a mood by means of a number of images.**
>
> REVISED
> **Joan Didion establishes a mood by means of a number of images,** showing readers passengers and tour directors, bright pink tour boats, and boys diving for coins.

You may use a dash if the closer expresses a sudden, dramatic break in thought. Be careful, however, not to overuse dashes. If a phrase or clause simply adds information to the sentence, use a comma.

> **The grocer as usual was sitting on the cot,** listening to the radio. —"Armistice"
>
> **Some of the prisoners were not with us in the afternoon**—they had been taken to the gas chamber.
> —*Survival in Auschwitz*

WRITING EXERCISE Rewrite the sentences below, adding a correctly punctuated sentence closer to each. Try to use a variety of grammatical structures in your closers.

1. A great deal of suffering has been caused by prejudice.
2. Some soldiers are boasters.
3. An explosion rocked the building.
4. In 1942 the federal government forced thousands of Japanese Americans living on the West Coast into internment camps.
5. Many death-camp survivors are haunted by unspeakable memories.
6. The scene was one of total confusion.
7. It was truly unforgettable; he remembered all the details.
8. The Vietnam War spurred acts of protest that took many forms.
9. Beneath the memorial, the remains of the battleship *Arizona* lie in the water.
10. Soldiers returning from war must live not only with their deeds and memories but with the probing questions of their children.

Integration and Disintegration

Postwar Society

American literature after World War II reflects the many changes that took place in society during that time. On the one hand, there were trends toward integration of African Americans, Latinos, women, and other groups previously excluded from political and cultural participation. On the other hand, there were trends toward the disintegration of structures and values that had been long upheld in the nation.

After the war, returning African-American veterans demanded the same rights and freedoms at home that they had fought to give to others abroad. In 1948 President Truman issued an executive order for integration of the armed forces and called for an end to discrimination in government hiring. Other civil rights advances followed, and in 1954 the Supreme Court's *Brown* v. *Board of Education* ruling struck down school segregation as unconstitutional. Martin Luther King, Jr., emerged as a civil rights leader during the 1955 Montgomery, Alabama, bus boycott, which ended segregation on city buses. In his 1963 "Letter from Birmingham Jail," he passionately defends the civil rights movement against critics who thought it was demanding too much, too soon.

The civil rights movement inspired other movements for justice. Mexican-American farmworkers and students, Native Americans, Asian Americans, feminists, the disabled, and many other Americans demanded basic rights and protested unfair laws, policies, and attitudes. Writers of literature called for inclusion and began to examine and celebrate their own particular cultural identities, as in Gary Soto's poem "Mexicans Begin Jogging" and Pat Mora's poem "Legal Alien."

As those barred from the mainstream demanded to join it, many within the mainstream wondered whether it was such a good place to be. American society in the 1950s was prosperous, consumerist, and conformist. Men striving to obtain "the good life" for their families were sometimes forced to suppress their individuality and desires as they worked for impersonal corporations. Works such as E. L. Doctorow's "The Writer in the Family," set in 1955, and Lanford Wilson's "Wandering" question the cost of such sacrifice.

In the 1960s, an influential youth counterculture arose, with the tenet, "Do your own thing." But as society became more permissive, the family as an institution seemed to weaken. Parents lost authority over children, and the divorce rate skyrocketed. Anne Tyler's "Teenage Wasteland," and John Updike's "Separating" are two stories that explore the breakup of a family.

Swearing-in ceremony of new U.S. citizens in New York City.

Voices from the TIMES

I have a dream that one day this nation will rise up and live out the true meaning of its creed, "We hold these truths to be self-evident; that all men are created equal." I have a dream that one day on the red hills of Georgia, sons of former slaves and the sons of former slave owners will be able to sit down together at the table of brotherhood. I have a dream that one day even the state of Mississippi, a state sweltering with the heat of injustice, sweltering with the heat of oppression, will be transformed into an oasis of freedom and justice. I have a dream that my four little children will one day live in a nation where they will not be judged by the color of their skin, but by the content of their character.

Martin Luther King, Jr.
from his "I Have a Dream" speech at
the 1963 March on Washington

For the first time in their history, women are becoming aware of an identity crisis in their own lives, a crisis which . . . has grown worse with each succeeding generation. . . . I think this is the crisis of women growing up—a turning point from an immaturity that has been called femininity to full human identity.

Betty Friedan
from *The Feminine Mystique*

They are the ones of our middle class who have left home, spiritually as well as physically, to take the vows of organization life . . .

William H. Whyte, Jr.
from *The Organization Man*

Voices *from the* TIMES

Come mothers and fathers
Throughout the land,
And don't criticize
What you can't understand.
Your sons and your daughters
Are beyond your command.
Your old road is rapidly agin'.
Please get out of the new one
If you can't lend a hand,
For the times they are a-changin'.

> **Bob Dylan**
> from "The Times
> They Are A-Changin"

We have allowed materialism to eclipse idealism, and overcompetitiveness to harm families and family values. Millions of people are in fear for the long-term security of their families, and a growing percentage is on the edge of poverty and despair.

> **Dr. Benjamin Spock**
> from *A Better World
> for Our Children*

My dream of America
is like dá bìn lòuh
with people of all persuasions and tastes
sitting down around a common pot
chopsticks and basket scoops here and
    there
some cooking squid and others beef
some tofu or watercress
all in one broth
like a stew that really isn't
as each one chooses what he wishes to eat
along with the good company
and the sweet soup
spooned out at the end of the meal.

> **Wing Tek Lum**
> "Chinese Hot Pot"

Traditions Across Time: Continuing Transformation

Trends toward further integration and disintegration have continued since the 1980s. Violence, particularly youth violence, is an issue that tears at the heart of American society. Joyce Carol Oates's story "Hostage" and Garrett Hongo's poem "The Legend" show the ripple effects of sudden, inexplicable acts of violence. The nation also struggles with issues of immigration and language. In "Mother Tongue," Amy Tan reflects on the richness of her Chinese mother's "broken" English, and in "The Latin Deli," Judith Ortiz Cofer portrays Latin American immigrants who miss the comfort of spoken Spanish. The last selection in this book, "Straw into Gold," is an inspiring essay by Sandra Cisneros. In it she tells how being different from the norm helped her achieve a rewarding career as a writer, teacher, and lecturer. In many ways, her success exemplifies the dramatic social changes in America during the last half of the 20th century.

Postwar Society

Martin Luther King, Jr.	*from* **Letter from Birmingham Jail** *An appeal for justice*	1136
	LITERARY LINK	
Nikki Giovanni	**Revolutionary Dreams** *Change will come naturally.*	1145
Lanford Wilson	**Wandering** *Why can't he be a man?*	1150
E. L. Doctorow	**The Writer in the Family** *Letters from beyond the grave*	1157
Anne Tyler	**Teenage Wasteland** *How much freedom does a teenager need?*	1168
John Updike	**Separating** *Breaking it to the children*	1180
Gary Soto	**Mexicans Begin Jogging** *Quick, over the fence!*	1194
Pat Mora	**Legal Alien** *Catching it from both sides*	1194

COMPARING LITERATURE
Traditions Across Time: Continuing Transformation

Joyce Carol Oates	**Hostage** (1991) *Criminal, victim, rescuer—who is who?*	1200
	LITERARY LINK	
Garrett Hongo	**The Legend** (1988) *The sudden theft of a life*	1210
Amy Tan	**Mother Tongue** (1990) *Different kinds of English*	1215
Judith Ortiz Cofer	**The Latin Deli: An Ars Poetica** (1991) *Reminders of home*	1223
Sandra Cisneros	**Straw into Gold: The Metamorphosis of the Everyday** (1987) *Doing the best with what you've got*	1227

from Letter from Birmingham Jail

by MARTIN LUTHER KING, JR.

Connect to Your Life

Personal Commitment What issue do you feel strongly about? How far would you go to support your convictions? Would you speak out, write to Congress, march in a demonstration, or take even stronger measures?

Build Background

Defending Civil Disobedience In 1963 the Reverend Martin Luther King, Jr., led a massive civil rights campaign in Birmingham, Alabama, involving drives for African-American voter registration and for desegregation in education and housing. During this nonviolent action, King was arrested and imprisoned several times. During one imprisonment, he wrote "Letter from Birmingham Jail," which has become a classic statement in support of civil disobedience. It was written in response to a published letter by eight local clergymen criticizing King's actions as "unwise and untimely." In the part of the letter that follows, King defends his actions by drawing upon the ideas of philosophers, religious scholars, biblical figures, and political thinkers with whom his audience, as clergymen, would have been familiar.

WORDS TO KNOW
Vocabulary Preview

affiliate	latent
appraisal	provocation
cognizant	retaliating
diligently	segregated
estrangement	statute

Focus Your Reading

LITERARY ANALYSIS **ALLUSION** An **allusion** is a reference to a person, place, event, or literary work with which the author believes the reader will be familiar. In his letter, King mentions the Boston Tea Party, a well-known event in American history, in which a group of rebels dumped 15,000 pounds of tea into Boston's harbor to protest the British Tea Act of 1773. This allusion reminds the reader that civil disobedience is a time-honored means of resisting unjust laws. Note other allusions in this letter, and consider why King uses them.

ACTIVE READING **LOGICAL ARGUMENT: DEDUCTION AND INDUCTION** In your own persuasive essays, you likely have used these processes of reasoning:

- When you use **induction,** you begin with specific facts and then reach a general conclusion based on them.
- When you use **deduction,** you begin with a general statement and then infer specific statements from it.

In this letter, King uses induction in the second paragraph to explain why he is in Birmingham. He presents facts about his role in the Southern Christian Leadership Conference (SCLC) and then concludes with the general statement "I am here because I have organizational ties here."

King uses deduction, beginning with the third paragraph, to justify his presence in the city. He begins with the general statement that "Injustice anywhere is a threat to justice everywhere." Then in three subsequent paragraphs, he gives specific instances of injustices in Birmingham, such as unsolved bombings of African-American homes.

READER'S NOTEBOOK Select a passage that appeals to you and identify the process of reasoning used in it. Write notes about King's general and specific statements.

Induction: specific ➡ general	**Deduction:** general ➡ specific

from LETTER FROM BIRMINGHAM JAIL

Martin Luther King, Jr.

APRIL 16, 1963

King in a jail cell at the Jefferson County Courthouse in Birmingham.

My Dear Fellow Clergymen:

While confined here in the Birmingham city jail, I came across your recent statement calling my present activities "unwise and untimely." Seldom do I pause to answer criticism of my work and ideas. If I sought to answer all the criticisms that cross my desk, my secretaries would have little time for anything other than such correspondence in the course of the day, and I would have no time for constructive work. But since I feel that you are men of genuine goodwill and that your criticisms are sincerely set forth, I want to try to answer your statement in what I hope will be patient and reasonable terms.

I think I should indicate why I am here in Birmingham, since you have been influenced by the view which argues against "outsiders coming in." I have the honor of serving as president of the Southern Christian Leadership Conference, an organization operating in every Southern state, with headquarters in Atlanta, Georgia. We have some eighty-five affiliated organizations across the South, and one of them is the Alabama Christian Movement for Human Rights. Frequently we share staff, educational, and financial resources with our affiliates. Several months ago the <u>affiliate</u> here in Birmingham asked us to be on call to engage in a nonviolent direct-action program if such were deemed necessary. We readily consented, and when the hour came, we lived up to our promise. So I, along with several members of my staff, am here because I was invited here. I am here because I have organizational ties here.

But more basically, I am in Birmingham because injustice is here. Just as the prophets of the eighth century B.C. left their villages and carried their "thus saith the Lord" far beyond the boundaries of their hometowns, and just as the Apostle Paul left his village of Tarsus and carried the gospel of Jesus Christ to the far corners of the Greco-Roman world, so am I compelled to carry the gospel of freedom beyond my own hometown. Like Paul, I must constantly respond to the Macedonian call for aid.[1]

Moreover, I am cognizant of the interrelatedness of all communities and states. I cannot sit idly by in Atlanta and not be concerned about what happens in Birmingham. Injustice anywhere is a threat to justice everywhere. We are caught in an inescapable network of mutuality, tied in a single garment of destiny. Whatever affects one directly, affects all indirectly. Never again can we afford to live with the narrow, provincial "outside agitator" idea. Anyone who lives inside the United States can never be considered an outsider anywhere within its bounds.

You deplore the demonstrations taking place in Birmingham. But your statement, I am sorry to say, fails to express a similar concern for the conditions that brought about the demonstrations. I am sure that none of you would want to rest content with the superficial kind of social analysis that deals merely with effects and does not grapple with underlying causes. It is unfortunate that demonstrations are taking place in Birmingham, but it is even more unfortunate that the city's white power structure left the Negro community with no alternative.

In any nonviolent campaign there are four basic steps: collection of the facts to determine whether injustices exist; negotiation; self-purification; and direct action. We have gone through all these steps in Birmingham. There can be no gainsaying[2] the fact that racial injustice engulfs this community. Birmingham is probably the most thoroughly segregated city in the United States. Its ugly record of brutality is widely known. Negroes have experienced grossly unjust treatment in the courts. There have been more unsolved bombings of Negro homes and

churches in Birmingham than in any other city in the nation. These are the hard, brutal facts of the case. On the basis of these conditions, Negro leaders sought to negotiate with the city fathers. But the latter consistently refused to engage in good-faith negotiations.

Then, last September, came the opportunity to talk with leaders of Birmingham's economic community. In the course of the negotiations, certain promises were made by the merchants—for example, to remove the stores' humiliating racial signs.[3] On the basis of these promises, The Reverend Fred Shuttlesworth and the leaders of the Alabama Christian Movement for Human Rights agreed to a moratorium[4] on all demonstrations. As the weeks and months went by, we realized that we were the victims of a broken promise. A few signs, briefly removed, returned; the others remained.

As in so many past experiences, our hopes had been blasted, and the shadow of deep disappointment settled upon us. We had no alternative except to prepare for direct action, whereby we would present our very bodies as a means of laying our case before the conscience of the local and the national community. Mindful of the difficulties involved, we decided to undertake a process of self-purification. We began a series of workshops on nonviolence, and we repeatedly asked ourselves: "Are you able to accept blows without retaliating?" "Are you able to endure the ordeal of jail?" We decided to schedule our direct-action program for the Easter season, realizing that except for Christmas, this is the main shopping period

---

1. **Macedonian** (măs´ĭ-dō'nē-ən) **call for aid:** According to the Bible (Acts 16), a man appeared to the apostle Paul in a vision, calling him to preach in Macedonia (at that time a Roman province north of Greece).

2. **gainsaying:** denying.

3. **racial signs:** signs marking segregated buildings and other facilities.

4. **moratorium** (môr´ə-tôr´ē-əm): temporary stoppage.

1138

of the year. Knowing that a strong economic-withdrawal program would be the by-product of direct action, we felt that this would be the best time to bring pressure to bear on the merchants for the needed change.

Then it occurred to us that Birmingham's mayoral election was coming up in March, and we speedily decided to postpone action until after election day. When we discovered that the Commissioner of Public Safety, Eugene "Bull" Connor, had piled up enough votes to be in the runoff, we decided again to postpone action until the day after the runoff so that the demonstrations could not be used to cloud the issues. Like many others, we waited to see Mr. Connor defeated, and to this end we endured postponement after postponement. Having aided in this community need, we felt that our direct-action program could be delayed no longer.

You may well ask: "Why direct action? Why sit-ins,[5] marches, and so forth? Isn't negotiation a better path?" You are quite right in calling for negotiation. Indeed, this is the very purpose of direct action. Nonviolent direct action seeks to create such a crisis and foster such a tension that a community which has constantly refused to negotiate is forced to confront the issue. It seeks so to dramatize the issue that it can no longer be ignored. My citing the creation of tension as part of the work of the nonviolent-resister may sound rather shocking. But I must confess that I am not afraid of the word "tension." I have earnestly opposed violent tension, but there is a type of constructive, nonviolent tension which is necessary for growth. Just as Socrates[6] felt that it was necessary to create a tension in the mind so that individuals could rise from the bondage of myths and half-truths to the unfettered realm of creative analysis and objective appraisal, so must

Birmingham police turn fire hoses on civil rights demonstrators.

we see the need for nonviolent gadflies[7] to create the kind of tension in society that will help men rise from the dark depths of prejudice and racism to the majestic heights of understanding and brotherhood.

The purpose of our direct-action program is to create a situation so crisis-packed that it will inevitably open the door to negotiation. I therefore concur with you in your call for negotiation. Too long has our beloved Southland been bogged down in a tragic effort to live in monologue rather than dialogue.

One of the basic points in your statement is that the action that I and my associates have taken in Birmingham is untimely. Some have asked: "Why didn't you give the new city administration time to act?" The only answer that I can give to this query is that the new Birmingham administration must be prodded about as much as the outgoing one before it

---

5. **sit-ins:** peaceful demonstrations in which protesters occupied, and refused to leave, seats in segregated lunch counters and other places of business.

6. **Socrates** (sŏk′rə-tēz′): a Greek philosopher of the fifth century B.C.—one of the major influences in the development of Western thought.

7. **gadflies:** critics.

WORDS
TO
KNOW   **appraisal** (ə-prā′zəl) *n.* evaluation

In 1968, civil-rights marchers in Memphis pass National Guard bayonets.

will act. . . . My friends, I must say to you that we have not made a single gain in civil rights without determined legal and nonviolent pressure. Lamentably, it is a historical fact that privileged groups seldom give up their privileges voluntarily. Individuals may see the moral light and voluntarily give up their unjust posture; but, as Reinhold Niebuhr[8] has reminded us, groups tend to be more immoral than individuals.

We know through painful experience that freedom is never voluntarily given by the oppressor; it must be demanded by the oppressed. Frankly, I have yet to engage in a direct-action campaign that was "well-timed" in the view of those who have not suffered unduly from the disease of segregation. For years now I have heard the word "Wait!" It rings in the ear of every Negro with piercing familiarity. This "Wait" has almost always meant "Never." We must come to see, with one of our distinguished jurists, that "justice too long delayed is justice denied."

We have waited for more than 340 years for our constitutional and God-given rights. The nations of Asia and Africa are moving with jetlike speed toward gaining political independence, but we still creep at horse-and-buggy pace toward gaining a cup of coffee at a lunch counter. Perhaps it is easy for those who

have never felt the stinging darts of segregation to say, "Wait." But when you have seen vicious mobs lynch your mothers and fathers at will and drown your sisters and brothers at whim; when you have seen hate-filled policemen curse, kick, and even kill your black brothers and sisters; when you see the vast majority of your twenty million Negro brothers smothering in an airtight cage of poverty in the midst of an affluent society; when you suddenly find your tongue twisted and your speech stammering as you seek to explain to your six-year-old daughter why she can't go to the public amusement park that has just been advertised on television, and see tears welling up in her eyes when she is told that Funtown is closed to colored children, and see ominous[9] clouds of inferiority beginning to form in her little mental sky, and see her beginning to distort her personality by developing an unconscious bitterness toward white people; when you have to concoct an answer for a five-year-old son who is asking: "Daddy, why do white people treat colored people so mean?"; when you take a cross-country drive and find it necessary to sleep night after night in the uncomfortable corners of your automobile because no motel will accept you; when you are humiliated day in and day out by nagging signs reading "white" and "colored"; when your first name becomes "nigger," your middle name becomes "boy" (however old you are) and your last name becomes "John," and your wife and mother are never given the respected title "Mrs."; when you are harried by day and haunted by night by the fact that you are a Negro, living constantly at tiptoe stance, never quite knowing what to expect next, and are

8. **Reinhold Niebuhr** (rĭn′hōld′ nē′bŏŏr′): a 20th-century American theologian whose writings deal mainly with moral and social problems.

9. **ominous** (ŏm′ə-nəs): threatening.

plagued with inner fears and outer resentments; when you are forever fighting a degenerating sense of "nobodiness"—then you will understand why we find it difficult to wait. There comes a time when the cup of endurance runs over, and men are no longer willing to be plunged into the abyss of despair. I hope, sirs, you can understand our legitimate and unavoidable impatience.

You express a great deal of anxiety over our willingness to break laws. This is certainly a legitimate concern. Since we so <u>diligently</u> urge people to obey the Supreme Court's decision of 1954 outlawing segregation in the public schools,[10] at first glance it may seem rather paradoxical[11] for us consciously to break laws. One may well ask: "How can you advocate breaking some laws and obeying others?" The answer lies in the fact that there are two types of laws: just and unjust. I would be the first to advocate obeying just laws. One has not only a legal but a moral responsibility to obey just laws. Conversely, one has a moral responsibility to disobey unjust laws. I would agree with St. Augustine[12] that "an unjust law is no law at all."

Now, what is the difference between the two? How does one determine whether a law is just or unjust? A just law is a man-made code that squares with the moral law or the law of God. An unjust law is a code that is out of harmony with the moral law. To put it in the terms of St. Thomas Aquinas:[13] An unjust law is a human law that is not rooted in eternal law and natural law. Any law that uplifts human personality is just. Any law that degrades human personality is unjust. All segregation <u>statutes</u> are unjust because segregation distorts the soul and damages the personality. It gives the segregator a false sense of superiority and the segregated a false sense of inferiority. Segregation, to use the terminology of the Jewish philosopher Martin Buber,[14] substitutes an "I-it" relationship for an "I-thou" relationship and ends up relegating

persons to the status of things. Hence segregation is not only politically, economically, and sociologically unsound, it is morally wrong and sinful. Paul Tillich[15] has said that sin is separation. Is not segregation an existential[16] expression of man's tragic separation, his awful <u>estrangement</u>, his terrible sinfulness? Thus it is that I can urge men to obey the 1954 decision of the Supreme Court, for it is morally right; and I can urge them to disobey segregation ordinances, for they are morally wrong.

Let us consider a more concrete example of just and unjust laws. An unjust law is a code that a numerical or power majority group compels a minority group to obey but does not make binding on itself. This is *difference* made legal. By the same token, a just law is a code that a majority compels a minority to follow and that it is willing to follow itself. This is *sameness* made legal.

Let me give another explanation. A law is unjust if it is inflicted on a minority that, as a result of being denied the right to vote, had no part in enacting or devising the law. Who can say that the legislature of Alabama which set up that state's segregation laws was democratically elected? Throughout Alabama all sorts of devious methods are used to prevent Negroes

---

10. **the Supreme Court's . . . public schools:** the U.S. Supreme Court's decision in the case *Brown* v. *Board of Education of Topeka, Kansas.*

11. **paradoxical** (păr′ə-dŏk′sĭ-kəl): self-contradictory.

12. **St. Augustine** (ô′gə-stēn′): a North African bishop of the fourth–fifth centuries, whose writings have been extremely influential throughout the history of Christianity.

13. **St. Thomas Aquinas** (ə-kwī′nəs): a noted medieval philosopher and theologian.

14. **Martin Buber** (boō′bər): an influential 20th-century Jewish philosopher.

15. **Paul Tillich** (tĭl′ĭk): a German-born American theologian of the 20th century.

16. **existential** (ĕg′zĭ-stĕn′shəl): existing in the real world.

1141

from becoming registered voters, and there are some counties in which, even though Negroes constitute a majority of the population, not a single Negro is registered. Can any law enacted under such circumstances be considered democratically structured?

Sometimes a law is just on its face and unjust in its application. For instance, I have been arrested on a charge of parading without a permit. Now, there is nothing wrong in having an ordinance which requires a permit for a parade. But such an ordinance becomes unjust when it is used to maintain segregation and to deny citizens the First Amendment privilege of peaceful assembly and protest.

I hope you are able to see the distinction I am trying to point out. In no sense do I advocate evading or defying the law, as would the rabid segregationist. That would lead to anarchy. One who breaks an unjust law must do so openly, lovingly, and with a willingness to accept the penalty. I submit that an individual who breaks a law that conscience tells him is unjust, and who willingly accepts the penalty of imprisonment in order to arouse the conscience of the community over its injustice, is in reality expressing the highest respect for law.

Of course, there is nothing new about this kind of civil disobedience. It was evidenced sublimely in the refusal of Shadrach, Meshach, and Abednego to obey the laws of Nebuchadnezzar,[17] on the ground that a higher moral law was at stake. It was practiced superbly by the early Christians, who were willing to face hungry lions and the excruciating pain of chopping blocks rather than submit to certain unjust laws of the Roman Empire. To a degree, academic freedom is a reality today because Socrates practiced civil disobedience. In our own nation, the Boston Tea Party represented a massive act of civil disobedience.

We should never forget that everything Adolf Hitler did in Germany was "legal" and everything the Hungarian freedom fighters[18]

did in Hungary was "illegal." It was "illegal" to aid and comfort a Jew in Hitler's Germany. Even so, I am sure that, had I lived in Germany at the time, I would have aided and comforted my Jewish brothers. If today I lived in a Communist country where certain principles dear to the Christian faith are suppressed, I would openly advocate disobeying that country's antireligious laws.

I must make two honest confessions to you, my Christian and Jewish brothers. First, I must confess that over the past few years I have been gravely disappointed with the white moderate. I have almost reached the regrettable conclusion that the Negro's great stumbling block in his stride toward freedom is not the White Citizen's Counciler or the Ku Klux Klanner,[19] but the white moderate, who is more devoted to "order" than to justice; who prefers a negative peace which is the absence of tension to a positive peace which is the presence of justice; who constantly says: "I agree with you in the goal you seek, but I cannot agree with your methods of direct action"; who paternalistically[20] believes he can set the timetable for another man's freedom; who lives by a mythical concept of time and who constantly advises the Negro to wait for a "more convenient season." Shallow understanding from people of goodwill is more frustrating than absolute misunderstanding from people of ill

---

17. **the refusal . . . Nebuchadnezzar** (nĕb´ə-kəd-nĕz´ər): In the Bible (Daniel 3), Shadrach (shăd´răk), Meshach (mē´shăk), and Abednego (ə-bĕd´nĭ-gō´) are three Hebrews condemned to death for refusing to worship an idol set up by Nebuchadnezzar, king of Babylon. When cast into a fiery furnace, they are miraculously protected from the fire and emerge unharmed.

18. **Hungarian freedom fighters:** Hungarians who participated in a 1956 rebellion against the Communist government of their homeland. (The uprising was crushed by troops sent into Hungary by the Soviet Union.)

19. **the White . . . Klanner:** the member of a group committed to the exclusion and persecution of African Americans and other minorities.

20. **paternalistically** (pə-tûr´nə-lĭs´tĭ-klē): in a manner that suggests a father's claim of protective authority over his children.

will. Lukewarm acceptance is much more bewildering than outright rejection.

I had hoped that the white moderate would understand that law and order exist for the purpose of establishing justice and that when they fail in this purpose, they become the dangerously structured dams that block the flow of social progress. I had hoped that the white moderate would understand that the present tension in the South is a necessary phase of the transition from an obnoxious negative peace, in which the Negro passively accepted his unjust plight, to a substantive and positive peace, in which all men will respect the dignity and worth of human personality. Actually, we who engage in nonviolent direct action are not the creators of tension. We merely bring to the surface the hidden tension that is already alive. We bring it out in the open, where it can be seen and dealt with. Like a boil that can never be cured so long as it is covered up but must be opened with all its ugliness to the natural medicines of air and light, injustice must be exposed, with all the tension its exposure creates, to the light of human conscience and the air of national opinion before it can be cured.

In your statement you assert that our actions, even though peaceful, must be condemned because they precipitate violence. But is this a logical assertion? Isn't this like condemning a robbed man because his possession of money precipitated[21] the evil act of robbery? Isn't this like condemning Socrates because his unswerving commitment to truth and his philosophical inquiries precipitated the act by the misguided populace in which they made him drink hemlock? Isn't this like condemning Jesus because his unique God-consciousness and never-ceasing devotion to God's will precipitated the evil act of crucifixion? We must come to see that, as the federal courts have consistently affirmed, it is wrong to urge an individual to cease his efforts to gain his basic constitutional rights because the quest may precipitate violence. Society must protect the robbed and punish the robber. . . .

Oppressed people cannot remain oppressed forever. The yearning for freedom eventually manifests itself, and that is what has happened to the American Negro. Something within has reminded him of his birthright of freedom, and something without has reminded him that it can be gained. Consciously or unconsciously, he has been caught up by the *Zeitgeist*,[22] and with his black brothers of Africa and his brown and yellow brothers of Asia, South America, and the Caribbean, the United States Negro is moving with a sense of great urgency toward the promised land of racial justice. If one recognizes this vital urge that has engulfed the Negro community, one should readily understand why public demonstrations are taking place. The Negro has many pent-up resentments and latent frustrations, and he must release them. So let him march; let him make prayer pilgrimages to the city hall; let him go on freedom rides— and try to understand why he must do so. If his repressed emotions are not released in nonviolent ways, they will seek expression through violence; this is not a threat but a fact of history. So I have not said to my people: "Get rid of your discontent." Rather, I have tried to say that this normal and healthy discontent can be channeled into the creative outlet of nonviolent direct action. And now this approach is being termed extremist.

> Oppressed people cannot remain oppressed forever.

---

21. **precipitated** (prĭ-sĭp′ĭ-tā′tĭd): brought about; caused.
22. **Zeitgeist** (tsīt′gīst′) *German*: spirit of the time—the beliefs and attitudes shared by most of the people living in a particular period.

WORDS TO KNOW

latent (lāt′nt) *adj.* existing in a hidden form

But though I was initially disappointed at being categorized as an extremist, as I continued to think about the matter, I gradually gained a measure of satisfaction from the label. Was not Jesus an extremist for love: "Love your enemies, bless them that curse you, do good to them that hate you, and pray for them which despitefully use you, and persecute you." Was not Amos[23] an extremist for justice: "Let justice roll down like waters and righteousness like an ever-flowing stream." Was not Paul an extremist for the Christian gospel: "I bear in my body the marks of the Lord Jesus." Was not Martin Luther[24] an extremist: "Here I stand; I cannot do otherwise, so help me God." And John Bunyan:[25] "I will stay in jail to the end of my days before I make a butchery of my conscience." And Abraham Lincoln: "This nation cannot survive half slave and half free." And Thomas Jefferson: "We hold these truths to be self-evident, that all men are created equal. . . ." So the question is not whether we will be extremists, but what kind of extremists we will be. Will we be extremists for hate or for love? Will we be extremists for the preservation of injustice or for the extension of justice? In that dramatic scene on Calvary's hill[26] three men were crucified. We must never forget that all three were crucified for the same crime— the crime of extremism. Two were extremists for immorality, and thus fell below their environment. The other, Jesus Christ, was an extremist for love, truth, and goodness, and thereby rose above his environment. Perhaps the South, the nation and the world are in dire need

James Meredith during his struggle to enter the University of Mississippi in 1962.

of creative extremists. . . .

I wish you had commended the Negro sit-inners and demonstrators of Birmingham for their sublime courage, their willingness to suffer, and their amazing discipline in the midst of great <u>provocation</u>. One day the South will recognize its real heroes. They will be the James Merediths,[27] with the noble sense of purpose that enables them to face jeering and hostile mobs, and with the agonizing loneliness that characterizes the life of the pioneer. They will be old, oppressed, battered Negro women, symbolized in a seventy-two-year-old woman in Montgomery, Alabama, who rose up with a sense of dignity and with her people decided not to ride segregated buses, and who responded with ungrammatical profundity to one who inquired about her weariness: "My feets is tired, but my soul is at rest." They will be the young high school and college students, the young ministers of the gospel and a host of their elders, courageously and nonviolently sitting in

---

23. **Amos:** a Hebrew prophet whose words are recorded in the Old Testament book bearing his name.

24. **Martin Luther:** a German monk who launched the Protestant Reformation with his condemnations of the wealth and corruption of the 16th-century Roman Catholic Church.

25. **John Bunyan:** a 17th-century English preacher and author of the famous religious allegory *The Pilgrim's Progress*. He was twice imprisoned for unlicensed preaching.

26. **Calvary's hill:** the site of Jesus's crucifixion.

27. **James Merediths:** people like James Meredith, who endured violent opposition from whites to become the first African American to attend the University of Mississippi.

WORDS
TO
KNOW

provocation (prŏv′ə-kā′shən) *n.* something that arouses anger

at lunch counters and willingly going to jail for conscience' sake. One day the South will know that when these disinherited children of God sat down at lunch counters, they were in reality standing up for what is best in the American dream and for the most sacred values in our Judaeo-Christian heritage, thereby bringing our nation back to those great wells of democracy which were dug deep by the founding fathers in their formulation of the Constitution and the Declaration of Independence.

Never before have I written so long a letter. I'm afraid it is much too long to take your precious time. I can assure you that it would have been much shorter if I had been writing from a comfortable desk, but what else can one do when he is alone in a narrow jail cell, other than write long letters, think long thoughts, and pray long prayers?

If I have said anything in this letter that overstates the truth and indicates an unreasonable impatience, I beg you to forgive me. If I have said anything that understates the truth and indicates my having a patience that allows me to settle for anything less than brotherhood, I beg God to forgive me.

I hope this letter finds you strong in the faith. I also hope that circumstances will soon make it possible for me to meet each of you, not as an integrationist or a civil-rights leader but as a fellow clergyman and a Christian brother. Let us all hope that the dark clouds of racial prejudice will soon pass away and the deep fog of misunderstanding will be lifted from our fear-drenched communities, and in some not too distant tomorrow the radiant stars of love and brotherhood will shine over our great nation with all their scintillating[28] beauty.

Yours for the cause of Peace and Brotherhood,

Martin Luther King, Jr.

---

28. **scintillating** (sĭn'tl-ā'tĭng): sparkling.

REVOLUTIONARY DREAMS Nikki Giovanni

On the Subway (1986), Elizabeth Catlett. Courtesy of Isobel Neal Gallery, Chicago.

i used to dream militant
dreams of taking
over america to show
these white folks how it should be
5   done
i used to dream radical dreams
of blowing everyone away with my perceptive powers
of correct analysis
i even used to think i'd be the one
10   to stop the riot and negotiate the peace
then i awoke and dug
that if i dreamed natural
dreams of being a natural
woman doing what a woman
15   does when she's natural
i would have a revolution

Connect to the Literature

1. **What Do You Think?** What ideas and emotions in the letter had the greatest impact on you?

Comprehension Check
- According to King, it is morally right to disobey what kind of laws?
- Name a figure King admires as an extremist.

Think Critically

2. How do you think the eight clergymen felt after reading King's letter? Point out specific passages that may have particularly influenced their reactions.

3. Explain whether you think King was wise to criticize the white moderate in his letter.

4. Do you agree with King's methods of standing up for his beliefs?

THINK ABOUT
- the four steps in a nonviolent campaign
- specific kinds of nonviolent direct action that he advocates
- his belief in the need to create "tension" to effect reform
- his distinction between just and unjust laws
- the measures you considered for the Connect to Your Life activity on page 1136

5. **ACTIVE READING** **LOGICAL ARGUMENT: DEDUCTION AND INDUCTION** Explain the process of reasoning King uses in one passage from this essay. Refer to the notes in your **READER'S NOTEBOOK**.

Extend Interpretations

6. **The Writer's Style** King sometimes uses a technique known as **parallelism**—the use of the same grammatical forms to express equivalent thoughts. For example, he uses a series of *when* clauses beginning with "But *when* you have seen vicious mobs. . . ." Find other examples of this technique in the letter, and describe the effect.

7. **Comparing Texts** What might King have said about Nikki Giovanni's views of revolution in "Revolutionary Dreams" (page 1145)?

8. **Connect to Life** How realistic do you find the vision of America that King strives to bring about? Explain.

Literary Analysis

ALLUSION An **allusion** is a reference to a historical or literary person, place, or event with which the reader is assumed to be familiar. Many works contain allusions to the Bible, classical mythology, Shakespeare's plays, or other works of literature. By using allusions, writers tap the knowledge and memory of the reader, drawing upon associations already in the reader's mind. For example, readers familiar with the Bible likely will recognize King's allusion to Shadrach, Meshach, and Abednego, the three Jews who risked death rather than worship an idol. By alluding to these biblical characters, King emphasizes the civil rights protesters' courage to die for their convictions.

Cooperative Learning Activity Work with three classmates to investigate King's allusions to these historical figures: Socrates, the Apostle Paul, Adolf Hitler, and James Meredith. Each member of the group should research one of these people in detail. After you have completed your research, write a note explaining the allusion and telling why you think King includes it in his argument. Pool your notes and share them with other groups.

Choices & CHALLENGES

Writing Options

1. Defining a Hero Near the end of his letter, King says, "One day the South will recognize its real heroes." What do you think are King's criteria for a hero? Write a review of the letter, supporting your answer.

2. Editorial About King's Ideas Write an editorial for your school newspaper in which you explain whether you find King's ideas and methods of standing up for his beliefs applicable today. Use both inductive and deductive reasoning to develop your argument.

Writing Handbook
See page 1285: Persuasive Writing.

3. Compare-and-Contrast Essay How would you compare King's methods of standing up for his beliefs with those described by Thoreau in "Civil Disobedience,"

on page 370? Write a compare-and-contrast essay to convey your ideas. Place this piece in your **Working Portfolio.**

Activities & Explorations

1. Poster Design In this letter King uses several **aphorisms**—brief statements, usually one sentence long, that express a general principle or truth about life. Design a poster to represent the message that one of these aphorisms conveys. ~ **ART**

2. Dramatic Skit With a classmate, role-play a dialogue in which King and Thoreau comment on social conditions in their times and the use of civil disobedience as a means of opposing injustice. ~ **PERFORMING**

3. Multimedia Presentation With your classmates, plan and

present a multimedia program in memory of King. Use tape recordings of his speeches, slides or videotapes of his life, music, original poems, essays, or skits. Then share your presentation with other classes. ~ **VIEWING AND REPRESENTING**

Inquiry & Research

Civil Rights Today With a small group of classmates, investigate some of the recent legislation—both state and federal—affecting civil rights. Some of the topics you might explore include fair housing laws, discrimination based on gender or age, rights of criminals, quotas in hiring practices, and harassment in the workplace. Present an oral report to the class to share your findings.

Vocabulary in Action

EXERCISE A: MEANING CLUES On your paper, write the Word to Know whose meaning is suggested by each sentence.

1. Martin Luther King, Jr., was well acquainted with the political situation in Birmingham.
2. The city was divided along racial lines.
3. King's followers avoided fighting back violently.
4. There was a great deal of hidden frustration in the lives of African Americans.
5. The protesters in Birmingham strove to ignore any attempt to make them furious and lure them into violence.

EXERCISE B: SYNONYMS Write the Word to Know that is a synonym of each word below.

1. rule
2. isolation
3. assessment
4. associate
5. industriously

Building Vocabulary
Several Words to Know come from Latin. For an in-depth lesson on root words, see page 1130.

See page 308 for the biography of Martin Luther King, Jr.

WORDS TO KNOW	affiliate	cognizant	estrangement	provocation	segregated
	appraisal	diligently	latent	retaliating	statute

Tone in Contemporary Literature

War has a way of changing a nation's literature because it usually affects an entire generation. Realism had risen from the ashes of the Civil War, while modernism had defined its vision from the ruins of World War I. After the development of the cold war, with its threat of nuclear destruction, the human losses of the Vietnam War, and the civil violence of the 1960s, American literature began to change again. And no place is this change more evident than in the tone of the literature itself.

Women marching to celebrate the 50th anniversary of the passage of the 19th Amendment

From Modern to Contemporary

Tone is the attitude that a writer takes toward a subject. For the modernist, the numbing effects of the early 20th century led to a detached, unemotional tone. For example, the pain that modernist characters feel—Prufrock's failure at the end of T. S. Eliot's poem (page 1025), Nick's silent suffering in Ernest Hemingway's "The End of Something" (page 1018), and Granny Weatherall's bitter disappointment in Katherine Anne Porter's story (page 1034)—is conveyed in a matter-of-fact tone that is sympathetic but distant.

Compare this modernist aloofness to Tim O'Brien's Vietnam story "Ambush" (page 1105). The tone of this contemporary story is one of engagement rather than detachment. From the narrator's opening exchange with his daughter to his conversation in flashback with his buddy after the killing and finally to his image of the dead soldier at the end, the story echoes with emotion. It even ends on a hopeful note, with the possibility of healing.

Understanding Tone

Contemporary American writers are more diverse than ever before, so it is difficult to generalize about characteristics of their writing. As you read the selections in this part of Unit Seven, however, you'll notice differences in tone from modernist works. The chart and text that follow explore the distinguishing features of tone in contemporary literature.

Differences in Tone	
Modernist	**Contemporary**
detached, unemotional	emotional
serious irony	humorous irony
concern with individual in isolation	concern with connections between people
no heroes	antiheroes

IRONIC HUMOR Modernist literature is, as a rule, utterly humorless. Flannery O'Connor, writing in the 1950s, was one of the first to introduce a new kind of humor in American literature. Her characters, such as Mr. Shiftlet in "The Life You Save May Be Your Own" (page 528), are funny, not because they do funny things but because the reader can recognize the faults and weaknesses that the characters are blind to. O'Connor's humor thus comes from her ironic presentation of characters rather than from comic situations.

Instead of being defeated by irony as many modernist writers had been, contemporary writers look at irony, and absurd situations in general, as cause for subtle humor. The tone becomes something like, "If you can't fight it, you might as well laugh."

IMPLIED SOCIAL CRITICISM With a few exceptions, modernist writers usually stayed out of politics and were not very concerned about social injustices. After the 1960s, however, with the influence of the civil rights and the women's movements, the attitude toward the individual and society began to change—the individual was no longer seen in isolation but in relation to others.

It is this awareness of the larger social context that distinguishes contemporary voices from modernist ones. And it is more often an implied criticism of the barriers between people that colors contemporary literature. Read the following description taken from Joyce Carol Oates's story "Hostage" (page 1200). The narrator, a shy teenage girl, explains one of the barriers between her and the boy, Bruno, for whom she shows a strange fascination.

> I didn't know him. I didn't belong to his world. Though my family lived only a block or so from his family in a neighborhood of row houses . . . , my grandparents had emigrated from Budapest in the early 1900s and Bruno's parents had come from Lublin, a Polish city near the Russian border, in the early 1930s, and that made a considerable difference.
>
> —Joyce Carol Oates, "Hostage"

YOUR TURN: Is the tone of this passage matter-of-fact, bitter, or sarcastic?

THE ANTI-HERO An **anti-hero** is a protagonist who has the opposite qualities of a hero: he or she may be insecure, ineffective, cowardly, sometimes dishonest or dishonorable, most often a failure. The character from the play *Wandering* (p. 1150), called simply Him, who wants nothing out of life, is an anti-hero; so is the father following his own desires over his family's needs in John Updike's story "Separating" (page 1180).

The point of an anti-hero is not necessarily to incur praise or criticism but to help understanding. After all, a contemporary writer might ask, who can really be heroic in this world, where irony rules and things are not what they seem? The passage below is from Anne Tyler's story "Teenage Wasteland" (page 1168). Daisy, the anti-hero, is the mother of a boy who's caused trouble at school; the principal, Mr. Lanham, has called her to his office to detail her son's offenses.

YOUR TURN: Would you describe the tone of this passage as happy, angry, or dispirited?

> In the past, before her children were born, Daisy had been a fourth-grade teacher. It shamed her now to sit before this principal as a parent, a delinquent parent, a parent who struck Mr. Lanham, no doubt, as unseeing or uncaring.
>
> —Anne Tyler, "Teenage Wasteland"

Strategies for Reading: Tone in Contemporary Literature

1. Identify the emotions conveyed in a work. Does the narrator express emotions, or does he or she seem detached from the action?
2. Notice any humor in the irony (both situational and dramatic).
3. Clarify what, if anything, is being criticized and what just needs to be understood and accepted.
4. **Monitor** your reading strategies and modify them when your understanding breaks down. Remember to use your Strategies for Active Reading: **predict, visualize, connect, question, clarify,** and **evaluate.**

Wandering

Drama by LANFORD WILSON

Connect to Your Life

Biography: Fast-Forward How would you present a person's life story in less than five minutes? Brainstorm with a small group to think of ways you could do this. Consider what events would be important to include and how you would show the passage of time. After your discussion, share your ideas with other groups

Build Background

Sixties Youth *Wandering* is a very brief play sketching the life story of a man who questions the roles society expects him to assume. In the 1960s many young Americans began to reject long-accepted codes of behavior and values that they felt unnecessarily restricted people. For example, Many young men wondered why they should register for the draft, become soldiers in the Vietnam War, and then enter professions—duties that were expected of men in the United States. For a variety of reasons, some dodged the draft or tried to make themselves ineligible. Some declined to compete for job promotions or to work at all, because they did not want to be forced down conventional career paths. Young people of the time often expressed a wish to live freely, according to their own values and desires, rather than those of others. The main character in *Wandering* (called only Him) is such a person.

WORDS TO KNOW
Vocabulary Preview

aggressor	regimentation
compulsory	specimen
indoctrination	

Focus Your Reading

LITERARY ANALYSIS **TONE AND DIALOGUE** In drama, **tone**—the attitude a writer takes towards a subject—is typically revealed through the **dialogue**—a conversation among characters. Note that in *Wandering*, the lines the characters deliver are often charged with emotional associations. Yet the playwright never states what those specific associations are. Instead, he leaves it to the reader to supply the viewpoint conveyed through the characters' spoken words.

ACTIVE READING **VISUALIZING STAGE DIRECTIONS** Imagine you are attending a theatrical production of *Wandering*. Seated in the audience, you await the curtains to rise. **Visualize,** or form a mental picture, of what you would see, based on the descriptive details given in the introductory **stage directions**—instructions for the director, actors, and stage crew. For example, try to picture the actors animated and gesturing when they are rapidly reciting their lines of dialogue and frozen at attention when they are not speaking.

READER'S NOTEBOOK After reading the stage directions, draw a rough floor plan, like the one below, to show what the stage might look like at the opening of the play. Include the placement of the furniture and the position of the actors. As you continue to read the play, refer to your floor plan to help you picture how scene changes and a 40-year time span might be presented with only three actors on a nearly barren stage.

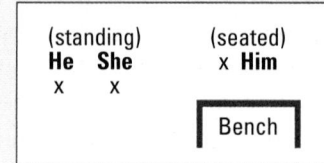

Wandering

Lanford Wilson

He, She, and Him *are all about twenty-five. The stage, which can be very small, should have a bench to be used as chair, bed, couch, bench, whatever.* He *and* She *are standing at attention, side by side.* Him *enters and sits. The actors should retire to the attention position when not speaking. Actions and props should be panto-mimed, and the play should be done very rapidly, without pause except toward the end, as indicated. The play runs through* Him's *life—a span of about forty years with several recaps[1] at the end. Actions and characterizations should be very simple.*

She. Where have you been?

Him. Wandering around.

She. Wandering around. I don't know why you can't be a man; you just wait till the army gets ahold of you, young man.

He. They'll make a man out of you.

She. Straighten you out.

He. A little regimentation.

She. Regulation.

He. Specification.

She. Indoctrination.

He. Boredom.

She. You'll get up and go to bed.

He. Drill, march.

She. Take orders.

He. Fight.

She. Do what they tell you.

He. Keep in step.

She. Do your part.

He. Kill a man.

She. You'll be a better person to live with, believe me. As a matter of fact your father and I are getting damn tired of having you around.

He. Looking after you.

She. Making your bed.

He. Keeping you out of trouble.

She. How old are you, anyway?

Him. Sixteen.

He. Sixteen, well, my God.

She. Shouldn't you be drafted before long?

Him. Two years.

She. You just better toe the mark.

He. How long at your present address?

Him. Six months.

He. Any previous experience as an apprentice?

Him. No sir.

He. Where did you live before that?

Him. I was just wandering around.

---

1. **recaps:** short for *recapitulations,* repetitions of the main point or points.

1151

He. Not good; draft status?

Him. Well, I haven't been called but—

He. We like fighters on our team, fellow.

Him. Well, actually I'm a conscientious—[2]

She. Sit down. Roll up your sleeve. Take off your shirt. Stick out your tongue. Bend over, open your mouth, make a fist, read the top line. Cough. (*The boy coughs.*) Very good.

Him. Thank you.

She. Perfect specimen.

Him. I do a considerable amount of walking.

He. I don't follow you.

Him. I don't believe in war.

He. There's no danger of war. Our country is never an aggressor.

Him. But armies, see, I don't believe in it.

He. Do you love your country?

Him. No more than any other, the ones I've seen.

He. That's treason.

Him. I'm sorry.

He. Quite all right; we'll take you.

Him. I won't go.

He. Service is compulsory.

Him. It's my right.

He. You'll learn.

Him. I don't believe in killing people.

He. For freedom?

Him. No.

He. For love?

Him. No.

He. For money?

Him. No.

He. We'll teach you.

Him. I know, but I won't.

He. You'll learn.

Him. I won't!

He. You're going.

Him. I'm not.

He. You'll see.

Him. I'm sure.

He. You'll see.

Him. I'm flat-footed.

He. You'll do.

Him. I'm queer.

He. Get lost.

She. I'm lost.

Him. I'm sorry.

She. Aren't you lost?

Him. I wasn't going anyplace in particular.

She. That's unnatural.

Him. I was just wandering.

She. What will become of you?

Him. I hadn't thought of it.

She. You don't believe in anything.

Him. But you see, I do.

He. I see.

Him. It's just that no one else seems to believe—not really.

He. I see.

Him. Like this pride in country.

He. I see.

Him. And this pride in blood.

He. I see.

Him. It just seems that pride is such a pointless thing; I can't believe in killing someone for it.

She. Oh, my God, honey, it isn't killing, it's merely nudging out of the way . . .

---

2. **conscientious—** : The young man is interrupted in the middle of saying "conscientious objector." This is a person whose conscience does not permit taking an active part in any effort associated with the conduct of war.

WORDS TO KNOW

specimen (spĕs′ə-mən) *n.* an example of a group

aggressor (ə-grĕs′ər) *n.* one that begins an attack or a quarrel

compulsory (kəm-pŭl′sə-rē) *adj.* required without exception; mandatory

A little regimentation.

Regulation.

Specification.

Indoctrination.

Boredom.

New recruit trying on a garrison hat during the
Vietnam War. Photo by Bob Gemel for *Life* Magazine.
Copyright © Time Inc.

1153

Him. But we don't need it.

She. Think of our position, think of me, think of the children.

Him. I am.

She. You're shiftless, is what it is.

Him. I'm really quite happy; I don't know why.

She. Well, how do you think I feel?

Him. Not too well really.

She. Where does it hurt?

Him. Nothing to worry about.

She. Yes sir.

Him. Thank you.

She. And that's all for the morning; Mr. Trader is on line six.

Him. Thank you; send Wheeler in.

He. How are you, old boy?

Him. Not well, I'm afraid.

She. Don't be, it isn't serious.

He. Just been working too hard.

She. Why don't you lie down?

He. Best thing for you.

She. I know, but he was quite handsome; a gentle man.

He. Bit of a radical though; not good for the family.

She. I know.

He. You're better off.

She. I have a life   **He.** You have a life
of my own.   of your own.

She. He was such a lost lamb.

He. Never agreed with anyone.

She. Arguments everywhere we went.

He. What kind of disposition is that?

She. I don't know what I ever saw in him.

He. You need someone who knows his way around.

She. I do.

He. I do.

(*A pause*)

She. I don't know why you can't be a man.

He. Keep in step.

She. Toe the mark.

He. Draft status?

She. Stick out your tongue.

He. You'll learn.

She. What'll become of you?

He. I see.

She. Think of the children.

He. Best thing for you.

She. I do.

(*A pause*)

He. I see.

Him. I mean, that can't be the way people want to spend their lives.

She. Trader on line six.

Him. Thank you.

He. Just been working too hard.

She. I do.

(*Pauses*)

She. Where?

Him. Wandering.

He. I see.

Him. They'll believe anything anyone tells them.

He. I see.

Him. I mean, that can't be the way people want to spend their lives.

She. That's all for the morning.

Him. Quite happy.

He. Best thing for you.

She. I do.

He. I do.

(*A pause*)

She. Where have you been?

(*A pause*)

Him. Can it?

Blackout

Connect to the Literature

1. What Do You Think? What questions do you want to ask about the characters and events in this play? Share them with a partner.

Comprehension Check
- How are stages of Him's life portrayed in the play?
- What is Him's view of military service?
- What happens to Him at the end of the play?

Think Critically

2. **ACTIVE READING** **VISUALIZING STAGE DIRECTIONS** Which scene from the play were you able to picture most vividly? As you read the play, did you experience the impression of continuous action? Explain.

3. What different people do He and She portray in the course of the play? In general, how would you say this pair of characters perceives Him?

4. How would you evaluate Him's life?

THINK ABOUT
- what he believes and what he does not believe
- why he says, "I'm really quite happy"
- how his life ends
- his final question, "That can't be the way people want to spend their lives. . . . Can it?"

5. What does the title of the play mean to you?

6. In what ways does Him remind you of anyone you know or have heard about?

Extend Interpretations

7. Comparing Texts Compare and contrast Him, She, and He in *Wandering* to the characters "anyone," "noone," "someones," and "everyones" in E. E. Cummings poem "anyone lived in a pretty how town" (page 410). How do you think naming characters as pronouns contributes to the meaning in each of these works?

8. The Writer's Style In what ways would you consider Lanford Wilson's approach to writing plays experimental?

9. Connect to Life Could Him represent most young people of your generation, or is he strictly a child of the 1960s? Support your opinion.

Literary Analysis

TONE AND DIALOGUE

Dialogue—written conversation between two or more characters—makes up most of the play's script. The dialogue in *Wandering* does not mimic ordinary conversation. It strings together clichéd, stock phrases in a highly rhythmic way. The lines are fragmentary and elliptical, forcing the audience to "fill in the blanks." Certain phrases are repeated, particularly in the recaps at the end. The style and topics of the dialogue reveal the play's **tone**—the writer's attitude toward the society of the time.

Cooperative Learning Activity
Listen for the tone revealed in the dialogue as you and two other students read the entire play rapidly, according to the playwright's stage directions. Then discuss the viewpoints that you think are conveyed through the dialogue.

Writing Options

1. Drama Review In a review of *Wandering*, tell whether you like the play, what it would be like when performed on-stage, and what the play's intended meaning might be.

2. Play Outline Write an outline of a play presenting the life story of a person, male or female, from your own generation. What title would you give it? What key events would you include? What important phrases might you repeat?

Inquiry & Research

Youth Counterculture Social changes in the 1960s spurred many of the nation's teenagers to defy mainstream culture. Find out how they expressed their new individuality through clothing styles and rock music. Report your findings in an oral report with audiovisual aids.

Vocabulary in Action

EXERCISE: CONTEXT CLUES Write the Word to Know that best completes each sentence.

1. During the 1960s, many people rebelled against what they considered rigid and unnecessary _____ in life in the United States.

2. They felt that short hair and a starched shirt made a man a _____ of conformity.

3. Some believed that in the Vietnam War, the United States was not the victim but the _____.

4. During this war, some men burned their draft cards to protest _____ military service.

5. Some who were drafted fled the country rather than undergo the _____ involved in basic training and the betrayal of their own beliefs.

Building Vocabulary
For an in-depth lesson on context clues, see page 326.

WORDS TO KNOW	aggressor compulsory indoctrination	regimentation specimen

Lanford Wilson
1937–

Other Works
Lemon Sky
Fifth of July
Burn This
Redwood Curtain
Balm in Gilead

Surprise Vocation Lanford Wilson began writing his first play during his lunch hour at the advertising agency where he was a graphic designer. He describes stumbling upon his vocation: "I was always very excited by theater. Growing up, I had no idea plays were written, for some reason. I started out writing stories, and then suddenly I realized something I was writing was a play. I thought, I don't know how to write a play. I don't even know what a play is."

Starving Artist In 1962 he moved to New York, where he lived in a rundown hotel. To gather material for his plays, he eavesdropped on conversations in all-night coffee shops. He produced his first play in 1963 at a coffeehouse theater that welcomed experimental works. To pay the rent, he worked as a complaint-department clerk, a hotel clerk, a dishwasher, and a waiter (he was fired after serving one meal). In 1966, when asked to contribute a two-minute play for a benefit evening, Wilson contributed a sketch he had written earlier. After the benefit, he felt "deprived of the challenge to write a two-minute play for a specific event." So he wrote *Wandering*.

Theatrical Success Story In 1969 Wilson cofounded the Circle Repertory Company, where he is still playwright-in-residence. More than 40 of his plays have been produced, and many enjoy frequent revivals. His plays depict real-life issues, yet they incorporate experimental presentational techniques. Wilson's awards include a Pulitzer Prize, two New York Drama Critics Circle Awards, an Emmy award nomination, and three Tony award nominations.

The Writer in the Family

Short Story by E. L. DOCTOROW

(**Connect to Your Life**)

The Meaning of Success What is *success?* For some people, success means being able to "follow their bliss," regardless of financial rewards or considerations about social status. For others, it means finding a job that pays well and demands a lot of responsibility. In your eyes, what makes someone successful? Discuss this question with classmates.

Build Background

Portrait of the Writer as a Young Man
"The Writer in the Family" appeared in E. L. Doctorow's only collection of short fiction to date, *Lives of the Poets* (1984). The collection's six loosely related stories and novella address the question of the writer's role in society. In essays and interviews, Doctorow has described the writer as a kind of witness, one whose biggest challenge is to understand his or her country as it really is and not as it wants to see itself. During most of the 1950s—the decade in which "The Writer in the Family" is set—the United States thought of itself as a place where anyone willing to work hard could achieve material comfort and personal success. Doctorow looks at this ideal through the eyes of Jonathan, the younger son of a "failure" named Jack.

WORDS TO KNOW
Vocabulary Preview

debilitated   robust
implicate   terminal
indestructible

Focus Your Reading

LITERARY ANALYSIS   PLOT DEVELOPMENT   As you know, **plot** is the sequence of events in a literary work. Usually, these events center on a **conflict** that is present at the beginning of the story and that is developed through **characters'** actions. In this story, the seeds of conflict are planted in the first sentence:

> *In 1955 my father died with his ancient mother still alive in a nursing home.*

Notice the chain of problems arising from this situation and how they are resolved.

ACTIVE READING   DRAWING CONCLUSIONS ABOUT CHARACTERS
Although Jonathan's father, Jack, dies at the beginning of the story, you will still learn much about him through the comments of other characters. As you read, pull together these sometimes conflicting pieces of information, and draw your own conclusions about Jack's life.

📖 **READER'S NOTEBOOK**
In a chart like this one, write down information you gain about Jack, under the name of the character who is the source of this information. After you finish the story, write what you believe is the truth about Jack's life.

JACK	
Jonathan says:	Mother says:
Aunt Frances says:	Harold says:

I say:

The WRITER IN THE FAMILY

E.L. DOCTOROW

In 1955 my father died with his ancient mother still alive in a nursing home. The old lady was ninety and hadn't even known he was ill. Thinking the shock might kill her, my aunts told her that he had moved to Arizona for his bronchitis. To the immigrant generation of my grandmother, Arizona was the American equivalent of the Alps, it was where you went for your health. More accurately, it was where you went if you had the money. Since my father had failed in all the business enterprises of his life, this was the aspect of the news my grandmother dwelled on, that he had finally had some success. And so it came about that as we mourned him at home in our stocking feet, my grandmother was bragging to her cronies about her son's new life in the dry air of the desert.

My aunts had decided on their course of action without consulting us. It meant neither my mother nor my brother nor I could visit Grandma because we were supposed to have moved west too, a family, after all. My brother Harold and I didn't mind—it was always a nightmare at the old people's home, where they all sat around staring at us while we tried to make conversation with Grandma. She looked terrible, had numbers of ailments, and her mind wandered. Not seeing her was no disappointment either for my mother, who had never gotten along with the old woman and did not visit when she could have. But what was disturbing was that my aunts had acted in the manner of that side of the family of making government on everyone's behalf, the true citizens by blood and the lesser citizens by marriage. It was exactly this attitude that had tormented my mother all her married life. She claimed Jack's family had never accepted her.

She had battled them for twenty-five years as an outsider.

A few weeks after the end of our ritual mourning my Aunt Frances phoned us from her home in Larchmont. Aunt Frances was the wealthier of my father's sisters. Her husband was a lawyer, and both her sons were at Amherst.[1] She had called to say that Grandma was asking why she didn't hear from Jack. I had answered the phone. "You're the writer in the family," my aunt said. "Your father had so much faith in you. Would you mind making up something? Send it to me and I'll read it to her. She won't know the difference."

That evening, at the kitchen table, I pushed my homework aside and composed a letter. I tried to imagine my father's response to his new life. He had never been west. He had never traveled anywhere. In his generation the great journey was from the working class to the professional class. He hadn't managed that either. But he loved New York, where he had been born and lived his life, and he was always discovering new things about it. He especially loved the old parts of the city below Canal Street, where he would find ships' chandlers[2] or firms that wholesaled in spices and teas. He was a salesman for an appliance jobber with accounts all over the city. He liked to bring home rare cheeses or exotic foreign vegetables that were sold only in certain neighborhoods. Once he brought home a barometer, another time an antique ship's telescope in a wooden case with a brass snap.

---

1. **Amherst:** A prestigious college in Massachusetts.
2. **ships' chandlers:** merchants dealing in nautical equipment.

"Dear Mama," I wrote. "Arizona is beautiful. The sun shines all day and the air is warm and I feel better than I have in years. The desert is not as barren as you would expect, but filled with wildflowers and cactus plants and peculiar crooked trees that look like men holding their arms out. You can see great distances in whatever direction you turn and to the west is a range of mountains maybe fifty miles from here, but in the morning with the sun on them you can see the snow on their crests."

My aunt called some days later and told me it was when she read this letter aloud to the old lady that the full effect of Jack's death came over her. She had to excuse herself and went out in the parking lot to cry. "I wept so," she said. "I felt such terrible longing for him. You're so right, he loved to go places, he loved life, he loved everything."

We began trying to organize our lives. My father had borrowed money against his insurance and there was very little left. Some commissions were still due but it didn't look as if his firm would honor them. There were a couple of thousand dollars in a savings bank that had to be maintained there until the estate was settled. The lawyer involved was Aunt Frances' husband and he was very proper. "The estate!" my mother muttered, gesturing as if to pull out her hair. "The estate!" She applied for a job part-time in the admissions office of the hospital where my father's <u>terminal</u> illness had been diagnosed, and where he had spent some months until they had sent him home to die. She knew a lot of the doctors and staff and she had learned "from bitter experience," as she told them, about the hospital routine. She was hired.

I hated that hospital, it was dark and grim and full of tortured people. I thought it was masochistic of[3] my mother to seek out a job there, but did not tell her so.

We lived in an apartment on the corner of 175th Street and the Grand Concourse, one flight up. Three rooms. I shared the bedroom with my brother. It was jammed with furniture because when my father had required a hospital bed in the last weeks of his illness we had moved some of the living-room pieces into the bedroom and made over the living room for him. We had to navigate bookcases, beds, a gateleg table, bureaus, a record player and radio console, stacks of 78 albums,[4] my brother's trombone and music stand, and so on. My mother continued to sleep on the convertible sofa in the living room that had been their bed before his illness. The two rooms were connected by a narrow hall made even narrower by bookcases along the wall. Off the wall were a small kitchen and dinette and a bathroom. There were lots of appliances in the kitchen—broiler, toaster, pressure cooker, counter-top dishwasher, blender—that my father had gotten through his job, at cost. A treasured phrase in our house: *at cost*. But most of these fixtures went unused because my mother did not care for them. Chromium devices with timers or gauges that required the reading of elaborate instructions were not for her. They were in part responsible for the awful clutter of our lives and now she wanted to get rid of them. "We're being buried," she said. "Who needs them!"

So we agreed to throw out or sell anything inessential. While I found boxes for the appliances and my brother tied the boxes with twine, my mother opened my father's closet and took out his clothes. He had several suits because as a salesman he needed to look his best.

---

3. **was masochistic** (măs′ə-kĭs′tĭk) **of:** showed a desire for suffering on the part of.

4. **78 albums:** phonograph records of a type that became obsolete in the mid-20th century, played at a speed of 78 revolutions per minute.

WORDS TO KNOW   **terminal** (tûr′mə-nəl) *adj.* final; fatal

1159

My mother wanted us to try on his suits to see which of them could be altered and used. My brother refused to try them on. I tried on one jacket which was too large for me. The lining inside the sleeves chilled my arms and the vaguest scent of my father's being came to me.

"This is way too big," I said.

"Don't worry," my mother said. "I had it cleaned. Would I let you wear it if I hadn't?"

It was the evening, the end of winter, and snow was coming down on the windowsill and melting as it settled. The ceiling bulb glared on a pile of my father's suits and trousers on hangers flung across the bed in the shape of a dead man. We refused to try on anything more, and my mother began to cry.

"What are you crying for?" my brother shouted. "You wanted to get rid of things, didn't you?"

A few weeks later my aunt phoned again and said she thought it would be necessary to have another letter from Jack. Grandma had fallen out of her chair and bruised herself and was very depressed.

"How long does this go on?" my mother said.

"It's not so terrible," my aunt said, "for the little time left to make things easier for her."

My mother slammed down the phone. "He can't even die when he wants to!" she cried. "Even death comes second to Mama! What are they afraid of, the shock will kill her? Nothing can kill her. She's <u>indestructible</u>! A stake through the heart couldn't kill her!"

When I sat down in the kitchen to write the letter I found it more difficult than the first one. "Don't watch me," I said to my brother. "It's hard enough."

"You don't have to do something just because someone wants you to," Harold said. He was two years older than me and had started at City College; but when my father became ill he had switched to night school and gotten a job in a record store.

"Dear Mama," I wrote. "I hope you're feeling well. We're all fit as a fiddle. The life here is good and the people are very friendly and informal. Nobody wears suits and ties here. Just a pair of slacks and a short-sleeved shirt. Perhaps a sweater in the evening. I have bought into a very successful radio and record business and I'm doing very well. You remember Jack's Electric, my old place on Forty-third Street? Well, now it's Jack's Arizona Electric and we have a line of television sets as well."

I sent that letter off to my Aunt Frances, and as we all knew she would, she phoned soon after. My brother held his hand over the mouthpiece. "It's Frances with her latest review," he said.

"Jonathan? You're a very talented young man. I just wanted to tell you what a blessing your letter was. Her whole face lit up when I read the part about Jack's store. That would be an excellent way to continue."

"Well, I hope I don't have to do this anymore, Aunt Frances. It's not very honest."

Her tone changed. "Is your mother there? Let me talk to her."

"She's not here," I said.

"Tell her not to worry," my aunt said. "A poor old lady who has never wished anything but the best for her will soon die."

I did not repeat this to my mother, for whom it would have been one more in the family anthology of unforgivable remarks. But then I had to suffer it myself for the possible truth it might embody. Each side defended its position with rhetoric,[5] but I, who wanted peace, rationalized the snubs and rebuffs each inflicted on the other, taking no stands, like my father himself.

---

5. **rhetoric** (rĕt′ər-ĭk): skillful talk.

WORDS TO KNOW	**indestructible** (ĭn′dĭ-strŭk′tə-bəl) *adj.* impossible to destroy

Years ago his life had fallen into a pattern of business failures and missed opportunities. The great debate between his family on the one side, and my mother Ruth on the other, was this: who was responsible for the fact that he had not lived up to anyone's expectations?

As to the prophecies, when spring came my mother's prevailed. Grandma was still alive.

One balmy Sunday my mother and brother and I took the bus to the Beth El cemetery in New Jersey to visit my father's grave. It was situated on a slight rise. We stood looking over rolling fields embedded with monuments. Here and there processions of black cars wound their way through the lanes, or clusters of people stood at open graves. My father's grave was planted with tiny shoots of evergreen but it lacked a headstone. We had chosen one and paid for it and then the stonecutters had gone on strike. Without a headstone my father did not seem to be honorably dead. He didn't seem to me properly buried.

My mother gazed at the plot beside his, reserved for her coffin. "They were always too fine for other people," she said. "Even in the old days on Stanton Street. They put on airs. Nobody was ever good enough for them. Finally Jack himself was not good enough for them. Except to get them things wholesale. Then he was good enough for them."

"Mom, please," my brother said.

"If I had known. Before I ever met him he was tied to his mama's apron strings. And Essie's apron strings were like chains, let me tell you. We had to live where we could be near them for the Sunday visits. Every Sunday, that was my life, a visit to mamaleh.[6] Whatever she knew I wanted, a better apartment, a stick of furniture, a summer camp for the boys, she spoke against it. You know your father, every decision had to be considered and reconsidered. And nothing changed. Nothing ever changed."

She began to cry. We sat her down on a nearby bench. My brother walked off and read the names on stones. I looked at my mother, who was crying, and I went off after my brother.

"Mom's still crying," I said. "Shouldn't we do something?"

"It's all right," he said. "It's what she came here for."

"Yes," I said, and then a sob escaped from my throat. "But I feel like crying too."

My brother Harold put his arm around me. "Look at this old black stone here," he said. "The way it's carved. You can see the changing fashion in monuments—just like everything else."

Somewhere in this time I began dreaming of my father. Not the robust father of my childhood, the handsome man with healthy pink skin and brown eyes and a mustache and the thinning hair parted in the middle. My dead father. We were taking him home from the hospital. It was understood that he had come back from death. This was amazing and joyous. On the other hand, he was terribly mysteriously damaged, or, more accurately, spoiled and unclean. He was very yellowed and debilitated by his death, and there were no guarantees that he wouldn't soon die again. He seemed aware of this and his entire personality was changed. He was angry and impatient with all of us. We were trying to help him in some way, struggling to get him home, but something prevented us, something we had to fix, a tattered suitcase that had sprung open, some mechanical thing: he had a car but it wouldn't start; or the car was made of wood; or his clothes, which had become too large for him, had caught in the door. In one version he was all bandaged and as we tried to lift him from his wheelchair into a taxi the bandage began to unroll and catch in the spokes

---

6. **mamaleh** (mä′mə-lə) *Yiddish:* mother.

| WORDS TO KNOW | **robust** (rō-bŭst′) *adj.* full of health and strength; vigorous |
| | **debilitated** (dĭ-bĭl′ĭ-tā′tĭd) *adj.* weakened; enfeebled |

of the wheelchair. This seemed to be some unreasonableness on his part. My mother looked on sadly and tried to get him to cooperate.

That was the dream. I shared it with no one. Once when I woke, crying out, my brother turned on the light. He wanted to know what I'd been dreaming but I pretended I didn't remember. The dream made me feel guilty. I felt guilty in the dream too because my enraged father knew we didn't want to live with him. The dream represented us taking him home, or trying to, but it was nevertheless understood by all of us that he was to live alone. He was this derelict[7] back from death, but what we were doing was taking him to some place where he would live by himself without help from anyone until he died again.

At one point I became so fearful of this dream that I tried not to go to sleep. I tried to think of good things about my father and to remember him before his illness. He used to call me "matey." "Hello, matey," he would say when he came home from work. He always wanted us to go someplace—to the store, to the park, to a ball game. He loved to walk. When I went walking with him he would say: "Hold your shoulders back, don't slump. Hold your head up and look at the world. Walk as if you meant it!" As he strode down the street his shoulders moved from side to side, as if he was hearing some kind of cakewalk.[8] He moved with a bounce. He was always eager to see what was around the corner.

Untitled (First Avenue) (about 1945), Fairfield Porter. Oil on canvas, 32" × 26¼". The Parrish Art Museum, Southampton, New York. Gift of the Estate of Fairfield Porter (1980.10.16).

The next request for a letter coincided with a special occasion in the house: My brother Harold had met a girl he liked and had gone out with her several times. Now she was coming to our house for dinner. We had prepared for this for days, cleaning everything in sight, giving the house a going-over, washing the dust of disuse from the glasses and good dishes. My mother came home early from work to get the dinner going. We opened the gateleg table in the living room and brought in the kitchen chairs. My mother spread the table with a laundered white cloth and put out her silver. It was the first family occasion since my father's illness.

I liked my brother's girlfriend a lot. She was a thin girl with very straight hair and she had a terrific smile. Her presence seemed to excite the air. It was amazing to have a living breathing girl in our house. She looked around and what she said was: "Oh, I've never seen so many books!" While she and my brother sat at the table my mother was in the kitchen putting the food into serving bowls and I was going from the kitchen to the living room, kidding around like a waiter, with a white cloth over my arm and a high style of service, placing the serving dish of green beans on the table with a flourish. In the kitchen my mother's eyes were sparkling. She looked at me and nodded and mimed the words: "She's adorable!"

---

7. **derelict:** a person rejected by society; tramp or vagrant.
8. **cakewalk:** music written to accompany a strutting dance.

My brother suffered himself to be waited on. He was wary of what we might say. He kept glancing at the girl—her name was Susan—to see if we met with her approval. She worked in an insurance office and was taking courses in accounting at City College. Harold was under a terrible strain but he was excited and happy too. He had bought a bottle of Concord-grape wine to go with the roast chicken. He held up his glass and proposed a toast. My mother said: "To good health and happiness," and we all drank, even I. At that moment the phone rang and I went into the bedroom to get it.

"Jonathan? This is your Aunt Frances. How is everyone?"

"Fine, thank you."

"I want to ask one last favor of you. I need a letter from Jack. Your grandma's very ill. Do you think you can?"

"Who is it?" my mother called from the living room.

"OK, Aunt Frances," I said quickly. "I have to go now, we're eating dinner." And I hung up the phone.

"It was my friend Louie," I said, sitting back down. "He didn't know the math pages to review."

The dinner was very fine. Harold and Susan washed the dishes and by the time they were done my mother and I had folded up the gateleg table and put it back against the wall and I had swept the crumbs up with the carpet sweeper. We all sat and talked and listened to records for a while and then my brother took Susan home. The evening had gone very well.

Once when my mother wasn't home my brother had pointed out something: the letters from Jack weren't really necessary. "What is this ritual?" he said, holding his palms up. "Grandma is almost totally blind, she's half deaf and crippled. Does the situation really call for a literary composition? Does it need verisimilitude?[9]

Would the old lady know the difference if she was read the phone book?"

"Then why did Aunt Frances ask me?"

"That is the question, Jonathan. Why did she? After all, she could write the letter herself—what difference would it make? And if not Frances, why not Frances' sons, the Amherst students? They should have learned by now to write."

"But they're not Jack's sons," I said.

"That's exactly the point," my brother said. "The idea is *service*. Dad used to get them things wholesale, getting them deals on things. Frances of Westchester[10] really needed things at cost. And Aunt Molly. And Aunt Molly's husband, and Aunt Molly's ex-husband. Grandma, if she needed an errand done. He was always on the hook for something. They never thought his time was important. They never thought every favor he got was one he had to pay back. Appliances, records, watches, china, opera tickets, any thing. Call Jack."

"It was a matter of pride to him to be able to do things for them," I said. "To have connections."

"Yeah, I wonder why," my brother said. He looked out the window.

Then suddenly it dawned on me that I was being <u>implicated</u>.

"You should use your head more," my brother said.

Yet I had agreed once again to write a letter from the desert and so I did. I mailed it off to Aunt Frances. A few days later, when I came home from school, I thought I saw her sitting in her car in front of our house. She drove a black Buick Roadmaster, a very large clean car with whitewall tires. It was Aunt Frances all right. She blew the horn when she saw me. I went over and leaned in at the window.

---

9. **verisimilitude** (vĕr′ə-sĭ-mĭl′ĭ-tōōd′): an appearance of reality; truth to life.

10. **Westchester:** an affluent county just north of New York City.

"Hello, Jonathan," she said. "I haven't long. Can you get in the car?"

"Mom's not home," I said. "She's working."

"I know that. I came to talk to you."

"Would you like to come upstairs?"

"I can't, I have to get back to Larchmont. Can you get in for a moment, please?"

I got in the car. My Aunt Frances was a very pretty white-haired woman, very elegant, and she wore tasteful clothes. I had always liked her and from the time I was a child she had enjoyed pointing out to everyone that I looked more like her son than Jack's. She wore white gloves and held the steering wheel and looked straight ahead as she talked, as if the car was in traffic and not sitting at the curb.

"Jonathan," she said, "there is your letter on the seat. Needless to say I didn't read it to Grandma. I'm giving it back to you and I won't ever say a word to anyone. This is just between us. I never expected cruelty from you. I never thought you were capable of doing something so deliberately cruel and perverse."

I said nothing.

"Your mother has very bitter feelings and now I see she has poisoned you with them. She has always resented the family. She is a very strong-willed, selfish person."

"No she isn't," I said.

"I wouldn't expect you to agree. She drove poor Jack crazy with her demands. She always had the highest aspirations and he could never fulfill them to her satisfaction. When he still had his store he kept your mother's brother, who drank, on salary. After the war when he began to make a little money he had to buy Ruth a mink jacket because she was so desperate to have one. He had debts to pay but she wanted a mink. He was a very special person, my brother, he should have accomplished something special, but he loved your mother and devoted his life to her. And all she ever thought about was keeping up with the Joneses."

I watched the traffic going up the Grand Concourse. A bunch of kids were waiting at the bus stop at the corner. They had put their books on the ground and were horsing around.

"I'm sorry I have to descend to this," Aunt Frances said. "I don't like talking about people this way. If I have nothing good to say about someone, I'd rather not say anything. How is Harold?"

"Fine."

"Did he help you write this marvelous letter?"

"No."

After a moment she said more softly: "How are you all getting along?"

"Fine."

"I would invite you up for Passover[11] if I thought your mother would accept."

I didn't answer.

She turned on the engine. "I'll say good-bye now, Jonathan. Take your letter. I hope you give some time to thinking about what you've done."

That evening when my mother came home from work I saw that she wasn't as pretty as my Aunt Frances. I usually thought my mother was a good-looking woman, but I saw now that she was too heavy and that her hair was undistinguished.

"Why are you looking at me?" she said.

"I'm not."

"I learned something interesting today," my mother said. "We may be eligible for a V.A. pension[12] because of the time your father spent in the Navy."

That took me by surprise. Nobody had ever told me my father was in the Navy.

"In World War I," she said, "he went to Webb's Naval Academy on the Harlem River. He was training to be an ensign. But the war ended and he never got his commission."

---

11. **Passover:** an important Jewish holiday, commemorating the Hebrew people's deliverance from slavery in Egypt.

12. **V.A. pension:** a pension paid by the Veterans Administration (now the Department of Veterans Affairs) to former members of the U.S. armed forces.

After dinner the three of us went through the closets looking for my father's papers, hoping to find some proof that could be filed with the Veterans Administration. We came up with two things, a Victory medal, which my brother said everyone got for being in the service during the Great War, and an astounding sepia photograph[13] of my father and his shipmates on the deck of a ship. They were dressed in bell-bottoms and T-shirts and armed with mops and pails, brooms and brushes.

"I never knew this," I found myself saying. "I never knew this."

"You just don't remember," my brother said.

I was able to pick out my father. He stood at the end of the row, a thin, handsome boy with a full head of hair, a mustache, and an intelligent smiling countenance.

"He had a joke," my mother said. "They called their training ship the *S.S. Constipation* because it never moved."

Neither the picture nor the medal was proof of anything, but my brother thought a duplicate of my father's service record had to be in Washington somewhere and that it was just a matter of learning how to go about finding it.

"The pension wouldn't amount to much," my mother said. "Twenty or thirty dollars. But it would certainly help."

I took the picture of my father and his shipmates and propped it against the lamp at my bedside. I looked into his youthful face and tried to relate it to the Father I knew. I looked at the picture a long time. Only gradually did my eye connect it to the set of Great Sea Novels in the bottom shelf of the bookcase a few feet away. My father had given that set to me: it was uniformly bound in green with gilt lettering and it included works by Melville, Conrad, Victor Hugo and Captain Marryat.[14] And lying across the top of the books, jammed in under the sagging shelf above, was his old ship's telescope in its wooden case with the brass snap.

I thought how stupid, and imperceptive, and self-centered I had been never to have understood while he was alive what my father's dream for his life had been.

On the other hand, I had written in my last letter from Arizona—the one that had so angered Aunt Frances—something that might allow me, the writer in the family, to soften my judgment of myself. I will conclude by giving the letter here in its entirety.

Dear Mama,

This will be my final letter to you since I have been told by the doctors that I am dying.

I have sold my store at a very fine profit and am sending Frances a check for five thousand dollars to be deposited in your account. My present to you, Mamaleh. Let Frances show you the passbook.

As for the nature of my ailment, the doctors haven't told me what it is, but I know that I am simply dying of the wrong life. I should never have come to the desert. It wasn't the place for me.

I have asked Ruth and the boys to have my body cremated and the ashes scattered in the ocean.

Your loving son,
Jack ❖

---

13. **sepia** (sē'pē-ə) **photograph:** a photograph printed in a brownish tint.

14. **Melville . . . Marryat** (măr'ē-ət): Herman Melville, an American writer who drew upon his experiences as a sailor in creating *Moby-Dick* and other novels; Joseph Conrad, a Polish-born English novelist (also a former sailor) whose works include *Lord Jim*; Victor Hugo, a French poet, novelist, and dramatist, among whose novels is the *Toilers of the Sea*; Captain Frederick Marryat, a British naval officer, an author of a number of novels dealing with life at sea.

Connect to the Literature

1. What Do You Think? Share your reaction to Jonathan's last letter. Do you agree with Aunt Frances that it was cruel?

Comprehension Check
- Why do the aunts lie to the grandmother about Jack's death?
- What does Aunt Frances ask Jonathan to do for the grandmother?
- At the end of the story, what does Jonathan learn about his father's past?

Think Critically

2. **ACTIVE READING** | **DRAWING CONCLUSIONS** | What do you think was Jack's dream for his life? What other conclusions did you draw about his life? Look over the chart you made in your **READER'S NOTEBOOK**, and state the information on which you based your conclusions.

3. How does Jonathan's mother's view of Jack's life compare with Aunt Frances's view?

4. Tell how you interpret Jonathan's dream.

THINK ABOUT
- his father's physical condition and attitude
- the obstacles that prevent the father from getting home
- the mother's attitude and actions
- Jonathan's feelings in the dream

5. Offer your final judgments of Jonathan, his mother, his Aunt Frances, and his brother Harold. Did these change from your earlier judgments?

Extend Interpretations

6. Different Perspectives Why might someone classify "The Writer in the Family" as a coming-of-age story?

7. Critic's Corner Respond to this comment by critic Paul Levine:

Jonathan's letters have a surprising effect on himself as well as others. To some family members, these fictions seem to make the dead man more real than when he was alive. To Jonathan, his constructions finally reveal something of his father's true nature which was hidden from him. The lies he creates disclose the truth about his own family situation.

8. Connect to Life Name a real person or a fictional character who reminds you of Jonathan's father, and explain what they have in common.

Literary Analysis

PLOT DEVELOPMENT As you recall, **plot** is based on **conflict,** a struggle between opposing forces. Conflict can be **external,** as when a character struggles with another character, a natural force, or a social circumstance. Conflict can also be **internal,** as when a character struggles with a moral dilemma. In "The Writer in the Family," external conflicts lead to internal conflicts for Jonathan. The letters that Aunt Frances requests create tension among the family members. As the plot develops, Jonathan must decide whether to keep writing. What other conflicts do you see in the story?

Cooperative Learning Activity Working in a small group, create a diagram of the conflicts in this story. Show which characters are in conflict with other characters, and which characters are in conflict with themselves. Be prepared to tell what the conflicts are about. The most important conflicts in the story are internal ones faced by Jonathan. Discuss how his final letter resolves these conflicts.

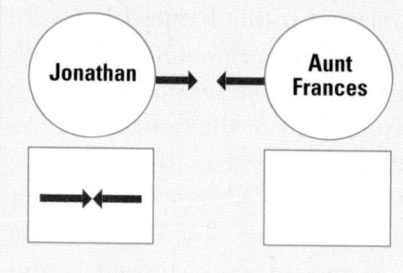

Writing Options

1. True Obituary Write an obituary that tells the *real* truth about Jack's life instead of following the standard formula. Mention his background, accomplishments, disappointments, and family.

2. Definition of Success Define *a successful life*, drawing on the ideas you had about success both before and after you read the story. In your definition, make reference to at least one of the characters from the story as a positive or negative example.

Inquiry & Research

Mourning Rituals When the story opens, Jonathan's family is observing *shiva*, the traditional seven-day period of mourning for Jews. Find out more or share what you already know about *shiva* rituals.

Vocabulary in Action

EXERCISE: CONTEXT CLUES On your paper, write the Word to Know that best completes each sentence.

1. The boy's father suffered from a _____ illness.

2. The image of his sick father contrasted with the boy's memory of the healthy, _____ father of his childhood.

3. His father was quite _____ by his illness.

4. Aunt Frances _____ Jonathan in a plot to deceive his grandmother.

5. Sometimes we forget that people are not _____, that even the healthiest can die suddenly.

Building Vocabulary
For an in-depth study of context clues, see page 326.

WORDS TO KNOW			
	debilitated	indestructible	terminal
	implicate	robust	

E(dgar) L(aurence) Doctorow
1931–

Other Works
Ragtime
World's Fair
Billy Bathgate

Serious Novelist E. L. Doctorow is one of the few bestselling American authors considered a "serious" writer by critics. Doctorow is known for the stylistic breadth of his fiction, which is alternately traditional and experimental, accessible and difficult. Many of his works blur the line separating fact from fiction. This strategy reflects Doctorow's belief, stated in the essay "False Documents," that "there is no fiction or nonfiction as we commonly understand the distinction: there is only narrative."

Mixing History with Fiction Such early novels as *The Book of Daniel* (1971) and *Ragtime* (1975) reimagine portions of this country's history, combining real-life events and figures with entirely fictitious ones. According to Doctorow, serious novelists use the power of the imagination to construct works of fiction "more valid, more real, more truthful than the 'true' documents of the politicians or the journalists or the psychologists." *The Book of Daniel*, for example, is based on the actual trial of Julius and Ethel Rosenberg, a communist couple executed for treason by the U.S. government during the Cold War period of the 1950s. Rather than merely dramatizing the facts of the case, Doctorow changes some facts and filters them through the highly subjective perspective of Daniel, the fictionalized couple's bitter and bewildered son.

A More Personal Collection When *Lives of the Poets* came out in 1984, its somewhat autobiographical flavor seemed like a departure for Doctorow, a writer who avoided drawing on his personal history in previous works of fiction. However, while this book is more personal than earlier works, it mixes fact and fiction in a similar way and displays the same fascination with the past.

Teenage Wasteland

Short Story by ANNE TYLER

(Connect to Your Life)

Troubled Teen In this story, Daisy and Matt learn that their teenage son, Donny, is having trouble in school. What advice would you give to parents in this situation? With a small group of classmates, discuss things you would do or rules you might enforce to help a teenager improve in school.

Build Background

Academic Reform Debate In keeping with other changes during the 1960s and 1970s, experimental theories of education were being tested in many U.S. schools and universities. Believing that teachers should act as assistants or helpers rather than as authority figures, supporters of "alternative schools" and "the open classroom" wanted to do away with traditional teaching methods. They wanted students to be free to discover their own learning styles, guide their own curriculum, and progress at their own pace. While quite successful in some schools, this academic reform movement met resistance from some educators and parents who felt that students, if left to themselves, would not be taught the basic skills of reading, writing, and arithmetic. In "Teenage Wasteland," Daisy and Matt, like many parents at the time, find themselves caught in the middle of this continuing debate. They receive conflicting advice from educators about how to help their son.

WORDS TO KNOW
Vocabulary Preview

amiably	qualm
forlorn	shamble
looming	subdued
morass	temporize
punitive	vindictive

Focus Your Reading

LITERARY ANALYSIS **CHARACTER: PROTAGONIST AND ANTAGONIST** The **protagonist** is the central character in a short story, novel, or play. The **antagonist** is the character or force that the protagonist is pitted against. Decide who is the protagonist and who is the antagonist in this story.

ACTIVE READING **RECOGNIZING IMPORTANT DETAILS**
In "Teenage Wasteland," Tyler uses many **details**—or specific pieces of information—to create an experience for your imagination. All of these details contribute to the total effect of the story, and you should savor them as you read. For example, notice the following details that reveal how Daisy imagines the principal's perception of herself and her husband: "an overweight housewife in a cotton dress and a too-tall, too-thin insurance agent in a baggy, frayed suit." These details provide a strong clue about Daisy's self-image. Still, some details are more compelling than others and deserve special attention as you read. In this story about a troubled teen, one cluster of important details concerns the different pieces of advice that the parents receive about how to help their son.

READER'S NOTEBOOK
To help you track the different kinds of advice that Daisy and Matt receive, keep a list of that advice in your notebook. As you read, write down what the principal, the teachers, and the tutor say about how to help Donny. Put a check mark beside each piece of advice that Daisy and Matt follow.

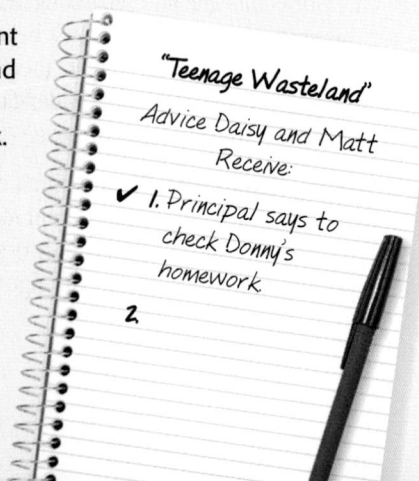

"Teenage Wasteland"
Advice Daisy and Matt
Receive:

✓ 1. Principal says to
check Donny's
homework

2.

Teenage Waste

He used to have very blond hair—almost white—cut shorter than other children's so that on his crown a little cowlick always stood up to catch the light. But this was when he was small. As he grew older, his hair grew darker, and he wore it longer —past his collar even. It hung in lank, taffy-colored ropes around his face, which was still an endearing face, fine-featured, the eyes an unusual aqua blue. But his cheeks, of course, were no longer round, and a sharp new Adam's apple jogged in his throat when he talked.

In October, they called from the private school he attended to request a conference with his parents. Daisy went alone; her husband was at work. Clutching her purse, she sat on the principal's couch and learned that Donny was noisy, lazy, and disruptive; always fooling around with his friends, and he wouldn't respond in class.

In the past, before her children were born, Daisy had been a fourth-grade teacher. It shamed her now to sit before this principal as a parent, a delinquent parent, a parent who struck Mr. Lanham, no doubt, as unseeing or uncaring. "It isn't that we're not concerned," she said. "Both of us are. And we've done what we could, whatever we could think of. We don't let him watch TV

Table with Fruit
(1951–1952), David Park.
Oil on canvas, 46″ × 35¼
collection of Mr. and Mr
R. Crosby Kemper. Photo
by Edward B. Bigelow.

on school nights. We don't let him talk on the phone till he's finished his homework. But he tells us he doesn't *have* any homework or he did it all in study hall. How are we to know what to believe?"

From early October through November, at Mr. Lanham's suggestion, Daisy checked Donny's assignments every day. She sat next to him as he worked, trying to be encouraging, sagging inwardly as she saw the poor quality of everything he did—the sloppy mistakes in math, the illogical leaps in his English themes, the history questions left blank if they required any research.

Daisy was often late starting supper, and she couldn't give as much attention to Donny's younger sister. "You'll never guess what happened at . . ." Amanda would begin, and Daisy would have to tell her, "Not now, honey."

By the time her husband Matt came home, she'd be snappish. She would recite the day's hardships—the fuzzy instructions in English, the botched history map, the <u>morass</u> of unsolvable algebra equations. Matt would look surprised and confused, and Daisy would gradually wind down. There was no way, really, to convey how exhausting all this was.

In December, the school called again. This time, they wanted Matt to come as well. She and Matt had to sit on Mr. Lanham's couch like two bad children and listen to the news: Donny had improved only slightly, raising a D in history to a C, and a C in algebra to a B-minus. What was worse, he had developed new problems. He had cut classes on at least three occasions. Smoked in the furnace room. Helped Sonny Barnett break into a freshman's locker. And last week, during athletics, he and three friends had been seen off the school grounds; when they returned, the coach had smelled beer on their breath.

Daisy and Matt sat silent, shocked. Matt rubbed his forehead with his fingertips. Imagine, Daisy thought, how they must look to Mr. Lanham: an overweight housewife in a cotton dress and a too-tall, too-thin insurance agent in a baggy, frayed suit. Failures, both of them—the kind of people who are always hurrying to catch up, missing the point of things that everyone else grasps at once. She wished she'd worn nylons instead of knee socks.

It was arranged that Donny would visit a psychologist for testing. Mr. Lanham knew just the person. He would set this boy straight, he said.

When they stood to leave, Daisy held her stomach in and gave Mr. Lanham a firm, responsible handshake.

Donny said the psychologist was a jackass and the tests were really dumb; but he kept all three of his appointments, and when it was time for the follow-up conference with the psychologist and both parents, Donny combed his hair and seemed unusually sober and <u>subdued</u>. The psychologist said Donny had no serious emotional problems. He was merely going through a difficult period in his life. He required some academic help and a better sense of self-worth. For this reason, he was suggesting a man named Calvin Beadle, a tutor with considerable psychological training.

In the car going home, Donny said he'd be damned if he'd let them drag him to some stupid fairy tutor. His father told him to watch his language in front of his mother.

That night, Daisy lay awake pondering the term "self-worth." She had always been free with her praise. She had always told Donny he had talent, was smart, was good with his hands. She had made a big to-do over every little gift he gave her. In fact, maybe she had gone too far, although, Lord knows, she had meant every word. Was that his trouble?

She remembered when Amanda was born. Donny had acted lost and bewildered. Daisy had been alert to that, of course, but still, a new baby keeps you so busy. Had she really done all she could have? She longed—she ached—for a time machine. Given one more chance, she'd do

She longed—

she ached—

for a time machine.

Given one more chance,

she'd do it perfectly—

hug him more,

praise him more,

or perhaps

praise him less.

Oh, who can say . . .

it perfectly—hug him more, praise him more, or perhaps praise him less. Oh, who can say . . .

The tutor told Donny to call him Cal. All his kids did, he said. Daisy thought for a second that he meant his own children, then realized her mistake. He seemed too young, anyhow, to be a family man. He wore a heavy brown handlebar mustache. His hair was as long and stringy as Donny's, and his jeans as faded. Wire-rimmed spectacles slid down his nose. He lounged in a canvas director's chair with his fingers laced across his chest, and he casually, <u>amiably</u> questioned Donny, who sat upright and glaring in an armchair.

"So they're getting on your back at school," said Cal. "Making a big deal about anything you do wrong."

"Right," said Donny.

"Any idea why that would be?"

"Oh, well, you know, stuff like homework and all," Donny said.

"You don't do your homework?"

"Oh, well, I might do it sometimes but not just exactly like they want it." Donny sat forward and said, "It's like a prison there, you know? You've got to go to every class, you can never step off the school grounds."

"You cut classes sometimes?"

"Sometimes," Donny said, with a glance at his parents.

Cal didn't seem perturbed. "Well," he said, "I'll tell you what. Let's you and me try working together three nights a week. Think you could handle that? We'll see if we can show that school of yours a thing or two. Give it a month; then if you don't like it, we'll stop. If *I* don't like it, we'll stop. I mean, sometimes people just don't get along, right? What do you say to that?"

"Okay," Donny said. He seemed pleased.

"Make it seven o'clock till eight, Monday, Wednesday, and Friday," Cal told Matt and Daisy. They nodded. Cal <u>shambled</u> to his feet, gave them a little salute, and showed them to the door.

This was where he lived as well as worked, evidently. The interview had taken place in the dining room, which had been transformed into a kind of office. Passing the living room, Daisy winced at the rock music she had been hearing, without registering it, ever since she had entered the house. She looked in and saw a boy about Donny's age lying on a sofa with a book. Another boy and a girl were playing Ping-Pong in front of the fireplace. "You have several here together?" Daisy asked Cal.

"Oh, sometimes they stay on after their sessions, just to rap. They're a pretty sociable group, all in all. Plenty of goof-offs like young Donny here."

He cuffed Donny's shoulder playfully. Donny flushed and grinned.

Climbing into the car, Daisy asked Donny, "Well? What did you think?"

But Donny had returned to his old evasive self. He jerked his chin toward the garage. "Look," he said. "He's got a basketball net."

Now on Mondays, Wednesdays, and Fridays, they had supper early—the instant Matt came home. Sometimes, they had to leave before they were really finished. Amanda would still be eating her dessert. "Bye, honey. Sorry," Daisy would tell her.

Cal's first bill sent a flutter of panic through Daisy's chest, but it was worth it, of course. Just look at Donny's face when they picked him up: alight and full of interest. The principal telephoned Daisy to tell her how Donny had improved. "Of course, it hasn't shown up in his grades yet, but several of the teachers have noticed how his attitude's changed. Yes, sir, I think we're onto something here."

At home, Donny didn't act much different. He still seemed to have a low opinion of his parents. But Daisy supposed that was unavoidable—part of being fifteen. He said his parents were too "controlling"—a word that made Daisy give him a sudden look. He said they acted like wardens.

WORDS TO KNOW   **amiably** (āʹmē-ə-blē) *adv.* in a pleasant and friendly manner; good-naturedly
shamble (shămʹbəl) *v.* to walk or move awkwardly or clumsily

On weekends, they enforced a curfew. And any time he went to a party, they always telephoned first to see if adults would be supervising. "For God's sake!" he said. "Don't you trust me?"

"It isn't a matter of trust, honey . . ." But there was no explaining to him.

His tutor called one afternoon. "I get the sense," he said, "that this kid's feeling . . . underestimated, you know? Like you folks expect the worst of him. I'm thinking we ought to give him more rope."

"But see, he's still so suggestible," Daisy said. "When his friends suggest some mischief—smoking or drinking or such—why, he just finds it hard not to go along with them."

"Mrs. Coble," the tutor said, "I think this kid is hurting. You know? Here's a serious, sensitive kid, telling you he'd like to take on some grown-up challenges, and you're giving him the message that he can't be trusted. Don't you understand how that hurts?"

"Oh," said Daisy.

"It undermines his self-esteem—don't you realize that?"

"Well, I guess you're right," said Daisy. She saw Donny suddenly from a whole new angle: his pathetically poor posture, that slouch so <u>forlorn</u> that his shoulders seemed about to meet his chin . . . oh, wasn't it awful being young? She'd had a miserable adolescence herself and had always sworn no child of hers would ever be that unhappy.

They let Donny stay out later, they didn't call ahead to see if the parties were supervised, and they were careful not to grill him about his evening. The tutor had set down so many rules! They were not allowed any questions at all about any aspect of school, nor were they to speak with his teachers. If a teacher had some complaint, she should phone Cal. Only one teacher disobeyed—the history teacher, Miss Evans. She called one morning in February. "I'm a little concerned about Donny, Mrs. Coble."

"Oh, I'm sorry, Miss Evans, but Donny's tutor handles these things now . . ."

"I always deal directly with the parents. You are the parent," Miss Evans said, speaking very slowly and distinctly. "Now, here is the problem. Back when you were helping Donny with his homework, his grades rose from a D to a C, but now they've slipped back, and they're closer to an F."

"They are?"

"I think you should start overseeing his homework again."

"But Donny's tutor says . . ."

"It's nice that Donny has a tutor, but you should still be in charge of his homework. With you, he learned it. Then he passed his tests. With the tutor, well, it seems the tutor is more of a crutch. 'Donny,' I say, 'a quiz is coming up on Friday. Hadn't you better be listening instead of talking?' 'That's okay, Miss Evans,' he says. 'I have a tutor now.' Like a talisman![1] I really think you ought to take over, Mrs. Coble."

"I see," said Daisy. "Well, I'll think about that. Thank you for calling."

Hanging up, she felt a rush of anger at Donny. A talisman! For a talisman, she'd given up all luxuries, all that time with her daughter, her evenings at home!

She dialed Cal's number. He sounded muzzy. "I'm sorry if I woke you," she told him, "but Donny's history teacher just called. She says he isn't doing well."

"She should have dealt with me."

"She wants me to start supervising his homework again. His grades are slipping."

"Yes," said the tutor, "but you and I both

> She'd had a miserable adolescence herself and had always sworn no child of hers would ever be that unhappy.

---

1. **talisman** (tăl′ĭs-mən): a thing believed to possess magic power or to bring good luck.

WORDS TO KNOW   **forlorn** (fər-lôrn′) *adj.* appearing sad or lonely

Portrait of Richard Freeman (1974), Fairfield Porter. Oil on panel, Bowdoin College Museum of Art, Brunswick, Maine, anonymous gift (1986,74.1).

"I care about

the *whole* child—

his happiness,

his self-esteem.

The grades will come.

Just give them time."

know there's more to it than mere grades, don't we? I care about the *whole* child—his happiness, his self-esteem. The grades will come. Just give them time."

When she hung up, it was Miss Evans she was angry at. What a narrow woman!

It was Cal this, Cal that, Cal says this, Cal and I did that. Cal lent Donny an album by the Who.[2] He took Donny and two other pupils to a rock concert. In March, when Donny began to talk endlessly on the phone with a girl named Miriam, Cal even let Miriam come to one of the tutoring sessions. Daisy was touched that Cal would grow so involved in Donny's life, but she was also a little hurt, because she had offered to have Miriam to dinner and Donny had refused. Now he asked them to drive her to Cal's house without a qualm.

This Miriam was an unappealing girl with blurry lipstick and masses of rough red hair. She wore a short, bulky jacket that would not have been out of place on a motorcycle. During the trip to Cal's she was silent, but coming back, she was more talkative. "What a neat guy, and what a house! All those kids hanging out, like a club. And the stereo playing rock . . . gosh, he's not like grown-up at all! Married and divorced and everything, but you'd think he was our own age."

"Mr. Beadle was married?" Daisy asked.

"Yeah, to this really controlling lady. She didn't understand him a bit."

"No, I guess not," Daisy said.

Spring came, and the students who hung around at Cal's drifted out to the basketball net above the garage. Sometimes, when Daisy and Matt arrived to pick up Donny, they'd find him there with the others—spiky and excited, jittering on his toes beneath the backboard. It was staying light much longer now, and the neighboring fence cast narrow bars across the bright grass. Loud music would be spilling from Cal's windows. Once it was the Who, which Daisy recognized from the time that Donny had borrowed the album. *"Teenage Wasteland,"*[3] she said aloud, identifying the song, and Matt gave a short, dry laugh. "It certainly is," he said. He'd misunderstood; he thought she was commenting on the scene spread before them. In fact, she might have been. The players looked like hoodlums, even her son. Why, one of Cal's students had recently been knifed in a tavern. One had been shipped off to boarding school in midterm; two had been withdrawn by their parents. On the other hand, Donny had mentioned someone who'd been studying with Cal for five years. "Five years!" said Daisy. "Doesn't anyone ever stop needing him?"

Donny looked at her. Lately, whatever she said about Cal was read as criticism. "You're just feeling competitive," he said. "And controlling."

She bit her lip and said no more.

In April, the principal called to tell her that Donny had been expelled. There had been a locker check, and in Donny's locker they found five cans of beer and half a pack of cigarettes. With Donny's previous record, this offense meant expulsion.

Daisy gripped the receiver tightly and said, "Well, where is he now?"

"We've sent him home," said Mr. Lanham. "He's packed up all his belongings, and he's coming home on foot."

Daisy wondered what she would say to him. She felt him looming closer and closer, bringing this brand-new situation that no one had prepared her to handle. What other place would take him? Could they enter him in public school? What were the rules? She stood at the living room window, waiting for him to show up. Gradually, she realized that he was taking too long. She checked the clock. She stared up the street again.

---

2. **the Who:** a British rock group formed in the early 1960s.

3. **"Teenage Wasteland":** The song is actually titled "Baba O'Riley" and can be found on the album *Who's Next* (1971).

WORDS TO KNOW	**qualm** (kwäm) *n.* a disturbing uneasiness or doubt **looming** (lōō'mǐng) *adj.* appearing to the mind in a large and threatening form **loom** *v.*

1175

When an hour had passed, she phoned the school. Mr. Lanham's secretary answered and told her in a grave, sympathetic voice that yes, Donny Coble had most definitely gone home. Daisy called her husband. He was out of the office. She went back to the window and thought awhile, and then she called Donny's tutor.

"Donny's been expelled from school," she said, "and now I don't know where he's gone. I wonder if you've heard from him?"

There was a long silence. "Donny's with me, Mrs. Coble," he finally said.

"With you? How'd he get there?"

"He hailed a cab, and I paid the driver."

"Could I speak to him, please?"

There was another silence. "Maybe it'd be better if we had a conference," Cal said.

"I don't *want* a conference. I've been standing at the window picturing him dead or kidnapped or something, and now you tell me you want a—"

"Donny is very, very upset. Understandably so," said Cal. "Believe me, Mrs. Coble, this is not what it seems. Have you asked Donny's side of the story?"

"Well, of course not, how could I? He went running off to you instead."

"Because he didn't feel he'd be listened to."

"But I haven't even—"

"Why don't you come out and talk? The three of us," said Cal, "will try to get this thing in perspective."

"Well, all right," Daisy said. But she wasn't as reluctant as she sounded. Already, she felt soothed by the calm way Cal was taking this.

Cal answered the doorbell at once. He said, "Hi, there," and led her into the dining room.

> He did his assignments, and he earned average grades, but he gathered no friends, joined no clubs. There was something exhausted and defeated about him.

Donny sat slumped in a chair, chewing the knuckle of one thumb. "Hello, Donny," Daisy said. He flicked his eyes in her direction.

"Sit here, Mrs. Coble," said Cal, placing her opposite Donny. He himself remained standing, restlessly pacing. "So," he said.

Daisy stole a look at Donny. His lips were swollen, as if he'd been crying.

"You know," Cal told Daisy, "I kind of expected something like this. That's a very <u>punitive</u> school you've got him in—you realize that. And any half-decent lawyer will tell you they've violated his civil rights. Locker checks! Where's their search warrant?"

"But if the rule is—" Daisy said.

"Well, anyhow, let him tell you his side."

She looked at Donny. He said, "It wasn't my fault. I promise."

"They said your locker was full of beer."

"It was a put-up job! See, there's this guy that doesn't like me. He put all these beers in my locker and started a rumor going, so Mr. Lanham ordered a locker check."

"What was the boy's *name*?" Daisy asked.

"Huh?"

"Mrs. Coble, take my word, the situation is not so unusual," Cal said. "You can't imagine how <u>vindictive</u> kids can be sometimes."

"What was the boy's name," said Daisy, "so that I can ask Mr. Lanham if that's who suggested he run a locker check."

"You don't believe me," Donny said.

"And how'd this boy get your combination in the first place?"

"Frankly," said Cal, "I wouldn't be surprised to learn the school was in on it. Any kid that marches to a different drummer,[4] why, they'd just love an excuse to get rid of him. The school is where I lay the blame."

"Doesn't *Donny* ever get blamed?"

"Now, Mrs. Coble, you heard what he—"

"Forget it," Donny told Cal. "You can see she doesn't trust me."

Daisy drew in a breath to say that of course she trusted him—a reflex. But she knew that bold-faced, wide-eyed look of Donny's. He had worn that look when he was small, denying some petty misdeed with the evidence plain as day all around him. Still, it was hard for her to accuse him outright. She temporized and said, "The only thing I'm sure of is that they've kicked you out of school, and now I don't know what we're going to do."

"We'll fight it," said Cal.

"We can't. Even you must see we can't."

"I could apply to Brantly," Donny said.

Cal stopped his pacing to beam down at him. "Brantly! Yes. They're really onto where a kid is coming from, at Brantly. Why, *I* could get you into Brantly. I work with a lot of their students."

Daisy had never heard of Brantly, but already she didn't like it. And she didn't like Cal's smile, which struck her now as feverish and avid—a smile of hunger.

On the fifteenth of April, they entered Donny in a public school, and they stopped his tutoring sessions. Donny fought both decisions bitterly. Cal, surprisingly enough, did not object. He admitted he'd made no headway with Donny and said it was because Donny was emotionally disturbed.

Donny went to his new school every morning, plodding off alone with his head down. He did his assignments, and he earned average grades, but he gathered no friends, joined no clubs. There was something exhausted and defeated about him.

The first week in June, during final exams, Donny vanished. He simply didn't come home one afternoon, and no one at school remembered seeing him. The police were reassuring, and for the first few days, they worked hard. They combed Donny's sad, messy room for clues; they visited Miriam and Cal. But then they started talking about the number of kids who ran away every year. Hundreds, just in this city. "He'll show up, if he wants to," they said. "If he doesn't, he won't."

Evidently, Donny didn't want to.

It's been three months now and still no word. Matt and Daisy still look for him in every crowd of awkward, heartbreaking teenage boys. Every time the phone rings, they imagine it might be Donny. Both parents have aged. Donny's sister seems to be staying away from home as much as possible.

At night, Daisy lies awake and goes over Donny's life. She is trying to figure out what went wrong, where they made their first mistake. Often, she finds herself blaming Cal, although she knows he didn't begin it. Then at other times she excuses him, for without him, Donny might have left earlier. Who really knows? In the end, she can only sigh and search for a cooler spot on the pillow. As she falls asleep, she occasionally glimpses something in the corner of her vision. It's something fleet[5] and round, a ball—a basketball. It flies up, it sinks through the hoop, descends, lands in a yard littered with last year's leaves and striped with bars of sunlight as white as bones, bleached and parched and cleanly picked. ❖

---

4. **marches to a different drummer:** thinks and acts independently; a reference to Henry David Thoreau's famous quotation (page 390).

5. **fleet:** swiftly moving; fast.

temporize (tĕm′pə-rīz′) *v.* to avoid immediate action or making a decision in order to gain time

Connect to the Literature

1. **What Do You Think?** How did you react to Donny's running away? Share your comments with your classmates.

Comprehension Check
- After the first conference with the principal, what does Daisy do at his suggestion?
- Why is Donny expelled from school?
- What does Donny do at the end of the story?

Think Critically

2. What do you think will happen to Donny?

3. Who or what do you think is most responsible for Donny's running away?

THINK ABOUT
- how Daisy tries to help him
- what Cal says and does
- Daisy's question, "Doesn't Donny ever get blamed?" (page 1177)

4. With whom do you sympathize more, Daisy or Donny? Explain why.

5. **ACTIVE READING** | **RECOGNIZING IMPORTANT DETAILS**
Consider the pieces of advice that Daisy and Matt follow, as listed in your **READER'S NOTEBOOK.** Do you think that Daisy and Matt could have handled the situation better if they had done something differently? Explain your opinion.

6. From the **tone** of this story, do you think Anne Tyler takes sides in the academic reform debate? Support your opinion.

Extend Interpretations

7. **Critic's Corner** Anne Tyler has said that she uses the family unit to show "how people manage to endure together—how they grate against each other, adjust, intrude, and protect themselves from intrusions, give up, and start all over again in the morning." How effectively do you think Tyler has portrayed the family in "Teenage Wasteland"?

8. **Comparing Texts** Compare "Teenage Wasteland" to another story of childhood troubles and parental guilt, "I Stand Here Ironing" (page 806). Which one do you think is sadder? Which mother do you think faces the greater difficulty in finding the right way to raise her child?

9. **Connect to Life** How would you describe a good parent?

Literary Analysis

PROTAGONIST AND ANTAGONIST The **protagonist** is the main character in a narrative or drama, usually the one with whom the audience identifies. The **antagonist** is usually the principal character in opposition to the protagonist. The antagonist can also be a force of nature. Both of these characters are involved in a story's central conflict, and after the climax, the protagonist often has a change in feelings, personality, or outlook.

Cooperative Learning Activity With a small group of classmates, share your views about which character is the protagonist and which is the antagonist in "Teenage Wasteland." Give specific reasons for your answers. Discuss whether the protagonist changes by the end of the story. If so, how? If not, what prevents that character from changing? Share your opinions with other pairs of students.

Writing Options

1. Rewritten Episode Retell an episode from this story—such as the meeting between Donny and his mother after his expulsion from school—from Donny's point of view.

2. Persuasive Speech Draft a persuasive speech that could be delivered to the PTA, explaining how much control parents should exert over their teenage children. Use examples from the story and from your own experience as support. Place this piece in your **Working Portfolio.**

Writing Handbook
See page 1285: Persuasive Writing.

Activities & Explorations

Dramatic Scene With a small group, act out one of the scenes from this story or imagine a related scene. For example, you might choose to show the first conversation between Daisy and the principal or Cal's interaction with his students. Stage your scene for your classmates.

Vocabulary in Action

EXERCISE: SYNONYMS AND ANTONYMS Identify each pair of words by writing "Synonyms" or "Antonyms."

1. temporize–delay
2. punitive–forgiving
3. shamble–stride
4. forlorn–sad
5. qualm–confidence
6. morass–predicament
7. subdued–excited
8. amiably–agreeably
9. looming–menacing
10. vindictive–spiteful

Building Vocabulary
One of the Words to Know, *looming,* has two meanings. For an in-depth lesson on homophones, homographs, and homonyms, see page 728.

Anne Tyler
1941–

Other Works
Celestial Navigation
Earthly Possessions
Saint Maybe
Ladder of Years
Patchwork Planet

Nomadic Childhood Shy, quiet, and keenly observant, Anne Tyler is the oldest of four children of Quaker parents. On a quest for the ideal community, her family moved frequently, living in several different Quaker communes throughout the Midwest and South. As Tyler later explained, this experience taught her to "look at the normal world with a certain amount of distance and surprise." This unusual point of view continues to influence her fiction.

Popular Novelist Tyler began writing while she was a student at Duke University, where she studied under the novelist Reynolds Price. In 1963 she married, and a few years later began both a family and a serious writing career. She did not receive national recognition until the publication of her sixth novel, *Searching for Caleb,* in 1976. Tyler first hit the bestseller list in 1982 with *Dinner at the Homesick Restaurant.* In 1988 another best-selling novel, *The Accidental Tourist,* was made into a movie, and a year later Tyler won a Pulitzer Prize for *Breathing Lessons.*

Her Fictional Characters In her more than 14 novels and 40 short stories, Tyler looks at the loneliness and isolation of middle-class family life. Many of her characters are comical and quirky—like the character who shelves her groceries in alphabetical order in *The Accidental Tourist.* Tyler portrays these characters with sympathy and gentle irony. She has said that the real heroes of her books are "first the ones who manage to endure and second the ones who are somehow able to grant other people the privacy of the space around them and yet still produce some warmth."

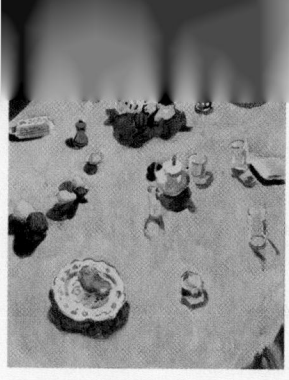

Separating

Short Story by JOHN UPDIKE

(Connect to Your Life)

Breaking Ties About half the marriages in the United States end in divorce. Before deciding to divorce, however, many married couples first agree to separate, or stop living together. What do you think are some reasons that married couples separate? How do you think a wife and husband feel once they have decided to separate? If they have children, how do you think the children feel? Jot down your responses to these questions, drawing from friends' experiences or your own.

Build Background

A Family Saga You are about to read a story about marital separation by John Updike, one of America's most acclaimed authors. Much of his writing concerns upper-middle-class people caught in what Updike has called "the despair of the daily." These characters lose touch with one another and, in doing so, put a strain on their marriages and their families. "Separating" is one in a series of 17 stories the author wrote about Joan and Richard Maple, which appear in his collection *Too Far To Go* (published in 1979). The Maples stories, written over a period of 23 years, depict the couple's youthful marriage in the 1950s, the birth and growth of four children, their separation after 21 years of marriage, and their eventual divorce. Though the stories depict the breakup of a marriage, they still chronicle lives "in many ways happy," according to Updike. "That a marriage fails is less than ideal; but all things end under heaven. . . . The moral of these stories is that all blessings are mixed."

WORDS TO KNOW **Vocabulary Preview**		
congruous	minutiae	precipitous
diaphanous	mollified	stiltedly
dissolution	opulent	succulent
elemental	palpable	tersely
garrulously	permeable	tumultuous

Focus Your Reading

LITERARY ANALYSIS **DRAMATIC IRONY** A stylistic element in this story is the use of dramatic irony. **Dramatic irony** occurs when a reader knows more about a situation than the story's characters know. In the beginning of "Separating," note the information you learn about the Maples that is still kept hidden from their children.

ACTIVE READING **MAKING PREDICTIONS** **Making predictions** involves using clues in a story and prior knowledge about a situation to predict events that might occur. In "Separating," try to predict the characters' reactions as the plot unfolds.

READER'S NOTEBOOK Read pages 1181 to 1182 until the narrative break, indicated by extra space in the text. Then create a questionnaire form like the one shown, and fill it in. As you continue reading, revise your predictions as necessary.

1. What do you already know about the children of divorce?

2. What do you know about the Maples's children?

3. What is Joan and Richard's strategy for breaking the news of their decision?

4. What might happen as a result of their strategy?

S E P A R A T I N G

J O H N U P D I K E

The day was fair. Brilliant. All that June the weather had mocked the Maples' internal misery with solid sunlight—golden shafts and cascades of green in which their conversations had wormed unseeing, their sad murmuring selves the only stain in Nature. Usually by this time of the year they had acquired tans; but when they met their elder daughter's plane on her return from a year in England they were almost as pale as she, though Judith was too dazzled by the sunny opulent jumble of her native land to notice. They did not spoil her homecoming by telling her immediately. Wait a few days, let her recover from jet lag, had been one of their formulations, in that string of gray dialogues—over coffee, over cocktails, over Cointreau[1]—that had shaped the strategy of their dissolution, while the earth performed its annual stunt of renewal unnoticed beyond their closed windows. Richard had thought to leave at Easter; Joan had insisted they wait until the four children were at last assembled, with all exams passed and ceremonies attended, and the bauble[2] of summer to console them. So he had drudged away, in love, in dread, repairing screens, getting the mowers sharpened, rolling and patching their new tennis court.

The court, clay, had come through its first winter pitted and windswept bare of redcoat. Years ago the Maples had observed how often, among their friends, divorce followed a dramatic home improvement, as if the marriage were making one last effort to live; their own worst crisis had come amid the plaster dust and exposed plumbing of a kitchen renovation. Yet, a summer ago, as canary-yellow bulldozers gaily churned a grassy, daisy-dotted knoll into a muddy plateau, and a crew of pigtailed young men raked and tamped clay into a plane, this transformation did not strike them as ominous, but festive in its

---

1. **Cointreau** (kwăn-trō′): brand name of an expensive, orange-flavored, syrupy alcoholic beverage.
2. **bauble:** a bright, showy thing.

impudence; their marriage could rend the earth for fun. The next spring, waking each day at dawn to a sliding sensation as if the bed were being tipped, Richard found the barren tennis court—its net and tapes still rolled in the barn—an environment congruous with his mood of purposeful desolation, and the crumbling of handfuls of clay into cracks and holes (dogs had frolicked on the court in a thaw; rivulets had eroded trenches) an activity suitably elemental and interminable. In his sealed heart he hoped the day would never come.

Now it was here. A Friday. Judith was re-acclimated; all four children were assembled, before jobs and camps and visits again scattered them. Joan thought they should be told one by one. Richard was for making an announcement at the table. She said, "I think just making an announcement is a cop-out. They'll start quarrelling and playing to each other instead of focusing. They're each individuals, you know, not just some corporate obstacle to your freedom."

"O.K., O.K. I agree." Joan's plan was exact. That evening, they were giving Judith a belated welcome-home dinner, of lobster and champagne. Then, the party over, they, the two of them, who nineteen years before would push her in a baby carriage along Fifth Avenue to Washington Square,[3] were to walk her out of the house, to the bridge across the salt creek, and tell her, swearing her to secrecy. Then Richard Jr., who was going directly from work to a rock concert in Boston, would be told, either late when he returned on the train or early Saturday morning before he went off to his job; he was seventeen and employed as one of a golf-course maintenance crew. Then the two younger children, John and Margaret, could, as the morning wore on, be informed.

"Mopped up, as it were," Richard said.

"Do you have any better plan? That leaves you the rest of Saturday to answer any questions, pack, and make your wonderful departure."

"No," he said, meaning he had no better plan, and agreed to hers, though to him it showed an edge of false order, a hidden plea for control, like Joan's long chore lists and financial accountings and, in the days when he first knew her, her too-copious lecture notes. Her plan turned one hurdle for him into four—four knife-sharp walls, each with a sheer blind drop on the other side.

All spring he had moved through a world of insides and outsides, of barriers and partitions. He and Joan stood as a thin barrier between the children and the truth. Each moment was a partition, with the past on one side and the future on the other, a future containing this unthinkable *now*. Beyond four knifelike walls a new life for him waited vaguely. His skull cupped a secret, a white face, a face both frightened and soothing, both strange and known, that he wanted to shield from tears, which he felt all about him, solid as the sunlight. So haunted, he had become obsessed with battening down the house against his absence, replacing screens and sash cords, hinges and latches—a Houdini[4] making things snug before his escape.

The lock. He had still to replace a lock on one of the doors of the screened porch. The task, like most such, proved more difficult than he had imagined. The old lock, aluminum frozen by corrosion, had been deliberately rendered obsolete by manufacturers. Three hardware stores had nothing that even approximately matched the mortised hole its removal (surprisingly easy) left. Another hole had to be gouged, with bits too small and saws too big, and the old hole fitted with a block of wood—the chisels dull, the saw rusty, his fingers thick with lack of sleep.

---

3. **Washington Square:** a fashionable area of Manhattan, in New York City.
4. **Houdini:** Harry Houdini (1874–1926), a famous American magician and escape artist.

WORDS TO KNOW

congruous (kŏng′grōō-əs) *adj.* fitting; suitable
elemental (ĕl′ə-mən′tl) *adj.* basic; like a natural force

Frank Wallace (1953),
Fairfield Porter. Oil on
canvas, 40″ × 30″,
Parrish Art Museum,
Southampton, New
York, gift of the Estate of
Fairfield Porter
(1980.10.59), photo
by Jim Strong.

Each
moment
was a
partition,
with the
past on
one side
and the future on the other.

The sun poured down, beyond the porch, on a world of neglect. The bushes already needed pruning, the windward side of the house was shedding flakes of paint, rain would get in when he was gone, insects, rot, death. His family, all those he would lose, filtered through the edges of his awareness as he struggled with screw holes, splinters, opaque instructions, <u>minutiae</u> of metal.

Judith sat on the porch, a princess returned from exile. She regaled them with stories of fuel shortages, of bomb scares in the Underground,[5] of Pakistani workmen loudly lusting after her as she walked past on her way to dance school. Joan came and went, in and out of the house, calmer than she should have been, praising his struggles with the lock as if this were one more and not the last of their long succession of shared chores. The younger of his sons for a few minutes held the rickety screen door while his father clumsily hammered and chiseled, each blow a kind of sob in Richard's ears. His younger daughter, having been at a slumber party, slept on the porch hammock through all the noise—heavy and pink, trusting and forsaken. Time, like the sunlight, continued relentlessly; the sunlight slowly slanted. Today was one of the longest days. The lock clicked, worked. He was through. He had a drink; he drank it on the porch, listening to his daughter. "It was so sweet," she was saying, "during the worst of it, how all the butchers and bakery shops kept open by candlelight. They're all so plucky and cute. From the papers, things sounded so much worse here—people shooting people in gas lines, and everybody freezing."

Richard asked her, "Do you still want to live in England forever?" *Forever:* the concept, now a reality upon him, pressed and scratched at the back of his throat.

"No," Judith confessed, turning her oval face to him, its eyes still childishly far apart, but the lips set as over something <u>succulent</u> and satisfactory. "I was anxious to come home. I'm an American." She was a woman. They had raised her; he and Joan had endured together to raise her, alone of the four. The others had still some raising left in them. Yet it was the thought of telling Judith—the image of her, their first baby, walking between them arm in arm to the bridge —that broke him. The partition between his face and the tears broke. Richard sat down to the celebratory meal with the back of his throat aching; the champagne, the lobster seemed phases of sunshine; he saw them and tasted them through tears. He blinked, swallowed, croakily joked about hay fever. The tears would not stop leaking through; they came not through a hole that could be plugged but through a <u>permeable</u> spot in a membrane, steadily, purely, endlessly, fruitfully. They became, his tears, a shield for himself against these others—their faces, the fact of their assembly, a last time as innocents, at a table where he sat the last time as head. Tears dropped from his nose as he broke the lobster's back; salt flavored his champagne as he sipped it; the raw clench at the back of his throat was delicious. He could not help himself.

His children tried to ignore his tears. Judith, on his right, lit a cigarette, gazed upward in the direction of her too energetic, too sophisticated exhalation; on her other side, John earnestly bent his face to the extraction of the last morsels— legs, tail segments—from the scarlet corpse. Joan, at the opposite end of the table, glanced at him surprised, her reproach displaced by a quick grimace, of forgiveness, or of salute to his superior gift of strategy. Between them, Margaret, no longer called Bean, thirteen and large for her age, gazed from the other side of his pane of tears as if into a shopwindow at something she coveted— at her father, a crystalline heap of splinters and

---

5. **the Underground:** London's subway system.

WORDS **minutiae** (mǐ-nōō′shē-ē′) *n.* tiny elements, details, or parts
TO   **succulent** (sŭk′yə-lənt) *adj.* tasty; delicious
KNOW   **permeable** (pûr′mē-ə-bəl) *adj.* able to be passed through

1184

memories. It was not she, however, but John who, in the kitchen, as they cleared the plates and carapaces[6] away, asked Joan the question: "*Why is Daddy crying?*"

Richard heard the question but not the murmured answer. Then he heard Bean cry, "Oh, no-oh!"—the faintly dramatized exclamation of one who had long expected it.

John returned to the table carrying a bowl of salad. He nodded <u>tersely</u> at his father and his lips shaped the conspiratorial words "She told."

"Told what?" Richard asked aloud, insanely.

The boy sat down as if to rebuke his father's distraction with the example of his own good manners. He said quietly, "The separation."

Joan and Margaret returned; the child, in Richard's twisted vision, seemed diminished in size, and relieved, relieved to have had the bogie-man at last proved real. He called out to her—the distances at the table had grown immense—"You knew, you always knew," but the clenching at the back of his throat prevented him from making sense of it. From afar he heard Joan talking, levelly, sensibly, reciting what they had prepared: it was a separation for the summer, an experiment. She and Daddy both agreed it would be good for them; they needed space and time to think; they liked each other but did not make each other happy enough, somehow.

Judith, imitating her mother's factual tone, but in her youth off-key, too cool, said, "I think it's silly. You should either live together or get divorced."

Richard's crying, like a wave that has crested and crashed, had become <u>tumultuous</u>; but it was overtopped by another tumult, for John, who had been so reserved, now grew larger and larger at the table. Perhaps his younger sister's being credited with knowing set him off. "Why didn't you *tell* us?" he asked, in a large round voice quite unlike his own. "You should have *told* us you weren't getting along."

Richard was startled into attempting to force words through his tears. "We *do* get along, that's the trouble, so it doesn't show even to us—" *That we do not love each other* was the rest of the sentence; he couldn't finish it.

Joan finished for him, in her style. "And we've always, *especially*, loved our children."

John was not <u>mollified</u>. "What do you care about *us*?" he boomed. "We're just little things you *had*." His sisters' laughing forced a laugh from him, which he turned hard and parodistic[7]:

---

6. **carapaces** (kăr′ə-pā′səz): hard outer coverings or shells of animals such as lobsters.

7. **parodistic**: mocking.

The Table (1970), Fairfield Porter. Collection of Elizabeth Feld.

WORDS TO KNOW	**tersely** (tûrs′lē) *adv.* briefly
	tumultuous (tŏŏ-mŭl′chŏŏ-əs) *adj.* wild and disorderly
	mollified (mŏl′ə-fīd′) *adj.* pacified; made calm **mollify** *v.*

1185

Claire White (1960), Fairfield Porter. Oil on canvas, 45½″ × 45″, collection of Stephen and Sheila Wald, Telluride, Colorado.

Joan came and went, . . .
calmer than she should have been.

"Ha ha *ha*." Richard and Joan realized simultaneously that the child was drunk, on Judith's homecoming champagne. Feeling bound to keep the center of the stage, John took a cigarette from Judith's pack, poked it into his mouth, let it hang from his lower lip, and squinted like a gangster.

"You're not little things we had," Richard called to him. "You're the whole point. But you're grown. Or almost."

The boy was lighting matches. Instead of holding them to his cigarette (for they had never seen him smoke; being "good" had been his way of setting himself apart), he held them to his mother's face, closer and closer, for her to blow out. Then he lit the whole folder—a hiss and then a torch, held against his mother's face. Prismed by tears, the flame filled Richard's vision; he didn't know how it was extinguished. He heard Margaret say, "Oh stop showing off," and saw John, in response, break the cigarette in two and put the halves entirely into his mouth and chew, sticking out his tongue to display the shreds to his sister.

Joan talked to him, reasoning—a fountain of reason, unintelligible. "Talked about it for years . . . our children must help us . . . Daddy and I both want . . ." As the boy listened, he carefully wadded a paper napkin into the leaves of his salad, fashioned a ball of paper and lettuce, and popped it into his mouth, looking around the table for the expected laughter. None came. Judith said, "Be mature," and dismissed a plume of smoke.

Richard got up from this stifling table and led the boy outside. Though the house was in twilight, the outdoors still brimmed with light, the lovely waste light of high summer. Both laughing, he supervised John's spitting out the lettuce and paper and tobacco into the pachysandra.[8] He took him by the hand—a square gritty hand, but for its softness a man's. Yet, it held on. They ran together up into the field, past the tennis court. The raw banking left by the bulldozers was dotted with daisies. Past the court and a flat stretch where they used to play family baseball stood a soft green rise glorious in the sun, each weed and species of grass distinct as illumination on parchment. "I'm sorry, so sorry," Richard cried. "You were the only one who ever tried to help me with all the damn jobs around this place."

Sobbing, safe within his tears and the champagne, John explained, "It's not just the separation, it's the whole crummy year, I *hate* that school, you can't make any friends, the history teacher's a scud."

They sat on the crest of the rise, shaking and warm from their tears but easier in their voices, and Richard tried to focus on the child's sad year—the weekdays long with homework, the weekends spent in his room with model airplanes, while his parents murmured down below, nursing their separation. How selfish, how blind, Richard thought; his eyes felt scoured. He told his son, "We'll think about getting you transferred. Life's too short to be miserable."

They had said what they could, but did not want the moment to heal, and talked on, about the school, about the tennis court, whether it would ever again be as good as it had been that first summer. They walked to inspect it and pressed a few more tapes more firmly down. A little stiltedly, perhaps trying now to make too much of the moment, Richard led the boy to the spot in the field where the view was best, of the metallic blue river, the emerald marsh, the scattered islands velvety with shadow in the low light, the white bits of beach far away. "See," he said. "It goes on being beautiful. It'll be here tomorrow."

"I know," John answered, impatiently. The moment had closed.

Back in the house, the others had opened

---

8. **pachysandra** (păk′ĭ-săn′drə): small, low-growing, leafy plants used as ground cover.

Stephen and Kathy (1965), Fairfield Porter. Oil on canvas.
Colby College Museum of Art, Waterville, Maine.

some white wine, the champagne being drunk, and still sat at the table, the three females, gossiping. Where Joan sat had become the head. She turned, showing him a tearless face, and asked, "All right?"

"We're fine," he said, resenting it, though relieved, that the party went on without him.

In bed she explained, "I couldn't cry I guess because I cried so much all spring. It really wasn't fair. It's your idea, and you made it look as though I was kicking you out."

"I'm sorry," he said. "I couldn't stop. I wanted to but couldn't."

"You *didn't* want to. You loved it. You were having your way, making a general announcement."

"I love having it over," he admitted. "God, those kids were great. So brave and funny." John, returned to the house, had settled to a model airplane in his room, and kept shouting down to them, "I'm O.K. No sweat." "And the way," Richard went on, cozy in his relief, "they never questioned the reasons we gave. No thought of a third person. Not even Judith."

"That *was* touching," Joan said.

He gave her a hug. "You were great too. Very reassuring to everybody. Thank you." Guiltily, he realized he did not feel separated.

"You still have Dickie to do," she told him. These words set before him a black mountain in the darkness; its cold breath, its near weight affected his chest. Of the four children, his elder son was most nearly his conscience. Joan did not need to add, "That's one piece of your dirty work I won't do for you."

"I know. I'll do it. You go to sleep."

Within minutes, her breathing slowed, became oblivious and deep. It was quarter to midnight. Dickie's train from the concert would come in at one-fourteen. Richard set the alarm for one. He had slept atrociously for weeks. But whenever he closed his lids some glimpse of the last hours scorched them—Judith exhaling toward the ceiling in a kind of aversion, Bean's mute staring, the sunstruck growth in the field where he and John had rested. The mountain before him moved closer, moved within him; he was huge, momentous. The ache at the back of his throat felt stale. His wife slept as if slain beside him. When, exasperated by his hot lids, his crowded heart, he rose from bed and dressed, she awoke enough to turn over. He told her then, "Joan, if I could undo it all, I would."

"Where would you begin?" she asked. There was no place. Giving him courage, she was always giving him courage. He put on shoes without socks in the dark. The children were breathing in their rooms, the downstairs was hollow. In their confusion they had left lights burning. He turned off all but one, the kitchen overhead. The car started. He had hoped it wouldn't. He met only moonlight on the road; it seemed a diaphanous companion, flickering in the leaves along the roadside, haunting his rearview mirror like a pursuer, melting under his headlights. The center of town, not quite deserted, was eerie at this hour. A young cop in uniform kept company with a gang of T-shirted kids on the steps of the bank. Across from the railroad station, several bars kept open. Customers, mostly young, passed in and out of the warm night, savoring summer's novelty. Voices shouted from cars as they passed; an immense conversation seemed in progress. Richard parked and in his weariness put his head on the passenger seat, out of the commotion and wheeling lights. It was as when, in the movies, an assassin grimly carries his mission through the jostle of a carnival—except the movies cannot show the precipitous, palpable slope you cling to within. You cannot climb back down; you can only fall. The synthetic fabric of the car seat, warmed by his cheek, confided to him an ancient, distant scent of vanilla.

A train whistle caused him to lift his head. It was on time; he had hoped it would be late. The slender drawgates descended. The bell of approach tingled happily. The great metal body, horizontally fluted, rocked to a stop, and sleepy teen-agers disembarked, his son among them. Dickie did not show surprise that this father was meeting him at this terrible hour. He sauntered to the car with two friends, both taller than he. He said "Hi" to his father and took the passenger's seat with an exhausted promptness that expressed gratitude. The friends got in the back, and Richard was grateful; a few more minutes' postponement would be won by driving them home.

He asked, "How was the concert?"

"Groovy," one boy said from the back seat.

"It bit," the other said.

"It was O.K.," Dickie said, moderate by nature, so reasonable that in his childhood the unreason of the world had given him headaches, stomach aches, nausea. When the second friend had been dropped off at his dark house, the boy blurted, "Dad, my eyes are killing me with hay fever! I'm out there cutting that grass all day!"

"Do we still have those drops?"

"They didn't do any good last summer."

"They might this." Richard swung a U-turn on the empty street. The drive home took a few minutes. The mountain was here, in his throat. "Richard," he said, and felt the boy, slumped and rubbing his eyes, go tense at his tone, "I didn't come to meet you just to make your life easier. I came because your mother and I have some news for you, and you're a hard man to get ahold of these days. It's sad news."

"That's O.K." The reassurance came out soft, but quick, as if released from the tip of a spring.

Richard had feared that his tears would return and choke him, but the boy's manliness set an example, and his voice issued forth steady and dry. "It's sad news, but it needn't be tragic news, at least for you. It should have no practical effect on your life, though it's bound to have an emotional effect. You'll work at your job, and go back to school in September. Your mother and I are really proud of what you're making of your life; we don't want that to change at all."

"Yeah," the boy said lightly, on the intake of his breath, holding himself up. They turned the corner; the church they went to loomed like a gutted fort. The home of the woman Richard hoped to marry stood across the green. Her bedroom light burned.

"Your mother and I," he said, "have decided to separate. For the summer. Nothing legal, no divorce yet. We want to see how it feels. For some years now, we haven't been doing enough for each other, making each other as happy as we should be. Have you sensed that?"

"No," the boy said. It was an honest, unemotional answer: true or false in a quiz.

WORDS	**diaphanous** (dĭ-ăf′ə-nəs) *adj.* light or fragile in an unearthly way
TO	**precipitous** (prĭ-sĭp′ĭ-təs) *adj.* steep; almost vertical
KNOW	**palpable** (păl′pə-bəl) *adj.* that can be touched or felt

Glad for the factual basis, Richard pursued, even garrulously, the details. His apartment across town, his utter accessibility, the split vacation arrangements, the advantages to the children, the added mobility and variety of the summer. Dickie listened, absorbing. "Do the others know?"

"Yes."

"How did they take it?"

"The girls pretty calmly. John flipped out; he shouted and ate a cigarette and made a salad out of his napkin and told us how much he hated school."

His brother chuckled. "He did?"

"Yeah. The school issue was more upsetting for him than Mom and me. He seemed to feel better for having exploded."

"He did?" The repetition was the first sign that he was stunned.

"Yes. Dickie, I want to tell you something. This last hour, waiting for your train to get in, has been about the worst of my life. I hate this. *Hate* it. My father would have died before doing it to me." He felt immensely lighter, saying this. He had dumped the mountain on the boy. They were home. Moving swiftly as a shadow, Dickie was out of the car, through the bright kitchen. Richard called after him, "Want a glass of milk or anything?"

"No thanks."

"Want us to call the course tomorrow and say you're too sick to work?"

"No, that's all right." The answer was faint, delivered at the door to his room; Richard listened for the slam that went with a tantrum. The door closed normally, gently. The sound was sickening.

Joan had sunk into that first deep trough of sleep and was slow to awake. Richard had to repeat, "I told him."

"What did he say?"

"Nothing much. Could you go say goodnight to him? Please."

She left their room, without putting on a bathrobe. He sluggishly changed back into his pajamas and walked down the hall. Dickie was already in bed, Joan was sitting beside him, and the boy's bedside clock radio was murmuring music. When she stood, an inexplicable light—the moon?—outlined her body through the nightie. Richard sat on the warm place she had indented on the child's narrow mattress. He asked him, "Do you want the radio on like that?"

"It always is."

"Doesn't it keep you awake? It would me."

"No."

"Are you sleepy?"

"Yeah."

"Good. Sure you want to get up and go to work? You've had a big night."

"I want to."

Away at school this winter he had learned for the first time that you can go short of sleep and live. As an infant he had slept with an immobile, sweating intensity that had alarmed his baby-sitters. In adolescence he had often been the first of the four children to go to bed. Even now, he would go slack in the middle of a television show, his sprawled legs hairy and brown. "O.K. Good boy. Dickie, listen. I love you so much, I never knew how much until now. No matter how this works out, I'll always be with you. Really."

Richard bent to kiss an averted face but his son, sinewy, turned and with wet cheeks embraced him and gave him a kiss, on the lips, passionate as a woman's. In his father's ear he moaned one word, the crucial, intelligent word: "*Why?*"

Why. It was a whistle of wind in a crack, a knife thrust, a window thrown open on emptiness. The white face was gone, the darkness was featureless. Richard had forgotten why. ❖

Connect to the Literature

1. **What Do You Think?** What was your reaction to the conversation that Richard and Dickie have in Dickie's bedroom?

Comprehension Check
- What question does Richard fear his children might ask about the cause of the separation?
- How did John, Margaret, and Judith each react to the news of their parents' breakup?

Think Critically

2. **ACTIVE READING** **MAKING PREDICTIONS** Review the questionnaire you filled out in your **READER'S NOTEBOOK.** Which of your predictions about what might happen in the story were accurate? What events, if any, in the story were a total surprise?

3. At the end of the story, did you feel sympathy for Richard? Point to things he says, does, or thinks that caused you to be sympathetic or not.

4. Think about Richard's and Joan's different plans for how to tell the children about the separation. What might Joan's plan reveal about her personality? What might Richard's plan reveal about his personality?

   THINK ABOUT
   - the explanations they offer their children
   - the "white face" in Richard's mind (pages 1182 and 1190)
   - Richard's remark, "Life's too short to be miserable" (page 1187)

5. Dickie asks his father, "Why?" and the narrator says, "Richard had forgotten why." What can you gather about why Richard and Joan are separating?

Extend Interpretations

6. **The Writer's Style** To reinforce his themes, Updike often uses **symbols,** things that represent something beyond their concrete meanings. For instance, at the table Richard cracks the lobster's back, as he has cracked apart his family. What symbolism do you find in other objects in the story, such as the Maples' house and tennis court?

7. **Connect to Life** Do you think the behavior of the people in this story is true to life? Explain. Refer to your responses in the Connect to Your Life activity on page 1180.

Literary Analysis

DRAMATIC IRONY Updike's use of **dramatic irony** in "Separating" establishes a relationship between the narrator and the reader from the very beginning of the story. The narrator of "Separating" confides that the Maples are going to separate. The reader holds privileged information, yet unknown to the characters who will most be affected by this decision—the children.

Cooperative Learning Activity
What do you think Updike's intentions were in sharing the news of the Maples' separation with the reader early in the story? What effect did this knowledge have on your involvement in the story? Meet with a small group to discuss these questions.

REVIEW **POINT OF VIEW**
Although Richard is not the narrator of "Separating," the narration focuses on his point of view. This focus on one character's thoughts, observations, and feelings is called **third-person limited point of view.** How might your response to the story have changed if it had been told from the third-person omniscient point of view, in which the narrator reports different characters' thoughts and feelings?

Choices & CHALLENGES

Writing Options

1. Diary Entry Write a diary entry from the perspective of a character in the story other than Richard—either Joan or one of the children.

2. Character Analysis Write a brief character analysis that examines Richard Maple's behavior and values. Make clear your final judgment of him.

Richard Maple

behavior | values

3. Story Forecast Updike wrote three other stories about the Maples after "Separating." What do you think happens to Joan, Richard, and each of their four children in the stories to come? Write a narrative summarizing your predictions.

Activities & Exploration

Staging a Scene Imagine that you are making a TV movie of "Separating." With a small group of classmates, select a scene from this story and write stage directions explaining how the actors should speak their lines. Also write notes about the props, lighting, scenery, costumes, and music you would use to bring this scene to life. Perform the scene for the class. ~ PERFORMING

Vocabulary in Action

EXERCISE A: SYNONYMS For each phrase in the first column, write the letter of the synonymous phrase from the second column.

1. a leaky depot
2. a primary need
3. luscious poultry
4. stiffly rejected
5. concisely discussing
6. a mollified minor
7. opulent quantities
8. makes dinky pieces
9. tumultuous water sports
10. garrulously complimenting

a. succulent duck
b. a soothed youth
c. chaotic aquatics
d. tersely conversing
e. bounteous amounts
f. stiltedly jilted
g. produces minutiae
h. chattily flattering
i. a permeable terminal
j. an elemental essential

EXERCISE B: ASSESSMENT PRACTICE Identify each pair of words as synonyms or antonyms.

1. diaphanous—solid
2. dissolution—union
3. palpable—concrete
4. congruous—appropriate
5. precipitous—flat

Building Vocabulary

Many of the Words to Know contain suffixes. For an in-depth lesson on word parts, see page 1130.

WORDS TO KNOW				
congruous	elemental	mollified	permeable	succulent
diaphanous	garrulously	opulent	precipitous	tersely
dissolution	minutiae	palpable	stiltedly	tumultuous

John Updike
1932–

Other Works
The Poorhouse Fair
Rabbit, Run
Pigeon Feathers and Other Stories
Couples
The Witches of Eastwick
Brazil

Boyhood Dreams John Updike's birthplace, Shillington, Pennsylvania, inspired the small-town settings of many of his early novels. His father taught high school algebra, while his mother, "a very sensitive and witty woman," wrote several unpublished stories and novels. Her talents influenced Updike's career ambitions. As a teenager, John Updike aspired to become a cartoonist or a humorist and to write for the *New Yorker*. By his mid-twenties, he had achieved these goals.

Literary Success Since then Updike has earned the reputation as a critically acclaimed fiction writer, poet, and essayist who keenly observes the American scene. He won a National Book Award for his novel *The Centaur,* a Pulitzer Prize for his

novels *Rabbit Is Rich* and *Rabbit at Rest,* and a National Book Critics Circle award for criticism for *Hugging the Shore.* Many of his novels and stories have been adapted as films, TV movies, and plays.

Flair for High Drama Much of Updike's work, like the short story "Separating," explores the tensions in middle-class American families. In an interview, he said, "I like middles. It is in middles that extremes clash, where ambiguity restlessly rules. . . . It seems to me that critics get increasingly querulous and impatient for madder music and stronger wine, when what we need is a greater respect for reality, its secrecy, its music."

Mexicans Begin Jogging

Poetry by GARY SOTO

Legal Alien

Poetry by PAT MORA

> ## Connect to Your Life
>
> Both of the following poems explore what happens when someone is prejudged or is treated differently on the basis of a stereotype. Think of a time when someone judged you without first getting to know you. What was assumed about you, and why? What was your attitude about being prejudged in that way? With a small group of classmates, discuss the difficulties that prejudging creates, both for the person judging and the person being judged.

Build Background

"Legal alien" is a term applied to an immigrant who has been granted legal permanent residence in the United States, even though he or she is not a U.S. citizen. The speaker in "Mexicans Begin Jogging" is a U.S. citizen who is mistakenly prejudged to be an "illegal alien"—an immigrant who enters the country illegally. An estimated 300,000 illegal aliens enter the United States each year. Many migrate north to cross the 1,952-mile-long border between the United States and Mexico. The Border Patrol, which was created in 1924, has thus far been unable to control illegal immigration from Mexico. Border Patrol activities include not only efforts to stop entry at the border but also searches to capture illegal immigrants in the United States in order to return them to their home countries.

Focus Your Reading

LITERARY ANALYSIS   TONE   **Tone** refers to the attitude a writer takes toward the subject he or she is writing about. In these two poems, the speakers can be identified as the poets themselves. As you read, watch for clues that indicate each poet's attitude toward being prejudged. Is the poet angry? hurt? amused? Notice images and individual words—nouns, verbs, and adjectives—that convey how each poet feels.

ACTIVE READING   COMPARING WRITERS' ATTITUDES   These poems are paired because both are by Mexican-American writers and both are about being prejudged. You might find it interesting to compare the two works.

READER'S NOTEBOOK   After you read the first poem, jot down one or two words to describe the writer's attitude, or tone. Then copy a word, phrase, or line that suggested this tone to you. As you read the second poem, compare or contrast its tone with that of the first poem. Again, copy a word, phrase, or line you found particularly revealing.

"Mexicans Begin Jogging"

Tone: _____

Suggested by: _____

MEXICANS BEGIN JOGGING

GARY SOTO

At the factory I worked
In the fleck of rubber, under the press
Of an oven yellow with flame,
Until the border patrol opened
5 Their vans and my boss waved for us to run.
"Over the fence, Soto," he shouted,
And I shouted that I was American.
"No time for lies," he said, and pressed
A dollar in my palm, hurrying me
10 Through the back door.

Since I was on his time, I ran
And became the wag to a short tail of Mexicans—
Ran past the amazed crowds that lined
The street and blurred like photographs, in rain.
15 I ran from that industrial road to the soft
Houses where people paled at the turn of an autumn sky.
What could I do but yell *vivas*[1]
To baseball, milkshakes, and those sociologists
Who would clock me
20 As I jog into the next century
On the power of a great, silly grin.

---

1. *vivas* (vē'väs) *Spanish:* cheers.

Illegal immigrants scaling the wall along
the U.S.-Mexican border near Tijuana.
AP/Wide World Photos.

Looking through a hole in the border wall.
Copyright © Paul Fusco/Magnum Photos, Inc.

Thinking Through the Literature

1. **Comprehension Check** Why does the boss want his workers to run?

2. Why do you think Soto runs even though he does not have to?

3. How would you describe Soto's apparent attitude toward being prejudged?

   THINK ABOUT
   - his indicating that he is an American (line 7)
   - the image he creates of the boss (lines 8–10)
   - his cheering for baseball, milkshakes, and sociologists (lines 17–18)
   - the image of himself in the last two lines

4. How do you interpret lines 15–16? Make inferences about the "soft / Houses where people paled at the turn of an autumn sky."

5. What does Soto suggest to you about the future direction of the United States in the line "As I jog into the next century"?

6. What **ironies** do you see in the **title** of this poem?

LEGAL ALIEN

PAT MORA

Bi-lingual, Bi-cultural,
able to slip from "How's life?"
to *"Me'stan volviendo loca,"*[1]
able to sit in a paneled office

5   drafting memos in smooth English,
able to order in fluent Spanish
at a Mexican restaurant,
American but hyphenated,
viewed by Anglos as perhaps exotic,

10 perhaps inferior, definitely different,
viewed by Mexicans as alien,
(their eyes say, "You may speak
Spanish but you're not like me")
an American to Mexicans

15 a Mexican to Americans
a handy token
sliding back and forth
between the fringes of both worlds
by smiling

20 by masking the discomfort
of being pre-judged
Bi-laterally.[2]

---

1. *"Me'stan volviendo loca"* (mĕ-stän′
   vôl-vē-ĕn′dô lô′kä) *Spanish:* "They're making
   me crazy."

2. **Bi-laterally:** in a way that is undertaken by
   two sides equally.

Illustration Copyright © Rob Colvin/Stock Illustration Source.

Thinking through the LITERATURE

Connect to the Literature

1. What Do You Think?
How do you visualize the writer of "Legal Alien"?

> **Comprehension Check**
> • How does the poet say she is viewed by Anglos? by Mexicans?

Think Critically

2. How do you think the poet feels about being bilingual and bicultural?

THINK ABOUT
{
• how she is viewed by Anglos
• how she is viewed by Mexicans
• her description of herself in lines 16–22
}

3. **ACTIVE READING** **COMPARING WRITERS' ATTITUDES** How did you describe the writer's attitude, or tone, in "Legal Alien" in your **READER'S NOTEBOOK**? Did you use the same word(s) to describe Gary Soto's attitude in "Mexicans Begin Jogging"? Explain how the tones are similar or different.

4. How do you interpret the **title** "Legal Alien"?

Extend Interpretations

5. Comparing Texts How similar are the poets' experiences in "Mexicans Begin Jogging" and "Legal Alien"? Tell what the poems suggest to you about some difficulties of being Mexican American.

6. Connect to Life For the Connect to Your Life activity on page 1194, you were asked to recall a time when you were prejudged. Was your reaction closer to Gary Soto's or Pat Mora's in these poems?

Literary Analysis

TONE As you know, **tone** is a writer's attitude toward a subject. A poet can communicate tone through **diction,** or choice of words. For example, elevated diction ("nerv'd Oppression's hand") and words with strong negative connotations ("toiling" and "anguish") help convey Frances E. W. Harper's serious, urgent tone in "Free Labor" (page 576). A poet can also state an attitude directly ("I celebrate myself, and sing myself"), as Walt Whitman does in "Song of Myself" (page 400). Often it is the **imagery** in a poem that suggests the writer's tone. In "Mexicans Begin Jogging," Gary Soto's amusement at being persistently and incorrectly prejudged is expressed through the humorous images of himself as "the wag to a short tail of Mexicans"; of himself cheering baseball, milkshakes, and sociologists; and of sociologists clocking him as he jogs, grinning, into the next century.

Paired Activity If someone were to tell you that Pat Mora's tone in "Legal Alien" was exactly the same as Gary Soto's in "Mexicans Begin Jogging," how would you prove this person wrong? What specific words and images would you point to in Mora's poem? Choose a classmate and convince him or her.

Choices & CHALLENGES

Writing Options

Guest Editorial In both these poems, people are prejudged because they are Mexican Americans. To express your opinion about being prejudged in general or about your own experience with being prejudged, draft a guest column for a student magazine or newspaper. Save this piece in your **Working Portfolio.**

Inquiry & Research

The title "Legal Alien" refers to a person who is authorized to live in the United States but is not a citizen of this country. In "Mexicans Begin Jogging" a worker is perceived to be an illegal alien, even though he is actually a U.S. citizen. Find out the different ways that a person can become a citizen of the United States. What requirements must someone meet?

Art Connection

Look at the photographs of a wall along the U.S.-Mexican border on pages 1195 and 1196, and also look at the illustration on page 1197. What ideas do these pictures suggest to you, and how well do you think they fit the Soto and Mora poems? What other visuals can you think of to illustrate the poems?

Gary Soto
1952–

Other Works
Black Hair
The Tale of Sunlight
Where Sparrows Work Hard
Small Faces

Pat Mora
1942–

Other Works
Borders
Chants
Nepantla
House of Houses

Working-Class Roots Gary Soto writes poetry that explores his childhood, his adolescence, and his ethnic identity. Growing up in a working-class Mexican-American family in the San Joaquin Valley in California, Soto worked as a migrant farm worker before entering college. When he encountered Donald Allen's anthology *The New American Poetry*, Soto decided to become a poet. "I discovered this poetry and thought, This is terrific; I'd like to do something like this."

Early Books Soto's first collection of poetry, *The Elements of San Joaquin*, is a bleak portrait of the lives of Mexican Americans. His prose memoirs include *Living up the Street*, which won an American Book Award.

A Teacher's Advice Soto has taught English and Chicano studies at the University of California, Berkeley. He has said that he wants his students "to understand how a writer puts things together, to see that it's not simply a mishmash of feelings."

Texas Treasure A poet, essayist, and children's book author, Pat Mora was born in the border city of El Paso, Texas. She graduated from Texas Western College and received her master's degree from the University of Texas at El Paso. Mora taught college English for ten years and acted as the host of a radio show, *Voices: The Mexican-American in Perspective*.

Awards and Anthologies Mora has received many awards for her works, including awards from the Southwest Council of Latin American Studies and the National Association for Chicano Studies. Her work appears in the anthologies *New Worlds of Literature, Hispanics in the United States*, and *Woman of Her Word: Hispanic Women Write*.

Why She Writes In an interview, Mora identified the sources of her poetic inspiration. "I write, in part, because Hispanic perspectives need to be part of our literary heritage; I want to be part of that validation process. I also write because I am fascinated by the pleasure and power of words."

Hostage

Short Story by JOYCE CAROL OATES

Comparing Literature

Traditions Across Time: Continuing Transformation

The narrator in "Hostage," by Joyce Carol Oates, is a ninth-grade girl who is strongly attracted to a boy at school. This boy, Bruno Sokolov, reputedly carries a switchblade in his pocket. Despite his aura of self-assurance, Bruno really is an outsider among his classmates.

Points of Comparison   As you read this story, think about the narrator's relationship with Bruno. Consider how you might compare and contrast Bruno with Donny, the troubled youth in "Teenage Wasteland."

Build Background

Oates's Fiction Joyce Carol Oates frequently writes about ordinary people affected by violence. In response to a reviewer who criticized her preoccupation with violence, Oates defended her work in this way: "As Flannery O'Connor—another writer frequently attacked for the 'darkness and violence' of her work—has said, No writer is a pessimist; the very act of writing is an optimistic act." By writing about violence in our society, Oates does not intend merely to mirror today's headlines but to "bring about a change of heart."

Focus Your Reading

LITERARY ANALYSIS | **CHARACTER**   The **characters** are the people who take part in the action of a story. In some stories, the characters' actions and decisions seem to control what happens. In other stories, the characters seem rather to be victims of forces beyond their control. Consider to what extent the characters in "Hostage" control what happens to them.

ACTIVE READING | **MAKING JUDGMENTS ABOUT CHARACTER**   In "Hostage," Joyce Carol Oates provides plentiful details to help you visualize the narrator's classmate Bruno. One way to understand the story better and to enjoy it more is to make judgments about Bruno's character as you read about his actions. Try these tips:

- List Bruno's actions in the story.
- For each action, state your judgment of Bruno. For example, ask yourself whether you admire or disapprove of him for that particular action.
- State the criterion, or the standard you used to make your judgment.

For example, one of Bruno's actions is that he carries a switchblade. You may disapprove of him for doing so. Your criterion might be that anyone carrying such a weapon is a threat to others.

READER'S NOTEBOOK On a chart like the one shown, list Bruno's actions, your judgments of him, and the criteria you used to make your judgments.

Bruno's Actions	My Judgments of Bruno	Criteria

Hostage

Joyce Carol Oates

BY the age of fourteen Bruno Sokolov had the heft and swagger of a near-grown man. His wide shoulders, sturdy neck, dark oily hair wetted and combed sleekly back from his forehead like a rooster's crest, above all his large head and the shrewd squint of his pebble-colored eyes gave him an air unnervingly adult, as if, in junior high school, in the company of children, he was in disguise, yet carelessly in disguise. He wore his older brothers' and even his father's cast-off clothing, <u>rakish</u> combinations that suited him, pin-striped shirts, sweater vests, suspenders, bulky tweed coats and corduroy trousers, cheap leather belts with enormous buckles, even, frequently, for there were always deaths in those big immigrant families, mourning bands around his upper arm that gave him a look both sinister and holy, to which none of our teachers could object. He was smart; he was tough; the natural leader of a neighborhood gang of boys; he carried a switchblade knife, or was believed to do so. He had a strangely scarred forehead—in one version of the story he'd overturned a pan of boiling water on himself as a small child, in another version his mother in a fit of emotion had overturned it on him. He spoke English with a strong accent, musical, yet mocking, as if these sounds were his own invention, these queer eliding vowels and diphthongs,[1] and he had remarkable self-confidence for a boy with his background, the son of Polish-Russian immigrants—out of bravado he ran for, and actually won, our ninth-grade presidency, in a fluke of an election that pitted our teachers' choice, a "good" boy, against a boy whom most of the teachers mistrusted, or feared. Even when Bruno Sokolov spoke intelligently in class there was an overtone of <u>subtle</u> mockery, if not contempt, in his voice. His grades were erratic and he was often absent from school—"family reasons" the usual excuse—and he was famous for intimidating, or harassing, or actually beating up certain of his classmates. His play at football and basketball was that of a steer loosed happily among heifers, and when, as our class president, a black snap-on

---

1. **eliding vowels and diphthongs:** vowels that are omitted or slurred over and combinations of vowel sounds within single syllables (as in *soil*).

1201

bow tie around his neck, he addressed the rowdy assemblage from the stage with the aplomb and drawling ease of a radio broadcaster or a politician, shrewd eyes glittering with a sense of his own power, we felt, aroused, laughing at his jokes, a shiver of certitude, rippling among even the dullest of us like a nervous reflex through a school of fish, that we were in the presence of someone distinctive; someone of whom, however we might dislike him, we might be proud.

I didn't know him. I didn't belong to his world. Though my family lived only a block or so from his family in a neighborhood of row houses built in the 1890s and hardly renovated since that time, my grandparents had emigrated from Budapest in the early 1900s and Bruno's parents had come from Lublin, a Polish city near the Russian border, in the early 1930s, and that made a considerable difference. And I was younger than Bruno, younger than most of my classmates—I had been skipped a grade in elementary school, a source of obscure pride and shame to me—so that if he happened to glance toward me, if his squinty amused stare drifted in my direction, there was nothing, it

I didn't belong to his world.

seemed, on which it might snag. I was small, I was brainy, I was invisible. For my part I observed Bruno Sokolov scrupulously, in classes, in the school corridors, making his way down the stairs, pushing ahead in the cafeteria line, actions he seemed to perform without thinking, as if the very size of his body had to be accommodated, his needs and impulses immediately discharged. Even to be teased by Bruno Sokolov was an

honor of a kind but it was not an honor casually granted, for the Sokolovs, poor as they were, crowded into their shabby row house with its rear yard lifting to a railway embankment, nonetheless took themselves seriously; they were displaced tradesmen, not Polish peasants.

The immigrants' world retained its taxonomical[2] distinctions of class, money, power, "breeding." In America, you were hungry to move up but you had no intention of helping others, outside the family, to move up with you.

The places where imagination takes root . . . There was an oversized winter coat Bruno Sokolov wore in bad weather, Cossack-style, navy blue, with upturned collar, deep pockets, and frayed sleeves, the mere sight of which made me feel confused, light-headed, panicked. There was the back of Bruno's big head, observed slantwise from me in English class, the springy oily dark hair often separating in quills, falling about his ears, and every few weeks a fresh haircut, done at home, crude and brutal, shaved at the neck. There was the sound of his suddenly uplifted voice, ringing and abrasive, often drawling in mockery, the give-and-take, foulmouthed, of young adolescent boys, and my immediate sense of alarm when I heard it, but also my envy: a sharp stabbing envy that cut me like a knife: for of course Bruno Sokolov never spoke my name, even in derision. He gave no sign of knowing it.

The infatuation was hardly love, not even affection, for I often fantasized Bruno Sokolov dying, a violent cinematic death, and took a vengeful pleasure in it; but there was about my feeling for him that sense, common to love, of futility and wild optimism conjoined, a quicken-

---

2. **taxonomical:** having to do with the science of classification.

WORDS
TO
KNOW

aplomb (ə-plŏm′) *n.* self-confidence
obscure (ŏb-skyoŏr′) *adj.* indistinct; not clearly understood
scrupulously (skroō′pyə-ləs-lē) *adv.* in an extremely careful and thorough manner; conscientiously
abrasive (ə-brā′sĭv) *adj.* harsh and rough
infatuation (ĭn-fǎch′oō-ā′shən) *n.* the state of being completely carried away by foolish or shallow love or affection

ing of the pulse even at the very instant that the quickening, the hope, is checked: *No. Don't.*

Midway in the school year when we were in ninth grade Bruno's father died a strange and much talked-of death and I waited for weeks to tell Bruno how sorry I was that it had happened, approaching him, one day, in the corridor outside our homeroom, with an aggressive sort of shyness, and Bruno stared down at me with a look of blank surprise as if a voice had sounded out of the very air beside him, a voice wrongly intimate and knowing. He was taller than I by more than a head, his height exaggerated by the springy thickness of his hair and the breadth of his shoulders. The shiny-smooth skin of his scar, disappearing under his hair, was serrated and would have been rough to the touch. His eyes were heavy-lidded from lack of sleep or grief and he stared at me for what seemed a long time before saying, with a shrug of his shoulders, "Yeah. Me too." And that was all.

My heart was beating rapidly, wildly. But that was all.

Even by the standards of our neighborhood Mr. Sokolov had died an unusual death. He was a large fleshy man with deep-set suspicious eyes and bushy but receding hair that gave him a perpetually affronted look; he dressed formally, in dark tight-fitting suits with old-fashioned wide lapels, starched white shirts, dark neckties. He and two brothers owned a small neighborhood grocery with a meat counter, a real butcher's shop as my mother spoke of it, and Mr. Sokolov so dominated the store, took such edgy excitable antagonistic pride in it, that many customers,

Illustration Copyright © Eric Dinyer.

including my mother, were offended by his manner. In Bruno's father Bruno's coarse sly charm was mere coarseness; he was in the habit of issuing commands, in Polish, to his brothers, in front of customers; the neighborhood belief was that he wasn't quite "right in the head"— and certainly the dislocations of language made for constant misunderstandings, and constant misunderstandings made for what is called, clinically, paranoia, that sense that the world's very tilt is in our disfavor, and that nothing, however accidental-seeming, is accidental. Mr. Sokolov's short temper led him into arguments and even into feuds with neighbors, customers, city authorities, local police; he was tyrannical

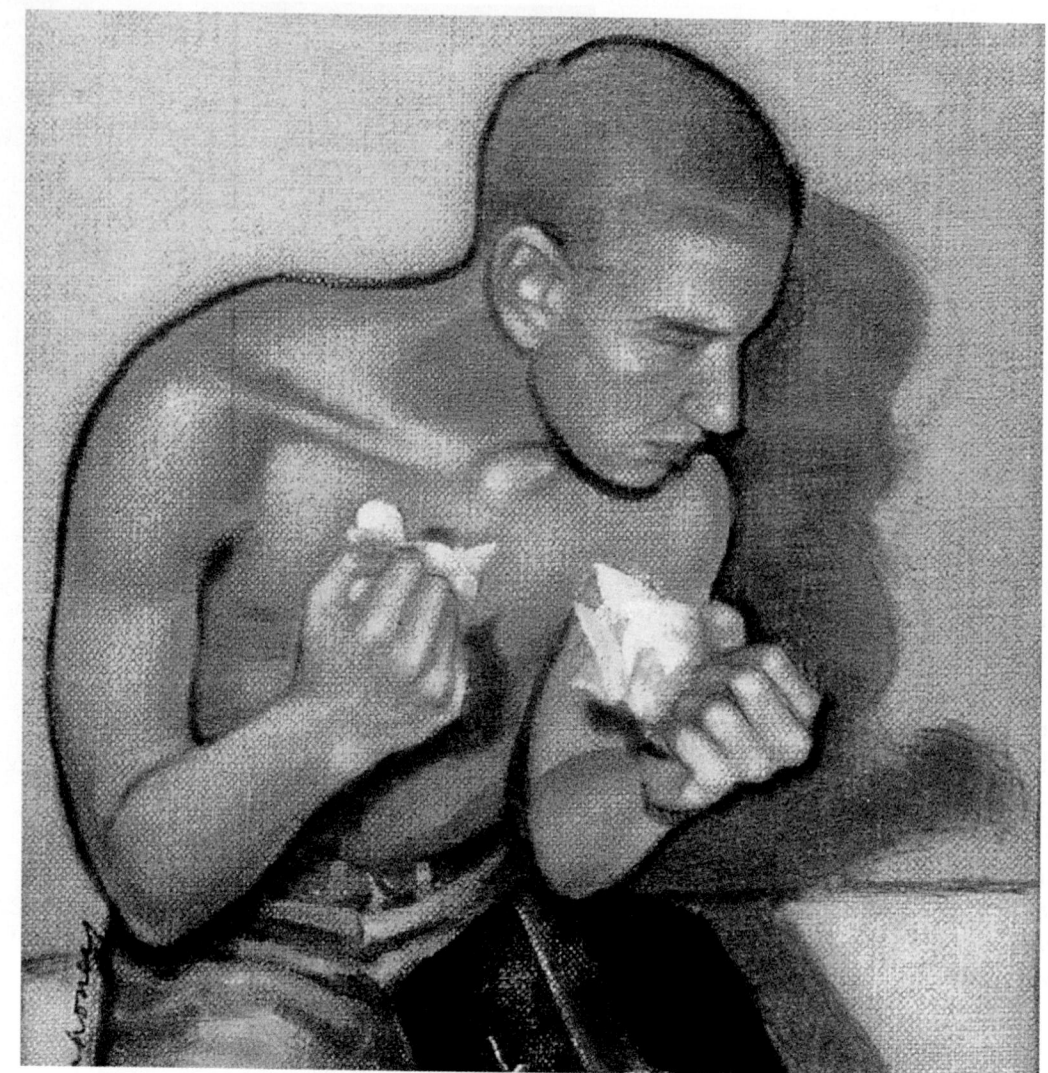

Illustration Copyright © 1987 Katherine Mahoney.

with his family—three sons, two daughters, a wife who spoke virtually no English; he was driven to fits of rage when his store was vandalized, and burglarized, and police failed to arrest the criminals, or even to give the Sokolovs the satisfaction that they were trying to find them. (All this was "Mafia"-related. It was an open secret that the small neighborhood tradesmen were being extorted or were engaged in some elaborate process of attempting to resist extortion.) Mr. Sokolov died, in fact, defending his store: he was hiding at the rear when someone broke in, and he attacked the intruder with a meat cleaver, but was himself shot in the leg, and when the man ran limping and bleeding out into the alley Mr. Sokolov pursued him with the cleaver, limping and bleeding too, and shouting wildly in Polish . . . and somehow Mr. Sokolov and the other man both disappeared. A trail of their commingled blood drops led to an intersection close by, then stopped. Police theorized that a van had been parked there, and that Mr. Sokolov was taken away in it: he was missing for several days, the object of a much-publicized local search, then his body, or rather parts of his body, began to be discovered . . . floating in the canal, carelessly buried at the city dump, tossed into the weedy vacant lot behind St. John the Evangelist Church, to which the Sokolovs belonged. The murderer or murderers were never found and twenty years later, long after Bruno Sokolov himself had died, in Korea, one of his cousins ran for mayor, and narrowly missed winning, on the strength of a passionate campaign against "organized crime" in the city.

On Saturday mornings in all but the worst winter weather I took two city buses downtown to the public library, where, in a windowless ground-floor room set aside for "young adult" readers I searched the shelves for books, especially novels, the search <u>invested</u> with a queer heart-stopping urgency as if the next book I chose, encased in its yellowing plastic cover, *YA* in tall black letters on its spine, might in some way change my life. I was of an age when any change at all seemed promising; I hadn't yet the temperament to conceive of change as fearful. I didn't doubt that *the* book, *the* revelation, awaited me, no matter that the books I actually did read were usually disappointing, too simplistically written and imagined, made up of characters too unswervingly good or bad to be believable. It was the search itself that excited me . . . the look and the feel of the books on their bracketed metal shelves, the smell of the room, a close, warm, stale mixture of floor wax, furniture polish, paper paste, the faint chemical scent of the middle-aged librarian's inky-black dyed hair. Sometimes the very approach to the library—my first glimpse of its Greek Revival portico and columns, its fanning stone steps—aroused me to a sickish apprehension, as if I understood beforehand that whatever I hoped to find there I would not find; or, by the act of finding it, making it my own, I would thereby lose it. The library was further invested with romance since every second or third Saturday I caught sight of Bruno Sokolov there too . . . and one day when I was sitting on the front steps,

waiting for the bus, Bruno stooped over me unannounced to ask, in his oddly breezy, brotherly manner, what I'd checked out, and to show me what he had—adult science fiction by Heinlein, Bradbury, Asimov. Did he have a card for upstairs? for adult books? I asked, surprised, and Bruno said, "Sure." Another time he showed me a book with a dark <u>lurid</u> cover, a ghoulish face with red-gleaming eyes, Bram Stoker's *Dracula*—he hadn't checked it out of the library but had simply taken it from a shelf and slipped it inside his coat. Not stealing exactly, Bruno said, because he'd bring it back, probably. "The kind of stuff I like, it's things that make you think, y'know, the weirder the better," he said, smiling and showing big damp yellowed teeth, "—stuff that scares you into thinking, y'know what I mean?" His eyes were heavy-lidded, his lips rather thick, the lower lip in particular; the curious scar high on his forehead gleamed with reflected light. I saw with surprise his thick stubby battered-looking fingers clutching the book, dirt-edged nails, the knuckles nicked and raw, as if he hurt himself casually without knowing what he did, or caring. Or maybe his hands were roughened from work at the grocery. Or from fighting.

I guessed he didn't know my name.

"Yes," I said, looking up at him, "—I know what you mean."

I watched him walk away, my eyes pinching, following his tall figure in its forward-plunging impatient stride until he was out of sight. *Thief,* I thought. *I could turn you in.* It was only the second or third time we'd spoken together and it would be the final time. And I guessed he didn't know my name. Or even know that he didn't know.

It wasn't long afterward, on another Saturday

morning, in late winter, in the library, downstairs, alone, emerging from the women's lavatory—that place of ancient toilets with chain-activated flushes, black-and-white-checked tile encrusted with decades of dirt, incongruously ornate plaster moldings—I heard someone say in a low insinuating voice, "Little girl? Eh? Little girl?—where're you going?" and was crudely awakened from my brooding trance, the usual spellbound state in which I walked about, when I was alone, in those days, dreaming not so much of Bruno Sokolov or one or another boy I knew as of the mysterious stab of emotions they aroused, the angry teasing hope they seemed to embody, and I'd just pushed through the heavy frosted-glass swinging door and saw, there, a few feet away, in the cavernous poorly lit corridor—this was in an alcove, not far from the young adults reading room—one of the hellish sights of my life: a man approaching me, smiling at me, intimate, derisive, accusatory. I had vaguely recalled this man following me down the stairs but I must have told myself, if I'd told myself anything, that he was simply headed for the men's lavatory. "Little girl—c'mon here," he said, less patiently. Did he know me? Was I expected to know him? I had seen him around the library and on the street outside, dressed shabbily yet flamboyantly in layers of mismatched clothing, overcoat, sweaters, shirt, filthy woolen scarf wound around his neck, unbuckled overshoes flapping on his feet; he was one of a number of oldish odd-looking and -behaving men who haunted the library, in cold weather especially, spending much of the day in the reference room, where they made a show of reading, or actually did read, the daily newspapers, turning the pages harshly, as if the world's events filled them with contempt. Sometimes they dozed, or muttered to themselves, or drank from pint bottles hidden in much-wrinkled paper bags, or forgot where they were,

the precariousness of their welcome, and addressed someone who didn't know them and who quickly edged away. If they caused much disruption one of the librarians, usually a stocky woman with pearl-framed glasses (whom I myself feared for her air of cold authority), ushered them outside, and shut the door behind them. Upon rare occasions police were called but I had never actually seen a policeman arrive.

But here, now, today, for no reason I could guess or would ever be explained to me, one of these men had followed me downstairs to the women's lavatory, speaking excitedly, scolding me, now walking straight at me as if he meant to run me down. He grabbed hold of my arm and wrestled me back against the wall, and the things I was carrying—my little beige leather army surplus purse, an armload of library books—went flying. I saw his coarse-veined face above me, and his white-rimmed rheumy mad eyes, felt his whiskers like wire brush against my skin, and must have screamed, though I don't remember screaming, and he panted, and cursed, and spoke to me with great urgency, now dragging me to the doorway of the men's lavatory, where, I suddenly knew, he would assault me, keep me hostage, kill me—there was no hope for me now. Had I not read of such horrors hinted in the newspaper, or heard of them, whispered, never fully articulated . . .

Yet I might have escaped my assailant, had I squirmed, ducked under his arm, twisted free. He outweighed me by more than one hundred pounds but I might have escaped him and run upstairs screaming for help except that I could not move; all the strength had drained from me. It was as if the mere touch of an adult, an adult's terrible authority, had paralyzed me.

But we were making noise, and the noises echoed in the high-ceilinged space. And then the frosted-glass window of the door to the lavatory shattered and fell in pieces around us. By now

Illustration Copyright © Greg Spalenka.

the librarian from the young adult room had emerged, and another woman was poking her head around a corner staring at us <u>incredulously</u>, and someone cried out for the madman to leave me alone, and the madman shouted back in a rage, and how many minutes passed in this way, or was it merely seconds, while I crouched unable to move yet trembling violently in a crook of a stranger's arm, breathing in the odors, the stench really, of his desperate being, a sharp smell of alcohol, and dirt-stiffened clothing, and I might have thought of praying, I might have thought of God, but all thoughts were struck from my brain, like shadows in a room blasted by light, and even the thought that I would be held hostage and mutilated and murdered and shamed before all the world had not the power to make me fight as I might have, and should have fought.

A number of people had gathered, but were shy of approaching us. The librarian with the pearl-framed glasses was trying to reason with my assailant, who, gripping me hard, with a kind of joy, kept saying, "No! No! No you don't—stay away!" His arm was crooked around my head, his elbow pinioning my neck, I half crouched in an awkward position, the side of my face against his coat, the rough material of his coat, and my hair bunched up fallen into my face; I did not think I was crying, for I had not the space or the breath for crying yet my face was wet with tears, my nose ran shamefully as a baby's—and all the while we swayed and lurched and staggered together, as in a comical dance, which, having begun, we could not end, for there was no way of ending, no way of escaping the corner we had backed into. Several times the word *police* was uttered and several times the madman threatened to "kill the little girl" if any police should so much as appear. Shouts and cries burst about us like birds' shrieks echoing in the passageway and then dipping abruptly to silence. My assailant had pulled me into the lavatory, the outer area of sinks and tall narrow mirrors and naked light bulbs, identical to the women's lavatory, it seemed, yet a forbidden space, and I was able to think clearly, for the first time since the madman had grabbed me, *He will have to kill me now to prove he can do it.*

And then the door was pushed open, and Bruno Sokolov appeared, crouched, unhesitating, moving swiftly—he had shoved his way past the witnesses in the corridor, paying no attention to them, drawn by the excitement, the upset, the prospect of a fight, not knowing who I was until he saw me and perhaps not even knowing then, for there wasn't time to think; in describing what happened I am trying to put into words quicksilver actions that took place within seconds, or split seconds: Bruno fierce and direct as on the basketball court when he deliberately ran down another player, pulling

the madman off me, yanking him away, the two of them screaming at each other, cursing, like men who know each other well, and there was Bruno of a height with my assailant fending off the man's frenzied windmill blows, the two of them now struggling by the sinks, Bruno punching, stabbing, kicking, a blade flashing in his right hand, and blood splashing on the floor, thick sinewy worms of red splashing on the tiled floor . . . Bruno had taken out his switchblade knife, and Bruno was using it, in wide sweeping furious strokes, cursing the man, saying repeatedly, "Die! Die! Die!" though the man had fallen to his knees shrieking in pain and terror, trying to shield his head with his arms. And there was Bruno in a pea-green army surplus jacket, bareheaded, sweating, crouched above him like a madman himself, his face so doughy-pale and distended in rage I would not have known it, eyes shining with moisture, "Die! *Die!*" with each stroke of the knife . . . but now I ran out of the lavatory and into the corridor, where someone caught me in her arms and walked me hurriedly down the hall to a cubicle of an office, the door shut, locked, a call placed to the emergency room of the closest hospital, the word *assault* uttered, and I saw it was the librarian with the pearl-framed glasses now as solicitous of me as a mother. And I knew I would be safe.

My assailant was a man of fifty-eight, an ex-mental patient now living on a disability pension from the U.S. Navy in a downtown hotel for transients. He did not die from Bruno Sokolov's attack but he was in critical condition for some weeks, semiconscious, and when conscious rarely coherent, unable to explain why he had assaulted me or even to recall that he had done so. Nor did he remember the junior high school boy who'd stabbed him with a wicked eight-inch switchblade knife, wounding him in the chest, belly, groin, arms, and face. His memories, such as they were, were concentrated upon late childhood spent in a rural settlement in western Pennsylvania half a century ago.

Following

this much-publicized incident things were never the same again for Bruno Sokolov. As a minor who had, in a sense, behaved heroically, he was not formally charged with any crime (possession of a deadly weapon, for instance, or "aggravated assault") and naturally witnesses testified in his behalf: he had rushed into the lavatory and thrown himself on the madman in order to save me, and then he had fought him, nearly killing him, in self-defense. (So I testified too. So I told everyone. Though I always knew that in the strictest sense it wasn't true.) But a juvenile-court judge placed him on six months' probation, during which time he was obliged to seek psychiatric therapy and to register as an outpatient at a state psychiatric facility, and the shame of that connection so qualified the glamour of Bruno's heroism, and what, literally, he had almost done—*killed a man! stabbed an adult man to death with a switchblade!*—that, in school, he became increasingly withdrawn and sullen, even among his pals, given to unpredictable displays of temper and childish violence, and his grades sharply declined, and he had to resign his class office, and there were intervals when he simply stayed away from school, and the psychiatric therapy was extended for another six months, and there were difficulties in the Sokolov family, and Bruno ran away, tried to enlist in the army, but failed, and came back home, working in the grocery after school and on Saturdays, and through the summer, and in the autumn, in high school; it could never have been the case that this hulking moody overgrown boy might have run for, let alone won, one of the class offices,

nor was he on any of the sports teams, hardly a schoolboy any longer but not a man either, bored, ironic, and truculent, out of scale in our classrooms and in our corridors, slamming his locker door shut as if he meant to break it . . . and should a textbook fall from his hand he'd be likely to give it a kick, but not out of clowning high spirits and not inviting you to laugh sharing a joke because there was no joke, only Bruno Sokolov's dangerous eyes shifting like water under wind, and then he'd be gone, no backward glance, hardly more than a tight ticlike grimace to acknowledge the tie, the bond, the secret between us, unspoken, that we were kin almost as blood relatives are kin who have virtually nothing to do with each other publicly and do not in a sense "know" each other at all, a phenomenon common with schoolchildren though perhaps not limited to them. *It's because of me,* I would think, staring after him, *what he is now—my fault.* Though at more sober moments I understood that what Bruno Sokolov had done had nothing to do with me, or no more to do with me than it had with the ex-mental patient he had nearly killed.

By sixteen Bruno Sokolov had quit school, by seventeen he had joined the army, by eighteen he'd been shipped overseas to die within a few months at the Battle of Taegu, Korea. Pvt. First Class Bruno J. Sokolov, his photograph, tough-jawed, squinty-eyed, hopeful, in the evening paper. And the other night I dreamt of him, a boy thirty-four years dead, remembering in the dream what I'd forgotten for years, that none of his friends had ever called him "Bruno" but always "Sokolov" or "Sokki"—"Sockie"—a harsh sibilant magical sound I had yearned to have the right to say, shouting it in the street as others did, and he would have turned, and he would have seen me, and he would have raised his hand in recognition. As if that might have made a difference. ❖

The Legend

Garrett Hongo

In Chicago, it is snowing softly
and a man has just done his wash for the week.
He steps into the twilight of early evening,
carrying a wrinkled shopping bag
5   full of neatly folded clothes,
and, for a moment, enjoys
the feel of warm laundry and crinkled paper,
flannellike against his gloveless hands.
There's a Rembrandt glow on his face,
10   a triangle of orange in the hollow of his cheek
as a last flash of sunset
blazes the storefronts and lit windows of the street.

He is Asian, Thai or Vietnamese,
and very skinny, dressed as one of the poor
15   in rumpled suit pants and a plaid mackinaw,
dingy and too large.
He negotiates the slick of ice
on the sidewalk by his car,
opens the Fairlane's back door,
20   leans to place the laundry in,
and turns, for an instant,
toward the flurry of footsteps
and cries of pedestrians
as a boy—that's all he was—
25   backs from the corner package store[1]
shooting a pistol, firing it,
once, at the dumbfounded man
who falls forward,
grabbing at his chest.

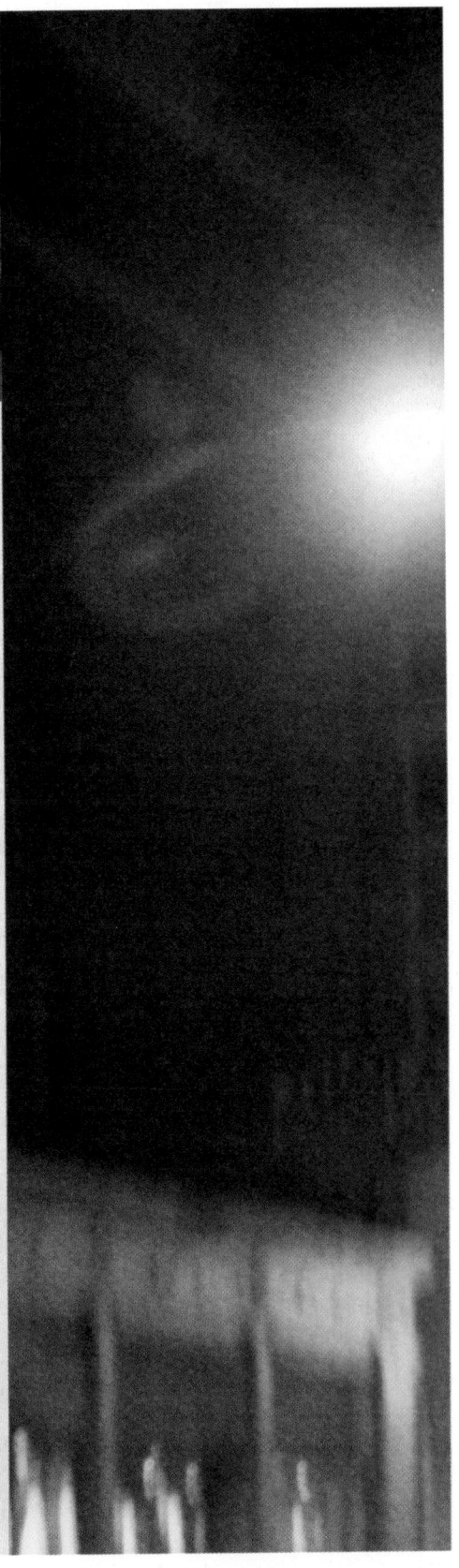

30 A few sounds escape from his mouth,
a babbling no one understands
as people surround him
bewildered at his speech.
The noises he makes are nothing to them.
35 The boy has gone, lost
in the light array of foot traffic
dappling the snow with fresh prints.

Tonight, I read about Descartes'[2]
grand courage to doubt everything
40 except his own miraculous existence
and I feel so distinct
from the wounded man lying on the concrete
I am ashamed.

Let the night sky cover him as he dies.
45 Let the weaver girl cross the bridge of heaven[3]
and take up his cold hands.

In Memory of Jay Kashiwamura

---

1. **package store:** a liquor store.
2. **Descartes** (dā-kärt′): René Descartes, a French
   philosopher, scientist, and mathematician of the 1600s
   who believed that the proof of human existence was the
   ability to think. His most famous statement was "I think,
   therefore I am."
3. **weaver girl . . . heaven:** In Chinese legend, the weaver girl
   and her beloved are separated by the "river of Heaven"—
   the Milky Way. Once a year, magpies spread their wings to
   form a bridge that allows her to cross the river.

Connect to the Literature

1. What Do You Think? How did you react to the violence in this story? Share your comments with your classmates.

> **Comprehension Check**
> - How is Bruno's father killed?
> - Where is the narrator attacked and by whom?
> - How does Bruno's personality change after his fight with the ex-mental patient?

Think Critically

2. How do you explain the narrator's feelings for Bruno at the end of the story?

3. **ACTIVE READING** | **MAKING JUDGMENTS ABOUT CHARACTER** | What judgments did you make about Bruno's character while reading this story? State the criteria you used to make your judgments. Refer to the chart in your **READER'S NOTEBOOK.**

4. How do you account for the change in Bruno after the stabbing?

> **THINK ABOUT**
> - the emotional effects of his violent act
> - how the juvenile-court judge and others perceive him
> - the narrator's comment that Bruno's violent act had "no more to do with me than it had with the ex-mental patient he had nearly killed" (page 1209)

5. How would you compare Bruno with his father?

Extend Interpretations

6. Critic's Corner One of our student board members, Katie McGuire, made this comment about the story: "At first, the author kept my interest by using a lot of description. . . . However, I think there was too much description. If the description was kept minimal, the story would have probably been more interesting." What do you think about the amount of description in Oates's story?

7. Connect to Life How would you explain why some people react violently in a threatening situation?

8. **Points of Comparison** Whom do you consider a more sympathetic character—Bruno in this story or Donny in "Teenage Wasteland"? Defend your answer.

Literary Analysis

CHARACTER: TRAGIC HERO One type of character sometimes found in drama and fiction is the tragic hero. Aristotle, an ancient Greek philosopher, was the first to define this character. According to Aristotle, a **tragic hero** is an exceptional character, often highly gifted. The hero's downfall is usually caused by a tragic flaw—an error in judgment or a defect in character—that leads to his or her destruction. Tragic heroes perceive how their own actions have brought about their ruin. The hero's fall arouses pity and fear in the audience—pity for the hero and fear for all humans, who share to some extent the hero's defects.

Cooperative Learning Activity Get together with a small group of classmates to discuss whether or not this definition of a tragic hero applies to Bruno. Then write a **summary** statement, stating your evaluation and supporting reasons. Share your statement with other groups.

Choices & CHALLENGES

Writing Options

1. Character Sketch How do you believe Bruno's life would have turned out if he had not stabbed the ex-mental patient in the library? Write a profile of Bruno that might eventually have appeared in the local newspaper. Be prepared to explain your predictions for him.

2. Expository Essay Draft an expository essay in which you explore the causes and effects of Bruno's actions. Ask a partner to read your work and to make suggestions. Use a chart like the following to organize your prewriting notes.

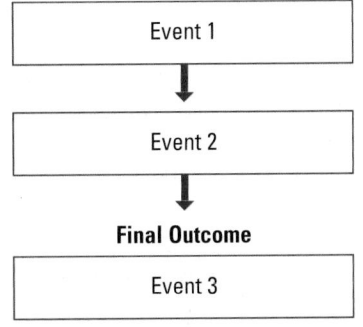

```
┌─────────────────────────┐
│         Event 1         │
└─────────────────────────┘
             ↓
┌─────────────────────────┐
│         Event 2         │
└─────────────────────────┘
             ↓
       Final Outcome
┌─────────────────────────┐
│         Event 3         │
└─────────────────────────┘
```

Writing Handbook
See page 1282: Cause and Effect

3. Literary Review In an interview, Joyce Carol Oates once argued that "all art is moral, educative, illustrative." To what extent do you think "Hostage" and Garrett Hongo's poem "The Legend" (page 1210) fit this description? What moral issues does each work raise? What does each work teach or show? Write a literary review to explore these questions. Place this piece in your **Working Portfolio.**

4. ▮ Points of Comparison
Write a dialogue in which the narrator of "Hostage" and Donny's mother in "Teenage Wasteland" (page 1169) exchange views about the needs of troubled youths.

Activities & Explorations

1. Role-Play Gather in groups of five and role-play each of the following characters, telling how the character views Bruno Sokolov and why:
- the narrator
- the madman in the library
- the juvenile-court judge
- one of Bruno's teachers
- Bruno himself

~ **PERFORMING**

2. Drawing Review the many visual details that Oates uses to describe Bruno, such as his scarred forehead. Then sketch a portrait of him. ~ **ART**

3. Debate Was the sentence Bruno received from the juvenile-court judge justified? With a small group of classmates, have a debate. ~ **SPEAKING AND LISTENING**

Inquiry & Research

Crime Statistics In "Hostage," both the narrator and Bruno are touched by violence. Find recent statistics on violent crime in the United States, and use them to answer the following questions and others that interest you: Has violent crime increased in recent years? What proportion of violent crime do teenagers commit? Has this proportion increased in recent years? You may also want to gather statistics for your own area from a local law-enforcement agency. Display your findings in line, bar, or pie graphs, and discuss with your classmates what these findings suggest about violence in this country.

More Online: Research Starter
www.mcdougallittell.com

Vocabulary in Action

EXERCISE A: SYNONYMS AND ANTONYMS Identify each pair of words as synonyms or antonyms. Afterward, choose a partner and take turns acting out the vocabulary word in each pair.

1. subtle–obvious
2. scrupulously–painstakingly
3. abrasive–soothing
4. rakish–drab
5. incredulously–doubtfully
6. infatuation–crush
7. antagonistic–agreeable
8. invest–supply
9. lurid–boring
10. affronted–offended

EXERCISE B: CONTEXT CLUES Choose one of these vocabulary words to complete each sentence: *aplomb, derisive, incongruously, obscure, sibilant.*

1. We often cannot know why people do the things they do; their motivations may be too _____ for anyone else to comprehend.

2. Sometimes the people whose behavior drives others away are those who are, _____, most in need of and eager for friends.

3. Similarly, those who are most _____ may be those who are most afraid of being made fun of.

4. Perhaps Bruno Sokolov was one of these people; perhaps his air of _____ masked deep doubts and insecurities.

5. When he boldly addressed the school assembly or spoke with seeming confidence in class, did he secretly fear _____ hisses of scorn from his listeners?

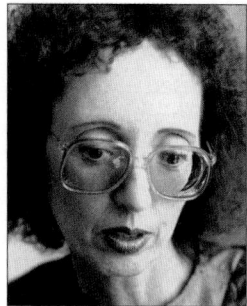

Joyce Carol Oates
1938–

Other Works
A Bloodsmoor Romance
Expensive People
The Time Traveler
Where Are You Going, Where Have You Been?

Prolific Writer Remarkable both for the quantity and the quality of her work, Joyce Carol Oates has published more than 25 novels, 15 volumes of short stories, and many collections of poems, essays, and plays. She has written an average of two books a year since she published her first collection of short stories, *By the North Gate*, when she was 25 years old. Many of her works hauntingly portray insanity and violence.

Academic Excellence Oates was raised in a rural community outside Lockport, New York. Her father was a tool-and-die designer, and her mother was a housewife. Oates attended a one-room school, where her determination and studious habits set her apart from her rowdy classmates. Her mother recalls, "She was always so hard-working, a perfectionist at everything." A brilliant student, Oates graduated Phi Beta Kappa from Syracuse University, where she was valedictorian of her class.

Literary Aims After winning the National Book Award for *them*, Oates described the aim of her fiction. She said, "I have tried to give a shape to certain obsessions of mid-century Americans—a confusion of love and money, of categories of public and private experience, of . . . an urge to violence as the answer to all problems, an urge to self-annihilation, suicide, the ultimate experience and the ultimate surrender. The use of language is all we have to pit against death and silence."

Author Activity

Oates often has been compared to Flannery O'Connor, author of "The Life You Save May Be Your Own" (page 529). In your view, what do the two writers have in common? How do they differ?

Mother Tongue

Essay by AMY TAN

Comparing Literature

Traditions Across Time: Continuing Transformation

The Mexican-American speaker of Pat Mora's poem "Legal Alien" is fluent in two languages—Spanish and English. In her essay "Mother Tongue," Amy Tan, a first generation Chinese American, describes her fluency in different kinds of "Englishes."

Points of Comparison As you read "Mother Tongue," compare Tan's examples of prejudgments based on language to the speaker's examples in "Legal Alien."

Build Background

Language, Family, and Culture Amy Tan's image of herself as a writer transcends her ethnic background: "I don't see myself writing about culture and the immigrant experience," she contends. "That's just part of the tapestry. What I believe my books are about is relationships and family. I've had women come up to me and say they felt the same way about their mothers, and they weren't immigrants."

In "Mother Tongue," Amy Tan focuses on how the communication between her and her mother shapes their relationship. The essay was originally delivered as a speech entitled "Englishes: Whose English Is It Anyway?" that Tan gave as a member of a panel on bilingualism.

WORDS TO KNOW
Vocabulary Preview

diagnosis	quandary
disobedient	transcribe
impeccable	

Focus Your Reading

LITERARY ANALYSIS **PERSONAL ESSAY** A **personal essay** is a brief nonfiction work that expresses the writer's thoughts, feelings, and opinions on a subject. Often this type of essay provides an opportunity for a writer to explore the meaning of events and issues in his or her own life. Note Tan's insights about the power of language and the influence of her mother.

ACTIVE READING **IDENTIFYING MAIN IDEAS AND SUPPORTING DETAILS** Amy Tan's essay is organized into a series of paragraphs, each usually developing one **main idea,** or central point. The sentences in a paragraph that provide information, such as facts, descriptions, and examples, related to the main idea are called **supporting details.** To figure out a main idea that is not directly stated, summarize how the supporting details fit together.

READER'S NOTEBOOK Create a diagram like the one shown. Record the main idea and supporting details for each of the following topics discussed in "Mother Tongue":

❶ different kinds of "Englishes"

❷ mother's spoken English

❸ limitations of mother's English

❹ standardized tests

❺ Tan's envisioned reader for her fiction

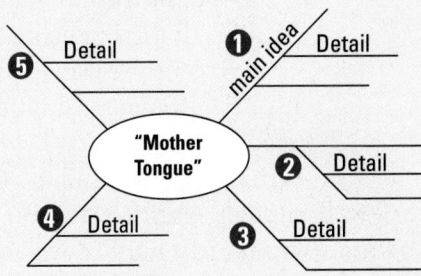

MOTHER TONGUE

母 語

AMY TAN

I am not a scholar of English or literature. I cannot give you much more than personal opinions on the English language and its variations in this country or others,

I am a writer. And by that definition, I am someone who has always loved language. I am fascinated by language in daily life. I spend a great deal of my time thinking about the power of language—the way it can evoke an emotion, a visual image, a complex idea, or a simple truth. Language is the tool of my trade. And I use them all—all the Englishes I grew up with.

Recently, I was made keenly aware of the different Englishes I do use. I was giving a talk to a large group of people, the same talk I had already given to half a dozen other groups. The nature of the talk was about my writing, my life, and my book, *The Joy Luck Club*. The talk was going along well enough, until I remembered one major difference that made the whole talk sound wrong. My mother was in the room. And it was perhaps the first time she had heard me give a lengthy speech, using the kind of English I have never used with her. I was saying things like, "The intersection of memory upon imagination" and "There is an aspect of my fiction that relates to thus-and-thus"—a speech filled with carefully wrought grammatical phrases, burdened, it suddenly seemed to me, with nominalized forms,[1] past perfect tenses, conditional phrases, all the forms of standard English that I had learned in school and through books, the forms of English I did not use at home with my mother.

Just last week, I was walking down the street with my mother, and I again found myself conscious of the English I was using, the English I do use with her. We were talking about the price of new and used furniture and I heard myself saying this: "Not waste money that way." My husband was with us as well, and he didn't notice any switch in my English. And then I realized why. It's because over the twenty years we've been together I've often used that same kind of English with him, and sometimes he even uses it with me. It has become our language of intimacy, a different sort of English that relates to family talk, the language I grew up with.

So you'll have some idea of what this family talk I heard sounds like, I'll quote what my mother said during a recent conversation which I videotaped and then transcribed. During this conversation, my mother was talking about a political gangster in Shanghai who had the same last name as her family's, Du, and how the gangster in his early years wanted to be adopted by her family, which was rich by comparison. Later, the gangster became more powerful, far richer than my mother's family, and one day showed up at my mother's wedding to

1. **nominalized** (nŏm′ə-nə-līzd′) **forms:** nouns formed from other parts of speech.

Amy Tan

WORDS TO KNOW

transcribe (trăn-skrīb′) *v.* to make a handwritten or typed copy of

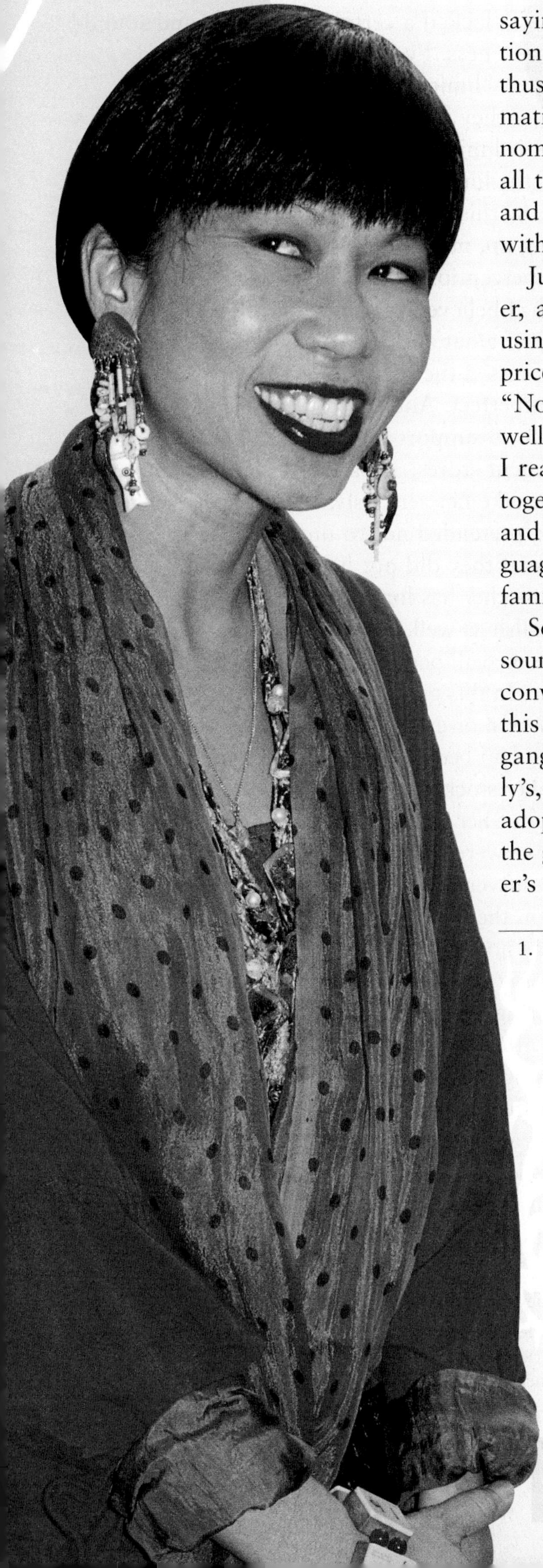

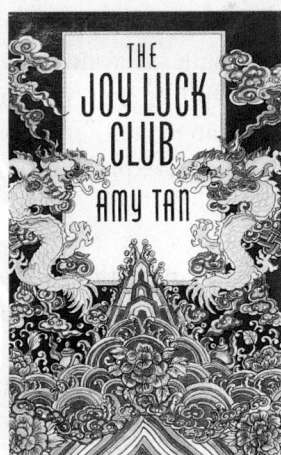

pay his respects. Here's what she said in part:

"Du Yusong having business like fruit stand. Like off the street kind. He is Du like Du Zong—but not Tsung-ming Island people. The local people call putong, the river east side, he belong to that side local people. That man want to ask Du Zong father take him in like become own family. Du Zong father wasn't look down on him, but didn't take seriously, until that man big like become a mafia. Now important person, very hard to inviting him. Chinese way, came only to show respect, don't stay for dinner. Respect for making big celebration, he shows up. Mean gives lots of respect. Chinese custom. Chinese social life that way. If too important won't have to stay too long. He come to my wedding. I didn't see, I heard it. I gone to boy's side, they have YMCA dinner. Chinese age I was nineteen."

You should know that my mother's expressive command of English belies[2] how much she actually understands. She reads the *Forbes* report, listens to *Wall Street Week*, converses daily with her stockbroker, reads all of Shirley MacLaine's books[3] with ease—all kinds of things I can't begin to understand. Yet some of my friends tell me they understand 50 percent of what my mother says. Some say they understand 80 to 90 percent. Some say they understand none of it, as if she were speaking pure Chinese. But to me, my mother's English is perfectly clear, perfectly natural. It's my mother tongue. Her language, as I hear it, is vivid, direct, full of observation and imagery. That was the language that helped shape the way I saw things, expressed things, made sense of the world.

Lately, I've been giving more thought to the kind of English my mother speaks. Like others, I have described it to people as "broken" or "fractured" English. But I wince when I say that. It has always bothered me that I can think of no way to describe it other than "broken," as if it were damaged and needed to be fixed, as if it

lacked a certain wholeness and soundness. I've heard other terms used, "limited English," for example. But they seem just as bad, as if everything is limited, including people's perceptions of the limited English speaker.

I know this for a fact, because when I was growing up, my mother's "limited" English limited my perception of her. I was ashamed of her English. I believed that her English reflected the quality of what she had to say. That is, because she expressed them imperfectly her thoughts were imperfect. And I had plenty of empirical[4] evidence to support me: the fact that people in department stores, at banks, and at restaurants did not take her seriously, did not give her good service, pretended not to understand her, or even acted as if they did not hear her.

My mother has long realized the limitations of her English as well. When I was fifteen, she used to have me call people on the phone to pretend I was she. In this guise, I was forced to ask for information or even to complain and yell at people who had been rude to her. One time it was a call to her stockbroker in New York. She had cashed out her small portfolio[5] and it just so happened we were going to go to New York the next week, our very first trip outside California. I had to get on the phone and say in an adolescent voice that was not very convincing, "This is Mrs. Tan."

And my mother was standing in the back whispering loudly, "Why he don't send me check, already two weeks late. So mad he lie to me, losing me money."

And then I said in perfect English, "Yes, I'm getting rather concerned. You had agreed to send the check two weeks ago, but it hasn't arrived."

Then she began to talk more loudly. "What he want, I come to New York tell him front of his

---

2. **belies** (bĭ-līz'): gives a misleading picture of.
3. **Shirley MacLaine's books:** works by the American actress Shirley MacLaine, many of which deal with reincarnation, or rebirth after death.
4. **empirical** (ĕm-pîr'ĭ-kəl): based on observation.
5. **portfolio** (pôrt-fō'lē-ō'): group of investments.

boss, you cheating me?" And I was trying to calm her down, make her be quiet, while telling the stockbroker, "I can't tolerate any more excuses. If I don't receive the check immediately, I am going to have to speak to your manager when I'm in New York next week." And sure enough, the following week there we were in front of this astonished stockbroker, and I was sitting there red-faced and quiet, and my mother, the real Mrs. Tan, was shouting at his boss in her impeccable broken English.

We used a similar routine just five days ago, for a situation that was far less humorous. My mother had gone to the hospital for an appointment, to find out about a benign[6] brain tumor a CAT scan[7] had revealed a month ago. She said she had spoken very good English, her best English, no mistakes. Still, she said, the hospital did not apologize when they said they had lost the CAT scan and she had come for nothing. She said they did not seem to have any sympathy when she told them she was anxious to know the exact diagnosis, since her husband and son had both died of brain tumors. She said they would not give her any more information until the next time and she would have to make another appointment for that. So she said she would not leave until the doctor called her daughter. She wouldn't budge. And when the doctor finally called her daughter, me, who spoke in perfect English—lo and behold—we had assurances the CAT scan would be found, promises that a conference call on Monday would be held, and apologies for any suffering my mother had gone through for a most regrettable mistake.

I think my mother's English almost had an effect on limiting my possibilities in life as well. Sociologists and linguists probably will tell you that a person's developing language skills are more influenced by peers. But I do think that the language spoken in the family, especially in immigrant families which are more insular, plays a large role in shaping the language of the child.

And I believe that it affected my results on achievement tests, IQ tests, and the SAT. While my English skills were never judged as poor, compared to math, English could not be considered my strong suit. In grade school I did moderately well, getting perhaps B's, sometimes B-pluses, in English and scoring perhaps in the sixtieth or seventieth percentile on achievement tests. But those scores were not good enough to override the opinion that my true abilities lay in math and science, because in those areas I achieved A's and scored in the ninetieth percentile or higher.

This was understandable. Math is precise; there is only one correct answer. Whereas, for me at least, the answers on English tests were always a judgment call, a matter of opinion and personal experience. Those tests were constructed around items like fill-in-the-blank sentence completion, such as, "Even though Tom was _____, Mary thought he was _____." And the correct answer always seemed to be the most bland combinations of thoughts, for example, "Even though Tom was shy, Mary thought he was charming," with the grammatical structure "even though" limiting the correct answer to some sort of semantic opposites,[8] so you wouldn't get answers like, "Even though Tom was foolish, Mary thought he was ridiculous." Well, according to my mother, there were very few limitations as to what Tom could have been and what Mary might have thought of him. So I never did well on tests like that.

The same was true with word analogies, pairs of words in which you were supposed to find some sort of logical, semantic relationship—for example, "*Sunset* is to *nightfall* as _____ is to _____." And here you would be presented

---

6. **benign** (bĭ-nīn′): not cancerous.

7. **CAT scan:** computerized axial tomography scan—a way of creating three-dimensional images of structures inside the human body.

8. **semantic** (sĭ-măn′tĭk) **opposites:** words opposite in meaning.

WORDS TO KNOW

impeccable (ĭm-pĕk′ə-bəl) *adj.* flawless; perfect

diagnosis (dī′əg-nō′sĭs) *n.* the identification of a physical disorder through an examination of its symptoms

with a list of four possible pairs, one of which showed the same kind of relationship: *red* is to *stoplight, bus* is to *arrival, chills* is to *fever, yawn* is to *boring.* Well, I could never think that way. I knew what the tests were asking, but I could not block out of my mind the images already created by the first pair, "sunset is to nightfall"—and I would see a burst of colors against a darkening sky, the moon rising, the lowering of a curtain of stars. And all the other pairs of words—red, bus, stoplight, boring—just threw up a mass of confusing images, making it impossible for me to sort out something as logical as saying: "A sunset precedes nightfall" is the same as "a chill precedes a fever." The only way I would have gotten that answer right would have been to imagine an associative[9] situation, for example, my being disobedient and staying out past sunset, catching a chill at night, which turns into feverish pneumonia as punishment, which indeed did happen to me.

I have been thinking about all this lately, about my mother's English, about achievement tests. Because lately I've been asked, as a writer, why there are not more Asian Americans represented in American literature. Why are there few Asian Americans enrolled in creative writing programs? Why do so many Chinese students go into engineering? Well, these are broad sociological questions I can't begin to answer. But I have noticed in surveys—in fact, just last week—that Asian students, as a whole, always do significantly better on math achievement tests than in English. And this makes me think that there are other Asian-American students whose English spoken in the home might also be described as "broken" or "limited." And perhaps they also have teachers who are steering them away from writing and into math and science, which is what happened to me.

Fortunately, I happen to be rebellious in nature and enjoy the challenge of disproving assumptions made about me. I became an English major my first year in college, after being enrolled as pre-med. I started writing nonfiction as a freelancer the week after I was told by my former boss that writing was my worst skill and I should hone[10] my talents toward account management.

But it wasn't until 1985 that I finally began to write fiction. And at first I wrote using what I thought to be wittily crafted sentences, sentences that would finally prove I had mastery over the English language. Here's an example from the first draft of a story that later made its way into *The Joy Luck Club,* but without this line: "That was my mental quandary in its nascent[11] state." A terrible line, which I can barely pronounce.

Fortunately, for reasons I won't get into today, I later decided I should envision a reader for the stories I would write. And the reader I decided upon was my mother, because these were stories about mothers. So with this reader in mind—and in fact she did read my early drafts—I began to write stories using all the Englishes I grew up with: the English I spoke to my mother, which for lack of a better term might be described as "simple"; the English she used with me, which for lack of a better term might be described as "broken"; my translation of her Chinese, which could certainly be described as "watered down"; and what I imagined to be her translation of her Chinese if she could speak in perfect English, her internal language, and for that I sought to preserve the essence, but neither an English nor a Chinese structure. I wanted to capture what language ability tests can never reveal: her intent, her passion, her imagery, the rhythms of her speech and the nature of her thoughts.

Apart from what any critic had to say about my writing, I knew I had succeeded where it counted when my mother finished reading my book and gave me her verdict: "So easy to read."

---

9. **associative:** based on mental connections.
10. **hone:** sharpen; focus.
11. **nascent:** (năs′ənt): emerging; beginning.

WORDS
TO
KNOW

disobedient (dĭs′ə-bē′dē-ənt) *adj.* not obeying instructions or orders
quandary (kwŏn′də-rē) *n.* a state of uncertainty

1220

Connect to the Literature

1. **What Do You Think?** What did you find most memorable about Amy Tan's mother? Share your thoughts with a partner.

Comprehension Check
- What are two kinds of "Englishes" that Amy Tan uses?
- In general, how do people react to the way Tan's mother speaks English?

Think Critically

2. How would you describe Tan's relationship with her mother?

3. How would you account for changes in Tan's attitude toward her mother's spoken English?

THINK ABOUT
- Tan's initial perceptions about her mother's "limited" English
- the qualities of the language Tan acquired from her mother
- the difference between her mother's understanding of English and her speaking ability
- Tan's identity as a writer

4. What do you consider the most important influences on Tan as a writer? Support your opinion.

5. Explain the significance of the title "Mother Tongue."

6. **ACTIVE READING** **IDENTIFYING MAIN IDEAS AND SUPPORTING DETAILS** Refer to the diagram you made in your **READER'S NOTEBOOK.** How would you summarize the main idea that Tan conveys about standardized tests and the details that she includes to support her point? What do you think is the main idea of the entire essay?

Extend Interpretations

7. **Connect to Life** How would you compare Tan's various "Englishes" with the ones that you or your friends speak in informal and formal situations?

8. **Points of Comparison** In what ways are Amy Tan, her mother, and the speaker in Pat Mora's poem "Legal Alien" all prejudged because of their spoken language? Support your response with evidence from each selection.

Literary Analysis

PERSONAL ESSAY The term **essay** is derived from the works of the 16th-century French writer Michel de Montaigne, who called his explorations of various subjects *essais*, the French word for "attempts." The essay writer does not presume to cover a subject completely. Following in this literary tradition, Amy Tan announces in the beginning of "Mother Tongue," "I am not a scholar of English or literature. I cannot give you much more than personal opinions on the English language. . . ." In this **personal essay,** Tan explores a topic that intrigues her and shares her own experiences and views. The reader, in turn, develops a more intimate awareness of what language means to Tan.

Cooperative Learning Activity With a small group of classmates, analyze Tan's personal essay. What do you think were Tan's main purposes for writing "Mother Tongue"? What issues and concerns does she raise? What is her attitude toward her subject? How would you describe the style of this essay? Create a chart like this one to record your thoughts and impressions.

"Mother Tongue"

Purpose	Theme	Tone	Style

Choices & CHALLENGES

Writing Options

1. Story Evaluation Tan states that she knew she had succeeded as a writer when her mother judged her work as "So easy to read." What criteria, or standards, do you use for evaluating a story? Write an evaluation of one of your favorite stories, explaining why you rate it so highly.

Writing Handbook
See page 1281: Explanatory Writing.

2. Points of Comparison Imagine a meeting between Amy Tan and the speaker of "Legal Alien." Write a dialogue in which they compare and contrast their views on how language shapes personal identity. Include details from the essay and the poem.

Vocabulary in Action

EXERCISE: CONTEXT CLUES In each sentence, identify the word that is used incorrectly. Then, on your paper, write the Word to Know that should replace it.

1. Amy Tan's mother demanded to know the grimace of her illness.
2. The author taped an interview with her mother so that she could later evade the conversation.
3. As immigrants, the family members were aware that their English was not despotic.
4. Were you a well-behaved or a pallid child?
5. Amy Tan was in a surfeit because she wanted to be a writer but was expected to become a doctor.

Building Vocabulary
For an in-depth lesson on context clues, see page 326.

WORDS TO KNOW			
diagnosis	impeccable	transcribe	
disobedient	quandary		

Amy Tan
1952–

Other Works
The Joy Luck Club
The Kitchen God's Wife
The Hundred Secret Senses

Dual Identity Amy Tan was born in Oakland, California, less than three years after her parents emigrated from China. At first, Tan turned away from her Chinese roots. "When I was growing up," Tan remarked, "I blamed everything on the fact that my mother was Chinese, while I thought of myself as totally American." After visiting China for the first time in 1987, she discovered another identity: "As soon as my feet touched China, I became Chinese."

Résumé Highlights Tan's parents had hoped that she would become a neurosurgeon or concert pianist, but she followed a different career path. Tan studied English and linguistics, then worked as a language development consultant for the disabled. She eventually became a business writer, preparing speeches for salespersons and corporate executives. Dissatisfied with business writing, Tan turned her talents to fiction writing.

Tan's Greatest Hits Tan's enormously successful novel, *The Joy Luck Club* (1989), appeared on *The New York Times* bestseller list for eight months and in 1993 was made into a feature film. She has since written two other popular novels as well as children's books. Tan has also performed with the "Rock Bottom Remainders"—a rock-and-roll band made up almost entirely of authors, including horror fiction writer Stephen King and humorist Dave Barry.

Author Activity

Tan's Short Stories Read one of Amy Tan's short stories and write a brief review to share with the class.

The Latin Deli: An Ars Poetica

Poetry by JUDITH ORTIZ COFER

Comparing Literature

Traditions Across Time: Continuing Transformation

Like Pat Mora's poem "Legal Alien," Judith Ortiz Cofer's poem "The Latin Deli: An Ars Poetica" expresses the sentiments of people caught between two cultures. And like Amy Tan's essay "Mother Tongue," Ortiz Cofer's poem explores how the interplay between the cultures influences a person's self-image and identity.

Points of Comparison   As you read "The Latin Deli: An Ars Poetica" compare its portrayal of the bicultural experience with the other portrayals you have read.

Build Background

Between Two Worlds In the 1950s, Judith Ortiz Cofer emigrated to the United States from Puerto Rico. Her family moved back and forth between Paterson, New Jersey, and Puerto Rico according to her father's assignments in the U.S. Navy. These two places shaped her writing.

In Puerto Rico, Ortiz Cofer listened to her grandmother's stories in Spanish under a giant mango tree, surrounded by her extended family. There, she says, "I first began to feel the power of words." In Paterson, she spent much of her time alone, building up "an arsenal of [English] words by becoming an insatiable reader of books." Like the immigrants in her poem, "The Latin Deli: An Ars Poetica" (which means the "art of poetry" in Latin), Ortiz Cofer's family continued to follow certain Puerto Rican traditions and customs while living in New Jersey. For example, they spoke Spanish at home, shopped for Puerto Rican foods at the local *bodega,* and practiced strict Catholicism.

Focus Your Reading

LITERARY ANALYSIS   IMAGERY   The descriptive words and phrases that a writer uses to re-create sensory experiences are called **imagery.** An image may appeal to one or more of the five senses: sight, sound, smell, taste, and touch. As you read "The Latin Deli: An Ars Poetica," note the sensory images and the impressions they leave on you as a reader.

ACTIVE READING   ANALYZING DESCRIPTIVE DETAILS   **Analyzing descriptive details** as you read involves recognizing the structure that a writer uses to bring the details of a description into sharper focus. The arrangement of the details helps you re-create in your own mind the people, places, objects, or events described. In "The Latin Deli: An Ars Poetica," Ortiz Cofer arranges the images in the order that someone would notice them. The "Patroness of Exiles"—the woman who runs the deli—is the focal point of the description.

READER'S NOTEBOOK Create a word web like the one shown to help you analyze the descriptive details in the poem. As you read each stanza, add descriptive words and phrases that are associated with the deli owner. Use these details to visualize the "Patroness of Exiles" as she gradually comes into focus.

The LATIN DELI: An Ars Poetica

JUDITH ORTIZ COFER

Presiding over a formica counter,
plastic Mother and Child magnetized
to the top of an ancient register,
the heady mix of smells from the open bins
5   of dried codfish, the green plantains
hanging in stalks like votive offerings,
she is the Patroness of Exiles,
a woman of no-age who was never pretty,
who spends her days selling canned memories
10 while listening to the Puerto Ricans complain
that it would be cheaper to fly to San Juan
than to buy a pound of Bustelo coffee here,
and to Cubans perfecting their speech
of a "glorious return" to Havana—where no one
15 has been allowed to die and nothing to change until then;
to Mexicans who pass through, talking lyrically
of *dólares* to be made in El Norte—
                              all wanting the comfort
of spoken Spanish, to gaze upon the family portrait
20 of her plain wide face, her ample bosom
resting on her plump arms, her look of maternal interest
as they speak to her and each other
of their dreams and their disillusions—
how she smiles understanding,
25 when they walk down the narrow aisles of her store
reading the labels of packages aloud, as if
they were the names of lost lovers: *Suspiros,*
Merengues, the stale candy of everyone's childhood.
                              She spends her days
30 slicing *jamón y queso* and wrapping it in wax paper
tied with string: plain ham and cheese
that would cost less at the A&P, but it would not satisfy
the hunger of the fragile old man lost in the folds
of his winter coat, who brings her lists of items
35 that he reads to her like poetry, or the others,
whose needs she must divine, conjuring up products
from places that now exist only in their hearts—
closed ports she must trade with.

2 Mother and Child: statue of the Virgin Mary with the baby Jesus.

5 plantains (plăn′tənz): tropical fruits resembling bananas.

6 votive (vō′tĭv) **offerings:** gifts placed before religious shrines as signs of gratitude or prayer.

11 San Juan (săn wän′): the capital of Puerto Rico.

14 Havana: the capital of Cuba.

17 *dólares* (dô′lä-rĕs) *Spanish:* dollars; ***El Norte*** (ĕl nôr′tĕ): a name by which some Latin Americans refer to the United States (literally, "the North").

30 *jamón y queso* (hä-môn′ ē kĕ′sô) *Spanish:* ham and cheese.

32 A&P: a supermarket.

36 divine: guess.

Connect to the Literature

1. What Do You Think?
What do you find most striking about the deli described in this poem?

Comprehension Check
- What does the sales counter at the deli look like?
- What are some of the items sold?
- What countries are the immigrants in the poem from?

Think Critically

2. **ACTIVE READING** **ANALYZING DESCRIPTIVE DETAILS** Review the word web you made in your **READER'S NOTEBOOK**. What details about the "Patroness of Exiles," the deli owner, capture attention? How does the way of organizing details in the poem give a "you are there" quality to the description?

3. How do you think the customers in the deli would describe their homesickness for the native countries? Support your answer with evidence from the poem.

4. What do think most draws the people to shop at the deli—the food, the other customers, or the deli owner? Defend your view.

5. Why do you think the customers in the deli value language and communication so highly?

THINK ABOUT
- the topics of the customers' conversations
- how the customers read labels on packages
- how the deli owner listens to her customers
- "the fragile old man" reading his grocery list like poetry

Extend Interpretations

6. Critic's Corner American poet Archibald Macleish writes in the opening line of his poem "Ars Poetica" that "a poem should be palpable," or easily perceived by the senses. Using this standard, how would you judge "The Latin Deli: An Ars Poetica"? Cite evidence from the poem as support.

7. Connect to Life What foods do you enjoy eating from your own ethnic or cultural heritage? What sorts of feelings or images do you associate with these foods?

8. **Points of Comparison** What similarities and differences do you see in the portrayals of the bicultural experience in "Legal Alien," "Mother Tongue," and "The Latin Deli: An Ars Poetica"?

Literary Analysis

IMAGERY Images—vivid "word pictures"—have the power to convey emotion, mood, and the immediacy of experience. "The Latin Deli: An Ars Poetica" is full of sensory images charged with feeling. For example, the reader overhears snippets of conversations, smells the heady odor of codfish, and sees the wide-faced deli owner who presides over this colorful scene.

Activity Create a five-senses chart like the one below and fill it in with examples of imagery from the poem.

Sense	Examples
Sight	
Sound	
Touch	
Smell	
Taste	

REVIEW **TITLE** The title of a literary work may suggest its subject, convey its tone, or reflect its meaning. The title of this poem, for example, refers to its setting—a deli that is frequented by Latin Americans. Its subtitle comes from the Latin term *ars poetica,* which means "the art of poetry." Why do you think Ortiz Cofer chose this subtitle?

Writing Options

1. Description of a Place Form a mental picture of an ethnic grocery, restaurant, or deli in your community and jot down your impressions of the foods, customers, and employees. Then write a vivid description with sensory details. If possible, visit this place before you begin to write.

2. Grocery List Like the "fragile old man" in the deli, write a grocery list and recite it aloud to the class, as though you were reading a beautiful poem.

3. Points of Comparison In a brief essay, contrast the ways the speaker in Gary Soto's poem "Mexicans Begin Jogging" and the people portrayed in "The Latin Deli: An Ars Poetica" define their personal and cultural identity.

Writing Handbook
See page 1281: Compare and Contrast

Activities & Explorations

1. Dramatic Skit With a small group of classmates, perform a skit dramatizing a conversation that might occur among the "Patroness of Exiles" and a few of her customers in the deli.
~ PERFORMING

2. Advertising Flyer Create an illustrated advertising flyer that features different products on sale at the deli. Try to appeal to the emotions of your potential customers. **~ ART**

Inquiry & Research

Latin American Cookbook The deli in this poem carries traditional Latin American foods, such as plantains and dried codfish. Locate information about popular Latin American dishes, and find a recipe for one of them in an ethnic cookbook. Work with your classmates to compile your recipes into a Latin American cookbook. Identify the country of origin for each dish.

Judith Ortiz Cofer
1952–

Other Works
An Island Like You
Silent Dancing
The Line of the Sun
The Latin Deli

Bridging Differences Judith Ortiz Cofer, an accomplished poet, essayist, and novelist, draws upon her memories of Puerto Rico in much of her work and often explores the immigrant experience. As a Puerto Rican-American writer, Ortiz Cofer remarks, "I believe my role as an artist is to build bridges. To unite us with the world and fellow beings."

Education and Teaching Ortiz Cofer earned a bachelor's degree from Augusta College in 1974 and received a master's degree from Florida Atlantic University in 1977. Before attending graduate school, she worked as a bilingual teacher at public schools in Florida. She has also taught at the University of Miami, Macon College, and the University of Georgia.

Literary Career In 1980 Ortiz Cofer published her first poetry collection, *Latin Women Pray*. She has since published several other books, including *The Latin Deli* (1993), a blending of prose and poetry; a collection of personal essays, *Silent Dancing: A Partial Remembrance of a Puerto Rican Childhood* (1990); and *An Island Like You: Stories of the Barrio* (1996). *The Line of the Sun* (1989), her semiautobiographical novel about a family caught between two cultures, was nominated for a Pulitzer Prize.

Author Activity

Poetry Slam Read another poem from Ortiz Cofer's anthology *The Latin Deli,* and think of an inventive way to present an oral interpretation of it. As a class project, organize a poetry slam, in which students perform oral readings of Ortiz Cofer's poems and compete for prizes.

Straw into Gold:
The Metamorphosis of the Everyday

Essay by SANDRA CISNEROS

Comparing Literature

Traditions Across Time: Continuing Transformation

In "Straw into Gold," Sandra Cisneros reviews the experiences that helped to shape her as a Latina writer. She chose to go her own way, defining herself instead of letting others define her.

Points of Comparison As you read this essay, think about ways to compare Cisneros's self-examination with Martin Luther King, Jr.'s in "Letter from Birmingham Jail" (page 1136).

Build Background

The Title of This Essay Sandra Cisneros is probably best known for *The House on Mango Street,* a book that has earned both popular and critical acclaim. She originally delivered the text of "Straw into Gold" as a speech. Her essay still retains some of the characteristics of an oral work—for example, a conversational tone and a distinctive voice. The phrase "Straw into Gold" refers to the challenge faced by the heroine in "Rumpelstiltskin." In this fairy tale, as you may recall, a miller's daughter will be put to death unless she can do the seemingly impossible—namely, spin gold out of mere straw. The word *metamorphosis* in the subtitle means "a change in form."

Focus Your Reading

LITERARY ANALYSIS **VOICE** The term **voice** refers to a writer's unique use of language that allows a reader to "hear" a human personality in his or her writing. For example, in "Straw into Gold," Cisneros writes:

I'd never seen anybody make corn tortillas. Ever.

The use of a contraction, the everyday words, the short sentence followed by a single word, and the pauses before and after the word *ever*—all contribute to create Cisneros's voice in this essay: one that is personal, informal, almost conversational in its natural sound. Note other instances in this essay when you "hear" Cisneros behind her words.

ACTIVE READING **ANALYZING STRUCTURE** The structure of a literary work is the way in which it is put together—how its parts are organized. The structure of an essay is related to its purpose. For example, King's purpose in "Letter from Birmingham Jail" (page 1136) is to justify nonviolent resistance, so he builds his essay around the points supporting his argument. Cisneros's purpose in "Straw into Gold," on the other hand, is to share some of her formative experiences. She builds her essay around her recollections of growing up. Fittingly, she begins with an anecdote—a brief story that makes a point.

READER'S NOTEBOOK Read the opening anecdote about making tortillas and write a summary of it. Continue to read, summarizing Cisneros's other recollections. Then write down the connections you see between the opening anecdote and the rest of the essay.

Sandra Cisneros

Straw into Gold: The Metamorphosis of the Everyday

When I was living in an artists' colony in the south of France, some fellow Latin-Americans who taught at the university in Aix-en-Provence invited me to share a home-cooked meal with them. I had been living abroad almost a year then on an NEA[1] grant, subsisting mainly on French bread and lentils so that my money could last longer. So when the invitation to dinner arrived, I accepted without hesitation. Especially since they had promised Mexican food.

What I didn't realize when they made this invitation was that I was supposed to be involved in preparing the meal. I guess they assumed I knew how to cook Mexican food because I am Mexican. They wanted specifically tortillas, though I'd never made a tortilla in my life.

It's true I had witnessed my mother rolling the little armies of dough into perfect circles, but my mother's family is from Guanajuato; they are *provincianos*, country folk. They only know how to make flour tortillas. My father's family, on the other hand, is *chilango*[2] from Mexico City. We ate corn tortillas but we didn't make them. Someone was sent to the corner tortilleria to buy some. I'd never seen anybody make corn tortillas. Ever.

Somehow my Latino hosts had gotten a hold of a packet of corn flour, and this is what they tossed my way with orders to produce tortillas. *Así como sea.* Any ol' way, they said and went back to their cooking.

Why did I feel like the woman in the fairy tale who was locked in a room and ordered to spin straw into gold? I had the same sick feeling when I was required to write my critical essay for the MFA[3] exam—the only piece of noncreative writing necessary in order to get my graduate degree. How was I to start? There were rules involved here, unlike writing a poem or story, which I did intuitively. There was a step by step process needed and I had better know it. I felt as if making tortillas—or writing a critical paper, for that matter—were tasks so impossible I wanted to break down into tears.

Somehow though, I managed to make tortillas —crooked and burnt, but edible nonetheless. My hosts were absolutely ignorant when it came to Mexican food; they thought my tortillas were delicious. (I'm glad my mama wasn't there.) Thinking back and looking at an old photograph documenting the three of us consuming those lopsided circles I am amazed. Just as I am amazed I could finish my MFA exam.

I've managed to do a lot of things in my life I didn't think I was capable of and which many others didn't think I was capable of either. Especially because I am a woman, a Latina, an only daughter in a family of six men. My father would've liked to have seen me married long ago. In our culture men and women don't leave their father's house except by way of marriage. I crossed my father's threshold with nothing carrying me but my own two feet. A woman whom no one came for and no one chased away.

---

1. **NEA:** National Endowment for the Arts—a federal agency that funds artistic projects of organizations and individuals.
2. **chilango** (chē-län′gō) Mexican slang: native to Mexico City.
3. **MFA:** master of fine arts (an academic degree).

WORDS TO KNOW

intuitively (ĭn-tōō′ĭ-tĭv-lē) *adv.* without thinking; instinctively
edible (ĕd′ə-bəl) *adj.* fit to eat

Olga (1940),
Rufino Tamayo.
Private Collection.

To make matters worse, I left before any of my six brothers had <u>ventured</u> away from home. I broke a terrible taboo.[4] Somehow, looking back at photos of myself as a child, I wonder if I was aware of having begun already my own quiet war.

I like to think that somehow my family, my Mexicanness, my poverty, all had something to do with shaping me into a writer. I like to think my parents were preparing me all along for my life as an artist even though they didn't know it. From my father I inherited a love of wandering. He was born in Mexico City but as a young man he traveled into the U.S. vagabonding. He eventually was drafted and thus became a citizen. Some of the stories he has told about his first months in the U.S. with little or no English surface in my stories in *The House on Mango Street* as well as others I have in mind to write in the future. From him I inherited a sappy heart. (He still cries when he watches Mexican soaps—especially if they deal with children who have forsaken their parents.)

My mother was born like me—in Chicago but of Mexican descent. It would be her tough street-wise voice that would haunt all my stories and poems. An amazing woman who loves to draw and read books and can sing an opera. A smart cookie.

---

4. **taboo:** a strict cultural rule forbidding something.

WORDS
TO
KNOW

venture (vĕn′chər) *v.* to dare to go

When I was a little girl we traveled to Mexico City so much I thought my grandparents' house on La Fortuna, number 12, was home. It was the only constant in our nomadic[5] ramblings from one Chicago flat to another. The house on Destiny Street, number 12, in the colonia Tepeyac would be perhaps the only home I knew, and that nostalgia[6] for a home would be a theme that would obsess me.

My brothers also figured greatly in my art. Especially the older two; I grew up in their shadows. Henry, the second oldest and my favorite, appears often in poems I have written and in stories which at times only borrow his nickname, Kiki. He played a major role in my childhood. We were bunk-bed mates. We were co-conspirators. We were pals. Until my oldest brother came back from studying in Mexico and left me odd woman out for always.

What would my teachers say if they knew I was a writer now? Who would've guessed it? I wasn't a very bright student. I didn't much like school because we moved so much and I was always new and funny looking. In my fifth-grade report card I have nothing but an <u>avalanche</u> of C's and D's, but I don't remember being that stupid. I was good at art and I read plenty of library books and Kiki laughed at all my jokes. At home I was fine, but at school I never opened my mouth except when the teacher called on me.

When I think of how I see myself it would have to be at age eleven. I know I'm thirty-two on the outside, but inside I'm eleven. I'm the girl in the picture with skinny arms and a crumpled skirt and crooked hair. I didn't like school because all they saw was the outside me. School was lots of rules and sitting with your hands folded and being very afraid all the time. I liked looking out the window and thinking. I liked staring at the girl across the way writing her name over and over again in red ink. I wondered why the boy with the dirty collar in front of me didn't have a mama who took better care of him.

I think my mama and papa did the best they could to keep us warm and clean and never hungry. We had birthday and graduation parties and things like that, but there was another hunger that had to be fed. There was a hunger I didn't even have a name for. Was this when I began writing?

In 1966 we moved into a house, a real one, our first real home. This meant we didn't have to change schools and be the new kids on the block every couple of years. We could make friends and not be afraid we'd have to say goodbye to them and start all over. My brothers and the flock of boys they brought home would become important characters eventually for my stories—Louie and his cousins, Meme Ortiz and his dog with two names, one in English and one in Spanish.

My mother flourished in her own home. She took books out of the library and taught herself to garden—to grow flowers so envied we had to put a lock on the gate to keep out the midnight flower thieves. My mother has never quit gardening.

This was the period in my life, that slippery age when you are both child and woman and neither, I was to record in *The House on Mango Street*. I was still shy. I was a girl who couldn't come out of her shell.

How was I to know I would be recording and <u>documenting</u> the women who sat their sadness on an elbow and stared out a window? It would be the city streets of Chicago I would later record, as seen through a child's eyes.

I've done all kinds of things I didn't think I could do since then. I've gone to a prestigious[7] university, studied with famous writers, and taken an MFA degree. I've taught poetry in schools in Illinois and Texas. I've gotten an NEA grant and run away with it as far as my courage would take

---

5. **nomadic:** moving from home to home; wandering.
6. **nostalgia** (nŏ-stăl′jə): a longing for things or people in the past.
7. **prestigious** (prĕ-stē′jəs): respected.

Street mural in a Latino neighborhood of Chicago

me. I've seen the bleached and bitter mountains of the Peloponnesus.[8] I've lived on an island. I've been to Venice twice. I've lived in Yugoslavia. I've been to the famous Nice[9] flower market behind the opera house. I've lived in a village in the pre-Alps and witnessed the daily parade of promenaders.

I've moved since Europe to the strange and wonderful country of Texas, land of polaroid-blue skies and big bugs. I met a mayor with my last name. I met famous Chicana and Chicano artists and writers and *políticos.*[10]

Texas is another chapter in my life. It brought with it the Dobie-Paisano Fellowship, a six-month residency on a 265-acre ranch. But most important, Texas brought Mexico back to me.

In the days when I would sit at my favorite people-watching spot, the snakey Woolworth's counter across the street from the Alamo[11] (the Woolworth's which has since been torn down to make way for progress), I couldn't think of anything else I'd rather be than a writer. I've traveled and lectured from Cape Cod to San Francisco, to Spain, Yugoslavia, Greece, Mexico, France, Italy, and now today to Texas. Along the way there has been straw for the taking. With a little imagination, it can be spun into gold. ❖

---

8. **Peloponnesus** (pĕl′ə-pə-nē′səs): the peninsula forming the southern part of mainland Greece.

9. **Nice** (nēs): a port city in southern France.

10. **políticos** (pô-lē′tē-kôs) Spanish: politicians.

11. **Alamo:** a mission chapel in San Antonio, Texas—site of a famous battle in Texas's war for independence from Mexico.

Connect to the Literature

1. What Do You Think? How would you describe Cisneros's personality? Share your comments with your classmates.

> **Comprehension Check**
> - What do Cisneros's Latin American friends assume she can do?
> - What family taboo does Cisneros break?
> - Near the end of her essay, Cisneros says, "I've done all kinds of things I didn't think I could do." Name one of the achievements she lists.

Think Critically

2. Why do you think Cisneros regards herself as a rebel?

3. What do you think was the greatest challenge Cisneros had to overcome to become a Latina writer?

- her poverty and rootlessness as a child
- her personal shyness
- her position as the only daughter in a male-dominated family
- her father's expectations of her

4. **ACTIVE READING** **ANALYZING STRUCTURE** Cisneros's essay begins with an anecdote about making tortillas. What connections do you see between this anecdote and her other recollections? Refer to what you wrote in your **READER'S NOTEBOOK.**

5. Why do you think Cisneros makes an **allusion** to the "Rumplestiltskin" tale in her essay?

Extend Interpretations

6. What If? How would the effect of this essay have been different if Cisneros had not mentioned her weaknesses, such as her inability to come out of her shell?

7. Connect to Life Cisneros comments, "I managed to do a lot of things in my life I didn't think I was capable of." What can you gain by attempting to do the seemingly impossible? Explain your answer.

8. **Points of Comparison** How would you compare Cisneros and King as outsiders or rebels, based on this essay and the excerpt from "Letter from Birmingham Jail" (page 1136)?

Literary Analysis

VOICE "Straw into Gold" reflects Cisneros's **voice,** or her unique way of using language to convey her personality in her writing. Among the elements that work together to create a writer's voice are sentence structure, diction, and tone.

For example, some writers rely on short, simple sentences, while others make use of long, complicated ones. Certain writers use concrete words; others prefer abstract terms. A writer's tone, or attitude toward the subject—for example, inviting, passionate, or sarcastic—also colors the voice.

Voice is similar to style, but not exactly the same. For instance, a textbook or manual might be written in a simple, direct style but might also lack a personal voice.

Cooperative Learning Activity With a small group of classmates, read aloud Cisneros's anecdote about making tortillas. Then analyze its sentence length, diction, and tone. Create a chart like the one shown to record your findings. Then choose a passage by another writer from the unit—analyze it, and jot down your findings on a second chart. Discuss how Cisneros's voice differs from this other writer's.

Cisneros's Voice

Sentence Length	Diction	Tone

Writing Options

1. Letter of Advice What advice do you think Cisneros might give to an aspiring writer? Based on what you learned about her from reading this essay, create her letter of advice, and share it with your classmates. Place this piece in your **Working Portfolio.**

2. Points of Comparison Write a dialogue in which Cisneros and Martin Luther King, Jr., share their views about self-definition. Use the ideas you discussed for question 8 on page 1232 to get started.

Art Connection

Look at the reproduction of the painting *Olga* by Rufino Tamayo on page 1229. What are your impressions of the woman in this painting? How would you compare them with your impressions of Cisneros?

Vocabulary in Action

EXERCISE: MEANING CLUES For each sentence, write **Sense** or **Nonsense** on your paper to indicate whether the statement does or does not make sense.

1. The tortillas were quite edible; no one could eat them.
2. She was discouraged by an avalanche of criticism.
3. The two boys decided to venture away from home and never came back.
4. Cisneros draws a distinction between writing according to rules and writing intuitively.
5. She tried to document the lives of Latino immigrants, ignoring them completely.

Building Vocabulary

For an in-depth lesson on word connotation and denotation, see page 908.

Sandra Cisneros
1954–

Other Works
The House on Mango Street
Woman Hollering Creek and
*   Other Stories*
My Wicked Wicked Ways

Lonely Childhood Born in Chicago, Sandra Cisneros was the only daughter of a Mexican father and a Mexican-American mother. Her family frequently moved between Mexico City and Chicago, so Cisneros seldom stayed long enough in one place to have close friends. To escape her loneliness, she turned to writing.

Finding Her Voice Cisneros wrote secretly at home, openly expressing her creativity only in high school where she edited a literary magazine. She took her first creative writing class in college. After completing college, Cisneros decided to attend graduate school. In the late 1970s, she enrolled in the Iowa Writers' Workshop at the University of Iowa. In these surroundings, she viewed herself as an outsider. "My classmates. . . had been bred as fine hothouse flowers," she has said. "I was a yellow weed among the city's cracks." Ironically, this realization was a blessing in disguise. It spurred Cisneros to write about her own experiences and to find her own voice: "I knew I was a Mexican woman. . . . My race, my gender, my class! That's when I decided I would write about something my classmates couldn't write about."

Achieving Success In 1984 Cisneros published *The House on Mango Street*, a series of 44 related prose vignettes narrated by Esperanza Cordero, a young girl growing up in a Latino neighborhood of Chicago. This book received the Before Columbus Foundation American Book Award in 1985. Since then, Cisneros has worked as a teacher to high school dropouts, a poet-in-residence at schools, and a visiting writer at colleges.

Comparing Literature: Assessment Practice

In writing assessments, you will often be asked to evaluate the quality or merit of a literary work. You are now going to practice writing an essay with an evaluative focus.

PART 1 Reading the Prompt

First, read the entire prompt carefully. Then read through it again, looking for key words that help you identify the purpose of the essay and decide how to approach it.

Writing Prompt

The selections in Unit 7, Part 2, illuminate social issues of the 1960s and afterward. Evaluate these selections and choose the two that you would rate as the most important to be studied. In an essay, explain the reasons for your choice of selections. Justify your ratings with evidence.

1
2
3
4

STRATEGIES
IN ACTION

1 **Evaluate,** or form a judgment.

2 Create a set of standards, or **criteria,** for judging a work's importance—for example, lasting relevance, broad appeal, original insights, and artistic quality.

3 **Explain**—tell how two selections fit your criteria.

4 Provide **examples** from the selections.

PART 2 Planning an Evaluative Essay

- Determine the key elements of important literary works, and use these elements as your criteria.

- For each selection, create an evaluation chart. If a criterion is applicable, mark the corresponding box and cite an example.

- Review your charts to see which two selections fit your criteria most closely. Flesh out the examples you noted.

Criteria	Present?	Example
Lasting relevance	☐	____
____	☐	____
____	☐	____
____	☐	____

PART 3 Drafting Your Essay

Introduction State your purpose—to evaluate literary works—and identify the selections you rated as most important to study. Summarize your criteria for importance.

Organization Discuss each selection as a whole, or apply one criterion at a time to both selections. Maintain the focus of your essay as you write. Support your judgments with details from the selections.

Conclusion Sum up the literary and social value of the two works you examined, and restate the key points that reinforce your evaluation.

Revision Allow time to review your work. Make sure it is clear, well-supported, and free from mistakes.

Writing Handbook See page 1283: Analysis

Fahrenheit 451

RAY BRADBURY

These thematically related readings are provided along with *Fahrenheit 451*:

"You Have Insulted Me"
KURT VONNEGUT, JR.

Burning a Book
WILLIAM STAFFORD

A Summer's Reading
BERNARD MALAMUD

Afterword to the Novel
RAY BRADBURY

The Portable Phonograph
WALTER VAN TILBURG CLARK

The Paterson Public Library
JUDITH ORTIZ COFER

The Phoenix
SYLVIA TOWNSEND WARNER

. . . And the Earth Did Not Devour Him

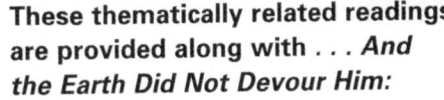

TOMÁS RIVERA

These thematically related readings are provided along with . . . *And the Earth Did Not Devour Him:*

from Fields of Toil: A Migrant Family's Journey
ISABEL VALLE

Latin Women Pray
JUDITH ORTIZ COFER

Napa, California
ANA CASTILLO

The Plan of Delano
NATIONAL FARM WORKERS ASSOCIATION

The Whistle
EUDORA WELTY

First Confession
FRANK O'CONNOR

Fourth Grade Ukus (1952)
MARIE HARA

In Answer to Their Questions
GIOVANNA (JANET) CAPONE

And Even *More* . . .

Books

Centaur
JOHN UPDIKE
A novel about a father and son coming to terms with life and each other.

What Manner of Man: A Biography of Martin Luther King, Jr.
LERONE BENNETT, JR.
A compelling profile of the celebrated civil rights leader.

The Disuniting of America: Reflections of a Multicultural Society
ARTHUR M. SCHLESINGER, JR.
A thoughtful analysis by the Pulitzer Prize–winning historian about the fragmentation of American society stemming from cultural diversity.

Other Media

Stand and Deliver
Film about an inspirational high school teacher in a barrio of Los Angeles, starring Edward James Olmos. (VIDEOCASSETTE)

The Accidental Tourist
Film adaptation of Anne Tyler's novel about a travel writer coping with the loss of his son and the breakup of his marriage. (VIDEOCASSETTE)

Eyes on the Prize
Documentary series chronicling the U.S. civil rights movement. PBS Video. (VIDEOCASSETTE)

Unsettling America: An Anthology of Contemporary Multicultural Poetry

EDITED BY MARIA MAZZIOTTI GILLAN AND JENNIFER GILLAN

A diverse chorus of poetic voices comment on ethnic pride and heritage, personal identity, and cultural stereotypes. Pat Mora, Lucille Clifton, Li-Young Lee, Louise Erdrich, and Lawrence Ferlinghetti are among the notable poets included in this collection.

War Abroad and Conflict at Home

The selections in this unit look at personal experiences related to battles overseas and struggles at home. How did this unit affect your understanding of World War II, the Vietnam War, and postwar American society? Explore your ideas by completing one or more of the options in each section.

Detail of *Ominous Omen* (1987), Rupert Garcia. Chalk, linseed oil, oil paint on canvas, 47″ × 130″, courtesy of Rupert Garcia; Rena Bransten Gallery, San Francisco; and Galerie Claude Samuel, Paris. Copyright © Rupert Garcia.

Reflecting on the Unit

OPTION 1

Pictures of War The selections in Part 1, "Remembering the Wars," deal with the effects of modern warfare on soldiers and civilians. For each selection you read, jot down a few phrases that describe the experiences it presents. Then choose the selection that presents war most vividly to you, and write a paragraph or draw a picture to show how that selection affected you.

OPTION 2

Issues for Today and the Future Review the selections in this unit, jotting down the social issues or problems they raise. Choose three or four issues that are most relevant to your own life and that you think will continue to be so in the future. Then do some freewriting about two of those issues. Explain why you think those issues are important to your life, whether you agree with how writers in this unit presented or interpreted the issues, and whether your opinions about the issues have changed as a result of reading the unit.

OPTION 3

Different Kinds of Courage How courageous are the characters and speakers presented in this unit? For each one that you can form an opinion about, assign a rating from 1 (very courageous) to 5 (not at all courageous) and describe in a few words the kind of courage shown. Then write a few paragraphs about a speaker or character who displays a kind of courage you admire.

Self ASSESSMENT

📖 READER'S NOTEBOOK

Make a list of the impressions you had before you read this unit about what people felt and thought during World War II, during the Vietnam War, and during the time between and after the wars. Then note whether your reading has confirmed your preconceptions or contradicted them.

Reviewing Literary Concepts

OPTION 1

Describing Tone Tone is the attitude that a writer takes toward a subject. Think back over the selections in Unit Seven, and describe the tone of each in a chart like the one begun here. In the third column, identify a feature of the content or style that helps convey this tone—for example, emphasis on emotions or personal relationships, an anti-hero as protagonist, comic irony, or implied social criticism.

Selection	Tone	Feature
Wandering	cynical, critical	anti-hero opposed to war and conformity

OPTION 2

Linking Title and Theme Review the selections in this unit to determine the theme, or central idea, of each. Then choose four or five selections and jot down a few phrases to evaluate how the title of each selection connects to its theme. Discuss your opinions with a small group of classmates—different people often discover different themes in the same work.

📁 Building Your Portfolio

- **Writing Options** Several writing options in this unit asked you to express your opinion of characters, situations, issues, or artistic qualities reflected in the selections. Choose one of the pieces in which you think you offered the most compelling argument to support your viewpoint. Attach a cover note to the assignment explaining what you learned about presenting a convincing case to your audience, then put the assignment in your **Presentation Portfolio.** 📁

- **Communication Workshop** In this unit you created a multimedia exhibit. Evaluate the quality of your exhibit, especially the print and audio-visual elements. Did the exhibit have a clear and unified focus? Did the media you included convey information in an interesting, creative way? Decide if you would like to keep your exhibit in your **Presentation Portfolio.** 📁

- **Additional Activities** Review the assignments you completed under **Activities & Explorations** and **Inquiry & Research.** Which one did you think was the most successful? Save it in your portfolio with a cover note explaining what you wanted to accomplish with the activity and why it succeeded.

Self ASSESSMENT

📕 **READER'S NOTEBOOK**

Copy the following list of literary terms discussed in Unit Seven. Which are more useful in understanding poetry? Which are more useful in analyzing prose? Create a Venn diagram to classify these terms. Review those you are not sure about in the **Glossary of Literary Terms** (page 1342).

point of view	plot development
imagery	protagonist
mood	antagonist
internal conflict	dramatic irony
speaker	tragic hero
style	personal essay
allusion	imagery
dialogue	voice

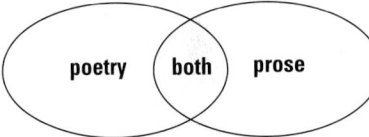

poetry   both   prose

Self ASSESSMENT

Look back over the work in your **Presentation Portfolio.** 📁 Which piece or pieces are you most proud of? In what ways has your writing improved during this year? In what ways do you want to improve your writing further?

Setting GOALS

You have read selections in this unit that raise important questions about political, cultural, social, and personal issues. Which of these issues would you like to learn more about? Consult with a librarian to help you compile a brief bibliography, and choose at least one title from your list to read on your own.

HENRY DAVID THOREAU

ROBERT FROST

TONI MORRISON

ARTHUR MILLER

PATRICK HENRY

SYLVIA PLATH

WALT WHITMAN

CARL SANDBURG

MARTIN LUTHER KING, JR.

EMILY DICKINSON

ZORA NEALE HURSTON

HENRY WADSWORTH LONGFELLOW

F. SCOTT FITZGERALD

JOYCE CAROL OATES

WASHINGTON IRVING

EDGAR ALLAN POE

RALPH WALDO EMERSON

JAMES BALDWIN

JOHN UPDIKE

NATHANIEL HAWTHORNE

E. E. CUMMINGS

T. S. ELIOT

WILLIAM FAULKNER

LANGSTON HUGHES

FLANNERY O'CONNOR

FREDERICK DOUGLASS

JOHN STEINBECK

MARK TWAIN

WILLA CATHER

1238

STEPHEN CRANE

ERNEST HEMINGWAY

Student *Resource Bank*

Reading Handbook 1240
Reading for Different Purposes 1240
Reading Different Genres 1242
Reading Different Formats 1243
Enriching Your Vocabulary 1244
Reading for Information 1250
Functional Reading 1260

Writing Handbook 1268
The Writing Process 1268
Building Blocks of Good Writing 1272
Descriptive Writing 1277
Narrative Writing 1279
Explanatory Writing 1281
Persuasive Writing 1285
Research Report Writing 1287
Business Writing 1293

Communication Handbook 1295
Inquiry and Research 1295
Study Skills and Strategies 1297
Critical Thinking 1299
Speaking and Listening 1300
Viewing and Representing 1302

Grammar Handbook 1305
Quick Reference: Parts of Speech 1305
Nouns 1306
Pronouns 1307
Verbs 1309

Modifiers 1312
Prepositions, Conjunctions, and Interjections 1314
Quick Reference: The Sentence and Its Parts 1316
The Sentence and Its Parts 1317
Phrases 1319
Verbals and Verbal Phrases 1319
Clauses 1321
The Structure of Sentences 1322
Writing Complete Sentences 1323
Subject-Verb Agreement 1324
Quick Reference: Punctuation 1327
Quick Reference: Capitalization 1329
Little Rules That Make a Big Difference 1330
Commonly Confused Words 1334
Grammar Glossary 1335

Glossary of Literary Terms 1332

Glossary of Words to Know in English and Spanish 1366

Pronunciation Key 1384

Index of Fine Art 1385

Index of Skills 1388

Index of Titles and Authors 1401

Acknowledgments 1405

Art Credits 1412

Reading for Different Purposes

You read for many different reasons. In a single day, you might read a short story for fun, a textbook for information to help you pass a test, and a weather map to find out if it will rain. For every type of reading, there are specific strategies that can help you understand and remember the material. This handbook will help you become a better reader in school, at home, and on the job.

Reading Literature

Before Reading

- **Set a purpose** for reading. Are you reading as part of an assignment or for fun? What do you want to learn? Establishing a purpose will help you focus.
- **Preview** the work by looking at the title and any images and captions. Try to **predict** what the work will be about.
- Ask yourself if you can **connect** the subject matter with what you already know.

During Reading

- **Check your understanding** of what you read. Can you restate the plot in your own words?
- Try to **connect** what you're reading to your own life. Have you experienced similar events or emotions?

- **Question** what's happening. You may wonder about events and characters' feelings.
- **Visualize,** or create a mental picture of, what the author describes.
- **Pause** from time to time to **predict** what will happen next.

After Reading

- **Review** your predictions. Were they correct?
- Try to **summarize** the work, expressing the **main idea** or the basic plot.
- **Reflect on** and evaluate what you have read. Did the reading fulfill your purpose?
- To **clarify** your understanding, write down opinions or thoughts about the work, or discuss it with someone.

Reading for Information

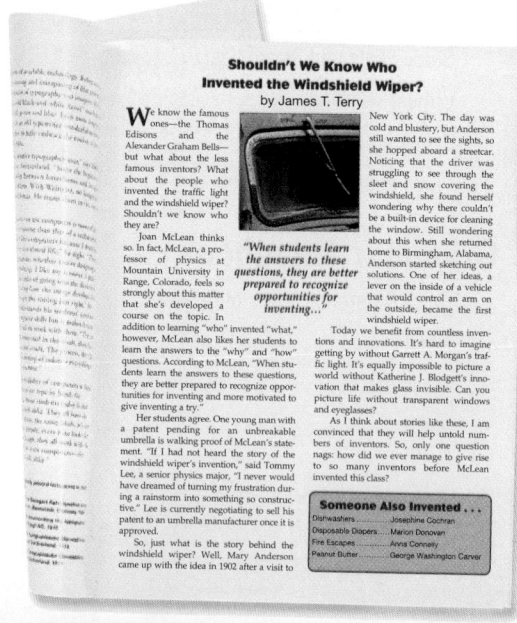

Set a Purpose for Reading
- Decide why you are reading the material—to study for a test, to do research, or to find out more about a topic that interests you.
- Use your **purpose** to determine how detailed your **notes** will be.

Look at Design Features
- Look at the **title** and **subheads** and at **boldfaced words** or phrases, **boxed text,** and any other text that is highlighted in some way.
- Use these **text organizers** for help in previewing the text and identifying the main ideas.
- Study photographs, maps, charts, and captions.

Notice Text Structures and Patterns
- Does the text make **comparisons?** Does it describe **causes and effects?** Is there a **sequence** of events?
- Look for **signal words** such as *same, different, because, first,* and *then.* They can reveal the material's organizational pattern.

Read Slowly and Carefully
- **Take notes** on the main ideas. State the information in your own words.
- Map the information by using a word web or another **graphic organizer.**
- Notice **unfamiliar words.** These are sometimes defined in the text.
- If there are **questions** accompanying the text, be sure that you can answer them.

Evaluate the Information
- Think about what you have read. Does the text make sense? Is it complete?
- **Summarize** the information—state the main points in just a few words.

Functional Reading

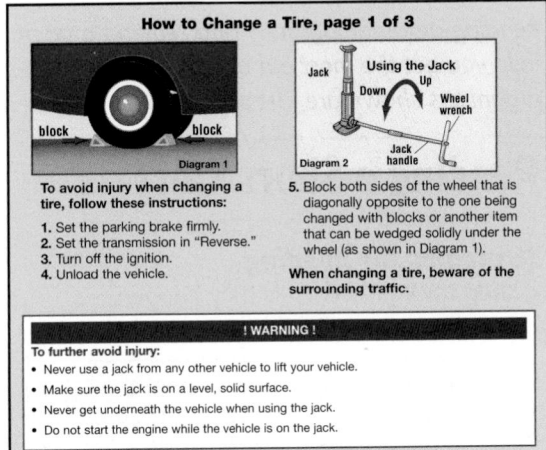

How to Change a Tire, page 1 of 3

To avoid injury when changing a tire, follow these instructions:
1. Set the parking brake firmly.
2. Set the transmission in "Reverse."
3. Turn off the ignition.
4. Unload the vehicle.

5. Block both sides of the wheel that is diagonally opposite to the one being changed with blocks or another item that can be wedged solidly under the wheel (as shown in Diagram 1).

When changing a tire, beware of the surrounding traffic.

! WARNING !

To further avoid injury:
- Never use a jack from any other vehicle to lift your vehicle.
- Make sure the jack is on a level, solid surface.
- Never get underneath the vehicle when using the jack.
- Do not start the engine while the vehicle is on the jack.

Identify the Audience, Source, and Purpose
- Look for clues that tell you whom the document is for. Is there an address or a title? Does the information in the document affect you?
- Look for clues that tell you who created the document. Is the source likely to be reliable?
- Think about the **purpose** of the document. Is it to show you how to do something? to warn you about something? to tell you about community events?

Read Carefully
- Notice **headings** or **rules** that separate one section from another.
- Look for numbers or letters that signal steps in a **sequence.** If you are reading directions, read them all the way through at least once before performing the steps.
- Examine any charts, photographs, or other **visuals** and their captions.
- **Reread** complex instructions if necessary.

Evaluate the Information
- Think about whether you have found the information you need.
- Look for telephone numbers, street addresses, or e-mail addresses of places where you could find more information.

Reading Different Genres

Reading an autobiography and reading a poem require different skills. Here are some tips to help you get the most out of the different genres, or types, of literature you read. The graphic organizers shown are just suggestions—use the note-taking method that works best for you.

Reading a Short Story

Strategies for Reading

- Keep track of events as they happen. Creating a chart like this one may help you.

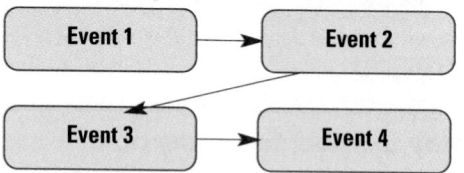

- From the details the writer provides, **visualize** the characters. **Predict** what they might do next.
- Look for specific adjectives that help you visualize the **setting**—the time and place in which events occur.

Reading a Poem

Strategies for Reading

- Notice the **form** of the poem, or the number of its lines and their shape on the page.
- Read the poem aloud a few times. Listen for **rhymes** and **rhythms.**
- **Visualize** the images and comparisons.
- **Connect** with the poem by asking yourself what message the poet is trying to send.
- Create a word web or other **graphic organizer** to record your reactions and questions.

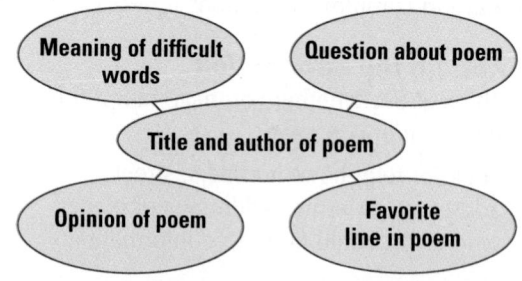

Reading a Speech

Strategies for Reading

- Think about the **historical context**—the occasion, the audience, and the purpose—of the speech.
- You may need to **clarify** certain terms and names by looking them up in a dictionary, an encyclopedia, or a glossary.
- Try to **visualize** the speaker giving the speech and the audience reacting to it.
- Notice the **style** of the speech. Are certain words and phrases repeated for effect? Does the speaker use **rhetorical questions** (questions to which no answer is expected because the answer is obvious)?
- **Evaluate** the effectiveness of the speech. Is the speech clear? Is it persuasive?

Reading Nonfiction

Strategies for Reading

- If you are reading a biography or autobiography, sketch a family tree or a word web to keep track of the people who are mentioned.
- When reading an essay, **evaluate** the writer's ideas and reasoning. Does the writer support opinions with facts and sound arguments?
- When reading an article or interview, **skim** it first to learn what its subject is. Look at any **headings** or **captions.** Then look for the **main idea.** Completing a chart like this one can help.

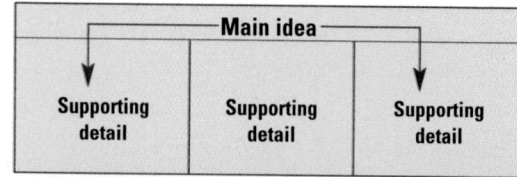

Reading Different Formats

These strategies will help you when you need to do research, learn about current events, or just find out more about a topic that interests you.

Reading Online Text

Strategies for Reading

- Notice the page's **Web address,** sometimes called a URL. You may want to make a note of it if you will need to return to that page. Most Web addresses begin with the coding http://www.

- Read the **title** of the page to get a general idea of what topics the page covers.

- Notice **links** to related pages. Links are often "buttons" or underlined words. Clicking on a link will take you to a different page—one that may or may not have been created by the same person or organization.

- Look for a **menu bar** along the top, bottom, or side of the page. This gives you links to other parts of the Web site.

- Notice any **source citations.** Some sites tell you where their information is from, enabling you to judge its reliability.

- Write down **important ideas and details.** Try to restate the text in your own words. Then decide whether you need to check other sources.

Reading a Newspaper or Magazine Article

Strategies for Reading

- Read the **headline** and any **subheads** to learn what the article is about and how it is organized.

- Notice any photographs, charts, graphs, or other **visuals.** Read their **captions.** Be sure you understand how the visuals and the main text are related.

- Notice any **quotations.** Think about whether the people who are quoted are likely to be reliable authorities on the topic.

Reading an Encyclopedia Article

Strategies for Reading

- Read the **headline** and any **subheads** to make sure that the article covers the topic of interest to you.

- Look at **visuals** and read their **captions.** Some online or CD-ROM encyclopedias also include sound files, animated maps, and short movies.

- Pay attention to how the article is organized. You may want to **skim** the article, or read it quickly, as you look for **key words** related to your topic. Once you find the information you need, read slowly and carefully.

- Watch for a **"see also"** or **"related articles"** section or—if the encyclopedia is online—for highlighted links. These features direct you to additional articles that include information on your subject.

Enriching Your Vocabulary

Context Clues

One way to figure out the meaning of a word you don't know is by using context clues. The context of a word is made up of the punctuation marks, other words, sentences, and paragraphs that surround the word.

General Context Sometimes you need to read all the information in the sentence or paragraph in order to infer the meaning of an unfamiliar word. The underlined words below give clues to the meaning of the word in the boldface type.

> I told my parents that I wanted <u>to quit playing</u> the violin, but they encouraged me to **persevere** instead.

> Brad was not used to the **turbulent** motion of the waves, so he felt ill when <u>the boat moved too much</u>.

Definition Clues Often a difficult word will be followed by its definition. Commas, dashes, or other punctuation marks may signal a definition.

> **Perennials**—<u>plants that live for more than two years</u>—make up only one-third of the garden's exhibit.

Restatement Clues Sometimes a writer restates a word or term in easier language. Commas, dashes, or other punctuation may signal restatement clues, as may expressions such as *that is, in other words,* and *or.*

> My sister is very **stingy;** that is, <u>she is unwilling to spend money</u>.

Example Clues Sometimes writers suggest the meaning of a word with one or two examples.

> Their new apartment was **arrayed** with many beautiful things, <u>such as a crystal lamp and a porcelain vase</u>.

Comparison Clues Sometimes a word's meaning is suggested by a comparison. *Like* and *as* are words that signal comparison clues.

> The prairie grasses **undulated** in the wind <u>like the waves of the ocean</u>.

Contrast Clues Sometimes writers point out differences between things or ideas. Contrast clues are often signaled by such words as *although, but, however, unlike,* and *in contrast to.*

> My dog is usually very calm, <u>unlike</u> our neighbor's dog, which is very **rowdy.**

Idioms and Slang An idiom is an expression whose overall meaning is different from the meaning of the individual words. Slang is informal language that comprises both made-up words and ordinary words that carry different meanings than in formal English. Use context clues to figure out the meaning of idioms and slang.

> If you're going to buy a house that has a garden, you'd better **have a green thumb!** (idiom)

> My parents **freaked out** when I told them that I went to the concert without their permission. (slang)

TIP One way to clarify your understanding of a word is to write a sentence using that word. Even better, use one of the context-clue strategies in your sentence. For example, include a restatement or definition clue.

For more about context clues, see page 326.

Word Parts

If you know base words, roots, and affixes—that is, prefixes and suffixes—you can figure out the meanings of many unfamiliar words.

Base Words A **base word** is a word that can stand alone. Other words or word parts can be added to base words to form new words.

Roots Many English words contain roots that come from older languages, such as Latin, Greek, and Old English. A **root** is a word part to which a prefix, a suffix, and/or another root must be added. Knowing the meaning of a word's root or roots can help you figure out the word's meaning.

Root	Meaning	Examples
agon (Greek)	struggle, contest	antagonist, agony
gon (Greek)	figure having angles	pentagon, polygon
circ (Latin)	around	circle, circumference
civ (Latin)	citizen	civilian, civilization
opt (Latin)	eye	optical, optometrist
hus (Old English)	house	husband, husbandry
mer(e) (Old English)	sea, pool	mermaid, merman

Prefixes A **prefix** is a word part that appears at the beginning of a base word or another word part. Attaching a prefix to an existing word usually changes the meaning of that word. Familiarizing yourself with the meanings of common prefixes can help you be prepared to figure out the meanings of unfamiliar words.

Prefix	Meaning	Examples
bi-	two	bicultural, bicycle
endo-	within	endoscope, endoskeleton
in-	not, without	inactive, insensitive
micro-	small	microbiology, microchip
pro-	before	proactive, prologue
trans-	over, across	transaction, transnational

Suffixes A **suffix** is a word part attached to the end of a base word or another word part. Attaching a suffix to an existing word may alter the word's meaning. However, a suffix does not change a word's meaning when it is added as follows:
- to a noun to change the number
- to a verb to change the tense
- to an adjective to change the degree of comparison
- to an adverb to show how

Suffix	Purpose	Examples
-s, -es	to change the number of a noun	elephant + *s*, elephants
-ed, -ing	to change verb tense	whisper + *ed*, whispered whisper + *ing*, whispering
-er, -est	to change the degree of comparison in modifiers	low + *er*, lower low + *est*, lowest
-ly	to show how	joyful + *ly*, joyfully

Other suffixes are added to a root or base word to change the word's meaning. These suffixes can also be used to change the word's part of speech.

Suffix	Meaning	Examples
-al	relating to	accidental, experimental
-ish	of, relating to, being	piggish, wolfish
-ize	to make	dramatize, philosophize

To infer the meaning of an unfamiliar word from it parts, follow these steps.
- Divide the word into parts. Think of other words you know that share the same root(s) or base word.
- Ask, Do these other words all have the same or similar meanings?
- Consider the meanings of any prefixes or suffixes in the unfamiliar word.
- From the meaning of the word's parts, predict what the word means.
- Check the context and a dictionary or glossary to find out whether your prediction is correct.

For more about roots, see page 444; for more about prefixes and suffixes, see page 1130.

Word Origins

When you study a word's origin and history, you find out when, where, and how the word came to be. A complete dictionary entry includes the word's history.

dra•ma (drä′mə) *n.* **1.** A work that is meant to be performed by actors. **2.** Theatrical works of a certain type or period in history. [Late Latin *drāma, drāmat-,* from Greek *drān,* to do or perform.]

This entry shows you that the earliest form of the word *drama* was the Greek word *drān.*

Word Families Words that have the same root have related meanings. Such words make up a word family. The charts below show common Greek and Latin roots. Notice how the meanings of the English words are related to the meanings of their roots.

Greek Root: `soph, wise`

English: **philosophy** "love of wisdom"; the study of logic and basic truths

sophisticated worldly, refined, or complex

sophomore "wise fool"; a student in the second year of high school or college

Latin Root: `port, to carry`

English: **import** to bring or carry in from an outside source

portable carried or moved easily

portfolio a portable case for holding materials

Latin Root: `struct, to build`

English: **construct** to build

destructive wanting to ruin or eliminate something

structure a building

TIP Once you recognize a root in one English word, you will notice the same root in other words—members of the same word family. Because these words developed from the same root, they are similar in meaning.

Foreign Words Some foreign words that enter the English language keep their original form.

Arabic	French	Japanese	Spanish
algebra	coupon	judo	bonanza
giraffe	gourmet	kimono	cargo
lime	memoir	ninja	guitar
mattress	rendezvous	samurai	patio
soda	sabotage	soy	stampede
zero	unique	tsunami	tuna

For more about word families and researching word origins, see page 206.

Synonyms and Antonyms

When you read, pay attention to the precise words a writer uses.

Synonyms A **synonym** is a word that has the same or almost the same meaning as another word. Read each set of synonyms listed below.

attempt/try

create/make

help/assist

labor/work

pledge/vow

occasionally/sometimes

smart/intelligent

wild/untamed

TIP You can find synonyms in a thesaurus or dictionary. In a dictionary, synonyms are often given following the definition of a word.

Antonyms An **antonym** is a word with a meaning opposite to that of another word. Read each set of antonyms listed below.

> arrive/depart
>
> cruel/kind
>
> different/similar
>
> fresh/stale
>
> noisy/silent
>
> polite/rude
>
> precede/follow
>
> timid/bold

Some antonyms are formed by adding one of the negative prefixes *anti-, in-,* or *un-* to a word, as in the chart below.

Word	Prefix	Antonym
bacterial	anti-	antibacterial
climax	anti-	anticlimax
consistent	in-	inconsistent
definite	in-	indefinite
install	un-	uninstall
true	un-	untrue

TIP You can find antonyms in dictionaries of synonyms and antonyms, as well as in some thesauruses.

TIP Some dictionaries contain notes that discuss synonyms and antonyms. These notes often include sentences that illustrate the relationships among the words.

Denotative and Connotative Meaning

Good writers choose just the right word to communicate a specific meaning.

Denotative Meaning A word's dictionary meaning is called its **denotation.** The denotation of the word *thin*, for example, is "having little flesh; spare; lean."

Connotative Meaning The images or feelings you connect to a word are called **connotations**. Connotative meaning stretches beyond a word's dictionary definition. Writers rely on connotations of words to communicate shades of meaning, as well as positive or negative feelings. Examples of similar words with different connotations are listed below.

Positive Connotations	Negative Connotations
aroma	stench
bold	reckless
cloud	smog
delicate	weak
desire	envy
gaze	glare
inquisitive	nosy
plant	weed
reproduce	forge
slender	scrawny

TIP Some dictionaries contain notes that discuss connotative meanings of the entry word and other related words.

For more information about denotative and connotative meanings, see page 908.

Homonyms, Multiple-Meaning Words, and Homophones

Homonyms, multiple-meaning words, and homophones can be confusing to readers and can plague writers.

Homonyms Words that have the same spelling and pronunciation but different meanings and in most cases different origins are called **homonyms**. Consider this example:

> The **pitcher** on our baseball team drank an entire **pitcher** of lemonade after the game!

Pitcher can mean "the player who throws the ball from the mound to the batter in baseball," but it can also mean "a container for liquids."

Words with Multiple Meanings Multiple-meaning words are ones that have over time acquired additional meanings based on the original meaning. Consider these examples:

> James ran one **block** so he could catch the bus.

> Did that tall woman **block** your view of the movie screen?

Block clearly has multiple meanings, but all of the additional meanings have developed from the same original meaning. You will find all the meanings for *block* under one entry in the dictionary.

Homophones Words that sound alike but have different meanings and spellings are called **homophones**. Consider these examples:

> The **weather** is supposed to be good this weekend.

> Please let me know **whether** you want to go to see *Othello* or *Hamlet*.

Many common words with Anglo-Saxon origins have homophones *(there, their; write, right)*. Check your writing to make sure you have used the right word and not its homophone.

For more about homonyms and homophones, see page 728; for more about multiple-meaning words, see page 630.

Analogies

Analogy An **analogy** is a comparison between two things that are similar in some way. Analogies often appear on tests, usually in a format like this:

> TRACTOR : VEHICLE :: A) wrench : tool
> B) lawnmower : lawn
> C) farmer : farm
> D) hay : barn
> E) car : driver

To determine the correct answer, follow these steps:

- Read the part in capital letters as "*Tractor* is to *vehicle* as . . . "
- Read the answer choices as "*wrench* is to *tool*," "*lawnmower* is to *lawn*," "*farmer* is to *farm*," and so on.
- Ask yourself how the first two words, *tractor* and *vehicle,* are related. (A tractor is a kind of vehicle. So *tractor* is an item in the larger category of *vehicles.*)
- Then look for the answer that best shows the same relationship. (Of these possible answers, only item A shows the relationship of an item to a category.)

Here are some relationships that are often expressed in analogies:

Relationship	Example
Part to whole	FINGER : HAND
Word to synonym	HARD : DIFFICULT
Word to antonym	RAINY : SUNNY
Degree of intensity	HAPPY : ECSTATIC
Item to category	LEMONADE : DRINK
Characteristic to object	STICKINESS : GLUE

For more about analogies, see page 254.

Specialized Vocabulary

Professionals who work in fields such as law, science, and sports use their own technical or specialized vocabulary. Use these strategies to help you figure out the meanings of specialized vocabulary.

Use Context Clues Often the surrounding text gives clues that help you infer the meaning of an unfamiliar term.

> After taxes are deducted you will **net** $680.

Use Reference Tools Textbooks often define a special term when it is first introduced. Look for definitions or restatements in parentheses. You may also find definitions in footnotes, a glossary, or a dictionary. If you need more information, refer to a specialized reference, such as one of the following:

- an encyclopedia
- a field guide
- an atlas
- a user's manual
- a technical dictionary

Decoding Multisyllabic Words

Many words that are familiar to you when you speak them or hear them may be unfamiliar to you when you see them in print. When you come across a word unfamiliar in print, first try to pronounce it to see if you might recognize it. The following syllabication generalizations can help you figure out a word's pronunciation.

Generalization 1: VCCV

When there are two consonants between two vowels, divide between the two consonants, unless they are a blend or a digraph.

    pic/ture   a/brupt   feath/er

Generalization 2: VCCCV

When there are three consonants between two vowels, divide between the blend or the digraph and the other consonant.

    an/gler   mush/room   emp/tied

Generalization 3: VCCV

When there are two consonants between two vowels, divide between the consonants, unless they are a blend or a digraph, the first syllable is a closed syllable, and the vowel is short.

    lath/er   ush/er   ten/der

Generalization 4: Common Vowel Clusters

Do not split common vowel clusters, such as long vowel digraphs, *r*-controlled vowels, and vowel diphthongs.

    par/ty   poi/son   fea/ture

Generalization 5: VCV

When you see a VCV pattern in the middle of a word, divide the word either before or after the consonant. If you divide the word after the consonant, the first vowel sound will be short. If you divide the word before the consonant, the first vowel sound will be long.

    box/ed   ro/bot   cra/zy

Generalization 6: Compound Words

Divide compound words between the individual words.

    grape/vine   life/guard

Generalization 7: Affixes

When a word includes an affix, divide between the base word and the affix.

    fast/er   rest/less

Reading for Information

Reading informational materials—such as textbooks, magazines, newspapers, and Web pages—requires the use of special strategies. For example, you need to study text organizers, such as headings and special type, to learn the main ideas, facts, terms, and names that are of importance. You also need to identify patterns of organization in the text. Using such strategies will help you to read informational materials with ease and quickly gain a clear understanding of their contents.

Reading a Textbook

Look for headings, large or dark type, pictures, and drawings. These special features, called **text organizers,** usually show the most important information on the page. Paying attention to them can help you understand and remember what you read.

Strategies for Reading

A First, look at the **title** and any **subheads.** These will tell you the main ideas of the lesson.

B Many textbooks list one or more **objectives** or **key terms** at the beginning of each lesson. These identify the most important facts and details in the lesson.

C **Key terms** are often boldfaced or underlined where they first appear in the text. Be sure that you understand what they mean.

D Notice any **special features,** such as extended quotations or sidebar quotations, questions, or articles. These provide important information.

E Look at the **visuals**—illustrations, photographs, graphs, maps, time lines—and read their **captions.** Visuals often present information that is not in the main text.

SECTION **2**

A The Civil War Begins

MAIN IDEA	WHY IT MATTERS NOW	**B** Terms & Names
Shortly after the nation's Southern states seceded from the Union, war began between the North and South.	The nation's identity was forged in part by the Civil War. Sectional divisions remain very strong today.	• Fort Sumter • Bull Run • Stonewall Jackson • Ulysses S. Grant • Robert E. Lee • Antietam • Emancipation Proclamation • conscription • Clara Barton • income tax

One American's Story

On April 18, 1861, Major Robert Anderson was traveling by ship from Charleston, South Carolina, to New York City. That day, Anderson wrote a report to the secretary of war in which he described his most recent command.

A PERSONAL VOICE ROBERT ANDERSON

"Having defended Fort Sumter for thirty-four hours, until the quarters were entirely burned, the main gates destroyed by fire, . . . the magazine surrounded by flames, . . . four barrels and three cartridges of powder only being available, and no provisions but pork remaining, I accepted terms of evacuation . . . and marched out of the fort . . . with colors flying and drums beating . . . and saluting my flag with fifty guns."

—quoted in *Fifty Basic Civil War Documents*

▲ **Major Robert Anderson** observes the firing at Fort Sumter in 1861.

C

Months earlier, as soon as the Confederacy was formed, Confederate soldiers in each secessionist state began seizing federal installations—especially forts. By the time of Lincoln's inauguration on March 4, 1861, only four Southern forts remained in Union hands. The most important was **Fort Sumter,** on an island in Charleston harbor.

Lincoln decided to neither abandon Fort Sumter nor reinforce it. He would merely send in "food for hungry men." At 4:30 A.M. on April 12, Confederate batteries began thundering away to the cheers of Charleston's citizens. The deadly struggle between North and South was under way.

A Union and Confederate Forces Clash

News of Fort Sumter's fall united the North. When Lincoln called for volunteers, the response throughout the Northern states was overwhelming. However, Lincoln's call for troops provoked a very different reaction in the states of the

More Strategies for Reading Textbooks

- Before you begin reading the text, read any **questions** that appear at the end of the lesson or chapter. These will help you focus your reading.

- Read slowly and carefully. If you see an unfamiliar word and can't find a definition in the text or in a marginal note, check the **glossary** or a dictionary. Look for **pronunciation guides** as you read.

- Take **notes** as you read. Doing this will help you understand new ideas and terms as well as remember what you are reading. Review your notes before a test to jog your memory.

- You may want to take notes in the form of a **graphic organizer,** such as a cause-and-effect chart or a comparison-and-contrast chart.

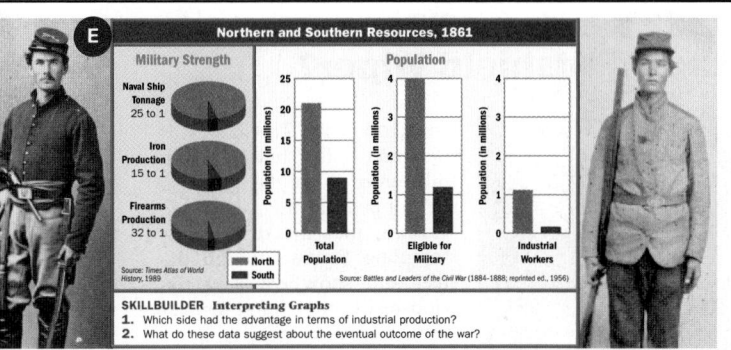

E

Northern and Southern Resources, 1861

Military Strength

Naval Ship Tonnage 25 to 1

Iron Production 15 to 1

Firearms Production 32 to 1

Source: *Times Atlas of World History,* 1989

Population

North
South

Total Population

Eligible for Military

Industrial Workers

Source: *Battles and Leaders of the Civil War* (1884–1888; reprinted ed., 1956)

SKILLBUILDER Interpreting Graphs
1. Which side had the advantage in terms of industrial production?
2. What do these data suggest about the eventual outcome of the war?

Most Union troops saw the war as a struggle to preserve the Union.

upper South. In April and May, Virginia, Arkansas, North Carolina, and Tennessee seceded, bringing the number of Confederate states to eleven. The western counties of Virginia opposed slavery, so they seceded from Virginia and were admitted into the Union as West Virginia in 1863. The four remaining slave states—Maryland, Delaware, Kentucky, and Missouri—remained in the Union.

Most Confederate soldiers fought to protect the South from Northern aggression.

STRENGTHS AND STRATEGIES The Union and the Confederacy were unevenly matched. The Union enjoyed enormous advantages in resources over the South—more people, more factories, greater food production, and a more extensive railroad system. The Confederacy's advantages included "King Cotton," first-rate generals, and highly motivated soldiers. **A**

Both sides adopted military strategies suited to their objectives and resources. The Union, which had to conquer the South to win, devised a three-part plan:

- The navy would blockade Southern ports, so they could neither export cotton nor import much-needed manufactured goods.
- Union riverboats and armies would move down the Mississippi River and split the Confederacy in two.
- Union armies would capture the Confederate capital at Richmond, Virginia.

The Confederacy's strategy was mostly defensive, although Southern leaders encouraged their generals to attack the North if the opportunity arose.

BULL RUN The first bloodshed on the battlefield occurred about three months after Fort Sumter fell, near the little creek of **Bull Run,** just 25 miles from Washington, D.C. The battle was a seesaw affair. In the morning the Union army gained the upper hand, but the Confederates held firm, inspired by General Thomas J. Jackson. "There stands Jackson like a stone wall!" another general shouted, coining the nickname **Stonewall Jackson.** In the afternoon Confederate reinforcements helped win the first Southern victory. Fortunately for the Union, the Confederates were too exhausted to follow up their victory with an attack on Washington. Still, Confederate morale soared. Many Confederate soldiers, confident that the war was over, left the army and went home.

UNION ARMIES IN THE WEST Lincoln responded to the defeat at Bull Run by stepping up enlistments. He also appointed General George McClellan to lead the Union forces encamped near Washington. While McClellan drilled his troops, the Union forces in the west began the fight for control of the Mississippi River.

MAIN IDEA

Making Inferences
D
A) Why were Northern factories and railroads so advantageous to the Union's war effort?

Reading a Magazine Article

Strategies for Reading

A Read the **title** and any other **headings** to get an idea of what the article is about and how it is organized.

B As you read the main text, notice any **quotations.** Who is quoted? Is the person a reliable authority on the subject?

C Notice text that is set off in some way, such as a passage in a **different typeface.** A quotation or statistic that sums up the article is sometimes presented in this way.

D Study **visuals,** such as photographs, graphs, charts, and maps. Make sure you know how they relate to the main text.

A Shouldn't We Know Who Invented the Windshield Wiper?

by James T. Terry

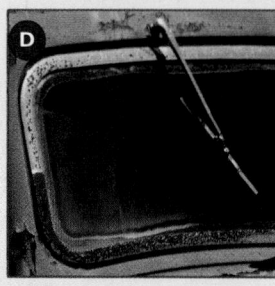

We know the famous ones—the Thomas Edisons and the Alexander Graham Bells— but what about the less famous inventors? What about the people who invented the traffic light and the windshield wiper? Shouldn't we know who they are?

Joan McLean thinks so. In fact, McLean, a professor of physics at Mountain University in Range, Colorado, feels so strongly about this matter that she's developed a course on the topic. In addition to learning "who" invented "what," however, McLean also likes her students to learn the answers to the "why" and "how" questions. According to McLean, "When students learn the answers to these questions, they are better prepared to recognize opportunities for inventing and more motivated to give inventing a try."

Her students agree. One young man with a patent pending for an unbreakable umbrella is walking proof of McLean's statement. **B** "If I had not heard the story of the windshield wiper's invention," said Tommy Lee, a senior physics major, "I never would have dreamed of turning my frustration during a rainstorm into something so constructive." Lee is currently negotiating to sell his patent to an umbrella manufacturer once it is approved.

So, just what is the story behind the windshield wiper? Well, Mary Anderson came up with the idea in 1902 after a visit to New York City. The day was cold and blustery, but Anderson still wanted to see the sights, so she hopped aboard a streetcar. Noticing that the driver was struggling to see through the sleet and snow covering the windshield, she found herself wondering why there couldn't be a built-in device for cleaning the window. Still wondering about this when she returned home to Birmingham, Alabama, Anderson started sketching out solutions. One of her ideas, a lever on the inside of a vehicle that would control an arm on the outside, became the first windshield wiper.

Today we benefit from countless inventions and innovations. It's hard to imagine getting by without Garrett A. Morgan's traffic light. It's equally impossible to picture a world without Katherine J. Blodgett's innovation that makes glass invisible. Can you picture life without transparent windows and eyeglasses?

As I think about stories like these, I am convinced that they will help untold numbers of inventors. So, only one question nags: how did we ever manage to give rise to so many inventors before McLean invented this class?

C *"When students learn the answers to these questions, they are better prepared to recognize opportunities for inventing...."*

C
Someone Also Invented . . .

Dishwashers .... Josephine Cochran
Disposable Diapers .... Marion Donovan
Fire Escapes .... Anna Connelly
Peanut Butter .... George Washington Carver

Reading a Web Page

Strategies for Reading

A Look for the page's **Web address,** sometimes called a URL. If you think you will need to return to the page, write down the address or use the Web browser to "bookmark" the page or log it as a favorite site.

B Read the **title** of the page to find out what the page covers.

C Look for a **menu bar** along the top, bottom, or side of the page. This tells you about other parts of the site.

D Notice any **links** to related pages. Links are often "buttons" or underlined words.

E Some sites have **interactive areas** where you can make a comment. This site has a "Forum" area where experts answer questions on different topics.

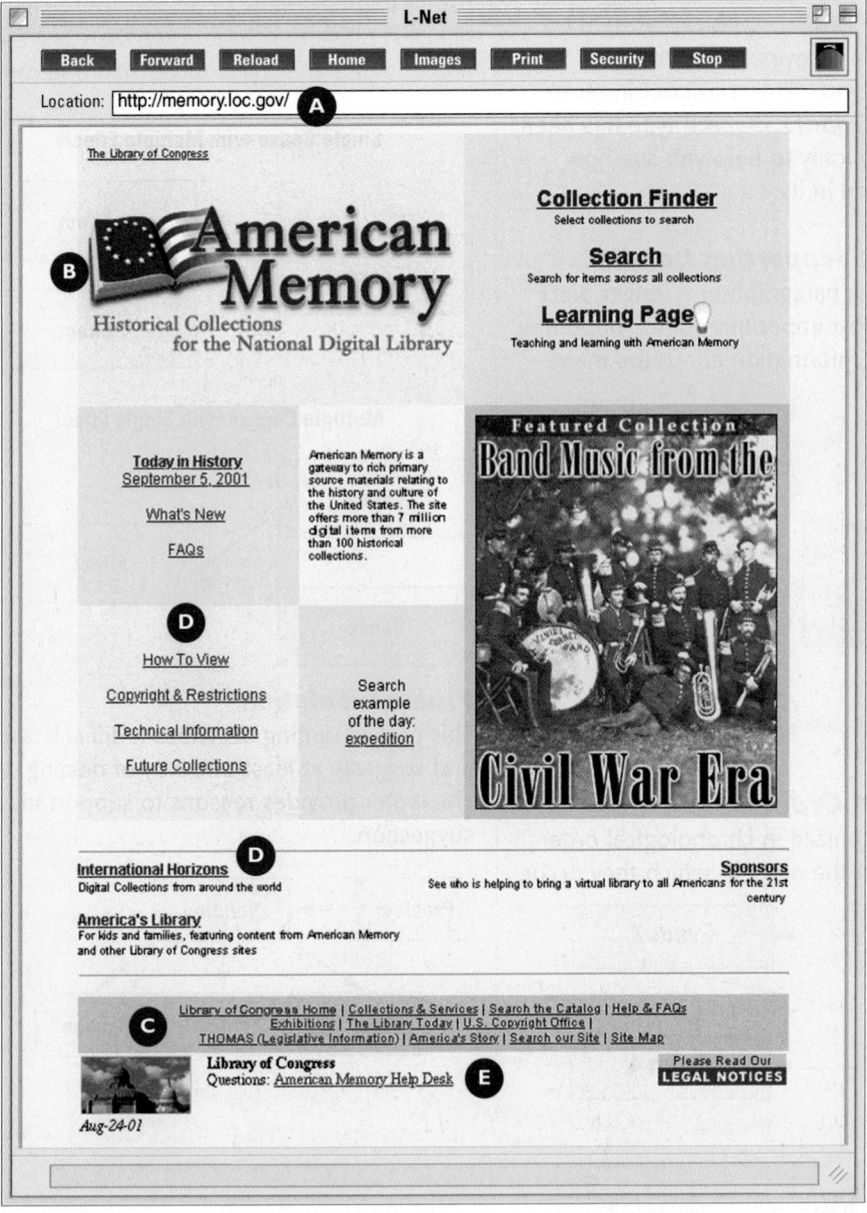

Patterns of Organization

Reading any type of writing is easier if you understand how it is organized. A writer organizes ideas in a sequence, or structure, that helps the reader see how the ideas are related. Five important structures are the following:

- main idea and supporting details
- chronological order
- comparison and contrast
- cause and effect
- problem-solution

This page contains an overview of the five structures, which you will learn about in more detail on pages *1255–1259*. Each type has been represented graphically to help you see how ideas are organized in it.

Main Idea and Supporting Details

The main idea of a paragraph or a longer piece of writing is its most important point. Supporting details give more information about the main idea.

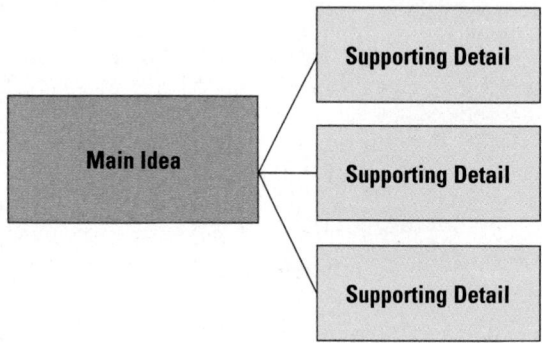

Chronological Order

Writing that is organized in chronological order presents events in the order in which they occur.

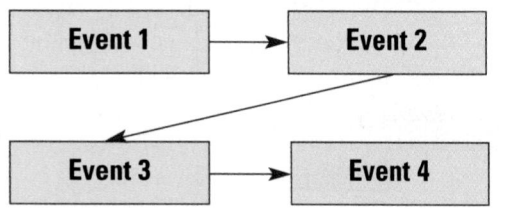

Comparison and Contrast

Comparison-and-contrast writing explains how two or more subjects are similar and how they are different.

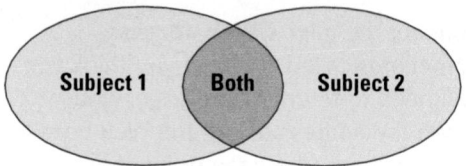

Cause and Effect

Cause-and-effect writing explains the relationship between events. A cause is an event that gives rise to another event, or a condition, called an effect. A cause may have more than one effect, and an effect may have more than one cause.

Single Cause with Multiple Effects

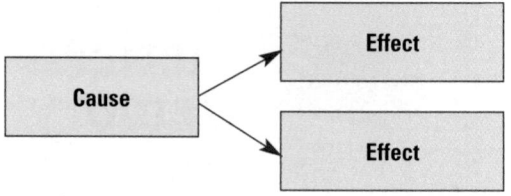

Multiple Causes with Single Effect

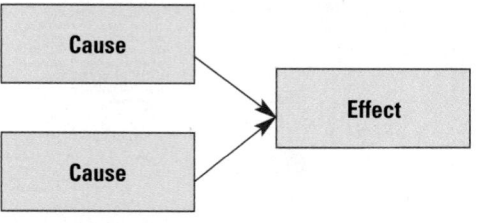

Problem-Solution

This type of writing describes a difficult issue and suggests at least one way of dealing with it. The writer provides reasons to support his or her suggestion.

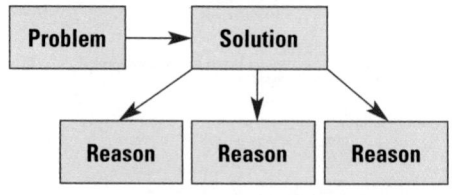

Main Idea and Supporting Details

The **main idea** of a paragraph is the basic point the writer is making in that paragraph. The **supporting details** give you additional information about the main idea. A main idea may be stated directly, or it may be implied. If it is stated, it may appear anywhere in the paragraph. Often it appears in the first or the last sentence. An implied main idea is suggested through the details that are provided.

Strategies for Reading

- To find the **main idea,** ask, What is this paragraph about?
- To find **supporting details,** ask, What else do I learn about the main idea?

MODEL

Main Idea in the First Sentence

Main idea

More than one factor caused the farmland of the Great Plains to become a dust bowl in the 1930s. Overgrazing and overplowing stripped the fields bare of natural grasses whose roots kept the soil in place. When the rains stopped coming as frequently as they had, the soil dried out. The dry topsoil was easily carried off by the wind. Then blowing clouds of dirt worsened problems by blocking out sunlight, burying gardens and chicken coops, and covering train tracks and roads.

Supporting details

MODEL

Main Idea in the Last Sentence

Supporting details

During the 1930s, many U.S. farmers needed help to survive. To aid them, Congress passed a soil-conservation act. This act allowed farmers to get government money for producing less of those crops that wear out the soil, such as cotton and wheat. Congress also created the Resettlement Administration, which loaned small farmers money to buy

Main idea

land. Many of Franklin D. Roosevelt's New Deal programs helped American farmers to recover from the economic and environmental crises of the 1930s.

MODEL

Implied Main Idea

Implied main idea: Wind erosion reduces the productivity of farm fields in many ways.

When farm fields are dry and bare, wind easily erodes them. The first thing the wind carries away is their nutrient-rich topsoil, leaving the fields less fertile. Blowing grit may, in turn, harm whatever plants are standing, resulting in the production of fewer seeds. Dust clouds may also blot out sunlight, which is vital to plant growth. For this reason, too, wind erosion can result in reduced crop production.

PRACTICE AND APPLY

During the 1930s, the Great Plains became a dust bowl of drifting dirt and sand. As a result, many Midwestern farmers lost, sold, or simply abandoned their land. After all, producing crops in such terrain was nearly impossible, and without crops to sell, most farmers could not afford to make their mortgage payments. So either farmers lost their farms when banks foreclosed on overdue mortgages or they sold their land at ridiculously low prices. Some farmers simply abandoned their land and went off to make better lives elsewhere.

Read the paragraph above and then do the following activities:

1. Identify the main idea of the paragraph and tell whether it is stated or implied.

2. List at least three details that support or expand on the main idea.

Chronological Order

Chronological order, also called time order, is the order in which events happen. It is also an order in which they may be presented. Historical events are usually presented in chronological order. Similarly, the steps of a process are often presented in the order in which they should happen.

Strategies for Reading

- Look for the **individual events** or **steps in the sequence.**
- Look for words and phrases that identify **time,** such as *in 1871, within the year, by 1872, on that day, earlier,* and *later.*
- Look for words that signal **order,** such as *first, afterward, then, before, during, eventually,* and *next.*

MODEL

> Time words and phrases
>
> Event
>
> **In 1871, Alexander Graham Bell came to Boston for a few weeks to lecture on his father's system for teaching speech to the deaf.** What he didn't know was that this brief trip would have a dramatic impact on his life. Bell's lectures amazed audiences, prompting other Bostonians to extend similar invitations to him. **Within the year,** the Scottish-born teacher and scientist found himself living in Boston—although he had moved with his parents from London, England, to Ontario, Canada, **just a**
>
> Order words
>
> **year before.**
> **By 1872,** Bell had opened a school in Boston for training teachers of the deaf. **In 1873,** he accepted a teaching position at Boston University as professor of vocal physiology.
> **During this period,** Bell also met Thomas Watson, a young repair mechanic and model maker. Inspired by Bell's ideas and eager to help the inventor, Watson teamed up with Bell. **For over two years** the men worked together to create an apparatus for transmitting sound by electricity. **Then, on April 6, 1875,** Bell acquired a patent for a multiple telegraph. A

little less than a year later, on the heels of their first success, the two created the first telephone.

The first "telephonic communication" took place on March 10, 1876. On that day, Bell called to his assistant over a new transmitter he was trying out, "Mr. Watson! Come here! I want you!" and Mr. Watson heard him.

There was more work to do before others would have actual telephone service, of course. By 1915, however, coast-to-coast telephone communication was a reality.

By then, the two had also succeeded in inventing many other useful devices. In fact, although Bell is best known for inventing the telephone, he was also the father of many other equally amazing devices and scientific advancements.

PRACTICE AND APPLY

Reread the model and then do the following activities:

1. List at least six words or phrases in the model that show time or order.

2. Draw a time line beginning with Bell's arrival in Ontario, Canada, in 1870 and ending with the availability of coast-to-coast phone service in 1915. Chart on the time line each major event described in the model.

Comparison and Contrast

Comparison-and-contrast writing explains how two subjects are alike and different. This type of writing is usually organized by subject or by feature. In **subject organization,** the writer discusses first one subject, then the other. In **feature organization,** the writer compares a feature of one subject with the same feature of the other, then compares another feature of both, and so on.

Strategies for Reading

- Look for words and phrases that signal **comparison,** such as *like, alike, similarly, both,* and *in the same way.*
- Look for words and phrases that signal **contrast,** such as *unlike, in contrast, differ,* and *different.*

MODEL

Subjects

Comparison words and phrases

Contrast words and phrases

Booker T. Washington and W. E. B. Du Bois were alike in many ways. Both were devoted to helping their fellow African Americans attain equal rights. Both were educated black men with university teaching positions. Both also worked passionately toward their goal at the beginning of the 20th century. Nevertheless, they were not allies. Why? They had very different ideas about how blacks should go about attaining equal rights.

Washington believed that for black people to achieve equal status and power as citizens they needed to focus on learning crafts, farming, and industrial skills. He argued that by gaining such vocational skills and the economic security that would surely follow, black people would naturally earn the respect and acceptance of the white community. In Washington's opinion, however, to earn an education and economic security, black people would need to let go temporarily of the fight for civil rights and political power.

In contrast to Washington, W. E. B. Du Bois believed that black people

could not afford to stop fighting for civil rights and political power. In his opinion, only agitation and protest would achieve social change. According to Du Bois, in the climate of extreme racism that existed in America at the time, Washington's approach would merely cause blacks to suffer even more oppression.

So although these two African-American contemporaries had the same goal, their different approaches to achieving this goal made them adversaries rather than allies.

PRACTICE AND APPLY

Reread the model and then answer the following questions:

1. Is the model organized by subject or by feature?

2. In a sentence or two, summarize Washington's approach to attaining civil rights. Then summarize Du Bois's approach.

3. List three words or phrases that the writer uses to signal comparison or contrast.

Cause and Effect

A **cause** is an event, or something that happens. An **effect** is a result of an event. A cause-and-effect relationship exists when one event brings about, or causes, another event or a condition. When writers want to explain cause-and-effect relationships, they usually arrange the cause(s) and effect(s) in one of three ways:

1. as a description of the cause(s) followed by an explanation of the effect(s)
2. as a description of the effect(s) followed by an explanation of the cause(s)
3. as a chain of causes and effects

These patterns of organization are all examples of **cause-and-effect order.**

Strategies for Reading

- To find the **effect(s),** ask, What happened?
- To find the **cause(s),** ask, Why did that happen?
- Look for **words and phrases that signal relationships between events,** such as *because, as a result, for that reason, so, consequently,* and *since.*

MODEL

Cause	In 1872 a group of tourists were awestruck by the deep canyons, dense pine forests, and refreshing rivers and waterfalls of Yellowstone, Montana.
Effect that in turn becomes a cause	They were so moved by the area's natural wonders, in fact, that they immediately wanted to protect them.
Signal words and phrases	So they trooped off to Washington, D.C., to demand that Yellowstone lands be set aside for public use. There, before Congress, with the help of breathtaking paintings and photographs by artists who had ventured to Yellowstone with government land surveyors, these passionate preservationists presented their case. Dazzled, Congress
Effect	responded to their pleas by creating the first national park, Yellowstone National Park.

The next several national parks owe their establishment primarily to the enthusiasm and persuasive abilities of one nature lover, John Muir.

Muir took influential friends such as Ralph Waldo Emerson and Theodore Roosevelt on spectacular hikes through the Sierras. While on these hikes, he expressed his love of nature in passionate arguments for its preservation. In 1890, largely as a result of Muir's efforts, Yosemite, Sequoia, and General Grant national parks were established.

Interestingly, however, about 25 percent of today's national parks owe their preservation to looters—or rather, to a Congress roused into action by looters. In 1906, because Congress was concerned that widespread plundering of precious Southwestern archaeological sites was destroying important artifacts, it enacted a law to prevent such plundering. This law, called the Antiquities Act, authorized the president to set aside as national monuments extremely precious or threatened lands. Consequently, by calling on the powers granted to him under this law, President Theodore Roosevelt was able to put under government protection many sites that might otherwise have been destroyed. These sites would eventually earn national-park status.

PRACTICE AND APPLY

Reread the model and then do the following activities:

1. In the cause-and-effect relationship of which they were a part, were looters a cause or an effect? On a cause-and-effect graphic organizer, show at least one cause-and-effect relationship in which looters were involved. To view samples of cause-and-effect graphic organizers, see page 1254 of this Reading Handbook.

2. List two cause-and-effect signal words or phrases that appear in the model.

Problem-Solution

Problem-solution writing describes a difficult issue or problem and offers a solution for it. In such writing, the writer uses logical arguments to convince readers that the proposed solution will solve the problem. The writer may also explain how to carry out the solution.

Strategies for Reading

- To find the **problem,** ask, What is this writing about?
- To find the **solution,** ask, What suggestion does the writer offer to remedy the problem?
- Look for the **reasons** the writer gives for choosing this solution. Is the thinking behind them logical? Is the evidence given to support them strong and convincing?
- Look for any **first steps** the writer recommends taking to carry out this solution. Ask, Are these steps clear and doable?

MODEL

You and some friends are interested in creating your own magazine. You also have several friends who want to start a band, and your sister wants to know more about Web-page design. You look in your textbooks for help, but you don't find the explanations you need. **Frustrated, you and**

Problem — **your friends find yourselves wondering how you can get the help you really need—the help of experts.**

Solution — **One solution is to establish a visiting-artists program at your school.** A visiting-artists program is a formal means of getting visual and performing artists, poets and writers, computer-graphics experts, and other kinds of professional artists to visit your school. Once such a program is established, a school official could schedule and pay for visits by professional artists and arrange for interested students to attend the workshops and lectures given by them. Consequently, **establishing such a**

Reasons — **program would enable you and your friends to get hands-on instruction from experts.**

A good first step toward establishing such a program is to form a committee of students interested in getting the program adopted at your school. At the start, the committee would just conduct research to learn the following:
- which community organizations provide schools with names of artists who will come to visit
- which organizations provide money to support visiting-artists programs at schools, and what the procedure for applying for this money is
- how well visiting-artists programs have worked at other schools
- how many students would be interested in having such a program
- which teacher(s) would be willing to volunteer time to help run the program

A good second step toward establishing such a program is to draft a proposal that you can give to the school faculty and administrators. In this proposal, you would need to do the following:
- give school officials reasons for establishing the program
- show officials how the program could be implemented easily
- support your claims with research

Establishing a visiting-artists program may seem like a lot of trouble just to solve the problems you and your friends face. However, once the program is in place, you and others will be able to continue benefiting from it, exploring new interests and career options. For example, maybe next year you'll want to learn how to produce your own video, create special effects for movies, or become a makeup artist. With a visiting-artists program in place, you can learn about all those endeavors and more.

PRACTICE AND APPLY

Reread the model and then answer the following questions:

1. What solution does the writer offer?

2. What reasons does she give for adopting it?

3. What steps does the writer suggest the students follow to enact this solution?

Functional Reading

Functional reading is reading to discover such information as instruction in how to do something. When you read a map, a memo, or an instruction manual, you are engaged in functional reading. These guidelines show how you can improve your functional-reading skills.

Instruction Manual

Strategies for Reading

A Look at the **title** on the page to discover what the text is about.

B Read the lists of **bulleted items** carefully. The bulleted points are usually the essential pieces of information.

C Be sure to read the text that immediately precedes a visual. This **lead-in text** can help you understand what the visual is intended to show.

D Pay attention to **captions** with pictures or drawings. These will help you interpret what you are seeing.

E Study **visuals** closely. These will help you interpret what you are reading and may even provide information not covered in the text.

A Rules of the Road: Passing

Always use caution when passing another vehicle. When passing via the left lane on a two-lane highway, make sure that all of the following are true:

- you can see the left lane clearly
- **B** the left lane is free of oncoming traffic for a distance great enough to allow you to pass
- you are sure that you will be able to return to your lane before you are within 200 feet of an oncoming vehicle

- you can see the car you have just passed in your rearview mirror before you re-enter the right-hand lane

Do not pass via the left lane of a two-lane highway in any of the situations shown on the diagram below.

C In each of the following situations, the red car is breaking the law.

In a no passing zone   On a hill   **D**   Within 100 feet of a bridge, viaduct, tunnel, or railroad crossing   On a curve where you cannot see oncoming vehicles

25

PRACTICE AND APPLY

Reread the page from the driving-instruction manual and then answer the following questions:

1. What essential piece of information does the lead-in text provide about the visual on this page?

2. What are the four driving situations described in which a driver should not pass another vehicle?

3. What do all of the bulleted items concern?

4. What information about lane markings can you gain from the visual that you do not learn from the text on this page?

Technical Manual

Strategies for Reading

A Read the **title** to learn what material the page covers. This page, from a car owner's manual, explains how to operate the radio that comes with the car.

B Examine **pictures** or other **graphics**. Pictures can help you familiarize yourself with the various parts of an item or a process.

C Read any **labels** or **captions** that identify parts of the picture. These labels can help you locate buttons or other components.

D Check **numbered** or **lettered text** to see if it is linked by corresponding numbers or letters to parts of a diagram or illustration. If it is, refer to the picture as you read.

E Read the **text** carefully to learn how to perform particular tasks. If the manual presents the steps of a process in paragraph form, look for signal words such as *first, next, then,* and *finally* to learn the order in which you should follow the instructions.

PRACTICE AND APPLY

Using the manual below, answer the questions.

1. How do you select scan-tuning mode? How do you deactivate this mode?

2. What steps must you follow to preset a station?

A How to Operate the Radio

The following diagram of your factory-installed radio shows the locations of its various features.

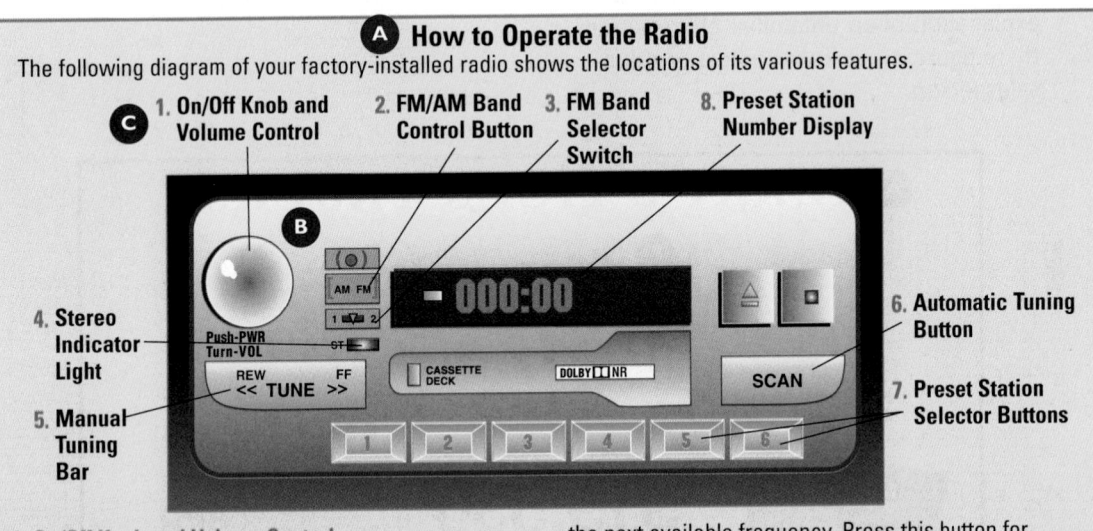

C 1. On/Off Knob and Volume Control 2. FM/AM Band Control Button 3. FM Band Selector Switch 8. Preset Station Number Display

4. Stereo Indicator Light 5. Manual Tuning Bar 6. Automatic Tuning Button 7. Preset Station Selector Buttons

D

1. On/Off Knob and Volume Control
Push this knob to turn the radio on or off. **E**

2. FM/AM Band Control Button
Press this button to select the AM band and a red light appears. Press this button a second time to deselect the AM band and tune in FM stations.

3. FM Band Selector Switch
Move this switch left to select FM band 1 or right to select FM band 2. *Note: This is inoperative when the AM band is selected.*

4. Stereo Indicator Light (ST)
When the radio receives an FM signal clear enough to produce in stereo, it does so and the light comes on.

5. Manual Tuning Bar
Press the left side of the button to select stations in descending order of frequency. Press the right side to select stations in ascending order.

6. Automatic Tuning Button
Press this button for less than 2 seconds to jump up to the next available frequency. Press this button for longer than 2 seconds to activate scan-tuning.

In scan-tuning mode, the radio jumps to the next station, remains there for 5 seconds, then jumps to the next station, remains there for 5 seconds, and so on, until the button is briefly pressed again.

7. Preset Station Selector Buttons
Use these buttons to preset 18 of your favorite radio stations (12 FM and 6 AM) by following these steps:

1. Select FM or AM with the FM/AM Band Control Button.

2. Select the station using manual tuning or scan-tuning.

3. Press and hold one of the preset station selector buttons until you hear a beep (about 3 seconds).

To change a preset station, repeat the steps above.

8. Preset Station Number Display
When a station or frequency is being broadcast, its number is displayed on this panel.

Product Advertisement

Strategies for Reading

(A) Read any **titles** or **subtitles** in the advertisement to find out what the product is and who is selling it.

(B) Study any **pictures** of the product. Does the product appear to fit your needs?

(C) Look for **essential information** such as price, features, and the location or phone number of the company selling the product.

(D) Make sure you understand any **abbreviations.** In the ad shown, *P/S, P/B,* and *P/W* stand for *power steering, power brakes,* and *power windows.* If there is no explanation of an unfamiliar abbreviation, try to figure it out from context or ask a salesperson.

(E) Look for **small print** in the advertisement. Small print often contains important information such as warnings, limitations, exclusions, end dates, and notice of extra fees.

PRACTICE AND APPLY

Reread the advertisement and then answer the following questions:

1. List at least four features of the truck that is advertised.
2. What does the abbreviation *APR* stand for?
3. Who qualifies for the rebate?
4. What four fees must a buyer pay in addition to the $15,530 purchase price?
5. When does the offer expire?

(A) TERRY'S TIGER TRUCKS

(B)

NEW TIGER TRUCK

(C) YOUR PRICE **$15,530***

0.9% APR (annual percentage rate) FINANCING

(D) • P/S, P/B, P/W
• Leather Seats
• Compact Spare Tire
• Halogen Headlights
• Air Bags
• 12.5-Gallon Fuel Tank
• Floor Mats
• AM/FM Radio

CALL **(C) 555-1769** TODAY

(E) *Plus tax, title, license, and $50.48 document fee. Qualified buyers with approved credit only. Must qualify for first-time buyer rebate; some customers will not qualify. One offer per purchase. Offer expires 3 days from publication.

Product Manual

Strategies for Reading

(A) Read the **title** to learn what material the page covers. This page is from the owner's manual of a car.

(B) Look for **numbered steps** or a **bulleted list** detailing how to perform a particular task.

(C) Notice any **subheads** that tell what a section of text is about. Also look for **labels,** such as *Diagram 1* or *Figure A.*

(D) Study any **pictures** or other **graphics** in the manual. If you are having trouble following the instructions, pictures can help you pinpoint where you are going wrong.

(E) Notice any **warning symbols,** such as exclamation points or stop signs. These symbols are meant to call your attention to special instructions that must be followed to complete the task safely and properly.

PRACTICE AND APPLY

Reread the manual page and then answer the following questions:

1. What does this page explain how to do?

2. According to the instructions, what should you do to the tire diagonally opposite to the one being changed?

3. If you turned the wheel wrench clockwise, would the jack go up or down?

4. Why is it important to not start the engine while the vehicle is on the jack and to make sure the jack is on a level and solid surface?

(A) How to Change a Tire, page 1 of 3

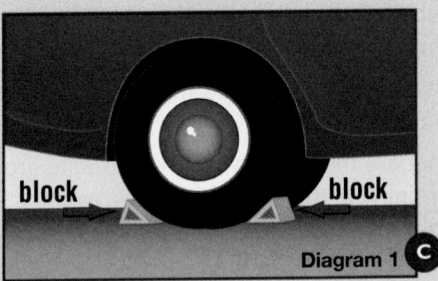

block   block

Diagram 1 (C)

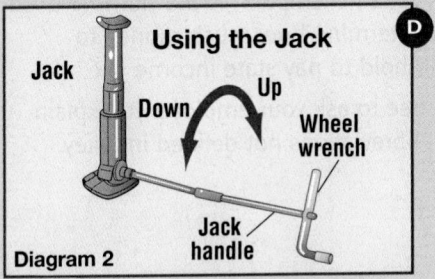

Using the Jack (D)

Jack   Down   Up   Wheel wrench

Diagram 2   Jack handle

To avoid injury when changing a tire, follow these instructions:

1. Set the parking brake firmly.
2. Set the transmission in "Reverse."
3. Turn off the ignition.
4. Unload the vehicle.

5. Block both sides of the wheel that is diagonally opposite to the one being changed with blocks or other items that can be wedged solidly under the wheel (as shown in Diagram 1).

When changing a tire, beware of the surrounding traffic.

! WARNING ! E

To further avoid injury:

- Never use a jack from any other vehicle to lift your vehicle.
- Make sure the jack is on a level, solid surface.
- Never get underneath the vehicle when using the jack.
- Do not start the engine while the vehicle is on the jack.

Pay Stub

Strategies for Reading

(A) Scan the entire pay stub to see whether the **personal information** and number of **hours** worked are correct. If anything is inaccurate, report it to your employer immediately.

(B) Look for explanations of **abbreviations** that are used on the stub. These may appear at the bottom of the stub or on the back. Some abbreviations are so commonly used, however, that they will probably not be defined in a key. These are

- *y.t.d.,* which means "year to date"—that is, up to the present date in this year
- *fed. ex.,* meaning "federal exemption," which is a number used to figure out how much of one's pay should be withheld to pay federal income tax
- *state ex.,* meaning "state exemption." The state exemption is the number used to determine how much money to withhold to pay state income tax

Feel free to ask your employer to explain any abbreviations not defined in a key.

(C) Pay particular attention to the **dollar amounts** listed as federal and state income-tax withholdings, health-insurance deductions, and other **types of deductions.** If any of these strike you as excessive, feel free to ask how they were calculated.

(D) See the **net pay** figure to learn the actual amount of money you are taking home.

(E) If you wish to see how many **vacation days, sick days,** or **personal days** you have earned, look at the **accumulations section.**

PRACTICE AND APPLY

Reread the pay stub and then answer the following questions:

1. How many hours did this employee work during this pay period?

2. What amount did she pay for union dues during this period?

3. For the entire year to the present date, how much money has been deducted from this employee's income?

4. What is this employee's net pay for this pay period?

5. What are this employee's year-to-date gross earnings? Is this figure the same as the employee's year-to-date taxable earnings?

LOCATION	EMPLOYEE NAME		SOC. SEC. NO.	FED. EX.	STATE EX.	PAY PERIOD ENDING	CHECK NO.
Park #87	Haley Allen Simpson	**(A)**	987-65-4320	S-000	S-000	07/27/01	552573

987-65-4320

STATEMENT OF EARNINGS & LEAVE - NON-NEGOTIABLE
THIS IS A STATEMENT OF YOUR EARNINGS, DEDUCTIONS AND LEAVE. DETACH AND RETAIN FOR YOUR RECORDS

DEDUCTIONS

TYPE	HOURS	AMOUNT	TYPE	AMOUNT	Y.T.D.	TYPE	AMOUNT	Y.T.D.
REG **(A)**	80.00	747.20	FIT	96.79 **(C)**	245.54			
			SIT	22.42	58.29			
			DUE	4.05	12.15			
						TOTAL	123.26	315.98
TOTAL	80.00	747.20						

EARNINGS	747.20
DEDUCTIONS **(D)**	123.26
NET PAY	623.94

Y.T.D. GROSS EARNINGS	1942.72
Y.T.D. TAXABLE EARNINGS	1942.72
Y.T.D. F.I.C.A. EARNINGS	

ACCUMULATIONS

VACATION	0.0001
(E) SICK/PERSONAL TIME	0.0001

EMPLOYEE #	12329

Union dues.................DUE	Medicare...............MED	Garnishments...............GAR	State Tax Levy...............STA
Park Pension ....PEN	Federal Witholdings.....FIT	Child Support...............CHS	Federal Tax Levy.............FED
Municipal Pension .....PEN	State Witholdings....**(B)**.SIT	Hospitalization-Dent. ...DEN	Illinois Student Loan ....STU
Laborers Pension.......PEN	Hamilton Insurance ......HAM	Education Loan ....EDU	Federal Student Loan ......FSL
Social Security...........SOC	Equitable Life Ins. ....EQU	Credit Union (Bank).........CRE	City Parking/Water...........PAR

Medicine Label

Strategies for Reading

(A) Check the **Uses** section to make sure the medication can be used to treat your symptoms.

(B) Study the **directions,** which tell how much of the medication you should take and how often to take it.

(C) Always study the **warnings** and **drug-interaction precautions** on any medicine label. It is important to familiarize yourself with these sections in case there is any reason you should not take the medication or anything you should not do while taking the medication.

(D) Read the lists of both **active** and **inactive ingredients** to see whether the medication contains any ingredients to which you know you react unfavorably. Also check these lists if you are surprised by a negative reaction to the medicine. Doing so may help you to discover ingredients you should avoid in the future.

PRACTICE AND APPLY

1. Name three symptoms that would be relieved by this product.

2. Should an 11-year-old child take this product to relieve hay-fever symptoms? Why or why not?

3. Name two active ingredients and two inactive ingredients. What are the purposes of the active ingredients you named?

4. What does the tampering warning say?

No-Sneeze
Allergy Sinus Tablets

(A) Uses

No-Sneeze can be used for the temporary relief of sinus congestion and pressure, sinus pain, nasal congestion, headache, runny nose, sneezing, itching of the nose or throat, itchy and watery eyes due to hay fever.

(B) Directions

Adults & children 12 years of age and older:
Take 2 tablets every 4–5 hours. Do not take more than 6 tablets in 24 hours except as directed by a doctor.

Children under 12 years:
Do not use this adult product in children under 12 years of age. This will provide more than the recommended dose (overdose) and could cause serious health problems.

(C) Warnings

Do not exceed maximum specified in directions. Do not take for pain for more than 7 days unless directed by a doctor. If pain or fever persists or worsens, if new symptoms develop, or if redness or swelling is present, consult a doctor. These could be signs of a serious condition. May cause excitability. If nervousness, dizziness, or sleeplessness occurs, discontinue use and consult a doctor. May cause drowsiness; alcohol, sedatives, and tranquilizers may increase the drowsiness effect. Avoid alcoholic beverages while taking this

product. Do not take this product if you are taking sedatives or tranquilizers without first consulting your doctor. Use caution when driving a motor vehicle or operating machinery. Do not take this product, unless directed by a doctor, if you have a breathing problem such as emphysema or chronic bronchitis, or if you have glaucoma, or difficulty in urination due to enlargement of the prostate gland. Do not take this product if you have heart disease, high blood pressure, thyroid disease, or diabetes, unless directed by a doctor. As with any drug, if you are pregnant or nursing a baby, seek the advice of a health professional before using this product.

Keep this and all drugs out of the reach of children. In case of accidental overdose, contact a doctor or a Poison Control Center immediately. Prompt medical attention is critical for adults as well as children even if you do not notice any signs or symptoms of overdose.

Drug Interaction Precautions Do not use with other products containing acetaminophen. Do not use this product if you are now taking a prescription monoamine oxidase inhibitor (MAOI) (certain drugs for depression, psychiatric or emotional conditions, or Parkinson's disease), or for 2 weeks after stopping the MAOI drug. If you are uncertain whether your prescription drug contains an MAOI, consult a health professional before using this product.

DO NOT USE IF CARTON IS OPEN, PROTECTIVE SEAL IS BROKEN, OR BLISTER UNIT IS BROKEN.

(D)

Active Ingredients: (in each tablet)	Purposes:
Acetaminophen, 500 mg	Pain reliever
Chlorpheniramine maleate, 2 mg	Antihistamine
Pseudoephedrine HCl, 30 mg	Nasal decongestant

Inactive Ingredients:
Benzyl Alcohol, Butylparaben, Castor Oil, Corn Starch, D&C

Yellow #10, Edetate Calcium Disodium, FD&C Blue #1, Hydroxypropyl Methylcellulose, Magnesium Stearate, Methylparaben, Propylparaben, Sodium Lauryl Sulfate, Sodium Propionate, Sodium Starch Glycolate, Titanium Dioxide.

Store at room temperature and avoid high humidity and excessive heat above 40°C (104°F).
See side panel for expiration date and lot number.

Passport Application

For most travel outside the United States, you must have a passport. Consequently, if you are a United States citizen, at some point you will likely need to fill out the passport application shown here. The instructions and other information on page 2 of this application will instruct you in how to do this. The strategies on the next page can also help.

A UNITED STATES DEPARTMENT OF STATE
APPLICATION FOR ☐ PASSPORT ☐ REGISTRATION
(Type or print all capital letters in blue or black ink in white areas only)

D

1. NAME (First and Middle)

LAST

2. MAIL PASSPORT TO: STREET / RFD # OR P.O. BOX   APT. #

CITY   STATE

ZIP CODE   COUNTRY / IN CARE OF (if applicable)

IMPORTANT
PLEASE READ
INSTRUCTIONS ON
PAGE 2!

☐ 5 Yr.   ☐ 10 Yr.   Issue Date

R   D   O   DP

End. # _____   Exp. _____

3. SEX ☐ M ☐ F

4. PLACE OF BIRTH (City & State or City & Country)

5. DATE OF BIRTH   Month   Day   Year

6. SOCIAL SECURITY NUMBER (SEE FEDERAL TAX LAW NOTICE ON PAGE 2)

7. HEIGHT Feet | Inches

8. HAIR COLOR

9. EYE COLOR

10. HOME TELEPHONE ( )

11. BUSINESS TELEPHONE ( )

12. OCCUPATION

13. PERMANENT ADDRESS (DO NOT LIST P.O. BOX)   STREET/RFD #   CITY   STATE   ZIP CODE

FOLD

14. FATHER'S FULL NAME Last   First | BIRTHPLACE | BIRTHDATE | U.S. CITIZEN ☐ Yes ☐ No

15. MOTHER'S FULL MAIDEN NAME Last   First | BIRTHPLACE | BIRTHDATE | U.S. CITIZEN ☐ Yes ☐ No

16. HAVE YOU EVER BEEN MARRIED? ☐ Yes ☐ No | SPOUSE'S OR FORMER SPOUSE'S FULL NAME AT BIRTH Last   First | BIRTHPLACE | BIRTHDATE | U.S. CITIZEN ☐ Yes ☐ No

DATE OF MOST RECENT MARRIAGE   Month   Day   Year | WIDOWED/DIVORCED? ☐ Yes Give Date ☐ No   Month   Day   Year | 17. OTHER NAMES YOU HAVE USED (1)   (2)

18. HAVE YOU EVER BEEN ISSUED A U.S. PASSPORT? ☐ Yes ☐ No   IF YES, COMPLETE NEXT LINE AND SUBMIT PASSPORT IF AVAILABLE.

NAME IN WHICH ISSUED   MOST RECENT PASSPORT NUMBER   APPROXIMATE ISSUE DATE Month   Day   Year

DISPOSITION ☐ Submitted ☐ Stolen ☐ Lost ☐ Other _____

C

S T A P L E

FROM 1" TO 1 - 3/8"

2" x 2"

S T A P L E

S T A P L E

SUBMIT TWO RECENT IDENTICAL PHOTOS

S T A P L E

D

FOLD

It is necessary to submit a statement with an application for a new passport when a previous valid or potentially valid passport cannot be presented. The statement must set forth in detail why the previous passport cannot be presented. Use Form DSP-64.

19. EMERGENCY CONTACT. If you wish, you may supply the name, address and telephone number of a person not traveling with you to be contacted in case of emergency.

NAME

STREET

CITY   STATE   ZIP CODE

TELEPHONE ( )   RELATIONSHIP

20. TRAVEL PLANS (not mandatory)   Month   Day   Year
Date of Trip
Length of Trip
COUNTRIES TO BE VISITED

21. STOP. DO NOT SIGN APPLICATION UNTIL REQUESTED TO DO SO BY PERSON ADMINISTERING OATH.
I have not, since acquiring United States citizenship, performed any of the acts listed under "Acts or Conditions" on the reverse of this application form (unless explanatory statement is attached). I solemnly swear (or affirm) that the statements made on this application are true and the photograph attached is a true likeness of me.

X _____   X _____
Parent's/Legal Guardian's Signature if identifying minor child   Applicant's Signature - age 13 or older

E

22. FOR ACCEPTANCE AGENT'S USE
Subscribed and sworn to (affirmed) before me   Month   Day   Year   (SEAL)

(Signature of person authorized to accept application)

☐ Clerk of Court; Location _____
☐ PASSPORT Agent
☐ Postal Employee
☐ (Vice) Consul USA

23. APPLICANT'S IDENTIFYING DOCUMENTS
☐ DRIVER'S LICENSE   ISSUE DATE: Month Day Year   EXPIRATION DATE: Month Day Year   ID No. _____
☐ PASSPORT
☐ OTHER (Specify) _____   PLACE OF ISSUE: _____   ISSUED IN THE NAME OF: _____

24. FOR ISSUING OFFICE USE ONLY (Applicant's evidence of citizenship)
☐ Birth Certificate   SR   CR   City   Filed/Issued:
☐ Passport   Bearer's Name:
☐ Report of Birth
☐ Naturalization/Citizenship Cert.   No.:   Issued:
☐ Other:
☐ Seen & Returned
☐ Attached

APPLICATION APPROVAL

25.
FEE _____   EXEC. _____   EF _____   OTHER _____

B

FORM DSP-11 (12-97)   (SEE INSTRUCTIONS ON PAGE 2)

Page 1
Form Approved OMB No. 1405-0004 (Exp. 5/31/2001) Estimated Burden - 20 Minutes*

Strategies for Reading

A Beginning at the top, scan the entire application to see what the different sections are. Watch for **headings** that identify the sections and **lines** that divide one section from another.

B Notice **sections you should not or need not fill in.**

C Look for **difficult words** or **abbreviations**—such as *disposition* ("present location or status"), *mandatory* ("required, necessary"), *M* ("male"), and *F* ("female")—and determine what they mean.

D Notice **instructions** that tell you how to fill out particular sections of the application. Also notice instructions about **other materials you may need to provide.**

E Pay special attention to any part of the application that calls for your **signature.** Be sure to read all statements carefully before signing your name to them.

PRACTICE AND APPLY

Reread the application and then answer the following questions:

1. When are you supposed to sign this application? If you are a minor child, who else must sign the form?

2. How many photos must you submit? What must each photograph show? What size must each be? How must you attach at least one of the photos?

3. What do all the areas of the application that you are not supposed to fill out have in common?

4. Which numbered item relates to travel plans? If you already have travel plans, do you have to include information about them?

5. If you had a valid passport before but cannot present it, what must you submit? On what form must you submit this?

UNITED STATES DEPARTMENT OF STATE
PASSPORT APPLICATION
HOW TO APPLY FOR A U.S. PASSPORT

FOR INQUIRIES (A fee is charged for this service.): National Passport Information Center, 1-900-225-5674, For TDD: 1-900-225-7778 **OR** For Credit Card Users: 1-888-362-8668, For TDD: 1-888-498-3648

U.S. passports are issued only to U.S. citizens or nationals. Each person must obtain his or her own passport. IF YOU ARE A FIRST-TIME APPLICANT, please complete and submit this application in person. (Applicants under 13 years of age usually need not appear in person unless requested. A parent or guardian may execute the application on the child's behalf.) Each application must be accompanied by (1) PROOF OF U.S. CITIZENSHIP, (2) PROOF OF IDENTITY, (3) TWO PHOTOGRAPHS, (4) FEES (as explained below) to one of the following acceptance agents: a clerk of any Federal or State court of record or a judge or clerk of any probate court accepting applications; a designated municipal or county official; a designated postal employee at an authorized post office; or an agent at a Passport Agency in Boston, Chicago, Honolulu, Houston, Los Angeles, Miami, New Orleans, New York, Philadelphia, San Francisco, Seattle, Stamford, or Washington, D.C.; or a U.S. consular official.

IF YOU HAVE HAD A PREVIOUS PASSPORT, inquire about eligibility to use Form DSP-82 (mail-in application). Address requests for passport amendment, extension of validity, or additional visa pages to a Passport Agency or a U.S. Consulate or Embassy abroad. Check visa requirements with consular officials of countries to be visited well in advance of your departure.

(1) PROOF OF U.S. CITIZENSHIP.
(a) APPLICANTS BORN IN THE UNITED STATES. Submit previous U.S. passport or **certified** birth certificate. A birth certificate must include your given name and surname, date and place of birth, date the birth record was filed, and seal or other certification of the official custodian of such records. A record filed more than 1 year after the birth is acceptable if it is supported by evidence described in the next paragraph.

IF NO BIRTH RECORD EXISTS, submit registrar's notice to that effect. Also submit an early baptismal or circumcision certificate, hospital birth record, early census, school, or family Bible records, newspaper or insurance files, or notarized affidavits of persons having knowledge of your birth (preferably with at least one record listed above). Evidence should include your given name and surname, date and place of birth, and seal or other certification of office (if customary) and signature of issuing official.

(b) APPLICANTS BORN OUTSIDE THE UNITED STATES. Submit previous U.S. passport or Certificate of Naturalization, or Certificate of Citizenship, or a Report of Birth Abroad, or evidence described below.

IF YOU CLAIM CITIZENSHIP THROUGH NATURALIZATION OF PARENT(S), submit the Certificate(s) of Naturalization of your parent(s), your foreign birth certificate, and proof of your admission to the United States for permanent residence.

IF YOU CLAIM CITIZENSHIP THROUGH BIRTH ABROAD TO U.S. CITIZEN PARENT(S), submit a Consular Report of Birth (Form FS-240) or Certification of Birth (Form DS-1350 or FS-545), or your foreign birth certificate, parents' marriage certificate, proof of citizenship of your parent(s), and affidavit of U.S. citizen parent(s) showing all periods and places of residence/physical presence in the United States and abroad before your birth.

(2) PROOF OF IDENTITY. If you are not personally known to the acceptance agent, you must establish your identity to the agent's satisfaction. You may submit items such as the following containing your signature AND physical description or photograph that is a good likeness of you: previous U.S. passport; Certificate of Naturalization or of Citizenship; driver's license (not temporary or learner's license); or government (Federal, State, municipal) identification card or pass. Temporary or altered documents are not acceptable.

IF YOU CANNOT PROVE YOUR IDENTITY as stated above, you must appear with an IDENTIFYING WITNESS who is a U.S. citizen or permanent resident alien who has known you for at least 2 years. Your witness must prove his or her identity and complete and sign an Affidavit of Identifying Witness (Form DSP-71) before the acceptance agent. You must also submit some identification of your own.

(3) TWO PHOTOGRAPHS. Submit two identical photographs of you alone, sufficiently recent to be a good likeness (normally taken within the last 6 months), 2 x 2 inches in size, with an image size from bottom of chin to top of head (including hair) of between 1 and 1-3/8 inches. Photographs must be clear, front view, full face, taken in normal street attire without a hat or dark glasses, and printed on thin paper with a plain light (white or off-white) background. They may be black and white or color. They must be capable of withstanding a mounting temperature of 225° Fahrenheit (107° Celsius). Photographs retouched so that your appearance is changed are unacceptable. Snapshots, most vending machine prints, and magazine or full-length photographs are unacceptable.

(4) FEES. Submit $60 if you are 16 years of age or older. The passport fee is $45. In addition, a fee of $15 is charged for the execution of the application. Your passport will be valid for 10 years from the date of issue except where limited by the Secretary of State to a shorter period. Submit $40 if you are 15 years of age or younger. The passport fee is $25 and the execution fee is $15. Your passport will be valid for 5 years from the date of issue, except where limited as above.

Expedited service is available only in the United States. Expedite requests will be processed in 3 workdays from receipt at a Passport Agency. This service is available only for early departure, generally with proof of travel. The additional fee is $35.

Pay the passport and execution fees in one of the following forms: Checks-personal, certified, traveler's; bank draft or cashier's check; money order-U.S. Postal, international, currency exchange; or if abroad, the foreign currency equivalent, or a check drawn on a U.S. bank.

Make passport and execution fees payable to Passport Services (except if applying at a designated acceptance facility, such as a State court or municipal office, pay execution fee as required) or the appropriate Embassy or Consulate, if abroad. Pay special postage if applicable.

An additional adjudication fee of $100 will be charged to previously undocumented passport customers who were born outside the United States and who have not been issued any of the following documents: a U.S. passport, a Consular Report of Birth Abroad, a Certification of Report of Birth, a Certificate of Naturalization or a Certificate of Citizenship.

An additional $15 fee will be charged when, upon request, the Department of State verifies issuance of a previous U.S. passport or Consular Report of Birth Abroad because the customer is unable to submit evidence of U.S. citizenship.

No fee is charged to applicants with U.S. Government or military authorization for no-fee passports (except designated acceptance facilities may collect the execution fee).

FEDERAL TAX LAW:
26 U.S.C. 6039E (Internal Revenue Code) requires a passport applicant to provide his/her name and social security number. If you have not been issued a social security

❶ The Writing Process

Different writers use different processes. Try out different strategies and figure out what works best for you. For some assignments, it is best to start by figuring out what you need to end up with, make a plan or outline, and stick to it. Other writing assignments may be more successful if you start by writing everything you know about the topic, allow things to get messy, and then reshape and revise the writing so it fits the assignment. Try both approaches and get to know yourself as a writer.

Also consider whether the assignment is high-stakes or low-stakes writing. When the success of the piece is very important, such as in a test, you might choose to focus on meeting the requirements or criteria of the assignment. When the purpose of the writing is to develop your ideas, there is more opportunity to experiment and take risks. Take into account the time factor as well. In a timed writing test, you may not have time to explore and revise.

Correct grammar and spelling are very important in your final product. You don't need to focus on these as you shape your ideas and draft your piece, but be sure you allow time for a careful edit before turning in your final piece.

⓵ Prewriting

In the prewriting stage, you explore your ideas and discover what you want to write about.

Finding Ideas for Writing
Try one or more of the following techniques to help you find a writing topic.

Personal Techniques
- Practice imaging, or trying to remember mainly sensory details about a subject—its look, sound, feel, taste, and smell.
- Complete a knowledge inventory to discover what you already know about a subject.
- Browse through magazines, newspapers, and on-line bulletin boards for ideas.
- Start a clip file of articles that you want to save for future reference. Be sure to label each clip with source information.

Sharing Techniques
- With a group, brainstorm a topic by trying to come up with as many ideas as you can without stopping to critique or examine them.
- Interview someone who knows a great deal about your topic.

Writing Techniques
- After freewriting on a topic, try looping, or choosing your best idea for more freewriting. Repeat the loop at least once.
- Make a list to help you organize ideas, examine them, or identify areas for further research.

Graphic Techniques
- Create a pro-and-con chart to compare the positive and negative aspects of an idea or a course of action.
- Use a cluster map or tree diagram to explore subordinate ideas that relate to your general topic or central idea.

Determining Your Purpose
Your purpose for writing may be to express yourself, to entertain, to describe, to explain, to analyze, or to persuade. To clarify it, ask questions like these:

- Why did I choose to write about my topic?
- What aspects of the topic mean the most to me?
- What do I want others to think or feel after they read my writing?

LINK TO LITERATURE One purpose for writing is to clarify a subject. For example, Toni Morrison wrote "Thoughts on the African-American Novel," page 973, to explain why these novels need to be a unique form, incorporating art and oral tradition, and not be simply new stories by and about African Americans.

Identifying Your Audience

Knowing who will read your writing can help you focus your topic and choose relevant details. As you think about your readers, ask yourself questions like these:

- What does my audience already know about my topic?
- What will they be most interested in?
- What language is most appropriate for this audience?

1.2 Drafting

In the drafting stage, you put your ideas on paper and allow them to develop and change as you write.

Two broad approaches in this stage are discovery drafting and planned drafting.

Discovery drafting is a good approach when you are not quite sure what you think about your subject. You just plunge into your draft and let your feelings and ideas lead you where they will. After finishing a discovery draft, you may decide to start another draft, do more prewriting, or revise your first draft.

Planned drafting may work better for research reports, critical reviews, and other kinds of formal writing. Try making a writing plan or a scratch outline before you begin drafting. Then, as you write, you can fill in the details.

LINK TO LITERATURE Some writers plan and outline; some write in a great flurry, without much previous planning as ideas occur to them. Of course, the ideas have been generating within them before they begin to write. Zora Neale Hurston who wrote "How It Feels to Be Colored Me," page 950, wrote her most popular novel, *Their Eyes Were Watching God,* "under internal pressure" in seven weeks. She says the story was "dammed up in me."

1.3 Revising, Editing, and Proofreading

The changes you make in your writing during this stage usually fall into three categories: revising for content, revising for structure, and proofreading to correct mistakes in mechanics.

Use the questions that follow to assess problems and determine what changes would improve your work.

Revising for Content

- Does my writing have a main idea or central focus? Is my thesis clear?
- Have I incorporated adequate detail? Where might I include a telling detail, revealing statistic, or vivid example?
- Is any material unnecessary, irrelevant, or confusing?

WRITING TIP Be sure to consider the needs of your audience as you answer the questions under Revising for Content and Revising for Structure. For example, before you can determine whether any of your material is unnecessary or irrelevant, you need to identify what your audience already knows.

Revising for Structure

- Is my writing unified? Do all ideas and supporting details pertain to my main idea or advance my thesis?
- Is my writing clear and coherent? Is the flow of sentences and paragraphs smooth and logical?
- Do I need to add transitional words, phrases, or sentences to make the relationships among ideas clearer?
- Are my sentences well constructed? What sentences might I combine to improve the grace and rhythm of my writing?

Proofreading to Correct Mistakes in Grammar, Usage, and Mechanics

When you are satisfied with your revision, proofread your paper, looking for mistakes in grammar, usage, and mechanics. You may want to do this several times, looking for different types of mistakes each time. The following checklist may help.

Sentence Structure and Agreement

- Are there any run-on sentences or sentence fragments?
- Do all verbs agree with their subjects?
- Do all pronouns agree with their antecedents?
- Are verb tenses correct and consistent?

Forms of Words

- Do adverbs and adjectives modify the appropriate words?
- Are all forms of *be* and other irregular verbs used correctly?
- Are pronouns used correctly?
- Are comparative and superlative forms of adjectives correct?

Capitalization, Punctuation, and Spelling

- Is any punctuation mark missing or not needed?
- Are all words spelled correctly?
- Are all proper nouns and all proper adjectives capitalized?

WRITING TIP For help identifying and correcting problems that are listed in the Proofreading Checklist, see the Grammar Handbook, pages 1305–1340.

You might wish to mark changes on your paper by using the proofreading symbols shown in the chart below.

Proofreading Symbols

∧	Add letters or words.	/	Make a capital letter lowercase.
⊙	Add a period.	¶	Begin a new paragraph.
≡	Capitalize a letter.	⌦	Delete letters or words.
⊂	Close up space.	∿	Switch the positions of letters or words.
⋏	Add a comma.		

1.4 Publishing and Reflecting

Always consider sharing your finished writing with a wider audience. Reflecting on your writing is another good way to bring closure to a project.

Creative Publishing Ideas

Following are some ideas for publishing and sharing your writing.

- Post your writing on an electronic bulletin board or send it to others via e-mail.
- Create a multimedia presentation and share it with classmates.
- Publish your writing in a school newspaper or literary magazine.
- Present your work orally in a report, a speech, a reading, or a dramatic performance.
- Submit your writing to a local newspaper or a magazine that publishes student writing.
- Form a writing exchange group with other students.

WRITING TIP You might work with other students to publish an anthology of class writing. Then exchange your anthology with another class or another school. Reading the work of other student writers will help you get ideas for new writing projects and find ways to improve your work.

Reflecting on Your Writing

Think about your writing process and whether you would like to add what you have written to your portfolio. You might attach a note in which you answer questions like these:

- What did I learn about myself and my subject through this writing project?
- Which parts of the writing process did I most and least enjoy?
- As I wrote, what was my biggest problem? How did I solve it?
- What did I learn that I can use the next time I write?

1.5 Using Peer Response

Peer response consists of the suggestions and comments your peers or classmates make about your writing.

You can ask a peer reader for help at any point in the writing process. For example, your peers can help you develop a topic, narrow your focus, discover confusing passages, or organize your writing.

Questions for Your Peer Readers

You can help your peer readers provide you with the most useful kinds of feedback by following these guidelines:

- Tell readers where you are in the writing process. Are you still trying out ideas, or have you completed a draft?

- Ask questions that will help you get specific information about your writing. Open-ended questions that require more than yes-or-no answers are more likely to give you information you can use as you revise.

- Give your readers plenty of time to respond thoughtfully to your writing.

- Encourage your readers to be honest when they respond to your work. It's OK if you don't agree with them—you always get to decide which changes to make.

Tips for Being a Peer Reader

Follow these guidelines when you respond to someone else's work:

- Respect the writer's feelings.

- Make sure you understand what kind of feedback the writer is looking for, and then respond accordingly.

- Use "I" statements, such as "I like . . . ," "I think . . . ," or "It would help me if . . . ." Remember that your impressions and opinions may not be the same as someone else's.

WRITING TIP Writers are better able to absorb criticism of their work if they first receive positive feedback. When you act as a peer reader, try to start your review by telling something you like about the piece.

The chart below explains different peer-response techniques to use when you are ready to share your work.

Peer-Response Techniques

Sharing Use this when you are just exploring ideas or when you want to celebrate the completion of a piece of writing.

- *Will you please read or listen to my writing without criticizing or making suggestions afterward?*

Summarizing Use this when you want to know if your main idea or goals are clear.

- *What do you think I'm saying? What's my main idea or message?*

Replying Use this strategy when you want to make your writing richer by adding new ideas.

- *What are your ideas about my topic? What do you think about what I have said in my piece?*

Responding to Specific Features Use this when you want a quick overview of the strengths and weaknesses of your writing.

- *Are the ideas supported with enough examples? Did I persuade you? Is the organization clear enough for you to follow the ideas?*

Telling Use this to find out which parts of your writing are affecting readers the way you want and which parts are confusing.

- *What did you think or feel as you read my words? Would you show me which passage you were reading when you had that response?*

❷ Building Blocks of Good Writing

Whatever your purpose in writing, you need to capture your readers' interest, organize your ideas well, and present your thoughts clearly. Giving special attention to some particular parts of a story or an essay can make your writing more enjoyable and more effective.

2.1 Introductions

When you flip through a magazine trying to decide which articles to read, the opening paragraph is often critical. If it does not grab your attention, you are likely to turn the page.

Kinds of Introductions

Here are some introduction techniques that can capture a reader's interest.

- Make a surprising statement
- Provide a description
- Pose a question
- Relate an anecdote
- Address the reader directly
- Begin with a thesis statement

Make a Surprising Statement Beginning with a startling statement or an interesting fact can capture your reader's curiosity about the subject, as in the model below.

> MODEL
> Although she wrote nearly 1,800 poems, Emily Dickinson probably did not want to publish any of them. Most of her poems were first published almost 100 years after they were written.

Provide a Description A vivid description sets a mood and brings a scene to life for your reader. Here, details about a horse's actions set the tone for an essay about horse training.

> MODEL
> Dust flew as the horse stomped the ground. The puffs of moisture blowing from his nostrils and the laid back ears let the spectators know the stomping was not some clever performance. As she approached cautiously, the trainer could see the wild look in the horse's eyes.

Pose a Question Beginning with a question can make your reader want to read on to find out the answer. The following introduction asks an important question about the fate of a well-known and respected writer.

> MODEL
> Zora Neale Hurston was one of the most successful writers of the Harlem Renaissance period. She wrote plays, novels, and essays that were enthusiastically received. How did it happen that such a talented and popular author died in poverty?

Relate an Anecdote Beginning with a brief anecdote, or story, can hook readers and help you make a point in a dramatic way. The anecdote below introduces an interview with a recently retired school teacher.

> MODEL
> "Down in the valley
> Where the green grass grows. . . ."
>   The words and rhythm of the chanting children on the playground brought tears to Clara Jones's eyes. Though she could barely see the forms of the youngsters, she knew exactly the structure of the old jump-rope game they played.
>   I began softly to ask her about her 55 years of teaching at Pleasant Hills Elementary School.

Address the Reader Directly Speaking directly to readers establishes a friendly, informal tone and involves them in your topic.

> MODEL
> Do you know how many trees will be cut down for the new shopping mall to be built? Do you know how many families will have to give up their homes so that some shoppers can have yet another department store that sells the same things as five others in our area?

Begin with a Thesis Statement A thesis statement expressing a paper's main idea may be woven into both the beginning and the end of nonfiction writing. The following is a thesis statement that introduces a literary analysis.

MODEL
In "Death of a Hired Man," Robert Frost uses the hushed conversation of a husband and wife to explore the meaning of a lonely person's life. The whole poem seems to take place in whispers, though the message is strong.

WRITING TIP In order to write the best introduction for your paper, you may want to try more than one of the methods and then decide which is the most effective for your purpose and audience.

2.2 Paragraphs

A paragraph is made up of sentences that work together to develop an idea or accomplish a purpose. Whether or not it contains a topic sentence stating the main idea, a good paragraph must have unity and coherence.

Unity
A paragraph has unity when all the sentences support and develop one stated or implied idea. Use the following techniques to create unity in your paragraphs.

Write a Topic Sentence A topic sentence states the main ideas of the paragraph; all other sentences in the paragraph provide supporting details. A topic sentence is often the first sentence in a paragraph. However, it may also appear later in the paragraph or at the end, to summarize or reinforce the main idea, as shown in the model that follows.

MODEL
Cats purr when they are being stroked by humans. Cats purr when they cuddle up with other cats. Many cats purr when they are in the veterinarian's office. Some cats purr when they are frightened. Since cats seem to purr in situations of both joy and stress, the cause of purring is still a mystery to humans.

Relate All Sentences to an Implied Main Idea A paragraph can be unified without a topic sentence as long as every sentence supports the implied, or unstated, main idea. In the model below, all the sentences work together to create a unified impression of a frustrated writer trying to begin writing.

MODEL
He picked up his pencil at 9:27 and set it down purposefully on the tablet. A minute or so passed. Well, maybe he should sharpen the pencil. That took 30 seconds—now 9:29. He set his pencil down again. He readjusted his chair. He raked his left hand through his thick hair. Was there a spot of thinning hair? He got up to go look in the mirror. No, not yet. At 9:31 he sat down again and took up the pencil. This time he moved the tablet a little to the right.

Coherence
A paragraph is coherent when all its sentences are related to one another and flow logically from one to the next. The following techniques will help you achieve coherence in paragraphs.

- Present your ideas in the most logical order.
- Use pronouns, synonyms, and repeated words to connect ideas.
- Use transitional devices to show the relationships among ideas.

In the model below, the writer used some of these techniques to create a unified paragraph.

MODEL
After you figure out how big to make the model ship for your film of a shipwreck, you will need to take some other factors into account as well. You will have to figure out how much to stir the water and what speed to set the film. Perhaps even more important is to be sure no real objects at full size can be seen by the camera. In other words, don't let your towels and soap dish sneak into the picture and be sure the cat is locked out of the bathroom.

Transitions are words and phrases that show the connections between details. Clear transitions help show how your ideas relate to each other.

Kinds of Transitions

Transitions can help readers understand several kinds of relationships:

- Time or sequence
- Spatial relationships
- Degree of importance
- Compare and contrast
- Cause and effect

Time or Sequence Some transitions help to clarify the sequence of events over time. When you are telling a story or describing a process, you can connect ideas with such transitional words as *first, second, always, then, next, later, soon, before, finally, after, earlier, afterward,* and *tomorrow.*

> MODEL
> **Before a blood donation can be used, it must be processed carefully. First, a sample is tested for infectious diseases and identified by blood type. Next, preservatives are added. Finally, a blood cell separator breaks up the blood into its parts, such as red blood cells, platelets, and plasma.**

Spatial Relationships Transitional words and phrases such as *in front, behind, next to, along, nearest, lowest, above, below, underneath, on the left,* and *in the middle* can help readers visualize a scene.

> MODEL
> **Two rows of corn grew along the south side of the garden. In front of them stood the tomatoes climbing on wire enclosures and a couple of okra plants. In the middle rows were medium-height plants—bush beans, peas, potatoes, and a few peppers. Low-growing plants filled the front of the garden—radishes on the right, then rows of lettuce, spinach, and onions. On the left squash and cucumber vines spread over the ground.**

Degree of Importance Transitional words such as *mainly, strongest, weakest, first, second, most important, least important, worst,* and *best* may be used to rank ideas or to show degree of importance.

> MODEL
> **There are several reasons to eat plenty of fresh fruits and vegetables. The best reason is that they taste so good!**

Compare and Contrast Words and phrases such as *similarly, likewise, also, like, as, neither . . . nor,* and *either . . . or* show similarity between details. *However, by contrast, yet, but, unlike, instead, whereas,* and *while* show difference. Note the use of both types of transitions in the model below.

> MODEL
> **Although I like to shop in the big stores in the mall, when I'm really serious about buying something I go to a small store. Like big stores, many small stores carry a good selection of merchandise. But whereas the big stores may have lower prices, the small stores have more personal service and clerks who know about the products they sell.**

WRITING TIP Both *but* and *however* may be used to join two independent clauses. When *but* is used as a coordinating conjunction, it is preceded by a comma. When *however* is used as a conjunctive adverb, it is preceded by a semicolon and followed by a comma.

Cause and Effect When you are writing about a cause-and-effect relationship, use transitional words and phrases such as *since, because, thus, therefore, so, due to, for this reason,* and *as a result* to help clarify that relationship and to make your writing coherent.

> MODEL
> **As a result of the unusual amount of rain this summer, the grass is still lush and green even now in August.**

Conclusions

A conclusion should leave readers with a strong final impression. Try any of these approaches.

Kinds of Conclusions

Here are some effective methods for bringing your writing to a conclusion:

- Restate your thesis
- Ask a question
- Make a recommendation
- Make a prediction
- Summarize your information

Restate Your Thesis A good way to conclude an essay is by restating your thesis, or main idea, in different words. The conclusion below restates the thesis introduced on page 1273.

> MODEL
> **In Robert Frost's "Death of a Hired Man," a sad human life unfolds in the whispered conversations between Mary and Warren. Quiet compassion is also evident and is the point of the poem.**

Ask a Question Try asking a question that sums up what you have said and gives readers something new to think about. The question below concludes an appeal for preventing unwanted kittens and puppies.

> MODEL
> **Considering how many kittens, puppies, cats, and dogs are put to sleep or die on the streets, don't you think it makes sense that all household pets should be neutered?**

Make a Recommendation When you are persuading your audience to take a position on an issue, you can conclude by recommending a specific course of action.

> MODEL
> **Help protect animals from careless humans. Volunteer at an animal shelter. Distribute literature around your neighborhood.**

Make a Prediction Readers are concerned about matters that may affect them and therefore are moved by a conclusion that predicts the future.

> MODEL
> **If the city council approves the new shopping mall, we will lose the woodlands that help make our neighborhood quiet and attractive. In their place, we will have traffic congestion, exhaust fumes, bright lights long into the night, and a source of danger to our children.**

Summarize Your Information Summarizing reinforces the writer's main ideas, leaving a strong, lasting impression. The model below concludes with a statement that summarizes a review of a book.

> MODEL
> **Patricia McKissack's biography gives a strong picture of W. E. B. Du Bois, who was a link between Frederick Douglass, whom he knew early in life, and Martin Luther King, Jr., whom he knew late in life.**

 ## Elaboration

Elaboration is the process of developing a writing idea by providing specific supporting details that are relevant and appropriate to the purpose and form of your writing.

- **Facts and Statistics** A fact is a statement that can be verified, while a statistic is a fact stated in numbers. Make sure the facts and statistics you supply are from a reliable, up-to-date source. As in the model below, the facts and statistics you use should strongly support the statements you make.

> MODEL
> **A student who has an eye for beautiful gardens might consider a career in landscape architecture. The American Society of Landscape Architects has over 12,000 members, up 20 percent in the last five years. The average income of landscape architects is $52,886, which is higher than that of building architects.**

- **Sensory Details** Details that show how something looks, sounds, tastes, smells, or feels can enliven a description, making readers feel they are actually experiencing what you are describing. Which senses does the writer appeal to in this paragraph?

Sliding along on her cross-country skis, Sasha felt she was truly on top of the world. The action of the snow, skis, and sturdy boots massaged her feet. She opened her mouth to taste the sprinkles of snow. The view was a rainbow of color as snowflakes made tiny speckled prisms on her goggles.

- **Incidents** From our earliest years, we are interested in hearing "stories." One way to illustrate a point powerfully is to relate an incident or tell a story, as shown in the example below.

The East India Company had a monopoly on supplying tea to the American Colonies. Tea shipments took on the symbolism of the increasing tyranny of the English government. On December 16, 1773, a group of about 150 colonists put burnt cork on their faces, dressed as Mohawk warriors, boarded the tea-carrying ships, and proceeded to dump the entire tea cargoes into Boston Harbor.

- **Examples** An example can help make an abstract or a complex idea concrete or can provide evidence to clarify a point for readers.

Many of the stars and galaxies we see at night are showing us light from ancient times. Who knows where they really are today? For example, the light from the galaxy Andromeda started its light travel over two million years ago. That's how long it's taken the light to get here—over two million light years!

- **Quotations** Choose quotations that clearly support your points and be sure that you copy each quotation word for word. Remember always to credit the source.

Do you know anyone who says "you all" to mean "the group of you"? "Have you all seen this movie?" McCrum, Cran, and MacNeil explain in *The Story of English* that this famous Southern expression comes from a Scots-Irish translation of the plural for you. They say the expression "is typical both of Ulster and of the (largely southern) states of America." Did you all know that?

2.6 Using Language Effectively

Effective use of language can help readers to recognize the significance of an issue, to visualize a scene, or to understand a character. The specific words and phrases that you use have everything to do with how effectively you communicate meaning. This is true of all kinds of writing, from novels to office memos. Keep these particular points in mind.

- **Specific Nouns** Nouns are specific when they refer to individual or particular things. If you refer to a *city*, you are being general. If you refer to *London*, you are being specific. Specific nouns help readers identify the *who*, *what*, and *where* of your message.

- **Specific Verbs** Verbs are the most powerful words in sentences. They convey the action, the movement, and sometimes the drama of thoughts and observations. Verbs such as *trudged*, *skipped*, and *sauntered* provide a more vivid picture of the action than the verb *walked*.

- **Specific Modifiers** Use modifiers sparingly, but when you use them, make them count. Is the building *big* or *towering*? Are your poodle's paws *small* or *petite*? Once again, it is the more specific word that carries the greater impact.

③ Descriptive Writing

Descriptive writing allows you to paint word pictures about anything and everything in the world, from events of global importance to the most personal feelings. It is an essential part of almost every piece of writing, including essays, poems, letters, field notes, newspaper reports, and videos.

RUBRIC **Standards for Writing**

A successful description should
- have a clear focus and sense of purpose.
- use sensory details and precise words to create a vivid image, establish a mood, or express emotion.
- present details in a logical order.

---

③.1 Key Techniques

Consider Your Goals What do you want to accomplish in writing your description? Do you want to show why something is important to you? Do you want to make a person or scene more memorable? Do you want to explain an event?

Identify Your Audience Who will read your description? How familiar are they with your subject? What background information will they need? Which details will they find most interesting?

Think Figuratively What figures of speech might help make your description vivid and interesting? What simile or metaphor comes to mind? What imaginative comparisons can you make? What living thing does an inanimate object remind you of?

MODEL
Into the room swooped the judge, black robe flapping like the ragged black feathers of a raven. With one menacing motion, he swished his robe and swirled the locks of his gray curly hair so that he could perch grimly behind the high bench of authority.

Gather Sensory Details Which sights, smells, tastes, sounds, and textures make your subject come alive? Which details stick in your mind when you observe or recall your subject? Which senses does it most strongly affect?

MODEL
At the first whiff of country air she was immediately transported to the scene of her grandmother's garden. Pungent tomato vines curled around splintery stakes, mushy tomatoes rotted on the ground in cheerful acknowledgment of plenty, and firm orangey fruit clung proudly to the vines soaking up the sweaty summer sun.

You might want to use a chart like the one shown here to collect sensory details about your subject.

Sights	Sounds	Textures	Smells	Tastes

Create a Mood What feelings do you want to evoke in your readers? Do you want to soothe them with comforting images? Do you want to build tension with ominous details? Do you want to evoke sadness or joy?

MODEL
After the soft rain passed, raindrops sparkled on the leaves of trillium and jack-in-the-pulpit. Sun dappled the forest floor as a gentle breeze stirred the leaves overhead. Lush green moss nestled among the spreading roots of sturdy oaks, and bright colors flashed among the trees as songbirds fluttered through the mild, peaceful air.

3.2 Options for Organization

Spatial Order Choose one of these options to show the spatial order of a scene.

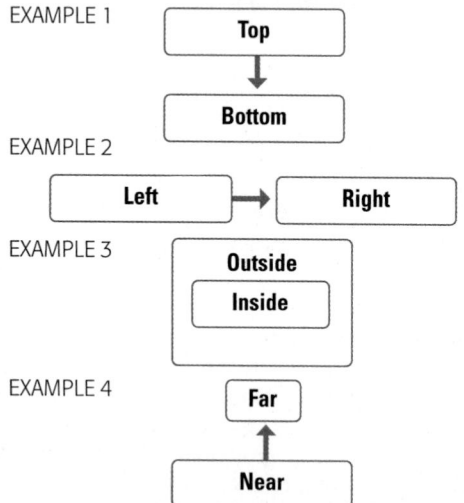

EXAMPLE 1

Top → Bottom

EXAMPLE 2

Left → Right

EXAMPLE 3

Outside / Inside

EXAMPLE 4

Far ← Near

MODEL
Peering through the goggles, the diver surveyed the reef. To the left, a school of silvery fish swam near the surface. Below them, the reef was a rainbow of color. In the middle of the scene bright, tiny fish nosed along the reef. Below them on the sand a crab looked for food. Further right a cluster of fan coral waved its purple fronds in the gentle current. Beyond it lay the barnacle-encrusted shape of a ship's propeller.

WRITING TIP Use transitions that help the reader picture the relationship among the objects you describe. Some useful transitions for showing spatial relationships are *behind, below, here, in the distance, on the left, over,* and *on top.*

Order of Impression Order of impression is how you notice details.

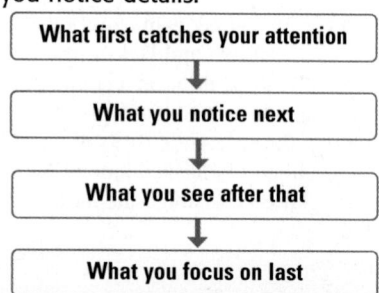

What first catches your attention
↓
What you notice next
↓
What you see after that
↓
What you focus on last

MODEL
Rain pelted against the windshield. Robbie narrowed his eyes to try to see the road in the brief clearing spasms between swipes of wiper blades. He could barely see that there was a little clearing far off in the horizon. Dark clouds made distinct shapes. Suddenly he noticed that against a small patch of lighter color was a swirling black cloud beginning to take the shape of a funnel.

WRITING TIP Use transitions that help readers understand the order of the impressions you are describing. Some useful transitions are *after, next, during, first, before, finally,* and *then.*

Order of Importance You might want to use order of importance as the organizing structure for your description.

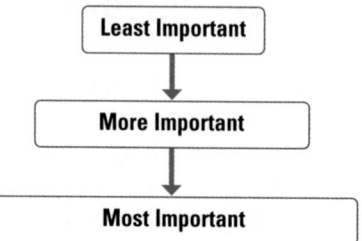

Least Important
↓
More Important
↓
Most Important

MODEL
I checked my backpack for the comforting essentials. Book? Yes. Journal and pencil? Yes. Water bottle? Yes. Tissues? Yes. Then I checked for the required essentials. Passport? Yes. Airline ticket? Yes. Map? Yes. Last of all, I checked the most important possession for this trip—a light heart and a sense of adventure. I was beginning my first real vacation in two years!

WRITING TIP Use transitions that help the reader understand the order of importance that you attach to the elements of your description. Some useful transitions are *first, second, mainly, more important, less important,* and *least important.*

❹ Narrative Writing

Narrative writing tells a story. If you write a story from your imagination, it is a fictional narrative. A true story about actual events is a nonfictional narrative. Narrative writing can be found in short stories, novels, news articles, and biographies.

RUBRIC Standards for Writing

A successful narrative should
- include descriptive details and dialogue to develop the characters, setting, and plot.
- have a clear beginning, middle, and end.
- have a logical organization with clues and transitions to help the reader understand the order of events.
- maintain a consistent tone and point of view.
- use language that is appropriate for the audience.
- demonstrate the significance of events or ideas.

❹.❶ Key Techniques

Identify the Main Events What are the most important events in your narrative? Is each event part of the chain of events needed to tell the story? In a fictional narrative, this series of events is the story's plot.

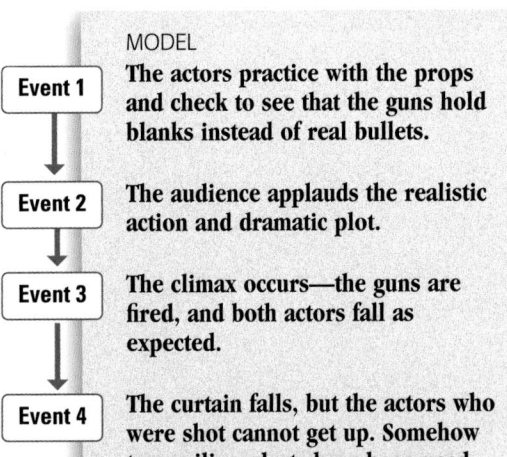

MODEL

Event 1 → The actors practice with the props and check to see that the guns hold blanks instead of real bullets.

Event 2 → The audience applauds the realistic action and dramatic plot.

Event 3 → The climax occurs—the guns are fired, and both actors fall as expected.

Event 4 → The curtain falls, but the actors who were shot cannot get up. Somehow tranquilizer darts have been used.

Describe the Setting When do the events occur? Where do they take place? How can you use setting to create mood and to set the stage for the characters and their actions?

MODEL
In the creaky old theater, the troupe of actors wander around working with their props. The air smells of phosphorus from the practice run of firing blank cartridges in the pistols.

Depict Characters Vividly What do your characters look like? What do they think and say? How do they act? What vivid details can show readers what the characters are like?

MODEL
A few minutes before curtain time, the stately actor who plays Norma opens and shuts her enormous pink and white umbrella as she takes short halting steps. The actors who play rivals Billy Jack and Spike work on spinning their pistols then crouching and aiming. Billy Jack adjusts his eye patch.

WRITING TIP Dialogue is an effective way of developing characters in a narrative. As you write dialogue, choose words that express your characters' personalities and show how the characters feel about one another and about the events in the plot.

MODEL
Norma strolls over to the poker table. "Hi, fellas," she says in a sultry voice.
  "Hey, Norma," answers Billy Jack, first to respond. "Come right here. Bring me luck."
  "Not so fast," complains Spike. "Come here, Norma. Or better yet, check out Billy Jack's hand on your way over."
  Billy Jack shifts his right hand from his cards to the gun on his hip.

4.2 Options for Organization

Option 1: Chronological Order One way to organize a piece of narrative writing is to arrange the events in chronological order, as shown below.

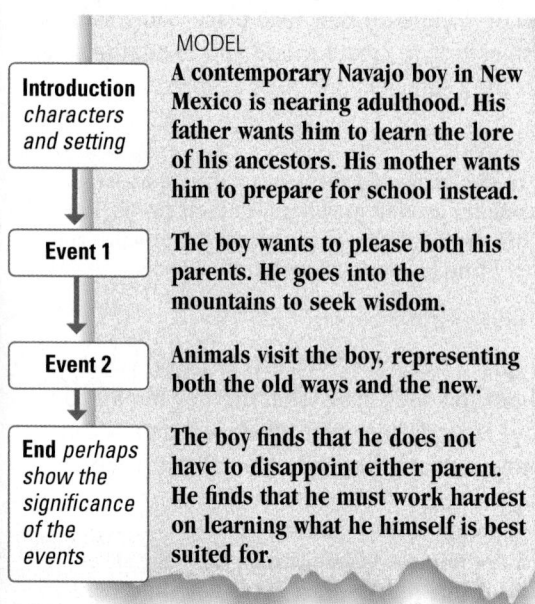

MODEL

Introduction *characters and setting* — A contemporary Navajo boy in New Mexico is nearing adulthood. His father wants him to learn the lore of his ancestors. His mother wants him to prepare for school instead.

Event 1 — The boy wants to please both his parents. He goes into the mountains to seek wisdom.

Event 2 — Animals visit the boy, representing both the old ways and the new.

End *perhaps show the significance of the events* — The boy finds that he does not have to disappoint either parent. He finds that he must work hardest on learning what he himself is best suited for.

Option 2: Flashback It is also possible in narrative writing to arrange the order of events by starting with an event that happened before the beginning of the story.

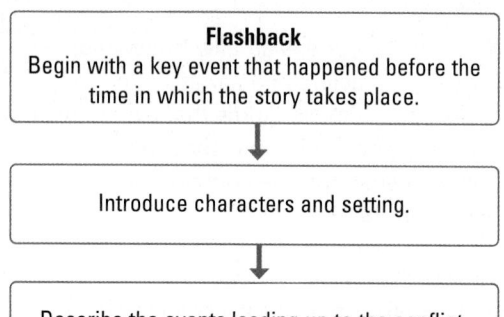

Flashback
Begin with a key event that happened before the time in which the story takes place.

↓

Introduce characters and setting.

↓

Describe the events leading up to the conflict.

Option 3: Focus on Conflict When the telling of a fictional narrative focuses on a central conflict, the story's plot may follow the model shown below.

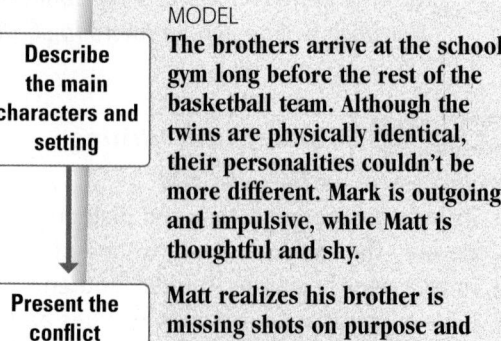

MODEL

Describe the main characters and setting — The brothers arrive at the school gym long before the rest of the basketball team. Although the twins are physically identical, their personalities couldn't be more different. Mark is outgoing and impulsive, while Matt is thoughtful and shy.

Present the conflict — Matt realizes his brother is missing shots on purpose and believes they will lose the championship.

Relate the events that make the conflict complex and cause the characters to change —
- Matt has a chance at a basketball scholarship if they win the championship.
- Mark needs money to buy a car.
- Matt and Mark have stood by each other no matter what.

Present the resolution or outcome of the conflict — Matt retells a family story in which their grandfather chose honor and integrity over easy money. Mark plays to win.

⑤ Explanatory Writing

Explanatory writing informs and explains. For example, you can use it to evaluate the effects of a new law, to compare two movies, to analyze a piece of literature, or to examine the problem of greenhouse gases in the atmosphere.

5.1 Types of Explanatory Writing

There are many types of explanatory writing. Think about your topic and select the type that presents the information most clearly.

Compare and Contrast How are two or more subjects alike? How are they different?

> MODEL
> **Leon and Father Paul have different beliefs about how to bury the dead, but they both have great affection for the old man who has died, Leon's grandfather. They both contribute their own rituals for the burial.**

Cause and Effect How does one event cause something else to happen? Why do certain conditions exist? What are the results of an action or a condition?

> MODEL
> **Because Leon and Ken did not ask for a funeral Mass for Teofilo, Father Paul did not think he should sprinkle holy water over the body.**

Analysis How does something work? How can it be defined? What are its parts?

> MODEL
> **The rituals of the Laguna people have strong cultural traditions. So also do the rituals of the Roman Catholic Church. Some groups of Native Americans believe deeply in both sets of rituals and find ways to incorporate both into their lives.**

Problem-Solution How can you identify and state a problem? How would you analyze the problem and its causes? How can it be solved?

> MODEL
> **Father Paul had to decide whether to go by the strict rules of his church or to help the family who wanted his help in a way that did not follow the rules.**

5.2 Compare and Contrast

Compare-and-contrast writing examines the similarities and differences between two or more subjects. You might, for example, compare and contrast two short stories, the main characters in a novel, or two movies.

RUBRIC	Standards for Writing

Successful compare-and-contrast writing should

- clearly identify the subjects that are being compared and contrasted.
- include specific, relevant details.
- follow a clear plan of organization dealing with the same features of both subjects under discussion.
- use language and details appropriate to the audience.
- use transitional words and phrases to clarify similarities and differences.

Options for Organization

Compare-and-contrast writing can be organized in different ways. The examples that follow demonstrate feature-by-feature organization and subject-by-subject organization.

Option 1: Feature-by-Feature Organization

MODEL

Feature 1 I. Different beliefs about burial practices.

Subject A. Leon: traditional Laguna way.

Subject B. Father Paul: Last Rites and a funeral Mass.

Feature 2 II. Both want a proper burial.

Subject A. Leon: painted face, feather in hair, body to graveyard, corn meal and pollen.

Subject B. Father Paul: decide whether to sprinkle holy water without full Catholic rites.

Option 2: Subject-by-Subject Organization

MODEL

Subject A I. Leon:

Feature 1. Believes in traditional Laguna burial.

Feature 2. Proper burial: painted face, feather in hair, body to graveyard, corn meal and pollen.

Subject B II. Father Paul:

Feature 1. Believes burial requires Last Rites and a funeral Mass.

Feature 2. Must decide whether to sprinkle holy water without full Catholic rites.

WRITING TIP Remember your purpose for comparing and contrasting your subjects, and support your purpose with expressive language and specific details.

5.3 Cause and Effect

Cause-and-effect writing explains why something happened, why certain conditions exist, or what resulted from an action or a condition. You might use cause-and-effect writing to explain a character's actions, the progress of a disease, or the outcome of a war.

Options for Organization

Your organization will depend on your topic and purpose for writing.

- If you want to explain the causes of an event such as the closing of a factory, you might first state the effect and then examine its causes.

Option 1: Effect to Cause Organization

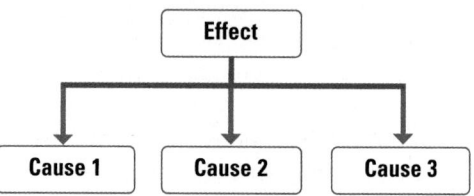

- If your focus is on explaining the effects of an event, such as the passage of a law, you might first state the cause and then explain the effects.

Option 2: Cause to Effect Organization

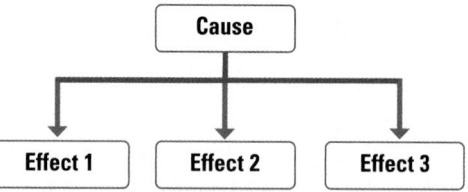

- Sometimes you'll want to describe a chain of cause-and-effect relationships to explore a topic such as the disappearance of tropical rain forests or the development of home computers.

Option 3: Cause-and-Effect Chain Organization

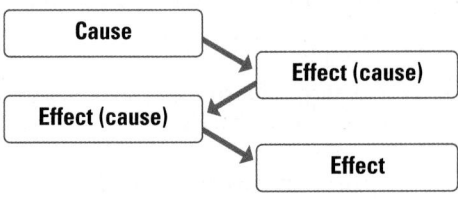

WRITING TIP Don't assume that a cause-and-effect relationship exists just because one event follows another. Look for evidence that the later event could not have happened if the first event had not caused it.

5.4 Problem-Solution

Problem-solution writing clearly states a problem, analyzes the problem, and proposes a solution to the problem. It can be used to identify and solve a conflict between characters, analyze a chemistry experiment, or explain why the home team keeps losing.

RUBRIC Standards for Writing

Successful problem-solution writing should
- identify the problem and help the reader understand the issues involved.
- analyze the causes and effects of the problem.
- integrate quotations, facts, and statistics into the text.
- explore possible solutions to the problem and recommend the best one(s).
- use language, tone, and details appropriate to the audience.

Options for Organization
Your organization will depend on the goal of your problem-solution piece, your intended audience, and the specific problem you choose to address. The organizational methods that follow are effective for different kinds of problem-solution writing.

Option 1: Simple Problem-Solution

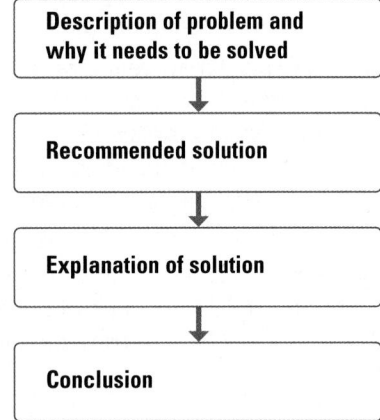

Option 2: Deciding Between Solutions

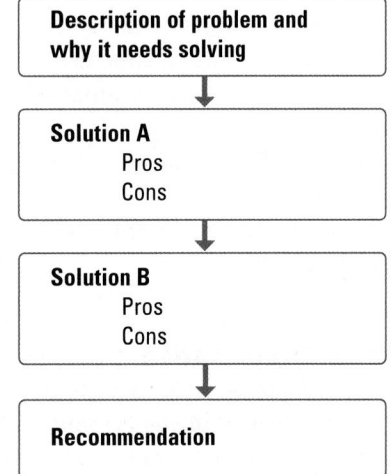

WRITING TIP Have a classmate read and respond to your problem-solution writing. Ask your peer reader: Is the problem clearly stated? Is the organization easy to follow? Do the proposed solutions seem logical?

5.5 Analysis

In writing an analysis, you explain how something works, how it is defined, or what its parts are. The details you include will depend upon the kind of analysis you write.

Process Analysis What are the major steps or stages in a process? What background information does the reader need to know—such as definitions of terms or a list of needed equipment—to understand the analysis? You might use process analysis to explain how Mark Twain learned to be a steamboat pilot.

Definition Analysis What are the most important characteristics of a subject? You might use definition analysis to explain the characteristics of a sonnet, the abilities of a physicist, or the skill of piloting a steamboat.

Parts Analysis What are the parts, groups, or types that make up a subject? Parts analysis could be used to explain the parts of the brain or the lessons learned by observing the river.

RUBRIC **Standards for Writing**

A successful analysis should

- hook the readers' attention with a strong introduction.
- clearly state the subject and its parts.
- use a specific organizing structure to provide a logical flow of information.
- show connections among facts and ideas through subordinate clauses and transitional words and phrases.
- use language and details appropriate for the audience.

Options for Organization

Organize your details in a logical order appropriate for the kind of analysis you're writing.

Option 1: Process Analysis A process analysis is usually organized chronologically, with steps or stages in the order they occur.

	MODEL
Introduction	**Navigating north from New Orleans**
Background	**Mark Twain follows this process for his first trip as a cub pilot.**
Explain Steps	**Step 1: Straighten out the boat.**
	Step 2: Stay close to the moored boats.
	Step 3: Pass Six-Mile, Nine-Mile, and Twelve-Mile points.
	Step 4: Cross the river when the calm water ends.

Option 2: Definition Analysis You can organize the details in a definition or parts analysis in order of importance or impression.

	MODEL
Introduce Term	**A successful riverboat pilot must be a keen observer.**
General Definition	**The riverboat pilot must observe the surface of the river, the landmarks along the shore, and signs of nature.**
Explain Qualities	**Quality 1: The surface can tell of rising water or hidden hazards.**
	Quality 2: Landmarks tell where the boat is; pilot must recall what dangers to avoid at that point.
	Quality 3: The sky can give hints about what weather may be coming.

Option 3: Parts Analysis The following parts analysis explores three skills a riverboat pilot needs.

	MODEL
Introduce Subject	**Piloting a riverboat required several skills.**
Explain Parts	**Part 1: recognize how weather might threaten the boat**
	Part 2: observe floating objects that could show a rising river, see ripples in the water surface that could indicate a hazard
	Part 3: use landmarks to know where boat is and where dangers lie

WRITING TIP Try to capture your readers' interest in your introduction. You might begin with a vivid description or an interesting fact, detail, or quotation. For example, an exciting excerpt from the narrative could open the process analysis.

An effective way to conclude an analysis is to return to your thesis and restate it in different words.

❻ Persuasive Writing

Persuasive writing allows you to use the power of language to inform and influence others. It can take many forms, including speeches, newspaper editorials, billboards, advertisements, and critical reviews.

❻⋅❶ Key Techniques

Clarify Your Position What do you believe about the issue? How can you express your opinion most clearly?

> MODEL
> Patients should not be so quick to request antibiotics for every sickness because the typical antibiotics are becoming less effective.

Know Your Audience Who will read your writing? What do they already know and believe about the issue? What objections to your position might they have? What additional information might they need? What tone and approach would be most effective?

> MODEL
> By overusing antibiotics, we are encouraging the development of microorganisms that can resist drugs. Sometimes it is best to let the body's natural defenses work on their own.

Support Your Opinion Why do you feel the way you do about the issue? What facts, statistics, examples, quotations, anecdotes, or opinions of authorities support your view? What reasons will convince your readers? What evidence can answer their objections?

> MODEL
> In explaining new research to combat microorganisms that cause dangerous diseases, authors of a *Business Week* article give this startling fact: "Killer microbes such as staph have evolved the ability to dice up penicillin and pump out tetracycline before either antibiotic has a chance to work."

Ways to Support Your Argument

Statistics	Facts that are stated in numbers
Examples	Specific instances that explain your point
Observations	Events or situations you yourself have seen
Anecdotes	Brief stories that illustrate your point
Quotations	Direct statements from authorities

Begin and End with a Bang How can you hook your readers and make a lasting impression? What memorable quotation, anecdote, or statistic will catch their attention at the beginning or stick in their minds at the end? What strong summary or call to action can you conclude with?

> BEGINNING
> Stop before you call your doctor for medicine to cure that cold or ease that sore throat. You might be doing your body more harm than good by taking an antibiotic.

> CONCLUSION
> Listen to doctors when they suggest that antibiotics should be reserved for serious illness. Take the doctor's advice to drink lots of liquids and get bed rest instead of taking drugs for less serious illness. Maybe humanity can win the battle with microbes by slowing their evolution into supermicrobes that resist antibiotics.

6.2 Options for Organization

In a two-sided persuasive essay, you want to show the weaknesses of other opinions as you explain the strengths of your own.

The example below demonstrates one method of organizing your persuasive essay to convince your audience.

Option 1: Reasons for Your Opinion

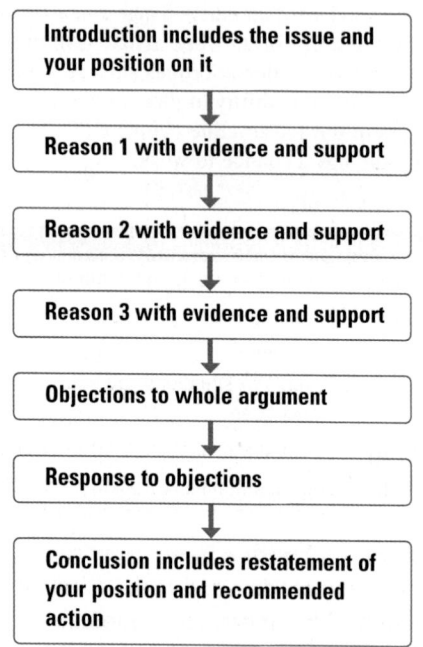

Introduction includes the issue and your position on it

Reason 1 with evidence and support

Reason 2 with evidence and support

Reason 3 with evidence and support

Objections to whole argument

Response to objections

Conclusion includes restatement of your position and recommended action

Option 2: Point-by-Point Basis

In the organization that follows, each reason and its objections are examined on a point-by-point basis.

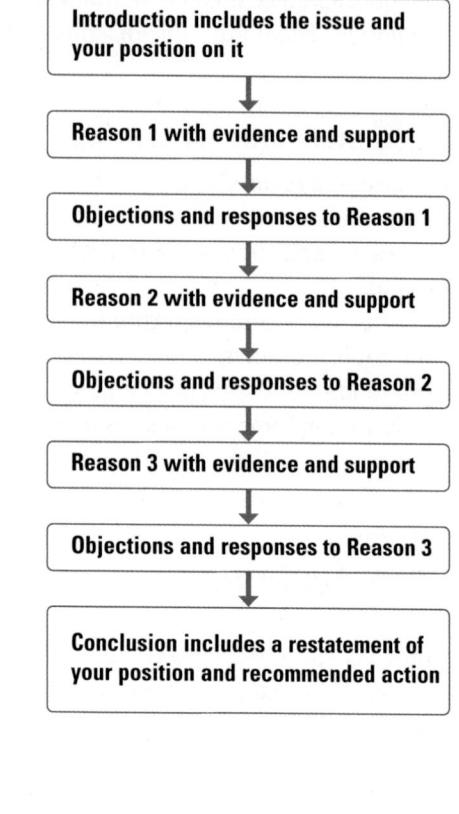

Introduction includes the issue and your position on it

Reason 1 with evidence and support

Objections and responses to Reason 1

Reason 2 with evidence and support

Objections and responses to Reason 2

Reason 3 with evidence and support

Objections and responses to Reason 3

Conclusion includes a restatement of your position and recommended action

---

Beware of Illogical Arguments Be careful about using illogical arguments. Opponents can easily attack your argument if you present illogical material.

Circular reasoning—trying to prove a statement by just repeating it in different words

> Antibiotics are being overused because people take them too often.

Overgeneralization—making a statement that is too broad to prove

> People are demanding antibiotics whenever they don't feel good.

Either-or fallacy—stating that there are only two alternatives when there are many

> If we don't set national limits on prescribing antibiotics, we will face worldwide epidemics caused by untreatable supermicrobes.

Cause-and-effect fallacy—falsely assuming that because one event follows another, the first event caused the second

> Supermicrobes are evolving because of the discovery of penicillin.

❼ Research Report Writing

A research report explores a topic in depth, incorporating information from a variety of sources.

❼.❶ Key Techniques

Develop Relevant, Interesting, and Researchable Questions Asking thoughtful questions is an ongoing part of research. Begin with a list of basic questions that are relevant to your topic. Focus on getting basic facts that answer the *who, what, where, when,* and *why* of your topic. If you were researching how Mark Twain's childhood experiences affected his attitudes, you might develop a set of questions similar to these.

> MODEL
> **What was frontier life like in the early 1800s?**
>
> **Did frontier humor of the time resemble the humor in Twain's writing?**
>
> **What other famous people grew up in similar surroundings?**

As you become more familiar with your topic, think of questions that might provide an interesting perspective that makes readers think.

> MODEL
> **Did frontier life have similar effects on Mark Twain and Abraham Lincoln?**

Check that your questions are researchable. Ask questions that will uncover facts, statistics, case studies, and other documentable evidence.

Clarify Your Thesis A thesis statement is one or two sentences clearly stating the main idea that you will develop in your report. A thesis may also indicate the organizational pattern you will follow and reflect your tone and point of view.

> MODEL
> **Mark Twain was born in Missouri in 1835. Abraham Lincoln was born in rural Kentucky in 1809. A similar geography shaped both men as well as shaping their beliefs and temperaments.**

Document Your Sources You need to document, or credit, the sources where you find your evidence. In the example below, the writer uses and documents a quotation from the introduction to a collection of Mark Twain's works.

> MODEL
> **Bernard DeVoto quotes William Dean Howells as calling Mark Twain "the Lincoln of our literature" (DeVoto 5).**

Support Your Ideas You should support your ideas with relevant evidence—facts, anecdotes, and statistics—from reliable sources. In the example below, the writer includes a fact about the style of both Twain and Lincoln.

> MODEL
> **DeVoto points out that both men saw the humor in everyday life and used humor from their earliest years (5).**

 ## Gathering Information: Sources

You will use a range of sources to collect the information you need to develop your research paper. These will include both print and electronic resources.

General Reference Works To clarify your thesis and begin your research, consult reference works that give quick, general overviews on a subject. General reference works include encyclopedias, almanacs and yearbooks, atlases, and dictionaries.

Specialized Reference Works Once you have a good idea of your specific topic, you are ready to look for detailed information in specialized reference works. In the library's reference section, specialized dictionaries and encyclopedias can be found for almost any field. For example, in the field of literature, you will find specialized reference sources such as *Contemporary Authors* and *Twentieth-Century Literary Criticism.*

Periodicals Journals and periodicals are a good source for detailed, up-to-date information. Periodical indexes, found in print and on-line catalogs in the library, will help you find articles on a topic. The *Readers' Guide to Periodical Literature* indexes many popular magazines. More specialized indexes include the *Humanities Index* and the *Social Sciences Index.*

Electronic Resources Commercial information services offer access to reference works such as dictionaries and encyclopedias, databases, and periodicals.

The **Internet** is a vast network of computer networks. News services, libraries, universities, researchers, organizations, and government agencies use the Internet to communicate and to distribute information. The Internet gives you access to the World Wide Web, which provides information on particular topics and links you to related topics and resources.

A **CD-ROM** is a research aid that stores information on a compact disk. Reference works on CD-ROMs may include text, sound, images, and video.

Databases are large collections of related information stored electronically. You can scan the information or search for specific facts.

RESEARCH TIP To find books on a specific topic, check the library's on-line catalog. Be sure to copy the correct call numbers of books that sound promising. Also look at books shelved nearby. They may relate to your topic.

Gathering Information: Validity of Sources

When you find source material, you must determine whether it is useful and accurate.

Credibility of Authorship Check whether an author has written several books or articles on the subject and has published in a well-respected newspaper or journal.

Objectivity Decide whether the information is fact, opinion, or propaganda. Reputable sources credit other sources of information.

Currency Check the publication date of the source to see whether the information is current.

Credibility of Publisher Seek information from a respected newspaper or journal, not from a tabloid newspaper or popular-interest magazine.

WEB TIP Be especially skeptical of information you locate on the Internet since virtually anyone can post anything there. Read the URL, or Internet address. Sites sponsored by a government agency (*.gov*) or an educational institution (*.edu*) are generally more reliable.

Taking Notes

As you find useful information, record the bibliographic information of each source on a separate index card. Then you are ready to take notes on your sources. You will probably use these three methods of note-taking.

Paraphrase, or restate in your own words, the main ideas and supporting details of the passage.

Summarize, or rephrase in fewer words, the original materials, trying to capture the key ideas.

Quote, or copy word for word, the original text, if you think the author's own words best clarify a particular point. Use quotation marks to signal the beginning and the end of the quotation.

For more details on making source cards and taking notes, see the Research Report Workshop on pages 980–988.

7.5 Options for Organization

Begin by reading over your note cards and sorting them into groups. The main-idea headings may help you find connections among the notes. Then arrange the groups of related note cards so that the ideas flow logically from one group to the next.

Like other forms of writing, research reports can be organized in several different ways. Some subjects may fit in chronological order. For other subjects, you may want to compare and contrast two topics. Other possibilities are a cause-and-effect organization or least-important to most-important evidence. If your material does not lend itself to any of the above organizations, try a general-to-specific approach.

Whatever your organizational pattern, making an outline can help guide the drafting process. The subtopics that you located in sorting your note cards will be the major topics of your outline, preceded by Roman numerals. Make sure that items of the same importance are parallel in form. For example, in the Option 1 Topic Outline below, topics I and II are both phrases. So are subtopics A and B.

A second kind of outline, shown below in Option 2, uses complete sentences instead of phrases for topics and subtopics.

Option 1: Topic Outline

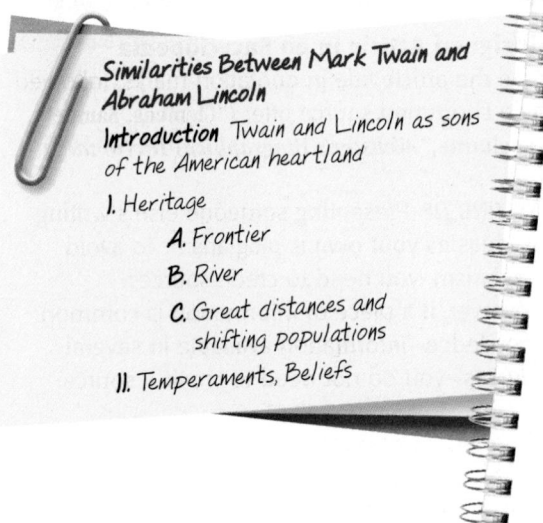

Similarities Between Mark Twain and Abraham Lincoln

Introduction Twain and Lincoln as sons of the American heartland

I. Heritage
    A. Frontier
    B. River
    C. Great distances and shifting populations
II. Temperaments, Beliefs

Option 2: Sentence Outline

Similarities Between Mark Twain and Abraham Lincoln

Introduction Both Mark Twain and Abraham Lincoln were sons of the American heartland.

I. Twain and Lincoln were shaped by the places where they were born and raised.
    A. Both men lived in the frontier area of the nation.
    B. Both men were river men.
    C. The area in which they lived was characterized by great distances and shifting populations.
II. In addition to similarities in their geographic heritage, Twain and Lincoln shared certain traits and beliefs.

7.6 Documenting Sources

When you quote, paraphrase, or summarize information from a source, you need to credit that source. Parenthetical documentation is the accepted method for crediting sources. You may choose to name the author in parentheses following the information, along with the page number on which the information is found.

> MODEL
> **Innocents Abroad** was not just independent of European influence, it was indifferent to it (DeVoto 5).

In parenthetical documentation, you may also use the author's name in the sentence, along with the information. If so, enclose, in parentheses after the sentence, only the page number on which the information is found.

> MODEL
> According to DeVoto, Lincoln expressed a culture that had turned its gaze from Europe to the continent (3).

In either case, your reader can find out more about the source by turning to your Works Cited page, which lists complete bibliographical information for each source.

PUNCTUATION TIP When only the author and page number appear in parentheses, there is no punctuation between the two items. Also notice that the parenthetical citation comes after the closing quotation marks of a quotation, if there is one, and before the end punctuation of the sentence.

The examples above show citations for books with one author. The list that follows shows the correct way to write parenthetical citations for several kinds of sources.

Guidelines for Parenthetical Documentation

Work by One Author
Put the author's last name and the page reference in parentheses: (DeVoto 34).

If you mention the author's name in the sentence, put only the page reference in parentheses: (34).

Work by Two or Three Authors
Put the authors' last names and the page reference in parentheses: (Baker and Gibson 84).

Work by More Than Three Authors
Give the first author's last name followed by *et al.* and the page reference: (Armento et al. 334-335).

Work with No Author Given
Give the title or a shortened version and (if appropriate) the page reference: ("Mark Twain's Portrait" 29).

One of Two or More Works by Same Author
Give the author's last name, the title or a shortened version, and the page reference: (Twain, Roughing It 47).

Selection from a Book of Collected Essays
Give the name of the author of the essay and the page reference: (Gerber 134).

Dictionary Definition
Give the entry title in quotation marks: ("jingo").

Unsigned Article in an Encyclopedia
Give the article title in quotation marks, followed by a shortened source title: ("Clemens, Samuel Langhorne," *Webster's Biographical Dictionary*)

WRITING TIP Presenting someone else's writing or ideas as your own is plagiarism. To avoid plagiarism, you need to credit sources. However, if a piece of information is common knowledge—information available in several sources—you do not need to credit a source.

7.7 Following MLA Manuscript Guidelines

The final copy of your report should follow the Modern Language Association (MLA) guidelines for manuscript preparation.

- The heading in the upper left-hand corner of the first page should include your name, your teacher's name, the course name, and the date, each on a separate line.
- Below the heading, center the title on the page.
- Number all the pages consecutively in the upper right-hand corner, one-half inch from the top. Also, include your last name before the page number.

- Double-space the entire paper.
- Except for the margins above the page numbers, leave one-inch margins on all sides of every page.

The Works Cited page at the end of your report is an alphabetized list of the sources you have used and documented. In each entry all lines after the first are indented an additional one-half inch.

WRITING TIP When your report includes a quotation that is longer than four lines, set it off from the rest of the text by indenting the entire quotation one inch from the left margin. In this case, you should not use quotation marks.

Works Cited

Models for Works Cited Entries

Works Cited

Armento, Beverly J., et al. A More Perfect Union. Boston: Houghton, 1991. 334–335.

❶ Book with more than three authors; note that publishers' names are shortened

Baker, Susan, and Curtis S. Gibson. "Lincoln." Gore Vidal: A Critical Companion. Westport: Greenwood, 1997. 87–92.

❷ Work with two authors

Gerber, John C. "Mark Twain's Use of the Comic Pose." Critical Essays on Mark Twain, 1910–1980. Ed. Louis J. Budd. Boston: Hall, 1983. 131–143.

❸ Selection from a book of collected essays

Park, Clara Claiborne. "The River and the Road: Fashions in Forgiveness." American Scholar 66 (1997): 43–62.

❹ Article in scholarly journal

Ravitch, Diane, ed. The American Reader: Words That Moved a Nation. New York: Harper, 1990.

❺ Book with an editor but no single author

Twain, Mark. Early Tales and Sketches. Ed. Edgar Marquess Branch and Robert H. Hirst. Berkeley: U of California P, 1979.

❻ Book with one author

---. Roughing It. Ed. Harriet E. Smith and Edgar M. Branch. Berkeley: U of California P, 1993.

❼ Second work by same author

MLA Documentation: Electronic Sources

As with print sources, information from electronic sources such as CD-ROMs or the Internet must be documented on your Works Cited page. You may find a reference to a source on the Internet and then use the print version of the article. If so, document it as you do other printed works. However, if you read or print out an article directly off the Internet, document it as shown below for an electronic source. Although electronic sources are shown separately below, they should be included on the Works Cited page with print sources.

Internet Sources Works Cited entries for Internet sources include the same kind of information as those for print sources. They also include the date you obtained the information and the electronic address of the source. Some of the information about the source may be unavailable. Include as much as you can. For more information on how to write Works Cited entries for Internet sources, see the MLA guidelines posted on the Internet or gain access to this document through the McDougal Littell website.

 More Online: Style Guidelines
www.mcdougallittell.com

CD-ROMs Entries for CD-ROMs include the publication medium (CD-ROM), the distributor, and the date of publication. Some of the information shown may not be always available. Include as much as you can.

Works Cited

Crisler, Vern. "The Comedy of Mark Twain." Home page.
    12 Aug. 1998 <http://www.geocities.com/Athens/
    6208/comedy.html>.

"Lincoln, Abraham." Grolier Multimedia Encyclopedia. 1998
    ed. CD-ROM. Danbury: Grolier Interactive.

"Mark Twain." Britannica Online. Vers. 98.2. Apr. 1998.
    Encyclopaedia Britannica. 22 Sept. 1998
    <http://www.eb.com:180>.

Newman, Rhoda. "Mark Twain, Internationalist." Foreign
    Service Journal Feb. 1996: 18–23. TwainWeb. Mark
    Twain Forum. 9 Sept. 1998 <http://web.mit.edu/
    linguistics/www/forum/filelist/intl01.html>.

Twain, Mark. "Correspondence with the San Francisco Alta
    California: 1867-1869." Mark Twain Quotations,
    Newspaper Collections, and Related Resources. Ed.
    Barbara Schmidt. Tarleton College. 9 Sept. 1998
    <http://www.tarleton.edu/activities/pages/facultypages/
    schmidt/altaindex.html>.

VanSpanckeren, Kathryn. "The Rise of Realism: 1860–1914."
    Chap. 5 of An Outline of American Literature. U.S.
    Information Agency. 9 Sept. 1998
    <http://odur.let.rug.nl/~usa/LIT/chap5.htm>.

Works Cited

Models for Works Cited entries for electronic sources

❶ Home page; shows date you accessed it

❷ Encyclopedia article from CD-ROM version

❸ Encyclopedia article from online version

❹ Article from a scholarly journal available on the Internet; includes page numbers and access date

❺ The complete text of the letters, available on the Internet; includes access date

⑧ Business Writing

The ability to write clearly and succinctly is an essential skill in the business world. As you prepare to enter the job market, you will need to know how to create letters, memos, and résumés.

8.1 Key Techniques

Think About Your Purpose Why are you doing this writing? Do you want to "sell" yourself to a college admissions committee or a job interviewer? Do you want to order or complain about a product? Do you want to set up a meeting or respond to someone's ideas?

Identify Your Audience Who will read your writing? What background information will they need? What questions might they have? What tone or language is appropriate?

Support Your Points What specific details clarify your ideas? What reasons do you have for your statements? What points most strongly support them?

Finish Strongly How can you best sum up your statements? What is your main point? What action do you want others to take?

8.2 Options

Model 1: Letter

84 Mariposa Lane
El Paso, TX 79935
April 16, _____

Heading *Where the letter comes from and when*

Inside Address *To whom the letter is being sent*

Dr. Larry Raines, Chair
English Department
Lincoln University
1127 University Drive
Tempe, AZ 85282

Salutation *Greeting*

Dear Dr. Raines:

As a high school junior, I am investigating colleges to visit during this summer. My special interest is in English literature, and I know that Lincoln University has a fine department in this field.

Body *Text of the message*

Please send me information about applying to Lincoln and also requirements for entering your department.

Thank you.

Sincerely,

Lianna Chavez

Closing

Model 2: Memo

Heading *Whom the memo is to and from, what it's about, and when it's being sent*	To: Jane Bakerman From: Larry Raines Re: Prospective Student Date: 4/20/___
Body	Jane, attached is a copy of a letter from a high school junior who is interested in our program. Will you please send her the English Department flyer and then forward to the dean's office the request for a catalog? Thanks.

Model 3: Résumé

A well-written résumé is invaluable when you apply for a part-time or full-time job or to college. It should highlight your skills, accomplishments, and experience. Proofread your résumé carefully to make sure it is clear and accurate and free of errors in grammar and spelling. It is a good idea to save a copy of your résumé on your computer or on a disk so that you can easily update it.

State your purpose. *This résumé is for a job application. A modified style can be used for a college application.*

JOSEPH L. JASPER
361 Alameda
Santa Fe, NM 87501

Objective A summer position as a department store clerk

Qualifications Ability to use computer
Excellent skills in mathematics
Cheerful, friendly disposition

List your previous employment experience *in reverse chronological order.*

Work Experience 1998–present—Part-time employment as cashier at college bookstore, Colorado College, Colorado Springs, CO
Summer 1998—Held clerk position at Drake's Department Store, Santa Fe, NM
Winter Vacation 1997, 1998—Part-time clerk at Big Four Drug Store, Colorado Springs, CO

Education Our Lady of Light High School, Class of 1998
Completing freshman year at Colorado College

Extracurricular activities and hobbies *can give a fuller picture of you and point out special job-related skills.*

Extracurricular Activities High School: Chorus, Math Club, first-string basketball
College: Chorus, Freshman Honor Society

Hobbies Puzzles, basketball, reading

References Available upon request

❶ Inquiry and Research

In this age of seemingly unlimited information, the ability to locate and evaluate resources efficiently can spell the difference between success and failure—in both the academic and the business worlds. Make use of print and nonprint information sources.

⓵ Finding Sources

Good research involves using the wealth of resources available to answer your questions and raise new questions. Knowing where to go and how to access information can lead you to interesting and valuable sources.

Reference Works

Reference works are print and nonprint sources of information that provide quick access to both general overviews and specific facts about a subject. These include

Dictionaries—word definitions, pronunciations, and origins

Thesauruses—lists of synonyms and antonyms for each entry

Glossaries—collections of specialized terms, such as those pertaining to literature, with definitions

Encyclopedias—detailed information on nearly every subject, arranged alphabetically (*Encyclopaedia Britannica*). Specialized encyclopedias deal with specific subjects, such as music, economics, and science (*Encyclopedia of Economics*).

Almanacs and Yearbooks—current facts and statistics (*World Almanac, Statistical Abstract of the United States*)

Atlases—maps and information about weather, agricultural and industrial production, and other geographical topics (*National Geographic Atlas of the World*)

Specialized Reference Works—biographical data (*Who's Who, Current Biography*), literary information (*Contemporary Authors, Book Review Digest, Cyclopedia of Literary Characters, The Oxford Companion to English Literature*), and quotations (*Bartlett's Familiar Quotations*)

Electronic Sources—Many of these reference works and databases are available on CD-ROMs, which may include text, sound, photographs, and video. CD-ROMs can be used on a home or library computer. You can subscribe to services that offer access to these sources on-line.

Periodicals and Indexes

One kind of specialized reference is a periodical.

- Some periodicals, such as *Atlantic Monthly* and *Psychology Today,* are intended for a general audience. They are indexed in the *Readers' Guide to Periodical Literature.*

- Many other periodicals, or journals, are intended for specialized or academic audiences. These include titles and subject matter as diverse as *American Psychologist* and *Studies in Short Fiction.* These are indexed in the *Humanities Index* and the *Social Sciences Index.* In addition, most fields have their own indexes. For example, articles on literature are indexed in the *MLA International Bibliography.*

- Many indexes are available in print, CD-ROM, and on-line forms.

Internet

The Internet is a vast network of computers. News services, libraries, universities, researchers, organizations, and government agencies use the Internet to distribute information and to communicate. The Internet can provide links to library catalogs, newspapers, government sources, and many of the reference sources described above. The Internet includes two key features:

World Wide Web—source of information on specific subjects and links to related topics

Electronic mail (e-mail)—communications link to other e-mail users worldwide

Other Resources

In addition to reference works found in the library and over the Internet, you can get information from the following sources: corporate publications, lectures, correspondence, and media such as films, television programs, and recordings. You can also observe directly, conduct your own interviews, and collect data from polls or questionnaires that you create yourself.

 Evaluating Sources

Not all information is equal. You need to be a discriminating consumer of information and evaluate the credibility of the source, the reliability of the specific information included, and its value in answering your research needs.

Credibility of Sources

You must determine the credibility and appropriateness of each source in order to write an effective report or speech. Ask yourself the following questions:

Is the writer an authority? A writer who has written several books on a subject or whose name is included in many bibliographies may be considered an authoritative source.

Is the source reliable and unbiased? What is the author's motivation? For example, a defense of an industry in which the author has a financial interest may be biased. A profile of a writer or scientist written by a close relative may also be biased.

WEB TIP Be especially skeptical of information you locate on the Internet, since virtually anyone can post anything there. Read the URL, or Internet address. Sites sponsored by a government agency (*.gov*) or an educational institution (*.edu*) are generally more reliable.

Is the source up-to-date? It is important to consult the most recent material, especially in fields such as medicine and technology that undergo constant research and development. Some authoritative sources have withstood the test of time, however, and should not be overlooked.

Is the source appropriate? What audience is the material written for? In general, look for information directed at the educated reader. Material geared to experts or to popular audiences may be too technical or too simplified and therefore not appropriate for most research projects.

Distinguishing Fact from Opinion

As you gather information, it is important to recognize facts and opinions. A **fact** can be proven to be true or false. You could verify the statement "Congress rejected the bill" by checking newspapers, magazines, or the *Congressional Record.* An **opinion** is a judgment based on facts. The statement "Congress should not have rejected the bill" is an opinion. To evaluate an opinion, check for evidence presented logically and validly to support it.

Recognizing Bias

A writer may have a particular bias. This does not automatically make his or her point of view unreliable. However, recognizing an author's bias can help you evaluate a source. Recognizing that the author of an article about immigration is a Chinese immigrant will help you understand that author's bias. In addition, an author may have a hidden agenda that makes him or her less than objective about a topic. To avoid relying on information that may be biased, check an author's background and gather a variety of viewpoints.

 Collecting Information

People use a variety of techniques to collect information during the research process. Try out several of those suggested below and decide which ones work best for you.

Paraphrasing and Summarizing

You can adapt material from other sources by quoting it directly or by paraphrasing or summarizing it. A paraphrase involves restating the information in your own words. It is often a simpler version but not necessarily a shorter version. A summary involves extracting the main ideas and supporting details and writing a shorter version of the information.

Remember to credit the source when you paraphrase or summarize. See the Writing Handbook—Research Report, pages 1287–1292.

Strategies for Paraphrasing

1. Select the portion of the article you want to record.

2. Read it carefully and think about those ideas you find most interesting and useful to your research. Often these will be the main ideas.

3. Retell the information in your own words.

Strategies for Summarizing

1. Read the article carefully. Determine the main ideas.

2. In your own words, write a shortened version of these main ideas.

Avoiding Plagiarism

Plagiarism is copying someone else's ideas or words and using them as if they were your own. This can happen inadvertently if you are sloppy about collecting information and documenting your sources. Plagiarism is intellectual stealing and can have serious consequences.

How to Avoid Plagiarism

1. When you paraphrase or summarize, be sure to change entirely the wording of the original by using your own words.

2. Both in notes and on your final report, enclose in quotation marks any material copied directly from other sources.

3. Indicate in your final report the sources of any ideas that are not general knowledge—including those in the visuals—that you have paraphrased or summarized.

4. Include a list of Works Cited with your finished report. See the Writing Handbook—Research Report, pages 1287–1292.

② Study Skills and Strategies

As you read an assignment for the first time, review material for a test, or search for information for a research report, you use different methods of reading and studying.

2.1 Skimming

When you run your eyes quickly over a text, paying attention to overviews, headings, topic sentences, highlighted words, and graphic features, you are skimming.

Skimming is a good technique for previewing material in a textbook or other source that you must read for an assignment. It is also useful when you are researching a self-selected topic. Skimming a source helps you determine whether it has pertinent information. For example, suppose you are writing a research report on Native American myths and legends. Skimming an essay or a book on myths and legends can help you quickly determine whether any part of it deals with your topic.

2.2 Scanning

To find a specific piece of information in a text, use scanning. To scan, place a card under the first line of a page and move it down slowly. Look for key words and phrases that signal the information you are looking for.

Scanning is useful in reviewing for a test or in finding a specific piece of information for a paper. Suppose you are looking for a discussion of the role of Coyote for your research report. You can scan a book chapter or an essay, looking for the key name *Coyote.*

In-Depth Reading

When you must thoroughly understand the material in a text, you use in-depth reading.

In-depth reading involves asking questions, taking notes, looking for main ideas, and drawing conclusions as you read slowly and carefully. For example, in researching your report on Native American myths and legends, you may find an essay on the common elements in tales of Coyote, the trickster, that are found in a number of Native American cultures. Since this is closely related to your topic, you will read it in depth and take notes. You also should use in-depth reading for reading textbooks and literary works.

2.4 Outlining

Outlining is an efficient way of organizing ideas and is useful in taking notes.

Outlining helps you retain information as you read in depth. For example, you might outline a chapter in a history textbook, listing the main subtopics and the ideas or details that support them. An outline can also be useful for taking notes for a research report or in reading a piece of literature. The following is an example of a topic outline that summarizes, in short phrases, part of a chapter.

MAIN IDEA: **Myths are concerned with fundamental issues.**
I. **The Cosmos**
   A. **Why things came to be**
   B. **How things work**
   C. **Power of nature**
II. **Past and Present**
   A. **Links historical events**
   B. **Builds hope**

2.5 Identifying Main Ideas

To understand and remember any material you read, identify its main idea.

In informative material, the main idea is often stated. The thesis statement of an essay or article and the topic sentence of each paragraph often state the main idea. In other material, especially literary works, the main idea is implied. After reading the piece carefully, analyze the important parts, such as characters and plot. Then try to sum up in one sentence the general point that the story makes.

 Taking Notes

As you listen or read in depth, take notes to help you understand the material. Look and listen for key words that point to main ideas.

One way to help you summarize the main idea and supporting details is to take notes in modified outline form. In using a modified outline form, you do not need to use numerals and letters. Unlike a formal outline, a modified outline does not require two or more points under each heading, and headings do not need to be grammatically parallel. Yet, like a formal outline, a modified outline organizes a text's main ideas and related details. The following modified outline lists some Native American groups in western North America.

Plains
- **Cheyenne**
- **Comanche**
- **Sioux**

Northwest Coast
- **Chinook**

California-Intermountain
- **Nez Perce**
- **Paiute**
- **Shoshone**

Southwest
- **Apache**
- **Hopi**
- **Navajo**

Use abbreviations and symbols to make note taking more efficient. Following are some commonly used abbreviations for note taking.

w/	with	re	regarding
w/o	without	=	is, equals
#	number	*	important
&, +	and	def	definition
>	more than	Amer	America
<	less than	tho	although

❸ Critical Thinking

Critical thinking includes the ability to analyze, evaluate, and synthesize ideas and information. Critical thinking goes beyond simply understanding something. It involves making informed judgments based on sound reasoning skills.

❸.❶ Avoiding Faulty Reasoning

When you write or speak for a persuasive purpose, you must make sure your logic is valid. Avoid these mistakes in reasoning, called **logical fallacies.**

Overgeneralization
Conclusions reached on the basis of too little evidence result in the fallacy called overgeneralization. A person who saw three cyclists riding bicycles without helmets might conclude, "Nobody wears bicycle helmets." That conclusion would be an overgeneralization.

Circular Reasoning
When you support an opinion by simply repeating it in different terms, you are using circular reasoning. For example, "Sport utility vehicles are popular because more people buy them than any other category of new cars." This is an illogical statement because the second part of the sentence simply uses different words to restate the first part of the sentence.

Either-Or Fallacy
Assuming that a complex question has only two possible answers is called the either-or fallacy. "Either we raise the legal driving age or accidents caused by teenage drivers will continue to increase" is an example of the either-or fallacy. The statement ignores other ways of decreasing the automobile accident rate of teenagers.

Cause-and-Effect Fallacy
The cause-and-effect fallacy occurs when you say that event B was caused by event A just because event B occurred after event A.

A person might conclude that because a city's air quality worsened two months after a new factory began operation, the new factory caused the air pollution. However, this cause-and-effect relationship would have to be supported by more specific evidence.

❸.❷ Identifying Modes of Persuasion

Understanding persuasive techniques can help you evaluate information, make informed decisions, and avoid persuasive techniques intended to deceive you. Some modes of persuasion appeal to your various emotions.

Loaded Language
Loaded language is words or phrases chosen to appeal to the emotions. It is often used in place of facts to shape opinion or to evoke a positive or negative reaction. For example, you might feel positive about a politician who has a *plan.* You might, however, feel negative about a politician who has a *scheme.*

Bandwagon Appeal
Bandwagon taps into the human desire to belong. This technique suggests that "everybody" is doing it, or buying it, or believing it. Phrases such as "Don't be the only one . . ." and "Everybody is . . . " signal the bandwagon appeal.

Testimonials
Testimonials present well-known people or satisfied customers who promote and endorse a product or idea. This technique taps into the appeal of celebrities or into people's need to identify with others just like themselves.

③·③ Logical Thinking

Persuasive writing and speaking require good reasoning skills. Two ways of creating logical arguments are deductive reasoning and inductive reasoning.

Deductive Arguments

A deductive argument begins with a generalization, or premise, and then advances with facts and evidence that lead to a conclusion. The conclusion is the logical outcome of the premise. A false premise leads to a false conclusion; a valid premise leads to a valid conclusion provided that the specific facts are correct and the reasoning is correct.

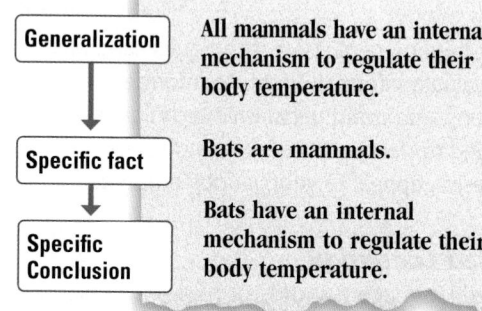

Generalization	All mammals have an internal mechanism to regulate their body temperature.
Specific fact	Bats are mammals.
Specific Conclusion	Bats have an internal mechanism to regulate their body temperature.

You may use deductive reasoning when writing a persuasive paper or speech. Your conclusion is the thesis of your paper. Facts in your paper supporting your premise should lead logically to that conclusion.

Inductive Arguments

An inductive argument begins with specific evidence that leads to a general conclusion.

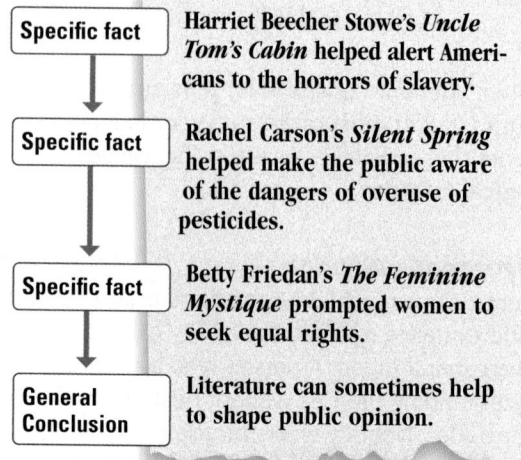

Specific fact	Harriet Beecher Stowe's *Uncle Tom's Cabin* helped alert Americans to the horrors of slavery.
Specific fact	Rachel Carson's *Silent Spring* helped make the public aware of the dangers of overuse of pesticides.
Specific fact	Betty Friedan's *The Feminine Mystique* prompted women to seek equal rights.
General Conclusion	Literature can sometimes help to shape public opinion.

The conclusion of an inductive argument often includes a qualifying term such as *some, often,* or *most.* This usage helps to avoid the fallacy of overgeneralization.

④ Speaking and Listening

Good speakers and listeners do more than just talk and hear. They use specific techniques to present their ideas effectively, and they are attentive and critical listeners.

④·① Giving a Speech

In school, in business, and in community life, giving a speech is one of the most effective ways of communicating. Whether to persuade, to inform, or to entertain, you may often speak before an audience.

Analyzing Audience and Purpose

In order to speak effectively, you need to know to whom you are speaking and why you are speaking. When preparing a speech, think about how much knowledge and interest your audience has in your subject. A speech has one of two main purposes: to inform or to persuade. A third purpose, to entertain, is often considered closely related to these two purposes.

A speech **to inform** gives the audience new information, provides a better understanding of information, or enables people to use information in a new way. An informative speech is presented in an objective way.

In a speech **to persuade,** a speaker tries to change the actions or beliefs of an audience.

Preparing and Delivering a Speech

There are four main methods of preparing and delivering a speech:

Manuscript When you speak from **manuscript,** you prepare a complete script of your speech in advance and use it to deliver your speech.

Memory When you speak from **memory,** you prepare a written text in advance and then memorize it so you can deliver it word for word.

Impromptu When you speak **impromptu,** you speak on the spur of the moment without any special preparation.

Extemporaneous When you give an **extemporaneous** speech, you research and prepare your speech and then deliver it with the help of notes.

Points for Effective Speech Delivery

- Avoid speaking either too fast or too slow. Vary your **speaking rate** depending on your material. Slow down for difficult concepts. Speed up to convince your audience that you are knowledgeable about your subject.

- Speak loud enough to be heard clearly, but not so loud that your voice is overwhelming.

- Use a **conversational tone.**

- Use a change of **pitch,** or inflection, to help make your tone and meaning clear.

- Let your **facial expression** reflect your message.

- Make **eye contact** with as many audience members as possible.

- Use **gestures** to emphasize your words. Don't make your gestures too small to be seen. On the other hand, don't gesture too frequently or wildly.

- Use **good posture**—not too relaxed and not too rigid. Avoid nervous mannerisms.

4.2 Analyzing, Evaluating and Critiquing a Speech

Evaluating speeches helps you make informed judgments about the ideas presented in a speech. It also helps you learn what makes an effective speech and delivery. Use these criteria to help you analyze, evaluate, and critique speeches.

CRITERIA **How to Evaluate a Persuasive Speech**

- Did the speaker have a clear goal or argument?
- Did the speaker take the audience's biases into account?
- Did the speaker support the argument with convincing facts?
- Did the speaker use sound logic in developing the argument?
- Did the speaker use voice, facial expression, gestures, and posture effectively?
- Did the speaker hold the audience's interest?

CRITERIA **How to Evaluate an Informative Speech**

- Did the speaker have a specific, clearly focused topic?
- Did the speaker take the audience's previous knowledge into consideration?
- Did the speaker cite sources for the information?
- Did the speaker communicate the information objectively?
- Did the speaker present the information in an organized manner?
- Did the speaker use visual aids effectively?
- Did the speaker use voice, facial expression, gestures, and posture effectively?

4.3 Using Active Listening Strategies

Listeners play an active part in the communication process. A listener has a responsibility just as a speaker does. Listening, unlike hearing, is a learned skill.

As you listen to a public speaker, use the following active listening strategies:

- Determine the **speaker's purpose.**
- Listen for the **main idea** of the message and not simply the individual details.
- **Anticipate the points** that will be made based on the speaker's purpose and main idea.
- Listen with an open mind, but **identify faulty logic, unsupported facts,** and **emotional appeals.**

4.4 Conducting Interviews

Conducting a personal interview can be an effective way to get information.

Preparing for the Interview

- Read any articles by or about the person you will interview. This background information will help you get to the point during the interview.
- Prepare a list of questions. Think of more questions than you will need. Include some yes/no questions and some open-ended questions. Order your questions from most important to least important.

Participating in the Interview

- Listen interactively. Be prepared to follow up on a response you find interesting.
- Avoid arguments. Be tactful and polite.

Following Up on the Interview

- Summarize your notes while they are still fresh in your mind.
- Send a thank-you note to the interviewee.

5 Viewing and Representing

In our media-saturated world, we are immersed in visual messages that convey ideas, information, and attitudes. To understand and use visual representations effectively, you need to be aware of the techniques and the range of visuals that are commonly used.

5.1 Understanding Visual Messages

Information is communicated not only with words but with graphic devices. A **graphic device** is a visual representation of data and ideas and the relations among them.

Reading Charts and Graphs

A chart organizes information by arranging it in rows and columns. It is helpful in showing complex information clearly. When interpreting a chart, first read the title. Then analyze how the information is presented. Charts can take many different forms. The following chart compares the transcendentalists and Gothic writers of the 1800s.

A Comparison of Transcendentalists and Gothic Writers of the 1800s	
Transcendentalists	**Gothic Writers**
Optimists	Pessimists
Emphasis on nature	Emphasis on human frailty
Emphasis on human/universe connection	Emphasis on flawed universe
Emphasis on light	Emphasis on the dark

There are several different types of **graphs,** visual aids that are often used to display numerical information.

- A **circle graph** shows proportions of the whole. The following circle graph shows the types of writing Zora Neale Hurston published.

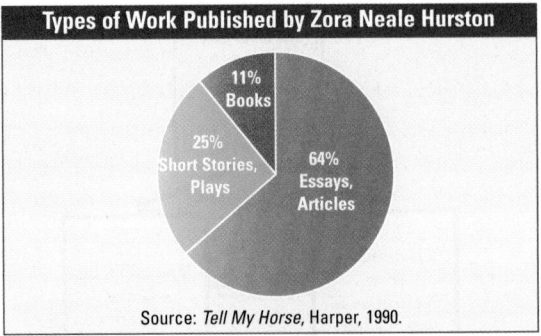

Types of Work Published by Zora Neale Hurston

11% Books
25% Short Stories, Plays
64% Essays, Articles

Source: *Tell My Horse,* Harper, 1990.

- A **line graph** shows the change in data over a period of time. The following line graph shows the expansion of land used for raising crops between 1850 and 1900.

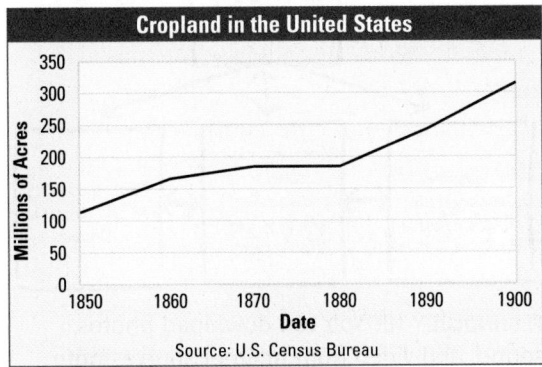

Cropland in the United States

Source: U.S. Census Bureau

- A **bar graph** compares amounts.

Interpreting Images

Speakers and writers often use visual aids to inform or persuade their audiences. These aids can be invaluable in helping you understand the information being communicated. However, you must interpret visual aids critically, as you do written material.

- **Examine photographs critically.** Does the camera angle or the background in the photo intentionally evoke a positive or negative response? Has the image been altered or manipulated?

- **Evaluate carefully the data presented in charts and graphs.** Some charts and graphs may exaggerate the facts. For example, a circle graph representing a sample of only ten people may be misleading if the speaker suggests that this data represents a trend.

5.2 Evaluating Visual Messages

When you view images, whether they are cartoons, advertising art, photographs, or paintings, there are certain elements to look for.

CRITERIA   How to Analyze Images

- Is color used realistically? Is it used to emphasize certain objects? To evoke a specific response?
- What tone is created by color and by light and dark in the picture?
- Do the background images intentionally evoke a positive or negative response?
- What is noticeable about the picture's composition, that is, the arrangement of lines, colors, and forms? Does the composition emphasize certain objects or elements in the picture?
- For graphs and charts, does the visual accurately represent the data?

5.3 Using Visual Representations

Tables, graphs, diagrams, pictures, and animations often communicate information more effectively than words alone do.

Use visuals with written reports to illustrate complex concepts and processes or to make a page look more interesting. Computer programs, CD-ROMs, and on-line services can help you generate

- **graphs** that present numerical information
- **charts** and **tables** that allow easy comparison of information
- **logos** and **graphic devices** that highlight important information
- **borders** and **tints** that signal different kinds of information
- **clip art** that adds useful pictures

- **interactive animations** that illustrate difficult concepts

You might want to explore ways of displaying data in more than one visual format before deciding which will work best for you.

5.4 Making Multimedia Presentations

A multimedia presentation is an electronically prepared combination of text, sound, and visuals such as photographs, videos, and animation. Your audience reads, hears, and sees your presentation at a computer, following different "paths" you create to lead the user through the information you have gathered.

Planning Presentations

To create a multimedia presentation, first choose your topic and decide what you want to include. Then plan how you want your user to move through your presentation. For a multimedia presentation on the American Dream, you might include the following items:

- text discussing aspects of the American Dream

- taped reading from the Declaration of Independence

- tape of Martin Luther King's "I Have a Dream" speech

- chart showing "Dreams Won" and "Dreams to Be Fulfilled"

- video of immigrants at Ellis Island

- video interview with a scholar on what ideas and ideals have changed from decade to decade and what have remained the same

- photos of people who embody some aspect of the American Dream

You can choose one of the following ways to organize your presentation:

a step-by-step, with only one path, or order, in which the user can see and hear the information

a branching path that allows users to make some choices about what they will see and hear, and in what order

A flow chart can help you figure out the paths a user can take through your presentation. Each box in the flow chart that follows represents something about the American Dream for the user to read, see, or hear. The arrows on the flow chart show the possible paths the user can follow.

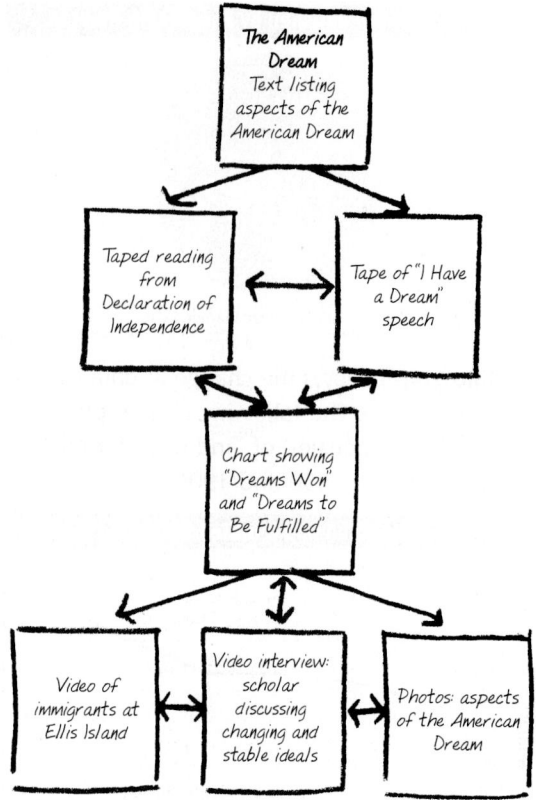

TECHNOLOGY TIP You can download photos, sound, and video from Internet sources onto your computer. This process allows you to add to your multimedia presentation various elements that would usually require complex editing equipment.

Guiding Your User

Your user will need directions to follow the path you have planned for your multimedia presentation.

Most multimedia authoring programs allow you to create screens that include text or audio directions that guide the user from one part of your presentation to the next.

If you need help creating your multimedia presentation, ask your school's technology adviser. You may also be able to get help from your classmates or your software manual.

Grammar Handbook

1 Quick Reference: Parts of Speech

Part of Speech	Definition	Examples
Noun	Names a person, place, thing, idea, quality, or action.	Silko, Rainy Mountain, churches, peace, honesty, hunting
Pronoun	Takes the place of a noun or another pronoun.	
Personal	Refers to the one speaking, spoken to, or spoken about.	I, me, my, mine, we, us, our, ours, you, your, yours, she, he, it, her, him, hers, his, its, they, them, their, theirs
Reflexive	Follows a verb or preposition and refers to a preceding noun or pronoun.	myself, yourself, herself, himself, itself, ourselves, yourselves, themselves
Intensive	Emphasizes a noun or another pronoun.	(Same as reflexives)
Demonstrative	Points to specific persons or things.	this, that, these, those
Interrogative	Signals questions.	who, whom, whose, which, what
Indefinite	Refers to person(s) or thing(s) not specifically mentioned.	both, all, most, many, anyone, everybody, several, none, some
Relative	Introduces subordinate clauses and relates them to words in the main clause.	who, whom, whose, which, that
Verb	Expresses action, condition, or state of being.	
Action	Tells what the subject does or did, physically or mentally.	run, reaches, listened, consider, decides, dreamt
Linking	Connects subjects to that which identifies or describes them.	am, is, are, was, were, sound, taste, appear, feel, become, remain, seem
Auxiliary	Precedes and introduces main verbs.	be, have, do, can, could, will, would, may, might
Adjective	Modifies nouns or pronouns.	**strong** women, **two** epics, **enough** time
Adverb	Modifies verbs, adjectives, or other adverbs.	walked **out**, **really** funny, **far** away
Preposition	Relates one word to another (following) word.	at, by, for, from, in, of, on, to, with
Conjunction	Joins words or word groups.	
Coordinating	Joins words or word groups used the same way.	and, but, or, for, so, yet, nor
Correlative	Join words or word groups used the same way and are used in pairs.	both . . . and, either . . . or, neither . . . nor
Subordinating	Joins word groups not used the same way.	although, after, as, before, because, when, if, unless
Interjection	Expresses emotion.	wow, ouch, hurrah

2 Nouns

A noun is a word used to name a person, place, thing, idea, quality, or action. Nouns can be classified in several ways. All nouns can be placed in at least two classifications. They are either common or proper. All are also either abstract or concrete. Some nouns can be classified as compound, collective, and possessive as well.

2.1 Common Nouns are general names, common to an entire group.
> EXAMPLES: *writer, song, bravery, hunter*

2.2 Proper Nouns name specific, one-of-a-kind things. (See Capitalization, page 1329.)
> EXAMPLES: *Mourning Dove, Mississippi, Granny*

2.3 Concrete Nouns name things that can be perceived by the senses.
> EXAMPLES: *windmill, turtle, clouds, canoe*

2.4 Abstract Nouns name things that cannot be observed by the senses.
> EXAMPLES: *intelligence, fear, joy, loneliness*

	Common	Proper
Abstract	democracy	Age of Exploration
Concrete	woman	Phoenix

2.5 Compound Nouns are formed from two or more words but express a single idea. They are written as single words, as separate words, or with hyphens. Use a dictionary to check the correct spelling of a compound noun.
> EXAMPLES: *birthright, folk tale, Sky-World*

2.6 Collective Nouns are singular nouns that refer to groups of people or things. (See Collective Nouns as Subjects, page 1326.)
> EXAMPLES: *army, flock, class, species*

2.7 Possessive Nouns show who or what owns something. Consult the chart below for the proper use of the possessive apostrophe.

Category	Possessive Nouns Rule	Examples
All singular nouns	Add apostrophe plus -s	Welty's, genius's, jury's, sister-in-law's
Plural nouns not ending in -s	Add apostrophe plus -s	children's women's people's
Plural nouns ending in -s	Add apostrophe only	witnesses' churches' males' Johnsons'

GRAMMAR PRACTICE

A. For each underlined noun, first tell whether it is common or proper. Then tell whether it is concrete or abstract.

1. My people named this knoll <u>Rainy Mountain</u>.
2. I returned there in July, just after my <u>grandmother</u> had died.
3. Grandmother used to sit by the window, crafting her <u>beadwork</u>.
4. The Kiowas surrendered before she was born, so my grandmother was spared the <u>humiliation</u> of imprisonment.
5. The <u>Kiowas</u> were on a long migration from the mountains.
6. Once a <u>group</u> of men had asked for one animal from the buffalo <u>herd</u>.
7. A <u>company</u> of soldiers carried out orders to disperse the tribe.
8. Born into the Sun Dance <u>culture</u>, my grandmother became a Christian in her later years.
9. Now I have her only in <u>memory</u>.
10. Kiowa legend tells how seven sisters became the stars of the <u>Big Dipper</u>.

B. 11–15. From the sentences above, write two compound nouns and three collective nouns.

C. Write the possessive form of the following nouns.

16. N. Scott Momaday
17. Kiowas
18. buffalo
19. companions
20. cross
21. gossip
22. cousins
23. people
24. council
25. grandmother

3 Pronouns

A pronoun is a word that is used in place of a noun or another pronoun. The word or word group to which the pronoun refers is called its antecedent.

3.1 ***Personal Pronouns*** are pronouns that change their form to express person, number, gender, and case. The forms of these pronouns are shown in the chart that follows.

	Nominative	Objective	Possessive
Singular			
First Person	I	me	my, mine
Second Person	you	you	your, yours
Third Person	she, he, it	her, him, it	her, hers, his, its
Plural			
First Person	we	us	our, ours
Second Person	you	you	your, yours
Third Person	they	them	their, theirs

3.2 ***Pronoun Agreement*** Pronouns should agree with their antecedents in number and person. Singular pronouns are used to replace singular nouns. Plural pronouns are used to replace plural nouns. Pronouns must also match the gender (masculine, feminine, or neuter) of the nouns they replace.

3.3 ***Pronoun Case*** Personal pronouns change form to show how they function in a sentence. This change of form is called *case.* The three cases are **nominative, objective,** and **possessive.**

A nominative pronoun is used as the subject or the predicate nominative of a sentence.

An objective pronoun is used as the direct or indirect object of a sentence or as the object of a preposition.

SUBJECT   OBJECT

He will lead them to us.

OBJECT OF PREPOSITION

A possessive pronoun shows ownership. The pronouns *mine, yours, hers, his, its, ours,* and *theirs* can be used in place of nouns.

> **EXAMPLE:** *This horse is mine.*

The pronouns *my, your, her, his, its, our,* and *their* are used before nouns.

> **EXAMPLE:** *This is my horse.*

USAGE TIP To decide which pronoun to use in a comparison, such as *He tells better tales than (I or me),* fill in the missing words: *He tells better tales than I tell.*

WATCH OUT! Many spelling errors can be avoided if you watch out for *its* and *their.* Don't confuse the possessive pronoun *its* with the contraction *it's,* meaning *it is* or *it has.* The homonyms *they're* (contraction for *they are*) and *there* (a place or an expletive) are often mistakenly used for *their.*

3.4 ***Reflexive and Intensive Pronouns***
These pronouns are formed by adding *-self* or *-selves* to certain personal pronouns. Their forms are the same, and they differ only in how they are used.

Reflexive pronouns follow verbs or prepositions and reflect back on an earlier noun or pronoun.

> **EXAMPLES:** *He likes himself too much. She is now herself again.*

Intensive pronouns intensify or emphasize the nouns or pronouns to which they refer.

> **EXAMPLES:** *They themselves will educate their children. You did it yourselves.*

Singular	
First Person	myself
Second Person	yourself
Third Person	herself, himself, itself

Plural	
First Person	ourselves
Second Person	yourselves
Third Person	themselves

WATCH OUT! Avoid using *hisself* or *theirselves.* Standard English does not include these forms.

> **NONSTANDARD**: *Did the pottery maker enjoy hisself?*
> **STANDARD**: *Did the pottery maker enjoy himself?*

USAGE TIP Reflexive and intensive pronouns should never be used without antecedents.

> **INCORRECT**: *Read a tale to my brother and myself.*
> **CORRECT**: *Read a tale to my brother and me.*

3.5 **Demonstrative Pronouns** point out things and persons near and far.

	Singular	Plural
Near	this	these
Far	that	those

WATCH OUT! Avoid using the objective pronoun *them* in place of the demonstrative *those.*

> **INCORRECT**: *Let's dramatize one of them tales.*
> **CORRECT**: *Let's dramatize one of those tales.*

3.6 **Indefinite Pronouns** do not refer to specific persons or things and usually have no antecedents. The chart shows some commonly used indefinite pronouns:

Singular	Plural	Singular or Plural	
each	both	all	half
either	few	any	plenty
neither	many	more	none
another	several	most	some

Here is another set of indefinite pronouns, all of which are singular. Notice that, with one exception, they are spelled as one word:

anyone	everyone	no one	someone
anybody	everybody	nobody	somebody
anything	everything	nothing	something

USAGE TIP Since all these are singular, pronouns referring to them should be singular.

> **INCORRECT**: *Did everybody play their part well?*
> **CORRECT**: *Did everybody play his or her part well?*

If the antecedent of the pronoun is both male and female, *his or her* may be used as an alternative, or the sentence may be recast:

> **EXAMPLES**: *Did everybody play his or her part well?*
> *Did all the students play their parts well?*

GRAMMAR PRACTICE

Write the correct form of all incorrect pronouns in the sentences below.

1. Most cross-country travelers today confine theirselves to interstate highways.
2. William Least Heat-Moon preferred them highways that were colored in blue on maps.
3. Only by traveling these routes can someone find their way to small towns and interesting people like Kendrick Fritz.
4. This Hopi Indian hisself tells Heat-Moon some fascinating things about Hopi culture.
5. Did anyone notice that one of them two rules of the Spider Grandmother is similar to the Christian Golden Rule?

3.7 **Interrogative Pronouns** tell a reader or listener that a question is coming. The interrogative pronouns are *who, whom, whose, which,* and *what.*

> **EXAMPLES**: *Who is going to rehearse with you? From whom did you receive the script?*

USAGE TIP *Who* is used for subjects, *whom* for objects. To find out which pronoun you need to use in a question, change the question to a statement:

> **QUESTION**: *(Who/Whom?) did you meet there?*
> **STATEMENT**: *You met (?) there.*

Since the verb has a subject *(you)*, the needed word must be the object form, *whom.*

> **EXAMPLE:** *Whom did you meet there?*

WATCH OUT! A special problem arises when you use an interrupter such as *do you think* within a sentence:

> **EXAMPLE:** *(Who/Whom) do you think will win?*

If you eliminate the interrupter, it is clear that the word you need is *who.*

3.8 *Relative Pronouns* relate, or connect, clauses to the words they modify in sentences. The noun or pronoun that the clause modifies is the antecedent of the relative pronoun. Here are the relative pronouns and their uses:

Replacing:	Subject	Object	Possessive
Persons	who	whom	whose
Things	which	which	whose
Things/Persons*	that	that	whose

* *That* generally will not replace specific names, such as *Mark Twain.*

Often short sentences with related ideas can be combined using relative pronouns to create a more effective sentence.

> **SHORT SENTENCE:** *Mark Twain may be America's greatest humorist.*
> **RELATED SENTENCE:** *Mark Twain wrote Huckleberry Finn.*
> **COMBINED SENTENCE:** *Mark Twain, who wrote Huckleberry Finn, may be America's greatest humorist.*

GRAMMAR PRACTICE

Choose the appropriate interrogative or relative pronoun from the words in parentheses.

1. "The Notorious Jumping Frog" was written by Samuel Clemens, (who/whom) wrote under the pseudonym Mark Twain.
2. The story gained national fame for Mark Twain, (who/that) first published it in 1865.
3. (Who/Whom) do you think is funnier, Jim Smiley or the storyteller Simon Wheeler?
4. Twain was an engaging storyteller (who/whom) large audiences came to see.
5. Smiley spent months educating his frog, (which/whose) fame as a jumper spread throughout the gold camps.

 Verbs

> *A verb is a word that expresses an action, a condition, or a state of being. There are two main kinds of verbs: action and linking. Other verbs, called auxiliary verbs, are sometimes used with action verbs and linking verbs.*

4.1 *Action Verbs* tell what action someone or something is performing, physically or mentally.

> **PHYSICAL ACTION:** *You hit the target.*
> **MENTAL ACTION:** *She dreamed of me.*

4.2 *Linking Verbs* do not express action. Linking verbs link subjects to complements that identify or describe them. Linking verbs may be divided into two groups:

> **FORMS OF *TO BE*:** *She is our queen.*
> **VERBS THAT EXPRESS CONDITION:** *The writer looked thoughtful.*

4.3 *Auxiliary Verbs,* sometimes called helping verbs, precede action or linking verbs and modify their meanings in special ways. The most commonly used auxiliary verbs are parts of the verbs *be, have,* and *do.*

> **Be:** *am, is, are, was, were, be, being, been*
> **Have:** *have, has, had*
> **Do:** *do, does, did*

Other common auxiliary verbs are *can, could, will, would, shall, should, may, might,* and *must.*

> **EXAMPLES:** *I always have admired her.*
> *You must listen to me.*

4.4 *Transitive and Intransitive Verbs*
Action verbs can be either transitive or intransitive. A transitive verb directs the action towards someone or something. The transitive verb has an object. An intransitive verb does not direct the action towards someone or something. It does not have an object. Since linking verbs convey no action, they are always intransitive.

> **Transitive:** *The storm sank the ship.*
> **Intransitive:** *The ship sank.*

4.5 *Principal Parts* Action and linking verbs typically have four principal parts, which are used to form verb tenses. The principal parts are the *present*, the *present participle*, the *past*, and the *past participle*.

If the verb is a regular verb, the past and past participle are formed by adding the ending *-d* or *-ed* to the present part. Here is a chart showing four regular verbs:

Present	Present Participle	Past	Past Participle
risk	(is) risking	risked	(have) risked
solve	(is) solving	solved	(have) solved
drop	(is) dropping	dropped	(have) dropped
carry	(is) carrying	carried	(have) carried

Note that the present participle and past participle forms are preceded by a form of *be* or *have*. These forms cannot be used alone as main verbs and always need an auxiliary verb.

> **EXAMPLES**: *The actors were dressing themselves.*
>
> *The playwright has stopped the rehearsal.*

The past and past participle of irregular verbs are not formed by adding *-d* or *-ed* to the present; they are formed in irregular ways.

Present	Present Participle	Past	Past Participle
begin	(is) beginning	began	(have) begun
break	(is) breaking	broke	(have) broken
bring	(is) bringing	brought	(have) brought
choose	(is) choosing	chose	(have) chosen
go	(is) going	went	(have) gone
lose	(is) losing	lost	(have) lost
see	(is) seeing	saw	(have) seen
swim	(is) swimming	swam	(have) swum
write	(is) writing	wrote	(have) written

4.6 *Verb Tense* The tense of a verb tells the time of the action or the state of being. An action or state of being can occur in the present, the past, or the future. There are six tenses, each expressing a different range of time.

Present tense expresses an action that is happening at the present time, occurs regularly, or is constant or generally true. Use the present part.

> **EXAMPLES**
> **NOW**: *That poet reads well.*
> **REGULAR**: *I swim every day.*
> **GENERAL**: *Time flies.*

Past tense expresses an action that began and ended in the past. Use the past part.

> **EXAMPLE**: *The storyteller finished his tale.*

Future tense expresses an action (or state of being) that will occur. Use *shall* or *will* with the present part.

> **EXAMPLE**: *They will attend the next festival.*

Present perfect tense expresses action (1) that was completed at an indefinite time in the past or (2) that began in the past and continues into the present. Use *have* or *has* with the past participle.

> **EXAMPLE**: *Poetry has inspired readers throughout the ages.*

Past perfect tense shows an action in the past that came before another action in the past. Use *had* before the past participle.

> **EXAMPLE**: *The witness had already testified before the defendant confessed.*

Future perfect tense shows an action in the future that will be completed before another action in the future. Use *shall have* or *will have* before the past participle.

> **EXAMPLE**: *They will have finished the novel before seeing the movie version of the tale.*

4.7 *Progressive Forms* The progressive forms of the six tenses show ongoing action. Use a form of *be* with the present participle of a verb.

> **PRESENT PROGRESSIVE**: *She is rehearsing her lines.*
> **PAST PROGRESSIVE**: *She was rehearsing her lines.*
> **FUTURE PROGRESSIVE**: *She will be rehearsing her lines.*

PRESENT PERFECT PROGRESSIVE: *She has been rehearsing her lines.*
PAST PERFECT PROGRESSIVE: *She had been rehearsing her lines.*
FUTURE PERFECT PROGRESSIVE: *She will have been rehearsing her lines.*

WATCH OUT! Do not shift tense needlessly. Watch out for these special cases.

- In most compound sentences and in sentences with compound predicates, keep the tenses the same.

  INCORRECT: *Every morning they get up and went to work.*
  CORRECT: *Every morning they get up and go to work.*

- If one past action happens before another, do shift tenses—from the past to the past perfect:

  INCORRECT: *They wished they started earlier.*
  CORRECT: *They wished they had started earlier.*

GRAMMAR PRACTICE

Identify the tense of the verb(s) in each of the following sentences. If you find an unnecessary tense shift, correct it.

1. The setting of *The Crucible* is the late 17th century in Salem, Massachusetts.
2. Before the witch trials ended, people had lost their ability to make objective judgments.
3. Miller knew that the play pertains to his own time.
4. People will read it far into the future, and many will apply its message to their own time.
5. In the play some accuse others of being witches, even though they knew the accusation was false.

4.8 *Active and Passive Voice* The voice of a verb tells whether the subject of a sentence performs or receives the action expressed by the verb. When the subject performs the action, the verb is in the active voice. When the subject is the receiver of the action, the verb is in the passive voice.

Compare these two sentences:

ACTIVE: *The Puritans did not celebrate Christmas.*
PASSIVE: *Christmas was not celebrated by the Puritans.*

To form the passive voice use a form of *be* with the past participle of the main verb.

WATCH OUT! Use the passive voice sparingly. It tends to make writing less forceful and less direct. It can also make the writing awkward.

AWKWARD: *The stories of hysterical witnesses were believed by gullible and fearful jurors.*
CORRECT: *Gullible and fearful jurors believed the stories of hysterical witnesses.*

There are occasions when you will choose to use the passive voice because

- you want to emphasize the receiver: *The king was shot.*
- the doer is unknown: *My books were stolen.*
- the doer is unimportant: *French is spoken here.*

4.9 *Mood* The mood identifies the manner in which the verb expresses an idea. There are three moods.

The indicative mood states a fact or asks a question. You use this mood most often.

EXAMPLE: *His trust was shattered by the betrayal.*

The imperative mood is used to give a command or make a request.

EXAMPLE: *Be there by eight o'clock sharp.*

The subjunctive mood is used to express a wish or a condition that is contrary to fact.

EXAMPLE: *If I were you, I wouldn't get my hopes up.*

GRAMMAR PRACTICE

For the first five items below, identify the boldfaced verb phrase as active or passive.

1. *The Crucible* **has played** in theaters throughout the world.
2. It **was written** by Arthur Miller, one of America's greatest dramatists.
3. Miller **did** not **approve** of Reverend Parris's greed for gold.
4. **Has** the reputation of the minister **been maligned?**
5. After the trials Parris **was voted** from office, and surviving victims **were awarded** compensation by the government.

For the following items, identify the boldfaced verb as indicative or subjunctive in mood.

6. If Parris **were** alive today, would he tell his side of the story?

7. The jurors expressed their regret to all citizens who **had suffered.**

8. Many people at that time **were** devout Puritans.

9. Some of the farms belonging to the victims **were abandoned.**

10. If there **were** court-appointed lawyers at the time, would justice have been served?

---

❺ Modifiers

Modifiers are words or groups of words that change or limit the meanings of other words. The two kinds of modifiers are adjectives and adverbs.

5.1 *Adjectives* An adjective is a word that modifies a noun or pronoun by telling *which one, what kind, how many,* or *how much.*

WHICH ONE: *this, that, these, those*
EXAMPLE: *Those actions were truly heroic.*

WHAT KIND: *large, beautiful, cowardly, innocent*
EXAMPLE: *Many innocent people suffered.*

HOW MANY: *ten, many, several, every*
EXAMPLE: *Every juror has to make up his or her own mind.*

HOW MUCH: *little, enough, less, abundant*
EXAMPLE: *Our farmers hope to have abundant rainfall this summer.*

The **articles** *a, an,* and *the* are usually classified as adjectives. These are the most common adjectives that you will use.

EXAMPLES: *The bridge was burned before the attack.*
A group of peasants led the procession in the town.

5.2 *Predicate Adjectives* Most adjectives come before the nouns they modify, as in the examples above. Predicate adjectives, however, follow linking verbs and describe the subject.

EXAMPLE: *My friends are very intelligent.*

Be especially careful to use adjectives (not adverbs) after such linking verbs as *look, feel, grow, taste,* and *smell.*

EXAMPLE: *The weather grows cold.*

5.3 *Adverbs* modify verbs, adjectives, or other adverbs by telling *where, when, how,* or *to what extent.*

WHERE: *The children played outside.*
WHEN: *The author spoke yesterday.*
HOW: *We walked slowly behind the leader.*
TO WHAT EXTENT: *He worked very hard.*

Unlike adjectives, adverbs tend to be mobile words; they may occur in many places in sentences.

EXAMPLES: *Suddenly the wind shifted. The wind suddenly shifted. The wind shifted suddenly.*

Changing the position of adverbs within sentences can vary the rhythm in your writing.

5.4 *Adjective or Adverb* Many adverbs are formed by adding *-ly* to adjectives.

EXAMPLES: *sweet, sweetly; gentle, gently*

However, *-ly* added to a noun will usually yield an adjective.

EXAMPLES: *friend, friendly; woman, womanly*

5.5 *Comparison of Modifiers* The form of an adjective or adverb indicates the degree of comparison that the modifier expresses. Both adjectives and adverbs have three forms, or degrees: the positive, comparative, and superlative.

The positive form is used to describe individual things, groups, or actions.

EXAMPLES: *Poe was a great writer. His descriptions are vivid.*

The comparative form is used to compare two things, groups, or actions.

EXAMPLES: *I think that Poe was a greater writer than Nathaniel Hawthorne. Poe's descriptions are more vivid.*

The superlative form is used to compare more than two things, groups, or actions.

> **EXAMPLES:** *I think that Poe was the greatest short story writer of his century. Poe's descriptions are the most vivid I have ever read.*

5.6 **Regular Comparisons** One-syllable and some two-syllable adjectives and adverbs form their comparative and superlative forms by adding *-er* or *-est*. All three-syllable and most two-syllable modifiers form their comparative and superlative by using *more* or *most*.

Positive	Comparative	Superlative
small	smaller	smallest
thin	thinner	thinnest
sleepy	sleepier	sleepiest
useless	more useless	most useless
precisely	more precisely	most precisely

WATCH OUT! Note that spelling changes must sometimes be made to form the comparative and superlative of modifiers.

> **EXAMPLES:** *friendly, friendlier* (change *y* to *i* and add the ending)
> *sad, sadder* (double the final consonant and add the ending)

5.7 **Irregular Comparisons** Some commonly used modifiers have irregular comparative and superlative forms. You may wish to memorize them.

Positive	Comparative	Superlative
good	better	best
bad	worse	worst
far	farther or further	farthest or furthest
little	less or lesser	least
many	more	most
well	better	best
much	more	most

5.8 **Using Modifiers Correctly** Study the tips that follow to avoid common mistakes.

Farther* and *Further *Farther* is used for distances; use *further* for everything else.

Avoiding double comparisons You make a comparison by using *-er/-est* or by using *more/most*. Using *-er* with *more* or using *-est* with *most* is incorrect.

> **INCORRECT:** *I like her more better than she likes me.*
> **CORRECT:** *I like her better than she likes me.*

Avoiding illogical comparisons An illogical or confusing comparison results if two unrelated things are compared or if something is compared with itself. The word *other* or the word *else* should be used in a comparison of an individual member with the rest of the group.

> **ILLOGICAL:** *"The Fall of the House of Usher" was as suspenseful as any Poe story.*
> (Did Poe write "The Fall of the House of Usher"?)
> **LOGICAL:** *"The Fall of the House of Usher" was as suspenseful as any other Poe story.*

Bad* vs. *Badly *Bad,* always an adjective, is used before nouns or after linking verbs to describe the subject. *Badly,* always an adverb, never modifies a noun. Be sure to use the right form after a linking verb.

> **INCORRECT:** *Ed felt badly after his team lost.*
> **CORRECT:** *Ed felt bad after his team lost.*

Good* vs. *Well *Good* is always an adjective. It is used before nouns or after a linking verb to modify the subject. *Well* is often an adverb meaning "expertly" or "properly." *Well* can also be used as an adjective after a linking verb, when it means "in good health."

> **INCORRECT:** *Helen writes very good.*
> **CORRECT:** *Helen writes very well.*
> **CORRECT:** *Yesterday I felt bad; today I feel well.*

Double negatives If you add a negative word to a sentence that is already negative, the result will be an error known as a double negative. When using *not* or *-n't* with a verb, use "any-" words, such as *anybody* or *anything*, rather than "*no-*" words, such as *nobody* or *nothing*, later in the sentence.

> **INCORRECT:** *I don't have no money.*
> **CORRECT:** *I don't have any money.*
>
> **INCORRECT:** *We haven't seen nobody.*
> **CORRECT:** *We haven't seen anybody.*

Using *hardly, barely,* or *scarcely* after a negative word is also incorrect.

> **INCORRECT:** *They couldn't barely see two feet ahead.*
> **CORRECT:** *They could barely see two feet ahead.*

Misplaced modifiers A misplaced modifier is one placed so far away from the word it modifies that the intended meaning of the sentence is unclear. Place modifiers as close as possible to the words they modify.

> **MISPLACED:** *We found the child in the park who was missing.* (The child was missing, not the park.)
>
> **CLEARER:** *We found the child who was missing in the park.*

GRAMMAR PRACTICE

Choose the correct word from each pair in parentheses.

1. Flannery O'Connor's story is (better/more better) than other stories I have read recently.
2. Mr. Shiftlet and Mrs. Crater (could/couldn't) hardly be less honest with each other.
3. Mr. Shiftlet says there isn't (any/no) broken thing on the farm that he can't fix.
4. He feels (good/well) about fixing the car.
5. Who do you think is the (stranger/strangest) person—Mr. Shiftlet or Mrs. Crater?
6. Mr. Shiftlet wouldn't have been able to hurt (anybody/nobody) if Mrs. Crater had not been so eager for Lucynell to get married.
7. As Mr. Shiftlet drove on alone he felt (depresseder/more depressed) than ever.
8. Shiftlet didn't feel very (well/good) about being alone, so he picked up a hitchhiker.

9. Shiftlet feels (bad/badly) about the rottenness of the world.
10. One wonders how many other great stories Flannery O'Connor would have written had she lived (longer/more longer).

---

6 Prepositions, Conjunctions, and Interjections

6.1 *Prepositions* A preposition is a word used to show the relationship between a noun or a pronoun and another word in the sentence.

Commonly Used Prepositions			
above	down	near	through
at	for	of	to
before	from	on	up
below	in	out	with
by	into	over	without

The preposition is always followed by a word or group of words that serves as its object. The preposition, its object, and modifiers of the object are called the **prepositional phrase.** In each example below, the prepositional phrase is underlined and the object of the preposition is in boldface type.

> **EXAMPLES**
> *The future of the entire **kingdom** is uncertain.*
> *We searched through the deepest **woods.***

Prepositional phrases may be used as adjectives or as adverbs. The phrase in the first example is used as an adjective modifying the noun *future*. In the second example, the phrase is used as an adverb modifying the verb *searched*.

WATCH OUT! Prepositional phrases must be as close as possible to the word they modify.

> **MISPLACED:** *We have clothes for leisure wear of many colors.*
> **CLEARER:** *We have clothes of many colors for leisure wear.*

6.2 *Conjunctions* A conjunction is a word used to connect words, phrases, or sentences. There are three kinds of conjunctions: **coordinating conjunctions, correlative conjunctions,** and **subordinating conjunctions.**

Coordinating conjunctions connect words or word groups that have the same function in a sentence. These include *and, but, or, for, so, yet,* and *nor.*

Coordinating conjunctions can join nouns, pronouns, verbs, adjectives, adverbs, prepositional phrases, and clauses in a sentence.

These examples show coordinating conjunctions joining words of the same function:

EXAMPLES

I have many friends <u>but</u> few enemies. (two noun objects)

We ran out the door <u>and</u> into the street. (two prepositional phrases)

They are pleasant <u>yet</u> seem aloof. (two predicates)

We have to go now, <u>or</u> we will be late. (two clauses)

Correlative conjunctions are similar to coordinating conjunctions. However, correlative conjunctions are always used in pairs.

Correlative Conjunctions		
both . . . and	neither . . . nor	whether . . . or
either . . . or	not only . . . but also	

Subordinating conjunctions introduce subordinate clauses—clauses that cannot stand by themselves as complete sentences. The subordinating conjunction shows how the subordinate clause relates to the rest of the sentence. The relationships include time, manner, place, cause, comparison, condition, and purpose.

SUBORDINATING CONJUNCTIONS	
TIME	*after, as, as long as, as soon as, before, since, until, when, whenever, while*
MANNER	*as, as if*
PLACE	*where, wherever*
CAUSE	*because, since*
COMPARISON	*as, as much as, than*
CONDITION	*although, as long as, even if, even though, if, provided that, though, unless, while*
PURPOSE	*in order that, so that, that*

In the example below, the boldface word is the conjunction, and the underlined words are called a subordinate clause:

EXAMPLE: *Walt Whitman was a man of the people,* **<u>although</u>** <u>many did not appreciate his poems.</u>

Walt Whitman was a man of the people is an independent clause because it can stand alone as a complete sentence. *Although many did not appreciate his poems* cannot stand alone as a complete sentence; it is a subordinate clause.

Conjunctive adverbs are used to connect clauses that can stand by themselves as sentences. Conjunctive adverbs include *also, besides, finally, however, moreover, nevertheless, otherwise,* and *then.*

EXAMPLE: *She loved the fall; <u>however,</u> she also enjoyed winter.*

6.3 *Interjections* are words used to show strong emotion, such as *wow* and *cool.* Often followed by an exclamation point, they have no grammatical relationship to the rest of a sentence.

EXAMPLE: *Thoreau lived in the woods by himself. <u>Amazing!</u>*

GRAMMAR PRACTICE

Label each of the boldface words as a preposition, conjunction, or interjection.

1. Thoreau's sojourn **at** Walden Pond lasted about two years, **yet** it made him famous.

2. Thoreau was determined that neither weather nor poverty would deter him, **since** his purpose was so important.

3. He lived just a few miles **from** Concord, **so** he was able to visit his friends and relatives frequently.

4. Thoreau left the woods **because** he thought **that** he might have other lives to live.

5. The cabin **in** which he lived has been re-created, **but** it is not **on** the site where he built it.

6. You're going to visit Walden Pond **with** us? **Great!**

7 Quick Reference: The Sentence and Its Parts

The diagrams that follow will give you a brief review of the essentials of the sentence—subjects and predicates—and of some of its parts.

Thoreau's original **cabin** | **cost** less than thirty dollars.

The **complete subject** includes all the words that identify the person, place, thing, or idea that the sentence is about.

The **complete predicate** includes all the words that tell or ask something about the subject.

cabin

cost

The **simple subject** tells exactly whom or what the sentence is about. It may be one word or a group of words, but it does not include modifiers.

The **simple predicate**, or **verb**, tells what the subject does or is. It may be one word or several, but it does not include modifiers.

In *Walden*, | Thoreau | **has offered** | readers his thoughts about living.

subject

A **prepositional phrase** consists of a preposition, its object, and any modifiers of the object. In this phrase, *in* is the preposition and *Walden* is its object.

Verbs often have more than one part. They may be made up of a **main verb,** like *offered,* and one or more **auxiliary,** or **helping, verbs,** like *has.*

A **direct object** is a word or group of words that tells who or what receives the action of the verb in the sentence.

An **indirect object** is a word or a group of words that tells *to whom* or *for whom* or *to what* or *for what* about the verb. A sentence can have an indirect object only if it has a direct object. The indirect object always comes before the direct object in a sentence.

8 The Sentence and Its Parts

A sentence is a group of words used to express a complete thought. A complete sentence has a subject and predicate.

8.1 Kinds of Sentences Sentences make statements, ask questions, give commands, and show feelings. There are four basic types of sentences.

Type	Definition	Example
Declarative	states a fact, wish, intent, or feeling	I read Porter's story recently.
Interrogative	asks a question	Did you read her story?
Imperative	gives a command, request, or direction	Read the story carefully.
Exclamatory	expresses strong feeling or excitement	This writer is good!

WRITING TIP One way to vary your writing is to employ a variety of different types of sentences. In the first example below, each sentence is declarative. Notice how much more interesting the revised paragraph is.

SAMPLE PARAGRAPH: *You have to see Niagara Falls in person. You can truly appreciate their awesome power in no other way. You should visit them on your next vacation. They are a spectacular sight.*

REVISED PARAGRAPH: *Have you ever seen Niagara Falls in person? You can truly appreciate their awesome power in no other way. Visit them on your next vacation. What a spectacular sight they are!*

WATCH OUT! Conversation frequently includes parts of sentences, or **fragments.** In formal writing, however, you need to be sure that every sentence is a complete thought and includes a subject and predicate. (See Correcting Fragments, page 1323.)

8.2 Complete Subjects and Predicates A sentence has two parts: a subject and a predicate. The complete subject includes all the words that identify the person, place, thing, or idea that the sentence is about. The complete predicate includes all the words that tell what the subject did or what happened to the subject.

Complete Subject	Complete Predicate
The poets of the time	wrote about nature.
This new approach	was extraordinary.

8.3 Simple Subjects and Predicates The simple subject is the key word in the complete subject. The simple predicate is the key word in the complete predicate. In the examples that follow, they are underlined.

Simple Subject	Simple Predicate
The <u>poets</u> of the time	<u>wrote</u> about nature.
This new <u>approach</u>	<u>was</u> extraordinary.

8.4 Compound Subjects and Predicates A compound subject consists of two or more subjects that share the same verb. They are typically joined by the coordinating conjunction *and* or *or*.

    EXAMPLE: <u>Short story writers and poets</u> will read from their work.

A compound predicate consists of two or more predicates that share the same subject. They, too, are usually joined by the coordinating conjunction *and, but,* or *or*.

    EXAMPLE: We <u>listened to the poets and discussed their work.</u>

8.5 Subjects and Predicates in Questions In many interrogative sentences, the subject may appear after the verb or between parts of a verb phrase.

    INTERROGATIVE: *<u>Was</u> the <u>reading</u> very interesting?*
    INTERROGATIVE: *Why <u>were</u> those particular writers <u>invited</u>?*

Grammar Handbook

8.6 Subjects and Predicates in Imperative Sentences Imperative sentences give commands, requests, or directions. The subject of an imperative sentence is the person spoken to, or *you*. While it is not stated, it is understood to be *you*.

EXAMPLE: *(You) Please tell me what you're thinking.*

8.7 Subjects in Sentences That Begin with There and Here When a sentence begins with *there* or *here*, the subject usually follows the verb. Remember that *there* and *here* are never the subjects of a sentence. The simple subjects in the example sentences are underlined.

EXAMPLES

Here is the solution to the mystery.
There is no time to waste now.
There were too many passengers on the boat.

GRAMMAR PRACTICE

Copy each of the following sentences. Then draw one line under the complete subject and two lines under the complete predicate.

1. Katherine Anne Porter published only six stories in her first collection.
2. "The Jilting of Granny Weatherall" was one of the six.
3. This story about a woman on her deathbed has been reprinted often.
4. Why is the main character called "Granny" rather than "Grandmother"?
5. Have you analyzed the symbolic meaning of her last name?
6. Both George and John probably died before Mrs. Weatherall.
7. There are memories of a former suitor that torment the dying woman.
8. The imagination of Katherine Anne Porter is evident in this portrait of an aged woman.
9. Five novelettes, three volumes of short stories, and only one novel comprise all of Miss Porter's works.
10. Her reputation is based on quality, not quantity.

8.8 Complements A complement is a word or group of words that completes the meaning of the sentence. Some sentences contain only a subject and a verb. Most sentences, however, require additional words placed after the verb to complete the meaning of the sentence. There are three kinds of complements: **direct objects, indirect objects,** and **subject complements.**

Direct objects are words or word groups that receive the action of action verbs. A direct object answers the question *what?* or *whom?* In the examples that follow, the direct objects are underlined.

EXAMPLES

The students asked many questions. (asked what?)

The teacher quickly answered them. (answered what?)

The school accepted girls and boys. (accepted whom?)

Indirect objects tell *to* or *for whom* or *what* the action of the verb is performed. Indirect objects come before direct objects. In the examples that follow, the indirect objects are underlined.

EXAMPLES

My sister usually gave her friends good advice. (gave to whom?)

Her brother sent the post office a heavy package. (sent to what?)

His kind grandfather mailed him a new tie. (mailed to whom?)

Subject complements come after linking verbs and identify or describe the subject. Subject complements that name or identify the subject of the sentence are called **predicate nominatives.** These include **predicate nouns** and **predicate pronouns.** In the examples that follow, the subject complements are underlined.

EXAMPLES

My friends are very hard workers.
The best writer in the class is she.

Other subject complements describe the subject of the sentence. These are called **predicate adjectives.**

EXAMPLE: *The pianist appeared very energetic.*

GRAMMAR PRACTICE

Write all of the complements in the following sentences, and label them as direct objects, indirect objects, predicate nouns, or predicate adjectives.

1. In "Armistice," by Bernard Malamud, Morris had seen terrible persecution in Russia.
2. Morris felt sympathetic toward others of his race.
3. Because of his childhood memories, Morris feared the Nazis.
4. Seeing his father's anxiety, Leonard became concerned.
5. Gus delivered Morris delicatessen meats.
6. Delighted with military power, Gus was a Nazi sympathizer.
7. Laughing, Gus asked Morris questions about the German armies in France.
8. The main characters in Malamud's story create an armistice at the end.
9. Their truce is not permanent, however.
10. In spite of what Gus imagines, his delivery truck is not really a German tank.

❾ Phrases

A phrase is a group of related words that does not have a subject and predicate and functions in a sentence as a single part of speech.

9.1 *Prepositional Phrases* A prepositional phrase is a phrase that consists of a preposition, its object, and any modifiers of the object. Prepositional phrases that modify nouns or pronouns are called **adjective phrases.** Prepositional phrases that modify a verb, an adjective, or another adverb are **adverb phrases.**

ADJECTIVE PHRASE: *The central character of the story is a wicked villain.*

ADVERB PHRASE: *He reveals his nature in the first scene.*

9.2 *Appositives and Appositive Phrases* An appositive is a noun or pronoun that usually comes directly after another noun or pronoun and identifies or provides further information about that word. An appositive phrase includes the appositive and all its modifiers. In the following examples, the appositive phrases are underlined.

> **EXAMPLES**
> *We were discussing Edward Hopper, the painter.*
>
> *Margaret Fuller, a well-known feminist, edited* The Dial.

Occasionally, an appositive phrase may precede the noun it tells about.

> **EXAMPLE:** *A well-known feminist, Margaret Fuller edited* The Dial.

❿ Verbals and Verbal Phrases

A verbal is a verb form that is used as a noun, an adjective, or an adverb. A verbal phrase consists of a verbal, all its modifiers, and all its complements. There are three kinds of verbals: infinitives, participles, and gerunds.

10.1 *Infinitives and Infinitive Phrases* An infinitive is a verb form that usually begins with *to* and functions as a noun, adjective, or adverb. The infinitive and its modifiers constitute an infinitive phrase. The examples that follow show several uses of infinitives and infinitive phrases. Each infinitive phrase is underlined.

> **NOUN:** *To know her is my only desire.* (subject)
>
> *I'm planning to walk with you.* (direct object)
>
> *Her goal was to promote women's rights.* (predicate nominative)
>
> **ADJECTIVE:** *We saw his need to be loved.* (adjective modifying *need*)
>
> **ADVERB:** *She wrote to voice her opinions.* (adverb modifying *wrote*)

Like verbs themselves, infinitives can take objects (*her* in the first noun example), be made passive (*to be loved* in the adjective example), and take modifiers (*with you* in the adverb example).

Because *to*, the sign of the infinitive, precedes infinitives, it is usually easy to recognize them. However, sometimes *to* may be omitted.

> **EXAMPLE:** *Let no one dare [to] enter this shrine.*

10.2 *Participles and Participial Phrases*

A participle is a verb form that functions as an adjective. Like adjectives, participles modify nouns and pronouns. Most participles use the present participle form, ending in *-ing*, or the past participle form, ending in *-ed* or *-en*. In the examples below, the participles are underlined.

> **MODIFYING A NOUN:** *The dying man had a smile on his face.*
> **MODIFYING A PRONOUN:** *Frustrated, everyone abandoned the cause.*

Participial phrases are participles with all their modifiers and complements.

> **MODIFYING A NOUN:** *The dogs searching for survivors are well trained.*
> **MODIFYING A PRONOUN:** *Having approved your proposal, we are ready to act.*

10.3 *Dangling and Misplaced Participles*

A participle or participial phrase should be placed as close as possible to the word that it modifies. Otherwise the meaning of the sentence may not be clear.

> **MISPLACED:** *The boys were looking for squirrels searching the trees.*
> **CLEARER:** *The boys searching the trees were looking for squirrels.*

A participle or participial phrase that does not clearly modify anything in a sentence is called a **dangling participle.** A dangling participle causes confusion because it appears to modify a word that it cannot sensibly modify.

Correct a dangling participle by providing a word for the participle to modify.

> **CONFUSING:** *Running like the wind, my hat fell off.* (The hat wasn't running.)
> **CLEARER:** *Running like the wind, I lost my hat.*

10.4 *Gerunds and Gerund Phrases*

A gerund is a verb form ending in *-ing* that functions as a noun. Gerunds may perform any function nouns perform.

> **SUBJECT:** *Running is my favorite pastime.*
> **DIRECT OBJECT:** *I truly love running.*
> **SUBJECT COMPLEMENT:** *My deepest passion is running.*
> **OBJECT OF PREPOSITION:** *Her love of running keeps her strong.*

Gerund phrases are gerunds with all their modifiers and complements. The gerund phrases are underlined in the following examples.

> **SUBJECT:** *Wishing on a star never got me far.*
> **OBJECT OF PREPOSITION:** *I will finish before leaving the office.*
> **APPOSITIVE:** *Her avocation, flying airplanes, finally led to full-time employment.*

GRAMMAR PRACTICE

Identify the underlined phrases as appositive phrases, infinitive phrases, participial phrases, or gerund phrases.

1. In "The Masque of the Red Death," Poe uses allegory, a device for representing abstract qualities.

2. To escape the plague, Prince Prospero seals himself and his courtiers in a walled abbey.

3. Feeling secure from the Red Death, Prospero holds a lavish masquerade ball.

4. Every hour he heard the chimes clanging mournfully.

5. There suddenly appeared in the last room a masked figure, the Red Death in a ghastly shroud.

6. The Prince unsheathed his dagger to kill the figure.

7. Killing the apparition was impossible.

11 Clauses

A clause is a group of words that contains a subject and a verb. There are two kinds of clauses: independent clauses and subordinate clauses.

11.1 Independent and Subordinate Clauses
An independent clause can stand alone as a sentence, as the word *independent* suggests.

INDEPENDENT CLAUSE: *Robert Hayden admired Frederick Douglass.*

A sentence may contain more than one independent clause.

EXAMPLE: *Robert Hayden admired Frederick Douglass, and he expressed his admiration in a poem.*

In the example above, the coordinating conjunction *and* joins the two independent clauses.

A subordinate clause cannot stand alone as a sentence. It is subordinate to, or dependent on, the main clause.

EXAMPLE: *Hayden did extensive research on Douglass before he wrote his poem.*

Before he wrote his poem depends on the independent clause. It cannot stand by itself.

11.2 Adjective Clauses
An adjective clause is a subordinate clause used as an adjective. It usually follows the noun or pronoun it modifies.

EXAMPLE: *The research that he did was very useful.*

Adjective clauses are typically introduced by the relative pronouns *who, whom, whose, which,* and *that* (see Relative Pronouns, page 1309). In the examples that follow, the adjective clauses are underlined.

EXAMPLES

The autobiographer whom I liked best was Frederick Douglass.

He was a man who was determined to find freedom.

I read novels that let me escape from daily life.

WATCH OUT! The relative pronouns *whom, which,* and *that* may sometimes be omitted when they are objects of their own clauses.

EXAMPLE: *The autobiographer [whom] I liked best was Frederick Douglass.*

11.3 Adverb Clauses
An adverb clause is a subordinate clause that is used as an adverb to modify a verb, an adjective, or another adverb. It is introduced by a subordinating conjunction (see Subordinating Conjunctions, page 1315).

Adverb clauses typically occur at the beginning or end of sentences. The clauses are underlined in these examples.

MODIFYING A VERB: *When we need you, we will call.*

MODIFYING AN ADVERB: *I'll stay here where there is shelter from the rain.*

MODIFYING AN ADJECTIVE: *Roman felt good when he finished his essay.*

11.4 Noun Clauses
A noun clause is a subordinate clause that is used in a sentence as a noun. A noun clause may be used as a subject, a direct object, an indirect object, a predicate nominative, or an object of a preposition. Noun clauses are often introduced by pronouns such as *that, what, who, whoever, which,* and *whose,* and by subordinating conjunctions, such as *how, when, where, why,* and *whether.* (See Subordinating Conjunctions, page 1315.)

USAGE TIP Because the same words may introduce adjective and noun clauses, you need to consider how the clause functions within its sentence.

To determine if a clause is a noun clause, try substituting *something* or *someone* for the clause. If you can do it, it is probably a noun clause.

EXAMPLES: *I know whose woods these are.* ("I know *something*." The clause is a noun clause, direct object of the verb *know*.)

Give a copy to whoever wants one. ("Give a copy to *someone*." The clause is a noun clause, object of the preposition *to*.)

GRAMMAR PRACTICE

Identify each underlined clause as an adjective clause, an adverb clause, or a noun clause.

1. Frederick Douglass's story illustrates <u>that a man can risk everything to be free.</u>
2. <u>When the slaves were working in the fields,</u> Covey often would sneak up on them.
3. Any man <u>who brutalizes others</u> is himself a brute.
4. Do you believe <u>that a slave breaker could be so mean</u>?
5. The institution of slavery brutalized slaves and masters <u>because it was so inhumane.</u>

⓬ The Structure of Sentences

When classified by their structure, there are four kinds of sentences: simple, compound, complex, and compound-complex.

12.1 **Simple Sentences** A simple sentence is a sentence that has one independent clause and no subordinate clauses. The fact that such sentences are called "simple" does not mean that they are uncomplicated. Various parts of simple sentences may be compound, and they may contain grammatical structures such as appositives and verbals.

EXAMPLES

Ambrose Bierce and Stephen Crane, two great American writers, both wrote during the latter half of the 19th century. (compound subject and an appositive)

Crane, best known for writing fiction, also wrote great poetry. (participial phrase containing a gerund phrase)

12.2 **Compound Sentences** A compound sentence has two or more independent clauses. The clauses are joined together with a comma and a coordinating conjunction (*and, but, or, nor, yet, for, so*), a semicolon, or a conjunctive adverb with a semicolon. Like simple sentences, compound sentences do not contain any dependent clauses.

EXAMPLES

Walt Whitman was a great poet, yet he made very little money from his writing.

Emily Dickinson lived a relatively quiet life; however, that did not prevent her from writing great poems.

WATCH OUT! Do not confuse compound sentences with simple sentences that have compound parts.

> **EXAMPLE:** *A subcommittee drafted a document and immediately presented it to the entire group.* (here *and* signals a compound predicate, not a compound sentence)

12.3 **Complex Sentences** A complex sentence has one independent clause and one or more subordinate clauses. Each subordinate clause can be used as a noun or as a modifier. If it is used as a modifier, a subordinate clause usually modifies a word in the main clause and the main clause can stand alone. However, when a subordinate clause is a noun clause, it is a part of the independent clause; the two cannot be separated.

> **MODIFIER:** *One should not complain, <u>unless she or he has a better solution.</u>*

> **NOUN CLAUSE:** *We sketched pictures of <u>whomever we wished.</u>* (noun clause is the object of the preposition *of* and cannot be separated from the rest of the sentence)

12.4 **Compound-Complex Sentences** A compound-complex sentence has two or more independent clauses and one or more subordinate clauses. Compound-complex sentences are, simply, both compound and complex. If you start with a compound sentence, all you need to do to form a compound-complex sentence is add a subordinate clause.

> **COMPOUND:** *All the students knew the answer, yet they were too shy to volunteer.*

> **COMPOUND-COMPLEX:** *All the students knew the answer that their teacher expected, yet they were too shy to volunteer.*

GRAMMAR PRACTICE

Tell whether each sentence is a simple sentence, a compound sentence, a complex sentence, or a compound-complex sentence.

1. Douglass first settled in Massachusetts with his wife, who was free.

2. He changed his original name, Frederick Bailey, to Frederick Douglass in order to avoid pursuit.

3. He taught himself to read and write, but his speaking skills, which made him famous, seemed to be innate.

4. The *Narrative of the Life of Frederick Douglass* contained a preface by William Lloyd Garrison and a prefatory letter by Wendell Phillips.

5. Garrison and Phillips were well known, and their names helped to sell the book.

⓭ Writing Complete Sentences

A sentence is a group of words that expresses a complete thought. In writing that you wish to share with a reader, try to avoid both sentence fragments and run-on sentences.

⓭.① Correcting Fragments A sentence fragment is a group of words that is only part of a sentence. It does not express a complete thought and may be confusing to the reader or the listener. A sentence fragment may be lacking a subject, a predicate, or both.

> **FRAGMENT:** *waited for the boat to arrive* (no subject)
> **CORRECTED:** *We waited for the boat to arrive.*
> **FRAGMENT:** *people of various races, ages, and creeds* (no predicate)
> **CORRECTED:** *People of various races, ages, and creeds gathered together.*
> **FRAGMENT:** *near the old cottage* (neither subject nor predicate)
> **CORRECTED:** *The burial ground is near the old cottage.*

In your own writing, fragments are usually the result of haste or incorrect punctuation. Sometimes fixing a fragment will be a matter of attaching it to a preceding or following sentence.

> **FRAGMENT:** *We saw the two girls. Waiting for the bus to arrive.*
> **CORRECTED:** *We saw the two girls waiting for the bus to arrive.*
> **FRAGMENT:** *Newspapers appeal to a wide audience. Including people of various races, ages, and creeds.*
> **CORRECTED:** *Newspapers appeal to a wide audience, including people of various races, ages, and creeds.*

⓭.② Correcting Run-on Sentences

A run-on sentence is made up of two or more sentences written as though they were one. Some run-ons have no punctuation within them. Others may use only a comma where a conjunction or stronger punctuation is necessary. Use your judgment in correcting run-on sentences, as you have choices. You can make two sentences if the thoughts are not closely connected. If the thoughts are closely related, you can keep the run-on as one sentence by adding a semicolon or a conjunction.

> **RUN-ON:** *We found a place by a small pond for the picnic it is three miles from the village.*
> **MAKE TWO SENTENCES:** *We found a place by a small pond for the picnic. It is three miles from the village.*
> **RUN-ON:** *We found a place by a small pond for the picnic it was perfect.*
> **USE A SEMICOLON:** *We found a place by a small pond for the picnic; it was perfect.*
> **ADD A CONJUNCTION:** *We found a place by a small pond for the picnic, and it was perfect.*

WATCH OUT! When you add a conjunction, make sure you use appropriate punctuation before it: a comma for a coordinating conjunction, a semicolon for a conjunctive adverb. (See Conjunctions, page 1315.) A very common mistake is to use a comma instead of a conjunction or an end mark. This error is called a **comma splice**.

> **INCORRECT:** *He finished the apprenticeship, then he left the village.*
> **CORRECT:** *He finished the apprenticeship, and then he left the village.*

GRAMMAR PRACTICE

Rewrite the following paragraph, correcting all fragments and run-ons.

The narrator in Charlotte Perkins Gilman's story "The Yellow Wallpaper" expects that her husband will laugh at her, that's an odd response, in my opinion. She could have lived more happily. If the relationship between her and her husband were an equal partnership. We can acknowledge that men and women may be different in some ways. Without believing that they are as different as this story suggests. The male character acts practical and "strong," the female character acts nervous and weak.

⑭ Subject-Verb Agreement

The subject and verb of a sentence must agree in number. Agreement means that when the subject is singular, the verb must be singular; when the subject is plural, the verb must be plural.

14.1 **Basic Agreement** Fortunately, agreement between subject and verb in English is simple. Most verbs show the difference between singular and plural only in the third person present tense. The present tense of the third person singular ends in *-s*.

Present Tense Verb Forms	
Singular	**Plural**
I sleep	we sleep
you sleep	you sleep
she, he, it sleeps	they sleep

14.2 **Agreement with Be** The verb *be* presents special problems in agreement because this verb does not follow the usual verb patterns.

Forms of *Be*			
Present Tense		**Past Tense**	
Singular	**Plural**	**Singular**	**Plural**
I am	we are	I was	we were
you are	you are	you were	you were
she, he, it is	they are	she, he, it was	they were

14.3 **Words Between Subject and Verb**
A verb agrees only with its subject. When words come between a subject and its verb, ignore them when considering proper agreement. Identify the subject and make sure the verb agrees with it.

EXAMPLES

A story in the newspapers tells about the 1890s.

Dad as well as Mom reads the paper daily.

14.4 **Agreement with Compound Subjects** Use a plural verb with most compound subjects joined by the word *and*.

EXAMPLE: *My father and his friends (they) read the paper daily.*

You could substitute the plural pronoun *they* for *my father and his friends*. This shows that you need a plural verb.

If the compound subject is thought of as a unit, you use the singular verb. Test this by substituting the singular pronoun *it*.

EXAMPLE: *Peanut butter and jelly [it] is my brother's favorite sandwich.*

Use a singular verb with a compound subject that is preceded by *each, every,* or *many a*.

EXAMPLE: *Each novel and short story seems grounded in personal experience.*

With *or, nor*, and the correlative conjunctions *either . . . or* and *neither . . . nor*, make the verb agree with the noun or pronoun nearest the verb.

EXAMPLES

Cookies or ice cream is my favorite dessert.

Either Cheryl or her friends are being invited.

Neither ice storms nor snow is predicted today.

14.5 **Personal Pronouns as Subjects**
When using a personal pronoun as a subject, make sure to match it with the correct form of the verb *be*. (See the chart in 14.2.) Note especially that the pronoun *you* takes the verbs *are* and *were*, regardless of whether it is referring to the singular *you* or to the plural *you*.

WATCH OUT! *You is* and *you was* are nonstandard forms and should be avoided in writing and speaking. *We was* and *they was* are also forms to be avoided.

> **INCORRECT:** *You was wrong that time. They was friends at one time.*
>
> **CORRECT:** *You were wrong that time. They were friends at one time.*

14.6 Indefinite Pronouns as Subjects

Some indefinite pronouns are always singular; some are always plural. Others may be either singular or plural.

Singular Indefinite Pronouns			
another	either	neither	other
anybody	everybody	nobody	somebody
anyone	everyone	no one	someone
anything	everything	nothing	something
each	much	one	

> **EXAMPLES**
> *Each of the writers was given an award.*
> *Somebody in the room upstairs is sleeping.*

The indefinite pronouns that are always plural include *both, few, many,* and *several.* These take plural verbs.

> **EXAMPLES**
> *Many of the books in our library are not in circulation.*
>
> *Few have been returned recently.*

Still other indefinite pronouns may be either singular or plural.

Singular or Plural Indefinite Pronouns			
all	enough	most	plenty
any	more	none	some

The number of the indefinite pronouns *any* and *none* depends on the intended meaning.

> **EXAMPLES**
> *Any of these topics has potential for a good article.* (any one topic)
>
> *Any of these topics have potential for a good article.* (all of the many topics)

The indefinite pronouns *all, some, more, most,* and *none* are singular when they refer to a quantity or part of something. They are plural when they refer to a number of individual things. Context will usually give a clue.

> **EXAMPLES**
> *All of the flour is gone.* (referring to a quantity)
>
> *All of the flowers are gone.* (referring to individual items)

14.7 Inverted Sentences

Problems in agreement often occur in inverted sentences beginning with *here* or *there*; in questions beginning with *why, where,* and *what*; and in inverted sentences beginning with a phrase. Identify the subject—wherever it is—before deciding on the verb.

> **EXAMPLES**
> *There clearly are far too many cooks in this kitchen.*
>
> *What is the correct ingredient for this stew?*
>
> *Far from the embroiled cooks stands the master chef.*

GRAMMAR PRACTICE

Locate the subject in each clause in the sentences below. Then choose the correct verb.

1. Many poets have written great poetry, but few (is/are) as talented as Emily Dickinson.

2. There (is/are) many lines in her work that all of her readers (treasures/treasure).

3. Some of her readers (appreciates/appreciate) her use of dashes, while others (finds/find) it confusing.

4. There (is/are) no question that she used unusual punctuation.

5. Each of the poems (presents/present) an idea to think about.

6. My favorite poems (was/were) "Much Madness is divinest Sense" and "Success is counted sweetest."

7. Neither of those poems (is/are) Felicia's favorite, though.

8. What (is/are) the dominant vowel sound in the last four lines of "Much Madness is divinest Sense"?

9. The consonant that prevails in the same poem (seems/seem) to be *s*.

10. I can't decide whether the sound or the ideas of the poems (is/are) more striking.

14.8 Sentences with Predicate Nominatives
When a predicate nominative serves as a complement in a sentence, use a verb that agrees with the subject, not the complement.

EXAMPLES
The poems of Emily Dickinson are a portrait of a free spirit. (*poems* is the subject—not *portrait*—and it takes the plural verb *are*.)

A portrait of a free spirit is the poems of Emily Dickinson. (Here, *portrait* is the subject, not the predicate nominative *poems*.)

14.9 Don't and Doesn't as Auxiliary Verbs
The auxiliary verb *doesn't* is used with singular subjects and with the personal pronouns *she, he*, and *it*. The auxiliary verb *don't* is used with plural subjects and with the personal pronouns *I, we, you*, and *they*.

SINGULAR
Her poetry doesn't always rhyme precisely.
She doesn't always use rhyme in a stanza.

PLURAL
Her lines don't always rhyme exactly.
They don't always use regular rhythm either.

14.10 Collective Nouns as Subjects
Collective nouns are singular nouns that name a group of persons or things. *Team*, for example, is the collective name of a group of individuals. A collective noun takes a singular verb when the group acts as a single unit. It takes a plural verb when the members of the group act separately.

EXAMPLES
Our team usually wins. (the team as a whole wins)

Our team vote differently on most issues. (the individual members vote)

14.11 Relative Pronouns as Subjects
When a relative pronoun is used as a subject of its clause—*who, which,* and *that* can serve as subjects—the verb of the clause must agree in number with the antecedent of the pronoun.

SINGULAR: *I didn't read the chapter on modern poets that was assigned.*

The antecedent of the relative pronoun *that* is the singular noun *chapter;* therefore, *that* is singular and must take the singular verb *was*.

PLURAL: *Emily Dickinson and Walt Whitman, who were 19th-century poets, are important poets in American literature.*

The antecedent of the relative pronoun *who* is the plural compound subject *Emily Dickinson and Walt Whitman*. Therefore, *who* is plural, and it takes the plural verb *were*.

GRAMMAR PRACTICE
Choose the correct verb for each of the following sentences.

1. Dickinson's daily life (don't/doesn't) seem to have been very exciting.
2. Her inner life, however, was a source of creativity that (have/has) amazed generations of readers.
3. Only a handful of her poems (were/was) published during her lifetime.
4. One wonders why more people (don't/doesn't) read her poetry today.
5. The speaker of one of the poems (compare/compares) hope to a bird.
6. A volume of her poems (weren't/wasn't) published until after her death.
7. A group of us (have/has) voted for our favorite Dickinson poem.
8. The poem about death as a gentleman caller, which we read two weeks ago, (are/is) my favorite.
9. We (don't/doesn't) agree that much madness is necessarily divinest sense.
10. Dickinson's letters to the world (seem/seems) largely to have gone unanswered.

Quick Reference: Punctuation

Punctuation	Function	Examples
End Marks period, question mark, exclamation point	to end sentences	Fitzgerald wrote *The Great Gatsby*. Was it the best novel of this century? What a tremendous novel it is!
	initials and other abbreviations	Dr. Margaret Mead, R. E. Lee, General Motors Inc., P.M., A.D., ft., Blvd., Rd.

	items in outlines	I. Volcanoes
		    A. Central-vent
		       1. Shield

	exception: P.O. states	NE (Nebraska), NV (Nevada)
Commas	before conjunction in compound sentence	I have never disliked poetry, but now I really love it.
	items in a series	She is brave, loyal, and kind. The slow, easy route is best.
	words of address	America, I love you. We think of you often, Dad.
	parenthetical expressions	Well, just suppose that we can't? Hard workers, as you know, don't quit. I'm not a quitter, believe me.
	introductory phrases and clauses	In the beginning of the day, I feel fresh. While she was out, I was here. Having finished my chores, I went out.
	nonessential phrases and clauses	Ed Pawn, captain of the chess team, won. Ed Pawn, who is the captain, won. The two leading runners, sprinting toward the finish line, ended in a tie.
	in dates and addresses	Send it by July 15, 2001, to Mercer Corporation, 12 Main Street, Minneapolis, Minnesota.
	in letter parts	Dear Jim, Sincerely yours,
	for clarity, or to avoid confusion	By noon, time had run out. What the minister does, does matter. While cooking, Jim burned his hand.
Semicolons	in compound sentences that are not joined by coordinators *and,* etc.	The last shall be first; the first shall be last. I read the Bible; however, I have not memorized it.
	with items in series that contain commas	We invited my sister, Jan; her friend, Don; my uncle Jack; and Mary Dodd.
	in compound sentences that contain commas	After I ran out of money, I called my parents; but only my sister was home, unfortunately.

Punctuation	Function	Examples
Colons	to introduce lists	**Correct:** Those we wrote were the following: Dana, John, and Will. **Incorrect:** Those we wrote were: Dana, John, and Will.
	before a long quotation	Thomas Jefferson wrote: "We the people of the United States, in order to form a more perfect union . . . ."
	after the salutation of a business letter	Dear Ms. Williams: Dear Senator Willey:
	with certain numbers	1:28 P.M., Genesis 2:5
Dashes	to indicate an abrupt break in thought	I was thinking of my mother—who is arriving tomorrow—just as you walked in.
Parentheses	to enclose less important material	Our holiday (over the July 4 weekend) ended too soon. New York City (Have you ever been there?) really is a wonderful town.
Hyphens	with a compound adjective before nouns	A rectangle is a four-sided figure.
	in compounds with *all-, ex-, self-, -elect*	He's an ex-mayor but all-American. Our senator-elect is too self-important.
	in compound numbers (to *ninety-nine*)	Today, I turn twenty-one.
	in fractions used as adjectives	My cup is one-third full.
	between prefixes and words beginning with capital letters	Life may have seemed simpler in pre-Civil War days. It's very chilly for mid-June.
	when dividing words at the end of a line	Did you know that school segrega-tion has been illegal since 1954?
Apostrophes	to form possessives of nouns and indefinite pronouns	my friend's book, my friends' book, anyone's guess, somebody else's problem
	for omitted letters in contractions or numbers in dates	don't (omitted **o**); he'd (omitted **woul**) the class of '99 (omitted **19**)
	to form plurals of letters and numbers	I had two A's and no 2's on my report card.
Quotation Marks	to set off a speaker's exact words	Sara said, "I'm finally ready." "I'm ready," Sara said, "finally." Did Sara say, "I'm ready"? Sara said, "I'm ready!"
	for titles of stories, short poems, essays, songs, book chapters	I liked Oates's "Hostage," Steinem's "Sisterhood," and Plath's "Mirror." Chapter II is titled "Our Gang's Dark Oath."
Ellipses	for material omitted from a quotation	"We the people . . . in order to form a more perfect union . . . ."
Italics	for titles of books, plays, magazines, long poems, operas, films, TV series, recordings, names of ships	*The Scarlet Letter, The Crucible, Time, The Death of the Hired Man, West Side Story, Citizen Kane, The X-Files, The Spirit of St. Louis, The Best of Frank Sinatra, Lusitania*

Quick Reference: Capitalization

Category/Rule	Examples
People and Titles	
Names and initials of people	Emily Dickinson, T. S. Eliot
Titles used with or in place of names	Professor Holmes, Senator Long, The President has arrived.
Deities and members of religious groups	Jesus, Allah, the Buddha, Zeus, Baptists, Roman Catholics
Names of ethnic and national groups	Hispanics, Jews, African Americans
Geographical Names	
Cities, states, countries, continents	New York, Maine, Haiti, Africa
Regions, bodies of water, mountains	the South, Lake Erie, Mount Katadin
Geographic features, parks	Great Plains, Everglades, Yellowstone
Streets and roads, planets	55 East Ninety-fifth Street, Maple Lane, Venus, Jupiter
Organizations and Events	
Companies, organizations, teams	General Motors, Lions Club, Utah Jazz
Buildings, bridges, monuments	World Trade Towers, Golden Gate Bridge, Lincoln Memorial
Documents, awards	the Constitution, Nobel Prize
Special named events	Super Bowl, World Series
Governmental bodies, historical periods and events	the Supreme Court, the U.S. Senate, Harlem Renaissance, World War II
Days and months, holidays	Friday, May, Easter, Memorial Day
Specific cars, boats, trains, planes	Mustang, *Titanic*, *California Zephyr*
Proper Adjectives	
Adjectives formed from proper nouns	American League, French cooking, Emersonian period, Atlantic coast
First Words and the Pronoun *I*	
The first word in a sentence or quote	This is it. He said, "Let's go."
Complete sentence in parentheses	(Consult the previous chapter.)
Salutation and closing of letters	Dear Madam, Very truly yours,
First lines of most poetry / The personal pronoun *I*	Then am I / A happy fly / If I live / Or if I die.
First, last, and all important words in titles	*A Tale of Two Cities,* "The World Is Too Much with Us"

Little Rules That Make A Big Difference

Sentences

Avoid sentence fragments. Make sure all your sentences express complete thoughts.

A sentence fragment is a group of words that does not express a grammatically complete thought. It may lack a subject, a predicate, or both. Fragments may be corrected by adding the missing element(s) or by changing the punctuation to make the fragment part of another sentence.

> **FRAGMENT:** *We admire Franklin Roosevelt. A man who prevailed over the serious handicap of polio.*

> **COMPLETE:** *We admire Franklin Roosevelt. He was a man who prevailed over the serious handicap of polio.* (adding a subject and a predicate verb)

> **COMPLETE:** *We admire Franklin Roosevelt, a man who prevailed over the serious handicap of polio.* (changing the punctuation)

Avoid run-on sentences. Make sure all clauses in a sentence have the proper punctuation and/or conjunctions between them.

A run-on sentence consists of two or more sentences written as though they were one or separated only by a comma. Correct run-ons by making two separate sentences, using a semicolon, adding a conjunction, or rewriting the sentence.

> **RUN-ON:** *James Galway is a great musician, he plays the flute.*

> **CORRECT:** *James Galway is a great musician. He plays the flute.*

> **CORRECT:** *James Galway is a great musician; he plays the flute.*

> **CORRECT:** *James Galway, who plays the flute, is a great musician.*

Use end marks correctly. Use a period, not a question mark, at the end of an indirect question.

An indirect question is a question that does not use the exact words of the original speaker. Note the difference between the following sentences, and observe that the second sentence ends in a period, not a question mark.

> **DIRECT:** *Lou asked, "What is that?"*

> **INDIRECT:** *Lou asked what it was.*

Do not use quotation marks with indirect quotations within a sentence.

A direct quotation uses the speaker's exact words. An indirect quotation puts the speaker's words in other words. Compare these sentences:

> **DIRECT:** *Jean said, "I'm going to be up all night writing my essay."* (quotation marks appropriate)

> **INDIRECT:** *Jean said that she was going to be up all night writing her essay.* (no quotation marks)

Phrases

Place participial and prepositional phrases as close as possible to the words they modify. Participial and prepositional phrases are modifiers; that is, they tell about some other word in a sentence. To avoid confusion, they should be placed as close as possible to the word that they modify.

> **INCORRECT:** *Tiny microphones are planted by agents called bugs.*

> **CORRECT:** *Tiny microphones called bugs are planted by agents.*

Avoid dangling participles. Make sure a participial phrase does modify a word in the sentence.

> **INCORRECT:** *Disappointed in love, a hermit's life seemed attractive.* (Who was disappointed?)

> **CORRECT:** *Disappointed in love, the man became a hermit.*

Clauses

Use commas to set off nonessential adjective clauses.

Do you need the clause in order to indicate precisely who or what is meant? If not, it is nonessential and should be set off by commas.

USE COMMAS: *Maya Angelou, who is a great role model for youth, spoke at the inauguration.*

NO COMMAS: *A poet who is a great role model for youth spoke at the inauguration.*

Verbs

Don't use past tense forms with an auxiliary verb or past participle forms without an auxiliary verb. (See Auxiliary Verbs, page 1309.)

INCORRECT: *I have saw her somewhere before.* (*saw* is past tense and shouldn't be used with *have*)

CORRECT: *I have seen her somewhere before.*

INCORRECT: *I seen her somewhere before.* (*seen* is a past participle and shouldn't be used without an auxiliary)

Shift tense only when necessary.

Usually, when you are writing in present tense, you should stay in present tense; when you are writing in past tense, you should stay in past tense.

INCORRECT: *When Mark Twain tells stories, everybody listened.*

CORRECT: *When Mark Twain told stories, everybody listened.*

Sometimes a shift in tense is necessary to show a logical sequence of actions or the relationship of one action to another.

CORRECT: *After he had told his story, everybody went to sleep.*

Subject-Verb Agreement

Make sure subjects and verbs agree in number.

INCORRECT: *The history of civil wars are tragic.*

CORRECT: *The history of civil wars is tragic.*

INCORRECT: *Robert Frost, like many other poets, experiment with rhyme.*

CORRECT: *Robert Frost, like many other poets, experiments with rhyme.*

Use a singular verb with nouns that look plural but have singular meaning.

Some nouns that end in -*s* are singular, even though they look plural. Examples are *measles, news, Wales,* and the names ending in -*ics* when they refer to a school subject, science, or general practice.

EXAMPLES: *The United States is a great democracy.*
Physics was Albert Einstein's specialty.

Use a singular verb with titles.

EXAMPLE: The House of Seven Gables *was Hawthorne's second novel.*
"Revolutionary Dreams" is an ironic poem.

Use a singular verb with words of weight, time, and measure.

EXAMPLES: *Two weeks is the typical length of a vacation.*
Five dollars and two cents was the exact cost.

Pronouns

Use personal pronouns correctly in compounds.

Don't be confused about case when *and* joins a noun and a personal pronoun; the case of the pronoun still depends upon its function.

INCORRECT: *Her and her friends joined a book club.*

CORRECT: *She and her friends joined a book club.*

INCORRECT: *The librarian suggested two good books to John and I.*

CORRECT: *The librarian suggested two good books to John and me.*

INCORRECT: *The library lent John and they some books.*

CORRECT: *The library lent John and them some books.*

Usually, if you remove the noun and *and,* the correct pronoun will be obvious.

Use *we* and *us* correctly with nouns.

When a noun directly follows *we* or *us*, the case of the pronoun depends upon its function.

INCORRECT: *Us readers really enjoy Frost's poetry.*

CORRECT: *We readers really enjoy Frost's poetry.* (*we* is the subject)

INCORRECT: *The drama coach assigned roles to we students.*

CORRECT: *The drama coach assigned roles to us students.* (*us* is the object of *to*)

Avoid unclear pronoun reference.

The reference of a pronoun is ambiguous when the reader cannot tell which of two preceding nouns is its antecedent. The reference is indefinite when the idea to which the pronoun refers is only weakly or vaguely expressed.

AMBIGUOUS: *After Cal started tutoring Donny, Daisy worried that he* [who—Cal or Donny?] *wasn't doing what he should.*

CLEARER: *After Cal started tutoring Donny, Daisy worried that Donny wasn't doing what he should.*

INDEFINITE: *Some of our greatest writers have not been recognized as such during their lifetimes, which is a pity.*

CLEARER: *It is a pity that some of our greatest writers have not been recognized as such during their lifetimes.*

Avoid change of person.

If you are writing in third person—using pronouns such as *she, he, it, they, them, his, her, its*—do not shift to second person—*you.*

INCORRECT: *The feudal laborer had to obey his lord, and you needed to obey the king as well.*

CORRECT: *The feudal laborer had to obey his lord, and he needed to obey the king as well.*

Use correct pronouns in elliptical comparisons.

An elliptical comparison is a comparison from which words have been omitted. In order to choose the proper pronoun, fill in the missing words. Note the difference below:

EXAMPLES: *I agree with my parents more often than (I agree with) her.*
I agree with my parents more often than she (agrees with them).

Don't confuse pronouns and contractions.

Personal pronouns are made possessive without the use of an apostrophe, as is the relative pronoun *whose.* Whenever you are unsure whether to write *it's* or *its, who's* or *whose*, ask if you mean *it is/has* or *who is/has.* If you do, write the contraction. Do the same for *you're* and *your, they're* and *their,* except that the contraction in this case is for the verb *are.*

Modifiers

Avoid double comparisons.

A double comparison is a comparison made twice. In general, if you use *-er* or *-est* on the end of a modifier, you would not also use *more* or *most* in front of it.

INCORRECT: *I like Miller's plays more better than Tennessee Williams's.*

CORRECT: *I like Miller's plays better than Tennessee Williams's.*

INCORRECT: *Hers was the most unkindest remark I have ever heard.*

CORRECT: *Hers was the most unkind remark I have ever heard.*

Avoid illogical comparisons.

Can you tell what is wrong with the following sentence?

Plays are more entertaining than any kind of performance art.

This sentence is difficult to understand. To avoid such illogical comparisons, use *other* when comparing an individual member with the rest of the group.

Plays are more entertaining than any other kind of performance art.

To avoid another kind of illogical comparison, use *than* or *as* after the first member in a compound comparison.

> **ILLOGICAL:** *Ramón wrote as many good poems if not more than Chidi. (Did Ramón write as many poems or as many good poems?)*

> **CLEARER:** *Ramón wrote as many good poems as Chidi, if not more.*

Avoid misplacing modifiers.

Modifiers of all kinds must be placed as close as possible to the words they modify. If you place them elsewhere, you risk being misunderstood.

> **MISPLACED:** *Tourists can discover many famous historical sites walking in downtown Philadelphia.*

> **CLEARER:** *Walking in downtown Philadelphia, tourists can discover many famous historical sites.*

Words Not to Capitalize

Do not capitalize *north, south, east,* and *west* when they are used to tell direction.

> **EXAMPLE:** *Chicago is north and west of Indianapolis.*
> **EXAMPLE:** *Did you know that North Carolina and West Virginia are virtually neighboring states?* (North and West are part of the names of the states.)

Do not capitalize *sun* and *moon,* and capitalize *earth* only when it is used with the names of other planets.

> **EXAMPLES:** *The sun and the moon are heavenly bodies in a solar system that includes Mars, Jupiter, and the Earth.*

> *We now live on the earth, not in heaven.*

Do not capitalize the names of seasons.

> **EXAMPLE:** *The summer will soon be over, and we'll return to school in the fall.*

Do not capitalize the names of most school subjects.

School subjects are capitalized only when they name a specific course, such as World History I. Otherwise, they are not capitalized.

> **EXAMPLE:** *I'm taking physics, social studies, and a foreign language this year.*

Note: English and the names of other languages are always capitalized.

> **EXAMPLE:** *Everybody takes English and either Spanish or French.*

GRAMMAR PRACTICE

Rewrite each sentence correctly.

1. my favorite story by Mark Twain
2. The frog wouldn't jump for Smiley, filled with buckshot.
3. Most stories of the Wild West is full of adventure.
4. When Mark Twain publishes his stories, he became famous.
5. His attitude in his autobiography appeals to Rachel and I.
6. This year my hardest subjects are Chemistry, Electronics, and English.
7. Having read most of *Walden,* Thoreau is my favorite writer.
8. Chief Joseph's speech is the most saddest I have read in a long time.
9. *The Crucible* has important ideas for we people today.
10. Throwing a hysterical fit, Judge Hathorne thinks the girls are possessed.

Commonly Confused Words

accept/except	The verb *accept* means "to receive or believe"; *except* is usually a preposition meaning "excluding."	Everyone except me had read *Beloved*. Toni Morrison accepted the Nobel Prize.
advice/advise	*Advise* is a verb; *advice* is a noun naming that which an *adviser* gives.	The doctor advised the narrator of "The Yellow Wallpaper" to stay in bed. Did he give her good advice?
affect/effect	As a verb, *affect* means "to influence." *Effect* as a verb means "to cause." If you want a noun, you will almost always want *effect*.	The Second World War affected the lives of millions. Do wars effect major changes? Their effects are unknown.
all ready/already	*All ready* is an adjective meaning "fully ready." *Already* is an adverb meaning "before or by this time."	The speaker in Gary Soto's poem is not all ready to run because he is already an American citizen.
allusion/illusion	An *allusion* is an indirect reference to something. An *illusion* is a false picture or idea.	Writers often make allusions to the Bible. He is under the illusion that he's a genius.
among/between	*Between* is used when you are speaking of only two things. *Among* is used for three or more.	There is no disagreement between you and me. "Adolescence—III" is among my favorite poems.
bring/take	*Bring* is used to denote motion toward a speaker or place. *Take* is used to denote motion away from such a person or place.	Bring the books over here, and I will take them to the library.
fewer/less	*Fewer* refers to the number of separate, countable units. *Less* refers to bulk quantity.	We have less literature and fewer selections in this year's curriculum.
leave/let	*Leave* means "to allow something to remain behind." *Let* means "to permit."	The librarian will leave some books on display but will not let us borrow any.
lie/lay	To *lie* is "to rest or recline." It does not take an object. To *lay* always takes an object.	Dogs love to lie in the sun. We always lay some bones next to him.
loose/lose	*Loose* (lo͞os) means "free, not restrained"; *lose* (lo͞oz) means "to misplace or fail to find."	Who turned the horses loose? I hope we won't lose any of them.
precede/proceed	*Precede* means "to go or come before." Use *proceed* for other meanings.	"A" precedes "b" in the alphabet. Everyone proceeded to the exit.
than/then	Use *than* in making comparisons; use *then* on all other occasions.	If you find Steinbeck's writing more vivid than Malamud's, then tell me.
two/too/to	*Two* is the number. *Too* is an adverb meaning "also" or "very." Use *to* before a verb or as a preposition.	Meg had to go to town, too. We had too much reading to do. Two chapters is too much.

Grammar Glossary

This glossary contains various terms you need to understand when you use the Grammar Handbook. Used as a reference source, this glossary will help you explore grammar concepts and the ways they relate to one another.

Abbreviation An abbreviation is a shortened form of a word or word group; it is often made up of initials. (B.C., A.M., *Maj.*)

Active voice. *See* **Voice.**

Adjective An adjective modifies, or describes, a noun or pronoun. (*happy* camper, she is *small*)

> A **predicate adjective** follows a linking verb and describes the subject. (The day seemed *long.*)
>
> A **proper adjective** is formed from a proper noun. (*Jewish* temple, *Alaskan* husky)
>
> The **comparative** form of an adjective compares two things. (*more alert, thicker*)
>
> The **superlative** form of an adjective compares more than two things. (*most abundant, weakest*)

What Adjectives Tell	Examples
How many	*some* writers *much* joy
What kind	*grand* plans *wider* streets
Which one(s)	*these* flowers *that* star

Adjective phrase. See **Phrase.**

Adverb An adverb modifies a verb, an adjective, or another adverb. (Clare sang *loudly.*)

> The **comparative** form of an adverb compares two actions. (*more generously, faster*)

The **superlative** form of an adverb compares more than two actions. (*most sharply, closest*)

What Adverbs Tell	Examples
How	climb *carefully* chuckle *merrily*
When	arrived *late* left *early*
Where	climbed *up* moved *away*
To what extent	*extremely* upset *hardly* visible

Adverb, conjunctive. *See* **Conjunctive adverb.**

Adverb phrase. *See* **Phrase.**

Agreement Sentence parts that correspond with one another are said to be in agreement.

> In **pronoun-antecedent agreement,** a pronoun and the word it refers to are the same in number, gender, and person. (*Bill* mailed *his* application. The *students* ate *their* lunches.)
>
> In **subject-verb agreement,** the subject and verb in a sentence are the same in number. (*A child cries* for help. *They cry* aloud.)

Ambiguous reference An ambiguous reference occurs when a pronoun may refer to more than one word. (Bud asked his brother if *he* had any mail.)

Antecedent An antecedent is the noun or pronoun to which a pronoun refers. (If *Adam* forgets *his* raincoat, *he* will be late for school. *She* learned *her* lesson.)

Appositive An appositive is a noun or phrase that explains one or more words in a sentence. (Cary Grant, *an Englishman,* spent most of his adult life in America.)

> An **essential appositive** is needed to make the sense of a sentence complete. (A comic strip inspired the musical *Annie.*)
>
> A **nonessential appositive** is one that adds information to a sentence but is not necessary to its sense. (O. Henry, *a short-story writer,* spent time in prison.)

Article Articles are the special adjectives *a, an,* and *the.* (*the* day, *a* fly)

> The **definite article** (the word *the*) is one that refers to a particular thing. (*the* cabin)
>
> An **indefinite article** is used with a noun that is not unique but refers to one of many of its kind. (*a* dish, *an* otter)

Auxiliary verb. *See* **Verb.**

Clause A clause is a group of words that contains a verb and its subject. (*they slept*)

> An **adjective clause** is a subordinate clause that modifies a noun or pronoun. (Hugh bought the sweater *that he had admired.*)
>
> An **adverb clause** is a subordinate clause used to modify a verb, an adjective, or an adverb. (Ring the bell *when it is time for class to begin.*)

A **noun clause** is a subordinate clause that is used as a noun. (*Whatever you say* interests me.)

An **elliptical clause** is a clause from which a word or words have been omitted. (We are not as lucky as *they*.)

A **main (independent) clause** can stand by itself as a sentence. (*the flashlight flickered*)

A **subordinate (dependent) clause** does not express a complete thought and cannot stand by itself. (*while the nation watched*)

Clause	Example
Main (independent)	The hurricane struck
Subordinate (dependent)	while we were preparing to leave.

Collective noun. *See* **Noun.**

Comma splice A comma splice is an error caused when two sentences are separated with a comma instead of a correct end mark. (*The band played a medley of show tunes, everyone enjoyed the show.*)

Common noun. *See* **Noun.**

Comparative. *See* **Adjective; Adverb.**

Complement A complement is a word or group of words that completes the meaning of a verb. (The kitten finished the *milk*.) *See also* **Direct object; Indirect object.**

An **objective complement** is a word or a group of words that follows a direct object and renames or describes that object. (The parents of the rescued child declared Gus a *hero*.)

A **subject complement** follows a linking verb and renames or describes the subject. (The coach seemed *anxious*.) *See also* **Noun (predicate noun); Adjective, (predicate adjective).**

Complete predicate The complete predicate of a sentence consists of the main verb plus any words that modify or complete the verb's meaning. (The student *produces work of high caliber*.)

Complete subject The complete subject of a sentence consists of the simple subject plus any words that modify or describe the simple subject. (*Students of history* believe that wars can be avoided.)

Sentence Part	Example
Complete subject	The man in the ten-gallon hat
Complete predicate	wore a pair of silver spurs.

Compound sentence part A sentence element that consists of two or more subjects, verbs, objects, or other parts is compound. (*Lou* and *Jay* helped. Laura *makes* and *models* scarves. Jill sings *opera* and *popular music*.)

Conjunction A conjunction is a word that links other words or groups of words.

A **coordinating conjunction** connects related words, groups of words, or sentences. (*and, but, or*)

A **correlative conjunction** is one of a pair of conjunctions that work together to connect sentence parts. (*either . . . or, neither . . . nor, not only . . . but also, whether . . . or, both . . . and*)

A **subordinating conjunction** introduces a subordinate clause. (*after, although, as, as if, as long as, as though, because, before, if, in order that, since, so that, than, though, till, unless, until, whatever, when, where, while*)

Conjunctive adverb A conjunctive adverb joins the clauses of a compound sentence. (*however, therefore, yet*)

Contraction A contraction is formed by joining two words and substituting an apostrophe for a letter or letters left out of one of the words. (*didn't, we've*)

Coordinating conjunction. *See* **Conjunction.**

Correlative conjunction. *See* **Conjunction.**

Dangling modifier A dangling modifier is one that does not clearly modify any word in the sentence. (*Dashing for the train, the barriers got in the way*.)

Demonstrative pronoun. *See* **Pronoun.**

Dependent clause. *See* **Clause.**

Direct object A direct object receives the action of a verb. Direct objects follow transitive verbs. (Jude planned the *party*.)

Direct quotation. *See* **Quotation.**

Divided quotation. *See* **Quotation.**

Double negative A double negative is the incorrect use of two negative words when only one is needed. (*Nobody didn't care.*)

End mark An end mark is one of several punctuation marks that can end a sentence. See the punctuation chart on page 1327.

Fragment. *See* **Sentence fragment.**

Future tense. *See* **Verb tense.**

Gender The gender of a personal pronoun indicates whether the person or thing referred to is male, female, or neuter. (My cousin plays the tuba; *he* often performs in school concerts.)

Gerund A gerund is a verbal that ends in *-ing* and functions as a noun. (*Making* pottery takes patience.)

Helping verb. *See* **Verb (auxiliary verb).**

Illogical comparison An illogical comparison is a comparison that does not make sense because words are missing or illogical. (My computer is *newer than Kay.*)

Indefinite pronoun. *See* **Pronoun.**

Indefinite reference Indefinite reference occurs when a pronoun is used without a clear antecedent. (My aunt hugged me in front of my friends, and *it* was embarrassing.)

Independent clause. *See* **Clause.**

Indirect object An indirect object tells to whom or for whom (sometimes to what or for what) something is done. (Arthur wrote *Kerry* a letter.)

Indirect question An indirect question tells what someone asked without using the person's exact words. (*My friend asked me if I could go with her to the dentist.*)

Indirect quotation. *See* **Quotation.**

Infinitive An infinitive is a verbal beginning with *to* that functions as a noun, an adjective, or an adverb. (He wanted *to go* to the play.)

Intensive pronoun. *See* **Pronoun.**

Interjection An interjection is a word or phrase used to express strong feeling. (*Wow! Good grief!*)

Interrogative pronoun. *See* **Pronoun.**

Intransitive verb. *See* **Verb.**

Inverted sentence An inverted sentence is one in which the subject comes after the verb. (*How was the movie? Here come the clowns.*)

Irregular verb. *See* **Verb.**

Linking verb. *See* **Verb.**

Main clause. *See* **Clause.**

Main verb. *See* **Verb.**

Modifier A modifier makes another word more precise. Modifiers most often are adjectives or adverbs; they may also be phrases, verbals, or clauses that function as adjectives or adverbs. (*small* box, smiled *broadly,* house *by the sea,* dog *barking loudly*)

An *essential modifier* is one that is necessary to the meaning of a sentence. (Everybody *who has a free pass* should enter now. None *of the passengers* got on the train.)

A *nonessential modifier* is one that merely adds more information to a sentence that is clear without the addition. (We will use the new dishes, *which are stored in the closet.*)

Noun A noun names a person, a place, a thing, or an idea. (*auditor, shelf, book, goodness*)

An *abstract noun* names an idea, a quality, or a feeling. (*joy*)

A *collective noun* names a group of things. (*bevy*)

A *common noun* is a general name of a person, a place, a thing, or an idea. (*valet, hill, bread, amazement*)

A *compound noun* contains two or more words. (*hometown, pay-as-you-go, screen test*)

A *noun of direct address* is the name of a person being directly spoken to. (*Lee,* do you have the package? No, *Suki,* your letter did not arrive.)

A *possessive noun* shows who or what owns or is associated with something. (*Lil's* ring, a *day's* pay)

A *predicate noun* follows a linking verb and renames the subject. (Karen is a *writer.*)

A *proper noun* names a particular person, place, or thing. (*John Smith, Ohio, Sears Tower, Congress*)

Number A word is **singular** in number if it refers to just one person, place, thing, idea, or action, and **plural** in number if it refers to more than one person, place, thing, idea, or action. (The words *he, waiter,* and *is* are singular. The words *they, waiters,* and *are* are plural.)

Object of a preposition The object of a preposition is the noun or pronoun that follows a preposition. (The athletes cycled along the *route.* Jane baked a cake for *her.*)

Object of a verb The object of a verb receives the action of the verb. (Sid told *stories.*)

Participle A participle is often used as part of a verb phrase. (had *written*) It can also be used as a verbal that functions as an adjective. (the *leaping* deer, the medicine *taken* for a fever)

The *present participle* is formed by adding *-ing* to the present form of a verb. (*Walking* rapidly, we reached the general store.)

The *past participle* of a regular verb is formed by adding *-d* or *-ed* to the present form. The past participles of irregular verbs do not follow this pattern. (*Startled,* they ran from the house. *Spun* glass is delicate. A *broken* cup lay there.)

Passive voice. *See* **Voice.**

Past tense. *See* **Verb tense.**

Perfect tenses. *See* **Verb tense.**

Person Person is a means of classifying pronouns.

A *first-person* pronoun refers to the person speaking. (*We* came.)

A *second-person* pronoun refers to the person spoken to. (*You* ask.)

A *third-person* pronoun refers to some other person(s) or thing(s) being spoken of. (*They* played.)

Personal pronoun. *See* **Pronoun.**

Phrase A phrase is a group of related words that does not contain a verb and its subject. (*noticing everything, under a chair*)

An *adjective phrase* modifies a noun or a pronoun. (The label *on the bottle* has faded.)

An *adverb phrase* modifies a verb, an adjective, or an adverb. (Come *to the fair.*)

An *appositive phrase* explains one or more words in a sentence. (Mary, *a champion gymnast,* won gold medals at the Olympics.)

A *gerund phrase* consists of a gerund and its modifiers and complements. (*Fixing the leak* will take only a few minutes.)

An *infinitive phrase* consists of an infinitive, its modifiers, and its complements. (*To prepare for a test,* study in a quiet place.)

A *participial phrase* consists of a participle and its modifiers and complements. (*Straggling to the finish line,* the last runners arrived.)

A *prepositional phrase* consists of a preposition, its object, and the object's modifiers. (The Saint Bernard does rescue work *in the Swiss Alps.*)

A *verb phrase* consists of a main verb and one or more helping verbs. (*might have ordered*)

Possessive A noun or pronoun that is possessive shows ownership or relationship. (*Dan's* story, *my* doctor)

Possessive noun. *See* **Noun.**

Possessive pronoun. *See* **Pronoun.**

Predicate The predicate of a sentence tells what the subject is or does. (The van *runs well even in winter.* The job *seems too complicated.*) *See also* **Complete predicate; Simple predicate.**

Predicate adjective. *See* **Adjective.**

Predicate nominative A predicate nominative is a noun or pronoun that follows a linking verb and renames or explains the subject. (Joan is a computer *operator.* The winner of the prize was *he.*)

Predicate pronoun. *See* **Pronoun.**

Preposition A preposition is a word that relates its object to another part of the sentence or to the sentence as a whole. (Alfredo leaped *onto* the stage.)

Prepositional phrase. *See* **Phrase.**

Present tense. *See* **Verb tense.**

Pronoun A pronoun replaces a noun or another pronoun. Some pronouns allow a writer or speaker to avoid repeating a proper noun. Other pronouns let a writer refer to an unknown or unidentified person or thing.

A *demonstrative pronoun* singles out one or more persons or things. (*This* is the letter.)

An *indefinite pronoun* refers to an unidentified person or thing. (*Everyone* stayed home. Will you hire *anybody?*)

An *intensive pronoun* emphasizes a noun or pronoun. (The teacher *himself* sold tickets.)

An *interrogative pronoun* asks a question. (*What* happened to you?)

A *personal pronoun* shows a distinction of person. (*I* came. *You* see. *He* knows.)

A *possessive pronoun* shows ownership. (*My* spaghetti is always good. Are *your* parents coming to the play?)

A ***predicate pronoun*** follows a linking verb and renames the subject. (The owners of the store were *they*.)

A ***reflexive pronoun*** reflects an action back on the subject of the sentence. (Joe helped *himself*.)

A ***relative pronoun*** relates a subordinate clause to the word it modifies. (The draperies, *which* had been made by hand, were ruined in the fire.)

Pronoun-antecedent agreement. *See* **Agreement.**

Pronoun forms

The ***subject form*** of a pronoun is used when the pronoun is the subject of a sentence or follows a linking verb as a predicate pronoun. (*She* fell. The star was *she*.)

The ***object form*** of a pronoun is used when the pronoun is the direct or indirect object of a verb or verbal or the object of a preposition. (We sent *him* the bill. We ordered food for *them*.)

Proper adjective. *See* **Adjective.**

Proper noun. *See* **Noun.**

Punctuation Punctuation clarifies the structure of sentences. See the punctuation chart below.

Quotation A quotation consists of words from another speaker or writer.

A ***direct quotation*** is the exact words of a speaker or writer. (Martin said, *"The homecoming game has been postponed."*)

A ***divided quotation*** is a quotation separated by words that identify the speaker. (*"The homecoming game,"* said Martin, *"has been postponed."*)

An ***indirect quotation*** reports what a person said without giving the exact words. (*Martin said that the homecoming game had been postponed.*)

Reflexive pronoun. *See* **Pronoun.**

Regular verb. *See* **Verb.**

Relative pronoun. *See* **Pronoun.**

Run-on sentence A run-on sentence consists of two or more sentences written incorrectly as one. (*The sunset was beautiful its brilliant colors lasted only a short time.*)

Sentence A sentence expresses a complete thought. The chart at the top of the next page shows the four kinds of sentences.

A ***complex sentence*** contains one main clause and one or more subordinate clauses. (*Open the windows before you go to bed. If she falls, I'll help her up.*)

Punctuation	Uses	Examples
Apostrophe (')	Shows possession	Lou's garage Alva's script
	Indicates a contraction	I'll help you. The baby's tired.
Colon (:)	Introduces a list or quotation	three colors: red, green, and yellow
	Divides some compound sentences	This was the problem: we had to find our own way home.
Comma (,)	Separates ideas	The glass broke, and the juice spilled all over.
	Separates modifiers	The lively, talented cheerleaders energized the team.
	Separates items in series	We visited London, Rome, and Paris.
Exclamation point (!)	Ends an exclamatory sentence	Have a wonderful time!
Hyphen (-)	Joins parts of some compound words	daughter-in-law, great-grandson
Period (.)	Ends a declarative sentence	Swallows return to Capistrano in spring.
	Indicates most abbreviations	min. qt. Blvd. Gen. Jan.
Question mark (?)	Ends an interrogative sentence	Where are you going?
Semicolon (;)	Divides some compound sentences	Marie is an expert dancer; she teaches a class in tap.
	Separates items in series that contain commas	Jerry visited Syracuse, New York; Athens, Georgia; and Tampa, Florida.

A **compound sentence** is made up of two or more independent clauses joined by a conjunction, a colon, or a semicolon. (*The ship finally docked, and the passengers quickly left.*)

A **simple sentence** consists of only one main clause. (*My friend volunteers at a nursing home.*)

Kind of Sentence	Example
Declarative (statement)	Our team won.
Exclamatory (strong feeling)	I had a great time!
Imperative (request, command)	Take the next exit.
Interrogative (question)	Who owns the car?

Sentence fragment A sentence fragment is a group of words that is only part of a sentence. (*When he arrived. Merrily yodeling.*)

Simple predicate A simple predicate is the verb in the predicate. (*John collects foreign stamps.*)

Simple subject A simple subject is the key noun or pronoun in the subject. (*The new house is empty.*)

Split infinitive A split infinitive occurs when a modifier is placed between the word *to* and the verb in an infinitive. (*to quickly speak*)

Subject The subject is the part of a sentence that tells whom or what the sentence is about. (*Lou swam.*) See **Complete subject; Simple subject.**

Subject-verb agreement. See **Agreement.**

Subordinate clause. See **Clause.**

Subordinating conjunction. See **Conjunction.**

Superlative. See **Adjective; Adverb.**

Transitive verb. See **Verb.**

Unidentified reference An unidentified reference usually occurs when the word *it, they, this, which,* or *that* is used. (In California *they* have good weather most of the time.)

Verb A verb expresses an action, a condition, or a state of being.

An **action verb** tells what the subject does, has done, or will do. The action may be physical or mental. (Susan *trains* guide dogs.)

An **auxiliary verb** is added to a main verb to express tense, add emphasis, or otherwise affect the meaning of the verb. Together the auxiliary and main verb make up a verb phrase. (*will* intend, *could have* gone)

A **linking verb** expresses a state of being or connects the subject with a word or words that describe the subject. (The ice *feels* cold.) Linking verbs include *appear, be (am, are, is, was, were, been, being), become, feel, grow, look, remain, seem, smell, sound,* and *taste.*

A **main verb** expresses action or state of being; it appears with one or more auxiliary verbs. (will be *staying*)

The **progressive form** of a verb shows continuing action. (She *is knitting.*)

The past tense and past participle of a **regular verb** are formed by adding *-d* or *-ed.* (*open, opened*) An **irregular verb** does not follow this pattern. (*throw, threw, thrown; shrink, shrank, shrunk*)

The action of a **transitive verb** is directed toward someone or something, called the object of the verb. (Leo *washed* the windows.) An **intransitive verb** has no object. (The leaves *scattered.*)

Verb phrase. See **Phrase.**

Verb tense Verb tense shows the time of an action or the time of a state of being.

The **present tense** places an action or condition in the present. (Jan *takes* piano lessons.)

The **past tense** places an action or condition in the past. (We *came* to the party.)

The **future tense** places an action or condition in the future. (You *will understand.*)

The **present perfect tense** describes an action in an indefinite past time or an action that began in the past and continues in the present. (*has called, have known*)

The **past perfect tense** describes one action that happened before another action in the past. (*had scattered, had mentioned*)

The **future perfect tense** describes an event that will be finished before another future action begins. (*will have taught, shall have appeared*)

Verbal A verbal is formed from a verb and acts as another part of speech, such as a noun, an adjective, or an adverb.

Verbal	Example
Gerund (used as a noun)	Lamont enjoys *swimming.*
Infinitive (used as an adjective, an adverb, or a noun)	Everyone wants *to help.*
Participle (used as an adjective)	The leaves *covering the drive* made it slippery.

Voice The voice of a verb depends on whether the subject performs or receives the action of the verb.

In the ***active voice*** the subject of the sentence performs the verb's action. (We *knew* the answer.)

In the ***passive voice*** the subject of the sentence receives the action of the verb. (The team *has been eliminated.*)

Glossary of Literary Terms

Act An act is a major unit of action in a play, similar to a chapter in a book. Depending on their lengths, plays can have as many as five acts. Arthur Miller's play *The Crucible* has four acts.

See also **Drama; Scene.**

Allegory An allegory is a work of literature in which people, objects, and events stand for abstract qualities. In an allegory, a bird might represent freedom, for example, or a child might represent innocence.

Example: Nathaniel Hawthorne's "Dr. Heidegger's Experiment" can be interpreted as an allegory with each of the characters representing an abstract quality—for instance, Mr. Medbourne might represent greed. In "The Masque of the Red Death," the main character Prospero, the sequence and the decorations of the rooms in the castle, and objects such as the ebony clock all have allegorical meaning.

See pages 462, 500.

Alliteration Alliteration is the repetition of consonant sounds at the beginnings of words. Poets use alliteration to impart a musical quality to their poems, to create mood, to reinforce meaning, to emphasize particular words, and to unify lines or stanzas. Note the examples of alliteration in the following line:

> **D**oubting, **d**reaming **d**reams no mortal ever
> **d**ared to **d**ream before.
> —**Edgar Allan Poe, from "The Raven"**

See pages 467–469.

Allusion An allusion is an indirect reference to a person, place, event, or literary work with which the author believes the reader will be familiar.

Example: In "Speech in the Virginia Convention," Patrick Henry warns colonists not to be "betrayed with a kiss"—an allusion to the Apostle Judas, who betrayed Jesus by kissing him.

See pages 267, 307, 1146.

Analogy An analogy is a point by point comparison between two things for the purpose of clarifying the less familiar of the two subjects.

Example: In "My Dungeon Shook," James Baldwin draws an analogy between his nephew's probable reaction to seeing the stars shining while the sun is out and white people's reaction to black people's moving out of their fixed places.

See pages 676, 863, 964.

Anapest *See* **Meter.**

Anaphora Anaphora is a repetition of a word or words at the beginning of successive lines, clauses, or sentences:

> **Blackness**
> **is a** title,
> **is a** preoccupation,
> **is a** commitment . . .
> —**Gwendolyn Brooks, from "Primer for Blacks"**

See page 971.
See also **Repetition.**

Anecdote An anecdote is a brief story that focuses on a single episode or event in a person's life and that is used to illustrate a particular point.

Example: In "Straw into Gold," Sandra Cisneros provides an anecdote about the challenge she faced when ordered to make corn tortillas, a task she had never done before. This anecdote illustrates Cisneros's pluck in attempting the seemingly impossible.

See page 1227.

Antagonist An antagonist is usually the principal character in opposition to the **protagonist,** or hero of a narrative or drama. The antagonist can also be a force of nature.

Example: In Bernard Malamud's "Armistice," the antagonist is Gus Wagner, the meat man, who haggles about the Nazis' war tactics with the protagonist, Morris Lieberman.

See page 1178.
See also **Character; Protagonist.**

Antihero An antihero is a protagonist who has the qualities opposite to those of a hero; he or she may be insecure, ineffective, cowardly, sometimes dishonest or dishonorable, most often a failure. The character Him in Lanford Wilson's *Wandering* is an antihero. A popular antihero in contemporary culture is the cartoon character Homer Simpson.

Aphorism An aphorism is a brief statement, usually one sentence long, that expresses a general principle or truth about life.

Example: Ralph Waldo Emerson's "Self-Reliance" is sprinkled with such memorable aphorisms as "A foolish consistency is the hobgoblin of little minds."

See page 367.

Assonance Assonance is the repetition of vowel sounds within words. Both poets and prose writers use assonance to impart a musical quality to their works, to create mood, to reinforce meaning, to emphasize particular words, and to unify lines, stanzas, or passages. Note examples of assonance in the following lines:

> Along the window-sill, the lipstick stubs
> Glittered in their steel shells.
> —Rita Dove, from "Adolescence—III"

See also **Alliteration; Consonance; Rhyme.**

Atmosphere *See* **Mood.**

Audience Audience is the person or persons who are intended to read a piece of writing. The intended audience of a work determines its form, style, tone, and the details included. For example, Cabeza de Vaca's audience for *La Relación* was the king of Spain. Hence *La Relación* took the form of a formal report with a patriotic tone that included details of the explorers' hardship and determination. Had the work been addressed to Cabeza de Vaca's wife, it would likely have been less formal and probably would have included details about his personal feelings.

See pages 78, 98.

Author's Purpose A writer usually writes for one or more of these purposes: to inform, to entertain, to express himself or herself, or to persuade readers to believe or do something. For example, the purpose of a news report is to inform; the purpose of an editorial is to persuade the readers or audience to do or believe something.

Example: In *The Interesting Narrative of the Life of Olaudah Equiano,* the author's purpose is primarily to inform readers about the horrors that captured Africans endured in the holds of slave ships during the Middle Passage. Thoreau's purpose in "Civil Disobedience," on the other hand, is to persuade his audience to use nonviolent resistance to oppose unjust laws.

See pages 107, 116, 562, 645.

Autobiographical Essay *See* **Essay.**

Autobiography An autobiography is the story of a person's life written by that person. Generally written from the first-person point of view, autobiographies can vary in style from straightforward chronological accounts to impressionistic narratives.

Example: Both *Narrative of the Life of Frederick Douglass, an American Slave* and *Coming of Age in Mississippi* are autobiographies.

See pages 116, 571.

Ballad A ballad is a narrative poem that was originally meant to be sung. Ballads often contain dialogue and repetition and suggest more than they actually state. Traditional **folk ballads,** composed by unknown authors and handed down orally, are written in four-line stanzas with regular rhythm and rhyme. A **literary ballad** is one that is modeled on the folk ballads but written by a single author—for example, Dudley Randall's "Ballad of Birmingham."

See page 620.
See also **Narrative Poem; Rhyme; Rhythm.**

Biography A biography is a type of nonfiction in which a writer gives a factual account of someone else's life. Written in the third person, a biography may cover a person's entire life or focus on only an important part of it. The poet Carl Sandburg wrote an acclaimed six-volume biography of Abraham Lincoln. Modern biography includes a popular form called **fictionalized biography** in which writers use their imaginations to re-create past conversations and to elaborate on some incidents.

Blank Verse A poem written in blank verse consists of unrhymed lines of iambic pentameter. In other words, each line of blank verse has five pairs of syllables. In most pairs, an unstressed syllable is followed by a stressed syllable. The most versatile of poetic forms, blank verse imitates the natural rhythms of English speech, as in the following lines:

> I let my neighbor know beyond the hill;
> And on a day we meet to walk the line
> And set the wall between us once again.
> —Robert Frost, from "Mending Wall"

See also **Meter; Rhythm.**
See page 1013.

Caesura (sĭ-zhŏŏr´ə) A caesura is a pause or a break in a line of poetry. Poets use a caesura to emphasize the word or phrase that precedes it or to vary the rhythmical effects. In the following line, a caesura follows the word *die:*

> If we must die, let it not be like hogs
> —Claude McKay, from "If We Must Die"

Cast of Characters The cast of characters is a list of all the characters in a play, usually in the order of appearance. This list is found at the beginning of a script.

See page 165.

Catalog A catalog is a list of people, things, or attributes. This technique, found in epics and in the Bible, also characterizes Whitman's style, as seen in the beginning of this line:

> Kanuck, Tuckahoe, Congressman, Cuff, I give them the same, I receive them the same.
> —Walt Whitman, from "Song of Myself"

See page 396.

Character Characters are the people, and sometimes animals or other beings, who take part in the action of a story or novel. Events center on the lives of one or more characters, referred to as **main characters.** The other characters, called **minor characters,** interact with the main characters and help move the story along. In Bernard Malamud's "Armistice," for example, Morris Lieberman and Gus Wagner are main characters, while Leonard, Morris's son, is a minor character.

Characters may also be classified as either static or dynamic. **Static characters** tend to stay in a fixed position over the course of the story. They do not experience life-altering moments and seem to act the same, even though their situations may change. In contrast, **dynamic characters** evolve as individuals, learning from their experiences and growing emotionally.

See pages 860, 892, 1212.
See also **Antagonist; Foil; Motivation; Protagonist.**

Characterization Characterization refers to the techniques a writer uses to develop characters. There are four basic methods of characterization:

1. A writer may use physical description. In F. Scott Fitzgerald's "Winter Dreams," Judy Jones is described as follows:

> She wore a blue gingham dress, rimmed at throat and shoulders with a white edging that accentuated her tan . . . She was arrestingly beautiful. The color in her cheeks was centered like the color in a picture—it was not a "high" color, but a sort of fluctuating and feverish warmth . . .

2. The character's own actions, words, thoughts, and feelings might be presented. In Fitzgerald's story, after Judy Jones tries to revive the romance between herself and Dexter, she cries and says, "I'm more beautiful than anybody else, . . . why can't I be happy?"

3. The actions, words, thoughts, and feelings of other characters provide another means of developing a character. Mr. Sandwood, in Fitzgerald's story, exclaims about Judy Jones: "My God, she's good-looking!" To which Mr. Hedrick replies: "Good looking! She always looks as if she wanted to be kissed! Turning those big cow-eyes on every calf in town!"

4. The narrator's own direct comments also serve to develop a character. The narrator of "Winter Dreams" says of Judy Jones:

> Whatever Judy wanted, she went after with the full pressure of her charm. There was no divergence of method, no jockeying for position or premeditation of effects—there was very little mental side to any of her affairs. She simply made men conscious to the highest degree of her physical loveliness.

See pages 525, 539, 833.
See also **Character; Narrator; Point of View.**

Cliché A cliché is an overused expression that has lost its freshness, force, and appeal. The phrase "happy as a lark" is an example of a cliché.

Climax In a plot structure, the climax, or **turning point,** is the moment when the reader's interest and emotional intensity reach a peak. The climax usually occurs toward the end of a story and often results in a change in the characters or a solution to the conflict.

Example: In Edgar Allan Poe's "The Masque of the Red Death," the climax occurs when the Red Death arrives at the masked ball and is confronted by Prince Prospero. Shortly afterward, Prospero and all of his guests die.

See also **Falling Action; Plot; Rising Action; Resolution.**

Comedy A comedy is a dramatic work that is light and often humorous in tone, usually ending happily with a peaceful resolution of the main conflict. A comedy differs from a **farce** by having a more believable plot, more realistic characters, and less boisterous behavior.

See also **Drama; Farce.**

Coming-of-Age Story In a coming-of-age story, the main character is an adolescent in the process of growing up. As the story unfolds, this character faces conflicts, makes difficult decisions, and gains new awareness of self and others. The **plot** describes a rite of passage, or the experiences that lead the main character to a new level of maturity.

Example: In "Seventeen Syllables," Rosie matures because of her relationship with Jesus Carrasco and her anguish over her parents' conflicts.

See page 800.

Conceit *See* **Extended Metaphor.**

Conflict A conflict is a struggle between opposing forces that is the basis of a story's plot. An **external conflict** pits a character against nature, society, or another character. An **internal conflict** is a conflict between opposing forces within a character.

Example: In "Coyote and the Buffalo," Coyote's struggle to keep Buffalo Bill from killing him is an external conflict, whereas Coyote's struggle to decide whether to kill and eat the buffalo cow is an internal conflict.

See pages 53, 88, 243, 1109, 1166.
See also **Antagonist; Plot.**

Connotation Connotation is the emotional response evoked by a word, in contrast to its **denotation,** which is its literal meaning. *Kitten,* for example, is defined as a "young cat." However, the word also suggests, or connotes, images of softness, warmth, and playfulness.

Consonance Consonance is the repetition of consonant sounds within and at the ends of words, as in the following line:

> Some late visitor entreating entrance at my chamber door.
> —Edgar Allan Poe, from "The Raven"

See also **Alliteration; Assonance.**

Contrast Contrast is a technique used to clarify something by showing it against its opposite. In "What Is an American?" for example, de Crèvecoeur contrasts America and Americans with Europe and Europeans.

Corrido A *corrido* is a fast-paced ballad that derives from the Mexican oral tradition. *Corridos* were first sung in Mexico in the mid-nineteenth century and soon spread to the border regions of South Texas. A *corrido* generally involves a cultural conflict.

Example: "The Legend of Gregorio Cortez," a prose retelling of a *corrido,* involves the struggle between Mexicans and Anglos in Texas at the beginning of the 20th century.

See also **Ballad; Narrative Poem.**

Couplet See **Sonnet.**

Creation Myth See **Myth.**

Cuento A *cuento* is a traditional folk tale that comes from the oral tradition of New Mexico and southern Colorado. First brought to the southwestern part of the United States by Spanish and Mexican settlers, *cuentos* were further influenced by Native American cultures in this area. Early settlers and their descendants told cuentos to entertain, reinforce cultural values, and teach traditional customs and beliefs to their children. "The Indian and the Hundred Cows" is an example of a *cuento.*

See page 643.
See also **Folk Tale; Oral Literature.**

Cultural Hero A cultural hero is a larger-than-life figure who reflects the values of a people. Rather than being the creation of a single writer, this kind of hero evolves from the telling of folk tales from one generation to the next. The role of the cultural hero is to provide a noble image that will inspire and guide the actions of all who share that culture.

Example: Gregorio Cortez, a Mexican–American cultural hero, exhibits family loyalty when he shoots the sheriff who shot Cortez's brother, Román.

See page 718.

Dactyl See **Meter.**

Denotation See **Connotation.**

Dénouement The dénouement is the final unraveling or outcome of the plot in drama or fiction during which the complications of the plot are resolved, any mysteries are solved, and any secrets are explained.

Example: In "The Devil and Tom Walker," the dénouement explains what becomes of Tom's ill-gained wealth after his death.

Description Description is writing that helps a reader to picture scenes, events, and characters. Effective description usually relies on imagery, figurative language, and precise diction, as in the following passage;

> I saw again the naked house on the prairie, black and grim as a wooden fortress; the black pond where I had learned to swim, its margin pitted with sun-dried cattle tracks; the rain gullied clay banks about the naked house, the four dwarf ash seedlings where the dish-cloths were always hung to dry before the kitchen door.
> —Willa Cather, from "A Wagner Matinee"

See page 676.
See also **Diction; Figurative Language; Imagery.**

Dialect A dialect is the distinct form of a language as it is spoken in one geographical area or by a particular social or ethnic group. A group's dialect is reflected in characteristic pronunciations, vocabulary, idioms, and grammatical constructions. When trying to reproduce a given dialect, writers often use unconventional spellings to suggest the way words actually sound. Writers use dialect to establish setting, to provide local color, and to develop characters. In the following passage, the use of dialect captures the sound and tang of frontier speech:

> And he had a little small bull-pup, that to look at him you'd think he warn't worth a cent but to set around and look ornery and lay for a chance to steal something.
>
> —Mark Twain, from "The Notorious Jumping Frog of Calaveras County"

See pages 593, 637, 685.
See also **Local Color Realism.**

Dialogue Dialogue is conversation between two or more characters in either fiction or nonfiction. In drama, the story is told almost exclusively through dialogue, which moves the plot forward and reveals character.

See pages 206, 1155.
See also **Drama.**

Diary A diary is a writer's personal day-to-day account of his or her experiences and impressions. Most diaries are private and not intended to be shared. Some, however, have been published because they are well written and provide useful perspectives on historical events or on the everyday life of particular eras. Two important American diaries, not included in this book, are Madame Sarah Kemble Knight's 18th-century diary of her journey on horseback from Boston to New York and Mary Boykin Chesnut's diary of the Civil War.

Diction A writer's or speaker's choice of words is called diction. Diction includes both vocabulary (individual words) and syntax (the order or arrangement of words). Diction can be formal or informal, technical or common, abstract or concrete. In the following complex sentence, the diction is formal:

> When, however, the mass movement repudiates violence while moving resolutely toward its goal, its opponents are revealed as the instigators and practitioners of violence if it occurs.
>
> —Martin Luther King, Jr., from *Stride Toward Freedom*

See pages 150, 1198.

Drama Drama is literature in which plot and character are developed through dialogue and action; in other words, drama is literature in play form. Dramas are meant to be performed by actors and actresses who appear on stage, before radio microphones, or in front of television or movie cameras.

Unlike other forms of literature, such as fiction or poetry, a work of drama requires the collaboration of many people in order to come to life. In an important sense, a drama in printed form is an incomplete work of art, a script that must be fleshed out by a director, actors, set designers, and others who interpret the work and stage a performance.

Most plays are divided into acts, with each act having an emotional peak, or climax, of its own. The acts sometimes are divided into scenes; each scene is limited to a single time and place. Most contemporary plays have two or three acts, although some have only one act.

See pages 161–162.
See also **Act; Dialogue; Scene; Stage Directions.**

Dramatic Irony See **Irony.**

Elegy An elegy is a poem written in tribute to a person, usually someone who has died recently. The tone of an elegy is usually formal and dignified. In "Gary Keillor," Gary gives a comic rendition of Walt Whitman's elegy for Abraham Lincoln, "O Captain! My Captain!"

Epic Poem An epic poem is a long narrative poem on a serious subject presented in an elevated or formal style. An epic traces the adventures of a hero whose actions consist of courageous, even superhuman deeds, which often represent the ideals and values of a group, nation, or race. *I Am Joaquín* is an epic poem.

See page 316.
See also **Narrative Poem**.

Epithet An epithet is a brief descriptive phrase that points out traits associated with a particular person or thing.

Example: Carl Sandburg's "Chicago" begins with a series of epithets, such as "Hog Butcher for the World."

Essay An essay is a short work of nonfiction that deals with a single subject. Essays are often informal, loosely structured, and highly personal. They can be descriptive, informative, persuasive, narrative, or any combination of these. Amy Tan's personal essay "Mother Tongue" combines all of these modes.

An **autobiographical essay** focuses on an aspect of a writer's life. Generally, writers of autobiographical essays use the first-person point of view, combining objective description with the expression of subjective feelings. Zora Neale Hurston's "How It Feels to Be Colored Me" is an example of an autobiographical essay.

See pages 369, 957, 1221.

Exaggeration See **Hyperbole**.

Experimental Poetry Poetry described as experimental is often full of surprises—comic situations, conversational speech, playful use of words, descriptions of ordinary objects, and other distinctive elements not found in traditional verse forms. William Carlos Williams belonged to a group of experimental poets known as the **Imagists.** Their poems contained sharp, clear images of striking beauty, similar to the ones found in haiku. E. E. Cummings's "anyone lived in pretty how town" reflects his

poetic experiments, such as altering the expected order of words.

See page 414.

Exposition Exposition is the part of a literary work that provides the background information necessary to understand characters and their actions. Typically found at the beginning of a work, the exposition introduces the characters, describes the setting, and summarizes significant events that took place before the action begins.

Example: In the exposition to "The Devil and Tom Walker," Washington Irving introduces the main characters—a miser and his wife—who dwell in a desolate house near a swamp and take wicked glee in hoarding things from each other.

See also **Plot; Rising Action.**

Extended Metaphor Like any metaphor, an extended metaphor is a comparison between two essentially unlike things that nevertheless have something in common. It does not contain the word *like* or *as*. An extended metaphor compares two things at some length and in various ways. Sometimes the comparison is carried throughout a paragraph, a stanza, or an entire selection. In the following stanza, notice the extended metaphor comparing hope to a bird:

> "Hope" is the thing with feathers—
> That perches in the soul—
> And sings the tune without the words—
> And never stops—at all— . . .
>
> —Emily Dickinson,
> from "'Hope' is the thing with feathers—"

Like an extended metaphor, a **conceit** compares two apparently dissimilar things in several ways. The word *conceit* usually implies a more elaborate, formal, and ingeniously clever comparison than the extended metaphor.

See page 948.

External Conflict See **Conflict**.

Eyewitness Report An eyewitness report is a firsthand account of an event written by someone who directly observed it or participated in it. (As such, an eyewitness account is a **primary source.**) Narrated from the first-person point of view, eyewitness reports almost always include the following:

- objective facts about an event
- a chronological (time-order) pattern of organization
- vivid sensory details
- quotations from people who were present
- description of the writer's feelings and interpretations.

The excerpt from Anne Moody's autobiography, *Coming of Age in Mississippi,* is an eyewitness report of a sit-in in 1963.

See page 616.
See also **Primary Source.**

Fable A fable is a brief tale that illustrates a clear, often directly stated, **moral,** or lesson. The characters in a fable are usually animals, but sometimes they are humans. The most well-known fables—for example, "The Fox and the Crow" and "The Tortoise and the Hare" are those of Aesop, a Greek slave who lived about 600 B.C. Traditionally, fables are handed down from generation to generation as oral literature.

See also **Oral Literature.**

Falling Action In a plot structure, the falling action, or **resolution,** occurs after the climax to reveal the final outcome of events and to tie up any loose ends.

Example: In Joyce Carol Oates's "Hostage," the falling action occurs after Bruno attacks the narrator's assailant, nearly killing him. We learn that Bruno is given six months' probation and psychiatric care. He withdraws from others, quits school, joins the army, and is shipped to Korea, where he dies in battle.

See also **Climax; Exposition; Plot; Rising Action.**

Farce A farce is a type of exaggerated comedy that features an absurd plot, ridiculous situations, and humorous dialogue. The main purpose of a farce is to keep an audience laughing. The characters are usually **stereotypes,** or simplified examples of different traits or qualities. Comic devices typically used in farces include mistaken identity, deception, wordplay—such as puns and double meanings—and exaggeration.

See also **Comedy; Stereotype.**

Fiction Fiction refers to works of prose that contain imaginary elements. Although fiction, like nonfiction, may be based on actual events and real people, it differs from nonfiction in that it is shaped primarily by the writer's imagination. For example, although Garrison Keillor's "Gary Keillor" is based on autobiographical experiences, it cannot be classified as nonfiction because it is imbued with imaginary events and exaggeration in order to hold the reader's interest. The two major types of fiction are novels and short stories. The four basic elements of a work of fiction are character, setting, plot, and theme.

See also **Novel; Short Story.**

Figurative Language Figurative language is language that communicates ideas beyond the literal meaning of words. Figurative language can make descriptions and unfamiliar or difficult ideas easier to understand. Note the figurative language in lines 3–5 below:

> Every few years
> Tía Chucha would visit the family
> in a tornado of song
> and open us up
> as if we were an overripe avocado.
>
> —Luis Rodriguez, from "Tía Chucha"

The most common types of figurative language, called **figures of speech,** are simile, metaphor, personification, and hyperbole.

See pages 287, 293, 392, 760, 943.
See also **Hyperbole; Metaphor; Personification; Simile.**

Figures of Speech *See* **Figurative Language**.

First-Person Point of View *See* **Point of View**.

Flashback A flashback is a scene that interrupts the action of a narrative to describe events that took place at an earlier time. It provides background helpful in understanding a character's present situation.

Example: William Faulkner's "A Rose for Emily" opens with Miss Emily's funeral, followed by a flashback that recounts how, when she was alive, Colonel Sartoris exempted her from paying taxes.

Foil A foil is a character whose traits contrast with those of another character. A writer might use a minor character as a foil to emphasize the positive traits of the main character.

Example: In "The Legend of Gregorio Cortez," the "loud-mouthed, discontented" Román is a foil for his heroic brother, Gregorio Cortez.

See page 228.
See also **Character**.

Folk Tale A folk tale is a short, simple story that is handed down, usually by word of mouth, from generation to generation. Folk tales include legends, fairy tales, myths, and fables. Folk tales often teach family obligations or societal values. "Coyote and the Buffalo" is an Okanogan folk tale and "The Indian and the Hundred Cows" is a Hispanic folk tale.

See also **Legend; Myth; Fable**.

Foot *See* **Meter**.

Foreshadowing Foreshadowing is a writer's use of hints or clues to indicate events that will occur in a story. Foreshadowing creates suspense and at the same time prepares the reader for what is to come.

Example: In Nathaniel Hawthorne's "Dr. Heidegger's Experiment," the former rivalry for the Widow Wycherly foreshadows the rivalry that occurs later in Dr. Heidegger's study.

See pages 514, 525.

Form At its simplest, form refers to the physical arrangement of words in a poem—the length and placement of the lines and the grouping of lines into stanzas. The term can also be used to refer to other types of patterning in poetry, anything from rhythm and other sound patterns to the design of a traditional poetic type, such as a sonnet or dramatic monologue. Finally, *form* can be used as a synonym for *genre,* which refers to literary categories, ranging from the broad (short story, novel) to the narrowly defined (sonnet).

See also **Genre, Stanza**.

Free Verse Free verse is poetry that does not have regular patterns of rhyme and meter. The lines in free verse often flow more naturally than do rhymed, metrical lines and thus achieve a rhythm more like that of everyday human speech. Walt Whitman is generally credited with bringing free verse to American poetry:

> I hear America singing, the varied carols I hear,
> Those of mechanics, each one singing his as it
>   should be blithe and strong,
> The carpenter singing his as he measures his
>   plank or beam,
> The mason singing his as he makes ready for
>   work, or leaves off work, . . .
>
> —Walt Whitman, from "I Hear America Singing"

See page 395, 404.
See also **Meter; Rhyme**.

Genre Genre refers to the distinct types into which literary works can be grouped. The four main literary genres are fiction, poetry, nonfiction, and drama.

Gothic Literature Gothic literature is characterized by grotesque characters, bizarre situations, and violent events. Originating in Europe, Gothic literature was a popular form of writing in the United States during the 19th century, especially in the hands of such notables as Edgar Allan Poe and Nathaniel Hawthorne. Interest in Gothic revived in the 20th century among southern writers such as William Faulkner and Flannery O'Connor.

See pages 446–448.

Haiku Haiku is a highly compressed form of Japanese poetry that creates a brief, clear picture in order to produce an emotional response. Haiku relies heavily on imagery, usually drawn from nature, and on the power of suggestion. When written in Japanese, a haiku has three lines of five, seven, and five syllables each. Here is a haiku written in English:

> Leaning out over
> The dreadful precipice,
> One contemptuous tree.
>
> —W. H. Auden

See page 790.

Historical Context The historical context of a literary work refers to the social conditions that inspired or influenced its creation. To understand and appreciate some works, the reader must relate them to particular events in history. For example, to understand fully Lincoln's "Gettysburg Address," the reader must imaginatively re-create the scene—Lincoln addressing a war-weary crowd on the very site where a horrific battle had recently been fought.

Example: Patrick Henry's "Speech in the Virginia Convention" was inspired by the British military buildup in America prior to the American Revolution; Martin Luther King's *Stride Toward Freedom* was inspired by the civil rights struggle of the 1950s to overturn segregation laws in the South.

See pages 307, 369, 605.

Historical Narratives Historical narratives are accounts of real-life historical experiences, given either by a person who experienced those events or by someone who has studied or observed them. Cabeza de Vaca's *La Relación,* William Bradford's *Of Plymouth Plantation,* and *The Interesting Narrative of the Life of Olaudah Equiano* all are historical narratives.

See page 70.
See also **Primary Sources; Secondary Sources.**

Humor is a term applied to a literary work whose purpose is to entertain and to evoke laughter—for example, Twain's "The Celebrated Jumping Frog of Calaveras County." In literature there are three basic types of humor, all of which may involve exaggeration or irony. **Humor of situation,** which is derived from the plot of a work, usually involves exaggerated events or situational irony. **Humor of character** is often based on exaggerated personalities or on characters who fail to recognize their own flaws, a form of dramatic irony. **Humor of language** may include sarcasm, exaggeration, puns, or verbal irony, which occurs when what is said is not what is meant.

See pages 434, 679, 685.
See also **Comedy; Farce; Irony.**

Hyperbole Hyperbole is a figure of speech in which the truth is exaggerated for emphasis or for humorous effect. The expression "I'm so hungry I could eat a horse" is a hyperbole.

Example: In Américo Paredes's "The Legend of Gregorio Cortez," the narrator, describing Cortez's abilities as a gunman, says, "He could put five bullets into a piece of board and not make but one hole, and quicker than you could draw a good deep breath."

See also **Understatement.**

Iamb See **Meter.**

Iambic Pentameter See **Blank Verse; Meter.**

Imagery The descriptive words and phrases that a writer uses to re-create sensory experiences are called imagery. By appealing to the five senses, imagery helps a reader imagine exactly what the characters and experiences being described are like. In the following passage, the imagery lets the reader experience the miserliness of the main character and his wife:

> They lived in a forlorn-looking house that stood alone and had an air of starvation. A few straggling savin trees, emblems of sterility, grew near it; no smoke ever curled from its chimney . . . A miserable horse, whose ribs were as articulate as the bars of a gridiron, stalked about a field, where a thin carpet of moss . . . tantalized and balked his hunger.
>
> —Washington Irving,
> from "The Devil and Tom Walker"

The term **synesthesia** refers to imagery that appeals to one sense when another is being stimulated; for example, description of sounds in terms of colors, as in this passage:

> Music. The great blobs of purple and red emotion have not touched him.
>
> —Zora Neale Hurston,
> from "How It Feels to Be Colored Me"

See pages 360, 496, 676, 779, 804, 1005, 1030, 1093, 1198, 1225.
See also **Description; Kinesthetic Imagery.**

Imagists *See* **Experimental Poetry; Style.**

Impressionism Impressionism refers to a technique of writing that reflects the ideals of a school of mid–19th-century French painters, including Manet, Monet, and Renoir. These painters believed that the artist should try to capture the impressions that an object makes rather than render it in precise, realistic detail. Impressionistic writers describe people, places, and events as they appear to an individual at a particular moment and from a particular angle of vision.

Example: In "A Mystery of Heroism," Crane uses an impressionistic technique to capture soldiers' sensations in battle.

Interior Monologue *See* **Monologue; Stream of Consciousness.**

Internal Conflict *See* **Conflict.**

Inverted Syntax Inverted syntax is a reversal in the expected order of words.

Example: In the first line of "Upon the Burning of Our House," Anne Bradstreet writes "when rest I took" rather than "when I took rest."

Irony Irony refers to a contrast between appearance and actuality. **Situational irony** is a contrast between what is expected to happen and what actually does happen, as in the poem "Richard Cory," when a gentleman who is admired and envied commits suicide. **Dramatic irony** occurs when readers know more about a situation or a character in a story than the characters do. In Flannery O'Connor's "The Life You Save May Be Your Own," for example, readers find out that Mr. Shiftlet is a scoundrel before the other characters do. **Verbal irony** occurs when someone states one thing and means another, as in the title of Stephen Crane's poem "Do Not Weep, Maiden, for War Is Kind."

See pages 539, 602, 667, 786, 1055, 1191.

Kinesthetic Imagery Kinesthetic imagery re-creates the tension felt through muscles, tendons, or joints in the body. In the following line, the phrase "the stiff Heart" creates a kinesthetic image:

> The stiff Heart questions was it He, that bore,
>
> —Emily Dickinson, from "After great pain, a formal feeling comes"

See also **Imagery.**

Legend A legend is a story passed down orally from generation to generation and popularly believed to have a historical basis. While some legends may be based on real people or situations, most of the events are either greatly exaggerated or fictitious. Like myths, legends may incorporate supernatural elements and magical deeds. But legends differ from myths in that they claim to be stories about real human beings and are often set in a particular time and place. "The Legend of Gregorio Cortez" is an example.

See page 718.

Literary Criticism Literary criticism refers to a piece of writing that focuses on a literary work or a genre, describing some aspect of it, such as its origin, its characteristics, or its effects. Toni Morrison's "Thoughts on the African-American Novel" is an example of literary criticism.

See page 976.

Literary Letter A literary letter is a letter that has been published and read by a wider audience because it was written by a well-known public figure or provides information about the period in which it was written. Abigail Adams's "Letter to John Adams" is an example of a literary letter.

See page 282.

Loaded Language Loaded language consists of words with strong connotations, or emotional associations. Writers and speakers use loaded language most often for persuasive purposes, as in this example:

> The God that holds you over the pit of hell, much as one holds a spider, or some loathsome insect over the fire, abhors you, and is dreadfully provoked.
> —Jonathan Edwards, from "Sinners in the Hands of an Angry God"

See also **Connotation.**

Local Color Realism Local color realism, especially popular in the late 18th century, is a style of writing that truthfully imitates ordinary life and brings a particular region alive by portraying the dialects, dress, mannerisms, customs, character types, and landscapes of that region. Mark Twain frequently uses local color realism in his writing for humorous effect.

See pages 636, 679.
See also **Dialect.**

Lyric Poem A lyric poem is a short poem in which a single speaker expresses thoughts and feelings in intensely emotional language. In a love lyric, a speaker expresses romantic love. In other lyrics, a speaker may meditate on nature or seek to resolve an emotional crisis. Anne Bradstreet's poem "To My Dear and Loving Husband" is a love lyric.

Magical Realism Magical realism is a style of writing that often includes exaggeration, unusual humor, magical and bizarre events, dreams that come true, and superstitions that prove warranted. Magical realism differs from pure fantasy in combining fantastic elements with realistic elements such as recognizable characters, believable dialogue, a true-to-life setting, a matter-of-fact tone, and a plot that sometimes contains historic events. This style characterizes some of the fiction of such influential South American writers as the late Jorge Luis Borges of Argentina and Gabriel Garcia Márquez of Colombia.

Main Character *See* **Character.**

Memoir A memoir is a form of auto-biographical writing in which a person recalls significant events in his or her life. Most memoirs share the following characteristics: (1) they usually are structured as narratives told by the writers themselves, using the first-person point of view; (2) although some names may be changed to protect privacy, memoirs are true accounts of actual events; (3) although basically personal, memoirs may deal with newsworthy events having a significance beyond the confines of the writer's life; (4) unlike strictly historical accounts, memoirs often include the writers' feelings and opinions about historical events, giving the reader insight into the impact of history on people's lives. Langston Hughes's "When the Negro Was in Vogue" is an example of a memoir.

Metaphor A metaphor is a figure of speech that compares two things that have something in common. Unlike similes, metaphors do not use the word *like* or *as,* but make comparisons directly.

Example: Abigail Adams's statement "our country is . . . the first and greatest parent" is a metaphor.

See pages 287, 347, 760, 815, 833.
See also **Figurative Language; Simile.**

Meter Meter is the repetition of a regular rhythmic unit in a line of poetry. Each unit, known as a **foot,** has one stressed syllable (indicated by a ´) and either one or two unstressed syllables (indicated by a ˘). The four basic types of metrical feet are the **iamb,** an unstressed syllable followed by a stressed syllable; the **trochee,** a stressed syllable followed by an unstressed syllable; the **anapest,** two unstressed syllables followed by a stressed syllable; and the **dactyl,** a stressed syllable followed by two unstressed syllables.

  Two words are used to describe the meter of a line. The first word identifies the type of metrical foot—iambic, trochaic, anapestic, or dactylic—and the second word indicates the number of feet in a line: **monometer** (one foot), **dimeter** (two feet), **trimeter** (three feet), **tetrameter** (four feet), **pentameter** (five feet), **hexameter** (six feet), and so forth.

Examples: In "To My Dear and Loving Husband," the meter is **iambic pentameter,** the most common form of meter in English poetry.

> If ev́ | er mán | were loved | by wife | then
>   thee.

In the following lines from Henry Wadsworth Longfellow's "A Psalm of Life," the meter is trochaic tetrameter:

> Tell me | not, in | mournful | numbers,
> Life is | but an | empty | dream!—

See pages 142, 394.
See also **Rhythm; Scansion.**

Minor Character *See* **Character.**

Modernism Modernism was a literary movement that roughly spanned the time period between the two world wars, 1914–1945. Modernist works are characterized by a high degree of experimentation and spare, elliptical prose. Modernist characters are most often alienated people searching unsuccessfully for meaning and love in their lives. For example, in Hemingway's "The End of Something," Nick Adams feels alienated from his girlfriend but cannot explain why. The question of what's bothering Nick remains unanswered. Departing from the usual detailed narrative comments of his predecessors, Hemingway gives little direct information about the characters' feelings or thoughts. Instead, the reader has to infer the characters' inner thoughts from their words and actions and from the symbolism in the description of the setting.

See pages 992–994, 1016–1017.

Monody A lyric poem in which a single mourner expresses grief. Herman Melville's "Monody" laments the death of Nathaniel Hawthorne.

See page 513.
See also **Elegy.**

Monologue In a drama, the speech of a character who is alone on stage, voicing his or her thoughts, is known as a monologue, or a **soliloquy.** In a short story or a poem, the direct presentation of a character's unspoken thoughts is called an **interior monologue.** An interior monologue may jump back and forth between past and present, displaying thoughts, memories, and impressions just as they might occur in a person's mind. "I Stand Here Ironing" is an example of an interior monologue.

See pages 162, 815.
See also **Stream of Consciousness.**

Mood Mood is the feeling or atmosphere that a writer creates for the reader. The writer's use of connotation, imagery, figurative language, sound and rhythm, and descriptive details all contribute to the mood. These elements help create a creepy, threatening mood in the following passage:

> The swamp was thickly grown with great gloomy pines and hemlocks, . . . It was full of pits and quagmires, partly covered with weeds and mosses, where the green surface often betrayed the traveler into a gulf of black, smothering mud; . . .
>
> —Washington Irving, from "The Devil and Tom Walker"

See pages 496, 514, 928, 1005, 1101.
See also **Connotation; Description; Diction; Figurative Language; Imagery; Style.**

Moral See **Fable.**

Motivation Motivation is the stated or implied reason behind a character's behavior. The grounds for a character's action may not be obvious, but they should be comprehensible and consistent, in keeping with the character as developed by the writer.

Example: In Richard Wright's story "The Man Who Was Almost a Man," Dave's motivation for wanting to own a gun is to gain a sense of power and control.

See page 877.
See also **Character.**

Myth A myth is a traditional story, passed down through generations, that explains why the world is the way it is. Myths are essentially religious, because they present supernatural events and beings and articulate the values and beliefs of a cultural group. A **creation myth** is a particular kind of myth that explains how the universe, the earth, and life on earth began. "The World on the Turtle's Back" is an Iroquois creation myth.

See page 31.

Narrative A narrative is any type of writing that is primarily concerned with relating an event or a series of events. A narrative can be imaginary, as is a short story or novel, or factual, as is a newspaper account or a work of history. The word *narration* can be used interchangeably with *narrative,* which comes from the Latin word meaning "tell."

See also **Fiction; Nonfiction; Novel; Plot; Short Story.**

Narrative Poem A narrative poem is a poem that tells a story using elements of character, setting, and plot to develop a theme. Edgar Allan Poe's "The Raven" is a narrative poem, as is Dudley Randall's "Ballad of Birmingham."

See pages 618, 833.
See also **Ballad.**

Narrator The narrator of a story is the character or voice that relates the story's events to the reader.

Example: The narrator of Joyce Carol Oates's "Hostage" is one of the main characters, a girl in junior high school. The narrator of William Faulkner's "A Rose for Emily" is an unidentified citizen of Jefferson, Mississippi, Emily Grierson's hometown.

See pages 360, 779.

Naturalism An offshoot of realism, naturalism was a literary movement that originated in France in the late 1800s. Like the realists, the naturalists sought to render common people and ordinary life accurately. However, the naturalists emphasized how instinct and environment affect human behavior. Strongly influenced by Charles Darwin's ideas, the naturalists believed that the fate of humans is determined by forces beyond individual control. Stephen Crane's story "A Mystery of Heroism" is an example of naturalism.

See page 602.

Nature Writing Nature writing refers to a type of essay in which the writer explores the relationship between humans and nature through firsthand observations. Henry David Thoreau, the father of American nature writing, was renowned for his patient, frequent, careful observations of Walden Pond and its environs. In *Walden,* he conveyed his observations and insights in richly poetic language.

See page 392.
See also **Essay.**

Nonfiction Nonfiction is writing about real people, places, and events. Unlike fiction, nonfiction is largely concerned with factual information, although the writer shapes the information according to his or her purpose and viewpoint. Biography, autobiography, and newspaper articles are examples of nonfiction.

See also **Autobiography; Biography; Essay.**

Novel A novel is an extended work of fiction. Like the short story, a novel is essentially the product of a writer's imagination. The most obvious difference between a novel and a short story is length. Because the novel is considerably longer, a novelist can develop a wider range of characters and a more complex plot.

Octave *See* **Sonnet.**

Off Rhyme *See* **Slant Rhyme.**

Omniscient *See* **Point of View.**

Onomatopoeia The word *onomatopoeia* literally means "name-making." It is the process of creating or using words that imitate sounds. The *buzz* of the bee, the *honk* of the car horn, the *peep* of the chick are all onomatopoetic, or echoic, words.

Onomatopoeia as a literary technique goes beyond the use of simple echoic words. Writers, particularly poets, choose words whose sounds suggest their denotative and connotative meanings: for example, *whisper, kick, gargle, gnash,* and *clatter.*

Open Letter An open letter is addressed to a specific person but published for a wider readership.

Example: James Baldwin's "My Dungeon Shook" is an open letter addressed to his nephew, but intended for the general public, particularly white Americans.

See page 964.

Oral Literature Oral literature is literature that is passed from one generation to another by performance or word of mouth. Folk tales, fables, myths, chants, and legends are part of the oral tradition of cultures throughout the world.

See pages 20–22, 652.
See also **Fable; Folk Tale; Legend; Myth.**

Oxymoron *See* **Paradox.**

Parable A parable is a brief story that is meant to teach a lesson or illustrate a moral truth. A parable is more than a simple story, however. Each detail of the parable corresponds to some aspect of the problem or moral dilemma to which it is directed. The story of the prodigal son in the Bible is a classic parable. In *Walden,* Thoreau's parable of the strong and beautiful bug that emerges from an old table is meant to show that, similarly, new life can awaken in human beings despite the deadness of society.

Paradox A paradox is a statement that seems to contradict itself but may nevertheless suggest an important truth.

Example: In *Walden,* Henry David Thoreau writes the paradox "I am not as wise as the day I was born." The statement suggests that civilization erases a child's innate wisdom and spiritual awareness.

A special kind of paradox is the **oxymoron,** which brings together two contradictory terms, as in the phrases "wise fool" and "feather of lead."

See pages 378, 392, 760, 959.

Parallelism When a speaker or writer expresses ideas of equal worth with the same grammatical form, the technique is called parallelism, or parallel construction. Note that in the following example, each line or independent clause begins with the word *I* followed by a verb—*sit, hear, see* (and in the rest of the poem, *mark, observe*).

> I sit and look out upon all the sorrows of the world, and upon all oppression and shame,
>
> I hear secret convulsive sobs from young men at anguish with themselves, remorseful after deeds done,
>
> I see in low life the mother misused by her children, dying, neglected, gaunt, desperate,
>
> I see the wife misused by her husband, I see the treacherous seducer of young women . . .
>
> —Walt Whitman, from "I Sit and Look Out"

This parallel construction creates a rolling rhythm, emphasizes the role of the speaker, and conveys that the ideas all relate to the same theme—that the speaker observes "all the sorrows of the world."
See pages 279, 404, 607.

Parody Parody is writing that imitates either the style or the subject matter of a literary work for the purpose of criticism or humorous effect or for flattering tribute.

Persona See **Speaker.**

Personal Essay See **Essay.**

Personification Personification is a figure of speech in which an object, animal, or idea is given human characteristics.

Example: In Emily Dickinson's poem "Because I could not stop for Death," death is personified as a gentleman of kindness and civility.
See pages 750, 760, 828.

Persuasive Writing Persuasive writing is intended to convince a reader to adopt a particular opinion or to perform a certain action. Effective persuasion usually appeals to both the reason and the emotions of an audience. Patrick Henry, Jonathan Edwards, Martin Luther King, Jr., and Malcolm X all use persuasion in their writing.
See pages 158, 260–261.

Petrarchan Sonnet See **Sonnet.**

Plain Style See **Style.**

Plot The plot is the sequence of actions and events in a literary work. Generally, plots are built around a **conflict**—a problem or struggle between two or more opposing forces. Plots usually progress through stages: exposition, rising action, climax, and falling action.

The **exposition** provides important background information and introduces the setting, characters, and conflict. During the **rising action,** the conflict becomes more intense and suspense builds as the main characters struggle to resolve their problem. The **climax** is the turning point in the plot when the outcome of the conflict becomes clear, usually resulting in a change in the characters or a solution to the conflict. After the climax, the **falling action** occurs and shows the effects of the climax. As the falling action begins, the suspense is over but the results of the decision or action that caused the climax are not yet fully worked out. The **resolution,** which often blends with the falling action, reveals the final outcome of events and ties up loose ends.

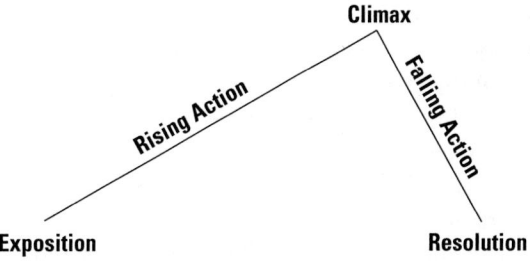

See pages 243, 786, 1166.
See also **Climax; Conflict; Exposition; Falling Action; Rising Action.**

Poetry Poetry is language arranged in lines. Like other forms of literature, poetry attempts to re-create emotions and experiences. Poetry, however, is usually more condensed and suggestive than prose. Because poetry frequently does not include the kind of detail and explanation common to the short story or the novel, poetry tends to leave more to the reader's imagination. Poetry also may require more work on the part of the reader to unlock meaning.

Poems often are divided into stanzas, or paragraph-like groups of lines. The stanzas in a poem may contain the same number of lines or may vary in length. Some poems have definite patterns of meter and rhyme. Others rely more on the sounds of words and less on fixed rhythms and rhyme schemes. The use of figurative language is also common in poetry.

The form and content of a poem combine to convey meaning. The way that a poem is arranged on the page, the impact of the images, the sounds of the words and phrases, and all the other details that make up a poem work together to help the reader grasp its central idea.

See pages 394–395, 1006.
See also **Experimental Poetry; Form; Free Verse; Meter; Rhyme; Rhythm; Stanza.**

Point of View Point of view refers to the narrative perspective from which events in a story or novel are told. In the **first-person** point of view, the narrator is a character in the work who tells everything in his or her own words and uses the pronouns *I, me, my.* Joyce Carol Oates's "Hostage" is narrated from the first-person point of view.

In the **third-person** point of view, events are related by a voice outside the action, not by one of the characters. A third-person narrator uses pronouns like *he, she,* and *they.* In the **third-person omniscient** point of view, the narrator is an all-knowing, objective observer who stands outside the action and reports what different characters are thinking. Flannery O'Connor's "The Life You Save May Be Your Own" is told from the third-person omniscient point of view. In the **third-person limited** point of view, the narrator stands outside the action and focuses on one character's thoughts, observations, and feelings. Richard Wright's "The Man Who Was

Almost a Man" is told from the third-person limited point of view, focusing on Dave's thoughts, observations, and feelings.

In the **second-person** point of view, rarely used, the narrator addresses the reader intimately as *you.* Much of John Steinbeck's essay "Why Soldiers Don't Talk" is narrated from the second-person point of view.

See pages 591, 1055, 1085, 1191.

Primary Sources Primary sources are those that offer direct, firsthand knowledge—such as diaries, memoirs, and personal histories. These sources often reveal the beliefs and motives of the people involved in a historical event, their ability to overcome obstacles, and the distinctive features of time and place in which they lived.

Example: *Of Plymouth Plantation* provides a glimpse of Plymouth colony through the eyes of William Bradford, its first governor and an eyewitness to the events he describes.

Secondary sources, on the other hand, offer indirect, secondhand knowledge—for example, "Women and Children First," which was written by a descendant of the Pilgrims more than 350 years after they landed.

See pages 88, 98.
See also **Eyewitness Report.**

Prop Prop, an abbreviation of *property,* refers to a physical object that is used in a stage production.

Example: In Arthur Miller's *The Crucible,* an important prop is the small rag doll that Mary Warren brings from the court and gives to Elizabeth Proctor.

Prose Generally, *prose* refers to all forms of written or spoken expression that are organized and that lack regular rhythmic patterns. Prose is characterized by logical order, continuity of thought, and individual style. Prose style varies from one writer to another, depending on such elements as word choice, sentence length and structure, use of figurative language, and tone.

Examples: Examples of the variety of prose styles can be seen in William Bradford's historical writing from the 17th century, Thomas Jefferson's political writing from the 18th century, Edgar Allan Poe's fiction from the 19th century, and Sandra Cisneros's fiction from the 20th century.

Protagonist The protagonist is the main character or hero in a narrative or drama, usually the one with whom the audience identifies.

Example: The young soldier, Fred Collins, is the protagonist of Stephen Crane's story "A Mystery of Heroism."

See page 1178.
See also **Antagonist; Character; Tragic Hero.**

Protest Poetry Protest poetry is poetry written primarily not to express personal feelings but to persuade readers to support a certain political cause or take a particular action.

Example: James Russell Lowell's "Stanzas on Freedom" and Frances Ellen Watkins Harper's "Free Labor" are both protest poems that speak out against slavery.

Psalm A psalm is a sacred song or hymn. Capitalized, the word refers to any of the sacred songs or hymns collected in the Old Testament *Book of Psalms.*

Purpose *See* **Author's Purpose.**

Quatrain A quatrain is a four-line stanza, as in the following example:

> This is my letter to the World
> That never wrote to Me—
> The simple News that Nature told—
> With tender Majesty
>
> —Emily Dickinson,
> from "This is my letter to the World"

See pages 750, 761.
See also **Poetry; Stanza.**

Rationalism Rationalism, a movement in 18th-century thought, emphasized the role of reason in human affairs. To the rationalists, the universe was a harmonious, carefully ordered place, in which each human being played a small role in the functioning of the whole—like a cog in a wheel. These thinkers also believed in human perfectibility, convinced that the exercise of reason would lead to scientific advances, better government, and eventually an ideal society. Thomas Jefferson's "Declaration of Independence," a masterpiece of political writing, reflects rationalist ideas about natural rights.

See pages 256–258, 270–276.

Realism In literature, realism has both a general and a special meaning. As a general term, *realism* refers to any effort to offer an accurate and detailed portrayal of actual life. Thus, critics talk about Shakespeare's realistic portrayals of his characters and praise the medieval poet Chaucer for his realistic descriptions of people from different social classes.

   More specifically, realism also refers to a literary method developed in the 19th century. The realists based their writing on careful observations of contemporary life, often focusing on the middle or lower classes. They attempted to present life objectively and honestly, without the sentimentality or idealism that had colored earlier literature. Typically, realists developed their settings in great detail in an effort to re-create a specific time and place for the reader. Willa Cather, Kate Chopin, and Mark Twain are all considered realists.

See pages 636–637.
See also **Local Color Realism; Naturalism.**

Refrain In poetry, a refrain is part of a stanza, consisting of one or more lines that are repeated regularly, sometimes with changes, often at the ends of succeeding stanzas. For example, in "The Raven," the line "Quoth the Raven, 'Nevermore'" is a refrain. Refrains are often found in **ballads.**

Repetition Repetition is the recurrence of words, phrases, or lines. For example, the first line of "Song of the Sky Loom" is the same as the last line. Sometimes repetition is **incremental:** the structure of a line or stanza is repeated a certain number of times, with a slight variation in wording each time.

Example: The sequence "May the warp be . . . / May the weft be . . . / May the border be . . ." is an example of incremental repetition.

See pages 37, 267, 404, 607, 1005.
See also **Anaphora.**

Resolution *See* **Falling Action.**

Rhetorical Question A rhetorical question is a question to which no answer is expected because the answer is obvious. Rhetorical questions are often used in persuasive writing to emphasize a point or create an emotional effect.

Example: Patrick Henry asks this rhetorical question in his "Speech in the Virginia Convention": "Is life so dear, or peace so sweet, as to be purchased at the price of chains and slavery?"

See page 262.
See also **Persuasive Writing.**

Rhyme Rhyme is the similarity of sound between two words. Words rhyme when the sounds of their accented vowels, and all succeeding sounds, are identical, as in *tether* and *together.* For true rhyme, the consonants that precede the vowels must be different.

Rhyme that occurs within a single line, as in the following example, is called **internal rhyme.**

> Ah, distinctly I <u>remember</u> it was in the bleak
> <u>December</u>;
>
> —Edgar Allan Poe, from "The Raven"

When rhyme comes at the end of a line of poetry, it is called **end rhyme.** The pattern of end rhyme in a poem is called the **rhyme scheme** and is charted by assigning a letter, beginning with the letter *a,* to each line. Lines that rhyme are given the same letter. The rhyme scheme of the following stanza is *aabbcc:*

> In silent night when rest I took   *a*
> For sorrow near I did not look   *a*
> I wakened was with thund'ring noise   *b*
> And piteous shrieks of dreadful voice.   *b*
> That fearful sound of "Fire!" and "Fire!"   *c*
> Let no man know is my desire.   *c*
>
> —Anne Bradstreet,
> from "Upon the Burning of Our House"

See pages 347, 471, 833.
See also **Slant Rhyme.**

Rhyme Scheme *See* **Rhyme.**

Rhythm Rhythm refers to the pattern or flow of sound created by the arrangement of stressed and unstressed syllables in a line of poetry. Some poems follow a regular pattern, or **meter,** of accented and unaccented syllables. Poets use rhythm to bring out the musical quality of language, to emphasize ideas, to create mood, and to reinforce subject matter.

See also **Meter.**
See pages 924, 1005.

Rising Action In a plot structure, the rising action refers to events that lead to the climax by adding complications or expanding the conflict. Suspense usually builds during the rising action.

See also **Climax; Exposition; Falling Action; Plot; Suspense.**

Romanticism Romanticism was a movement in the arts that flourished in Europe and America throughout much of the 19th century. Romantic writers glorified nature and celebrated individuality. Their treatment of subject was emotional rather than rational, intuitive rather than analytic. Washington Irving and Henry Wadsworth Longfellow were popular American romantic writers.

See pages 340–342.

Sarcasm Sarcasm, a type of **verbal irony,** refers to a critical, contemptuous remark expressed in a statement in which literal meaning is the opposite of actual meaning. Sarcasm is mocking, and its intention is to hurt.

See also **Irony.**

Satire Satire is a literary technique in which foolish ideas or customs are ridiculed for the purpose of improving society. Satire may be gently witty, mildly abrasive, or bitterly critical. Short stories, poems, novels, essays, and plays all may be vehicles for satire.

Example: In the excerpt from *The Autobiography of Mark Twain,* Twain satirizes the gullibility of the people in his hometown who are easily duped by impostors, like the mesmerizer and himself.

Scansion The process of determining meter is known as scansion. When you scan a line of poetry, you mark its stressed and unstressed syllables in order to identify the rhythm.
See also **Meter.**

Scene A scene is a subdivision of an act in a drama. Each scene usually establishes a different time or place.
See also **Act; Drama.**

Science Fiction Science fiction is prose writing that presents the possibilities of the past or the future, using known scientific data and theories as well as the creative imagination of the writer. Most science fiction comments on present-day society through the writer's fictional conception of a past or future society. Ray Bradbury and Kurt Vonnegut, Jr., are two popular writers of science fiction.

Secondary Sources *See* **Primary Sources.**

Sermon A sermon is a form of religious persuasion in which a speaker exhorts the audience to behave in a more spiritual and moral fashion. "Sinners in the Hands of an Angry God" is a sermon.

Setting The setting of a literary work refers to the time and place in which the action occurs. A story can be set in an imaginary place, such as an enchanted castle, or a real place, such as New York City or Tombstone, Arizona. The time can be the past, the present, or the future.

Example: Willa Cather's story "A Wagner Matinee" is set in Boston around the turn of the 20th century.
See pages 62, 78, 636–637, 697.

Sestet *See* **Sonnet.**

Short Story A short story is a work of fiction that can be read in one sitting. It usually focuses on one or two major characters and one major conflict.
A short story must be unified; all the elements must work together to produce a total effect. This unity of effect is reinforced through an appropriate title and through the use of symbolism, irony, and other literary devices.
See also **Character; Conflict; Fiction; Novel; Plot; Setting; Theme.**

Simile A simile is a figure of speech that compares two things that have something in common, using a word such as *like* or *as.*

Example: Abigail Adams's statement "power and liberty are like heat and moisture" and Thoreau's statement "we live meanly, like ants" contain similes.
See pages 287, 750, 760.
See also **Figurative Language; Metaphor.**

Situational Irony *See* **Irony.**

Slant Rhyme Rhymes that are not exact but only approximate are known as slant rhymes, or **off rhymes:**

> "Hope" is the thing with feathers—
> That perches in the <u>soul</u>—
> And sings the tune without the words—
> And never stops—at <u>all</u>—
>
> —Emily Dickinson,
> from "'Hope' is the thing with feathers—"

See page 750.
See also **Rhyme.**

Slave Narrative A slave narrative is an autobiographical account written by someone who endured the miseries of slavery. Olaudah Equiano's and Frederick Douglass's auto-biographies are examples of slave narratives. These writers often use sensory details to re-create their experiences. For example, to re-create the horror of confinement in the hold of a slave ship, Equiano gives the reader such details as "the galling of the chains" and "the groans of the dying."

See page 98.
See also **Autobiography.**

Soliloquy See **Monologue.**

Sonnet A sonnet is a 14-line lyric poem, commonly written in iambic pentameter. The **Petrarchan sonnet** consists of two parts. The first eight lines, called the **octave,** usually have the rhyme scheme *abbaabba.* In the last six lines, called the **sestet,** the rhyme scheme may be *cdecde, cdcdcd,* or another variation. The octave generally presents a problem or raises a question, and the sestet resolves or comments on the problem. James Weldon Johnson's "My City" is a Petrarchan sonnet. A **Shakespearean sonnet** is divided into three quatrains (groups of four lines) and a couplet (two rhyming lines). Its rhyme scheme is *abab cdcd efef gg.* The couplet usually expresses a response to the important issue developed in the three quatrains. Claude McKay's "If We Must Die" is a Shakespearean sonnet.

See pages 943, 948.
See also **Meter; Quatrain; Rhyme.**

Sound Devices See **Alliteration; Assonance; Consonance; Meter; Onomatopoeia; Repetition; Rhyme; Rhyme Scheme; Rhythm.**

Speaker The speaker of a poem, like the narrator of a story, is the voice that talks to the reader. In some poems, the speaker can be identified with the poet, as in the case of "Tía Chucha," Luis J. Rodriguez's tribute to his aunt. In other poems, the poet invents a fictional character, or a **persona,** to play the role of the speaker. *Persona* is a Latin word meaning "actor's mask." In Sylvia Plath's poem "Mirror," the persona is an inanimate object capable of speech and thought.

See pages 421, 1061, 1116.

Stage Directions Stage directions are the playwright's instructions for the director, performers, and stage crew. Usually set in italics, they are located at the beginning of and throughout a script. Stage directions usually tell the time and place of the action and explain how characters move and speak. They also describe scenery, props, lighting, costumes, music, or sound effects.

See pages 162, 190.
See also **Drama.**

Stanza A stanza is a group of lines that form a unit in a poem. A stanza is usually characterized by a common pattern of meter, rhyme, and number of lines. Longfellow's "A Psalm of Life" is written in four-line stanzas. During the 20th century, poets experimented more freely with stanza form than did earlier poets, sometimes writing poems without any stanza breaks.

See page 347.

Stereotype A stereotype is an over-simplified image of a person, group, or institution. Sweeping generalizations about "all Southerners" or "every used-car dealer" are stereotypes. Simplified or stock characters in literature are often called stereotypes. Such characters do not usually demonstrate the complexities of real people.

Example: In Washington Irving's "The Devil and Tom Walker," Tom Walker's wife is a stereotype of a greedy and shrewish wife.

Stream of Consciousness Stream of consciousness is a technique that was developed by modernist writers to present the flow of a character's seemingly unconnected thoughts, responses, and sensations. The term was coined by American psychologist William James to characterize the unbroken flow of thought that occurs in the waking mind.

Example: In "The Love Song of J. Alfred Prufrock," T. S. Eliot uses this technique to reveal the jumble of thoughts that flow through Prufrock's mind.

See page 1043.
See also **Modernism.**

Structure The structure of a literary work is the way in which it is put together—the arrangement of its parts. In poetry, structure refers to the arrangement of words and lines to produce a desired effect. A common structural unit in poetry is the stanza, of which there are numerous types. In prose, structure is the arrangement of larger units or parts of a selection. Paragraphs, for example, are a basic unit in prose, as are chapters in novels and acts in plays. The structure of a poem, short story, novel, play, or nonfiction selection usually emphasizes certain important aspects of content.

Examples: F. Scott Fitzgerald's "Winter Dreams" is divided into six sections, each section reflecting another stage in Dexter Green's relationship with Judy Jones. Gish Jen's "In the American Society" is divided into two sections. The first section focuses on the father's own society, while the second section focuses on the American society into which the mother aspires to fit.

See pages 580, 892.
See also **Form; Stanza.**

Style Style is the distinctive way in which a work of literature is written. Style refers not so much to what is said but how it is said. Word choice, sentence length, tone, imagery, and use of dialogue all contribute to a writer's style. A group of writers might exemplify common stylistic characteristics; for example, the Puritans who wrote in the **plain style**—a simple direct way of expressing ideas—or the **Imagists** whose poems are marked by compression and rich sensory images.

Example: E. E. Cummings's style is decidedly unconventional, breaking rules of capitalization, punctuation, diction, and syntax.

See pages 497, 571, 606, 686, 761, 938, 971, 1014, 1023, 1120.

Surprise Ending A surprise ending is an unexpected plot twist at the end of a story.

Example: "Story of an Hour" ends with a surprise when Mrs. Mallard drops dead after her husband, presumed to be dead, reappears.

See page 786.
See also **Irony.**

Surrealism Surrealism, a movement in art and literature, sought to express freely the creations of the imagination as revealed in dreams. This movement, which developed in France during the 1920s, reached the United States after World War II. The roots of this movement go back to Baudelaire, and it reflects Sigmund Freud's theories about the subconscious mind.

Suspense Suspense is the excitement or tension that readers feel as they become involved in a story and eagerly await the outcome.

Example: In Ambrose Bierce's "An Occurrence at Owl Creek Bridge," the suspense builds as the reader awaits the outcome of Peyton Farquhar's attempted escape from hanging at the hands of Union troops.

See page 514.
See also **Rising Action.**

Symbol A symbol is a person, place, or object that has a concrete meaning in itself and also stands for something beyond itself, such as an idea or feeling.

Example: In "Dr. Heidegger's Experiment," the blooming and fading rose symbolizes human mortality.

See pages 578, 838, 860.

Synesthesia *See* **Imagery.**

Tall Tale A tall tale is a distinctively American type of humorous story characterized by exaggeration. Tall tales and practical jokes have similar kinds of humor. In both, someone gets fooled, to the amusement of the person or persons who know the truth, as in Twain's "The Notorious Jumping Frog of Calaveras County."

See page 685.
See also **Humor; Hyperbole.**

Theme Theme is the central idea or ideas the writer intends to share with the reader. The idea may be a lesson about life or about people and their actions. Most themes are not obvious and must be inferred by the reader. At times, different readers discover different themes in the same work.

Example: One theme of "The Masque of the Red Death" could be stated, "No one, not even the wealthiest person, has the power to escape death."

See pages 293, 298, 763–764, 898, 1085.

Third-Person Point of View *See* **Point of View.**

Title The title of a literary work introduces readers to the piece and usually reveals something about its subject or theme. Often, a poet uses the title to provide information necessary for understanding a poem.

Examples: "A Worn Path," the title of Eudora Welty's short story, suggests the main character, Phoenix, herself: the path of her life is worn with age and struggle, and her life has centered on a single routine motivated by love. The title of Sylvia Plath's poem "Mirror" provides a necessary clue as to the identity of the speaker.

See pages 898, 1085, 1109, 1225.

Tone Tone is a writer's attitude toward his or her subject. A writer can communicate tone through **diction,** choice of details, and direct statements of his or her position. Unlike **mood,** which refers to the emotional response of the reader to a work, tone reflects the feelings of the writer. To identify the tone of a work of literature, you might find it helpful to read the work aloud, as if giving a dramatic reading before an audience. The emotions that you convey in an oral reading should give you hints as to the tone of the work.

Examples: Red Jacket's tone is serious and respectful in "Lecture to a Missionary"; Claude McKay's tone in "If We Must Die" is proud, defiant, and urgent.

See pages 298, 421, 828, 838, 937, 957, 1093, 1148–1149, 1155, 1198.

See also **Connotation; Diction; Mood; Style.**

Tragedy A tragedy is a dramatic work that presents the downfall of a dignified character who is involved in historically, morally, or socially significant events. The main character, or tragic hero, has a tragic flaw, a quality that leads to his or her destruction. The events in a tragic plot are set in motion by a decision that is often an error in judgment caused by the tragic flaw. Succeeding events are linked in a cause-and-effect relationship and lead inevitably to a disastrous conclusion, usually death. Arthur Miller's *The Crucible* could be classified as a tragedy.

Tragic Hero The ancient Greek philosopher Aristotle defined a tragic hero as a character whose basic goodness and superiority are marred by a tragic flaw that brings about or contributes to his or her downfall. The flaw may be poor judgment, pride, weakness, or an excess of an admirable quality. The tragic hero recognizes his or her own flaw and its consequences, but only after it is too late to change the course of events.

Example: Bruno, the hero of Joyce Carol Oates's "Hostage," might be considered a tragic hero because his excessively violent defense of a young girl leads to his ruin.

See page 1212.
See also **Character.**

Transcendentalism The philosophy of transcendentalism, an American offshoot of German romanticism, was based on a belief that "transcendent forms" of truth exist beyond reason and experience. Ralph Waldo Emerson, the leader of the movement, asserted that every individual is capable of discovering this higher truth through intuition. Henry David Thoreau and Walt Whitman are two well-known transcendentalist writers.

See pages 341–342.
See also **Romanticism.**

Transcript   A transcript is a written record of words originally spoken aloud. For example, "The Examination of Sarah Good" provides the actual questions posed by the examiner and Sarah Good's responses to them during her interrogation for witchcraft in 1692.

See page 148.

Trickster Tale   A trickster tale is a folk tale about an animal or person who engages in trickery, violence, and magic. Neither all good nor all bad, a trickster may be foolish yet clever, greedy yet helpful, immoral yet moral. "Coyote and the Buffalo" and "Fox and Coyote and Whale" are both trickster tales.

See page 46.
See also **Folk Tale.**

Trochee   *See* **Meter.**

Understatement   Understatement is a description of a person, an event, or an idea from a perspective that greatly plays down the importance of the subject, often to add humor or to make a point ironically.

Example: In "Letter to John Adams," Abigail Adams points out the tyranny of male power by gently saying, "I cannot say that I think you very generous to the ladies."

See also **Hyperbole.**

Verbal Irony   *See* **Irony.**

Voice   The term *voice* refers to a writer's unique use of language that allows a reader to "hear" a human personality in his or her writing. The elements of style that determine a writer's voice include sentence structure, diction, and tone. For example, some writers are noted for their reliance on short, simple sentences, while others make use of long, complicated ones. Certain writers use concrete words, such as *lake* or *cold,* which name things that you can see, hear, feel, taste, or smell. Others prefer abstract terms like *memory,* which name things that cannot be perceived with the senses. A writer's tone also leaves its imprint on his or her personal voice. The term can be applied to the narrator of a selection, as well as the writer.

In the following passage, the diction and tone help establish the narrator as a witty, sarcastic character:

> Tom's wife was a tall termagant, fierce of temper, loud of tongue, and strong of arm. Her voice was often heard in wordy warfare with her husband; and his face sometimes showed signs that their conflicts were not confined to words.
>
> —Washington Irving,
> "The Devil and Tom Walker"

See pages 873, 1128.
See also **Diction, Tone.**

Word Choice   *See* **Diction.**

Glossary of Words to Know
In English and Spanish

A

abdicate (ăb′dĭ-kāt′) *v.* to give up responsibility for
abdicar *v.* renunciar a un cargo o responsabilidad

abhor (ăb-hôr′) *v.* to regard with disgust
aborrecer *v.* odiar; tener aversión

abide (e-bīd′) *v.* to put up with
soportar *v.* aguantar; tolerar

abject (ăb′jĕkt′) *adj.* low; contemptible; wretched
abyecto *adj.* bajo; ruin; despreciable

abode (ə-bōd′) *n.* a dwelling place; home
morada *n.* sitio donde se vive; hogar

abominable (ə-bŏm′ə-nə-bəl) *adj.* thoroughly detestable
abominable *adj.* totalmente detestable

abrasive (ə-brā′sĭv) *adj.* harsh and rough
abrasivo *adj.* áspero e irritante

absolve (əb-zŏlv′) *v.* to clear of guilt or blame
absolver *v.* limpiar de culpa

acquiescing (ăk′wē-ĕs′ĭng) *adj.* consenting passively or without protest **acquiesce** *v.*
conforme *adj.* que acepta pasivamente o sin protestar **conformarse** *v.*

adamant (ăd′ə-mənt) *adj.* stubborn; not giving in
obstinado *adj.* terco; que no cede

adversary (ăd′vər-sĕr′ē) *n.* an opponent
adversario *s.* opositor

affiliate (ə-fĭl′ē-ĭt) *n.* a person or organization associated with another
afiliado *s.* persona u organización asociada a otra

affinity (ə-fĭn′ĭ-tē) *n.* a kinship or likeness
afinidad *s.* parentesco o semejanza

afflict (ə-flĭkt′) *v.* to trouble or attack, causing physical or mental suffering
afligir *v.* aquejar; afectar o atacar, causando daño físico o sufrimiento mental

affronted (ə-frŭn′tĭd) *adj.* intentionally insulted **affront** *v.*
afrontado *adj.* insultado con intención **afrontar** *v.*

aggressor (ə-grĕs′ər) *n.* one that begins an attack or a quarrel
agresor *s.* el que inicia un ataque o pleito

aghast (ə-găst′) *adj.* overcome with fear; terrified
horrorizado *adj.* aterrorizado; lleno de miedo

alleviation (ə-lē′vē-ā′shən) *n.* a decrease in severity; relief
alivio *s.* disminución de gravedad; mejoría

allurement (ə-lŏŏr′mənt) *n.* attraction; enticement
fascinación *s.* atracción; encanto

aloof (ə-lōōf′) *adj.* distant
distante *adj.* indiferente

amiably (ā′mē-ə-blē) *adv.* in a pleasant and friendly manner; good-naturedly
amigablemente *adv.* de forma agradable y amable; cordialmente

amicably (ăm′ĭ-kə-blē) *adv.* in a friendly way
amigablemente *adv.* de forma amistosa

anarchy (ăn′ər-kē) *n.* absence of any form of political authority
anarquía *s.* ausencia total de autoridad política

anguish (ăng′gwĭsh) *n.* agonizing physical or mental pain
angustia *s.* gran dolor físico o mental

annihilate (ə-nī′ə-lāt′) *v.* to destroy completely; wipe out
aniquilar *v.* destruir por completo; eliminar; arrasar

anonymity (ăn′ə-nĭm′ĭ-tē) *n.* a state of being unknown or unrecognized, without special or distinguishing qualities
anonimato *s.* estado en que no se es reconocido o identificado, sin cualidades distintivas o especiales

antagonistic (ăn-tăg′ə-nĭs′tĭk) *adj.* openly hostile and aggressive toward another
antagónico *adj.* abiertamente hostily agresivo hacia otro

aplomb (ə-plŏm′) *n.* self-confidence
aplomo *s.* confianza en sí mismo

appease (ə-pēz′) *v.* to bring peace, quiet, or calm to; soothe
apaciguar *v.* aquietar, tranquilizar o calmar; confortar

appraisal (ə-prā′zəl) *n.* evaluation
avalúo *s.* evaluación

apprehension (ăp′rĭ-hĕn′shən) *n.* a suspicion of future evil; dread
aprensión *s.* sospecha de un mal futuro; recelo

apprise (ə-prīz′) *v.* to give notice to; inform
informar *v.* avisar; advertir

arbitrary (är′bĭ-trĕr′ē) *adj.* based on unpredictable decisions rather than on reason or law
arbitrario *adj.* basado en decisiones inesperadas o caprichosas, no en la razón o en la ley

arbitrate (är′bĭ-trāt) *v.* to judge or act as referee
arbitrar *v.* juzgar o actuar como árbitro

arroyo (ə-roi′ō) *n.* a deep gully cut by an intermittent stream; a dry gulch
arroyo *s.* barranco profundo cortado por un riachuelo intermitente; quebrada seca (este término se usa en inglés con el significado dado, que es distinto al significado en español: río pequeño)

articulate (är-tĭk′yə-lĭt) *adj.* clear and effective in speech
elocuente *adj.* que se expresa con claridad y convicción

ascertain (ăs′ər-tān′) *v.* to find out
averiguar *v.* investigar

ascribe (ə-skrīb′) *v.* to attribute to a specified cause or source
atribuir *v.* achacar a una causa u origen específico

aspire (ə-spīr′) *v.* to seek to achieve; strive
aspirar *v.* desear la realización de algo; empeñarse

assurance (ə-shoŏr′əns) *n.* self-confidence
seguridad *s.* confianza en sí mismo

atrocious (ə-trō′shəs) *adj.* shockingly bad or lacking in taste; awful
atroz *adj.* muy malo o carente de gusto; horrible

avalanche (ăv′ə-lănch′) *n.* an overwhelming amount
avalancha *s.* cantidad abrumadora

avarice (ăv′ə-rĭs) *n.* greed
avaricia *s.* codicia

aversion (ə-vûr′zhən) *n.* a strong dislike
aversión *s.* antipatía profunda

avid (ăv′ĭd) *adj.* having an intense desire or craving
ávido *adj.* con deseo o necesidad intensa

B

basely (bās′lē) *adv.* dishonorably; meanly
bajamente *adv.* ruinmente; con maldad

begrudge (bĭ-grŭj′) *v.* to resent another person's possession of something
envidiar *v.* resentir que otra persona posea algo

beguiling (bĭ-gī′lĭng) *adj.* charming or delighting **beguile** *v.*
encantador *adj.* seductor; fascinante **encantar** *v.*

Glossary of Words to Know

beholden (bĭ hōl′ dən) *adj.* obliged to feel grateful; indebted
agradecido *adj.* obligado a sentir gratitud; endeudado

beseech (bĭ-sēch′) *v.* to implore; beg
suplicar *v.* implorar; rogar

bestowed (bĭ-stōd′) *adj.* applied; used
bestow *v.*
otorgado *adj.* aplicado; usado **otorgar** *v.*

blatantly (blāt′nt-lē) *adv.* in an extremely obvious way; conspicuously
evidentemente *adv.* de forma sumamente obvia; conspicuamente

blunder (blŭn′dər) *n.* a mistake
torpeza *s.* metedura de pata

C

cajole (kə-jōl′) *v.* to persuade by pleasant words or flattery; coax
engatusar *v.* persuadir con bellas palabras; convencer con halagos o falsas promesas

calamity (kə-lăm′ĭ-tē) *n.* disaster
calamidad *s.* desastre

callow (kăl′ō) *adj.* lacking adult maturity or experience; immature
inmaduro *adj.* carente de madurez o experiencia; inexperto

careen (kə-rēn′) *v.* to swerve, or cause to swerve, from side to side while in motion
carenar *v.* dar bandazos; ir de un lado a otro mientras se avanza

cassock (kăs′ək) *n.* an ankle-length garment, with close-fitting waist and sleeves, worn by clergymen
sotana *s.* prenda que llega al tobillo, de talle ajustado y mangas, usada por religiosos

cauterize (kô′tə-rīz′) *v.* to burn or sear to destroy abnormal tissue
cauterizar *v.* quemar o chamuscar para destruir tejido anormal

cavorting (kə-vôr′tĭng) *adj.* prancing about; capering **cavort** *v.*
retozador *adj.* que da cabriolas; que se divierte ruidosamente **retozar** *v.*

censurer (sĕn′shər-ər) *n.* one who expresses strong disapproval or harsh criticism
censor *s.* el que expresa fuerte desaprobación o crítica dura

circumvent (sûr′kəm-vĕnt′) *v.* to avoid or get around by clever maneuvering
evitar *v.* salvar o rodear; evadir mediante maniobras ingeniosas

cloister (kloi′stər) *n.* a place devoted to religious seclusion; a monastery or convent
claustro *s.* lugar dedicado al encierro religioso; monasterio o convento

cognizant (kŏg′nĭ-zənt) *adj.* aware
conocido *adj.* sabido

coherent (kō-hîr′ənt) *adj.* understandable; logically consistent
coherente *adj.* comprensible; uniforme y lógico

collusion (kə-lōō′zhən) *n.* a secret agreement for a deceitful purpose
colusión *s.* acuerdo secreto con fines engañosos

commission (kə-mĭsh′ən) *v.* to assign a task or duty to
comisionar *v.* asignar una tarea u obligación

commodity (kə-mŏd′ĭ-tē) *n.* something useful; an article of commerce
mercancía *s.* producto útil; artículo comercial

comply (kəm-plī′) *v.* to obey another's command, request, rule, or wish
cumplir *v.* obedecer la orden, solicitud, regla o deseo de otro

composed (kəm-pōzd′) *adj.* calm; cool and collected
sosegado *adj.* calmado; tranquilo y sereno

compound (kŏm-pound′) *v.* to form or make up; compose
componer *v.* formar o inventar; crear

compulsory (kəm-pŭl′sə-rē) *adj.* required without exception; mandatory
obligatorio *adj.* requerido sin excepciones; forzoso

conceived (kən-sēvd′) *adj.* originated
conceive *v.*
concebido *adj.* originado **concebir** *v.*

conclude (kən-klōōd´) *v.* to arrive at a judgment or decision
concluir *v.* llegar a un juicio o decisión

confederate (kən-fěd´ər-ĭt) *n.* one who assists in a plot; associate
confederado *s.* alguien que participa en una conjura; socio

confront (kən-frŭnt´) *v.* to come up against; meet face to face
confrontar *v.* enfrentarse; encarar

congenial (kən-gēn´yəl) *adj.* suited to one's needs or nature; agreeable
compatible *adj.* adecuado a las necesidades o naturaleza de uno; agradable

congruous (kŏng´grōō-əs) *adj.* fitting; suitable
congruente *adj.* conveniente; oportuno

conjecture (kən-jěk´chər) *v.* to make a judgment on the basis of uncertain evidence; guess
conjeturar *v.* formarse un juicio con evidencia incierta; adivinar

conscientious (kŏn´shē-ěn´shəs) *adj.* guided by conscience; honest
concienzudo *adj.* guiado por la conciencia; honesto

consecrate (kŏn´sĭ-krāt´) *v.* to declare sacred
consagrar *v.* declarar sagrado

consternation (kŏn´stər-nā´shən) *n.* a state of paralyzing dismay; fear
consternación *s.* estado de profundo dolor emocional; miedo

constitute (kŏn´stĭ-tōōt´) *v.* to amount to; equal
constituir *v.* representar; formar

contagion (kən-tā´jən) *n.* the spreading of disease
contagio *s.* difusión de una enfermedad

contempt (kən-těmpt´) *n.* scorn; disdain
desdén *s.* burla; desprecio

contemptuously (kən-těmp´chōō-əs-lē) *adv.* in a way that shows disdain or disgust; scornfully
desdeñosamente *adv.* con desprecio

contend (kən-těnd´) *v.* to compete; vie
contender *v.* competir; luchar

contentious (kən-těn´shəs) *adj.* quarrelsome
contencioso *adj.* discutidor; conflictivo

contrite (kən-trīt´) *adj.* sorrowful for one's wrongdoing; repentant
contrito *adj.* afligido por errores propios; arrepentido

copious (kō´pē-əs) *adj.* in large amounts; abundant
copioso *adj.* en grandes cantidades; abundante

coquettish (kō-kět´ĭsh) *adj.* flirtatious
coqueto *adj.* seductor

corroding (kə-rō´dĭng) *adj.* gradually destructive **corrode** *v.*
corrosivo *adj.* que causa destrucción gradual **corroer** *v.*

countenance (koun´tə-nəns) *n.* the face, especially as an indicator of emotion
semblante *s.* cara, especialmente como indicador de emoción

countenance (koun´tə-nəns) *v.* to give or express approval; support
aprobar *s.* apoyar

courtier (kôr´tē-ər) *n.* a member of a royal court
cortesano *s.* miembro de una corte real

credulity (krĭ-dōō´lĭ-tē) *n.* an inclination to believe too readily
credulidad *s.* inclinación a creer fácilmente

D

dank (dăngk) *adj.* unpleasantly damp; moist and chilly
húmedo *adj.* mojado y malsano; frío y mojado

daunted (dôn´tĭd) *adj.* intimidated or frightened **daunt** *v.*
atemorizado *adj.* intimidado o asustado **atemorizar** *v*

dauntless (dônt´lĭs) *adj.* fearless
temerario *adj.* sin miedo

debilitated (dĭ-bĭl´ĭ-tā´tĭd) *adj.* weakened; enfeebled
debilitado *adj.* frágil; endeble

decorum (dǐ-kôr'əm) *n.* proper and dignified behavior
decoro *s.* conducta adecuada y digna

decrepit (dǐ-krĕp'ĭt) *adj.* weakened, worn out, or broken down by old age or hard use
decrépito *adj.* débil, desgastado o roto por el tiempo o por mucho uso

deferential (dĕf'ə-rĕn'shəl) *adj.* extremely respectful
deferente *adj.* muy respetuoso

deficiency (dǐ-fǐsh'ən-sē) *n.* a lack
deficiencia *s.* carencia

delectable (dǐ-lĕk'tə-bəl) *adj.* highly pleasing; delightful
deleitable *adj.* muy agradable; delicioso

deliberately (dǐ-lǐb'ər-ĭt-lē) *adv.* in an unhurried and thoughtful manner
deliberadamente *adv.* de manera pensada y sin precipitación

deliverance (dǐ-lǐv'ər-əns) *n.* rescue from danger
salvación *s.* rescate de un peligro

delve (dĕlv) *v.* to conduct an investigation; search
indagar *v.* realizar una investigación; buscar

denunciation (dǐ-nŭn'sē-ā'shən) *n.* an act of condemning or accusing another; accusation
denuncia *s.* acto de condena o acusación

deplore (dǐ-plôr') *v.* to feel strong disapproval of or deeply regret
deplorar *v.* desaprobar fuertemente; lamentar profundamente

deposition (dĕp'ə-zǐsh'ən) *n.* a written statement by a witness
declaración *s.* testimonio escrito de un testigo

derision (dǐ-rǐzh'ən) *n.* harsh ridicule or mockery; scorn
humillación *s.* desprecio o desdén profundo; escarnio; burla aguda

derisive (dǐ-rī'sǐv) *adj.* mocking or ridiculing; scornful
humillante *adj.* desdeñable; despreciable

derive (dǐ-rīv') *v.* to obtain; get; receive
derivar *v.* obtener; recibir

desolate (dĕs'ə-lǐt) *adj.* without inhabitants; barren
desolado *adj.* inhabitado; vacío; yermo

despotic (dǐ-spŏt'ĭk) *adj.* like a dictator
despótico *adj.* como un dictador

detract (dǐ-trăkt') *v.* to take away; diminish
detractar *v.* quitar; disminuir

devastation (dĕv'ə-stā'shən) *n.* complete destruction
devastación *s.* destrucción total

devious (dē'vē-əs) *adj.* shifty; not straightforward
taimado *adj.* engañoso; deshonesto

devotion (dǐ-vō'shən) *n.* earnest dedication
devoción *s.* dedicación honesta

diagnosis (dī'əg-nō'sǐs) *n.* the identification of a physical disorder through an examination of its symptoms
diagnóstico *s.* identificación de un mal o enfermedad física mediante el examen de sus síntomas

diaphanous (dī-ăf'ə-nəs) *adj.* light or fragile in an unearthly way
diáfano *adj.* claro y limpio

diffident (dǐf'ǐ-dənt) *adj.* shy and timid; lacking self-confidence
tímido *adj.* turbado; inseguro

digress (dī-grĕs') *v.* to wander away from the main subject in a conversation or in writing; ramble
desviarse *v.* alejarse del tema central de una conversación; irse por las ramas

dilapidated (dǐ-lăp'ĭ-dā'tĭd) *adj.* in a state of disrepair; rundown
dilapidado *adj.* ruinoso; desgastado

diligently (dǐl'ə-jənt-lē) *adv.* in a persevering, painstaking manner
diligentemente *adv.* de manera perseverante, cuidadosa

dirge (dûrj) *n.* a slow, mournful piece of music; a funeral hymn
canto fúnebre *s.* pieza musical lenta y dolida; himno fúnebre

discourse (dĭ-skôrs') *v.* to speak
disertar *v.* hablar en público

disobedient (dĭs'ə-bē'dē-ənt) *adj.* not obeying instructions or orders
desobediente *adj.* que no obedece indicaciones u órdenes

dispensation (dĭs'pən-sā'shən) *n.* distribution; giving out
dispensación *s.* distribución; reparto

disproportionate (dĭs'prə-pôr'shə-nĭt) *adj.* out of proportion; of an unequal size or amount
desproporcionado *adj.* que no tiene la proporción debida

dispute (dĭ-spyōōt') *v.* to question or doubt
disputar *v.* discutir; cuestionar o dudar

disreputable (dĭs-rĕp'yə-tə-bəl) *adj.* lacking respectability of character or behavior
desprestigiado *adj.* carente de carácter o conducta respetable

dissemble (dĭ-sĕm'bəl) *v.* to disguise or conceal behind a false appearance
disimular *v.* disfrazar u ocultar detrás de una apariencia falsa

dissipation (dĭs'ə-pā'shən) *n.* a reckless waste of resources; wastefulness
disipación *s.* gasto descuidado de recursos; desperdicio

dissolution (dĭs'ə-lōō'shən) *n.* a breaking up; disintegration
disolución *s.* ruptura; desintegración

divining (dĭ-vī'nĭng) *adj.* finding out through intuition; guessing from incomplete evidence **divine** *v.*
adivinado *adv.* descubierto a través de la intuición; intuido sin tener todos los elementos **adivinar** *v.*

divulge (dĭ-vŭlj') *v.* to make known something private
divulgar *v.* dar a conocer algo privado

document (dŏk'yə-mənt) *v.* to provide a detailed account of
documentar *v.* dar información detallada

dolefully (dōl'fə-lē) *adv.* mournfully
lúgubremente *adv.* tristemente

dredge (drĕj) *v.* to dig into; unearth
escarbar *v.* sacar a la luz; desenterrar

dubious (dōō'bē-əs) *adj.* doubtful; suspicious
dudoso *adj.* sospechoso; oscuro

E

edible (ĕd'ə-bəl) *adj.* fit to eat
comestible *adj.* que se puede comer

edict (ē'dĭkt') *n.* an order put out by a person in authority
edicto *s.* orden de una persona de autoridad

efface (ĭ-fās') *v.* to rub or wipe out; erase
tachar *v.* tallar o limpiar; borrar

effrontery (ĭ-frŭn'tə-rē) *n.* disrespectful and insulting boldness
desvergüenza *s.* descaro irrespetuoso e insultante

elemental (ĕl'ə-mən'tl) *adj.* basic; like a natural force
elemental *adj.* básico; como una fuerza natural

eloquence (ĕl'ə-kwəns) *n.* expressiveness
elocuencia *s.* expresividad

emaciated (ĭ-mā'shē-ā'tĭd) *adj.* excessively thin; wasted away **emaciate** *v.*
emaciado *adj.* en los huesos; muy delgado por pasar hambre **emaciarse** *v.*

emancipate (ĭ-măn'sə-pāt') *v.* to free; liberate
emancipar *v.* liberar; dejar libre

embody (ĕm-bŏd'ē) *v.* to represent in bodily form
encarnar *v.* representar en forma corporal

embroidered (ĕm-broi'dərd) *adj.* decorated with stitched designs **embroider** *v.*
bordado *adj.* decorado con puntadas **bordar** *v.*

emergence (ĭ-mûr'jəns) *n.* the process of coming forth or coming into existence
emergencia *s.* proceso de surgir o de nacer

empower (ĕm-pou'ər) *v.* to invest with authority
autorizar *v.* investir de autoridad

encroach (ĕn-krōch') *v.* to advance beyond original limits; intrude
traspasar *v.* ir más allá de los límites; cometer una intrusión

endeavor (ĕn-dĕvʹər) *v.* to make an earnest effort; strive
esforzarse *v.* hacer un esfuerzo honesto; empeñarse

engender (ĕn-jĕnʹdər) *v.* to produce; bring about
engendrar *v.* producir; crear

enterprising (ĕnʹtər-prīʹzĭng) *adj.* possessing imagination and initiative
emprendedor *adj.* que posee imaginación e iniciativa

environs (ĕn-vīʹrənz) *n.* a surrounding region
alrededores *s.* región cercana

estrangement (ĭ-strānjʹmənt) *n.* separation; alienation
alejamiento *s.* distanciamiento; separación

ethical (ĕthʹĭ-kəl) *adj.* dealing with principles of right and wrong; moral
ético *adj.* relacionado con principios del bien y el mal; moral

evade (ĭ-vādʹ) *v.* to escape or avoid
evadir *v.* escapar o evitar

evolve (ĭ-vŏlvʹ) *v.* to develop gradually
evolucionar *v.* desarrollar gradualmente

excommunication (ĕksʹkə-myoōʹnĭ-kāʹshən) *n.* banishment from a church
excomunión *s.* expulsión de una iglesia

excruciatingly (ĭk-skroōʹshē-āʹtĭng-lē) *adv.* in a way that causes great pain or distress
atrozmente *adv.* de forma que causa gran dolor o malestar

exhilaration (ĭg-zĭlʹə-rāʹshən) *n.* a lively delight
regocijo *s.* dicha vivaz

exploitation (ĕkʹsploi-tāʹshən) *n.* use of another person or group for selfish purposes
explotación *s.* uso de otra persona o grupo con fines egoístas

extenuating (ĭk-stĕnʹyoō-āʹtĭng) *adj.* lessening a fault by serving as a partial excuse **extenuate** *v.*
atenuante *adj.* que reduce una falta al servir como excusa parcial **atenuar** *v.*

exultingly (ĭg-zŭlʹtĭng-lē) *adv.* in a joyful and triumphant way
exultantemente *adv.* de manera gozosa y triunfal

F

faculty (făkʹəl-tē) *n.* a natural power or ability
facultad *s.* capacidad o habilidad natural

fanatic (fē-nătʹĭk) *n.* a person possessed by an excessive and irrational zeal, especially for a religious or political cause
fanático *s.* persona poseída por un fervor excesivo e irracional, especialmente por una causa religiosa o política

feigned (fānd) *adj.* not real; pretended
fingido *adj.* irreal; aparentado

felicity (fĭ-lĭsʹĭ-tē) *n.* happiness; bliss
felicidad *s.* alegría; dicha

fitfully (fĭtʹfə-lē) *adv.* in an irregular way; unsteadily
espasmódicamente *adv.* de manera irregular; a intervalos

flourish (flûrʹĭsh) *v.* to thrive
florecer *v.* prosperar

forlorn (fər-lôrnʹ) *adj.* appearing sad or lonely
abandonado *adj.* con aspecto triste o desolado por la soledad

formidable (fôrʹmĭ-də-bəl) *adj.* difficult to defeat
formidable *adj.* difícil de derrotar

forte (fôrt) *n.* something in which a person excels
fuerte *s.* tema o habilidad en que una persona destaca

furtive (fûrʹtĭv) *adj.* secret; sneaky
furtivo *adj.* secreto; disimulado

futile (fyoōtʹl) *adj.* useless
fútil *adj.* inútil

futility (fyoō-tĭlʹĭ-tē) *n.* uselessness
futilidad *s.* inutilidad

G

garrulously (găr'ə-ləs-lē) *adv.* talking too much about trifles; talkative
gárrulamente *adv.* con mucha labia; locuazmente

gaunt (gônt) *adj.* thin and bony
demacrado *adj.* flaco y huesudo

genetic (jə-nĕt'ĭk) *adj.* relating to genes, the units that determine and transmit hereditary characteristics
genético *adj.* relacionado con los genes, las unidades que determinan y transmiten características hereditarias

genial (jēn'yəl) *adj.* having a friendly disposition
cordial *adj.* de disposición amable

glib (glĭb) *adj.* showing little thought, preparation, or concern
superficial *adj.* que muestra poca reflexión, preparación o interés

grimace (grĭm'ĭs) *n.* a twisting or distortion of the face
mueca *s.* torcimiento o distorsión de la cara

grotesque (grō-tĕsk') *adj.* having a bizarre, fantastic appearance
grotesco *adj.* de apariencia extraña, fantástica

gullible (gŭl'ə-bəl) *adj.* easily deceived or tricked
crédulo *adj.* fácil de engañar

H

harbor (här'bər) *v.* to shelter; protect
refugiar *v.* amparar; proteger

hue (hyōō) *n.* appearance; color
tinte *s.* apariencia; color

I

immaculate (ĭ-măk'yə-lĭt) *adj.* without stain; pure
inmaculado *adj.* sin mancha; puro

impeccable (ĭm-pĕk'ə-bəl) *adj.* flawless; perfect
impecable *adj.* sin fallas; perfecto

impel (ĭm-pĕl') *v.* to drive forward; force
impeler *v.* obligar; forzar

impertinence (ĭm-pûr'tn-əns) *n.* improper boldness; rudeness
impertinencia *s.* franqueza inadecuada; rudeza

impertinent (ĭm-pûr' tn ənt) *adj.* rude, ill-mannered
impertinente *adj.* rudo, grosero

impervious (ĭm-pûr'vē-əs) *adj.* incapable of being affected
insensible *adj.* que nada le afecta

impetuosity (ĭm-pĕch'ōō-ŏs'ĭ-tē) *n.* unthinking action
impetuosidad *s.* acción no pensada

implacable (ĭm-plăk'ə-bəl) *adj.* impossible to satisfy
implacable *adj.* imposible de satisfacer

implicate (ĭm'plĭ-kāt') *v.* to connect to an activity, especially one of an unsavory or criminal nature
implicar *v.* conectar con una actividad, especialmente si es dudosa o criminal

implore (ĭm-plôr') *v.* to beg; earnestly ask for
implorar *v.* rogar; pedir urgentemente

inaccessible (ĭn'ăk-sĕs'ə-bəl) *adj.* not obtained easily, if at all; unreachable
inaccesible *adj.* difícil de obtener; inalcanzable

inanimate (ĭn-ăn'ə-mĭt) *adj.* not alive; lifeless
inanimado *adj.* sin vida; muerto

inaudibly (ĭn-ô'də-blē) *adv.* unable to be heard clearly
inaudiblemente *adv.* que no se oye claramente

incense (ĭn-sĕns') *v.* to cause to be extremely angry
encolerizar *v.* causar enojo extremo

incessant (ĭn-sĕs'ənt) *adj.* ceaseless; continual
incesante *adj.* que no para; continuo

inclination (ĭn'klə-nā'shən) *n.* a favorable disposition; desire
inclinación *s.* disposición favorable; deseo

inconceivable (ĭn′kən-sē′və-bəl) *adj.* not able to be understood or imagined
inconcebible *adj.* que no se puede entender o imaginar

incongruously (ĭn-kŏng′grōō-əs-lē) *adv.* in a manner that is not fitting, suitable, or in agreement; incompatibly
incongruentemente *adv.* de forma inadecuada o inapropiada; incompatiblemente

incorrigible (ĭn-kôr′ĭ-jə-bəl) *adj.* impossible to correct or reform; uncontrollable
incorregible *adj.* imposible de corregir o reformar; incontrolable

incredulously (ĭn-krĕj′ə-ləs-lē) *adv.* in a manner showing a lack of belief
incrédulamente *adv.* sin fe o confianza

indestructible (ĭn′dĭ-strŭk′tə-bəl) *adj.* impossible to destroy
indestructible *adj.* imposible de destruir

indictment (ĭn-dīt′mənt) *n.* accusation
denuncia *s.* acusación

indignant (ĭn-dĭg′nənt) *adj.* filled with anger caused by something unjust or mean
indignado *adj.* lleno de ira causada por algo injusto o malo

indiscretion (ĭn′dĭ-skrĕsh′ən) *n.* a lack of good judgment in speech or behavior
indiscreción *s.* falta de juicio al hablar o actuar

indiscriminately (ĭn′dĭ-skrĭm′ə-nĭt-lē) *adv.* randomly
indiscriminadamente *adv.* al azar

indoctrination (ĭn-dŏk′trə-nā′shən) *n.* the process of being taught fundamentals, especially of military customs and discipline
adoctrinamiento *s.* proceso de enseñar los aspectos fundamentales, especialmente de las costumbres y la disciplina militar

indomitable (ĭn-dŏm′ĭ-tə-bəl) *adj.* not easily discouraged or defeated
indomable *adj.* que no se deja desalentar o vencer

ineffable (ĭn-ĕf′ə-bəl) *adj.* unable to be expressed in words
inefable *adj.* que no se puede expresar en palabras

inexpedient (ĭn′ĭk-spē′dē-ənt) *adj.* not useful for achieving a goal
inoportuno *adj.* inservible para alcanzar una meta

inexplicable (ĭn-ĕk′splĭ-kə-bəl) *adj.* difficult or impossible to explain
inexplicable *adj.* difícil o imposible de explicar

infamous (ĭn′fə-məs) *adj.* notorious
infame *adj.* de mala reputación; tristemente célebre

infatuation (ĭn-făch′ōō-ā′shən) *n.* the state of being completely carried away by foolish or shallow love or affection
encaprichamiento *s.* amor o afecto necio o superficial que domina el pensamiento

infirmity (ĭn-fûr′mĭ-tē) *n.* a sickness or weakness
enfermedad *s.* dolencia o debilidad

inflict (ĭn-flĭkt′) *v.* to cause to have or suffer; impose
infligir *v.* producir un daño; imponer

ingenuous (ĭn-jĕn′yōō-əs) *adj.* innocent; naive
ingenuo *adj.* inocente; candoroso

ingratiate (ĭn-grā′shē-āt′) *v.* to gain another's favor by deliberate effort
congraciar *v.* ganarse la aprobación de otro con un esfuerzo deliberado

inherently (ĭn-hîr′ənt-lē) *adv.* essentially
inherentemente *adv.* esencialmente

iniquity (ĭ-nĭk′wĭ-tē) *n.* wickedness; immorality
iniquidad *s.* maldad; inmoralidad

insidious (ĭn-sĭd′ē-əs) *adj.* treacherous
insidioso *adj.* traicionero

insipid (ĭn-sĭp′ĭd) *adj.* lacking in flavor; bland
insípido *adj.* sin sabor; aburrido

insoluble (ĭn-sŏl′yə-bəl) *adj.* having no solution; unsolvable
insoluble *adj.* que no tiene solución; irresoluble

insurrection (ĭn′sə-rĕk′shən) *n.* rebellion
insurrección *s.* rebelión

intently (ĭn-tĕnt′lē) *adv.* with concentrated attention
atentamente *adv.* con atención concentrada

intercede (ĭn′tər-sēd′) *v.* to plead on behalf of another or mediate in a dispute
interceder *v.* pedir a nombre de otro o mediar en una disputa

interment (ĭn-tûr′mənt) *n.* burial
entierro *s.* sepelio

interminable (ĭn-tûr′mə-nə-bəl) *adj.* endless
interminable *adj.* sin fin

interpose (ĭn′tər-pōz′) *v.* to interfere in order to help; intervene
interponerse *v.* interferir para ayudar; intervenir

intimate (ĭn′tə-māt) *v.* to make known indirectly; hint
intimar *v.* dar a conocer de manera indirecta; sugerir

intuitively (ĭn-tōō′ĭ-tĭv-lē) *adv.* without thinking; instinctively
intuitivamente *adv.* sin pensar; instintivamente

inundate (ĭn′ŭn-dāt′) *v.* to cover with water; overwhelm
inundar *v.* cubrir de agua; rebasar

invest (ĭn-vĕst′) *v.* to provide with a certain quality
investir *v.* dar cierta cualidad

invincible (ĭn-vĭn′sə-bəl) *adj.* unbeatable
invencible *adj.* que no se deja derrotar

irresolution (ĭ-rĕz′ə-lōō′shən) *n.* uncertainty; indecision
irresolución *s.* incertidumbre; indecisión

irrevocable (ĭ-rĕv′ə-kə-bəl) *adj.* impossible to take back or undo
irrevocable *adj.* imposible de retirar o deshacer

J

jubilant (jōō′bə-lənt) *adj.* joyful and triumphant
jubiloso *adj.* gozoso y triunfal

K

kindred (kĭn′drĭd) *n.* relatives or family
parentela *s.* parientes o familiares

L

laceration (lăs′ə-rā′shən) *n.* a physical, mental, or emotional wound
laceración *s.* herida física, mental o emocional

lament (lə-mĕnt′) *v.* to grieve; wail
lamentarse *v.* dolerse; quejarse

languish (lăng′gwĭsh) *v.* to become weak
languidecer *v.* debilitar

largesse (lär-zhĕs′) *n.* generosity
larqueza *s.* generosidad

latent (lāt′nt) *adj.* existing in a hidden form
latente *adj.* que existe en forma oculta

lattice (lăt′ĭs) *n.* an open framework made of spaced, crisscrossed strips
rejilla *s.* marco abierto hecho con tiras cruzadas

legacy (lĕg′ə-sē) *n.* something handed down from an ancestor or a predecessor or from the past
legado *s.* lo que se deja o transmite a los sucesores

lethargy (lĕth′ər-jē) *n.* a state of sluggishness and inactivity
letargo *s.* estado de sopor e inactividad

license (lī′səns) *n.* a lack of restrictions on behavior; freedom
licencia *s.* facultad o permiso para hacer una cosa; libertad

linear (lĭn′ē-ər) *adj.* resembling or arranged in a line
lineal *adj.* organizado en líneas

list (lĭst) *v.* to lean or tilt to one side
inclinarse *v.* hacerse hacia un lado

loathsome (lōth′səm) *adj.* arousing great dislike
odioso *adj.* que provoca mucho disgusto o rechazo; despreciado

looming (lōō'mǐng) *adj.* appearing to the mind in a large and threatening form **loom** *v.*
imponente *adj.* que parece grande y amenazante **imponer** *v.*

ludicrous (lōō'dǐ-krəs) *adj.* laughably absurd; ridiculous
risible *adj.* tan absurdo que causa risa; ridículo

lurid (lōōr'ǐd) *adj.* startling and sensational
chillón *adj.* llamativo y sensacional

luxuriant (lŭg-zhōōr'ē-ənt) *adj.* characterized by abundant growth
exuberante *adj.* que crececon lozanía

M

magnanimity (măg'nə-nǐm'ǐ-tē) *n.* generosity
magnanimidad *s.* generosidad

malicious (mə-lǐsh'əs) *adj.* wicked; spiteful
malicioso *adj.* maligno; malo

malinger (mə-lǐng'gər) *v.* to pretend illness in order to avoid duty or work
hacerse el enfermo *v.* fingir enfermedad para evitar obligaciones o trabajo

martial (mär'shəl) *adj.* warlike
marcial *adj.* bélico; de guerra

materialism (mə-tîr'ē-ə-lǐz'əm) *n.* a preoccupation with worldly rather than spiritual concerns
materialismo *s.* preocupación por lo mundano en vez de lo espiritual

mean (mēn) *adj.* inferior in quality, value, or importance
inferior *adj.* de menor calidad, valor, o importancia

mediocrity (mē'dē-ŏk'rǐ-tē) *n.* a state of being only average in quality; moderate inferiority
mediocridad *s.* de calidad apenas promedio; inferioridad moderada

meditation (mĕd'ǐ-tā'shən) *n.* a thought or reflection
meditación *s.* pensamiento o reflexión profunda

melancholy (mĕl'ən-kŏl'ē) *adj.* gloomy; sad
melancólico *adj.* triste

mercenary (mûr'sə-nĕr'ē) *n.* a professional soldier hired to fight in a foreign army
mercenario *s.* soldado profesional contratado para pelear en un ejército extranjero

mesa (mā' sə) *n.* a broad, flat-topped hill with clifflike sides
meseta *s.* planicie en lo alto de una montaña

meticulous (mǐ-tǐk'yə-ləs) *adj.* extremely careful and precise about details
meticuloso *adj.* sumamente cuidadoso, preciso y detallado

mincing (mǐn'sǐng) *adj.* acting refined or dainty
remilgado *adj.* refinado o afectado

minutiae (mǐ-nōō'shē-ē') *n.* tiny elements, details, or parts
minucias *s.* elementos, detalles o piezas pequeñas

misgiving (mǐs-gǐv'ǐng) *n.* a feeling of doubt, mistrust, or uncertainty
recelo *s.* sentimiento de duda, desconfianza o incertidumbre

mitigation (mǐt'ǐ-gā'shən) *n.* lessening of something that causes suffering
mitigación *s.* lo que modera o suaviza algo que causa sufrimiento

mollified (mŏl'ə-fīd') *adj.* pacified; made calm **mollify** *v.*
apaciguado *adj.* pacificado; calmado **apaciguar** *v.*

monumental (mŏn'yə-mĕn'tl) *adj.* great and lasting
monumental *adj.* grande y duradero

morass (mə-răs') *n.* a difficult, confused, or entangled state of affairs; puzzling mess
marisma *s.* algo difícil, confuso o enredado; enredo incomprensible

morose (mə-rōs') *adj.* gloomy and ill-tempered
moroso *adj.* triste y malhumorado

multitude (mŭl'tǐ-tōōd') *n.* a great number of people
multitud *s.* gran cantidad de personas

N

narrative (năr'ə-tĭv) *n.* a story
  narrativa *s.* narración

nomadic (nō-măd'ĭk) *adj.* without a fixed
  home; wandering
  nómada *adj.* sin hogar fijo; que va de un lugar
  a otro

nominal (nŏm'ə-nəl) *adj.* in name but not in
  reality
  nominal *adj.* de nombre pero no en la
  realidad

nonconformist (nŏn'kən-fôr'mĭst) *n.* one
  who does not follow generally accepted
  beliefs, customs, or practices
  inconformista *s.* el que no acepta los
  principios, costumbres y creencias de la
  sociedad en que vive

O

obliterate (ə-blĭt'ə-rāt') *v.* to wipe out, leaving
  no trace
  borrar *v.* eliminar sin dejar huella

obscure (ŏb-skyŏŏr') *adj.* indistinct; not clearly
  understood
  oscuro *adj.* indistinto; que no se entiende
  claramente

obscure (ŏb-skyŏŏr') *v.* to cover over; hide
  oscurecer *v.* ocultar; confundir

obstinate (ŏb'stə-nĭt) *adj.* stubborn
  obstinado *adj.* terco

obtuse (ŏb-tōōs') *adj.* slow to understand; dull
  obtuso *adj.* lento para comprender; tonto

odious (ō'dē-əs) *adj.* arousing, or worthy of,
  strong dislike
  odioso *adj.* digno de odio; fastidioso

ominous (ŏm'ə-nəs) *adj.* threatening;
  menacing
  ominoso *adj.* amenazante; de mal agüero

opaque (ō-pāk') *adj.* not allowing light to pass
  through
  opaco *adj.* que no permite el paso de la luz

oppressed (ə-prĕst') *adj.* kept down by severe
  and unjust use of force or authority **oppress** *v.*
  oprimido *adj.* sometido por una fuerza o
  autoridad injusta **oprimir** *v.*

opulent (ŏp'yə-lənt) *adj.* characterized by
  abundance, extravagance, or wealth
  opulento *adj.* de gran abundancia,
  extravagancia o riqueza

ostentation (ŏs'tĕn-tā'shən) *n.* display meant
  to impress others; boastful showiness
  ostentación *s.* despliegue que tiene el fin de
  impresionar; alarde presuntuoso

overwrought (ō'vər-rôt') *adj.* excessively
  nervous or excited
  sobreexcitado *adj.* nerviosísimo; agotado por
  la emoción

P

pallid (păl'ĭd) *adj.* abnormally pale
  pálido *adj.* descolorido

palpable (păl'pə-bəl) *adj.* that can be touched
  or felt
  palpable *adj.* que puede ser tocado o sentido

panache (pə-năsh') *n.* a sense of style; flair
  brío *s.* garbo; elegancia

paradox (păr'ə-dŏks') *n.* a seemingly
  contradictory statement that may
  nevertheless be true
  paradoja *s.* declaración que parece
  contradictoria pero que es verdadera

parsimony (pär'sə-mō'nē) *n.* extreme
  economy; stinginess
  parsimonia *s.* extrema economía; tacañería

patent (păt'nt) *adj.* obvious; apparent
  patente *adj.* obvio; aparente

pathetic (pə-thĕt'ĭk) *adj.* arousing pity or
  compassion
  patético *adj.* que despierta piedad o
  compasión

peculiar (pĭ-kyōōl'yər) *adj.* belonging
  particularly or primarily to one person, group,
  or kind
  peculiar *adj.* propio de una persona, grupo o
  clase

perceptibly (pər-sĕp'tə-blē) *adv.* in a way that can be perceived by the senses or the mind; noticeably
perceptiblemente *adv.* de forma que puede ser percibido por los sentidos o la mente; evidentemente

perennial (pə-rĕn'ē-əl) *adj.* lasting through the year or through many years; enduring
perenne *adj.* que dura todo el año o muchos años; duradero

permeable (pûr'mē-ə-bəl) *adj.* able to be passed through
permeable *adj.* que deja pasar

perseverance (pûr'sə-vîr'əns) *n.* persistence in the face of difficulty; determination
perseverancia *s.* persistencia frente a las dificultades; determinación

perspective (pər-spĕk'tĭv) *n.* a mental view or outlook; point of view
perspectiva *s.* visión mental o panorámica; punto de vista

perturbation (pûr'tər-bā'shən) *n.* a disturbance of the emotions; agitation; uneasiness
perturbación *s.* alteración de las emociones; agitación; incomodidad

pervade (pər-vād') *v.* to spread throughout
penetrar *v.* saturar por completo

perverse (pər-vûrs') *adj.* stubbornly opposed to what is right or reasonable; wrong-headed
perverso *adj.* opuesto tercamente a lo que es correcto o razonable; obstinado

pestilence (pĕs'tə-ləns) *n.* any epidemic disease that is usually fatal
peste *s.* enfermedad epidémica que suele ser mortal

pestilential (pĕs'tə-lĕn'shəl) *adj.* deadly; poisonous
pestilente *adj.* mortal; venenoso

petulance (pĕch'ə-ləns) *n.* ill temper; annoyance
petulancia *s.* mal humor; arrogancia

piety (pī'ĭ-tē) *n.* religious devotion; reverence for God
piedad *s.* devoción religiosa; reverencia a Dios

pious (pī'əs) *adj.* having or showing reverence for God
piadoso *adj.* que tiene o muestra reverencia a Dios

placate (plā'kāt') *v.* to soothe another's feelings; appease
aplacar *v.* calmar los sentimientos de otro; apaciguar

placid (plăs'ĭd) *adj.* undisturbed; calm or quiet
plácido *adj.* tranquilo; calmado o callado

plague (plāg) *v.* to annoy; harass
plagar *v.* molestar; fastidiar

plaintiff (plān'tĭf) *n.* the party that institutes a suit in court
demandante *s.* parte que inicia una demanda judicial

poignant (poin'yənt) *adj.* emotionally touching or moving
conmovedor *adj.* emotivo; enternecedor

precarious (prĭ-kâr'ē-əs) *adj.* risky; uncertain
precario *adj.* peligroso; incierto

precept (prē'sĕpt') *n.* a rule or principle prescribing a particular course of action
precepto *s.* regla o principio que dicta un curso de acción

precipitately (prĭ-sĭp'ĭ-tĭt-lē) *adv.* steeply
precipitadamente *adv.* empinadamente

precipitous (prĭ-sĭp'ĭ-təs) *adj.* steep; almost vertical
escarpado *adj.* empinado; casi vertical

predilection (prĕd'l-ĕk'shən) *n.* a personal preference
predilección *s.* preferencia personal

predominate (prĭ-dŏm'ə-nāt') *v.* to have controlling power or influence
predominar *v.* tener poder o influencia para controlar

preeminently (prē-ĕm'ə-nənt-lē) *adv.* above all; most importantly
preeminentemente *adv.* por encima de todo; con suma importancia

preening (prē'nĭng) *n.* dressing and grooming oneself with excessive care; primping **preen** *v.*
acicalamiento *s.* vestirse y arreglarse con cuidado excesivo **acicalar** *v.*

preoccupied (prē-ŏk'yə-pīd') *adj.* lost in thought; intensely concerned
preocupado *adj.* distraído; absorto

prestige (prĕ-stēzh') *n.* honor; admiration
prestigio *s.* honor; admiración

presume (prĭ-zoōm') *v.* to act overconfidently; go beyond the proper limits; dare
presumir *v.* actuar con demasiada seguridad; ir más allá de lo adecuado

pretense (prē'tĕns') *n.* the act of pretending; a false appearance or action intended to deceive
fingimiento *s.* acto de fingir; falsa apariencia o acción con el propósito de engañar

preternaturally (prē'tər-nǎch'ər-əl-ē) *adv.* more than naturally; extraordinarily
sobrenaturalmente *adv.* de modo sobrenatural; extraordinariamente

probity (prō'bĭ-tē) *n.* honesty; integrity
probidad *s.* honestidad; integridad

procure (prō-kyoōr') *v.* to get by special effort; obtain
adquirir *v.* conseguir por medio de esfuerzos especiales; obtener

profoundly (prə-found'lē) *adv.* deeply; intensely
profundamente *adv.* hondamente; intensamente

profusion (prə-fyoō'zhən) *n.* abundance; lavishness
profusión *s.* abundancia

propitious (prə-pĭsh'əs) *adj.* helpful or advantageous; favorable
propicio *adj.* que ayuda o es ventajoso; favorable

providence (prŏv'ĭ-dəns) *n.* an instance of divine care or guidance
providencia *s.* ejemplo de cuidado o guía divina

provisional (prə-vĭzh'ə-nəl) *adj.* temporary
provisional *adj.* temporal

provocation (prŏv'ə-kā'shən) *n.* something that arouses anger
provocación *s.* algo que despierta ira

prowess (prou'ĭs) *n.* superior strength, courage, or daring, especially in battle
valentía *s.* gran fuerza, valentía y arrojo, especialmente en la batalla

punitive (pyoō'nĭ-tĭv) *adj.* punishing or having to do with punishment
punitivo *adj.* que castiga o que se relaciona con el castigo

purging (pûr'jĭng) *n.* getting rid of something unwanted; cleansing **purge** *v.*
purga *s.* eliminación de algo no deseado; limpieza **purgar** *v.*

Q

qualm (kwäm) *n.* a disturbing uneasiness or doubt
remordimiento *s.* duda que perturba

quandary (kwŏn'də-rē) *n.* a state of uncertainty
dilema *s.* estado de incertidumbre

querulous (kwĕr'ə-ləs) *adj.* given to complaining
quejumbroso *adj.* dado a quejarse

R

rakish (rā'kĭsh) *adj.* dashingly or sportingly stylish; jaunty
gallardo *adj.* brioso o elegante; garboso

rapt (rǎpt) *adj.* deeply moved, delighted, or absorbed
extasiado *adj.* profundamente conmovido, encantado o absorto

ravaged (rǎv'ĭjd) *adj.* devastated; ruined **ravage** *v.*
destruido *adj.* devastado; arruinado **destruir** *v.*

rebuff (rĭ-bŭf') *v.* to reject bluntly; snub
desairar *v.* rechazar abiertamente; desdeñar

recalcitrant (rĭ-kǎl'sĭ-trənt) *adj.* stubborn; hard to deal with
recalcitrante *adj.* terco; obstinado

recommence (rē′kə-mĕns′) *v.* to begin again
reiniciar *v.* comenzar de nuevo

regimentation (rĕj′ə-mən-tā′shən) *n.* the process of using discipline and control to organize into a rigid system
reglamentación *s.* proceso de organizarun sistema estricto con disciplina y control

rend (rĕnd) *v.* to tear or split apart violently
desgarrar *v.* romper o dividir violentamente

repercussion (rē′pər-kŭsh′ən) *n.* a far-reaching effect
repercusión *s.* efecto de largo alcance

repose (rĭ-pōz′) *v.* to rest or relax
reposar *v.* descansar o relajarse

reproach (rĭ-prōch′) *n.* an expression of blame or disapproval
reproche *s.* expresión de culpa o desaprobación

repudiate (rĭ-pyōo′dē-āt′) *v.* to reject the validity or authority of
repudiar *v.* rechazar la validez o autoridad

resignation (rĕz′ĭg-nā′shən) *n.* an acceptance of something as unavoidable
resignación *s.* aceptación; conformidad

resolute (rĕz′ə-lōot′) *adj.* firm or determined; unwavering
resuelto *adj.* firme o decidido; sin dudas

resolve (rĭ-zŏlv′) *v.* to make a firm decision
resolver *v.* tomar una decisión firme

respite (rĕs′pĭt) *n.* a brief period of rest or relief from pain or labor
respiro *s.* breve período de descanso o alivio de dolor o trabajo

retaliating (rĭ-tăl′ē-ā′tĭng) *n.* taking revenge **retaliate** *v.*
represalia *s.* venganza **vengarse** *v.*

retraction (rĭ-trăk′shən) *n.* a taking back of something said
retractación *s.* anulación de lo dicho

reverberate (rĭ-vûr′bə-rāt′) *v.* to echo
reverberar *v.* hacer eco

ritual (rĭch′ōo-əl) *n.* a ceremonial act or a series of such acts
ritual *s.* acto ceremonial o serie de dichos actos

robust (rō-bŭst′) *adj.* full of health and strength; vigorous
robusto *adj.* lleno de salud y fuerza; vigoroso

rudiment (rōo′də-mənt) *n.* an imperfect or undeveloped form
rudimento *s.* forma imperfecta o subdesarrollada

rue (rōo) *v.* to regret
lamentar *v.* arrepentirse

ruminating (rōo′mə-nā-tĭng) *adj.* turning a matter over and over in the mind **ruminate** *v.*
rumión *adj.* que da muchas vueltas a un asunto en la mente **rumiar** *v.*

rummage (rŭm′ĭj) *v.* to search through a confusion of objects
hurgar *v.* buscar revolviéndolo todo

S

sagacious (sə-gā′shəs) *adj.* wise
sagaz *adj.* sabio

scoff (skŏf) *v.* to mock
mofarse *v.* burlarse

scrupulously (skrōo′pyə-ləs-lē) *adv.* in an extremely careful and thorough manner; conscientiously
escrupulosamente *adv.* de manera extremadamente cuidadosa y a fondo; concienzudamente

scrutinize (skrōot′n-īz′) *v.* to look over carefully; study
escudriñar *v.* revisar cuidadosamente; inspeccionar

segregated (sĕg′rĭ-gā′tĭd) *adj.* separated according to race **segregate** *v.*
segregado *adj.* separado por razas **segregar** *v.*

sentinel (sĕn′tə-nəl) *n.* a guard
centinela *s.* guardia

serenity (sə-rĕn′ĭ-tē) *n.* a mental and spiritual calm; tranquillity
serenidad *s.* calma mental y espiritual; tranquilidad

servile (sur′vəl) *adj.* humbly submissive; slavish
servil *adj.* humildemente sumiso; abyecto

servitude (sûr'vĭ-tōōd') *n.* the condition of one who is subject to a master; lack of freedom
　servidumbre *s.* condición de quien está sujeto a un amo; falta de libertad

shamble (shăm'bəl) *v.* to walk or move awkwardly or clumsily
　arrastrar los pies *v.* caminar o moverse con dificultad o torpeza

sibilant (sĭb'ə-lənt) *adj.* hissing
　sibilante *adj.* que silba o suena a manera de silbido

simper (sĭm'pər) *v.* to smile in a shy or self-conscious way
　sonreír tontamente *v.* sonreír con vergüenza o timidez

singular (sĭng'gyə-lər) *adj.* unusual or remarkable; unique
　singular *adj.* inusual o notable; único

solace (sŏl'ĭs) *n.* comfort in sorrow or distress
　solaz *s.* consuelo en la pena o la desgracia

solicitous (sə-lĭs'ĭ-təs) *adj.* full of desire; eager
　solícito *adj.* lleno de deseo; atento

sordid (sôr'dĭd) *adj.* wretched; dirty; morally degraded
　sórdido *adj.* miserable; sucio; degradado moralmente

specimen (spĕs'ə-mən) *n.* an example of a group
　espécimen *s.* ejemplar de un grupo

specter (spĕk'tər) *n.* a ghostly vision; phantom
　espectro *s.* visión fantasmagórica; fantasma

spurn (spûrn) *v.* to reject scornfully
　desdeñar *v.* rechazar con desdén

statute (stăch'ōōt) *n.* a law
　estatuto *s.* ley

stench (stĕnch) *n.* a strong, foul odor
　hedor *s.* olor desagradable y penetrante

stigma (stĭg'mə) *n.* a mark of disgrace
　estigma *s.* marca de desgracia

stiltedly (stĭl'tĭd-lē) *adv.* in a stiffly dignified manner
　circunspectamente *adv.* con dignidad tiesa

stupendous (stōō-pĕn'dəs) *adj.* of amazing size; enormous
　estupendo *adj.* de sorprendente tamaño; enorme

subdued (səb-dōōd') *adj.* made submissive; reduced in intensity; toned down **subdue** *v.*
　disminuido *adj.* hecho sumiso; de menor intensidad o tono **disminuir** *v.*

subjugation (sŭb'jə-gā'shən) *n.* control by conquering
　subyugación *s.* control por medio de la conquista

sublime (sə-blīm') *adj.* of high spiritual, moral, or intellectual worth; noble
　sublime *adj.* de elevado valor espiritual, moral o intelectual; noble

subordinate (sə-bôr'dn-ĭt) *n.* one who is lower in rank
　subordinado *s.* el que es de rango inferior

subservient (səb-sûr'vē-ənt) *adj.* acting like a servant
　servil *adj.* que se comporta como sirviente

subsistence (səb-sĭs'təns) *n.* livelihood
　subsistencia *s.* forma de ganarse la vida

subtle (sŭt'l) *adj.* so slight as to be difficult to detect
　sutil *adj.* delicado; tenue; difícil de detectar

succulent (sŭk'yə-lənt) *adj.* tasty; delicious
　suculento *adj.* sabroso; delicioso

succumb (sə-kŭm') *v.* to give up or give in; yield
　sucumbir *v.* ceder o aceptar; rendirse

suffuse (sə-fyōōz') *v.* to spread through
　difundir *v.* bañar; cubrir

sullenly (sŭl'ən-lē) *adv.* resentfully; sulkily
　enfurruñadamente *adv.* con mal humor y resentimiento

sully (sŭl'ē) *v.* to spoil; tarnish
　manchar *v.* arruinar; ensuciar

summarily (sə-mĕr'ə-lē) *adv.* in a way that is quick and bypasses usual procedures
　sumariamente *adv.* con rapidez y sin seguir los trámites normales

sundry (sŭn'drē) *adj.* various; miscellaneous
  diversos *adj.* varios; misceláneos

superficially (soo'pər-fĭsh'ə-lē) *adv.* in a shallow way; concerned with only what is obvious
  superficialmente *adv.* de manera ligera; con interés sólo en lo obvio

surfeit (sûr'fĭt) *n.* a fullness beyond the point of satisfaction
  hartura *s.* saciedad más allá del punto de satisfacción

surmise (sər-mīz') *v.* to guess
  suponer *v.* adivinar

surreptitious (sûr'əp-tĭsh'əs) *adj.* secret; stealthy
  subrepticio *adj.* secreto; oculto

synthesis (sĭn'thĭ-sĭs) *n.* the combining of separate elements or substances to form a coherent whole
  síntesis *s.* combinación de elementos o sustancias separadas para formar un todo coherente

T

tacitly (tăs'ĭt-lē) *adv.* silently
  tácitamente *adv.* silenciosamente

tactful (tăkt'fəl) *adj.* careful of others' feelings; considerate
  prudente *adj.* cuidadoso de los sentimientos de otros; considerado

tangible (tăn'jə-bəl) *adj.* able to be touched or felt
  tangible *adj.* que puede ser tocado o sentido

taut (tôt) *adj.* pulled tight; straight
  tirante *adj.* estirado

tedious (tē'dē-əs) *adj.* boring because of dullness
  tedioso *adj.* aburridor

temerity (tə-měr'ĭ-tē) *n.* foolish boldness
  temeridad *s.* valentía tonta

tempest (těm'pĭst) *n.* a violent storm
  tempestad *s.* tormenta violenta

temporize (těm'pə-rīz') *v.* to avoid immediate action or making a decision in order to gain time
  contemporizar *v.* evitar acción inmediata; tomar una decisión a fin de ganar tiempo

terminal (tûr'mə-nəl) *adj.* final; fatal
  terminal *adj.* final; fatal

terrestrial (tə-rĕs'trē-əl) *adj.* on the ground; earthly
  terrestre *adj.* relativo al suelo o a la Tierra

tersely (tûrs'lē) *adv.* briefly
  concisamente *adv.* brevemente

theology (thē-ŏl'ə-jē) *n.* a system of religious beliefs
  teología *s.* sistema de creencias religiosas

thwart (thwôrt) *v.* to block or hinder; prevent the fulfillment of
  frustrar *v.* bloquear u obstaculizar; impedir

tousled (tou'zəld) *adj.* messy; rumpled **tousle** *v.*
  desarreglado *adj.* en desorden; revuelto
  desarreglar *v.*

tranquil (trăng'kwəl) *adj.* undisturbed; peaceful
  tranquilo *adj.* imperturbable; pacífico

transcribe (trăn-skrīb') *v.* to make a handwritten or typed copy of
  transcribir *v.* hacer una copia manuscrita o mecanografiada

transient (trăn'shənt) *adj.* lasting or existing for only a short time
  transitorio *adj.* que dura o existe sólo por breve tiempo

tremulous (trěm'yə-ləs) *adj.* marked by trembling, quivering, or shaking
  trémulo *adj.* que tiembla o se sacude

trepidation (trěp'ĭ-dā'shən) *n.* fearful uncertainty or worry
  trepidación *s.* incertidumbre o preocupación que causa miedo

truculent (trŭk'yə-lənt) *adj.* eager for a fight; fierce
  agresivo *adj.* deseoso de pelear; fiero

tumultuous (too-mŭl'choo-əs) *adj.* wild and disorderly
  tumultuoso *adj.* alborotado y desordenado

tyrannical (tĭ-răn′ĭ-kəl) *adj.* harsh; oppressive
tiránico *adj.* cruel; opresivo

U

unassailable (ŭn′ə-sā′lə-bəl) *adj.* impossible to dispute or disprove; undeniable
indiscutible *adj.* imposible de disputar o desaprobar; innegable

undulating (ŭn′jə-lā′tĭng) *adj.* moving with a wavelike motion **undulate** *v.*
ondulante *adj.* con movimiento similar al de las olas **ondular** *v.*

unintelligible (ŭn′ĭn-tĕl′ĭ-jə-bəl) *adj.* incomprehensible; unable to be understood
ininteligible *adj.* incomprensible; imposible de ser entendido

unobtrusive (ŭn′əb-trōō′sĭv) *adj.* not noticeable; not calling attention to oneself
discreto *adj.* que no se nota; que no llama la atención hacia sí

unrelenting (ŭn′rĭ-lĕn′tĭng) *adj.* not stopping or weakening
inexorable *adj.* que no para ni se debilita

unscrupulous (ŭn-skrōō′pyə-ləs) *adj.* without principles; dishonorable
inescrupuloso *adj.* sin principios; deshonesto

untenanted (ŭn-tĕn′ən-tĭd) *adj.* not occupied
desocupado *adj.* vacío

untoward (ŭn-tôrd′) *n.* inappropriate
adverso *s.* inapropiado

usurping (yōō-sur′pĭng) *n.* taking another's place wrongfully **usurp** *v.*
usurpador *s.* el que toma el lugar de otro sin derecho **usurpar** *v.*

V

vacillating (văs′ə-lā′tĭng) *adj.* swinging from one course of action or opinion to another; indecisive **vacillate** *v.*
vacilante *adj.* que cambia de opinión o de curso; indeciso **vacilar** *v.*

vagabond (văg′ə-bŏnd′) *n.* a wanderer; drifter
vagabundo *s.* persona que anda errante de un lugar a otro

vanquish (văng′kwĭsh) *v.* to defeat in battle
vencer *v.* derrotar en la batalla

variant (vâr′ē-ənt) *n.* something that differs slightly from others of its kind
variante *s.* algo que difiere un poco de otros de su tipo

veneer (və-nîr′) *n.* a thin surface layer that conceals what is below
chapa *s.* capa delgada en la superficie que oculta lo que está debajo; barniz

venerable (vĕn′ər-ə-bəl) *adj.* worthy of respect because of age, dignity, or character
venerable *adj.* digno de respeto por la edad, dignidad o carácter

venture (vĕn′chər) *v.* to dare to go
aventurar *v.* atreverse a ir

vigilant (vĭj′ə-lənt) *adj.* alert; watchful
vigilante *adj.* alerta; atento

vindication (vĭn′dĭ-kā′shən) *n.* the defense or justification of something, such as one's rights
vindicación *s.* defensa o justificación de algo, como los derechos propios

vindictive (vĭn-dĭk′tĭv) *adj.* wanting revenge; bearing a grudge
vengador *adj.* que desea venganza; que guarda resentimiento

virulent (vîr′yə-lənt) *adj.* extremely poisonous or harmful
virulento *adj.* extremadamente venenoso o dañino

vivacious (vĭ-vā′shəs) *adj.* full of energy; lively
vivaz *adj.* lleno de energía; vital

void (void) *n.* an empty space
vacío *s.* espacio sin nada

vulgar (vŭl′gər) *adj.* coarse; common
vulgar *adj.* rudo; común

W

wane (wān) *v.* to decrease in size, intensity, or degree
decaer *v.* disminuir de tamaño, intensidad o grado

whence (hwĕns) *adv.* from where
  dónde *adv.* de dónde

wrath (răth) *n.* fierce anger, or punishment
  resulting from such anger
  ira *s.* cólera fuerte o castigo resultante de
  esa ira

wretched (rĕch′ĭd) *adj.* miserable
  desgraciado *adj.* miserable

Pronunciation Key

Symbol	Examples	Symbol	Examples	Symbol	Examples
ă	at, gas	m	man, seem	v	van, save
ā	ape, day	n	night, mitten	w	web, twice
ä	father, barn	ng	sing, anger	y	yard, lawyer
âr	fair, dare	ŏ	odd, not	z	zoo, reason
b	bell, table	ō	open, road, grow	zh	treasure, garage
ch	chin, lunch	ô	awful, bought, horse	ə	awake, even, pencil,
d	dig, bored	oi	coin, boy		pilot, focus
ĕ	egg, ten	ŏŏ	look, full	ər	perform, letter
ē	evil, see, meal	o͞o	root, glue, through		
f	fall, laugh, phrase	ou	out, cow		**Sounds in Foreign Words**
g	gold, big	p	pig, cap	KH	*German* ich, auch;
h	hit, inhale	r	rose, star		*Scottish* loch
hw	white, everywhere	s	sit, face	N	*French* entre, bon, fin
ĭ	inch, fit	sh	she, mash	œ	*French* feu, cœur;
ī	idle, my, tried	t	tap, hopped		*German* schön
îr	dear, here	th	thing, with	ü	*French* utile, rue;
j	jar, gem, badge	*th*	then, other		*German* grün
k	keep, cat, luck	ŭ	up, nut		
l	load, rattle	ûr	fur, earn, bird, worm		

Stress Marks

′ This mark indicates that the preceding syllable receives the primary stress. For
  example, in the word *language,* the first syllable is stressed: lăng′gwĭj.

′ This mark is used only in words in which more than one syllable is stressed. It
  indicates that the preceding syllable is stressed, but somewhat more weakly
  than the syllable receiving the primary stress. In the word *literature,* for example, the first syllable receives the primary stress, and the last syllable receives a
  weaker stress: lĭt′ər-ə-cho͝or′.

Adapted from *The American Heritage Dictionary of the English Language, Third
Edition;* Copyright © 1992 by Houghton Mifflin Company. Used with the permission of Houghton Mifflin Company.

Index of Fine Art

viii *right*, 16–17   Giovanni da Verrazano becoming the first European to enter New York Bay, 1524 (1868), unknown American artist.

x *top*, 130–131   *A Morning View of Blue Hill Village* (1824), Jonathan Fisher.

xii *left*, 336–337   *The Wanderer* (1818), Caspar David Friedrich.

xiii, 398   *Cliff Dwellers* (1913), George Bellows.

xv, 554–555   Pictorial quilt (1895–1898), Harriet Powers.

xvii, 712   *Cliffs Beyond Abiquiu, Dry Waterfall* (1943), Georgia O'Keeffe.

xviii *top right*, 739   *Mr. and Mrs. Isaac Newton Phelps Stokes* (1897), John Singer Sargent.

xix, 836   *Three Folk Musicians* (1967), Romare Bearden.

xx, 920 *top*   *Langston Hughes*, Winold Reiss.

xxii, 1068–1069   *Ominous Omen* (1987), Rupert Garcia.

6–7   *Child and Her Mother, Wapato, Yakima Valley, Washington* (1939), Dorothea Lange.

8   Detail of *Sharecropper* (1970), Elizabeth Catlett.

12   *Georgia Landscape* (about 1934–1935), Hale Woodruff.

27   *Creation Legend*, Tom (Two Arrows) Dorsey.

36   *Born Free*, Edwin Salomon.

51   *Between Heaven and Earth; Earth and Sky* (1976), Frank LaPena.

56   *Wun-Pan-To-Mee, The White Weasel* (1836), George Catlin.

60   *Kiowa Sun Dance*, Sharron Ahtone.

66   Detail of *The Landing of Columbus at San Salvador (Guanahani) in the Bahamas, 12 October 1492* (17th century), unknown artist.

74   Indians forced to carry baggage and supplies of the Spanish invaders (1590), Theodor de Bry.

75   *Indian Man of Florida* (about 1585–1593), John White, after Jacques Le Moyne de Morgues.

84   Detail of *View of Plymouth* (1627), Carl Sachs.

96   Detail of *The Slave Ship* (1956), Robert Riggs.

101   *Road Past the View I* (1964), Georgia O'Keeffe.

111   *Afi Negble, Asenema, Ghana* (1964), Paul Strand.

113   *Samuel J. K. Essoun, Shama, Ghana* (1963), Paul Strand.

114   *Nana Oparabea, High Priestess, Larteh, Ghana* (1963), Paul Strand.

135   *Mrs. Freake and Baby Mary* (1674), unknown artist.

155   *Un quadro di fuochi preziosi* [A painting of precious fires] (1983), Enzo Cucchi.

256 *left*   *Portrait of Thomas Jefferson* (1805), Gilbert Stuart.

256 *right*   *John Locke*, John Michael Rysbrack.

257 *top*   *Silhouette of Abigail Adams* (1829), Jarvis F. Hanks.

265   *Patrick Henry Before the Virginia House of Burgesses* (1851), Peter F. Rothermel.

273   *Signing the Declaration of Independence*, John Trumbull.

281   *Thomas Jefferson*, Charles Févret de Saint-Mémin.

290–291   Van Bergen Overmantel (1732–1733), attributed to John Heaten.

311   Detail of *The Farmworkers of Guadalupe* (1990), Judith F. Baca.

313 *top*   *Viva La Raza, Long Live Humanity* (1969), Salvador Roberto Torres.

314   *Farm Workers' Altar* (1967), Emanuel Martinez.

339 *bottom left*   *The Trail of Tears* (1942), Robert Lindneux.

345   *En Mer* [At sea] (1898), Max Bohm.

365   *Kindred Spirits* (1849), Asher B. Durand.

413   *Icarus* (1947), Henri Matisse.

417   *Untitled (The Wedding Quilt)* (1981), Rosario Morales.

418   *In My Grandmother's Garden* (1982), Rosario Morales.

419   *Woman with Turban* (1985), Gilberto Ruiz.

427   Detail of *Play Within a Play* (1963), David Hockney.

446   Gargoyles on the Cathedral of Notre Dame, Paris.

455   *Il ridotto* [The foyer] (about 1757–1760), Pietro Longhi.

459	Detail of *Adoration of the Magi: Lorenzo il Magnifico as Youngest of Magi* (1459), Benozzo Gozzoli.
461	Detail of wood skull (19th or 20th century), artist unknown.
479	*Self-Portrait*, Bertalan Székely.
482	*Head of Ophelia*, study (about 1897), Edwin Austin Abbey.
505	*Déjeuner* [Luncheon] (1876), Gustave Caillebotte.
511	*La danse à la campagne* [The country dance] (1883), Pierre Auguste Renoir.
518	*German Teapot* (1994), Charles Warren Mundy.
524	*Woman in Distress* (1882), James Ensor.
531	*Mrs. Gamely* (1930), George Luks.
535	*The Interloper* (1958), Billy Morrow Jackson.
537	*Road to Rhome* (1938), Alexander Hogue.
558 *bottom*	*Battle of Franklin, Tennessee, 30 November 1864* (1891), Kurz and Allison.
564	*A Load of Brush* (1912), Louis Paul Dessar.
567	*Head of a Negro* (1777–1778), John Singleton Copley.
594	*Battle of Chancellorsville*, unknown artist.
619	*Flip Flops and Lace* (1991), Stephen Scott Young.
636	*The Jolly Flatboatmen in Port* (1857), George Caleb Bingham.
640	*Castle Mission*, John Runne.
646–647	*Wild Horses of Nevada* (1927), Maynard Dixon.
649	*Home Is the Hunter* (1994), Gary Kapp.
650	*Night Horse* (1992), C. J. Wells.
691	*Mrs. Stewart, Housewife and Singer, Brasstown, North Carolina*, Doris Ulmann.
693	*The Opera, Paris* (about 1924), Raoul Dufy.
696	*House in Winter* (1941), Wright Morris.
701	*Westly Potato Camp, Edison, California*, Dorothea Lange.
705	*New Mexico Peon* (1945), Ernest L. Blumenschein.
709	*Chama Running Red* (1925), John Sloan.
767	*A Woman Sewing in an Interior* (about 1900), Vilhelm Hammershøi.
771	*Stairway* (1949), Edward Hopper.
785	*Morning Glories* (1873), Winslow Homer.
789	*Consolation* (1961), Ruth Gikow.
797	*Returning Sails to Gyotoku* (about 1837–1838), Ichiryusai Hiroshige.
803	*Theresa* (1987), Romare Bearden.
810	*Girl Skipping Rope* (1943), Ben Shahn.
813	*The Brown Sweater* (1952), Raphael Soyer.
825	*City Building* (1930), Thomas Hart Benton.
827	*Country Dance* (1928), Thomas Hart Benton.
853	*Autoportrait* (about 1925), Tamara de Lempicka.
859	*The Shelton with Sunspots* (1926), Georgia O'Keeffe.
881	*Diner Interior with Coffee Urns* (1984), Ralph Goings.
889	*The Splash* (1966), David Hockney.
895	*Analogía IV* (1972), Victor Grippo.
897	*Femme Violette*, Wilfredo Lam.
912–913	*Rush Hour, New York* (1915), Max Weber.
914 *left*	*Nude Descending a Staircase, No. 2* (1912), Marcel Duchamp.
923	*The Negro Looks Ahead* (1940), Richmond Barthe.
925	*Jim*, Selma Burke.
926–927	*Black Manhattan* (1969), Romare Bearden.
941	*New York Harbor/Paris* (about 1925), Jan Matulka.
942	*Shotgun, Third Ward #1* (1966), John T. Biggers.
952	*Skipping Along*, Stephen Scott Young.
954	*Bal Jeunesse* (about 1927), Palmer Hayden.
962	*My Brother* (1942), John Wilson.
969	*110th Street*, Romare Bearden.
992	*Weeping Woman* (1937), Pablo Picasso.
1007	*Philo Bound* (about 1965), Billy Morrow Jackson.

1020   *Canoe* (1957), David Park.

1031   Detail of *David* (1501–1504), Michelangelo.

1035   *La mére morte de l'artiste* [The artist's mother in death], James Ensor.

1036   *Portrait of Ambroise Vollard* (1909), Pablo Picasso.

1041   *Yvonne and Magdaleine Torn in Tatters* (1911), Marcel Duchamp.

1089   *A.F.T.A.D.—"Memphis Belle" B-17* (1943), Stow Wengenroth.

1099 *left*   *Evacuation Day, May 8, 1942* (1942), Dorothea Lange.

1100 *top right*   *Pledge of Allegiance at Rafael Weill Elementary* (1942), Dorothea Lange.

1100 *bottom*   *Manzanar Relocation Center* (1942), Dorothea Lange.

1107   *Fenixes* (1984), Rupert Garcia.

1145   *On the Subway* (1986), Elizabeth Catlett.

1162   *Untitled (First Avenue)* (about 1945), Fairfield Porter.

1169   *Table with Fruit* (1951–1952), David Park.

1171   *Girl Looking at Landscape* (1957), Richard Diebenkorn.

1174   *Portrait of Richard Freeman* (1974), Fairfield Porter.

1183   *Frank Wallace* (1953), Fairfield Porter.

1185   *The Table* (1970), Fairfield Porter.

1186   *Claire White* (1960), Fairfield Porter.

1188   *Stephen and Kathy* (1965), Fairfield Porter.

1229   *Olga* (1940), Rufino Tamayo.

Index of Skills

Literary Concepts

Act, 161, 1342. *See also* Drama.

Allegory, 454, 462, 500, 1342

Alliteration. *See* Poetic elements.

Allusion, 262, 267, 307, 1005, 1025, 1136, 1146, 1232, 1342

Analogy, 254, 676, 863, 964, 1342

Anapest, 142, 1342. *See also* Poetic elements, meter.

Anaphora. *See* Figurative language.

Anecdote, 323, 806, 1227, 1342

Antagonist, 161, 329, 1168, 1178, 1343

Antihero, 1149, 1237, 1343

Aphorism, 340, 363, 367, 381, 1147, 1343

Archaic language, 138

Argumentation, 260–261, 1136

Aside, 162

Assonance. *See* Poetic elements.

Audience, 72, 78, 98, 152, 158, 323, 620, 959, 1178, 1343

Author's attitude. *See* Tone. *See also* Tone, recognizing *under* Reading and Critical Thinking Skills.

Author's perspective, 932, 937

Author's purpose (motivation), 100, 107, 116, 360, 562, 645, 950, 1343. *See also* Author's purpose (motivation) *under* Reading and Critical Thinking Skills.

Autobiographical essay. *See* Essay.

Autobiography, 70, 71, 99, 109, 116, 319, 381, 438, 562, 571, 1343

Ballad, 394, 618, 620, 731, 1344

Bias, 88, 144, 150

Biography, 70, 1344

Blank verse. *See* Poetic elements.

Caesura, 1344

Cast of characters, 161, 165, 1344

Catalog, 396, 404, 1344

Character(s), 48, 161, 190, 206, 228, 243, 251, 329, 360, 434, 516, 528, 544, 602, 637, 765, 788, 800, 804, 830, 833, 840, 860, 892, 1105, 1157, 1168, 1178, 1200, 1212, 1344

Characterization, 360, 516, 525, 539, 830, 833, 1345

Cliché, 442, 1345

Climax, 161, 243, 329, 1178, 1345. *See also* Plot.

Comedy, 161, 1345

Coming-of-age story, 788, 800, 1345

Conceit, 1345

Conflict, 48, 53, 88, 129, 161, 243, 544, 783, 788, 800, 894, 911, 1109, 1157, 1166, 1178, 1345
    external and internal, 53, 88, 243, 329, 1105, 1109, 1166, 1345, 1348, 1254

Connotation, 150, 152, 908, 1346

Consonance. *See* Poetic elements.

Contrast, 289, 1346

Corrido, 702, 1346

Couplet. *See* Poetic elements.

Creation myth, 21, 24, 31, 1346

Cuento, 638, 643, 702, 1346

Cultural hero, 46, 702, 718, 1346

Dactyl, 142, 1346. *See also* Poetic elements, meter.

Deduction, 1136

Denotation, 908, 1346

Dénouement, 1346. *See also* Plot.

Description, 669, 676, 1223, 1346

Details, 70, 78, 93, 98, 100, 123, 251, 299, 300, 369, 438, 544, 669, 676, 824, 894, 973, 1168, 1215, 1221, 1223

Dialect, 593, 637, 679, 685, 1014, 1055, 1347

Dialogue, 162, 206, 329, 438, 544, 548, 562, 571, 620, 1006, 1014, 1018, 1023, 1095, 1150, 1155, 1347

Diary, 70, 81, 88, 1033, 1347

Diction, 78, 150, 421, 497, 571, 824, 863, 873, 967, 1025, 1198, 1232, 1347. *See also* Word choice.

Drama, 161–162, 329, 1347

Dramatic monologue, 162

Dynamic character, 840, 860, 892. *See also* Character.

Elegy, 394, 513, 1347

End rhyme, 344, 347, 466, 471, 620, 1360. *See also* Rhyme scheme.

Epic poem. *See* Poetry.

Epigram, 678

Epithet, 98, 829, 1348

Essay, 289, 369, 378, 950, 1221, 1348
    autobiographical, 950, 957, 1343
    critical, 973
    nature writing, 381, 392, 1356
    personal, 1215, 1221, 1357

Exaggeration, 685, 1348

Experimental poetry. *See* Poetry.

Exposition, 161, 1348. *See also* Plot.

Extended metaphor. *See* Figurative language.

External conflict. *See* Conflict.

Eyewitness report, 81, 120, 123, 609, 616, 1349

Fable, 21, 441, 1349

Falling action, 161, 1349. *See also* Plot.

Farce, 1349

Fiction, 62, 702, 1349

Figurative language, 282, 287, 293, 392, 438, 497, 562, 602, 750, 760, 860, 911, 943, 945, 1095, 1349
    anaphora, 395, 971, 1342
    extended metaphor, 760, 945, 948, 1348
    hyperbole, 1351
    metaphor, 287, 293, 347, 392, 497, 750, 757, 760, 815, 860, 911, 948, 1014, 1354
    personification, 392, 602, 750, 760, 828, 860, 911, 1357
    simile, 287, 392, 497, 602, 750, 760, 860, 911, 1361

Figures of speech, 602, 828

Flashback, 516, 548, 1350

Foil, 161, 228, 329, 1350

Folk tale, 39, 46, 638, 643, 644, 1350

Foot, 138, 142, 1013, 1350. *See also* Poetic elements, meter.

Foreshadowing, 500, 514, 525, 1350

Form, 394, 416, 553, 1006, 1350

Free verse. *See* Poetic elements.

Genre, 1350. *See also* Drama; Fiction; Nonfiction; Poetry.

Gothic literature, 446–448, 1350

Haiku, 790, 1351

Hero. *See* Cultural hero; Tragic hero.

Historical context, influence on literature, 300, 307, 369, 605, 1351

    African slave trade, 109, 117

    alienation of the individual, 992–994, 997–999, 1000, 1006, 1012, 1018, 1024, 1025, 1034, 1044, 1045, 1056, 1057, 1063

    American dream, 820–822, 824, 829, 830, 834, 835, 839, 840, 862, 863, 874, 875–876, 877, 893, 894, 899

    conflict and expansion, 556–557, 558–560, 562, 573, 574, 579, 580, 592, 593, 604, 605, 608, 609, 617, 618, 621, 632–634, 638, 644, 645, 653, 654–657, 658, 669, 679, 684, 688, 699, 702, 719

    individualism, 338–339, 340–342, 344, 348, 349, 362, 363, 368, 369, 380, 381, 396, 405, 410, 415, 416, 423, 424, 435, 446–448, 450–453, 454, 464, 466, 473, 500, 515, 516, 527, 528

    integration and disintegration, 1132-1134, 1136, 1150, 1156, 1157, 1167, 1168, 1179, 1180, 1193, 1194, 1199, 1200, 1214, 1215, 1222, 1223, 1226, 1227, 1232

    modern age, 914–915, 916–918, 920–923, 924, 931, 932, 940, 944, 945, 949, 950, 958, 959, 966, 967, 972, 973, 977

    Native American traditions, 18–19, 20–27, 33, 39, 47, 48, 54, 55, 63, 66–68, 72, 80, 81, 90, 91–92, 93, 99, 100, 108, 295, 299

    Puritan tradition, 132–133, 134–136, 138, 143, 144, 152, 160, 163, 244

    racial justice, 300, 307, 308, 309, 317

    revolutionary times, 256–258, 262, 269, 270, 281, 282, 288, 289, 294

    war, 1070–1071, 1072–1074, 1076, 1087, 1088, 1094, 1095, 1102, 1103–1104, 1105, 1110, 1111, 1117, 1118, 1121

    women's voices, 740–741, 742–744, 746–748, 750, 755, 763, 765, 781, 782, 783, 787, 788, 801, 802, 805, 806, 817

Historical narrative. *See* Narrative.

Humor, 349, 424, 434, 679, 685, 1351

Hyperbole. *See* Figurative language.

Iamb, 142, 1351. *See also* Poetic elements, meter.

Iambic pentameter. *See* Poetic elements.

Imagery, 349, 360, 496, 528, 553, 607, 676, 750, 779, 786, 802, 804, 805, 971, 1000, 1005, 1018, 1025, 1030, 1088, 1093, 1095, 1118, 1120, 1198, 1223, 1225, 1351

    kinesthetic, 1254

Impressionism, 1254

Induction, 1136

Informal language, 990

Interior monologue, 806, 815, 1254. *See also* Stream of consciousness.

Internal conflict. *See* Conflict.

Internal rhyme, 466, 471

Inverted syntax, 138

Irony, 528, 539, 602, 658, 667, 786, 1017, 1055, 1067, 1098, 1148, 1196, 1237, 1254

    dramatic, 434, 528, 539, 786, 1055, 1180, 1191, 1254

    situational, 360, 434, 528, 539, 667, 786, 1055, 1254

    verbal, 434, 1254

Legend, 702, 718, 1254

Literary criticism, 973, 976, 1353

Literary letter, 282, 287, 1353

Loaded language, 144, 152, 1353

Local color realism, 636, 679, 1353

Lyric poem. *See* Poetry.

Magical realism, 1353

Main character, 161, 788, 800, 833, 840, 1105, 1178, 1353. *See also* Character.

Memoir, 438, 669, 1353

Metaphor. *See* Figurative language.

Meter. *See* Poetic elements.

Minor character, 161, 1354. *See also* Character.

Modernism, 992–994, 1016–1017, 1025, 1055, 1067, 1148, 1354

Monody, 513, 514, 1354

Monologue, 162, 806, 815, 816, 1354. *See also* Soliloquy.

Mood, 62, 473, 496, 514, 924, 928, 1000, 1001, 1005, 1095, 1101, 1111, 1225, 1355

Moral, 638, 1355

Motivation, 877, 1076, 1355

Myth, 21, 24, 31, 1355

Narrative, 1355

    historical, 70–71, 129, 1351

    slave, 70, 93, 98, 562, 1362

Narrative poem. *See* Poetry.

Narrator, 360, 496, 765, 779, 804, 815, 1355

    first-person, 765, 779, 873

    omniscient, 360

Naturalism, 593, 602, 603, 1355

Nature writing. *See* Essay.

Nonfiction, 62, 950, 1356

Novel, elements of, 973, 1356

Objectivity, 562, 571, 957

Octave. *See* Poetic elements.

Ode, 394, 406

Off rhyme. *See* Poetic elements, rhyme scheme.

Onomatopoeia. *See* Poetic elements.

Open letter, 959, 964, 1356

Oral literature, 20–22, 645, 652, 1356

Oxymoron, 1356

Parable, 1356

Paradox, 378, 392, 760, 959, 1356

Parallelism, 261, 270, 279, 607, 1146, 1357. *See also* Poetic elements.

Parody, 1357

Performance reviews. *See* Performance reviews *under* Reading and Critical Thinking Skills.

Persona, 1057, 1061, 1357

Personal essay. *See* Essay.

Personification. *See* Figurative language.

Plain style, 1357. *See also* Style.

Play. *See* Drama.

Plot, 48, 129, 161, 206, 243, 251, 329, 360, 638, 688, 783, 786, 800, 830, 833, 1157, 1166, 1357

Poetic elements. *See also* Figurative language; Imagery; Rhythm; Speaker.
  alliteration, 971, 1342
  assonance, 1343
  blank verse, 394, 1006, 1013, 1014, 1344
  consonance, 1346
  conventional form, 394
  couplet, 948, 1346
  free verse, 395, 396, 404, 1111, 1350
  iambic pentameter, 142, 943, 1006, 1013, 1351
  meter, 138, 142, 344, 347, 394, 395, 553, 620, 833, 1354
  octave, 943, 1356
  onomatopoeia, 1356
  organic form, 394
  parallelism, 396, 404, 1357
  quatrain, 620, 750, 761, 1359
  repetition, 33, 37, 396, 404, 620, 971, 1000, 1005, 1014, 1360
  rhyme, 347, 466, 471, 833, 971, 1360
  rhyme scheme, 142, 344, 347, 466, 471, 553, 750, 1360
  sestet, 943, 1361
  slant rhyme, 750, 761, 1361
  sound devices, 466, 471, 971, 1362
  stanza, 37, 344, 347, 553, 620, 1006, 1111, 1362
  structure, 416, 421, 1111, 1116, 1363
Poetry, 394–395, 1006
  epic, 309, 316, 394, 1348
  experimental, 410, 414, 1348
  lyric, 143, 838, 1353
  narrative, 316, 618, 830, 833, 1355
  protest, 578, 621, 731, 1359
Point of view, 88, 497, 580, 591, 833, 834, 1045, 1055, 1085, 1260
  first-person, 438, 580, 591, 731, 816, 1006, 1350
  limited, 580, 1045, 1055, 1191
  omniscient, 580, 591, 1085, 1191
  second-person, 1006
  third-person, 580, 591, 731, 815, 1006, 1045, 1055, 1085, 1191
Primary source. *See* Source.
Prop, 162, 163, 190, 1260
Prose, 423, 1260
Protest poem. *See* Poetry.
Protagonist, 161, 329, 1168, 1178, 1237, 1359
Quatrain. *See* Poetic elements.
Rationalism, 256–258, 270–276, 340, 446, 1359
Realism, 448, 636–637, 1359
Refrain, 414, 1359
Regional literature, 636
Repetition, 267, 497, 605, 607, 1018, 1360. *See also* Poetic elements.
Resolution, 129, 161, 329, 1360. *See also* Plot.
Rhetorical questions, 261–262, 1360
Rhyme. *See* Poetic elements.
Rhyme scheme. *See* Poetic elements.
Rhythm, 37, 138, 344, 394, 395, 396, 551, 750, 924, 928, 1000, 1005, 1013, 1014, 1095, 1118, 1120, 1360
Rising action, 161, 1360. *See also* Plot.

Romanticism, 340–342, 446, 1025, 1360
Sarcasm, 162
Satire, 1361
Scansion, 142, 943, 1013, 1361. *See also* Poetic elements, meter.
Scene, 161, 1361
Science fiction, 1361
Secondary source. *See* Source.
Sequence. *See* Chronological order *under* Reading and Critical Thinking Skills.
Sermon, 152, 1361
Sestet. *See* Poetic elements.
Setting, 55, 62, 78, 161, 162, 163, 251, 329, 544, 636–637, 669, 688, 697, 731, 830, 833, 1095, 1361
Short story, 117, 544–549, 1361
Simile. *See* Figurative language.
Slant rhyme. *See* Poetic elements, slant rhyme.
Slave narrative. *See* Narrative.
Social criticism, 1148–1149
Soliloquy, 162, 815, 1362
Song, 33
Sonnet, 940, 943, 948, 1362
  Italian (Petrarchan), 943, 1362
  Shakespearean (English or Elizabethan), 948, 1362
Sound devices. *See* Poetic elements.
Source
  primary, 81, 88, 91, 98, 616, 1260
  secondary, 91, 98, 1361
Speaker, 416, 421, 471, 804, 898, 967, 968, 1001, 1003, 1005, 1057, 1061, 1089, 1098, 1101, 1111, 1116, 1194, 1362
Stage directions, 162, 163, 190, 329, 1150
Stanza. *See* Poetic elements.
Static character, 840, 860, 892. *See also* Character.
Stereotype, 1362
Stream of consciousness, 1017, 1025, 1034, 1043, 1067, 1362
Structure, 55, 580, 591, 877, 892, 1227, 1232, 1363. *See also* Poetic elements.
Style, 62, 109, 497, 562, 571, 605, 607, 686, 750, 761, 938, 967, 971, 1014, 1018, 1023, 1067, 1118, 1120, 1363
Supernatural element, 24
Surprise ending, 786, 1363
Surrealism, 1363
Suspense, 496, 514, 1363
Symbol, 62, 404, 574, 578, 835, 838, 860, 1191, 1363
Synesthesia, 1363
Tall tale, 679, 685, 702, 1363
Theme, 2, 5, 62, 251, 289, 293, 298, 330, 347, 360, 638, 643, 763–764, 786, 830, 831, 894, 898, 967, 1057, 1058, 1061, 1076, 1085, 1191, 1237, 1364
Time frame. *See* Setting.
Title, 243, 330, 602, 894, 898, 1057, 1058, 1061, 1076, 1085, 1109, 1111, 1196, 1198, 1225, 1237, 1364
Tone, 295, 298, 307, 421, 497, 562, 571, 607, 824, 828, 838, 863, 932, 937, 957, 967, 971, 1018, 1023, 1088, 1093, 1148–1149, 1150, 1155, 1178, 1194, 1198, 1232, 1237, 1364. *See also* Tone *under* Reading and Critical Thinking Skills.
Tragedy, 161, 1364

Tragic hero, 1212, 1364
Transcendentalism, 340–342, 363, 1364
Transcript, 144, 148, 1365
Trickster tale, 21, 39, 46, 1365
Trochee, 142, 1365. *See also* Poetic elements, meter.
True rhyme. *See* Poetic elements, slant rhyme.
Understatement, 1365
Voice, 863, 873, 1227, 1232, 1365
Word choice, 150, 562, 571, 607, 971, 1000, 1005, 1018, 1118, 1120, 1365. *See also* Diction.

Reading and Critical Thinking Skills

Analogies. *See also* Analogies *under* Vocabulary Skills.
 formulating, 254
 reading and understanding, 190, 964
Analyzing, 93, 129, 151, 158, 289, 293, 307, 360, 367, 378, 578, 580, 591, 760, 786, 932, 964, 971, 972, 1000, 1030, 1061, 1103, 1155, 1198, 1212, 1223, 1225, 1232
Arguments, evaluating, 300, 700, 1104, 1146
Author's attitude. *See* Tone, recognizing.
Author's purpose (motivation)
 analyzing, 571, 1241
 identifying, 100, 107, 562, 645, 652, 1241
Author's style. *See* Style, analyzing.
Bias, identifying, 144, 150
Brainstorming, 593, 932, 1095, 1150
Cause and effect, analyzing, 24, 31, 1093, 1254, 1258
Characterization, analyzing, 516, 525, 830, 833
Chronological order, 609, 1034, 1043, 1254, 1256
Classifying and categorizing
 chart, 24, 31, 37, 46, 48, 53, 55, 64, 88, 93, 109, 152, 163, 190, 228, 251, 268, 287, 289, 309, 318, 349, 369, 410, 421, 462, 471, 496, 500, 516, 562, 578, 593, 616, 658, 667, 669, 676, 688, 783, 802, 804, 806, 824, 830, 835, 863, 877, 892, 894, 928, 932, 940, 945, 973, 1000, 1006, 1018, 1025, 1076, 1095, 1157, 1200, 1221, 1225, 1232
 cluster diagram, 62, 81, 100, 940, 950, 967, 1057, 1120
 graph, 79, 602, 840, 875
 other diagram, 243, 279, 282, 498, 609, 638, 702, 705, 824, 1034, 1045, 1215
 Venn diagram, 148, 243, 294, 1005
 word web, 39, 289, 562, 605, 765, 875, 1223
Comparison and contrast
 characters, 55, 410, 528, 1056, 1200, 1215
 conflicts, 1061
 elements of literature, 31, 37, 46, 48, 78, 98, 100, 158, 228, 279, 293, 298, 309, 316, 342, 347, 367, 378, 392, 404, 414, 416, 421, 424, 434, 462, 496, 514, 516, 525, 539, 571, 578, 591, 602, 618, 620, 643, 652, 676, 685, 779, 782, 786, 804, 815, 828, 833, 838, 873, 876, 928, 937, 943, 948, 957, 959, 967, 973, 1005, 1043, 1055, 1085, 1093, 1101, 1105, 1111, 1118, 1155, 1194, 1198, 1215, 1223, 1225, 1227
 organizational pattern, 1254, 1257
Conclusions, drawing, 55, 62, 78, 158, 293, 295, 347, 360, 367, 434, 462, 471, 496, 514, 528, 667, 676, 685, 688, 697, 760, 815, 828, 833, 838, 894, 898, 932, 937, 957,

1013, 1055, 1061, 1076, 1085, 1101, 1116, 1120, 1146, 1155, 1157, 1166, 1178, 1191, 1212, 1215, 1225, 1232
Connections
 to current events, 150, 243, 287, 307, 574, 616, 620, 765, 783, 1136
 to historical events, 81, 243, 562, 605, 1095, 1105
 to personal experiences, 24, 33, 39, 53, 72, 93, 138, 144, 152, 262, 270, 282, 289, 295, 344, 363, 381, 396, 414, 454, 466, 473, 500, 580, 593, 645, 652, 658, 679, 688, 750, 830, 835, 840, 863, 924, 945, 950, 1000, 1006, 1025, 1034, 1045, 1168, 1180, 1194, 1240
Credibility of information sources, 1296
Critical analysis, 378, 404, 414, 471, 496, 525, 607, 760, 957, 1061, 1166, 1178, 1212, 1225
Cultural understanding
 connections, 77, 1083
 discussing themes and connections across cultures, 48, 377, 495, 702, 718, 1033
 shared characteristics, 718
Current events. *See* Connections, to current events.
Design features, 1241
Details
 analyzing, 93, 99, 107, 676, 697, 824, 838, 1178, 1225
 interpreting, 496, 828, 1101
Details, supporting, 93, 107, 496, 697, 786, 824, 973, 1061, 1215, 1221, 1254, 1255
Diagramming. *See* Classifying and categorizing.
Dialect, analyzing, 679
Fact and opinion, distinguishing, 150
Functional reading, 1241, 1260–1267
 instruction manual, 1260
 medicine label, 1265
 passport application, 1266–1267
 pay stub, 1264
 product advertisement, 1262
 product manual, 1263
 technical manual, 1261
Graphic organizers, interpreting, 875. *See also* Classifying and categorizing.
Images, interpreting, 779
Inferences, making, 48, 62, 63, 190, 206, 287, 298, 378, 410, 765, 779, 786, 877, 892, 971, 1018, 1023, 1118, 1120. *See also* Conclusions, drawing; Strategies for reading, predicting.
Interpretation, 31, 37, 46, 53, 62, 78, 88, 98, 107, 116, 142, 148, 158, 190, 206, 228, 243, 267, 279, 287, 293, 298, 316, 347, 360, 367, 378, 390, 404, 414, 434, 462, 471, 496, 514, 525, 539, 571, 578, 591, 602, 607, 620, 643, 652, 667, 676, 685, 697, 718, 760, 779, 786, 800, 804, 815, 828, 833, 838, 860, 873, 892, 898, 928, 937, 943, 948, 957, 964, 971, 1005, 1013, 1023, 1030, 1043, 1055, 1061, 1085, 1093, 1101, 1109, 1116, 1120, 1146, 1155, 1166, 1178, 1191, 1198, 1212, 1221, 1225, 1232. *See also* Judgments, making; Opinions, forming.
Judgments, making, 46, 78, 88, 107, 116, 148, 190, 206, 228, 243, 267, 293, 347, 434, 514, 602, 616, 643, 667, 676, 697, 702, 718, 760, 806, 815, 828, 830, 840, 937, 948, 964, 971, 1013, 1030, 1045, 1055, 1061, 1085, 1101, 1109, 1116, 1178, 1200, 1212, 1221

Main idea and supporting details, 1254, 1255
Main ideas, recognizing, 473, 943, 948, 973, 976, 1215, 1242
Modes of reasoning
    deductive, 1136
    inductive, 1136
Opinions, forming, 46, 53, 88, 148, 206, 242, 243, 279, 316, 347, 414, 471, 607, 616, 620, 652, 667, 676, 718, 779, 828, 873, 892, 964, 971, 1023, 1030, 1061, 1093, 1178, 1221
Oral reading, 38, 54. *See also* Oral report/presentation, delivering, *under* Speaking and Listening.
Paraphrasing, 270, 279, 578
Patterns of organization, 1254–1259. *See also* Organization *under* Writing Skills, Modes, and Formats.
Peer discussion, 24, 31, 46, 54, 62, 81, 89, 93, 99, 149, 152, 228, 243, 262, 267, 279, 282, 289, 295, 347, 349, 363, 381, 396, 414, 434, 454, 462, 496, 500, 525, 539, 572, 580, 591, 593, 605, 645, 646, 669, 679, 685, 765, 783, 800, 804, 835, 863, 924, 928, 943, 950, 1006, 1018, 1030, 1034, 1045, 1055, 1076, 1085, 1088, 1093, 1095, 1109, 1120, 1150, 1157, 1168, 1194, 1198
Personal experience. *See* Connections to personal experiences.
Personal response, 31, 46, 53, 62, 78, 88, 98, 107, 116, 142, 148, 158, 190, 206, 228, 243, 267, 279, 287, 293, 298, 316, 347, 360, 367, 378, 392, 404, 414, 434, 462, 471, 496, 514, 525, 539, 571, 578, 591, 602, 607, 616, 620, 643, 652, 667, 676, 685, 697, 718, 760, 779, 786, 800, 804, 815, 828, 833, 860, 873, 892, 898, 928, 937, 943, 948, 957, 964, 971, 1005, 1013, 1023, 1030, 1043, 1055, 1061, 1085, 1093, 1101, 1116, 1120, 1146, 1155, 1166, 1178, 1191, 1194, 1198, 1212, 1221, 1225, 1232, 1240
Persuasive techniques, 1285
    elevated language, using, 261
    evaluating, 260
    identifying, 158, 260, 261
    parallelism, using, 270, 279
    repetition, 261, 262
    rhetorical questions, 261, 262, 267
Prior knowledge, activating, 24, 31, 46, 53, 78, 88, 98, 107, 116, 142, 148, 158, 163, 190, 206, 228, 243, 267, 279, 287, 293, 298, 347, 360, 367, 378, 392, 404, 414, 424, 434, 462, 471, 514, 525, 539, 571, 578, 602, 607, 616, 620, 643, 652, 667, 676, 685, 697, 718, 760, 786, 800, 804, 815, 828, 833, 860, 873, 898, 928, 937, 943, 957, 964, 971, 1005, 1013, 1023, 1030, 1043, 1055, 1061, 1085, 1093, 1101, 1116, 1120, 1146, 1155, 1166, 1178, 1191, 1194, 1198, 1212, 1221, 1225, 1232, 1240
Problem-Solution, 1254, 1259
Purposes for reading, 1240, 1241. *See also* Prior knowledge, activating.
Reader's experiences. *See* Connections to personal experiences.
Silent reading (reinforced throughout)
Strategies for reading, 1240–1243. *See also* Connections.
    clarifying, 6–7, 9, 11, 12, 13, 14, 15, 72, 138, 142, 454, 462, 788, 1240, 1242
    connecting, 6–7, 9, 10, 11, 14, 15, 1240, 1242
    evaluating, 6–7, 9, 10, 11, 14, 15, 1240, 1242
    predicting, 6–7, 10, 658, 667, 783, 786, 1180, 1191, 1240, 1242

    previewing, 1240
    questioning, 6–7, 9, 10, 11, 14, 15, 760, 1240
    visualizing, 6–7, 9, 10, 11, 33, 349, 360, 593, 602, 669, 676, 802, 804, 1240, 1242
Strategies for reading types of literature. *See also* Functional reading.
    autobiography, 109
    drama, 162
    encyclopedia article, 1243
    epic poetry, 309
    essays, 369
    fiction, 1242
    fiction with social themes, 764
    free verse, 396, 404
    historical narrative, 71
    information, 1240–1241, 1250, 1251
    magazine articles, 1242, 1252
    modernist literature, 1149
    narrative poetry, 618
    Native American songs, 33
    newspaper, 1242
    non-fiction, 1242
    online text, 1243
    persuasive rhetoric, 261, 262
    poetry, 344, 395, 416, 574, 750, 924, 938, 1242
    regional literature, 637
    speech, 1242
    web page, 1252
Structure, analyzing, 307, 591
Study strategies
    identifying main idea, 71, 81, 88, 107, 363, 473, 943, 948, 972, 973, 976, 1061, 1215, 1221, 1298
    in-depth reading, suggestions for, 71, 162, 261, 395, 637, 764, 1017, 1149, 1298
    outlining, 653, 893, 986, 987, 1086, 1156, 1298
    scanning, 98, 279, 287, 378, 392, 514, 620, 676, 697, 779, 1297
    skimming, 330, 332, 333, 732, 735, 1297
    study guide questions, 34, 42, 139, 284, 304, 398, 399, 411, 418, 575, 751, 752, 753, 754, 756, 757, 758, 826, 831, 836, 896, 925, 926, 941, 946, 968, 1001, 1003, 1058, 1089, 1098, 1113, 1196
    taking notes, 24, 33, 39, 48, 55, 72, 93, 109, 163, 307, 309, 349, 369, 410, 473, 562, 574, 580, 679, 750, 788, 830, 932, 940, 973, 1000, 1006, 1018, 1034, 1045, 1298
Style, analyzing, 496, 602, 643, 686, 760, 779, 838, 860, 938, 1013, 1101, 1109, 1146, 1155, 1191, 1227, 1232
Summarizing, 81, 88, 363, 367, 1240
Text organizers, using, 72
Text structures
    cause and effect, 1241
    chronological, 609, 1034, 1043
    compare and contrast, 1241
    main idea and supporting details, 1242
    sequence, 1241
Tone. *See also* Tone *under* Literary Concepts.
    analyzing, 289, 1198
    recognizing, 957
    word choice, 1198

Vocabulary. *See* Vocabulary Skills.
Writer's motivation, stance, position. *See* Author's purpose (motivation).

Vocabulary Skills

Affixes, 550, 1130
Analogies, 63, 254, 361, 541, 1044, 1248
Antonyms, 159, 380, 393, 515, 1179, 1192, 1214, 1246–1247
Base words, 1130, 1245
Building vocabulary, 32, 54, 63, 80, 90, 99, 108, 117, 126, 159, 245, 254, 268, 280, 288, 294, 308, 326, 361, 368, 380, 393, 444, 463, 472, 499, 515, 527, 541, 550, 573, 592, 604, 608, 630, 668, 698, 780, 801, 817, 862, 874, 893, 908, 958, 966, 990, 1015, 1032, 1044, 1087, 1147, 1156, 1167, 1179, 1192, 1214, 1222, 1233
Connotation, 268, 908, 1247
Context clues
    comparison, 1244
    contrast, 1244
    definition or restatement, 326, 1244
    example, 1244
    general context, 1244
    idioms, 1244
    inference, 80, 280, 294, 326, 368, 380, 499, 527, 608, 630, 679, 698, 780, 801, 874, 966, 1087, 1156, 1167, 1214, 1222
    slang, 1244
Decoding multisyllabic words, 1249
Denotation, 245, 908, 1247
Dialect, 593, 637, 679, 685, 1014, 1055, 1347
Etymology. *See* Word origins.
Figurative language. *See* Figurative language *under* Literary Concepts.
Foreign words, 1246
History of English, 317
Homographs, 728
Homonyms, 728, 1248
Homophones, 728, 1248
Idioms, 393, 893
Informal language, 990
Meaning clues, 90, 117, 361, 472, 496, 573, 604, 687, 780, 817, 958, 1147, 1233. *See also* Context clues.
Multiple meanings, 1248
Portmanteau, 990
Prefixes, 444, 1130, 1245
Reference materials, using dictionaries, 126, 550, 630, 728, 990
Related words, 54, 108
Roots, 444, 550, 1130, 1245
Specialized vocabulary, 1249
Suffixes, 444, 1130, 1245
Synonyms, 32, 99, 159, 288, 380, 592, 668, 862, 893, 908, 1015, 1032, 1147, 1179, 1192, 1214, 1246
Word families, 1246
Word meaning, 308, 463
Word origins
    derivation, 54, 288, 463, 550, 817, 893, 1032, 1147, 1246
    influences on English language, 317
Word parts, 1245

Grammar, Usage, and Mechanics

Abbreviations, 1335
Active voice, 1335
Adjective, 445, 1305, 1312, 1335
    clause, 1321, 1331
    comparative form of, 906, 907, 1312, 1313, 1335
    phrase, 445, 1319, 1335
    predicate, 1312, 1335, 1336
    proper, 1335
    superlative form of, 1313, 1335
Adverb, 551, 1305, 1312, 1335
    clause, 1321
    comparative form of, 1312, 1313, 1335
    conjunctive, 1335
    phrase, 551, 1319, 1335
    superlative form of, 1313, 1335
Agreement, 1335
    pronoun-antecedent, 324, 325, 549, 1335
    subject-verb, 325, 1324, 1331, 1335
Ambiguous reference, 1332, 1335
Antecedent, 324, 325, 549, 1335
Apostrophe, 1328
Appositive, 1319, 1335
    essential, 1335
    nonessential, 1335
    phrase, 1319
Article, 1335
    definite, 1335
    indefinite, 1335
Capitalization, 253, 443, 906, 907, 1329, 1333
Clause, 1321, 1335
    adjective, 1321, 1335
    adverb, 1321, 1335
    dependent, 1336
    elliptical, 1336
    independent, 1321, 1336
    noun, 909, 1321, 1335
    subordinate, 1321, 1336
Colon, 1328
Comma, 253, 629, 727, 989, 1327
    in addresses, 1327
    with adjective clauses, 1327, 1330
    with adverb clauses, 1327
    in compound sentences, 1327
    in dates, 1327
    after introductory phrases, 1327
    in letter parts, 1327
    in series, 1327
Comma splice, 1323, 1336
Commonly confused words
    Accept and *except*, 1334
    Advice and *advise*, 1334
    Affect and *effect*, 1334
    All ready and *already*, 1334
    Allusion and *illusion*, 1334
    Among and *between*, 1334
    Bad and *badly*, 1313
    Good and *well*, 1313
    Leave and *let*, 1334

Lie and *lay*, 1334
Loose and *lose*, 1334
Precede and *proceed*, 1334
Than and *then*, 1334
Two, too, and *to,* 1334
Who and *whom,* 909
Comparison
double, 1313
illogical, 1313
irregular, 906, 907, 1313
regular, 1312, 1313
Complement, 1318, 1336
direct object, 1318
indirect object, 1318
subject complement, 1318
Complex sentence, 127
Compound-complex sentence, 127
Compound noun, 1306, 1337
Compound sentence, 127, 631, 1336
Compound subject, 1317
Compound verb, 1403
Conjunction, 1305, 1315, 1336
coordinating, 1315, 1336
correlative, 1315, 1336
subordinating, 1315, 1336
Conjunctive adverb, 1315, 1336
Contraction, 1336
Coordinating conjunction, 1336
Correlative conjunction, 1315
Dangling modifier, 1314, 1336
Dash, 1328
Dependent clause, 1336
Direct object, 1318, 1336
Double comparison, 1313, 1332
Double negative, 125, 1314, 1336
Ellipse, 1328
Elliptical clause, 1336
End marks, 1327, 1336
in quotation, 1327
Exclamation point, 1327
Fragment, sentence, 253, 727, 1129, 1323, 1330, 1337
Gender, 1337
Gerund, 255, 1320, 1337
phrase, 1320
Hyphen, 1328
Illogical comparison, 1337
Indefinite pronoun, 1324, 1337
Indefinite reference, 1337
Independent clause, 1321, 1336, 1337
Indirect object, 1318, 1337
Indirect question, 1330, 1337
Infinitive, 1319, 1337
phrase, 1319
split, 1340
Intensive pronoun, 1337
Interjection, 1305, 1315, 1337
Irregular verb, 1337
Italics, 1328
Modifier, 1337. *See also* Adjective; Adverb.
dangling, 1314

essential, 1337
misplaced, 125, 549, 1314, 1333
nonessential, 1337
placement of, 1333
Noun, 1305, 1337
abstract, 1306, 1337
clause, 909, 1321
collective, 1306, 1336, 1337
common, 1306, 1337
compound, 1306, 1337
concrete, 1306
of direct address, 1337
plural, 443
possessive, 443, 989, 1129, 1306, 1337
predicate, 1337
proper, 1306, 1337
Number, 1337
Object
direct, 1318, 1336
indirect, 1318, 1337
of preposition, 1337
Parallel structure, 906, 907, 991
Participial phrase, 1320
Participle, 1320, 1338
dangling, 1320
misplaced, 1320
past, 1338
present, 1338
Passive voice, 1338
Period, 1327
Person, 1338
first, 1338
second, 1338
third, 1338
Personal pronoun, 1324, 1338
Phrase, 1319, 1330, 1338
adjective, 445, 1319, 1338
adverb, 55, 1319, 1338
appositive, 1319, 1338
gerund, 1320, 1338
infinitive, 1319, 1338
participial, 1320, 1338
prepositional, 1319, 1338
Possessives, 1338
noun, 443, 989, 1129, 1338
pronoun, 1338
Predicate, 1338
complete, 1317, 1336, 1338
compound, 1317
simple, 1316, 1338, 1340
Predicate adjective, 1312, 1336
Predicate nominative, 1318, 1326, 1336, 1338
Preposition, 1305, 1314, 1338
Prepositional phrase, 1314, 1319, 1338
Pronoun, 1305, 1307, 1338
agreement with antecedent, 324, 325, 549, 1307
ambiguous reference of, 1332
case of, 1307, 1331
demonstrative, 1308, 1336, 1338
indefinite, 1308, 1338

intensive, 1307, 1338
interrogative, 1308, 1338
nominative, 1307
object form of, 1332
objective case, 1307, 1339
person, 1332
personal, 1307, 1338
possessive, 1307, 1338
reflexive, 1307, 1338
relative, 1309, 1339
as subject, 1332, 1339
subject form of, 1332
unidentified reference of, 1332
Punctuation, 549, 1327, 1339
apostrophe, 1328, 1339
colon, 1328, 1339
comma, 1327, 1339
dash, 1328
exclamation point, 1327, 1339
hyphen, 1328, 1339
parentheses, 1328
period, 1327, 1339
question mark, 1327, 1339
quotation marks, 549, 1328
semicolon, 1327, 1339
Question mark, 1327
Quotation, 1339
direct, 1330, 1339
divided, 1339
indirect, 1330, 1339
Quotation marks, 1328
Regular verb, 1339
Relative pronoun, 1326, 1339
Run-on sentence, 907, 1323, 1330, 1339
Semicolon, 1327, 1339
Sentence, 1339
closer, 1131
complex, 127, 1322, 1339
compound, 127, 631, 1322, 1336, 1339
compound-complex, 127, 1322
declarative, 1317
exclamatory, 1317
fragment, 253, 727, 1129, 1323, 1330, 1337
imperative, 1317
interrogative, 1317
inverted, 1325
run-on, 907, 1323, 1330, 1339
simple, 127, 1322, 1339
Sentence fragment, 1340
Sentence structure, 1316
Split infinitive, 1340
Subject, 1340
agreement of verb with, 325, 1324, 1331, 1340
collective noun as, 1326
complement, 1318
complete, 1317, 1336
compound, 1317
in imperative sentences, 1318
indefinite pronoun as, 1325
personal pronoun as, 1324
in questions, 1317

relative pronoun as, 1326
in sentences that begin with *There* and *Here,* 1318
simple, 1316, 1340
Subordinate clause, 1321, 1336, 1340
Tense, 327, 443, 628, 727, 989, 1310, 1340. *See also* Verb.
future, 327, 1310, 1340
future perfect, 327, 1310, 1340
past, 327, 443, 727, 1310, 1340
past perfect, 327, 1129, 1310, 1340
present, 327, 443, 628, 989, 1310, 1340
present perfect, 327, 1310, 1340
progressive, 1310–1311
Unidentified reference, 1340
Verb, 1309, 1340. *See also* Tense; Voice.
action, 1309, 1340
agreement with subject, 1324, 1331
auxiliary, 1309, 1331, 1340
compound, 1403
intransitive, 1309, 1340
irregular, 1340
linking, 1309, 1340
main, 1340
mood of, 1311
phrase, 1340
principal parts, 1310
progressive form of, 1310, 1311, 1340
regular, 1340
tense, 327, 443, 628, 727, 1129, 1310, 1331, 1340
transitive, 1309, 1340
voice, 1311, 1340
Verbal, 1319, 1340
gerund, 1340
infinitive, 1319, 1340
infinitive phrase, 1319
participle, 1340
Voice, 1340
active, 1311, 1340
passive, 1311, 1340

Writing Skills, Modes, and Formats

Analysis, 603, 698, 1283
Audience, identifying, 323, 547, 983, 1269
Brainstorming, 47, 1126
Business writing, 1293
Cause-and-effect writing, 1213
Characters, depicting, 268, 1212
Classificatory writing. *See also* Compare-and-contrast writing.
cause-and-effect writing, 1213
problem-solution writing, 949
Classifying and diagramming. *See also* Classifying and categorizing *under* Reading and Critical Thinking Skills.
chart, 422, 572, 603, 816, 818, 929, 978, 1213
diagram, 244, 542, 900, 1064, 1122
Venn diagram, 246
word web, 294
Compare-and-contrast writing, 64, 159, 244, 246, 317, 378, 498, 526, 540, 572, 592, 621, 719, 801, 805, 816, 829, 893, 899, 929, 965, 977, 978, 1110, 1117, 1121, 1147, 1213, 1222, 1226, 1233, 1281

Conclusion, 628, 1275
Descriptive writing, 54, 117, 463, 472, 1226, 1277
Dialogue, 108, 117, 422, 435, 719, 801, 977, 1117, 1213, 1233
Drafting, 118, 123, 246, 252, 318, 323, 441, 547, 627, 905, 987, 1269
Editing. *See* Proofreading; Revising and editing.
Elaboration, 123, 124, 252, 323, 324, 441–442, 547–548, 627, 905, 988, 1275
Essay, 32, 38, 64, 79, 108, 118, 149, 246, 317, 328, 379, 415, 422, 542, 617, 787, 893, 899, 948, 965, 1062, 1064, 1110, 1122, 1147, 1213, 1222, 1226, 1234
Evaluation. *See* Standards for evaluating writing.
Explanatory writing. *See* Expository writing.
Expository writing, 1213, 1281
    abstract, 972
    analysis, 603, 698
    analytical essay, 542, 617, 1122
    book review, 317
    character analysis, 1192
    comparative analysis, 64, 540
    comparison-and-contrast essay, 159, 244, 317, 378, 540, 572, 592, 622, 805, 816, 829, 893, 899, 902, 929, 965, 978, 1062, 1110, 1147, 1222, 1226
    critical essay, 621
    documentary plan, 939
    essay, 32, 38, 64, 79, 108, 118, 149, 246, 317, 328, 368, 379, 415, 422, 540, 542, 617, 787, 893, 899, 948, 965, 1062, 1064, 1110, 1122, 1147, 1213, 1222, 1234
    evaluative essay, 436, 592, 720, 818, 900, 1222, 1234
    expository essay, 1213
    eyewitness report, 89, 120, 617
    instruction manual, 668
    interpretive essay, 393
    lecture notes, 526
    literary review, 405, 435, 1213
    magazine article, 47, 294, 677
    multimedia outline, 1086
    news article/report, 268, 515, 668
    obituary, 526, 1167
    police report, 526
    research report, 687
    review, 899, 944, 1147, 1156
    synopsis, 498
    synthesis essay, 1064
    warning label, 515
Facts and statistics, using, 123
Firsthand and expressive writing
    advertising copy, 780
    advice, 861, 1024, 1031, 1233
    announcement, 159
    archaeological report, 463
    autobiographical sketch, 422, 572, 939, 958
    character sketch, 268, 801, 1213
    closing statement, 572
    comic tale, 644
    critical essay, 893
    definition of adulthood, 1056
    definition of success, 1167

diary entry, 89, 415, 472, 526, 677, 805, 1062, 1192
dream analysis, 1086
editorial, 244, 463, 572, 1015, 1056, 1147, 1199
epitaph, 415, 1094
evaluative essay, 318, 436
eventful paragraph, 1086
firsthand account, 79
grocery list, 1226
interview, 698, 834
letter, 148, 159, 288, 294, 328, 393, 498, 540, 602, 608, 617, 719, 834, 874, 929, 977, 1024, 1031, 1056, 1121, 1233
letter to editor, 780, 1086
memoir, 874, 1102
nature log, 393
performance review, 54
personal ad, 1024
personal narrative, 280, 1094
personal response, 816, 965
play outline, 1156
prediction, 1192
problem-solving essay, 949
proposal, 958, 972, 1110
psychological evaluation, 861, 1044
questions and answers, 89
recommendations, 299
reflective essay, 38, 378, 415, 438
report card, 108
report to the president, 79
responding as a character, 299, 572, 617, 644, 687, 816, 834, 1121
résumé, 861
sermon, 644
slogan, 944
social commentary, 1031
speech, 1179
teenager's declaration, 280
telegram, 698
tips for newcomers, 874
yearbook biography, 972
Focus, determining, 1126
Goals, setting, 983
Information, collecting, 984, 1126, 1288
Informative writing. *See* Expository writing.
Introduction, 1272
Language use, 1276
Literary interpretation, 624–628
Mood, creating, 1277
Narrative and literary writing, 1279. *See also* Writing about literature.
    alternative ending, 32, 603, 787
    alternative outline, 653
    ballads, 463, 621
    comic tale, 644
    dialogue, 108, 117, 422, 435, 719, 801, 977, 1117, 1213, 1233
    diary entry, 89, 415, 472, 526, 677, 805, 1062, 1192
    eulogy, 1044
    folk tale rewrite, 687
    imaginary interview, 816

missing scene, 244
monologue, 787, 834
narrative sequel, 839
new story ending, 32, 603
parody, 348, 472
personal narrative, 280
poem, 117, 348, 405, 463, 579, 829, 929, 949
poetic riddle, 1062
rewritten episode, 1179
script, 149, 668, 1024, 1121
sermon, 644
short story summary, 99, 498
song, 38, 99, 839
sonnet, 949
speech 268, 1179
storyboard, 1121
story sequel, 435, 540, 780, 816
stream-of-consciousness narrative, 1031
trickster tale, 47
Organization, 905, 985, 1278
analysis, 542, 603, 1284
cause-and-effect, 698, 1213, 1282
chronological order, 436, 1280
conflict-focused, 1280
feature-by-feature, 905, 1282
flashback, 1280
order of importance, 1156, 1278
order of impression, 1278
problem-solving writing, 948, 1283
spatial order, 1278
subject-by-subject, 905, 1282
Outlining, 653, 893, 986, 1086, 1156, 1288
Paragraphs, composing, 1273
Paraphrasing, 280, 368, 608
Peer response, 123, 252, 323, 442, 548, 627, 726, 905, 987, 1128, 1271. See also Peer discussion under Reading and Critical Thinking Skills.
Persuasion
bandwagon appeal, 323
cause-and-effect fallacy, 323, 1286
circular reasoning, 323, 1286
either-or fallacy, 323, 1286
elevated language, 261
emotional appeal, 158, 261
ethical appeal, 261
faulty reasoning, 1299
loaded language, 144, 152, 1299
logical appeal, 158, 260–261
name-calling, 323, 1286
over-generalization, 323, 1286
repetition, 261
rhetorical question, 261, 262, 267
testimonial, 1299
Persuasive writing, 320, 1285
closing statement, 572
essay, 308, 320, 787
literary review, 405, 435
newspaper editorial, 244, 463, 572, 1015, 1056, 1147, 1199
proposal, 958, 972

review, 244, 248
sermon, 152, 158
speech, 1179
Portfolio, 5, 38, 54, 63, 79, 89, 120, 124, 129, 149, 244, 248, 252, 268, 288, 308, 317, 320, 324, 329, 348, 361, 368, 422, 438, 442, 472, 498, 515, 540, 544, 548, 553, 592, 603, 624, 628, 644, 653, 668, 722, 726, 731, 762, 780, 816, 829, 893, 899, 902, 906, 911, 939, 949, 965, 972, 977, 980, 988, 1015, 1031, 1044, 1062, 1086, 1110, 1121, 1124, 1126, 1128, 1147, 1179, 1199, 1213, 1233
Prewriting, 123, 251, 323, 324, 441, 547, 627, 905, 983, 1269
Problem-solution writing, 949
Proofreading, 124, 252, 324, 422, 548, 628, 1269
Publishing and reflecting, 124, 324, 548, 628, 726, 906, 988, 1126, 1270
Purpose, determining, 723, 1269
Quotations, using, 548, 985
Research report writing, 980, 983–985, 1287. See also Reports and research projects, types of, written under Inquiry and Research.
Revising and editing, 124, 125, 252, 324, 325, 442, 443, 548, 549, 628, 629, 727, 906, 907, 988, 989, 1129, 1269
rewriting and extending, 988
Rubric. See Standards for evaluating writing.
Sensory details, using, 1277
Short story, 544
Sources. See also Sources of Information under Inquiry and Research.
citing, 1291
documenting, 984, 1290
Standards for evaluating writing
comparison-and-contrast essay, 902, 903–904, 1281, 1282
critical review, 248, 249–250
description, 1277
eyewitness report, 120, 121–122
literary interpretation, 624, 625–626
multimedia exhibit, 1124, 1125
narrative writing, 1279
persuasion, 320, 321–322, 1285
problem-solution, 1283
reflective essay, 438, 439–440
research report, 980, 981–982
short story, 544, 545–546
storytelling, 722, 724
Summarizing, 122, 248, 249, 250, 626, 904, 972, 1289, 1296–1297, 1298
Thesis statement, 624, 980, 981, 983, 987, 1287
Topic sentence, 1273
Transitions, 902, 904, 905, 980, 982, 1274
Works cited list, 982, 1291, 1292
Writing about literature
alternative ending, 32, 603, 787
analytical essay, 603
argument outline, 593
character sketch, 268
comparative analysis, 159, 244, 317, 378

concluding paragraph, 515
interpretation, 393
literary review, 405, 435, 1213
missing scene, 244
new stanza, 579
new story ending, 32, 787
responding as a character, 299, 572, 617, 644, 687, 816, 834
review, 805
rewriting and extending, 1179
Writing from experience
analysis, 603
nature log, 405

Inquiry and Research

Authority of sources
appropriateness, 1295, 1296
credibility, 984, 1296
Bibliography. *See* Works cited list.
Databases. *See* Electronic resources.
Dictionaries, 644
Documentary, 621
Electronic resources. *See also* LaserLinks *under* Viewing and Representing.
CD-ROMs, 379, 608, 687, 1288
online resources, 79, 149, 268, 379, 422, 452, 463, 572, 603, 657, 668, 677, 687, 748, 762, 816, 923, 929, 939, 945, 966, 977, 999, 1015, 1045, 1074, 1110, 1111, 1146
Encyclopedias, 268, 379, 608, 668, 939
Graphic organizers. *See also* Classifying and categorizing *under* Reading and Critical Thinking Skills.
chart, 24, 31, 37, 46, 48, 53, 55, 64, 88, 93, 109, 152, 163, 190, 228, 251, 268, 287, 289, 309, 318, 349, 369, 410, 462, 471, 496, 500, 516, 562, 578, 593, 616, 658, 667, 669, 676, 688, 783, 802, 804, 806, 824, 830, 835, 863, 877, 892, 894, 928, 932, 940, 945, 973, 1000, 1006, 1018, 1025, 1057, 1076, 1095, 1120, 1157, 1200, 1221, 1225, 1232
diagram, 62, 81, 100, 243, 279, 282, 498, 609, 702, 705, 824, 950, 967, 1034, 1045, 1057, 1120, 1215
graph, 79, 840, 875
Information organization and recording
chart, 24, 31, 37, 46, 48, 53, 55, 64, 88, 93, 109, 152, 163, 190, 228, 251, 268, 287, 289, 309, 318, 349, 369, 410, 462, 471, 496, 500, 516, 562, 578, 593, 616, 658, 667, 669, 676, 688, 783, 802, 804, 806, 824, 830, 835, 863, 877, 892, 894, 928, 932, 940, 945, 973, 1000, 1006, 1018, 1025, 1057, 1076, 1095, 1120, 1157, 1200, 1221, 1225, 1232
cluster diagram, 62, 81, 100, 940, 950, 967, 1057, 1120
graph, 79, 602, 840, 875
map, 677, 1117
notes, 985
other diagram, 243, 279, 282, 498, 609, 638, 702, 705, 824, 1034, 1045, 1215
Venn diagram, 148, 242, 294, 1005
word web, 39, 289, 562, 605, 765, 875, 1223

Internet, 79, 149, 268, 379, 422, 452, 463, 572, 603, 657, 668, 677, 748, 762, 816, 923, 929, 939, 945, 966, 977, 999, 1015, 1045, 1074, 1110, 1111, 1118, 1146, 1288, 1295
Interviewing, 816, 1062
Logical thinking, 1300
deductive arguments, 1300
inductive arguments, 1300
MLA guidelines, 1291
Note-taking, 985, 1288
Outlining, 986
Paraphrasing, 985, 1296
Plagiarism, avoiding, 987, 1297
Reports and research projects, topics for
anti-Semitism, 1086
antisocial personalities, 540
artistic visions, 159
Battle of Gettysburg, 608
Birmingham bombing, 621
the blues, 929
Brady, Mathew, 603
civil rights today, 1147
clothing styles, 861
con artists, 540
corridos, 719
creation myth, 32
Depression, 780
environmental effects of war, 1117
farm life, 1015
guerrilla tactics, 1101
Harlem Renaissance, 939
Harlem Renaissance artists, 944
hunting, 38
hypnosis, 668
impact of antiwar protests, 1121
inspirational speakers, 159
Japanese-American internment, 1102
Latin American cookbook, 1226
legal alien, 1198
Mayflower, 89
McCarthyism, 224
Michelangelo, 1031
Mississippi River, 667
mourning rituals, 1167
Native American music, 38
New Mexico, 38
"New South," 526
19th-century New England, 762
nonviolent resistance, 379
origin of the novel, 977
plague, 463
psychology, 472
Puerto Rico, 422
Puritan homes, 143
Puritan women, 143
Salem memorials, 149
Salem witch trials, 149, 244
shell shock, 1094
sibling rivalry, 816

Sioux culture, 653
slave laws, 572
slave narrative, 572
Spanish explorers, 79
Spanish word translation, 644
spirituals, 965
twins, 498
violent crime, 1213
Wagner, Richard, 698
Walden Pond, 393
women's roles, 1062
youth counterculture, 1156
Reports and research projects, types of
art display, 944
booklet, 834
bulletin-board display, 939
case study, 540
debate, 79
drama, 1015
fashion show, 861
graph, 79, 1213
illustration, 861
map, 38, 677, 1117
mock interview, 541
multimedia, 687, 939
musical recording, 38, 698, 719, 839, 861, 929, 939,
    965, 1032
oral, 38, 244, 368, 463, 498, 572, 653, 762, 929, 965,
    977, 1086, 1094, 1102, 1110, 1121, 1147, 1156
photo exhibit, 603
poster, 572
time line, 89
written, 540, 1031
Source cards, 984
Sources of information. *See also* Credibility of information
    sources *under* Reading and Critical Thinking Skills.
documenting, 987, 1291
electronic, 1288, 1295
evaluating, 91, 984, 1288, 1296
identifying, 1288, 1296
primary, 81, 88, 91, 98, 616, 1260
secondary, 91, 98, 1361
Web site. *See* Internet.
Works cited list, 982, 1291, 1292
World Wide Web, 499, 687, 762, 939, 1015, 1295

Speaking and Listening

Cooperative learning, 31, 37, 53, 107, 158, 190, 206, 287,
    307, 316, 367, 378, 392, 404, 471, 571, 607, 643, 652,
    718, 779, 815, 892, 898, 937, 971, 973, 1023, 1116,
    1146, 1155, 1166, 1178, 1191, 1212, 1215, 1232
Creative reader response
audio recordings, 415, 435, 472, 541, 603, 719, 839,
    1032
conversation, 816, 1062
discussion, 268, 379, 572, 816, 965
music, 143, 621, 834, 939
newscast, 149, 719, 780
oral reading, 38, 929

oral report. *See* Reports and research projects, types of,
    oral, *under* Inquiry and Research.
role-play, 1213
soundtrack, 89
speeches, 79, 965
TV shows, 244, 288, 653, 1031
videotape, 617
Debate, 78, 280, 1121, 1213
Dramatic reading/presentation, 719, 958
choral reading, 317
dramatic dialogue, 463, 1147
improvisation, 1031
poem, 422, 435, 472, 621, 762, 805, 929, 1226
scene from a play, 244
scene from a story, 379, 526, 780, 1032, 1056, 1086,
    1178, 1192
sermon, 159
skit, 280, 1226
soliloquy, 299
speech, 268, 572
Interview, 603, 1094, 1302
Literary performance. *See* Performance presentations.
Multimedia presentation, 939, 1304
Oral reading. *See* Dramatic reading/presentations.
Oral report/presentation, delivering, 677
Peer response, 24, 46, 54, 62, 81, 89, 93, 99, 149, 152, 228,
    243, 262, 267, 279, 282, 289, 295, 347, 349, 363, 381,
    396, 414, 434, 454, 462, 496, 500, 525, 539, 572, 580,
    591, 593, 605, 645, 646, 669, 679, 685, 765, 783, 800,
    804, 835, 863, 924, 1006, 1013, 1018, 1030, 1034,
    1045, 1055, 1076, 1085, 1088, 1093, 1095, 1109,
    1120, 1150, 1157, 1168, 1194, 1198
Performance presentation
analyzing, 762, 1300
delivering, 762, 1301
evaluating, 762, 1301
planning and presenting, 762, 1301
Persuasion. *See* Persuasion *under* Writing Skills, Modes, and
    Formats.
Role-playing, 1213
Technology
audio recording, 472, 541, 603, 719, 839, 1032
CD-ROMs, 1288
Internet, 79, 149, 268, 379, 422, 452, 463, 572, 603,
    657, 668, 677, 748, 762, 816, 923, 929, 939, 945,
    966, 977, 999, 1015, 1045, 1074, 1110, 1111,
    1118, 1146, 1288, 1295
multimedia program, 939
video, 46, 415, 526, 676, 787, 1056
Vocabulary. *See* Vocabulary Skills.

Viewing and Representing

Art, responding to, 32, 79, 89, 149, 268, 422, 435, 526, 572,
    616, 816, 861, 965, 1086, 1199, 1233
Creative reader response
advertisement, 268, 698
bar graph, 79
board game, 361
bumper sticker, 348

calendar, 861
caricature, 540, 1031
cartoon, 288, 1102
collage, 348, 405, 422, 1015
dance, 405, 939
expense chart, 1056
flow chart, 498
flyer, 668, 1226
food chain diagram, 32
historical fashions, 244, 861
illustrations, 38, 54, 63, 149, 299, 415, 422, 435, 472,
    603, 644, 697, 805, 834, 929, 1024, 1044, 1061,
    1086, 1213
jacket cover, 159
map, 719, 929
mask, 839
model plane, 1094
movie score, 1110
museum exhibit, 99
narrative pictograph, 32
pantomime, 47, 90, 472, 498, 698, 780
photo essay, 393
photo research, 965
picture book, 572
Pilgrim memorial, 89
poster, 268, 379, 498, 540, 579, 698, 816, 949, 977,
    1121, 1147
product chart, 515
set design, 244, 463
stage directions, 668
storyboard, 79, 143
time line, 89
T-shirt emblem, 972
wallpaper design, 781
Multimedia presentation, 939, 1147
Technology
    CD-ROMs, 1288
    creating visuals with, 762
    e-mail, 1295
    Internet, 79, 149, 268, 379, 422, 452, 463, 572, 603,
        657, 668, 677, 748, 762, 816, 923, 929, 939, 945,
        966, 977, 999, 1015, 1045, 1074, 1110, 1111,
        1118, 1146, 1288, 1295
    LaserLinks, 22, 24, 33, 39, 48, 68, 72, 79, 81, 93, 100,
        109, 136, 138, 144, 224, 258, 262, 282, 289, 295,
        300, 308, 309, 342, 344, 349, 368, 379, 381, 396,
        422, 448, 453, 454, 560, 562, 574, 580, 609, 634,
        645, 657, 658, 688, 698, 702, 744, 748, 765, 783,
        788, 806, 817, 824, 829, 840, 862, 863, 877, 918,
        923, 944, 994, 999, 1025, 1032, 1086, 1088,
        1102, 1105, 1134, 1146, 1147, 1193, 1213, 1215,
        1223
    multimedia program, 939
    video, 46, 415, 526, 676, 787, 1056
    World Wide Web, 1295
View and compare
    The Crucible, 163, 242
Visual literacy, 1303
Visuals, using, 1303

Assessment
Assessment practice
    analogies, 254, 361, 1044
    grammar, 125, 127, 255, 325, 445, 549, 551, 631, 727,
        729, 907, 909, 991
    revising and editing, 125, 443, 549, 629, 727, 907, 988
    vocabulary, 32, 54, 63, 80, 90, 99, 108, 117, 159, 245,
        280, 288, 294, 308, 361, 368, 380, 393, 472, 499,
        515, 527, 541, 573, 592, 604, 608, 668, 687, 698,
        780, 801, 817, 862, 874, 893, 958, 966, 1015,
        1032, 1044, 1087, 1147, 1156, 1167, 1179, 1192,
        1214, 1222, 1233
Criteria, using to analyze, evaluate, and critique
    comparison-and-contrast essay, 902–904
    critical review, 248–250
    eyewitness report, 120–122
    images, 1303
    literary interpretation, 624–626
    multimedia exhibit, 1124–1125
    persuasive writing, 320–322
    reflective essay, 438–440
    research report, 980–982
    short story, 544–546
    speech, 1301
    storytelling presentation, 722, 724
Goals, setting, 129, 329, 553, 731, 911, 1067, 1237
Literary concepts, identifying and analyzing
    conflict, 53, 88, 129, 243, 911, 1109, 1166
    drama, 329
    figurative language, 287, 293, 392, 497, 602, 760, 860,
        911, 943
    form, 553
    historical narrative, 129
    imagery, 360, 553, 779, 786, 804, 805, 1005, 1030,
        1093, 1120, 1198, 1225
    modernist characters and techniques, 1055, 1067
    oral literature, 129, 652
    persuasion, 158, 329
    point of view, 88, 497, 591, 731, 1055, 1085, 1191
    setting, 62, 78, 329, 697, 731
    style, 62, 497, 571, 607, 686, 761, 938, 971, 1014,
        1023, 1067, 1120
    theme, 62, 293, 298, 347, 360, 643, 786, 831, 898,
        1058, 1061, 1085, 1237
    tone, 298, 307, 421, 828, 838, 937, 957, 1093, 1155,
        1178, 1198, 1232, 1237
Portfolio, 129, 329, 553, 731, 911, 1067, 1236
Reading and writing strategies for assessment
    answering essay questions, 334, 736
    answering multiple-choice questions, 333, 735
    reading a test selection, 330–332, 732–734
    responding to short-answer questions, 334, 736
    revising, editing, and proofreading, 335, 737
Reflecting and assessing
    connecting to history, 328, 730, 910, 1236
    insight into human nature, 128, 552, 1066, 1236
    literary terms, understanding of, 129, 329, 553, 731,
        911, 1067, 1236
    modern literature, understanding of, 1067
    responses to literature, 129

Index of Titles and Authors

Page numbers that appear in italics refer to biographical information.

A

Acquainted with the Night, 1001
Adams, Abigail, 282, *288*
Adolescence—III, 802
After great pain, a formal feeling comes—, 757
Alvarez, Julia, 814
Ambush, 1105
America and I, 863
Anaya, Rudolfo A., 638, *644*
Angelou, Maya, 109, *117*
Any Human to Another, 940
anyone lived in a pretty how town, 410
Armistice, 1076
At the Justice Department, November 15, 1969, 1118
Autobiography of Mark Twain, The, from, 658

B

Baldwin, James, 959, *966*
Ballad of Birmingham, 618
Ballou, Sullivan, 590
Baudelaire, Charles, 495
Because I could not stop for Death—, 759
Bierce, Ambrose, 580, *592*
Black Elk, 645, *653*
Black Elk Speaks, from, 645
Black Man Talks of Reaping, A, 945
Blue Highways, from, 100
Bontemps, Arna, 945, *949*
Bradford, William, 81, *90*
Bradstreet, Anne, 138, *143*
Brooks, Gwendolyn, 967, *972*

C

Cabeza de Vaca, Álvar Nuñez, 72, *80*
Camouflaging the Chimera, 1111
Cather, Willa, 688, *699*
Cervantes, Lorna Dee, 894, *899*
Chicago, 824
Chief Joseph, 651
Chopin, Kate, 783, *787*

Cisneros, Sandra, 1227, *1233*
Civil Disobedience, from, 369
Coming of Age in Mississippi, from, 609
Complaints and Disorders, from, 782
Coyote and the Buffalo, 40
Crane, Stephen, 593, *604*
Crèvecoeur, Michel-Guillaume Jean de, 289, *294*
Crucible, The, 163
Cullen, Countee, 940, *944*
Cummings, E. E., 410, *415*

D

Danse Macabre, from, 464
Danse Russe, 410
Death of the Ball Turret Gunner, The, 1088
Death of the Hired Man, The, 1007
Deciding, 1111
Declaration of Independence, The, 270
Declaration of the Rights of Woman, The, from, 277
Defining the Grateful Gesture, 894
Devil and Tom Walker, The, 349
Diaries, The, from, 1033
Dickinson, Emily, 746, 750, 755
Didion, Joan, 1095, *1102*
Dr. Heidegger's Experiment, 500
Doctorow, E. L., 1157, *1167*
Douglass, Frederick, 562, *573*
Dove, Rita, 802, *805*
Dunbar, Paul Laurence, 835, *839*

E

Edwards, Jonathan, 152, *160*
Eliot, T. S., 1025, *1032*
Emerson, Ralph Waldo, 363, *368*
Ending Poem, 416
End of Something, The, 1018
Epigrams, 678
Equiano, Olaudah, 93, *99*
Examination of Sarah Good, The, 144

F

Fall of the House of Usher, The, 473
Faulkner, William, 516, *527*

First Jumping Frog, The, 684
Fitzgerald, F. Scott, 840, *862*
Flute Players, 930
Fox and Coyote and Whale, 43
Franklin, Benjamin, 292
Frederick Douglass, 615
Free Labor, 574
Frost, Robert, 996, 1000, 1006
Fuller, Margaret, 366

G

Gandhi, Mohandas K., 377
Gary Keillor, 424
Gettysburg Address, The, 605
Gilman, Charlotte Perkins, 765, *781*
Giovanni, Nikki, 1145
Glanton, Dahleen, 931
Gonzales, Rodolfo, 309, *317*
Gouges, Olympe de, 277
Griego y Maestas, José, 638, *644*

H

Harlem, 926
Harper, Frances Ellen Watkins, 574, *579*
Hawthorne, Nathaniel, 500, *515*
Hayden, Robert, 615
Heat-Moon, William Least, 100, *108*
Hemingway, Ernest, 1018, *1024*
Henry, Patrick, 262, *269*
High Horse's Courting, 645
History Clashes with Commercialism, 150
Hongo, Garrett, 1210
"Hope" is the thing with feathers—, 752
Hostage, 1200
How It Feels to Be Colored Me, 950
Hughes, Langston, *920, 924, 932*
Hunting Song/Dinni-e Sin, 33
Hurston, Zora Neale, 950, *958*

I

I Am Joaquín/Yo Soy Joaquín, from, 309
If We Must Die, 945
I Hear America Singing, 397
I Heard a Fly buzz—when I died—, 758
In Praise of Robert Frost, 1012
In Response to Executive Order 9066, 1095
In the American Society, 877
Indian and the Hundred Cows, The / El Indito de las Cien Vacas, 638

Interesting Narrative of the Life of Olaudah Equiano, The, from, 93
Ironing Their Clothes, 814
Iroquois, 24
Irving, Washington, 349, *362*
I Sit and Look Out, 399
I Stand Here Ironing, 806
I, Too, 925
I Will Fight No More Forever, 651

J

Jarrell, Randall, 1088, *1094*
Jefferson, Thomas, 270, *281*
Jen, Gish 877, *893*
Jilting of Granny Weatherall, The, 1035
Johnson, James Weldon, 940, *944*

K

Kafka, Franz, 1033
Keillor, Garrison, 424, *435*
Kennedy, John F., 1012
King, Martin Luther, Jr., 300, *308*, 1136
King, Stephen, 464
Komunyakaa, Yusef, 1111, *1117*

L

Larsen, Wendy Wilder, 1111, *1117*
Latin Deli: An Ars Poetica, The, 1223
Lecture to a Missionary, 295
Legal Alien, 1194
Legend, The, 1210
Legend of Gregorio Cortez, The, 702
Letter from Birmingham Jail, 1136
Letter from Paradise, 21° 19' N., 157° 52' W., 1095
Letter to John Adams, 282
Letter to Sarah Ballou, 590
Letter to the Rev. Samson Occom, 282
Letter to Thomas Wentworth Higginson (April 15, 1862), 755
Levertov, Denise, 1118, *1121*
Levi, Primo, 1083
Life for My Child Is Simple, 967
Life on the Mississippi, from, 669
Life You Save May Be Your Own, The, 528
Lincoln, Abraham, 605, *608*
Longfellow, Henry Wadsworth, 344, *348*
Love, Langston, from, 931
Love Song of J. Alfred Prufrock, The, 1025

Lowell, James Russell, 574, *579*
Lucinda Matlock, 824

M

Malamud, Bernard, 1076, *1087*
Malcolm X, 300, *308*
Man to Send Rain Clouds, The, 48
Man Who Was Almost a Man, The, 1045
Masque of the Red Death, The, 454
Masters, Edgar Lee, 824, *829*
McKay, Claude, 945, *949*
Melville, Herman, 513
Memoirs, from, 366
Mending Wall, 1002
Mexicans Begin Jogging, 1194
Miller, Arthur, 163, *245*
Miniver Cheevy, 830
Mirror, 1057
Momaday, N. Scott, 55, *63*
Monody (Elegy for Nathaniel Hawthorne), 513
Moody, Anne, 609, *617*
Mora, Pat, 1194, *1199*
Morales, Aurora Levins, 416, *423*
Morales, Rosario, 416, *423*
Morrison, Toni, 973, *977*
Mother Tongue, 1215
Mourning Dove, 39, *47*
Much Madness is divinest Sense—, 754
My City, 940
My Dungeon Shook: Letter to My Nephew, 959
My Father and the Figtree, 891
My life closed twice before its close—, 756
My Sojourn in the Lands of My Ancestors, 109
Mystery of Heroism, A, 593

N

Narrative of the Life of Frederick Douglass, an American Slave, from, 562
Navajo, 33
Necessary to Protect Ourselves, 300
Neihardt, John G., 645, *653*
Neruda, Pablo, 406
New Immigrants, The, 875
Nga, Tran Thi, 1111, *1117*
Notorious Jumping Frog of Calaveras County, The, 679
Nye, Naomi Shihab, 891

O

Oates, Joyce Carol, 1200, *1214*
O'Brien, Tim, 1105, *1110*
Occurrence at Owl Creek Bridge, An, 580
O'Connor, Flannery, 528, *541*
Ode to Walt Whitman, 406
Of *Plymouth Plantation,* from, 81
Okanogan, 40, 43
Okita, Dwight, 1095, *1102*
Olsen, Tillie, 806, *817*
On Civil Disobedience, 377
Ortiz Cofer, Judith, 1223, *1226*
"Out, Out—", 1004

P

Paredes, Américo, 702, *719*
Plath, Sylvia, 1057, *1063*
Poe, Edgar Allan, *450,* 454, 466, 473
Point/Counterpoint; The Japanese-American Internment, 1103
Polo, Marco, 77
Poor Richard's Almanack, from, 292
Porter, Katherine Anne, 1035, *1044*
Primer for Blacks, 967
Psalm of Life, A, 344

R

Rabéarivelo, Jean Joseph, 930
Randall, Dudley, 618, *621*
Raven, The, 466
Red Jacket, 295, *299*
Refugee Ship, 894
Relación, La, from, 72
Revolutionary Dreams, 1145
Richard Cory, 830
Robinson, Edwin Arlington, 830, *834*
Rodriguez, Luis J., 416, *423*
Rose for Emily, A, 516

S

Salem Court Documents, 1692, 144
Sandburg, Carl, 824, *829*
Sapia, Yvonne, 894, *899*
Self in 1958, 1057
Self-Reliance, from, 363
Separating, 1180
Seventeen Syllables, 788
Sexton, Anne, 1057, *1063*

Silko, Leslie Marmon, 48, *54*
Sinners in the Hands of an Angry God, from, 152
Song of Myself, from, 400
Song of the Sky Loom, 33
Soto, Gary, 1194, *1199*
Speech in the Virginia Convention, 262
Spleen LXXXI, 495
Stanzas on Freedom, 574
Steinbeck, John, 1088, *1094*
Story of an Hour, The, 783
Straw into Gold: The Metamorphosis of the Everyday, 1227
Stride Toward Freedom, from, 300
Success is counted sweetest, 753
Survival in Auschwitz, from, 1083
Sympathy, 835

T

Tan, Amy, 1215, *1222*
Teenage Wasteland, 1168
Tewa, 33
This is my letter to the World, 751
Thoreau, Henry David, 369, *380*, 381
Thoughts on the African-American Novel, 973
Tía Chucha, 416
To My Dear and Loving Husband, 138
Travels of Marco Polo, The, from, 77
Twain, Mark, *654*, 658, 669, 678, 679
Tyler, Anne, 1168, *1179*

U

Updike, John, 1180, *1193*
Upon the Burning of Our House, July 10th, 1666, 138

W

Wagner Matinee, A, 688
Walden, from, 381
Walker, Alice, 955
Wandering, 1150
Way to Rainy Mountain, The, from, 55
Weary Blues, The, 927
Welty, Eudora, 8
We Wear the Mask, 835
What Is an American?, 289
Wheatley, Phillis, 282, *288*
When the Negro Was in Vogue, 932
Whitman, Walt, 396, *405*
Why Soldiers Won't Talk, 1088
Williams, William Carlos, 410, *415*
Wilson, Lanford, 1150, *1156*
Winter Dreams, 840
Women and Children First: The Mayflower Pilgrims, 91
World on the Turtle's Back, The, 24
Worn Path, A, 8
Wright, Richard, 1045, *1056*
Writer in the Family, The, 1157

Y

Yamamoto, Hisaye, 788, *801*
Yellow Wallpaper, The, 765
Yezierska, Anzia, 863, *874*

Z

Zora Neale Hurston: A Cautionary Tale and a Partisan View, from, 955

Acknowledgments *(continued)*

Wylie Agency: "The Man to Send Rain Clouds" by Leslie Marmon Silko. Copyright © 1981 by Leslie Marmon Silko. Reprinted with the permission of The Wylie Agency, Inc.

N. Scott Momaday: Excerpt from *The Way to Rainy Mountain* by N. Scott Momaday. Copyright © by N. Scott Momaday. Reprinted by permission of the author.

Simon & Schuster: Excerpts from *Cabeza de Vaca's Adventures in the Unknown Interior,* translated and annotated by Cyclone Covey. Copyright © 1961 by Macmillan Publishing Company. Reprinted with the permission of Simon & Schuster.

Alfred A. Knopf: Excerpts from *Of Plymouth Plantation* by William Bradford, edited by Samuel Eliot Morison. Copyright © 1952 by Samuel Eliot Morison, renewed 1980 by Emily M. Beck. Reprinted by permission of Alfred A. Knopf, Inc.

Cowles Enthusiast Media: "Women and Children First" by Alicia Crane Williams, *American History Illustrated,* November/December 1993. Copyright © American History Illustrated magazine. Reprinted with the permission of Cowles Enthusiast Media, Inc. (History Group), a PRIMEDIA publication.

Little, Brown and Company: Excerpt from *Blue Highways* by William Least Heat-Moon. Copyright © 1982 by William Least Heat-Moon. Reprinted by permission of Little, Brown and Company.

Random House: "My Sojourn in the Land of My Ancestors," from *All God's Children Need Traveling Shoes* by Maya Angelou. Copyright © 1986 by Maya Angelou. Reprinted by permission of Random House, Inc.

The 21st Century: "Vacation to Hell" by Joseph Saroufim, *The 21st Century,* November 1996. Copyright © The 21st Century newspaper. Reprinted through the courtesy of The 21st Century, Box 30, Newton, MA 02161.

Unit Two

USA Today: "History Clashes with Commercialism" by Craig Wilson, *USA Today,* 24 October 1997. Copyright © 1997 USA Today. Reprinted with permission.

Viking Penguin: *The Crucible* by Arthur Miller. Copyright © 1952, 1953, 1954, renewed © 1980, 1981, 1982 by Arthur Miller. Used by permission of Viking Penguin, a division of Penguin Putnam Inc.

Scott Renshaw: *"The Crucible:* A Film Review by Scott Renshaw." Copyright © 1996 by Scott Renshaw. Reprinted by permission of the author.

University of Illinois Press: "The Declaration of the Rights of Woman" by Olympe de Gouges, from *Women in Revolutionary Paris, 1789–1795,* edited by Darline Levy, Harriet Applewhite, and Mary Johnson. Copyright © 1979 by the Board of Trustees of the University of Illinois. Reprinted by permission of the University of Illinois Press.

University of Oklahoma Press: "Lecture to a Missionary" by Red Jacket, from *American Indian Literature: An Anthology,* revised edition, edited by Alan R. Velie. Copyright © 1979, 1991 by the University of Oklahoma Press. Reprinted by permission of the University of Oklahoma Press.

Writers House: Excerpt from *Stride Toward Freedom* by Martin Luther King, Jr. Copyright © 1958 by Martin Luther King, Jr., renewed 1986 by Coretta Scott King. Reprinted by arrangement with the Heirs to the Estate of Martin Luther King, Jr., c/o Writers House Inc. as agent for the proprietor.

Pathfinder Press: Excerpt from "Necessary to Protect Ourselves" by Malcolm X, from *Malcolm X: The Last Speeches.* Copyright © 1989 by Betty Shabazz, Bruce Perry, and Pathfinder Press. Reprinted by permission of Pathfinder Press.

Rodolfo Gonzales: Excerpts from *I Am Joaquín/Yo Soy Joaquín* by Rodolfo Gonzales. Reprinted by permission of the author.

New York Times: "A Boy's School Project Aims to Revise History" by Lizette Alvarez, *New York Times*, 1 May 1998. Copyright © 1998 by The New York Times. Reprinted by permission.

Unit Three

Navajivan Trust: Excerpt from "Readiness for Satyagraha" by Mohandas K. Gandhi, from *The Essential Writings of Mahatma Gandhi*, edited by Raghavan Iyer. Used with the permission of the trustees of the Navajivan Trust.

University of Alabama Press: "Ode to Walt Whitman" by Pablo Neruda, from *Homage to Walt Whitman: A Collection of Poems from the Spanish*, translated by Didier Tisdel Jaén. Copyright © 1969 by the University of Alabama Press. Reprinted by permission of the University of Alabama Press.

New Directions Publishing Corporation: "Danse Russe" from *Collected Poems, 1909–1939*, vol. 1, by William Carlos Williams. Copyright © 1938 by New Directions Publishing Corp. Reprinted by permission of New Directions Publishing Corp.

"Spleen" by Charles Baudelaire (poem LXXXI from *The Flowers of Evil*), translated by Sir John Squires. Copyright © 1965 by New Directions Publishing Corp. Reprinted by permission of New Directions Publishing Corp.

Liveright Publishing Corporation: "anyone lived in a pretty how town," from *Complete Poems, 1904–1962* by E. E. Cummings, edited by George J. Firmage. Copyright 1940, © 1968, 1991 by the Trustees for the E. E. Cummings Trust. Reprinted by permission of Liveright Publishing Corporation.

Firebrand Books: "Ending Poem," from *Getting Home Alive* by Aurora Levins Morales and Rosario Morales. Copyright © 1986 by Aurora Levins Morales and Rosario Morales. Reprinted by permission of Firebrand Books, Ithaca, New York.

Curbstone Press: "Tía Chucha," from *The Concrete River* by Luis J. Rodriguez. Copyright © 1993 by Luis J. Rodriguez. Reprinted with permission of Curbstone Press. Distributed by Consortium.

Ellen Levine Literary Agency: "Gary Keillor," from *The Book of Guys* by Garrison Keillor. Copyright © 1993 by Garrison Keillor. Reprinted by permission of Ellen Levine Literary Agency on behalf of the author.

Merlyn's Pen: "Eternally Slow" by Stephanie Lauer. First appeared in *Merlyn's Pen* magazine. Copyright © by Merlyn's Pen, Inc. All rights reserved. Reprinted by permission of Merlyn's Pen, Inc.

Stephen King: Excerpt from *Danse Macabre* by Stephen King. Copyright © Stephen King. All rights reserved. Reprinted with permission.

Random House: "A Rose for Emily" by William Faulkner, from *The Collected Stories of William Faulkner*. Copyright © 1930 and renewed 1958 by William Faulkner. Reprinted by permission of Random House, Inc.

Harcourt Brace & Company: "The Life You Save May Be Your Own," from *A Good Man Is Hard to Find and Other Stories* by Flannery O'Connor. Copyright 1953 by Flannery O'Connor and renewed © 1981 by Regina O'Connor. Reprinted by permission of Harcourt Brace & Company.

Sarah Mossberger: "Reunited" by Sarah Mossberger, *Voices of Youth*, vol. 4. Used with permission of Sarah Mossberger.

Unit Four

Doubleday: Excerpt from *Coming of Age in Mississippi* by Anne Moody. Copyright © 1968 by Anne Moody. Used by permission of Doubleday, a division of Bantam Doubleday Dell Publishing Group, Inc.

Liveright Publishing Corporation: "Frederick Douglass," from *Angle of Ascent: New and Selected Poems* by Robert Hayden. Copyright © 1975, 1972, 1970, 1966 by Robert Hayden. Reprinted by permission of Liveright Publishing Corporation.

Dudley Randall: "Ballad of Birmingham" by Dudley Randall. Reprinted by permission of the author.

Molly Ball: *The Red Badge of Courage* by Molly Ball, *Statement,* Spring 1997. Reprinted with the permission of Molly Ball.

Museum of New Mexico Press: "The Indian and the Hundred Cows"/"El indito de las cien vacas" from *Cuentos: Tales from the Hispanic Southwest,* retold by José Griego y Maestas and translated by Rudolfo A. Anaya. Copyright © 1980 by the Museum of New Mexico Press. Reprinted with permission of the Museum of New Mexico Press.

University of Nebraska Press: "High Horse's Courting," from *Black Elk Speaks* by Black Elk and John G. Neihardt. Copyright © 1932, 1959, 1972 by John G. Neihardt, copyright © 1961 by the John G. Neihardt Trust. Reprinted by permission of the University of Nebraska Press.

HarperCollins Publishers: Chapter 11 from *The Autobiography of Mark Twain,* edited by Charles Neider. Copyright © 1917, 1940, 1958, 1959 by The Mark Twain Company, copyright 1924, 1945, 1952 by Clara Clemens Samossoud, copyright © 1959 by Charles Neider. Reprinted by permission of HarperCollins Publishers, Inc.

University of Texas Press: "The Legend of Gregorio Cortez," from *With His Pistol in His Hand: A Border Ballad and Its Hero* by Américo Paredes. Copyright © 1958, renewed 1986 by the University of Texas Press. Reprinted by permission of the author and the University of Texas Press.

Unit Five

Little, Brown and Company; Harvard University Press; and the Trustees of Amherst College: "After great pain, a formal feeling comes—" by Emily Dickinson, from *The Complete Poems of Emily Dickinson,* edited by Thomas Johnson. Copyright © 1929 by Martha Dickinson Bianchi, copyright © renewed 1957, 1963 by Mary L. Hampson. Used by permission of Little, Brown and Company. Reprinted by permission of the publishers and the Trustees of Amherst College from *The Poems of Emily Dickinson,* edited by Thomas H. Johnson (Cambridge: The Belknap Press of Harvard University Press). Copyright © 1951, 1955, 1979, 1983 by the President and Fellows of Harvard College.

Feminist Press: Excerpt from *Complaints and Disorders: The Sexual Politics of Sickness* by Barbara Ehrenreich and Deirdre English (New York: The Feminist Press at The City University of New York, 1973). Copyright © 1973 by Barbara Ehrenreich and Deirdre English. Reprinted by permission of The Feminist Press at The City University of New York.

Rutgers University Press: "Seventeen Syllables," from *Seventeen Syllables and Other Stories* by Hisaye Yamamoto. Copyright © by Hisaye Yamamoto. Reprinted by permission of Rutgers University Press.

Rita Dove: "Adolescence—III," from *The Yellow House on the Corner* by Rita Dove, published by Carnegie-Mellon University Press. Copyright © 1980 by Rita Dove. Reprinted by permission of the author.

Delacorte Press/Seymour Lawrence: "I Stand Here Ironing," from *Tell Me a Riddle* by Tillie Olsen, introduction by John Leonard. Copyright © 1956, 1957, 1960, 1961 by Tillie Olsen. Used by permission of Delacorte Press/Seymour Lawrence, a division of Bantam Doubleday Dell Publishing Group, Inc.

Susan Bergholz Literary Services: "Ironing Their Clothes," from *Homecoming* by

Viking Penguin: "My City," from *Saint Peter Relates an Incident* by James Weldon Johnson. Copyright 1935 by James Weldon Johnson, © renewed 1963 by Grace Nail Johnson. Used by permission of Viking Penguin, a division of Penguin Putnam Inc.

GRM Associates: "Any Human to Another," from *The Medea and Some Poems* by Countee Cullen. Copyright © 1935 by Harper & Brothers, copyright renewed 1963 by Ida M. Cullen. Reprinted by permission of GRM Associates, Inc., agents for the Estate of Ida M. Cullen.

Archives of Claude McKay: "If We Must Die" by Claude McKay, from *Selected Poems of Claude McKay.* Copyright © 1957 by Harcourt Brace. Used by permission of The Archives of Claude McKay, Carl Cowl, Administrator.

Estate of Zora Neale Hurston: "How It Feels to Be Colored Me" by Zora Neale Hurston, from *I Love Myself When I Am Laughing: A Zora Neale Hurston Reader,* edited by Alice Walker. Reprinted by permission of the Estate of Zora Neale Hurston.

University of Illinois Press: Excerpts from "Zora Neale Hurston: A Cautionary Tale and a Partisan View" by Alice Walker, foreword to *Zora Neale Hurston: A Literary Biography* by Robert E. Hemenway. Copyright © 1977 by the Board of Trustees of the University of Illinois. Used with the permission of the University of Illinois Press.

James Baldwin Estate: "My Dungeon Shook" by James Baldwin, originally published in *The Progressive.* Copyright © 1962 by James Baldwin, copyright renewed. Collected in *The Fire Next Time,* published by Vintage Books. Reprinted with the permission of the James Baldwin Estate.

Gwendolyn Brooks: "Life for My Child Is Simple," from *Blacks* by Gwendolyn Brooks (Chicago: Third World Press, 1991). Copyright © 1991 by Gwendolyn Brooks. Reprinted by permission of the author.

"Primer for Blacks," from *Primer for Blacks* by Gwendolyn Brooks (Chicago: Third World Press, 1991). Copyright © 1991 by Gwendolyn Brooks. Reprinted by permission of the author.

Doubleday: "Thoughts on the African-American Novel" by Toni Morrison, from *Black Women Writers (1950–1980)* by Mari Evans. Copyright © 1983 by Toni Morrison. Used by permission of Doubleday, a division of Bantam Doubleday Dell Publishing Group, Inc.

Henry Holt & Company: "Acquainted with the Night," "Mending Wall," and "'Out, Out—,'" from *The Poetry of Robert Frost,* edited by Edward Connery Lathem. Copyright 1944, 1956, 1958 by Robert Frost, copyright 1967 by Lesley Frost Ballantine, copyright 1916, 1928, 1930, 1939, © 1969 by Henry Holt and Company, Inc. Reprinted with the permission of Henry Holt and Company, Inc.

"The Death of the Hired Man" by Robert Frost, from *The Poetry of Robert Frost,* edited by Edward Connery Lathem. Copyright © 1958 by Robert Frost, copyright © 1967 by Lesley Frost Ballantine. Copyright 1930, 1939, © 1969 by Henry Holt & Company. Reprinted by permission of Henry Holt & Company, Inc.

Excerpts from "Some Science Fiction," "The Gift Outright," "After Apple-Picking," "Nothing Gold Can Stay," and "Fire and Ice," from *The Poetry of Robert Frost,* edited by Edward Connery Lathem. Copyright 1942, 1951, 1955, 1958, 1962 by Robert Frost, copyright © 1967, 1970 by Lesley Frost Ballantine, copyright 1923, 1930, 1939, © 1969 by Henry Holt & Company. Reprinted by permission of Henry Holt & Company, Inc.

Scribner: "The End of Something," from *In Our Time* by Ernest Hemingway. Copyright 1925 Charles Scribner's Sons, copyright renewed 1953 by Ernest Hemingway. Reprinted with the permission of Scribner, a division of Simon & Schuster.

Faber and Faber: "The Love Song of J. Alfred Prufrock," from *Collected Poems, 1909–1962* by T. S. Eliot. Reprinted by permission of Faber and Faber Ltd.

Harcourt Brace & Company: "The Jilting of Granny Weatherall," from *Flowering Judas and Other Stories* by Katherine Anne Porter. Copyright 1930 and renewed 1958 by Katherine Anne Porter. Reprinted by permission of Harcourt Brace & Company.

HarperCollins Publishers: "The Man Who Was Almost a Man," from *Eight Men* by Richard Wright. Copyright © 1961 by Richard Wright. Reprinted by permission of HarperCollins Publishers, Inc.

HarperCollins Publishers and Faber and Faber: "Mirror," from *Crossing the Water* by Sylvia Plath. Copyright © 1963 by Ted Hughes. Originally appeared in *The New Yorker*. Reprinted by permission of HarperCollins Publishers, Inc., and Faber and Faber Ltd.

Houghton Mifflin Company: "Self in 1958," from *Live or Die* by Anne Sexton. Copyright © 1966 by Anne Sexton. Reprinted by permission of Houghton Mifflin Company. All rights reserved.

Unit Seven

Pantheon Books: Excerpts from *The Good War* by Studs Terkel. Copyright © 1984 by Studs Terkel. Reprinted by permission of Pantheon Books, a division of Random House, Inc.

Russell & Volkening: "Armistice," from *The People and Uncollected Stories* by Bernard Malamud. Copyright © 1989 by Ann Malamud. Reprinted by permission of Russell & Volkening as agents for the author.

"Teenage Wasteland" by Anne Tyler, from *Seventeen* magazine, November 1983. Copyright © 1983 by Anne Tyler. Reprinted by permission of Russell & Volkening as agents for the author.

Viking Penguin: Excerpt from *If This Is a Man (Survival in Auschwitz)* by Primo Levi, translated by Stuart Woolf. Translation copyright © 1959 by Orion Press, Inc., © 1958 by Giulio Einaudi Editore SpA. Used by permission of Viking Penguin, a division of Penguin Putnam Inc.

"Symptoms" ("Why Soldiers Won't Talk"), from *Once There Was a War* by John Steinbeck. Copyright 1943, 1958 by John Steinbeck, renewed © 1971 by Elaine Steinbeck, John Steinbeck IV, and Thomas Steinbeck. Used by permission of Viking Penguin, a division of Penguin Putnam Inc.

Farrar, Straus & Giroux: "The Death of the Ball Turret Gunner," from *The Complete Poems* by Randall Jarrell. Copyright © 1969 by Mrs. Randall Jarrell. Reprinted by permission of Farrar, Straus & Giroux, Inc.

Excerpt from "Letter from Paradise, 21° 19' N., 157° 52' W.," from *Slouching Towards Bethlehem* by Joan Didion. Copyright © 1966, 1968 by Joan Didion. Reprinted by permission of Farrar, Straus & Giroux, Inc.

Dwight Okita: "In Response to Executive Order 9066," from *Crossing with the Light* by Dwight Okita (Chicago: Tía Chucha Press). Copyright © 1992 by Dwight Okita. Used by permission of the author.

Houghton Mifflin Company/Seymour Lawrence: "Ambush," from *The Things They Carried* by Tim O'Brien. Copyright © 1990 by Tim O'Brien. Reprinted by permission of Houghton Mifflin Co./Seymour Lawrence. All rights reserved.

University Press of New England: "Camouflaging the Chimera," from *Dien Cai Dau* by Yusef Komunyakaa, published by Wesleyan University Press. Copyright © 1988 by Yusef Komunyakaa. Reprinted by permission of the University Press of New England.

Leona P. Schecter Literary Agency: "Deciding," from *Shallow Graves* by Wendy Wilder Larsen and Tran Thi Nga. Reprinted by permission of the Leona P. Schecter Literary Agency.

New Directions Publishing Corporation: "At the Justice Department, November 15, 1969," from *Poems, 1968–1972* by Denise Levertov. Copyright © 1969 by Denise Levertov. Reprinted by permission of New Directions Publishing Corp.

Wing Tek Lum: "Chinese Hot Pot" by Wing Tek Lum, from *Chinese American Poetry,* edited by L. Ling-chi Wang and Henry Yiheng Zhao. Reprinted by permission of Wing Tek Lum.

Writers House: Excerpts from "Letter from Birmingham Jail" by Martin Luther King, Jr. Copyright © 1963 by Martin Luther King, Jr., renewed 1991 by Coretta Scott King. Reprinted by arrangement with the Heirs to the Estate of Martin Luther King, Jr., c/o Writers House Inc. as agent for the proprietor.

William Morrow & Company: "Revolutionary Dreams," from *The Women and the Men* by Nikki Giovanni. Copyright © 1970, 1974, 1975 by Nikki Giovanni. Reprinted by permission of William Morrow & Company, Inc.

International Creative Management: *Wandering* by Lanford Wilson. Copyright © 1967 by Lanford Wilson, renewed 1993. Reprinted by permission of International Creative Management, Inc.

Random House: "The Writer in the Family," from *Lives of the Poets* by E. L. Doctorow. Copyright © 1984 by E. L. Doctorow. Reprinted by permission of Random House, Inc.

Alfred A. Knopf: "Separating," from *Problems and Other Stories* by John Updike. Copyright © 1975 by John Updike. Reprinted by permission of Alfred A. Knopf, Inc.

"The Legend," from *The River of Heaven* by Garrett Hongo. Copyright © 1988 by Garrett Hongo. Reprinted by permission of Alfred A. Knopf, Inc.

Chronicle Books: "Mexicans Begin Jogging" by Gary Soto, from *Gary Soto: New & Selected Poems,* published by Chronicle Books, San Francisco. Copyright © 1995 by Gary Soto. Reprinted by permission of Chronicle Books.

Arte Público Press: "Legal Alien," from *Chants* by Pat Mora (Houston: Arte Público Press—University of Houston, 1985). Copyright © 1985 by Pat Mora. Reprinted by permission of the publisher.

"The Latin Deli" by Judith Ortiz Cofer, *The Americas Review* 19.1 (Houston: Arte Público Press—University of Houston, 1991). Reprinted by permission of the publisher.

John Hawkins & Associates: "Hostage," from *Heat and Other Stories* by Joyce Carol Oates, published by Plume. Copyright © 1992 The Ontario Review, Inc. Reprinted by permission of John Hawkins & Associates, Inc.

Sandra Dijkstra Literary Agency: "Mother Tongue" by Amy Tan. First appeared in *The Threepenny Review,* Fall 1990. Copyright © 1990 by Amy Tan. Reprinted by permission of Amy Tan and the Sandra Dijkstra Literary Agency.

Susan Bergholz Literary Services: "Straw into Gold: The Metamorphosis of the Everyday" by Sandra Cisneros. First published in *The Texas Observer,* 25 September 1987. Copyright © 1987 by Sandra Cisneros. Reprinted by permission of Susan Bergholz Literary Services, New York. All rights reserved.

The editors have made every effort to trace the ownership of all copyrighted material found in this book and to make full acknowledgment for its use. Omissions brought to our attention will be corrected in a subsequent edition.

Art Credits

Cover, Frontispiece

Illustration copyright © 1998 Michael Steirnagle.

Front Matter

viii *left* Courtesy, University of Texas at Austin. Photo by Donald Codry, from *Mexican Masks* by Donald Codry, copyright © 1980. By permission of the University of Texas Press; *right* The Granger Collection, New York; **x** *top, A Morning View of Blue Hill Village* (1824), Jonathan Fisher. William A. Farnsworth Library and Art Museum, Rockland, Maine, museum purchase, 1965 (1965.134); *bottom* Teapot (about 1799) by Paul Revere. Silver, 7¼″. Courtesy of the Museum of Fine Arts, Boston, gift of James Longley; **x–xi** Photofest; **xii** *left, The Wanderer* (1818), Caspar David Friedrich. Kunsthalle, Hamburg, Germany/Bridgeman/Art Resource, New York; *right* Smithsonian Institution, Washington, D.C.; **xiii** *Cliff Dwellers* (1913), George Bellows. Oil on canvas, 40³⁄₁₆″ × 42¹⁄₁₆″. Los Angeles County Museum of Art, Los Angeles County Fund. Copyright © 1995 Museum Associates, Los Angeles County Museum of Art, all rights reserved; **xiv** Corbis; **xv** Pictorial quilt (1895–1898), Harriet Powers. Pieced and appliquéd cotton embroidered with plain and metallic yarns, 69″ × 105″. Courtesy of Museum of Fine Arts, Boston, bequest of Maxim Karolik; **xvi** The Granger Collection, New York; **xviii** *left* Amherst College Library, Archives and Special Collections; *top right, Mr. and Mrs. Isaac Newton Phelps Stokes* (1897), John Singer Sargent. Oil on canvas, 85¼″ × 39¾″. The Metropolitan Museum of Art, bequest of Edith Minturn Phelps (Mrs. I. N.) Stokes, 1938 (38.104). Copyright © 1989 The Metropolitan Museum of Art, New York; **xx** Langston Hughes, Winold Reiss. National Portrait Gallery, Washington, D.C./Art Resource, New York; **xxi** The Granger Collection, New York; **xxii** *Ominous Omen* (1987), Rupert Garcia. Chalk, linseed oil, and oil paint on canvas, 47″ × 130″. Courtesy of the artist, Rena Bransten Gallery, San Francisco, and Galerie Claude Samuel, Paris. Copyright © Rupert Garcia; **2** *left* National Archives; *top right* From the collections of the Library of Congress; *bottom right* Photo by John Olson for *Life* magazine. Copyright © Time Inc.; **3** *top left, right* The Granger Collection, New York; *bottom left* Photo by Howard Sochurek for *Life* magazine. Copyright © Time Inc.; **6–7** *Child and Her Mother, Wapato, Yakima Valley, Washington* (1939), Dorothea Lange. From the collections of the Library of Congress.

Unit One

18 *corn* The Granger Collection, New York; *cliff dwellings* Copyright © 1993 North Wind Pictures; **19** *compass* Copyright © Robert Frerck/Odyssey/Chicago; *foot warmer* Copyright © Winterthur Museum; **20** *top left* Colter Bay Indian Arts Museum at Grand Teton National Park, Wyoming; **21** Illustration by Rebecca McClellan; **22** *left* Copyright © 1993 Allen Russell/Profiles West; *right* AP/Wide World Photos; **28, 29** Details of *Creation Legend,* Tom (Two Arrows) Dorsey. Philbrook Museum of Art, Tulsa, Oklahoma (46.24); **32** *right* Illustration by David Cunningham; **39** Courtesy, University of Texas at Austin. Photo by Donald Codry, from *Mexican Masks* by Donald Codry, copyright © 1980. By permission of the University of Texas Press; **45** From *Mexican Masks* by Donald Codry, copyright © 1980. By permission of the University of Texas Press; **47** Historical Photograph Collections, Washington State University Libraries, Pullman, Washington; **54** Photo by Lee H. Marmon; **56** *initial M,* **58** *map* Illustrations by Gary Antonetti/Ortelius Design, Inc.; **58** *left* Dean Conger/Corbis; *right* Copyright © Gene Moore/Phototake, New York/PNI; **63** AP/Wide World Photos; **65** *left* From *Fool's Crow* by James Welch. Copyright © 1986 by James Welch. Used by permission of Viking Penguin, a division of Penguin Putnam Inc.; *right* Reprinted by permission of Random House, Inc.; **66–67** Photo by Sharon Hoogstraten; **68** Newberry Library, Chicago; **79** *bottom* Detail of Indians forced to carry baggage and supplies of the Spanish invaders (1590), Theodor de Bry. Rare Books and Manuscripts Division, The New York Public Library, Astor, Lenox and Tilden Foundations; **80** The Granger Collection, New York; **82** *background* Copyright © D. Bowen/Westlight; *inset* Wood River Gallery, Mill Valley, California; **89** Detail of *View of Plymouth* (1627), Carl Sachs. American Heritage Picture Collection, New York; **90** Copyright © Culver Pictures; **93** Courtesy of Les Mansfield, Cincinnati, Ohio; **99** The Granger Collection, New York; **103, 105** From *Blue Highways* by William Least Heat-Moon. Copyright © 1982 by William Least Heat-Moon. By permission of Little, Brown and Company; **108** AP/Wide World Photos; **110, 110–111, 111, 112, 115** *fabrics* Photos by Sharon Hoogstraten; **117** UPI/Bettmann; **119** *left* From *The Great Explorers: The European Discovery of America* by Samuel Eliot Morison. Copyright © 1986 by Samuel Eliot Morison. Used by permission of Oxford University Press, Inc.; *right* Cover of *Blue Highways* by William Least Heat-Moon. Cover photograph copyright © Chuck Kuhn/The Image Bank. Cover reprinted by permission of Houghton Mifflin Company. All rights reserved; **120–124** Photos by Sharon Hoogstraten; **128** The Granger Collection, New York.

Unit Two
132 *war* Copyright © 1993 North Wind Pictures; *Sir Isaac Newton* (18th century), unknown artist. Trinity College, Cambridge, U.K./Erich Lessing/Art Resource, New York; **133** *teapot* (about 1799) by Paul Revere. Silver, 7¼″. Courtesy of the Museum of Fine Arts, Boston, gift of James Longley; *wig* Corbis-Bettmann; *watch* Copyright © Christie's Images; *statue* Copyright © Philip Jon Bailey; **137** Detail of chair seat cover (about 1725), embroidered by a member of the Bradstreet family. Cotton threads, linen warp, wool embroidery, 43 cm × 47 cm. Courtesy, Museum of Fine Arts, Boston, gift of Samuel Bradstreet; **138, 140–141** Copyright © David Fitzgerald/Tony Stone Images; **145, 149** Copyright © Culver Pictures; **151** Lee Snider/Corbis; **153, 157** Copyright © David Fitzgerald/Tony Stone Images; **159** The Granger Collection, New York; **160** Stock Montage; **161** The Granger Collection, New York; **164–165** Photofest; **166** Photo by Kim Britt; **169, 171, 176** Photofest; **179** Lee Snider/Corbis; **182** Photofest; **191** Copyright © Martin Rogers/National Geographic Image Collection; **193** Photofest; **207** Lee Snider/Corbis; **209, 220, 222–223** Photofest; **222** *bottom* Robbie Jack/Corbis; **225, 227** Photofest; **229** Copyright © ZEE/PNI; **238, 241** Photofest; **242** *bottom left* The Granger Collection, New York; *top right* Copyright © Twentieth Century Fox/Shooting Star. All rights reserved; **245** AP/Wide World Photos; **248–252** Photos by Sharon Hoogstraten; **256** *left, Portrait of Thomas Jefferson* (1805), Gilbert Stuart. Gift of the Regents of the Smithsonian Institution, the Thomas Jefferson Memorial Foundation, and the Enid and Crosby Kemper Foundation. National Portrait Gallery, Smithsonian Institution, Washington, D.C./Art Resource, New York; **257** *top, Abigail Adams* (1829), Jarvis F. Hanks. Courtesy, Charles Ames, Esq.; *bottom* The Granger Collection, New York; **260** *top* The Granger Collection, New York; *bottom* Howard Sochurek/*Life* magazine. Copyright © Time Inc.; **262** Detail of *Patrick Henry Before the Virginia House of Burgesses* (1851), Peter F. Rothermel. Red Hill, The Patrick Henry National Memorial, Brookneal, Virginia; **269** Stock Montage; **271** *left* Photo courtesy School Division, Houghton Mifflin Company; *right* Copyright © 1995 Smithsonian Institution; **274** Photo courtesy School Division, Houghton Mifflin Company; **275** Independence National Historical Park Collection; **281** *Thomas Jefferson*, Charles Févret de Saint-Mémin. Black chalk on paper, 23¹³/₁₆″ × 17″. Worcester Art Museum, Worcester, Massachusetts (1954.82); **284, 286** *signatures* The

Granger Collection, New York; **288** *top* From the collections of the Library of Congress; *bottom* National Gallery of Art, Washington, D.C.; **289** Detail of the Van Bergen Overmantel (1732–1733), attributed to John Heaten. Oil on wood (fireboard), 15¼″ × 73½″. Copyright © New York State Historical Association, Cooperstown, New York; **294** Stock Montage; **295** The Granger Collection, New York; **299** Courtesy of the Bureau of American Ethnology, Smithsonian Institution, Washington, D.C.; **308** *left* Stock Montage; *right* The Granger Collection, New York; **309, 313** *bottom* From the collections of the Library of Congress (LC-USF34-24829-D); **319** *left* Reprinted by permission of Dover Publications, Inc., Philip Smith, editor. Copyright © 1996 by Dover Publications, Inc.; *right* Reprinted by permission of HarperCollins Publishers, New York, from *The American Revolutionaries: A History in Their Own Words, 1750–1800* by Milton Meltzer. Copyright © 1987 by Milton Melzer; **320–324, 330** Photos by Sharon Hoogstraten.

Unit Three
338 Smithsonian Institution, Washington, D.C.; **339** *cotton gin, telegraph* Smithsonian Institution, Washington, D.C.; *Levi's jeans* Courtesy of the Bancroft Library; *clock* Private collection/Art Resource, New York; *The Trail of Tears* (1942), Robert Lindneux. Oil on canvas. The Granger Collection, New York; **344** Detail of *En Mer* [At sea] (1898), Max Bohm. Courtesy of Alfred J. Walker Fine Art, Boston; **345, 346** *background* Copyright © D. Bowen/Westlight; **348** Stock Montage; **349, 350–351, 352, 353, 356, 359** Illustrations by Marlene Kay Goodman; **362** FPG International; **363** Detail of *Kindred Spirits* (1849), Asher B. Durand. Oil on canvas. Collection of The New York Public Library, Astor, Lenox and Tilden Foundations; **368** The New-York Historical Society; **370** Copyright © David Turnley/Corbis; **371** *top* AP/Wide World Photos; *bottom* Copyright © 1990 Joseph Cempa/Black Star/PNI; **374, 375** *left* UPI/Corbis-Bettmann; **375** *right* Copyright © Hulton Getty Picture Collection/Tony Stone Images; **380** National Portrait Gallery, Smithsonian Institution, Washington, D.C./Art Resource, New York; **381** Corbis-Bettmann; **382** *leaf* Copyright © John Shaw; **386** Copyright © Art Wolfe/Tony Stone Images; **387** Copyright © Jake Wyman/Photonica; **391** Copyright © John Shaw; **395** Copyright © 1993 Magnetic Poetry, Inc. All rights reserved. Photo by Sharon Hoogstraten; **397** Detail of *Cliff Dwellers* (1913), George Bellows. Oil on canvas. 40³⁄₁₆″ × 42¹⁄₁₆″. Los Angeles County Museum of Art, Los Angeles County Fund. Copyright © 1995 Museum Associates, Los Angeles County Museum of Art. All rights reserved; **405** Museum of The City of New York; **415** *left* National Archives; *right* By permission of the Houghton Library, Harvard University; **416** Detail of *Woman with Turban* (1985), Gilberto Ruiz. Mixed media on fabric, 36″ × 52″. Courtesy of Barbara Gillman Gallery, Miami Beach, Florida; **423** Copyright © 1986 Linda Haas; **435** FPG International; **437** *left* From *My First Summer in the Sierra* by John Muir, introduction by Gretel Ehrlich. Copyright © 1987 by Gretel Ehrlich. Used by permission of Viking Penguin, a division of Penguin Putnam Inc.; *right* Reprinted by permission of Harper & Row, Publishers, Inc., New York, from *Pilgrim at Tinker Creek* by Annie Dillard. Copyright © 1974 by Annie Dillard; **438–442, 450–454** *border* Photos by Sharon Hoogstraten; **450** *top* Corbis; *bottom* Corbis-Bettmann; **451** Hulton Deutsch Collection/Corbis; **452** *top* Weidenfeld and Nicolson Archive; *bottom* Edgar Allan Poe Museum, Richmond, Virginia; **453** *left* Copyright © Archive Photos; *right* AP/Wide World Photos; **454** *top* Copyright © 1986 Alberto Baudo/The Stock Market; **462–463** *border* Photo by Sharon Hoogstraten; **464–465** Copyright © 1986 Alberto Baudo/The Stock Market; **471–473** *border* Photo by Sharon Hoogstraten; **473, 474** *bottom left* Copyright © PhotoDisc; **474–475** Copyright © Anthony Howarth/Woodfin Camp/PNI; **476** Copyright © Gary L. Benson/AllStock/PNI; **479**

background Copyright © 1984 William Johnson/Stock Boston/PNI; **483** Copyright © PhotoDisc; **487** Copyright © Angelo Hornak/Corbis; **488** Copyright © Manuel Bellver/Corbis; **491** Copyright © Ann Rhoney/nonstøck Inc./PNI. All rights reserved; **494** Copyright © William Johnson/Stock Boston/PNI; **496–499** *border* Photo by Sharon Hoogstraten; **497, 499** Courtesy of the collections of the Library of Congress; **500** Photo by Sharon Hoogstraten; **501** Detail of *La danse à la campagne* [The country dance] (1883), Pierre Auguste Renoir. Private collection; **502, 505** *bottom*, **506, 508, 511** *bottom left*, **512** Photos by Sharon Hoogstraten; **515** National Archives; **517** *background* Photo by Sharon Hoogstraten; **527** The Granger Collection, New York; **541** AP/Wide World Photos; **543** *left* From *Billy Budd* by Herman Melville. Copyright © 1948, 1956 by The President and Fellows of Harvard College. Used by permission of Viking Penguin, a division of Penguin Putnam Inc.; *right* Reprinted by permission of Random House, Inc; **544–548** Photos by Sharon Hoogstraten.

Unit Four
556 *book* The Granger Collection, New York; **557** *money, poster* The Granger Collection, New York; *locomotive* Copyright © Chuck Place Photography; *clock* Bridgeman/Art Resource, New York; **558** *bottom, Battle of Franklin, Tennessee, 30 November 1864* (1891), Kurz and Allison. Lithograph. The Granger Collection, New York; **559** *bottom*, **560** *left* Courtesy of the U.S. Postal Service; **560** *right* Courtesy of Chicago Historical Society; **561** The Granger Collection, New York; **563** Corbis-Bettmann; **570** National Archives of Canada (C-28186); **573, 574** *top left* From the collections of the Library of Congress; **575** *background* Photograph by Sharon Hoogstraten; *left, right* The Granger Collection, New York; **576–577** Collection of The New-York Historical Society; **579** *left*, **580** From the collections of the Library of Congress; **587** Copyright © H. Abernathy/H. Armstrong Roberts; **590** *man* Chicago Historical Society; *woman* Merserve Collection, Library of Congress; **592** Culver Pictures; **593, 600** South Carolina Confederate Relic Room & Museum; **603** Corbis-Bettmann; **604** The Granger Collection, New York; **606** Gettysburg Historic Park/ NARA Special Media Archives, Services Division (Still Pictures); **608** From the collections of the Library of Congress; **609** AP/Wide World Photos; **610–611** Illustration by Robert Tanenbaum; **612, 614** Photos by Sharon Hoogstraten; **621** Copyright © Layle Silbert; **624–628** Photos by Sharon Hoogstraten; **632** *center right* Collection of the New York Historical Society; **632–633** South Dakota State Historical Society; **633** *top* From the collections of the Library of Congress; **634–635** Photo by Sharon Hoogstraten; **636** *top* Library of Congress/Corbis; *bottom* The Granger Collection, New York; **642** Copyright © John Runne. Evergreen Art Company, Evergreen, Colorado; **653** *left* Smithsonian Institution, Washington, D.C.; *right* Photo by Ron Nicodemus; **654–658** *border* Photo by Sharon Hoogstraten; **654** *signature* Christie's Images; *top right* The Granger Collection, New York; *bottom center* Corbis-Bettmann; **655** *top* Copyright © Kelly Mooney Photography/Corbis; *bottom* The Granger Collection, New York; **656** *left, center* The Granger Collection, New York; *right* Charles E. Rotkin/Corbis; **657** *top* The Granger Collection, New York; *bottom* Corbis-Bettmann; **667–669, 670–671** David Muench/Corbis; **672, 675, 677** *left* The Granger Collection, New York; **677** *right* Copyright © Buddy Mays/Travel Stock; **684** The Granger Collection, New York; **685–687** *border* Photo by Sharon Hoogstraten; **687** The Granger Collection, New York; **689, 690, 694** Illustrations by Judith DuFour Love; **698** The Granger Collection, New York; **699** National Archives; **703, 717** Photo by Sharon Hoogstraten; **719** Arte Público Press; **722–726, 732** Photos by Sharon Hoogstraten.

Unit Five

740 *Susan B. Anthony, statue* The Granger Collection, New York; **741** *poster, washing machine, automobile* The Granger Collection, New York; *watch* From *Pocket Watches* by Leonardo Leonardi and Gabriele Ribolini. Copyright © 1994, published by Chronicle Books; **742** *top* Copyright © Hulton Deutsch Collection; *bottom* The Granger Collection, New York; **743** *top* Culver Pictures; **744** *left* Courtesy of Chicago Historical Society; *right* The Granger Collection, New York; **746–750** *border* Photo by Sharon Hoogstraten; **746** *signature* The Granger Collection, New York; *top right* Amherst College Library, Archives and Special Collections; *bottom center* By permission of the Houghton Library, Harvard University; *bottom right* Corbis-Bettmann; **747** Jones Library, Special Collections, Amherst, Massachussetts; **748** *left* Corbis-Bettmann; *right* Amherst College Library, Archives and Special Collections; **749** Photofest; **757** *background* Corbis; **760–762** *border* Photo by Sharon Hoogstraten; **761, 762** Culver Pictures; **763** *top* Cover of *The Scarlet Letter* by Nathaniel Hawthorne. Used by permission of Dover Publications, Inc., New York; *bottom* Courtesy, Picture Research Consultants & Archive; **765** Detail of *A Woman Sewing in an Interior* (about 1900), Vilhelm Hammershøi. Christie's, London/Bridgeman/Art Resource, New York; **781** Stock Montage; **782** Culver Pictures; **787** Missouri Historical Society, St. Louis; **788** Photo by Russell Lee. Underwood Photo Archives, San Francisco; **801** Karen Huie; **805** Fred Viebahn; **816** Illustration copyright © 1990 by Mike Dooling, reprinted by permission of Scholastic Inc.; **817** AP/Wide World Photos; **819** *right* Reprinted by permission of Avon Books/Morrow, Inc.; **820** *bottom center,* **820–821** The Granger Collection, New York; **821** *top* Corbis-Bettmann; **822** The Granger Collection, New York; **824** *top left* Copyright © 1996 T. H. Benton & R. P. Benton Testamentary Trusts/Licensed by VAGA, New York; **829** *left* Stock Montage; *right* Illinois State Historical Library, Springfield; **834** Bettmann; **839** Moorland-Spingarn Research Center; **840** Illustration by Chuck Wilkinson; **862** National Archives; **864** Photo by Lewis W. Hine. Courtesy of George Eastman House, Rochester, New York; **867, 868** The Granger Collection, New York; **871** Photo by Lewis W. Hine. Courtesy of George Eastman House, Rochester, New York; **877, 885** Illustration by Roseann Litzinger; **893** Photo by Jerry Bauer; **901** *right* Book cover from *The Great Gatsby* (Authorized Text Edition) by F. Scott Fitzgerald (New York: Simon & Schuster, 1995). Reprinted with permission of Scribner, a division of Simon & Schuster; **902–906** Photos by Sharon Hoogstraten.

Unit Six

914 *Nude Descending a Staircase, No. 2* (1912), Marcel Duchamp. Oil on canvas, 58″ × 35″. Philadelphia Museum of Art, Louise and Walter Arensberg Collection (50-134-59); *Louis Armstrong* The Bettmann Archive; **915** *woman* Corbis-Bettmann; *wristwatch* Private collection. Photo by Sharon Hoogstraten; *Charles Lindbergh* The Bettmann Archive; **916** *center left* Copyright © 1969 James Vander Zee. All rights reserved; *bottom* UPI/Bettmann; **917** UPI/Bettmann; **918** *top, bottom* AP/Wide World Photos; **920–924** *border* Photo by Sharon Hoogstraten; **920** *top, Langston Hughes,* Winold Reiss. National Portrait Gallery, Washington, D.C./Art Resource, New York; *bottom center* UPI/Corbis-Bettmann; *bottom right* The Granger Collection, New York; **921** *left* Corbis-Bettmann; *right* The Granger Collection, New York; **922** UPI/Corbis-Bettmann; **928–929** *border* Photo by Sharon Hoogstraten; **929** Copyright © 1995 Archive Photos/PNI; **931** Copyright © Chicago Tribune. Photo by Milbert Orlando Brown; **932** Copyright © Frank Driggs/Archive Photos/PNI; **934–935** *background* UPI/Corbis-Bettmann; **934** *left* Copyright © Culver Pictures; *center, right* Copyright © Frank Driggs/Archive Photos/PNI; **935** *left* Copyright © Archive Photos; *right*

UPI/Corbis-Bettmann; **937–939** *border* Photo by Sharon Hoogstraten; **938** The Granger Collection, New York; **939** National Portrait Gallery, Smithsonian Institution, Washington, D.C./Art Resource, New York; **944** *left* Fisk University; *right* National Portrait Gallery, Smithsonian Institution, Washington, D.C./Art Resource, New York; **945** Photo by Arthur Rothstein. From the collections of the Library of Congress; **949** *left* Yale Collection of American Literature, Beinecke Rare Book and Manuscript Library, Estate of Carl van Vechten, Joseph Solomon, Executor; *right* Fisk University; **950** Detail of *Bal Jeunesse* (about 1927), Palmer Hayden. Watercolor on paper, 14″ × 17″. Collection of Meredith and Gail Wright Sirmans; **955** *Mules and Men* by Zora Neale Hurston. Copyright © 1935 Zora Neale Hurston. Cover design by Suzanne Noli. Cover illustration copyright © David Diaz. Reproduced by permission of HarperCollins. All rights reserved; **958** Yale Collection of American Literature, Beinecke Rare Book and Manuscript Library, Estate of Carl van Vechten, Joseph Solomon, Executor; **960–963** *background* Photo by Sharon Hoogstraten; **965** Smith College Museum of Art, Northampton, Massachusetts, purchased 1943; **966** The Granger Collection, New York; **968** Copyright © 1992 Ron Rovtar/FPG International; **972** Howard Simmons; **975** *top left* Cover of *The Bluest Eye* by Toni Morrison. Copyright © 1989 Plume. Used with permission of Dutton Signet, a division of Penguin Books U.S.A. Cover illustration by Thomas Blackshear; *bottom left* Cover of *Beloved* by Toni Morrison. Copyright © 1988 New American Library. Used with permission of Dutton Signet, a division of Penguin Books U.S.A.; *right* Cover of *Song of Solomon* by Toni Morrison. Copyright © 1978 New American Library. Used with permission of Dutton Signet, a division of Penguin Books U.S.A.; **977** Copyright © Layle Silbert; **980–988** Photos by Sharon Hoogstraten; **992** *bottom* Copyright © Imperial War Museum; **993** The Bettmann Archive; **994** *left* National Archives; **996–1000** *border* Photo by Sharon Hoogstraten; **996** *signature* The Granger Collection, New York; *top* Copyright © Burt Glinn/Magnum Photos; *bottom right* Corbis-Bettmann; **997** *left* Hulton Deutsch Collection/Corbis; *right* From *New Hampshire* by Robert Frost (Henry Holt, Inc.); **998** *top* Copyright © Archive Photos; *bottom* Copyright © William Johnson/Stock Boston; **999** *top* UPI/Corbis-Bettmann; *bottom* John F. Kennedy Library/Corbis; **1002** Copyright © 1993 Thayer Syne/FPG International; **1005–1006** *border* Photo by Sharon Hoogstraten; **1012** *background* Photo by Emily Kling; **1013–1015** *border* Photo by Sharon Hoogstraten; **1014** The Granger Collection, New York; **1015** Copyright © Burt Glinn/Magnum Photos; **1016** The Granger Collection, New York; **1022** Copyright © D. J. McKay; **1024** National Archives; **1031, 1032, 1033, 1044** The Granger Collection, New York; **1045** AP/Wide World Photos; **1046–1047** Courtesy of *Life* magazine. Copyright © Margaret Bourke-White Estate; **1048** Courtesy of Sears, Roebuck and Co.; **1056** National Archives; **1057** Copyright © 1991 Photoworld/FPG International; **1059** *kitchen* Copyright © 1995 FPG International; **1059** *doll,* **1060** Photo by Sharon Hoogstraten; **1062** Copyright © Archive Photos; **1063** *left, right* AP/Wide World Photos; **1065** *left* Book cover of *The Nick Adams Stories* by Ernest Hemingway (New York: Charles Scribner's Sons, 1972). Reprinted with permission of Scribner, a division of Simon & Schuster; *right* Reprinted by permission of Random House, Inc.

Unit Seven

1070 *mushroom cloud* AP/Wide World Photos; *John F. Kennedy* Copyright © 1960 Bob Henriques/Magnum Photos; **1071** *television* AP/Wide World Photos; *Twiggy, Richard Nixon* Copyright © Archive Photos; *watch* Private collection. Photo by Sharon Hoogstraten; **1072** *bottom* National Archives; **1073** Copyright © 1944 Robert Capa/Magnum Photos; **1074** Copyright © Donald J. Weber; **1076** Photo by Victor

Laredo; **1086** *top* Photo by George Skrigin; *bottom* UPI/Bettmann; **1087** AP/Wide World Photos; **1088, 1090, 1091, 1092** Copyright © 1968 Donald McCullin/Magnum Photos; **1094** *left* Copyright © 1995 Elliott Erwitt/Magnum Photos; *right* AP/Wide World Photos; **1095, 1099** *left, Evacuation Day, May 8, 1942,* Dorothea Lange. War Relocation Authority; **1099** *top right* AP/Wide World Photos; *bottom right* UPI/ Bettmann Newsphotos; **1100** *top left* UPI/Bettmann; *top right, Pledge of Allegiance at Rafael Weill Elementary* (1942), Dorothea Lange; *center right* Charles Mace/War Relocation Authority; *bottom, Manzanar Relocation Center* (1942), Dorothea Lange. War Relocation Authority; **1102** *left* AP/Wide World Photos; **1104** Corbis; **1108** *background* Copyright © Art Wolfe/Tony Stone Images; *woman* Copyright © 1969 Marc Riboud/Magnum Photos; *man* Copyright © Howard Grey/Tony Stone Images; **1110** Photo by Jerry Bauer; **1111** Photo by John Olson for *Life* magazine. Copyright © Time Inc.; **1117** *bottom left* Carolyn Wright; **1118** Photo by John Olson for *Life* magazine. Copyright © Time Inc.; **1124** Photo by Sharon Hoogstraten; **1125** *top* Copyright © Cantigny First Division Foundation; *bottom left, bottom right* Copyright © 1993 The Peace Museum; **1126-1128** Photos by Sharon Hoogstraten; **1132, 1133** AP/Wide World Photos; **1134** Illustration by J. W. Stewart; **1137, 1139, 1140, 1144** UPI/Corbis-Bettmann; **1148** Photo by John Olson for *Life* magazine. Copyright © Time Inc.; **1156** Photofest; **1158, 1159, 1160, 1165** Copyright © 1998 Curt Teich Postcard Archives, Lake County Museum, Illinois; **1167** Wyatt Counts/AP/Wide World Photos; **1168** *Portrait of Richard Freeman* (1974), Fairfield Porter. Oil on panel. Bowdoin College Museum of Art, Brunswick, Maine, anonymous gift (1986.74.1); **1179** AP/Wide World Photos; **1180** *The Table* (1970), Fairfield Porter. Collection of Elizabeth Feld; **1193, 1194** AP/Wide World Photos; **1199** *right* Arte Público Press; **1210–1211** Photos by Amy Ahlstrom; **1214, 1216–1217** AP/Wide World Photos; **1217** *bottom right* From *The Joy Luck Club* by Amy Tan. Copyright © 1989 by Amy Tan. Used by permission of Viking Penguin, a division of Penguin Putnam, Inc. Photo by Sharon Hoogstraten; **1222** Tom Herde/*The Boston Globe;* **1223, 1224** Copyright © William Schemmel/Stock South/PNI; **1226** Arte Público Press; **1231** Corbis; **1233** Photo by Rubén Guzmán.

Reading Handbook
1240 right, 1252 Copyright © Corbis.

Multicultural Advisory Board *(continued)*

Teacher Review Panels *(continued)*

CALIFORNIA (continued)

Karen Buxton, English Department Chairperson, Winston Churchill Middle School, San Juan School District

Bonnie Garrett, Davis Middle School, Compton School District

Sally Jackson, Madrona Middle School, Torrance Unified School District

Sharon Kerson, Los Angeles Center for Enriched Studies, Los Angeles Unified School District

Gail Kidd, Center Middle School, Azusa School District

Corey Lay, ESL Department Chairperson, Chester Nimitz Middle School, Los Angeles Unified School District

Myra LeBendig, Forshay Learning Center, Los Angeles Unified School District

Dan Manske, Elmhurst Middle School, Oakland Unified School District

Joe Olague, Language Arts Department Chairperson, Alder Middle School, Fontana School District

Pat Salo, 6th Grade Village Leader, Hidden Valley Middle School, Escondido Elementary School District

FLORIDA

Judith H. Briant, English Department Chairperson, Armwood High School, Hillsborough County School District

Beth Johnson, Polk County English Supervisor, Polk County School District

Sharon Johnston, Learning Resource Specialist, Evans High School, Orange County School District

Eileen Jones, English Department Chairperson, Spanish River High School, Palm Beach County School District

Jan McClure, Winter Park High School, Orange County School District

Wanza Murray, English Department Chairperson (retired), Vero Beach Senior High School, Indian River City School District

Shirley Nichols, Language Arts Curriculum Specialist Supervisor, Marion County School District

Debbie Nostro, Ocoee Middle School, Orange County School District

Barbara Quinaz, Assistant Principal, Horace Mann Middle School, Dade County School District

OHIO

Glyndon Butler, English Department Chairperson, Glenville High School, Cleveland City School District

Ellen Geisler, English/Language Arts Department Chairperson, Mentor Senior High School, Mentor School District

Dr. Paulette Goll, English Department Chairperson, Lincoln West High School, Cleveland City School District

Lorraine Hammack, Executive Teacher of the English Department, Beachwood High School, Beachwood City School District

Marguerite Joyce, English Department Chairperson, Woodridge High School, Woodridge Local School District

Sue Nelson, Shaw High School, East Cleveland School District

Dee Phillips, Hudson High School, Hudson Local School District

Carol Steiner, English Department Chairperson, Buchtel High School, Akron City School District

Nancy Strauch, English Department Chairperson, Nordonia High School, Nordonia Hills City School District

Ruth Vukovich, Hubbard High School, Hubbard Exempted Village School District

TEXAS

Dana Davis, English Department Chairperson, Irving High School, Irving Independent School District

Susan Fratcher, Cypress Creek High School, Cypress Fairbanks School District

Yolanda Garcia, Abilene High School, Abilene Independent School District

Patricia Helm, Lee Freshman High School, Midland Independent School District

Joanna Huckabee, Moody High School, Corpus Christi Independent School District

Josie Kinard, English Department Chairperson, Del Valle High School, Ysleta Independent School District

Mary McFarland, Amarillo High School, Amarillo Independent School District

Gwen Rutledge, English Department Chairperson, Scarborough High School, Houston Independent School District

Bunny Schmaltz, Assistant Principal, Ozen High School, Beaumont Independent School District

Michael Urick, A. N. McCallum High School, Austin Independent School District

Manuscript Reviewers *(continued)*

Kathleen M. Anderson-Knight, United Township High School, East Moline, Illinois

Susan Arabie, Marshall High School, Marshall, Texas

Anita Arnold, Thomas Jefferson High School, San Antonio, Texas

Cassandra L. Asberry, Dean of Instruction, Carter High School, Dallas, Texas

Jolene Auderer, Pine Tree High School, Longview, Texas

Don Baker, English Department Chairperson, Peoria High School, Peoria, Illinois

Beverly Ann Barge, Wasilla High School, Wasilla, Alaska

Louann Bohman, Wilbur Cross High School, New Haven, Connecticut

Rose Mary Bolden, Justin F. Kimball High School, Dallas, Texas

Lydia C. Bowden, Boca Ciega High School, St. Petersburg, Florida

Angela Boyd, Andrews High School, Andrews, Texas

Hugh Delle Broadway, McCullough High School, The Woodlands, Texas

Glyndon B. Butler, English Department Chairperson, Glenville High School, Cleveland, Ohio

Stephan P. Clarke, Spencerport High School, Spencerport, New York

Kathleen D. Crapo, South Fremont High School, St. Anthony, Idaho

Dr. Shawn Eric DeNight, Miami Edison Senior High School, Miami, Florida

JoAnna R. Exacoustas, La Serna High School, Whittier, California

Linda Ferguson, English Department Head, Tyee High School, Seattle, Washington

Ellen Geisler, English Department Chairperson, Mentor Senior High School, Mentor, Ohio

Ricardo Godoy, English Department Chairman, Moody High School, Corpus Christi, Texas

Meredith Gunn, Secondary Language Arts Instructional Specialist, Katy, Texas

Judy Hammack, English Department Chairperson, Milton High School, Alpharetta, Georgia

Robert Henderson, West Muskingum High School, Zanesville, Ohio

Martha Watt Hosenfeld, English Department Chairperson, Churchville-Chili High School, Churchville, New York

Janice M. Johnson, Assistant Principal, Union High School, Grand Rapids, Michigan

Eileen S. Jones, English Department Chair, Spanish River Community High School, Boca Raton, Florida

Paula S. L'Homme, West Orange High School, Winter Garden, Florida

Bonnie J. Mansell, Downey Adult School, Downey, California

Linda Maxwell, MacArthur High School, Houston, Texas

Ruth McClain, Paint Valley High School, Bainbridge, Ohio

Rebecca Miller, Taft High School, San Antonio, Texas

Deborah Lynn Moeller, Western High School, Fort Lauderdale High School

Bobbi Darrell Montgomery, Batavia High School, Batavia, Ohio

Bettie Moody, Leesburg High School, Leesburg, Florida

Margaret L. Mortenson, English Department Chairperson, Timpanogos High School, Orem, Utah

Marjorie M. Nolan, Language Arts Department Head, William M. Raines Sr. High School, Jacksonville, Florida

Julia Pferdehirt, Free-lance writer, former Special Education teacher, Middleton, Wisconsin

Cindy Rodgers, MacArthur High School, Houston, Texas

Pauline Sahakian, English Department Chairperson, San Marcos High School, San Marcos, Texas

Jacqueline Y. Schmidt, Department Chairperson and Coordinator of English, San Marcos High School, San Marcos, Texas

David Schultz, East Aurora High School, East Aurora, New York

Milinda Schwab, Judson High School, Converse, Texas

John Sferro, Butler High School, Vandalia, Ohio

Brad R. Smedley, English Department Chairperson, Hudtloff Middle School, Lakewood, Washington

Faye S. Spangler, Versailles High School, Versailles, Ohio

Rita Stecich, Evergreen Park Community High School, Evergreen Park, Illinois

GayleAnn Turnage, Abiline High School, Abiline, Texas

Ruth Vukovich, Hubbard High School, Hubbard, Ohio

Kevin Walsh, Dondero High School, Royal Oak, Michigan

Charlotte Washington, Westwood Middle School, Grand Rapids, Michigan

Tom Watson, Westbridge Academy, Grand Rapids, Michigan

Linda Weatherby, Deerfield High School, Deerfield, Illinois